QPB
science
ENCYCLOPEDIA

QPB
science
ENCYCLOPEDIA

Quality Paperback Book Club
New York

Printed in the United States of America

contents

featured essays

appendices

A symbol for ◊mass number, the number of neutrons and protons in an atomic nucleus.

A in physics, symbol for ◊ampere, a unit of electrical current.

aardvark ***Afrikaans 'earth pig'*** nocturnal mammal *Orycteropus afer*, the only species in the order Tubulidentata, found in central and southern Africa. A timid, defenceless animal about the size of a pig, it has a long head, a piglike snout, large ears, sparse body hair, a thick tail, and short legs.

It can burrow rapidly with its clawed front feet. It spends the day in its burrow, and at night digs open termite and ant nests, licking up the insects with its long sticky tongue. Its teeth are unique, without enamel, and are the main reason for the aardvark being placed in its own order. When fully grown, it is about 1.5 m/5 ft long and its tongue is 30 cm/12 in long.

AARDVARK

http://www.oit.itd.umich.edu/bio108/Chordata/Mammalia/Tubulidentata.shtml

Detailed description of this strange-looking, insectivorous mammal. There is information about the aardvark's skeletal and dental structure, and links to explain unfamiliar terms.

aardwolf nocturnal mammal *Proteles cristatus* of the ◊hyena family, Hyaenidae. It is yellowish grey with dark stripes and, excluding its bushy tail, is around 70 cm/30 in long. It is found in eastern and southern Africa, usually in the burrows of the ◊aardvark. It feeds almost exclusively on termites, eating up to 300,000 per day, but may also eat other insects and small mammals.

Males mate monogamously but females, which have a much larger range, will mate with other males.

abacus ancient calculating device made up of a frame of parallel wires on which beads are strung. The method of calculating with a handful of stones on a 'flat surface' (Latin *abacus*) was familiar to the Greeks and Romans, and used by earlier peoples, possibly even in ancient Babylon; it survives in the more sophisticated bead-frame form of the Russian *schoty* and the Japanese *soroban*. The abacus has been superseded by the electronic calculator.

ABACUS: THE ART OF CALCULATING WITH BEADS

http://members.aol.com/stubbs3/abacus.htm

Clear explanation of how the abacus works – with demonstrations of how to add and subtract. This site requires a Java-enabled Web browser or Netscape 2.0+.

The wires of a bead-frame abacus define place value (for example, in the decimal number system each successive wire, counting from right to left, would stand for ones, tens, hundreds, thousands, and so on) and beads are slid to the top of each wire in order to represent the digits of a particular number. On a simple decimal abacus, for example, the number 8,493 would be entered by sliding three beads on the first wire (three ones), nine beads on the second wire (nine tens), four beads on the third wire (four hundreds), and eight beads on the fourth wire (eight thousands).

abalone edible marine snail of the worldwide genus *Haliotis*, family Haliotidae. Abalones have flattened, oval, spiralled shells, which have holes around the outer edge and a bluish mother-of-pearl lining. This lining is used in ornamental work.

abdomen in vertebrates, the part of the body below the ◊thorax, containing the digestive organs; in insects and other arthropods, it is the hind part of the body. In mammals, the abdomen is separated from the thorax by the ◊diaphragm, a sheet of muscular tissue; in arthropods, commonly by a narrow constriction. In mammals, the female reproductive organs are in the abdomen. In insects and spiders, it is characterized by the absence of limbs.

aberration of starlight apparent displacement of a star from its true position, due to the combined effects of the speed of light and the speed of the Earth in orbit around the Sun (about 30 km per second/18.5 mi per second).

Aberration, discovered in 1728 by English astronomer James Bradley (1693–1762), was the first observational proof that the Earth orbits the Sun.

aberration, optical any of a number of defects that impair the image in an optical instrument. Aberration occurs because of minute variations in lenses and mirrors, and because different

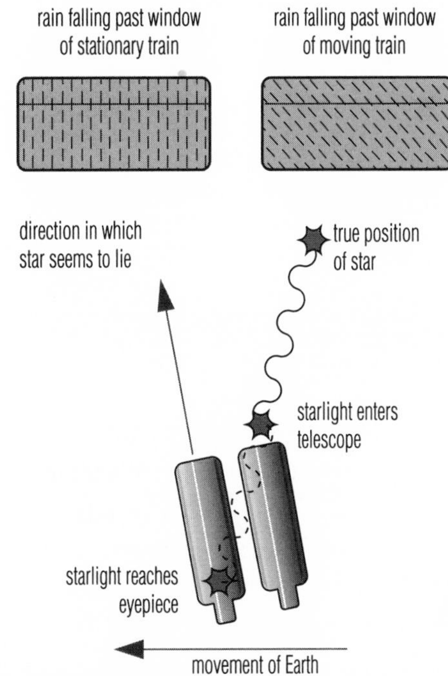

aberration of starlight *The aberration of starlight is an optical illusion caused by the motion of the Earth. Rain falling appears vertical when seen from the window of a stationary train; when seen from the window of a moving train, the rain appears to follow a sloping path. In the same way, light from a star 'falling' down a telescope seems to follow a sloping path because the Earth is moving. This causes an apparent displacement, or aberration, in the position of the star.*

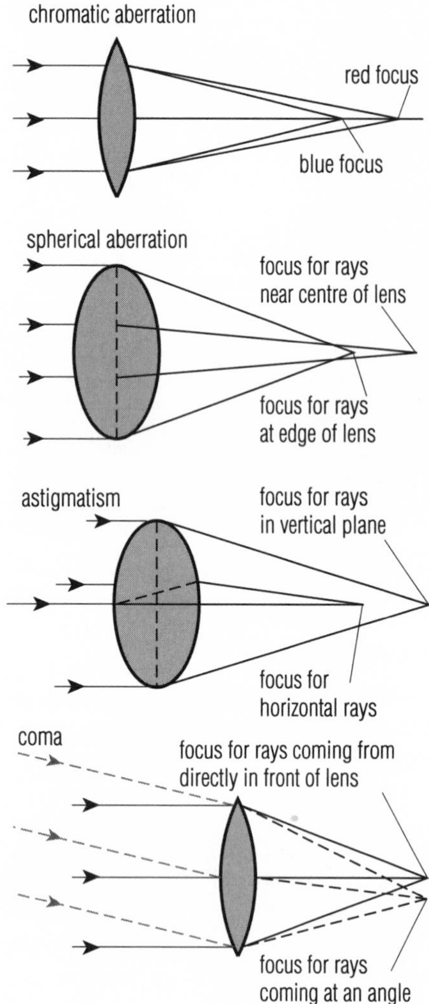

aberration, optical *The main defects, or aberrations, of optical systems. Chromatic aberration, or coloured fringes around images, arises because light of different colours is focused at different points by a lens, causing a blurred image. Spherical aberration arises because light that passes through the centre of the lens is focused at a different point from light passing through the edge of the lens. Astigmatism arises if a lens has different curvatures in the vertical and horizontal directions. Coma arises because light passing directly through a lens is focused at a different point to light entering the lens from an angle.*

parts of the light ◊spectrum are reflected or refracted by varying amounts.

In **chromatic aberration** the image is surrounded by coloured fringes, because light of different colours is brought to different focal points by a lens. In **spherical aberration** the image is blurred because different parts of a spherical lens or mirror have different focal lengths. In **astigmatism** the image appears elliptical or cross-shaped because of an irregularity in the curvature of the lens. In **coma** the images appear progressively elongated towards the edge of the field of view. Elaborate computer programs are now used to design lenses in which the aberrations are minimized.

abiotic factor a nonorganic variable within the ecosystem, affecting the life of organisms. Examples include temperature, light, and soil structure. Abiotic factors can be harmful to the environment, as when sulphur dioxide emissions from power stations produce acid rain.

abortion ***Latin*** ***aborire 'to miscarry'*** ending of a pregnancy before the fetus is developed sufficiently to survive outside the uterus. Loss of a fetus at a later gestational age is termed premature stillbirth. Abortion may be accidental (◊miscarriage) or deliberate (termination of pregnancy).

deliberate termination In the first nine weeks of pregnancy, medical termination may be carried out using the 'abortion pill' (◊mifepristone) in conjunction with a ◊prostaglandin. There are also various procedures for surgical termination, such as ◊dilatation and curettage, depending on the length of the pregnancy.

Worldwide, an estimated 150,000 unwanted pregnancies are terminated each day by induced abortion. One-third of these abortions are performed illegally and unsafely, and cause one in eight of all maternal deaths.

abortion as birth control Abortion as a means of birth control has long been controversial. The argument centres largely upon whether a woman should legally be permitted to have an abortion and, if so, under what circumstances. Another aspect is whether, and to what extent, the law should protect the fetus.

Those who oppose abortion generally believe that human life begins at the moment of conception, when a sperm fertilizes an egg. This is the view held, for example, by the Roman Catholic Church. Those who support unrestricted legal abortion may believe in a woman's right to choose whether she wants a child, and may take into account the large numbers of deaths and injuries from unprofessional back-street abortions.

Others approve abortion for specific reasons. For example, if a woman's life or health is jeopardized, abortion may be recommended; and if there is a strong likelihood that the child will be born with severe mental or physical disability. Other grounds for abortion include pregnancy resulting from sexual assault such as rape or incest.

abrasive ***Latin 'to scratch away'*** substance used for cutting and polishing or for removing small amounts of the surface of hard materials. There are two types: natural and artificial abrasives, and their hardness is measured using the ◊Mohs' scale. Natural abrasives include quartz, sandstone, pumice, diamond, emery, and corundum; artificial abrasives include rouge, whiting, and carborundum.

abscess collection of ◊pus in solid tissue forming in response to infection. Its presence is signalled by pain and inflammation.

abscissa in ◊coordinate geometry, the x-coordinate of a point – that is, the horizontal distance of that point from the vertical or y-axis. For example, a point with the coordinates (4, 3) has an abscissa of 4. The y-coordinate of a point is known as the ◊ordinate.

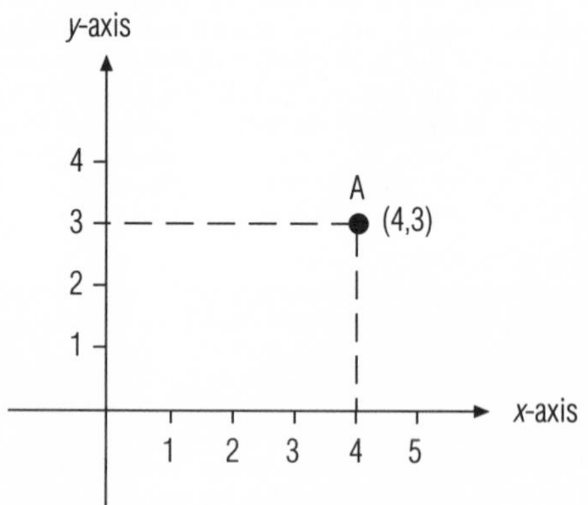

abscissa

abscissin or ***abscissic acid*** plant hormone found in all higher plants. It is involved in the process of ◊abscission and also inhibits stem elongation, germination of seeds, and the sprouting of buds.

abscission in botany, the controlled separation of part of a plant from the main plant body – most commonly, the falling of leaves or the dropping of fruit controlled by ◊abscissin. In ◊deciduous plants the leaves are shed before the winter or dry season, whereas ◊evergreen plants drop their leaves continually throughout the year. Fruitdrop, the abscission of fruit while still immature, is a naturally occurring process.

Abscission occurs after the formation of an abscission zone at the point of separation. Within this, a thin layer of cells, the abscission layer, becomes weakened and breaks down through the conversion of pectic acid to pectin. Consequently the leaf, fruit, or other part can easily be dislodged by wind or rain. The process is thought to be controlled by the amount of ◊auxin present. Fruitdrop is particularly common in fruit trees such as apples, and orchards are often sprayed with artificial auxin as a preventive measure.

absolute (of a value) in computing, real and unchanging. For example, an **absolute address** is a location in memory and an **absolute cell reference** is a single fixed cell in a spreadsheet display. The opposite of absolute is ◊relative.

absolute value or ***modulus*** in mathematics, the value, or magnitude, of a number irrespective of its sign. The absolute value of a number n is written $|n|$ (or sometimes as mod n), and is defined as the positive square root of n^2. For example, the numbers –5 and 5 have the same absolute value:

$$|5| = |-5| = 5$$

For a ◊complex number, the absolute value is its distance to the origin when it is plotted on an Argand diagram, and can be calculated (without plotting) by applying ◊Pythagoras' theorem. By definition, the absolute value of any complex number $a + ib$ (where a and b are real numbers and i is $\sqrt{-1}$) is given by the expression:

$$|a + ib| = \sqrt{(a^2 + b^2)}$$

absolute zero lowest temperature theoretically possible according to kinetic theory, zero kelvin (0 K), equivalent to –273.15°C/–459.67°F, at which molecules are in their lowest energy state. Although the third law of ◊thermodynamics indicates the impossibility of reaching absolute zero in practice, a temperature of 2.8×10^{-10} K (0.28 billionths of a degree above absolute zero) has been produced in 1993 at the Low Temperature Laboratory in Helsinki, Finland, using a technique called nuclear demagnetization. Near absolute zero, the physical properties of some materials change substantially; for example, some metals lose their electrical resistance and become superconducting.

absorption the taking up of one substance by another, such as a liquid by a solid (ink by blotting paper) or a gas by a liquid (ammonia by water). In physics, absorption is the phenomenon by which a substance retains radiation of particular wavelengths; for example, a piece of blue glass absorbs all visible light except the wavelengths in the blue part of the spectrum; it also refers to the partial loss of energy resulting from light and other electromagnetic waves passing through a medium. In nuclear physics, absorption is the capture by elements, such as boron, of neutrons produced by fission in a reactor.

absorption lines in astronomy, dark line in the spectrum of a hot object due to the presence of absorbing material along the line of sight. Absorption lines are caused by atoms absorbing light from the source at sharply defined wavelengths. Numerous absorption lines in the spectrum of the Sun (Fraunhofer lines) allow astronomers to study the composition of the Sun's outer layers. Absorption lines in the spectra of stars give clues to the composition of interstellar gas.

absorption spectroscopy or ***absorptiometry*** in analytical chemistry, a technique for determining the identity or amount present of a chemical substance by measuring the amount of electromagnetic radiation the substance absorbs at specific wavelengths; see ◊spectroscopy.

abutilon one of a group of 90 related species of tropical or semitropical ornamental plants. The Indian mallow or velvet leaf (*Abutilon theophrastus*) is one of the more common; it has bell-shaped yellow flowers and is the source of a jutelike fibre. Many of the species are pollinated by hummingbirds. (Genus *Abutilon*, family Malvaceae.)

abyssal plain broad expanse of sea floor lying 3–6 km/2–4 mi below sea level. Abyssal plains are found in all the major oceans, and they extend from bordering continental rises to mid-oceanic ridges.

abyssal zone dark ocean region 2,000–6,000 m/6,500–19,500 ft deep; temperature 4°C/39°F. Three-quarters of the area of the deep-ocean floor lies in the abyssal zone, which is too far from the surface for photosynthesis to take place. Some fish and crustaceans living there are blind or have their own light sources. The region above is the bathyal zone; the region below, the hadal zone.

Abyssinian cat or ***rabbit cat*** breed of domestic shorthaired cat, possibly descended from antiquity. In modern times, it was imported from Abyssinia (now Ethiopia) to Britain in the 1860s. The coat of the usual variety is ruddy brown (similar to a rabbit or hare) with each hair ringed with two or three darker coloured bands. It has a medium-length body, long, slender legs, large wideset ears, and deep gold or green eyes. It resembles cats that appear in ancient Egyptian wall paintings.

The breed was recognized in Britain 1882 and is now most widely bred in the USA. There are many varieties.

abzyme in biotechnology, an artificially created antibody that can be used like an enzyme to accelerate reactions.

AC in physics, abbreviation for ◊alternating current.

> To remember the order of items in an AC circuit:
>
> THE **VOLTAGE** (V) ACROSS A **CAPACITOR** (C) LAGS THE **CURRENT** (I) BY 90 DEGREES. THE VOLTAGE ACROSS THE **INDUCTOR** (L) LEADS THE CURRENT BY 90 DEGREES. THIS IS GIVEN BY THE WORD CIVIL, WHEN SPLIT INTO CIV AND VIL.

acacia any of a large group of shrubs and trees that includes the thorn trees of the African savanna and the gum arabic tree (*Acacia senegal*) of N Africa, and several North American species of the southwestern USA and Mexico. The hardy tree commonly known as acacia is the false acacia (*Robinia pseudacacia*, of the subfamily Papilionoideae). True acacias are found in warm regions of the world, particularly Australia. (Genus *Acacia*, family Leguminosae.)

A. dealbata is grown in the open air in some parts of France and the warmer European countries, and is remarkable for its clusters of fluffy, scented yellow flowers, sold by florists as mimosa. The leaves of the genus are normally bipinnate (leaflets on both sides of each stem and stems growing on both sides of a larger stem), and the flowers grow in a head.

acanthus herbaceous plant with handsome lobed leaves. Twenty species are found in the Mediterrranean region and Old World tropics, including bear's-breech (*Acanthus mollis*) whose leaves were used as a motif in classical architecture, especially on Corinthian columns. (Genus *Acanthus*, family Acanthaceae.)

accelerated freeze drying common method of food preservation. See ◊food technology.

acceleration rate of change of the velocity of a moving body. It is usually measured in metres per second per second (m s^{-2}) or feet per second per second (ft s^{-2}). Because velocity is a ◊vector quantity (possessing both magnitude and direction) a body travelling at constant speed may be said to be accelerating if its direction of motion changes. According to Newton's second law of motion, a body will accelerate only if it is acted upon by an unbalanced, or resultant, ◊force.

Acceleration due to gravity is the acceleration of a body falling freely under the influence of the Earth's gravitational field; it varies slightly at different latitudes and altitudes. The value adopted internationally for gravitational acceleration is 9.806 m s^{-2}/32.174 ft s^{-2}.

acceleration, secular in astronomy, the continuous and nonperiodic change in orbital velocity of one body around another, or the axial rotation period of a body.

An example is the axial rotation of the Earth. This is gradually slowing down owing to the gravitational effects of the Moon and the resulting production of tides, which have a frictional effect on the Earth. However, the angular ◊momentum of the Earth–Moon system is maintained, because the momentum lost by the Earth is passed to the Moon. This results in an increase in the Moon's orbital period and a consequential moving away from the Earth. The overall effect is that the Earth's axial rotation period is increasing by about 15 millionths of a second a year, and the Moon is receding from the Earth at about 4 cm/1.5 in a year.

acceleration, uniform in physics, acceleration in which the velocity of a body changes by equal amounts in successive time intervals. Uniform acceleration is represented by a straight line on a ◊speed–time graph.

accelerator in physics, a device to bring charged particles (such as protons and electrons) up to high speeds and energies, at which they can be of use in industry, medicine, and pure physics. At low energies, accelerated particles can be used to produce the image on a television screen and generate X-rays (by means of a ◊cathode-ray tube), destroy tumour cells, or kill bacteria. When high-energy particles collide with other particles, the fragments formed reveal the nature of the fundamental forces.

The first accelerators used high voltages (produced by ◊van de Graaff generators) to generate a strong, unvarying electric field. Charged particles were accelerated as they passed through the electric field. However, because the voltage produced by a generator is limited, these accelerators were replaced by machines where the particles passed through regions of alternating electric fields, receiving a succession of small pushes to accelerate them.

The first of these accelerators was the **linear accelerator** or **linac**. The linac consists of a line of metal tubes, called drift tubes, through which the particles travel. The particles are accelerated by electric fields in the gaps between the drift tubes.

Another way of making repeated use of an electric field is to bend the path of a particle into a circle so that it passes repeatedly through the same electric field. The first accelerator to use this idea was the **cyclotron** pioneered in the early 1930s by US physicist Ernest Lawrence. A cyclotron consists of an electromagnet with two hollow metal semicircular structures, called dees, supported between the poles of an electromagnet. Particles such as protons are introduced at the centre of the machine and travel outwards in a spiral path, being accelerated by an oscillating electric field each time they pass through the gap between the dees. Cyclotrons can accelerate particles up to energies of 25 MeV (25 million electron volts); to produce higher energies, new techniques are needed.

In the ◊synchrotron, particles travel in a circular path of constant radius, guided by electromagnets. The strengths of the electromagnets are varied to keep the particles on an accurate path. Electric fields at points around the path accelerate the particles.

ACCELERATOR PHYSICS PAGE

http://www-laacg.atdiv.lanl.gov/accphys.html

Virtual library dedicated to accelerator physics, with pages on design and components, as well as direct links to laboratories throughout the world.

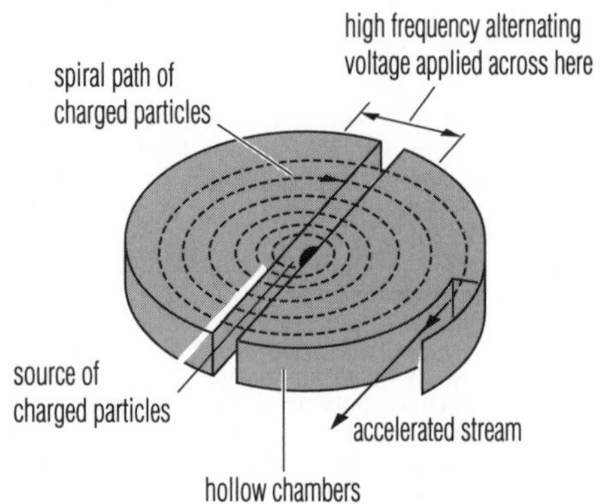

***accelerator** The cyclotron, an early accelerator, consisted of two D-shaped hollow chambers enclosed in a vacuum. An alternating voltage was applied across the gap between the hollows. Charged particles spiralled outward from the centre, picking up energy and accelerating each time they passed through the gap.*

Early accelerators directed the particle beam onto a stationary target; large modern accelerators usually collide beams of particles that are travelling in opposite directions. This arrangement doubles the effective energy of the collision.

The world's most powerful accelerator is the 2 km/1.25 mi diameter machine at ◊Fermilab near Batavia, Illinois, USA. This machine, the Tevatron, accelerates protons and antiprotons and then collides them at energies up to a thousand billion electron volts (or 1 TeV, hence the name of the machine). The largest accelerator is the ◊Large Electron Positron Collider at ◊CERN near Geneva, which has a circumference of 27 km/16.8 mi around which electrons and positrons are accelerated before being allowed to collide. The world's longest linac is also a colliding beam machine: the Stanford Linear Collider, in California, in which electrons and positrons are accelerated along a straight track, 3.2 km/2 mi long, and then steered to a head-on collision with other particles, such as protons and neutrons. Such experiments have been instrumental in revealing that protons and neutrons are made up of smaller elementary particles called ◊quarks.

accelerator board type of ◊expansion board that makes a computer run faster. It usually contains an additional processor (see ◊central processing unit).

accelerometer apparatus, either mechanical or electromechanical, for measuring ◊acceleration or deceleration – that is, the rate of increase or decrease in the ◊velocity of a moving object.

The mechanical types have a spring-supported mass with a damper system, with indication of acceleration on a scale on which a light beam is reflected from a mirror on the mass. The electromechanical types use (1) a slide wire, (2) a strain gauge, (3) variable inductance, or (4) a piezoelectric or similar device that produces electrically measurable effects of acceleration.

Accelerometers are used to measure the efficiency of the braking systems on road and rail vehicles; those used in aircraft and spacecraft can determine accelerations in several directions simultaneously. There are also accelerometers for detecting vibrations in machinery.

acceptable use in computing, set of rules enforced by a service provider or backbone network restricting the use to which their facilities may be put. Every organization on the Internet has its own **acceptable use policy** (AUP); schools, for example, may ban the use of their facilities to find or download pornography from the Internet.

Originally, when the Internet was publicly funded, acceptable use banned advertising, and although funding is moving to private enterprise and advertising has now become commonplace, some service providers still do not allow commercial exploitation. The US National Science Foundation's NSFnet, for example, imposes a strict AUP to prohibit commercial organizations from using the network.

access in computing, the way in which ◊file access is provided so that the data can be stored, retrieved, or updated by the computer.

access privilege in computer networking, authorized access to files. The ability to authorize or restrict access selectively to files or directories, including separate privileges such as reading, writing, or changing data, is a key element in computer security systems. This kind of system ensures that, for example, a company's employees cannot read its personnel files or alter payroll data unless they work for the appropriate departments, or that freelance or temporary staff can be given access to some areas of the computer system but not others.

Certain types of restrictions may be applied by users themselves to files on their own desktop machines, such as private e-mail; others may be granted only by the system administrator.

On all client–server systems, all data, even private e-mail and personal letters, can be accessed by the system administrator, who needs system-wide privileges in order to manage the network properly. Data which is encrypted, however, will not be readable unless the system administrator knows the user's individual password.

The privacy of employee e-mail is a contentious issue, as many employees assume their e-mail is private, while many companies presume ownership of all data stored on company systems.

access provider in computing, another term for ◊Internet Service Provider.

access time or ***reaction time*** in computing, the time taken by a computer, after an instruction has been given, to read from or write to ◊memory.

acclimation or ***acclimatization*** the physiological changes induced in an organism by exposure to new environmental conditions. When humans move to higher altitudes, for example, the number of red blood cells rises to increase the oxygen-carrying capacity of the blood in order to compensate for the lower levels of oxygen in the air.

In evolutionary terms, the ability to acclimate is an important adaptation as it allows the organism to cope with the environmental changes occurring during its lifetime.

accommodation in biology, the ability of the ◊eye to focus on near or far objects by changing the shape of the lens.

For an object to be viewed clearly its image must be precisely focused on the retina, the light-sensitive layer of cells at the rear of the eye. Close objects can be seen when the lens takes up a more spherical shape, distant objects when the lens is flattened. These changes in shape are caused by the movement of ligaments attached to a ring of ciliary muscles lying beneath the iris.

From about the age of 40, the lens in the human eye becomes less flexible, causing the defect of vision known as **presbyopia** or lack of accommodation. People with this defect need different spectacles for reading and distance vision.

account on a computer network, a ◊user-ID issued to a specific individual to enable access to the system for purposes of billing, administration, or private messaging. The existence of accounts allows system administrators to assign ◊access privileges to specific individuals (which in turn enables those individuals to receive private messages such as e-mail) and also to track the use of the computer system and its resources.

On commercial systems such as CompuServe or America Online, users are given an account when they dial up the system and give the number of a credit card to which usage may be billed. On other types of systems, accounts are typically issued by the system administrator. In all cases, accounts are protected by a password, which should be carefully chosen.

accretion in astrophysics, a process by which an object gathers up surrounding material by gravitational attraction, so simultaneously increasing in mass and releasing gravitational energy. Accretion on to compact objects such as ◊white dwarfs, ◊neutron stars and ◊black holes can release large amounts of gravitational energy, and is believed to be the power source for active galaxies. Accreted material falling towards a star may form a swirling disc of material known as an ◊accretion disc that can be a source of X-rays.

accretion disc in astronomy, a flattened ring of gas and dust orbiting an object in space, such as a star or ◊black hole. The orbiting material is accreted (gathered in) from a neighbouring object such as another star. Giant accretion discs are thought to exist at the centres of some galaxies and ◊quasars.

If the central object of the accretion disc has a strong gravitational field, as with a neutron star or a black hole, gas falling onto the accretion disc releases energy, which heats the gas to extreme temperatures and emits short-wavelength radiation, such as X-rays.

accumulator in computing, a special register, or memory location, in the ◊arithmetic and logic unit of the computer processor. It is used to hold the result of a calculation temporarily or to store data that is being transferred.

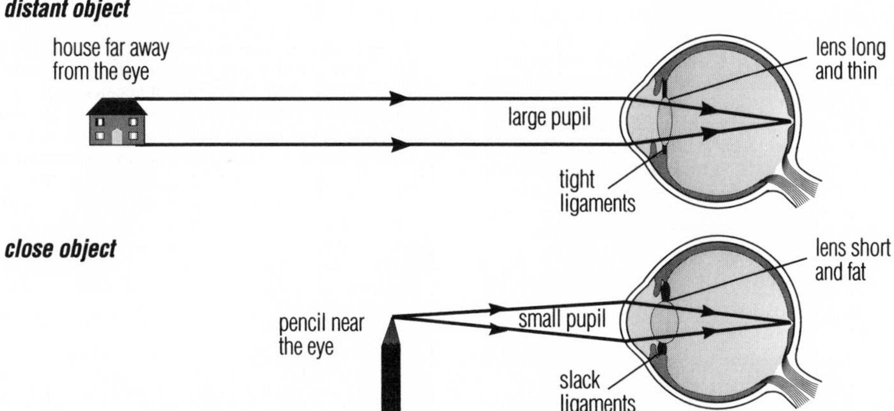

accommodation *The mechanism by which the shape of the lens in the eye is changed so that clear images of objects, whether distant or near, can be focused on the retina.*

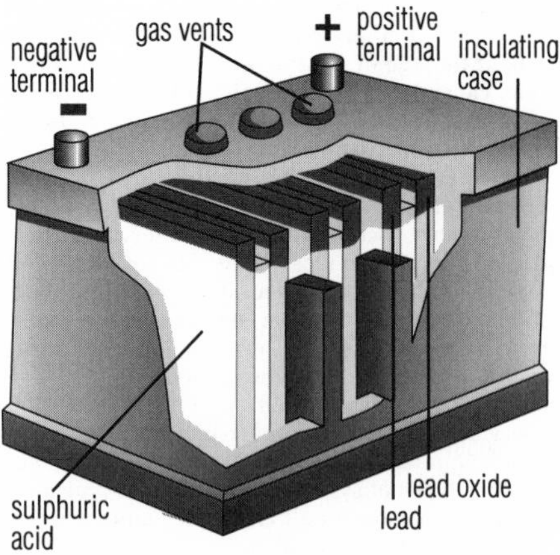

accumulator *The lead–acid car battery is a typical example of an accumulator. The battery has a set of grids immersed in a sulphuric acid electrolyte. One set of grids is made of lead (Pb) and acts as the anode and the other set made of lead oxide (PbO_2) acts as the cathode.*

accumulator in electricity, a storage ◊battery – that is, a group of rechargeable secondary cells. A familiar example is the lead–acid car battery.

An ordinary 12-volt car battery consists of six lead–acid cells which are continually recharged when the motor is running by the car's alternator or dynamo. It has electrodes of lead and lead oxide in an electrolyte of sulphuric acid. Another common type of accumulator is the 'nife' or Ni Fe cell, which has electrodes of nickel and iron in a potassium hydroxide electrolyte.

accuracy in mathematics, a measure of the precision of a number. The degree of accuracy depends on how many figures or decimal places are used in rounding off the number. For example, the result of a calculation or measurement (such as 13.429314) might be rounded off to three decimal places (13.429), to two decimal places (13.43), to one decimal place (13.4), or to the nearest whole number (13). The first answer is more accurate than the second, the second more accurate than the third, and so on.

Accuracy also refers to a range of errors. For example, an accuracy of ± 5% means that a value may lie between 95% and 105% of a given answer.

acer group of over 115 related species of trees and shrubs of the temperate regions of the northern hemisphere, many of them popular garden specimens. They include ◊sycamore and ◊maple. Some species have pinnate leaves (leaflets either side of a stem), including the box elder (*Acer negundo*) of North America. (Genus *Acer*.)

That is the essence of science: ask an impertinent question, and you are on the way to a pertinent answer.

JACOB BRONOWSKI Polish-born scientist, broadcaster, and writer. *Ascent of Man*

acesulfame-K noncarbohydrate sweetener that is up to 300 times as sweet as sugar. It is used in soft drinks and desserts.

acetaldehyde common name for ◊ethanal.

acetate common name for ◊ethanoate.

acetic acid common name for ◊ethanoic acid.

acetone common name for ◊propanone.

acetylcholine (ACh) chemical that serves as a ◊neuro-transmitter, communicating nerve impulses between the cells of the nervous system. It is largely associated with the transmission of impulses across the ◊synapse (junction) between nerve and muscle cells, causing the muscles to contract.

ACh is produced in the synaptic knob (a swelling at the end of a nerve cell) and stored in vesicles until a nerve impulse triggers its discharge across the synapse. When the ACh reaches the membrane of the receiving cell it binds with a specific site and brings about depolarization – a reversal of the electric charge on either side of the membrane – causing a fresh impulse (in nerve cells) or a contraction (in muscle cells). Its action is shortlived because it is quickly destroyed by the enzyme cholinesterase.

Anticholinergic drugs have a number of uses in medicine to block the action of ACh, thereby disrupting the passage of nerve impulses and relaxing certain muscles, for example in premedication before surgery.

acetylene common name for ◊ethyne.

acetylsalicylic acid chemical name for the painkilling drug ◊aspirin.

achene dry, one-seeded ◊fruit that develops from a single ◊ovary and does not split open to disperse the seed. Achenes commonly occur in groups – for example, the fruiting heads of buttercup *Ranunculus* and clematis. The outer surface may be smooth, spiny, ribbed, or tuberculate, depending on the species.

Achernar or ***Alpha Eridani*** brightest star in the constellation Eridanus, and the ninth brightest star in the sky. It is a hot, luminous, blue star with a true luminosity 250 times that of the Sun. It is 125 light years away.

Achilles tendon tendon at the back of the ankle attaching the calf muscles to the heel bone. It is one of the largest tendons in the human body, and can resist great tensional strain, but is sometimes ruptured by contraction of the muscles in sudden extension of the foot.

Ancient surgeons regarded wounds in this tendon as fatal, probably because of the Greek legend of Achilles, which relates how the mother of the hero Achilles dipped him when an infant into the river Styx, so that he became invulnerable except for the heel by which she held him.

achondrite type of ◊meteorite. They comprise about 15% of all meteorites and lack the **chondrules** (silicate spheres) found in ◊chondrites.

achromatic lens combination of lenses made from materials of different refractive indexes, constructed in such a way as to minimize chromatic aberration (which in a single lens causes coloured fringes around images because the lens diffracts the different wavelengths in white light to slightly different extents).

acid compound that, in solution in an ionizing solvent (usually water), gives rise to hydrogen ions (H^+ or protons). In modern chemistry, acids are defined as substances that are proton donors and accept electrons to form ◊ionic bonds. Acids react with ◊bases to form salts, and they act as solvents. Strong acids are corrosive; dilute acids have a sour or sharp taste, although in some organic acids this may be partially masked by other flavour characteristics.

Acids can be detected by using coloured indicators such as ◊litmus and methyl orange. The strength of an acid is measured by its hydrogen-ion concentration, indicated by the ◊pH value. Acids are classified as monobasic, dibasic, tribasic, and so forth, according to the

To remember how to mix acid and water safely:

ADD ACID TO WATER, JUST AS YOU OUGHTA!

number of hydrogen atoms, replaceable by bases, in a molecule. The first known acid was vinegar (ethanoic or acetic acid). Inorganic acids include boric, carbonic, hydrochloric, hydrofluoric, nitric, phosphoric, and sulphuric. Organic acids include acetic, benzoic, citric, formic, lactic, oxalic, and salicylic, as well as complex substances such as ◊nucleic acids and ◊amino acids.

acidic oxide oxide of a ◊nonmetal. Acidic oxides are covalent compounds. Those that dissolve in water, such as sulphur dioxide, give acidic solutions.

$$SO_2 + H_2O \leftrightarrow H_2SO_{3(aq)} \leftrightarrow H^+_{(aq)} + HSO_3{}^-{}_{(aq)}$$

All acidic oxides react with alkalis to form salts.

$$CO_2 + NaOH \rightarrow NaHCO_3$$

acid rain acidic precipitation thought to be caused principally by the release into the atmosphere of sulphur dioxide (SO_2) and oxides of nitrogen. Sulphur dioxide is formed by the burning of fossil fuels, such as coal, that contain high quantities of sulphur; nitrogen oxides are contributed from various industrial activities and from car exhaust fumes.

Acid deposition occurs not only as wet precipitation (mist, snow, or rain), but also comes out of the atmosphere as dry particles or is absorbed directly by lakes, plants, and masonry as gases. Acidic gases can travel over 500 km/310 mi a day so acid rain can be considered an example of transboundary pollution.

Acid rain is linked with damage to and the death of forests and lake organisms in Scandinavia, Europe, and eastern North America. It also results in damage to buildings and statues. US and European power stations that burn fossil fuels release about 8 g/0.3 oz of sulphur dioxide and 3 g/0.1 oz of nitrogen oxides per kilowatt-hour.

ACID RAIN

http://www.environment-agency.gov.uk/s-enviro/states/3-2.html

Britain's Environmental Agency report on the environmental consequences of acid rain. This well-written article, supported by graphs and statistics, gives a good understanding of the scale of the problems caused by acid rain.

acid salt chemical compound formed by the partial neutralization of a dibasic or tribasic ◊acid (one that contains two or three hydrogen atoms). Although a salt, it contains replaceable hydrogen, so it may undergo the typical reactions of an acid. Examples are sodium hydrogen sulphate ($NaHSO_4$) and acid phosphates.

ack radio-derived term for 'acknowledge'. It is used on the Internet as a brief way of indicating agreement with or receipt of a message or instruction.

aclinic line the magnetic equator, an imaginary line near the Equator, where a compass needle balances horizontally, the attraction of the north and south magnetic poles being equal.

ACM abbreviation for the US ◊Association for Computing Machinery.

acne skin eruption, mainly occurring among adolescents and young adults, caused by inflammation of the sebaceous glands which secrete an oily substance (sebum), the natural lubricant of the skin. Sometimes the openings of the glands become blocked, causing the formation of pus-filled swellings. Teenage acne is seen mainly on the face, back, and chest.

There are other, less common types of acne, sometimes caused by contact with irritant chemicals (chloracne).

aconite or ***monkshood*** or ***wolfsbane*** herbaceous plant belonging to the buttercup family, with hooded blue–mauve flowers, native to

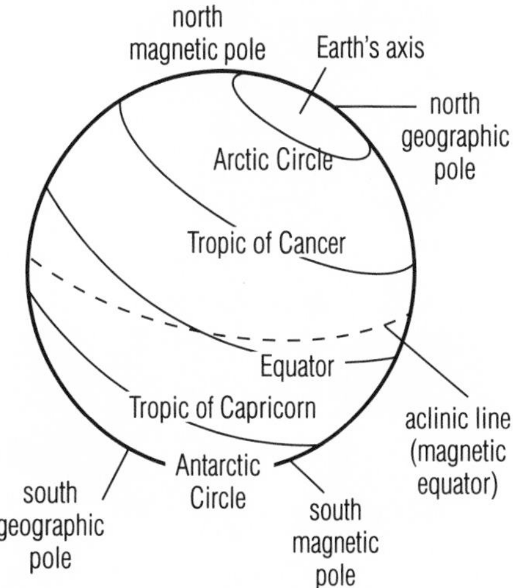

***aclinic line** The magnetic equator, or the line at which the attraction of both magnetic poles is equal. Along the aclinic line, a compass needle swinging vertically will settle in a horizontal position.*

Europe and Asia. It produces aconitine, a poison with pain-killing and sleep-inducing properties. (*Aconitum napellus,* family Ranunculaceae.)

There are about 100 species throughout the northern temperate regions, all hardy ◊herbaceous plants containing poison. Summer aconite (*Aconitum uncinatum*) is a common North American flower. Winter aconite (*Eranthis hyemalis*) belongs to another genus of the buttercup family; it has yellow buttercuplike flowers with six petals which appear in February and March; the leaves follow later.

acorn fruit of the ◊oak tree, a ◊nut growing in a shallow cup.

Acorn UK computer manufacturer. In the early 1980s, Acorn produced a series of home microcomputers, including the Electron and the Atom. Its most successful computer, the BBC Microcomputer, was produced in conjunction with the BBC. Subsequent computers (the Master and the Archimedes) were less successful. Acorn was rescued by the Italian company Olivetti in 1985 but it has since sold off its majority shareholding.

acouchi any of several small South American rodents, genus *Myoprocta.* They have white-tipped tails, and are smaller relatives of the ◊agouti.

acoustic coupler device that enables computer data to be transmitted and received through a normal telephone handset; the handset rests on the coupler to make the connection. A small speaker within the device is used to convert the computer's digital output data into sound signals, which are then picked up by the handset and transmitted through the telephone system. At the receiving telephone, a second acoustic coupler or modem converts the sound signals back into digital data for input into a computer.

Unlike a ◊modem, an acoustic coupler does not require direct connection to the telephone system. However, interference from background noise means that the quality of transmission is poorer than with a modem, and more errors are likely to arise.

acoustic ohm c.g.s. unit of acoustic impedance (the ratio of the sound pressure on a surface to the sound flux through the surface). It is analogous to the ohm as the unit of electrical ◊impedance.

acoustics in general, the experimental and theoretical science of sound and its transmission; in particular, that branch of the science that has to do with the phenomena of sound in a particular space such as a room or theatre. In architecture, the sound-reflecting character of an internal space.

Acoustical engineering is concerned with the technical control of sound, and involves architecture and construction, studying control

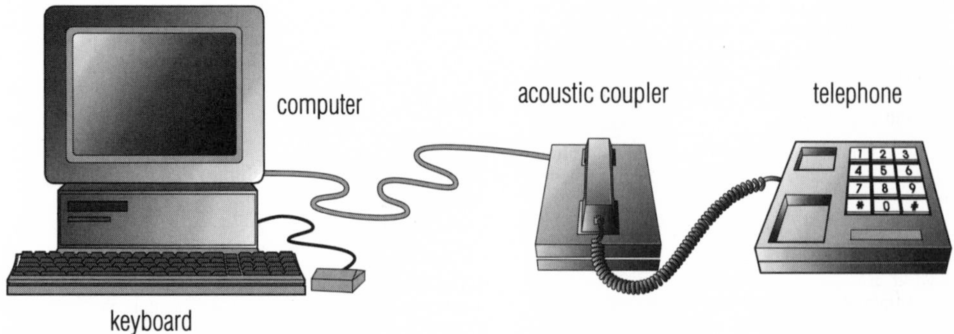

acoustic coupler *The acoustic coupler converts digital output from a computer to sound signals that can be sent via a telephone line.*

of vibration, soundproofing, and the elimination of noise. It also includes all forms of sound recording and reinforcement, the hearing and perception of sounds, and hearing aids.

ACOUSTIC ILLUSIONS

http://www.uni-bonn.de/~uzs083/akustik.html

Dedicated to the Shepard effect: a scale that gives the listener the impression of an endlessly rising melody, when in fact the pitch of the tones does not rise. Sound files illustrate this, and accompany an account of an experiment in which the Shepard effect was applied to J S Bach's *Das Musikalische Opfer/Musical Offering.*

acquired character feature of the body that develops during the lifetime of an individual, usually as a result of repeated use or disuse, such as the enlarged muscles of a weightlifter.

French naturalist Jean Baptiste ◊Lamarck's theory of evolution assumed that acquired characters were passed from parent to offspring. Modern evolutionary theory does not recognize the inheritance of acquired characters because there is no reliable scientific evidence that it occurs, and because no mechanism is known whereby bodily changes can influence the genetic material. The belief that this does not occur is known as ◊central dogma.

acquired immune deficiency syndrome full name for the disease ◊AIDS.

acre traditional English land measure equal to 4,840 square yards (4,047 sq m/0.405 ha). Originally meaning a field, it was the size that a yoke of oxen could plough in a day.

As early as Edward I's reign, (1272–1307) the acre was standardized by statute for official use, although local variations in Ireland, Scotland, and some English counties continued. It may be subdivided into 160 square rods (one square rod equalling 25.29 sq m/30.25 sq yd).

acre-foot unit sometimes used to measure large volumes of water, such as the capacity of a reservoir (equal to its area in acres multiplied by its average depth in feet). One acre-foot equals 1,233.5 cu m/43,560 cu ft or the amount of water covering one acre to a depth of one foot.

acridine $C_{13}H_9N$, a heterocyclic organic compound that occurs in coal tar. It is crystalline, melting at 108°C/226.4°F. Acridine is extracted by dilute acids but can also be obtained synthetically. It is used to make dyes and drugs.

Acrobat program developed by Adobe to allow users of different types of computers to view the same documents complete with graphics and layout. Launched in 1993, Acrobat was designed to get around the limitations of existing systems when transferring data between different types of computers, which typically required all formatting to be stripped from the documents. The program to generate the code that makes the documents transferable with formatting intact must be bought, but the program for reading the documents is available free of charge.

By 1996 Acrobat was in common use on the World Wide Web for distributing certain types of company documents, and the program had been enhanced to integrate with Web ◊browsers.

acrolein or ***acraldehyde*** CH_2:CHCHO, a colourless liquid formed during the partial combustion of fats. It is an unsaturated aldehyde, boils at 52°C/125.6°F, has an irritating action on the skin, and its vapours cause a copious flow of tears. It was used in gas form as a chemical weapon in World War I by the French under the codename *Papite.*

acronym abbreviation that can be pronounced as a word, for example **RISC** (Reduced Instruction Set Computer) and **MUD** (multi-user dungeon). People in the computer industry often incorrectly refer to all abbreviations as acronyms. Both are frequently used as industry jargon and as shorthand to save typing on the Net. See also ◊TLA (three letter acronym).

acrylic acid common name for ◊propenoic acid.

ACTH (abbreviation for ***adrenocorticotrophic hormone***) ◊hormone secreted by the anterior lobe of the ◊pituitary gland. It controls the production of corticosteroid hormones by the ◊adrenal gland and is commonly produced as a response to stress.

actinide any of a series of 15 radioactive metallic chemical elements with atomic numbers 89 (actinium) to 103 (lawrencium). Elements 89 to 95 occur in nature; the rest of the series are synthesized elements only. Actinides are grouped together because of their chemical similarities (for example, they are all bivalent), the properties differing only slightly with atomic number. The series is set out in a band in the ◊periodic table of the elements, as are the ◊lanthanides.

actinium ***Greek aktis 'ray'*** white, radioactive, metallic element, the first of the actinide series, symbol Ac, atomic number 89, relative atomic mass 227; it is a weak emitter of high-energy alpha particles.

Actinium occurs with uranium and radium in ◊pitchblende and other ores, and can be synthesized by bombarding radium with neutrons. The longest-lived isotope, Ac-227, has a half-life of 21.8 years (all the other isotopes have very short half-lives). Chemically, it is exclusively trivalent, resembling in its reactions the lanthanides and the other actinides. Actinium was discovered 1899 by the French chemist André Debierne (1874–1949).

actinium K original name of the radioactive element ◊francium, given 1939 by its discoverer, the French scientist Marguerite Perey (1909–1975).

action and reaction in physical mechanics, equal and opposite forces which act together. For example, the pressure of expanding gases from the burning of fuel in a rocket engine produces an equal and opposite reaction, which causes the rocket to move. This is Newton's third law of motion (see ◊Newton's laws of motion.

action potential in biology, a change in the ◊potential difference (voltage) across the membrane of a nerve cell when an impulse passes along it. A change in potential (from about –60 to +45 millivolts) accompanies the passage of sodium and potassium ions across the membrane.

activation analysis in analytical chemistry, a technique used to reveal the presence and amount of minute impurities in a substance or element. A sample of a material that may contain traces of a certain element is irradiated with ◊neutrons, as in a reactor. Gamma rays emitted by the material's radioisotope have unique energies and relative intensities, similar to the spectral lines from a luminous gas. Measurements and interpretation of the gamma-ray spectrum, using data from standard samples for comparison, provide information on the amount of impurities present.

activation energy in chemistry, the energy required in order to start a chemical reaction. Some elements and compounds will react together merely by bringing them into contact (spontaneous reaction). For others it is necessary to supply energy in order to start the reaction, even if there is ultimately a net output of energy. This initial energy is the activation energy.

active galaxy in astronomy, a type of galaxy that emits vast quantities of energy from a small region at its centre called the active galactic nucleus (AGN). Active galaxies are subdivided into ◊radio galaxies, ◊Seyfert galaxies, ◊BL Lacertae objects, and ◊quasars.

Active galaxies are thought to contain black holes with a mass some 108 times that of the Sun, drawing stars and interstellar gas towards it in a process of accretion. The gravitational energy released by the in-falling material is the power source for the AGN. Some of the energy may appear as a pair of opposed jets emerging from the nucleus. The orientation of the jets to the line of sight and their interaction with surrounding material determines the type of active galaxy that is seen by observers. See also ◊starburst galaxy.

active matrix LCD (or ***TFT (thin film transistor) display***) type of colour ◊liquid crystal display (LCD) commonly used in laptop computers. Active matrix displays are made by sandwiching a film containing tiny transistors between two plates of glass. They achieve high contrast and brightness by applying voltage across the horizontal and vertical wires between the two glass plates, balanced by using a small transistor inside each ◊pixel to amplify the voltage when so instructed.

To create ◊VGA colour, each pixel must also integrate colour filters; essentially, each logical pixel is made up of three physical pixels, one for each of red, blue, and green, the primary colours of light. The consequence of this – and the reason active matrix screens are such expensive options – is that a VGA display requires approximately a billion transistors, and even minute imperfections render the screens useless for computing purposes. A high refresh rate means that the screens are extremely responsive, so the cursor does not disappear as a mouse is moved quickly across the screen.

Active matrix displays began to appear on laptops in 1992, and are expected by many to eventually replace the older cathode-ray technology for television sets as well as display monitors.

active transport in cells, the use of energy to move substances, usually molecules or ions, across a membrane.

Energy is needed because movement occurs against a concentration gradient, with substances being passed into a region where they are already present in significant quantities. Active transport thus differs from ◊diffusion, the process by which substances move towards a region where they are in lower concentration, as when oxygen passes into the blood vessels of the lungs. Diffusion requires no input of energy.

active window on graphical operating systems, the ◊window containing the program actually in use at any given time. Usually active windows are easily identified by the use of colour schemes which assign a different colour to the window's title bar (a thin strip along the top of each window bearing the name of the window's specific program or function) from that of the title bars of inactive windows.

On a true ◊multitasking system, each window may represent an active program, but the active window is the one into which the user may enter data. A user might, for example, be typing a document into a word processor in the active window while in the background other programs back up files or sort data in a database.

ActiveX in computing, Microsoft's umbrella name for a collection of technologies used to create applications that run on the World Wide Web or on ◊intranets.

ActiveX is based on DCOM (Microsoft's Distributed Component Object Model) and uses ActiveX Controls, which are a lightweight version of OLE (◊object linking and embedding) Custom Controls or OCXs. It also includes scripting languages such as JavaScript and VB Script (Visual Basic Script), and a ◊Java Virtual Machine (JVM).

ActiveX was announced in 1996, and later that year was handed to the ◊Open Group, to manage its development and turn it into a cross-platform industry standard.

activity in physics, the number of particles emitted in one second by a radioactive source. The term is used to describe the radioactivity or the potential danger of that source. The unit of activity is the becquerel (Bq), named after the French physicist Henri Becquerel.

activity series in chemistry, alternative name for ◊reactivity series.

acupuncture in alternative medicine, a system of inserting long, thin metal needles into the body at predetermined points to relieve pain, as an anaesthetic in surgery, and to assist healing. The needles are rotated manually or electrically. The method, developed in ancient China and increasingly popular in the West, is thought to work by stimulating the brain's own painkillers, the ◊endorphins.

Acupuncture is based on a theory of physiology that posits a network of life-energy pathways, or 'meridians', in the human body and some 800 'acupuncture points' where metal needles may be inserted to affect the energy flow for purposes of preventative or remedial therapy or to produce a local anaesthetic effect. Numerous studies and surveys have attested the efficacy of the method, which is widely conceded by orthodox practitioners despite the lack of an acceptable scientific explanation.

ACUPUNCTURE.COM

http://acupuncture.com/

Thorough introduction to the alternative world of acupuncture with descriptions of the main notions and powers of herbology, yoga, Qi Gong, and Chinese nutrition. Consumers are given access to lists of practitioners and an extensive section on acupuncture research. Practitioners can browse through journal listings and the latest industry news and announcements.

acute in medicine, term used to describe a disease of sudden and severe onset which resolves quickly; for example, pneumonia and meningitis. In contrast, a **chronic** condition develops and remains over a long period.

acute angle an angle between 0° and 90°; that is, an amount of turn that is less than a quarter of a circle.

Ada high-level computer-programming language, developed and owned by the US Department of Defense, designed for use in situations in which a computer directly controls a process or machine, such as a military aircraft. The language took more than five years to specify, and became commercially available only in the late 1980s. It is named after English mathematician Ada Augusta Byron.

adaptation ***Latin adaptare 'to fit to'*** in biology, any change in the structure or function of an organism that allows it to survive and reproduce more effectively in its environment. In ◊evolution, adaptation is thought to occur as a result of random variation in the genetic make-up of organisms coupled with ◊natural selection. Species become extinct when they are no longer adapted to their environment – for instance, if the climate suddenly becomes colder.

adaptive radiation in evolution, the formation of several species, with ◊adaptations to different ways of life, from a single ancestral type. Adaptive radiation is likely to occur whenever members of a species migrate to a new habitat with unoccupied ecological niches. It is thought that the lack of competition in such niches allows sections of the migrant population to develop new adaptations, and eventually to become new species.

The colonization of newly formed volcanic islands has led to the development of many unique species. The 13 species of Darwin's finch on the Galápagos Islands, for example, are probably descended from a single species from the South American mainland. The parent stock evolved into different species that now occupy a range of diverse niches.

ADC in electronics, abbreviation for ◊analogue-to-digital converter.

addax light-coloured ◊antelope *Addax nasomaculatus* of the family Bovidae. It lives in N Africa around the Sahara Desert where it exists on scanty vegetation without drinking. It is about 1.1 m/3.5 ft at the shoulder, and both sexes have spirally twisted horns. Its hooves are broad, enabling it to move easily on soft sand.

adder electronic circuit in a computer or calculator that carries out the process of adding two binary numbers. A separate adder is needed for each pair of binary ◊bits to be added. Such circuits are essential components of a computer's ◊arithmetic and logic unit (ALU).

adder ***Anglo-Saxon naedre 'serpent'*** European venomous snake, the common ◊viper *Vipera berus*. Growing on average to about 60 cm/24 in in length, it has a thick body, triangular head, a characteristic V-shaped mark on its head and, often, zigzag markings along the back. It feeds on small mammals and lizards. The puff adder *Bitis arietans* is a large, yellowish, thick-bodied viper up to 1.6 m/5 ft long, living in Africa and Arabia.

addiction state of dependence caused by habitual use of drugs, alcohol, or other substances. It is characterized by uncontrolled craving, tolerance, and symptoms of withdrawal when access is denied. Habitual use produces changes in body chemistry and treatment must be geared to a gradual reduction in dosage.

Initially, only opium and its derivatives (morphine, heroin, codeine) were recognized as addictive, but many other drugs, whether therapeutic (for example, tranquillizers) or recreational (such as cocaine and alcohol), are now known to be addictive.

Research points to a genetic predisposition to addiction; environment and psychological make-up are other factors. Although physical addiction always has a psychological element, not all psychological dependence is accompanied by physical dependence. A carefully controlled withdrawal programme can reverse the chemical changes of habituation. Cure is difficult because of the many other factors contributing to addiction.

adding machine device for adding (and usually subtracting, multiplying, and dividing) numbers, operated mechanically or electromechanically; now largely superseded by electronic ◊calculators.

addition in arithmetic, the operation of combining two numbers to form a sum; thus, 7 + 4 = 11. It is one of the four basic operations of arithmetic (the others are subtraction, multiplication, and division).

addition polymerization ◊polymerization reaction in which a single monomer gives rise to a single polymer, with no other reaction products.

addition reaction chemical reaction in which the atoms of an element or compound react with a double bond or triple bond in an organic compound by opening up one of the bonds and becoming attached to it, for example

$$CH_2{=}CH_2 + HCl \rightarrow CH_3CH_2Cl$$

An example is the addition of hydrogen atoms to ◊unsaturated compounds in vegetable oils to produce margarine. Addition reactions are used to make useful polymers from ◊alkenes.

add-on small program written to extend the features of a larger one. The earliest successful add-on for personal computer users in the UK was a small routine which allowed the original version of the spreadsheet Lotus 1-2-3 to print out a pound sign (£), something the program's US developers had thought unnecessary.

address in a computer memory, a number indicating a specific location.

At each address, a single piece of data can be stored. For microcomputers, this normally amounts to one ◊byte (enough to represent a single character, such as a letter or digit).

The maximum capacity of a computer memory depends on how many memory addresses it can have. This is normally measured in units of 1,024 bytes (known as kilobytes, or K).

address means of specifying either a computer or a person for the purpose of directing messages or other data across a network. Addressing e-mail to a person across the Internet involves typing in a string of characters such as 'userID@machine.system.type.country'. To send mail to Jane Doe, for example, whose user ID is 'janed' and who works at a company called Anyco in the UK, a user would type in 'janed@anyco.co.uk'.

Computers do not, however, use these named addresses in routing data. The portion after the address is known as a ◊domain, and the domain name is an easy-to-remember alias for a numbered address that is understandable by a computer. This numbered address, which takes a form similar to 127.000.000.001, is known as an IP (Internet protocol) address. Both the numbered IP addresses and domain names are assigned by the ◊InterNIC.

address book facility in most e-mail software that allows the storage and retrieval of e-mail addresses. Address books remove the problem of trying to remember a particular user's exact e-mail address – and it must be exact, as computers are unable to correct human errors. The best address-book software allows a user to type in just the correspondent's name and fills in the rest automatically.

address bus in computing, the electrical pathway or ◊bus used to select the route for any particular data item as it is moved from one part of a computer to another.

adenoids masses of lymphoid tissue, similar to ◊tonsils, located in the upper part of the throat, behind the nose. They are part of a child's natural defences against the entry of germs but usually shrink and disappear by the age of ten.

Adenoids may swell and grow, particularly if infected, and block the breathing passages. If they become repeatedly infected, they may be removed surgically (**adenoidectomy**), usually along with the tonsils.

ADH (abbreviation for ***antidiuretic hormone***) in biology, part of the system maintaining a correct salt/water balance in vertebrates.

Its release is stimulated by the ◊hypothalamus in the brain, which constantly receives information about salt concentration from receptors situated in the neck. In conditions of water shortage increased ADH secretion from the brain will cause more efficient conservation of water in the kidney, so that fluid is retained by the body. When an animal is able to take in plenty of water, decreased ADH secretion will cause the urine to become dilute and plentiful. The system allows the body to compensate for a varying fluid intake and maintain a correct balance.

Adhara star 600 light years from Earth. It plays a greater part in ionizing hydrogen in our region of the Galaxy than all the other 3 million stars lying closer to our local cloud, according to US astronomers in 1995.

Most of space contains unionized hydrogen in tiny amounts but Adhara is connected to our local cloud by a tunnel of almost hydrogen-free space. This means its ionizing radiation reaches our local cloud without obstacle.

The surface temperature of Adhara is 21,000 K (almost four times that of the Sun) and it is the brightest source of extreme UV radiation apart from the Sun.

ADHESIVE

The Florida leaf beetle *Hemisphaerota cyanen* has 60,000 adhesive pads on its feet. These enable it to resist the pull of a 2 g/0.07 oz weight (the equivalent of a human hanging on to 200 grand pianos). Ant predators are unable to move the beetle.

adhesive substance that sticks two surfaces together. Natural adhesives (glues) include gelatin in its crude industrial form (made from bones, hide fragments, and fish offal) and vegetable gums. Synthetic adhesives include thermoplastic and thermosetting resins, which are often stronger than the substances they join; mixtures of ◊epoxy resin and hardener that set by chemical reaction; and elastomeric (stretching) adhesives for flexible joints. Superglues are fast-setting adhesives used in very small quantities.

adiabatic in physics, a process that occurs without loss or gain of heat, especially the expansion or contraction of a gas in which a change takes place in the pressure or volume, although no heat is allowed to enter or leave.

adipose tissue type of ◊connective tissue of vertebrates that serves as an energy reserve, and also pads some organs. It is commonly called fat tissue, and consists of large spherical cells filled with fat. In mammals, major layers are in the inner layer of skin and around the kidneys and heart.

Fatty acids are transported to and from it via the blood system. An excessive amount of adipose tissue is developed in the course of some diseases, especially obesity.

adit in mining, a horizontal shaft from the surface to reach a mineral seam. It was a common method of mining in hilly districts, and was also used to drain water. The mineral-bearing rock is excavated by digging horizontally into the side of a valley. It is used, for example, in ◊coal mining.

adjacent angles pair of angles meeting at a common vertex (corner) and sharing a common arm. Two adjacent angles lying on the same side of a straight line add up to 180° and are said to be supplementary.

adjacent side in a ◊right-angled triangle, the side that is next to a given angle but is not the hypotenuse (the side opposite the right angle). The third side is the **opposite side** to the given angle.

admiral any of several species of butterfly in the same family (Nymphalidae) as the tortoiseshells. The red admiral *Vanessa atalanta,* wingspan 6 cm/2.5 in, is found worldwide in the northern hemisphere. It either hibernates, or migrates south each year from northern areas to subtropical zones.

Adobe US company specializing in graphics and desktop publishing software. Founded in 1982 by former Xerox PARC researchers John Warnock and Chuck Geschke, Adobe was the inventor of ◊PostScript and is the publisher of ◊Acrobat and Pagemaker. Adobe's enduring contribution to the computer industry is that it facilitated the use of computers to produce the fancy fonts without which desktop publishing would not have been possible.

Adobe Type Manager in computing, program from Adobe that manages fonts under Windows 3.1 and allows the printing and display of ◊PostScript fonts.

adolescence in the human life cycle, the period between the beginning of puberty and adulthood.

The four stages of man are infancy, childhood, adolescence and obsolescence.

ART LINKLETTER US writer and broadcaster.
Child's Garden of Misinformation

ADP abbreviation for ***adenosine diphosphate***, the chemical product formed in cells when ◊ATP breaks down to release energy.

adrenal gland or ***suprarenal gland*** triangular gland situated on top of the ◊kidney. The adrenals are soft and yellow, and consist of two parts: the cortex and medulla. The **cortex** (outer part) secretes various steroid hormones and other hormones that control salt and water metabolism and regulate the use of carbohydrates, proteins, and fats. The **medulla** (inner part) secretes the hormones adrenaline and noradrenaline which, during times of stress, cause the heart to beat faster and harder, increase blood flow to the heart and muscle cells, and dilate airways in the lungs, thereby delivering more oxygen to cells throughout the body and in general preparing the body for 'fight or flight'.

adrenaline or ***epinephrine*** hormone secreted by the medulla of the ◊adrenal glands. Adrenaline is synthesized from a closely related substance, noradrenaline, and the two hormones are released into the bloodstream in situations of fear or stress.

Adrenaline's action on the ◊liver raises blood-sugar levels by stimulating glucose production and its action on adipose tissue raises blood fatty-acid levels; it also increases the heart rate, increases blood flow to muscles, reduces blood flow to the skin with the production of sweat, widens the smaller breathing tubes (bronchioles) in the lungs, and dilates the pupils of the eyes.

adrenocorticotrophic hormone hormone secreted by the anterior lobe of the ◊pituitary gland; see ◊ACTH.

ADSL (abbreviation for ***asymmetric digital subscriber loop***) standard for transmitting video data through existing copper telephone wires. ADSL was developed by US telephone companies as a way of competing with cable television companies in delivering both TV and phone services. By 1996 it was developing into a possible alternative means for high-speed Internet access. ADSL is one of several types of digital subscriber loops (DSLs) in progress.

adsorption taking up of a gas or liquid at the surface of another substance, most commonly a solid (for example, activated charcoal adsorbs gases). It involves molecular attraction at the surface, and should be distinguished from ◊absorption (in which a uniform solution results from a gas or liquid being incorporated into the bulk structure of a liquid or solid).

Advanced Earth Observing Satellite (ADEOS) Japanese ◊remote sensing satellite launched August 1996. It gathers data on climate change, the environment, and Earth and ocean processes.

ADEOS is carrying eight instruments: Ocean Color and Temperature Scanner (OCTS); Advanced Visible and Near-Infrared Radiometer (AVNIR), Interferometric Monitor for Greenhouse Gases, Improved Limb Atmospheric Spectrometer (ILAS), Retroreflector in Space (RIS), Scatterometer (NSCAT), Total Ozone Mapping Spectrometer (TOMS), and Polarization and Directionality of the Earth's Reflectances (POLDER). NSCAT and TOMS are NASA instruments and POLDER is French, the rest are Japanese.

advanced gas-cooled reactor (AGR) type of ◊nuclear reactor used in W Europe. The AGR uses a fuel of enriched uranium dioxide in stainless-steel cladding and a moderator of graphite. Carbon dioxide gas is pumped through the reactor core to extract the heat produced by the ◊fission of the uranium. The heat is transferred to water in a steam generator, and the steam drives a turbogenerator to produce electricity.

Advanced Technology Attachment Packet Interface in computing, enhancement to integrated drive electronics (IDE), usually abbreviated to ◊ATAPI.

adventitious in botany, arising in an abnormal position, as in roots developing on the stem of a cutting or buds developing on roots.

advertising in computing, practice of paying to place information about a company's services or products in front of consumers. The earliest advertisers on the Net used to distribute their information as widely as possible in a practice quickly dubbed 'spamming'. By 1996 the practice of advertising on the World Wide Web was becoming commonplace.

Much Web advertising is sold in the same way as advertising in traditional media such as the print and broadcasting industries. Advertisers pay to place a small graphic known as an 'advertising banner' on a particular Web page in a spot (usually the top) where users are expected to see it clearly and click on it to follow the link to the advertiser's own site for more information. More sophisticated systems are under development which allow an advertising agency to track users' interests by watching which Web sites they visit and using that information to choose banners to insert which match those users' interests.

The US-based research company Jupiter Communications puts the value of online advertising at $940 million for 1997, up from $55 million in 1995. It is expected to reach $4.4 billion in 2000.

Aepyornis genus of large, extinct, flightless birds living in Madagascar until a few thousand years ago. Some stood 3 m/10 ft high and laid eggs with a volume of 43 l/9.5 gal. They had long, thick legs, four-toed feet, and rudimentary wings.

aerated water water that has had air (oxygen) blown through it. Such water supports aquatic life and prevents the growth of putrefying bacteria. Polluted waterways may be restored by artificial aeration.

aerenchyma plant tissue with numerous air-filled spaces between the cells. It occurs in the stems and roots of many aquatic plants where it aids buoyancy and facilitates transport of oxygen around the plant.

aerial or ***antenna*** in radio and television broadcasting, a conducting device that radiates or receives electromagnetic waves. The design of an aerial depends principally on the wavelength of the signal. Long waves (hundreds of metres in wavelength) may employ long wire aerials; short waves (several centimetres in wavelength) may employ rods and dipoles; microwaves may also use dipoles – often with reflectors arranged like a toast rack – or highly directional parabolic dish aerials. Because microwaves travel in straight lines, requiring line-of-sight communication, microwave aerials are usually located at the tops of tall masts or towers.

aerial oxidation in chemistry, a rection in which air is used to oxidize another substance, as in the contact process for the manufacture of sulphuric acid:

$$2SO_2 + O_2 \leftrightarrow 2SO_3$$

and in the ◊souring of wine.

aerobic in biology, term used to describe those organisms that require oxygen (usually dissolved in water) for the efficient release of energy contained in food molecules, such as glucose. They include almost all organisms (plants as well as animals) with the exception of certain bacteria, yeasts, and internal parasites.

Aerobic reactions occur inside every cell and lead to the formation of energy-rich ◊ATP, subsequently used by the cell for driving its metabolic processes. Oxygen is used to convert glucose to carbon dioxide and water, thereby releasing energy.

Most aerobic organisms die in the absence of oxygen, but certain organisms and cells, such as those found in muscle tissue, can function for short periods anaerobically (without oxygen). ◊Anaerobic organisms can survive without oxygen.

aerodynamics branch of fluid physics that studies the forces exerted by air or other gases in motion. Examples include the airflow around bodies moving at speed through the atmosphere (such as land vehicles, bullets, rockets, and aircraft), the behaviour of gas in engines and furnaces, air conditioning of buildings, the deposition of snow, the operation of air-cushion vehicles (hovercraft), wind loads on buildings and bridges, bird and insect flight, musical wind instruments, and meteorology. For maximum efficiency, the aim is usually to design the shape of an object to produce a streamlined flow, with a minimum of turbulence in the moving air. The behaviour of aerosols or the pollution of the atmosphere by foreign particles are other aspects of aerodynamics.

aerogel light, transparent, highly porous material composed of more than 90% air. Such materials are formed from silica, metal oxides, and organic chemicals, and are produced by drying gels – networks of linked molecules suspended in a liquid – so that air fills the spaces previously occupied by the liquid. They are excellent heat insulators and have unusual optical, electrical, and acoustic properties.

Aerogels were first produced by US scientist Samuel Kristler in the early 1930s by drying silica gels at high temperatures and pressures.

aeronautics science of travel through the Earth's atmosphere, including aerodynamics, aircraft structures, jet and rocket propulsion, and aerial navigation.

In **subsonic aeronautics** (below the speed of sound), aerodynamic forces increase at the rate of the square of the speed.

Transsonic aeronautics covers the speed range from just below to just above the speed of sound and is crucial to aircraft design. Ordinary sound waves move at about 1,225 kph/760 mph at sea level, and air in front of an aircraft moving slower than this is 'warned' by the waves so that it can move aside. However, as the flying speed approaches that of the sound waves, the warning is too late for the air to escape, and the aircraft pushes the air aside, creating shock waves, which absorb much power and create design problems. On the ground the shock waves give rise to a ◊sonic boom. It was once thought that the speed of sound was a speed limit to aircraft, and the term ◊sound barrier came into use.

Supersonic aeronautics concerns speeds above that of sound and in one sense may be considered a much older study than aeronautics itself, since the study of the flight of bullets, known as ◊ballistics, was undertaken soon after the introduction of firearms. **Hypersonics** is the study of airflows and forces at speeds above five times that of sound (Mach 5); for example, for guided missiles, space rockets, and advanced concepts such as ◊HOTOL (horizontal takeoff and landing). For all flight speeds streamlining is necessary to reduce the effects of air resistance.

Aeronautics is distinguished from astronautics, which is the science of travel through space. Astronavigation (navigation by reference to the stars) is used in aircraft as well as in ships and is a part of aeronautics.

aeroplane (US ***airplane***) powered heavier-than-air craft supported in flight by fixed wings. Aeroplanes are propelled by the thrust of a jet engine or airscrew (propeller). They must be designed aerodynamically, since streamlining ensures maximum flight efficiency. The Wright brothers flew the first powered plane (a biplane) in Kitty Hawk, North Carolina, USA in 1903. For the history of aircraft and aviation, see ◊flight.

design Efficient streamlining prevents the formation of shock waves over the body surface and wings, which would cause instability and power loss. The wing of an aeroplane has the cross-sectional shape of an aerofoil, being broad and curved at the front, flat underneath (sometimes slightly curved), curved on top, and tapered to a sharp point at the rear. It is so shaped that air passing above it is speeded up, reducing pressure below atmospheric pressure and air passing below it is slower thus increasing pressure and providing a double effect. This follows from ◊Bernoulli's principle and results in a force acting vertically upwards, called lift, which counters the plane's weight. In level flight lift equals weight. The wings develop sufficient lift to support the plane when they move quickly through the air. The thrust that causes propulsion comes from the reaction to the air stream accelerated backwards by the propeller or the gases shooting backwards from the jet exhaust. In flight the engine thrust must overcome the air resistance, or ◊drag. Drag depends on frontal area (for example, large, airliner; small, fighter plane) and shape (drag coefficient); in level

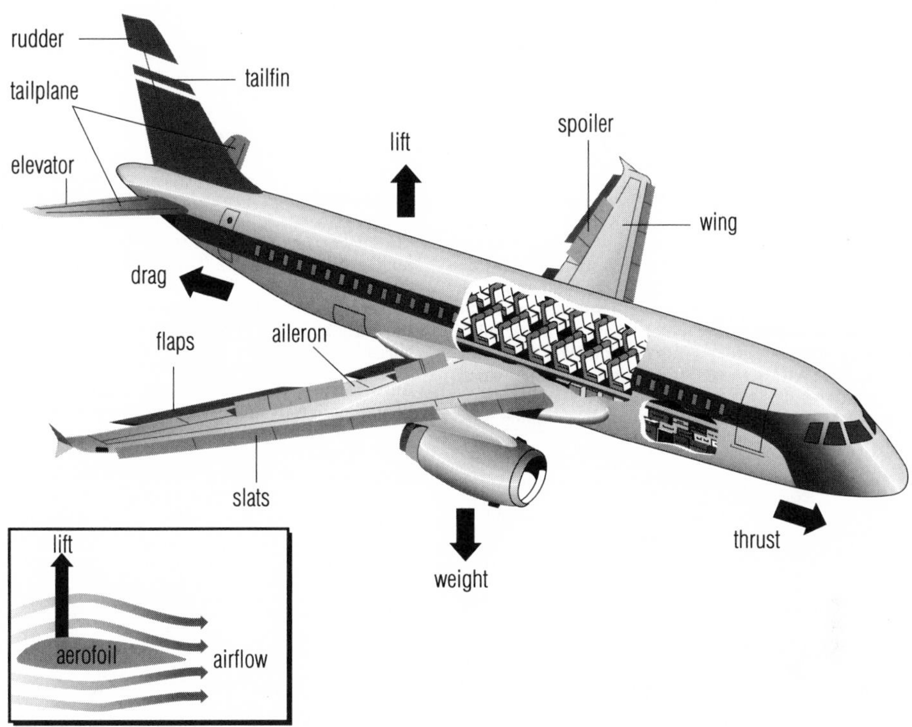

aeroplane *In flight, the forces on an aeroplane are lift, weight, drag, and thrust. The lift is generated by the air flow over the wings, which have the shape of an aerofoil. The engine provides the thrust. The drag results from the resistance of the air to the aeroplane's passage through it. Various moveable flaps on the wings and tail allow the aeroplane to be controlled. The rudder is moved to turn the aeroplane. The elevators allow the craft to climb or dive. The ailerons are used to bank the aeroplane while turning. The flaps, slats, and spoilers are used to reduce lift and speed during landing.*

flight, drag equals thrust. The drag is reduced by streamlining the plane, resulting in higher speed and reduced fuel consumption for a given power. Less fuel need be carried for a given distance of travel, so a larger payload (cargo or passengers) can be carried.

aerosol particles of liquid or solid suspended in a gas. Fog is a common natural example. Aerosol cans contain a substance such as scent or cleaner packed under pressure with a device for releasing it as a fine spray. Most aerosols used chlorofluorocarbons (CFCs) as propellants until these were found to cause destruction of the ◊ozone layer in the stratosphere.

The international community has agreed to phase out the use of CFCs, but most so-called 'ozone-friendly' aerosols also use ozone-depleting chemicals, although they are not as destructive as CFCs. Some of the products sprayed, such as pesticides, can be directly toxic to humans.

aestivation in zoology, a state of inactivity and reduced metabolic activity, similar to ◊hibernation, that occurs during the dry season in species such as lungfish and snails. In botany, the term is used to describe the way in which flower petals and sepals are folded in the buds. It is an important feature in ◊plant classification.

aether alternative form of ◊ether, the hypothetical medium once believed to permeate all of space.

AFD abbreviation for ***accelerated freeze drying***, a common method of food preservation. See ◊food technology.

affine geometry geometry that preserves parallelism and the ratios between intervals on any line segment.

affinity in chemistry, the force of attraction (see ◊bond) between atoms that helps to keep them in combination in a molecule. The

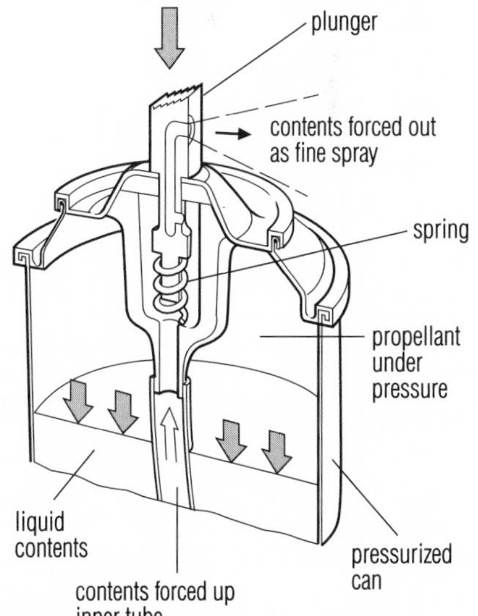

aerosol *The aerosol can produces a fine spray of liquid particles, called an aerosol. When the top button is pressed, a valve is opened, allowing the pressurized propellant in the can to force out a spray of the liquid contents. As the liquid sprays from the can, the small amount of propellant dissolved in the liquid vaporizes, producing a fine spray of small droplets.*

term is also applied to attraction between molecules, such as those of biochemical significance (for example, between ◊enzymes and substrate molecules). This is the basis for affinity ◊chromat-ography, by which biologically important compounds are separated.

The atoms of a given element may have a greater affinity for the atoms of one element than for another (for example, hydrogen has a great affinity for chlorine, with which it easily and rapidly combines to form hydrochloric acid, but has little or no affinity for argon).

afforestation planting of trees in areas that have not previously held forests. (**Reafforestation** is the planting of trees in deforested areas.) Trees may be planted (1) to provide timber and wood pulp; (2) to provide firewood in countries where this is an energy source; (3) to bind soil together and prevent soil erosion; and (4) to act as windbreaks.

Afforestation is a controversial issue because while many ancient woodlands of mixed trees are being lost, the new plantations consist almost exclusively of conifers. It is claimed that such plantations acidify the soil and conflict with the interests of ◊biodiversity (they replace more ancient and ecologically valuable species and do not sustain wildlife).

Afghan hound breed of fast hunting dog resembling the ◊saluki in build, though slightly smaller.

African palm squirrel smallish rodent *Epixerus ebii* living in dense tropical rainforest in western Africa and little known, having seldom been seen alive. The species has probably always been quite scarce, but is now threatened by rainforest destruction over a large part of its range.

African violet herbaceous plant from tropical central and E Africa, with velvety green leaves and scentless purple flowers. Different colours and double-flowered varieties have been bred. (*Saintpaulia ionantha,* family Gesneriaceae.)

afterbirth in mammals, the placenta, umbilical cord, and ruptured membranes, which become detached from the uterus and expelled soon after birth.

afterburning method of increasing the thrust of a gas turbine (jet) aeroplane engine by spraying additional fuel into the hot exhaust duct between the turbojet and the tailpipe where it ignites. Used for short-term increase of power during takeoff, or during combat in military aircraft.

afterimage persistence of an image on the retina of the eye after the object producing it has been removed. This leads to persistence of vision, a necessary phenomenon for the illusion of continuous movement in films and television. The term is also used for the persistence of sensations other than vision.

after-ripening process undergone by the seeds of some plants before germination can occur. The length of the after-ripening period in different species may vary from a few weeks to many months.

It helps seeds to germinate at a time when conditions are most favourable for growth. In some cases the embryo is not fully mature at the time of dispersal and must develop further before germination can take place. Other seeds do not germinate even when the embryo is mature, probably owing to growth inhibitors within the seed that must be leached out or broken down before germination can begin.

agama small central African lizard. It lives in groups of up to 25 in tropical forest and feeds mainly on insects.
classification The agama *Agama agama* is in the Old World family Agamidae, order Squamata.

agamid lizard in the family Agamidae, containing about 300 species.

Agamids include the common ◊agama; the Australian frilled lizard *Chlamydosaurus,* which runs on its hind legs and has a frill on each side of its neck; the thorny devil *Moloch horridus,* whose body is covered with large spikes; and the Malaysia flying dragon *Draco volans.*
classification Agamids are in family Agamidae, suborder Sauria, order Squamata, class Reptilia.

agar jellylike carbohydrate, obtained from seaweeds. It is used mainly in microbiological experiments as a culture medium for growing bacteria and other microorganisms. The agar is resistant to breakdown by microorganisms, remaining a solid jelly throughout the course of the experiment.

agaric any of a group of fungi (see ◊fungus) of typical mushroom shape. Agarics include the field mushroom *Agaricus campestris* and the cultivated edible mushroom *A. brunnesiens.* Closely related is the often poisonous *Amanita,* ◊which includes the fly agaric *A. muscaria.* (Genus *Agaricus,* family Agaricaceae.)

agate cryptocrystalline (with crystals too small to be seen with an optical microscope) silica, SiO_2, composed of cloudy and banded ◊chalcedony, sometimes mixed with ◊opal, that forms in rock cavities.

Agate stones, being hard, are also used to burnish and polish gold applied to glass and ceramics and as clean vessels for grinding rock samples in laboratories.

agave any of several related plants with stiff, sword-shaped, spiny leaves arranged in a rosette. All species come from the warmer parts of the New World. They include *Agave sisalina,* whose fibres are used for rope making, and the Mexican century plant *A. americana,* which may take many years to mature (hence its common name). Alcoholic drinks such as tequila and pulque are made from the sap of agave plants. (Genus *Agave,* family Agavaceae.)

ageing in common usage, the period of deterioration of the physical condition of a living organism that leads to death; in biological terms, the entire life process.

Three current theories attempt to account for ageing. The first suggests that the process is genetically determined, to remove individuals that can no longer reproduce. The second suggests that it is due to the accumulation of mistakes during the replication of ◊DNA at cell division. The third suggests that it is actively induced by fragments of DNA that move between cells, or by cancer-causing viruses; these may become abundant in old cells and induce them to produce unwanted ◊proteins or interfere with the control functions of their DNA.

agent software that mimics intelligence by automating tasks according to user-defined rules. The most visible agent on the Internet in 1995 was Firefly, which recommends music that users might like based on information they have already given about their favourite artists. Agents might also select news stories of

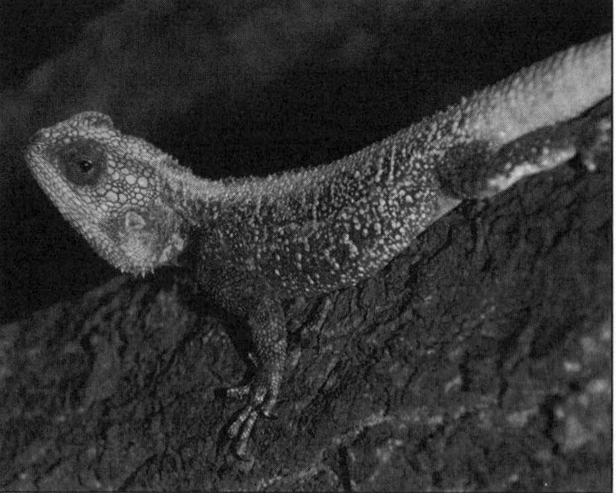

agama *During the breeding season male agamids usually develop bright colours, especially on the head. The male of this* Agama atricollis, *a widespread species in the savannas of S and E Africa, is able to fade out his conspicuous blue hues and change to a camouflage brown coloration within a minute or two of sensing danger. Premaphotos Wildlife*

agave Agaves are desert plants from the New World. They normally flower once when they reach maturity – which in some species may take as long as 60 years – and then die. Fibres such as sisal can be produced from some species, and the alcoholic drink tequila is made from others. Premaphotos Wildlife

interest, arrange scheduling with other agents, and filter out unwanted junk e-mail.

Much research on agents is proceeding at the ◊MIT Media Lab, where Professor Pattie Maes directs the group studying the capability and potential of autonomous agents. See also ◊crawler and ◊bot.

Agent Orange selective ◊weedkiller, notorious for its use in the 1960s during the Vietnam War by US forces to eliminate ground cover which could protect enemy forces. It was subsequently discovered to contain highly poisonous ◊dioxin. Thousands of US troops who had handled it, along with many Vietnamese people who came into contact with it, later developed cancer or produced deformed babies.

Agent Orange, named after the distinctive orange stripe on its packaging, combines equal parts of 2,4-D (2,4-dichlorophenoxyacetic acid) and 2,4,5-T (2,4,5-trichlorophenoxyacetic acid), both now banned in the USA. Companies that had manufactured the chemicals faced an increasing number of lawsuits in the 1970s. All the suits were settled out of court in a single class action, resulting in the largest ever payment of its kind ($180 million) to claimants.

age–sex graph graph of the population of an area showing age and sex distribution.

aggression in biology, behaviour used to intimidate or injure another organism (of the same or of a different species), usually for the purposes of gaining territory, a mate, or food. Aggression often involves an escalating series of threats aimed at intimidating an opponent without having to engage in potentially dangerous physical contact. Aggressive signals include roaring by red deer, snarling by dogs, the fluffing-up of feathers by birds, and the raising of fins by some species of fish.

agonist in biology, a ◊muscle that contracts and causes a movement. Contraction of an agonist is complemented by relaxation of its ◊antagonist. For example, the biceps (in the front of the upper arm) bends the elbow whilst the triceps (lying behind the biceps) straightens the arm.

agoraphobia ◊phobia involving fear of open spaces and public places. The anxiety produced can be so severe that some sufferers are unable to leave their homes for many years.

Agoraphobia affects 1 person in 20 at some stage in their lives. The most common time of onset is between the ages of 18 and 28.

agouti small rodent of the genus *Dasyprocta*, family Dasyproctidae. It is found in the forests of Central and South America. The agouti is herbivorous, swift-running, and about the size of a rabbit.

AGR abbreviation for ◊advanced gas-cooled reactor, **a type of nuclear reactor**.

agribusiness commercial farming on an industrial scale, often financed by companies whose main interests lie outside agriculture; for example, multinational corporations. Agribusiness farms are mechanized, large in size, highly structured, and reliant on chemicals.

agriculture ***Latin ager 'field', colere 'to cultivate'*** the practice of farming, including the cultivation of the soil (for raising crops) and the raising of domesticated animals. The units for managing agricultural production vary from smallholdings and individually owned farms to corporate-run farms and collective farms run by entire communities.

Crops are for human or animal food, or commodities such as cotton and sisal. For successful production, the land must be prepared (ploughed, cultivated, harrowed, and rolled). Seed must be planted and the growing plants nurtured. This may involve ◊fertilizers, ◊irrigation, pest control by chemicals, and monitoring of acidity or nutrients. When the crop has grown, it must be harvested and, depending on the crop, processed in a variety of ways before it is stored or sold.

Greenhouses allow cultivation of plants that would otherwise find the climate too harsh. ◊Hydroponics allows commercial cultivation of crops using nutrient-enriched solutions instead of soil. Special methods, such as terracing, may be adopted to allow cultivation in hostile terrain and to retain topsoil in mountainous areas with heavy rainfall.

Animals are raised for wool, milk, leather, dung (as fuel), or meat. They may be semidomesticated, such as reindeer, or fully domesticated but nomadic (where naturally growing or cultivated food supplies are sparse), or kept in one location. Animal farming involves accommodation (buildings, fencing, or pasture), feeding, breeding, gathering the produce (eggs, milk, or wool), slaughtering, and further processing such as tanning.

agrimony herbaceous plant belonging to the rose family, with small yellow flowers on a slender spike. It grows along hedges and in fields. (*Agrimonia eupatoria,* family Rosaceae.)

agronomy study of crops and soils, a branch of agricultural science. Agronomy includes such topics as selective breeding (of plants and animals), irrigation, pest control, and soil analysis and modification.

AI abbreviation for ◊artificial intelligence.

Aichi Japanese aircraft of World War II, principally used by the navy.

The **B7A**, known to the Allies as 'Grace', was a torpedo-bomber produced in small numbers. The **D3A**, known as 'Val', was a carrier dive bomber of great strength and efficiency; it was the principal dive bomber used at Pearl Harbor Dec 1941, and sank numerous Allied warships throughout the war. The **E13A**, 'Jake', was a floatplane used for reconnaissance; it was used in this role to prepare the way for the Pearl Harbor raid, and was carried by almost all Japanese warships.

AIDS acronym for ***acquired immune deficiency syndrome***, the gravest of the sexually transmitted diseases, or ◊STDs. It is caused by the human immunodeficiency virus (◊HIV), now known to be a ◊retrovirus, an organism first identified in 1983. HIV is transmitted in body fluids, mainly blood and genital secretions.

diagnosis of AIDS The effect of the virus in those who become ill is the devastation of the immune system, leaving the victim sus-

AIDS AND HIV INFORMATION

http://www.thebody.com/

AIDS/HIV site offering safe sex and AIDS prevention advice, information about treatments and testing, and health/nutritional guidance for those who have contracted the disease.

Agriculture: chronology

10000–8000 BC	Holocene (post-glacial) period of hunters and gatherers. Harvesting and storage of wild grains in southwest Asia. Herding of reindeer in northern Eurasia. Domestic sheep in northern Iraq.
8000	Neolithic revolution with cultivation of domesticated wheats and barleys, sheep, and goats in southwest Asia. Domestication of pigs in New Guinea.
7000–6000	Domestic goats, sheep, and cattle in Anatolia, Greece, Persia, and the Caspian basin. Planting and harvesting techniques transferred from Asia Minor to Europe.
5000	Beginning of Nile valley civilization. Millet cultivated in China.
3400	Flax used for textiles in Egypt. Widespread corn production in the Americas.
3200	Records of ploughing, raking, and manuring by Egyptians.
c. 3100	River Nile dammed during the rule of King Menes.
3000	First record of asses used as beasts of burden in Egypt. Sumerian civilization used barley as main crop with wheat, dates, flax, apples, plums, and grapes.
2900	Domestication of pigs in eastern Asia.
2640	Reputed start of Chinese silk industry.
2500	Domestic elephants in the Indus valley. Potatoes a staple crop in Peru.
2350	Wine-making in Egypt.
2250	First known irrigation dam.
1600	Important advances in the cultivation of vines and olives in Crete.
1500	*Shadoof* (mechanism for raising water) used for irrigation in Egypt.
1400	Iron ploughshares in use in India.
1300	Aqueducts and reservoirs used for irrigation in Egypt.
1200	Domestic camels in Arabia.
1000–500	Evidence of crop rotation, manuring, and irrigation in India.
600	First windmills used for corn grinding in Persia.
350	Rice cultivation well established in parts of western Africa. Hunting and gathering in the east, central, and south parts of the continent.
c. 200	Use of gears to create ox-driven water wheel for irrigation. Archimedes screw used for irrigation.
100	Cattle-drawn iron ploughs in use in China.
AD 65	*De Re Rustica/On Rural Things*, Latin treatise on agriculture and irrigation.
500	'Three fields in two years' rotation used in China.
630	Cotton introduced into Arabia.
800	Origins of the 'open field' system in northern Europe.
900	Wheeled ploughs in use in western Europe. Horse collar, originating in China, allowed horses to be used for ploughing as well as carrying.
1000	Frisians (NW Netherlanders) began to build dykes and reclaim land. Chinese began to introduce Champa rice which cropped much more quickly than other varieties.
11th century	Three-field system replaced the two-field system in western Europe. Concentration on crop growing.
1126	First artesian wells, at Artois, France.
12th century	Increasing use of water mills and windmills. Horses replaced oxen for pulling work in many areas.
12th–14th centuries	Expansion of European population brought more land into cultivation. Crop rotations, manuring, and new crops such as beans and peas helped increase productivity. Feudal system at its height.
13th–14th centuries	Agricultural recession in western Europe with a series of bad harvests, famines, and pestilence.
1347	Black Death killed about a third of the European population.
16th century	Decline of the feudal system in western Europe. More specialist forms of production were now possible with urban markets. Manorial estates and serfdom remained in eastern Europe. Chinese began cultivation of non-indigenous crops such as corn, sweet potatoes, potatoes, and peanuts.
17th century	Potato introduced into Europe. Norfolk crop rotation became widespread in England, involving wheat, turnips, barley and then ryegrass/clover.
1700–1845	Agricultural revolution began in England. Two million hectares of farmland in England enclosed. Removal of open fields in other parts of Europe followed.
c. 1701	Jethro Tull developed the seed drill and the horse-drawn hoe.
1747	First sugar extracted from sugar beet in Prussia.
1762	Veterinary school founded in Lyon, France.
1783	First plough factory in England.
1785	Cast-iron ploughshare patented.
1793	Invention of the cotton gin.
1800	Early threshing machines developed in England.
1820s	First nitrates for fertilizer imported from South America.
1830	Reaping machines developed in Scotland and the US. Steel plough made by John Deere in Illinois, US.
1840s	Extensive potato blight in Europe.
1850s	Use of clay pipes for drainage well established throughout Europe.
1862	First steam plough used in the Netherlands.
1850–1890s	Major developments in transport and refrigeration technology altered the nature of agricultural markets with crops, dairy products, and wheat being shipped internationally.
1890s	Development of stationary engines for ploughing.
1892	First petrol-driven tractor in the USA.
1921	First attempt at crop dusting with pesticides from an aeroplane near Dayton, Ohio, US.
1938	First self-propelled grain combine harvester used in the USA.
1942–62	Huge increase in the use of pesticides, later curbed by disquiet about their effects and increasing resistance of pests to standard controls such as DDT.
1945 onwards	Increasing use of scientific techniques, crop specialization and larger scale of farm enterprises.
1985	First cases of bovine spongiform encephalopathy (BSE) recorded by UK vets.
1992	Number of cases of BSE in cattle was at its peak (700 cases per week).
1995	Increase in the use of genetic engineering with nearly 3,000 transgenic crops being field-tested.
1996	Organic farming was on the increase in EU countries. The rise was 11% per year in Britain, 50% in Germany, and 40% in Italy.

ceptible to diseases that would not otherwise develop. Diagnosis of AIDS is based on the appearance of rare tumours or opportunistic infections in unexpected candidates. *Pneumocystis carinii* pneumonia, for instance, normally seen only in the malnourished or those whose immune systems have been deliberately suppressed, is common among AIDS victims and, for them, a leading cause of death.

treatment In the West the time-lag between infection with HIV and the development of AIDS seems to be about ten years, but progression is far more rapid in developing countries. Some AIDS victims die within a few months of the outbreak of symptoms, some survive for several years; roughly 50% are dead within three years. There is no cure for the disease and the four antivirals currently in use against AIDS have not lived up to expectations. Trials began in 1994 using a new AIDS drug called 3TC in conjunction with ◊zidovudine (formerly ◊AZT). Although individually the drugs produce little effect, when the drugs were used together in 1995, the levels of virus in the blood were ten times lower than at the beginning of the trial. Treatment of opportunistic infections extended the average length of survival with AIDS (in Western countries) from about 11 months in 1985 to 23 months in 1994.

HIV/AIDS – worldwide statistics Allowing for under-diagnosis, incomplete reporting, and reporting delay, and based on the available data on HIV infections around the world, it is estimated (1997) that approximately 8.4 million AIDS cases in adults and children have occurred worldwide since the pandemic began. WHO estimate that of these cases, which include active AIDS cases and people

AIDS – Recent Developments

BY PAUL MOSS

The global count of people infected with the human immunodeficiency virus (HIV) continues to increase at an alarming rate. Despite some notable successes with health education campaigns, millions are infected, with the worst infection rates being in the developing world. Nevertheless, there are signs that the enormous scientific effort that has been mobilized against the disease is now paying dividends. Current drug regimes are able to prolong life and are even allowing scientists to debate the prospect of cure.

When HIV enters the body, the main cell type infected is the CD4+ T lymphocyte, a circulating white cell that plays an important role in controlling immune responses. In addition, the virus can enter a variety of other cell types that have the CD4 molecule on their surface. The net result of infection is a relentless fall in the number of CD4+ T cells and a gradual dismantling of the immune system's ability to fight off infectious agents such as bacteria, fungi, and other viruses. This process leaves patients very susceptible to a wide variety of infections, many of which are virtually never seen in people with a normally functioning immune system. One important advance in the last few years has been the use of molecular assays to measure the amount of virus in the blood of infected patients. This procedure is valuable in predicting how rapidly they are likely to progress to an advanced state of the disease.

Early treatment

The initial successes in the drug treatment of HIV infection were with agents that could treat or prevent the infectious complications of the disease. These drugs remain very valuable but do not have any activity against HIV itself. The first drug with proven activity against HIV was zidovudine (AZT). Zidovudine resembles one of the building blocks of DNA, and when HIV undergoes replication, zidovudine can bind to an essential HIV enzyme and prevent the virus from completing its life cycle. Zidovudine can improve the symptoms of HIV infection, is valuable in asymptomatic patients with low CD4+ lymphocyte counts, and is effective at reducing the rate of transmission of HIV from pregnant women to their babies. However, when zidovudine is used alone, the virus is usually able to escape from the effects of zidovudine by mutating its DNA sequence. There is now an increasing appreciation of the need to use zidovudine in combination with some of the new antiviral drugs.

New developments

At the moment, probably the most exciting class of drugs that inhibit HIV replication is the protease inhibitors. When HIV replicates inside a cell it has to make a copy of its DNA, and then this genetic message is decoded into a protein. Some HIV proteins need to be broken down into smaller pieces in order to function, and this is done by a protease molecule. Normal function of the HIV protease appears to be vital for efficient replication of the virus, and over the last few years researchers have spent a great deal of effort in developing drugs that can block its function.

At least four protease inhibitors have been tried in clinical practice: saquinavir, ritonavir, nelfinavir, and indinavir. All have slightly different properties and different side effects. In clinical trials, these drugs have demonstrated a spectacular ability to reduce the amount of virus in the body. Sensitive molecular assays such as the polymerase chain reaction (PCR) have shown that the amount of HIV in blood can be reduced by over a thousandfold and sometimes may reach undetectable levels. Although effective on their own, most of the current drive in HIV therapeutics is to use these agents in combination with other anti-HIV agents. Typically this would include zidovudine, a protease inhibitor, and another agent such as didanosine. In a recent trial this combination led to the virus being undetectable in 60 % of patients after 24 weeks of treatment. A very encouraging observation with protease inhibitors is that they can be used at a very advanced state of the disease. It seems that the drugs should be used at quite large doses, to avoid the development of a resistant virus, and unfortunately they do have several side effects. Although most of these effects are not serious, many patients are unable to tolerate a particular drug combination; in these cases a change to another combination is indicated.

The role of combination therapy

The exact role of combination therapy in the overall management of HIV infection is a subject of considerable debate at present. In an attempt to achieve consensus, a panel of the International AIDS Society-USA met in 1996. After results from many clinical trials, the group suggested that combination therapy was now the treatment of choice. It remains unclear, however, whether or not protease inhibitors should be used with all patients or just those at particular risk of rapid progression to full-blown AIDS based on measurement of the amount of HIV in their blood. Patients with symptoms should be offered treatment, but for those who are asymptomatic the situation is less clear and the decision will be based on the CD4+ count and the viral load in the blood. There are relatively little data to recommend how to treat patients who have been infected in the last month or two and are suffering from the typical symptoms of acute infection: fever, swollen lymph nodes, and headaches. As this is a time of intense viral replication, there is a theoretical advantage in using the strongest available treatment to limit the initial multiplication of the virus. This may also reduce the chance of the virus making mutations that would allow it to resist drug treatment.

The last few years have seen valuable advances in the treatment of HIV infection. Several powerful drugs are now available and are being tested in trials around the world. The human immunodeficiency virus has an astounding ability to mutate itself in order to evade drugs, and there are likely to be setbacks ahead. It is too soon to say whether or not some patients may be offered the prospect of complete cure. Nevertheless, many AIDS researchers are hoping that they can now maintain the upper hand in the battle against this formidable virus.

---

who have died of AIDS, not HIV infections, more than 70% were in Africa, with about 9% in the USA, 9% in the rest of the Americas, 6% in Asia, and 4% in Europe. Of the total number of AIDS cases reported, 39% were in the USA, 34% in Africa, 20% in Asia, 12.5% in Europe, and 12% in the Americas.

Estimates released by WHO in Nov 1996 and Jan 1997 revealed that 22.6 million men, women, and children had been infected by HIV. Of these, 21.8 million were adults and 830,000 children. Approximately 42% of adult sufferers were female, with the proportion of women infected by HIV/AIDS steadily increasing. The majority of newly infected adults were under 25 years of age. WHO estimated that by the year 2000 30–40 million people would have been infected by the virus. The United Nations AIDS programme (UNAIDS) concluded in 1997 that the world total number of HIV infections was just under 30 million.

sub-Saharan Africa The worst affected area is sub-Saharan Africa, where the United Nations AIDS programme (UNAIDS) estimated that 20 million people had been infected. About two-thirds of this total were in east and central Africa, an area that accounts for only about one-sixth of the total population of the sub-Saharan region. In Kenya, Malawi, Rwanda, Uganda, Tanzania, Zambia, and Zimbabwe, surveys showed that over 10% of women attending antenatal clinics in urban areas were HIV-infected, with rates exceeding 40% in some surveillance sites. The number of AIDS cases in Africa has also continued to increase. An estimated 5 million people in sub-Saharan Africa have developed AIDS.

S and SE Asia The most alarming trends of HIV infection are in south and southeast Asia, where the epidemic is spreading as fast as it was a decade ago in sub-Saharan Africa. The majority of the 6 million HIV infections estimated to have occurred in adults in these regions (1997) appeared in India, Thailand, and Myanmar (Burma), but high rates of HIV spread have been seen elsewhere too.

Latin America and the Caribbean WHO estimated (1996) that about 1.6 million HIV infections had occurred in Latin America and the Caribbean since the epidemic began. In these regions epidemics are increasingly occurring among women and adolescents. The future course of the epidemic in the region depends greatly on the rate at which the virus spreads in Brazil, which has more AIDS cases than any other country outside Africa and the USA.

Middle East and north Africa About 200,000 HIV infections were estimated to have occurred so far in the Middle East and north Africa (1996). These figures are of particular concern because other factors – the presence of other sexually transmitted diseases and intravenous drug use, for example – suggest that there is an increased exposure to the risk of HIV infection.

E Europe and central Asia It was estimated (1996) that over 50,000 adults in eastern Europe and central Asia had been infected with HIV. HIV is spreading in these regions – sometimes quite rapidly – to communities and countries that were hardly affected by the epidemic only a few years ago. Ukraine recently reported a substantial increase in newly infected drug users in cities bordering the Black Sea. The Russian Federation may experience a similar progression.

North America In 1993 AIDS for the first time became the USA's leading cause of death among all people aged between 25 and 44. By Nov 1996, 565,097 cumulative AIDS cases had been reported in the USA. However, in 1996 the AIDS death rate in the USA fell from 15.6 per 100,000 people to 11.6 (26%, which was the first decline in the 15 years since the pandemic had began. In 1996 AIDS was no longer the main killer of adults between the ages of 25 to 44 but it remained so for African Americans in that age group. Although the overall number of new HIV infections in the USA has decreased, results from several studies suggest that the HIV epidemic has now spread to a new generation of homosexual and bisexual men. In Jan 1997, AIDS experts reported a 30% drop in AIDS deaths in New York. The actual count fell from 7,046 to 4,944. The researchers said this was as a result of improved treatments and better access to care. An estimated 860,000 adults in North America were living with HIV infection at the end of 1997.

W Europe The United Nations AIDS programme (UNAIDS) estimated in 1997 that 150,000 HIV infections had occurred in western Europe. As of mid-1996, 167,021 AIDS cases had been reported throughout the European Union (EU). The highest rate of reported AIDS cases within the EU was in Spain. Information from the UK indicates that the declining trend in male-to-male transmission observed in the late 1980s may have begun to reverse as early as 1990.

E Asia and the Pacific WHO estimated that by the end of 1996 over 113,000 HIV infections had occurred in east Asia and the Pacific. An estimated 15,100 AIDS cases had occurred in these regions, 11,700 of these in Australia and New Zealand. There was evidence that HIV infection rates had reached a plateau in Australia and were declining in New Zealand. However, an HIV epidemic recently developed in Papua New Guinea. By the end of 1994, this island of about 4 million people had an estimated 4,000 adults living with HIV, overtaking Australia as the country with the highest number of HIV cases per head of population in the Pacific region.

The cumulative direct and indirect costs of HIV and AIDS in the 1980s have been conservatively estimated at $240 billion. The global cost – direct and indirect – of HIV and AIDS by the year 2000 could be as high as $500 billion a year – equivalent to more than 2% of global GDP.

ailanthus any of several trees or shrubs with compound leaves made up of pointed leaflets and clusters of small greenish flowers with an unpleasant smell. The tree of heaven (*Ailanthus altissima*), native to E Asia, is grown worldwide as an ornamental; it can grow to 30 m/100 ft in height and the trunk can reach 1 m/3 ft in diameter. (Genus *Ailanthus,* family Simaroubaceae.)

air the mixture of gases making up the Earth's ◊atmosphere.

airbrush small fine spray-gun used by artists, graphic designers, and photographic retouchers. Driven by air pressure from a compressor or pressurized can, it can apply a thin, very even layer of ink or paint, allowing for subtle gradations of tone.

air conditioning system that controls the state of the air inside a building or vehicle. A complete air-conditioning unit controls the temperature and humidity of the air, removes dust and odours from it, and circulates it by means of a fan. US inventor Willis Haviland Carrier (1876–1950) developed the first effective air-conditioning unit in 1902 for a New York printing plant.

The air in an air conditioner is cooled by a type of ◊refrigeration unit comprising a compressor and a condenser. The air is cleaned by means of filters and activated charcoal. Moisture is extracted by condensation on cool metal plates. The air can also be heated by electrical wires or, in large systems, pipes carrying hot water or steam; and cool, dry air may be humidified by circulating it over pans of water or through a water spray.

The first air conditioners were used in 19th century textile mills, where a fine water spray was used to cool and humidify the atmosphere.

A specialized air-conditioning system is installed in spacecraft as part of the life-support system. This includes the provision of oxygen to breathe and the removal of exhaled carbon dioxide.

Outdoor spaces may also be cooled using overhead cool air jets.

aircraft any aeronautical vehicle capable of flying through the air. It may be lighter than air (supported by buoyancy) or heavier than air (supported by the dynamic action of air on its surfaces). ◊Balloons and ◊airships are lighter-than-air craft. Heavier-than-air craft include the ◊aeroplane, glider, autogiro, and helicopter.

air-cushion vehicle (ACV) craft that is supported by a layer, or cushion, of high-pressure air. The ◊hovercraft is one form of ACV.

Airedale terrier breed of large terrier, about 60 cm/24 in tall, with a wiry red-brown coat and black saddle patch. It originated about 1850 in England, as a cross between the otterhound and Irish and Welsh terriers.

airlock airtight chamber that allows people to pass between areas of different pressure; also an air bubble in a pipe that impedes fluid flow. An airlock may connect an environment at ordinary pressure and an environment that has high air pressure (such as a submerged caisson used for tunnelling or building dams or bridge foundations).

An airlock may also permit someone wearing breathing apparatus to pass into an airless environment (into water from a submerged submarine or into the vacuum of space from a spacecraft).

air passages in biology, the nose, pharynx, larynx, trachea, and bronchi. When a breath is taken, air passes through high narrow passages on each side of the nose where it is warmed and moistened and particles of dust are removed. Food and air passages meet and cross in the pharynx. The larynx lies in front of the lower part of the pharynx and it is the organ where the voice is produced using the vocal cords. The air passes the glottis (the opening between the vocal cords) and enters the trachea. The trachea leads into the chest and divides above the heart into two bronchi. The bronchi carry the air to the lungs and they subdivide to form a succession of fine tubes and, eventually, a network of capillaries that allow the exchange of gases between the inspired air and the blood.

air pollution contamination of the atmosphere caused by the discharge, accidental or deliberate, of a wide range of toxic airborne substances. Often the amount of the released substance is relatively high in a certain locality, so the harmful effects become more noticeable. The cost of preventing any discharge of pollutants into the air is prohibitive, so attempts are more usually made to reduce the amount of discharge gradually and to disperse it as quickly as possible by using a very tall chimney, or by intermittent release.

Possibly the world's worst ever human-made air pollution disas-

Air pollution: major pollutants

pollutant	sources	effects
sulphur dioxide SO_2	oil, coal combustion in power stations	acid rain formed, which damages plants, trees, buildings, and lakes
oxides of nitrogen NO, NO_2	high-temperature combustion in cars, and to some extent power stations	acid rain formed
lead compounds	from leaded petrol used by cars	nerve poison
carbon dioxide CO_2	oil, coal, petrol, diesel combustion	greenhouse effect
carbon monoxide CO	limited combustion of oil, coal, petrol, diesel fuels	poisonous, leads to photochemical smog in some areas
nuclear waste	nuclear power plants, nuclear weapon testing, war	radioactivity, contamination of locality, cancers, mutations, death

ter occurred in Indonesia in September 1997. It was caused by forest clearance fires. Smoke pollution in the city of Palangkaraya reached 7.5 mg per cu m (nearly 3 mg more than in the London smog of 1952 in which 4,000 people died). The pollutants spread to Malaysia and other countries of the region.

The 1997 Kyoto protocol commits the industrialized nations of the world to cutting their levels of harmful gas emissions to 5.2% by 2012. Europe is expected to take the biggest cut of 8%, the USA 7%, and Japan 6%. The agreement covers Russia and Eastern Europe as well.

AIR POLLUTION – COMMITTEE ON THE MEDICAL ASPECTS OF AIR POLLUTANTS

http://www.open.gov.uk/doh/hef/airpol/airpolh.htm

Comprehensive report on the state of Britain's air from the Ministry of Health. There is a large amount of textual and statistical information on all aspects of air pollution, description of improved warning and detection measures, and details of how the general public may access advice and information.

air sac in birds, a thin-walled extension of the lungs. There are nine of these and they extend into the abdomen and bones, effectively increasing lung capacity. In mammals, it is another name for the alveoli in the lungs, and in some insects, for widenings of the trachea.

The sacs subdivide into further air spaces which partially replace the marrow in many of the bird's bones. The air space in these bones assists flight by making them lighter.

airship or ***dirigible*** any aircraft that is lighter than air and power-driven, consisting of an ellipsoidal balloon that forms the streamlined envelope or hull and has below it the propulsion system (propellers), steering mechanism, and space for crew, passengers, and/or cargo. The balloon section is filled with lighter-than-air gas, either the nonflammable helium or, before helium was industrially available in large enough quantities, the easily ignited and flammable hydrogen. The envelope's form is maintained by internal pressure in the nonrigid (blimp) and semirigid (in which the nose and tail sections have a metal framework connected by a rigid keel) types. The rigid type (zeppelin) maintains its form using an internal metal framework. Airships have been used for luxury travel, polar exploration, warfare, and advertising.

AIRSHIP AND BLIMP RESOURCES

http://www.hotairship.com/index.html

Information about airships – with the main focus on contemporary development. This site includes sections such as 'hot news', 'manufacturer database', 'homebuilding', and 'museums'.

Rigid airships predominated from about 1900 until 1940. As the technology developed, the size of the envelope was increased from about 45 m/150 ft to more than 245 m/800 ft for the last two zeppelins built. In 1852 the first successful airship was designed and flown by Henri Giffard of France. In 1900 the first rigid type was designed by Count (*Graf*) Ferdinand von ◊Zeppelin of Germany (though he did not produce a successful model till his L-24 in1908). Airships were used by both sides during World War I, but they were not seriously used for military purposes after that as they were largely replaced by aeroplanes. The British mainly used small machines for naval reconnaissance and patrolling the North Sea; Germany used Schutte-Lanz and Zeppelin machines for similar patrol work and also for long-range bombing attacks against English and French cities, mainly Paris and London.

air transport means of conveying goods or passengers by air from one place to another. See ◊flight.

ajolote Mexican reptile of the genus *Bipes*. It and several other tropical burrowing species are placed in the Amphisbaenia, a group separate from lizards and snakes among the Squamata. Unlike the others, however, which have no legs, it has a pair of short but well-developed front legs. In line with its burrowing habits, the skull is very solid, the eyes small, and external ears absent.

The scales are arranged in rings, giving the body a wormlike appearance.

AKITA

http://club.infocom.net/~akita/index.html

Profile of the Akita from the American Kennel Club. There is a history of the breed, description of the ideal breed standard, a note on the dog's temperament, and some quirky facts about the breed. There is also a high resolution photo of this large and powerful dog.

Akita breed of guard dog from the prefecture of Akita in NW Japan. It is strongly built and stands about 69 cm/27 in tall. It has small, pointed ears, a thick coat, which may be beige, grey, brindled or black, and carries its tail curled over its back.

alabaster naturally occurring fine-grained white or light-coloured translucent form of gypsum, often streaked or mottled. A soft material, it is easily carved, but seldom used for outdoor sculpture.

Alamogordo town in New Mexico, USA, associated with nuclear testing. The first atom bomb was exploded nearby at Trinity Site 16 July 1945.

It is now a test site for guided missiles.

Alaskan malamute breed of dog. It is a type of ◊husky.

albacore name loosely applied to several species of fish found in warm regions of the Atlantic and Pacific oceans, in particular to a large tuna, *Thunnus alalunga*, and to several other species of the mackerel family.

albatross large seabird, genus *Diomedea,* with long narrow wings adapted for gliding and a wingspan of up to 3 m/10 ft, mainly found in the southern hemisphere. It belongs to the family Diomedeidae, order Procellariiformes, the same group as petrels and shearwaters. The external nostrils of birds in this order are more or less tubular, and the bills are hooked.

Albatrosses feed mainly on squid and fish, and nest on remote oceanic islands. Albatrosses can cover enormous distances, flying as far as 16,100 km/10,000 mi in 33 days, or up to 640 km/600 mi in one day. They continue flying even after dark, at speeds of up to 53.5 kph/50 mph, though they may stop for an hour's rest and to feed during the night. They are sometimes called 'gooney birds', probably because of their clumsy way of landing. Albatrosses are becoming increasingly rare, and are in danger of extinction. In the southern hemisphere, more than 40,000 albatrosses drown each year as a result of catching squid attached to bait lines.

The Diomedeidae family contains 14 species of albatross found in the Southern Atlantic and the Pacific oceans. The **wandering albatross** *D. exulans,* which has a wingspan of up to 3.4 m/11 ft, is the largest oceanic bird and can live for up to 80 years. Its huge wingspan means that it has difficulty in taking off unless there are strong winds. For this reason it nests on cliffs on islands. A single white egg is laid. The chick's full weight is 12 kg/26 lb, heavier than the parents, which typically weigh around 9 kg/20 lb. The chick needs this extra body weight to survive the Antarctic winter; the parents only return to the chick if and when they can find food for it.

albedo the fraction of the incoming light reflected by a body such as a planet. A body with a high albedo, near 1, is very bright, while a body with a low albedo, near 0, is dark. The Moon has an average albedo of 0.12, Venus 0.76, Earth 0.37.

albinism rare hereditary condition in which the body has no tyrosinase, one of the enzymes that form the pigment ◊melanin, normally found in the skin, hair, and eyes. As a result, the hair is white and the skin and eyes are pink. The skin and eyes are abnormally sensitive to light, and vision is often impaired. The condition occurs among all human and animal groups.

albumin or ***albumen*** any of a group of sulphur-containing ◊proteins. The best known is in the form of egg white; others occur in milk, and as a major component of serum. They are soluble in water and dilute salt solutions, and are coagulated by heat.

The presence of serum albumin in the urine, termed albuminuria or proteinuria, may be indicative of kidney or heart disease.

Alcan Canadian aluminium-producing company. Alcan Aluminium was founded in Montréal 1928 as the Canadian subsidiary of **Alcoa**, the US aluminium company founded in Pittsburgh, Pennsylvania, 1888. Alcan became independent from Alcoa 1945 and is the fifth largest company in Canada today, second in the world in aluminium production only to Alcoa.

ALCHEMICAL SUBSTANCES

http://www.levity.com/alchemy/substanc.html

Modern explanations of the lyrical names alchemists gave to their substances. Part of the huge Virtual Alchemy Library Web site this section is slightly disorganized, not being listed in alphabetical or any other particular order. Some of the exotic substances described include the bizarrely named 'Thion hudor' and the rather poetic 'Purple of Cassius'.

alchemy ***Arabic** al-Kimya* supposed technique of transmuting base metals, such as lead and mercury, into silver and gold by the philosopher's stone, a hypothetical substance, to which was also attributed the power to give eternal life.

This aspect of alchemy constituted much of the chemistry of the Middle Ages. More broadly, however, alchemy was a system of philosophy that dealt both with the mystery of life and the formation of inanimate substances. Alchemy was a complex and indefinite conglomeration of chemistry, astrology, occultism, and magic, blended with obscure and abstruse ideas derived from various religious systems and other sources. It was practised in Europe from ancient times to the Middle Ages but later fell into disrepute when ◊chemistry and ◊physics developed.

What is accomplished with fire is alchemy, whether in the furnace or the kitchen stove.

PARACELSUS Swiss physician, alchemist, and scientist.
In J Bronowski *The Ascent of Man* 1975

alcohol any member of a group of organic compounds characterized by the presence of one or more aliphatic OH (hydroxyl) groups

Alkane	Alcohol	Aldehyde	Ketone	Carboxylic acid	Alkene
CH_4 methane	CH_3OH methanol	HCHO methanal	—	HCO_2H methanoic acid	—
CH_3CH_3 ethane	CH_3CH_2OH ethanol	CH_3CHO ethanal	—	CH_3CO_2H ethanoic acid	CH_2CH_2 ethene
$CH_3CH_2CH_3$ propane	$CH_3CH_2CH_2OH$ propanol	CH_3CH_2CHO propanal	CH_3COCH_3 propanone	$CH_3CH_2CO_2H$ propanoic acid	CH_2CHCH_3 propene
methane	methanol	methanal	propanone	methanoic acid	ethene

alcohol *The systematic naming of simple straight-chain organic molecules.*

in the molecule, and which form ◊esters with acids. The main uses of alcohols are as solvents for gums, resins, lacquers, and varnishes; in the making of dyes; for essential oils in perfumery; and for medical substances in pharmacy. The alcohol produced naturally in the ◊fermentation process and consumed as part of alcoholic beverages is called ◊ethanol.

Alcohols may be liquids or solids, according to the size and complexity of the molecule. The five simplest alcohols form a series in which the number of carbon and hydrogen atoms increases progressively, each one having an extra CH_2 (methylene) group in the molecule: methanol or wood spirit (methyl alcohol, CH_3OH); ethanol (ethyl alcohol, C_2H_5OH); propanol (propyl alcohol, C_3H_7OH); butanol (butyl alcohol, C_4H_9OH); and pentanol (amyl alcohol, $C_5H_{11}OH$). The lower alcohols are liquids that mix with water; the higher alcohols, such as pentanol, are oily liquids immiscible with water; and the highest are waxy solids – for example, hexadecanol (cetyl alcohol, $C_{16}H_{33}OH$) and melissyl alcohol ($C_{30}H_{61}OH$), which occur in sperm-whale oil and beeswax respectively. Alcohols containing the CH_2OH group are primary; those containing CHOH are secondary; while those containing COH are tertiary.

alcoholic solution solution produced when a solute is dissolved in ethanol.

alcoholism dependence on alcohol. It is characterized as an illness when consumption of alcohol interferes with normal physical or emotional health. Excessive alcohol consumption, whether through sustained ingestion or irregular drinking bouts or binges, may produce physical and psychological addiction and lead to nutritional and emotional disorders. Long-term heavy consumption of alcohol leads to diseases of the heart, liver, and peripheral nerves. Support groups such as Alcoholics Anonymous are helpful.

Aldebaran or ***Alpha Tauri*** brightest star in the constellation Taurus and the 14th brightest star in the sky; it marks the eye of the 'bull'. Aldebaran is a red giant 60 light years away, shining with a true luminosity of about 100 times that of the Sun.

aldehyde any of a group of organic chemical compounds prepared by oxidation of primary alcohols, so that the OH (hydroxyl) group loses its hydrogen to give an oxygen joined by a double bond to a carbon atom (the aldehyde group, with the formula CHO).

alder any of a group of trees or shrubs belonging to the birch family, found mainly in cooler parts of the northern hemisphere and characterized by toothed leaves and catkins. (Genus *Alnus,* family Betulaceae.)

alewife fish *Alosa pseudoharengus* of the ◊herring group, up to 30 cm/1 ft long, found in the NW Atlantic and in the Great Lakes of North America.

alexanders strong-smelling tall ◊herbaceous plant belonging to the carrot family. It is found along hedgerows and on cliffs throughout S Europe. Its yellow flowers appear in spring and early summer. (*Smyrnium olusatrum,* family Umbelliferae.)

Alexander technique in alternative medicine, a method of correcting bad habits of posture, breathing, and muscular tension, which Australian therapist F M Alexander maintained cause many ailments. The technique is also used to promote general health and relaxation and enhance vitality.

Back troubles, migraine, asthma, hypertension, and some gastric and gynaecological disorders are among the conditions said to be alleviated by the technique, which is also said to be effective in the prevention of disorders, particularly those of later life.

alfalfa or ***lucerne*** perennial tall ◊herbaceous plant belonging to the pea family. It is native to Europe and Asia and has spikes of small purple flowers in late summer. It is now a major fodder crop, commonly processed into hay, meal, or silage. Alfalfa sprouts, the sprouted seeds, have become a popular salad ingredient. (*Medicago sativa,* family Leguminosae.)

algae (singular ***alga***) highly varied group of plants, ranging from single-celled forms to large and complex seaweeds. They live in both fresh and salt water, and in damp soil. Algae do not have true roots, stems, or leaves.

Marine algae help combat ◊global warming by removing carbon dioxide from the atmosphere during ◊photosynthesis.

Alembert, Jean le Rond d' (1717–1783)

French mathematician, encyclopedist, and theoretical physicist. In association with Denis Diderot, he helped plan the great Encyclopédie, for which he also wrote the 'Discours préliminaire' 1751. He framed several theorems and principles – notably d'Alembert's principle – in dynamics and celestial mechanics, and devised the theory of partial differential equations.

The principle that now bears his name was first published in his *Traité de dynamique* 1743, and was an extension of the third of Isaac ◊Newton's laws of motion. D'Alembert maintained that the law was valid not merely for a static body, but also for mobile bodies. Within a year he had found a means of applying the principle to the theory of equilibrium and the motion of fluids. Using also the theory of partial differential equations, he studied the properties of sound, and air compression, and also managed to relate his principle to an investigation of the motion of any body in a given figure.

Mary Evans Picture Library

algebra branch of mathematics in which the general properties of numbers are studied by using symbols, usually letters, to represent variables and unknown quantities. For example, the algebraic statement $(x + y)^2 = x^2 + 2xy + y^2$ is true for all values of x and y. If $x = 7$ and $y = 3$, for instance:

$$(7 + 3)^2 = 7^2 + 2(7 \times 3) + 3^2 = 100$$

An algebraic expression that has one or more variables (denoted by letters) is a ◊polynomial equation. Algebra is used in many areas of mathematics – for example, matrix algebra and Boolean algebra (the latter is used in working out the logic for computers).

In ordinary algebra the same operations are carried on as in arithmetic, but, as the symbols are capable of a more generalized and extended meaning than the figures used in arithmetic, it facilitates calculation where the numerical values are not known, or are inconveniently large or small, or where it is desirable to keep them in an analysed form.

Within an algebraic equation the separate calculations involved must be completed in a set order. Any elements in brackets should always be calculated first, followed by multiplication, division, addition, and subtraction.

quadratic equation This is a polynomial equation of second degree (that is, an equation containing as its highest power the square of a variable, such as x^2). The general formula of such equations is $ax^2 + bx + c = 0$, in which a, b, and c are real numbers, and only the coefficient a cannot equal 0.

Some quadratic equations can be solved by factorization, or the values of x can be found by using the formula for the general solution

$$x = [-b \pm \sqrt{(b^2 - 4ac)}]/2a$$

Depending on the value of the discriminant $b^2 - 4ac$, a quadratic equation has two real, two equal, or two complex roots (solutions). When $b^2 - 4ac > 0$ there are two distinct real roots. When $b^2 - 4ac = 0$ there are two equal real roots. When $b^2 - 4ac < 0$ there are two distinct complex roots.

simultaneous equations If there are two or more algebraic equations that contain two or more unknown quantities that may have

To remember the order of operations in complex algebraic or numerical expression:

BLESS MY DEAR AUNT SALLY!

BRACKETS, MULTIPLY, DIVIDE, ADD, SUBTRACT

a unique solution they can be solved simultaneously. For example, in the case of two linear equations with two unknown variables, such as:

$$\text{(i) } x + 3y = 6 \text{ and (ii) } 3y - 2x = 4$$

the solution will be those unique values of x and y that are valid for both equations. Linear simultaneous equations can be solved by using algebraic manipulation to eliminate one of the variables. For example, both sides of equation (i) could be multiplied by 2, which gives $2x + 6y = 12$. This can be added to equation (ii) to get $9y = 16$, which is easily solved: $y = \frac{16}{9}$. The variable x can now be found by inserting the known y value into either original equation and solving for x.

'Algebra' was originally the name given to the study of equations. In the 9th century, the Arab mathematician Muhammad ibn-Mūsā al-Khwārizmī used the term *al-jabr* for the process of adding equal quantities to both sides of an equation. When his treatise was later translated into Latin, *al-jabr* became 'algebra' and the word was adopted as the name for the whole subject.

algebraic fraction fraction in which letters are used to represent numbers – for example, $\frac{a}{b}$, $\frac{xy}{z}2$, and $\frac{1}{x+y}$. Like numerical fractions, algebraic f\ractions may be simplified or factorized. Two equivalent algebraic fractions can be cross-multiplied; for example, if $\frac{a}{b} = \frac{b}{c}$ then $ad = bc$

(In the same way, the two equivalent numerical fractions $\frac{2}{3}$ and $\frac{4}{6}$ can be cross-multiplied to give cross-products that are both 12.)

alginate salt of alginic acid, $(C_6H_8O_6)_n$, obtained from brown seaweeds and used in textiles, paper, food products, and pharmaceuticals.

ALGOL (acronym for **algo*rithmic* language**) in computing, an early high-level programming language, developed in the 1950s and 1960s for scientific applications. A general-purpose language, ALGOL is best suited to mathematical work and has an algebraic style. Although no longer in common use, it has greatly influenced more recent languages, such as Ada and PASCAL.

Algol or **Beta Persei** ◊eclipsing binary, a pair of orbiting stars in the constellation Perseus, one of which eclipses the other every 69 hours, causing its brightness to drop by two-thirds.

The brightness changes were first explained in 1782 by English amateur astronomer John Goodricke (1764–1786). He pointed out that the changes between magnitudes 2.2 and 3.5 repeated themselves exactly after an interval of 2.867 days and supposed this to be due to two stars orbiting round and eclipsing each other.

Algonquin Radio Observatory site in Ontario, Canada, of the radio telescope, 46 m/150 ft in diameter, of the National Research Council of Canada, opened 1966.

algorithm procedure or series of steps that can be used to solve a problem.

In computer science, it describes the logical sequence of operations to be performed by a program. A ◊flow chart is a visual representation of an algorithm.

The word derives from the name of 9th-century Arab mathematician Muhammad ibn-Mūsā al-Khwārizmī.

alias name representing a particular user or group of users in e-mail systems. This feature, which is not available on all systems, is a matter of convenience as it allows a user to substitute shorter or easier-to-remember real names for e-mail addresses. In 1995 CompuServe announced a system of named aliases for its long, numbered addresses.

aliasing or *jaggies* effect seen on computer screen or printer output, when smooth curves appear to be made up of steps because the resolution is not high enough. The steps are caused by clumps of pixels that become visible when the monitor's definition is lower than that of the image that it is trying to show. ◊Anti-aliasing is a software technique that reduces this effect by using intermediate shades of colour to create an apparently smoother curve.

ALife in computing, contraction of ◊artificial life.

alimentary canal in animals, the tube through which food passes; it extends from the mouth to the anus. It is a complex organ, adapted for ◊digestion. In human adults, it is about 9 m/30 ft long, consisting of the mouth cavity, pharynx, oesophagus, stomach, and the small and large intestines.

A constant stream of enzymes from the canal wall and from the pancreas assists the breakdown of food molecules into smaller, soluble nutrient molecules, which are absorbed through the canal wall into the bloodstream and carried to individual cells. The muscles of the alimentary canal keep the incoming food moving, mix it with the enzymes and other juices, and slowly push it in the direction of the anus, a process known as ◊peristalsis. The wall of the canal receives an excellent supply of blood and is folded so as to increase its surface area. These two adaptations ensure efficient absorption of nutrient molecules.

aliphatic compound any organic chemical compound in which the carbon atoms are joined in straight chains, as in hexane (C_6H_{14}), or in branched chains, as in 2-methylpentane $(CH_3CH(CH_3)CH_2CH_2CH_3)$.

Aliphatic compounds have bonding electrons localized within the vicinity of the bonded atoms. ◊Cyclic compounds that do not have delocalized electrons are also aliphatic, as in the alicyclic compound cyclohexane (C_6H_{12}) or the heterocyclic piperidine $(C_5H_{11}N)$. Compare ◊aromatic compound.

alkali in chemistry, a compound classed as a ◊base that is soluble in water. Alkalis neutralize acids and are soapy to the touch.

The hydroxides of metals are alkalis; those of sodium and potassium being chemically powerful; both were historically derived from the ashes of plants.

The four main alkalis are sodium hydroxide (caustic soda, NaOH); potassium hydroxide (caustic potash, KOH); calcium hydroxide (slaked lime or limewater, $Ca(OH)_2$); and aqueous ammonia $(NH_{3\,(aq)})$. Their solutions all contain the hydroxide ion OH^-, which gives them a characteristic set of properties.

Alkalis react with acids to form a salt and water (neutralization).

$$KOH + HNO_3 \rightarrow KNO_3 + H_2OOH^- + H^+ \rightarrow H_2O$$

They give a specific colour reaction with indicators; for example, litmus turns blue.

alkali metal any of a group of six metallic elements with similar chemical properties: lithium, sodium, potassium, rubidium, caesium, and francium. They form a linked group (Group One) in the ◊periodic table of the elements. They are univalent (have a valency of one) and of very low density (lithium, sodium, and potassium float on water); in general they are reactive, soft, low-melting-point metals. Because of their reactivity they are only found as compounds in nature.

alkaline-earth metal any of a group of six metallic elements with similar bonding properties: beryllium, magnesium, calcium, strontium, barium, and radium. They form a linked group in the ◊periodic table of the elements. They are strongly basic, bivalent (have a valency of two), and occur in nature only in compounds.

alkaloid any of a number of physiologically active and frequently poisonous substances contained in some plants. They are usually organic bases and contain nitrogen. They form salts with acids and, when soluble, give alkaline solutions.

Substances in this group are included by custom rather than by scientific rules. Examples include morphine, cocaine, quinine, caffeine, strychnine, nicotine, and atropine.

In 1992, epibatidine, a chemical extracted from the skin of an Ecuadorian frog, was identified as a member of an entirely new

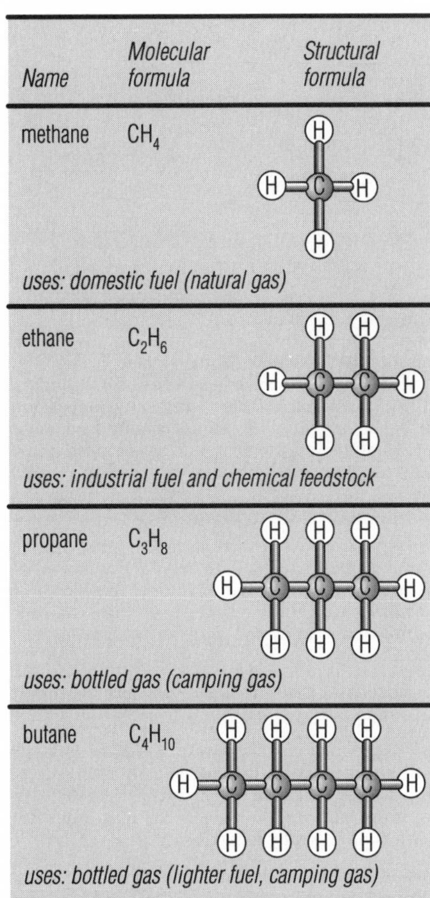

***alkane** The lighter alkanes methane, ethane, propane, and butane, showing the aliphatic chains. A hydrogen atom bonds to a carbon atom at all available sites.*

class of alkaloid. It is an organochlorine compound, which is rarely found in animals, and a powerful painkiller, about 200 times as effective as morphine.

alkane member of a group of ◊hydrocarbons having the general formula C_nH_{2n+2}, commonly known as **paraffins**. As they contain only single ◊covalent bonds, alkanes are said to be saturated. Lighter alkanes, such as methane, ethane, propane, and butane, are colourless gases; heavier ones are liquids or solids. In nature they are found in natural gas and petroleum.

alkene member of the group of ◊hydrocarbons having the general formula C_nH_{2n}, formerly known as **olefins**. Alkenes are unsaturated compounds, characterized by one or more double bonds between adjacent carbon atoms. Lighter alkenes, such as ethene and propene, are gases, obtained from the ◊cracking of oil fractions. Alkenes react by addition, and many useful compounds, such as poly(ethene) and bromoethane, are made from them.

alkyne member of the group of ◊hydrocarbons with the general formula C_nH_{2n-2}, formerly known as the **acetylenes**. They are unsaturated compounds, characterized by one or more triple bonds between adjacent carbon atoms. Lighter alkynes, such as ethyne, are gases; heavier ones are liquids or solids.

allele one of two or more alternative forms of a ◊gene at a given position (locus) on a chromosome, caused by a difference in the ◊DNA. Blue and brown eyes in humans are determined by different alleles of the gene for eye colour.

Organisms with two sets of chromosomes (diploids) will have two copies of each gene. If the two alleles are identical the individual is said to be ◊homozygous at that locus; if different, the individual is ◊heterozygous at that locus. Some alleles show ◊dominance over others.

ALLERGY FACTS

http://www.sig.net/~allergy/facts.html

Extended fact sheet about allergies. It provides basic information about the causes, symptoms, and treatment of allergy attacks, and helps clarify typical misunderstandings about allergy sufferers. It also provides tips for the everyday life of an allergy sufferer and an extended list of allergy symptoms.

allergy special sensitivity of the body that makes it react with an exaggerated response of the natural immune defence mechanism to the introduction of an otherwise harmless foreign substance **(allergen)**.

alligator ***Spanish el lagarto 'the lizard'*** reptile of the genus *Alligator*, related to the crocodile. There are only two living species: *A. mississipiensis*, the Mississippi alligator of the southern states of the USA, and *A. sinensis* from the swamps of the lower Chang Jiang River in China. The former grows to about 4 m/12 ft, but the latter only to 1.5 m/5 ft. Alligators lay their eggs in waterside nests of mud and vegetation and are good mothers. They swim well with lashing movements of the tail and feed on fish and mammals but seldom attack people.

The skin is of value for fancy leather, and alligator farms have been established in the USA. Closely related are the caymans of South America; these belong to the genus *Caiman*. Alligators ranged across N Europe from the Upper Cretaceous to the Pliocene period.

AMERICAN ALLIGATOR

http://www.seaworld.org/animal_bytes/alligatorab.html

Illustrated guide to the American alligator including information about genus, size, life span, habitat, gestation, diet, and a series of fun facts.

alligator clip small metal clip wired to other similar clips to allow temporary connections. Today's modular phone jacks generally make it easy to hook up modems and telephones. However, in some situations, such as a hotel room where a telephone is hard-wired to the wall or in a foreign country where a visitor's modem plug is incompatible with the local telephone network, the only answer is to take the phone apart and hook the modem directly to the phone line using these small clips.

allium any of a group of plants of the lily family, usually strong-smelling with a sharp taste; they form bulbs in which sugar is stored. Cultivated species include onion, garlic, chive, and leek. Some species are grown in gardens for their decorative globular heads of white, pink, or purple flowers. (Genus *Allium*, family Liliaceae.)

allometry in biology, a regular relationship between a given feature (for example, the size of an organ) and the size of the body as a whole, when this relationship is not a simple proportion of body size. Thus, an organ may increase in size proportionately faster, or slower, than body size does. For example, a human baby's head is much larger in relation to its body than is an adult's.

alloparental care in animal behaviour, the care of another animal's offspring. 'Fostering' is common in some birds, such as pigeons, and social mammals, such as meerkats. Usually both the adoptive parent and the young benefit.

allopathy *Greek allos 'other', pathos 'suffering'* in ◊homoeopathy a term used for orthodox medicine, using therapies designed to counteract the manifestations of the disease. In strict usage, allopathy is the opposite of homoeopathy.

allotropy property whereby an element can exist in two or more forms (allotropes), each possessing different physical properties but the same state of matter (gas, liquid, or solid). The allotropes of carbon are diamond and graphite. Sulphur has several allotropes (flowers of sulphur, plastic, rhombic, and monoclinic). These solids have different crystal structures, as do the white and grey forms of tin and the black, red, and white forms of phosphorus.

Oxygen exists as two gaseous allotropes: one used by organisms for respiration (O_2), and the other a poisonous pollutant, ozone (O_3).

alloy metal blended with some other metallic or nonmetallic substance to give it special qualities, such as resistance to corrosion, greater hardness, or tensile strength. Useful alloys include bronze, brass, cupronickel, duralumin, German silver, gunmetal, pewter, solder, steel, and stainless steel.

Among the oldest alloys is bronze (mainly an alloy of copper and tin), the widespread use of which ushered in the Bronze Age. Complex alloys are now common; for example, in dentistry, where a cheaper alternative to gold is made of chromium, cobalt, molybdenum, and titanium. Among the most recent alloys are superplastics: alloys that can stretch to double their length at specific temperatures, permitting, for example, their injection into moulds as easily as plastic.

allspice spice prepared from the dried berries of the evergreen pimento tree, also known as the West Indian pepper tree, (*Pimenta dioica*) of the myrtle family, cultivated chiefly in Jamaica. It has an aroma similar to that of a mixture of cinnamon, cloves, and nutmeg.

alluvial deposit layer of broken rocky matter, or sediment, formed from material that has been carried in suspension by a river or stream and dropped as the velocity of the current decreases. River plains and deltas are made entirely of alluvial deposits, but smaller pockets can be found in the beds of upland torrents.

Alluvial deposits can consist of a whole range of particle sizes, from boulders down through cobbles, pebbles, gravel, sand, silt, and clay. The raw materials are the rocks and soils of upland areas that are loosened by erosion and washed away by mountain streams. Much of the world's richest farmland lies on alluvial deposits. These deposits can also provide an economic source of minerals. River currents produce a sorting action, with particles of heavy material deposited first while lighter materials are washed downstream.

Hence heavy minerals such as gold and tin, present in the original rocks in small amounts, can be concentrated and deposited on stream beds in commercial quantities. Such deposits are called 'placer ores'.

Almagest *Arabic al 'the' and a corruption of the Greek megiste 'greatest'* book compiled by the Greek astronomer ◊Ptolemy during the 2nd century AD, which included the idea of an Earth-centred universe; it was translated into Arabic in the 9th century. Some medieval books on astronomy, astrology, and alchemy were given the same title.

Each of the 13 sections of the book deals with a different branch of astronomy. The introduction describes the universe as spherical and contains arguments for the Earth being stationary at the centre. From this mistaken assumption, it goes on to describe the motions of the Sun, Moon, and planets; eclipses; and the positions, brightness, and precession of the 'fixed stars'. The book drew on the work of earlier astronomers such as Hipparchus.

almond tree related to the peach and apricot. Dessert almonds are the kernels of the fruit of the sweet variety *Prunus amygdalus dulcis,* which is also used to produce a low-cholesterol cooking oil. Oil of bitter almonds, from the variety *P. amygdalus amara,* is used in flavouring. Almond oil is also used for cosmetics, perfumes, and fine lubricants. (*Prunus amygdalus,* family Rosaceae.)

aloe *Aloes vary in size from dwarf species, no more than a few centimetres in diameter (such as the popular houseplant* Aloe variegata*), to species as large as a small tree. This* Aloe arborescens *from South Africa is of intermediate size. In their natural habitat most aloes flower during winter. Premaphotos Wildlife*

aloe one of a group of plants native to southern Africa, with long, fleshy, spiny-edged leaves. The drug usually referred to as 'bitter aloes' is a powerful purgative (agent that causes the body to expel impurities) prepared from the juice of the leaves of several of the species. (Genus *Aloe,* family Liliaceae.)

alpaca domesticated South American hoofed mammal *Lama pacos* of the camel family, found in Chile, Peru, and Bolivia, and herded at high elevations in the Andes. It is bred mainly for its long, fine, silky wool, and stands about 1 m/3 ft tall at the shoulder with neck and head another 60 cm/2 ft.

The alpaca is also used for food at the end of its fleece-producing years. Like the ◊llama, it was probably bred from the wild ◊guanaco and is a close relative of the ◊vicuna.

alpha in computing, the first version of a new software program. Developing modern software requires much testing and many versions before the definitive product is achieved. The first versions of any new product are typically full of ◊bugs, and are tested by the developers and their assistants. Later versions, known as ◊beta versions, are given to outside users to test.

Alpha Centauri or **Rigil Kent** brightest star in the constellation Centaurus and the third-brightest star in the sky. It is actually a triple star (see ◊binary star); the two brighter stars orbit each other every 80 years, and the third, Proxima Centauri, is the closest star to the Sun, 4.2 light years away, 0.1 light years closer than the other two.

alpha channel in ◊24-bit colour, a channel for controlling colour information. Describing colour for a computer display requires three channels of information per ◊pixel, one for each of the primary colours of light: red, blue, and green. A 24-bit graphics adapter with a 32-bit ◊bus can use the remaining 8 bits to send control information for the remaining 24 bits.

alpha decay disintegration of the nucleus of an atom to produce an ◊alpha particle. See also ◊radioactivity.

alphanumeric data data made up of any of the letters of the alphabet and any digit from 0 to 9. The classification of data according to the type or types of character contained enables computer ◊validation systems to check the accuracy of data: a computer can be programmed to reject entries that contain the wrong type of character. For example, a person's name would be rejected if it contained any numeric data, and a bank-account number would be rejected if it contained any alphabetic data. A car's registration number, by comparison, would be expected to contain alphanumeric data but no punctuation marks.

alpha particle positively charged, high-energy particle emitted from the nucleus of a radioactive atom. It is one of the products of the spontaneous disintegration of radioactive elements (see ◊radioactivity) such as radium and thorium, and is identical with the nucleus of a helium atom – that is, it consists of two protons and two neutrons. The process of emission, **alpha decay**, transforms one element into another, decreasing the atomic (or proton) number by two and the atomic mass (or nucleon number) by four.

Because of their large mass alpha particles have a short range of only a few centimetres in air, and can be stopped by a sheet of paper. They have a strongly ionizing effect (see ◊ionizing radiation) on the molecules that they strike, and are therefore capable of damaging living cells. Alpha particles travelling in a vacuum are deflected slightly by magnetic and electric fields.

Alps, Lunar conspicuous mountain range on the Moon, NE of the Sea of Showers (Mare Imbrium), cut by a valley 150 km/93 mi long. The highest peak is Mont Blanc, about 3,660 m/12,000 ft.

Alsatian another name for the ◊German shepherd dog.

Altair or ***Alpha Aquilae*** brightest star in the constellation Aquila and the 12th brightest star in the sky. It is a white star 16 light years away and forms the so-called Summer Triangle with the stars Deneb (in the constellation Cygnus) and Vega (in Lyra).

AltaVista search engine on the World Wide Web run by DEC (Digital Equipment Corporation). AltaVista runs an automated program to index all the pages it can find on the Web, enabling visitors to enter search terms such as a name or subject and quickly retrieve a list of pages to visit to look for specific information. It has a similar indexing program for UseNet.

In mid-1996 DEC claimed the service indexed 30 million pages on 275,600 servers, as well as 3 million articles from 14,000 USENET newsgroups, and was accessed over 16 million times per weekday.

alternate angles a pair of angles that lie on opposite sides and at opposite ends of a transversal (a line that cuts two or more lines in the same plane). The alternate angles formed by a transversal of two parallel lines are equal.

alternating current (AC) electric current that flows for an interval of time in one direction and then in the opposite direction, that is, a current that flows in alternately reversed directions through or around a circuit. Electric energy is usually generated as alternating current in a power station, and alternating currents may be used for both power and lighting.

The advantage of alternating current over direct current (DC), as from a battery, is that its voltage can be raised or lowered economically by a transformer: high voltage for generation and transmission, and low voltage for safe utilization. Railways, factories, and domestic appliances, for example, use alternating current.

My personal desire would be to prohibit entirely the use of alternating currents. They are unnecessary as they are dangerous ... I can therefore see no justification for the introduction of a system which has no element of permanency and every element of danger to life and property.

Thomas Alva Edison US scientist and inventor.
Quoted in R L Weber, *A Random Walk in Science*

alternation of generations typical life cycle of terrestrial plants and some seaweeds, in which there are two distinct forms occurring alternately: **diploid** (having two sets of chromosomes) and **haploid** (one set of chromosomes). The diploid generation produces haploid spores by ◊meiosis, and is called the sporophyte, while the haploid generation produces gametes (sex cells), and is called the gametophyte. The gametes fuse to form a diploid ◊zygote which develops into a new sporophyte; thus the sporophyte and gametophyte alternate.

alternative energy see ◊energy, alternative.

alternative medicine see ◊medicine, alternative.

alternator electricity ◊generator that produces an alternating current.

alt hierarchy on USENET, the 'alternative' set of ◊newsgroups, set up so that anyone can start a newsgroup on any topic. Most areas of USENET, such as the ◊Big Seven hierarchies, allow the creation of newsgroups only after structured discussion and a vote to demonstrate that demand for the newsgroup exists. The alt hierarchy was created to allow users to bypass this process.

altimeter instrument used in aircraft that measures altitude, or height above sea level. The common type is a form of aneroid ◊barometer, which works by sensing the differences in air pressure at different altitudes. This must continually be recalibrated because of the change in air pressure with changing weather conditions. The ◊radar altimeter measures the height of the aircraft above the ground, measuring the time it takes for radio pulses emitted by the aircraft to be reflected. Radar altimeters are essential features of automatic and blind-landing systems.

altimetry method of measuring changes in sea level using an ◊altimeter attached to a satellite. The altimeter measures the distance between the satellite and water surface.

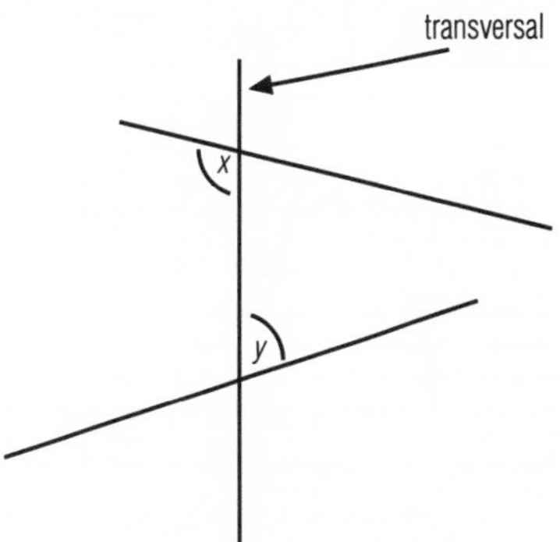

x and *y* are alternate angles

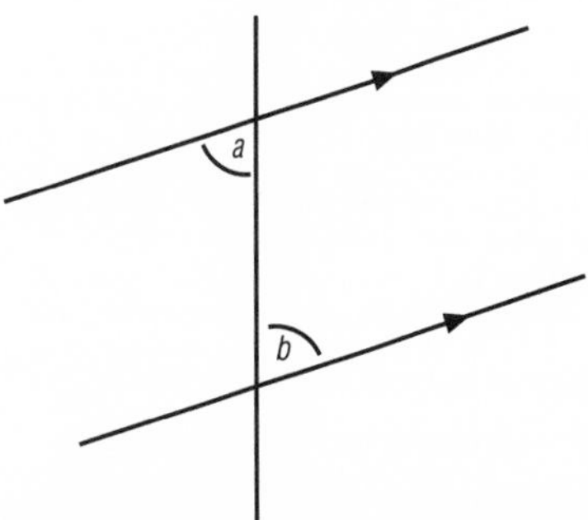

where a transversal cuts through a pair of parallel lines the alternate angles *a* and *b* are equal

alternate angles

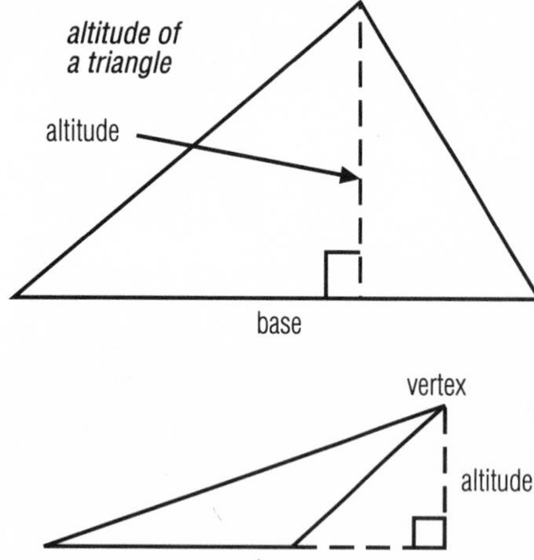

two altitudes of a quadrilateral

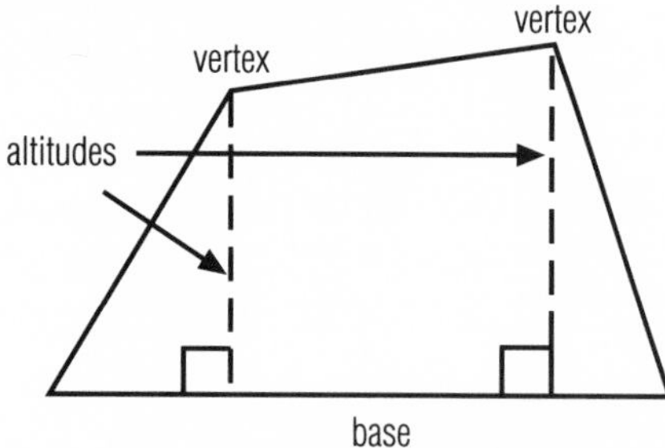

***altitude** The altitude of a figure is the perpendicular distance from a vertex (corner) to the base (the side opposite the vertex).*

altitude or ***elevation*** in astronomy, the angular distance of an object above the horizon, ranging from 0° on the horizon to 90° at the zenith. Together with ◊azimuth, it forms the system of horizontal coordinates for specifying the positions of celestial bodies.

altitude in geometry, the perpendicular distance from a ◊vertex (corner) of a figure, such as a triangle, to the base (the side opposite the vertex).

altitude measurement of height, usually given in metres above sea level.

altricial animals born in a very dependent state and in need of a high degree of parental care. Examples include those mammals that are born naked and blind, such as mice and most other rodents, and most baby birds.

altruism in biology, helping another individual of the same species to reproduce more effectively, as a direct result of which the altruist may leave fewer offspring itself. Female honey bees (workers) behave altruistically by rearing sisters in order to help their mother, the queen bee, reproduce, and forgo any possibility of reproducing themselves.

ALU abbreviation for ◊arithmetic and logic unit.

alum any double sulphate of a monovalent metal or radical (such as sodium, potassium, or ammonium) and a trivalent metal (such as aluminium, chromium, or iron). The commonest alum is the double sulphate of potassium and aluminium, $K_2Al_2(SO_4)_4.24H_2O$, a white crystalline powder that is readily soluble in water. It is used in curing animal skins. Other alums are used in papermaking and to fix dye in the textile industry.

alumina or ***corundum*** Al_2O_3 oxide of aluminium, widely distributed in clays, slates, and shales. It is formed by the decomposition of the feldspars in granite and used as an abrasive. Typically it is a white powder, soluble in most strong acids or caustic alkalis but not in water. Impure alumina is called 'emery'. Rubies, sapphires, and topaz are corundum gemstones.

aluminium lightweight, silver-white, ductile and malleable, metallic element, symbol Al, atomic number 13, relative atomic mass 26.9815, melting point 658°C. It is the third most abundant element (and the most abundant metal) in the Earth's crust, of which it makes up about 8.1% by mass. It is non-magnetic, an excellent conductor of electricity, and oxidizes easily, the layer of oxide on its surface making it highly resistant to tarnish. In the USA the original name suggested by the scientist Humphry Davy, 'aluminum', is retained.

pure aluminium Aluminium is a reactive element with stable compounds, so a great deal of energy is needed in order to separate aluminium from its ores, and the pure metal was not readily obtainable until the middle of the 19th century. Commercially, it is prepared by the electrolysis of alumina (aluminium oxide), which is obtained from the ore ◊bauxite. In its pure state aluminium is a weak metal, but when combined with elements such as copper, silicon, or magnesium it forms alloys of great strength.

uses Aluminium is widely used in the shipbuilding and aircraft industries because of its light weight (relative density 2.70). It is also used in making cooking utensils, cans for beer and soft drinks, and foil. It is much used in steel-cored overhead cables and for canning uranium slugs for nuclear reactors. Aluminium is an essential constituent in some magnetic materials; and, as a good conductor of electricity, is used as foil in electrical capacitors. A plastic form of aluminium, developed 1976, which moulds to any shape and extends to several times its original length, has uses in electronics, cars, and building construction.

aluminium chloride $AlCl_3$ white solid made by direct combination of aluminium and chlorine.

$$2Al + 3Cl_2 \rightarrow 2AlCl_3$$

The anhydrous form is a typical covalent compound.

aluminium hydroxide or ***alumina cream*** $Al(OH)_3$ gelatinous precipitate formed when a small amount of alkali solution is added to a solution of an aluminium salt.

$$Al_{(aq)} + 3OH_{(aq)} \rightarrow Al(OH)_{3(s)}$$

It is an ◊amphoteric compound as it readily reacts with both acids and alkalis.

aluminium oxide or ***alumina*** Al_2O_3 white solid formed by heating aluminium hydroxide. It is an ◊amphoteric oxide, since it reacts readily with both acids and alkalis, and it is used as a refractory (furnace lining) and in column ◊chromatography.

alveolus (plural ***alveoli***) one of the many thousands of tiny air sacs in the ◊lungs in which exchange of oxygen and carbon dioxide takes place between air and the bloodstream.

Alzheimer's disease common manifestation of ◊dementia, thought to afflict one in 20 people over 65. After heart disease, cancer, and strokes it is the most common cause of death in the Western world. Attacking the brain's 'grey matter', it is a disease of mental processes rather than physical function, characterized by memory loss and progressive intellectual impairment. It was first

ALZHEIMER'S DISEASE WEB PAGE

http://med-www.bu.edu/Alzheimer/home.html

Although some of the pages on this site are aimed at the local community, there is much to interest those further afield – with information for families, caregivers, and investigators.

The Ageing Brain and Alzheimer's Disease

BY A D SMITH

'Omnia fert aetas, animum quoque; saepe ego longas cantando puerum memini me condere soles: nunc oblita mihi tot carmina ...'

'Time wastes all things, the mind too: often I remember how in boyhood I outwore long sunlit days in singing: now I have forgotten so many a song ...'

(Virgil, 'Eclogue IX', translation by Mackail)

Was Virgil right? Is it really true that dementia, a decline in our mental and cognitive functions illustrated here by a declining memory, is an inevitable part of ageing? If so, then we will be facing a very serious problem in the next 30 years because the world's population is ageing rapidly as advances in medicine, surgery and nutrition help to extend the human life span. The future demographic predictions are alarming. Between 1990 and 2030 the proportion of people over 60 will grow by about 75% in OECD countries, with a dramatic rise of almost 100% in Japan. It has been known for a long time that the incidence of dementia increases with age, so we can expect the proportion with dementia to increase by similar amount. Dementia, of which Alzheimer's disease is by far the most common cause, is a dreadful devastation of the human mind and spirit; it involves a progressive loss of those very features that make us human: the mind, normal behaviour and even our very personality disintegrates. Modern medicine has followed Virgil in the view that dementia is an inevitable consequence of the ageing of the brain. However, recent discoveries have cast serious doubt on this view and have led to a different idea, that dementia is a true disease, which, if its causes can be identified, should be possible to treat or even to prevent. In other words, to understand dementia we do not have to unravel the secrets of ageing but should consider it just like any other common disease such as cancer, heart disease or diabetes.

Alzheimer's disease (AD) was first described in a woman in her 50s by Alois Alzheimer in 1907. He examined the brain after she died and found in the microscope two kinds of structures that were stained by silver salts. One is called the amyloid plaque and lies outside the cells, while the other is called the neurofibrillary tangle and is found mainly within nerve cells in the cerebral cortex. Both these silver-staining structures are composed of highly insoluble proteins in a fibrillar form. The amyloid plaque is mainly composed of a protein called beta-amyloid peptide which has 40–43 amino acid residues per molecule but which is normally completely insoluble because the individual molecules aggregate together to form fibrils. The protein that makes up the neurofibrillary tangle is different and is derived from a protein called tau whose normal function is to stabilize the microtubules in the nerve's axon, so maintaining the function of this long process of the nerve cell.

Most research into dementia has concentrated on these two proteins and on the question: 'What causes them to accumulate in the brain in people with AD?' However, it has been realized that the deposition of these proteins might not be the primary cause of the symptoms of dementia; perhaps they are the end products of a process that is more closely related to the loss of normal functioning of the brain. This process is in fact the loss of nerve cells and, in particular, the loss of the connections between nerve cells that occur at synapses. The long nerve fibres in the cerebral cortex that pass from one part of the cortex to another die back in AD and so the different functional parts of the cortex are no longer connected to each other. The disease first strikes in the part of the brain that is known to be crucial for memory, the medial temporal lobe which lies deep in the middle of the brain. Nerve cells in some parts of the medial temporal lobe (the hippocampus) die earliest, so that more than 70% of them have disappeared by the time the patient dies. This process of continual death of nerve cells (neurodegeneration) can be followed in life by a simple brain scan, using computed tomography or magnetic resonance imaging. The loss of tissue in the medial temporal lobe occurs at 15% per year and correlates very well with the decline in cognitive function as measured by standard neuropsychological tests. No such rapid loss of tissue occurs with normal ageing and healthy individuals followed each year also show no obvious loss in cognitive function. It is likely that the finding that old people on average have a lower performance in some cognitive tests is mainly explained by the fact that any group of elderly people will include some in whom AD has already begun even though the symptoms are not readily detected.

The nerve cells of the medial temporal lobe are connected to almost all other parts of the cerebral cortex and must serve some kind of integrative role, such as the consolidation of memory. The loss of these connections as the neurons die may be one of the causes of the different symptoms of AD, which arise from abnormal functioning of different parts of the cortex. The death of nerve cells in the medial temporal lobe is accompanied by the death of another small group of nerve cells that lie in the basal nucleus of the forebrain. These basal forebrain neurons make the transmitter called acetylcholine and their main function is to regulate all parts of the cerebral cortex. The only available current treatments for AD act by inhibiting the enzyme that normally destroys acetylcholine, but they are not very effective and they do not slow down the progression of the disease. What is this disease process that strikes at nerve cells in the middle of the cerebral cortex and in the base of the forebrain? Why are these nerve cells particularly vulnerable? These are crucial questions for current research. If we can find the answers to these questions we should be able to devise drugs that slow down or stop the death of cells from occurring and so slow down the decline in cognitive function. There are several current views about what causes the nerve cells to die. One is that the cells are killed by the accumulation of beta-amyloid, and it has indeed been found that beta-amyloid peptide is toxic to nerve cells under certain circumstances. However, the paradox is that amyloid plaques occur most densely in parts of the brain where relatively few cells die. Nevertheless, several of the next generation of drugs being developed for AD are based on the view that if we can stop beta-amyloid being generated from its precursor protein (amyloid precursor protein) then we may be able to slow down progression of the disease. Another view is that the nerve cells die because they are 'strangled' from within by the accumulation of abnormal tau protein. Again, if ways can be found to prevent this from occurring then the disease might be treatable. A third view is that the nerve cells die because there is an excessive production of free radicals in the brain. Free radicals are molecules that have an extra electron and so they are very reactive and combine readily with many of the cell's important proteins. The consequence is that the protein's normal functioning is disturbed. Because free radicals are so reactive, they cannot readily be detected in brain tissue but the damaged proteins have been found in larger amounts than normal in the brains of people with AD. Even if we cannot identify the origin of these free radicals it might be possible to 'capture' them by administering drugs to which they combine in preference to the proteins of cells. Indeed, one such 'drug' is vitamin E and clinical trials are in progress to see whether feeding large amounts of vitamin E can slow down the progression of AD.

A major breakthrough in our understanding of AD was made at St Mary's Hospital Medical School, London, in 1991 where scientists discovered that one of the rare forms of familial AD (i.e. AD that is inherited in a classical Mendelian manner) is due to a mutation in the gene for amyloid precursor protein on chromosome 21. People with this mutation develop the symptoms of AD before the age of 60, so-called early-onset AD. Other forms of early-onset AD have also been found to be due to mutations in specific genes on chromosomes 1 and 14, but these familial forms of AD are quite rare, comprising about 5 % of all cases. It seems likely that these familial forms of AD are all due to abnormalities in the way the body handles the amyloid precursor protein, leading to excessive production of the toxic beta-amyloid. The common sporadic form of AD is usually later in onset, over the age of 65. Sporadic AD and familial AD show the same pathological changes in the brain and yet they must have very different causes. The causes of sporadic AD are now known to be multi-factorial, which means that several factors have to come together in one person before the disease develops. A discovery by scientists at Duke University, North Carolina in 1993 has transformed our understanding of AD; they found that people who carry a common variant (*E4*) of the gene for apolipoprotein E had a five-fold greater risk of developing AD than people who do not carry this variant. This is the first of many 'susceptibility genes' discovered for AD. A susceptibility gene only increases the risk of the disease developing; having this gene does not mean that the person will inevitably get AD. Clearly, other risk factors have to be present. As well as genetic risk factors, a variety of nongenetic factors may influence our risk of getting AD. A lot of current research is directed to identifying these risk factors because some of them may turn out to be modifiable by drugs, life style or diet. Some of these have obvious social and medical implications. Thus, if low education really is a risk factor, we must clearly do our best to give everyone the same high level of schooling. If dietary deficiencies are a risk then we must make sure that everyone has an adequate diet. The possibility of preventing AD from developing in a proportion of the elderly must be pursued with as much vigour as the search for drug treatments for those who are unfortunate enough to develop the disease. These are two of medicine's major challenges for the 21st century.

described by Alois Alzheimer 1906. It affects up to 4 million people in the USA and around 600,000 in Britain.

causes Various factors have been implicated in causing Alzheimer's disease including high levels of aluminium in drinking water and the presence in the brain of an abnormal protein, known as beta-amyloid.

In 1993 the gene coding for apolipoprotein (APOE) was implicated. US researchers established that people who carry a particular version of this gene (APOE-E4) are at greatly increased risk of developing the disease. It is estimated that one person in thirty carries this protein mutation; in the USA the figure is as high as 15%. The suspect gene can be detected with a test, so it is technically possible to identify those most at risk. As no cure is available such testing is unlikely to be widespread.

A second Alzheimer's gene was identified in 1997. The gene, HLA-A2, increases the speed at which the disease begins. The *Neurology* report stated that if a person had both HLA-A2 and APOE-E4, he or she may reach dementia a decade earlier than those with only one of the genes.

diagnosis US researchers began trialling a simple eye test in 1994 that could be used to diagnose sufferers. The drug tropicamide causes marked pupil dilation in those with the disease, and only slight dilation in healthy individuals.

treatment Some researchers are convinced that, whatever its cause, Alzheimer's disease is essentially an inflammatory condition, similar to rheumatoid arthritis. Although there is no cure, trials of anti-inflammatory drugs have shown promising results. Also under development are drugs which block the toxic effects of beta-amyloid. A 1996 study by US neuroscientists found that oestrogen skin patches were also beneficial in the treatment of female Alzheimer's patients, improving concentration and memory.

AM abbreviation for ◊amplitude modulation.

amalgam any alloy of mercury with other metals. Most metals will form amalgams, except iron and platinum. Amalgam is used in dentistry for filling teeth, and usually contains copper, silver, and zinc as the main alloying ingredients. This amalgam is pliable when first mixed and then sets hard, but the mercury leaches out and may cause a type of heavy-metal poisoning.

Amalgamation, the process of forming an amalgam, is a technique sometimes used to extract gold and silver from their ores. The ores are ground to a fine sand and brought into contact with mercury, which dissolves the gold and silver particles. The amalgam is then heated to distil the mercury, leaving a residue of silver and gold. The mercury is recovered and reused.

Almagamation to extract gold from its ore has been in use since Roman times.

amanita any of a group of fungi (see ◊fungus) distinguished by a ring (or volva) around the base of the stalk, warty patches on the cap, and the clear white colour of the gills. Many of the species are brightly coloured and highly poisonous. (Genus *Amanita,* family Agaricaceae.)

amatol explosive consisting of ammonium nitrate and TNT (trinitrotoluene) in almost any proportions.

amber fossilized ◊resin from coniferous trees of the Middle ◊Tertiary period. It is often washed ashore on the Baltic coast with plant and animal specimens preserved in it; many extinct species have been found preserved in this way. It ranges in colour from red to yellow, and is used to make jewellery.

When amber is rubbed with cloth, it attracts light objects, such as feathers. The effect, first noticed by the ancient Greeks, is due to acquisition of negative electric charge, hence the adaptation of the Greek word for amber, *elektron,* for electricity (see ◊static electricity).

Amber has been coveted for its supposed special properties since prehistoric times. Archaeologists have found amulets made of amber dating back as far as 35000 BC.

Amber's preservative properties were demonstrated 1992 when DNA was extracted from insects estimated to be around 30 million years old which were found fossilized in amber, and in 1995 US scientists succeeded in extracting bacterial spores from a bee in amber that was 40 million years old. Despite their lengthy dormancy, the bacterial spores were successfully germinated.

ambergris fatty substance, resembling wax, found in the stomach and intestines of the sperm ◊whale. It is found floating in warm seas, and is used in perfumery as a fixative.

Basically intestinal matter, ambergris is not the result of disease, but the product of an otherwise normal intestine. The name derives from the French *ambre gris* (grey amber).

American Association for the Advancement of Science (AAAS) US scientific society founded in 1848 with the aim of informing the public of the progress of science, and furthering scientific responsibility; its headquarters are in Washington, DC. It holds a large annual meeting, with many speakers describing the latest scientific developments, publishes journals, and sponsors awards.

It was modelled on the British Association for the Advancement of Science.

American National Standards Institute (ANSI) US national standards body. It sets official procedures in (among other areas) computing and electronics. The ANSI ◊character set is the standard set of characters used by Windows-based computers.

America Online (AOL) US market-leading commercial information service. America Online was launched 1986 with a bright, colourful graphical interface and a marketing campaign that issued free discs on almost every US magazine cover. In 1995 it overtook the then market leader, CompuServe, and by 1996 had more than 5 million users worldwide. America Online combined with the German publishing conglomerate Bertelsmann to launch a UK version of the service, known as AOL, in early 1996.

Because a number of America Online users, many of them using temporary accounts set up from the many free discs, acted in breach of ◊netiquette when America Online opened its Internet ◊gateway 1994, America Online users are held in contempt by many parts of the Net.

americium radioactive metallic element of the ◊actinide series, symbol Am, atomic number 95, relative atomic mass 243.13; it was first synthesized 1944. It occurs in nature in minute quantities in ◊pitchblende and other uranium ores, where it is produced from the decay of neutron-bombarded plutonium, and is the element with the highest atomic number that occurs in nature. It is synthesized in quantity only in nuclear reactors by the bombardment of plutonium with neutrons. Its longest-lived isotope is Am-243, with a half-life of 7,650 years.

The element was named by Glenn Seaborg, one of the team who first synthesized it in 1944, after the United States of America. Ten isotopes are known.

Ames Research Center US space-research (NASA) installation at Mountain View, California, USA, for the study of aeronautics and life sciences. It has managed the Pioneer series of planetary probes and is involved in the search for extraterrestrial life.

amethyst variety of ◊quartz, SiO_2, coloured violet by the presence of small quantities of impurities such as manganese or iron; used as a semiprecious stone. Amethysts are found chiefly in the Ural Mountains, India, the USA, Uruguay, and Brazil.

amide any organic chemical derived from a fatty acid by the replacement of the hydroxyl group (–OH) by an amino group ($-NH_2$).

One of the simplest amides is acetamide (CH_3CONH_2), which has a strong mousy odour.

Amiga microcomputer produced by US company Commodore 1985 to succeed the Commodore C64 home computer. The original Amiga was based on the Motorola 68000 microprocessor and achieved significant success in the domestic market.

Despite a failure to sell to the general business market, the latest versions of the Amiga are widely used in the film and video industries, where the Amiga's specialized graphics capabilities are used to create a variety of visual effects.

amine any of a class of organic chemical compounds in which one or more of the hydrogen atoms of ammonia (NH_3) have been replaced by other groups of atoms.

alanine $CH_3CH{\cdot}(NH_2){\cdot}COOH$

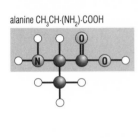

cysteine $SH{\cdot}CH_2CH{\cdot}(NH_2){\cdot}COOH$

glycine NH_2CH_2COOH

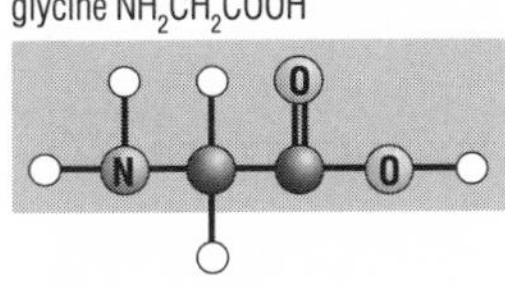

tyrosine $C_6H_4OH{\cdot}CH_2CH{\cdot}(NH_2){\cdot}COOH$

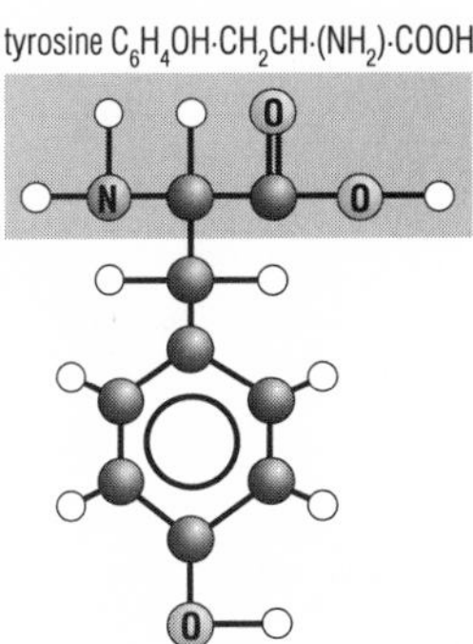

— covalent bond
○ hydrogen atom
carbon atom
oxygen atom
nitrogen atom
sulphur atom

***amino acid** Amino acids are natural organic compounds that make up proteins and can thus be considered the basic molecules of life. There are 20 different common amino acids. They consist mainly of carbon, oxygen, hydrogen, and nitrogen. Each amino acid has a common core structure (consisting of two carbon atoms, two oxygen atoms, a nitrogen atom, and four hydrogen atoms) to which is attached a variable group, known as the R group. In glycine, the R group is a single hydrogen atom; in alanine, the R group consists of a carbon and three hydrogen atoms.*

Methyl amines have unpleasant ammonia odours and occur in decomposing fish. They are all gases at ordinary temperature.

Aromatic amine compounds include aniline, which is used in dyeing.

AMINO ACIDS

http://www.chemie.fu-berlin.de/chemistry/bio/amino-acids.html

Small but interesting site giving the names and chemical structures of all the amino acids.

amino acid water-soluble organic ◊molecule, mainly composed of carbon, oxygen, hydrogen, and nitrogen, containing both a basic amino group (NH_2) and an acidic carboxyl (COOH) group. They are small molecules able to pass through membranes. When two or more amino acids are joined together, they are known as ◊peptides; ◊proteins are made up of peptide chains folded or twisted in characteristic shapes.

Many different proteins are found in the cells of living organisms, but they are all made up of the same 20 amino acids, joined together in varying combinations (although other types of amino acid do occur infrequently in nature). Eight of these, the **essential amino acids**, cannot be synthesized by humans and must be obtained from the diet. Children need a further two amino acids that are not essential for adults. Other animals also need some preformed amino acids in their diet, but green plants can manufacture all the amino acids they need from simpler molecules, relying on energy from the Sun and minerals (including nitrates) from the soil.

To remember the ten essential amino acids:

THESE TEN VALUABLE AMINO ACIDS HAVE LONG PRESERVED LIFE IN MAN.

THREONINE / TRYPTOPHAN / VALINE / ARGENINE / HISTIDINE / LYSINE / PHENYLALANINE / LEUCINE / ISOLEUCINE / METHIONINE

ammeter instrument that measures electric current, usually in ◊amperes. The ammeter is placed in series with the component through which current is to be measured, and is constructed with a low internal resistance in order to prevent the reduction of that current as it flows through the instrument itself. A common type is the ◊moving-coil meter, which measures direct current (DC), but can, in the presence of a rectifier, measure alternating current (AC) also. Hot-wire, moving-iron and dynamometer ammeters can be used for both DC and AC.

ammonia NH_3 colourless, pungent-smelling gas, lighter than air and very soluble in water. It is made on an industrial scale by the ◊Haber (or Haber–Bosch) process, and used mainly to produce nitrogenous fertilizers, nitric acid, and some explosives.

In aquatic organisms and some insects, nitrogenous waste (from the breakdown of amino acids and so on) is excreted in the form of ammonia, rather than as urea in mammals.

ammoniacal solution in chemistry, a solution produced by dissolving a solute in aqueous ammonia.

ammonite extinct marine ◊cephalopod mollusc of the order Ammonoidea, related to the modern nautilus. The shell was curled in a plane spiral and made up of numerous gas-filled chambers, the outermost containing the body of the animal. Many species flourished between 200 million and 65 million years ago, ranging in size from that of a small coin to 2 m/6 ft across.

ammonium carbonate $(NH_4)_2CO_3$ white, crystalline solid that readily sublimes at room temperature into its constituent gases: ammonia, carbon dioxide, and water. It was formerly used in ◊smelling salts.

ammonium chloride or ***sal ammoniac*** NH_4Cl a volatile salt that forms white crystals around volcanic craters. It is prepared synthetically for use in 'dry-cell' batteries, fertilizers, and dyes.

ammonium nitrate NH_4NO_3 colourless, crystalline solid, prepared by ◊neutralization of nitric acid with ammonia; the salt is crystallized from the solution. It sublimes on heating.

amnesia loss or impairment of memory. As a clinical condition it may be caused by disease or injury to the brain, by some drugs, or by shock; in some cases it may be a symptom of an emotional disorder.

amniocentesis sampling the amniotic fluid surrounding a fetus in the womb for diagnostic purposes. It is used to detect Down's syn-

AMNIOCENTESIS

http://www.aomc.org/amnio.html#_wmh4_822004218

Comprehensive plain English guide to amniocentesis. For a pregnant woman considering the procedure, this is an invaluable source of information. The advantages and the risks of sampling the amniotic fluid are clearly presented.

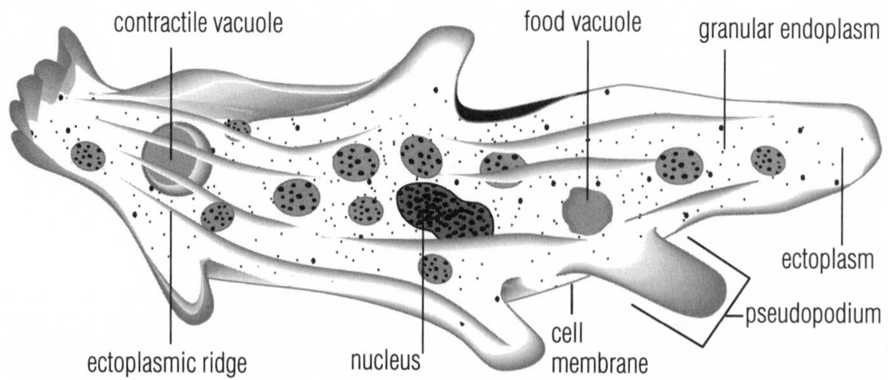

***amoeba** The amoebae are among the simplest living organisms, consisting of a single cell. Within the cell, there is a nucleus, which controls cell activity, and many other microscopic bodies and vacuoles (fluid-filled spaces surrounded by a membrane) with specialized functions. Amoebae eat by flowing around food particles, engulfing the particle, a process called phagocytosis.*

drome and other genetic abnormalities. The procedure carries a 1 in 200 risk of miscarriage.

amnion innermost of three membranes that enclose the embryo within the egg (reptiles and birds) or within the uterus (mammals). It contains the amniotic fluid that helps to cushion the embryo.

amoeba (plural ***amoebae***) one of the simplest living animals, consisting of a single cell and belonging to the ◊protozoa group. The body consists of colourless protoplasm. Its activities are controlled by the nucleus, and it feeds by flowing round and engulfing organic debris. It reproduces by ◊binary fission. Some species of amoeba are harmful parasites.

amp in physics, abbreviation for **ampere**, a unit of electrical current. Its use is deprecated.

ampere SI unit (symbol A) of electrical current. Electrical current is measured in a similar way to water current, in terms of an amount per unit time; one ampere represents a flow of about 6.28 $\times 10^{18}$ ◊electrons per second, or a rate of flow of charge of one coulomb per second.

The ampere is defined as the current that produces a specific magnetic force between two long, straight, parallel conductors placed 1m/3.3 ft apart in a vacuum. It is named after the French scientist André Ampère.

Ampère's rule rule developed by French physicist André Ampère connecting the direction of an electric current and its associated magnetic currents. It states that if a person were travelling along a current-carrying wire in the direction of conventional current flow (from the positive to the negative terminal), and carrying a magnetic compass, then the north pole of the compass needle would be deflected to the left-hand side.

amphetamine or ***speed*** powerful synthetic ◊stimulant. Benzedrine was the earliest amphetamine marketed, used as a 'pep pill' in World War II to help soldiers overcome fatigue, and until the 1970s amphetamines were prescribed by doctors as an appetite suppressant for weight loss; as an antidepressant, to induce euphoria; and as a stimulant, to increase alertness.

Indications for its use today are very restricted because of severe side effects, including addiction. Amphetamine is a sulphate or phosphate form of $C_9H_{13}N$.

amphibian ***Greek 'double life'*** member of the vertebrate class Amphibia, which generally spend their larval (tadpole) stage in

Ampère, André Marie
(1775–1836)

French physicist and mathematician who made many discoveries in electromagnetism and electrodynamics. He followed up the work of Hans Oersted on the interaction between magnets and electric currents, developing a rule for determining the direction of the magnetic field associated with an electric current. The unit of electric current, the **ampere**, is named after him.

Ampère's law is an equation that relates the magnetic force produced by two parallel current-carrying conductors to the product of their currents and the distance between the conductors. Today Ampère's law is usually stated in the form of calculus: the line integral of the magnetic field around an arbitrarily chosen path is proportional to the net electric current enclosed by the path.

Mary Evans Picture Library

***amphibian** Toads are among the commonest amphibians. This striking green toad* Bufo viridis *is distributed in a number of habitats in the E Mediterranean area, such as these coastal sand flats on the island of Corfu.   Premaphotos Wildlife*

AMPHIBIAN

Frogs and toads never eat with their eyes open. When eating, they have to push down with the back of the eyeball in order to force food into the stomach.

fresh water, transferring to land at maturity (after ◊metamorphosis) and generally returning to water to breed. Like fish and reptiles, they continue to grow throughout life, and cannot maintain a temperature greatly differing from that of their environment. The class contains 4,553 known species, 4,000 of which are frogs and toads, 390 salamanders, and 163 caecilians (wormlike in appearance).

Amphioxus genus name of the ◊lancelet.

amphoteric term used to describe the ability of some chemical compounds to behave either as an ◊acid or as a ◊base depending on their environment. For example, the metals aluminium and zinc, and their oxides and hydroxides, act as bases in acidic solutions and as acids in alkaline solutions.

Amino acids and proteins are also amphoteric, as they contain both a basic (amino, $-NH_2$) and an acidic (carboxyl, $-COOH$) group.

amplifier electronic device that magnifies the strength of a signal, such as a radio signal. The ratio of output signal strength to input signal strength is called the **gain** of the amplifier. As well as achieving high gain, an amplifier should be free from distortion and able to operate over a range of frequencies. Practical amplifiers are usually complex circuits, although simple amplifiers can be built from single transistors or valves.

amplitude or ***argument*** in mathematics, the angle in an ◊Argand diagram between the line that represents the complex number and the real (positive horizontal) axis. If the complex number is written in the form $r(\cos\theta + i\sin\theta)$, where r is radius and $i = \sqrt{-1}$, the amplitude is the angle θ (theta). The amplitude is also the peak value of an oscillation.

amplitude maximum displacement of an oscillation from the equilibrium position. For a wave motion, it is the height of a crest (or the depth of a trough). With a sound wave, for example, amplitude corresponds to the intensity (loudness) of the sound. In AM (amplitude modulation) radio broadcasting, the required audio-frequency signal is made to modulate (vary slightly) the amplitude of a continuously transmitted radio carrier wave.

amplitude modulation (AM) method by which radio waves are altered for the transmission of broadcasting signals. AM waves are constant in frequency, but the amplitude of the transmitting wave varies in accordance with the signal being broadcast.

ampulla in the inner ◊ear, a slight swelling at the end of each semicircular canal, able to sense the motion of the head.

The sense of balance depends largely on sensitive hairs within the ampullae responding to movements of fluid within the canal.

amygdala almond-shaped region of the ◊brain adjacent to the hippocampus, that links the cortex, responsible for conscious thought, with the regions controlling emotions. A 1994 US study showed that it was involved in interpreting fear-provoking information and linking it to fear responses. For example, where the amygdala is damaged patients are unable to recognize fearful expressions.

Emotionally charged events are more easily recalled than neutral events, and in 1996 US researchers demonstrated a link between the amygdala and the memorizing of emotionally loaded images.

amyl alcohol former name for ◊pentanol.

amylase one of a group of ◊enzymes that break down starches into their component molecules (sugars) for use in the body. It occurs widely in both plants and animals. In humans, it is found in saliva and in pancreatic juices.

Human amylase has an optimum pH of 7.2–7.4. Like most enzymes amylase is denatured by temperatures above 60°C.

anabolic steroid any ◊hormone of the ◊steroid group that stimulates tissue growth. Its use in medicine is limited to the treatment of some anaemias and breast cancers; it may help to break up blood clots. Side effects include aggressive behaviour, masculinization in women, and, in children, reduced height.

anabolism process of building up body tissue, promoted by the influence of certain hormones. It is the constructive side of ◊metabolism, as opposed to ◊catabolism.

anaconda South American snake *Eunectes murinus*, a member of the python and boa family, the Boidae. One of the largest snakes, growing to 9 m/30 ft or more, it is found in and near water, where it lies in wait for the birds and animals on which it feeds. The anaconda is not venomous, but kills its prey by coiling round it and squeezing until the creature suffocates.

Females are up to 5 times larger than males. They have litters of up to 80 babies, born live, and each weighing only 250–300 g. The gestation period last six to eight months, during which time the female will not eat at all.

anaemia condition caused by a shortage of haemoglobin, the oxygen-carrying component of red blood cells. The main symptoms are fatigue, pallor, breathlessness, palpitations, and poor resistance to infection. Treatment depends on the cause.

Anaemia arises either from abnormal loss or defective production of haemoglobin. Excessive loss occurs, for instance, with chronic slow bleeding or with accelerated destruction (◊haemolysis) of red blood cells. Defective production may be due to iron deficiency, vitamin B_{12} deficiency (pernicious anaemia), certain blood diseases (sickle-cell disease and thalassaemia), chronic infection, kidney disease, or certain kinds of poisoning. Untreated anaemia taxes the heart and may prove fatal.

anaerobic (of living organisms) not requiring oxygen for the release of energy from food molecules such as glucose. Anaerobic organisms include many bacteria, yeasts, and internal parasites.

Obligate anaerobes, such as certain primitive bacteria, cannot function in the presence of oxygen; but **facultative anaerobes**, like the fermenting yeasts and most bacteria, can function with or without oxygen. Anaerobic organisms release much less of the available energy from their food than do ◊aerobic organisms.

anaesthetic drug that produces loss of sensation or consciousness; the resulting state is **anaesthesia**, in which the patient is insensitive to stimuli. Anaesthesia may also happen as a result of nerve disorder.

Ever since the first successful operation in 1846 on a patient rendered unconscious by ether, advances have been aimed at increasing safety and control. Sedatives may be given before the anaesthetic to make the process easier. The level and duration of unconsciousness are managed precisely. Where general anaesthesia may be inappropriate (for example, in childbirth, for a small procedure, or in the elderly), many other techniques are available. A topical substance may be applied to the skin or tissue surface; a local agent may be injected into the tissues under the skin in the area to be treated; or a regional block of sensation may be achieved by injection into a nerve. Spinal anaesthetic, such as epidural, is injected into the tissues surrounding the spinal cord, producing loss of feeling in the lower part of the body.

ANAESTHETIC

Although the science of anaesthetics is 150 years old, it is only comparatively recently that safe doses have begun to be calculated correctly. It is said that when the Japanese bombed Pearl Harbor in 1941, more US servicemen were killed by anaesthetists than by bombs.

History of Anaesthesia

BY PAULETTE PRATT

While the need for some form of anaesthesia had been recognized since earliest times, for centuries all that was available to deaden the pain of surgery was a copious draft of alcohol. As late as 1839 a leading French surgeon predicted: 'To escape pain in surgical operations is a chimera which we cannot expect in our time.' Mercifully, he was mistaken for the first use of anaesthesia in surgery was recorded only seven years later.

By this time there had been some experimentation with volatile agents such as ether, chloroform and nitrous oxide. Ether, for example, enjoyed a certain notoriety arising from medical students' 'ether frolics'. But this was the substance used in what is credited as the first operation undertaken in an anaesthetized patient – in the famous 'ether dome' at Massachusetts General Hospital in Boston on October 16, 1846. Its use was demonstrated by the dentist William Thomas Green Morton (1819–68).

The following day, not content with the apparatus he had used to administer the ether, Morton commissioned an improved version. Later he abandoned this, too, in favour of a simple sponge. 'This should be about the size of the open hand, or a little larger, and concave, to suit over the nose and mouth,' he wrote in the *Lancet* (June 30, 1847).

'The sponge is then thoroughly saturated with ether, applied to the nose and mouth, and, with the latter open, the patient directed to inhale as fully and freely as possible. In this way, I have found the result more sure and satisfactory, and the difficulty of inhalation very much reduced, or entirely removed. The most delicate or nervous females, or aged persons, as well as young children, are thus rapidly and almost imperceptibly narcotized...'

Only a month after its Boston debut, ether anaesthesia was first used in Britain, at London's University College Hospital. In January 1847, James Young Simpson (1811–70), Professor of Obstetrics at Edinburgh, was the first to introduce its use for women in childbirth, initially for forceps or operative deliveries but soon also for uncomplicated cases.

However, disliking ether's 'disagreeable and very persistent smell', Simpson soon began casting around for an alternative and decided to try chloroform. In November 1847, to the consternation of his household, he and two junior colleagues were accidentally exposed to chloroform when a bottle was knocked over at his house in Queen Street. He later wrote: 'The first night we took chloroform, Dr Duncan, Dr Keith and I all tried it simultaneously and were under the table in a minute or two.'

The first obstetric delivery under chloroform took place the day after this mishap and, ten days later, Simpson published his first pamphlet on its use. A forceful figure, he insisted that liberal administration of chloroform on the corner of a towel or handkerchief was harmless.

Not surpisingly, however, since it had gone from first testing to clinical use within the space of little more than a week, the safety of chloroform as an anaesthetic agent was never established. In fact the first UK death from chloroform anaesthesia took place only three months after its introduction.

Elsewhere, once its toxicity became apparent, chloroform fell out of favour. Predictably its use was banned at Massachusetts General, the birthplace of ether anaesthesia. But in Britain Simpson had done such a good job of publicizing chloroform that its popularity grew regardless. Here controversy centred not on safety but on the morality of using anaesthesia at all to relieve the pain of childbirth. There were those who pointed to its apparent biblical proscription – 'In pain shalt thou bear offspring.'

However, the role of anaesthesia in childbirth was confirmed when, on April 7 1853, the well-known London physician John Snow held out a chloroform-soaked handkerchief to assist the birth of Queen Victoria's ninth child, Prince Leopold. The Queen subsequently noted in her diary: 'Dr Snow administered that blessed chloroform and the effect was soothing, quieting and delightful beyond measure.'

Despite a rising death toll (and the appointment of various commissions to investigate the action of chloroform), the drug remained in use until well into the new century.

Meanwhile a third volatile agent, nitrous oxide, had surfaced at around the same time as ether and chloroform. Its pain-killing properties were discovered in 1800 by the British chemist Humphry Davy (1778–1829), who foresaw that 'it may probably be used with advantage in surgical operations'. In 1845, nitrous oxide was first used for pain relief, also at Massachusetts General Hospital, in what proved to be a disastrous demonstration by another dentist, Horace Wells (1815–48). Then it was lost to view for more than two decades.

Nitrous oxide – popularly known as 'laughing gas' because of the excitement it induces – was finally adopted as an anaesthetic agent by way of its use by travelling salesmen. One of these, Gardner Quincy Colton (1814–98), founder of the New York Dental Institute, demonstrated use of the gas at the 1867 International Exhibition in Paris. It was taken up by an influential US dental surgeon, Thomas Wiltberger (1823–97), who in due course introduced it to British dentists. Nitrous oxide is still used as an inhalation agent in surgery today.

There were to be further colourful chapters in the development of safe, effective anaesthesia, including the loss of a few surgical patients to exploding gases. Also memorable was the era of 'twilight sleep' in obstetrics, when a light state of scopolamine–morphine narcosis was used to ease pain and eradicate unpleasant recollections. The main effect of this, in addition to prolonging labour and expunging any memory on the part of the mother of her child's birth, was to produce babies almost too dopey to breathe.

While some specialist training was initiated in the 1930s, it was only after World War 2 – a century after the first use of anaesthesia in surgery – that the speciality really came into its own. Today it is the biggest UK medical speciality, practised with a precision unimaginable in the early days under the 'ether dome'.

analgesic agent for relieving ◊pain. Opiates alter the perception or appreciation of pain and are effective in controlling 'deep' visceral (internal) pain. Non-opiates, such as ◊aspirin, ◊paracetamol, and NSAIDs (nonsteroidal anti-inflammatory drugs), relieve musculoskeletal pain and reduce inflammation in soft tissues.

Pain is felt when electrical stimuli travel along a nerve pathway, from peripheral nerve fibres to the brain via the spinal cord.

An anaesthetic agent acts either by preventing stimuli from being sent (local), or by removing awareness of them (general). Analgesic drugs act on both.

Temporary or permanent analgesia may be achieved by injection of an anaesthetic agent into, or the severing of, a nerve. Implanted devices enable patients to deliver controlled electrical stimulation to block pain impulses. Production of the body's natural opiates, ◊endorphins, can be manipulated by techniques such as relaxation and biofeedback. However, for the severe pain of, for example, terminal cancer, opiate analgesics are required.

US researchers found 1996 that some painkillers were more effective and provided longer-lasting relief for women than men.

analogous in biology, term describing a structure that has a similar function to a structure in another organism, but not a similar evolutionary path. For example, the wings of bees and of birds have the same purpose – to give powered flight – but have different origins.

Compare ◊homologous.

analogue (of a quantity or device) changing continuously; by contrast a ◊digital quantity or device varies in series of distinct steps. For example, an analogue clock measures time by means of a continuous movement of hands around a dial, whereas a digital clock measures time with a numerical display that changes in a series of discrete steps.

Most computers are digital devices. Therefore, any signals and data from an analogue device must be passed through a suitable ◊analogue-to-digital converter before they can be received and processed by computer. Similarly, output signals from digital computers must be passed through a digital-to-analogue converter before they can be received by an analogue device.

analogue computer computing device that performs calculations through the interaction of continuously varying physical quantities, such as voltages (as distinct from the more common ◊digital computer, which works with discrete quantities). An analogue computer is said to operate in real time (corresponding to time in the real world), and can therefore be used to monitor and control other events as they happen.

Although common in engineering since the 1920s, analogue computers are not general-purpose computers, but specialize in solving ◊differential calculus and similar mathematical problems. The earliest analogue computing device is thought to be the flat, or planispheric, astrolabe, which originated in about the 8th century.

analogue signal in electronics, current or voltage that conveys or stores information, and varies continuously in the same way as the information it represents (compare ◊digital signal). Analogue signals are prone to interference and distortion.

The bumps in the grooves of a vinyl record form a mechanical analogue of the sound information stored, which is then is converted into an electrical analogue signal by the record player's pick-up device.

analogue-to-digital converter (ADC) electronic circuit that converts an analogue signal into a digital one. Such a circuit is needed to convert the signal from an analogue device into a digital signal for input into a computer. For example, many ◊sensors designed to measure physical quantities, such as temperature and pressure, produce an analogue signal in the form of voltage and this must be passed through an ADC before computer input and processing. A ◊digital-to-analogue converter performs the opposite process.

analogy in mathematics and logic, a form of argument or process of reasoning from one case to another parallel case. Arguments from analogy generally have the following form: if some event or thing has the properties *a* and *b*, and if another event or thing has the properties *b* and *c*, then the former event or thing has the property *c*, too. Arguments from analogy are not always sound and can mislead. False analogies arise when the cases are insufficiently similar to support the reasoning. For example, a whale lives in water and resembles a fish, but we cannot conclude from this that it is a fish. When arguments from analogy are compressed, they are called metaphors.

analysis in chemistry, the determination of the composition of substances; see ◊analytical chemistry.

analysis branch of mathematics concerned with limiting processes on axiomatic number systems; ◊calculus of variations and infinitesimal calculus is now called analysis.

analyst job classification for ◊computer personnel. An analyst prepares a report on an existing data processing system and makes proposals for changes and improvements.

ANALYTICAL CHEMISTRY BASICS

http://www.scimedia.com/chem-ed/analytic/ac-basic.htm

Detailed online course, designed for those at undergraduate level, that provides the user with an introduction to some of the fundamental concepts and methods of analytical chemistry. Some of the sections included are gravimetric analysis, titration and spectroscopy.

analytical chemistry branch of chemistry that deals with the determination of the chemical composition of substances. **Qualitative analysis** determines the identities of the substances in a given sample; **quantitative analysis** determines how much of a particular substance is present.

Simple qualitative techniques exploit the specific, easily observable properties of elements or compounds – for example, the flame test makes use of the different flame colours produced by metal cations when their compounds are held in a hot flame. More sophisticated methods, such as those of ◊spectroscopy, are required where substances are present in very low concentrations or where several substances have similar properties.

Most quantitative analyses involve initial stages in which the substance to be measured is extracted from the test sample, and purified. The final analytical stages (or 'finishes') may involve measurement of the substance's mass (gravimetry) or volume (volumetry, titrimetry), or a number of techniques initially developed for qualitative analysis, such as fluorescence and absorption spectroscopy, chromatography, electrophoresis, and polarography. Many modern methods enable quantification by means of a detecting device that is integrated into the extraction procedure (as in gas–liquid chromatography).

For him [the scientist], truth is so seldom the sudden light that shows new order and beauty; more often, truth is the uncharted rock that sinks his ship in the dark.

JOHN CORNFORTH Australian chemist.
Nobel prize address 1975

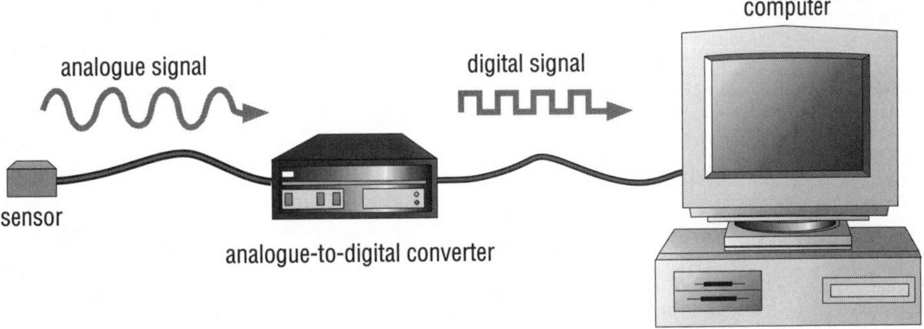

analogue-to-digital converter *An analogue-to-digital converter, or ADC, converts a continuous analogue signal produced by a sensor to a digital ('off and on') signal for computer processing.*

analytical engine programmable computing device designed by English mathematician Charles ◊Babbage in 1833.

It was based on the ◊difference engine but was intended to automate the whole process of calculation. It introduced many of the concepts of the digital computer but, because of limitations in manufacturing processes, was never built.

Among the concepts introduced were input and output, an arithmetic unit, memory, sequential operation, and the ability to make decisions based on data. It would have required at least 50,000 moving parts. The design was largely forgotten until some of Babbage's writings were rediscovered in 1937.

The whole of the developments and operations of analysis are now capable of being executed by machinery. ... As soon as an Analytical Engine exists, it will necessarily guide the future course of science.

CHARLES BABBAGE English mathematician. *Passages from the Life of a Philosopher* 1864

analytical geometry another name for ◊coordinate geometry.

anamorphic projection technique used in film and in ◊virtual reality to squeeze wide-frame images so that they fit into the dimensions of a 35-mm frame of film. In film projection, the projector has a complementary lens which reverses the process. In virtual reality, the computer must calculate the amount of deformation and reverse it.

anatomy study of the structure of the body and its component parts, especially the ◊human body, as distinguished from physiology, which is the study of bodily functions.

Herophilus of Chalcedon (c. 330–c. 260 BC) is regarded as the founder of anatomy. In the 2nd century AD, the Graeco-Roman physician Galen produced an account of anatomy that was the only source of anatomical knowledge until *On the Working of the Human Body* 1543 by Belgian physician Andreas Vesalius. In 1628, English physician William Harvey published his demonstration of the circulation of the blood. With the invention of the microscope, Italian physiologist Marcello Malpighi and Dutch microscopist Anton van Leeuwenhoek were able to found the study of ◊histology. In 1747, Albinus (1697–1770), with the help of the artist Wandelaar (1691–1759), produced the most exact account of the bones and muscles, and in 1757–65 Swiss biologist Albrecht von Haller gave the most complete and exact description of the organs that had yet appeared. Among the anatomical writers of the early 19th century are the surgeon Charles Bell (1774–1842), Jonas Quain (1796–1865), and Henry Gray (1825–1861). Radiographic anatomy (using X-rays; see ◊radiography) has been one of the triumphs of the 20th century, which has also been marked by immense activity in embryological investigation.

anchor in computing, an HTML (hypertext markup language) tag that turns ordinary text into a ◊hyperlink. Anchors are used to enable easy navigation within a single large document or to link to remote documents on distant computers. On the World Wide Web, anchor text is underlined, coloured differently, or surrounded by a dotted line in order to mark it out from normal text.

anchovy small fish *Engraulis encrasicholus* of the ◊herring family. It is fished extensively, being abundant in the Mediterranean, and is also found on the Atlantic coast of Europe and in the Black Sea. It grows to 20 cm/8 in.

Pungently flavoured, it is processed into fish pastes and essences, and used as a garnish, rather than eaten fresh.

andesite volcanic igneous rock, intermediate in silica content between rhyolite and basalt. It is characterized by a large quantity of feldspar ◊minerals, giving it a light colour. Andesite erupts from volcanoes at destructive plate margins (where one plate of the Earth's surface moves beneath another; see ◊plate tectonics), including the Andes, from which it gets its name.

AND gate in electronics, a type of ◊logic gate.

Anderson, Elizabeth Garrett (1836–1917)

English physician, the first English woman to qualify in medicine. Unable to attend medical school, Anderson studied privately and was licensed by the Society of Apothecaries in London in 1865. She was physician to the Marylebone Dispensary for Women and Children (later renamed the Elizabeth Garrett Anderson Hospital), a London hospital now staffed by women and serving female patients.

She became the first woman member of the British Medical Association in 1873 and the first woman mayor in Britain. She lectured at the London School of Medicine for Women (1875–97), and was its dean (1883–1903).

Mary Evans Picture Library

androecium male part of a flower, comprising a number of ◊stamens.

androgen general name for any male sex hormone, of which ◊testosterone is the most important.

They are all ◊steroids and are principally involved in the production of male ◊secondary sexual characteristics (such as beard growth).

Andromeda major constellation of the northern hemisphere, visible in autumn. Its main feature is the Andromeda galaxy. The star Alpha Andromedae forms one corner of the Square of Pegasus. It is named after the princess of Greek mythology.

Andromeda galaxy galaxy 2.2 million light years away from Earth in the constellation Andromeda, and the most distant object visible to the naked eye. It is the largest member of the ◊Local Group of galaxies.

Like the Milky Way, it is a spiral orbited by several companion galaxies but contains about twice as many stars. It is about 200,000 light years across.

AND rule rule used for finding the combined probability of two or more independent events both occurring. If two events E_1 and E_2 are independent (have no effect on each other) and the probabilities of their taking place are p_1 and p_2, respectively, then the combined probability p that both E_1 and E_2 will happen is given by:

$$p = p_1 \times p_2$$

For example, if a blue die and a red die are thrown together, the probability of a blue six is $\frac{1}{6}$, and the probability of a red six is $\frac{1}{6}$. Therefore, the probability of both a red six and a blue six being thrown is $\frac{1}{6} \times \frac{1}{6} = \frac{1}{36}$.

By contrast, the **OR rule** is used for finding the probability of either one event or another taking place.

anechoic chamber room designed to be of high sound absorbency. All surfaces inside the chamber are covered by sound-absorbent materials such as rubber. The walls are often covered with inward-facing pyramids of rubber, to minimize reflections. It is used for experiments in ◊acoustics and for testing audio equipment.

anemometer device for measuring wind speed and liquid flow. The most basic form, the **cup-type anemometer**, consists of cups at the ends of arms, which rotate when the wind blows. The speed of rotation indicates the wind speed.

Vane-type anemometers have vanes, like a small windmill or propeller, that rotate when the wind blows. **Pressure-tube anemometers** use the pressure generated by the wind to indicate speed. The wind blowing into or across a tube develops a pressure, proportional to the wind speed, that is measured by a manometer or pressure gauge. **Hot-wire anemometers** work on the principle that the rate at which heat is transferred from a hot wire to the surrounding air is a measure of the air speed. Wind speed is determined by measuring either the electric current required to maintain a hot wire at a constant temperature, or the variation of resistance while a constant current is maintained.

ANEMONE

http://www.actwin.com/fish/species/anemone.html

Article on keeping anemones in an aquarium environment. The site offers information on species, feeding, and tank maintenance practices to help these creatures thrive in captivity.

anemone flowering plant belonging to the buttercup family, found in northern temperate regions, mainly in woodland. It has ◊sepals which are coloured to attract insects. (Genus *Anemone*, family Ranunculaceae.)

The garden anemone (*Anemone coronaria*) is blue, purple, red, or white. The European and Asian white wood anemone (*A. nemorosa*), or windflower, grows in shady woods, flowering in spring. *Hepatica nobilis*, once included within the genus *Anemone*, is common in the Alps. The ◊pasqueflower is now placed in a separate genus.

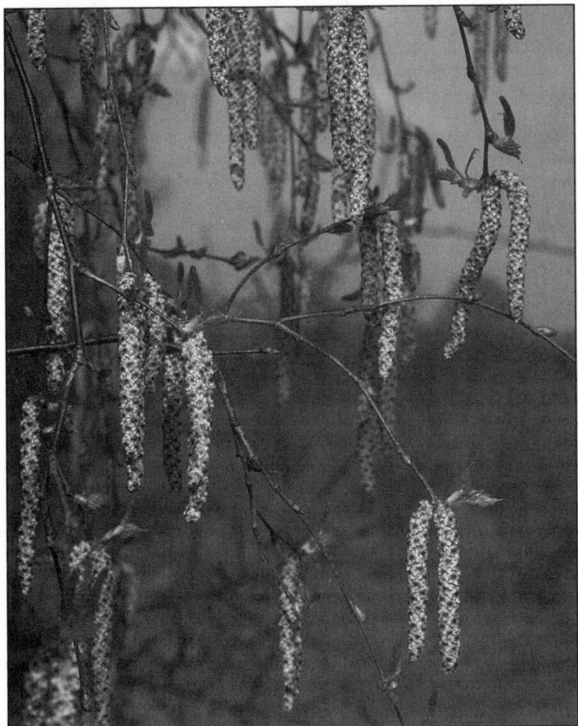

anemophily *A familiar example of anemophily (wind pollination) is provided by the silver birch* Betula pendula, *whose pendant male catkins produce vast amounts of pollen. The much slimmer and shorter female catkins point upwards.* *Premaphotos Wildlife*

anemophily type of ◊pollination in which the pollen is carried on the wind. Anemophilous flowers are usually unscented, have either very reduced petals and sepals or lack them altogether, and do not produce nectar. In some species they are borne in ◊catkins. Male and female reproductive structures are commonly found in separate flowers. The male flowers have numerous exposed stamens, often on long filaments; the female flowers have long, often branched, feathery stigmas.

aneroid barometer kind of ◊barometer.

aneurysm weakening in the wall of an artery, causing it to balloon outwards with the risk of rupture and serious, often fatal, blood loss. If detected in time, some accessible aneurysms can be repaired by bypass surgery, but such major surgery carries a high risk for patients in poor health.

angel dust popular name for the anaesthetic **phencyclidine**, a depressant drug.

angelfish any of a number of unrelated fish. The freshwater **angelfish**, genus *Pterophyllum*, of South America, is a tall, side-to-side flattened fish with a striped body, up to 26 cm/10 in long, but usually smaller in captivity. The **angelfish** or **monkfish** of the genus *Squatina* is a bottom-living shark up to 1.8 m/6 ft long with a body flattened from top to bottom. The **marine angelfishes**, *Pomacanthus* and others, are long narrow-bodied fish with spiny fins, often brilliantly coloured, up to 60 cm/2 ft long, living around coral reefs in the tropics.

ANGELFISH

http://www.actwin.com/fish/species/angelfish.html

Angelfish page by Cindy Hawley. This site includes details of angelfish breeds, feeding, keeping in an aquarium, and possible diseases. Images and multimedia clips are also downloadable from this site.

angelica any of a group of tall, perennial herbs with divided leaves and clusters of white or greenish flowers, belonging to the carrot family. Most are found in Europe and Asia. The roots and fruits have long been used in cooking and in medicine. (Genus *Angelica*, family Umbelliferae.)

angina or ***angina pectoris*** severe pain in the chest due to impaired blood supply to the heart muscle because a coronary artery is narrowed. Faintness and difficulty in breathing accompany the pain. Treatment is by drugs or bypass surgery.

angiosperm flowering plant in which the seeds are enclosed within an ovary, which ripens into a fruit. Angiosperms are divided into ◊monocotyledons (single seed leaf in the embryo) and ◊dicotyledons (two seed leaves in the embryo). They include the majority of flowers, herbs, grasses, and trees except conifers.

There are over 250,000 different species of angiosperm, found in a wide range of habitats. Like ◊gymnosperms, they are seed plants, but differ in that ovules and seeds are protected within the

ANGIOSPERM ANATOMY

http://www.botany.uwc.ac.za:80/sci_ed/std8/anatomy/

Good general guide to angiosperms. The differences between monocotyledons and dicotyledons are set out here. The functions of roots, stems, leaves, and flowers are explained by readily understandable text and good accompanying diagrams.

carpel. Fertilization occurs by male gametes passing into the ovary from a pollen tube. After fertilization the ovule develops into the seed while the ovary wall develops into the fruit.

Angkor site of the ancient capital of the Khmer Empire in NW Cambodia, north of Tonle Sap. The remains date mainly from the 10th–12th centuries AD, and comprise temples originally dedicated to the Hindu gods, shrines associated with Theravāda Buddhism, and royal palaces. Many are grouped within the enclosure called **Angkor Thom**, but the great temple of **Angkor Wat** (early 12th century) lies outside.

Angkor was abandoned in the 15th century, and the ruins were overgrown by jungle and not adequately described until 1863. Buildings on the site suffered damage during the civil war 1970–75; restoration work is in progress.

angle in mathematics, the amount of turn or rotation; it may be defined by a pair of rays (half-lines) that share a common endpoint but do not lie on the same line. Angles are measured in ◊degrees (°) or ◊radians (rads) – a complete turn or circle being 360° or 2π rads.

Angles are classified generally by their degree measures: **acute angles** are less than 90°; **right angles** are exactly 90° (a quarter turn); **obtuse angles** are greater than 90° but less than 180°; **reflex angles** are greater than 180° but less than 360°.

<> in documentation, brackets that indicate places where the user should input information of the type described between the brackets. Angled brackets are also used in online services and on the Internet to indicate that the name used is a user-ID rather than a real name, and on CompuServe as part of certain ◊emoticons.

<g> on CompuServe, an indicator that the message writer is smiling. The 'g', which stands for 'grin', is similar to an ◊emoticon in that it helps to identify an online writer's state of mind in the absence of facial expressions, tone of voice, and other real-world clues. Variants include <vbg> for 'very big grin'.

angle of declination angle at a particular point on the Earth's surface between the direction of the true or geographic North Pole and the magnetic north pole. The angle of declination has varied over time because of the slow drift in the position of the magnetic north pole.

angle of dip or ***angle of inclination*** angle at a particular point on the Earth's surface between the direction of the Earth's magnetic field and the horizontal; see ◊magnetic dip.

angle of incidence angle between a ray of light striking a mirror (incident ray) and the normal to that mirror. It is equal to the ◊angle of reflection.

angle of reflection angle between a ray of light reflected from a mirror and the normal to that mirror. It is equal to the ◊angle of incidence.

angle of refraction angle between a refracted ray of light and the normal to the surface at which ◊refraction occurred. When a ray passes from air into a denser medium such as glass, it is bent towards the normal so that the angle of refraction is less than the ◊angle of incidence.

angler any of an order of fish Lophiiformes, with flattened body and broad head and jaws. Many species have small, plantlike tufts on their skin. These act as camouflage for the fish as it waits, either

ANGLER

The parasitic male anglerfish stays with his partner for life – literally. Once the tiny male is attached to the much larger female, his tissues fuse with hers, he loses his senses of sight and smell, and receives his nourishment from her bloodstream.

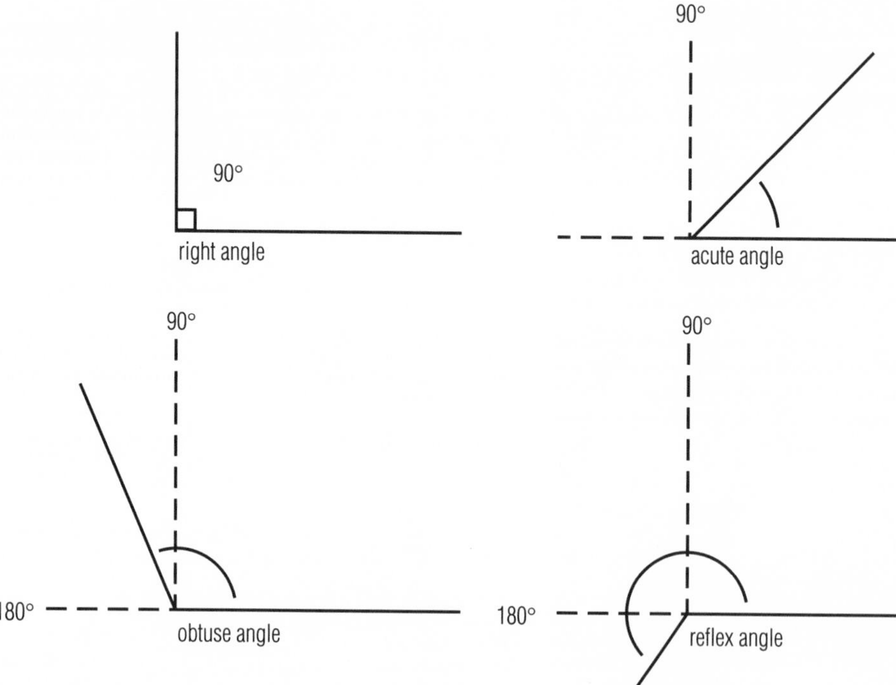

angle *The four types of angle, as classified by their degree measures. No angle is classified as having a measure of 180°, as by definition such an 'angle' is actually a straight line.*

floating among seaweed or lying on the sea bottom, twitching the enlarged tip of the threadlike first ray of its dorsal fin to entice prey.

There are over 200 species of angler fish, living in both deep and shallow water in temperate and tropical seas. The males of some species have become so small that they live as parasites on the females.

Anglo-Australian Telescope large telescope on ◊Siding Spring Mountain, New South Wales.

angstrom unit (symbol Å) of length equal to 10^{-10} metres or one-ten-millionth of a millimetre, used for atomic measurements and the wavelengths of electromagnetic radiation.

It is named after the Swedish scientist A J Ångström.

Anguilliformes order of bony fish comprising the ◊eels. All Anguilliformes have snakelike bodies and no pelvic fins. The order includes freshwater eels (Anguillidae), moray eels (Muraenidae), and conger eels (Congridae).

Anguis genus of legless lizards containing the ◊slow-worm.
classification *Anguis* is in family Anguidae, suborder Sauria,order Squamata, class Reptilia.

angular momentum in physics, a type of ◊momentum.

anhydride chemical compound obtained by the removal of water from another compound; usually a dehydrated acid. For example, sulphur(VI) oxide (sulphur trioxide, SO_3) is the anhydride of sulphuric acid (H_2SO_4).

anhydrite naturally occurring anhydrous calcium sulphate ($CaSO_4$).

It is used commercially for the manufacture of plaster of Paris and builders' plaster.

anhydrous of a chemical compound, containing no water. If the water of crystallization is removed from blue crystals of copper(II) sulphate, a white powder (anhydrous copper sulphate) results. Liquids from which all traces of water have been removed are also described as being anhydrous.

aniline ***Portuguese anil 'indigo'*** $C_6H_5NH_2$ or ***phenylamine*** one of the simplest aromatic chemicals (a substance related to benzene, with its carbon atoms joined in a ring). When pure, it is a colourless oily liquid; it has a characteristic odour, and turns brown on contact with air. It occurs in coal tar, and is used in the rubber industry and to make drugs and dyes.

It is highly poisonous.

Aniline was discovered 1826, and was originally prepared by the dry distillation of ◊indigo, hence its name.

> *What is man without the beasts? If all the beasts were gone, man would die from a great loneliness of spirit.*
>
> CHIEF SEATTLE Native American chief.
> Reputed letter to US President Franklin Pierce 1854, shown 1992 to have been largely a forgery created 1971 by TV scriptwriter Ted Perry

animal or ***metazoan Latin anima 'breath', 'life'*** member of the ◊kingdom Animalia, one of the major categories of living things, the science of which is **zoology**. Animals are all ◊heterotrophs (they obtain their energy from organic substances produced by other organisms); they have eukaryotic cells (the genetic material is contained within a distinct nucleus) bounded by a thin cell membrane rather than the thick cell wall of plants. Most animals are capable of moving around for at least part of their life cycle.

In the past, it was common to include the single-celled ◊protozoa with the animals, but these are now classified as protists, together with single-celled plants. Thus all animals are multicellular. The oldest land animals known date back 440 million years. Their remains were found 1990 in a sandstone deposit near Ludlow, Shropshire, UK, and included fragments of two centipedes a few centimetres long and a primitive spider measuring about 1 mm.

Speeds of Animals

Animal	*Speed*	
	kph	*mph*
Cheetah	103	64
Wildebeest	98	61
Lion	81	50
Quarterhorse	76	47.5
Elk	72	45
Cape hunting dog	72	45
Coyote	69	43
Grey fox	68	42
Hyena	64	40
Zebra	64	40
Greyhound	63	39
Whippet	57	35.5
Rabbit (domestic)	56	35
Jackal	56	35
Reindeer	51	32
Giraffe	51	32
White-tailed deer	48	30
Wart hog	48	30
Grizzly bear	48	30
Cat (domestic)	48	30
Human	45	28
Elephant	40	25
Black mamba snake	32	20
Squirrel	19	12
Pig (domestic)	18	11
Chicken	14	9
Giant tortoise	0.27	0.17
Three-toed sloth	0.24	0.15
Garden snail	0.05	0.03

animal behaviour scientific study of the behaviour of animals, either by comparative psychologists (with an interest mainly in the psychological processes involved in the control of behaviour) or by ethologists (with an interest in the biological context and relevance of behaviour; see ◊ethology).

animal, domestic in general, a tame animal. In agriculture, it is an animal brought under human control for exploitation of its labour; use of its feathers, hide, or skin; or consumption of its eggs, milk, or meat. Common domestic animals include poultry, cattle (including buffalo), sheep, goats, and pigs. Starting about 10,000 years ago, the domestication of animals has only since World War II led to intensive ◊factory farming.

Increasing numbers of formerly wild species have been domesticated, with stress on scientific breeding for desired characteristics. At least 60% of the world's livestock is in developing countries, but the Third World consumes only 20% of all meat and milk produced. Most domestic animals graze plants that are not edible to humans, and 40% of the world's cereal production becomes animal feed; in the USA it is 90%.

animation, computer computer-generated graphics that appear to move across the screen. Traditional animation involves a great deal of drudgery in creating the 24 frames per second needed to deceive the human eye into seeing a moving picture on film. In computer-generated animation, while humans still create the key frames that specify the starting and ending points of a particular sequence – a character running through a landscape, for example – computers are faster and more accurate at calculating the in-between positions and generating the frames.

first achievements The first completely computer-generated character to appear in a major motion picture was the sea-water creature in James Cameron's film *The Abyss* 1990, developed at the leading special effects shop ◊Industrial Light & Magic. It was quickly followed by the liquid-metal man in Cameron's *Terminator 2* 1991. The first entirely computer-animated full-length feature film was ◊Pixar's *Toy Story* 1995, which was the first film ever to

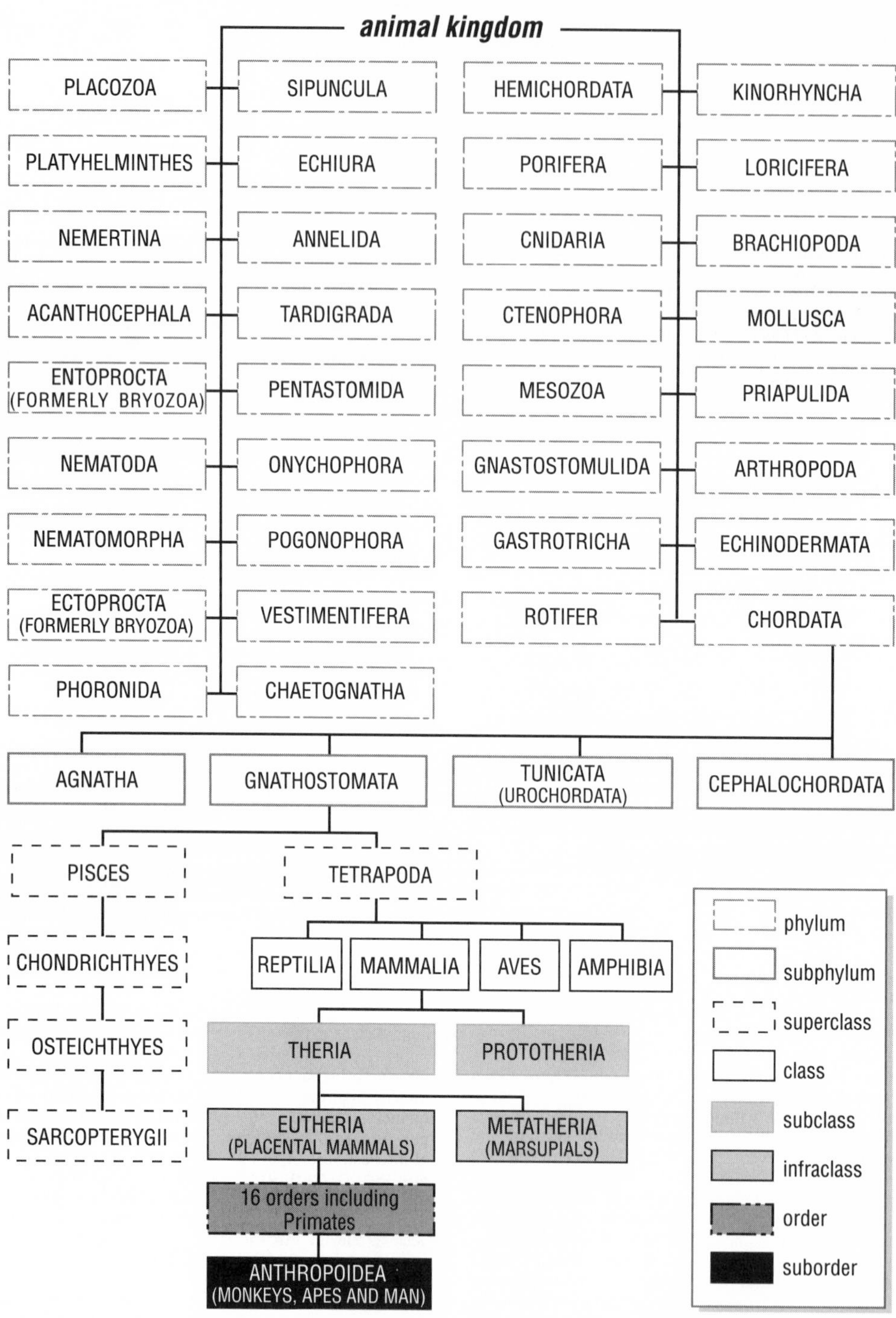

animal *The animal kingdom is divided into 34 major groups or phyla. The large phylum Chordata (animals that have, at some time in their life, a notochord, or stiff rod of cells running along the length of their body) is subdivided into four subphyla, of which two, the Agnatha and the Gnathostomata, are vertebrates (animals with backbones). The subphyla are divided into classes and subclasses.*

achieve independent motion of characters and backgrounds in the same sequence.

algorithms and initial image creation The basis of computer animation is ◊algorithms developed by academic researchers. These are used to develop software routines that handle the complex calculations needed to work out the precise colour of each ◊pixel in each of the finished frames; the process demands exceptionally powerful hardware with massive storage capacity. For the animator, an image begins as an on-screen collection of lines that look much like a wire frame. There are a variety of techniques the animator can use to develop 3-D objects – they can be extruded from a cross section, or 'swept', which is the on-screen equivalent of turning a cross section on a lathe to produce an evenly curved surface. Less symmetrical objects may be defined by a series of ◊Bezier curves.

adding solidity and colour The object then has to be **rendered**, which essentially means making it into an image of a solid object. To do this, the computer needs four types of information. First, the object has to be located in space. Second, it has to be assigned a colour, specified either by levels of red, blue, and green or by levels of hue, saturation, and brightness. Third, the location and focal point of the camera photographing the object have to be specified – these determine how the object appears on screen, in perspective. Fourth, the location and type of light sources must be specified: colour, brightness and, in the case of spotlighting, the size of the cone-shaped pool of illumination. ◊Ray-tracing, meanwhile, calculates how the light directed at the object reaches it, with what intensity, and in what areas. From all this information, the computer can calculate the colour intensity of each pixel making up the object.

light reflection There is another element, too: how the object itself reflects light. Two techniques model this, each named after its creator. If the object's surface can be described as a mosaic of polygons, **Gouraud shading** works by measuring the colour and brightness at the vertices of the polygons and mixing these to get values for the areas inside them. **Phong shading** extends this by taking into account the angle of reflection; it is therefore a more accurate technique for creating spectacular highlights. Gouraud, because it is simpler, is faster, and there is specialized hardware available for it; Phong has to be implemented in software. Both methods produce an object that looks as though it is made of soft, smooth plastic – the smoothness comes from **anti-aliasing**, a process that removes the jagged edges or stepped effect which mars the edges of diagonal lines on a computer display screen.

mapping for realism **Mappings** are what make the objects look as though they are made of real-world materials. There are four main types of mapping: texture, environment, bump, and transparency. Texture is the actual texture of the material the object is made of: brick, water, wood, and so on. The system essentially wraps the object in the texture the animator chooses. Environment mapping adds the reflections on the object's surface of its surroundings; a shiny, round, metal object rolling down a hill, for example, must show accurate reflections of the trees and other objects it rolls past. Bump mapping takes into account the shape of the object itself and the way this affects reflections and shadings in its surface colour. Transparency mapping defines what can be seen through the object, and the distortion caused by the substance of the object; this was a key element in animating the monster in *The Abyss*, which was made of sea water.

fog and haze Finally, fog and haze are important elements of computer animation, particularly for backgrounds, as computerized images tend to look too flat and sharp. The introduction of a little fog hides the sharp edges and makes the scene look more realistic. This is vital for one of the largest growth areas in computer animation for film and video: simulated flyovers, which are impossible in live action and expensive and difficult in model work.

animism in anthropology, the belief that everything, whether animate or inanimate, possesses a soul or spirit. It is a fundamental system of belief in certain religions, particularly those of some pre-industrial societies. Linked with this is the worship of natural objects such as stones and trees, thought to harbour spirits (naturism); fetishism; and ancestor worship.

In psychology and physiology, animism is the view of human personality that attributes human life and behaviour to a force distinct from matter. In developmental psychology, an animistic stage in the early thought and speech of the child has been described, notably by Swiss psychologist Jean Piaget.

In philosophy, the view that in all things consciousness or something mindlike exists.

In religious theory, the conception of a spiritual reality behind the material one: for example, beliefs in the soul as a shadowy duplicate of the body capable of independent activity, both in life and death.

anion ion carrying a negative charge. During electrolysis, anions in the electrolyte move towards the anode (positive electrode).

An electrolyte, such as the salt zinc chloride ($ZnCl_2$), is dissociated in aqueous solution or in the molten state into doubly charged Zn^{2+} zinc ◊cations and singly-charged Cl^- anions. During electrolysis, the zinc cations flow to the cathode (to become discharged and liberate zinc metal) and the chloride anions flow to the anode.

anise Mediterranean plant belonging to the carrot family, with small creamy-white flowers in clusters; its fragrant seeds, similar to liquorice in taste, are used to flavour foods. Aniseed oil is used in cough medicines. (*Pimpinella anisum,* family Umbelliferae.)

annealing controlled cooling of a material to increase ductility and strength. The process involves first heating a material (usually glass or metal) for a given time at a given temperature, followed by slow cooling. It is a common form of ◊heat treatment.

annelid any segmented worm of the phylum Annelida. Annelids include earthworms, leeches, and marine worms such as lugworms.

They have a distinct head and soft body, which is divided into a number of similar segments shut off from one another internally by membranous partitions, but there are no jointed appendages. Annelids are noted for their ability to regenerate missing parts of their bodies.

annihilation in nuclear physics, a process in which a particle and its 'mirror image' particle called an **antiparticle** collide and disappear, with the creation of a burst of energy.

The energy created is equivalent to the mass of the colliding particles in accordance with the ◊mass–energy equation. For example, an electron and a positron annihilate to produce a burst of high-energy X-rays.

Not all particle–antiparticle interactions result in annihilation; the exception concerns the group called ◊mesons, which are composed of ◊quarks and their antiquarks. See ◊antimatter.

annotate to add one's own comments to Web pages or graphical computerized documents such as stored faxes.

annual percentage rate (APR) the true annual rate of interest charged for a loan. Lenders usually increase the return on their money by compounding the interest payable on a loan to that loan on a monthly or even daily basis. This means that each time that interest is payable on a loan it is charged not only on the initial sum (principal) but also on the interest previously added to that principal. As a result, APR is usually approximately double the flat rate of interest, or simple interest.

annual plant plant that completes its life cycle within one year, during which time it germinates, grows to maturity, bears flowers, produces seed, and then dies.

annual rings or ***growth rings*** concentric rings visible on the wood of a cut tree trunk or other woody stem. Each ring represents a period of growth when new ◊xylem is laid down to replace tissue being converted into wood (secondary xylem). The wood formed from xylem produced in the spring and early summer has larger and more numerous vessels than the wood formed from xylem produced in autumn when growth is slowing down. The result is a clear boundary between the pale spring wood and the denser, darker autumn wood. Annual rings may be used to estimate the age of the plant (see ◊dendrochronology), although occasionally more than one growth ring is produced in a given year.

annular eclipse solar ◊eclipse in which the Moon does not completely obscure the Sun and a thin ring of sunlight remains visible. Annular eclipses occur when the Moon is at its furthest point from the Earth.

annulus ***Latin 'ring'*** in geometry, the plane area between two concentric circles, making a flat ring.

anode in chemistry, the positive electrode of an electrolytic ◊cell, towards which negative particles (anions), usually in solution, are attracted. See ◊electrolysis.

anode in electronics, the positive electrode of a thermionic valve, cathode ray tube, or similar device, towards which electrons are drawn after being emitted from the ◊cathode.

anodizing process that increases the resistance to ◊corrosion of a metal, such as aluminium, by building up a protective oxide layer on the surface. The natural corrosion resistance of aluminium is provided by a thin film of aluminium oxide; anodizing increases the thickness of this film and thus the corrosion protection.

It is so called because the metal becomes the ◊anode in an electrolytic bath containing a solution of, for example, sulphuric or chromic acid as the ◊electrolyte. During ◊electrolysis oxygen is produced at the anode, where it combines with the metal to form an oxide film.

anomalocaris prehistoric marine predator resembling a crustacean but with a softer exoskeleton. Up to 2 m in length, it was the largest animal on Earth when it thrived around 525 million years ago. See ◊prehistoric life.

anomalous expansion of water expansion of water as it is cooled from 4°C to 0°C. This behaviour is unusual because most substances contract when they are cooled. It means that water has a greater density at 4°C than at 0°C. Hence ice floats on water, and the water at the bottom of a pool in winter is warmer than at the surface. As a result lakes and ponds freeze slowly from the surface downwards, usually remaining liquid near the bottom, where aquatic life is more likely to survive.

anonymous FTP (***file transfer protocol***) method of retrieving a file from a remote computer without having an account on that computer. Many organizations, such as universities and software companies, maintain publicly accessible archives of files that may be retrieved across the Internet via ◊FTP. An ordinary user who is not affiliated to the organization may retrieve files by entering the FTP address and then typing in either 'anonymous' or 'ftp' when asked for a user-ID or log-in name, followed by the user's e-mail address in place of a password. These users are typically offered ◊access privileges to only a small part of the company's stored files, and the rest may be cordoned off from access by a ◊firewall.

anonymous remailer service that allows Internet users to post to USENET and send e-mail without revealing their true identity or e-mail address. To send an anonymous message, a user first sends the message to the remailer, which strips all identifying information from the message before sending it on to its specified destination, identified only as coming from the anonymous server.

The ability to post anonymously also removes user accountability, and so these servers are controversial. However, they provide a useful function on the Net in support groups and other areas where the ability to post anonymously allows people to speak freely about confidential matters without the risk of being identified by friends, family, or anyone else.

The best-known anonymous server, the Finnish **anon.penet.fi** was closed down in Aug 1996 as it could no longer guarantee anonymity following a court case ordering the operator to reveal a user's name. The more elaborate servers use encryption to make the message even more difficult to trace.

anorak term used interchangeably with **geek**, **techie**, or **nerd**. It derives from the stereotype that all technical people resemble the stereotypical anorak-wearing trainspotter; in other words, that they are obsessive, slightly antisocial, and overly knowledgeable about matters that interest very few other people.

anorexia lack of desire to eat, or refusal to eat, especially the pathological condition of **anorexia nervosa**, most often found in adolescent girls and young women. Compulsive eating, or ◊bulimia, distortions of body image, and depression often accompany anorexia.

Anorexia nervosa is characterized by severe self-imposed restriction of food intake. The consequent weight loss may lead, in women, to absence of menstruation. Anorexic patients sometimes commit suicide. Anorexia nervosa is often associated with increased physical activity and symptoms of mental disorders. Psychotherapy is an important part of the treatment.

anoxia or ***hypoxia*** in biology, deprivation of oxygen, a condition that rapidly leads to collapse or death, unless immediately reversed.

ANSI abbreviation for **American National Standards Institute**, ◊a US national standards body.

ant insect belonging to the family Formicidae, and to the same order (Hymenoptera) as bees and wasps. Ants are characterized by a conspicuous waist and elbowed antennae. About 10,000 different species are known; all are social in habit, and all construct nests of various kinds. Ants are found in all parts of the world, except the polar regions. It is estimated that there are about 10 million billion ants.

Ant behaviour is complex, and serves the colony rather than the individual. Ants find their way by light patterns, gravity (special sense organs are located in the joints of their legs), and chemical trails between food areas and the nest.

specialized roles Communities include **workers**, sterile, wingless females, often all alike, although in some species large-headed 'soldiers' are differentiated; **fertile females**, fewer in number and usually winged; and **males**, also winged and smaller than their consorts, with whom they leave the nest on a nuptial flight at certain times of the year. After aerial mating, the males die, and the fertilized queens lose their wings when they settle, laying eggs to found their own new colonies. The eggs hatch into wormlike larvae, which then pupate in silk cocoons before emerging as adults.

remarkable species Some species conduct warfare. Others are pastoralists, tending herds of ◊aphids and collecting a sweet secretion ('honeydew') from them. Army (South American) and driver (African) ants march nomadically in huge columns, devouring even tethered animals in their path. Leaf-cutter ants, genus *Atta*, use pieces of leaf to grow edible fungus in underground 'gardens' which can be up to 5 m/16 ft deep and cover hundreds of square metres. Weaver ants, genus *Oecophylla*, use their silk-producing larvae as living shuttles to bind the edges of leaves together to form the nest. Eurasian robber ants *Formica sanguinea* raid the nests of

ant *With a length of over 30 mm/1.2 in, this* Diponera *species ant from the rainforests of South America is among the giants of its kind. Like most members of its primitive subfamily Ponerinae, it forages singly rather than in bands and the nests generally contain only a few dozen individuals. Premaphotos Wildlife*

another ant species, *Formica fusca,* for pupae, then use the adults as 'slaves' when they hatch. Among honey ants, some workers serve as distended honey stores.

antacid any substance that neutralizes stomach acid, such as sodium bicarbonate or magnesium hydroxide ('milk of magnesia').

Antacids are weak ◊bases, swallowed as solids or emulsions. They may be taken between meals to relieve symptoms of hyperacidity, such as pain, bloating, nausea, and 'heartburn'. Excessive or prolonged need for antacids should be investigated medically.

antagonist in biology, a ◊muscle that relaxes in response to the contraction of its agonist muscle. The biceps, in the front of the upper arm, bends the elbow whilst the triceps, lying behind the biceps, straightens the arm.

antagonistic muscles in the body, a pair of muscles allowing coordinated movement of the skeletal joints. The extension of the arm, for example, requires one set of muscles to relax, while another set contracts. The individual components of antagonistic pairs can be classified into extensors (muscles that straighten a limb) and flexors (muscles that bend a limb).

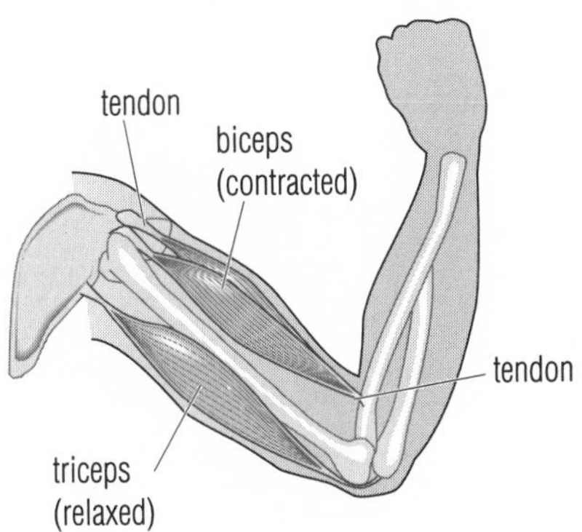

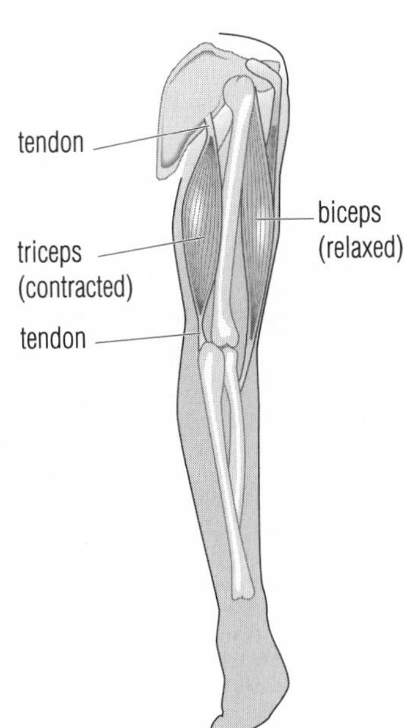

antagonistic muscle *Even simple movements such as bending and straightening the arm require muscle pairs to contract and relax synchronously.*

Antarctic Circle imaginary line that encircles the South Pole at latitude 66° 32' S. The line encompasses the continent of Antarctica and the Antarctic Ocean.

The region south of this line experiences at least one night in the southern summer during which the Sun never sets, and at least one day in the southern winter during which the Sun never rises.

Antares or ***Alpha Scorpii*** brightest star in the constellation Scorpius and the 15th brightest star in the sky. It is a red supergiant several hundred times larger than the Sun and perhaps 10,000 times as luminous, lies about 300 light years away, and fluctuates slightly in brightness.

anteater mammal of the family Myrmecophagidae, order Edentata, native to Mexico, Central America, and tropical South America. The anteater lives almost entirely on ants and termites. It has toothless jaws, an extensile tongue, and claws for breaking into the nests of its prey.

Species include the giant anteater *Myrmecophaga tridactyla,* about 1.8 m/6 ft long including the tail, the tamandua or collared anteater *Tamandua tetradactyla,* about 90 cm/3.5 ft long, and the silky anteater *Cyclopes didactyla,* about 35 cm/14 in long. The name is also incorrectly applied to the aardvark, the echidna, and the pangolin.

antelope any of numerous kinds of even-toed, hoofed mammals belonging to the cow family, Bovidae. Most antelopes are lightly built and good runners. They are grazers or browsers, and chew the cud. They range in size from the dik-diks and duikers, only 30 cm/1 ft high, to the eland, which can be 1.8 m/6 ft at the shoulder.

The majority of antelopes are African, including the eland, wildebeest, kudu, springbok, and waterbuck, although other species live in parts of Asia, including the deserts of Arabia and the Middle East. The pronghorn antelope *Antilocapra americana* of North America belongs to a different family, the Antilocapridae.

antenatal in medicine, before birth. Antenatal care refers to health services provided to ensure the health of pregnant women and their babies.

antenna in radio and television, another name for ◊aerial.

antenna in zoology, an appendage ('feeler') on the head. Insects, centipedes, and millipedes each have one pair of antennae but there are two pairs in crustaceans, such as shrimps. In insects, the antennae are involved with the senses of smell and touch; they are frequently complex structures with large surface areas that increase the ability to detect scents.

anterior in biology, the front of an organism, usually the part that goes forward first when the animal is moving. The anterior end of the nervous system, over the course of evolution, has developed into a brain with associated receptor organs able to detect stimuli including light and chemicals.

anther in a flower, the terminal part of a stamen in which the ◊pollen grains are produced. It is usually borne on a slender stalk or filament, and has two lobes, each containing two chambers, or pollen sacs, within which the pollen is formed.

antheridium organ producing the male gametes, ◊antherozoids, in algae, bryophytes (mosses and liverworts), and pteridophytes (ferns, club mosses, and horsetails). It may be either single-celled, as in most algae, or multicellular, as in bryophytes and pteridophytes.

antherozoid motile (or independently moving) male gamete produced by algae, bryophytes (mosses and liverworts), pteridophytes (ferns, club mosses, and horsetails), and some gymnosperms (notably the cycads). Antherozoids are formed in an antheridium and, after being released, swim by means of one or more ◊flagella, to the female gametes. Higher plants have nonmotile male gametes contained within ◊pollen grains.

anthracene white, glistening, crystalline, tricyclic, aromatic hydrocarbon with a faint blue fluorescence when pure. Its melting point is about 216°C/421°F and its boiling point 351°C/664°F. It occurs in the high-boiling-point fractions of coal tar, where it was discovered in 1832 by the French chemists Auguste Laurent (1808–1853) and Jean Dumas (1800–1884).

anthracite *from Greek anthrax, 'coal'* hard, dense, shiny variety of ◊coal, containing over 90% carbon and a low percentage of ash and impurities, which causes it to burn without flame, smoke, or smell. Because of its purity, anthracite gives off relatively little sulphur dioxide when burnt.

Anthracite gives intense heat, but is slow-burning and slow to light; it is therefore unsuitable for use in open fires. Its characteristic composition is thought to be due to the action of bacteria in disintegrating the coal-forming material when it was laid down during the ◊Carboniferous period.

Among the chief sources of anthracite coal are Pennsylvania in the USA; S Wales, UK; the Donbas, Ukraine and Russia; and Shanxi province, China.

anthrax disease of livestock, occasionally transmitted to humans, usually via infected hides and fleeces. It may develop as black skin pustules or severe pneumonia. Treatment is with antibiotics. Vaccination is effective.

Anthrax is caused by a bacillus (*Bacillus anthracis*). In the 17th century, some 60,000 cattle died in a European pandemic known as the Black Bane, thought to have been anthrax. The disease is described by the Roman poet Virgil and may have been the cause of the biblical fifth plague of Egypt.

ANTHRAX

http://www.outbreak.org/cgi-unreg/dynaserve.exe/cb/anthrax.html

Basic medical details of the livestock disease and biological weapon anthrax. The Web site contains brief sections covering characteristics of the disease, the symptoms it causes, cautions and precautions, first aid therapy for victims of the disease, and a list of neutralization and decontamination methods.

anthropic principle in science, the idea that 'the universe is the way it is because if it were different we would not be here to observe it'. The principle arises from the observation that if the laws of science were even slightly different, it would have been impossible for intelligent life to evolve. For example, if the electric charge on the electron were only slightly different, stars would have been unable to burn hydrogen and produce the chemical elements that make up our bodies. Scientists are undecided whether the principle is an insight into the nature of the universe or a piece of circular reasoning.

Man appears to be the missing link between anthropoid apes and human beings.

KONRAD LORENZ Austrian zoologist.
The New York Times Magazine 11 April 1965

anthropoid *Greek anthropos 'man', eidos 'resemblance'* any primate belonging to the suborder Anthropoidea, including monkeys, apes, and humans.

You will die but the carbon will not; its career does not end with you ... it will return to the soil, and there a plant may take it up again in time, sending it once more on a cycle of plant and animal life.

JACOB BRONOWSKI Polish-born British scientist, broadcaster, and writer.
'Biography of an Atom – and the Universe *New York Times* 13 Oct 1968

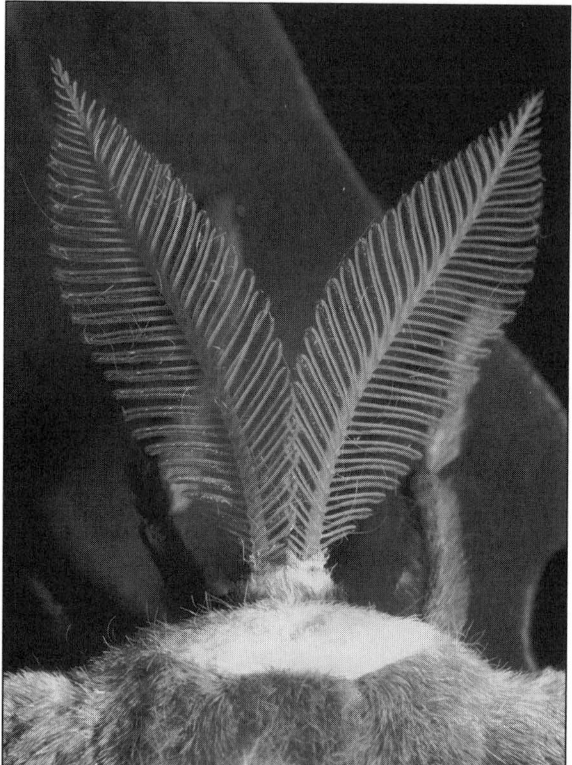

antenna *The antennae of some male moths are capable of picking up incredibly low concentrations of airborne female sex pheromones at distances of several kilometres. This picture shows the enormous antennae of the American moon moth* Actias luna (Saturniidae) *Premaphotos Wildlife*

anthropology *Greek anthropos 'man', logos 'discourse'* the study of humankind. It investigates the cultural, social, and physical diversity of the human species, both past and present. It is divided into two broad categories: biological or physical anthropology, which attempts to explain human biological variation from an evolutionary perspective; and the larger field of social or cultural anthropology, which attempts to explain the variety of human cultures. This differs from sociology in that anthropologists are concerned with cultures and societies other than their own.

biological anthropology Biological anthropology is concerned with human ◊palaeontology, primatology, human adaptation, demography, ◊population genetics, and human growth and development.

social anthropology Social or cultural anthropology is divided into three subfields: social or cultural anthropology proper, ◊prehistory or prehistoric archaelogy, and anthropological linguistics. The term 'anthropology' is frequently used to refer solely to social anthropology. With a wide range of theoretical perspectives and topical interests, it overlaps with many other disciplines. It is a uniquely Western social science.

participant observation Anthropology's primary method involves the researcher living for a year or more in another culture, speaking the local language and participating in all aspects of everyday life; and writing about it afterwards. By comparing these accounts, anthropologists hope to understand who we are.

anthropometry science dealing with the measurement of the human body, particularly stature, body weight, cranial capacity, and length of limbs, in samples of living populations, as well as the remains of buried and fossilized humans.

anti-aliasing in computer graphics, a software technique for diminishing ◊aliasing ('jaggies') – steplike lines that should be smooth. Jaggies occur because the output device, the monitor or printer, does not have a high enough resolution to represent a smooth line. Anti-aliasing reduces the prominence of jaggies by surrounding the steps with intermediate shades of grey (for grey-scaling devices) or colour (for colour devices). Although this reduces the jagged appearance of the lines, it also makes them fuzzier.

ANTIBIOTICS: HOW DO ANTIBIOTICS WORK

http://ericir.syr.edu/Projects/Newton/12/Lessons/antibiot.html

Introduction to the use and importance of antibiotics in easy to understand language. The site also includes a glossary of scientific and difficult terms, a further reading list, and an activities sheet.

antibiotic drug that kills or inhibits the growth of bacteria and fungi. It is derived from living organisms such as fungi or bacteria, which distinguishes it from synthetic antimicrobials.

The earliest antibiotics, the ◊penicillins, came into use from 1941 and were quickly joined by chloramphenicol, the ◊cephalosporins, erythromycins, tetracyclines, and aminoglycosides. A range of broad-spectrum antibiotics, the 4-quinolones, was developed 1989, of which ciprofloxacin was the first. Each class and individual antibiotic acts in a different way and may be effective against either a broad spectrum or a specific type of disease-causing agent. Use of antibiotics has become more selective as side effects, such as toxicity, allergy, and resistance, have become better understood. Bacteria have the ability to develop resistance following repeated or subclinical (insufficient) doses, so more advanced and synthetic antibiotics are continually required to overcome them.

ANTIBODY RESOURCE PAGE

http://www.antibodyresource.com/

Fascinating annotated access site for all you could ever want to know about antibodies and some you'd rather not! This site contains several educational resources (aimed at university level), but also contains images, animations, and descriptions of research into many different types of antibodies.

antibody protein molecule produced in the blood by ◊lymphocytes in response to the presence of foreign or invading substances (◊antigens); such substances include the proteins carried on the surface of infecting microorganisms. Antibody production is only one aspect of ◊immunity in vertebrates.

Each antibody acts against only one kind of antigen, and combines with it to form a 'complex'. This action may render antigens harmless, or it may destroy microorganisms by setting off chemical changes that cause them to self-destruct.

In other cases, the formation of a complex will cause antigens to form clumps that can then be detected and engulfed by white blood cells, such as ◊macrophages and ◊phagocytes.

Each bacterial or viral infection will bring about the manufacture of a specific antibody, which will then fight the disease. Many diseases can only be contracted once because antibodies remain in the blood after the infection has passed, preventing any further invasion. Vaccination boosts a person's resistance by causing the production of antibodies specific to particular infections.

Antibodies were discovered 1890 by German physician Emil von Behring and Japanese bacteriologist Shibasaburo Kitasato.

Large quantities of specific antibodies can now be obtained by the monoclonal technique (see ◊monoclonal antibody).

anticline in geology, rock layers or beds folded to form a convex arch (seldom preserved intact) in which older rocks comprise the core. Where relative ages of the rock layers, or stratigraphic ages, are not known, convex upward folded rocks are referred to as **antiforms**.

The fold of an anticline may be undulating or steeply curved. A steplike bend in otherwise gently dipping or horizontal beds is a **monocline**. The opposite of an anticline is a ◊syncline.

anticlockwise direction of rotation, opposite to the way the hands of a clock turn.

anticoagulant substance that inhibits the formation of blood clots. Common anticoagulants are heparin, produced by the liver and some white blood cells, and derivatives of coumarin. Anticoagulants are used medically in the prevention and treatment of thrombosis and heart attacks. Anticoagulant substances are also produced by blood-feeding animals, such as mosquitoes, leeches, and vampire bats, to keep the victim's blood flowing.

Most anticoagulants prevent the production of thrombin, an enzyme that induces the formation from blood plasma of fibrinogen, to which blood platelets adhere and form clots.

anticyclone area of high atmospheric pressure caused by descending air, which becomes warm and dry. Winds radiate from a calm centre, taking a clockwise direction in the northern hemisphere and an anticlockwise direction in the southern hemisphere. Anticyclones are characterized by clear weather and the absence of rain and violent winds. In summer they bring hot, sunny days and in winter they bring fine, frosty spells, although fog and low cloud are not uncommon in the UK. **Blocking anticyclones**, which prevent the normal air circulation of an area, can cause summer droughts and severe winters.

antidepressant any drug used to relieve symptoms in depressive illness. The two main groups are the tricyclic antidepressants (TCADs) and the monoamine oxidase inhibitors (MAOIs), which act by altering chemicals available to the central nervous system. Both may produce serious side effects and are restricted.

anti-emetic any substance that counteracts nausea or vomiting.

antiferromagnetic material material with a very low magnetic ◊susceptibility that increases with temperature up to a certain temperature, called the ◊Néel temperature. Above the Néel temperature, the material is only weakly attracted to a strong magnet.

antifreeze substance added to a water-cooling system (for example, that of a car) to prevent it freezing in cold weather.

antigen any substance that causes the production of ◊antibodies by the body's immune system. Common antigens include the proteins carried on the surface of bacteria, viruses, and pollen grains. The proteins of incompatible blood groups or tissues also act as antigens, which has to be taken into account in medical procedures such as blood transfusions and organ transplants.

antihistamine any substance that counteracts the effects of ◊histamine. Antihistamines may occur naturally or they may be synthesized.

H_1 antihistamines are used to relieve allergies, alleviating symptoms such as runny nose, itching, swelling, or asthma. H_2 antihistamines suppress acid production by the stomach, and are used in the treatment of peptic ulcers, often making surgery unnecessary.

antiknock substance added to ◊petrol to reduce knocking in car engines. It is a mixture of dibromoethane and tetraethyl lead. Its use in leaded petrol has resulted in atmospheric pollution by lead compounds.

antilogarithm or *antilog* the inverse of ◊logarithm, or the number whose logarithm to a given base is a given number. If $y = \log a\ x$, then $x = \text{antilog}\ a\ y$.

antimatter in physics, a form of matter in which most of the attributes (such as electrical charge, magnetic moment, and spin) of ◊elementary particles are reversed. Such particles (◊antiparticles) can be created in particle accelerators, such as those at ◊CERN in Geneva, Switzerland, and at ◊Fermilab in the USA. In 1996 physicists at CERN created the first atoms of antimatter: nine atoms of antihydrogen survived for 40 nanoseconds.

Antibiotic Resistance: a Rising Toll

BY PAULETTE PRATT

When, in 1969, the US Surgeon-General announced that we could soon 'close the book' on infectious diseases, he was speaking prematurely. For already, two years earlier, first reports had surfaced of penicillin resistance developing in *Pneumococcus*, a bacterium which causes a number of potentially fatal diseases, including pneumonia and meningitis. Within little more than a decade, epidemics of pneumococcal disease were breaking out in many countries.

In 1995, when workers from the Centers for Disease Control in Atlanta looked at samples taken from patients with severe pneumonia, they found that a quarter had been hit by pneumococcal (*Staphylococcus pneumoniae*) strains resistant to penicillin; some 15 % were also resistant to erythromycin. Today, growing resistance of this and other organisms to antibiotics is a global public health problem.

Rise of the superbugs

Bacteria vary greatly in their sensitivity to antibiotics, and there is no such thing as a 'magic bullet' with blanket activity against all pathogens. The trouble is that, after more than half a century of antibiotic use, bacteria are mutating faster than new drugs can be found. The growth of super-resistance is being hastened by the indiscriminate use of antibiotics, including over-prescribing.

In the developed world, the danger is greatest in hospitals, where people are already very sick. Currently some 14,000 Americans are dying each year from hospital-acquired infections caused by resistant bacteria. Most at risk are people whose immune systems are in some way impaired, including the very young or the frail elderly, AIDS patients, organ transplant recipients, and patients receiving chemotherapy for cancer.

Most notorious of the so-called 'superbugs' stalking hospital floors is methicillin-resistant *Staphylococcus aureus* (MRSA), a pathogen with an awesome talent for acquiring resistance traits from its microscopic neighbours. So far outbreaks of MRSA, which can cause temporary closure of operating rooms and intensive care units, have been met with vancomycin, a 'last resort' antibiotic normally reserved for life-threatening infections. But in spring of 1997, the Japanese reported the most convincing evidence yet of the appearance of vancomycin-resistant strains.

The Japanese report brings one step closer the spectre of the unstoppable 'superbug' overrunning hospitals. In fact, microbiologists have been predicting just this scenario, not least because strains of the intestinal bacterium *Enterococcus* have for some time been defying all existing antibiotics, including vancomycin and the closely related teicoplanin. In the laboratory, it has been shown that genes for resistance can pass from *Enterococcus* to the more deadly *S. aureus* by plasmid transfer.

It was fear of an epidemic of untreatable infections that prompted the recent European ban on avoparcin, a drug administered to farm animals to promote growth. The rationale for antibiotic use in this context is that it improves feeding efficiency. However, avoparcin is close in chemical structure to vancomycin, and many scientists argue that its use as a growth promoter in livestock creates a potential reservoir of vancomycin-resistant bacteria that would be transmissible to human beings.

Return of old-time diseases

The phenomenon of super-resistance means also that many one-time killer diseases, including tuberculosis (TB), typhoid, cholera, and diphtheria, are returning in force. TB, always a major problem in the Third World, is the biggest threat, since now it is making a comeback in countries where previously it had been brought under control. Moreover, some strains of the bacterium have become resistant. Parts of the US worst affected are deprived inner-city areas such as Newark, New Jersey, and Brooklyn, the Bronx, and Harlem in New York, where resistance is widespread.

A big factor in the spread of multi-drug-resistant tuberculosis (MDRTB) has been the failure of control programs in the industrialized countries, including the US. This has meant that many patients starting out on medication lapse before the six-month course is completed. If a patient carrying a resistant strain takes only one drug instead of the prescribed combination, or fails to complete the course, the effect is to promote resistant strains.

Fresh strategies

Bacteria developing the ability to foil an antibiotic can become permanently resistant, according to researchers at Emory University in Atlanta. They demonstrated this in another rising superbug, *Escherichia coli*, which causes gastrointestinal infections. This finding implies that, contrary to what many doctors previously believed, reducing antibiotic use will not eliminate resistant strains.

While the quest for new drugs to fight infection is now paramount, many researchers are developing fresh strategies. These include: tinkering with the structure of antibiotics to add in helper molecules; seeking to disable genes for resistance; and developing laser-activated chemical compounds to blitz the superbugs. Some teams, too, are reviving the old idea of turning bacteriophages (bacteria-eating viruses) loose on resistant bacteria.

All these strategies and more may be needed to overcome the rising toll exacted by antibiotic resistance. Certainly, with infectious diseases claiming more than 17 million lives a year worldwide, we are still no nearer to 'closing the book'.

Mechanisms of resistance

Bacteria may be naturally resistant to some antibiotics, or resistance may be acquired, mostly by the phenomenon of plasmid transfer. A plasmid is a free-floating fragment of DNA adrift in the cell cytoplasm. It carries some genetic material, including data governing the cell's resistance to antibiotics. Plasmids can be transmitted from one bacterium to another.

Occasionally resistance may be due to spontaneous mutation, which is the result of an error in replication of the cell's nuclear material during reproduction. Further reproduction causes the development of a resistant strain.

Bacteria demonstrate resistance in two ways. One way is by producing enzymes that disable drugs. A drug-defying enzyme is not always expressed by the organism targeted by therapy. The normally innocuous *Staphylococcus epidermidis* produces an enzyme that disables penicillin before it can act against harmful staphylococcal species; or some bacteria can contrive metabolic changes that foil the action of drugs. Sulphonamides – antibacterials introduced before the discovery of antibiotics – are often defeated by these metabolic readjustments on the part of bacteria.

antimony silver-white, brittle, semimetallic element (a metalloid), symbol Sb (from Latin *stibium*), atomic number 51, relative atomic mass 121.75. It occurs chiefly as the ore stibnite, and is used to make alloys harder; it is also used in photosensitive substances in colour photography, optical electronics, fireproofing, pigment, and medicine. It was employed by the ancient Egyptians in a mixture to protect the eyes from flies.

antinode in physics, the position in a ◊standing wave pattern at which the amplitude of vibration is greatest (compare ◊node). The standing wave of a stretched string vibrating in the fundamental mode has one antinode at its midpoint. A vibrating air column in a pipe has an antinode at the pipe's open end and at the place where the vibration is produced.

anti-oxidant any substance that prevents deterioration of fats, oils, paints, plastics, and rubbers by oxidation. When used as food additives, anti-oxidants prevent fats and oils from becoming rancid when exposed to air, and thus extend their shelf life.

Vegetable oils contain natural anti-oxidants, such as vitamin E, which prevent spoilage, but anti-oxidants are nevertheless added to most oils. They are not always listed on food labels because if a food manufacturer buys an oil to make a food product, and the oil has anti-oxidant already added, it does not have to be listed on the label of the product.

antiparticle in nuclear physics, a particle corresponding in mass and properties to a given ◊elementary particle but with the opposite electrical charge, magnetic properties, or coupling to other fundamental forces. For example, an electron carries a negative charge whereas its antiparticle, the positron, carries a positive one. When a particle and its antiparticle collide, they destroy each other, in the process called 'annihilation', their total energy being converted to lighter particles and/or photons. A substance consisting entirely of antiparticles is known as ◊antimatter.

antipodes ***Greek 'opposite feet'*** places at opposite points on the globe.

antipyretic any drug, such as aspirin, used to reduce fever.

antirrhinum any of several plants in the figwort family, including the snapdragon (*Antirrhinum majus*). Foxgloves and toadflax are relatives. Antirrhinums are native to the Mediterranean region and W North America. (Genus *Antirrhinum,* family Scrophulariaceae.)

antiseptic any substance that kills or inhibits the growth of microorganisms. The use of antiseptics was pioneered by Joseph Lister. He used carbolic acid (◊phenol), which is a weak antiseptic; antiseptics such as TCP are derived from this.

antitussive any substance administered to suppress a cough. Coughing, however, is an important reflex in clearing secretions from the airways; its suppression is usually unnecessary and possibly harmful, unless damage is being done to tissue during excessive coughing spasms.

antivirus software computer program that detects ◊viruses and/or cleans viruses from an infected computer system. There are many types of antivirus software. Scanners check a computer system and detect viruses; these must be updated regularly, as new viruses are written and released. Other utilities allow a user to edit the data on hard and floppy discs directly or repair system damage. Still other types, which may come with specialized hardware, function by detecting and blocking changes to files or system activities which are typical of how viruses behave.

antler 'horn' of a deer, often branched, and made of bone rather than horn. Antlers, unlike true horns, are shed and regrown each year. Reindeer of both sexes grow them, but in all other types of deer, only the males have antlers.

During growth the antler is covered by a sensitive, hairy skin, known as 'velvet', which dries up and is rubbed off when maturity is attained. The number and complexity of the branches increase year by year.

ant lion larva of one of the insects of the family Myrmeleontidae, order Neuroptera, which traps ants by waiting at the bottom of a pit dug in loose, sandy soil. Ant lions are mainly tropical, but also occur in parts of Europe, where there are more than 40 species, and in the USA, where they are called doodlebugs.

anus or **anal canal** the opening at the end of the alimentary canal that allows undigested food and other waste materials to pass out of the body, in the form of faeces. In humans, the term is also used to describe the last 4 cm/1.5 in of the alimentary canal. The anus is found in all types of multicellular animal except the coelenterates (sponges) and the platyhelminths (flatworms), which have a mouth only.

It is normally kept closed by rings of muscle called sphincters. The commonest medical condition associated with the anus is haemorrhoids (piles).

anxiety unpleasant, distressing emotion usually to be distinguished from fear. Fear is aroused by the perception of actual or threatened danger; anxiety arises when the danger is imagined or cannot be identified or clearly perceived. It is a normal response in stressful situations, but is frequently experienced in many mental disorders.

Anxiety is experienced as a feeling of suspense, helplessness, or alternating hope and despair together with excessive alertness and characteristic bodily changes such as tightness in the throat, disturbances in breathing and heartbeat, sweating, and diarrhoea.

In psychiatry, an anxiety state is a type of neurosis in which the anxiety either seems to arise for no reason or else is out of proportion to what may have caused it. 'Phobic anxiety' refers to the irrational fear that characterizes ◊phobia.

AOL abbreviation for ◊America Online; the UK version of the US service.

aorta the body's main ◊artery, arising from the left ventricle of the heart in birds and mammals. Carrying freshly oxygenated blood, it arches over the top of the heart and descends through the trunk, finally splitting in the lower abdomen to form the two iliac arteries. Loss of elasticity in the aorta provides evidence of ◊atherosclerosis, which may lead to heart disease.

In fish a ventral aorta carries deoxygenated blood from the heart to the ◊gills, and the dorsal aorta carries oxygenated blood from the gills to other parts of the body.

a.p. in physics, abbreviation for **atmospheric pressure**.

Apache Point Observatory US observatory in the Sacramento Mountains of New Mexico containing a 3.5-m/138-in reflector, opened 1994, and operated by the Astrophysical Research Consortium (the universities of Washington, Chicago, Princeton, New Mexico, and Washington State).

apastron the point at which an object travelling in an elliptical orbit around a star is at its furthest from the star. The term is usually applied to the position of the minor component of a ◊binary star in relation to the primary. Its opposite is ◊periastron.

apatite common calcium phosphate mineral, $Ca_5(PO_4)_3(F,OH,Cl)$. Apatite has a hexagonal structure and occurs widely in igneous rocks, such as pegmatite, and in contact metamorphic rocks, such as marbles. It is used in the manufacture of fertilizer and as a source of phosphorus. Carbonate hydroxylapatite, $Ca_5(PO_4,CO_3)_3(OH)_2$, is the chief constituent of tooth enamel and, together with other related phosphate minerals, is the inorganic constituent of bone. Apatite ranks 5 on the ◊Mohs' scale of hardness.

apatosaurus large plant-eating dinosaur, formerly called **brontosaurus**, which flourished about 145 million years ago. Up to 21 m/69 ft long and 30 tonnes in weight, it stood on four elephantlike legs and had a long tail, long neck, and small head. It probably snipped off low-growing vegetation with peglike front teeth, and swallowed it whole to be ground by pebbles in the stomach.

ape ◊primate of the family Pongidae, closely related to humans, including gibbon, orang-utan, chimpanzee, and gorilla.

> *If it is true that we have sprung from the ape, there are occasions when my own spring appears not to have been very far.*
>
> CORNELIA OTIS SKINNER US writer and actress. *The Ape in Me*, title essay

Ape City Yerkes Regional Primate Center, Atlanta, Georgia, where large numbers of primates are kept for physiological and psychological experiment. A major area of research at Ape City is language.

aperture in photography, an opening in the camera that allows light to pass through the lens to strike the film. Controlled by the iris diaphragm, it can be set mechanically or electronically at various diameters.

The **aperture ratio** or **relative aperture**, more commonly known as the ◊f-number, is a number defined as the focal length of the lens divided by the effective diameter of the aperture. A smaller f-number implies a larger diameter lens and therefore more light available for high-speed photography, or for work in poorly illuminated areas. However, small f-numbers involve small depths of focus.

aperture synthesis in astronomy, a technique used in ◊radio astronomy in which several small radio dishes are linked together to simulate the performance of one very large radio telescope, which can be many kilometres in diameter. See ◊radio telescope.

apex the highest point of a triangle, cone, or pyramid – that is, the vertex (corner) opposite a given base.

NATIONAL APHASIA ASSOCIATION

http://www.aphasia.org/

US-based site with a lot of straightforward information about aphasia; for example, there is a page of important facts and a true/false quiz. The site also contains information about current research and links to support groups for sufferers, their friends, and families.

aphasia general term for the many types of disturbance in language that are due to brain damage, especially in the speech areas of the dominant hemisphere.

aphelion the point at which an object, travelling in an elliptical orbit around the Sun, is at its furthest from the Sun. The Earth is at its aphelion on 5 July.

aphid any of the family of small insects, Aphididae, in the order Hemiptera, suborder Homoptera, that live by sucking sap from plants. There are many species, often adapted to particular plants; some are agricultural pests.

aphid *A colony of aphids* Cavariella konoi, *commonly known as greenfly, feeding on green stems of the almond willow. Ants often attend such colonies to feed on the honeydew (a sweet, sticky substance) that aphids excrete.* *Premaphotos Wildlife*

In some stages of their life cycle, wingless females rapidly produce large numbers of live young by ◊parthenogenesis, leading to enormous infestations, and numbers can approach 2 billion per hectare/1 billion per acre. They can also cause damage by transmitting viral diseases. An aphid that damages cypress and cedar trees appeared in Malawi in 1985 and by 1991 was attacking millions of trees in central and E Africa. Some research suggests, however, that aphids may help promote fertility in the soil through the waste they secrete, termed 'honeydew'. Aphids are also known as plant lice, greenflies, or blackflies.

aphrodisiac ***from Aphrodite, the Greek goddess of love*** any substance that arouses or increases sexual desire.

API abbreviation for ◊Applications Program Interface, a standard environment in which computer programs are written.

apogee the point at which an object, travelling in an elliptical orbit around the Earth, is at its furthest from the Earth.

Apollo asteroid member of a group of ◊asteroids whose orbits cross that of the Earth. They are named after the first of their kind, Apollo, discovered in 1932 and then lost until 1973. Apollo asteroids are so small and faint that they are difficult to see except when close to Earth (Apollo is about 2 km/1.2 mi across).

Apollo project US space project to land a person on the Moon, achieved 20 July 1969, when Neil Armstrong was the first to set foot there. He was accompanied on the Moon's surface by 'Buzz' Aldrin; Michael Collins remained in the orbiting command module.

The programme was announced in 1961 by President Kennedy. The world's most powerful rocket, *Saturn V*, was built to launch the Apollo spacecraft, which carried three astronauts. When the spacecraft was in orbit around the Moon, two astronauts would descend to the surface in a lunar module to take samples of rock and set up experiments that would send data back to Earth. After three other preparatory flights, *Apollo 11* made the first lunar landing. Five more crewed landings followed, the last in 1972. The total cost of the programme was over $24 billion.

APOLLO 11

http://www.nasa.gov/hqpao/apollo_11.html

This NASA page relives the excitement of the *Apollo 11* mission, with recollections from the participating astronauts, images, audio clips, access to key White House documents, and a bibliography.

Apollo–Soyuz test project joint US–Soviet space mission in which an Apollo and a Soyuz craft docked while in orbit around the Earth on 17 July 1975. The craft remained attached for two days and crew members were able to move from one craft to the other through an airlock attached to the nose of the Apollo. The mission was designed to test rescue procedures as well as having political significance.

apoptosis or ***cell suicide*** a cell's destruction of itself. All cells contain genes that cause them to self-destruct if damaged, diseased, or as part of the regulation of cell numbers during the organism's normal development. Many cancer cells have mutations in genes controlling apoptosis, so understanding apoptosis may lead to new cancer treatments where cells can be instructed to destroy themselves.

During apoptosis, a cell first produces the enzymes needed for self-destruction before shrinking to a characteristic spherical shape with balloon-like bumps on its outer surface. The enzymes break down its contents into small fragments which are easily digestible by surrounding cells.

aposematic coloration in biology, the technical name for **warning coloration** markings that make a dangerous, poisonous, or foul-tasting animal particularly conspicuous and recognizable to a predator. Examples include the yellow and black stripes of bees and wasps, and the bright red or yellow colours of many poisonous frogs. See also ◊mimicry.

apothecaries' weights obsolete units of mass, formerly used in pharmacy: 20 grains equal one scruple; three scruples equal one dram; eight drams equal an apothecary's ounce (oz apoth.), and 12 such ounces equal an apothecary's pound (lb apoth.). There are 7,000 grains in one pound avoirdupois (0.454 kg).

apparent depth depth that a transparent material such as water or glass appears to have when viewed from above. This is less than its real depth because of the ◊refraction that takes place when light passes into a less dense medium. The ratio of the real depth to the apparent depth of a transparent material is equal to its ◊refractive index.

appendicitis inflammation of the appendix, a small, blind extension of the bowel in the lower right abdomen. In an acute attack, the pus-filled appendix may burst, causing a potentially lethal spread of infection. Treatment is by removal (appendicectomy).

appendix a short, blind-ended tube attached to the ◊caecum. It has no known function in humans, but in herbivores it may be large, containing millions of bacteria that secrete enzymes to digest grass (as no vertebrate can secrete enzymes that will digest cellulose, the main constituent of plant cell walls).

apple fruit of several species of apple tree. There are several hundred varieties of cultivated apples, grown all over the world, which may be divided into eating, cooking, and cider apples. All are derived from the wild ◊crab apple. (Genus *Malus,* family Rosaceae.)

Apple trees grow best in temperate countries with a cool climate and plenty of rain during the winter. The desired variety is grafted onto rootstocks, and the tree must grow for six to eight years before it produces a good crop of fruit. The tree requires a winter period, in which it is dormant, in order to fruit in the spring, but must be protected from frost while the flowers and fruit are young. Pruning is necessary to produce strong branches, and sprays are used to protect the fruit from pests and to influence its development. The apple has been an important food plant in Europe and Asia for thousands of years.

Apple US computer company, manufacturer of the ◊Macintosh range of computers.

applet mini-software application. Examples of applets include Microsoft WordPad, the simple word processor in Windows 95, or the single-purpose applications that in 1996 were beginning to appear on the World Wide Web, written in Java. These include small animations, such as a moving ticker tape of stock prices.

Appleton layer or ***F layer*** band containing ionized gases in the Earth's upper atmosphere, at a height of 150–1,000 km/94–625 mi, above the ◊E layer (formerly the Kennelly–Heaviside layer). It acts as a dependable reflector of radio signals as it is not affected by atmospheric conditions, although its ionic composition varies with the sunspot cycle.

The Appleton layer has the highest concentration of free electrons and ions of the atmospheric layers. It is named after the English physicist Edward Appleton.

application in computing, a program or job designed for the benefit of the end user, such as a payroll system or a ◊word processor. The term is used to distinguish such programs from those that control the computer (◊systems programs) or assist the programmer, such as a ◊compiler.

application in mathematics, a curved line that connects a series of points (or 'nodes') in the smoothest possible way. The shape of the curve is governed by a series of complex mathematical formulae. Applications are used in ◊computer graphics and ◊CAD.

applications package in computing, the set of programs and related documentation (such as instruction manuals) used in a particular application. For example, a typical payroll applications package would consist of separate programs for the entry of data, updating the master files, and printing the pay slips, plus documentation in the form of program details and instructions for use.

Applications Program Interface (API) in computing, standard environment, including tools, protocols, and other routines, in which programs can be written. An API ensures that all applications are consistent with the operating system and have a similar ◊user interface.

appropriate technology simple or small-scale machinery and tools that, because they are cheap and easy to produce and maintain, may be of most use in the developing world; for example, hand ploughs and simple looms. This equipment may be used to supplement local crafts and traditional skills to encourage small-scale industrialization.

Many countries suffer from poor infrastructure and lack of capital but have the large supplies of labour needed for this level of technology. The use of appropriate technology was one of the recommendations of the Brandt Commission.

approximation rough estimate of a given value. For example, for ◊pi (which has a value of 3.1415926 correct to seven decimal places), 3 is an approximation to the nearest whole number.

APR abbreviation for ◊annual percentage rate.

apricot yellow-fleshed fruit of the apricot tree, which is closely related to the almond, peach, plum, and cherry. Although native to the Far East, it has long been cultivated in Armenia, from where it was introduced into Europe and the USA. (Genus *Prunus armeniaca,* family Rosaceae.)

aquaculture the cultivation of fish and shellfish for human consumption; see ◊fish farming.

aqualung or ***scuba*** underwater breathing apparatus worn by divers, developed in the early 1940s by French diver Jacques Cousteau. Compressed-air cylinders strapped to the diver's back are regulated by a valve system and by a mouth tube to provide air to the diver at the same pressure as that of the surrounding water (which increases with the depth).

aquamarine blue variety of the mineral ◊beryl. A semiprecious gemstone, it is used in jewellery.

aquaplaning phenomenon in which the tyres of a road vehicle cease to make direct contact with the road surface, owing to the presence of a thin film of water. As a result, the vehicle can go out of control (particularly if the steered wheels are involved).

aqua regia ***Latin 'royal water'*** mixture of three parts concentrated hydrochloric acid and one part concentrated nitric acid, which dissolves all metals except silver.

aquarium tank or similar container used for the study and display of living aquatic plants and animals. The same name is used for institutions that exhibit aquatic life. These have been common since Roman times, but the first modern public aquarium was opened in Regent's Park, London in 1853. A recent development is the oceanarium or seaquarium, a large display of marine life forms.

Aquarius zodiacal constellation a little south of the celestial equator near Pegasus. Aquarius is represented as a man pouring water from a jar. The Sun passes through Aquarius from late February to early March. In astrology, the dates for Aquarius, the 11th sign of the zodiac, are between about 20 January and 18 February (see ◊precession).

aquatic living in water. All life on Earth originated in the early oceans, because the aquatic environment has several advantages for organisms. Dehydration is almost impossible, temperatures usually remain stable, and the density of water provides physical support.

Life forms that cannot exist out of water, amphibians that take to the water on occasions, animals that are also perfectly at home on land, and insects that spend a stage of their life cycle in water can all be described as aquatic. Aquatic plants are known as ◊hydrophytes.

aquatic insect insect that spends all or part of its life in water. Of the 29 insect orders, 11 members have some aquatic stages. Most of these have aquatic, immature stages, which usually take place in fresh water, sometimes in brackish water (very few species are truly marine); the adults are terrestrial, but in some orders there are species where all stages (egg, larva, and adult) live in the water.
partially aquatic Three orders, Ephemeroptera (mayflies), Odonata (dragonflies), and Plecoptera (stone-flies) have aquatic larvae, but the adults are terrestrial. In the orders Neuroptera (alder flies), Tricoptera (caddis flies), Lepidoptera (butterflies and moths), and Diptera (true flies), some species have aquatic larvae, but the adults of all species are terrestrial. Hymenoptera, the social insect order which includes the ants and bees, has some aquatic species of ichneumon fly: immature stages of *Agriotypus* are aquatic, and adults of *Caraphractus* and *Prestwitchia*.
totally aquatic The order Collembola (springtails) has two species in which all stages are aquatic: *Hydropodura aquatica* and *Isotoma palustris*. In Hemiptera (bugs), and Coleoptera (beetles), some members, for example the water bugs, spend all stages of the life-cycle in the water.

aqueduct any artificial channel or conduit for water, originally applied to water supply tunnels, but later used to refer to elevated structures of stone, wood, or ironcarrying navigable canals across valleys.One of the first great aqueducts was built in 691 BC, carrying water for 80 km/50 mi to Ninevah, capital of the ancient Assyrian Empire. Many Roman aqueducts are still standing, for example the one carried by the Pont du Gard at Nîmes in S France, built about 8 BC (48 m/160 ft high).

The largest Roman aqueduct, at Carthage in Tunisia, is 141 km/87 mi long and was built during the reign of Publius Aelius Hadrianus between AD 117 and 138. A recent aqueduct is the California State Water Project taking water from Lake Oroville in the north, through two power plants and across the Tehachapi Mountains, more than 177 km/110 mi to S California.

aqueous humour watery fluid found in the chamber between the cornea and lens of the vertebrate eye. Similar to blood serum in composition, it is constantly renewed.

aqueous solution solution in which the solvent is water.

aquifer a body of rock through which appreciable amounts of water can flow. The rock of an aquifer must be porous and permeable (full of interconnected holes) so that it can conduct water. Aquifers are an important source of fresh water, for example, for drinking and irrigation, in many arid areas of the world, and are exploited by the use of ◊artesian wells.

An aquifer may be underlain, overlain, or sandwiched between less permeable layers, called aquicludes or **aquitards**, which impede water movement. Sandstones and porous limestones make the best aquifers.

Aquila constellation on the celestial equator (see ◊celestial sphere). Its brightest star is first-magnitude ◊Altair, flanked by the stars Beta and Gamma Aquilae. It is represented by an eagle.

Nova Aquilae, which appeared June 1918, shone for a few days nearly as brightly as Sirius.

arable farming cultivation of crops, as opposed to the keeping of animals. Crops may be ◊cereals, vegetables, or plants for producing oils or cloth. Arable farming generally requires less attention than livestock farming. In a ◊mixed farming system, crops may therefore be found farther from the farm centre than animals.

arachnid or ***arachnoid*** type of arthropod of the class Arachnida, including spiders, scorpions, ticks, and mites. They differ from insects in possessing only two main body regions, the cephalothorax and the abdomen, and in having eight legs.

araucaria coniferous tree related to the firs, with flat, scalelike needles. Once widespread, it is now native only to the southern hemisphere. Some grow to gigantic size. Araucarias include the monkey-puzzle tree (*Araucaria araucana*), the Australian bunya bunya pine (*A. bidwillii*), and the Norfolk Island pine (*A. heterophylla*). (Genus *Araucaria*, family Araucariaceae.)

ARACHNOLOGY

http://dns.ufsia.ac.be/Arachnology/Arachnology.html

Largely a collection of annotated links, organized under headings such as taxonomy and classification, palaeontology, poison, bites, diseases, pests, and phobia. The site also contains spider-related myths, stories, poems, songs, and art.

arboretum collection of trees. An arboretum may contain a wide variety of species or just closely related species or varieties – for example, different types of pine tree.

arbor vitae any of several coniferous trees or shrubs belonging to the cypress family, with flattened branchlets covered in overlapping aromatic green scales. The northern white cedar (*Thuja occidentalis*) and the western red cedar (*T. plicata*) are found in North America. The Chinese or Oriental species *T. orientalis*, reaching 18 m/60 ft in height, is widely grown as an ornamental. (Genus *Thuja*, family Cupressaceae.)

arbutus any of a group of evergreen shrubs belonging to the heath family, found in temperate regions. The strawberry tree (*Arbutus unedo*) is grown for its ornamental, strawberrylike fruit. (Genus *Arbutus*, family Ericaceae.)

arc in geometry, a section of a curved line or circle. A circle has three types of arc: a **semicircle**, which is exactly half of the circle; **minor arcs**, which are less than the semicircle; and **major arcs**, which are greater than the semicircle.

An arc of a circle is measured in degrees, according to the angle formed by joining its two ends to the centre of that circle. A semicircle is therefore 180°, whereas a minor arc will always be less than 180° (acute or obtuse) and a major arc will always be greater than 180° but less than 360° (reflex).

Archaea group of microorganisms that are without a nucleus and have a single chromosome. All are strict anaerobes, that is, they are killed by oxygen. This is thought to be a primitive condition and to indicate that Archaea are related to the earliest life forms, which appeared about 4 billion years ago, when there was little oxygen in the Earth's atmosphere. They are found in undersea vents, hot springs, the Dead Sea, and salt pans, and have even adapted to refuse tips.

Archaea was originally classified as bacterial, but in 1996 when the genome of *Methanococcus jannaschii* (an archaeaon that lives in undersea vents at temperatures around 100°C/212°F) was sequenced, US geneticists found that 56% of its genes were unlike those of any other organism, making Archaea unique.

In 1994 US biologists detected archaeans in the Antarctic (where they make up 30% of the single-celled marine biomass), Arctic, Mediterranean, and Baltic Sea.

Archaean or ***Archaeozoic*** widely used term for the earliest era of geological time; the first part of the Precambrian **Eon**, spanning the interval from the formation of Earth to about 2,500 million years ago.

archaeology ***Greek archaia 'ancient things', logos 'study'*** study of prehistory and history, based on the examination of physical remains. Principal activities include preliminary field (or site) surveys, ◊excavation (where necessary), and the classification, ◊dating, and interpretation of finds.
history A museum found at the ancient Sumerian city of Ur indicates that interest in the physical remains of the past stretches back into prehistory. In the Renaissance this interest gained momentum among dealers in and collectors of ancient art and was further stimulated by discoveries made in Africa, the Americas, and Asia by Europeans during the period of imperialist colonization in the 16th–19th centuries, such as the antiquities discovered during Napoleon's Egyptian campaign in the 1790s. Romanticism in Europe stimulated an enthusiasm for the mouldering skull, the

ARCHAEOLOGY

http://www.archaeology.org/

Online edition of the prestigious journal of the Archaeological Institute of America. The well-written articles give a glimpse of the range of archaeological research being done around the globe. The full texts of short articles are available online, together with abstracts (and often the full text) of a large number of longer articles. Two years of back issues can be accessed.

ancient potsherds, ruins, and dolmens; relating archaeology to a wider context of art and literature.

Towards the end of the 19th century archaeology became an academic study, making increasing use of scientific techniques and systematic methodologies such as aerial photography. Since World War II new developments within the discipline include medieval, postmedieval, landscape, and industrial archaeology; underwater reconnaissance enabling the excavation of underwater sites; and rescue archaeology (excavation of sites risking destruction).

related disciplines Useful in archaeological studies are ◊dendrochronology (tree-ring dating), ◊geochronology (science of measuring geological time), ◊stratigraphy (study of geological strata), palaeobotany (study of ancient pollens, seeds, and grains), archaeozoology (analysis of animal remains), epigraphy (study of inscriptions), and numismatics (study of coins).

archaeopteryx *Greek archaios 'ancient', pterux 'wing'* extinct primitive bird, known from fossilized remains, about 160 million years old, found in limestone deposits in Bavaria, Germany. It is popularly known as 'the first bird', although some earlier bird ancestors are now known. It was about the size of a crow and had feathers and wings, with three clawlike digits at the end of each wing, but in many respects its skeleton is reptilian (teeth and a long, bony tail) and very like some small meat-eating dinosaurs of the time.

archegonium *Greek arche 'origin', gonos 'offspring'* female sex organ found in bryophytes (mosses and liverworts), pteridophytes (ferns, club mosses, and horsetails), and some gymnosperms. It is a multicellular, flask-shaped structure consisting of two parts: the swollen base or venter containing the egg cell, and the long, narrow neck. When the egg cell is mature, the cells of the neck dissolve, allowing the passage of the male gametes, or ◊antherozoids.

archerfish surface-living fish of the family Toxotidae, such as the genus *Toxotes*, native to SE Asia and Australia. The archerfish grows to about 25 cm/10 in and is able to shoot down insects up to 1.5 m/5 ft above the water by spitting a jet of water from its mouth.

Archie software tool for locating information on the ◊Internet. It can be difficult to locate a particular file because of the relatively unstructured nature of the Internet. Archie uses indexes of files and their locations on the Internet to find them quickly.

Archimedes
(c. 287–212 BC)

Greek mathematician who made major discoveries in geometry, hydrostatics, and mechanics, and established the sciences of statics and hydrostatics. He formulated a law of fluid displacement (Archimedes' principle), and is credited with the invention of the Archimedes screw, a cylindrical device for raising water. His method of finding mathematical proof to substantiate experiment and observation became the method of modern science in the High Renaissance.

Hydrostatics and Archimedes' principle The best-known result of Archimedes' work on hydrostatics is Archimedes' principle, which states that a body immersed in water will displace a volume of fluid that weighs as much as the body would weigh in air. It is alleged that Archimedes' principle was discovered when he stepped into the public bath and saw the water overflow. He was so delighted that he rushed home naked, crying 'Eureka! Eureka!' ('I have found it! I have found it!').

He used his discovery to prove that the goldsmith of Hieron II, King of Syracuse, had adulterated a gold crown with silver. Archimedes realized that if the gold had been mixed with silver (which is less dense than gold), the crown would have a greater volume and therefore displace more water than an equal weight of pure gold. The story goes that the crown was found to be impure, and that the unfortunate goldsmith was executed.

Statics and the lever In the field of statics, he is credited with working out the rigorous mathematical proofs behind the law of the lever. The lever had been used by other scientists, but it was Archimedes who demonstrated mathematically that the ratio of the effort applied to the load raised is equal to the inverse ratio of the distances of the effort and load from the pivot or fulcrum of the lever. Archimedes is credited with having claimed that if he had a sufficiently distant place to stand, he could use a lever to move the world.

This claim is said to have given rise to a challenge from King Hieron to Archimedes to show how he could move a truly heavy object with ease, even if he could not move the world. In answer to this, Archimedes developed a system of compound pulleys. According to Plutarch's Life of Marcellus (who sacked Syracuse), Archimedes used this to move with ease a ship that had been lifted with great effort by many men out of the harbour on to dry land. The ship was laden with passengers, crew and freight, but Archimedes – sitting at a distance from the ship – was reportedly able to pull it over the land as though it were gliding through water.

Mathematics Archimedes wrote many mathematical treatises, some of which still exist in altered forms in Arabic. Archimedes' approximation for the value for π was more accurate than any previous estimate – the value lying between $\frac{223}{71}$ and $\frac{220}{70}$. The average of these two numbers is less than 0.0003 different from the modern approximation for π. He also examined the expression of very large numbers, using a special notation to estimate the number of grains of sand in the Universe. Although the result, 10^{63}, was far from accurate, Archimedes demonstrated that large numbers could be considered and handled effectively.

Archimedes also evolved methods to solve cubic equations and to determine square roots by approximation. His formulae for the determination of the surface areas and volumes of curved surfaces and solids anticipated the development of integral calculus, which did not come for another 2,000 years. Archimedes had decreed that his gravestone be inscribed with a cylinder enclosing a sphere together with the formula for the ratio of their volumes – a discovery that he regarded as his greatest achievement.

Mary Evans Picture Library

Eureka! I have found it!

ARCHIMEDES Greek mathematician.
Remark, quoted in Vitruvius Pollio *De Architectura* IX

Archimedes' principle in physics, the principle that the weight of the liquid displaced by a floating body is equal to the weight of the body. The principle is often stated in the form: 'an object totally or partially submerged in a fluid displaces a volume of fluid that weighs the same as the apparent loss in weight of the object (which, in turn, equals the upwards force, or upthrust, experienced by that object).' It was discovered by the Greek mathematician Archimedes.

Archimedes screw one of the earliest kinds of pump, associated with the Greek mathematician Archimedes. It consists of an enormous spiral screw revolving inside a close-fitting cylinder. It is used, for example, to raise water for irrigation.

The lowest portion of the screw just dips into the water, and as the cylinder is turned a small quantity of water is scooped up. The inclination of the cylinder is such that at the next revolution the water is raised above the next thread, whilst the lowest thread scoops up another quantity. The successive revolutions, therefore, raise the water thread by thread until it emerges at the top of the cylinder.

archipelago group of islands, or an area of sea containing a group of islands. The islands of an archipelago are usually volcanic in origin, and they sometimes represent the tops of peaks in areas around continental margins flooded by the sea.

Volcanic islands are formed either when a hot spot within the Earth's mantle produces a chain of volcanoes on the surface, such as the Hawaiian Archipelago or at a destructive plate margin (see ◊plate tectonics) where the subduction of one plate beneath another produces an arc-shaped island group called an 'island arc', such as the Aleutian Archipelago. Novaya Zemlya in the Arctic Ocean, the northern extension of the Ural Mountains, resulted from continental flooding.

architecture in computing, the overall design of a computer system, encompassing both hardware and software. The architecture of a particular system includes the specifications of individual components and the ways they interact. Because the operating system defines how these elements interact with each other and with application software, it is also included in the term.

archive collection of computer files. The term is commonly used to refer to the files created by ◊data compression programs, such as the popular PKZIP, which contain one or more files. On the Internet it is also used to refer to a large store of files from which visitors can select the ones they want.

***Archimedes screw** The Archimedes screw, a spiral screw turned inside a cylinder, was once commonly used to lift water from canals. The screw is still used to lift water in the Nile delta in Egypt, and is often used to shift grain in mills and powders in factories.*

arc lamp or ***arc light*** electric light that uses the illumination of an electric arc maintained between two electrodes. The English chemist Humphry Davy demonstrated the electric n arc in 1802 and electric arc lighting was first introduced by English electrical engineer W E Staite (1809–1854) in 1846. The lamp consists of two carbon electrodes, between which a very high voltage is maintained. Electric current arcs (jumps) between the two electrolytes, creating a brilliant light. Its main use in recent years has been in cinema projectors.

arc minute, arc second units for measuring small angles, used in geometry, surveying, map-making, and astronomy. An arc minute (symbol ') is one-sixtieth of a degree, and an arc second (symbol ') is one-sixtieth of an arc minute. Small distances in the sky, as between two close stars or the apparent width of a planet's disc, are expressed in minutes and seconds of arc.

arctic animals animals inhabiting the Arctic. The birds are chiefly sea birds, such as petrels, eider ducks, cormorants, auks, gulls, puffins, and guillemots; all are migratory. The mammals include the walrus, seals, and several varieties of whale; the polar bear, reindeer, elk, fox, wolf, ermine, and musk-ox are the principal terrestrial mammals.

Insectivorous and herbivorous habits are almost absent in arctic animals, which are either fish- or meat-eating. Many of them become snowy white in winter; among these are birds, such as the ptarmigan, and mammals, such as the hare and lemming, which are brown in summer, and the arctic fox, which is salty-blue in summer; the polar bear is white all year round.

Molluscs, annelids, and jellyfish are common to all the northern seas, while such fish as salmon, cod, and halibut are plentiful. Insects found in the far north include bees, flies, and butterflies, but as the flora is scanty they do not occur in great abundance.

ARCTIC CIRCLE

http://www.lib.uconn.edu/ArcticCircle/

Well-written site with excellent information about all aspects of life in the Arctic. There are sections on history, natural resources, the rights of indigenous peoples, and issues of environmental concern.

Arctic Circle imaginary line that encircles the North Pole at latitude 66° 33' north. Within this line there is at least one day in the summer during which the Sun never sets, and at least one day in the winter during which the Sun never rises.

Arcturus or ***Alpha Boötis*** brightest star in the constellation Boötes and the fourth-brightest star in the sky. Arcturus is a red giant about 28 times larger than the Sun and 70 times more luminous, 36 light years away from Earth.

are metric unit of area, equal to 100 square metres (119.6 sq yd); 100 ares make one ◊hectare.

area the size of a surface. It is measured in square units, usually square centimetres (cm^2), square metres (m^2), or square kilome-

Areas: Common Areas

figure	*rule for calculating area*
rectangle	lengthx breadth
triangle	half base length × vertical height
parallelogram	base length × vertical height
trapezium	average length of parallel sides × perpendicular distance between them
circle	πr^2, where r is the radiussector $\frac{x\pi r^2}{360}$ where x is the angle of the sector

tres (km^2). Surface area is the area of the outer surface of a solid.

The areas of geometrical plane shapes with straight edges are determined using the area of a rectangle. Integration may be used to determine the area of shapes enclosed by curves.

areca any of a group of palm trees native to Asia and Australia. The ◊betel nut comes from the species *Areca catechu.* (Genus *Areca.*)

Arecibo site in Puerto Rico of the world's largest single-dish ◊radio telescope, 305 m/1,000 ft in diameter. It is built in a natural hollow and uses the rotation of the Earth to scan the sky. It has been used both for radar work on the planets and for conventional radio astronomy, and is operated by Cornell University, USA.

In 1996 it received a $25 million upgrade, increasing the sensitivity of the disc tenfold. Two new mirrors were also added and the observation frequency increased from 3,000 megahertz to up to 10,000 megahertz. Another upgrade took place in 1997, when a new receiver capable of monitoring 168 million radio channels, SERENDIP IV, was added to the facility.

Water, water, everywhere, / Nor any drop to drink.

SAMUEL COLERIDGE English poet.
The Ancient Mariner pt 2

---

arête (***German*** **grat;** ***North American*** **combe-ridge)** sharp narrow ridge separating two ◊glacial troughs (valleys), or ◊corries. The typical U-shaped cross sections of glacial troughs give arêtes very steep sides. Arêtes are common in glaciated mountain regions such as the Rockies, the Himalayas, and the Alps.

argali wild sheep from the mountains of central Asia. It is the largest species of sheep with a shoulder height of up to 1.2 m/4 ft.
classification Argali *Ovis ammon* is in family Bovidae, order Artiodactyla.

Argand diagram in mathematics, a method for representing complex numbers by Cartesian coordinates (x, y). Along the x-axis (horizontal axis) are plotted the real numbers, and along the y-axis (vertical axis) the nonreal, or ◊imaginary, numbers.

argon ***Greek argos 'idle'*** colourless, odourless, nonmetallic, gaseous element, symbol Ar, atomic number 18, relative atomic mass 39.948. It is grouped with the ◊inert gases, since it was long believed not to react with other substances, but observations now indicate that it can be made to combine with boron fluoride to form compounds. It constitutes almost 1% of the Earth's atmosphere, and was discovered in 1894 by British chemists John Rayleigh (1842–1919) and William Ramsay after all oxygen and nitrogen had been removed chemically from a sample of air. It is used in electric discharge tubes and argon lasers.

argonaut or ***paper nautilus*** octopus living in the open sea, genus *Argonauta.* The female of the common paper nautilus, *A. argo,* is 20 cm/8 in across, and secretes a spiralled papery shell for her eggs from the web of the first pair of arms. The male is a shell-less dwarf, 1 cm/0.4 in across.

argument in computing, the value on which a ◊function operates. For example, if the argument 16 is operated on by the function 'square root', the answer 4 is produced.

argument in mathematics, a specific value of the independent variable of a ◊function of x. It is also another name for ◊amplitude.

Ariane launch vehicle built in a series by the European Space Agency (first flight 1979). The launch site is at Kourou in French Guiana. Ariane is a three-stage rocket using liquid fuels. Small solid-fuel and liquid-fuel boosters can be attached to its first stage to increase carrying power.

Since 1984 it has been operated commercially by Arianespace, a private company financed by European banks and aerospace industries. A more powerful version, *Ariane 5,* was launched 4 June 1996, and was intended to carry astronauts aboard the Hermes spaceplane. However, it went off course immediately after takeoff , turned on its side, broke into two and disintegrated. A fault in the software controlling the takeoff trajectory was to blame.

A mostly successful test flight for *Ariane 5* was completed in November 1997.

arid region in earth science, a region that is very dry and has little vegetation. Aridity depends on temperature, rainfall, and evaporation, and so is difficult to quantify, but an arid area is usually defined as one that receives less than 250 mm/10 in of rainfall each year. (By comparison, New York City receives 1,120 mm/44 in per year.) There are arid regions in North Africa, Pakistan, Australia, the USA, and elsewhere. Very arid regions are ◊deserts.

Ariel series of six UK satellites launched by the USA 1962–79, the most significant of which was *Ariel 5* in 1974, which made a pioneering survey of the sky at X-ray wavelengths.

Aries zodiacal constellation in the northern hemisphere between Pisces and Taurus, near Auriga, represented as the legendary ram whose golden fleece was sought by Jason and the Argonauts.

Its most distinctive feature is a curve of three stars of decreasing brightness. The brightest of these is Hamal or Alpha Arietis, 65 light years from Earth.

The Sun passes through Aries from late April to mid-May. In astrology, the dates for Aries, the first sign of the zodiac, are between about 21 March and 19 April (see ◊precession). The spring ◊equinox once lay in Aries, but has now moved into Pisces through the effect of the Earth's precession (wobble).

aril accessory seed cover other than a ◊fruit; it may be fleshy and sometimes brightly coloured, woody, or hairy. In flowering plants (◊angiosperms) it is often derived from the stalk that originally attached the ovule to the ovary wall. Examples of arils include the bright-red, fleshy layer surrounding the yew seed (yews are ◊gymnosperms so they lack true fruits), and the network of hard filaments that partially covers the nutmeg seed and yields the spice known as mace.

Another aril, the horny outgrowth found towards one end of the seed of the castor-oil plant *Ricinus communis,* is called a caruncle. It is formed from the integuments (protective layers enclosing the ovule) and develops after fertilization.

arithmetic branch of mathematics concerned with the study of numbers and their properties. The fundamental operations of arithmetic are addition, subtraction, multiplication, and division. Raising to powers (for example, squaring or cubing a number), the extraction of roots (for example, square roots), percentages, fractions, and ratios are developed from these operations.

Forms of simple arithmetic existed in prehistoric times. In China, Egypt, Babylon, and early civilizations generally, arithmetic was used for commercial purposes, records of taxation, and astronomy. During the Dark Ages in Europe, knowledge of arithmetic was preserved in India and later among the Arabs. European mathematics revived with the development of trade and overseas exploration. Hindu-Arabic numerals replaced Roman numerals, allowing calculations to be made on paper, instead of by the ◊abacus.

The essential feature of this number system was the introduction of zero, which allows us to have a **place–value** system. The decimal numeral system employs ten numerals (0,1,2,3,4,5,6,7,8,9) and is said to operate in 'base ten'. In a base-ten number, each position has a value ten times that of the position to its immediate right; for example, in the number 23 the numeral 3 represents three units (ones), and the numeral 2 represents two tens. The Babylonians, however, used a complex base-sixty system, residues of which are found today in the number of minutes in each hour and in angular measurement (6 × 60 degrees). The Mayas used a base-twenty system.

There have been many inventions and developments to make the manipulation of the arithmetic processes easier, such as the invention of ◊logarithms by Scottish mathematician John ◊Napier in 1614 and of the slide rule in the period 1620–30. Since then, many forms of ready reckoners, mechanical and electronic calculators, and computers have been invented.

Modern computers fundamentally operate in base two, using only two numerals (0,1), known as a binary system. In binary, each position has a value twice as great as the position to its immediate right, so that for example binary 111 (or 111_2) is equal to 7 in the decimal system, and binary 1111 (or 1111_2) is equal to 15. Because the main operations of subtraction, multiplication, and division can be reduced mathematically to addition, digital computers carry out calculations by adding, usually in binary numbers in which the numerals 0 and 1 can be represented by off and on pulses of electric current.

Modular or modulo arithmetic, sometimes known as residue arithmetic or clock arithmetic, can take only a specific number of digits, whatever the value. For example, in modulo 4 (mod 4) the only values any number can take are 0, 1, 2, or 3. In this system, 7 is written as 3 mod 4, and 35 is also 3 mod 4. Notice 3 is the residue, or remainder, when 7 or 35 is divided by 4. This form of arithmetic is often illustrated on a circle. It deals with events recurring in regular cycles, and is used in describing the functioning of petrol engines, electrical generators, and so on. For example, in the mod 12, the answer to a question as to what time it will be in five hours if it is now ten o'clock can be expressed 10 + 5 = 3.

arithmetic and logic unit (ALU) in a computer, the part of the ◊central processing unit (CPU) that performs the basic arithmetic and logic operations on data.

arithmetic mean the average of a set of *n* numbers, obtained by adding the numbers and dividing by *n*. For example, the arithmetic mean of the set of 5 numbers 1, 3, 6, 8, and 12 is (1 + 3 + 6 + 8 + 12)/5 = 30/5 = 6.

The term 'average' is often used to refer only to the arithmetic mean, even though the mean is in fact only one form of average (the others include ◊median and ◊mode).

arithmetic progression or ***arithmetic sequence*** sequence of numbers or terms that have a common difference between any one term and the next in the sequence. For example, 2, 7, 12, 17, 22, 27, ... is an arithmetic sequence with a common difference of 5.

The *n*th term in any arithmetic progression can be found using the formula:

$$n\text{th term} = a + (n - 1)d$$

where a is the first term and d is the common difference.

An **arithmetic series** is the sum of the terms in an arithmetic sequence. The sum S of n terms is given by:

$$S = \tfrac{n}{2}[2a + (n - 1)d]$$

ARM (abbreviation for ***Advanced RISC Machine***) microprocessor developed by Acorn in 1985 for use in the Archimedes microcomputer. In 1990 the company Advanced RISC Machines was formed to develop the ARM microprocessor. The ARM is the microprocessor in Apple's ◊Newton.

armadillo mammal of the family Dasypodidae, with an armour of bony plates along its back or, in some species, almost covering the entire body. Around 20 species live between Texas and Patagonia and range in size from the fairy armadillo, or pichiciego, *Chlamyphorus truncatus,* at 13 cm/5 in, to the giant armadillo *Priodontes giganteus,* 1.5 m/4.5 ft long. Armadillos feed on insects, snakes, fruit, and carrion. Some can roll into an armoured ball if attacked; others defend themselves with their claws or rely on rapid burrowing for protection.

ARMADILLO

Nine-banded armadillos almost always produce litters of quadruplets. The one fertilized egg divides into four to produce a single-sex litter of identical babies. If times are hard, the female armadillo can delay the implantation of her egg for up to three years to maximize the chances of her offspring's survival.

They belong to the order Edentata ('without teeth') which also includes sloths and anteaters. However, only the latter are toothless. Some species of armadillos can have up to 90 peglike teeth.

armature in a motor or generator, the wire-wound coil that carries the current and rotates in a magnetic field. (In alternating-current machines, the armature is sometimes stationary.) The pole piece of a permanent magnet or electromagnet and the moving, iron part of a ◊solenoid, especially if the latter acts as a switch, may also be referred to as armatures.

armillary sphere earliest known astronomical device, in use from the 3rd century BC. It showed the Earth at the centre of the universe, surrounded by a number of movable metal rings representing the Sun, Moon, and planets. The armillary sphere was originally used to observe the heavens and later for teaching navigators about the arrangements and movements of the heavenly bodies.

aromatherapy in alternative medicine, use of oils and essences derived from plants, flowers, and wood resins. Bactericidal properties and beneficial effects upon physiological functions are attributed to the oils, which are sometimes ingested but generally massaged into the skin.

Aromatherapy was first used in ancient Greece and Egypt, but became a forgotten art until the 1930s, when a French chemist accidentally spilt lavender over a cut and found that the wound healed without a scar. However, it was not until the 1970s that it began to achieve widespread popularity.

aromatic compound organic chemical compound in which some of the bonding electrons are delocalized (shared among several atoms within the molecule and not localized in the vicinity of the atoms involved in bonding). The commonest aromatic compounds have ring structures, the atoms comprising the ring being either all carbon or containing one or more different atoms (usually nitrogen, sulphur, or oxygen). Typical examples are benzene (C_6H_6) and pyridine (C_6H_5N).

ARPANET (acronym for ***Advanced Research Projects Agency Network***) early US network that forms the basis of the ◊Internet. It was set up in 1969 by ARPA to provide services to US academic institutions and commercial organizations conducting computer science research.

ARPANET pioneered many of today's networking techniques.

It was renamed DARPANET when ARPA changed its name to Defense Advanced Research Projects Agency. In 1975 responsibility for DARPANET was passed on to the Defense Communication Agency.

array in computer programming, a list of values that can all be referred to by a single ◊variable name. Separate values are distinguished by using a **subscript** with each variable name.

Arrays are useful because they allow programmers to write general routines that can process long lists of data. For example, if every price stored in an accounting program used a different variable name, separate program instructions would be needed to process each price. However, if all the prices were stored in an array, a general routine could be written to process, say, 'price (*J*)', and, by allowing *J* to take different values, could then process any individual price.

For example, consider this list of highest daily temperatures: day 1 – 22°C; day 2 – 23°C; day 3 – 19°C; day 4 – 21°C. This array might be stored with the single variable name 'temp'. Separate elements of the array would then be identified with subscripts. So, for example, the array element '$\text{temp}(_1)$' would store the value '22', and the array element '$\text{temp}(_3)$' would store the value '19'.

array collection of numbers (or letters representing numbers) arranged in rows and columns. A ◊matrix is an array shown inside a pair of brackets; it indicates that the array should be treated as a single entity.

arrhythmia disturbance of the normal rhythm of the heart. There are various kinds of arrhythmia, some benign, some indicative of heart disease. In extreme cases, the heart may beat so fast as to be potentially lethal and surgery may be used to correct the condition.

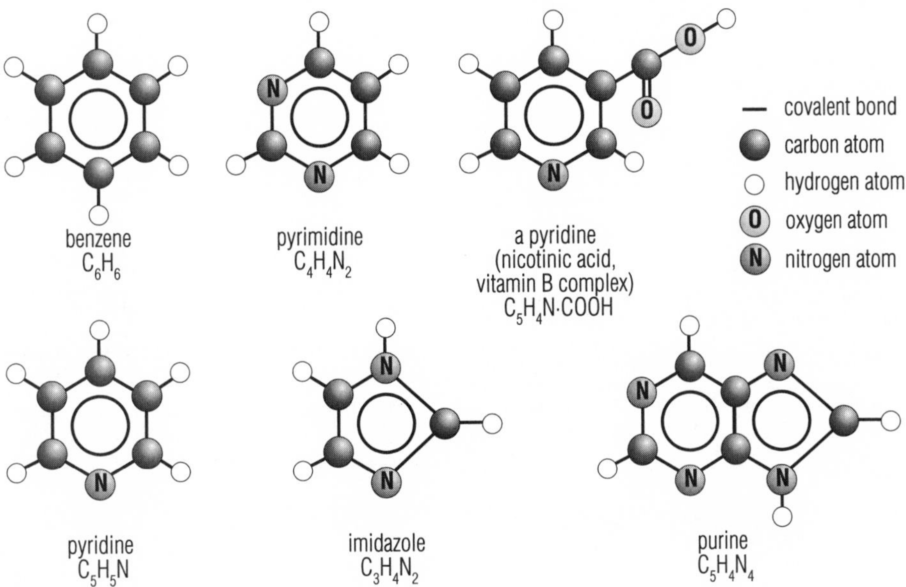

aromatic compound *Compounds whose molecules contain the benzene ring, or variations of it, are called aromatic. The term was originally used to distinguish sweet-smelling compounds from others.*

Extra beats between the normal ones are called **extrasystoles**; abnormal slowing is known as **bradycardia** and speeding up is known as **tachycardia**.

arrowroot starchy substance used as a thickener in cooking, produced from the clumpy roots of various tropical plants. The true arrowroot (*Maranta arundinacea*) was used by native South Americans as an antidote against the effects of poisoned arrows.

The West Indian island of St Vincent is the main source of supply today. The plant roots and tubers are dried, finely powdered, and filtered. Because of the small size of the starch particles, the powder becomes translucent when cooked.

arrowwood any of various North American trees and shrubs, especially of the genus *Viburnum*, named for their long, straight branches, which were used by American Indians to make arrows.

arsenic brittle, greyish-white, semimetallic element (a metalloid), symbol As, atomic number 33, relative atomic mass 74.92. It occurs in many ores and occasionally in its elemental state, and is widely distributed, being present in minute quantities in the soil, the sea, and the human body. In larger quantities, it is poisonous. The chief source of arsenic compounds is as a by-product from metallurgical processes. It is used in making semiconductors, alloys, and solders.

As it is a cumulative poison, its presence in food and drugs is very dangerous. The symptoms of arsenic poisoning are vomiting, diarrhoea, tingling and possibly numbness in the limbs, and collapse. It featured in some drugs, including Salvarsan, the first specific treatment for syphilis. Its name derives from the Latin *arsenicum*.

arteriosclerosis hardening of the arteries, with thickening and loss of elasticity. It is associated with smoking, ageing, and a diet high in saturated fats. The term is used loosely as a synonym for ◊atherosclerosis.

artery vessel that carries blood from the heart to the rest of the body. It is built to withstand considerable pressure, having thick walls which contain smooth muscle fibres. During contraction of the heart muscle, arteries expand in diameter to allow for the sudden increase in pressure that occurs; the resulting ◊pulse or pressure wave can be felt at the wrist. Not all arteries carry oxygenated (oxygen-rich) blood; the pulmonary arteries convey deoxygenated (oxygen-poor) blood from the heart to the lungs.

Arteries are flexible, elastic tubes, consisting of three layers, the middle of which is muscular; its rhythmic contraction aids the pumping of blood around the body. In middle and old age, the walls degenerate and are vulnerable to damage by the build-up of fatty deposits. These reduce elasticity, hardening the arteries and decreasing the internal bore. This condition, known as ◊atherosclerosis, can lead to high blood pressure, loss of circulation, heart disease, and death.

Research indicates that a typical Western diet, high in saturated fat, increases the chances of arterial disease developing.

artesian well well that is supplied with water rising naturally from an underground water-saturated rock layer (◊aquifer). The water rises from the aquifer under its own pressure. Such a well may be drilled into an aquifer that is confined by impermeable rocks both above and below. If the water table (the top of the region of water saturation) in that aquifer is above the level of the well head, hydrostatic pressure will force the water to the surface.

Artesian wells are often overexploited because their water is fresh and easily available, and they eventually become unreliable. There is also some concern that pollutants such as pesticides or nitrates can seep into the aquifers.

arthritis inflammation of the joints, with pain, swelling, and restricted motion. Many conditions may cause arthritis, including gout, infection, and trauma to the joint. There are three main forms of arthritis: ◊rheumatoid arthritis; osteoarthritis; and septic arthritis.

arthropod member of the phylum Arthropoda; an invertebrate animal with jointed legs and a segmented body with a horny or chitinous casing (exoskeleton), which is shed periodically and replaced as the animal grows. Included are arachnids such as spiders and mites, as well as crustaceans, millipedes, centipedes, and insects.

artichoke either of two plants belonging to the sunflower family, parts of which are eaten as vegetables. The **common** or **globe artichoke** (*Cynara scolymus*) is a form of thistle native to the Mediterranean. It is tall, with purplish-blue flowers; the leaflike structures (bracts) around the unopened flower are eaten. The **Jerusalem artichoke** (*Helianthus tuberosus*), which has edible tubers, is a native of North America (its common name is a corruption of the Italian for sunflower, *girasole*). (Family Compositae.)

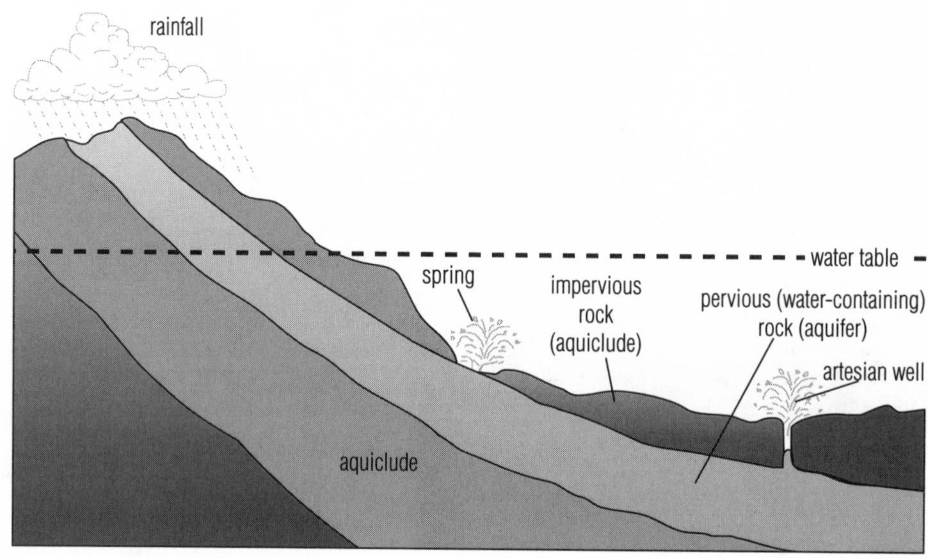

artesian well *In an artesian well, water rises from an underground water-containing rock layer under its own pressure. Rain falls at one end of the water-bearing layer, or aquifer, and percolates through the layer. The layer fills with water up to the level of the water table. Water will flow from a well under its own pressure if the well head is below the level of the water table.*

article or ***posting*** on USENET, an individual public message.

artificial insemination (AI) introduction by instrument of semen from a sperm bank or donor into the female reproductive tract to bring about fertilization. Originally used by animal breeders to improve stock with sperm from high-quality males, in the 20th century it has been developed for use in humans, to help the infertile. See ◊in vitro fertilization.

> *The whole thinking process is rather mysterious to us, but I believe that the attempt to make a thinking machine will help us greatly in finding out how we think ourselves.*
>
> Alan Mathison Turing English mathematician. Quoted in A Hodges *Alan Turing: The Enigma of Intelligence* 1985

artificial intelligence (AI) branch of science concerned with creating computer programs that can perform actions comparable with those of an intelligent human. Current AI research covers such areas as planning (for robot behaviour), language understanding, pattern recognition, and knowledge representation.

The possibility of artificial intelligence was first proposed by the English mathematician Alan ◊Turing in 1950. Early AI programs, developed in the 1960s, attempted simulations of human intelligence or were aimed at general problem-solving techniques. By the mid-1990s, scientists were concluding that AI was more difficult to create than they had imagined. It is now thought that intelligent behaviour depends as much on the knowledge a system possesses as on its reasoning power. Present emphasis is on ◊knowledge-based systems, such as ◊expert systems, while research projects focus on ◊neural networks, which attempt to mimic the structure of the human brain.

On the ◊Internet, small bits of software that automate common routines or attempt to predict human likes or behaviour based on past experience are called intelligent agents or bots.

artificial life (contracted to ***ALife***) in computing, area of scientific research that attempts to simulate biological phenomena via computer programs. The first ALife workshop was held at Los Alamos, USA, in 1987. Research in this area is being conducted all around the world; one of the most significant centres is the ◊MIT Media Lab.

artificial limb device to replace a limb that has been removed by surgery or lost through injury, or one that is malformed because of genetic defects. It is one form of ◊prosthesis.

artificial radioactivity natural and spontaneous radioactivity arising from radioactive isotopes or elements that are formed when elements are bombarded with subatomic particles – protons, neutrons, or electrons – or small nuclei.

artificial respiration emergency procedure to restart breathing once it has stopped; in cases of electric shock or apparent drowning, for example, the first choice is the expired-air method, the **kiss of life** by mouth-to-mouth breathing until natural breathing is restored.

artificial selection in biology, selective breeding of individuals that exhibit the particular characteristics that a plant or animal breeder wishes to develop. In plants, desirable features might include resistance to disease, high yield (in crop plants), or attractive appearance. In animal breeding, selection has led to the development of particular breeds of cattle for improved meat production (such as the Aberdeen Angus) or milk production (such as Jerseys).

Artificial selection was practised by the Sumerians at least 5,500 years ago and carried on through the succeeding ages, with the result that all common vegetables, fruit, and livestock are long modified by selective breeding. Artificial selection, particularly of pigeons, was studied by the English evolutionist Charles Darwin who saw a similarity between this phenomenon and the processes of natural selection.

Artiodactyla order of even-toed mammals containing pigs, camels, hippos, and ruminant animals, such as antelope, deer, and sheep.

The order is divided into nine living families (the other 20 families are all extinct). Suidae includes the eight species of pig; Tayassuidae, the two species of peccary; and Hippopotamidae, the two species of hippopotamuses. Camelidae has three to five species of camels and the guanaco. The five ruminant (cud-chewing) families are Tragulidae, with four species of chevrotain; Cervidae, 41 species of deer; Bovidae, 128 species of cattle, sheep, and

arum *Arum dioscoridis comes from the Mediterranean region, where arum lilies grow in abundance. What appears to be a single flower is in fact a flower head, the spadix, bearing separate rings of male and female flowers enclosed in a leaflike spathe. Premaphotos Wildlife*

antelopes; Antilocapridae, one species, the pronghorn, often misnamed antelope, of North America; and Giraffidae, two species of giraffe.

arum any of a group of mainly European plants with narrow leaves and a single, usually white, special leaf (spathe) surrounding the spike of tiny flowers. The ornamental arum called the trumpet lily (*Zantedeschia aethiopica*) is a native of South Africa. (Genus *Arum*, family Araceae.)

asbestos any of several related minerals of fibrous structure that offer great heat resistance because of their nonflammability and poor conductivity. Commercial asbestos is generally either made from serpentine ('white' asbestos) or from sodium iron silicate ('blue' asbestos). The fibres are woven together or bound by an inert material. Over time the fibres can work loose and, because they are small enough to float freely in the air or be inhaled, asbestos usage is now strictly controlled; exposure to its dust can cause cancer.

ASCII (acronym for ***American standard code for information interchange***) in computing, a coding system in which numbers are assigned to letters, digits, and punctuation symbols. Although computers work in code based on the ◊binary number system, ASCII numbers are usually quoted as decimal or ◊hexadecimal numbers. For example, the decimal number 45 (binary 0101101) represents a hyphen, and 65 (binary 1000001) a capital A. The first 32 codes are used for control functions, such as carriage return and backspace.

Strictly speaking, ASCII is a 7-bit binary code, allowing 128 different characters to be represented, but an eighth bit is often used to provide ◊parity or to allow for extra characters. The system is widely used for the storage of text and for the transmission of data between computers.

ASCII art pictures or fancy graphics created entirely out of ◊ASCII characters such as letters of the alphabet or punctuation marks. ASCII art has existed since the invention of computers. Today it is found in USENET ◊signatures (.sigs), special ◊newsgroups such as alt.art.ascii, and occasionally in messages, both public and private.

ascorbic acid $C_6H_8O_6$ or ***vitamin C*** a relatively simple organic acid found in citrus fruits and vegetables. It is soluble in water and destroyed by prolonged boiling, so soaking or overcooking of vegetables reduces their vitamin C content. Lack of ascorbic acid results in scurvy.

In the human body, ascorbic acid is necessary for the correct synthesis of ◊collagen. Lack of vitamin C causes skin sores or ulcers, tooth and gum problems, and burst capillaries (scurvy symptoms) owing to an abnormal type of collagen replacing the normal type in these tissues.

The Australian billygoat plum, *Terminalia ferdiandiana*, is the richest natural source of vitamin C, containing 100 times the concentration found in oranges.

asepsis practice of ensuring that bacteria are excluded from open sites during surgery, wound dressing, blood sampling, and other medical procedures. Aseptic technique is a first line of defence against infection.

asexual reproduction in biology, reproduction that does not involve the manufacture and fusion of sex cells, nor the necessity for two parents. The process carries a clear advantage in that there is no need to search for a mate nor to develop complex pollinating mechanisms; every asexual organism can reproduce on its own. Asexual reproduction can therefore lead to a rapid population build-up.

In evolutionary terms, the disadvantage of asexual reproduction arises from the fact that only identical individuals, or clones, are produced – there is no variation.

In the field of horticulture, where standardized production is needed, this is useful, but in the wild, an asexual population that cannot adapt to a changing environment or evolve defences against a new disease is at risk of extinction. Many asexually reproducing organisms are therefore capable of reproducing sexually as well.

Amoeba divides after it has grown to a certain size.
The pseudopodia are pulled in and the nucleus divides.
The cell body begins to divide when the nucleus has split.
Two daughter amoebae are formed.

Asexual processes include ◊binary fission, in which the parent organism splits into two or more 'daughter' organisms, and ◊budding, in which a new organism is formed initially as an out-

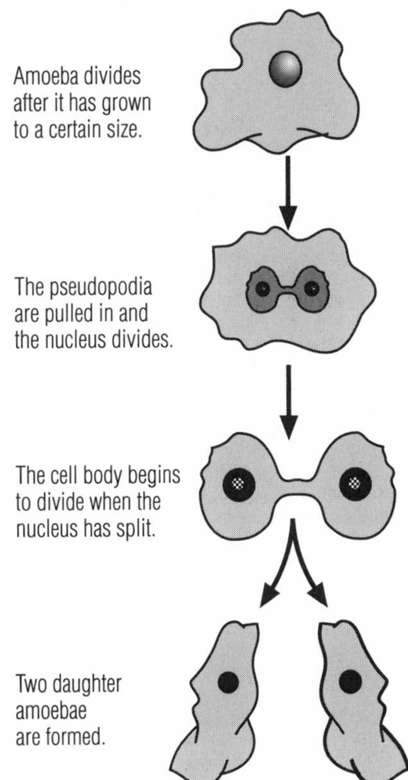

asexual reproduction *Asexual reproduction is the simplest form of reproduction, occurring in many simple plants and animals. Binary fission, shown here occurring in an amoeba, is one of a number of asexual reproduction processes.*

growth of the parent organism. The asexual reproduction of spores, as in ferns and mosses, is also common and many plants reproduce asexually by means of runners, rhizomes, bulbs, and corms; see also ◊vegetative reproduction.

ash any tree of a worldwide group belonging to the olive family, with winged fruits. The ◊mountain ash **or rowan**, which resembles the ash, belongs to the family Rosaceae. (Genus *Fraxinus*, family Oleaceae.)

ashen light in astronomy, a faint glow occasionally reported in the dark hemisphere of ◊Venus when the planet is in a crescent phase. Its origin is unknown, but it may be related to the terrestrial airglow caused by interaction of high-energy solar radiation with the upper atmosphere of the Earth.

Asiatic wild ass alternative name for both the ◊kiang and the ◊onager.

ASIC (abbreviation for ***application-specific integrated circuit***) integrated circuit built for a specific application.

asp any of several venomous snakes, including *Vipera aspis* of S Europe, allied to the adder, and the Egyptian cobra *Naja haje*, reputed to have been used by the Egyptian queen Cleopatra for her suicide.

asparagus any of a group of plants with small scalelike leaves and many fine, feathery branches. Native to Europe and Asia, *Asparagus officinalis* is cultivated and the tender young shoots (spears) are greatly prized as a vegetable. (Genus *Asparagus*, family Liliaceae.)

aspartame noncarbohydrate sweetener used in foods under the tradename Nutrasweet. It is about 200 times as sweet as sugar and, unlike saccharine, has no aftertaste.

The aspartame molecule consists of two amino acids (aspartic acid and phenylalanine) linked by a methylene ($-CH_2-$) group. It breaks down slowly at room temperature and rapidly at higher temperatures. It is not suitable for people who suffer from phenylketonuria.

aspen any of several species of ◊poplar tree. The European quaking aspen (*Populus tremula*) has flattened leafstalks that cause the leaves to flutter in the slightest breeze. The soft, light-coloured wood is used for matches and paper pulp. (Genus *Populus*.)

asphalt mineral mixture containing semisolid brown or black ◊bitumen, used in the construction industry. Asphalt is mixed with rock chips to form paving material, and the purer varieties are used for insulating material and for waterproofing masonry. It can be produced artificially by the distillation of ◊petroleum.

The availability of recycled coloured glass led in 1988 to the invention of **glassphalt**, asphalt that is 15% crushed glass. It is used to pave roads in New York.

Considerable natural deposits of asphalt occur around the Dead Sea and in the Philippines, Cuba, Venezuela, and Trinidad. Bituminous limestone occurs at Neufchâtel, France.

asphodel either of two related Old World plants of the lily family. The white asphodel or king's spear (*Asphodelus albus*) is found in Italy and Greece, sometimes covering large areas, and providing grazing for sheep. The other asphodel is the yellow asphodel (*Asphodeline lutea*). (Genera *Asphodelus* and *Asphodeline*, family Liliaceae.)

The ancient Greeks connected the beautiful plants of *A. lutea* with the dead, and they were supposed to grow in the mythological Elysian fields where heroes enjoyed new life after death.

asphyxia suffocation; a lack of oxygen that produces a potentially lethal build-up of carbon dioxide waste in the tissues.

Asphyxia may arise from any one of a number of causes, including inhalation of smoke or poisonous gases, obstruction of the windpipe (by water, food, vomit, or a foreign object), strangulation, or smothering. If it is not quickly relieved, brain damage or death ensues.

aspidistra any of several Asiatic plants of the lily family. The Chinese *Aspidistra elatior* has broad leaves which taper to a point and, like all aspidistras, grows well in warm indoor conditions. (Genus *Aspidistra*, family Liliaceae.)

aspirin acetylsalicylic acid, a popular pain-relieving drug (◊analgesic) developed in the late 19th century as a household remedy for aches and pains. It relieves pain and reduces inflammation and fever. It is derived from the white willow tree *Salix alba*, and is the world's most widely used drug.

Aspirin was first refined from salicylic acid by German chemist Felix Hoffman, and marketed in 1899. Although salicylic acid occurs naturally in willow bark (and has been used for pain relief since 1763) the acetyl derivative is less bitter and less likely to cause vomiting.

ass any of several horselike, odd-toed, hoofed mammals of the genus *Equus*, family Equidae. Species include the African wild ass *E. asinus*, and the Asian wild ass *E. hemionus*. They differ from horses in their smaller size, larger ears, tufted tail, and characteristic bray. Donkeys and burros are domesticated asses.

assassin bug member of a family of blood-sucking bugs that contains about 4,000 species. Assassin bugs are mainly predators, feeding on other insects, but some species feed on birds and mammals, including humans. They are found, mainly in tropical regions, although some have established themselves in Europe and North America.

classification Assassin bugs are in family Reduviidae, suborder Heteroptera, order Hemiptera (true bugs), class Insecta, phylum Arthropoda.

The general characteristics of the family include bright coloration, a long four-segmented antenna, and a cone-shaped proboscis which, when the insect is not feeding, is folded under the head. Because of this they are sometimes called **cone-nosed** bugs.

species *Reduvius personatus* is about 15 mm/0.5 in long and dark brown. In the wild it inhabits hollow trees where it feeds on the blood of other insects. It can invade houses, where it hides in holes and crevices in the wall. Like other assassin bugs, it is nocturnal, emerging at night to feed on ◊bedbugs and other insects. It is widely distributed in Europe and North America.

Kissing bugs comprise several Central and South American genera that have earned their name from their habit of biting sleeping people on the face. *Rhodnius*, *Triatoma*, and *Panstrongylus*, are vectors for the parasite that causes ◊Chagas's disease.

assay in chemistry, the determination of the quantity of a given substance present in a sample. Usually it refers to determining the purity of precious metals.

The assay may be carried out by 'wet' methods, when the sample is wholly or partially dissolved in some reagent (often an acid), or by 'dry' or 'fire' methods, in which the compounds present in the sample are combined with other substances.

assembler in computing, a program that translates a program written in an assembly language into a complete ◊machine code program that can be executed by a computer. Each instruction in the assembly language is translated into only one machine-code instruction.

assembly industry manufacture that involves putting together many prefabricated components to make a complete product; for example, a car or television set. The inputs for this type of industry are therefore outputs from others. Some assembly industries are surrounded by their suppliers; others use components from far afield.

assembly language low-level computer-programming language closely related to a computer's internal codes. It consists chiefly of a set of short sequences of letters (mnemonics), which are translated, by a program called an assembler, into ◊machine code for the computer's ◊central processing unit (CPU) to follow directly. In assembly language, for example, 'JMP' means 'jump' and 'LDA' means 'load accumulator'. Assembly code is used by programmers who need to write very fast or efficient programs.

Because they are much easier to use, high-level languages are normally used in preference to assembly languages. An assembly language may still be used in some cases, however, particularly when no suitable high-level language exists or where a very efficient machine-code program is required.

assembly line method of mass production in which a product is built up step-by-step by successive workers adding one part at a time. It is commonly used in industries such as the car industry.

US inventor Eli Whitney pioneered the concept of industrial assembly in the 1790s, when he employed unskilled labour to assemble muskets from sets of identical precision-made parts produced by machine tools. In 1901 Ransome Olds in the USA began mass-producing motor cars on an assembly-line principle, a method further refined by the introduction of the moving conveyor belt by Henry Ford in 1913 and the time-and-motion studies of Fredriech Winslow Taylor. On the assembly line human workers now stand side by side with ◊robots.

assimilation in animals, the process by which absorbed food molecules, circulating in the blood, pass into the cells and are used for growth, tissue repair, and other metabolic activities. The actual destiny of each food molecule depends not only on its type, but also on the body requirements at that time.

Association for Computing Machinery (ACM) US organization made up of computer professionals of all types. Its monthly journal, the *Communications of the Association for Computing Machinery*, is peer-reviewed. Its subsidiary special interest groups, or **SIGs**, focus on areas such as graphics and human–computer interaction. Several of these run major conferences for their areas such as SIGGRAPH (graphics) and SIGCHI (human–computer interaction).

The equivalent UK organization is the **British Computer Society** (BCS).

associative operation in mathematics, an operation in which the outcome is independent of the grouping of the numbers or symbols concerned. For example, multiplication is associative, as $4 \times (3 \times 2) = (4 \times 3) \times 2 = 24$; however, division is not, as $12 \div (4 \div 2) = 6$, but $(12 \div 4) \div 2 = 1.5$. Compare ◊commutative operation and ◊distributive operation.

assortative mating in ◊population genetics, selective mating in a population between individuals that are genetically related or have similar characteristics. If sufficiently consistent, assortative mating can theoretically result in the evolution of new species without geographical isolation (see ◊speciation).

astatine ***Greek astatos 'unstable'*** nonmetallic, radioactive element, symbol At, atomic number 85, relative atomic mass 210. It is a member of the ◊halogen group, and is very rare in nature. Astatine is highly unstable, with at least 19 isotopes; the longest lived has a half-life of about eight hours.

aster any plant of a large group belonging to the same subfamily as the daisy. All asters have starlike flowers with yellow centres and outer rays (not petals) varying from blue and purple to white. Asters come in many sizes. Many are cultivated as garden flowers, including the Michaelmas daisy (*Aster nova-belgii*). (Genus *Aster*, family Compositae.)

The China aster (*Callistephus chinensis*) belongs to a closely related genus; it was introduced to Europe and the USA from China in the early 18th century.

asterisk (*) or ***star*** wild card character standing for multiple characters in most operating systems. It allows a user to specify a group of files for mass handling. Typing 'dir *.bat' in DOS, for example, will return a list of all files with the extension .BAT in the current directory. On USENET, * is used to denote a group of ◊newsgroups; the phrase 'alt.music.*' means all the newsgroups in the alt.music hierarchy, such as alt.music.pop, alt.music.jazz, and so on. On the Internet, an asterisk before and after a word is a way of indicating emphasis.

asteroid or ***minor planet*** any of many thousands of small bodies, composed of rock and iron, that orbit the Sun. Most lie in a belt between the orbits of Mars and Jupiter, and are thought to be fragments left over from the formation of the ◊Solar System. About 100,000 may exist, but their total mass is only a few hundredths the mass of the Moon.

They include ◊Ceres (the largest asteroid, 940 km/584 mi in diameter), Vesta (which has a light-coloured surface, and is the brightest as seen from Earth), ◊Eros, and ◊Icarus. Some asteroids are in orbits that bring them close to Earth, and some, such as the ◊Apollo asteroids, even cross Earth's orbit; at least some of these may be remnants of former comets. One group, the Trojans, moves along the same orbit as Jupiter, 60° ahead and behind the planet. One unusual asteroid, ◊Chiron, orbits beyond Saturn.

NASA's Near Earth Asteroid Rendezvous (NEAR) was launched in February 1996 to study Eros to ascertain what asteroids are made of and whether they are similar in structure to meteorites. In 1997 it flew past asteroid Mathilde, revealing a 25 km crater covering the 53-km asteroid. The Near Earth Asteroid Tracking (NEAT) system had detected more than 10,000 asteroids by August 1997.

The first asteroid was discovered by the Italian astronomer Giuseppe Piazzi at the Palermo Observatory, Sicily, 1 January 1801. The first asteroid moon was observed by the space probe *Galileo* ◊in 1993 orbiting asteroid Ida.

Bifurcated asteroids, first discovered 1990, are in fact two chunks of rock that touch each other. It may be that at least 10% of asteroids approaching the Earth are bifurcated.

asthenosphere a layer within Earth's ◊mantle lying beneath the ◊lithosphere, typically beginning at a depth of approximately 100 km/63 mi and extending to depths of approximately 260 km/160 mi. Sometimes referred to as the 'weak sphere', it is characterized by being weaker and more elastic than the surrounding mantle.

The asthenosphere's elastic behaviour and low viscosity allow the overlying, more rigid plates of lithosphere to move laterally in a process known as ◊plate tectonics. Its elasticity and viscosity also allow overlying crust and mantle to move vertically in response to gravity to achieve **isostatic equilibrium** (see ◊isostasy).

asthma chronic condition characterized by difficulty in breathing due to spasm of the bronchi (air passages) in the lungs. Attacks may be provoked by allergy, infection, and stress. The incidence of asthma may be increasing as a result of air pollution and occupational hazard. Treatment is with ◊bronchodilators to relax the bronchial muscles and thereby ease the breathing, and in severe cases by inhaled ◊steroids that reduce inflammation of the bronchi.

Extrinsic asthma, which is triggered by exposure to irritants such as pollen and dust, is more common in children and young adults. In February 1997 Brazilian researchers reported two species of dust mite actually living on children's scalps. This explains why vacuuming of bedding sometimes fails to prevent asthma attacks. The use of antidandruff shampoo should keep numbers of mites down by reducing their food supply. Less common, intrinsic asthma tends to start in the middle years.

Approximately 5–10% of children suffer from asthma, but about a third of these will show no symptoms after adolescence, while another 5–10% of people develop the condition as adults. Growing evidence that the immune system is involved in both

ASTHMA – TUTORIAL FOR CHILDREN AND PARENTS

http://sln.fi.edu/inquirer/warming.html

Online tutorial for parents and children on asthma. It provides an explanation of what happens during an asthma attack, a description of the symptoms normally registered during an attack, and a discussion of the available medications. Movies and sound clips of asthmatic breathing are also included.

ASTHMA

Dust mites live in large numbers on the human scalp, feeding on skin flakes – an activity which causes allergic reactions in asthmatic children. This discovery was announced by Brazilian researchers in 1997, and may explain why repeated vacuuming of bedding does not get rid of dust mites.

forms of asthma has raised the possibility of a new approach to treatment.

Although the symptoms are similar to those of bronchial asthma, **cardiac asthma** is an unrelated condition and is a symptom of heart deterioration.

astigmatism aberration occurring in the lens of the eye. It results when the curvature of the lens differs in two perpendicular planes, so that rays in one plane may be in focus while rays in the other are not. With astigmatic eyesight, the vertical and horizontal cannot be in focus at the same time; correction is by the use of a cylindrical lens that reduces the overall focal length of one plane so that both planes are seen in sharp focus.

astrolabe ancient navigational instrument, forerunner of the sextant. Astrolabes usually consisted of a flat disc with a sighting rod that could be pivoted to point at the Sun or bright stars.

From the altitude of the Sun or star above the horizon, the local time could be estimated.

ASTROLABE – AN INSTRUMENT WITH A PAST AND A FUTURE

http://myhouse.com/mc/planet/astrodir/astrolab.htm

Good guide to this ancient astronomical computer. The long history of the instrument, and its importance in the history of astrology and astronomy, is explained with the help of good photographs. A section on the parts of the astrolabe explains how the instrument works and its uses.

astrometry measurement of the precise positions of stars, planets, and other bodies in space. Such information is needed for practical purposes including accurate timekeeping, surveying and navigation, and calculating orbits and measuring distances in space. Astrometry is not concerned with the surface features or the physical nature of the body under study.

Before telescopes, astronomical observations were simple astrometry. Precise astrometry has shown that stars are not fixed in position, but have a ◊proper motion caused as they and the Sun orbit the Milky Way Galaxy. The nearest stars also show ◊parallax (apparent change in position), from which their distances can be calculated. Above the distorting effects of the atmosphere, satellites such as ◊Hipparcos *can make even more precise measurements than ground telescopes, so refining the distance scale of space.*

astronaut person making flights into space; the term **cosmonaut** is used in the West for any astronaut from the former Soviet Union.

ASTRONAUT

Astronauts in space cannot belch. It is gravity that causes bubbles to rise to the top of a liquid, so space shuttle crews were forced to request less gas in their fizzy drinks to avoid discomfort.

ASK AN ASTRONAUT

http://www.nss.org/askastro/

Apollo 17 multimedia archive with video and audio files, plus mission details and astronaut biographies. Sponsored by the National Space Society, this site includes numerous images, a list of questions and answers, and links to related sites.

astronautics science of space travel. See ◊rocket; ◊satellite; ◊space probe.

Astronomer Royal honorary post in British astronomy. Originally it was held by the director of the Royal Greenwich Observatory; since 1972 the title of Astronomer Royal has been awarded separately as an honorary title to an outstanding British astronomer. The Astronomer Royal from 1995 is Martin Rees. There is a separate post of Astronomer Royal for Scotland.

Astronomical Almanac in astronomy, an international work of reference published jointly every year by the ◊Royal Greenwich Observatory and the ◊US Naval Observatory containing detailed tables of planetary motions, ◊eclipses, and other astronomical phenomena.

astronomical unit unit (symbol AU) equal to the mean distance of the Earth from the Sun: 149,597,870 km/92,955,800 mi. It is used to describe planetary distances. Light travels this distance in approximately 8.3 minutes.

astronomy science of the celestial bodies: the Sun, the Moon, and the planets; the stars and galaxies; and all other objects in the universe. It is concerned with their positions, motions, distances, and physical conditions and with their origins and evolution. Astronomy thus divides into fields such as astrophysics, celestial mechanics, and ◊cosmology. See also ◊gamma-ray astronomy, ◊infrared astronomy, ◊radio astronomy, ◊ultraviolet astronomy, and ◊X-ray astronomy.

Greek astronomers Astronomy is perhaps the oldest recorded science; there are observational records from ancient Babylonia, China, Egypt, and Mexico. The first true astronomers, however, were the Greeks, who deduced the Earth to be a sphere and attempted to measure its size. Ancient Greek astronomers included Thales and ◊Pythagoras. Eratosthenes of Cyrene measured the size of the Earth with considerable accuracy. Star catalogues were drawn up, the most celebrated being that of Hipparchus. The *Almagest*, by ◊Ptolemy of Alexandria, summarized Greek astronomy and survived in its Arabic translation. The Greeks still regarded the Earth as the centre of the universe, although this was doubted by some philosophers, notably Aristarchus of Samos, who maintained that the Earth moves around the Sun.

Ptolemy, the last famous astronomer of the Greek school, died about AD 180, and little progress was made for some centuries.

Arab revival The Arabs revived the science, developing the astrolabe and producing good star catalogues. Unfortunately, a general belief in the pseudoscience of astrology continued until the end of the Middle Ages (and has been revived from time to time).

the Sun at the centre The dawn of a new era came in 1543, when a Polish canon, ◊Copernicus, published a work entitled *De revolutionibus orbium coelestium/On the Revolutions of the Heavenly Spheres*, in which he demonstrated that the Sun, not the Earth, is the centre of our planetary system. (Copernicus was wrong in many respects – for instance, he still believed that all celestial orbits must be perfectly circular.) Tycho ◊Brahe, a Dane, increased the accuracy of observations by means of improved instruments allied to his own personal skill, and his observations were used by German mathematician Johannes ◊Kepler to prove the validity of the Copernican system. Considerable opposition existed, however, for removing the Earth from its central position in the universe; the Catholic church was openly hostile to the idea, and, ironically, Brahe never accepted the idea that the Earth could move around the Sun. Yet before the end of the 17th century, the theoretical work of Isaac ◊Newton had established celestial mechanics.

Astronomy: chronology

2300 BC	Chinese astronomers made their earliest observations.
2000	Babylonian priests made their first observational records.
1900	Stonehenge was constructed: first phase.
434	Anaxagoras claims the Sun is made up of hot rock.
365	The Chinese observed the satellites of Jupiter with the naked eye.
3rd century	Aristarchus argued that the Sun is the centre of the Solar System.
2nd century AD	Ptolemy's complicated Earth-centred system was promulgated, which dominated the astronomy of the Middle Ages.
1543	Copernicus revived the ideas of Aristarchus in *De Revolutionibus*.
1608	Hans Lippershey invented the telescope, which was first used by Galileo in 1609.
1609	Johannes Kepler's first two laws of planetary motion were published (the third appeared in 1619).
1632	The world's first official observatory was established in Leiden in the Netherlands.
1633	Galileo's theories were condemned by the Inquisition.
1675	The Royal Greenwich Observatory was founded in England.
1687	Isaac Newton's *Principia* was published, including his 'law of universal gravitation'.
1705	Edmond Halley correctly predicted that the comet that had passed the Earth in 1682 would return in 1758; the comet was later to be known by his name.
1781	William Herschel discovered Uranus and recognized stellar systems beyond our Galaxy.
1796	Pierre Laplace elaborated his theory of the origin of the solar system.
1801	Giuseppe Piazzi discovered the first asteroid, Ceres.
1814	Joseph von Fraunhofer first studied absorption lines in the solar spectrum.
1846	Neptune was identified by Johann Galle, following predictions by John Adams and Urbain Leverrier.
1859	Gustav Kirchhoff explained dark lines in the Sun's spectrum.
1887	The earliest photographic star charts were produced.
1889	Edward Barnard took the first photographs of the Milky Way.
1908	Fragment of comet fell at Tunguska, Siberia.
1920	Arthur Eddington began the study of interstellar matter.
1923	Edwin Hubble proved that the galaxies are systems independent of the Milky Way, and by 1930 had confirmed the concept of an expanding universe.
1930	The planet Pluto was discovered by Clyde Tombaugh at the Lowell Observatory, Arizona, USA.
1931	Karl Jansky founded radio astronomy.
1945	Radar contact with the Moon was established by Z Bay of Hungary and the US Army Signal Corps Laboratory.
1948	The 5-m/200-in Hale reflector telescope was installed at Mount Palomar, California, USA.
1957	The Jodrell Bank telescope dish in England was completed.
1957	The first Sputnik satellite (USSR) opened the age of space observation.
1962	The first X-ray source was discovered in Scorpius.
1963	The first quasar was discovered.
1967	The first pulsar was discovered by Jocelyn Bell and Antony Hewish.
1969	The first crewed Moon landing was made by US astronauts.
1976	A 6 m/240 in reflector telescope was installed at Mount Semirodniki, USSR.
1977	Uranus was discovered to have rings.
1977	The spacecraft *Voyager* 1 and 2 were launched, passing Jupiter and Saturn 1979–1981.
1978	The spacecraft *Pioneer Venus* 1 and 2 reached Venus.
1978	A satellite of Pluto, Charon, was discovered by James Christy of the US Naval Observatory.
1986	Halley's comet returned. *Voyager 2* flew past Uranus and discovered six new moons.
1987	Supernova SN1987A flared up, becoming the first supernova to be visible to the naked eye since 1604. The 4.2-m/165-in William Herschel Telescope on La Palma, Canary Islands, and the James Clerk Maxwell Telescope on Mauna Kea, Hawaii, began operation.
1988	The most distant individual star was recorded – a supernova, 5 billion light years away, in the AC118 cluster of galaxies.
1989	*Voyager 2* flew by Neptune and discovered eight moons and three rings.
1990	Hubble Space Telescope was launched into orbit by the US space shuttle.
1991	The space probe *Galileo* flew past the asteroid Gaspra, approaching it to within 26,000 km/16,200 mi.
1992	COBE satellite detected ripples from the Big Bang that mark the first stage in the formation of galaxies.
1994	Fragments of comet Shoemaker–Levy struck Jupiter.
1996	US astronomers discovered the most distant galaxy so far detected. It is in the constellation Virgo and is 14 billion light years from Earth.
1997	Data from the satellite *Hipparicos* improved estimates of the age of the universe, and the distances to many nearby stars.

Galileo and the telescope The refracting telescope was invented about 1608, by Hans Lippershey in Holland, and was first applied to astronomy by Italian scientist ◊Galileo in the winter of 1609–10. Immediately, Galileo made a series of spectacular discoveries. He found the four largest satellites of Jupiter, which gave strong support to the Copernican theory; he saw the craters of the Moon, the phases of Venus, and the myriad faint stars of our ◊Galaxy, the Milky Way.

Galileo's most powerful telescope magnified only 30 times, but it was not long before larger telescopes were built and official observatories were established.

Galileo's telescope was a refractor; that is to say, it collected its light by means of a glass lens or object glass. Difficulties with his design led Newton, in 1671, to construct a reflector, in which the light is collected by means of a curved mirror.

further discoveries In the 17th and 18th centuries astronomy was mostly concerned with positional measurements. Uranus was discovered 1781 by William ◊Herschel, and this was soon followed by the discovery of the first four asteroids, Ceres in 1801, Pallas in 1802, Juno in 1804, and Vesta in 1807. In 1846 Neptune was located by Johann Galle, following calculations by British astronomer John Couch Adams and French astronomer Urbain Jean Joseph Leverrier. Also significant was the first measurement of the distance of a star, when in 1838 the German astronomer Friedrich Bessel measured the ◊parallax of the star 61 Cygni, and calculated that it lies at a distance of about 6 light years (about half the correct value).

Astronomical spectroscopy was developed, first by Fraunhofer in Germany and then by people such as Pietro Angelo Secchi and William Huggins, while Gustav ◊Kirchhoff successfully interpreted the spectra of the Sun and stars. By the 1860s good photographs of the Moon had been obtained, and by the end of the century photographic methods had started to play a leading role in research.

galaxies William Herschel, probably the greatest observer in the history of astronomy, investigated the shape of our Galaxy during the latter part of the 18th century and concluded that its stars are arranged roughly in the form of a double-convex lens. Basically Herschel was correct, although he placed our Sun near the centre of the system; in fact, it is well out towards the edge, and lies 25,000 light years from the galactic nucleus. Herschel also studied the luminous 'clouds' or nebulae, and made the tentative suggestion that those nebulae capable of resolution into stars might be separate galaxies, far outside our own Galaxy.

It was not until 1923 that US astronomer Edwin Hubble, using the 2.5 m/100 in reflector at the Mount Wilson Observatory, was able to verify this suggestion. It is now known that the 'spiral nebulae' are galaxies in their own right, and that they lie at immense distances. The most distant galaxy visible to the naked eye, the Great Spiral in ◊Andromeda, is 2.2 million light years away; the most remote galaxy so far measured lies over 10 billion light years away. It was also found that galaxies tended to form groups, and that the groups were apparently receding from each other at speeds proportional to their distances.

a growing universe This concept of an expanding and evolving universe at first rested largely on Hubble's law, relating the distance of objects to the amount their spectra shift towards red – the ◊red shift. Subsequent evidence derived from objects studied in other parts of the ◊electromagnetic spectrum, at radio and X-ray wavelengths, has provided confirmation. ◊Radio astronomy established its place in probing the structure of the universe by demonstrating in 1954 that an optically visible distant galaxy was identical with a powerful radio source known as Cygnus A. Later analysis of the comparative number, strength, and distance of radio sources suggested that in the distant past these, including the ◊quasars discovered in 1963, had been much more powerful and numerous than today. This fact suggested that the universe has been evolving from an origin, and is not of infinite age as expected under a ◊steady-state theory.

The discovery in 1965 of microwave background radiation was evidence for the enormous temperature of the giant explosion, or Big Bang, that brought the universe into existence.

further exploration Although the practical limit in size and efficiency of optical telescopes has apparently been reached, the siting of these and other types of telescope at new observatories in the previously neglected southern hemisphere has opened fresh areas of the sky to search. Australia has been in the forefront of these developments. The most remarkable recent extension of the powers of astronomy to explore the universe is in the use of rockets, satellites, space stations, and space probes. Even the range and accuracy of the conventional telescope may be greatly improved free from the Earth's atmosphere. When the USA launched the Hubble Space Telescope into permanent orbit in 1990, it was the most powerful optical telescope yet constructed, with a 2.4 m/94.5 in mirror. It detects celestial phenomena seven times more distant (up to 14 billion light years) than any Earth-based telescope.

See also ◊black hole and ◊infrared radiation.

We now have direct evidence of the birth of the Universe and its evolution ... ripples in space-time laid down earlier than the first billionth of a second. If you're religious it's like seeing God.

GEORGE SMOOT US astrophysicist.
Attributed remark 1992

astrophotography use of photography in astronomical research. The first successful photograph of a celestial object was the daguerreotype plate of the Moon taken by John W Draper (1811–1882) of the USA in March 1840. The first photograph of a star, Vega, was taken by US astronomer William C Bond (1789–1859) in 1850. Modern-day astrophotography uses techniques such as ◊charge-coupled devices (CCDs).

astrophysics study of the physical nature of stars, galaxies, and the universe. It began with the development of spectroscopy in the 19th century, which allowed astronomers to analyse the composition of stars from their light. Astrophysicists view the universe as a vast natural laboratory in which they can study matter under conditions of temperature, pressure, and density that are unattainable on Earth.

asymmetric digital subscriber loop in computing, standard for transmitting video data; see ◊ADSL.

asymptote in ◊coordinate geometry, a straight line that a curve approaches progressively more closely but never reaches. The x and y axes are asymptotes to the graph of xy = constant (a rectangular ◊hyperbola).

If a point on a curve approaches a straight line such that its distance from the straight line is d, then the line is an asymptote to the curve if limit d tends to zero as the point moves towards infinity. Among ◊conic sections (curves obtained by the intersection of a plane and a double cone), a hyperbola has two asymptotes, which in the case of a rectangular hyperbola are at right angles to each other.

asynchronous irregular or not synchronized. In computer communications, the term is usually applied to data transmitted irregularly rather than as a steady stream. Asynchronous communication uses ◊start bits and ◊stop bits to indicate the beginning and end of each piece of data. Most personal computer communications are asynchronous, including connections across the Internet.

asynchronous transfer mode (ATM) in computing, high-speed computer ◊networking standard suitable for all types of data, including voice and video, that can be used on both private and public networks. ATM is used mainly on the core 'backbones' of large communications networks and in wide-area networks.

The basic technology was developed as part of the Cambridge Ring in the late 1970s, and is now being adopted by companies such as IBM and AT&T.

ATAPI (abbreviation for ***Advanced Technology Attachment Packet Interface***) in computing, enhancement to integrated drive electronics (IDE) that allows easier installation and support of CD-ROM drives and other devices. Part of the Enhanced IDE standard introduced by hard disc manufacturer Western Digital in 1994, ATAPI uses a standard software device driver and does away with the need for older, proprietary interfaces.

atavism (***Latin atavus 'ancestor'***) in genetics, the reappearance of a characteristic not apparent in the immediately preceding generations; in psychology, the manifestation of primitive forms of behaviour.

ataxia loss of muscular coordination due to neurological damage or disease.

AT command set (abbreviation for ***attention command set***) set of standard commands allowing a ◊modem to be controlled via software. These commands are used via special communications software to control a modem's actions from the computer console. The most common are ATZ to reset the modem and ATH to hang the modem up at the end of a call. The set was invented by Hayes Computer Products for its earliest modems.

Ateles genus of ◊spider monkey.

atheroma furring-up of the interior of an artery by deposits, mainly of cholesterol, within its walls.

Associated with atherosclerosis, atheroma has the effect of narrowing the lumen (channel) of the artery, thus restricting blood flow. This predisposes to a number of conditions, including thrombosis, angina, and stroke.

atherosclerosis thickening and hardening of the walls of the arteries, associated with ◊atheroma.

Atlas rocket US rocket, originally designed and built as an intercontinental missile, but subsequently adapted for space use. Atlas rockets launched astronauts in the Mercury series into orbit, as well as numerous other satellites and space probes.

ATM in computing, abbreviation for ◊asynchronous transfer mode, **automated teller machine**, or ◊Adobe Type Manager, depending on context.

atmosphere mixture of gases surrounding a planet. Planetary atmospheres are prevented from escaping by the pull of gravity. On Earth, atmospheric pressure decreases with altitude. In its lowest layer, the atmosphere consists of 78% nitrogen and 21% oxygen, both in molecular form (two atoms bonded together), and 1% argon. Small quantities of other gases, including water and carbon dioxide, are important in the chemistry and physics of Earth's atmosphere. The atmosphere plays a major part in the various cycles of nature (the ◊water cycle, the ◊carbon cycle, and the ◊nitrogen cycle). It is the principal industrial source of nitrogen, oxygen, and argon, which are obtained by the fractional distillation of liquid air.

The combination of gases, moisture, and dust particles in the Earth's atmosphere filter, reflect, refract, and scatter the rays of

◊light energy travelling from the Sun. Visible light varies in colour, the shorter wavelengths being blue and the longer wavelengths being red. Blue light waves are readily scattered by tiny particles of matter in the atmosphere, while the remaining light waves travel on uninterrupted unless they meet up with larger particles. Thus, the clearer and less polluted the atmosphere, the bluer the sky will appear; when there are smoke particles or other pollutants in the atmosphere, more of the colour rays are scattered and the sky will appear greyer and darker. Water droplets reflect the light rays rather than scatter them, and so in a moist atmosphere the sky will appear a paler blue. Hence, the sky will appear deepest blue where the atmosphere is driest and least polluted, and when the sun is directly overhead. At sunrise or sunset, when sunlight has further to travel through the atmosphere, more of the light waves are scattered, and any undisturbed red light waves will give the sun and sky near the horizon a red or orange appearance. At higher altitudes, as the atmosphere thins, there are fewer particles to scatter the light rays and so more are absorbed, and the sky

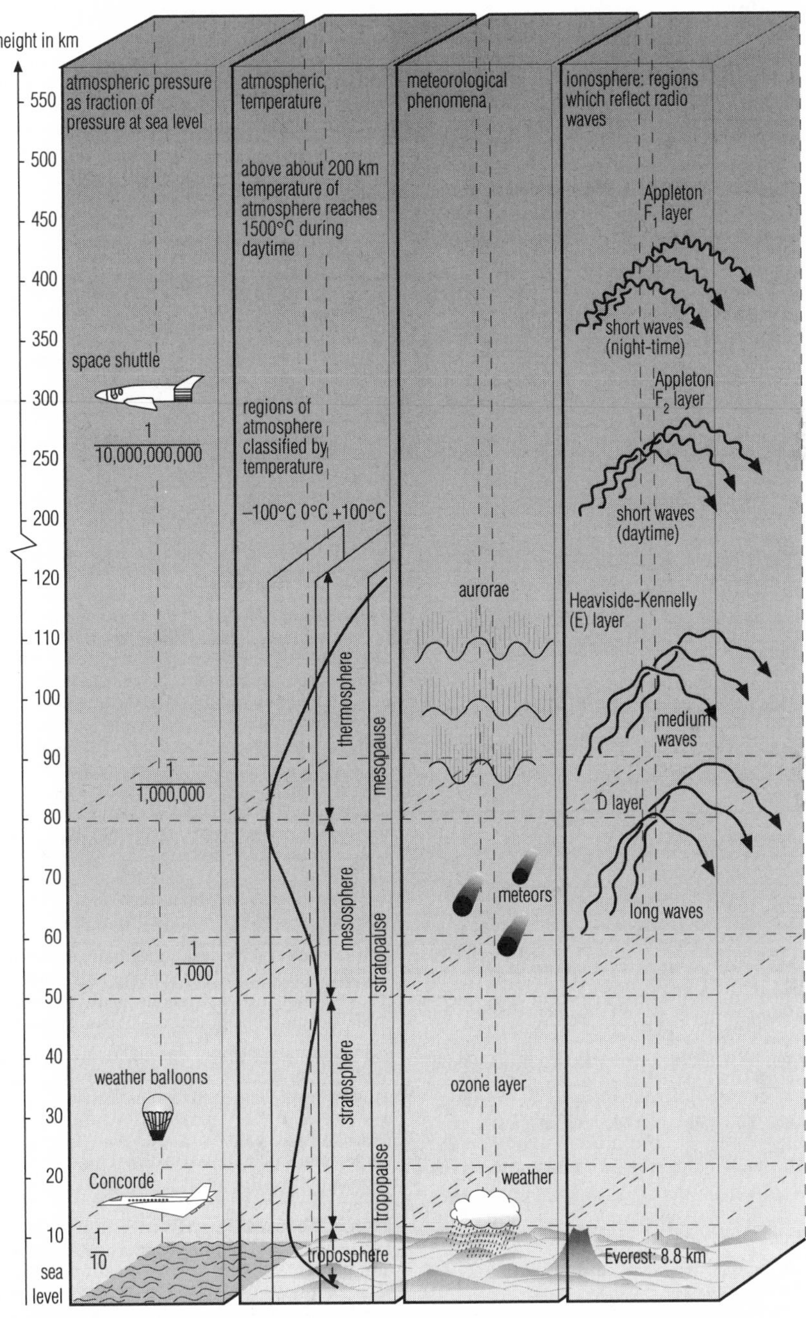

atmosphere *All but 1% of the Earth's atmosphere lies in a layer 30 km/19 mi above the ground. At a height of 5,500 m/18,000 ft, air pressure is half that at sea level. The temperature of the atmosphere varies greatly with height; this produces a series of layers, called the troposphere, stratosphere, mesosphere, and thermosphere.*

Atmosphere: composition

gas	*symbol*	*volume (%)*	*role*
nitrogen	N_2	78.08	cycled through human activities and through the action of microorganisms on animal and plant waste
oxygen	O_2	20.94	cycled mainly through the respiration of animals and plants and through the action of photosynthesis
carbon dioxide	CO_2	0.03	cycled through respiration and photosynthesis in exchange reactions with oxygen. It is also a product of burning fossil fuels
argon	Ar	0.093	chemically inert and with only a few industrial uses
neon	Ne	0.0018	as argon
helium	He	0.0005	as argon
krypton	Kr	trace	as argon
xenon	Xe	trace	as argon
ozone	O_3	0.00006	a product of oxygen molecules split into single atoms by the Sun's radiation and unaltered oxygen molecules
hydrogen	H_2	0.00005	unimportant; it is so light it escapes into space

tends to lose its colour and appear darker. The phenomenon of why the sky appears blue was first demonstrated by British physicist John Tyndall in the mid-19th century, and later explained theoretically by Lord Rayleigh.

atmosphere or ***standard atmosphere*** in physics, a unit (symbol atm) of pressure equal to 760 torr, 1013.25 millibars, or 1.01325×10^5 newtons per square metre. The actual pressure exerted by the atmosphere fluctuates around this value, which is assumed to be standard at sea level and 0°C/32°F, and is used when dealing with very high pressures.

atmospheric pressure the pressure at any point on the Earth's surface that is due to the weight of the column of air above it; it therefore decreases as altitude increases. At sea level the average pressure is 101 kilopascals (1,013 millibars, 760 mmHg, or 14.7 lb per sq in).

Changes in atmospheric pressure, measured with a barometer, are used in weather forecasting. Areas of relatively high pressure are called ◊anticyclones; areas of low pressure are called ◊depressions.

To remember the effects of falling and rising atmospheric pressure:

WHEN PRESSURE IS FALLING, STORMS MAY COME A'CALLING. WHEN PRESSURE IS HIGH, EXPECT CLEAR BLUE SKY.

atoll continuous or broken circle of ◊coral reef and low coral islands surrounding a lagoon.

atom ***Greek atomos 'undivided'*** smallest unit of matter that can take part in a chemical reaction, and which cannot be broken down chemically into anything simpler. An atom is made up of protons and neutrons in a central nucleus surrounded by electrons (see ◊atomic structure). The atoms of the various elements differ in atomic number, relative atomic mass, and chemical behaviour.

Atoms are much too small to be seen even by even the most powerful optical microscope (the largest, caesium, has a diameter of 0.0000005 mm/0.00000002 in), and they are in constant motion. However, modern electron microscopes, such as the ◊scanning tunnelling microscope (STM) and the ◊atomic force microscope (AFM), can produce images of individual atoms and molecules.

The unleashed power of the atom has changed everything save our modes of thinking and we thus drift toward unparalleled catastrophe.

ALBERT EINSTEIN German-born US physicist. Telegram sent to prominent Americans 24 May 1946

sodium 2.8.1

sulphur 2.8.6

atom, electronic structure *The arrangement of electrons in a sodium atom and a sulphur atom. The number of electrons in a neutral atom gives that atom its atomic number: sodium has an atomic number of 11 and sulphur has an atomic number of 16.*

atom, electronic structure of the arrangement of electrons around the nucleus of an atom, in distinct energy levels, also called orbitals or shells (see ◊orbital, ◊atomic). These shells can be regarded as a series of concentric spheres, each of which can contain a certain maximum number of electrons; the noble gases have an arrangement in which every shell contains this number (see ◊noble gas structure). The energy levels are usually numbered beginning with the shell nearest to the nucleus. The outermost shell is known as the ◊valency shell as it contains the valence electrons.

The lowest energy level, or innermost shell, can contain no more than two electrons. Outer shells are considered to be stable when they contain eight electrons but additional electrons can sometimes be accommodated provided that the outermost shell has a stable configuration. Electrons in unfilled shells are available to take part in chemical bonding, giving rise to the concept of valency. In ions, the electron shells contain more or fewer electrons than are required for a neutral atom, generating negative or positive charges.

The atomic number of an element indicates the number of electrons in a neutral atom. From this it is possible to deduce its electronic structure. For example, sodium has atomic number 11 ($Z = 11$) and its electronic arrangement (configuration) is two electrons in the first energy level, eight electrons in the second energy level and one electron in the third energy level – generally written as 2.8.1. Similarly for sulphur ($Z = 16$), the electron arrangement will be 2.8.6. The electronic structure dictates whether two elements will combine by ionic or covalent bonding (see ◊bond) or not at all.

atomic absorption spectrometry technique used in archaeology to determine quantitatively the chemical composition of artefactual metals, minerals, and rocks, in order to identify raw material sources, to relate artefacts of the same material, or to trace trade routes. A sample of the material is atomized in a flame, and its light intensity measured. The method is slow and destroys the sample.

atomic clock timekeeping device regulated by various periodic processes occurring in atoms and molecules, such as atomic vibration or the frequency of absorbed or emitted radiation.

The first atomic clock was the **ammonia clock**, invented at the US National Bureau of Standards in 1948. It was regulated by measuring the speed at which the nitrogen atom in an ammonia molecule vibrated back and forth. The rate of molecular vibration is not affected by temperature, pressure, or other external influences, and can be used to regulate an electronic clock.

A more accurate atomic clock is the **caesium clock**. Because of its internal structure, a caesium atom produces or absorbs radiation of a very precise frequency (9,192,631,770 Hz) that varies by less than one part in 10 billion. This frequency has been used to define the second, and is the basis of atomic clocks used in international timekeeping.

Hydrogen maser clocks, based on the radiation from hydrogen atoms, are the most accurate. The hydrogen maser clock at the US Naval Research Laboratory, Washington DC, is estimated to lose one second in 1,700,000 years. Cooled hydrogen maser clocks could theoretically be accurate to within one second in 300 million years.

Atomic clocks are so accurate that minute adjustments must be made periodically to the length of the year to keep the calendar exactly synchronized with the Earth's rotation, which has a tendency to slow down. There have been 17 adjustments made since 1972 addding a total of 20 seconds to the calendar. In 1997 the northern hemisphere's summer was longer than usual – by one second. An extra second was added to the world's time at precisely 23 hours, 59 minutes, and 60 seconds on 30 June 1997. The adjustment was called for by the International Earth Rotation Service in Paris, which monitors the difference between Earth time and atomic time.

atomic energy another name for ◊nuclear energy.

atomic force microscope (AFM) microscope developed in the late 1980s that produces a magnified image using a diamond probe, with a tip so fine that it may consist of a single atom, dragged over the surface of a specimen to 'feel' the contours of the surface. In effect, the tip acts like the stylus of a record player, reading the surface. The tiny up-and-down movements of the probe are converted to an image of the surface by computer and displayed on a screen. The AFM is useful for examination of biological specimens since, unlike the ◊scanning tunnelling microscope, the specimen does not have to be electrically conducting.

atomicity number of atoms of an ◊element that combine together to form a molecule. A molecule of oxygen (O_2) has atomicity 2; sulphur (S_8) has atomicity 8.

atomic mass see ◊relative atomic mass.

atomic mass unit or ***dalton unit*** (symbol amu or u) unit of mass that is used to measure the relative mass of atoms and molecules. It is equal to one-twelfth of the mass of a carbon-12 atom, which is equivalent to the mass of a proton or 1.66×10^{-27} kg. The ◊relative atomic mass of an atom has no units; thus oxygen-16 has an atomic mass of 16 daltons but a relative atomic mass of 16.

atomic number or ***proton number*** the number (symbol Z) of protons in the nucleus of an atom. It is equal to the positive charge on the nucleus.

In a neutral atom, it is also equal to the number of electrons surrounding the nucleus. The chemical elements are arranged in the ◊periodic table of the elements according to their atomic number. See also ◊nuclear notation.

atomic radiation energy given out by disintegrating atoms during ◊radioactive decay, whether natural or synthesized. The energy may be in the form of fast-moving particles, known as ◊alpha particles and ◊beta particles, or in the form of high-energy electromagnetic waves known as ◊gamma radiation. Overlong exposure to atomic radiation can lead to ◊radiation sickness.

Radiation biology studies the effect of radiation on living organisms. Exposure to atomic radiation is linked to chromosomal damage, cancer, and, in laboratory animals at least, hereditary disease.

atomic size or ***atomic radius*** size of an atom expressed as the radius in ◊angstroms or other units of length.

The sodium atom has an atomic radius of 1.57 angstroms (1.57×10^{-8} cm). For metals, the size of the atom is always greater than the size of its ion. For non-metals the reverse is true.

atomic structure internal structure of an ◊atom.

the nucleus The core of the atom is the **nucleus**, a dense body only one ten-thousandth the diameter of the atom itself. The simplest nucleus, that of hydrogen, comprises a single stable positively charged particle, the **proton**. Nuclei of other elements contain more protons and additional particles, called **neutrons**, of about the same mass as the proton but with no electrical charge. Each element has its own characteristic nucleus with a unique number of protons, the atomic number. The number of neutrons may vary. Where atoms of a single element have different numbers of neutrons, they are called ◊isotopes. Although some isotopes tend to be unstable and exhibit ◊radioactivity, they all have identical chemical properties.

electrons The nucleus is surrounded by a number of moving **electrons**, each of which has a negative charge equal to the positive charge on a proton, but which weighs only $\frac{1}{1839}$ times as much. In a neutral atom, the nucleus is surrounded by the same number of electrons as it contains protons. According to ◊quantum theory, the position of an electron is uncertain; it may be found at any point. However, it is more likely to be found in some places than others. The region of space in which an electron is most likely to be found is called an orbital (see ◊orbital, atomic). The chemical properties of an element are determined by the ease with which its atoms can gain or lose electrons from its outer orbitals.

attraction and repulsion Atoms are held together by the electrical forces of attraction between each negative electron and the positive protons within the nucleus. The latter repel one another with enormous forces; a nucleus holds together only because an even stronger force, called the **strong nuclear force**, attracts the protons and neutrons to one another. The strong force acts over a very short range – the protons and neutrons must be in virtual contact with one another (see ◊forces, fundamental). If, therefore, a fragment of a complex nucleus, containing some protons, becomes only slightly loosened from the main group of neutrons and protons, the natural repulsion between the protons will cause this fragment to fly apart from the rest of the nucleus at high speed. It is by such fragmentation of atomic nuclei (nuclear ◊fission) that nuclear energy is released.

atomic time time as given by ◊atomic clocks, which are regulated by natural resonance frequencies of particular atoms, and display a continuous count of seconds.

In 1967 a new definition of the second was adopted in the SI system of units: the duration of 9,192,631,770 periods of the radiation corresponding to the transition between two hyperfine levels of the ground state of the caesium-133 atom. The International Atomic Time Scale is based on clock data from a number of countries; it is a continuous scale in days, hours, minutes, and seconds from the origin on 1 January 1958, when the Atomic Time Scale was made 0 h 0 min 0 sec when Greenwich Mean Time was at 0 h 0 min 0 sec.

atomic weight another name for ◊relative atomic mass.

atomizer device that produces a spray of fine droplets of liquid. A vertical tube connected with a horizontal tube dips into a bottle of liquid, and at one end of the horizontal tube is a nozzle, at the other a rubber bulb. When the bulb is squeezed, air rushes over the top of the vertical tube and out through the nozzle. Following ◊Bernoulli's principle, the pressure at the top of the vertical tube is reduced, allowing the liquid to rise. The air stream picks up the liquid, breaks it up into tiny drops, and carries it out of the nozzle as a spray. Scent spray, paint spray guns, and carburettors all use the principle of the atomizer.

ATP (abbreviation for ***adenosine triphosphate***), a nucleotide molecule found in all cells. It can yield large amounts of energy, and is used to drive the thousands of biological processes needed to sustain life, growth, movement, and reproduction. Green plants use light energy to manufacture ATP as part of the process of ◊photosynthesis. In animals, ATP is formed by the breakdown of glucose molecules, usually obtained from the carbohydrate component of a diet, in a series of reactions termed ◊respiration. It is the driving force behind muscle contraction and the synthesis of complex molecules needed by individual cells.

atrium either of the two upper chambers of the heart. The left atrium receives freshly oxygenated blood from the lungs via the pulmonary vein; the right atrium receives deoxygenated blood from the ◊vena cava. Atrium walls are thin and stretch easily to allow blood into the heart. On contraction, the atria force blood into the thick-walled ventricles, which then give a second, more powerful beat.

atrophy in medicine, a diminution in size and function, or output, of a body tissue or organ. It is usually due to nutritional impairment, disease, or disuse (muscle).

atropine alkaloid derived from ◊belladonna, a plant with toxic properties. It acts as an anticholinergic, inhibiting the passage of certain nerve impulses. It is used in premedication, to reduce bronchial and gastric secretions. It is also administered as a mild antispasmodic drug, and to dilate the pupil of the eye.

attachment way of incorporating a file into an e-mail message for transmission. Within a single system, such as a corporate local area network (LAN) or a commercial online service, ◊binary files can be sent intact. Over the Internet, attached files must be encoded into ◊ASCII characters and then decoded by the receiver. See ◊MIME.

attar of roses perfume derived from the essential oil of roses (usually damask roses), obtained by crushing and distilling the petals of the flowers.

attention-deficit hyperactivity disorder (ADHD) psychiatric condition occurring in young children characterized by impaired attention and hyperactivity. The disorder, associated with disruptive behaviour, learning difficulties, and under-achievement, is more common in boys. It is treated with methylphenidate (Ritalin). There was a 50% increase in the use of the drug in the USA 1994–96, with an estimated 5% of school-age boys diagnosed as suffering from ADHD.

In 1996, US researchers found that 50% of children diagnosed as ADHD sufferers carry a gene that affects brain cell response to the neurotransmitter dopamine. The same gene has also been linked to impulsiveness in adults. Diagnosis requires the presence, for at least six months, of eight behavioural problems, first developing before the age of seven. In addition to their hyperactivity, such children are found to be reckless, impulsive, and accident prone; they are often aggressive and tend to be unpopular with other children. The outlook for ADHD sufferers varies, with up to a quarter being diagnosed with antisocial personality disorder as adults.

aubergine or ***eggplant*** plant belonging to the nightshade family, native to tropical Asia. Its purple-skinned, sometimes white, fruits are eaten as a vegetable. (*Solanum melongena,* family Solanaceae.)

aubrieta any of a group of spring-flowering dwarf perennial plants native to the Middle East. All are trailing plants with showy, purple flowers. They are widely cultivated in rock gardens. (Genus *Aubrieta,* family Cruciferae.)

audio file computer file that encodes sounds which can be played back using the appropriate software and hardware. On the World Wide Web, the latest types of audio files can be played on the user's computer system in real time while they are being downloaded. Apple Macintosh computers have sound capabilities built in, as do multimedia personal computers (MPCs). Older PCs need to have a ◊sound card installed in order to achieve good playback quality.

audio–video interleave in computing, ◊file format for video clips.

auditory canal tube leading from the outer ◊ear opening to the eardrum. It is found only in animals whose eardrums are located inside the skull, principally mammals and birds.

audit trail record of computer operations, showing what has been done and, if available, who has done it. The term is taken from accountancy, but audit trails are now widely used to check many aspects of computer security, in addition to use in accounts programs.

auger tool for boring holes. Originally, a carpenter's tool, with a cutting edge and a screw point, manipulated by means of a handle at right angles to the shank. In archaeology a large auger is used to collect sediment and soil samples below ground without hand excavation, or to determine the depth and type of archaeological deposits. The auger may be hand- or machine-powered.

auk *The Atlantic, or common, puffin* Fratercula arctica *lives in the open seas and breeds on the rocky coasts of the N Atlantic. With its short tail and narrow wings, which beat rapidly in flight, the puffin is a typical auk. Like all of the auks, the puffin spends most of its life at sea, coming ashore only during the breeding season. Its colourful striped beak has serrated edges to allow it to catch and grip many small fish before flying back to the nest.* *Premaphotos Wildlife*

augmented reality use of computer systems and data to overlay video or other real-life representations. For example, a video of a car engine with the mechanical drawings overlaid.

auk oceanic bird belonging to the family Alcidae, order Charadriiformes, consisting of 22 species of marine diving birds including razorbills, puffins, murres, and guillemots. Confined to the northern hemisphere, their range extends from well inside the Arctic Circle to the lower temperate regions. They feed on fish, and use their wings to 'fly' underwater in pursuit.

Most auks are colonial, breeding on stack tops or cliff edges, although some nest in crevices or holes. With the exception of one species they all lay a single large, very pointed egg.

AUP abbreviation for **acceptable use policy**; see ◊acceptable use.

auricula species of ◊primrose, *a* plant whose leaves are said to resemble a bear's ears. It grows wild in the Alps but is popular in cool-climate areas and often cultivated in gardens. *(Primula auricula.)*

Auriga constellation of the northern hemisphere, represented as a charioteer. Its brightest star is the first-magnitude ◊Capella, about 45 light years from Earth; Epsilon Aurigae is an ◊eclipsing binary star with a period of 27 years, the longest of its kind (last eclipse 1983).

aurochs (plural ***aurochs***) extinct species of long-horned wild cattle *Bos primigenius* that formerly roamed Europe, SW Asia, and N Africa. It survived in Poland until 1627. Black to reddish or grey, it was up to 1.8 m/6 ft at the shoulder. It is depicted in many cave paintings, and is considered the ancestor of domestic cattle.

aurora coloured light in the night sky near the Earth's magnetic poles, called **aurora borealis** ('northern lights') in the northern hemisphere and **aurora australis** in the southern hemisphere. Although aurorae are usually restricted to the polar skies, fluctuations in the ◊solar wind occasionally cause them to be visible at lower latitudes. An aurora is usually in the form of a luminous arch with its apex towards the magnetic pole followed by arcs, bands, rays, curtains, and coronas, usually green but often showing shades of blue and red, and sometimes yellow or white. Aurorae are caused at heights of over 100 km/60 mi by a fast stream of charged particles from solar flares and low-density 'holes' in the Sun's corona.

These are guided by the Earth's magnetic field towards the north and south magnetic poles, where they enter the upper atmosphere and bombard the gases in the atmosphere, causing them to emit visible light.

auscultation evaluation of internal organs by listening, usually with the aid of a stethoscope.

AUSSAT organization formed in 1981 by the federal government of Australia and Telecom Australia to own and operate Australia's domestic satellite system. The first stage, *Aussat 1*, was launched by the US space shuttle *Discovery* in 1985 and the third and final stage was launched from French Guiana, South America, in 1987. The AUSSAT satellite system enables people in remote outback areas of Australia to receive television broadcasts.

Australian cattle dog breed of herding dog known also as a 'heeler' from its technique of controlling cattle by nipping their heels. It has a short coat flecked with red or blue, pricked ears, and a long tail, and stands about 51 cm/20 in tall.

Bred from imported collies, Australian cattle dogs are also claimed to have ◊dingo blood.

Australian Museum the original museum of Australia, which dates from 1827, when it was known as the Colonial Museum. Housed in Sydney, New South Wales, its collection covers anthropology, geology, palaeontology, and the natural sciences (with the exception of botany). It is rated as one of the major natural history museums in the world.

Australian sheepdog breed of dog. See ◊kelpie.

Australian terrier small low-set dog with a long body and straight back. Its straight, rough coat is about 5–6.5 cm/2–2.5 in long, and blue or silver-grey, and tan or clear red or sandy in colour. It has a long head with a topknot of soft hair and ears either pricked or dropped forwards towards the front. Australian terriers are about 25 cm/10 in high and weigh 4.5–5 kg/10–11 lb

The Australian terrier traces its ancestry to the Cairn, Norwich, and Yorkshire terriers.

Australia Prize annual award for achievement internationally in science and technology, established 1990 and worth £115,000.

The first winners were Allan Kerr of Adelaide University, Australia; Eugene Nester of Washington University, USA; and Jeff Schell of the Max Planck Institute in Cologne, Germany. Their studies of the genetic systems of the crown-gall bacterium *Agrobacterium tumefaciens* led to the creation of genetically engineered plants resistant to herbicides, pests, and viruses.

Australia Telescope giant radio telescope in New South Wales, Australia, operated by the Commonwealth Scientific and Industrial Research Organization (CSIRO). It consists of six 22-m/72-ft antennae at Culgoora, a similar antenna at Siding Spring Mountain, and the 64-m/210-ft ◊Parkes radio telescope – the whole simulating a dish 300 m/186 mi across.

Australopithecus the first hominid, living 3.5–4 million years ago; see ◊human species, ◊origins of.

authentication system for certifying the origin of an electronic communication. In the real world, a handwritten signature authenticates a document, for example a contract, as coming from a particular person. In the electronic world, encryption systems provide the same function via ◊digital signatures and other techniques.

In ◊public-key cryptography, for example, the ability to decrypt a message with a particular user's public key authenticates the message as coming from that user and no one else. Authentication is an essential requirement for electronic commerce.

authoring development of multimedia presentations. Authoring includes pulling together the necessary audio, video, graphics, and text files and formatting them for display.

authoring tool software that allows developers to create multimedia presentations or World Wide Web pages. Typically, these tools automate some of the more difficult parts of generating program source codes so that developers can work on a higher, more abstract level. Popular authoring tools for the World Wide Web include Hot Metal and HTML Assistant, both available in ◊shareware versions.

authorization permission to access a particular system. Unauthorized access to private computer systems was made illegal in many countries during the late 1980s.

autism, infantile rare disorder, generally present from birth, characterized by a withdrawn state and a failure to develop normally in language or social behaviour. Although the autistic child may, rarely, show signs of high intelligence (in music or with numbers, for example), many have impaired intellect. The cause is unknown, but is thought to involve a number of factors, possibly including an inherent abnormality of the child's brain. Special education may bring about some improvement.

Autism was initially defined by four common traits – preference for aloneness; insistence on sameness; need for elaborate routines; and the possession of some abilities that seem exceptional compared with other deficits – but current clinical diagnosis involves wider criteria.

AutoCAD the leading computer-aided design (CAD) software package. It is published by the specialist US company AutoDesk (founded 1982). Users include engineers, architects, and designers.

autochrome in photography, a single-plate additive colour process devised by the ◊Lumière brothers in 1903. It was the first commercially available process, in use 1907–35.

autoclave pressurized vessel that uses superheated steam to sterilize materials and equipment such as surgical instruments. It is similar in principle to a pressure cooker.

autoexec.bat in computing, a file in the ◊MS-DOS operating system that is automatically run when the computer is ◊booted.

autogiro or ***autogyro*** heavier-than-air craft that supports itself in the air with a rotary wing, or rotor. The Spanish aviator Juan de la Cierva designed the first successful autogiro in 1923. The autogiro's rotor provides only lift and not propulsion; it has been superseded by the helicopter, in which the rotor provides both. The autogiro is propelled by an orthodox propeller.

The three- or four-bladed rotor on an autogiro spins in a horizontal plane on top of the craft, and is not driven by the engine. The blades have an aerofoil cross section, as a plane's wings. When the autogiro moves forward, the rotor starts to rotate by itself, a state known as autorotation. When travelling fast enough, the rotor develops enough lift from its aerofoil blades to support the craft.

autoimmunity in medicine, condition where the body's immune responses are mobilized not against 'foreign' matter, such as invading germs, but against the body itself. Diseases considered to be of autoimmune origin include ◊myasthenia gravis, ◊rheumatoid arthritis, and ◊lupus erythematous.

In autoimmune diseases T-lymphocytes reproduce to excess to home in on a target (properly a foreign disease-causing molecule); however, molecules of the body's own tissue that resemble the target may also be attacked, for example insulin-producing cells, resulting in insulin-dependent diabetes; if certain joint membrane cells are attacked, then rheumatoid arthritis may result; and if myelin, the basic protein of the nervous system, then multiple sclerosis results. In 1990 in Israel a T-cell vaccine was produced that arrests the excessive reproduction of T-lymphocytes attacking healthy target tissues.

autolysis in biology, the destruction of a ◊cell after its death by the action of its own ◊enzymes, which break down its structural molecules.

automatic fallback in computing, feature allowing ◊modems to drop to a slower speed if conditions such as line noise make it necessary. Modem speeds are typically rated according to one or another ◊CCITT standard (known as a **V number**). All modems rated for a specific standard are ◊backwards compatible.

automatic pilot control device that keeps an aeroplane flying automatically on a given course at a given height and speed.

The automatic pilot contains a set of gyroscopes that provide references for the plane's course. Sensors detect when the plane deviates from this course and send signals to the control surfaces – the ailerons, elevators, and rudder – to take the appropriate action. Autopilot is also used in missiles. Most airliners cruise on automatic pilot, also called autopilot and gyropilot, for much of the time.

US business executive Lawrence Sperry first used a ◊gyroscope in 1912 to create an artificial horizon. This entered production in 1924 and was soon linked to aircraft controls to increase stability. More gyroscopes were added later to control altitude and course. The first automatic pilot was introduced in the 1930s using pneumatic power.

automation widespread use of self-regulating machines in industry. Automation involves the addition of control devices, using electronic sensing and computing techniques, which often follow the pattern of human nervous and brain functions, to already mechanized physical processes of production and distribution; for example, steel processing, mining, chemical production, and road, rail, and air control.

automation *Industrial automation has led to greater productivity and improved quality control. On this production line at a Rover car plant in England car bodies are welded by computer-controlled robots, a task that is complex yet boring and potentially hazardous for human workers.* *Rover Group*

Civilization advances by extending the number of important operations which we can perform without thinking about them.

Alfred North Whitehead English philosopher and mathematician.
An Introduction to Mathematics

automatism performance of actions without awareness or conscious intent. It is seen in sleepwalking and in some (relatively rare) psychotic states.

automaton mechanical figure imitating human or animal performance. Automatons are usually designed for aesthetic appeal as opposed to purely functional robots. The earliest recorded automaton is an Egyptian wooden pigeon of 400 BC.

autonomic nervous system in mammals, the part of the nervous system that controls those functions not controlled voluntarily, including the heart rate, activity of the intestines, and the production of sweat.

There are two divisions of the autonomic nervous system. The **sympathetic** system responds to stress, when it speeds the heart rate, increases blood pressure, and generally prepares the body for action. The **parasympathetic** system is more important when the body is at rest, since it slows the heart rate, decreases blood pressure, and stimulates the digestive system.

At all times, both types of autonomic nerves carry signals that bring about adjustments in visceral organs. The actual rate of heartbeat is the net outcome of opposing signals. Today, it is known that the word 'autonomic' is misleading – the reflexes managed by this system are actually integrated by commands from the brain and spinal cord (the central nervous system).

autopsy or ***postmortem*** examination of the internal organs and tissues of a dead body, performed to try to establish the cause of death.

autoradiography in biology, a technique for following the movement of molecules within an organism, especially a plant, by labelling with a radioactive isotope that can be traced on photographs. It is used to study ◊photosynthesis, where the pathway of radioactive carbon dioxide can be traced as it moves through the various chemical stages.

autoresponder on the Internet, a ◊server that responds automatically to specific messages or input. A common use for autoresponders is to automate the dispatch of sales information via e-mail. A user requesting such information typically sends a message with specified words such as 'send info' in the subject line or the body of the message. The words trigger the autoresponder to send the prepared information file.

Autoresponders are also used in e-mail systems which can be configured to notify correspondents that the user is on holiday.

autosome any ◊chromosome in the cell other than a sex chromosome. Autosomes are of the same number and kind in both males and females of a given species.

autosuggestion conscious or unconscious acceptance of an idea as true, without demanding rational proof, but with potential subsequent effect for good or ill. Pioneered by French psychotherapist Emile Coué (1857–1926) in healing, it is sometimes used in modern psychotherapy to conquer nervous habits and dependence on addictive substances such as tobacco and alcohol.

autotroph any living organism that synthesizes organic substances from inorganic molecules by using light or chemical energy. Autotrophs are the **primary producers** in all food chains since the materials they synthesize and store are the energy sources of all other organisms. All green plants and many planktonic organisms are autotrophs, using sunlight to convert carbon dioxide and water into sugars by ◊photosynthesis.

The total ◊biomass of autotrophs is far greater than that of animals, reflecting the dependence of animals on plants, and the ultimate dependence of all life on energy from the Sun – green plants convert light energy into a form of chemical energy (food) that animals can exploit. Some bacteria use the chemical energy of sulphur compounds to synthesize organic substances. It is estimated that 10% of the energy in autotrophs can pass into the next stage of the ◊food chain, the rest being lost as heat or indigestible matter. See also ◊heterotroph.

autumnal equinox see ◊equinox.

autumn crocus any of a group of late-flowering plants belonging to the lily family. The mauve **meadow saffron** (*Colchicum autumnale*) yields **colchicine**, which is used in treating gout and in plant breeding. (Genus *Colchicum*, family Liliaceae.)

Colchicine causes plants to double the numbers of their chromosomes, forming ◊polyploids)

auxin plant ◊hormone that promotes stem and root growth in plants. Auxins influence many aspects of plant growth and development, including cell enlargement, inhibition of development of axillary buds, ◊tropisms, and the initiation of roots. **Synthetic auxins** are used in rooting powders for cuttings, and in some weedkillers, where high auxin concentrations cause such rapid growth that the plants die. They are also used to prevent premature fruit-drop in orchards. The most common naturally occurring auxin is known as indoleacetic acid, or IAA. It is produced in the shoot apex and transported to other parts of the plant.

avalanche ***from French avaler 'to swallow'*** fall or flow of a mass of snow and ice down a steep slope under the force of gravity. Avalanches occur because of the unstable nature of snow masses in mountain areas.

Changes of temperature, sudden sound, or earth-borne vibrations may trigger an avalanche, particularly on slopes of more than 35°. The snow compacts into ice as it moves, and rocks may be carried along, adding to the damage caused.

Avalanches leave slide tracks, long gouges down the mountainside that can be up to 1 km/0.6 mi long and 100 m/330 ft wide. These slides have a similar beneficial effect on biodiversity as do forest fires, clearing the land of snow and mature mountain forest enabling plants and shrubs that cannot grow in shade, to recolonize and creating wildlife corridors.

AVALANCHE AWARENESS

http://www-nsidc.colorado.edu/NSIDC/EDUCATION/AVALANCHE/

Excellent description of avalanches, what causes them, and how to minimize dangers if caught in one. There is advice on how to determine the stability of a snowpack, what to do if caught out, and how to locate people trapped under snow. Nobody skiing off piste should set off without reading this.

avatar computer-generated character that represents a human in on-screen interaction. In the mid-1990s, avatars were primarily used in computer games, but because they take up much less memory or bandwidth than full video, companies such as British Telecom were researching the possibility of building multiparty videoconferencing systems using this technology.

Avebury Europe's largest stone circle (diameter 412 m/1,350 ft), in Wiltshire, England. This megalithic henge monument, probably a ritual complex, contains 650 massive blocks of stone, arranged in circles and avenues. It was probably constructed around 3,500 years ago, and is linked with nearby ◊Silbury Hill.

The henge, an earthen bank and interior ditch with opposed entrances, originally rose 15 m/49 ft above the bottom of the ditch. This earthwork and an outer ring of stones surround the inner circles. The stones vary in size from 1.5 m/5 ft to 5.5 m/18 ft high and 1 m/3 ft to 3.65 m/12 ft broad. They were erected by a late Neolithic or early Bronze Age culture. Visible remains seen today may cover an earlier existing site – a theory applicable to a number of prehistoric sites.

avens any of several low-growing plants found throughout Europe, Asia, and N Africa. (Genus *Geum*, family Rosaceae.)

Mountain avens (*Dryas octopetala*) belongs to a different genus and grows in mountain and arctic areas of Europe, Asia, and North America. A creeping perennial, it has white flowers with yellow stamens.

average in statistics, a term used inexactly to indicate the typical member of a set of data. It usually refers to the ◊arithmetic mean. The term is also used to refer to the middle member of the set when it is sorted in ascending or descending order (the Gmedian), and the most commonly occurring item of data (the ◊mode), as in 'the average family'.

AVI (abbreviation for ***Audio-Visual Interleave***) file format capable of storing moving images (such as video) with accompanying sound. AVI files can be replayed by any multimedia PC with Microsoft ◊Windows and a ◊sound card. AVI files are frequently very large (around 50 Mbyte for a five-minute rock video, for example), so they are usually stored on ◊CD-ROM.

aviation term used to describe the science of powered ◊flight.

AVIATION ENTHUSIASTS' CORNER

http://www.brooklyn.cuny.edu/rec/air/air.html

Forum dedicated to furthering interest in aviation-related hobbies. It includes links to museums and displays, features on key events in aviation history, and indexes of aircraft by type and manufacturer.

avocado tree belonging to the laurel family, native to Central America. Its dark-green, thick-skinned, pear-shaped fruit has buttery-textured flesh and is used in salads. (*Persea americana*, family Lauraceae.)

avocet wading bird, with a characteristic long, narrow, upturned bill, which it uses to sift water as it feeds in the shallows. It is about 45 cm/18 in long, has long legs, partly webbed feet, and black and white plumage. There are four species of avocet, genus *Recurvirostra*, family Recurvirostridae, order Charadriiformes. They are found in Europe, Africa, and central and southern Asia. Stilts belong to the same family.

Avogadro, Amedeo, Conte di Quaregna (1776–1856) Italian physicist, one of the founders of physical chemistry, who proposed ◊Avogadro's hypothesis on gases in 1811. His work enabled scientists to calculate ◊Avogadro's number, and still has relevance for atomic studies.

Avogadro made it clear that the gas particles need not be individual atoms but might consist of molecules, the term he introduced to describe combinations of atoms. No previous scientist had made this fundamental distinction between the atoms of a substance and its molecules.

Avogadro's hypothesis in chemistry, the law stating that equal volumes of all gases, when at the same temperature and pressure,

AVOGADRO'S HYPOTHESIS OF 1811

http://dbhs.wvusd.k12.ca.us/Chem-History/Avogadro.html

Avogadro's hypothesis was contained in the *Essay on a Manner of Determining the Relative Masses of the Elementary Molecules of Bodies, and the Proportions in Which They Enter Into These Compounds* from the *Journal de physique*, 73: 58-76 (1811). This Web site is a transcript of a translation of that essay taken from Alembic Club Reprints, No. 4, *Foundations of the Molecular Theory: Comprising Papers and Extracts by John Dalton, Joseph Louis Gay-Lussac, and Amadeo Avogadro (1808–11).*

have the same numbers of molecules. It was first propounded by Amedeo Avogadro.

Avogadro's number or *Avogadro's constant* the number of carbon atoms in 12 g of the carbon-12 isotope (6.022045×10^{23}). The relative atomic mass of any element, expressed in grams, contains this number of atoms. It is named after Amedeo Avogadro.

avoirdupois system of units of mass based on the pound (0.45 kg), which consists of 16 ounces (each of 16 drams) or 7,000 grains (each equal to 65 mg).

axil upper angle between a leaf (or bract) and the stem from which it grows. Organs developing in the axil, such as shoots and buds, are termed axillary, or lateral.

axiom in mathematics, a statement that is assumed to be true and upon which theorems are proved by using logical deduction; for example, two straight lines cannot enclose a space. The Greek mathematician Euclid used a series of axioms that he considered could not be demonstrated in terms of simpler concepts to prove his geometrical theorems.

axis (plural *axes*) in geometry, one of the reference lines by which a point on a graph may be located. The horizontal axis is usually referred to as the x-axis, and the vertical axis as the y-axis. The term is also used to refer to the imaginary line about which an object may be said to be symmetrical (**axis of symmetry**) – for example, the diagonal of a square – or the line about which an object may revolve (**axis of rotation**).

axis deer or *chital* species of deer found in India and the East Indies. It is profusely spotted with white on a fawn background, shading from almost black on the back to white on the underparts.

classification The axis deer *Axis axis* is in family Cervidae, order Artiodactyla.

axolotl *Aztec 'water monster'* aquatic larval form ('tadpole') of the Mexican salamander *Ambystoma mexicanum,* belonging to the family Ambystomatidae. Axolotls may be up to 30 cm/12 in long. They are remarkable because they can breed without changing to the adult form, and will metamorphose into adults only in response to the drying-up of their ponds. The adults then migrate to another pond.

Axolotls resemble a newt in shape, having a powerful tail, two pairs of weak limbs, and three pairs of simple external gills. They lay eggs like a frog's in strings attached to water plants by a viscous substance, and the young, hatched in two to three weeks, resemble the parents. See also ◊neoteny.

axon long threadlike extension of a ◊nerve cell that conducts electrochemical impulses away from the cell body towards other nerve cells, or towards an effector organ such as a muscle. Axons terminate in ◊synapses, junctions with other nerve cells, muscles, or glands.

aye-aye nocturnal tree-climbing prosimian *Daubentonia madagascariensis* of Madagascar, related to the lemurs. It is just over 1 m/3 ft long, including a tail 50 cm/20 in long.

It has an exceptionally long middle finger with which it probes for insects and their larvae under the bark of trees, and gnawing, rodentlike front teeth, with which it tears off the bark to get at its prey. The aye-aye has become rare through loss of its forest habitat, and is now classified as an endangered species.

Ayurveda basically naturopathic system of medicine widely practised in India and based on principles derived from the ancient Hindu scriptures, the Vedas. Hospital treatments and remedial prescriptions tend to be nonspecific and to coordinate holistic therapies for body, mind, and spirit.

azalea any of a group of deciduous flowering shrubs belonging to the heath family. Several species are native to Asia and North America, and many cultivated varieties have been derived from these. Azaleas are closely related to the mostly evergreen ◊rhododendrons. (Genus *Rhododendron,* family Ericaceae.)

Azaleas, particularly the Japanese varieties, make fine ornamental shrubs. Several species are highly poisonous.

Azilian archaeological period following the close of the Old Stone (Palaeolithic) Age and regarded as the earliest culture of the Mesolithic Age in W Europe. It was first recognized at Le Mas d'Azil, a cave in Ariège, France.

azimuth in astronomy, the angular distance of an object eastwards along the horizon, measured from due north, between the astronomical ◊meridian (the vertical circle passing through the centre of the sky and the north and south points on the horizon) and the vertical circle containing the celestial body whose position is to be measured.

azo dye synthetic dye containing the azo group of two nitrogen atoms (N=N) connecting aromatic ring compounds. Azo dyes are usually red, brown, or yellow, and make up about half the dyes produced. They are manufactured from aromatic ◊amines.

AZT drug used in the treatment of AIDS; see ◊zidovudine.

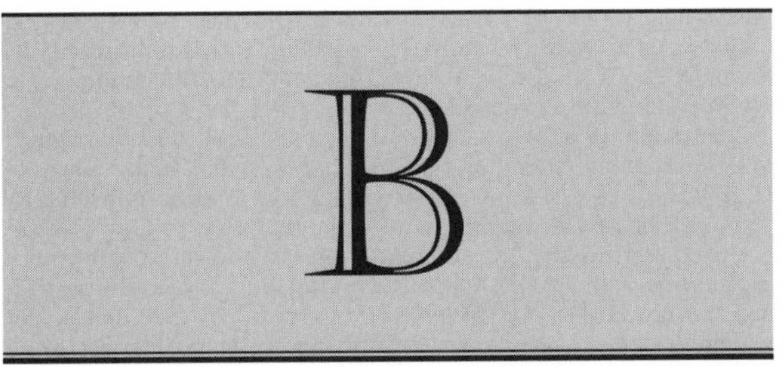

Babbage, Charles
(1792–1871)

English mathematician who devised a precursor of the computer. He designed an analytical engine, a general-purpose mechanical computing device for performing different calculations according to a program input on punched cards (an idea borrowed from the Jacquard loom). This device was never built, but it embodied many of the principles on which digital computers are based.

Mary Evans Picture Library

BABBAGE, CHARLES

Charles Babbage, who was perhaps the first person to conceive the idea of a mechanical computer, was a stickler for accuracy. He once wrote to the poet Tennyson to object to the poet's lines 'Every moment dies a man, every moment one is born'. According to Babbage, Tennyson's recipe gave zero population growth, and should be corrected to:'Every moment one and one-sixteenth is born'.

Babbit metal soft, white metal, an ◊alloy of tin, lead, copper, and antimony, used to reduce friction in bearings, developed by the US inventor Isaac Babbit in 1839.

babbler bird of the thrush family Muscicapidae with a loud babbling cry. Babblers, subfamily Timaliinae, are found in the Old World, and there are some 250 species in the group.

babirusa wild pig *Babirousa babyrussa,* becoming increasingly rare, found in the moist forests and by the water of Sulawesi, Buru, and nearby Indonesian islands. The male has large upper tusks which grow upwards through the skin of the snout and curve back towards the forehead. The babirusa is up to 80 cm/2.5 ft at the shoulder. It is nocturnal, and swims well.

baboon large monkey of the genus *Papio,* with a long doglike muzzle and large canine teeth, spending much of its time on the ground in open country. Males, with head and body up to 1.1 m/3.5 ft long, are larger than females, and dominant males rule the 'troops' in which baboons live. They inhabit Africa and SW Arabia.

Species include the **olive baboon** *P. anubis* from W Africa to Kenya, the **chacma** *P. ursinus* from S Africa, and the **sacred baboon** *P. hamadryas* from NE Africa and SW Arabia. The male sacred baboon has a 'cape' of long hair.

bacille Calmette-Guérin tuberculosis vaccine ◊BCG.

bacillus member of a group of rodlike ◊bacteria that occur everywhere in the soil and air. Some are responsible for diseases such as ◊anthrax or for causing food spoilage.

backbone in networking, a high-◊bandwidth trunk to which smaller networks connect. The original backbone of the Internet was NSFnet, funded by the US National Science Foundation, which linked together the five regional supercomputing centres.

backcross breeding technique used to determine the genetic makeup of an individual organism.

background radiation radiation that is always present in the environment. By far the greater proportion (87%) of it is emitted from natural sources. Alpha and beta particles, and gamma radiation are radiated by the traces of radioactive minerals that occur naturally in the environment and even in the human body, and by radioactive gases such as radon and thoron, which are found in soil and may seep upwards into buildings. Radiation from space (◊cosmic radiation) also contributes to the background level.

backing storage in computing, memory outside the ◊central processing unit used to store programs and data that are not in current use. Backing storage must be nonvolatile – that is, its contents must not be lost when the power supply to the computer system is disconnected.

back pain aches in the region of the spine. Low back pain can be caused by a very wide range of medical conditions. About half of all episodes of back pain will resolve within a week, but severe back pain can be chronic and disabling. The causes include muscle sprain, a prolapsed intervertebral disc, and vertebral collapse due to ◊osteoporosis or cancer. Treatment methods include rest, analgesics, physiotherapy, osteopathy, and exercises.

backswimmer or ***water boatman*** aquatic predatory bug living mostly in fresh water. The adults are about 15 mm/0.5 in long and rest upside down at the water surface to breathe. When disturbed they dive, carrying with them a supply of air trapped under the wings. They have piercing beaks, used in feeding on tadpoles and small fish.

classification Backswimmers belong to the genus *Notonecta,* family Notonectidae in suborder Heteroptera, order Hemiptera (true bugs), class Insecta, phylum Arthropoda.

Females have a sharp ovipositor to pierce the stems of aquatic plants. In each notch one egg is laid; each female lays a total of approximately 60 eggs over a period of a few weeks. Backswimmers fly readily from pond to pond.

backup in computing, a copy file that is transferred to another medium, usually a ◊floppy disc or tape. The purpose of this is to have available a copy of a file that can be restored in case of a fault in the system or the file itself. Backup files are also created by many applications (with the extension .BAC or .BAK); a version is therefore available of the original file before it was modified by the current application.

backup system in computing, a duplicate computer system that can take over the operation of a main computer system in the event of equipment failure. A large interactive system, such as an airline's ticket-booking system, cannot be out of action for even a few hours without causing considerable disruption. In such cases a complete duplicate computer system may be provided to take over and run the system should the main computer develop a fault or need maintenance.

Backup systems include **incremental backup** and **full backup**.

backwards compatible in computing, term describing a product that is designed to be compatible with its predecessors. In software, a word processor is backwards compatible if it can read and write the files of earlier versions of the same software, and an operating system is backwards compatible if it can run programs designed for earlier versions of the operating system. Similarly, all modems are compatible with all the standards (V numbers) which precede the fastest one they can handle.

bacon beetle destructive species of beetle that attacks bacon, dried foods, and hides. It is related to the ◊carpet beetles.

classification The bacon beetle *Dermestes lardarius* is in the family Dermestidae, order Coleoptera, class Insecta, phylum Arthropoda.

bacteria (singular ***bacterium***) microscopic single-celled organisms lacking a nucleus. Bacteria are widespread, present in soil, air, and water, and as parasites on and in other living things. Some parasitic bacteria cause disease by producing toxins, but others are harmless and may even benefit their hosts. Bacteria usually reproduce by ◊binary fission (dividing into two equal parts), and this may occur approximately every 20 minutes. It is thought that 1–10% of the world's bacteria have been identified.

classification Bacteria are now classified biochemically, but their varying shapes provide a rough classification; for example, **cocci** are round or oval, **bacilli** are rodlike, **spirilla** are spiral, and **vibrios** are shaped like commas. Exceptionally, one bacterium has been found, *Gemmata obscuriglobus,* that does have a nucleus. Unlike ◊viruses, bacteria do not necessarily need contact with a live cell to become active.

Bacteria can be classified into two broad classes (called Gram positive and negative) according to their reactions to certain stains, or dyes, used in microscopy. The staining technique, called the Gram test after Danish bacteriologist Hans Gram, allows doctors to identify many bacteria quickly.

Bacteria have a large loop of ◊DNA, sometimes called a bacterial chromosome. In addition there are often small, circular pieces of DNA known as ◊plasmids that carry spare genetic information. These plasmids can readily move from one bacterium to another, even though the bacteria may be of different species. In a sense, they are parasites within the bacterial cell, but they survive by coding characteristics that promote the survival of their hosts. For example, some plasmids confer antibiotic resistance on the bacteria they inhabit. The rapid and problematic spread of antibiotic resistance among bacteria is due to plasmids, but they are also useful to humans in ◊genetic engineering. There are ten times more bacterial cells than human cells in the human body.

functions Certain types of bacteria are vital in many food and industrial processes, while others play an essential role in the ◊nitrogen cycle, which maintains soil fertility. For example, bacteria are used to break down waste products, such as sewage; make butter, cheese, and yoghurt; cure tobacco; tan leather; and (by virtue of the ability of certain bacteria to attack metal) clean ships' hulls and derust their tanks, and even extract minerals from mines. Several species of bacteria in the stomach of a bowhead whale are

Phages

BY DAVID EVANS

Introduction

Phages, or bacteriophages (literally 'bacteria eaters'), are viruses that infect bacteria. They were first identified by F W Twort in 1905 and, independently, by F d'Herelle in 1917 as filterable infectious agents that caused the lysis (disintegration) of *Shigella dynsenteriae*, the bacterium that causes dysentery. They were initially of interest for their specificity, they would not infect other bacteria, and potential therapeutic use, and have become some of the best characterized viruses.

Life cycle of phages

Phages, like other viruses, are obligate intracellular parasites. They cannot reproduce independently and must instead infect a host bacterium within which they replicate, usually resulting in the lysis of the bacteria and release of progeny phage particles. The phage particle is a metabolically inert entity consisting of a protein coat (capsid) surrounding the genome which consists of single- or double-stranded DNA or RNA. Two distinct replication patterns exist; lytic, in which genome replication, transcription and translation of phage genes and the subsequent assembly of progeny phage particles occurs immediately (so called virulent phages) and lysogenic, in which the phage genome becomes integrated into the host chromosome (the temperate phages). In the latter case the phage genome is replicated as part of the bacterial chromosome, remaining latent as a prophage until induction at which point the phage enters a normal lytic cycle.

Phage structure and classification

The diverse range of phages are primarily classified according to their capsid structure (filamentous – e.g. M13, tailless icosahedral – e.g. [phgr]X174, phages with noncontractile tails – e.g. [lambda] and phages with contractile tails – e.g. T2) and the type of genetic material. The T-even phages of *Escherichia coli* (T2, T4, T6) possess large double-stranded DNA genomes within an icosahedral capsid bearing a contractile tail, and are some of the most complex of all viruses.

Phages in research

The short replication cycle (as little as 15 min) and ease of manipulation in the laboratory have meant that phages have been used for some of the most significant biological, and in particular genetic, experiments of the last 50 years. The identification of DNA as the genetic material was based on a study of phage T2 infection of *E. coli* by Alfred Hershey and Martha Chase in 1952. Phage [phgr]X174, a single-stranded DNA phage was the first complete genome to be sequenced (1977), leading to the discovery of overlapping genes, and the switch between lytic and lysogenic life cycles by phage lambda ([lambda]) is the paradigm for a 'genetic switch', which has broad similarities with similar controlling events in many other organisms (including humans). The natural ability of phages to exchange genetic material between bacteria has led to them being exploited for experiments in molecular genetics –both phage M13 and [lambda] are widely used DNA cloning vectors.

Phages and human disease

The specificity of bacterial infection by phages means that they can be used to distinguish between different strains of bacteria (particularly *Salmonella* sp.), a technique called 'phage typing' widely used in reference laboratories. Furthermore, phages may have a role in causing human disease as well as diagnosing it. *Vibrio cholerae*, the bacterium that causes cholera, requires two factors for full virulence; the cholera toxin (CT) and a toxin-coregulated pili (TCP) required for intestinal colonization. Recent research has shown that the genes encoding both CT and TCP are carried by the filamentous phage CTXθ, which can transfer them to apathogenic strains of *V. cholerae* and so lead to the formation of novel virulent strains capable of causing cholera.

d'Herelle suggested that the specific lysis of bacteria by phages could be exploited in the development of therapeutic treatments for bacterial infections. The intervening 80 years have seen the discovery and widespread use of antibiotics for treating bacterial infection. Although very effective, there are an increasing number of multiply drug-resistant bacteria, e.g. *Mycobacterium tuberculosis* (TB) and *Staphylococcus aureus* (septicaemia) as a direct consequence of the widespread use of antibiotics, and there has been a resurgence in the interest in the use of phages for treating bacterial infection.

capable of digesting pollutants (naphthalene and anthracene, two carcinogenic fractions of oil difficult to break down, and PCBs, also carcinogenic).

Bacteria cannot normally survive temperatures above 100°C/212°F, such as those produced in pasteurization, but those in deep-sea hot vents in the eastern Pacific are believed to withstand temperatures of 350°C/662°F. *Thermus aquaticus,* or taq, grows freely in the boiling waters of hot springs, and an enzyme derived from it is used in genetic engineering to speed up the production of millions of copies of any DNA sequence, a reaction requiring very high temperatures.

interaction Certain bacteria can influence the growth of others; for example, lactic acid bacteria will make conditions unfavourable for salmonella bacteria. Other strains produce nisin, which inhibits growth of listeria and botulism organisms. Plans in the food industry are underway to produce super strains of lactic acid bacteria to avoid food poisoning.

An estimated 99% of bacteria live in **biofilms** rather than in single-species colonies. These are complex colonies made up of a number of different species of bacteria structured on a layer of slime produced by the bacteria. Fungi, algae, and protozoa may also inhabit the biofilms.

prehistoric bacteria Bacterial spores 40 million years old were extracted from a fossilized bee and successfully germinated by US scientists in 1995. It is hoped that prehistoric bacteria can be tapped as a source of new chemicals for use in the drugs industry. Any bacteria resembling extant harmful pathogens will be destroyed, and all efforts are being to made to ensure no bacteria escape the laboratory.

bacteriology the study of ◊bacteria.

bacteriophage virus that attacks ◊bacteria. Such viruses are now of use in genetic engineering.

Bactrian species of ◊camel *Camelus bactrianus* found in the Gobi Desert in Central Asia. Body fat is stored in two humps on the back. It has very long winter fur which is shed in ragged lumps. The head and body length is about 3 m/10 ft, and the camel is up to 2.1 m/6.8 ft tall at the shoulder. Most Bactrian camels are domesticated and are used as beasts of burden in W Asia.

badger large mammal of the weasel family with molar teeth of a crushing type adapted to a partly vegetable diet, and short strong legs with long claws suitable for digging. The Eurasian **common badger** *Meles meles* is about 1 m/3 ft long, with long, coarse, greyish hair on the back, and a white face with a broad black stripe along each side. Mainly a woodland animal, it is harmless and nocturnal, and spends the day in a system of burrows called a 'sett'. It feeds on roots, a variety of fruits and nuts, insects, worms, mice, and young rabbits.

The Eurasian badger lives for up to 15 years. It mates February to March, and again July to Septemebr if the earlier mating has not resulted in fertilization. Implantation of the ◊blastocyst (early embryo) is however delayed until December. Cubs are born January to March, and remain below ground for eight weeks. They remain with the sow at least until autumn.

The **American badger** *Taxidea taxus* is slightly smaller than the Eurasian badger, and lives in open country in North America. Various species of hog badger, ferret badger, and stink badger occur in S and E Asia, the last having the well-developed anal scent glands characteristic of the weasel family.

badlands barren landscape cut by erosion into a maze of ravines, pinnacles, gullies and sharp-edged ridges. Areas in South Dakota and Nebraska, USA, are examples.

Baikonur launch site for spacecraft, located at Tyuratam, Kazakhstan, near the Aral Sea: the first satellites and all Soviet space probes and crewed Soyuz missions were launched from here. It covers an area of 12,200 sq km/4,675 sq mi, much larger than its US equivalent, the ◊Kennedy Space Center in Florida.

Bailey bridge prefabricated bridge developed by the British Army in World War II; made from a set of standardized components so that bridges of varying lengths and load-carrying ability could be assembled to order. They were used in every theatre of the war and many remained in place for several years after the war until the civil authorities could replace them with more permanent structures.

Baily's beads bright spots of sunlight seen around the edge of the Moon for a few seconds immediately before and after a total ◊eclipse of the Sun, caused by sunlight shining between mountains at the Moon's edge. Sometimes one bead is much brighter than the others, producing the so-called **diamond ring** effect. The effect was described in 1836 by the English astronomer Francis Baily (1774–1844), a wealthy stockbroker who retired in 1825 to devote himself to astronomy.

Bakelite first synthetic ◊plastic, created by Leo Baekeland in 1909. Bakelite is hard, tough, and heatproof, and is used as an

Baird, John Logie (1888–1946)

Scottish electrical engineer who pioneered television. In 1925 he gave the first public demonstration of television, transmitting an image of a recognizable human face. The following year, he gave the world's first demonstration of true television before an audience of about 50 scientists at the Royal Institution, London. By 1928 Baird had succeeded in demonstrating colour television.

Baird used a mechanical scanner which temporarily changed an image into a sequence of electronic signals that could then be reconstructed on a screen as a pattern of half-tones. The neon discharge lamp Baird used offered a simple means for the electrical modulation of light at the receiver. His first pictures were formed of only 30 lines repeated approximately 10 times a second. The results were crude but it was the start of television as a practical technology.

By 1927, Baird had transmitted television over 700 km/435 mi of telephone line between London and Glasgow and soon after made the first television broadcast using radio, between London and the *SS Berengaria*, halfway across the Atlantic Ocean. He also made the first transatlantic television broadcast between Britain and the United States when signals transmitted from the Baird station in Coulson, Kent, were picked up by a receiver in Hartsdale, New York.

Baird's black-and-white system was used by the BBC in an experimental television service in 1929. In 1936, when the public television service was started, his system was threatened by one promoted by Marconi-EMI. The following year the Baird system was dropped in favour of the Marconi electronic system, which gave a better definition.

Mary Evans Picture Library

BADLANDS NATIONAL PARK

http://www.nps.gov/badl/htmlfiles/expanded.htm

Impressive US National Park Service guide to the Badlands National Park. There is comprehensive information on the geology, flora and fauna, and history of the Badlands. Hikers are provided with detailed guidance on routes and there is a listing of the park's educational activities.

electrical insulator. It is made by the reaction of phenol with formaldehyde, producing a powdery resin that sets solid when heated. Objects are made by subjecting the resin to compression moulding (simultaneous heat and pressure in a mould).

It is one of the thermosetting plastics, which do not remelt when heated, and is often used for electrical fittings.

baking powder mixture of ◊bicarbonate of soda, an acidic compound, and a nonreactive filler (usually starch or calcium sulphate), used in baking as a raising agent. It gives a light open texture to cakes and scones, and is used as a substitute for yeast in making soda bread.

Several different acidic compounds (for example, tartaric acid, cream of tartar, sodium or calcium acid phosphates, and glucono-delta-lactone) may be used, any of which will react with the sodium hydrogencarbonate, in the presence of water and heat, to release the carbon dioxide that causes the cake mix or dough to rise.

balance apparatus for weighing or measuring mass. The various types include the **beam balance**, consisting of a centrally pivoted lever with pans hanging from each end, and the **spring balance**, in which the object to be weighed stretches (or compresses) a vertical coil spring fitted with a pointer that indicates the weight on a scale. Kitchen and bathroom scales are balances.

balanced diet diet that includes carbohydrate, protein, fat, vitamins, water, minerals, and fibre (roughage). Although all these substances are needed if a person is to be healthy, there is disagreement over how much of each type a person needs.

balance of nature in ecology, the idea that there is an inherent equilibrium in most ◊ecosystems, with plants and animals interacting so as to produce a stable, continuing system of life on Earth. The activities of human beings can, and frequently do, disrupt the balance of nature.

Organisms in the ecosystem are adapted to each other – for example, waste products produced by one species are used by another and resources used by some are replenished by others; the oxygen needed by animals is produced by plants while the waste product of animal respiration, carbon dioxide, is used by plants as a raw material in photosynthesis. The nitrogen cycle, the water cycle, and the control of animal populations by natural predators are other examples.

BALDNESS

The best way for a man to know whether he will go bald is to look at his mother's father. Baldness is hereditary, but the gene controlling it is on the sex-linked chromosome and skips one generation.

baldness loss of hair from the scalp, common in older men. Its onset and extent are influenced by genetic make-up and the level of male sex ◊hormones. There is no cure, and expedients such as hair implants may have no lasting effect. Hair loss in both sexes may also occur as a result of ill health or radiation treatment, such as for cancer. **Alopecia**, a condition in which the hair falls out, is different from the 'male-pattern baldness' described above.

Experience is a comb which nature gives to men when they are bald.

ANONYMOUS Eastern proverb

Balistidae family of fish containing the ◊triggerfish.

ball-and-socket joint joint allowing considerable movement in three dimensions, for instance the joint between the pelvis and the femur. To facilitate movement, such joints are rimmed with cartilage and lubricated by synovial fluid. The bones are kept in place by ligaments and moved by muscles.

ballistics study of the motion and impact of projectiles such as bullets, bombs, and missiles. For projectiles from a gun, relevant exterior factors include temperature, barometric pressure, and wind strength; and for nuclear missiles these extend to such factors as the speed at which the Earth turns.

balloon lighter-than-air craft that consists of a gasbag filled with gas lighter than the surrounding air and an attached basket, or gondola, for carrying passengers and/or instruments. In 1783, the first successful human ascent was in Paris, in a hot-air balloon designed by the Montgolfier brothers Joseph Michel and Jacques Etienne. In 1785, a hydrogen-filled balloon designed by French physicist Jacques Charles travelled across the English Channel.

balloon help small cartoon-style bubble which pops up in a graphical computer system to convey ◊online help. In many new products, balloon help is activated by holding the mouse over an icon or other type of control for a few seconds. Such help is context-sensitive.

ball valve valve that works by the action of external pressure raising a ball and thereby opening a hole.

balm, lemon garden herb, see ◊lemon balm.

balsam any of various garden plants belonging to the balsam family. They are usually annuals with spurred red or white flowers and pods that burst and scatter their seeds when ripe. (Genus *Impatiens*, family Balsaminaceae.)

In medicine and perfumery, balsam refers to various oily or gummy aromatic plant ◊resins, such as balsam of Peru from the Central American tree *Myroxylon pereirae*.

bamboo any of a large group of giant grass plants, found mainly in tropical and subtropical regions. Some species grow as tall as 36 m/

***bamboo** The tall, closely packed stems of many bamboos, such as this example from the tropical rainforest of Brazil, frequently form dense clumps in the forest understorey. Bamboo grows rapidly and has a wide variety of uses. Premaphotos Wildlife*

120 ft. The stems are hollow and jointed and can be used in furniture, house, and boat construction. The young shoots are edible; paper is made from the stems. (Genus *Bambusa,* family Gramineae.)

Bamboos flower and seed only once before the plant dies, sometimes after growing for as long as 120 years.

banana any of several treelike tropical plants which grow up to 8 m/25 ft high. The edible banana is the fruit of a sterile hybrid form. (Genus *Musa,* family Musaceae.)

The curved yellow fruits of the commercial banana, arranged in clusters known as 'hands', form cylindrical masses of a hundred or more fruits.

They are picked and exported green and ripened aboard refrigerated ships. The plant is destroyed after cropping. The **plantain**, a larger, coarser hybrid variety that is used green as a cooked vegetable, is a dietary staple in many countries. In the wild, bananas depend on bats for pollination.

banded brush beetle type of ◊rose chafer.
classification The banded brush beetle *Trichius fasciatus,* in the subfamily Trichiinae, family Scarabaeidae, order Coleoptera, class Insecta, phylum Arthropoda.

bandfish marine bony fish. It is elongated with very long dorsal fins that run the length of its body. Bandfish spend most of their time on the sea bed, occasionally swimming to midwater to feed on small planktonic crustacea.

bandicoot small marsupial mammal inhabiting Australia and New Guinea. There are about 11 species, family Peramelidae, rat- or rabbit-sized, and living in burrows. They have long snouts, eat insects, and are nocturnal. A related group, the rabbit bandicoots or bilbies, is reduced to a single species that is now endangered and protected by law.

bandwidth in computing and communications, the rate of data transmission, measured in ◊bits per second (bps).

bandy-bandy venomous Australian snake *Vermicella annulata* of the cobra family, which grows to about 75 cm/2.5 ft. It is banded in black and white. It is not aggressive toward humans.

bang in UNIX, an exclamation mark (!). It appears in some older types of Internet addresses and is used in dictating the commands necessary to run UNIX systems.

__banyan__ This banyan tree in the Ranthambhore National Park in N India is reputed to be the second largest specimen in the country. Its shade provides a midday resting place for many people and animals. As a result, banyans are planted along roadsides over much of India. Premaphotos Wildlife

bang path list of routing that appears in the header of a message sent across the Internet, showing how it travelled from the sender to its destination. It is named after the ◊bangs separating the sites in the list.

banksia any shrub or tree of a group native to Australia, including the honeysuckle tree. They are named after the British naturalist and explorer Joseph Banks. (Genus *Banksia,* family Proteaceae.)

Banksias have spiny evergreen leaves and large flower spikes, made up of about 1,000 individual flowers formed around a central axis. The colours of the flower spikes can be gold, red, brown, purple, greenish-yellow, and grey.

banner in computing, advertisement on a World Wide Web page, usually but not always in the form of a horizontal rectangle. Clicking on a banner usually takes the user to the advertised Web site. Noncommercial sites display one another's banners via organizations like LinkExchange and BannerExchange.

bantam small ornamental variety of domestic chicken weighing about 0.5–1 kg/1–2 lb. Bantams can either be a small version of one of the larger breeds, or a separate type. Some are prolific egg layers. Bantam cocks have a reputation as spirited fighters.

banteng wild species of cattle *Bos banteng,* now scarce, but formerly ranging from Myanmar (Burma) through SE Asia to Malaysia and Java, inhabiting hilly forests. Its colour varies from pale brown to blue-black, usually with white stockings and rump patch, and it is up to 1.5 m/5 ft at the shoulder.

banyan tropical Asian fig tree. It produces aerial roots that grow down from its spreading branches, forming supporting pillars that look like separate trunks. (*Ficus benghalensis,* family Moraceae.)

baobab tree with rootlike branches, hence the nickname 'upside-down tree', and a disproportionately thick girth, up to 9 m/30 ft in diameter. The pulp of its fruit is edible and is known as monkey bread. (Genus *Adansonia,* family Bombacaceae.)

bar unit of pressure equal to 10^5 pascals or 10^6 dynes/cm^2, approximately 750 mmHg or 0.987 atm. Its diminutive, the **millibar** (one-thousandth of a bar), is commonly used by meteorologists.

barb general name for fish of the genus *Barbus* and some related genera of the family Cyprinidae. As well as the ◊barbel, barbs include many small tropical Old World species, some of which are familiar aquarium species. They are active egg-laying species, usually of 'typical' fish shape and with barbels at the corner of the mouth.

Barbary ape tailless, yellowish-brown macaque monkey *Macaca sylvanus,* 55–75 cm/20–30 in long. Barbary apes are found in the mountains and wilds of Algeria and Morocco, especially in the forests of the Atlas Mountains. They were introduced to Gibraltar, where legend has it that the British will leave if the ape colony dies out.

The macaque is threatened by illegal logging, which is devastating some of the ancient forests in the area. Although it is breeding well in captivity, forest loss may confound attempts to reintroduce this species into the wild.

Barbary sheep or ***aoudad*** or ***udad*** species of bovid related to the goat and sheep. It has powerful horns and a goatlike odour, but is distinguished from goats by its longer tail and the mane of long hair on the throat and upper parts of the forelegs. It is found in North Africa and parts of the Sudan.
classification The Barbary sheep *Ammotragus lervia* is in family Bovidae, order Artiodactyla

barbastelle insect-eating bat *Barbastella barbastellus* with hairy cheeks and lips, 'frosted' black fur, and a wingspan of about 25 cm/10 in. It lives in hollow trees and under roofs, and is occasionally found in the UK but more commonly in Europe.

barbed wire cheap fencing material made of strands of galvanized wire (see ◊galvanizing), twisted together with sharp barbs at close intervals. In 1873 an American, Joseph Glidden, devised a machine to mass-produce barbed wire. Its use on the open grasslands of 19th-century America led to range warfare between farmers and cattle ranchers; the latter used to drive their herds cross-country.

barbel freshwater fish *Barbus barbus* found in fast-flowing rivers with sand or gravel bottoms in Britain and Europe. Long-bodied, and up to 1 m/3 ft long in total, the barbel has four **barbels** ('little beards' – sensory fleshy filaments) near the mouth.

barberry any spiny shrub belonging to the barberry family, with sour red berries and yellow flowers. These shrubs are often used as hedges. (Genus *Berberis,* family Berberidaceae.)

barbet ***Latin barbatus, 'bearded'*** small, tropical bird, often brightly coloured. There are about 78 species of barbet in the family Capitonidae, order Piciformes, common to tropical Africa, Asia, and America. Barbets eat insects and fruit and, being distant relations of woodpeckers, drill nest holes with their beaks. The name comes from the 'little beard' of bristles about the mouth that assists them in catching insects.

barbiturate hypnosedative drug, commonly known as a 'sleeping pill', consisting of any salt or ester of barbituric acid $C_4H_4O_3N_2$. It works by depressing brain activity. Most barbiturates, being highly addictive, are no longer prescribed and are listed as controlled substances.

Tolerance develops quickly in the user so that increasingly large doses are required to induce sleep. A barbiturate's action persists for hours or days, causing confused, aggressive behaviour or disorientation. Overdosage causes death by inhibiting the breathing centre in the brain. Short-acting barbiturates are used as ◊anaesthetics to induce general anaesthesia; slow-acting ones may be prescribed for epilepsy.

bar chart in statistics, a way of displaying data, using horizontal or vertical bars. The heights or lengths of the bars are proportional to the quantities they represent.

bar code pattern of bars and spaces that can be read by a computer. Bar codes are widely used in retailing, industrial distribution, and public libraries. The code is read by a scanning device; the computer determines the code from the widths of the bars and spaces.

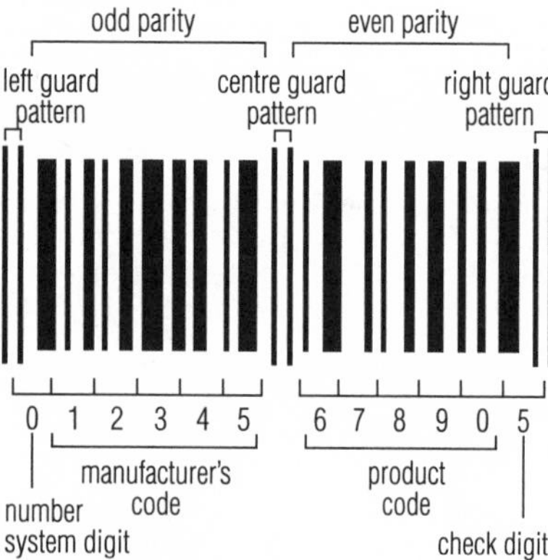

***bar code** The bars of varying thicknesses and spacings represent two series of numbers, identifying the manufacturer and the product. Two longer, thinner bars mark the beginning and end of the manufacturer and product codes. The bar code is used on most articles for sale in shops.*

The technique was patented in 1949 but became popular only in 1973, when the food industry in North America adopted the Universal Product Code system.

barium ***Greek barytes 'heavy'*** soft, silver-white, metallic element, symbol Ba, atomic number 56, relative atomic mass 137.33. It is one of the alkaline-earth metals, found in nature as barium carbonate and barium sulphate. As the sulphate it is used in medicine: taken as a suspension (a 'barium meal'), its movement along the gut is followed using X-rays. The barium sulphate, which is opaque to X-rays, shows the shape of the gut, revealing any abnormalities of the alimentary canal. Barium is also used in alloys, pigments, and safety matches and, with strontium, forms the emissive surface in cathode-ray tubes. It was first discovered in barytes or heavy spar.

bark protective outer layer on the stems and roots of woody plants, composed mainly of dead cells. To allow for expansion of the stem, the bark is continually added to from within, and the outer surface often becomes cracked or is shed as scales. Trees deposit a variety of chemicals in their bark, including poisons. Many of these chemical substances have economic value because they can be used in the manufacture of drugs. Quinine, derived from the bark of the *Cinchona* tree, is used to fight malarial infections; curare, an anaesthetic used in medicine, comes from the *Strychnus toxifera* tree in the Amazonian rainforest.

Bark technically includes all the tissues external to the vascular ◊cambium (the ◊phloem, cortex, and periderm), and its thickness may vary from 2.5 mm/0.1 in to 30 cm/12 in or more, as in the giant redwood *Sequoia* where it forms a thick, spongy layer.

bark beetle any one of a number of species of mainly wood-boring beetles. Bark beetles are cylindrical, brown or black, and 1–9 mm/0.04–0.4 in long. Some live just under the bark and others bore deeper into the hardwood. The detailed tunnelling pattern that they make within the trunk varies with the species concerned, and is used for identification.

Most bark beetles live in forest trees; some, however, attack fruit trees. Generally, but not always, dead or dying timber is attacked. Some species transmit pathogens, for example, the fungus that causes ◊Dutch elm disease.

Examples include the **birch bark beetle** *Scolytus ratzeburgi* and the **greater fruit-tree bark beetle** *S. meli.*

classification Bark beetles are in the families Curculionidae or Scolytidae, order Coleoptera, class Insecta, phylum Arthropoda.

barking deer another name for the ◊muntjac.

barley cereal belonging to a family of grasses. It resembles wheat but is more tolerant of cold and draughts. Cultivated barley (*Hordeum vulgare*) comes in three main varieties – six-rowed, four-rowed, and two-rowed. (Family Gramineae.)

Barley was one of the earliest cereals to be cultivated, about 5000 BC in Egypt, and no other cereal can thrive in so wide a range of climatic conditions; polar barley is sown and reaped well within the Arctic Circle in Europe. Barley is no longer much used in bread making, but it is used in soups and stews and as a starch. Its high-protein form is widely used as animal feed, and its low-protein form is used in brewing and distilling alcoholic drinks.

barley midge another name for the ◊hessian fly.

barn farm building traditionally used for the storage and processing of cereal crops and hay. On older farmsteads, the barn is usually the largest building. It is often characterized by ventilation openings rather than windows and has at least one set of big double doors for access. Before mechanization, wheat was threshed by hand on a specially prepared floor inside these doors.

barnacle marine crustacean of the subclass Cirripedia. The larval form is free-swimming, but when mature, it fixes itself by the head to rock or floating wood. The animal then remains attached, enclosed in a shell through which the cirri (modified legs) protrude to sweep food into the mouth. Barnacles include the stalked **goose barnacle** *Lepas anatifera* found on ships' bottoms, and the **acorn barnacles**, such as *Balanus balanoides,* common on rocks.

barnacle Acorn barnacles, such as Chthalamus stellatus, *are a familiar sight on rocky seashores between the tidemarks, where they are the most abundant life form. Identification of the various species is based on the arrangement of the calcareous plates and requires the use of a powerful hand lens or microscope. Premaphotos Wildlife*

Barnard's star second-closest star to the Sun, six light years away in the constellation Ophiuchus. It is a faint red dwarf of 10th magnitude, visible only through a telescope. It is named after the US astronomer Edward E Barnard (1857–1923), who discovered in 1916 that it has the fastest proper motion of any star, crossing 1 degree of sky every 350 years.

Some observations suggest that Barnard's star may be accompanied by planets.

BARNACLE

The parasitic barnacle *Loxothylacus panopaei* uses a crab as its host. The barnacle larva attaches itself to a crab and injects it with a squirming worm-shaped bag of cells. One of these cells develops into the adult barnacle that spends its life as a lump on the crab's carapace.

Barnard, Christiaan Neethling (1922–)

South African surgeon who performed the first human heart transplant 1967 at Groote Schuur Hospital in Cape Town. The 54-year-old patient lived for 18 days.

Barnard also discovered that intestinal artresia – a congenital deformity in the form of a hole in the small intestine – is the result of an insufficient supply of blood to the fetus during pregnancy. It was a fatal defect before he developed the corrective surgery.

barograph device for recording variations in atmospheric pressure. A pen, governed by the movements of an aneroid ◊barometer, makes a continuous line on a paper strip on a cylinder that rotates over a day or week to create a **barogram**, or permanent record of variations in atmospheric pressure.

barometer instrument that measures atmospheric pressure as an indication of weather. Most often used are the **mercury barometer** and the **aneroid barometer**.

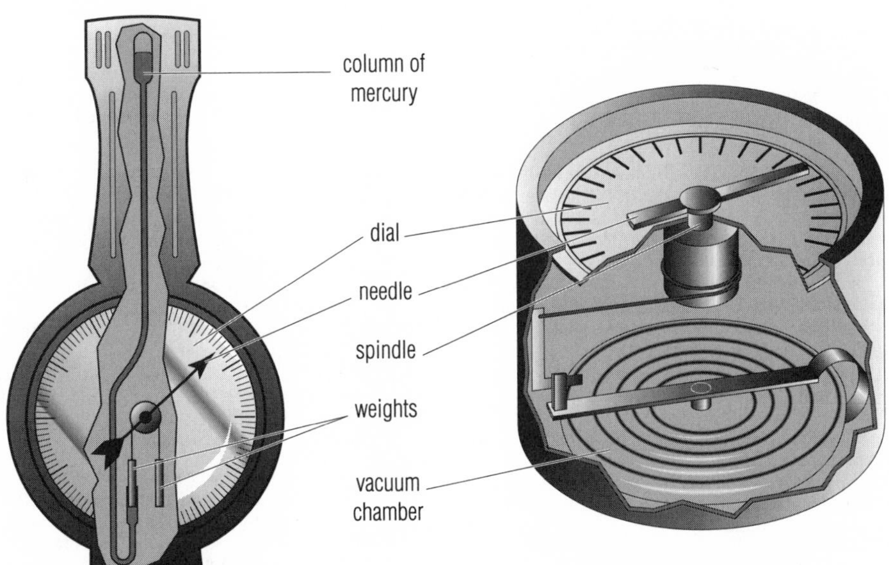

***barometer** (left) The mercury barometer and (right) the aneroid barometer. In the mercury barometer, the weight of the column of mercury is balanced by the pressure of the atmosphere on the lower end. A change in height of the column indicates a change in atmospheric pressure. In the aneroid barometer, any change of atmospheric pressure causes the metal box which contains the vacuum to be squeezed or to expand slightly. The movements of the box sides are transferred to a pointer and scale via a chain of levers.*

In a mercury barometer a column of mercury in a glass tube, roughly 0.75 m/2.5 ft high (closed at one end, curved upwards at the other), is balanced by the pressure of the atmosphere on the open end; any change in the height of the column reflects a change in pressure. In an aneroid barometer, a shallow cylindrical metal box containing a partial vacuum expands or contracts in response to changes in pressure.

baroreceptor in biology, a specialized nerve ending that is sensitive to pressure. There are baroreceptors in various regions of the heart and circulatory system (carotid sinus, aortic arch, atria, pulmonary veins, and left ventricle). Increased pressure in these structures stimulates the baroreceptors, which relay information to the medulla providing an important mechanism in the control of blood pressure.

barracuda large predatory fish *Sphyraena barracuda* found in the warmer seas of the world. It can grow over 2 m/6 ft long and has a superficial resemblance to a pike. Young fish shoal, but the older ones are solitary. The barracuda has very sharp shearing teeth and may attack people.

BARRACUDA

Barracudas are mysteriously attracted to all things yellow. This means that they may be caught by the use of yellow-feathered lines.

barrel cylindrical container, tapering at each end, made of thick strips of wood bound together by metal hoops. Barrels are used for the bulk storage of fine wines and spirits.

Barrels were made by craftsmen known as coopers, whose main skill was the shaping and bending of the wooden strips (staves) so that they fitted together without gaps when secured by the hoops. Barrels were widely used for storing liquids and dry goods until the development of plastic containers.

barrel unit of liquid capacity, the value of which depends on the liquid being measured. It is used for petroleum, a barrel of which contains 159 litres/35 imperial gallons; a barrel of alcohol contains 189 litres/41.5 imperial gallons.

barrier island long island of sand, lying offshore and parallel to the coast.

Some are over 100 km/60 mi in length. Most barrier islands are derived from marine sands piled up by shallow longshore currents that sweep sand parallel to the seashore. Others are derived from former spits, connected to land and built up by drifted sand, that were later severed from the mainland.

Often several islands lie in a continuous row offshore. Coney Island and Jones Beach near New York City are well-known examples, as is Padre Island, Texas. The Frisian Islands are barrier islands along the coast of the Netherlands.

barrier reef ◊coral reef that lies offshore, separated from the mainland by a shallow lagoon.

Barringer Crater or ***Arizona Meteor Crater*** or ***Coon Butte*** impact crater near Winslow in Arizona caused by the impact of a 50 m/165 ft iron ◊meteorite some 25,000 years ago. It is 1.2 km/0.7 mi in diameter, 200 m/660 ft deep and the walls are raised 50–60 m/165–198 ft above the surrounding desert.

It is named after the US mining engineer Daniel Barringer who proposed in 1902 that it was an impact crater rather than a volcanic feature, an idea confirmed in the 1960s by US geologist Eugene Shoemaker.

barrow *Old English beorgh 'hill or mound'* burial mound, usually composed of earth but sometimes of stones. Examples are found in many parts of the world. The two main types are **long**, dating from the Neolithic (New Stone Age), and **round**, dating from the early Bronze Age. Barrows made entirely of stones are known as cairns.

long barrow Long barrows may be mere mounds, typically higher and wider at one end. They usually contain a chamber of wood or stone slabs, or a turf-lined cavity, in which the body or bodies of the deceased were placed. Secondary chambers may be added in the sides of the mound. They are common in South England from Sussex to Dorset. Earthen (or unchambered) long barrows belong to the early and middle Neolithic, whereas others were constructed over megalithic (great stone) tombs which generally served as collective burial chambers. The stones are arranged to form one, often large, chamber with a single entrance, and are buried under a mound of earth. The remains of these stone chambers, once their earth covering has disappeared, are known as **dolmens**, and in Wales as **cromlechs**.

round barrow Round barrows belong mainly to the Bronze Age, although in historic times there are examples from the Roman period, and some of the Saxon and most of the Danish invaders were barrow-builders. In northern Europe, round barrows were sometimes built above a tree-trunk coffin in which waterlogged conditions have preserved nonskeletal material, such as those found in Denmark dating from around 1000 BC.

In Britain the most common type is the bell barrow, consisting of a circular mound enclosed by a ditch and an outside bank of earth. Other types include the bowl barrow, pond barrow, saucer barrow, ring barrow, and disc barrow, all of which are associated with the Wessex culture (early Bronze Age culture of S England dating from approximately 2000–1500 BC).

Barrows from the Roman era have a distinctive steep and conical outline, and in SE Britain usually cover the graves of wealthy merchant traders. They are also found in Belgic Gaul, where the traders had commercial links. Not all burials in the Roman era were in barrows; cemeteries were also used.

In eastern European and Asiatic areas where mobility was afforded by the horse and wagon, a new culture developed of pit graves marked by a *kurgan,* or round mound, in which a single body lay, often accompanied by grave goods which might include a wagon. These date from around 3000 BC.

boat burial The placing of a great person's body in a ship is seen in Viking burials, such as the Oseberg ship in Norway, which was buried and sealed around AD 800. Barrows were erected over boat burials during the Saxon period, and the Sutton Hoo boat burial excavated in Suffolk, England during 1938–39 was that of an East Anglian king of Saxon times.

baryon in nuclear physics, a heavy subatomic particle made up of three indivisible elementary particles called quarks. The baryons form a subclass of the ◊hadrons and comprise the nucleons (protons and neutrons) and hyperons.

basal metabolic rate (BMR) minimum amount of energy needed by the body to maintain life. It is measured when the subject is awake but resting, and includes the energy required to keep the heart beating, sustain breathing, repair tissues, and keep the brain and nerves functioning. Measuring the subject's consumption of oxygen gives an accurate value for BMR, because oxygen is needed to release energy from food.

A cruder measure of BMR estimates the amount of heat given off, some heat being released when food is used up. BMR varies from one species to another, and from males to females. In humans, it is highest in children and declines with age. Disease, including mental illness, can make it rise or fall. Hormones from the ◊thyroid gland control the BMR.

basalt commonest volcanic ◊igneous rock in the solar system. Much of the surfaces of the terrestrial planets Mercury, Venus, Earth, and Mars, as well as the Moon, are composed of basalt. Earth's ocean floor is virtually entirely made of basalt. Basalt is mafic, that is, it contains relatively little ◊silica: about 50% by weight. It is usually dark grey but can also be green, brown, or black. Its essential constituent minerals are calcium-rich ◊feldspar and calcium and magnesium-rich ◊pyroxene.

The groundmass may be glassy or finely crystalline, sometimes with large ◊crystals embedded. Basaltic lava tends to be runny and flows for great distances before solidifying. Successive eruptions of basalt have formed the great plateaus of Colorado and the Deccan plateau region of southwest India. In some places, such as Fingal's

Cave in the Inner Hebrides of Scotland and the Giant's Causeway in Antrim, Northern Ireland, shrinkage during the solidification of the molten lava caused the formation of hexagonal columns.

The dark-coloured lowland maria regions (see ◊mare) of the Moon are underlain by basalt. Lunar mare basalts have higher concentrations of titanium and zirconium and lower concentrations of volatile elements like potassium and sodium relative to terrestrial basalts. Martian basalts are characterized by low ratios of iron to manganese relative to terrestrial basalts, as judged from some martian meteorites (shergottites, a class of the **SNC** meteorites) and spacecraft analyses of rocks and soils on the Martian surface.

bascule bridge type of drawbridge in which one or two counterweighted deck members pivot upwards to allow shipping to pass underneath. One example is the double bascule Tower Bridge, London.

base in chemistry, a substance that accepts protons, such as the hydroxide ion (OH^-) and ammonia (NH_3). Bases react with acids to give a salt. Those that dissolve in water are called alkalis.

Inorganic bases are usually oxides or hydroxides of metals, which react with dilute acids to form a salt and water. A number of carbonates also react with dilute acids, additionally giving off carbon dioxide. Many organic compounds that contain nitrogen are bases.

Binary (Base 2)	*Octal (Base 8)*	*Decimal (Base 10)*	*Hexadecimal (Base 16)*
0	0	0	0
1	1	1	1
10	2	2	2
11	3	3	3
100	4	4	4
101	5	5	5
110	6	6	6
111	7	7	7
1000	10	8	8
1001	11	9	9
1010	12	10	A
1011	13	11	B
1100	14	12	C
1101	15	13	D
1110	16	14	E
1111	17	15	F
10000	20	16	10
11111111	377	255	FF
11111010001	3721	2001	7D1

base in mathematics, the number of different single-digit symbols used in a particular number system. In our usual (decimal) counting system of numbers (with symbols 0, 1, 2, 3, 4, 5, 6, 7, 8, 9) the base is 10. In the ◊binary number system, which has only the symbols 1 and 0, the base is two. A base is also a number that, when raised to a particular power (that is, when multiplied by itself a particular number of times as in $10^2 = 10 \times 10 = 100$), has a ◊logarithm equal to the power. For example, the logarithm of 100 to the base ten is 2.

In geometry, the term is used to denote the line or area on which a polygon or solid stands.

Science is an essentially anarchistic enterprise: theoretical anarchism is more humanitarian and more likely to encourage progress than its law-and-order alternatives.

Paul K Feyerabend Austrian-born US philosopher of science. *Against Method* 1975

Binary (base 2)	*Octal (base 8)*	*Decimal (base 10)*	*Hexadecimal (base 16)*
0	0	0	0
1	1	1	1
10	2	2	2
11	3	3	3
100	4	4	4
101	5	5	5
110	6	6	6
111	7	7	7
1000	10	8	8
1001	11	9	9
1010	12	10	A
1011	13	11	B
1100	14	12	C
1101	15	13	D
1110	16	14	E
1111	17	15	F
10000	20	16	10
11111111	377	255	FF
11111010001	3721	2001	7D1

base *Four different numerical systems showing the numbers 1–16, with some examples of greater numbers. In the hexadecimal (base 16) system, all numbers up to 15 must be represented by a single character. To achieve this the decimal values 10–15 are represented by the letters A–F.*

baseband in computing, type of ◊network that transmits a computer signal without modulation (conversion of ◊digital signals to ◊analogue). To be able to send a computer's signal over the analogue telephone network, a ◊modem is required to convert – or modulate – the signal. On baseband networks, which include the most popular standards such as ◊Ethernet, the signal can be sent directly, without such processing.

basenji breed of dog originating in Central Africa, where it is used for hunting. About 41 cm/16 in tall, it has pointed ears, curled tail, and short glossy coat of black or red, often with white markings. It is remarkable because it has no true bark.

base pair in biochemistry, the linkage of two base (purine or pyrimidine) molecules in ◊DNA. They are found in nucleotides, and form the basis of the genetic code.

One base lies on one strand of the DNA double helix, and one on the other, so that the base pairs link the two strands like the rungs of a ladder. In DNA, there are four bases: adenine and guanine (purines) and cytosine and thymine (pyrimidines). Adenine always pairs with thymine, and cytosine with guanine.

BASIC (acronym for ***beginner's all-purpose symbolic instruction code***) high-level computer-programming language, developed 1964, originally designed to take advantage of ◊multiuser systems (which can be used by many people at the same time). The language is relatively easy to learn and is popular among microcomputer users.

Most versions make use of an ◊interpreter, which translates BASIC into ◊machine code and allows programs to be entered and run with no intermediate translation. Some more recent versions of BASIC allow a ◊compiler to be used for this process.

basicity number of replaceable hydrogen atoms in an acid. Nitric acid (HNO_3) is monobasic, sulphuric acid (H_2SO_4) is dibasic, and phosphoric acid (H_3PO_4) is tribasic.

basic–oxygen process most widely used method of steelmaking, involving the blasting of oxygen at supersonic speed into molten pig iron.

Pig iron from a blast furnace, together with steel scrap, is poured into a converter, and a jet of oxygen is then projected into the mixture. The excess carbon in the mix and other impurities

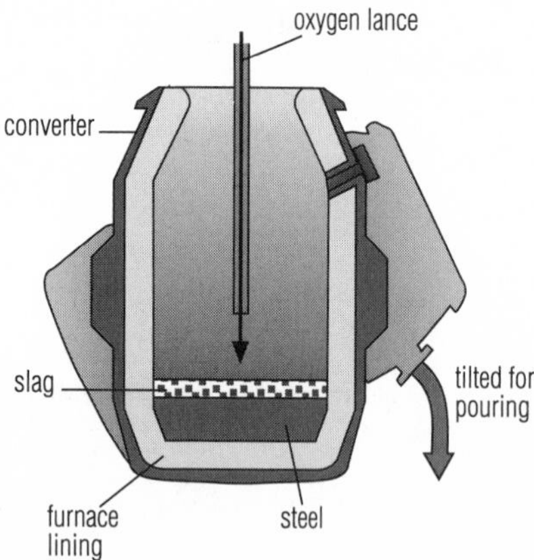

***basic–oxygen process** The basic–oxygen process is the primary method used to produce steel. Oxygen is blown at high pressure through molten pig iron and scrap steel in a converter lined with basic refractory materials. The impurities, principally carbon, quickly burn out, producing steel.*

quickly burn out or form a slag, and the converter is emptied by tilting. It takes only about 45 minutes to refine 350 tonnes/400 tons of steel. The basic–oxygen process was developed 1948 at a steelworks near the Austrian towns of Linz and Donawitz. It is a version of the ◊Bessemer process.

basidiocarp spore-bearing body, or 'fruiting body', of all basidiomycete fungi (see ◊fungus), except the rusts and smuts. A well known example is the edible mushroom *Agaricus brunnescens.* Other types include globular basidiocarps (puffballs) or flat ones that project from tree trunks (brackets). They are made up of a mass of tightly packed, intermeshed ◊hyphae.

The tips of these hyphae develop into the reproductive cells, or **basidia**, that form a fertile layer known as the hymenium, or **gills**, of the basidiocarp. Four spores are budded off from the surface of each basidium.

basil or ***sweet basil*** plant with aromatic leaves, belonging to the mint family. A native of the tropics, it is cultivated in Europe as a herb and used to flavour food. Its small white flowers appear on spikes. (Genus *Ocimum basilicum,* family Labiatae.)

basilisk Central and South American lizard, genus *Basiliscus.* It is about 50 cm/20 in long and weighs about 90 g/0.2 lb. Its rapid speed (more than 2 m/6.6 ft per second) and the formation of air pockets around the feet enable it to run short distances across the surface of water. The male has a well-developed crest on the head, body, and tail.

basket-star any ◊brittle-star of the order Phrynaphiurida, whose spiny arms branch repeatedly to form a coiled mass. Unlike other brittle-stars, which tend to be carnivorous, the hundred or so species of basket-star are suspension feeders, trapping large particles in their extended arms.

bass long-bodied scaly sea fish *Morone labrax* found in the N Atlantic and Mediterranean. They grow to 1 m/3 ft, and are often seen in shoals.

Other fish of the same family (Serranidae) are also called bass, as are North American freshwater fishes of the family Centrarchidae, such as black bass and small-mouthed bass.

basset any of several breeds of hound with a long low body and long pendulous ears, of a type originally bred in France for hunting hares by scent.

BAT CONSERVATION INTERNATIONAL

http://www.batcon.org/

Articles, photographs, and miscellaneous bat trivia, plus sound files of bat echolocation signals. As well as promoting membership of their bat society, this page contains plenty of bat-related information, including US and European species' lists and tips on photographing these elusive animals.

bat any mammal of the order Chiroptera, related to the Insectivora (hedgehogs and shrews), but differing from them in being able to fly. Bats are the only true flying mammals. Their forelimbs are developed as wings capable of rapid and sustained flight. There are two main groups of bats: **megabats**, which eat fruit, and **microbats**, which mainly eat insects. Although by no means blind, many microbats rely largely on ◊echolocation for navigation and finding prey, sending out pulses of high-pitched sound and listening for the echo. Bats are nocturnal, and those native to temperate countries hibernate in winter. There are about 977 species forming the order Chiroptera, making this the second-largest mammalian order; bats make up nearly one-quarter of the world's mammals. Although bats are widely distributed, populations have declined alarmingly and many species are now endangered.
megabats The Megachiroptera live in the tropical regions of the Old World, Australia, and the Pacific, and feed on fruit, nectar, and pollen. The hind feet have five toes with sharp hooked claws which suspend the animal head downwards when resting. There are 162 species of Megachiroptera. Relatively large, weighing up to 900 g/2 lb and with a wingspan as great as 1.5 m/5 ft, they have large eyes and a long face, earning them the name 'flying fox'. Most orient by sight.

Many rainforest trees depend on bats for pollination and seed dispersal, and around 300 bat-dependent plant species yield more than 450 economically valuable products. Some bats are keystone species on whose survival whole ecosystems may depend. Bat-pollinated flowers tend to smell of garlic, rotting vegetation, or fungus.
microbats Most bats are Microchiroptera, mainly small and insect-eating. Some eat fish as well as insects; others consume small rodents, frogs, lizards, or birds; a few feed on the blood of mammals (◊vampire bats). There are about 750 species. They roost in caves, crevices, and hollow trees. A single bat may eat 3,000

***bat** The Gambian epauletted bat* Epomophorus gambianus *is a common species in W Africa. It often roosts quite low in trees during the day, undisturbed by the presence of people. Like many tropical bats, it feeds on fruit. A young bat is visible tucked under the wing of one of the females pictured. Premaphotos Wildlife*

insects in one night. The bumblebee bat, inhabiting SE Asian rainforests, is the smallest mammal in the world.

Many microbats have poor sight and orientation and hunt their prey principally by echolocation. They have relatively large ears and many have nose-leaves, fleshy appendages around the nose and mouth, that probably help in sending or receiving the signals, which are squeaks pitched so high as to be inaudible to the human ear.

ancestors The difference in the two bat groups is so marked that many biologists believe that they must have had different ancestors: microbats descending from insectivores and megabats descending from primates. Analysis of the proteins in blood serum from megabats and primates by German biologists in 1994 showed enough similarities to suggest a close taxonomic relationship between the two groups.

biology A bat's wings consist of a thin hairless skin expansion, stretched between the four fingers of the hand, from the last finger down to the hindlimb, and from the hindlimb to the tail. The thumb is free and has a sharp claw to help in climbing. The shoulder girdle and breastbone are large, the latter being keeled, and the pelvic girdle is small. The bones of the limbs are hollow, other bones are slight, and the ribs are flattened.

An adult female bat usually rears only one pup a year, which she carries with her during flight. In species that hibernate, mating may take place before hibernation, the female storing the sperm in the genital tract throughout the winter and using it to fertilize her egg on awakening in spring.

batch file file that runs a group (batch) of commands. The most commonly used batch file is the ◊DOS start-up file ◊AUTOEXEC.BAT.

batch processing in computing, a system for processing data with little or no operator intervention. Batches of data are prepared in advance to be processed during regular 'runs' (for example, each night). This allows efficient use of the computer and is well suited to applications of a repetitive nature, such as a company payroll.

In ◊interactive computing, by contrast, data and instructions are entered while the processing program is running.

bat-eared fox small African fox *Otocyon megalotis,* with huge ears, sandy or greyish coat, black legs, and black-tipped bushy tail. They measure about 80 cm/31.5 in in length, including tail, and are 30 cm/12 in at the shoulder; weight 3–5 kg/6.5–11 lb. Bat-eared foxes feed on insects, particularly termites. There are East African and South African subspecies.

Litters of two to five cubs are born after a gestation period of 60 days. Both parents help to raise the young, sometimes aided by a cub from the previous year, but cub mortality is high as they are vulnerable to predators and disease. Cubs are fully grown at four months.

Bates eyesight training method developed by US ophthalmologist William Bates (1860–1931) to enable people to correct problems of vision without wearing glasses. The method is of proven effectiveness in relieving all refractive conditions, correcting squints, lazy eyes, and similar problems, but does not claim to treat eye disease.

bat fly wingless parasitic fly. Bat flies are tiny, bloodsucking, external parasites of bats and look rather spiderlike.

Penicillidia dufouri measures about 5 mm/0.2 in in length, is rust-brown in colour and parasitizes mouse-eared bats.

classification Bat flies are in the families Nycteribiidae and Streblidae, order Diptera, class Insecta, phylum Arthropoda.

batholith large, irregular, deep-seated mass of intrusive ◊igneous rock, usually granite, with an exposed surface of more than 100 sq km/40 sq mi. The mass forms by the intrusion or upswelling of magma (molten rock) through the surrounding rock. Batholiths form the core of some large mountain ranges like the Sierra Nevada of western North America.

According to ◊plate tectonic theory, magma rises in subduction zones along continental margins where one plate sinks beneath another. The solidified magma becomes the central axis of a rising mountain range, resulting in the deformation (folding and overthrusting) of rocks on either side. Gravity measurements indicate that the downward extent or thickness of many batholiths is some 6–9 mi/10–15 km.

Bates, H(enry) W(alter) (1825–1892)

English naturalist and explorer. He spent 11 years collecting animals and plants in South America and identified 8,000 new species of insects. He made a special study of camouflage in animals, and his observation of insect imitation of species that are unpleasant to predators is known as 'Batesian mimicry'.

Mary Evans Picture Library

bathyal zone upper part of the ocean, which lies on the continental shelf at a depth of between 200 m/650 ft and 2,000 m/6,500 ft.

Bathyal zones (both temperate and tropical) have greater biodiversity than coral reefs, according to a 1995 study by the Natural History Museum in London. Maximum biodiversity occurs between 1,000 m/3,280 ft and 3,000 m/9,800 ft.

bathyscaph or ***bathyscaphe*** or ***bathyscape*** deep-sea diving apparatus used for exploration at great depths in the ocean. In 1960, Jacques Piccard and Don Walsh took the bathyscaph *Trieste* to a depth of 10,917 m/35,820 ft in the Challenger Deep in the ◊Mariana Trench off the island of Guam in the Pacific Ocean.

battery any energy-storage device allowing release of electricity on demand. It is made up of one or more electrical ◊cells. Primary-cell batteries are disposable; secondary-cell batteries, or ◊accumulators, are rechargeable. Primary-cell batteries are an extremely uneconomical form of energy, since they produce only 2% of the power used in their manufacture. It is dangerous to try to recharge a primary-cell battery.

The common **dry cell** is a primary-cell battery based on the Leclanché cell and consists of a central carbon electrode immersed

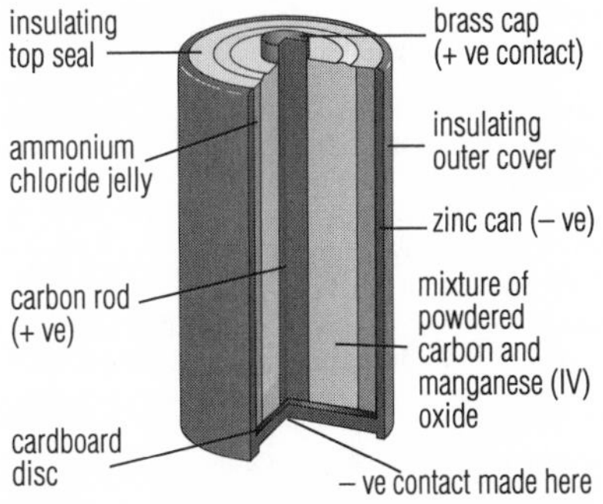

battery *The common dry cell relies on chemical changes occurring between the electrodes – the central carbon rod and the outer zinc casing – and the ammonium chloride electrolyte to produce electricity. The mixture of carbon and manganese is used to increase the life of the cell.*

in a paste of manganese dioxide and ammonium chloride as the electrolyte. The zinc casing forms the other electrode.

The lead–acid **car battery** is a secondary-cell battery. The car's generator continually recharges the battery when the engine is running. It consists of sets of lead (positive) and lead peroxide (negative) plates in an electrolyte of sulphuric acid (◊battery acid). Hydrogen cells and sodium–sulphur batteries were developed in 1996 to allow cars to run entirely on battery power for up to 60 km/100 mi.

The introduction of rechargeable nickel–cadmium batteries has revolutionized portable electronic news gathering (sound recording, video) and information processing (computing). These batteries offer a stable, short-term source of power free of noise and other electrical hazards.

battery acid ◊sulphuric acid of approximately 70% concentration used in lead–acid cells (as found in car batteries).

The chemical reaction within the battery that is responsible for generating electricity also causes a change in the acid's composition. This can be detected as a change in its specific gravity: in a fully charged battery the acid's specific gravity is 1.270–1.290; in a half-charged battery it is 1.190–1.210; in a flat battery it is 1.110–1.130.

baud in engineering, a unit of electrical signalling speed equal to one pulse per second, measuring the rate at which signals are sent between electronic devices such as telegraphs and computers; 300 baud is about 300 words a minute.

Bauds were used as a measure to identify the speed of ◊modems until the early 1990s because at the lower modem speeds available then the baud rate generally equalled the rate of transmission measured in ◊bps (bits per second). At higher speeds, this is not the case, and modem speeds now are generally quoted in bps.

Baudot code five-bit code developed in France by engineer Emil Baudot (1845–1903) in the 1870s. It is still in use for telex.

bauxite principal ore of ◊aluminium, consisting of a mixture of hydrated aluminium oxides and hydroxides, generally contaminated with compounds of iron, which give it a red colour. It is formed by the ◊chemical weathering of rocks in tropical climates. Chief producers of bauxite are Australia, Guinea, Jamaica, Russia, Kazakhstan, Surinam, and Brazil.

To extract aluminium from bauxite, high temperatures (about 800°C/1,470°F) are needed to make the ore molten. Strong electric currents are then passed through the molten ore. The process is only economical if cheap electricity is readily available, usually from a hydroelectric plant.

bay any of various species of ◊laurel tree. The aromatic evergreen leaves are used for flavouring in cookery. There is also a golden-leaved variety. (Genus *Laurus,* family Lauraceae.)

Bayesian statistics form of statistics that uses the knowledge of prior probability together with the probability of actual data to determine posterior probabilities, using Bayes' theorem.

Bayes' theorem in statistics, a theorem relating the ◊probability of particular events taking place to the probability that events conditional upon them have occurred.

For example, the probability of picking an ace at random out of a pack of cards is $\frac{4}{52}$. If two cards are picked out, the probability of the second card being an ace is conditional on the first card: if the first card is an ace the probability of drawing a second ace will be $\frac{3}{51}$; if not it will be $\frac{4}{51}$. Bayes' theorem gives the probability that given that the second card is an ace, the first card is also.

BCE abbreviation for **before the Common Era**, used with dates instead of BC.

B cell or ***B lymphocyte*** immune cell that produces antibodies. Each B cell produces just one type of ◊antibody, specific to a single ◊antigen. Lymphocytes are related to ◊T cells.

BCG (abbreviation for ***bacille Calmette-Guérin***), bacillus injected as a vaccine to confer active immunity to ◊tuberculosis (TB).

BCG was developed by Albert Calmette and Camille Guérin in France in 1921 from live bovine TB bacilli. These bacteria were bred in the laboratory over many generations until they became attenuated (weakened). Each inoculation contains just enough live, attenuated bacilli to provoke an immune response: the formation of specific antibodies. The vaccine provides protection for 50–80% of infants vaccinated.

beach strip of land bordering the sea, normally consisting of boulders and pebbles on exposed coasts or sand on sheltered coasts. It is usually defined by the high- and low-water marks. A berm, a ridge of sand and pebbles, may be found at the farthest point that the water reaches.

The material of the beach consists of a rocky debris eroded from exposed rocks and headlands, or carried in by rivers. The material is transported to the beach, and along the beach, by waves that hit the coastline at an angle, resulting in a net movement of the material in one particular direction. This movement is known as **longshore drift**. Attempts are often made to halt longshore drift by erecting barriers (groynes), at right angles to the movement. Pebbles are worn into round shapes by being battered against one another by wave action and the result is called **shingle**. The finer material, the **sand**, may be subsequently moved about by the wind, forming sand dunes.

Apart from the natural process of longshore drift, a beach may be threatened by the commercial use of sand and aggregate, by the mineral industry – since particles of metal ore are often concentrated into workable deposits by the wave action – and by pollution (for example, by oil spilled or dumped at sea).

beagle short-haired hound with pendant ears, sickle tail, and a bell-like voice, bred for hunting hares on foot ('beagling').

beak horn-covered projecting jaws of a bird (see ◊bill), or other horny jaws such as those of the octopus, platypus, or tortoise.

Beaker people prehistoric people thought to have been of Iberian origin, who spread out over Europe from the 3rd millennium BC. They were skilled in metalworking, and are identified by their use of distinctive earthenware drinking vessels with various designs.

A type of beaker with an inverted bell-shaped profile was widely distributed throughout Europe. These bell beakers are associated with the spread of alcohol consumption, probably mead. The Beaker people favoured individual inhumation (burial of the intact body), often in round ◊barrows, with an associated set of small stone and metal artefacts, or secondary burials in some form of chamber tomb. A beaker typically accompanied male burials, possibly to hold a drink for the deceased on their final journey. The inclusion of flint, later metal, daggers in grave goods may signify a warrior, and suggests that the incursion of Bell Beaker culture may have come as an intrusion into traditional pre-existing cultures.

beam balance instrument for measuring mass (or weight). A simple form consists of a beam pivoted at its midpoint with a pan hanging at each end. The mass to be measured, in one pan, is compared with a variety of standard masses placed in the other. When the beam is balanced, the masses' turning effects or moments under gravity, and hence the masses themselves, are equal.

beam engine engine that works by providing an up and down motion to one end of a beam, which is translated into working machinery at the other end. Beam machines may be powered by a number of sources, including steam and water.

beam weapon weapon capable of destroying a target by means of a high-energy beam. Beam weapons similar to the 'death ray' of science fiction have been explored, most notably during Ronald Reagan's presidential term in the 1980s in the USA.

The **high-energy laser** (HEL) produces a beam of high accuracy that burns through the surface of its target. The **charged particle beam** uses either electrons or protons, which have been accelerated almost to the speed of light, to slice through its target.

bean seed of a large number of leguminous plants (see ◊legume). Beans are rich in nitrogen compounds and proteins and are grown both for human consumption and as food for cattle and horses. Varieties of bean are grown throughout Europe, the USA, South America, China, Japan, SE Asia, and Australia.

The broad bean (*Vicia faba*) has been cultivated in Europe since prehistoric times. The French bean, kidney bean, or haricot (*Phaseolus vulgaris*) is probably of South American origin; the runner bean (*P. coccineus*) is closely related to it, but differs in its climbing habit. Among beans of warmer countries are the lima or butter bean (*P. lunatus*) of South America; the soya bean (*Glycine max*), extensively used in China and Japan; and the winged bean (*Psophocarpus tetragonolobus*) of SE Asia. The tuberous root of the winged bean has potential as a main crop in tropical areas where protein deficiency is common. The Asian mung bean (*Phaseolus mungo*) yields the bean sprouts used in Chinese cookery. Canned baked beans are usually a variety of (*P. vulgaris*), which grows well in the USA.

BEAR DEN

http://www.nature-net.com/bears/index.html

Invaluable resource for information on all types of bears. As well as general information on the evolution and history of bears in general, there are more specific details on each of the eight species of bear, including habitat, reproduction, food, and much more. The site also has photographs and sound effects.

bear large mammal with a heavily built body, short powerful limbs, and a very short tail. Bears breed once a year, producing one to four cubs. In northern regions they hibernate, and the young are born in the winter den. They are found mainly in North America and N Asia. The skin of the polar bear is black to conserve 80–90% of the solar energy trapped and channelled down the hollow hairs of its fur.

Bears walk on the soles of the feet and have long, nonretractable claws. The bear family, Ursidae, is related to carnivores such as dogs and weasels, and all are capable of killing prey. (The panda is probably related to both bears and raccoons.)

species There are seven species of bear. The **brown bear** *Ursus arctos* formerly ranged across most of Europe, N Asia, and North America, but is now reduced in number. It varies in size from under 2 m/7 ft long in parts of the Old World to 2.8 m/9 ft long and 780 kg/1,700 lb in Alaska. The **grizzly bear** is a North American variety of this species, and another subspecies, the **Kodiak bear** of Alaska, is the largest living land carnivore. The white **polar bear** *Thalarctos maritimus* is up to 2.5 m/8 ft long, has furry undersides to the feet, and feeds mainly on seals. It is found in the north polar region. The North American **black bear** *Euarctos americanus* and the **Asian black bear** *Selenarctos thibetanus* are smaller, only about 1.6 m/5 ft long. The latter has a white V-mark on its chest. The **spectacled bear** *Tremarctos ornatus* of the Andes is similarly sized, as is the **sloth bear** *Melursus ursinus* of India and Sri Lanka, which has a shaggy coat and uses its claws and protrusile lips to obtain termites, one of its preferred foods. The smallest bear is the Malaysian **sun bear** *Helarctos malayanus*, rarely more than 1.2 m/4 ft long, a good climber, whose favourite food is honey.

threat of extinction Of the seven species of bear, five are currently reckoned to be endangered and all apart from the polar bear and the American black bear are in decline. The population of brown bears in the Pyrenees was estimated at eight in 1994, and it is feared they will be extinct in 20 years unless new bears are introduced. In May 1996 two female Slovenian brown bears were released into the central Pyrenees; the Slovenian brown bear is closest genetically to the Pyrenean one.

In 1992, American black bears were upgraded to Appendix 2 of CITES (Convention on International Trade in Endangered Species) to stem the trade in their gall bladders, which are used in Asian traditional medicine to treat liver disease. The gall bladders contain an active substance, ursodiol, which is tapped through surgically-implanted tubes. Although an inexpensive synthetic version of ursodiol is available, in 1995 there were at least 10,000 bears being kept in farms in China for their gall bladders, for which many people still prefer to pay thousands of dollars. Trade in Asian black bears and their parts is illegal.

bearberry any of a group of evergreen trailing shrubs belonging to the heath family, found in high and rocky places. Most bearberries are North American but *Arctostaphylos uva-ursi* is also found in Asia and Europe in northern mountainous regions. It has small pink flowers in spring, followed by red berries that are dry but edible. (Genus *Arctostaphylos*, family Ericaceae.)

bearded collie breed of British ◊sheepdog with shaggy hair on its muzzle. Standing about 53 cm/21 in tall, it has a long coat, which is often grey, or sometimes sandy, with white on the head, chest, and feet.

Bear, Great and Little common names (and translations of the Latin) for the constellations ◊Ursa Major and ◊Ursa Minor respectively.

bearing device used in a machine to allow free movement between two parts, typically the rotation of a shaft in a housing.

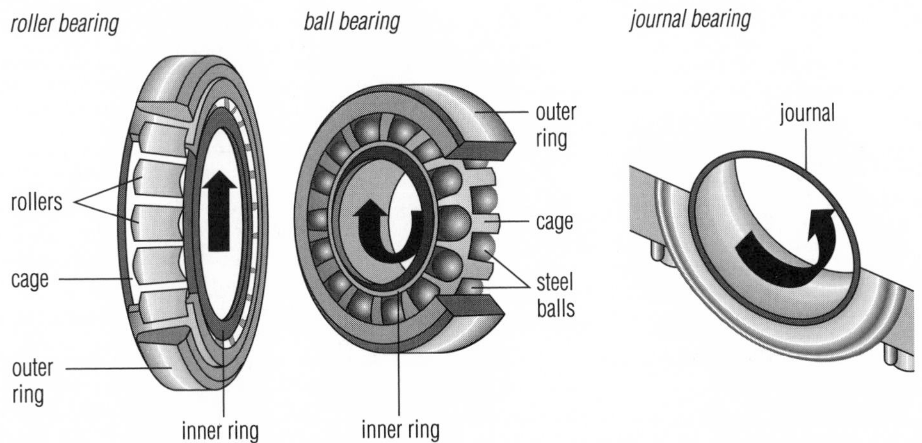

bearing *Three types of bearing. The roller and the ball bearing are similar, differing only in the shape of the parts that roll when the middle shaft turns. The simpler journal bearing consists of a sleeve, or journal, lining the surface of the rotating shaft. The bearing is lubricated to reduce friction and wear.*

Ball bearings consist of two rings, one fixed to a housing, one to the rotating shaft. Between them is a set, or race, of steel balls. They are widely used to support shafts, as in the spindle in the hub of a bicycle wheel.

The **sleeve**, or **journal bearing**, is the simplest bearing. It is a hollow cylinder, split into two halves. It is used for the big-end and main bearings on a car ◊crankshaft.

In some machinery the balls of ball bearings are replaced by cylindrical rollers or thinner **needle bearings**.

In precision equipment such as watches and aircraft instruments, bearings may be made from material such as ruby and are known as **jewel bearings**.

For some applications bearings made from nylon and other plastics are used. They need no lubrication because their surfaces are naturally waxy.

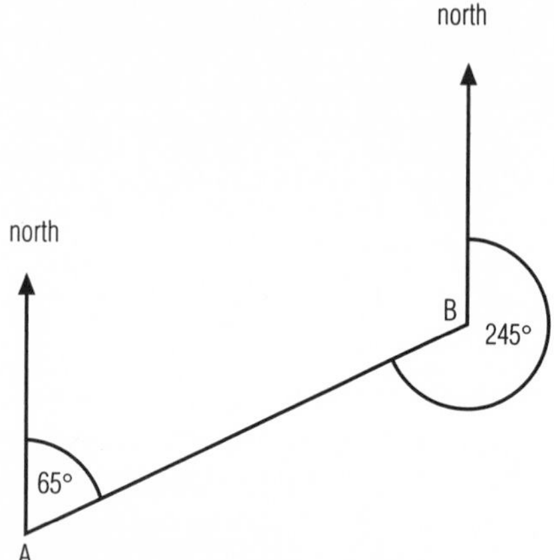

the bearing of B from A is 065°
the backbearing, or bearing of A from B, is 245°

***bearing** A bearing is the direction of a fixed point, or the path of a moving object, from a point of observation on the Earth's surface, expressed as an angle from the north. In the diagram, the bearing of a point A from an observer at B is the angle between the line BA and the north line through B, measured in a clockwise direction from the north line.*

bearing the direction of a fixed point, or the path of a moving object, from a point of observation on the Earth's surface, expressed as an angle from the north. Bearings are taken by ◊compass and are measured in degrees (°), given as three-digit numbers increasing clockwise. For instance, north is 000°, northeast is 045°, south is 180°, and southwest is 225°.

True north differs slightly from magnetic north (the direction in which a compass needle points), hence NE may be denoted as 045M or 045T, depending on whether the reference line is magnetic (M) or true (T) north. True north also differs slightly from grid north since it is impossible to show a spherical Earth on a flat map.

beat frequency in musical acoustics, fluctuation produced when two notes of nearly equal pitch or ◊frequency are heard together. Beats result from the ◊interference between the sound waves of the notes. The frequency of the beats equals the difference in frequency of the notes.

Beaufort scale system of recording wind velocity (speed), devised by Francis Beaufort in 1806. It is a numerical scale ranging from 0 to 17, calm being indicated by 0 and a hurricane by 12; 13–17 indicate degrees of hurricane force.

In 1874 the scale received international recognition; it was modified in 1926. Measurements are made at 10 m/33 ft above ground level.

BEAVER

By building dams, beavers create extremely fertile living conditions for other animals. The ponds formed by the dams trap a wealth of nourishing minerals. They are also full of zooplankton, the combined mass of which is a thousand times greater than that found elsewhere.

beaver aquatic rodent with webbed hind feet, a broad flat scaly tail, and thick waterproof fur. It has very large incisor teeth and fells trees to feed on the bark and to use the logs to construct the 'lodge', in which the young are reared, food is stored, and much of the winter is spent. There are two species, the Canadian *Castor canadensis* and the European *C. fiber.* They grow up to 1.4 m/4.6 ft in length and weigh about 20 kg/44 lb.

Beavers are monogamous and a pair will produce a litter of twins each year. Their territory consists of about 3 km/2 mi of river. Beavers can construct dams on streams, and thus modify the environment considerably; beaver ponds act as traps for minerals and provide fertile living conditions for other species – zooplankton biomass may be 1,000 times greater within a beaver pond than elsewhere. Beavers once ranged across Europe, N Asia, and North America, but in Europe now only survive where they are protected, and are reduced elsewhere, partly through trapping for their fur.

becquerel SI unit (symbol Bq) of ◊radioactivity, equal to one radioactive disintegration (change in the nucleus of an atom when a particle or ray is given off) per second.

Beaufort Scale

Number and description	*Features*	*Air speed*	
		kph	*mph*
0 calm	smoke rises vertically; water smooth	0–2	0–1
1 light air	smoke shows wind direction; water ruffled	2–5	1–3
2 light breeze	leaves rustle; wind felt on face	6–11	4–7
3 gentle breeze	loose paper blows around	12–19	8–12
4 moderate breeze	branches sway	20–29	13–18
5 fresh breeze	small trees sway, leaves blown off	30–39	19–24
6 strong breeze	whistling in telephone wires; sea spray from waves	40–50	25–31
7 near gale	large trees sway	51–61	32–38
8 gale	twigs break from trees	62–74	39–46
9 strong gale	branches break from trees	75–87	47–54
10 storm	trees uprooted; weak buildings collapse	88–101	55–63
11 violent storm	widespread damage	102–117	64–73
12 hurricane	widespread structural damage	above 118	above 74

Becquerel, (Antoine) Henri (1852–1908)

French physicist. He discovered penetrating radiation coming from uranium salts, the first indication of radioactivity, and shared a Nobel prize with Marie and Pierre Curie in 1903.

Mary Evans Picture Library

The becquerel is much smaller than the previous standard unit, the ◊curie (3.7×10^{10} Bq). It is named after French physicist Henri Becquerel.

bed in geology, a single ◊sedimentary rock unit with a distinct set of physical characteristics or contained fossils, readily distinguishable from those of beds above and below. Well-defined partings called **bedding planes** separate successive beds or strata.

The depth of a bed can vary from a fraction of a centimetre to several metres or yards, and can extend over any area. The term is also used to indicate the floor beneath a body of water (lake bed) and a layer formed by a fall of particles (ash bed).

bedbug flattened wingless red-brown insect *Cimex lectularius* with piercing mouthparts. It hides by day in crevices or bedclothes and emerges at night to suck human blood.

Bedlington breed of ◊terrier with a short body, long legs, and curly hair, usually grey, named after a district of Northumberland, England.

bee four-winged insect of the superfamily Apoidea in the order Hymenoptera, usually with a sting. There are over 12,000 species, of which fewer than 1 in 20 are social in habit. The **hive bee** or **honeybee** *Apis mellifera* establishes perennial colonies of about 80,000, the majority being infertile females (workers), with a few larger fertile males (drones), and a single very large fertile female (the queen). Worker bees live for no more than a few weeks, while a drone may live a few months, and a queen several years. Queen honeybees lay two kinds of eggs: fertilized, female eggs, which have two sets of chromosomes and develop into workers or queens, and unfertilized, male eggs, which have only one set of chromosomes and develop into drones.

Bees transmit information to each other about food sources by 'dances', each movement giving rise to sound impulses which are picked up by tiny hairs on the back of the bee's head, the orientation of the dance also having significance. They use the Sun in navigation (see ◊migration). Besides their use in crop pollination and production of honey and wax, bees (by a measure of contaminants brought back to their hives) can provide an inexpensive and effective monitor of industrial and other pollution of the atmosphere and soil.

The most familiar species is the ◊bumblebee, genus *Bombus,* which is larger and stronger than the hive bee and so is adapted to fertilize plants in which the pollen and nectar lie deep, as in red clover; they can work in colder weather than the hive bee.

Social bees, apart from the bumblebee and the hive bee, include the stingless South American **vulture bee** *Trigona hypogea,* **discovered in 1982, which is solely carnivorous.**

Solitary bees include species useful in pollinating orchards in spring, and may make their nests in tunnels under the ground or in hollow plant stems; 'cuckoo' bees lay their eggs in the nests of bumblebees, which they closely resemble.

The killer bees of South America are a hybrid type, created when an African subspecies of honeybee escaped from a research establishment in Brazil in 1957. They mated with, and supplanted, the honeybees of European origin in most of South and Central America, and by 1990 had spread as far north as Texas, USA. As well as being more productive and resistant to disease than European honeybees, they also defend their hives more aggressively, in larger numbers, and for a greater length of time than other honeybees. However, their stings are no more venomous, and although they have killed hundreds of thousands of animals and probably more than 1,000 people, most individuals survive an attack, and almost all deaths have occurred where the victim has somehow been prevented from fleeing.

Most bees are passive unless disturbed, but some species are aggressive. One bee sting may be fatal to a person who is allergic to them, but this is comparatively rare (about 1.5% of the population), and most adults can survive 300–500 stings without treatment. A vaccine treatment against bee stings, which uses concentrated venom, has been developed.

BEEKEEPING

http://weber.u.washington.edu/~jlks/bee.html

Everything you could possibly wish to know about beekeeping is here. There are, for example, sections on the diseases afflicting bees, as well as advice on honey and mead-making. The site also includes an archived list of articles and some multimedia items.

beech one of several European hardwood trees or related trees growing in Australasia and South America. The common beech (*Fagus sylvaticus*), found in European forests, has a smooth grey trunk and edible nuts, or 'mast', which are used as animal feed or processed for oil. The timber is used in furniture. (Genera *Fagus* and *Nothofagus,* family Fagaceae.)

bee-eater brightly-coloured bird *Merops apiaster,* family Meropidae, order Coraciiformes, found in Africa, S Europe, and Asia. Bee-eaters are slender, with chestnut, yellow, and blue-green plumage, a long bill and pointed wings, and a flight like that of the swallow, which they resemble in shape. They feed on bees, wasps, and other insects, and nest in colonies in holes dug out with their long bills in sandy river banks.

bee louse any of a number of species of wingless flies parasitic on bees. They look more like lice than flies. Most have claws at the ends of their legs.

classification Bee lice are in the family Braulidae, order Diptera (suborder Cyclorrhapha), class Insecta, phylum Arthropoda.

Bee lice lay their eggs on the walls or under the cappings of honey cells. The larvae work their way from one cell to the next, feeding on the honey. In small numbers the bee louse is insignificant; if many are present however, they can be serious pests to bees and beekeepers.

Braula caeca is rust-brown and about 1.5 mm/0.06 in long. It is a parasite of honeybees.

beet any of several plants belonging to the goosefoot family, used as food crops. One variety of the common beet (*Beta vulgaris*) is used in to produce sugar and another, the mangelwurzel, is grown as a cattle feed. The beetroot, or red beet (*B. rubra*), is a salad plant. (Genus *Beta,* family Chenopodiaceae.)

beetfly small grey fly with black hairs. Its maggots feed on beet leaves. As soon as the maggots hatch they begin to feed, continuing for one month, when they turn into chestnut-brown pupae. The flies emerge a fortnight later.

classification The beet fly *Anthomyia betae* is in the family Anthomyiidae, order Diptera, class Insecta, phylum Arthropoda.

beetle common name of insects in the order Coleoptera (Greek 'sheath-winged') with leathery forewings folding down in a protective sheath over the membranous hindwings, which are those used for flight. They pass through a complete metamorphosis. They include some of the largest and smallest of all insects: the largest is the **Hercules beetle** *Dynastes hercules* of the South American rainforests, 15 cm/6 in long; the smallest is only 0.05 cm/0.02 in long. Comprising more than 50% of the animal kingdom, beetles number some 370,000 named species, with many not yet described.

BEETLE

When it jumps, the flea beetle accelerates at 260 times more than gravity while spinning head over heels about 70 times per second. Flea beetles always land the right way up.

Beetles are found in almost every land and freshwater habitat, and feed on almost anything edible. Examples include **click beetle** or **skipjack** species of the family Elateridae, so called because if they fall on their backs they right themselves with a jump and a loud click; the larvae, known as **wireworms**, feed on the roots of crops. In some tropical species of Elateridae the beetles have luminous organs between the head and abdomen and are known as **fireflies**. The potato pest **Colorado beetle** *Leptinotarsa decemlineata* is striped in black and yellow. The **blister beetle** *Lytta vesicatoriaf,* a shiny green species from S Europe, was once sold pulverized as an aphrodisiac and contains the toxin cantharidin. The larvae of the **furniture beetle** *Anobium punctatum* and the **deathwatch beetle** *Xestobium rufovillosum* and their relatives are serious pests of structural timbers and furniture (see ◊woodworm).

begonia any of a group of tropical and subtropical plants. They have fleshy and succulent leaves, and some have large, brilliant flowers. There are numerous species in the tropics, especially in South America and India. (Genus *Begonia,* family Begoniaceae.)

behaviourism school of psychology originating in the USA, of which the leading exponent was John B Watson.

Behaviourists maintain that all human activity can ultimately be explained in terms of conditioned reactions or reflexes and habits formed in consequence. Leading behaviourists include Ivan ◊Pavlov and B F Skinner.

It is a good morning exercise for a research scientist to discard a pet hypothesis every day before breakfast. It keeps him young.

KONRAD LORENZ Austrian zoologist. *The So-Called Evil*

behaviour therapy in psychology, the application of behavioural principles, derived from learning theories, to the treatment of clinical conditions such as ◊phobias, ◊obsessions, and sexual and interpersonal problems.

The symptoms of these disorders are regarded as learned patterns of behaviour that therapy can enable the patient to unlearn. For example, in treating a phobia, the patient is taken gradually into the feared situation in about 20 sessions until the fear noticeably reduces.

bel unit of sound measurement equal to ten ◊decibels. It is named after Scottish scientist Alexander Graham Bell.

belemnite extinct relative of the squid, with rows of little hooks rather than suckers on the arms. The parts of belemnites most frequently found as fossils are the bullet-shaped shells that were within the body. Like squid, these animals had an ink sac which could be used to produce a smokescreen when attacked.

Belgian sheepdog any of four varieties of herding and guarding dog developed in Belgium: the Groenedael, Turvuren, Malinois, and Lakenois. Similar in build and size, they stand about 62 cm/24 in tall, the main difference between them being the variations in colour and type of coat.

The Groenedael has a long all-black coat; the Tervuren has a long tawny coat with black markings on the face; the Malinois is similar to the Tervuren in colour, but with a short coat; the Lakenois also shares the Tervuren's colouring, but with a short, coarse, wavy coat.

Bell, Alexander Graham (1847–1922)

Scottish-born US scientist and inventor. He was the first person ever to transmit speech from one point to another by electrical means. This invention – the telephone – was made in 1876. Later Bell experimented with a type of phonograph and, in aeronautics, invented the tricycle undercarriage.

Bell also invented a photophone, which used selenium crystals to apply the telephone principle to transmitting words in a beam of light. He thus achieved the first wireless transmission of speech.

Mary Evans Picture Library

BELL, ALEXANDER GRAHAM

Alexander Graham Bell's invention of the telephone stemmed from his interest in hearing defects. His wife was profoundly deaf. On the day that Bell was buried in 1922, the entire telephone network in the USA was closed down for one minute in tribute.

belladonna or ***deadly nightshade*** poisonous plant belonging to the nightshade family, found in Europe and Asia. It grows to 1.5 m/5 ft in height, with dull green leaves growing in unequal pairs, up to 20 cm/8 in long, and single purplish flowers that produce deadly black berries. Drugs are made from the leaves. (*Atropa belladonna,* family Solanaceae.)

The dried powdered leaves are used to produce the drugs atropine and hyoscine. Belladonna extract acts medicinally as an anticholinergic (blocking the passage of certain nerve impulses), and is highly poisonous in large doses.

Bell Burnell, (Susan) Jocelyn (1943–) British astronomer. In 1967 she discovered the first ◊pulsar (rapidly flashing star) with Antony Hewish and colleagues at Cambridge University, England.

bellflower general name for many plants with bell-shaped flowers. The ◊harebell (*Campanula rotundifolia*) is a wild bellflower. The Canterbury bell (*C. medium*) is the garden variety, originally from S Europe. (Genus *Campanula,* family Campanulaceae.)

bells nautical term applied to half-hours of watch. A day is divided into seven watches, five of four hours each and two, called dogwatches, of two hours. Each half-hour of each watch is indicated by the striking of a bell, eight bells signalling the end of the watch.

benchmark in computing, a measure of the performance of a piece of equipment or software, usually consisting of a standard program or suite of programs. Benchmarks can indicate whether a computer is powerful enough to perform a particular task, and so enable machines to be compared. However, they provide only a very rough guide to practical performance, and may lead manufacturers to design systems that get high scores with the artificial benchmark programs but do not necessarily perform well with day-to-day programs or data.

bends or ***compressed-air sickness*** or ***caisson disease*** popular name for a syndrome seen in deep-sea divers, arising from too rapid a release of nitrogen from solution in their blood. If a diver surfaces too quickly, nitrogen that had dissolved in the blood under increasing water pressure is suddenly released, forming bubbles in the bloodstream and causing pain (the 'bends') and paralysis. Immediate treatment is gradual decompression in a decompression chamber, whilst breathing pure oxygen.

Benioff zone seismically active zone inclined from a deep sea trench beneath a continent or continental margin. Earthquakes along Benioff zones define the top surfaces of plates of ◊lithosphere that descend in to the mantle beneath another, overlying plate. The zone is named after Hugo Benioff, a US seismologist who first described this feature.

bent or **bent grass** any of a group of grasses. Creeping bent grass (*Agrostis stolonifera*), also known as fiorin, is common in N North America, Europe, and Asia, including lowland Britain. It spreads by ◊runners and has large attractive clusters (panicles) of yellow or purple flowers on thin stalks, like oats. It is often used on lawns and golf courses. (Genus *Agrostris,* family Gramineae.)

benzaldehyde C_6H_5CHO colourless liquid with the characteristic odour of almonds. It is used as a solvent and in the making of perfumes and dyes. It occurs in certain leaves, such as the cherry, laurel, and peach, and in a combined form in certain nuts and kernels. It can be extracted from such natural sources, but is usually made from ◊toluene.

Benzedrine trade name for ◊amphetamine, a stimulant drug.

benzene C_6H_6 clear liquid hydrocarbon of characteristic odour, occurring in coal tar. It is used as a solvent and in the synthesis of many chemicals.

The benzene molecule consists of a ring of six carbon atoms, all of which are in a single plane, and it is one of the simplest ◊cyclic compounds. Benzene is the simplest of a class of compounds collectively known as **aromatic compounds**. Some are considered carcinogenic (cancer-inducing).

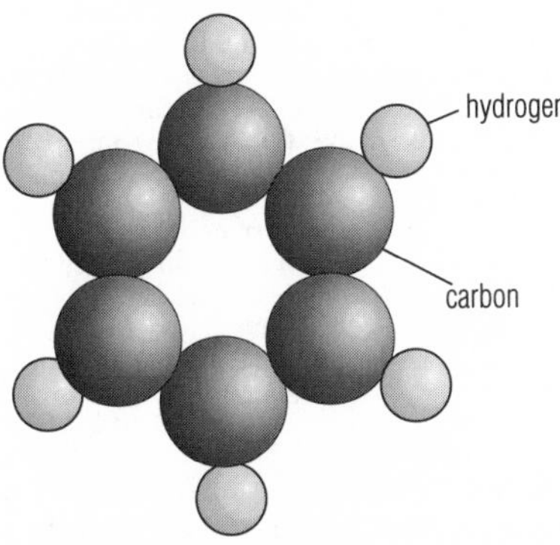

***benzene** The molecule of benzene consists of six carbon atoms arranged in a ring, with six hydrogen atoms attached. The benzene ring structure is found in many naturally occurring organic compounds.*

benzodiazepine any of a group of mood-altering drugs (tranquillizers), for example Librium and Valium. They are addictive and interfere with the process by which information is transmitted between brain cells, and various side effects arise from continued use. They were originally developed as muscle relaxants, and then excessively prescribed in the West as anxiety-relieving drugs.

Today the benzodiazepines are recommended only for short-term use in alleviating severe anxiety or insomnia.

benzoic acid C_6H_5COOH white crystalline solid, sparingly soluble in water, that is used as a preservative for certain foods and as an antiseptic. It is obtained chemically by the direct oxidation of benzaldehyde and occurs in certain natural resins, some essential oils, and as hippuric acid.

benzoin resin (thick liquid that hardens in the air) obtained by making cuts in the bark of the tree *Styrax benzoin,* which grows in the East Indies. Benzoin is used in cosmetics, perfumes, and incense.

benzpyrene one of a number of organic compounds associated with a particular polycyclic ring structure. Benzpyrenes are present in coal tar at low levels and are considered carcinogenic (cancer-inducing). Traces of benzpyrenes are present in wood smoke, and this has given rise to some concern about the safety of naturally smoked foods.

bergamot small evergreen tree belonging to the rue family. A fragrant citrus-scented essence is obtained from the rind of its fruit and used as a perfume and food flavouring, for example in Earl Grey tea. The sole source of supply is S Calabria, Italy, but the name comes from the town of Bergamo, in Lombardy. (*Citrus bergamia,* family Rutaceae.)

Bergmann musquete ***Machine Pistol 18*** German automatic weapon of World War I, the forerunner of the modern submachine gun. A simple automatic weapon with a short barrel and wooden stock, it fired the standard 9 mm pistol cartridge at 400 rounds per minute.

It was first issued in 1916 for trench defence, but the adoption of the infiltration tactic by General von Hutier led to the weapon being issued to 'Storm Troops' since it provided the ideal combination of firepower and portability demanded in this role.

beriberi nutritional disorder occurring mostly in the tropics and resulting from a deficiency of vitamin B_1 (◊thiamine). The disease takes two forms: in one ◊oedema (waterlogging of the tissues) occurs; in the other there is severe emaciation. There is nerve degeneration in both forms and many victims succumb to heart failure.

Beringia or **Bering Land Bridge** former land bridge 1,600 km/1,000 mi wide between Asia and North America; it existed during the ice ages that occurred before 35,000 BC and during the period 24,000–9,000 BC. It is now covered by the Bering Strait and Chukchi Sea.

berkelium synthesized, radioactive, metallic element of the actinide series, symbol Bk, atomic number 97, relative atomic mass 247.

It was first produced in 1949 by Glenn Seaborg and his team, at the University of California at Berkeley, USA, after which it is named.

Bernoulli's principle law stating that the pressure of a fluid varies inversely with speed, an increase in speed producing a decrease in pressure (such as a drop in hydraulic pressure as the fluid speeds up flowing through a constriction in a pipe) and vice versa. The principle also explains the pressure differences on each surface of an aerofoil, which gives lift to the wing of an aircraft. The principle was named after Swiss mathematician and physicist Daniel Bernoulli.

berry fleshy, many-seeded ◊fruit that does not split open to release the seeds. The outer layer of tissue, the exocarp, forms an outer skin that is often brightly coloured to attract birds to eat the fruit and thus disperse the seeds. Examples of berries are the tomato and the grape.

A **pepo** is a type of berry that has developed a hard exterior, such as the cucumber fruit. Another is the **hesperidium**, which has a thick, leathery outer layer, such as that found in citrus fruits, and fluid-containing vesicles within, which form the segments.

beryl mineral, beryllium aluminium silicate, $Be_3Al_2Si_6O_{18}$, which forms crystals chiefly in granite. It is the chief ore of beryllium. Two of its gem forms are aquamarine (light-blue crystals) and emerald (dark-green crystals).

beryllium hard, light-weight, silver-white, metallic element, symbol Be, atomic number 4, relative atomic mass 9.012. It is one of the ◊alkaline-earth metals, with chemical properties similar to those of magnesium. In nature it is found only in combination with other elements and occurs mainly as beryl ($3BeO.Al_2O_3.6SiO_2$). It is used to make sturdy, light alloys and to control the speed of neutrons in nuclear reactors. Beryllium oxide was discovered in 1798 by French chemist Louis-Nicolas Vauquelin (1763–1829), but the element was not isolated until 1828, by Friedrich Wöhler and Antoine-Alexandre-Brutus Bussy independently.

In 1992 large amounts of beryllium were unexpectedly discovered in six old stars in the Milky Way.

Berzelius, Jöns Jakob (1779–1848)

Swedish chemist. He accurately determined more than 2,000 relative atomic and molecular masses. In 1813–14, he devised the system of chemical symbols and formulae now in use and proposed oxygen as a reference standard for atomic masses. His discoveries include the elements cerium 1804, selenium 1817, and thorium 1828; he was the first to prepare silicon in its amorphous form and to isolate zirconium. The words 'isomerism', 'allotropy', and 'protein' were coined by him.

Berzelius noted that some reactions appeared to work faster in the presence of another substance which itself did not appear to change, and postulated that such a substance contained a catalytic force. Platinum, for example, was capable of speeding up reactions between gases. Although he appreciated the nature of catalysis, he was unable to give any real explanation of the mechanism.

Mary Evans Picture Library

Bessemer process the first cheap method of making ◊steel, invented by Henry Bessemer in England 1856. It has since been superseded by more efficient steel-making processes, such as the ◊basic–oxygen process. In the Bessemer process compressed air is blown into the bottom of a converter, a furnace shaped like a cement mixer, containing molten pig iron. The excess carbon in the iron burns out, other impurities form a slag, and the furnace is emptied by tilting.

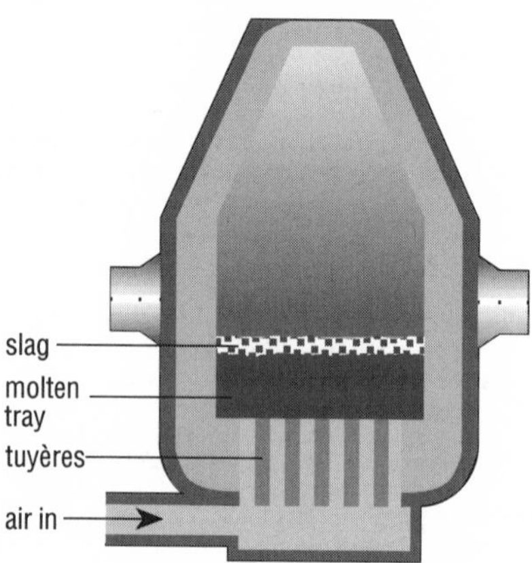

Bessemer process *In a Bessemer converter, a blast of high-pressure air oxidizes impurities in molten iron and converts it to steel.*

Bessemer, Henry (1813–1898)

British engineer and inventor who developed a method of converting molten pig iron into steel (the Bessemer process) in 1856. Knighted in 1879.

Mary Evans Picture Library

beta pre-release version of a new software program still in development, which is handed out to users for testing. The worst ◊bugs are usually eliminated at the earlier alpha stage of development. Beta testers use the software to do real work and report any bugs or badly implemented features they find to the developers, who incorporate this information in refining the product for release. Companies that assist with such testing are known as beta sites.

beta-blocker any of a class of drugs that block impulses that stimulate certain nerve endings (beta receptors) serving the heart muscle. This reduces the heart rate and the force of contraction, which in turn reduces the amount of oxygen (and therefore the blood supply) required by the heart. Beta-blockers may be useful in the treatment of angina, arrhythmia (abnormal heart rhythms), and raised blood pressure, and following heart attacks. They must be withdrawn from use gradually.

beta decay the disintegration of the nucleus of an atom to produce a beta particle, or high-speed electron, and an electron-antineutrino. During beta decay, a neutron in the nucleus changes into a proton, thereby increasing the atomic number by one while the mass number stays the same. The mass lost in the change is converted into kinetic (movement) energy of the beta particle.

Beta decay is caused by the weak nuclear force, one of the fundamental ◊forces of nature operating inside the nucleus.

beta index mathematical measurement of the connectivity of a transport network. If the network is represented as a simplified topological map, made up of nodes (junctions or places) and edges (links), the beta index may be calculated by dividing the number of nodes by the number of edges. If the number of nodes is n and the number of edges is e, then the beta index ß is given by the formula:

$$ß = n/e$$

The higher the index number, the better connected the network is. If ß is greater than 1, then a complete circuit exists.

beta particle electron ejected with great velocity from a radioactive atom that is undergoing spontaneous disintegration. Beta particles do not exist in the nucleus but are created on disintegration, beta decay, when a neutron converts to a proton to emit an electron.

Beta particles are more penetrating than ◊alpha particles, but less so than ◊gamma radiation; they can travel several metres in air, but are stopped by 2–3 mm of aluminium. They are less strongly ionizing than alpha particles and, like cathode rays, are easily deflected by magnetic and electric fields.

beta version in computing, a pre-release version of ◊software or an ◊application program, usually distributed to a limited number of expert users (and often reviewers). Distribution of beta versions allows user testing and feedback to the developer, so that any necessary modifications can be made before release.

Betelgeuse or ***Alpha Orionis*** red supergiant star in the constellation of ◊Orion. It is the tenth brightest star in the night sky, although its brightness varies. It is 1,100 million km/700 million mi across, about 800 times larger than the Sun, roughly the same size as the orbit of Mars. It is over 10,000 times as luminous as the Sun, and lies 650 light years from Earth. Light takes 60 minutes to travel across the giant star.

Its magnitude varies irregularly between 0.4 and 1.3 in a period of 5.8 years. It was the first star whose angular diameter was measured with the Mount Wilson ◊interferometer in 1920. The name is a corruption of the Arabic, describing its position in the shoulder of Orion.

betel nut fruit of the areca palm (*Areca catechu*), which is chewed together with lime and betel pepper as a stimulant by peoples of the East and Papua New Guinea. Chewing it blackens the teeth and stains the mouth deep red.

betony plant belonging to the mint family, formerly used in medicine and dyeing. It has a hairy stem and leaves, and dense heads of reddish-purple flowers. (*Stachys* (formerly *Betonica*) *officinalis,* family Labiatae.)

Bezier curve curved line invented by Pierre Bézier that connects a series of points (or 'nodes') in the smoothest possible way. The shape of the curve is governed by a series of complex mathematical formulae. They are used in ◊computer graphics and ◊CAD.

bezoar or **bezoar stone** hardened mass occasionally found in the stomach or intestines of ruminating animals, such as goats, llamas, antelopes, and cows. They appear to be formed through the presence of some irritating substance in the alimentary tract.

bhang name for a weak form of the drug ◊cannabis used in India.

bhp abbreviation for **brake horsepower**.

bicarbonate common name for ◊hydrogencarbonate

bicarbonate indicator pH indicator sensitive enough to show a colour change as the concentration of the gas carbon dioxide increases. The indicator is used in photosynthesis and respiration experiments to find out whether carbon dioxide is being liberated. The initial red colour changes to yellow as the pH becomes more acidic.

Carbon dioxide, even in the concentrations found in exhaled air, will dissolve in the indicator to form a weak solution of carbonic acid, which will lower the pH and therefore give the characteristic colour change.

bicarbonate of soda or ***baking soda*** (technical name **sodium hydrogencarbonate**) $NaHCO_3$ white crystalline solid that neutralizes acids and is used in medicine to treat acid indigestion. It is also used in baking powders and effervescent drinks.

bichir African fish, genus *Polypterus,* found in tropical swamps and rivers. Cylindrical in shape, some species grow to 70 cm/2.3 ft or more. They show many 'primitive' features, such as breathing air by using the swimbladder, having a spiral valve in the intestine, having heavy bony scales, and having larvae with external gills. These, and the fleshy fins, lead some scientists to think they are related to lungfish and coelacanths.

bichon frise breed of small dog probably originating in France or Spain and characterized by its pure white, softly curling coat. Compactly built, it carries its tail curved over its back and stands 23–8 cm/9–11 in at the shoulder.

bicuspid valve or ***mitral valve*** in the left side of the ◊heart, a flap of tissue that prevents blood flowing back into the atrium when the ventricle contracts.

bicycle pedal-driven two-wheeled vehicle used in cycling. It consists of a metal frame mounted on two large wire-spoked wheels, with handlebars in front and a seat between the front and back wheels. The bicycle is an energy-efficient, nonpolluting form of transport, and it is estimated that 800 million bicycles are in use throughout the world – outnumbering cars three to one. China, India, Denmark, and the Netherlands are countries with a high use of bicycles. More than 10% of road spending in the Netherlands is on cycleways and bicycle parking.

history The first bicycle was seen in Paris in 1791 and was a form of hobby-horse (though there are versions of the hobby-horse that date back even earlier) that had to be propelled by pushing the feet against the ground. The first treadle-propelled cycle was designed by the Scottish blacksmith Kirkpatrick Macmillan in 1839. The Rover 'safety bike' of 1885 may be considered the forerunner of the modern bicycle, with a chain and sprocket drive on the rear wheel. By the end of the 19th century wire wheels, metal frames (replacing wood), and pneumatic tyres (invented by the Scottish veterinary surgeon John B Dunlop 1888) had been added. Among the bicycles of that time was the front-wheel-driven penny farthing with a large front wheel.

technology Recent technological developments have been related to reducing wind resistance caused by the frontal area and the turbulent drag of the bicycle. Most of an Olympic cyclist's energy is taken up in fighting wind resistance in a sprint. The first major innovation was the solid wheel, first used in competitive cycling 1984, but originally patented as long ago as 1878. Further developments include handlebars that allow the cyclist to crouch and use the shape of the hands and forearms to divert air away from the chest. Modern racing bicycles now have a monocoque structure produced by laying carbon fibre around an internal mould and then baking them in an oven. Using all these developments, Chris Boardman set a speed record of 54.4 kph (34 mph) on his way to winning a gold medal at the 1992 Barcelona Olympics. To manufacture a bicycle requires only 1% of the energy and materials used to build a car.

When I see an adult on a bicycle, I have hope for the human race.

H G Wells English writer.
Attributed remark

---

biennial plant plant that completes its life cycle in two years. During the first year it grows vegetatively and the surplus food produced is stored in its ◊perennating organ, usually the root. In the following year these food reserves are used for the production of leaves, flowers, and seeds, after which the plant dies. Many root vegetables are biennials, including the carrot *Daucus carota* and parsnip *Pastinaca sativa.* Some garden plants that are grown as biennials are actually perennials, for example, the wallflower *Cheiranthus cheiri.*

Big Bang in astronomy, the hypothetical 'explosive' event that marked the origin of the universe as we know it. At the time of the Big Bang, the entire universe was squeezed into a hot, superdense state. The Big Bang explosion threw this compact material outwards, producing the expanding universe (see ◊red shift). The cause of the Big Bang is unknown; observations of the current rate of expansion of the universe suggest that it took place about 10–20 billion years ago. The Big Bang theory began modern ◊cosmology.

According to a modified version of the Big Bang, called the **inflationary theory**, the universe underwent a rapid period of expansion shortly after the Big Bang, which accounts for its current large size and uniform nature. The inflationary theory is supported by the most recent observations of the ◊cosmic background radiation.

Scientists have calculated that one 10^{-36} second (equivalent to one million-million-million-million-million-millionth of a second) after the Big Bang, the universe was the size of a pea, and the temperature was 10 billion million million million°C (18 billion million million million°F). One second after the Big Bang, the temperature was about 10 billion°C (18 billion°F).

Big Blue popular name for ◊IBM, derived from the company's size and its blue logo.

Big Crunch in cosmology, a possible fate of the universe in which it ultimately collapses to a point following the halting and reversal of the present expansion. See also ◊Big Bang and ◊critical density.

Big Dipper North American name for the Plough, the seven brightest and most prominent stars in the constellation ◊Ursa Major.

big horn sheep or ***Rocky Mountain sheep*** species of large North American sheep with a brown coat, which turns to bluish-grey in winter. It is so named from the size of the horns of the ram, which often measure over 1 m/3.3 ft round the curve.
classification The big horn sheep *Ovis canadensis* is in family Bovidae, order Artiodactyla

bight coastal indentation, crescent-shaped or gently curving, such as the Bight of Biafra in W Africa and the Great Australian Bight.

Big Seven hierarchies on UseNet, the original seven ◊hierarchies of ◊newsgroups. They are: comp (computing), misc (miscellaneous), news, rec (recreation), sci (science), soc (social issues), and talk (debate). These categories of newsgroups are managed according to specific rules which govern the creation of new groups, in contrast to the ◊alt hierarchy.

bilberry any of several shrubs belonging to the heath family, closely related to North American blueberries. They have blue or black edible berries. (Genus *Vaccinium*, family Ericaceae.)

bilby rabbit-eared bandicoot *Macrotis lagotis*, a lightly built marsupial with big ears and long nose. This burrowing animal is mainly carnivorous, and its pouch opens backwards.

bile brownish alkaline fluid produced by the liver. Bile is stored in the gall bladder and is intermittently released into the duodenum (small intestine) to aid digestion. Bile consists of bile salts, bile pigments, cholesterol, and lecithin. **Bile salts** assist in the breakdown and absorption of fats; **bile pigments** are the breakdown products of old red blood cells that are passed into the gut to be eliminated with the faeces.

> To remember the properties of bile:
>
> BILE FROM THE LIVER EMULSIFIES GREASES
> TINGES THE URINE AND COLOURS THE FAECES
> AIDS PERISTALSIS, PREVENTS PUTREFACTION
>
> IF YOU REMEMBER ALL THIS YOU'LL GIVE SATISFACTION.

bilharzia or ***schistosomiasis*** disease that causes anaemia, inflammation, formation of scar tissue, dysentery, enlargement of the spleen and liver, cancer of the bladder, and cirrhosis of the liver. It is contracted by bathing in water contaminated with human sewage. Some 200 million people are thought to suffer from this disease in the tropics, and 750,000 people a year die.

Freshwater snails act as host to the first larval stage of blood flukes of the genus *Schistosoma*; when these larvae leave the snail in their second stage of development, they are able to pass through human skin, become sexually mature, and produce quantities of eggs, which pass to the intestine or bladder. Numerous eggs are excreted from the body in urine or faeces to continue the cycle. Treatment is by means of drugs, usually containing antimony, to kill the parasites.

bill in birds, the projection of the skull bones covered with a horny sheath. It is not normally sensitive, except in some aquatic birds, rooks, and woodpeckers, where the bill is used to locate food that is not visible. The bills of birds are adapted by shape and size to specific diets, for example, shovellers use their bills to sieve mud in order to extract food; birds of prey have hooked bills adapted to tearing flesh; the bills of the avocet, and the curlew are long and narrow for picking tiny invertebrates out of the mud; and those of woodpeckers are sharp for pecking holes in trees and plucking out insects. The bill is also used by birds for preening, fighting, display, and nest-building.

billion the cardinal number represented by a 1 followed by nine zeros (1,000,000,000 or 10^9), equivalent to a thousand million.

bimetallic strip strip made from two metals each having a different coefficient of ◊thermal expansion; it therefore bends when subjected to a change in temperature. Such strips are used widely for temperature measurement and control, for instance in the domestic thermostat.

bimodal in statistics, having two distinct peaks of ◊frequency distribution.

binary file any file that is not plain text. Program (.EXE or .COM), sound, video, and graphics files are all types of binary files. Such files require special treatment for inclusion in e-mail sent across the Internet, which can transmit only ◊ASCII text and imposes a size limit of 64Kb per message. Several programs have been developed to code binary files into ASCII for transmission, splitting them into smaller parts as necessary. The most commonly used such program is ◊UUencode, but there are others including base64 and BinHex. See also ◊MIME.

binary fission in biology, a form of ◊asexual reproduction, whereby a single-celled organism, such as the amoeba, divides into two smaller 'daughter' cells. It can also occur in a few simple multicellular organisms, such as sea anemones, producing two smaller sea anemones of equal size.

binary large object (contracted to ***BLOB***) in computing, any large single block of data stored in a database, such as a picture or sound file. A BLOB does not include record fields, and so cannot be directly searched by the database's search engine.

binary newsgroup any UseNet ◊newsgroup set up for the transmission of picture and other nontext files. The binary newsgroups have their own sub-hierarchy, alt.binaries, and include groups such as alt.binaries.pictures.fine-art.digitized and alt.binaries.pictures.erotica.

Because newsgroups are subject to the same restrictions as Internet e-mail for the transmission of ◊binary files, pictures, programs, and other files posted to these newsgroups are ◊UUencoded and split into sections. To view the pictures, all the parts must be downloaded and then UUdecoded and stitched back together to form the original file, which can then be viewed using the appropriate graphics program.

Other binary newsgroups distribute sound files (alt.binaries.sound.*) or user-contributed new levels for games such as *Doom* (alt.binaries.doom). These newsgroups take up a lot of ◊bandwidth and therefore not all sites elect to carry them; blocking software typically bars access to many of these groups. It is considered a breach of ◊netiquette to post binary files to nonbinary newsgroups.

binary number system system of numbers to ◊base two, using combinations of the digits 1 and 0. Codes based on binary numbers are used to represent instructions and data in all modern digital computers, the values of the binary digits (contracted to 'bits') being stored or transmitted as, for example, open/closed switches, magnetized/unmagnetized discs and tapes, and high/low voltages in circuits.

The value of any position in a binary number increases by powers of 2 (doubles) with each move from right to left (1, 2, 4, 8, 16, and so on). For example, 1011 in the binary number system means $(1 \times 8) + (0 \times 4) + (1 \times 2) + (1 \times 1)$, which adds up to 11 in the decimal system.

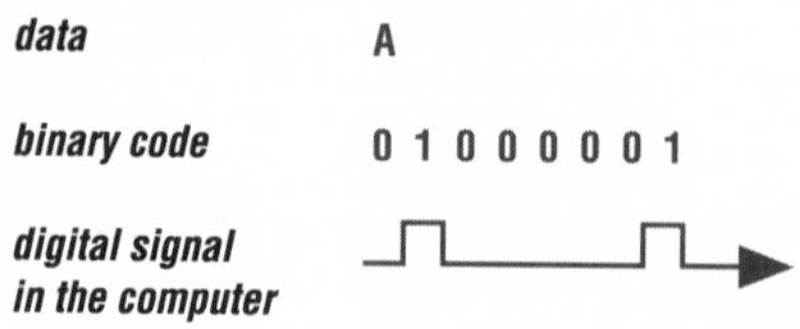

binary number system The capital letter A represented in binary form.

binary search in computing, a rapid technique used to find any particular record in a list of records held in sequential order. The computer is programmed to compare the record sought with the record in the middle of the ordered list. This being done, the computer discards the half of the list in which the record does not appear, thereby reducing the number of records left to search by half. This process of selecting the middle record and discarding the unwanted half of the list is repeated until the required record is found.

binary star pair of stars moving in orbit around their common centre of mass. Observations show that most stars are binary, or even multiple – for example, the nearest star system to the Sun, ◊Alpha Centauri.

One of the stars in the binary system Epsilon Aurigae may be the largest star known. Its diameter is 2,800 times that of the Sun. If it were in the position of the Sun, it would engulf Mercury, Venus, Earth, Mars, Jupiter, and Saturn. A spectroscopic binary is a binary in which two stars are so close together that they cannot be seen separately, but their separate light spectra can be distinguished by a spectroscope.

Another type is the ◊eclipsing binary.

binding energy in physics, the amount of energy needed to break the nucleus of an atom into the neutrons and protons of which it is made.

BinHex program for coding ◊binary files into ◊ASCII for transmission over the Internet via e-mail.

binoculars optical instrument for viewing an object in magnification with both eyes; for example, field glasses and opera glasses. Binoculars consist of two telescopes containing lenses and prisms, which produce a stereoscopic effect as well as magnifying the image.

Use of prisms has the effect of 'folding' the light path, allowing for a compact design.

The first binocular telescope was constructed by the Dutch inventor Hans Lippershey in 1608. Later development was largely due to the German Ernst Abbe of Jena, who at the end of the 19th century designed prism binoculars that foreshadowed the instruments of today, in which not only magnification but also stereoscopic effect is obtained.

binomial in mathematics, an expression consisting of two terms, such as $a + b$ or $a - b$.

binomial system of nomenclature in biology, the system in which all organisms are identified by a two-part Latinized name. Devised by the biologist ◊Linnaeus, it is also known as the Linnaean system. The first name is capitalized and identifies the ◊genus; the second identifies the ◊species within that genus.

binomial theorem formula whereby any power of a binomial quantity may be found without performing the progressive multiplications.

It was discovered by Isaac ◊Newton and first published in 1676.

binturong shaggy-coated mammal *Arctitis binturong*, the largest member of the mongoose family, nearly 1 m/3 ft long excluding a long muscular tail with a prehensile tip. Mainly nocturnal and tree-dwelling, the binturong is found in the forests of SE Asia, feeding on fruit, eggs, and small animals.

biochemistry science concerned with the chemistry of living organisms: the structure and reactions of proteins (such as enzymes), nucleic acids, carbohydrates, and lipids.

Its study has led to an increased understanding of life processes, such as those by which organisms synthesize essential chemicals from food materials, store and generate energy, and pass on their characteristics through their genetic material. A great deal of medical research is concerned with the ways in which these processes are disrupted. Biochemistry also has applications in agriculture and in the food industry (for instance, in the use of enzymes).

biodegradable capable of being broken down by living organisms, principally bacteria and fungi. In biodegradable substances, such as food and sewage, the natural processes of decay lead to compaction and liquefaction, and to the release of nutrients that are then recycled by the ecosystem.

This process can have some disadvantageous side effects, such as the release of methane, an explosive greenhouse gas. However, the technology now exists for waste tips to collect methane in

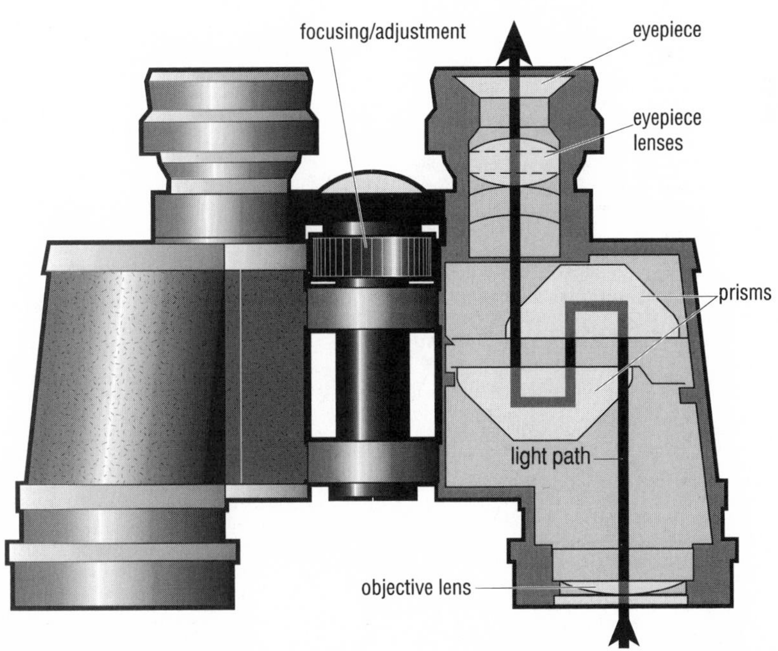

binoculars *An optical instrument that allows the user to focus both eyes on the magnified image at the same time. The essential components of binoculars are objective lenses, eyepieces, and a system of prisms to invert and reverse the image. A focusing system provides a sharp image by adjusting the relative positions of these components.*

underground pipes, drawing it off and using it as a cheap source of energy. Nonbiodegradable substances, such as glass, heavy metals, and most types of plastic, present serious problems of disposal.

biodiversity (contraction of ***biological diversity***) measure of the variety of the Earth's animal, plant, and microbial species; of genetic differences within species; and of the ecosystems that support those species. Its maintenance is important for ecological stability and as a resource for research into, for example, new drugs and crops. In the 20th century, the destruction of habitats is believed to have resulted in the most severe and rapid loss of biodiversity in the history of the planet.

Estimates of the number of species vary widely because many species-rich ecosystems, such as tropical forests, contain unexplored and unstudied habitats. Especially among small organisms, many are unknown; for instance, it is thought that only 1–10% of the world's bacterial species have been identified.

The most significant threat to biodiversity comes from the destruction of rainforests and other habitats in the southern hemisphere. It is estimated that 7% of the Earth's surface hosts 50–75% of the world's biological diversity. Costa Rica, for example, has an area less than 10% of the size of France but possesses three times as many vertebrate species.

biodynamic farming agricultural practice based on the principle of ◊homeopathy: tiny quantities of a substance are applied to transmit vital qualities to the soil. It is a form of ◊organic farming, and was developed by the Austrian holistic mystic Rudolf Steiner and Ehrenfried Pfiffer.

bioengineering the application of engineering to biology and medicine. Common applications include the design and use of artificial limbs, joints, and organs, including hip joints and heart valves.

biofeedback in medicine, the use of electrophysiological monitoring devices to 'feed back' information about internal processes and thus facilitate conscious control. Developed in the USA in the 1960s, independently by neurophysiologist Barbara Brown and neuropsychiatrist Joseph Kamiya, the technique is effective in alleviating hypertension and preventing associated organic and physiological dysfunctions.

biofuel any solid, liquid, or gaseous fuel produced from organic (once living) matter, either directly from plants or indirectly from industrial, commercial, domestic, or agricultural wastes. There are three main methods for the development of biofuels: the burning of dry organic wastes (such as household refuse, industrial and agricultural wastes, straw, wood, and peat); the fermentation of wet wastes (such as animal dung) in the absence of oxygen to produce biogas (containing up to 60% methane), or the fermentation of sugar cane or corn to produce alcohol and esters; and energy forestry (producing fast-growing wood for fuel).

Fermentation produces two main types of biofuels: alcohols and esters. These could theoretically be used in place of fossil fuels but, because major alterations to engines would be required, biofuels are usually mixed with fossil fuels. The EU allows 5% ethanol, derived from wheat, beet, potatoes, or maize, to be added to fossil fuels. A quarter of Brazil's transportation fuel in 1994 was ethanol.

biogenesis biological term coined in 1870 by English scientist Thomas Henry Huxley to express the hypothesis that living matter always arises out of other similar forms of living matter. It superseded the opposite idea of ◊spontaneous generation or abiogenesis (that is, that living things may arise out of nonliving matter).

biogeography study of how and why plants and animals are distributed around the world, in the past as well as in the present; more specifically, a theory describing the geographical distribution of ◊species developed by Robert MacArthur and US zoologist Edward O Wilson. The theory argues that for many species, ecological specializations mean that suitable habitats are patchy in their occurrence. Thus for a dragonfly, ponds in which to breed are separated by large tracts of land, and for edelweiss adapted to alpine peaks the deep valleys between cannot be colonized.

biological clock regular internal rhythm of activity, produced by unknown mechanisms, and not dependent on external time signals. Such clocks are known to exist in almost all animals, and also in many plants, fungi, and unicellular organisms; the first biological clock gene in plants was isolated in 1995 by a US team of researchers. In higher organisms, there appears to be a series of clocks of graded importance. For example, although body temperature and activity cycles in human beings are normally 'set' to 24 hours, the two cycles may vary independently, showing that two clock mechanisms are involved.

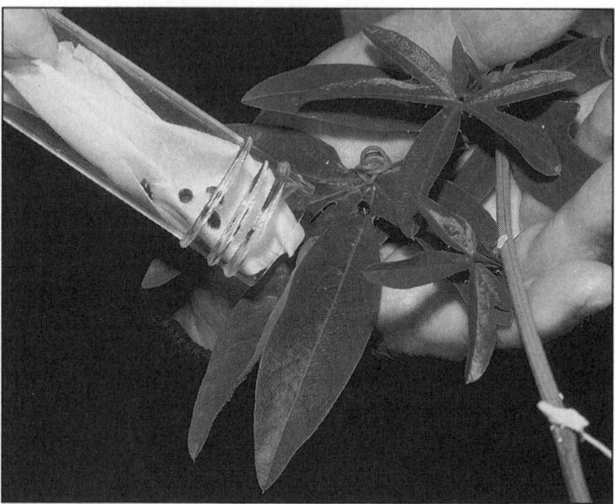

biological control *The beetle* Cryptolaemus montrouzieri *being released on to a mealybug-infested passion flower. Because mealybugs, which are a serious pest, have a waxy coating and so are resistant to insecticides, biological control agents are used against them.* *Premaphotos Wildlife*

biological control control of pests such as insects and fungi through biological means, rather than the use of chemicals. This can include breeding resistant crop strains; inducing sterility in the pest; infecting the pest species with disease organisms; or introducing the pest's natural predator. Biological control tends to be naturally self-regulating, but as ecosystems are so complex, it is difficult to predict all the consequences of introducing a biological controlling agent.

The introduction of the cane toad to Australia 50 years ago to eradicate a beetle that was destroying sugar beet provides an example of the unpredictability of biological control. Since the cane toad is poisonous it has few Australian predators and it is now a pest, spreading throughout eastern and northern Australia at a rate of 35 km/22 mi a year.

BIOLOGICAL CONTROL

http://www.nysaes.cornell.edu:80/ent/biocontrol/

University-based site on the various methods of biological control used by farmers in the USA. This includes sections on parasitoids, predators, pathogens, and weed feeders. Each sections contains images and sections on 'relative effectiveness' and 'pesticide susceptibility'.

biological oxygen demand (BOD) the amount of dissolved oxygen taken up by microorganisms in a sample of water. Since these microorganisms live by decomposing organic matter, and the amount of oxygen used is proportional to their number and metabolic rate, BOD can be used as a measure of the extent to which the water is polluted with organic compounds.

biological shield shield around a nuclear reactor that is intended to protect personnel from the effects of ◊radiation. It usually consists of a thick wall of steel and concrete.

biology ***Greek bios 'life', logos 'discourse'*** science of life. Biology includes all the life sciences – for example, anatomy and physiology (the study of the structure of living things), cytology (the study of cells), zoology (the study of animals) and botany (the study of plants), ecology (the study of habitats and the interaction of living species), animal behaviour, embryology, and taxonomy, and plant breeding. Increasingly in the 20th century biologists have concentrated on molecular structures: biochemistry, biophysics, and genetics (the study of inheritance and variation).

Biological research has come a long way towards understanding the nature of life, and during the 1990s our knowledge will be further extended as the international ◊Human Genome Project attempts to map the entire genetic code contained in the 23 pairs of human chromosomes.

The greatest stride in biology, in our century, was its shift to the molecular dimension. The next will be its shift toward the submolecular, electronic dimension.

Albert Szent-Györgyi Hungarian-born US biochemist.
Bioelectronics 1968

bioluminescence production of light by living organisms. It is a feature of many deep-sea fishes, crustaceans, and other marine animals. On land, bioluminescence is seen in some nocturnal insects such as glow-worms and fireflies, and in certain bacteria and fungi. Light is usually produced by the oxidation of luciferin, a reaction catalysed by the ◊enzyme luciferase. This reaction is unique, being the only known biological oxidation that does not produce heat. Animal luminescence is involved in communication, camouflage, or the luring of prey, but its function in other organisms is unclear.

biomass the total mass of living organisms present in a given area. It may be specified for a particular species (such as earthworm biomass) or for a general category (such as herbivore biomass). Estimates also exist for the entire global plant biomass. Measurements of biomass can be used to study interactions between organisms, the stability of those interactions, and variations in population numbers. Where dry biomass is measured, the material is dried to remove all water before weighing.

Some two-thirds of the world's population cooks and heats water by burning biomass, usually wood. Plant biomass can be a renewable source of energy as replacement supplies can be grown relatively quickly. Fossil fuels however, originally formed from biomass, accumulate so slowly that they cannot be considered renewable. The burning of biomass (defined either as natural areas of the ecosystem or as forest, grasslands, and fuelwoods) produces 3.5 million tonnes of carbon in the form of carbon dioxide each year, accounting for up to 40% of the world's annual carbon dioxide production.

BIOMASS

http://www.nrel.gov/research/industrial_tech/biomass.html

Well-presented information on biomass from the US Department of Energy. A graph supports the textual explanation of the fact that the world is only using 7 % of annual biomass production. There is a clear explanation of the chemical composition of biomass and development of technologies to transform it into usable fuel sources.

biome broad natural assemblage of plants and animals shaped by common patterns of vegetation and climate. Examples include the tundra biome and the desert biome.

biomechanics application of mechanical engineering principles and techniques in the field of medicine and surgery, studying natural structures to improve those produced by humans. For example, mother-of-pearl is structurally superior to glass fibre, and deer antlers have outstanding durability because they are composed of microscopic fibres. Such natural structures may form the basis of high-tech composites. Biomechanics has been responsible for many recent advances in ◊orthopaedics, anaesthesia, and intensive care. Biomechanical assessment of the requirements for replacement of joints, including evaluation of the stresses and strains between parts, and their reliability, has allowed development of implants with very low friction and long life.

biometrics in computing, biometrics is applied loosely to the measurement of biological (human) data, usually for security purposes, rather than the statistical analysis of biological data. For example, when someone wants to enter a building or cash a cheque, their finger or eyeball may be scanned and compared with a fingerprint or eyeball scan stored earlier. Biometrics saves people from having to remember PINs (personal identification numbers) and passwords.

biometry literally, the measurement of living things, but generally used to mean the application of mathematics to biology. The term is now largely obsolete, since mathematical or statistical work is an integral part of most biological disciplines.

bionics ***from 'biological electronics'*** design and development of electronic or mechanical artificial systems that imitate those of living things. The bionic arm, for example, is an artificial limb (◊prosthesis) that uses electronics to amplify minute electrical signals generated in body muscles to work electric motors, which operate the joints of the fingers and wrist.

The first person to receive two bionic ears was Peter Stewart, an Australian journalist, 1989. His left ear was fitted with an array of 22 electrodes, replacing the hairs that naturally convert sounds into electrical impulses. Five years previously he had been fitted with a similar device in his right ear.

biophysics application of physical laws to the properties of living organisms. Examples include using the principles of ◊mechanics to calculate the strength of bones and muscles, and ◊thermodynamics to study plant and animal energetics.

biopsy removal of a living tissue sample from the body for diagnostic examination.

biorhythm rhythmic change, mediated by ◊hormones, in the physical state and activity patterns of certain plants and animals that have seasonal activities. Examples include winter hibernation, spring flowering or breeding, and periodic migration. The hormonal changes themselves are often a response to changes in day length (◊photoperiodism); they signal the time of year to the animal or plant. Other biorhythms are innate and continue even if external stimuli such as day length are removed. These include a 24-hour or ◊circadian rhythm, a 28-day or circalunar rhythm (corresponding to the phases of the Moon), and even a year-long rhythm in some organisms.

Such innate biorhythms are linked to an internal or ◊biological clock, whose mechanism is still poorly understood.

Often both types of rhythm operate; thus many birds have a circalunar rhythm that prepares them for the breeding season, and a photoperiodic response. There is also a nonscientific and unproven theory that human activity is governed by three biorhythms: the **intellectual** (33 days), the **emotional** (28 days), and the **physical** (23 days). Certain days in each cycle are regarded as 'critical', even more so if one such day coincides with that of another cycle.

BIOS (acronym for ***basic input/output system***) in computing, the part of the ◊operating system that handles input and output. The term is also used to describe the programs stored in ◊ROM (and called ROM BIOS), which are automatically run when a computer is switched on allowing it to ◊boot. BIOS is unaffected by upgrades to the operating system stored on disc.

biosensor device based on microelectronic circuits that can directly measure medically significant variables for the purpose of diagnosis or monitoring treatment. One such device measures the blood sugar level of diabetics using a single drop of blood, and shows the result on a liquid crystal display within a few minutes.

biosphere the narrow zone that supports life on our planet. It is limited to the waters of the Earth, a fraction of its crust, and the lower regions of the atmosphere.

BioSphere 2 (BS2) ecological test project, a 'planet in a bottle', in Arizona, USA. Under a sealed glass and metal dome, different habitats are recreated, with representatives of nearly 4,000 species, to test the effects that various environmental factors have on ecosystems. Simulated ecosystems, or 'mesocosms', include savanna, desert, rainforest, marsh and Caribbean reef. The response of such systems to elevated atmospheric concentrations of carbon dioxide gas (CO_2) are among the priorities of Biosphere 2 researchers.
BioSphere 1 Experiments with biospheres that contain relatively simple life forms have been carried out for decades, and a 21-day trial period in 1989 that included humans preceded the construction of BS2. However, BS2 is not in fact the second in a series: the Earth is considered to be Biosphere 1.
human inhabitants Originally, people, called 'Biospherians', were sealed in the dome. The people within were self-sufficient, except for electricity, which was supplied by a 3.7 megawatt power station on the outside (solar panels were considered too expensive). The original team of eight in residence 1991–1993 was replaced March 1994 with a new team of seven people sealed in for six-and-a-half months. In 1995 it was decided that further research would not involve sealing people within the biosphere. Researchers, students, and visitors routinely go in and out of the Biosphere 2 facility.
organization Biosphere 2 was originally run by a private company partly funded by ecology-minded oil millionaire Edward P Bass (1945–) and was called Space Biosphere Ventures. Space Biosphere Ventures investors expected to find commercial applications for the techniques developed in the course of the project. As of 1 January 1996 Columbia University, USA, joined Space Bisphere Ventures to form Biosphere 2 Center, Inc.. The purpose of the joint venture is to use the facility for conferences and classes as well as further short-term experiments with the artificial ecosystems that do not involve isolating humans inside.

biosynthesis synthesis of organic chemicals from simple inorganic ones by living cells – for example, the conversion of carbon dioxide and water to glucose by plants during ◊photosynthesis.

Other biosynthetic reactions produce cell constituents including proteins and fats.

biotechnology industrial use of living organisms to manufacture food, drugs, or other products. The brewing and baking industries have long relied on the yeast microorganism for ◊fermentation purposes, while the dairy industry employs a range of bacteria and fungi to convert milk into cheeses and yoghurts. ◊Enzymes, whether extracted from cells or produced artificially, are central to most biotechnological applications.

Recent advances include ◊genetic engineering, in which single-celled organisms with modified ◊DNA are used to produce insulin and other drugs.

In 1993 two-thirds of biotechnology companies were concentrating on human health developments, whilst only 1 in 10 were concerned with applications for food and agriculture.

biotic factor organic variable affecting an ecosystem – for example, the changing population of elephants and its effect on the African savanna.

biotin or ***vitamin H*** vitamin of the B complex, found in many different kinds of food; egg yolk, liver, legumes, and yeast contain large amounts. Biotin is essential to the metabolism of fats. Its absence from the diet may lead to dermatitis.

birch any of a group of slender trees with small leaves and fine, peeling bark. About 40 species are found in cool temperate parts of the northern hemisphere. Birches grow rapidly, and their hard, beautiful wood is used for veneers and cabinet work. (Genus *Betula*, family Betulaceae.)

bird backboned animal of the class Aves, the biggest group of land vertebrates, characterized by warm blood, feathers, wings, breathing through lungs, and egg-laying by the female. Birds are bipedal; feet are usually adapted for perching and never have more than four toes. Hearing and eyesight are well developed, but the sense of smell is usually poor. No existing species of bird possesses teeth.

Most birds fly, but some groups (such as ostriches) are flightless, and others include flightless members. Many communicate by sounds (nearly half of all known species are songbirds) or by visual displays, in connection with which many species are brightly coloured, usually the males. Birds have highly developed patterns of instinctive behaviour. There are nearly 8,500 species of birds.

According to the Red List of endangered species published by the World Conservation Union (IUCN) for 1996, 11% of bird species are threatened with extinction.
wing structure The wing consists of the typical bones of a forelimb, the humerus, radius and ulna, carpus, metacarpus, and digits. The first digit is the pollex, or thumb, to which some feathers, known as ala spuria, or bastard wing, are attached; the second digit is the index, which bears the large feathers known as the primaries or manuals, usually ten in number. The primary feathers, with the secondaries or cubitals, which are attached to the ulna, form the large wing-quills, called remiges, which are used in flight.
anatomy The sternum, or breastbone, of birds is affected by their powers of flight: those birds which are able to fly have a keel projecting from the sternum and serving as the basis of attachment of the great pectoral muscles which move the wings. In birds that do not fly the keel is absent or greatly reduced. The vertebral column is completed in the tail region by a flat plate known as the pygostyle, which forms a support for the rectrices, or steering tailfeathers.

The legs are composed of the femur, tibia and fibula, and the bones of the foot; the feet usually have four toes, but in many cases there are only three. In swimming birds the legs are placed well back.

BIRD

Rifleman, short-tailed pygmy tyrant, frilled coquette, bobwhite, tawny frogmouth, trembler, wattle-eye, fuscous honeyeater, dickcissel, common grackle, and forktailed drongo are all common names for species of bird.

The uropygial gland on the pygostyle (bone in the tail) is an oil gland used by birds in preening their feathers, as their skin contains no sebaceous glands. The eyes have an upper and a lower eyelid and a semi-transparent nictitating membrane with which the bird can cover its eyes at will.

The **vascular system** contains warm blood, which is kept usually at a higher temperature (about 41°C/106°F) than that of mammals; death from cold is rare unless the bird is starving or ill. The aortic arch (main blood vessel leaving the heart) is on the right side of a bird, whereas it is on the left in a mammal. The heart of a bird consists of a right and a left half with four chambers.

The **lungs** are small and prolonged into air-sacs connected to a number of air-spaces in the bones. These air-spaces are largest in powerful fliers, but they are not so highly developed in young, small, aquatic, and terrestrial birds. These air-spaces increase the efficiency of the respiratory system and reduce the weight of the bones. The lungs themselves are more efficient than those of mammals; the air is circulated through a system of fine capillary tubes, allowing continuous gas exchange to take place, whereas in mammals the air comes to rest in blind air sacs.

The organ of voice is not the larynx, but usually the syrinx, a peculiarity of this class formed at the bifurcation of the trachea (windpipe) and the modulations are effected by movements of the adjoining muscles.

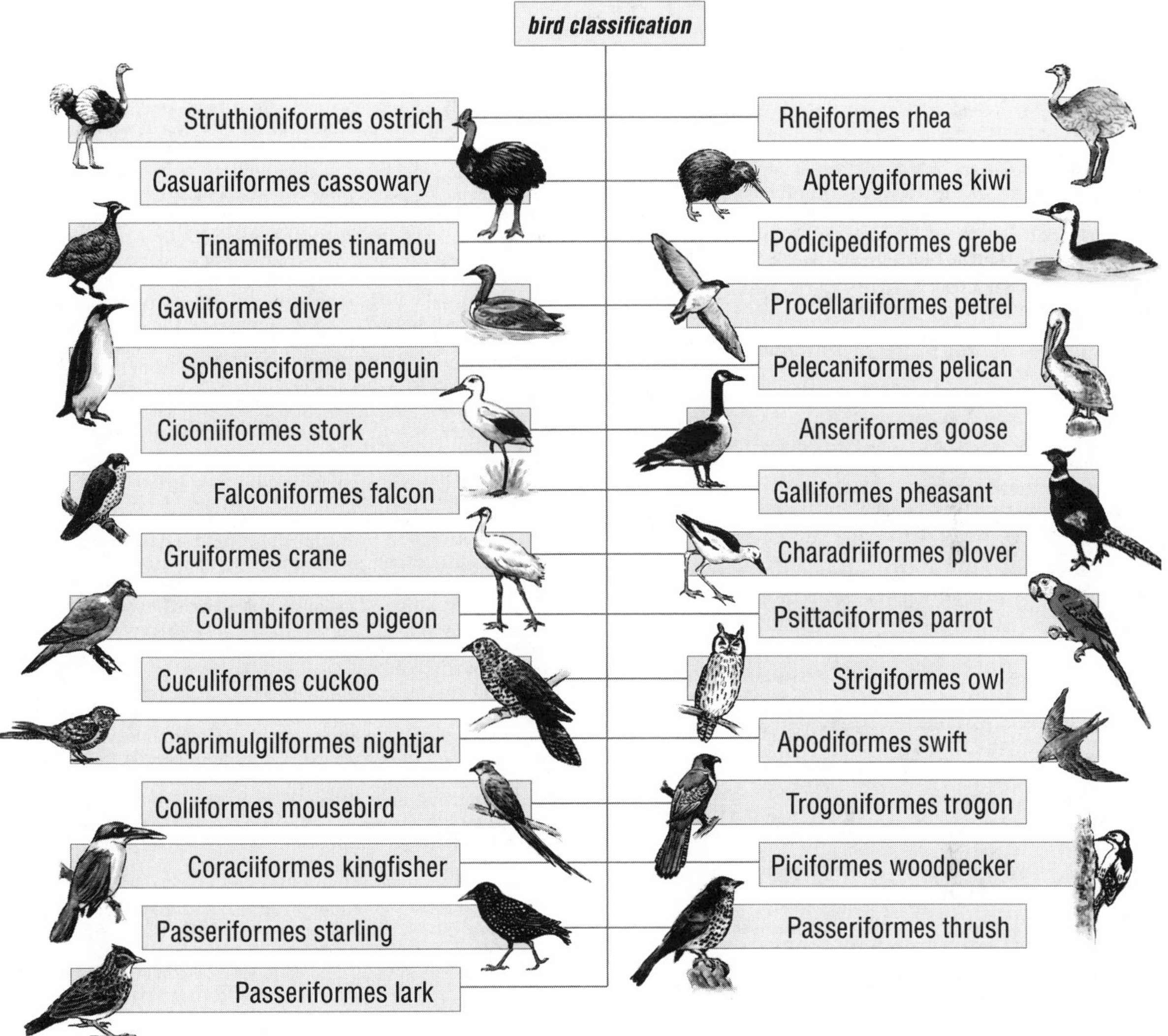

bird *This diagram shows a representative species from each of the 29 orders. There are nearly 8,500 species of birds, of which the largest is the N African ostrich, reaching a height of 2.74 m/9 ft and weighing 156 kg/345 lb. The smallest bird, the bee hummingbird of Cuba and the Isle of Pines, measures 57 mm/2.24 in in length and weighs a mere 1.6 g/0.056 oz.*

digestion Digestion takes place in the oesophagus, stomach, and intestines in a manner basically similar to mammals. The tongue aids in feeding, and there is frequently a **crop**, a dilation of the oesophagus, where food is stored and softened. The stomach is small with little storage capacity and usually consists of the proventriculus, which secretes digestive juices, and the gizzard, which is tough and muscular and grinds the food, sometimes with the aid of grit and stones retained within it. Digestion is completed, and absorption occurs, in the intestine and the digestive caeca. The intestine ends in a cloaca through which both urine and faeces are excreted.

nesting and eggs Typically eggs are brooded in a nest and, on hatching, the young receive a period of parental care. The collection of nest material, nest building, and incubation may be carried out by the male, female, or both. The cuckoo neither builds a nest nor rears its own young, but places the eggs in the nest of another bird and leaves the foster parents to care for them.

The study of birds is called ◊ornithology.

bird louse parasitic biting louse, found mainly on birds, less frequently on mammals. Bird lice are wingless ectoparasites (living on the skin of their hosts), have biting mouthparts (as opposed to true lice which have sucking mouthparts), and reduced eyes.

classification Bird lice are in the order Mallophaga, class Insecta, phylum Arthropoda.

The **chicken body louse** *Menacanthus stramineus* is small, yellowish, and about 2.8–3.3 mm/0.1–0.13 in long. The parasite feeds on the skin debris and feathers of the chicken. A heavily infested bird can carry over 8,000 lice on its body. The host appears to withstand the usual degree of infestation without apparent ill-effects, but heavy infestation can result in loss of plumage and a decline in the bird's health.

bird of paradise one of 40 species of crowlike birds in the family Paradiseidae, native to New Guinea and neighbouring islands. Females are generally drably coloured, but the males have bright and elaborate plumage used in courtship display. Hunted almost to extinction for their plumage, they are now subject to conservation.

They are smallish birds, extremely active, and have compressed beaks, large toes, and strong feet. Their food consists chiefly of fruits, seeds, and nectar, but it may also include insects and small animals, such as worms. The Australian ◊bowerbirds are closely related.

Birman or ***'sacred cat of Burma'*** breed of domestic cat with medium-length fur, possibly originating in the temples of Burma. Similar to a ◊Colourpoint Longhair or Himalayan cat, the Birman has shorter hair, legs with a longer body. In Britain, the Blue-point variety's fur is beige-gold with blue-grey points (dark face, tail, and legs), with white paws; the US standard calls for bluish-white fur and deep blue points. It has brilliant blue eyes. There are several other varieties.

Birmans were recognized as a breed in France in 1925 and in the USA in 1926.

birth act of producing live young from within the body of female animals. Both viviparous and ovoviviparous animals give birth to young. In viviparous animals, embryos obtain nourishment from the mother via a ◊placenta or other means.

In ovoviviparous animals, fertilized eggs develop and hatch in the oviduct of the mother and gain little or no nourishment from maternal tissues. See also ◊pregnancy.

There's a time when you have to explain to your children why they're born, and it's a marvelous thing if you know the reason by then.

HAZEL SCOTT US entertainer.
Quoted in *Ms.* Nov 1974

birth control another name for ◊family planning; see also ◊contraceptive.

bisect to divide a line or angle into two equal parts.

bisector a line that bisects an angle or another line (known as a **perpendicular bisector** when it bisects at right angles).

bismuth hard, brittle, pinkish-white, metallic element, symbol Bi, atomic number 83, relative atomic mass 208.98. It has the highest atomic number of all the stable elements (the elements from atomic number 84 up are radioactive). Bismuth occurs in ores and occasionally as a free metal (◊native metal). It is a poor conductor of heat and electricity, and is used in alloys of low melting point and in medical compounds to soothe gastric ulcers. The name comes from the Latin *besemutum,* from the earlier German *Wismut.*

bison large, hoofed mammal of the bovine family. There are two species, both brown. The **European bison** or **wisent** *Bison bonasus,* of which only a few protected herds survive, is about 2 m/7 ft high and weighs up to 1,100 kg/2,500 lb. The **North American bison** (often known as 'buffalo') *Bison bison* is slightly smaller, with a heavier mane and more sloping hindquarters. Formerly roaming the prairies in vast numbers, it was almost exterminated in the 19th century, but survives in protected areas. There were about 14,000 bison in North American reserves in 1994.

Crossed with domestic cattle, the latter has produced a hardy hybrid, the 'beefalo', producing a lean carcass on an economical grass diet.

bistable circuit or ***flip-flop*** simple electronic circuit that remains in one of two stable states until it receives a pulse (logic 1 signal) through one of its inputs, upon which it switches, or 'flips', over to the other state. Because it is a two-state device, it can be used to store binary digits and is widely used in the ◊integrated circuits used to build computers.

bisulphate another term for ◊hydrogen sulphate.

bit (contraction of ***binary digit***) in computing, a single binary digit, either 0 or 1. A bit is the smallest unit of data stored in a computer; all other data must be coded into a pattern of individual bits. A ◊byte represents sufficient computer memory to store a single ◊character of data, and usually contains eight bits. For example, in the ◊ASCII code system used by most microcomputers the capital letter A would be stored in a single byte of memory as the bit pattern 01000001.

The maximum number of bits that a computer can normally process at once is called a **word**. Microcomputers are often described according to how many bits of information they can handle at once. For instance, the first microprocessor, the Intel 4004 (launched 1971), was a 4-bit device. In the 1970s several different 8-bit computers, many based on the Zilog Z80 or Rockwell 6502 processors, came into common use. In 1981, the IBM Personal Computer (PC) was introduced, using the Intel 8088 processor, which combined a 16-bit processor with an 8-bit ◊data bus. Business micros of the later 1980s began to use 32-bit processors such as the Intel 80386 and Motorola 68030. Machines based on the first 64-bit microprocessor appeared in 1993.

The higher the number of bits a computer can process simultaneously, the more powerful the computer is said to be. However, other factors influence the overall speed of a computer system, such as the ◊clock rate of the processor and the amount of ◊RAM available. Tasks that require a high processing speed include sorting a data-

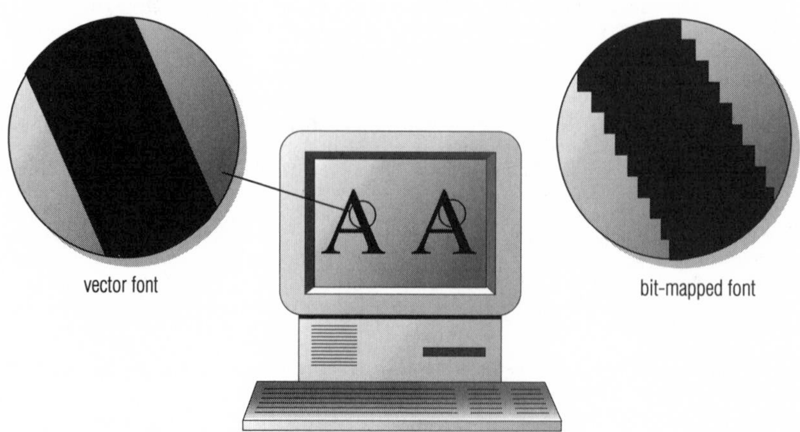

bit map *The difference in close-up between a bit-mapped and vector font. As separate sets of bit maps are required for each different type size, scaleable vector graphics (outline) is the preferred medium for fonts.*

base or doing long, complex calculations in spreadsheets. A system running slowly with a ◊graphical user interface may benefit more from the addition of extra RAM than from a faster processor.

In the PC industry, new hardware is most readily adopted when it is compatible with old software, which slows the adoption of new software. For example, most people were still using Microsoft's 16-bit Windows 3 program with 16-bit applications in 1995–96, a decade after 32-bit processors like Intel's 80386 became widely available. This was true even though 32-bit operating systems – Unix, IBM's OS/2 and Microsoft's Windows NT – had been available for some years.

bit map in computing, a pattern of ◊bits used to describe the organization of data. Bit maps are used to store typefaces or graphic images (bit-mapped or ◊raster graphics), with 1 representing black (or a colour) and 0 white.

Bit maps may be used to store a typeface or ◊font, but a separate set of bit maps is required for each typesize. A vector font, by contrast, can be held as one set of data and scaled as required. Bit-mapped graphics are not recommended for images that require scaling (compare ◊vector graphics – those stored in the form of geometric formulas).

bit-mapped font ◊font held in computer memory as sets of bit maps.

Bitnet (acronym for ***Because It's Time Network***) news ◊network developed in 1983 at the City University of New York, USA. Bitnet operates as a collection of mailing lists using ◊Listserv, which was picked up by the rest of the Internet and is widely used, although Bitnet itself is falling into disuse.

bit pad computer input device; see ◊graphics tablet.

bits per second (bps) commonly used measure of the speed of transmission of a ◊modem. In 1997 the fastest modems readily available were rated at 33,600 bps, with two incompatible 56K systems also competing for sales. Modem speeds should conform to standards, known as ◊V numbers, laid down by the ◊Comité Consultatif International Téléphonique et Télégraphique (CCITT) so that modems from different manufacturers can connect to each other. Many modems transfer data much faster than their nominal speeds via techniques such as ◊data compression.

bitterling freshwater fish *Rhodeus sericeus* of Northern Europe, introduced to North America. It grows to a length of 90 mm/3.5 in, and has an attractive bluish stripe along each side towards the tail. It is found in lakes and slow-moving rivers.

Having selected a mate, the female bitterling deposits her eggs inside a freshwater mussel via a long tube protruding from her body, and the male then deposits his sperm into the mussel. The eggs are nurtured safe from predators (and unharmed by the mussel) within the mussel's gills for two to three weeks before hatching and swimming away.

bittern any of several species of small herons, in particular the common bittern *Botaurus stellaris* of Europe and Asia. It is shy, stoutly built, buff-coloured, speckled with black and tawny brown, with a long bill and a loud, booming call. Its habit of holding its neck and bill in a vertical position conceals it among the reeds, where it rests by day, hunting for frogs, reptiles, and fish towards nightfall. An inhabitant of marshy country, it is now quite rare in Britain.

bittersweet alternative name for the woody ◊nightshade plant.

bitumen impure mixture of hydrocarbons, including such deposits as petroleum, asphalt, and natural gas, although sometimes the term is restricted to a soft kind of pitch resembling asphalt.

Solid bitumen may have arisen as a residue from the evaporation of petroleum. If evaporation took place from a pool or lake of petroleum, the residue might form a pitch or asphalt lake, such as Pitch Lake in Trinidad. Bitumen was used in ancient times as a mortar, and by the Egyptians for embalming.

bivalent in biology, a name given to the pair of homologous chromosomes during reduction division (◊meiosis). In chemistry, the term is sometimes used to describe an element or group with a ◊valency of two, although the term 'divalent' is more common.

bivalve marine or freshwater mollusc whose body is enclosed between two shells hinged together by a ligament on the dorsal side of the body.

The shell is closed by strong 'adductor' muscles. Ventrally, a retractile 'foot' can be put out to assist movement in mud or sand. Two large platelike gills are used for breathing and also, with the ◊cilia present on them, make a mechanism for collecting the small particles of food on which bivalves depend. The bivalves form one of the five classes of molluscs, the Lamellibranchiata, otherwise known as Bivalvia or Pelycypoda, containing about 8,000 species.

black beetle another name for ◊cockroach, although cockroaches belong to an entirely different order of insects (Dictyoptera) from the beetles (Coleoptera).

blackberry prickly shrub, closely related to raspberries and dewberries. Native to northern parts of Europe, it produces pink or white blossom and edible black compound fruits. (*Rubus fruticosus,* family Rosaceae.)

blackbird bird *Turdus merula* of the thrush family, Muscicapidae, order Passeriformes, about 25 cm/10 in long. The male is black with a yellow bill and eyelids, the female dark brown with a dark beak. It lays three to five blue-green eggs with brown spots in a nest of grass and moss, plastered with mud, built in thickets or creeper-clad trees. The blackbird feeds on fruit, seeds, worms, grubs, and snails. Its song is rich and flutelike.

Found across Europe, Asia, and North Africa, the blackbird adapts well to human presence and gardens, and is one of the most common British birds. North American 'blackbirds' belong to a different family of birds, the Icteridae.

black body in physics, a hypothetical object that completely absorbs all electromagnetic radiation striking it. It is also a perfect emitter of thermal radiation.

Although a black body is hypothetical, a practical approximation can be made by using a small hole in the wall of a constant-temperature enclosure. The radiation emitted by a black body is of all wavelengths, but with maximum radiation at a particular wavelength that depends on the body's temperature. As the temperature increases, the wavelength of maximum intensity becomes shorter (see ◊Wien's displacement law). The total energy emitted at all wavelengths is proportional to the fourth power of the temperature (see ◊Stefan–Boltzmann law). Attempts to explain these facts failed until the development of ◊quantum theory in 1900.

black box popular name for the unit containing an aeroplane's flight and voice recorders. These monitor the plane's behaviour and the crew's conversation, thus providing valuable clues to the cause of a disaster. The box is nearly indestructible and usually painted orange for easy recovery. The name also refers to any compact electronic device that can be quickly connected or disconnected as a unit.

The maritime equivalent is the **voyage recorder**, installed in ships from 1989. It has 350 sensors to record the performance of engines, pumps, navigation lights, alarms, radar, and hull stress.

blackbuck antelope *Antilope cervicapra* found in central and NW India. It is related to the gazelle, from which it differs in having spirally-twisted horns. The male is black above and white beneath, whereas the female and young are fawn-coloured above.

It is about 76 cm/2.5 ft in height.

blackcap ◊warbler *Sylvia atricapilla,* family Muscicapidae, order Passeriformes. The male has a black cap, the female a reddish-brown one. The general colour of the bird is an ashen-grey, turning to an olive-brown above and pale or whitish-grey below. About 14 cm/5.5 in long, the blackcap likes wooded areas, and is a summer visitor to N Europe, wintering in Africa.

blackcock or ***heathcock*** large grouse *Lyrurus tetrix* found on moors and in open woods in N Europe and Asia. The male is mainly black with a lyre-shaped tail, and grows up to 54 cm/1.7 ft in height. The female is speckled brown and only 40 cm/1.3 ft tall.

Their food consists of buds, young shoots, berries, and insects.

Blackcocks are polygamous, and in the spring males attract females by curious crowings. In males a piece of bright red skin above the eyes also becomes more intense during the pairing season.

They are related to the quail, partridge, and capercaillie, in the order Galliformes.

blackcurrant variety of ◊currant.

Black Death great epidemic of bubonic ◊plague that ravaged Europe in the mid-14th century, killing between one-third and half of the population (about 75 million people). The cause of the plague was the bacterium *Yersinia pestis,* transmitted by fleas borne by migrating Asian black rats. The name Black Death was first used in England in the early 19th century.

black earth exceedingly fertile soil that covers a belt of land in NE North America, Europe, and Asia.

In Europe and Asia it extends from Bohemia through Hungary, Romania, S Russia, and Siberia, as far as Manchuria, having been deposited when the great inland ice sheets melted at the close of the last ◊ice age. In North America, it extends from the Great Lakes east through New York State, having been deposited when the last glaciers melted and retreated from the terminal moraine.

blackfly plant-sucking insect, a type of ◊aphid.

blackfly small but stoutly built blood-sucking flies with short antennae. Blackflies have broad wings with all the obvious veins in the anterior part of the wing. The family is widely distributed, the adults often occurring in such large numbers as to make them a nuisance. They are most abundant in north temperate and subarctic regions.

classification Blackflies are in family Simuliidae, order Diptera, class Insecta, phylum Arthropoda.

There are six larval stages that are found in running water, including cascades and waterfalls; they have a well capsulated head, a solitary thoracic proleg and a posterior sucker composed of small hooks by which they anchor themselves against the current. They are found on stones, reeds, mayfly larvae, and other aquatic forms. The pupae usually rest in a tent of silk in similar situations to the larvae.

Simulium species are the vectors of ◊onchocerciasis in Central and South America, Africa, and the Yemen. They also transmit other filarial worms to cattle and to ducks. Blackflies are vectors of a large number of avian malarias to many birds including domestic stock, turkeys, ducks, and geese in North America and Canada. In addition, number of blackflies attacking livestock can be so great, and the attacks so fierce, as to kill the livestock, and human deaths have also occurred.

black hole object in space whose gravity is so great that nothing can escape from it, not even light. Thought to form when massive stars shrink at the end of their lives, a black hole sucks in more matter, including other stars, from the space around it. Matter that falls into a black hole is squeezed to infinite density at the centre of the hole. Black holes can be detected because gas falling towards them becomes so hot that it emits X-rays.

Black holes containing the mass of millions of stars are thought to lie at the centres of ◊quasars. Satellites have detected X-rays from a number of objects that may be black holes, but only four likely black holes in our Galaxy had been identified by 1994.

blacksnake any of several species of snake. The blacksnake *Pseudechis porphyriacus* is a venomous snake of the cobra family found in damp forests and swamps in E Australia. The blacksnake, *Coluber constrictor* from the eastern USA, is a relative of the European grass snake, growing up to 1.2 m/4 ft long, and without venom.

blackthorn densely branched spiny European bush. It produces white blossom on bare black branches in early spring. Its sour plumlike blue-black fruit, the sloe, is used to make sloe gin. (*Prunus spinosa,* family Rosaceae.)

Blackwell, Elizabeth (1821–1910) English-born US physician, the first woman to qualify in medicine in the USA in 1849, and the first woman to be recognized as a qualified physician in the UK in 1869.

black widow The term 'black widow' covers a number of different species of Latrodectus *spiders including* L. mactans, *the southern black widow from the New World. The name derives from the generally held belief that the female spider invariably eats the male after mating. Recent observations indicate that this may be the case in only a few species. Premaphotos Wildlife*

black widow North American spider *Latrodectus mactans.* The male is small and harmless, but the female is 1.3 cm/0.5 in long with a red patch below the abdomen and a powerful venomous bite. The bite causes pain and fever in human victims, but they usually recover.

bladder hollow elastic-walled organ which stores the urine produced in the kidneys. It is present in the ◊urinary systems of some fishes, most amphibians, some reptiles, and all mammals. Urine enters the bladder through two ureters, one leading from each kidney, and leaves it through the urethra.

bladderwort any of a large group of carnivorous aquatic plants. They have leaves with bladders (hollow sacs) that trap small animals living in the water. (Genus *Utricularia,* family Lentibulariaceae.)

blast freezing industrial method of freezing substances such as foods by blowing very cold air over them.

blast furnace smelting furnace used to extract metals from their ores, chiefly pig iron from iron ore. The temperature is raised by the injection of an air blast.

In the extraction of iron the ingredients of the furnace are iron ore, coke (carbon), and limestone. The coke is the fuel and provides the carbon monoxide for the reduction of the iron ore; the limestone acts as a flux, removing impurities.

blastocyst in mammals, the hollow ball of cells which is an early stage in the development of the ◊embryo, roughly equivalent to the ◊blastula of other animal groups.

blastomere in biology, a cell formed in the first stages of embryonic development, after the splitting of the fertilized ovum, but before the formation of the ◊blastula or blastocyst.

blastula early stage in the development of a fertilized egg, when the egg changes from a solid mass of cells (the morula) to a hollow ball of cells (the blastula), containing a fluid-filled cavity (the blastocoel). See also ◊embryology.

bleaching decolorization of coloured materials. The two main types of bleaching agent are the **oxidizing bleaches**, which bring about the ◊oxidation of pigments and include the ultraviolet rays in sunshine, hydrogen peroxide, and chlorine in household bleaches, and the **reducing bleaches**, which bring about ◊reduction and include sulphur dioxide.

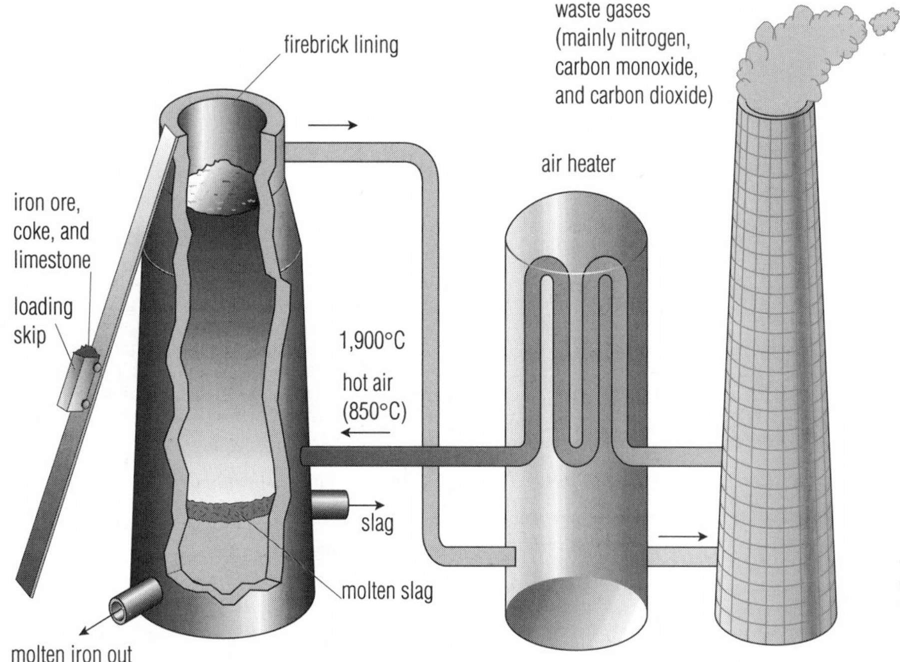

blast furnace *The blast furnace is used to extract iron from a mixture of iron ore, coke, and limestone. The less dense impurities float above the molten iron and are tapped off as slag. The molten iron sinks to the bottom of the furnace and is tapped off into moulds referred to as pigs. The iron extracted this way is also known as pig iron.*

blenny *Blennies are normally found in coastal rockpools. However, the E African species* Omobranchus striatus, *seen here, spends much of its time out of water, in groups on rocks beside the pool, ready to flip quickly into the water when danger threatens.* *Premaphotos Wildlife*

Bleaching processes have been known from antiquity, mainly those acting through sunlight. Both natural and synthetic pigments usually possess highly complex molecules, the colour property often being due only to a part of the molecule. Bleaches usually attack only that small part, yielding another substance similar in chemical structure but colourless.

bleak freshwater fish *Alburnus alburnus* of the carp family. It is up to to 20 cm/8 in long, and lives in still or slow-running clear water in Britain and Europe.

In Eastern Europe its scales are used in the preparation of artificial pearls.

bleeding loss of blood from the circulation; see ◊haemorrhage.

blenny any fish of the family Blenniidae, mostly small fish found near rocky shores, with elongated slimy bodies tapering from head to tail, no scales, and long pelvic fins set far forward.

blesbok African antelope *Damaliscus albifrons,* about 1 m/3 ft high, with curved horns, brownish body, and a white blaze on the face. It was seriously depleted in the wild at the end of the 19th century. A few protected herds survive in South Africa. It is farmed for meat.

blesbok *Blesbok antelopes, which live on the African savanna, are now scarce. Blesbok males are highly territorial and spend a great deal of time standing near a central dung-heap, attracting females to their harem and driving off rival males.* *Premaphotos Wildlife*

blight any of a number of plant diseases caused mainly by parasitic species of ◊fungus, which produce a whitish appearance on leaf and stem surfaces; for example, **potato blight** *Phytophthora infestans*. General damage caused by aphids or pollution is sometimes known as blight.

In 1998 a new virulent strain of *P. infestans*, US-8, was decimating potato and tomato crops throughout the US and eastern Canada, proving to be resistant to previously effective fungicides.

blind carbon copy e-mail message sent to multiple recipients who do not know each other's identities. The facility for blind carbon copies is built into some e-mail software, and is useful in eliminating long lists of recipients which clutter up a mass-distribution message; it also protects the confidentiality of a particular user's contact list.

blindness complete absence or impairment of sight. It may be caused by heredity, accident, disease, or deterioration with age.

Age-related macular degeneration (AMD), the commonest form of blindness, occurs as the retina gradually deteriorates with age. It affects 1% of people over the age of 70, with many more experiencing marked reduction in sight.

Retinitis pigmentosa, a common cause of blindness, is a hereditary disease affecting 1.2 million people worldwide.

Education of the blind was begun by Valentin Haüy, who published a book with raised lettering in 1784, and founded a school. Aids to the blind include the use of the Braille and Moon alphabets in reading and writing. Guide dogs for the blind were first trained in Germany for soldiers blinded in World War I.

> *Science without religion is lame. Religion without science is blind.*
>
> ALBERT EINSTEIN German-born US scientist. Quoted in A Pais *'Subtle is the Lord...': The Science and the Life of Albert Einstein* 1982

blind signature encryption technique that authenticates a message without revealing any information about the sender. Blind signatures are one element in the attempt to develop technology that protects individual privacy as more and more transactions take place over public networks where users' activities can be tracked.

blind spot area where the optic nerve and blood vessels pass through the retina of the ◊eye. No visual image can be formed as there are no light-sensitive cells in this part of the retina.

Thus the organism is blind to objects that fall in this part of the visual field.

blindworm another name for a ◊slow-worm.

blink in communications, to ◊log on using an offline reader or other software that uses automated ◊scripts. Blinking saves on communications and telephone charges, but it changes the nature of online interaction because users cannot use chat facilities.

Blinking also encourages repetition, since users replying off-line are unlikely to realize they are echoing each others' comments.

On Americal OnLine, a blink is called a **flashsession**.

blister beetle or *oil beetle* any of a small group of medium sized (3–20 mm/0.1–0.8 in) often brightly coloured beetles. Most give off an evil-smelling liquid, containing the irritant cantharidin, from the joints of their legs as a defence mechanism. When in contact with human skin, the liquid causes inflammation and blisters.

classification Blister beetles are members of the family Meloidae, order Coleoptera, class Insecta, phylum Arthropoda.

The general characteristics of the group include: head strongly bent downwards, narrow neck, and cylindrical and fairly soft body.

The **Spanish fly** *Lytta vesicatoria* was used to produce cantharidin for medicinal purposes, when blistering was a common medical treatment.

BL Lacertae object starlike object that forms the centre of a distant galaxy, with a prodigious energy output. BL Lac objects, as they are called, seem to be related to ◊quasars and are thought to be the brilliant nuclei of elliptical galaxies. They are so named because the first to be discovered lies in the small constellation Lacerta.

BLOB in computing, contraction of ◊binary large object.

block in computing, a group of records treated as a complete unit for transfer to or from ◊backing storage. For example, many disc drives transfer data in 512-byte blocks.

block and tackle type of ◊pulley.

blocking software any of various software programs that work on the World Wide Web to block access to categories of information considered offensive or dangerous. Typically used by parents or teachers to ensure that children do not see pornographic or other adult material, some blocking products additionally allow the blocking of personal information such as home addresses and telephone numbers; some people regard this as censorship.

Blocking software became even more controversial in mid-1996 when Washington DC-based reporters Brock Meeks and Declan McCullagh revealed that the list of banned sites in some popular products included political material and that some sites were blocked indiscriminately.

Popular blocking software products include Net Nanny, SurfWatch, CyberPatrol, and CyberSitter.

blood fluid circulating in the arteries, veins, and capillaries of vertebrate animals; the term also refers to the corresponding fluid in those invertebrates that possess a closed ◊circulatory system. Blood carries nutrients and oxygen to each body cell and removes waste products, such as carbon dioxide. It is also important in the immune response and, in many animals, in the distribution of heat throughout the body.

In humans blood makes up 5% of the body weight, occupying a volume of 5.5 l/10 pt in the average adult. It is composed of a colourless, transparent liquid called **plasma**, in which are suspended microscopic cells of three main varieties:

Red cells (erythrocytes) form nearly half the volume of the blood, with about 6 million red cells in every millilitre of an adult's blood. Their red colour is caused by ◊haemoglobin.

White cells (leucocytes) are of various kinds. Some (phagocytes) ingest invading bacteria and so protect the body from disease; these also help to repair injured tissues. Others (lymphocytes) produce antibodies, which help provide immunity.

Blood **platelets** (thrombocytes) assist in the clotting of blood.

Blood cells constantly wear out and die and are replaced from the bone marrow. Red blood cells die at the rate of 200 billion per day but the body produces new cells at an average rate of 9,000 million per hour.

> To remember the functions of the blood:
>
> OLD CHARLIE FOSTER HATES WOMEN HAVING DULL CLOTHES.
>
> OXYGEN (TRANSPORT) / CARBON DIOXIDE (TRANSPORT) / FOOD / HEAT / WASTE / HORMONES / DISEASE / CLOTTING

blood clotting complex series of events (known as the blood clotting cascade) that prevents excessive bleeding after injury. It is triggered by ◊vitamin K. The result is the formation of a meshwork of protein fibres (fibrin) and trapped blood cells over the cut blood vessels.

When platelets (cell fragments) in the bloodstream come into contact with a damaged blood vessel, they and the vessel wall itself release the enzyme **thrombokinase**, which brings about the conversion of the inactive enzyme **prothrombin** into the active **thrombin**. Thrombin in turn catalyses the conversion of the soluble protein **fibrinogen**, present in blood plasma, to the insoluble **fibrin**. This fibrous protein forms a net over the wound that traps red blood cells and seals the wound; the resulting jellylike clot hardens on exposure to air to form a scab. Calcium, vitamin K, and a variety of enzymes called factors are also necessary for efficient blood clotting. ◊Haemophilia is one of several diseases in which the clotting mechanism is impaired.

blood group any of the types into which blood is classified according to the presence or otherwise of certain ◊antigens on the surface of its red cells. Red blood cells of one individual may carry molecules on their surface that act as antigens in another individual whose red blood cells lack these molecules. The two main antigens are designated A and B. These give rise to four blood groups: having A only (A), having B only (B), having both (AB), and having neither (O). Each of these groups may or may not contain the ◊rhesus factor. Correct typing of blood groups is vital in transfusion, since incompatible types of donor and recipient blood will result in coagulation, with possible death of the recipient.

The ABO system was first described by Austrian scientist Karl Landsteiner in 1902. Subsequent research revealed at least 14 main types of blood group systems, 11 of which are involved with induced ◊antibody production. Blood typing is also of importance in forensic medicine, cases of disputed paternity, and in anthropological studies.

bloodhound breed of dog that originated as a hunting dog in Belgium in the Middle Ages. Black and tan in colour, it has long, pendulous ears and distinctive wrinkled head and face. It grows to a height of about 65 cm/26 in. Its excellent powers of scent have been employed in tracking and criminal detection from very early times.

blood poisoning presence in the bloodstream of quantities of bacteria or bacterial toxins sufficient to cause serious illness.

blood pressure pressure, or tension, of the blood against the inner walls of blood vessels, especially the arteries, due to the muscular pumping activity of the heart. Abnormally high blood pressure (◊hypertension) may be associated with various conditions or arise with no obvious cause; abnormally low blood pressure (hypotension) occurs in ◊shock and after excessive fluid or blood loss from any cause.

In mammals, the left ventricle of the ◊heart pumps blood into the arterial system. This pumping is assisted by waves of muscular contraction by the arteries themselves, but resisted by the elasticity of the inner and outer walls of the same arteries. Pressure is greatest when the heart ventricle contracts **(systole)** and lowest when the ventricle relaxes (**diastole**), and pressure is solely maintained by the elasticity of the arteries. Blood pressure is measured in millimetres of mercury (the height of a column on the measuring instrument, a sphygmomanometer). Normal human blood pressure varies with age, but in a young healthy adult it is around 120/80 mm Hg; the first number represents the systolic pressure and the second the diastolic. Large deviations from this reading usually indicate ill health.

blood test laboratory evaluation of a blood sample. There are numerous blood tests, from simple typing to establish the ◊blood group to sophisticated biochemical assays of substances, such as hormones, present in the blood only in minute quantities.

The majority of tests fall into one of three categories: **haematology** (testing the state of the blood itself), **microbiology** (identifying infection), and **blood chemistry** (reflecting chemical events elsewhere in the body). Before operations, a common test is haemoglobin estimation to determine how well a patient might tolerate blood loss during surgery.

blood transfusion see ◊transfusion.

blood vessel tube that conducts blood either away from or towards the heart in multicellular animals. Freshly oxygenated blood is carried in the arteries – major vessels which give way to the arterioles (small arteries) and finally capillaries; deoxygenated blood is returned to the heart by way of capillaries, then venules (small veins) and veins.

bloodworm larvae of the ◊midge. They are red because their blood plasma contains haemoglobin like human blood, which increases its ability to take up oxygen. This is of value to the larvae, which commonly burrow in the oxygen-poor mud bottom of pools and rivers. They feed on algae and detritus.

Bloodworms are long, with a distinct head, and segmentation of the abdomen. Prolegs (leglike projections) are found on the first thoracic and last abdominal segments. Gills are present on the last abdominal segment, and often on the segment preceding it. On average they measure 6 mm/0.2 in in length.

Bloodworms frequently build tubes of mud around themselves, which may be attached to stones. They constitute a major part of the diet of fish, hence they are often used as bait by anglers.

Not all midge larvae are red. Those that do not live in mud tubes, but frequent the surface waters, are green, and some species have blue bands.

bloom whitish powdery or waxlike coating over the surface of certain fruits that easily rubs off when handled. It often contains ◊yeasts that live on the sugars in the fruit. The term bloom is also used to describe a rapid increase in number of certain species of algae found in lakes, ponds, and oceans.

Such blooms may be natural but are often the result of nitrate pollution, in which artificial fertilizers, applied to surrounding fields, leach out into the waterways. This type of bloom can lead to the death of almost every other organism in the water; because light cannot penetrate the algal growth, the plants beneath can no longer photosynthesize and therefore do not release oxygen into the water. Only those organisms that are adapted to very low levels of oxygen survive.

BLOWFLY

Blowfly larvae develop in less than two weeks. During this time they can gain 5% of their final larval weight each hour.

blowfly any fly of the genus *Calliphora,* also known as bluebottle, or of the related genus *Lucilia,* when it is greenbottle. It lays its eggs in dead flesh, on which the maggots feed.

blowfly *Bluebottles* Calliphora vicina, *commonly known as blowfly, lay eggs on rotting flesh.* *Premaphotos Wildlife*

blubber thick layer of ◊fat under the skin of marine mammals, which provides an energy store and an effective insulating layer, preventing the loss of body heat to the surrounding water. Blubber has been used (when boiled down) in engineering, food processing, cosmetics, and printing, but all of these products can now be produced synthetically.

bluebell name given in Scotland to the ◊harebell (*Campanula rotundifolia*), and in England to the wild hyacinth (*Endymion non-scriptus*), belonging to the lily family (Liliaceae).

blueberry any of various North American shrubs belonging to the heath family, growing in acid soil. The genus also includes huckleberries, bilberries, deerberries, and cranberries, many of which resemble each other and are difficult to tell apart from blueberries. All have small oval short-stalked leaves, slender green or reddish twigs, and whitish bell-like blossoms. Only true blueberries, however, have tiny granular speckles on their twigs. Blueberries have black or blue edible fruits, often covered with a white bloom. (Genus *Vaccinium*, family Ericaceae.)

bluebird or ***blue robin*** or ***blue warbler*** three species of a North American bird, genus *Sialia*, belonging to the thrush subfamily, Turdinae, order Passeriformes. The eastern bluebird *Sialia sialis* is regarded as the herald of spring as it returns from migration. About 18 cm/7 in long, it has a reddish breast, the upper plumage being sky-blue, and a distinctive song. It lays about six pale-blue eggs.

bluebottle another name for ◊blowfly.

bluebuck any of several species of antelope, including the blue ◊duiker *Cephalophus monticola* of South Africa, about 33 cm/13 in high. The male of the Indian ◊nilgai antelope is also known as the bluebuck.

The bluebuck or blaubok, *Hippotragus leucophaeus*, was a large blue-grey South African antelope. Once abundant, it was hunted to extinction, the last being shot in 1800.

bluegrass dense spreading grass, which is blue-tinted and grows in clumps. Various species are known from the northern hemisphere. Kentucky bluegrass (*Poa pratensis*), introduced to the USA from Europe, provides pasture for horses. (Genus *Poa*, family Gramineae.)

blue-green algae or ***cyanobacteria*** single-celled, primitive organisms that resemble bacteria in their internal cell organization, sometimes joined together in colonies or filaments. Blue-green algae are among the oldest known living organisms and, with bacteria, belong to the kingdom Monera; remains have been found in rocks up to 3.5 billion years old. They are widely distributed in aquatic habitats, on the damp surfaces of rocks and trees, and in the soil.

Blue-green algae and bacteria are prokaryotic organisms. Some can fix nitrogen and thus are necessary to the nitrogen cycle, while others follow a symbiotic existence – for example, living in association with fungi to form lichens. Fresh water can become polluted by nitrates and phosphates from fertilizers and detergents. This eutrophication, or overenrichment, of the water causes multiplication of the algae in the form of algae blooms. The algae multiply and cover the water's surface, remaining harmless until they give off toxins as they decay. These toxins kill fish and other wildlife and can be harmful to domestic animals, cattle, and people.

blue gum either of two Australian trees: Tasmanian blue gum (*Eucalyptus globulus*) of the myrtle family, with bluish bark, a chief source of eucalyptus oil; or the tall, straight Sydney blue gum (*E. saligna*). The former is widely cultivated in California and has also been planted in South America, India, parts of Africa, and S Europe.

blueprint photographic process used for copying engineering drawings and architectural plans, so called because it produces a white copy of the original against a blue background.

The plan to be copied is made on transparent tracing paper, which is placed in contact with paper sensitized with a mixture of iron ammonium citrate and potassium hexacyanoferrate. The paper is exposed to ◊ultraviolet radiation and then washed in water. Where the light reaches the paper, it turns blue (Prussian blue). The paper underneath the lines of the drawing is unaffected, so remains white.

blue-ribbon campaign campaign for free speech on the Internet. It was launched to protest against various international moves towards censorship on the Internet, especially the ◊Communications Decency Act in 1996. Participation in the campaign is indicated by the small graphic of a looped blue ribbon displayed on many sites on the World Wide Web and available from the campaign's Web site http://www.eff.org/blueribbon.html.

blue shark species of ◊shark with a blue back and white underside. It grows to a length of at least 7 m/23 ft and is found in all oceanic waters except the polar seas.
classification The blue shark *Odontaspis glaucas* belongs in the family Odontaspididae, order Lamniformes (typical sharks), subclass Elasmobranchii, class Chondrichthyes.

blue shift in astronomy, a manifestation of the ◊Doppler effect in which an object appears bluer when it is moving towards the observer or the observer is moving towards it (blue light is of a higher frequency than other colours in the spectrum). The blue shift is the opposite of the ◊red shift.

blue whale the world's largest animal; see ◊whale.

BMP in Windows, a file extension indicating a graphics file in ◊bitmap format. Bit-mapped files are commonly used for icons and wallpaper.

BMR abbreviation for ◊basal metabolic rate.

boa any of various nonvenomous snakes of the family Boidae, found mainly in tropical and subtropical parts of the New World. Boas feed mainly on small mammals and birds. They catch these in their teeth or kill them by constriction (crushing the creature within their coils until it suffocates). The boa constrictor *Constrictor constrictor* can grow up to 5.5 m/18.5 ft long, but rarely reaches more than 4 m/12 ft. Other boas include the anaconda and the emerald tree boa *Boa canina*, about 2 m/6 ft long and bright green.

Some small burrowing boas live in N Africa and W Asia, while other species live on Madagascar and some Pacific islands, but the majority of boas live in South and Central America. The name boa is sometimes used loosely to include the pythons of the Old World, which also belong to the Boidae family, and which share with boas vestiges of hind limbs and constricting habits.

boar wild member of the pig family, such as the Eurasian wild boar *Sus scrofa*, from which domestic pig breeds derive. The wild boar is sturdily built, being 1.5 m/4.5 ft long and 1 m/3 ft high, and possesses formidable tusks. Of gregarious nature and mainly woodland-dwelling, it feeds on roots, nuts, insects, and some carrion.

The dark coat of the adult boar is made up of coarse bristles with varying amounts of underfur, but the young are striped. The male domestic pig is also known as a boar, the female as a sow.

boarfish marine bony fish found chiefly in the Mediterranean and northeast Atlantic. It has a flat oval body that is reddish coloured with seven transverse orange bands on the back. Boarfish are related to the dory.
classification Boarfish *Capros aper* belongs to the order Zeiformes, class Osteichthyes.

The name boarfish is derived from its projecting hoglike snout.

bobcat wild cat *Lynx rufus* living in a variety of habitats from S Canada through to S Mexico. It is similar to the lynx, but only 75 cm/2.5 ft long, with reddish fur and less well-developed ear tufts.

bobolink North American songbird *Dolichonyx oryzivorus*, family Icteridae, order Passeriformes, that takes its common name from the distinctive call of the male. It has a long middle toe and pointed tailfeathers. Breeding males are mostly black, with a white rump; females are buff-coloured with dark streaks. Bobolinks are about 18 cm/7 in long and build their nests on the ground in hayfields and weedy meadows.

Bode's law numerical sequence that gives the approximate distances, in astronomical units (distance between Earth and Sun = one astronomical unit), of the planets from the Sun by adding 4 to each term of the series 0, 3, 6, 12, 24, ... and then dividing by 10. Bode's law predicted the existence of a planet between ◊Mars and ◊Jupiter, which led to the discovery of the asteroids.

The 'law' breaks down for ◊Neptune and ◊Pluto. The relationship was first noted in 1772 by the German mathematician Johann Titius (1729–1796) (it is also known as the Titius–Bode law).

Bohr, Niels Henrik David (1885–1962)

Danish physicist whose theoretical work established the structure of the atom and the validity of quantum theory by showing that the nuclei of atoms are surrounded by shells of electrons, each assigned particular sets of quantum numbers according to their orbits. For this work he was awarded the Nobel Prize for Physics in 1922. He explained the structure and behaviour of the nucleus, as well as the process of nuclear fission. Bohr also proposed the doctrine of complementarity, the theory that a fundamental particle is neither a wave nor a particle, because these are complementary modes of description.

quantum theory and atomic structure Bohr's first model of the atom was developed working in Manchester, UK with Ernest Rutherford, who had proposed a nuclear theory of atomic structure from his work on the scattering of alpha rays in 1911. It was not, however, understood how electrons could continually orbit the nucleus without radiating energy, as classical physics demanded.

Mary Evans Picture Library

In 1913, Bohr developed his theory of atomic structure by applying quantum theory to the observations of radiation emitted by atoms. Ten years earlier, Max Planck had proposed that radiation is emitted or absorbed by atoms in discrete units, or quanta, of energy. Bohr postulated that an atom may exist in only a certain number of stable states, each with a certain amount of energy in which electrons orbit the nucleus without emitting or absorbing energy. He proposed that emission or absorption of energy occurs only with a transition from one stable state to another. When a transition occurs, an electron moving to a higher orbit absorbs energy and an electron moving to a lower orbit emits energy. In so doing, a set number of quanta of energy are emitted or absorbed at a particular frequency. Bohr's atomic theory was validated in 1922 by the discovery of an element he had predicted, hafnium.

the liquid-droplet model In 1939, Bohr proposed his liquid-droplet model for the nucleus, in which nuclear particles are pulled together by short-range forces, similar to the way in which molecules in a drop of liquid are attracted to one another. The extra energy produced by the absorption of a neutron causes the nuclear particles to separate into two groups of approximately the same size, thus breaking the nucleus into two smaller nuclei – as happens in nuclear fission. The model was vindicated when Bohr correctly predicted the differing behaviour of nuclei of uranium-235 and uranium-238 from the fact that the number of neutrons in each nucleus is odd and even respectively.

BODMAS (mnemonic for **brackets**, **of**, **division**, **multiplication**, **addition**, **subtraction**) – the order in which an arithmetical expression should be calculated.

Boeing US military and commercial aircraft manufacturer. Among the models Boeing has produced are the B-17 Flying Fortress, 1935; the B-52 Stratofortress, 1952; the Chinook helicopter, 1961; the first jetliner, the Boeing 707, 1957; the ◊jumbo jet or Boeing 747, 1969; the ◊jetfoil, 1975; and the 777-300 jetliner, 1997.

The company was founded in 1916 near Seattle, Washington, by William E Boeing (1881–1956) as the Pacific Aero Products Company. Renamed the following year, the company built its first seaplane and in 1919 set up an airmail service between Seattle and Victoria, British Columbia. The company announced in December 1996 that they would merge with US aircraft manufacturers McDonnell Douglas to create the world's largest aerospace company, with sales of $48 billion/£29 billion, some 200,000 employees, and an order book of civil and military aircraft worth $100 billion/£60 billion. The new US group would manufacture about three-quarters of the world's commercial airliners. It would operate under the Boeing name and with its principal headquarters in Seattle, WA. The single aerospace giant would transform the whole industry and threaten all of its rivals, including the European consortium Airbus Industrie, which had a 20% share of the commercial airline market. The merger of Boeing and McDonnell Douglas was approved by the European Union in 1997. Also in 1997 Boeing unveiled its 777-300 jetliner, the world's longest and largest twin-engine aircraft of its kind at the time, which would replace the four-engine Boeing 747.

bog type of wetland where decomposition is slowed down and dead plant matter accumulates as ◊peat. Bogs develop under conditions of low temperature, high acidity, low nutrient supply, stagnant water, and oxygen deficiency. Typical bog plants are sphagnum moss, rushes, and cotton grass; insectivorous plants such as sundews and bladderworts are common in bogs (insect prey make up for the lack of nutrients).

bogbean or ***buckbean*** aquatic or bog plant belonging to the gentian family, with a creeping rhizome (underground stem) and leaves and pink flower spikes held above water. It is found over much of the northern hemisphere. (*Menyanthes trifoliata*, family Gentianaceae.)

bohrium synthesized, radioactive element of the ◊transactinide series, symbol Bh, atomic number 107, relative atomic mass 262. It was first synthesized by the Joint Institute for Nuclear Research in Dubna, Russia in 1976; in 1981 the Laboratory for Heavy Ion Research in Darmstadt, Germany, confirmed its existence. It was named in 1997 after Danish physicist Niels ◊Bohr. Its temporary name was unnilseptium.

Bohr model model of the atom conceived by Danish physicist Neils Bohr in 1913. It assumes that the following rules govern the behaviour of electrons: (1) electrons revolve in orbits of specific radius around the nucleus without emitting radiation; (2) within each orbit, each electron has a fixed amount of energy; electrons in orbits farther away from the nucleus have greater energies; (3) an electron may 'jump' from one orbit of high energy to another of lower energy causing the energy difference to be emitted as a ◊photon of electromagnetic radiation such as light. The Bohr model has been superseded by wave mechanics (see ◊quantum theory).

boiler any vessel that converts water into steam. Boilers are used in conventional power stations to generate steam to feed steam ◊turbines, which drive the electricity generators. They are also used in steamships, which are propelled by steam turbines, and in steam locomotives. Every boiler has a furnace in which fuel (coal, oil, or gas) is burned to produce hot gases, and a system of tubes in which heat is transferred from the gases to the water.

The common kind of boiler used in ships and power stations is the **water-tube** type, in which the water circulates in tubes surrounded by the hot furnace gases. The water-tube boilers at power stations produce steam at a pressure of up to 300 atmospheres and at a temperature of up to 600°C/1,100°F to feed to the steam turbines. It is more efficient than the **fire-tube** type that is used in steam locomotives. In this boiler the hot furnace gases are drawn through tubes surrounded by water.

boiling process of changing a liquid into its vapour, by heating it at the maximum possible temperature for that liquid (see ◊boiling point) at atmospheric pressure.

boiling point for any given liquid, the temperature at which the application of heat raises the temperature of the liquid no further, but converts it into vapour.

The boiling point of water under normal pressure is 100°C/ 212°F. The lower the pressure, the lower the boiling point and vice versa.

boletus any of several fleshy fungi (see ◊fungus) with thick stems and caps of various colours. The European *Boletus edulis* is edible, but some species are poisonous. (Genus *Boletus,* class Basidiomycetes.)

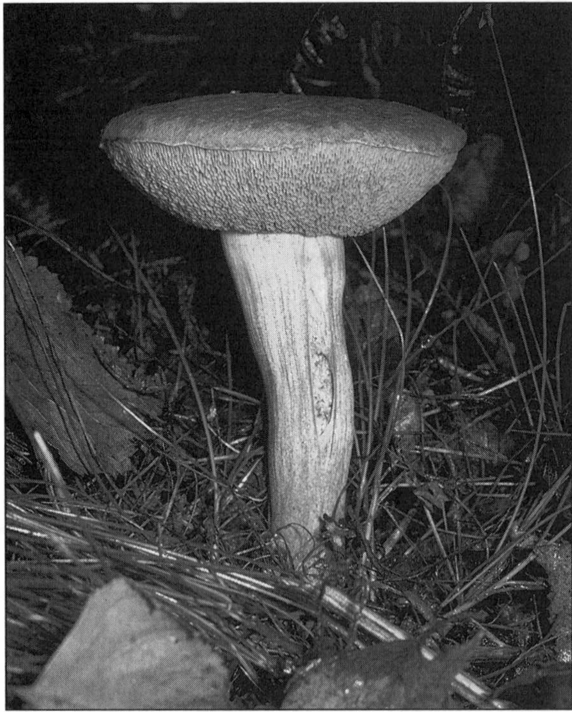

***boletus** The red crack boletus* Boletus chrysenteron. *Like other members of the genus, it releases its spores through a mass of pores beneath the cap, rather than from the more familiar gills seen beneath the cap of an edible mushroom. Premaphotos Wildlife*

boll weevil small American beetle *Anthonomus grandis* of the weevil group. The female lays her eggs in the unripe pods or 'bolls' of the cotton plant, and on these the larvae feed, causing great destruction.

bolometer sensitive ◊thermometer that measures the energy of radiation by registering the change in electrical resistance of a fine wire when it is exposed to heat or light.

The US astronomer Samuel Langley devised it in 1880 for measuring radiation from stars.

bolometric magnitude in astronomy, a measure of the brightness of a star over all wavelengths. Bolometric magnitude is related the total radiation output of the star. See ◊magnitude.

Boltzmann, Ludwig Eduard (1844–1906) Austrian physicist who studied the kinetic theory of gases, which explains the properties of gases by reference to the motion of their constituent atoms and molecules. He established the branch of physics now known as statistical mechanics.

He derived a formula, the **Boltzmann distribution**, which gives the number of atoms or molecules with a given energy at a specific temperature. The constant in the formula is called the **Boltzmann constant**.

BOLTZMANN, LUDWIG

http://www-history.mcs.st-and.ac.uk/~history/Mathematicians/Boltzmann.html

Biography of the physicist and mathematician. The site contains a description of the work of Boltzmann, and also describes his working relationships with his contemporaries, which due to the radical nature of his work were often strained. Also included are several literature references for further reading, and a photograph of Boltzmann.

Boltzmann constant in physics, the constant (symbol k) that relates the kinetic energy (energy of motion) of a gas atom or molecule to temperature. Its value is 1.38066×10^{-23} joules per kelvin. It is equal to the gas constant R, divided by ◊Avogadro's number.

bolus mouthful of chewed food mixed with saliva, ready for swallowing. Most vertebrates swallow food immediately, but grazing mammals chew their food a great deal, allowing a mechanical and chemical breakdown to begin.

bombardier beetle beetle that emits an evil-smelling fluid from its abdomen, as a defence mechanism. This fluid rapidly evaporates into a gas, which appears like a minute jet of smoke when in contact with air, and blinds the predator about to attack.
classification Bombardier beetles in genus *Brachinus,* family Carabidae, order Coleoptera, class Insecta, phylum Arthropoda.

Bombay duck or ***bummalow*** small fish *Harpodon nehereus* found in the Indian Ocean. It has a thin body, up to 40 cm/16 in long, and sharp, pointed teeth. It feeds on shellfish and other small fish. It is valuable as a food fish, and is eaten, salted and dried, with dishes such as curry.

bond in chemistry, the result of the forces of attraction that hold together atoms of an element or elements to form a molecule. The principal types of bonding are ◊ionic, ◊covalent, ◊metallic, and ◊intermolecular (such as hydrogen bonding).

bone hard connective tissue comprising the ◊skeleton of most vertebrate animals. Bone is composed of a network of collagen fibres impregnated with mineral salts (largely calcium phosphate and calcium carbonate), a combination that gives it great density and strength, comparable in some cases with that of reinforced concrete. Enclosed within this solid matrix are bone cells, blood vessels, and nerves. The interior of the long bones of the limbs consists of a spongy matrix filled with a soft marrow that produces blood cells.

There are two types of bone: those that develop by replacing ◊cartilage and those that form directly from connective tissue. The latter, which includes the bones of the cranium, are usually plate-like in shape and form in the skin of the developing embryo. Humans have about 206 distinct bones in the skeleton, of which the smallest are the three ossicles in the middle ear.

To remember the bones of the upper limb:

SOME CRIMINALS HAVE UNDERESTIMATED ROYAL CANADIAN MOUNTED POLICE.

SCAPULA / CLAVICLE / HUMERUS / ULNA / RADIUS / CARPALS / METACARPALS / PHALANGES

bone marrow substance found inside the cavity of bones. In early life it produces red blood cells but later on lipids (fat) accumulate and its colour changes from red to yellow.

Bone marrow may be transplanted in the treatment of some diseases, such as leukaemia, using immunosuppressive drugs in the recipient to prevent rejection. Transplants to adult monkeys from early aborted monkey fetuses have successfully bypassed rejection.

bone *Bone is a network of fibrous material impregnated with mineral salts and as strong as reinforced concrete. The upper end of the thighbone or femur is made up of spongy bone, which has a fine lacework structure designed to transmit the weight of the body. The shaft of the femur consists of hard compact bone designed to resist bending. Fine channels carrying blood vessels, nerves, and lymphatics interweave even the densest bone.*

bongo Central African antelope *Boocercus eurycerus,* living in dense humid forests. Up to 1.4 m/4.5 ft at the shoulder, it has spiral horns which may be 80 cm/2.6 ft or more in length. The body is rich chestnut, with narrow white stripes running vertically down the sides, and a black belly.

bonito any of various species of medium-sized tuna, predatory fish of the genus *Sarda,* in the mackerel family. The ocean bonito *Katsuwonus pelamis* grows to 1 m/3 ft and is common in tropical seas. The Atlantic bonito *Sarda sarda* is found in the Mediterranean and tropical Atlantic and grows to the same length but has a narrower body.

bonobo species of ◊chimpanzee.

boobook owl *Ninox novaeseelandiae* found in Australia, so named because of its call.

booby tropical seabird of the genus *Sula,* in the same family, Sulidae, as the northern ◊gannet, order Pelicaniformes. There are six species, including the circumtropical brown booby *S. leucogaster.* Plumage is white and black or brown, with no feathers on the throat and lower jaw. They inhabit coastal waters, and dive to catch fish. The name was given by sailors who saw the bird's tameness as stupidity.

One species, **Abbott's booby**, breeds only on Christmas Island, in the western Indian Ocean. Unlike most boobies and gannets, it nests high up in trees. Large parts of its breeding ground have been destroyed by phosphate mining, but conservation measures now protect the site.

booklouse any of numerous species of tiny wingless insects of the order Psocoptera, especially *Atropus pulsatoria,* which lives in books and papers, feeding on starches and moulds.

Most of the other species live in bark, leaves, and lichens. They thrive in dark, damp conditions.

bookmark facility for marking a specific place in electronic documentation to enable easy return to it. It is used in several types of software, including electronic help files and tutorials. Bookmarks are especially important on the World Wide Web, where it can be difficult to remember a uniform resource locator (◊URL) in order to

Boole, George
(1815–1864)

English mathematician. His work *The Mathematical Analysis of Logic 1847* established the basis of modern mathematical logic, and his Boolean algebra can be used in designing computers.

Boole's system is essentially two-valued. By subdividing objects into separate classes, each with a given property, his algebra makes it possible to treat different classes according to the presence or absence of the same property. Hence it involves just two numbers, 0 and 1 – the binary system used in the computer.

Mary Evans Picture Library

BOOLE, GEORGE

http://www-history.mcs.st-and.ac.uk/~history/Mathematicians/Boole.html

Extensive biography of the mathematician. The site contains a clear description of his working relationship with his contemporaries, and also includes the title page of his famous book *Investigation of the Laws of Thought*. Several literature references for further reading on the mathematician are also listed, and the Web site also features a portrait of Boole.

return to it. Most Web browsers therefore have built-in bookmark facilities, whereby the browser stores the URL with the page name attached. To return directly to the site, the user picks the page name from the list of saved bookmarks.

Boolean algebra set of algebraic rules, named after mathematician George Boole, in which TRUE and FALSE are equated to 0 and 1. Boolean algebra includes a series of operators (AND, OR, NOT, NAND (NOT AND), NOR, and XOR (exclusive OR)), which can be used to manipulate TRUE and FALSE values (see ◊truth table). It is the basis of computer logic because the truth values can be directly associated with ◊bits.

These rules are used in searching databases either locally or across the ◊Internet via services like AltaVista to limit the number of hits to those which most closely match a user's requirements. A search instruction such as 'tennis NOT table' would retrieve articles about tennis and reject those about ping-pong.

boomslang rear-fanged venomous African snake *Dispholidus typus,* often green but sometimes brown or blackish, and growing to a length of 2 m/6 ft. It lives in trees, and feeds on tree-dwelling lizards such as chameleons. Its venom can be fatal to humans; however, boomslangs rarely attack people.

boot or ***bootstrap*** in computing, the process of starting up a computer. Most computers have a small, built-in boot program that starts automatically when the computer is switched on – its only task is to load a slightly larger program, usually from a hard disc, which in turn loads the main ◊operating system.

In microcomputers the operating system is often held in the permanent ◊ROM memory and the boot program simply triggers its operation.

Some boot programs can be customized so that, for example, the computer, when switched on, always loads and runs a program from a particular backing store or always adopts a particular mode of screen display.

boot disc (also known as an ***emergency disc***) floppy disc containing the necessary files to ◊boot a computer without needing to access its hard disc. Boot discs are vital in recovering from virus attacks, when it is not known which files on a computer's hard disc may be infected; in recovering from a system crash which has corrupted existing files; or in correcting mistakes introduced into files necessary for starting up the computer by newly installed software programs.

Boötes constellation of the northern hemisphere represented by a herdsman driving a bear (◊Ursa Major) around the pole. Its brightest star is ◊Arcturus (or Alpha Boötis), which is about 37 light years from Earth. The herdsman is assisted by the neighbouring ◊Canes Venatici, 'the Hunting Dogs'.

borage plant native to S Europe, used in salads and in medicine. It has small blue flowers and hairy leaves. (*Borago officinalis,* family Boraginaceae.)

borax hydrous sodium borate, $Na_2B_4O_7.10H_2O$, found as soft, whitish crystals or encrustations on the shores of hot springs and in the dry beds of salt lakes in arid regions, where it occurs with other borates, halite, and gypsum. It is used in bleaches and washing powders.

A large industrial source is Borax Lake, California. Borax is also used in glazing pottery, in soldering, as a mild antiseptic, and as a metallurgical flux.

Bordeaux mixture a solution made up of equal quantities of copper(II) sulphate and lime in water, used in horticulture and in the wine industry as a ◊fungicide.

border collie breed of ◊sheepdog originating in the Borders region of Scotland and still much prized as a versatile working dog with a powerful herding instinct. It has a smooth or fairly long, dense, black and white coat and stands about 53 cm/21 in tall.

border terrier small, hardy, short-tailed dog with an otterlike head, moderately broad skull and short, strong muzzle. Its small, V-shaped ears drop forward. The coat is hard and dense with a close undercoat and is red, beige, and tan, or blue and tan. Dogs weigh 6–7 kg/13–15.5 lb; bitches 5–6.5 kg/ 11–14.5 lb.

bore surge of tidal water up an estuary or a river, caused by the funnelling of the rising tide by a narrowing river mouth. A very high tide, possibly fanned by wind, may build up when it is held back by a river current in the river mouth. The result is a broken wave, a metre or a few feet high, that rushes upstream.

Famous bores are found in the rivers Severn (England), Seine (France), Hooghly (India), and Chiang Jiang (China), where bores of over 4 m/13 ft have been reported.

boric acid or ***boracic acid*** $B(OH)_3$ acid formed by the combination of hydrogen and oxygen with nonmetallic boron. It is a weak antiseptic and is used in the manufacture of glass and enamels. It is also an efficient insecticide against ants and cockroaches.

boron nonmetallic element, symbol B, atomic number 5, relative atomic mass 10.811. In nature it is found only in compounds, as with sodium and oxygen in borax. It exists in two allotropic forms (see ◊allotropy): brown amorphous powder and very hard, brilliant crystals. Its compounds are used in the preparation of boric acid, water softeners, soaps, enamels, glass, and pottery glazes. In alloys it is used to harden steel. Because it absorbs slow neutrons, it is used to make boron carbide control rods for nuclear reactors. It is a necessary trace element in the human diet. The element was named by Humphry Davy, who isolated it in 1808, from *bor*ax + -on, as in carb*on*.

borzoi ***Russian 'swift'*** breed of large dog originating in Russia. It is of the greyhound type, white with darker markings, with a thick, silky coat, and stands 75 cm/30 in or more at the shoulder.

The borzoi's original quarry was hares and foxes, but it was selectively bred in the 19th century to produce a larger, stronger dog suitable for hunting wolves.

Bosch, Carl
(1874–1940)

Mary Evans Picture Library

German metallurgist and chemist. He developed the GHaber process from a small-scale technique for the production of ammonia into an industrial high-pressure process that made use of water gas as a source of hydrogen. He shared the Nobel Prize for Chemistry in 1931 with Friedrich Bergius.

Bose–Einstein condensate hypothesis put forward 1925 by Albert Einstein and Indian physicist Satyendra Bose, suggesting that when a dense gas is cooled to a little over absolute zero it will condense and its atoms will lose their individuality and act as an organized whole. The first Bose–Einstein condensate was produced in June 1995 by US physicists cooling rubidinum atoms to 10 billionths of a degree above zero. The condensate existed for about a minute before becoming rubidinum ice.

boson in physics, an elementary particle whose spin can only take values that are whole numbers or zero. Bosons may be classified as ◊gauge bosons (carriers of the four fundamental forces) or ◊mesons. All elementary particles are either bosons or ◊fermions.

Unlike fermions, more than one boson in a system (such as an atom) can possess the same energy state. When developed mathematically, this statement is known as the Bose–Einstein law, after its discoverers Indian physicist Satyendra Bose and Albert Einstein.

Boston terrier breed of dog developed in the USA for dog fighting during the second half of the 19th century from crosses of English and French ◊bulldogs. It is bred in three sizes, ranging from 7 kg/15 lb to 11 kg/24 lb in weight, has a brindled or black coat with symmetrical white markings on face, chest, and legs, and carries its ears upright.

The name 'Boston terrier' is misleading as it is related to the bulldog breeds rather than terriers.

'bot (short for ***robot***) on the Internet, automated piece of software that performs specific tasks. 'Bots are commonly found on multi-user dungeons (◊MUDs) and other multi-user role-playing game sites, where they maintain a constant level of activity even when few human users are logged on. On the World Wide Web, 'bots automate maintenance tasks such as indexing Web pages and tracing broken links.

botanical garden place where a wide range of plants is grown, providing the opportunity to see a botanical diversity not likely to be encountered naturally. Among the earliest forms of botanical garden was the **physic garden**, devoted to the study and growth of medicinal plants; an example is the Chelsea Physic Garden in London, established in 1673 and still in existence. Following increased botanical exploration, botanical gardens were used to test the commercial potential of new plants being sent back from all parts of the world.

Today a botanical garden serves many purposes: education, science, and conservation. Many are associated with universities and also maintain large collections of preserved specimens (see ◊herbarium), libraries, research laboratories, and gene banks. There are 1,600 botanical gardens worldwide.

botany ***Greek botane 'herb'*** the study of living and fossil ◊plants, including form, function, interaction with the environment, and classification.

Botany is subdivided into a number of specialized studies, such as the identification and classification of plants (taxonomy), their external formation (plant morphology), their internal arrangement (plant anatomy), their microscopic examination (plant histology), their functioning and life history (plant physiology), and their distribution over the Earth's surface in relation to their surroundings (plant ecology). Palaeobotany concerns the study of fossil plants, while economic botany deals with the utility of plants. ◊Horticulture, ◊agriculture, and ◊forestry are branches of botany.

botfly any fly of the family Oestridae. The larvae are parasites that feed on the skin (warblefly of cattle) or in the nasal cavity (nostrilflies of sheep and deer). The horse botfly belongs to another family, the Gasterophilidae. It has a parasitic larva that feeds in the horse's stomach.

bo tree or ***peepul*** Indian ◊fig tree, said to be the tree under which the Buddha became enlightened. (*Ficus religiosa*, family Moraceae.)

bottlebrush any of several trees or shrubs common in Australia, belonging to the myrtle family. They have cylindrical, composite flower heads in green, yellow, white, various shades of red, and violet. (Genus *Callistemon*, family Myrtaceae.)

bottlenose species of ◊dolphin.

botulism rare, often fatal type of ◊food poisoning. Symptoms include vomiting, diarrhoea, muscular paralysis, breathing difficulties and disturbed vision.

It is caused by a toxin produced by the bacterium *Clostridium botulinum*, found in soil and sometimes in improperly canned foods.

Thorough cooking destroys the toxin, which otherwise suppresses the cardiac and respiratory centres of the brain. In neurology, botulinum toxin is sometimes used to treat rare movement disorders.

bougainvillea any plant of a group of South American tropical vines of the four o'clock family, now cultivated in warm countries around the world for the colourful red and purple bracts (leaflike structures) that cover the flowers. They are named after the French navigator Louis de Bougainville. (Genus *Bougainvillea*, family Nyctaginaceae.)

bounce in computing, system by which an electronic mail message that cannot be delivered to its addressee is returned ('bounced back') to the sender, with a note advising of its failure to reach its destination. Failed delivery is usually due to an incorrect e-mail address or a network problem.

boundary a line around the edge of an area; a perimeter. The boundary of a circle is known as the **circumference**. The boundary which marks the limit of land may be indicated by a post, ditch, hedge, march of stones, road, or river, or it may be indicated by reference to a plan, or to possession of tenants, or by actual measurement.

Bourbaki, Nicolas pseudonym adopted by a group of mathematicians, most of them French, who, collectively and anonymously, published a definitive survey of mathematics 1939–67. The group, which at any one time contained about 20 members, was centred at the Ecole Normale Supérieure in Paris. The group's founder was André Weil.

Bourdon gauge instrument for measuring pressure, patented by French watchmaker Eugène Bourdon in 1849. The gauge contains a C-shaped tube, closed at one end. When the pressure inside the tube increases, the tube uncurls slightly causing a small movement at its closed end. A system of levers and gears magnifies this movement and turns a pointer, which indicates the pressure on a circular scale. Bourdon gauges are often fitted to cylinders of compressed gas used in industry and hospitals.

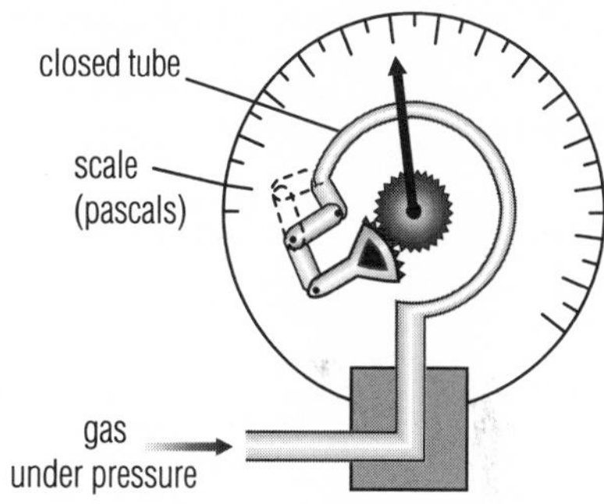

Bourdon gauge *The most common form of Bourdon gauge is the C-shaped tube. However, in high-pressure gauges spiral tubes are used; the spiral rotates as pressure increases and the tip screws forwards.*

Bovidae mammal family that consists of 128 species of antelopes, sheep, goats, and cattle. They are ruminants (chew the cud) and also artiodactylate (even-toed); all the males and some of the females have horns consisting of solid bony extensions of the skull encased in a sheath of true horn.

Bovids occur in all parts of the Old World and in North America, but are not native to Australia and South America.

classification Bovidae is a family in order Artiodactyla.

bovine somatotropin (BST) hormone that increases an injected cow's milk yield by 10–40%. It is a protein naturally occurring in milk and breaks down within the human digestive tract into harmless amino acids. However, doubts have arisen recently as to whether such a degree of protein addition could in the long term be guaranteed harmless either to cattle or to humans.

Although no evidence of adverse side effects to consumers have been found, BST was banned in Europe 1993 until the year 2000. In the USA genetically engineered BST has been in use since February 1994; in Vermont a law requiring milk containing BST to be labelled as such was passed September 1995.

The incidence of mastitis in herds injected with BST is 15–45% higher.

Facts do not cease to exist because they are ignored.

ALDOUS HUXLEY English novelist.
Proper Studies, 'Note on Dogma'

bovine spongiform encephalopathy (BSE) or ***mad cow disease*** disease of cattle, related to ◊scrapie in sheep, which attacks the nervous system, causing aggression, lack of coordination, and collapse. First identified in 1986, it is almost entirely confined to the UK. By 1996 it had claimed 158,000 British cattle.

BSE is one of a group of diseases known as the transmissible spongiform encephalopathies, since they are characterized by the appearance of spongy changes in brain tissue. Some scientists believe that all these conditions, including Creutzfeldt–Jakob disease (CJD) in humans, are in effect the same disease, and in 1996 a link was established between the deaths of 10 young people from CJD and the consumption of beef products.

The cause of these universally fatal diseases is not fully understood, but they may be the result of a rogue protein called a prion. A prion may be inborn or it may be transmitted in contaminated tissue.

According to an official European Commission Report released in Mar 1997, consumers throughout Europe were being exposed to BSE-infected meat. The report also highlighted lax health controls, and supported the view that the extent of BSE throughout the EU was much wider then governments were prepared to admit.

It was also revealed in 1997 that the British government had allowed more than 6,000 carcasses suspected of having BSE to be buried in landfill sites across Britain – in direction contravention of its own regulations. Because of fears that BSE could get into drinking water, or the food chain, both the British government and the EU have insisted the carcasses should be incinerated.

bower bird New Guinean and N Australian bird of the family Ptilonorhynchidae, order Passeriformes, related to the ◊bird of paradise. The males are dull-coloured, and build elaborate bowers of sticks and grass, decorated with shells, feathers, or flowers, and even painted with the juice of berries, to attract the females. There are 17 species.

bowfin North American fish *Amia calva* with a swim bladder highly developed as an air sac, enabling it to breathe air. It is the only surviving member of a primitive group of bony fishes.

bowhead Arctic whale *Balaena mysticetus* with strongly curving upper jawbones supporting the plates of baleen with which it sifts planktonic crustaceans from the water. Averaging 15 m/50 ft long and 90 tonnes/100 tons in weight, these slow-moving, placid whales were once extremely common, but by the 17th century were already becoming scarce through hunting. Only an estimated 3,000 remain, and continued hunting by the Inuit may result in extinction.

Bowman's capsule in the vertebrate kidney, a cup-shaped structure enclosing the glomerulus, which is the initial site of filtration of the blood leading to urine formation.

There are approximately a million of these capsules in a human kidney, each containing a tight knot of capillaries and leading into a kidney tubule or nephron where unwanted fluid and waste molecules are filtered from the blood to be excreted in the form of urine.

box any of several small evergreen trees and shrubs, with small, leathery leaves. Some species are used as hedging plants and for shaping into garden ornaments. (Genus *Buxus,* family Buxaceae.)

boxer breed of dog, about 60 cm/24 in tall, with a smooth coat and a set-back nose. The tail is usually docked. A boxer is usually brown, often with white markings, but may be fawn or brindled.

boxfish or ***trunkfish***, any fish of the family Ostraciodontidae, with scales that are hexagonal bony plates fused to form a box covering the body, only the mouth and fins being free of the armour. Boxfish swim slowly. The cowfish, genus *Lactophrys,* with two 'horns' above the eyes, is a member of this group.

Boyle, Robert
(1627–1691)

Irish chemist and physicist who published the seminal The Sceptical Chymist 1661. He formulated Boyle's law in 1662. He was a pioneer in the use of experiment and scientific method.

Boyle questioned the alchemical basis of the chemical theory of his day and taught that the proper object of chemistry was to determine the compositions of substances. The term 'analysis' was coined by Boyle and many of the reactions still used in qualitative work were known to him. He introduced certain plant extracts, notably litmus, for the indication of acids and bases. He was also the first chemist to collect a sample of gas.

Mary Evans Picture Library

Father of Chemistry and Uncle of the Earl of Cork.

ROBERT BOYLE Irish chemist.
On his tombstone in Dublin, quoted in
R L Weber *More Random Walks in Science*

Boyle's law law stating that the volume of a given mass of gas at a constant temperature is inversely proportional to its pressure. For example, if the pressure of a gas doubles, its volume will be reduced by a half, and vice versa. The law was discovered in 1662 by Irish physicist and chemist Robert Boyle. See also ◊gas laws.

bozo filter facility to eliminate messages from irritating users. It is also known as a ◊killfile.

BP abbreviation for ***British Pharmacopoeia***; **British Petroleum**.

bps abbreviation for **bits per second**, measure used in specifying data transmission rates.

brachiopod or ***lamp shell*** any member of the phylum Brachiopoda, marine invertebrates with two shells, resembling but totally unrelated to bivalves.

There are about 300 living species; they were much more numerous in past geological ages. They are suspension feeders, ingesting minute food particles from water. A single internal organ, the lophophore, handles feeding, aspiration, and excretion.

Brachyteles primate genus consisting of the single species commonly called the woolly ◊spider monkey.

bracken any of several large ferns (especially *Pteridium aquilinum*) which grow abundantly in the northern hemisphere. The rootstock produces coarse fronds each year, which die down in autumn.

bracket fungus any of a group of fungi (see ◊fungus) with fruiting bodies that grow like shelves from the trunks and branches of trees. (Class Basidiomycetes.)

braconid small parasitic wasp closely related to the ◊ichneumon flies, but differing from them mainly by having fewer wing veins. Braconids chiefly parasitize caterpillars, but also some beetle and fly larvae, so they are selectively used in ◊biological control programmes.

bracket fungus This varicoloured Coriolus versicolor *is one of a large number of often unrelated fungi referred to collectively as bracket fungi because they form bracketlike growths on trees and timber. The fruiting body is the only part that is immediately visible. The mass of hyphae, which form its mycelium, penetrates and feeds upon the dead wood on which the fungus is living. The spore-producing fruiting body is derived from the mycelium. Premaphotos Wildlife*

classification Braconids are in the family Braconidae, order Hymenoptera, class Insecta, phylum Arthropoda.

Apanteles glomeratus is a tiny black braconid that parasitizes the cabbage white butterfly. The female lays her eggs in the caterpillar. About autumn, masses of sulphur-yellow cocoons of the parasite can be seen attached to the skin casts of the dead (pupated) caterpillar.

Brahe, Tycho
(1546–1601)

Danish astronomer. His accurate observations of the planets enabled German astronomer and mathematician Johannes Kepler to prove that planets orbit the Sun in ellipses. Brahe's discovery and report of the 1572 supernova brought him recognition, and his observations of the comet of 1577 proved that it moved in an orbit among the planets, thus disproving Aristotle's view that comets were in the Earth's atmosphere.

Brahe was a colourful figure who wore a silver nose after his own was cut off in a duel, and who took an interest in alchemy. In 1576 Frederick II of Denmark gave him the island of Hven, where he set up an observatory. Brahe was the greatest observer in the days before telescopes, making the most accurate measurements of the positions of stars and planets. He moved to Prague as imperial mathematician in 1599, where he was joined by Kepler, who inherited his observations when he died.

Mary Evans Picture Library

BRAHE, TYCHO

Tycho Brahe, the 16th-century Danish astronomer, wore a false nose made of silver. His own had been cut off in a duel while he was a student in Rostock.

bract leaflike structure in whose ◊axil a flower or inflorescence develops. Bracts are generally green and smaller than the true leaves. However, in some plants they may be brightly coloured and conspicuous, taking over the role of attracting pollinating insects to the flowers, whose own petals are small; examples include poinsettia *Euphorbia pulcherrima* and bougainvillea.

A whorl of bracts surrounding an ◊inflorescence is termed an **involucre**. A **bracteole** is a leaf-like organ that arises on an individual flower stalk, between the true bract and the ◊calyx.

brain in higher animals, a mass of interconnected ◊nerve cells forming the anterior part of the ◊central nervous system, whose activities it coordinates and controls. In ◊vertebrates, the brain is contained by the skull. At the base of the ◊brainstem, the **medulla oblongata** contains centres for the control of respiration, heartbeat rate and strength, and blood pressure. Overlying this is the **cerebellum**, which is concerned with coordinating complex muscular processes such as maintaining posture and moving limbs.

The cerebral hemispheres (**cerebrum**) are paired outgrowths of the front end of the forebrain, in early vertebrates mainly concerned with the senses, but in higher vertebrates greatly developed and involved in the integration of all sensory input and motor output, and in thought, emotions, memory, and behaviour.

In vertebrates, many of the nerve fibres from the two sides of the body cross over as they enter the brain, so that the left cerebral hemisphere is associated with the right side of the body and vice versa. In humans, a certain asymmetry develops in the two halves of the cerebrum. In right-handed people, the left hemisphere seems to play a greater role in controlling verbal and some mathematical skills, whereas the right hemisphere is more involved in spatial perception. In general, however, skills and abilities are not closely localized. In the brain, nerve impulses are passed across ◊synapses by neurotransmitters, in the same way as in other parts of the nervous system.

In mammals the cerebrum is the largest part of the brain, carrying the **cerebral cortex**. This consists of a thick surface layer of cell bodies (grey matter), below which fibre tracts (white matter) connect various parts of the cortex to each other and to other points in the central nervous system. As cerebral complexity grows, the surface of the brain becomes convoluted into deep folds. In higher mammals, there are large unassigned areas of the brain that seem to be connected with intelligence, personality, and higher mental faculties. Language is controlled in two special regions usually in the left side of the brain: **Broca's area** governs the ability to talk, and **Wernicke's area** is responsible for the comprehension of spoken and written words. In 1990, scientists at Johns Hopkins University, Baltimore, succeeded in culturing human brain cells.

If the cells and fibre of the human brain were stretched out end to end, they would certainly reach to the moon and back. Yet the fact that they are not arranged end to end enabled man to go there himself. The astonishing tangle within our heads makes us what we are.

COLIN BLAKEMORE English physiologist.
BBC Reith Lecture 1976

brain damage impairment which can be caused by trauma (for example, accidents) or disease (such as encephalitis), or which may be present at birth. Depending on the area of the brain that is affected, language, movement, sensation, judgement, or other abilities may be impaired.

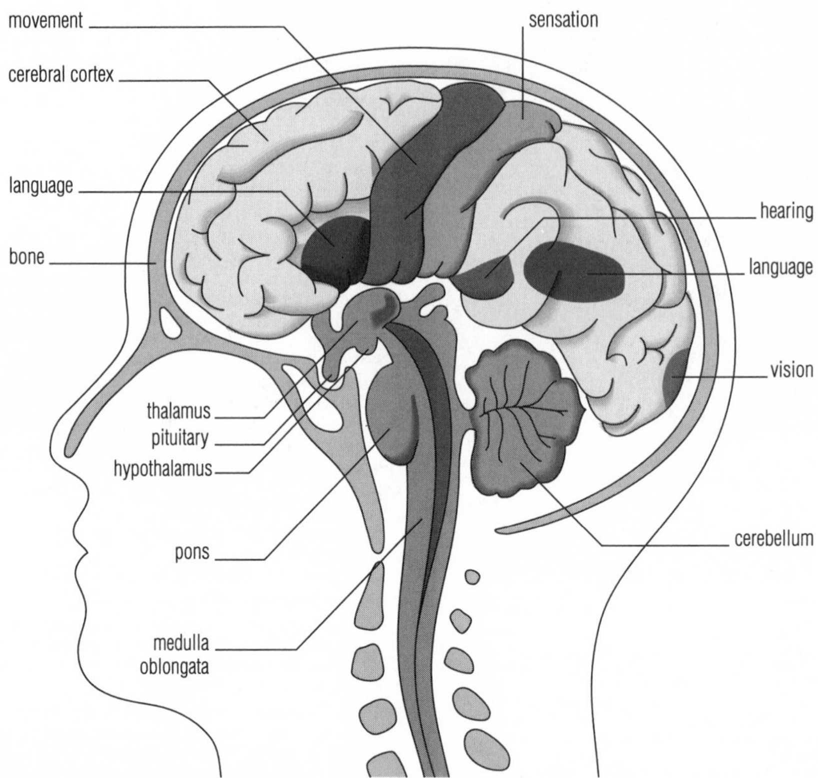

brain *The structure of the human brain. At the back of the skull lies the cerebellum, which coordinates reflex actions that control muscular activity. The medulla controls respiration, heartbeat, and blood pressure. The hypothalamus is concerned with instinctive drives and emotions. The thalamus relays signals to and from various parts of the brain. The pituitary gland controls the body's hormones. Distinct areas of the large convoluted cerebral hemispheres that fill most of the skull are linked to sensations, such as hearing and sight, and voluntary activities, such as movement.*

brainstem region where the top of the spinal cord merges with the undersurface of the brain, consisting largely of the medulla oblongata and midbrain.

The oldest part of the brain in evolutionary terms, the brainstem is the body's life-support centre, containing regulatory mechanisms for vital functions such as breathing, heart rate, and blood pressure. It is also involved in controlling the level of consciousness by acting as a relay station for nerve connections to and from the higher centres of the brain.

In many countries, death of the brainstem is now formally recognized as death of the person as a whole. Such cases are the principal donors of organs for transplantation. So-called 'beating-heart donors' can be maintained for a limited period by life-support equipment.

brake device used to slow down or stop the movement of a moving body or vehicle. The mechanically applied calliper brake used on bicycles uses a scissor action to press hard rubber blocks against the wheel rim. The main braking system of a car works hydraulically: when the driver depresses the brake pedal, liquid pressure forces pistons to apply brakes on each wheel.

Two types of car brakes are used. **Disc brakes** are used on the front wheels of some cars and on all wheels of sports and performance cars, since they are the more efficient and less prone to fading (losing their braking power) when they get hot. Braking pressure forces brake pads against both sides of a steel disc that rotates with the wheel. **Drum brakes** are fitted on the rear wheels of some cars and on all wheels of some passenger cars. Braking pressure forces brake shoes to expand outwards into contact with a drum rotating with the wheels. The brake pads and shoes have a tough ◊friction lining that grips well and withstands wear.

Many trucks and trains have **air brakes**, which work by compressed air. On landing, jet planes reverse the thrust of their engines to reduce their speed quickly. Space vehicles use retro-rockets for braking in space and use the air resistance, or drag of the atmosphere, to slow down when they return to Earth.

bramble any of a group of prickly bushes belonging to the rose family. Examples are ◊blackberry, raspberry, and dewberry. (Genus *Rubus*, family Rosaceae.)

brambling or ***bramble finch*** bird *Fringilla montifringilla* belonging to the finch family Fringillidae, order Passeriformes. It is about 15 cm/6 in long, and breeds in N Europe and Asia.

brass metal ◊alloy of copper and zinc, with not more than 5% or 6% of other metals. The zinc content ranges from 20% to 45%, and the colour of brass varies accordingly from coppery to whitish yellow. Brasses are characterized by the ease with which they may be shaped and machined; they are strong and ductile, resist many forms of corrosion, and are used for electrical fittings, ammunition cases, screws, household fittings, and ornaments.

Brasses are usually classed into those that can be worked cold (up to 25% zinc) and those that are better worked hot (about 40% zinc).

brassica any of a group of plants, many of which are cultivated as vegetables. The most familiar is the common cabbage (*Brassica*

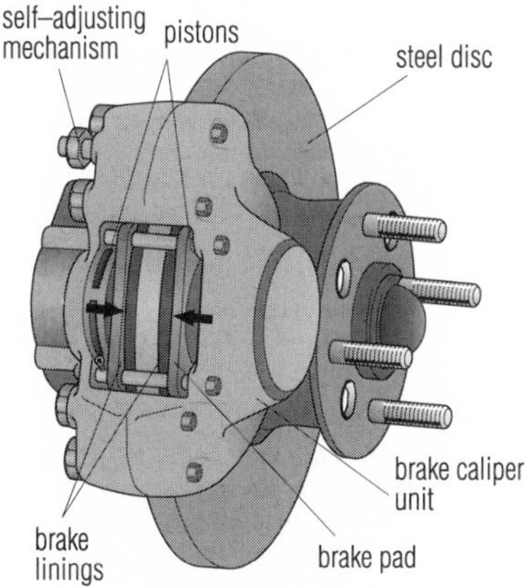

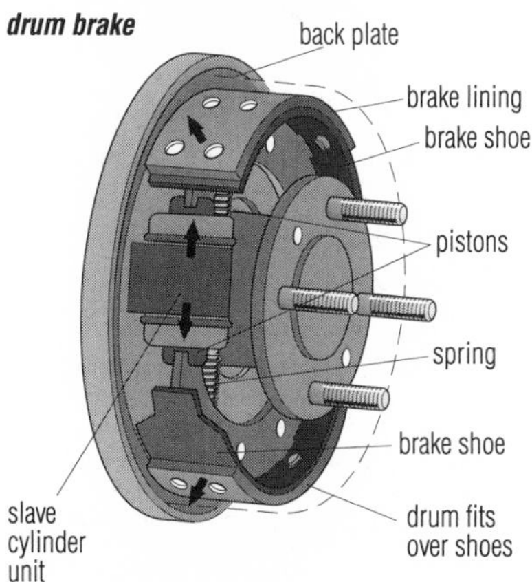

brake *Two common braking systems: the disc brake (left) and the drum brake (right). In the disc brake, increased hydraulic pressure of the brake fluid in the pistons forces the brake pads against the steel disc attached to the wheel. A self-adjusting mechanism balances the force on each pad. In the drum brake, increased pressure of the brake fluid within the slave cylinder forces the brake pad against the brake drum attached to the wheel.*

oleracea), with its varieties broccoli, cauliflower, kale, and Brussels sprouts. (Genus *Brassica*, family Cruciferae.)

In 1990 US experiments in cross-pollinating the wild cabbage (*B. campestris*) with related varieties of cultivated cabbage, turnip, and swede produced a new plant with a life cycle of only five weeks. This is now being used in US schools to enable pupils to carry out plant-breeding experiments that can produce ten generations in one year.

Braun AEG German company, manufacturer of sound equipment and domestic appliances, founded 1921 by Max Braun and based in Frankfurt.

The factory was rebuilt 1945 and in 1951 when Max Braun died his son Artur (1925–) began commissioning a number of young and highly innovative German industrial designers associated with the new design school (Hochschüle für Gestaltung) at Ulm – among them Dieter Rams and Hans Gugelot (1920–1965) – to update the company's product range. Their radically new designs quickly became hallmarks of the stark, geometric design style that developed in Germany at that time.

Brazil nut gigantic South American tree; also its seed, which is rich in oil and highly nutritious. The seeds (nuts) are enclosed in a hard outer casing, each fruit containing 10–20 seeds arranged like the segments of an orange. The timber of the tree is also valuable. (*Bertholletia excelsa*, family Lecythidaceae.)

brazing method of joining two metals by melting an ◊alloy or metal into the joint. It is similar to soldering (see ◊solder) but takes place at a much higher temperature. Copper and silver alloys are widely used for brazing, at temperatures up to about 900°C/1,650°F.

Where high precision is needed, as in space technology, nickel based filters are used in the temperature range 1,000–1,200°C/ 1,832–2,192°F.

breadfruit fruit of two tropical trees belonging to the mulberry family. It is highly nutritious and when baked is said to taste like bread. It is native to many South Pacific islands. (*Artocarpus communis* and *A. altilis*, family Moraceae.)

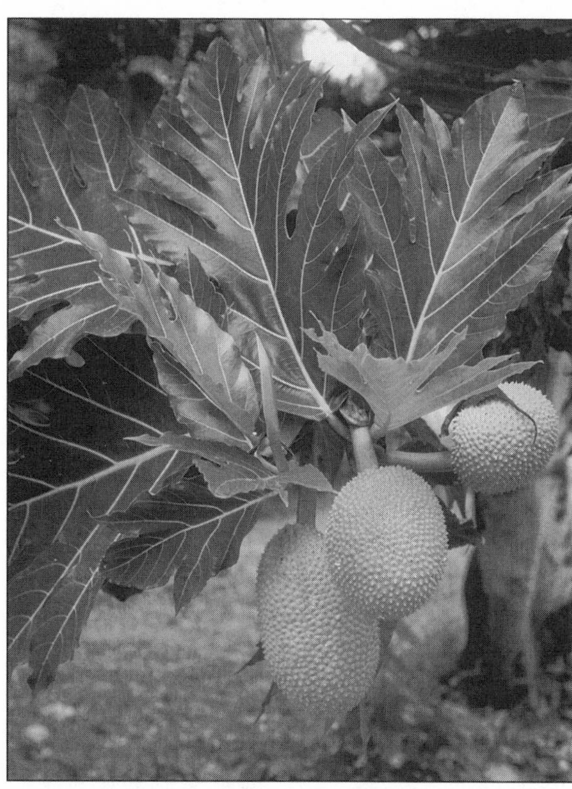

breadfruit *Breadfruit trees, native to Polynesia, are now a familiar sight in many tropical countries around the world, where they have been planted for their large nutritious fruits. When cooked, the fruit has a breadlike texture, hence the name.* *Premaphotos Wildlife*

breadth thickness, another name for width. The area of a rectangle is given by the formula: area = length times breadth.

bream deep-bodied, flattened fish *Abramis brama* of the carp family, growing to about 50 cm/1.6 ft, typically found in lowland rivers across Europe.

breast one of a pair of organs on the chest of the human female, also known as a ◊mammary gland. Each of the two breasts contains milk-producing cells and a network of tubes or ducts that lead to openings in the nipple.

Milk-producing cells in the breast do not become active until a woman has given birth to a baby. Breast milk is made from sub-

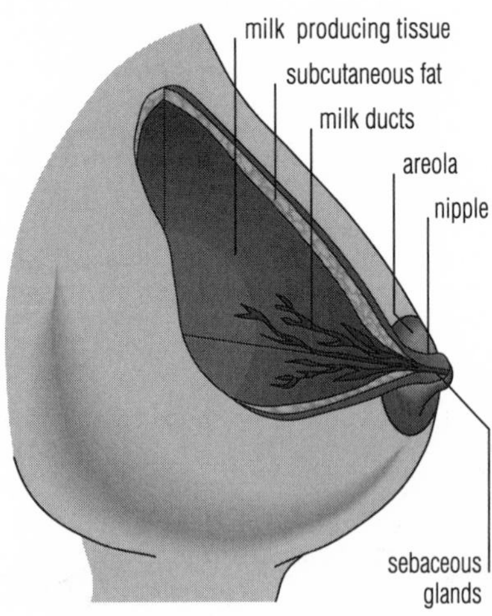

***breast** The human breast or mammary gland. Milk produced in the tissue of the breast to feed a baby after a woman has given birth passes along ducts which lead to openings in the nipple.*

stances extracted from the mother's blood as it passes through the breasts, and contains all the nourishment a baby needs. Breast-fed newborns develop fewer infections than bottle-fed babies because of the antibodies and white blood cells contained in breast milk. These are particularly abundant in the colostrum produced in the first few days of breast-feeding.

breast cancer in medicine, ◊cancer of the ◊breast. It is usually diagnosed following the detection of a painless lump in the breast (either through self-examination or ◊mammography). Other, less common symptoms, include changes in the shape or texture of the breast and discharge from the nipple. It is the commonest cancer amongst women: there are 28,000 new cases of breast cancer in Britain each year and 185,700 in the USA.

treatment If the tumour is caught early, only it and the immediate surrounding tissue needs removing, in a process called lumpectomy, usually accompanied by radiotherapy. In more advanced cases a mastectomy is performed. Chemotherapy or hormone-blocking drugs (such as tamoxifen) may also accompany either procedure. The average survival rate after 5 years was 83.2% in 1996.

risk factors Possible risk factors include a family history of breast cancer (mutations in the genes *BRCA1* and *BRCA2* were found to cause more than 50% of inherited breast cancer cases in the 1990s); childlessness or late childbearing; early onset of menstruation and late menopause.

breast screening in medicine, examination of the breast to detect the presence of breast cancer at an early stage. Screening methods include self-screening by monthly examination of the breasts and formal programmes of screening by palpation (physical examination) and mammography in special clinics. Screening may be offered to older women on a routine basis and it is important in women with a family history of breast cancer.

BREAST CANCER AWARENESS

http://avon.avon.com/showpage.asp?thepage=crusade

Promotes awareness of this disease through a library of frequently asked questions about breast cancer and mammograms, as well as a glossary of common terms and access to support groups. There is also information here about their fundraising activities and recipients of awards for people and groups seen to be contributing the most to the fight against this disease. It is sponsored by the make-up company Avon.

Breathalyzer trademark for an instrument for on-the-spot checking by police of the amount of alcohol consumed by a suspect driver. The driver breathes into a plastic bag connected to a tube containing a chemical (such as a diluted solution of potassium dichromate in 50% sulphuric acid) that changes colour in the presence of alcohol. Another method is to use a gas chromatograph, again from a breath sample.

breathing in terrestrial animals, the muscular movements whereby air is taken into the lungs and then expelled, a form of ◊gas exchange. Breathing is sometimes referred to as external respiration, for true respiration is a cellular (internal) process.

Lungs are specialized for gas exchange but are not themselves muscular, consisting of spongy material. In order for oxygen to be passed to the blood and carbon dioxide removed, air is drawn into the lungs (inhaled) by the contraction of the diaphragm and intercostal muscles; relaxation of these muscles enables air to be breathed out (exhaled). The rate of breathing is controlled by the brain. High levels of activity lead to a greater demand for oxygen and an increased rate of breathing.

breathing rate the number of times a minute the lungs inhale and exhale. The rate increases during exercise because the muscles require an increased supply of oxygen and nutrients. At the same time very active muscles produce a greater volume of carbon dioxide, a waste gas that must be removed by the lungs via the blood.

The regulation of the breathing rate is under both voluntary and involuntary control, although a person can only forcibly stop breathing for a limited time. The regulatory system includes the use of chemoreceptors, which can detect levels of carbon dioxide in the blood. High concentrations of carbon dioxide, occurring for example during exercise, stimulate a fast breathing rate.

breccia coarse-grained clastic ◊sedimentary rock, made up of broken fragments (clasts) of pre-existing rocks held together in a fine-grained matrix. It is similar to ◊conglomerate but the fragments in breccia are jagged in shape.

breed recognizable group of domestic animals, within a species, with distinctive characteristics that have been produced by ◊artificial selection.

breeder reactor or ***fast breeder*** alternative names for ◊fast reactor, a type of nuclear reactor.

breeding in biology, the crossing and selection of animals and plants to change the characteristics of an existing ◊breed or ◊cultivar (variety), or to produce a new one.

Cattle may be bred for increased meat or milk yield, sheep for thicker or finer wool, and horses for speed or stamina. Plants, such as wheat or maize, may be bred for disease resistance, heavier and more rapid cropping, and hardiness to adverse weather.

breeding in nuclear physics, a process in a reactor in which more fissionable material is produced than is consumed in running the reactor.

For example, plutonium-239 can be made from the relatively plentiful (but nonfissile) uranium-238, or uranium-233 can be produced from thorium. The Pu-239 or U-233 can then be used to fuel other reactors.

brewing making of beer, ale, or other alcoholic beverage, from ◊malt and ◊barley by steeping (mashing), boiling, and fermenting.

Mashing the barley releases its sugars. Yeast is then added, which contains the enzymes needed to convert the sugars into ethanol (alcohol) and carbon dioxide. Hops are added to give a bitter taste.

brewster unit (symbol B) for measuring the reaction of optical materials to stress, defined in terms of the slowing down of light passing through the material when it is stretched or compressed.

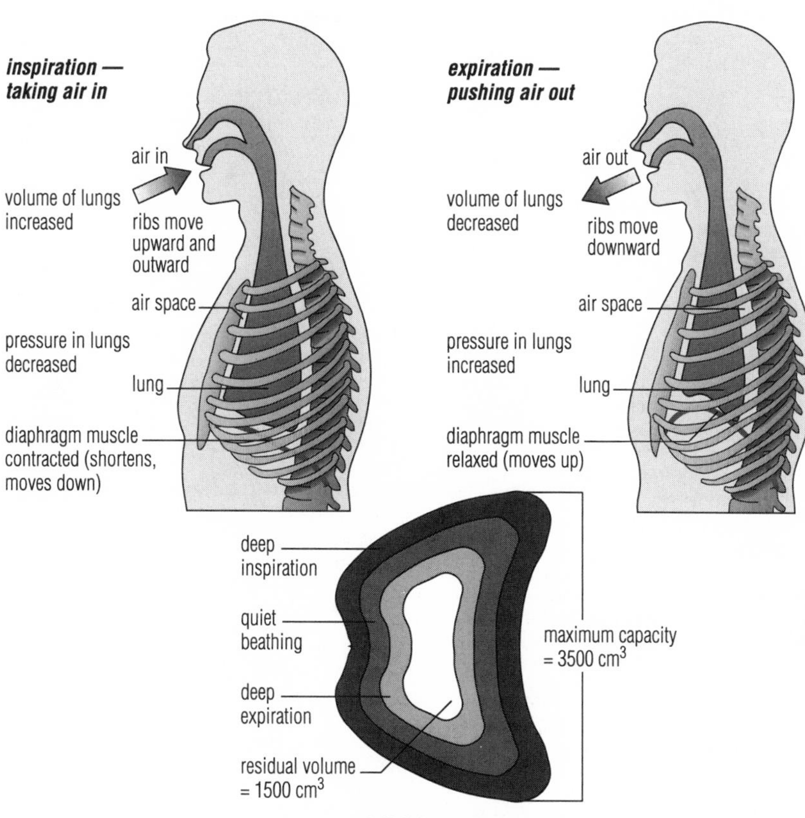

breathing *The two phases of the process of breathing, or respiration. Gas exchange occurs in the alveoli, tiny air tubes in the lungs.*

brick common block-shaped building material, with all opposite sides parallel. It is made of clay that has been fired in a kiln. Bricks are made by kneading a mixture of crushed clay and other materials into a stiff mud and extruding it into a ribbon. The ribbon is cut into individual bricks, which are fired at a temperature of up to about 1,000°C/1,800°F. Bricks may alternatively be pressed into shape in moulds.

Refractory bricks used to line furnaces are made from heat-resistant materials such as silica and dolomite. They must withstand operating temperatures of 1,500°C/2,700°F or more.

Facing bricks are designed to be visually more attractive than than common bricks, and include specially moulded bricks.

Sun-dried bricks of mud reinforced with straw were first used in Mesopotamia some 8,000 years ago. Similar mud bricks, called adobe, are still used today in Mexico and other areas where the climate is warm and dry.

brickwork method of construction using bricks made of fired clay or sun-dried earth. In wall building, bricks are either laid out as stretchers (long side facing out) or as headers (short side facing out). The two principal patterns of brickwork are **English bond** in which alternate courses, or layers, are made up of stretchers or headers only, and **Flemish bond** in which stretchers and headers alternate within courses.

Some evidence exists of the use of fired bricks in ancient Mesopotamia and Egypt, although the Romans were the first to make extensive use of this technology. Today's mass production of fired bricks tends to be concentrated in temperate regions where there are plentiful supplies of fuel available.

bridge in computing, a device that connects two similar local area networks (LANs). Bridges transfer data in packets between the two networks, without making any changes or interpreting the data in any way. See also ◊router and ◊brouter.

bridge structure that provides a continuous path or road over water, valleys, ravines, or above other roads. The basic designs and composites of these are based on the way they bear the weight of the structure and its load. **Beam**, or **girder**, bridges are supported at each end by the ground with the weight thrusting downwards. **Cantilever** bridges are a complex form of girder in which only one end is supported. **Arch** bridges thrust outwards and downwards at their ends. **Suspension** bridges use cables under tension to pull inwards against anchorages on either side of the span, so that the roadway hangs from the main cables by the network of vertical cables. The **cable-stayed** bridge relies on diagonal cables connected directly between the bridge deck and supporting towers at each end. Some bridges are too low to allow traffic to pass beneath easily, so they are designed with movable parts, like swing and draw bridges.
history In prehistory, people used logs or wove vines into ropes that were thrown across the obstacle. Clapper bridges, made from flat stones simply laid across or supported by piles of stones, were some of the earliest bridges. By 4000 BC arched structures of stone and/or brick were used in the Middle East, and the Romans built long arched spans, many of which are still standing. Cast iron bridges were introduced in 1779. The ◊Bessemer process produced steel that made it possible to build long-lived framed structures that support great weight over long spans.

brill flatfish *Scophthalmus laevis,* living in shallow water over sandy bottoms in the NE Atlantic and Mediterranean. It is a freckled sandy brown, and grows to 60 cm/2 ft.

brine common name for a solution of sodium chloride (NaCl) in water.

Brines are used extensively in the food-manufacturing industry for canning vegetables, pickling vegetables (sauerkraut manufacture), and curing meat. Industrially, brine is the source from which chlorine, caustic soda (sodium hydroxide), and sodium carbonate are made.

Brinell hardness test test of the hardness of a substance according to the area of indentation made by a 10 mm/0.4 in hardened steel or sintered tungsten carbide ball under standard loading conditions in a test machine. The resulting Brinell number is equal to the load (kg) divided by the surface area (mm^2) and is named after its inventor, Swedish metallurgist Johann Brinell.

brisling processed form of sprat *Sprattus sprattus* a small herring, fished in Norwegian fjords, then seasoned and canned.

bristlecone pine the oldest living species of ◊pine tree.

bristletail primitive wingless insect of the order Thysanura. Up to 2 cm/0.8 in long, bristletails have a body tapering from front to back, two long antennae, and three 'tails' at the rear end. They include the **silverfish** *Lepisma saccharina* and the **firebrat** *Thermobia domestica*. Two-tailed bristletails constitute another insect order, the Diplura. They live under stones and fallen branches, feeding on decaying material.

bristle-worm or ***polychaete*** segmented worm of the class Polychaeta, characterized by having a pair of fleshy paddles (parapodia) on each segment, together with prominent bristles (setae), and a well-developed head with a pair each of eyes, antennae, and palps. Most bristle-worms are marine, and live in burrows in sand and mud or in rock crevices and under stones. More than 5,300 species are recognized.

The bristle-worms can be conveniently divided into two loosely defined groups: the **Errantia**, which are free-living (that is swimming, crawling, or actively burrowing), and the **Sedentaria**, which live within a tube or a permanent burrow.

British Blue breed of domestic shorthaired cat. It has a fuller face than the ◊Russian Blue, a more compact body, and shorter legs. The coat is a solid blue-grey colour and the eyes should be either orange or copper.

British Standards Institute (BSI) UK national standards body. Although government funded, the institute is independent. The BSI interprets international technical standards for the UK, and also sets its own.

For consumer goods, it sets standards which products should reach (the BS standard), as well as testing products to see that they conform to that standard (as a result of which the product may be given the BSI 'kite' mark).

British Telecom (BT) British ◊telecommunications company. Its principal activity is the supply of local, long-distance, and international telecommunications services and equipment in the UK, serving 27 million exchange lines. BT also offers an international direct-dialled telephone service to more than 200 countries and other overseas territories – covering 99% of the world's 800 million telephones. One of the world's leading providers of telecommunications services and one of the largest private-sector companies in Europe, in 1997 BT had a market capitalization in excess of £28 billion and had established operations in more than 30 countries worldwide, with joint ventures in Spain, Germany, Italy, the Netherlands, Sweden, South Africa, New Zealand, Japan, and India.

BT formed part of the Post Office until 1980, and was privatized in 1984. Previously a monopoly, it now faces commercial competition for some of its services. BT is not allowed to offer other cable services apart from telephones.

British thermal unit imperial unit (symbol Btu) of heat, now replaced in the SI system by the ◊joule (one British thermal unit is approximately 1,055 joules). Burning one cubic foot of natural gas releases about 1,000 Btu of heat.

One British thermal unit is defined as the amount of heat required to raise the temperature of 0.45 kg/1 lb of water by 1°F. The exact value depends on the original temperature of the water.

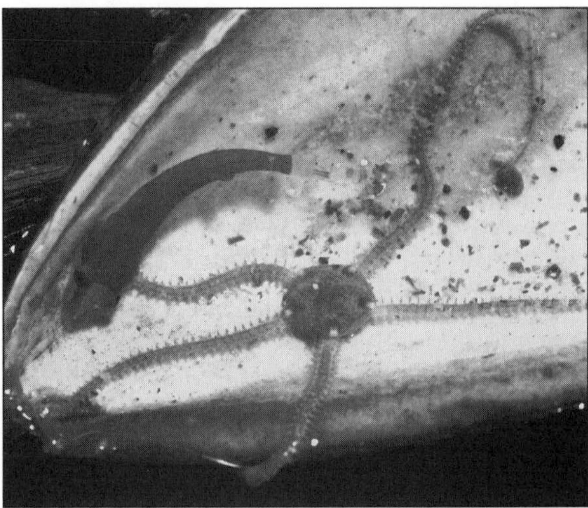

brittle-star *Living mostly on soft seabeds, the brittle-star* Ophiothrix fragilis *feeds on small crustaceans and molluscs. Brittle-stars are distinguished from starfish by the more or less clear demarcation between the five arms and the body. Both starfish and brittle-stars have the ability to regrow their arms if they are broken off. Premaphotos Wildlife*

brittle material material that breaks suddenly under stress at a point just beyond its elastic limit (see ◊elasticity). Brittle materials may also break suddenly when given a sharp knock. Pottery, glass, and cast iron are examples of brittle materials. Compare ◊ductile material.

brittle-star any member of the echinoderm class Ophiuroidea. A brittle-star resembles a starfish, and has a small, central, rounded body and long, flexible, spiny arms used for walking. The small brittle-star *Amphipholis squamata* is greyish, about 4.5 cm/2 in across, and found on sea bottoms worldwide. It broods its young, and its arms can be luminous.

About 2,000 species of brittle-stars and basket-stars, whose arms are tangled and rootlike, are included in this group.

broadband in computing, term indicating a high ◊bandwidth.

broadbill primitive perching bird of the family Eurylaimidae, found in Africa and S Asia. Broadbills are forest birds and are often found near water. They are gregarious and noisy, have brilliant coloration and wide bills, and feed largely on insects.

broadcasting the transmission of sound and vision programmes by ◊radio and ◊television. Broadcasting may be organized under private enterprise, as in the USA, or may operate under a compromise system, as in Britain, where a television and radio service controlled by the state-regulated British Broadcasting Corporation (BBC) operates alongside the commercial ◊Independent Television Commission (known as the Independent Broadcasting Authority before 1991).

In the USA, broadcasting is limited only by the issue of licences from the Federal Communications Commission to competing commercial companies; in Britain, the BBC is a centralized body appointed by the state and responsible to Parliament, but with policy and programme content not controlled by the state; in Japan, which ranks next to the USA in the number of television sets owned, there is a semigovernmental radio and television broadcasting corporation (NHK) and numerous private television companies.

Television broadcasting entered a new era with the introduction of high-powered communications satellites in the 1980s. The signals broadcast by these satellites are sufficiently strong to be picked up by a small dish aerial located, for example, on the roof of a house. Direct broadcast by satellite thus became a feasible alternative to land-based television services. See also ◊cable television. A similar revolution will take place when digital television becomes widely available.

broad-leaved tree another name for a tree belonging to the ◊angiosperms, such as ash, beech, oak, maple, or birch. The leaves are generally broad and flat, in contrast to the needlelike leaves of most ◊conifers. See also ◊deciduous tree.

broccoli variety of ◊cabbage. It contains high levels of the glucosinolate compound glucoraphanin. A breakdown product of this was found to neutralize damage to cells and so help to prevent cancer.

brocket name for a male European red deer in its second year, when it has short, straight, pointed antlers. Brocket deer, genus *Mazama,* include a number of species of small, shy, solitary deer found in Central and South America. They are up to 1.3 m/4 ft in body length and 65 cm/2 ft at the shoulder, and have similar small, straight antlers even when adult.

brolga or ***native companion***, Australian crane *Grus rubicunda,* about 1.5 m/5 ft tall, mainly grey with a red patch on the head.

brome grass any of several annual grasses found in temperate regions; some are used as food for horses and cattle, but many are weeds. (Genus *Bromus,* family Gramineae.)

bromeliad any tropical or subtropical plant belonging to the pineapple family, usually with stiff leathery leaves, which are often coloured and patterned, and bright, attractive flower spikes. There are about 1,400 species in tropical America; several are cultivated as greenhouse plants. (Family Bromeliaceae.)

Some grow in habitats ranging from scrub desert to tropical forest floor. Many, however, grow on rainforest trees. These are epiphytes: they are supported by the tree but do not take nourishment from it, using rain and decayed plant and animal remains for independent sustenance.

bromeliad The large Bromelia balansae, *shown here, is one of numerous terrestrial bromeliads present on the sand dunes of the Brazilian coast near Rio; it is also widespread in dry areas inland. The flower spikes are regularly visited by hummingbirds, which are the main pollinators of many members of the family. Premaphotos Wildlife*

bromide salt of the halide series containing the Br^- ion, which is formed when a bromine atom gains an electron.

The term 'bromide' is sometimes used to describe an organic compound containing a bromine atom, even though it is not ionic. Modern naming uses the term 'bromo-' in such cases. For example, the compound C_2H_5Br is now called bromoethane; its traditional name, still used sometimes, is ethyl bromide.

bromine ***Greek bromos 'stench'*** dark, reddish-brown, nonmetallic element, a volatile liquid at room temperature, symbol Br, atomic number 35, relative atomic mass 79.904. It is a member of the ◊halogen group, has an unpleasant odour, and is very irritating to mucous membranes. Its salts are known as bromides.

Bromine was formerly extracted from salt beds but is now mostly obtained from sea water, where it occurs in small quantities. Its compounds are used in photography and in the chemical and pharmaceutical industries.

bronchiole small-bore air tube found in the vertebrate lung responsible for delivering air to the main respiratory surfaces. Bronchioles lead off from the larger bronchus and branch extensively before terminating in the many thousand alveoli that form the bulk of lung tissue.

bronchitis inflammation of the bronchi (air passages) of the lungs, usually caused initially by a viral infection, such as a cold or flu. It is aggravated by environmental pollutants, especially smoking, and results in a persistent cough, irritated mucus-secreting glands, and large amounts of sputum.

bronchodilator drug that relieves obstruction of the airways by causing the bronchi and bronchioles to relax and widen. It is most useful in the treatment of ◊asthma.

bronchus one of a pair of large tubes (bronchi) branching off from the windpipe and passing into the vertebrate lung. Apart from their size, bronchi differ from the bronchioles in possessing cartilaginous rings, which give rigidity and prevent collapse during breathing movements.

Numerous glands in the wall of the bronchus secrete a slimy mucus, which traps dust and other particles; the mucus is constantly being propelled upwards to the mouth by thousands of tiny hairs or cilia. The bronchus is adversely effected by several respiratory diseases and by smoking, which damages the cilia and therefore the lung-cleansing mechanism.

brontosaurus former name of a type of large, plant-eating dinosaur, now better known as ◊apatosaurus.

bronze alloy of copper and tin, yellow or brown in colour. It is harder than pure copper, more suitable for ◊casting, and also resists ◊corrosion. Bronze may contain as much as 25% tin, together with small amounts of other metals, mainly lead.

Bronze is one of the first metallic alloys known and used widely by early peoples during the period of history known as the ◊Bronze Age. The first bronze objects date from 3000 BC.

Bell metal, the bronze used for casting bells, contains 15% or more tin. **Phosphor bronze** is hardened by the addition of a small percentage of phosphorus. **Silicon bronze** (for telegraph wires) and **aluminium bronze** are similar alloys of copper with silicon or aluminium and small amounts of iron, nickel, or manganese, but usually no tin.

Bronze Age stage of prehistory and early history when copper and bronze (an alloy of tin and copper) became the first metals worked extensively and used for tools and weapons. One of the classifications of the Danish archaeologist Christian Thomsen's Three Age System, it developed out of the Stone Age and generally preceded the Iron Age. It first began in the Far East and may be dated 5000–1200 BC in the Middle East and about 2000–500 BC in Europe.

Mining and metalworking were the first specialized industries, and the invention of the wheel during this time revolutionized transport.

Agricultural productivity (which began during the New Stone Age, or Neolithic period, about 6000 BC) was transformed by the ox-drawn plough, increasing the size of the population that could be supported by farming.

In some areas, including most of Africa, there was no Bronze Age, and ironworking was introduced directly into the Stone Age economy.

broom any of a group of shrubs (especially species of *Cytisus* and *Spartium*), often cultivated for their bright yellow flowers. (Family Leguminosae.)

brouter device for connecting computer networks that incorporates the facilities of both a ◊bridge and a ◊router. Brouters usually offer routing over a limited number of ◊protocols, operating by routing where possible and bridging the remaining protocols.

Brown, Robert
(1773–1858)

Scottish botanist who in 1827 discovered Brownian motion. As a botanist, his more lasting work was in the field of plant morphology. He was the first to establish the real basis for the distinction between gymnosperms (pines) and angiosperms (flowering plants).

On an expedition to Australia in 1801–05 Brown collected 4,000 plant species and later classified them using the 'natural' system of Bernard de Jussieu (1699–1777) rather than relying upon the system of Carolus Linnaeus.

Mary Evans Picture Library

brown bear species of ◊bear found in N Europe.

brown dwarf in astronomy, an object less massive than a star, but heavier than a planet. Brown dwarfs do not have enough mass to ignite nuclear reactions at their centres, but shine by heat released during their contraction from a gas cloud. Some astronomers believe that vast numbers of brown dwarfs exist throughout the Galaxy. Because of the difficulty of detection, none were spotted until 1995, when US astronomers discovered a brown dwarf, GI229B, in the constellation Lepus. It is about 20–40 times as massive as Jupiter but emits only 1% of the radiation of the smallest known star. In 1996 UK astronomers discovered four possible brown dwarfs within 150 light years of the Sun.

Brownian movement the continuous random motion of particles in a fluid medium (gas or liquid) as they are subjected to impact from the molecules of the medium. The phenomenon was explained by German physicist Albert Einstein in 1905 but was probably observed as long ago as 1827 by the Scottish botanist Robert Brown. It provides evidence for the ◊kinetic theory of matter.

BROWNIAN MOTION

http://dbhs.wvusd.k12.ca.us/Chem-History/Brown-1829.html

Transcript of 'Remarks on Active Molecules' by Robert Brown from *Additional Remarks on Active Molecules* (1829). The text describes Robert Brown's observations of the random motion of particles, which in turn led to the placement of the subject on millions of school exam papers.

brown ring test in analytical chemistry, a test for the presence of ◊nitrates.

To an aqueous solution containing the test substance is added iron(II) sulphate. Concentrated sulphuric acid is then carefully poured down the inside wall of the test tube so that it forms a distinct layer at the bottom. The formation of a brown colour at the boundary between the two layers indicates the presence of nitrate.

browse to explore a computer system or network for particular files or information. To browse in Windows is to search for a particular file to open or run. On the World Wide Web, browsing is the activity of moving from site to site to view information. This is sometimes also called 'surfing'.

browser in computing, any program that allows the user to search for and view data. Browsers are usually limited to a particular type of data, so, for example, a graphics browser will display graphics files stored in many different file formats. Browsers usually do not permit the user to edit data, but are sometimes able to convert data from one file format to another.

Web browsers allow access to the ◊World Wide Web. Netscape Navigator and Microsoft's Internet Explorer were the leading Web browsers in 1996–97. They act as a graphical interface to information available on the Internet – they read ◊HTML (hypertext markup language) documents and display them as graphical documents which may include images, video, sound, and ◊hypertext links to other documents.

The first widespread browser for personal computers (PCs) was the text-based program Lynx, which is still used via ◊gateways from text-based online systems such as Delphi and CIX. Browsers using ◊graphical user interfaces became widely available from 1993 with the release of ◊Mosaic, written by Marc Andreessen and Eric Bina. For some specialist applications such as viewing the virtual reality sites beginning to appear on the Web, a special virtual reality modelling language (◊VRML) browser is needed.

brucellosis disease of cattle, goats, and pigs, also known when transmitted to humans as **undulant fever** since it remains in the body and recurs. It was named after Australian doctor David Bruce (1855–1931), and is caused by bacteria (genus *Brucella*). It is transmitted by contact with an infected animal or by drinking contaminated milk.

Brunel, Isambard Kingdom
(1806–1859)

British engineer and inventor. In 1833 he became engineer to the Great Western Railway, which adopted the 2.1-m/7-ft gauge on his advice. He built the Clifton Suspension Bridge over the river Avon at Bristol and the Saltash Bridge over the river Tamar near Plymouth. His shipbuilding designs include the *Great Western* 1837, the first steamship to cross the Atlantic regularly; the *Great Britain* 1843, the first large iron ship to have a screw propeller; and the *Great Eastern* 1858, which laid the first transatlantic telegraph cable.

Mary Evans Picture Library

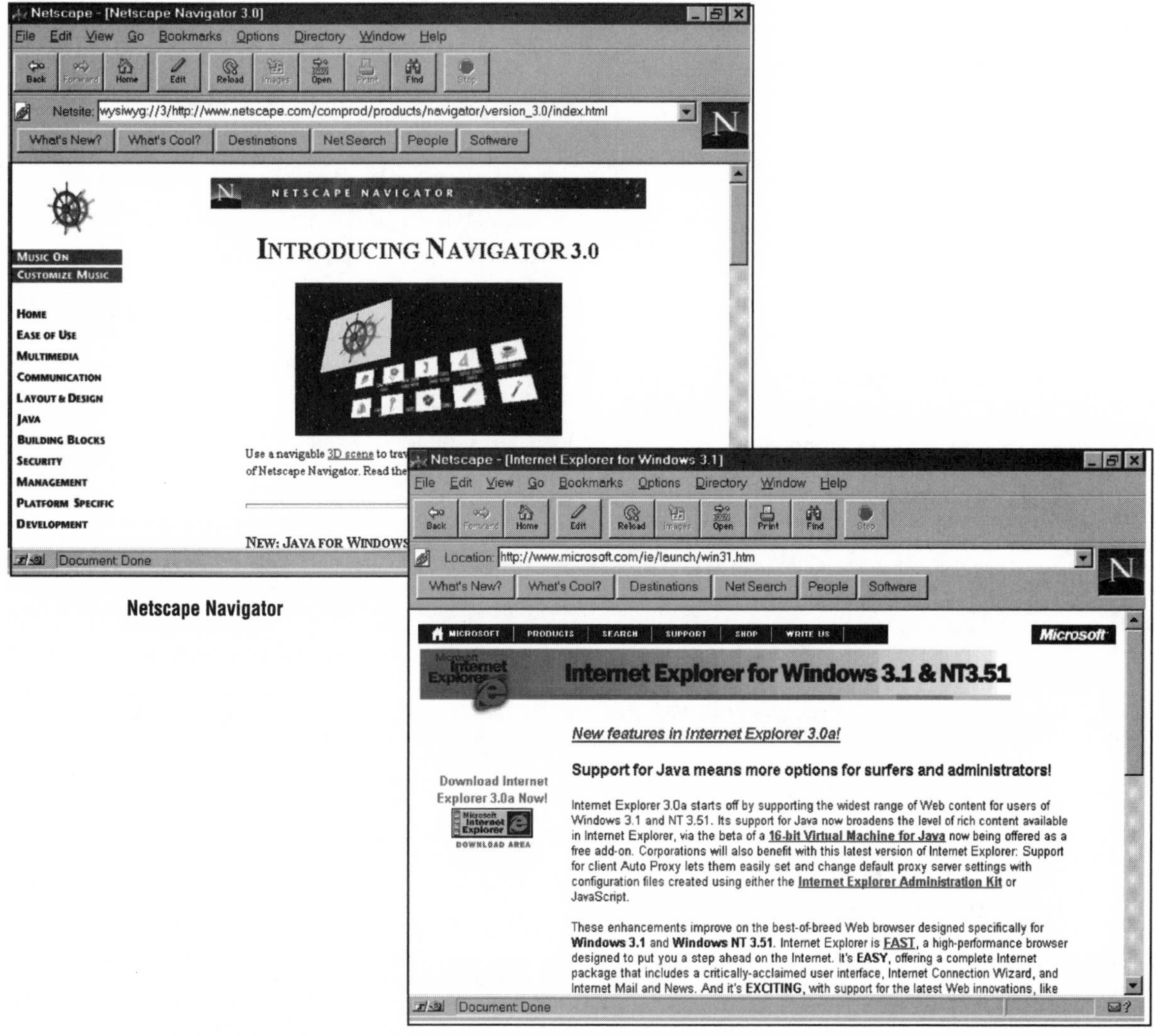

Netscape Navigator

Microsoft Internet Explorer

browser *Two popular World Wide Web browsers, Netscape Navigator and Microsoft Internet Explorer, which provide the user with a straightforward method of accessing information available online.*

It has largely been eradicated in the West through vaccination of livestock and pasteurization of milk. Brucellosis is especially prevalent in the Mediterranean and in Central and South America. It can be treated with antibacterial drugs.

brush in certain electric motors, one of a pair of contacts that pass electric current into and out of the rotating coils by means of a device known as a ◊commutator. The brushes, which are often replaceable, are usually made of a soft, carbon material to reduce wear of the copper contacts on the rotating commutator.

Brussels sprout one of the small edible buds along the stem of a variety of ◊cabbage. (*Brassica oleracea* var. *gemmifera*.) They are high in the glucosinolate compound sinigrin. Sinigrin was found to destroy precancerous cells in laboratory rats in 1996.

bryony either of two climbing hedgerow plants found in Britain: **white bryony** (*Bryonia dioca*) belonging to the gourd family (Cucurbitaceae), and **black bryony** (*Tamus communis*) of the yam family (Dioscoreaceae).

bryophyte member of the Bryophyta, a division of the plant kingdom containing three classes: the Hepaticae (◊liverwort), Musci (◊moss), and Anthocerotae (◊hornwort). Bryophytes are generally small, low-growing, terrestrial plants with no vascular (water-conducting) system as in higher plants. Their life cycle shows a marked ◊alternation of generations. Bryophytes chiefly occur in damp habitats and require water for the dispersal of the male gametes (◊antherozoids).

In bryophytes, the ◊sporophyte, consisting only of a spore-bearing capsule on a slender stalk, is wholly or partially dependent on the ◊gametophyte for water and nutrients. In some liverworts the plant body is a simple ◊thallus, but in the majority of bryophytes it is differentiated into stem, leaves, and ◊rhizoids.

BSI abbreviation for ◊British Standards Institute.

BST abbreviation for ***British Summer Time*** and ◊bovine somatotropin.

> To remember when we lose an hour, and when we gain an hour:
>
> SPRING FORWARD, FALL BACK
>
> OR
>
> REMEMBER THAT CLOCKS GO FORWARD AN HOUR IN SPRING, SINCE THEY ARE EAGER FOR THE SUMMER; CLOCKS GO BACK AN HOUR IN AUTUMN, SINCE THEY ARE SHYING AWAY FROM THE BITTER CHILL OF WINTER

BT abbreviation for ◊British Telecom.

Btu symbol for ◊British thermal unit.

bubble chamber in physics, a device for observing the nature and movement of atomic particles, and their interaction with radiation. It is a vessel filled with a superheated liquid through which ionizing particles move and collide. The paths of these particles are shown by strings of bubbles, which can be photographed and studied. By using a pressurized liquid medium instead of a gas, it overcomes drawbacks inherent in the earlier ◊cloud chamber. It was invented by US physicist Donald Glaser in 1952. See ◊particle detector.

bubble-jet printer in computing, an ◊ink-jet printer in which the ink is heated to boiling point so that it forms a bubble at the end of a nozzle. When the bubble bursts, the ink is transferred to the paper.

bubble memory in computing, a memory device based on the creation of small 'bubbles' on a magnetic surface. Bubble memories typically store up to 4 megabits (4 million ◊bits) of information. They are not sensitive to shock and vibration, unlike other memory devices such as disc drives, yet, like magnetic discs, they are nonvolatile and do not lose their information when the computer is switched off.

bubbleshell marine mollusc with a tiny shell. It burrows in the sand and feeds on animal matter.

bubble sort in computing, a technique for ◊sorting data. Adjacent items are continually exchanged until the data are in sequence.

bubonic plague epidemic disease of the Middle Ages; see ◊plague and ◊Black Death.

buckminsterfullerene form of carbon, made up of molecules (buckyballs) consisting of 60 carbon atoms arranged in 12 pentagons and 20 hexagons to form a perfect sphere. It was named after the US architect and engineer Richard Buckminster Fuller because of its structural similarity to the geodesic dome that he designed. See ◊fullerene.

buckthorn any of several thorny shrubs. The buckthorn (*Rhamnus catharticus*) is native to Britain, but is also found throughout Europe, W Asia, and N Africa. Its berries were formerly used in medicine as a purgative, to clean out the bowels. (Genus *Rhamnus*, family Rhamnaceae.)

buckwheat any of a group of cereal plants. The name usually refers to *Fagopyrum esculentum*, which reaches about 1 m/3 ft in height and can grow on poor soil in a short summer. The highly nutritious black triangular seeds (groats) are eaten by both animals and humans. They can be cooked and eaten whole or as a cracked meal (kasha), or ground into flour, often made into pancakes. (Genus *Fagopyrum*, family Polygonaceae.)

buckyballs popular name for molecules of ◊buckminsterfullerene.

bud undeveloped shoot usually enclosed by protective scales; inside is a very short stem and numerous undeveloped leaves, or flower parts, or both. Terminal buds are found at the tips of shoots, while axillary buds develop in the ◊axils of the leaves, often remaining dormant unless the terminal bud is removed or damaged. Adventitious buds may be produced anywhere on the plant, their formation sometimes stimulated by an injury, such as that caused by pruning.

budding type of ◊asexual reproduction in which an outgrowth develops from a cell to form a new individual. Most yeasts reproduce in this way.

In a suitable environment, yeasts grow rapidly, forming long chains of cells as the buds themselves produce further buds before being separated from the parent. Simple invertebrates, such as ◊hydra, can also reproduce by budding.

In horticulture, the term is used for a technique of plant propagation whereby a bud (or scion) and a sliver of bark from one plant are transferred to an incision made in the bark of another plant (the stock). This method of ◊grafting is often used for roses.

buddleia any of a group of ornamental shrubs or trees with spikes of fragrant flowers. The purple or white flower heads of the butterfly bush (*Buddleia davidii*) attract large numbers of butterflies. (Genus *Buddleia*, family Buddleiaceae.)

budgerigar small Australian parakeet *Melopsittacus undulatus* of the parrot family, Psittacidae, order Psittaciformes, that feeds mainly on grass seeds. Normally it is bright green, but yellow, white, blue, and mauve varieties have been bred for the pet market. It breeds freely in captivity.

buffalo either of two species of wild cattle. The Asiatic water buffalo *Bubalis bubalis* is found domesticated throughout S Asia and wild in parts of India and Nepal. It likes moist conditions. Usually grey or black, up to 1.8 m/6 ft high, both sexes carry large horns. The African buffalo *Syncerus caffer* is found in Africa, south of the Sahara, where there is grass, water, and cover in which to retreat. There are a number of subspecies, the biggest up to 1.6 m/5 ft high, and black, with massive horns set close together over the head. The name is also commonly applied to the American ◊bison.

buffer in chemistry, mixture of compounds chosen to maintain a steady ◊pH. The commonest buffers consist of a mixture of a weak organic acid and one of its salts or a mixture of acid salts of phosphoric acid. The addition of either an acid or a base causes a shift in the ◊chemical equilibrium, thus keeping the pH constant.

buffer in computing, a part of the ◊memory used to store data temporarily while it is waiting to be used. For example, a program might store data in a printer buffer until the printer is ready to print it.

bug in computing, an ◊error in a program. It can be an error in the logical structure of a program or a syntax error, such as a spelling mistake. Some bugs cause a program to fail immediately; others remain dormant, causing problems only when a particular combination of events occurs. The process of finding and removing errors from a program is called **debugging**.

bug in entomology, an insect belonging to the order Hemiptera. All these have two pairs of wings with forewings partly thickened.

They also have piercing mouthparts adapted for sucking the juices of plants or animals, the 'beak' being tucked under the body when not in use.

They include: the bedbug, which sucks human blood; the shieldbug, or stinkbug, which has a strong odour and feeds on plants; and the water boatman and other water bugs.

bugle any of a group of low-growing plants belonging to the mint family, with spikes of white, pink, or blue flowers. The leaves may be smooth-edged or slightly toothed, the lower ones with a long stalk. They are often grown as ground cover. (Genus *Ajuga*, family Labiatae.)

bugloss any of several plants native to Europe and Asia, distinguished by their rough, bristly leaves and small blue flowers. (Genera *Anchusa*, *Lycopsis*, and *Echium*, family Boraginaceae.)

bulb underground bud with fleshy leaves containing a reserve food supply and with roots growing from its base. Bulbs function in vegetative reproduction and are characteristic of many monocotyledonous plants such as the daffodil, snowdrop, and onion. Bulbs are grown on a commercial scale in temperate countries, such as England and the Netherlands.

Millennium Bug: Preparing Computers for the Year 2000

BY SCOTT KIRSNER

Digital Disarray

It sounds like a bad riddle: how will two missing digits create a $600 billion industry when the calendar flips from 1999 to 2000?

Unfortunately, it's not a riddle; it's reality. As the 20th century draws to a close, an expensive computer problem dubbed 'the millennium bug' has emerged. In brief, most computers handle dates using a two-digit shorthand: 98 instead of the four-digit 1998. When presented with a date like 00, they become hopelessly confused. Since they're missing the two digits that indicate what millennium and century the date is in (19 or 20), computers tend to assume that 00 is actually 1900. So they'll either begin making errors of calculation or they'll stop working altogether. Reprogramming them to be capable of comprehending dates in the new millennium is expected to cost as much as $600 billion worldwide.

The origins of the problem are simple. First, the programmers who wrote software in the 1960s for the first generation of commercial mainframe computers were shortsighted. They didn't imagine that the programs they were creating – or the machines they were creating them for – would still be in service in the far-off year of 2000. So they conserved the computers' memory by using a two-digit shorthand for the year. Every byte of memory was precious in those days, and lopping off 19 from dates was an obvious way to save a few bytes here and there.

Banks were among the first institutions to notice the downside to that approach. When they began writing long-term mortgages and approving loans that lasted past 1999, they were forced to confront the millennium bug. But the problem received little widespread attention until the mid-1990s. Technology consultants began writing articles and giving speeches about 'the year 2000 problem'. Business executives began to take notice, and even consumers couldn't ignore the problem when credit card issuers and driver's licence organizations began to renew cards and licences for shorter periods of time, because their systems couldn't handle an expiration date past 1999.

How might businesses and consumers be affected by the millennium bug? Computers, both new and old, in every industry are vulnerable. They might shut down as a result of being asked to process the date 00. Some say that is the best-case scenario, because at least businesses will know something is wrong. Worse would be if computers continued to operate, making numerous date-related errors that would be difficult to identify and fix.

The areas of greatest concern are defence, health care, transportation, telecommunications, financial services, and national and local governments. Technology experts warn of the hazards of air travel if the Federal Aviation Administration's computers can't manage data properly, the danger of hospital stays if the computers that monitor patients go awry, and the possibility of social unrest if the federal government can't provide services in 2000.

Date Expansion or Windowing?

Fixing the millennium bug is a labour-intensive endeavour. An organization can opt to replace its systems entirely with new ones that can function in the 21st century, or it may pursue one of two basic repair strategies – 'date expansion' or 'windowing'.

Date expansion involves changing the two-digit dates to four. That entails converting all of the data an organization has stored from one format to the other, and reprogramming systems to handle four-digit dates like 2001.

Windowing is considered a simpler, less expensive solution, but it's only a temporary patch. Rather than converting all of a company's data, the windowing approach merely adds logic to a program to help it determine whether a two-digit date belongs in the 20th century or the 21st. Programmers might create a 'window' of time – from 00 to 30, for example – and then instruct the computer to assume that those dates should all be preceded by 20, whereas dates between 31 and 99 should be preceded by 19. But when 2031 rolls around, that hypothetical company would have a new problem on its hands. Windowing assumes that an organization will either replace its older systems before the window of time closes, or reprogram them yet again.

Eradicating the millennium bug is a multi-stage process. An organization must first assess which of its systems will be unable to handle dates in the 21st century. Then, it must convert those systems, either through expansion or windowing. Finally, it has to test the systems to ensure that they will work after the clock ticks past midnight on 31 December, 1999.

Ripple Effects

But even if companies successfully repair their own systems, they're still vulnerable to what has been dubbed 'the ripple effect'. One of their suppliers or customers, or a government regulator, could send them unconverted data and contaminate their systems. Or even worse, a key supplier might be unable to provide services or raw materials as a result of the bug, hamstringing its customers. For those reasons, organizations must make sure that everyone else with whom they do business is solving their own year 2000 problems. Certain sectors of the economy, like the financial services arena, are even coordinating massive, interorganizational tests to make sure that stock exchanges, banks, regulators, and clearing houses will be able to work together in the new millennium.

And waiting in the wings are the lawyers. If software or hardware fails, they'll be scrutinizing contracts to see who is liable. If a conversion project turns out to have been defective, they may bring litigation against the service provider that was contracted to perform the fix. And if a company's stock takes a dive as a result of year 2000-related failures, lawyers may file negligence lawsuits against the Board of Directors. Once litigation and damages are figured into the cost of the millennium bug, some analysts believe the total worldwide cost could skyrocket to as much as $3.6 trillion.

The sudden emergence of the year 2000 problem has created an entire mini-economy. Programmers and technology managers are finding that they can demand and receive higher salaries, computer consultants have more work than they can handle, and software companies have begun to market tools aimed at making assessment, conversion, and testing more efficient. There are dozens of Web sites and books devoted to the problem. The American Stock Exchange has even created an options index that enables investors to speculate on the fortunes of 18 companies selling software or services intended to solve the year 2000 problem.

Few participants in this mini-economy are willing to speculate about the extent to which the world will be affected by the millennium bug. Will 1 January, 2000, arrive without a hitch, or will, as some technology experts predict, the front pages of every major newspaper be filled with stories about date-related computer crises? All that's certain is that programmers and their technology managers won't be among the celebrants on New Year's Eve, 1999; they'll be huddled over their mainframes, fingers crossed.

bulbil small bulb that develops above ground from a bud. Bulbils may be formed on the stem from axillary buds, as in members of the saxifrage family, or in the place of flowers, as seen in many species of onion *Allium*. They drop off the parent plant and develop into new individuals, providing a means of ◊vegetative reproduction and dispersal.

bulbul fruit-eating bird of the family Pycnonotidae, order Passeriformes, that ranges in size from that of a sparrow to a blackbird. They are mostly rather dull coloured and very secretive, living in dense forests. They are widely distributed throughout Africa and Asia; there are about 120 species.

bulimia ***Greek 'ox hunger'*** eating disorder in which large amounts of food are consumed in a short time ('binge'), usually followed by depression and self-criticism. The term is often used for **bulimia nervosa**, an emotional disorder in which eating is followed by deliberate vomiting and purging. This may be a chronic stage in ◊anorexia nervosa.

Bulinus large genus of tiny freshwater and land snails, comprising over 1,000 species. They have external shells, and are related to the hedge- and grass-snails.

Certain species of this snail act as the intermediate host for the microscopic worm that causes ◊bilharzia, one of the most common parasitic diseases.

classification *Bulinus* is in class Gastropoda of phylum Mollusca.

bulldog British breed of dog of ancient but uncertain origin, formerly bred for bull-baiting. The head is broad and square, with deeply wrinkled cheeks, small folded ears, very short muzzle, and massive jaws, the peculiar set of the lower jaw making it difficult for the dog to release its grip. Thickset in build, the bulldog grows to about 45 cm/18 in and has a smooth beige, tawny, or brindle coat. The French bulldog is much lighter in build and has large upright ears.

bulldozer earth-moving machine widely used in construction work for clearing rocks and tree stumps and levelling a site. The bulldozer is a kind of tractor with a powerful engine and a curved, shovel-like blade at the front, which can be lifted and forced down by hydraulic rams. It usually has ◊caterpillar tracks so that it can move easily over rough ground.

bulletin board in computing, a centre for the electronic storage of messages, usually accessed over the telephone network via a ◊modem but also sometimes accessed via ◊Telnet across the Internet. Bulletin board systems (often abbreviated to BBSs) are usually dedicated to specific interest groups, and may carry public and private messages, notices, and programs.

bullfinch Eurasian finch with a thick head and neck, and short heavy bill, genus *Pyrrhula pyrrhula*, family Fringillidae, order Passeriformes. It is small and blue-grey or black in colour, the males being reddish and the females brown on the breast. Bullfinches are 15 cm/6 in long, and usually seen in pairs. They feed on tree buds as well as seeds and berries, and are usually seen in woodland. They also live in the Aleutians and on the Alaska mainland.

bullfrog North American species of ◊frog.

bullhead or ***miller's thumb*** small fish *Cottus gobio* found in fresh water in the northern hemisphere, often under stones. It has a large head, a spine on the gill cover, and grows to 10 cm/4 in.

Related bullheads, such as the **father lasher** *Myxocephalus scorpius*, live in coastal waters. They are up to 30 cm/1 ft long. The male guards the eggs and fans them with his tail.

bull terrier breed of dog, originating as a cross between a terrier and a bulldog. Very powerfully built, it grows to about 40 cm/16 in tall, and has a short, usually white, coat, narrow eyes, and distinctive egg-shaped head. It was formerly used in bull-baiting. Pit bull terriers are used in illegal dog fights. The ◊Staffordshire bull terrier is a distinct breed.

bulrush either of two plants: the great reed mace or cat's tail (*Typha latifolia*) with velvety chocolate-brown spikes of tightly packed flowers reaching up to 15 cm/6 in long; and a type of sedge (*Scirpus lacustris*) with tufts of reddish-brown flowers at the top of a rounded, rushlike stem.

bumblebee any large ◊bee, 2–5 cm/1–2 in, usually dark-coloured but banded with yellow, orange, or white, belonging to the genus *Bombus*.

Most species live in small colonies, usually underground, often in an old mousehole. The queen lays her eggs in a hollow nest of moss or grass at the beginning of the season. The larvae are fed on pollen and honey, and develop into workers. All the bees die at the end of the season except fertilized females, which hibernate and produce fresh colonies in the spring. Bumblebees are found naturally all over the world, with the exception of Australia, where they have been introduced to facilitate the pollination of some cultivated varieties of clover.

bundling computer industry practice of selling different, often unrelated, products in a single package. Bundles may consist of hardware or software or both; for example, a modem or a selection of software may be bundled with a personal computer to make the purchase of the computer seem more attractive.

Bunsen burner gas burner used in laboratories, consisting of a vertical metal tube through which a fine jet of fuel gas is directed. Air is drawn in through airholes near the base of the tube and the mixture is ignited and burns at the tube's upper opening.

The invention of the burner is attributed to German chemist Robert von Bunsen in 1855 but English chemist and physicist Michael Faraday is known to have produced a similar device at an earlier date. A later refinement was the metal collar that can be turned to close or partially close the airholes, thereby regulating the amount of air sucked in and hence the heat of the burner's flame.

bunting any of a number of sturdy, finchlike birds with short, thick bills, of the family Emberizidae, order Passeriformes, especially the genera *Passerim* and *Emberiza*. Most of these brightly coloured birds are native to the New World.

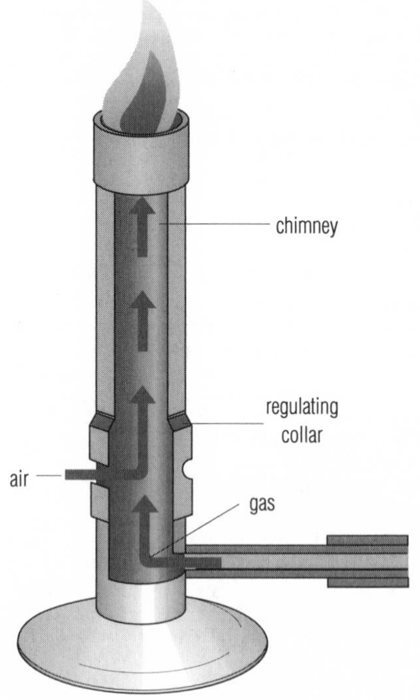

***Bunsen burner** The Bunsen burner, used for heating laboratory equipment and chemicals. The flame can reach temperatures of 1,500°C/2,732°F and is at its hottest when the collar is open.*

Bunsen, Robert Wilhelm
(1811–1899)

German chemist credited with the invention of the Bunsen burner. His name is also given to the carbon–zinc electric cell, which he invented in 1841 for use in arc lamps. In 1860 he discovered two new elements, caesium and rubidium.

Mary Evans Picture Library

buoy floating object used to mark channels for shipping or warn of hazards to navigation. Buoys come in different shapes, such as a pole (spar buoy), cylinder (car buoy), and cone (nun buoy). Light buoys carry a small tower surmounted by a flashing lantern, and bell buoys house a bell, which rings as the buoy moves up and down with the waves. Mooring buoys are heavy and have a ring on top to which a ship can be tied.

buoyancy lifting effect of a fluid on a body wholly or partly immersed in it. This was studied by ◊Archimedes in the 3rd century BC.

bur or ***burr*** in botany, a type of 'false fruit' or ◊pseudocarp, surrounded by numerous hooks; for instance, that of burdock *Arctium*, where the hooks are formed from bracts surrounding the flowerhead. Burs catch in the feathers or fur of passing animals, and thus may be dispersed over considerable distances.

burbot or **eelpout** long, rounded fish *Lota lota* of the cod family, the only one living entirely in fresh water. Up to 1 m/3 ft long, it lives on the bottom of clear lakes and rivers, often in holes or under rocks, throughout Europe, Asia, and North America.

burdock any of several bushy herbs characterized by hairy leaves and ripe fruit enclosed in ◊burs with strong hooks. (Genus *Arctium*, family Compositae.)

burette in chemistry, a piece of apparatus, used in ◊titration, for the controlled delivery of measured variable quantities of a liquid.

It consists of a long, narrow, calibrated glass tube, with a tap at the bottom, leading to a narrow-bore exit.

Burmese cat breed of domestic shorthaired cat of ancient origin. The modern breed is descended for a cat introduced into the USA in 1930 from Burma and crossed with a Siamese. The original Burmese has a sable brown coat with lighter shading on the underside; the medium-length body is muscular and more rounded than a Siamese.

It was first recognized as a true breed in the USA in 1936 and in the UK in 1952. The standards vary for the Burmese in the USA and Britain; for instance, the British eye shape is specified as oval, while the American standard demands a rounder look. There are many varieties.

burn in medicine, destruction of body tissue by extremes of temperature, corrosive chemicals, electricity, or radiation. **First-degree burns** may cause reddening; **second-degree burns** cause blistering and irritation but usually heal spontaneously; **third-degree burns** are disfiguring and may be life-threatening.

Burns cause plasma, the fluid component of the blood, to leak from the blood vessels, and it is this loss of circulating fluid that engenders ◊shock. Emergency treatment is needed for third-degree burns in order to replace the fluid volume, prevent infection (a serious threat to the severely burned), and reduce the pain. Plastic, or reconstructive, surgery, including skin grafting, may be required to compensate for damaged tissue and minimize disfigurement. If a skin graft is necessary, dead tissue must be removed from a burn (a process known as debridement) so that the patient's blood supply can nourish the graft.

burnet herb belonging to the rose family, also known as **salad burnet**. It smells of cucumber and can be used in salads. The name is also used for other members of the genus. (*Sanguisorba minor*, family Rosaceae.)

burning common name for ◊combustion.

burying beetle another name for the ◊sexton beetle.

bus in computing, the electrical pathway through which a computer processor communicates with some of its parts and/or peripherals. Physically, a bus is a set of parallel tracks that can carry digital signals; it may take the form of copper tracks laid down on the computer's ◊printed circuit boards (PCBs), or of an external cable or connection.

A computer typically has three internal buses laid down on its main circuit board: a **data bus**, which carries data between the components of the computer; an **address bus**, which selects the route to be followed by any particular data item travelling along the data bus; and a **control bus**, which is used to decide whether data is written to or read from the data bus. An external **expansion bus** is used for linking the computer processor to peripheral devices, such as modems and printers.

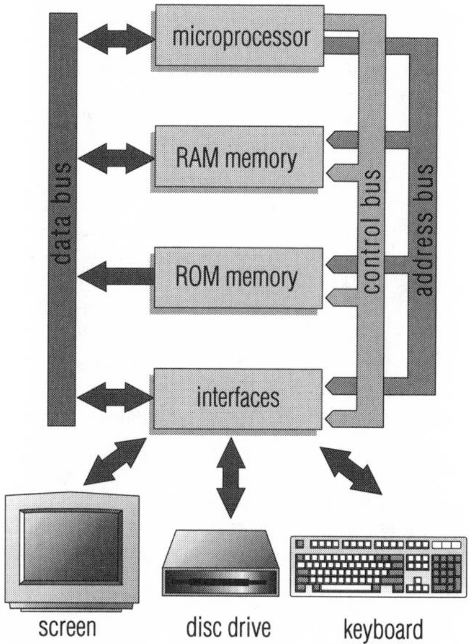

bus *The communication path used between the component parts of a computer.*

Bush, Vannevar
(1890–1974)

US electrical engineer and scientist. During the 1920s and 1930s he developed several mechanical and mechanical–electrical analogue computers which were highly effective in the solution of differential equations. The standard electricity meter is based on one of his designs.

bushbaby small nocturnal African prosimian with long feet, long, bushy tail, and large ears. Bushbabies are active tree dwellers and feed on fruit, insects, eggs, and small birds.
classification Bushbabies are members of the loris family Lorisidae, order Primates.

bushbuck antelope *Tragelaphus scriptus* found over most of Africa south of the Sahara. Up to 1 m/3 ft high, the males have keeled horns twisted into spirals, and are brown to blackish. The females are generally hornless, lighter, and redder. All have white markings, including stripes or vertical rows of dots down the sides. Rarely far from water, bushbuck live in woods and thick brush.

bushel dry or liquid measure equal to eight gallons or four pecks (2,219.36 cu in/36.37 litres) in the UK; some US states have different standards according to the goods measured.

bushman's rabbit or ***riverine rabbit*** a wild rodent *Bunolagus monticularis* found in dense riverine bush in South Africa. It lives in small populations, and individuals are only seen very occasionally; it is now at extreme risk of extinction owing to loss of habitat to agriculture. Very little is known about its life or habits.

bushmaster large snake *Lachesis muta.* It is a type of pit viper, and is related to the rattlesnakes. Up to 4 m/12 ft long, it is found in wooded areas of South and Central America, and is the largest venomous snake in the New World. When alarmed, it produces a noise by vibrating its tail among dry leaves.

bush pig wild pig found in forested regions of Africa. Typically it is dark brown in colour, about 60 cm/24 in high and has short tusks no more than 15 cm/6 in long.

The **red river hog** is a West African variety of the same species but is rusty red in colour with prominent black and white markings on the face.
classification The bush pig *Potamochoerus porcus* is in family Suidae, order Artiodactyla.

bustard bird of the family Otididae, order Gruiformes, related to ◊cranes but with a rounder body, thicker neck, and a relatively short beak. Bustards are found on the ground on open plains and fields.

The great bustard *Otis tarda* is one of the heaviest flying birds at 18 kg/40 lb, and the larger males may have a length of 1 m/3 ft and wingspan of 2.3 m/7.5 ft. It is found in N Asia and Europe, although there are fewer than 30,000 great bustards left in Europe; two-thirds of these live on the Spanish steppes.

butadiene or ***buta-1,3-diene*** CH_2:CHCH:CH_2 inflammable gas derived from petroleum, used in making synthetic rubber and resins.

butane C_4H_{10} one of two gaseous alkanes (paraffin hydrocarbons) having the same formula but differing in structure. Normal butane is derived from natural gas; isobutane is a by-product of petroleum manufacture. Liquefied under pressure, it is used as a fuel for industrial and domestic purposes (for example, in portable cookers).

butcherbird another name for a ◊shrike.

butene C_4H_8 fourth member of the ◊alkene series of hydrocarbons. It is an unsaturated compound, containing one double bond.

buttercup any plant of the buttercup family with divided leaves and yellow flowers. (Genus *Ranunculus,* family Ranunculaceae.)

butterfly insect belonging, like moths, to the order Lepidoptera, in which the wings are covered with tiny scales, often brightly coloured. There are some 15,000 species of butterfly, many of which are under threat throughout the world because of the destruction of habitat.

Butterflies have a tubular proboscis through which they suck up nectar, or, in some species, carrion, dung, or urine. ◊Metamorphosis is complete; the pupa, or chrysalis, is usually without the protection of a cocoon. Adult lifespan may be only a few weeks, but some species hibernate and lay eggs in the spring.

The largest family, Nymphalidae, has some 6,000 species; it includes the peacock, tortoiseshells, and fritillaries. The family Pieridae includes the **cabbage white**, one of the few butterflies injurious to crops. The Lycaenidae are chiefly small, often with metallic coloration, for example the blues, coppers, and hairstreaks. The **large blue** *Lycaena arion* has a complex life history: it lays its eggs on wild thyme, and the caterpillars are then taken by Myrmica ants to their nests. The ants milk their honey glands, while the caterpillars feed on the ant larvae. In the spring, the caterpillars finally pupate and emerge as butterflies. The mainly tropical Papilionidae, or swallowtails, are large and very beautiful, especially the South American species. The world's largest butterfly is Queen Alexandra's birdwing *Ornithoptera alexandrae* of Papua New Guinea, with a body 7.5 cm/3 in long and a wingspan of 25 cm/10 in. The most spectacular migrant is the orange and black monarch butterfly *Danaus plexippus,* which may fly from N Canada to Mexico in the autumn.

Butterflies usually differ from moths in having the antennae club-shaped rather than plumed or feathery, no 'lock' between the fore- and hindwing, and resting with the wings in the vertical position rather than flat or sloping.

BUTTERFLY

The sensors on the feet of a red admiral butterfly are 200 times more sensitive to sugar than the human tongue.

butterfly fish any of several fishes, not all related. They include the freshwater butterfly fish *Pantodon buchholzi* of western Africa and the tropical marine butterfly fishes in family Chaetodontidae.

P. buchholzi can leap from the water and glide for a short distance on its large winglike pectoral fins. Up to 10 cm/4 in long, it lives in stagnant water, at the water surface during the day, lying beneath floating leaves. At night it hunts for insects, jumping out of the water to catch them.

The members of Chaetodontidae are brightly coloured with laterally flattened bodies, often with long snouts which they poke into crevices in rocks and coral when feeding. They have a flattened narrow body with one dorsal fin and a fairly long snout. Their bristlelike teeth are closely set in rows for feeding on small animals and green algae. The commonest colours are black, yellow, and brilliant metallic blues and greens.
classification Chaetodontidae is in order Perciformes; *Pantodon buchholzi* is in order Osteoglossiformes; both are in class Osteichthyes.

butterwort insectivorous plant belonging to the bladderwort family, with purplish flowers and a rosette of flat leaves covered with a sticky substance that traps insects. (Genus *Pinguicula,* family Lentibulariaceae.)

buzzard species of medium-sized hawk with broad wings, often seen soaring. Buzzards are in the falcon family, Falconidae, order Falconiformes. The **common buzzard** *Buteo buteo* of Europe and Asia is about 55 cm/1.8 ft long with a wingspan of over 1.2 m/4 ft. It preys on a variety of small animals up to the size of a rabbit.

The **rough-legged buzzard** *B. lagopus* lives in the northern tundra and eats lemmings. The **honey buzzard** *Pernis apivora* feeds largely, as its name suggests, on honey and insect larvae. It spends the summer in Europe and W Asia and winters in Africa. The **red-shouldered hawk** *B. lineatus* and **red-tailed hawk** *B. jamaicensis* occur in North America.

by-product substance formed incidentally during the manufacture of some other substance; for example, slag is a by-product of the production of iron in a ◊blast furnace. For industrial processes to be economical, by-products must be recycled or used in other ways as far as possible; in this example, slag is used for making roads.

Often, a poisonous by-product is removed by transforming it into another substance, which although less harmful is often still inconvenient. For example, the sulphur dioxide produced as a by-product of electricity generation can be removed from the smoke stack using ◊flue-gas desulphurization. This process produces large amounts of gypsum, some of which can be used in the building industry.

byssus tough protein fibres secreted by the foot of sessile (fixed) bivalves, such as ◊mussels, as a means of attachment to rocks.

The byssus of some rock creatures can be woven into fabrics. A delicate silk called byssus is made from the byssus of mussels found in the Mediterranean.

byte sufficient computer memory to store a single ◊character of data. The character is stored in the byte of memory as a pattern of ◊bits (binary digits), using a code such as ◊ASCII. A byte usually contains eight bits – for example, the capital letter F can be stored as the bit pattern 01000110.

A single byte can specify 256 values, such as the decimal numbers from 0 to 255; in the case of a single-byte ◊pixel (picture element), it can specify 256 different colours. Three bytes (24 bits) can specify 16,777,216 values. Computer memory size is measured in **kilobytes** (1,024 bytes) or **megabytes** (1,024 kilobytes).

°C symbol for degrees ◊Celsius, sometimes called centigrade.

C++ in computing, a high-level programming language used in ◊object-oriented applications. It is derived from the language C.

C in computing, a high-level, general-purpose programming language popular on minicomputers and microcomputers. Developed in the early 1970s from an earlier language called BCPL, C was first used as the language of the operating system ◊UNIX, though it has since become widespread beyond UNIX. It is useful for writing fast and efficient systems programs, such as operating systems (which control the operations of the computer).

cabbage vegetable plant related to the turnip and wild mustard, or charlock. It was cultivated as early as 2000 BC, and the many commercial varieties include kale, Brussels sprouts, common cabbage, savoy, cauliflower, sprouting broccoli, and kohlrabi. (*Brassica oleracea,* family Cruciferae.)

cabbage butterfly one of several butterfly species, the caterpillars of which feed on the leaves of members of the cabbage family, particularly as pests on cabbages. ◊Ichneumon flies parasitize the caterpillars, thereby controlling their numbers.
classification Cabbage butterflies are in genus *Pieris* in order Lepidoptera, class Insecta, phylum Arthropoda.
species The **large white** *Pieris brassicae* is found in Europe and North Africa. The expanded wings measure 7.5 cm/3 in across, and are white with black edgings. The female, which has black spots on the upper surfaces of the wings, lays her yellow eggs in clusters on cabbage leaves. The fully grown caterpillar sometimes measures 4 cm/1.5 in, and will eat twice its own weight of leaf in 24 hours. After it has hung for some time by its tail from a ledge, it changes into a shining pale green chrysalis. The butterfly, which in the case of the autumn brood waits till winter is past before emerging, lives on nectar.

The **small white butterfly** *Pieris rapae,* has a wing expansion of about 5 cm/2 in, lays its eggs singly on the underside of vegetable leaves, and produces a velvety caterpillar which devours the hearts, instead of merely the leaves, of cabbages. The chrysalis is brownish-yellow with black spots.

A third species, the **green-veined white butterfly** *Pieris napi,* which is similar to the small white, cannot multiply so fast, because both the butterfly and its caterpillar are a favourite food of small birds.

cabbage-tree palm tall, fan-leaf palm *Livistona australis* of the coastal areas of E Australia. Aborigines eat the cabbagelike hearts of the young leaves.

cable unit of length, used on ships, originally the length of a ship's anchor cable or 120 fathoms (219 m/720 ft), but now taken as one-tenth of a ◊nautical mile (185.3 m/608 ft).

cable car method of transporting passengers up steep slopes by cable. In the **cable railway**, passenger cars are hauled along rails by a cable wound by a powerful winch. A pair of cars usually operates together on the funicular principle, one going up as the other goes down. The other main type is the **aerial cable car**, where the passenger car is suspended from a trolley that runs along an aerial cableway.

A cable-car system has operated in San Francisco since 1873. The streetcars travel along rails and are hauled by moving cables under the ground.

cable modem box supplied by cable companies to provide television and telephone services, including Internet. The advantages of cable modems over traditional ◊modems, which operate over standard telephone lines, are greatly increased speed of communications as well as the ability to transmit video and two-way audio, and lower costs.

cable television distribution of broadcast signals through cable relay systems.

Narrow-band systems were originally used to deliver services to areas with poor regular reception; systems with wider bands, using coaxial and fibreoptic cable, are increasingly used for distribution and development of home-based interactive services, typically telephones.

In 1997, the USA had 65 million cable television subscribers using more than 11,000 cable systems. The systems were to spend more than $3.5 billion on basic programming in 1997, up 14% from 1996. In 1998, the 65 million US subscribers paid an average of more than $31 a month. The cost for 1998 represented the third straight year the price has increased by 8%, four times the inflation rate.

cacao tropical American evergreen tree, now also cultivated in W Africa and Sri Lanka. Its seeds are cocoa beans, from which cocoa and chocolate are prepared. (*Theobroma cacao,* family Sterculiaceae.)

The trees mature at five to eight years and produce two crops a year. The fruit is 17–25 cm/6.5–9.5 in long, hard, and ridged, with the beans inside. The seeds are called cocoa nibs; when left to ferment, then roasted and separated from the husks, they contain about 50% fat, part of which is removed to make chocolate and cocoa.

The Aztecs revered cacao and made a drink exclusively for the nobility from cocoa beans and chillies, which they called chocolatl. In the 16th century Spanish traders brought cacao to Europe. It was used to make a drink, which came to rival coffee and tea in popularity.

cachalot alternative name for the sperm whale; see ◊whale.

cache memory in computing, a reserved area of the ◊immediate access memory used to increase the running speed of a computer program.

The cache memory may be constructed from ◊SRAM, which is faster but more expensive than the normal ◊DRAM. Most programs access the same instructions or data repeatedly. If these frequently used instructions and data are stored in a fast-access SRAM memory cache, the program will run more quickly. In other cases, the memory cache is normal DRAM, but is used to store frequently used instructions and data that would normally be accessed from ◊backing storage. Access to DRAM is faster than access to backing storage so, again, the program runs more quickly. This type of cache memory is often called a **disc cache**.

cactus (plural *cacti*) strictly, any plant of the family Cactaceae, although the word is commonly used to describe many different succulent and prickly plants. True cacti have a woody axis (central core) surrounded by a large fleshy stem, which takes various forms and is usually covered with spines (actually reduced leaves). They are all specially adapted to growing in dry areas.

Cactus flowers are often large and brightly coloured; the fruit is fleshy and often edible, as in the case of the prickly pear. The Cactaceae are a New World family and include the treelike saguaro and the night-blooming cereus with blossoms 30 cm/12 in across.

CACTUS AND SUCCULENT PLANT MALL

http://www.cactus-mall.com/index.html

Huge source of information on cacti and how to grow them. There are also reports on conservation of cacti and succulents. There are links to a large number of international cacti associations.

CAD (acronym for ***computer-aided design***) the use of computers in creating and editing design drawings. CAD also allows such things as automatic testing of designs and multiple or animated three-dimensional views of designs. CAD systems are widely used in architecture, electronics, and engineering, for example in the motor-vehicle industry, where cars designed with the assistance of computers are now commonplace.

A related development is ◊CAM (computer-assisted manufacturing).

Cadarache French nuclear research site, NE of Aix-en-Provence.

caddis fly insect of the order Trichoptera. Adults are generally dull brown, mothlike, with wings covered in tiny hairs. Mouthparts are poorly developed, and many caddis flies do not feed as adults. They are usually found near water.

The larvae are aquatic, and many live in cases, open at both ends, which they make out of sand or plant remains. Some species make silk nets among aquatic vegetation to help trap food.

caddis fly *Caddis fly adults are generally rather drab insects most likely to be seen by ponds, lakes, and rivers where they may form dense mating swarms. The larvae fashion intricate cases from materials such as sand grains, twigs, empty snail shells, or other debris. Premaphotos Wildlife*

cadmium soft, silver-white, ductile, and malleable metallic element, symbol Cd, atomic number 48, relative atomic mass 112.40. Cadmium occurs in nature as a sulphide or carbonate in zinc ores. It is a toxic metal that, because of industrial dumping, has become an environmental pollutant. It is used in batteries, electroplating, and as a constituent of alloys used for bearings with low coefficients of friction; it is also a constituent of an alloy with a very low melting point.

Cadmium is also used in the control rods of nuclear reactors, because of its high absorption of neutrons. It was named in 1817 by the German chemist Friedrich Strohmeyer (1776–1835) after the Greek mythological character Cadmus.

caecilian tropical amphibian of wormlike appearance. There are about 170 species known in the family Caeciliidae, forming the amphibian order Apoda (also known as Caecilia or Gymnophiona). Caecilians have a grooved skin that gives a 'segmented' appearance; they have no trace of limbs or pelvis. The body is 20–130 cm/8–50 in long, beige to black in colour. The eyes are very small and weak or blind. They eat insects and small worms. Some species bear live young, others lay eggs.

Caecilians live in burrows in damp ground in the tropical Americas, Africa, Asia, and the Seychelles Islands.

CAECILIANS WEB SITE

http://www.sfo.com/~morriss/eels.html

Many facts about these legless amphibians, especially *Typhlonectes natans*, an aquatic caecilian often found in aquariums in the USA. Tips on care, health, and breeding can also be found at this site.

caecum in the ◊digestive system of animals, a blind-ending tube branching off from the first part of the large intestine, terminating in the appendix. It has no function in humans but is used for the digestion of cellulose by some grass-eating mammals.

The rabbit caecum and appendix contains millions of bacteria that produce cellulase, the enzyme necessary for the breakdown of cellulose to glucose. In order to be able to absorb nutrients released by the breakdown of cellulose, rabbits pass food twice down the intestine. They egest soft pellets which are then re-eaten. This is known as coprophagy.

Caesarean section surgical operation to deliver a baby by way of an incision in the mother's abdominal and uterine walls. It may be recommended for almost any obstetric complication implying a threat to mother or baby.

Caesarean section was named after the Roman emperor Julius Caesar, who was born this way. In medieval Europe, it was performed mostly in attempts to save the life of a child whose mother had died in labour. The Christian Church forbade cutting open the mother before she was dead.

caesium ***Latin*** *caesius* ***'bluish-grey'*** soft, silvery-white, ductile metallic element, symbol Cs, atomic number 55, relative atomic mass 132.905. It is one of the ◊alkali metals, and is the most electropositive of all the elements. In air it ignites spontaneously, and it reacts vigorously with water. It is used in the manufacture of photocells. The name comes from the blueness of its spectral line.

The rate of vibration of caesium atoms is used as the standard of measuring time. Its radioactive isotope Cs-137 (half-life 30.17 years) is a product of fission in nuclear explosions and in nuclear reactors; it is one of the most dangerous waste products of the nuclear industry, being a highly radioactive biological analogue for potassium.

caffeine ◊alkaloid organic substance found in tea, coffee, and kola nuts; it stimulates the heart and central nervous system. When isolated, it is a bitter crystalline compound, $C_8H_{10}N_4O_2$. Too much caffeine (more than six average cups of tea or coffee a day) can be detrimental to health.

caiman or **cayman** large reptile, related to the ◊alligator.

All caimans are found only in Central and South America.

types of caiman The black caiman *Melanosuchus niger* is the largest South American predator, reaching 6 m in length. Cuvier's dwarf caiman *Paleosuchus palpebrosus* may be as little as 1.2 m in length when fully grown (females). Schneider's dwarf caiman *Paleosuchus trigonatus* reaches 1.7 m and is reasonably common in the Amazonian rainforests. Broad-snouted caiman *Caiman latirostris* is found is found mainly in freshwater swamps and grows up to 3.5 m. Common caiman *Caiman crocodilus* is found from southern Mexico to northern Argentina and can grow up to 3 m.

cairn Scottish breed of ◊terrier. Shaggy, short-legged, and compact, it can be sandy, greyish brindle, or red. It was formerly used for flushing out foxes and badgers.

caisson hollow cylindrical or boxlike structure, usually of reinforced ◊concrete, sunk into a riverbed to form the foundations of a bridge.

An **open caisson** is open at the top and at the bottom, where there is a wedge-shaped cutting edge. Material is excavated from inside, allowing the caisson to sink. A **pneumatic caisson** has a pressurized chamber at the bottom, in which workers carry out the excavation. The air pressure prevents the surrounding water entering; the workers enter and leave the chamber through an airlock, allowing for a suitable decompression period to prevent ◊decompression sickness (the so-called bends).

cal symbol for ◊calorie.

CAL (acronym for ***computer-assisted learning***) the use of computers in education and training: the computer displays instructional material to a student and asks questions about the information given; the student's answers determine the sequence of the lessons.

calabash tropical South American evergreen tree with gourds (fruits) 50 cm/20 in across, whose dried skins are used as water containers. The Old World tropical-vine bottle gourd (*Lagenaria siceraria*, of the gourd family Cucurbitaceae) is sometimes also called a calabash, and it produces equally large gourds. (*Crescentia cujete*, family Bignoniaceae.)

calamine $ZnCO_3$ zinc carbonate, an ore of zinc. The term also refers to a pink powder made of a mixture of zinc oxide and iron(II) oxide used in lotions and ointments as an astringent for treating, for example, sunburn, eczema, measles rash, and insect bites and stings.

In the USA the term refers to zinc silicate $Zn_4Si_2O_7(OH)_2.H_2O$.

calceolaria plant with brilliantly coloured slipper-shaped flowers. Native to South America, calceolarias were introduced to Europe and the USA in the 1830s. (Genus *Calceolaria*, family Scrophulariaceae.)

calcination ◊oxidation of metals by burning in air.

calcite colourless, white, or light-coloured common rock-forming mineral, calcium carbonate, $CaCO_3$. It is the main constituent of ◊limestone and marble and forms many types of invertebrate shell.

Calcite often forms ◊stalactites and stalagmites in caves and is also found deposited in veins through many rocks because of the ease with which it is dissolved and transported by groundwater; ◊oolite is a rock consisting of spheroidal calcite grains. It rates 3 on the ◊Mohs' scale of hardness. Large crystals up to 1 m/3 ft have been found in Oklahoma and Missouri, USA. Iceland spar is a transparent form of calcite used in the optical industry; as limestone it is used in the building industry.

calcium ***Latin** calcis* ***'lime'*** soft, silvery-white metallic element, symbol Ca, atomic number 20, relative atomic mass 40.08. It is one of the ◊alkaline-earth metals. It is the fifth most abundant element (the third most abundant metal) in the Earth's crust. It is found mainly as its carbonate $CaCO_3$, which occurs in a fairly pure condition as chalk and limestone (see ◊calcite). Calcium is an essential component of bones, teeth, shells, milk, and leaves, and it forms 1.5% of the human body by mass.

Calcium ions in animal cells are involved in regulating muscle contraction, blood clotting, hormone secretion, digestion, and glycogen metabolism in the liver. It is acquired mainly from milk and cheese, and its uptake is facilitated by vitamin D. Calcium deficiency leads to chronic muscle spasms (tetany); an excess of calcium may lead to the formation of stones in the kidney or gall bladder.

The element was discovered and named by the English chemist Humphry Davy in 1808. Its compounds include slaked lime (calcium hydroxide, $Ca(OH)_2$); plaster of Paris (calcium sulphate, $CaSO_4.2H_2O$); calcium phosphate ($Ca_3(PO_4)_2$), the main constituent of animal bones; calcium hypochlorite ($CaOCl_2$), a bleaching agent; calcium nitrate ($Ca(NO_3)_2.4H_2O$), a nitrogenous fertilizer; calcium carbide (CaC_2), which reacts with water to give ethyne (acetylene); calcium cyanamide ($CaCN_2$), the basis of many pharmaceuticals, fertilizers, and plastics, including melamine; calcium cyanide ($Ca(CN)_2$), used in the extraction of gold and silver and in electroplating; and others used in baking powders and fillers for paints.

calcium carbonate $CaCO_3$ white solid, found in nature as limestone, marble, and chalk. It is a valuable resource, used in the making of iron, steel, cement, glass, slaked lime, bleaching powder, sodium carbonate and bicarbonate, and many other industrially useful substances.

calcium hydrogencarbonate $Ca(HCO_3)_2$ substance found in ◊hard water, formed when rainwater passes over limestone rock.

$$CaCO_{3\,(s)} + CO_{2\,(g)} + H_2O_{(l)} \rightarrow Ca(HCO_3)_{2\,(aq)}$$

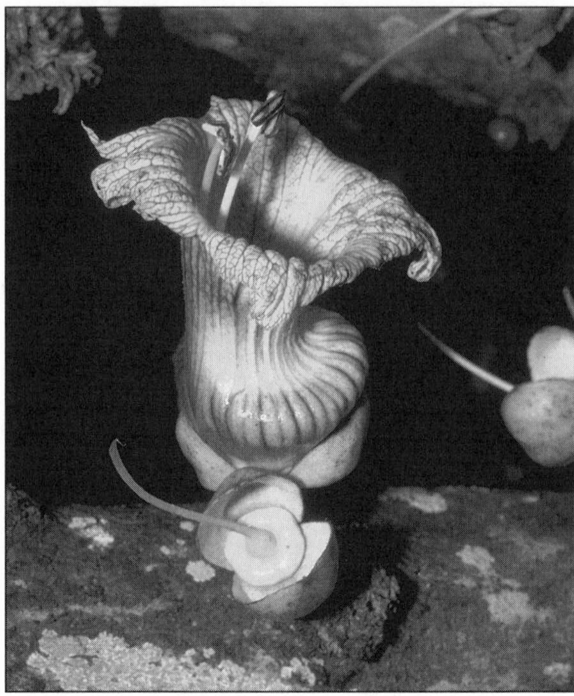

calabash *Like many tropical trees, the flowers of the calabash tree grow directly from the wood of the trunk and branches. At night the flowers give off an unpleasant odour, attracting numerous pollinating bats.* *Premaphotos Wildlife*

When this water is boiled it reforms calcium carbonate, removing the hardness; this type of hardness is therefore known as temporary hardness.

calcium hydrogenphosphate $Ca(H_2PO_4)_2$ substance made by heating calcium phosphate with 70% sulphuric acid. It is more soluble in water than calcium phosphate, and is used as a fertilizer.

calcium hydroxide $Ca(OH)_2$ or ***slaked lime*** white solid, slightly soluble in water. A solution of calcium hydroxide is called ◊limewater and is used in the laboratory to test for the presence of carbon dioxide. It is manufactured industrially by adding water to calcium oxide (quicklime) in a strongly exothermic reaction.

$$CaO + H_2O \rightarrow Ca(OH)_2$$

It is used to reduce soil acidity and as a cheap alkali in many industrial processes.

calcium nitrate $Ca(NO_3)_2$ white, crystalline compound that is very soluble in water. The solid decomposes on heating to form oxygen, brown nitrogen(IV) oxide gas, and the white solid calcium oxide.

$$2Ca(NO_3)_2 \rightarrow 2CaO + 4NO_2 + O_2$$

calcium oxide or ***quicklime*** CaO white solid compound, formed by heating ◊calcium carbonate.

$$CaCO_3 \rightarrow CaO + CO_2$$

When water is added it forms calcium hydroxide (slaked lime) in an ◊exothermic reaction.

$$CaO + H_2O \rightarrow Ca(OH)_2$$

It is a typical basic oxide, turning litmus blue.

calcium phosphate $Ca_3(PO_4)_2$ or ***calcium orthophosphate*** white solid, the main constituent of animal bones. It occurs naturally as the mineral apatite and in rock phosphate, and is used in the preparation of phosphate fertilizers.

calcium sulphate $CaSO_4$ white, solid compound, found in nature as gypsum and anhydrite. It dissolves slightly in water to form ◊hard water; this hardness is not removed by boiling, and hence is sometimes called permanent hardness.

calcium superphosphate common name for ◊calcium hydrogenphosphate.

calculator pocket-sized electronic computing device for performing numerical calculations. It can add, subtract, multiply, and divide; many calculators also compute squares and roots and have advanced trigonometric and statistical functions. Input is by a small keyboard and results are shown on a one-line computer screen, typically a ◊liquid-crystal display (LCD) or a light-emitting diode (LED). The first electronic calculator was manufactured by the Bell Punch Company in the USA in 1963.

calculus ***Latin 'pebble'*** branch of mathematics which uses the concept of a derivative (see ◊differentiation) to analyse the way in which the values of a ◊function vary. Calculus is probably the most widely used part of mathematics. Many real-life problems are analysed by expressing one quantity as a function of another – position of a moving object as a function of time, temperature of an object as a function of distance from a heat source, force on an object as a function of distance from the source of the force, and so on – and calculus is concerned with such functions.

There are several branches of calculus. Differential and integral calculus, both dealing with small quantities which during manipulation are made smaller and smaller, compose the **infinitesimal calculus. Differential equations** relate to the derivatives of a set of variables and may include the variables. Many give the mathematical models for physical phenomena such as ◊simple harmonic ◊motion. Differential equations are solved generally by ◊integration, depending on their degree. If no analytical processes are available, integration can be performed numerically. Other branches of calculus include calculus of variations and calculus of errors.

caldera in geology, a very large basin-shaped ◊crater. Calderas are found at the tops of volcanoes, where the original peak has collapsed into an empty chamber beneath. The basin, many times larger than the original volcanic vent, may be flooded, producing a crater lake, or the flat floor may contain a number of small volcanic cones, produced by volcanic activity after the collapse.

Typical calderas are Kilauea, Hawaii; Crater Lake, Oregon, USA; and the summit of Olympus Mons, on Mars. Some calderas are wrongly referred to as craters, such as Ngorongoro, Tanzania.

calendar division of the ◊year into months, weeks, and days and the method of ordering the years. From year one, an assumed date of the birth of Jesus, dates are calculated backwards (BC 'before Christ' or BCE 'before common era') and forwards (AD, Latin *anno Domini* 'in the year of the Lord', or CE 'common era'). The **lunar month** (period between one new moon and the next) naturally averages 29.5 days, but the Western calendar uses for convenience a **calendar month** with a complete number of days, 30 or 31 (February has 28). For adjustments, since there are slightly fewer than six extra hours a year left over, they are added to Feb as a 29th day every fourth year (**leap year**), century years being excepted unless they are divisible by 400. For example, 1896 was a leap year; 1900 was not.

The **month names** in most European languages were probably derived as follows: January from Janus, Roman god; February from *Februar,* Roman festival of purification; March from Mars, Roman god; April from Latin *aperire,* 'to open'; May from Maia, Roman goddess; June from Juno, Roman goddess; July from Julius Caesar, Roman general; August from Augustus, Roman emperor; September, October, November, December (originally the seventh to tenth months) from the Latin words meaning seventh, eighth, ninth, and tenth, respectively.

The **days of the week** are Monday named after the Moon; Tuesday from Tiu or Tyr, Anglo-Saxon and Norse god; Wednesday from Woden or Odin, Norse god; Thursday from Thor, Norse god; Friday from Freya, Norse goddess; Saturday from Saturn, Roman god; and Sunday named after the Sun.

All early calendars except the ancient Egyptian were lunar. The word calendar comes from the Latin *Kalendae* or *calendae,* the first day of each month on which, in ancient Rome, solemn proclamation was made of the appearance of the new moon.

The **Western** or **Gregorian calendar** derives from the **Julian calendar** instituted by Julius Caesar 46 BC. It was adjusted by Pope Gregory XIII 1582, who eliminated the accumulated error caused by a faulty calculation of the length of a year and avoided its recurrence by restricting century leap years to those divisible by 400. Other states only gradually changed from Old Style to New Style; Britain and its colonies adopted the Gregorian calendar 1752, when the error amounted to 11 days, and 3 September 1752 became 14 September (at the same time the beginning of the year was put back from 25 March to 1 January). Russia did not adopt it until the October Revolution of 1917, so that the event (then 25 October) is currently celebrated 7 November.

The **Jewish calendar** is a complex combination of lunar and solar cycles, varied by considerations of religious observance. A year may have 12 or 13 months, each of which normally alternates between 29 and 30 days; the New Year (Rosh Hashanah) falls between 5 September and 5 October. The calendar dates from the hypothetical creation of the world (taken as 7 October 3761 BC).

The **Chinese calendar** is lunar, with a cycle of 60 years. Both the traditional and, from 1911, the Western calendar are in use in China.

The **Muslim calendar**, also lunar, has 12 months of alternately 30 and 29 days, and a year of 354 days. This results in the calendar rotating around the seasons in a 30-year cycle. The era is counted as beginning on the day Muhammad fled from Mecca AD 622.

calibration the preparation of a usable scale on a measuring instrument. A mercury ◊thermometer, for example, can be calibrated with a Celsius scale by noting the heights of the mercury column at two standard temperatures – the freezing point (0°C) and boiling point (100°C) of water – and dividing the distance between them into 100 equal parts and continuing these divisions above and below.

Science is all those things which are confirmed to such a degree that it would be unreasonable to withhold one's provisional consent.

STEPHEN JAY GOULD US palaeontologist and writer.
Lecture on Evolution

California current cold ocean ◊current in the E Pacific Ocean flowing southwards down the West coast of North America. It is part of the North Pacific ◊gyre (a vast, circular movement of ocean water).

californium synthesized, radioactive, metallic element of the actinide series, symbol Cf, atomic number 98, relative atomic mass 251. It is produced in very small quantities and used in nuclear reactors as a neutron source. The longest-lived isotope, Cf-251, has a half-life of 800 years.

It is named after the state of California, where it was first synthesized 1950 by US nuclear chemist Glenn Seaborg and his team at the University of California at Berkeley.

calla alternative name for ◊arum lily.

call for votes in computing, on ◊USENET, process by which the nature and scope of a new ◊newsgroup is determined. Calls for votes are posted to **news.announce.newgroups**. In the case of the ◊Big Seven hierarchies, the call for votes is a requirement; it is recommended but not compulsory for ◊alt hierarchy groups. The point is to ensure that newsgroup names follow a consistent pattern and that new newsgroups are formed in response to genuine interest.

Callichthys genus of South American ◊catfish. Its body is protected by large, hard, scaly plates.
classification *Callichthys* belongs to the family Callichthydae (armoured catfish), order Siluriformes, class Osteichthyes.

callipers measuring instrument used, for example, to measure the internal and external diameters of pipes. Some callipers are made like a pair of compasses, having two legs, often curved, pivoting about a screw at one end. The ends of the legs are placed in contact with the object to be measured, and the gap between the ends is then measured against a rule. The slide calliper looks like an adjustable spanner, and carries a scale for direct measuring, usually with a ◊vernier scale for accuracy.

callistemon the genus of the Australian ◊bottlebrush.

Callisto second-largest moon of Jupiter, 4,800 km/3,000 mi in diameter, orbiting every 16.7 days at a distance of 1.9 million km/1.2 million mi from the planet. Its surface is covered with large craters.

The space probe *Galileo* detected molecules containing both carbon and nitrogen atoms on the surface of Callisto, US astronomers announced in March 1997. Their presence may indicate that Callisto harboured life at some time.

callus in botany, a tissue that forms at a damaged plant surface. Composed of large, thin-walled ◊parenchyma cells, it grows over and around the wound, eventually covering the exposed area.

In animals, a callus is a thickened pad of skin, formed where there is repeated rubbing against a hard surface. In humans, calluses often develop on the hands and feet of those involved in heavy manual work.

calomel Hg_2Cl_2 (technical name ***mercury(I) chloride***) white, heavy powder formerly used as a laxative, now used as a pesticide and fungicide.

calorie c.g.s. unit of heat, now replaced by the ◊joule (one calorie is approximately 4.2 joules). It is the heat required to raise the temperature of one gram of water by 1°C. In dietetics, the Calorie or kilocalorie is equal to 1,000 calories.

The kilocalorie measures the energy value of food in terms of its heat output: 28 g/1 oz of protein yields 120 kilocalories, of carbohydrate 110, of fat 270, and of alcohol 200.

calorific value the amount of heat generated by a given mass of fuel when it is completely burned. It is measured in joules per kilogram. Calorific values are measured experimentally with a bomb calorimeter.

calorimeter instrument used in physics to measure various thermal properties, such as heat capacity or the heat produced by fuel. A simple calorimeter consists of a heavy copper vessel that is polished (to reduce heat losses by radiation) and covered with insulating material (to reduce losses by convection and conduction).

In a typical experiment, such as to measure the heat capacity of a piece of metal, the calorimeter is filled with water, whose temperature rise is measured using a thermometer when a known mass of the heated metal is immersed in it. Chemists use a bomb calorimeter to measure the heat produced by burning a fuel completely in oxygen.

calotype paper-based photograph using a wax paper negative, the first example of the ◊negative/positive process invented by the English photographer Fox Talbot around 1834.

calyptra in mosses and liverworts, a layer of cells that encloses and protects the young ◊sporophyte (spore capsule), forming a sheathlike hood around the capsule. The term is also used to describe the root cap, a layer of ◊parenchyma cells covering the end of a root that gives protection to the root tip as it grows through the soil. This is constantly being worn away and replaced by new cells from a special ◊meristem, the calyptrogen.

calyx collective term for the ◊sepals of a flower, forming the outermost whorl of the ◊perianth. It surrounds the other flower parts and protects them while in bud. In some flowers, for example, the campions *Silene,* the sepals are fused along their sides, forming a tubular calyx.

CAM (acronym for ***computer-aided manufacturing***) the use of computers to control production processes; in particular, the control of machine tools and ◊robots in factories. In some factories, the whole design and production system has been automated by linking ◊CAD (computer-aided design) to CAM.

Linking flexible CAD/CAM manufacturing to computer-based sales and distribution methods makes it possible to produce semi-customized goods cheaply and in large numbers.

Calvin, Melvin (1911–1997)

US chemist who, using radioactive carbon-14 as a tracer, determined the biochemical processes of photosynthesis, in which green plants use chlorophyll to convert carbon dioxide and water into sugar and oxygen. Nobel prize 1961.

Mary Evans Picture Library

cam part of a machine that converts circular motion to linear motion or vice versa. The **edge cam** in a car engine is in the form of a rounded projection on a shaft, the camshaft. When the camshaft turns, the cams press against linkages (plungers or followers) that open the valves in the cylinders.

A **face cam** is a disc with a groove in its face, in which the follower travels. A **cylindrical cam** carries angled parallel grooves, which impart a to-and-fro motion to the follower when it rotates.

Camberwell beauty species of ◊butterfly.

cambium in botany, a layer of actively dividing cells (lateral ◊meristem), found within stems and roots, that gives rise to ◊secondary growth in perennial plants, causing an increase in girth. There are two main types of cambium: **vascular cambium**, which gives rise to secondary ◊xylem and ◊phloem tissues, and **cork cambium** (or phellogen), which gives rise to secondary cortex and cork tissues (see ◊bark).

Cambrian period of geological time 570–510 million years ago; the first period of the Palaeozoic era. All invertebrate animal life appeared, and marine algae were widespread. The **Cambrian Explosion** 530–520 million years ago saw the first appearance in the fossil record of all modern animal phyla; the earliest fossils with hard shells, such as trilobites, date from this period.

The name comes from Cambria, the medieval Latin name for Wales, where Cambrian rocks are typically exposed and were first described.

camcorder another name for a ◊video camera.

camel large cud-chewing mammal of the even-toed hoofed order Artiodactyla. Unlike typical ruminants, it has a three-chambered stomach. It has two toes which have broad soft soles for walking on sand, and hooves resembling nails. There are two species, the single-humped **Arabian camel** *Camelus dromedarius* and the twin-humped **Bactrian camel** *C. bactrianus* from Asia. They carry a food reserve of fatty tissue in the hump, can go without drinking for long periods, can feed on salty vegetation, and withstand extremes of heat and cold, thus being well adapted to desert conditions.

The Arabian camel has long been domesticated, so that its original range is not known. It is used throughout Arabia and N Africa, and has been taken to other places such as North America and Australia, in the latter country playing a crucial part in the development of the interior. The **dromedary** is, strictly speaking, a lightly built, fast, riding variety of the Arabian camel, but often the name is applied to all one-humped camels. Arabian camels can be used as pack animals, for riding, racing, milk production, and for meat. The Bactrian camel is native to the central Asian deserts, where a small number still live wild, but most are domestic animals. With a head and body length of 3 m/10 ft and shoulder height of about 2 m/6 ft, the Bactrian camel is a large animal, but not so long in the leg as the Arabian. It has a shaggy winter coat. In 1995 there were only about 730–880 Bactrian camels remaining in the wild. Smaller, flat-backed members of the camel family include the ◊alpaca, the ◊guanaco, the ◊llama, and the ◊vicuna.

camellia any oriental evergreen shrub with roselike flowers belonging to the tea family. Many species, including *Camellia japonica* and *C. reticulata,* have been introduced into Europe, the USA, and Australia; they are widely cultivated as ornamental shrubs. (Genus *Camellia,* family Theaceae.)

CAMERAS: THE TECHNOLOGY OF PHOTOGRAPHIC IMAGING

http://www.mhs.ox.ac.uk/cameras/index.htm

General presentation of the camera collection at the Museum of the History of Science, Oxford, UK. Of the many highlights perhaps the most distinguished are some very early photographs, the photographic works of Sarah A Acland, and the cameras of T E Lawrence.

camera apparatus used in ◊photography, consisting of a lens system set in a light-proof box inside of which a sensitized film or plate can be placed. The lens collects rays of light reflected from the subject and brings them together as a sharp image on the film. The opening or hole at the front of the camera, through which light enters, is called an ◊aperture. The aperture size controls the amount of light that can enter. A shutter controls the amount of time light has to affect the film. There are small-, medium-, and large-format cameras; the format refers to the size of recorded image and the dimensions of the image obtained.

A simple camera has a fixed shutter speed and aperture, chosen so that on a sunny day the correct amount of light is admitted. More complex cameras allow the shutter speed and aperture to be adjusted; most have a built-in exposure meter to help choose the correct combination of shutter speed and aperture for the ambient conditions and subject matter. The most versatile camera is the single lens reflex (◊SLR) which allows the lens to be removed and special lenses attached. A pin-hole camera has a small (pin-sized) hole instead of a lens. It must be left on a firm support during exposures, which are up to ten seconds with slow film, two seconds with fast film and five minutes for paper negatives in daylight. The pinhole camera gives sharp images from close-up to infinity.

camera obscura darkened box with a tiny hole for projecting the inverted image of the scene outside on to a screen inside. For its development as a device for producing photographs, see ◊photography.

camouflage colours or structures that allow an animal to blend with its surroundings to avoid detection by other animals. Camouflage can take the form of matching the background colour, of countershading (darker on top, lighter below, to counteract natural shadows), or of irregular patterns that break up the outline of the animal's body. More elaborate camouflage involves closely resembling a feature of the natural environment, as with the stick insect; this is closely akin to ◊mimicry. Camouflage is also important as a military technique, disguising either equipment, troops, or a position in order to conceal them from an enemy.

camphor $C_{10}H_{16}O$ volatile, aromatic ◊ketone substance obtained from the camphor tree *Cinnamomum camphora.* It is distilled from chips of the wood, and is used in insect repellents and medicinal inhalants and liniments, and in the manufacture of celluloid.

The camphor tree, a member of the family Lauraceae, is native to China, Taiwan, and Japan.

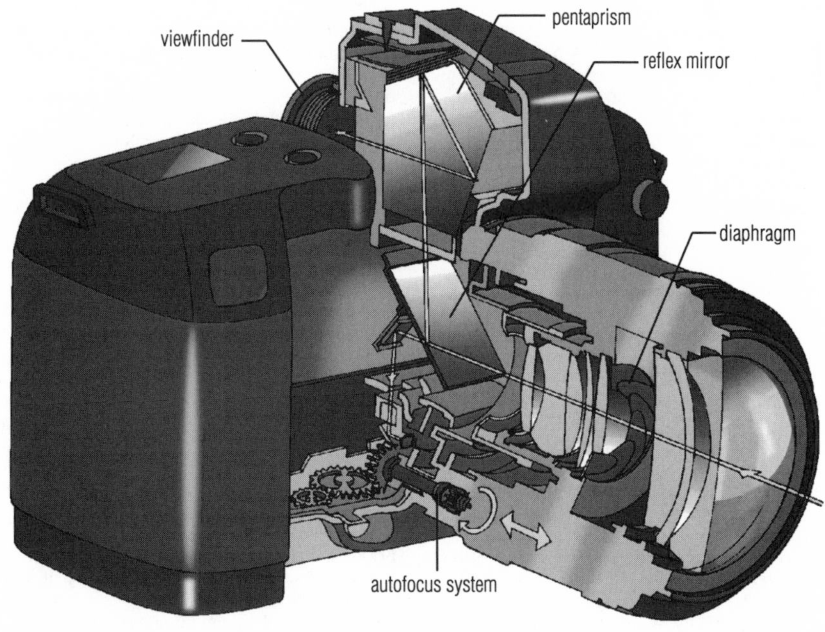

***camera** The single-lens reflex (SLR) camera in which an image can be seen through the lens before a picture is taken. The reflex mirror directs light entering the lens to the viewfinder. The SLR allows different lenses, such as close-up or zoom, to be used because the photographer can see exactly what is being focused on.*

campion any of several plants belonging to the pink family. They include the garden campion (*Lychnis coronaria*), the wild white and red campions (*Silene alba* and *S. dioica*), and the bladder campion (*S. vulgaris*). (Genera *Lychnis* and *Silene,* family Caryophyllaceae.)

campus-wide information system (CWIS) computerized information service used on US university campuses, often hooked to the Internet. These systems typically include local events listings, general campus information, access to the library catalogue, weather reports, directories, and even ◊bulletin-board and messaging services.

One of the first such systems was Cornell University's CUINFO, developed by a team led by technical administrator Steve Worona 1982. The development of ◊Gopher servers 1991 made these systems much easier to navigate, and many systems were redesigned to take advantage of the new technology. In the mid-1990s these systems began moving to the World Wide Web.

Campylobacter genus of bacteria that cause serious outbreaks of gastroenteritis. They grow best at 43°C, and so are well suited to the digestive tract of birds. Poultry is therefore the most likely source of a *Campylobacter* outbreak, although the bacteria can also be transmitted via beef or milk. *Campylobacter* can survive in water for up to 15 days, so may be present in drinking water if supplies are contaminated by sewage or reservoirs are polluted by seagulls.

canal artificial waterway constructed for drainage, irrigation, or navigation. **Irrigation canals** carry water for irrigation from rivers, reservoirs, or wells, and are designed to maintain an even flow of water over the whole length. **Navigation and ship canals** are constructed at one level between ◊locks, and frequently link with rivers or sea inlets to form a waterway system. The Suez Canal in 1869 and the Panama Canal in 1914 eliminated long trips around continents and dramatically shortened shipping routes.

irrigation canals The river Nile has fed canals to maintain life in Egypt since the earliest times. The division of the waters of the Upper Indus and its tributaries, which form an extensive system in Pakistan and Punjab, India, was, for more than ten years, a major cause of dispute between India and Pakistan, settled by a treaty 1960. The Murray basin, Victoria, Australia, and the Imperial and Central Valley projects in California, USA, are examples of 19th- and 20th-century irrigation-canal development. Excessive extraction of water for irrigation from rivers and lakes can cause environmental damage.

ship canals Probably the oldest ship canal to be still in use, as well as the longest, is the Grand Canal in China, which links Tianjin and Hangzhou and connects the Huang He (Yellow River) and Chang Jiang. It was originally built in three stages 485 BC–AD 283, reaching a total length of 1,780 km/1,110 mi. Large sections silted up in later years, but the entire system was dredged, widened, and rebuilt between 1958 and 1972 in conjunction with work on flood protection, irrigation, and hydroelectric schemes. It carries millions of tonnes of freight every year.

Where speed is not a prime factor, the cost-effectiveness of transporting goods by canal has encouraged a revival; Belgium, France, Germany, and the states of the former USSR are among countries that have extended and streamlined their canals. The Baltic–Volga waterway links the Lithuanian port of Klaipeda with Kahovka, at the mouth of the Dnieper on the Black Sea, a distance of 2,430 km/1,510 mi. A further canal cuts across the north Crimea, thus shortening the voyage of ships from the Dnieper through the Black Sea to the Sea of Azov. In Central America, the Panama Canal 1904–14 links the Atlantic and Pacific oceans (64 km/40 mi). In North America, the Erie Canal 1825 links the Great Lakes with the Hudson River and opened up the northeast and Midwest to commerce; the St Lawrence Seaway 1954–59 extends from Montréal to Lake Ontario (290 km/180 mi) and, with the deepening of the Welland Ship Canal and some of the river channels, provides a waterway that enables ocean going vessels to travel (during the ice-free months) between the Atlantic and Duluth, Minnesota, USA, at the western end of Lake Superior, some 3,770 km/2,342 mi.

Canaries current cold ocean current in the North Atlantic Ocean flowing SW from Spain along the NW coast of Africa. It meets the northern equatorial current at a latitude of 20° N.

canary bird *Serinus canaria* of the finch family Fringillidae, found wild in the Canary Islands and Madeira. In its wild state the plumage is green, sometimes streaked with brown. The wild canary builds its nest of moss, feathers, and hair in thick high shrubs or trees, and produces two to four broods in a season.

Canaries have been bred as cage birds in Europe since the 15th century, and many domestic varieties are yellow or orange as a result of artificial selection.

Some canaries were used in mines as detectors of traces of poison gas in the air.

CANARY FAQ

http://www2.upatsix.com/faq/canary.htm

Answers to frequently asked questions about canaries provide a wealth of information on all breeds of these cage birds. Every conceivable aspect of caring for canaries is covered and there are useful links to other canary sites.

cancel in mathematics, to simplify a fraction or ratio by dividing both numerator and denominator by the same number (which must be a ◊common factor of both of them). For example, $\frac{5x}{25}$ cancels to $\frac{x}{5}$ when divided top and bottom by 5.

cancelbot automated software program (see ◊bot) that cancels messages on UseNet. The arrival of ◊spamming (advertising) on the Net prompted the development of technology to use features built into UseNet to cancel messages. While single messages are easily cancelled manually, an automated routine is needed to handle mass postings, which may go out to more than 14,000 newsgroups. Cancelbot is activated by the ◊CancelMoose.

CancelMoose anonymous individual who fires off the ◊cancelbot. The CancelMoose (usually written as 'CancelMoose™' on the Net) monitors newsgroups such as alt.current-events.net-abuse and news.admin.net-abuse for complaints about ◊spamming (advertising), usually defined as messages posted to more than 25 newsgroups of widely varying content. The CancelMoose's identity is kept secret for reasons of personal safety.

cancer group of diseases characterized by abnormal proliferation of cells. Cancer (malignant) cells are usually degenerate, capable only of reproducing themselves (tumour formation). Malignant cells tend to spread from their site of origin by travelling through the bloodstream or lymphatic system. Cancer kills about 6 million people a year worldwide.

causes There are more than 100 types of cancer. Some, like lung or bowel cancer, are common; others are rare. The likely causes remain unexplained. Triggering agents (◊carcinogens) include chemicals such as those found in cigarette smoke, other forms of smoke, asbestos dust, exhaust fumes, and many industrial chemicals. Some viruses can also trigger the cancerous growth of cells (see ◊oncogenes), as can X-rays and radioactivity. Dietary factors are important in some cancers; for example, lack of fibre in the diet may predispose people to bowel cancer and a diet high in animal fats and low in fresh vegetables and fruit increases the risk of breast cancer. Psychological ◊stress may increase the risk of cancer, more so if the person concerned is not able to control the source of the stress.

cancer genes In some families there is a genetic tendency towards a particular type of cancer. In 1993 researchers isolated the first gene that predisposes individuals to cancer. About 1 in 200 people in the West carry the gene. If the gene mutates, those with the altered gene have a 70% chance of developing colon cancer, and female carriers have a 50% chance of developing cancer of the uterus. This accounts for an estimated 10% of all colon cancer.

In 1994 a gene that triggers breast cancer was identified. **BRCA1** was found to be responsible for almost half the cases of inherited breast cancer, and most cases of ovarian cancer. In 1995 a link between BRCA1 and non-inherited breast cancer was discovered. Women with the gene have an 85% chance of developing breast or ovarian cancer during their lifetime. A second breast cancer gene **BRCA2** was identified later in 1995.

The commonest cancer in young men is testicular cancer, the incidence of which has been rising by 3% a year since 1974 (1998).

Cancer faintest of the zodiacal constellations (its brightest stars are fourth magnitude). It lies in the northern hemisphere between ◊Leo and ◊Gemini, and is represented as a crab. The Sun passes through the constellation during late July and early August. In astrology, the dates for Cancer are between about 22 June and 22 July (see ◊precession).

Cancer's most distinctive feature is the open star cluster Praesepe, popularly known as the Beehive, visible to the naked eye as a nebulous patch.

candela SI unit (symbol cd) of luminous intensity, which replaced the old units of candle and standard candle. It measures the brightness of a light itself rather than the amount of light falling on an object, which is called **illuminance** and measured in ◊lux.

One candela is defined as the luminous intensity in a given direction of a source that emits monochromatic radiation of frequency 540×10^{-12} Hz and whose radiant energy in that direction is 1/683 watt per steradian.

Candida albicans yeastlike fungus present in the human digestive tract and in the vagina, which causes no harm in most healthy people. However, it can cause problems if it multiplies excessively, as in vaginal candidiasis or ◊thrush, the main symptom of which is intense itching.

The most common form of thrush is oral, which often occurs in those taking steroids or prolonged courses of antibiotics.

Newborn babies may pick up the yeast during birth and suffer an infection of the mouth and throat. There is also some evidence that overgrowth of *Candida* may occur in the intestines, causing diarrhoea, bloating, and other symptoms such as headache and fatigue, but this is not yet proven. Occasionally, *Candida* can infect immunocompromised patients, such as those with AIDS. Treatment for candidiasis is based on antifungal drugs.

candle cylinder of wax (such as tallow or paraffin wax) with a central wick of string. A flame applied to the end of the wick melts the wax, thereby producing a luminous flame. The wick is treated with a substance such as alum so that it carbonizes but does not rapidly burn out.

Candles and oil lamps were an early form of artificial lighting. Accurately made candles – which burned at a steady rate – were calibrated along their lengths and used as a type of clock. The candle was also the name of a unit of luminous intensity, replaced in 1940 by the ◊candela (cd), equal to $\frac{1}{60}$ of the luminance of 1 sq cm of a black body radiator at a temperature of 2,042K (the temperature of solidification of platinum).

CANDLE MAKING

http://www.southwest.com.au/~snorth/crafts.htm#contents

Mainly text guide to making and designing your own candles. There are a few general pictures of the finished product, but the text is very instructive.

cane reedlike stem of various plants such as the sugar cane, bamboo, and, in particular, the group of palms called rattans, consisting of the genus *Calamus* and its allies. Their slender stems are dried and used for making walking sticks, baskets, and furniture.

Canes Venatici constellation of the northern hemisphere near ◊Ursa Major, identified with the hunting dogs of ◊Boötes, the herder. Its stars are faint, and it contains the Whirlpool galaxy (M51), the first spiral galaxy to be recognized.

It contains many objects of telescopic interest, including the relatively bright ◊globular cluster M3. The brightest star, a third magnitude double, is called Cor Caroli or Alpha Canum Venaticorum.

cane toad toad of the genus *Bufo marinus*, family Bufonidae. Also known as the giant or marine toad, the cane toad is the largest in the world. It acquired its name after being introduced to Australia during the 1930s to eradicate the cane beetle, which had become a serious pest there. However, having few natural enemies, the cane toad itself has now become a pest in Australia.

The cane toad's defence system consists of highly developed glands on each side of its neck which can squirt a poisonous fluid to a distance of around 1 m/3.3 ft.

CANE TOAD

http://share.jcu.edu.au/dept/PHTM/staff/rsbufo.htm

Profile of the world's largest toad, its unwise introduction to Australia, and the damage it has wrought. There's a photo of a cane toad, another of the massive number of eggs it can produce, and a complete bibliography of books and articles written about *Bufo marinus*.

canine in mammalian carnivores, any of the long, often pointed teeth found at the front of the mouth between the incisors and premolars. Canine teeth are used for catching prey, for killing, and for tearing flesh. They are absent in herbivores such as rabbits and sheep, and are much reduced in humans.

Canis Major brilliant constellation of the southern hemisphere, represented (with Canis Minor) as one of the two dogs following at the heel of ◊Orion. Its main star, ◊Sirius, is the brightest star in the night sky.

Epsilon Canis Majoris is also of the first magnitude, and there are three second magnitude stars.

Canis Minor small constellation along the celestial equator (see ◊celestial sphere), represented as the smaller of the two dogs of ◊Orion (the other dog being ◊Canis Major). Its brightest star is the first magnitude ◊Procyon.

Procyon and Beta Canis Minoris form what the Arabs called 'the Short Cubit', in contrast to 'the Long Cubit' formed by ◊Castor and ◊Pollux (Alpha and Beta Geminorum).

cannabis dried leaves and female flowers (marijuana) and ◊resin (hashish) of certain varieties of ◊hemp, which are smoked or swallowed to produce a range of effects, including feelings of great happiness and altered perception. (*Cannabis sativa*, family Cannabaceae.)

Cannabis is a soft drug in that any dependence is psychological rather than physical. It is illegal in many countries and has not been much used in medicine since the 1930s. However, recent research has led to the discovery of cannabis receptors (sensory nerve endings) in the brain, and the discovery of a naturally occurring brain chemical which produces the same effects as smoking cannabis. Researchers believe this work could lead to the use of cannabislike compounds to treat physical illness without affecting the mind. Cannabis is claimed to have beneficial effects in treating chronic diseases such as AIDS and ◊multiple sclerosis. The main psychoactive ingredient in cannabis is delta-9-tetrahydrocannabinol (THC) which is available legally as a prescribed drug in capsule form.

canning food preservation in hermetically sealed containers by the application of heat. Originated by Nicolas Appert in France 1809 with glass containers, it was developed by Peter Durand in

England in 1810 with cans made of sheet steel thinly coated with tin to delay corrosion. Cans for beer and soft drinks are now generally made of aluminium.

Canneries were established in the USA before 1820, but the US canning industry expanded considerably in the 1870s when the manufacture of cans was mechanized and factory methods of processing were used. The quality and taste of early canned food was frequently inferior but by the end of the 19th century, scientific research made greater understanding possible of the food-preserving process, and standards improved. More than half the aluminium cans used in the USA are now recycled.

Canopus or ***Alpha Carinae*** second brightest star in the night sky (after Sirius), lying in the southern constellation Carina. It is a first-magnitude yellow-white supergiant about 120 light years from Earth, and thousands of times more luminous than the Sun.

cantaloupe any of several small varieties of muskmelon *Cucumis melo*, distinguished by their round, ribbed fruits with orange-coloured flesh.

cantilever beam or structure that is fixed at one end only, though it may be supported at some point along its length; for example, a diving board. The cantilever principle, widely used in construction engineering, eliminates the need for a second main support at the free end of the beam, allowing for more elegant structures and reducing the amount of materials required. Many large-span bridges have been built on the cantilever principle.

A typical cantilever bridge consists of two beams cantilevered out from either bank, each supported part way along, with their free ends meeting in the middle. The multiple-cantilever Forth Rail Bridge (completed 1890) across the Firth of Forth in Scotland has twin main spans of 521 m/1,710 ft.

canyon ***Spanish cañon 'tube'*** deep, narrow valley or gorge running through mountains. Canyons are formed by stream down-cutting, usually in arid areas, where the rate of down-cutting is greater than the rate of weathering, and where the stream or river receives water from outside the area.

There are many canyons in the western USA and in Mexico, for example the Grand Canyon of the Colorado River in Arizona, the canyon in Yellowstone National Park, and the Black Canyon in Colorado.

cap another name for a ◊diaphragm contraceptive.

capacitance, electrical property of a capacitor that determines how much charge can be stored in it for a given potential difference between its terminals. It is equal to the ratio of the electrical charge stored to the potential difference. It is measured in ◊farads.

capacitor or ***condenser*** device for storing electric charge, used in electronic circuits; it consists of two or more metal plates separated by an insulating layer called a dielectric.

Its **capacitance** is the ratio of the charge stored on either plate to the potential difference between the plates. The SI unit of capacitance is the farad, but most capacitors have much smaller capacitances, and the microfarad (a millionth of a farad) is the commonly used practical unit.

capacity alternative term for ◊volume, generally used to refer to the amount of liquid or gas that may be held in a container. Units of capacity include litre and millilitre (metric); pint and gallon (imperial).

Cape Canaveral promontory on the Atlantic coast of Florida, USA, 367 km/228 mi N of Miami, used as a rocket launch site by ◊NASA.

Cape gooseberry plant *Physalis peruviana* of the potato family. Originating in South America, it is grown in South Africa, from where it takes its name. It is cultivated for its fruit, a yellow berry surrounded by a papery ◊calyx.

Capella or ***Alpha Aurigae*** brightest star in the constellation ◊Auriga and the sixth brightest star in the night sky. It is a visual and spectroscopic binary that consists of a pair of yellow-giant stars 45 light years from Earth, orbiting each other every 104 days.

It is a first-magnitude star, whose Latin name means the 'the Little Nanny Goat': its kids are the three adjacent stars Epsilon, Eta, and Zeta Aurigae.

Cape mountain zebra ◊zebra subspecies *Equus zebra zebra*, confined to South Africa. It almost became extinct in the 1940s, and in 1993 had a population of only 450, despite attempts at conservation. The main population is in Mountain Zebra Park in the east of the country, although some zebras have been moved to other parks in an attempt to build up other viable breeding herds.

caper trailing shrub native to the Mediterranean. Its flower buds are preserved in vinegar as a condiment. (*Capparis spinosa*, family Capparidaceae.)

capercaillie or ***wood-grouse*** or ***cock of the wood*** (***Gaelic capull coille, 'cock of the wood'***) large bird *Tetrao uroqallus* of the ◊grouse type, family Tetraonidae, order Galliformes. Found in coniferous woodland in Europe and N Asia, it is about the size of the turkey and resembles the ◊blackcock in appearance and polygamous habit. The general colour of the male is blackish-grey above, black below, with a dark green chest, and rounded tail which is fanned out in courtship. The female is smaller, mottled, and has a reddish breast barred with black. The feathers on the legs and feet are longest in winter time, and the toes are naked. The capercaillie feeds on insects, worms, berries, and young pine-shoots. At nearly 1 m/3 ft long, the male is the biggest gamebird in Europe. The female is about 60 cm/2 ft long.

Hunted to extinction in Britain in the 18th century, the capercaillie was reintroduced from Sweden in the 1830s and has re-established itself in Scotland.

capillarity spontaneous movement of liquids up or down narrow tubes, or capillaries. The movement is due to unbalanced molecular attraction at the boundary between the liquid and the tube. If liquid molecules near the boundary are more strongly attracted to molecules in the material of the tube than to other nearby liquid molecules, the liquid will rise in the tube. If liquid molecules are less attracted to the material of the tube than to other liquid molecules, the liquid will fall.

capillary in biology, narrowest blood vessel in vertebrates, 0.008–0.02 mm in diameter, barely wider than a red blood cell. Capillaries are distributed as **beds**, complex networks connecting arteries and veins. Capillary walls are extremely thin, consisting of a single layer of cells, and so nutrients, dissolved gases, and waste products can easily pass through them. This makes the capillaries the main area of exchange between the fluid (◊lymph) bathing body tissues and the blood.

> To remember the principles of capillary action:
>
> WATER RISES TO THE TOPS OF PLANTS BY CAPILLARY ACTION (CA), WHICH DEPENDS UPON COHESIVE AND ADHESIVE (C+A) PROPERTIES OF WATER

capillary in physics, a very narrow, thick-walled tube, usually made of glass, such as in a thermometer. Properties of fluids, such as surface tension and viscosity, can be studied using capillary tubes.

capitulum in botany, a flattened or rounded head (inflorescence) of numerous, small, stalkless flowers. The capitulum is surrounded by a circlet of petal-like bracts and has the appearance of a large, single flower.

Capricorn alternative term for Capricornus.

Capricornus zodiacal constellation in the southern hemisphere next to ◊Sagittarius. It is represented as a fish-tailed goat, and its brightest stars are third magnitude. The Sun passes through it late January to mid-February. In astrology, the dates for Capricornus (popularly known as Capricorn) are between about 22 December and 19 January(see ◊precession).

capsicum any of a group of pepper plants belonging to the nightshade family, native to Central and South America. The different species produce green to red fruits that vary in size. The small ones are used whole to give the hot flavour of chilli, or ground to produce cayenne or red pepper; the large pointed or squarish pods, known as sweet peppers or pimientos (green, red, or yellow peppers), are mild-flavoured and used as a vegetable. (Genus *Capsicum,* family Solanaceae.)

Capstone long-term US government project to develop a set of standards for publicly available ◊cryptography as authorized by the Computer Security Act 1987. The initiative has four elements: a data encryption ◊algorithm (Skipjack), a ◊hash function, a key exchange protocol, and a ◊digital signature algorithm.

The project is managed primarily by the National Security Agency (NSA) and the National Institute of Standards and Technology (NIST).

capsule in botany, a dry, usually many-seeded fruit formed from an ovary composed of two or more fused ◊carpels, which splits open to release the seeds. The same term is used for the spore-containing structure of mosses and liverworts; this is borne at the top of a long stalk or seta.

Capsules burst open (dehisce) in various ways, including lengthwise, by a transverse lid – for example, scarlet pimpernel *Anagallis arvensis* – or by a number of pores, either towards the top of the capsule, as in the poppy *Papaver,* or near the base, as in certain species of bellflower *Campanula.*

capture saving of user actions as digital data that can be read by a computer. In real-time data communications, it refers to using software to log a session so that the session can be saved to a file. The term is also used with reference to screens, where the graphical material displayed on a computer screen may be saved as a picture file. In the study of ◊human–computer interaction, the data captured are user keystrokes, mouse movements, and even facial expressions and muttered complaints so that developers can replay the session to help them design better ◊user interfaces.

captured rotation or ***synchronous rotation*** in astronomy, the circumstance in which one body in orbit around another, such as the moon of a planet, rotates on its axis in the same time as it takes to complete one orbit. As a result, the orbiting body keeps one face permanently turned towards the body about which it is orbiting. An example is the rotation of our own ◊Moon, which arises because of the tidal effects of the Earth over a long period of time.

capuchin monkey of the genus *Cebus* found in Central and South America, so called because the hairs on the head resemble the cowl of a Capuchin monk. Capuchins live in small groups, feed on fruit and insects, and have a long tail that is semiprehensile and can give support when climbing through the trees.

There are now thought to be only 800 yellow-breasted capuchins left in the wild, found only in the Atlantic forest in Bahia state, Brazil.

capybara world's largest rodent *Hydrochoerus hydrochaeris,* up to 1.3 m/4 ft long and 50 kg/110 lb in weight. It is found in South America, and belongs to the guinea-pig family. The capybara inhabits marshes and dense vegetation around water. It has thin, yellowish hair, swims well, and can rest underwater with just eyes, ears, and nose above the surface.

car small, driver-guided, passenger-carrying motor vehicle; originally the automated version of the horse-drawn carriage, meant to convey people and their goods over streets and roads.

Over 50 million motor cars are produced each year worldwide. The number of cars in the world in 1997 exceeded 500 million. Most are four-wheeled and have water-cooled, piston-type internal-combustion engines fuelled by petrol or diesel. Variations have existed for decades that use ingenious and often nonpolluting power plants, but the motor industry long ago settled on this general formula for the consumer market. Experimental and sports models are streamlined, energy-efficient, and hand-built.

origins Although it is recorded that in 1479 Gilles de Dom was paid 25 livres (the equivalent of 25 pounds of silver) by the treasurer of Antwerp in the Low Countries for supplying a self-propelled vehicle, the ancestor of the automobile is generally agreed to be the cumbersome steam carriage made by Nicolas-Joseph Cugnot in 1769, still preserved in Paris. Steam was an attractive form of power to the English pioneers, and in 1803 Richard Trevithick built a working steam carriage. Later in the 19th century, practical steam coaches were used for public transport until stifled out of existence by punitive road tolls and legislation.

the first motorcars Although a Frenchman, Jean Etienne Lenoir, patented the first internal-combustion engine (gas-driven but immobile) in 1860, and an Austrian, Siegfried Marcus, built a vehicle which was shown at the Vienna Exhibition (1873), two Germans, Gottleib Daimler and Karl Benz are generally regarded as the creators of the motorcar. In 1885 Daimler and Benz built and ran the first petrol-driven motorcar (they worked independently with Daimler building a very efficient engine and Benz designing a car but with a poor engine). The pattern for the modern motorcar was set by Panhard in 1891 (front radiator, Daimler engine under bonnet, sliding-pinion gearbox, wooden ladder-chassis) and Mercedes in 1901 (honeycomb radiator, in-line four-cylinder engine, gate-change gearbox, pressed-steel chassis) set the pattern for the modern car. Emerging with Haynes and Duryea in the early 1890s, US demand was so fervent that 300 makers existed by 1895; only 109 were left by 1900.

In Britain, cars were still considered to be light locomotives in the eyes of the law and, since the Red Flag Act 1865, had theoretically required someone to walk in front with a red flag (by night, a lantern). Despite these obstacles, which put UK development another ten years behind all others, in 1896 (after the Red Flag Act had been repealed) Frederick Lanchester produced an advanced and reliable vehicle, later much copied.

motorcars as an industry The period 1905–06 inaugurated a world motorcar boom continuing to the present day. Among the legendary cars of the early 20th century are: De Dion Bouton, with the first practical high-speed engines; Mors, notable first for racing and later as a silent tourer; Napier, the 24-hour record-holder at Brooklands 1907, unbeaten for 17 years; the incomparable Rolls-Royce Silver Ghost; the enduring Model T Ford; and the many types of Bugatti and Delage, from record-breakers to luxury tourers. After World War I popular motoring began with the era of cheap, light (baby) cars made by Citroên, Peugeot, and Renault (France); Austin, Morris, Clyno, and Swift (England); Fiat (Italy); Volkswagen (Germany); and the cheap though bigger Ford, Chevrolet, and Dodge in the USA. During the interwar years a great deal of racing took place, and the experience gained benefited the everyday motorist in improved efficiency, reliability, and safety. There was a divergence between the lighter, economical European car, with its good handling, and the heavier US car, cheap, rugged, and well adapted to long distances on straight roads at speed. By this time motoring had become a universal pursuit.

After World War II small European cars tended to fall into three categories, in about equal numbers: front engine and rear drive, the classic arrangement; front engine and front-wheel drive; rear engine and rear-wheel drive. Racing cars have the engine situated in the middle for balance. From the 1950s a creative resurgence produced in practical form automatic transmission for small cars, rubber suspension, transverse engine mounting, self-levelling ride, disc brakes, and safer wet-weather tyres.

By the mid-1980s, Japan was building 8 million cars a year, on par with the US. The largest Japanese manufacturer, Toyota, was producing 2.5 million cars per year.

The car has become the carapace, the protective and aggressive shell, of urban and suburban man.

Marshall McLuhan Canadian communications theorist. *Understanding Media* ch 22

---

caracal cat *Felis caracal* related to the ◊lynx. It has long black ear tufts, a short tail, and short reddish-fawn fur. It lives in bush and desert country in Africa, Arabia, and India, hunting birds and small mammals at night. Head and body length is about 75 cm/2.5 ft.

carambola small evergreen tree of SE Asia. The fruits, called **star fruit**, are yellowish, about 12 cm/4 in long, with a five-pointed star-shaped cross-section. They can be eaten raw, cooked, or pickled, and are juicily acidic. The juice is also used to remove stains from hands and clothes. (*Averrhoa carambola,* family Averrhoaceae.)

caramel complex mixture of substances produced by heating sugars, without charring, until they turn brown. Caramel is used as colouring and flavouring in foods. Its production in the manufacture of sugar confection gives rise to a toffeelike sweet of the same name.

The intricate chemical reactions involved in the production of caramel (caramelization) are not fully understood, but are known to result in the formation of a number of compounds. Two compounds in particular (acetylformoin and 4-hydroxy-2,5-dimethyl-3-furanone) are thought to contribute to caramel's characteristic flavour.

Commercially, the caramelization process is speeded up by the addition of selected ◊amino acids.

carapace protective covering of many animals, particularly the arched bony plate characteristic of the order Chelonia (tortoises, terrapins, and turtles), and the shield that protects the fore parts of crustaceans, such as crabs.

carat ***Arabic quirrat 'seed'*** unit for measuring the mass of precious stones; it is equal to 0.2 g/0.00705 oz, and is part of the troy system of weights. It is also the unit of purity in gold (US karat). Pure gold is 24-carat; 22-carat (the purest used in jewellery) is 22 parts gold and two parts alloy (to give greater strength).

Originally, one carat was the weight of a carob seed.

caraway herb belonging to the carrot family. Native to northern temperate regions of Europe and Asia, it is grown for its spicy, aromatic seeds, which are used in cookery, medicine, and perfumery. (*Carum carvi,* family Umbelliferae.)

carbide compound of carbon and one other chemical element, usually a metal, silicon, or boron.

Calcium carbide (CaC_2) can be used as the starting material for many basic organic chemical syntheses, by the addition of water and generation of ethyne (acetylene). Some metallic carbides are used in engineering because of their extreme hardness and strength. Tungsten carbide is an essential ingredient of carbide tools and high-speed tools. The 'carbide process' was used during World War II to make organic chemicals from coal rather than from oil.

carbohydrate chemical compound composed of carbon, hydrogen, and oxygen, with the basic formula $C_m(H_2O)_n$, and related compounds with the same basic structure but modified ◊functional groups. As sugar and starch, carbohydrates form a major energy-providing part of the human diet.

The simplest carbohydrates are sugars (**monosaccharides**, such as glucose and fructose, and **disaccharides**, such as sucrose), which are soluble compounds, some with a sweet taste. When these basic sugar units are joined together in long chains or branching structures they form **polysaccharides**, such as starch and glycogen, which often serve as food stores in living organisms. Even more complex carbohydrates are known, including ◊chitin, which is found in the cell walls of fungi and the hard outer skeletons of insects, and ◊cellulose, which makes up the cell walls of plants. Carbohydrates form the chief foodstuffs of herbivorous animals.

carbolic acid common name for the aromatic compound ◊phenol.

CHEMISTRY OF CARBON

http://cwis.nyu.edu/pages/mathmol/modules/carbon/carbon1.html

Excellent introduction to carbon, the element at the heart of life as we know it. This site is illustrated throughout and explains the main basic forms of carbon and the importance of the way scientists choose to represent these various structures.

carbon ***Latin carbo, carbonaris 'coal'*** nonmetallic element, symbol C, atomic number 6, relative atomic mass 12.011. It occurs on its own as diamond, graphite, and as fullerenes (the allotropes), as compounds in carbonaceous rocks such as chalk and limestone, as carbon dioxide in the atmosphere, as hydrocarbons in petroleum, coal, and natural gas, and as a constituent of all organic substances.

In its amorphous form, it is familiar as coal, charcoal, and soot. The atoms of carbon can link with one another in rings or chains, giving rise to innumerable complex compounds. Of the inorganic carbon compounds, the chief ones are **carbon dioxide**, a colourless gas formed when carbon is burned in an adequate supply of air; and **carbon monoxide** (CO), formed when carbon is oxidized in a limited supply of air. **Carbon disulphide** (CS_2) is a dense liquid with a sweetish odour. Another group of compounds is the **carbon halides**, including ◊carbon tetrachloride (tetrachloromethane, CCl_4).

When added to steel, carbon forms a wide range of alloys with useful properties. In pure form, it is used as a moderator in nuclear reactors; as colloidal graphite it is a good lubricant and, when deposited on a surface in a vacuum, reduces photoelectric and secondary emission of electrons. Carbon is used as a fuel in the form of coal or coke. The radioactive isotope carbon-14 (half-life 5,730 years) is used as a tracer in biological research and in radiocarbon dating. Analysis of interstellar dust has led to the discovery of discrete carbon molecules, each containing 60 carbon atoms. The C_{60} molecules have been named ◊buckminsterfullerenes because of their structural similarity to the geodesic domes designed by US architect and engineer Buckminster Fuller.

> *Life exists in the universe only because the carbon atom possesses certain exceptional properties.*
>
> JAMES HOPWOOD JEANS English mathematician and scientist. *Mysterious Universe*

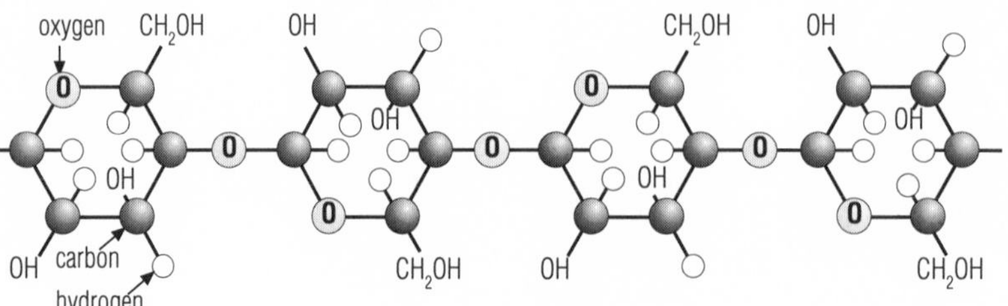

carbohydrate *A molecule of the polysaccharide glycogen (animal starch) is formed from linked glucose ($C_6H_{12}O_6$) molecules. A typical glycogen molecule has 100–1,000 glucose units.*

carbonate CO_3^{2-} ion formed when carbon dioxide dissolves in water; any salt formed by this ion and another chemical element, usually a metal.

Carbon dioxide (CO_2) dissolves sparingly in water (for example, when rain falls through the air) to form carbonic acid (H_2CO_3), which unites with various basic substances to form carbonates. Calcium carbonate ($CaCO_3$) (chalk, limestone, and marble) is one of the most abundant carbonates known, being a constituent of mollusc shells and the hard outer skeletons of crustaceans.

carbonated water water in which carbon dioxide is dissolved under pressure. It forms the basis of many fizzy soft drinks such as soda water and lemonade.

carbon copy in e-mail, a duplicate copy of a message sent to multiple recipients; a nod to traditional office systems. It is often abbreviated in software and on line to 'cc'.

carbon cycle sequence by which ◊carbon circulates and is recycled through the natural world. The carbon element from carbon dioxide, released into the atmosphere by living things as a result of ◊respiration, is taken up by plants during ◊photosynthesis and converted into carbohydrates; the oxygen component is released back into the atmosphere. Some of this carbon becomes locked up in coal and petroleum and other sediments. The simplest link in the carbon cycle occurs when an animal eats a plant and carbon is transferred from, say, a leaf cell to the animal body. The oceans absorb 25–40% of all carbon dioxide released into the atmosphere.

Today, the carbon cycle is in danger of being disrupted by the increased consumption and burning of fossil fuels, and the burning of large tracts of tropical forests, as a result of which levels of carbon dioxide are building up in the atmosphere and probably contributing to the ◊greenhouse effect.

carbon cycle in astrophysics, a sequence of nuclear fusion reactions in which carbon atoms act as a catalyst to convert four hydrogen atoms into one helium atom with the release of energy. The carbon cycle is the dominant energy source for ordinary stars of mass greater than about 1.5 times the mass of the Sun.

Nitrogen and oxygen are also involved in the sequence so it is sometimes known as the **carbon-nitrogen-oxygen cycle** or **CNO cycle**.

carbon dating alternative name for ◊radiocarbon dating.

carbon dioxide CO_2 colourless, odourless gas, slightly soluble in water and denser than air. It is formed by the complete oxidation of carbon.

It is produced by living things during the processes of respiration and the decay of organic matter, and plays a vital role in the carbon cycle. It is used as a coolant in its solid form (known as 'dry ice'), and in the chemical industry. Its increasing density contributes to the ◊greenhouse effect and ◊global warming. Britain has 1% of the world's population, yet it produces 3% of CO_2 emissions; the USA has 5% of the world's population and produces 25% of CO_2 emissions. Annual releases of carbon dioxide reached 23 billion tones in 1997. According to a 1997 estimate by the World Energy council, carbon dioxide emissions rose by 7.8% between 1986 and 1996.

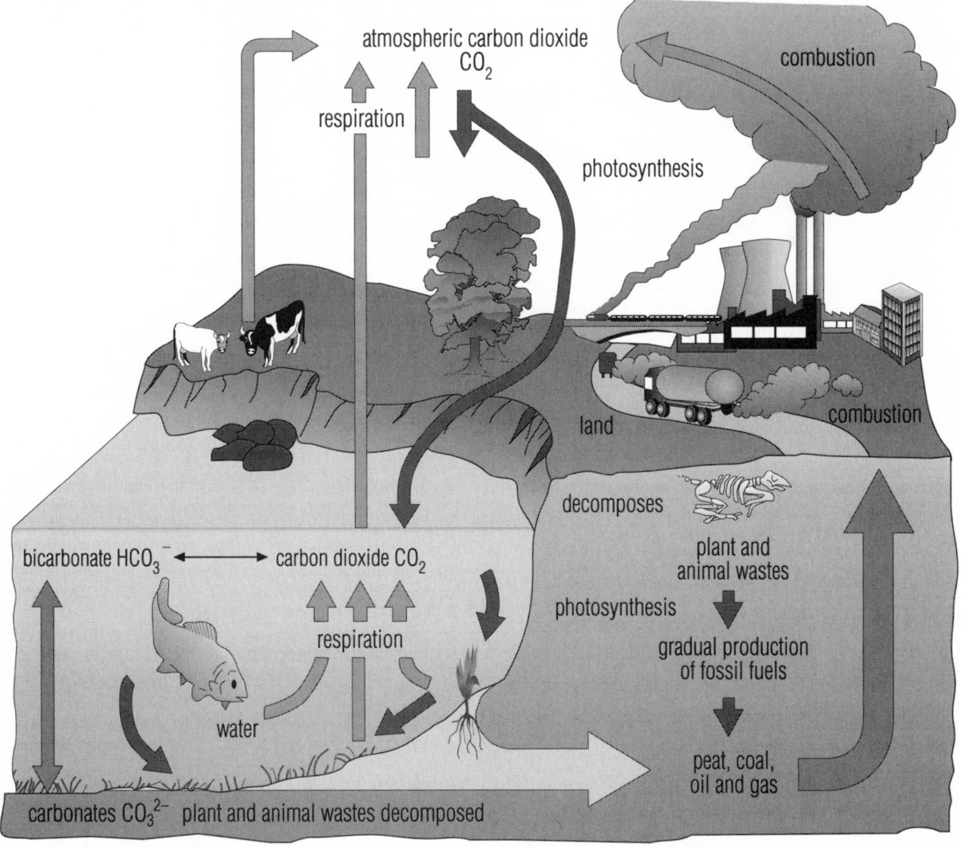

carbon cycle *The carbon cycle is necessary for the continuation of life. Since there is only a limited amount of carbon in the Earth and its atmosphere, carbon must be continuously recycled if life is to continue. Other chemicals necessary for life – nitrogen, sulphur, and phosphorus, for example – also circulate in natural cycles.*

carbon fibre fine, black, silky filament of pure carbon produced by heat treatment from a special grade of Courtelle acrylic fibre and, used for reinforcing plastics. The resulting composite is very stiff and, weight for weight, has four times the strength of high-tensile steel. It is used in the aerospace industry, cars, and electrical and sports equipment.

carbonic acid H_2CO_3 weak, dibasic acid formed by dissolving carbon dioxide in water.

$$H_2O + CO_2 \leftrightarrow H_2CO_3$$

It forms two series of salts: ◊carbonates and ◊hydrogencarbonates. Fizzy drinks are made by dissolving carbon dioxide in water under pressure; soda water is a solution of carbonic acid.

Carboniferous period of geological time 362.5–290 million years ago, the fifth period of the Palaeozoic era. In the USA it is divided into two periods: the Mississippian (lower) and the Pennsylvanian (upper).

Typical of the lower-Carboniferous rocks are shallow-water ◊limestones, while upper-Carboniferous rocks have ◊delta deposits with ◊coal (hence the name). Amphibians were abundant, and reptiles evolved during this period.

carbon monoxide CO colourless, odourless gas formed when carbon is oxidized in a limited supply of air. It is a poisonous constituent of car exhaust fumes, forming a stable compound with haemoglobin in the blood, thus preventing the haemoglobin from transporting oxygen to the body tissues.

In industry, carbon monoxide is used as a reducing agent in metallurgical processes – for example, in the extraction of iron in ◊blast furnaces – and is a constituent of cheap fuels such as water gas. It burns in air with a luminous blue flame to form carbon dioxide.

carbon sequestration disposal of carbon dioxide waste in solid or liquid form. From 1993 energy conglomerates such as Shell, Exxon, and British coal have been researching ways to reduce their carbon dioxide emissions by developing efficient technologies to trap the gas and store it securely – for example, by burying it or dumping it in the oceans. See also ◊greenhouse effect.

carbon tetrachloride former name for the chlorinated organic compound ◊tetrachloromethane.

Carborundum trademark for a very hard, black abrasive, consisting of silicon carbide (SiC), an artificial compound of carbon and silicon. It is harder than ◊corundum but not as hard as ◊diamond.

It was first produced 1891 by US chemist Edward Acheson (1856–1931).

carboxyl group –COOH in organic chemistry, the acidic functional group that determines the properties of fatty acids (carboxylic acids) and amino acids.

carboxylic acid organic acid containing the carboxyl group (–COOH) attached to another group (R), which can be hydrogen (giving methanoic acid, HCOOH) or a larger molecule (up to 24 carbon atoms). When R is a straight-chain alkyl group (such as CH_3 or CH_3CH_2), the acid is known as a ◊fatty acid.

Examples of carboxylic acids include acetic acid, found in vinegar, malic acid, found in rhubarb, and citric acid, contained in oranges and lemons.

To remember the (alpha, omega) dicarboxylic acids from $C_2 - C_{10}$:

OH MY, SUCH GOOD APPLE PIE, SWEET AS SUGAR

OXALIC, MALONIC, SUCCINIC, GLUTARIC, ADIPIC, PIMELIC, SUBERIC, AZELAIC, SEBACIC

carburation mixing of a gas, such as air, with a volatile hydrocarbon fuel, such as petrol, kerosene, or fuel oil, in order to form an explosive mixture. The process, which ensures that the maximum amount of heat energy is released during combustion, is used in internal-combustion engines. In most petrol engines the liquid fuel is atomized and mixed with air by means of a device called a **carburettor**.

carcinogen any agent that increases the chance of a cell becoming cancerous (see ◊cancer), including various chemical compounds, some viruses, X-rays, and other forms of ionizing radiation. The term is often used more narrowly to mean chemical carcinogens only.

carcinoma malignant ◊tumour arising from the skin, the glandular tissues, or the mucous membranes that line the gut and lungs.

cardinal number in mathematics, one of the series of numbers 0, 1, 2, 3, 4, … . Cardinal numbers relate to quantity, whereas ordinal numbers (first, second, third, fourth, … .) relate to order.

cardioid heart-shaped curve traced out by a point on the circumference of a circle, resulting from the circle rolling around the edge of another circle of the same diameter.

The polar equation of the cardioid is of the form:

$$r = a(1 + \cos\theta)$$

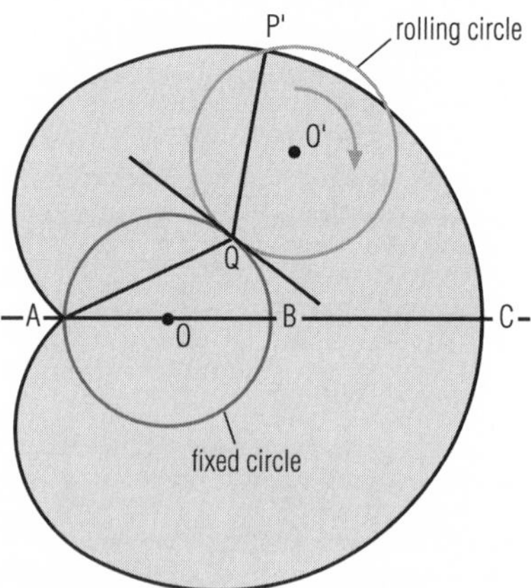

cardioid The cardioid is the curve formed when one circle rolls around the edge of another circle of the same size. It is named after its heart shape.

caribou the ◊reindeer of North America.

caries decay and disintegration, usually of the substance of teeth (cavity) or bone, caused by acids produced when the bacteria that live in the mouth break down sugars in the food. Fluoride, a low sugar intake, and regular brushing are all protective. Caries form mainly in the 45 minutes following consumption of sugary food.

Carina constellation of the southern hemisphere, represented as a ship's keel. Its brightest star is ◊Canopus, the second brightest in the night sky; it also contains Eta Carinae, a massive and highly luminous star embedded in a gas cloud, perhaps 8,000 light years away.

Carina was formerly regarded as part of Argo, and is situated in one of the brightest parts of the ◊Milky Way.

Carnac site of prehistoric ◊megaliths in Brittany, France, where remains of tombs and stone alignments of the period 2000–1500 BC (Neolithic and early Bronze Age) are found. Stones removed for local building have left some gaps in the alignments.

There are various groups of menhirs round the village of Carnac in the *département* of Morbihan, situated at Kermario (place of the dead), Kerlescan (place of burning), Erdeven, and St-Barbe. The largest of the stone alignments has 1,000 blocks of grey granite up to 4 m/13 ft high, extending over 2 km/1.2 mi. These ◊menhirs (standing stones) are arranged in 11 parallel rows, with a circle at the western end.

Stone circles and alignments are thought to be associated with astronomical and religious ritual, and those at Carnac may possibly have been used for calculating the phases of the moon.

carnassial tooth one of a powerful scissorlike pair of molars, found in all mammalian carnivores except seals. Carnassials are formed from an upper premolar and lower molar, and are shaped to produce a sharp cutting surface. Carnivores such as dogs transfer meat to the back of the mouth, where the carnassials slice up the food ready for swallowing.

carnation any of a large number of double-flowered cultivated varieties of a plant belonging to the ◊pink family. The flowers smell like cloves; they are divided into flake, bizarre, and picotees, according to whether the petals have one or more colours on their white base, have the colour appearing in strips, or have a coloured border to the petals. (*Dianthus caryophyllus,* family Carophyllaceae.)

carnauba palm tree native to South America, especially Brazil. It produces fine timber and a hard wax, used for polishes and lipsticks. (*Copernicia cerifera.*)

carnivore in zoology, mammal of the order Carnivora. Although its name describes the flesh-eating ancestry of the order, it includes pandas, which are herbivorous, and civet cats, which eat fruit.

Carnivores have the greatest range of body size of any mammalian order, from the 100 g/3.5 oz weasel to the 800 kg/1,764 lb polar bear.

The characteristics of the Carnivora are sharp teeth, small incisors, a well-developed brain, a simple stomach, a reduced or absent caecum, and incomplete or absent clavicles (collarbones); there are never less than four toes on each foot; the scaphoid and lunar bones are fused in the hand; and the claws are generally sharp and powerful.

Carnot, (Nicolas Leonard) Sadi (1796–1832) French scientist and military engineer who founded the science of thermodynamics. His pioneering work was *Reflexions sur la puissance motrice du feu/On the Motive Power of Fire,* which considered the changes that would take place in an idealized, frictionless steam engine.

Carnot's theorem showed that the amount of work that an engine can produce depends only on the temperature difference that occurs in the engine. He described the maximum amount of heat convertible into work by the formula $(T_1 - T_2)/T_2$, where T_1 is the temperature of the hottest part of the machine and T_2 is the coldest part.

Carnot cycle series of changes in the physical condition of a gas in a reversible heat engine, necessarily in the following order: (1) isothermal expansion (without change of temperature), (2) adiabatic expansion (without change of heat content), (3) isothermal compression, and (4) adiabatic compression.

The principles derived from a study of this cycle are important in the fundamentals of heat and ◊thermodynamics.

carob small Mediterranean tree belonging to the ◊legume family. Its pods, 20 cm/8 in long, are used as an animal feed; they are also the source of a chocolate substitute. (*Ceratonia siliqua,* family Leguminosae.)

carotene naturally occurring pigment of the ◊carotenoid group. Carotenes produce the orange, yellow, and red colours of carrots, tomatoes, oranges, and crustaceans.

carotenoid any of a group of yellow, orange, red, or brown pigments found in many living organisms, particularly in the ◊chloroplasts of plants. There are two main types, the **carotenes** and the **xanthophylls**. Both types are long-chain lipids (◊fats).

Some carotenoids act as accessory pigments in ◊photosynthesis, and in certain algae they are the principal light-absorbing pigments functioning more efficiently than ◊chlorophyll in low-intensity light. Carotenoids can also occur in organs such as petals, roots, and fruits, giving them their characteristic colour, as in the yellow and orange petals of wallflowers *Cheiranthus.* They are also responsible for the autumn colours of leaves, persisting longer than the green chlorophyll, which masks them during the summer.

carotid artery one of a pair of major blood vessels, one on each side of the neck, supplying blood to the head.

carp fish *Cyprinus carpio* found all over the world. It commonly grows to 50 cm/1.8 ft and 3 kg/7 lb, but may be even larger. It lives in lakes, ponds, and slow rivers. The wild form is drab, but cultivated forms may be golden, or may have few large scales (mirror carp) or be scaleless (leather carp). **Koi** carp are highly prized and can grow up to 1 m/3 ft long with a distinctive pink, red, white, or black colouring.

A large proportion of European freshwater fish belong to the carp family, Cyprinidae, and related fishes are found in Asia, Africa, and North America. The carp's fast growth, large size, and ability to live in still water with little oxygen have made it a good fish to farm, and it has been cultivated for hundreds of years and spread by human agency. Members of this family have a single non-spiny dorsal fin, pelvic fins well back on the body, and toothless jaws, although teeth in the throat form an efficient grinding apparatus. Minnows, roach, rudd, and many others, including goldfish, belong to this family. Chinese **grass carp** *Ctenopharyngodon idella* have been introduced (one sex only) to European rivers for weed control.

carpel female reproductive unit in flowering plants (◊angiosperms). It usually comprises an ◊ovary containing one or more ovules, the stalk or style, and a ◊stigma at its top which receives the pollen. A flower may have one or more carpels, and they may be separate or fused together. Collectively the carpels of a flower are known as the ◊gynoecium.

carpet beetle small black or brown beetle. The larvae are covered with hairs and often known as **woolly bears**; they feed on carpets, fabrics, and hides causing damage.

The **common carpet beetle** *Anthrenus scrophularia* measures 3–4 mm/0.1–0.2 in long. It is oval, black, and has yellow scales on the shield (pronotum) and ginger red on the wing cases (elytra). This species prefers fabrics to carpets, and the larvae, which are brownish, hairy grubs, eat holes into fabrics or make slits in the carpet.

Larvae of *Anthrenus museorum* can do extensive damage to museum collections. Specimens of stuffed animals or entire insect collections, which have been inadequately treated prior to storage, can be destroyed.

classification Carpet beetles are in the genus *Anthrenus* and *Attagenus* in the family Dermestidae of order Coleoptera, class Insecta, phylum Arthropoda.

carragheen species of deep-reddish branched seaweed. Named after Carragheen, near Waterford, in the Republic of Ireland, it is found on rocky shores on both sides of the Atlantic. It is exploited commercially in food and medicines and as cattle feed. (*Chondrus crispus.*)

carriage return (CR) in computing, a special code (◊ASCII value 13) that moves the screen cursor or a print head to the beginning of the current line. Most word processors and the ◊MS-DOS operating system use a combination of CR and line feed (LF – ASCII value 10) to represent a hard return. The ◊UNIX system, however, uses only LF and therefore files transferred between MS-DOS and UNIX require a conversion program.

carrier in medicine, anyone who harbours an infectious organism without ill effects but can pass the infection to others. The term is also applied to those who carry a recessive gene for a disease or defect without manifesting the condition.

carrion crow British bird *Corvus corone* of family Corvidae, order Passeriformes, closely related to *C. cornix,* the hooded crow. In the USA the name refers to the black vulture.

carrot hardy European biennial plant with feathery leaves and an orange tapering root that is eaten as a vegetable. It has been cultivated since the 16th century. The root has a high sugar content and also contains ◊carotene, which is converted into vitamin A by the human liver. (*Daucus carota,* family Umbelliferae.)

carrying capacity in ecology, the maximum number of animals of a given species that a particular area can support. When the carrying capacity is exceeded, there is insufficient food (or other resources) for the members of the population. The population may then be reduced by emigration, reproductive failure, or death through starvation.

Cartesian coordinates in ◊coordinate geometry, components used to define the position of a point by its perpendicular distance from a set of two or more axes, or reference lines. For a two-dimensional area defined by two axes at right angles (a horizontal x-axis and a vertical y-axis), the coordinates of a point are given by its perpendicular distances from the y-axis and x-axis, written in the form (x,y). For example, a point P that lies three units from the y-axis and four units from the x-axis has Cartesian coordinates (3,4) (see ◊abscissa and ◊ordinate). In three-dimensional coordinate geometry, points are located with reference to a third, z-axis, mutually at right angles to the x and y axes.

The Cartesian coordinate system can be extended to any finite number of dimensions (axes), and is used thus in theoretical mathematics. It is named after the French mathematician, René Descartes. The system is useful in creating technical drawings of machines or buildings, and in computer-aided design (◊CAD).

cartilage flexible bluish-white ◊connective tissue made up of the protein collagen. In cartilaginous fish it forms the skeleton; in other vertebrates it forms the greater part of the embryonic skeleton, and is replaced by ◊bone in the course of development, except in areas of wear such as bone endings, and the discs between the backbones. It also forms structural tissue in the larynx, nose, and external ear of mammals.

Cartilage does not heal itself, so where injury is severe the joint may need to be replaced surgically. In a 1994 trial, Swedish doctors repaired damaged knee joints by implanting cells cultured from the patient's own cartilage.

cartography art and practice of drawing ◊maps.

caryopsis dry, one-seeded ◊fruit in which the wall of the seed becomes fused to the carpel wall during its development. It is a type of ◊achene, and therefore develops from one ovary and does not split open to release the seed. Caryopses are typical of members of the grass family (Gramineae), including the cereals.

casein main protein of milk, from which it can be separated by the action of acid, the enzyme rennin, or bacteria (souring); it is also the main protein in cheese. Casein is used as a protein supplement in the treatment of malnutrition. It is used commercially in cosmetics, glues, and as a sizing for coating paper.

case-sensitive term describing a system that distinguishes between capitals and lower-case letters. Domain names and Internet addresses are typically not case-sensitive; however, a particular system may be case-sensitive for user IDs. On most systems, the software controlling passwords is case-sensitive, making it harder for an unauthorized user to guess a password.

cash crop crop grown solely for sale rather than for the farmer's own use, for example, coffee, cotton, or sugar beet. Many Third World countries grow cash crops to meet their debt repayments rather than grow food for their own people. The price for these crops depends on financial interests, such as those of the multinational companies and the International Monetary Fund.

In 1990 Uganda, Rwanda, Nicaragua, and Somalia were the countries most dependent on cash crops for income.

cashew tropical American tree. Widely cultivated in India and Africa, it produces poisonous kidney-shaped nuts that become edible after being roasted. (*Anacardium occidentale,* family Anacardiaceae.)

cassava or **manioc** plant belonging to the spurge family. Native to South America, it is now widely grown throughout the tropics for its starch-containing roots, from which tapioca and bread are made. (*Manihot utilissima,* family Euphorbiaceae.)

Cassava is grown as a staple crop in rural Africa, Asia, and South America. Altogether, it provides a staple crop for approximately 200 million people. The root cells contain the poison cyanoglucoside (converted to hydrogen cyanide in the body) but the plant's latex (milky fluid) contains enzymes that break down the poison. During the processing of cassava the two must mix; the commonest method is by fermentation, although some poison may remain. In Congo (formerly Zaire) and Mozambique at least 10,000 women and children suffered from chronic poisoning between 1985 and 1995.

Cassegrain telescope or ***Cassegrain reflector*** type of reflecting ◊telescope in which light collected by a concave primary mirror is reflected on to a convex secondary mirror, which in turn directs it back through a hole in the primary mirror to a focus behind it. As a result, the telescope tube can be kept short, allowing equipment for analyzing and recording starlight to be mounted behind the main mirror. All modern large astronomical telescopes are of the Cassegrain type.

It is named after the 17th century French astronomer, Cassegrain who first devised it as an improvement to the simpler ◊Newtonian telescope.

cassia bark of an aromatic SE Asian plant (*Cinnamomum cassia*) belonging to the laurel family (Lauraceae). It is very similar to cinnamon, and is often used as a substitute for it. *Cassia* is also a genus of pod-bearing tropical plants of the family Caesalpiniaceae, many of which have strong purgative (cleansing) properties; *C. senna* is the source of the laxative drug senna (which causes the bowels to empty).

Cassini joint space probe of the US agency NASA and the European Space Agency to the planet Saturn. *Cassini* was launched in October1997, to go into orbit around Saturn 2004, dropping off a sub-probe, *Huygens,* to land on Saturn's largest moon, Titan.

It was launched on a Titan 4 rocket, with its electricity supplied by 32 kg/70 lb of plutonium. This is the largest amount of plutonium ever to be sent into space, and provoked fears of contamination should Cassini, or its rocket, malfunction. A Titan 4 exploded in flight 1993.

CASSINI MISSION TO SATURN

http://miranda.colorado.edu/cassini/

Well-presented information on the purposes of the Cassini space probe. The complexities of designing the probe and its instruments and navigating it to the distant planet are explained in easy to understand language with the aid of good graphics. There are also interesting details of what is already known about Saturn's moons.

Cassiopeia prominent constellation of the northern hemisphere, named after the mother of Andromeda. It has a distinctive W-shape, and contains one of the most powerful radio sources in the sky, Cassiopeia A. This is the remains of a ◊supernova (star explosion) that occurred c. AD 1702, too far away to be seen from Earth.

It was in Cassiopeia that Tycho ◊Brahe observed a new star 1572, probably a supernova, since it was visible in daylight and outshone ◊Venus for ten days.

cassiterite or ***tinstone*** mineral consisting of reddish-brown to black stannic oxide (SnO_2), usually found in granite rocks. It is the chief ore of tin. When fresh it has a bright ('adamantine') lustre. It was formerly extensively mined in Cornwall, England; today Malaysia is the world's main supplier. Other sources of cassiterite are Africa, Indonesia, and South America.

cassowary large flightless bird, genus *Casuarius,* of the family Casuariidae, order Casuariiformes, found in New Guinea and N Australia, usually in forests. Related to the emu, the cassowary has a bare head with a horny casque, or helmet, on top, and brightly-coloured skin on the neck. Its loose plumage is black and its wings tiny, but it can run and leap well and defends itself by kicking.

Cassowaries stand up to 1.5 m/5 ft tall. They live in pairs and the male usually incubates the eggs, about six in number, which the female lays in a nest of leaves and grass.

casting process of producing solid objects by pouring molten material into a shaped mould and allowing it to cool. Casting is used to shape such materials as glass and plastics, as well as metals and alloys.

The casting of metals has been practised for more than 6,000 years, using first copper and bronze, then iron, and now alloys of zinc and other metals. The traditional method of casting metal is **sand casting**. Using a model of the object to be produced, a hollow mould is made in a damp sand and clay mix. Molten metal is then poured into the mould, taking its shape when it cools and solidifies. The sand mould is broken to release the casting. Permanent metal moulds called **dies** are also used for casting, in particular, small items in mass-production processes where molten metal is injected under pressure into cooled dies. **Continuous casting** is a method of shaping bars and slabs that involves pouring molten metal into a hollow, water-cooled mould of the desired cross section.

cast iron cheap but invaluable constructional material, most commonly used for car engine blocks. Cast iron is partly refined pig (crude) ◊iron, which is very fluid when molten and highly suitable for shaping by casting; it contains too many impurities (for example, carbon) to be readily shaped in any other way. Solid cast iron is heavy and can absorb great shock but is very brittle.

Castor or ***Alpha Geminorum*** second brightest star in the constellation ◊Gemini and the 23rd brightest star in the night sky. Along with the brighter ◊Pollux, it forms a prominent pair at the eastern end of Gemini, representing the head of the twins.

Second-magnitude Castor is 45 light years from Earth, and is one of the finest ◊binary stars in the sky for small telescopes. The two main components orbit each other over a period of 467 years. A third, much fainter, star orbits the main pair over a period probably exceeding 10,000 years. Each of the three visible components is a spectroscopic binary, making Castor a sextuple star system.

castoreum preputial follicles of the beaver, abbreviated as 'castor', and used in perfumery.

castor-oil plant tall tropical and subtropical shrub belonging to the spurge family. The seeds, called 'castor beans' in North America, yield the purgative castor oil (which cleans out the bowels) and also ricin, one of the most powerful poisons known. Ricin can be used to destroy cancer cells, leaving normal cells untouched. (*Ricinus communis,* family Euphorbiaceae.)

castration removal of the sex glands (either ovaries or testes). Male domestic animals may be castrated to prevent reproduction, to make them larger or more docile, or to eradicate disease.

Castration of humans was used in ancient and medieval times and occasionally later to preserve the treble voice of boy singers or, by Muslims, to provide eunuchs, trustworthy harem guards. If done in childhood, it inhibits sexual development: for instance, the voice remains high, and growth of hair on the face and body is reduced, owing to the absence of the hormones normally secreted by the testes.

CASTRATION

Exceptional boy singers used to be castrated to preserve their very high voices. Many of these **castrati** earned very high fees as opera singers.

casuarina any of a group of trees or shrubs with many species in Australia and New Guinea, also found in Africa and Asia. Commonly known as she-oaks, casuarinas have taken their Latin name from the similarity of their long, drooping branchlets to the feathers of the cassowary bird (whose genus is *Casuarius*). (Genus *Casuarina,* family Casuarinaceae.)

cat small, domesticated, carnivorous mammal *Felis catus,* often kept as a pet or for catching small pests such as rodents. Found in many colour variants, it may have short, long, or no hair, but the general shape and size is constant. Cats have short muzzles, strong limbs, and flexible spines which enable them to jump and climb. All walk on the pads of their toes (**digitigrade**) and have retractile claws, so are able to stalk their prey silently. They have large eyes and an acute sense of hearing. The canine teeth are long and well-developed, as are the shearing teeth in the side of the mouth.
origins Domestic cats have a common ancestor, the **African wild cat** *Felis libyca,* found across Africa and Arabia. This is similar to the **European wild cat** *F. silvestris.* Domestic cats can interbreed with either of these wild relatives. Various other species of small wild cat live in all continents except Antarctica and Australia. Large cats such as the lion, tiger, leopard, puma, and jaguar also belong to the cat family Felidae.

CAT

A tenth of the diet of feral cats is made up of vegetable material.

catabolism in biology, the destructive part of ◊metabolism where living tissue is changed into energy and waste products.

It is the opposite of ◊anabolism. It occurs continuously in the body, but is accelerated during many disease processes, such as fever, and in starvation.

catalpa any of a group of trees belonging to the trumpet creeper family, found in North America, China, and the West Indies. The northern catalpa (*Catalpa speciosa*) of North America grows to 30 m/100 ft and has heart-shaped deciduous leaves and tubular white flowers with purple borders. (Genus *Catalpa,* family Bignoniaceae.)

catalyst substance that alters the speed of, or makes possible, a chemical or biochemical reaction but remains unchanged at the end of the reaction. ◊Enzymes are natural biochemical catalysts. In practice most catalysts are used to speed up reactions.

catalytic converter device fitted to the exhaust system of a motor vehicle in order to reduce toxic emissions from the engine. It converts harmful exhaust products to relatively harmless ones by passing the exhaust gases over a mixture of catalysts coated on a metal or ceramic honeycomb (a structure that increases the surface area and therefore the amount of active catalyst with which the exhaust gases will come into contact). **Oxidation catalysts** (small amounts of precious palladium and platinum metals) convert hydrocarbons (unburnt fuel) and carbon monoxide into carbon dioxide and water, but do not affect nitrogen oxide emissions. **Three-way catalysts** (platinum and rhodium metals) convert nitrogen oxide gases into nitrogen and oxygen.

Over the lifetime of a vehicle, a catalytic converter can reduce hydrocarbon emissions by 87%, carbon monoxide emissions by 85%, and nitrogen oxide emissions by 62%, but will cause a slight increase in the amount of carbon dioxide emitted. Catalytic converters are standard in the USA, where a 90% reduction in pollution from cars was achieved without loss of engine performance or fuel economy. Only 10% of cars in Britain had catalytic converters in 1993.

Catalytic converters are destroyed by emissions from leaded petrol and work best at a temperature of 300°C. The benefits of catalytic converters are offset by any increase in the number of cars in use.

catamaran ***Tamil 'tied log'*** twin-hulled sailing vessel, based on the native craft of South America and the Indies, made of logs lashed together, with an outrigger. A similar vessel with three hulls is known as a trimaran. Car ferries with a wave-piercing catamaran design are also in use in parts of Europe and North America. They have a pointed main hull and two outriggers and travel at a speed of 35 knots (84.5 kph/52.5 mph).

cataract eye disease in which the crystalline lens or its capsule becomes cloudy, causing blindness. Fluid accumulates between the fibres of the lens and gives place to deposits of ◊albumin. These coalesce into rounded bodies, the lens fibres break down, and areas of the lens or the lens capsule become filled with opaque products of degeneration. The condition is estimated to have blinded more than 25 million people worldwide, and 150,000 in the UK.

The condition nearly always affects both eyes, usually one more than the other. In most cases, the treatment is replacement of the opaque lens with an artificial implant.

catarrh inflammation of any mucous membrane, especially of the nose and throat, with increased production of mucus.

Catarrhini Old World monkeys and apes, including macaques and baboons (Cercopithecidae) and chimpanzees and orang-utans (Pongidae). The term is now rarely used.

Catarrhines are characterized by having their nostrils close to each other and facing downwards. Many species have cheek pouches and brightly coloured buttocks. They have 32 teeth and do not have prehensile tails. Compare with the New World ◊Platyrrhini.

catastrophe theory mathematical theory developed by René Thom 1972, in which he showed that the growth of an organism proceeds by a series of gradual changes that are triggered by, and in turn trigger, large-scale changes or 'catastrophic' jumps. It also has applications in engineering – for example, the gradual strain on the structure of a bridge that can eventually result in a sudden collapse – and has been extended to economic and psychological events.

It is characteristic of science that the full explanations are often seized in their essence by the percipient scientist long in advance of any possible proof.

JOHN DESMOND BERNAL
The Origin of Life 1967

catecholamine chemical that functions as a ◊neurotransmitter or a ◊hormone. Dopamine, adrenaline (epinephrine), and noradrenaline (norepinephrine) are catecholamines.

catenary curve taken up by a flexible cable suspended between two points, under gravity; for example, the curve of overhead suspension cables that hold the conductor wire of an electric railway or tramway.

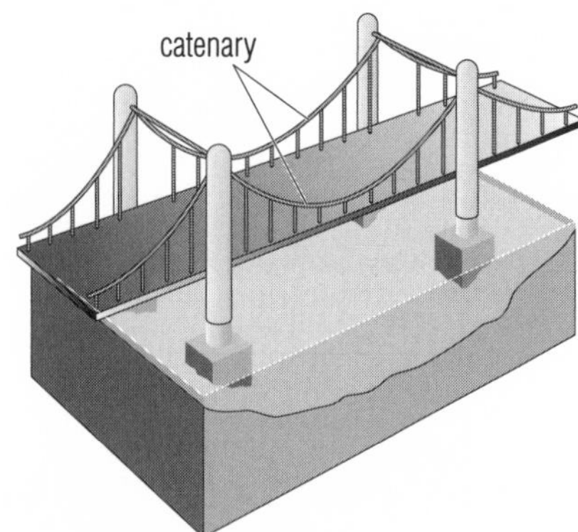

catenary *Construction utilizing the form of a catenary can be seen in this suspension bridge.*

caterpillar larval stage of a ◊butterfly or ◊moth. Wormlike in form, the body is segmented, may be hairy, and often has scent

caterpillar *A caterpillar of a notodontid moth from the rainforest of New Guinea. Its aposematic (warning) coloration is a signal to potential predators that it has an unpleasant taste. Premaphotos Wildlife*

glands. The head has strong biting mandibles, silk glands, and a spinneret.

Many caterpillars resemble the plant on which they feed, dry twigs, or rolled leaves. Others are highly coloured and rely for their protection on their irritant hairs, disagreeable smell, or on their power to eject a corrosive fluid. Yet others take up a 'threat attitude' when attacked. Caterpillars emerge from eggs that have been laid by the female insect on the food plant and feed greedily, increasing greatly in size and casting their skins several times, until the pupal stage is reached. The abdominal segments bear a varying number of 'prolegs' as well as the six true legs on the thoracic segments.

CATERPILLAR

The caterpillars of some swallowtail butterflies deter predators by their uncanny resemblance to fresh bird droppings.

caterpillar track trade name for an endless flexible belt of metal plates on which certain vehicles such as tanks and bulldozers run, which takes the place of ordinary tyred wheels and improves performance on wet or uneven surfaces.

A track-laying vehicle has a track on each side, and its engine drives small cogwheels that run along the top of the track in contact with the ground. The advantage of such tracks over wheels is that they distribute the vehicle's weight over a wider area and are thus ideal for use on soft and waterlogged as well as rough and rocky ground.

catfish fish belonging to the order Siluriformes, in which barbels (feelers) on the head are well-developed, so giving a resemblance to the whiskers of a cat. Catfishes are found worldwide, mainly but not exclusively in fresh water, and are plentiful in South America.

The E European **giant catfish** or **wels** *Silurus glanis* grows to 1.5 m/5 ft long or more. It has been introduced to several places in Britain. The unrelated marine **wolffish** *Anarhicas lupus*, a deep-sea relative of the blenny, growing 1.2 m/4 ft long, is sometimes called a catfish.

catheter fine tube inserted into the body to introduce or remove fluids. The urinary catheter, passed by way of the urethra (the duct that leads urine away from the bladder) was the first to be used. In today's practice, catheters can be inserted into blood vessels, either in the limbs or trunk, to provide blood samples and local pressure measurements, and to deliver drugs and/or nutrients directly into the bloodstream.

cathode in chemistry, the negative electrode of an electrolytic ◊cell, towards which positive particles (cations), usually in solution, are attracted. See ◊electrolysis.

A cathode is given its negative charge by connecting it to the negative side of an external electrical supply. This is in contrast to the negative electrode of an electrical (battery) cell, which acquires its charge in the course of a spontaneous chemical reaction taking place within the cell.

cathode in electronics, the part of an electronic device in which electrons are generated. In a thermionic valve, electrons are produced by the heating effect of an applied current; in a photocell, they are produced by the interaction of light and a semiconducting material. The cathode is kept at a negative potential relative to the device's other electrodes (anodes) in order to ensure that the liberated electrons stream away from the cathode and towards the anodes.

cathode-ray oscilloscope (CRO) instrument used to measure electrical potentials or voltages that vary over time and to display the waveforms of electrical oscillations or signals. Readings are displayed graphically on the screen of a ◊cathode-ray tube.

cathode-ray tube vacuum tube in which a beam of electrons is produced and focused onto a fluorescent screen. It is an essential component of television receivers, computer visual display units, and oscilloscopes.

The electrons' kinetic energy is converted into light energy as they collide with the screen.

cation ◊ion carrying a positive charge. During electrolysis, cations in the electrolyte move to the cathode (negative electrode).

To remember that cations are atoms that have lost an electron:

CAT LOST AN EYE

catkin in flowering plants (◊angiosperms), a pendulous inflorescence, bearing numerous small, usually unisexual flowers. The tiny flowers are stalkless and the petals and sepals are usually absent or much reduced in size. Many types of trees bear catkins, including willows, poplars, and birches. Most plants with catkins are wind-pollinated, so the male catkins produce large quantities of pollen. Some ◊gymnosperms also have catkin-like structures that produce pollen, for example, the swamp cypress *Taxodium*.

CAT scan or *CT scan* (acronym for ***computerized axial tomography scan***) sophisticated method of X-ray imaging. Quick and non-invasive, CAT scanning is used in medicine as an aid to diagnosis, helping to pinpoint problem areas without the need for exploratory surgery. It is also used in archaeology to investigate mummies.

The CAT scanner passes a narrow fan of X-rays through successive slices of the suspect body part. These slices are picked up by crystal detectors in a scintillator and converted electronically into cross-sectional images displayed on a viewing screen. Gradually, using views taken from various angles, a three-dimensional picture of the organ or tissue can be built up and irregularities analysed.

cattle any large, ruminant, even-toed, hoofed mammal of the genus *Bos,* family Bovidae, including wild species such as the yak, gaur, gayal, banteng, and kouprey, as well as domestic breeds. Asiatic water buffaloes *Bubalus,* African buffaloes *Syncerus,* and American bison *Bison* are not considered true cattle. Cattle are bred for meat (beef cattle) or milk (dairy cattle).

Cattle were first domesticated in the Middle East during the Neolithic period, about 8000 BC. They were brought north into Europe by migrating Neolithic farmers. Fermentation in the four-chambered stomach allows cattle to make good use of the grass that is normally the main part of the diet. There are two main types of domesticated cattle: the European breeds, variants of *Bos taurus* descended from the ◊aurochs, **and the various breeds of zebu** *Bos indicus,* the humped cattle of India, which are useful in the tropics for their ability to withstand the heat and diseases to which European breeds succumb. The old-established beef breeds are mostly British in origin. The Hereford, for example, is the premier English breed, ideally suited to rich lowland pastures but it will also thrive on poorer land such as that found in the US Midwest and the Argentine pampas.

Of the Scottish beef breeds, the Aberdeen Angus, a black and hornless variety, produces high-quality meat through intensive feeding methods. Other breeds include the Devon, a hardy early-maturing type, and the Beef Shorthorn, now less important than formerly, but still valued for an ability to produce good calves when crossed with less promising cattle. In recent years, more interest has been shown in other European breeds, their tendency to have less fat being more suited to modern tastes. Examples include the Charolais and the Limousin from central France, and the Simmental, originally from Switzerland. In the USA, four varieties of zebus, called Brahmans, have been introduced. They interbreed with *B. taurus* varieties and produce valuable hybrids that resist heat, ticks, and insects. For dairying purposes, a breed raised in many countries is variously known as the Friesian, Holstein, or Black and White. It can give enormous milk yields, up to 13,000 l/3,450 gal in a single lactation, and will produce calves ideally suited for intensive beef production. Other dairying types include the Jersey and Guernsey, whose milk has a high butterfat content, and the Ayrshire, a smaller breed capable of staying outside all year.

cauda tail, or taillike appendage; part of the *cauda equina,* a bundle of nerves at the bottom of the spinal cord in vertebrates.

cauliflower variety of ◊cabbage, with a large edible head of fleshy, cream-coloured flowers which do not fully mature. It is similar to broccoli but less hardy. (*Brassica oleracea botrytis,* family Cruciferae.)

caustic soda former name for ◊sodium hydroxide (NaOH).

cauterization in medicine, the use of special instruments to burn or fuse small areas of body tissue to destroy dead cells, prevent the spread of infection, or seal tiny blood vessels to minimize blood loss during surgery.

Cavalier King Charles spaniel breed of toy dog very similar to the related ◊King Charles spaniel. It is slightly larger (up to 8 kg/18 lb) and with a longer muzzle, and may be black and tan, tricoloured, ruby (a rich red) or Blenheim (chestnut and white).

cave roofed-over cavity in the Earth's crust usually produced by the action of underground water or by waves on a seacoast. Caves of the former type commonly occur in areas underlain by limestone, such as Kentucky and many Balkan regions, where the rocks are soluble in water. A **pothole** is a vertical hole in rock caused by water descending a crack; it is thus open to the sky.

Cave animals often show loss of pigmentation or sight, and under isolation, specialized species may develop. The scientific study of caves is called **speleology**. During the ◊ice age, humans began living in caves leaving many layers of debris that archaeologists have unearthed and dated in the Old World and the New. They also left cave art, paintings of extinct animals often with hunters on their trail. Celebrated caves include the Mammoth Cave in Kentucky, USA, 6.4 km/4 mi long and 38 m/125 ft high; the Caverns of Adelsberg (Postumia) near Trieste, Italy, which extend for many miles; Carlsbad Cave, New Mexico, the largest in the USA; the Cheddar Caves, England; Fingal's Cave, Scotland, which has a range of basalt columns; and Peak Cavern, England.

VIRTUAL CAVE

http://www.vol.it/MIRROR2/EN/CAVE/virtcave.html

Browse the mineral wonders unique to the cave environment – from bell canopies and bottlebrushes to splattermites and stalactites.

cave animal animal that has adapted to life within caves. The chief characteristics of cave animals are reduced or absent eyes and consequently other well-developed sense organs, such as antennae and feelers, and their lack of colour. Most are predators, owing to the lack of vegetable matter in this dark habitat.

Cave-dwellers include several species of snails found in Austrian caves that have developed blindness as a result of their mode of life and a genus of small cockroaches in caves of the Philippine Islands where the females are blind and flightless. There are numerous species of ◊cavefish including *Amblyopsis*, which occurs in the Mammoth Cave of Kentucky, USA. Cave-dwelling amphibians include several blind salamanders, such as the ◊olm.

cavefish cave-dwelling fish, which may belong to one of several quite unrelated groups, independently adapted to life in underground waters. Cavefish have in common a tendency to blindness and atrophy of the eye, enhanced touch-sensitive organs in the skin, and loss of pigment.

The **Kentucky blindfish** *Amblyopsis spelaea*, which lives underground in limestone caves, has eyes that are vestigial and beneath the skin, and a colourless body. The Mexican **cave characin** is a blind, colourless form of *Astyanax fasciatus* found in surface rivers of Mexico.

Cavendish experiment measurement of the gravitational attraction between lead spheres, which enabled English physicist and chemist Henry Cavendish to calculate 1798 a mean value for the mass and density of Earth, using Isaac Newton's law of universal gravitation.

cave spider small spider *Meta menardi* found in caves, cellars, and other dark places. It spins a small open web to catch insects. Its presence can be detected by its spherical egg sacs suspended by thick silk.

cavitation formation of partial vacuums (or cavities) in fluids at high velocities, produced by propellers or other machine parts in hydraulic engines, in accordance with Bernoulli's principle. When these vacuums collapse, pitting, vibration, and noise can occur in the metal parts in contact with the fluids.

cavy short-tailed South American rodent, family Caviidae, of which the guinea-pig *Cavia porcellus* is an example. Wild cavies are greyish or brownish with rather coarse hair. They live in small groups in burrows, and have been kept for food since ancient times.

cayenne pepper or ***red pepper*** spice produced from the dried fruits of several species of ◊capsicum (especially *Capsicum frutescens*), a tropical American group of plants. Its origins are completely different from black or white pepper, which comes from an East Indian plant (*Piper nigrum*).

cc symbol for ***cubic centimetre***; abbreviation for **carbon copy/copies**.

CCITT abbreviation for ◊Comité Consultatif International Téléphonique et Télégraphique, an organization that sets international communications standards.

CD abbreviation for ◊compact disc; **Corps Diplomatique** (French 'Diplomatic Corps'); **certificate of deposit**.

CD-I or **CD-i** (abbreviation for ***compact disc-interactive***) ◊compact disc developed by Philips for storing a combination of video, audio, text, and pictures. It was intended principally for the consumer market to be used in systems using a combination of computer and television. It flopped as a consumer system but is still used in education and training.

CD-quality sound digitized sound at 44.1 KHz and 16 bits, the standard defined in ISO 10149, known as the Red Book. CD-quality sound was designed to be the minimum standard required to reproduce every sound the human ear can hear. Most audio CDs are recorded to this level.

CD-R (abbreviation for ***compact disc-recordable***) compact disc on which data can be overwritten (compare ◊CD-ROM, compact disc

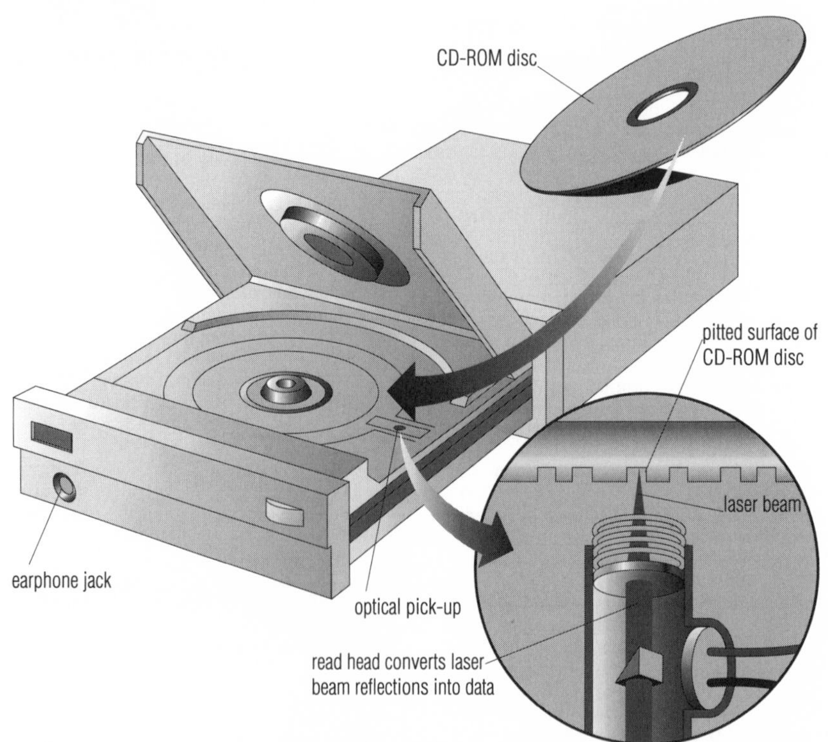

CD-ROM drive *Data is obtained by the CD-ROM drive by converting the reflections from a disc's surface into digital form.*

read-only memory). The disc combines magnetic and optical technology: during the writing process, a laser melts the surface of the disc, thereby allowing the magnetic elements of the surface layer to be realigned.

CD-ROM (abbreviation for ***compact-disc read-only memory***) computer storage device developed from the technology of the audio ◊compact disc. It consists of a plastic-coated metal disc, on which binary digital information is etched in the form of microscopic pits. This can then be read optically by passing a laser beam over the disc. CD-ROMs typically hold about 650 ◊megabytes of data, and are used in distributing large amounts of text, graphics, audio, and video, such as encyclopedias, catalogues, technical manuals, and games.

Standard CD-ROMs cannot have information written onto them by computer, but must be manufactured from a master, although recordable CDs, called CD-R discs, have been developed for use as computer discs. A compact disc, CD-RW, that can be overwritten repeatedly by a computer has also been developed. The compact disc, with its enormous storage capability, may eventually replace the magnetic disc as the most common form of backing store for computers.

The technology is being developed rapidly: a standard CD-ROM disc spins at between 240–1170 rpm, but faster discs have been introduced which speed up data retrieval to many times the standard speed. Research is being conducted into high-density CDs capable of storing many ◊gigabytes of data, made possible by using multiple layers on the surface of the disc, and by using double-sided discs. The first commercial examples of this research include DVD players and DVD-ROM computer discs launched in 1997.

PhotoCD, developed by Kodak and released in 1992, transfers ordinary still photographs onto CD-ROM discs.

CD-ROM drive in computing, a disc drive for reading CD-ROM discs. The vast majority of CD-ROM drives conform to the Yellow Book standard, defined by Philips and Sony. Because of this, all drives are essentially interchangeable. CD-ROM drives are available either as stand-alone or built-in units with a variety of interfaces (connections) and access times. (*See illustration on page 140.*)

CD-ROM XA (***CD-ROM extended architecture***) in computing, a set of standards for storing multimedia information on CD-ROM. Developed by Philips, Sony, and Microsoft, it is a partial development of the ◊CD-I standard. It interleaves data (as in CD-I) so that blocks of audio data are sandwiched between blocks of text, graphics, or video. This allows parallel streams of data to be handled, so that information can be seen and heard simultaneously.

Cebidae largest family of South American monkeys. The Cebidae is divided into five subfamilies represented by titis, squirrel monkeys, sakis, howlers, capuchins, and spider monkeys. They are all tree-living and are found in the rainforest where they feed on vegetable matter and small animals.

Cebus genus of South American monkey. The species have a well-developed big toe, a hairy prehensile tail, and 36 teeth. They include the ◊capuchin monkeys.

classification *Cebus* monkeys are typical of the family Cebidae in the order Primates.

cedar any of an Old World group of coniferous trees belonging to the pine family. The cedar of Lebanon (*Cedrus libani*) grows to great height and age in the mountains of Syria and Asia Minor. Of the historic forests on Mount Lebanon itself, only a few groups of trees remain. (Genus *Cedrus*, family Pinaceae.)

Ceefax ***'see facts'*** one of Britain's two ◊teletext systems (the other is Teletext), or 'magazines of the air', developed by the BBC and first broadcast in 1973.

In 1995 the BBC began testing a scheme to allow Ceefax (repackaged in HTML, hypertext markup language, to enable it to behave like Web pages) to be viewed on a PC by connecting a DAB (digital audio broadcasting) radio to the PC like a modem.

CEGB abbreviation for the former (until 1990) UK ***Central Electricity Generating Board***. For current industry structure see ◊electricity.

celandine either of two plants belonging to different families, the only similarity being their bright yellow flowers. The **greater celandine** (*Chelidonium majus*) belongs to the poppy family and is common in hedgerows. The **lesser celandine** (*Ranunculus ficaria*) is a member of the buttercup family and is a common wayside and meadow plant in Europe.

celeriac variety of garden celery belonging to the carrot family, with an edible turniplike root and small bitter stems. (*Apium graveolens* var. *rapaceum*, family Umbelliferae.)

celery Old World plant belonging to the carrot family. It grows wild in ditches and salt marshes and has a coarse texture and sharp taste. Cultivated varieties of celery are grown under cover to make the edible stalks less bitter. (*Apium graveolens*, family Umbelliferae.)

celestial mechanics the branch of astronomy that deals with the calculation of the orbits of celestial bodies, their gravitational attractions (such as those that produce the Earth's tides), and also the orbits of artificial satellites and space probes. It is based on the laws of motion and gravity laid down by Isaac ◊Newton.

celestial sphere imaginary sphere surrounding the Earth, on which the celestial bodies seem to lie. The positions of bodies such as stars, planets, and galaxies are specified by their coordinates on the celestial sphere. The equivalents of latitude and longitude on the celestial sphere are called ◊declination and ◊right ascension (which is measured in hours from 0 to 24). The **celestial poles** lie directly above the Earth's poles, and the **celestial equator** lies over the Earth's Equator. The celestial sphere appears to rotate once around the Earth each day, actually a result of the rotation of the Earth on its axis.

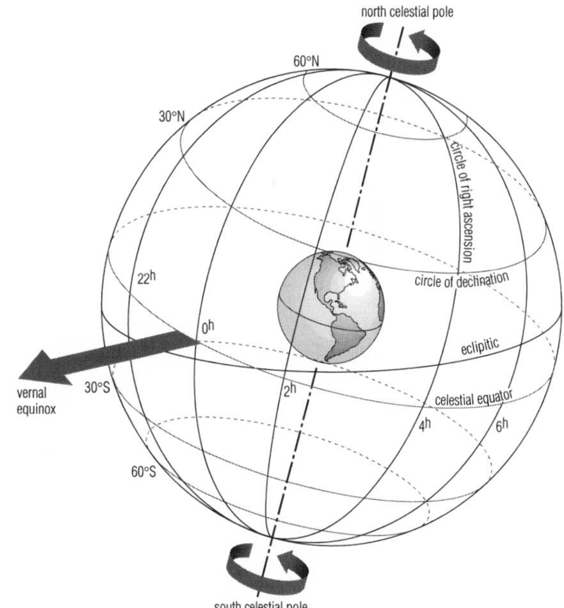

celestial sphere *The main features of the celestial sphere. The equivalents of latitude and longitude on the celestial sphere are declination and right ascension. Declination runs from 0° at the celestial equator to 90° at the celestial poles. Right ascension is measured in hours eastwards from the vernal equinox, one hour corresponding to 15° of longitude.*

cell in biology, a discrete, membrane-bound portion of living matter, the smallest unit capable of an independent existence. All living organisms consist of one or more cells, with the exception of

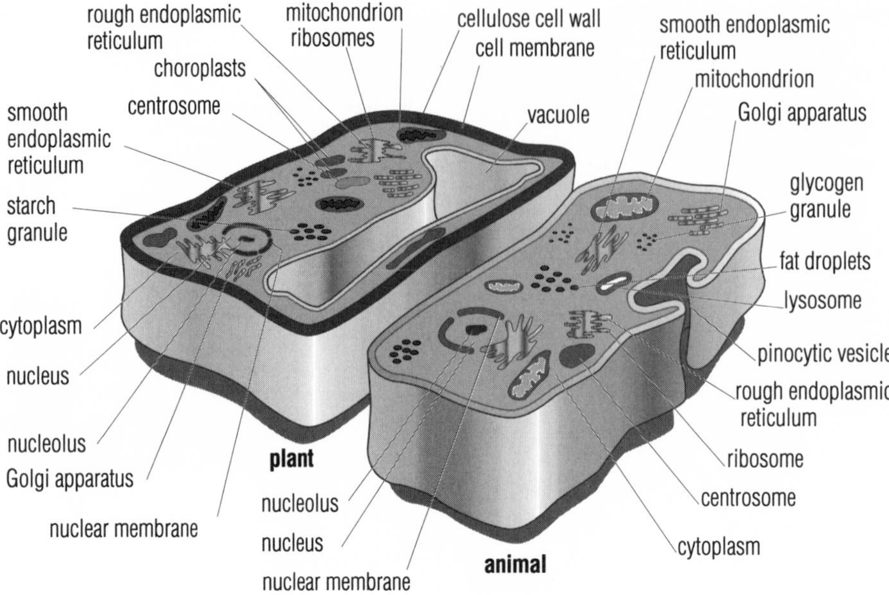

***cell** Typical plant and animal cell. Plant and animal cells share many structures, such as ribosomes, mitochondria, and chromosomes, but they also have notable differences: plant cells have chloroplasts, a large vacuole, and a cellulose cell wall. Animal cells do not have a rigid cell wall but have an outside cell membrane only.*

◊viruses. Bacteria, protozoa, and many other microorganisms consist of single cells, whereas a human is made up of billions of cells. Essential features of a cell are the membrane, which encloses it and restricts the flow of substances in and out; the jellylike material within, the ◊cytoplasm; the ◊ribosomes, which carry out protein synthesis; and the ◊DNA, which forms the hereditary material.

> *Truth is ever to be found in simplicity, and not in the multiplicity and confusion of things ... He is the God of order and not of confusion.*
>
> Isaac Newton English physicist and mathematician. Quoted in R L Weber, *More Random Walks in Science*

cell differentiation in developing embryos, the process by which cells acquire their specialization, such as heart cells, muscle cells, skin cells, and brain cells. The seven-day-old human pre-embryo consists of thousands of individual cells, each of which is destined to assist in the formation of individual organs in the body.

Research has shown that the eventual function of a cell, in for example, a chicken embryo, is determined by the cell's position. The embryo can be mapped into areas corresponding with the spinal cord, the wings, the legs, and many other tissues. If the embryo is relatively young, a cell transplanted from one area to another will develop according to its new position. As the embryo develops the cells lose their flexibility and become unable to change their destiny.

CELLS ALIVE

http://www.cellsalive.com/

Lively and attractive collection of microscopic and computer-generated images of living cells and microorganisms. It includes sections on HIV infection, penicillin, and how antibodies are made.

To remember the phases of cell division:

PRIME MINISTER – A TOAD!

PROPHASE, METAPHASE, ANAPHASE, TELOPHASE

cell division the process by which a cell divides, either ◊meiosis, associated with sexual reproduction, or ◊mitosis, associated with growth, cell replacement, or repair. Both forms involve the duplication of DNA and the splitting of the nucleus.

cell, electrical or ***voltaic cell*** or ***galvanic cell*** device in which chemical energy is converted into electrical energy; the popular name is ◊'battery', but this actually refers to a collection of cells in one unit. The reactive chemicals of a **primary cell** cannot be replenished, whereas **secondary cells** – such as storage batteries – are rechargeable: their chemical reactions can be reversed and the original condition restored by applying an electric current. It is dangerous to attempt to recharge a primary cell.

cell, electrolytic device to which electrical energy is applied in order to bring about a chemical reaction; see ◊electrolysis.

cell membrane or ***plasma membrane*** thin layer of protein and fat surrounding cells that controls substances passing between the cytoplasm and the intercellular space. The cell membrane is semipermeable, allowing some substances to pass through and some not.

Generally, small molecules such as water, glucose, and amino acids can penetrate the membrane, while large molecules, such as starch, cannot. Membranes also play a part in ◊active transport, hormonal response, and cell metabolism.

cellophane transparent wrapping film made from wood ◊cellulose, widely used for packaging, first produced by Swiss chemist Jacques Edwin Brandenberger in 1908.

Cellophane is made from wood pulp, in much the same way that the artificial fibre ◊rayon is made: the pulp is dissolved in chemicals to form a viscose solution, which is then pumped through a long narrow slit into an acid bath where the emergent viscose stream turns into a film of pure cellulose.

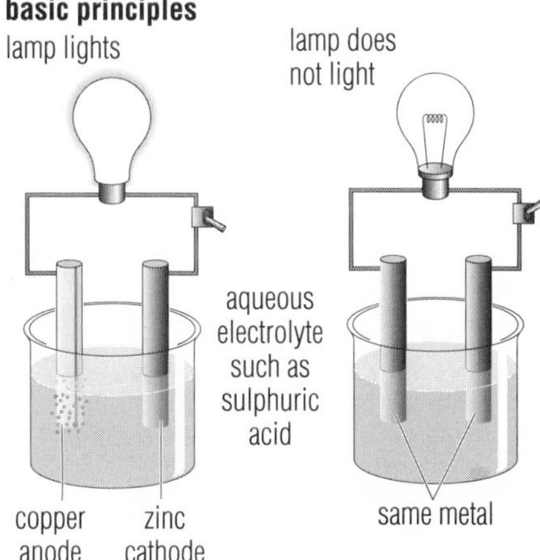

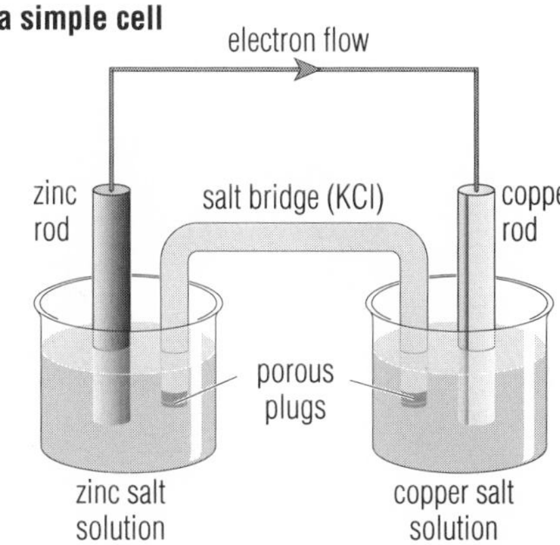

***cell, electrical** When electrical energy is produced from chemical energy using two metals acting as electrodes in a aqueous solution, it is sometimes known as a galvanic cell or voltaic cell. Here the two metals copper (+) and zinc (–) are immersed in dilute sulphuric acid, which acts as an electrolyte. If a light bulb is connected between the two, an electric current will flow with bubbles of gas being deposited on the electrodes in a process known as polarization.*

cellphone short for ◊cellular phone.

cell sap dilute fluid found in the large central vacuole of many plant cells. It is made up of water, amino acids, glucose, and salts. The sap has many functions, including storage of useful materials, and provides mechanical support for non-woody plants.

cellular modem type of ◊modem that connects to a ◊cellular phone for the wireless transmission of data.

cellular phone or ***cellphone*** mobile radio telephone, one of a network connected to the telephone system by a computer-controlled communication system. Service areas are divided into small 'cells', about 5 km/3 mi across, each with a separate low-power transmitter.

The cellular system allows the use of the same set of frequencies with the minimum risk of interference. Nevertheless, in crowded city areas, cells can become overloaded. This has led to a move away from analogue transmissions to digital methods that allow more calls to be made within a limited frequency range.

cellular phone wireless phone that operates over radio frequencies and links calls to the public telephone system via a base station; the area covered by each base station is called a cell. Unlike phones connected up by telephone lines, cellular phones allow mobility, as calls can be made while moving from one radio cell to another. A network of connected base stations and exchanges connects the cellular calls to the public telephone system.

cellulite fatty compound alleged by some dietitians to be produced in the body by liver disorder and to cause lumpy deposits on the hips and thighs. Medical opinion generally denies its existence, attributing the lumpy appearance to a type of subcutaneous fat deposit.

celluloid transparent or translucent, highly flammable, plastic material (a ◊thermoplastic) made from cellulose nitrate and camphor. It was once used for toilet articles, novelties, and photographic film, but has now been replaced by the nonflammable substance ◊cellulose acetate.

cellulose complex ◊carbohydrate composed of long chains of glucose units, joined by chemical bonds called glycosidic links. It is the principal constituent of the cell wall of higher plants, and a vital ingredient in the diet of many ◊herbivores. Molecules of cellulose are organized into long, unbranched microfibrils that give support to the cell wall. No mammal produces the enzyme cellulase, necessary for digesting cellulose; mammals such as rabbits and cows are only able to digest grass because the bacteria present in their gut can manufacture it.

Cellulose is the most abundant substance found in the plant kingdom. It has numerous uses in industry: in rope-making; as a source of textiles (linen, cotton, viscose, and acetate) and plastics (cellophane and celluloid); in the manufacture of nondrip paint; and in such foods as whipped dessert toppings.

Japanese chemists produced the first synthetic cellulose in 1996 and the gene for the plant enzyme that makes cellulose was identified by Australian biologists in 1998.

cellulose acetate or **cellulose ethanoate** chemical (an ◊ester) made by the action of acetic acid (ethanoic acid) on cellulose. It is used in making transparent film, especially photographic film; unlike its predecessor, celluloid, it is not flammable.

cellulose nitrate or ***nitrocellulose*** series of esters of cellulose with up to three nitrate (NO_3) groups per monosaccharide unit. It is made by the action of concentrated nitric acid on cellulose (for example, cotton waste) in the presence of concentrated sulphuric acid. Fully nitrated cellulose (gun cotton) is explosive, but esters with fewer nitrate groups were once used in making lacquers, rayon, and plastics, such as coloured and photographic film, until replaced by the nonflammable cellulose acetate. ◊Celluloid is a form of cellulose nitrate.

cell wall in plants, the tough outer surface of the cell. It is constructed from a mesh of ◊cellulose and is very strong and relatively inelastic. Most living cells are turgid (swollen with water; see ◊turgor) and develop an internal hydrostatic pressure (wall pressure) that acts against the cellulose wall. The result of this turgor pressure is to give the cell, and therefore the plant, rigidity. Plants that are not woody are particularly reliant on this form of support.

The cellulose in cell walls plays a vital role in global nutrition. No vertebrate is able to produce cellulase, the enzyme necessary for the breakdown of cellulose into sugar. Yet most mammalian herbivores rely on cellulose, using secretions from microorganisms living in the gut to break it down. Humans cannot digest the cellulose of the cell walls; they possess neither the correct gut microorganisms nor the necessary grinding teeth. However, cellulose still forms a necessary part of the human diet as ◊fibre (roughage).

Celsius scale of temperature, previously called centigrade, in which the range from freezing to boiling of water is divided into 100 degrees, freezing point being 0 degrees and boiling point 100 degrees.

The degree centigrade (°C) was officially renamed Celsius in 1948 to avoid confusion with the angular measure known as the centigrade (one hundredth of a grade). The Celsius scale is named after the Swedish astronomer Anders Celsius (1701–1744), who devised it in 1742 but in reverse (freezing point was 100°; boiling point 0°).

Celsius, Anders (1701–1744)

Swedish astronomer, physicist, and mathematician who introduced the Celsius scale of temperature. His other scientifc works include a paper on accurately determining the shape and size of the Earth, some of the first attempts to gauge the magnitude of the stars in the constellation Aries, and a study of the falling water level of the Baltic Sea.

Mary Evans Picture Library

CELSIUS, ANDERS (1701–1744)

http://www.astro.uu.se/history/Celsius_eng.html

Biography of Swedish astronomer Anders Celsius. Famous for his creation of the Celsius temperature scale, the astronomer was also the first to realise that the aurora phenomenon was magnetic in nature. A portrait of Celsius is also available from this page.

cement any bonding agent used to unite particles in a single mass or to cause one surface to adhere to another. **Portland cement** is a powder obtained from burning together a mixture of lime (or chalk) and clay, which when mixed with water and sand or gravel turns into mortar or concrete.

In geology, cement refers to a chemically precipitated material such as carbonate that occupies the interstices of clastic rocks.

The term 'cement' covers a variety of materials, such as fluxes and pastes, and also bituminous products obtained from tar. In 1824 English bricklayer Joseph Aspdin (1779–1855) created and patented the first Portland cement, so named because its colour in the hardened state resembled that of Portland stone, a limestone used in building.

Cenozoic or *Caenozoic* era of geological time that began 65 million years ago and continues to the present day. It is divided into the Tertiary and Quaternary periods. The Cenozoic marks the emergence of mammals as a dominant group, including humans, and the formation of the mountain chains of the Himalayas and the Alps.

censorship banning of certain types of information from public access. Concerns over the ready availability of material such as bomb recipes and pornography have led a number of countries to pass laws attempting to censor the Internet. The best known of these is the US ◊Communications Decency Act 1996, but initiatives have been taken in other countries, for example Singapore, which announced 1996 new regulations bringing the Internet under the Singapore Broadcasting Authority and requiring all access providers and users to be registered and licensed. Less formal pressures have been applied against ◊Internet Service Providers in Germany and the UK to block specific types of material.

centaur in astronomy, cometlike object with an unstable orbit of less than 200 years. They are 100–400 km in diameter and are redder than other asteroids. The six known centaurs originated in the ◊Kuiper belt. ◊Chiron and ◊Pholus are centaurs.

Centaurus large, bright constellation of the southern hemisphere, represented as a centaur. Its brightest star, ◊Alpha Centauri, is a triple star, and contains the closest star to the Sun, Proxima Centauri, which is only 4.3 light years away. Omega Centauri, which is just visible to the naked eye as a hazy patch, is the largest and brightest ◊globular cluster of stars in the sky, 16,000 light years away.

Alpha and Beta Centauri are both of the first magnitude and, like Alpha and Beta Ursae Majoris, are known as 'the Pointers', as a line joining them leads to ◊Crux. Centaurus A, a galaxy 15 million light years away, is a strong source of radio waves and X-rays.

centigrade former name for the ◊Celsius temperature scale.

centipede jointed-legged animal of the group Chilopoda, members of which have a distinct head and a single pair of long antennae. Their bodies are composed of segments (which may number nearly 200), each of similar form and bearing a single pair of legs. Most are small, but the tropical *Scolopendra gigantea* may reach 30 cm/1 ft in length. **Millipedes**, class Diplopoda, have fewer segments (up to 100), but have two pairs of legs on each.

Nocturnal, frequently blind, and all carnivorous, centipedes live in moist, dark places, and protect themselves by a poisonous secretion. They have a pair of poison claws, and strong jaws with poison fangs. The bite of some tropical species is dangerous to humans. Several species live in Britain, *Lithobius forficatus* being the most common.

centipede *A giant centipede of the species* Scolopendra, *active at night in the forests of Madagascar. Unlike millipedes, which have two pairs of legs to each body segment, centipedes have one pair of legs to a segment. They also have venomous fangs with which to immobilize their prey, mostly worms and insects but occasionally small vertebrates.* *Premaphotos Wildlife*

central dogma in genetics and evolution, the fundamental belief that ◊genes can affect the nature of the physical body, but that changes in the body (◊acquired character, for example, through use or accident) cannot be translated into changes in the genes.

central heating system of heating from a central source, typically of a house, larger building, or group of buildings, as opposed to heating each room individually. Steam heat and hot-water heat are the most common systems in use. Water is heated in a furnace burning oil, gas, or solid fuel, and, as steam or hot water, is then pumped through radiators in each room. The level of temperature can be selected by adjusting a ◊thermostat on the burner or in a room.

Central heating has its origins in the hypocaust heating system introduced by the Romans nearly 2,000 years ago. From the 18th century, steam central heating, usually by pipe, was available in the West and installed in individual houses on an ad hoc basis. The Scottish engineer James ◊Watt heated his study with a steam pipe connected to a boiler, and Matthew Boulton installed steam heating in a friend's Birmingham house. Not until the latter half of the

20th century was central heating in general use. Central heating systems are usually switched on and off by a time switch. Another kind of central heating system uses hot air, which is pumped through ducts (called risers) to grills in the rooms. Underfloor heating (called radiant heat) is used in some houses, the heat coming from electric elements buried in the floor. New energy-efficient houses use heat from the Sun and good insulation to replace some central heating.

central nervous system (CNS) the brain and spinal cord, as distinct from other components of the ◊nervous system. The CNS integrates all nervous function.

In invertebrates it consists of a paired ventral nerve cord with concentrations of nerve-cell bodies, known as ◊ganglia in each segment, and a small brain in the head. Some simple invertebrates, such as sponges and jellyfishes, have no CNS but a simple network of nerve cells called a nerve net.

central processing unit (CPU) main component of a computer, the part that executes individual program instructions and controls the operation of other parts. It is sometimes called the central processor or, when contained on a single integrated circuit, a microprocessor.

The CPU has three main components: the **arithmetic and logic unit** (ALU), where all calculations and logical operations are carried out; a **control unit**, which decodes, synchronizes, and executes program instructions; and the **immediate access memory**, which stores the data and programs on which the computer is currently working. All these components contain ◊registers, which are memory locations reserved for specific purposes.

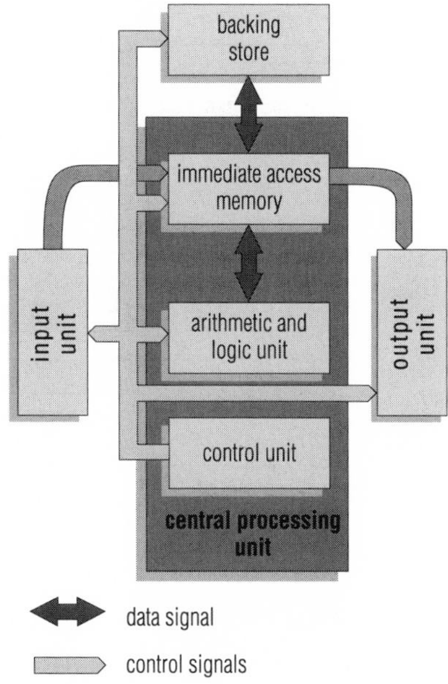

central processing unit *The relationship between the three main areas of a computer's central processing unit. The arithmetic and logic unit (ALU) does the arithmetic, using the registers to store intermediate results, supervised by the control unit. Input and output circuits connect the ALU to external memory, input, and output devices.*

centre of gravity the point in an object about which its weight is evenly balanced. In a uniform gravitational field, this is the same as the centre of mass.

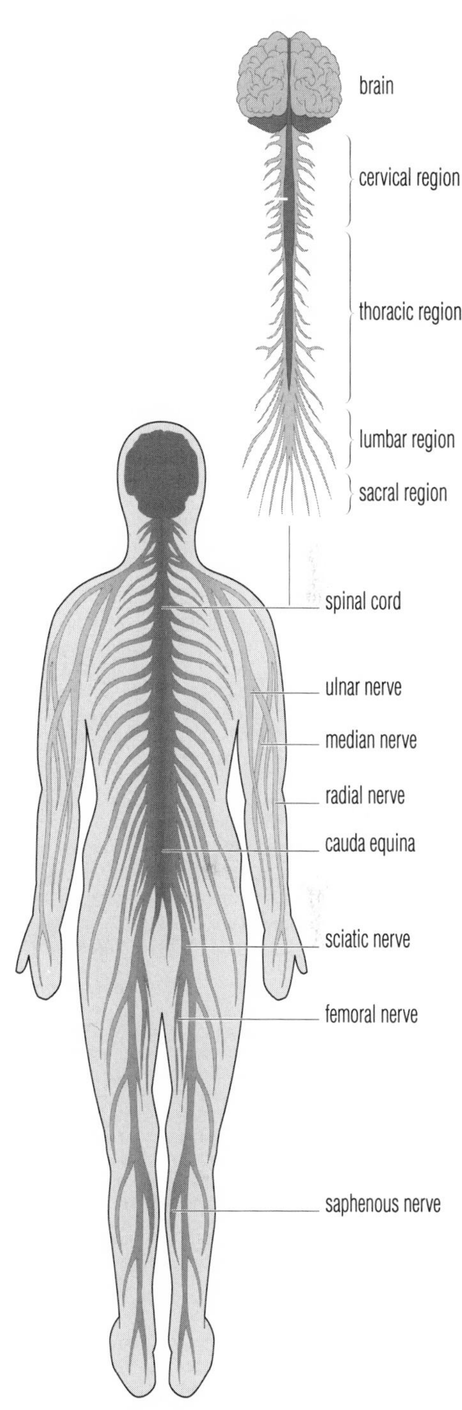

central nervous system *The central nervous system (CNS) with its associated nerves. The CNS controls and integrates body functions. In humans and other vertebrates it consists of a brain and a spinal cord, which are linked to the body's muscles and organs by means of the peripheral nervous system.*

Were it not for gravity one man might hurl another by a puff of his breath into the depths of space, beyond recall for all eternity.

RUGGERIO GIUSEPPE BOSCOVICH Croatian-born Italian scientist. *Theoria*

centre of mass point in or near an object at which the whole mass of the object may be considered to be concentrated. A symmetrical homogeneous object such as a sphere or cube has its centre of mass at its geometrical centre; a hollow object (such as a cup) may have its centre of mass in space inside the hollow.

For an object to be in stable equilibrium, a vertical line down through its centre of mass must run within the boundaries of its base; if tilted until this line falls outside the base, the object becomes unstable and topples over.

centrifugal force useful concept in physics, based on an apparent (but not real) force. It may be regarded as a force that acts radially outward from a spinning or orbiting object, thus balancing the ◊centripetal force (which is real). For an object of mass m moving with a velocity v in a circle of radius r, the centrifugal force F equals mv^2/r (outward).

centrifuge apparatus that rotates containers at high speeds, creating centrifugal forces. One use is for separating mixtures of substances of different densities.

The mixtures are usually spun horizontally in balanced containers ('buckets'), and the rotation sets up centrifugal forces, causing their components to separate according to their densities. A common example is the separation of the lighter plasma from the heavier blood corpuscles in certain blood tests. The **ultracentrifuge** is a very high-speed centrifuge, used in biochemistry for separating ◊colloids and organic substances; it may operate at several million revolutions per minute. The centrifuges used in the industrial separation of cream from milk, and yeast from fermented wort (infused malt), operate by having mixtures pumped through a continually rotating chamber, the components being tapped off at different points. Large centrifuges are used for physiological research – for example, in astronaut training where bodily responses to gravitational forces many times the normal level are tested.

centriole structure found in the ◊cells of animals that plays a role in the processes of ◊meiosis and ◊mitosis (cell division).

centripetal force force that acts radially inward on an object moving in a curved path. For example, with a weight whirled in a circle at the end of a length of string, the centripetal force is the tension in the string. For an object of mass m moving with a velocity v in a circle of radius r, the centripetal force F equals mv^2/r (inward). The reaction to this force is the ◊centrifugal force.

centromere part of the ◊chromosome where there are no ◊genes. Under the microscope, it usually appears as a constriction in the strand of the chromosome, and is the point at which the spindle fibres are attached during ◊meiosis and ◊mitosis (cell division).

Centronics interface standard type of computer ◊interface, used to connect computers to ◊parallel devices, usually printers. (Centronics was an important printer manufacturer in the early days of microcomputing.)

centrosome cell body that contains the ◊centrioles. During cell division the centrosomes organize the microtubules to form the spindle that divides the chromosomes into daughter cells. Centrosomes were first described in 1887, independently by German biologist Theodor Boveri (1862–1915) and Edouard van Beneden.

cephalopod any predatory marine mollusc of the class Cephalopoda, with the mouth and head surrounded by tentacles. Cephalopods are the most intelligent, the fastest-moving, and the largest of all animals without backbones, and there are remarkable luminescent forms which swim or drift at great depths. They have the most highly developed nervous and sensory systems of all invertebrates, the eye in some closely paralleling that found in vertebrates. Examples include squid, ◊octopus, and ◊cuttlefish. Shells are rudimentary or absent in most cephalopods.

Typically, they move by swimming with the mantle (fold of outer skin) aided by the arms, but can squirt water out of the siphon (funnel) to propel themselves backwards by jet propulsion. Squid, for example, can escape predators at speeds of 11 kph/7mph. Cephalopods grow very rapidly and may be mature in a year. The female common octopus lays 150,000 eggs after copulation, and stays to brood them for as long as six weeks. After they hatch the female dies, and, although reproductive habits of many cephalopods are not known, it is thought that dying after spawning may be typical.

CEPHALOPOD PAGE

http://is.dal.ca/~ceph/wood.html

Introduction to the world of cephalopods, the class which includes the squids, cuttlefish, and octopuses, maintained by a graduate student at Dalhousie University, Canada. As well as some excellent images of marine life, this site also contains biological information about each subgroup.

cephalosporin any of a class of broad-spectrum antibiotics derived from a fungus (genus *Cephalosporium*). They are similar to penicillins and are used on penicillin-resistant infections.

The first cephalosporin was extracted from sewage-contaminated water, and other naturally occurring ones have been isolated from moulds taken from soil samples. Side effects include allergic reactions and digestive upsets. Synthetic cephalosporins can be designed to be effective against a particular ◊pathogen.

Cepheid variable yellow supergiant star that varies regularly in brightness every few days or weeks as a result of pulsations. The time that a Cepheid variable takes to pulsate is directly related to its average brightness; the longer the pulsation period, the brighter the star.

This relationship, the **period luminosity law** (discovered by US astronomer Henrietta Leavitt), allows astronomers to use Cepheid variables as 'standard candles' to measure distances in our Galaxy and to nearby galaxies. They are named after their prototype, Delta Cephei, whose light variations were observed 1784 by English astronomer John Goodricke (1764–1786).

Cepheus constellation of the north polar region, named after King Cepheus of Greek mythology, husband of Cassiopeia and father of Andromeda. It contains the Garnet Star (Mu Cephei), a red supergiant of variable brightness that is one of the reddest-coloured stars known, and Delta Cephei, prototype of the Cepheid ◊variables, which are important both as distance indicators and for the information they give about stellar evolution.

Cerberus genus of viviparous (bearing their young live) and aquatic snakes. They are common to the rivers and estuaries of the East Indies from Bengal to Australia.

C. rhynchops has large ventral scales. None of the species is fatally poisonous to humans.

classification *Cerberus* is in family Colubridae, suborder Serpentes, order Squamata, class Reptilia.

Cercopithecus genus of monkeys consisting of the guenons.

cereal grass grown for its edible, nutrient-rich, starchy seeds. The term refers primarily to wheat, oats, rye, and barley, but may also refer to maize (corn), millet, and rice. Cereals contain about 75% complex carbohydrates and 10% protein, plus fats and fibre (roughage). They store well. If all the world's cereal crop were consumed as whole-grain products directly by humans, everyone could obtain adequate protein and carbohydrate; however, a large proportion of cereal production in affluent nations is used as animal feed to boost the production of meat, dairy products, and eggs.

The term also refers to breakfast foods prepared from the seeds of cereal crops. Some cereals require cooking (porridge oats), but most are ready to eat. Mass-marketed cereals include refined and sweetened varieties as well as whole cereals such as muesli. Whole cereals are more nutritious and provide more fibre than the refined cereals, which often have vitamins and flavourings added to replace those lost in the refining process.

cerebellum part of the brain of ◊vertebrate animals which controls muscle tone, movement, balance, and coordination. It is relatively small in lower animals such as newts and lizards, but large in birds since flight demands precise coordination. The human cerebellum is also well developed, because of the need for balance when walking or running, and for finely coordinated hand movements.

cerebral haemorrhage or ***apoplectic fit*** in medicine, a form of ◊stroke in which there is bleeding from a cerebral blood vessel into the surrounding brain tissue. It is generally caused by degenerative disease of the arteries and high blood pressure. Depending on the site and extent of bleeding, the symptoms vary from transient weakness and numbness to deep coma and death. Damage to the brain is permanent, though some recovery can be made. Strokes are likely to recur.

cerebral hemisphere one of the two halves of the ◊cerebrum.

cerebral palsy any nonprogressive abnormality of the brain occurring during or shortly after birth. It is caused by oxygen deprivation, injury during birth, haemorrhage, meningitis, viral infection, or faulty development. Premature babies are at greater risk of being born with cerebral palsy, and in 1996 US researchers linked this to low levels of the thyroid hormone thyroxine. The condition is characterized by muscle spasm, weakness, lack of coordination, and impaired movement; or there may be spastic paralysis, with fixed deformities of the limbs. Intelligence is not always affected.

CEREBRAL PALSY TUTORIAL

http://galen.med.virginia.edu/~smb4v/tutorials/cp/cp.htm

Multimedia tutorial on cerebral palsy for children and parents. It discusses the causes and different kinds of the disorder, describes a series of therapeutic interventions, and presents equipment of different kinds that can prove useful for children with this debilitating disease.

cerebrum part of the vertebrate ◊brain, formed from the two paired cerebral hemispheres, separated by a central fissure. In birds and mammals it is the largest and most developed part of the brain. It is covered with an infolded layer of grey matter, the cerebral cortex, which integrates brain functions. The cerebrum coordinates all voluntary activity.

Ceres the largest asteroid, 940 km/584 mi in diameter, and the first to be discovered (by Italian astronomer Giuseppe Piazzi 1801). Ceres orbits the Sun every 4.6 years at an average distance of 414 million km/257 million mi. Its mass is about one-seventieth of that of the Moon.

cerium malleable and ductile, grey, metallic element, symbol Ce, atomic number 58, relative atomic mass 140.12. It is the most abundant member of the lanthanide series, and is used in alloys, electronic components, nuclear fuels, and lighter flints. It was discovered 1804 by the Swedish chemists Jöns Berzelius and Wilhelm Hisinger (1766–1852), and, independently, by Martin Klaproth. The element was named after the then recently discovered asteroid Ceres.

cermet (contraction of ***ceramics and metal***) bonded material containing ceramics and metal, widely used in jet engines and nuclear reactors. Cermets behave much like metals but have the great heat resistance of ceramics. Tungsten carbide, molybdenum boride, and aluminium oxide are among the ceramics used; iron, cobalt, nickel, and chromium are among the metals.

CERN particle physics research organization founded 1954 as a cooperative enterprise among European governments. It has laboratories at Meyrin, near Geneva, Switzerland. It was originally known as the **Conseil Européen pour la Recherche Nucléaire** but subsequently renamed **Organisation Européenne pour la Recherche Nucléaire**, although still familiarly known as CERN. It houses the world's largest particle ◊accelerator, the ◊Large Electron Positron Collider (LEP), with which notable advances have been made in ◊particle physics.

In 1965 the original laboratory was doubled in size by extension across the border from Switzerland into France. In 1994 the 19 member nations of CERN approved the construction of the Large Hadron Collider. It is expected to cost £1.25 million and to be fully functional in 2005.

Cerro Tololo Inter-American Observatory observatory on Cerro Tololo mountain in the Chilean Andes operated by AURA (the Association of Universities for Research into Astronomy). Its main instrument is a 4-m/158-in reflector, opened in 1974, a twin of that at Kitt Peak, Arizona, USA.

CERT abbreviation for ◊Computer Emergency Response Team.

cervical cancer in medicine, ◊cancer of the cervix (neck of the womb).

cervical smear in medicine, removal of a small sample of tissue from the cervix (neck of the womb) to screen for changes implying a likelihood of cancer. The procedure is also known as the **Pap test** after its originator, George Papanicolau.

CET abbreviation for ***Central European Time***.

Cetus ***Latin 'whale'*** large constellation on the celestial equator (see ◊celestial sphere), represented as a sea monster or a whale. Cetus contains the long-period variable star ◊Mira, and Tau Ceti, one of the nearest stars, which is visible with the naked eye.

It is named after the sea monster sent to devour Andromeda. Mira is sometimes the most conspicuous object in the constellation, but it is more usually invisible to the naked eye.

CFC abbreviation for ◊chlorofluorocarbon.

CGA (abbreviation for ***colour graphics adapter***) in computing, first colour display system for IBM PCs and compatible machines. It has been superseded by ◊EGA, ◊VGA, ◊SVGA, and◊ XGA.

CGI abbreviation for ◊common gateway interface.

c.g.s. system system of units based on the centimetre, gram, and second, as units of length, mass, and time, respectively. It has been replaced for scientific work by the ◊SI units to avoid inconsistencies in definition of the thermal calorie and electrical quantities.

chacma species of ◊baboon.

Chaetodon genus of spiny-rayed fishes known as ◊butterfly fishes.

Chaetopterus large sedentary bristle-worm (polychaete) that inhabits U-shaped tubes in sand or mud. The tube can be 23 cm/9 in long and the two ends protrude from the surface and can be seen at a very low spring tide.

The worm's body, which is phosphorescent, is divided into three regions with various sizes of fans and bristles. These aid in spinning a mucous net, which filters out particles suspended in the sea water and is then eaten by the worm, another being spun in its place about once an hour.

classification *Chaetopterus* is a member of class Polychaeta in phylum Annelida.

chafer beetle of the family Scarabeidae. The adults eat foliage or flowers, and the underground larvae feed on roots, chiefly those of grasses and cereals, and can be very destructive. Examples are the ◊cockchafer **and the rose chafer** *Cetonia aurata,* about 2 cm/0.8 in long and bright green.

chaffinch bird *Fringilla coelebs* of the finch family, common throughout much of Europe and W Asia. About 15 cm/6 in long, the male is olive-brown above, with a bright chestnut breast, a bluish-grey cap, and two white bands on the upper part of the wing; the female is duller. During winter they form single-sex flocks.

Chagas's disease disease common in Central and South America, infecting approximately 18 million people worldwide. It is caused by a trypanosome parasite, *Trypanosoma cruzi,* transmitted by several species of blood-sucking insect; it results in incurable damage to the heart, intestines, and brain. It is named after Brazilian doctor Carlos Chagas (1879–1934).

It is the world's third most prevalent parasitic disease, after malaria and schistosomiasis. In its first stage symptoms resemble flu but 20–30% of sufferers develop inflammation of the heart muscles up to 20 years later.

chain reaction in chemistry, a succession of reactions, usually involving ◊free radicals, where the products of one stage are the reactants of the next. A chain reaction is characterized by the continual generation of reactive substances.

A chain reaction comprises three separate stages: **initiation** – the initial generation of reactive species; **propagation** – reactions that involve reactive species and generate similar or different reactive species; and **termination** – reactions that involve the reactive species but produce only stable, nonreactive substances. Chain reactions may occur slowly (for example, the oxidation of edible oils) or accelerate as the number of reactive species increases, ultimately resulting in explosion.

chain reaction in nuclear physics, a fission reaction that is maintained because neutrons released by the splitting of some atomic nuclei themselves go on to split others, releasing even more neutrons. Such a reaction can be controlled (as in a nuclear reactor) by using moderators to absorb excess neutrons. Uncontrolled, a chain reaction produces a nuclear explosion (as in an atom bomb).

chalaza glutinous mass of transparent albumen supporting the yolk inside birds' eggs. The chalaza is formed as the egg slowly passes down the oviduct, when it also acquires its coiled structure.

chalcedony form of the mineral quartz, SiO_2, in which the crystals are so fine-grained that they are impossible to distinguish with a microscope (cryptocrystalline). Agate, onyx, and carnelian are ◊gem varieties of chalcedony.

chalcopyrite copper iron sulphide mineral, $CuFeS_2$, the most common ore of copper. It is brassy yellow in colour and may have an iridescent surface tarnish. It occurs in many different types of mineral vein, in rocks ranging from basalt to limestone.

chalk soft, fine-grained, whitish sedimentary rock composed of calcium carbonate, $CaCO_3$, extensively quarried for use in cement, lime, and mortar, and in the manufacture of cosmetics and toothpaste. **Blackboard chalk** in fact consists of gypsum (calcium sulphate, $CaSO_4.2H_2O$).

Chalk was once thought to derive from the remains of microscopic animals or foraminifera. In 1953, however, it was seen under the electron microscope to be composed chiefly of ◊coccolithophores, unicellular lime-secreting algae, and hence primarily of plant origin. It is formed from deposits of deep-sea sediments called oozes.

Challenger orbiter used in the US ◊space shuttle programme which on 28 January 1986 exploded on takeoff, killing all seven crew members.

chameleon any of 80 or so species of lizard of the family Chameleontidae. Some species have highly developed colour-changing abilities, caused by stress and changes in the intensity of light and temperature, which alter the dispersal of pigment granules in the layers of cells beneath the outer skin.

The tail is long and highly prehensile, assisting the animal when climbing. Most chameleons live in trees and move very slowly.

The tongue is very long, protrusile, and covered with a viscous secretion; it can be shot out with great rapidity to 20 cm/8 in for the capture of insects. The eyes are on 'turrets', move independently, and can swivel forward to give stereoscopic vision for 'shooting'. Most live in Africa and Madagascar, but the **common chameleon** *Chameleo chameleon* is found in Mediterranean countries; two species live in SW Arabia, and one species in India and Sri Lanka.

Some species of chameleon, such as the African species *C. bitaeniatus* give birth to live young; the female 'gives birth' to a fully-formed young enclosed in a membrane, which is immediately shed.

chamois goatlike mammal *Rupicapra rupicapra* found in mountain ranges of S Europe and Asia Minor. It is brown, with dark patches running through the eyes, and can be up to 80 cm/2.6 ft high. Chamois are very sure-footed, and live in herds of up to 30 members.

Both sexes have horns which may be 20 cm/8 in long. These are set close together and go up vertically, forming a hook at the top. Chamois skin is very soft, and excellent for cleaning glass, but the chamois is now comparatively rare and 'chamois leather' is often made from the skin of sheep and goats.

champignon any of a number of edible fungi (see ◊fungus). The fairy ring champignon (*Marasmius oreades*) has this name because its fruiting bodies (mushrooms) grow in rings around the outer edge of the underground mycelium (threadlike body) of the fungus. (Family Agaricaceae.)

chance likelihood, or ◊probability, of an event taking place, expressed as a fraction or percentage. For example, the chance that a tossed coin will land heads up is 50%.

As a science, it originated when the Chevalier de Méré consulted Blaise ◊Pascal about how to reduce his gambling losses. In 1664, in correspondence with another mathematician, Pierre de ◊Fermat, Pascal worked out the foundations of the theory of chance. This underlies the science of statistics.

> *I have been trying to point out that in our lives chance may have an astonishing influence and, if I may offer advice to the young laboratory worker, it would be this – never to neglect an extraordinary appearance or happening. It may be – usually is, in fact – a false alarm that leads to nothing, but it may on the other hand be the clue provided by fate to lead you to some important advance.*
>
> ALEXANDER FLEMING Scottish bacteriologist.
> Lecture at Harvard

chancroid or ***soft sore*** acute localized, sexually transmitted ulcer on or about the genitals caused by the bacterium *Haemophilus ducreyi.*

It causes painful enlargement and suppuration of lymph nodes in the groin area.

Chandrasekhar limit or ***Chandrasekhar mass*** in astrophysics, the maximum possible mass of a ◊white dwarf star. The limit depends slightly on the composition of the star but is equivalent to 1.4 times the mass of the Sun. A white dwarf heavier than the Chandrasekhar limit would collapse under its own weight to form a ◊neutron star or a ◊black hole. The limit is named after the

CHAMELEONS

http://www.skypoint.com/members/mikefry/chams.html

Excellent guide to the expensive and time-consuming business of looking after a pet chameleon. Would-be owners are warned not to support the trade in endangered species. Dietary and housing requirements are well-explained, together with advice on what to do if your lizard is stressed, goes on hunger strike, has parasites, or does not get enough unfiltered sunlight. There are links to a number of specialist sites related to chameleons in the wild or in captivity.

Indian-US astrophysicist Subrahmanyan Chandrasekhar who developed the theory of white dwarfs in the 1930s.

change of state in science, a change in the physical state (solid, liquid, or gas) of a material. For instance, melting, boiling, evaporation, and their opposites, solidification and condensation, are changes of state. The former set of changes are brought about by heating or decreased pressure; the latter by cooling or increased pressure.

These changes involve the absorption or release of heat energy, called ◊latent heat, even though the temperature of the material does not change during the transition between states.

See also ◊states of matter. In the unusual change of state called **sublimation**, a solid changes directly to a gas without passing through the liquid state. For example, solid carbon dioxide (dry ice) sublimes to carbon dioxide gas.

channel in computing, path connecting a computer to peripheral devices along which data can be transferred.

channel efficiency measure of the ability of a river channel to discharge water. Channel efficiency can be assessed by calculating the channel's ◊hydraulic radius. The most efficient channels are generally semicircular in cross-section, and it is this shape that water engineers try to create when altering a river channel to reduce the risk of flooding.

Surely John Bull will not endanger his birthright, his liberty, his property, simply in order that men and women may cross between England and France without running the risk of sea-sickness.

GARNET WOLSELEY English soldier.
On the Channel Tunnel proposals of 1882

Channel Tunnel tunnel built beneath the English Channel, linking Britain with mainland Europe. It comprises twin rail tunnels, 50 km/31 mi long and 7.3 m/24 ft in diameter, located 40 m/130 ft beneath the seabed. Construction began in 1987, and the French and English sections were linked in December 1990. It was officially opened on 6 May 1994. The shuttle train service, Le Shuttle, opened to lorries in May 1994 and to cars in December 1994. The tunnel's high-speed train service, Eurostar, linking London to Paris and Brussels, opened in November 1994.

The estimated cost of the tunnel has continually been revised upwards to a figure of £8 billion (1995). In 1995 Eurotunnel plc, the Anglo-French company that built the tunnel, made a loss of £925 million.

chanterelle edible ◊fungus that is bright yellow and funnel-shaped. It grows in deciduous woodland. (*Cantharellus cibarius*, family Cantharellaceae.)

Chaos Theory: The Mathematics of Chaos

BY IAN STEWART

The mathematics of chaos

Why are tides predictable years ahead, whereas weather forecasts often go wrong within a few days?

Both tides and weather are governed by natural laws. Tides are caused by the gravitational attraction of the Sun and Moon; the weather by the motion of the atmosphere under the influence of heat from the Sun. The law of gravitation is not noticeably simpler than the laws of fluid dynamics; yet for weather the resulting behaviour seems to be far more complicated.

The reason for this is 'chaos', which lies at the heart of one of the most exciting and most rapidly expanding areas of mathematical research, the theory of nonlinear dynamic systems.

Random behaviour in dynamic systems

It has been known for a long time that dynamic systems – systems that change with time according to fixed laws – can exhibit regular patterns, such as repetitive cycles. Thanks to new mathematical techniques, emphasizing shape rather than number, and to fast and sophisticated computer graphics, we now know that dynamic systems can also behave randomly. The difference lies not in the complexity of the formulae that define their mathematics, but in the geometrical features of the dynamics. This is a remarkable discovery: random behaviour in a system whose mathematical description contains no hint whatsoever of randomness.

Simple geometric structure produces simple dynamics. For example, if the geometry shrinks everything towards a fixed point, then the motion tends towards a steady state. But if the dynamics keep stretching things apart and then folding them together again, the motion tends to be chaotic – like food being mixed in a bowl. The motion of the Sun and Moon, on the kind of timescale that matters when we want to predict the tides, is a series of regular cycles, so prediction is easy. The changing patterns of the weather involve a great deal of stretching and folding, so here chaos reigns.

Fractals

The geometry of chaos can be explored using theoretical mathematical techniques such as topology – 'rubber-sheet geometry' – but the most vivid pictures are obtained using computer graphics. The geometric structures of chaos are 'fractals': they have detailed form on all scales of magnification. Order and chaos, traditionally seen as opposites, are now viewed as two aspects of the same basic process, the evolution of a system in time. Indeed, there are now examples where both order and chaos occur naturally within a single geometrical form.

Predicting the unpredictable

Does chaos make randomness predictable? Sometimes. If what looks like random behaviour is actually governed by a dynamic system, then short-term prediction becomes possible. Long-term prediction is not as easy, however. In chaotic systems any initial error of measurement, however small, will grow rapidly and eventually ruin the prediction. This is known as the butterfly effect: if a butterfly flaps its wings, a month later the air disturbance created may cause a hurricane.

Chaos can be applied to many areas of science, such as chemistry, engineering, computer science, biology, electronics, and astronomy. For example, although the short-term motions of the Sun and Moon are not chaotic, the long-term motion of the Solar System **is** chaotic. It is impossible to predict on which side of the Sun Pluto will lie in 200 million years' time. Saturn's satellite Hyperion tumbles chaotically. Chaos caused by Jupiter's gravitational field can fling asteroids out of orbit, towards the Earth. Disease epidemics, locust plagues, and irregular heartbeats are more down-to-earth examples of chaos, on a more human timescale.

Making sense of chaos

Chaos places limits on science: it implies that even when we know the equations that govern a system's behaviour, we may not in practice be able to make effective predictions. On the other hand, it opens up new avenues for discovery, because it implies that apparently random phenomena may have simple, nonrandom explanations. So chaos is changing the way scientists think about what they do: the relation between determinism and chance, the role of experiment, the computability of the world, the prospects for prediction, and the interaction between mathematics, science, and nature. Chaos cuts right across traditional subject boundaries, and distinctions between pure and applied mathematicians, between mathematicians and physicists, between physicists and biologists, become meaningless when compared to the unity revealed by their joint efforts.

chaos theory or ***chaology*** or ***complexity theory*** branch of mathematics that attempts to describe irregular, unpredictable systems – that is, systems whose behaviour is difficult to predict because there are so many variable or unknown factors. Weather is an example of a chaotic system.

Chaos theory, which attempts to predict the *probable* behaviour of such systems, based on a rapid calculation of the impact of as wide a range of elements as possible, emerged in the 1970s with the development of sophisticated computers. First developed for use in meteorology, it has also been used in such fields as economics.

char or **charr** fish *Salvelinus alpinus* related to the trout, living in the Arctic coastal waters, and also in Europe and North America in some upland lakes. It is one of Britain's rarest fish, and is at risk from growing acidification.

Numerous variants have been described, but they probably all belong to the same species.

characin freshwater fish belonging to the family Characidae. There are over 1,300 species, mostly in South and Central America, but also in Africa. Most are carnivores. In typical characins, unlike the somewhat similar carp family, the mouth is toothed, and there is a small dorsal adipose fin just in front of the tail.

Characins are small fishes, often colourful, and they include ◊tetras and ◊piranhas.

character one of the symbols that can be represented in a computer. Characters include letters, numbers, spaces, punctuation marks, and special symbols.

characteristic in mathematics, the integral (whole-number) part of a ◊logarithm. The fractional part is the ◊mantissa.

For example, in base ten, $10^0 = 1$, $10^1 = 10$, $10^2 = 100$, and so on; the powers to which 10 is raised are the characteristics. To determine the power to which 10 must be raised to obtain a number between 10 and 100, say 20 (2×10, or log 2 + log 10), the logarithm for 2 is found (0.3010), and the characteristic 1 added to make 1.3010.

character printer computer ◊printer that prints one character at a time.

character set in computing, the complete set of symbols that can be used in a program or recognized by a computer. It may include letters, digits, spaces, punctuation marks, and special symbols.

extended character set in PC-based computing, the set of 254 characters stored in ◊ROM. Besides the 128 ◊ASCII characters, the set includes block graphics and foreign language characters.

character type check in computing, a ◊validation check to ensure that an input data item does not contain invalid characters. For example, an input name may be checked to ensure that it contains only letters of the alphabet or an input six-figure date may be checked to ensure it contains only numbers.

charcoal black, porous form of ◊carbon, produced by heating wood or other organic materials in the absence of air. It is used as a fuel in the smelting of metals such as copper and zinc, and by artists for making black line drawings. **Activated charcoal** has been powdered and dried so that it presents a much increased surface area for adsorption; it is used for filtering and purifying liquids and gases – for example, in drinking-water filters and gas masks.

Charcoal was traditionally produced by burning dried wood in a kiln, a process lasting several days. The kiln was either a simple hole in the ground, or an earth-covered mound. Today kilns are of brick or iron, both of which allow the waste gases to be collected and used. Charcoal had many uses in earlier centuries. Because of the high temperature at which it burns (2,012°F/1,100°C), it was used in furnaces and blast furnaces before the development of ◊coke. It was also used in an industrial process for obtaining ethanoic acid (acetic acid), in producing wood tar and ◊wood pitch, and (when produced from alder or willow trees) as a component of gunpowder.

charge see ◊electric charge.

charge-coupled device (CCD) device for forming images electronically, using a layer of silicon that releases electrons when struck by incoming light. The electrons are stored in ◊pixels and read off into a computer at the end of the exposure. CCDs have now almost entirely replaced photographic film for applications such as astrophotography where extreme sensitivity to light is paramount.

charged particle beam high-energy beam of electrons or protons. Such beams are being developed as weapons.

Charles, Jacques Alexandre César (1746–1823)

French physicist who studied gases and made the first ascent in a hydrogen-filled balloon in 1783. His work on the expansion of gases led to the formulation of Charles's law.

Hearing of the hot-air balloons of the Montgolfier brothers, Charles and his brothers began experimenting with hydrogen balloons and made their ascent only ten days after the Montgolfiers' first flight. In later flights Charles ascended to an altitude of 3,000 m/10,000 ft.

Mary Evans Picture Library

Charles's law law stating that the volume of a given mass of gas at constant pressure is directly proportional to its absolute temperature (temperature in kelvin). It was discovered by French physicist Jacques Charles 1787, and independently by French chemist Joseph Gay-Lussac in 1802.

The gas increases by 1/273 of its volume at 0°C for each °C rise of temperature. This means that the coefficient of expansion of all gases is the same. The law is only approximately true and the coefficient of expansion is generally taken as 0.003663 per °C.

charlock or ***wild mustard*** annual plant belonging to the cress family, found in Europe and Asia. It has hairy stems and leaves and yellow flowers. (*Sinapis arvensis*, family Cruciferae.)

charm in physics, a property possessed by one type of ◊quark (very small particles found inside protons and neutrons), called the charm quark. The effects of charm are only seen in experiments with particle ◊accelerators. See ◊elementary particles.

chat real-time exchange of messages between users of a particular system. Chat allows people who are geographically far apart to type messages to each other which are sent and received instantly. On a system like ◊America Online, users may chat while playing competitive games or while reading messages, as well as joining public or private 'rooms' to talk with a variety of other users. The biggest chat system is Internet Relay Chat (IRC), which is used for the exchange of information and software as well as for social interaction.

check box small, square box used as a control in ◊dialog boxes. Check boxes ◊toggle functions and are operated by moving the cursor over the box and clicking the mouse button to check or clear the box.

check digit in computing, a digit attached to an important code number as a ◊validation check.

checksum in computing, a ◊control total of specific items of data. A checksum is used as a check that data have been input or transmitted correctly. It is used in communications and in, for example, accounts programs. See also ◊validation.

cheetah large wild cat *Acinonyx jubatus* native to Africa, Arabia, and SW Asia, but now rare in some areas. Yellowish with black spots, it has a slim lithe build. It is up to 1 m/3 ft tall at the shoulder, and up to 1.5 m/5 ft long. It can reach 103 kph/64 mph, but tires after about 400 yards. Cheetahs live in open country where they hunt small antelopes, hares, and birds.

A cheetah's claws do not retract as fully as in most cats. It is the world's fastest mammal. Cheetahs face threats both from ranchers who shoot them as vermin and from general habitat destruction that is reducing the prey on which they feed, especially gazelles. As a result the wild population is thought to have fallen by over half since the 1970s; there are now thought to be no more than 5,000–12,000 left.

CHEETAH

The cheetah can accelerate from zero to 72 kmph/ 45 mph in two seconds.

chelate chemical compound whose molecules consist of one or more metal atoms or charged ions joined to chains of organic residues by coordinate (or dative covalent) chemical ◊bonds.

The parent organic compound is known as a **chelating agent** – for example, EDTA (ethylene-diaminetetraacetic acid), used in chemical analysis. Chelates are used in analytical chemistry, in agriculture and horticulture as carriers of essential trace metals, in water softening, and in the treatment of thalassaemia by removing excess iron, which may build up to toxic levels in the body. Metalloproteins (natural chelates) may influence the performance of enzymes or provide a mechanism for the storage of iron in the spleen and plasma of the human body.

Chelonia order of reptiles containing some 250 species of ◊tortoises, ◊terrapins, and ◊turtles. Members possess a shell made up of bony plates. The upper part of the shell, the carapace, may be fused to the vertebrae and ribs. Chelonians are toothless, with a hardened horny beak.

chemical change change that occurs when two or more substances (reactants) interact with each other, resulting in the production of different substances (products) with different chemical compositions. A simple example of chemical change is the burning of carbon in oxygen to produce carbon dioxide.

chemical element alternative name for ◊element.

chemical equation method of indicating the reactants and products of a chemical reaction by using chemical symbols and formulae. A chemical equation gives two basic pieces of information: (1) the reactants (on the left-hand side) and products (right-hand side); and (2) the reacting proportions (stoichiometry) – that is, how many units of each reactant and product are involved. The equation must balance; that is, the total number of atoms of a particular element on the left-hand side must be the same as the number of atoms of that element on the right-hand side.

$$Na_2CO_3 + 2HCl \rightarrow 2NaCl + CO_2 + H_2O$$

$$\text{reactants} \rightarrow \text{products}$$

This equation states that one molecule of sodium carbonate combines with two molecules of hydrochloric acid to form two molecules of sodium chloride, one of carbon dioxide, and one of water. Double arrows indicate that the reaction is reversible – in the formation of ammonia from hydrogen and nitrogen, the direction depends on the temperature and pressure of the reactants.

$$3H_2 + N_2 \leftrightarrow 2NH_3$$

chemical equilibrium condition in which the products of a reversible chemical reaction are formed at the same rate at which they decompose back into the reactants, so that the concentration of each reactant and product remains constant.

The amounts of reactant and product present at equilibrium are defined by the **equilibrium constant** for that reaction and specific temperature.

chemical family collection of elements that have very similar chemical and physical properties. In the ◊periodic table of the elements such collections are to be found in the vertical columns (groups). The groups that contain the most markedly similar elements are group I, the ◊alkali metals; group II, the ◊alkaline-earth metals; group VII, the ◊halogens; and group 0, the noble or ◊inert gases.

chemical oxygen demand (COD) measure of water and effluent quality, expressed as the amount of oxygen (in parts per million) required to oxidize the reducing substances present.

Under controlled conditions of time and temperature, a chemical oxidizing agent (potassium permanganate or dichromate) is added to the sample of water or effluent under consideration, and the amount needed to oxidize the reducing materials present is measured. From this the chemically equivalent amount of oxygen can be calculated. Since the reducing substances typically include remains of living organisms, COD may be regarded as reflecting the extent to which the sample is polluted. Compare ◊biological oxygen demand.

chemical weathering form of ◊weathering brought about by chemical attack of rocks, usually in the presence of water. Chemical weathering involves the 'rotting', or breakdown, of the original minerals within a rock to produce new minerals (such as ◊clay minerals, ◊bauxite, and ◊calcite). Some chemicals are dissolved and carried away from the weathering source.

A number of processes bring about chemical weathering, such as carbonation (breakdown by weakly acidic rainwater), hydrolysis (breakdown by water), hydration (breakdown by the absorption of water), and oxidation (breakdown by the oxygen in water). The reaction of carbon dioxide gas in the atmosphere with ◊silicate minerals in rocks to produce carbonate minerals (see ◊calcite) is called the 'Urey reaction' after the chemist who proposed it, Harold Urey. The Urey reaction is an important link between Earth's climate and the geology of the planet. It has been proposed that chemical weathering of large mountain ranges like the Himalayas of Nepal can remove carbon dioxide from the atmosphere by the Urey reaction (or other more complicated reactions like it) , leading to a cooler climate as the ◊greenhouse effects of the lost carbon dioxide are diminished.

chemiluminescence the emission of light from a substance as a result of a chemical reaction (rather than raising its temperature). See ◊luminescence.

chemisorption the attachment, by chemical means, of a single layer of molecules, atoms, or ions of gas to the surface of a solid or, less frequently, a liquid. It is the basis of catalysis (see ◊catalyst) and is of great industrial importance.

chemistry branch of science concerned with the study of the structure and composition of the different kinds of matter, the changes which matter may undergo and the phenomena which occur in the course of these changes.

Organic chemistry is the branch of chemistry that deals with carbon compounds. **Inorganic chemistry** deals with the description, properties, reactions, and preparation of all the elements and their compounds, with the exception of carbon compounds. **Physical chemistry** is concerned with the quantitative explanation of chemical phenomena and reactions, and the measurement of data required for such explanations. This branch studies in particular the movement of molecules and the effects of temperature and pressure, often with regard to gases and liquids.

molecules, atoms, and elements All matter can exist in three states: gas, liquid, or solid. It is composed of minute particles termed **molecules**, which are constantly moving, and may be further divided into ◊atoms.

Molecules that contain atoms of one kind only are known as **elements**; those that contain atoms of different kinds are called **compounds**.

compounds and mixtures Chemical compounds are produced by a chemical action that alters the arrangement of the atoms in the

Chemistry: chronology

c. 3000 BC Egyptians were producing bronze – an alloy of copper and tin.
c. 450 BC Greek philosopher Empedocles proposed that all substances are made up of a combination of four elements – Earth, air, fire, and water – an idea that was developed by Plato and Aristotle and persisted for over 2,000 years.
c. 400 BC Greek philosopher Democritus theorized that matter consists ultimately of tiny, indivisible particles, *atomos*.
AD 1 Gold, silver, copper, lead, iron, tin, and mercury were known.
200 The techniques of solution, filtration, and distillation were known.
7th–17th centuries Chemistry was dominated by alchemy, the attempt to transform nonprecious metals such as lead and copper into gold. Though misguided, it led to the discovery of many new chemicals and techniques, such as sublimation and distillation.
12th century Alcohol was first distilled in Europe.
1242 Gunpowder introduced to Europe from the Far East.
1620 Scientific method of reasoning expounded by Francis Bacon in his *Novum Organum*.
1650 Leyden University in the Netherlands set up the first chemistry laboratory.
1661 Robert Boyle defined an element as any substance that cannot be broken down into still simpler substances and asserted that matter is composed of 'corpuscles' (atoms) of various sorts and sizes, capable of arranging themselves into groups, each of which constitutes a chemical substance.
1662 Boyle described the inverse relationship between the volume and pressure of a fixed mass of gas (Boyle's law).
1697 Georg Stahl proposed the erroneous theory that substances burn because they are rich in a certain substance, called phlogiston.
1755 Joseph Black discovered carbon dioxide.
1774 Joseph Priestley discovered oxygen, which he called 'dephlogisticated air'. Antoine Lavoisier demonstrated his law of conservation of mass.
1777 Lavoisier showed air to be made up of a mixture of gases, and showed that one of these – oxygen – is the substance necessary for combustion (burning) and rusting to take place.
1781 Henry Cavendish showed water to be a compound.
1792 Alessandra Volta demonstrated the electrochemical series.
1807 Humphry Davy passed electric current through molten compounds (the process of electrolysis) in order to isolate elements, such as potassium, that had never been separated by chemical means. Jöns Berzelius proposed that chemicals produced by living creatures should be termed 'organic'.
1808 John Dalton published his atomic theory, which states that every element consists of similar indivisible particles – called atoms – which differ from the atoms of other elements in their mass; he also drew up a list of relative atomic masses. Joseph Gay-Lussac announced that the volumes of gases that combine chemically with one another are in simple ratios.
1811 Publication of Amedeo Avogadro's hypothesis on the relation between the volume and number of molecules of a gas, and its temperature and pressure.
1813–14 Berzelius devised the chemical symbols and formulae still used to represent elements and compounds.
1828 Franz Wöhler converted ammonium cyanate into urea – the first synthesis of an organic compound from an inorganic substance.
1832–33 Michael Faraday expounded the laws of electrolysis, and adopted the term 'ion' for the particles believed to be responsible for carrying current.
1846 Thomas Graham expounded his law of diffusion.
1853 Robert Bunsen invented the Bunsen burner.
1858 Stanislao Cannizzaro differentiated between atomic and molecular weights (masses).
1861 Organic chemistry was defined by German chemist Friedrich Kekulé as the chemistry of carbon compounds.
1864 John Newlands devised the first periodic table of the elements.
1869 Dmitri Mendeleyev expounded his periodic table of the elements (based on atomic mass), leaving gaps for elements that had not yet been discovered.
1874 Jacobus van't Hoff suggested that the four bonds of carbon are arranged tetrahedrally, and that carbon compounds can therefore be three-dimensional and asymmetric.
1884 Swedish chemist Svante Arrhenius suggested that electrolytes (solutions or molten compounds that conduct electricity) dissociate into ions, atoms or groups of atoms that carry a positive or negative charge.
1894 William Ramsey and Lord Rayleigh discovered the first inert gases, argon.
1897 The electron was discovered by J J Thomson.
1901 Mikhail Tsvet invented paper chromatography as a means of separating pigments.
1909 Sören Sörensen devised the pH scale of acidity.
1912 Max von Laue showed crystals to be composed of regular, repeating arrays of atoms by studying the patterns in which they diffract X-rays.
1913–14 Henry Moseley equated the atomic number of an element with the positive charge on its nuclei, and drew up the periodic table, based on atomic number, that is used today.
1916 Gilbert Newton Lewis explained covalent bonding between atoms as a sharing of electrons.
1927 Nevil Sidgwick published his theory of valency, based on the numbers of electrons in the outer shells of the reacting atoms.
1930 Electrophoresis, which separates particles in suspension in an electric field, was invented by Arne Tiselius.
1932 Deuterium (heavy hydrogen), an isotope of hydrogen, was discovered by Harold Urey.
1940 Edwin McMillan and Philip Abelson showed that new elements with a higher atomic number than uranium can be formed by bombarding uranium with neutrons, and synthesized the first transuranic element, neptunium.
1942 Plutonium was first synthesized by Glenn T Seaborg and Edwin McMillan.
1950 Derek Barton deduced that some properties of organic compounds are affected by the orientation of their functional groups (the study of which became known as conformational analysis).
1954 Einsteinium and fermium were synthesized.
1955 Ilya Prigogine described the thermodynamics of irreversible processes (the transformations of energy that take place in, for example, many reactions within living cells).
1962 Neil Bartlett prepared the first compound of an inert gas, xenon hexafluoroplatinate; it was previously believed that inert gases could not take part in a chemical reaction.
1965 Robert B Woodward synthesized complex organic compounds.
1981 Quantum mechanics applied to predict course of chemical reactions by US chemist Roald Hoffmann and Kenichi Fukui of Japan.
1982 Element 109, unnilennium, synthesized.
1985 Fullerenes, a new class of carbon solids made up of closed cages of carbon atoms, were discovered by Harold Kroto and David Walton at the University of Sussex, England.
1987 US chemists Donald Cram and Charles Pederson, and Jean-Marie Lehn of France created artificial molecules that mimic the vital chemical reactions of life processes.
1990 Jean-Marie Lehn, Ulrich Koert, and Margaret Harding reported the synthesis of a new class of compounds, called nucleohelicates, that mimic the double helical structure of DNA, turned inside out.
1993 US chemists at the University of California and the Scripps Institute synthesized rapamycin, one of a group of complex, naturally occurring antibiotics and immunosuppressants that are being tested as anticancer agents.
1994 Elements 110 (ununnilium) and 111 (unununium) discovered at the GSI heavy-ion cyclotron, Darmstadt, Germany.
1995 German chemists built the largest ever wheel molecule made up of 154 molybdenum atoms surrounded by oxygen atoms. It has a relative molecular mass of 24,000 and is soluble in water.
1996 Element 112 discovered at the GSI heavy-ion cyclotron, Darmstadt, Germany.
1997 The International Union of Pure and Applied Chemistry (IUPAC) stated that elements 104–109 should be named rutherfordium (104), dubnium (105), seaborgium (106), bohrium (107), hassium (108), and meitnerium (109).

reacting molecules. Heat, light, vibration, catalytic action, radiation, or pressure, as well as moisture (for ionization), may be necessary to produce a chemical change. Examination and possible breakdown of compounds to determine their components is **analysis**, and the building up of compounds from their components is **synthesis**. When substances are brought together without changing their molecular structures they are said to be **mixtures**.

formulas and equations Symbols are used to denote the elements. The symbol is usually the first letter or letters of the English or Latin name of the element – for example, C for carbon; Ca for calcium; Fe for iron (*ferrum*). These symbols represent one atom of the element; molecules containing more than one atom of an element are denoted by a subscript figure – for example, water is H_2O. In some substances a group of atoms acts as a single entity, and these are enclosed in parentheses in the symbol – for example $(NH_4)_2SO_4$ denotes ammonium sulphate. The symbolic representation of a molecule is known as a **formula**. A figure placed before a formula represents the number of molecules of a substance taking part in, or being produced by, a chemical reaction – for example, $2H_2O$ indicates two molecules of water. Chemical reactions are expressed by means of **equations** as in:

$$NaCl + H_2SO_4 \rightarrow NaHSO_4 + HCl$$

This equation states the fact that sodium chloride (NaCl) on being treated with sulphuric acid (H_2SO_4) is converted into sodium bisulphate (sodium hydrogensulphate, $NaHSO_4$) and hydrogen chloride (HCl). See also ◊chemical equation.

metals, nonmetals, and the periodic system Elements are divided into **metals**, which have lustre and conduct heat and electricity, and **nonmetals**, which usually lack these properties. The **periodic system**, developed by John Newlands in 1863 and established by Dmitri ◊Mendeleyev in 1869, classified elements according to their relative atomic masses. Those elements that resemble each other in general properties were found to bear a relation to one another by weight, and these were placed in groups or families. Certain anomalies in this system were later removed by classifying the elements according to their atomic numbers. The latter is equivalent to the positive charge on the nucleus of the atom.

The true use of chemistry is not to make gold but to prepare medicines.

PARACELSUS Swiss physician, alchemist, and scientist. Attributed remark

chemosynthesis method of making ◊protoplasm (contents of a cell) using the energy from chemical reactions, in contrast to the use of light energy employed for the same purpose in ◊photosynthesis. The process is used by certain bacteria, which can synthesize organic compounds from carbon dioxide and water using the energy from special methods of ◊respiration.

Nitrifying bacteria are a group of chemosynthetic organisms which change free nitrogen into a form that can be taken up by plants; nitrobacteria, for example, oxidize nitrites to nitrates. This is a vital part of the ◊nitrogen cycle. As chemosynthetic bacteria can survive without light energy, they can live in dark and inhospitable regions, including the hydrothermal vents of the Pacific ocean. Around these vents, where temperatures reach up to 350°C/662°F, the chemosynthetic bacteria are the basis of a food web supporting fishes and other marine life.

chemotaxis in biology, the property that certain cells have of attracting or repelling other cells. For example, white blood cells are attracted to the site of infection by the release of substances during certain types of immune response.

chemotherapy any medical treatment with chemicals. It usually refers to treatment of cancer with cytotoxic and other drugs. The term was coined by the German bacteriologist Paul Ehrlich for the use of synthetic chemicals against infectious diseases.

chemotropism movement by part of a plant in response to a chemical stimulus. The response by the plant is termed 'positive' if the growth is towards the stimulus or 'negative' if the growth is away from the stimulus.

Fertilization of flowers by pollen is achieved because the ovary releases chemicals that produce a positive chemotropic response from the developing pollen tube.

Cherenkov radiation a type of electromagnetic radiation emitted by charged particles entering a transparent medium at a speed greater than the speed of light in the medium. It appears as a bluish light. Cherenkov radiation can be detected from high-energy cosmic rays entering the Earth's atmosphere. It is named after Pavel Alexseevich Cherenkov, the Russian physicist who first observed it.

Chernobyl town in northern Ukraine, 100 km/62 mi north of Kiev; site of a nuclear power station. On 26 April 1986, two huge explosions occurred at the plant, destroying a central reactor and breaching its 1,000-tonne roof. In the immediate vicinity of Chernobyl, 31 people died (all firemen or workers at the plant) and 135,000 were permanently evacuated. It has been estimated that there will be an additional 20–40,000 deaths from cancer in the following 60 years; 600,000 are officially classified as at risk. According to WHO figures of 1995, the incidence of thyroid cancer in children has increased 200-fold in Belarus as a result of fallout from the disaster.

The Chernobyl disaster occurred as the result of an unauthorized test being conducted, in which the recactor was run while its cooling system was inoperative. The resulting clouds of radioactive isotopes spread all over Europe, from Ireland to Greece. A total of 9 tonnes of radioactive material were released into the atmosphere, 90 times the amount produced by the Hiroshima A-bomb. In all, 5 million people are thought to have been exposed to radioactivity following the blast. In Ukraine, Belarus, and Russia more than 500,000 people were displaced from affected towns and villages and thousands of square miles of land were contaminated.

cherry any of a group of fruit-bearing trees distinguished from plums and apricots by their fruits, which are round and smooth and not covered with a bloom. They are cultivated in temperate regions with warm summers and grow best in deep fertile soil. (Genus *Prunus*, family Rosaceae.)

chervil any of several plants belonging to the carrot family. The garden chervil (*Anthriscus cerefolium*) has leaves with a sweetish smell, similar to parsley. It is used as a garnish and in soups. Chervil originated on the borders of Europe and Asia and was introduced to W Europe by the Romans. (Genus *Anthriscus*, family Umbelliferae.)

chestnut any of a group of trees belonging to the beech family. The Spanish or sweet chestnut (*Castanea sativa*) produces edible nuts inside husks; its timber is also valuable. ◊Horse chestnuts are quite distinct, belonging to the genus *Aesculus*, family Hippocastanaceae. (True chestnut genus *Castanea*, family Fagaceae.)

chevrotain or ***mouse deer*** small forest-dwelling mammals resembling deer. Horns are absent and they reach a maximum height at the shoulder of about 35 cm/14 in. They are active at night and feed mainly on plants and fruit.

There are four species in two genera, *Tragulus* and *Hyemoschus*. *Tragulus* contains three species of small animals, which have more or less the characteristics and habits of some rodents. They inhabit Asia, Malaysia, Sri Lanka, and India. *Hyemoschus* contains only one species, the African **water chevrotain**.

classification Chevrotains are members of the family Tragulidae in the mammalian order Artiodactyla.

chicken domestic fowl; see under ◊poultry.

chickenpox or ***varicella*** common, usually mild disease, caused by a virus of the ◊herpes group and transmitted by airborne droplets. Chickenpox chiefly attacks children under the age of ten. The incubation period is two to three weeks. One attack normally gives immunity for life.

The temperature rises and spots (later inflamed blisters) develop on the torso, then on the face and limbs. The sufferer recovers within a week, but remains infectious until the last scab disappears.

The US Food and Drug Administration approved a chickenpox vaccine in March 1995. Based on a weakened form of the live virus, the vaccine is expected to be 70–90% effective. A vaccine is available in Europe, but is only used in children with an impaired immune system.

chickpea annual leguminous plant (see ◊legume), grown for food in India and the Middle East. Its short hairy pods contain edible seeds similar to peas. (*Cicer arietinum,* family Leguminosae.)

chickweed any of several low-growing plants belonging to the pink family, with small white starlike flowers. (Genera *Stellaria* and *Cerastium,* family Caryophyllaceae.)

chicle milky juice from the sapodilla tree *Achras zapota* of Central America; it forms the basis of chewing gum.

chicory plant native to Europe and W Asia, with large, usually blue, flowers. Its long taproot is used dried and roasted as a coffee substitute. As a garden vegetable, grown under cover, its blanched leaves are used in salads. It is related to ◊endive. (*Cichorium intybus,* family Compositae.)

chiffchaff small songbird *Phylloscopus collybita* of the warbler family, Muscicapidae, order Passeriformes. It is found in woodlands and thickets in Europe and N Asia during the summer, migrating south for winter. About 11 cm/4.3 in long, olive above, greyish below, with yellow-white nether parts, an eyestripe, and usually dark legs, it looks similar to a willow warbler but has a distinctive song.

chigger or ***harvest mite*** scarlet or rusty brown ◊mite genus *Trombicula,* family Trombiculidae, in the order Acarina, common in summer and autumn. Chiggers are parasitic, and their tiny red larvae cause intensely irritating bites in places where the skin is thin, such as behind the knees or between the toes. After a time they leave their host and drop to the ground where they feed upon minute insects.

Chiggers are medically important and can be harmful to humans in two ways: either by the feeding activities of the larval mite, on folds of skin or the edges of hair follicles resulting in painful lesions 0.4–2 cm/0.16–0.8 in long, or by acting as carriers of disease, for example scrub ◊typhus or haemorrhagic fever.

chihuahua smallest breed of dog, 15 cm/10 in high, developed in the USA from Mexican origins. It may weigh only 1 kg/2.2 lb. The domed head and wide-set ears are characteristic, and the skull is large compared to the body. It can be almost any colour, and occurs in both smooth (or even hairless) and long-coated varieties.

chilblain painful inflammation of the skin of the feet, hands, or ears, due to cold. The parts turn red, swell, itch violently, and are very tender. In bad cases, the skin cracks, blisters, or ulcerates.

childbirth the expulsion of a baby from its mother's body following ◊pregnancy. In a broader sense, it is the period of time involving labour and delivery of the baby.

chilli (***North American* chili**) pod, or powder made from the pod, of a variety of ◊capsicum (***Capsicum frutescens***), a small, hot, red pepper. It is widely used in cooking. The hot ingredient of chilli is capsaicin. It causes a burning sensation in the mouth by triggering nerve branches in the eyes, nose, tongue, and mouth.

Capsaicin does not activate the taste buds and therefore has no flavour. It is claimed that people can become physically addicted to it.

CHILLI!

http://www.tpoint.net/~wallen/chili.html

Online adulation of the hottest food in the world with personal recommendations on the many varieties and recipes, as well as how to prepare the chillies themselves.

chimaera fish of the group Holocephali. Chimaeras have thick bodies that taper to a long thin tail, large fins, smooth skin, and a cartilaginous skeleton. They can grow to 1.5 m/4.5 ft. Most chimaeras are deep-water fish, and even *Chimaera monstrosa,* a relatively shallow-living form caught around European coasts, lives at a depth of 300–500 m/1,000–1,600 ft.

chimera or ***chimaera*** in biology, an organism composed of tissues that are genetically different. Chimeras can develop naturally if a ◊mutation occurs in a cell of a developing embryo, but are more commonly produced artificially by implanting cells from one organism into the embryo of another.

CHIMPANZEE

http://www.seaworld.org/animal_bytes/chimpanzeeab.html

Illustrated guide to the chimpanzee including information about genus, size, life span, habitat, gestation, diet, and a series of fun facts.

chimpanzee highly intelligent African ape *Pan troglodytes* that lives mainly in rain forests but sometimes in wooded savanna. Chimpanzees are covered in thin but long black body hair, except for the face, hands, and feet, which may have pink or black skin. They normally walk on all fours, supporting the front of the body on the knuckles of the fingers, but can stand or walk upright for a short distance. They can grow to 1.4 m/4.5 ft tall, and weigh up to 50 kg/110 lb. They are strong and climb well, but spend time on the ground, living in loose social groups. The bulk of the diet is fruit, with some leaves, insects, and occasional meat. Chimpanzees can use 'tools', fashioning twigs to extract termites from their nests.

The **bonobo** or pygmy chimpanzee, *Pan paniscus* is found only in a small area of rainforest in Congo (formerly Zaire). Bonobos are about the same height as 'common' chimpanzees, but they are of a slighter build, with less hair, and stand upright more frequently. They are a distinct species, numbering approximately 10,000.

Chimpanzees are found in an area from W Africa to W Uganda and Tanzania in the east. Studies of chromosomes suggest that chimpanzees are the closest apes to humans, perhaps sharing 99% of the same genes. Trained chimpanzees can learn to communicate with humans with the aid of machines or sign language, but are probably precluded from human speech by the position of the voicebox.

CHIMPANZEE

Sick chimpanzees use natural remedies to heal themselves. Internal parasites are purged by eating certain leaves, and stomach upsets are treated with mouthfuls of earth rich in clay minerals, sodium, iron, and aluminium.

china clay commercial name for ◊kaolin.

chincherinchee poisonous plant *Ornithogalum thyrsoides* of the lily family Liliaceae. It is native to South Africa, and has spikes of long-lasting, white or yellow, waxlike flowers.

chinchilla South American rodent *Chinchilla laniger* found in high, rather barren areas of the Andes in Bolivia and Chile. About the size of a small rabbit, it has long ears and a long bushy tail, and shelters in rock crevices. These gregarious animals have thick, soft, silver-grey fur, and were hunted almost to extinction for it. They are now farmed and protected in the wild.

Chinese crested dog breed of toy dog developed in China, notable for being hairless except for large plumes on its head, feet and tail. Its skin has a blue or pink tinge, sometimes with black spots. Lightly built, it weighs up to 5.5 kg/12 lb.

The 'Powder Puff' variety has long, plume-like, very fine hair all over its body.

chip or ***silicon chip*** another name for an ◊integrated circuit, a complete electronic circuit on a slice of silicon (or other semiconductor) crystal only a few millimetres square.

chipmunk any of several species of small ground squirrel with characteristic stripes along its side. Chipmunks live in North America and E Asia, in a variety of habitats, usually wooded, and take shelter in burrows. They have pouches in their cheeks for carrying food. They climb well but spend most of their time on or near the ground.

The **Siberian chipmunk** *Eutamias sibiricus,* about 13 cm/5 in long, is found in N Russia, N China, and Japan.

chip-set in computing, group of ◊chips that work together to perform a particular set of functions. Standard chip-sets, for example, manage graphics or form the working parts of a modem.

Chiron unusual Solar-System object orbiting between Saturn and Uranus, discovered 1977 by US astronomer Charles T Kowal (1940–).

Initially classified as an asteroid, it is now believed to be a giant cometary nucleus about 200 km/120 mi across, composed of ice with a dark crust of carbon dust. It has a 51-year orbit and a coma (cloud of gas and dust) caused by evaporation from its surface, resembling that of a comet. It is classified as a ◊centaur.

chiropractic in alternative medicine, technique of manipulation of the spine and other parts of the body, based on the principle that physical disorders are attributable to aberrations in the functioning of the nervous system, which manipulation can correct.

Developed in the 1890s by US practitioner Daniel David Palmer, chiropractic is widely practised today by accredited therapists, although orthodox medicine remains sceptical of its efficacy except for the treatment of back problems.

chiru Tibetan species of antelope. It is pale fawn in colour with coarse hair; the male alone has horns, and these are long, straight, ringed and gazellelike. It is nearly 1 m/3.3 ft in height.
classification The chiru *Pantholops hodgsoni* is in the family Bovidae (cattle and antelopes) of order Artiodactyla.

chital another name for the ◊axis deer.

chitin complex long-chain compound, or ◊polymer; a nitrogenous derivative of glucose. Chitin is widely found in invertebrates. It forms the ◊exoskeleton of insects and other arthropods. It combines with protein to form a covering that can be hard and tough, as in beetles, or soft and flexible, as in caterpillars and other insect larvae. It is insoluble in water and resistant to acids, alkalis, and many organic solvents. In crustaceans such as crabs, it is impregnated with calcium carbonate for extra strength.

Chitin also occurs in some ◊protozoans and coelenterates (such as certain jellyfishes), in the jaws of annelid worms, and as the cell-wall polymer of fungi. Its uses include coating apples (still fresh after six months), coating seeds, and dressing wounds. In 1993 chemists at North Carolina State University found that it can be used to filter pollutants from industrial waste water.

chiton group of marine molluscs, ranging in size from 1 cm/0.4 in to 15 cm/6 in; some are littoral (intertidal) whilst others live at greater depths. They live on vegetable matter and are like limpets in habit; they usually attach themselves to rocks, but can crawl by means of their long foot, and are capable of rolling themselves up.

All the species are bilaterally symmetrical, have eight shell-plates embedded partially or entirely in the mantle, and are covered with spicules.
classification Chitons are in class Polyplacophora, phylum Mollusca.

chive or ***chives*** perennial European plant belonging to the lily family, related to onions and leeks. It has an underground bulb, long hollow tubular leaves, and globe-shaped purple flower heads. The leaves are used as a garnish for salads. (*Allium schoenoprasum,* family Liliaceae.)

chlamydia viruslike bacteria which live parasitically in animal cells, and cause disease in humans and birds. Chlamydiae are thought to be descendants of bacteria that have lost certain metabolic processes. In humans, a strain of chlamydia causes ◊trachoma, a disease found mainly in the tropics (a leading cause of blindness); venereally transmitted chlamydiae cause genital and urinary infections.

Protein from *C. Pneumoniae* (which accounts for 10% of pneumonia cases) has been found in 79% of cases of atheroma (furring up of the arteries) in a US study, and it has also been cultured from a diseased coronary artery, providing a possible link between chlamydia infection and heart disease. A link has also been established between *C. Pneumoniae* infection and chronic high blood pressure.

chloral or ***trichloroethanal*** CCl_3CHO oily, colourless liquid with a characteristic pungent smell, produced by the action of chlorine on ethanol. It is soluble in water and its compound chloral hydrate is a powerful sleep-inducing agent.

chlorate any salt derived from an acid containing both chlorine and oxygen and possessing the negative ion ClO^-, ClO_2^-, ClO_3^-, or ClO_4^-. Common chlorates are those of sodium, potassium, and barium. Certain chlorates are used in weedkillers.

chlorella any single-celled, green, freshwater alga of the genus *Chlorella,* 3–10 micrometres in diameter, which can increase its weight by four times in 12 hours. Nutritive content: 50% protein, 20% fat, 20% carbohydrate, 10% phosphate, calcium, and ◊trace elements.

chloride Cl^- negative ion formed when hydrogen chloride dissolves in water, and any salt containing this ion, commonly formed by the action of hydrochloric acid (HCl) on various metals or by direct combination of a metal and chlorine. Sodium chloride (NaCl) is common table salt.

chlorinated solvent any liquid organic compound that contains chlorine atoms, often two or more. These compounds are very effective solvents for fats and greases, but many have toxic properties.

They include trichloromethane (chloroform, $CHCl_3$), tetrachloromethane (carbon tetrachloride, CCl_4), and trichloroethene ($CH_2ClCHCl_2$).

chlorination the treatment of water with chlorine in order to disinfect it; also, any chemical reaction in which a chlorine atom is introduced into a chemical compound.

chlorine *Greek* ***chloros*** ***'green'*** greenish-yellow, gaseous, non-metallic element with a pungent odour, symbol Cl, atomic number 17, relative atomic mass 35.453. It is a member of the ◊halogen group and is widely distributed, in combination with the ◊alkali metals, as chlorates or chlorides.

Chlorine was discovered in 1774 by the German chemist Karl Scheele, but English chemist Humphry Davy first proved it to be an element in 1810 and named it after its colour. In nature it is always found in the combined form, as in hydrochloric acid, produced in the mammalian stomach for digestion. Chlorine is obtained commercially by the electrolysis of concentrated brine and is an important bleaching agent and ermicide, used for sterilizing both drinking water and swimming-pools. As an oxidizing agent it finds many

CHLORINE

http://c3.org/

Designed to promote better understanding of the science of chlorine chemistry, examining how it contributes to an enhancement of our standard of living and quality of life.

applications in organic chemistry. The pure gas (Cl_2) is a poison and was used in gas warfare in World War I, where its release seared the membranes of the nose, throat, and lungs, producing pneumonia. Chlorine is a component of chlorofluorocarbons (CFCs) and is partially responsible for the depletion of the ◊ozone layer; it is released from the CFC molecule by the action of ultraviolet radiation in the upper atmosphere, making it available to react with and destroy the ozone. The concentration of chlorine in the atmosphere in 1997 reached just over 3 parts per billion. It is expected to reach its peak in 1999 and then start falling rapidly due to international action to curb ozone-destroying chemicals.

PROBLEM OF CHLOROFLUOROCARBONS

http://pooh.chem.wm.edu/chemWWW/courses/chem105/projects/group2/page5.html

Excellent graphical presentation of the effect of CFCs on the ozone layer. The information can be readily understood by a general reader wishing to learn more about the chemistry of ozone depletion and why more ultraviolet radiation is reaching the surface of the earth.

chlorofluorocarbon (CFC) a class of synthetic chemicals that are odourless, nontoxic, nonflammable, and chemically inert. The first CFC was synthesized in 1892, but no use was found for it until the 1920s. Since then their stability and apparently harmless properties have made CFCs popular as propellants in ◊aerosol cans, as refrigerants in refrigerators and air conditioners, as degreasing agents, and in the manufacture of foam packaging. They are partly responsible for the destruction of the ◊ozone layer. In June 1990 representatives of 93 nations, including the UK and the USA, agreed to phase out production of CFCs and various other ozone-depleting chemicals by the end of the 20th century.

When CFCs are released into the atmosphere, they drift up slowly into the stratosphere, where, under the influence of ultraviolet radiation from the Sun, they react with ozone (O_3) to form free chlorine (Cl) atoms and molecular oxygen (O_2), thereby destroying the ozone layer that protects Earth's surface from the Sun's harmful ultraviolet rays. The chlorine liberated during ozone breakdown can react with still more ozone, making the CFCs particularly dangerous to the environment. CFCs can remain in the atmosphere for more than 100 years. Replacements for CFCs are being developed, and research into safe methods for destroying existing CFCs is being carried out. In 1996 it was reported that US chemists at Yale University had developed a process for breaking down freons and other gases containing CFCs into nonhazardous compounds.

Since their initial introduction, different CFC compounds have been introduced into the environment as new applications have evolved. Comparisons of the concentrations of different CFC compounds can therefore be used to date ground water flows and even ocean circulation patterns. Ironically, CFC dating provides the environmental industry and research scientists with a powerful new tool for understanding the factors that affect Earth's environment.

The European Union agreed to ban by the end of 1995 the five 'full hydrogenated' CFCs that are restricted under the ◊Montréal Protocol and a range of CFCs used as industrial solvents, refrigerants, and in fire extinguishers.

The tragedy of a scientific man is that he has found no way to guide his own discoveries to a constructive end.

CHARLES A LINDBERGH US aviator. Attributed remark

chloroform (technical name ***trichloromethane***) $CHCl_3$ clear, colourless, toxic, carcinogenic liquid with a characteristic pungent, sickly sweet smell and taste, formerly used as an anaesthetic (now superseded by less harmful substances).

It is used as a solvent and in the synthesis of organic chemical compounds.

chlorophyll green pigment present in most plants; it is responsible for the absorption of light energy during ◊photosynthesis.

The pigment absorbs the red and blue-violet parts of sunlight but reflects the green, thus giving plants their characteristic colour.

Chlorophyll is found within chloroplasts, present in large numbers in leaves. Cyanobacteria (blue-green algae) and other photosynthetic bacteria also have chlorophyll, though of a slightly different type. Chlorophyll is similar in structure to ◊haemoglobin, but with magnesium instead of iron as the reactive part of the molecule.

chloroplast structure (◊organelle) within a plant cell containing the green pigment chlorophyll. Chloroplasts occur in most cells of the green plant that are exposed to light, often in large numbers. Typically, they are flattened and disclike, with a double membrane enclosing the stroma, a gel-like matrix. Within the stroma are stacks of fluid-containing cavities, or vesicles, where ◊photosynthesis occurs.

It is thought that the chloroplasts were originally free-living cyanobacteria (blue-green algae) which invaded larger, non-photosynthetic cells and developed a symbiotic relationship with them. Like ◊mitochondria, they contain a small amount of DNA and divide by fission. Chloroplasts are a type of ◊plastid.

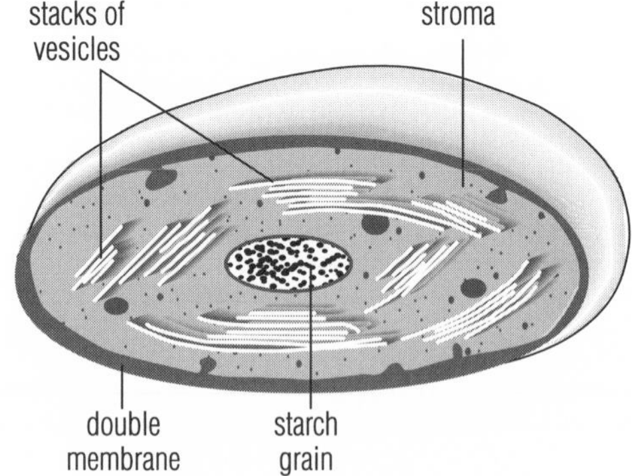

chloroplast *Green chlorophyll molecules on the membranes of the vesicle stacks capture light energy to produce food by photosynthesis.*

chlorosis abnormal condition of green plants in which the stems and leaves turn pale green or yellow. The yellowing is due to a reduction in the levels of the green chlorophyll pigments. It may be caused by a deficiency in essential elements (such as magnesium, iron, or manganese), a lack of light, genetic factors, or viral infection.

choke coil in physics, a coil employed to limit or suppress alternating current without stopping direct current, particularly the type used as a 'starter' in the circuit of fluorescent lighting.

cholecalciferol or ***vitamin D*** fat-soluble chemical important in the uptake of calcium and phosphorous for bones. It is found in liver, fish oils and margarine. It can be produced in the skin, provided that the skin is adequately exposed to sunlight. Lack of vitamin D leads to rickets and other bone diseases.

cholecystectomy surgical removal of the ◊gall bladder. It is carried out when gallstones or infection lead to inflammation of the gall bladder, which may then be removed either by conventional surgery or by a 'keyhole' procedure (see ◊endoscopy).

cholera disease caused by infection with various strains of the bacillus *Vibrio cholerae,* transmitted in contaminated water and characterized by violent diarrhoea and vomiting. It is prevalent in many tropical areas.

The formerly high death rate during epidemics has been much reduced by treatments to prevent dehydration and loss of body salts, together with the use of antibiotics. There is an effective vaccine that must be repeated at frequent intervals for people exposed to continuous risk of infection. The worst epidemic in the Western hemisphere for 70 years occurred in Peru in 1991, with 55,000 confirmed cases and 258 deaths. It was believed to have been spread by the consumption of seafood contaminated by untreated sewage. 1991 was also the worst year on record for cholera in Africa with 13,000 deaths.

cholesterol white, crystalline ◊sterol found throughout the body, especially in fats, blood, nerve tissue, and bile; it is also provided in the diet by foods such as eggs, meat, and butter. A high level of cholesterol in the blood is thought to contribute to atherosclerosis (hardening of the arteries).

Cholesterol is an integral part of all cell membranes and the starting point for steroid hormones, including the sex hormones. It is broken down by the liver into bile salts, which are involved in fat absorption in the digestive system, and it is an essential component of **lipoproteins**, which transport fats and fatty acids in the blood. **Low-density lipoprotein cholesterol** (LDL-cholesterol), when present in excess, can enter the tissues and become deposited on the surface of the arteries, causing ◊atherosclerosis. **High-density lipoprotein cholesterol** (HDL-cholesterol) acts as a scavenger, transporting fat and cholesterol from the tissues to the liver to be broken down. The composition of HDL-cholesterol can vary and some forms may not be as effective as others. Blood cholesterol levels can be altered by reducing the amount of alcohol and fat in the diet and by substituting some of the saturated fat for polyunsaturated fat, which gives a reduction in LDL-cholesterol. HDL-cholesterol can be increased by exercise.

CHOLESTEROL

The Inuit people rarely suffer from heart disease. One explanation for this may be the high amount of fish, notably salmon, in their diet, which reduces the level of blood cholesterol.

chondrite type of ◊meteorite characterized by **chondrules**, small spheres, about 1 mm in diameter, made up of the silicate minerals olivine and orthopyroxene.

chondrule in astronomy a small, round mass of ◊silicate material found. Chondrites (stony ◊meteorites) are characterized by the presence of chondrules.

Chondrules are thought to be mineral grains that condensed from hot gas in the early Solar System, most of which were later incorporated into larger bodies from which the ◊planets formed.

chord in geometry, a straight line joining any two points on a curve. The chord that passes through the centre of a circle (its longest chord) is the diameter. The longest and shortest chords of an ellipse (a regular oval) are called the major and minor axes, respectively.

Chordata phylum of animals, members of which are called ◊chordates.

chordate animal belonging to the phylum Chordata, which includes vertebrates, sea squirts, amphioxi, and others. All these animals, at some stage of their lives, have a supporting rod of tissue (notochord or backbone) running down their bodies.

Chordates are divided into three major groups: ◊tunicates, cephalochordates (see ◊lancelet), and craniates (including all vertebrates).

chorea condition featuring involuntary movements of the face muscles and limbs. It is seen in a number of neurological diseases, including ◊Huntington's chorea.

chorion outermost of the three membranes enclosing the embryo of reptiles, birds, and mammals; the ◊amnion is the innermost membrane.

chorionic villus sampling (CVS) ◊biopsy of a small sample of placental tissue, carried out in early pregnancy at 10–12 weeks' gestation. Since the placenta forms from embryonic cells, the tissue obtained can be tested to reveal genetic abnormality in the fetus. The advantage of CVS over ◊amniocentesis is that it provides an earlier diagnosis, so that if any abnormality is discovered, and the parents opt for an abortion, it can be carried out more safely.

choroid layer found at the rear of the ◊eye beyond the retina. By absorbing light that has already passed through the retina, it stops back-reflection and so prevents blurred vision.

chough bird *Pyrrhocorax pyrrhocorax* of the crow family, Corvidae, order Passeriformes, about 38 cm/15 in long, black-feathered, with red bill and legs, and long hooked claws. Choughs are frugivorous and insectivorous. They make mud-walled nests and live on sea cliffs and mountains from Europe to E Asia, but are now rare.

The **alpine chough** *Pyrrhocorax graculus* is similar, but has a shorter yellow bill and is found up to the snowline in mountains from the Pyrenees to Central Asia.

chow chow breed of dog originating in China in ancient times. About 45 cm/1.5 ft tall, it has a broad neck and head, round catlike feet, a soft woolly undercoat with a coarse outer coat, and a mane. Its coat should be of one colour, and it has an unusual blue-black tongue.

Christmas rose decorative species of ◊hellebore.

Christmas tree any evergreen tree brought indoors and decorated for Christmas. The custom was a medieval German tradition and is now practised in many Western countries.

chroma key in television, technique for substituting backgrounds. For example, the empty studio behind a newscaster may be replaced with an outdoor scene or a frame of video footage. This technique is commonly used on news programmes and other shows that feature 'talking heads'.

A computer analyses the image of the newscaster, who is placed in front of a plain background, usually blue, to identify the exact ◊pixels where the talking figure begins and ends. It can then substitute a new image for just the area specified. The technique allows broadcasters to add visual interest while keeping costs down.

chromatography ***Greek chromos 'colour'*** technique for separating or analysing a mixture of gases, liquids, or dissolved substances. This is brought about by means of two immiscible substances, one of which (**the mobile phase**) transports the sample mixture through the other (**the stationary phase**). The mobile phase may be a gas or a liquid; the stationary phase may be a liquid or a solid, and may be in a column, on paper, or in a thin layer on a glass or plastic support. The components of the mixture are absorbed or impeded by the stationary phase to different extents

CHROMATOGRAPHY

http://www.eng.rpi.edu/dept/chem-eng/Biotech-Environ/CHROMO/chromintro.html

Explanation of the theory and practice of chromatography. Designed for school students (and introduced by a Biotech Bunny), the contents include equipment, analysing a chromatogram, and details of the various kinds of chromatography.

and therefore become separated. The technique is used for both qualitative and quantitive analyses in biology and chemistry.

In **paper chromatography**, the mixture separates because the components have differing solubilities in the solvent flowing through the paper and in the chemically bound water of the paper.

In **thin-layer chromatography**, a wafer-thin layer of adsorbent medium on a glass plate replaces the filter paper. The mixture separates because of the differing solubilities of the components in the solvent flowing up the solid layer, and their differing tendencies to stick to the solid (adsorption). The same principles apply in **column chromatography**.

In **gas–liquid chromatography**, a gaseous mixture is passed into a long, coiled tube (enclosed in an oven) filled with an inert powder coated in a liquid. A carrier gas flows through the tube. As the mixture proceeds along the tube it separates as the components dissolve in the liquid to differing extents or stay as a gas. A detector locates the different components as they emerge from the tube. The technique is very powerful, allowing tiny quantities of substances (fractions of parts per million) to be separated and analysed.

Preparative chromatography is carried out on a large scale for the purification and collection of one or more of a mixture's constituents; for example, in the recovery of protein from abattoir wastes.

Analytical chromatography is carried out on far smaller quantities, often as little as one microgram (one-millionth of a gram), in order to identify and quantify the component parts of a mixture. It is used to determine the identities and amounts of amino acids in a protein, and the alcohol content of blood and urine samples. The technique was first used in the separation of coloured mixtures into their component pigments.

chromite $FeCr_2O_4$, iron chromium oxide, the main chromium ore. It is one of the ◊spinel group of minerals, and crystallizes in dark-coloured octahedra of the cubic system. Chromite is usually found in association with ultrabasic and basic rocks; in Cyprus, for example, it occurs with ◊serpentine, and in South Africa it forms continuous layers in a layered ◊intrusion.

chromium ***Greek chromos 'colour'*** hard, brittle, grey-white, metallic element, symbol Cr, atomic number 24, relative atomic mass 51.996. It takes a high polish, has a high melting point, and is very resistant to corrosion. It is used in chromium electroplating, in the manufacture of stainless steel and other alloys, and as a catalyst. Its compounds are used for tanning leather and for ◊alums. In human nutrition it is a vital trace element. In nature, it occurs chiefly as chrome iron ore or chromite ($FeCr_2O_4$). Kazakhstan, Zimbabwe, and Brazil are sources.

The element was named 1797 by the French chemist Louis Vauquelin (1763–1829) after its brightly coloured compounds.

chromium ore essentially the mineral chromite, $FeCr_2O_4$, from which chromium is extracted. South Africa and Zimbabwe are major producers.

chromogranin protein released by the ◊adrenal gland, along with the hormone adrenaline, during times of stress. There are three types, chromagranin A, B, and C. The function of chromagranins is poorly understood, but they do have an antibacterial affect that could boost the immune system when it is suppressed during times of stress. Chromagranin A also stimulates ◊insulin release and relaxes blood vessels – functions similarly reduced by adrenaline during stress.

chromosome structure in a cell nucleus that carries the ◊genes. Each chromosome consists of one very long strand of DNA, coiled and folded to produce a compact body. The point on a chromosome where a particular gene occurs is known as its locus. Most higher organisms have two copies of each chromosome (they are ◊diploid) but some have only one (they are ◊haploid). There are 46 chromosomes in a normal human cell. See also ◊mitosis and ◊meiosis.

Chromosomes are only visible during cell division; at other times they exist in a less dense form called chromatin.

The first artificial human chromosome was built by US geneticists in 1997. They constructed telomeres, centromeres, and DNA containing genetic information, which they removed from white blood cells, and inserted them into human cancer cells. The cells assembled the material into chromosomes. The artificial chromosome was successfully passed onto all daughter cells.

XY

chromosome The 23 pairs of chromosomes of a normal human male.

chromosphere ***Greek 'colour' and 'sphere'*** layer of mostly hydrogen gas about 10,000 km/6,000 mi deep above the visible surface of the Sun (the photosphere). It appears pinkish red during ◊eclipses of the Sun.

chronic in medicine, term used to describe a condition that is of slow onset and then runs a prolonged course, such as rheumatoid arthritis or chronic bronchitis. In contrast, an **acute** condition develops quickly and may be of relatively short duration.

chronic fatigue syndrome a common debilitating condition also known as myalgic encephalomyelitis (ME), postviral fatigue syndrome, or 'yuppie flu'. It is characterized by a diffuse range of symptoms present for at least six months including extreme fatigue, muscular pain, weakness, depression, poor balance and coordination, joint pains, and gastric upset. It is usually diagnosed after exclusion of other diseases and frequently follows a flulike illness.

CHRONIC FATIGUE SYNDROME FAQ

http://www.cais.com/cfs-news/faq.htm

Extensive answer sheet shedding light on the hottest questions regarding chronic fatigue syndrome. The site deals with issues such as the relation to stress and depression, the possible causes and duration of the illness, and the onset and clinical symptoms of the disease. It also discuss a series of common misunderstandings related to the syndrome.

The cause of CFS remains unknown, but it is believed to have its origin in a combination of viral, social, and psychological factors. Theories based on one specific cause (such as Epstein-Barr virus) have been largely discredited. There is no definitive treatment, but with time the symptoms become less severe. Depression is treated if present, and recent research has demonstrated the effectiveness of ◊cognitive therapy.

chronometer instrument for measuring time precisely, originally used at sea. It is designed to remain accurate through all conditions of temperature and pressure. The first accurate marine chronometer, capable of an accuracy of half a minute a year, was made in 1761 by John Harrison in England.

chrysalis pupa of an insect, but especially that of a ◊butterfly or ◊moth. It is essentially a static stage of the creature's life, when the adult insect, benefiting from the large amounts of food laid down by the actively feeding larva, is built up from the disintegrating larval tissues. The chrysalis may be exposed or within a cocoon.

chrysanthemum any of a large group of plants with colourful, showy flowers, containing about 200 species. There are hundreds of cultivated varieties, whose exact wild ancestry is uncertain. In the Far East the common chrysanthemum has been cultivated for more than 2,000 years and is the imperial emblem of Japan. Chrysanthemums can be grown from seed, but new plants are more commonly produced from cuttings or by dividing up established plants. (Genus *Chrysanthemum,* family Compositae.)

chrysotile mineral in the ◊serpentine group, $Mg_3Si_2O_5(OH)_4$. A soft, fibrous, silky mineral, the primary source of asbestos.

chub freshwater fish *Leuciscus cephalus* of the carp family. Thickset and cylindrical, it grows up to 60 cm/2 ft, is dark greenish or grey on the back, silvery yellow below, with metallic flashes on the flanks. It lives generally in clean rivers throughout Europe.

chyme general term for the stomach contents. Chyme resembles a thick creamy fluid and is made up of partly digested food, hydrochloric acid, and a range of enzymes.

The muscular activity of the stomach churns this fluid constantly, continuing the mechanical processes initiated by the mouth. By the time the chyme leaves the stomach for the duodenum, it is a smooth liquid ready for further digestion and absorption by the small intestine.

Cibachrome in photography, a process of printing directly from transparencies. It can be home-processed and the rich, saturated colours are highly resistant to fading. It was introduced 1963.

cicada any of several insects of the family Cicadidae. Most species are tropical, but a few occur in Europe and North America. Young cicadas live underground, for up to 17 years in some species. The adults live on trees, whose juices they suck. The males produce a loud, almost continuous, chirping by vibrating membranes in resonating cavities in the abdomen.

CICHLID HOME PAGE

http://trans4.neep.wisc.edu/~gracy/fish/opener.html

Comprehensive source of information on cichlidae, their habitats, and how to keep them in an aquarium. There are a large number of photographs. Fish can be searched for by scientific or common names.

cichlid any freshwater fish of the family Cichlidae. Cichlids are somewhat perchlike, but have a single nostril on each side instead of two. They are mostly predatory, and have deep, colourful bodies, flattened from side to side so that some are almost disc-shaped. Many are territorial in the breeding season and may show care of the young. There are more than 1,000 species found in South and Central America, Africa, and India.

The **discus fish** *Symphysodon* produces a skin secretion on which the young feed. Other cichlids, such as those of the genus *Tilapia,* brood their young in the mouth.

cigarette beetle small beetle that feeds preferentially on tobacco products, such as cigarettes and cigars. It may, however, feed on a wide range of other products for example, raisins, ginger, cocoa, drugs, and even straw.
classification The cigarette beetle *Lasioderma serricorne* is a member of the family Anobiidae (furniture beetles) in order Coleoptera, class Insecta, phylum Arthropoda.

cilia (singular ***cilium***) small hairlike organs on the surface of some cells, particularly the cells lining the upper respiratory tract. Their wavelike movements waft particles of dust and debris towards the exterior. Some single-celled organisms move by means of cilia. In multicellular animals, they keep lubricated surfaces clear of debris. They also move food in the digestive tracts of some invertebrates.

ciliary muscle ring of muscle surrounding and controlling the lens inside the vertebrate eye, used in ◊accommodation (focusing). Suspensory ligaments, resembling spokes of a wheel, connect the lens to the ciliary muscle and pull the lens into a flatter shape when the muscle relaxes. When the muscle is relaxed the lens has its longest ◊focal length and focuses rays from distant objects. On contraction, the lens returns to its normal spherical state and therefore has a shorter focal length and focuses images of near objects.

cinchona any of a group of tropical American shrubs or trees belonging to the madder family. The drug ◊quinine is produced from the bark of some species, and these are now cultivated in India, Sri Lanka, the Philippines, and Indonesia. (Genus *Chinchona,* family Rubiaceae.)

cine camera camera that takes a rapid sequence of still photographs called frames. When the frames are projected one after the other on to a screen, they appear to show movement, because our eyes hold on to the image of one picture until the next one appears.

The cine camera differs from an ordinary still camera in having a motor that winds the film on. The film is held still by a claw mechanism while each frame is exposed. When the film is moved between frames, a semicircular disc slides between the lens and the film and prevents exposure.

CinePak in computing, software method of compressing and decompressing ◊QuickTime 'movies', also called a software codec. CinePak takes a recorded QuickTime file and reduces it in size, frame by frame. This is a slow process, but the result is a file that can be played back efficiently by computers with QuickTime installed.

cinnabar mercuric sulphide mineral, HgS, the only commercially useful ore of mercury. It is deposited in veins and impregnations near recent volcanic rocks and hot springs. The mineral itself is used as a red pigment, commonly known as **vermilion**. Cinnabar is found in the USA (California), Spain (Almadén), Peru, Italy, and Slovenia.

cinnamon dried inner bark of a tree belonging to the laurel family, grown in India and Sri Lanka. The bark is ground to make the spice used in curries and confectionery. Oil of cinnamon is obtained from waste bark and is used as flavouring in food and medicine. (*Cinnamomum zeylanicum,* family Lauraceae.)

cinquefoil any of a group of plants that usually have five-lobed leaves and brightly coloured flowers. They is widespread in northern temperate regions. (Genus *Potentilla,* family Rosaceae.)

circadian rhythm metabolic rhythm found in most organisms, which generally coincides with the 24-hour day. Its most obvious manifestation is the regular cycle of sleeping and waking, but body temperature and the concentration of ◊hormones that influence mood and behaviour also vary over the day. In humans, alteration of habits (such as rapid air travel round the world) may result in the circadian rhythm being out of phase with actual activity patterns, causing malaise until it has had time to adjust.

In mammals the circadian rhythm is controlled by the suprachiasmatic nucleus in the ◊hypothalamus. US researchers discovered a second circadian control mechanism in 1996; they found that cells within the retina also produced the hormone melatonin. In 1997, US geneticists identified a gene, *clock*, in chromosome 5 in mice, that regulated the circadian rhythm.

circle perfectly round shape, the path of a point that moves so as to keep a constant distance from a fixed point (the centre). Each circle has a **radius** (the distance from any point on the circle to the centre), a **circumference** (the boundary of the circle), **diameters** (straight lines crossing the circle through the centre), **chords** (lines joining two points on the circumference), **tangents** (lines that touch the circumference at one point only), **sectors** (regions inside the circle between two radii), and **segments** (regions between a chord and the circumference).

The ratio of the distance all around the circle (the circumference) to the diameter is an ◊irrational number called π (**pi**), roughly equal to 3.1416. A circle of radius r and diameter d has a circumference $C = \pi d$, or $C = 2\pi r$, and an area $A = \pi r^2$. The area of a circle can be shown by dividing it into very thin sectors and reassembling them to make an approximate rectangle. The proof of $A = \pi r^2$ can be done only by using ◊integral calculus.

> To remember the circumference and area of a circle:
>
> FIDDLEDEDUM, FIDDLEDEDEE, A RING ROUND THE MOON IS π TIMES D. IF A HOLE IN YOUR SOCK YOU WANT REPAIRED, YOU USE THE FORMULA πR SQUARED.

circuit in physics or electrical engineering, an arrangement of electrical components through which a current can flow. There are two basic circuits, series and parallel. In a ◊series circuit, the components are connected end to end so that the current flows through all components one after the other. In a ◊parallel circuit, components are connected side by side so that part of the current passes through each component. A circuit diagram shows in graphical form how components are connected together, using standard symbols for the components.

circuit breaker switching device designed to protect an electric circuit by breaking the circuit if excessive current flows. It has the same action as a ◊fuse, and many houses now have a circuit breaker between the incoming mains supply and the domestic circuits. Circuit breakers usually work by means of ◊solenoids. Those at electricity-generating stations have to be specially designed to prevent dangerous arcing (the release of luminous discharge) when the high-voltage supply is switched off. They may use an air blast or oil immersion to quench the arc.

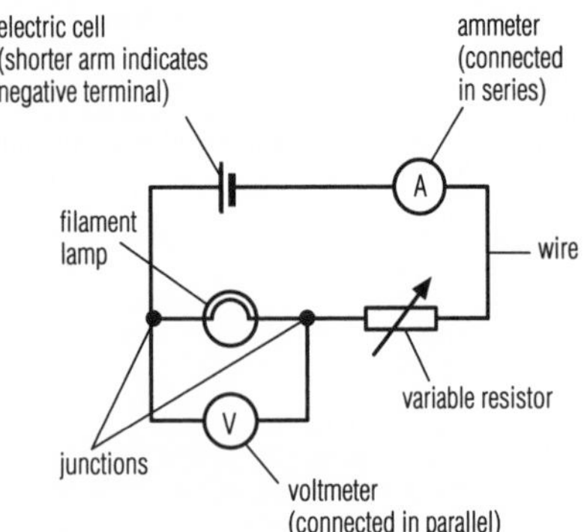

***circuit diagram** A circuit diagram shows in graphical form how the components of an electric circuit are connected together. Each component is represented by an internationally recognized symbol, and the connecting wires are shown by straight lines. A dot indicates where wires join.*

circuit diagram simplified drawing of an electric circuit. The circuit's components are represented by internationally recognized symbols, and the connecting wires by straight lines. A dot indicates where wires join.

circulatory system system of vessels in an animal's body that transports essential substances (blood or other circulatory fluid) to and from the different parts of the body. Except for simple animals such as sponges and coelenterates (jellyfishes, sea anemones, corals), all animals have a circulatory system.

In fishes, blood passes once around the body before returning to a two-chambered heart (single circulation). In birds and mammals, blood passes to the lungs and back to the heart before circulating around the remainder of the body (double circulation). In all vertebrates, blood flows in one direction. Valves in the heart, large arteries, and veins prevent backflow, and the muscular walls of the arteries assist in pushing the blood around the body.

Although most animals have a heart or hearts to pump the blood, normal body movements circulate the fluid in some small invertebrates. In the **open system**, found in snails and other mol-

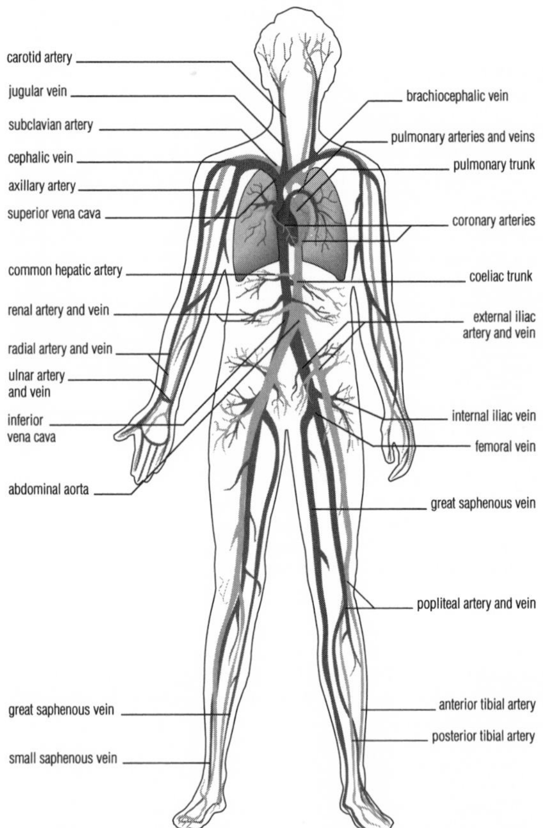

***circulatory system** Blood flows through 96,500 km/60,000 mi of arteries and veins, supplying oxygen and nutrients to organs and limbs. Oxygen-poor blood (blue) circulates from the heart to the lungs where oxygen is absorbed. Oxygen-rich blood (red) flows back to the heart and is then pumped round the body through the aorta, the largest artery, to smaller arteries and capillaries. Here oxygen and nutrients are exchanged with carbon dioxide and waste products and the blood returns to the heart via the veins. Waste products are filtered by the liver, spleen, and kidneys, and nutrients are absorbed from the stomach and small intestine.*

Blood: the Discovery of Circulation

BY JULIAN ROWE

Background
After completing a preliminary medical course at the University of Cambridge, where would an ambitious young man in the 17th century go to get a really good medical training? To the University of Padua in Italy, where the great Italian anatomist Hieronymous Fabricius (1537–1619) taught. So this is where English physician William Harvey (1578–1657) naturally went.

William Harvey had a consuming interest in the movement of the blood in the body. In 1579, Fabricius had publicly demonstrated the valves, which he termed 'sluice gates', in the veins: his principal anatomical work was an accurate and detailed description of them.

Galen's theory
Galen, a Greek physician (c. 130–c. 200), had 1,500 years previously written a monumental treatise covering every aspect of medicine. In this work, he asserted that food turned to blood in the liver, ebbed and flowed in vessels and, on reaching the heart, flowed through pores in the septum (the dividing wall) from the right to left side, and was sent on its way by heart spasms. The blood did not circulate. This doctrine was still accepted and taught well into the 16th century.

One-way flow
Harvey was unconvinced. He had done a simple calculation. He worked out that for each human heart beat, about 60 cm^3 of blood left the heart, which meant that the heart pumped out 259 litres every hour. This is more than three times the weight of the average man.

Harvey examined the heart and blood vessels of 128 mammals and found that the valve which separated the left side of the heart from the right ventricle is a one-way structure, as were the valves in the veins discovered by his tutor Fabricius. For this reason he decided that the blood in the veins must flow only towards the heart.

Harvey's experiment
Harvey was now in a position to do his famous experiment. He tied a tourniquet round the upper part of his arm. It was just tight enough to prevent the blood from flowing through the veins back into his heart – but not so tight that arterial blood could not enter the arms. Below the tourniquet, the veins swelled up; above it, they remained empty. This showed that the blood could be entering the arm only through the arteries. Further, by carefully stroking the blood out of a short length of vein, Harvey showed that it could fill up only when blood was allowed to enter it from the end that was furthest away from the heart. He had proved that blood in the veins must flow only towards the heart.

A new theory of circulation
Galen's pores in the septum of the heart had never been found. Belgian physician Andreas Versalius (1514–1564) was another alumnus of Padua University. Although brought up in the Galen tradition, he had carried out secret dissections to discover the pores, and had failed. He did, however, show that men and women had the same number of ribs!

Harvey clinched his researches into the movement of the blood when he demonstrated that no blood seeps through the septum of the heart. He reasoned that blood must pass from the right side of the heart to the left through the lungs. He had discovered the circulation of the blood, and thus, some 20 years after he left Padua, became the father of modern physiology. In 1628 Harvey published his proof of the circulation of the blood in his classic book

On the Motion of the Heart and Blood in Animals. A new age in medicine and biology had begun.

luscs, the blood (more correctly called ◊haemolymph) passes from the arteries into a body cavity (haemocoel), and from here is gradually returned to the heart, via the gills, by other blood vessels. Insects and other arthropods have an open system with a heart. In the **closed system** of earthworms, blood flows directly from the main artery to the main vein, via smaller lateral vessels in each body segment. Vertebrates, too, have a closed system with a network of tiny ◊capillaries carrying the blood from arteries to veins.

circumcision surgical removal of all or part of the foreskin (prepuce) of the penis, usually performed on the newborn; it is practised among Jews and Muslims. In some societies in Africa and the Middle East, female circumcision or clitoridectomy (removal of the labia minora and/or clitoris) is practised on adolescents as well as babies; it is illegal in the West.

Female circumcision has no medical benefit and often causes disease and complications in childbirth; in 1994 there were at least 90 million women and girls worldwide who had undergone circumcision. Male circumcision too is usually carried out for cultural reasons and not as a medical necessity, apart from cases where the opening of the prepuce is so small as to obstruct the flow of urine. Some evidence indicates that it protects against the development of cancer of the penis later in life and that women with circumcised partners are at less risk from cancer of the cervix.

circumference in geometry, the curved line that encloses a curved plane figure, for example a ◊circle or an ellipse. Its length varies according to the nature of the curve, and may be ascertained by the appropriate formula. The circumference of a circle is πd or $2\pi r$, where d is the diameter of the circle, r is its radius, and π is the constant pi, approximately equal to 3.1416.

circumpolar in astronomy, a description applied to celestial objects that remain above the horizon at all times and do not set as seen from a given location. The amount of sky that is circumpolar depends on the observer's latitude on Earth. At the Earth's poles, all the visible sky is circumpolar, but at the Earth's equator none of it is circumpolar.

circumscribe in geometry, to surround a figure with a circle which passes through all the vertices of the figure. Any triangle may be circumscribed and so may any regular polygon. Only certain quadrilaterals may be circumscribed (their opposite angles must add up to 180°).

cirque French name for a ◊corrie, a steep-sided hollow in a mountainside.

cirrhosis any degenerative disease in an organ of the body, especially the liver, characterized by excessive development of connective tissue, causing scarring and painful swelling. Cirrhosis of the liver may be caused by an infection such as viral hepatitis, chronic obstruction of the common bile duct, chronic alcoholism or drug use, blood disorder, heart failure, or malnutrition. However, often no cause is apparent. If cirrhosis is diagnosed early, it can be arrested by treating the cause; otherwise it will progress to coma and death.

CIS, CI$ abbreviations for ***CompuServe Information Service***; see ◊CompuServe.

CISC (acronym for ***complex instruction-set computer***) in computing, a microprocessor (processor on a single chip) that can carry out a large number of ◊machine code instructions – for example, the Intel 80386. The term was introduced to distinguish them from the more rapid ◊RISC (reduced instruction-set computer) processors, which handle only a smaller set of instructions.

cistron in genetics, the segment of ◊DNA that is required to synthesize a complete polypeptide chain. It is the molecular equivalent of a ◊gene.

CITES (abbreviation for ***Convention on International Trade in Endangered Species***) international agreement under the auspices of the IUCN with the aim of regulating trade in ◊endangered species of animals and plants. The agreement came into force 1975 and by 1997 had been signed by 138 states. It prohibits any trade in a category of 8,000 highly endangered species and controls trade in a further 30,000 species.

Animals and plants listed in Appendix 1 of CITES are classified endangered; those listed in Appendix 2 are classified vulnerable.

citizens' band (CB) short-range radio communication facility (around 27 MHz) used by members of the public in the USA and many European countries to talk to one another or call for emergency assistance.

citric acid $HOOCCH_2C(OH)(COOH)CH_2COOH$ organic acid widely distributed in the plant kingdom; it is found in high concentrations in citrus fruits and has a sharp, sour taste. At one time it was commercially prepared from concentrated lemon juice, but now the main source is the fermentation of sugar with certain moulds.

citronella lemon-scented oil used in cosmetics and insect repellents, obtained from a S Asian grass (*Cymbopogon nardus*).

citrus any of a group of evergreen and aromatic trees or shrubs, found in warm parts of the world. Several species – the orange, lemon, lime, citron, and grapefruit – are cultivated for their fruit. (Genus *Citrus*, family Rutaceae.)

civet small to medium-sized carnivorous mammal found in Africa and Asia, belonging to the family Viverridae, which also includes ◊mongooses **and** ◊**genets**. Distant relations of cats, they generally have longer jaws and more teeth. All have a scent gland in the inguinal (groin) region. Extracts from this gland are taken from the ◊**African civet** *Civettictis civetta* and used in perfumery.

As well as eating animal matter, many species, for example, the SE Asian **palm civet** *Arctogalidia trivirgata*, are fond of fruit.

civil aviation operation of passenger and freight transport by air. With increasing traffic, control of air space is a major problem, and in 1963 Eurocontrol was established by Belgium, France, West Germany, Luxembourg, the Netherlands, and the UK to supervise both military and civil movement in the air space over member countries. There is also a tendency to coordinate services and other facilities between national airlines; for example, the establishment of Air Union in 1963 by France (Air France), West Germany (Lufthansa), Italy (Alitalia), and Belgium (Sabena).

In the UK there are about 170 airports. Heathrow, City, Gatwick, and Stansted (all serving London), Prestwick, and Edinburgh are managed by the British Airports Authority (founded 1965). Close cooperation is maintained with authorities in other countries, including the Federal Aviation Agency, which is responsible for regulating development of aircraft, air navigation, traffic control, and communications in the USA. The Civil Aeronautics Board is the US authority prescribing safety regulations and investigating accidents. There are no state airlines in the USA, although many of the private airlines are large. The world's largest airline was the USSR's government-owned Aeroflot (split among republics in 1992), which operated 1,300 aircraft over 1 million km/620,000 mi of routes. It once carried over 110 million passengers a year, falling to 62 million by 1992.

civil engineering branch of engineering that is concerned with the construction of roads, bridges, airports, aqueducts, waterworks, tunnels, canals, irrigation works, and harbours.

The term is thought to have been used for the first time by British engineer John Smeaton in about 1750 to distinguish civilian from military engineering projects.

Civil Engineers, Institution of the first national body concerned with the engineering profession in England, founded in 1818. The celebrated builder of roads, bridges and canals, Thomas Telford, became its first president.

CIX abbreviation for ◊Compulink Information eXchange.

cladistics method of biological ◊classification (taxonomy) that uses a formal step-by-step procedure for objectively assessing the extent to which organisms share particular characters, and for assigning them to taxonomic groups. Taxonomic groups (for example, ◊species, ◊genus, family) are termed **clades**.

cladode in botany, a flattened stem that is leaflike in appearance and function. It is an adaptation to dry conditions because a stem contains fewer ◊stomata than a leaf, and water loss is thus minimized. The true leaves in such plants are usually reduced to spines or small scales. Examples of plants with cladodes are butcher's-broom *Ruscus aculeatus*, asparagus, and certain cacti. Cladodes may bear flowers or fruit on their surface, and this distinguishes them from leaves.

clam common name for a ◊bivalve mollusc. The giant clam *Tridacna gigas* of the Indopacific can grow to 1 m/3 ft across in 50 years and weigh, with the shell, 500 kg/1,000 lb.

A giant clam produces a billion eggs in a single spawning.

The term is usually applied to edible species, such as the North American hard clam *Venus mercenaria*, used in clam chowder, and whose shells were formerly used as money by North American Indians. A giant clam may produce a billion eggs in a single spawning.

ClariNet commercial news service distributed via USENET. It is not available on all sites since companies must pay to receive ClariNet, which is owned by Clarinet Communications Corp. Under the service's terms and conditions, professional media personnel are banned from using ClariNet news as a source in their work.

Clarke orbit alternative name for ◊geostationary orbit, an orbit 35,900 km/22,300 mi high, in which satellites circle at the same speed as the Earth turns. This orbit was first suggested by space writer Arthur C Clarke in 1945.

class in biological classification, a group of related ◊orders. For example, all mammals belong to the class Mammalia and all birds to the class Aves. Among plants, all class names end in 'idae' (such as Asteridae) and among fungi in 'mycetes'; there are no equivalent conventions among animals. Related classes are grouped together in a ◊phylum.

class in mathematics another name for a ◊set.

classification in biology, the arrangement of organisms into a hierarchy of groups on the basis of their similarities in biochemical, anatomical, or physiological characters. The basic grouping is a ◊species, several of which may constitute a ◊genus, which in turn are grouped into families, and so on up through orders, classes, phyla (in plants, sometimes called divisions), to kingdoms.

> To remember the order of taxonomic classification:
>
> KRAKATOA POSITIVELY CASTS OFF FUMES GENERATING SULPHUROUS VAPOURS.
>
> OR
>
> KINDLY PLACE COVER ON FRESH GREEN SPRING VEGETABLES.
>
> KINGDOM / PHYLUM / CLASS / ORDER / FAMILY / GENUS / SPECIES / VARIETY

Classification of Living Things

Classification is the grouping of organisms based on similar traits and evolutionary histories. Taxonomy and systematics are the two sciences that attempt to classify living things. In taxonomy, organisms are generally assigned to groups based on their characteristics. In modern systematics, the placement of organisms into groups is based on evolutionary relationships among organisms. Thus, the groupings are based on evolutionary relatedness or family histories called phylogenies.

The groups into which organisms are classified are called taxa (singular, taxon). The taxon that includes the fewest members is the species, which consists of a single organism. Closely related species are placed into a genus (plural, genera). Related genera are placed into families, families into orders, orders into classes, classes into phyla (singular, phylum) or, in the case of plants and fungi, into divisions, and phyla into divisions or kingdoms. The kingdom level, of which five are generally recognized, is the broadest taxonomic group and includes the greatest number of species. The table below provides an example of the classification of an organism representative of the animal kingdom and the plant kingdom.

Taxonomic Groups[1]	*Common name Genus*[3]	*Kingdom*	*Phylum/division*[2]	*Class*	*Order*	*Family Species*[3]
human	Animalia	Chordata	Mammalia	Primates	Hominoidea	*Homo sapiens*
Douglas fir	Plantae	Tracheophyta	Gymnospermae	Coniferales	Pinaceae	*Pseudotsuga douglasii*

[1] Intermediate taxonomic levels can be created by adding the prefixes 'super-' or 'sub-' to the name of any taxonomic level.

[2] The term division is generally used in place of phylum/phyla for the classification of plants and fungi.

[3] An individual organism is given a two-part name made up of its genus and species names. For example, Douglas fir is correctly known as *Pseudotsuga douglasii*.

It takes a very unusual mind to undertake the analysis of the obvious.

ALFRED NORTH WHITEHEAD English philosopher and mathematician. *Science and the Modern World*

classify in mathematics, to put into separate classes, or ◊sets, which may be uniquely defined.

class interval in statistics, the range of each class of data, used when dealing with large amounts of data. To obtain an idea of the distribution, the data are broken down into convenient classes, which must be mutually exclusive and are usually equal. The class interval defines the range of each class; for example, if the class interval is five and the data begin at zero, the classes are 0–4, 5–9, 10–14, and so on.

clathrate compound formed when the small molecules of one substance fill in the holes in the structural lattice of another, solid, substance – for example, sulphur dioxide molecules in ice crystals. Clathrates are therefore intermediate between mixtures and true compounds (which are held together by ◊ionic or covalent chemical bonds).

clathration in chemistry, a method of removing water from an aqueous solution, and therefore increasing the solution's concentration, by trapping it in a matrix with inert gases such as freons.

clausius in engineering, a unit of ◊entropy (the loss of energy as heat in any physical process). It is defined as the ratio of energy to temperature above absolute zero.

claustrophobia ◊phobia involving fear of enclosed spaces.

clavicle ***Latin clavis 'key'*** the collar bone of many vertebrates. In humans it is vulnerable to fracture, since falls involving a sudden force on the arm may result in very high stresses passing into the chest region by way of the clavicle and other bones. It is connected at one end with the sternum (breastbone), and at the other end with the shoulder-blade, together with which it forms the arm socket. The wishbone of a chicken is composed of its two fused clavicles.

claw hard, hooked, pointed outgrowth of the digits of mammals, birds, and most reptiles. Claws are composed of the protein keratin, and grow continuously from a bundle of cells in the lower skin layer. Hooves and nails are modified structures with the same origin as claws.

clay very fine-grained ◊sedimentary deposit that has undergone a greater or lesser degree of consolidation. When moistened it is plastic, and it hardens on heating, which renders it impermeable. It may be white, grey, red, yellow, blue, or black, depending on its composition. Clay minerals consist largely of hydrous silicates of aluminium and magnesium together with iron, potassium, sodium, and organic substances. The crystals of clay minerals have a layered structure, capable of holding water, and are responsible for its plastic properties. According to international classification, in mechanical analysis of soil, clay has a grain size of less than 0.002 mm/0.00008 in.

clay mineral one of a group of hydrous silicate minerals that form most of the fine-grained particles in clays. Clay minerals are normally formed by weathering or alteration of other silicate minerals. Virtually all have sheet silicate structures similar to the micas. They exhibit the following useful properties: loss of water on heating; swelling and shrinking in different conditions;, cation exchange with other media; and plasticity when wet. Examples are kaolinite, illite, and montmorillonite.

Kaolinite $Al_2Si_2O_5(OH)_4$ is a common white clay mineral derived from alteration of aluminium silicates, especially feldspars. Illite contains the same constituents as kaolinite, plus potassium, and is the main mineral of clay sediments, mudstones, and shales; it is a weathering product of feldspars and other silicates. Montmorillonite contains the constituents of kaolinite plus sodium and magnesium; along with related magnesium- and iron-bearing clay minerals, it is derived from alteration and weathering of mafic igneous rocks. Kaolinite (the mineral name for kaolin or china clay) is economically important in the ceramic and paper industries. Illite, along with other clay minerals, may also be used in ceramics. Montmorillonite is the chief constituent of fuller's earth, and is also used in drilling muds (muds used to cool and lubricate drilling equipment). Vermiculite (similar to montmorillonite) will expand on heating to produce a material used in insulation.

cleanliness unit unit for measuring air pollution: the number of particles greater than 0.5 micrometres in diameter per cubic foot of air. A more usual measure is the weight of contaminants per cubic metre of air.

cleartext or ***plaintext*** in encryption, the original, unencrypted message.

cleavage in mineralogy, the tendency of a mineral to split along defined, parallel planes related to its internal structure. It is a useful distinguishing feature in mineral identification. Cleavage occurs where bonding between atoms is weakest, and cleavages may be perfect, good, or poor, depending on the bond strengths; a given mineral may possess one, two, three, or more orientations along which it will cleave.

Some minerals have no cleavage, for example, quartz will fracture to give curved surfaces similar to those of broken glass. Some other minerals, such as apatite, have very poor cleavage that is sometimes known as a parting. Micas have one perfect cleavage and therefore split easily into very thin flakes. Pyroxenes have two good cleavages and break (less perfectly) into long prisms. Galena has three perfect cleavages parallel to the cube edges, and readily breaks into smaller and smaller cubes. Baryte has one perfect cleavage plus good cleavages in other orientations.

cleg another name for ◊horsefly.

cleistogamy production of flowers that never fully open and that are automatically self-fertilized. Cleistogamous flowers are often formed late in the year, after the production of normal flowers, or during a period of cold weather, as seen in several species of violet *Viola*.

It frequently happens that in the ordinary affairs ... of life opportunities present themselves of contemplating the most curious operations of nature.

BENJAMIN THOMPSON, COUNT RUMFORD RUMFORD US-born British physicist. Addressing the Royal Society 1798

clematis any of a group of temperate woody climbing plants with colourful showy flowers. They belong to the buttercup family. (Genus *Clematis*, family Ranunculaceae.)

click in computing, to press down and then immediately release a button on a ◊mouse. The phrase 'to click on' means to select an ◊icon on a computer screen by moving the mouse cursor to the icon's position and clicking a mouse button. See also ◊double click.

click beetle ◊beetle that can regain its feet from lying on its back by jumping into the air and turning over, clicking as it does so.

clickstream unedited log of mouse-clicks that records visitor actions on a site on the World Wide Web. This data is analysed to create feedback for advertisers, enabling them to check whether their strategies are successful in attracting user attention.

client in ◊client–server architecture, software that enables a user to access a store of data or programs on a ◊server. On the Internet, client software is the software that users need to run on home computers in order to be able to use services such as the World Wide Web.

client–server architecture in computing, a system in which the mechanics of looking after data are separated from the programs that use the data. For example, the 'server' might be a central database, typically located on a large computer that is reserved for this purpose. The 'client' would be an ordinary program that requests data from the server as needed.

Most Internet services are examples of client–server applications, including the World Wide Web, FTP, Telnet, and Gopher.

climactichnite flat, soft-bodied animal of the Cambrian period, about 25 cm/10 in in length. Climactichnites pulled themselves along the sand, possibly using flaps on either side of the body, feeding on microorganisms. Although an evolutionary dead end, they may have been some of the first animals to move on land.

climate combination of weather conditions at a particular place over a period of time – usually a minimum of 30 years. A classification of climate encompasses the averages, extremes, and frequencies of all meteorological elements such as temperature, atmospheric pressure, precipitation, wind, humidity, and sunshine, together with the factors that influence them. The primary factors involved are: the Earth's rotation and latitudinal effects; ocean currents; large-scale movements of wind belts and air masses over the Earth's surface; temperature differences between land and sea surfaces; and topography. Climatology , the scientific study of climate, includes the construction of computer-generated models, and considers not only present-day climates, their effects and their classification, but also long-term climate changes, covering both past climates (paleoclimates) and future predictions. Climatologists are especially concerned with the influence of human activity on climate change, among the most important of which, at both a local and global level, are those currently linked with ◊ozone depleters and the ◊greenhouse effect.

climate classification The word climate comes from the Greek *klima*, meaning an inclination or slope (referring to the angle of the Sun's rays, and thus latitude) and the earliest known classification of climate was that of the ancient Greeks, who based their system on latitudes. In recent times, many different systems of classifying climate have been devised, most of which follow that formulated by the German climatologist Wladimir Köppen (1846–1940) in 1900.

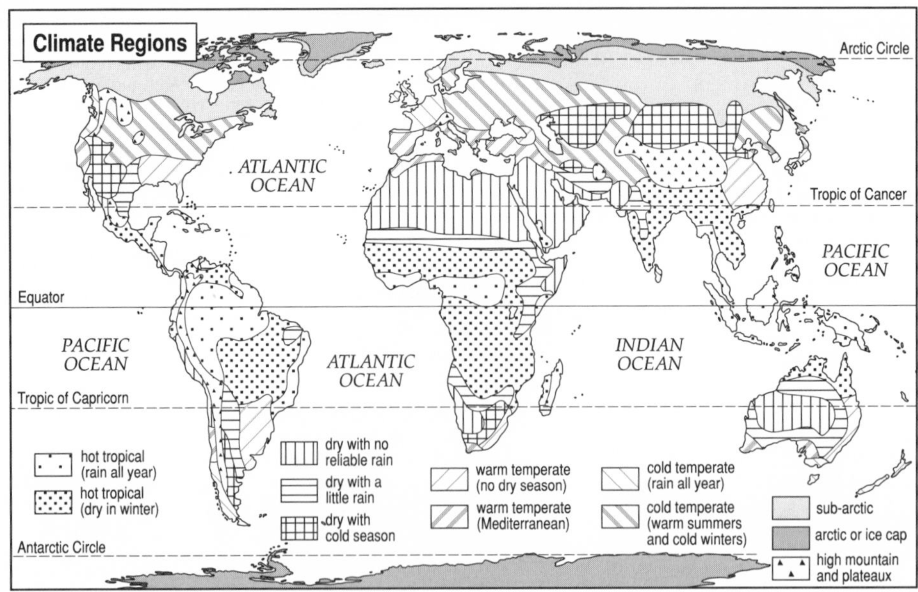

climate *The world's climatic zones. There are many systems of classifying climate. One system, that of Wladimir Köppen, was based on temperature and plant type. Other systems take into account the distribution of global winds.*

These systems use vegetation-based classifications such as desert, tundra, and rainforest. Classification by air mass is used in conjunction with this method. This idea was first introduced in 1928 by the Norwegian meteorologist Tor Bergeron, and links the climate of an area with the movement of the air masses it experiences.

In the 18th century, the British scientist George Hadley developed a model of the general circulation of atmosphere based on convection. He proposed a simple pattern of cells of warm air rising at the Equator and descending at the poles. In fact, due to the rotation of the Earth, there are three such cells in each hemisphere. The first two of these consist of air that rises at the Equator and sinks at latitudes north and south of the tropics; the second two exist at the mid-latitudes where the rising air from the sub-tropics flows towards the cold air masses of the third pair of cells circulating from the two polar regions. Thus, in this model, there are six main circulating cells of air above ground producing seven terrestrial zones – three rainy regions (at the Equator and the temperate latitudes) resulting from the moisture-laden rising air, interspersed and bounded by four dry or desert regions (at the poles and subtropics) resulting from the dry descending air.

climax community assemblage of plants and animals that is relatively stable in its environment. It is brought about by ecological ◊succession, and represents the point at which succession ceases to occur.

In temperate or tropical conditions, a typical climax community comprises woodland or forest and its associated fauna (for example, an oak wood in the UK). In essence, most land management is a series of interferences with the process of succession.

The theory, created by Frederic Clement in 1916, has been criticized for not explaining 'retrogressive' succession, when some areas revert naturally to pre-climax vegetation.

climax vegetation the plants in a ◊climax community.

clinical psychology branch of psychology dealing with the understanding and treatment of health problems, particularly mental disorders. The main problems dealt with include anxiety, phobias, depression, obsessions, sexual and marital problems, drug and alcohol dependence, childhood behavioural problems, psychoses (such as schizophrenia), mental disability, and brain disease (such as dementia) and damage. Other areas of work include forensic psychology (concerned with criminal behaviour) and health psychology.

Assessment procedures assess intelligence and cognition (for example, in detecting the effects of brain damage) by using psychometric tests. **Behavioural approaches** are methods of treatment that apply learning theories to clinical problems. **Behaviour therapy** helps clients change unwanted behaviours (such as phobias, obsessions, sexual problems) and to develop new skills (such as improving social interactions). **Behaviour modification** relies on operant conditioning, making selective use of rewards (such as praise) to change behaviour. This is helpful for children, the mentally disabled, and for patients in institutions, such as mental hospitals. **Cognitive therapy** is a new approach to treating emotional problems, such as anxiety and depression, by teaching clients how to deal with negative thoughts and attitudes. **Counselling**, developed by Carl Rogers, is widely used to help clients solve their own problems. **Psychoanalysis**, as developed by Sigmund Freud and Carl Jung, is little used by clinical psychologists today. It emphasizes childhood conflicts as a source of adult problems.

clinometer hand-held surveying instrument for measuring angles of slope.

clip art small graphics used to liven up documents and presentations. Many software packages such as word processors and presentation graphics packages come with a selection of clip art.

clipboard in computing, a temporary file or memory area where data can be stored before being copied into an application file. It is used, for example, in cut-and-paste operations.

Clipper chip controversial encryption hardware system that contains built-in facilities to allow authorized third parties access to the encrypted data. Adopted as a US government standard in 1994, the Clipper chip was a chip that used ◊public-key cryptography and a proprietary ◊algorithm called Skipjack, and could be built into any communications device, such as a telephone or modem. It was developed by the US National Security Agency as part of its ◊Capstone project.

Clipper was instantly unpopular on the Net because of privacy concerns: it contained a system for depositing a copy of the user's private key in escrow (see ◊key escrow), from where it could be obtained by law enforcement officials equipped with an appropriate court order.

Clipper suffered further defeat when Matt Blaze, a researcher at AT&T Bell Labs cracked the technology in 1995. In 1996, the US government proposed the development of a network of trusted third parties to hold keys in escrow; the initiative was dubbed 'Clipper III'.

clo unit of thermal insulation of clothing. Standard clothes have an insulation of about 1 clo; the warmest clothing is about 4 clo per 2.5 cm/1 in of thickness. See also ◊tog.

cloaca the common posterior chamber of most vertebrates into which the digestive, urinary, and reproductive tracts all enter; a cloaca is found in most reptiles, birds, and amphibians; many fishes; and, to a reduced degree, marsupial mammals. Placental mammals, however, have a separate digestive opening (the anus) and urinogenital opening. The cloaca forms a chamber in which products can be stored before being voided from the body via a muscular opening, the cloacal aperture.

clock any device that measures the passage of time, usually shown by means of pointers moving over a dial or by a digital display. Traditionally a timepiece consists of a train of wheels driven by a spring or weight controlled by a balance wheel or pendulum. Many clocks now run by batteries rather than clockwork. The watch is a portable clock.

history In ancient Egypt the time during the day was measured by a shadow clock, a primitive form of ◊sundial, and at night the water clock was used. Up to the late 16th century the only clock available for use at sea was the sand clock, of which the most familiar form is the hourglass. During the Middle Ages various types of sundial were widely used, and portable sundials were in use from the 16th to the 18th century. Watches were invented in the 16th century – the first were made in Nürnberg, Germany, shortly after 1500 – but it was not until the 19th century that they became cheap enough to be widely available. The first known public clock was set up in Milan, Italy, in 1353. The timekeeping of both clocks and watches was revolutionized in the 17th century by the application of pendulums to clocks and of balance springs to watches.

types of clock The **marine chronometer** is a precision timepiece of special design, used at sea for giving Greenwich mean time (GMT). **Electric timepieces** were made possible by the discovery early in the 19th century of the magnetic effects of electric currents. One of the earliest and most satisfactory methods of electrical control of a clock was invented by Matthaeus Hipp in 1842. In one kind of electric clock, the place of the pendulum or spring-controlled balance wheel is taken by a small synchronous electric motor, which counts up the alternations (frequency) of the incoming electric supply and, by a suitable train of wheels, records the time by means of hands on a dial. The **quartz crystal clock** (made possible by the ◊piezoelectric effect of certain crystals) has great precision, with a short-term variation in accuracy of about one-thousandth of a second per day. More accurate still is the ◊atomic clock. This utilizes the natural resonance of certain atoms (for example, caesium) as a regulator controlling the frequency of a quartz crystal ◊oscillator. Atomic clocks can be accurate to within one second in 300 million years.

clock interrupt in computing, an ◊interrupt signal generated by the computer's internal electronic clock.

clock rate the frequency of a computer's internal electronic clock. Every computer contains an electronic clock, which produces a sequence of regular electrical pulses used by the control unit to synchronize the components of the computer and regulate the ◊fetch–execute cycle by which program instructions are processed.

A fixed number of time pulses is required in order to execute each particular instruction. The speed at which a computer can process instructions therefore depends on the clock rate: increasing the clock rate will decrease the time required to complete each particular instruction.

Clock rates are measured in **megahertz** (MHz), or millions of pulses a second. Microcomputers commonly have a clock rate of 8–50 MHz.

clockwise the direction in which the hands of a traditional clock turn.

clone in genetics, any one of a group of genetically identical cells or organisms. An identical ◊twin is a clone; so, too, are bacteria living in the same colony. The term 'clone' has also been adopted by computer technology to describe a (nonexistent) device that mimics an actual one to enable certain software programs to run correctly.

In August 1996, scientists in Oregon, USA, cloned two rhesus monkeys from embryo cells. President Clinton announced in March 1997 a ban on using federal funds to support human cloning research, and called for a moratorium on this type of scientific research. He also asked the National Bioethics Advisory Commission to review and issue a report on the ramifications that cloning would have on humans.

British scientists confirmed in February 1997 that they had cloned an adult sheep from a single cell to produce a lamb with the same genes as its mother. A cell was taken from the udder of the mother sheep, and its DNA combined with an unfertilized egg that had had its DNA removed. The fused cells were grown in the laboratory and then implanted into the uterus of a surrogate mother sheep. The resulting lamb, Dolly, came from an animal that was six years old, whose genes have already been damaged by environmental toxins and cosmic rays; the sheep could therefore develop cancers abnormally early.

It was the first time cloning had been achieved using cells other then reproductive cells. The cloning breakthrough has ethical implications, as the same principle could be used with human cells and eggs. The news was met with international calls to prevent the cloning of humans. The UK, Spain, Germany, Canada, and Denmark already have laws against cloning humans, as do some individual states in the USA (legislators introduced bills to ban human cloning and associated research nationally March 1997). France and Portugal also have very restrictive laws on cloning.

In June 1997, in response to the recommendations of the National Bioethics Advisory Commission, President Clinton proposed a five-year ban on cloning a human being. He said this would not stop the cloning of animals or of human DNA. The first binding international ban on human cloning was signed in January 1998 by 19 European countries. The text, which was an addition to the European Convention on Human Rights and Biomedicine, placed a total ban on human cloning although it allowed the cloning of cells for research purposes. The 40-member Council of Europe called the protocol 'Europe's response to the threat' of human cloning.

Britain did not sign the protocol because it was not yet a signatory to the convention of which it was a part. The cloning protocol, agreed to by European leaders at a summit October 1997, would also not include Germany, which claimed the measure was weaker than the current German law that forbids all research on human embryos.

A calf cloned from fetal muscle cells by French geneticists was born near Paris in 1998. She only survived for about a month.

> *People must understand that science is inherently neither a potential for good nor for evil. It is a potential to be harnessed by man to do his bidding.*
>
> GLENN T SEABORG US physicist. Associated Press interview with Alton Blakeslee, 29 Sept 1964

clone in computing, copy of hardware or software that may not be identical to the original design but provides the same functions. All personal computers (PCs) are to some extent clones of the original IBM PC and PC AT launched by IBM in 1981 and 1984, respectively – including IBM's current machines. Clones typically compete by being cheaper and are sometimes less well made than the branded product but this is not always the case. Compaq, for example, competed with IBM by producing the first portable PC and by building better desktop machines, while Dell competed by building PCs to individual orders and supplying customers direct.

Cloning a disc drive or workstation, however, means making an exact copy of all the files or software so that the new drive or machine functions identically to the original one.

closed in mathematics, descriptive of a set of data for which an operation (such as addition or multiplication) done on any members of the set gives a result that is also a member of the set.

For example, the set of even numbers is closed with respect to addition, because two even numbers added to each other always give another even number.

closed-circuit television (CCTV) localized television system in which programmes are sent over relatively short distances, the camera, receiver, and controls being linked by cable. Closed-circuit TV systems are used in department stores and large offices as a means of internal security, monitoring people's movements.

clothes moth moth whose larvae feed on clothes, upholstery, and carpets. The adults are small golden or silvery moths. The natural

Dolly – the Cloning Debate

BY STEPHEN WEBSTER

On Sunday, 23 February 1997, the *New York Times* announced the existence of a new kind of animal. Dolly, a 7-month-old Finn Dorset sheep, was alive and well and living in a guarded pen in the Roslin Institute, a research station just outside Edinburgh, Scotland. What made Dolly uniquely interesting to the newspapers, and soon after to almost everyone, was that she arose not by the union of egg and sperm but by cloning. For the first time a mammal had been cloned from an adult cell: a tiny fleck of skin, scraped from the udder of another sheep and stored for months in a refrigerator, had been treated in such a way that it started to grow. As reported in the newspapers, the embryo, implanted in a surrogate mother, became a fetus and was born in the ordinary way. These were the facts of Dolly's life; yet why Dolly had come and whether any good could come from her were issues largely ignored in the ensuing media frenzy. Along with many others, President Clinton was quick to see the popular significance: if Dolly proves that clones can be made from the cells of adult mammals, then presumably the technique can be used on that other well-known mammal, *Homo sapiens*. On the day following the announcement, Clinton declared that Dolly 'raises serious ethical questions, particularly with respect to the possible use of this technology to clone human embryos'. Meanwhile, across the Atlantic in the UK, a House of Commons committee summoned Ian Wilmut, the team leader of Roslin's Dolly project, to explain the meaning of his work. Wilmut confirmed that his technology could be applied to humans and that, given the resources, it might lead to cloned humans 'within a couple of years'. He said, however, that such a use of the technique would be 'pointless', and declared himself glad that there were laws in the UK banning the cloning of humans.

Advantages of cloning

It is important, therefore, in assessing the significance of Dolly, to understand the background to cloning, and to appreciate why Wilmut's small agricultural research institute persisted for so long in its attempts to clone an adult mammal. The motive is simple, and relates to the commercial breeding of animals. If a farmer has a successful animal, for example a cow that produces a great quantity of excellent milk, similar cows would also be welcome. Normally, breeders obtain the animals they want by mating one favoured individual with another. Yet sexual reproduction produces variation among animals, so the offspring are always a little different from the parents. If it were possible to reproduce an animal without using sex, then the offspring would be identical to its single parent: a clone. Any useful characteristics in the parent would then be found in its genetically identical offspring.

With plants the application was obvious: tomatoes, strawberries, and carrots can all be cloned from individuals judged successful by farmer and consumer – and have been. It is harder to clone animals, yet soon another scientific development made cloning even more attractive: genetic engineering. Much time and money has been invested in making transgenic animals: creatures that contain one or more genes from another species, particularly humans. The Roslin Institute, with its commercial links to the pharmaceutical company PPL Therapeutics, was interested in making sheep with genes that altered the composition of the milk, so that it contained valuable medicines. Clones of such sheep would be guaranteed to have the same ability, and the investment would be secure.

The basis of cloning is that all the cells of an organism, with the exception of the sex cells, contain a full set of genes. A liver cell, for example, contains all the genes for making a brain, the skin, the skeleton, and indeed every other part of the body, yet when a liver cell reproduces it only ever makes other liver cells. It is as if all the other genes it contains were permanently switched off. Therefore, in order to grow an animal from a single cell, a way had to be found to switch back on every gene.

Early cloning attempts

Early cloning experiments, unsurprisingly, used cells taken from an embryo. The method followed was always this: take the nucleus (where the genes are found) out of a cell and then inject it into a fertilized egg – one that has been prepared by having its own nucleus removed. Success came in 1952 in Philadelphia, Pennsylvania, when Robert Briggs and Tom King took a frog embryo, separated out all the cells, and inserted each nucleus into a prepared egg. Twenty-seven tadpoles developed, each genetically identical. It was a world first: an animal had been experimentally cloned.

Frogs are not economically important; mammals are. If a sheep or cow could be cloned after its excellence had been established, in other words when it was fully developed, the technique would be highly lucrative. However, efforts to clone mammals were at first unsuccessful. Then, in the mid-1980s scientists at the University of Wisconsin, funded by the US beef giant W R Grace and Company, made a breakthrough – they managed to clone cow embryo cells, with the cloned embryos growing into adults. The same procedure was followed: take the nucleus from an embryo cell, inject it into a prepared egg, and look for signs of development. If all went well the growing egg, now itself an embryo, would be implanted into a surrogate mother and after the normal gestation period the cow would be born. Venture capitalists saw an opportunity here, related to the beef industry's requirements for productive, disease-resistant cows. Yet while the technique worked, the cloned cows were expensive. The quality of American beef was good enough using ordinary breeding techniques. Cloning cattle was an expensive luxury and within just a few years, research money for cloning was once more in short supply.

Recent experiments

Researchers at the Roslin Institute had meanwhile been developing their interest in transgenic sheep. Sheep embryos were being injected with human genes, and some of these genes were finding their way into the sheep genetic apparatus. One such gene caused the sheep to produce in their milk the drug alpha-1 antitrypsin, used in treating some lung diseases. However, the technique is hit-and-miss: the sheep embryos only incorporate the human genes occasionally. Yet if it were possible to clone transgenic sheep, especially from those individuals with a proven drug-producing history, then the offspring would be guaranteed to contain the gene, and there would be no need for those gene injections with their low success rates. Ian Wilmut had already had success with cloning from embryonic cells, but believed that it should be possible to use adult cells instead. He argued that all the genes contained within an adult nucleus could be reactivated; it was just a matter of finding the right method. Oddly enough, a period of starvation was found to produce the desired effect. Cells taken from a sheep's udder were starved for a short period and this produced in the nucleus a change: the genes became active again. Egg cells were prepared by having their own nuclei removed and replaced by the udder nuclei. Out of 277 eggs that received the nuclei, just 29 developed into embryos, all of which were implanted in surrogate mothers. Fourteen pregnancies began, but most miscarried; only one pregnancy went through to term – this was Dolly.

Ethical issues

It is no exaggeration to say that the scientific world was astonished by the achievement. Scientists' widespread feeling had been that cloning from adult mammals was impossible; indeed, throughout the long-running but sporadic debate about the ethics of cloning, running since the 1970s, scientific commentators tended to downplay the possibility of cloning from adults. In any event, with the attention of the media focused on the concept of human cloning, scientists have had little opportunity to explain that Dolly is not simply an example of scientists in white coats 'playing God' but might constitute instead a serious medical advance.

Following the birth of Dolly, the public debate focused entirely on this question: will humans be cloned? The prospect of dictators cloning themselves and of women giving birth to their father were all discussed as serious possibilities. One reader, writing to the UK newspaper *The Times*, suggested that if his son, who had died in a car accident, were cloned 'he would be able to resume his relationship with my wife and myself and our younger son in a meaningful way and our family would be complete again'. Yet a clone of a person would have their own personality, wrought by the environment. They would have their own identity. In reality no-one could clone themselves and predict the outcome, any more than one can predict the future. Controlling the outcome of human cloning, in any civilized society, would most likely be illegal, as human clones would have the same rights as any other human. The scientific reasons commonly given for cloning humans all fail when considered alonside the social and ethical problems. However, if research into human cloning gets under way, there are useful applications that involve the cloning of tissues, not individuals. Cloned bone marrow, genetically identical to the patient in need, would save lives. More lives would be saved if whole organs could be grown, genetically matched to someone with heart or kidney disease. For the moment research in such areas is banned in the UK. In the USA federal funds cannot be used for human embryo research, but private laboratories have greater freedom. Research into mammal cloning, if not human cloning, is bound to continue. The debate too will continue, and will raise the most profound of questions about human and animal rights, about the question of personal identity, and about the purposes and methods of science. Meanwhile, Dolly the sheep thrives in her pen in Scotland, the centre of attention, but a reminder that the end of the century has seen the arrival of another troubling scientific development.

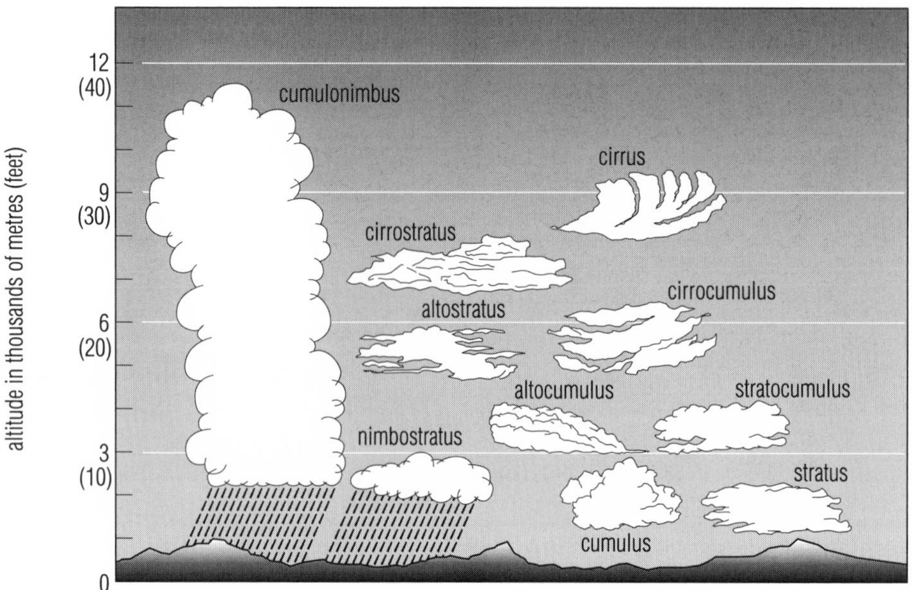

cloud *Standard types of cloud. The height and nature of a cloud can be deduced from its name. Cirrus clouds are at high levels and have a wispy appearance. Stratus clouds form at low level and are layered. Middle-level clouds have names beginning with 'alto'. Cumulus clouds, ball or cottonwool clouds, occur over a range of height.*

habitat of the larvae is in the nests of animals, feeding on remains of hair and feathers, but they have adapted to human households and can cause considerable damage, for example, the common clothes moth *Tineola bisselliella.*

cloud water vapour condensed into minute water particles that float in masses in the atmosphere. Clouds, like fogs or mists, which occur at lower levels, are formed by the cooling of air containing water vapour, which generally condenses around tiny dust particles.

Clouds are classified according to the height at which they occur and their shape. **Cirrus** and **cirrostratus** clouds occur at around 10 km/33,000 ft. The former, sometimes called mares'-tails, consist of minute specks of ice and appear as feathery white wisps, while cirrostratus clouds stretch across the sky as a thin white sheet. Three types of cloud are found at 3–7 km/10,000–23,000 ft: cirrocumulus, altocumulus, and altostratus. **Cirrocumulus** clouds occur in small or large rounded tufts, sometimes arranged in the pattern called mackerel sky. **Altocumulus** clouds are similar, but larger, white clouds, also arranged in lines. **Altostratus** clouds are like heavy cirrostratus clouds and may stretch across the sky as a grey sheet. **Stratocumulus** clouds are generally lower, occurring at 2–6 km/6,500–20,000 ft. They are dull grey clouds that give rise to a leaden sky that may not yield rain. Two types of clouds, **cumulus** and **cumulonimbus**, are placed in a special category because they are produced by daily ascending air currents, which take moisture into the cooler regions of the atmosphere. Cumulus clouds have a flat base generally at 1.4 km/4,500 ft where condensation begins, while the upper part is dome-shaped and extends to about 1.8 km/6,000ft. Cumulonimbus clouds have their base at much the same level, but extend much higher, often up to over 6 km/20,000 ft. Short heavy showers and sometimes thunder may accompany them. **Stratus** clouds, occurring below 1–2.5 km/3,000–8,000 ft, have the appearance of sheets parallel to the horizon and are like high fogs.

In addition to their essential role in the water cycle, clouds are important in the regulation of radiation in the Earth's atmosphere. They reflect short-wave radiation from the Sun, and absorb and re-emit long-wave radiation from the Earth's surface.

CLOUD CATALOGUE

http://covis.atmos.uiuc.edu/guide/clouds/html/cloud.home.html

Illustrated guide to how clouds form and to the various different types. The site contains plenty of images and a glossary of key terms.

cloud chamber apparatus for tracking ionized particles. It consists of a vessel fitted with a piston and filled with air or other gas, saturated with water vapour. When the volume of the vessel is suddenly expanded by moving the piston outwards, the vapour cools and a cloud of tiny droplets forms on any nuclei, dust, or ions present. As fast-moving ionizing particles collide with the air or gas molecules, they show as visible tracks.

Much information about interactions between such particles and radiations has been obtained from photographs of these tracks.

The system has been improved upon in recent years by the use of liquid hydrogen or helium instead of air or gas (see ◊particle detector). The cloud chamber was devised in 1897 by Charles Thomson Rees Wilson (1869–1959) at Cambridge University.

clove dried, unopened flower bud of the clove tree. A member of the myrtle family, the tree is a native of the Maluku Islands, Indonesia. Cloves are used for flavouring in cookery and confectionery. Oil of cloves, which has tonic qualities and relieves wind, is used in medicine. The aroma of cloves is also shared by the leaves, bark, and fruit of the tree. (*Eugenia caryophyllus,* family Myrtaceae.)

clover any of an Old World group of low-growing leguminous plants (see ◊legume), usually with leaves consisting of three leaflets and small flowers in dense heads. Sweet clover refers to various species belonging to the related genus *Melilotus.* (True clover genus *Trifolium,* family Leguminosae.)

club moss or **lycopod** any of a group of mosslike plants that do not produce seeds but reproduce by ◊spores. They are related to the ferns and horsetails. (Order Lycopodiales, family Pteridophyta.)

These plants have a wide distribution, but were far more numerous in Palaeozoic times, especially the Carboniferous period

(363–290 million years ago), when members of the group were large trees. The species that exist now are all small in size.

clubroot disease affecting cabbages, turnips, and allied plants of the Cruciferae family. It is caused by a ◊slime mould, *Plasmodiophora brassicae.* This attacks the roots of the plant, which send out knotty outgrowths. Eventually the whole plant decays.

clubshell or ***watering-pot shell*** bivalve shelled mollusc. It is hermaphrodite and usually lives on corals and rocks.
classification Clubshells are in genus *Clavagella,* order Pholadomyoida, class Bivalvia, phylum Mollusca.

Clumber spaniel breed of medium-sized gundog (a dog trained to aid in hunting) that takes its name from Clumber Park, Nottinghamshire, the estate of the dukes of Newcastle who imported the dogs into England from France probably in the late 18th century. Its thick, soft coat is white with lemon-coloured flecks. One of the largest spaniels, it weighs up to 36 kg/80 lb.

clusec unit for measuring the power of a vacuum pump.

Cluster a ◊European Space Agency project to study the interaction of the solar wind with the Earth's ◊magnetosphere from an array of four identical satellites. Cluster works in conjunction with *SOHO* (Solar and Heliospheric Observatory).

clutch any device for disconnecting rotating shafts, used especially in a car's transmission system. In a car with a manual gearbox, the driver depresses the clutch when changing gear, thus disconnecting the engine from the gearbox.

The clutch consists of two main plates, a pressure plate and a driven plate, which is mounted on a shaft leading to the gearbox. When the clutch is engaged, the pressure plate presses the driven plate against the engine ◊flywheel, and drive goes to the gearbox. Depressing the clutch springs the pressure plate away, freeing the driven plate. Cars with **automatic transmission** have no clutch. Drive is transmitted from the flywheel to the automatic gearbox by a liquid coupling or ◊torque converter.

cm symbol for **centimetre**.

CMOS (abbreviation for ***complementary metal-oxide semiconductor***) family of integrated circuits (chips) widely used in building electronic systems.

CMYK (abbreviation for ***cyan–magenta–yellow–black***) four-colour separation used in most (subtractive) colour printing processes. Representation on computer screens normally uses the additive ◊RGB method and so conversion is usually necessary on output for printing either on colour printers or as separations.

CNC abbreviation for ◊computer numerical control.

CNO cycle in astrophysics, alternative name for ◊carbon cycle.

coachwood tree *Ceratopetalum apetalum* with light, easily worked timber, found in gullies in E Australia.

coal black or blackish mineral substance formed from the compaction of ancient plant matter in tropical swamp conditions. It is used as a fuel and in the chemical industry. Coal is classified according to the proportion of carbon it contains. The main types are ◊anthracite **(shiny, with about 90% carbon), bituminous coal** (shiny and dull patches, about 75% carbon), and **lignite** (woody, grading into peat, about 50% carbon). Coal burning is one of the main causes of ◊acid rain.

coal gas gas produced when coal is destructively distilled or heated out of contact with the air. Its main constituents are methane, hydrogen, and carbon monoxide. Coal gas has been superseded by ◊natural gas for domestic purposes.

coal mining extraction of coal from the Earth's crust. Coal mines may be opencast ◊adit, or deepcast. The least expensive is opencast but this may result in scars on the landscape.

coal tar black oily material resulting from the destructive distillation of bituminous coal.

Further distillation of coal tar yields a number of fractions: light oil, middle oil, heavy oil, and anthracene oil; the residue is called pitch. On further fractionation a large number of substances are obtained, about 200 of which have been isolated. They are used as dyes and in medicines.

coastal erosion the erosion of the land by the constant battering of the sea's waves. This produces two effects. The first is a hydraulic effect, in which the force of the wave compresses air pockets in coastal rocks and cliffs, and the air then expands explosively. The second is the effect of ◊corrasion, in which rocks and pebbles are flung against the cliffs, wearing them away. Frost shattering (or freeze-thaw), caused by the expansion of frozen seawa-

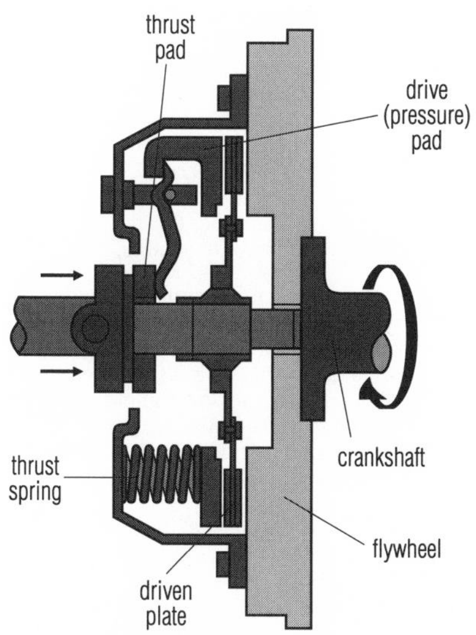

disengaged (pedal pressed down)

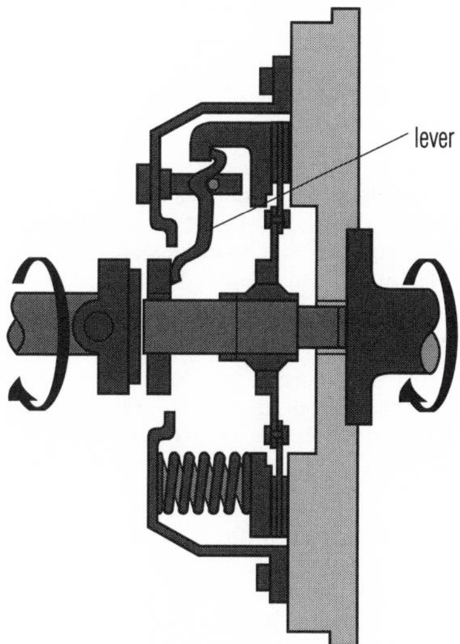

engaged (pedal up)

***clutch** The clutch consists of two main plates: a drive plate connected to the engine crankshaft and a driven plate connected to the wheels. When the clutch is disengaged, the drive plate does not press against the driven plate. When the clutch is engaged, the two plates are pressed into contact and the rotation of the crankshaft is transmitted to the wheels.*

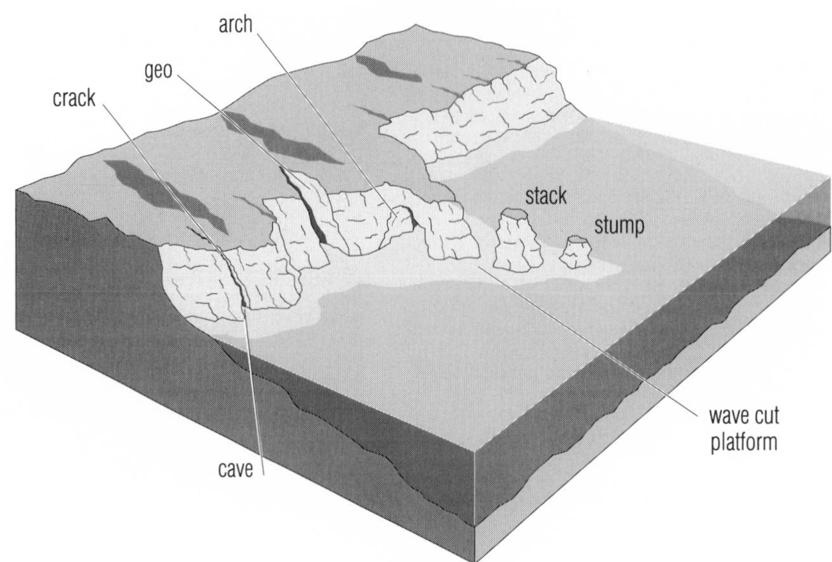

coastal erosion *Typical features of coastal erosion: from the initial cracks in less resistant rock through to arches, stacks, and stumps that can occur as erosion progresses.*

ter in cavities, and biological weathering, caused by the burrowing of rock-boring molluscs, also result in the breakdown of the rock.

In areas where there are beaches, the waves cause longshore drift, in which sand and stone fragments are carried parallel to the shore, causing buildups (sandspits) in some areas and beach erosion in others.

coastal protection measures taken to prevent ◊coastal erosion. Many stretches of coastline are so severely affected by erosion that beaches are swept away, threatening the livelihood of seaside resorts, and buildings become unsafe.

To reduce erosion, several different forms of coastal protection may be employed. Structures such as sea walls attempt to prevent waves reaching the cliffs by deflecting them back to sea. Such structures are expensive and of limited success. Adding sediment (beach nourishment) to make a beach wider causes waves to break early so that they have less power when they reach the cliffs. Wooden or concrete barriers called groynes may also be constructed at right angles to the beach in order to block the movement of sand along the beach (longshore drift).

coati or ***coatimundi*** any of several species of carnivores of the genus *Nasua*, in the same family, Procyonidae, as the raccoons. A coati is a good climber and has long claws, a long tail, a good sense of smell, and a long, flexible piglike snout used for digging. Coatis live in packs in the forests of South and Central America.

The common coati *Nasua nasua* of South America is about 60 cm/2 ft long, with a tail about the same length.

coaxial cable electric cable that consists of a solid or stranded central conductor insulated from and surrounded by a solid or braided conducting tube or sheath. It can transmit the high-frequency signals used in television, telephone, and other telecommunications transmissions.

cobalt ***German Kobalt 'evil spirit'*** hard, lustrous, grey, metallic element, symbol Co, atomic number 27, relative atomic mass 58.933. It is found in various ores and occasionally as a free metal, sometimes in metallic meteorite fragments. It is used in the preparation of magnetic, wear-resistant, and high-strength alloys; its compounds are used in inks, paints, and varnishes.

The isotope Co-60 is radioactive (half-life 5.3 years) and is produced in large amounts for use as a source of gamma rays in industrial radiography, research, and cancer therapy. Cobalt was named in 1730 by Swedish chemist Georg Brandt (1694–1768); the name derives from the fact that miners considered its ore malevolent because it interfered with copper production.

cobalt-60 radioactive (half-life 5.3 years) isotope produced by neutron radiation of cobalt in heavy-water reactors, used in large amounts for gamma rays in cancer therapy, industrial radiography, and research, substituting for the much more costly radium.

cobalt chloride $CoCl_2$ compound that exists in two forms: the hydrated salt ($CoCl_2.6H_2O$), which is pink, and the anhydrous salt, which is blue. The anhydrous form is used as an indicator because it turns pink if water is present. When the hydrated salt is gently heated the blue anhydrous salt is reformed.

cobalt ore cobalt is extracted from a number of minerals, the main ones being **smaltite**, $(CoNi)As_3$; **linnaeite**, Co_3S_4; **cobaltite**, CoAsS; and **glaucodot**, (CoFe)AsS.

All commercial cobalt is obtained as a by-product of other metals, usually associated with other ores, such as copper. Congo (formerly Zaire) is the largest producer of cobalt, and it is obtained there as a byproduct of the copper industry. Other producers include Canada and Morocco. Cobalt is also found in the manganese nodules that occur on the ocean floor, and was successfully refined in 1988 from the Pacific Ocean nodules, although this process has yet to prove economic.

COBOL (acronym for ***common business-oriented language***) high-level computer-programming language, designed in the late 1950s for commercial data-processing problems; it has become the major language in this field. COBOL features powerful facilities for file handling and business arithmetic. Program instructions written in this language make extensive use of words and look very much like English sentences. This makes COBOL one of the easiest languages to learn and understand.

cobra any of several poisonous snakes, especially the genus *Naja*, of the family Elapidae, found in Africa and southern Asia, species of which can grow from 1 m/3 ft to over 4.3 m/14 ft. The neck stretches into a hood when the snake is alarmed. Cobra venom contains nerve toxins powerful enough to kill humans.

The Indian cobra *Naja naja* is about 1.5 m/5 ft long, and found over most of southern Asia. Some individuals have 'spectacle' markings on the hood. The hamadryad *N. hannah* of southern and southeast Asia can be 4.3 m/14 ft or more, and eats snakes. The ringhals *Hemachatus hemachatus* of S Africa and the black-necked cobra

N. nigricollis, of the African savanna are both about 1 m/3 ft long. Both are able to spray venom towards the eyes of an attacker.

coca South American shrub belonging to the coca family, whose dried leaves are the source of the drug cocaine. It was used as a holy drug by the Andean Indians. (*Erythroxylon coca*, family Erythroxylaceae.)

cocaine alkaloid $C_{17}H_{21}NO_4$ extracted from the leaves of the coca tree. It has limited medical application, mainly as a local anaesthetic agent that is readily absorbed by mucous membranes (lining tissues) of the nose and throat. It is both toxic and addictive. Its use as a stimulant is illegal. ◊Crack is a derivative of cocaine.

Cocaine was first extracted from the coca plant in Germany in the 19th century. Most of the world's cocaine is produced from coca grown in Peru, Bolivia, Colombia, and Ecuador. Estimated annual production totals 215,000 tonnes, with most of the processing done in Colombia. Long-term use may cause mental and physical deterioration.

coccolithophorid microscopic, planktonic marine alga, which secretes a calcite shell. The shells (coccoliths) of coccolithophores are a major component of deep sea ooze. Coccolithophores were particularly abundant during the late ◊Cretaceous period and their remains form the northern European chalk deposits, such as the white cliffs of Dover.

coccus (plural *cocci*) member of a group of globular bacteria, some of which are harmful to humans. The cocci contain the subgroups **streptococci**, where the bacteria associate in straight chains, and **staphylococci**, where the bacteria associate in branched chains.

cochineal red dye obtained from the cactus-eating Mexican ◊scale insect *Dactylopius coccus*, used in colouring food and fabrics.

cochlea part of the inner ◊ear. It is equipped with approximately 10,000 hair cells, which move in response to sound waves and thus stimulate nerve cells to send messages to the brain. In this way they turn vibrations of the air into electrical signals.

cockatiel Australian parrot *Nymphicus hollandicus*, about 20 cm/8 in long, with greyish or yellow plumage, yellow cheeks, a long tail, and a crest like a cockatoo. Cockatiels are popular as pets and aviary birds.

cockatoo any of several crested parrots, especially of the genus *Cacatua*, family Psittacidae, of the order Psittaciformes. They usually have light-coloured plumage with tinges of red, yellow, or orange on the face, and an erectile crest on the head. They are native to Australia, New Guinea, and nearby islands.

There are about 17 species, one of the most familiar being the sulphur-crested cockatoo *C. galerita* of Australia and New Guinea, about 50 cm/20 in long, white with a yellow crest and dark beak.

cockchafer or ***maybug*** European beetle *Melolontha melolontha*, of the scarab family, up to 3 cm/1.2 in long, with clumsy, buzzing flight, seen on early summer evenings. Cockchafers damage trees by feeding on the foliage and flowers.

cocker spaniel breed of small gundog developed in Britain for hunting woodcock (hence its name). It stands about 40 cm/15 in tall and weighs about 14 kg/30 lb. The American cocker is recognized as distinct from the English breed but both have a long, dense coat, which may be a solid colour (red, gold, black) or bi-coloured (black and white).

cockle any of over 200 species of bivalve mollusc with ribbed, heart-shaped shells. Some are edible and are sold in W European markets.

cock-of-the-rock South American bird of the genus *Rupicola*. It belongs to the family Cotingidae, which also includes the cotingas and umbrella birds. There are two species: *R. peruviana*, the Andean cock-of-the-rock, and *R. rupicola*, the Guyanan cock-of-the-rock. The male has brilliant orange plumage including the head crest, the female is a duller brown. Males display at a communal breeding area.

***cockroach** The so-called Australian cockroach* Periplaneta australasiae. *Mostly of African origin, cockroaches have become a cosmopolitan pest, infesting in particular kitchens and food stores, and often being linked to outbreaks of food poisoning. Premaphotos Wildlife*

cockroach any of numerous insects of the family Blattidae, distantly related to mantises and grasshoppers. There are 3,500 species, mainly in the tropics. They have long antennae and biting mouthparts. They can fly, but rarely do so.

The common cockroach, or black-beetle *Blatta orientalis*, is found in human dwellings, is nocturnal, omnivorous, and contaminates food. The German cockroach *Blattella germanica* and American cockroach *Periplaneta americana* are pests in kitchens, bakeries, and warehouses. In Britain only two innocuous species are native, but several have been introduced with imported food and have become severe pests. They are very difficult to eradicate. Cockroaches have a very high resistance to radiation, making them the only creatures likely to survive a nuclear holocaust.

COCKROACHES

http://www.ex.ac.uk/~gjlramel/blatodea.html

General information about the cockroach from its original arrival on Earth to the present day. Includes life history, its relationship with humans, and even how to keep a cockroach as a pet!

cocktail effect the effect of two toxic, or potentially toxic, chemicals when taken together rather than separately. Such effects are known to occur with some mixtures of drugs, with the active ingredient of one making the body more sensitive to the other.

This sometimes occurs because both drugs require the same ◊enzyme to break them down. Chemicals such as pesticides and food additives are only ever tested singly, not in combination with other chemicals that may be consumed at the same time, so no allowance is made for cocktail effects.

'Gulf War syndrome' may have resulted from the cocktail effect of an anti-nerve gas drug and two different insecticides.

coconut fruit of the coconut palm, which grows throughout the lowland tropics. The fruit has a large outer husk of fibres, which is removed and used to make coconut matting and ropes. Inside this is the nut which is exported to temperate countries. Its hard shell contains white flesh and clear coconut milk, both of which are tasty and nourishing. (*Cocos nucifera*, family Arecaceae.)

The white flesh of the coconut can be eaten fresh, or it can be dried before extracting the oil which makes up nearly two-thirds of it. The oil is used to make soap and margarine and in cooking; the remains are used in cattle feed.

cocoon pupa-case of many insects, especially of ◊moths and ◊silkworms. This outer web or ball is spun from the mouth by caterpillars before they pass into the ◊chrysalis state.

cod any fish of the family Gadidae, especially the Atlantic cod, *Gadus morhua* found in the N Atlantic and Baltic. It is brown to grey with spots, white below, and can grow to 1.5 m/5 ft.

The main cod fisheries are in the North Sea, and off the coasts of Iceland and Newfoundland, Canada. Much of the catch is salted and dried. Formerly one of the cheapest fish, decline in numbers from overfishing has made it one of the most expensive.

COD abbreviation for ◊chemical oxygen demand, a measure of water and effluent quality.

code the expression of an ◊algorithm in a ◊programming language. The term is also used as a verb, to describe the act of programming.

codec device that codes and decodes an ◊analogue stream to or from ◊digital data. It is used in applications such as remote broadcast-quality voiceovers recorded in a remote studio and transmitted via codecs and ◊Integrated Services Digital Network (ISDN) lines to a central studio for final mixing.

codeine opium derivative that provides ◊analgesia in mild to moderate pain. It also suppresses the cough centre of the brain. It is an alkaloid, derived from morphine but less toxic and addictive.

codominance in genetics, the failure of a pair of alleles, controlling a particular characteristic, to show the classic recessive-dominant relationship. Instead, aspects of both alleles may show in the phenotype.

The snapdragon shows codominance in respect to colour. Two alleles, one for red petals and the other for white, will produce a pink colour if the alleles occur together as a heterozygous form.

codon in genetics, a triplet of bases (see ◊base pair) in a molecule of DNA or RNA that directs the placement of a particular amino acid during the process of protein (polypeptide) synthesis. There are 64 codons in the ◊genetic code.

coefficient the number part in front of an algebraic term, signifying multiplication. For example, in the expression $4x^2 + 2xy - x$, the coefficient of x^2 is 4 (because $4x^2$ means $4 \times x^2$), that of xy is 2, and that of x is -1 (because $-1 \times x = -x$).

In general algebraic expressions, coefficients are represented by letters that may stand for numbers; for example, in the equation $ax^2 + bx + c = 0$, a, b, and c are coefficients, which can take any number.

coefficient of relationship the probability that any two individuals share a given gene by virtue of being descended from a common ancestor. In sexual reproduction of diploid species, an individual shares half its genes with each parent, with its offspring, and (on average) with each sibling; but only a quarter (on average) with its grandchildren or its siblings' offspring; an eighth with its great-grandchildren, and so on.

In certain species of insects (for example honey bees), females have only one set of chromosomes (inherited from the mother), so that sisters are identical in genetic make-up; this produces a different set of coefficients. These coefficients are important in calculations of ◊inclusive fitness.

coelacanth large dark brown to blue-grey fish that lives in the deep waters (200 m/650 ft) of the western Indian Ocean around the Comoros Islands. They can grow to about 2 m/6 ft in length, and weigh up to 73 kg/160 lb. They have bony, overlapping scales, and muscular lobe (limblike) fins sometimes used like oars when swimming and for balance while resting on the sea floor. They feed on other fish, and give birth to live young rather than shedding eggs as most fish do. Coelacanth fossils exist dating back over 400 million years and coelacanth were believed to be extinct until one was caught in 1938 off the coast of South Africa. For this reason they are sometimes referred to as 'living fossils'.

classification Coelacanths belong to the animal phylum Chordata, superclass Pisces (fish), class Sarcopterygii, subclass Crossopterygii, order Actinistia or coelacanthiformes, represented by a single family Lateimeriidae. There is only one known surviving species of coelacanth, *Latimeria chalumnae*. Coelacanths are now threatened, and have been listed as endangered by ◊CITES since 1991.

Nature's oddities are more than good theories. They are material for probing the limits of interesting theories about life's history and meaning.

STEPHEN JAY GOULD US palaeontologist and writer. *The Panda's Thumb* 1980

coelenterate any freshwater or marine organism of the phylum Coelenterata, having a body wall composed of two layers of cells. They also possess stinging cells. Examples are jellyfish, hydra, and coral.

coeliac disease disease in which the small intestine fails to digest and absorb food. The disease can appear at any age but has a peak incidence in the 30–50 age group; it is more common in women. It is caused by an intolerance to gluten (a constituent of wheat, rye and barley) and characterized by diarrhoea and malnutrition. Treatment is by a gluten-free diet.

coelom in all but the simplest animals, the fluid-filled cavity that separates the body wall from the gut and associated organs, and allows the gut muscles to contract independently of the rest of the body.

coevolution evolution of those structures and behaviours within a species that can best be understood in relation to another species. For example, insects and flowering plants have evolved together: insects have produced mouthparts suitable for collecting pollen or drinking nectar, and plants have developed chemicals and flowers that will attract insects to them.

Coevolution occurs because both groups of organisms, over millions of years, benefit from a continuing association, and will evolve structures and behaviours that maintain this association.

coffee drink made from the roasted and ground beanlike seeds found inside the red berries of any of several species of shrubs, originally native to Ethiopia and now cultivated throughout the tropics. It contains a stimulant, ◊caffeine. (Genus *Coffea*, family Rubiaceae.)

cultivation The shrub, naturally about 5 m/17 ft high, is pruned to about 2 m/7 ft; it is fully fruit-bearing in 5 or 6 years, and lasts for 30 years. Coffee grows best on frost-free hillsides with moderate rainfall. The world's largest producers are Brazil, Colombia, and Côte d'Ivoire; others include Indonesia (Java), Ethiopia, India, Hawaii, and Jamaica. In recent years the world coffee market has suffered from over-supply, and in the early 1990s the price of coffee was well below the cost of production.

history Coffee drinking began in Arab regions in the 14th century but did not become common in Europe until three hundred years later, when the first coffee houses were opened in Vienna, and soon after in Paris and London. In the American colonies, coffee became the substitute for tea when tea was taxed by the British.

coffee machine on the Internet, the coffee machine at Cambridge University, England, whose supplies may be monitored via the World Wide Web. It derives from an idea originally developed at a US university, where the Coke machine was some distance from the programming lab. A system of switches was installed so that a programmer could check the machine's supply of Cokes and their temperature before going to collect a drink.

cognition in psychology, a general term covering the functions involved in synthesizing information – for example, perception (seeing, hearing, and so on), attention, memory, and reasoning.

cognitive therapy or ***cognitive behaviour therapy*** treatment for emotional disorders such as ◊depression and ◊anxiety states. It encourages the patient to challenge the distorted and unhelpful thinking that is characteristic of depression, for example. The treatment may include ◊behaviour therapy.

coherence in physics, property of two or more waves of a beam of light or other electromagnetic radiation having the same frequency and the same ◊phase, or a constant phase difference.

cohesion in physics, a phenomenon in which interaction between two surfaces of the same material in contact makes them cling together (with two different materials the similar phenomenon is called adhesion). According to kinetic theory, cohesion is caused by attraction between particles at the atomic or molecular level. ◊Surface tension, which causes liquids to form spherical droplets, is caused by cohesion.

coil in medicine, another name for an ◊intrauterine device.

coke clean, light fuel produced, along with town gas, when coal is strongly heated in an airtight oven. Coke contains 90% carbon and makes a useful domestic and industrial fuel (used, for example in the iron and steel industries).

The process was patented in England 1622, but it was only in 1709 that Abraham Darby devised a commercial method of production.

cola or ***kola*** any of several tropical trees, especially *Cola acuminata.* In W Africa the nuts are chewed for their high ◊caffeine content, and in the West they are used to flavour soft drinks. (Genus *Cola,* family Sterculiaceae.)

cold, common minor disease of the upper respiratory tract, caused by a variety of viruses. Symptoms are headache, chill, nasal discharge, sore throat, and occasionally cough. Research indicates that the virulence of a cold depends on psychological factors and either a reduction or an increase of social or work activity, as a result of stress, in the previous six months.

There is little immediate hope of an effective cure since the viruses transform themselves so rapidly.

cold-blooded of animals, dependent on the surrounding temperature; see ◊poikilothermy.

cold dark matter theory in cosmology, a theory in which the bulk of the matter in the universe is in the form of dark, unseen material consisting of slow-moving particles. The gravitational clumping of this dark matter in the early universe is may have lead to the formation of clusters and superclusters of ◊galaxies.

cold fusion in nuclear physics, the fusion of atomic nuclei at room temperature. If cold fusion were possible it would provide a limitless, cheap, and pollution-free source of energy, and it has therefore been the subject of research around the world.

In 1989, Martin Fleischmann (1927–) and Stanley Pons (1943–) of the University of Utah, USA, claimed that they had achieved cold fusion in the laboratory, but their results could not be substantiated. The University of Utah announced in 1998 that they would allow the cold fusion patent to elapse, given that the work of Pons and Fleischmann has never been reproduced.

> *An important scientific innovation rarely makes its way by gradually winning over and converting its opponents: it rarely happens that Saul becomes Paul. What does happen is that its opponents gradually die out, and that the growing generation is familiarized with the ideas from the beginning.*
>
> MAX PLANCK German physicist.
> In G Holton *Thematic Origins of Scientific Thought* 1973, *Scientific Autobiography* 1949

cold-working method of shaping metal at or near atmospheric temperature.

coleoptile the protective sheath that surrounds the young shoot tip of a grass during its passage through the soil to the surface. Although of relatively simple structure, most coleoptiles are very sensitive to light, ensuring that seedlings grow upwards.

colic spasmodic attack of pain in the abdomen, usually coming in waves. Colicky pains are caused by the painful muscular contraction and subsequent distension of a hollow organ; for example, the bowels, gall bladder (biliary colic), or ureter (renal colic).

Intestinal colic is due to partial or complete blockage of the intestine, or constipation; **infantile colic** is usually due to wind in the intestine.

colitis inflammation of the colon (large intestine) with diarrhoea (often bloody). It is usually due to infection or some types of bacterial dysentery.

collagen protein that is the main constituent of ◊connective tissue. Collagen is present in skin, cartilage, tendons, and ligaments. Bones are made up of collagen, with the mineral calcium phosphate providing increased rigidity.

It was identified in a yeastlike fungus in 1996, the first time it has been found in a nonanimal source.

collective farm ***Russian*** **kolkhoz** farm in which a group of farmers pool their land, domestic animals, and agricultural implements, retaining as private property enough only for the members' own requirements. The profits of the farm are divided among its members. In cooperative farming, farmers retain private ownership of the land.

Collective farming was first developed in the USSR in 1917, where it became general after 1930. Stalin's collectivization drive 1929–33 wrecked a flourishing agricultural system and alienated the Soviet peasants from the land: 15 million people were left homeless, 1 million of whom were sent to labour camps and some 12 million deported to Siberia. In subsequent years, millions of those peasants forced into collectives died. Collective farming is practised in other countries; it was adopted from 1953 in China, and Israel has a large number of collective farms.

collective unconscious in psychology, a shared pool of memories, ideas, modes of thought, and so on, which, according to the Swiss psychiatrist Carl Jung, comes from the life experience of one's ancestors, indeed from the entire human race. It coexists with the personal ◊unconscious, which contains the material of individual experience, and may be regarded as an immense depository of ancient wisdom.

Primal experiences are represented in the collective unconscious by archetypes, symbolic pictures, or personifications that appear in dreams and are the common element in myths, fairy tales, and the literature of the world's religions. Examples include the serpent, the sphinx, the Great Mother, the anima (representing the nature of woman), and the mandala (representing balanced wholeness, human or divine).

collenchyma plant tissue composed of relatively elongated cells with thickened cell walls, in particular at the corners where adjacent cells meet.

It is a supporting and strengthening tissue found in nonwoody plants, mainly in the stems and leaves.

collie any of several breeds of sheepdog originally bred in Britain. They include the ◊border collie, the ◊bearded collie, and the ◊rough collie and its smooth-haired counterpart.

colligative property property that depends on the concentration of particles in a solution. Such properties include osmotic pressure (see ◊osmosis), elevation of ◊boiling point, depression of ◊freezing point, and lowering of ◊vapour pressure.

collimator (1) small telescope attached to a larger optical instrument to fix its line of sight; (2) optical device for producing a nondivergent beam of light; (3) any device for limiting the size and angle of spread of a beam of radiation or particles.

collinear in mathematics, lying on the same straight line.

collision detection in ◊virtual reality, the ability of software to detect when two on-screen objects make contact.

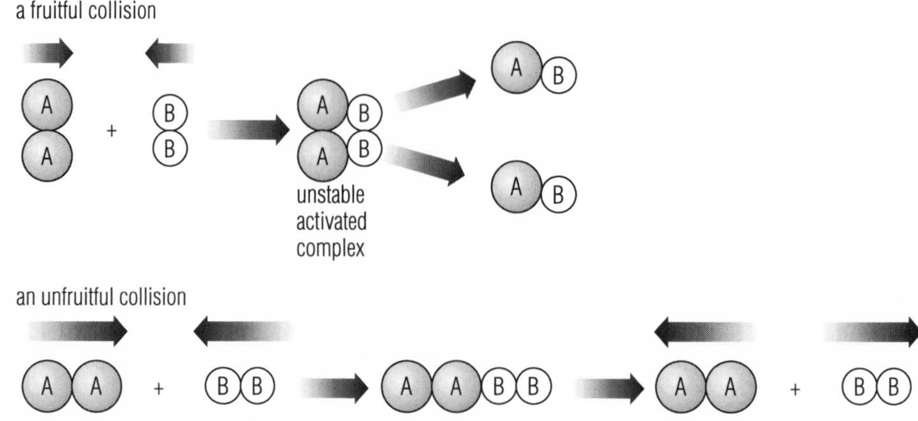

collision theory *Collision theory explains how chemical reactions occur and why rates of reaction differ. For a reaction to occur, particles must collide. If the collision causes a chemical change it is referred to as a fruitful collision.*

collision theory theory that explains how chemical reactions take place and why rates of reaction alter. For a reaction to occur the reactant particles must collide. Only a certain fraction of the total collisions cause chemical change; these are called **fruitful collisions**. The fruitful collisions have sufficient energy (activation energy) at the moment of impact to break the existing bonds and form new bonds, resulting in the products of the reaction. Increasing the concentration of the reactants and raising the temperature bring about more collisions and therefore more fruitful collisions, increasing the rate of reaction.

When a ◊catalyst undergoes collision with the reactant molecules, less energy is required for the chemical change to take place, and hence more collisions have sufficient energy for reaction to occur. The reaction rate therefore increases.

colloid substance composed of extremely small particles of one material (the dispersed phase) evenly and stably distributed in another material (the continuous phase). The size of the dispersed particles (1–1,000 nanometres across) is less than that of particles in suspension but greater than that of molecules in true solution. Colloids involving gases include **aerosols** (dispersions of liquid or solid particles in a gas, as in fog or smoke) and **foams** (dispersions of gases in liquids).

Those involving liquids include **emulsions** (in which both the dispersed and the continuous phases are liquids) and **sols** (solid particles dispersed in a liquid). Sols in which both phases contribute to a molecular three-dimensional network have a jellylike form and are known as **gels**; gelatin, starch 'solution', and silica gel are common examples.

Milk is a natural emulsion of liquid fat in a watery liquid; synthetic emulsions such as some paints and cosmetic lotions have chemical emulsifying agents to stabilize the colloid and stop the two phases from separating out. Colloids were first studied thoroughly by the British chemist Thomas Graham, who defined them as substances that will not diffuse through a semipermeable membrane (as opposed to what he termed crystalloids, solutions of inorganic salts, which will diffuse through).

colobus or ***guereza*** large tree-dwelling African monkey characterized by the almost complete suppression of the thumb. There six species divided into two groups: the black-and-white colobus and the red colobus. They live in groups and feed on fruit, leaves, flowers, and twigs.

Black-and-white colobus monkeys are slightly larger, with a head and body length of 62.5 cm/24.5 in and a long tail (80 cm/31.5 in).

classification Colobuses are in the genus *Colobus,* family Cercopithecidae, order Primates.

colon in anatomy, the main part of the large intestine, between the caecum and rectum. Water and mineral salts are absorbed from undigested food in the colon, and the residue passes as faeces towards the rectum.

colonization in ecology, the spread of species into a new habitat, such as a freshly cleared field, a new motorway verge, or a recently flooded valley. The first species to move in are called **pioneers**, and may establish conditions that allow other animals and plants to move in (for example, by improving the condition of the soil or by providing shade). Over time a range of species arrives and the habitat matures; early colonizers will probably be replaced, so that the variety of animal and plant life present changes. This is known as ◊succession.

Colorado beetle or ***potato beetle*** North American black and yellow striped beetle that is a pest on potato crops. Although it was once a serious pest, it can now usually be controlled by using insecticides. It has also colonized many European countries.

classification Colarado beetles *Leptinotarsa decemlineata* are in the family Chrysomelidae, order Coleoptera, class Insecta, phylum Arthropoda.

colour quality or wavelength of light emitted or reflected from an object. Visible white light consists of electromagnetic radiation of various wavelengths, and if a beam is refracted through a prism, it can be spread out into a spectrum, in which the various colours correspond to different wavelengths. From long to short wavelengths (from about 700 to 400 nanometres) the colours are red, orange, yellow, green, blue, indigo, and violet.

The light entering our eyes is either reflected from the objects we see, or emitted by hot or luminous objects.

> TO REMEMBER THE ADDITIVE AND SUBTRACTIVE MIXTURES OF COLOURS:
>
> BETTER GET READY WHILE YOUR MISTRESS COMES BACK.
>
> BLUE + GREEN + RED = WHITE (ADDITIVE) YELLOW + MAGENTA + CYAN = BLACK (SUBTRACTIVE)

emitted light Sources of light have a characteristic ◊spectrum or range of wavelengths. Hot solid objects emit light with a broad range of wavelengths, the maximum intensity being at a wavelength which depends on the temperature. The hotter the object, the shorter the wavelengths emitted, as described by ◊Wien's displacement law. Hot gases, such as the vapour of sodium street lights, emit light at discrete wavelengths. The pattern of wavelengths emitted is unique to each gas and can be used to identify the gas (see ◊spectroscopy).
reflected light When an object is illuminated by white light, some of the wavelengths are absorbed and some are reflected to the eye of an observer. The object appears coloured because of the mixture of wavelengths in the reflected light. For instance, a red object absorbs all wavelengths falling on it except those in the red end of the spectrum. This process of subtraction also explains why certain mixtures of paints produce different colours. Blue and yellow paints when mixed together produce green because between them the yellow and blue pigments absorb all wavelengths except those around green. A suitable combination of three pigments – cyan (blue-green), magenta (blue-red), and yellow – can produce any colour when mixed. This fact is used in colour printing, although additional black pigment is also added.
primary colours In the light-sensitive lining of our eyeball (the ◊retina), cells called cones are responsible for colour vision. There are three kinds of cones. Each type is sensitive to one colour only, either red, green, or blue. The brain combines the signals sent from the set of cones to produce a sensation of colour. When all cones are stimulated equally the sensation is of white light. The three colours to which the cones respond are called the **primary colours**. By mixing lights of these three colours, it is possible to produce any colour. This process is called colour mixing by addition, and is used to produce the colour on a television screen, where glowing phosphor dots of red, green, and blue combine.
complementary colours Pairs of colours that produce white light, such as yellow and blue, are called complementary colours.
classifying colours Many schemes have been proposed for classifying colours. The most widely used is the Munsell scheme, which classifies colours according to their hue (dominant wavelength), saturation (the degree of whiteness), and brightness (intensity).

colour in particle physics, a property of ◊quarks analogous to electric charge but having three states, denoted by red, green, and blue. The colour of a quark is changed when it emits or absorbs a ◊gluon. The term has nothing to do with colour in its usual sense. See ◊quantum chromodynamics.

colour blindness hereditary defect of vision that reduces the ability to discriminate certain colours, usually red and green. The condition is sex-linked, affecting men more than women.

colour depth in computing, the maximum number of colours that can be displayed simultaneously in an image by a particular computer system.

The most common modes are 16, 256, 32K, 64K and 16.7 million (true colour). The greater the colour depth, the larger the size of the picture file but the more detailed and realistic the quality of the picture.

colour index in astronomy, a measure of the colour of a star made by comparing its brightness through different coloured filters. It is defined as the difference between the ◊magnitude of the star measured through two standard photometric filters. Colour index is directly related to the surface temperature of a star and its spectral classification.

colouring food additive used to alter or improve the colour of processed foods. Colourings include artificial colours, such as tartrazine and amaranth, which are made from petrochemicals, and the 'natural' colours such as chlorophyll, caramel, and carotene. Some of the natural colours are actually synthetic copies of the naturally occurring substances, and some of these, notably the synthetically produced caramels, may be injurious to health.

Colourpoint Longhair or ***Himalayan*** breed of domestic longhaired cat originally developed in the 1920s in America and Sweden from a cross between Persian and Siamese cats. The Sealpoint was one of the first varieties to be developed and has a warm cream coat with contrasting deep brown markings on the face, ears, feet, paws, and tail. It has small ears, blue eyes, and short legs.

The breed was recognized in 1955 in Europe and in the USA in 1957 where it is most widely bred. It has many varieties.

colour vision the ability of the eye to recognize different frequencies in the visible spectrum as colours. In most vertebrates, including humans, colour vision is due to the presence on the ◊retina of three types of light-sensitive cone cell, each of which responds to a different primary colour (red, green, or blue).

Colour vision is one of the ways in which the brain can acquire knowledge of the unchanging characteristics of objects. Colours are constructs of the brain, rather than physical features of objects or their surface. They remain more or less stable, and objects remain recognizable, in spite of the continuously changing illumination in which they are seen, a phenomenon known as **colour constancy**.

Colt, Samuel (1814–1862)

US gunsmith who invented the revolver in 1835 that bears his name. With its rotating cylinder which turned, locked, and unlocked by cocking the hammer, the Colt was superior to other revolving pistols, and it revolutionized military tactics.

mass production for war Colt built a large factory in Hartford, Connecticut in 1854. He introduced mass-production techniques, and his weapons had interchangeable parts, making them easy to maintain and repair. During the Crimean War 1853–56 he also manufactured arms in Pimlico, London. By 1855 he had the largest private armoury in the world. When the American Civil War broke out in 1861, he supplied thousands of guns to the US government.

Mary Evans Picture Library

coltsfoot perennial plant belonging to the daisy family. The single yellow flower heads have many narrow rays (not petals), and the stems have large purplish scales. The large leaf, up to 22 cm/9 in across, is shaped like a horse's foot and gives the plant its name. Coltsfoot grows in Europe, N Asia, and N Africa, often on bare ground and in waste places, and has been introduced to North America. It was formerly used in medicine. (*Tussilago farfara*, family Compositae.)

colugo or ***flying lemur*** SE Asian climbing mammal of the genus *Cynocephalus*, order Dermoptera, about 60 cm/2 ft long including the tail. It glides between forest trees using a flap of skin that extends from head to forelimb to hindlimb to tail. It may glide 130 m/425 ft or more, losing little height. It feeds largely on buds and leaves, and rests hanging upside down under branches.

There are two species, *C. variegatus* of Indochina and Indonesia, and *C. volans* of the Philippines.

columbine any of a group of plants belonging to the buttercup family. All are perennial herbs with divided leaves and hanging flower heads with spurred petals. (Genus *Aquilegia*, family Ranunculaceae.)

The wild columbine (*Aquilegia vulgaris*), with blue flowers, has been developed by repeated crossing to produce modern garden species (*A. x hybrida*), with larger flowers and a wider range of colours. The eastern columbine (*A. canadensis*), with red flowers, is native to E North America.

columbium (Cb) former name for the chemical element ◊niobium. The name is still used occasionally in metallurgy.

column a vertical list of numbers or terms, especially in matrices.

COM acronym for ◊computer output on microfilm/microfiche.

coma in astronomy, the hazy cloud of gas and dust that surrounds the nucleus of a ◊comet.

coma in medicine, a state of deep unconsciousness from which the subject cannot be roused. Possible causes include head injury, brain disease, liver failure, cerebral haemorrhage, and drug overdose.

coma in optics, one of the geometrical aberrations of a lens, whereby skew rays from an object make a comet-shaped spot on the image plane instead of meeting at a point.

combe or ***coombe*** steep-sided valley found on the scarp slope of a chalk ◊escarpment. The inclusion of 'combe' in a placename usually indicates that the underlying rock is chalk.

combination in mathematics, a selection of a number of objects from some larger number of objects when no account is taken of order within any one arrangement. For example, 123, 213, and 312 are regarded as the same combination of three digits from 1234. Combinatorial analysis is used in the study of ◊probability.

The number of ways of selecting r objects from a group of n is given by the formula:

$$n!/[r!(n - r)!]$$

(see ◊factorial). This is usually denoted by ^nCr.

combine in ◊probability theory, to work out the chances of two or more events occurring at the same time.

combined cycle generation system of electricity generation that makes use of both a gas turbine and a steam turbine. Combined cycle plants are more efficient than conventional generating plants.

In combined cycle generation, the gas turbine is powered by burning gas fuel, and turns an electric generator. The exhaust gases are then used to heat water to produce steam. The steam powers a steam turbine attached to an electric generator, producing additional electricity.

combined heat and power generation (CHP generation) simultaneous production of electricity and useful heat in a power station. The heat is often in the form of hot water or steam, which can be used for local district heating or in industry. The electricity output from a CHP plant is lower than from a conventional station, but the overall efficiency of energy conversion is higher. A typical CHP plant may convert 80% of the original fuel energy into a mix of electricity and useful heat, whereas a conventional power station rarely even manages a 40% conversion rate.

combine harvester or ***combine*** machine used for harvesting cereals and other crops, so called because it combines the actions of reaping (cutting the crop) and threshing (beating the ears so that the grain separates).

A combine, drawn by horses, was first built in Michigan in 1836. Today's mechanical combine harvesters are capable of cutting a swath of up to 9 m/30 ft or more.

combustion burning, defined in chemical terms as the rapid combination of a substance with oxygen, accompanied by the evolution of heat and usually light. A slow-burning candle flame and the explosion of a mixture of petrol vapour and air are extreme examples of combustion.

comet small, icy body orbiting the Sun, usually on a highly elliptical path. A comet consists of a central nucleus a few kilometres across, and has been likened to a dirty snowball because it consists mostly of ice mixed with dust. As a comet approaches the Sun its nucleus heats up, releasing gas and dust which form a tenuous coma, up to 100,000 km/60,000 mi wide, around the nucleus. Gas and dust stream away from the coma to form one or more tails, which may extend for millions of kilometres. US astronomers concluded in 1996 that there are two distinct types of comet: one rich in methanol and one low in methanol. Evidence for this comes in part from observations of the spectrum of Comet Hyakutake.

Comets are believed to have been formed at the birth of the Solar System. Billions of them may reside in a halo (the ◊Oort cloud) beyond Pluto. The gravitational effect of passing stars pushes some towards the Sun, when they eventually become visible from Earth. Most comets swing around the Sun and return to distant space, never to be seen again for thousands or millions of years, although some, called periodic comets, have their orbits altered by the gravitational pull of the planets so that they reappear every 200 years or less. Periodic comets are thought to come from the ◊Kuiper belt, a zone just beyond Neptune. Of the 800 or so comets whose orbits have been calculated, about 160 are periodic. The one with the shortest known period is ◊Encke's comet, which orbits the Sun every 3.3 years. A dozen or more comets are discovered every year, some by amateur astronomers.

Comet Hale-Bopp (C/1995–01) large and exceptionally active comet, which in March 1997 made its closest flyby to Earth since 2000 BC, coming within 190 million km/118 million mi. It has a diameter of approximately 40 km/25 mi and an extensive gas coma (when close to the Sun Hale-Bopp released 10 tonnes of gas every second). Unusually, Hale-Bopp has three tails: one consisting of dust particles, one of charged particles, and a third of sodium particles.

Comet Hale-Bopp was discovered independently in July 1995 by two amateur US astronomers, Alan Hale and Thomas Bopp.

Comet Shoemaker-Levy 9 a ◊comet that crashed into ◊Jupiter in July 1994. The fragments crashed into Jupiter at 60 kps/37 mps over the period 16–22 July 1994. The impacts occurred on the far side of Jupiter, but the impact sites came into view of Earth about 25 minutes later. Analysis of the impacts shows that most of the pieces were solid bodies about 1 km/0.6 mi in diameter, but that at least three of them were clusters of smaller objects.

When first sighted in 24 March 1993 by US astronomers Carolyn and Eugene Shoemaker and David Levy, it was found to consist of at least 21 fragments in an unstable orbit around Jupiter. It is believed to have been captured by Jupiter in about 1930 and fragmented by tidal forces on passing within 21,000 km/ 13,050 mi of the planet in July 1992.

COMET SHOEMAKER-LEVY HOME PAGE

http://www.jpl.nasa.gov/sl9/

Description of the comet's collision with Jupiter 1994, the first collision of two Solar System bodies ever to be observed. There is background information, latest theories about the effects of the collision, and even some animations of Jupiter and the impact.

comfort index estimate of how tolerable conditions are for humans in hot climates. It is calculated as the temperature in degrees Fahrenheit plus a quarter of the relative ◊humidity, expressed as a percentage. If the sum is less than 95, conditions are tolerable for those unacclimatized to the tropics.

comfrey any of a group of plants belonging to the borage family, with rough, hairy leaves and small bell-shaped flowers (blue, purple-pink, or white). They are found in Europe and W Asia. (Genus *Symphytum*, family Boraginaceae.)

The European species (*Symphytum officinale*) was once used to make ointment for treating wounds and various ailments, and is still sometimes used as a poultice which is applied to the skin to treat inflammation. It grows up to 1.2 m/4 ft tall and has hairy,

Comet Hale-Bopp

BY CHARLES ARTHUR

The appearance of the Hale-Bopp comet in the skies of the northern hemisphere in February 1997 excited scientists and the public alike; but nobody could have foreseen that by the time it had disappeared from our skies, 41 people would have taken their lives because of its presence.

Comets throughout history

Comets have been viewed as harbingers of doom for thousands of years: their inexplicable appearance in an otherwise orderly sky perplexed ancient astronomers. Now they are known to be chunks of rock, dust, ice, and other chemicals, following enormously elliptical orbits around the Sun, which take them within the Earth's orbit before they swing past into the darkness of space beyond the most distant planet, Pluto. As a comet nears the Sun, its body is heated by solar radiation causing some of its constituent chemicals to boil off into space, producing the characteristic 'tail'. This tail is pushed away from the Sun by the pressure of the 'solar wind': thus the tail's direction is not related to the direction of travel, only to the position of the Sun.

This elliptical orbit means that a comet travels through a regular path; each comet differs only in how long it takes to appear. Halley's Comet, for example, turns up every 76 years; its last visit was in 1986. In 1996, many people were disappointed when Comet Hyakutake, discovered by an amateur Japanese astronomer, turned out to be a drab show.

Hale-Bopp, also discovered by amateur astronomers, takes roughly 4,000 years to complete its orbit. It first became visible in the northern hemisphere in February 1997, because its orbit is tilted compared to ours – so that it approached from 'above' the plane of the solar system.

Ablaze in the night sky

Astronomers and the general public were delighted. 'The comet of the century', commented the scientists. It quickly became so bright that outside the light pollution of cities it was easily visible at night without telescopes or binoculars, and most notably early in the morning.

Beautiful time-lapse photographs – taken in deserts, over monuments such as Stonehenge (which was seeing the comet for at least the second time), and open country – filled newspapers, showing off its dual blue (dust) and yellow (gas) tails stretching for up to 20 million miles. It was, astronomers agreed, one of the brightest comets in the past 500 years. On the Internet, the discussion about the comet drew outlandish comments from some people – including some who said that the comet was being shadowed by a UFO that was hiding behind it in order to approach the Earth. Scientists laughed it off as the sort of misconception that can be commonplace on the global network. 'If I was in a UFO and wanted to sneak up on earth, I wouldn't do it behind the most-watched celestial object for years', said one.

Comet Hale-Bopp grew brighter by the day. Its closest approach to the Earth was on 22 March, when it flew by just 123 million miles away from us; its closest approach to the Sun was on 1 April, when it was just 85 million miles away from it. (The Earth is 93 million miles from the Sun.)

Heaven's gate

However, on Wednesday, March 26, the idea that Hale-Bopp was simply a cosmic phenomenon all changed. It was late in the afternoon when San Diego police drove to a five-bedroom Spanish mansion at 18241 Colina Norte, after receiving two anonymous phone calls telling them to check on the residents.

They had no reason to be suspicious: anyone who knew the house had heard that it was the centre for a group of people who made their living programming Web pages for corporate customers: not unusual for San Diego.

Arriving there, the police found the front doors locked, the windows shut and blinds drawn. A side door was unlocked – and through there they found ten dead men on the floor. The bodies were already decomposing. In all, the corpses of 21 women and 18 men, passports and IDs tucked in the top pockets of their shirts, were discovered. It had been a mass suicide, timed to coincide with Hale-Bopp's closest approach to Earth.

Videotapes made by the suicides, who had dressed in matching black with crewcut hair, showed that despite the name of their business – WWW Higher Source – they were quite simply a cult. They believed their leader, who told them that the comet was really the cloak for a UFO; they believed the time had come to 'shed their earthly containers' (bodies) and regain their true identities as angels from another planet. They died in a mass suicide carried out in three waves over a period of days, using a mixture of alcohol and phenobarbitol (swallowed with pudding or apple sauce) and plastic bags over their heads; the last survivors took the bags off the earlier dead and draped them with purple scarves. Each had videotaped a statement saying they were 'going to a better place'. The cult called themselves 'Heaven's Gate', and had its own Web site, which had been crammed with invisible text to give it a high profile on the Internet for anyone searching for information about UFOs. The site invited people to join them in their mission. Sadly, two more people did, committing suicide in April and May, in the belief that they would join the group in leaving on the comet.

Yet away from the obsessed, the comet brought good news to makers of binoculars and telescopes, and of camera tripods: people wanted to get pictures of the comet of the century. Undoubtedly, it fulfilled all expectations.

winged stems, lanceolate (tapering) leaves, and white, yellowish, purple, or pink flowers in drooping clusters.

Comité Consultatif International Téléphonique et Télégraphique (CCITT) international organization that determines international communications standards and protocols for data communications, including ◊fax. It was subsumed into the International Telecommunications Union (ITU) in 1993.

Natura non nisi parendo vincitur.
Nature, to be commanded, must be obeyed.

FRANCIS BACON English politician, philosopher, and essayist. *Novum Organum* 1620 Aphorism 43

command language in computing, a set of commands and the rules governing their use, by which users control a program. For example, an ◊operating system may have commands such as SAVE and DELETE, or a payroll program may have commands for adding and amending staff records.

command line interface (CLI) in computing, a character-based interface in which a prompt is displayed on the screen at which the user types a command, followed by ◊carriage return, at which point the command, if valid, is executed.

commensalism in biology, a relationship between two ◊species whereby one (the commensal) benefits from the association, whereas the other neither benefits nor suffers. For example, certain species of millipede and silverfish inhabit the nests of army ants and live by scavenging on the refuse of their hosts, but without affecting the ants.

Commercial Internet eXchange (CIX) US-based international nonprofit-making organization of ◊Internet Service Providers and other data network suppliers. It is part of the Internet's US ◊backbone funded by commercial service providers.

Common Agricultural Policy (CAP) system of financial support for farmers in European Union (EU) countries. The most important way in which EU farmers are supported is through guaranteeing them minimum prices for part of what they produce. The CAP has been criticized for its role in creating overproduction, and consequent environmental damage, and for the high price of food subsidies. ***aims*** The CAP permits the member countries of the EU jointly to organize and control agricultural production within their boundaries. The objectives of the CAP were outlined in the Treaty of Rome: to increase agricultural productivity, to provide a fair standard of living for farmers and their employees, to stabilize markets, and to assure the availability of supply at a price that was reasonable to the consumer.
history The policy, applied to most types of agricultural product, was evolved and introduced between 1962 and 1967, and has since been amended to take account of changing conditions and the entry of additional member states. At the heart of the CAP is a price support system based on setting a target price for a commodity, imposing a levy on cheaper imports, and intervening to buy produce at a predetermined level to maintain the stability of the internal market. When the CAP was devised, the six member states were net importers of most essential agricultural products, and the intervention mechanism was aimed at smoothing out occasional surpluses caused by an unusually productive season.
overproduction The CAP became extremely expensive in the 1970s and 1980s due to overproduction of those agricultural products that were subsidized. In many years, far more was produced than could be sold and it had to be stored, creating 'mountains' and 'lakes' of produce. This put the CAP under intense financial and political strain, and led to mounting pressure for reform.

common denominator denominator that is a common multiple of, and hence exactly divisible by, all the denominators of a set of fractions, and which therefore enables their sums or differences to be found.

For example, $\frac{2}{3}$ and $\frac{3}{4}$ can both be converted to equivalent fractions of denominator 12, $\frac{2}{3}$ being equal to $\frac{8}{12}$ and $\frac{3}{4}$ to $\frac{9}{12}$. Hence their sum is $\frac{17}{12}$ and their difference is $\frac{1}{12}$. The **lowest common denominator** (lcd) is the smallest common multiple of the denominators of a given set of fractions.

common difference the difference between any number and the next in an ◊arithmetic progression. For example, in the set 1, 4, 7, 10, ... , the common difference is 3.

common factor number that will divide two or more others without leaving a remainder. For example, 3 is a common factor of 15, 21, and 24.

common gateway interface (CGI) on the World Wide Web, a facility for adding scripts to handle user input. It allows a Web ◊server to communicate with other programs running on the same server in order to process data input by visitors to the Web site. CGI scripts 'parse' the input data, identifying each element and feeding it to the correct program for action, normally a ◊search engine or e-mail program. The results are then fed back to the user in the form of search results or sent e-mail.

common logarithm another name for a ◊logarithm to the base ten.

comms program contraction of ◊communications program.

communication in biology, the signalling of information by one organism to another, usually with the intention of altering the recipient's behaviour. Signals used in communication may be **visual** (such as the human smile or the display of colourful plumage in birds), **auditory** (for example, the whines or barks of a dog), **olfactory** (such as the odours released by the scent glands of a deer), **electrical** (as in the pulses emitted by electric fish), or **tactile** (for example, the nuzzling of male and female elephants).

> *What hath God wrought?*
>
> SAMUEL FINLEY BREESE MORSE US inventor.
> First message sent on his electric telegraph 24 May 1844

communications in computing, see ◊data communications.

Communications Decency Act 1996 rider (supplement) to the US Telecommunications Bill seeking to prohibit the transmission of indecent material to minors via the Internet.

Within hours of the bill's passage into law on 8 February 1996, suits were filed by 46 plaintiffs including the American Civil Liberties Union, Voter Telecom Watch, the Electronic Frontier Foundation, and the Center for Democracy and Technology to block the law's enforcement. On 12 June the Philadelphia federal court struck the law down with a judgement that read in part: 'Just as the strength of the Internet is chaos, so the strength of our liberty depends upon the chaos and cacophony of the unfettered speech the First Amendment (to the US Constitution) protects'. A second judgement from a New York court agreed. The government was expected to appeal both rulings to the Supreme Court.

communications program or ***comms program*** general-purpose program for accessing older ◊online systems and ◊bulletin board systems which use a ◊command-line interface; also known as a terminal emulator.

Most operating systems include a trimmed-down comms program, but full-featured programs include facilities to store phone numbers and settings for frequently called services, address books, and the ability to write scripts to automate logging on. Popular comms programs include ProComm, Smartcom, Qmodem, and Odyssey.

communications satellite relay station in space for sending telephone, television, telex, and other messages around the world. Messages are sent to and from the satellites via ground stations. Most communications satellites are in ◊geostationary orbit, appearing to hang fixed over one point on the Earth's surface.

The first satellite to carry TV signals across the Atlantic Ocean was *Telstar* in July 1962. The world is now linked by a system of communications satellites called Intelsat. Other satellites are used by individual countries for internal communications, or for business or military use. A new generation of satellites, called **direct broadcast satellites**, are powerful enough to transmit direct to small domestic aerials. The power for such satellites is produced by solar cells (see ◊solar energy). The total energy requirement of a satellite is small; a typical communications satellite needs about 2 kW of power, the same as an electric heater.

community in ecology, an assemblage of plants, animals, and other organisms living within a circumscribed area. Communities are usually named by reference to a dominant feature such as characteristic plant species (for example, a beech-wood community), or a prominent physical feature (for example, a freshwater-pond community).

commutative operation in mathematics, an operation that is independent of the order of the numbers or symbols concerned. For example, addition is commutative: the result of adding 4 + 2 is the same as that of adding 2 + 4; subtraction is not as 4 – 2 = 2, but 2 – 4 = –2. Compare ◊associative operation and ◊distributive operation.

commutator device in a DC (direct-current) electric motor that reverses the current flowing in the armature coils as the armature rotates.

A DC generator, or ◊dynamo, uses a commutator to convert the AC (alternating current) generated in the armature coils into DC. A commutator consists of opposite pairs of conductors insulated from one another, and contact to an external circuit is provided by carbon or metal brushes.

compact disc (CD) disc for storing digital information, about 12 cm/4.5 in across, mainly used for music, when it can have over an hour's playing time. The compact disc is etched by a ◊laser beam

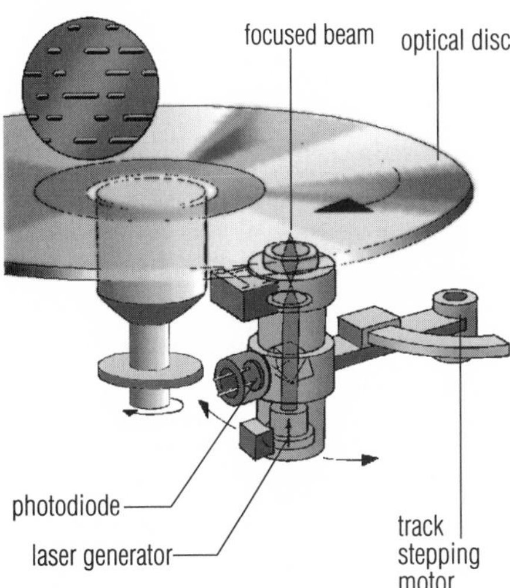

***compact disc** The compact disc is a digital storage device; music is recorded as a series of etched pits representing numbers in digital code. During playing, a laser scans the pits and the pattern of reflected light reveals the numbers representing the sound recorded. The optical signal is converted to electrical form by a photocell and sent to the amplifiers and loudspeakers.*

with microscopic pits that carry a digital code representing the sounds; the pitted surface is then coated with aluminium. During playback, a laser beam reads the code and produces signals that are changed into near-exact replicas of the original sounds.

CD-ROM, or **Compact-Disc Read-Only Memory**, is used to store written text, pictures, and video clips in addition to music. The discs are ideal for large works, such as catalogues and encyclopedias. CD-I, or **Compact-Disc Interactive**, is a form of CD-ROM used with a computerized reader, which responds intelligently to the user's instructions. Recordable CDs, called **WORMs** ('write once, read many times'), are used as computer discs, but are as yet too expensive for home use. **Video CDs**, on sale since 1994, store an hour of video. High-density video discs, first publicly demonstrated in 1995, can hold full-length features. Erasable CDs, which can be erased and recorded many times, are also used by the computer industry. These are coated with a compound of cobalt and the rare earth metal gadolinium, which alters the polarization of light falling on it. In the reader, the light reflected from the disc is passed through polarizing filters and the changes in polarization are converted into electrical signals.

Multi-layer CDs with increased storage capacity were developed in 1996. Two layers are enough to store a film 2 hours long, and up to 16 layers have been reliably read.

comparative anatomy study of the similarity and differences in the anatomy of different groups of animals. It helps to reveal how animals are related to each other and how they have changed through evolution.

Structures are **homologous** if they have arisen from the same ancestral structure through evolution, but perform either similar or different functions in modern animals. Examples of homologous structures are the wings of birds, the human arm, and the forelimb of whales.

Analogous structures have developed from different ancestral structures, but perform similar functions, such as the wings of insects and those of birds.

compass any instrument for finding direction. The most commonly used is a magnetic compass, consisting of a thin piece of magnetic material with the north-seeking pole indicated, free to rotate on a pivot and mounted on a compass card on which the points of the compass are marked. When the compass is properly adjusted and used, the north-seeking pole will point to the magnetic north,

To remember the points of the compass, in the correct order:

NOBODY EVER SWALLOWS WHALES

OR

NEVER EAT SHREDDED WHEAT

OR

NEVER EAT SLIMY WORMS

OR

NEVER EAT SOGGY WAFFLES

OR

NEVER EAT SOUR WATERMELON

PLACE THE FIRST LETTER OF EACH WORD IN A CLOCKWISE CIRCLE STARTING AT THE 12 O'CLOCK (NORTH) POSITION

from which true north can be found from tables of magnetic corrections.

Compasses not dependent on the magnet are gyrocompasses, dependent on the ◊gyroscope, and radiocompasses, dependent on the use of radio. These are unaffected by the presence of iron and by magnetic anomalies of the Earth's magnetic field, and are widely used in ships and aircraft. See ◊navigation.

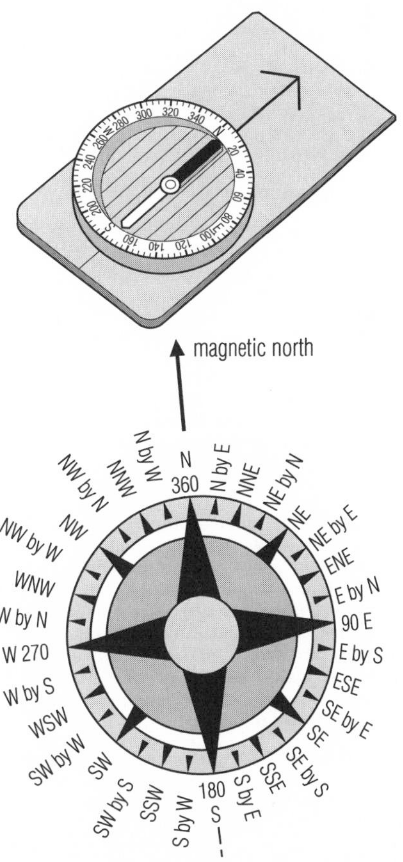

***compass** As early as 2500 BC, the Chinese were using pieces of magnetic rock, magnetite, as simple compasses. By the 12th century, European navigators were using compasses consisting of a needle-shaped magnet floating in a bowl of water.*

compensation point in biology, the point at which there is just enough light for a plant to survive. At this point all the food produced by ◊photosynthesis is used up by ◊respiration. For aquatic plants, the compensation point is the depth of water at which there is just enough light to sustain life (deeper water = less light = less photosynthesis).

competition in ecology, the interaction between two or more organisms, or groups of organisms (for example, species), that use a common resource which is in short supply. Competition invariably results in a reduction in the numbers of one or both competitors, and in ◊evolution contributes both to the decline of certain species and to the evolution of ◊adaptations.

Thus plants may compete with each other for sunlight, or nutrients from the soil, while animals may compete amongst themselves for food, water, or refuge.

compiler computer program that translates programs written in a ◊high-level language into machine code (the form in which they can be run by the computer). The compiler translates each high-level instruction into several machine-code instructions – in a process called **compilation** – and produces a complete independent program that can be run by the computer as often as required, without the original source program being present.

Different compilers are needed for different high-level languages and for different computers. In contrast to using an ◊interpreter, using a compiler adds slightly to the time needed to develop a new program because the machine-code program must be recompiled after each change or correction. Once compiled, however, the machine-code program will run much faster than an interpreted program.

complement in mathematics, the set of the elements within the universal set that are not contained in the designated set. For example, if the universal set is the set of all positive whole numbers and the designated set *S* is the set of all even numbers, then the complement of *S* (denoted *S*') is the set of all odd numbers.

complementary angles two angles that add up to 90°.

complementary medicine in medicine, systems of care based on methods of treatment or theories of disease that differ from those taught in most western medical schools. See ◊medicine, ◊alternative.

complementary metal-oxide semiconductor (CMOS) in electronics, a particular way of manufacturing integrated circuits (chips). The main advantage of CMOS chips is their low power requirement and heat dissipation, which enables them to be used in electronic watches and portable microcomputers. However, CMOS circuits are expensive to manufacture and have lower operating speeds than have circuits of the ◊transistor–transistor logic (TTL) family.

complementary number in number theory, the number obtained by subtracting a number from its base. For example, the complement of 7 in numbers to base 10 is 3. Complementary numbers are necessary in computing, as the only mathematical operation of which digital computers (including pocket calculators) are directly capable is addition. Two numbers can be subtracted by adding one number to the complement of the other; two numbers can be divided by using successive subtraction (which, using complements, becomes successive addition); and multiplication can be performed by using successive addition.

complementation in genetics, the interaction that can occur between two different mutant alleles of a gene in a ◊diploid organism, to make up for each other's deficiencies and allow the organism to function normally.

completing the square method of converting a quadratic expression such as $x^2 + px + q$ into a perfect square by adding $\frac{p^2}{4}$ and subtracting q in order to solve the quadratic equation $x^2 + px + q = 0$. The steps are:

$$x^2 + px = -q$$

$$x^2 + px + \frac{p^2}{4} = \frac{p^2}{4} - q$$

$$(x^2 + \frac{p}{2})^2 = \frac{p^2}{4} - q$$

$$x + \frac{p}{2} = \pm \frac{p^2}{4} - q$$

$$x = -\frac{p}{2} \pm \frac{p^2}{4} - q$$

complex in psychology, a group of ideas and feelings that have become repressed because they are distasteful to the person in whose mind they arose, but are still active in the depths of the person's unconscious mind, continuing to affect his or her life and actions, even though he or she is no longer fully aware of their existence. Typical examples include the ◊Oedipus complex and the ◊inferiority complex.

complex number in mathematics, a number written in the form $a + ib$, where a and b are ◊real numbers and i is the square root of -1 (that is, $i^2 = -1$); i used to be known as the 'imaginary' part of the complex number. Some equations in algebra, such as those of the form $x^2 + 5 = 0$, cannot be solved without recourse to complex numbers, because the real numbers do not include square roots of negative numbers.

The sum of two or more complex numbers is obtained by adding separately their real and imaginary parts, for example:

$$(a + bi) + (c + di) = (a + c) + (b + d)i$$

Complex numbers can be represented graphically on an Argand diagram, which uses rectangular ◊Cartesian coordinates in which the x-axis represents the real part of the number and the y-axis the imaginary part. Thus the number $z = a + bi$ is plotted as the point (a, b). Complex numbers have applications in various areas of science, such as the theory of alternating currents in electricity.

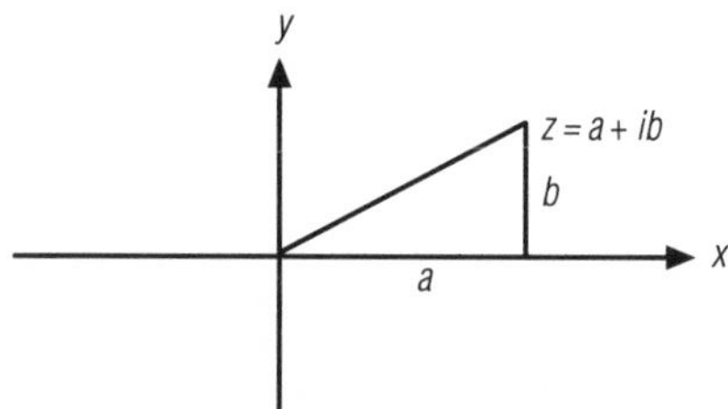

complex number *A complex number can be represented graphically as a line whose end-point coordinates equal the real and imaginary parts of the complex number. This type of diagram is called an Argand diagram after the French mathematician Jean Argand (1768–1822) who devised it.*

component in physics, one of two or more vectors, normally at right angles to each other, that add together to produce the same effect as a single resultant vector. Any ◊vector quantity, such as force, velocity, or electric field, can be resolved into components chosen for ease of calculation. For example, the weight of a body resting on a slope can be resolved into two force components (see ◊resolution of forces); one normal to the slope and the other parallel to the slope.

COM port (contraction of ***communication port*** on a personal computer (PC), one of the serial ◊ports through which ◊data communications take place. PCs may have up to four COM ports. However, these cannot all be used simultaneously as COM1 and COM3 share an ◊interrupt, as do COM2 and COM4. A modem added to a machine with a mouse on COM1 must be attached to COM2 or COM4.

Compositae daisy family, comprising dicotyledonous flowering plants characterized by flowers borne in composite heads (see ◊capitulum). It is the largest family of flowering plants, the majority being herbaceous. Birds seem to favour the family for use in nest 'decoration', possibly because many species either repel or kill insects (see ◊pyrethrum). Species include the daisy and dandelion; food plants such as the artichoke, lettuce, and safflower; and the garden varieties of chrysanthemum, dahlia, and zinnia.

composite in industry, any purpose-designed engineering material created by combining materials with complementary properties into a composite form. Most composites have a structure in which one component consists of discrete elements, such as fibres, dispersed in a continuous matrix. For example, lengths of asbestos, glass, or carbon steel, or 'whiskers' (specially grown crystals a few millimetres long) of substances such as silicon carbide may be dispersed in plastics, concrete, or steel.

composite function in mathematics, a function made up of two or more other functions carried out in sequence, usually denoted by * or ^, as in the relation $(f * g)\ x = f\ [g(x)]$.

Usually, composition is not commutative: $(f * g)$ is not necessarily the same as $(g * f)$.

compost organic material decomposed by bacteria under controlled conditions to make a nutrient-rich natural fertilizer for use in gardening or farming. A well-made compost heap reaches a high temperature during the composting process, killing most weed seeds that might be present.

compound chemical substance made up of two or more ◊elements bonded together, so that they cannot be separated by physical means. Compounds are held together by ionic or covalent bonds.

compound document in Windows, a document containing elements that have been created using other programs. Usually managed through a word processor, such a document might include a table created in a spreadsheet and pictures created in a drawing program. These items may be linked using ◊object linking and embedding (OLE), so that any changes made to the table in the word processor will also be made to the original table developed in the spreadsheet.

Compressed Serial Line Internet Protocol in computing, protocol usually abbreviated to ◊CSLIP.

compression in computing, see ◊data compression.

compressor machine that compresses a gas, usually air, commonly used to power pneumatic tools, such as road drills, paint sprayers, and dentist's drills.

Reciprocating compressors use pistons moving in cylinders to compress the air. Rotary compressors use a varied rotor moving eccentrically inside a casing. The air compressor in jet and ◊gas turbine engines consists of a many-varied rotor rotating at high speed within a fixed casing, where the rotor blades slot between fixed, or stator, blades on the casing.

Compton effect in physics, the increase in wavelength (loss of energy) of a photon by its collision with a free electron **(Compton scattering)**. The Compton effect was first demonstrated with X-rays and provided early evidence that electromagnetic waves consisted of particles – photons – which carried both energy and momentum. It is named after US physicist Arthur Compton.

Compulink Information eXchange (CIX) London-based electronic conferencing system founded in 1987. Owned by Frank and Sylvia Thornley, CIX is the oldest and largest native British conferencing system. In 1996 it had approximately 16,000 users, including most of the country's technology journalists.

CompuServe large (US-based) public online information service. It is widely used for ◊electronic mail and ◊bulletin boards, as well as ◊gateway access to large periodical databases.

CompuServe was established in 1979. It is easier to use than the Internet and most computer hardware and software suppliers provide support for their products on CompuServe. Worldwide subscribers to CompuServe have risen from half a million in 1988 to about 5.2 million in 1997 CompuServe started moving some of its services to the ◊World Wide Web in 1996 and was taken over by rival ◊America Online in 1997.

COMPUTER MUSEUM

http://www.net.org/

Well-designed interactive museum, examining the history, development, and future of computer technology. As well as plenty of illustrations and detailed explanations, it is possible to change your route through the museum by indicating whether you are a kid, student, adult, or educator.

computer programmable electronic device that processes data and performs calculations and other symbol-manipulation tasks. There are three types: the ◊digital computer, which manipulates information coded as binary numbers (see ◊binary number

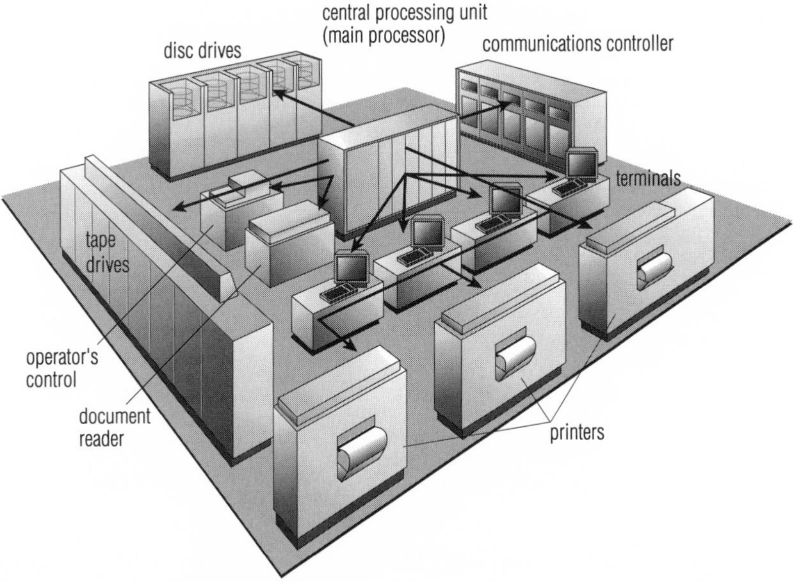

***computer** A mainframe computer. Functionally, it has the same component parts as a microcomputer, but on a much larger scale. The central processing unit is at the hub, and controls all the attached devices.*

Computer: chronology

1614	John Napier invented logarithms.
1615	William Oughtred invented the slide rule.
1623	Wilhelm Schickard (1592–1635) invented the mechanical calculating machine.
1645	Blaise Pascal produced a calculator.
1672–74	Gottfried Leibniz built his first calculator, the Stepped Reckoner.
1801	Joseph-Marie Jacquard developed an automatic loom controlled by punch cards.
1820	The first mass-produced calculator, the Arithometer, was developed by Charles Thomas de Colmar (1785–1870).
1822	Charles Babbage completed his first model for the difference engine.
1830s	Babbage created the first design for the analytical engine.
1890	Herman Hollerith developed the punched-card ruler for the US census.
1936	Alan Turing published the mathematical theory of computing.
1938	Konrad Zuse constructed the first binary calculator, using Boolean algebra.
1939	US mathematician and physicist J V Atanasoff (1903–1995) became the first to use electronic means for mechanizing arithmetical operations.
1943	The Colossus electronic code-breaker was developed at Bletchley Park, England. The Harvard University Mark I or Automatic Sequence Controlled Calculator (partly financed by IBM) became the first program-controlled calculator.
1946	ENIAC (acronym for electronic numerator, integrator, analyser, and computer), the first general purpose, fully electronic digital computer, was completed at the University of Pennsylvania, USA.
1948	Manchester University (England) Mark I, the first stored-program computer, was completed. William Shockley of Bell Laboratories invented the transistor.
1951	Launch of Ferranti Mark I, the first commercially produced computer. Whirlwind, the first real-time computer, was built for the US air-defence system. Grace Murray Hopper of Remington Rand invented the compiler computer program.
1952	EDVAC (acronym for electronic discrete variable computer) was completed at the Institute for Advanced Study, Princeton, USA (by John Von Neumann and others).
1953	Magnetic core memory was developed.
1958	The first integrated circuit was constructed.
1963	The first minicomputer was built by Digital Equipment (DEC). The first electronic calculator was built by Bell Punch Company.
1964	Launch of IBM System/360, the first compatible family of computers. John Kemeny and Thomas Kurtz of Dartmouth College invented BASIC (Beginner's All-purpose Symbolic Instruction Code), a computer language similar to FORTRAN.
1965	The first supercomputer, the Control Data CD6600, was developed.
1971	The first microprocessor, the Intel 4004, was announced.
1974	CLIP-4, the first computer with a parallel architecture, was developed by John Backus at IBM.
1975	Altair 8800, the first personal computer (PC), or microcomputer, was launched.
1981	The Xerox Star system, the first WIMP system (acronym for windows, icons, menus, and pointing devices), was developed. IBM launched the IBM PC.
1984	Apple launched the Macintosh computer.
1985	The Inmos T414 transputer, the first 'off-the-shelf' microprocessor for building parallel computers, was announced.
1988	The first optical microprocessor, which uses light instead of electricity, was developed.
1989	Wafer-scale silicon memory chips, able to store 200 million characters, were launched.
1990	Microsoft released Windows 3, a popular windowing environment for PCs.
1992	Philips launched the CD-I (Compact-Disc Interactive) player, based on CD audio technology, to provide interactive multimedia programs for the home user.
1993	Intel launched the Pentium chip containing 3.1 million transistors and capable of 100 MIPs (millions of instructions per second). The Personal Digital Assistant (PDA), which recognizes user's handwriting, went on sale.
1995	Intel launched the Pentium Pro microprocessor (formerly codenamed P6).
1996	IBM's computer Deep Blue beat grand master Gary Kaspanov at chess, the first time a computer has beaten a human grand master.
1997	In the USA, an attempt to bring legislation to control the Internet, intended to prevent access to sexual material, is rejected as unconstitutional.

system); the ◊analogue computer, which works with continuously varying quantities; and the hybrid computer, which has characteristics of both analogue and digital computers.

There are four types of digital computer, corresponding roughly to their size and intended use. **Microcomputers** are the smallest and most common, used in small businesses, at home, and in schools. They are usually single-user machines. **Minicomputers** are found in medium-sized businesses and university departments. They may support from around 10 to 200 users at once. **Mainframes**, which can often service several hundred users simultaneously, are found in large organizations, such as national companies and government departments. **Supercomputers** are mostly used for highly complex scientific tasks, such as analysing the results of nuclear physics experiments and weather forecasting.

We do not need to have an infinity of different machines doing different jobs. A single one will suffice. The engineering problem of producing various machines for various jobs is replaced by the office work of 'programming' the universal machine to do these jobs.

ALAN MATHISON TURING English mathematician.
Quoted in A Hodges *Alan Turing: The Enigma of Intelligence* 1985

computer-aided design use of computers to create and modify design drawings; see ◊CAD.

computer-aided manufacturing use of computers to regulate production processes in industry; see ◊CAM.

computer art art produced with the help of a computer.

Since the 1950s the aesthetic use of computers has been increasingly evident in most artistic disciplines, including film animation, architecture, and music. ◊Computer graphics has been the most developed area, with the 'paint-box' computer liberating artists from the confines of the canvas. It is now also possible to programme computers in advance to generate graphics, music, and sculpture, according to 'instructions' which may include a preprogrammed element of unpredictability. In this last function, computer technology has been seen as a way of challenging the elitist nature of art by putting artistic creativity within relatively easy reach of anyone owning a computer.

computer-assisted learning use of computers in education and training; see ◊CAL.

computer-assisted reporting use of computers to do journalistic research. At its simplest, computer-assisted reporting involves searching an online database for basic information such as addresses and phone numbers. At their most sophisticated, computer systems allow journalists to sift through large quantities of data to find patterns of behaviour or connections that would not be visible by other means.

computer crime broad term applying to any type of crime committed via a computer, including unauthorized access to files. Most computer crime is committed by disgruntled former employees or subcontractors. Examples include the releasing of ◊viruses, ◊hacking, and computer fraud. Many countries, including the USA and the UK, have specialized law enforcement units to supply the technical knowledge needed to investigate computer crime.

Computer Emergency Response Team (CERT) team of engineers based at Carnegie-Mellon University in Pittsburgh, Pennsylvania, USA, that issues security advice and helps resolve emergencies on the Internet by providing technical expertise.

In 1996 the US government announced the formation of a national emergency response team.

computer engineer job classification for ◊computer personnel. A computer engineer repairs and maintains computer hardware.

computer game or *video game* any computer-controlled game in which the computer (sometimes) opposes the human player. Computer games typically employ fast, animated graphics on a ◊VDU (visual display unit) and synthesized sound.

Commercial computer games became possible with the advent of the ◊microprocessor in the mid-1970s and rapidly became popular as amusement-arcade games, using dedicated chips. Available games range from chess to fighter-plane simulations.

Some of the most popular computer games in the early 1990s were id Software's *Wolfenstein 3D* and *Doom*, which were designed to be played across networks including the Internet. A whole subculture built up around those particular games, as users took advantage of id's help to create their own additions to the game.

The computer games industry has been criticized for releasing many violent games with little intellectual content.

computer generation any of the five broad groups into which computers may be classified: **first generation** the earliest computers, developed in the 1940s and 1950s, made from valves and wire circuits; **second generation** from the early 1960s, based on transistors and printed circuits; **third generation** from the late 1960s, using integrated circuits and often sold as families of computers, such as the IBM 360 series; **fourth generation** using ◊microprocessors, large-scale integration (LSI), and sophisticated programming languages, still in use in the 1990s; and **fifth generation** based on parallel processing and very large-scale integration, currently under development.

computer graphics use of computers to display and manipulate information in pictorial form. Input may be achieved by scanning an image, by drawing with a mouse or stylus on a graphics tablet, or by drawing directly on the screen with a light pen.

The output may be as simple as a pie chart, or as complex as an animated sequence in a science-fiction film, or a seemingly three-dimensional engineering blueprint. The drawing is stored in the computer as raster graphics or vector graphics.

Vector graphics are stored in the computer memory by using geometric formulas. They can be transformed (enlarged, rotated, stretched, and so on) without loss of picture resolution. It is also possible to select and transform any of the components of a vector-graphics display because each is separately defined in the computer memory. In these respects vector graphics are superior to raster graphics. They are typically used for drawing applications, allowing the user to create and modify technical diagrams such as designs for houses or cars.

Raster graphics are stored in the computer memory by using a map to record data (such as colour and intensity) for every ◊pixel that makes up the image. When transformed (enlarged, rotated, stretched, and so on), raster graphics become ragged and suffer loss of picture resolution, unlike vector graphics. They are typically used for painting applications, which allow the user to create artwork on a computer screen much as if they were painting on paper or canvas.

Computer graphics are increasingly used in computer-aided design (◊CAD), and to generate models and simulations in engineering, meteorology, medicine and surgery, and other fields of science.

computerized axial tomography medical technique, usually known as ◊CAT scan, for noninvasive investigation of disease or injury.

computer-mediated communication umbrella term for all types of communication via computers, such as ◊electronic conferencing and chat.

Computer Misuse Act British law passed in 1990 which makes it illegal to hack into computers (see ◊hacking). The first prosecution under the Act was that of British hacker Paul Bedworth, who in 1993 was acquitted on the grounds that he was addicted to computing.

computer numerical control control of machine tools, most often milling machines, by a computer. The pattern of work for the machine to follow, which often involves performing repeated sequences of actions, is described using a special-purpose programming language.

computer operator job classification for ◊computer personnel. Computer operators work directly with the computer, running the programs, changing discs and tapes, loading paper into printers, and ensuring all ◊data security procedures are followed.

computer output on microfilm/microfiche (COM) technique for producing computer output in very compact, photographically reduced form (◊microform).

computer personnel people who work with or are associated with computers. In a large computer department the staff may work under the direction of a **data processing manager**, who supervises and coordinates the work performed. Computer personnel can be broadly divided into two categories: those who run and maintain existing ◊applications programs (programs that perform a task for the benefit of the user) and those who develop new applications.

Personnel who run existing applications programs: **data control staff** receive information from computer users (for instance, from the company's wages clerks), ensure that it is processed as required, and return it to them in processed form; **data preparation staff**, or **keyboard operators**, prepare the information received by the data control staff so that it is ready for processing by computer. Once the information has been typed at the keyboard of a VDU (or at a ◊key-to-disc or key-to-tape station), it is placed directly onto a medium such as disc or tape; **computer operators** work directly with computers, running the programs, changing discs and tapes, loading paper into printers, and ensuring that all ◊data security procedures are followed; **computer engineers** repair and maintain computer hardware; **file librarians**, or **media librarians**, store and issue the data files used by the department; an **operations manager** coordinates all the day-to-day activities of these staff. Personnel who develop new applications: **systems analysts** carry out the analysis of an existing system (see ◊systems analysis), whether already computerized or not, and prepare proposals for a new system; **programmers** write the software needed for new systems.

Computer Professionals for Social Responsibility (CPSR) US organization advocating the responsible use of computers. Based in Washington DC, it was one of the first organizations to oppose President Reagan's Strategic Defense Initiative on the grounds that the many billions of lines of code it would take to program it could never be debugged successfully.

computer program coded instructions for a computer; see ◊program.

computer simulation representation of a real-life situation in a computer program. For example, the program might simulate the flow of customers arriving at a bank. The user can alter variables, such as the number of cashiers on duty, and see the effect.

More complex simulations can model the behaviour of chemical reactions or even nuclear explosions. The behaviour of solids and liquids at high temperatures can be simulated using ◊quantum simulation. Computers also control the actions of machines – for example, a ◊flight simulator models the behaviour of real aircraft and allows training to take place in safety. Computer simulations are very useful when it is too dangerous, time consuming, or simply impossible to carry out a real experiment or test.

computer-supported collaborative work (CSCW) work undertaken by individuals who, using computers, are able to function together as a group on a project despite being geographically separated. The technology to facilitate CSCW is still under development. Early initiatives include video and data conferencing so that two users can talk on the telephone while simultaneously viewing a document in progress. Changes made by either participant affect both participants' displays.

computer terminal the device whereby the operator communicates with the computer; see ◊terminal.

Computer Underground Digest widely distributed ◊e-zine covering such issues as ◊hacking, freedom of speech, and security risks.

computing device any device built to perform or help perform computations, such as the ◊abacus, ◊slide rule, or ◊computer.

The earliest known example is the abacus. Mechanical devices with sliding scales (similar to the slide rule) date from ancient Greece. In 1642, French mathematician Blaise Pascal built a mechanical adding machine and in 1671 German mathematician Gottfried Leibniz produced a machine to carry out multiplication. The first mechanical computer, the ◊analytical engine, was designed by British mathematician Charles Babbage in 1835. For the subsequent history of computing, see ◊computer.

concave of a surface, curving inwards, or away from the eye. For example, a bowl appears concave when viewed from above. In geometry, a concave polygon is one that has an interior angle greater than 180°. Concave is the opposite of ◊convex.

concave lens lens that possesses at least one surface that curves inwards. It is a diverging lens, spreading out those light rays that have been refracted through it. A concave lens is thinner at its centre than at its edges, and is used to correct short-sightedness.

Common forms include the **biconcave** lens (with both surfaces curved inwards) and the **plano-concave** (with one flat surface and one concave). The whole lens may be further curved overall, making a **convexo-concave** or diverging meniscus lens, as in some lenses used for corrective purposes.

concave mirror curved mirror that reflects light from its inner surface. It may be either circular or parabolic in section. A concave mirror converges light rays to form a reduced, inverted, real image in front, or an enlarged, upright, virtual image seemingly behind it, depending on how close the object is to the mirror.

Only a parabolic concave mirror has a true, single-point ◊principal focus for parallel rays. For this reason, parabolic mirrors are used as reflectors to focus light in telescopes, or to focus microwaves in satellite communication systems. The reflector behind a spot lamp or car headlamp is parabolic.

concentration in chemistry, the amount of a substance (◊solute) present in a specified amount of a solution. Either amount may be specified as a mass or a volume (liquids only). Common units used are ◊moles per cubic decimetre, grams per cubic decimetre, grams per 100 cubic centimetres, and grams per 100 grams.

The term also refers to the process of increasing the concentration of a solution by removing some of the substance (◊solvent) in which the solute is dissolved. In a **concentrated solution**, the solute is present in large quantities. Concentrated brine is around 30% sodium chloride in water; concentrated caustic soda (caustic liquor) is around 40% sodium hydroxide; and concentrated sulphuric acid is 98% acid.

concentration gradient change in the concentration of a substance from one area to another. Particles, such as sugar molecules, in a fluid move over time so that they become evenly distributed throughout the fluid. In particular, they move from an area of high concentration to an area of low concentration; that is, they diffuse along the concentration gradient (see ◊diffusion).

This explains why oxygen in the lungs will diffuse into the blood supply. The oxygen molecules are more concentrated in the lungs than they are in the capillaries surrounding the ◊alveoli (air sacs). As it diffuses along the concentration gradient, oxygen will tend to pass into the blood. Gas exchange therefore depends on the maintenance of a concentration gradient, so that oxygen will continue to diffuse across the respiratory surface.

concentric circles two or more circles that share the same centre.

conceptacle flask-shaped cavities found in the swollen tips of certain brown seaweeds, notably the wracks, *Fucus*. The gametes are formed within them and released into the water via a small pore in the conceptacle, known as an ostiole.

conch name applied to various shells, but especially to the fountain shell, a species of gastropod mollusc in the order Mesogastropoda.

conchology branch of zoology that studies molluscs with reference to their shells.

Concorde the only supersonic airliner, which cruises at Mach 2, or twice the speed of sound, about 2,170 kph/1,350 mph. Concorde, the result of Anglo-French cooperation, made its first flight 1969 and entered commercial service seven years later. It is 62 m/202 ft long and has a wing span of nearly 26 m/84 ft. Developing Concorde cost French and British taxpayers £2 billion.

concrete building material composed of cement, stone, sand, and water. It has been used since Egyptian and Roman times. Since the late 19th century, it has been increasingly employed as an economical alternative to materials such as brick and wood, and has been combined with steel to increase its tension capacity.

Reinforced concrete and prestressed concrete are strengthened by combining concrete with another material, such as steel rods or glass fibres. The addition of carbon fibres to concrete increases its conductivity. The electrical resistance of the concrete changes with increased stress or fracture, so this 'smart concrete' can be used as an early indicator of structural damage.

concurrent lines two or more lines passing through a single point; for example, the diameters of a circle are all concurrent at the centre of the circle.

concussion temporary unconsciousness resulting from a blow to the head. It is often followed by amnesia for events immediately preceding the blow.

condensation conversion of a vapour to a liquid. This is frequently achieved by letting the vapour come into contact with a cold surface. It is the process by which water vapour turns into fine water droplets to form ◊cloud.

Condensation in the atmosphere occurs when the air becomes completely saturated and is unable to hold any more water vapour. As air rises it cools and contracts – the cooler it becomes the less water it can hold. Rain is frequently associated with warm weather fronts because the air rises and cools, allowing the water vapour to condense as rain. The temperature at which the air becomes saturated is known as the ◊dew point. Water vapour will not condense in air if there are not enough condensation nuclei (particles of dust, smoke or salt) for the droplets to form on. It is then said to be supersaturated. Condensation is an important part of the ◊water cycle.

condensation in organic chemistry, a reaction in which two organic compounds combine to form a larger molecule, accompanied by the removal of a smaller molecule (usually water). This is also known as an addition–elimination reaction. Polyamides (such as nylon) and polyesters (such as Terylene) are made by condensation ◊polymerization.

condensation number in physics, the ratio of the number of molecules condensing on a surface to the total number of molecules touching that surface.

condensation polymerization ◊polymerization reaction in which one or more monomers, with more than one reactive functional group, combine to form a polymer with the elimination of water or another small molecule.

condenser laboratory apparatus used to condense vapours back to liquid so that the liquid can be recovered. It is used in ◊distillation and in reactions where the liquid mixture can be kept boiling without the loss of solvent.

condenser in electronic circuits, a former name for a ◊capacitor.

condenser in optics, a ◊lens or combination of lenses with a short focal length used for concentrating a light source onto a small area, as used in a slide projector or microscope substage lighting unit. A condenser can also be made using a concave mirror.

conditioning in psychology, two major principles of behaviour modification.

In **classical conditioning**, described by Russian psychologist Ivan Pavlov, a new stimulus can evoke an automatic response by being repeatedly associated with a stimulus that naturally provokes that response. For example, the sound of a bell repeatedly associated with food will eventually trigger salivation, even if sounded without food being presented. In **operant conditioning**, described by US psychologists Edward Lee Thorndike (1874–1949) and B F Skinner, the frequency of a voluntary response can be increased by following it with a reinforcer or reward.

School yourself to demureness and patience. Learn to innure yourself to drudgery in science. Learn, compare, collect the facts.

IVAN PAVLOV Russian physiologist.
Bequest to the Academic Youth of Soviet Russia 27 Feb 1936

condom or ***sheath*** or ***prophylactic*** barrier contraceptive, made of rubber, which fits over an erect penis and holds in the sperm produced by ejaculation. It is an effective means of preventing pregnancy if used carefully, preferably with a ◊spermicide. A condom with spermicide is 97% effective; one without spermicide is 85% effective as a contraceptive. Condoms can also give some protection against sexually transmitted diseases, including AIDS.

In 1996 the European Union agreed a standard for condoms, which is 17 cm/6.7 in long; although the width can be variable, a regular width was agreed as 5.2 cm/2 in.

condor name given to two species of birds in separate genera. The **Andean condor** *Vultur gryphus,* has a wingspan up to 3 m/10 ft, weighs up to 13 kg/28 lb, and can reach up to 1.2 m/3.8 ft in length. It is black, with some white on the wings and a white frill at the base of the neck. It lives in the Andes at heights of up to 4,500 m/14,760 ft, and along the South American coast, and feeds mainly on carrion. The **Californian condor** *Gymnogyps californianus* is a similar bird, with a wingspan of about 3 m/10 ft. It feeds entirely on carrion, and is on the verge of extinction.

The Californian condor lays only one egg at a time and may not breed every year. In 1994, only 89 Californian condors remained, of which only four were in the wild. It became the subject of a special conservation effort, and by July 1995 the number had increased to 104.

conductance ability of a material to carry an electrical current, usually given the symbol G. For a direct current, it is the reciprocal of ◊resistance: a conductor of resistance R has a conductance of $1/R$. For an alternating current, conductance is the resistance R divided by the ◊impedance Z: $G = R/Z$. Conductance was formerly expressed in reciprocal ohms (or mhos); the SI unit is the ◊siemens (S).

conduction, electrical flow of charged particles through a material giving rise to electric current. Conduction in metals involves the flow of negatively charged free ◊electrons. Conduction in gases and some liquids involves the flow of ◊ions that carry positive charges in one direction and negative charges in the other. Conduction in a ◊semiconductor such as silicon involves the flow of electrons and positive holes.

TO REMEMBER THE PRINCIPLES OF HEAT TRANSFER:

CONDUCTION – IMAGINE A LINE OF PASSENGERS ON A BUS BEING ASKED TO MOVE DOWN BY THE **CONDUCTOR**, EACH PASSENGER CAUSING THE NEXT TO BUSTLE ALONG (ANALOGY FOR THE MOVEMENT/VIBRATION OF ATOMS THAT IS PASSED ALONG, CAUSING HEAT TO BE TRANSFERRED) **CONVECTION** – CONSIDER **VECTOR**, A DISEASE-CARRYING INSECT, FOR EXAMPLE A MOSQUITO, WHICH TRAVELS IN SWARMS (VERY MUCH LIKE THE MOVEMENT OF CONVECTION CURRENTS) **RADIATION** – HEAT RADIATION IS A FORM OF **RADIATION** –(THINK OF NUCLEAR FALLOUT OR THE SUN'S RADIATION) AND THUS TRAVELS IN WAVES UNDETECTED UNTIL THEY FALL UPON ANOTHER BODY

conduction, heat flow of heat energy through a material without the movement of any part of the material itself (compare ◊conduction, ◊electrical). Heat energy is present in all materials in the form of the kinetic energy of their vibrating molecules, and may be conducted from one molecule to the next in the form of this mechanical vibration. In the case of metals, which are particularly good conductors of heat, the free electrons within the material carry heat around very quickly.

conductivity, thermal (unit W m^{-1} K^{-1}) measure of how well a material conducts heat. A good conductor, such as a metal, has a high conductivity; a poor conductor, called an insulator, has a low conductivity. See also ◊U-value.

conductor any material that conducts heat or electricity (as opposed to an insulator, or nonconductor). A good conductor has a high electrical or heat conductivity, and is generally a substance rich in free electrons such as a metal. A poor conductor (such as the nonmetals, glass and porcelain) has few free electrons. Carbon is exceptional in being nonmetallic and yet (in some of its forms) a relatively good conductor of heat and electricity. Substances such as silicon and germanium, with intermediate conductivities that are improved by heat, light, or impurities, are known as ◊semiconductors.

cone in botany, the reproductive structure of the conifers and cycads; also known as a ◊strobilus. It consists of a central axis surrounded by numerous, overlapping, scalelike, modified leaves

cone *The western yellow or ponderosa pine* Pinus ponderosa *var.* arizonica *exhibits the needlelike leaves and cones typical of gymnosperms. These are female cones which have shed their seeds; male cones are smaller and shed vast quantities of pollen into the air. Premaphotos Wildlife*

(sporophylls) that bear the reproductive organs. Usually there are separate male and female cones, the former bearing pollen sacs containing pollen grains, and the larger female cones bearing the ovules that contain the ova or egg cells. The pollen is carried from male to female cones by the wind (◊anemophily). The seeds develop within the female cone and are released as the scales open in dry atmospheric conditions, which favour seed dispersal.

In some groups (for example, the pines) the cones take two or even three years to reach maturity. The cones of ◊junipers have fleshy cone scales that fuse to form a berrylike structure. One group of ◊angiosperms, the alders, also bear conelike structures; these are the woody remains of the short female catkins, and they contain the alder ◊fruits.

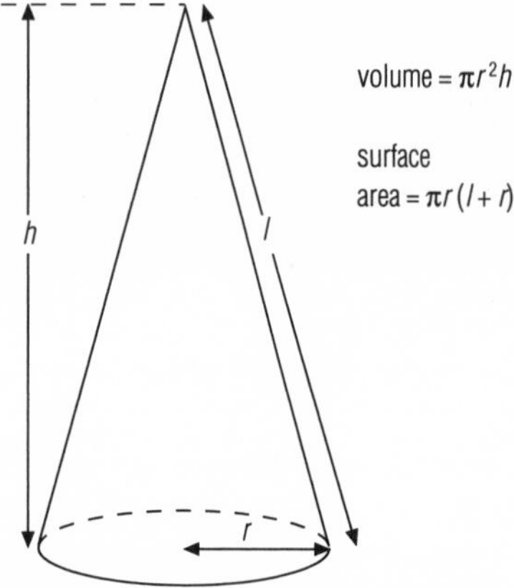

cone The volume and surface area of a cone are given by formulae involving a few simple dimensions.

cone in geometry, a solid or surface consisting of the set of all straight lines passing through a fixed point (the vertex) and the points of a circle or ellipse whose plane does not contain the vertex.

A circular cone of perpendicular height, with its apex above the centre of the circle, is known as a **right circular cone**; it is generated by rotating an isosceles triangle or framework about its line of symmetry. A right circular cone of perpendicular height h and base of radius r has a volume $V = \frac{1}{3}\pi r^2 h$.

The distance from the edge of the base of a cone to the vertex is called the slant height. In a right circular cone of slant height l, the curved surface area is πrl, and the area of the base is πr^2. Therefore the total surface area $A = \pi rl + \pi r^2 = \pi r(l + r)$.

cone in zoology, type of light-sensitive cell found in the retina of the ◊eye.

config.sys in computing, the ◊configuration file used by the MS-DOS and OS/2 ◊operating systems. It is read when the system is ◊booted.

configuration in chemistry, the arrangement of atoms in a molecule or of electrons in atomic orbitals.

configuration in computing, the way in which a system, whether it be ◊hardware and/or ◊software, is set up. A minimum configuration is often referred to for a particular application, and this will usually include a specification of processor, disc and memory size, and peripherals required.

congenital disease in medicine, a disease that is present at birth. It is not necessarily genetic in origin; for example, congenital herpes may be acquired by the baby as it passes through the mother's birth canal.

conger any large marine eel of the family Congridae, especially the genus *Conger*. Conger eels live in shallow water, hiding in crevices during the day and active by night, feeding on fish and crabs. They are valued for food and angling.

conglomerate in geology, coarse-grained clastic ◊sedimentary rock, composed of rounded fragments (clasts) of pre-existing rocks cemented in a finer matrix, usually sand.

The fragments in conglomerates are pebble- to boulder-sized, and the rock can be regarded as the lithified equivalent of gravel. A ◊bed of conglomerate is often associated with a break in a sequence of rock beds (an unconformity), where it marks the advance of the sea over an old eroded landscape. An **oligomict conglomerate** contains one type of pebble; a **polymict conglomerate** has a mixture of pebble types. If the rock fragments are angular, it is called a ◊breccia.

congruent in geometry, having the same shape and size, as applied to two-dimensional or solid figures. With plane congruent figures, one figure will fit on top of the other exactly, though this may first require rotation and/or rotation of one of the figures.

conic section curve obtained when a conical surface is intersected by a plane. If the intersecting plane cuts both extensions of the cone, it yields a ◊hyperbola; if it is parallel to the side of the cone, it produces a ◊parabola. Other intersecting planes produce ◊circles or ◊ellipses.

The Greek mathematician Apollonius wrote eight books with the title *Conic Sections,* which superseded previous work on the subject by Aristarchus and Euclid.

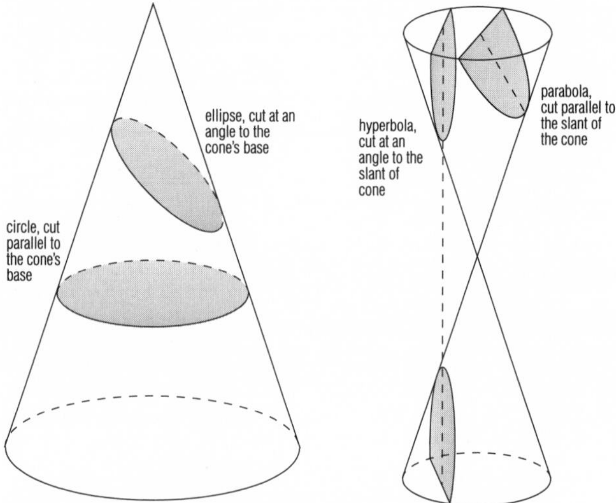

conic section The four types of curve that may be obtained by cutting a single or double right-circular cone with a plane (two-dimensional surface).

conidium (plural ***conidia***) asexual spore formed by some fungi at the tip of a specialized ◊hypha or conidiophore. The conidiophores grow erect, and cells from their ends round off and separate into conidia, often forming long chains. Conidia easily become detached and are dispersed by air movements.

conifer any of a large number of cone-bearing trees or shrubs. They are often pyramid-shaped, with leaves that are either scaled or needle-shaped; most are evergreen. Conifers include pines, spruces, firs, yews, junipers, monkey puzzles, and larches. (Order Coniferales.)

Conifers belong to the ◊gymnosperm or naked-seed-bearing group of plants. The reproductive organs are the male and female cones, and pollen is scattered in the wind. The seeds develop in the female cones. The processes of reaching maturity, fertilization, and seed ripening may take several years. Most conifers grow quickly and can survive in poor soil, on steep slopes, and in short growing seasons. Coniferous forests are widespread in Scandinavia and upland areas of the UK such as the Scottish Highlands, and are often planted in ◊afforestation schemes. Conifers also grow in ◊woodland.

conjugate in mathematics, a term indicating that two elements are connected in some way; for example, $(a + ib)$ and $(a - ib)$ are conjugate complex numbers.

conjugate angles two angles that add up to 360°.

conjugation in biology, the bacterial equivalent of sexual reproduction. A fragment of the ◊DNA from one bacterium is passed along a thin tube, the pilus, into another bacterium.

conjugation in organic chemistry, the alternation of double (or triple) and single carbon–carbon bonds in a molecule – for example, in penta-1,3-diene, $H_2C{=}CH{-}CH{=}CH{-}CH_3$. Conjugation imparts additional stability as the double bonds are less reactive than isolated double bonds.

conjunction in astronomy, the alignment of two celestial bodies as seen from Earth. A ◊superior planet (or other object) is in conjunction when it lies behind the Sun. An ◊inferior planet (or other object) comes to **inferior conjunction** when it passes between the Earth and the Sun; it is at **superior conjunction** when it passes behind the Sun.

Planetary conjunction takes place when a planet is closely aligned with another celestial object, such as the Moon, a star, or another planet.

Because the orbital planes of the inferior planets are tilted with respect to that of the Earth, they usually pass either above or below the Sun at inferior conjunction. If they line up exactly, a ◊transit will occur.

conjunctiva membrane covering the front of the vertebrate ◊eye. It is continuous with the epidermis of the eyelids, and lies on the surface of the cornea.

conjunctivitis inflammation of the conjunctiva, the delicate membrane that lines the inside of the eyelids and covers the front of the eye. Symptoms include redness, swelling, and a watery or pus-filled discharge. It may be caused by infection, allergy, or other irritant.

connective tissue in animals, tissue made up of a noncellular substance, the ◊extracellular matrix, in which some cells are embedded. Skin, bones, tendons, cartilage, and adipose tissue (fat) are the main connective tissues. There are also small amounts of connective tissue in organs such as the brain and liver, where they maintain shape and structure.

conodont extinct eel-like organism 520–240 million years old. Several thousand species have been described, ranging from 1–40 cm/0.4–15.8 in in length. They were predators, and, following the discovery of a large fossil in South Africa in 1995, are believed to be the first ◊vertebrates. This fossil of a 40-cm/15.8-in conodont shows fossilized soft tissue including muscle and eyes. It has eye muscles, an exclusively vertebrate feature, and 'real teeth'.

Conodont fossils consist mainly of teeth, and are often abundant, especially in Upper ◊Cambrian and ◊Triassic limestone. They were first discovered by Russian naturalist Christian Pander (1794–1865).

Conservation must come before recreation.

PRINCE OF WALES CHARLES Heir to the throne of Great Britain and Northern Ireland.
The Times 5 July 1989

conservation in the life sciences, action taken to protect and preserve the natural world, usually from pollution, overexploitation, and other harmful features of human activity. The late 1980s saw a great increase in public concern for the environment, with membership of conservation groups, such as ◊Friends of the Earth, ◊Greenpeace, and the US Sierra Club, rising sharply. Globally the most important issues include the depletion of atmospheric ozone by the action of ◊chlorofluorocarbons (CFCs), the build-up of carbon dioxide in the atmosphere (thought to contribute to an intensification of the ◊greenhouse effect), and ◊deforestation.

Conservation: chronology

1627	Last surviving aurochs, long-horned wild cattle that previously roamed Europe, southwest Asia, and North Africa, became extinct in Poland.
1664	A Dutch mandate drawn up to protect forest in Cape Colony, South Africa.
1681	The last dodo died on the island of Mauritius.
1764	The British established forest reserves on Tobago, after deforestation in Barbados and Jamaica resulted in widespread soil erosion.
1769	The French passed conservation laws in Mauritius.
1868	First laws passed in the UK to protect birds.
1948	The International Union for Conservation of Nature and Natural Resources (IUCN) was founded, with its sister organization, the World Wildlife Fund (WWF).
1970	The Man and the Biosphere Programme was initiated by UNESCO, providing for an international network of biosphere reserves.
1971	The Convention on Wetlands of International Importance (especially concerned with wildfowl habitat) signed in Ramsar, Iran, and started a List of Wetlands of International Importance.
1972	The Convention Concerning the Protection of the World Cultural and Natural Heritage adopted in Paris, France, providing for the designation of World Heritage Sites.
1972	The UN Conference on the Human Environment held in Stockholm, Sweden, lead to the creation of the UN Environment Programme (UNEP).
1973	The Convention on International Trade in Endangered Species of Wild Fauna and Flora (CITES) signed in Washington, DC.
1974	The world's largest protected area, the Greenland National Park covering 97 million hectares, created.
1980	The World Conservation Strategy launched by the IUCN, with the WWF and UNEP, showed how conservation contributes to development.
1982	The first herd of ten Arabian oryx bred from a 'captive breeding' programme released into the wild in Oman. The last wild oryx had been killed 1972.
1986	The first 'Red List' of endangered animal species compiled by IUCN.
1989	International trade in ivory banned under CITES legislation in an effort to protect the African elephant from poachers.
1992	The UN convened the 'Earth Summit' in Rio de Janeiro, Brazil, to discuss global planning for a sustainable future. The Convention on Biological Diversity and the Convention on Climate Change were opened for signing.
1993	The Convention on Biological Diversity came into force.
1995	The Arabian oryx conservation programme (began 1962), the most successful attempt at reintroducing zoo-bred animals to the wild, came to an end as the last seven animals were flown from the USA to join the 228-strong herd in Oman.
1996	The World Wide Fund for Nature had 5 million members in 28 countries.
1997	The world ban on the ivory trade was lifted in June 1997 at the tenth CITES convention. Trade is scheduled to resume in 1999 with Zimbabwe, Botswana, and Namibia the only countries allowed to export.

conservation of energy in chemistry, the principle that states that in a chemical reaction, the total amount of energy in the system remains unchanged.

For each component there may be changes in energy due to change of physical state, changes in the nature of chemical bonds, and either an input or output of energy. However, there is no net gain or loss of energy.

conservation of mass in chemistry, the principle that states that in a chemical reaction the sum of all the masses of the substances involved in the reaction (reactants) is equal to the sum of all of the masses of the substances produced by the reaction (products) – that is, no matter is gained or lost.

conservation of momentum in mechanics, a law that states that total ◊momentum is conserved (remains constant) in all collisions, providing no external resultant force acts on the colliding bodies. The principle may be expressed as an equation used to solve numerical problems: total momentum before collision = total momentum after collision.

console in computing, a combination of keyboard and screen (also described as a terminal). For a multiuser system, such as ◊UNIX, there is only one system console from which the system can be administered, while there may be many user terminals. See also ◊games console.

constant in mathematics, a fixed quantity or one that does not change its value in relation to ◊variables. For example, in the algebraic expression $y^2 = 5x - 3$, the numbers 3 and 5 are constants. In physics, certain quantities are regarded as universal constants, such as the speed of light in a vacuum.

constantan or ***eureka*** high-resistance alloy of approximately 40% nickel and 60% copper with a very low coefficient of ◊thermal expansion (measure of expansion on heating). It is used in electrical resistors.

constant composition, law of in chemistry, the law that states that the proportions of the amounts of the elements in a pure compound are always the same and are independent of the method by which the compound was produced.

constellation one of the 88 areas into which the sky is divided for the purposes of identifying and naming celestial objects. The first

CONSTELLATIONS AND THEIR STARS

http://www.vol.it/mirror/constellations/

Notes on the constellations (listed alphabetically, by month, and by popularity), plus lists of the 25 brightest stars and the 32 nearest stars, and photographs of the Milky Way.

Constellations

Constellation	*Abbreviation*	*Popular name(s)*
Andromeda	And	–
Antlia Ant	Airpump	
Apus Aps	Bird of Paradise	
Aquarius	Aqr	Water-Bearer
Aquila Aqi	Eagle	
Ara Ara	Altar	
Aries Ari	Ram	
Auriga Aur	Charioteer	
BoötesBoo	Herdsman	
Caelum	Cae	Chisel
Camelopardalis	Cam	Giraffe
CancerCnc	Crab	
Canes Venatici	CVn	Hunting Dogs
Canis Major	CMa	Great Dog
Canis Minor	CMi	Little Dog
Capricornus	Cap	Goat, Sea-Goat
Carina	Car	Keel
Cassiopeia	Cas	–
Centaurus	Cen	Centaur
Cepheus	Cep	–
Cetus	Cet	Whale
Chamaeleon	Cha	Chameleon
Circinus	Cir	Compasses
Columba	Col	Dove
Coma Berenices	Com	Berenice's Hair
Corona Australis	CrA	Southern Crown
Corona Borealis	CrB	Northern Crown
Corvus	Crv	Crow, Raven
Crater	Crt	Cup
Crux	Cru	Southern Cross
Cygnus	Cyn	Swan
Delphinus	Del	Dolphin
Dorado	Dor	Goldfish, Swordfish
Draco	Dra	Dragon
Equuleus	Equ	Filly, Foal
Eridanus	Eri	River
Fornax	For	Furnace
Gemini	Gem	Twins
Grus	Gru	Crane
Hercules	Her	–
Horologium	Hor	Clock
Hydra	Hya	Sea Serpent
Hydrus	Hyi	Watersnake
Indus	Ind	Indian
Lacerta	Lac	Lizard
Leo	Leo	Lion
Leo Minor	LMi	Little Lion
Lepus	Lep	Hare
Libra	Lib	Scales
Lupus	Lup	Wolf
Lynx	Lyn	–
Lyra	Lyr	Lyre, Harp
Mensa	Men	Table, Mountain
Microscopium	Mic	Microscope
Monoceros	Mon	Unicorn
Musca	Mus	Southern Fly
Norma	Nor	Rule, Straightedge
Octans	Oct	Octant
Ophiuchus	Oph	Serpent-Bearer
Orion	Ori	–
Pavo	Pav	Peacock
Pegasus	Peg	Flying Horse
Perseus	Per	–
Phoenix	Phe	–
Pictor	Pic	Painter, Easel
Pisces	Psc	Fishes
Piscis Austrinus	PsA	Southern Fish
Puppis	Pup	Poop
Pyxis	Pyx	Compass
Reticulum	Ret	Net
Sagitta	Sge	Arrow
Sagittarius	Sgr	Archer
Scorpius	Sco	Scorpion
Sculptor	Scl	–
Scutum	Sct	Shield
Serpens	Ser	Serpent
Sextans	Sex	Sextant
Taurus	Tau	Bull
Telescopium	Tel	Telescope
Triangulum	Tri	Triangle
Triangulum Australe	TrA	Southern Triangle
Tucana	Tuc	Toucan
Ursa Major	UMa	Big Dipper
Ursa Minor	UMi	Little Dipper
Vela	Vel	Sail
Virgo	Vir	Virgin
Volans	Vol	Flying Fish
Vulpecula	Vul	Fox

constellations were simple, arbitrary patterns of stars in which early civilizations visualized gods, sacred beasts, and mythical heroes.

The constellations in use today are derived from a list of 48 known to the ancient Greeks, who inherited some from the Babylonians. The current list of 88 constellations was adopted by the International Astronomical Union, astronomy's governing body, in 1930.

constipation in medicine, the infrequent emptying of the bowel. The intestinal contents are propelled by peristaltic contractions of the intestine in the digestive process. The faecal residue collects in the rectum, distending it and promoting defecation. Constipation may be due to illness, alterations in food consumption, stress, or as an adverse effect of certain drugs. An increased intake of dietary fibre (see ◊fibre, ◊dietary) can alleviate constipation. Laxatives may be used to relieve temporary constipation but they should not be used routinely.

contact force force or push produced when two objects are pressed together and their surface atoms try to keep them apart. Contact forces always come in pairs – for example, the downwards force exerted on a floor by the sole of a person's foot is matched by an equal upwards force exerted by the floor on that sole.

contact lens lens, made of soft or hard plastic, that is worn in contact with the cornea and conjunctiva of the eye, beneath the eyelid, to correct defective vision. In special circumstances, contact lenses may be used as protective shells or for cosmetic purposes, such as changing eye colour.

The earliest use of contact lenses in the late 19th century was protective, or in the correction of corneal malformation. It was not until the 1930s that simplification of fitting technique by taking eye impressions made general use possible. Recent developments are a type of soft lens that can be worn for lengthy periods without removal, and a disposable soft lens that needs no cleaning but should be discarded after a week of constant wear.

contact process the main industrial method of manufacturing the chemical ◊sulphuric acid. Sulphur dioxide (produced by burning sulphur) and air are passed over a hot (450°C) ◊catalyst of vanadium (V) oxide. The sulphur trioxide produced is absorbed in concentrated sulphuric acid to make fuming sulphuric acid (oleum), which is then diluted with water to give concentrated sulphuric acid (98%). Unreacted gases are recycled.

content provider organization or individual who creates intellectual property, such as information databases, which may be distributed via traditional media or via the World Wide Web.

context-sensitive help type of help built into software that displays information related to the particular function in use.

continent any one of the seven large land masses of the Earth, as distinct from the oceans. They are Asia, Africa, North America, South America, Europe, Australia, and Antarctica. Continents are constantly moving and evolving (see ◊plate tectonics). A continent does not end at the coastline; its boundary is the edge of the shallow continental shelf, which may extend several hundred kilometres out to sea.

At the centre of each continental mass lies a shield or ◊craton, a deformed mass of old ◊metamorphic rocks dating from Precambrian times. The shield is thick, compact, and solid (the Canadian Shield is an example), having undergone all the mountain-building activity it is ever likely to, and is usually worn flat. Around the shield is a concentric pattern of fold mountains, with older ranges, such as the Rockies, closest to the shield, and younger ranges, such as the coastal ranges of North America, farther away. This general concentric pattern is modified when two continental masses have drifted together and they become welded with a great mountain range along the join, the way Europe and N Asia are joined along the Urals. If a continent is torn apart, the new continental edges have no fold mountains; for instance, South America has fold mountains (the Andes) along its western flank, but none along the east where it tore away from Africa 200 million years ago.

> To remember the seven continents:
>
> EAT AN ASPIRIN AFTER A NIGHT-TIME SNACK
>
> EUROPE, ANTARCTICA, ASIA, AFRICA, AUSTRALIA, NORTH AMERICA, SOUTH AMERICA (THE SECOND LETTER IN THE FIRST THREE 'A' WORDS HELPS TO REMEMBER THE 'A' CONTINENTS)

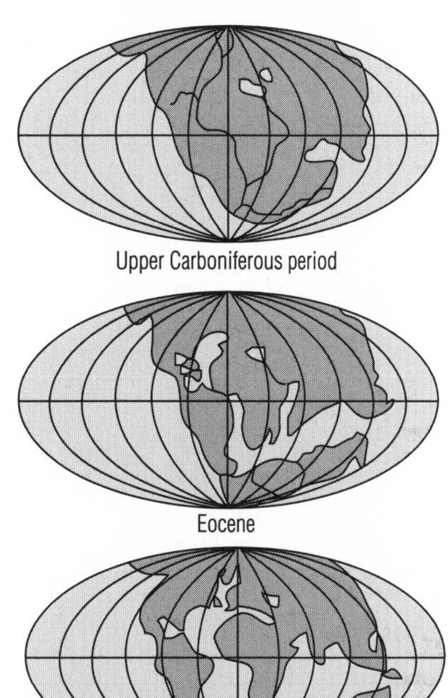

***continental drift** The continents are slowly shifting their positions, driven by fluid motion beneath the Earth's crust. Over 200 million years ago, there was a single large continent called Pangaea. By 200 million years ago, the continents had started to move apart. By 50 million years ago, the continents were approaching their present positions.*

continental drift in geology, the theory that, about 250–200 million years ago, the Earth consisted of a single large continent (◊Pangaea), which subsequently broke apart to form the continents known today. The theory was proposed 1912 by German meteorologist Alfred Wegener, but such vast continental movements could not be satisfactorily explained until the study of ◊plate tectonics in the 1960s.

The term 'continental drift' is not strictly correct, since land masses do not drift through the oceans. The continents form part of a plate, and the amount of crust created at divergent plate margins must equal the amount of crust destroyed at subduction zones.

continental shelf the submerged edge of a continent, a gently sloping plain that extends into the ocean. It typically has a gradient of less than 1°. When the angle of the sea bed increases to 1°–5° (usually several hundred kilometres away from land), it becomes known as the **continental slope**.

continuity in mathematics, property of functions of a real variable that have an absence of 'breaks'. A function f is said to be continuous at a point a if $\lim f(x) = f(a)$.

continuous data data that can take any of an infinite number of values between whole numbers and so may not be measured completely accurately. This type of data contrasts with ◊discrete data, in which the variable can only take one of a finite set of values. For example, the sizes of apples on a tree form continuous data, whereas the numbers of apples form discrete data.

continuous variation the slight difference of an individual character, such as height, across a sample of the population. Although there are very tall and very short humans, there are also many people with an intermediate height. The same applies to weight. Continuous variation can result from the genetic make-up of a population, or from environmental influences, or from a combination of the two.

continuum in mathematics, a ◊set that is infinite and everywhere continuous, such as the set of points on a line.

> *I have continued my work on the continuum problem last summer and I finally succeeded in proving the consistency of the continuum hypothesis (even the generalized form) with respect to generalized set theory. But for the time being please do not tell anyone of this.*
>
> KURT GÖDEL Austrian-born US mathematician. Letter to his teacher Karl Menger 1937

contouring in ◊computer graphics, a technique for enhancing the outline of a particular shape. This technique is used in applications such as mapping (see ◊animation, ◊computer), where a computer following the contours of an object ◊pixel by pixel can be much more precise than a human.

contraceptive any drug, device, or technique that prevents pregnancy. The contraceptive pill (the ◊Pill) contains female hormones that interfere with egg production or the first stage of pregnancy. The 'morning-after' pill can be taken up to 72 hours after unprotected intercourse. Barrier contraceptives include ◊condoms (sheaths) and ◊diaphragms, also called caps or Dutch caps; they prevent the sperm entering the cervix (neck of the womb).

◊Intrauterine devices, also known as IUDs or coils, cause a slight inflammation of the lining of the womb; this prevents the fertilized egg from becoming implanted. See also ◊family planning.

Other contraceptive methods include ◊sterilization (women) and ◊vasectomy (men); these are usually nonreversible. 'Natural' methods include withdrawal of the penis before ejaculation (coitus interruptus), and avoidance of intercourse at the time of ovulation (◊rhythm method). These methods are unreliable and normally only used on religious grounds. A new development is a sponge impregnated with spermicide that is inserted into the vagina. The use of any contraceptive (birth control) is part of family planning. The effectiveness of a contraceptive method is often given as a percentage. To say that a method has 95% effectiveness means that, on average, out of 100 healthy couples using that method for a year, 95 will not conceive.

contractile root in botany, a thickened root at the base of a corm, bulb, or other organ that helps position it at an appropriate level in the ground. Contractile roots are found, for example, on the corms of plants of the genus *Crocus*. After they have become anchored in the soil, the upper portion contracts, pulling the plant deeper into the ground.

contractile vacuole tiny organelle found in many single-celled fresh-water organisms. It slowly fills with water, and then contracts, expelling the water from the cell.

Fresh-water protozoa such as *Amoeba* absorb water by the process of ◊osmosis, and this excess must be eliminated. The rate of vacuole contraction slows as the external salinity is increased, because the osmotic effect weakens; marine protozoa do not have a contractile vacuole.

control in biology, the process by which a tissue, an organism, a population, or an ecosystem maintains itself in a balanced, stable state. Blood sugar must be kept at a stable level if the brain is to function properly, and this steady-state is maintained by an interaction between the liver, the hormone insulin, and a detector system in the pancreas.

In the ecosystem, the activities of the human race are endangering the balancing mechanisms associated with the atmosphere in general and the ◊greenhouse effect in particular.

control bus in computing, the electrical pathway, or ◊bus, used to communicate control signals.

control character in computing, any character produced by depressing the control key (Ctrl) on a keyboard at the same time as another (usually alphabetical) key. The control characters form the first 32 ◊ASCII characters and most have specific meanings according to the operating system used. They are also used in combination to provide formatting control in many word processors, although the user may not enter them explicitly.

control experiment essential part of a scientifically valid experiment, designed to show that the factor being tested is actually responsible for the effect observed. In the control experiment all factors, apart from the one under test, are exactly the same as in the test experiments, and all the same measurements are carried out. In drug trials, a placebo (a harmless substance) is given alongside the substance being tested in order to compare effects.

control total in computing, a ◊validation check in which an arithmetic total of a specific field from a group of records is calculated. This total is input together with the data to which it refers. The program recalculates the control total and compares it with the one entered to ensure that no entry errors have been made.

control unit the component of the ◊central processing unit that decodes, synchronizes, and executes program instructions.

convection heat energy transfer that involves the movement of a fluid (gas or liquid). Fluid in contact with the source of heat expands and tends to rise within the bulk of the fluid. Cooler fluid sinks to take its place, setting up a convection current. This is the principle of natural convection in many domestic hot-water systems and space heaters.

convection current current caused by the expansion of a liquid or gas as its temperature rises. The expanded material, being less dense, rises above colder and therefore denser material. Convection currents arise in the atmosphere above warm land masses or seas, giving rise to sea breezes and land breezes, respectively. In some heating systems, convection currents are used to carry hot water upwards in pipes.

Convection currents in the viscous rock of the Earth's mantle help to drive the movement of the rigid plates making up the Earth's surface (see ◊plate tectonics).

conventional current direction in which an electric current is considered to flow in a circuit. By convention, the direction is that in which positive-charge carriers would flow – from the positive terminal of a cell to its negative terminal. It is opposite in direction to the flow of electrons. In circuit diagrams, the arrows shown on symbols for components such as diodes and transistors point in the direction of conventional current flow.

convergence in mathematics, the property of a series of numbers in which the difference between consecutive terms gradually decreases. The sum of a converging series approaches a limit as the number of terms tends to ◊infinity.

> *What can be more curious than that the hand of a man, formed for grasping, that of a mole for digging, [...] and the wing of a bat, should all be constructed on the same pattern, and should include the same bones, in the same relative positions?*
>
> CHARLES DARWIN British naturalist. *On the Origin of Species* 1859

convergent evolution in biology, the independent evolution of similar structures in species (or other taxonomic groups) that are not closely related, as a result of living in a similar way. Thus, birds and bats have wings, not because they are descended from a com-

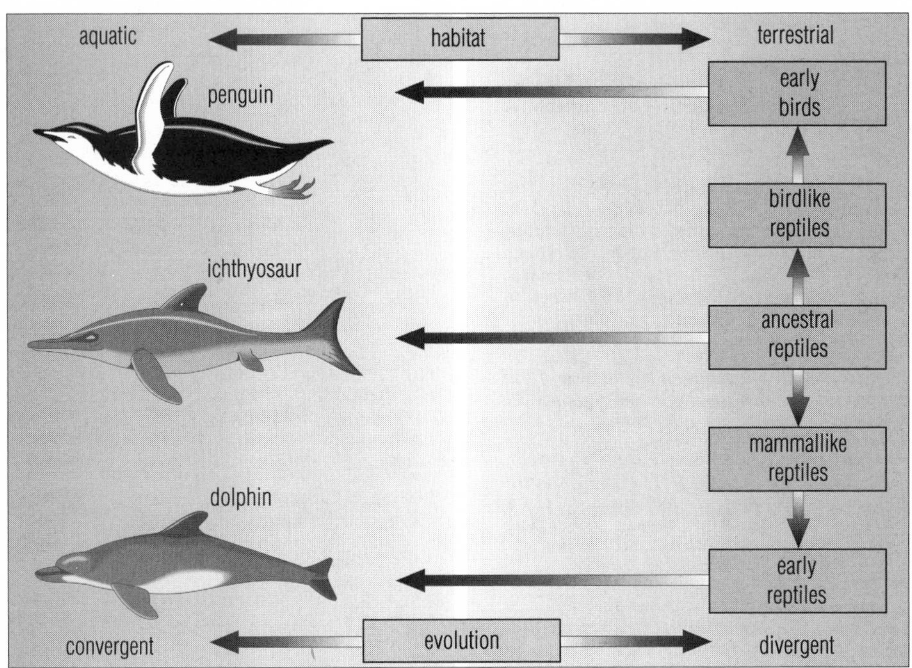

convergent evolution *Convergent evolution produced the superficially similar streamlined bodies of the dolphin and penguin. Despite their very different evolutionary paths – one as a mammal, the other as a bird – both have evolved and adapted to the aquatic environment they now inhabit.*

mon winged ancestor, but because their respective ancestors independently evolved flight.

converging lens lens that converges or brings to a focus those light rays that have been refracted by it. It is a ◊convex lens, with at least one surface that curves outwards, and is thicker towards the centre than at the edge. Converging lenses are used to form real images in many ◊optical instruments, such as cameras and projectors. A converging lens that forms a virtual, magnified image may be used as a ◊magnifying glass or to correct ◊long-sightedness.

converse in mathematics, the reversed order of a conditional statement; the converse of the statement 'if *a*, then *b*' is 'if *b*, then *a*'. The converse does not always hold true; for example, the converse of 'if $x = 3$, then $x^2 = 9$' is 'if $x^2 = 9$, then $x = 3$', which is not true, as x could also be -3.

convertiplane ◊vertical takeoff and landing craft (VTOL) with rotors on its wings that spin horizontally for takeoff, but tilt to spin in a vertical plane for forward flight.

At takeoff it looks like a two-rotor helicopter, with both rotors facing skywards. As forward speed is gained, the rotors tilt slowly forward until they are facing directly ahead. There are several different forms of convertiplane. The LTV-Hillier-Ryan XC-142, designed in the USA, had wings, carrying the four engines and propellers, that rotated. The German VC-400 had two rotors on each of its wingtips. Neither of these designs went into production. A Bell/Boeing design, the V-22 Osprey, uses a pair of tilting engines, with propellers 11.5 m/38 ft across, mounted at the end of the wings. It was originally intended to carry about 50 passengers direct to city centres. Crashes of two prototypes led to design changes 1994, but the project continues.

convex of a surface, curving outwards, or towards the eye. For example, the outer surface of a ball appears convex. In geometry, the term is used to describe any polygon possessing no interior angle greater than 180°. Convex is the opposite of ◊concave.

convex lens lens that possesses at least one surface that curves outwards. It is a ◊converging lens, bringing rays of light to a focus. A convex lens is thicker at its centre than at its edges, and is used to correct long-sightedness.

Common forms include the **biconvex** lens (with both surfaces curved outwards) and the **plano-convex** (with one flat surface and one convex). The whole lens may be further curved overall, making a **concavo-convex** or converging meniscus lens, as in some lenses used in corrective eyewear.

convex mirror curved mirror that reflects light from its outer surface. It diverges reflected light rays to form a reduced, upright, virtual image. Convex mirrors give a wide field of view and are therefore particularly suitable for car wing mirrors and surveillance purposes in shops.

conveyor device used for transporting materials. Widely used throughout industry is the **conveyor belt**, usually a rubber or fabric belt running on rollers. Trough-shaped belts are used, for example in mines, for transporting ores and coal. **Chain conveyors** are also used in coal mines to remove coal from the cutting machines. Overhead endless chain conveyors are used to carry components and bodies in car-assembly works. Other types include **bucket conveyors** and **screw conveyors**, powered versions of the ◊Archimedes screw.

convolvulus or ***bindweed*** any of a group of plants belonging to the morning-glory family. They are characterized by their twining stems and by their petals, which are joined into a funnel-shaped tube. (Genus *Convolvulus*, family Convolvulaceae.)

convulsion series of violent contractions of the muscles over which the patient has no control. It may be associated with loss of consciousness. Convulsions may arise from any one of a number of causes, including brain disease (such as ◊epilepsy), injury, high fever, poisoning, and electrocution.

cookie on the World Wide Web, a short piece of text that a Web site stores in a Cookies folder or a cookie.txt file on the user's computer, either for tracking or configuration purposes, for example, to improve the targeting of banner advertisements. Cookies can also store user preferences and passwords. The cookie is sent back to the server when the browser requests a new page.

Cookies are derived from 'magic cookies', the identification tokens used by some UNIX systems.

Originally, a cookie was an aphorism or short, witty saying obtained by typing 'cookie' at a computer's main system prompt. A cookie was then chosen at random – like a 'fortune cookie' – from a database called a 'cookie file'.

cookie recipe urban legend that circulates around the Net. The story is about a protagonist who ate some delicious cookies for dessert after a meal in a fancy department store or restaurant. When asked for the recipe, the waiter refuses, but finally relents saying it will cost 'two fifty'. When the bill comes, the protagonist discovers the restaurant has charged $250. Feeling stung, he/she posts the recipe to the Net to ensure the maximum distribution (and therefore revenge) possible. A cookie recipe is attached.

coolabah Australian riverside tree *Eucalyptus microtheca* of the myrtle family Myrtaceae. It is common in the inland and usually associated with areas subject to occasional inundation.

coonhound breed of large hound developed from European hounds imported into in Virginia, USA, at the start of the 17th century, and used for hunting various types of small game. It has a short black coat with red markings on muzzle, chest, and feet; long drooping ears; and a long tail. It stands up to 68 cm/27 in tall.

cooperative farming system in which individual farmers pool their resources (excluding land) to buy commodities such as seeds and fertilizers, and services such as marketing. It is a system of farming found throughout the world and is particularly widespread in Denmark and the ex-Soviet republics. In a ◊collective farm, land is also held in common.

coordinate in geometry, a number that defines the position of a point relative to a point or axis (reference line). ◊Cartesian coordinates define a point by its perpendicular distances from two or more axes drawn through a fixed point mutually at right angles to each other. ◊Polar coordinates define a point in a plane by its distance from a fixed point and direction from a fixed line.

coordinate geometry or ***analytical geometry*** system of geometry in which points, lines, shapes, and surfaces are represented by algebraic expressions. In plane (two-dimensional) coordinate geometry, the plane is usually defined by two axes at right angles to each other, the horizontal x-axis and the vertical y-axis, meeting at O, the origin. A point on the plane can be represented by a pair of ◊Cartesian coordinates, which define its position in terms of its distance along the x-axis and along the y-axis from O. These distances are respectively the x and y coordinates of the point.

Lines are represented as equations; for example, $y = 2x + 1$ gives a straight line, and $y = 3x^2 + 2x$ gives a ◊parabola (a curve). The graphs of varying equations can be drawn by plotting the coordinates of points that satisfy their equations, and joining up the points. One of the advantages of coordinate geometry is that geometrical solutions can be obtained without drawing but by manipulating algebraic expressions. For example, the coordinates of the point of intersection of two straight lines can be determined by finding the unique values of x and y that satisfy both of the equations for the lines, that is, by solving them as a pair of ◊simultaneous equations. The curves studied in simple coordinate geometry are the ◊conic sections (circle, ellipse, parabola, and hyperbola), each of which has a characteristic equation.

coot freshwater bird of the genus *Fulica* in the rail family, order Gruiformes. Coots are about 38 cm/1.2 ft long, and mainly black. They have a white bill, extending up the forehead in a plate, and big feet with four lobed toes.

copepod ◊crustacean of the subclass Copepoda, mainly microscopic and found in plankton.

coplanar in geometry, describing lines or points that all lie in the same plane.

copper orange-pink, very malleable and ductile, metallic element, symbol Cu (from Latin *cuprum*), atomic number 29, relative atomic mass 63.546. It is used for its durability, pliability, high thermal and electrical conductivity, and resistance to corrosion.

It was the first metal used systematically for tools by humans; when mined and worked into utensils it formed the technological basis for the Copper Age in prehistory. When alloyed with tin it forms bronze, which is stronger than pure copper and may hold a sharp edge; the systematic production and use of this alloy was the basis for the prehistoric Bronze Age. Brass, another hard copper alloy, includes zinc. The element's name comes from the Greek for Cyprus (*Kyprios*), where copper was mined.

cartesian coordinates

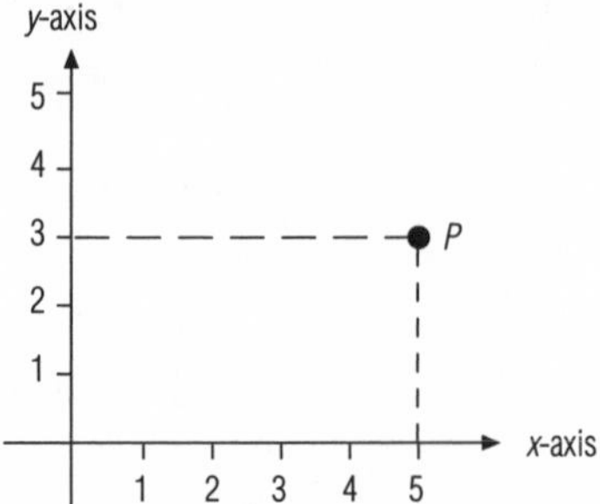

the cartesian coordinates of *P* are (5,3)

polar coordinates

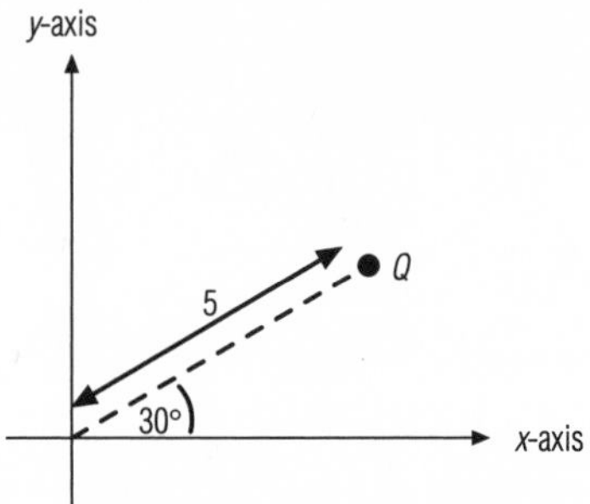

the polar coordinates of *Q* are (5,30°)

***coordinate** Coordinates are numbers that define the position of points in a plane or in space. In the Cartesian coordinate system, a point in a plane is charted based upon its location along intersecting horizontal and vertical axes. In the polar coordinate system, a point in a plane is defined by its distance from a fixed point and direction from a fixed line.*

COPPER PAGE

http://www.copper.org/

guide to copper and copper alloys, providing a wealth of information ranging from a historical overview of the copper industry to a database of literary resources about copper technology.

copper(II) carbonate $CuCO_3$ green solid that readily decomposes to form black copper(II) oxide on heating.

$$CuCO_3 \rightarrow CuO + CO_2$$

It dissolves in dilute acids to give blue solutions with effervescence caused by the giving off of carbon dioxide.

$$CuCO_3 + H_2SO_4 \rightarrow CuSO_4 + CO_2 + H_2O$$

Copernicus, Nicolaus
(1473–1543)

Latinized form of Mikolaj Kopernik Polish astronomer who believed that the Sun, not the Earth, is at the centre of the Solar System, thus defying the Christian church doctrine of the time. For 30 years, he worked on the hypothesis that the rotation and the orbital motion of the Earth are responsible for the apparent movement of the heavenly bodies. His great work De revolutionibus orbium coelestium/On the Revolutions of the Heavenly Spheres was the important first step to the more accurate picture of the Solar System built up by Tycho Brahe, Kepler, Galileo, and later astronomers.

Copernicus proposed replacing Ptolemy's ideas with a model in which the planets (including the Earth) orbited a centrally situated Sun. He proposed that the Earth described one full orbit of the Sun in a year, whereas the Moon orbited the Earth. The Earth rotated daily about its axis (which was inclined at 23.5° to the plane of orbit), thus accounting for the apparent daily rotation of the sphere of the fixed stars.

This model was a distinct improvement on the Ptolemaic system for a number of reasons. It explained why the planets Mercury and Venus displayed only 'limited motion'; their orbits were inside that of the Earth's. Similarly, it explained that the planets Mars, Jupiter, and Saturn displayed such curious patterns in their movements ('retrograde motion', loops, and kinks) because they travel in outer orbits at a slower pace than the Earth. The movement of the Earth on its axis accounted for the precession of the equinoxes, previously discovered by Hipparchus.

Copernicus' model represents a complete reformation of astronomy by replacing the anthropocentric view of the universe with the heliocentric viewpoint. Unable to free himself from the constraints of classical thinking, however, Copernicus was able to imagine only circular planetary orbits. This forced him to retain the system of epicycles, with the Earth revolving around a centre that revolved around another centre, which in turn orbited the Sun. Kepler rescued the model by introducing the concept of elliptical orbits. Copernicus also held to the notion of spheres, in which the planets were supposed to travel. It was Brahe who finally rid astronomy of that concept.

French mathematician, encyclopedist, and theoretical physicist. In association with Denis Diderot, he helped plan the great Encyclopédie, for which he also wrote the 'Discours préliminaire' 1751. He framed several theorems and principles – notably d'Alembert's principle – in dynamics and celestial mechanics, and devised the theory of partial differential equations.

The principle that now bears his name was first published in his Traité de dynamique 1743, and was an extension of the third of Isaac Newton's laws of motion. D'Alembert maintained that the law was valid not merely for a static body, but also for mobile bodies. Within a year he had found a means of applying the principle to the theory of equilibrium and the motion of fluids. Using also the theory of partial differential equations, he studied the properties of sound, and air compression, and also managed to relate his principle to an investigation of the motion of any body in a given figure.

Mary Evans Picture Library

copper ore any mineral from which copper is extracted, including native copper, Cu; chalcocite, Cu_2S; chalcopyrite, $CuFeS_2$; bornite, Cu_5FeS_4; azurite, $Cu_3(CO_3)_2(OH)_2$; malachite, $Cu_2CO_3(OH)_2$; and chrysocolla, $CuSiO_3.2H_2O$.

Native copper and the copper sulphides are usually found in veins associated with igneous intrusions. Chrysocolla and the carbonates are products of the weathering of copper-bearing rocks. Copper was one of the first metals to be worked, because it occurred in native form and needed little refining. Today the main producers are the USA, Russia, Kazakhstan, Georgia, Uzbekistan, Armenia, Zambia, Chile, Peru, Canada, and Congo (formerly Zaire).

copper(II) oxide CuO black solid that is readily reduced to copper by carbon, carbon monoxide, or hydrogen if heated with any of these.

$$CuO + C \rightarrow Cu + CO \quad CuO + CO \rightarrow Cu + CO_2$$

$$CuO + H_2 \rightarrow Cu + H_2O$$

It is usually made in the laboratory by heating copper(II) carbonate, nitrate, or hydroxide.

$$2Cu(NO_3)_2 \rightarrow 2CuO + 4NO_2 + O_2$$

Copper(II) oxide is a typical basic oxide, dissolving readily in most dilute acids.

copper(II) sulphate $CuSO_4$ substance usually found as a blue, crystalline, hydrated salt $CuSO_4.5H_2O$ (also called blue vitriol). It is made from the action of dilute sulphuric acid on copper(II) oxide, hydroxide, or carbonate.

$$CuO + H_2SO_4 + 4H_2O \rightarrow CuSO_4.5H_2O$$

When the hydrated salt is heated gently it loses its water of crystallization and the blue crystals turn to a white powder. The reverse reaction is used as a chemical test for water.

$$CuSO_4.5H_2O \leftrightarrow CuSO_4 + 5H_2O$$

coppicing woodland management practice of severe pruning where trees are cut down to near ground level at regular intervals, typically every 3–20 years, to promote the growth of numerous shoots from the base.

This form of ◊forestry was once commonly practised in Europe, principally on hazel and chestnut, to produce large quantities of thin branches for firewood, fencing, and so on; alder, eucalyptus, maple, poplar, and willow were also coppiced. The resulting thicket was known as a coppice or copse. See also ◊pollarding.

coprocessor in computing, an additional ◊processor that works with the main ◊central processing unit to carry out a specific function. The two most common coprocessors are the **mathematical coprocessor**, used to speed up calculations, and the **graphic coprocessor**, used to improve the handling of graphics.

copulation act of mating in animals with internal ◊fertilization. Male mammals have a ◊penis or other organ that is used to introduce spermatozoa into the reproductive tract of the female. Most birds transfer sperm by pressing their cloacas (the openings of their reproductive tracts) together.

copy protection techniques used to prevent illegal copying of computer programs. Copy protection is not as common as it used to be because it also prevents legal copying (for backup purposes). Alternative techniques to prevent illegal use include ◊dongles, passwords and the need to uninstall a program before it can be installed on another machine.

coral marine invertebrate of the class Anthozoa in the phylum Cnidaria, which also includes sea anemones and jellyfish. It has a

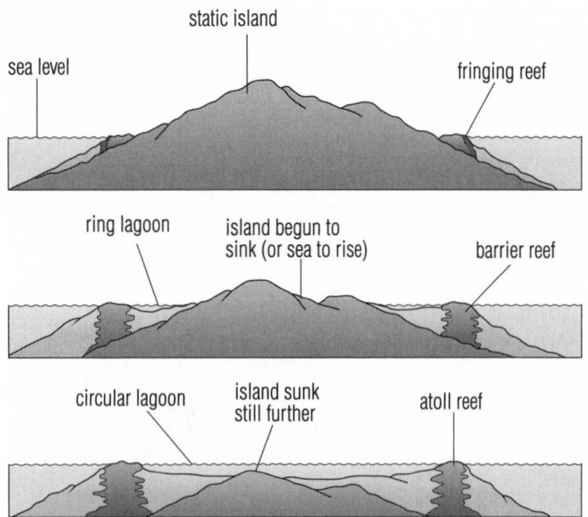

***coral atoll** The formation of a coral atoll by the gradual sinking of a volcanic island. The reefs fringing the island build up as the island sinks, eventually producing a ring of coral around the spot where the island sank.*

skeleton of lime (calcium carbonate) extracted from the surrounding water. Corals exist in warm seas, at moderate depths with sufficient light. Some coral is valued for decoration or jewellery, for example, Mediterranean red coral *Corallum rubrum.*

Corals live in a symbiotic relationship with microscopic ◊algae (zooxanthellae), which are incorporated into the soft tissue. The algae obtain carbon dioxide from the coral polyps, and the polyps receive nutrients from the algae. Corals also have a relationship to the fish that rest or take refuge within their branches, and which excrete nutrients that make the corals grow faster. The majority of corals form large colonies although there are species that live singly. Their accumulated skeletons make up large coral reefs and atolls. The Great Barrier Reef, to the NE of Australia, is about 1,600 km/1,000 mi long, has a total area of 20,000 sq km/7,700 sq mi, and adds 50 million tonnes of calcium to the reef each year. The world's reefs cover an estimated 620,000 sq km/240,000 sq mi.

Coral reefs provide a habitat for a diversity of living organisms. In 1997, some 93,000 species were identified. One third of the world's marine fishes live in reefs. The world's first global survey of coral reefs, carried out in 1997, found around 95% of reefs had experienced some damage from overfishing, pollution, dynamiting, poisoning, and the dragging of ships' anchors.

diseases Since the 1990s, coral reefs have been destroyed by previously unknown diseases. The **white plague** attacked 17 species of coral in the Florida Keys, USA, in 1995. The **rapid wasting disease**, discovered in 1997, affects coral reefs from Mexico to Trinidad. In the Caribbean, the fungus *Aspergillus* attacks sea fans, a soft coral. It was estimated in 1997 that around 90% of the coral around the Galapagos islands had been destroyed as a result of 'bleaching', a whitening of coral reefs which occurs when the coloured algae evacuate the coral. This happens either because the corals produce toxins that are harmful to the algae or because they do not produce sufficient nutrients. Without the algae, the coral crumbles and dies away. Bleaching is widespread all over the Caribbean and the Indo-Pacific.

WELCOME TO CORAL FOREST

http://www.blacktop.com/coralforest/

Site dedicated to explaining the importance of coral reefs for the survival of the planet. It is an impassioned plea on behalf of the world's endangered coral reefs and includes a full description of their biodiversity, maps of where coral reefs are to be found (no less than 109 countries), and many photos.

coralroot any leafless orchid of the genus *Corallorhiza,* having branched coral-colored roots and small yellowish or purplish flowers. These orchids are either parasitic on the roots of other plants, or saprophytes, living on decaying organic matter.

coral snake venomous snake. *Elaps corallinus* is a typical specimen; it occurs in the tropical forests of South America, and its small body, less than 1 m/3.3 ft in length, is ringed with coral-red. It is highly poisonous.

classification Coral snakes are in the family Elapidae, suborder Serpentes, order Squamata, class Reptilia.

coral tree any of several tropical trees with bright red or orange flowers and producing a very lightweight wood. (Genus *Erythrina,* family Fabaceae.)

Corba (acronym for ***Common object request broker architecture***) in computing, agreed specification that enables software components or 'objects' from different suppliers running on different computers using different operating systems to interoperate with one another. Corba has been extended via the Internet Inter-Orb Protocol (IIOP) to work over the Internet. Corba is promulgated as a standard by the Object Management Group (OMG).

cord unit for measuring the volume of wood cut for fuel. One cord equals 128 cubic feet (3.456 cubic metres), or a stack 8 feet (2.4 m) long, 4 feet (1.2 m) wide, and 4 feet high.

cordillera group of mountain ranges and their valleys, all running in a specific direction, formed by the continued convergence of two tectonic plates (see ◊plate tectonics) along a line. The term is applied especially to the principal mountain belt of a continent. The Andes of South America are an example.

core in earth science, the innermost part of Earth. It is divided into an outer core, which begins at a depth of 2,898 km/1,800 mi, and an inner core, which begins at a depth of 4,982 km/3,095 mi. Both parts are thought to consist of iron-nickel alloy. The outer core is liquid and the inner core is solid.

The fact that seismic shear waves (see ◊seismic wave) disappear at the mantle–outer core boundary indicates that the outer core is molten, since shear waves cannot travel through fluid. Scientists infer the iron-nickel rich composition of the core from Earth's density and its ◊moment of inertia. The temperature of the core, as estimated from the melting point of iron at high pressure, is thought to be at least 4,000°C/7,232°F, but remains controversial. Earth's magnetic field is believed to be the result of the motions involving the inner and outer cores.

Corel Canadian software company founded in 1983 by British citizen Michael Cowpland. Its drawing program Corel Draw led the market from its first release. Corel bought the desktop publishing package Ventura Publisher 1995 and then the word processor WordPerfect 1996.

corgi breed of dog. See ◊Welsh corgi.

coriander pungent fresh herb belonging to the parsley family, native to Europe and Asia; also a spice made from its dried ripe seeds. The spice is used commercially as a flavouring in meat products, bakery goods, tobacco, gin, liqueurs, chilli, and curry powder. Both are commonly used in cooking in the Middle East, India, Mexico, and China. (*Coriandrum sativum,* family Umbelliferae.)

Coriolis effect the effect of the Earth's rotation on the atmosphere and on all objects on the Earth's surface. In the northern hemisphere it causes moving objects and currents to be deflected to the right; in the southern hemisphere it causes deflection to the left. The effect is named after its discoverer, French mathematician Gaspard de Coriolis (1792–1843).

cork light, waterproof outer layers of the bark covering the branches and roots of almost all trees and shrubs. The cork oak (*Quercus suber*), a native of S Europe and N Africa, is cultivated in Spain and Portugal; the exceptionally thick outer layers of its bark provide the cork that is used commercially.

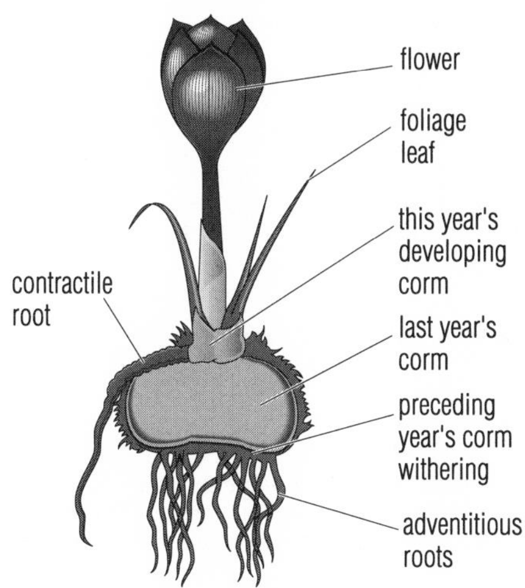

corm *Corms, found in plants such as the gladiolus and crocus, are underground storage organs. They provide the food for growth during adverse conditions such as cold or drought.*

corm short, swollen, underground plant stem, surrounded by protective scale leaves, as seen in the genus *Crocus.* It stores food, provides a means of ◊vegetative reproduction, and acts as a ◊perennating organ.

During the year, the corm gradually withers as the food reserves are used for the production of leafy, flowering shoots formed from axillary buds. Several new corms are formed at the base of these shoots, above the old corm.

cormorant any of various diving seabirds, mainly of the genus *Phalacrocorax,* order Pelecaniformes, about 90 cm/3 ft long, with webbed feet, a long neck, hooked beak, and glossy black plumage. Cormorants generally feed on fish and shellfish, which they catch by swimming and diving under water, sometimes to a considerable depth. They collect the food in a pouch formed by the dilatable skin at the front of the throat. Some species breed on inland lakes and rivers.

P. carbo has a bright shiny head and neck, with bluish-black feathers, speckled with white. The general colour above is a greenish black, the throat white, and the bill and feet are dark grey. It is found in all parts of the world in coastal regions.

There are about 30 species of cormorant worldwide, including a flightless form *Nannopterum harrisi* in the Galápagos Islands; the **shag**, or **green cormorant**, *P. aristotelis*; and the **small European cormorant**, *Halietor pygmaeus,* which is a freshwater bird. The **guanay cormorant** *P. bougainvillei,* of the Peruvian coast, is the main producer of the ◊guano of those regions.

corn general term for the main ◊cereal crop of a region – for example, wheat in the UK, oats in Scotland and Ireland, maize in the USA. Also, another word for ◊maize.

corncrake or landrail bird *Crex crex* of the rail family Rallidae, order Gruiformes. About 25 cm/10 in long, the bill and tail are short, the legs long and powerful, and the toes have sharp claws. It is drably coloured, shy, and has a persistent rasping call. The corncrake can swim and run easily, but its flight is heavy. It lives in meadows and crops in temperate regions, but has become rare where mechanical methods of cutting corn are used.

cornea transparent front section of the vertebrate ◊eye. The cornea is curved and behaves as a fixed lens, so that light entering the eye is partly focused before it reaches the lens.

There are no blood vessels in the cornea and it relies on the fluid in the front chamber of the eye for nourishment. Further protection for the eye is provided by the ◊conjunctiva. In humans, diseased or opaque parts may be replaced by grafts of corneal tissue from a donor.

cornflower native European and Asian plant belonging to the same genus as the ◊knapweeds but distinguished from them by its deep azure-blue flowers. Formerly a common weed in N European wheat fields, it is now widely grown in gardens as a ◊herbaceous plant with flower colours ranging from blue through shades of pink and purple to white. (*Centaurea cyanus,* family Compositae.)

cornified layer the upper layer of the skin where the cells have died, their cytoplasm being replaced by keratin, a fibrous protein also found in nails and hair. Cornification gives the skin its protective waterproof quality.

corolla collective name for the petals of a flower. In some plants the petal margins are partly or completely fused to form a **corolla tube**, for example in bindweed *Convolvulus arvensis.*

corona faint halo of hot (about 2,000,000°C/3,600,000°F) and tenuous gas around the Sun, which boils from the surface. It is visible at solar ◊eclipses or through a **coronagraph**, an instrument that blocks light from the Sun's brilliant disc. Gas flows away from the corona to form the ◊solar wind.

Corona Australis or ***Southern Crown*** small constellation of the southern hemisphere, located near the constellation ◊Sagittarius. It is similar in size and shape to ◊Corona Borealis but is not as bright.

Corona Borealis or ***Northern Crown*** small but easily recognizable constellation of the northern hemisphere, between ◊Hercules and ◊Boötes, traditionally identified with the jewelled crown of Ariadne that was cast into the sky by Bacchus in Greek mythology. Its brightest star is Alphecca (or Gemma), which is 78 light years from Earth.

It contains several variable stars. R Coronae Borealis is normally fairly constant in brightness but fades at irregular intervals and stays faint for a variable length of time. T Coronae Borealis is normally faint, but very occasionally blazes up and for a few days may be visible to the naked eye. It is a recurrent ◊nova.

coronary artery disease ***Latin*** *corona* ***'crown', from the arteries encircling the heart*** condition in which the fatty deposits of ◊atherosclerosis form in the coronary arteries that supply the heart muscle, narrowing them and restricting the blood flow.

These arteries may already be hardened (arteriosclerosis). If the heart's oxygen requirements are increased, as during exercise, the blood supply through the narrowed arteries may be inadequate, and the pain of ◊angina results. A ◊heart attack occurs if the blood supply to an area of the heart is cut off, for example because a blood clot (thrombus) has blocked one of the coronary arteries. The subsequent lack of oxygen damages the heart muscle (infarct), and if a large area of the heart is affected, the attack may be fatal. Coronary artery disease tends to run in families and is linked to smoking, lack of exercise, and a diet high in saturated (mostly animal) fats, which tends to increase the level of blood ◊cholesterol. It is a common cause of death in many industrialized countries; older men are the most vulnerable group. The condition is treated with drugs or bypass surgery.

Coronella genus of snakes inhabiting Europe, Asia, and America. All are harmless.

corpuscular theory hypothesis about the nature of light championed by Isaac Newton, who postulated that it consists of a stream of particles or corpuscles. The theory was superseded at the beginning of the 19th century by English physicist Thomas Young's wave theory. ◊Quantum theory and wave mechanics embody both concepts.

corpus luteum glandular tissue formed in the mammalian ◊ovary after ovulation from the Graafian follicle, a group of cells associated with bringing the egg to maturity. It secretes the hormone progesterone in anticipation of pregnancy.

After the release of an egg the follicle enlarges under the action of luteinizing hormone, released from the pituitary. The corpus luteum secretes the hormone progesterone, which maintains the uterus wall ready for pregnancy. If pregnancy occurs, the corpus luteum continues to secrete progesterone until the fourth month; if pregnancy does not occur the corpus luteum breaks down.

corrasion the grinding away of solid rock surfaces by particles carried by water, ice, and wind. It is generally held to be the most significant form of ◊erosion. As the eroding particles are carried along they become eroded themselves due to the process of attrition.

correlation the degree of relationship between two sets of information. If one set of data increases at the same time as the other, the relationship is said to be positive or direct. If one set of data increases as the other decreases, the relationship is negative or inverse. Correlation can be shown by plotting a best-fit line on a ◊scatter diagram.

In statistics, such relations are measured by the calculation of ◊coefficients of correlation. These generally measure correlation on a scale with 1 indicating perfect positive correlation, 0 no correlation at all, and –1 perfect inverse correlation. Correlation coefficients for assumed linear relations include the Pearson product moment correlation coefficient (known simply as the correlation coefficient), Kendall's tau correlation coefficient, or Spearman's rho correlation coefficient, which is used in nonparametric statistics (where the data are measured on ordinal rather than interval scales). A high correlation does not always indicate dependence between two variables; it may be that there is a third (unstated) variable upon which both depend.

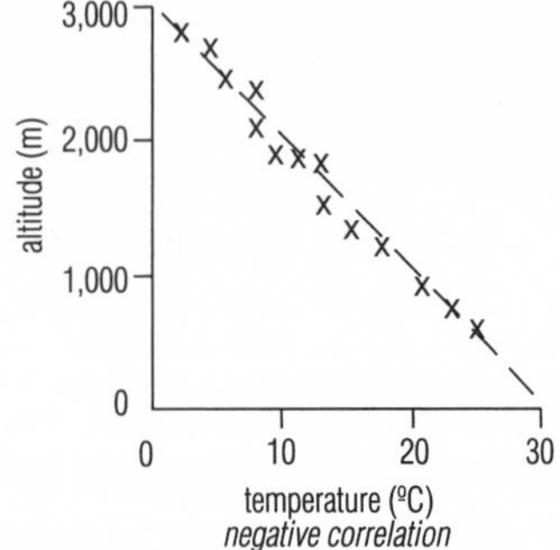

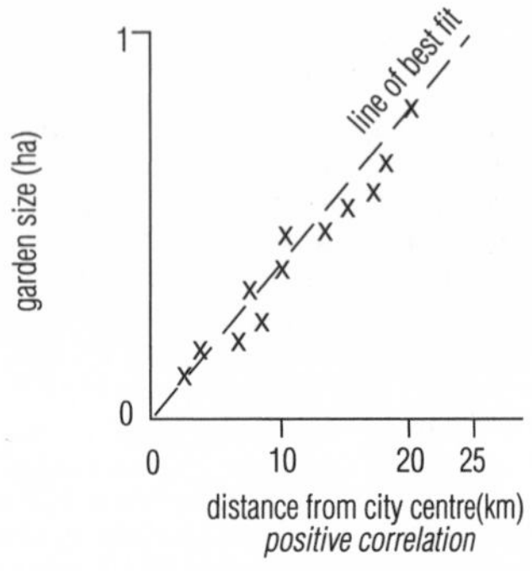

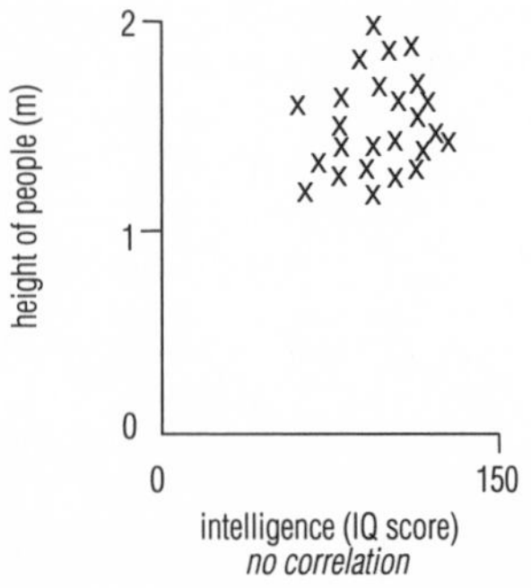

correlation Scattergraphs showing different kinds of correlation. In this way, a causal relationship between two variables may be proved or disproved, provided there are no hidden factors.

correspondence in mathematics, the relation between two sets where an operation on the members of one set maps some or all of them onto one or more members of the other. For example, if *A* is the set of members of a family and *B* is the set of months in the year, *A* and *B* are in correspondence if the operation is: '...has a birthday in the month of...'.

corresponding angles a pair of equal angles lying on the same side of a transversal (a line that cuts through two or more lines in the same plane), and making an interior and exterior angle with the intersected lines.

corrie (***Welsh*** **cwm**; ***French, North American*** **cirque**) Scottish term for a steep-sided hollow in the mountainside of a glaciated area. The weight and movement of the ice has ground out the bottom and worn back the sides. A corrie is open at the front, and its sides and back are formed of ◊arêtes. There may be a lake in the bottom, called a tarn.

A corrie is formed as follows: (1) snow accumulates in a hillside hollow (enlarging the hollow by nivation), and turns to ice; (2) the hollow is deepened by abrasion and plucking; (3) the ice in the corrie rotates under the influence of gravity, deepening the hollow still further; (4) since the ice is thinner and moves more slowly at the foot of the hollow, a rock lip forms; (5) when the ice melts, a lake or tarn may be formed in the corrie. The steep back wall may be severely weathered by freeze-thaw, weathering providing material for further abrasion.

corrosion in chemistry, the eating away and eventual destruction of metals and alloys by chemical attack. The rusting of ordinary iron and steel is the most common form of corrosion. Rusting takes place in moist air, when the iron combines with oxygen and water to form a brown-orange deposit of ◊rust (hydrated iron oxide). The rate of corrosion is increased where the atmosphere is polluted with sulphur dioxide. Salty road and air conditions accelerate the rusting of car bodies.

Corrosion is largely an electrochemical process, and acidic and salty conditions favour the establishment of electrolytic cells on the metal, which cause it to be eaten away. Other examples of corrosion include the green deposit that forms on copper and bronze, called verdigris, a basic copper carbonate. The tarnish on silver is a corrosion product, a film of silver sulphide.

corrosion in earth science, an alternative name for ◊solution, the process by which water dissolves rocks such as limestone.

corruption of data introduction or presence of errors in data. Most computers use a range of ◊verification and ◊validation routines to prevent corrupt data from entering the computer system or detect corrupt data that are already present.

cortex in biology, the outer part of a structure such as the brain, kidney, or adrenal gland. In botany the cortex includes nonspecialized cells lying just beneath the surface cells of the root and stem.

corticosteroid any of several steroid hormones secreted by the cortex of the ◊adrenal glands; also synthetic forms with similar properties. Corticosteroids have anti-inflammatory and ◊immunosuppressive effects and may be used to treat a number of conditions, including rheumatoid arthritis, severe allergies, asthma, some skin diseases, and some cancers. Side effects can be serious, and therapy must be withdrawn very gradually.

The two main groups of corticosteroids include **glucocorticoids** (◊cortisone, hydrocortisone, prednisone, and dexamethasone), which are essential to carbohydrate, fat, and protein metabolism, and to the body's response to stress; and **mineralocorticoids** (aldosterone, fluorocortisone), which control the balance of water and salt in the body.

corticotrophin-releasing hormone (CRH) hormone produced by the ◊hypothalamus that stimulates the adrenal glands to produce the steroid cortisol, essential for normal ◊metabolism. CRH is also produced by the ◊placenta and a surge in CRH may trigger the beginning of labour.

cortisol hormone produced by the ◊adrenal glands. It plays a role in helping the body combat stress and is at its highest level in the blood at dawn.

cortisone natural corticosteroid produced by the ◊adrenal gland, now synthesized for its anti-inflammatory qualities and used in the treatment of rheumatoid arthritis.

Cortisone was discovered by Tadeus Reichstein of Basel, Switzerland, and put to practical clinical use for rheumatoid arthritis by Philip Hench (1896–1965) and Edward Kendall (1886–1972) in the USA (all three shared a Nobel prize 1950).

A product of the adrenal gland, it was first synthesized from a constituent of ox bile, and is now produced commercially from a Mexican yam and from a by-product of the sisal plant. It is used for treating allergies and certain cancers, as well as rheumatoid arthritis. The side effects of cortisone steroids include muscle wasting, fat redistribution, diabetes, bone thinning, and high blood pressure.

corundum native aluminium oxide, Al_2O_3, the hardest naturally occurring mineral known apart from diamond (corundum rates 9 on the Mohs' scale of hardness); lack of ◊cleavage also increases its durability. Its crystals are barrel-shaped prisms of the trigonal system. Varieties of gem-quality corundum are **ruby** (red) and **sapphire** (any colour other than red, usually blue). Poorer-quality and synthetic corundum is used in industry, for example as an ◊abrasive.

Corundum forms in silica-poor igneous and metamorphic rocks. It is a constituent of emery, which is metamorphosed bauxite.

cosecant in trigonometry, a ◊function of an angle in a right-angled triangle found by dividing the length of the hypotenuse (the longest side) by the length of the side opposite the angle. Thus the cosecant of an angle A, usually shortened to cosec A, is always greater than (or equal to) 1. It is the reciprocal of the sine of the angle, that is, cosec $A = 1/\sin A$.

cosine in trigonometry, a ◊function of an angle in a right-angled triangle found by dividing the length of the side adjacent to the angle by the length of the hypotenuse (the longest side). It is usually shortened to **cos**.

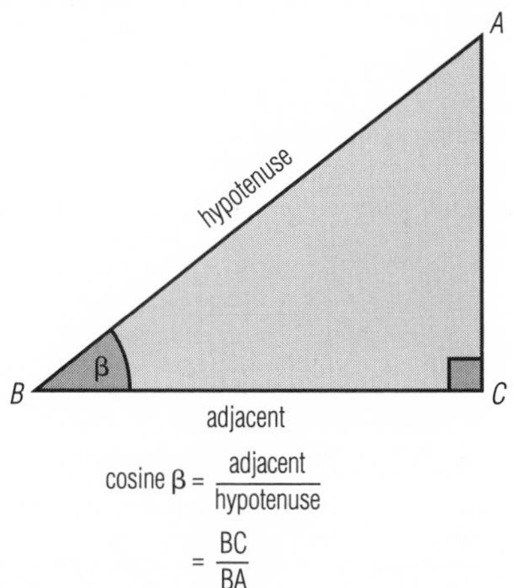

***cosine** The cosine of angle β is equal to the ratio of the length of the adjacent side to the length of the hypotenuse (the longest side, opposite to the right angle).*

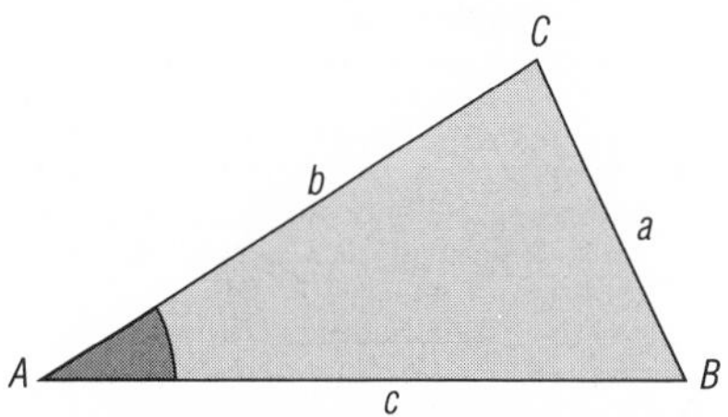

***cosine rule** The cosine rule is a rule of trigonometry that relates the sides and angles of triangles. It can be used to find a missing length or angle in a triangle.*

cosine rule in trigonometry, a rule that relates the sides and angles of triangles. The rule has the formula:

$$a^2 = b^2 + c^2 - 2bc \cos A$$

where a, b, and c are the sides of the triangle, and A is the angle opposite a.

cosmic background radiation or **3° radiation** electromagnetic radiation left over from the original formation of the universe in the Big Bang around 15 billion years ago. It corresponds to an overall background temperature of 3K (–270°C/–454°F), or 3°C above absolute zero. In 1992 the Cosmic Background Explorer satellite, COBE, detected slight 'ripples' in the strength of the background radiation that are believed to mark the first stage in the formation of galaxies.

Cosmic background radiation was first detected in 1965 by US physicists Arno Penzias (1933–) and Robert Wilson (1936–), who in 1978 shared the Nobel Prize for Physics for their discovery.

cosmic radiation streams of high-energy particles from outer space, consisting of protons, alpha particles, and light nuclei, which collide with atomic nuclei in the Earth's atmosphere, and produce secondary nuclear particles (chiefly ◊mesons, such as pions and muons) that shower the Earth.

Those of low energy seem to be galactic in origin, and those of high energy of extragalactic origin. The galactic particles may come from ◊supernova explosions or ◊pulsars. At higher energies, other sources are necessary, possibly the giants jets of gas which are emitted from some galaxies.

cosmid fragment of ◊DNA from the human genome inserted into a bacterial cell. The bacterium replicates the fragment along with its own DNA. In this way the fragments are copied for a gene library. Cosmids are characteristically 40,000 base pairs in length. The most commonly used bacterium is *Escherichia coli.* A ◊yeast artificial chromosome works in the same way.

cosmogony ***Greek 'universe' and 'creation'*** study of the origin and evolution of cosmic objects, especially the Solar System.

cosmological principle in astronomy, a hypothesis that any observer anywhere in the ◊universe has the same view that we

BRIEF HISTORY OF COSMOLOGY

http://www-history.mcs.st-and.ac.uk/~history/HistTopics/Cosmology.html

Based at St Andrews University, Scotland, a site chronicling the history of cosmology from the time of the Babylonians to the Hubble Space Telescope. It includes links to the biographies of the key historical figures responsible for the advancement of the subject, and in addition has a brief list of references for further reading.

have; that is, that the universe is not expanding from any centre but all galaxies are moving away from one another.

cosmology branch of astronomy that deals with the structure and evolution of the universe as an ordered whole. Its method is to construct 'model universes' mathematically and compare their large-scale properties with those of the observed universe.

Modern cosmology began in the 1920s with the discovery that the universe is expanding, which suggested that it began in an explosion, the ◊Big Bang. An alternative – now discarded – view, the ◊steady-state theory, claimed that the universe has no origin, but is expanding because new matter is being continually created.

cosmonaut term used in the West for any astronaut from the former Soviet Union.

Cosmos name used from the early 1960s for nearly all Soviet artificial satellites. Over 2,300 Cosmos satellites had been launched by mid 1995.

> *Our loyalties are to the species and the planet. We speak for Earth. Our obligation to survive is owed not just to ourselves but also to that Cosmos, ancient and vast, from which we spring.*
>
> CARL SAGAN US astronomer. *Cosmos* 1980

CoSy (contraction of ***conferencing system***) ◊command-line interface electronic conferencing software developed at the University of Guelph in the Canadian province of Ontario. It is used on London's ◊Compulink Information eXchange (CIX) service and for the Open University's conferencing, as well as many others worldwide.

cotangent in trigonometry, a ◊function of an angle in a right-angled triangle found by dividing the length of the side adjacent to the angle by the length of the side opposite it. It is usually written as cotan, or cot and it is the reciprocal of the tangent of the angle, so that cot A = 1/tan A, where A is the angle in question.

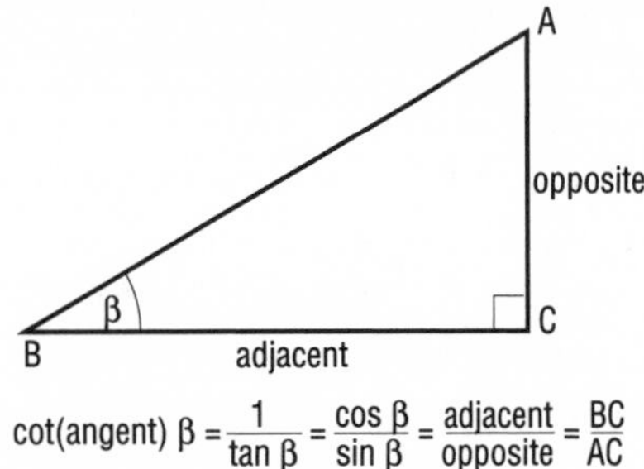

$$\cot(\text{angent})\ \beta = \frac{1}{\tan\beta} = \frac{\cos\beta}{\sin\beta} = \frac{\text{adjacent}}{\text{opposite}} = \frac{BC}{AC}$$

cotangent *The cotangent of angle β is equal to the ratio of the length of the adjacent side to the length of the opposite side.*

cot death or ***sudden infant death syndrome*** (SIDS) death of an apparently healthy baby, almost always during sleep. It is most common in the winter months, and strikes more boys than girls. The cause is not known but risk factors that have been identified include prematurity, respiratory infection, overheating, and sleeping position.

There was a 60% reduction in the number of cot deaths in the UK in the first nine months of 1993, following a massive advertising campaign advising parents to put their babies to sleep on their backs, ensure they do not overheat, and avoid smoking near them. Earlier, in New Zealand (1991), where the cot death rate had been the highest in the world, the rate was halved by a similar campaign.

cotoneaster any of a group of shrubs or trees found in Europe and Asia, belonging to the rose family and closely related to the hawthorn and medlar. The fruits, though small and unpalatable, are usually bright red and conspicuous, often surviving through the winter. Some of the shrubs are cultivated for their attractive appearance. (Genus *Cotoneaster*, family Rosaceae.)

cotton tropical and subtropical ◊herbaceous plant belonging to the mallow family. Fibres surround the seeds inside the ripened fruits, or bolls, and these are spun into yarn for cloth. (Genus *Gossypium*, family Malvaceae.)

The fibres are separated from the seeds in a machine called a ◊cotton gin. The seeds are used to produce cooking oil and livestock feed, and the pigment gossypol may be useful as a male contraceptive in a modified form. Cotton disease (byssinosis), caused by cotton dust, affects the lungs of those working in the industry.

Cotton production uses 50% of world pesticides and represents 5% of world agricultural output.

cotton gin machine that separates cotton fibres from the seed boll. Production of the gin (then called an en**gin**e) by US inventor Eli Whitney in 1793 was a milestone in textile history.

The modern gin consists of a roller carrying a set of circular saws. These project through a metal grill in a hopper containing the seed bolls. As the roller rotates, the saws pick up the cotton fibres, leaving the seeds behind.

cotton grass or ***bog cotton*** any grasslike plant of a group belonging to the sedge family. White tufts cover the fruiting heads in midsummer; these break off and are carried long distances on the wind. Cotton grass is found in wet places throughout the Arctic and temperate regions of the northern hemisphere, most species growing in acid bogs. (Genus *Eriophorum*, family Cyperaceae.)

cotton spinning creating thread or fine yarn from the cotton plant by spinning the raw fibre contained within the seed-pods. The fibre is separated from the pods by a machine called a ◊cotton gin. It is then cleaned and the fibres are separated out (carding). Finally the fibres are drawn out to the desired length and twisted together to form strong thread.

cotton stainer any plant-feeding ◊bug of the family Pyrrhocoridae that pierces and stains cotton bolls; see also ◊Hemiptera.

cottonwood any of several North American ◊poplar trees with seeds topped by a thick tuft of silky hairs. The eastern cottonwood (*Populus deltoides*), growing to 30 m/100 ft, is native to the eastern USA. The name 'cottonwood' is also given to the downy-leaved Australian tree *Bedfordia salaoina*. (True cottonwood genus *Populus*, family Salicaceae.)

cotton-worm caterpillar of the owlet moth, closely allied to the army worm. Cotton-worms are found in both North and South America, where they ravage the cotton crops whilst ignoring other plants.

classification The cotton-worm *Aletia xylinae* is in the family Noctuidae, order Lepidoptera, class Insecta, phylum Arthropoda.

cotyledon structure in the embryo of a seed plant that may form a 'leaf' after germination and is commonly known as a seed leaf. The number of cotyledons present in an embryo is an important character in the classification of flowering plants (◊angiosperms).

Monocotyledons (such as grasses, palms, and lilies) have a single cotyledon, whereas dicotyledons (the majority of plant species) have two. In seeds that also contain ◊endosperm (nutritive tissue), the cotyledons are thin, but where they are the primary food-storing tissue, as in peas and beans, they may be quite large. After germination the cotyledons either remain below ground (hypogeal) or, more commonly, spread out above soil level (epigeal) and become the first green leaves. In gymnosperms there may be up to a dozen cotyledons within each seed.

couch grass European grass that spreads rapidly by underground stems. It is considered a troublesome weed in North America, where it has been introduced. (*Agropyron repens*, family Gramineae.)

cougar another name for the ◊puma, a large North American cat.

coulomb SI unit (symbol C) of electrical charge. One coulomb is the quantity of electricity conveyed by a current of one ◊ampere in one second.

Coulomb, Charles Augustin de (1736–1806) French scientist, inventor of the ◊torsion balance for measuring the force of electric and magnetic attraction. The coulomb was named after him. In the fields of structural engineering and friction, Coulomb greatly influenced and helped to develop engineering in the 19th century.

Coulomb's law of 1787 states that the force between two electric charges is proportional to the product of the charges and inversely proportional to the square of the distance between them.

count rate in physics, the number of particles emitted per unit time by a radioactive source. It is measured by a counter, such as a ◊Geiger counter, or ◊ratemeter.

couple in mechanics, a pair of forces acting on an object that are equal in magnitude and opposite in direction, but do not act along the same straight line. The two forces produce a turning effect or moment that tends to rotate the object; however, no single resultant (unbalanced) force is produced and so the object is not moved from one position to another.

The moment of a couple is the product of the magnitude of either of the two forces and the perpendicular distance between those forces. If the magnitude of the force is F newtons and the distance is d metres then the moment, in newton-metres, is given by:

$$\text{moment} = Fd$$

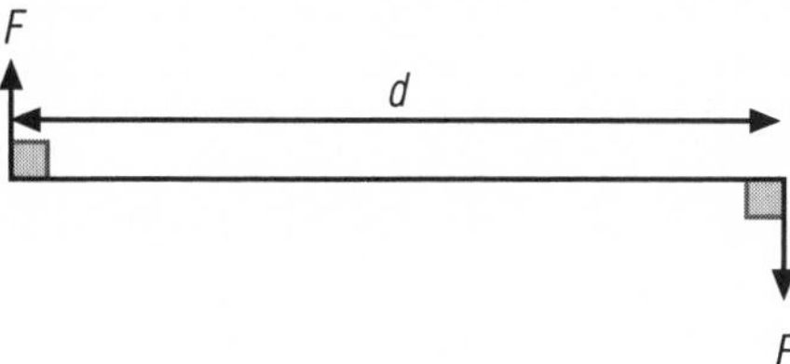

couple *Two equal but opposite forces (F) will produce a turning effect on a rigid body, provided that they do not act through the same straight line. The turning effect, or moment, is equal to the magnitude of one of the turning forces multiplied by the perpendicular distance (d) between those two forces.*

courgette small variety of ◊marrow, belonging to the gourd family. It is cultivated as a vegetable and harvested before it is fully mature, at 15–20 cm/6–8 in. In the USA and Canada it is known as a zucchini. (*Cucurbita pepo,* family Cucurbitaceae.)

courtship behaviour exhibited by animals as a prelude to mating. The behaviour patterns vary considerably from one species to another, but are often ritualized forms of behaviour not obviously related to courtship or mating (for example, courtship feeding in birds).

Courtship ensures that copulation occurs with a member of the opposite sex of the right species. It also synchronizes the partners' readiness to mate and allows each partner to assess the suitability of the other.

Cousteau, Jacques Yves (1910–1997) French oceanographer who pioneered the invention of the aqualung 1943 and techniques in underwater filming. In 1951 he began the first of many research voyages in the ship *Calypso.* His film and television documentaries and books established him as a household name.

covalent bond chemical ◊bond produced when two atoms share one or more pairs of electrons (usually each atom contributes an electron). The bond is often represented by a single line drawn between the two atoms. Covalently bonded substances include hydrogen (H_2), water (H_2O), and most organic substances.

cowfish type of ◊boxfish.

cow parsley or ***keck*** tall perennial plant belonging to the carrot family, found in Europe, N Asia, and N Africa. It grows up to 1 m/3 ft tall and has pinnate leaves (leaflets growing either side of a stem), hollow furrowed stems, and heads of delicate white flowers. (*Anthriscus sylvestris,* family Umbelliferae.)

cowrie marine snail of the family Cypreidae, in which the interior spiral form is concealed by a double outer lip. The shells are hard, shiny, and often coloured. Most cowries are shallow-water forms, and are found in many parts of the world, particularly the tropical Indo-Pacific. Cowries have been used as ornaments and fertility charms, and also as currency, for example the Pacific money cowrie *Cypraea moneta.*

cow shark species of shark. Cow sharks have six or seven gill openings, are about 5 m/16.5 ft long, and are found in most parts of the oceans.

classification Cow sharks are in family Hexanchidae, order Hexanchiformes, subclass Elasmobranchii, class Chondrichthyes.

cowslip European plant related to the primrose, with several small deep-yellow fragrant flowers growing from a single stem. It is native to temperate regions of the Old World. The oxlip (*Primula elatior*) is also closely related. (*Primula veris,* family Primulaceae.)

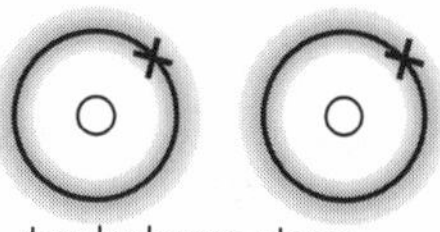

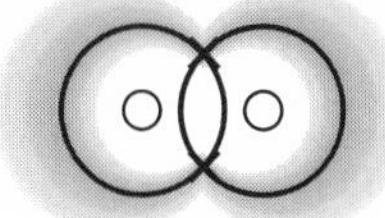

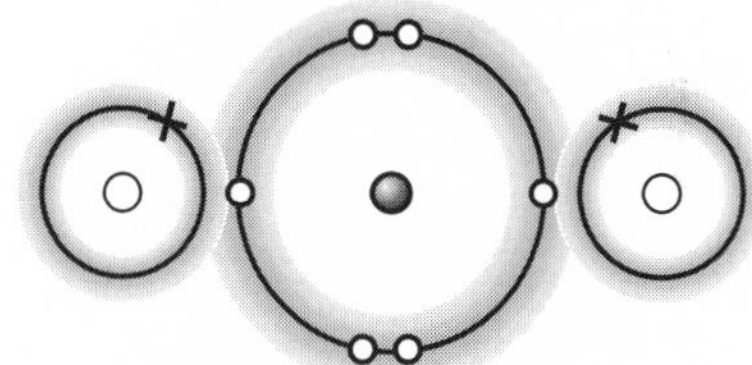

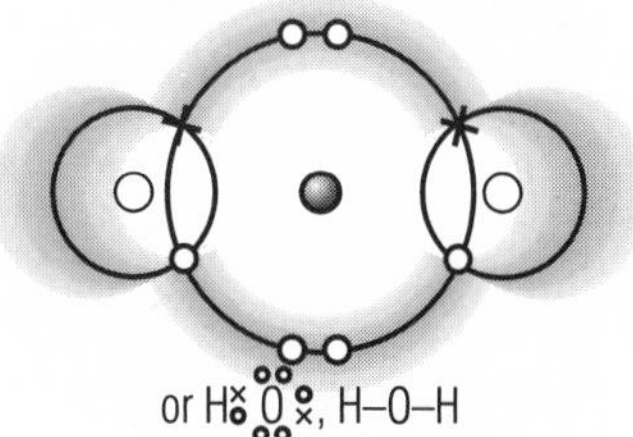

covalent bond *The formation of a covalent bond between two hydrogen atoms to form a hydrogen molecule (H_2), and between two hydrogen atoms and an oxygen atom to form a molecule of water (H_2O). The sharing means that each atom has a more stable arrangement of electrons (its outer electron shells are full).*

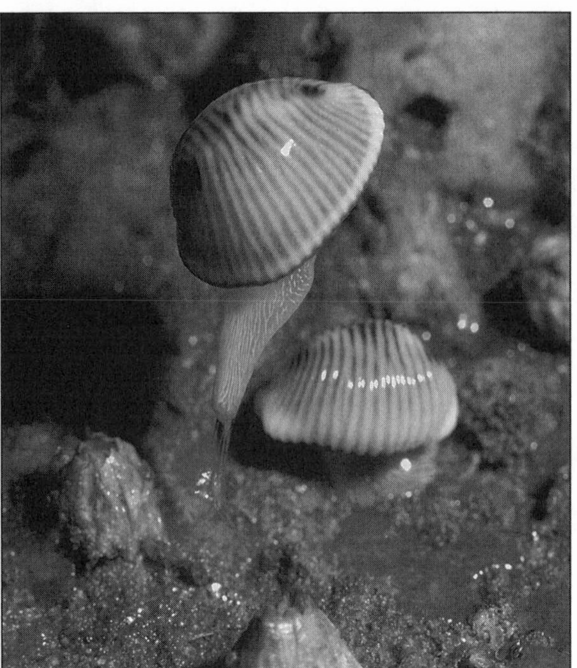

cowrie *Although most species of cowrie are tropical, there are several European species. This European cowrie* Trivia monacha *is one of two species which can be found along the coast of the British Isles; they are likely to be found only at low water during periods of spring tides. Premaphotos Wildlife*

coyote wild dog *Canis latrans,* in appearance like a small wolf, living in North and Central America. Its head and body are about 90 cm/3 ft long and brown, flecked with grey or black. Coyotes live in open country and can run at 65 kph/40 mph. Their main foods are rabbits and rodents. Although persecuted by humans for over a century, the species is very successful.

coypu South American water rodent *Myocastor coypus,* about 60 cm/2 ft long and weighing up to 9 kg/20 lb. It has a scaly, ratlike tail, webbed hind feet, a blunt-muzzled head, and large orange incisors. The fur ('nutria') is reddish brown. It feeds on vegetation, and lives in burrows in rivers and lake banks.

Taken to Europe and then to North America to be farmed for their fur, many escaped or were released. In Britain, coypus escaped from fur farms and became established on the Norfolk Broads where their adult numbers reached 5,000. They destroyed crops and local vegetation, and undermined banks and dykes. After a 10-year campaign they were eradicated in 1989 at a cost of over £2 million. In 1993 escaped coypu in Louisiana, USA, were causing serious damage to coastal marshland.

CP/M (abbreviation for ***control program/monitor*** or ***control program for microcomputers***) one of the earliest ◊operating systems for microcomputers. It was written by Gary Kildall, who founded Digital Research. In the 1970s it became a standard for microcomputers based on the Intel 8080 and Zilog Z80 8-bit microprocessors. In the 1980s it was superseded by Microsoft's ◊MS-DOS, written for Intel's 16-bit 8086/88 microprocessors.

CPSR abbreviation for ◊Computer Professionals for Social Responsibility.

CPU in computing, abbreviation for ◊central processing unit.

crab any decapod (ten-legged) crustacean of the division Brachyura, with a broad, rather round, upper body shell (carapace) and a small ◊abdomen tucked beneath the body. Crabs are related to lobsters and crayfish. Mainly marine, some crabs live in fresh water or on land. They are alert carnivores and scavengers. They have a typical sideways walk, and strong pincers on the first pair of legs, the other four pairs being used for walking. Periodically, the outer shell is cast to allow for growth. The name 'crab' is sometimes used for similar arthropods, such as the horseshoe crab, which is neither a true crab nor a crustacean.

CRAB

Female crabs can only mate just after moulting, when their shells are still soft. This is a vulnerable time, particularly for female paddle crabs, as some large male paddle crabs are cannibalistic. Most males, however, are keener to mate than to eat. Having found a female that is about to moult, the male paddle crab carries her around until she is ready, then mates with her and protects her until her shell hardens again.

crab apple any of 25 species of wild apple trees, native to temperate regions of the northern hemisphere. Numerous varieties of cultivated apples have been derived from *Malus pumila,* the common native crab apple of SE Europe and central Asia. The fruit of native species is smaller and more bitter than that of cultivated varieties and is used in crab-apple jelly. (Genus *Malus,* family Rosaceae.)

crab louse human pubic ◊louse.
classification The crab louse *Phtirus pubis* is in suborder Anoplura, order Phthiraptera, class Insecta, phylum Arthropoda.

Crab nebula cloud of gas 6,000 light years from Earth, in the constellation ◊Taurus. It is the remains of a star that according to Chinese records, exploded as a ◊supernova observed as a brilliant point of light on 4 July 1054. At its centre is a ◊pulsar that flashes 30 times a second. It was named by Lord Rosse after its crablike shape.

crack street name for a chemical derivative (bicarbonate) of ◊cocaine in hard, crystalline lumps; it is heated and inhaled (smoked) as a stimulant. Crack was first used in San Francisco in the early 1980s, and is highly addictive.

Its use has led to numerous deaths, but it is the fastest-growing sector of the illegal drug trade, since it is less expensive than cocaine.

cracker a hacker (see ◊hacking); the term distinguishes criminal hacking ('cracking') from those who explore to satisfy their intellectual curiosity. The term is used much less than most hackers would like.

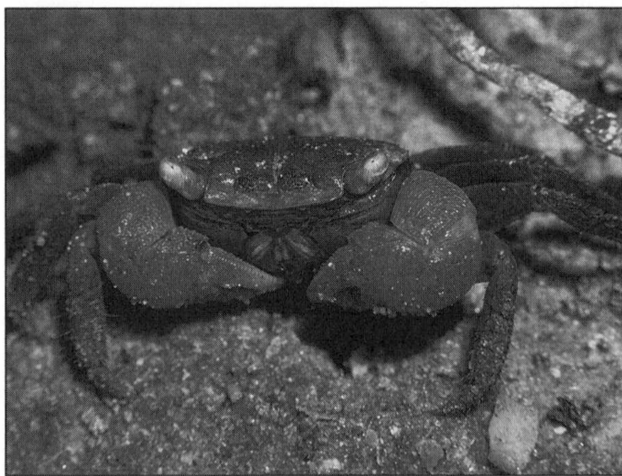

crab *Crabs have adapted to many habitats. This* Sesarma *species crab from Kenya, E Africa, is adapted to the muddy tidal regions dominated by mangroves. Premaphotos Wildlife*

cracking reaction in which a large ◊alkane molecule is broken down by heat into a smaller alkane and a small ◊alkene molecule. The reaction is carried out at a high temperature (600°C or higher) and often in the presence of a catalyst. Cracking is a commonly used process in the ◊petrochemical industry.

It is the main method of preparation of alkenes and is also used to manufacture petrol from the higher-boiling-point ◊fractions that are obtained by fractional ◊distillation (fractionation) of crude oil.

crag in previously glaciated areas, a large lump of rock that a glacier has been unable to wear away. As the glacier passed up and over the crag, weaker rock on the far side was largely protected from erosion and formed a tapering ridge, or **tail**, of debris.

An example of a crag-and-tail feature is found in Edinburgh in Scotland; Edinburgh Castle was built on the crag (Castle Rock), which dominates the city beneath.

crake any of several small birds of the family Rallidae, order Gruiformes, related to the ◊corncrake.

cranberry any of several trailing evergreen plants belonging to the heath family, related to bilberries and blueberries. They grow in marshy places and bear small, acid, crimson berries, high in vitamin C content, used for making sauce and jelly. (Genus *Vaccinium,* family Ericaceae.)

crane in engineering, a machine for raising, lowering, or placing in position heavy loads. The three main types are the jib crane, the overhead travelling crane, and the tower crane. Most cranes have the machinery mounted on a revolving turntable. This may be mounted on trucks or be self-propelled, often being fitted with ◊caterpillar tracks.

The main features of a **jib crane** are a power winch, a rope or cable, and a movable arm or jib. The cable, which carries a pulley block, hangs from the end of the jib and is wound up and down by the winch. The **overhead travelling crane**, chiefly used in workshops, consists of a fixed horizontal arm, along which runs a trolley carrying the pulley block. **Tower cranes**, seen on large building sites, have a long horizontal arm able to revolve on top of a tall tower. The arm carries the trolley.

Cranes can also be mounted on barges or large semisubmersibles for marine construction work.

crane in zoology, a large, wading bird of the family Gruidae, order Gruiformes, with long legs and neck, short powerful wings, a naked or tufted head, and unwebbed feet. The hind toe is greatly elevated, and has a sharp claw. Cranes are marsh- and plains-dwelling birds, feeding on plants as well as insects and small animals. They fly well and are usually migratory. Their courtship includes frenzied, leaping dances. They are found in all parts of the world except South America.

The **common crane** *Grus grus* is still numerous in many parts of Europe, and winters in Africa and India. It stands over 1 m/3ft high. The plumage of the adult bird is grey, varied with black and white, with a red patch of bare skin on the head and neck. All cranes have suffered through hunting and loss of wetlands; the population of the North American **whooping crane** *G. americana* fell to 21 wild birds in 1944. Through careful conservation, numbers have now risen to about 200.

crane fly or ***daddy-longlegs*** any fly of the family Tipulidae, with long, slender, fragile legs. They look like giant mosquitoes, but the adults are quite harmless. The larvae live in soil or water.

cranesbill any of a group of plants containing about 400 species. The plants are named after the long beaklike protrusion attached to the seed vessels. When ripe, this splits into coiling spirals which jerk the seeds out, helping to scatter them. (Genus *Geranium,* family Geraniaceae.)

cranium the dome-shaped area of the vertebrate skull that protects the brain. It consists of eight bony plates fused together by sutures (immovable joints). Fossil remains of the human cranium have aided the development of theories concerning human evolution.

The cranium has been studied as a possible indicator of intelligence or even of personality. The Victorian argument that a large cranium implies a large brain, which in turn implies a more profound intelligence, has been rejected.

crank handle bent at right angles and connected to the shaft of a machine; it is used to transmit motion or convert reciprocating (backwards-and-forwards or up-and-down) movement into rotary movement, or vice versa.

Although similar devices may have been employed in antiquity and as early as the 1st century in China and the 8th century in Europe, the earliest recorded use of a crank in a water-raising machine is by Arab mathematician al-Jazari in the 12th century. Not until the 15th century, however, did the crank become fully assimilated into developing European technology.

crankshaft essential component of piston engines that converts the up-and-down (reciprocating) motion of the pistons into useful rotary motion. The car crankshaft carries a number of cranks. The pistons are connected to the cranks by connecting rods and ◊bearings; when the pistons move up and down, the connecting rods force the offset crank pins to describe a circle, thereby rotating the crankshaft.

crater bowl-shaped depression in the ground, usually round and with steep sides. Craters are formed by explosive events such as the eruption of a volcano, the explosion of bomb, or the impact of a meteorite.

The Moon has more than 300,000 craters over 1 km/6 mi in diameter, formed by meteorite bombardment; similar craters on Earth have mostly been worn away by erosion. Craters are found on many other bodies in the Solar System.

Studies at the Jet Propulsion Laboratory in California, USA, have shown that craters produced by impact or by volcanic activity have distinctive shapes, enabling astronomers to distinguish likely methods of crater formation on planets in the Solar System. Unlike volcanic craters, impact craters have a raised rim and central peak and are almost always circular, irrespective of the meteorite's angle of incidence.

We used to think that if we knew one, we knew two, because one and one are two. We are finding that we must learn a great deal more about 'and'.

ARTHUR STANLEY EDDINGTON British astrophysicist.
Attributed remark

---

craton or ***shield*** core of a continent, a vast tract of highly deformed ◊metamorphic rock around which the continent has been built. Intense mountain-building periods shook these shield areas in Precambrian times before stable conditions set in.

Cratons exist in the hearts of all the continents, a typical example being the Canadian Shield.

crawler on the World Wide Web, automated indexing software that scours the Web for new or updated sites. See also ◊'bot, ◊spider, and ◊agent.

crayfish freshwater decapod (ten-limbed) crustacean belonging to several families structurally similar to, but smaller than, the lobster. Crayfish are brownish-green scavengers and are found in all parts of the world except Africa. They are edible, and some species are farmed.

Accurate reckoning – the entrance into the knowledge of all existing things and all obscure secrets.

AHMES THE SCRIBE Ancient Egyptian Scribe.
Rhind Papyrus

---

creationism theory concerned with the origins of matter and life, claiming, as does the Bible in Genesis, that the world and humanity were created by a supernatural Creator, not more than 6,000 years ago. It was developed in response to Darwin's theory of

crayfish The spectacular blue mountain crayfish Euastacus ontanus *inhabits clear, swiftly-flowing mountain streams in the subtropical forests of S Queensland, Australia. Premaphotos Wildlife*

◊evolution; it is not recognized by most scientists as having a factual basis.

After a trial 1981–82 a US judge ruled unconstitutional an attempt in Arkansas schools to enforce equal treatment of creationism and evolutionary theory. In Alabama from 1996 all biology textbooks must contain a statement that evolution is a controversial theory and not a proven fact.

Creative Labs name of the US and British subsidiaries of the parent computing company Creative Technology, which was founded in Singapore in 1981. Creative Labs manufactures the leading ◊sound card, the SoundBlaster, which it markets alongside the Internet telephony, video, and multimedia products that make up the company's product range.

By the company claimed 20 million users of its products and had 4,400 staff worldwide, 400 of them in research and development.

creep in civil and mechanical engineering, the property of a solid, typically a metal, under continuous stress that causes it to deform below its ◊yield point (the point at which any elastic solid normally stretches without any increase in load or stress). Lead, tin, and zinc, for example, exhibit creep at ordinary temperatures, as seen in the movement of the lead sheeting on the roofs of old buildings.

Copper, iron, nickel, and their alloys also show creep at high temperatures.

creeper any small, short-legged passerine bird of the family Certhidae. They spiral with a mouselike movement up tree trunks, searching for insects and larvae with their thin, down-curved beaks.

The brown creeper *Certhia familiaris* is 12 cm/5 in long, brown above, white below, and is found across North America and Eurasia.

creosote black, oily liquid derived from coal tar, used as a wood preservative. Medicinal creosote, which is transparent and oily, is derived from wood tar.

crescent curved shape of the Moon when it appears less than half illuminated. It also refers to any object or symbol resembling the crescent Moon. Often associated with Islam, it was first used by the Turks on their standards after the capture of Constantinople in 1453, and appears on the flags of many Muslim countries. The **Red Crescent** is the Muslim equivalent of the Red Cross.

cress any of several plants of the cress family, characterized by a pungent taste. The common European garden cress (*Lepidium sativum*) is cultivated worldwide. (Genera include *Lepidium, Cardamine,* and *Arabis*; family Cruciferae.)

Cretaceous ***Latin creta 'chalk'*** period of geological time approximately 144.2–65 million years ago. It is the last period of the Mesozoic era, during which angiosperm (seed-bearing) plants evolved, and dinosaurs reached a peak before their extinction at the end of the period. The north European chalk, which forms the white cliffs of Dover, was deposited during the latter half of the Cretaceous.

crevasse deep crack in the surface of a glacier; it can reach several metres in depth. Crevasses often occur where a glacier flows over the break of a slope, because the upper layers of ice are unable to stretch and cracks result. Crevasses may also form at the edges of glaciers owing to friction with the bedrock.

Crick, Francis Harry Compton (1916–)

English molecular biologist. From 1949 he researched the molecular structure of DNA, and the means whereby characteristics are transmitted from one generation to another. For this work he was awarded a Nobel prize (with Maurice Wilkins and James Watson) in 1962.

Using Wilkins's and others' discoveries, Crick and Watson postulated that DNA consists of a double helix consisting of two parallel chains of alternate sugar and phosphate groups linked by pairs of organic bases. They built molecular models which also explained how genetic information could be coded – in the sequence of organic bases. Crick and Watson published their work on the proposed structure of DNA in 1953. Their model is now generally accepted as correct.

Mary Evans Picture Library

cricket in zoology, an insect belonging to any of various families, especially the Gryllidae, of the order Orthoptera. Crickets are related to grasshoppers. They have somewhat flattened bodies and long antennae. The males make a chirping noise by rubbing together special areas on the forewings. The females have a long needlelike

cricket Most crickets are drably coloured in brown, grey, or black – this Kenyan species Rhicnogryllus lepidus *is an exception. Its bright livery is probably an example of aposematic (warning) coloration. Premaphotos Wildlife*

egglaying organ (ovipositor). There are around 900 species known worldwide.

Crinoidea class of echinoderms containing about 600 living species and more than 2,000 fossil forms; the extinct crinoids are commonly called stone lilies, and the existing species ◊sea lilies and ◊feather stars.

Crinoids retain many primitive features, notably in the use of the hydraulic water-vascular system for powering the capture and transportation of food rather than for locomotion. Uniquely amongst living echinoderms, the mouth is on the upper surface. Food particles are collected by the waving arms, and directed to the mouth along food grooves lined with cilia. Most of the living species are non-sessile (free-living), although a stalked stage may occur in development.

classification Crinoidea is in phylum Echinodermata.

crith unit of mass used for weighing gases. One crith is the mass of one litre of hydrogen gas (H_2) at standard temperature and pressure.

critical angle in optics, for a ray of light passing from a denser to a less dense medium (such as from glass to air), the smallest angle of incidence at which the emergent ray grazes the surface of the denser medium – at an angle of refraction of 90°.

When the angle of incidence is less than the critical angle, the ray passes out (is refracted) into the less dense medium; when the angle of incidence is greater than the critical angle, the ray is reflected back into the denser medium (see ◊total internal reflection).

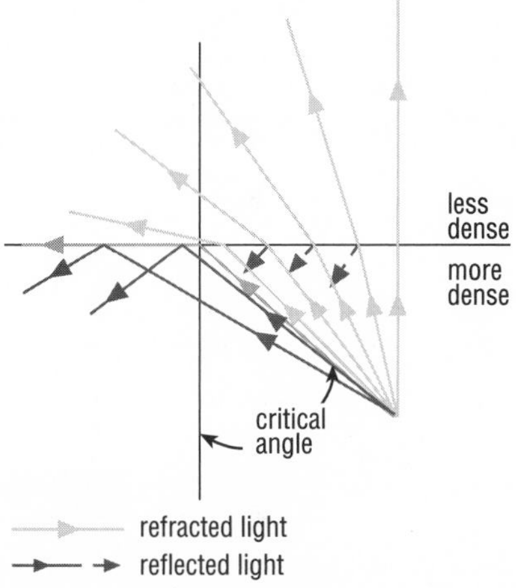

critical angle The critical angle is the angle at which light from within a transparent medium just grazes the surface of the medium. In the diagram, the red beam is at the critical angle. Blue beams escape from the medium, at least partially. Green beams are totally reflected from the surface.

critical density in cosmology, the minimum average density that the universe must have for it to stop expanding at some point in the future.

The precise value depends on ◊Hubble's constant and so is not fixed, but it is approximately between 10^{-29} and 2×10^{-29}g/cm^3, equivalent to a few hydrogen atoms per cubic metre. The density parameter (symbol Ω) is the ratio of the actual density to the critical density. If $\Omega < 1$, the universe is open and will expand forever (see heat death). If $\Omega > 1$, the universe is closed and the expansion will eventually halt, to be followed by a contraction (see Big Crunch). Current estimates from visible matter in the universe indicate that Ω is about 0.01, well below critical density, but unseen dark matter may be sufficient to raise Ω to somewhere between 0.1 and 2.

critical mass in nuclear physics, the minimum mass of fissile material that can undergo a continuous ◊chain reaction. Below this mass, too many ◊neutrons escape from the surface for a chain reaction to carry on; above the critical mass, the reaction may accelerate into a nuclear explosion.

critical path analysis procedure used in the management of complex projects to minimize the amount of time taken. The analysis shows which subprojects can run in parallel with each other, and which have to be completed before other subprojects can follow on.

By identifying the time required for each separate subproject and the relationship between the subprojects, it is possible to produce a planning schedule showing when each subproject should be started and finished in order to complete the whole project most efficiently. Complex projects may involve hundreds of subprojects, and computer ◊applications packages for critical path analysis are widely used to help reduce the time and effort involved in their analysis.

critical reaction in a nuclear reactor, a self-sustaining chain reaction in which the number of neutrons being released by the fission of uranium-235 nuclei and the number of neutrons being absorbed by uranium-238 nuclei and by control rods are balanced. If balance is not achieved the reaction will either slow down and cease to generate enough power, or will build up and go out of control, as in a nuclear explosion. Control rods are used to adjust the rate of reaction and maintain balance.

critical temperature temperature above which a particular gas cannot be converted into a liquid by pressure alone. It is also the temperature at which a magnetic material loses its magnetism (the Curie temperature or point).

CRO abbreviation for ◊cathode-ray oscilloscope.

crocodile large scaly-skinned ◊reptile with a long, low cigar-shaped body and short legs. Crocodiles can grow up to 7 m/23 ft in length, and have long, powerful tails that propel them when swimming. They are found near swamps, lakes, and rivers in Asia, Africa, Australia, and Central America, where they are often seen floating in the water like logs, with only their nostrils, eyes, and ears above the surface. They are fierce hunters and active mainly at night. Young crocodiles eat worms and insects, but as they mature they add frogs and small fish to their diet. Adult crocodiles will attack animals the size of antelopes and even, occasionally, people. They can live up to 100 years and are related to the ◊alligator and the smaller cayman.

behaviour In some species, the female lays over 100 hard-shelled eggs in holes or nest mounds of vegetation, which she guards until the eggs hatch, before carrying the hatchlings down to the water in her mouth. When in the sun, crocodiles cool themselves by opening their mouths wide, which also enables scavenging birds to pick their teeth. They can stay underwater for long periods, but must surface to breathe. The nostrils can be closed underwater. They ballast themselves with stones to adjust their buoyancy. Crocodiles have remained virtually unchanged for 200 million years.

types of crocodile There are 15 species of crocodile, all of them endangered, found in tropical parts of Africa, Asia, Australia, and Central America. The largest is the saltwater (indopacific) crocodile *Crocodylus porosus*, which can grow to 7 m/23 ft or more, and is found in E India, Australia, and the W Pacific, in both freshwater and saltwater habitats. The Nile crocodile *C. niloticus* is found in Africa and reaches 6 m/20 ft. The American crocodile *C. acutus*, about 4.6 m/15 ft long, is found from S Florida to Ecuador. The

CROCODILE

Over short distances on land, the crocodile can move at 48 kmph/30 mph, lifting itself up on its legs like a lizard. In the water, it can move at 32 kmph/20 mph.

◊gavial, or gharial, *Gavialis gangeticus* is sometimes placed in a family of its own. It is an Indian species that grows to 6.5 m/21 ft or more, and has a very long narrow snout specialized for capturing and eating fish. The Cuban crocodile *C. rhombifer* has a short snout, grows up to 3.5 m/11.5 ft, and lives in freshwater swamps in Cuba. Morelet's crocodile *C. moreletti* is found in Central America, where it is overhunted, and grows up to 3.5 m/11.5 ft. Johnston's crocodile *C. johnsoni* is an Australian crocodile that feeds mainly on fish and reaches up to 3 m/9.75 ft in length. The Siamese crocodile *C. siamensis* is probably found only in captivity and grows up to 4 m/13 ft in length. The Philippine crocodile *C. mindorensis* is found in the Philippine Islands and grows to just under 3 m/9.75 ft. The mugger *C. palustris* is an Indian crocodile resembling the Nile crocodile but smaller, reaching up to 4 m/13 ft. The Orinoco crocodile *C. intermedius* grows up to 6 m/19.5 ft. False gharial *Tomistoma schlegelli* is found in rivers in India and Indochina and grows up to 4 m/13 ft. African slender-snouted crocodile *C. cataphractus* grows up to 4 m/13 ft and is found in western and central Africa. Dwarf crocodile *Osteolaemus tetraspis* reaches only 2 m/6.6 ft in length and is found in the tropical forests of west and central Africa. New Guinea crocodile *C. novaguineae* reaches 7 m/23 ft in length.

differences between crocodiles and alligators Crocodiles differ from alligators in that they have a narrower, more pointed snout and their fourth tooth on the lower jaw can always be seen, even when their mouth is shut. On average, they are larger.

classification Crocodiles are in the phylum Chordata, subphylum Vertebrata, class Reptilia, subclass Archosauria, order Crocodilia. There are 13 species in the Crocodylidae family, including the Nile crocodile (*Crocodylus niloticus*) and the saltwater crocodile (*C. porosus*).

The crocodile cannot turn its head. Like science, it must always go forward with all-devouring jaws.

PETER KAPITZA Russian physicist.
In A S Eve *Rutherford* 1933

Crocodylia order of the class Reptilia that includes crocodiles, alligators, gavials, and caimans.

There are about 20 living species in three families. The **Gavialidae family** includes only the ◊gavial, a fish-eating reptile found in India. The **Alligatoridae family** includes two living species of ◊alligators and several ◊caimans.The **Crocodylidae family** contains the true ◊crocodiles, comprising rather less than a dozen species ranging over Africa, Asia, northern Australia, and tropical America. The Indian crocodile, known as the mugger and erroneously as the alligator, ranges over India, Sri Lanka, Myanmar, and Malaysia. It is a freshwater variety inhabiting only rivers, lakes, and marshes, and in its characteristics most nearly approaches the caiman and the alligator.

crocus any of a group of plants belonging to the iris family, with single yellow, purple, or white flowers and narrow, pointed leaves. They are native to northern parts of the Old World, especially S Europe and Asia Minor. (Genus *Crocus*, family Iridaceae.)

During the dry season of the year crocuses remain underground in the form of a corm (underground storage organ), and produce fresh shoots and flowers in spring or autumn. At the end of the season of growth new corms are produced. Several species are cultivated as garden plants, the familiar mauve, white, and orange forms being varieties of *Crocus vernus, C. versicolor,* and *C. aureus.* The saffron crocus *C. sativus* belongs to the same genus. The so-called ◊autumn crocus or meadow saffron (*Colchicum autumnale*) is not a true crocus but belongs to the lily family.

Crohn's disease or ***regional ileitis*** chronic inflammatory bowel disease. It tends to flare up for a few days at a time, causing diarrhoea, abdominal cramps, loss of appetite, weight loss, and mild fever. The cause of Crohn's disease is unknown, although stress may be a factor.

Crohn's disease may occur in any part of the digestive system but usually affects the small intestine. It is characterized by ulceration, abscess formation, small perforations, and the development of adhesions binding the loops of the small intestine. Affected segments of intestine may constrict, causing obstruction, or may perforate. It is treated by surgical removal of badly affected segments, and by corticosteroids. Mild cases respond to rest, bland diet, and drug treatment. Crohn's disease first occurs most often in adults aged 20–40.

crop in birds, the thin-walled enlargement of the digestive tract between the oesophagus and stomach. It is an effective storage organ especially in seed-eating birds; a pigeon's crop can hold about 500 cereal grains. Digestion begins in the crop, by the moisturizing of food. A crop also occurs in insects and annelid worms.

crop in computing, to cut away unwanted portions of a picture. The term comes from traditional manual methods of layout and paste-up; cropping is an option made available via photo-finishing and graphics software.

crop circle circular area of flattened grain found in fields especially in SE England, with increasing frequency every summer since 1980. More than 1,000 such formations were reported in the UK in 1991. The cause is unknown.

Most of the research into crop circles has been conducted by dedicated amateur investigators rather than scientists. Physicists who have studied the phenomenon have suggested that an electromagnetic whirlwind, or 'plasma vortex', can explain both the crop circles and some UFO sightings, but this does not account for the increasing geometrical complexity of crop circles, nor for the fact that until 1990 they were unknown outside the UK. Crop circles began to appear in the USA only after a US magazine published an article about them. A few people have confessed publicly to having made crop circles that were accepted as genuine by investigators.

crop rotation system of regularly changing the crops grown on a piece of land. The crops are grown in a particular order to utilize and add to the nutrients in the soil and to prevent the build-up of insect and fungal pests. Including a legume crop, such as peas or beans, in the rotation helps build up nitrate in the soil, because the roots contain bacteria capable of fixing nitrogen from the air.

A simple seven-year rotation, for example, might include a three-year ley followed by two years of wheat and then two years of barley, before returning the land to temporary grass once more. In this way, the cereal crops can take advantage of the build-up of soil fertility that occurs during the period under grass. In the 18th century, a four-year rotation was widely adopted with autumn-sown cereal, followed by a root crop, then spring cereal, and ending with a leguminous crop. Since then, more elaborate rotations have been devised with two, three, or four successive cereal crops, and with the root crop replaced by a cash crop such as sugar beet or potatoes, or by a legume crop such as peas or beans.

crossbill species of ◊finch, genus *Loxia*, family Fringillidae, order Passeriformes, in which the hooked tips of the upper and lower beak cross one another, an adaptation for extracting the seeds from conifer cones. The red or common crossbill *Loxia curvirostra* is found in parts of Eurasia and North America, living chiefly in pine forests.

The parrot crossbill *L. pytopsittacus* of Europe, and the white-winged crossbill *L. leucoptera* of N Asia and North America, feed on pine and larch respectively.

crossing over in biology, a process that occurs during ◊meiosis. While the chromosomes are lying alongside each other in pairs, each partner may twist around the other and exchange corresponding chromosomal segments. It is a form of genetic ◊recombination, which increases variation and thus provides the raw material of evolution.

cross-linking in chemistry, lateral linking between two or more long-chain molecules in a ◊polymer. Cross-linking gives the polymer a higher melting point and makes it harder. Examples of cross-linked polymers include Bakelite and vulcanized rubber.

cross-posting on USENET, the practice of sending a message to more than one ◊newsgroup. A small amount of cross-posting is acceptable if the message is on a topic that is relevant to more than one newsgroup. For example, a message about top tennis player André Agassi's personal life might be posted to both rec.sport.tennis and alt.showbiz.gossip. Large amounts of cross-posting are called spam (see ◊spamming) and may lead to ◊flames and the attention of the ◊CancelMoose.

cross-section the surface formed when a solid is cut through by a plane at right angles to its axis.

croup inflammation of the larynx in small children, with harsh, difficult breathing and hoarse coughing. Croup is most often associated with viral infection of the respiratory tract.

crow any of 35 species of omnivorous birds in the genus *Corvus*, family Corvidae, order Passeriformes, which also includes choughs, jays, and magpies. Crows are usually about 45 cm/1.5 ft long, black, with a strong bill feathered at the base. The tail is long and graduated, and the wings are long and pointed, except in the jays and magpies, where they are shorter. Crows are considered to be very intelligent. The family is distributed throughout the world, though there are very few species in eastern Australia or South America. The common crows are *C. brachyrhynchos* in North America, and *C. corone* in Europe and Asia.

crowfoot any of several white-flowered aquatic plants belonging to the buttercup family, with a touch of yellow at the base of the petals. The divided leaves are said to resemble the feet of a crow. (Genus *Ranunculus*, family Ranunculaceae.)

CRT abbreviation for ◊cathode-ray tube.

crude oil the unrefined form of ◊petroleum.

crumple zone region at the front and rear of a motor vehicle that is designed to crumple gradually during a collision, so reducing the risk of serious injury to passengers. The progressive crumpling absorbs the kinetic energy of the vehicle more gradually than a rigid structure would, thereby diminishing the forces of deceleration acting on the vehicle and on the people inside.

crust the outermost part of the structure of Earth, consisting of two distinct parts, the oceanic crust and the continental crust. The **oceanic** crust is on average about 10 km/6.2 mi thick and consists mostly of basaltic types of rock. By contrast, the **continental** crust is largely made of granite and is more complex in its structure. Because of the movements of ◊plate tectonics, the oceanic crust is in no place older than about 200 million years. However, parts of the continental crust are over 3 billion years old.

Beneath a layer of surface sediment, the oceanic crust is made up of a layer of basalt, followed by a layer of gabbro. The composition of the oceanic crust overall shows a high proportion of **si**licon and **ma**gnesium oxides, hence named **sima** by geologists. The continental crust varies in thickness from about 40 km/25 mi to 70 km/45 mi, being deeper beneath mountain ranges. The surface layer consists of many kinds of sedimentary and igneous rocks. Beneath lies a zone of metamorphic rocks built on a thick layer of granodiorite. **Si**licon and **al**uminium oxides dominate the composition and the name **sial** is given to continental crustal material.

crustacean one of the class of arthropods that includes crabs, lobsters, shrimps, woodlice, and barnacles. The external skeleton is made of protein and chitin hardened with lime. Each segment bears a pair of appendages that may be modified as sensory feelers (antennae), as mouthparts, or as swimming, walking, or grasping structures.

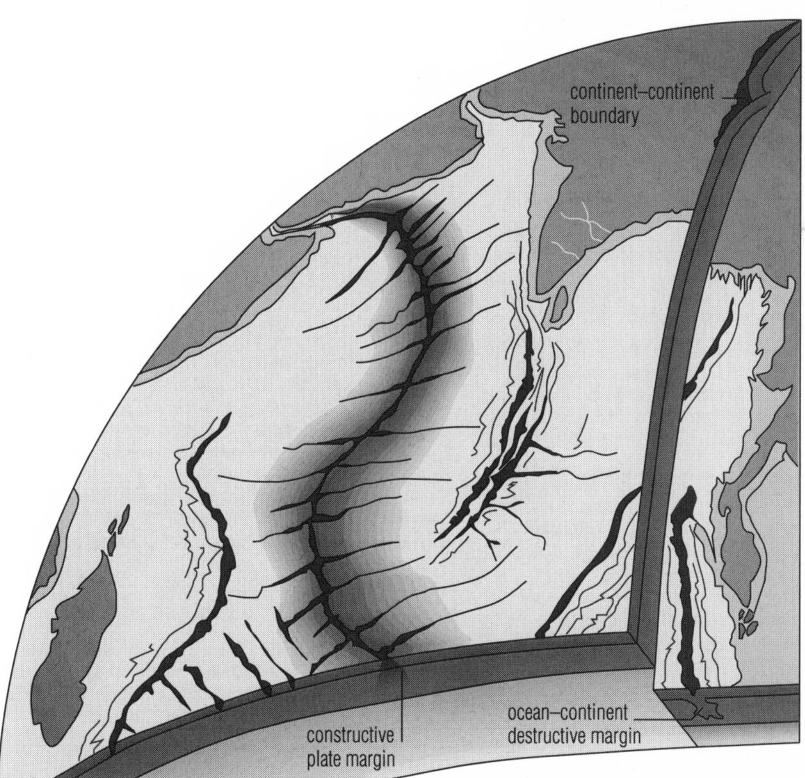

***crust** The crust of the Earth is made up of plates with different kinds of margins. In mid-ocean, there are constructive plate margins, where magma wells up from the Earth's interior, forming new crust. On continent–continent margins, mountain ranges are flung up by the collision of two continents. At an ocean–continent destructive margin, ocean crust is forced under the denser continental crust, forming an area of volcanic instability.*

Crux constellation of the southern hemisphere, popularly known as the Southern Cross, the smallest of the 88 constellations but one of the brightest, and one of the best known as it is represented on the flags of Australia and New Zealand. Its brightest stars are Alpha Crucis (or Acrux), a ◊double star about 400 light years from Earth, and Beta Crucis (or Mimosa).

Near Beta Crucis lies a glittering star cluster known as the Jewel Box, named by John Herschel. The constellation also contains the Coalsack, a dark nebula silhouetted against the bright starry background of the Milky Way.

cryogenics science of very low temperatures (approaching ◊absolute zero), including the production of very low temperatures and the exploitation of special properties associated with them, such as the disappearance of electrical resistance (◊superconductivity).

Low temperatures can be produced by the Joule–Thomson effect (cooling a gas by making it do work as it expands). Gases such as oxygen, hydrogen, and helium may be liquefied in this way, and temperatures of 0.3K can be reached. Further cooling requires magnetic methods; a magnetic material, in contact with the substance to be cooled and with liquid helium, is magnetized by a strong magnetic field. The heat generated by the process is carried away by the helium. When the material is then demagnetized, its temperature falls; temperatures of around 10^{-3}K have been achieved in this way. At temperatures near absolute zero, materials can display unusual properties. Some metals, such as mercury and lead, exhibit superconductivity. Liquid helium loses its viscosity and becomes a 'superfluid' when cooled to below 2K; in this state it flows up the sides of its container. Cryogenics has several practical applications. **Cryotherapy** is a process used in eye surgery, in which a freezing probe is briefly applied to the outside of the eye to repair a break in the retina. Electronic components called ◊Josephson junctions, which could be used in very fast computers, need low temperatures to function. Magnetic levitation (◊maglev) systems must be maintained at low temperatures. Food can be frozen for years, and freezing eggs, sperm and pre-embryos is now routine. In September 1996 South African researchers resuscitated a rat's heart that had been frozen to –196°C.

CRYONICS FREQUENTLY ASKED QUESTION LIST

http://www.cs.cmu.edu/afs/cs/user/tsf/Public-Mail/cryonics/html/overview.html

Answers to all the questions you could possibly ask about the controversial practice of cryonics. If, after reading this, you are tempted to give it a go, be warned. Of the sixty people who have been suspended, forty have been thawed out and buried, as the cryonics companies they had paid went bankrupt.

cryolite rare granular crystalline mineral (sodium aluminium fluoride), Na_3AlF_6, used in the electrolytic reduction of ◊bauxite to aluminium. It is chiefly found in Greenland.

cryptogam obsolete name applied to the lower plants. It included the algae, liverworts, mosses, and ferns (plus the fungi and bacteria in very early schemes of classification). In such classifications seed plants were known as ◊phanerogams.

cryptography science of creating and reading codes; for example, those produced by the Enigma coding machine used by the Germans in World War II and those used in commerce by banks encoding electronic fund-transfer messages, business firms sending computer-conveyed memos between headquarters, and in the growing field of electronic mail. The breaking and decipherment of such codes is known as 'cryptanalysis'. No method of encrypting is completely unbreakable, but decoding can be made extremely complex and time consuming.

CRYPTOGRAPHY

http://rschp2.anu.edu.au:8080/crypt.html

Introduction to the whys and wherefores of encrypting messages, particularly within an Internet framework. The author introduces various common encrypting systems and explains their relative weaknesses. The site also includes a good page on public-key cryptography which is becoming increasingly important as more and more information is transmitted electronically.

cryptosporidium waterborne parasite that causes disease in humans and other animals. It has been found in drinking water in the UK and USA, causing diarrhoea, abdominal cramps, vomiting, and fever, and can be fatal in people with damaged immune systems, such as AIDS sufferers or those with leukaemia. Just 30 cryptosporidia are enough to cause prolonged diarrhoea.

Conventional filtration and chlorine disinfection are ineffective at removing the parasite. Slow sand filtration is the best method of removal, but the existing systems were dismantled in the 1970s because of their slowness.

crystal substance with an orderly three-dimensional arrangement of its atoms or molecules, thereby creating an external surface of clearly defined smooth faces having characteristic angles between them. Examples are table salt and quartz.

Each geometrical form, many of which may be combined in one crystal, consists of two or more faces – for example, dome, prism, and pyramid. A mineral can often be identified by the shape of its crystals and the system of crystallization determined. A single crystal can vary in size from a submicroscopic particle to a mass some 30 m/100 ft in length. Crystals fall into seven crystal systems or groups, classified on the basis of the relationship of three or four imaginary axes that intersect at the centre of any perfect, undistorted crystal.

crystallization formation of crystals from a liquid, gas, or solution.

crystallography the scientific study of crystals. In 1912 it was found that the shape and size of the repeating atomic patterns (unit cells) in a crystal could be determined by passing X-rays through a sample. This method, known as ◊X-ray diffraction, opened up an entirely new way of 'seeing' atoms. It has been found that many substances have a unit cell that exhibits all the symmetry of the whole crystal; in table salt (sodium chloride, NaCl), for instance, the unit cell is an exact cube.

Many materials were not even suspected of being crystals until they were examined by X-ray crystallography. It has been shown that purified biomolecules, such as proteins and DNA, can form crystals, and such compounds may now be studied by this method. Other applications include the study of metals and their alloys, and of rocks and soils.

CRYSTALLOGRAPHY AND MINERALOGY

http://www.iumsc.indiana.edu/docs/crystmin.htm

Understand the shapes and symmetries of crystallography, with these interactive drawings of cubic, tetrahedral, octahedral, and dodecahedral solids (just drag your mouse over the figures to rotate them).

CSCW abbreviation for ◊computer-supported collaborative work.

CSH abbreviation for **corticotrophin-releasing hormone**.

CSLIP (abbreviation for ***Compressed Serial Line Internet Protocol***) in computing, newer version of ◊SLIP allowing slightly faster dial-up connections to the Internet.

CT scanner medical device used to obtain detailed X-ray pictures of the inside of a patient's body. See ◊CAT scan.

CTS/RTS (abbreviation for ***Clear To Send/Ready To Send***) in computing, hardware handshaking (see ◊handshake) used in high-speed modems. In most communications software this is an option that can be ◊toggled on or off. The alternative, software handshaking, is considered less reliable at high speeds.

cu abbreviation for **cubic** (measure).

CUA (abbreviation for ***common user access***) standard designed by ◊Microsoft to ensure that identical actions, such as saving a file or accessing help, can be carried out using the same keystrokes in any piece of software. For example, in programs written to the CUA standard, help is always summoned by pressing the F1 function key. New programs should be easier to use because users will not have to learn new commands to perform standard tasks.

cube in geometry, a regular solid figure whose faces are all squares. It has 6 equal-area faces and 12 equal-length edges.

If the length of one edge is *l*, the volume *V* of the cube is given by:

$$V = l^3$$

and its surface area *A* by:

$$A = 6l^2$$

cube to multiply a number by itself and then by itself again. For example, 5 cubed = $5^3 = 5 \times 5 \times 5 = 125$. The term also refers to a number formed by cubing; for example, 1, 8, 27, 64 are the first four cubes.

cubic centimetre (or metre) the metric measure of volume, corresponding to the volume of a cube whose edges are all 1 cm (or 1 metre) in length.

cubic decimetre metric measure (symbol dm^3) of volume corresponding to the volume of a cube whose edges are all 1 dm (10 cm) long; it is equivalent to a capacity of one litre.

cubic equation any equation in which the largest power of x is x^3. For example, $x^3 + 3x^2y + 4y^2 = 0$ is a cubic equation.

cubic measure measure of volume, indicated either by the word 'cubic' followed by a linear measure, as in 'cubic foot', or the word 'cubed' after a linear measure, as in 'metre cubed'.

cubit earliest known unit of length, which originated between 2800 and 2300 BC. It is approximately 50.5 cm/20.6 in long, which is about the length of the human forearm measured from the tip of the middle finger to the elbow.

cuboid six-sided three-dimensional prism whose faces are all rectangles. A brick is a cuboid.

cuckoo species of bird, any of about 200 members of the family Cuculidae, order Cuculiformes, especially the Eurasian cuckoo *Cuculus canorus*, whose name derives from its characteristic call. Somewhat hawklike, it is about 33 cm/1.1 ft long, bluish-grey and barred beneath (females are sometimes reddish), and typically has a long, rounded tail. Cuckoos feed on insects, including hairy caterpillars that are distasteful to most birds. It is a 'brood parasite', laying its eggs singly, at intervals of about 48 hours, in the nests of small insectivorous birds. As soon as the young cuckoo hatches, it ejects all other young birds or eggs from the nest and is tended by its 'foster parents' until fledging. American species of cuckoo hatch and rear their own young.

The North American **roadrunner** *Geococcyx californianus* is a member of the cuckoo family, and the yellow-billed cuckoo, *Coccysus americanus*, incubates its own eggs.

cuckoo flower or ***lady's smock*** perennial meadow plant of northern temperate regions. From April to June it bears pale lilac flowers, which later turn white. (*Cardamine pratensis*, family Cruciferae.)

cuckoopint or ***lords-and-ladies*** perennial European plant, a wild arum. It has large arrow-shaped leaves that appear in early spring and flower-bearing stalks enclosed by a bract, or spathe (specialized leaf). The bright red berrylike fruits, which are poisonous, appear in late summer. (*Arum maculatum*, family Araceae.)

cuckoo spit the frothy liquid surrounding and exuded by the larvae of the ◊froghopper.

cuckoo-spit insect another name for ◊froghopper.

cucumber trailing annual plant belonging to the gourd family, producing long, green-skinned fruit with crisp, translucent, edible flesh. Small cucumbers, called gherkins, usually the fruit of Cucurbitaceae.)

There are about 735 species belonging to the cucumber family.

cultivar variety of a plant developed by horticultural or agricultural techniques. The term derives from '**culti**vated **var**iety'.

culture in biology, the growing of living cells and tissues in laboratory conditions.

cumin seedlike fruit of the herb cumin, which belongs to the carrot family. It has a bitter flavour and is used as a spice in cooking. (*Cuminum cyminum*, family Umbelliferae.)

cumulative frequency in statistics, the total frequency of a given value up to and including a certain point in a set of data. It is used to draw the cumulative frequency curve, the ogive.

cuprite Cu_2O ore (copper(I) oxide), found in crystalline form or in earthy masses. It is red to black in colour, and is often called ruby copper.

cupronickel copper alloy (75% copper and 25% nickel), used in hardware products and for coinage.

curare black, resinous poison extracted from the bark and juices of various South American trees and plants. Originally used on arrowheads by Amazonian hunters to paralyse prey, it blocks nerve stimulation of the muscles. Alkaloid derivatives (called curarines) are used in medicine as muscle relaxants during surgery.

curie former unit (symbol Ci) of radioactivity, equal to 3.7×10^{10} ◊becquerels. One gram of radium has a radioactivity of about one curie. It was named after French physicist Pierre Curie.

Curie temperature the temperature above which a magnetic material cannot be strongly magnetized. Above the Curie temperature, the energy of the atoms is too great for them to join together to form the small areas of magnetized material, or ◊domains, which combine to produce the strength of the overall magnetization.

curing method of preserving meat by soaking it in salt (sodium chloride) solution, with saltpetre (sodium nitrate) added to give the meat its pink colour and characteristic taste. The nitrates in cured meats are converted to nitrites and nitrosamines by bacteria, and these are potentially carcinogenic to humans.

curium synthesized, radioactive, metallic element of the *actinide* series, symbol Cm, atomic number 96, relative atomic mass 247. It is produced by bombarding plutonium or americium with neutrons. Its longest-lived isotope has a half-life of 1.7×10^7 years.

curlew wading bird of the genus *Numenius* of the sandpiper family, Scolopacidae, order Charadriiformes. The curlew is between 36 cm/14 in and 55 cm/1.8 ft long, and has pale brown plumage with dark bars and mainly white underparts, long legs, and a long, thin, downcurved bill. It feeds on a variety of insects and other invertebrates. Several species live in N Europe, Asia, and North America. The name derives from its haunting flutelike call.

One species, the Eskimo curlew, is almost extinct, never having recovered from relentless hunting in the late 19th century.

currant berry of a small seedless variety of cultivated grape (*Vitis vinifera*). Currants are grown on a large scale in Greece and California and are dried for use in cooking and baking. Because of the similarity of the fruit, the name 'currant' is also given to several species of shrubs (genus *Ribes*, family Grossulariaceae).

Curie, Marie
(1867–1934)

(born *Manya Sklodowska)* Polish scientist who, with husband Pierre Curie, discovered in 1898 two new radioactive elements in pitchblende ores: polonium and radium. They isolated the pure elements in 1902. Both scientists refused to take out a patent on their discovery and were jointly awarded the Nobel Prize for Physics 1903, with Henri Becquerel. Marie Curie was also awarded the Nobel Prize for Chemistry 1911.

From 1896 the Curies worked together on radioactivity, building on the results of Wilhelm Röntgen (who had discovered X-rays) and Becquerel (who had discovered that similar rays are emitted by uranium salts). Marie Curie discovered that thorium emits radiation and found that the mineral pitchblende was even more radioactive than could be accounted for by any uranium and thorium content. In July 1898, the Curies announced the discovery of polonium, followed by the discovery of radium five months later. They eventually prepared 1 g/ 0.04 oz of pure radium chloride – from 8 tonnes of waste pitchblende from Austria.

They also established that beta rays (now known to consist of electrons) are negatively charged particles. In 1910 with André Debierne (1874–1949), who had discovered actinium in pitchblende 1899, Marie Curie isolated pure radium metal in 1911.

Curie, Pierre (1859–1906) French scientist. He shared the Nobel Prize for Physics 1903 with his wife Marie ◊Curie and Henri ◊Becquerel. From 1896 the Curies had worked together on ◊radioactivity, discovering two radioactive elements.

Mary Evans Picture Library

current flow of a body of water or air, or of heat, moving in a definite direction. Ocean currents are fast-flowing currents of seawater generated by the wind or by variations in water density between two areas. They are partly responsible for transferring heat from the Equator to the poles and thereby evening out the global heat imbalance. There are three basic types of ocean current: **drift currents** are broad and slow-moving; **stream currents** are narrow and swift-moving; and **upwelling currents** bring cold, nutrient-rich water from the ocean bottom.

Stream currents include the ◊Gulf Stream and the ◊Japan (or Kuroshio) Current. Upwelling currents, such as the Gulf of Guinea Current and the Peru (Humboldt) current, provide food for plankton, which in turn supports fish and sea birds. At approximate five-to-eight-year intervals, the Peru Current that runs from the Antarctic up the W coast of South America, turns warm, with heavy rain and rough seas, and has disastrous results (as in 1982–83) for Peruvian wildlife and for the anchovy industry. The phenomenon is called **El Niño** (Spanish 'the Child') because it occurs towards Christmas.

current directory in a computer's file system, the ◊directory in which the user is positioned. As users move around a computer system, opening, reading, writing, and storing files, they navigate through that computer's directory structure. Most file commands are assumed to apply to the files in the current directory.

In DOS, adding the command 'prompt pg' to the ◊autoexec.bat file sets the computer to display the name and path of the current directory at the system prompt. On an FTP (file transfer protocol) site, the command 'pwd' will print the name of the current directory on the remote machine.

current, electric see ◊electric current.

cursor on a computer screen, the symbol that indicates the current entry position (where the next character will appear). It usually consists of a solid rectangle or underline character, flashing on and off.

curve in geometry, the ◊locus of a point moving according to specified conditions. The circle is the locus of all points equidistant from a given point (the centre). Other common geometrical curves are the ◊ellipse, ◊parabola, and ◊hyperbola, which are also produced when a cone is cut by a plane at different angles.

Many curves have been invented for the solution of special problems in geometry and mechanics – for example, the cissoid (the inverse of a parabola) and the ◊cycloid.

cuscus tree-dwelling marsupial found in Australia, New Guinea, and Sulawesi. There are five species, all about the size of a cat. They have a prehensile tail and an opposable big toe.

Phalanger spilocuscus is known as the spotted cuscus or tiger cat; *P. ursinus* and *P. celebensis* are natives of the Celebes.

classification Cuscuses are in genus *Phalanger,* in the family Phalangeridae (possums), order Marsupialia, class Mammalia.

CU-SeeMe in computing, software that enables ◊videoconferencing across the Internet. Developed by US computer scientist Richard Cogger, CU-SeeMe was bought in 1996 by US videoconferencing specialist White Pine Software of Nashua, New Hampshire, and is now a commercial product.

Early experiments with CU-SeeMe included broadcasts by the North American Space Agency (NASA) of live and prerecorded video footage of shuttle missions, New Year parties held at cybercafes around the world, and live hook-ups between schools.

cusp point where two branches of a curve meet and the tangents to each branch coincide.

custard apple any of several large edible heart-shaped fruits produced by a group of tropical trees and shrubs which are often cultivated. Bullock's heart (*Annona reticulata*) produces a large dark-brown fruit containing a sweet reddish-yellow pulp; it is a native of the West Indies. (Family Annonaceae.)

cuticle the horny noncellular surface layer of many invertebrates such as insects; in botany, the waxy surface layer on those parts of plants that are exposed to the air, continuous except for ◊stomata and ◊lenticels. All types are secreted by the cells of the ◊epidermis. A cuticle reduces water loss and, in arthropods, acts as an ◊exoskeleton.

cutting technique of vegetative propagation involving taking a section of root, stem, or leaf and treating it so that it develops into a new plant.

> *He that uses many words for the explaining of any subject, doth, like the cuttle fish, hide himself for the most part in his own ink.*
>
> John Ray English naturalist. *On the Creation*

cuttlefish any of a family, Sepiidae, of squidlike cephalopods with an internal calcareous shell (cuttlebone). The common cuttle *Sepia officinalis* of the Atlantic and Mediterranean is up to 30 cm/1 ft long. It swims actively by means of the fins into which the sides of its oval, flattened body are expanded, and jerks itself backwards by shooting a jet of water from its 'siphon'.

It is capable of rapid changes of colour and pattern. The large head has conspicuous eyes, and the ten arms are provided with suckers. Two arms are very much elongated, and with them the cuttlefish seizes its prey. It has an ink sac from which a dark fluid can be discharged into the water, distracting predators from the cuttle itself. The dark brown pigment sepia is obtained from the ink sacs of cuttlefish.

cutworm common name for the larva of many species of owlet-moth. They cut off the young shoots of cultivated plants. They are related to the army-worm and ◊cotton-worm.
classification Cutworms belong to several genera, including *Agrotis, Prodenia,* and *Euxoa* in the family Noctuidae, class Insecta, phylum Arthropoda.

CWIS in computing, abbreviation for ◊campus-wide information service.

cwt symbol for ◊hundredweight, a unit of weight equal to 112 pounds (50.802 kg); 100 lb (45.36 kg) in the USA.

cyanamide process process used in the manufacture of calcium cyanamide ($CaCN_2$), a colourless crystalline powder used as a fertilizer under the tradename Nitrolime. Calcium carbide is reacted with nitrogen in an electric furnace.

$$CaC_2 + N_2 \rightarrow CaCN_2 + C$$

The calcium cyanamide reacts with water in the soil to form the ammonium ion and calcium carbonate. The ammonium is then oxidized to nitrate, which is taken up by plants. Calcium cyanamide can also be converted commercially into ammonia.

cyanide CN^- ion derived from hydrogen cyanide (HCN), and any salt containing this ion (produced when hydrogen cyanide is neutralized by alkalis), such as potassium cyanide (KCN). The principal cyanides are potassium, sodium, calcium, mercury, gold, and copper. Certain cyanides are poisons.

cyanobacteria (singular ***cyanobacterium***) alternative name for ◊blue-green algae.

cyanocobalamin chemical name for vitamin B_{12}, which is normally produced by microorganisms in the gut. The richest sources are liver, fish, and eggs. It is essential to the replacement of cells, the maintenance of the myelin sheath which insulates nerve fibres, and the efficient use of folic acid, another vitamin in the B complex. Deficiency can result in pernicious anaemia (defective production of red blood cells), and possible degeneration of the nervous system.

cybercafe coffeehouse equipped with public-access Internet terminals. Typically, users pay a small sum to use the terminals for short periods. Cafes usually supply brief tutorials for newcomers. By 1996 many major cities around the world had such cafes. There were more than 1,200 cybercafes in 78 countries by the end of 1997.

CyberCash in computing, one of several schemes for electronic money that can be used to trade on the Internet. Founded in 1994, CyberCash uses the RSA encryption ◊algorithm to protect customer financial information in transit.

The system stores customers' payment information, such as credit card numbers, in an electronic wallet, software which is downloaded from the company's site on the World Wide Web. When a customer wishes to buy something at a commercial Web site, the site generates a payment request, the customer adds a payment method, and the CyberCash server authenticates the transaction. Future plans are to add electronic cheques and cash or debit cards to the choice of payment instruments. See also ◊DigiCash.

cyberlaw in computing, relatively new field of Internet and computer law. Still being defined, the field includes new areas such as the responsibility of ◊Internet Service Providers and ◊bulletin-board system operators for the material that passes through or is stored on their systems and the framework for international electronic commerce, and a new look at traditional areas such as intellectual property rights and copyright and censorship.

cybernetics ***Greek kubernan 'to steer'*** science concerned with how systems organize, regulate, and reproduce themselves, and also how they evolve and learn. In the laboratory, inanimate objects are created that behave like living systems. Applications range from the creation of electronic artificial limbs to the running of the fully automated factory where decisionmaking machines operate up to managerial level.

Cybernetics was founded and named in 1947 by US mathematician Norbert Wiener. Originally, it was the study of control systems using feedback to produce automatic processes.

> *We should take care not to make the intellect our god; it has, of course, powerful muscles, but no personality.*
>
> ALBERT EINSTEIN German-born US physicist. *Out of My Later Life*

cyberpunk in computing, term coined by US science-fiction writer and editor Gardner Dozois for a particular type of modern science fiction that combines high-technology landscapes with countercultural social and political ideas. Leading writers in this genre include William Gibson, Bruce Sterling, Pat Cadigan, Greg Bear, and Rudy Rucker.

cybersex in computing, online sexual fantasy spun by two or more participants via live, online chat. Futurists hypothesize about a future where 'virtual' sex will take place in ◊virtual reality via body suits and other hardware input devices. In 1996, however, cybersex is limited to text-based systems such as IRC (◊Internet Relay Chat) or the shared worlds created in ◊MUDs (Multiuser dungeons) and ◊MOOs (MUD, object-oriented), both shared role-playing game worlds.

cyberspace the imaginary, interactive 'worlds' created by networked computers; often used interchangeably with 'virtual world'. The invention of the word 'cyberspace' is generally credited to US science-fiction writer William Gibson (1948–) and his first novel *Neuromancer* 1984.

As well as meaning the interactive environment encountered in a virtual reality system, cyberspace is 'where' the global community of computer-linked individuals and groups lives. From the mid-1980s, the development of computer networks and telecommunications, both international (such as the ◊Internet) and local (such as the services known as 'bulletin board' or conferencing systems), made possible the instant exchange of messages using ◊electronic mail and electronic conferencing systems directly from the individual's own home.

cycad any of a group of plants belonging to the ◊gymnosperms, whose seeds develop in cones. Some are superficially similar to palms, others to ferns. Their large cones contain fleshy seeds. There are ten genera and about 80–100 species, native to tropical and subtropical countries. Cycads were widespread during the Mesozoic era (245–65 million years ago). (Order Cycadales.)

The stems of many species yield an edible starchy substance resembling ◊sago. In 1993 cycads were discovered to be pollinated by insects, not by wind as had been previously thought; their cones produce heat that vaporizes a sweet minty odour to attract insects to a supply of nectarlike liquid.

cyclamate derivative of cyclohexysulphamic acid, formerly used as an artificial ◊sweetener, 30 times sweeter than sugar. It was first synthesized 1937.

Its use in foods was banned in the USA and the UK from 1970, when studies showed that massive doses caused cancer in rats.

cyclamen any of a group of perennial plants belonging to the primrose family, with heart-shaped leaves and petals that are twisted at the base and bent back, away from the centre of the downward-facing flower. The flowers are usually white or pink, and several species are cultivated. (Genus *Cyclamen,* family Primulaceae.)

cycle in physics, a sequence of changes that moves a system away from, and then back to, its original state. An example is a vibration that moves a particle first in one direction and then in the opposite direction, with the particle returning to its original position at the end of the vibration.

cyclic compound any of a group of organic chemicals that have rings of atoms in their molecules, giving them a closed-chain structure.

cyclic polygon in geometry, a polygon in which each vertex (corner) lies on the circumference of a circle.

cyclic quadrilateral four-sided figure with all four of its vertices lying on the circumference of a circle. The opposite angles of cyclic quadrilaterals add up to 180°, and are therefore said to be supplementary; each external angle (formed by extending a side of the quadrilateral) is equal to the opposite interior angle.

Cycliophora invertebrate phylum containing only one known species *Symbion pandora.* The phylum was discovered in 1995. *S. pandora* are minute (347 µm) bottle-shaped invertebrates living amongst the mouthparts of lobsters. They have threadlike cilia for gathering food and are attached by an adhesive disc. They have a reproductive cycle consisting of both asexual and sexual forms. The cycliophoran's nearest known relatives are bryozoans.

cyclodextrin ring-shaped ◊glucose molecule chain created in 1993 at Osaka University, Japan. Cyclodextrins are commonly used in food additives, and can also be used as capsules to deliver drugs, as cutters to separate ions and molecules, and as catalysts for chemical reactions.

They generally consist of 6–8 glucose molecules linked together in a ring, leaving a central hole of 0.45–0.8 nanometres, which can hold a small molecule such as benzene. They can be joined together to form tubes even smaller than DNA, the length and width of which can be controlled. They could hypothetically be used in the production of large scale integrated computer systems.

cycloid in geometry, a curve resembling a series of arches traced out by a point on the circumference of a circle that rolls along a straight line. Its applications include the study of the motion of wheeled vehicles along roads and tracks.

cyclone alternative name for a ◊depression, an area of low atmospheric pressure. A severe cyclone that forms in the tropics is called a tropical cyclone or ◊hurricane.

cyclotron circular type of particle ◊accelerator.

Cygnus large prominent constellation of the northern hemisphere, represented as a swan. Its brightest star is first-magnitude Alpha Cygni or ◊Deneb.

Beta Cygni (Albireo) is a yellow and blue ◊double star, visible through small telescopes. The constellation contains the North America nebula (named after its shape), the Veil nebula (the remains of a ◊supernova that exploded about 50,000 years ago), Cygnus A (apparently a double galaxy, a powerful radio source, and the first radio star to be discovered), and the X-ray source Cygnus X-1, thought to mark the position of a black hole. The area is rich in high luminosity objects, nebulae, and clouds of obscuring matter. Deneb marks the tail of the swan, which is depicted as flying along the Milky Way. Some of the brighter stars form the Northern Cross, the upright being defined by Alpha, Gamma, Eta, and Beta, and the crosspiece by Delta, Gamma, and Epsilon Cygni.

cylinder in computing, combination of the tracks on all the platters making up a hard drive or fixed disc that can be accessed without moving the read/write heads.

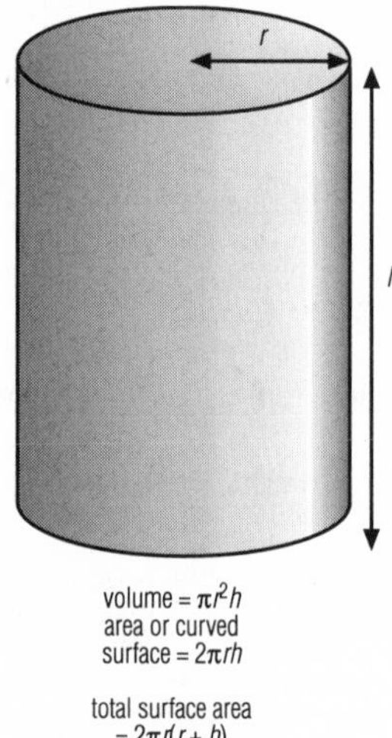

cylinder *The volume and area of a cylinder are given by simple formulae relating the dimensions of the cylinder.*

cylinder in geometry, a tubular solid figure with a circular base. In everyday use, the term applies to a **right cylinder**, the curved surface of which is at right angles to the base.

The volume V of a cylinder is given by the formula $V = \pi r^2 h$, where r is the radius of the base and h is the height of the cylinder. Its total surface area A has the formula $A = 2\pi r(h + r)$, where $2\pi rh$ is the curved surface area, and $2\pi r^2$ is the area of both circular ends.

cymbidium genus of generally epiphytic orchids found in Africa, Asia, and Australia, producing numerous showy flowers. The three Australian species are popular subjects for hybridization.

cypherpunk (contraction of *'cipher'* and *'cyberpunk'*) in computing, a passionate believer in the importance of free access to strong encryption on the Net, in the interests of guarding privacy and free speech.

cypress any of a group of coniferous trees or shrubs containing about 20 species, originating from temperate regions of the northern hemisphere. They have tiny scalelike leaves and cones made up of woody, wedge-shaped scales containing an aromatic ◊resin. (Genera *Cupressus* and *Chamaecyparis,* family Cupressaceae.)

cystic fibrosis hereditary disease involving defects of various tissues, including the sweat glands, the mucous glands of the bronchi (air passages), and the pancreas. The sufferer experiences repeated chest infections and digestive disorders and generally fails to thrive. In 1989 a gene for cystic fibrosis was identified by teams of researchers in Michigan, USA, and Toronto, Canada. This discovery enabled the development of a screening test for carriers; the disease can also be detected in the unborn child.

inheriting the disease One person in 22 is a carrier of the disease. If two carriers have children, each child has a one-in-four chance of having the disease, so that it occurs in about one in 2,000 pregnancies. Around 10% of newborns with cystic fibrosis develop an intestinal blockage (meconium ileus) which requires surgery.

treatment Cystic fibrosis was once universally fatal at an early age; now, although there is no definitive cure, treatments have

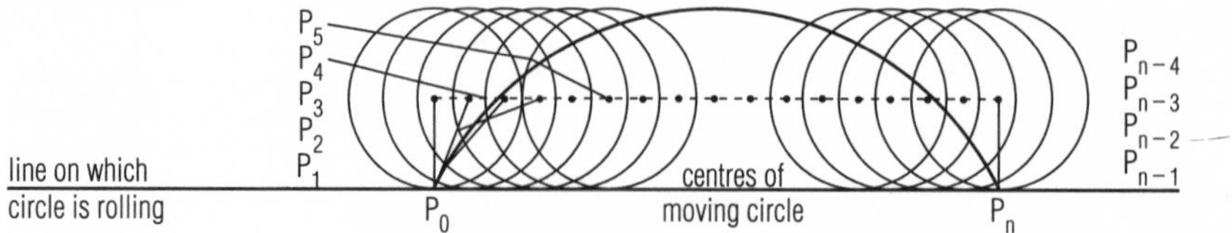

cycloid *The cycloid is the curve traced out by a point on a circle as it rolls along a straight line. The teeth of gears are often cut with faces that are arcs of cycloids so that there is rolling contact when the gears are in use.*

raised both the quality and expectancy of life. Results in 1995 from a four-year US study showed that the painkiller ibuprofen, available over the counter, slowed lung deterioration in children by almost 90% when taken in large doses.

Management of cystic fibrosis is by diets and drugs, physiotherapy to keep the chest clear, and use of antibiotics to combat infection and minimize damage to the lungs. Some sufferers have benefited from heart-lung transplants.

gene therapy In 1993, UK researchers (at the Imperial Cancer Research Fund, Oxford, and the Wellcome Trust, Cambridge) successfully introduced a corrective version of the gene for cystic fibrosis into the lungs of mice with induced cystic fibrosis, restoring normal function (in 1992, US researchers had introduced such a gene into the lungs of healthy laboratory rats, greatly improving the prospect of a cure). Trials in human subjects began in 1993, and the cystic fibrosis defect in the nasal cavities of three patients in the USA was successfully corrected, though a later trial was halted after a patient became ill following a dose of the genetically altered virus. Patients treated by gene therapy administered in the form of a nasal spray were showing signs of improvement following a preliminary trial in 1996. Cystic fibrosis is seen as a promising test case for ◊gene therapy. It is the commonest fatal hereditary disease amongst white people.

cystitis inflammation of the bladder, usually caused by bacterial infection, and resulting in frequent and painful urination. It is more common in women. Treatment is by antibiotics and copious fluids with vitamin C.

cytochrome protein responsible for part of the process of ◊respiration by which food molecules are broken down in aerobic organisms. Cytochromes are part of the electron transport chain, which uses energized electrons to reduce molecular oxygen (O_2) to oxygen ions (O^{2-}). These combine with hydrogen ions (H^+) to form water (H_2O), the end product of aerobic respiration. As electrons are passed from one cytochrome to another, energy is released and used to make ◊ATP.

cytokine in biology, chemical messenger that carries information from one cell to another, for example the ◊lymphokines.

cytokinin ◊plant hormone that stimulates cell division. Cytokinins affect several different aspects of plant growth and development, but only if ◊auxin is also present. They may delay the process of senescence, or ageing, break the dormancy of certain seeds and buds, and induce flowering.

cytology the study of ◊cells and their functions. Major advances have been made possible in this field by the development of ◊electron microscopes.

cytoplasm the part of the cell outside the ◊nucleus. Strictly speaking, this includes all the ◊organelles (mitochondria, chloroplasts, and so on), but often cytoplasm refers to the jellylike matter in which the organelles are embedded (correctly termed the cytosol). The cytoplasm is the site of protein synthesis.

In many cells, the cytoplasm is made up of two parts: the **ectoplasm** (or plasmagel), a dense gelatinous outer layer concerned with cell movement, and the **endoplasm** (or plasmasol), a more fluid inner part where most of the organelles are found.

cytoskeleton in a living cell, a matrix of protein filaments and tubules that occurs within the cytosol (the liquid part of the cytoplasm). It gives the cell a definite shape, transports vital substances around the cell, and may also be involved in cell movement.

cytotoxic drug any drug used to kill the cells of a malignant tumour; it may also damage healthy cells. Side effects include nausea, vomiting, hair loss, and bone-marrow damage. Some cytotoxic drugs are also used to treat other diseases and to suppress rejection in transplant patients.

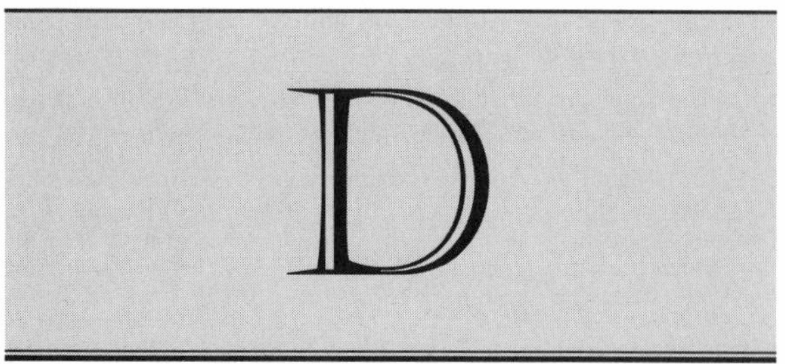

dab small marine flatfish of the flounder family, especially the genus *Limanda*. Dabs live in the North Atlantic and around the coasts of Britain and Scandinavia.

Species include *L. limanda* which grows to about 40 cm/16 in, and the American dab *L. proboscida*, which grows to 30 cm/12 in. Both have both eyes on the right side of their bodies. The left, or blind, side is white, while the rough-scaled right side is light-brown or grey, with dark-brown spots.

DAC abbreviation for ◊digital-to-analogue converter.

dace freshwater fish *Leuciscus leuciscus* of the carp family. Common in England and mainland Europe, it is silvery and grows up to 30 cm/1 ft.

dachshund ***German 'badger-dog'*** small dog of German origin, bred originally for digging out badgers. It has a long body and short legs. Several varieties are bred: standard size (up to 10 kg/22 lb), miniature (5 kg/11 lb or less), long-haired, smooth-haired, and wire-haired.

daddy-longlegs popular name for a ◊crane fly.

Daedalus in space travel, a futuristic project proposed by the British Interplanetary Society to send a ◊robot probe to nearby stars. The probe, 20 times the size of the Saturn V moon rocket, would be propelled by thermonuclear fusion; in effect, a series of small hydrogen-bomb explosions. Interstellar cruise speed would be about 40,000 km/25,000 mi per second.

daffodil any of several Old World species of bulbous plants belonging to the amaryllis family, characterized by their trumpet-shaped yellow flowers which appear in spring. The common daffodil of northern Europe (*Narcissus pseudonarcissus*) has large yellow flowers and grows from a large bulb. There are numerous cultivated forms in which the colours range from white to deep orange. (Genus *Narcissus*, family Amaryllidaceae.)

DAGUERREIAN SOCIETY

http://abell.austinc.edu/dag/home.html

Information about the process involved in this early form of photography, 19th- and 20th-century texts about it, an extensive bibliography of related literature, plenty of daguerreotypes to look at, and information about this society itself can be found here.

daguerreotype in photography, a single-image process using mercury vapour and an iodine-sensitized silvered plate; it was invented by Louis Daguerre 1838.

dahlia any of a group of perennial plants belonging to the daisy family, comprising 20 species and many cultivated forms. Dahlias are stocky plants with tuberous roots and showy flowers that come in a wide range of colours. They are native to Mexico and Central America. (Genus *Dahlia*, family Compositae.)

daisy any of numerous species of perennial plants belonging to the daisy family, especially the field daisy of Europe and North America (*Chrysanthemum leucanthemum*) and the English common daisy (*Bellis perennis*), with a single white or pink flower rising from a rosette of leaves. (Family Compositae.)

daisy bush any of several Australian and New Zealand shrubs with flowers like daisies and felted or hollylike leaves. (Genus *Olearia*, family Compositae.)

daisywheel printing head in a computer printer or typewriter that consists of a small plastic or metal disc made up of many spokes (like the petals of a daisy). At the end of each spoke is a character in relief. The daisywheel is rotated until the spoke bearing the required character is facing an inked ribbon, then a hammer strikes the spoke against the ribbon, leaving the impression of the character on the paper beneath.

The daisywheel can be changed to provide different typefaces; however, daisywheel printers cannot print graphics nor can they print more than one typeface in the same document. For these reasons, they are rapidly becoming obsolete.

DALMATIAN CLUB OF AMERICA

http://www.cet.com/~bholland/dca/

Absolute must for Dalmatian lovers. The site is filled with information about the history of the breed, the breed standard, shows, veterinary advice, and many tips for owners. There is a comprehensive listing of other Dalmatian sites and a useful bibliography. This well-organized site even has a search engine.

Dalmatian breed of dog, about 60 cm/24 in tall, with a distinctive smooth white coat with spots that are black or brown. Dalmatians are born white; the spots appear later. They were formerly used as coach dogs, running beside horse-drawn carriages to fend off highwaymen.

DALMATIAN

Three out of ten dalmatian dogs suffer from some form of hearing disability, and 8% of all dalmations are entirely deaf. Their beautiful spotty coats are caused by intense inbreeding, which has the side-effect of increasing genetic disorders – such as deafness.

Dalton, John
(1766–1844)

English chemist who proposed the theory of atoms, which he considered to be the smallest parts of matter. He produced the first list of relative atomic masses in 'Absorption of Gases' 1805 and put forward the law of partial pressures of gases (Dalton's law).

Mary Evans Picture Library

dam structure built to hold back water in order to prevent flooding, to provide water for irrigation and storage, and to provide

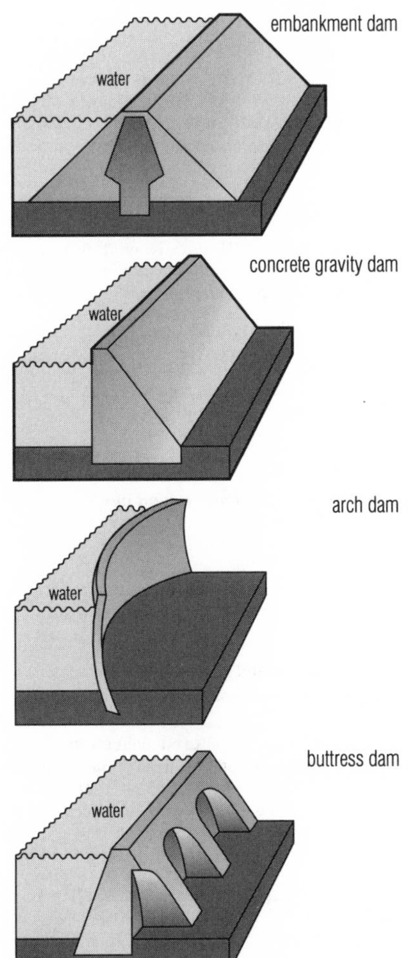

dam *There are two basic types of dam: the gravity dam and the arch dam. The gravity dam relies upon the weight of its material to resist the forces imposed upon it; the arch dam uses an arch shape to take the forces in a horizontal direction into the sides of the river valley. The largest dams are usually embankment dams. Buttress dams are used to hold back very wide rivers or lakes.*

hydroelectric power. The biggest dams are of the earth- and rock-fill type, also called **embankment dams**. Early dams in Britain, built before and about 1800, had a core made from puddled clay (clay which has been mixed with water to make it impermeable). Such dams are generally built on broad valley sites. Deep, narrow gorges dictate a **concrete dam**, where the strength of reinforced concrete can withstand the water pressures involved.

concrete dams A valuable development in arid regions, as in parts of Brazil, is the **underground dam**, where water is stored on a solid rock base, with a wall to ground level, so avoiding rapid evaporation. Many concrete dams are triangular in cross section, with their vertical face pointing upstream. Their sheer weight holds them in position, and they are called **gravity dams**. They are no longer favoured for very large dams, however, because they are expensive and time-consuming to build. Other concrete dams are built in the shape of an arch, which transfers the horizontal force into the sides of the river valley: the **arch dam** derives its strength from the arch shape, just as an arch bridge does, and has been widely used in the 20th century. They require less construction material than other dams and are the strongest type.

buttress dams are used when economy of construction is important or foundation conditions preclude any other type. The upstream portion of a buttress dam may comprise series of cantilevers, slabs, arches or domes supported from the back by a line of buttresses. They are usually made from reinforced and prestressed concrete.

earth dams Earth dams have a watertight core wall, formerly made of puddle clay but nowadays constructed of concrete. Their construction is very economical even for very large structures. **Rock-fill dams** are a variant of the earth dam in which dumped rock takes the place of compacted earth fill.

major dams Rogun (Tajikistan) is the world's highest at 335 m/1,099 ft. New Cornelia Tailings (USA) is the world's biggest in volume, 209 million cu m/7.4 billion cu ft. Owen Falls (Uganda) has the world's largest reservoir capacity, 204.8 billion cu m/7.2 trillion cu ft. Itaipu (Brazil/Paraguay) is the world's most powerful, producing 12,700 megawatts of electricity. The Three Gorges Dam on the Chang Jiang was officially inaugurated in 1994 and is due for completion 2009. A treaty between Nepal and India, ratified by Nepal in 1996, included plans to construct the 315-m/1,035-ft Pancheshwar dam.

In 1997 there were approximately 40,000 large dams (more than 15 m in height) and 800,000 small ones worldwide.

damask textile of woven linen, cotton, wool, or silk, with a reversible figured pattern. It was first made in the city of Damascus, Syria.

damper any device that deadens or lessens vibrations or oscillations; for example, one used to check vibrations in the strings of a piano. The term is also used for the movable plate in the flue of a stove or furnace for controlling the draught.

damselfly long, slender, colourful ◊dragonfly of the suborder Zygoptera, with two pairs of similar wings that are generally held vertically over the body when at rest, unlike those of other dragonflies.

damselfly *As in all members of the suborder Zygoptera, this common blue damselfly* Enallagma cyathigerum *male holds his wings closed above his back. Dragonflies (suborder Anisoptera) hold their wings out to their sides at 90 degrees to the body when at rest, and are generally stouter than damselflies. Premaphotos Wildlife*

damson cultivated variety of plum tree, distinguished by its small oval edible fruits, which are dark purple or blue-black in colour. (*Prunus domestica* var. *institia.*)

dandelion common plant throughout Europe and Asia, belonging to the same family as the daisy. The stalk rises from a rosette of leaves that are deeply indented like a lion's teeth, hence the name (from French *dent de lion*). The flower heads are bright yellow, and the fruit is covered with fine hairs, known as the dandelion 'clock'. (*Taraxacum officinale*, family Compositae.)

The milky juice of the dandelion has laxative properties (causing the bowels to empty), and the young leaves are sometimes eaten in salads. In the Russian species (*Taraxacum koksaghyz*), the juice forms an industrially usable ◊latex, relied upon especially during World War II when Malaysian rubber supplies were blocked by the Japanese (see also ◊rubber).

Dandie Dinmont breed of ◊terrier that originated in the Scottish border country. It is about 25 cm/10 in tall, short-legged and long-bodied, with drooping ears and a long tail. Its hair, about 5 cm/2 in long, can be greyish or yellowish. It is named after the character Dandie Dinmont in Walter Scott's novel *Guy Mannering* 1815.

darcy c.g.s. unit (symbol D) of permeability, used mainly in geology to describe the permeability of rock (for example, to oil, gas, or water).

dark cloud in astronomy, a cloud of cold dust and gas seen in silhouette against background stars or an ◊HII region.

dark matter matter that, according to current theories of ◊cosmology, makes up 90–99% of the mass of the universe but so far remains undetected. Dark matter, if shown to exist, would explain many currently unexplained gravitational effects in the movement of galaxies.

Theories of the composition of dark matter include unknown atomic particles (cold dark matter) or fast-moving neutrinos (hot dark matter) or a combination of both.

In 1993 astronomers identified part of the dark matter in the form of stray planets and ◊brown dwarfs, and possibly, stars that have failed to light up. These objects are known as MACHOs (massive astrophysical compact halo objects) and, according to US astronomers 1996, make up approximately half of the dark matter in the Milky Way's halo.

DARPANET early US computer network. See ◊ARPANET.

dasyure any ◊marsupial of the family Dasyuridae, also known as a 'native cat', found in Australia and New Guinea. Various species have body lengths from 25 cm/10 in to 75 cm/2.5 ft. Dasyures have long, bushy tails and dark coats with white spots. They are agile, nocturnal carnivores, able to move fast and climb.

DARWIN, CHARLES ROBERT

The English naturalist Charles Darwin, who developed the theory of evolution, was once told by his father: 'You care for nothing but shooting, dogs, and rat-catching, and you will be a disgrace to yourself and all your family'.

DAT abbreviation for ◊digital audio tape.

data (singular ***datum***) facts, figures, and symbols, especially as stored in computers. The term is often used to mean raw, unprocessed facts, as distinct from information, to which a meaning or interpretation has been applied.

> *... mathematics is a natural and a fundamental language. It may well be that it's a property of human beings, that only human beings can think maths. But I think it's probably true that any intelligence in the universe would have this language as well. So maybe it's even greater than – no, not greater than, but more universal than – the human race.*
>
> Erik Christopher Zeeman English mathematician.
> L Wolpert and A Richards *A Passion for Science* 1988

database in computing, a structured collection of data, which may be manipulated to select and sort desired items of information. For example, an accounting system might be built around a database containing details of customers and suppliers. In larger computers, the database makes data available to the various programs that need it, without the need for those programs to be aware of

Darwin, Charles Robert
(1809–1882)

English naturalist who developed the modern theory of evolution and proposed, with Alfred Russel Wallace, the principle of natural selection. After research in South America and the Galápagos Islands as naturalist on HMS Beagle 1831–36, Darwin published On the Origin of Species *by Means of Natural Selection or the Preservation of Favoured Races in the Struggle for Life 1859.* This book explained the evolutionary process through the principles of natural selection and aroused bitter controversy because it disagreed with the literal interpretation of the Book of Genesis in the Bible.

Mary Evans Picture Library

Darwin's work marked a turning point in many of the sciences, including physical anthropology and palaeontology. But, before the voyage of the Beagle, Darwin, like everyone else at that time, did not believe in the mutability of species. In South America, he saw fossil remains of giant sloths and other animals now extinct, and on the Galápagos Islands he found a colony of finches that he could divide into at least 14 similar species, none of which existed on the mainland. It was obvious to him that one type must have evolved into many others, but how they did so eluded him. Two years after his return he read Malthus's 'An Essay on the Principle of Population' 1798, which proposed that the human population was growing too fast for it to be adequately fed, and that something would have to reduce it, such as war or natural disaster. This work inspired Darwin to see that the same principle could be applied to animal populations.

Darwin's theory of natural selection concerned the variation existing between members of a sexually reproducing population. Those members with variations better fitted to the environment would be more likely to survive and breed, subsequently passing on these favourable characteristics to their offspring. He avoided the issue of human evolution, however, remarking at the end of The Origin of Species that 'much light will be thrown on the origin of man and his history'. It was not until his publication of The *Descent of Man and Selection in Relation to Sex* 1871, that Darwin argued that people evolved just like other organisms. He did not seek the controversy he caused but his ideas soon caught the public imagination. The popular press soon published articles about the 'missing link' between humans and apes.

Darwin also made important discoveries in many other areas, including the fertilization mechanisms of plants, the classification of barnacles, and the formation of coral reefs. He was the first to propose a link between coral reefs and volcanic islands. His ideas remain the primary theory of atoll growth formation.

how the data are stored. The term is also sometimes used for simple record-keeping systems, such as mailing lists, in which there are facilities for searching, sorting, and producing records.

There are three main types (or 'models') of database: hierarchical, network, and relational, of which relational is the most widely used. In a **relational database** data are viewed as a collection of linked tables. A **free-text database** is one that holds the unstructured text of articles or books in a form that permits rapid searching.

A collection of databases is known as a **databank**. A database-management system (DBMS) program ensures that the integrity of the data is maintained by controlling the degree of access of the ◊applications programs using the data. Databases are normally used by large organizations with mainframes or minicomputers.

A telephone directory stored as a database might allow all the people whose names start with the letter B to be selected by one program, and all those living in Chicago by another.

database program Databases are usually created using a database program that enables a user to define the database structure by selecting the number of fields, naming those fields, and allocating the type and amount of data that will valid for each field. Data programs also determine how data can be viewed on screen or extracted into files.

data bus in computing, the electrical pathway, or ◊bus, used to carry data between the components of the computer.

data capture collecting information for computer processing and analysis. Data may be captured automatically – for example, by a ◊sensor that continuously monitors physical conditions such as temperature – or manually; for example, by reading electricity meters.

data communications sending and receiving data via any communications medium, such as a telephone line. The term usually implies that the data are digital (such as computer data) rather than analogue (such as voice messages). However, in the ISDN (◊Integrated Services Digital Network) system, all data – including voices and video images – are transmitted digitally.

See also ◊telecommunications.

data compression in computing, techniques for reducing the amount of storage needed for a given amount of data. They include word tokenization (in which frequently used words are stored as shorter codes), variable bit lengths (in which common characters are represented by fewer ◊bits than less common ones), and run-length encoding (in which a repeated value is stored once along with a count).

In **lossless compression** the original file is retrieved unchanged after decompression. Some types of data (sound and pictures) can be stored by **lossy compression** where some detail is lost during compression, but the loss is not noticeable. Lossy compression allows a greater level of compression. The most popular compression program is ◊PKZIP, widely available as ◊shareware.

data dictionary in computing, a file that holds data about data – for example, lists of files, number of records in each file, and types of fields. Data dictionaries are used by database software to enable access to the data; they are not normally accessible to the user.

Data Encryption Standard (DES) in computing, widely used US government standard for encryption, adopted in 1977 and recertified for five more years 1993. DES was developed by IBM and adopted as a government standard by the National Security Agency. It is a private-key system, so that the sender and recipient encrypt and decrypt the message using the same key.

This means that a secure way has to be found to send the key from one party to the other; any third party who has the key can decrypt the encoded transmissions. Concerns over the long-term security of DES in the face of increasingly available cheap hardware have been somewhat mitigated by new techniques such as triply encrypted DES.

data flow chart diagram illustrating the possible routes that data can take through a system or program; see ◊flow chart.

DataGlove in ◊virtual reality, a glove wired to the computer that allows it to take input from a user's hand gestures. Sensors in the glove detect the wearer's hand movements, and transmit these to the computer in a digital format which the computer can interpret.

DataGlove is a trademark of VPL Research; the general term for such devices is **wired glove**.

data logging in computing, the process, usually automatic, of capturing and recording a sequence of values for later processing and analysis by computer. For example, the level in a water-storage tank might be automatically logged every hour over a seven-day period, so that a computer could produce an analysis of water use. The monitoring is carried out through ◊sensors or similar instruments, connected to the computer via an ◊interface.

The computer logging the data samples the readings at regular time intervals. Data is analysed either continuously (displayed on a changing screen display or as a graph on a ◊plotter) or at the end of the logging period.

data mining analysis of computer data to determine trends. It is used by retailers to find out those items often purchased together. For example, one supermarket chain found that purchases of nappies and beer were linked, and so increased sales by putting beer next to nappies. Store 'loyalty cards' enable retailers to profile customers' week-by-week shopping against their age, sex, and address.

data preparation preparing data for computer input by transferring it to a machine-readable medium. This usually involves typing the data at a keyboard (or at a ◊key-to-disc or key-to-tape station) so that it can be transferred directly to tapes or discs. Various methods of direct data capture, such as ◊bar codes, ◊optical mark recognition (OMR), and ◊optical character recognition (OCR), have been developed to reduce or eliminate lengthy data preparation before computer input.

data processing (DP) or ***electronic data processing*** (EDP) use of computers for performing clerical tasks such as stock control, payroll, and dealing with orders. DP systems are typically ◊batch systems, running on mainframe computers.

data processing cycle For data to be processed the following cycle of operations must be undergone: data are collected, then input into a computer where they are processed to produce the output. As the output may also be the input of a subsequent process the process is deemed cyclical. Whilst being processed data may undergo other operations such as storage and ◊validation.

data protection safeguarding of information about individuals stored on computers, to protect privacy.

data recovery in computing, any of several possible procedures for restoring a computer system and its data after a system crash, burglary, or other damage. The first line of defence in any computer system is ◊backups.

Every system fails at some point, and typically the data on the system is more valuable than the hardware on which it resides. The best course of action depends on the cause of the damage, which may be due to an outside agent, such as a virus, or a simple mistake, such as accidentally deleting important files. Some antivirus software comes with tools to assist users to clean up their systems; for deleted files, utility software such as Norton Utilities may be able to restore ('undelete') the data. In worse cases, specialists may still be able to restore the information by reading the hard disc's platters directly.

data security in computing, precautions taken to prevent the loss or misuse of data, whether accidental or deliberate. These include measures that ensure that only authorized personnel can gain entry to a computer system or file, and regular procedures for storing and 'backing up' data, which enable files to be retrieved or recreated in the event of loss, theft, or damage.

A number of ◊verification and ◊validation techniques may also be used to prevent data from being lost or corrupted by misprocessing.

Encryption involves the translation of data into a form that is meaningless to unauthorized users who do not have the necessary decoding software.

Passwords can be chosen by, or issued to, individual users. These secret words (or combinations of alphanumeric characters) may have to be entered each time a user logs on to a computer system or attempts to access a particular protected file within the system.

Physical access to the computer facilities can be restricted by locking entry doors and storage cabinets.

Master files (files that are updated periodically) can be protected by storing successive versions, or **generations**, of these files and of the transaction files used to update them. The most recent version of the master file may then be recreated, if necessary, from a previous generation. It is common practice to store the three most recent versions of a master file (often called the grandfather, father, and son generations).

Direct-access files are protected by making regular **dumps**, or back-up copies. Because the individual records in direct-access files are constantly being accessed and updated, specific generations of these files cannot be said to exist. The files are therefore dumped at fixed time intervals onto a secure form of backing store. A record, or log, is also kept of all the changes made to a file between security dumps.

Fireproof safes are used to store file generations or sets of security dumps, so that the system can be restarted on a new computer in the event of a fire in the computer department.

Write-protect mechanisms on discs or tapes allow data to be read but not deleted, altered, or overwritten. For example, the protective case of a $3\frac{1}{2}$-inch floppy disc has a write-protect tab that can be slid back with the tip of a pencil or pen to protect the disc's contents.

data terminator or **rogue value** in computing, a special value used to mark the end of a list of input data items. The computer must be able to detect that the data terminator is different from the input data in some way – for instance, a negative number might be used to signal the end of a list of positive numbers, or 'XXX' might be used to terminate the entry of a list of names.

date palm tree, also known as the date palm. The female tree produces the brown oblong fruit, dates, in bunches weighing 9–11 kg/20–25 lb. Dates are an important source of food in the Middle East, being rich in sugar; they are dried for export. The tree also supplies timber and materials for baskets, rope, and animal feed. (Genus *Phoenix.*)

The most important species is *Phoenix dactylifera*; native to northern Africa, southwest Asia, and parts of India, it grows up to 25 m/80 ft high. A single bunch can contain as many as 1,000 dates. Their juice is made into a kind of wine.

dating science of determining the age of geological structures, rocks, and fossils, and placing them in the context of geological time. The techniques are of two types: relative dating and absolute dating. **Relative dating** can be carried out by identifying fossils of creatures that lived only at certain times (marker fossils), and by looking at the physical relationships of rocks to other rocks of a known age.

Absolute dating is achieved by measuring how much of a rock's radioactive elements have changed since the rock was formed, using the process of ◊radiometric dating.

datura any of a group of plants belonging to the nightshade family, such as the ◊thorn apple, with handsome trumpet-shaped blooms. They have narcotic (pain-killing and sleep-inducing) properties. (Genus *Datura,* family Solanaceae.)

daughterboard in computing, small printed circuit board that plugs into a ◊motherboard to give it new capabilities.

David Dunlap Observatory Canadian observatory at Richmond Hill, Ontario, operated by the University of Toronto, with a 1.88-m/74-in reflector, the largest optical telescope in Canada, opened in 1935.

day time taken for the Earth to rotate once on its axis. The **solar day** is the time that the Earth takes to rotate once relative to the Sun. It is divided into 24 hours, and is the basis of our civil day. The **sidereal day** is the time that the Earth takes to rotate once relative to the stars. It is 3 minutes 56 seconds shorter than the solar day, because the Sun's position against the background of stars as seen from Earth changes as the Earth orbits it.

Thought is only a flash between two long nights, but this flash is everything.

JULES HENRI POINCARÉ French mathematician.

dayflower any plant of the genus *Commelina* of the spiderwort family. All have pointed leaves and creeping stems that form roots. The flowers, usually blue, open in the morning and wither by day's end throughout the summer and fall.

dBASE family of microcomputer programs used for manipulating large quantities of data; also, a related ◊fourth-generation language. The first version, dBASE II, was published by Ashton-Tate in 1981; it has since become the basis for a recognized standard for database applications, known as xBase.

DBS in computing, abbreviation for ◊direct broadcast system.

DC in physics, abbreviation for ***direct current*** (electricity).

DCC abbreviation for ◊digital compact cassette.

DCE (abbreviation for ***data communications equipment***) in computing, another name for a ◊modem.

DDE in computing, abbreviation for ◊dynamic data exchange, a form of communication between processes used in Microsoft Windows.

DDT abbreviation for ***dichloro-diphenyl-trichloroethane***) $(ClC_6H_5)_2CHC(HCl_2)$ insecticide discovered in 1939 by Swiss chemist Paul Müller. It is useful in the control of insects that spread malaria, but resistant strains develop. DDT is highly toxic and persists in the environment and in living tissue. Its use is now banned in most countries, but it continues to be used on food plants in Latin America.

deadly nightshade another name for ◊belladonna, a poisonous plant.

deafness partial or total deficit of hearing in either ear. Of assistance are hearing aids, lip-reading, a cochlear implant in the ear in combination with a special electronic processor, sign language, and 'cued speech' (manual clarification of ambiguous lip movement during speech).

Conductive deafness is due to faulty conduction of sound inwards from the external ear, usually due to infection (see ◊otitis), or a hereditary abnormality of the bones of the inner ear (see ◊otosclerosis).

Perceptive deafness may be inborn or caused by injury or disease of the cochlea, auditory nerve, or the hearing centres in the brain. It becomes more common with age.

deamination removal of the amino group ($-NH_2$) from an unwanted ◊amino acid. This is the nitrogen-containing part, and it is converted into ammonia, uric acid, or urea (depending on the type of animal) to be excreted in the urine.

In vertebrates, deamination occurs in the ◊liver.

death cessation of all life functions, so that the molecules and structures associated with living things become disorganized and indistinguishable from similar molecules found in nonliving things. In medicine, a person is pronounced dead when the brain ceases to control the vital functions, even if breathing and heartbeat are maintained artificially.

medical definition Death used to be pronounced with the permanent cessation of heartbeat, but the advent of life-support equipment has made this point sometimes difficult to determine. For removal of vital organs in transplant surgery, the World Health Organization in 1968 set out that a potential donor should exhibit

no brain–body connection, muscular activity, blood pressure, or ability to breathe spontaneously.
religious belief In religious belief, death may be seen as the prelude to rebirth (as in Hinduism and Buddhism); under Islam and Christianity, there is the concept of a day of judgement and consignment to heaven or hell; Judaism concentrates not on an afterlife but on survival through descendants who honour tradition.

death cap fungus of the ◊amanita group, the most poisonous mushroom known. The fruiting body, or mushroom, has a scaly white cap and a collarlike structure (volva) near the base of the stalk. (*Amanita phalloides,* family Agaricaceae.)

death's-head moth largest British ◊hawk moth with downy wings measuring 13 cm/5 in from tip to tip, and its thorax is marked as though with a skull.

When it is at rest it sometimes gives out a squeaking noise, produced probably by rubbing the palpi (sense organs close to the mouthparts) upon the proboscis.

The caterpillar is about 10 cm/4 in long and is brightly coloured. It feeds on potato plants.
classification Hawk moths *Acherontia atropos* are in the family Sphingidae in order Lepidoptera, class Insecta, phylum Arthropoda.

deathwatch beetle any wood-boring beetle of the family Anobiidae, especially *Xestobium rufovillosum.* The larvae live in oaks and willows, and sometimes cause damage by boring in old furniture or structural timbers. To attract the female, the male beetle produces a ticking sound by striking his head on a wooden surface, and this is taken by the superstitious as a warning of approaching death.

debt-for-nature swap agreement under which a proportion of a country's debts are written off in exchange for a commitment by the debtor country to undertake projects for environmental protection. Debt-for-nature swaps were set up by environment groups in the 1980s in an attempt to reduce the debt problem of poor countries, while simultaneously promoting conservation.

Most debt-for-nature swaps have concentrated on setting aside areas of land, especially tropical rainforest, for protection and have involved private conservation foundations. The first swap took place in 1987, when a US conservation group bought $650,000 of Bolivia's national debt from a bank for $100,000, and persuaded the Bolivian government to set aside a large area of rainforest as a nature reserve in exchange for never having to pay back the money owed. Other countries participating in debt-for-nature swaps are the Philippines, Costa Rica, Ecuador, and Poland. However, the debtor country is expected to ensure that the area of land remains adequately protected, and in practice this does not always happen. The practice has also produced complaints of neocolonialism.

debugging finding and removing errors, or ◊bugs, from a computer program or system.

DEC (acronym for ***Digital Equipment Corporation***) US computer manufacturer. DEC was founded by US computer engineers, Kenneth Olsen and Harlan Anderson, and was the first ◊minicomputer manufacturer. It became the world's second largest computer manufacturer, after ◊IBM, but made huge losses in the early 1990s. DEC's most successful computers were the PDP-11 and the VAX (Virtual Address eXtension). The former was used in the creation of the ◊UNIX operating system.

The original aim was to make the first small computers for engineering and departmental use, and the PDP (Programmed Data Processor) range became known as minicomputers to contrast them with giant mainframes. The success of its 32-bit VAX minis in the 1980s made DEC one of the world's largest computer manufacturers. The company – now called **Digital** – has still to recover, but has developed the world's fastest microprocessor, the Alpha chip, and has a popular search engine called ◊AltaVista on the Internet's World Wide Web.

decagon in geometry, a ten-sided ◊polygon.

decay, radioactive see ◊radioactive decay.

Decca navigation system radio-based aid to marine navigation, available in many parts of the world. The system consists of a master radio transmitter and two or three secondary transmitters situated within 100–200 km/60–120 mi from the master. The signals from the transmitters are detected by the ship's navigation receiver, and slight differences (phase differences) between the master and secondary transmitter signals indicate the position of the receiver. It was first used 1944 for the D-Day landings.

decibel unit (symbol dB) of measure used originally to compare sound intensities and subsequently electrical or electronic power outputs; now also used to compare voltages. An increase of 10 dB is equivalent to a 10-fold increase in intensity or power, and a 20-fold increase in voltage. The decibel scale is used for audibility measurementsi, as one decibel, representing an increase of about 25%, is about the smallest change the human ear can detect. A whisper has an intensity of 20 dB; 140 dB (a jet aircraft taking off nearby) is the threshold of pain.

The difference in decibels between two levels of intensity (or power) L_1 and L_2 is 10 $\log_{10}(L_1/L_2)$; a difference of 1 dB thus corresponds to a change of about 25%. For two voltages V_1 and V_2, the difference in decibels is 20 $\log_{10}(V_1/V_2)$; 1 dB corresponding in this case to a change of about 12%.

Decibel scale

The decibel scale is used primarily to compare sound intensities although it can be used to compare voltages.

Decibels	*Typical sound*
0	threshold of hearing
10	rustle of leaves in gentle breeze
10	quiet whisper
20	average whisper
20–50	quiet conversation
40–45	hotel; theatre (between performances)
50–65	loud conversation
65–70	traffic on busy street
65–90	train
75–80	factory (light/medium work)
90	heavy traffic
90–100	thunder
110–140	jet aircraft at take-off
130	threshold of pain
140–190	space rocket at take-off

deciduous of trees and shrubs, that shed their leaves at the end of the growing season or during a dry season to reduce ◊transpiration (the loss of water by evaporation).

Most deciduous trees belong to the ◊angiosperms, plants in which the seeds are enclosed within an ovary, and the term 'deciduous tree' is sometimes used to mean 'angiosperm tree', despite the fact that many angiosperms are evergreen, especially in the tropics, and a few ◊gymnosperms, plants in which the seeds are exposed, are deciduous (for example, larches). The term **broad-leaved** is now preferred to 'deciduous' for this reason.

decimal fraction a ◊fraction in which the denominator is any higher power of 10. Thus $\frac{3}{10}$, $\frac{51}{100}$, and $\frac{23}{1000}$ are decimal fractions and are normally expressed as 0.3, 0.51, and 0.023. The use of decimals greatly simplifies addition and multiplication of fractions, though not all fractions can be expressed exactly as decimal fractions.

The regular use of the decimal point appears to have been introduced about 1585, but the occasional use of decimal fractions can be traced back as far as the 12th century.

decimal number system or ***denary number system*** the most commonly used number system, to the base ten. Decimal numbers do not necessarily contain a decimal point; 563, 5.63, and –563 are all decimal numbers. Other systems are mainly used in computing and include the ◊binary number system, ◊octal number system, and ◊hexadecimal number system.

Decimal numbers may be thought of as written under column headings based on the number ten. For example, the number 2,567 stands for 2 thousands, 5 hundreds, 6 tens, and 7 ones. Large decimal numbers may also be expressed in ◊floating-point notation.

decimal point the dot dividing a decimal number's whole part from its fractional part (the digits to the left of the point are unit digits). It is usually printed on the line but hand written above the line, for example 3.5. Some European countries use a comma to denote the decimal point, for example 3,56.

decision table in computing, a method of describing a procedure for a program to follow, based on comparing possible decisions and their consequences. It is often used as an aid in systems design.

The top part of the table contains the conditions for making decisions (for example, if a number is negative rather than positive and is less than 1), and the bottom part describes the outcomes when those conditions are met. The program either ends or repeats the operation.

declarative programming computer programming that does not describe how to solve a problem, but rather describes the logical structure of the problem. It is used in the programming language PROLOG. Running such a program is more like proving an assertion than following a ◊procedure.

declination in astronomy, the coordinate on the ◊celestial sphere (imaginary sphere surrounding the Earth) that corresponds to latitude on the Earth's surface. Declination runs from 0° at the celestial equator to 90° at the north and south celestial poles.

decoder in computing, an electronic circuit used to select one of several possible data pathways. Decoders are, for example, used to direct data to individual memory locations within a computer's immediate access memory.

decomposer in biology, any organism that breaks down dead matter. Decomposers play a vital role in the ◊ecosystem by freeing important chemical substances, such as nitrogen compounds, locked up in dead organisms or excrement. They feed on some of the released organic matter, but leave the rest to filter back into the soil as dissolved nutrients, or pass in gas form into the atmosphere, for example as nitrogen and carbon dioxide.

The principal decomposers are bacteria and fungi, but earthworms and many other invertebrates are often included in this group. The ◊nitrogen cycle relies on the actions of decomposers.

decomposition process whereby a chemical compound is reduced to its component substances. In biology, it is the destruction of dead organisms either by chemical reduction or by the action of decomposers, such as bacteria and fungi.

decompression sickness illness brought about by a sudden and substantial change in atmospheric pressure. It is caused by a too rapid release of nitrogen that has been dissolved into the bloodstream under pressure; when the nitrogen forms bubbles it causes the ◊bends. The condition causes breathing difficulties, joint and muscle pain, and cramps, and is experienced mostly by deep-sea divers who surface too quickly.

After a one-hour dive at 30 m/100 ft, 40 minutes of decompression are needed, according to US Navy tables.

decontamination factor in radiological protection, a measure of the effectiveness of a decontamination process. It is the ratio of the original contamination to the remaining radiation after decontamination: 1,000 and above is excellent; 10 and below is poor.

decrepitation in crystallography, unusual features that accompany the thermal decomposition of some crystals, such as lead(II) nitrate. When these are heated, they spit and crackle and may jump out of the test tube before they decompose.

dedicated computer computer built into another device for the purpose of controlling or supplying information to it. Its use has increased dramatically since the advent of the ◊microprocessor: washing machines, digital watches, cars, and video recorders all now have their own processors.

A dedicated system is a general-purpose computer system confined to performing only one function for reasons of efficiency or convenience. A word processor is an example.

Deep Blue name given to the IBM chess-playing computer that first defeated a human grandmaster, the Russian Gary Kasparov, in 1996.

The architect and principal designer of Deep Blue is Feng-Hsiung Hsu, who joined IBM in 1989. Deep Blue's award-winning precursor, Deep Thought, was developed by Hsu and other graduate students at Carnegie-Mellon University in Pittsburgh. In 1988 it was the first computer to achieve a grandmaster rating.

KASPAROV V. DEEP BLUE – THE REMATCH

http://www.chess.ibm.com/

Official site of the team that produced the first computer able to beat a world chess champion. This is a complete account of the tussle between Deep Blue and Gary Kasparov. There are some thought provoking articles on the consequences of Deep Blue's victory. There is also some video footage of the games.

deep-sea trench another term for ◊ocean trench.

deer any of various ruminant, even-toed, hoofed mammals belonging to the family Cervidae. The male typically has a pair of antlers, shed and regrown each year. Most species of deer are forest-dwellers and are distributed throughout Eurasia and North America, but are absent from Australia and Africa south of the Sahara.

deerhound breed of large, rough-coated dog, formerly used in Scotland for hunting and killing deer. Slim and long-legged, it grows to 75 cm/30 in or more, usually with a bluish-grey coat.

default in computing, a factory setting for user-configurable options. Default settings appear in all areas of computing, from the on-screen colour scheme in a ◊graphical user interface to the directories where software programs store data.

defibrillation use of electrical stimulation to restore a chaotic heartbeat to a rhythmical pattern. In fibrillation, which may occur in most kinds of heart disease, the heart muscle contracts irregularly; the heart is no longer working as an efficient pump. Paddles are applied to the chest wall, and one or more electric shocks are delivered to normalize the beat.

In patients suffering with ◊arrhythmia, implantable defibrillators are inserted into the chest with leads threading through veins into the right side of the heart. The first was implanted in 1980 and by 1996 around 50,000–80,000 had been implanted worldwide.

In nature there are neither rewards nor punishments – there are consequences.

ROBERT INGERSOLL US lawyer and orator. *Lectures and Essays*, 'Some Reasons Why'

deforestation destruction of forest for timber, fuel, charcoal burning, and clearing for agriculture and extractive industries, such as mining, without planting new trees to replace those lost (reafforestation) or working on a cycle that allows the natural forest to regenerate. Deforestation causes fertile soil to be blown away or washed into rivers, leading to ◊soil erosion, drought, flooding, and loss of wildlife. It may also increase the carbon dioxide content of the atmosphere and intensify the ◊greenhouse effect, because there are fewer trees absorbing carbon dioxide from the air for photosynthesis.

Many people are concerned about the rate of deforestation as great damage is being done to the habitats of plants and animals.

Deforestation ultimately leads to famine, and is thought to be partially responsible for the flooding of lowland areas – for example, in Bangladesh – because trees help to slow down water movement.

defragmentation program or ***disc optimizer*** in computing, a program that rearranges data on disc so that files are not scattered in many small sections. See also ◊fragmentation.

degaussing neutralization of the magnetic field around a body by encircling it with a conductor through which a current is maintained. Ships were degaussed in World War II to prevent them from detonating magnetic mines.

degeneration in biology, a change in the structure or chemical composition of a tissue or organ that interferes with its normal functioning. Examples of degeneration include fatty degeneration, fibroid degeneration (cirrhosis), and calcareous degeneration, all of which are part of natural changes that occur in old age.

The causes of degeneration are often unknown. Heredity often has a role in the degeneration of organs; for example, fibroid changes in the kidney can be seen in successive generations. Defective nutrition and continued stress on particular organs can cause degenerative changes. Alcoholism can result in cirrhosis of the liver and tuberculosis causes degeneration of the lungs.

de Gennes, Pierre-Gilles 1932 French physicist who worked on liquid crystals and polymers. He showed how mathematical models, developed for studying simpler systems, are applicable to such complicated systems. He won the Nobel Prize for Physics in 1991.

It had been known for a long time that liquid crystals scatter light in an unusual way but all early explanations failed. De Gennes found the explanation in the special way that the molecules of a liquid crystal are arranged. According to de Gennes, the molecules are arranged in a similar way to the molecules of a magnet, so that they point in the same direction. De Gennes found similar analogies between the behaviour of molecules in magnetic materials and polymers. This led to the formulation of laws from which simple relations between different properties of polymers can be deduced. In this way, predictions can be made about unknown properties – predictions which have been confirmed by experiment.

degree in mathematics, a unit (symbol °) of measurement of an angle or arc. A circle or complete rotation is divided into 360°. A degree may be subdivided into 60 minutes (symbol '), and each minute may be subdivided in turn into 60 seconds (symbol ‘).

Temperature is also measured in degrees, which are divided on a decimal scale. See also ◊Celsius, and ◊Fahrenheit.

A degree of latitude is the length along a meridian such that the difference between its north and south ends subtend an angle of 1° at the centre of the Earth. A degree of longitude is the length between two meridians making an angle of 1° at the centre of the Earth.

dehydration in chemistry, the removal of water from a substance to give a product with a new chemical formula; it is not the same as drying.

There are two types of dehydration. For substances such as hydrated copper sulphate ($CuSO_4.5H_2O$) that contain ◊water of crystallization, dehydration means removing this water to leave the anhydrous substance. This may be achieved by heating, and is reversible.

Some substances, such as ethanol, contain the elements of water (hydrogen and oxygen) joined in a different form. **Dehydrating agents** such as concentrated sulphuric acid will remove these elements in the ratio 2:1.

dehydration process to preserve food. Moisture content is reduced to 10–20% in fresh produce, and this provides good protection against moulds. Bacteria are not inhibited by drying, so the quality of raw materials is vital.

The process was developed commercially in France about 1795 to preserve sliced vegetables, using a hot-air blast. The earliest large-scale application was to starch products such as pasta, but after 1945 it was extended to milk, potatoes, soups, instant coffee, and prepared baby and pet foods. A major benefit to food manufacturers is reduction of weight and volume of the food products, thus lowering distribution cost.

Deimos one of the two moons of Mars. It is irregularly shaped, 15 × 12 × 11 km/9 × 7.5 × 7 mi, orbits at a height of 24,000 km/15,000 mi every 1.26 days, and is not as heavily cratered as the other moon, Phobos. Deimos was discovered in 1877 by US astronomer Asaph Hall (1829–1907), and is thought to be an asteroid captured by Mars's gravity.

delete remove or erase. In computing, the deletion of a character removes it from the file; the deletion of a file normally means removing its directory entry, rather than actually deleting it from the disc. Many systems now have an ◊undelete facility that allows the restoration of the directory entry. While deleted files may not have been removed from the disc, they can be overwritten.

deliquescence phenomenon of a substance absorbing so much moisture from the air that it ultimately dissolves in it to form a solution.

Deliquescent substances make very good drying agents and are used in the bottom chambers of ◊desiccators. Calcium chloride ($CaCl_2$) is one of the commonest.

delirium in medicine, a state of acute confusion in which the subject is incoherent, frenzied, and out of touch with reality. It is often accompanied by delusions or hallucinations.

Delirium may occur in feverish illness, some forms of mental illness, brain disease, and as a result of drug or alcohol intoxication. In chronic alcoholism, attacks of **delirium tremens** (DTs), marked by hallucinations, sweating, trembling, and anxiety, may persist for several days.

Delphi in computing, text-based UK and US national online information service. In 1992, Delphi was the first national US service to open a ◊gateway to the Internet. Founded 1982 as the world's first online encyclopedia, Delphi was bought by News International 1993, and launched its UK service in 1994. In 1996 the US arm of Delphi was sold back to one of its original owners. The UK service continues in the hands of News International.

delphinium any of a group of plants containing about 250 species, including the butterfly or Chinese delphinium (*Delphinium grandiflorum*), an Asian form and one of the ancestors of the garden delphinium. Most species have blue, purple, or white flowers on a long spike. (Genus *Delphinium,* family Ranunculaceae.)

delta tract of land at a river's mouth, composed of silt deposited as the water slows on entering the sea. Familiar examples of large deltas are those of the Mississippi, Ganges and Brahmaputra, Rhône, Po, Danube, and Nile; the shape of the Nile delta is like the Greek letter *delta* Δ, and thus gave rise to the name.

The **arcuate delta** of the Nile is only one form. Others are **bird-foot deltas**, like that of the Mississippi which is a seaward extension of the river's ◊levee system; and **tidal deltas**, like that of the Mekong, in which most of the material is swept to one side by sea currents.

Delta rocket US rocket used to launch many scientific and communications satellites since 1960, based on the Thor ballistic missile. Several increasingly powerful versions produced as satellites became larger and heavier. Solid-fuel boosters were attached to the first stage to increase lifting power.

delta wing aircraft wing shaped like the Greek letter *delta* Δ. Its design enables an aircraft to pass through the ◊sound barrier with little effect. The supersonic airliner ◊Concorde and the US ◊space shuttle have delta wings.

dementia mental deterioration as a result of physical changes in the brain. It may be due to degenerative change, circulatory disease, infection, injury, or chronic poisoning. **Senile dementia**, a progressive loss of mental faculties such as memory and orientation, is typically a disease process of old age, and can be accompanied by ◊depression.

Dementia is distinguished from amentia, or severe congenital mental insufficiency.

demo or ***demonstration software*** in computing, preview version of software that allows users to try out the main features of a particular program before buying it. Especially common among ◊shareware producers, demo software usually blocks some features of the full version, so that a demo database might be able to handle only a small number of records.

The word 'demo' is also used to refer to fancy graphics and sound routines which are created by young programmers to demonstrate their skills to friends, admirers, and potential employers such as computer game publishers.

demodulation in radio, the technique of separating a transmitted audio frequency signal from its modulated radio carrier wave. At the transmitter, the audio frequency signal (representing speech or music, for example) may be made to modulate the amplitude (AM broadcasting) or frequency (FM broadcasting) of a continuously transmitted radio-frequency carrier wave. At the receiver, the signal from the aerial is demodulated to extract the required speech or sound component. In early radio systems, this process was called detection. See ◊modulation.

Demon Internet in computing, Britain's first and largest mass-market ◊Internet Service Provider. Founded 1992 by English hardware salesman Cliff Stanford with 200 founding subscribers who each paid £120 in advance for a year's service, Demon set the price (£10 a month plus VAT) for Internet access in the UK. By 1996, Demon Internet had 65,000 customers.

demonstration software in computing, see ◊demo.

denaturation irreversible changes occurring in the structure of proteins such as enzymes, usually caused by changes in pH or temperature, by radiation or chemical treatments. An example is the heating of egg albumen resulting in solid egg white.

The enzymes associated with digestion and metabolism become inactive if given abnormal conditions. Heat will damage their complex structure so that the usual interactions between enzyme and substrate can no longer occur.

dendrite part of a ◊nerve cell or neuron. The dendrites are slender filaments projecting from the cell body. They receive incoming messages from many other nerve cells and pass them on to the cell body.

If the combined effect of these messages is strong enough, the cell body will send an electrical impulse along the axon (the thread-like extension of a nerve cell). The tip of the axon passes its message to the dendrites of other nerve cells.

dendrochronology or ***tree-ring dating*** analysis of the ◊annual rings of trees to date past events by determining the age of timber. Since annual rings are formed by variations in the water-conducting cells produced by the plant during different seasons of the year, they also provide a means of establishing past climatic conditions in a given area.

Samples of wood are obtained by driving a narrow metal tube into a tree to remove a core extending from the bark to the centre. Samples taken from timbers at an archaeological site can be compared with a master core on file for that region or by taking cores from old living trees; the year when they were felled can be determined by locating the point where the rings of the two samples correspond and counting back from the present.

Moisture levels will affect growth, the annual rings being thin in dry years, thick in moist ones, although in Europe ring growth is most affected by temperature change and insect defoliation.

In North America, studies are now extremely extensive, covering many wood types, including sequoia, juniper, and sagebrush. Sequences of tree rings extending back over 8,000 years have been obtained for the southwest USA and northern Mexico by using cores from the bristle-cone pine *Pinus aristata* of the White Mountains, California, which can live for over 4,000 years in that region. The dryness of the southwest USA has preserved wood in its archaeological sites. In wet temperate regions, wood is usually absorbed by soil acidity so that this dating technique cannot be used.

Deneb or ***Alpha Cygni*** brightest star in the constellation ◊Cygnus, and the 19th brightest star in the night sky. It is one of the greatest supergiant stars known, with a true luminosity of about 60,000 times that of the Sun. Deneb is about 1,800 light years from Earth.

The name Deneb is derived from the Arabic word for tail.

denier unit used in measuring the fineness of yarns, equal to the mass in grams of 9,000 metres of yarn. Thus 9,000 metres of 15 denier nylon, used in nylon stockings, weighs 15 g/0.5 oz, and in this case the thickness of thread would be 0.00425 mm/0.0017 in. The term is derived from the French silk industry; the *denier* was an old French silver coin.

denitrification process occurring naturally in soil, where bacteria break down ◊nitrates to give nitrogen gas, which returns to the atmosphere.

denominator in mathematics, the bottom number of a fraction, so called because it names the family of the fraction. The top number, or numerator, specifies how many unit fractions are to be taken.

density measure of the compactness of a substance; it is equal to its mass per unit volume and is measured in kg per cubic metre/lb per cubic foot. Density is a ◊scalar quantity. The average density D of a mass m occupying a volume V is given by the formula:

$$D = m/V$$

◊Relative density is the ratio of the density of a substance to that of water at 4°C/32.2°F.

In photography, density refers to the degree of opacity of a negative; in population studies, it is the quantity or number per unit of area; in electricity, current density is the amount of current passing through a cross-sectional area of a conductor (usually given in amperes per sq in or per sq cm).

density wave in astrophysics, a concept proposed to account for the existence of spiral arms in ◊galaxies. In the density wave theory, stars in a spiral galaxy move in elliptical orbits in such a way that they crowd together in waves of temporarily enhanced density that appear as spiral arms. The idea was first proposed by Swedish astronomer Bertil Lindblad in the 1920s and developed by US astronomers C C Lin and Frank Shu in the 1960s.

dental caries in medicine, another name for ◊caries.

dental formula way of showing the number of teeth in an animal's mouth. The dental formula consists of eight numbers separated by a line into two rows. The four above the line represent the teeth on one side of the upper jaw, starting at the front. If this reads 2 1 2 3 (as for humans) it means two incisors, one canine, two premolars, and three molars (see ◊tooth). The numbers below the line represent the lower jaw. The total number of teeth can be calculated by adding up all the numbers and multiplying by two.

dentistry care and treatment of the teeth and gums. **Orthodontics** deals with the straightening of the teeth for aesthetic and clinical reasons, and **periodontics** with care of the supporting tissue (bone and gums).

The bacteria that start the process of dental decay are normal, nonpathogenic members of a large and varied group of microorganisms present in the mouth. They are strains of oral streptococci, and it is only in the presence of sucrose (from refined sugar) in the mouth that they become damaging to the teeth. ◊Fluoride in the water supply has been one attempted solution to prevent decay,

DENTISTRY NOW

http://www.DentistryNow.com/Mainpage.htm#Main Part

Canadian-based site that includes an index of dentists worldwide. There is also an index of university courses where dentistry can be studied. In addition, there is a section on common dental problems and a good site for kids called 'tooth fairy' to introduce them to the importance of cleaning their teeth.

and in 1979 a vaccine was developed from a modified form of the bacterium *Streptococcus mutans*.

dentition type and number of teeth in a species. Different kinds of teeth have different functions; a grass-eating animal will have large molars for grinding its food, whereas a meat-eater will need powerful canines for catching and killing its prey. The teeth that are less useful to an animal's lifestyle may be reduced in size or missing altogether. An animal's dentition is represented diagramatically by a ◊dental formula.

Young children have **deciduous dentition**, popularly known as 'milk teeth', the first ones erupting at about six months of age. **Mixed dentition** is present from the ages of about six (when the first milk teeth are shed) to about 12. **Permanent dentition** (up to 32 teeth) is usually complete by the mid-teens, although the third molars (wisdom teeth) may not appear until around the age of 21.

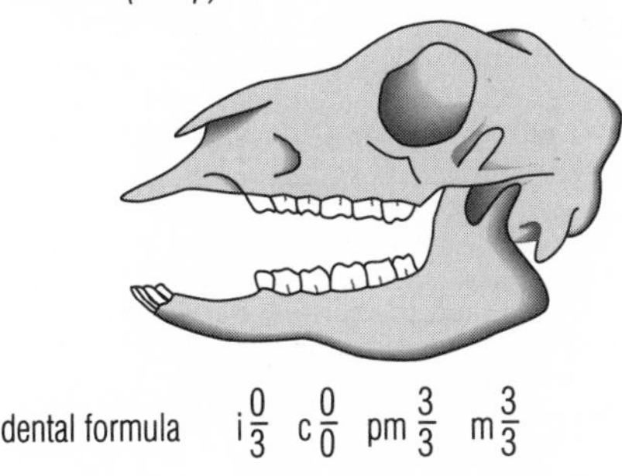

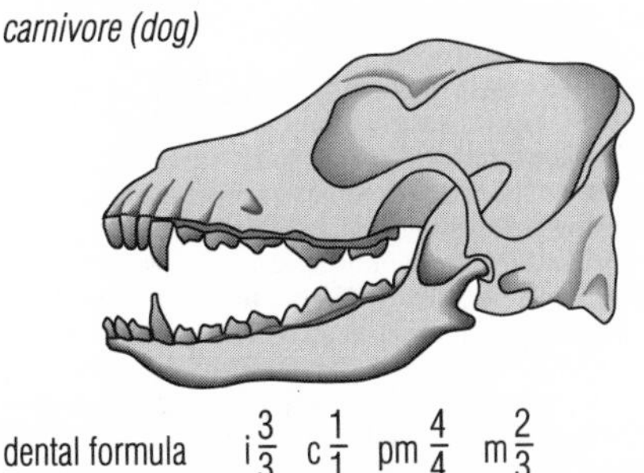

***dentition** The dentition and dental formulae of a typical herbivore (sheep) and carnivore (dog). The dog has long pointed canines for puncturing and gripping its prey and has modified premolars and molars (carnassials) for shearing flesh. In the sheep, by contrast, there is a wide gap, or diastema, between the incisors, developed for cutting through blades of grass, and the grinding premolars and molars; the canines are absent.*

denudation natural loss of soil and rock debris, blown away by wind or washed away by running water, laying bare the rock below. Over millions of years, denudation causes a general lowering of the landscape.

deodar Himalayan ◊cedar tree, often planted as a rapid-growing ornamental. Its fragrant, durable wood is valuable as timber. (*Cedrus deodara*, family Pinaceae.)

deoxyribonucleic acid full name of ◊DNA.

depolarizer oxidizing agent used in dry-cell batteries that converts hydrogen released at the negative electrode into water. This prevents the build-up of gas, which would otherwise impair the efficiency of the battery. ◊Manganese(IV) oxide is used for this purpose.

depression or ***cyclone*** or ***low*** in meteorology, a region of low atmospheric pressure. In mid latitudes a depression forms as warm, moist air from the tropics mixes with cold, dry polar air, producing warm and cold boundaries (◊fronts) and unstable weather – low cloud and drizzle, showers, or fierce storms. The warm air, being less dense, rises above the cold air to produce the area of low pressure on the ground. Air spirals in towards the centre of the depression in an anticlockwise direction in the northern hemisphere, clockwise in the southern hemisphere, generating winds up to gale force. Depressions tend to travel eastwards and can remain active for several days.

depression in medicine, an emotional state characterized by sadness, unhappy thoughts, apathy, and dejection. Sadness is a normal response to major losses such as bereavement or unemployment. After childbirth, ◊postnatal depression is common. However, clinical depression, which is prolonged or unduly severe, often requires treatment, such as antidepressant medication, ◊cognitive therapy, or, in very rare cases, electroconvulsive therapy (ECT), in which an electrical current is passed through the brain.

Periods of depression may alternate with periods of high optimism, over-enthusiasm, and confidence. This is the manic phase in a disorder known as **manic depression** or **bipolar disorder**. A manic depressive state is one in which a person switches repeatedly from one extreme to the other. Each mood can last for weeks or months. Typically, the depressive state lasts longer than the manic phase.

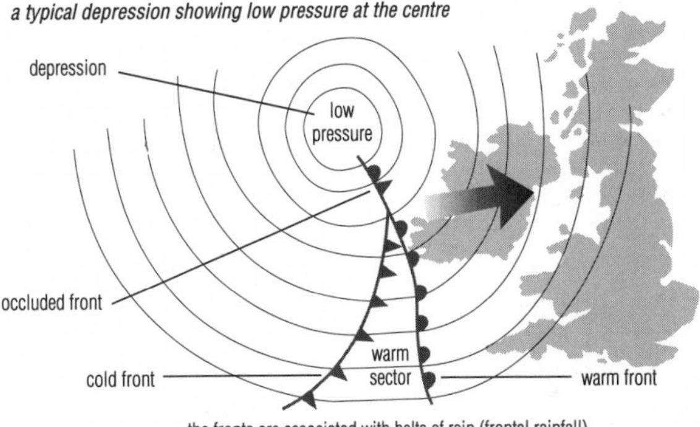

depression

derivative or ***differential coefficient*** in mathematics, the limit of the gradient of a chord linking two points on a curve as the distance between the points tends to zero; for a function of a single variable, $y = f(x)$, it is denoted by $f'(x)$, $Df(x)$, or dy/dx, and is equal to the gradient of the curve.

dermatitis inflammation of the skin (see ◊eczema), usually related to allergy. **Dermatosis** refers to any skin disorder and may be caused by contact or systemic problems.

dermatology medical speciality concerned with the diagnosis and treatment of skin disorders.

derrick simple lifting machine consisting of a pole carrying a block and tackle. Derricks are commonly used on ships that carry freight. In the oil industry the tower used for hoisting the drill pipes is known as a derrick.

derris climbing leguminous plant (see ◊legume) of southeast Asia. Its roots contain rotenone, a strong insecticide. (*Derris elliptica*, family Fabaceae.)

DES in computing, abbreviation for ◊Data Encryption Standard.

desalination removal of salt, usually from sea water, to produce fresh water for irrigation or drinking. Distillation has usually been the method adopted, but in the 1970s a cheaper process, using certain polymer materials that filter the molecules of salt from the water by reverse osmosis, was developed.

Desalination plants occur along the shores of the Middle East where fresh water is in short supply.

DESCARTES, RENÉ

http://www.knight.org/advent/cathen/04744b.htm

Extensive treatment of the life and philosophical, scientific, and mathematical achievements of Renatus Cartesius. The restless travels of the young savant are described before a detailed discussion of his contribution to learning.

Descartes, René (1596–1650)

French philosopher and mathematician. He believed that commonly accepted knowledge was doubtful because of the subjective nature of the senses, and attempted to rebuild human knowledge using as his foundation the dictum cogito ergo sum ('I think, therefore I am'). He also believed that the entire material universe could be explained in terms of mathematical physics, and founded coordinate geometry as a way of defining and manipulating geometrical shapes by means of algebraic expressions. Cartesian coordinates, the means by which points are represented in this system, are named after him. Descartes also established the science of optics, and helped to shape contemporary theories of astronomy and animal behaviour.

Descartes identified the 'thinking thing' (res cogitans), or mind, with the human soul or consciousness; the body, though somehow interacting with the soul, was a physical machine, secondary to, and in principle separable from, the soul. He held that everything has a cause; nothing can result from nothing. He believed that, although all matter is in motion, matter does not move of its own accord; the initial impulse comes from God. He also postulated two quite distinct substances: spatial substance, or matter, and thinking substance, or mind. This is called 'Cartesian dualism', and it preserved him from serious controversy with the church.

Mary Evans Picture Library

Cogito, ergo sum.
I think, therefore I am.

RENÉ DESCARTES French philosopher and mathematician.
Le discours de la méthode

desert arid area with sparse vegetation (or, in rare cases, almost no vegetation). Soils are poor, and many deserts include areas of shifting sands. Deserts can be either hot or cold. Almost 33% of the Earth's land surface is desert, and this proportion is increasing.

The **tropical desert** belts of latitudes from 5° to 30° are caused by the descent of air that is heated over the warm land and therefore has lost its moisture. Other natural desert types are the **continental deserts**, such as the Gobi, that are too far from the sea to receive any moisture; **rain-shadow deserts**, such as California's Death Valley, that lie in the lee of mountain ranges, where the ascending air drops its rain only on the windward slopes; and **coastal deserts**, such as the Namib, where cold ocean currents cause local dry air masses to descend. Desert surfaces are usually rocky or gravelly, with only a small proportion being covered with sand. Deserts can be created by changes in climate, or by the human-aided process of desertification.

Largest deserts in the world

Desert	Location	Area[1] sq km	sq mi
Sahara	northern Africa	9,065,000	3,500,000
Gobi	Mongolia/northeastern China	1,295,000	500,000
Patagonian	Argentina	673,000	260,000
Rub al-Khali	southern Arabian peninsula	647,500	250,000
Chihuahuan	Mexico/southwestern USA	362,600	140,000
Taklimakan	northern China	362,600	140,000
Great Sandy	northwestern Australia	338,500	130,000
Great Victoria	southwestern Australia	338,500	130,000
Kalahari	southwestern Africa	260,000	100,000
Kyzyl Kum	Uzbekistan	259,000	100,000
Thar	India/Pakistan	259,000	100,000
Sonoran	Mexico/southwestern USA	181,300	70,000
Simpson	Australia	103,600	40,000
Mojave	southwestern USA	51,800	20,000

[1]Desert areas are very approximate, because clear physical boundaries may not occur.

Characteristics common to all deserts include irregular rainfall of less than 250 mm/19.75 in per year, very high evaporation rates often 20 times the annual precipitation, and low relative humidity and cloud cover. Temperatures are more variable; tropical deserts have a big diurnal temperature range and very high daytime temperatures (58°C/136.4°F) has been recorded at Azizia in Libya), whereas mid-latitude deserts have a wide annual range and much lower winter temperatures (in the Mongolian desert the mean temperature is below freezing point for half the year).

Desert soils are infertile, lacking in ◊humus and generally grey or red in colour. The few plants capable of surviving such conditions are widely spaced, scrubby and often thorny. Long-rooted plants (phreatophytes) such as the date palm and musquite commonly grow along dry stream channels. Salt-loving plants (◊halophytes) such as saltbushes grow in areas of highly saline soils and near the edges of playas (dry saline lakes). Others, such as the ◊xerophytes are drought-resistant and survive by remaining leafless during the dry season or by reducing water losses with small waxy leaves. They frequently have shallow and widely branching root systems and store water during the wet season (for example, succulents and cacti with pulpy stems).

desertification spread of deserts by changes in climate, or by human-aided processes. Desertification can sometimes be reversed by special planting (marram grass, trees) and by the use of water-absorbent plastic grains, which, added to the soil, enable crops to be grown.

The processes leading to desertification include overgrazing, destruction of forest belts, and exhaustion of the soil by intensive cultivation without restoration of fertility – all of which may be prompted by the pressures of an expanding population or by concentration in land ownership. About 135 million people are directly affected by desertification, mainly in Africa, the Indian subcontinent, and South America.

desiccator airtight vessel, traditionally made of glass, in which materials may be stored either to dry them or to prevent them, once dried, from reabsorbing moisture.

The base of the desiccator is a chamber in which is placed a substance with a strong affinity for water (such as calcium chloride or silica gel), which removes water vapour from the desiccator atmosphere and from substances placed in it.

desktop in computing, a graphical representation of file systems, in which applications and files are represented by pictures (icons), which can be triggered by a single or double click with a ◊mouse button. Such a ◊graphical user interface can be compared with the ◊command line interface, which is character-based.

desktop publishing (DTP) use of microcomputers for small-scale typesetting and page makeup. DTP systems are capable of producing camera-ready pages (pages ready for photographing and printing), made up of text and graphics, with text set in different typefaces and sizes. The page can be previewed on the screen before final printing on a laser printer.

A DTP program is able to import text and graphics from other packages; run text as columns, over pages, and around artwork and other insertions; enable a wide range of ◊fonts; and allow accurate positioning of all elements required to make a page.

desktop video in computing, a ◊videoconferencing system that can be used by an individual from a desktop computer. A desktop conferencing system needs a computer, an attached video camera, microphone, and speakers, and a telephone or network connection.

Early videoconferencing systems required such expensive equipment that participants had to gather in the room where the equipment was kept. Systems introduced in the mid-1990s, however, made videoconferencing as convenient, private, and easy to use as ordinary telephone calls.

The first desktop videoconferencing system on the Internet was ◊CU-SeeMe.

destination page in computing, page designated by a ◊hypertext link.

detergent surface-active cleansing agent. The common detergents are made from ◊fats (hydrocarbons) and sulphuric acid, and their long-chain molecules have a type of structure similar to that of ◊soap molecules: a salt group at one end attached to a long hydrocarbon 'tail'. They have the advantage over soap in that they do not produce scum by forming insoluble salts with the calcium and magnesium ions present in hard water.

To remove dirt, which is generally attached to materials by means of oil or grease, the hydrocarbon 'tails' (soluble in oil or grease) penetrate the oil or grease drops, while the 'heads' (soluble in water but insoluble in grease) remain in the water and, being salts, become ionized. Consequently the oil drops become negatively charged and tend to repel one another; thus they remain in suspension and are washed away with the dirt.

Detergents were first developed from coal tar in Germany during World War I, and synthetic organic detergents were increasingly used after World War II.

Domestic powder detergents for use in hot water have alkyl benzene as their main base, and may also include bleaches and fluorescers as whiteners, perborates to free stain-removing oxygen, and water softeners. Environment-friendly detergents contain no phosphates or bleaches. Liquid detergents for washing dishes are based on epoxyethane (ethylene oxide). Cold-water detergents consist of a mixture of various alcohols, plus an ingredient for breaking down the surface tension of the water, so enabling the liquid to penetrate fibres and remove the dirt. When these surface-active agents (surfactants) escape the normal processing of sewage, they cause troublesome foam in rivers; phosphates in some detergents can also cause the excessive enrichment (◊eutrophication) of rivers and lakes.

determinant in mathematics, an array of elements written as a square, and denoted by two vertical lines enclosing the array. For a 2 × 2 matrix, the determinant is given by the difference between the products of the diagonal terms. Determinants are used to solve sets of ◊simultaneous equations by matrix methods.

When applied to transformational geometry, the determinant of a 2 × 2 matrix signifies the ratio of the area of the transformed shape to the original and its sign (plus or minus) denotes whether the image is direct (the same way round) or indirect (a mirror image).

For example, the determinant of the matrix

$$(a\ b) = |\ a\ b\ | = ad - bc(c\ d)\ |\ c\ d\ |$$

detonator or ***blasting cap*** or ***percussion cap*** small explosive charge used to trigger off a main charge of high explosive. The relatively unstable compounds mercury fulminate and lead azide are often used in detonators, being set off by a lighted fuse or, more commonly, an electric current.

detritus in biology, the organic debris produced during the ◊decomposition of animals and plants.

deuterium naturally occurring heavy isotope of hydrogen, mass number 2 (one proton and one neutron), discovered by Harold Urey in 1932. It is sometimes given the symbol D. In nature, about one in every 6,500 hydrogen atoms is deuterium. Combined with oxygen, it produces 'heavy water' (D_2O), used in the nuclear industry.

deuteron nucleus of an atom of deuterium (heavy hydrogen). It consists of one proton and one neutron, and is used in the bombardment of chemical elements to synthesize other elements.

developer in computing, designer of a computer system, most commonly used to mean a software developer.

developing in photography, the process that produces a visible image on exposed photographic ◊film, involving the treatment of the exposed film with a chemical developer.

The developing liquid consists of a reducing agent that changes the light-altered silver salts in the film into darker metallic silver. The developed image is made permanent with a fixer, which dissolves away any silver salts which were not affected by light. The developed image is a negative, or reverse image: darkest where the strongest light hit the film, lightest where the least light fell. To produce a positive image, the negative is itself photographed, and the development process reverses the shading, producing the final print. Colour and black-and-white film can be obtained as direct reversal, slide, or transparency material. Slides and transparencies are used for projection or printing with a positive-to-positive process such as Cibachrome.

development in biology, the process whereby a living thing transforms itself from a single cell into a vastly complicated multicellular organism, with structures, such as limbs, and functions, such as respiration, all able to work correctly in relation to each other. Most of the details of this process remain unknown, although some of the central features are becoming understood.

Apart from the sex cells (◊gametes), each cell within an organism contains exactly the same genetic code. Whether a cell develops into a liver cell or a brain cell depends therefore not on which ◊genes it contains, but on which genes are allowed to be expressed. The development of forms and patterns within an organism, and the production of different, highly specialized cells, is a problem of control, with genes being turned on and off according to the stage of development reached by the organism.

developmental psychology study of development of cognition and behaviour from birth to adulthood.

device driver in computing, small piece of software required to tell the operating system how to interact with a particular input or output device or peripheral.

Much work has been done to standardize devices and their interfaces to eliminate the need for individual device drivers. Peripherals such as CD-ROM drives, for example, work with a single standard device driver (in Microsoft Windows, MSCDEX.EXE). Other devices, such as modems and printers, still need an individual driver tailored to work with that specific model.

devil ray any of several large rays of the genera *Manta* and *Mobula,* in which two 'horns' project forwards from the sides of the huge mouth. These flaps of skin guide the plankton, on which the fish feed, into the mouth.

The largest of these rays can be 7 m/23 ft across, and weigh 1,000 kg/2,200 lb. They live in warm seas.

devil's coach horse large, black, long-bodied, omnivorous beetle *Ocypus olens,* about 3 cm/1.2 in long. It has powerful jaws and is capable of giving a painful bite. It emits an unpleasant smell when threatened.

devil's coach horse *The devil's coach horse beetle (family Staphylinidae) adopts a threatening posture with its tail raised and emits an unpleasant smell when it senses danger. Premaphotos Wildlife*

Devonian period of geological time 408–360 million years ago, the fourth period of the Palaeozoic era. Many desert sandstones from North America and Europe date from this time. The first land plants flourished in the Devonian period, corals were abundant in the seas, amphibians evolved from air-breathing fish, and insects developed on land.

The name comes from the county of Devon in southwest England, where Devonian rocks were first studied.

dew precipitation in the form of moisture that collects on the ground. It forms after the temperature of the ground has fallen below the ◊dew point of the air in contact with it. As the temperature falls during the night, the air and its water vapour become chilled, and condensation takes place on the cooled surfaces.

dew point temperature at which the air becomes saturated with water vapour. At temperatures below the dew point, the water vapour condenses out of the air as droplets. If the droplets are large they become deposited on the ground as dew; if small they remain in suspension in the air and form mist or fog.

dewpond drinking pond for farm animals on arid hilltops such as chalk downs. In the UK, dewponds were excavated in the 19th century and lined with mud and clay. It is uncertain where the water comes from but it may be partly rain, partly sea mist, and only a small part dew.

dhole wild dog *Cuon alpinus* found in Asia from Siberia to Java. With head and body up to 1 m/39 in long, variable in colour but often reddish above and lighter below, the dhole lives in groups of from 3 to 30 individuals. The species is becoming rare and is protected in some areas.

Dholes can chase prey for long distances; a pack is capable of pulling down deer and cattle as well as smaller prey. They are even known to have attacked tigers and leopards.

diabase alternative name for ◊dolerite (a form of basalt that contains very little silica), especially dolerite that has metamorphosed.

diabetes disease *diabetes mellitus* in which a disorder of the islets of Langerhans in the ◊pancreas prevents the body producing the hormone ◊insulin, so that sugars cannot be used properly.

Treatment is by strict dietary control and oral or injected insulin, depending on the type of diabetes.

There are two forms of diabetes: Type 1, or insulin-dependent diabetes, which usually begins in childhood (early onset) and is an autoimmune condition; and Type 2, or noninsulin-dependent diabetes, which occurs in later life (late onset).

diagenesis in geology, the physical and chemical changes by which a sediment becomes a ◊sedimentary rock. The main processes involved include compaction of the grains, and the cementing of the grains together by the growth of new minerals deposited by percolating groundwater.

dialler in computing, element of an Internet software package that makes the connection to the ◊online service or ◊Internet Service Provider. In Windows systems, this is usually the WINSOCK.DLL file, with or without a front end (part of the program that interacts with the user) to make configuration easier.

dialog box in ◊graphical user interfaces, a small on-screen window with blanks for user input.

dial-up connection in computing, connection to an ◊online system or ◊Internet Service Provider made by dialling via a ◊modem over a telephone line.

dialysis technique for removing waste products from the blood suffering chronic or acute kidney failure. There are two main methods, haemodialysis and peritoneal dialysis.

In **haemodialysis**, the patient's blood is passed through a pump, where it is separated from sterile dialysis fluid by a semipermeable membrane. This allows any toxic substances which have built up in the bloodstream, and which would normally be filtered out by the kidneys, to diffuse out of the blood into the dialysis fluid. Haemodialysis is very expensive and usually requires the patient to attend a specialized unit.

Peritoneal dialysis uses one of the body's natural semipermeable membranes for the same purpose. About two litres of dialysis fluid is slowly instilled into the peritoneal cavity of the abdomen, and drained out again, over about two hours. During that time toxins from the blood diffuse into the peritoneal cavity across the peritoneal membrane. The advantage of peritoneal dialysis is that the patient can remain active while the dialysis is proceeding. This is known as continuous ambulatory peritoneal dialysis (CAPD).

In the long term, dialysis is expensive and debilitating, and ◊transplants are now the treatment of choice for patients in chronic kidney failure.

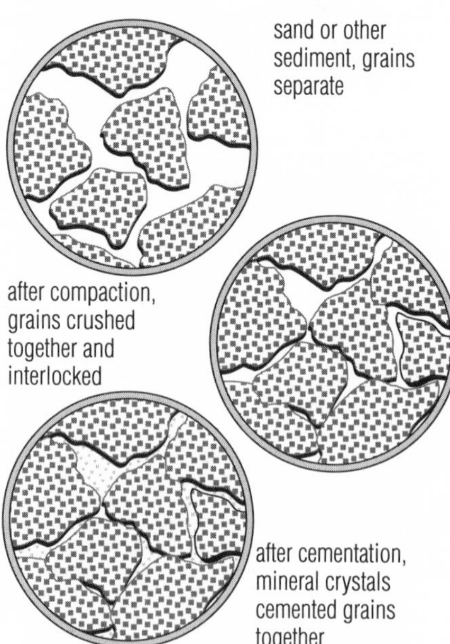

diagenesis *The formation of sedimentary rock by diagenesis. Sand and other sediment grains are compacted and cemented together.*

diamagnetic material a material weakly repelled by a magnet. All substances are diamagnetic but the behaviour is often masked by stronger forms of magnetism such as ◊paramagnetic or ◊ferromagnetic behaviour.

Diamagnetism is caused by changes in the orbits of electrons in the substance induced by the applied field. Diamagnetic materials have a small negative magnetic ◊susceptibility.

diameter straight line joining two points on the circumference of a circle that passes through the centre of that circle. It divides a circle into two equal halves.

diamond generally colourless, transparent mineral, an ◊allotrope of carbon. It is regarded as a precious gemstone, and is the hardest substance known (10 on the ◊Mohs' scale). Industrial diamonds, which may be natural or synthetic, are used for cutting, grinding, and polishing.

Diamond crystallizes in the cubic system as octahedral crystals, some with curved faces and striations. The high refractive index of 2.42 and the high dispersion of light, or 'fire', account for the spectral displays seen in polished diamonds.

history Diamonds were known before 3000 BC and until their discovery in Brazil in 1725, India was the principal source of supply. Present sources are Australia, Congo (formerly Zaire), Botswana, Russia (Yakut), South Africa, Namibia, and Angola; the first two produce large volumes of industrial diamonds. Today, about 80% of the world's rough gem diamonds are sold through the De Beers Central Selling Organization in London.

sources Diamonds may be found as alluvial diamonds on or close to the Earth's surface in riverbeds or dried watercourses; on the sea bottom (off southwest Africa); or, more commonly, in diamond-bearing volcanic pipes composed of 'blue ground', ◊kimberlite or lamproite, where the original matrix has penetrated the Earth's crust from great depths. They are sorted from the residue of crushed ground by X-ray and other recovery methods.

varieties There are four chief varieties of diamond: well-crystallized transparent stones, colourless or only slightly tinted, valued as gems; **boart**, poorly crystallized or inferior diamonds; **balas**, an industrial variety, extremely hard and tough; and **carbonado**, or industrial diamond, also called black diamond or carbon, which is opaque, black or grey, and very tough. Industrial diamonds are also produced synthetically from graphite. Some synthetic diamonds conduct heat 50% more efficiently than natural diamonds and are five times greater in strength. This is a great advantage in their use to disperse heat in electronic and telecommunication devices and in the production of laser components.

practical uses Because diamonds act as perfectly transparent windows and do not absorb infrared radiation, they were used aboard NASA space probes to Venus in 1978. The tungsten-carbide tools used in steel mills are cut with industrial diamond tools.

cutting Rough diamonds are often dull or greasy before being polished; around 50% are considered 'cuttable' (all or part of the diamond may be set into jewellery). Gem diamonds are valued by weight (◊carat), cut (highlighting the stone's optical properties), colour, and clarity (on a scale from internally flawless to having a large inclusion clearly visible to the naked eye). They are sawn and polished using a mixture of oil and diamond powder. The two most popular cuts are the brilliant, for thicker stones, and the marquise, for shallower ones. India is the world's chief cutting centre.

Noted rough diamonds include the Cullinan, or Star of Africa (3,106 carats, over 500 g/17.5 oz before cutting, South Africa, 1905); Excelsior (995.2 carats, South Africa, 1893); and Star of Sierra Leone (968.9 carats, Yengema, 1972).

experiments a moderate force applied to the small tips of two opposing diamonds can be used to attain extreme pressures of millions of atmospheres or more, allowing scientists to subject small amounts of material to conditions that exist deep within planet interiors.

diamorphine technical term for ◊heroin.

DIANE (acronym for ***direct information access network for Europe***) collection of information suppliers, or 'hosts', for the European computer network.

diapause period of suspended development that occurs in some species of insects, characterized by greatly reduced metabolism. Periods of diapause are often timed to coincide with the winter months, and improve the insect's chances of surviving adverse conditions.

diaphragm in mammals, a thin muscular sheet separating the thorax from the abdomen. It is attached by way of the ribs at either side and the breastbone and backbone, and a central tendon. Arching upwards against the heart and lungs, the diaphragm is important in the mechanics of breathing. It contracts at each inhalation, moving downwards to increase the volume of the chest cavity, and relaxes at exhalation.

diaphragm or ***cap*** or ***Dutch cap*** barrier ◊contraceptive that is passed into the vagina to fit over the cervix (neck of the uterus), preventing sperm from entering the uterus. For a cap to be effective, a ◊spermicide must be used and the diaphragm left in place for 6–8 hours after intercourse. This method is 97% effective if practised correctly.

diarrhoea frequent or excessive action of the bowels so that the faeces are liquid or semiliquid. It is caused by intestinal irritants (including some drugs and poisons), infection with harmful organisms (as in dysentery, salmonella, or cholera), or allergies.

Diarrhoea is the biggest killer of children in the world. In 1996 the World Health Organization reported that 3.1 million deaths had been caused by diarrhoeal disease during 1995. The commonest cause of dehydrating diarrhoea is human rotavirus infection, responsible for about 870,000 infant deaths annually. Dehydration as a result of diarrhoeal disease can be treated by giving a solution of salt and glucose by mouth in large quantities (to restore the electrolyte balance in the blood). Since most diarrhoea is viral in origin, antibiotics are ineffective.

diastole in biology, the relaxation of a hollow organ. In particular, the term is used to indicate the resting period between beats of the heart when blood is flowing into it.

diastolic pressure in medicine, measurement due to the pressure of blood against the arterial wall during diastole (relaxation of the heart). It is the lowest ◊blood pressure during the cardiac cycle. The average diastolic pressure in healthy young adults is about 80 mmHg. The variation of diastolic pressure due to changes in body position and mood is greater than that of systolic pressure. Diastolic pressure is also a more accurate predictor of hypertension (high blood pressure).

diatom microscopic ◊alga found in all parts of the world in either fresh or marine waters. Diatoms consist of single cells that secrete a hard cell wall made of ◊silica. (Division Bacillariophyta.)

The cell wall of a diatom is made up of two overlapping valves known as **frustules**, which are impregnated with silica, and which fit together like the lid and body of a pillbox. Diatomaceous earths (diatomite) are made up of the valves of fossil diatoms, and are used in the manufacture of dynamite and in the rubber and plastics industries.

diatomic molecule molecule composed of two atoms joined together. In the case of an element such as oxygen (O_2), the atoms are identical.

dichloro-diphenyl-trichloroethane full name of the insecticide ◊DDT.

dichotomous key method of identifying an organism. The investigator is presented with pairs of statements, for example 'flower has less than five stamens' and 'flower has five or more stamens'. By successively eliminating statements the field naturalist moves closer to a positive identification. Dichotomous keys assume a good knowledge of the subject under investigation.

dicotyledon major subdivision of the ◊angiosperms, containing the great majority of flowering plants. Dicotyledons are characterized by the presence of two seed leaves, or ◊cotyledons, in the embryo, which is usually surrounded by the ◊endosperm. They generally have broad leaves with netlike veins.

diecasting form of ◊casting in which molten metal is injected into permanent metal moulds or dies.

dielectric an insulator or nonconducter of electricity, such as rubber, glass, and paraffin wax. An electric field in a dielectric material gives rise to no net flow of electricity. However, the applied field causes electrons within the material to be displaced, creating an electric charge on the surface of the material. This reduces the field strength within the material by a factor known as the dielectric constant (or relative permittivity) of the material. Dielectrics are used in capacitors, to reduce dangerously strong electric fields, and have optical applications.

diesel engine ◊internal-combustion engine that burns a lightweight fuel oil. The diesel engine operates by compressing air until it becomes sufficiently hot to ignite the fuel. It is a piston-in-cylinder engine, like the ◊petrol engine, but only air (rather than an air-and-fuel mixture) is taken into the cylinder on the first piston stroke (down). The piston moves up and compresses the air until it is at a very high temperature. The fuel oil is then injected into the hot air, where it burns, driving the piston down on its power stroke. For this reason the engine is called a compression-ignition engine.

Diesel engines have sometimes been marketed as 'cleaner' than petrol engines because they do not need lead additives and produce fewer gaseous pollutants. However, they do produce high levels of the tiny black carbon particles called particulates, which are believed to be carcinogenic and may exacerbate or even cause asthma.

The principle of the diesel engine was first explained in England by Herbert Akroyd (1864–1937) in 1890, and was applied practically by Rudolf Diesel in Germany in 1892.

diesel oil lightweight fuel oil used in diesel engines. Like petrol, it is a petroleum product. When used in vehicle engines, it is also known as **derv** (diesel-engine road vehicle).

diet range of foods eaten by an animal each day; it is also a particular selection of food, or the total amount and choice of food for a specific person or people. Most animals require seven kinds of food in their diet: proteins, carbohydrates, fats, vitamins, minerals, water, and roughage. A diet that contains all of these things in the correct amounts and proportions is termed a balanced diet. The amounts and proportions required varies with different animals, according to their size, age, and lifestyle. The ◊digestive systems of animals have evolved to meet particular needs; they have also adapted to cope with the foods available in the surroundings in which they live. The necessity of finding and processing an appropriate diet is a very basic drive in animal evolution. **Dietetics** is the science of feeding individuals or groups; a dietition is a specialist in this science.

Dietary requirements may vary over the lifespan of an animal, according to whether it is growing, reproducing, highly active, or approaching death. For instance, increased carbohydrate for additional energy, or increased minerals, may be necessary during periods of growth.

An adequate diet for humans is one that supplies the body's daily nutritional needs (see ◊nutrition), and provides sufficient energy to meet individual levels of activity. The average daily requirement for men is 2,500 calories, but this will vary with age, occupation, and weight; in general, women need fewer calories than men. The energy requirements of active children increase steadily with age, reaching a peak in the late teens. At present, about 450 million people in the world – mainly living in famine or poverty stricken areas, especially in Third World countries – subsist on fewer than 1,500 calories per day. The average daily intake in developed countries is 3,300 calories.

> *The act of putting into your mouth what the earth has grown is perhaps your most direct interaction with the earth.*
>
> Frances Lappé US ecologist. *Diet for a Small Planet* pt 1

dietetics specialized branch of human nutrition, dealing with the promotion of health through the proper kinds and quantities of food.

Therapeutic dietetics has a large part to play in the treatment of certain illnesses, such as allergies, arthritis, and diabetes; it is sometimes used alone, but often in conjunction with drugs. The preventative or curative effects of specific diets, such as the 'grape cure' or raw vegetable diets sometimes prescribed for cancer patients, are disputed by orthodox medicine.

difference in mathematics, the result obtained when subtracting one number from another. Also, those elements of one ◊set that are not elements of another.

difference engine mechanical calculating machine designed (and partly built in 1822) by the British mathematician Charles ◊Babbage to produce reliable tables of life expectancy. A precursor of the ◊analytical engine, it was to calculate mathematical functions by solving the differences between values given to ◊variables within equations. Babbage designed the calculator so that once the initial values for the variables were set it would produce the next few thousand values without error.

differential arrangement of gears in the final drive of a vehicle's transmission system that allows the driving wheels to turn at different speeds when cornering. The differential consists of sets of bevel gears and pinions within a cage attached to the crown wheel. When cornering, the bevel pinions rotate to allow the outer wheel to turn faster than the inner.

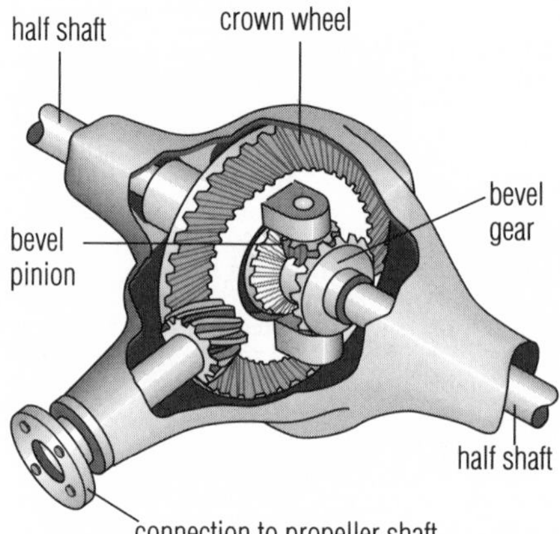

***differential** The differential lies midway between the driving wheels of a motorcar. When the car is turning, the bevel pinions spin, allowing the outer wheel to turn faster than the inner wheel.*

differential calculus branch of ◊calculus involving applications such as the determination of maximum and minimum points and rates of change.

differentiation in embryology, the process by which cells become increasingly different and specialized, giving rise to more complex structures that have particular functions in the adult organism. For instance, embryonic cells may develop into nerve, muscle, or bone cells.

differentiation in mathematics, a procedure for determining the ◊derivative or gradient of the tangent to a curve $f(x)$ at any point x.

Diffie-Hellman key exchange system in computing, the basis of ◊public-key cryptography, proposed by researchers Whitfield Diffie and Martin Hellman 1976.

diffraction the slight spreading of a light beam into a pattern of light and dark bands when it passes through a narrow slit or past

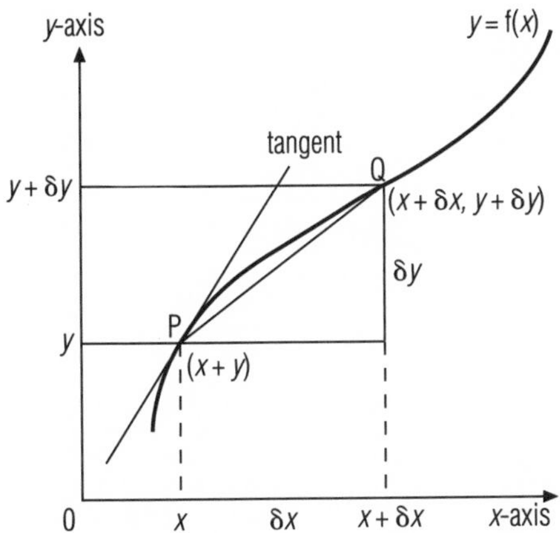

***differentiation** A mathematical procedure for determining the gradient, or slope, of the tangent to any curve f(x) at any point x. Part of a branch of mathematics called differential calculus, it is used to solve problems involving continuously varying quantities (such as the change in velocity or altitude of a rocket), to find the rates at which these variations occur and to obtain maximum and minimum values for the quantities.*

the edge of an obstruction. A **diffraction grating** is a plate of glass or metal ruled with close, equidistant parallel lines used for separating a wave train such as a beam of incident light into its component frequencies (white light results in a spectrum).

The regular spacing of atoms in crystals are used to diffract X-rays, and in this way the structure of many substances has been elucidated, including that of proteins (see ◊X-ray diffraction). Sound waves can also be diffracted by a suitable array of solid objects.

diffusion spontaneous and random movement of molecules or particles in a fluid (gas or liquid) from a region in which they are at a high concentration to a region of lower concentration, until a uniform concentration is achieved throughout. No mechanical mixing or stirring is involved. For instance, if a drop of ink is added to water, its molecules will diffuse until their colour becomes evenly distributed throughout.

In biological systems, diffusion plays an essential role in the transport, over short distances, of molecules such as nutrients, respiratory gases, and neurotransmitters. It provides the means by which small molecules pass into and out of individual cells and microorganisms, such as amoebae, that possess no circulatory system. Diffusion of water across a semi-permeable membrane is termed ◊osmosis.

One application of diffusion is the separation of isotopes, particularly those of uranium. When uranium hexafluoride diffuses through a porous plate, the ratio of the 235 and 238 isotopes is changed slightly. With sufficient number of passages, the separation is nearly complete. There are large plants in the USA and UK for obtaining enriched fuel for fast nuclear reactors and the fissile uranium-235, originally required for the first atom bombs. Another application is the diffusion pump, used extensively in vacuum work, in which the gas to be evacuated diffuses into a chamber from which it is carried away by the vapour of a suitable medium, usually oil or mercury.

Laws of diffusion were formulated by Thomas Graham in 1829 (for gases) and Adolph Fick 1829–1901 (for solutions).

digestion process whereby food eaten by an animal is broken down mechanically, and chemically by ◊enzymes, mostly in the stomach and ◊intestines, to make the nutrients available for absorption and cell metabolism.

In some single-celled organisms, such as amoebae, a food particle is engulfed by the cell and digested in a ◊vacuole within the cell.

digestive system in the body, all the organs and tissues involved in the digestion of food. In animals, these consist of the mouth, stomach, intestines, and their associated glands. The process of digestion breaks down the food by physical and chemical means into the different elements that are needed by the body for energy and tissue building and repair. Digestion begins in the mouth and is completed in the ◊stomach; from there most nutrients are absorbed into the small intestine from where they pass through the intestinal wall into the bloodstream; what remains is stored and concentrated into faeces in the large intestine. Birds have two additional digestive organs – the ◊crop and ◊gizzard. In smaller, simpler animals such as jellyfish, the digestive system is simply a cavity (coelenteron or enteric cavity) with a 'mouth' into which food is taken; the digestible portion is dissolved and absorbed in this cavity, and the remains are ejected back through the mouth.

The digestive system of humans consists primarily of the ◊alimentary canal, a tube which starts at the mouth, continues with the pharynx, oesophagus (or gullet), stomach, large and small intestines, and rectum, and ends at the anus. The food moves through this canal by ◊peristalsis whereby waves of involuntary muscular contraction and relaxation produced by the muscles in the wall of the gut cause the food to be ground and mixed with various digestive juices. Most of these juices contain digestive enzymes, chemicals that speed up reactions involved in the breakdown of food. Other digestive juices empty into the alimentary canal from the salivary glands, gall bladder, and pancreas, which are also part of the digestive system.

The fats, proteins, and carbohydrates (starches and sugars) in foods contain very complex molecules that are broken down (see ◊diet; ◊nutrition) for absorption into the bloodstream: starches and complex sugars are converted to simple sugars; fats are converted to fatty acids and glycerol; and proteins are converted to amino acids and peptides. Foods such as vitamins, minerals, and water do not need to undergo digestion prior to absorption into the bloodstream. The small intestine, which is the main site of digestion and absorption, is subdivided into the duodenum, jejunum, and ileum.

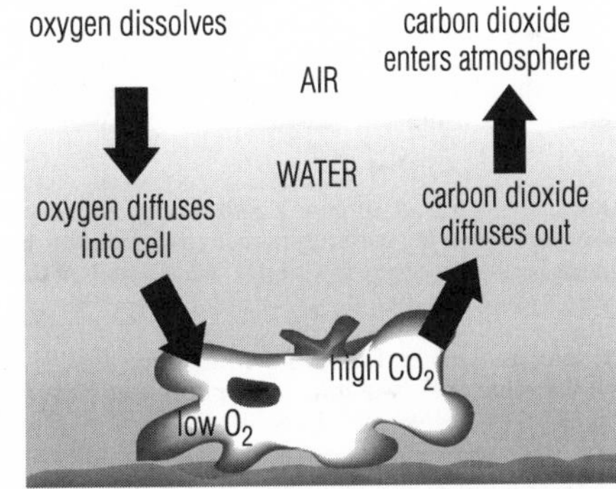

***diffusion** Diffusion is the movement of molecules from a region of high concentration into a region of lower concentration.*

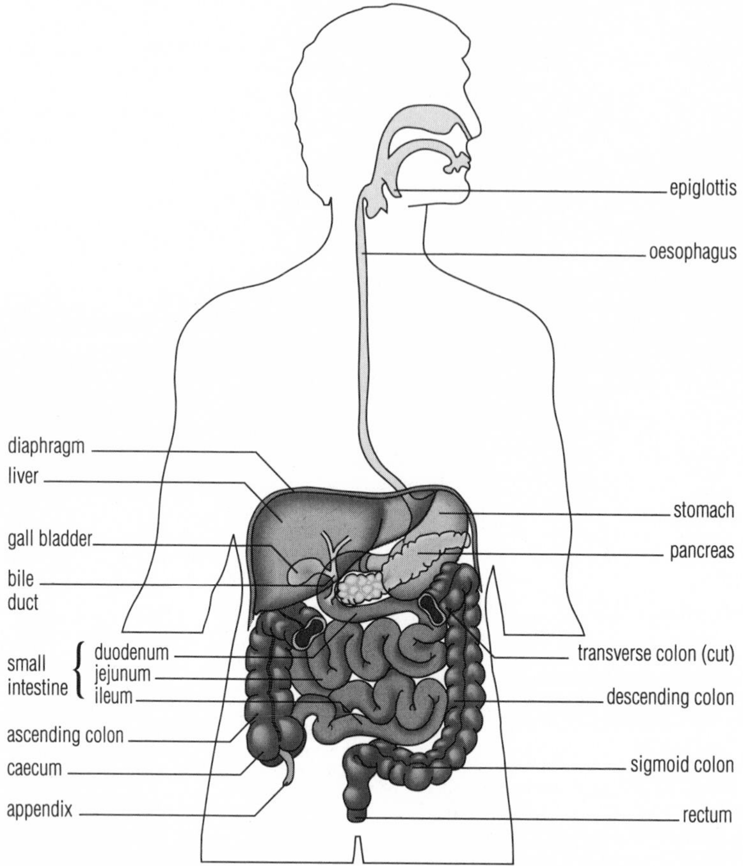

digestive system *The human digestive system. When food is swallowed, it is moved down the oesophagus by the action of muscles (peristalsis) into the stomach. Digestion starts in the stomach as the food is mixed with enzymes and strong acid. After several hours, the food passes to the small intestine. Here more enzymes are added and digestion is completed. After all nutrients have been absorbed, the indigestible parts pass into the large intestine and thence to the rectum. The liver has many functions, such as storing minerals and vitamins and making bile, which is stored in the gall bladder until needed for the digestion of fats. The pancreas supplies enzymes. The appendix appears to have no function in human beings.*

Covering the surface of its mucous membrane lining are a large number of small prominences called villi which increase the surface for absorption and allow the digested nutrients to diffuse into small blood-vessels lying immediately under the epithelium.

DigiCash in computing, one of several competing systems for electronic money suitable for use on the Internet. Invented by Belgian-based US cryptographer David Chaum, DigiCash uses ◊public-key cryptography techniques to assure anonymity. Trials of the system began in 1994 using software developed for Windows, UNIX, and the Mac.

digit in mathematics, any of the numbers from 0 to 9 in the decimal system. Different bases have different ranges of digits. For example, the ◊hexadecimal system has digits 0 to 9 and A to F, whereas the binary system has two digits (or ◊bits), 0 and 1.

digital in electronics and computing, a term meaning 'coded as numbers'. A digital system uses two-state, either on/off or high/low voltage pulses, to encode, receive, and transmit information. A **digital display** shows discrete values as numbers (as opposed to an analogue signal, such as the continuous sweep of a pointer on a dial).

Digital electronics is the technology that underlies digital techniques. Low-power, miniature, integrated circuits (chips) provide the means for the coding, storage, transmission, processing, and reconstruction of information of all kinds.

digital audio tape (DAT) digitally recorded audio tape produced in cassettes that can carry up to two hours of sound on each side and are about half the size of standard cassettes. DAT players/recorders were developed in 1987. Prerecorded cassettes are copy-protected. The first DAT for computer data was introduced in 1988.

DAT machines are constructed like video cassette recorders (though they use metal audio tape), with a movable playback head, the tape winding in a spiral around a rotating drum. The tape can also carry additional information; for example, a time code for instant location of any point on the track. The music industry delayed releasing prerecorded DAT cassettes because of fears of bootlegging, but a system has now been internationally agreed whereby it is not possible to make more than one copy of any prerecorded compact disc or DAT. DAT is mainly used in recording studios for making master tapes. The system was developed by Sony.

By 1990, DATs for computer data had been developed to a capacity of around 2.5 gigabytes per tape, achieved by using helical scan recording (in which the tape covers about 90% of the total head area of the rotating drum). This enables data from the tape to be read over 200 times faster than it can be written. Any file can be located within 60 seconds.

Digestive System: Pioneering Experiments on the Digestive System

BY JULIAN ROWE

An army marches on its stomach

On 6 June 1822 at Fort Mackinac, Michigan, USA, an 18-year-old French Canadian was accidentally wounded in the abdomen by the discharge of a musket. He was brought to the army surgeon, US physician William Beaumont (1785–1853), who noted several serious wounds and, in particular, a hole in the abdominal wall and stomach. The surgeon observed that through this hole in the patient 'was pouring out the food he had taken for breakfast'.

The patient, Alexis St Martin, a trapper by profession, was serving with the army as a porter and general servant. Not surprisingly, St Martin was at first unable to keep food in his stomach. As the wound gradually healed, firm dressings were needed to retain the stomach contents. Beaumont tended his patient assiduously and tried during the ensuing months to close the hole in his stomach, without success. After 18 months, a small, protruding fleshy fold had grown to fill the aperture (fistula). This 'valve' could be opened simply by pressing it with a finger.

Digestion ... inside and outside

At this point, it occurred to Beaumont that here was an ideal opportunity to study the process of digestion. His patient must have been an extremely tough character to have survived the accident at all. For the next nine years he was the subject of a remarkable series of pioneering experiments, in which Beaumont was able to vary systematically the conditions under which digestion took place and discover the chemical principles involved.

Beaumont attacked the problem of digestion in two ways. He studied how various substances were actually digested in the stomach, and also how they were 'digested' outside the stomach in the digestive juices he extracted from St Martin. He found it was easy enough to drain out the digestive juices from his fortuitously wounded patient 'by placing the subject on his left side, depressing the valve within the aperture, introducing a gum elastic tube and then turning him ... on introducing the tube the fluid soon began to run.'

A typical experiment

Beaumont was basically interested in the rate and temperature of digestion, and also the chemical conditions that favoured different stages of the process of digestion. He describes a typical experiment (he performed hundreds), where (a) digestion in the stomach is contrasted (b) with artificial digestion in glass containers kept at suitable temperatures, like this:

(a) 'At 9 o'clock he breakfasted on bread, sausage, and coffee, and kept exercising. 11 o'clock, 30 minutes, stomach two-thirds empty, aspects of weather similar, thermometer 298°F, temperature of stomach $101\frac{1}{28}$ and $100\frac{3}{48}$. The appearance of contraction and dilation and alternative piston motions were distinctly observed at this examination. 12 o'clock, 20 minutes, stomach empty.'

(b) 'February 7. At 8 o'clock, 30 minutes a.m. I put twenty grains of boiled codfish into three drachms of gastric juice and placed them on the bath.'

'At 1 o'clock, 30 minutes, p.m., the fish in the gastric juice on the bath was almost dissolved, four grains only remaining: fluid opaque, white, nearly the colour of milk. 2 o'clock, the fish in the vial all completely dissolved.'

All a matter of chemistry

Beaumont's research showed clearly for the first time just what happens during digestion and that digestion, as a process, can take place independently outside the body. He wrote that gastric juice: 'so far from being inert as water as some authors assert, is the most general solvent in nature of alimentary matter – even the hardest bone cannot withstand its action. It is capable, even out of the stomach, of effecting perfect digestion, with the aid of due and uniform degree of heat (100°Fahrenheit) and gentle agitation ... I am impelled by the weight of evidence ... to conclude that the change effected by it on the aliment, is purely chemical.'

Our modern understanding of the physiology of digestion as a process whereby foods are gradually broken down into their basic components follows logically from his work. An explanation of how the digestive juices flowed in the first place came in 1889, when Russian physiologist Ivan Pavlov (1849–1936) showed that their secretion in the stomach was controlled by the nervous system. By preventing the food eaten by a dog from actually entering the stomach, he found that the secretions of gastric juices began the moment the dog started eating, and continued as long as it did so. Since no food had entered the stomach, the secretions must be mediated by the nervous system.

Later, it was found that the further digestion that takes place beyond the stomach was hormonally controlled. But it was Beaumont's careful scientific work, which was published in 1833 with the title *Experiments and Observations on the Gastric Juice and Physiology of Digestion*, that triggered subsequent research in this field.

digital camera camera that uses a ◊charge-coupled device (CCD) to take pictures which are stored as digital data rather than on film. The output from digital cameras can be downloaded onto a computer for retouching or storage, and can be readily distributed as computer files. Leading manufacturers of digital cameras include Canon and Kodak.

digital city in computing, area in ◊cyberspace, either text-based or graphical, that uses the model of a city to make it easy for visitors and residents to find specific types of information.

digital compact cassette (DCC) digitally recorded audio cassette that is roughly the same size as a standard cassette. It cannot be played on a normal tape recorder, though standard tapes can be played on a DCC machine; this is known as 'backwards compatibility'. The playing time is 90 minutes.

A DCC player has a stationary playback and recording head similar to that in ordinary tape decks, though the tape used is chrome video tape. The cassettes are copy-protected and can be individually programmed for playing order. Some DCC decks have a liquid-crystal digital-display screen, which can show track titles and other information encoded on the tape.

digital composition or **compositing** in computing, computerized film editing. Some film special effects require shots to be cut together – composited. A sequence showing an actor hanging off the edge of a skyscraper, for example, may be put together out of footage of the actor in a safe location inserted into a shot looking down the side of the skyscraper, which may itself be a model. Traditional techniques for creating such a shot involved photographing the foreground shot with the background shot playing behind it, with an inevitable degradation of quality in the background material. In digital compositing, the same footage is digitized, and the work of merging the two sequences is done by manipulating computer files. The composite image is then transferred back onto film with no loss of quality.

digital computer computing device that operates on a two-state system, using symbols that are internally coded as binary numbers (numbers made up of combinations of the digits 0 and 1); see ◊computer.

digital data transmission in computing, a way of sending data by converting all signals (whether pictures, sounds, or words) into numeric (normally binary) codes before transmission, then reconverting them on receipt. This virtually eliminates any distortion or degradation of the signal during transmission, storage, or processing.

digitalis in botany, any of a group of plants belonging to the figwort family, which includes the ◊foxgloves. The leaves of the common foxglove (*Digitalis purpurea*) are the source of the drug **digitalis** used in the treatment of heart disease. (Genus *Digitalis,* family Scrophulariaceae.)

digitalis in medicine, drug that increases the efficiency of the heart by strengthening its muscle contractions and slowing its rate. It is derived from the leaves of the common European woodland plant *Digitalis purpurea* (foxglove).

It is purified to digoxin, digitoxin, and lanatoside C, which are effective in cardiac regulation but induce the side effects of nausea, vomiting, and pulse irregularities. Pioneered in the late 1700s by William Withering, an English physician and botanist, digitalis was the first cardiac drug.

digital monitor in computing, display ◊monitor using standard cathode-ray tube technology that converts a ◊digital signal from the computer into an ◊analogue signal for display.

Digital monitors are unable to display the continuously variable range of colours offered by analogue monitors.

digital recording technique whereby the pressure of sound waves is sampled more than 30,000 times a second and the values converted by computer into precise numerical values. These are recorded and, during playback, are reconverted to sound waves.

This technique gives very high-quality reproduction. The numerical values converted by computer represent the original sound-wave form exactly and are recorded on compact disc. When this is played back by ◊laser, the exact values are retrieved.

When the signal is fed via an amplifier to a loudspeaker, sound waves exactly like the original ones are reproduced.

digital retouching in computing, technique for touching up digital photographs, similar to airbrushing in the analogue world. It is commonly used in the film industry to remove scratches or to cover up filming mistakes.

The retoucher points out the error to the computer and the computer calculates new colour values for the affected ◊pixels from the colours of neighbouring pixels.

digital sampling electronic process used in ◊telecommunications for transforming a constantly varying (analogue) signal into one composed of discrete units, a digital signal. In the creation of recorded music, sampling enables the composer, producer, or remix engineer to borrow discrete vocal or instrumental parts from other recorded work (it is also possible to sample live sound).

A telephone microphone changes sound waves into an analogue signal that fluctuates up and down like a wave. In the digitizing process the waveform is sampled thousands of times a second and each part of the sampled wave is given a binary code number (made up of combinations of the digits 0 and 1) related to the height of the wave at that point, which is transmitted along the telephone line. Using digital signals, messages can be transmitted quickly, accurately, and economically.

digital signal processor (DSP) in computing, special-purpose integrated circuit that handles voice. DSPs are used in voice modems, which add answering machine facilities to a personal computer, and also in computer dictation systems.

digital signature in computing, method of using encryption to certify the source and integrity of a particular electronic document. Because all ◊ASCII characters look the same no matter who types them, methods have to be found to certify the origins of particular messages if they are to be legally binding for electronic commerce or other transactions. One type of digital signature commonly seen on the Net is generated by the program ◊Pretty Good Privacy (PGP), which adds a digest of the message to the signature.

digital-to-analogue converter electronic circuit that converts a digital signal into an ◊analogue (continuously varying) signal. Such a circuit is used to convert the digital output from a computer into the analogue voltage required to produce sound from a conventional loudspeaker.

digital versatile disc or ***digital video disc*** (DVD) disc format for storing digital information. DVDs can hold 14 times the data stored on current CDs. Pre-recorded CVDs have a storage capacity of 4.7 gigabytes and can hold a full-length feature film. As with CDs, information is etched in the form of microscopic pits onto a plastic disc (though the pits are half the size), which is then coated with aluminium. DVDs may have two pitted surfaces per side whereas CDs have only one. The data is read optically using a laser as the disc rotates. A double layer disc can hold 4 hours of video. The Japanese company TDK produced the rewriteable DVD-RAM, capable of holding 2.6 gigabytes, in 1996.

digital video interactive powerful compression system used for storing video images on computer; see ◊DVI.

digitize in computing, to turn ◊analogue signals into the binary data a computer can read. Any type of analogue signal can be digitized, including pictures, sound, video, or film. The result is files that can be manipulated, stored, or transmitted by computers.

digitizer in computing, a device that converts an analogue video signal into a digital format so that video images can be input, stored, displayed, and manipulated by a computer. The term is sometimes used to refer to a ◊graphics tablet.

dihybrid inheritance in genetics, a pattern of inheritance observed when two characteristics are studied in succeeding generations.

The first experiments of this type, as well as in ◊monohybrid inheritance, were carried out by Austrian biologist Gregor ◊Mendel using pea plants.

dik-dik any of several species of tiny antelope, genus *Madoqua,* found in Africa south of the Sahara in dry areas with scattered brush. Dik-diks are about 60 cm/2 ft long and 35 cm/1.1 ft tall, and are often seen in pairs. Males have short, pointed horns. The dik-dik is so named because of its alarm call.

dilatation and curettage (D and C) common gynaecological procedure in which the cervix (neck of the womb) is widened, or dilated, giving access so that the lining of the womb can be scraped away (curettage). It may be carried out to terminate a pregnancy, treat an incomplete miscarriage, discover the cause of heavy menstrual bleeding, or for biopsy.

dill herb belonging to the carrot family, whose bitter seeds and aromatic leaves are used in cooking and in medicine. (*Anethum graveolens,* family Umbelliferae.)

dilution process of reducing the concentration of a solution by the addition of a solvent.

The extent of a dilution normally indicates the final volume of solution required. A fivefold dilution would mean the addition of sufficient solvent to make the final volume five times the original.

dimension in science, any directly measurable physical quantity such as mass (M), length (L), and time (T), and the derived units obtainable by multiplication or division from such quantities.

For example, acceleration (the rate of change of velocity) has dimensions (LT^{-2}), and is expressed in such units as km s^{-2}. A quantity that is a ratio, such as relative density or humidity, is dimensionless.

In geometry, the dimensions of a figure are the number of measures needed to specify its size. A point is considered to have zero dimension, a line to have one dimension, a plane figure to have two, and a solid body to have three.

dimethyl sulphoxide (DMSO) $(CH_3)_2SO$ colourless liquid used as an industrial solvent and an antifreeze. It is obtained as a by-product of the processing of wood to paper.

DIN (abbreviation for ***Deutsches Institut für Normung***) German national standards body, which has set internationally accepted standards for (among other things) paper sizes and electrical connectors.

dingbat non-alphanumeric character, such as a star, bullet, or arrow. Dingbats have been combined into ◊PostScript and ◊TrueType fonts for use with word processors and graphics programs.

dingo wild dog of Australia. Descended from domestic dogs brought from Asia by Aborigines thousands of years ago, it belongs to the same species *Canis familiaris* as other domestic dogs. It is reddish brown with a bushy tail, and often hunts at night. It cannot bark.

dinitrogen oxide alternative name for ◊nitrous oxide, or 'laughing gas', one of the nitrogen oxides.

Dinorwig location of Europe's largest pumped-storage hydroelectric scheme, completed 1984, in Gwynedd, North Wales. It is used as a backup to meet heavy demands for electricity. Six turbogenerators are installed, with a maximum output of some 1,880 megawatts. The working head of water for the station is 530 m/1,740 ft.

The main machine hall is twice as long as a football field and as high as a 16-storey building.

dinosaur *Greek deinos 'terrible', sauros 'lizard'* any of a group (sometimes considered as two separate orders) of extinct reptiles living between 205 million and 65 million years ago. Their closest living relations are crocodiles and birds. Many species of dinosaur evolved during the millions of years they were the dominant large land animals. Most were large (up to 27 m/90 ft), but some were as small as chickens. They disappeared 65 million years ago for reasons not fully understood, although many theories exist.

classification Dinosaurs are divisible into two unrelated stocks, the orders **Saurischia** ('lizard-hip') and **Ornithischia** ('bird-hip'). Members of the former group possess a reptile-like pelvis and are mostly bipedal and carnivorous, although some are giant amphibious quadrupedal herbivores. Members of the latter group have a bird-like pelvis, are mainly four-legged, and entirely herbivorous.

The Saurischia are divided into: **theropods** ('beast-feet'), including all the bipedal carnivorous forms with long hindlimbs and short forelimbs (◊tyrannosaurus, megalosaurus); and **sauropodomorphs** ('lizard-feet forms'), including sauropods, the large quadrupedal herbivorous and amphibious types with massive limbs, long tails and necks, and tiny skulls (diplodocus, brontosaurus).

The Ornithischia were almost all plant-eaters, and eventually outnumbered the Saurischia. They are divided into four suborders: **ornithopods** ('bird-feet'), Jurassic and Cretaceous bipedal forms (Iguanodon) and Cretaceous hadrosaurs with duckbills; **stegosaurs** ('plated' dinosaurs), Jurassic quadrupedal dinosaurs with a double row of triangular plates along the back and spikes on the tail (stegosaurus); **ankylosaurs** ('armoured' dinosaurs), Cretaceous quadrupedal forms, heavily armoured with bony plates (nodosaurus); and **ceratopsians** ('horned' dinosaurs), Upper Cretaceous quadrupedal horned dinosaurs with very large skulls bearing a neck frill and large horns (triceratops).

These two main dinosaur orders form part of the superorder Archosaurus ('ruling reptiles'), comprising a total of five orders. The other three are **Pterosaurs** ('winged lizards'), including ◊pterodactyls, of which no examples exist today, **crocodilians**, and **birds**. All five orders are thought to have evolved from a 'stem-order', the **Thecondontia**.

species Brachiosaurus, a long-necked plant-eater of the sauropod group, was about 12.6 m/40 ft to the top of its head, and weighed 80 tonnes. Compsognathus, a meat-eater, was only the size of a chicken, and ran on its hind legs. Stegosaurus, an armoured plant-eater 6 m/20 ft long, had a brain only about 3 cm/1.25 in long. Not all dinosaurs had small brains. At the other extreme, the hunting dinosaur stenonychosaurus, 2 m/6 ft long, had a brain size comparable to that of a mammal or bird of today, stereoscopic vision, and grasping hands. Many dinosaurs appear to have been equipped for a high level of activity. ◊Tyrannosaurus was a huge, two-footed, meat-eating theropod dinosaur of the Upper Cretaceous in North America and Asia. The largest carnivorous dinosaur was *Giganotosaurus carolinii.* It lived in Patagonia about 97 million years ago, was 12.5 m/41 ft long, and weighed 6–8 tonnes. Its skeleton was discovered 1995.

theories of extinction A popular theory of dinosaur extinction suggests that the Earth was struck by a giant meteorite or a swarm of comets 65 million years ago and this sent up such a cloud of debris and dust that climates were changed and the dinosaurs could not adapt quickly enough. The evidence for this includes a bed of rock rich in ◊iridium – an element rare on Earth but common in extraterrestrial bodies – dating from the time.

An alternative theory suggests that changes in geography brought about by the movements of continents and variations in sea level led to climate changes and the mixing of populations between previously isolated regions. This resulted in increased competition and the spread of disease.

archaeological findings The term 'dinosaur' was coined 1842 by Richard Owen, although there were findings of dinosaur bones as far back as the 17th century. In 1822 G A Mantell (1790–1852) found teeth of iguanodon in a quarry in Sussex. The first dinosaur to be described in a scientific journal was in 1824, when William Buckland, professor of geology at Oxford University, published his finding of a 'megalosaurus or great fossil lizard' found at Stonesfield, a village northwest of Oxford, although a megalosaurus bone had been found in 1677.

One of the largest dinosaur species found in the UK was a Sauropod, *Cetiosaurus oxoniensis,* discovered in 1870 near Bletchingdon, north of Oxford. It was around 15 m/49 ft long, although specimens have been discovered in North Africa up to 18 m/60 ft long. In 1992 another large dinosaur, *Iguanodon bernissartensis,* was discovered near Ockley in Surrey, England, by amateur fossil hunters.

An almost complete fossil of a dinosaur skeleton was found in 1969 in the Andean foothills, South America; it had been a two-legged carnivore 2 m/6 ft tall and weighed more than 100 kg/220 lb. More than 230 million years old, it is the oldest known dinosaur. In 1982 a number of nests and eggs were found in 'colonies' in Montana, suggesting that some bred together like modern seabirds. In 1987 finds were made in China that may add much to the traditional knowledge of dinosaurs, chiefly gleaned from North American specimens. In 1989 and 1990 an articulated *Tyrannosaurus rex* was unearthed by a palaeontological team in Montana, with a full skull, one of only six known. Short stretches of dinosaur DNA were extracted in 1994 from unfossilized bone retrieved from coal deposits approximately 80 million years old.

recent discoveries The discovery of a small dinosaur was announced in China in 1996. Sinosauropteryx lived about 120 million years old and was 0.5 m/1.6 ft tall. It had short forelegs, a long tail, and short feathers, mainly on its neck and shoulders.

In 1997 US scientists claimed that 65 million-year-old remains discovered in the Atlantic Ocean were proof that a massive asteroid impact on Earth killed the dinosaurs. A sea-drilling expedition discovered three samples that have the signature of an asteroid impact. Previous evidence from sediment suggested that the dinosaurs did not become extinct at exactly the same time as an impact occurred. The new evidence appeared to substantiate the theories of geologists such as Walter Alvarez, who championed the theory that the dinosaurs disappeared from fossil history because of such an impact.

US palaeontologists discovered in 1997 a dinosaur wishbone in place in the skeleton of a velociraptor. This was the first time a wishbone had been found in place and scientists claimed that this constitutes strong evidence for birds having evolved from dinosaurs.

diode combination of a cold anode and a heated cathode, or the semiconductor equivalent, which incorporates a *p–n* junction; see ◊semiconductor diode. Either device allows the passage of direct current in one direction only, and so is commonly used in a ◊rectifier to convert alternating current (AC) to direct current (DC).

dioecious of plants with male and female flowers borne on separate individuals of the same species. Dioecism occurs, for example, in the willows *Salix.* It is a way of avoiding self-fertilization.

dioptre optical unit in which the power of a ◊lens is expressed as the reciprocal of its focal length in metres. The usual convention is that convergent lenses are positive and divergent lenses negative. Short-sighted people need lenses of power about –0.7 dioptre; a typical value for long sight is about +1.5 dioptre.

diorite igneous rock intermediate in composition between mafic (consisting primarily of dark-coloured minerals) and felsic (consisting primarily of light-coloured minerals) – the coarse-grained plutonic equivalent of ◊andesite. Constituent minerals include ◊feldspar and amphibole or pyroxene with only minor amounts of ◊quartz.

dioxin any of a family of over 200 organic chemicals, all of which are heterocyclic hydrocarbons (see ◊cyclic compounds).

The term is commonly applied, however, to only one member of the family, 2,3,7,8-tetrachlorodibenzo-*p*-dioxin (2,3,7,8-TCDD), a highly toxic chemical that occurs, for example, as an impurity in the defoliant Agent Orange, used in the Vietnam War, and sometimes in the weedkiller 2,4,5-T. It has been associated with a disfiguring skin complaint (chloracne), birth defects, miscarriages, and cancer.

Disasters involving accidental release of large amounts of dioxin into the environment have occurred at Seveso, Italy, and Times Beach, Missouri, USA. Small amounts of dioxins are released by the burning of a wide range of chlorinated materials (treated wood, exhaust fumes from fuels treated with chlorinated additives, and plastics) and as a side-effect of some techniques of paper-making. The possibility of food becoming contaminated by dioxins in the environment has led the European Community to decrease significantly the allowed levels of dioxin emissions from incinerators. Dioxin may be produced as a by-product in the manufacture of the bactericide ◊hexachlorophene.

DIP abbreviation for ◊document image processing.

diphtheria acute infectious disease in which a membrane forms in the throat (threatening death by ◊asphyxia), along with the production of a powerful toxin that damages the heart and nerves. The organism responsible is a bacterium (*Corynebacterium diphtheriae*). It is treated with antitoxin and antibiotics.

Although its incidence has been reduced greatly by immunization, an epidemic in the former Soviet Union resulted in 47,802 cases and 1,746 deaths in 1994, and 1,500 deaths in 1995. In 1995 the World Health Organization (WHO) declared the epidemic 'an international public health emergency' after 20 linked cases were identified in other parts of Europe. The epidemic showed signs of abating in 1996, with a 59% decrease in the number of cases for the first three months, compared with the same period in 1995.

diploblastic in biology, having a body wall composed of two layers. The outer layer is the **ectoderm**, the inner layer is the **endoderm**. This pattern of development is shown by ◊coelenterates.

diplodocus plant-eating sauropod dinosaur that lived about 145 million years ago, the fossils of which have been found in the western USA. Up to 27 m/88 ft long, most of which was neck and tail, it weighed about 11 tonnes. It walked on four elephantine legs, had nostrils on top of the skull, and peglike teeth at the front of the mouth.

diploid having paired ◊chromosomes in each cell. In sexually reproducing species, one set is derived from each parent, the ◊gametes, or sex cells, of each parent being ◊haploid (having only one set of chromosomes) due to ◊meiosis (reduction cell division).

diplomonad single-celled organisms with two nuclei and no mitochondria. They produce energy by anaerobic metabolism, such as glycolysis. The human intestinal parasite *Giardia lamblia* is a diplomonad.

dip, magnetic angle at a particular point on the Earth's surface between the direction of the Earth's magnetic field and the horizontal. It is measured using a **dip circle**, which has a magnetized needle suspended so that it can turn freely in the vertical plane of the magnetic field. In the northern hemisphere the needle dips below the horizontal, pointing along the line of the magnetic field towards its north pole. At the magnetic north and south poles, the needle dips vertically and the angle of dip is 90°. See also ◊angle of declination.

dipole the uneven distribution of magnetic or electrical characteristics within a molecule or substance so that it behaves as though it possesses two equal but opposite poles or charges, a finite distance apart.

The uneven distribution of electrons within a molecule composed of atoms of different ◊electronegativities may result in an apparent concentration of electrons towards one end of the molecule and a deficiency towards the other, so that it forms a dipole consisting of apparently separated but equal positive and negative charges. The product of one charge and the distance between them is the **dipole moment**. A bar magnet has a magnetic dipole and behaves as though its magnetism were concentrated in separate north and south magnetic poles.

dipole in radio, a rod aerial, usually one half-wavelength or a whole wavelength long.

dipole, magnetic see ◊magnetic dipole.

dipper or ***water ouzel*** any of various birds of the genus *Cinclus*, family Cinclidae, order Passeriformes, found in hilly and mountainous regions across Eurasia and North America, where there are clear, fast-flowing streams. It can swim, dive, or walk along the bottom, using the pressure of water on its wings and tail to keep it down, while it searches for insect larvae and other small animals. Both wings and tail are short, the beak is fairly short and straight, and the general colour of the bird is brown, the throat and part of the breast being white.

diprotodon extinct giant Australian marsupial. It was about the size of a large rhinoceros, with well developed incisor teeth and huge skull. It is the largest known marsupial and lived during the Pleistocene epoch.

DIP switch (abbreviation of ***dual in-line package***) in computing, tiny switch that controls settings on devices such as printers and modems. The owner's manual will usually specify how DIP switches should be set.

On printers, these switches are typically used to specify which emulation to use; on modems, they set the modem to match the ◊COM port to which it is connected. They should not need to be changed once the device has been installed and is working properly.

Diptera order consisting of the two-winged 'true' ◊flies. The order contains some 75,000 species arranged in approximately 100 families.

Diptera is divided into three suborders.

suborder Nematocera The adults are usually long-legged delicate flies. Their long filamentous antennae have many segments. The larvae usually have a well-defined chitinous head. The pupae are usually free and active. This suborder includes: midges, mosquitoes, gnats, and craneflies

suborder Brachycera These are more robust flies than the nematocerans, with various types of antennae, usually made up of vari-

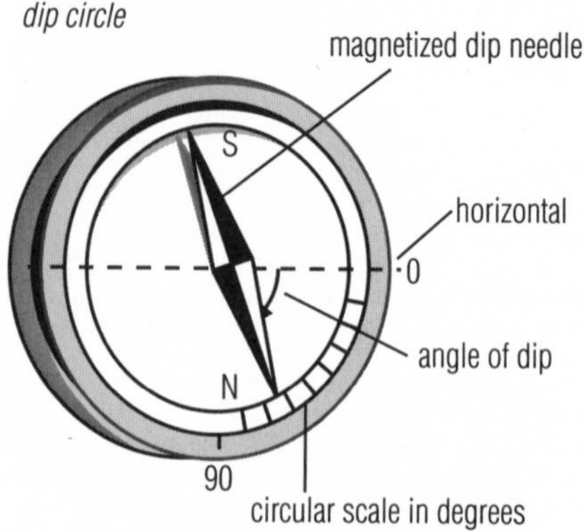

dip *A dip circle is used to measure the angle between the direction of the Earth's magnetic field and the horizontal at any point on the Earth's surface.*

ous, dissimilar segments. The larva has a less heavily chitinized head which is retractile. The pupa is usually free. This suborder includes: assassin flies, bee flies, and horse flies.

suborder Cyclorrhapha The antennae are usually of two small segments with a larger, pendulous third segment; an arista (bristle-like extension) is usually present. The palps usually consist of one segment. The larva is a maggot without a head capsule. The pupa usually has a puparium which is formed from the last-stage larval skin. This suborder includes: house flies, blowflies, botflies, tsetse flies, and fruit flies.

classification Diptera is in the subclass Pterygota, class Insecta, phylum Arthropoda.

direct access or ***random access*** type of ◊file access. A direct-access file contains records that can be accessed by the computer directly because each record has its own address on the storage disc.

direct broadcast system (DBS) in computing, combination of a small satellite dish and receiver which allows consumers to receive television and radio broadcasts from a satellite rather than via terrestrial broadcasting towers and repeaters.

direct connection in computing, connection between two computers via cable to transfer files without the intermediary of a network or online service. Each computer must be running communications software using the same protocols for file transfers. If the computers are in the same room, they can be connected using a special type of serial cable known as a null modem cable; if they are connected via telephone lines each must have a modem so that one can dial the other.

There are several software packages designed for this purpose; the market leader is Laplink.

direct current (DC) electric current that flows in one direction, and does not reverse its flow as ◊alternating current does. The electricity produced by a battery is direct current.

directed number a number with a positive (+) or negative (–) sign attached, for example +5 or –5. On a graph, a positive sign shows a movement to the right or upwards; a negative sign indicates movement downwards or to the left.

direct memory access (DMA) in computing, a technique used for transferring data to and from external devices without going through the ◊central processing unit (CPU) and thus speeding up transfer rates. DMA is used for devices such as ◊scanners.

direct memory access channel in computing, channel used for the fast transfer of data; usually abbreviated as ◊DMA channel.

Director in computing, multimedia software ◊authoring tool published by Macromedia, a company of multimedia software specialists based in San Francisco, USA.

directory in computing, a list of file names, together with information that enables a computer to retrieve those files from ◊backing storage. The computer operating system will usually store and update a directory on the backing storage to which it refers. So, for example, on each ◊disc used by a computer a directory file will be created listing the disc's contents.

directory tree in computing, collective name for a ◊directory and all its subdirectories.

dirigible another name for ◊airship.

disaccharide ◊sugar made up of two monosaccharides or simple sugars. Sucrose, $C_{12}H_{22}O_{11}$, or table sugar, is a disaccharide.

disc in astronomy, the flat, roughly circular region of a spiral or lenticular ◊galaxy containing stars, ◊nebulas, and dust clouds orbiting about the nucleus. Discs contain predominantly young stars and regions of star formation. The disc of our own Galaxy is seen from Earth as the band of the ◊Milky Way.

disc or ***disk*** in computing, a common medium for storing large volumes of data (an alternative is ◊magnetic tape). A **magnetic disc** is rotated at high speed in a disc-drive unit as a read/write (playback or record) head passes over its surfaces to record or read the magnetic variations that encode the data. Recently, **optical discs,**

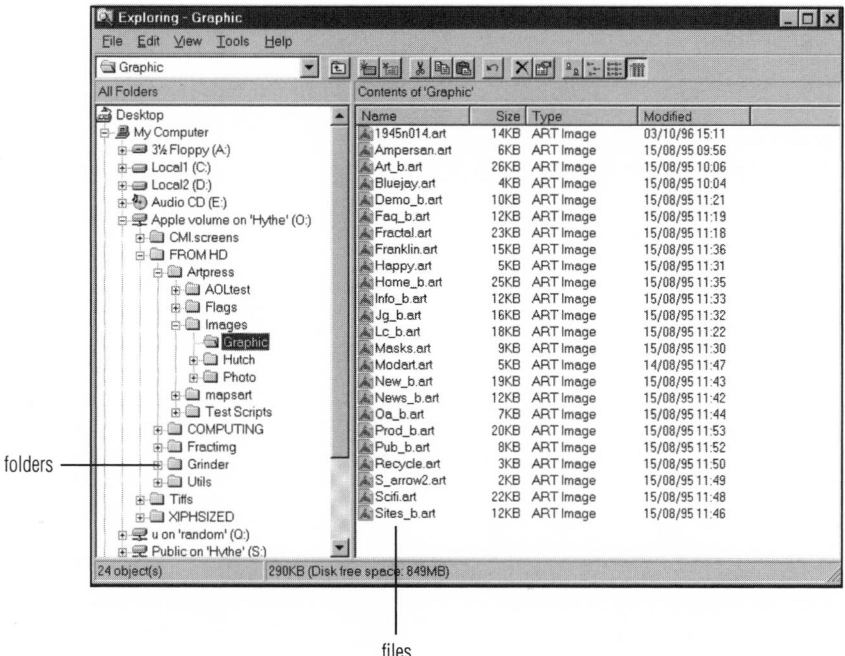

directory *A graphical illustration of the directory filing system on a computer. On the left hand side of the screen are the sub-directories available from the root; on the right are the files contained within the active directory.*

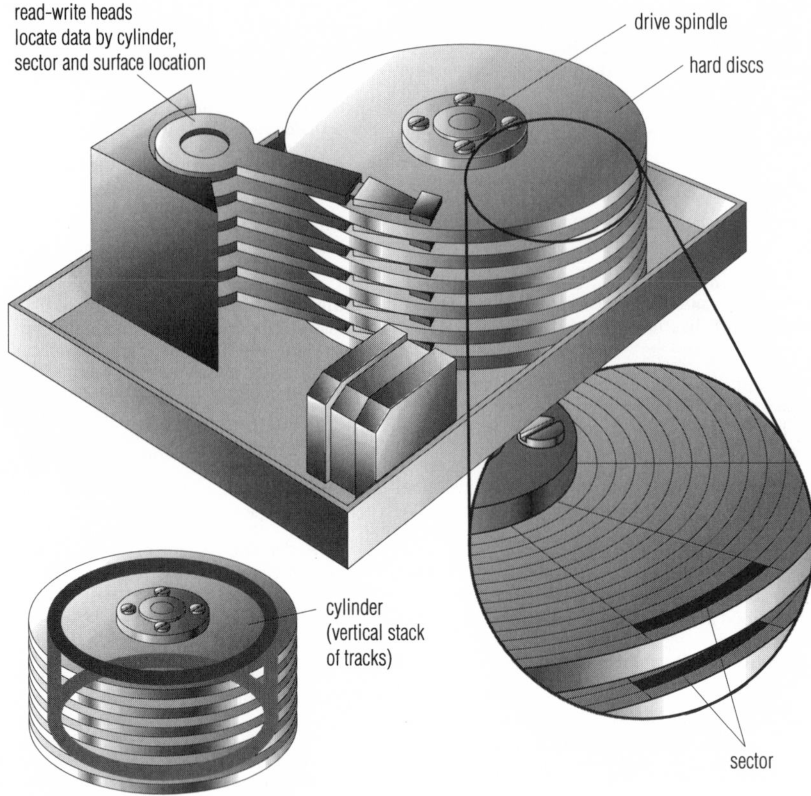

***disc** A hard disc. Data is stored in sectors within cylinders and is read by a head which passes over the spinning surface of each disc.*

such as ◊CD-ROM (compact-disc read-only memory) and ◊WORM (write once, read many times), have been used to store computer data. Data are recorded on the disc surface as etched microscopic pits and are read by a laser-scanning device. Optical discs have an enormous capacity – about 550 megabytes (million ◊bytes) on a compact disc, and thousands of megabytes on a full-size optical disc.

Magnetic discs come in several forms: **fixed hard discs** are built into the disc-drive unit, occasionally stacked on top of one another. A fixed disc cannot be removed: once it is full, data must be deleted in order to free space or a complete new disc drive must be added to the computer system in order to increase storage capacity. In 1997, small hard drives typically stored two thousand megabytes or 2 gigabytes (GB) of data, but could store up to 9 GB or more. Arrays of such discs were also used to store minicomputer and mainframe data in RAID storage systems, replacing large fixed discs and removable hard discs.

Removable hard discs are still found in minicomputer and mainframe systems. The discs are contained, individually or as stacks (disc packs), in a protective plastic case, and can be taken out of the drive unit and kept for later use. By swapping such discs around, a single hard-disc drive can be made to provide a potentially infinite storage capacity. However, access speeds and capacities tend to be lower that those associated with large fixed hard discs. A **floppy disc** (or diskette) is the most common form of backing store for microcomputers. It is much smaller in size and capacity than a hard disc, normally holding 0.5–2 megabytes of data. The floppy disc is so called because it is manufactured from thin flexible plastic coated with a magnetic material. The earliest form of floppy disc was packaged in a card case and was easily damaged; more recent versions are contained in a smaller, rigid plastic case and are much more robust. All floppy discs can be removed from the drive unit.

disc compression technique, based on ◊data compression, that makes hard discs and floppy discs appear to have more storage capacity than is normally available. If the data stored on a disc can be compressed to occupy half the original amount of disc space, it will appear that the disc is twice its original size. The processes of compression (to store data) and decompression (so that data can be used) are hidden from the user by the software.

Several commercial disc compression products are available, for example DoubleSpace in ◊MS-DOS 6.0 and Stacker.

disc drive mechanical device that reads data from, and writes data to, a magnetic ◊disc.

disc formatting in computing, preparing a blank magnetic disc in order that data can be stored on it. Data are recorded on a disc's surface on circular tracks, each of which is divided into a number of sectors. In formatting a disc, the computer's operating system adds control information such as track and sector numbers, which enables the data stored to be accessed correctly by the disc-drive unit.

Some floppy discs, called **hard-sectored discs**, are sold already formatted. However, because different makes of computer use different disc formats, discs are also sold unformatted, or **soft-sectored**, and computers are provided with the necessary ◊utility program to format these discs correctly before they are used.

discharge in a river, the volume of water passing a certain point per unit of time. It is usually expressed in cubic metres per second (cumecs). The discharge of a particular river channel may be calculated by multiplying the channel's cross-sectional area (in square metres) by the velocity of the water (in metres per second).

discharge tube device in which a gas conducting an electric current emits visible light. It is usually a glass tube from which virtually all the air has been removed (so that it 'contains' a near vacu-

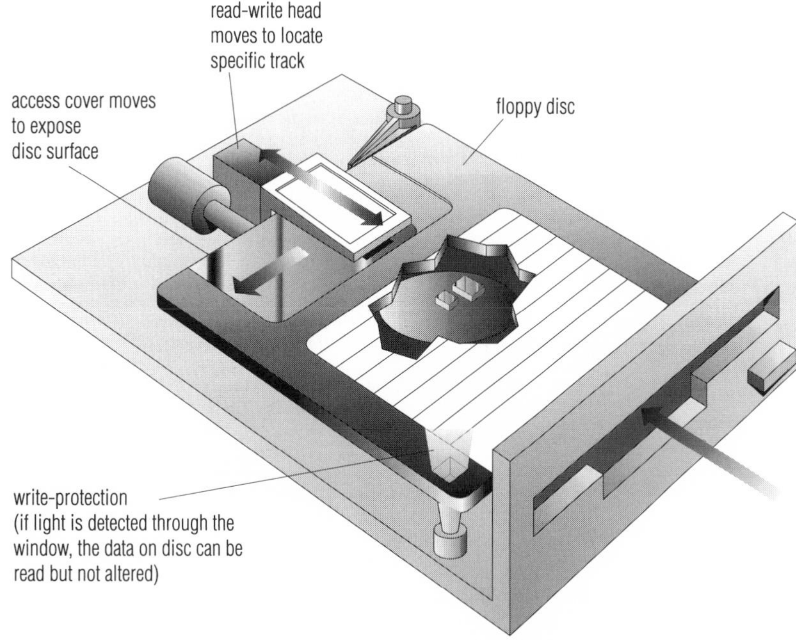

***disc drive** A floppy disc drive. As the disc is inserted into the drive, its surface is exposed to the read-write head, which moves over the spinning disc surface to locate a specific track.*

um), with electrodes at each end. When a high-voltage current is passed between the electrodes, the few remaining gas atoms in the tube (or some deliberately introduced ones) ionize and emit coloured light as they conduct the current along the tube. The light originates as electrons change energy levels in the ionized atoms.

By coating the inside of the tube with a phosphor, invisible emitted radiation (such as ultraviolet light) can produce visible light; this is the principle of the fluorescent lamp.

Discman Sony trademark for a portable compact-disc player; the equivalent of a ◊Walkman, it also comes in a model with a liquid-crystal display for data discs.

disc optimizer in computing, another name for a ◊defrag-mentation program, a program that gathers together files that have become fragmented for storage on different areas of a disc. See also ◊fragmentation.

discrete data data that can take only whole-number or fractional values. The opposite is ◊continuous data, which can take all in-between values. Examples of discrete data include frequency and population data. However, measurements of time and other dimensions can give rise to continuous data.

disease condition that disturbs or impairs the normal state of an organism. Diseases can occur in all life forms, and normally affect the functioning of cells, tissues, organs, or systems. Diseases are usually characterized by specific symptoms and signs, and can be mild and short-lasting – such as the common cold – or severe enough to decimate a whole species – such as ◊Dutch elm disease. Diseases can be classified as infectious or noninfectious. Infectious diseases are caused by microorganisms, such as bacteria and viruses, invading the body; they can be spread across a species, or transmitted between one or more species. All other diseases can be grouped together as noninfectious diseases. These can have many causes: they may be inherited (◊congenital diseases); they may be caused by the ingestion or absorption of harmful substances, such as toxins; they can result from poor nutrition or hygiene; or they may arise from injury or ageing. The causes of some diseases are still unknown.

Some diseases occur mainly in certain climates or geographical regions of the world. These are **endemic** diseases. For example, African sleeping sickness, which is carried by the tsetse fly, is found mainly in the very hot, humid regions of Africa. Similarly, malaria, a disease spread by mosquitoes, is usually found in or near the marsh or stagnant water which provide breeding grounds for the insect. Other diseases may be seasonal – such as influenza, which tends to occur mainly in winter, or intestinal illnesses that result from food contamination in summer.

Some age groups may be more prone to certain diseases, such as measles in children, meningitis in young adults, and coronary heart disease in the elderly. Other diseases may tend to occur only in certain racial types and are usually genetic in origin, such as sickle-cell disease which is found mainly among people of black African descent. Other diseases, such as black lung, or coal-workers' pneumoconiosis, result from occupational hazards; some of the 'new' diseases that have appeared in recent years – such as ◊sick building syndrome and legionnaire's disease, result from modern building designs, while the cause of ME (myalgic encephalomyelitis), or chronic fatigue syndrome, is still unknown.

CRIMEAN WAR

In the Crimean War more soldiers died from disease than in the fighting. Disease (mainly typhus, cholera, and dysentery) accounted for many the deaths of 104,494 soldiers compared with 63,261 from wounds; 662,917 were out of action through illness compared with 150,533 wounded.

disinfectant agent that kills, or prevents the growth of, bacteria and other microorganisms. Chemical disinfectants include carbolic acid (phenol, used by Joseph Lister in surgery in the 1870s), ethanol, methanol, chlorine, and iodine.

dispersal phase of reproduction during which gametes, eggs, seeds, or offspring move away from the parents into other areas. The result is that overcrowding is avoided and parents do not find themselves in competition with their own offspring. The mechanisms are various, including a reliance on wind or water currents and, in the case of animals, locomotion. The ability of a species to spread widely through an area and to colonize new habitats has survival value in evolution.

dispersion in chemistry, the distribution of the microscopic particles of a ◊colloid. In colloidal sulphur the dispersion is the tiny particles of sulphur in the aqueous system.

dispersion in physics, the separation of waves of different frequencies by passage through a dispersive medium, in which the speed of the wave depends upon its frequency or wavelength. In optics, the splitting of white light into a spectrum; for example, when it passes through a prism or diffraction grating. It occurs because the prism or grating bends each component wavelength through a slightly different angle. A rainbow is formed when sunlight is dispersed by raindrops.

dispersion in statistics, the extent to which data are spread around a central point (typically the ◊arithmetic mean).

displacement activity in animal behaviour, an action that is performed out of its normal context, while the animal is in a state of stress, frustration, or uncertainty. Birds, for example, often peck at grass when uncertain whether to attack or flee from an opponent; similarly, humans scratch their heads when nervous.

displacement reaction chemical reaction in which a less reactive element is replaced in a compound by a more reactive one.

For example, the addition of powdered zinc to a solution of copper(II) sulphate displaces copper metal, which can be detected by its characteristic colour. See also ◊electrochemical series.

display in computing, an ◊output device that looks like a television set and displays commands to the computer and their results.

display control interface in computing, standard developed by Microsoft and Intel for the ◊device drivers that control ◊graphics cards.

dissection cutting apart of bodies to study their organization, or tissues to gain access to a site in surgery. Postmortem dissection was considered a sin in the Middle Ages. In the UK before 1832, hanged murderers were the only legal source of bodies, supplemented by graverobbing (Burke and Hare were the most notorious grave robbers). The Anatomy Act of 1832 authorized the use of deceased institutionalized paupers unclaimed by next of kin, and by the 1940s bequests of bodies had been introduced.

dissociation in chemistry, the process whereby a single compound splits into two or more smaller products, which may be capable of recombining to form the reactant.

Where dissociation is incomplete (not all the compound's molecules dissociate), a ◊chemical equilibrium exists between the compound and its dissociation products. The extent of incomplete dissociation is defined by a numerical value (dissociation constant).

distance learning form of education using technology to teach pupils who are dispersed geographically. Britain's Open University, founded in 1969, is the oldest and most successful distance-learning institution in the world, using a mixture of postal mail, television, electronic conferencing, and the Internet to offer degree courses to students all over the world. Experiments in the 1990s used ◊videoconferencing and other multimedia techniques to widen the university's range.

distance modulus in astronomy, a method of finding the distance to an object in the universe, such as a star or ◊galaxy, using the difference between the actual and observed brightness of the object. The actual brightness is deduced from the object's type and its size. The apparent brightness is obtained by direct observation.

distance ratio in a machine, the distance moved by the input force, or effort, divided by the distance moved by the output force, or load. The ratio indicates the movement magnification achieved, and is equivalent to the machine's ◊velocity ratio.

distance-time graph graph used to describe the motion of a body by illustrating the relationship between the distance that it travels and the time taken. Plotting distance (on the vertical axis) against time (on the horizontal axis) produces a graph the gradient of which is the body's speed. If the gradient is constant (the graph is a straight line), the body has uniform or constant speed; if the gradient varies (the graph is curved), then so does the speed and the body may be said to be accelerating or decelerating.

distemper any of several infectious diseases of animals characterized by catarrh, cough, and general weakness. Specifically, it refers to a virus disease in young dogs, also found in wild animals, which can now be prevented by vaccination. In 1988 an allied virus killed over 10,000 common seals in the Baltic and North seas.

distillation technique used to purify liquids or to separate mixtures of liquids possessing different boiling points. **Simple distillation** is used in the purification of liquids (or the separation of substances in solution from their solvents) – for example, in the production of pure water from a salt solution.

The solution is boiled and the vapours of the solvent rise into a separate piece of apparatus (the condenser) where they are cooled and condensed. The liquid produced (the distillate) is the pure solvent; the non-volatile solutes (now in solid form) remain in the distillation vessel to be discarded as impurities or recovered as required. Mixtures of liquids (such as ◊petroleum or aqueous ethanol) are separated by **fractional distillation**, or fractionation. When the mixture is boiled, the vapours of its most volatile component rise into a vertical ◊fractionating column where they condense to liquid form. However, as this liquid runs back down the column it is reheated to boiling point by the hot rising vapours of the next-most-volatile component and so its vapours ascend the column once more. This boiling-condensing process occurs repeatedly inside the column, eventually bringing about a temperature gradient along its length. The vapours of the more volatile components therefore reach the top of the column and enter the condenser for collection before those of the less volatile components. In the fractional distillation of petroleum, groups of compounds (fractions) possessing similar relative molecular masses and boiling points are tapped off at different points on the column.

The earliest-known reference to the process is to the distillation of wine in the 12th century by Adelard of Bath. The chemical retort used for distillation was invented by Muslims, and was first seen in the West about 1570.

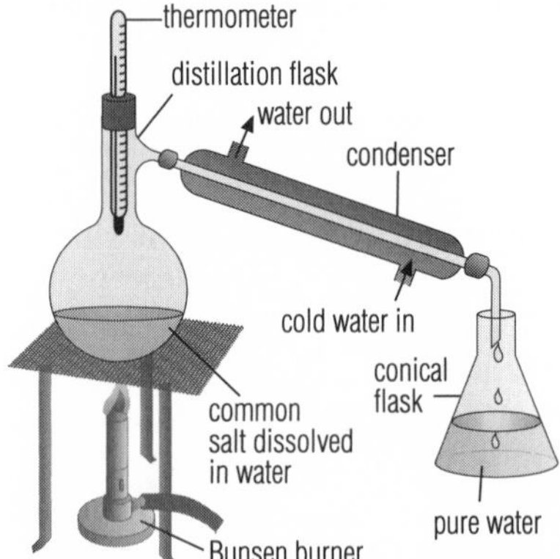

distillation Laboratory apparatus for simple distillation. Other forms of distillation include steam distillation, in which steam is passed into the mixture being distilled, and vacuum distillation, in which air is removed from above the mixture to be distilled.

distributed processing computer processing that uses more than one computer to run an application. ◊Local area networks, ◊client–server architecture, and ◊parallel processing involve distributed processing.

distribution in statistics, the pattern of ◊frequency for a set of data.

distributive operation in mathematics, an operation, such as multiplication, that bears a relationship to another operation, such as addition, such that $a \times (b + c) = (a \times b) + (a \times c)$. For example, $3 \times (2 + 4) = (3 \times 2) + (3 \times 4) = 18$. Multiplication may be said to be distributive over addition. Addition is not, however, distributive over multiplication because $3 + (2 \times 4) \rightarrow (3 + 2) \times (3 + 4)$.

distributor device in the ignition system of a piston engine that distributes pulses of high-voltage electricity to the ◊spark plugs in the cylinders. The electricity is passed to the plug leads by the tip of a rotor arm, driven by the engine camshaft, and current is fed to the rotor arm from the ignition coil. The distributor also houses the contact point or breaker, which opens and closes to interrupt the battery current to the coil, thus triggering the high-voltage pulses. With electronic ignition the distributor is absent.

dithering in computer graphics, a technique for varying the patterns of dots in an image in order to give the impression of shades of grey. Each dot, however, is of the same size and the same intensity, unlike grey scaling (where each dot can have a different shade) and photographically reproduced half-tones (where the dot size varies).

diuretic any drug that increases the output of urine by the kidneys. It may be used in the treatment of high blood pressure and to relieve ◊oedema associated with heart, lung, kidney or liver disease, and some endocrine disorders.

diver or ***loon*** any of four species of marine bird of the order Gaviiformes, specialized for swimming and diving, found in northern regions of the northern hemisphere. The legs are set so far back that walking is almost impossible, but they are powerful swimmers and good flyers, and only come ashore to nest. They have straight bills, short tail-feathers, webbed feet, and long bodies; they feed on fish, crustaceans, and some water plants. During the breeding period they live inland and the female lays two eggs which hatch into down-covered chicks. Of the four species, the largest is the white-billed diver *Gavia adamsii*, an Arctic species 75 cm/2.5 ft long.

diversification in agriculture and business, the development of distinctly new products or markets. A company or farm may diversify in order to spread its risks or because its original area of operation is becoming less profitable. In the UK agricultural diversification has included offering accommodation and services to tourists – for example, bed and breakfast, camping and caravanning sites, and pony trekking.

diverticulitis inflammation of diverticula (pockets of herniation) in the large intestine. It is usually triggered by infection and causes diarrhoea or constipation, and lower abdominal pain. Usually it can be controlled by diet and antibiotics.

diving apparatus any equipment used to enable a person to spend time underwater. Diving bells were in use in the 18th century, the diver breathing air trapped in a bell-shaped chamber. This was followed by cumbersome diving suits in the early 19th century. Complete freedom of movement came with the ◊aqualung, invented by Jacques ◊Cousteau in the early 1940s. For work at greater depths the technique of saturation diving was developed in the 1970s in which divers live for a week or more breathing a mixture of helium and oxygen at the pressure existing on the seabed where they work (as in work on North Sea platforms and tunnel building).

The first diving suit, with a large metal helmet supplied with air through a hose, was invented in the UK by the brothers John and Charles Deane in 1828. Saturation diving was developed for working in offshore oilfields. Working divers are ferried down to the work site by a lock-out ◊submersible. By this technique they avoid the need for lengthy periods of decompression after every dive. Slow decompression is necessary to avoid the dangerous consequences of an attack of the bends, or ◊decompression sickness.

division basic operation of arithmetic, the inverse of ◊multiplication.

dizziness another word for ◊vertigo.

DLL in computing, the abbreviation for ◊dynamic link library.

DMA channel (abbreviation for ***direct memory access channel***) in computing, type of channel used for the fast transfer of data between a computer and peripherals such as CD-ROM drives. Most ISA (industry standard architecture) personal computers (PCs) have eight DMA channels, of which typically six are available for use by add-on peripherals, most of which require dedicated channels.

DNA (abbreviation for ***deoxyribonucleic acid***) complex giant molecule that contains, in chemically coded form, the information needed for a cell to make proteins. DNA is a ladderlike double-stranded ◊nucleic acid which forms the basis of genetic inheritance in all organisms, except for a few viruses that have only ◊RNA. DNA is organized into ◊chromosomes and, in organisms other than bacteria, it is found only in the cell nucleus.

If you want to understand function, study structure.

FRANCIS CRICK English molecular biologist.
What Mad Pursuit 1988

DNA fingerprinting or ***DNA profiling*** another name for ◊genetic fingerprinting.

DNS in computing, abbreviation for domain ◊name server.

Dobermann or ***Dobermann pinscher*** breed of smooth-coated dog with a docked tail, much used as a guard dog. It stands up to 70 cm/27.5 in tall, has a long head with a flat, smooth skull, and is often black with brown markings. It takes its name from the man who bred it in 19th-century Germany.

dock or ***sorrel*** in botany, any of a number of plants belonging to the buckwheat family. They are tall, annual or perennial herbs, often with lance-shaped leaves and small greenish flowers. Native to temperate regions, there are 30 North American and several British species. (Genus *Rumex*, family Polygonaceae.)

dock port accommodation for commercial and naval vessels, usually simple linear quayage (wharfs or piers) adaptable to ships of any size, but with specialized equipment for handling bulk cargoes, refrigerated goods, container traffic, and oil tankers.

document in computing, data associated with a particular application. For example, a **text document** might be produced by a ◊word processor and a graphics document might be produced with a ◊CAD package. An ◊OMR or ◊OCR document is a paper document containing data that can be directly input to the computer using a ◊document reader.

documentation in computing, the written information associated with a computer program or ◊applications package. Documentation is usually divided into two categories: program documentation and user documentation.

Program documentation is the complete technical description of a program, drawn up as the software is written and intended to support any later maintenance or development of that program. It typically includes details of when, where, and by whom the software was written; a general description of the purpose of the software, including recommended input, output, and storage methods; a detailed description of the way the software functions, including full program listings and ◊flow charts; and details of software testing, including sets of ◊test data with expected results. **User documentation** explains how to operate the software. It typically includes a nontechnical explanation of the purpose of the software; instructions for loading, running, and using the software; instructions for preparing any necessary input data; instructions for requesting and interpreting output data; and explanations of any error messages that the program may produce.

document image processing (DIP) scanning documents for storage on ◊CD-ROM. The scanned images are indexed electronically,

DNA: Discovery of the Structure of DNA

BY JULIAN ROWE

The first announcement

'We wish to suggest a structure for the salt of deoxyribose nucleic acid (DNA). This structure has novel features which are of considerable biological interest.'

So began a 900-word article that was published in the journal *Nature* in April 1953. Its authors were British molecular biologist Francis Crick (1916–) and US biochemist James Watson (1928–). The article described the correct structure of DNA, a discovery that many scientists have called the most important since Austrian botanist and monk Gregor Mendel (1822–1884) laid the foundations of the science of genetics. DNA is the molecule of heredity, and by knowing its structure, scientists can see exactly how forms of life are transmitted from one generation to the next.

The problem of inheritance

The story of DNA really begins with British naturalist Charles Darwin (1809–1882). When, in November 1859, he published 'On the Origin of Species by Means of Natural Selection' outlining his theory of evolution, he was unable to explain exactly how inheritance came about. For at that time it was believed that offspring inherited an average of the features of their parents. If this were so, as Darwin's critics pointed out, any remarkable features produced in a living organism by evolutionary processes would, in the natural course of events, soon disappear.

The work of Gregor Mendel, only rediscovered 18 years after Darwin's death, provided a clear demonstration that inheritance was not a 'blending' process at all. His description of the mathematical basis to genetics followed years of careful plant-breeding experiments. He concluded that each of the features he studied, such as colour or stem length, was determined by two 'factors' of inheritance, one coming from each parent. Each egg or sperm cell contained only one factor of each pair. In this way a particular factor, say for the colour red, would be preserved through subsequent generations.

Genes

Today, we call Mendel's factors **genes**. Through the work of many scientists, it came to be realized that genes are part of the chromosomes located in the nucleus of living cells and that DNA, rather than protein as was first thought, was a hereditary material.

The double helix

In the early 1950s, scientists realized that X-ray crystallography, a method of using X-rays to obtain an exact picture of the atoms in a molecule, could be successfully applied to the large and complex molecules found in living cells.

It had been known since 1946 that genes consist of DNA. At King's College, London, New Zealand–British biophysicist Maurice Wilkins (1916–) had been using X-ray crystallography to examine the structure of DNA, together with his colleague, British X-ray crystallographer Rosalind Franklin (1920–1958), and had made considerable progress.

While in Copenhagen, US scientist James Watson had realized that one of the major unresolved problems of biology was the precise structure of DNA. In 1952, he came as a young postdoctoral student to join the Medical Research Council Unit at the Cavendish Laboratory, Cambridge, where Francis Crick was already working. Convinced that a gene must be some kind of molecule, the two scientists set to work on DNA.

Helped by the work of Wilkins, they were able to build an accurate model of DNA. They showed that DNA had a double helical structure, rather like a spiral staircase. Because the molecule of DNA was made from two strands, they envisaged that as a cell divides, the strands unravel, and each could serve as a template as new DNA was formed in the resulting daughter cells. Their model also explained how genetic information might be coded in the sequence of the simpler molecules of which DNA is comprised. Here for the first time was a complete insight into the basis of heredity. James Watson commented that this result was 'too pretty not to be true!'

Cracking the code

Later, working with South African–British molecular biologist Sidney Brenner (1927–), Crick went on to work out the genetic code, and so ascribe a precise function to each specific region of the molecule of DNA. These triumphant results created a tremendous flurry of scientific activity around the world. The pioneering work of Crick, Wilkins, and Watson was recognized in the award of the Nobel Prize for Physiology or Medicine in 1962.

The unravelling of the structure of DNA lead to a new scientific discipline, molecular biology, and laid the foundation stones for genetic engineering – a powerful new technique that is revolutionizing biology, medicine, and food production through the purposeful adaptation of living organisms.

---

which provides much faster access than is possible with either paper or ◊microform. See also ◊optical character recognition.

document reader in computing, an input device that reads marks or characters, usually on preprepared forms and documents. Such devices are used to capture data by ◊optical mark recognition (OMR), ◊optical character recognition (OCR), and ◊mark sensing.

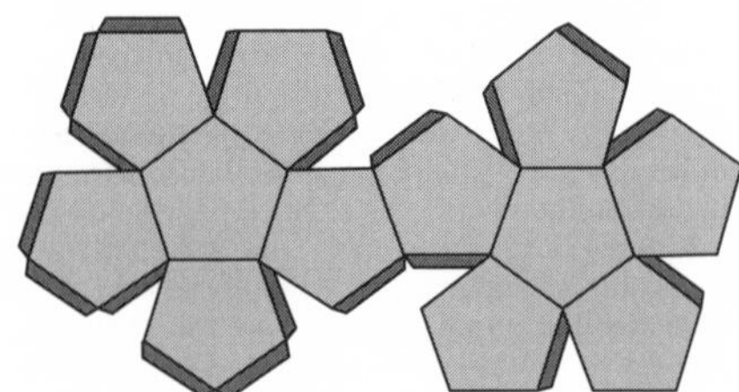

dodecahedron *A dodecahedron is a solid figure which has 12 pentagonal faces and 12 vertices. It is one of the five regular polyhedra (with all faces the same size and shape).*

dodder parasitic plant belonging to the morning-glory family, without leaves or roots. The thin stem twines around the host plant, and penetrating suckers withdraw nourishment. (Genus *Cuscuta,* family Convolvulaceae.)

dodecahedron regular solid with 12 pentagonal faces and 12 vertices. It is one of the five regular ◊polyhedra, or Platonic solids.

dodo extinct flightless bird *Raphus cucullatus,* order Columbiformes, formerly found on the island of Mauritius, but

DODO

Most pictures of the dodo show a bird with two right legs. This is because the only person to paint a live dodo, the Belgian artist Roelandt Savery, made an elementary error in drawing the parts that he could not see.

exterminated by early settlers around 1681. Although related to the pigeons, it was larger than a turkey, with a bulky body, rudimentary wings, and short curly tail-feathers. The bill was blackish in colour, forming a horny hook at the end.

dog any carnivorous mammal of the family Canidae, including wild dogs, wolves, jackals, coyotes, and foxes. Specifically, the domestic dog *Canis familiaris,* the earliest animal descended from the wolf. Dogs were first domesticated around 14,000 years ago, and migrated with humans to all the continents. They have been selectively bred into many different varieties for use as working animals and pets.

characteristics The dog has slender legs and walks on its toes (**digitigrade**). The forefeet have five toes, the hind feet four, with non-retractile claws. The head is small and the muzzle pointed, but the shape of the head differs greatly in various breeds. The average life of a dog is from 10 to 14 years, though some live to be 20. The dog has a very acute sense of smell and can readily be trained, for it has a good intelligence.

wild dogs Of the wild dogs, some are solitary, such as the long-legged maned wolf *Chrysocyon brachurus* of South America, but others hunt in groups, such as the African hunting dog *Lycaonpictus* (classified as a vulnerable species) and the ◊wolf. ◊Jackals scavenge for food, and the raccoon dog *Nyctereutes procyonoides* of east Asia includes plant food as well as meat in its diet. The Australian wild dog is the ◊dingo.

DOG LOVERS' PAGE

`http://www.petnet.com.au/dogs/dogbreedindex.html`

Information on breeds, ranging from the world's smallest breed (the Chihuahua) to the tallest (the Irish Wolfhound). This Australian-based site includes photographs and details of over 100 breeds of dog.

dog in computing, reference to a cartoon published in *The New Yorker* that showed a dog poised over a computer keyboard remarking to another dog, 'On the Internet, no one knows you're a dog.' It is used to illustrate the point that the Internet gives users the opportunity to adopt a different persona, for example many women surf using a male identity.

dogbane any sometimes poisonous herbaceous North American plant of the genus *Apocynum,* with opposite leaves, small white or pink flowers, and milky juice.

dogfish any of several small sharks found in the northeast Atlantic, Pacific, and Mediterranean.

dog's mercury plant belonging to the spurge family, common in woods of Europe and southwest Asia. It grows to 30 cm/1 ft, has oval, light-green leaves, and spreads over woodland floors in patches of plants of a single sex. Male flowers are small, greenish yellow, and held on an upright spike above the leaves; female flowers droop below the upper leaves. (*Mercurialis perennis,* family Euphorbiaceae.)

dogwhelk marine mollusc, some of which live on rocky shores whilst others burrow. The shell aperture is grooved to house the inhalant siphon keeping it clear of the mud.

The **common dogwhelk** *Thais lapillus* is a predator of barnacles and mussels and the coloured bands in the shell are believed to be influenced by the food material. The egg capsules are attached singly in crevices and have the appearance of corn grains.

The **netted dogwhelk** *Nassarius reticulatus* is recognizable by the crenulations on the shell. The egg capsules are flat and are deposited in eel-grass. Like the closely related thick-lipped dogwhelk *N. incrassatus,* it is a scavenger.

classifiation Dogwhelks are in order Neogastropoda, subclass Prosobranchia, class Gastropoda, phylum Mollusca.

dogwood any of a group of trees and shrubs belonging to the dogwood family, native to temperate regions of North America, Europe, and Asia. The flowering dogwood (*Cornus florida*) of the eastern USA is often cultivated as an ornamental for its beautiful blooms consisting of clusters of small greenish flowers surrounded by four large white or pink petal-like bracts (specialized leaves). (Genus *Cornus,* family Cornaceae.)

Heads of small white flowers, each with four petals joined as a tube, are produced in midsummer, followed by black berries. The dogwood is characteristic of lime soils in southern England, and is found over much of southern Europe. *C. sanguinea* is native to Britain and common in old hedgerows and woods. It takes its name from the redness of the twigs. The introduced red-osier dogwood (*C. sericea*) has longer twigs of a brighter red, with white berries rather than black. Various other species of dogwood are planted in gardens.

Dolby system electronic circuit that reduces the background high-frequency noise, or hiss, during replay of magnetic tape recordings. The system was developed by US engineer Raymond Dolby (1933–) in 1966.

doldrums area of low atmospheric pressure along the Equator, in the intertropical convergence zone where the northeast and southeast trade winds converge. The doldrums are characterized by calm or very light winds, during which there may be sudden squalls and stormy weather. For this reason the areas are avoided as far as possible by sailing ships.

dolerite igneous rock formed below the Earth's surface, a form of basalt, containing relatively little silica (mafic in composition).

Dolerite is a medium-grained (hypabyssal) basalt and forms in shallow intrusions, such as dykes, which cut across the rock strata, and sills, which push between beds of sedimentary rock. When exposed at the surface, dolerite weathers into spherical lumps.

dolmen prehistoric ◊megalith in the form of a chamber built of three or more large upright stone slabs, capped by a horizontal flat stone. Dolmens are the burial chambers of Neolithic (New Stone Age) chambered tombs and passage graves, revealed by the removal of the covering burial mound. They are found in Europe and Africa, and occasionally in Asia as far east as Japan.

dolomite in mineralogy, white mineral with a rhombohedral structure, calcium magnesium carbonate ($CaMg(CO_3)_2$). Dolomites are common in geological successions of all ages and are often formed when ◊limestone is changed by the replacement of the mineral calcite with the mineral dolomite.

dolphin any of various highly intelligent aquatic mammals of the family Delphinidae, which also includes porpoises. There are about 60 species. Most inhabit tropical and temperate oceans, but there are some freshwater forms in rivers in Asia, Africa, and South America. The name 'dolphin' is generally applied to species having a beaklike snout and slender body, whereas the name 'porpoise' is reserved for the smaller species with a blunt snout and stocky body. Dolphins use sound (◊echolocation) to navigate, to find prey, and for communication. The common dolphin *Delphinus delphis* is found in all temperate and tropical seas. It is up to 2.5 m/8 ft long, and is dark above and white below, with bands of grey, white, and yellow on the sides. It has up to 100 teeth in its jaws, which make the 15 cm/6 in 'beak' protrude forward from the rounded head. The corners of its mouth are permanently upturned, giving the appearance of a smile, though dolphins cannot actually smile. Dolphins feed on fish and squid.

river dolphins There are five species of river dolphin, two South American and three Asian, all of which are endangered. The two South American species are the **Amazon river dolphin** or **boto** *Inia geoffrensis,* the largest river dolphin (length 2.7 m/8.9 ft, weight 180 kg/396 lb) and the **La Plata river dolphin** *Pontoporia blainvillei* (length 1.8 m/5.9 ft, weight 50 kg/110 lb). The **tucuxi** *Sotalia fluviatilis* is not a true river dolphin, but lives in the Amazon and Orinoco rivers, as well as in coastal waters.

The Asian species are the **Ganges river dolphin** *Platanista gangetica,* the **Indus river dolphin** *Platanista minor* (length 2 m/6.6 ft, weight 70 kg/154 lb) (fewer than 500 remaining), and the

Yangtze river dolphin or ***baiji Lipotes vexillifer*** (length 2 m/6.6 ft, weight 70 kg/154 lb) (fewer than 100 remaining).

As a result of living in muddy water, river dolphins' eyes have become very small. They rely on echolocation to navigate and find food. Some species of dolphin can swim at up to 56 kph/35 mph, helped by special streamlining modifications of the skin.

All dolphins power themselves by beating the tail up and down, and use the flippers to steer and stabilize. The flippers betray dolphins' land-mammal ancestry with their typical five-toed limb-bone structure. Dolphins have great learning ability and are popular performers in aquariums. The species most frequently seen is the bottle-nosed dolphin *Tursiops truncatus,* found in all warm seas, mainly grey in colour and growing to a maximum 4.2 m/14 ft. The US Navy began training dolphins for military purposes in 1962, and in 1987 six dolphins were sent to detect mines in the Persian Gulf. Marine dolphins are endangered by fishing nets, speedboats, and pollution. In 1990 the North Sea states agreed to introduce legislation to protect them.

Also known as **dolphin** is the totally unrelated true fish *Coryphaena hippurus,* up to 1.5 m/5 ft long.

dolphinfish carnivorous marine fish. Dolphinfish are large and brilliantly coloured, with hues of metallic yellow, blue, and silver; their bodies are elongated, compressed, and covered with small scales. They are usually about 2 m/6.6 ft in length and feed largely on flying fish.

classification Dolphinfish are in the genus *Coryphaena,* family Corphaenidae, belonging to the order Perciformes, class Osteichthyes.

domain on the Internet, segment of an address that specifies an organization, its type, or its country of origin. Domain names are read backwards, starting at the end. All countries except the USA use a final two-letter code such as **ca** for Canada and **uk** for the UK. US addresses end in one of seven 'top-level' domains, which specify the type of organization: **com** (commercial), **mil** (military), **org** (usually a nonprofit-making organization), and so on.

These names are for humans; to enable mail and other messages to be sorted by machine, computers use IP (Internet protocol) numbers. To route a message, the computer looks up the domain name on a domain name server (DNS), which tells the computer the number.

In 1998 there were 30 million domains on the Internet.

domain small area in a magnetic material that behaves like a tiny magnet. The magnetism of the material is due to the movement of electrons in the atoms of the domain. In an unmagnetized sample of material, the domains point in random directions, or form closed loops, so that there is no overall magnetization of the sample. In a magnetized sample, the domains are aligned so that their magnetic effects combine to produce a strong overall magnetism.

domain name server in computing, see ◊name server.

dominance in genetics, the masking of one allele (an alternative form of a gene) by another allele. For example, if a ◊heterozygous person has one allele for blue eyes and one for brown eyes, his or her eye colour will be brown. The allele for blue eyes is described as ◊recessive and the allele for brown eyes as dominant.

The preservation of favourable variations and the rejection of injurious variations, I call Natural Selection, or Survival of the Fittest. Variations neither useful nor injurious would not be affected by natural selection and would be left a fluctuating element.

CHARLES DARWIN British naturalist.
On the Origin of Species 1859

Dominion Astrophysical Observatory Canadian observatory near Victoria, British Columbia, the site of a 1.85-m/73-in reflector opened in 1918, operated by the National Research Council of Canada. The associated Dominion Radio Astrophysical Observatory at Penticton, British Columbia, operates a 26-m/84-ft radio dish and an aperture synthesis radio telescope.

dongle in computing, a device that ensures the legal use of an application program. It is usually attached to the printer port of the computer (between the port and the printer cable) and the program will not run in its absence.

donkey another name for ◊ass.

Doom popular computer game released in 1994. It is one of a series of games from the Texas-based company id Software, which specializes in 3-D graphics, alien monsters, and complex mazes which players must navigate to find secret treasures and hidden keys along the way. *Doom* can be played competitively over a network as well as on a single computer.

Because the company has encouraged players to create their own additional levels for *Doom* (and its other games) by releasing the necessary source code, a whole culture has grown up around *Doom* and id's other games.

dopamine neurotransmitter, hydroxytyramine $C_8H_{11}NO_2$, an intermediate in the formation of adrenaline. There are special nerve cells (neurons) in the brain that use dopamine for the transmission of nervous impulses. One such area of dopamine neurons lies in the basal ganglia, a region that controls movement. Patients suffering from the tremors of Parkinson's disease show nerve degeneration in this region. Another dopamine area lies in the limbic system, a region closely involved with emotional responses. It has been found that schizophrenic patients respond well to drugs that limit dopamine excess in this area.

Doppler, Christian Johann
(1803–1853)

Austrian physicist who in 1842 described the **Doppler effect** and derived the observed frequency mathematically in Doppler's principle.

Doppler effect change in the observed frequency (or wavelength) of waves due to relative motion between the wave source and the observer. The Doppler effect is responsible for the perceived change in pitch of a siren as it approaches and then recedes, and for the ◊red shift of light from distant galaxies. It is named after the Austrian physicist Christian Doppler.

Dorado constellation of the southern hemisphere, represented as a goldfish. It is easy to locate, since the Large ◊Magellanic Cloud marks its southern border. Its brightest star is Alpha Doradus, just under 200 light years from Earth.

One of the most conspicuous objects in the Large Magellanic Cloud is the 'Great Looped Nebula' that surrounds 30 Doradus.

dor beetle oval-shaped, stout beetle measuring on average 20 mm/0.8 in, and with a metallic sheen. In general, dor beetles feed on dung, mostly of herbivorous animals.

They usually build burrows almost 50 cm/19.5 in deep under an accumulation of dung. The blind end of each burrow is sealed with a portion of dung into which the female deposits a single egg. The developing larva feeds on the dung. Both adults and larvae possess stridulating (sound-producing) organs.

classification Dor beetles are in the family Geotrupidae (superorder Scarabaeoidea), order Coleoptera, class Insecta, phylum Arthropoda.

dormancy in botany, a phase of reduced physiological activity exhibited by certain buds, seeds, and spores. Dormancy can help a plant to survive unfavourable conditions, as in annual plants that pass the cold winter season as dormant seeds, and plants that form dormant buds.

For various reasons many seeds exhibit a period of dormancy even when conditions are favourable for growth. Sometimes this

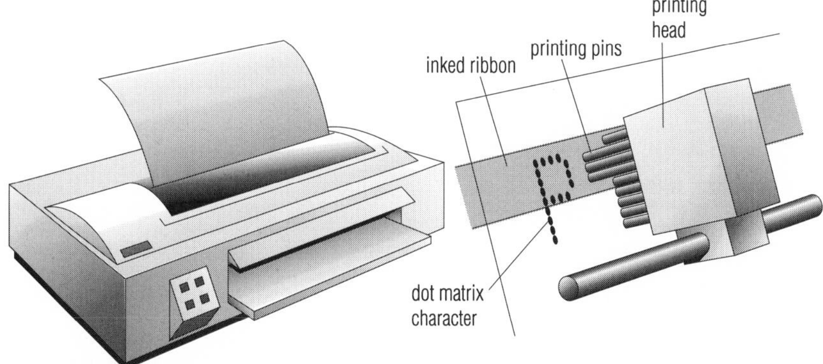

dot matrix printer *Characters and graphics printed by a dot matrix printer are produced by a block of pins which strike the ribbon and make up a pattern using many small dots.*

dormancy can be broken by artificial methods, such as penetrating the seed coat to facilitate the uptake of water (chitting) or exposing the seed to light. Other seeds require a period of ◊after-ripening.

dormouse small rodent, of the family Gliridae, with a hairy tail. There are about ten species, living in Europe, Asia, and Africa. They are arboreal (live in trees) and nocturnal, hibernating during winter in cold regions. They eat berries, nuts, pollen, and insects.

dorsal in vertebrates, the surface of the animal closest to the backbone. For most vertebrates and invertebrates this is the upper surface, or the surface furthest from the ground. For bipedal primates such as humans, where the dorsal surface faces backwards, then the word is 'back'.

Not all animals can be said to have a dorsal surface, just as many animals cannot be said to have a front; for example, jellyfish, anemones, and sponges do not have a dorsal surface.

dory marine fish *Zeus faber* found in the Mediterranean and Atlantic. It grows up to 60 cm/2 ft, and has nine or ten long spines at the front of the dorsal fin, and four at the front of the anal fin. It is considered to be an excellent food fish and is also known as **John Dory**.

The dory is olive brown or grey, with a conspicuous black spot ringed with yellow on each side. A stalking predator, it shoots out its mobile jaws to catch fish.

DOS (acronym for ***disc operating system***) computer ◊operating system specifically designed for use with disc storage; also used as an alternative name for a particular operating system, ◊MS-DOS.

dot in computing, full stop that separates ◊IP addresses, sections of ◊domain names, and the hierarchies in ◊newsgroup names, as well as file names and their extensions.

dot matrix printer computer printer that produces each character individually by printing a pattern, or matrix, of very small dots. The printing head consists of a vertical line or block of either 9 or 24 printing pins. As the printing head is moved from side to side across the paper, the pins are pushed forwards selectively to strike an inked ribbon and build up the dot pattern for each character on the paper beneath.

A dot matrix printer is more flexible than a ◊daisywheel printer because it can print graphics and text in many different typefaces. It is cheaper to buy and maintain than a ◊laser printer or ◊ink-jet printer, and, because its pins physically strike the paper, is capable of producing carbon copies. However, it is noisy in operation and cannot produce the high-quality printing associated with the non-impact printers.

dot pitch in computing, distance between the dots which make up the picture on a computer monitor. The smaller the dot pitch, the better and finer-grained the picture.

dotterel bird *Eudromias morinellus* of the plover family, in order Charadriiformes, nesting on high moors and tundra in Europe and Asia, and migrating south for the winter. About 23 cm/9 in long, its plumage is patterned with black, brown, and white in summer, duller in winter, but always with white eyebrows and breastband. The female is larger than the male, and mates up to five times with different partners, each time laying her eggs and leaving them in the sole care of the male, who incubates and rears the brood. Three pale-green eggs with brown markings are laid in hollows in the ground.

double bond two covalent bonds between adjacent atoms, as in the ◊alkenes (–C=C–) and ◊ketones (–C=O–).

double click in computing, to click (press and release a ◊mouse button) twice in quick succession. Double clicking on an ◊icon shown on a ◊graphical user interface (GUI) is used to start an application. In most GUIs it is possible to set the maximum time interval between the two clicks.

double coconut treelike ◊palm plant, also known as **coco de mer**, of the Seychelles. It produces a two-lobed edible nut, one of the largest known fruits. (*Lodoicea maldivica.*)

double decomposition reaction between two chemical substances (usually ◊salts in solution) that results in the exchange of a constituent from each compound to create two different compounds.

For example, if silver nitrate solution is added to a solution of sodium chloride, there is an exchange of ions yielding sodium nitrate and silver chloride.

double precision in computing, a type of floating-point notation that has higher precision, that is, more significant decimal places. The term 'double' is not strictly correct, deriving from such numbers using twice as many ◊bits as standard floating-point notation.

double star two stars that appear close together. Many stars that appear single to the naked eye appear double when viewed through a telescope. Some double stars attract each other due to gravity, and orbit each other, forming a genuine ◊binary star, but other double stars are at different distances from Earth, and lie in the same line of sight only by chance. Through a telescope both types look the same.

Double stars of the second kind, which are of little astronomical interest, are referred to as 'optical pairs'; those of the first as 'physical pairs' or, more usually, 'visual binaries'. They are the principal source from which is derived our knowledge of stellar masses.

dough mixture consisting primarily of flour, water, and yeast, which is used in the manufacture of bread.

The preparation of dough involves thorough mixing (kneading) and standing in a warm place to 'prove' (increase in volume) so that the ◊enzymes in the dough can break down the starch from the flour into smaller sugar molecules, which are then fermented by the yeast. This releases carbon dioxide, which causes the dough to rise.

Douglas fir any of some six species of coniferous evergreen tree belonging to the pine family. The most common is *Pseudotsuga menziesii*, native to western North America and east Asia. It grows up to 60–90 m/200–300 ft in height, has long, flat, spirally-arranged needles and hanging cones, and produces hard, strong timber. *P. glauca* has shorter, bluish needles and grows to 30 m/100 ft in mountainous areas. (Genus *Pseudotsuga*, family Pinaceae.)

douroucouli or ***night monkey*** or ***owl monkey*** nocturnal South American monkey. Its eyes are very large and its thick coat is a grey brown. Douroucoulis sleep in tree holes or thick vegetation and feed mainly on fruit and leaves, and some insects. They are the only nocturnal monkeys.

Unlike most South American monkeys, their long tails are not prehensile. The incisors in the lower jaw project forwards and they have a total of 36 teeth.

classification Douroucoulis are in the genus *Aotus* in the family Cebidae, order Primates.

dove another name for ◊pigeon.

Down's syndrome condition caused by a chromosomal abnormality (the presence of an extra copy of chromosome 21), which in humans produces mental retardation; a flattened face; coarse, straight hair; and a fold of skin at the inner edge of the eye (hence the former name 'mongolism'). The condition can be detected by prenatal testing.

Those afflicted are usually born to mothers over 40 (one in 100), and in 1995 French researchers discovered a link between Down's syndrome incidence and paternal age, with men over 40 having an increased likelihood of fathering a Down's syndrome baby.

The syndrome is named after J L H Down (1828–1896), an English physician who studied it. All people with Down's syndrome who live long enough eventually develop early-onset ◊Alzheimer's disease, a form of dementia. This fact led to the discovery in 1991 that some forms of early-onset Alzheimer's disease are caused by a gene defect on chromosome 21.

DOWN'S SYNDROME WEB PAGE

http://www.nas.com/downsyn/

Well-organized source of information about the syndrome – with articles, essays, lists of organizations worldwide, toy catalogues, the 'Brag Book' photo gallery, and links to other helpful Web sites.

downtime in computing, time when a computer system is unavailable for use, due to maintenance or a system crash. Some downtime is inevitable on almost all systems.

dowsing ascertaining the presence of water or minerals beneath the ground with a forked twig or a pendulum. Unconscious muscular action by the dowser is thought to move the twig, usually held with one fork in each hand, possibly in response to a local change in the pattern of electrical forces. The ability has been known since at least the 16th century and, though not widely recognized by science, it has been used commercially and in archaeology.

INTRODUCTION TO DOWSING

http://home.interstat.net/~slawcio/dowsing.html

American Association of Dowsers site that includes all the information you might need to make some dowsing rods and how to use them.

dpi abbreviation for ***dots per inch***, measure of the ◊resolution of images produced by computer screens and printers.

Draco in astronomy, a large but faint constellation represented as a dragon coiled around the north celestial pole. Due to ◊precession the star Alpha Draconis (Thuban) was the pole star 4,800 years ago.

This star seems to have faded, for it is no longer the brightest star in the constellation as it was at the beginning of the 17th century. Gamma Draconis is more than a magnitude brighter. It was extensively observed by James Bradley, who from its apparent changes in position discovered the ◊aberration of starlight and ◊nutation.

drag resistance to motion a body experiences when passing through a fluid – gas or liquid. The aerodynamic drag aircraft experience when travelling through the air represents a great waste of power, so they must be carefully shaped, or streamlined, to reduce drag to a minimum. Cars benefit from ◊streamlining, and aerodynamic drag is used to slow down spacecraft returning from space. Boats travelling through water experience hydrodynamic drag on their hulls, and the fastest vessels are ◊hydrofoils, whose hulls lift out of the water while cruising.

drag and drop in computing, in ◊graphical user interfaces, feature that allows users to select a file name or icon using a mouse and move it to the name or icon representing a program so that the computer runs the program using that file as input data.

This method is convenient for computer users, as it eliminates unnecessary typing. Moving the name of a text file, for example, to a copy of a word processor will start up the word processor with that file loaded and ready for editing.

dragon name popularly given to various sorts of lizard. These include the ◊flying dragon *Draco volans* of southeast Asia; the komodo dragon *Varanus komodoensis* of Indonesia, at over 3 m/10 ft the largest living lizard; and some Australian lizards with bizarre spines or frills.

dragonet small, spiny-rayed fish that lives in temperate and tropical seas. The males are larger and brightly coloured with filamentlike rays extending from the first dorsal fin. Females are dull in colour. Dragonets have smooth bodies without scales.

The gill openings are reduced to a single small hole near the nape of the neck and the ventral fins are under the throat. The **sculpin** *Callionymus draco* is about 30 cm/12 in long, and is brown and white in colour; the common dragonet *C. lyra* is yellow, sapphire, and violet in hue.

classification Dragonets are in the genus *Callionymus*, order Perciformes, class Osteichthyes.

dragonfly any of numerous insects of the order Odonata, including the ◊damselfly. They all have long narrow bodies, two pairs of almost equal-sized, glassy wings with a network of veins; short, bristlelike antennae; powerful, 'toothed' mouthparts; and very large compound eyes which may have up to 30,000 facets. They can fly at speeds of up to 64–96 kph/40–60 mph.

Dragonflies hunt other insects by sight, both as adults and as aquatic nymphs. The largest species have a wingspan of 18 cm/7 in, but fossils related to dragonflies have been found with wings of up to 70 cm/2.3 ft across.

DRAM (acronym for ***dynamic random-access memory***) computer memory device in the form of a silicon chip commonly used to provide the ◊immediate-access memory of microcomputers. DRAM loses its contents unless they are read and rewritten every 2 milliseconds or so. This process is called **refreshing** the memory. DRAM is slower but cheaper than ◊SRAM, an alternative form of silicon-chip memory.

drawing program in computing, software that allows a user to draw freehand and create complex graphics. Additional features may include special ◊fonts, ◊clip art, or painting facilities that allow a user to simulate on the computer the drawing characteristics of specific real-world implements such as charcoal, watercolours, or pastels. The market-leading drawing package is Corel Draw.

dream series of events or images perceived through the mind during sleep. Their function is unknown, but Sigmund ◊Freud saw them as wish fulfilment (nightmares being failed dreams prompted by fears of 'repressed' impulses). Dreams occur in periods of rapid eye movement (REM) by the sleeper, when the cortex of the brain is approximately as active as in waking hours. Dreams occupy about a fifth of sleeping time.

If a high level of acetylcholine (chemical responsible for transmission of nerve impulses) is present, dreams occur too early in sleep, causing wakefulness, confusion, and ◊depression, which suggests that a form of memory search is involved. Prevention of dreaming, by taking sleeping pills, for example, has similar unpleasant results. For the purposes of (allegedly) foretelling the future, dreams fell into disrepute in the scientific atmosphere of the 18th century.

drill large Old World monkey *Mandrillus leucophaeus* similar to a baboon and in the same genus as the ◊mandrill. Drills live in the forests of Cameroon and Nigeria. Brownish-coated, black-faced, and stoutly built, with a very short tail, the male can have a head and body up to 75 cm/2.5 ft long, although females are much smaller.

drilling common woodworking and metal machinery process that involves boring holes with a drill bit. The commonest kind of drill bit is the fluted drill, which has spiral grooves around it to allow the cut material to escape. In the oil industry, rotary drilling is used to bore oil wells. The drill bit usually consists of a number of toothed cutting wheels, which grind their way through the rock as the drill pipe is turned, and mud is pumped through the pipe to lubricate the bit and flush the ground-up rock to the surface.

In rotary drilling, a drill bit is fixed to the end of a length of drill pipe and rotated by a turning mechanism, the rotary table. More lengths of pipe are added as the hole deepens. The long drill pipes are handled by lifting gear in a steel tower or ◊derrick.

drinking water water that has been subjected to various treatments, including ◊filtration and ◊sterilization, to make it fit for human consumption; it is not pure water.

DRINKING WATER

Darkling beetles living in the Namib desert in Africa drink by standing on their heads at the crests of sand dunes at dawn. Mists rolling in from the coast condense to form water on their bodies; the water then trickles down into their mouths.

drive bay in computing, slot in a computer designed to hold a disc drive such as a hard drive, floppy drive, or CD-ROM drive. Like most computer components, disc drives have decreased in size. Older drives were $5\frac{1}{4}$ inches in size, but most newer drives are $3\frac{1}{2}$ inches. Kits to fit a $3\frac{1}{2}$ inch drive into a $5\frac{1}{4}$ inch bay are readily available.

driver in computing, a program that controls a peripheral device. Every device connected to the computer needs a driver program.

The driver ensures that communication between the computer and the device is successful.

For example, it is often possible to connect many different types of printer, each with its own special operating codes, to the same type of computer. This is because driver programs are supplied to translate the computer's standard printing commands into the special commands needed for each printer.

dromedary variety of Arabian ◊camel. The dromedary or one-humped camel has been domesticated since 400 BC. During a long period without water, it can lose up to one-quarter of its body weight without ill effects.

DROMEDARY CAMEL

http://www.seaworld.org/animal_bytes/dromedary_camelab.html

Illustrated guide to the dromedary camel including information about genus, size, life span, habitat, gestation, diet, and a series of fun facts.

drop-down list in computing, in a ◊graphical user interface, a list of options that hangs down from a blank space in a ◊dialog box or other on-screen form when a computer awaits user input.

To select one of the choices, highlight it and click. The list will disappear and the selected item will appear in the blank. If the list is longer than the space available, small arrows and a scroll bar will appear on the right-hand side.

drug any of a range of substances, natural or synthetic, administered to humans and animals as therapeutic agents: to diagnose, prevent, or treat disease, or to assist recovery from injury. Traditionally many drugs were obtained from plants or animals; some minerals also had medicinal value. Today, increasing numbers of drugs are synthesized in the laboratory.

Drugs are administered in various ways, including: orally, by injection, as a lotion or ointment, as a ◊pessary, by inhalation, or by transdermal patch.

A miracle drug is any drug that will do what the label says it will do.

ERIC HODGINS
Episode

drug, generic any drug produced without a brand name that is identical to a branded product. Usually generic drugs are produced when the patent on a branded drug has expired, and are cheaper than their branded equivalents.

drug misuse illegal use of drugs for nontherapeutic purposes. Under the UK Misuse of Drugs regulations drugs used illegally include: narcotics, such as heroin, morphine, and the synthetic opioids; barbiturates; amphetamines and related substances; ◊benzodiazepine tranquillizers; cocaine, LSD, and cannabis. **Designer drugs**, for example ecstasy, are usually modifications of the amphetamine molecule, altered in order to evade the law as well as for different effects, and may be many times more powerful and dangerous. Crack, a highly toxic derivative of cocaine, became available to drug users in the 1980s. Some athletes misuse drugs such as ephedrine and ◊anabolic steroids.

Sources of traditional drugs include the 'Golden Triangle' (where Myanmar, Laos, and Thailand meet), Mexico, Colombia, China, and the Middle East.

drupe fleshy ◊fruit containing one or more seeds which are surrounded by a hard, protective layer – for example cherry, almond, and plum. The wall of the fruit (◊pericarp) is differentiated into the outer skin (exocarp), the fleshy layer of tissues (mesocarp), and the hard layer surrounding the seed (endocarp).

The coconut is a drupe, but here the pericarp becomes dry and fibrous at maturity. Blackberries are an aggregate fruit composed of a cluster of small drupes.

dry-cleaning method of cleaning textiles based on the use of volatile solvents, such as trichloroethene (trichloroethylene), that dissolve grease. No water is used. Dry-cleaning was first developed in France 1849.

Some solvents are known to damage the ozone layer and one, tetrachloroethene (perchloroethylene), is toxic in water and gives off toxic fumes when heated.

dry ice solid carbon dioxide (CO_2), used as a refrigerant. At temperatures above –79°C/–110.2°F, it sublimes (turns into vapour without passing through a liquid stage) to gaseous carbon dioxide.

dry rot infection of timber in damp conditions by fungi (see ◊fungus), such as *Merulius lacrymans*, that form a threadlike surface. Whitish at first, the fungus later reddens as reproductive spores are formed. Tentacles from the fungus also work their way into the timber, making it dry-looking and brittle. Dry rot spreads rapidly through a building.

Commonly abused drugs

The two main laws about drugs are the Medicines Act and the Misuse of Drugs Act. The Medicines Act controls the way medicines are made and supplied. The Misuse of Drugs Act bans the non-medical use of certain drugs. The Misuse of Drugs Act places drugs in different classes – A, B, and C. The penalties for offences involving a drug depend on the class it is in and will also vary according to individual circumstances. Class A drugs carry the highest penalty, class C the lowest.

Name	Source	Forms and appearance	Legal position	Methods of use°
Amphetamine (also called speed, uppers, whizz, billy, sulphate)	a totally synthetic product	powder form; tablets and capsules	class B, schedule 2 controlled substance	taken orally in drink or licking off the finger; sniffed; smoked; dissolved in water for injecting
Anabolic steroids	synthetic products designed to imitate certain natural hormones within the human body	capsules and tablets; liquid	not controlled	injections; also taken orally
Cannabis (also called dope, grass, hash, ganja, shit, blow, weed)	plants of the genus *Cannabis saliva*	herbal: dried plant material, similar to a coarse cut tobacco (marijuana); resin: blocks of various colours and texture (hashish); oil: extracted from resin, with a distinctive smell	class B, schedule 1 controlled substance	smoked in a variety of ways; can be put into cooking or made into a drink; occasionally eaten on its own
Cocaine (also called coke, charlie, snow, white lady)	leaves of the coca bush, *Erythroxylum coca*	white crystalline powder; very rarely in paste form	class A, schedule 2 controlled substance	sniffed; injected; smoked (paste)
Crack and freebase cocaine (also called rock, wash, cloud nine; base, freebase)	derived from cocaine hydrochloride	crystals (crack cocaine); powder (freebase cocaine)	class A, schedule 2 controlled substances	smoking
Ecstasy (also called disco burgers, Dennis the Menace, diamonds, New Yorkers, E, Adam, XTC, Fantasy, Doves, rhubarb and custard (red and yellow capsules))	a totally synthetic product	tablets and capsules; rarely, powder; ecstasy is not always available in pure form, which increases the risks	class A, schedule 1	orally; occasionally injections
Heroin (also called smack, junk, H, skag, brown, horse, gravy)	from raw opium produced by the opium poppy	powder	class A, schedule 2 controlled substance	smoking; injections; also sniffed or taken orally
Lysergic acid diethylamide (LSD) (also called acid, trips, tab, blotters, dots)	derived from ergot (a fungus of certain cereal grains)	colourless crystals; for street use, mainly impregnated into squares of blotted paper or into squares of clear gelatine; or into tiny pills	class A, schedule 1 controlled substance	orally (paper squares and pills); under the eyelid (gelatine squares)
Magic (hallucinogenic) mushrooms (also called shrooms, mushies)	natural mushrooms (mainly fly agaric and liberty cap)	several varieties; identification is difficult	possession and eating of fresh mushrooms is not an offence; preparation is[1]	eaten; infused to make a drink
Methadone (also called doll, dolly, red rock, tootsie roll; phy-amps, phy (ampoules))	a totally synthetic product	powder; tablets, ampoules, linctus, mixture	class A, schedule 2 controlled substance	orally; injections
Methylamphetamine (also called ice, meth, crystal, glass, ice-cream (crystal form); meth, methedrine (powder or tablets))	a totally synthetic drug, closely related to amphetamine sulphate	crystals or, less commonly, tablets or powder	class B, schedule 2 controlled substance	burning crystals and inhaling the fumes; drinking, sniffing, licking off the finger (powder and tablets)
Nitrites (poppers) (also called nitro, nitrite)	various synthetic volatile chemicals	in small glass bottles under trade names of Liquid Gold, Hi-Tech, Rave, Locker Room, Ram, Rush, etc	controlled by the Medicines Act	inhalation
Solvents (also called glue, gas, can, cog (depending on substance and container))	domestic and commercial products	liquid petroleum gases (LPGs): aerosols, camping gas cylinders, lighter gas refills; liquid solvents: fire extinguisher fluid, corrective fluids, certain paints and removers, nail polish and remover, anti-freeze, petrol; solvent-based glues: impact adhesives used for wood, plastic, laminate surfaces, vinyl floor tiles	not controlled	sprayed into the mouth and inhaled (LPGs); sniffing
Tranquillizers (also called tranx, barbs, barbies, blockers, tueys, traffic lights, golf balls (tranquillizers); jellies, jelly beans, M&Ms, rugby balls (temazepam in jelly capsules))	pharmaceutical drugs aimed at treating patients with problems of anxiety, insomnia, and depression; based on benzodiazepine or barbiturate	tablets or capsules	benzodiazepine based: class C controlled substances; barbiturate based: class B controlled substances	taken orally or injected

[1] Preparation (such as crushing, slicing, drying, etc) is punishable as an offence relating to psilocin and psilocybin – the active ingredients of most hallucinogenic mushrooms, both class A, schedule 1 controlled substances.

Effects of use	Adverse effects	Tolerance potential	Habituation potential	Withdrawal effects	Overdose potential
increased energy, strength, concentration, euphoria and elation; suppression of appetite; wakefulness	increased blood pressure with risk of stroke; diarrhoea or increased urination; disturbance of sleep patterns; weight loss; depression; paranoia; psychosis	tolerance develops rapidly	physical dependence: rare; psychological dependence: common	mental agitation, depression, panic	fatal overdose possible, even at low doses
increase in body bulk and muscle growth; feelings of stamina and strength	bone growth abnormalities; hypertension and heart disease; liver and kidney malfunction; hepatitis; sexual abnormalities and impotence	tolerance may develop	no physical dependence; profound psychological dependence	sudden collapse of muscle strength and stamina; irritability, violent mood swings	overdose can lead to collapse, convulsions, coma, and death
relaxation, feelings of happiness, congeniality, increased concentration, sexual arousal	impaired judgement; loss of short-term memory; dizziness; confusion; anxiety; paranoia; potential for cancer and breathing disorders	tolerance develops rapidly	true physical dependence: rare; psychological dependence: common	disturbed sleep patterns; anxiety, panic	it is not thought possible to overdose fatally
feelings of energy, strength, exhilaration, confidence; talkativeness	agitation, panic, feelings of being threatened; damage to nasal passages, exhaustion, weight loss; collapsed veins, ulceration; delusions, violence	tolerance develops rapidly	strong physical and psychological dependence	severe cravings; feelings of anxiety and panic; depression	it is possible to overdose fatally
elation and euphoria, feelings of power, strength, and well-being	depression, feelings of being threatened; paranoia, psychosis; violence	some tolerance develops	strong physical and psychological dependence	severe depression; aggression, panic; risk of suicide	overdose can lead to coma and death
feelings of euphoria, energy, stamina, sociability, sexual arousal	mood swings, nausea and vomiting, overheating, dehydration, convulsions, sudden death	tolerance develops	physical dependence: none; physiological dependence: low	no physical symptoms; irritability, depression	overdose can lead to coma and death
feelings of euphoria, inner peace, freedom from fear and deprivation	depressed breathing, severe constipation, nausea, and vomiting; effect on general state of health, lower immunity; vein collapse and ulceration; risk of infection from needles	tolerance develops rapidly	profound physical and psychological dependence	sweating, flu-like symptoms 'going cold turkey'; severe cravings; professional assistance necessary	overdose can lead to coma and death
hallucinations	risk of accident while hallucinating; flashbacks; risk of developing a latent psychiatric disorder	tolerance develops and disappears rapidly	no physical dependence; some psychological dependence	no physical effect; few psychological effects	it is not thought possible to overdose
hallucinations; feelings of euphoaria, well-being, gaiety	long-term mental problems; risk of poisoning	tolerance develops rapidly	no dependence	few withdrawal effects	little overdose potential
feelings of relaxation, bodily warmth, freedom from pain and worry	sweating, nausea, itching, tiredness; disruption of menstrual cycle in women	tolerance develops slowly	strong physical and psychological dependence	fever, flu-like symptoms; diarrhoea; aggression	overdose can lead to respiratory depression, collapse, coma, and death
feelings of euphoria, great strength and energy, sustained for long periods without rest or food	increased blood pressure with risk of stroke and heart failure, diarrhoea or increased urination, disturbance of sleep, hallucinations, aggression, psychosis, delusions, paranoia	tolerance develops rapidly	physical dependence: not uncommon; psychological dependence: profound	severe cravings; depression; fear; panic and mental agitation	serious risk of fatal overdose, even at very low levels
feelings of excitement and exhilaration; sexual arousal and increased sensitivity of sexual organs	nausea and vomiting; headaches and dizziness; skin problems; damage to vision if touches the eyes; poisonous if swallowed	tolerance develops quickly	no significant physical or psychological dependence	no significant effects	little risk of overdose
deep intoxication, hallucinations, excitability	over-stimulation of the heart, and death; asphyxiation from swelling of throat tissues or inhalation of vomit; problems with speech, balance, short-term memory, cognitive skills; possible personality changes	tolerance may develop	no physical dependence; strong psychological dependence	no physical symptoms; anxiety and mood swings	overdose can lead to collapse, coma, and death
in higher doses: feelings of euphoria, elimination of fear and feeling of deprivation	violent mood swings, bizarre sexual behaviour, deep depression, disorientation, lethargy	tolerance develops rapidly	profound physical and psychological tolerance	confusion, head-aches, depression; sudden withdrawal may lead to con-vulsions and death	overdose can lead to convulsions, depression of breathing, collapse, coma, and death

DSP in computing, abbreviation for ◊digital signal processor.

DTP abbreviation for ◊desktop publishing.

dubnium synthesized, radioactive, metallic element of the ◊transactinide series, symbol Db, atomic number 105, relative atomic mass 261. Six isotopes have been synthesized, each with very short (fractions of a second) half-lives. Two institutions claim to have been the first to produce it: the Joint Institute for Nuclear Research in Dubna, Russia, 1967; and the University of California at Berkeley, USA, who disputed the Soviet claim, 1970. Its temporary name was unnilpentium.

duck any of about 50 species of short-legged waterbirds with webbed feet and flattened bills, of the family Anatidae, order Anseriformes, which also includes the larger geese and swans. Ducks were domesticated for eggs, meat, and feathers by the ancient Chinese and the ancient Maya (see ◊poultry). Most ducks live in fresh water, feeding on worms and insects as well as vegetable matter. They are generally divided into dabbling ducks and diving ducks.
anatomy The three front toes of a duck's foot are webbed and the hind toe is free; the legs are scaly. The broad rounded bill is skin-covered with a horny tip provided with little plates (lamellae) through which the duck is able to strain its food from water and mud.
species of duck The mallard *Anas platyrhynchos,* 58 cm/1.9 ft, found over most of the northern hemisphere, is the species from which all domesticated ducks originated. The male (drake) has a glossy green head, brown breast, grey body, and yellow bill. The female (duck) is speckled brown, with a duller bill. The male moults and resembles the female for a while just after the breeding season. There are many other species of duck including ◊teal, ◊eider, mandarin duck, ◊merganser, muscovy duck, pintail duck, ◊shelduck, and ◊shoveler. They have different-shaped bills according to their diet and habitat; for example, the shoveler has a wide spade-shaped bill for scooping insects off the surface of water.

duck-billed platypus another name for the ◊platypus.

duckweed any of a family of tiny plants found floating on the surface of still water throughout most of the world, except the polar regions and tropics. Each plant consists of a flat, circular, leaflike structure 0.4 cm/0.15 in or less across, with a single thin root up to 15 cm/6 in long below. (Genus chiefly *Lemna,* family Lemnaceae.)

The plants bud off new individuals and soon cover the surface of the water. Flowers rarely appear, but when they do, they are extremely small and are found in a pocket at the edge of the plant.

ductile material material that can sustain large deformations beyond its elastic limit (see ◊elasticity) without fracture. Metals are very ductile, and may be pulled out into wires, or hammered or rolled into thin sheets without breaking. Compare ◊brittle material.

ductless gland alternative name for an ◊endocrine gland.

dugong marine mammal *Dugong dugong* of the order Sirenia (sea cows), found in the Red Sea, the Indian Ocean, and western Pacific. It can grow to 3.6 m/11 ft long, and has a tapering body with a notched tail and two fore-flippers. It has a very long hind gut (30 m/98 ft in adults) which functions similarly to the rumen in ◊ruminants. It is largely herbivorous, feeding mostly on sea grasses and seaweeds, and is thought to have given rise to the mermaid myth.

Previously thought to be the only truly herbivorous marine mammal, Australian research 1995 showed that some dugongs eat sea squirts, which make up 25.5% of the wet weight of faeces from dugongs in Moreton Bay, eastern Australia.

duiker ***Afrikaans diver*** any of several antelopes of the family Bovidae, common in Africa. Duikers are shy and nocturnal, and grow to 30–70 cm/12–28 in tall.

duikerbok small African antelope with crested head, large muzzle, and short, conical horns in the males only.
classification Duikerboks are in genus *Cephalophus* in the family Bovidae (cattle and antelopes) of order Artiodactyla.

dulse any of several edible red seaweeds, especially *Rhodymenia palmata,* found on middle and lower shores of the north Atlantic. They may have a single broad blade up to 30 cm/12 in long rising directly from the holdfast which attaches them to the sea floor, or may be palmate (with five lobes) or fan-shaped. The frond is tough and dark red, sometimes with additional small leaflets at the edge.

Dumas, Jean Baptiste André
(1800–1884)

French chemist. He made contributions to organic analysis and synthesis, and to the determination of atomic weights (relative atomic masses) through the measurement of vapour densities. In 1833, Dumas worked out an absolute method for the estimation of the amount of nitrogen in an organic compound, which still forms the basis of modern methods of analysis. He went on to correct the atomic masses of 30 elements – half the total number known at that time – referring to the hydrogen value as 1.

In 1826, Dumas began working on atomic theory, and concluded that 'in all elastic fluids observed under the same conditions, the molecules are placed at equal distances' – that is, they are present in equal numbers. His theory of substitution in organic compounds, which he proved by experiments, established that atoms of apparently opposite electrical charge replaced each other. This refuted the dualistic theory of chemistry proposed by Swedish chemist Jöns Berzelius.

Studying blood, Dumas showed that urea is present in the blood of animals from which the kidneys have been removed, proving that one of the functions of the kidneys is to remove urea from the blood, not to produce it.

Mary Evans Picture Library

dumb terminal in computing, a ◊terminal that has no processing capacity of its own. It works purely as a means of access to a main ◊central processing unit. Compare with a ◊personal computer used as an intelligent terminal – for example in ◊client–server architecture.

dump in computing, the process of rapidly transferring data to external memory or to a printer. It is usually done to help with debugging (see ◊bug) or as part of an error-recovery procedure designed to provide ◊data security. A ◊screen dump makes a printed copy of the current screen display.

dune mound or ridge of wind-drifted sand common on coasts and in sandy deserts. Loose sand is blown and bounced along by the wind, up the windward side of a dune. The sand particles then fall to rest on the lee side, while more are blown up from the windward side. In this way a dune moves gradually downwind.

In sandy deserts, the typical crescent-shaped dune is called a **barchan**. **Seif dunes** are longitudinal and lie parallel to the wind direction, and **star-shaped dunes** are formed by irregular winds.

dung waste matter excreted by living animals. Dung may also serve as a marker through the addition of scents from the anal glands, whether for determining territorial boundaries or as an indication of status within a group.

Some animals, such as rabbits, may reingest dung immediately

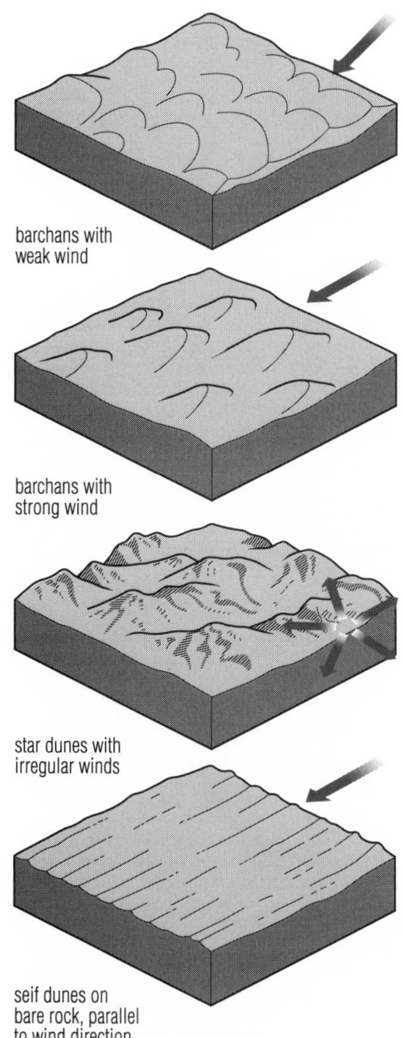

***dune** The shape of a dune indicates the prevailing wind pattern. Crescent-shaped dunes form in sandy desert with winds from a constant direction. Seif dunes form on bare rocks, parallel to the wind direction. Irregular star dunes are formed by variable winds.*

after excretion and continue digesting it, a process known as **refection**. In addition to being broken down by bacteria, animal dung provides food for many invertebrates, especially beetles and flies, and provides a habitat for certain species of fungi and plants such as stinging nettles.

dunlin small gregarious shore bird *Calidris alpina* of the sandpiper family Scolopacidae, order Charadriformes, about 18 cm/7 in long, nesting on moors and marshes in the far northern regions of Eurasia and North America. Chestnut above and black below in summer, it is greyish in winter; the bill and feet are black.

Dunnite US high explosive named after Major Dunn, its developer; also called 'Explosive D'. Made of ammonium picrate powder, it was relatively insensitive, and so was widely used in armour-piercing shells as it withstood the shock of impact against armour without detonating, allowing the shell to pierce the armour before the fuse initiated the explosive.

dunnock or ***hedge sparrow*** European bird *Prunella modularis* family Prunellidae, similar in size and colouring to the sparrow, but with a slate-grey head and breast, and more slender bill. It is characterized in the field by a hopping gait, with continual twitches of the wings whilst feeding. It nests in bushes and hedges.

duodecimal system system of arithmetic notation using 12 as a base, at one time considered superior to the decimal number system in that 12 has more factors (2, 3, 4, 6) than 10 (2, 5).

It is now superseded by the universally accepted decimal system.

duodenum in vertebrates, a short length of ◊alimentary canal found between the stomach and the small intestine. Its role is in digesting carbohydrates, fats, and proteins. The smaller molecules formed are then absorbed, either by the duodenum or the ileum.

Entry of food to the duodenum is controlled by the pyloric sphincter, a muscular ring at the outlet of the stomach. Once food has passed into the duodenum it is mixed with bile released from the gall bladder and with a range of enzymes secreted from the pancreas, a digestive gland near the top of the intestine. The bile neutralizes the acidity of the gastric juices passing out of the stomach and aids fat digestion.

duplex or *echo* in printing, the ability to print on both sides of the page; in computer communications, setting that ◊toggles the ability to send and receive signals simultaneously. **Full duplex** means two-way communication is enabled; **half duplex** means it is disabled.

duralumin lightweight aluminium ◊alloy widely used in aircraft construction, containing copper, magnesium, and manganese.

durra or ***doura*** grass, also known as Indian millet, grown as a cereal in parts of Asia and Africa. *Sorghum vulgare* is the chief cereal in many parts of Africa. See also ◊sorghum. (Genus *Sorghum*.)

dust bowl area in the Great Plains region of North America (Texas to Kansas) that suffered extensive wind erosion as the result of drought and poor farming practice in once-fertile soil. Much of the topsoil was blown away in the droughts of the 1930s and the 1980s.

Similar dust bowls are being formed in many areas today, noticeably across Africa, because of overcropping and overgrazing.

Dutch cap common name for a barrier method of contraception; see ◊diaphragm.

Dutch elm disease disease of elm trees *Ulmus*, principally Dutch, English, and American elm, caused by the fungus *Certocystis ulmi*. The fungus is usually spread from tree to tree by the elm-bark beetle, which lays its eggs beneath the bark. The disease has no cure, and control methods involve injecting insecticide into the trees annually to prevent infection, or the destruction of all elms in a broad band around an infected area, to keep the beetles out.

The disease was first described in the Netherlands and by the early 1930s had spread across Britain and continental Europe, as well as North America.

DVD abbreviation for ◊digital versatile disc or **digital video disc**.

DVI (abbreviation for ***digital video interactive***) in computing, a powerful compression and decompression system for digital video and audio. DVI enables 72 minutes of full-screen, full-motion video and its audio track to be stored on a CD-ROM. Originally developed by the US firm RCA, DVI is now owned by Intel and has active support from IBM and Microsoft. It can be used on the hard disc of a PC as well as on a CD-ROM.

Dvorak keyboard alternative keyboard layout to the normal typewriter keyboard layout (◊QWERTY). In the Dvorak layout the most commonly used keys are situated in the centre, so that keying is faster.

DWANGO (acronym for ***Dial-up Wide Area Network Game Operation***) in computing, server that enables computer users with modems to play each other at action games such as DOOM, Duke Nuken 3D, and Monster Truck Madness without the variable delays involved in moving data over the Internet.

dye substance that, applied in solution to fabrics, imparts a colour resistant to washing. **Direct dyes** combine with the material of the fabric, yielding a coloured compound; **indirect dyes** require the presence of another substance (a mordant), with which the fabric must first be treated; **vat dyes** are colourless soluble substances that on exposure to air yield an insoluble coloured compound.

Naturally occurring dyes include indigo, madder (alizarin), logwood, and cochineal, but industrial dyes (introduced in the 19th century) are usually synthetic: acid green was developed 1835 and bright purple in 1856.

Industrial dyes include ◊azo dyestuffs, ◊acridine, ◊anthracene, and ◊aniline.

dyke in earth science, a sheet of ◊igneous rock created by the intrusion of magma (molten rock) across layers of pre-existing rock. (By contrast, a sill is intruded *between* layers of rock.) It may form a ridge when exposed on the surface if it is more resistant than the rock into which it intruded. A dyke is also a human-made embankment built along a coastline (for example, in the Netherlands) to prevent the flooding of lowland coastal regions.

dynamic data exchange (DDE) in computing, a form of interprocess communication used in Microsoft ◊Windows, providing exchange of commands and data between two applications. DDE was used principally to include live data from one application in another – for example, spreadsheet data in a word-processed report. After Windows 3.1 DDE was replaced by ◊object linking and embedding.

DDE links between files rely on the files remaining in the same locations in the computer's directory.

Dynamic HTML in computing, the fourth version of hypertext markup language (◊HTML), the language used to create Web pages. It is called Dynamic HTML because it enables dynamic effects to be incorporated in pages without the delays involved in downloading Java ◊applets and without referring back to the server.

dynamic IP address in computing, a temporary ◊IP address assigned from a pool of available addresses by an ◊Internet Service Provider when a customer logs on to begin an online session.

Companies and other organizations which have their own networks typically have their own permanent IP addresses. Customers of a dial-up service provider, however, only need addresses for the length of time that they are actually on line. This method allows the finite number of available IP addresses to be used most efficiently.

dynamic link library (DLL) in computing, files of executable functions that can be loaded on demand in Microsoft ◊Windows and linked at run time. Windows itself uses DLL files for handling international keyboards, for example, and Windows word-processing programs use DLL files for functions such as spelling and hyphenation checks, and thesaurus.

dynamics or ***kinetics*** in mechanics, the mathematical and physical study of the behaviour of bodies under the action of forces that produce changes of motion in them.

dynamite explosive consisting of a mixture of nitroglycerine and diatomaceous earth (diatomite, an absorbent, chalklike material). It was first devised by Alfred Nobel.

dynamo simple generator or machine for transforming mechanical energy into electrical energy. A dynamo in basic form consists of a powerful field magnet between the poles of which a suitable conductor, usually in the form of a coil (armature), is rotated. The mechanical energy of rotation is thus converted into an electric current in the armature.

Present-day dynamos work on the principles described by English physicist Michael Faraday in 1830, that an ◊electromotive force is developed in a conductor when it is moved in a magnetic field.

dyne c.g.s. unit (symbol dyn) of force. 10^5 dynes make one newton. The dyne is defined as the force that will accelerate a mass of one gram by one centimetre per second per second.

dysentery infection of the large intestine causing abdominal cramps and painful ◊diarrhoea with blood. There are two kinds of dysentery: **amoebic** (caused by a protozoan), common in the tropics, which may lead to liver damage; and **bacterial**, the kind most often seen in the temperate zones.

Both forms are successfully treated with antibacterials and fluids to prevent dehydration.

DYSLEXIA

Hans Christian Andersen, the Danish writer of fairy tales, was a bad speller and was probably dyslexic.

dyslexia ***Greek 'bad', 'pertaining to words'*** malfunction in the brain's synthesis and interpretation of written information, popularly known as 'word blindness'.

Dyslexia may be described as specific or developmental to distinguish it from reading or writing difficulties which are acquired. It results in poor ability in reading and writing, though the person may excel in other areas, for example, in mathematics. A similar disability with figures is called **dyscalculia**. **Acquired dyslexia** may occur as a result of brain injury or disease.

dysprosium ***Greek dusprositos 'difficult to get near'*** silver-white, metallic element of the ◊lanthanide series, symbol Dy, atomic number 66, relative atomic mass 162.50. It is among the most magnetic of all known substances and has a great capacity to absorb neutrons.

It was discovered in 1886 by French chemist Paul Lecoq de Boisbaudran (1838–1912).

EAR ANATOMY

http://weber.u.washington.edu/~otoweb/ear_anatomy.html

Concise medical information on the anatomy and function of the ear. It includes separate sections on perforated eardrums and their treatment, ear tubes and their use, tinnitus, and a series of different hearing tests.

2E abbreviation for *east*.

eagle any of several genera of large birds of prey of the family Accipitridae, order Falconiformes, including the golden eagle *Aquila chrysaetos* of Eurasia and North America, which has a 2 m/6 ft wingspan. Eagles occur worldwide, usually building eyries or nests in forests or mountains, and all are fierce and powerful birds of prey. The harpy eagle is the largest eagle.

The white-headed bald eagle *Haliaetus leucocephalus* is the symbol of the USA; rendered infertile through the ingestion of agricultural chemicals, it is now rare, except in Alaska.

Another endangered species is the Philippine eagle, sometimes called the Philippine monkey-eating eagle (although its main prey is the flying lemur). Loss of large tracts of forest, coupled with hunting by humans, have greatly reduced its numbers.

ear organ of hearing in animals. It responds to the vibrations that constitute sound, which are translated into nerve signals and passed to the brain. A mammal's ear consists of three parts: outer ear, middle ear, and inner ear. The **outer ear** is a funnel that collects sound, directing it down a tube to the **ear drum** (tympanic membrane), which separates the outer and **middle ears**. Sounds vibrate this membrane, the mechanical movement of which is transferred to a smaller membrane leading to the **inner ear** by three small bones, the auditory ossicles. Vibrations of the inner ear membrane move fluid contained in the snail-shaped cochlea, which vibrates hair cells that stimulate the auditory nerve connected to the brain. There are approximately 30,000 sensory hair cells (**stereocilia**). Exposure to loud noise and the process of ageing damages the stereocilia, resulting in hearing loss. Three fluid-filled canals of the inner ear detect changes of position; this mechanism, with other sensory inputs, is responsible for the sense of balance.

When a loud noise occurs, muscles behind the eardrum contract automatically, suppressing the noise to enhance perception of sound and prevent injury.

earth electrical connection between an appliance and the ground. In the event of a fault in an electrical appliance, for example, involving connection between the live part of the circuit and the outer casing, the current flows to earth, causing no harm to the user.

In most domestic installations, earthing is achieved by a connection to a metal water-supply pipe buried in the ground.

Earth third planet from the Sun. It is almost spherical, flattened slightly at the poles, and is composed of three concentric layers: the ◊core, the ◊mantle, and the ◊crust. About 70% of the surface (including the north and south polar icecaps) is covered with water. The Earth is surrounded by a life-supporting atmosphere and is the only planet on which life is known to exist.
mean distance from the Sun 149,500,000 km/92,860,000 mi
equatorial diameter 12,756 km/7,923 mi
circumference 40,070 km/24,900 mi
rotation period 23 hr 56 min 4.1 sec

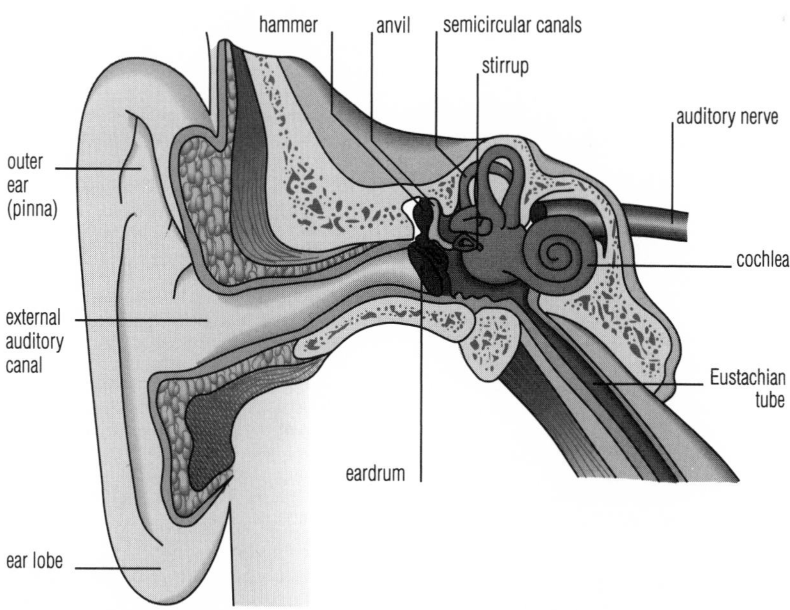

ear *The structure of the ear. The three bones of the middle ear – hammer, anvil, and stirrup – vibrate in unison and magnify sounds about 20 times. The spiral-shaped cochlea is the organ of hearing. As sound waves pass down the spiral tube, they vibrate fine hairs lining the tube, which activate the auditory nerve connected to the brain. The semicircular canals are the organs of balance, detecting movements of the head.*

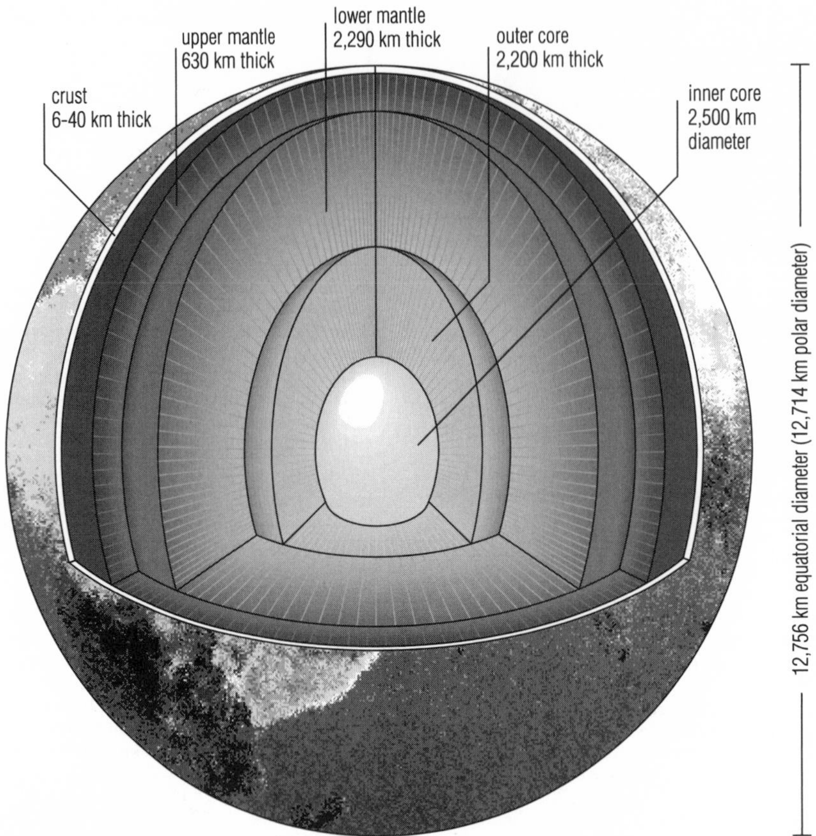

Earth *Inside the Earth. The surface of the Earth is a thin crust about 6 km/4 mi thick under the sea and 40 km/25 mi thick under the continents. Under the crust lies the mantle about 2,900 km/1,800 mi thick and with a temperature of 1,500–3,000°C/2,700–5,400°F. The inner core is probably solid iron and nickel at about 5,000°C/9,000°F.*

year (complete orbit, or sidereal period) 365 days 5 hr 48 min 46 sec. Earth's average speed around the Sun is 30 kps/18.5 mps; the plane of its orbit is inclined to its equatorial plane at an angle of 23.5°, the reason for the changing seasons
atmosphere nitrogen 78.09%; oxygen 20.95%; argon 0.93%; carbon dioxide 0.03%; and less than 0.0001% neon, helium, krypton, hydrogen, xenon, ozone, radon
surface land surface 150,000,000 sq km/57,500,000 sq mi (greatest height above sea level 8,872 m/29,118 ft Mount Everest); water surface 361,000,000 sq km/139,400,000 sq mi (greatest depth 11,034 m/36,201 ft ◊Mariana Trench in the Pacific). The interior is thought to be an inner core about 2,600 km/1,600 mi in diameter, of solid iron and nickel; an outer core about 2,250 km/1,400 mi thick, of molten iron and nickel; and a mantle of mostly solid rock about 2,900 km/1,800 mi thick, separated from the Earth's crust by the ◊Mohorovičić discontinuity. The crust and the topmost layer of the mantle form about twelve major moving plates, some of which carry the continents. The plates are in constant, slow motion, called tectonic drift. US geophysicists announced in 1996 that they had detected a difference in the spinning time of the Earth's core and the rest of the planet; the core is spinning slightly faster.
satellite the Moon
age 4.6 billion years. The Earth was formed with the rest of the ◊Solar System by consolidation of interstellar dust. Life began 3.5–4 billion years ago

To remember the most common elements of the planet's crust, in descending order:

ONLY SILLY ASSES IN COLLEGE STUDY PAST MIDNIGHT

OXYGEN, SILICON, ALUMINIUM, IRON, CALCIUM, SODIUM, POTASSIUM, MAGNESIUM

EARTH AND MOON VIEWER

http://www.fourmilab.ch/earthview/vplanet.html

View a map of the Earth showing the day and night regions at this moment, or view the Earth from the Sun, the Moon, or any number of other locations. Alternatively, take a look at the Moon from the Earth or the Sun, or from above various formations on the lunar surface.

The earth only has so much bounty to offer and inventing ever larger and more notional prices for that bounty does not change its real value.

BEN ELTON English writer and comedian.
Stark, 'Dinner in Los Angeles'

earthquake abrupt motion that propagates through the Earth and along its surfaces. Earthquakes are caused by the sudden release in rocks of strain accumulated over time as a result of ◊tectonics. The study of earthquakes is called ◊seismology. Most earthquakes occur along ◊faults (fractures or breaks) and ◊Benioff zones. Plate tectonic movements generate the major proportion: as two plates move past each other they can become jammed. When sufficient strain has accumulated, the rock breaks, releasing a series of elastic waves (◊seismic waves) as the plates spring free. The force of earthquakes (magnitude) is measured on the ◊Richter scale, and their effect (intensity) on the ◊Mercalli scale. The point at which an earthquake originates is the **seismic focus** or **hypocentre**; the point on the Earth's surface directly above this is the **epicentre**.

The Alaskan (USA) earthquake of 27 March 1964 ranks as one of the greatest ever recorded, measuring 8.3 to 8.8 on the Richter scale. The 1906 San Francisco earthquake is among the most famous in history. Its magnitude was 8.3 on the Richter scale. The deadliest, most destructive earthquake in historical times is thought to have been in China in 1556. In 1987, a California earthquake was successfully predicted by measurement of underground pressure waves; prediction attempts have also involved the study of such phenomena as the change in gases issuing from the ◊crust, the level of water in wells, slight deformation of the rock surface, a sequence of minor tremors, and the behaviour of animals. The possibility of earthquake prevention is remote. However, rock slippage might be slowed at movement points, or promoted at stoppage

Earth science: chronology

10000–8000 BC	Holocene (post-glacial) period of hunters and gatherers. Harvesting and storage of wild grains in southwest Asia. Herding of reindeer in northern Eurasia. Domestic sheep in northern Iraq.
8000	Neolithic revolution with cultivation of domesticated wheats and barleys, sheep, and goats in southwest Asia. Domestication of pigs in New Guinea.
7000–6000	Domestic goats, sheep, and cattle in Anatolia, Greece, Persia, and the Caspian basin. Planting and harvesting techniques transferred from Asia Minor to Europe.
5000	Beginning of Nile valley civilization. Millet cultivated in China.
3400	Flax used for textiles in Egypt. Widespread corn production in the Americas.
3200	Records of ploughing, raking, and manuring by Egyptians.
c. 3100	River Nile dammed during the rule of King Menes.
3000	First record of asses used as beasts of burden in Egypt. Sumerian civilization used barley as main crop with wheat, dates, flax, apples, plums, and grapes.
2900	Domestication of pigs in eastern Asia.
2640	Reputed start of Chinese silk industry.
2500	Domestic elephants in the Indus valley. Potatoes a staple crop in Peru.
2350	Wine-making in Egypt.
2250	First known irrigation dam.
1600	Important advances in the cultivation of vines and olives in Crete.
1500	*Shadoof* (mechanism for raising water) used for irrigation in Egypt.
1400	Iron ploughshares in use in India.
1300	Aqueducts and reservoirs used for irrigation in Egypt.
1200	Domestic camels in Arabia.
1000–500	Evidence of crop rotation, manuring, and irrigation in India.
600	First windmills used for corn grinding in Persia.
350	Rice cultivation well established in parts of western Africa. Hunting and gathering in the east, central, and south parts of the continent.
c. 200	Use of gears to create ox-driven water wheel for irrigation. Archimedes screw used for irrigation.
100	Cattle-drawn iron ploughs in use in China.
AD 65	*De Re Rustica/On Rural Things*, Latin treatise on agriculture and irrigation.
500	'Three fields in two years' rotation used in China.
630	Cotton introduced into Arabia.
800	Origins of the 'open field' system in northern Europe.
900	Wheeled ploughs in use in western Europe. Horse collar, originating in China, allowed horses to be used for ploughing as well as carrying.
1000	Frisians (NW Netherlanders) began to build dykes and reclaim land. Chinese began to introduce Champa rice which cropped much more quickly than other varieties.
11th century	Three-field system replaced the two-field system in western Europe. Concentration on crop growing.
1126	First artesian wells, at Artois, France.
12th century	Increasing use of water mills and windmills. Horses replaced oxen for pulling work in many areas.
12th–14th centuries	Expansion of European population brought more land into cultivation. Crop rotations, manuring, and new crops such as beans and peas helped increase productivity. Feudal system at its height.
13th–14th centuries	Agricultural recession in western Europe with a series of bad harvests, famines, and pestilence.
1347	Black Death killed about a third of the European population.
16th century	Decline of the feudal system in western Europe. More specialist forms of production were now possible with urban markets. Manorial estates and serfdom remained in eastern Europe. Chinese began cultivation of non-indigenous crops such as corn, sweet potatoes, potatoes, and peanuts.
17th century	Potato introduced into Europe. Norfolk crop rotation became widespread in England, involving wheat, turnips, barley and then ryegrass/clover.
1700–1845	Agricultural revolution began in England. Two million hectares of farmland in England enclosed. Removal of open fields in other parts of Europe followed.
c. 1701	Jethro Tull developed the seed drill and the horse-drawn hoe.
1747	First sugar extracted from sugar beet in Prussia.
1762	Veterinary school founded in Lyon, France.
1783	First plough factory in England.
1785	Cast-iron ploughshare patented.
1793	Invention of the cotton gin.
1800	Early threshing machines developed in England.
1820s	First nitrates for fertilizer imported from South America.
1830	Reaping machines developed in Scotland and the US. Steel plough made by John Deere in Illinois, US.
1840s	Extensive potato blight in Europe.
1850s	Use of clay pipes for drainage well established throughout Europe.
1862	First steam plough used in the Netherlands.
1850–1890s	Major developments in transport and refrigeration technology altered the nature of agricultural markets with crops, dairy products, and wheat being shipped internationally.
1890s	Development of stationary engines for ploughing.
1892	First petrol-driven tractor in the USA.
1921	First attempt at crop dusting with pesticides from an aeroplane near Dayton, Ohio, US.
1938	First self-propelled grain combine harvester used in the USA.
1942–62	Huge increase in the use of pesticides, later curbed by disquiet about their effects and increasing resistance of pests to standard controls such as DDT.
1945 onwards	Increasing use of scientific techniques, crop specialization and larger scale of farm enterprises.
1985	First cases of bovine spongiform encephalopathy (BSE) recorded by UK vets.
1992	Number of cases of BSE in cattle was at its peak (700 cases per week).
1995	Increase in the use of genetic engineering with nearly 3,000 transgenic crops being field-tested.
1996	Organic farming was on the increase in EU countries. The rise was 11% per year in Britain, 50% in Germany, and 40% in Italy.

points, by the extraction or injection of large quantities of water underground, since water serves as a lubricant. This would ease overall pressure.

earth science scientific study of the planet Earth as a whole. The mining and extraction of minerals and gems, the prediction of weather and earthquakes, the pollution of the atmosphere, and the forces that shape the physical world all fall within its scope of study. The emergence of the discipline reflects scientists' concern that an understanding of the global aspects of the Earth's structure and its past will hold the key to how humans affect its future, ensuring that its resources are used in a sustainable way. It is a synthesis of several traditional subjects such as ◊geology, ◊meteorology, ◊oceanography, ◊geophysics, ◊geochemistry, and ◊palaeontology.

Earth Summit (official name ***United Nations Conference on Environment and Development***) international meetings aiming at drawing measures towards environmental protection of the world. The first summit took place in Rio de Janeiro, Brazil, in June 1992. Treaties were made to combat global warming and protect wildlife ('biodiversity') (the latter was not signed by the USA). The second Earth Summit was held in New York in June 1997 to review progress on the environment. The meeting agreed to work towards a global forest convention in 2000 with the aim of halting the destruction of tropical and old-growth forests.

The Rio summit, which cost $23 million to stage (of which 60% was spent on security), was attended by 10,000 official delegates, 12,000 representatives of nongovernmental organizations, and 7,000 journalists.

In 1993, the Clinton administration overturned certain decisions made by George Bush at the Earth Summit. The USA, which had failed to ratify the Convention of Biological Diversity pact along with other nations, came under renewed pressure to endorse it in April 1995 after India threatened to prevent US pharmaceutical and cosmetic companies from gaining access to its natural resources.

By 1996 most wealthy nations estimated that they would exceed their emissions targets, including Spain by 24%, Australia by 25%, and the USA by 3%. Britain and Germany were expected to meet their targets.

The second summit (1997) failed to agree a new deal to address the world's escalating environmental crisis. Dramatic falls in aid to the so-called Third World countries, which the 1992 Earth Summit promised to increase, were at the heart of the breakdown. British prime minister Tony Blair condemned the USA, Japan, Canada and Australia for failing to deliver on commitments to stabilise rising emissions of climate-changing greenhouse gases. The European Community as a whole was on target to meet its stabilisation commitment because of cuts in emissions in Germany and the UK.

Deforestation was the main problem tackled at the second summit. The World Bank and the World Wide Fund for Nature signed an agreement aimed at protecting 250 million hectares/617 million acres of forest (10% of the world's forests). The importance of the issue was highlighted by the fact that deforestation progressed rapidly in developing countries since the first summit, with 15,000 sq km/9,300 sq mi a year lost in the Amazon region alone.

earthworm ◊annelid worm of the class Oligochaeta. Earthworms are hermaphroditic and deposit their eggs in cocoons. They live by burrowing in the soil, feeding on the organic matter it contains. They are vital to the formation of humus, aerating the soil and levelling it by transferring earth from the deeper levels to the surface as castings.

EARWIG

In the 18th century, earwigs were prescribed for hearing difficulties. Dr James' *Medicinal Dictionary* of 1743, comments: 'These insects, being dried, pulverized, and mixed with the urine of a hare, are esteemed to be good for deafness, being introduced into the ear.'

earwig nocturnal insect of the order Dermaptera. The forewings are short and leathery and serve to protect the hindwings, which are large and are folded like a fan when at rest. Earwigs seldom fly. They have a pincerlike appendage in the rear. The male is distinguished by curved pincers; those of the female are straight. Earwigs are regarded as pests because they feed on flowers and fruit, but they also eat other insects, dead or alive. Eggs are laid beneath the soil, and the female cares for the young even after they have hatched. The male dies before the eggs have hatched.

Easter Island or ***Rapa Nui, Spanish Isla de Pascua*** Chilean island in the south Pacific Ocean, part of the Polynesian group, about 3,500 km/2,200 mi west of Chile; area about 166 sq km/64 sq mi; population (1994) 2,800. It was first reached by Europeans on Easter Sunday 1722. On it stand over 800 huge carved statues (*moai*) and the remains of boat-shaped stone houses, the work of Neolithic peoples from Polynesia. The chief centre is Hanga-Roa.

In 1996, following seven years of work, a New Zealand linguist, Dr Steven Fischer, deciphered a script discovered on the island. This script showed the inhabitants were the first in Oceania to write. According to Dr Fischer, the script, known as 'rongorongo', was made up of chants in Rapanui, the island's Polynesian tongue, and tell the story of creation.

The carved statues are believed to have been religious icons. However, archaeological evidence suggests that, prior to European contact, the island suffered an environmental or cultural crisis resulting in the inhabitants renouncing their earlier religious values, which caused them to damage or overturn many of the statues.

Eastman, George (1854–1932)

US entrepreneur and inventor who founded the Eastman Kodak photographic company in 1892. He patented flexible film 1884, invented the Kodak box camera 1888, and introduced daylight-loading film in 1892. By 1900 his company was selling a pocket camera for as little as one dollar.

eau de cologne refreshing toilet water (weaker than perfume), made of alcohol and aromatic oils. Its invention is ascribed to Giovanni Maria Farina (1685–1766), who moved from Italy to Cologne 1709 to manufacture it.

EBCDIC (abbreviation for ***extended binary-coded decimal interchange code***) in computing, a code used for storing and communicating alphabetic and numeric characters. It is an 8-bit code, capable of holding 256 different characters, although only 85 of these

***ecdysis** A bush cricket or katydid (family Tettigoniidae) sheds its skin at night in a rainforest in Costa Rica. The insect is very vulnerable to attack at this time, so it is an advantage for ecdysis to take place during the hours of darkness. Premaphotos Wildlife*

Did We Save the World at Rio de Janeiro?

BY NIGEL DUDLEY

The Earth Summit

The United Nations Conference on Environment and Development – usually called UNCED or the Earth Summit – took place in Rio de Janeiro, Brazil, in June 1992. It was the largest gathering of heads of state in history and almost certainly also the largest assembly of professional environmentalists and non-governmental organizations. In a historic meeting, the world's leaders agreed two important conventions to combat environmental destruction – on climate change and biodiversity – along with a comprehensive environmental strategy called 'Agenda 21' and a carefully-worded set of 'Forest Principles'. The meeting raised high expectations. It was hailed as a new start for the environment – indeed as a step towards a safer, more equitable world. Yet did anything really change? Five years on, in June 1997, a follow-up meeting took place in New York. Some of the results make depressing reading.

The Climate Change Convention has made extremely slow progress. After agreeing targets for reducing greenhouse gases that many experts believed were too low, several of the richer countries have failed to meet even these aims, and, instead, pollution continues to increase. The Convention on Biological Diversity has, in turn, become mired in infighting about rights to genetic material and has suffered chronic underfunding: if anything, threats of widespread extinctions are greater now than they were in 1992. Debates about a global forest convention – rejected at the time of the Earth Summit – are still going on today, against a background of continuing deforestation and forest degradation. Worse still, there has been a well-orchestrated backlash against the environment, promoted by some business interests intent on preventing their short-term profits being affected by long-term environmental planning.

Decisions into practice

Yet the bad news has to be balanced by some good. While global negotiations have sometimes seemed like little more than an excuse for a handful of people to fly around the world for talking sessions, changes at the national, regional, and grassroots levels have been more encouraging. A 'Local Agenda 21' initiative has challenged community groups, non-governmental organizations, individuals, and local authorities to put the principles of the Earth Summit into practice. Literally thousands of projects have sprung up around the world, ranging from neighbourhood energy conservation schemes to community forest management and introduction of new techniques to enable resources to be used sustainably. These are important not only because of their practical impact, but because they have enabled the environmental message to be carried into thousands of schools and colleges, women's groups, religious organizations, trade unions, and so on.

Indeed, if there is one fundamental change that can be identified since the Rio meeting, it is that social issues have become much more fundamentally related to environmental concerns. Whereas early environmental projects sometimes virtually ignored people – leading to circumstances such as local people being expelled from their traditional areas to establish nature reserves – today there is increasing effort to integrate human and environmental needs, leading to stronger and more durable solutions. Rather than impose solutions from above, experience has also shown that results are likely to be far better if local people are involved in both the planning and the management of conservation projects, instead of being left to gaze at them from the outside. Such changes make the conservationist's role more complicated, and involve some inevitable give and take, but ultimately result in ways of reducing our impact on the environment that invite general support rather than opposition.

Things are working better at a regional level as well. Although we have no global forest convention, there have been several regional initiatives to define and implement 'sustainable forest management', where timber needs are balanced with other requirements, such as biodiversity conservation, environmental services such as control of soil erosion, production of food, medicinal herbs, and a range of non-timber forest products, recreational uses of forests, and even the spiritual and religious importance of particular forests.

Global partnerships

In the absence of global leadership, local and national partnerships have been developing to fill the vacuum. Some of them are unexpected. For example, sections of the timber trade have been working with non-governmental organizations in several countries to develop 'certification of good forest management'; a forest gains a certificate if it is judged to be well-managed by an independent inspector against an agreed set of standards. Consumers have the chance to buy timber that they know has been produced without damaging the environment or local human communities. Efforts are being co-ordinated by the Forest Stewardship Council, an international organization based in Mexico which had not even been thought of at Rio, and already over 5 million hectares of forest have been certified around the world.

Conditions are still getting worse

These and other similar developments are certainly signs of hope. But down at the sharp end of environmental problems, it is hard to avoid the conclusion that, for many countries, conditions are still getting worse. Almost every developing country is still losing its forests. Desertification – the creation of new deserts as a result of overgrazing, poor irrigation schemes, climate change, and forest loss – is occurring in over a hundred countries. Forest fires are increasing in intensity, particularly in the tropical moist forests that should almost never burn under natural conditions. Commercially important fish species have, in many cases, been over-caught to the extent that stocks have collapsed, and the loss of mangroves in coastal regions has resulted in a similar rapid decline in the coastal species that rely on them to provide cover for breeding. The ozone hole continues to grow, and the evidence for climate change is increasing: extreme weather events appear to be growing in strength and frequency. At the moment we stand at a crossroads. Awareness of the importance of environmental issues has never been stronger. Governments and local communities are becoming increasingly willing to take action. But at the same time, ground continues to be lost – literally – and efforts at conservation and restoration will, in the future, be played out against a backdrop of a planet that will probably be far poorer in species and habitats than it was when the 20th century began.

are defined in the standard version. It is still used in many mainframe computers, but almost all mini-and microcomputers now use ◊ASCII code.

ebony any of a group of hardwood trees belonging to the ebony family, especially some tropical ◊persimmons native to Africa and Asia. (Genus chiefly *Diospyros*, family Ebenaceae.)

e-cash (contraction of ***electronic cash***) generic name for new electronic money systems such as Mondex, ◊CyberCash, and ◊DigiCash.

eccentricity in geometry, a property of a ◊conic section (circle, ellipse, parabola, or hyperbola). It is the distance of any point on the curve from a fixed point (the focus) divided by the distance of that point from a fixed line (the directrix). A circle has an eccentricity of zero; for an ellipse it is less than one; for a parabola it is equal to one; and for a hyperbola it is greater than one.

ecdysis periodic shedding of the ◊exoskeleton by insects and other arthropods to allow growth. Prior to shedding, a new soft and expandable layer is laid down underneath the existing one. The old layer then splits, the animal moves free of it, and the new layer expands and hardens.

ECG abbreviation for ◊electrocardiogram.

echidna or ***spiny anteater*** toothless, egg-laying, spiny mammal of the order Monotremata, found in Australia and New Guinea. There are two species: *Tachyglossus aculeatus,* the short-nosed echidna, and the rarer *Zaglossus bruijni,* the long-nosed echidna. They feed entirely upon ants and termites, which they dig out with their powerful claws and lick up with their prehensile tongues. When attacked, an echidna rolls itself into a ball, or tries to hide by burrowing in the earth.

echinoderm marine invertebrate of the phylum Echinodermata ('spiny-skinned'), characterized by a five-radial symmetry. Echinoderms have a water-vascular system which transports substances around the body. They include starfishes (or sea stars), brittle-stars, sea lilies, sea urchins, and sea cucumbers. The skeleton is external, made of a series of limy plates. Echinoderms generally move by using tube-feet, small water-filled sacs that can be protruded or pulled back to the body.

Echinodermata phylum of invertebrate animals, members of which are called echinoderms.

echo in computing, user input that is printed to the screen so the user can read it.

echo repetition of a sound wave, or of a radar or sonar signal, by reflection from a surface. By accurately measuring the time taken for an echo to return to the transmitter, and by knowing the speed of a radar signal (the speed of light) or a sonar signal (the speed of sound in water), it is possible to calculate the range of the object causing the echo (◊echolocation).

echolocation or ***biosonar*** method used by certain animals, notably bats, whales, and dolphins, to detect the positions of objects by using sound. The animal emits a stream of high-pitched sounds, generally at ultrasonic frequencies (beyond the range of human hearing), and listens for the returning echoes reflected off objects to determine their exact location.

The location of an object can be established by the time difference between the emitted sound and its differential return as an echo to the two ears. Echolocation is of particular value under conditions when normal vision is poor (at night in the case of bats, in murky water for dolphins). A few species of bird can also echolocate, including cave-dwelling birds such as some species of swiftlets and the South American Oil Bird.

The frequency range of bats' echolocation calls is 20–215 kHz. Many species produce a specific and identifiable pattern of sound. Bats vary in the way they use echolocation: some emit pure sounds lasting up to 150 milliseconds, while others use a series of shorter 'chirps'. Sounds may be emitted through the mouth or nostrils depending on species.

Echolocation was first described in the 1930s, though it was postulated by Italian biologist Lazzaro Spallanzani (1729–1799).

echo sounder or ***sonar device*** device that detects objects under water by means of ◊sonar – by using reflected sound waves. Most boats are equipped with echo sounders to measure the water depth beneath them. An echo sounder consists of a transmitter, which emits an ultrasonic pulse, and a receiver, which detects the pulse after reflection from the seabed. The time between transmission and receipt of the reflected signal is a measure of the depth of water. Fishing boats use echo sounders to detect shoals of fish and navies use them to find enemy submarines.

eclampsia convulsions occurring during pregnancy following ◊pre-eclampsia.

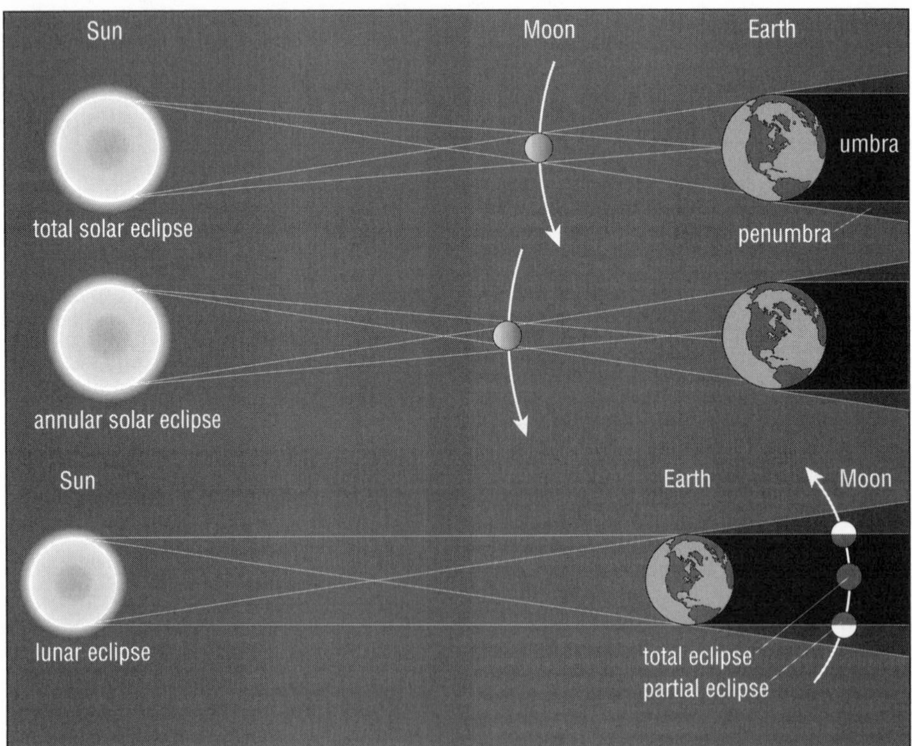

eclipse *The two types of eclipse: lunar and solar. A lunar eclipse occurs when the Moon passes through the shadow of the Earth. A solar eclipse occurs when the Moon passes between the Sun and the Earth, blocking out the Sun's light. During a total solar eclipse, when the Moon completely covers the Sun, the Moon's shadow sweeps across the Earth's surface from west to east at a speed of 3,200 kph/2,000 mph.*

Solar and Lunar Eclipses

Table does not include partial eclipses of the Moon.

Month	Day	Type of eclipse	Duration of maximum eclipse	Region for observation
1998				
February	26	solar total	17 hr 29 min	southern and eastern USA, Central America, northern South America
August	22	solar annular	2 hr 7 min	Southeast Asia, Oceania, Australasia
1999				
February	16	solar annular	6 hr 35 min	southern Indian Ocean, Antarctica, Australia
August	11	solar total	11 hr 4 min	Europe, North Africa, Arabia, western Asia
2000				
January	21	lunar total	4 hr 44 min	the Americas, Europe, Africa, western Asia
February	5	solar partial	12 hr 50 min	Antarctica
July	1	solar partial	19 hr 34 min	southeastern Pacific Ocean
July	16	lunar total	13 hr 56 min	southeastern Asia, Australasia
July	31	solar partial	2 hr 14 min	Arctic regions
December	25	solar partial	17 hr 36 min	USA, eastern Canada, Central America, Caribbean
2001				
January	9	lunar total	20 hr 21 min	Africa, Europe, Asia
June	21	solar total	12 hr 4 min	central and southern Africa
December	14	solar annular	20 hr 52 min	Pacific Ocean

eclipse passage of an astronomical body through the shadow of another.

The term is usually employed for solar and lunar eclipses, which may be either partial or total, but also, for example, for eclipses by Jupiter of its satellites. An eclipse of a star by a body in the Solar System is called an occultation.

A **solar eclipse** occurs when the Moon passes in front of the Sun as seen from Earth, and can happen only at new Moon. During a total eclipse the Sun's ◊corona can be seen. A total solar eclipse can last up to 7.5 minutes. When the Moon is at its farthest from Earth it does not completely cover the face of the Sun, leaving a ring of sunlight visible. This is an **annular eclipse** (from the Latin word *annulus* 'ring'). Between two and five solar eclipses occur each year.

A **lunar eclipse** occurs when the Moon passes into the shadow of the Earth, becoming dim until emerging from the shadow. Lunar eclipses may be partial or total, and they can happen only at full Moon. Total lunar eclipses last for up to 100 minutes; the maximum number each year is three.

eclipsing binary binary (double) star in which the two stars periodically pass in front of each other as seen from Earth.

When one star crosses in front of the other the total light received on Earth from the two stars declines. The first eclipsing binary to be noticed was ◊Algol.

ecliptic path, against the background of stars, that the Sun appears to follow each year as it is orbited by the Earth. It can be thought of as the plane of the Earth's orbit projected on to the ◊celestial sphere (imaginary sphere around the Earth).

The ecliptic is tilted at about 23.5° with respect to the celestial equator, a result of the tilt of the Earth's axis relative to the plane of its orbit around the Sun.

ecliptic coordinates in astronomy, a system for measuring the position of astronomical objects on the ◊celestial sphere with reference to the plane of the Earth's orbit, the ◊ecliptic.

Ecliptic latitude (symbol ß) is measured in degrees from the ecliptic (ß = 0°) to the north (ß = 90°) and south (ß = – 90°) ecliptic poles.

Ecliptic longitude (symbol λ) is measured in degrees eastward along the ecliptic (λ = 0° to 360°) from a fixed point known as the first point of ◊Aries or the ◊vernal equinox. Ecliptic coordinates are often used to measure the positions of the Sun and planets with respect to the Earth.

Ecliptic latitude and longitude are sometimes known as celestial latitude and longitude or ◊declination and ◊ascension. The ecliptic longitude of the Sun (solar longitude) is a convenient measure of the position of the Earth in its orbit.

WHAT THE HECK IS AN E. COLI?

http://falcon.cc.ukans.edu/~jbrown/ecoli.html

Explains the basics behind this bacterium, including information on the dangerous strain of the bacterium and how it developed. It contains guidelines to reduce the risk of infection. There are a number of links throughout the article to sites expanding on issues raised.

E. coli abbreviation for *Escherichia coli.*

ecology ***Greek oikos 'house'*** study of the relationship among organisms and the environments in which they live, including all living and nonliving components. The chief environmental factors governing the distribution of plants and animals are temperature, humidity, soil, light intensity, daylength, food supply, and interaction with other organisms. The term was coined by the biologist Ernst Haeckel in 1866.

Ecology may be concerned with individual organisms (for example, behavioural ecology, feeding strategies), with populations (for example, population dynamics), or with entire communities (for example, competition between species for access to resources in an ecosystem, or predator–prey relationships). Applied ecology is concerned with the management and conservation of habitats and the consequences and control of pollution.

We are unravelling nature like an old jumper.

PENNY KEMP English ecologist. *A Green Manifesto for the 1990s* ch 4

EcoNet in computing, one of several international computer networks dedicated to environmental issues.

Ecology: chronology

c. 325 BC	Greek scholar Theophrastus wrote about the relationship between organisms, and between organisms and their environment – the first ecological study.
1735	Swedish naturalist Carl Linnaeus developed his system for classifying and naming plants and animals.
1798	English cleric Thomas Malthus produced the earliest theoretical study of population dynamics.
1859	English naturalist Charles Darwin published his 'On the Origin of Species'.
1869	German zoologist Ernst Haeckel first defined the term 'ecology'.
1899	US botanist Henry Cowles published his classic paper on succession in sand dunes on Lake Michigan, USA.
1913	British Ecological Society founded.
1915	Ecological Society of America founded.
1916	US ecologist Frederic Clements coined the phrase 'climax communities' for large areas of rather uniform vegetation which he attributed to climactic factors.
1926	Russian botanist N I Vavilov published *Centres of Origin of Cultivated Plants*, concluding that there are relatively few such centres, many of which are located in mountainous areas.
1934	Russian ecologist G F Gause first stated the principles of competitive exclusion, related to a species' niche.
1935	British ecologist Arthur Tansley first coined the term 'ecosystem'.
1938	The coelacanth, a marine fish believed to have become extinct 65 million years ago, was 'rediscovered' in the Indian Ocean.
1940	Population biologist Charles Elton developed the idea of trophic levels in a community of organisms.
1950	The theory that natural selection may favour either individuals with high reproductive rates and rapid development (*r*-selection) or individuals with low reproductive rates and better competitive ability (*k*-selection) was first discussed.
1967	US biologists MacArthur and Wilson proposed their 'Theory of Island Biogeography' which related population and community size to island size. The theory is still widely used in the design of nature reserves today.
1979	English naturalist James Lovelock proposed his Gaia hypothesis, viewing the planet as a single organism.
1993	UN Convention on Biological Diversity came into force.

ecosystem in ecology, an integrated unit consisting of the ◊community of living organisms and the nonliving, or physical, environment in a particular area. The relationships among species in an ecosystem are usually complex and finely balanced, and removal of any one species may be disastrous. The removal of a major predator, for example, can result in the destruction of the ecosystem through overgrazing by herbivores.

Ecosystems can be identified at different scales – for example, the global ecosystem consists of all the organisms living on Earth, the Earth itself (both land and sea), and the atmosphere above; a freshwater-pond ecosystem consists of the plants and animals living in the pond, the pond water and all the substances dissolved or suspended in that water, and the rocks, mud, and decaying matter that make up the pond bottom.

Energy and nutrients pass through organisms in an ecosystem in a particular sequence (see ◊food chain): energy is captured through ◊photosynthesis, and nutrients are taken up from the soil or water by plants; both are passed to herbivores that eat the plants and then to carnivores that feed on herbivores. These nutrients are returned to the soil through the ◊decomposition of excrement and dead organisms, thus completing a cycle that is crucial to the stability and survival of the ecosystem.

ECSTASY.ORG

http://www.ecstasy.org/

Huge clearing house for information on this popular recreational drug. Contents of this much-visited site include instructions for paramedics and hospital staff, how to get an ecstasy sample chemically assessed, how to recognise danger signs, notes on the dance drug scene, and what to do if arrested for possession. On the question of the dangers of the drug, the site is noncommittal, presenting a huge sample of contradictory scientific opinion assessing the toxicity and long-term dangers of MDMA.

ecstasy or ***MDMA*** (3,4-methylenedioxymethamphetamine) illegal drug in increasing use from the 1980s. It is a modified ◊amphetamine with mild psychedelic effects, and works by depleting serotonin (a neurotransmitter) in the brain. Its long-term effects are unknown, but animal experiments have shown brain damage.

Ecstasy was first synthesized in 1914 by the Merck pharmaceutical company in Germany, and was one of eight psychedelics tested by the US army in 1953, but was otherwise largely forgotten until the mid-1970s. It can be synthesized from nutmeg oil. Since 1996 chemical recipes for making the drug have been circulated on the Internet.

ECT abbreviation for ◊electroconvulsive therapy.

ectoparasite ◊parasite that lives on the outer surface of its host.

ectopic in medicine, term applied to an anatomical feature that is displaced or found in an abnormal position. An ectopic pregnancy is one occurring outside the womb, usually in a Fallopian tube.

ectoplasm outer layer of a cell's ◊cytoplasm.

ectotherm 'cold-blooded' animal (see ◊poikilothermy), such as a lizard, that relies on external warmth (ultimately from the Sun) to raise its body temperature so that it can become active. To cool the body, ectotherms seek out a cooler environment.

eczema inflammatory skin condition, a form of dermatitis, marked by dryness, rashes, itching, the formation of blisters, and the exudation of fluid. It may be allergic in origin and is sometimes complicated by infection.

eddy current electric current induced, in accordance with ◊Faraday's laws, in a conductor located in a changing magnetic field. Eddy currents can cause much wasted energy in the cores of transformers and other electrical machines.

edelweiss perennial alpine plant belonging to the daisy family, with a white, woolly, star-shaped flower, found in the high mountains of Europe and Asia. (*Leontopodium alpinum*, family Compositae.)

edge connector in computing, an electrical connection formed by taking some of the metallic tracks on a ◊printed circuit board to the edge of the board and using them to plug directly into a matching socket.

EDISON, THOMAS

http://hfm.umd.umich.edu/histories/edison/tae.html

Short, illustrated biography of the US inventor, plus a chronology and bibliography. It includes sections on such topics as his childhood and the electric light.

Edison, Thomas Alva
(1847–1931)

US scientist and inventor, whose work in the fields of communications and electrical power greatly influenced the world in which we live. With more than 1,000 patents, Edison produced his most important inventions in Menlo Park, New Jersey 1876–87, including the phonograph and the electric light bulb in 1879. He also constructed a system of electric power distribution for consumers, the telephone transmitter, and the megaphone.

telegraphy and telephony Edison's first success came in the area of telegraphy. Perceiving the need for rapid communications after the Civil War, his first invention was an automatic repeater for telegraphic messages. He then invented a tape machine called a 'ticker', which communicated stock exchange prices across the country.

Turning his attention to the transmission of the human voice over long distances in 1876, he patented an electric transmitter system that proved to be less commercially successful than the telephone of Bell and Gray, patented a few months later. Undeterred, Edison set about improving their system, culminating in his invention of the carbon transmitter, which so increased the volume of the telephone signal that it was used as a microphone in the Bell telephone.

the light bulb While experimenting with the carbon microphone in the 1870s, Edison had toyed briefly with the idea of using a thin carbon filament as a light source in an incandescent electric lamp. He returned to the idea in 1879. His first major success came on 19 October of that year when, using carbonized sewing cotton mounted on an electrode in a vacuum (one millionth of an atmosphere), he obtained a source that remained aglow for 45 hours without overheating – a major problem with all other materials used. He and his assistants tried 6,000 other organic materials before finding a bamboo fibre that gave a bulb life of 1,000 hours.

generators and the first power stations To produce a serious rival to gas illumination, a power source was required as well as a cheap and reliable lamp. The alternatives were either generators or heavy and expensive batteries. At that time, the best generators rarely converted more than 40% of the mechanical energy into electrical energy. Edison's first generator consisted of a drum armature of soft iron wire and a simple bi-polar magnet, and was designed to operate one arc lamp and some incandescent lamps in series.

A few months later he built a much more ambitious generator, the largest built to date; weighing 500 kg/1,103 lb and with an efficiency of 82%. Edison's team were at the forefront of development in generator technology over the next decade, during which efficiency was raised above 90%. To complete his electrical system he designed cables to carry power into the home from small (by modern standards) generating stations, and also invented an electricity meter to record its use.

the phonograph In 1877 he began the era of recorded sound by inventing the phonograph, a device in which the vibrations of the human voice were engraved by a needle on a revolving cylinder coated with tin foil.

Mary Evans Picture Library

Edge connectors are often used to connect the computer's main circuit board, or motherboard, to the expansion boards that provide the computer with extra memory or other facilities.

EDI in computing, abbreviation for ◊electronic data interchange.

EDIFACT (acronym from ***electronic data interchange for administration, commerce, and trade***) in computing, the ISO and ANSI standard system for handling EDI transactions.

editing in computing, act of creating, changing, and formatting word processor documents or pages for distribution on the World Wide Web.

EDO RAM (abbreviation for ***extended data out random-access memory***) in computing, faster type of ◊RAM introduced in the mid-1990s.

EDP in computing, abbreviation for **electronic** ◊data processing.

Educational Resources Information Center in computing, database of resources for education available on the Internet. See ◊ERIC.

edutainment (contraction of ***education and entertainment***) ◊multimedia-related term, used to describe computer software that is both educational and entertaining. Examples include educational software for children that teaches them to spell or count while playing games, and ◊CD-ROMs about machines that contain animations showing how the machines work. Compare ◊infotainment.

Edwards Air Force Base military USAF centre in California, situated on a dry lake bed, often used as a landing site by the Space Shuttle.

EEG abbreviation for ◊electroencephalogram.

eel any fish of the order Anguilliformes. Eels are snakelike, with elongated dorsal and anal fins. They include the freshwater eels of Europe and North America (which breed in the Atlantic), the marine conger eels, and the morays of tropical coral reefs.

A new species of moray eel was discovered 1995 off the coasts of Oman and Somalia. It is up to 60 cm/2 ft in length with a large black blotch around the gill openings.

eelgrass or ***tape grass*** **or** ***glass wrack*** any of several aquatic plants, especially *Zostera marina*. Eelgrass is found in tidal mud flats and is one of the few flowering plants to adapt to marine conditions, being completely submerged at high tide. (Genus *Zostera*, family Zosteraceae.)

eelpout freshwater fish also called a ◊burbot.

EEPROM (acronym for ***electrically erasable programmable read-only memory***) computer memory that can record data and retain it indefinitely. The data can be erased with an electrical charge and new data recorded.

Some EEPROM must be removed from the computer and erased and reprogrammed using a special device. Other EEPROM, called **flash memory**, can be erased and reprogrammed without removal from the computer.

EFF abbreviation for ◊***Electronic Frontier Foundation***.

Effelsberg site, near Bonn, Germany, of the world's largest fully steerable radio telescope, the 100-m/328-ft radio dish of the Max Planck Institute for Radio Astronomy, opened in 1971.

efficiency in physics, a general term indicating the degree to which a process or device can convert energy from one form to another without loss. It is normally expressed as a fraction or percentage, where 100% indicates conversion with no loss. The efficiency of a machine, for example, is the ratio of the work done by the machine to the energy put into the machine; in practice it is always less than 100% because of frictional heat losses. Certain electrical machines with no moving parts, such as transformers, can approach 100% efficiency.

Since the ◊mechanical advantage, or force ratio, is the ratio of the load (the output force) to the effort (the input force), and the ◊velocity ratio is the distance moved by the effort divided by the distance moved by the load, for certain machines the efficiency can also be defined as the mechanical advantage divided by the velocity ratio.

efflorescence loss of water or crystallization of crystals exposed to air, resulting in a dry powdery surface.

EFTPOS (acronym for ***electronic funds transfer at point of sale***), a form of electronic funds transfer.

EGA (abbreviation for ***enhanced graphics array***) computer colour display system superior to ◊CGA (colour graphics adapter), providing 16 colours on screen and a resolution of 640 x 350, but not as good as ◊VGA.

egestion the removal of undigested food or faeces from the gut. In most animals egestion takes place via the anus, although the invertebrate flatworms must use the mouth because their gut has no exit. Egestion is the last part of a complex feeding process that starts with food capture and continues with digestion and assimilation.

egg in animals, the ovum, or female ◊gamete (reproductive cell).

After fertilization by a sperm cell, it begins to divide to form an embryo. Eggs may be deposited by the female (◊ovipary) or they may develop within her body (◊vivipary and ◊ovovivipary). In the oviparous reptiles and birds, the egg is protected by a shell, and well supplied with nutrients in the form of yolk.

Section through a fertilized egg

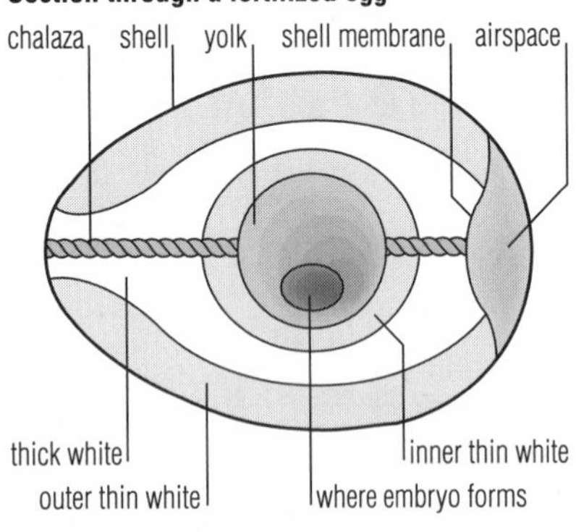

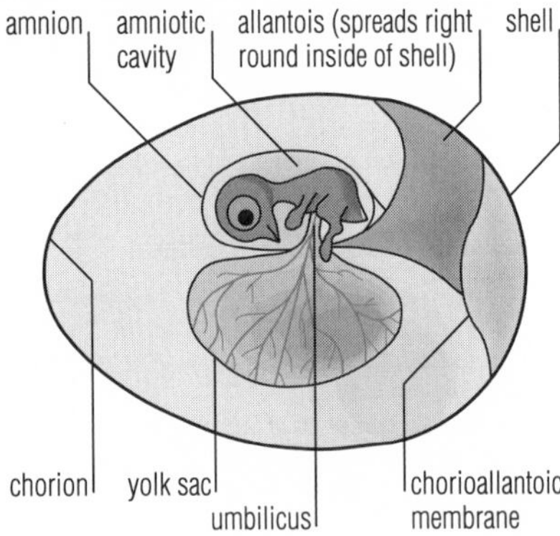

egg Section through a fertilized bird egg. Inside a bird's egg is a complex structure of liquids and membranes designed to meet the needs of the growing embryo. The yolk, which is rich in fat, is gradually absorbed by the embryo. The white of the egg provides protein and water. The chalaza is a twisted band of protein which holds the yolk in place and acts as a shock absorber. The airspace allows gases to be exchanged through the shell. The allantois contains many blood vessels which carry gases between the embryo and the outside.

eggar-moth large reddish-brown moth with a highly developed hindwing. The length across the wings is 3.8–11.5 cm/1.5–4.5 in.

The walls of the cocoons sometimes have a smooth, shell-like appearance, hence the name.

classification The eggar-moth in the family Lasiocampidae, order Lepidoptera, class Insecta, phylum Arthropoda.

eggplant another name for ◊aubergine.

ego *Latin 'I'* in psychology, the processes concerned with the self and a person's conception of himself or herself, encompassing values and attitudes. In Freudian psychology, the term refers specifically to the element of the human mind that represents the conscious processes concerned with reality, in conflict with the ◊id (the instinctual element) and the ◊superego (the ethically aware element).

No other manmade device since the shields and lances of the ancient knights fulfils a man's ego like an automobile.

ROOTES English car manufacturer.
Quoted in 'Who Said That?', BBC TV, 14 Jan 1958

egret any of several ◊herons with long tufts of feathers on the head or neck. They belong to the order Ciconiiformes.

eider large marine ◊duck of the genus *Somateria,* family Anatidae, order Anseriformes. They are found on the northern coasts of the Atlantic and Pacific Oceans. The **common eider** *S. molissima* is highly valued for its soft down, which is used in quilts and cushions for warmth. The adult male has a black cap and belly and a green nape. The rest of the plumage is white with a pink breast and throat, while the female is a mottled brown. The bill is large and flattened and both bill and feet are olive green.

Other species are the **king eider-duck** *S. spectablis,* **Steller's eider** *Polysticta stelleri,* and the **spectacled eider** *S. fischeri.*

eidophor television projection system that produces pictures up to 10 m/33 ft square, at sports events or rock concerts, for example. The system uses three coloured beams of light, one of each primary colour (red, blue, and green), which scan the screen. The intensity of each beam is controlled by the strength of the corresponding colour in the television picture.

Imagination is more important than knowledge.

ALBERT EINSTEIN German-born US physicist.
On Science

EINSTEIN'S LEGACY

http://www.ncsa.uiuc.edu/Cyberia/NumRel/EinsteinLegacy.html

Illustrated introduction to the man and his greatest legacy – relativity and the concept of space-time. There is a film and audio clip version of the page courtesy of a US scientist and details about how current research is linked to Einstein's revolutionary ideas.

Einstein, Albert (1879–1955)

German-born US physicist whose theories of relativity revolutionized our understanding of matter, space, and time. Einstein established that light may have a particle nature and deduced the **photoelectric law**, for which he was awarded the Nobel Prize for Physics in 1921. He also investigated Brownian motion, confirming the existence of atoms. His last conception of the basic laws governing the universe was outlined in his unified field theory, made public in 1953.

Brownian motion Einstein's first major achievement concerned Brownian movement, the random movement of fine particles that can be seen through a microscope, which was first observed in 1827 by Robert Brown when studying a suspension of pollen grains in water. The motion of the pollen grains increased when the temperature increased but decreased if larger particles were used. Einstein explained this phenomenon as being the effect of large numbers of molecules (in this case, water molecules) bombarding the particles. He was able to make predictions of the movement and sizes of the particles, which were later verified experimentally by the French physicist Jean Perrin (1870–1942).

Einstein's explanation of Brownian motion and its subsequent experimental confirmation was one of the most important pieces of evidence for the hypothesis that matter is composed of atoms. Experiments based on this work were used to obtain an accurate value of Avogadro's number (the number of atoms in one mole of a substance) and the first accurate values of atomic size.

the photoelectric effect and the Nobel Prize Einstein's work on photoelectricity began with an explanation of the radiation law proposed in 1901 by Max Planck: $E=h\nu$, where E is the energy of radiation, h is Planck's constant, and ν is the frequency of radiation. Einstein suggested that packets of light energy are capable of behaving as particles called 'light quanta' (later called photons). Einstein used this hypothesis to explain the photoelectric effect, proposing that light particles striking the surface of certain metals cause electrons to be emitted.

It had been found experimentally that electrons are not emitted by light of less than a certain frequency ν^0; that when electrons are emitted, their energy increases with an increase in the frequency of the light; and that an increase in light intensity produces more electrons but does not increase their energy. Einstein suggested that the kinetic energy of each electron, $\frac{1}{2}mv^2$, is equal to the difference in the incident light energy $h\nu$ and the light energy needed to overcome the threshold of emission, $h\nu^0$. This can be written mathematically as:

$$\tfrac{1}{2}mv^2 = h\nu - h\nu^0$$

the speed of light and the special theory of relativity The **special theory of relativity** started with the premises that (1) the laws of nature are the same for all observers in unaccelerated motion, and (2) the speed of light is independent of the motion of its source. Until then, there had been a steady accumulation of knowledge that suggested that light and other electromagnetic radiation do not behave as predicted by classical physics. It proved impossible, for example, to measure the expected changes in the speed of light relative to the motion of the Earth. The **Michelson–Morley experiment** demonstrated that the velocity of light is constant and does not vary with the motion of either the source or the observer. Their experiment also confirmed that no 'ether' exists in the Universe as a medium to carry light waves, as was required by classical physics.

Mary Evans Picture Library

These findings did not worry Einstein, who viewed light as behaving like particles. He recognized that light, being different from waves that travel in a medium, has a measured speed that is independent of the speed of the observer. Thus, contrary to everyday experience with phenomena such as sound waves, the velocity of light is the same for an observer travelling at high speed *towards* a light source as it is for an observer travelling rapidly *away* from the light source. To Einstein it followed that, if the speed of light is the same for both these observers, the time and distance framework they use to measure the speed of light cannot be the same. Time and distance vary, depending on the velocity of each observer.

From the notions of relative motion and the constant velocity of light, Einstein derived that, in a system in motion relative to an observer, length would be observed to decrease, time would slow down, and mass would increase. The magnitude of these effects is negligible at ordinary velocities and Newton's laws still held good. But at velocities approaching that of light, they become substantial. If a system were to move at the velocity of light, to an observer carried with it, its length would be zero, time would be at a stop, and its mass would be infinite. Einstein therefore concluded that no system can move at a velocity equal to or greater than the velocity of light.

Einstein's conclusions regarding time dilation and mass increase were later verified with observations of fast-moving atomic clocks and cosmic rays. Einstein went on to show in 1907 that mass is related to energy by the famous equation $E = mc^2$, which indicates the enormous amount of energy that is stored as mass, some of which is released in radioactivity and nuclear reactions, for example in the Sun.

gravity and the general theory of relativity In the **general theory of relativity**, the properties of space–time were to be conceived as modified locally by the presence of a body with mass; and light rays should bend when they pass by a massive object. A planet's orbit around the Sun arises from its natural trajectory in modified space–time – there is no need to invoke, as Isaac Newton did, a force of gravity. General relativity theory was inspired by the simple idea that it is impossible in a small region to distinguish between acceleration and gravitation effects (as in a lift one feels heavier when it accelerates upwards).

Einstein used the general theory to account for an anomaly in the orbit of the planet Mercury that could not be explained by Newtonian mechanics. Furthermore, the general theory made two predictions concerning light and gravitation. The first was that a red shift is produced if light passes through an intense gravitational field, and this was subsequently detected in astronomical observations in 1925. The second was a prediction that the apparent positions of stars would shift when they are seen near the Sun because the Sun's intense gravity would bend the light rays from the stars as they pass the Sun. Einstein was triumphantly vindicated when observations of a solar eclipse in 1919 showed apparent shifts of exactly the amount he had predicted.

einsteinium synthesized, radioactive, metallic element of the actinide series, symbol Es, atomic number 99, relative atomic mass 254.09.

It was produced by the first thermonuclear explosion, in 1952, and discovered in fallout debris in the form of the isotope Es-253 (half-life 20 days). Its longest-lived isotope, Es-254, with a half-life of 276 days, allowed the element to be studied at length. It is now synthesized by bombarding lower-numbered ◊transuranic elements in particle accelerators. It was first identified by A Ghiorso and his team who named it in 1955 after Albert Einstein, in honour of his theoretical studies of mass and energy.

EIS (abbreviation for ***executive information systems***) software applications that extract information from an organization's computer applications and data files and present the data in a form required by management.

EISA (abbreviation for ***extended industry standard architecture***) in computing, one of several types of ◊data bus created to improve on the original ISA (industry standard architecture) design introduced with the IBM PC AT microcomputer in 1984. The EISA bus adds speed and capacity because it is a 32-bit bus (ISA is a 16-bit bus), although it can still accept ISA-compatible expansion cards.

The EISA bus was developed by a consortium of PC manufacturers to counter IBM's proprietary MCA (micro channel architecture) bus in 1987, but it has since been superseded by the ◊PCI (peripheral component interconnect) bus designed by Intel. See also ◊local bus.

ejecta in astronomy, any material thrown out of a ◊crater due to volcanic eruption or the impact of a ◊meteorite or other object. Ejecta from impact craters on the ◊Moon often form long bright streaks known as rays, which in some cases can be traced for thousands of kilometres across the lunar surface.

ejector seat device for propelling an aircraft pilot out of the plane to parachute to safety in an emergency, invented by the British engineer James Martin (1893–1981). The first seats of 1945 were powered by a compressed spring; later seats used an explosive charge. By the early 1980s, 35,000 seats had been fitted worldwide, and the lives of 5,000 pilots saved by their use.

Seats that can be ejected on takeoff and landing or at low altitude were a major breakthrough of the 1980s. They are as effective as those originally designed for parachuting from high altitudes.

Ekman spiral effect in oceanography, theoretical description of a consequence of the ◊Coriolis effect on ocean currents, whereby currents flow at an angle to the winds that drive them. It derives its name from the Swedish oceanographer Vagn Ekman (1874–1954).

In the northern hemisphere, surface currents are deflected to the right of the wind direction. The surface current then drives the subsurface layer at an angle to its original deflection. Consequent subsurface layers are similarly affected, so that the effect decreases with increasing depth. The result is that most water is transported at about right-angles to the wind direction. Directions are reversed in the southern hemisphere.

eland largest species of ◊antelope, *Taurotragus oryx*. Pale fawn in colour, it is about 2 m/6 ft high, and both sexes have spiral horns about 45 cm/18 in long. It is found in central and southern Africa.

Elasmobranchii subclass of class Chondrichthyes (cartilaginous fish), which includes the ◊sharks and ◊rays. They are characterized by having five to seven pairs of gill clefts that open separately to the exterior and are not covered by a protective fold of skin.

elastic collision in physics, a collision between two or more bodies in which the total ◊kinetic energy of the bodies is conserved (remains constant); none is converted into any other form of energy. The molecules of a gas may be considered to collide elastically, but large objects may not because some of their kinetic energy will be converted on collision to heat and sound, or used to deform the object.

elasticity in physics, the ability of a solid to recover its shape once deforming forces (stresses modifying its dimensions or shape) are removed. An elastic material obeys ◊Hooke's law, which states that its deformation is proportional to the applied stress up to a certain point, called the **elastic limit**, beyond which additional stress will deform it permanently. Elastic materials include metals and rubber; however, all materials have some degree of elasticity.

elastomer any material with rubbery properties that stretches easily and then quickly returns to its original length when released.

Natural and synthetic rubbers and such materials as polychloroprene and butadiene copolymers are elastomers. The convoluted molecular chains making up these materials are uncoiled by a stretching force, but return to their original position when released because there are relatively few crosslinks between the chains.

elater beetle another name for ◊click beetle.

E layer (formerly called the Kennelly–Heaviside layer) the lower regions (90–120 km/56–75 mi) of the ◊ionosphere, which reflect radio waves, allowing their reception around the surface of the Earth. The E layer approaches the Earth by day and recedes from it at night.

elder in botany, any of a group of small trees or shrubs belonging to the honeysuckle family, native to North America, Europe, Asia, and North Africa. Some are grown as ornamentals for their showy yellow or white flower clusters and their colourful black or scarlet berries. (Genus *Sambucus*, family Caprifoliaceae.)

The American elder (*Sambucus canadensis*) reaches tree size and has blue berries. The common elder (*S. nigra*) of Europe, North Africa, and western Asia has pinnate leaves (leaflets growing either side of a stem) and heavy heads of small, sweet-scented, white flowers in early summer. These are followed by clusters of small, black, shiny berries. The scarlet-berried *S. racemosa* is found in parts of Europe, Asia, and North America.

electrical energy form of energy carried by an electric current. It may be converted into other forms of energy such as heat, light, and motion.

The electrical energy W watts converted in a circuit component through which a current I amperes passes and across which there is a potential difference of V volts is given by the formula:

$$W = IV$$

electrical relay an electromagnetic switch; see ◊relay.

electrical safety measures taken to protect human beings from electric shock or from fires caused by electrical faults. They are of paramount importance in the design of electrical equipment. Safety measures include the fitting of earth wires, and fuses or circuit breakers; the insulation of wires; the double insulation of portable equipment; and the use of residual-current devices (RCDs), which will break a circuit and cut off all currents if there is any imbalance between the currents in the live and neutral wires connected to an appliance (caused, for example, if some current is being conducted through a person).

The effects of electric shock vary from a tingling sensation to temporary paralysis and even death, and depend upon the amount of current passing through the body, and upon whether it passes through the central nervous system thereby affecting brain and heart function. Fires are usually caused by overheated cables or loose connections.

electric arc a continuous electric discharge of high current between two electrodes, giving out a brilliant light and heat. The phenomenon is exploited in the carbon-arc lamp, once widely used in film projectors. In the electric-arc furnace an arc struck between very large carbon electrodes and the metal charge provides the heating. In arc ◊welding an electric arc provides the heat to fuse the metal. The discharges in low-pressure gases, as in neon and sodium lights, can also be broadly considered as electric arcs.

electric bell a bell that makes use of electromagnetism. At its heart is a wire-wound coil on an iron core (an electromagnet) which, when a direct current (from a battery) flows through it, attracts an iron ◊armature. The armature acts as a switch, whose movement causes contact with an adjustable contact point to be broken, so breaking the circuit. A spring rapidly returns the armature to the contact point, once again closing the circuit, and so bringing about the oscillation. The armature oscillates back and forth, and the clapper or hammer fixed to the armature strikes the bell.

electric charge property of some bodies that causes them to exert forces on each other. Two bodies both with positive or both with negative charges repel, each other, whereas bodies with opposite or 'unlike' charges attract each other, since each is in the ◊electric field of the other. In atoms, ◊electrons possess a negative charge, and ◊protons an equal positive charge. The ◊SI unit of electric charge is the coulomb (symbol C).

A body can be charged by friction, induction, or chemical change and shows itself as an accumulation of electrons (negative charge) or loss of electrons (positive charge) on an atom or body. Atoms have no charge but can sometimes gain electrons to become negative ions or lose them to become positive ions. So-called ◊static electricity, seen in such phenomena as the charging of nylon shirts when they are pulled on or off, or in brushing hair, is in fact the gain or loss of electrons from the surface atoms. A flow of charge (such as electrons through a copper wire) constitutes an electric current; the flow of current is measured in amperes (symbol A).

electric current the flow of electrically charged particles through a conducting circuit due to the presence of a ◊potential difference. The current at any point in a circuit is the amount of charge flowing per second; its SI unit is the ampere (coulomb per second).

Current carries electrical energy from a power supply, such as a battery of electrical cells, to the components of the circuit, where it is converted into other forms of energy, such as heat, light, or motion. It may be either ◊direct current or ◊alternating current.

heating effect When current flows in a component possessing resistance, electrical energy is converted into heat energy. If the resistance of the component is R ohms and the current through it is I amperes, then the heat energy W (in joules) generated in a time t seconds is given by the formula:

$$W = I^2Rt$$

magnetic effect A magnetic field is created around all conductors that carry a current. When a current-bearing conductor is made into a coil it forms an electromagnet with a ◊◊magnetic field that is similar to that of a bar magnet, but which disappears as soon as the current is switched off. The strength of the magnetic field is directly proportional to the current in the conductor – a property that allows a small ◊electromagnet to be used to produce a pattern of magnetism on recording tape or disc that accurately represents the sound or data to be stored. The direction of the field created around a conducting wire may be predicted by using ◊Maxwell's screw rule.

motor effect A conductor carrying current in a magnetic field experiences a force, and is impelled to move in a direction perpendicular to both the direction of the current and the direction of the magnetic field. The direction of motion may be predicted by Fleming's left-hand rule (see ◊Fleming's rules). The magnitude of the force experienced depends on the length of the conductor and on the strengths of the current and the magnetic field, and is greatest when the conductor is at right angles to the field. A conductor wound into a coil that can rotate between the poles of a magnet forms the basis of an ◊electric motor.

electric eel South American freshwater bony fish. It grows to almost 3 m/10 ft and the electric shock produced, normally for immobilizing prey, is enough to stun an adult human. Electric eels are not true eels.

classification *Electrophorus electricus* is in the order Cypriniformes, class Osteichthyes.

electric field in physics, a region in which a particle possessing electric charge experiences a force owing to the presence of another electric charge. The strength of an electric field, E, is measured in volts per metre (V m^{-1}). It is a type of ◊electromagnetic field.

electric fish any of several unrelated fishes that have electricity-producing powers, including the South American 'electric eel'. These include *Electrophorus electricus,* which is not a true eel, and in which the lateral tail muscles are modified to form electric organs capable of generating 650 volts; the current passing from tail to head is strong enough to stun another animal. Not all electric fishes produce such strong discharges; most use weak electric fields to navigate and to detect nearby objects.

electricity all phenomena caused by ◊electric charge, whether static or in motion. Electric charge is caused by an excess or deficit of electrons in the charged substance, and an electric current is the movement of charge through a material. Substances may be electrical conductors, such as metals, that allow the passage of electricity through them readily, or insulators, such as rubber, that are extremely poor conductors. Substances with relatively poor conductivities that can be improved by the addition of heat or light are known as ◊semiconductors.

> **BEE**
>
> Bees exposed to the electrical fields of high-voltage power cables produce their honey in an erratic manner. As a consequence, bee-keepers have learned not to place their hives under power cables.

electrical properties of solids The first artificial electrical phenomenon to be observed was that some naturally occurring materials such as amber, when rubbed with a piece of cloth, would then attract small objects such as dust and pieces of paper. Rubbing the object caused it to become electrically charged so that it had an excess or deficit of electrons. When the amber is rubbed with a piece of cloth electrons are transferred from the cloth to the amber so that the amber has an excess of electrons and is negatively charged, and the cloth has a deficit of electrons and is positively charged. This accumulation of charge is called ◊static electricity.

This charge on the object exerts an electric field in the space around itself that can attract or repel other objects. It was discovered that there are only two types of charge, positive and negative, and that they neutralize one another. Objects with a like charge always repel one another while objects with an unlike charge attract each other. Neutral objects (such as pieces of paper) can be attracted to charged bodies by electrical induction. For example, the charge on a negatively charged body causes a separation of charge across the neutral body. The positive charges tend to move towards the side near the negatively charged body and the negative charges tend to move towards the opposite side so that the neutral body is weakly attracted to the charged body by ◊induction.

The ◊electroscope is a device used to demonstrate the presence of electric charges and to measure its size and whether it is positive or negative. The electroscope was invented by Michael Faraday.

current, charge, and energy An ◊electric current in a material is the passage of charge through it. In metals and other conducting materials, the charge is carried by free electrons that are not bound tightly to the atoms and are thus able to move through the material. For charge to flow in a circuit there must be a ◊potential difference (pd) applied across the circuit. This is often supplied in the form of a battery that has a positive terminal and a negative terminal. Under the influence of the potential difference, the electrons are repelled from the negative terminal side of the circuit and attracted to the positive terminal of the battery. A steady flow of electrons around the circuit is produced.

Current flowing through a circuit can be measured using an ◊ammeter and is measured in ◊amperes (or amps). A ◊coulomb (C) is the unit of charge, defined as the charge passing a point in a wire each second when the current is exactly 1 amp. The unit of charge is named after Charles Augustin de ◊Coulomb. Direct current (DC) flows continuously in one direction; ◊alternating current (AC) flows alternately in each direction.

In a circuit the battery provides energy to make charge flow through the circuit. The amount of energy supplied to each unit of charge is called the electromotive force (emf). The unit of emf is the ◊volt (V). A battery has an emf of 1 volt when it supplies I joule of energy to each coulomb of charge flowing through it. The energy carried by flowing charges can be used to do work, for example to light a bulb, to cause current to flow through a resistor, to emit radiation, or to produce heat. When the energy carried by a current is made to do work in this way, a potential difference can be measured across the circuit component concerned by a voltmeter or a ◊cathode-ray oscilloscope. The potential difference is also measured in volts. Power, measured in ◊watts, is the product of current and voltage.

Although potential difference and current measure different things, they are related to one another. This relationship was discovered by Georg ◊Ohm, and is expressed by ◊Ohm's law: the current through a wire is proportional to the potential difference across its ends. The potential difference divided by the current is a constant for a given piece of wire. This constant for a given material is called the ◊resistance.

conduction in liquids and gases In liquids, current can flow by the movement of charged ions through a solution or molten salt (the electrolyte), resulting in the migration of ions to the electrodes: positive ions (cations) to the negative electrode (cathode) and negative ions (anions) to the positive electrode (anode). This process is called ◊electrolysis and represents bi-directional flow of charge as opposite charges move to oppositely charged electrodes. In metals, charges are only carried by free electrons and therefore move in only one direction.

electromagnetism ◊Magnetic fields are produced either by current-carrying conductors or by permanent magnets. In current-carrying wires, the magnetic field lines are concentric circles around the wire. Their direction depends on the direction of the current and their strength on the size of the current.

If a conducting wire is moved within a magnetic field, the magnetic field acts on the free electrons within the conductor, displacing them and causing a current to flow. The force acting on the electrons and causing them to move is greatest when the wire is perpendicular to the magnetic field lines. The direction of the current is given by the ◊left-hand rule. The generation of a current by the relative movement of a conductor in a magnetic field is called ◊electromagnetic induction. This is the basis of how a ◊dynamo works.

generation of electricity Electricity is the most useful and most convenient form of energy, readily convertible into heat and light and used to power machines. Electricity can be generated in one place and distributed anywhere because it readily flows through wires. It is generated at power stations where a suitable energy source is harnessed to drive ◊turbines that spin electricity generators. Current energy sources are coal, oil, water power (hydroelectricity), natural gas, and ◊nuclear energy. Research is under way to increase the contribution of wind, tidal, solar, and geothermal power. Nuclear fuel has proved a more expensive source of electricity than initially anticipated and worldwide concern over radioactivity may limit its future development.

Electricity is generated at power stations at a voltage of about 25,000 volts, which is not a suitable voltage for long-distance transmission. For minimal power loss, transmission must take place at very high voltage (400,000 volts or more). The generated voltage is therefore increased ('stepped up') by a ◊transformer. The resulting high-voltage electricity is then fed into the main arteries of the grid system, an interconnected network of power stations and distribution centres covering a large area. After transmission to a local substation, the line voltage is reduced by a step-down transformer and distributed to consumers.

Among specialized power units that convert energy directly to electrical energy without the intervention of any moving mechanisms, the most promising are thermionic converters. These use conventional fuels such as propane gas, as in portable military power packs, or, if refuelling is to be avoided, radioactive fuels, as in uncrewed navigational aids and spacecraft.

UK electricity generation was split into four companies in 1990 in preparation for privatization. The nuclear power stations remain in the hands of the state through Nuclear Electric (accounting for 20% of electricity generated); National Power (50%) and PowerGen (30%) generate electricity from fossil-fuel and renewable sources. Transmission lines and substations are owned by the National Grid, which was privatized in 1996.

Electricity generated on a commercial scale was available from the early 1880s and used for electric motors driving all kinds of machinery, and for lighting, first by carbon arc, but later by incandescent filaments (first of carbon and then of tungsten), enclosed in glass bulbs partially filled with inert gas under vacuum. Light is also produced by passing electricity through a gas or metal vapour or a fluorescent lamp. Other practical applications include telephone, radio, television, X-ray machines, and many other applications in ◊electronics.

An important consideration in the design of electrical equipment is ◊electrical safety. This includes measures to minimize the risk of electric shock or fire caused by electrical faults. Safety measures include the fitting of earth wires, and fuses or circuit breakers, and the insulation of wires.

history The fact that amber has the power, after being rubbed, of attracting light objects, such as bits of straw and feathers, is said to have been known to Thales of Miletus and to the Roman naturalist Pliny. William Gilbert, Queen Elizabeth I's physician, found that many substances possessed this power, and he called it 'electric' after the Greek word meaning 'amber'.

In the early 1700s, it was recognized that there are two types of electricity and that unlike kinds attract each other and like kinds repel. The charge on glass rubbed with silk came to be known as positive electricity, and the charge on amber rubbed with wool as negative electricity. These two charges were found to cancel each other when brought together.

In 1800 Alessandro ◊Volta found that a series of cells containing brine, in which were dipped plates of zinc and copper, gave an electric current, which later in the same year was shown to evolve hydrogen and oxygen when passed through water (see ◊electrolysis). Humphry Davy, in 1807, decomposed soda and potash (both thought to be elements) and isolated the metals sodium and potassium, a discovery that led the way to ◊electroplating. Other properties of electric currents discovered were the heating effect, now used in lighting and central heating, and the deflection of a magnetic needle, described by Hans Oersted in 1820 and elaborated by André ◊Ampère in 1825. This work made possible the electric telegraph.

For Michael Faraday, the fact that an electric current passing through a wire caused a magnet to move suggested that moving a wire or coil of wire rapidly between the poles of a magnet would induce an electric current. He demonstrated this in 1831, producing the first dynamo, which became the basis of electrical engineering. The characteristics of currents were crystallized about 1827 by Georg ◊Ohm, who showed that the current passing along a wire was equal to the electromotive force across the wire multiplied by a constant, which was the conductivity of the wire. The unit of resistance (ohm) is named after Ohm, the unit of emf (volt) is named after Volta, and the unit of current (amp) after Ampère.

The work of the late 1800s indicated the wide interconnections of electricity (with magnetism, heat, and light), and about 1855 James Clerk ◊Maxwell formulated a single electromagnetic theory. The universal importance of electricity was decisively proved by the discovery that the atom, until then thought to be the ultimate particle of matter, is composed of a positively charged central core, the nucleus, about which negatively charged electrons rotate in various orbits.

electric motor a machine that converts electrical energy into mechanical energy. There are various types, including direct-current and induction motors, most of which produce rotary motion. A linear induction motor produces linear (in a straight line) rather than rotary motion.

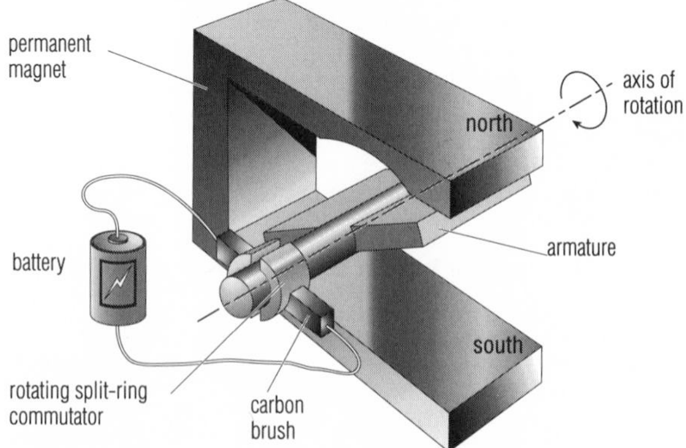

electric motor *In an electric motor, magnetic fields generated by electric currents push against each other, causing a shaft (the armature) to rotate.*

A simple **direct-current motor** consists of a horseshoe-shaped permanent ◊magnet with a wire-wound coil (◊armature) mounted so that it can rotate between the poles of the magnet. A ◊commutator reverses the current (from a battery) fed to the coil on each half-turn, which rotates because of the mechanical force exerted on a conductor carrying a current in a magnetic field.

An **induction motor** employs ◊alternating current. It comprises a stationary current-carrying coil (stator) surrounding another coil (rotor), which rotates because of the current induced in it by the magnetic field created by the stator; it thus requires no commutator.

electric organs specialized organs that discharge electricity and occur only in fish; see ◊electric fish.

electric power the rate at which an electrical machine uses electrical ◊energy or converts it into other forms of energy – for example, light, heat, mechanical energy. Usually measured in watts (equivalent to joules per second), it is equal to the product of the voltage and the current flowing.

An electric lamp that passes a current of 0.4 amperes at 250 volts uses 100 watts of electrical power and converts it into light and heat – in ordinary terms it is a 100-watt lamp. An electric motor that requires 6 amperes at the same voltage consumes 1,500 watts (1.5 kilowatts), equivalent to delivering about 2 horsepower of mechanical power.

electric ray another name for the ◊torpedo.

electrocardiogram (ECG) graphic recording of the electrical activity of the heart, as detected by electrodes placed on the skin. Electrocardiography is used in the diagnosis of heart disease.

electrochemical series or ***electromotive series*** list of chemical elements arranged in descending order of the ease with which they can lose electrons to form cations (positive ions). An element can be displaced (◊displacement reaction) from a compound by any element above it in the series.

electrochemistry the branch of science that studies chemical reactions involving electricity. The use of electricity to produce chemical effects, ◊electrolysis, is employed in many industrial processes, such as the manufacture of chlorine and the extraction of aluminium. The use of chemical reactions to produce electricity is the basis of electrical ◊cells, such as the dry cell and the Leclanché cell.

Since all chemical reactions involve changes to the electronic structure of atoms, all reactions are now recognized as electrochemical in nature. Oxidation, for example, was once defined as a process in which oxygen was combined with a substance, or hydrogen was removed from a compound; it is now defined as a process in which electrons are lost.

Electrochemistry is also the basis of new methods of destroying toxic organic pollutants. For example, the development of electrochemical cells that operate with supercritical water (see ◊fluid, supercritical) to combust organic waste materials.

electroconvulsive therapy (ECT) or ***electroshock therapy*** treatment mainly for severe ◊depression, given under anaesthesia and with a muscle relaxant. An electric current is passed through one or both sides of the brain to induce alterations in its electrical activity. The treatment can cause distress and loss of concentration and memory, and so there is much controversy about its use and effectiveness.

ECT was first used in 1938 but its success in treating depression lead to its excessive use for a wide range of mental illnesses against which it was ineffective. Its side effects included broken bones and severe memory loss.

The procedure in use today is much improved, using the minimum shock necessary to produce a seizure, administered under general anaesthetic with muscle relaxants to prevent spasms and fractures. It is the seizure rather than the shock itself that produces improvement. The smaller the shock administered the less damage there is to memory.

electrode any terminal by which an electric current passes in or out of a conducting substance; for example, the anode or cathode in a battery or the carbons in an arc lamp. The terminals that emit and collect the flow of electrons in thermionic ◊valves (electron tubes) are also called electrodes: for example, cathodes, plates, and grids.

electrodynamics the branch of physics dealing with electric charges, electric currents and associated forces. ◊Quantum electrodynamics (QED) studies the interaction between charged particles and their emission and absorption of electromagnetic radiation. This field combines quantum theory and relativity theory, making accurate predictions about subatomic processes involving charged particles such as electrons and protons.

electroencephalogram (EEG) graphic record of the electrical discharges of the brain, as detected by electrodes placed on the scalp. The pattern of electrical activity revealed by electroencephalography is helpful in the diagnosis of some brain disorders, in particular epilepsy.

electrolysis in chemistry, the production of chemical changes by passing an electric current through a solution or molten salt (the electrolyte), resulting in the migration of ions to the electrodes: positive ions (cations) to the negative electrode (cathode) and negative ions (anions) to the positive electrode (anode).

During electrolysis, the ions react with the electrode, either receiving or giving up electrons. The resultant atoms may be liberated as a gas, or deposited as a solid on the electrode, in amounts that are proportional to the amount of current passed, as discovered by English chemist Michael Faraday. For instance, when acidified water is electrolysed, hydrogen ions (H^+) at the cathode receive electrons to form hydrogen gas; hydroxide ions (OH^-) at the anode give up electrons to form oxygen gas and water.

One application of electrolysis is **electroplating**, in which a solution of a salt, such as silver nitrate ($AgNO_3$), is used and the object to be plated acts as the negative electrode, thus attracting silver ions (Ag^+). Electrolysis is used in many industrial processes, such as coating metals for vehicles and ships, and refining bauxite into aluminium; it also forms the basis of a number of electrochemical analytical techniques, such as polarography.

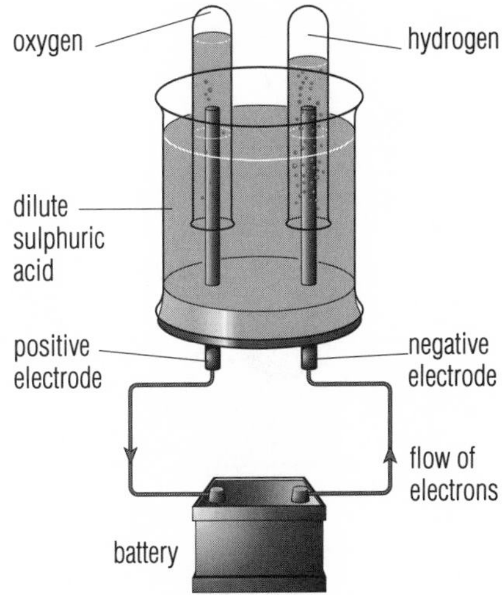

electrolysis *Passing an electric current through acidified water (such as diluted sulphuric acid) breaks down the water into its constituent elements – hydrogen and oxygen.*

electrolyte solution or molten substance in which an electric current is made to flow by the movement and discharge of ions in accordance with Faraday's laws of ◊electrolysis.

The term 'electrolyte' is frequently used to denote a substance that, when dissolved in a specified solvent, usually water, dissociates into ◊ions to produce an electrically conducting medium.

In medicine the term is often used for the ion itself (sodium or potassium, for example). Electrolyte balance may be severely disrupted in illness or injury.

electromagnet coil of wire wound around a soft iron core that acts as a magnet when an electric current flows through the wire. Electromagnets have many uses: in switches, electric bells, solenoids, and metal-lifting cranes.

electromagnetic field in physics, the region in which a particle with an ◊electric charge experiences a force. If it does so only when moving, it is in a pure **magnetic field**; if it does so when stationary, it is in an **electric field**. Both can be present simultaneously.

electromagnetic force one of the four fundamental ◊forces of nature, the other three being gravity, the strong nuclear force, and the weak nuclear force. The ◊elementary particle that is the carrier for the electromagnetic force is the photon.

electromagnetic induction in electronics, the production of an ◊electromotive force (emf) in a circuit by a change of magnetic flux through the circuit or by relative motion of the circuit and the magnetic flux. In a closed circuit an ◊induced current will be produced. All dynamos and generators make use of this effect. When magnetic tape is driven past the playback head (a small coil) of a tape-recorder, the moving magnetic field induces an emf in the head, which is then amplified to reproduce the recorded sounds.

If the change of magnetic flux is due to a variation in the current flowing in the same circuit, the phenomenon is known as self-induction; if it is due to a change of current flowing in another circuit it is known as mutual induction.

electromagnetic spectrum the complete range, over all wavelengths, of ◊electromagnetic waves.

To remember the different categories of radiation, in order of increasing wavelength:

CARY GRANT EXPECTS UNANIMOUS VOTES IN MOVIE REVIEWS TONIGHT

COSMIC, GAMMA, X-RAYS, ULTRAVIOLET, VISIBLE, INFRARED, MICROWAVE, RADIO, TELEVISION

electromagnetic system of units former system of absolute electromagnetic units (emu) based on the ◊c.g.s. system and having, as its primary electrical unit, the unit magnetic pole. It was replaced by ◊SI units.

electromagnetic waves oscillating electric and magnetic fields travelling together through space at a speed of nearly 300,000 km/186,000 mi per second. The (limitless) range of possible wavelengths or ◊frequencies of electromagnetic waves, which can be thought of as making up the **electromagnetic spectrum**, includes radio waves, infrared radiation, visible light, ultraviolet radiation, X-rays, and gamma rays.

electromotive force (emf) loosely, the voltage produced by an electric battery or generator in an electrical circuit or, more precisely, the energy supplied by a source of electric power in driving a unit charge around the circuit. The unit is the ◊volt.

electron stable, negatively charged ◊elementary particle; it is a constituent of all atoms, and a member of the class

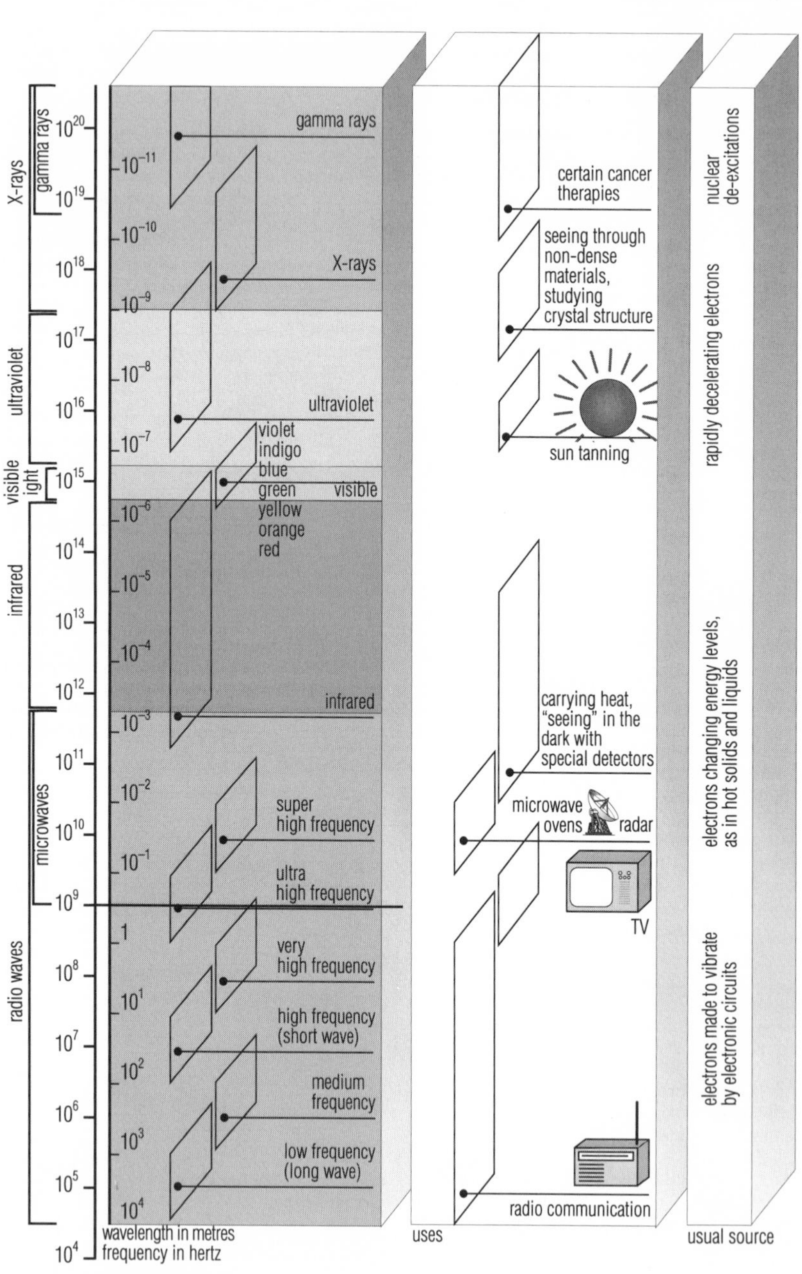

electromagnetic waves Radio waves have the lowest frequency. Infrared radiation, visible light, ultraviolet radiation, X-rays, and gamma rays have progressively higher frequencies.

of particles known as leptons. The electrons in each atom surround the nucleus in groupings called shells; in a neutral atom the number of electrons is equal to the number of protons in the nucleus. This electron structure is responsible for the chemical properties of the atom (see atomic structure).

Electrons carry a charge of 1.602192×10^{-19} coulomb and have a mass of 9.109×10^{-31} kg, which is $\frac{1}{1836}$ times the mass of a ◊proton. A beam of electrons will undergo ◊diffraction (scattering) and produce interference patterns in the same way as ◊electromagnetic waves such as light; hence they may be regarded as waves as well as particles.

The electron is not as simple as it looks.

WILLIAM HENRY BRAGG British physicist.
Recounted by Sir George Paget Thompson
at electron diffraction conference 1967

---

electronegativity the ease with which an atom can attract electrons to itself. Electronegative elements attract electrons, so forming negative ions.

Linus Pauling devised an electronegativity scale to indicate the relative power of attraction of elements for electrons. Fluorine, the most nonmetallic element, has a value of 4.0 on this scale; oxygen, the next most nonmetallic, has a value of 3.5.

In a covalent bond between two atoms of different electronegativities, the bonding electrons will be located close to the more electronegative atom, creating a ◊dipole.

electron gun a part in many electronic devices consisting of a series of ◊electrodes, including a cathode for producing an electron beam. It plays an essential role in ◊cathode-ray tubes (television tubes) and ◊electron microscopes.

electronic banking in computing, system whereby a user can execute banking transactions via a modem, either directly or through an online service or the Internet.

electronic book in computing, software with or without specialized hardware that provides the equivalent of a book's worth of information. The term is used generally to apply even to simple text files created by scanning printed books or manuals such as those created and archived by ◊Project Gutenberg.

'Electronic Book' refers to a specific product released by Sony, a special player for small-sized CD-ROMs containing educational and reference material.

electronic cash in computing, see ◊e-cash.

electronic commerce in computing, business-to-business use of networks such as the Internet to handle legally binding transactions. Traditionally, electronic commerce has required expensive membership of an electronic data interchange (EDI) service. In the mid-1990s, electronic commerce began to shift to the Internet to take advantage of its global reach and inexpensive connections. By 1996 many legal issues remained to be resolved.

Electronic Communications Privacy Act in computing, US law passed in 1986 that protects the privacy of e-mail and other electronic communications.

electronic conferencing in computing, public discussions conducted on an online service or via ◊USENET; any participant may log in at any time and read the collected messages and add new ones.

Because of its time-independent, many-to-many nature, electronic conferencing can be used to provide some of the same functions as real-life meetings, classrooms, and unstructured socializing without requiring the participants to meet face-to-face. While electronic conferencing is no substitute for live interaction, it does allow people who are widely geographically separated or who might otherwise never meet to exchange ideas.

electronic data interchange (EDI) in computing, system for managing business-to-business transactions such as invoicing and ordering to eliminate the wastefulness of paper-based transaction systems.

Traditionally, most EDI systems relied on proprietary protocols and private data networks, with the disadvantages that individual systems were incompatible. The growth of the Intenet is now opening the way for the rapid adoption of global electronic commerce.

electronic flash discharge tube that produces a high-intensity flash of light, used for photography in dim conditions. The tube contains an inert gas such as krypton. The flash lasts only a few thousandths of a second.

Electronic Frontier Foundation (EFF) US organization that lobbies for the extension of civil liberties and constitutional rights into ◊cyberspace. It was founded by former Grateful Dead lyricist John Perry Barlow and Lotus founder Mitch Kapor in 1991 after a series of US raids on suspected computer hackers. Its offices are in San Francisco.

electronic mail or ***E-mail*** messages sent electronically from computer to computer via network connections such as ◊Ethernet or the Internet, or via telephone lines to a host system. Messages once sent are stored on the network or by the host system until the recipient picks them up.

Subscribers to an electronic mail system type messages in ordinary letter form on a word processor, or microcomputer, and 'drop' the letters into a central computer's memory bank by means of a computer/telephone connector (a ◊modem). The recipient 'collects' the letter by calling up the central computer and feeding a unique password into the system.

electronic point of sale (EPOS) system used in retailing in which a bar code on a product is scanned at the cash till and the information relayed to the store computer. The computer will then relay back the price of the item to the cash till. The customer can then be given an itemized receipt while the computer removes the item from stock figures.

EPOS enables efficient computer stock control and reordering as well as giving a wealth of information about turnover, profitability on different lines, stock ratios, and other important financial indicators.

electronic publishing the distribution of information using computer-based media such as ◊multimedia and ◊hypertext in the creation of electronic 'books'. Critical technologies in the development of electronic publishing were ◊CD-ROM, with its massive yet compact storage capabilities, and the advent of computer networking with its ability to deliver information instantaneously anywhere in the world.

electronics branch of science that deals with the emission of◊ electrons from conductors and ◊semiconductors, with the subsequent manipulation of these electrons, and with the construction of electronic devices. The first electronic device was the thermionic ◊valve, or vacuum tube, in which electrons moved in a vacuum, and led to such inventions as ◊radio, television, radar, and the digital ◊computer. Replacement of valves with the comparatively tiny and reliable ◊transistor from 1948 revolutionized electronic development. Modern electronic devices are based on minute ◊integrated circuits (silicon chips), wafer-thin crystal slices holding tens of thousands of electronic components.

By using solid-state devices such as integrated circuits, extremely complex electronic circuits can be constructed, leading to the development of ◊digital watches, pocket ◊calculators, powerful ◊microcomputers, and ◊word processors.

electronic shopping in computing, using an online service or Internet service such as the World Wide Web to select and buy merchandise.

electron microscope instrument that produces a magnified image by using a beam of ◊electrons instead of light rays, as in an optical ◊microscope. An **electron lens** is an arrangement of electromagnetic coils that control and focus the beam. Electrons are not visible to the eye, so instead of an eyepiece there is a fluorescent screen or a photographic plate on which the electrons form an

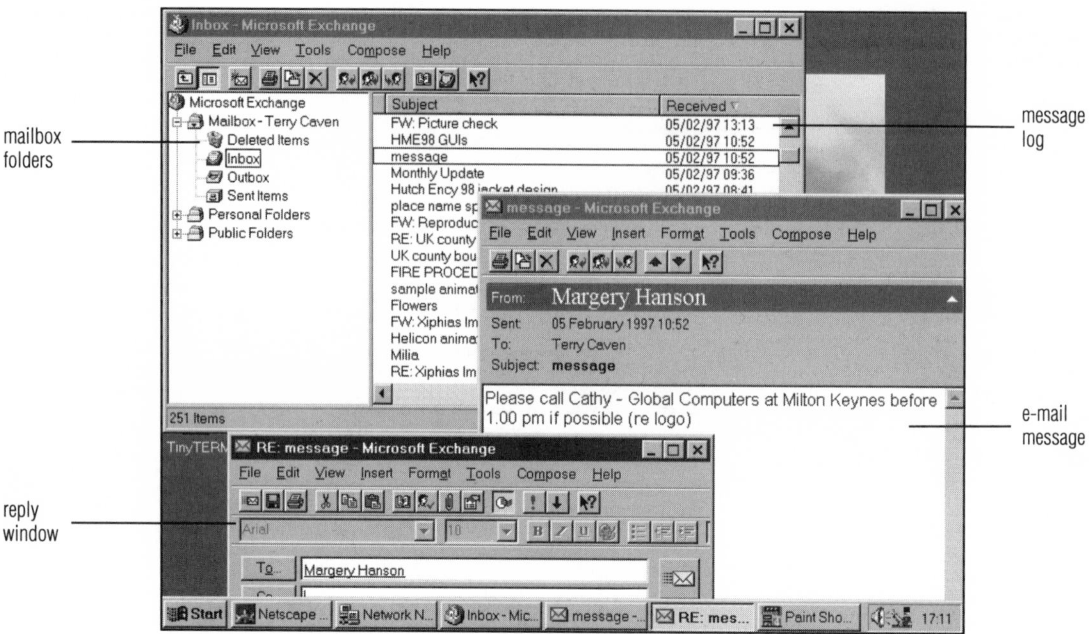

electronic mail *A typical E-mail user interface. Because messages can be created 'off-line' and are sent at high speed, line connection time, and therefore costs, can be kept to a minimum.*

image. The wavelength of the electron beam is much shorter than that of light, so much greater magnification and resolution (ability to distinguish detail) can be achieved. The development of the electron microscope has made possible the observation of very minute organisms, viruses, and even large molecules.

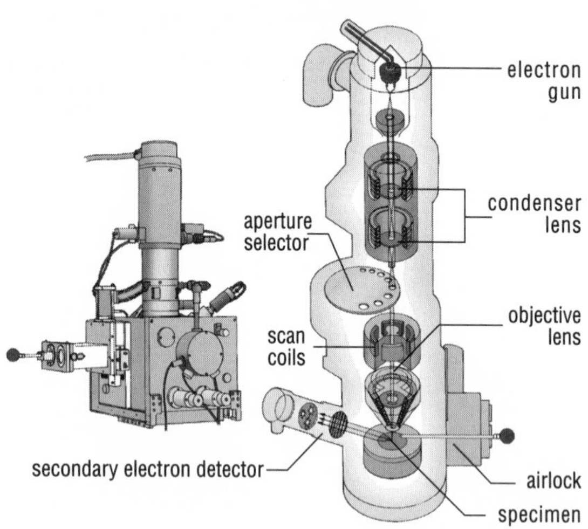

electron microscope *The scanning electron microscope. Electrons from the electron gun are focused to a fine point on the specimen surface by the lens systems. The beam is moved across the specimen by the scan coils. Secondary electrons are emitted by the specimen surface and pass through the detector, which produces an electrical signal. The signal is passed to an electronic console, and produces an image on a screen.*

A transmission electron ◊microscope passes the electron beam through a very thin slice of a specimen. A ◊scanning electron microscope looks at the exterior of a specimen. A ◊scanning transmission electron microscope (STEM) can produce a magnification of 90 million times. See also ◊atomic force microscope.

electron probe microanalyser modified ◊electron microscope in which the target emits X-rays when bombarded by electrons. Varying X-ray intensities indicate the presence of different chemical elements. The composition of a specimen can be mapped without the specimen being destroyed.

electrons, delocalized electrons that are not associated with individual atoms or identifiable chemical bonds, but are shared collectively by all the constituent atoms or ions of some chemical substances (such as metals, graphite, and ◊aromatic compounds).

A metallic solid consists of a three-dimensional arrangement of metal ions through which the delocalized electrons are free to travel. Aromatic compounds are characterized by the sharing of delocalized electrons by several atoms within the molecule.

electrons, localized a pair of electrons in a ◊covalent bond that are located in the vicinity of the nuclei of the two contributing atoms. Such electrons cannot move beyond this area.

electron volt unit (symbol eV) for measuring the energy of a charged particle (◊ion or ◊electron) in terms of the energy of motion an electron would gain from a potential difference of one volt. Because it is so small, more usual units are mega-(million) and giga-(billion) electron volts (MeV and GeV).

electrophoresis the ◊diffusion of charged particles through a fluid under the influence of an electric field. It can be used in the biological sciences to separate ◊molecules of different sizes, which diffuse at different rates. In industry, electrophoresis is used in paint-dipping operations to ensure that paint reaches awkward corners.

electroplating deposition of metals upon metallic surfaces by electrolysis for decorative and/or protective purposes. It is used in the preparation of printers' blocks, 'master' audio discs, and in many other processes.

A current is passed through a bath containing a solution of a salt of the plating metal, the object to be plated being the cathode (negative terminal); the anode (positive terminal) is either an inert substance or the plating metal. Among the metals most commonly used for plating are zinc, nickel, chromium, cadmium, copper, silver, and gold.

In **electropolishing**, the object to be polished is made the anode in an electrolytic solution and by carefully controlling conditions the high spots on the surface are dissolved away, leaving a high-quality stain-free surface. This technique is useful in polishing irregular stainless-steel articles.

electroporation in biotechnology, technique of introducing foreign DNA into pollen with a strong burst of electricity, used in creating genetically engineered plants.

electropositivity in chemistry, a measure of the ability of elements (mainly metals) to donate electrons to form positive ions. The greater the metallic character, the more electropositive the element.

electrorheological fluid another name for ◊smart fluid, a liquid suspension that gels when an electric field is applied across it.

electroscope apparatus for detecting ◊electric charge. The simple gold-leaf electroscope consists of a vertical conducting (metal) rod ending in a pair of rectangular pieces of gold foil, mounted inside and insulated from an earthed metal case or glass jar. An electric charge applied to the end of the metal rod makes the gold leaves diverge, because they each receive a similar charge (positive or negative) and so repel each other.

The polarity of the charge can be found by bringing up another charge of known polarity and applying it to the metal rod. A like charge has no effect on the gold leaves, whereas an opposite charge neutralizes the charge on the leaves and causes them to collapse.

electrostatic precipitator device that removes dust or other particles from air and other gases by electrostatic means. An electric discharge is passed through the gas, giving the impurities a negative electric charge. Positively charged plates are then used to attract the charged particles and remove them from the gas flow. Such devices are attached to the chimneys of coal-burning power stations to remove ash particles.

electrostatics the study of stationary electric charges and their fields (not currents). See ◊static electricity.

electrovalent bond another name for an ◊ionic bond, a chemical bond in which the combining atoms lose or gain electrons to form ions.

electrum naturally occurring alloy of gold and silver used by early civilizations to make the first coins, about the 6th century BC.

element substance that cannot be split chemically into simpler substances. The atoms of a particular element all have the same number of protons in their nuclei (their ◊atomic number). Elements are classified in the ◊periodic table of the elements. Of the known elements, 92 are known to occur in nature (those with atomic numbers 1–92). Those elements with atomic numbers above 92 do not occur in nature and are synthesized only, produced in particle accelerators. Of the elements, 81 are stable; all the others, which include atomic numbers 43, 61, and from 84 up, are radioactive.

Elements are classified as metals, nonmetals, or metalloids (weakly metallic elements) depending on a combination of their physical and chemical properties; about 75% are metallic. Some elements occur abundantly (oxygen, aluminium); others occur moderately or rarely (chromium, neon); some, in particular the radioactive ones, are found in minute (neptunium, plutonium) or very minute (technetium) amounts.

Symbols (devised by Swedish chemist Jöns ◊Berzelius) are used to denote the elements; the symbol is usually the first letter or letters of the English or Latin name (for example, C for carbon, Ca for calcium, Fe for iron, from the Latin *ferrum*). The symbol represents one atom of the element.

According to current theories, hydrogen and helium were produced in the ◊Big Bang at the beginning of the universe. Of the other elements, those up to atomic number 26 (iron) are made by nuclear fusion within the stars. The more massive elements, such as lead and uranium, are produced when an old star explodes; as its centre collapses, the gravitational energy squashes nuclei together to make new elements.

Two or more elements bonded together form a **compound** so that they cannot be separated by physical means. Compounds are held together by ionic or covalent bonds. The number of atoms of an element that combine together to form a molecule is it **atomicity**. A molecule of oxygen (O_2) has atomicity 2; sulphur (S_8) has atomicity 8.

element in mathematics, a member of a ◊set.

elementary particle in physics, a subatomic particle that is not made up of smaller particles, and so can be considered one of the fundamental units of matter. There are three groups of elementary particles: quarks, leptons, and gauge bosons.

Quarks, of which there are 12 types (up, down, charm, strange, top, and bottom, plus the antiparticles of each), combine in groups of three to produce heavy particles called baryons, and in groups of two to produce intermediate-mass particles called mesons. They and their composite particles are influenced by the strong nuclear force.

Leptons are light particles. Again, there are 12 types: the electron, muon, tau; their neutrinos, the electron neutrino, muon neutrino, and tau neutrino; and the antiparticles of each. These particles are influenced by the weak nuclear force.

Gauge bosons carry forces between other particles. There are four types: gluon, photon, weakon, and graviton. The gluon carries the strong nuclear force, the photon the electromagnetic force, the weakons the weak nuclear force, and the graviton the force of gravity (see ◊forces, fundamental).

elements, the four earth, air, fire, and water. The Greek philosopher Empedocles believed that these four elements made up the fundamental components of all matter and that they were destroyed and renewed through the action of love and discord.

This belief was shared by Aristotle who also claimed that the elements were mutable and contained specific qualities: cold and dry for earth, hot and wet for air, hot and dry for fire, and cold and wet for water. The transformation of the elements formed the basis of medieval alchemy, and the belief that base metals could be turned into gold. The theory of the elements prevailed until the 17th century when Robert Boyle redefined an element as a substance 'simple or unmixed, not made of other bodies' and proposed the existence of a greater number than four.

elephant large grazing mammal with thick, grey wrinkled skin, large ears, a long flexible trunk, and huge curving tusks. There are fingerlike projections at the end trunk used for grasping food and carrying it to its mouth. The trunk is also used for carrying water to the mouth. The elephant is herbivorous and, because of its huge size, much of its time must be spent feeding on leaves, shoots, bamboo, reeds, grasses and fruits and, where possible, cultivated crops such as maize and bananas. They are the largest living land animal.

Elephants usually live in herds containing between 20–40 females (cows), led by a mature, experienced cow. Most bull elephants live alone or in small groups; young males remain with the herd until they reach sexual maturity. Elephants have the longest gestation period of any animal (18–23 months between conception and birth) and usually produce one calf , which takes between 10–15 years to reach maturity. Elephants can live up to 60 years in

To distinguish between Indian and African elephants:

Indian elephants have little ears, African elephants have large ears

ELEPHANT

http://www.fws.gov/~r9extaff/biologues/bio_elep.html

Presentation on the Asian and African elephant with details about their physical appearance, food, social life, status of protection, and more. It is a useful, quick reference tool for all those concerned about wildlife and its protection.

the wild, but those in captivity have been known to reach over 65. There are two species of elephant, the African and the Indian or Asian elephant.

Elephants have one of the lowest metabolic rates among placental mammals. Their tusks, which are initially tipped with enamel but later consist entirely of ivory, continue growing throughout life. They are preceded by milk tusks, which are shed at an early age.

species differences The African elephant is much the larger of the two specie, growing to heights of 4 m/13 ft and weighing up to 8 tonnes compared with the 2.7 m/9 ft and 4 tonnes of the Indian elephant. The African elephant has larger ears and longer tusks than its Asian relative (many Asian elephants, particularly the females are tuskless). The African elephant has a sloping forehead and a hollow back, whereas the Asian elephant has two domes on its forehead just above its ears, and an arched back. The trunk of the African elephant is ridged with two fingerlike projections; the Asian species only has a smooth trunk with one finger. The African species has four nails on its front foot and three on its hind (back) foot, whereas the Asian elephant has five on its front foot and four on its hind. African elephants live only in Africa, south of the Sahara desert. The Indian or Asian elephant can be found in parts of India and Southeast Asia.

Young Asian elephants are hairy, and in this respect somewhat resemble the extinct mammoth genus; the adults have smooth, nearly naked skin. The African species is of fiercer disposition and can move rapidly over rough ground.

endangered species Elephants are slaughtered for ivory, and this, coupled with the fact that they reproduce slowly and do not breed readily in captivity, is leading to their extinction. In Africa, overhunting caused numbers to collapse during the 1980s and the elephant population of E Africa is threatened with extinction. There were 1.3 million African elephants in 1981; fewer than 700,000 in 1988; 600,000 in 1990; and fewer than 580,000 in 1997. They were placed on the CITES list of most endangered species in 1989, and a world ban on trade in ivory was imposed in 1990, resulting in an apparent drop in poaching. In 1997, at the 10th CITES convention, the elephant was downlisted to CITES Appendix II (vulnerable) and the ban on ivory exportation was lifted.

The Asian elephant was also listed on the CITES endangered list; its wild population in 1996 was only 35,000–54,000. There are about 10,000 working elephants in Asia, most of which are caught from the wild and 'tamed' by starvation and brutality.

It was estimated in 1997 that in Sri Lanka alone elephants might be extinct within ten years. The country's government maintained that there were 4,000 animals left, whereas the Wildlife and Nature Protection Society of Sri Lanka claimed there were only 2,500.

classification Elephants belong to the phylum Chordata, class Mammalia (mammals), order Proboscidea, family Elephantidae. There are two species, the African elephant(*Loxodonta africana*), and the Indian or Asian elephant (*Elephas maximus*).

elephant bird another name for extinct members of the genus ◊Aepyornis.

elephantiasis in the human body, a condition of local enlargement and deformity, most often of a leg, though the scrotum, vulva, or breast may also be affected.

The commonest form of elephantiasis is the tropical variety (filariasis) caused by infestation by parasitic roundworms (filaria); the enlargement is due to damage of the lymphatic system which impairs immunity. This leaves sufferers susceptible to infection from bacteria and fungi, entering through skin splits. The swelling reduces dramatically if the affected area is kept rigorously clean and treated with antibiotic cream, combined with rest, after drug treatment has killed all filarial worms.

elephant's tusk shell burrowing marine mollusc with a tusk-shaped shell open at both ends, from the larger of which the long foot appears and is used in creeping movements. The elephant's tusk shell has tentacles around its mouth, lacks eyes and heart, and lives in muddy sand sometimes at great depths of the sea.

classification Elephant's tusk shells are in genus *Dentalium*, class Scaphopoda, phylum Mollusca.

elephant-trunk fish African freshwater fish *Gnathonemus petersii* in the order Mormyriformes. They grow to about 23 cm/9 in in length, have small eyes and fins and are mainly nocturnal. They generate an electric field which they use to detect obstacles. Elephant-trunk fish live in lakes in West and Central Africa.

Their brains are very large in proportion to their bodies: 3.1% of body mass compared with less than 1% for most fish and 2.3% for humans.

elevation a drawing to scale of one side of an object or building.

elevation of boiling point raising of the boiling point of a liquid above that of the pure solvent, caused by a substance being dissolved in it. The phenomenon is observed when salt is added to boiling water; the water ceases to boil because its boiling point has been elevated.

How much the boiling point is raised depends on the number of molecules of substance dissolved. For a single solvent, such as pure water, all substances in the same molecular concentration produce the same elevation of boiling point. The elevation e produced by the presence of a solute of molar concentration C is given by the equation $e = KC$, where K is a constant (called the ebullioscopic constant) for the solvent concerned.

elevator any mechanical device for raising or lowering goods or materials. Such a device used for lifting people in buildings is known as an elevator in the USA and as a lift in Britain.

elk large deer *Alces alces* inhabiting northern Europe, Asia, Scandinavia, and North America, where it is known as the moose. It is brown in colour, stands about 2 m/6 ft at the shoulders, has very large palmate antlers, a fleshy muzzle, short neck, and long legs. It feeds on leaves and shoots. In North America, the ◊wapiti is called an elk.

elkhound Norwegian dog resembling the ◊husky but much smaller. Its coat is thick, with a full undercoat and the tail is bushy. Elkhounds are grey, with a darker shade on the back, and are about 50 cm/20 in high, weighing approximately 22 kg/48 lb.

elk, Irish extinct Pleistocene species of deer *Cervus megaceros*, the bones of which are found in Irish bogs and also in certain parts of Great Britain and mainland Europe. It stood about 2 m/6.6 ft in height, and is characterized by the enormous size of its antlers, which sometimes had a spread of almost 3.3 m/11 ft.

classification The Irish Elk is in family Cervidae, order Artiodactyla.

It is closely allied to the present day fallow deer and became extinct after the coming of humans to Europe.

ellipse curve joining all points (loci) around two fixed points (foci) such that the sum of the distances from those points is always constant. The diameter passing through the foci is the major axis, and the diameter bisecting this at right angles is the minor axis. An ellipse is one of a series of curves known as ◊conic sections. A slice across a cone that is not made parallel to, and does not pass through, the base will produce an ellipse.

elliptical galaxy in astronomy, one of the main classes of ◊galaxy in the Hubble classification and characterized by a featureless elliptical profile. Unlike spiral galaxies, elliptical galaxies have very little gas or dust and no stars have recently formed within them. They range greatly in size from giant ellipticals, which are often found at the centres of clusters of galaxies and may be strong radio

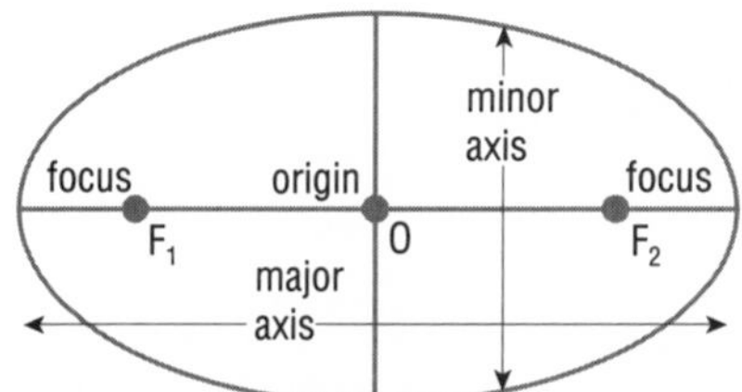

ellipse *Technical terms used to describe the ellipse; for all points on the ellipse, the sum of the distances from the two foci, F_1 and F_2, is the same.*

sources, to tiny dwarf ellipticals, containing about a million stars, which are the most common galaxies of any type. More than 60% of known galaxies are elliptical.

elm any of a group of trees found in temperate regions of the northern hemisphere and in mountainous parts of the tropics. All have doubly-toothed leaf margins and clusters of small flowers. (Genus *Ulmus,* family Ulmaceae.)

Species include the wych elm (*Ulmus glabra*), native to Britain; the North American white elm (*U. americana*); and the red or slippery elm (*U. fulva*). Most elms (apart from the wych elm) reproduce not by seed but by suckering (new shoots arising from the root system). This nonsexual reproduction results in an enormous variety of forms.

The fungus disease *Ceratocystis ulmi,* known as **Dutch elm disease** because of a severe outbreak in the Netherlands in 1924, has reduced the numbers of elm trees in Europe and North America. It is carried from tree to tree by beetles. Elms were widespread throughout Europe to about 4000 BC, when they suddenly disappeared and were not common again until the 12th century. This may have been due to an earlier epidemic of Dutch elm disease. In 1997 the US National Arboretum developed a Valley Forge elm that is resistant to the disease. It is expected to be available to the public in 2000.

Elm in computing, mail reader commonly used on online systems. It is typically found on older, text-based systems running under UNIX.

El Niño ***Spanish 'the child'*** warm ocean surge of the ◊Peru Current, so called because it tends to occur at Christmas, recurring about every 5–8 years in the eeastern Pacific off South America. It involves a change in the direction of ocean currents, which prevents the upwelling of cold, nutrient-rich waters along the coast of Ecuador and Peru, killing fishes and plants. It is an important factor in global weather.

El Niño is believed to be caused by the failure of trade winds and, consequently, of the ocean currents normally driven by these winds. Warm surface waters then flow in from the east. The phenomenon can disrupt the climate of the area disastrously, and has played a part in causing famine in Indonesia, drought and bush fires in the Galápagos Islands, rainstorms in California and South America, and the destruction of Peru's anchovy harvest and wildlife in 1982–83. El Niño contributed to algal blooms in Australia's drought-stricken rivers and an unprecedented number of typhoons in Japan in 1991. It is also thought to have caused the 1997 drought in Australia and contributed to certain ecological disasters such as bush fires in Indonesia.

El Niño usually lasts for about 18 months, but the 1990 occurrence lasted until June 1995; US climatologists estimated this duration to be the longest in 2,000 years. The last prolonged El Niño of 1939–41 caused extensive drought and famine in Bengal. It is understood that there might be a link between El Niño and ◊global warming.

EL NINO THEME PAGE

http://www.pmel.noaa.gov/toga-tao/el-nino/home.html

Wealth of scientific information about El Nino (a 'disruption of the ocean-atmosphere system in the tropical Pacific') with animated views of the monthly sea changes brought about by it, El Nino-related climate predictions, and forecasts from meteorological centres around the world. It also offers an illuminating FAQ section with basic and more advanced questions as well as an interesting historical overview of the phenomenon starting from 1550.

elongation in astronomy, the angular distance between the Sun and a planet or other solar-system object. This angle is 0° at ◊conjunction, 90° at ◊quadrature, and 180° at ◊opposition.

elution in chemistry, washing of an adsorbed substance from the adsorbing material; it is used, for example, in the separation processes of chromatography and electrophoresis.

elytra horny wing cases characteristic of beetles. The elytra are adapted from the beetles' forewings (only the hindwings are used for flight). They fold over the back, generally meeting in the middle in a straight line, and serve to protect the hindwings and the soft posterior parts of the body.

Elytra are also to be found in ◊earwigs.

In Hemiptera (true ◊bugs) the forewings are hardened over half their length and are known as **hemelytra**. In Orthoptera (crickets, grasshoppers, and locusts) the forewings are greatly thickened and are known as **tegmina**.

EMACS or, more properly, ***GNU EMACS*** in computing, a heavyweight ◊text editor used mainly by UNIX hackers. The name is dervied from Editing Macros, but is humorously, and recursively, said to stand for EMACS Makes A Computer Slow. EMACS was written by Richard Stallman at the MIT AI Lab and is published as ◊public-domain software, Emacs was created by the US Free Software Foundation.

e-mail (abbreviation for ***electronic mail***) in computing, a system that enables the users of a computer network to send messages to other users. The messages (which may contain enclosed text files, artwork, or multimedia clips) are usually placed in a reserved area ('mailbox') on a central computer until they are retrieved by the receiving user. Passwords are frequently used to prevent unauthorized access to stored messages (see ◊data security). The high speed of transmission for e-mail messages means that they cost less than comparable phone calls or faxes.

embolism blockage of a blood vessel by an obstruction called an embolus (usually a blood clot, fat particle, or bubble of air).

VISIBLE EMBRYO

http://visembryo.ucsf.edu/

Learn about the first four weeks of human development.

embryo early developmental stage of an animal or a plant following fertilization of an ovum (egg cell), or activation of an ovum by ◊parthenogenesis. In humans, the term embryo describes the fertilized egg during its first seven weeks of existence; from the eighth week onwards it is referred to as a fetus.

In animals the embryo exists either within an egg (where it is nourished by food contained in the yolk), or in mammals, in the ◊uterus of the mother. In mammals (except marsupials) the embryo is fed through the ◊placenta. The plant embryo is found within the seed in higher plants. It sometimes consists of only a few cells, but usually includes a root, a shoot (or primary bud), and one or two ◊cotyledons, which nourish the growing seedling.

embryology study of the changes undergone by an organism from its conception as a fertilized ovum (egg) to its emergence into the world at hatching or birth. It is mainly concerned with the

El Niño – The Christmas Child

BY NIGEL DUDLEY

In 1997, more tropical forest burned than at any other time in recorded history. Vast fires in Indonesia and the Amazon appeared on television screens all over the world, but fires also blazed throughout Africa, Papua New Guinea, and Australia. Unlike some temperate and boreal forests, most tropical moist forests do not readily burn under natural conditions. Reasons for the increase are complex, and include changes to the forest through over-logging and uncontrolled use of fire as a land management tool. However, the 1997 fires were given a fresh impetus by a catastrophic drought that affected vast areas of Africa, Asia, and South America. This drought was, in turn, associated with a hitherto fairly obscure climatic event known as El Niño (literally 'The Child') that principally affects large parts of the Pacific coast of South America.

Theory

El Niño is a current of warm water in the southeastern Pacific, which usually reaches the Pacific coast of South America around Christmas – hence the name. Although normally benign, it can periodically become extremely damaging when it is associated with another climatic phenomenon known as the Southern Oscillation, a complex series of events including changes in wind temperature, ocean currents, and sea levels. The combination, often known as an El Niño/Southern Oscillation or ENSO event, creates an invasion of warm water into usually cool areas, causing wet and stormy weather in the west Pacific and sometimes as far as North America, and drought conditions in Africa, Brazil, Australia, and parts of Asia and the Pacific.

Immediate impact

The immediate impact on the Latin American coastline can be catastrophic. Warmer water kills plankton, squid, and smaller fish such as anchovy and sardine. Lack of food in turn kills larger fish such as herring and hake. This also sometimes causes extreme short-term declines in the seabird colonies found along the coast and on offshore islands – which may also have their nests inundated by rising waters. Coral reefs sometimes suffer bleaching, perhaps as a result of warmer water. In human terms, fisheries face extreme hardship and agricultural crops are likely to collapse. Along the coasts of Chile and off the southern USA, sardine populations can virtually disappear for a period. Particularly spectacular ENSO events occurred in 1940–41, 1957–58, and 1982–83. Loss of sardines caused a collapse in the industry in California during the 1940s, as recorded in John Steinbeck's *Cannery Row*.

Wider implications

The wider climatic conditions have other impacts. Increased forest fires have been mentioned above, but it is only in recent years that their full significance has been recognized. For example, over several months in the summer of 1997, an area of Southeast Asia from the Philippines to Australia was enveloped in smog caused by forest fires on the Indonesian islands of Java, Borneo, Sulawesi, Irian Jaya, and Sumatra. Over 2 million hectares of forests and other land were destroyed. More than 40,000 Indonesians became ill as a result and over a million suffered eye infections; smog also resulted in plane crashes and shipping accidents. Primary forest and at least 19 protected areas were damaged in Indonesia, and endangered species such as the orang-utan were threatened further. Rains after the fire caused soil erosion and consequent damage to offshore fisheries as coral was smothered with debris. Business, including tourism, suffered badly and initial estimates put costs at a massive US$20 billion. Although most fires were set deliberately – often illegally – by commercial interests such as plantation owners, impacts were exacerbated by the El Niño climatic effect. ENSO events are also associated with particularly bad burning seasons in Australia and the Amazon.

Drought also causes direct human hardship as a result of crop failures. At the end of 1997, hundreds of thousands of people in the Indonesian-controlled area of Irian Jaya and in neighbouring Papua New Guinea faced starvation after the worst drought for 50 years. Associated fires in Papua New Guinea created such a dense pall of smoke that pilots bringing in emergency food supplies were sometimes unable to land.

The future

Currently, El Niño and the associated ENSO events appear to be growing both more frequent and more severe. An increasing number of scientists are linking this to changes caused by pollution-related climatic change, although others think that it may be largely the result of natural fluctuations that will reverse later. Whatever the cause, the impacts are becoming more intense, and off the coast of western South America and the southern USA marine life seems to be undergoing longer-term changes. Since the 1950s, there has been an 80 percent decline in zooplankton along California's coast between San Diego and San Francisco, accompanied by a 1.2–1.6°C temperature rise. This decline is affecting seabird populations, particularly the sooty shearwater, which has declined by 90 %.

Timing of ENSO events is also becoming more erratic. In the past, severe El Niño events tended to last around 18 months, and would be separated by long breaks so that marine and bird life could become re-established. However, the 1990 ENSO event appears to be continuing, with a series of unpredictable peaks and troughs. It apparently reached maturity in early 1992 and started to decline in the expected manner, but untypically increased in strength again the following November. It stayed through 1994 and it appears as if the 1997 events may be simply another continuation. A link between climate change and changes in ENSO events is suspected but is as yet unproven.

Climate change specialists are also interested in El Niño because the main oceanic effects – a rise in sea level, higher water temperatures, and reduced offshore flow – are those most often associated with predictions relating to climate change. Scientists and fisheries experts have studied El Niño to find out what might happen under conditions of global warming.

Given their importance there is a strong incentive to predict ENSO events. For example, scientists are currently using the occurrence of a temperature-sensitive algae, *Emiliana huxleyi*, in layers of sediment to create an accurate profile of changing sea temperatures in the eastern Pacific between 1915 and 1988. However, many aspects of this extremely important phenomenon remain as elusive as when early settlers named the warming after the birth of the Christ child, which they were celebrating when it arrived.

changes in cell organization in the embryo and the way in which these lead to the structures and organs of the adult (the process of ◊differentiation).

Applications of embryology include embryo transplants, both commercial (for example, in building up a prize dairy-cow herd quickly at low cost) and in obstetric medicine (as a method for helping couples with fertility problems to have children).

embryo sac large cell within the ovule of flowering plants that represents the female ◊gametophyte when fully developed. It typically contains eight nuclei. Fertilization occurs when one of these nuclei, the egg nucleus, fuses with a male ◊gamete.

emerald a clear, green gemstone variety of the mineral ◊beryl. It occurs naturally in Colombia, the Ural Mountains in Russia,

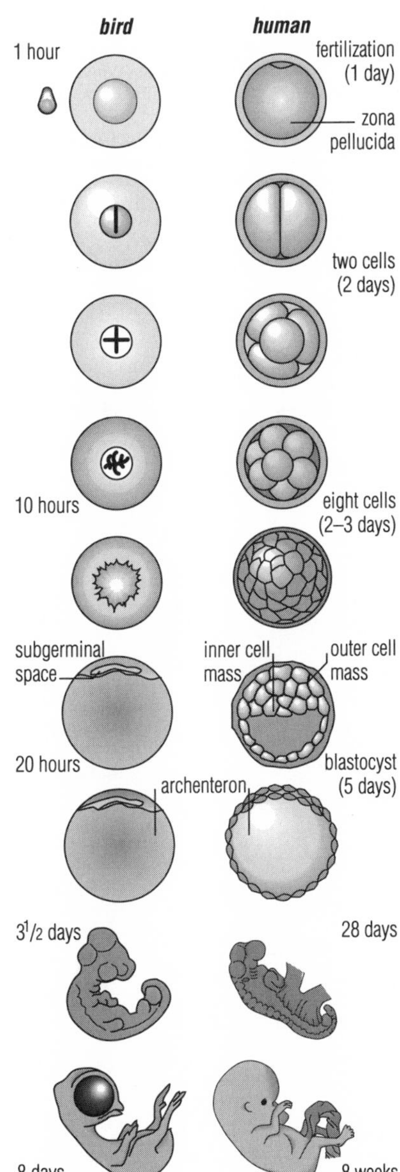

***embryo** The development of a bird and a human embryo. In the human, division of the fertilized egg, or ovum, begins within hours of conception. Within a week, a hollow, fluid-containing ball – a blastocyte – with a mass of cells at one end has developed. After the third week, the embryo has changed from a mass of cells into a recognizable shape. At four weeks, the embryo is 3 mm/0.1 in long, with a large bulge for the heart and small pits for the ears. At six weeks, the embryo is 1.5 cm/0.6 in long with a pulsating heart and ear flaps. By the eighth week, the embryo (now technically a fetus) is 2.5 cm/1 in long and recognizably human, with eyelids and small fingers and toes.*

Zimbabwe, and Australia. The green colour is caused by the presence of the element chromium in the beryl.

emergent properties features of a system that are due to the way in which its components are structured in relation to each other, rather than to the individual properties of those components. Thus the distinctive characteristics of ◊chemical compounds are emergent properties of the way in which the constituent elements are organized, and cannot be explained by the particular properties of those elements taken in isolation. In biology, ◊ecosystem stability is an emergent property of the interaction between the constituent species, and not a property of the species themselves.

emery black to greyish form of impure ◊corundum that also contains the minerals magnetite and hematite. It is used as an ◊abrasive.

emetic any substance administered to induce vomiting. Emetics are used to empty the stomach in many cases of deliberate or accidental drug overdose. The most frequently used is ipecacuanha.

emf in physics, abbreviation for ◊electromotive force.

emission line in astronomy, bright line in the spectrum of a luminous object caused by ◊atoms emitting light at sharply defined ◊wavelengths.

emission spectroscopy in analytical chemistry, a technique for determining the identity or amount present of a chemical substance by measuring the amount of electromagnetic radiation it emits at specific wavelengths; see ◊spectroscopy.

emoticon **(contraction of *emotion and icon*)** in computing, symbol composed of punctuation marks designed to express some form of emotion in the form of a human face. Emoticons were invented by ◊e-mail users to overcome the fact that communication using text only cannot convey nonverbal information (body language or vocal intonation) used in ordinary speech.

The following examples should be viewed sideways::-) smiling :-O shouting :-(glum 8-) wearing glasses and smiling.

emotion in psychology, a powerful feeling; a complex state of body and mind involving, in its bodily aspect, changes in the viscera (main internal organs) and in facial expression and posture, and in its mental aspect, heightened perception, excitement and, sometimes, disturbance of thought and judgement. The urge to action is felt and impulsive behaviour may result.

emphysema incurable lung condition characterized by disabling breathlessness. Progressive loss of the thin walls dividing the air spaces (alveoli) in the lungs reduces the area available for the exchange of oxygen and carbon dioxide, causing the lung tissue to expand. The term 'emphysema' can also refer to the presence of air in other body tissues.

Emphysema is most often seen at an advanced stage of chronic ◊bronchitis, although it may develop in other long-standing diseases of the lungs. It destroys lung tissue, leaving behind scar tissue in the form of air blisters called bullae. As the disease progresses, the bullae occupy more and more space in the chest cavity, inflating the lungs and causing severe breathing difficulties. The bullae may be removed surgically, and since early 1994 US trials have achieved measured success using lasers to eliminate them in a procedure called lung-reduction pneumenoplasty (LRP). Lasers are particularly useful where the emphysema is diffuse and bullae are interspersed within healthy tissue. As LRP is a less invasive process, survival rates are improved (90% compared with 75% for conventional surgery) and patients recover quicker.

EMS in computing, abbreviation for ◊***expanded memory specification***.

emu flightless bird *Dromaius novaehollandiae*, family Dromaiidae, order Casuariidae, native to Australia. It stands about 1.8 m/6 ft high and has coarse brown plumage, small rudimentary

EMU

While a male emu is incubating his eggs, he cannot move from the nest to eat or drink. He must survive on his existing fat reserves for eight weeks. When the chicks are hatched they remain in their father's care for at least seven months.

wings, short feathers on the head and neck, and powerful legs, which are well adapted for running and kicking.

The female has a curious bag or pouch in the windpipe that enables her to emit a characteristic loud booming note. Emus are monogamous, and the male wholly or partially incubates the eggs.

In Western Australia emus are farmed for their meat, skins, feathers, and oil.

emulator in computing, an item of software or firmware that allows one device to imitate the functioning of another. Emulator software is commonly used to allow one make of computer to run programs written for a different make of computer. This allows a user to select from a wider range of ◊applications programs, and perhaps to save money by running programs designed for an expensive computer on a cheaper model.

Many printers contain emulator firmware that enables them to imitate Hewlett Packard and Epson printers, because so much software is written to work with these widely used machines.

emulsifier food additive used to keep oils dispersed and in suspension, in products such as mayonnaise and peanut butter. Egg yolk is a naturally occurring emulsifier, but most of the emulsifiers in commercial use today are synthetic chemicals.

emulsion a stable dispersion of a liquid in another liquid – for example, oil and water in some cosmetic lotions.

encapsulate in computing, term used to describe the technique that uses one ◊protocol as an envelope for another for transmission across a network.

encapsulated PostScript (EPS) computer graphics file format used by the ◊PostScript page-description language. It is essentially a PostScript file with a special structure designed for use by other applications.

encephalin a naturally occurring chemical produced by nerve cells in the brain that has the same effect as morphine or other derivatives of opium, acting as a natural painkiller. Unlike morphine, encephalins are quickly degraded by the body, so there is no build-up of tolerance to them, and hence no addiction. Encephalins are a variety of ◊peptides, as are ◊endorphins, which have similar effects.

encephalitis inflammation of the brain, nearly always due to viral infection but it may also occur in bacterial and other infections. It varies widely in severity, from shortlived, relatively slight effects of headache, drowsiness, and fever to paralysis, coma, and death.

Encke's comet comet with the shortest known orbital period, 3.3 years. It is named after German mathematician and astronomer Johann Franz Encke (1791–1865), who calculated its orbit in 1819 from earlier sightings.

It was first seen in 1786 by the French astronomer Pierre Méchain (1744–1804). It is the parent body of the Taurid meteor shower and a fragment of it may have hit the Earth in the ◊Tunguska Event in 1908.

In 1913, it became the first comet to be observed throughout its entire orbit when it was photographed near ◊aphelion (the point in its orbit furthest from the Sun) by astronomers at Mount Wilson Observatory in California, USA.

endangered species plant or animal species whose numbers are so few that it is at risk of becoming extinct. Officially designated endangered species are listed by the ◊International Union for the Conservation of Nature (IUCN).

Endangered species are not a new phenomenon; extinction is an integral part of evolution. The replacement of one species by another usually involves the eradication of the less successful form, and ensures the continuance and diversification of life in all forms. However, extinctions induced by humans are thought to be destructive, causing evolutionary dead-ends that do not allow for succession by a more fit species. The great majority of recent extinctions have been directly or indirectly induced by humans; most often by the loss, modification, or pollution of the organism's habitat, but also by hunting for 'sport' or for commercial purposes.

According to a 1995 report to Congress by the US Fish and Wildlife Service, although seven of the 893 species listed as endangered under the US Endangered Species Act 1968–93 have become extinct, 40% are no longer declining in number. In February 1996, a private conservation group, Nature Conservancy, reported around 20,000 native US plant and animal species to be rare or imperilled.

According to the Red Data List of endangered species, published in 1996 by the IUCN, 25% of all mammal species (including 46% of primates, 36% of insectivores, and 33% of pigs and antelopes), and 11% of all bird species are threatened with extinction.

endive cultivated annual plant, the leaves of which are used in salads and cooking. One variety has narrow, curled leaves; another has wide, smooth leaves. It is related to ◊chicory. (*Cichorium endivia,* family Compositae.)

endocrine gland gland that secretes hormones into the bloodstream to regulate body processes. Endocrine glands are most highly developed in vertebrates, but are also found in other animals, notably insects. In humans the main endocrine glands are the pituitary, thyroid, parathyroid, adrenal, pancreas, ovary, and testis.

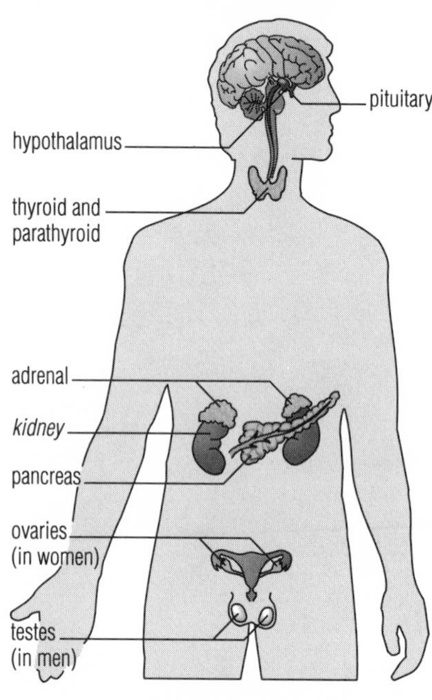

endocrine gland The main human endrocrine glands. These glands produce hormones – chemical messengers – which travel in the bloodstream to stimulate certain cells.

endolymph fluid found in the inner ◊ear, filling the central passage of the cochlea as well as the semicircular canals.

Sound waves travelling into the ear pass eventually through the three small bones of the middle ear and set up vibrations in the endolymph. These vibrations are detected by receptors in the cochlea, which send nerve impulses to the hearing centres of the brain.

endometriosis common gynaecological complaint in which patches of endometrium (the lining of the womb) are found outside the uterus.

This ectopic (abnormally positioned) tissue is present most often in the ovaries, although it may invade any pelvic or abdominal site, as well as the vagina and rectum. Endometriosis may be treated with analgesics, hormone preparations, or surgery. Between 30 and 40% of women treated for infertility are suffering from the condition.

endoparasite ◊parasite that lives inside the body of its host.

endoplasm inner, liquid part of a cell's ◊cytoplasm.

endoplasmic reticulum (ER) a membranous system of tubes, channels, and flattened sacs that form compartments within ◊eukaryotic cells. It stores and transports proteins within cells and also carries various enzymes needed for the synthesis of ◊fats. The ◊ribosomes, or the organelles that carry out protein synthesis, are attached to parts of the ER.

Under the electron microscope, ER looks like a series of channels and vesicles, but it is in fact a large, sealed, baglike structure crumpled and folded into a convoluted mass. The interior of the 'bag', the ER lumen, stores various proteins needed elsewhere in the cell, then organizes them into transport vesicles formed by a small piece of ER membrane budding from the main membrane.

endorphin natural substance (a polypeptide) that modifies the action of nerve cells. Endorphins are produced by the pituitary gland and hypothalamus of vertebrates. They lower the perception of pain by reducing the transmission of signals between nerve cells.

Endorphins not only regulate pain and hunger, but are also involved in the release of sex hormones from the pituitary gland. Opiates act in a similar way to endorphins, but are not rapidly degraded by the body, as natural endorphins are, and thus have a long-lasting effect on pain perception and mood. Endorphin release is stimulated by exercise.

endoscopy examination of internal organs or tissues by an instrument allowing direct vision. An endoscope is equipped with an eyepiece, lenses, and its own light source to illuminate the field of vision. The endoscope used to examine the digestive tract is a flexible fibreoptic instrument swallowed by the patient.

There are various types of endoscope in use – some rigid, some flexible – with names prefixed by their site of application (for example, bronchoscope and laryngoscope). The value of endoscopy is in permitting diagnosis without the need for exploratory surgery. Biopsies (tissue samples) and photographs may be taken by way of the endoscope as an aid to diagnosis, or to monitor the effects of treatment. Some surgical procedures can be performed using fine instruments introduced through the endoscope. Keyhole surgery is increasingly popular as a cheaper, safer option for some conditions than conventional surgery.

endoskeleton the internal supporting structure of vertebrates, made up of cartilage or bone. It provides support, and acts as a system of levers to which muscles are attached to provide movement. Certain parts of the skeleton (the skull and ribs) give protection to vital body organs.

Sponges are supported by a network of rigid, or semirigid, spiky structures called spicules; a bath sponge is the proteinaceous skeleton of a sponge.

endosperm nutritive tissue in the seeds of most flowering plants. It surrounds the embryo and is produced by an unusual process that parallels the ◊fertilization of the ovum by a male gamete. A second male gamete from the pollen grain fuses with two female nuclei within the ◊embryo sac. Thus endosperm cells are triploid (having three sets of chromosomes); they contain food reserves such as starch, fat, and protein that are utilized by the developing seedling.

In 'non-endospermic' seeds, absorption of these food molecules by the embryo is completed early, so that the endosperm has disappeared by the time of germination.

endotherm **'warm-blooded'**, or ***homeothermic***, animal. Endotherms have internal mechanisms for regulating their body temperatures to levels different from the environmental temperature. See ◊homeothermy.

endothermic reaction chemical reaction that requires an input of energy in the form of heat for it to proceed; the energy is absorbed from the surroundings by the reactants.

The dissolving of sodium chloride in water and the process of photosynthesis are both endothermic changes. See ◊energy of reaction.

endotoxin in biology, heat stable complex of protein and lipopolysaccharide that is produced following the death of certain bacteria. Endotoxins are typically produced by the Gram negative bacteria and can cause fever. They can also cause shock by rendering the walls of the blood vessels permeable so that fluid leaks into the tissues and blood pressure falls sharply.

end user the user of a computer program; in particular, someone who uses a program to perform a task (such as accounting or playing a computer game), rather than someone who writes programs (a programmer).

Energiya most powerful Soviet space rocket, first launched 15 May 1987.

Used to launch the Soviet space shuttle, the Energiya booster is capable, with the use of strap-on boosters, of launching payloads of up to 190 tonnes into Earth orbit.

energy capacity for doing ◊work. Energy can exist in many different forms. For example, potential energy (PE) is energy deriving from position; thus a stretched spring has elastic PE, and an object raised to a height above the Earth's surface, or the water in an elevated reservoir, has gravitational PE. Moving bodies possess kinetic energy (KE). Energy can be converted from one form to another, but the total quantity in a system stays the same (in accordance with the ◊conservation of energy principle). Energy cannot be created or destroyed. For example, as an apple falls it loses gravitational PE but gains KE.

Although energy is never lost, after a number of conversions it tends to finish up as the kinetic energy of random motion of molecules (of the air, for example) at relatively low temperatures. This is 'degraded' energy that is difficult to convert back to other forms.

energy is the capacity to do work A body with no energy can do no ◊work. For example, a flat battery in a torch will not light the torch. If the battery is fully charged, it should contain enough chemical energy to do the work involved in illuminating the torch bulb. When one body A does work on another body B, A transfers energy to B. The energy transferred is equal to the work done by A on B. Energy is therefore measured in ◊joules. The rate of doing work or consuming energy is called power and is measured in ◊watts (joules per second).

energy types and transfer Energy can be converted from any form into another. A ball resting on a slope possesses ◊potential energy that is gradually changed into ◊kinetic energy of rotation and translation as the ball rolls down. As a pendulum swings, energy is constantly being changed from a potential form at the highest points of the swing to kinetic energy at the lowest point. At positions in between these two extremes, the system possesses both kinetic and potential energy in varying proportions.

A weightlifter changes chemical energy from his muscles into potential energy of the weight when the weight is lifted. If the weightlifter releases the weight, the potential energy is converted to kinetic energy as it falls, and this in turn is converted to heat energy and sound energy as it hits the floor. A lump of coal and a tank of petrol, together with the oxygen needed for their combustion, have chemical energy. Other sorts of energy include electrical and nuclear energy, and light and sound.

resources So-called energy resources are stores of convertible energy. Nonrenewable resources include the fossil fuels (coal, oil, and gas) and nuclear-fission 'fuels' – for example, uranium 235. The term 'fuel' is used for any material from which energy can be obtained. We use up fuel reserves such as coal and oil, and convert the energy they contain into other, useful forms. The chemical energy released by burning fuels can be used to do work.

Renewable resources, such as wind, tidal, and geothermal power, have so far been less exploited. Hydroelectric projects are well established, and wind turbines and tidal systems are being developed.

energy conservation and efficiency All forms of energy are interconvertible by appropriate processes. Energy is transferred from one form to another, but the sum total of the energy after the conversion is always the same as the initial energy. This is the principle of conservation of energy. This principle can be illustrated by the use of energy flow diagrams, called Sankey diagrams, which show the energy transformations that take place.

Energy Resources

BY PETER LAFFERTY

Humans are using up the world's energy resources in a way no other animal has ever done. We use them to provide light and heating in our homes, to plough the land, to cook our food, to travel, to run our factories, and in countless other ways. Whether we are rural workers in a developing country or urban workers in a wealthy industrial country, we all need energy, although the sources of the energy and the amounts used vary greatly from one society to another.

Sources of energy

There are different forms or types of energy. Fuels such as coal, oil (petroleum), and wood contain chemical energy. When these fuels are burnt, the chemical energy changes to heat and light energy. Electricity is the most important form of energy in the industrialized world, because it can be transported over long distances via cables and transmission lines. It is also a very convenient form of energy, since it can power a wide variety of household appliances and industrial machinery. It is produced by converting the chemical energy from coal, oil, or natural gas in power stations.

Energy resources fall into two broad groups: renewable and nonrenewable. Renewable resources are those which replenish themselves naturally and will either always be available – hydroelectric power, solar energy, wind and wave power, tidal energy, and geothermal energy – or will continue to be available provided supplies are given sufficient time to replenish themselves – peat and firewood. Nonrenewable resources are those of which there are limited supplies and which once used are gone forever. These include coal, oil, natural gas, and uranium.

Fossil fuels

Coal, oil, and natural gas are called fossil fuels because they are the fossilized remains of plants and animals that lived hundreds of millions of years ago. Burning fossil fuels releases chemicals that cause acid rain, and is gradually increasing the carbon dioxide in the atmosphere, causing global warming.

Fossil fuel resources are not evenly distributed around the world. Over half the world's known oil reserves are in the Middle East; about 40% of the reserves of natural gas are in the Commonwealth of Independent States (CIS), and 25% in the Middle East. About two-thirds of the world's coal is shared between North America, the CIS, and China.

Uranium

Uranium is a radioactive metallic element and a very concentrated source of energy; large reserves are found in Australia, North America, and South Africa. Used to produce electricity in a nuclear power station, a single ton of uranium can produce as much energy as 15,000 tons of coal, or 10,000 tons of oil. Used in the type of nuclear power station now in operation, the world's known uranium supplies have about the same energy content as the known oil reserves. However, these power stations, known as thermal stations or reactors, use only a small part of the energy available in uranium. The next generation of reactors, known as fast or breeder reactors, release virtually all its energy. These reactors would increase the world's uranium energy reserves by sixty times. However, although nuclear power stations do not produce carbon dioxide or cause acid rain, they do produce radioactive waste that is dangerous and difficult to process or store safely.

Solar energy

Many renewable resources take advantage of the energy in sunlight. The Sun's energy can be tapped directly by photovoltaic cells that convert light into electricity. Other solar energy plants use mirrors to direct sunlight onto pipes containing a liquid. The liquid boils and is used to drive an electricity generator. The Sun's energy also drives the wind and waves, so energy produced by wind farms and wave-driven generators is also derived from the Sun.

Gravitational energy

Hydroelectricity and tidal power stations make use of gravitational forces. The Earth's gravity pulls water downward through the turbines in a hydroelectric power station. In a tidal power station, the Moon's gravity lifts water as the tides rise, giving the water potential energy (energy due to position) which is released as the water flows through a turbine. Geothermal energy (the heat energy of hot rocks deep beneath the Earth's surface) is due to gravity compressing and heating the rocks when the Earth formed.

The worldwide energy pie

Globally, the largest contributions to current energy resources come from oil (31%), coal (26%), and natural gas (19%). Renewable energy currently supplies about 20% of the world's energy needs, with hydroelectricity supplying 6% of the world's needs and traditional biofuels (firewood, crop wastes, peat, and dung) supplying 12%. A small contribution is made by new renewables, such as the conversion of crops such as sugar into alcohol fuel and the burning of waste material.

The contribution solar, wave, tidal, and geothermal power can make to the world's energy resources is currently limited. This is because renewable energy depends on the development of means of capturing and concentrating it. In addition, renewable energy is not always available when needed – rivers can dry up, the wind does not always blow.

Future demands

It is clear that, in the future, demand for energy will be higher than at present, due to population growth and increased industrialization. Furthermore, the energy available must be at a reasonable cost or economic growth will be held back. This is especially important for developing countries, where the inability to meet high-energy costs hinders development.

Future solutions

In principle, known resources of nonrenewable energy should be sufficient for several hundred years or more. At the present rate of consumption, oil reserves will last about 40 years; gas reserves will last about 60 years; coal reserves will last about 250 years; and uranium reserves, if used in fast reactors, would last for more than 1,000 years. It is also likely that further fossil-fuel reserves will be discovered as currently known supplies run out. However, in practice, the outlook is uncertain. Increasing concern about pollution might make dirty coal-fired power stations unacceptable in the future.

One alternative is to make greater use of nuclear power, moving to fast reactors and then developing nuclear fusion plants that would mimic the power production process found in the Sun. However, anxiety about safety and waste disposal is already limiting the use of nuclear energy, so it is unlikely to provide an answer in the future.

There is considerable room for development in the use of renewable resources, but with most of the world's energy production based around nonrenewable fuel supplies, the widespread introduction of efficient renewable energy will require a complete restructuring of the ways we produce and use energy.

When a petrol engine is used to power a car, about 75% of the energy from the fuel is wasted. The total energy input equals the total energy output, but a lot of energy is wasted as heat so that the engine is only about 25% efficient. The combustion of the petrol-air mixture produces heat energy as well as kinetic energy. All forms of energy tend to be transformed into heat and can not then readily be converted into other, useful forms of energy.

heat transfer A difference in temperature between two objects in thermal contact leads to the transfer of energy as ◊heat. Heat is energy transferred due to a temperature difference. Heat is transferred by the movement of particles (that possess kinetic energy) by conduction, convection, and radiation. ◊Conduction involves the movement of heat through a solid material by the movement of free electrons. For example, thermal energy is lost from a house by conduction through the walls and windows. ◊Convection involves the transfer of energy by the movement of fluid particles. All objects radiate heat in the form of radiation of electromagnetic waves. Hotter objects emit more energy than cooler objects.

Methods of reducing energy transfer as heat through the use of ◊insulation are important because the world's fuel reserves are limited and heating homes costs a lot of money in fuel bills. Heat transfer from the home can be reduced by a variety of methods, such as loft insulation, cavity wall insulation, and double glazing. The efficiency of insulating materials in the building industry are compared by measuring their heat-conducting properties, represented by a ◊U-value. A low U-value indicates a good insulating material.

$E = mc^2$ It is now recognised that mass can be converted into energy under certain conditions, according to Einstein's theory of relativity. This conversion of mass into energy is the basis of atomic power. ◊Einstein's special theory of ◊relativity 1905 correlates any gain, E, in energy with a gain, m, in mass, by the equation $E = mc^2$, in which c is the speed of light. The conversion of mass into energy in accordance with this equation applies universally, although it is only for nuclear reactions that the percentage change in mass is large enough to detect.

energy, alternative energy from sources that are renewable and ecologically safe, as opposed to sources that are nonrenewable with toxic by-products, such as coal, oil, or gas (fossil fuels), and uranium (for nuclear power). The most important alternative energy source is flowing water, harnessed as ◊hydroelectric power. Other sources include the oceans' tides and waves (see ◊tidal power station and ◊wave power), ◊wind power (harnessed by windmills and wind turbines), the Sun (◊solar energy), and the heat trapped in the Earth's crust (◊geothermal energy) (see also ◊cold fusion).

energy conservation methods of reducing energy use through insulation, increasing energy efficiency, and changes in patterns of use. Profligate energy use by industrialized countries contributes greatly to air pollution and the ◊greenhouse effect when it draws on nonrenewable energy sources.

It has been calculated that increasing energy efficiency alone could reduce carbon dioxide emissions in several high-income countries by 1–2% a year. The average annual decrease in energy consumption in relation to gross national product 1973–87 was 1.2% in France, 2% in the UK, 2.1% in the USA, and 2.8% in Japan.

energy level the permitted energy that an electron can have in any particular atom. Energy levels can be calculated using ◊quantum theory. The permitted energy levels depend mainly on the distance of the electron from the nucleus. See ◊orbital, atomic.

energy of reaction energy released or absorbed during a chemical reaction, also called **enthalpy of reaction** or **heat of reaction**. In a chemical reaction, the energy stored in the reacting molecules is rarely the same as that stored in the product molecules. Depending on which is the greater, energy is either released (an exothermic reaction) or absorbed (an endothermic reaction) from the surroundings (see ◊conservation of energy). The amount of energy released or absorbed by the quantities of substances represented by the chemical equation is the energy of reaction.

Energy Star in computing, US programme requiring all computer equipment to conserve electrical power. Key features of Energy Star-compliant hardware include a built-in function to put the computer and monitor into suspended animation after a specified period of disuse and limits on the amount of power computers and printers can draw.

engine device for converting stored energy into useful work or movement. Most engines use a fuel as their energy store. The fuel is burnt to produce heat energy – hence the name 'heat engine' – which is then converted into movement. Heat engines can be classified according to the fuel they use (◊petrol engine or ◊diesel engine), or according to whether the fuel is burnt inside (◊internal combustion engine) or outside (◊steam engine) the engine, or according to whether they produce a reciprocating or rotary motion (◊turbine or ◊Wankel engine).

engine in computing, core piece of software around which other features and functions are built. A database ◊search engine, for example, accepts user input and handles the processing necessary to find matches between the user input and the database records.

In a computer game, the term 'engine' is also used to refer to the core software that allows users to move around the game's levels and pick up weapons and treasure.

The scientist describes what is: the engineer creates what never was.

THEODORE VON KÁRMÁN Hungarian-born US aerodynamicist.
Biogr. Mem. FRS 1980 26 110

engineering the application of science to the design, construction, and maintenance of works, machinery, roads, railways, bridges, harbour installations, engines, ships, aircraft and airports, spacecraft and space stations, and the generation, transmission, and use of electrical power. The main divisions of engineering are aerospace, chemical, civil, computer, electrical, electronic, gas, marine, materials, mechanical, mining, production, radio, and structural.

Did you know that if a beaver two feet long with a tail a foot and a half long can build a dam twelve feet high and six feet wide in two days, all you would need to build the Kariba Dam is a beaver sixty-eight feet long with a fifty-one foot tail?

NORTON JUSTER US writer.
The Phantom Tollbooth ch 14

TO REMEMBER THAT TO TIGHTEN A BOLT OR NUT YOU TURN IT CLOCKWISE (RIGHT), AND TO TAKE IT OFF YOU TURN IT ANTI-CLOCKWISE (LEFT):

RIGHTY TIGHTY, LEFTY LOOSIE

engineering drawing technical drawing that forms the plans for the design and construction of engineering components and structures. Engineering drawings show different projections, or views of objects, with the relevant dimensions, and show how all the separate parts fit together. They are often produced by computers using computer-aided design (◊CAD).

English toy terrier or ***black-and-tan terrier*** breed of toy dog closely resembling the ◊Manchester terrier but smaller and with erect ears. It weighs no more than 3.5 kg/8 lb and is 25–30 cm/10–12 in high.

enset *Ensete ventricosum* relative of the banana with edible corms and stems. It was domesticated between 5,000 and 10,000 years ago but is now grown only in southern Ethiopia. It is resistant to drought and when mashed and fermented can be kept for months, or even years, before being made into a wide variety of foods. Its fibre can also be used to produce material.

Wild enset grows over much of western and southern Africa. In 1993 a US research team was set up to explore the possibility of cultivating enset in the drought-stricken north of Ethiopia.

enthalpy in chemistry, alternative term for ◊energy of reaction, the heat energy associated with a chemical change.

entomology study of insects.

entropy in ◊thermodynamics, a parameter representing the state of disorder of a system at the atomic, ionic, or molecular level; the greater the disorder, the higher the entropy. Thus the fast-moving disordered molecules of water vapour have higher entropy than those of more ordered liquid water, which in turn have more entropy than the molecules in solid crystalline ice.

In a closed system undergoing change, entropy is a measure of the amount of energy unavailable for useful work. At ◊absolute zero (–273.15°C/–459.67°F/0 K), when all molecular motion ceases and order is assumed to be complete, entropy is zero.

... a living organism ... feeds upon negative entropy ... Thus the device by which an organism maintains itself stationary at a fairly high level of orderliness (fairly low level of entropy) really consists in continually sucking orderliness from its environment.

Erwin Schrödinger Austrian physicist.
What is Life? 1944

E number code number for additives that have been approved for use by the European Commission (EC). The E written before the number stands for European. E numbers do not have to be displayed on lists of ingredients, and the manufacturer may choose to list additives by their name instead. E numbers cover all categories of additives apart from flavourings.

Additives, other than flavourings, that are not approved by the European Commission, but are still used in Britain, are represented by a code number without an E.

envelope in geometry, a curve that touches all the members of a family of lines or curves. For example, a family of three equal circles all touching each other and forming a triangular pattern (like a clover leaf) has two envelopes: a small circle that fits in the space in the middle, and a large circle that encompasses all three circles.

environment in ecology, the sum of conditions affecting a particular organism, including physical surroundings, climate, and influences of other living organisms. See also ◊biosphere and ◊habitat.

In common usage, 'the environment' often means the total global environment, without reference to any particular organism. In genetics, it is the external influences that affect an organism's development, and thus its ◊phenotype.

The sun, the moon and the stars would have disappeared long ago ... had they happened to be within the reach of predatory human hands.

Havelock Ellis British psychologist.
The Dance of Life ch 7

environmental audit another name for ◊green audit, the inspection of a company to assess its environmental impact.

environmentalism theory emphasizing the primary influence of the environment on the development of groups or individuals. It stresses the importance of the physical, biological, psychological, or cultural environment as a factor influencing the structure or behaviour of animals, including humans.

In politics this has given rise in many countries to Green parties, which aim to 'preserve the planet and its people'.

Environmentally Sensitive Area (ESA) scheme introduced by the UK Ministry of Agriculture in 1984, as a result of EC legislation, to protect some of the most beautiful areas of the British countryside from the loss and damage caused by agricultural change. The first areas to be designated ESAs were in the Pennine Dales, the North Peak District, the Norfolk Broads, the Breckland, the Suffolk River Valleys, the Test Valley, the South Downs, the Somerset Levels and Moors, West Penwith, Cornwall, the Shropshire Borders, the Cambrian Mountains, and the Lleyn Peninsula.

The total area designated as ESA's was estimated 1993 at 785,600 hectares. The scheme is voluntary, with farmers being encouraged to adapt their practices so as to enhance or maintain the natural features of the landscape and conserve wildlife habitat. A farmer who joins the scheme agrees to manage the land in this way for at least five years. In return for this agreement, the Ministry of Agriculture pays the farmer a sum that reflects the financial losses incurred as a result of reconciling conservation with commercial farming.

Environmental Protection Agency (EPA) US agency set up 1970 to control water and air quality, industrial and commercial wastes, pesticides, noise, and radiation. In its own words, it aims to protect 'the country from being degraded, and its health threatened, by a multitude of human activities initiated without regard to long-ranging effects upon the life-supporting properties, the economic uses, and the recreational value of air, land, and water'.

environment–heredity controversy see ◊nature–nurture controversy.

enzyme biological ◊catalyst produced in cells, and capable of speeding up the chemical reactions necessary for life. They are large, complex ◊proteins, and are highly specific, each chemical reaction requiring its own particular enzyme. The enzyme's specificity arises from its **active site**, an area with a shape corresponding to part of the molecule with which it reacts (the substrate). The enzyme and the substrate slot together forming an enzyme–substrate complex that allows the reaction to take place, after which the enzyme falls away unaltered.

The activity and efficiency of enzymes are influenced by various factors, including temperature and pH conditions. Temperatures above 60°C/140°F damage (denature) the intricate structure of enzymes, causing reactions to cease. Each enzyme operates best within a specific pH range, and is denatured by excessive acidity or alkalinity.

Digestive enzymes include amylases (which digest starch), lipases (which digest fats), and proteases (which digest protein). Other enzymes play a part in the conversion of food energy into ◊ATP; the manufacture of all the molecular components of the body; the replication of ◊DNA when a cell divides; the production of hormones; and the control of movement of substances into and out of cells.

Enzymes have many medical and industrial uses, from washing powders to drug production, and as research tools in molecular biology. They can be extracted from bacteria and moulds, and ◊genetic engineering now makes it possible to tailor an enzyme for a specific purpose.

ENZYME

The reason that pigs never suffer from gout is because of an enzyme. In humans, this painful disease is caused by a build-up of uric acid. Pigs have an enzyme that breaks uric acid into soluble components. Humans do not have this enzyme, so they suffer from gout and pigs do not.

Eocene second epoch of the Tertiary period of geological time, 56.5–35.5 million years ago. Originally considered the earliest division of the Tertiary, the name means 'early recent', referring to the early forms of mammals evolving at the time, following the extinction of the dinosaurs.

eotvos unit unit (symbol E) for measuring small changes in the intensity of the Earth's ◊gravity with horizontal distance.

ephemeral plant plant with a very short life cycle, sometimes as little as six to eight weeks. It may complete several generations in one growing season.

epicentre the point on the Earth's surface immediately above the seismic focus of an ◊earthquake. Most damage usually takes place at an earthquake's epicentre. The term sometimes refers to a point directly above or below a nuclear explosion ('at ground zero').

epicyclic gear or ***sun-and-planet gear*** gear system that consists of one or more gear wheels moving around another. Epicyclic gears are found in bicycle hub gears and in automatic gearboxes.

epicycloid in geometry, a curve resembling a series of arches traced out by a point on the circumference of a circle that rolls around another circle of a different diameter. If the two circles have the same diameter, the curve is a ◊cardioid.

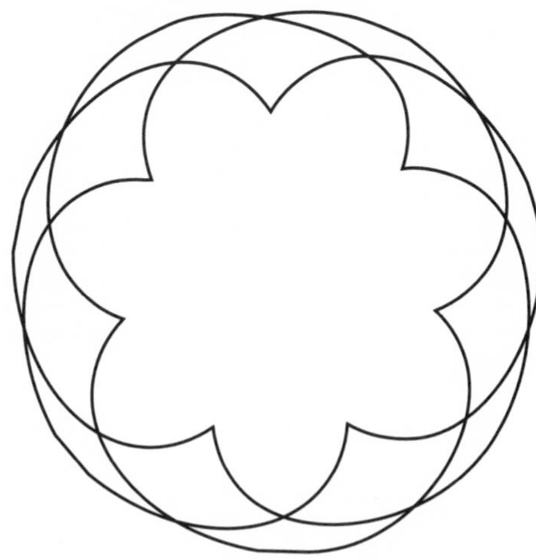

epicycloid A seven-cusped epicycloid, formed by a point on the circumference of a circle (of diameter d*) that rolls around another circle (of diameter 7d/3).*

epidemic outbreak of infectious disease affecting large numbers of people at the same time. A widespread epidemic that sweeps across many countries (such as the ◊Black Death in the late Middle Ages) is known as a **pandemic**.

epidermis outermost layer of ◊cells on an organism's body. In plants and many invertebrates such as insects, it consists of a single layer of cells. In vertebrates, it consists of several layers of cells.

The epidermis of plants and invertebrates often has an outer noncellular ◊cuticle that protects the organism from desiccation.

epididymis in male vertebrates, a long coiled tubule in the ◊testis, in which sperm produced in the seminiferous tube are stored. In men, it is a duct about 6 m/20 ft long, convoluted into a small space.

epigeal seed germination in which the ◊cotyledons (seed leaves) are borne above the soil.

epiglottis small flap located behind the root of the tongue in mammals. It closes off the end of the windpipe during swallowing to prevent food from passing into it and causing choking.

The action of the epiglottis is a highly complex reflex process involving two phases. During the first stage a mouthful of chewed food is lifted by the tongue towards the top and back of the mouth. This is accompanied by the cessation of breathing and by the blocking of the nasal areas from the mouth. The second phase involves the epiglottis moving over the larynx while the food passes down into the oesophagus.

epilepsy medical disorder characterized by a tendency to develop fits, which are convulsions or abnormal feelings caused by abnormal electrical discharges in the cerebral hemispheres of the ◊brain. Epilepsy can be controlled with a number of anticonvulsant drugs.

The term epilepsy covers a range of conditions from mild 'absences', involving momentary loss of awareness, to major convulsions. In some cases the abnormal electrical activity is focal (confined to one area of the brain); in others it is generalized throughout the cerebral cortex. Fits are classified according to their clinical type. They include: the **grand mal** seizure with convulsions and loss of consciousness; the fleeting absence of awareness **petit mal**, almost exclusively a disorder of childhood; **Jacksonian** seizures, originating in the motor cortex; and **temporal-lobe** fits, which may be associated with visual hallucinations and bizarre disturbances of the sense of smell.

Epilepsy affects 1–3% of the world's population. It may arise spontaneously or may be a consequence of brain surgery, organic brain disease, head injury, metabolic disease, alcoholism or withdrawal from some drugs. Almost a third of patients have a family history of the condition.

Most epileptics have infrequent fits that have little impact on their daily lives. Epilepsy does not imply that the sufferer has any impairment of intellect, behaviour, or personality.

UNDERSTANDING EPILEPSY

http://www.epinet.org.au/efvunder.html

Clear and concise guide to epilepsy provided by EpiNet courtesy of the Epilepsy Foundation of Victoria, Australia. It covers the basics of the subject under the headings of 'What is Epilepsy?', 'Diagnosis', and 'Recognizing Seizures'. It also provides a guide to the different types of seizure and suggests first aid measures for each.

epiphyte any plant that grows on another plant or object above the surface of the ground, and has no roots in the soil. An epiphyte does not parasitize the plant it grows on but merely uses it for support. Its nutrients are obtained from rainwater, organic debris such as leaf litter, or from the air.

The greatest diversity of epiphytes is found in tropical areas and includes many orchids.

epithelium in animals, tissue of closely packed cells that forms a surface or lines a cavity or tube. Epithelium may be protective (as in the skin) or secretory (as in the cells lining the wall of the gut).

epoch subdivision of a geological period in the geological time scale. Epochs are sometimes given their own names (such as the

TO REMEMBER THE DIFFERENT EPOCHS, IN DESCENDING ORDER OF AGE:

TO REMEMBER THE DIFFERENT EPOCHS, IN ASCENDING ORDER:

HEAVY PEOPLE PUT MORE ON EVERY PLATE

OR

HAPPY PLUMP PREGNANT MOTHERS ONLY EAT PICKLES

OR

HAPPY PEOPLE PLAY MUSIC, OTHERS EAT PIZZA

PUT EGGS ON MY PLATE PLEASE HONEY

OR

PLEASE ELIMINATE OLD MEN PLAYING POKER HONESTLY

HOLOCENE, PLEISTOCENE, PLIOCENE, MIOCENE, OLIGOCENE, EOCENE, PALEOCENE

PALAEOCENE, EOCENE, OLIGOCENE, MIOCENE, PLIOCENE, PLEISTOCENE, HOLOCENE

Palaeocene, Eocene, Oligocene, Miocene, and Pliocene epochs comprising the Tertiary period), or they are referred to as the late, early, or middle portions of a given period (as the Late Cretaceous or the Middle Triassic epoch).

Geological time is broken up into **geochronological units** of which epoch is just one level of division. The hierarchy of geochronological divisions is eon, era, period, epoch, age, and chron. Epochs are subdivisions of periods and ages are subdivisions of epochs. Rocks representing an epoch of geological time comprise a **series**.

epoxy resin synthetic ◊resin used as an ◊adhesive and as an ingredient in paints. Household epoxy resin adhesives come in component form as two separate tubes of chemical, one tube containing resin, the other a curing agent (hardener). The two chemicals are mixed just before application, and the mix soon sets hard.

EPROM (acronym for ***erasable programmable read-only memory***) computer memory device in the form of an ◊integrated circuit (chip) that can record data and retain it indefinitely. The data can be erased by exposure to ultraviolet light, and new data recorded. Other kinds of computer memory chips are ◊ROM (read-only memory), ◊PROM (programmable read-only memory), and ◊RAM (random-access memory).

EPS in computing, abbreviation for ◊encapsulated PostScript.

Epsilon Aurigae ◊eclipsing binary star in the constellation Auriga. One of the pair is an 'ordinary' star, but the other seems to be an enormous distended object whose exact nature remains unknown. The period (time between eclipses) is 27 years, the longest of its kind. The last eclipse was in 1982–84.

Epsom salts $MgSO_4.7H_2O$ hydrated magnesium sulphate, used as a relaxant and laxative and added to baths to soothe the skin. The name is derived from a bitter saline spring at Epsom, Surrey, England, which contains the salt in solution.

equation in chemistry, representation of a chemical reaction by symbols and numbers; see ◊chemical equation.

equation in mathematics, expression that represents the equality of two expressions involving constants and/or variables, and thus usually includes an equals (=) sign. For example, the equation $A = \pi r^2$ equates the area A of a circle of radius r to the product πr^2.

The algebraic equation $y = mx + c$ is the general one in coordinate geometry for a straight line.

If a mathematical equation is true for all variables in a given domain, it is sometimes called an identity and denoted by ≡.

Thus $(x + y)^2 = x^2 + 2xy + y^2$ for all $x, y \in R$.

An **indeterminate equation** is an equation for which there is an infinite set of solutions – for example, $2x = y$. A **diophantine equation** is an indeterminate equation in which both the solution and the terms must be whole numbers (after Diophantus of Alexandria, c. AD 250).

equation of motion mathematical equation that gives the position and velocity of a moving object at any time. Given the mass of an object, the forces acting on it, and its initial position and velocity, an equation of motion is used to calculate its position and velocity at any later time. The equation must be based on ◊Newton's laws of motion or, if speeds near that of light are involved, on the theory of relativity.

equations of motion or ***kinematic equations*** mathematical equations that give the position or velocity at any time of an object moving with constant acceleration. The five common equations are:

$$v = u + ats = \tfrac{1}{2}(u + v)ts = ut + \tfrac{1}{2}at^2v^2 = u^2 + 2$$

as in which *a* is the object's constant acceleration, *u* is its initial velocity, *v* is its velocity after a time *t*, and *s* is the distance travelled by it in that time.

Equator or ***terrestrial equator*** the ◊great circle whose plane is perpendicular to the Earth's axis (the line joining the poles). Its length is 40,092 km/24,901.8 mi, divided into 360 degrees of longitude. The Equator encircles the broadest part of the Earth, and represents 0° latitude. It divides the Earth into two halves, called the northern and the southern hemispheres.

The **celestial equator** is the circle in which the plane of the Earth's Equator intersects the ◊celestial sphere.

equatorial coordinates in astronomy, a system for measuring the position of astronomical objects on the ◊celestial sphere with reference to the plane of the Earth's equator.

◊Declination (symbol Δ), analogous to latitude, is measured in degrees from the equator to the north (Δ = 90°) or south (Δ =–90°) celestial poles. Right ◊ascension (symbol α), analogous to longitude, is normally measured in hours of time (α = 0 h to 24 h) eastward along the equator from a fixed point known as the first point of ◊Aries or the ◊vernal equinox.

equatorial mounting in astronomy, a method of mounting a telescope to simplify the tracking of celestial objects. One axis (the polar axis) is mounted parallel to the rotation axis of the Earth so that the ◊telescope can be turned about it to follow objects across the sky. The declination axis moves the telescope in ◊declination and is clamped before tracking begins. Another advantage over the simpler altazimuth mounting is that the orientation of the image is fixed, permitting long-exposure photography.

Equidae horse family in the order Perissodactyla, which includes the odd-toed hoofed animals. Besides the domestic horse, wild asses, wild horses, onagers, and zebras, there are numerous extinct species known from fossils.

All species in the family are inhabitants of flat, open country, except the mountain zebra from the hills of southern Africa. They have long legs, adapted to carry the animals at speed over firm ground; only one toe, terminating in a hoof, is present on each limb. They are all herbivorous and have keen senses to detect their enemies. Their jaws are strong and able to chew the tough grasses and herbs on which they feed in the wild state.

equilateral geometrical figure, having all sides of equal length.

equilibrium in physics, an unchanging condition in which an undisturbed system can remain indefinitely in a state of balance. In a **static equilibrium**, such as an object resting on the floor, there is no motion. In a **dynamic equilibrium**, in contrast, a steady state is maintained by constant, though opposing, changes. For example, in a sealed bottle half-full of water, the constancy of the water level is a result of molecules evaporating from the surface and condensing on to it at the same rate.

equinox the points in spring and autumn at which the Sun's path, the ◊ecliptic, crosses the celestial equator, so that the day and night are of approximately equal length. The **vernal equinox** occurs about 21 March and the **autumnal equinox**, 23 September.

era any of the major divisions of geological time, each including several periods, but smaller than an eon. The currently recognized eras all fall within the Phanerozoic eon – or the vast span of time, starting about 570 million years ago, when fossils are found to become abundant. The eras in ascending order are the Palaeozoic, Mesozoic, and Cenozoic. We are living in the Recent epoch of the Quaternary period of the Cenozoic era.

Geological time is broken up into **geochronological units** of which era is just one level of division. The hierarchy of geochronological divisions is eon, era, period, ◊epoch, age, and chron. Eras are subdivisions of eons and periods are subdivisions of eras. Rocks representing an era of geological time comprise an **erathem**.

erasable optical disc in computing, another name for a ◊floptical disc.

Eratosthenes' sieve a method for finding ◊prime numbers. It involves writing in sequence all numbers from 2. Then, starting with 2, cross out every second number (but not 2 itself), thus eliminating numbers that can be divided by 2. Next, starting with 3, cross out every third number (but not 3 itself), and continue the process for 5, 7, 11, 13, and so on. The numbers that remain are primes.

erbium soft, lustrous, greyish, metallic element of the ◊lanthanide series, symbol Er, atomic number 68, relative atomic mass 167.26. It occurs with the element yttrium or as a minute part of various minerals. It was discovered in 1843 by Carl Mosander (1797–1858), and named after the town of Ytterby, Sweden, near which the lanthanides (rare-earth elements) were first found.

Erbium has been used since 1987 to amplify data pulses in optical fibre, enabling faster transmission. Erbium ions in the fibreglass, charged with infrared light, emit energy by amplifying the data pulse as it moves along the fibre.

erg c.g.s. unit of work, replaced in the SI system by the◊ joule. One erg of work is done by a force of one ◊dyne moving through one centimetre.

ergonomics study of the relationship between people and the furniture, tools, and machinery they use at work. The object is to improve work performance by removing sources of muscular stress and general fatigue: for example, by presenting data and control panels in easy-to-view form, making office furniture comfortable, and creating a generally pleasant environment.

Good ergonomic design makes computer systems easier to use and minimizes the health hazards and physical stresses of working with computers for many hours a day: it helps data entry workers to avoid conditions like ◊strain injury (RSI), eyestrain, and back and muscle aches.

ergot any of a group of parasitic fungi (especially of the genus *Claviceps*), whose brown or black grainlike masses replace the kernels of rye or other cereals. *C. purpurea* attacks the rye plant. Ergot poisoning is caused by eating infected bread, resulting in burning pains, gangrene, and convulsions.

The large grains of the fungus contain the poison ergotamine.

ERIC (abbreviation for ***Educational Resources Information Center***) in computing, database of resources for education available on the Internet. Established 1966, ERIC is a federally funded network of educational information. Sixteen clearing houses index educational materials for the database, which is housed at the University of Saskatchewan, Canada. The database is distributed in a variety of formats including printed books, CD-ROM, and microfiche.

erica any plant of a large group that includes the heathers. There are about 500 species, distributed mainly in South Africa with some in Europe. (Genus *Erica,* family Ericaceae.)

Eridanus in astronomy, the sixth largest constellation, which meanders from the celestial equator (see ◊celestial sphere) deep into the southern hemisphere of the sky. Eridanus is represented as a river. Its brightest star is ◊Achernar, a corruption of the Arabic for 'the end of the river'.

ermine the ◊stoat during winter, when its coat becomes white.

In northern latitudes the coat becomes completely white, except for a black tip on the tail, but in warmer regions the back may remain brownish. The fur is used commercially.

ERNIE acronym for ***electronic random number indicator***, machine designed and produced by the UK Post Office Research Station to select a series of random 9-figure numbers to indicate prizewinners among Premium Bond holders.

Eros in astronomy, an asteroid, discovered in 1898, that can pass 22 million km/14 million mi from the Earth, as observed in 1975. Eros was the first asteroid to be discovered that has an orbit coming within that of Mars. It is elongated, measures about 36 × 12 km/22 × 7 mi, rotates around its shortest axis every 5.3 hours, and orbits the Sun every 1.8 years.

The Near Earth Asteroid Rendezvous (NEAR) launched February 1996 is estimated to take three years to reach Eros. It will spend a year circling the asteroid in an attempt to determine what it is made of.

erosion wearing away of the Earth's surface, caused by the breakdown and transportation of particles of rock or soil (by contrast, ◊weathering does not involve transportation). Agents of erosion include the sea, rivers, glaciers, and wind.

Water, consisting of sea waves and currents, rivers, and rain; ice, in the form of glaciers; and wind, hurling sand fragments against exposed rocks and moving dunes along, are the most potent forces of erosion.

People also contribute to erosion by bad farming practices and the cutting down of forests, which can lead to the formation of dust bowls.

There are several processes of erosion including hydraulic action, ◊corrosion, attrition, and ◊solution.

erratic in geology, a displaced rock that has been transported by a glacier or some other natural force to a site of different geological composition.

error in computing, a fault or mistake, either in the software or on the part of the user, that causes a program to stop running (crash) or produce unexpected results. Program errors, or bugs, are largely eliminated in the course of the programmer's initial testing procedure, but some will remain in most programs. All computer operating systems are designed to produce an **error message** (on the display screen, or in an error file or printout) whenever an error is detected, reporting that an error has taken place and, wherever possible, diagnosing its cause.

Truth comes out of error more easily than out of confusion.

FRANCIS BACON English politician, philosopher, and essayist.
Quoted in R L Weber, *A Random Walk in Science*

---

error detection in computing, the techniques that enable a program to detect incorrect data. A common method is to add a check digit to important codes, such as account numbers and product codes. The digit is chosen so that the code conforms to a rule that the program can verify. Another technique involves calculating the sum (called the ◊hash total) of each instance of a particular item of data, and storing it at the end of the data.

error message message produced by a computer to inform the user that an error has occurred.

erythroblast in biology, a series of nucleated cells that go through various stages of development in the bone marrow until they form red blood cells (erythrocytes). This process is known as erythropoiesis. Erythroblasts can appear in the blood of people with blood cancers.

erythrocyte another name for ◊red blood cell.

Eryx genus of egg-laying snakes, closely allied to the ◊boa constrictor. The species of *Eryx* differ from boas in having a very short, obtuse tail and narrower ventral plates. They occur in Asia and Africa.

ESA abbreviation for ◊European Space Agency.

escalator automatic moving staircase that carries people between floors or levels. It consists of treads linked in an endless belt arranged to form strips (steps), powered by an electric motor that moves both steps and handrails at the same speed. Towards the top and bottom the steps flatten out for ease of passage. The first escalator was exhibited in Paris in 1900.

escape sequence in computing, string of characters sent to a ◊modem to switch it from sending data to a state in which it can accept and act upon commands.

Most modems use the escape sequence patented by Hayes, which consists of three plus signs (+++) with a brief pause on either side to distinguish the characters from data.

escape velocity in physics, minimum velocity with which an object must be projected for it to escape from the gravitational pull of a planetary body. In the case of the Earth, the escape velocity is 11.2 kps/6.9 mps; the Moon, 2.4 kps/1.5 mps; Mars, 5 kps/3.1 mps; and Jupiter, 59.6 kps/37 mps.

escarpment or ***cuesta*** large ridge created by the erosion of dipping sedimentary rocks. It has one steep side (scarp) and one gently sloping side (dip). Escarpments are common features of chalk landscapes, such as the Chiltern Hills and the North Downs in England. Certain features are associated with chalk escarpments, including dry valleys (formed on the dip slope), combes (steep-sided valleys on the scarp slope), and springs.

Escherichia coli rod-shaped Gram-negative ◊bacterium (see bacteria) that lives, usually harmlessly, in the colon of most warm-blooded animals. It is the commonest cause of urinary tract infections in humans. It is sometimes found in water or meat where faecal contamination has occurred and can cause severe gastric problems.

The mapping of the genome of *E. coli,* consisting of 4,403 genes, was completed in 1997.

classification *Escherichia coli* is the only species in the bacterial family Enterobacteriaceae.

ESP abbreviation for ◊extrasensory perception.

esparto species of grass native to southern Spain, southern Portugal, and the Balearics, but now widely grown in dry, sandy locations throughout the world. The plant is just over 1 m/3 ft high, producing greyish-green leaves, which are used for making paper, ropes, baskets, mats, and cables. (*Stipa tenacissima.*)

ESPRIT (abbreviation for ***European Strategic Programme for Research and Development in Information Technology***) European Union programme that funds technology research at an early stage of development. ESPRIT's goals include encouraging the development of international standards and cooperation between European companies, universities, and research centres in order to develop the infrastructure necessary for Europe to be able to compete with Japan and the USA.

essential amino acid water-soluble organic molecule vital to a healthy diet; see ◊amino acid.

essential fatty acid organic compound consisting of a hydrocarbon chain and important in the diet; see ◊fatty acid.

ester organic compound formed by the reaction between an alcohol and an acid, with the elimination of water. Unlike ◊salts, esters are covalent compounds.

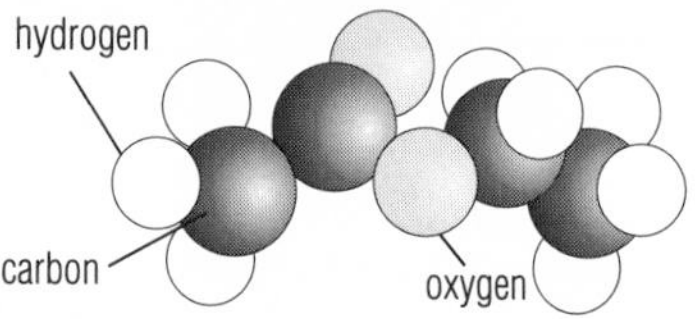

ester Molecular model of the ester ethyl ethanoate (ethyl acetate) $CH_3CH_2COOCH_3$

estradiol alternative spelling of oestradiol, a type of ◊oestrogen (female sex hormone).

ethanal common name ***acetaldehyde*** CH_3CHO one of the chief members of the group of organic compounds known as ◊aldehydes. It is a colourless inflammable liquid boiling at 20.8°C/69.6°F. Ethanal is formed by the oxidation of ethanol or ethene and is used to make many other organic chemical compounds.

ethanal trimer common name ***paraldehyde*** $(CH_3CHO)_3$ colourless liquid formed from ethanal. It is soluble in water.

ethane CH_3CH_3 colourless, odourless gas, the second member of the alkane series of hydrocarbons (paraffins).

ethane-1,2-diol technical name for ◊glycol.

ethanoate common name ***acetate*** $CH_3CO_2^-$ negative ion derived from ethanoic (acetic) acid; any salt containing this ion. In textiles, acetate rayon is a synthetic fabric made from modified cellulose (wood pulp) treated with ethanoic acid; in photography, acetate film is a non-flammable film made of cellulose ethanoate.

ethanoic acid common name ***acetic acid*** CH_3CO_2H one of the simplest fatty acids (a series of organic acids). In the pure state it is a colourless liquid with an unpleasant pungent odour; it solidifies to an icelike mass of crystals at 16.7°C/62.4°F, and hence is often called glacial ethanoic acid. Vinegar contains 5% or more ethanoic acid, produced by fermentation.

Cellulose (derived from wood or other sources) may be treated with ethanoic acid to produce a cellulose ethanoate (acetate) solution, which can be used to make plastic items by injection moulding or extruded to form synthetic textile fibres.

ethanol common name ***ethyl alcohol*** C_2H_5OH alcohol found in beer, wine, cider, spirits, and other alcoholic drinks. When pure, it is a colourless liquid with a pleasant odour, miscible with water or ether; it burns in air with a pale blue flame. The vapour forms an explosive mixture with air and may be used in high-compression internal combustion engines.

It is produced naturally by the fermentation of carbohydrates by yeast cells. Industrially, it can be made by absorption of ethene and subsequent reaction with water, or by the reduction of ethanal in the presence of a catalyst, and is widely used as a solvent.

Ethanol is used as a raw material in the manufacture of ether, chloral, and iodoform. It can also be added to petrol, where it improves the performance of the engine, or be used as a fuel in its own right (as in Brazil). Crops such as sugar cane may be grown to provide ethanol (by fermentation) for this purpose.

ethene common name ***ethylene*** C_2H_4 colourless, flammable gas, the first member of the ◊alkene series of hydrocarbons. It is the most widely used synthetic organic chemical and is used to produce the plastics polyethene (polyethylene), polychloroethene, and polyvinyl chloride (PVC). It is obtained from natural gas or coal gas, or by the dehydration of ethanol.

Ethene is produced during plant metabolism and is classified as a plant hormone. It is important in the ripening of fruit and in ◊abscission. Small amounts of ethene are often added to the air surrounding fruit to artificially promote ripening. Tomato and marigold plants show distorted growth in concentrations as low as 0.01 parts per million. Plants also release ethene when they are under stress. German physicists invented a device in 1997 that measures stress levels in plants by measuring surrounding ethene levels.

ether in chemistry, any of a series of organic chemical compounds having an oxygen atom linking the carbon atoms of two hydrocarbon radical groups (general formula R-O-R'); also the common name for ethoxyethane $C_2H_5OC_2H_5$ (also called diethyl ether).

This is used as an anaesthetic and as an external cleansing agent before surgical operations. It is also used as a solvent, and in the extraction of oils, fats, waxes, resins, and alkaloids.

Ethoxyethane is a colourless, volatile, inflammable liquid, slightly soluble in water, and miscible with ethanol. It is prepared by treatment of ethanol with excess concentrated sulphuric acid at 140°C/284°F.

ether or ***aether*** in the history of science, a hypothetical medium permeating all of space. The concept originated with the Greeks, and has been revived on several occasions to explain the properties and propagation of light. It was supposed that light and other electromagnetic radiation – even in outer space – needed a medium, the ether, in which to travel. The idea was abandoned with the acceptance of ◊relativity.

Ethernet in computing, the most popular protocol for ◊local area networks. Ethernet was developed principally by the Xerox Corporation, but can now be used on most computers. It normally allows data transfer at rates up to 10 Mbps. but 100 Mbps Fast Ethernet – often called 100Base-T – is already in widespread use while Gigabit Ethernet is being tipped for future success.

Ethernet and Fast Ethernet are IEEE standards, and Gigabit Ethernet should become a standard in 1998.

Ethiopian wolf ***Simien jackal*** or ***Abyssinian wolf*** member of the family Canidae, *Canis simensis,* and genetically close to the grey wolf and coyote. They are found mainly in Ethiopia's Bale and Simien Mountains, but numbers are seriously in decline with only about 400 left in 1997.

ethnography study of living cultures, using anthropological techniques like participant observation (where the anthropologist lives in the society being studied) and a reliance on informants. Ethnography has provided much data of use to archaeologists as analogies.

ethnology study of contemporary peoples, concentrating on their geography and culture, as distinct from their social systems. Ethnologists make a comparative analysis of data from different cultures to understand how cultures work and why they change, with a view to deriving general principles about human society.

ethnopaediatrics in anthropology, the study of child-rearing practices in different cultures. Areas studied include the comparison of feeding regimes, sleeping arrangements, and degree of verbal stimulation.

ethology comparative study of animal behaviour in its natural setting. Ethology is concerned with the causal mechanisms (both the stimuli that elicit behaviour and the physiological mechanisms controlling it), as well as the development of behaviour, its function, and its evolutionary history.

Ethology was pioneered during the 1930s by the Austrians Konrad Lorenz and Karl von Frisch who, with the Dutch zoologist Nikolaas Tinbergen, received the Nobel prize in 1973. Ethologists believe that the significance of an animal's behaviour can be understood only in its natural context, and emphasize the importance of field studies and an evolutionary perspective. A recent development within ethology is ◊sociobiology, the study of the evolutionary function of ◊social behaviour.

ethyl alcohol common name for ethanol.

ethylene common name for ethene.

ethylene glycol alternative name for glycol.

ethyne common name ***acetylene*** CHCH colourless inflammable gas produced by mixing calcium carbide and water. It is the simplest member of the ◊alkyne series of hydrocarbons. It is used in the manufacture of the synthetic rubber neoprene, and in oxyacetylene welding and cutting.

Ethyne was discovered by Edmund Davy in 1836 and was used in early gas lamps, where it was produced by the reaction between water and calcium carbide. Its combustion provides more heat, relatively, than almost any other fuel known (its calorific value is five times that of hydrogen). This means that the gas gives an intensely hot flame; hence its use in oxyacetylene torches.

etiolation in botany, a form of growth seen in plants receiving insufficient light. It is characterized by long, weak stems, small leaves, and a pale yellowish colour (◊chlorosis) owing to a lack of chlorophyll. The rapid increase in height enables a plant that is surrounded by others to quickly reach a source of light, after which a return to normal growth usually occurs.

Etruscan art the art of the inhabitants of Etruria, central Italy, a civilization that flourished 8th–2nd centuries BC. The Etruscans produced sculpture, painting, pottery, metalwork, and jewellery. Etruscan terracotta coffins (sarcophagi), carved with reliefs and topped with portraits of the dead reclining on one elbow, were to influence the later Romans and early Christians.

painting Most examples of Etruscan painting come from excavated tombs, whose frescoes depict scenes of everyday life, mythology, and mortuary rites, typically in bright colours and a vigorous, animated style. Scenes of feasting, dancing, swimming, fishing, and playing evoke a confident people who enjoyed life to the full, and who even in death depicted themselves in a joyous and festive manner. The decline of their civilization, in the shadow of Rome's expansion, is reflected in their later art, which loses its original *joie de vivre* and becomes sombre.

influences Influences from archaic Greece and the Middle East are evident, as are those from the preceding Iron Age Villanovan culture, but the full flowering of Etruscan art represents a unique synthesis of existing traditions and artistic innovation, which was to have a profound influence on the development of Western art.

eucalyptus any tree of a group belonging to the myrtle family, native to Australia, where they are commonly known as gumtrees. About 90% of Australian timber belongs to the eucalyptus genus, which contains about 500 species. The trees have dark hardwood timber which is used for heavy construction work such as railway and bridge building. They are mostly tall, aromatic, evergreen trees with pendant leaves and white, pink, or red flowers. (Genus *Eucalyptus,* family Myrtaceae.)

Compounds isolated from eucalyptus leaves were found in 1996 to be highly effective in killing *Streptococcus mutans,* the bacteria found in the mouth that cause dental decay.

EUCALYPTUS

The tallest tree ever measured was an Australian eucalyptus (*Eucalyptus regnans*), reported in 1872. It was 132 m/435 ft tall.

Eudora in computing, popular program for handling and receiving Internet e-mail. Published by the Californian company Qualcomm, Eudora uses ◊POP3, and by the mid-1990s was one of the most commonly used e-mail programs on the Net.

eugenics ***Greek eugenes 'well-born'*** study of ways in which the physical and mental characteristics of the human race may be improved. The eugenic principle was abused by the Nazi Party in Germany during the 1930s and early 1940s to justify the attempted extermination of entire social and ethnic groups and the establishment of selective breeding programmes. Modern eugenics is concerned mainly with the elimination of genetic disease.

The term was coined by the English scientist Francis Galton in 1883, and the concept was originally developed in the late 19th century with a view to improving human intelligence and behaviour.

In 1986 Singapore became the first democratic country to adopt an openly eugenic policy by guaranteeing pay increases to female university graduates when they give birth to a child, while offering grants towards house purchases for nongraduate married women on condition that they are sterilized after the first or second child. In China in June 1995, a law was passed making it illegal for carriers of certain genetic diseases to marry unless they agree to sterilization or long-term contraception. All couples wishing to marry must undergo genetic screening.

Knowledge is the death of research.

WALTHER NERNST German physical chemist.
On examinations, in C G Gillespie (ed)
The Dictionary of Scientific Biography 1981

Euglena genus of single-celled organisms in the ◊protozoan phylum Sarcomastigophora that live in fresh water. They are usually oval or cigar-shaped, less than 0.5 mm/0.2 in long, and have a nucleus, green pigment in chloroplasts, a contractile vacuole, a light-sensitive eyespot, and one or two ◊flagella, with which they swim. A few species are colourless or red.

classification Euglena are members of the order Euglenida in class Phytomastigophora, subphylum Mastigophora, phylum Sarcomastigophora.

This organism combines animal and plant characteristics. Its plantlike characteristics include the chloroplasts and its consequent ability to photosynthesize, and the rigid cellulose wall of some species. Its main animal characteristic is its motility, but it can also absorb food from its environment, and many species have a flexible body covering.

eukaryote in biology, one of the two major groupings into which all organisms are divided. Included are all organisms, except bacteria and cyanobacteria (◊blue-green algae), which belong to the ◊prokaryote grouping.

The cells of eukaryotes possess a clearly defined nucleus, bounded by a membrane, within which DNA is formed into distinct chromosomes. Eukaryotic cells also contain mitochondria, chloroplasts, and other structures (organelles) that, together with a defined nucleus, are lacking in the cells of prokaryotes.

Euratom acronym for ◊European Atomic Energy Community, forming part of the ***European Union organization***.

eureka in chemistry, alternative name for the copper–nickel alloy ◊constantan, which is used in electrical equipment.

eureka *Greek 'I've got it!'* exclamation supposedly made by ◊Archimedes on his discovery of fluid displacement.

Eurocodes series of codes giving design rules for all types of engineering structures, except certain very specialized forms, such as nuclear reactors. The codes will be given the status of ENs (European standards) and will be administered by CEN (European Committee for Standardization). ENs will eventually replace national codes, in Britain currently maintained by the BSI (British Standards Institute), and will include parameters to reflect local requirements.

Europa in astronomy, the fourth-largest moon of the planet Jupiter, diameter 3,140 km/1,950 mi, orbiting 671,000 km/417,000 mi from the planet every 3.55 days. It is covered by ice and criss-crossed by thousands of thin cracks, each some 50,000 km/30,000 mi long.

NASA's robot probe, *Galileo*, began circling Europa in February 1997 and is expected to send back around 800 images from 50 different sites by 1999. NASA plans to send a $250 million robot probe in 2001 or 2002 to circle 100 km/60 mi above the surface, using radar and lasers to establish whether water exists beneath the icy surface. If found, a lander would be launched by 2006 to release a robot that would melt its way through the ice and release a submarine to take pictures. This operation is also billed at $250 million. One of the first discoveries was that what were thought to be cracks covering the surface of the moon are in fact low ridges. Further investigation is needed to determine their origin.

European Atomic Energy Community (Euratom) organization established by the second Treaty of Rome 1957, which seeks the cooperation of member states of the European Union in nuclear research and the rapid and large-scale development of nonmilitary nuclear energy.

European corn borer moth whose larvae are a serious menace in countries, such as the USA, where maize is an important crop.

European Southern Observatory observatory operated jointly by Belgium, Denmark, France, Germany, Italy, the Netherlands, Sweden, and Switzerland with headquarters near Munich. Its telescopes, located at La Silla, Chile, include a 3.6-m/142-in reflector opened 1976 and the 3.58-m/141-in New Technology Telescope opened in 1990. By 1988 work began on the Very Large Telescope, consisting of four 8-m/315-in reflectors mounted independently but capable of working in combination.

European Space Agency (ESA) organization of European countries (Austria, Belgium, Denmark, Finland, France, Germany, Ireland, Italy, the Netherlands, Norway, Spain, Sweden, Switzerland, and the UK) that engages in space research and technology. It was founded in 1975, with headquarters in Paris.

ESA has developed various scientific and communications satellites, the *Giotto* space probe, and the ◊Ariane *rockets. ESA built* ◊Spacelab, *and plans to build its own space station, Columbus,* for attachment to a US space station.

The ESA's earth-sensing satellite ERS-2 was launched successfully in 1995. It will work in tandem with ERS-1 launched in 1991, and should improve measurements of global ozone.

European Strategic Programme for Research and Development in Information Technology full name for ◊ESPRIT.

europium soft, greyish, metallic element of the ◊lanthanide series, symbol Eu, atomic number 63, relative atomic mass 151.96. It is used in lasers and as the red phosphor in colour televisions; its compounds are used to make control rods for nuclear reactors. It was named in 1901 by French chemist Eugène Demarçay (1852–1904) after the continent of Europe, where it was first found.

eusociality form of social life found in insects such as honey bees and termites, in which the colony is made up of special castes (for example, workers, drones, and reproductives) whose membership is biologically determined. The worker castes do not usually reproduce. Only one mammal, the naked mole rat, has a social organization of this type. A eusocial shrimp was discovered in 1996 living in the coral reefs of Belize. *Synalpheus regalis* lives in colonies of up to 300 individuals, all the offspring of a single reproductive female. See also ◊social behaviour.

Eustachian tube small air-filled canal connecting the middle ◊ear with the back of the throat. It is found in all land vertebrates and equalizes the pressure on both sides of the eardrum.

Eutelsat acronym for ***European Telecommunications Satellite Organization***.

euthanasia in medicine, mercy killing of someone with a severe and incurable condition or illness. Euthanasia is an issue that creates much controversy on medical and ethical grounds.

In Australia, a bill legalizing voluntary euthanasia for terminally ill patients was passed by the Northern Territory state legislature in May 1995.

In the Netherlands, where approximately 2,700 patients formally request it each year, euthanasia is technically illegal. However, provided guidelines issued by the Royal Dutch Medical Association are followed, doctors are not prosecuted.

In the USA, the Supreme Court ruled in June 1997 that the terminally ill do not have the fundamental right to have doctors help them to die. The Court upheld state laws in Washington and New York that forbid assisted suicides.

A patient's right to refuse life-prolonging treatment is recognized in several countries, including the UK.

Eutheria former division of class Mammalia, comprising all ◊mammals mammals with a placenta.

eutrophication excessive enrichment of rivers, lakes, and shallow sea areas, primarily by nitrate fertilizers washed from the soil by rain, by phosphates from fertilizers, and from nutrients in municipal sewage, and by sewage itself. These encourage the growth of algae and bacteria which use up the oxygen in the water, thereby making it uninhabitable for fishes and other animal life.

evaporation process in which a liquid turns to a vapour without its temperature reaching boiling point. A liquid left to stand in a saucer eventually evaporates because, at any time, a proportion of its molecules will be fast enough (have enough kinetic energy) to escape through the attractive intermolecular forces at the liquid surface into the atmosphere. The temperature of the liquid tends to fall because the evaporating molecules remove energy from the liquid. The rate of evaporation rises with increased temperature because as the mean kinetic energy of the liquid's molecules rises, so will the number possessing enough energy to escape.

A fall in the temperature of the liquid, known as the **cooling effect**, accompanies evaporation because as the faster molecules escape through the surface the mean energy of the remaining molecules falls. The effect may be noticed when wet clothes are worn, and sweat evaporates from the skin. ◊Refrigeration makes use of the cooling effect to extract heat from foodstuffs, and in the body it plays a part in temperature control.

Euthanasia

BY ROY PORTER

Euthanasia literally means a good or an easy death. Within traditional Christian culture, a good death (as prescribed by the *ars moriendi* – the art of dying well) was a Christian death, departing in a state of grace, denouncing Satan, praying to God, repenting one's sins and (for Roman Catholics) receiving the sacraments.

In the 17th century Francis Bacon argued that relief of suffering was a desideratum in terminal care and that the physician may sometimes hasten death. The idea of dying well was gradually secularized. Dying, it was said, should be like sleep, for a peaceful death betokened a serene conscience, a life well lived. In the new idea of euthanasia emerging in the 19th century, it was the duty of the doctor to ensure a peaceful death, by careful management and judicious application of opiates. At the wishes of family or patient, the family doctor was doubtless the frequent agent of informal (and strictly illegal) euthanasia.

This unofficial trend has been rendered more problematic in recent times. The Nazi 'final solution' perverted euthanasia for supremely evil purposes and created suspicion that any legalization of euthanasia would lead in time to (possibly compulsory) public euthanasia programmes for problem people and the senile. Moreover, death now increasingly occurs in public institutions, notably hospitals and hospices. This may make humane euthanasia more difficult, as physicians and nursing staff involved in such practices may fear exposure and legal prosecution from Christian pressure groups such as 'Life'.

Yet the circumstances of modern death have also increased backing for euthanasia. Thanks to life-support systems, it is now relatively easy to keep many 'dead' people artificially alive, with respirators and support systems. Repugnance is widespread for the 'cruelty' of this meaningless prolongation of life amongst those in a 'permanent vegetative state'. Hence there is a growing desire to devise acceptable procedures for mercy killing, promoted by bodies such as 'Exit'. Euthanasia may be squared with the professional ethics of the physician and with normal morality through the argument that while it is the doctor's duty to save life, that duty does not run so far as to prolong life through artificial means in all circumstances.

Change has been most marked in The Netherlands, where since 1984 the medical colleges have accepted medical euthanasia under strictly controlled circumstances. By 1995 a survey suggested that active euthanasia (a physician humanely intervening to end a terminally ill patient's life at the request of that patient) was taking place in around 1.8% of all deaths. Public acceptance of this practice had been facilitated by the development of 'living wills'. Since 1994 Dutch physicians have been legally obliged to honour such 'living wills'. 'Living wills' have been legally binding in South Australia since the 'Natural Death Act' of 1983.

Such proposals have met with a much more divided reception elsewhere. In Britain, euthanasia remains illegal, living wills have no standing, and 'Exit' has been subject to prosecution – as has the maverick American pathologist, Dr Jack Kevorkian, who has practised doctor-assisted suicide at the patient's request. A law (1996) in Australia's Northern Territories permitting voluntary euthanasia has since been overturned by the Federal Government. In 1997 the British Medical Association came out against voluntary euthanasia.

The advance of modern medicine presents deep ethical dilemmas in the case of death. There is no easy way to balance the sanctity of human life against the right of personal autonomy. Fundamental legal and moral questions are also raised.

evening primrose any of a group of plants that typically have pale yellow flowers which open in the evening. About 50 species are native to North America, several of which now also grow in Europe. Some are cultivated for their oil, which is rich in gamma-linoleic acid (GLA). The body converts GLA into substances which resemble hormones, and **evening primrose oil** is beneficial in relieving the symptoms of ◊premenstrual tension. It is also used in treating eczema and chronic fatigue syndrome. (Genus *Oenothera*, family Onagraceae.)

event-driven in computing, computer system that does not do anything until events are detected, such as mouse-clicks. Microsoft Windows is an event-driven operating environment.

evergreen in botany, a plant such as pine, spruce, or holly, that bears its leaves all year round. Most ◊conifers are evergreen. Plants that shed their leaves in autumn or during a dry season are described as ◊deciduous.

everlasting flower any flower head with coloured bracts that retains its colour when cut and dried.

> *Nature does not make jumps.*
>
> CAROLUS LINNAEUS Swedish naturalist and physician. *Philosophia Botanica*

evolution the slow, gradual process of change from one form to another, as in the evolution of the universe from its formation to its present state, or in the evolution of life on Earth. In biology, it is the process by which life has developed by stages from single-celled organisms into the multiplicity of animal and plant life, extinct and existing, that inhabit the Earth. The development of the concept of evolution is usually associated with the English naturalist Charles ◊Darwin who attributed the main role in evolutionary change to ◊natural selection acting on randomly occurring variations. However, these variations in species are now known to be ◊adaptations produced by spontaneous changes or ◊mutations in the genetic material of organisms.

evolution and creationism Organic evolution traces the development of simple unicellular forms to more complex forms, ultimately to the flowering plants and vertebrate animals, including humans. The Earth contains an immense diversity of living organisms: about a million different species of animals and half a million species of plants have so far been described. Some religions deny the theory of evolution considering it conflicts with their belief that God created all things (see ◊creationism). But most people accept that there is overwhelming evidence the diversity of life arose by a gradual process of evolutionary divergence and not by individual acts of divine creation. There are several lines of evidence: the fossil record, the existence of similarities or homologies between different groups of organisms, embryology, and geographical distribution.

EVOLUTION: THEORY AND HISTORY

http://www.ucmp.berkeley.edu/history/evolution.html

Dedicated to the study of the history and theories associated with evolution, this site explores topics on classification, taxonomy, and dinosaur discoveries, and then looks at the key figures in the field and reviews their contributions.

We must, however, acknowledge, as it seems to me, that man with all his noble qualities, still bears in his bodily frame the indelible stamp of his lowly origin.

CHARLES DARWIN British naturalist.
Last words of *Descent of Man* 1871

evolutionary stable strategy (ESS) in ◊sociobiology, an assemblage of behavioural or physical characters (collectively termed a 'strategy') of a population that is resistant to replacement by any forms bearing new traits, because the new traits will not be capable of successful reproduction.

ESS analysis is based on ◊game theory and can be applied both to genetically determined physical characters (such as horn length), and to learned behavioural responses (for example, whether to fight or retreat from an opponent). An ESS may be conditional on the context, as in the rule 'fight if the opponent is smaller, but retreat if the opponent is larger'.

evolutionary toxicology study of the effects of pollution on evolution. A polluted habitat may cause organisms to select for certain traits, as in **industrial melanism** for example, where some insects, such as the peppered moth, are darker in polluted areas, and therefore better camouflaged against predation.

Pollutants may also trigger mutations, for example, voles living around the Chernobyl exploded nuclear reactor have a very high mutation rate despite appearing healthy and reproducing successfully. Fish in polluted rivers also exhibit mutations.

excavation or ***dig*** in archaeology, the systematic recovery of data through the exposure of buried sites and artefacts. Excavation is destructive, and is therefore accompanied by a comprehensive recording of all material found and its three-dimensional locations (its context). As much material and information as possible must be recovered from any dig. A full record of all the techniques employed in the excavation itself must also be made, so that future archaeologists will be able to evaluate the results of the work accurately.

Besides being destructive, excavation is also costly. For both these reasons, it should be used only as a last resort. It can be partial, with only a sample of the site investigated, or total. Samples are chosen either intuitively, in which case excavators investigate those areas they feel will be most productive, or statistically, in which case the sample is drawn using various statistical techniques, so as to ensure that it is representative.

An important goal of excavation is a full understanding of a site's stratigraphy; that is, the vertical layering of a site.

These layers or levels can be defined naturally (for example, soil changes), culturally (for example, different occupation levels), or arbitrarily (for example, 10 cm/4 in levels). Excavation can also be done horizontally, to uncover larger areas of a particular layer and reveal the spatial relationships between artefacts and features in that layer. This is known as open-area excavation and is used especially where single-period deposits lie close to the surface, and the time dimension is represented by lateral movement rather than by the placing of one building on top of the preceding one.

Most excavators employ a flexible combination of vertical and horizontal digging adapting to the nature of their site and the questions they are seeking to answer.

excavator machine designed for digging in the ground, or for earth-moving in general. Diggers with hydraulically powered digging arms are widely used on building sites. They may run on wheels or on ◊caterpillar tracks. The largest excavators are the draglines used in mining to strip away earth covering the coal or mineral deposit.

Excel ◊spreadsheet program produced by ◊Microsoft in 1985. Versions are available for PC-compatibles running ◊Windows and for the Apple Macintosh. Excel pioneered many advanced features in the ease of use of spreadsheets, and has displaced ◊Lotus 1–2–3 as the standard spreadsheet program.

exclusion principle in physics, a principle of atomic structure originated by Austrian–US physicist Wolfgang ◊Pauli. It states that no two electrons in a single atom may have the same set of ◊quantum numbers.

Hence, it is impossible to pack together certain elementary particles, such as electrons, beyond a certain critical density, otherwise they would share the same location and quantum number. A white dwarf star, which consists of electrons and other elementary particles, is thus prevented from contracting further by the exclusion principle and never collapses.

excretion in biology, the removal of waste products from the cells of living organisms. In plants and simple animals, waste products are removed by diffusion, but in higher animals they are removed by specialized organs. In mammals the kidneys are the principle organs of excretion. Water and metabolic wastes are also excreted in the faeces and, in humans, through the sweat glands; carbon dioxide and water are removed via the lungs.

TO REMEMBER THE EXCRETORY ORGANS OF THE BODY:

SKILLSKIN / KIDNEYS / INTESTINES / LIVER / LUNGS

executable file in computing, a file – always a program of some kind – that can be run by the computer directly. The file will have been generated from a ◊source program by an ◊assembler or ◊compiler. It will therefore not be coded in ◊ASCII and will not be readable as text. On ◊MS-DOS systems executable files have an .EXE or .COM extension.

exfoliation in biology, the separation of pieces of dead bone or skin in layers.

exobiology study of life forms that may possibly exist elsewhere in the universe, and of the effects of extraterrestrial environments on Earth organisms. Techniques include space probe experiments designed to detect organic molecules, and the monitoring of radio waves from other star systems.

exocrine gland gland that discharges secretions, usually through a tube or a duct, on to a surface. Examples include sweat glands which release sweat on to the skin, and digestive glands which release digestive juices on to the walls of the intestine. Some animals also have ◊endocrine glands (ductless glands) that release hormones directly into the bloodstream.

exon in genetics, a sequence of bases in ◊DNA that codes for a protein. Exons make up only 2% of the body's total DNA. The remainder is made up of ◊introns. During RNA processing the introns are cut out of the molecule and the exons spliced together.

exoskeleton the hardened external skeleton of insects, spiders, crabs, and other arthropods. It provides attachment for muscles and protection for the internal organs, as well as support. To permit growth it is periodically shed in a process called ◊ecdysis.

exosphere the uppermost layer of the ◊atmosphere. It is an ill-defined zone above the thermosphere, beginning at about 700 km/435 mi and fading off into the vacuum of space. The gases are extremely thin, with hydrogen as the main constituent.

exothermic reaction a chemical reaction during which heat is given out (see ◊energy of reaction).

expanded memory in computing, additional memory in an ◊MS-DOS-based computer, usually installed on an expanded-memory board. Expanded memory requires an expanded-memory manager, which gives access to a limited amount of memory at any one time, and is slower to use than ◊extended memory. Software is available under both MS-DOS and ◊Windows to simulate expanded memory for those applications that require it.

expansion in physics, the increase in size of a constant mass of substance caused by, for example, increasing its temperature

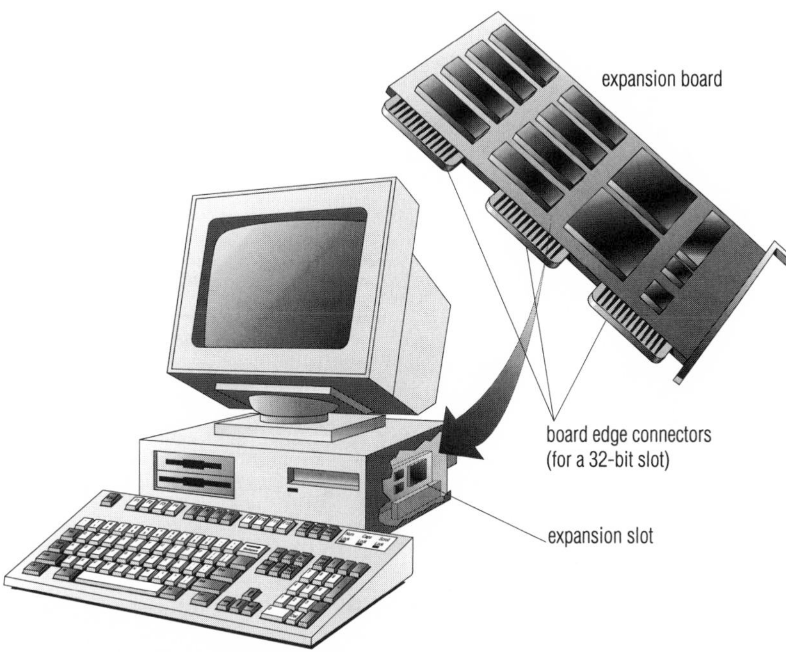

***expansion board** An expansion board may be fitted into any free expansion slot in a computer to provide additional facilities or functionality.*

This covers a wide range of fields of study, including: **human and animal learning**, in which learning theories describe how new behaviours are acquired and modified; **cognition**, the study of a number of functions, such as perception, attention, memory, and language; and **physiological psychology**, which relates the study of cognition to different regions of the brain. **Artificial intelligence** refers to the computer simulation of cognitive processes, such as language and problem-solving.

expert system computer program for giving advice (such as diagnosing an illness or interpreting the law) that incorporates knowledge derived from human expertise. It is a kind of ◊knowledge-based system containing rules that can be applied to find the solution to a problem. It is a form of ◊artificial intelligence.

expire in computing, function for removing old USENET articles from an off-line reader program. Sometimes also called 'prune' or 'purge', this function is necessary to make room for new articles.

explanation in science, an attempt to make clear the cause of any natural event by reference to physical laws and to observations.

The extent to which any explanation can be said to be true is one of the chief concerns of philosophy, partly because observations may be wrongly interpreted, partly because explanations should help us predict how nature will behave. Although it may be reasonable to expect that a physical law will hold in the future, that expectation is problematic in that it relies on induction, a much criticized feature of human thought; in fact no explanation, however 'scientific', can be held to be true for all time, and thus the difference between a scientific and a common-sense explanation remains the subject of intense philosophical debate.

(◊thermal expansion) or its internal pressure. The **expansivity**, or coefficient of thermal expansion, of a material is its expansion (per unit volume, area, or length) per degree rise in temperature.

expansion board or ***expansion card*** printed circuit board that can be inserted into a computer in order to enhance its capabilities (for example, to increase its memory) or to add facilities (such as graphics).

expectorant any substance, often added to cough mixture, to encourage secretion of mucus in the airways to make it easier to cough up. It is debatable whether expectorants have an effect on lung secretions.

experiment in science, a practical test designed with the intention that its results will be relevant to a particular theory or set of theories. Although some experiments may be used merely for gathering more information about a topic that is already well understood, others may be of crucial importance in confirming a new theory or in undermining long-held beliefs.

The manner in which experiments are performed, and the relation between the design of an experiment and its value, are therefore of central importance. In general, an experiment is of most value when the factors that might affect the results (variables) are carefully controlled; for this reason most experiments take place in a well-managed environment such as a laboratory or clinic.

experimental psychology the application of scientific methods to the study of mental processes and behaviour.

EXPERIMENTAL PSYCHOLOGY LAB

http://www.uni-tuebingen.de/uni/sii/Ulf/Lab/WebExpPsyLab.html

Take part in online psychology experiments carried out by the University of Tübingen's Psychology Institute. There are a variety of experiments here, some requiring Java and ActiveX, and some only in German.

Explorer series of US scientific satellites. *Explorer 1,* launched January 1958, was the first US satellite in orbit and discovered the Van Allen radiation belts around the Earth.

explosive any material capable of a sudden release of energy and the rapid formation of a large volume of gas, leading, when compressed, to the development of a high-pressure wave (blast).

types of explosive Combustion and explosion differ essentially only in rate of reaction, and many explosives (called **low explosives**) are capable of undergoing relatively slow combustion under suitable conditions. **High explosives** produce uncontrollable blasts. The first low explosive was ◊gunpowder; the first high explosive was ◊nitroglycerine.

exponent or ***index*** in mathematics, a number that indicates the number of times a term is multiplied by itself; for example $x^2 = x \times x$, $4^3 = 4 \times 4 \times 4$.

Exponents obey certain rules. Terms that contain them are multiplied together by adding the exponents; for example, $x^2 \times x^5 = x^7$. Division of such terms is done by subtracting the exponents; for example, $y^5 \div y^3 = y^2$. Any number with the exponent 0 is equal to 1; for example, $x^0 = 1$ and $99^0 = 1$.

exponential in mathematics, descriptive of a ◊function in which the variable quantity is an exponent (a number indicating the power to which another number or expression is raised).

Exponential functions and series involve the constant e = 2.71828.... . Scottish mathematician John Napier devised natural ◊logarithms in 1614 with e as the base.

Exponential functions are basic mathematical functions, written as ex or exp x. The expression ex has five definitions, two of which are: (i) ex is the solution of the differential equation $dx/dt = x$ (x =

1 if $t = 0$); (ii) ex is the limiting sum of the infinite series $1 + x + (x2/2!) + (x3/3!) + ... + (xn/n!)$.

export file in computing, a file stored by the computer in a standard format so that it can be accessed by other programs, possibly running on different makes of computer.

For example, a word-processing program running on an Apple ◊Macintosh computer may have a facility to save a file on a floppy disc in a format that can be read by a word-processing program running on an IBM PC-compatible computer. When the file is being read by the second program or computer, it is often referred to as an **import file**.

exposure meter instrument used in photography for indicating the correct exposure – the length of time the camera shutter should be open under given light conditions. Meters use substances such as cadmium sulphide and selenium as light sensors. These materials change electrically when light strikes them, the change being proportional to the intensity of the incident light. Many cameras have a built-in exposure meter that sets the camera controls automatically as the light conditions change.

extended memory in computing, memory in an ◊MS-DOS-based system that exceeds the 1 Mbyte that DOS supports. Extended memory is not accessible to the ◊operating system and requires an extended memory manager.

extensor a muscle that straightens a limb.

exterior angle one of the four external angles formed when a straight line or transveral cuts through a pair of (usually parallel) lines. Also, an angle formed by extending a side of a polygon.

external modem in computing, a ◊modem that is a self-contained unit sitting outside a personal computer (PC) and connected to it by a cable. There are two main types of external modem: mains-powered desktop modems and: credit-card sized modems that fit the PCMCIA slots in notebook and handheld computers.

External modems have the advantage over internal ones in that they are easy to move from computer to computer as needed. However, high-speed modems outstrip the capabilities of the serial ports on older and cheaper PCs by taking in data too fast for the computer to be able to read it.

extinction in biology, the complete disappearance of a species or higher taxon. Extinctions occur when an animal becomes unfit for survival in its natural habitat usually to be replaced by another, better-suited animal. An organism becomes ill-suited for survival because its environment is changed or because its relationship to other organisms is altered. For example, a predator's fitness for survival depends upon the availability of its prey.

past extinctions Mass extinctions are episodes during which large numbers of species have become extinct virtually simultaneously, the best known being that of the dinosaurs, other large reptiles, and various marine invertebrates about 65 million years ago between the end of the ◊Cretaceous period and the beginning of the Tertiary period. The latter, known as the **K–T extinction**, has been attributed to catastrophic environmental changes following a meteor impact or unusually prolonged and voluminous volcanic eruptions.

Another mass extinction occurred about 10,000 years ago when many giant species of mammal died out. This is known as the 'Pleistocene overkill' because their disappearance was probably hastened by the hunting activities of prehistoric humans. The greatest mass extinction occurred about 250 million years ago, marking the Permian–Triassic boundary (see ◊geological time), when up to 96% of all living species became extinct. Mass extinctions apparently occur at periodic intervals of approximately 26 million years.

current extinctions Humans have the capacity to profoundly influence many habitats and today a large number of extinctions are attributable to human activity. Some species, such as the ◊dodo of Mauritius, the ◊moas of New Zealand, and the passenger ◊pigeon of North America, were exterminated by hunting. Others became extinct when their habitat was destroyed. ◊Endangered species are close to extinction. The rate of extinction is difficult to estimate, but appears to have been accelerated by humans. Conservative estimates put the rate of loss due to deforestation alone at 4,000 to 6,000 species a year. Overall, the rate could be as high as one species an hour, with the loss of one species putting those dependent on it at risk. Australia has the worst record for extinction: 18 mammals have disappeared since Europeans settled there, and 40 more are threatened.

> *If we are still here to witness the destruction of our planet [by the Sun] some five billion years or more hence, then we will have achieved something so unprecedented in the history of life that we should be willing to sing our swan song with joy.*
>
> STEPHEN JAY GOULD US palaeontologist and writer. *The Panda's Thumb* 1980

extracellular matrix strong material naturally occurring in animals and plants, made up of protein and long-chain sugars (polysaccharides) in which cells are embedded. It is often called a 'biological glue', and forms part of ◊connective tissues such as bone and skin.

The cell walls of plants and bacteria, and the ◊exoskeletons of insects and other arthropods, are also formed by types of extracellular matrix.

extrasensory perception (ESP) any form of perception beyond and distinct from the known sensory processes. The main forms of ESP are clairvoyance (intuitive perception or vision of events and situations without using the senses); precognition (the ability to foresee events); and telepathy or thought transference (communication between people without using any known visible, tangible, or audible medium). Verification by scientific study has yet to be achieved.

extroversion or ***extraversion*** personality dimension described by the psychologists Carl ◊Jung and, later, Hans Eysenck. The typical extrovert is sociable, impulsive, and carefree. The opposite of extroversion is ◊introversion.

extruded shape in computer graphics, a three-dimensional shape created by extending a two-dimensional shape along a third dimension.

extrusion common method of shaping metals, plastics, and other materials. The materials, usually hot, are forced through the hole in a metal die and take its cross-sectional shape. Rods, tubes, and sheets may be made in this way.

extrusive rock or ***volcanic rock*** ◊igneous rock formed on the surface of the Earth by volcanic activity. The term includes fine-grained crystalline or glassy rocks formed from hot lava quenched at or near Earth's surface and rocks composed of solid debris, called pyroclastics, depostcd by explosive eruptions.

Large amounts of extrusive rock called ◊basalt form at the Earth's ◊ocean ridges from lava that fills the void formed when two tectonic plates spread apart. Explosive volcanoes that deposit pyroclastics generally occur where one tectonic plate descends beneath another. ◊Andesite is often formed by explosive volcanoes. Magmas that give rise to pyroclastic extrusive rocks are explosive because they are viscous. The island of Montserrat, West Indies, is an example of an explosive volcano that spews pyroclastics of andesite composition. Magmas that produce crystalline or glassy volcanic rocks upon cooling are less viscous. The low viscosity allows the extruding lava to flow easily. Fluid-like lavas that flow from the volcanoes of the Hawaiian Islands have low viscosity and cool to form basalt.

eye the organ of vision. In the human eye, the light is focused by the combined action of the curved **cornea**, the internal fluids, and the **lens**. The insect eye is compound – made up of many separate facets – known as ommatidia, each of which collects light and directs it separately to a receptor to build up an image. Invertebrates have much simpler eyes, with no lenses. Among molluscs, cephalopods have complex eyes similar to those of vertebrates.

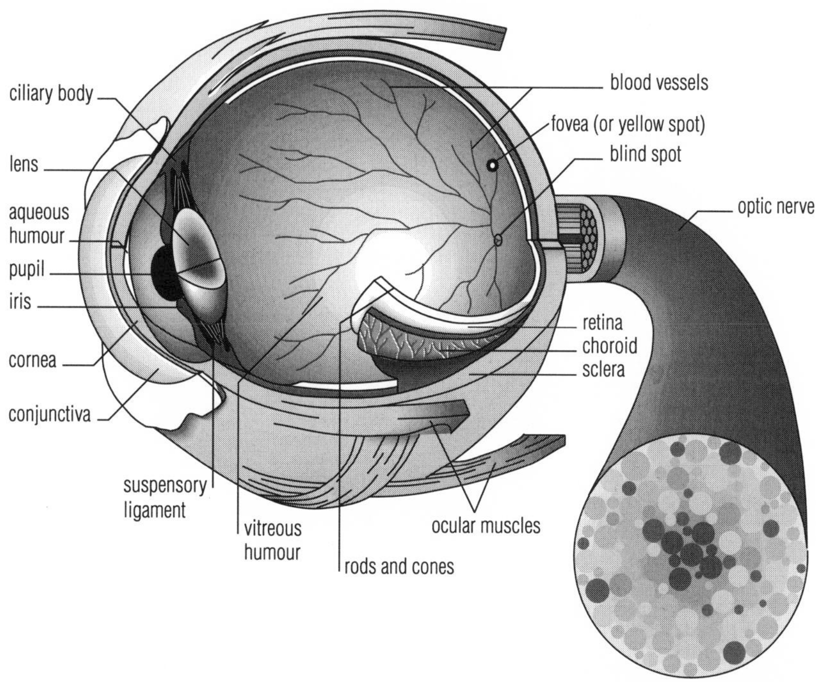

eye *The human eye. The retina of the eye contains about 137 million light-sensitive cells in an area of about 650 sq mm/1 sq in. There are 130 million rod cells for black and white vision and 7 million cone cells for colour vision. The optic nerve contains about 1 million nerve fibres. The focusing muscles of the eye adjust about 100,000 times a day. To exercise the leg muscles to the same extent would need an 80 km/50 mi walk.*

The mantis shrimp's eyes contain ten colour pigments with which to perceive colour; some flies and fishes have five, while the human eye has only three.

human eye This is a roughly spherical structure contained in a bony socket. Light enters it through the cornea, and passes through the circular opening (**pupil**) in the iris (the coloured part of the eye).

The ciliary muscles act on the lens (the rounded transparent structure behind the iris) to change its shape, so that images of objects at different distances can be focused on the retina. This is at the back of the eye, and is packed with light-sensitive cells (rods and cones), connected to the brain by the optic nerve.

Don't believe what your eyes are telling you, all they show is limitation. Look with your understanding, find out what you already know, and you'll see the way to fly.

RICHARD BACH US writer.
Jonathan Livingstone Seagull

eyebright any of a group of annual plants belonging to the figwort family. They are 2–30 cm/1–12 in high and have whitish flowers streaked with purple. The name indicates their traditional use as an eye-medicine. (Genus *Euphrasia,* family Scrophulariaceae.)

eye, defects of the abnormalities of the eye that impair vision. Glass or plastic lenses, in the form of spectacles or contact lenses, are the usual means of correction. Common optical defects are ◊short-sightedness or myopia; farsightedness or hypermetropia; lack of ◊accommodation or presbyopia; and ◊astigmatism. Other eye defects include ◊colour blindness.

e-zine (contraction of ***electronic magazine***) in computing, periodical sent by ◊e-mail. E-zines can be produced very cheaply, as there are no production costs for design and layout, and minimal costs for distribution. Like printed magazines, e-zines typically have multiple contributors and an editor responsible for selecting content.

One of the best-known e-zines is the ◊*Computer Underground Digest,* which tracks battles over freedom of speech online and issues concerning hacking and computer crime.

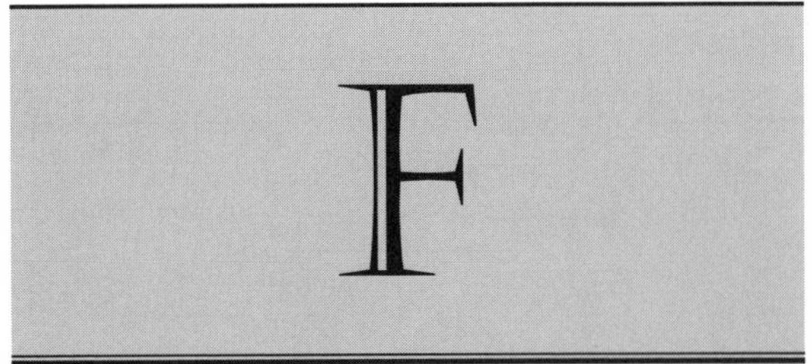

Many things about our bodies would not seem so filthy and obscene if we did not have the idea of nobility in our heads.

G C Lichtenberg German physicist and philosopher. *Aphorisms*, 'Notebook D' 6

°F symbol for degrees ◊Fahrenheit.

F1 on personal computers (PCs), the key to access ◊online help.

face in geometry, a plane surface of a solid enclosed by edges. A cube has six square faces, a cuboid has six rectangular faces, and a tetrahedron has four triangular faces.

facies in geology, body of rock strata possessing unifying characteristics indicative of the environment in which the rocks were formed. The term is also used to describe the environment of formation itself or unifying features of the rocks that comprise the facies.

Features that define a facies can include collections of fossils, sequences of rock layers, or the occurrence of specific minerals. Sedimentary rocks deposited at the same time, but representing different facies belong to a single **chronostratigraphic unit** (see ◊stratigraphy). But these same rocks may belong to different **lithostratigraphic units**. For example, beach sand is deposited at the same time that mud is deposited further offshore. The beach sand eventually turns to sandstone while the mud turns to shale. The resulting ◊sandstone and ◊shale **strata** comprise two different facies, one representing the beach environment and the other the offshore environment, formed at the same time; the sandstone and shale belong to the same chronostratigraphic unit but distinct lithostratigraphic units.

facsimile transmission full name for ◊fax **or telefax**.

factor a number that divides into another number exactly. For example, the factors of 64 are 1, 2, 4, 8, 16, 32, and 64. In algebra, certain kinds of polynomials (expressions consisting of several or many terms) can be factorized. For example, the factors of $x^2 + 3x + 2$ are $x + 1$ and $x + 2$, since $x^2 + 3x + 2 = (x + 1)(x + 2)$. This is called factorization. See also ◊number.

factorial of a positive number, the product of all the whole numbers (integers) inclusive between 1 and the number itself. A factorial is indicated by the symbol '!'. Thus $6! = 1 \times 2 \times 3 \times 4 \times 5 \times 6 = 720$. Factorial zero, 0!, is defined as 1.

factory farming intensive rearing of poultry or other animals for food, usually on high-protein foodstuffs in confined quarters. Chickens for eggs and meat, and calves for veal are commonly factory farmed. Some countries restrict the use of antibiotics and growth hormones as aids to factory farming because they can persist in the flesh of the animals after they are slaughtered. The emphasis is on productive yield rather than animal welfare so that conditions for the animals are often very poor. For this reason, many people object to factory farming on moral as well as health grounds.

Egg-laying hens are housed in 'batteries' of cages arranged in long rows. If caged singly, they lay fewer eggs, so there are often four to a cage with a floor area of only 2,400 sq cm/372 sq in. In the course of a year, battery hens average 261 eggs each, whereas for free-range chickens the figure is 199.

faeces remains of food and other waste material eliminated from the digestive tract of animals by way of the anus. Faeces consist of quantities of fibrous material, bacteria and other microorganisms, rubbed-off lining of the digestive tract, bile fluids, undigested food, minerals, and water.

Fahrenheit, Gabriel Daniel (1686–1736) Polish-born Dutch physicist who invented the first accurate thermometer in 1724 and devised the Fahrenheit temperature scale. Using his thermometer, Fahrenheit was able to determine the boiling points of liquids and found that they vary with atmospheric pressure.

Fahrenheit scale temperature scale invented in 1714 by Gabriel Fahrenheit which was commonly used in English-speaking countries until the 1970s, after which the ◊Celsius scale was generally adopted, in line with the rest of the world. In the Fahrenheit scale, intervals are measured in degrees (°F); °F = (°C x 9/5) + 32.

Fahrenheit took as the zero point the lowest temperature he could achieve anywhere in the laboratory, and, as the other fixed point, body temperature, which he set at 96°F. On this scale, water freezes at 32°F and boils at 212°F.

fainting sudden, temporary loss of consciousness caused by reduced blood supply to the brain. It may be due to emotional shock or physical factors, such as pooling of blood in the legs from standing still for long periods.

falcon any bird of prey of the genus *Falco,* family Falconidae, order Falconiformes. Falcons are the smallest of the hawks (15–60 cm/6–24 in). They have short curved beaks with one tooth in the upper mandible; the wings are long and pointed, and the toes elongated. They nest in high places and kill their prey on the wing by 'stooping' (swooping down at high speed). They include the peregrine and kestrel.

The peregrine falcon *F. peregrinus,* up to about 50 cm/1.8 ft long, has become re-established in North America and Britain after near extinction (by pesticides, gamekeepers, and egg collectors). When stooping on its intended prey, it is the fastest creature in the world, timed at 240 kph/150 mph. The US government announced preliminary measures to remove the American peregrine falcon from the endangered species list in 1995 following a successful breeding programme.

Fallopian tube or ***oviduct*** in mammals, one of two tubes that carry eggs from the ovary to the uterus. An egg is fertilized by sperm in the Fallopian tubes, which are lined with cells whose ◊cilia move the egg towards the uterus.

fallout harmful radioactive material released into the atmosphere in the debris of a nuclear explosion and descending to the surface of the Earth. Such material can enter the food chain, cause◊radiation sickness, and last for hundreds of thousands of years (see ◊half-life).

fallow land ploughed and tilled, but left unsown for a season to allow it to recuperate. In Europe, it is associated with the medieval three-field system. It is used in some modern ◊crop rotations and in countries that do not have access to fertilizers to maintain soil fertility.

fallow deer one of two species of deer. Fallow deer are characterized by the expansion of the upper part of their antlers in palmate form. Usually they stand about 1 m/3.3 ft high, and have small heads, large ears, and rather long tails. In colour they are fawn, with a number of large white spots, or they may be yellowish-brown or, more rarely, dark brown.

The commonest species *Dama dama* is a native of North Africa and the countries bordering the Mediterranean, but was introduced into Britain at an early period. *D. mesopotamica* is a native of the mountains of Iran.

classification The fallow deer is in genus *Dama* in the Cervidae family of the mammalian order Artiodactyla.

false of a statement, untrue. Falseness is used in proving propositions by considering the negative of the proposition to be true, then making deductions until a contradiction is reached which proves the negative to be false and the proposition to be true.

false-colour imagery graphic technique that displays images in false (not true-to-life) colours so as to enhance certain features. It is widely used in displaying electronic images taken by spacecraft; for example, Earth-survey satellites such as *Landsat*. Any colours can be selected by a computer processing the received data.

falsificationism in philosophy of science, the belief that a scientific theory must be under constant scrutiny and that its merit lies only in how well it stands up to rigorous testing. It was first expounded by philosopher Karl Popper in his *Logic of Scientific Discovery* 1934.

Such thinking also implies that a theory can be held to be scientific only if it makes predictions that are clearly testable. Critics of this belief acknowledge the strict logic of this process, but doubt whether the whole of scientific method can be subsumed into so narrow a programme. Philosophers and historians such as Thomas Kuhn and Paul Feyerabend have attempted to use the history of science to show that scientific progress has resulted from a more complicated methodology than Popper suggests.

family in biological classification, a group of related genera (see ◊genus). Family names are not printed in italic (unlike genus and species names), and by convention they all have the ending -idae (animals) or -aceae (plants and fungi). For example, the genera of hummingbirds are grouped in the hummingbird family, Trochilidae. Related families are grouped together in an ◊order.

family planning spacing or preventing the birth of children. Access to family-planning services (see ◊contraceptive) is a significant factor in women's health as well as in limiting population growth. If all those women who wished to avoid further childbirth were able to do so, the number of births would be reduced by 27% in Africa, 33% in Asia, and 35% in Latin America; and the number of women who die during pregnancy or childbirth would be reduced by about 50%.

The average number of pregnancies per woman is two in the industrialized countries, where 71% use family planning, as compared to six or seven pregnancies per woman in the Third World. According to a World Bank estimate, doubling the annual $2 billion spent on family planning would avert the deaths of 5.6 million infants and 250,000 mothers each year.

fanjet another name for ◊turbofan, the jet engine used by most airliners.

fantail variety of domestic ◊pigeon, often white, with a large, widely fanning tail.

FAQ (abbreviation for ***frequently asked questions***) in computing, file of answers to commonly asked questions on any topic. First used on USENET, where regular posters to ◊newsgroups got tired of answering the same questions over and over and wrote these information files to end the repetition. 'Newbies' are recommended to read the FAQ for any newsgroup they join before posting. Most FAQs are available via FTP from rtfm.mit.edu or via the World-Wide Web from **http://www.cis.ohio-state.edu/htbin/search-usenet-faqs**. By 1996 FAQ was a common term for any information file, on line or off line.

farad SI unit (symbol F) of electrical capacitance (how much electric charge a ◊capacitor can store for a given voltage). One farad is a capacitance of one ◊coulomb per volt. For practical purposes the microfarad (one millionth of a farad, symbol μF) is more commonly used.

faraday unit of electrical charge equal to the charge on one mole of electrons. Its value is 9.648×10^4 coulombs.

Faraday's constant constant (symbol *F*) representing the electric charge carried on one mole of electrons. It is found by multiplying Avogadro's constant by the charge carried on a single electron, and is equal to 9.648×10^4 coulombs per mole.

One **faraday** is this constant used as a unit. The constant is used to calculate the electric charge needed to discharge a particular quantity of ions during ◊electrolysis.

Faraday's laws three laws of electromagnetic induction, and two laws of electrolysis, all proposed originally by English scientist Michael Faraday:

induction (1) a changing magnetic field induces an electromagnetic force in a conductor; (2) the electromagnetic force is proportional to the rate of change of the field; (3) the direction of the induced electromagnetic force depends on the orientation of the field.

electrolysis (1) the amount of chemical change during electrolysis is proportional to the charge passing through the liquid; (2) the amount of chemical change produced in a substance by a given amount of electricity is proportional to the electrochemical equivalent of that substance.

far point the farthest point that a person can see clearly. The eye is unable to focus a sharp image on the retina of an object beyond this point. The far point for a normal eye should be at infinity; any eye that has a far point nearer than this is short-sighted (see ◊short-sightedness).

fast breeder or ***breeder reactor*** alternative names for ◊fast reactor, a type of nuclear reactor.

fasting the practice of voluntarily going without food. It can be undertaken as a religious observance, a sign of mourning, a political protest (hunger strike), or for slimming purposes.

Fasting or abstinence from certain types of food or beverages occurs in most religious traditions. It is seen as an act of self-discipline that increases spiritual awareness by lessening dependence on the material world. In the Roman Catholic church, fasting is seen as a penitential rite, a means to express repentance for sin. The most commonly observed Christian fasting is in Lent, from Ash Wednesday to Easter Sunday, and recalls the 40 days Jesus spent in the wilderness. Roman Catholics and Orthodox Christians usually fast before taking communion and monastic communities observe regular weekly fasts. Devout Muslims go without food or water between sunrise and sunset during the month of Ramadan. Jews fast for *Yom Kippur* and before several other festivals. Many devout Hindus observe a weekly day of partial or total fast.

Total abstinence from food for a limited period is prescribed by some ◊naturopaths to eliminate body toxins or make available for recuperative purposes the energy normally used by the digestive system. Prolonged fasting can be dangerous. The liver breaks up its fat stores, releasing harmful by-products called ketones, which results in a condition called ketosis, which develops within three days. An early symptom is a smell of pear drops on the breath. Other symptoms include nausea, vomiting, fatigue, dizziness, severe depression, and irritability. Eventually the muscles and other body tissues become wasted, and death results.

fast reactor or ***fast breeder reactor*** ◊nuclear reactor that makes use of fast neutrons to bring about fission. Unlike other reactors used by the nuclear-power industry, it has little or no ◊moderator, to slow down neutrons. The reactor core is surrounded by a 'blanket' of uranium carbide. During operation, some of this uranium is converted into plutonium, which can be extracted and later used as fuel.

Fast breeder reactors can extract about 60 times the amount of energy from uranium that thermal reactors do. In the 1950s, when uranium stocks were thought to be dwindling, the fast breeder was considered to be the reactor of the future. Now, however, when new uranium reserves have been found and because of various technical difficulties in their construction, development of the fast breeder has slowed in most parts of the world.

fat in the broadest sense, a mixture of ◊lipids – chiefly triglycerides (lipids containing three ◊fatty acid molecules linked to a molecule of glycerol). More specifically, the term refers to a lipid mixture that is solid at room temperature (20°C); lipid mixtures that are liquid at room temperature are called **oils**. The higher the proportion of saturated fatty acids in a mixture, the harder the fat.

Boiling fats in strong alkali forms soaps (saponification). Fats are essential constituents of food for many animals, with a calorific value twice that of carbohydrates; however, eating too much fat, especially fat of animal origin, has been linked with heart disease

Faraday, Michael
(1791–1867)

English chemist and physicist. In 1821, he began experimenting with electromagnetism, and discovered the induction of electric currents and made the first dynamo, the first electric motor, and the first transformer. Faraday isolated benzene from gas oils and produced the basic laws of electrolysis in 1834. He also pointed out that the energy of a magnet is in the field around it and not in the magnet itself, extending this basic conception of field theory to electrical and gravitational systems.

chemistry and the discovery of benzene Faraday was mainly interested in chemistry during his early years at the Royal Institution. He investigated the effects of including precious metals in steel in 1818, producing high-quality alloys that later stimulated the production of special high-grade steels. In 1823, Faraday produced liquid chlorine by heating crystals of chlorine hydrate in an inverted U-tube, one limb of which was heated and the other placed in a freezing mixture. After the production of liquid carbon dioxide in 1835, he used this coolant to liquefy other gases. In the same year, Faraday isolated benzene from gas oils and demonstrated the use of platinum as a catalyst. He also demonstrated the importance in chemical reactions of surfaces and inhibitors, foreshadowing a huge area of the modern chemical industry.

laws of electrolysis Faraday's laws of electrolysis established the link between electricity and chemical affinity, one of the most fundamental concepts in science. Electrolysis is the production of chemical changes by passing an electric current through a solution. It was Faraday who coined the terms anode, cathode, cation, anion, electrode, and electrolyte. He postulated that, during the electrolysis of an aqueous electrolyte, positively-charged cations move towards the negatively-charged cathode and negatively-charged anions migrate to the positively-charged anode. Faraday demonstrated that the ions are discharged at each electrode according to the following rules:

(a) the quantity of a substance produced is proportional to the amount of electricity passed;

(b) the relative quantities of different substances produced by the same amount of electricity are proportional to their equivalent weights (that is, the relative atomic mass divided by the oxidation state or valency).

electromagnetism and the electric motor In 1821, only one year after Hans Oersted had discovered with a compass needle that a current of electricity flowing through a wire produces a magnetic field, Faraday was asked to investigate the phenomenon of electromagnetism by the editor of the *Philosophical Magazine*. Faraday conceived that circular lines of magnetic force are produced around the wire to explain the orientation of Oersted's compass needle.

Faraday's conviction that an electric current gives rise to lines of magnetic force arose from his idea that electricity was a form of vibration and not a moving fluid. He believed that electricity was a state of varying strain in the molecules of the wire conductor, and that this gave rise to a similar strain in the medium surrounding the conductor. It was reasonable to consider therefore that the transmitted strain might set up a similar strain in the molecules of another nearby conductor.

private collection

Faraday set about devising an apparatus that would demonstrate the conversion of electrical energy into motive force. His device consisted of two vessels of mercury connected to a battery. Above the vessels and connected to each other were suspended a magnet and a wire, which were free to move and dipped just below the surface of the mercury. In the mercury were fixed a wire and a magnet respectively. When the current was switched on, it flowed through both the fixed and free wires, generating a magnetic field in them. This caused the free magnet to revolve around the fixed wire, and the free wire to revolve around the fixed magnet.

The experiment demonstrated the basic principles governing the electric motor. Although the practical motors that subsequently developed had a very different form to Faraday's apparatus, he is usually credited with the invention of the electric motor.

electromagnetic induction and the transformer Faraday hunted for the effect of electromagnetic induction from 1824 onwards, expecting to find that a magnetic field would induce a steady electric current in a conductor. Faraday eventually succeeded in producing induction in 1831. He wound two coils around an iron bar and connected one to a battery and the other to a galvanometer (an instrument for detecting small electric currents by their magnetic effect). Nothing happened when the current flowed through the first coil, but Faraday noticed that the galvanometer responded whenever the current was switched on or off. Faraday found an immediate explanation with his lines of force. If the lines of force were cut – that is, if the magnetic field changed – then an electric current would be induced in a conductor placed within the magnetic field. The iron bar helped to concentrate the magnetic field, as Faraday later came to understand, and a current was induced in the second coil by the magnetic field momentarily set up as current entered or left the first coil. With this device, Faraday had discovered the transformer, a modern transformer being no different in essence even though the alternating current required had not then been discovered.

Faraday is thus also credited with the simultaneous discovery of electromagnetic induction, although the same discovery had been made in the same way by Joseph Henry in 1830. However, busy teaching, Henry had not been able to publish his findings before Faraday did, although both men are now credited with the independent discovery of induction.

Arago's wheel and the electric generator In 1824, Francois Arago found that a rotating non-magnetic disc, specifically of copper, caused the deflection of a magnetic needle placed above it. This was in fact a demonstration of electromagnetic induction, but nobody at that time could explain 'Arago's wheel'. Faraday realized that the motion of the copper wheel relative to the magnet in Arago's experiment caused an electric current to flow in the disc, which in turn set up a magnetic field and deflected the magnet. He set about constructing a similar device in which the current produced could be led off, and built the first electric generator in 1831. It consisted of a copper disc that was rotated between the poles of a magnet; Faraday touched wires to the edge and centre of the disc and connected them to a galvanometer, which registered a steady current.

electrostatic charge In 1832 Faraday showed that an electrostatic charge gives rise to the same effects as current electricity. He demonstrated in 1837 that electrostatic force consists of a field of curved lines of force, and that different substances have specific inductive capacities – that is, they take up different amounts of electric charge when subjected to an electric field.

In 1838, he proposed a theory of electricity elaborating his idea of varying strain in molecules. In a good conductor, a rapid build-up and breakdown of strain took place, transferring energy quickly from one molecule to the next. This also accounted for the decomposition of compounds in electrolysis. At the same time, Faraday wrongly rejected the notion that electricity involved the movement of any kind of electrical fluid (the motion of electrons is involved). However, in that this motion causes a rapid transfer of electrical energy through a conductor, Faraday's ideas were valid.

polarization of light Finally, Faraday considered the nature of light and in 1846 arrived at a form of the electromagnetic theory of light that was later developed by Scottish physicist James Clerk Maxwell. In 1845, Lord Kelvin suggested that Faraday investigate the action of electricity on polarized light. Faraday had in fact already carried out such experiments with no success, but this could have been because electrical forces were not strong. Faraday now used an electromagnet to give a strong magnetic field instead and found that it causes the plane of polarization to rotate, the angle of rotation being proportional to the strength of the magnetic field.

paramagnetism and diamagnetism Several further discoveries resulted from this experiment. Faraday realized that the glass block used to transmit the beam of light must also transmit the magnetic field, and he noticed that the glass tended to set itself at right-angles to the poles of the magnet rather than lining up with it as an iron bar would. He showed that the differing responses of substances to a magnetic field depended on the distribution of the lines of force through them. He called materials that are attracted to a magnetic field paramagnetic, and those that are repulsed diamagnetic. Faraday then went on to point out that the energy of a magnet is in the field around it and not in the magnet itself, and he extended this basic conception of field theory to electrical and gravitational systems.

in humans. In many animals and plants, excess carbohydrates and proteins are converted into fats for storage. Mammals and other vertebrates store fats in specialized connective tissues (◊adipose tissues), which not only act as energy reserves but also insulate the body and cushion its organs.

As a nutrient, fat serves five purposes: it is a source of energy (9 kcal/g); makes the diet palatable; provides basic building blocks for cell structure; provides essential fatty acids (linoleic and linolenic); and acts as a carrier for fat-soluble vitamins (A, D, E, and K). Foods rich in fat are butter, lard, margarine, and cooking oils. Products high in monounsaturated or polyunsaturated fats are thought to be less likely to contribute to cardiovascular disease.

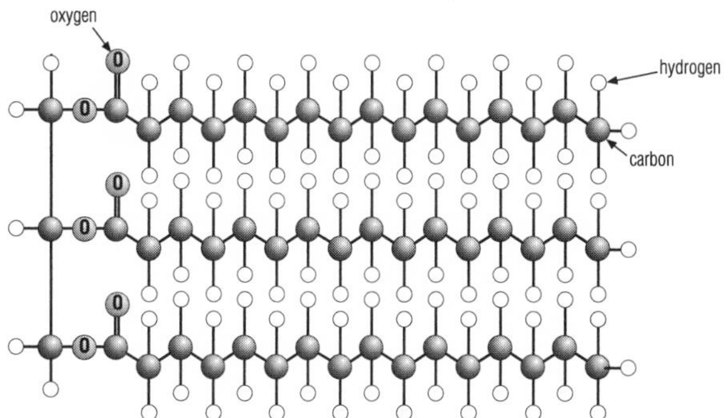

fat The molecular structure of typical fat. The molecule consists of three fatty acid molecules linked to a molecule of glycerol.

FAT in computing, abbreviation for ◊file allocation table.

fat hen plant belonging to the goosefoot family, widespread in temperate regions. It grows up to 1 m/3 ft tall and has lance- or diamond-shaped leaves and compact heads of small inconspicuous flowers. Now considered a weed, fat hen was once valued for its fatty seeds and edible leaves. (*Chenopodium album,* family Chenopodiaceae.)

fathom ***Anglo-Saxon faethm 'to embrace'*** in mining, seafaring, and handling timber, a unit of depth measurement (1.83 m/6 ft) used prior to metrication; it approximates to the distance between an adult man's hands when the arms are outstretched.

fatigue in muscle, reduced response brought about by the accumulation of lactic acid in muscle tissue due to excessive cellular activity.

fatty acid or ***carboxylic acid*** organic compound consisting of a hydrocarbon chain, up to 24 carbon atoms long, with a carboxyl group (–COOH) at one end. The covalent bonds between the carbon atoms may be single or double; where a double bond occurs the carbon atoms concerned carry one instead of two hydrogen atoms. Chains with only single bonds have all the hydrogen they can carry, so they are said to be **saturated** with hydrogen. Chains with one or more double bonds are said to be **unsaturated** (see ◊polyunsaturate). Fatty acids are produced in the small intestine when fat is digested.

Saturated fatty acids include palmitic and stearic acids; unsaturated fatty acids include oleic (one double bond), linoleic (two double bonds), and linolenic (three double bonds). Linoleic acid accounts for more than one third of some margarines. Supermarket brands that say they are high in polyunsaturates may contain as much as 39%. Fatty acids are generally found combined with glycerol in ◊lipids such as tryglycerides.

fault in geology, a fracture in the Earth either side of which rocks have moved past one another. Faults involve displacements, or offsets, ranging from the microscopic scale to hundreds of kilometres. Large offsets along a fault are the result of the accumulation of smaller movements (metres or less) over long periods of time. Large motions cause detectable ◊earthquakes.

Faults are planar features. Fault orientation is described by the inclination of the fault plane with respect to horizontal and its direction in the horizontal plane (see ◊strike). Faults at high angle with respect to horizontal (in which the fault plane is steep) are classified as either **normal faults**, where one block has apparently moved downhill along the inclined fault plane, or **reverse faults**, where one block appears to have moved uphill along the fault

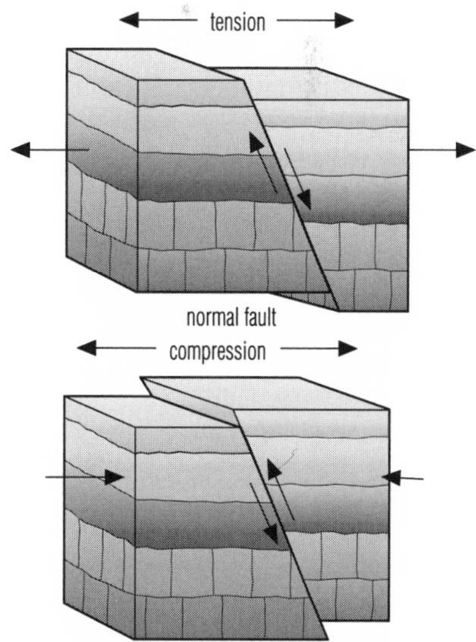

fault Faults are caused by the movement of rock layers, producing such features as block mountains and rift valleys. A normal fault is caused by a tension or stretching force acting in the rock layers. A reverse fault is caused by compression forces. Faults can continue to move for thousands or millions of years.

plane. Normal faults occur where rocks on either side have moved apart. Reverse faults occur where rocks on either side have been forced together. A reverse fault that forms a low angle with the horizontal plane is called a **thrust fault**.

A **lateral fault**, or **tear fault**, occurs where the relative movement along the fault plane is sideways. A particular kind of fault found only in ocean ridges is the **transform fault** (a term coined by Canadian geophysicist John Tuzo Wilson in 1965). On a map, an ocean ridge has a stepped appearance. The ridge crest is broken into sections, each section offset from the next. Between each section of the ridge crest the newly generated plates are moving past one another, forming a transform fault.

Faults produce lines of weakness on the Earth's surface (along their strike) that are often exploited by processes of ◊weathering and ◊erosion. Coastal caves and geos (narrow inlets) often form along faults and, on a larger scale, rivers may follow the line of a fault.

favourites menu option on Microsoft's Internet Explorer Web browser that allows users to go quickly to sites that have been ◊bookmarked, as with the bookmarks feature in Netscape Navigator. The access software for the AOL and CompuServe online services uses Favourite Places to provide the same feature.

fax (common name for ***facsimile transmission*** or ***telefax***) the transmission of images over a ◊telecommunications link, usually the telephone network. When placed on a fax machine, the original image is scanned by a transmitting device and converted into coded signals, which travel via the telephone lines to the receiving fax machine, where an image is created that is a copy of the original. Photographs as well as printed text and drawings can be sent. The standard transmission takes place at 4,800 or 9,600 bits of information per second.

The world's first fax machine, the *pantélégraphe,* was invented by Italian physicist Giovanni Caselli in 1866, over a century before the first electronic model came on the market. Standing over 2 m/6.5 ft high, it transmitted by telegraph nearly 5,000 handwritten documents and drawings between Paris and Lyon in its first year.

fax modem ◊modem capable of transmitting and receiving data in the form of a fax.

A normal fax machine sends data in binary form down a telephone line, in a similar way to a modem. A modem can therefore act as a fax machine, given suitable software. This means a document does not need to be printed before faxing and an incoming fax can be viewed before printing out on a plain-paper printer. However, the computer must be permanently turned on in order to receive faxes.

FDDI (abbreviation for ***fibre-optic digital device interface***) in computing, a series of network protocols, developed by the ◊American National Standards Institute, concerned with high-speed networks using ◊fibre optic cable.

FDDI supports data transmission rates of up to 100 Mb per second and is being introduced in many sites as a replacement for ◊Ethernet. FDDI not only makes possible transmission of large amounts of data, for example colour pictures, but also allows the transmission of voice and video data. See also ◊optical fibres.

feather rigid outgrowth of the outer layer of the skin of birds, made of the protein keratin. Feathers provide insulation and facilitate flight. There are several types, including long quill feathers on

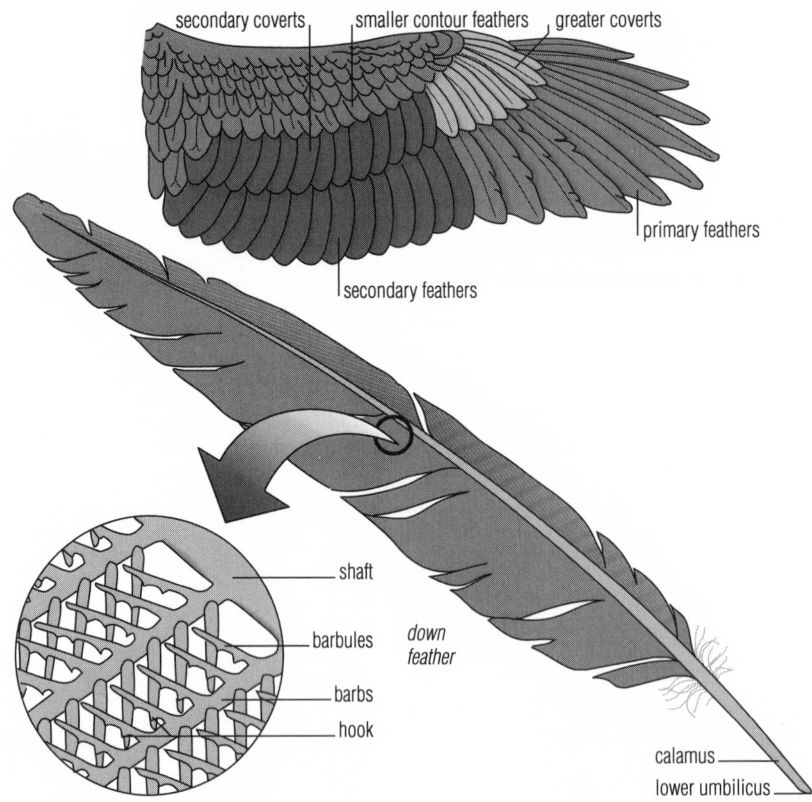

feather *Types of feather. A bird's wing is made up of two types of feather: contour feathers and flight feathers. The primary and secondary feathers are flight feathers. The coverts are contour feathers, used to streamline the bird. Semi-plume and down feathers insulate the bird's body and provide colour.*

the wings and tail, fluffy down feathers for retaining body heat, and contour feathers covering the body. The colouring of feathers is often important in camouflage or in courtship and other displays. Feathers are normally replaced at least once a year.

There is an enormous variation between species in the number of feathers, for example a whistling swan has over 25,000 contour feathers, whereas a ruby-throated hummingbird has less than 950.

Feathers generally consist of two main parts, axis and barbs, the former of which is divided into the quill, which is bare and hollow, and the shaft, which bears the barbs. The quill is embedded in the skin, and has at its base a small hole through which the nourishment passes during the growth of the feather. The barbs which constitute the vane are lath-shaped and taper to a point, and each one supports a series of outgrowths known as barbules, so that each barb is like a tiny feather. Adjacent barbs are linked to each other by hooks on the barbules.

feather star any of an unattached, free-swimming group of sea lilies, order Comatulida. The arms are branched into numerous projections (hence 'feather' star), and grow from a small cup-shaped body. Below the body are appendages that can hold on to a surface, but the feather star is not permanently attached.

fecundity the rate at which an organism reproduces, as distinct from its ability to reproduce (◊fertility). In vertebrates, it is usually measured as the number of offspring produced by a female each year.

Federal Aviation Administration (FAA) agency of the US Department of Transportation that controls air traffic. Its responsibilities include regulating air transportation, aviation safety, developing and operating a system of air-traffic control, requiring airports and airlines to provide antihijacking security, and conducting aviation research. The agency is also responsible for investigating aeroplane accidents. It was established in 1958 as the Federal Aviation Agency and was renamed upon its assignment to Transportation in 1967. It is directed by an administrator (assistant secretary) appointed directly by the president.

feedback in biology, another term for biofeedback.

feedback general principle whereby the results produced in an ongoing reaction become factors in modifying or changing the reaction; it is the principle used in self-regulating control systems, from a simple ◊thermostat and steam-engine ◊governor to automatic computer-controlled machine tools. A fully computerized control system, in which there is no operator intervention, is called a **closed-loop feedback** system. A system that also responds to control signals from an operator is called an **open-loop feedback** system.

In self-regulating systems, information about what *is* happening in a system (such as level of temperature, engine speed, or size of workpiece) is fed back to a controlling device, which compares it with what *should* be happening. If the two are different, the device takes suitable action (such as switching on a heater, allowing more steam to the engine, or resetting the tools). The idea that the Earth is a self-regulating system, with feedback operating to keep nature in balance, is a central feature of the ◊Gaia hypothesis.

Fehling's test chemical test to determine whether an organic substance is a reducing agent (substance that donates electrons to other substances in a chemical reaction). It is usually used to detect reducing sugars (monosaccharides, such as glucose, and the disaccharides maltose and lactose) and aldehydes.

If the test substance is heated with a freshly prepared solution containing copper(II) sulphate, sodium hydroxide and sodium potassium tartrate, the production of a brick-red precipitate indicates the presence of a reducing agent.

feldspar a group of ◊silicate minerals. Feldspars are the most abundant mineral type in the Earth's crust. They are the chief constituents of ◊igneous rock and are present in most metamorphic and sedimentary rocks. All feldspars contain silicon, aluminium, and oxygen, linked together to form a framework. Spaces within this framework structure are occupied by sodium, potassium, calcium, or occasionally barium, in various proportions. Feldspars form white, grey, or pink crystals and rank 6 on the ◊Mohs' scale of hardness.

The four extreme compositions of feldspar are represented by the minerals **orthoclase**, $KAlSi_3O_8$; **albite**, $NaAlSi_3O_8$; **anorthite**, $CaAl_2Si_2O_8$; and **celsian**, $BaAl_2Si_2O_8$. **Plagioclase feldspars** contain variable amounts of sodium (as in albite) and calcium (as in anorthite) with a negligible potassium content. **Alkali feldspars** (including orthoclase) have a high potassium content, less sodium, and little calcium.

The type known as moonstone has a pearl-like effect and is used in jewellery. Approximately 4,000 tonnes of feldspar are used in the ceramics industry annually.

feldspathoid any of a group of silicate minerals resembling feldspars but containing less silica. Examples are nepheline ($NaAlSiO_4$ with a little potassium) and leucite ($KAlSi_2O_6$). Feldspathoids occur in igneous rocks that have relatively high proportions of sodium and potassium. Such rocks may also contain alkali feldspar, but they do not generally contain quartz because any free silica would have combined with the feldspathoid to produce more feldspar instead.

felsic rock a ◊plutonic rock composed chiefly of light-coloured minerals, such as quartz, feldspar and mica. It is derived from **feldspar**, **lenad** (meaning feldspathoid), and **silica**. The term **felsic** also applies to light-coloured minerals as a group, especially quartz, feldspar, and feldspathoids.

femtosecond ◊SI unit of time. It is 10^{-15} seconds (one millionth of a billionth).

femur the ***thigh-bone***; also the upper bone in the hind limb of a four-limbed vertebrate.

fence lizard or ***swift*** name given to several species of lizard found in North and Central America. They are viviparous (the young develop in the mother before birth).

Fermat, Pierre de (1601–1665)

French mathematician who, with Blaise Pascal, founded the theory of probability and the modern theory of numbers. Fermat also made contributions to analytical geometry. In 1657, Fermat published a series of problems as challenges to other mathematicians, in the form of theorems to be proved.

Fermat's last theorem states that equations of the form *xn + yn = zn where x, y, z,* and *n* are all integers have no solutions if *n* > 2. Fermat scribbled the theorem in the margin of a mathematics textbook and noted that he could have shown it to be true had he enough space in which to write the proof. The theorem remained unproven for 300 years (and therefore, strictly speaking, constituted a conjecture rather than a theorem). In 1993, Andrew Wiles, the English mathematician of Princeton University, USA, announced a proof; this turned out to be premature, but he put forward a revised proof in 1994. Fermat's last theorem was finally laid to rest in June 1997 when Wiles collected the Wolfskehl prize (the legacy bequeathed in the 19th century for the problem's solution).

Mary Evans Picture Library

classification Fence lizards are all in genus *Sceloporus,* family Iguanidae, suborder Sauria, order Squamata, class Reptilia.

fennec small nocturnal desert ◊fox *Fennecus zerda* found in North Africa and Arabia. It has a head and body only 40 cm/1.3 ft long, and its enormous ears act as radiators to lose excess heat. It eats insects and small animals.

fennel any of several varieties of a perennial plant with feathery green leaves, belonging to the carrot family. Fennels have an aniseed (liquorice) flavour, and the leaves and seeds are used in seasoning. The thickened leafstalks of sweet fennel (*F. vulgare dulce*) are eaten as a vegetable. (*Foeniculum vulgare,* family Umbelliferae.)

Fermat's principle in physics, the principle that a ray of light, or other radiation, moves between two points along the path that takes the minimum time.

The principle is named after French mathematician Pierre de Fermat, who used it to deduce the laws of ◊reflection and ◊refraction.

FERMAT'S LAST THEOREM

http://www-groups.dcs.st-and.ac.uk/~history/HistTopics/Fermat's_last_theorem.html

Account of Fermat's last theorem and of the many attempts made to prove it. It is extensively hyperlinked to related mathematicians and also includes a list of 17 references for further reading.

fermentation the breakdown of sugars by bacteria and yeasts using a method of respiration without oxygen (◊anaerobic). Fermentation processes have long been utilized in baking bread, making beer and wine, and producing cheese, yoghurt, soy sauce, and many other foodstuffs.

In baking and brewing, yeasts ferment sugars to produce ◊ethanol and carbon dioxide; the latter makes bread rise and puts bubbles into beers and champagne. Many antibiotics are produced by fermentation; it is one of the processes that can cause food spoilage.

Wine is the most healthful and most hygienic of beverages.

LOUIS PASTEUR French chemist and microbiologist.
Etudes sur la Vin Pt 1 Ch 2

fermi unit of length equal to 10^{-15}m, used in atomic and nuclear physics. The unit is named after Enrico Fermi.

Fermilab (shortened form of ***Fermi National Accelerator Laboratory***)

US centre for ◊particle physics at Batavia, Illinois, near Chicago. It is named after Italian–US physicist Enrico Fermi. Fermilab was opened in 1972, and is the home of the Tevatron, the world's most powerful particle ◊accelerator. It is capable of boosting protons and antiprotons to speeds near that of light (to energies of 20 TeV).

fermion in physics, a subatomic particle whose spin can only take values that are half-integers, such as $\frac{1}{2}$ or $\frac{3}{2}$. Fermions may be classified as leptons, such as the electron, and baryons, such as the proton and neutron. All elementary particles are either fermions or ◊bosons.

The exclusion principle, formulated by Austrian–US physicist Wolfgang Pauli in 1925, asserts that no two fermions in the same system (such as an atom) can possess the same position, energy state, spin, or other quantized property.

fermium synthesized, radioactive, metallic element of the ◊actinide series, symbol Fm, atomic number 100, relative atomic mass 257.10. Ten isotopes are known, the longest-lived of which, Fm-257, has a half-life of 80 days. Fermium has been produced only in minute quantities in particle accelerators.

Fermi, Enrico (1901–1954)

Italian-born US physicist who proved the existence of new radioactive elements produced by bombardment with neutrons, and discovered nuclear reactions produced by low-energy neutrons. This research won him the Nobel Prize for Physics in 1938 and was the basis for studies leading to the atomic bomb and nuclear energy. Fermi built the first nuclear reactor in 1942 at Chicago University and later took part in the Manhattan Project to construct an atom bomb. His theoretical work included the study of the weak nuclear force, one of the fundamental forces of nature, and beta decay.

neutron bombardment and the Nobel Prize Following the work of the Joliot-Curies, who discovered artificial radioactivity in 1934 using alpha particle bombardment, Fermi began producing new radioactive isotopes by neutron bombardment. Unlike the alpha particle, which is positively charged, the neutron is charge neutral. Fermi realized that less energy would be wasted when a bombarding neutron encounters a positively charged target nucleus.

He also found that a block of paraffin wax or a jacket of water around the neutron source produced slow, or 'thermal', neutrons. Slow-neutrons are more effective at producing artificial radioactive elements because they remain longer near the target nucleus and have a greater chance of being absorbed.

He did, however, misinterpret the results of experiments involving neutron bombardment of uranium, failing to recognize that nuclear fission had occurred. Instead, he maintained that the bombardment produced two new transuranic elements. It was left to Lise Meitner and Otto Frisch to explain nuclear fission in 1938.

nuclear reactors and the atomic bomb In the USA, Fermi continued the work on the fission of uranium (initiated by neutrons) by building the first nuclear reactor, then called an **atomic pile,** because it had a moderator consisting of a pile of purified graphite blocks (to slow the neutrons) with holes drilled in them to take rods of enriched uranium. Other neutron-absorbing rods of cadmium, called control rods, could be lowered into or withdrawn from the pile to limit the number of slow-neutrons available to initiate the fission of uranium. The reactor was built on the squash court of Chicago University. On the afternoon of 2 December 1942, the control rods were withdrawn for the first time and the reactor began to work, using a self-sustaining nuclear chain reaction. Two years later, the USA, through a team led by Arthur Compton and Fermi, had constructed an atomic bomb, which used the same reaction but without control, resulting in a nuclear explosion.

beta decay and the neutrino Fermi's experimental work on beta decay in radioactive materials provided further evidence for the existence of the neutrino, predicted by Austrian physicist Wolfgang Pauli. The decay, which takes place spontaneously in the unstable nuclei of radioactive elements, results from the conversion of a neutron into a proton, an electron (beta particle) and an antineutrino:

$$n \rightarrow p + e^- + \nu$$

Mary Evans Picture Library

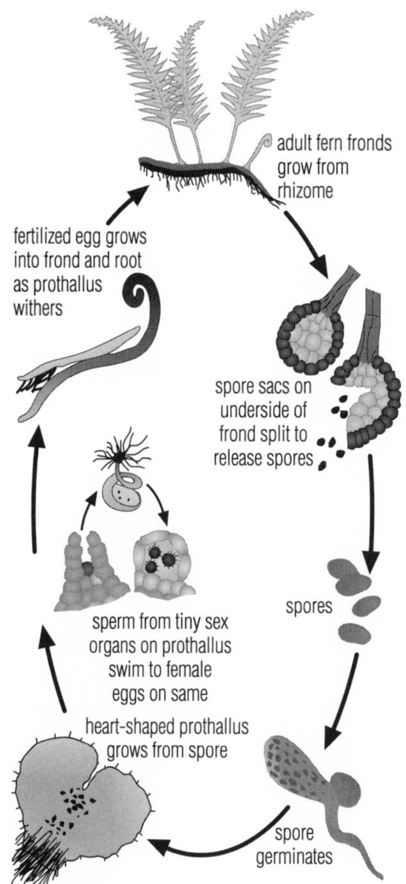
adult fern fronds grow from rhizome
fertilized egg grows into frond and root as prothallus withers
spore sacs on underside of frond split to release spores
spores
sperm from tiny sex organs on prothallus swim to female eggs on same
heart-shaped prothallus grows from spore
spore germinates

fern The life cycle of a fern. Ferns have two distinct forms that alternate during their life cycle. For the main part of its life, a fern consists of a short stem (or rhizome) from which roots and leaves grow. The other part of its life is spent as a small heart-shaped plant called a prothallus.

It was discovered in 1952 in the debris of the first thermonuclear explosion. The element was named in 1955 in honour of US physicist Enrico ◊Fermi.

fern any of a group of plants related to horsetails and clubmosses. Ferns are spore-bearing, not flowering, plants and most are perennial, spreading by slow-growing roots. The leaves, known as fronds, vary widely in size and shape. Some taller types, such as tree ferns, grow in the tropics. There are over 7,000 species. (Order Filicales.)

ferret domesticated variety of the Old World ◊polecat.

About 35 cm/1.2 ft long, it usually has yellowish-white fur and pink eyes, but may be the dark brown colour of a wild polecat.

Ferrets may breed with wild polecats. They have been used since ancient times to hunt rabbits and rats.

ferric ion traditional name for the trivalent condition of iron, Fe^{3+}; the modern name is iron(III). Ferric salts are usually reddish or yellow in colour and form reddish-yellow solutions. $Fe_2(SO_4)_3$ is iron(III) sulphate (ferric sulphate).

ferrimagnetism form of ◊magnetism in which adjacent molecular magnets are aligned anti-parallel, but have unequal strength, producing a strong overall magnetization. Ferrimagnetism is found in certain inorganic substances, such as ◊ferrites.

ferrite ceramic ferrimagnetic material. Ferrites are iron oxides to which small quantities of ◊transition metal oxides (such as cobalt and nickel oxides) have been added. They are used in transformer cores, radio antennae, and, formerly, in computer memories.

ferro-alloy alloy of iron with a high proportion of elements such as manganese, silicon, chromium, and molybdenum. Ferro-alloys are used in the manufacture of alloy steels. Each alloy is generally named after the added metal – for example, ferrochromium.

ferroelectric material ceramic dielectric material that, like ferromagnetic materials, has a ◊domain structure that makes it exhibit magnetism and usually the ◊piezoelectric effect. An example is Rochelle salt (potassium sodium tartrate tetrahydrate, $KNaC_4H_4O_6.4H_2O$).

ferromagnetism form of ◊magnetism in which magnetism can be acquired in an external magnetic field and usually retained in its absence, so that ferromagnetic materials are used to make permanent magnets. A ferromagnetic material may therefore be said to have a high magnetic ◊permeability and ◊susceptibility (which depends upon temperature). Examples are iron, cobalt, nickel, and their alloys.

Ultimately, ferromagnetism is caused by spinning electrons in the atoms of the material, which act as tiny weak magnets. They align parallel to each other within small regions of the material to form ◊domains, or areas of stronger magnetism. In an unmagnetized material, the domains are aligned at random so there is no overall magnetic effect. If a magnetic field is applied to that material, the domains align to point in the same direction, producing a strong overall magnetic effect. Permanent magnetism arises if the domains remain aligned after the external field is removed. Ferromagnetic materials exhibit ◊hysteresis.

ferrous ion traditional name for the divalent condition of iron, Fe^{2+}; the modern name is iron(II). Ferrous salts are usually green, and form yellow-green solutions. $FeSO_4$ is iron(II) sulphate (ferrous sulphate).

fertility an organism's ability to reproduce, as distinct from the rate at which it reproduces (◊fecundity). Individuals become infertile (unable to reproduce) when they cannot generate gametes (eggs or sperm) or when their gametes cannot yield a viable ◊embryo after fertilization.

fertility drug any of a range of drugs taken to increase a female's fertility, developed in Sweden in the mid-1950s. They increase the chances of a multiple birth.

The most familiar is gonadotrophin, which is made from hormone extracts taken from the human pituitary gland: follicle-stimulating hormone and luteinizing hormone. It stimulates ovulation in women. As a result of a fertility drug, in 1974 the first sextuplets to survive were born to Susan Rosenkowitz of South Africa.

fertilization in ◊sexual reproduction, the union of two ◊gametes (sex cells, often called egg and sperm) to produce a ◊zygote, which combines the genetic material contributed by each parent. In self-fertilization the male and female gametes come from the same plant; in cross-fertilization they come from different plants. Self-fertilization rarely occurs in animals; usually even ◊hermaphrodite animals cross-fertilize each other.

In terrestrial insects, mammals, reptiles, and birds, fertilization occurs within the female's body. In humans it usually takes place in the ◊Fallopian tube. In the majority of fishes and amphibians, and most aquatic invertebrates, fertilization occurs externally, when both sexes release their gametes into the water. In most fungi, gametes are not released, but the hyphae of the two parents grow towards each other and fuse to achieve fertilization. In higher plants, ◊pollination precedes fertilization.

fertilizer substance containing some or all of a range of about 20 chemical elements necessary for healthy plant growth, used to compensate for the deficiencies of poor or depleted soil. Fertilizers may be **organic**, for example farmyard manure, composts, bonemeal, blood, and fishmeal; or **inorganic**, in the form of compounds, mainly of nitrogen, phosphate, and potash, which have been used on a very much increased scale since 1945.

Because externally applied fertilizers tend to be in excess of

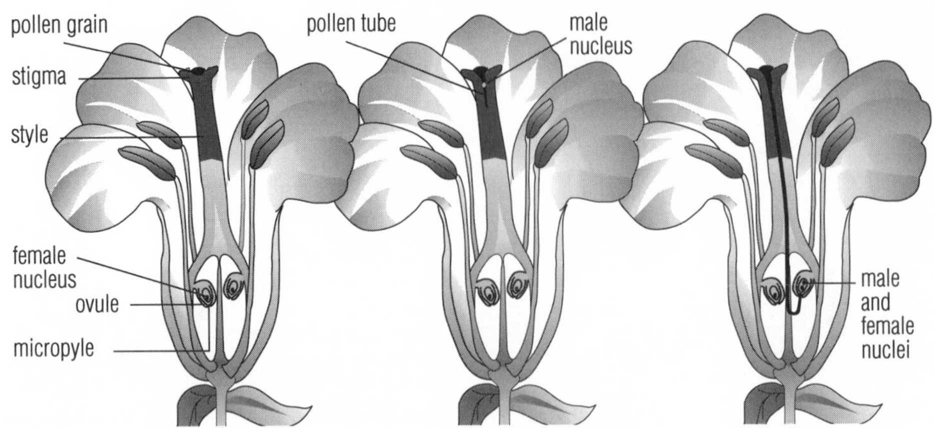

fertilization *In a flowering plant pollen grains land on the surface of the stigma, and if conditions are acceptable the pollen grain germinates, forming a pollen tube, through which the male gametes pass, entering the ovule via the micropyle in order to reach the female egg.*

plant requirements and drain away to affect lakes and rivers (see ◊eutrophication), attention has turned to the modification of crop plants themselves. Plants of the legume family, including the bean, clover, and lupin, live in symbiosis with bacteria located in root nodules, which fix nitrogen from the atmosphere. Research is now directed to producing a similar relationship between such bacteria and crops such as wheat.

fescue any grass of a widely distributed group. Many are used in temperate regions for lawns and pasture. Many upland species are viviparous, producing young plantlets instead of flowers. (Genus *Festuca*, family Gramineae.)

fetal therapy diagnosis and treatment of conditions arising in the unborn child. While some anomalies can be diagnosed antenatally, fetal treatments are only appropriate in a few cases – mostly where the development of an organ is affected.

Fetal therapy was first used 1963 with exchange transfusion for haemolytic disease of the newborn, once a serious problem (see also ◊rhesus factor). Today the use of fetal therapy remains limited. Most treatments involve 'needling': introducing fine instruments through the mother's abdominal and uterine walls under ultrasound guidance. Open-womb surgery (hysterotomy) remains controversial because of the risks involved. It is available only in some centres in the United States.

fetch-execute cycle or ***processing cycle*** in computing, the two-phase cycle used by the computer's central processing unit to process the instructions in a program. During the **fetch phase**, the next program instruction is transferred from the computer's immediate-access memory to the instruction register (memory location used to hold the instruction while it is being executed). During the **execute phase**, the instruction is decoded and obeyed. The process is repeated in a continuous loop.

fetishism in psychology, the transfer of erotic interest to an object, such as an item of clothing, whose real or fantasized presence is necessary for sexual gratification. The fetish may also be a part of the body not normally considered erogenous, such as the feet.

fetus or ***foetus*** stage in mammalian ◊embryo development. The human embryo is usually termed a fetus after the eighth week of development, when the limbs and external features of the head are recognizable.

fever condition of raised body temperature, usually due to infection.

fibre, dietary or ***roughage*** plant material that cannot be digested by human digestive enzymes; it consists largely of cellulose, a carbohydrate found in plant cell walls. Fibre adds bulk to the gut contents, assisting the muscular contractions that force food along the intestine. A diet low in fibre causes constipation and is believed to increase the risk of developing diverticulitis, diabetes, gall-bladder disease, and cancer of the large bowel – conditions that are rare in nonindustrialized countries, where the diet contains a high proportion of unrefined cereals.

Soluble fibre consists of indigestible plant carbohydrates (such as pectins, hemicelluloses, and gums) that dissolve in water. A high proportion of the fibre in such foods as oat bran, pulses, and

Feynman, Richard P(hillips) (1918–1988)

US physicist whose work laid the foundations of quantum electrodynamics. For his work on the theory of radiation he shared the Nobel Prize for Physics 1965 with Julian Schwinger and Sin-Itiro Tomonaga (1906–1979). He also contributed to many aspects of particle physics, including quark theory and the nature of the weak nuclear force.

For his work on quantum electrodynamics, he developed a simple and elegant system of **Feynman diagrams** to represent interactions between particles and how they moved from one space-time point to another. He had rules for calculating the probability associated with each diagram.

His other major discoveries are the theory of superfluidity (frictionless flow) in liquid helium, developed in the early 1950s; his work on the weak interaction (with US physicist Murray Gell-Mann) and the strong force; and his prediction that the proton and neutron are not elementary particles. Both particles are now known to be composed of quarks.

Californian Institute of Technology

vegetables is of this sort. Its presence in the diet has been found to reduce the amount of cholesterol in blood over the short term, although the mechanism for its effect is disputed.

fibreglass glass that has been formed into fine fibres, either as long continuous filaments or as a fluffy, short-fibred glass wool. Fibreglass is heat- and fire-resistant and a good electrical insulator. It has applications in the field of fibre optics and as a strengthener for plastics in ◊GRP (glass-reinforced plastics).

The long filament form is made by forcing molten glass through the holes of a spinneret, and is woven into textiles. Glass wool is made by blowing streams of molten glass in a jet of high-pressure steam, and is used for electrical, sound, and thermal insulation, especially for the roof space in houses.

fibre optics branch of physics dealing with the transmission of light and images through glass or plastic fibres known as ◊optical fibres.

fibrin insoluble protein involved in blood clotting. When an injury occurs fibrin is deposited around the wound in the form of a mesh, which dries and hardens, so that bleeding stops. Fibrin is developed in the blood from a soluble protein, fibrinogen.

The conversion of fibrinogen to fibrin is the final stage in blood clotting. Platelets, a type of cell found in blood, release the enzyme thrombin when they come into contact with damaged tissue, and the formation of fibrin then occurs. Calcium, vitamin K, and a variety of enzymes called factors are also necessary for efficient blood clotting.

fibula the rear lower bone in the hind leg of a vertebrate. It is paired and often fused with a smaller front bone, the tibia.

Fidonet in computing, early network of ◊bulletin board systems (BBSs) which sends mail and news around the world via an arrangement whereby the individual systems call each other to exchange data every night. Such systems are called 'store-and-forward'.

field in computing, a specific item of data. A field is usually part of a **record**, which in turn is part of a ◊file.

field in physics, a region of space in which an object exerts a force on another separate object because of certain properties they both possess. For example, there is a force of attraction between any two objects that have mass when one is in the gravitational field of the other.

Other fields of force include ◊electric fields (caused by electric charges) and ◊magnetic fields (caused by circulating electric currents), either of which can involve attractive or repulsive forces.

field enclosed area of land used for farming. Traditionally fields were measured in ◊acres; the current unit of measurement is the hectare (2.47 acres).

In Britain, regular field systems were functioning before the Romans' arrival. The open-field system was in use at the time of the Norman Conquest. Enclosure began in the 14th century and continued into the 19th century.

In the Middle Ages, the farmland of an English rural community was often divided into three large fields (the **open-field system**). These were worked on a simple rotation basis of one year wheat, one year barley, and one year ◊fallow. The fields were divided into individually owned strips of the width that one plough team with oxen could plough (about 20 m/66 ft). At the end of each strip would be a turning space, either a road or a **headland**. Through repeated ploughing a **ridge-and-furrow** pattern became evident. A farmer worked a number of strips, not necessarily adjacent to each other, in one field.

The open-field communities were subsequently reorganized, the land enclosed, and the farmers' holdings redistributed into individual blocks which were then divided into separate fields. This enclosure process reached its peak during the 18th century. 20th-century developments in agricultural science and technology have encouraged farmers to amalgamate and enlarge their fields, often to as much as 40 hectares/100 acres.

The open field system was also found in France, Germany, Greece, and Slavonic lands.

fieldfare gregarious thrush *Turdus pilaris* of the family Muscicapidae, order Passeriformes; it has chestnut upperparts with a pale-grey lower back and neck, and a dark tail. The bird's underparts are a rich ochre colour, spotted with black. Its nest is of long fine grass with an intervening layer of mud; it may be built in birch or fir trees at a height of 5 m/16 ft or less. It feeds on berries, insects, and other invertebrates.

field-length check ◊validation check in which the characters in an input field are counted to ensure that the correct number of characters have been entered. For example, a six-figure date field may be checked to ensure that it does contain exactly six digits.

field of view angle over which an image may be seen in a mirror or an optical instrument such as a telescope. A wide field of view allows a greater area to be surveyed without moving the instrument, but has the disadvantage that each of the objects seen is smaller. A ◊convex mirror gives a larger field of view than a plane or flat mirror. The field of view of an eye is called its **field of vision** or visual field.

A telephoto lens has a small field of view, around 14°, and produces a highly magnified image. A 'fish-eye' lens has a very wide angle of view, around 180°. Our eyes have a field of vision of around 45°.

field studies study of ecology, geography, geology, history, archaeology, and allied subjects, in the natural environment as opposed to the laboratory.

The most exciting phrase to hear in science, the one that heralds new discoveries, is not 'Eureka!' (I've found it!) but 'That's funny...'

ISAAC ASIMOV Russian-born US writer.

fifth-generation computer anticipated new type of computer based on emerging microelectronic technologies with high computing speeds and ◊parallel processing. The development of very large-scale integration (◊VLSI) technology, which can put many more circuits on to an integrated circuit (chip) than is currently possible, and developments in computer hardware and software design may produce computers far more powerful than those in current use.

It has been predicted that such a computer will be able to communicate in natural spoken language with its user; store vast knowledge databases; search rapidly through these databases, making intelligent inferences and drawing logical conclusions; and process images and 'see' objects in the way that humans do.

In 1981 Japan's Ministry of International Trade and Industry launched a ten-year project to build the first fifth-generation computer, the 'parallel inference machine', consisting of over a thousand microprocessors operating in parallel with each other. By 1992, however, the project was behind schedule and had only produced 256-processor modules. It has since been suggested that research into other technologies, such as ◊neural networks, may present more promising approaches to artificial intelligence. Compare earlier ◊computer generations.

fig any of a group of trees belonging to the mulberry family, including the many cultivated varieties of *F. carica*, originally from W Asia. They produce two or three crops of fruit a year. Eaten fresh or dried, figs have a high sugar content and laxative properties. (Genus *Ficus*, family Moraceae.)

In the wild, *F. carica* is dependent on the fig wasp for pollination, and the wasp in turn is parasitic on the flowers. The tropical **banyan** (*F. benghalensis*) has less attractive edible fruit, and roots that grow down from its branches. The **bo tree** under which Buddha became enlightened is the Indian peepul or wild fig (*F. religiosa*).

fighting fish any of a southeast Asian genus *Betta* of fishes of the gourami family, especially *B. splendens*, about 6 cm/2 in long and a popular aquarium fish. It can breathe air, using an accessory breathing organ above the gill, and can live in poorly oxygenated water. The male has large fins and various colours, including shining greens, reds, and blues. The female is yellowish brown with short fins.

The male builds a nest of bubbles at the water's surface and displays to a female to induce her to lay. Rival males are attacked, and in a confined space, fights may occur. In Thailand, public contests are held.

figwort any of a group of Old World plants belonging to the figwort family, which also includes foxgloves and snapdragons. Members of the genus have square stems, opposite leaves, and open two-lipped flowers in a cluster at the top of the stem. (Genus *Scrophularia*, family Scrophulariaceae.)

filament in astronomy, a dark, winding feature occasionally seen on images of the Sun in hydrogen light. Filaments are clouds of relatively cool gas suspended above the Sun by magnetic fields and seen in silhouette against the hotter ◊photosphere below. During total ◊eclipses they can be seen as bright features against the sky at the edge of the Sun where they are known as ◊prominences.

file in computing, a collection of data or a program stored in a computer's external memory (for example, on ◊disc). It might include anything from information on a company's employees to a program for an adventure game. **Serial files** hold information as a sequence of characters, so that, to read any particular item of data, the program must read all those that precede it. **Random-access files** allow the required data to be reached directly. Files are usually located via a ◊directory.

file access in computing, the way in which the records in a file are stored, retrieved, or updated by computer. There are four main types of file organization, each of which allows a different form of access to the records.

Records in a **serial file** are not stored in any particular order, so a specific record can be accessed only by reading through all the previous records.

Records in a **sequential file** are sorted by reference to a key field (see ◊sorting) and the computer can use a searching technique, such as a binary search, to access a specific record.

An **indexed sequential file** possesses an index, which records the position of each block of records and is created and updated with that file. By consulting the index, the computer can obtain the address of the block containing the required record, and search just that block rather than the whole file.

A **direct-access** or **random-access file** contains records that can be accessed directly by the computer.

file allocation table (FAT) in computing, a table used by the operating system to record the physical arrangement of files on disc. As a result of ◊fragmentation, files can be split into many parts sited at different places on the disc.

file extension in computing, the last three letters of a file name in DOS or Windows, which indicate the type of data the file contains. Extensions in common use include .TXT for 'text', .GIF for 'graphics interchange format', and .EXE for 'executable'.

In Windows, the operating system may be configured to associate specific file extensions with specific programs, so that double-clicking on a file name starts the right program and opens the file for editing.

file format in computing, specific way data is stored in a file. Most computer programs use proprietary file formats which cannot be read by other programs. As this is inconvenient for users, in recent years software publishers have developed filters which convert older file formats into the ones the program in use can read.

Often ◊file extensions are used to indicate which program was used to create a particular file. Some formats, such as GIF (graphics interchange format), have become so popular and widely used that they are supported by many programs.

Before transmitting data over a public network to another user, it is important to check that the receiving user can read the format the data is in. For this purpose, the most commonly readable format is plain ◊ASCII for text and either GIF or ◊JPEG (Joint Photographic Experts Group) for graphics.

file generation in computing, a specific version of a file. When ◊file updating takes place, a new generation of the file is created, containing accurate, up-to-date information. The old generation of the file will often be stored to provide ◊data security in the event that the new generation of the file is lost or damaged.

file librarian or ***media librarian*** job classification for ◊computer personnel. A file librarian stores and issues the data files used by the computer department.

file merging in computing, combining two or more sequentially ordered files into a single sequentially ordered file.

file searching ◊searching a computer memory (usually ◊backing storage) for a file.

file server computer on a ◊network that handles (and usually stores) the data used by other computers on the network. See also ◊client–server architecture.

file sorting arranging files in sequence; see ◊sorting.

file transfer in computing, the transmission of a file (data stored on disc, for example) from one machine to another. Both machines must be physically linked (for example, by a telephone line via a ◊modem or ◊acoustic coupler) and both must be running appropriate communications software.

file updating in computing, reviewing and altering the records in a file to ensure that the information they contain is accurate and up-to-date. Three basic processes are involved: adding new records, deleting existing records, and amending existing records.

The updating of a **direct-access file** is a continuous process because records can be accessed individually and changed at any time. This type of updating is typical of large interactive database systems, such as airline ticket-booking systems. Each time a ticket is booked, files are immediately updated so that double booking is impossible.

In large commercial applications, however, millions of customer records may be held in a large sequentially ordered file, called the **master file**. Each time the records in the master file are to be updated (for example, when quarterly bills are being drawn up), a **transaction file** must be prepared. This will contain all the additions, deletions, and amendments required to update the master file. The transaction file is sorted into the same order as the master file, and then the computer reads both files and produces a new updated **generation** of the master file, which will be stored until the next file updating takes place.

film, photographic strip of transparent material (usually cellulose acetate) coated with a light-sensitive emulsion, used in cameras to take pictures. The emulsion contains a mixture of light-sensitive silver halide salts (for example, bromide or iodide) in gelatin. When the emulsion is exposed to light, the silver salts are invisibly altered, giving a latent image, which is then made visible by the process of ◊developing. Films differ in their sensitivities to light, this being indicated by their speeds. Colour film consists of several layers of emulsion, each of which records a different colour in the light falling on it.

In **colour film** the front emulsion records blue light, then comes a yellow filter, followed by layers that record green and red light respectively. In the developing process the various images in the layers are dyed yellow, magenta (red), and cyan (blue), respectively.

When they are viewed, either as a transparency or as a colour print, the colours merge to produce the true colour of the original scene photographed.

filter in chemistry, a porous substance, such as blotting paper, through which a mixture can be passed to separate out its solid constituents.

filter in computing, a program that transforms data. Filters are often used when data output from one ◊application program is input into a different program, which requires a different data format. For example files transferred between two different word-processing programs are run through either an output filter supplied with the first program or an input filter supplied with the second program.

Filters are also used to expand coding structures, which have been simplified for keyboard input, into the often more verbose form required by such standards as SGML (◊Standard Generalized Markup Language).

filter in electronics, a circuit that transmits a signal of some frequencies better than others. A low-pass filter transmits signals of low frequency and direct current; a high-pass filter transmits high-frequency signals; a band-pass filter transmits signals in a band of frequencies.

filter in optics, a device that absorbs some parts of the visible ◊spectrum and transmits others. For example, a green filter will absorb or block all colours of the spectrum except green, which it allows to pass through. A yellow filter absorbs only light at the blue and violet end of the spectrum, transmitting red, orange, green, and yellow light.

filtrate liquid or solution that has passed through a filter.

filtration technique by which suspended solid particles in a fluid are removed by passing the mixture through a filter, usually porous paper, plastic, or cloth. The particles are retained by the filter to form a residue and the fluid passes through to make up the filtrate. For example, soot may be filtered from air, and suspended solids from water.

fin in aquatic animals, flattened extension from the body that aids balance and propulsion through the water.

In fish they may be paired, such as the pectoral and ventral fins, or singular, such as the caudal and dorsal fins, all being supported by a series of cartilaginous or bony rays.

The fins in cetaceans (whales and dolphins) are simple extensions of the soft tissue and have no bony rays. The flippers of seals are modified five-fingered limbs and contain the same bones as the limbs of other vertebrates.

finch any of various songbirds of the family Fringillidae, in the order Passeriformes (perching birds). They are seed-eaters with stout conical beaks. The name may also be applied to members of the Emberizidae (buntings), and Estrildidae (weaver-finches).

FINCHWORLD

http://www.finchworld.com/

Huge source of information on finches. Contents include practical advice for those buying a finch for the first time, tips on diet, housing, recreation activities, and avian illnesses. There are links to finch sites around the world and news of ornithological research on these songbirds.

finite having a countable number of elements, the opposite of infinite.

finsen unit unit (symbol FU) for measuring the intensity of ultraviolet (UV) light; for instance, UV light of 2 FUs causes sunburn in 15 minutes.

fiord alternative spelling of ◊fjord.

fir any of a group of ◊conifer trees belonging to the pine family. The true firs include the balsam fir (*A. balsamea*) of northern North America and the silver fir (*A. alba*) of Europe and Asia. Douglas firs of the genus *Pseudotsuga* are native to western North America and the Far East. (True fir genus *Abies*, family Pinaceae.)

fireball in astronomy, a very bright ◊meteor, often bright enough to be seen in daylight and occasionally leading to the fall of a ◊meteorite. Some fireballs are caused by ◊satellites or other space debris burning up in the Earth's atmosphere.

firebrat any insect of the order Thysanura (◊bristletail).

fire clay a ◊clay with refractory characteristics (resistant to high temperatures), and hence suitable for lining furnaces (firebrick). Its chemical composition consists of a high percentage of silicon and aluminium oxides, and a low percentage of the oxides of sodium, potassium, iron, and calcium.

firedamp gas that occurs in coal mines and is explosive when mixed with air in certain proportions. It consists chiefly of methane (CH_4, natural gas or marsh gas) but always contains small quantities of other gases, such as nitrogen, carbon dioxide, and hydrogen, and sometimes ethane and carbon monoxide.

fire-danger rating unit index used by the UK Forestry Commission to indicate the probability of a forest fire. 0 means a fire is improbable, 100 shows a serious fire hazard.

fire extinguisher device for putting out a fire. Fire extinguishers work by removing one of the three conditions necessary for fire to continue (heat, oxygen, and fuel), either by cooling the fire or by excluding oxygen.

The simplest fire extinguishers contain water, which when propelled onto the fire cools it down. Water extinguishers cannot be used on electrical fires, as there is a danger of electrocution, or on burning oil, as the oil will float on the water and spread the blaze.

Many domestic extinguishers contain liquid carbon dioxide under pressure. When the handle is pressed, carbon dioxide is released as a gas that blankets the burning material and prevents oxygen from reaching it. Dry extinguishers spray powder, which then releases carbon dioxide gas. Wet extinguishers are often of the soda-acid type; when activated, sulphuric acid mixes with sodium bicarbonate, producing carbon dioxide. The gas pressure forces the solution out of a nozzle, and a foaming agent may be added.

Some extinguishers contain halons (hydrocarbons with one or more hydrogens substituted by a halogen such as chlorine, bromine, or fluorine). These are very effective at smothering fires, but cause damage to the ozone layer, and their use is now restricted.

firefly any winged nocturnal beetle of the family Lampyridae. They all emit light through the process of ◊bioluminescence.

fire protection methods available for fighting fires. Industrial and commercial buildings are often protected by an automatic sprinkler system: heat or smoke opens the sprinkler heads on a network of water pipes which spray the source of the fire. In circumstances where water is ineffective and may be dangerous, for example, for oil and petrol storage-tank fires, foam systems are used; for industrial plants containing flammable vapours, carbon dioxide is used; where electricity is involved, vaporizing liquids create a nonflammable barrier; for some chemicals only various dry powders can be used.

firewall in computing, security system built to block access to a particular computer or network while still allowing some types of data to flow in and out onto the Internet.

A firewall allows a company's employees to access sites on the World Wide Web or exchange e-mail while at the same time preventing hackers from gaining access to the company's data.

firewheel Australian tree *Stenocarpus sinuatus* native to rainforests of New South Wales and Queensland, which bears wheel-like whorls of bright red flowers.

FireWire in computing, Apple's implementation of the IEEE ◊1394 serial connection system.

firewood the principal fuel for some 2 billion people, mainly in the Third World. In principle a renewable energy source, firewood is being cut far faster than the trees can regenerate in many areas of Africa and Asia, leading to ◊deforestation.

In Mali, for example, wood provides 97% of total energy consumption, and deforestation is running at an estimated 9,000 hectares a year. The heat efficiency of firewood can be increased by use of well-designed stoves, but for many people they are either unaffordable or unavailable. With wood for fuel becoming scarcer the UN Food and Agricultural Organization has estimated that by the year 2000 3 billion people worldwide will face chronic problems in getting food cooked.

firmware computer program held permanently in a computer's ◊ROM (read-only memory) chips, as opposed to a program that is read in from external memory as it is needed.

First Amendment amendment to the US Constitution that guarantees freedom of religion, of speech, of assembly, and of the press. Adopted in 1791, the First Amendment is often quoted on the Internet, even by non-US citizens, in arguments over international attempts at censorship.

First Virtual Bank joint project with the bank FirstUSA which allows shoppers on the World Wide Web to open a central account using credit cards. Shoppers use their account numbers to make purchases at any of a number of participating merchants.

FISH FAQ

http://www.wh.whoi.edu/homepage/faq.html

Answers to hundreds of questions about fish and shellfish. Unfortunately the questions are not grouped, or searchable, in any way, but they do include answers to such things as 'Do fish sleep?' and 'Are Hawaiian monk seals coming back?'.

fish aquatic vertebrate that uses gills to obtain oxygen from fresh or sea water. There are three main groups: the bony fishes or Osteichthyes (goldfish, cod, tuna); the cartilaginous fishes or Chondrichthyes (sharks, rays); and the jawless fishes or Agnatha (hagfishes, lampreys).

Fishes of some form are found in virtually every body of water in the world except for the very salty water of the Dead Sea and some of the hot larval springs. Of the 30,000 fish species, approximately 2,500 are freshwater.

bony fishes These constitute the majority of living fishes (about 20,000 species). The skeleton is bone, movement is controlled by mobile fins, and the body is usually covered with scales. The gills are covered by a single flap. Many have a ◊swim bladder with

FISH

Spurdog, alewife, twaite shad, jollytail, tadpole madtom, bummalow, walleye pollock, wrestling halfbeak, mummichog, jolthead porgy, sweetlip emperor, and slippery dick are all common names for species of fish.

which the fish adjusts its buoyancy. Most lay eggs, sometimes in vast numbers; some ◊cod can produce as many as 28 million. These are laid in the open sea, and probably no more than 28 of them will survive to become adults. Those species that produce small numbers of eggs very often protect them in nests, or brood them in their mouths. Some fishes are internally fertilized and retain eggs until hatched inside the body, then giving birth to live young. Most bony fishes are ray-finned fishes, but a few, including lungfishes and coelacanths, are fleshy-finned.

cartilaginous fishes These are efficient hunters. There are fewer than 600 known species of sharks and rays. The skeleton is cartilage, the mouth is generally beneath the head, the nose is large and sensitive, and there is a series of open gill slits along the neck region. They have no swimbladder and, in order to remain buoyant, must keep swimming. They may lay eggs ('mermaid's purses') or bear live young. Some types of cartilaginous fishes, such as sharks, retain the shape they had millions of years ago.

jawless fishes Jawless fish have a body plan like that of some of the earliest vertebrates that existed before true fishes with jaws evolved. There is no true backbone but a ◊notochord. The lamprey attaches itself to the fishes on which it feeds by a suckerlike rasping mouth. Hagfishes are entirely marine, very slimy, and feed on carrion and injured fishes.

The world's largest fish is the whale shark *Rhineodon typus,* more than 20 m/66 ft long; the smallest is the dwarf pygmy goby *Pandaka pygmaea*), 7.5–9.9 mm long. The study of fishes is called ichthyology.

fish as food The nutrient composition of fish is similar to that of meat, except that there are no obvious deposits of fat. Examples of fish comparatively high in fat are salmon, mackerel, and herring. White fish such as cod, haddock, and whiting contain only 0.4–4% fat. Fish are good sources of B vitamins and iodine, and the fatty fish livers are good sources of A and D vitamins. Calcium can be obtained from fish with soft skeletons, such as sardines. Roe and caviar have a high protein content (20–25%).

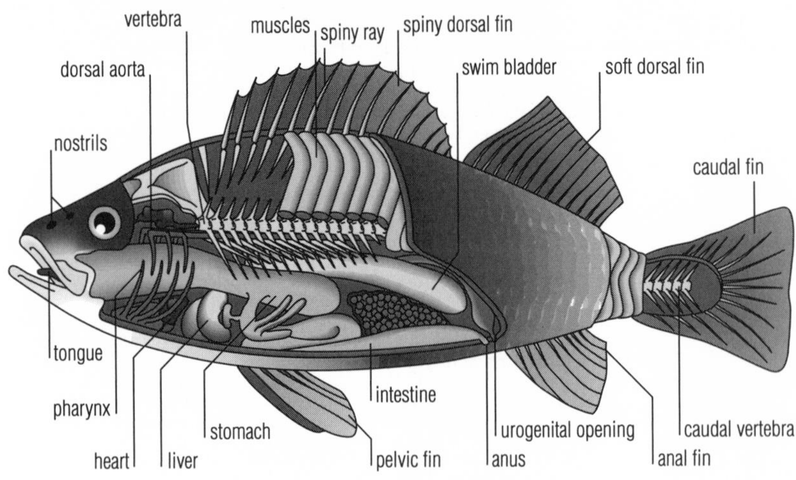

fish The anatomy of a fish. All fishes move through water using their fins for propulsion. The bony fishes, like the specimen shown here, constitute the largest group of fishes with about 20,000 species.

fisher or ***pekan*** North American ◊marten *Martes pennanti,* dark brown with greyish foreparts and blackish rump and tail. It is less arboreal than the smaller American marten *M. americana.*

fish farming or ***aquaculture*** raising fish (including molluscs and crustaceans) under controlled conditions in tanks and ponds, sometimes in offshore pens. It has been practised for centuries in the Far East, where Japan today produces some 100,000 tonnes of fish a year; the US, Norway, and Canada are also big producers. In the 1980s 10% of the world's consumption of fish was farmed, notably carp, catfish, trout, Atlantic salmon, turbot, eel, mussels, clams, oysters, and shrimp.

A total 600,000 tonnes of salmon was produced by world fish in 1995, accounting for 37% of salmon consumed. Fish farms are environmentally controversial because of the risk of escapees that could spread disease and alter the genetic balance of wild populations. In 1995 1,500,000 fish escaped from Norwegian fish farms.

By 1998 shrimp farms worldwide were producing 3 million tonnes of shrimps per year.

fishing and fisheries fisheries can be classified by (1) type of water: freshwater (lake, river, pond); marine (inshore, midwater, deep sea); (2) catch: for example, salmon fishing; (3) fishing method: diving, stunning or poisoning, harpooning, trawling, drifting. The world's total fish catch is about 100 million tonnes a year (1995).

marine fishing Most of the world's catch comes from the oceans, and marine fishing accounts for around 20% of the world's animal-based protein. A wide range of species is included in the landings of the world's marine fishing nations, but the majority belong to the herring and cod groups. The majority of the crustaceans landed are shrimps, and squid and bivalves, such as oysters, are dominant among the molluscs.

Almost all marine fishing takes place on or above the continental shelf, in the photic zone, the relatively thin surface layer (50 m/165 ft) of water that can be penetrated by light, allowing photosynthesis by plant ◊plankton to take place. **Pelagic fishing** exploits not only large fish such as tuna, which live near the surface in the open sea and are caught in purse-seine nets, with an annual catch of over 30 million tonnes, but also small, shoaling and plankton-feeding fish that live in the main body of the water.

Examples are herring, sardines, anchovies, and mackerel, which are caught with drift nets, purse seines, and pelagic trawls. The fish are often used for fish meal rather than for direct human consumption. **Demersal fishes**, such as haddock, halibut, plaice, and cod, live primarily on or near the ocean floor, and feed on various invertebrate marine animals. Over 20 million tonnes of them are caught each year by trawling.

freshwater fishing Such species as salmon and eels, which migrate to and from fresh and salt water for spawning, may be fished in either system. About a third of the total freshwater catch comes from ◊fish farming methods, which are better developed in freshwater than in marine systems. There is large demand for a , trout, carp, eel, bass, pike, perch, and catfish. These are caught in ponds, lakes, rivers, or swamps. In Africa, although marine fishing is generally more important, certain areas have significant freshwater fisheries; Lake Victoria annually yields a catch of 100,000 tonnes, which is four times the total catch from the whole eastern African seaboard. In western Europe there is very little food production from fresh water; instead the fish are usually exploited for recreational purposes or sport.

methods The gear and methods used to catch fish are very varied and show much geographical and historical variation. The method chosen for a particular situation will depend on the species being hunted and the nature of the habitat (for example, the speed of the current, the depth of water, and the roughness of the sea bed). It is often useful to divide gear types into active (for example trawls, seines, harpoons, dredges) and passive (drift nets, traps, hooks and lines). Passive gear relies on the fish's own movements to bring them into contact with it, and may involve some method of artificial attraction such as baits or lights. Most fishing gear is operated from boats, ranging from one-person canoes to trawlers about 100 m/330 ft long.

trawling Much of the world's fish catch is caught by trawls. These may be used on the sea bed (demersal) or in midwater (pelagic), but in all cases the equipment consists essentially of a tapered bag of netting which is towed through the water. The mouth of the net is kept open in the vertical plane by having floats on the headline and weights on the footrope. On bottom trawls these weights are usually hollow iron spheres that roll over the sea bed. In addition there may be tickler chains which help to dislodge or disturb fish from the sea bed in advance of the trawl so that they are more likely to be caught. There are three methods of keeping the net open in the horizontal plane: (1) pair trawling, in which the two trawl warps are towed by separate vessels; (2) beam trawling, in which the net is supported on a rigid frame consisting of a horizontal wooden or metal beam with a shoe at either end; and (3) otter trawling, in which an otter board (a weighted board with lines and baited hooks attached) is incorporated into each warp and acts as a hydroplane to push the warp out sideways. Most modern trawlers are otter trawlers, and many haul the net up over the stern rather than the side. The main problem with pelagic trawls is to control the depth of fishing and to relate this to the concentrations of fish. The most effective means of tracking fish for this purpose is by using an ◊echo sounder.

seine nets Seine nets operate by trapping fish within encircling gear. The **Danish seine** resembles a light trawl with very long side pieces, or wings, but is operated differently. The method consists of dropping a large buoy and then paying out up to 4 km/2.5 mi of warp in dogleg shape, then the net, followed by a further length of rope warp in reverse dogleg, bringing the boat back to the buoy, which is then picked up before hauling in the rope warps. As the ropes straighten on the sea bed, they channel the fish into a narrow path between them. The fish are then swept up by the net as it is hauled towards the boat. This method requires smooth sandy ground. **Beach seines** are similar to Danish seines but may consist simply of a wall of netting. They are set in a line or semicircle parallel to a beach and can then be hauled onto the beach, trapping the fish between the net and the shore. Salmon are often caught this way in estuaries. **Purse seines**, nets that close like a purse, are used to catch pelagic fish such as herring, mackerel, and tuna, which form dense shoals near the surface. Once a shoal has been located, usually by echo sounder, the net is shot around it by one vessel and later hauled in towards another. The nets are large, often as long as 30 nautical miles, and are not usually hauled aboard like trawls. Instead the fish are scooped or pumped out of the net into the ship's hold. They have caused a crisis in the South Pacific where Japan, Taiwan, and South Korea fish illegally in other countries' fishing zones.

gill nets Gill nets passively depend on the fish entangling themselves in the meshes of the net, usually being held fast by their gill covers. An example is the drift net used for pelagic fish, but in many areas it is now superseded by purse seines and pelagic trawls. Drift nets are walls of netting suspended from floats on the surface. Those used in the East Anglian herring fishery were only 70 m/230 ft long but were set in fleets up to 4 km/2.5 mi long. Herring were caught in them as they came up to the surface at night to feed. Other types of gill net can be used near the sea bed, and one, the trammel, is still used quite commonly in inshore fisheries along the south coast of England. This typically consists of a curtain of large- and small-mesh netting into which the fish swim, forcing the small-mesh net into the large and becoming trapped in a net bag.

traps Netting panels can be arranged to form traps into which fish are guided or attracted; those used on the northeast coast of England to catch salmon are good examples. Many crustaceans, such as lobsters and crabs, are normally taken in baited baskets set in strings of several hundred laid over suitable ground. Earthenware jars are used as octopus traps in the Mediterranean.

lines and hooks Although a distinct method of catching fish, lines and hooks can be regarded as a special type of trap. Natural or artificial baits are used and the gear may be fished anywhere from the sea bed to the surface. Hooks and lines fished off the sea bed may be towed from moving boats, which is called trolling. The largest lines, called long lines, are those used by the Japanese to catch tuna in ocean areas. These are up to 80 km/50 mi long and the baited hooks hang well below the surface from the buoyed lines.

dredges Dredges act like small trawls to collect molluscs and other sluggish or sessile organisms; some are hydraulic and use jets of water to dislodge the molluscs from the bottom and wash them into the dredge bag or directly onto the boat via a conveyor belt.

other methods Molluscs may also be gathered by hand, either on foot at low water or by divers below the shoreline. Rakes may be used to dig out cockles from within the sand. Other methods include dip, lift and cast nets, harpoons, and spears.

fission in physics, the splitting of a heavy atomic nucleus into two or more major fragments. It is accompanied by the emission of two or three neutrons and the release of large amounts of ◊nuclear energy.

Fission occurs spontaneously in nuclei of uranium-235, the main fuel used in nuclear reactors. However, the process can also be induced by bombarding nuclei with neutrons because a nucleus that has absorbed a neutron becomes unstable and soon splits. The neutrons released spontaneously by the fission of uranium nuclei may therefore be used in turn to induce further fissions, setting up a ◊chain reaction that must be controlled if it is not to result in a nuclear explosion.

Anyone who expects a source of power from the transformation of these atoms is talking moonshine.

ERNEST RUTHERFORD New Zealand physicist. *Physics Today* Oct 1970

fistula in medicine, an abnormal pathway developing between adjoining organs or tissues, or leading to the exterior of the body. A fistula developing between the bowel and the bladder, for instance, may give rise to urinary-tract infection by intestinal organisms.

fit in medicine, popular term for ◊convulsion.

fitness in genetic theory, a measure of the success with which a genetically determined character can spread in future generations. By convention, the normal character is assigned a fitness of one, and variants (determined by other ◊alleles) are then assigned fitness values relative to this. Those with fitness greater than one will spread more rapidly and will ultimately replace the normal allele; those with fitness less than one will gradually die out.

fixed font in computing, a ◊font that uses fixed, rather than proportional, spacing. It is a necessary option in off-line reader software and e-mail programs, since some ASCII art and tables do not display correctly without it.

fixed point temperature that can be accurately reproduced and used as the basis of a temperature scale. In the Celsius scale, the fixed points are the temperature of melting ice, defined to be 0°C (32°F), and the temperature of boiling water (at standard atmospheric pressure), defined to be 100°C (212°F).

fixed-point notation system in which numbers are represented using a set of digits with the decimal point always in its correct position. For very large and very small numbers this requires a lot of digits. In computing, the size of the numbers that can be handled in this way is limited by the capacity of the computer, and so the slower ◊floating-point notation is often preferred.

fjord or ***fiord*** narrow sea inlet enclosed by high cliffs. Fjords are found in Norway, New Zealand, and western parts of Scotland. They are formed when an overdeepened U-shaped glacial valley is drowned by a rise in sea-level. At the mouth of the fjord there is a characteristic lip causing a shallowing of the water. This is due to reduced glacial erosion and the deposition of moraine at this point.

Fiordland is the deeply indented southwest coast of South Island, New Zealand; one of the most beautiful inlets is Milford Sound.

flaccidity in botany, the loss of rigidity (turgor) in plant cells, caused by loss of water from the central vacuole so that the cytoplasm no longer pushes against the cellulose cell wall. If this condition occurs throughout the plant then wilting is seen.

Flaccidity can be induced in the laboratory by immersing the plant cell in a strong saline solution. Water leaves the cell by ◊osmosis causing the vacuole to shrink. In extreme cases the actual cytoplasm pulls away from the cell wall, a phenomenon known as plasmolysis.

flag in botany, another name for ◊iris, especially yellow flag (*Iris pseudacorus*), which grows wild in damp places throughout Europe; it is a true water plant but adapts to garden borders. It has a thick rhizome (underground stem), stiff bladelike leaves, and stems up to 150 cm/5 ft high. The flowers are large and yellow.

flag in computing, an indicator that can be set or unset in order to signal whether a particular condition is true – for example, whether the end of a file has been reached, or whether an overflow error has occurred. The indicator usually takes the form of a single binary digit, or bit (either 0 or 1).

flagellum small hairlike organ on the surface of certain cells. Flagella are the motile organs of certain protozoa and single-celled algae, and of the sperm cells of higher animals. Unlike ◊cilia, flagella usually occur singly or in pairs; they are also longer and have a more complex whiplike action.

Each flagellum consists of contractile filaments producing snakelike movements that propel cells through fluids, or fluids past cells. Water movement inside sponges is also produced by flagella.

flame angry public or private ◊electronic mail message. Users of the ◊Internet use flames to express disapproval of breaches of ◊netiquette or the voicing of an unpopular opinion. An offensive message posted to, for example, a USENET ◊newsgroup, will cause those offended to flame the culprit. Such flames maintain a level of discipline among the Internet's users.

flame test in chemistry, the use of a flame to identify metal ◊cations present in a solid.

A nichrome or platinum wire is moistened with acid, dipped in a compound of the element, either powdered or in solution, and then held in a hot flame. The colour produced in the flame is characteristic of metals present; for example, sodium burns with an orange-yellow flame, and potassium with a lilac one.

Flame test

element	*colour of flame*
sodium	orange-yellow
potassium	lilac
calcium	red or yellow-red
strontium, lithium	crimson
barium, manganese (manganese chloride)	pale green
copper, thallium, boron (boric acid)	bright green
lead, arsenic, antimony	livid blue
copper (copper (II) chloride)	bright blue

flame tree any of various trees with brilliant red flowers, including the smooth-stemmed semi-deciduous *Brachychiton acerifolium* with scarlet bell-shaped flowers, native to Australia, but spread throughout the tropics.

flame war in computing, heated electronic argument where few good points are made and most of the participants ◊flame each other repeatedly.

Several flame wars have passed into USENET legend, including the deliberate 1994 invasion of the **rec.pets.cats** newsgroup by the **alt.tasteless** newsgroup.

flamingo long-legged and long-necked wading bird, family Phoenicopteridae, of the stork order Ciconiiformes. Largest of the family is the greater or roseate flamingo *Phoenicopterus ruber*, found in Africa, the Caribbean, and South America, with delicate pink plumage and 1.25 m/4 ft tall. They sift the mud for food with their downbent bills, and build colonies of high, conelike mud nests, with a little hollow for the eggs at the top.

flannel flower Australian flower *Actinotus helianthi* found in New South Wales and Queensland, having white flannel-like bracts below the flower.

flare, solar brilliant eruption on the Sun above a ◊sunspot, thought to be caused by release of magnetic energy. Flares reach maximum brightness within a few minutes, then fade away over about an hour. They eject a burst of atomic particles into space at up to 1,000 kps/600 mps. When these particles reach Earth they can cause radio blackouts, disruptions of the Earth's magnetic field, and ◊aurorae.

flash flood flood of water in a normally arid area brought on by a sudden downpour of rain. Flash floods are rare and usually occur in mountainous areas. They may travel many kilometres from the site of the rainfall.

Because of the suddenness of flash floods, little warning can be given of their occurrence. In 1972 a flash flood at Rapid City, South Dakota, USA, killed 238 people along Rapid Creek.

flash memory type of ◊EEPROM memory that can be erased and reprogrammed without removal from the computer.

flashover small fire that erupts suddenly into a much larger one. They can occur if there is sufficient build up of heat from a small fire to ignite the mixture of gas and smoke produced. This increases temperatures further igniting surroundings. Flashovers can occur extremely rapidly with temperatures of 1,100°C being reached in seconds.

FlashPix in computing, a ◊file format for digital imaging intended as a universal standard for both individual multimedia applications and external communications over online services. It was developed collaboratively by Kodak, Hewlett-Packard, Live Picture, and Microsoft in 1996.

flash point in physics, the lowest temperature at which a liquid or volatile solid heated under standard conditions gives off sufficient vapour to ignite on the application of a small flame.

The **fire point** of a material is the temperature at which full combustion occurs. For safe storage of materials such as fuel or oil, conditions must be well below the flash and fire points to reduce fire risks to a minimum.

flash upgrade in computing, technique for upgrading firmware by updating the software embedded in it. It is used particularly for modems and ◊EPROMs.

flatfish bony fishes of the order Pleuronectiformes, having a characteristically flat, asymmetrical body with both eyes (in adults) on the upper side. Species include flounders, turbots, halibuts, plaice, and the European soles.

flat screen type of display suitable for portable computers such as LCD (◊liquid crystal display) or gas plasma screens (see ◊plasma display). Flat-screen, or flat-panel, displays are compact and lightweight compared to traditional cathode-ray tube monitors and TV sets.

It is predicted that eventually all TV screens will be made using this type of technology.

flatworm invertebrate of the phylum Platyhelminthes. Some are free-living, but many are parasitic (for example, tapeworms and flukes). The body is simple and bilaterally symmetrical, with one opening to the intestine. Many are hermaphroditic (with both male and female sex organs) and practise self-fertilization.

flax any of a group of plants including the cultivated *L. usitatissimum;* **linen** is produced from the fibre in its stems. The seeds yield **linseed oil**, used in paints and varnishes. The plant, of almost worldwide distribution, has a stem up to 60 cm/24 in high, small leaves, and bright blue flowers. (Genus *Linum,* family Linaceae.)

After extracting the oil, what is left of the seeds is fed to cattle. The stems are retted (soaked) in water after harvesting, and then dried, rolled, and scutched (pounded), separating the fibre from the central core of woody tissue. The long fibres are spun into linen thread, twice as strong as cotton, yet more delicate, and suitable for lace; shorter fibres are used to make string or paper.

Annual world production of flax fibre amounts to approximately 60,000 tonnes, with Russia, Ukraine, Belarus, and Latvia accounting for half of the total. Other producers are Belgium, the Netherlands, and Northern Ireland.

> *Colour possessed me. I didn't have to pursue it. It will possess me always ... This is the meaning of this happy hour: colour and I are one. I am a painter.*
>
> PAUL KLEE Swiss artist. *The Diaries of Paul Klee*, April 1914

FLEA

As a flea jumps, its rate of acceleration is 20 times that of the space shuttle during launching. It reaches a speed of 100 m per sec within the first 500th of a second.

flea wingless insect of the order Siphonaptera, with blood-sucking mouthparts. Fleas are parasitic on warm-blooded animals. Some fleas can jump 130 times their own height.

Species include the human flea *Pulex irritans;* the rat flea *Xenopsylla cheopsis,* the transmitter of plague and typhus; and (fostered by central heating) the cat and dog fleas *Ctenocephalides felis* and *C. canis.*

fleabane any of several plants of two related groups, belonging to the daisy family. Common fleabane (*P. dysenterica*) has golden-yellow flower heads and grows in wet and marshy places throughout Europe. (Genera *Pulicaria* and *Erigeron,* family Compositae.)

Fleming, Alexander (1881–1955) Scottish bacteriologist who discovered the first antibiotic drug, ◊penicillin, in 1928. In 1922 he had discovered lysozyme, an antibacterial enzyme present in saliva, nasal secretions, and tears. While studying this, he found an unusual mould growing on a neglected culture dish, which he isolated and grew into a pure culture; this led to his discovery of penicillin. It came into use in 1941. In 1945 he won the Nobel Prize for Physiology or Medicine with Howard W Florey and Ernst B Chain, whose research had brought widespread realization of the value of penicillin.

Fleming, (John) Ambrose (1849–1945)

English electrical physicist and engineer who invented the thermionic valve in 1904 and devised Fleming's rules. Knighted 1929.

Mary Evans Picture Library

Fleming's rules memory aids used to recall the relative directions of the magnetic field, current, and motion in an electric generator or motor, using one's fingers. The three directions are represented by the thu*m*b (for *m*otion), *f*orefinger (for *f*ield), and second finger (for ◊conventional ◊current), all held at right angles to each other. The right hand is used for generators and the left for motors.

The rules were devised by the English physicist John Fleming.

flesh fly medium-sized fly varying from golden-brown to dark grey. The larvae feed on carrion and animal waste, though the larvae of *Wohlfahrtia* often invade the skin of children and young animals and other larvae will cause myiasis (invasion of the tissues) when the skin is already broken by a cut or abrasion.

classification Flesh flies are members of the genera *Sarcophaga* and *Wohlfahrtia* in the family Sarcophagidae of the insect order Diptera, class Insecta, phylum Arthropoda.

flexor any muscle that bends a limb. Flexors usually work in opposition to other muscles, the extensors, an arrangement known as antagonistic.

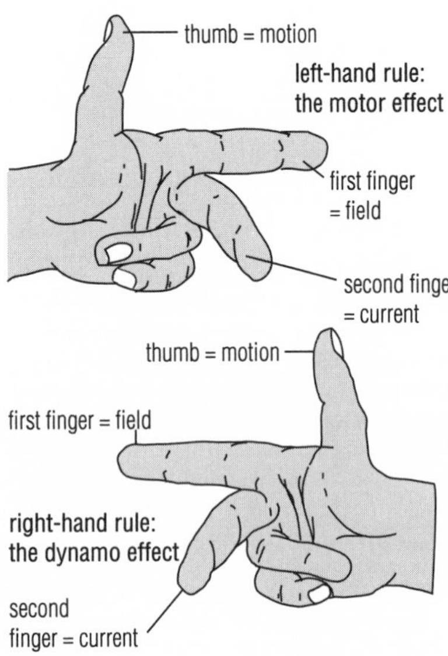

Fleming's rules *Fleming's rules give the direction of the magnetic field, motion, and current in electrical machines. The left hand is used for motors, and the right hand for generators and dynamos.*

flight or ***aviation*** method of transport in which aircraft carry people and goods through the air. People first took to the air in ◊balloons and began powered flight in 1852 in ◊airships, but the history of flying, both for civilian and military use, is dominated by the ◊aeroplane. The earliest planes were designed for gliding; the advent of the petrol engine saw the first powered flight by the ◊Wright brothers in 1903 in the USA. This inspired the development of aircraft throughout Europe. Biplanes were succeeded by monoplanes in the 1930s. The first jet plane (see ◊jet propulsion) was produced in 1939, and after the end of World War II the development of jetliners brought about a continuous expansion in passenger air travel. In 1969 came the supersonic aircraft ◊Concorde.

history In the 14th century the English philosopher Roger Bacon spoke of constructing an aircraft by means of a hollow globe and liquid fire. He was followed in the 15th century by Albert of Saxony, who also spoke of balloon flight by means of fire in a light sphere. During the 16th and 17th centuries a number of fantastic ideas were put forward; one was that swans' eggs be filled with sulphur or mercury and thereby drawn up to the Sun.

early ideas Francisco de Lana in 1670 proposed that four hollow balls made of very thin brass should be emptied of air. To them should be attached a small boat and sail, and in that way a balloon would be contrived which could carry a person. The idea was not feasible, since the globes, made of brass only 0.1 mm thick, would have collapsed by reason of their own weight. But although de Lana saw this difficulty, he argued that their shape would prevent that.

balloons It was not until the next century that the real ◊balloon was invented. The beginning of the development of the balloon was the work of two brothers, Joseph and Etienne Montgolfier, who came to the conclusion that a paper bag filled with a 'substance of a cloud-like nature' would float in the atmosphere. They made a number of experiments which attracted attention and further efforts from others. Progress was made gradually, and the first person-carrying ascent took place in October 1783, when Pilatre de Rozier went up in a Montgolfier captive balloon. The first woman to ascend was Madame Thible, who went up from Lyons in 1784. In 1859 a flight of over 1,600 km/994 mi was made in the USA.

adding power It had long been recognized that the difficulty with balloons was navigating through the air. Oars were tried, but were not successful. The first attempt to navigate the balloon by means of a small, light engine came in 1852, the experiment being made by Henri Giffard. From 1897 the development of the airship was the special work of Ferdinand ◊Zeppelin. In 1900 he made his first flight with a dirigible balloon carrying five men. It was made of aluminium, supported by gas-bags, and driven by two motors, each of about 12 kW. His first experiment met with some success, a second, more powerful version was wrecked, and a third met with great success. This airship carried 11 passengers and attained a speed of about 55 kph/34 mph, travelling about 400 km/248 mi in 11 hours, but was wrecked by a storm in 1908, caught fire, and was completely destroyed.

powered flight In the late 19th century experiments were being made with soaring machines and hang gliders, chiefly by Otto Lilienthal, who, with an arrangement formed on the plan of birds' wings, attempted to imitate their 'soaring flight'. Following up Lilienthal's ideas, the Wright brothers produced their first powered aeroplane in 1903. Their first successful machine was simply an aeroplane that flew in a straight line, but this received many modifications; and in 1908 they went to France to carry on experiments, during which Wilbur Wright created a record by remaining in the air for over an hour while carrying a passenger. He also attained a speed of 60 kph/37 mph.

In Europe, at the beginning of the 20th century, France led in aeroplane design and Louis Blériot brought aviation much publicity by crossing the English Channel in 1909, as did the Reims air races of that year. The first powered flight in the UK was made by Samuel Franklin Cody 1908. In 1912 Sopwith and Bristol both built small biplanes. The first big twin-engined aeroplane was the Handley Page bomber 1917. The stimulus of World War I (1914–18) and rapid development of the petrol engine led to increased power, and speeds rose to 320 kph/200 mph. Streamlining the body of planes became imperative: the body, wings, and exposed parts were reshaped to reduce drag. Eventually the biplane was superseded by the internally braced monoplane structure, for example, the Hawker Hurricane and Supermarine Spitfire fighters and Avro Lancaster and Boeing Flying Fortress bombers of World War II (1939–45).

jet aircraft The German Heinkel 178, built in 1939, was the first jet plane; it was driven, not by a ◊propeller as all planes before it, but by a jet of hot gases. The first British jet aircraft, the Gloster E.28/39, flew from Cranwell, Lincolnshire, on 15 May 1941, powered by a jet engine invented by British engineer Frank Whittle. Twin-jet Meteor fighters were in use by the end of WWII. The rapid development of the jet plane led to enormous increases in power and speed until air-compressibility effects were felt near the speed of sound, which at first seemed to be a flight speed limit (the sound barrier). The sound barrier was first broken in the USA in 1947 by a rocket-powered aircraft piloted by Chuck Yeager. To attain ◊supersonic speed, streamlining the aircraft body became insufficient: wings were swept back, engines buried in wings and tail units, and bodies were even eliminated in all-wing delta designs. In the 1950s the first jet airliners, such as the Comet (first introduced in 1949), were introduced into service. Today jet planes dominate both military and civilian aviation, although many light planes still use piston engines and propellers. The late 1960s saw the introduction of the ◊jumbo jet, and in 1976 the Anglo-French Concorde, which makes a transatlantic crossing in under three hours, came into commercial service.

other developments During the 1950s and 1960s research was done on V/STOL (vertical and/or short takeoff and landing) aircraft. The British Harrier jet fighter has been the only VTOL aircraft to achieve commercial success, but STOL technology has fed into subsequent generations of aircraft. The 1960s and 1970s also saw the development of variable geometry ('swing-wing') aircraft, the wings of

HOW DO PLANES FLY?

http://observe.ivv.nasa.gov/nasa/exhibits/planes/planes_1a.html

Lucid exposition of the whys and hows connected with the flight of an aeroplane. Kids are invited to perform a number of related experiments and the answers are given with a series of fun interactive steps.

which can be swept back in flight to achieve higher speeds. In the 1980s much progress was made in 'fly-by-wire' aircraft with computer-aided controls. International partnerships have developed both civilian and military aircraft. The airbus is a wide-bodied airliner built jointly by companies from France, Germany, the UK, the Netherlands, and Spain. The Eurofighter 2000 is a joint project between the UK, Italy, Germany, and Spain. The B-2 bomber, (a stealth bomber) developed by the US Air Force in 1989, is invisible to radar. The altitude record for a solar-powered plane was set in 1997 by Pathfinder, a 30-m/98-ft wingspan aircraft, which reached 20,528 m/67,349 ft above sea level over Hawaii.

flight simulator computer-controlled pilot-training device, consisting of an artificial cockpit mounted on hydraulic legs, that simulates the experience of flying a real aircraft. Inside the cockpit, the trainee pilot views a screen showing a computer-controlled projection of the view from a real aircraft, and makes appropriate adjustments to the controls. The computer monitors these adjustments, changes both the alignment of the cockpit on its hydraulic legs, and the projected view seen by the pilot. In this way a trainee pilot can progress to quite an advanced stage of training without leaving the ground.

flint compact, hard, brittle mineral (a variety of chert), brown, black, or grey in colour, found as nodules in limestone or shale deposits. It consists of cryptocrystalline (grains too small to be visible even under a light microscope) ◊silica, SiO_2, principally in the crystalline form of quartz. Implements fashioned from flint were widely used in prehistory.

The best flint, used for Neolithic tools, is **floorstone**, a shiny black flint that occurs deep within chalk.

Because of their hardness (7 on the ◊Mohs' scale), flint splinters are used for abrasive purposes and, when ground into powder, added to clay during pottery manufacture. Flints have been used for making fire by striking the flint against steel, which produces a spark, and for discharging guns. Flints in cigarette lighters are made from cerium alloy.

flip-flop in computing, another name for a ◊bistable circuit.

floating state of equilibrium in which a body rests on or is suspended in the surface of a fluid (liquid or gas). According to ◊Archimedes' principle, a body wholly or partly immersed in a fluid will be subjected to an upward force, or upthrust, equal in magnitude to the weight of the fluid it has displaced.

If the ◊density of the body is greater than that of the fluid, then its weight will be greater than the upthrust and it will sink. However, if the body's density is less than that of the fluid, the upthrust will be the greater and the body will be pushed upwards towards the surface. As the body rises above the surface the amount of fluid that it displaces (and therefore the magnitude of the upthrust) decreases. Eventually the upthrust acting on the submerged part of the body will equal the body's weight, equilibrium will be reached, and the body will float.

floating-point notation system in which numbers are represented by means of a decimal fraction and an exponent. For example, in floating-point notation, 123,000,000,000 would be represented as 0.123×10^{12}, where 0.123 is the fraction, or mantissa, and 12 the exponent. The exponent is the power of 10 by which the fraction must be multiplied in order to obtain the true value of the number.

In computing, floating-point notation enables programs to work with very large and very small numbers using only a few digits; however, it is slower than ◊fixed-point notation and suffers from small rounding errors.

flocculation in soils, the artificially induced coupling together of particles to improve aeration and drainage. Clay soils, which have very tiny particles and are difficult to work, are often treated in this way. The method involves adding more lime to the soil.

floppy disc in computing, a storage device consisting of a light, flexible disc enclosed in a cardboard or plastic jacket. The disc is placed in a disc drive, where it rotates at high speed. Data are recorded magnetically on one or both surfaces.

Floppy discs were invented by IBM in 1971 as a means of loading programs into the computer. They were originally 20 cm/8 in in diameter and typically held about 240 ◊kilobytes of data. Present-day floppy discs, widely used on ◊microcomputers, are usually either 13.13 cm/5.25 in or 8.8 cm/3.5 in in diameter, and generally hold 0.5–2 ◊megabytes, depending on the disc size, recording method, and whether one or both sides are used.

Floppy discs are inexpensive, and light enough to send through the post, but have slower access speeds and are more fragile than hard discs. (See also ◊disc).

FLOPS (abbreviation for ***floating point operations per second***) measure of the speed at which a computer program can be run.

floptical disc or ***erasable optical disc*** in computing, a type of optical disc that can be erased and loaded with new data, just like a magnetic disc. By contrast, most optical discs are read-only. A single optical disc can hold as much as 1,000 megabytes of data, about 800 times more than a typical floppy disc. Floptical discs need a special disc drive, but some such drives are also capable of accepting standard 3.5 inch floppy discs.

floral diagram diagram showing the arrangement and number of parts in a flower, drawn in cross section. An ovary is drawn in the centre, surrounded by representations of the other floral parts, indicating the position of each at its base. If any parts such as the petals or sepals are fused, this is also indicated. Floral diagrams allow the structure of different flowers to be compared, and are usually shown with the floral formula.

floral formula symbolic representation of the structure of a flower. Each kind of floral part is represented by a letter (K for calyx, C for corolla, P for perianth, A for androecium, G for gynoecium) and a number to indicate the quantity of the part present, for example, C5 for a flower with five petals. The number is in brackets if the parts are fused. If the parts are arranged in distinct whorls within the flower, this is shown by two separate figures, such as A5 + 5, indicating two whorls of five stamens each.

A flower with radial symmetry is known as **actinomorphic**; a flower with bilateral symmetry as **zygomorphic**.

floret small flower, usually making up part of a larger, composite flower head. There are often two different types present on one flower head: disc florets in the central area, and ray florets around the edge which usually have a single petal known as the ligule. In the common daisy, for example, the disc florets are yellow, while the ligules are white.

flotation, law of law stating that a floating object displaces its own weight of the fluid in which it floats. See ◊Archimedes principle.

flotation process common method of preparing mineral ores for subsequent processing by making use of the different wetting properties of various components. The ore is finely ground and then mixed with water and a specially selected wetting agent. Air is bubbled through the mixture, forming a froth; the desired ore particles attach themselves to the bubbles and are skimmed off, while unwanted dirt or other ores remain behind.

flounder small flatfish *Platychthys flesus* of the NE Atlantic and Mediterranean, although it sometimes lives in estuaries. It is dull in colour and grows to 50 cm/1.6 ft.

FLOUNDER

Flounders attempt to merge into any background. They will even assume an approximate chequered pattern if the floor of their tank resembles a chess-board.

flour beetle beetle that is a major pest of stored agricultural products, such as flour. They are found worldwide in granaries and stores where both the adult beetles and the larvae feed on damaged grain or flour. Neither adults nor larvae can eat intact grains.

classification Flour beetles are in the genus *Tribolium,* family Tenebrionidae, class Insecta, phylum Arthropoda.

flow chart diagram, often used in computing, to show the possible paths that data can take through a system or program.

A **system flow chart**, or **data flow chart**, is used to describe the flow of data through a complete data-processing system. Different graphic symbols represent the clerical operations involved and the different input, storage, and output equipment required. Although the flow chart may indicate the specific programs used, no details are given of how the programs process the data.

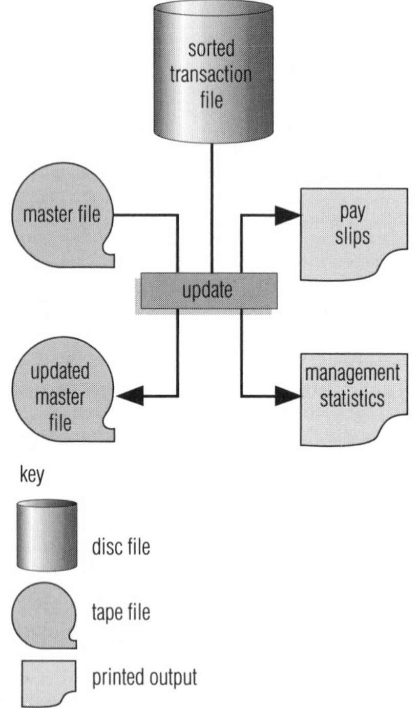

flow chart *A system flow chart describes the flow of data through a data-processing system. This chart shows the data flow in a basic accounting system.*

A **program flow chart** is used to describe the flow of data through a particular computer program, showing the exact sequence of operations performed by that program in order to process the data. Different graphic symbols are used to represent data input and output, decisions, branches, and ◊subroutines.

flow control in data communications, hardware or software signals that control the flow of data to ensure that it is not transmitted too quickly for the receiving computer to handle.

flower the reproductive unit of an angiosperm or flowering plant, typically consisting of four whorls of modified leaves: ◊sepals, ◊petals, ◊stamens, and ◊carpels. These are borne on a central axis or ◊receptacle. The many variations in size, colour, number, and arrangement of parts are closely related to the method of pollination. Flowers adapted for wind pollination typically have reduced or absent petals and sepals and long, feathery ◊stigmas that hang outside the flower to trap airborne pollen. In contrast, the petals of insect-pollinated flowers are usually conspicuous and brightly coloured.

structure The sepals and petals form the **calyx** and **corolla** respectively and together comprise the **perianth** with the function of protecting the reproductive organs and attracting pollinators.

The stamens lie within the corolla, each having a slender stalk, or filament, bearing the pollen-containing anther at the top. Collectively they are known as the **androecium** (male organs). The

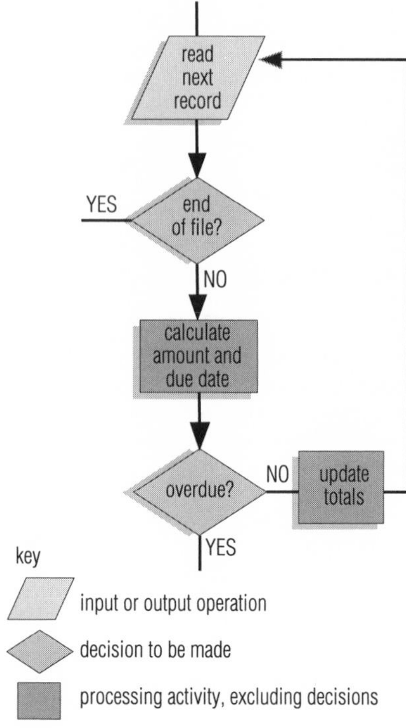

flow chart *A program flow chart shows the sequence of operations needed to achieve a task, in this case reading customer accounts and calculating the amount due for each customer. After an account has been processed, the program loops back to process the next one.*

inner whorl of the flower comprises the carpels, each usually consisting of an ovary in which are borne the ◊ovules, and a stigma borne at the top of a slender stalk, or style. Collectively the carpels are known as the **gynoecium** (female organs).

types of flower In size, flowers range from the tiny blooms of duckweeds scarcely visible to the naked eye to the gigantic flowers of the Malaysian *Rafflesia,* which can reach over 1 m/3 ft across. Flowers may either be borne singly or grouped together in inflorescences. The stalk of the whole ◊inflorescence is termed a **peduncle**, and the stalk of an individual flower is termed a **pedicel**. A

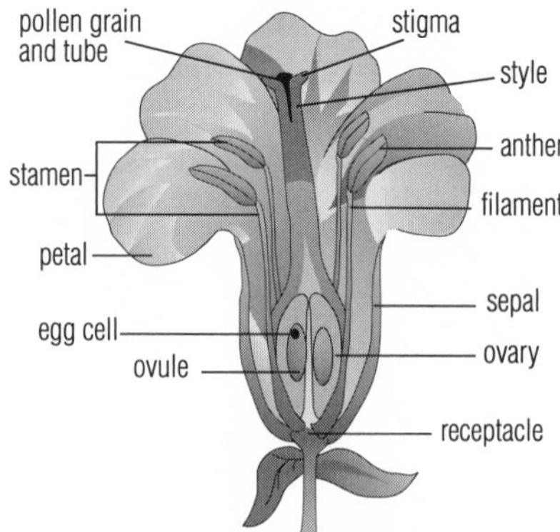

flower *Cross section of a typical flower showing its basic components: sepals, petals, stamens (anthers and filaments), and carpel (ovary and stigma). Flowers vary greatly in the size, shape, colour, and arrangement of these components.*

flower is termed hermaphrodite when it contains both male and female reproductive organs. When male and female organs are carried in separate flowers, they are termed **monoecious**; when male and female flowers are on separate plants, the term **dioecious** is used.

flowering plant term generally used for ◊angiosperms, which bear flowers with various parts, including sepals, petals, stamens, and carpels.

Sometimes the term is used more broadly, to include both angiosperms and ◊gymnosperms, in which case the ◊cones of conifers and cycads are referred to as 'flowers'. Usually, however, the angiosperms and gymnosperms are referred to collectively as ◊seed plants, or spermatophytes.

In 1996 UK palaeontologists found fossils in southern England of what may be the world's oldest flowering plant. *Bevhalstia pebja,* a wetland herb about 25 cm/10 in high, has been dated as early Cretaceous, about 130 million years old.

flue-gas desulphurization process of removing harmful sulphur pollution from gases emerging from a boiler. Sulphur compounds such as sulphur dioxide are commonly produced by burning ◊fossil fuels, especially coal in power stations, and are the main cause of ◊acid rain.

The process is environmentally beneficial but expensive, adding about 10% to the cost of electricity generation.

fluid any substance, either liquid or gas, in which the molecules are relatively mobile and can 'flow'.

fluid mechanics the study of the behaviour of fluids (liquids and gases) at rest and in motion. Fluid mechanics is important in the study of the weather, the design of aircraft and road vehicles, and in industries, such as the chemical industry, which deal with flowing liquids or gases.

fluid, supercritical fluid brought by a combination of heat and pressure to the point at which, as a near vapour, it combines the properties of a gas and a liquid. Supercritical fluids are used as solvents in chemical processes, such as the extraction of lubricating oil from refinery residues or the decaffeination of coffee, because they avoid the energy-expensive need for phase changes (from liquid to gas and back again) required in conventional distillation processes.

fluke any of various parasitic flatworms of the classes Monogenea and Digenea, that as adults live in and destroy the livers of sheep, cattle, horses, dogs, and humans. Monogenetic flukes can complete their life cycle in one host; digenetic flukes require two or more hosts, for example a snail and a human being, to complete their life cycle.

An estimated 40 million people worldwide are infected by foodborne flukes, mostly from undercooked or raw fish or shellfish, according to a 1994 WHO report.

fluorescence in scientific usage, very short-lived ◊luminescence (a glow not caused by high temperature). Generally, the term is used for any luminescence regardless of the persistence. ◊Phosphorescence lasts a little longer.

Fluorescence is used in strip and other lighting, and was developed rapidly during World War II because it was a more efficient means of illumination than the incandescent lamp. Recently, small bulb-size fluorescence lamps have reached the market. It is claimed that, if widely used, their greater efficiency could reduce demand for electricity. Other important applications are in fluorescent screens for television and cathode-ray tubes.

fluorescence microscopy technique for examining samples under a ◊microscope without slicing them into thin sections. Instead, fluorescent dyes are introduced into the tissue and used as a light source for imaging purposes. Fluorescent dyes can also be bonded to monoclonal antibodies and used to highlight areas where particular cell proteins occur.

fluoridation addition of small amounts of fluoride salts to drinking water by certain water authorities to help prevent tooth decay. Experiments in Britain, the USA, and elsewhere have indicated that a concentration of fluoride of 1 part per million in tap water retards the decay of children's teeth by more than 50%.

Much concern has been expressed about the risks of medicating the population at large by the addition of fluoride to the water supply, but the medical evidence demonstrates conclusively that there is no risk to the general health from additions of 1 part per million of fluoride to drinking water.

fluoride negative ion (F^-) formed when hydrogen fluoride dissolves in water; compound formed between fluorine and another element in which the fluorine is the more electronegative element (see ◊electronegativity, halide).

In parts of India, the natural level of fluoride in water is 10 parts per million. This causes fluorosis, or chronic fluoride poisoning, mottling teeth and deforming bones.

fluorine pale yellow, gaseous, nonmetallic element, symbol F, atomic number 9, relative atomic mass 19. It is the first member of the halogen group of elements, and is pungent, poisonous, and highly reactive, uniting directly with nearly all the elements. It occurs naturally as the minerals fluorite (CaF_2) and cryolite (Na_3AlF_6). Hydrogen fluoride is used in etching glass, and the freons, which all contain fluorine, are widely used as refrigerants.

Fluorine was discovered by the Swedish chemist Karl Scheele in 1771 and isolated by the French chemist Henri Moissan in 1886. Combined with uranium as UF_6, it is used in the separation of uranium isotopes.

The Infrared Space Observatory detected hydrogen fluoride molecules in an interstellar gas cloud in the constellation Sagittarius in 1997. It was the first time fluorine had been detected in space.

fluorite or ***fluorspar*** a glassy, brittle halide mineral, calcium fluoride CaF_2, forming cubes and octahedra; colourless when pure, otherwise violet, blue, yellow, brown, or green.

Fluorite is used as a flux in iron and steel making; colourless fluorite is used in the manufacture of microscope lenses. It is also used for the glaze on pottery, and as a source of fluorine in the manufacture of hydrofluoric acid.

fluorocarbon compound formed by replacing the hydrogen atoms of a hydrocarbon with fluorine. Fluorocarbons are used as inert coatings, refrigerants, synthetic resins, and as propellants in aerosols.

There is concern that the release of fluorocarbons – particularly those containing chlorine (chlorofluorocarbons, CFCs) – depletes the ◊ozone layer, allowing more ultraviolet light from the Sun to penetrate the Earth's atmosphere, and increasing the incidence of skin cancer in humans.

FLY

Fruit flies (*Drosophila*) reach sexual maturity in less than two weeks. This means that there are 25 generations a year. Every female can lay 100 eggs or more.

fly any insect of the order Diptera. A fly has a single pair of wings, antennae, and compound eyes; the hind wings have become modified into knoblike projections (halteres) used to maintain equilibrium in flight. There are over 90,000 species.

The mouthparts project from the head as a proboscis used for sucking fluids, modified in some species, such as mosquitoes, to pierce a victim's skin and suck blood. Discs at the ends of hairs on their feet secrete a fluid enabling them to walk up walls and across ceilings. Flies undergo complete metamorphosis; their larvae (maggots) are without true legs, and the pupae are rarely enclosed in a cocoon. The sexes are similar and coloration is rarely vivid, though some are metallic green or blue. The fruitfly, genus *Drosophila,* is much used in genetic experiments as it is easy to keep, fast-breeding, and has easily visible chromosomes.

flying dragon lizard *Draco volans* of the family Agamidae. It lives in sotheast Asia, and can glide on flaps of skin spread and

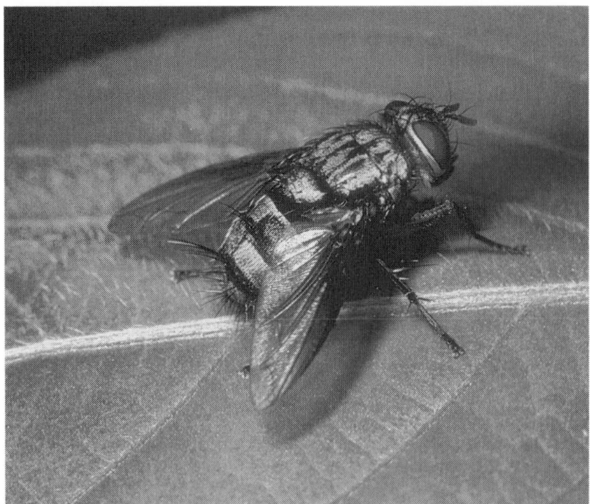

fly A tachinid fly Blepharella snyderi *in Kakamega Forest, Kenya. The females of the family Tachinidae lay their eggs on or near the bodies of other arthropods (future hosts), or on food which is likely to be eaten by a host at some point. The fly's larvae eventually live as internal parasites in other insects.*

supported by its ribs. This small (7.5 cm/3 in head and body) arboreal lizard can glide between trees for 6m/20 ft or more.

flying fish any marine bony fishes of the family Exocoetidae, order Beloniformes, best represented in tropical waters. They have winglike pectoral fins that can be spread to glide over the water.

flying fox another name for the fruit bat, a fruit-eating ◊bat of the suborder Megachiroptera.

flying gurnard any of various marine fishes of the order Dactylopteriformes (especially the genus *Dactylopterus*), having wing-like pectoral fins and capable of gliding for short distances.

They are not related to flying fishes.

flying lemur commonly used, but incorrect, name for ◊colugo.

It cannot fly, and it is not a lemur.

flying lizard another name for ◊flying dragon.

flying squirrel any of 43 known species of squirrel, not closely related to the true squirrels. They are characterized by a membrane along the side of the body from forelimb to hindlimb (in some species running to neck and tail) which allows them to glide through the air. Several genera of flying squirrel are found in the Old World; the New World has the genus *Glaucomys*. Most species are eastern Asian.

The giant flying squirrel *Petaurista* grows up to 1.1 m/3.5 ft including tail.

flystrike or ***blowfly strike*** or ***sheep strike*** infestation of the flesh of living sheep by blowfly maggots, especially those of the blue blowfly. It is one of the most costly sheep diseases in Australia, affecting all the grazing areas of New South Wales. Control has mainly been by insecticide, but non-chemical means, such as docking of tails and mulesing, are increasingly being encouraged. Mulesing involves an operation to remove the wrinkles of skin which trap moisture and lay the sheep open to infestation.

flythrough in ◊virtual reality, animation allowing users to view a model of a proposed or actual site as if they were inside it and moving through it.

For the 1996 Olympics in Atlanta, USA, flythroughs assisted site planners to identify areas in the main stadium where camera positions would be blocked by the audience, allowing solutions to be found in advance of construction.

flywheel heavy wheel in an engine that helps keep it running and smooths its motion. The ◊crankshaft in a petrol engine has a flywheel at one end, which keeps the crankshaft turning in between the intermittent power strokes of the pistons. It also comes into contact with the ◊clutch, serving as the connection between the engine and the car's transmission system.

FM in physics, abbreviation for ◊frequency modulation.

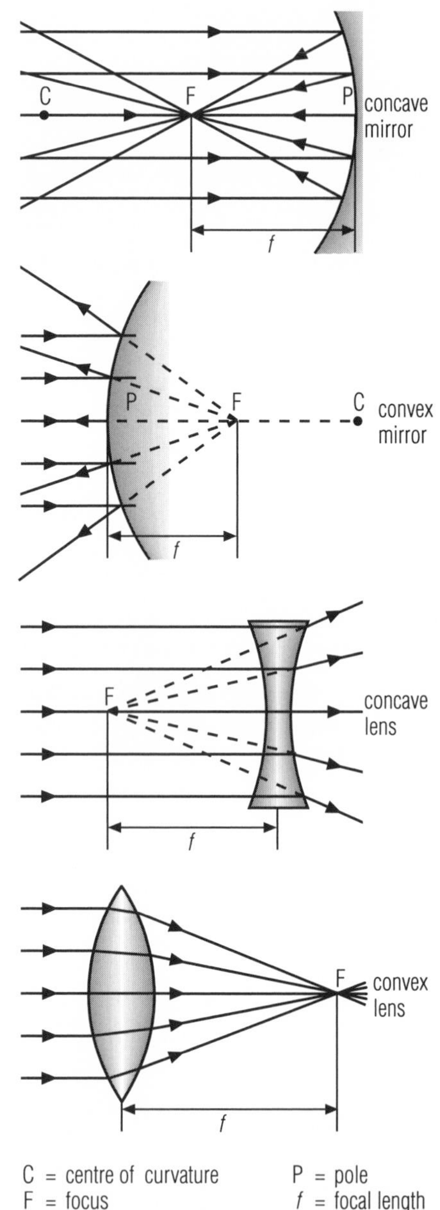

focal length The distance from the pole (P), or optical centre, of a lens or spherical mirror to its principal focus (F). The focal length of a spherical mirror is equal to half the radius of curvature ($f = \frac{CP}{2}$). *The focal length of a lens is inversely proportional to the power of that lens (the greater the power the shorter the focal length).*

FM synthesizer (abbreviation for ***frequency modulation synthesizer***) in computing, method for generating synthetic sounds based on techniques used to transmit FM radio signals.

FMV abbreviation for ◊full-motion video.

f-number or ***f-stop*** measure of the relative aperture of a telescope or camera lens; it indicates the light-gathering power of the lens. In photography, each successive f-number represents a halving of exposure speed.

focal length or ***focal distance*** the distance from the centre of a lens or curved mirror to the focal point. For a concave mirror or convex lens, it is the distance at which rays of light parallel to the principal axis of the mirror or lens are brought to a focus (for a mirror, this is half the radius of curvature). For a convex mirror or concave lens, it is the distance from the centre to the point from which rays of light parallel to the principal axis of the mirror or lens diverge.

With lenses, the greater the power (measured in dioptres) of the lens, the shorter its focal length. The human eye has a lens of adjustable focal length to allow the light from objects of varying distance to be focused on the retina.

focus in astronomy, either of two points lying on the major axis of an elliptical ◊orbit on either side of the centre. One focus marks the centre of mass of the system and the other is empty. In a circular orbit the two foci coincide at the centre of the circle and in a parabolic orbit the second focus lies at infinity. See ◊Kepler's Laws.

focus or ***focal point*** in optics, the point at which light rays converge, or from which they appear to diverge. Other electromagnetic rays, such as microwaves, and sound waves may also be brought together at a focus. Rays parallel to the principal axis of a lens or mirror are converged at, or appear to diverge from, the ◊principal focus.

focus in photography, the distance that a lens must be moved in order to focus a sharp image on the light-sensitive film at the back of the camera. The lens is moved away from the film to focus the image of closer objects. The focusing distance is often marked on a scale around the lens; however, some cameras now have an automatic focusing (autofocus) mechanism that uses an electric motor to move the lens.

fog cloud that collects at the surface of the Earth, composed of water vapour that has condensed on particles of dust in the atmosphere. Cloud and fog are both caused by the air temperature falling below ◊dew point. The thickness of fog depends on the number of water particles it contains. Officially, fog refers to a condition when visibility is reduced to 1 km/0.6 mi or less, and mist or haze to that giving a visibility of 1–2 km or about 1 mi.

There are two types of fog. An **advection fog** is formed by the meeting of two currents of air, one cooler than the other, or by warm air flowing over a cold surface. Sea fogs commonly occur where warm and cold currents meet and the air above them mixes. A **radiation fog** forms on clear, calm nights when the land surface loses heat rapidly (by radiation); the air above is cooled to below its dew point and condensation takes place. A **mist** is produced by condensed water particles, and a haze by smoke or dust.

In drought areas, for example, Baja California, Canary Islands, Cape Verde Islands, Namib Desert, Peru, and Chile, coastal fogs enable plant and animal life to survive without rain and are a potential source of water for human use (by means of water collectors exploiting the effect of condensation).

Industrial areas uncontrolled by pollution laws have a continual haze of smoke over them, and if the temperature falls suddenly, a dense yellow smog forms. At some airports since 1975 it has been possible for certain aircraft to land and take off blind in fog, using radar navigation.

fold in geology, a bend in ◊beds or layers of rock. If the bend is arched up in the middle it is called an **anticline**; if it sags downwards in the middle it is called a **syncline**. The line along which a bed of rock folds is called its axis. The axial plane is the plane joining the axes of successive beds.

folder in computing, name for a computer directory in Windows 95 and on the Macintosh operating system.

folic acid a ◊vitamin of the B complex. It is found in liver and green leafy vegetables, and is also synthesized by the intestinal bacteria. It is essential for growth, and plays many other roles in the body. Lack of folic acid causes anaemia because it is necessary for the synthesis of nucleic acids and the formation of red blood cells.

follicle in botany, a dry, usually many-seeded fruit that splits along one side only to release the seeds within. It is derived from a single ◊carpel. Examples include the fruits of the larkspurs *Delphinium* and columbine *Aquilegia*. It differs from a pod, which always splits open (dehisces) along both sides.

follicle in zoology, a small group of cells that surround and nourish a structure such as a hair (hair follicle) or a cell such as an egg (Graafian follicle; see ◊menstrual cycle).

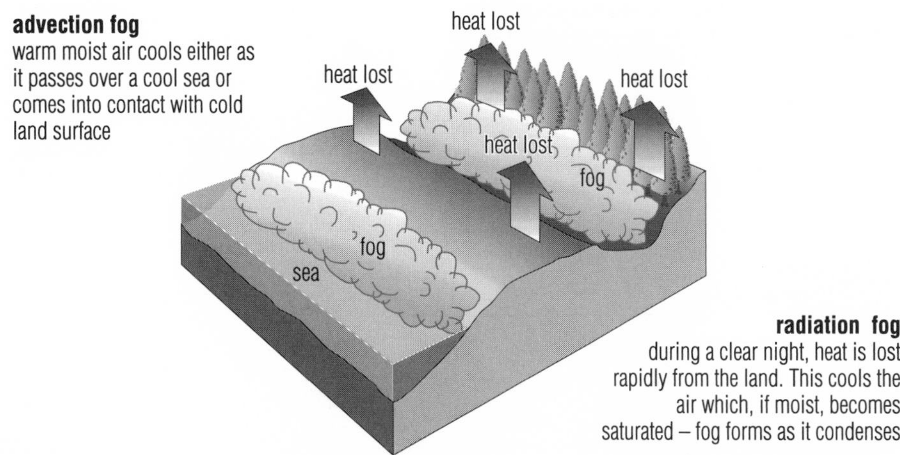
advection fog
warm moist air cools either as it passes over a cool sea or comes into contact with cold land surface
heat lost
heat lost
heat lost
heat lost
fog
fog
sea
radiation fog
during a clear night, heat is lost rapidly from the land. This cools the air which, if moist, becomes saturated – fog forms as it condenses

fog *Advection fog occurs when two currents of air, one cooler than the other meet, or by warm air flowing over a cold surface. Radiation fog forms through rapid heat loss from the land, causing condensation to take place and a mist to appear.*

follicle-stimulating hormone (FSH) a ◊hormone produced by the pituitary gland. It affects the ovaries in women, stimulating the production of an egg cell.

Luteinizing hormone is needed to complete the process. In men, FSH stimulates the testes to produce sperm. It is used to treat some forms of infertility.

follow-up post in computing, publicly posted reply to a USENET message; unlike a personal e-mail reply, follow-up post can be read by anyone.

Full-featured ◊newsreaders include a facility for setting the names of the newsgroups to which follow-ups should be posted. If, for example, an original message was posted to a number of groups, several of which were inappropriate, the person posting the follow-up might want to restrict further replies to only those groups where the message actually belongs.

Fomalhaut or ***Alpha Piscis Austrini*** the brightest star in the southern constellation ◊Piscis Austrinus and the 18th brightest star in the night sky. It is 22 light years from Earth, with a true luminosity 13 times that of the Sun.

Fomalhaut is one of a number of stars around which ◊IRAS (the Infra-Red Astronomy Satellite) detected excess infrared radiation, presumably from a region of solid particles around the star. This material may be a planetary system in the process of formation.

font or ***fount*** complete set of printed or display characters of the same typeface, size, and style (bold, italic, underlined, and so on).

Fonts used in computer setting are of two main types: bit-mapped and outline. **Bit-mapped fonts** are stored in the computer memory as the exact arrangement of ◊pixels or printed dots required to produce the characters in a particular size on a screen or printer. **Outline fonts** are stored in the computer memory as a set of instructions for drawing the circles, straight lines, and curves that make up the outline of each character. They require a powerful computer because each character is separately generated from a set of instructions and this requires considerable computation. Bit-mapped fonts become very ragged in appearance if they are enlarged and so a separate set of bit maps is required for each font size. In contrast, outline fonts can be scaled to any size and maintain exactly the same appearance.

food anything eaten by human beings and other animals and plants to sustain life and health. The building blocks of food are nutrients, and humans can utilize the following nutrients: **carbohydrates**, as starches found in bread, potatoes, and pasta; as simple sugars in sucrose and honey; as fibres in cereals, fruit, and vegetables; **proteins** as from nuts, fish, meat, eggs, milk, and some vegetables; **fats** as found in most animal products (meat, lard, dairy products, fish), also in margarine, nuts and seeds, olives, and edible oils; **vitamins**, found in a wide variety of foods, except for vitamin B_{12}, which is found mainly in foods of animal origin; **minerals**, found in a wide variety of foods (for example, calcium from milk and broccoli, iodine from seafood, and iron from liver and green vegetables); **water** ubiquitous in nature; **alcohol**, found in fermented distilled beverages, from 40% in spirits to 0.01% in low-alcohol lagers and beers.

Food is needed both for energy, measured in ◊calories or kilojoules, and nutrients, which are converted to body tissues. Some nutrients, such as fat, carbohydrate, and alcohol, provide mainly energy; other nutrients are important in other ways; for example, fibre is an aid to metabolism. Proteins provide energy and are necessary for building cell and tissue structure.

> *Food probably has a very great influence on the condition of men ... . Who knows if a well-prepared soup was not responsible for the pneumatic pump or a poor one for a war?*
>
> G C Lichtenberg German physicist and philosopher. *Aphorisms*, 'Notebook A' 14

Food and Agriculture Organization (FAO) United Nations specialized agency that coordinates activities to improve food and timber production and levels of nutrition throughout the world. It is also concerned with investment in agriculture and dispersal of emergency food supplies. It has headquarters in Rome and was founded in 1945.

The USA cut its FAO funding in 1990 from $61.4 million to $18 million because of its alleged politicization.

WORLD FOOD PROGRAMME

http://www.unicc.org/wfp/

Information on the work of the UN agency charged with addressing the needs of the one out of seven people on Earth who are starving. This is a good source of frequently updated information on international efforts to assist the victims of artificially created and natural disasters and of disaster mitigation initiatives.

food chain in ecology, a sequence showing the feeding relationships between organisms in a particular ◊ecosystem. Each organism depends on the next lowest member of the chain for its food.

Energy in the form of food is shown to be transferred from ◊autotrophs, or producers, which are principally plants and photosynthetic microorganisms, to a series of ◊heterotrophs, or consumers. The heterotrophs comprise the ◊herbivores, which feed on the producers; ◊carnivores, which feed on the herbivores; and ◊decomposers, which break down the dead bodies and waste products of all four groups (including their own), ready for recycling.

In reality, however, organisms have varied diets, relying on different kinds of foods, so that the food chain is an oversimplification. The more complex **food web** shows a greater variety of relationships, but again emphasizes that energy passes from plants to herbivores to carnivores.

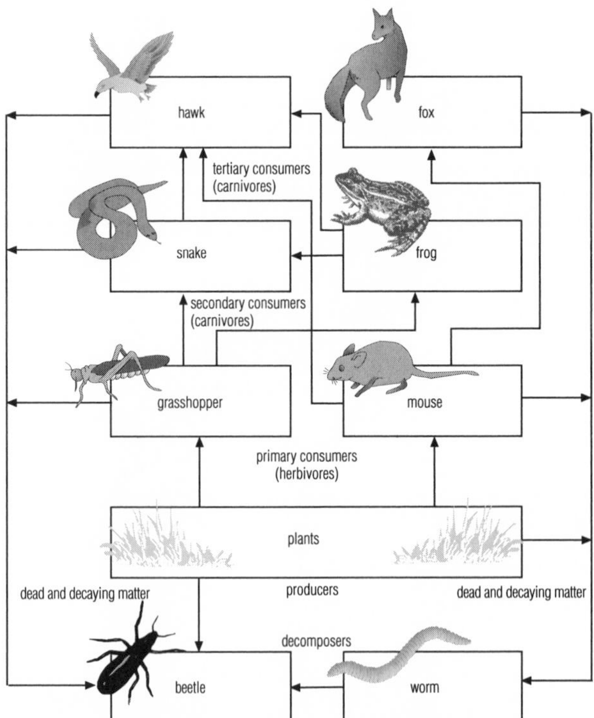

food chain *The complex interrelationships between animals and plants in a food chain. Food chains are normally only three or four links long. This is because most of the energy at each link is lost in respiration, and so cannot be passed on to the next link.*

Environmentalists have used the concept of the food chain to show how poisons and other forms of pollution can pass from one animal to another, threatening rare species. For example, the pesticide DDT has been found in lethal concentrations in the bodies of animals at the top of the food chain, such as the golden eagle *Aquila chrysaetos.*

food irradiation the exposure of food to low-level ◊irradiation to kill microorganisms; a technique used in ◊food technology. Irradiation is highly effective, and does not make the food any more radioactive than it is naturally. Irradiated food is used for astronauts and immunocompromised patients in hospitals. Some vitamins are partially destroyed, such as vitamin C, and it would be unwise to eat only irradiated fruit and vegetables.

The main cause for concern is that it may be used by unscrupulous traders to 'clean up' consignments of food, particularly shellfish, with high bacterial counts. Bacterial toxins would remain in the food, so that it could still cause illness, although irradiation would have removed signs of live bacteria. Stringent regulations would be needed to prevent this happening. Other damaging changes may take place in the food, such as the creation of ◊free radicals, but research so far suggests that the process is relatively safe.

food poisoning any acute illness characterized by vomiting and diarrhoea and caused by eating food contaminated with harmful bacteria (for example, ◊listeriosis), poisonous food (for example, certain mushrooms, puffer fish), or poisoned food (such as lead or arsenic introduced accidentally during processing). A frequent cause of food poisoning is ◊Salmonella bacteria. Salmonella comes in many forms, and strains are found in cattle, pigs, poultry, and eggs.

Deep freezing of poultry before the birds are properly cooked is a common cause of food poisoning. Attacks of salmonella also come from contaminated eggs that have been eaten raw or cooked only lightly. Pork may carry the roundworm *Trichinella,* and rye the parasitic fungus ergot. The most dangerous food poison is the bacillus that causes ◊botulism. This is rare but leads to muscle paralysis and, often, death. ◊Food irradiation is intended to prevent food poisoning.

food technology the application of science to the commercial processing of foodstuffs. Food is processed to make it more palatable or digestible, for which the traditional methods include boiling, frying, flour-milling, bread-, yoghurt-, and cheese-making, and brewing; or to prevent the growth of bacteria, moulds, yeasts, and other microorganisms; or to preserve it from spoilage caused by the action of ◊enzymes within the food that change its chemical composition, resulting in changes in flavour, odour, colour, and texture. These changes are not always harmful or undesirable; examples of desirable changes are the ripening of cream in butter manufacture, flavour development of cheese, and the hanging of meat to tenderize the muscle fibres. Fatty or oily foods suffer oxidation of the fats, which makes them rancid.

Preservation enables foods that are seasonally produced to be available all the year. Traditional forms of **food preservation** include salting, smoking, pickling, drying, bottling, and preserving in sugar. Modern food technology also uses many novel processes and additives, which allow a wider range of foodstuffs to be preserved. All foods undergo some changes in quality and nutritional value when subjected to preservation processes. No preserved food is identical in quality to its fresh counterpart, hence only food of the highest quality should be preserved.

In order to grow, bacteria, yeasts, and moulds need moisture, oxygen, a suitable temperature, and food. The various methods of food preservation aim to destroy the microorganisms within the food, to remove one or more of the conditions essential for their growth, or to make the foods unsuitable for their growth. Adding large amounts of salt or sugar reduces the amount of water available to microorganisms, because the water tied up by these solutes cannot be used for microbial growth. This is the principle in salting meat and fish, and in the manufacture of jams and jellies. These conditions also inhibit the enzyme activity in food. Preservatives may also be developed in the food by the controlled growth of microorganisms to produce fermentation that may make alcohol, or acetic or lactic acid. Examples of food preserved in this way are vinegar, sour milk, yoghurt, sauerkraut, and alcoholic beverages.

Refrigeration below 5°C/41°F (or below 3°C/37°F for cooked foods) slows the processes of spoilage, but is less effective for foods with a high water content. This process cannot kill microorganisms, nor stop their growth completely, and a failure to realize its limitations causes many cases of food poisoning. Refrigerator temperatures should be checked as the efficiency of the machinery (see ◊refrigeration) can decline with age, and higher temperatures are dangerous.

Deep freezing (–18°C/–1°F or below) stops almost all spoilage processes, except residual enzyme activity in uncooked vegetables and most fruits, which are blanched (dipped in hot water to destroy the enzymes) before freezing. Preservation by freezing works by rendering the water in foodstuffs unavailable to microorganisms by converting it to ice. Microorganisms cannot grow or divide while frozen, but most remain alive and can resume activity once defrosted. Some foods are damaged by freezing, notably soft fruits and salad vegetables, the cells of which are punctured by ice crystals, leading to loss of crispness. Fatty foods such as cow's milk and cream tend to separate. Freezing has little effect on the nutritive value of foods, though a little vitamin C may be lost in the blanching process for fruit and vegetables. Various processes are used for deep freezing foods commercially.

Pasteurization is used mainly for milk. By holding the milk at 72°C/161.6°F for 15 seconds, all disease-causing bacteria can be destroyed. Less harmful bacteria survive, so the milk will still go sour within a few days.

Ultra-heat treatment is used to produce UHT milk. This process uses higher temperatures than pasteurization, and kills all bacteria present, giving the milk a long shelf life but altering the flavour.

Drying is effective because both microorganisms and enzymes need water to be active. This is one of the oldest, simplest, and most effective way of preserving foods. In addition, drying concentrates the soluble ingredients in foods, and this high concentration prevents the growth of bacteria, yeasts, and moulds. Dried food will deteriorate rapidly if allowed to become moist, but provided they are suitably packaged, products will have a long shelf life. Traditionally, foods were dried in the sun and wind, but commercially today, products such as dried milk and instant coffee are made by spraying the liquid into a rising column of dry, heated air; solid foods, such as fruit, are spread in layers on a heated surface.

Freeze-drying is carried out under vacuum. It is less damaging to food than straight dehydration in the sense that foods reconstitute better, and is used for quality instant coffee and dried vegetables. The foods are fast frozen, then dried by converting the ice to vapour under very low pressure. The foods lose much of their weight, but retain the original size and shape. They have a spongelike texture, and rapidly reabsorb liquid when reconstituted. Refrigeration is unnecessary during storage; the shelf life is similar to dried foods, provided the product is not allowed to become moist. The success of the method is dependent on a fast rate of freezing, and rapid conversion of the ice to vapour. Hence, the most acceptable results are obtained with thin pieces of food, and the method is not recommended for pieces thicker than 3 cm/1 in. Fruit, vegetables, meat, and fish have proved satisfactory. This method of preservation is commercially used but the products are most often used as constituents of composite dishes, such as packet meals.

Canning relies on high temperatures to destroy microorganisms and enzymes. The food is sealed in a can to prevent recontamination. The effect of heat processing on the nutritive value of food is variable. For instance, the vitamin-C content of green vegetables is much reduced, but, owing to greater acidity, in fruit juices vitamin C is quite well retained. There is also a loss of 25–50% of water-soluble vitamins if the liquor is not used. Vitamin B (thiamine) is easily destroyed by heat treatment, particularly in alkaline conditions. Acid products retain thiamine well, because they require only minimum heat during sterilization. The sterilization process seems to have little effect on retention of vitamins A and B_2. During storage of canned foods, the proportion of vitamins B and C decreases gradually. Drinks may be canned to preserve the carbon dioxide that makes them fizzy.

Pickling utilizes the effect of acetic (ethanoic) acid, found in vinegar, in stopping the growth of moulds. In sauerkraut, lactic acid, produced by bacteria, has the same effect. Similar types of nonharmful, acid-generating bacteria are used to make yoghurt and cheese.

Curing of meat involves soaking in salt (sodium chloride) solution, with saltpetre (sodium nitrate) added to give the meat its pink colour and characteristic taste. Bacteria convert the nitrates in cured meats to nitrites and nitrosamines, which are potentially carcinogenic to humans.

Irradiation is a method of preserving food by subjecting it to low-level radiation (see ◊food irradiation).

Puffing is a method of processing cereal grains. They are subjected to high pressures, then suddenly ejected into a normal atmospheric pressure, causing the grain to expand sharply. This is used to make puffed wheat cereals and puffed rice cakes.

Chemical treatments are widely used, for example in margarine manufacture, in which hydrogen is bubbled through vegetable oils in the presence of a ◊catalyst to produce a more solid, spreadable fat. The catalyst is later removed. Chemicals introduced in processing that remain in the food are known as **food additives** and include flavourings, preservatives, anti-oxidants, emulsifiers, and colourings.

food test any of several types of simple test, easily performed in the laboratory, used to identify the main classes of food.
starch–iodine test Food is ground up in distilled water and iodine is added. A dense black colour indicates that starch is present.
sugar–Benedict's test Food is ground up in distilled water and placed in a test tube with Benedict's reagent. The tube is then heated in a boiling water bath. If glucose is present the colour changes from blue to brick-red.
protein–Biuret test Food is ground up in distilled water and a mixture of copper(II) sulphate and sodium hydroxide is added. If protein is present a mauve colour is seen.

foot in geometry, point where a line meets a second line to which it is perpendicular.

foot imperial unit of length (symbol ft), equivalent to 0.3048 m, in use in Britain since Anglo-Saxon times. It originally represented the length of a human foot. One foot contains 12 inches and is one-third of a yard.

foot-and-mouth disease contagious eruptive viral disease of cloven-hoofed mammals, characterized by blisters in the mouth and around the hooves. In cattle it causes deterioration of milk yield and abortions. It is an airborne virus, which makes its eradication extremely difficult.

foot-candle unit of illuminance, now replaced by the ◊lux. One foot-candle is the illumination received at a distance of one foot from an international candle. It is equal to 10.764 lux.

foot-pound imperial unit of energy (ft-lb), defined as the work done when a force of one pound moves through a distance of one foot. It has been superseded for scientific work by the joule: one foot-pound equals 1.356 joule.

footprint in computing, the area on the desk or floor required by a computer or other peripheral device.

footprint of a satellite, the area of the Earth over which its signals can be received.

footrot contagious disease of sheep caused by a bacterium and spreading easily in warm, wet conditions. It is characterized by inflammation and lameness and is controlled by vaccination, foot-bathing, and segregation.

forage crop plant that is grown to feed livestock; for example, grass, clover, and kale (a form of cabbage). Forage crops cover a greater area of the world than food crops, and grass, which dominates this group, is the world's most abundant crop, though much of it is still in an unimproved state.

foraminifera any marine protozoan of the order Foraminiferida, with shells of calcium carbonate. Their shells have pores through which filaments project. Some form part of the ◊plankton, others live on the sea bottom.

The many-chambered *Globigerina* is part of the plankton. Its shells eventually form much of the chalky ooze of the ocean floor.

forbidden line in astronomy, emission line seen in the spectra of certain astronomical objects that are not seen under the conditions prevailing in laboratory experiments. They indicate that the hot gas emitting them is at extremely low density. Forbidden lines are seen, for example, in the tenuous gas of the Sun's ◊corona, in ◊HII regions, and in the nucleuses of certain active galaxies.

force any influence that tends to change the state of rest or the uniform motion in a straight line of a body. The action of an unbalanced or resultant force results in the acceleration of a body in the direction of action of the force, or it may, if the body is unable to move freely, result in its deformation (see ◊Hooke's law). Force is a vector quantity, possessing both magnitude and direction; its SI unit is the newton.

According to Newton's second law of motion the magnitude of a resultant force is equal to the rate of change of ◊momentum of the body on which it acts; the force F producing an acceleration a m s^{-2} on a body of mass m kilograms is therefore given by: $F = ma$ See also ◊Newton's laws of motion.

force feedback in ◊virtual reality, realistic simulation of the physical sense of touch. This is an area of active research, as many applications of virtual reality are useless or impossible without it.

For example, force feedback is essential in medical training systems to teach the students how hard to press with a scalpel in delicate areas of the human body. Even simulated games need force feedback in order to allow objects to respond realistically to falling or being hit.

force multiplier machine designed to multiply a small effort in order to move a larger load. The number of times a machine multiplies the effort is called its ◊mechanical advantage. Examples of a force multiplier include crowbar, wheelbarrow, nutcrackers, and bottle opener.

force ratio the magnification of a force by a machine; see ◊mechanical advantage.

forces, fundamental in physics, the four fundamental interactions believed to be at work in the physical universe. There are two long-range forces: **gravity**, which keeps the planets in orbit around the Sun, and acts between all particles that have mass; and the **electromagnetic force**, which stops solids from falling apart, and acts between all particles with ◊electric charge. There are two very short-range forces which operate only inside the atomic nucleus: the **weak nuclear force**, responsible for the reactions that fuel the Sun and for the emission of ◊beta particles from certain nuclei; and the **strong nuclear force**, which binds together the protons and neutrons in the nuclei of atoms. The relative strengths of the four forces are: strong, 1; electromagnetic, 10^{-2}; weak, 10^{-6}; gravitational, 10^{-40}. By 1971, US physicists Steven Weinberg and Sheldon Glashow, Pakistani physicist Abdus Salam, and others had developed a theory that suggested that the weak and electromagnetic forces were aspects of a single force called the **electroweak force**; experimental support came from observation at ◊CERN in the 1980s. Physicists are now working on theories to unify all four forces.

People can have the Model T in any colour – so long as it's black.

HENRY FORD US automobile manufacturer.
A Nevins *Ford*

Fordism mass production characterized by a high degree of job specialization, as typified by the Ford Motor Company's early use of assembly lines. Mass-production techniques were influenced by US management consultant F W Taylor's book *Principles of Scientific Management* 1911.

Post-Fordism management theory and practice emphasize flexibility and autonomy of decisionmaking for nonmanagerial staff. It is concerned more with facilitating and coordinating tasks than with control.

forensic entomology branch of ◊forensic science, involving the study of insects on and around the corpse. Insects rapidly infest a corpse, and do so in an accepted sequence beginning with flies laying eggs. Further insects follow to feed on the decomposing flesh and fly maggots. Forensic entomologists are able to determine time of death by analysing insect colonization. They can also tell whether or not a corpse has been moved by examining the faunal community in the 'seepage area' beneath the body.

FORENSIC ENTOMOLOGY

Cocaine speeds up the growth of certain insects. This enables forensic entomologists to determine if a corpse is that of a cocaine user.

forensic medicine in medicine, branch of medicine concerned with the resolution of crimes. Examples of forensic medicine include the determination of the cause of death in suspicious circumstances or the identification of a criminal by examining tissue found at the scene of a crime. Forensic psychology involves the establishment of a psychological profile of a criminal that can assist in identification.

forensic science the use of scientific techniques to solve criminal cases. A multidisciplinary field embracing chemistry, physics, botany, zoology, and medicine, forensic science includes the identification of human bodies or traces. Ballistics (the study of projectiles, such as bullets), another traditional forensic field, makes use of such tools as the comparison microscope and the electron microscope.

Traditional methods such as fingerprinting are still used, assisted by computers; in addition, blood analysis, forensic dentistry, voice and speech spectrograms, and ◊genetic fingerprinting are increasingly applied. Chemicals, such as poisons and drugs, are analysed by ◊chromatography. ESDA (electrostatic document analysis) is a technique used for revealing indentations on paper, which helps determine if documents have been tampered with. ◊Forensic entomology is also a branch of forensic science.

forest area where trees have grown naturally for centuries, instead of being logged at maturity (about 150–200 years). A natural, or old-growth, forest has a multistorey canopy and includes young and very old trees (this gives the canopy its range of heights). There are also fallen trees contributing to the very complex ecosystem, which may support more than 150 species of mammals and many thousands of species of insects.

The Pacific forest of the west coast of North America is one of the few remaining old-growth forests in the temperate zone.

It consists mainly of conifers and is threatened by logging – less than 10% of the original forest remains.

forest fly external blood-sucking parasite, chiefly of horses. It is about 8 mm/0.3 in long and bears brown and yellow flecks.
classification The forest fly *Hippobosca equina* is a member of the insect family Hippoboscidae in order Diptera, class Insecta, phylum Arthropoda.

forestry the science of forest management. Recommended forestry practice aims at multipurpose crops, allowing the preservation of varied plant and animal species as well as human uses (lumbering, recreation). Forestry has often been confined to the planting of a single species, such as a rapid-growing conifer providing softwood for paper pulp and construction timber, for which world demand is greatest. In tropical countries, logging contributes to the destruction of ◊rainforests, causing global environmental problems. Small unplanned forests are ◊woodland.

The earliest planned forest dates from 1368 at Nürnberg, Germany; in Britain, planning of forests began in the 16th century. In the UK, Japan, and other countries, forestry practices have been criticized for concentration on softwood conifers to the neglect of native hardwoods.

forgery in computing, the art of falsifying either the contents or the origins of a message. On the Internet, where a person's

Forensic Science: Recent Advances

BY JOHN BROAD

The scientific support for Inspector Morse

The forensic scientist has to provide evidence that will stand scrutiny in a court of law. This is why crime laboratories need to keep up with the latest research and maintain the highest standards.

Every contact leaves a trace. The ordinary microscope is still a vital instrument for examining trace evidence – hairs, fibres, fragments of glass or paint – but the scanning electron microscope is also used. It provides high magnification with good resolution, and can also incorporate a **microprobe** that identifies the actual elements, particularly metallic ones, in the surface being examined.

Surface elements absorb electrons and emit X-rays, which the microprobe converts into an X-ray emission spectrum with a characteristic pattern that reveals the elements present. In this way, it is possible to detect and identify particles invisible to the optical microscope, such as those scattered from a firearm when discharged. These particles can indicate the type and make of ammunition used.

Anti-crime antibodies

Advances have also been made in analytical techniques called **immunoassays**, which use antibodies to detect and measure drugs, poisons, proteins, and even explosives such as TNT and Semtex. When a foreign chemical, such as a disease organism, enters the human body, antibodies are produced that recognize and react with the foreign substance.

The same process occurs in animals, which can be used to produce antibodies against a wide variety of chemicals. An animal is injected with a target substance, such as cocaine, and the resulting antibodies can be separated and used to recognize the substance against a background of body fluids, or in a body swab.

When trying to detect a target compound, such as the presence of explosive residue on a person's hands, it is vital to take account of possible contamination, since the substance might have been picked up casually. Also, it is important that the method used detects the target compound and no other. The value of antibodies is that they are specific to the compound that triggered their production. With other analytical methods, such as **thin-layer chromatography**, care has to be taken to eliminate other compounds that could show the same experimental result.

DNA fingerprinting

One impressive recent scientific advance is DNA fingerprinting, or DNA profiling. This has been used effectively in assault, rape, and murder cases and in paternity disputes. It figured prominently in the O J Simpson trial. For forensic purposes two DNA fingerprints are necessary – one from the suspect and another taken from the crime scene. There must be a convincing match to establish a link.

DNA profiling involves using special enzymes to cut up precisely a sample of DNA extracted from body cells. Only a very small amount of DNA – from just a few cells – is needed; the polymerase chain reaction (PCR) can amplify it into sufficient material to profile. The resulting 'bits' are separated by gel electrophoresis and can be blotted onto a special membrane, marked radioactively with specialized probes and then visualized as the familiar sequence of bars (known as an autoradiograph). Alternatively, the DNA bands can be labelled or highlighted in the actual gel then scanned with a laser. The result is a graphical print out showing peaks where the bands occur. These peaks can be converted into digital codes for storage on a computer. This is the method employed in building up national DNA databases, which store, for rapid recall, the DNA profiles of known offenders, suspects, and tissue samples taken from crime scenes. Rapid comparison can establish that a suspect could be linked with a number of scenes.

Controversies

Should blood for DNA profiling purposes be taken not only from suspects but from suspicious persons, unwanted persons, even undesirable persons? If a person refuses to submit to supplying a sample for DNA analysis (as is their entitlement) what inference should be drawn from this refusal? Should everyone be DNA profiled shortly after birth so that the ordinary citizen can more easily be monitored? Despite refinements and increased effectiveness, DNA profiling must be treated with caution. If two profiles convincingly match, they may not come from the same person. The chances of this are very small – but not as small as once thought. Identical twins have the same DNA profile, but DNA profiles of people from small communities with significant in-breeding can be deceptively similar. If two bands on adjacent profiles correspond, but not exactly, statistical analysis may be needed to decide if there is a match. In the end, despite the statistical back-up, the matching of two DNA profiles is a matter of expert opinion.

Electrostatic document analysis

Electrostatic document analysis (ESDA) is a recent technique used for revealing indentations on paper. Left on an underlying sheet, these indicate what has been written on the paper above.

The method uses a high electrostatic voltage to transfer the indentations onto imaging film where they are visualized by photographic toner. If the resulting impressions are markedly uneven – perhaps one half is more heavily indented than the other – then the writing under examination (on the top sheet) may have been written at two different times, showing that the document has been tampered with. The release of the 'Guildford Four' and the 'Birmingham Six' in the UK was clinched when the ESDA machine revealed 'doctored' written evidence at the original trial.

Computers on the beat

The increasing power of computers has been responsible for great advances in forensic science, as in other sciences. Computers have revolutionized the storage and retrieval of information. For example, all car registration numbers and owners' names are stored on computer for almost instant access. Information can be rapidly communicated to police officers in the field. This has increased the power of those who hold the information and, in addition to speeding the response to crime, has helped in the monitoring of 'undesirables' and in maintaining order on the streets.

Identification of a suspect fingerprint, by comparison with thousands stored on file, was once a time-consuming process. Nowadays, with a computer, the process takes minutes, even seconds. Even so, the final decision on fingerprint identification is still made visually by a trained expert. No matter how sophisticated the hardware, the human senses are still vital in forensic work.

The carnage on the roads

A vast amount of police time is consumed by road traffic problems. It would be correct to say that two scientific instruments – the Breathalyser and the Radar Speed Device (or gun) have had more impact on the general public than all other forensic scientific hardware put together. Scientific evidence presented in a court of law must be accurate, reliable, and based on thorough research in order to convince a Magistrate or jury. Confirmatory or back-up tests must be available when necessary. Scientific efforts designed to reduce the number of deaths and injuries caused by the drunk driver have resulted in the development of a roadside breath screening device; an evidential breath alcohol testing instrument; and a confirmatory blood test. The Breathalyser relies on a fuel cell to estimate the level of alcohol in a driver's breath. The intoximeter, used in the police station, is based on the absorption of infra red light (at 3.4 microns) by alcohol molecules and accurately establishes the breath alcohol level. The confirmatory blood test employs headspace gas chromatography to find the blood alcohol concentration or BAC. All these procedures use a different scientific principle for their method of operation.

The radar speed device has aimed to bring about some reduction in the devastation caused by speeding, particularly on modern motorways and highways. Its operation depends upon the Doppler effect and its output – often a photograph and accompanying data when it is linked to a camera – is valid as evidence in a court of law. All radar speed devices are checked rigorously in order to maintain the required accuracy and reliability. More efficient, but much more expensive, is the laser speed device that relies on the reflection of impulses of light from a moving source to calculate speed. Both these devices are easy to operate and to carry around.

If public pressure results in the legislation of some, or maybe all, recreational drugs then scientists will be obliged to design roadside screening tests for particular, or all, drugs with back-up evidential and confirmatory procedures. Apparently it is much more dangerous to drive a vehicle when 'stoned' with drugs than when drunk. Work has already begun on these problems. Trials are due to start in the UK on the use of absorbent pads impregnated with special chemicals. When pressed against the skin, sweat diffuses into the pad and a colour reaction denotes the presence of a particular drug. This is a noninvasive technique, but for evidential testing, blood or urine would be required and subjected to an immune assay and perhaps chromatography or even mass spectrometry. In the USA, efforts have so far centred on urine testing and the opinion has been expressed that eventually each police car will be followed closely by a 'urine bus' or 'slash van'.

Surveillance techniques

The recent developments and use of sophisticated surveillance techniques seen in car parks, town centres, business premises and around the residences of the rich and powerful, bear testimony to the trend. Most notable is CCTV (closed circuit television). Whether this actually reduces crime or merely drives the criminals elsewhere is open to debate. However the concern raised about such techniques, which extend to telephone tapping, is about the invasion of privacy. This could represent one or many steps down the slippery slope of monitoring the innocent and the guilty going about their daily business. Apart from the implications of 'Big Brother', there is the perennial vexed question of who monitors those who do the monitoring?

A dream or a nightmare?

The aim of the forensic scientist is to link a suspect with a crime scene, victim or incident, using the very latest in scientific technology. If there is no suspect then data can be collected and stored only as far as time and money allow. Nothing further can be done until the breakthrough occurs as a result of a stroke of luck or a tip-off. In the end, all that is required for a watertight case might be available – a suspect whose name and address is known and an impressive array of evidence and statements. But if the suspect has gone to ground and all enquiries are met with a wall of silence, no amount of scientific evidence will find someone determined to 'melt away'. Maybe it would be wise to tag everybody electronically at birth and monitor their every move on a central computer. This would solve the problem of the vanishing suspect and the missing person, but is it a dream or a ghastly nightmare?

identity is shaped by his/her words as sent out via e-mail or public conferencing systems such as USENET, sending out a forged message in another person's name can seriously damage them. Forged messages are, however, used by the ◊CancelMoose to manage ◊spamming and keep it from spreading.

forget-me-not any of a group of plants belonging to the borage family, including *M. sylvatica* and *M. scorpioides*, with small bright blue flowers. (Genus *Myosotis*, family Boraginaceae.)

forging one of the main methods of shaping metals, which involves hammering or a more gradual application of pressure. A blacksmith hammers red-hot metal into shape on an anvil, and the traditional place of work is called a forge. The blacksmith's mechanical equivalent is the drop forge. The metal is shaped by the blows from a falling hammer or ram, which is usually accelerated by steam or air pressure. Hydraulic presses forge by applying pressure gradually in a squeezing action.

formaldehyde common name for ◊methanal.

formalin aqueous solution of formaldehyde (methanal) used to preserve animal specimens.

formatting in computing, short for ◊disc formatting.

Formica trademark of the Formica Corporation for a heat-proof plastic laminate, widely used as a veneer on wipe-down kitchen surfaces and children's furniture. It is made from formaldehyde resins similar to ◊Bakelite. It was first put on the market in 1913.

formic acid common name for ◊methanoic acid.

forms on the World Wide Web, facility for accepting structured user input and inserting it into a program such as a database. Most newer graphical Web browsers can handle forms, as can the older, text-based browser Lynx. Forms are needed to manage database queries at sites such as ◊AltaVista, and to fill out registration forms for those sites that require them.

Web page designers implement forms by using a special set of hypertext markup language (HTML) tags and attaching a script, which parses the data and feeds it to the program specified in a form the program can use. The results, such as a user name and password or a list of matches, are sent back to the user.

formula in chemistry, a representation of a molecule, radical, or ion, in which the component chemical elements are represented by their symbols. An **empirical formula** indicates the simplest ratio of the elements in a compound, without indicating how many of them there are or how they are combined. A **molecular formula** gives the number of each type of element present in one molecule. A **structural formula** shows the relative positions of the atoms and the bonds between them. For example, for ethanoic acid, the empirical formula is CH_2O, the molecular formula is $C_2H_4O_2$, and the structural formula is CH_3COOH.

formula in mathematics, a set of symbols and numbers that expresses a fact or rule. $A = \pi r^2$ is the formula for calculating the area of a circle. Einstein's famous formula relating energy and mass is $E = mc^2$.

forsythia any of a group of temperate eastern Asian shrubs, which bear yellow bell-shaped flowers in early spring before the leaves appear. (Genus *Forsythia*, family Oleaceae.)

FORTRAN (or *fortran*, acronym for ***formula translation***) high-level computer-programming language suited to mathematical and scientific computations. Developed by John Backus at IBM in 1956, it is one of the earliest computer languages still in use. A recent version, Fortran 90, is now being used on advanced parallel computers. ◊BASIC was strongly influenced by FORTRAN and is similar in many ways.

fossil ***Latin fossilis 'dug up'*** a cast, impression, or the actual remains of an animal or plant preserved in rock. Fossils were created during periods of rock formation, caused by the gradual accumulation of sediment over millions of years at the bottom of the sea bed or an inland lake. Fossils may include footprints, an internal cast, or external impression. A few fossils are preserved intact, as with ◊mammoths fossilized in Siberian ice, or insects trapped in tree resin that is today amber. The study of fossils is called ◊palaeontology. Palaeontologists are able to deduce much of the geological history of a region from fossil remains.

About 250,000 fossil species have been discovered – a figure that is believed to represent less than 1 in 20,000 of the species that ever lived. **Microfossils** are so small they can only be seen with a microscope. They include the fossils of pollen, bone fragments, bacteria, and the remains of microscopic marine animals and plants, such as foraminifera and diatoms.

FOSSIL HOMINIDS FAQ

http://earth.ics.uci.edu:8080/faqs/fossil-hominids.html

Basic information about hominid species, the most important hominid fossils, and creationist arguments, plus links to related sites.

If A is a success in life, then A equals x plus y plus z. Work is x; y is play; and z is keeping your mouth shut.

ALBERT EINSTEIN German-born US physicist. *Observer* 15 Jan 1950

fossil fuel fuel, such as coal, oil, and natural gas, formed from the fossilized remains of plants that lived hundreds of millions of years ago. Fossil fuels are a ◊nonrenewable resource and will eventually run out. Extraction of coal and oil causes considerable environmental pollution, and burning coal contributes to problems of ◊acid rain and the ◊greenhouse effect.

four-colour process colour ◊printing using four printing plates, based on the principle that any colour is made up of differing proportions of the primary colours blue, red, and green. The first stage in preparing a colour picture for printing is to produce separate films, one each for the blue, red, and green respectively in the picture (colour separations). From these separations three printing plates are made, with a fourth plate for black (for shading or outlines and type). Ink colours complementary to those represented on the plates are used for printing – yellow for the blue plate, cyan for the red, and magenta for the green.

Fourdrinier machine papermaking machine patented by the Fourdrinier brothers Henry and Sealy in England in 1803. On the machine, liquid pulp flows onto a moving wire-mesh belt, and water drains and is sucked away, leaving a damp paper web. This is passed

Fourier, Jean Baptiste Joseph (1768–1830)

French applied mathematician whose formulation of heat flow in 1807 contains the proposal that, with certain constraints, any mathematical function can be represented by trigonometrical series. This principle forms the basis of **Fourier analysis**, used today in many different fields of physics. His idea, not immediately well received, gained currency and is embodied in his *Théorie analytique de la chaleur/The Analytical Theory of Heat* 1822.

Light, sound, and other wavelike forms of energy can be studied using Fourier's method, a developed version of which is now called harmonic analysis.

first through a series of steam-heated rollers, which dry it, and then between heavy calendar rollers, which give it a smooth finish.

Such machines can measure up to 90 m/300 ft in length, and are still in use.

four-stroke cycle the engine-operating cycle of most petrol and ◊diesel engines. The 'stroke' is an upward or downward movement of a piston in a cylinder. In a petrol engine the cycle begins with the induction of a fuel mixture as the piston goes down on its first stroke. On the second stroke (up) the piston compresses the mixture in the top of the cylinder. An electric spark then ignites the mixture, and the gases produced force the piston down on its third, power, stroke. On the fourth stroke (up) the piston expels the burned gases from the cylinder into the exhaust.

fourth-generation language in computing, a type of programming language designed for the rapid programming of ◊applications but often lacking the ability to control the individual parts of the computer. Such a language typically provides easy ways of designing screens and reports, and of using databases. Other 'generations' (the term implies a class of language rather than a chronological sequence) are ◊machine code (first generation); ◊assembly languages, or low-level languages (second); and conventional high-level languages such as ◊BASIC and ◊PASCAL (third).

fowl chicken or chickenlike bird. Sometimes the term is also used for ducks and geese. The red jungle fowl *Gallus gallus* is the ancestor of all domestic chickens. It is a forest bird of Asia, without the size or egg-laying ability of many domestic strains. ◊Guinea fowl are of African origin.

FOX

The average British fox obtains only about a third of its food from hunting. The remainder is acquired by scavenging.

fox one of the smaller species of wild dog of the family Canidae, which live in Africa, Asia, Europe, North America, and South America. Foxes feed on a wide range of animals from worms to rabbits, scavenge for food, and also eat berries. They are very adaptable, maintaining high populations close to urban areas.

Most foxes are nocturnal, and make an underground den, or 'earth'. The common or red fox *Vulpes vulpes* is about 60 cm/2 ft long plus a tail ('brush') 40 cm/1.3 ft long. The fur is reddish with black patches behind the ears and a light tip to the tail. Other foxes include the Arctic fox *Alopex lagopus*, the ◊fennec, the grey foxes genus *Urocyon* of North and Central America, and the South American genus *Dusicyon*, to which the extinct Falkland Islands dog belonged.

ADAM'S FOX BOX

http://tavi.acomp.usf.edu/foxbox

Beautifully designed site providing an impressive amount of information about foxes: articles, songs, stories, poems, images, and a video clip. The site also provides many pointers to other fox-related sites, including one explaining how to dance the foxtrot!

foxglove any of a group of flowering plants found in Europe and the Mediterranean region. They have showy spikes of bell-like flowers, and grow up to 1.5 m/5 ft high. (Genus *Digitalis*, family Scrophulariaceae.)

The wild species (*D. purpurea*), native to Britain, produces purple to reddish flowers. Its leaves were the original source of digitalis, a drug used for some heart problems.

foxhound small, keen-nosed hound, up to 60 cm/2 ft tall and black, tan, and white in colour. There are two recognized breeds: the English foxhound, bred for some 300 years to hunt foxes, and the American foxhound, not quite as stocky, used for foxes and other game.

fox terrier breed of ◊terrier evolved for use in foxhunts to attack foxes in their earths (dens) where the larger foxhound was unable to reach them. Two types are distinguished – the smooth- and wire-haired; but both have a mainly white coat with large brown and/or black markings. They weigh about 8 kg/17.5 lb, stand up to 39 cm/15 in tall, and carry their short, usually docked, tails upright.

f.p.s. system system of units based on the foot, pound, and second as units of length, mass, and time, respectively. It has now been replaced for scientific work by the ◊SI system.

fractal ***from Latin fractus 'broken'*** irregular shape or surface produced by a procedure of repeated subdivision. Generated on a computer screen, fractals are used in creating models of geographical or biological processes (for example, the creation of a coastline by erosion or accretion, or the growth of plants).

Sets of curves with such discordant properties were developed in the 19th century in Germany by Georg Cantor and Karl Weierstrass. The name was coined by the French mathematician Benoit Mandelbrod. Fractals are also used for computer art.

TO REMEMBER THE RULE OF DIVISION OF FRACTIONS:

THE NUMBER YOU ARE DIVIDING BY
TURN UPSIDE DOWN AND MULTIPLY.

fraction in chemistry, a group of similar compounds, the boiling points of which fall within a particular range and which are separated during fractional ◊distillation (fractionation).

fraction ***from Latin fractus 'broken'*** in mathematics, a number that indicates one or more equal parts of a whole. Usually, the number of equal parts into which the unit is divided (denominator) is written below a horizontal line, and the number of parts comprising the fraction (numerator) is written above; thus $\frac{2}{3}$ or $\frac{3}{4}$. Such fractions are called **vulgar** or **simple** fractions. The denominator can never be zero.

A **proper fraction** is one in which the numerator is less than the denominator. An **improper fraction** has a numerator that is larger than the denominator, for example $\frac{3}{2}$. It can therefore be expressed as a mixed number, for example, $1\frac{1}{2}$. A combination such as $\frac{5}{0}$ is not regarded as a fraction (an object cannot be divided into zero equal parts), and mathematically any number divided by 0 is equal to infinity. A **decimal fraction** has as its denominator a power of 10, and these are omitted by use of the decimal point and notation, for example 0.04, which is $\frac{4}{100}$. The digits to the right of the decimal point indicate the numerators of vulgar fractions whose denominators are 10, 100, 1,000, and so on. Most fractions can be expressed exactly as decimal fractions ($\frac{1}{3}$ = 0.333...). Fractions are also known as the **rational numbers**; that is, numbers formed by a ratio. **Integers** may be expressed as fractions with a denominator of 1.

fractionating column device in which many separate ◊distillations can occur so that a liquid mixture can be separated into its components.

Various designs exist but the primary aim is to allow maximum contact between the hot rising vapours and the cooling descending liquid. As the mixture of vapours ascends the column it becomes progressively enriched in the lower-boiling-point components, so these separate out first.

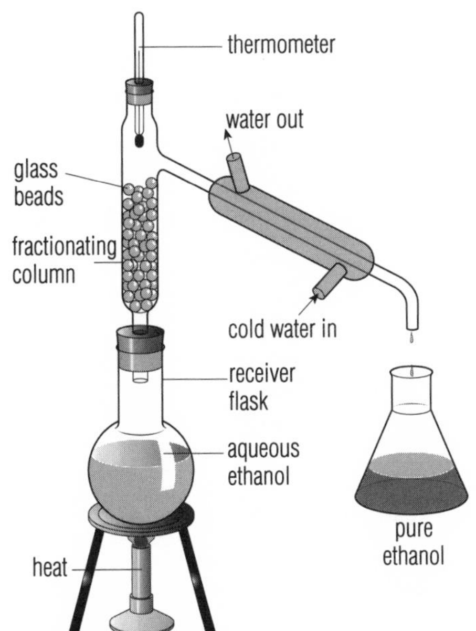

fractionating column Laboratory apparatus for fractional distillation. Fractional distillation is the main means of separating the components of crude oil.

This tomb holds Diophantus. Ah, how great a marvel! the tomb tells scientifically the measure of his life. God granted him to be a boy for the sixth part of his life, and adding a twelfth part to this, He clothed his cheeks with down; He lit him the light of wedlock after a seventh part, and five years after his marriage He granted him a son. Alas! late-born wretched child; after attaining the measure of half his father's life, chill Fate took him. After consoling his grief by this science of numbers for four years he ended his life.

DIOPHANTUS Greek mathematician.
Arithmetical riddle supposedly inscribed on Diophantus' tombstone, quoted in *The Greek Anthology V*

fractionation or ***fractional distillation*** process used to split complex mixtures (such as crude oil) into their components, usually by repeated heating, boiling, and condensation; see ◊distillation.

fragmentation in computing, the breaking up of files into many smaller sections stored on different parts of a disc. The computer ◊operating system stores files in this way so that maximum use can be made of disc space. Each section contains a pointer to where the next section is stored. The ◊file allocation table keeps a record of this.

Fragmentation slows down access to files. It is possible to defragment a disc by copying files. In addition, ◊defragmentation programs, or disc optimizers, allow discs to be defragmented without the need for files to be copied to a second storage device.

frame a single photograph in a sequence representing motion, or movement, on film; in a ◊network, a unit of data; in word processing or desktop publishing, a marked-out area on a page that can contain text or graphics.

What appears to be motion on a cinema or TV screen is actually a rapid sequence of single shots. Because of limitations in the human eye – known as the Phi phenomenon – those individual shots, if played in sequence at a rate of 24 to 30 frames per second, make the motion thus captured appear continuous.

frame buffer in computing, a ◊buffer used to store a screen image.

frame relay in ◊wide-area networks, a standard for the transmission of data that is optimized for high speeds up to about 1.5 Mbits/second.

francium radioactive metallic element, symbol Fr, atomic number 87, relative atomic mass 223. It is one of the alkali metals and occurs in nature in small amounts as a decay product of actinium. Its longest-lived isotope has a half-life of only 21 minutes. Francium was discovered and named in 1939 by Marguérite Perey to honour her country.

frangipani any of a group of tropical American trees, especially the species *P. rubra*, belonging to the dogbane family. Perfume is made from the strongly scented waxy flowers. (Genus *Plumeria*, family Apocynaceae.)

frankincense resin of various African and Asian trees, burned as incense. Costly in ancient times, it is traditionally believed to be one of the three gifts brought by the Magi to the infant Jesus. (Genus *Boswellia*, family Burseraceae.)

Frasch process process used to extract underground deposits of sulphur. Superheated steam is piped into the sulphur deposit and melts it. Compressed air is then pumped down to force the molten sulphur to the surface. The process was developed in the USA in 1891 by German-born Herman Frasch (1851–1914).

free fall the state in which a body is falling freely under the influence of ◊gravity, as in freefall parachuting (skydiving). In a vacuum, a freely falling body accelerates at a rate of 9.806 m sec^{-2}/32.174 ft sec^{-2}; the value varies slightly at different latitudes and altitudes. A body falling through air, accelerates until it reaches a maximum speed called the ◊terminal velocity; thereafter, there is no further acceleration.

In orbit, astronauts and spacecraft are still held by gravity and are in fact falling freely toward the Earth. Because of their speed (orbital velocity), the amount they fall towards the Earth just equals the amount the Earth's surface curves away; in effect they remain at the same height, apparently weightless.

Free-Net free community-based online system such as a network of public ◊bulletin boards and/or municipally owned systems. Free-Net is a registered service mark of the National Public Telecomputing Network. The first Free-Net was set up in 1986 in Cleveland, Ohio, USA.

free radical in chemistry, an atom or molecule that has an unpaired electron and is therefore highly reactive. Most free radicals are very short-lived. They are by-products of normal cell chemistry and rapidly oxidize other molecules they encounter. Free radicals are thought to do considerable damage. They are neutralized by protective enzymes.

Free radicals are often produced by high temperatures and are found in flames and explosions.

freesia any of a South African group of plants belonging to the iris family, commercially grown for their scented, funnel-shaped flowers. (Genus *Freesia*, family Iridaceae.)

Free Software Foundation (FSF) US organization, based in Boston, which creates and distributes good-quality free software and utilities. FSF is the publisher of the ◊GNU software, which includes compilers, operating systems, utilities, editors, databases, and PostScript viewers. All the software is free of licensing fees and restrictions.

The FSF was founded in 1983 by US artificial intelligence specialist Richard Stallman as a way of bringing back the cooperative spirit of the computing community's early days that had vanished by the early 1980s with the advent of widely sold proprietary software. The project's ultimate goal is to make commercial software obsolete by providing free software to do everything computer users want to do.

freeware in computing, free software which may or may not be in the public domain (see ◊public-domain software). One of the best-known examples of freeware is the encryption program ◊Pretty Good Privacy (PGP).

freeze-drying method of preserving food; see ◊food technology. The product to be dried is frozen and then put in a vacuum chamber that forces out the ice as water vapour, a process known as sublimation.

Many of the substances that give products such as coffee their typical flavour are volatile, and would be lost in a normal drying process because they would evaporate along with the water. In the freeze-drying process these volatile compounds do not pass into the ice that is to be sublimed, and are therefore largely retained.

freeze-thaw form of physical ◊weathering, common in mountains and glacial environments, caused by the expansion of water as it freezes. Water in a crack freezes and expands in volume by 9% as it turns to ice. This expansion exerts great pressure on the rock causing the crack to enlarge. After many cycles of freeze-thaw, rock fragments may break off to form ◊scree slopes.

For freeze-thaw to operate effectively the temperature must fluctuate regularly above and below 0°C/32°F. It is therefore uncommon in areas of extreme and perpetual cold, such as the polar regions.

freezing change from liquid to solid state, as when water becomes ice. For a given substance, freezing occurs at a definite temperature, known as the **freezing point**, that is invariable under similar conditions of pressure, and the temperature remains at this point until all the liquid is frozen. The amount of heat per unit mass that has to be removed to freeze a substance is a constant for any given substance, and is known as the latent heat of fusion.

freezing point for any given liquid, the temperature at which any further removal of heat will convert the liquid into the solid state. The temperature remains at this point until all the liquid has solidified. It is invariable under similar conditions of pressure – for example, the freezing point of water under standard atmospheric pressure is 0°C/32°F.

freezing point, depression of lowering of a solution's freezing point below that of the pure solvent; it depends on the number of molecules of solute dissolved in it. For a single solvent, such as pure water, all solute substances in the same molar concentration produce the same lowering of freezing point. The depression d produced by the presence of a solute of molar concentration C is given by the equation $d = KC$, where K is a constant (called the cryoscopic constant) for the solvent concerned.

Antifreeze mixtures for car radiators and the use of salt to melt ice on roads are common applications of this principle. Animals in arctic conditions, for example insects or fish, cope with the extreme cold either by manufacturing natural 'antifreeze' and staying active, or by allowing themselves to freeze in a controlled fashion, that is, they manufacture proteins to act as nuclei for the formation of ice crystals in areas that will not produce cellular damage, and so enable themselves to thaw back to life again.

Measurement of freezing-point depression is a useful method of determining the molecular weights of solutes. It is also used to detect the illicit addition of water to milk.

frequency in physics, the number of periodic oscillations, vibrations, or waves occurring per unit of time. The SI unit of frequency is the hertz (Hz), one hertz being equivalent to one cycle per second.

Human beings can hear sounds from objects vibrating in the range 20–15,000 Hz. Ultrasonic frequencies well above 15,000 Hz can be detected by such mammals as bats. Infrasound (low frequency sound) can be detected by some animals and birds. Pigeons can detect sounds as low as 0.1 Hz; elephants communicate using sounds as low as 1 Hz.

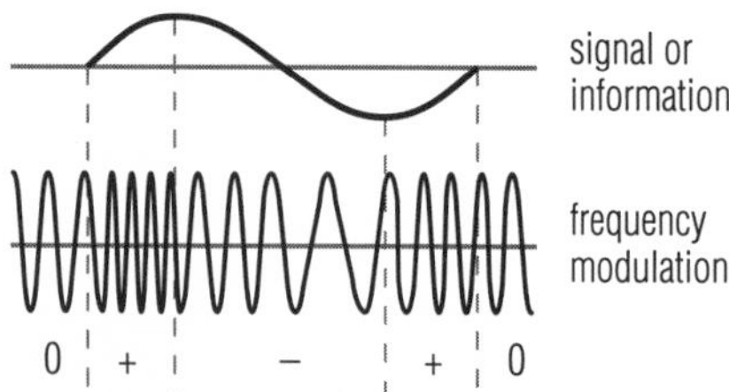

frequency modulation *In FM radio transmission, the frequency of the carrier wave is modulated, rather than its amplitude (as in AM broadcasts). The FM system is not affected by the many types of interference which change the amplitude of the carrier wave, and so provides better quality reception than AM broadcasts.*

Freud, Sigmund
(1856–1939)

Austrian physician who pioneered the study of the unconscious mind. He developed the methods of free association and interpretation of dreams that are basic techniques of psychoanalysis. The influence of unconscious forces on people's thoughts and actions was Freud's discovery, as was his controversial theory of the repression of infantile sexuality as the root of neuroses in the adult. His books include *Die Traumdeutung/The Interpretation of Dreams* 1900, *Jenseits des Lustprinzips/Beyond the Pleasure Principle* 1920, *Das Ich und das Es/The Ego and the Id* 1923, and *Das Unbehagen in der Kultur/Civilization and its Discontents* 1930. His influence has permeated the world to such an extent that it may be discerned today in almost every branch of thought.

From 1886 to 1938 Freud had a private practice in Vienna, and his theories and writings drew largely on case studies of his own patients, who were mainly upper-middle-class, middle-aged women. Much of the terminology of psychoanalysis was coined by Freud, and many terms have passed into popular usage, not without distortion. His theories have changed the way people think about human nature and brought about a more open approach to sexual matters. Antisocial behaviour is now understood to result in many cases from unconscious forces, and these new concepts have led to wider expression of the human condition in art and literature. Nevertheless, Freud's theories have caused disagreement among psychologists and psychiatrists, and his methods of psychoanalysis cannot be applied in every case.

Mary Evans Picture Library

frequency in statistics, the number of times an event occurs. For example, when two dice are thrown repeatedly and the two scores added together, each of the numbers 2 to 12 may have a frequency of occurrence. The set of data including the frequencies is called a **frequency distribution**, usually presented in a frequency table or shown diagramatically, by a frequency polygon.

frequency modulation (FM) method by which radio waves are altered for the transmission of broadcasting signals. FM varies the frequency of the carrier wave in accordance with the signal being transmitted. Its advantage over AM (◊amplitude modulation) is its better signal-to-noise ratio. It was invented by the US engineer Edwin Armstrong.

frequently asked questions in computing, expansion of the abbreviation ◊FAQ.

The ideas of Freud were popularized by people who only imperfectly understood them, who were incapable of the great effort required to grasp them in their relationship to larger truths, and who therefore assigned to them a prominence out of all proportion to their true importance.

ALFRED NORTH WHITEHEAD English philosopher and mathematician. *Dialogues* Dialogue XXVIII 3 June 1943

friction in physics, the force that opposes the relative motion of two bodies in contact. The **coefficient of friction** is the ratio of the force required to achieve this relative motion to the force pressing the two bodies together.

Friction is greatly reduced by the use of lubricants such as oil, grease, and graphite. Air bearings are now used to minimize friction in high-speed rotational machinery. In other instances friction is deliberately increased by making the surfaces rough – for example, brake linings, driving belts, soles of shoes, and tyres.

FRIENDS OF THE EARTH HOME PAGE

http://www.foe.co.uk/

Appeal for raised awareness of environmental issues with masses of information and tips for action from Friends of the Earth. The site hosts lengthy accounts of several campaigns undertaken by FoE on climate, industry, transport, and sustainable development. It also maintains an archive of press releases from FoE on some of the most controversial environmental problems encountered in the course of last year around the world.

Friends of the Earth (FoE or FOE) environmental pressure group, established in the UK 1971, that aims to protect the environment and to promote rational and sustainable use of the Earth's resources. It campaigns on such issues as acid rain; air, sea, river, and land pollution; recycling; disposal of toxic wastes; nuclear power and renewable energy; the destruction of rainforests; pesticides; and agriculture. FoE has branches in 30 countries.

Green consumerism is a target for exploitation. There's a lot of green froth on top, but murkiness lurks underneath.

Jonathon Porritt English environmental campaigner. Speech at a Friends of the Earth Conference 1989

frilled lizard yellowish-brown Australian lizard with a large frill of skin to the sides of the neck and throat. The lizard is about 90 cm/35 in long.

When the lizard is angry or alarmed it erects its frill, which may be as much as 25cm/10 in in diameter, thus giving itself the appearance of being larger than it really is. Frilled lizards are generally tree-living but may spend some time on the ground, where they run with their forelimbs in the air.

classification The frilled lizard *Chlamydosaurus kingi* belongs to the family Agamidae, suborder Sauria, order Squamata, class Reptilia.

Frisch–Peierls memorandum document revealing, for the first time, how small the critical mass (the minimum quantity of substance required for a nuclear chain reaction to begin) of uranium needed to be if the isotope uranium-235 was separated from naturally occurring uranium; the memo thus implied the feasibility of using this isotope to make an atom bomb. It was written by Otto Frisch and Rudolf Peierls at the University of Birmingham in 1940.

fritillary in botany, any of a group of plants belonging to the lily family. The snake's head fritillary (*F. meleagris*) has bell-shaped flowers with purple-chequered markings. (Genus *Fritillaria,* family Liliaceae.)

fritillary in zoology, any of a large grouping of butterflies of the family Nymphalidae. Mostly medium-sized, fritillaries are usually orange and reddish with a black criss-cross pattern or spots above and with silvery spots on the underside of the hindwings.

They take their name from the Latin word *fritillus* ('dice box') because of their spotted markings.

frog any amphibian of the order Anura (Greek 'tailless'). There are about 24 different families of frog, containing more than 3,800 species. There are no clear rules for distinguishing between frogs and ◊toads.

Frogs usually have squat bodies, with hind legs specialized for jumping, and webbed feet for swimming. Most live in or near water, though as adults they are air-breathing. A few live on land or even in trees. Their colour is usually greenish in the genus *Rana,* but other Ranidae are brightly coloured, for instance black and orange or yellow and white. Many use their long, extensible tongues to capture insects. The eyes are large and bulging. Frogs vary in size from the North American little grass frog *Limnaoedus ocularis,* 12 mm/0.5 in long, to the giant aquatic frog *Telmatobius culeus,* 50 cm/20 in long, of Lake Titicaca, South America. Frogs are widespread, inhabiting all continents except Antarctica, and they have adapted to a range of environments including deserts, forests, grasslands, and even high altitudes, with some species in the Andes and Himalayas existing above 5,000 m/19,600 ft.

courtship and reproduction In many species the males attract the females in great gatherings, usually by croaking. In some tropical species, the male's inflated vocal sac may exceed the rest of his body in size. Other courtship 'lures' include thumping on the ground and 'dances'.

Some lay eggs in large masses (spawn) in water. The jelly surrounding the eggs provides support and protection and retains warmth. Some South American frogs build mud-pool 'nests', and African tree frogs make foam nests from secreted mucus. In other species, the eggs may be carried in pockets on the mother's back, brooded by the male in his vocal sac or, as with the Eurasian midwife toad *Alytes obstetricans,* wrapped round the male's hind legs until hatching.

life cycle The tadpoles hatch from the eggs in about a fortnight. At first they are fishlike animals with external gills and a long swimming tail, but no limbs. The first change to take place is the disappearance of the external gills and the development of internal gills, which are still later supplanted by lungs. The hind legs appear before the front legs, and the last change to occur is the diminution and final disappearance of the tail. The tadpole stage lasts about three or four months. At the end of this time the animal leaves the water. Some species, such as the edible frog, are always aquatic. By autumn the frog grows big and sluggish. It stores fat in a special gland in the abdomen; it is this fat that it lives on during hibernation.

species Certain species of frog have powerful skin poisons (alkaloids) to deter predators. 'True frogs' are placed in the worldwide family Ranidae, with 800 species, of which the genus *Rana* is the best known. The North American bullfrog *Rana catesbeiana,* with a croak that carries for miles, is able to jump nine times its own length. The flying frogs, genus *Rhacophorus,* of Malaysia, using webbed fore and hind feet, can achieve a 12 m/40 ft glide. The hairy frog *Astylosternus robustus* is found in West Africa; it has long outgrowths on its flanks, which seem to aid respiration. A four-year rainforest study in E Madagascar revealed 106 new frog species in 1995. Indian zoologists discovered the first known leaf-eating frog in 1996, in Tamil Nadu, southern India. *R. hexadactyla* feeds mainly on leaves, flowers, and algae. New species are constantly being discovered. In 1997 a species *Eleutherodactylus pluvicanorus* was discovered in Bolivia; it is 4 cm long and ground-dwelling.

FROG

Certain frogs do not spend time as tadpoles. The female of a species of tiny Brazilian frog lays a single egg which hatches as a single froglet, rather than going through a tadpole phase first.

SOMEWHAT AMUSING WORLD OF FROGS

http://www.csu.edu.au/faculty/commerce/account/frogs/frog.htm

Fascinating facts about frogs – did you know, for example, that most frogs will drown eventually if denied access to land?

frogbit small water plant *Hydrocharis morsus-ranae* with submerged roots, floating leaves, and small green and white flowers.

froghopper or ***spittlebug*** leaping plant-bug, of the family Cercopidae, in the same order (Homoptera) as leafhoppers and aphids. Froghoppers live by sucking the juice from plants. The pale green larvae protect themselves (from drying out and from predators) by secreting froth ('cuckoo spit') from their anuses.

frogmouth nocturnal bird, related to the nightjar, of which the commonest species, the tawny frogmouth *Podargus strigoides,* is found throughout Australia, including Tasmania. Well camouflaged, it sits and awaits its prey.

frond large leaf or leaflike structure; in ferns it is often pinnately divided. The term is also applied to the leaves of palms and less commonly to the plant bodies of certain seaweeds, liverworts, and lichens.

front in meteorology, the boundary between two air masses of different temperature or humidity. A **cold front** marks the line of advance of a cold air mass from below, as it displaces a warm air mass; a **warm front** marks the advance of a warm air mass as it rises up over a cold one. Frontal systems define the weather of the mid-latitudes, where warm tropical air is constantly meeting cold air from the poles.

Warm air, being lighter, tends to rise above the cold; its moisture is carried upwards and usually falls as rain or snow, hence the changeable weather conditions at fronts. Fronts are rarely stable and move with the air mass. An **occluded front** is a composite form, where a cold front catches up with a warm front and merges with it.

front-end processor small computer used to coordinate and control the communications between a large mainframe computer and its input and output devices.

frost condition of the weather that occurs when the air temperature is below freezing, 0°C/32°F. Water in the atmosphere is deposited as ice crystals on the ground or exposed objects. As cold air is heavier than warm, ground frost is more common than hoar frost, which is formed by the condensation of water particles in the same way that dew collects.

frostbite the freezing of skin or flesh, with formation of ice crystals leading to tissue damage. The treatment is slow warming of the affected area; for example, by skin-to-skin contact or with lukewarm water. Frostbitten parts are extremely vulnerable to infection, with the risk of gangrene.

FRS abbreviation for ***Fellow of the ◊Royal Society***.

fructose $C_6H_{12}O_6$ a sugar that occurs naturally in honey, the nectar of flowers, and many sweet fruits; it is commercially prepared from glucose.

It is a monosaccharide, whereas the more familiar cane or beet sugar is a disaccharide, made up of two monosaccharide units: fructose and glucose. It is sweeter than cane sugar and can be used to sweeten foods for people with diabetes.

fruit ***from Latin frui 'to enjoy'*** in botany, the ripened ovary in flowering plants that develops from one or more seeds or carpels and encloses one or more seeds. Its function is to protect the seeds during their development and to aid in their dispersal. Fruits are often edible, sweet, juicy, and colourful. When eaten they provide vitamins, minerals, and enzymes, but little protein. Most fruits are borne by perennial plants.

Fruits are divided into three agricultural categories on the basis of the climate in which they grow. **Temperate fruits** require a cold season for satisfactory growth; the principal temperate fruits are apples, pears, plums, peaches, apricots, cherries, and soft fruits, such as strawberries. **Subtropical fruits** require warm conditions but can survive light frosts; they include oranges and other citrus fruits, dates, pomegranates, and avocados. **Tropical fruits** cannot tolerate temperatures that drop close to freezing point; they include bananas, mangoes, pineapples, papayas, and litchis. Fruits can also be divided botanically into **dry** (such as the ◊capsule, ◊follicle, ◊schizocarp, ◊nut, ◊caryopsis, pod or legume, ◊lomentum, and ◊achene) and those that become **fleshy** (such as the ◊drupe and the ◊berry). The fruit structure consists of the pericarp or fruit wall, which is usually divided into a number of distinct layers. Sometimes parts other than the ovary are incorporated into the fruit structure, resulting in a false fruit or ◊pseudocarp, such as the apple and strawberry. True fruits include the tomato, orange, melon, and banana. Fruits may be dehiscent, which open to shed their seeds, or indehiscent, which remain unopened and are dispersed as a single unit. Simple fruits (for example, peaches) are derived from a single ovary, whereas compositae or multiple fruits (for example, blackberries) are formed from the ovaries of a number of flowers. In ordinary usage, 'fruit' includes only sweet, fleshy items; it excludes many botanical fruits such as acorns, bean pods, thistledown, and cucumbers.

methods of seed dispersal Efficient seed dispersal is essential to avoid overcrowding and enable plants to colonize new areas; the natural function of a fruit is to aid in the dissemination of the seeds which it contains. A great variety of dispersal mechanisms exist: winged fruits are commonly formed by trees, such as ash and elm, where they are in an ideal position to be carried away by the wind; some wind-dispersed fruits, such as clematis and cotton, have plumes of hairs; others are extremely light, like the poppy, in which the capsule acts like a pepperpot and shakes out the seeds as it is blown about by the wind. Some fruits float on water; the coconut can be dispersed across oceans by means of its buoyant fruit. Geraniums, gorse, and squirting cucumbers have explosive mechanisms, by which seeds are forcibly shot out at dehiscence. Animals often act as dispersal agents either by carrying hooked or sticky fruits (burs) attached to their bodies, or by eating succulent fruits, the seeds passing through the alimentary canal unharmed.

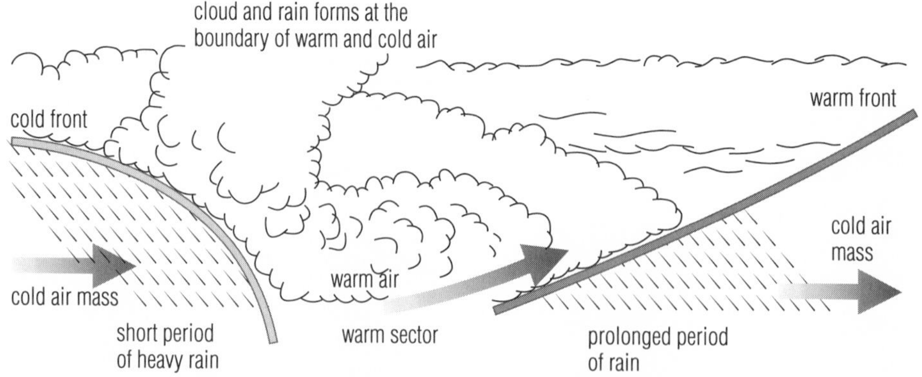

front *The boundaries between two air masses of different temperature and humidity. A warm front is when warm air displaces cold air; if cold air replaces warm air, it is a cold front.*

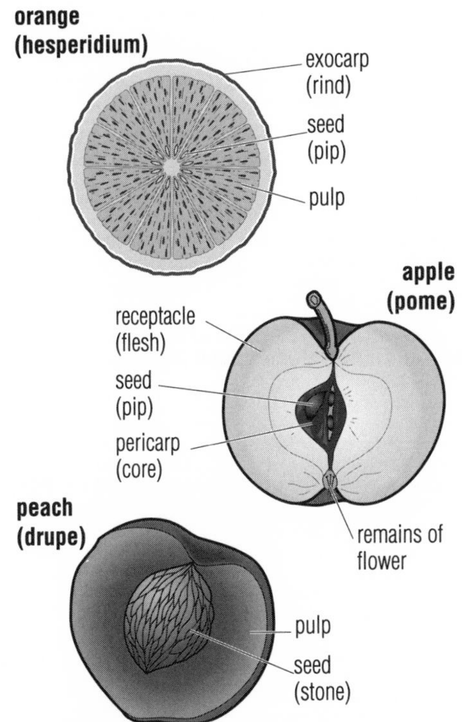

***fruit** A fruit contains the seeds of a plant. Its outer wall is the exocarp, or epicarp; its inner layers are the mesocarp and endocarp. The orange is a hesperidium, a berry having a leathery rind and containing many seeds. The peach is a drupe, a fleshy fruit with a hard seed, or 'stone', at the centre. The apple is a pome, a fruit with a fleshy outer layer and a core containing the seeds.*

Recorded world fruit production in the mid-1980s was approximately 300 million tonnes per year. Technical advances in storage and transport have made tropical fruits available to consumers in temperate areas, and fresh temperate fruits available all year in major markets.

frustule the cell wall of a ◊diatom (microscopic alga). Frustules are intricately patterned on the surface with spots, ridges, and furrows, each pattern being characteristic of a particular species.

frustum ***from Latin for 'a piece cut off'*** in geometry, a 'slice' taken out of a solid figure by a pair of parallel planes. A conical frustum, for example, resembles a cone with the top cut off. The volume and area of a frustum are calculated by subtracting the volume or area of the 'missing' piece from those of the whole figure.

FSF in computing, abbreviation for the ◊Free Software Foundation.

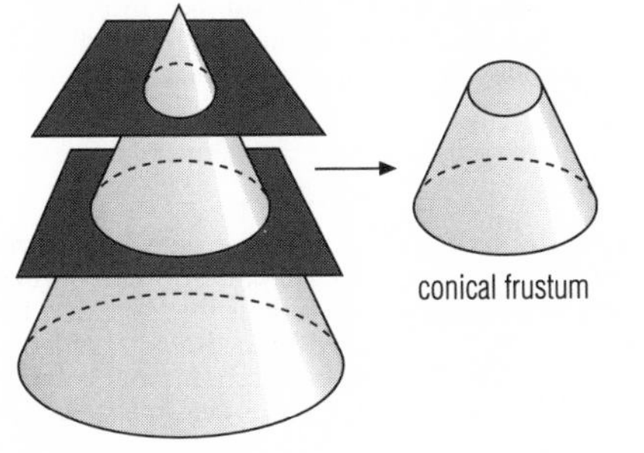

***frustum** The frustum, a slice taken out of a cone.*

FSH abbreviation for ◊follicle-stimulating hormone.

f-stop in photography, another name for ◊f-number.

ft symbol for ◊foot, **a measure of distance**.

FTP (abbreviation for ***File Transfer Protocol***) in computing, rules for transferring files between computers on the ◊Internet. The use of FTP avoids incompatibility between individual computers. To use FTP over the Internet, a user must have an Internet connection, an FTP client or World Wide Web◊ browser, and an account on the system holding the files. Many commercial and noncommercial systems allow anonymous FTP either to distribute new versions of software products or as a public service.

FTPmail in computing, an ◊FTP server that can be operated by e-mail. This service is useful for people with only limited access to the Internet.

fuchsia any shrub or ◊herbaceous plant of a group belonging to the evening-primrose family. Species are native to South and Central America and New Zealand, and bear red, purple, or pink bell-shaped flowers that hang downwards. (Genus *Fuchsia*, family Onagraceae.)

The genus was named in 1703 after German botanist Leonhard Fuchs (1501–1566).

fuel any source of heat or energy, embracing the entire range of materials that burn in air (combustibles). A **nuclear fuel** is any material that produces energy by nuclear fission in a nuclear reactor.

fuel cell cell converting chemical energy directly to electrical energy.

It works on the same principle as a battery but is continually fed with fuel, usually hydrogen. Fuel cells are silent and reliable (no moving parts) but expensive to produce.

Hydrogen is passed over an ◊electrode (usually nickel or platinum) containing a ◊catalyst, which strips electrons off the atoms. These pass through an external circuit while hydrogen ions (charged atoms) pass through an ◊electrolyte to another electrode, over which oxygen is passed. Water is formed at this electrode (as a by-product) in a chemical reaction involving electrons, hydrogen ions, and oxygen atoms. If the spare heat also produced is used for hot water and space heating, 80% efficiency in fuel is achieved.

fuel injection injecting fuel directly into the cylinders of an internal combustion engine, instead of by way of a carburettor. It is the standard method used in ◊diesel engines, and is now becoming standard for petrol engines. In the diesel engine, oil is injected into the hot compressed air at the top of the second piston stroke and explodes to drive the piston down on its power stroke. In the petrol engine, fuel is injected into the cylinder at the start of the first induction stroke of the ◊four-stroke cycle.

full duplex in computing, modem setting which means that two-way communication is enabled, so that everything you type is echoed back to the screen. See ◊duplex.

fullerene form of carbon, discovered in 1985, based on closed cages of carbon atoms. The molecules of the most symmetrical of the fullerenes are called ◊buckminsterfullerenes (or buckyballs). They are perfect spheres made up of 60 carbon atoms linked together in 12 pentagons and 20 hexagons fitted together like those of a spherical football. Other fullerenes, with 28, 32, 50, 70, and 76 carbon atoms, have also been identified.

Fullerenes can be made by arcing electricity between carbon rods. They may also occur in candle flames and in clouds of interstellar gas. Fullerene chemistry may turn out to be as important as organic chemistry based on the benzene ring. Already, new molecules based on the buckyball enclosing a metal atom, and 'buckytubes' (cylinders of carbon atoms arranged in hexagons), have been made. Applications envisaged include using the new molecules as lubricants, semiconductors, and superconductors, and as the starting point for making new drugs.

fuller's earth soft, greenish-grey rock resembling clay, but without clay's plasticity. It is formed largely of clay minerals, rich in montmorillonite, but a great deal of silica is also present. Its absorbent properties make it suitable for removing oil and grease, and it was formerly used for cleaning fleeces ('fulling'). It is still used in the textile industry, but its chief application is in the purification of oils. Beds of fuller's earth are found in the southern USA, Germany, Japan, and the UK.

full-motion video (FMV) in computing, video system that can display continuous motion. Some slow-speed CD-ROM drives and low-bandwidth networks are unable to handle the mass of data required for full-motion video, so video playback tends to jerk unevenly.

fulmar any of several species of petrels of the family Procellariidae, which are similar in size and colour to herring gulls. The northern fulmar *Fulmarus glacialis* is found in the North Atlantic and visits land only to nest, laying a single egg.

fulminate any salt of fulminic (cyanic) acid (HOCN), the chief ones being silver and mercury. The fulminates detonate (are exploded by a blow); see ◊detonator.

FULMAR

The world's official oldest wild bird is over 50 years old. It is a female fulmar, which nests each year on an uninhabited Orkney island. She has been monitored

fumitory any of a group of plants native to Europe and Asia. The common fumitory (*F. officinalis*) grows to 50 cm/20 in and produces pink flowers tipped with blackish red; it has been used in medicine for stomach and liver complaints. (Genus *Fumeria,* family Fumariaceae.)

function in computing, a small part of a program that supplies a specific value – for example, the square root of a specified number, or the current date. Most programming languages incorporate a number of built-in functions; some allow programmers to write their own. A function may have one or more arguments (the values on which the function operates). A **function key** on a keyboard is one that, when pressed, performs a designated task, such as ending a program.

function in mathematics, a function f is a non-empty set of ordered pairs $(x, f(x))$ of which no two can have the same first element. Hence, if $f(x) = x^2$ two ordered pairs are (–2,4) and (2,4). The set of all first elements in a function's ordered pairs is called the **domain**; the set of all second elements is the **range**. In the algebraic expression $y = 4x^3 + 2$, the dependent variable y is a function of the independent variable x, generally written as $f(x)$.

Functions are used in all branches of mathematics, physics, and science generally; for example, the formula $t = 2\pi\sqrt{(l/g)}$ shows that for a simple pendulum the time of swing t is a function of its length l and of no other variable quantity (π and g, the acceleration due to gravity, are ◊constants).

Form and function are a unity, two sides of one coin. In order to enhance function, appropriate form must exist or be created.

IDA ROLF US biochemist and physical therapist.
Rolfing, Preface

functional group in chemistry, a small number of atoms in an arrangement that determines the chemical properties of the group and of the molecule to which it is attached (for example, the carboxyl group COOH, or the amine group NH_2). Organic compounds can be considered as structural skeletons, with a high carbon content, with functional groups attached.

functional programming computer programming based largely on the definition of ◊functions. There are very few functional programming languages, HOPE and ML being the most widely used, though many more conventional languages (for example, C) make extensive use of functions.

function key key on a keyboard that, when pressed, performs a designated task, such as ending a computer program.

fundamental constant physical quantity that is constant in all circumstances throughout the whole universe. Examples are the electric charge of an electron, the speed of light, Planck's constant, and the gravitational constant.

Physical constants, or fundamental constants, are standardized values whose parameters do not change.

Constant	*Symbol*	*Value in SI units*
acceleration of free fall	g	$9.80665\ m\ s^{-2}$
Avogadro's constant	N_A	$6.0221367 \times 10^{23}\ mol^{-1}$
Boltzmann's constant	k	$1.380658 \times 10^{-23}\ J\ K^{-1}$
elementary charge	e	$1.60217733 \times 10^{-19}\ C$
electronic rest mass	m_e	$9.1093897 \times 10^{-31}\ kg$
Faraday's constant	F	$9.6485309 \times 10^{4}\ C\ mol^{-1}$
gas constant	R	$8.314510\ J\ K^{-1}\ mol^{-1}$
gravitational constant	G	$6.672 \times 10^{-11}\ N\ m^2\ kg^{-2}$
Loschmidt's number	N_L	$2.686763 \times 10^{25}\ m^{-3}$
neutron rest mass	m_n	$1.6749286 \times 10^{-27}\ kg$
Planck's constant	h	$6.6260755 \times 10^{-34}\ J\ s$
proton rest mass	m_p	$1.6726231 \times 10^{-27}\ kg$
speed of light in a vacuum	c	$2.99792458 \times 10^{8}\ m\ s^{-1}$
standard atmosphere	atm	$1.01325 \times 10^{5}\ Pa$
Stefan–Boltzmann constant	θ	$5.67051 \times 10^{-8}\ W\ m^{-2}\ K^{-4}$

fundamental forces see ◊forces, fundamental.

fundamental particle another term for ◊elementary particle.

fundamental vibration standing wave of the longest wavelength that can be established on a vibrating object such as a stretched string or air column. The sound produced by the fundamental vibration is the lowest-pitched (usually dominant) note heard.

The fundamental vibration of a string has a stationary ◊node at each end and a single ◊antinode at the centre where the amplitude of vibration is greatest.

fungicide any chemical ◊pesticide used to prevent fungus diseases in plants and animals. Inorganic and organic compounds containing sulphur are widely used.

fungus (plural ***fungi***) any of a unique group of organisms that includes moulds, yeasts, rusts, smuts, mildews, mushrooms, and toadstools. About 50,000 species have been identified. They are not considered to be plants for three main reasons: they have no leaves or roots; they contain no chlorophyll (green colouring) and are therefore unable to make their own food by ◊photosynthesis; and they reproduce by ◊spores. Some fungi are edible but many are highly poisonous; they often cause damage and sometimes disease

FUNGUS

Leaf-cutter ants feed their larvae on a fungus that they cultivate themselves in underground gardens. The ants depend on the fungus for food, and the fungus cannot reproduce without the ants. When a new queen takes flight to establish another colony, she takes some of the fungus with her in a special mouth pouch.

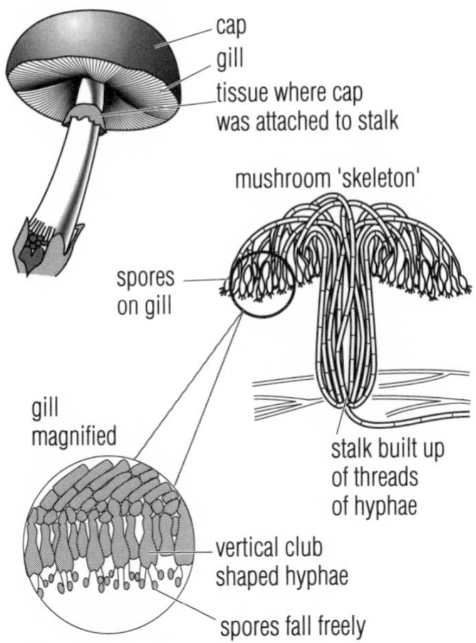

***fungus** Fungi grow from spores as fine threads, or hyphae. These have no distinct cellular structure. Mushrooms and toadstools are the fruiting bodies formed by the hyphae. Gills beneath the caps of these aerial structures produce masses of spores.*

to the organic matter they live and feed on, but some fungi are exploited in the production of food and drink (for example, yeasts in baking and brewing) and in medicine (for example, penicillin). (Kingdom Fungi.)

Fungi are either ◊parasites, existing on living plants or animals, or ◊saprotrophs, living on dead matter. Many of the most serious plant diseases are caused by fungi, and several fungi attack humans and animals. Athlete's foot, ◊thrush, and ◊ringworm are fungal diseases.

Before the classification Fungi came into use, they were included within the division Thallophyta, along with ◊algae and ◊bacteria. Two familiar fungi are bread mould, which illustrates the typical many-branched body (mycelium) of the organism, made up of threadlike chains of cells called hyphae; and mushrooms, which are the sexually reproductive fruiting bodies of an underground mycelium.

The mycelium of a true fungus is made up of many intertwined hyphae. When the fungus is ready to reproduce, the hyphae become closely packed into a solid mass called the fruiting body, which is usually small and inconspicuous but can be very large; mushrooms, toadstools, and bracket fungi are all examples of large fruiting bodies. These carry and distribute the spores. Most species of fungi reproduce both asexually (on their own) and sexually (involving male and female parents).

FUNGI

http://www.herb.lsa.umich.edu/kidpage/factindx.htm

University-run network of hyperlinked pages on fungi from their earliest fossil records to their current ecology and life cycles, from how they are classified systematically to how they are studied. Although this page is not shy of technical terms, there are clear explanations and pictures to help the uninitiated.

fur the ◊hair of certain animals. Fur is an excellent insulating material and so has been used as clothing. This is, however, vociferously criticized by many groups on humane grounds, as the methods of breeding or trapping animals are often cruel. Mink, chinchilla, and sable are among the most valuable, the wild furs being finer than the farmed.

Fur such as mink is made up of a soft, thick, insulating layer called underfur and a top layer of longer, lustrous guard hairs.

Furs have been worn since prehistoric times and have long been associated with status and luxury (ermine traditionally worn by royalty, for example), except by certain ethnic groups like the Inuit. The fur trade had its origin in North America, where in the late 17th century the Hudson's Bay Company was established. The chief centres of the fur trade are New York, London, St Petersburg, and Kastoria in Greece. It is illegal to import furs or skins of endangered species listed by ◊CITES (such as the leopard). Many synthetic fibres are widely used as substitutes.

furlong unit of measurement, originating in Anglo-Saxon England, equivalent to 220 yd (201.168 m).

A furlong consists of 40 rods, poles, or perches; 8 furlongs equal one statute ◊mile. Its literal meaning is 'furrow-long', and refers to the length of a furrow in the common field characteristic of medieval farming.

furnace structure in which fuel such as coal, coke, gas, or oil is burned to produce heat for various purposes. Furnaces are used in conjunction with ◊boilers for heating, to produce hot water, or steam for driving turbines – in ships for propulsion and in power stations for generating electricity. The largest furnaces are those used for smelting and refining metals, such as the ◊blast furnace, electric furnace, and ◊open-hearth furnace.

furniture beetle wood-boring beetle. See ◊woodworm

FurryMUCK in computing, popular ◊MUD site where the players take on the imaginary shapes and characters of furry, anthropomorphic animals.

furze another name for ◊gorse, a shrub.

fuse in electricity, a wire or strip of metal designed to melt when excessive current passes through. It is a safety device that halts surges of current which would otherwise damage equipment and cause fires. In explosives, a fuse is a cord impregnated with chemicals so that it burns slowly at a predetermined rate. It is used to set off a main explosive charge, sufficient length of fuse being left to allow the person lighting it to get away to safety.

fusel oil liquid with a characteristic unpleasant smell, obtained as a by-product of the distillation of the product of any alcoholic fermentation, and used in paints, varnishes, essential oils, and plastics. It is a mixture of fatty acids, alcohols, and esters.

fusion in physics, the fusing of the nuclei of light elements, such as hydrogen, into those of a heavier element, such as helium. The resultant loss in their combined mass is converted into energy. Stars and thermonuclear weapons are powered by nuclear fusion.

FUSION

http://www.pppl.gov/~rfheeter/

All-text site, but packed with information about fusion research and its applications. It is quite well-organized and it includes a glossary of commonly used terms to aid the uninitiated.

fuzzy logic in mathematics and computing, a form of knowledge representation suitable for notions (such as 'hot' or 'loud') that cannot be defined precisely but depend on their context. For example, a jug of water may be described as too hot or too cold, depending on whether it is to be used to wash one's face or to make tea.

The central idea of fuzzy logic is **probability of set membership**. For instance, referring to someone 175 cm/5 ft 9 in tall, the statement 'this person is tall' (or 'this person is a member of the set of tall people') might be about 70% true if that person is a man, and about 85% true if that person is a woman.

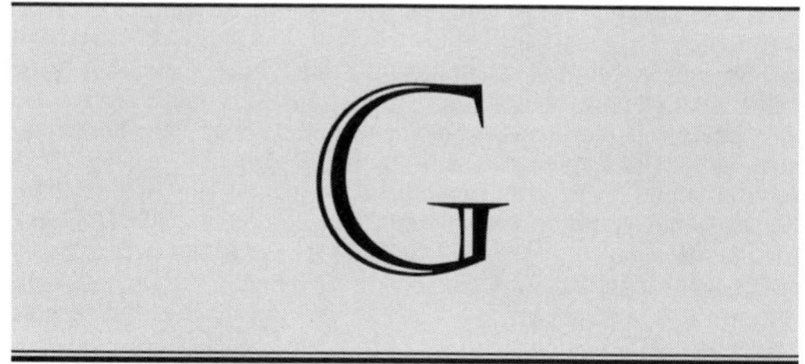

g symbol for ◊gram.

gabbro mafic (consisting primarily of dark-coloured crystals) igneous rock formed deep in the Earth's crust. It contains pyroxene and calcium-rich feldspar, and may contain small amounts of olivine and amphibole. Its coarse crystals of dull minerals give it a speckled appearance.

Gabbro is the plutonic version of basalt (that is, derived from magma that has solidified below the Earth's surface), and forms in large, slow-cooling intrusions.

Gabcikovo Dam hydroelectric dam on the river Danube, at the point where it crosses the frontier between Hungary and the Slovak Republic. A treaty agreeing to its construction was signed by Hungary and Czechoslovakia in 1977, but work was suspended in 1989 after Hungary withdrew its support for a scheme to divert water from the river. Czechoslovakia resumed work 1991, despite warnings from scientists and environmentalists that the scheme would destroy valuable wetlands in the Danube valley.

A dramatic reduction in river flow resulted from Czechoslovakia's first attempts to divert water November 1992, prompting the setting-up of an investigative committee, under the auspices of the European Community, and involving both parties concerned, to reassess the project.

gadfly fly that bites cattle, such as a ◊botfly or ◊horsefly.

gadolinium silvery-white metallic element of the lanthanide series, symbol Gd, atomic number 64, relative atomic mass 157.25. It is found in the products of nuclear fission and used in electronic components, alloys, and products needing to withstand high temperatures.

Gaia hypothesis theory that the Earth's living and nonliving systems form an inseparable whole that is regulated and kept adapted for life by living organisms themselves. The planet therefore functions as a single organism, or a giant cell. The hypothesis was elaborated by British scientist James Lovelock and first published in 1968.

> *The only laws of matter are those which our minds must fabricate, and the only laws of mind are fabricated by matter.*
>
> JAMES CLERK MAXWELL Scottish physicist. Attributed remark

gain in audio, the volume control.

gain in electronics, the ratio of the amplitude of the output signal produced by an amplifier to that of the input signal.

In a ◊voltage amplifier the voltage gain is the ratio of the output voltage to the input voltage; in an inverting ◊operational amplifier (op-amp) it is equal to the ratio of the resistance of the feedback resistor to that of the input resistor.

gal symbol for ◊gallon, ◊galileo.

galactic coordinates in astronomy, a system for measuring the position of astronomical objects on the ◊celestial sphere with reference to the galactic equator (or ◊great circle).

Galactic latitude (symbol b) is measured in degrees from the galactic equator (b = 0°) to the north (b = 90°) and south (b = – 90°) galactic poles.

Galactic longitude (symbol l) is measured in degrees eastward (l = 0° to 360°) from a fixed point in the constellation of ◊Sagittarius that approximates to the centre of the Galaxy. Galactic coordinates are often used when astronomers are studying the distribution of material in the ◊Galaxy.

galactic halo in astronomy, the outer, sparsely populated region of a galaxy, roughly spheroid in shape and extending far beyond the bulk of the visible stars. In our own Galaxy, the halo contains the globular clusters, and may harbour large quantities of ◊dark matter.

galactic plane in astronomy, a plane passing through the ◊Sun and the centre of the ◊Galaxy defining the mid-plane of the galactic disc. Viewed from the Earth, the galactic plane is a ◊great circle (galactic equator) marking the approximate centre line of the ◊Milky Way.

galago small African prosimian also known as ◊bushbaby.

galaxy congregation of millions or billions of stars, held together by gravity. **Spiral galaxies**, such as the ◊Milky Way, are flattened in shape, with a central bulge of old stars surrounded by a disc of younger stars, arranged in spiral arms like a Catherine wheel.

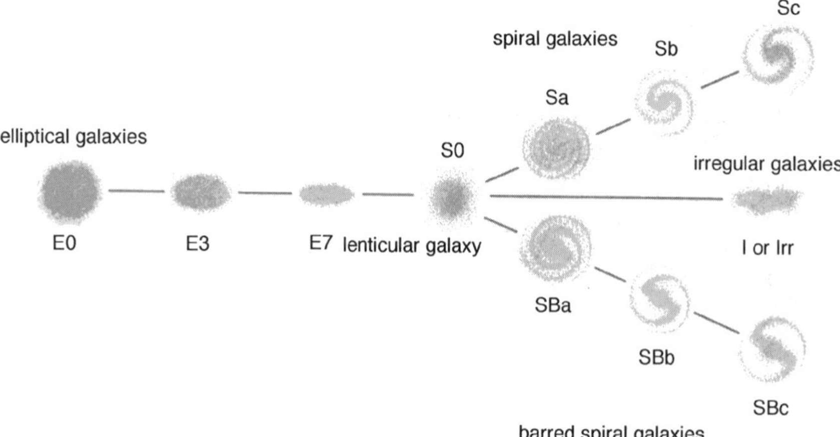

galaxy Galaxies were classified by US astronomer Edwin Hubble in 1925. He placed the galaxies in a 'tuning-fork' pattern, in which the two prongs correspond to the barred and non-barred spiral galaxies.

Barred spirals are spiral galaxies that have a straight bar of stars across their centre, from the ends of which the spiral arms emerge. The arms of spiral galaxies contain gas and dust from which new stars are still forming.

Elliptical galaxies contain old stars and very little gas. They include the most massive galaxies known, containing a trillion stars. At least some elliptical galaxies are thought to be formed by mergers between spiral galaxies. There are also irregular galaxies. Most galaxies occur in clusters, containing anything from a few to thousands of members.

Our own Galaxy, the Milky Way, is about 100,000 light years in diameter, and contains at least 100 billion stars. It is a member of a small cluster, the ◊Local Group. The Sun lies in one of its spiral arms, about 25,000 light years from the centre.

By the end of a five-year study in 1995, US astronomers had identified 600 previously uncatalogued galaxies, mostly 200–400 million light years away, leading to the conclusion that there may be 30–100% more galaxies than previously estimated. Two galaxies were discovered obscured by galactic dust at the edge of the Milky Way. One, named MB1, is a spiral galaxy 17,000 light years across; the other, MB2, is an irregular-shaped dwarf galaxy about 4,000 light years across. In 1996 US astronomers discovered a further new galaxy 17 million light years away. The galaxy NGC2915 is a blue compact dwarf galaxy and 95% of its mass is in the form of dark matter. In 1997 an international team of astronomers detected the furthest known object in the universe, which is a galaxy lying 13 billion light years away.

galena mineral consisting of lead sulphide, PbS, the chief ore of lead. It is lead-grey in colour, has a high metallic lustre and breaks into cubes because of its perfect cubic cleavage. It may contain up to 1% silver, and so the ore is sometimes mined for both metals. Galena occurs mainly among limestone deposits in Australia, Mexico, Russia, Kazakhstan, the UK, and the USA.

galileo unit (symbol gal) of acceleration, used in geological surveying. One galileo is 10^{-2} metres per second per second. The

Galileo
(1564–1642)

properly Galileo Galilei Italian mathematician, astronomer, and physicist. He developed the astronomical telescope and was the first to see sunspots, the four main satellites of Jupiter, and the appearance of Venus going through phases, thus proving it was orbiting the Sun. Galileo discovered that freely falling bodies, heavy or light, have the same, constant acceleration and that this acceleration is due to gravity. He also determined that a body moving on a perfectly smooth horizontal surface would neither speed up nor slow down. He invented a thermometer, a hydrostatic balance, and a compass, and discovered that the path of a projectile is a parabola.

Galileo's work founded the modern scientific method of deducing laws to explain the results of observation and experiment, although the story of his dropping cannonballs from the Leaning Tower of Pisa is questionable. His observations were an unwelcome refutation of the ideas of the Greek philosopher Aristotle taught at the church-run universities, largely because they made plausible for the first time the Sun-centred theory of Polish astronomer Nicolaus Copernicus. Galileo's persuasive *Dialogo sopra i due massimi sistemi del mondo/Dialogues on the Two Chief Systems of the World* 1632 was banned by the church authorities in Rome and he was made to recant by the Inquisition. Evangelista Torricelli is the most famous of his pupils.

astronomy and the invention of the telescope In July 1609, hearing that a Dutch scientist had made a telescope, Galileo worked out the principles involved and made a number of telescopes. He compiled fairly accurate tables of the orbits of four of Jupiter's satellites and proposed that their frequent eclipses could serve as a means of determining longitude on land and at sea. His observations on sunspots and Venus going through phases supported Copernicus's theory that the Earth rotated and orbited the Sun. Galileo's results published in *Sidereus Nuncius/The Starry Messenger* 1610 were revolutionary.

Mary Evans Picture Library

He believed, however – following both Greek and medieval tradition – that orbits must be circular, not elliptical, in order to maintain the fabric of the cosmos in a state of perfection. This preconception prevented him from deriving a full formulation of the law of inertia, which was later to be attributed to the contemporary French mathematician René Descartes.

the pendulum Galileo made several fundamental contributions to mechanics. He rejected the impetus theory that a force or push is required to sustain motion. While watching swinging lamps in Pisa cathedral, Galileo determined that each oscillation of a pendulum takes the same amount of time despite the difference in amplitude, and recognized the potential importance of this observation to timekeeping. In a later publication, he presented his derivation that the square of the period of a pendulum varies with its length (and is independent of the mass of the pendulum bob).

mechanics and the law of falling bodies Galileo discovered before Newton that two objects of different weights – an apple and a melon, for instance – falling from the same height would hit the ground at the same time. He realized that gravity not only causes a body to fall, but also determines the motion of rising bodies and, furthermore, that gravity extends to the centre of the Earth. Galileo then showed that the motion of a projectile is made up of two components: one component consists of uniform motion in a horizontal direction, and the other component is vertical motion under acceleration or deceleration due to gravity.

Galileo used this explanation to refute objections to Copernicus. The Church argued that a turning Earth would not carry along birds and clouds. Galileo explained that motion of a bird, like a projectile, has a horizontal component that is provided by the motion of the Earth and that this horizontal component of motion always exists to keep such objects in position even though they are not attached to the ground.

Galileo came to an understanding of uniform velocity and uniform acceleration by measuring the time it takes for bodies to move various distances. He had the brilliant idea of slowing vertical motion by measuring the movement of balls rolling down inclined planes, realizing that the vertical component of this motion is a uniform acceleration due to gravity. It took Galileo many years to arrive at the correct expression of the law of falling bodies, which he presented in *Discorsi e dimostrazioni matematiche intorno a due nove scienze/Discourses and Mathematical Discoveries Concerning Two New Sciences* 1638 as:

$$s=1/2at^2$$

where s is speed, a is the acceleration due to gravity, and t is time. He found that the distance travelled by a falling body is proportional to the square of the time of descent.

A summation of his life's work, *Discourses* also included the facts that the trajectory of a projectile is a parabola, and that the law of falling bodies is perfectly obeyed only in a vacuum, and that air resistance always causes a uniform terminal velocity to be reached.

Earth's gravitational field often differs by several milligals (thousandths of gals) in different places, because of the varying densities of the rocks beneath the surface.

GALILEO PROJECT INFORMATION

http://nssdc.gsfc.nasa.gov/planetary/galileo.html

Site dedicated to the Galileo Project and the opportunities it has offered scientists and astronomers to enhance our understanding of the universe. The site includes information about the mission's objectives, scientific results, images, and links to other relevant sites on the Web.

Galileo spacecraft launched from the space shuttle *Atlantis* October 1989, on a six-year journey to Jupiter. *Galileo's* probe entered the atmosphere of Jupiter December 1995. It radioed information back to the orbiter for 57 minutes before it was destroyed by atmospheric pressure. The orbiter will continue circling Jupiter until 1997. Despite technical problems data is still being relayed to Earth, but very slowly. The first pictures of Jupiter are due July 1996.

It flew past Venus February 1990 and passed within 970 km/600 mi of Earth December 1990, using the gravitational fields of these two planets to increase its velocity. It flew past the asteroids Gaspra in 1991 and Ida in 1993, taking close-up photographs.

At the end of July 1995, and 55 million km/34 million mi from Jupiter, *Galileo* entered a dust storm and began detecting up to 20,000 particles a day (previously the maximum detected was 200). The dust is associated with Jupiter, and may come from the planet itself, its rings, or its satellites.

Galileo The Galileo *spacecraft about to be detached from the Earth-orbiting space shuttle* Atlantis *at the beginning of its six-year journey to Jupiter. National Aeronautical Space Agency*

gall abnormal outgrowth on a plant that develops as a result of attack by insects or, less commonly, by bacteria, fungi, mites, or nematodes. The attack causes an increase in the number of cells or an enlargement of existing cells in the plant. Gall-forming insects generally pass the early stages of their life inside the gall.

Gall wasps are responsible for the conspicuous bud galls forming on oak trees, 2.5–4 cm/1–1.5 in across, known as 'oak apples'. The organisms that cause galls are host-specific. Thus, for example, gall wasps tend to parasitize oaks, and ◊sawflies willows.

gall bladder small muscular sac, part of the digestive system of most, but not all, vertebrates. In humans, it is situated on the underside of the liver and connected to the small intestine by the bile duct. It stores bile from the liver.

galley ship powered by oars, and usually also equipped with sails. Galleys typically had a crew of hundreds of rowers arranged in banks. They were used in warfare in the Mediterranean from antiquity until the 18th century.

France maintained a fleet of some 40 galleys, crewed by over 10,000 convicts, until 1748. The maximum speed of a galley is estimated to have been only four knots (7.5 kph/4.5 mph), because only 20% of the rower's effort was effective, and galleys could not be used in stormy weather because of their very low waterline.

gallium grey metallic element, symbol Ga, atomic number 31, relative atomic mass 69.72. It is liquid at room temperature. Gallium arsenide (GaAs) crystals are used in microelectronics, since electrons travel a thousand times faster through them than through silicon. The element was discovered in 1875 by Lecoq de Boisbaudran (1838–1912).

gallium arsenide compound of gallium and arsenic, formula GaAs, used in lasers, photocells, and microwave generators. Its semiconducting properties make it a possible rival to ◊silicon for use in microprocessors. Chips made from gallium arsenide require less electric power and process data faster than those made from silicon.

gall midge minute and fragile long-legged flies, with longish hairy antennae. The larvae are small maggots, ranging in colour from white or yellow, to orange and bright red, that feed on developing fruits which become deformed and decay, and frequently produce ◊galls on plants.

Some forms live within galls formed by other insects, such as beetles, or other species of Cecidomyiidae. The ◊hessian fly of North America and New Zealand, is a pest of wheat. The **pearl midge** *Contarinia pyrivota* is a serious fruit pest in Europe.

classification Gall midges are in the family Cecidomyiidae (suborder Nematocera) of the insect order Diptera, class Insecta, phylum Arthropoda.

gallon imperial liquid or dry measure, equal to 4.546 litres, and subdivided into four quarts or eight pints. The US gallon is equivalent to 3.785 litres.

gallstone pebblelike, insoluble accretion formed in the human gall bladder or bile ducts from cholesterol or calcium salts present in bile. Gallstones may be symptomless or they may cause pain, indigestion, or jaundice. They can be dissolved with medication or removed, either by means of an endoscope or, along with the gall bladder, in an operation known as cholecystectomy.

gall wasp small (only a few millimetres long), dark-coloured insect with a compressed abdomen. Most gall wasps form ◊galls, though a few live within the galls formed by other species; these are called **inquilines**. Others feed on gall-formers and inquilines.

classification Gall wasps are in the family Cynipidae, order Hymenoptera, class Insecta, phylum Arthropoda.

The exact reactions which lead to gall formation in the host plant are little understood. Basically it is a reaction of the cells of the plant to the presence of the larva.

complex life history The oak-apple gall is caused by species *Biorhiza pallida* and both winged males and wingless or vestigial-winged females emerge from these galls. After mating the females lay their eggs in the root of the same host plant, thus producing root galls. In the following spring only wingless females are produced. These females climb up the oak tree and produce the characteristic oak-apples, thus repeating the life cycle.

Rose galls are often produced by *Diplolepis rosae*. These gall wasps usually reproduce asexually; the females are about 4 mm/0.2 in long; parts of their abdomens and legs are yellow-red, while the rest of the body is black. Males of this species have been observed only rarely. The galls are a mass of reddish filaments within which are found a number of sealed chambers enclosing larvae. The larvae feed on the gall tissue.

galvanizing process for rendering iron rust-proof, by plunging it into molten zinc (the dipping method), or by electroplating it with zinc.

galvanometer instrument for detecting small electric currents by their magnetic effect.

games console computer capable only of playing games, which are supplied as cartridges or CD-ROM discs that slot directly into the console.

gamete cell that functions in sexual reproduction by merging with another gamete to form a ◊zygote. Examples of gametes include sperm and egg cells. In most organisms, the gametes are haploid (they contain half the number of chromosomes of the parent), owing to reduction division or ◊meiosis.

In higher organisms, gametes are of two distinct types: large immobile ones known as eggs or egg cells (see ◊ovum) and small ones known as ◊sperm. They come together at ◊fertilization. In some lower organisms the gametes are all the same, or they may belong to different mating strains but have no obvious differences in size or appearance.

game theory group of mathematical theories, developed in 1944 by Oscar Morgenstern (1902–1977) and John Von Neumann, that seeks to abstract from invented game-playing scenarios and their outcome the essence of situations of conflict and/or cooperation in the real political, business, and social world.

A feature of such games is that the rationality of a decision by one player will depend on what the others do; hence game theory has particular application to the study of oligopoly (a market largely controlled by a few producers).

> *A theory is a good theory if it satisfies two requirements: it must accurately describe a large class of observations on the basis of a model that contains only a few arbitrary elements, and it must make definite predictions about the results of future predictions.*
>
> STEPHEN HAWKING English physicist. *A Brief History of Time* 1988

gametophyte the ◊haploid generation in the life cycle of a plant that produces gametes; see ◊alternation of generations.

gamma radiation very high-frequency electromagnetic radiation, similar in nature to X-rays but of shorter wavelength, emitted by the nuclei of radioactive substances during decay or by the interactions of high-energy electrons with matter. Cosmic gamma rays have been identified as coming from pulsars, radio galaxies, and quasars, although they cannot penetrate the Earth's atmosphere.

Gamma rays are stopped only by direct collision with an atom and are therefore very penetrating; they can, however, be stopped by about 4 cm/1.5 in of lead or by a very thick concrete shield. They are less ionizing in their effect than alpha and beta particles, but are dangerous nevertheless because they can penetrate deeply into body tissues such as bone marrow. They are not deflected by either magnetic or electric fields.

Gamma radiation is used to kill bacteria and other microorganisms, sterilize medical devices, and change the molecular structure of plastics to modify their properties (for example, to improve their resistance to heat and abrasion).

gamma-ray astronomy the study of gamma rays from space. Much of the radiation detected comes from collisions between hydrogen gas and cosmic rays in our Galaxy. Some sources have been identified, including the Crab nebula and the Vela pulsar (the most powerful gamma-ray source detected).

Gamma rays are difficult to detect and are generally studied by use of balloon-borne detectors and artificial satellites. The first gamma-ray satellites were *SAS II* (1972) and *COS B* (1975), although gamma-ray detectors were carried on the *Apollo 15* and *16* missions. *SAS II* failed after only a few months, but *COS B* continued working until 1982, carrying out a complete survey of the galactic disc.

ganglion (plural *ganglia*) solid cluster of nervous tissue containing many cell bodies and ◊synapses, usually enclosed in a tissue sheath; found in invertebrates and vertebrates.

In many invertebrates, the central nervous system consists mainly of ganglia connected by nerve cords. The ganglia in the head (cerebral ganglia) are usually well developed and are analogous to the brain in vertebrates. In vertebrates, most ganglia occur outside the central nervous system.

gangrene death and decay of body tissue (often of a limb) due to bacterial action; the affected part gradually turns black and causes blood poisoning.

Gangrene sets in as a result of loss of blood supply to the area. This may be due to disease (diabetes, atherosclerosis), an obstruction of a major blood vessel (as in ◊thrombosis), injury, or frostbite. Bacteria colonize the site unopposed, and a strong risk of blood poisoning often leads to surgical removal of the tissue or the affected part (amputation).

gannet any of three species of North Atlantic seabirds; the largest is *Sula bassana*. When fully grown, it is white with buff colouring on the head and neck; the beak is long and thick and compressed at the point; the wings are black-tipped with a span of 1.7 m/5.6 ft. It breeds on cliffs in nests made of grass and seaweed, laying a single white egg. Gannets feed on fish that swim near the surface, such as herrings and pilchards. (Family Sulidae, order Pelecaniformaes.)

Diving swiftly and sometimes from a considerable height upon their prey, they enter the water with closed wings and neck outstretched. They belong to the same family as the ◊booby.

The gannets are the largest seabirds of the North Atlantic; they are found also in the southeast Pacific and in temperate waters off Africa.

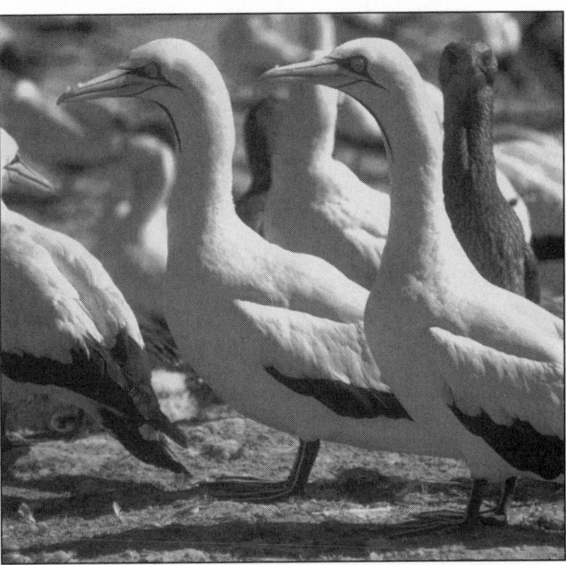

gannet *The Cape gannet* Morus capensis. *It forms dense breeding colonies around the coasts of S Africa, incubating its single egg with its feet. Gannets are accomplished 'plunge divers' and make a spectacular sight when fishing. Premaphotos Wildlife*

Ganymede in astronomy, the largest moon of the planet Jupiter, and the largest moon in the Solar System, 5,260 km/3,270 mi in diameter (larger than the planet Mercury). It orbits Jupiter every 7.2 days at a distance of 1.1 million km/700,000 mi. Its surface is a mixture of cratered and grooved terrain. Molecular oxygen was identified on Ganymede's surface in 1994.

The space probe *Galileo* detected a magnetic field around Ganymede in 1996; this suggests it may have a molten core. *Galileo* photographed Ganymede at a distance of 7,448 km/4,628 mi. The resulting images were 17 times clearer than those taken by *Voyager 2* in 1979, and show the surface to be extensively cratered and ridged, probably as a result of forces similar to those that create mountains on Earth. *Galileo* also detected molecules containing both carbon and nitrogen on the surface March 1997. Their presence may indicate that Ganymede harboured life at some time.

gar any of a group of primitive bony fishes, which also includes ◊sturgeons. Gar have long, beaklike snouts and elongated bodies covered in heavy, bony scales. All four species of gar live in freshwater rivers and lakes of the Mississippi drainage. See also ◊needlefish. (Order Semionotiformes.)

gardenia any of a group of subtropical and tropical trees and shrubs found in Africa and Asia, belonging to the madder family, with evergreen foliage and flattened rosettes of fragrant waxen-looking flowers, often white in colour. (Genus *Gardenia*, family Rubiaceae.)

garfish European marine fish with a long spearlike snout. The common garfish (*Belone belone*) has an elongated body measuring 75 cm/2.5 ft in length. (Family Belonidae, order Beloniformes.)

garlic perennial Asian plant belonging to the lily family, whose strong-smelling and sharp-tasting bulb, made up of several small segments, or cloves, is used in cooking. The plant has white flowers. It is widely cultivated and has been used successfully as a fungicide in the cereal grass ◊sorghum. It also has antibacterial properties. (*Allium sativum*, family Liliaceae.)

In tests carried out in 1994, US doctors found freshly pressed garlic extract killed a number of bacteria, including drug-resistant strains, even when diluted to one part in 250. Its effectiveness is probably due to allicin, a simple organic disulphide.

garnet group of ◊silicate minerals with the formula $X_3Y_3(SiO_4)_3$, where X is calcium, magnesium, iron, or manganese, and Y is usually aluminium or sometimes iron or chromium. Garnets are used as semiprecious gems (usually pink to deep red) and as abrasives. They occur in metamorphic rocks such as gneiss and schist.

Garnets consisting of neodymium, yttrium, and aluminium (referred to as Nd-YAG) produce infrared laser light when sufficiently excited. Nd-YAG lasers are inexpensive and used widely in industry and scientific research.

garpike freshwater bony fish. It has an elongated snout and its body is covered with thick scales. Garpikes are predators found in North America.

classification Garpikes are in the family Lepisosteidae, order Lepisosteiformes, class Osteichthyes.

gas in physics, a form of matter, such as air, in which the molecules move randomly in otherwise empty space, filling any size or shape of container into which the gas is put.

A sugar-lump sized cube of air at room temperature contains 30 trillion molecules moving at an average speed of 500 metres per second (1,800 kph/1,200 mph). Gases can be liquefied by cooling, which lowers the speed of the molecules and enables attractive forces between them to bind them together.

GAS UTILITIES HISTORY

http://www.geocities.com/Athens/Acropolis/4007/gsframe.htm

Despite the irritating frames layout of this web site it does contain plenty of information on the origins of the natural gas industry. The information database held here is searchable by country, time, or company, and the information pops up in another frame.

gas collection method used to collect a gas in a laboratory preparation. The properties of the gas, and whether it is required dry, dictate the method used. Dry ammonia is collected by downward displacement of air.

gas constant in physics, the constant R that appears in the equation $PV = nRT$, which describes how the pressure P, volume V, and temperature T of an ideal gas are related (n is the amount of gas in moles). This equation combines ◊Boyle's law and ◊Charles's law.

R has a value of 8.3145 joules per kelvin per mole.

gas-cooled reactor type of nuclear reactor; see ◊advanced gas-cooled reactor.

gas engine internal-combustion engine in which a gas (coal gas, producer gas, natural gas, or gas from a blast furnace) is used as the fuel.

The first practical gas engine was built in 1860 by Jean Etienne Lenoir, and the type was subsequently developed by Nikolaus August Otto, who introduced the ◊four-stroke cycle.

gas exchange movement of gases between an organism and the atmosphere, principally oxygen and carbon dioxide. All aerobic organisms (most animals and plants) take in oxygen in order to burn food and manufacture ◊ATP. The resultant oxidation reactions release carbon dioxide as a waste product to be passed out into the environment. Green plants also absorb carbon dioxide during ◊photosynthesis, and release oxygen as a waste product.

Specialized respiratory surfaces have evolved during evolution to make gas exchange more efficient. In humans and other tetrapods (four-limbed vertebrates), gas exchange occurs in the ◊lungs, aided by the breathing movements of the ribs. Many adult amphibia and terrestrial invertebrates can absorb oxygen directly through the skin. The bodies of insects and some spiders contain a system of air-filled tubes known as ◊tracheae. Fish have ◊gills as their main respiratory surface. In plants, gas exchange generally takes place via the ◊stomata and the air-filled spaces between the cells in the interior of the leaf.

gas giant in astronomy, any of the four large outer ◊planets of the Solar System, ◊Jupiter, ◊Saturn, ◊Uranus, and ◊Neptune, which consist largely of gas and have no solid surface.

gas laws physical laws concerning the behaviour of gases. They include ◊Boyle's law and ◊Charles's law, which are concerned with the relationships between the pressure, temperature, and volume of an ideal (hypothetical) gas. These two laws can be combined to give the **general** or **universal gas law**, which may be expressed as:

$$(\text{pressure} \times \text{volume})/\text{temperature} = \text{constant}$$

Van der Waals' law includes corrections for the nonideal behaviour of real gases.

gasohol motor fuel that is 90% petrol and 10% ethanol (alcohol). The ethanol is usually obtained by fermentation, followed by distillation, using maize, wheat, potatoes, or sugar cane. It was used in early cars before petrol became economical, and its use was revived during the 1940s war shortage and the energy shortage of the 1970s, for example in Brazil.

gasoline the US term for ◊petrol.

gas syringe graduated piece of glass apparatus used to measure accurately the volumes of gases.

gastroenteritis inflammation of the stomach and intestines, giving rise to abdominal pain, vomiting, and diarrhoea. It may be caused by food or other poisoning, allergy, or infection. Dehydration may be severe and it is a particular risk in infants.

gastrolith stone that was once part of the digestive system of a dinosaur or other extinct animal. Rock fragments were swallowed to assist in the grinding process in the dinosaur digestive tract, much as some birds now swallow grit and pebbles to grind food in their crop. Once the animal has decayed, smooth round stones remain – often the only clue to their past use is the fact that they are geologically different from their surrounding strata.

gastropod any member of a very large group of ◊molluscs (soft-bodied invertebrate animals). Gastropods have a single shell (in a spiral or modified spiral form) and eyes on stalks, and they move on a flattened, muscular foot. They have well-developed heads and rough, scraping tongues called radulae. Some are marine, some freshwater, and others land creatures, but they all tend to live in damp places. (Class Gastropoda.)

gas turbine engine in which burning fuel supplies hot gas to spin a ◊turbine. The most widespread application of gas turbines has been in aviation. All jet engines (see under ◊jet propulsion) are modified gas turbines, and some locomotives and ships also use gas turbines as a power source.

They are also used in industry for generating and pumping purposes.

In a typical gas turbine a multivaned compressor draws in and compresses air. The compressed air enters a combustion chamber at high pressure, and fuel is sprayed in and ignited. The hot gases produced escape through the blades of (typically) two turbines and spin them around. One of the turbines drives the compressor; the other provides the external power that can be harnessed.

gate, logic in electronics, see ◊logic gate.

Gates, Bill (William) Henry, III (1955–) US businessman and computer programmer. He co-founded ◊Microsoft Corporation in 1975 and was responsible for supplying MS-DOS, the operating system and the Basic language that ◊IBM used in the IBM PC.

In 1997 Gates controlled a $39.8 billion shareholding in Microsoft, making him the world's richest individual.

When the IBM deal was struck in 1980, Microsoft did not actually have an operating system, but Gates bought one from another company, renamed it MS-DOS, and modified it to suit IBM's new computer. Microsoft also retained the right to sell MS-DOS to other computer manufacturers, and because the IBM PC was not only successful but easily copied by other manufacturers, MS-DOS found its way onto the vast majority of PCs. The revenue from MS-DOS helped Microsoft to expand into other areas of software, guided by Gates.

gateway in computing, the point of contact between two ◊wide-area networks.

gauge any scientific measuring instrument – for example, a wire gauge or a pressure gauge. The term is also applied to the width of a railway or tramway track.

gauge boson or ***field particle*** any of the particles that carry the four fundamental forces of nature (see ◊forces, fundamental).

Gauge bosons are ◊elementary particles that cannot be subdivided, and include the photon, the graviton, the gluons, and the weakons.

gaur Asiatic wild ox, dark grey-brown in colour with white 'socks' and standing 2 m/6 ft tall at the shoulders. It originally roamed across a vast area of land stretching from India to SE Asia and Malaysia, but population numbers and the area where it can be found are now much smaller. (Species *Bos gaurus.*)

gauss c.g.s. unit (symbol Gs) of magnetic induction or magnetic flux density, replaced by the SI unit, the ◊tesla, but still commonly used. It is equal to one line of magnetic flux per square centimetre. The Earth's magnetic field is about 0.5 Gs, and changes to it over time are measured in gammas (one gamma equals 10^{-5} gauss).

gavial large reptile related to the crocodile. It grows to about 7 m/23 ft long, and has a very long snout with about 100 teeth in its jaws. Gavials live in rivers in northern India, where they feed on fish and frogs. They have been extensively hunted for their skins, and are now extremely rare. (Species *Gavialis gangeticus.*)

gayal species of ox found in the highland regions of east India and Burma. The animal is often found wild, but just as frequently in a semi-domesticated condition. It is smaller than the ◊gaur, and its horns are much straighter.

The gayal and the gaur frequently interbreed.

classification The gayal *Bos frontalis* is in family Bovidae (cattle and antelopes) of order Artiodactyla.

GAVIAL

http://www.sdcs.k12.ca.us/roosevelt/gavialhome.html

Well-presented information about the gavial. Intended to educate children about this harmless reptile, the site has information on habitat, diet, interaction with humans, and reproduction.

Gay-Lussac, Joseph Louis (1778–1850)

French physicist and chemist who investigated the physical properties of gases, and discovered new methods of producing sulphuric and oxalic acids. In 1802 he discovered the approximate rule for the expansion of gases now known as Charles's law; see also gas laws.

Mary Evans Picture Library

gazelle any of a number of lightly built, fast-running antelopes found on the open plains of Africa and southern Asia. (Especially species of the genus *Gazella.*)

gear toothed wheel that transmits the turning movement of one shaft to another shaft. Gear wheels may be used in pairs, or in threes if both shafts are to turn in the same direction. The gear ratio – the ratio of the number of teeth on the two wheels – determines the torque ratio, the turning force on the output shaft compared with the turning force on the input shaft. The ratio of the angular velocities of the shafts is the inverse of the gear ratio.

The common type of gear for parallel shafts is the **spur gear**, with straight teeth parallel to the shaft axis. The **helical gear** has teeth cut along sections of a helix or corkscrew shape; the double form of the helix gear is the most efficient for energy transfer. **Bevel gears**, with tapering teeth set on the base of a cone, are used to connect intersecting shafts.

gecko any of a group of lizards. Geckos are common worldwide in warm climates, and have large heads and short, stout bodies. Many have no eyelids. Their sticky toe pads enable them to climb vertically and walk upside down on smooth surfaces in their search for flies, spiders, and other prey. (Family Gekkonidae.)

There are about 850 known species of gecko. There are 102 Australian species, 17 new species having been discovered there

GECKO

One species of Hawaiian gecko reproduces without sex to create all-female populations. These females have fewer parasites (and thus better health) than their mixed-gender neighbours.

1986–96. A new species of gecko *Tarentola mindiae* was identified in Egypt's Western Desert in 1997.

geebung Australian shrub or tree of the genus *Persoonia* of the Proteaceae family with small bell-shaped cream or yellow flowers.

geek in computing, stereotypical exceptionally bright, obsessive computer user or programmer. See also ◊anorak and ◊nerd.

Geiger, Hans (Wilhelm) (1882–1945)

German physicist who produced the Geiger counter. He spent the period 1906–12 in Manchester, England, working with Ernest Rutherford on radioactivity. In 1908 they designed an instrument to detect and count alpha particles, positively charged ionizing particles produced by radioactive decay.

In 1928 Geiger and Walther Müller produced a more sensitive version of the counter, which could detect all kinds of ionizing radiation.

Geiger counter any of a number of devices used for detecting nuclear radiation and/or measuring its intensity by counting the number of ionizing particles produced (see ◊radioactivity). It detects the momentary current that passes between ◊electrodes in a suitable gas when a nuclear particle or a radiation pulse causes the ionization of that gas. The electrodes are connected to electronic devices that enable the number of particles passing to be measured. The increased frequency of measured particles indicates the intensity of radiation. The device is named after the German physicist Hans ◊Geiger.

The Geiger–Müller, Geiger–Klemperer, and Rutherford–Geiger counters are all devices often referred to loosely as Geiger counters.

Geissler tube high-voltage ◊discharge tube in which traces of gas ionize and conduct electricity. Since the electrified gas takes on a luminous colour characteristic of the gas, the instrument is also used in ◊spectroscopy. It was developed in 1858 by the German physicist Heinrich Geissler.

gel solid produced by the formation of a three-dimensional cage structure, commonly of linked large-molecular-mass polymers, in which a liquid is trapped. It is a form of ◊colloid. A gel may be a jellylike mass (pectin, gelatin) or have a more rigid structure (silica gel).

gelignite type of ◊dynamite.

gem mineral valuable by virtue of its durability (hardness), rarity, and beauty, cut and polished for ornamental use, or engraved. Of 120 minerals known to have been used as gemstones, only about 25 are in common use in jewellery today; of these, the diamond, emerald, ruby, and sapphire are classified as precious, and all the others semiprecious; for example, the topaz, amethyst, opal, and aquamarine.

Among the synthetic precious stones to have been successfully produced are rubies, sapphires, emeralds, and diamonds (first produced by General Electric in the USA in 1955). Pearls are not technically gems.

Gemini prominent zodiacal constellation in the northern hemisphere represented as the twins Castor and Pollux. Its brightest star is ◊Pollux; Castor is a system of six stars. The Sun passes through Gemini from late June to late July. Each December, the Geminid meteors radiate from Gemini. In astrology, the dates for Gemini are between about 21 May and 21 June (see ◊precession).

Gemini project US space programme (1965–66) in which astronauts practised rendezvous and docking of spacecraft, and working outside their spacecraft, in preparation for the Apollo Moon landings.

Gemini spacecraft carried two astronauts and were launched by Titan rockets.

gemma (plural ***gemmae***) unit of ◊vegetative reproduction, consisting of a small group of undifferentiated green cells. Gemmae are found in certain mosses and liverworts, forming on the surface of the plant, often in cup-shaped structures, or gemmae cups. Gemmae are dispersed by splashes of rain and can then develop into new plants. In many species, gemmation is more common than reproduction by ◊spores.

gemsbok species of antelope that inhabits the desert regions of southern Africa. It stands about 1.2 m/4 ft in height, and its general colour is greyish. Its horns are just over 1 m/3.3 ft long.
classification The gemsbok *Oryx gazella* is in family Bovidae, order Artiodactyla.

gene unit of inherited material, encoded by a strand of ◊DNA and transcribed by ◊RNA. In higher organisms, genes are located on the ◊chromosomes. A gene consistently affects a particular character in an individual – for example, the gene for eye colour. Also termed a Mendelian gene, after Austrian biologist Gregor ◊Mendel, it occurs at a particular point, or locus, on a particular chromosome and may have several variants, or ◊alleles, each specifying a particular form of that character – for example, the alleles for blue or brown eyes. Some alleles show ◊dominance. These mask the effect of other alleles, known as ◊recessive.

In the 1940s, it was established that a gene could be identified with a particular length of DNA, which coded for a complete protein molecule, leading to the 'one gene, one enzyme' principle. Later it was realized that proteins can be made up of several ◊polypeptide chains, each with a separate gene, so this principle was modified to 'one gene, one polypeptide'. However, the fundamental idea remains the same, that genes produce their visible effects simply by coding for proteins; they control the structure of those proteins via the genetic code, as well as the amounts produced and the timing of production.

In modern genetics, the gene is identified either with the ◊cistron (a set of ◊codons that determines a complete polypeptide) or with the unit of selection (a Mendelian gene that determines a particular character in the organism on which ◊natural selection can act). Genes undergo ◊mutation and ◊recombination to produce the variation on which natural selection operates.

We are survival machines – robot vehicles blindly programmed to preserve the selfish molecules known as genes. This is a truth which still fills me with astonishment.

Richard Dawkins English zoologist.
The Selfish Gene Preface

gene amplification technique by which selected DNA from a single cell can be duplicated indefinitely until there is a sufficient amount to analyse by conventional genetic techniques.

Gene amplification uses a procedure called the polymerase chain reaction. The sample of DNA is mixed with a solution of enzymes called polymerases, which enable it to replicate, and with a plentiful supply of nucleotides, the building blocks of DNA. The mixture is repeatedly heated and cooled. At each warming, the double-stranded DNA present separates into two single strands, and with each cooling the polymerase assembles a new paired strand for each single strand. Each cycle takes approximately 30 minutes to complete, so that after 10 hours there is one million times more DNA present than at the start.

The technique has been used to analyse DNA from a man who died in 1959, showing the presence of sequences from the HIV virus in his cells. It can also be used to test for genetic defects in a single cell taken from an embryo, before the embryo is reimplanted in ◊in vitro fertilization.

gene bank collection of seeds or other forms of genetic material, such as tubers, spores, bacterial or yeast cultures, live animals and plants, frozen sperm and eggs, or frozen embryos. These are stored for possible future use in agriculture, plant and animal breeding, or in medicine, genetic engineering, or the restocking of wild habitats where species have become extinct. Gene banks will be increasingly used as the rate of extinction increases, depleting the Earth's genetic variety (biodiversity).

gene imprinting genetic phenomenon whereby a small number of genes function differently depending on whether they were inherited from the father or the mother. If two copies of an imprinted gene are inherited from one parent and none from the other, a genetic abnormality results, whereas no abnormality occurs if, as is normal, a copy is inherited from both parents. Gene imprinting is known to play a part in a number of genetic disorders and childhood diseases, for example, the Prader–Willi syndrome (characterized by mild mental retardation and compulsive eating).

gene pool total sum of ◊alleles (variants of ◊genes) possessed by all the members of a given population or species alive at a particular time.

General Electric US electrical and electronics company founded in 1878 in New Jersey as the ◊Edison Electric Light Company to back the experiments of the inventor Thomas Edison. In 1892 the company merged with a competitor to form General Electric. Its headquarters are in Fairfield, Connecticut.

general MIDI (***musical instrument digital interface***) or GM standard set of 96 instrument and percussion 'voices' that can be used to encode musical tracks which can be reproduced on any GM-compatible synthesizer, or ◊MIDI.

general protection fault computing error message; see ◊GPF.

generate in mathematics, to produce a sequence of numbers from either the relationship between one number and the next or the relationship between a member of the sequence and its position. For example, $un+1 = 2un$ generates the sequence 1, 2, 4, 8, ... ; $an = n(n+1)$ generates the sequence of numbers 2, 6, 12, 20, ...

generation in computing, stage of development in computer electronics (see ◊computer generation) or a class of programming language (see ◊fourth-generation language).

generator machine that produces electrical energy from mechanical energy, as opposed to an ◊electric motor, which does the opposite. A simple generator (dynamo) consists of a wire-wound coil (◊armature) that is rotated between the poles of a permanent magnet. The movement of the wire in the magnetic field induces a current in the coil by ◊electromagnetic induction, which can be fed by means of a ◊commutator as a continuous direct current into an external circuit. Slip rings instead of a commutator produce an alternating current, when the generator is called an alternator.

genet any of several small, nocturnal, carnivorous mammals belonging to the mongoose and civet family. Most species live in Africa, but *G. genetta* is also found in Europe and the Middle East. It is about 50 cm/1.6 ft long with a 45 cm/1.5 ft tail, and greyish yellow in colour with rows of black spots. It is a good climber. (Genus *Genetta,* family Viverridae.)

gene therapy medical technique for curing or alleviating inherited diseases or defects; certain infections, and several kinds of cancer in which affected cells from a sufferer would be removed from the body, the ◊DNA repaired in the laboratory (◊genetic engineering), and the functioning cells reintroduced. In 1990 a genetically engineered gene was used for the first time to treat a patient.

The first human being to undergo gene therapy, in 1990, was one of the so-called 'bubble babies' – a four-year-old American girl suffering from a rare enzyme (ADA) deficiency that cripples the immune system. Unable to fight off infection, such children are nursed in a germ-free bubble; they usually die in early childhood.

Cystic fibrosis is the commonest inherited disorder and the one most keenly targeted by genetic engineers; it has been pioneered in patients in the USA and UK. Gene therapy is not the final answer to inherited disease; it may cure the patient but it cannot prevent him or her from passing on the genetic defect to any children. However, it does hold out the promise of a cure for various other conditions, including heart disease and some cancers; US researchers have successfully used a gene gun to target specific tumour cells. In 1995 tumour growth was halted in mice when DNA-coated gold bullets were fired into tumour cells.

By the end of 1995, although 600 people had been treated with gene therapy, nobody had actually been cured. Even in the ADA trials, the most successful to date, the children were still receiving injections of synthetic ADA, possibly the major factor in their improvement.

genetic code the way in which instructions for building proteins, the basic structural molecules of living matter, are 'written' in the genetic material ◊DNA. This relationship between the sequence of bases (the subunits in a DNA molecule) and the sequence of ◊amino acids (the subunits of a protein molecule) is the basis of heredity. The code employs ◊codons of three bases each; it is the same in almost all organisms, except for a few minor differences recently discovered in some protozoa.

Only 2% of DNA is made up of base sequences, called **exons**, that code for proteins. The remaining DNA is known as 'junk' DNA or **introns**.

genetic disease any disorder caused at least partly by defective genes or chromosomes. In humans there are some 3,000 genetic diseases, including cystic fibrosis, Down's syndrome, haemophilia, Huntington's chorea, some forms of anaemia, spina bifida, and Tay-Sachs disease.

genetic engineering deliberate manipulation of genetic material by biochemical techniques. It is often achieved by the introduction of new ◊DNA, usually by means of a virus or ◊plasmid. This can be for pure research, ◊gene therapy, or to breed functionally specific plants, animals, or bacteria. These organisms with a foreign gene added are said to be transgenic (see ◊transgenic organism). At the beginning of 1995 more than 60 plant species had been genetically engineered, and nearly 3,000 transgenic crops had been field-tested.

practical uses In genetic engineering, the splicing and reconciliation of genes is used to increase knowledge of cell function and reproduction, but it can also achieve practical ends. For example, plants grown for food could be given the ability to fix nitrogen, found in some bacteria, and so reduce the need for expensive fertilizers, or simple bacteria may be modified to produce rare drugs. A foreign gene can be inserted into laboratory cultures of bacteria to generate commercial biological products, such as synthetic insulin, hepatitis-B vaccine, and interferon. Gene splicing was invented in 1973 by the US scientists Stanley Cohen and Herbert Boyer, and patented in the USA in 1984.

new developments Developments in genetic engineering have led to the production of growth hormone, and a number of other bone-marrow stimulating hormones. New strains of animals have also been produced; a new strain of mouse was patented in the USA in 1989 (the application was rejected in the European Patent Office). A ◊vaccine against a sheep parasite (a larval tapeworm) has been developed by genetic engineering; most existing vaccines protect against bacteria and viruses.

The first genetically engineered food went on sale in 1994; the 'Flavr Savr' tomato, produced by the US biotechnology company Calgene, was available in California and Chicago.

safety measures There is a risk that when transplanting genes between different types of bacteria (*Escherichia coli,* which lives in the human intestine, is often used) new and harmful strains might be produced. For this reason strict safety precautions are observed, and the altered bacteria are disabled in some way so they are unable to exist outside the laboratory.

genetic fingerprinting or ***genetic profiling*** technique used for determining the pattern of certain parts of the genetic material ◊DNA that is unique to each individual. Like conventional fingerprinting, it can accurately distinguish humans from one another, with the exception of identical siblings from multiple births. It can be applied to as little material as a single cell.

Genetic fingerprinting involves isolating DNA from cells, then comparing and contrasting the sequences of component chemicals between individuals. The DNA pattern can be ascertained from a sample of skin, hair, or semen. Although differences are minimal (only 0.1% between unrelated people), certain regions of DNA, known as **hypervariable regions**, are unique to individuals.

genetics branch of biology concerned with the study of ◊heredity and variation; it attempts to explain how characteristics of living organisms are passed on from one generation to the next. The science of genetics is based on the work of Austrian biologist Gregor ◊Mendel whose experiments with the cross-breeding (hybridization) of peas showed that the inheritance of characteristics and traits takes place by means of discrete 'particles' (◊genes). These are present in the cells of all organisms, and are now recognized as being the basic units of heredity. All organisms possess ◊genotypes (sets of variable genes) and ◊phenotypes (characteristics produced by certain genes). Modern geneticists investigate the structure, function, and transmission of genes.

Before the publication of Mendel's work in 1865, it had been assumed that the characteristics of both parents were blended during inheritance, but Mendel showed that the genes remain intact, although their combinations change. As a result of his experiments with the cultivation of the common garden pea, Mendel introduced the concept of hybridization (see ◊monohybrid inheritance). Since Mendel, the study of genetics has advanced greatly, first through ◊breeding experiments and light-microscope observations (classical genetics), later by means of biochemical and electron microscope studies (molecular genetics).

In 1944, Canadian-born bacteriologist Oswald Avery, together with his colleagues at the Rockefeller Institute, Colin McLeod and Maclyn McCarty, showed that the genetic material was deoxyribonucleic acid ((◊DNA), and not protein as was previously thought. A further breakthrough was made in 1953 when James ◊Watson and Francis ◊Crick published their molecular model for the structure of DNA, the double helix, based on X-ray diffraction photographs. The following decade saw the cracking of the genetic code. The ◊genetic code is said to be universal since the same code applies to all organisms from bacteria and viruses to higher plants and animals, including humans. Today the deliberate manipulation of genes by biochemical techniques, or ◊genetic engineering, is commonplace.

genetic screening in medicine, the determination of the genetic make-up of an individual to determine if he or she is at risk of developing a hereditary disease later in life. Genetic screening can also be used to determine if an individual is a carrier for a particular genetic disease and, hence, can pass the disease on to any children. Genetic counselling should be undertaken at the same time as genetic screening of affected individuals. Diseases that can be screened for include cystic fibrosis, Huntington's chorea, and certain forms of cancer.

genitalia reproductive organs of sexually reproducing animals, particularly the external/visible organs of mammals: in males, the penis and the scrotum, which contains the testes, and in females, the clitoris and vulva.

genome the full complement of ◊genes carried by a single (haploid) set of ◊chromosomes. The term may be applied to the genetic information carried by an individual or to the range of genes found in a given species. The human genome is made up of 75,000 genes.

The first fully decoded genome in a life domain to which humans belong was announced in 1997. Scientists completed a genetic blueprint for *Saccharomyces cerevisiae*, common brewer's yeast, which shares a high number with genetic sequences with humans. The scientists produced a map of all the yeast's genes and the full genetic coding. Genomes have been identified for seven organisms, including the bacteria *Haemofilus influenzae* and *Escherichia coli*, and the mycoplasmas *Mycoplasma genitalium* and *Mycoplasma pneumoniae*.

GENE

There are more than 80,000 genes in human DNA.

We are built to make mistakes, coded for error.

LEWIS THOMAS US physician and educator.
The Medusa and the Snail, 'To Err is Human'

genotype the particular set of ◊alleles (variants of genes) possessed by a given organism. The term is usually used in conjunction with ◊phenotype, which is the product of the genotype and all environmental effects. See also ◊nature–nurture controversy.

genus (plural ***genera***) group of ◊species with many characteristics in common.

Thus all doglike species (including dogs, wolves, and jackals) belong to the genus *Canis* (Latin 'dog').

Species of the same genus are thought to be descended from a common ancestor species. Related genera are grouped into ◊families.

geochemistry science of chemistry as it applies to geology. It deals with the relative and absolute abundances of the chemical elements and their ◊isotopes in the Earth, and also with the chemical changes that accompany geologic processes.

geochronology the branch of geology that deals with the dating of the Earth by studying its rocks and contained fossils. The ◊geological time chart is a result of these studies. Absolute dating methods involve the measurement of radioactive decay over time in certain chemical elements found in rocks, whereas relative dating methods establish the sequence of deposition of various rock layers by identifying and comparing their contained fossils.

geode in geology, a subspherical cavity into which crystals have grown from the outer wall into the centre. Geodes often contain very well-formed crystals of quartz (including amethyst), calcite, or other minerals.

geodesic dome hemispherical dome, a type of space-frame, whose surface is formed out of short rods arranged in triangles. The rods lie on geodesics (the shortest lines joining two points on a curved surface). This type of dome allows large spaces to be enclosed using the minimum of materials, and was patented by US engineer Buckminster Fuller in 1954.

geodesy methods of surveying the Earth for making maps and correlating geological, gravitational, and magnetic measurements. Geodesic surveys, formerly carried out by means of various measuring techniques on the surface, are now commonly made by using radio signals and laser beams from orbiting satellites (see ◊global positioning system).

geographical information system (GIS) computer software that makes possible the visualization and manipulation of spatial data, and links such data with other information such as customer records.

geography the study of the Earth's surface; its topography, climate, and physical conditions, and how these factors affect people and society. It is usually divided into **physical geography**, dealing with landforms and climates, and **human geography**, dealing with the distribution and activities of peoples on Earth.

history Early preclassical geographers concentrated on map-making, surveying, and exploring. In classical Greece theoretical ideas first became a characteristic of geography. Aristotle and ◊Pythagoras believed the Earth to be a sphere, Eratosthenes was the first to calculate the circumference of the world, and Herodotus investigated the origin of the Nile floods and the relationship between climate and human behaviour.

During the medieval period the study of geography progressed little in Europe, but the Muslim world retained much of the Greek tradition, embellishing the 2nd-century maps of ◊Ptolemy. During the early Renaissance the role of the geographer as an explorer and surveyor became important once again.

The foundation of modern geography as an academic subject stems from the writings of Friedrich Humboldt and Johann Ritter, in the late 18th and early 19th centuries, who for the first time defined geography as a major branch of scientific inquiry.

TO REMEMBER THE GEOLOGICAL PERIODS IN DESCENDING ORDER OF AGE:

CAMELS OFTEN SIT DOWN CAREFULLY. PERHAPS THEIR JOINTS CREAK? EARLY OILING MIGHT PREVENT PERMANENT RHEUMATISM.

OR

CHINA OWLS SELDOM DECEIVE CLAY PIGEONS. THEY JUST CHASE EACH OTHER MAKING PREPOSTEROUS PUNS.

CAMBRIAN, ORDOVICIAN, SILURIAN, DEVONIAN, CARBONIFEROUS, PERMIAN, TRIASSIC, JURASSIC, CRETACEOUS, EOCENE, OLIGOCENE, MIOCENE, PLIOCENE, PLEISTOCENE (RECENT)

geological time time scale embracing the history of the Earth from its physical origin to the present day. Geological time is traditionally divided into eons (Archaean or Archaeozoic, Proterozoic, and Phanerozoic in ascending chronological order), which in turn are subdivided into eras, periods, epochs, ages, and finally chrons.

The terms eon, era, period, epoch, age and chron are **geochronological units** representing intervals of geological time. Rocks representing an interval of geological time comprise a **chronostratigraphic unit**. Each of the hierarchical geochronological terms has a chronostratigraphic equivalent. Thus, rocks formed during an eon (a geochronological unit) are members of an eonothem (the chronostratigraphic unit equivalent of eon). Rocks of an era belong to an erathem. The chronostratigraphic equivalents of period, epoch, age, and chron are system, series, stage, and chronozone, repectively.

Having in the natural history of this earth, seen a succession of worlds, we may conclude that there is a system in nature. ... The result, therefore of our present enquiry is, that we find no vestige of a beginning – no prospect of an end.

JAMES HUTTON Scottish geologist.
Transactions of the Royal Society of Edinburgh 1788

geology science of the Earth, its origin, composition, structure, and history. It is divided into several branches: **mineralogy** (the minerals of Earth), **petrology** (rocks), **stratigraphy** (the deposition of successive beds of sedimentary rocks), **palaeontology** (fossils), and **tectonics** (the deformation and movement of the Earth's crust).

Geology is regarded as part of earth science, a more widely embracing subject that brings in meteorology, oceanography, geophysics, and geochemistry.

GEOLOGYLINK

http://www.geologylink.com/

Comprehensive information on geology that features a daily update on current geologic events, virtual classroom tours, and virtual field trips to locations around the world. You will also find an in-depth look at a featured event, geologic news and reports, an image gallery, glossary, maps, and an area for asking geology professors your most perplexing questions, plus a list of references and links.

geomagnetic reversal another term for ◊polar reversal.

geometric mean in mathematics, the *n*th root of the product of *n* positive numbers. The geometric mean *m* of two numbers *p* and *q* is such that $m = \sqrt{(p \times q)}$. For example, the mean of 2 and 8 is $\sqrt{(2 \times 8)} = \sqrt{16} = 4$.

geometric progression or ***geometric sequence*** in mathematics, a sequence of terms (progression) in which each term is a constant multiple (called the **common ratio**) of the one preceding it. For example, 3, 12, 48, 192, 768, ... is a geometric progression with a common ratio 4, since each term is equal to the previous term multiplied by 4. Compare ◊arithmetic progression.

The sum of *n* terms of a **geometric series**

$$1 + r + r^2 + r^3 + ... + rn^{-1}$$

is given by the formula

$$Sn = (_1 - rn)/(^1 - r)$$

for all $r \neq 1$. For $r = 1$, the geometric series can be summed to infinity:

$$S\infty = 1/(1 - r).$$

In nature, many single-celled organisms reproduce by splitting in two so that one cell gives rise to 2, then 4, then 8 cells, and so on, forming a geometric sequence 1, 2, 4, 8, 16, 32, ..., in which the common ratio is 2.

geometric tortoise South African tortoise *Psammobates geometricus* which grows to only 10–12 cm/4–5 in in length. It is acutely threatened by the loss of its habitat, which has shrunk to just 4% of the reptile's original range. Remaining areas are mainly fragmented and have been invaded by alien plant species that the tortoise is unable to eat.

geometry branch of mathematics concerned with the properties of space, usually in terms of plane (two-dimensional) and solid (three-dimensional) figures. The subject is usually divided into **pure geometry**, which embraces roughly the plane and solid geometry dealt with in Greek mathematician Euclid's *Stoicheia/ Elements*, and **analytical** or ◊coordinate geometry, in which problems are solved using algebraic methods. A third, quite distinct, type includes the non-Euclidean geometries.

pure geometry This is chiefly concerned with properties of figures that can be measured, such as lengths, areas, and angles and is therefore of great practical use. An important idea in Euclidean geometry is the idea of **congruence**. Two figures are said to be congruent if they have the same shape and size (and area). If one figure is imagined as a rigid object that can be picked up, moved and placed on top of the other so that they exactly coincide, then the two figures are congruent. Some simple rules about congruence may be stated: two line segments are congruent if they are of equal length; two triangles are congruent if their corresponding sides are equal in length or if two sides and an angle in one is equal to those in the other; two circles are congruent if they have the same radius; two polygons are congruent if they can be divided into congruent triangles assembled in the same order.

The idea of picking up a rigid object to test congruence can be expressed more precisely in terms of elementary 'movements' of figures: a translation (or glide) in which all points move the same distance in the same direction (that is, along parallel lines); a rotation through a defined angle about a fixed point; a reflection (equivalent to turning the figure over).

Two figures are congruent to each other if one can be transformed into the other by a sequence of these elementary movements. In Euclidean geometry a fourth kind of movement is also studied; this is the enlargement in which a figure grows or shrinks in all directions by a uniform scale factor. If one figure can be transformed into another by a combination of translation, rotation, reflection, and enlargement then the two are said to be similar. All circles are similar. All squares are similar. Triangles are similar if corresponding angles are equal.

coordinate geometry A system of geometry in which points, lines, shapes, and surfaces are represented by algebraic expressions. In plane (two-dimensional) coordinate geometry, the plane is usually defined by two axes at right angles to each other, the horizontal x-axis and the vertical y-axis, meeting at 0, the origin. A point on the plane can be represented by a pair of ◊Cartesian coordinates, which define its position in terms of its distance along the x-axis and along the y-axis from 0. These distances are respectively the x and y coordinates of the point.

Lines are represented as equations; for example, $y = 2x + 1$ gives a straight line, and $y = 3x^2 + 2x$ gives a ◊parabola (a curve). The graphs of varying equations can be drawn by plotting the coordinates of points that satisfy their equations, and joining up the points. One of the advantages of coordinate geometry is that geometrical solutions can be obtained without drawing but by manipulating algebraic expressions. For example, the coordinates of the point of intersection of two straight lines can be determined by finding the unique values of x and y that satisfy both of the equations for the lines, that is, by solving them as a pair of ◊simultaneous equations. The curves studied in simple coordinate geometry are the ◊conic sections (circle, ellipse, parabola, and hyperbola), each of which has a characteristic equation.

Geometry probably originated in ancient Egypt, in land measurements necessitated by the periodic inundations of the river Nile, and was soon extended into surveying and navigation. Early geometers were the Greek mathematicians Thales, Pythagoras, and Euclid. Analytical methods were introduced and developed by the French philosopher René ◊Descartes in the 17th century. From the 19th century, various non-Euclidean geometries were devised by Carl Friedrich Gauss, János Bolyai, and Nikolai Lobachevsky. These were later generalized by Bernhard Riemann and found to have applications in the theory of relativity.

Ubi materia, ibi geometria.
Where there is matter, there is geometry.

JOHANNES KEPLER German astronomer and mathematician. Attributed remark

geomorphology branch of geology that deals with the nature and origin of surface landforms such as mountains, valleys, plains, and plateaus.

geophagy eating soil. It is a practice found in many animal species but the reasons for geophagy are poorly understood. Canadian and Japanese researchers established 1996, that chimpanzees eat earth containing clay minerals to combat diarrhoea and other digestive ailments. Other primates are also thought to eat earth for health reasons.

geophysics branch of earth science using physics to study the Earth's surface, interior, and atmosphere. Studies also include winds, weather, tides, earthquakes, volcanoes, and their effects.

geostationary orbit circular path 35,900 km/22,300 mi above the Earth's Equator on which a ◊satellite takes 24 hours, moving from west to east, to complete an orbit, thus appearing to hang stationary over one place on the Earth's surface. Geostationary orbits are used particularly for communications satellites and weather satellites. They were first thought of by the author Arthur C Clarke. A **geosynchronous orbit** lies at the same distance from Earth but is inclined to the Equator.

geothermal energy energy extracted for heating and electricity generation from natural steam, hot water, or hot dry rocks in the Earth's crust. Water is pumped down through an injection well where it passes through joints in the hot rocks. It rises to the surface through a recovery well and may be converted to steam or run through a heat exchanger. Dry steam may be directed through turbines to produce electricity. It is an important source of energy in volcanically active areas such as Iceland and New Zealand.

geraldton wax shrub *Chamelaucium uncinatum* with delicate needle leaves and waxy pink myrtle flowers. It is endemic to Western Australia and widely cultivated in other states

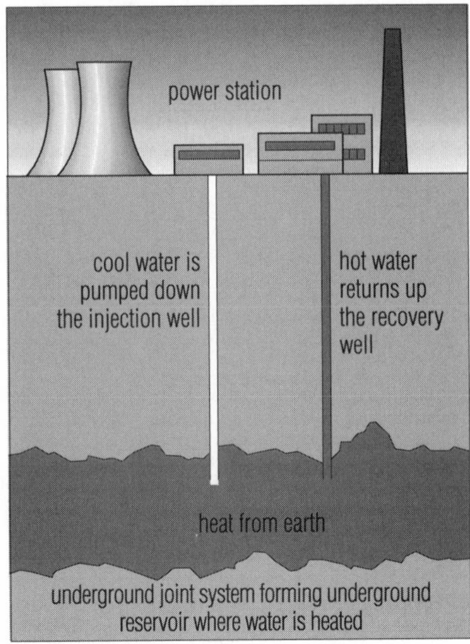

geothermal energy Geothermal energy is derived from the natural heat present below the surface of the Earth. Cool water is pumped down where it is heated up in large underground reservoirs before being pumped back to the surface.

geranium any of a group of plants either having divided leaves and white, pink, or purple flowers (geraniums), or having a hairy stem, and white, pink, red, or black-purple flowers (◊pelarg-oniums). Some geraniums are also called ◊cranesbill. (Genera *Geranium* and *Pelargonium*, family Geraniaceae.)

gerbil any of numerous rodents with elongated back legs, good at hopping or jumping. Gerbils range from mouse- to rat-size, and have hairy tails. Many of the 13 genera live in dry, sandy, or sparsely vegetated areas of Africa and Asia. (Family Cricetidae.)

The Mongolian jird or gerbil (*Meriones unguiculatus*) is a popular pet.

***gerbil** A hairy-footed gerbil* Gerbillurus paeba *foraging across the sands of the Kalahari Desert in Southern Africa. Found in Africa and Asia, gerbils live in burrows and feed at night, mostly on seeds and roots. Premaphotos Wildlife*

gerenuk antelope about 1 m/3 ft high at the shoulder, with a very long neck. It browses on leaves, often balancing on its hind legs to do so. Sandy brown in colour, it is well camouflaged in its East African habitat of dry scrub. (Species *Litocranius walleri.*)

geriatrics medical speciality concerned with diseases and problems of the elderly.

germ colloquial term for a microorganism that causes disease, such as certain ◊bacteria and ◊viruses. Formerly, it was also used to mean something capable of developing into a complete organism (such as a fertilized egg, or the ◊embryo of a seed).

germanium brittle, grey-white, weakly metallic (◊metalloid) element, symbol Ge, atomic number 32, relative atomic mass 72.6. It belongs to the silicon group, and has chemical and physical properties between those of silicon and tin. Germanium is a semiconductor material and is used in the manufacture of transistors and integrated circuits. The oxide is transparent to infrared radiation, and is used in military applications. It was discovered in 1886 by German chemist Clemens Winkler (1838–1904).

In parts of Asia, germanium and plants containing it are used to treat a variety of diseases, and it is sold in the West as a food supplement despite fears that it may cause kidney damage.

German measles or ***rubella*** mild, communicable virus disease, usually caught by children. It is marked by a sore throat, pinkish rash, and slight fever, and has an incubation period of two to three weeks. If a woman contracts it in the first three months of pregnancy, it may cause serious damage to the unborn child.

German shepherd or ***Alsatian*** breed of dog. It is about 63 cm/25 in tall and has a wolflike appearance, a thick coat with many varieties of colouring, and a distinctive way of moving. German shepherds are used as police dogs because of their courage and intelligence.

They were introduced from Germany into Britain and the USA after World War I.

German silver or ***nickel silver*** silvery alloy of nickel, copper, and zinc. It is widely used for cheap jewellery and the base metal for silver plating. The letters EPNS on silverware stand for **e**lectro**p**lated **n**ickel **s**ilver.

germination in botany, the initial stages of growth in a seed, spore, or pollen grain. Seeds germinate when they are exposed to favourable external conditions of moisture, light, and temperature, and when any factors causing dormancy have been removed.

The process begins with the uptake of water by the seed. The embryonic root, or radicle, is normally the first organ to emerge, followed by the embryonic shoot, or plumule. Food reserves, either within the ◊endosperm or from the ◊cotyledons, are broken down to nourish the rapidly growing seedling. Germination is considered to have ended with the production of the first true leaves.

germ layer in ◊embryology, a layer of cells that can be distinguished during the development of a fertilized egg. Most animals have three such layers: the inner, middle, and outer. These differentiate to form the various body tissues.

The inner layer (**endoderm**) gives rise to the gut, the middle one (**mesoderm**) develops into most of the other organs, while the outer one (**ectoderm**) gives rise to the skin and nervous system. Simple animals, such as sponges, lack a mesoderm.

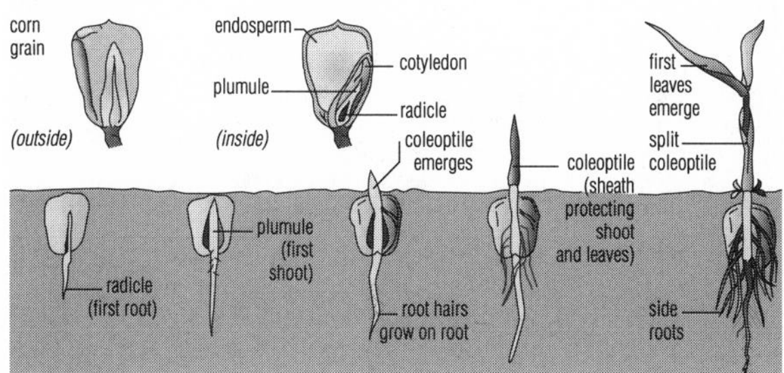

***germination** The germination of a corn grain. The plumule and radicle emerge from the seed coat and begin to grow into a new plant. The coleoptile protects the emerging bud and the first leaves.*

germ-line therapy hypothetical application of ◊gene therapy to sperm and egg cells to remove the risk of an inherited disease being passed to offspring. It is controversial because of the fear it will be used to produce 'designer babies', and may result in unforseen side effects.

Gestalt *German 'form'* concept of a unified whole that is greater than, or different from, the sum of its parts; that is, a complete structure whose nature is not explained simply by analysing its constituent elements. A chair, for example, will generally be recognized as a chair despite great variations between individual chairs in such attributes as size, shape, and colour.

Gestalt psychology regards all mental phenomena as being arranged in organized, structured wholes, as opposed to being composed of simple sensations. For example, learning is seen as a reorganizing of a whole situation (often involving insight), as opposed to the behaviourists' view that it consists of associations between stimuli and responses. Gestalt psychologists' experiments show that the brain is not a passive receiver of information, but that it structures all its input in order to make sense of it, a belief that is now generally accepted; however, other principles of Gestalt psychology have received considerable criticism.

The term 'Gestalt' was first used in psychology by the Austrian philosopher and psychologist Christian von Ehrenfels in 1890. Max Wertheimer, Wolfgang Köhler, and Kurt Koffka (1886–1941) were cofounders of Gestalt psychology.

gestation in all mammals except the ◊monotremes (platypus and spiny anteaters), the period from the time of implantation of the embryo in the uterus to birth. This period varies among species; in humans it is about 266 days, in elephants 18–22 months, in cats about 60 days, and in some species of marsupial (such as opossum) as short as 12 days.

gesture recognition in computing, technique whereby a computer accepts human gestures transmitted via hardware such as a ◊DataGlove as meaningful input to which it can respond. Gesture recognition is a key technology needed in the development of ◊virtual reality systems if they are to allow humans to interact fully and naturally with objects in computerized worlds.

geyser natural spring that intermittently discharges an explosive column of steam and hot water into the air due to the build-up of steam in underground chambers. One of the most remarkable geysers is Old Faithful, in Yellowstone National Park, Wyoming, USA. Geysers also occur in New Zealand and Iceland.

g-force force that pilots and astronauts experience when their craft accelerate or decelerate rapidly. One *g* is the ordinary pull of gravity.

Early astronauts were subjected to launch and reentry forces of up to six *g* or more; in the space shuttle, more than three *g* is experienced on liftoff. Pilots and astronauts wear *g*-suits that prevent their blood pooling too much under severe *g*-forces, which can lead to unconsciousness.

gherkin young or small green ◊cucumber, used for pickling.

ghost gum inland Australian species of gum *Eucalyptus papuana* with a smooth white trunk; made familiar by the paintings of Albert Namatjira.

giant molecular structure or ***macromolecular structure*** solid structure made up of many similar molecules; examples include diamond, graphite, silica, and polymers.

giant star in astronomy, a class of stars to the top right of the ◊Hertzsprung– Russell diagram characterized by great size and ◊luminosity. Giants have exhausted their supply of hydrogen fuel and derive their energy from the fusion of helium and heavier elements. They are roughly 10–300 times bigger than the Sun with 30–1,000 times the luminosity. The cooler giants are known as red giants.

gibberellin plant growth substance (see also ◊auxin) that promotes stem growth and may also affect the breaking of dormancy in certain buds and seeds, and the induction of flowering. Application of gibberellin can stimulate the stems of dwarf plants to additional growth, delay the ageing process in leaves, and promote the production of seedless fruit (◊parthenocarpy).

gibbon any of a group of several small southern Asian apes. The **common** or **lar gibbon** (*H. lar*) is about 60 cm/2 ft tall, with a body that is hairy except for the buttocks, which distinguishes it from other types of apes. Gibbons have long arms and no tail. They spend most of their time in trees and are very agile when swinging from branch to branch. On the ground they walk upright, and are more easily caught by predators. (Genus *Hylobates,* including the subgenus *Symphalangus.*)

The **siamang** (*S. syndactylus*) is the largest of the gibbons, growing to 90 cm/36 in tall; it is entirely black. Gibbons are found from Assam through the Malay peninsula to Borneo, but are becoming rare, with certain species classified as endangered.

Gibbs' function in ◊thermodynamics, an expression representing part of the energy content of a system that is available to do external work, also known as the free energy G. In an equilibrium system at constant temperature and pressure, $G = H–TS$, where H is the enthalpy (heat content), T the temperature, and S the ◊entropy (decrease in energy availability). The function was named after US physicist Josiah Willard Gibbs.

gidgee small Australian tree *Acacia cambagei* which gives off an unpleasant odour at the approach of rain; also known as stinking wattle.

GIF (acronym for ***Graphics Interchange Format***) in computing, popular and economical picture file format developed by CompuServe. GIF (pronounced with a hard 'g') is one of the two most commonly used file formats for pictures on the World Wide Web (the other is ◊JPEG) because pictures saved in this format take up a relatively small amount of space. The term is often used simply to mean 'pictures'.

giga- prefix signifying multiplication by 10^9 (1,000,000,000 or 1 billion), as in **gigahertz**, a unit of frequency equivalent to 1 billion hertz.

gigabyte in computing, a measure of ◊memory capacity, equal to 1,024 ◊megabytes. It is also used, less precisely, to mean 1,000 billion ◊bytes.

Giganotosaurus carolinii carnivorous dinosaur of the ◊Cretaceous period. They weighed 6–8 tonnes and were about 12.5 m/40 ft in length, making them the largest predators ever to walk the Earth. *Giganotosaurus* lived in Patagonia about 97 million years ago. Argentinian palaeontologists discovered about 70% of its skeleton in 1995.

GIGO (acronym for ***garbage in, garbage out***) expression used in computing to emphasize that inaccurate input data will result in inaccurate output data.

GII abbreviation for the ◊Global Information Infrastructure.

gila monster lizard native to the southwestern USA and Mexico. It is one of the only two existing venomous lizards, the other being the Mexican beaded lizard of the same genus. It has poison glands in its lower jaw, but its bite is not usually fatal to humans. (Species *Heloderma suspectum.*)

gill in biology, the main respiratory organ of most fishes and immature amphibians, and of many aquatic invertebrates. In all types, water passes over the gills, and oxygen diffuses across the gill membranes into the circulatory system, while carbon dioxide passes from the system out into the water.

In aquatic insects, these gases diffuse into and out of air-filled canals called tracheae.

gill imperial unit of volume for liquid measure, equal to one-quarter of a pint or 5 fluid ounces (0.142 litre). It is used in selling alcoholic drinks.

In S England it is also called a noggin, but in N England the large noggin is used, which is two gills.

gillyflower old name for the ◊carnation and related plants, used in the works of Chaucer, Shakespeare, and Spenser.

ginger southeast Asian reedlike perennial plant; the hot-tasting spicy underground root is used as a food flavouring and in preserves. (*Zingiber officinale,* family Zingiberaceae.)

ginkgo or ***maidenhair tree*** tree belonging to the ◊gymnosperm (or naked-seed-bearing) division of plants. It may reach a height of 30 m/100 ft by the time it is 200 years old. (*Ginkgo biloba.*)

The only living member of its group (Ginkgophyta), widespread in Mesozoic times (245–65 million years ago), it has been cultivated in China and Japan since ancient times, and is planted in many parts of the world. Its leaves are fan-shaped, and it bears fleshy, yellow, foul-smelling fruit enclosing edible kernels.

ginseng plant with a thick forked aromatic root used in alternative medicine as a tonic. (*Panax ginseng,* family Araliaceae.)

Giotto space probe built by the European Space Agency to study ◊Halley's comet. Launched by an Ariane rocket in July 1985, *Giotto* passed within 600 km/375 mi of the comet's nucleus on 13 March 1986. On 2 July 1990, it flew 23,000 km/14,000 mi from Earth, which diverted its path to encounter another comet, Grigg-Skjellerup, on 10 July 1992.

giraffe world's tallest mammal. It stands over 5.5 m/18 ft tall, the neck accounting for nearly half this amount. The giraffe has two to four small, skin-covered, hornlike structures on its head and a long, tufted tail. The fur has a mottled appearance and is reddish brown and cream. Giraffes are found only in Africa, south of the Sahara Desert. They eat leaves and vegetation that is out of reach of smaller mammals, and are ruminants; that is, they chew the cud. (Species *Giraffa camelopardalis,* family Giraffidae.)

GIRAFFE

http://www.seaworld.org/animal_bytes/giraffeab.html

Illustrated guide to the giraffe including information about genus, size, life span, habitat, gestation, diet, and a series of fun facts.

GIS in computing, abbreviation for ◊geographical information system.

gizzard muscular grinding organ of the digestive tract, below the ◊crop of birds, earthworms, and some insects, and forming part of the ◊stomach. The gizzard of birds is lined with a hardened horny layer of the protein keratin, preventing damage to the muscle layer during the grinding process. Most birds swallow sharp grit which aids maceration of food in the gizzard.

glacial trough or ***U-shaped valley*** steep-sided, flat-bottomed valley formed by a glacier. The erosive action of the glacier and of the debris carried by it results in the formation not only of the trough itself but also of a number of associated features, such as truncated spurs (projections of rock that have been sheared off by the ice) and hanging valleys (smaller glacial valleys that enter the trough at a higher level than the trough floor). Features characteristic of glacial deposition, such as drumlins and eskers, are commonly found on the floor of the trough, together with linear lakes called ribbon lakes.

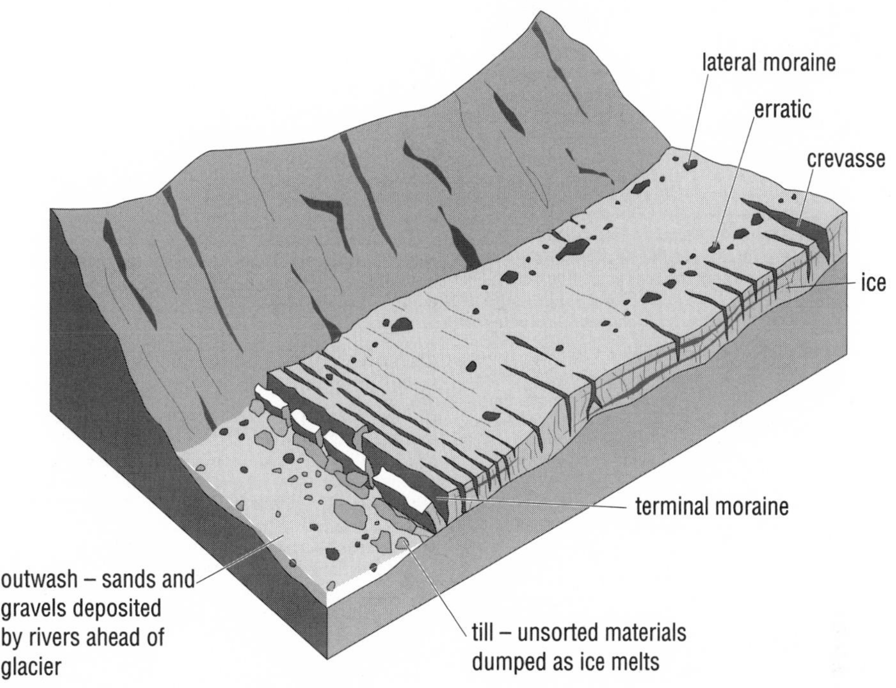

***glacial deposition** A glacier picks up large boulders and rock debris from the valley and deposits them at the snout of the glacier when the ice melts. Some deposited material is carried great distances by the ice to form erratics.*

glacier tongue of ice, originating in mountains in snowfields above the snowline, which moves slowly downhill and is constantly replenished from its source. The geographic features produced by the erosive action of glaciers are characteristic and include ◊glacial troughs (U-shaped valleys), ◊corries, and ◊arêtes. In lowlands, the laying down of ◊moraine (rocky debris once carried by glaciers) produces a variety of landscape features.

Glaciers form where annual snowfall exceeds annual melting and drainage. The snow compacts to ice under the weight of the layers above.

Under pressure the ice moves plastically (changing its shape permanently). When a glacier moves over an uneven surface, deep crevasses are formed in rigid upper layers of the ice mass; if it reaches the sea or a lake, it breaks up to form icebergs. A glacier that is formed by one or several valley glaciers at the base of a mountain is called a **piedmont** glacier. A body of ice that covers a large land surface or continent, for example Greenland or Antarctica, and flows outward in all directions is called an **ice sheet**.

In Oct 1996 a volcano erupted under Europe's largest glacier, Vatnajökull in Iceland, causing flooding.

GLACIERS

http://www-nsidc.colorado.edu/NSIDC/EDUCATION/GLACIERS/

Comprehensive information about glaciers from the US National Snow and Ice Data Centre. There are explanations of why glaciers form, different kinds of glaciers, and what they may tell us about climate change. There are a number of interesting facts and a bibliography about the compacted tongues of ice which cover 10% of the land surface of our planet.

gladiolus any plant of a group of southern European and African cultivated perennials belonging to the iris family, with brightly coloured funnel-shaped flowers borne on a spike; the swordlike leaves spring from a corm (swollen underground stem). (Genus *Gladiolus*, family Iridaceae.)

gland specialized organ of the body that manufactures and secretes enzymes, hormones, or other chemicals. In animals, glands vary in size from small (for example, tear glands) to large (for example, the pancreas), but in plants they are always small, and may consist of a single cell. Some glands discharge their products internally, ◊endocrine glands, and others, ◊exocrine glands, externally. Lymph nodes are sometimes wrongly called glands.

glandular fever or ***infectious mononucleosis*** viral disease characterized at onset by fever and painfully swollen lymph nodes; there may also be digestive upset, sore throat, and skin rashes. Lassitude persists for months and even years, and recovery can be slow. It is caused by the Epstein–Barr virus.

glass transparent or translucent substance that is physically neither a solid nor a liquid. Although glass is easily shattered, it is one of the strongest substances known. It is made by fusing certain types of sand (silica); this fusion occurs naturally in volcanic glass (see ◊obsidian).

In the industrial production of common types of glass, the type of sand used, the particular chemicals added to it (for example, lead, potassium, barium), and refinements of technique determine the type of glass produced. Types of glass include: soda glass; flint glass, used in cut-crystal ware; optical glass; stained glass; heat-resistant glass; and glasses that exclude certain ranges of the light spectrum. Blown glass is either blown individually from molten glass (using a tube up to 1.5 m/4.5 ft long), as in the making of expensive crafted glass, or blown automatically into a mould – for example, in the manufacture of light bulbs and bottles; pressed glass is simply pressed into moulds, for jam jars, cheap vases, and light fittings; while sheet glass, for windows, is made by putting the molten glass through rollers to form a 'ribbon', or by floating molten glass on molten tin in the 'float glass' process; ◊fibreglass is made from fine glass fibres. Metallic glass is produced by treating alloys so that they take on the properties of glass while retaining the malleability and conductivity characteristic of metals.

glass lizard another name for ◊glass snake.

glass-reinforced plastic (GRP) a plastic material strengthened by glass fibres, sometimes erroneously called ◊fibreglass. Glass-reinforced plastic is a favoured material for boat hulls and for the bodies and some structural components of high-performance cars and aircraft; it is also used in the manufacture of passenger cars.

Products are usually moulded, mats of glass fibre being sandwiched between layers of a polyester plastic, which sets hard when mixed with a curing agent.

glass snake or *glass lizard* any of a worldwide group of legless lizards. Their tails are up to three times the head–body length and are easily broken off. (Genus *Ophisaurus,* family Anguidae.)

Glauber's salt crystalline sodium sulphate decahydrate $Na_2SO_4.10H_2O$, produced by the action of sulphuric acid on common salt. It melts at 87.8°F/31°C; the latent heat stored as it solidifies makes it a convenient thermal energy store. It is used in medicine as a laxative.

glaucoma condition in which pressure inside the eye (intraocular pressure) is raised abnormally as excess fluid accumulates. It occurs when the normal outflow of fluid within the chamber of the eye (aqueous humour) is interrupted. As pressure rises, the optic nerve suffers irreversible damage, leading to a reduction in the field of vision and, ultimately, loss of eyesight.

The most common type, **chronic glaucoma**, usually affects people over the age of 40, when the trabecular meshwork (the filtering tissue at the margins of the eye) gradually becomes blocked and drainage slows down. The condition cannot be cured, but, in many cases, it is controlled by drug therapy. Laser treatment to the trabecular meshwork often improves drainage for a time; surgery to create an artificial channel for fluid to leave the eye offers more long-term relief. A tiny window may be cut in the iris during the same operation.

Acute glaucoma is a medical emergency. A precipitous rise in pressure occurs when the trabecular meshwork suddenly becomes occluded (blocked). This is treated surgically to remove the cause of the obstruction. Acute glaucoma is extremely painful. Treatment is required urgently since damage to the optic nerve begins within hours of onset.

GLAUCOMA RESEARCH FOUNDATION

http://www.glaucoma.org/

Excellent source of well-presented information on glaucoma. There is an informative list of frequently asked questions about the disease and the latest research findings. There are links to a number of optometric and opthalmological organizations and a search engine.

Global Information Infrastructure (GII) in computing, planned worldwide high-bandwidth network. US vice president Al Gore proposed the GII in a 1994 speech to the International Telecommunications Union, saying that it would promote the functioning of democracy, help nations to cooperate with each other, and be the key to economic growth for national and international economies.

Global Network Navigator (GNN) in computing, subscription-based online service for the World Wide Web, pioneered by US book publishers O'Reilly & Associates and bought by ◊America Online in 1995. Its Virtual Places software, released in 1996, allows users to interact with each other using avatars and live messages at any Virtual Places-enabled site on the Web. GNN also offers news and resource listings.

global positioning system (GPS) US satellite-based navigation system, a network of 24 satellites in six orbits, each circling the Earth once every 24 hours. Each satellite sends out a continuous time signal, plus an identifying signal. To fix position, a user needs to be within range of four satellites, one to provide a reference signal and three to provide directional bearings. The user's receiver can then calculate the position from the difference in time between receiving the signals from each satellite.

The position of the receiver can be calculated to better than 0.5 m/1.6 ft, although only the US military can tap the full potential of the system. Other users can obtain a position to within 100 m/330 ft. This is accurate enough to be of use to boats, walkers, and motorists, and suitable receivers are on the market.

global variable in computing, a ◊variable that can be accessed by any program instruction. See also ◊local variable.

global warming an increase in average global temperature of approximately 1°F/0.5°C over the past century. Global temperature has been highly variable in Earth history and many fluctuations in global temperature have occurred in historical times, but this most recent episode of warming coincides with the spread of industralization, prompting the hypothesis that it is the result of an accelerated ◊greenhouse effect caused by atmospheric pollutants, especially carbon dioxide gas. Recent melting and collapse of the Larsen Ice Shelf, Antarctica, is a consequence of global warming. Melting of ice is expected to raise sea level in the coming decades.

Natural, perhaps chaotic, climatic variations have not been ruled out as the cause of the current global rise in temperature, but scientists are still assessing the likely influence of anthropogenic (human-made) pollutants. Assessing the impact of humankind on global climate is complicated by the natural variability on both geological and human time scales. The present episode of global warming has thus far still left England approximately 1°C cooler than during the peak of the so-called Medieval Warm Period (1000 to 1400 AD). The latter was part of a purely natural climatic fluctuation on a global scale. With respect to historical times, the interval between the Medieval Warm Period and the rise in temperatures we see today was unusually cold throughout the world.

In addition to a rise in average global temperature, global warming as caused seasonal variations to be more pronounced in recent decades. Examples are the most severe winter on record in the eastern US in 1976–77 and the record heat waves in the Netherlands and Denmark the following year.

A 1995 United Nations summit in Berlin agreed to take action to reduce gas emissions harmful to the environment. Delegates at the summit, from more than 120 countries, approved a two-year negotiating process aimed at setting specific targets and timetables for reducing nations' emissions of carbon dioxide and other greenhouse gases after the year 2000. The Kyoto Protocol of 1997 commits the world's industrialized countries to cut their annual emissions of harmful gases by 5.2% by 2012.

GLOBAL WARMING

http://pooh.chem.wm.edu/chemWWW/courses/chem105/projects/group1/page1.html

Interesting step-by-step explanation of the chemistry behind global warming. There is information on the causes of global warming, the environmental effects, and the social and economic consequences. The views of those who challenge the assertion that the world is warming up are also presented. The graphics accompanying the site are attractive and easy to follow.

globefish another name for the ◊puffer fish.

Global Positioning System

BY EDWARD YOUNG

Satellites

The Global Positioning System, or GPS, has become indispensable as a tool for navigation and scientific discovery. It relies on 24 ◊satellites that can be accessed for accurate positioning by users all over the world. GPS is funded and controlled by the United States Department of Defense. Essential to the satellites are on-board ◊atomic clocks accurate to 3 billionths of one second.

A Master Control site at Falcon Air Force Base in Colorado Springs, USA, sends data to each satellite. Ephemeris data consists of satellite positions. Almanac data consists of the projected orbits of each satellite and information about their overall status. Clock corrections are also transmitted as necessary. In turn the satellites routinely send signals to five monitor stations so that their positions can be tracked. The monitor stations also 'downlink' the Almanac information sent to the satellites from the Master Control site.

GPS satellites transmit two ◊microwave carrier signals. The first high-frequency signal carries position and time data for civilian users worldwide. The US Department of Defense to limit horizontal and vertical accuracy to 100 and 156 meters respectively degrades this signal. A second lower-frequency signal can be used to correct for the effects of the ◊ionosphere for more precise positioning by authorized users, including allied military, government agencies and approved civilian users.

Receivers

GPS receivers search for the coded high-frequency radio signals transmitted by the satellites. Once located, complete transmission from a satellite takes 12.5 minutes. The signal includes the position of the satellite and time at which the signal was sent. Transit time of the satellite radio signal gives the distance, or range, of the satellite from the receiver because the speed of electromagnetic radiation (◊radio waves) is known. Time passes more quickly for the satellites than on Earth, as predicted by Einstein's theory of general ◊relativity, and so 'relativistic' corrections to the transit time must be made. Signals from four satellites are required for precise positioning and time measurement.

Applications

GPS receivers are used or navigation of ships, motor vehicles, aircraft, space vehicles, and persons on the ground. In addition, the precise time information and radio signals that carry the information are useful for scientific experiments.

◊Geodetics is one example of a scientific discipline benefiting from GPS technology. The relative motions of Earth's ◊tectonic plates cause ◊mountains and ◊earthquakes. Plate tectonic motions are in the order of millimetres per year. The small displacements over long time periods makes measuring tectonic motions by traditional geodetic methods laborious and time consuming. Scientists are now using signals by GPS satellites to track Earth's tectonic plates and to establish how they deform to form mountains, depressions, and earthquakes as they move. Measurements that might have taken months or years to perform by traditional geodetic methods can be obtained in just a few days with greater accuracy using GPS. In this application, referred to as space geodesy, the characteristics of the satellite radio waves themselves are used rather than the data they transmit. Slight differences in the phase, or wave-crest positions, of GPS radio waves detected by two receiver stations can be converted into the distance between the stations. In this way distances between points can be measured with millimeter accuracy if receivers are within approximately 30 kilometers of one another.

As part of one space geodesy study, changing ◊topography and relative motions measured by GPS reveal where strain is building in the tectonically active Aegean region. This information is helping scientists to identify potential earthquake hazards. In a similar study, GPS is being used to establish the ever-changing elevation and position of the worlds highest peak, Mount Everest.

globular cluster spherical or near-spherical ◊star cluster containing from approximately 10,000 to millions of stars. More than a hundred globular clusters are distributed in a spherical halo around our Galaxy. They consist of old stars, formed early in the Galaxy's history. Globular clusters are also found around other galaxies.

glomerulus in the kidney, the cluster of blood capillaries at the threshold of the renal tubule, or nephron, responsible for filtering out the fluid that passes down the tubules and ultimately becomes urine. In the human kidney there are approximately one million tubules, each possessing its own glomerulus.

The structure of the glomerulus allows a wide range of substances including amino acids and sugar, as well as a large volume of water, to pass out of the blood. As the fluid moves through the tubules, most of the water and all of the sugars are reabsorbed, so that only waste remains, dissolved in a relatively small amount of water. This fluid collects in the bladder as urine.

glottis in medicine, narrow opening at the upper end of the larynx that contains the vocal cords.

glove box in high technology, a protective device used when handling toxic, radioactive, or sterile materials within an enclosure containing a window for viewing. Gloves fixed to ports in the walls of a box allow manipulation of objects within the box. The risk that the operator might inhale fine airborne particles of poisonous materials is removed by maintaining a vacuum inside the box, so that any airflow is inwards.

glow-worm wingless female of any of a large number of luminous beetles (fireflies). The luminous organs, situated under the abdomen, at the end of the body, give off a greenish glow at night and attract winged males for mating. There are about 2,000 species of glow-worms, distributed worldwide. (Family Lampyridae.)

glucagon in biology, a hormone secreted by the alpha cells of the islets of Langerhans in the ◊pancreas, which increases the concentration of glucose in the blood by promoting the breakdown of glycogen in the liver. Secretion occurs in response to a lowering of blood glucose concentrations.

Glucagon injections can be issued to close relatives of patients with ◊diabetes who are being treated with insulin. Hypoglycaemia may develop in such patients in the event of inadequate control of diabetes. An injection of glucagon can be used to reverse hypoglycaemia before serious symptoms, such as unconsciousness, develop.

glucose or ***dextrose*** or ***grape sugar*** $C_6H_{12}O_6$ sugar present in the blood and manufactured by green plants during ◊photosynthesis. The ◊respiration reactions inside cells involves the oxidation of glucose to produce ◊ATP, the 'energy molecule' used to drive many of the body's biochemical reactions.

In humans and other vertebrates optimum blood glucose levels are maintained by the hormone ◊insulin.

GLOW-WORM

The simplest way to tell the sex of a glow-worm is by measuring the rate at which its emits light pulses. A male flashes once every 5.8 seconds, a female every 2.1 seconds.

Glucose is prepared in syrup form by the hydrolysis of cane sugar or starch, and may be purified to a white crystalline powder. Glucose is a monosaccharide sugar (made up of a single sugar unit), unlike the more familiar sucrose (cane or beet sugar), which is a disaccharide (made up of two sugar units: glucose and fructose).

glue type of ◊adhesive.

glue ear or ***secretory otitis media*** condition commonly affecting small children, in which the Eustachian tube, which normally drains and ventilates the middle ear, becomes blocked with mucus. The resulting accumulation of mucus in the middle ◊ear muffles hearing. It is the leading cause of deafness (usually transient) in children.

Glue ear resolves spontaneously after some months, but because the loss of hearing can interfere with a child's schooling the condition is often treated by a drainage procedure (myringotomy) and the surgical insertion of a small ventilating tube, or **grommet**, into the eardrum (tympanic membrane). This allows air to enter the middle ear, thereby enabling the mucus to drain freely once more along the Eustachian tube and into the back of the throat. The grommet is gradually extruded from the eardrum over several months, and the eardrum then heals naturally.

glue-sniffing or ***solvent misuse*** inhalation of the fumes from organic solvents of the type found in paints, lighter fuel, and glue, for their hallucinatory effects. As well as being addictive, solvents are dangerous for their effects on the user's liver, heart, and lungs. It is believed that solvents produce hallucinations by dissolving the cell membrane of brain cells, thus altering the way the cells conduct electrical impulses.

I am now convinced that theoretical physics is actual philosophy.

MAX BORN German-born British physicist.
Autobiography

---

gluon in physics, a ◊gauge boson that carries the ◊strong nuclear force, responsible for binding quarks together to form the strongly interacting subatomic particles known as ◊hadrons. There are eight kinds of gluon.

Gluons cannot exist in isolation; they are believed to exist in balls ('glueballs') that behave as single particles.

Glueballs may have been detected at CERN in 1995 but further research is required to confirm their existence.

gluten protein found in cereal grains, especially wheat and rye. Gluten enables dough to expand during rising. Sensitivity to gliadin, a type of gluten, gives rise to ◊coeliac disease.

glyceride ◊ester formed between one or more acids and glycerol (propan-1,2,3-triol). A glyceride is termed a mono-, di-, or triglyceride, depending on the number of hydroxyl groups from the glycerol that have reacted with the acids.

Glycerides, chiefly triglycerides, occur naturally as esters of ◊fatty acids in plant oils and animal fats.

glycerine another name for ◊glycerol.

glycerol or ***glycerine*** or ***propan-1,2,3-triol*** $HOCH_2CH(OH)CH_2OH$ thick, colourless, odourless, sweetish liquid. It is obtained from vegetable and animal oils and fats (by treatment with acid, alkali, superheated steam, or an enzyme), or by fermentation of glucose, and is used in the manufacture of high explosives, in antifreeze solutions, to maintain moist conditions in fruits and tobacco, and in cosmetics.

glycine $CH_2(NH_2)COOH$ the simplest amino acid, and one of the main components of proteins. When purified, it is a sweet, colourless crystalline compound.

Glycine was found in 1994 in the star-forming region Sagittarius B2. The discovery is important because of its bearing on the origins of life on Earth.

glycogen polymer (a polysaccharide) of the sugar ◊glucose made and retained in the liver as a carbohydrate store, for which reason it is sometimes called animal starch. It is a source of energy when needed by muscles, where it is converted back into glucose by the hormone ◊insulin and metabolized.

glycol or **ethylene glycol** or **ethane-1,2-diol** $HOCH_2CH_2OH$ thick, colourless, odourless, sweetish liquid. It is used in antifreeze solutions, in the preparation of ethers and esters (used for explosives), as a solvent, and as a substitute for glycerol.

glycoside in biology, compound containing a sugar and a non-sugar unit. Many glycosides occur naturally, for example, ◊digitalis is a preparation of dried and powdered foxglove leaves that contains a mixture of cardiac glycosides. One of its constituents, digoxin, is used in the treatment of congestive heart failure and cardiac arrhythmias.

GM synthesizer in computing, synthesizer standard; see ◊general MIDI.

GMT abbreviation for ◊Greenwich Mean Time.

gnat any of a group of small two-winged biting insects belonging to the mosquito family. The eggs are laid in water, where they hatch into wormlike larvae, which pass through a pupal stage (see ◊pupa) to emerge as adults. (Family Culicidae.)

Species include *Culex pipiens*, abundant in England; the carrier of malaria *Anopheles maculipennis;* and the banded mosquito *Aedes aegypti*, which transmits yellow fever.

Only the female is capable of drawing blood; the male does not have piercing jaws.

gneiss coarse-grained ◊metamorphic rock, formed under conditions of high temperature and pressure, and often occurring in association with schists and granites. It has a foliated, or layered, structure consisting of thin bands of micas and/or amphiboles dark in colour alternating with bands of granular quartz and feldspar that are light in colour. Gneisses are formed during regional ◊metamorphism; **paragneisses** are derived from metamorphism of sedimentary rocks and **orthogneisses** from metamorphism of granite or similar igneous rocks.

GNN in computing, abbreviation for ◊Global Network Navigator.

gnu another name for ◊wildebeest.

GNU in computing, suite of free UNIX-like software distributed by the ◊Free Software Foundation. The software includes operating systems, compilers, text editors (such as EMACS), and other useful utilities.

goat ruminant mammal (it chews the cud), closely related to sheep. Both male and female goats have horns and beards. They are sure-footed animals, and feed on shoots and leaves more than on grass. (Genus *Capra*, family Bovidae.)

Domestic varieties are descended from the **scimitar-horned wild goat** (*C. aegagrus*) and have been kept for over 9,000 years in southern Europe and Asia. They are kept for milk or for mohair (angora and cashmere goats). Wild species include the **ibex** (*C. ibex*) of the Alps and **markhor** (*C. falconeri*) of the Himalayas, 1 m/3 ft high and with long twisted horns. The **Rocky Mountain goat** (*Oreamnos americanus*) is a 'goat antelope' and is not closely related to true goats.

goat moth large yellowish-grey or brown moth with irregular markings of white and black on the upper wings and a wingspan of about 7–8 cm/2.8–3 in. It is common in Europe and the Middle East.

When the moth is frightened it emits a disagreeable odour like that of a male goat hence its name.

classification The goat moth *Cossus ligniperda* is in order Lepidoptera, class Insecta, phylum Arthropoda.

goblet cell in biology, cup-shaped cell present in the epithelium of the respiratory and gastrointestinal tracts. Goblet cells secrete mucin, the main constituent of mucous, which lubricates the mucous membranes of these tracts.

goby small marine bony fish. Nearly all gobies are found in the shallow coastal waters of the temperate and tropical oceans.

The first dorsal fin consists of a few flexible spines and the second dorsal fin is opposed to the anal fin. The caudal fin is generally rounded, with the pelvic fins united to form a cup-shaped sucker.

classification Gobies are in the family Gobiidae, order Perciformes, class Osteichthyes.

ABOUT GODDARD SPACE FLIGHT CENTRE

http://pao.gsfc.nasa.gov/gsfc/welcome/history/history.htm

Primarily composed of a biography and achievement history of the American rocket pioneer, the web site also describes the Goddard Space Flight Centre and details the type of mission they are responsible for undertaking. As part of NASA's huge Internet resources there are of course many links to related topics.

Goddard Space Flight Center NASA installation at Greenbelt, Maryland, USA, responsible for the operation of NASA's unmanned scientific satellites, including the ◊Hubble Space Telescope. It is also home of the National Space Science Data centre, a repository of data collected by satellites.

goitre enlargement of the thyroid gland seen as a swelling on the neck. It is most pronounced in simple goitre, which is caused by iodine deficiency. More common is toxic goitre or ◊hyperthyroidism, caused by overactivity of the thyroid gland.

According to a World Health Organization's survey of 1997 up to 60% of people in some Indian states were suffering with goitre.

gold heavy, precious, yellow, metallic element; symbol Au, atomic number 79, relative atomic mass 197.0. It is unaffected by temperature changes and is highly resistant to acids. For manufacture, gold is alloyed with another strengthening metal (such as copper or silver), its purity being measured in ◊carats on a scale of 24.

In 1990 the three leading gold-producing countries were South Africa, 605.4 tonnes; USA, 295 tonnes; and Russia, 260 tonnes. In 1989 gold deposits were found in Greenland with an estimated yield of 12 tonnes per year.

Gold occurs naturally in veins, but following erosion it can be transported and redeposited. It has long been valued for its durability, malleability, and ductility, and its uses include dentistry and jewellery. As it will not corrode, it is also used in the manufacture of electric contacts for computers and other electrical devices.

goldcrest smallest European bird, about 9 cm/3.5 in long and weighing 5 g/0.011 lb; a ◊warbler. It is olive green, with a bright orange-yellow streak running from the beak to the back of the head and a black border above the eye. The tail is brown, marked with black and white, and the cheeks, throat, and breast are a greyish white. (Species *Regulus regulus,* family Muscicapidae, order Passeriformes.)

The goldcrest builds its nest in conifers. It is found all over Europe, particularly frequenting fir woods. In winter it can be found feeding with tit flocks, moving through deciduous woodlands.

golden-eye fly alternative name for green ◊lacewing.

golden retriever breed of dog. See ◊retriever.

goldenrod one of several tall and leafy North American perennial plants, belonging to the daisy family. Flower heads are mostly composed of many small yellow flowers, or florets. (Genus *Solidago,* family Compositae.)

goldenseal North American plant *Hydrastis canadensis* of the buttercup family whose thick yellow root is used medicinally as an astringent and a tonic. The root contains the alkaloid hydrastine, employed by herbalists to stop uterine bleeding.

golden section visually satisfying ratio, first constructed by the Greek mathematician Euclid and used in art and architecture. It is found by dividing a line AB at a point O such that the rectangle produced by the whole line and one of the segments is equal to the square drawn on the other segment. The ratio of the two segments is about 8:13 or 1:1.618, and a rectangle whose sides are in this ratio is called a **golden rectangle**. The ratio of consecutive Fibonacci numbers tends to the golden ratio.

In van Gogh's picture *Mother and Child,* for example, the Madonna's face fits perfectly into a golden rectangle.

goldfinch songbird found in Eurasia, North Africa, and North America. (Species *Carduelis carduelis,* family Fringillidae, order Passeriformes.)

goldfish fish belonging to the ◊carp family, found in East Asia. It is greenish-brown in its natural state, but has been bred by the Chinese for centuries, taking on highly coloured and sometimes freakishly shaped forms. Goldfish can occur in a greater range of colours than any other animal tested. (Species *Carassius auratus,* family Cyprinidae.)

Golgi apparatus or ***Golgi body*** stack of flattened membranous sacs found in the cells of ◊eukaryotes. Many molecules travel through the Golgi apparatus on their way to other organelles or to the endoplasmic reticulum. Some are modified or assembled inside the sacs. The Golgi apparatus is named after the Italian physician Camillo Golgi.

Goliath beetle large beetle found only in tropical countries. The biggest Goliath beetle *Goliathus giganteus,* found in equatorial Africa, may be more than 150 mm/6 in long and is one of the largest insects.

They lay their eggs in the rotting wood of trees, and most adults feed on the tender floral parts or suck the sap exuded from trees. Its 'brushed velvet' wingcases are maroon and the pronotum (shield) is black with roughly longitudinal white stripes.

classification Goliath beetles belong to the subfamily Cetoniinae of the family Scarabaeidae in order Coleoptera, class Insecta, phylum Arthropoda.

gonad the part of an animal's body that produces the sperm or egg cells (ova) required for sexual reproduction. The sperm-producing gonad is called a ◊testis, and the egg-producing gonad is called an ◊ovary.

gonadotrophin any hormone that supports and stimulates the function of the gonads (sex glands); some gonadotrophins are used as fertility drugs.

Gondwanaland or ***Gondwana*** southern landmass formed 200 million years ago by the splitting of the single world continent ◊Pangaea. (The northern landmass was ◊Laurasia.) It later fragmented into the continents of South America, Africa, Australia, and Antarctica, which then drifted slowly to their present positions. The baobab tree found in both Africa and Australia is a relic of this ancient land mass.

A database of the entire geology of Gondwanaland has been constructed by geologists in South Africa. The database, known as

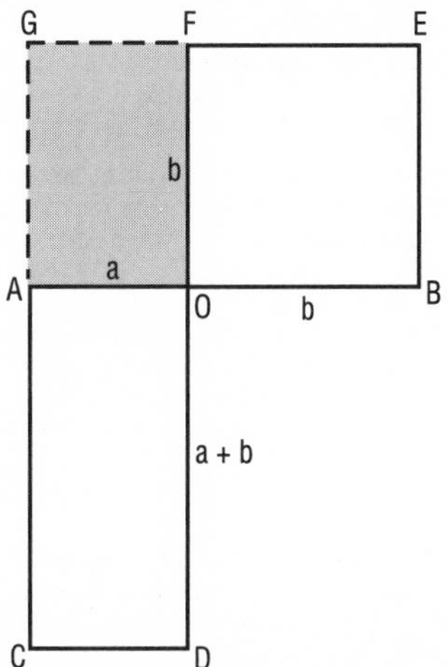

golden section *The golden section is the ratio a:b, equal to 8:13. A golden rectangle is one, like that shaded in the picture, that has its length and breadth in this ratio. These rectangles are said to be pleasant to look at and have been used instinctively by artists in their pictures.*

Golgi, Camillo
(1843–1926)

Italian cell biologist who produced the first detailed knowledge of the fine structure of the nervous system. He shared the 1906 Nobel Prize for Physiology or Medicine with Santiago Ramón y Cajal, who followed up Golgi's work.

Golgi's use of silver salts in staining cells proved so effective in showing up the components and fine processes of nerve cells that even the synapses – tiny gaps between the cells – were visible. The Golgi apparatus, a series of flattened membranous cavities found in the cytoplasm of cells, was first described by him in 1898.

Mary Evans Picture Library

Gondwana Geoscientific Indexing Database (GO-GEOID), displays information as a map of Gondwana 155 million years ago, before the continents drifted apart.

gonorrhoea common sexually transmitted disease arising from infection with the bacterium *Neisseria gonorrhoeae,* which causes inflammation of the genito-urinary tract. After an incubation period of two to ten days, infected men experience pain while urinating and a discharge from the penis; infected women often have no external symptoms.

Untreated gonorrhoea carries the threat of sterility to both sexes; there is also the risk of blindness in a baby born to an infected mother. The condition is treated with antibiotics, though ever-increasing doses are becoming necessary to combat resistant strains.

Good King Henry perennial plant belonging to the goosefoot family, growing to 50 cm/1.6 ft, with triangular leaves which are mealy when young. Spikes of tiny greenish-yellow flowers appear above the leaves in midsummer. (*Chenopodium bonus-henricus,* family Chenopodiaceae.)

Goonhilly British Telecom satellite-tracking station in Cornwall, England. It is equipped with a communications-satellite transmitter–receiver in permanent contact with most parts of the world.

goose any of several large aquatic birds belonging to the same family as ducks and swans. There are about 12 species, found in North America, Greenland, Europe, North Africa, and Asia north of the Himalayas. Both sexes are similar in appearance: they have short, webbed feet, placed nearer the front of the body than in other members of the family, and a slightly hooked beak. Geese feed entirely on grass and plants, build nests of grass and twigs on the ground, and lay 5–9 eggs, white or cream-coloured, according to the species. (Genera mainly *Anser* and *Branta,* family Anatidae, order Anseriformes.)

The **barnacle goose** (*B. leucopsis*) is about 60 cm/2 ft long and weighs about 2 kg/4.5 lb. It is black and white, marbled with blue and grey, and the beak is black. The **bean goose** (*A. fabalis*) is a grey species of European wild goose with an orange or yellow and black beak. It breeds in northern Europe and Siberia. The **Brent goose** (*B. bernicla*) is a small goose, black or brown, white, and grey in colour. It is almost completely herbivorous, feeding on eel grass and algae. The world population of Brent geese was 25,000 in 1996. The **greylag goose** (*A. anser*) is the ancestor of domesticated geese.

Other species include the **Canada goose** (*B. canadensis*) (common to North America and introduced into Europe in the 18th century), the **pink-footed goose** (*A. brachyrhynchus*), the **white-fronted goose** (*A. albifrons*), and the **ne-ne** or **Hawaiian goose** (*B. sandvicensis*).

gooseberry edible fruit of a low-growing bush (*Ribes uva-crispa*) found in Europe and Asia, related to the ◊currant. It is straggling in its growth, and has straight sharp spines in groups of three and rounded, lobed leaves. The flowers are green and hang on short stalks. The sharp-tasting fruits are round, hairy, and generally green, but there are reddish and white varieties.

goosefoot any of a group of plants belonging to the goosefoot family, closely related to spinach and beets. The seeds of white goosefoot (*C. album*) were used as food in Europe from Neolithic times, and also from early times in the Americas. White goosefoot grows to 1 m/3 ft tall and has lance- or diamond-shaped leaves and packed heads of small inconspicuous flowers. The green part is eaten as a spinach substitute. (Genus *Chenopodium,* family Chenopodiaceae.)

gopher any of a group of burrowing rodents. Gophers are a kind of ground squirrel represented by some 20 species distributed across western North America, Europe, and Asia. Length ranges from 15 cm/6 in to 90 cm/16 in, excluding the furry tail; colouring ranges from plain yellowish to striped and spotted species. (Genus *Citellus,* family Sciuridae.)

The name **pocket gopher** is applied to the eight genera of the North American family Geomyidae.

Gopher (derived from ***go for***; alternatively, named for the mascot of the University of Minnesota, where it was invented) menu-based server on the ◊Internet that indexes resources and retrieves them according to user choice via any one of several built-in methods such as ◊FTP or ◊Telnet. Gopher servers can also be accessed via the World Wide Web and searched via special servers called ◊Veronica.

Gopherspace in computing, name for the knowledge base composed of all the documents indexed on all the ◊Gophers in the world.

gopher tortoise land tortoise occurring in the southern USA. It has a domed shell and scaly legs. Its forelegs are flattened for digging the burrow where it lives. Gopher tortoises reach lengths of up to 37 cm/14.5 in.

classification The gopher tortoise *Gopherus polyphemus* is in family Cheloniidae, order Testudinae, class Reptilia.

Gordon setter breed of dog. See ◊setter.

gorge narrow steep-sided valley (or canyon) that may or may not have a river at the bottom. A gorge may be formed as a ◊waterfall retreats upstream, eroding away the rock at the base of a river valley; or it may be caused by rejuvenation, when a river begins to cut downwards into its channel once again (for example, in response to a fall in sea level). Gorges are common in limestone country, where they may be formed by the collapse of the roofs of underground caverns.

gorilla largest of the apes, found in the dense forests of West Africa and mountains of central Africa. The male stands about 1.8 m/6 ft high and weighs about 200 kg/450 lbs. Females are about half this size. The body is covered with blackish hair, silvered on the back in older males. Gorillas live in family groups; they are vegetarian, highly intelligent, and will attack only in self-defence. They are dwindling in numbers, being shot for food by some local people, or by poachers taking young for zoos, but protective measures

GORILLA

http://www.seaworld.org/animal_bytes/gorillaab.html

Illustrated guide to the gorilla including information about genus, size, life span, habitat, gestation, diet, and a series of fun facts.

are having some effect. (Species *Gorilla gorilla.*)

Gorillas construct stoutly built nests in trees for overnight use. The breast-beating movement, once thought to indicate rage, actually signifies only nervous excitement. There are three races – western lowland, eastern lowland, and mountain gorillas – and US scientists suggested in 1994 that there may be two separate species of gorilla.

gorse or ***furze*** or ***whin*** any of a group of plants native to Europe and Asia, consisting of thorny shrubs with spine-shaped leaves growing thickly along the stems and bright-yellow coconut-scented flowers. (Genus *Ulex,* family Leguminosae.)

GOSHAWK

The male goshawk mates up to 600 times with his partner for every clutch of eggs. This ensures that the sperm of any rival are completely swamped.

goshawk or ***northern goshawk*** woodland hawk similar in appearance to the peregrine falcon, but with shorter wings and legs. It is native to most of Europe, Asia, and North America, and is used in falconry. The male is much smaller than the female. It is ash grey on the upper part of the body and whitish underneath with brown horizontal stripes; it has a dark head and cheeks with a white stripe above the eye. The tail has dark bands across it. (Species *Accipiter gentilis,* order Falconiformes.)

Gossamer Albatross the first human-powered aircraft to fly across the English Channel, in June 1979. It was designed by Paul MacCready and piloted and pedalled by Bryan Allen. The Channel crossing took 2 hours 49 minutes. The same team was behind the first successful human-powered aircraft (*Gossamer Condor*) two years earlier.

Gouraud shading in computer animation, technique for calculating the correct colours and intensity of lighting playing on an on-screen three-dimensional object.

Gouraud shading works by measuring the colour and brightness at the vertices of the polygons that make up the object and mixing these to get values for the areas inside the polygons. Specialized hardware makes this process relatively fast. The technique is named after its inventor, Henri Gouraud and was developed 1973.

gourd any of a group of plants that includes melons and pumpkins. In a narrower sense, the name applies only to the genus *Lagenaria,* of which the bottle gourd or ◊calabash (*L. siceraria*) is best known. (Family Cucurbitaceae.)

gout hereditary form of ◊arthritis, marked by an excess of uric acid crystals in the tissues, causing pain and inflammation in one or more joints (usually of the feet or hands). Acute attacks are treated with anti-inflammatories.

The disease, ten times more common in men, poses a long-term threat to the blood vessels and the kidneys, so ongoing treatment may be needed to minimize the levels of uric acid in the bloodstream. It is aggravated by heavy drinking.

governor in engineering, any device that controls the speed of a machine or engine, usually by regulating the intake of fuel or steam.

Scottish inventor James ◊Watt invented the steam-engine governor in 1788. It works by means of heavy balls, which rotate on the end of linkages and move in or out because of ◊centrifugal force according to the speed of rotation. The movement of the balls closes or opens the steam valve to the engine. When the engine speed increases too much, the balls fly out, and cause the steam valve to close, so the engine slows down. The opposite happens when the engine speed drops too much.

GP in medicine, abbreviation for ***general practitioner***.

GPF (abbreviation for ***general protection fault***) in Windows 3.1, error message returned by a computer when it crashes. A GPF is the same as a UAE (unexpected application error) in Windows 3.0. It often indicates that one application has tried to use memory reserved for another.

Graafian follicle fluid-filled capsule that surrounds and protects the developing egg cell inside the ovary during the ◊menstrual cycle. After the egg cell has been released, the follicle remains and is known as a corpus luteum.

gradient on a graph, the slope of a straight or curved line. The slope of a curve at any given point is represented by the slope of the ◊tangent at that point.

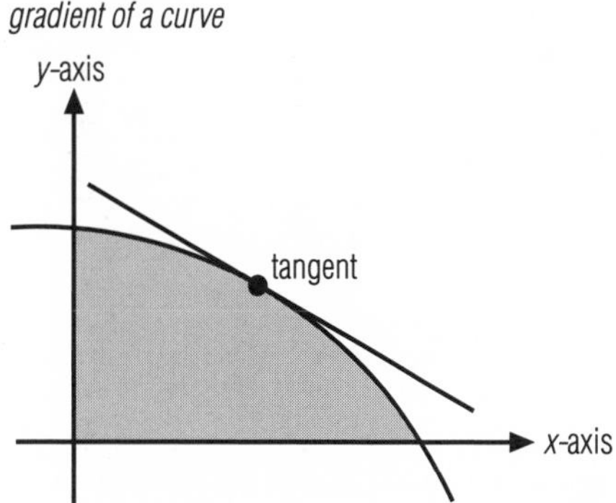

the gradient to a curve at any point is equal to the gradient of the tangent drawn touching that point

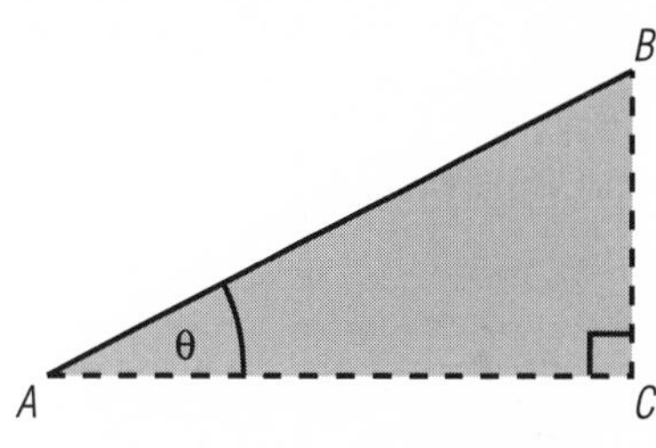

$$\text{gradient of } AB = \frac{\text{vertical distance}}{\text{horizontal distance}}$$

$$\frac{BC}{AC} = \tan\theta$$

gradient *The gradient of a curve keeps changing, so in order to calculate the gradient you have to draw a straight line that touches a point on the curve (the tangent). The gradient for that point on the curve will then be the same as the gradient of the straight line.*

grafting in medicine, the operation by which an organ or other living tissue is removed from one organism and transplanted into the same or a different organism.

In horticulture, it is a technique widely used for propagating plants, especially woody species. A bud or shoot on one plant, termed the **scion**, is inserted into another, the **stock**, so that they continue growing together, the tissues combining at the point of union. In this way some of the advantages of both plants are obtained.

Grafting is usually only successful between species that are closely related and is most commonly practised on roses and fruit trees. The grafting of nonwoody species is more difficult but it is sometimes used to propagate tomatoes and cacti. See also ◊transplant.

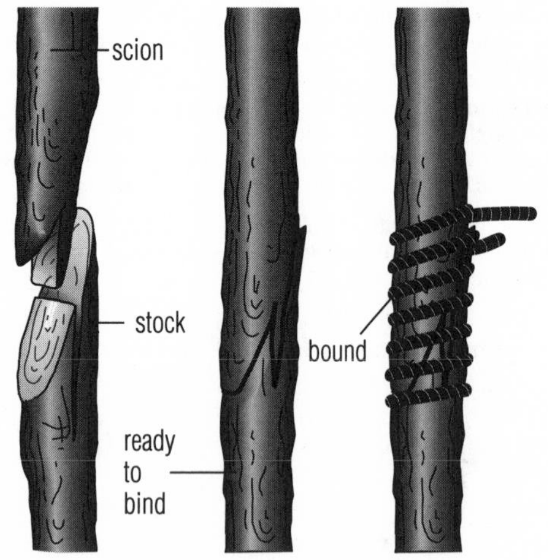

grafting Grafting, a method of artificial propagation in plants, is commonly used in the propagation of roses and fruit trees. A relatively small part, the scion, of one plant is attached to another plant so that growth continues. The plant receiving the transplanted material is called the stock.

grain the smallest unit of mass in the three English systems (avoirdupois, troy, and apothecaries' weights) used in the UK and USA, equal to 0.0648 g. It was reputedly the weight of a grain of wheat. One pound avoirdupois equals 7,000 grains; one pound troy or apothecaries' weight equals 5,760 grains.

gram metric unit of mass; one-thousandth of a kilogram.

gramophone old-fashioned name for a record player or stereo. It was developed from US inventor Thomas Edison's **phonograph**, which remains the traditional US name.

grampus common name for Risso's dolphin, a slate-grey dolphin found in tropical and temperate seas. These dolphins live in large schools and can reach 4 m/13 ft in length. They have blunt snouts with only a few teeth, and feed on squid and small fish. The name grampus is sometimes also used for the killer ◊whale. (Species *Grampus griseus.*)

Grande Dixence dam the world's highest dam, located in Switzerland, which measures 285 m/935 ft from base to crest. Completed in 1961, it contains 6 million cu m/8 million cu yd of concrete.

grand unified theory in physics, a sought-for theory that would combine the theory of the strong nuclear force (called ◊quantum chromodynamics) with the theory of the weak nuclear and electromagnetic forces. The search for the grand unified theory is part of a larger programme seeking a unified field theory, which would combine all the forces of nature (including gravity) within one framework.

granite coarse-grained intrusive ◊igneous rock, typically consisting of the minerals quartz, feldspar, and biotite mica. It may be pink or grey, depending on the composition of the feldspar. Granites are chiefly used as building materials.

Granites often form large intrusions in the core of mountain ranges, and they are usually surrounded by zones of ◊metamorphic rock (rock that has been altered by heat or pressure). Granite areas have characteristic moorland scenery. In exposed areas the bedrock may be weathered along joints and cracks to produce a tor, consisting of rounded blocks that appear to have been stacked upon one another.

grape fruit of any grape ◊vine, especially *V. vinifera.* (Genus *Vitis,* family Vitaceae.)

grapefruit round, yellow, juicy, sharp-tasting fruit of the evergreen grapefruit tree. The tree grows up to 10 m/more than 30 ft and has dark shiny leaves and large white flowers. The large fruits grow in grapelike clusters (hence the name). Grapefruits were first established in the West Indies and subsequently cultivated in Florida by the 1880s; they are now also grown in Israel and South Africa. Some varieties have pink flesh. (*Citrus paradisi,* family Rutaceae.)

graph pictorial representation of numerical data, such as statistical data, or a method of showing the mathematical relationship between two or more variables by drawing a diagram.

There are often two axes, or reference lines, at right angles intersecting at the origin – the zero point, from which values of the variables (for example, distance and time for a moving object) are assigned along the axes. Pairs of simultaneous values (the distance moved after a particular time) are plotted as points in the area between the axes, and the points then joined by a smooth curve to produce a graph. The horizontal axis is usually referred to as the x-axis, and the vertical axis as the y-axis.

Cartesian coordinates On a line graph values are plotted using coordinates, components used to define the position of a point by its perpendicular distance from a set of two or more axes, or reference lines. For a two-dimensional area defined by two axes at right angles, the coordinates of a point are given by its perpendicular distances from the y-axis and x-axis, written in the form (x,y). For example, a point P that lies three units from the y-axis and four units from the x-axis has Cartesian coordinates (3,4).

straight-line graph This type of graph is produced by plotting the variables of a ◊linear equation with the general form

$$y = mx + c$$

where m is the slope of the line represented by the equation and c is the y-intercept, or the value of y where the line crosses the y-axis in the ◊Cartesian coordinate system.

histogram These are graphs used in statistics, showing frequency of data, in which the horizontal axis details discrete units or class boundaries, and the vertical axis represents the frequency. Blocks are drawn such that their areas (rather than their height as in a ◊bar chart) are proportional to the frequencies within a class or across several class boundaries. There are no spaces between blocks.

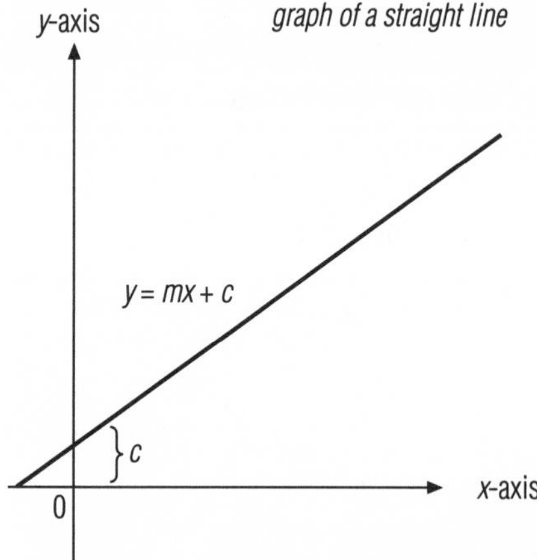

the equation of the straight-line graph takes the form $y = mx + c$, where m is the gradient (slope) of the line, and c is the y-intercept (the value of y where the line cuts the y-axis)for example, a graph of the equation $y = x\ 4$ will have a gradient of –1 and will cut the y-axis at $y = 4$

graph A graph is pictorial illustration of numerical data. It is a useful tool for interpreting data and is often used to spot trends or approximate a solution.

applications Graphs have many practical applications in all disciplines, for example **distance–time graphs** are used to describe the motion of a body by illustrating the relationship between the distance that it travels and the time taken. Plotting distance (on the vertical axis) against time (on the horizontal axis) produces a graph the gradient of which is the body's speed. If the gradient is constant (the graph is a straight line), the body has uniform or constant speed; if the gradient varies (the graph is curved), then so does the speed and the body may be said to be accelerating or decelerating.

Speed–time graphs are used to describe the motion of a body by illustrating how its speed or velocity changes with time. The gradient of the graph gives the object's acceleration: if the gradient is zero (the graph is horizontal) then the body is moving with constant speed or uniform velocity; if the gradient is constant, the body is moving with uniform acceleration. The area under the graph gives the total distance travelled by the body.

Conversion graphs are used for changing values from one unit to another, for example from Celsius to Fahrenheit, with the two axes representing the different units.

graphical user interface (GUI) or ***WIMP*** in computing, a type of ◊user interface in which programs and files appear as icons (small pictures), user options are selected from pull-down menus, and data are displayed in windows (rectangular areas), which the operator can manipulate in various ways. The operator uses a pointing device, typically a ◊mouse, to make selections and initiate actions.

The concept of the graphical user interface was developed by the Xerox Corporation in the 1970s, was popularized with the Apple Macintosh computers in the 1980s, and is now available on many types of computer – most notably as Windows, an operating system for IBM PC-compatible microcomputers developed by the software company Microsoft.

graphic equalizer control used in hi-fi systems that allows the distortions introduced in the sound output by unequal amplification of different frequencies to be corrected.

The frequency range of the signal is divided into separate bands, usually third-octave bands. The amplification applied to each band is adjusted by a sliding contact; the position of the contact indicates the strength of the amplification applied to each frequency range.

graphic file format format in which computer graphics are stored and transmitted. There are two main types: ◊raster graphics in which the image is stored as a ◊bit map (arrangement of dots), and ◊vector graphics, in which the image is stored using geometric formulas. There are many different file formats, some of which are used by specific computers, operating systems or applications. Some formats use file compression, particularly those that are able to handle more than one colour.

graphics used with computers, see ◊computer graphics.

graphics board in computing, another name for ◊graphics card.

graphics card in computing, a peripheral device that processes and displays graphics.

Graphics Interchange Format in computing, picture file format usually abbreviated to ◊GIF.

graphics tablet or ***bit pad*** in computing, an input device in which a stylus or cursor is moved, by hand, over a flat surface. The computer can keep track of the position of the stylus, so enabling the operator to input drawings or diagrams into the computer.

A graphics tablet is often used with a form overlaid for users to mark boxes in positions that relate to specific registers in the computer, although recent developments in handwriting recognition may increase its future versatility.

graphite blackish-grey, laminar, crystalline form of ◊carbon. It is used as a lubricant and as the active component of pencil lead.

The carbon atoms are strongly bonded together in sheets, but the bonds between the sheets are weak, allowing other atoms to enter regions between the layers causing them to slide over one another. Graphite has a very high melting point (3,500°C/6,332°F), and is a good conductor of heat and electricity. It absorbs neutrons and is therefore used to moderate the chain reaction in nuclear reactors.

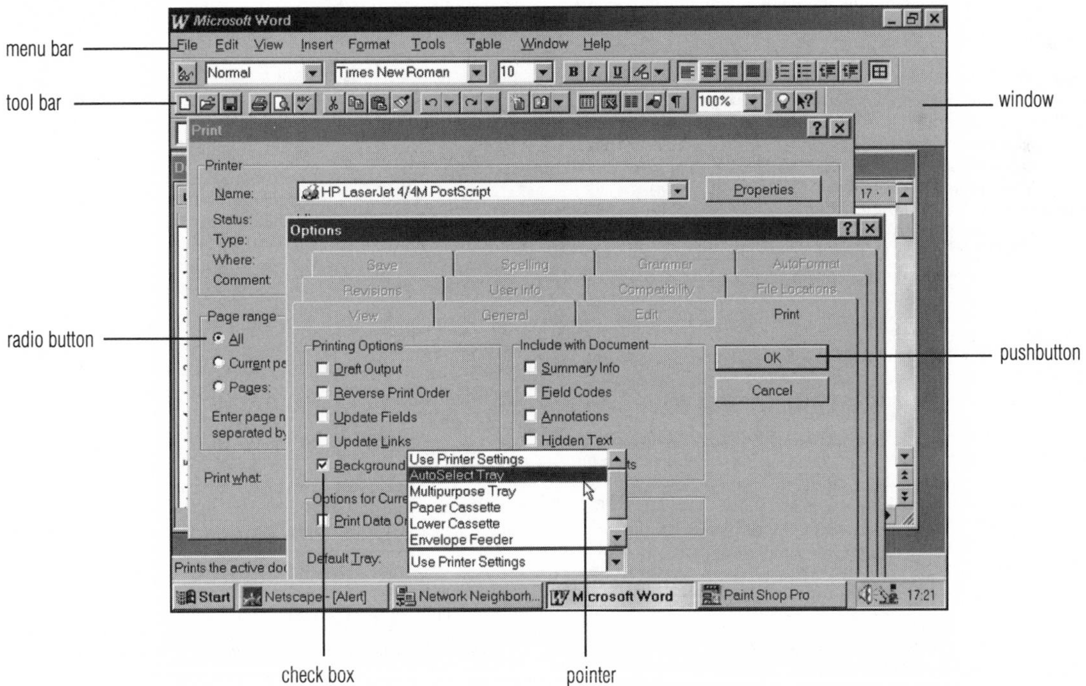

graphical user interface *A typical GUI, where the user is taken around the system by simply clicking on representative buttons or icons using the mouse.*

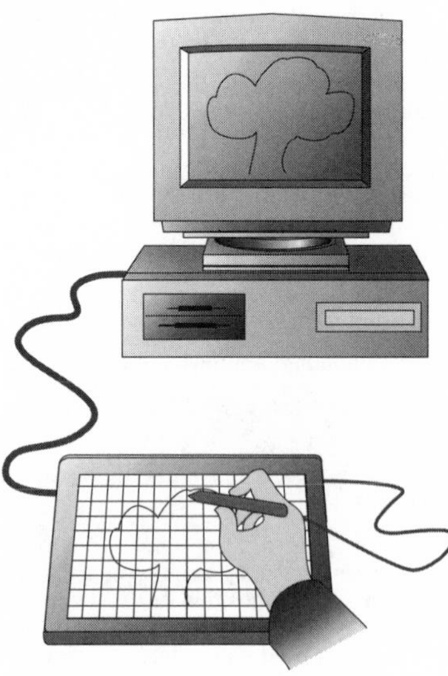

graphics tablet A graphics tablet enables images drawn freehand to be translated directly to the computer screen.

graph plotter alternative name for a ◊plotter.

grass any of a very large family of plants, many of which are economically important because they provide grazing for animals and food for humans in the form of cereals. There are about 9,000 species distributed worldwide except in the Arctic regions. Most are perennial, with long, narrow leaves and jointed, hollow stems; flowers with both male and female reproductive organs are borne on spikelets; the fruits are grainlike. Included in the family are bluegrass, wheat, rye, maize, sugarcane, and bamboo. (Family Gramineae.)

grasshopper any of several insects with strongly developed hind legs, enabling them to leap into the air. The hind leg in the male usually has a row of protruding joints that produce the characteristic chirping sound when rubbed against the hard wing veins. ◊Locusts, ◊crickets, and katydids are related to grasshoppers. (Families Acrididae and Tettigoniidae, order Orthoptera.)

The **short-horned grasshoppers** constitute the family Acrididae, and include locusts. All members of the family feed voraciously on vegetation. Eggs are laid in a small hole in the ground, and the unwinged larvae become adult after about six moults.

grass of Parnassus plant, unrelated to grasses, found growing in marshes and on wet moors in Europe and Asia. It is low-growing, with a rosette of heart-shaped stalked leaves, and has five-petalled white flowers with conspicuous veins growing singly on stem tips in late summer. (*Parnassia palustris*, family Parnassiaceae.)

grass snake olive-green, grey or brownish non-venomous snake *Natrix natrix* found near water in lowland areas with woodland. They are about 80 cm/32 in long and feed mainly on frogs, toads, and newts, which they hunt in the water. They are the largest British reptiles. There is also a grass snake in the USA.

The female lays 10–40 eggs within a pile of rotting vegetation, where they are incubated by the heat generated by the rotting process. Eggs are elongated, white, leathery, and about 3 cm/1.2 in long.

grass tree Australian plant belonging to the lily family. The tall, thick stems have a grasslike tuft at the top above which rises a flower spike resembling a spear; this often appears after bushfires and in some species can grow to a height of 3 m/10 ft. (Genus *Xanthorrhoea*, family Liliaceae.)

gravel coarse ◊sediment consisting of pebbles or small fragments of rock, originating in the beds of lakes and streams or on beaches. Gravel is quarried for use in road building, railway ballast, and for an aggregate in concrete. It is obtained from quarries known as gravel pits, where it is often found mixed with sand or clay.

Some gravel deposits also contain placer deposits of metal ores (chiefly tin) or free metals (such as gold and silver).

gravimetric analysis in chemistry, a technique for determining, by weighing, the amount of a particular substance present in a sample. It usually involves the conversion of the test substance into a compound of known molecular weight that can be easily isolated and purified.

gravimetry study of the Earth's gravitational field. Small variations in the gravitational field (gravimetric anomalies) can be caused by varying densities of rocks and structure beneath the surface. Such variations are measured by a device called a gravimeter, which consists of a weighted spring that is pulled further downwards where the gravity is stronger (at a Bouguer anomaly). Gravimetry is used by geologists to map the subsurface features of the Earth's crust, such as underground masses of heavy rock such as granite, or light rock such as salt.

gravitational field the region around a body in which other bodies experience a force due to its gravitational attraction. The gravitational field of a massive object such as the Earth is very strong and easily recognized as the force of gravity, whereas that of an object of much smaller mass is very weak and difficult to detect. Gravitational fields produce only attractive forces.

gravitational field strength (symbol g) the strength of the Earth's gravitational field at a particular point. It is defined as the gravitational force in newtons that acts on a mass of one kilogram. The value of g on the Earth's surface is taken to be 9.806 N kg^{-1}.

The symbol g is also used to represent the acceleration of a freely falling object in the Earth's gravitational field.

Near the Earth's surface and in the absence of friction due to the air, all objects fall with an acceleration of 9.806 m s^{-2}.

gravitational lensing bending of light by a gravitational field, predicted by Einstein's general theory of relativity. The effect was first detected in 1917 when the light from stars was found to be bent as it passed the totally eclipsed Sun. More remarkable is the splitting of light from distant quasars into two or more images by intervening galaxies. In 1979 the first double image of a quasar produced by gravitational lensing was discovered and a quadruple image of another quasar was later found.

gravitational potential energy energy possessed by an object when it is placed in a position from which, if it were free to do so, it would fall under the influence of gravity. The gravitational potential energy E_p of an object of mass m kg placed at a height h m above the ground is given by the formula:

$$E_p = mgh$$

where g is the gravitational field strength in N kg^{-1} of the Earth at the place.

In a ◊hydroelectric power station, gravitational potential energy of water held in a high-level reservoir is used to drive turbines to produce electricity.

graviton in physics, the ◊gauge boson that is the postulated carrier of the gravitational force.

gravity force of attraction that arises between objects by virtue of their masses. On Earth, gravity is the force of attraction between

GRAVITY

The maximum speed with which a falling raindrop can hit you is about 29 kmph/18 mph. In a vacuum, the further an object falls, the more speed it gains, but in the real world, air resistance eventually balances out the accelerating effect of gravity.

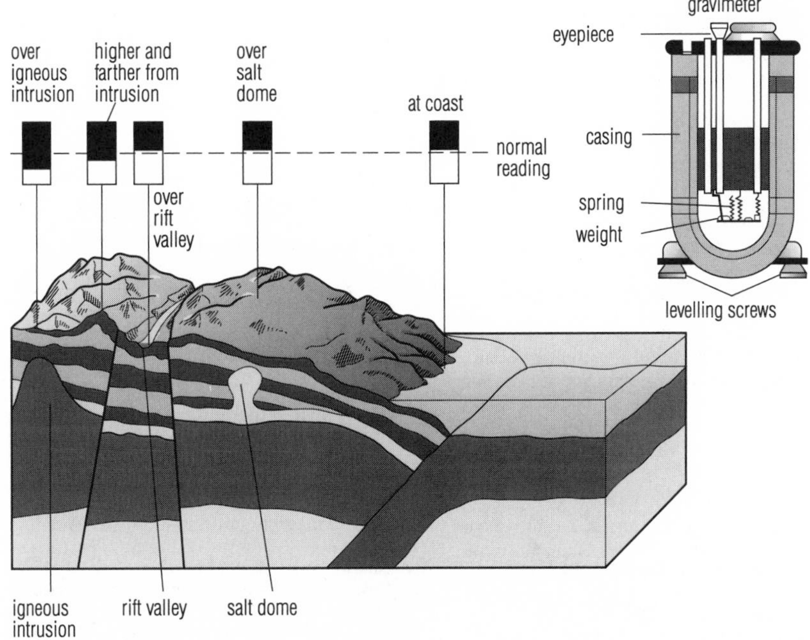

gravimetry *The gravimeter is an instrument for measuring the force of gravity at a particular location. Variations in the force of gravity acting on a weight suspended by a spring cause the spring to stretch. The gravimeter is used in aerial surveys. Geological features such as intrusions and salt domes are revealed by the stretching of the spring.*

any object in the Earth's gravitational field and the Earth itself. It is regarded as one of the four fundamental ◊forces of nature, the other three being the ◊electromagnetic force, the ◊strong nuclear force, and the ◊weak nuclear force. The gravitational force is the weakest of the four forces, but it acts over great distances. The particle that is postulated as the carrier of the gravitational force is the ◊graviton.

One of the earliest gravitational experiments was undertaken by Nevil Maskelyne in 1774 and involved the measurement of the attraction of Mount Schiehallion (Scotland) on a plumb bob.

measuring forces of attraction An experiment for determining the force of attraction between two masses was first planned in the mid-18th century by the Reverend J Mitchell, who did not live to work on the apparatus he had designed and completed. After Mitchell's death the apparatus came into the hands of Henry Cavendish, who largely reconstructed it but kept to Mitchell's original plan. The attracted masses consisted of two small balls, connected by a stiff wooden beam suspended at its middle point by a long, fine wire. The whole of this part of the apparatus was enclosed in a case, carefully coated with tinfoil to secure, as far as possible, a uniform temperature within the case. Irregular distribution of temperature would have resulted in convection currents of air which would have had a serious disturbing effect on the suspended system. To the beam was attached a small mirror with its plane vertical. A small glazed window in the case allowed any motion of the mirror to be observed by the consequent deviations of a ray of light reflected from it. The attracting masses consisted of two equal, massive lead spheres. Using this apparatus, Cavendish, in 1797, obtained for the gravitational constant G the value 6.6×10^{-11} N m^2 kg^{-2}. The apparatus was refined by Charles Vernon Boys and he obtained the improved value 6.6576×10^{-11} N m^2 kg^{-2}. The value generally used today is 6.6720×10^{-11} N m^2 kg^{-2}.

gravure one of the three main ◊printing methods, in which printing is done from a plate etched with a pattern of recessed cells in which the ink is held. The greater the depth of a cell, the greater the strength of the printed ink. Gravure plates are expensive to make, but the process is economical for high-volume printing and reproduces illustrations well.

gray SI unit (symbol Gy) of absorbed radiation dose. It replaces the rad (1 Gy equals 100 rad), and is defined as the dose absorbed when one kilogram of matter absorbs one joule of ionizing radiation. Different types of radiation cause different amounts of damage for the same absorbed dose; the SI unit of **dose equivalent** is the ◊sievert.

grayling freshwater fish with a long multirayed dorsal (back) fin and silver to purple body colouring. It is found in northern parts of Europe, Asia, and North America, where it was once common in the Great Lakes. (Species *Thymallus thymallus,* family Salmonidae.)

grayling butterfly butterfly widely distributed over the British Isles. It has dark brown wings with two black eye-spots on each of the forewings and one black eyespot centred with white on the hindwings. It is found on heaths and in dry stony places, especially on chalk and in clearings in woods.

classification The grayling butterfly *Hipparchia semele* is in order Lepidoptera, class Insecta, phylum Arthropoda.

Great Artesian Basin the largest area of artesian water in the world. It underlies much of Queensland, New South Wales, and South Australia, and in prehistoric times formed a sea. It has an area of 1,750,000 sq km/676,250 sq mi.

Great Bear popular name for the constellation ◊Ursa Major.

great circle circle drawn on a sphere such that the diameter of the circle is a diameter of the sphere. On the Earth, all meridians of longitude are half great circles; among the parallels of latitude, only the Equator is a great circle.

The shortest route between two points on the Earth's surface is along the arc of a great circle. These are used extensively as air routes although on maps, owing to the distortion brought about by ◊projection, they do not appear as straight lines.

Great Dane breed of large, short-haired dog, often fawn or brindle in colour, standing up to 76 cm/30 in tall, and weighing up to 70 kg/154 lb. It has a large head and muzzle, and small, erect ears. It was formerly used in Europe for hunting boar and stags.

Great Red Spot prominent oval feature, 14,000 km/8,500 mi wide and some 30,000 km/20,000 mi long, in the atmosphere of the planet ◊Jupiter, south of the Equator. It was first observed in the 19th century. Space probes show it to be an anticlockwise vortex of cold clouds, coloured possibly by phosphorus.

Great Wall array of galaxies arranged almost in a perfect plane, consisting of some 2,000 galaxies (about 500 million × 200 million light years across). It was discovered by US astronomers in Cambridge, Massachusetts, in 1989.

grebe any of a group of 19 species of water birds. The **great crested grebe** (*Podiceps cristatus*) is the largest of the Old World grebes. It feeds on fish, and lives on ponds and marshes in Europe, Asia, Africa, and Australia. It grows to 50 cm/20 in long and has a white breast, with chestnut and black feathers on its back and head. Dark ear tufts and a prominent collar or crest of feathers around the base of the head appear during the breeding season; these are lost in winter. (Family Podicipedidae, order Podicipediformes.)

Grebes have broad, flat feet, and the toes are partially webbed, the legs being set extremely far back on the body. The wings are short and rounded, there is practically no tail, and flight is low. Both sexes are similar in appearance.

greeking method used in ◊desktop publishing and other page make-up systems for showing type below a certain size on screen. Rather than the actual characters being displayed, either a grey bar or graphics symbols are used. Greeking is usually employed when a general impression of the page lay-out is required.

green audit inspection of a company to assess the total environmental impact of its activities or of a particular product or process.

For example, a green audit of a manufactured product looks at the impact of production (including energy use and the extraction of raw materials used in manufacture), use (which may cause pollution and other hazards), and disposal (potential for recycling, and whether waste causes pollution).

Such 'cradle-to-grave' surveys allow a widening of the traditional scope of economics by ascribing costs to variables that are usually ignored, such as despoliation of the countryside or air pollution.

Green Bank site in West Virginia, USA, of the National Radio Astronomy Observatory. Its main instruments are a 43-m/140-ft fully steerable dish, opened in 1965, and three 26-m/85-ft dishes. A 90-m/300-ft partially steerable dish, opened in 1962, collapsed 1988 because of metal fatigue; a replacement dish, 100 m/330 ft across, was under construction in 1995.

greenbottle type of ◊blowfly.

greenbrier or ***catbrier*** any of several climbing woody vines of the genus *Smilax* of the lily family, having smooth, shiny green oval leaves and usually black berries. The prickly stems of these plants often form impenetrable thickets.

green computing the gradual movement by computer companies toward incorporating energy-saving measures in the design of systems and hardware. The increasing use of energy-saving devices, so that a computer partially shuts down during periods of inactivity, but can reactivate at the touch of a key, could play a significant role in ◊energy conservation.

It is estimated that worldwide electricity consumption by computers amounts to 240 billion kilowatt hours per year, equivalent to the entire annual consumption of Brazil. In the USA, carbon dioxide emissions could be reduced by 20 million tonnes per year – equivalent to the carbon dioxide output of 5 million cars – if all computers incorporated the latest 'sleep technology' (which shuts down most of the power-consuming features of a computer if it is unused for any length of time).

Although it was initially predicted that computers would mean 'paperless offices', in practice the amount of paper consumed continues to rise. Other environmentally-costly features of computers include their rapid obsolescence, health problems associated with monitors and keyboards, and the unfavourable economics of component recycling.

greenfinch olive-green songbird common in Europe and North Africa. It has bright-yellow markings on the outer tail feathers and wings; males are much brighter in colour than females. (Species *Carduelis chloris*, family Fringillidae, order Passeriformes.)

greenfly plant-sucking insect, a type of ◊aphid.

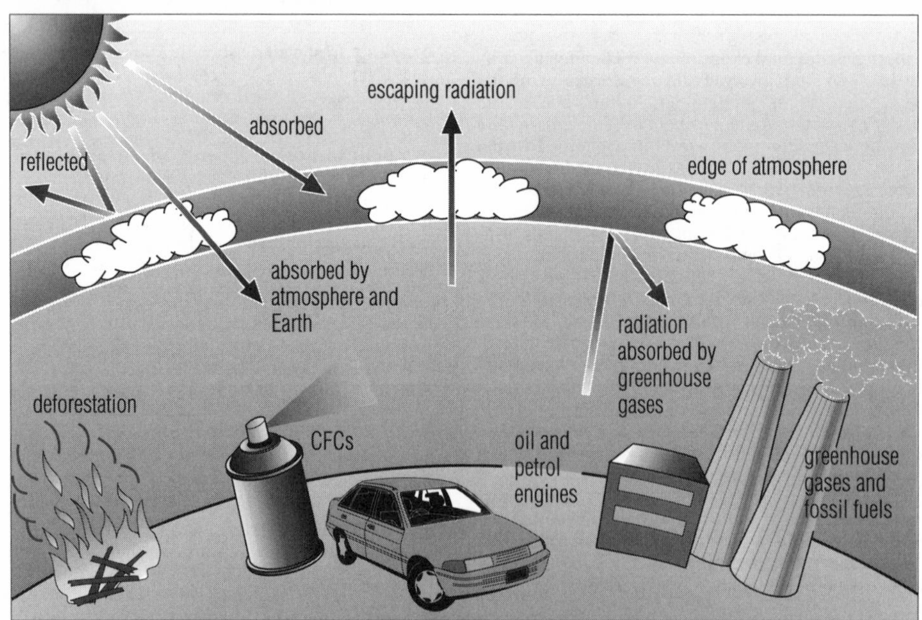

greenhouse effect *The warming effect of the Earth's atmosphere is called the greenhouse effect. Radiation from the Sun enters the atmosphere but is prevented from escaping back into space by gases such as carbon dioxide (produced for example, by the burning of fossil fuels), nitrogen oxides (from car exhausts), and CFCs (from aerosols and refrigerators). As these gases build up in the atmosphere, the Earth's average temperature is expected to rise.*

greenhouse effect phenomenon of the Earth's atmosphere by which solar radiation, trapped by the Earth and re-emitted from the surface as infrared radiation, is prevented from escaping by various gases in the air. Greenhouse gases trap heat because they readily absorb infrared radiation. The result is a rise in the Earth's temperature (◊global warming). The main greenhouse gases are carbon dioxide, methane, and ◊chlorofluorocarbons (CFCs) as well as water vapour. Fossil-fuel consumption and forest fires are the principal causes of carbon dioxide build-up; methane is a byproduct of agriculture (rice, cattle, sheep).

The United Nations Environment Programme estimates that by 2025, average world temperatures will have risen by 1.5°C/2.7°F with a consequent rise of 20 cm/7.9 in in sea level. Low-lying areas and entire countries would be threatened by flooding and crops would be affected by the change in climate. However, predictions about global warming and its possible climatic effects are tentative and often conflict with each other.

At the 1992 Earth Summit it was agreed that by 2000 countries would stabilize carbon dioxide emissions at 1990 levels, but to halt the acceleration of global warming, emissions would probably need to be cut by 60%. Any increases in carbon dioxide emissions are expected to come from transport. The Berlin Mandate, agreed unanimously at the climate conference in Berlin in 1995, committed industrial nations to the continuing reduction of greenhouse gas emissions after 2000, when the existing pact to stabilize emissions runs out. The stabilization of carbon dioxide emissions at 1990 levels by 2000 will not be achieved by a number of developed countries, including Spain, Australia, and the USA, according to 1997 estimates. Australia is in favour of different targets for different nations, and refused to sign a communiqué at the South Pacific Forum meeting in the Cook Islands in 1997 which insisted on legally binding reductions in greenhouse gas emissions.

Dubbed the 'greenhouse effect' by Swedish scientist Svante Arrhenius, it was first predicted in 1827 by French mathematician Joseph Fourier.

> *Our planet is not fragile at its own time scale, and we, pitiful latecomers in the last microsecond of our planetary year, are stewards of nothing in the long run. Yet no political movement is more vital and timely than modern environmentalism – because we must save ourselves (and our neighbor species) from our own immediate folly.*
>
> STEPHEN JAY GOULD US palaeontologist and writer.
> *Bully for Brontosaurus* 1991

green movement collective term for the individuals and organizations involved in efforts to protect the environment. The movement encompasses political parties such as the Green Party and organizations like ◊Friends of the Earth and ◊Greenpeace.

Despite a rapid growth of public support, and membership of environmental organizations running into many millions worldwide, political green groups have failed to win significant levels of the vote in democratic societies.

GreenNet in computing, international computer network used by environmental activists to exchange information and news.

Greenpeace international environmental pressure group, founded in 1971, with a policy of nonviolent direct action backed by scientific research. During a protest against French atmospheric nuclear testing in the South Pacific in 1985, its ship *Rainbow Warrior* was sunk by French intelligence agents, killing a crew member. In 1995 it played a prominent role in opposing the disposal of waste from an oil rig in the North Sea, and again attempted to disrupt French nuclear tests in the Pacific. In 1997 Greenpeace had a membership in 43 'chapters' worldwide.

green revolution in agriculture, the change in methods of arable farming instigated in the 1940s and 1950s in Third World countries. The intent was to provide more and better food for their populations, albeit with a heavy reliance on chemicals and machinery. It was abandoned by some countries in the 1980s. Much of the food produced was exported as ◊cash crops, so that local diet did not always improve.

The green revolution tended to benefit primarily those land-owners who could afford the investment necessary for such intensive agriculture. Without a dosage of 70–90 kg/154–198 lb of expensive nitrogen fertilizers per hectare, the high-yield varieties will not grow properly. Hence, rich farmers tended to obtain bigger yields while smallholders were unable to benefit from the new methods.

In terms of production, the green revolution was initially successful in southeast Asia; India doubled its wheat yield in 15 years, and the rice yield in the Philippines rose by 75%. However, yields have levelled off in many areas; some countries that cannot afford the dams, fertilizers, and machinery required, have adopted ◊intermediate technologies.

greenshank greyish shorebird of the sandpiper group. It has long olive-green legs and a long, slightly upturned bill, with white underparts and rump and dark grey wings. It breeds in northern Europe and regularly migrates through the Aleutian Islands, southwest of Alaska. (Species *Tringa nebularia,* family Scolopacidae, order Charadriiformes.)

Greenwich Mean Time (GMT) local time on the zero line of longitude (the ***Greenwich meridian***), which passes through the Old Royal Observatory at Greenwich, London. It was replaced in 1986 by coordinated universal time (UTC), but continued to be used to measure longitudes and the world's standard time zones; see ◊time.

grenadier another name for ◊rat-tail, a deep-sea fish.

grep in computing, UNIX command that allows full-text searching within files. On the Net, grep is sometimes used as an all-purpose synonym for 'search'.

grevillea genus of almost exclusively Australian trees and shrubs of the family Proteaceae bearing attractive spider-flowers. There are some 250 species widely distributed throughout the continent.

greyhound ancient breed of dog, with a long narrow head, slight build, and long legs. It stands up to 75 cm/30 in tall. It is renowned for its swiftness, and can exceed 60 kph/40 mph. Greyhounds were bred to hunt by sight, their main quarry being hares. Hunting hares with greyhounds is the basis of the ancient sport of coursing. Track-based greyhound racing is a popular spectator sport.

The Italian greyhound is similar in build to the ordinary greyhound, but very much smaller, weighing only about 3.6 kg/8 lb.

grey matter in biology, those parts of the brain and spinal cord that are made up of interconnected and tightly packed nerve cell nucleuses. The outer layers of the cerebellum contains most of the grey matter in the brain. It is the region of the brain that is responsible for advanced mental functions. Grey matter also constitutes the inner core of the spinal cord. This is in contrast to white matter, which is made of the axons of nerve cells.

grey scales method of representing continuous tone images on a screen or printer. Each dot in the ◊bit map is represented by a number of bits and can have a different shade of grey. Compare with ◊dithering when shades are simulated by altering the density and the pattern of black dots on a white background.

grid network of crossing parallel lines. **Rectangular grids** are used for drawing graphs. **Isometric grids** are used for drawing representations of solids in two dimensions in which lengths in the drawing match the lengths of the object.

grid network by which electricity is generated and distributed over a region or country. It contains many power stations and switching centres and allows, for example, high demand in one area to be met by surplus power generated in another.

The term is also used for any grating system, as in a cattle grid for controlling the movement of livestock across roads, and a conductor in a storage battery or electron gun.

grid reference a cadastral numbering system to specify location on a map. The numbers representing grid lines at the bottom of the map (eastings) are given before those at the side (northings). Successive decimal digits refine the location within the grid system.

griffon small breed of dog originating in Belgium. Red, black, or black and tan in colour and weighing up to 5 kg/11 lb, griffons are square-bodied and round-headed. There are rough- and smooth-coated varieties.

The name is also applied to several larger breeds of hunting dogs with rough coats, including two bred in northern France to pursue wild boar.

griffon Bruxelloise breed of terrierlike toy dog originally bred in Belgium. It weighs up to 4.5 kg/10 lb and has a harsh and wiry coat that is red or black in colour. The smooth-haired form of the breed is called the **petit Brabançon**.

The griffon Bruxelloise has a large rounded head with semi-erect ears; large black eyes with black eye-rims; and a short nose surrounded with black hair that converges upwards to meet the hair round the eyes. Its chest is wide and deep; legs are straight and of medium length; the tail is traditionally docked and carried upwards.

griffon vulture Old World vulture found in southern Europe, west and central Asia, and parts of Africa. It has a bald head with a neck ruff, and is 1.1 m/3.5 ft long with a wingspan of up to 2.7 m/9 ft. (Species *Gyps fulvus*, family Accipitridae.)

grooming in biology, the use by an animal of teeth, tongue, feet, or beak to clean fur or feathers. Grooming also helps to spread essential oils for waterproofing. In many social species, notably monkeys and apes, grooming of other individuals is used to reinforce social relationships.

Groom Lake or ***Area 51*** dry lake-bed site in Nevada, USA, of US Air Force base used for the development of secret projects. In the 1980s it was used for testing of Stealth aircraft and Star Wars (Strategic Defense Initiative) projects and later for studying ex-Soviet aircraft purchased from Russia.

The base was established in the 1950s as a testing ground for the U-2 spy plane. In 1984 it was designated so secret that it no longer appeared on maps, and its existence was officially denied until 1992. Because of the strangely shaped aircraft and lights to be seen, the nearest public vantage point to Groom Lake has since 1989 attracted UFO watchers.

grosbeak any of various thick-billed ◊finches. The **pine grosbeak** (*Pinicola enucleator*) breeds in Arctic forests. Its plumage is similar to that of the pine ◊crossbill. (Family Fringillidae, order Passeriformes.)

ground beetle large, adorned, brilliantly metallic beetle. Ground beetles are mainly terrestrial with few species being capable of flight. About 20,000 species are known to exist; nearly all are carnivorous as adults and larvae.

The larvae are of particular economic importance, destroying large numbers of soil insects and worms.

classification Ground beetles are in the family Carabidae, order Coleoptera, class Insecta, phylum Arthropoda.

ground controlled interception GCI British term for the ground command of fighter aircraft during and after the Battle of Britain 1940.

Using advanced ◊radar, the British could see German air formations at considerable ranges which enabled ground controllers to direct fighter aircraft into the path of the enemy, doing away with the need to fly standing patrols across likely approaches.

groundnut another name for ◊peanut.

ground water water collected underground in porous rock strata and soils; it emerges at the surface as springs and streams. The groundwater's upper level is called the **water table**. Sandy or other kinds of beds that are filled with groundwater are called **aquifers**. Recent estimates are that usable ground water amounts to more than 90% of all the fresh water on Earth; however, keeping such supplies free of pollutants entering the recharge areas is a critical environmental concern.

Most groundwater near the surface moves slowly through the ground while the water table stays in the same place. The depth of the water table reflects the balance between the rate of infiltration, called recharge, and the rate of discharge at springs or rivers or pumped water wells. The force of gravity makes underground water run 'downhill' underground just as it does above the surface. The greater the slope and the permeability, the greater the speed. Velocities vary from 100 cm/40 in per day to 0.5 cm/0.2 in.

group in chemistry, a vertical column of elements in the ◊periodic table. Elements in a group have similar physical and chemical properties; for example, the group I elements (the alkali metals: lithium, sodium, potassium, rubidium, caesium, and francium) are all highly reactive metals that form univalent ions. There is a gradation of properties down any group: in group I, melting and boiling points decrease, and density and reactivity increase.

group in mathematics, a finite or infinite set of elements that can be combined by an operation; formally, a group must satisfy certain conditions. For example, the set of all integers (positive or negative whole numbers) forms a group with regard to addition because: (1) addition is associative, that is, the sum of two or more integers is the same regardless of the order in which the integers are added; (2) adding two integers gives another integer; (3) the set includes an identity element 0, which has no effect on any integer to which it is added (for example, $0 + 3 = 3$); and (4) each integer has an inverse (for instance, 7 has the inverse −7), such that the sum of an integer and its inverse is 0. **Group theory** is the study of the properties of groups.

grouper any of several species of large sea perch (spiny-finned fish), found in warm waters. Some species grow to 2 m/6.5 ft long, and can weigh 300 kg/660 lbs. (Family Serranidae.)

The spotted **giant grouper** (*Promicrops itaiara*) is 2–2.5 m/6–8 ft long, may weigh over 300 kg/700 lb and is sluggish in movement. Formerly game fish, groupers are now commercially exploited as food.

groupware in computing, software designed to be used collaboratively by a small group of users, each with his/her own computer and a copy of the software. Examples of groupware are Lotus Notes and Novell GroupWise, both of which provide facilities for sending e-mail and sharing documents.

Standard business applications such as word processors are spoken of as 'groupware-enabled' if they provide facilities for a number of users to make revisions and incorporate them all into a final version. See also ◊computer-supported collaborative work.

grouse plump fowl-like game bird belonging to a subfamily of the pheasant family, which also includes the ptarmigan, capercaillie, and prairie chicken. Grouse are native to North America and northern Europe. They spend most of their time on the ground. During the mating season the males undertake elaborate courtship displays in small individual territories (◊leks). (Subfamily Tetraonidae, family Phasianidae, order Galliformes.)

growth in biology, the increase in size and weight during the development of an organism. Growth is an increase in biomass (mass of organic material, excluding water) and is associated with cell division.

All organisms grow, although the rate of growth varies over a lifetime. Typically, an organism shows an S-shaped curve, in which growth is at first slow, then fast, then, towards the end of life, nonexistent. Growth may even be negative during the period before death, with decay occurring faster than cellular replacement.

The concept of an average, the equation to a curve, the description of a froth or cellular tissue, all come within the scope of mathematics for no other reason than that they are summations of more elementary principles or phenomena. Growth and Form are throughout of this composite nature; therefore the laws of mathematics are bound to underlie them, and her methods to be peculiarly fitted to interpret them.

D'ARCY WENTWORTH THOMPSON British zoologist.
On Growth and Form

growth and decay curve graph showing exponential change (growth where the increment itself grows at the same rate) as occurs with compound interest and populations.

growth ring another name for ◊annual ring.

GRP abbreviation for ◊glass-reinforced plastic.

grub legless larval stages of Coleoptera (beetles) and Hymenoptera (bees, ants and wasps). See ◊larvae.

g-scale scale for measuring force by comparing it with the force due to ◊gravity (*g*), often called ◊g-force.

guan any of several large, pheasantlike birds native to the forests of South and Central America. They are sociable birds, almost the size of a turkey, with long, strong legs. Their colour is olive-green or brown. The family also includes the curassows. (Family Cracidae.)

guanaco hoofed ruminant (cud-chewing) mammal belonging to the camel family, found in South America on the pampas and mountain plateaux. It grows up to 1.2 m/4 ft at the shoulder, with the head and body measuring about 1.5 m/5 ft in length. It is sandy brown in colour, with a blackish face, and has fine wool. It lives in small herds and is the ancestor of the domestic ◊llama and ◊alpaca. It is also related to the other wild member of the camel family, the ◊vicuna. (Species *Lama guanacoe,* family Camelidae.)

guano dried excrement of fish-eating birds that builds up under nesting sites. It is a rich source of nitrogen and phosphorous, and is widely collected for use as fertilizer. Some 80% comes from the sea cliffs of Peru.

guarana Brazilian woody climbing plant. A drink with a high caffeine content is made from its roasted seeds, and it is the source of the drug known as zoom in the USA. Starch, gum, and several oils are extracted from it for commercial use. (*Paullinia cupana,* family Sapindaceae.)

guard cell in plants, a specialized cell on the undersurface of leaves for controlling gas exchange and water loss. Guard cells occur in pairs and are shaped so that a pore, or stomata, exists between them. They can change shape with the result that the pore disappears. During warm weather, when a plant is in danger of losing excessive water, the guard cells close, cutting down evaporation from the interior of the leaf.

guava tropical American tree belonging to the myrtle family; the astringent yellow pear-shaped fruit is used to make guava jelly, or it can be stewed or canned. It has a high vitamin C content. (*Psidium guajava,* family Myrtaceae.)

gudgeon any of an Old World group of freshwater fishes of the carp family, especially the species *G. gobio* found in Europe and northern Asia on the gravel bottoms of streams. It is olive-brown, spotted with black, and up to 20 cm/8 in long, with a distinctive barbel (sensory bristle, or 'whisker') at each side of the mouth. (Genus *Gobio,* family Cyprinidae.)

guelder rose or ***snowball tree*** cultivated shrub or small tree, native to Europe and North Africa, with round clusters of white flowers which are followed by shiny red berries. (*Viburnum opulus,* family Caprifoliaceae.)

guenon African monkey with characteristically greenish, yellow, or brown coat with brilliant markings. Guenons are slim and graceful in movement with very long tails that are not prehensile.

classification Guenons are in the genus *Cercopithecus,* family Cercopithecidae, order Primates.

GUI in computing, abbreviation for ◊graphical user interface.

guillemot any of several diving seabirds belonging to the auk family that breed on rocky North Atlantic and Pacific coasts. The **common guillemot** (*U. aalge*) has a long straight beak and short tail and wings; the feet are three-toed and webbed, the feathers are sooty brown and white. It breeds in large colonies on sea cliffs. The **black guillemot** (*C. grylle*) of northern coasts is much smaller and mostly black in summer, with orange legs when breeding. Guillemots build no nest, but lay one large, almost conical egg. (Genera *Uria* and *Cepphus,* family Alcidae, order Charadriiformes.)

guiltware or ***nagware*** in computing, variety of ◊shareware software that attempts to make the user register (and pay for) the software by exploiting the user's sense of guilt.

On-screen messages are displayed, usually when the program is started, reminding users that they have an unregistered version of the program that they should pay for if they intend to continue using it. Some programs will also display the message at random intervals while the program is in use.

guinea fowl any of a group of chickenlike African birds, including the **helmet guinea fowl** (*Numida meleagris*), which has a horny growth on the head, white-spotted feathers, and fleshy cheek wattles (loose folds of skin). It is the ancestor of the domestic guinea fowl. Guinea fowl are mostly gregarious ground-feeders, eating insects, leaves, and snails; at night they roost in trees. (Family Numididae, order Galliformes.)

guinea pig species of ◊cavy, a type of rodent.

Guinea worm parasitic, microscopic ◊nematode worm found in India and Africa, affecting some 650,000 people in Nigeria alone. It enters the body via drinking water and migrates to break out through the skin. (Species *Dracunculus medinensis.*)

> **GUINEA PIG CARE**
>
> http://www.bcyellowpages.com/advert/b/BCHES/guinea.htm
>
> From housing to health, this site contains lots of useful information for guinea pig lovers, including a health chart to help you diagnose illnesses.

Gulf Stream warm ocean ◊current that flows north from the warm waters of the Gulf of Mexico. Part of the current is diverted east across the Atlantic, where it is known as the **North Atlantic Drift**, and warms what would otherwise be a colder climate in the British Isles and northwestern Europe.

gull any of a group of seabirds that are usually 25–75 cm/10–30 in long, white with grey or black on the back and wings, and have large beaks. Immature birds are normally a mottled brown colour. Gulls are sociable, noisy birds and they breed in colonies. (Genus principally *Larus,* subfamily Larinae, family Laridae, order Charadriiformes.)

gull *The sharp, heavy beak typical of gulls can be clearly seen on this lesser black-backed gull. Premaphotos Wildlife*

The **common black-headed gull** (*L. ridibundus*), common on both sides of the Atlantic Ocean, is grey and white with (in summer) a dark-brown head and a red beak; it breeds in large colonies on wetlands, making a nest of dead rushes and laying, on average, three eggs. The **great black-headed gull** (*L. ichthyaetus*) is native to Asia. The **herring gull** (*L. argentatus*), common in the northern hemisphere, has white and pearl-grey plumage and a yellow beak. The **oceanic great black-backed gull** (*L. marinus*), found in the Atlantic, is over 75 cm/2.5 ft long.

The **kelp gull** or **Southern black-backed gull** (*L. dominicanus*) is common throughout the southern hemisphere. It feeds mainly on limpets, which are swallowed whole, with the shell later spat out and left in a heap around the nest area.

gum in botany, complex polysaccharides (carbohydrates) formed by many plants and trees, particularly by those from dry regions. They form four main groups: plant exudates (gum arabic); marine plant extracts (agar); seed extracts; and fruit and vegetable extracts. Some are made synthetically.

Gums are tasteless and odourless, insoluble in alcohol and ether but generally soluble in water. They are used for adhesives, fabric sizing, in confectionery, medicine, and calico printing.

gum in mammals, the soft tissues surrounding the base of the teeth. Gums are liable to inflammation (gingivitis) or to infection by microbes from food deposits (periodontal disease).

gum arabic substance obtained from certain species of ◊acacia trees, especially *A. senegal,* with uses in medicine, confectionery, and adhesive manufacture.

gumtree common name for the ◊eucalyptus tree.

gun any kind of firearm or any instrument consisting of a metal tube from which a projectile is discharged; see also ◊pistol and ◊small arms.

gun metal type of ◊bronze, an alloy high in copper (88%), also containing tin and zinc, so-called because it was once used to cast cannons. It is tough, hard-wearing, and resists corrosion.

gunpowder or ***black powder*** the oldest known ◊explosive, a mixture of 75% potassium nitrate (saltpetre), 15% charcoal, and 10% sulphur. Sulphur ignites at a low temperature, charcoal burns readily, and the potassium nitrate provides oxygen for the explosion. As gunpowder produces lots of smoke and burns quite slowly, it has progressively been replaced since the late 19th century by high explosives, although it is still widely used for quarry blasting, fuses, and fireworks. Gunpowder has high ◊activation energy; a gun based on gunpowder alone requires igniting by a flint or a match.

Gunpowder is believed to have been invented in China in the 10th century, but may also have been independently discovered by the Arabs. Certainly the Arabs produced the first known working gun, in 1304. Gunpowder was used in warfare from the 14th century but it was not generally adapted to civil purposes until the 17th century, when it began to be used in mining.

guppy brightly coloured fish *Poecilia reticulata,* with an elongated body and round tail fin, measuring about 6 cm/2.25 in in length. It occurs naturally in fresh and brackish water in parts of South America and the West Indies. Guppies have also been introduced into many other tropical areas as a natural pest control because they feed on mosquito and other insect larvae. The guppy gives birth to live young, and is a popular aquarium species.

gurnard any of a group of coastal fish that creep along the sea bottom with the help of three fingerlike appendages detached from the pectoral fins. Gurnards are both tropical and temperate zone fish. (Genus *Trigla,* family Trigilidae.)

gut or ***alimentary canal*** in the ◊digestive system, the part of an animal responsible for processing food and preparing it for entry into the blood.

The gut consists of a tube divided into segments specialized to perform different functions. The front end (the mouth) is adapted for food intake and for the first stages of digestion. The stomach is a storage area, although digestion of protein by the enzyme pepsin starts here; in many herbivorous mammals this is also the site of cellulose digestion. The small intestine follows the stomach and is specialized for digestion and for absorption. The large intestine, consisting of the colon, caecum, and rectum, has a variety of functions, including cellulose digestion, water absorption, and storage of faeces. From the gut nutrients are carried to the liver via the hepatic portal vein, ready for assimilation by the cells.

Gutenberg, Johannes (Gensfleisch) (c. 1398–1468)

German printer, the inventor of printing from movable metal type (although Laurens Janszoon Coster has a rival claim), based on the Chinese wood-block-type method.

Gutenberg began work on the process in the 1440s and in 1450 set up a printing business in Mainz. By 1456 he had produced the first printed Bible (known as the Gutenberg Bible). It is not known what other books he printed.

Mary Evans Picture Library

He punched and engraved a steel character (letter shape) into a piece of copper to form a mould which he filled with molten metal. The letters were in the Gothic style and of equal height. By 1500, more than 180 European towns had working presses of this kind.

gutta-percha juice of various tropical trees of the sapodilla family (such as the Malaysian *Palaquium gutta*), which can be hardened to form a flexible, rubbery substance used for electrical insulation, dentistry, and golf balls; it has now been largely replaced by synthetic materials.

guttation secretion of water on to the surface of leaves through specialized pores, or ◊hydathodes. The process occurs most frequently during conditions of high humidity when the rate of transpiration is low. Drops of water found on grass in early morning are often the result of guttation, rather than dew. Sometimes the water contains minerals in solution, such as calcium, which leaves a white crust on the leaf surface as it dries.

gymnosperm Greek ***'naked seed'*** in botany, any plant whose seeds are exposed, as opposed to the structurally more advanced ◊angiosperms, where they are inside an ovary. The group includes conifers and related plants such as cycads and ginkgos, whose seeds develop in ◊cones. Fossil gymnosperms have been found in rocks about 350 million years old.

gynaecology medical speciality concerned with disorders of the female reproductive system.

gynoecium or **gynaecium** collective term for the female reproductive organs of a flower, consisting of one or more ◊carpels, either free or fused together.

gyre circular surface rotation of ocean water in each major sea (a type of ◊current). Gyres are large and permanent, and occupy the northern and southern halves of the three major oceans. Their movements are dictated by the prevailing winds and the ◊Coriolis effect. Gyres move clockwise in the northern hemisphere and anticlockwise in the southern hemisphere.

gyroscope mechanical instrument, used as a stabilizing device and consisting, in its simplest form, of a heavy wheel mounted on an axis fixed in a ring that can be rotated about another axis, which is also fixed in a ring capable of rotation about a third axis.

Applications of the gyroscope principle include the gyrocompass, the gyropilot for automatic steering, and gyro-directed torpedoes.

The components of the gyroscope are arranged so that the three axes of rotation in any position pass through the wheel's centre of gravity. The wheel is thus capable of rotation about three mutually perpendicular axes, and its axis may take up any direction. If the axis of the spinning wheel is displaced, a restoring movement develops, returning it to its initial direction.

GZip in computing, compression software, properly called ◊GNU Zip, commonly used on the Internet. Files compressed using GZip can be recognized by the file extension '.GZ'. The software is published by the ◊Free Software Foundation and was originally developed for UNIX, although a DOS version is readily available.

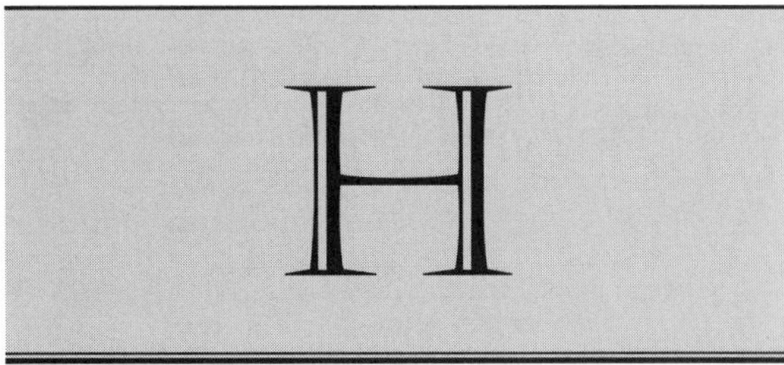

H

ha symbol for ◊hectare.

Haber process or ***Haber–Bosch process*** industrial process by which ammonia is manufactured by direct combination of its elements, nitrogen and hydrogen. The reaction is carried out at 400–500°C/752–932°F and at 200 atmospheres pressure. The two gases, in the proportions of 1:3 by volume, are passed over a ◊catalyst of finely divided iron.

Around 10% of the reactants combine, and the unused gases are recycled. The ammonia is separated either by being dissolved in water or by being cooled to liquid form.

$$N_2 + 3H_2 \leftrightarrow 2NH_3$$

habitat localized ◊environment in which an organism lives, and which provides for all (or almost all) of its needs. The diversity of habitats found within the Earth's ecosystem is enormous, and they are changing all the time. Many can be considered inorganic or physical; for example, the Arctic ice cap, a cave, or a cliff face. Others are more complex; for instance, a woodland or a forest floor. Some habitats are so precise that they are called **microhabitats**, such as the area under a stone where a particular type of insect lives. Most habitats provide a home for many species.

hacking unauthorized access to a computer, either for fun or for malicious or fraudulent purposes. Hackers generally use microcomputers and telephone lines to obtain access. In computing, the term is used in a wider sense to mean using software for enjoyment or self-education, not necessarily involving unauthorized access. The most destructive form of hacking is the introduction of a computer ◊virus.

Hacking can be divided into four main areas: ◊viruses, phreaking, software piracy (stripping away the protective coding that should prevent the software being copied), and accessing operating systems.

A 1996 US survey co-sponsored by the FBI showed 41% of academic, corporate, and government organizations interviewed had had their computer systems hacked into during 1995.

haddock marine fish belonging to the cod family and found off the N Atlantic coastline. It is brown with silvery underparts and black markings above the pectoral fins. It can grow up to 1 m/3 ft in length. Haddock are important food fish; about 45 million kg/100 million lb are taken annually off the New England fishing banks alone. (Species *Melanogrammus aeglefinus,* family Gadidae.)

Hadrian's Wall Roman frontier system built AD 122–26 to mark England's northern boundary and abandoned about 383; its ruins run 185 km/115 mi from Wallsend on the river Tyne to Maryport, W Cumbria. In some parts, the wall was covered with a glistening, white coat of mortar. The fort at South Shields, Arbeia, built to defend the eastern end, has been under reconstruction.

hadron in physics, a subatomic particle that experiences the strong nuclear force. Each is made up of two or three indivisible particles called ◊quarks. The hadrons are grouped into the ◊baryons (protons, neutrons, and hyperons) and the ◊mesons (particles with masses between those of electrons and protons).

Hadron–Electron Ring Accelerator (HERA) particle ◊accelerator built under the streets of Hamburg, Germany, occupying a tunnel 6.3 km/3.9 mi in length. It is the world's most powerful collider of protons and electrons, designed to accelerate protons to energies of 820 GeV (billion electron volts), and electrons to 30 GeV. HERA began operating 1992.

HERA can propel electrons into the proton interior, where they interact with the proton's constituent particles: three ◊quarks and a number of ◊gluons.

Haber, Fritz
(1868–1934)

German chemist whose conversion of atmospheric nitrogen to ammonia opened the way for the synthetic fertilizer industry. His study of the combustion of hydrocarbons led to the commercial 'cracking' or fractional distillation of natural oil (petroleum) into its components (for example, diesel, petrol, and paraffin). In electrochemistry, he was the first to demonstrate that oxidation and reduction take place at the electrodes; from this he developed a general electrochemical theory.

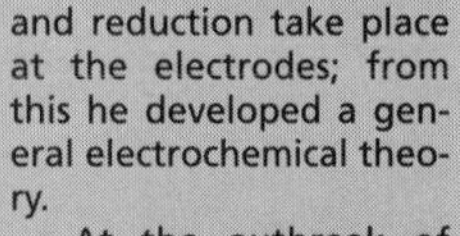

At the outbreak of World War I in 1914, Haber was asked to devise a method of producing nitric acid for making high explosives. Later he became one of the principals in the German chemical-warfare effort, devising weapons and gas masks, which led to protests against his Nobel prize in 1918.

Mary Evans Picture Library

haematology medical speciality concerned with disorders of the blood.

haemoglobin protein used by all vertebrates and some invertebrates for oxygen transport because the two substances combine reversibly. In vertebrates it occurs in red blood cells (erythrocytes), giving them their colour.

In the lungs or gills where the concentration of oxygen is high, oxygen attaches to haemoglobin to form **oxyhaemoglobin**. This process effectively increases the amount of oxygen that can be carried in the bloodstream. The oxygen is later released in the body tissues where it is at a low concentration, and the deoxygenated blood returned to the lungs or gills. Haemoglobin will combine also with carbon monoxide to form carboxyhaemoglobin, but in this case the reaction is irreversible.

haemolymph circulatory fluid of those molluscs and insects that have an 'open' circulatory system. Haemolymph contains water, amino acids, sugars, salts, and white cells like those of blood. Circulated by a pulsating heart, its main functions are to transport digestive and excretory products around the body. In molluscs, it also transports oxygen and carbon dioxide.

haemolysis destruction of red blood cells. Aged cells are constantly being lysed (broken down), but increased wastage of red cells is seen in some infections and blood disorders. It may result in ◊jaundice (through the release of too much haemoglobin) and in ◊anaemia.

haemophilia any of several inherited diseases in which normal blood clotting is impaired. The sufferer experiences prolonged bleeding from the slightest wound, as well as painful internal bleeding without apparent cause.

Haemophilias are nearly always sex-linked, transmitted through the female line only to male infants; they have afflicted a number of European royal households. Males affected by the most common form are unable to synthesize Factor VIII, a protein involved in the clotting of blood. Treatment is primarily with Factor VIII (now mass-produced by recombinant techniques), but the haemophiliac remains at risk from the slightest incident of bleeding. The disease is a painful one that causes deformities of joints.

haemorrhage loss of blood from the circulatory system. It is 'manifest' when the blood can be seen, as when it flows from a wound, and 'occult' when the bleeding is internal, as from an ulcer or internal injury.

Rapid, profuse haemorrhage causes ◊shock and may prove fatal if the circulating volume cannot be replaced in time. Slow, sustained bleeding may lead to ◊anaemia. Arterial bleeding is potentially more serious than blood lost from a vein. It may be stemmed by applying pressure directly to the wound.

haemorrhoids distended blood vessels (◊varicose veins) in the area of the anus, popularly called **piles**.

haemostasis natural or surgical stoppage of bleeding. In the natural mechanism, the damaged vessel contracts, restricting the flow, and blood ◊platelets plug the opening, releasing chemicals essential to clotting.

hafnium Latin *Hafnia* 'Copenhagen' silvery, metallic element, symbol Hf, atomic number 72, relative atomic mass 178.49. It occurs in nature in ores of zirconium, the properties of which it resembles. Hafnium absorbs neutrons better than most metals, so it is used in the control rods of nuclear reactors; it is also used for light-bulb filaments.

It was named in 1923 by Dutch physicist Dirk Coster (1889–1950) and Hungarian chemist Georg von Hevesy after the city of Copenhagen, where the element was discovered.

hail precipitation in the form of pellets of ice (hailstones). It is caused by the circulation of moisture in strong convection currents, usually within cumulonimbus ◊clouds.

Water droplets freeze as they are carried upwards. As the circulation continues, layers of ice are deposited around the droplets until they become too heavy to be supported by the currents and they fall as a hailstorm.

HAIL

Hailstones can kill. In the Gopalganji region of Bangladesh in 1988, 92 people died after being hit by huge hailstones weighing up to 1 kg/2.2 lb.

hair fine filament growing from mammalian skin. Each hair grows from a pit-shaped follicle embedded in the second layer of the skin, the dermis. It consists of dead cells impregnated with the protein keratin.

The average number of hairs on a human head varies from 98,000 (red-heads) to 120,000 (blondes). Each grows at the rate of 5–10 mm/0.2–0.4 in per month, lengthening for about three years before being replaced by a new one. A coat of hair helps to insulate land mammals by trapping air next to the body. The thickness of this layer can be varied at will by raising or flattening the coat. In some mammals a really heavy coat may be so effective that it must be shed in summer and a thinner one grown. Hair also aids camouflage, as in the zebra and the white winter coats of Arctic animals; and protection, as in the porcupine and hedgehog; bluffing enemies by apparently increasing the size, as in the cat; sexual display, as in humans and the male lion; and its colouring or erection may be used for communication. In 1990 scientists succeeded for the first time in growing human hair in vitro.

hairstreak any of a group of small butterflies, related to blues and coppers. Hairstreaks live in both temperate and tropical regions. Most of them are brownish or greyish-blue with hairlike tips streaked with white at the end of their hind wings. (Genera *Callophrys* and other related genera, family Lycaenidae.)

hake any of various marine fishes belonging to the cod family, found in N European, African, and American waters. They have silvery elongated bodies and grow up to 1 m/3 ft in length. They have two dorsal fins and one long anal fin. The silver hake (*M. bilinearis*) is an important food fish. (Genera *Merluccius* and *Urophycis*, family Gadidae.)

hakea shrub or tree of the Australian genus *Hakea*, family Proteaceae, characterized by hard woody fruit with winged seeds.

Hale-Bopp, Comet see ◊Comet Hale-Bopp.

half duplex in computing, a ◊modem setting which controls whether or not characters echo to (appear on) the screen. See ◊full duplex.

half-life during ◊radioactive decay, the time in which the strength of a radioactive source decays to half its original value. In theory, the decay process is never complete and there is always some residual radioactivity. For this reason, the half-life of a radioactive isotope is measured, rather than the total decay time. It may vary from millionths of a second to billions of years.

Radioactive substances decay exponentially; thus the time taken for the first 50% of the isotope to decay will be the same as the time taken by the next 25%, and by the 12.5% after that, and so on.

For example, carbon-14 takes about 5,730 years for half the material to decay; another 5,730 for half of the remaining half to decay; then 5,730 years for half of that remaining half to decay, and so on. Plutonium-239, one of the most toxic of all radioactive substances, has a half-life of about 24,000 years.

halftone in computing, term used in the publishing industry for a black-and-white photograph, indicating the many shades of grey that must be reproduced.

halftone process technique used in printing to reproduce the full range of tones in a photograph or other illustration. The intensity of the printed colour is varied from full strength to the lightest shades, even if one colour of ink is used. The picture to be reproduced is photographed through a screen ruled with a rectangular mesh of fine lines, which breaks up the tones of the original into areas of dots that vary in frequency according to the intensity of the tone. In the darker areas the dots run together; in the lighter areas they have more space between them.

halibut any of a group of large flatfishes found in the Atlantic and Pacific oceans. The largest of the flatfishes, they may grow up to 2 m/6 ft in length and weigh 90–135 kg/200–300 lb. They are a very dark mottled brown or green above and pure white on the underside. The Atlantic halibut (*H. hippoglossus*) is caught offshore at depths from 180 m/600 ft to 730 m/2,400 ft. (Genus *Hippoglossus*, family Pleuronectidae.)

halide any compound produced by the combination of a ◊halogen, such as chlorine or iodine, with a less electronegative element (see ◊electronegativity). Halides may be formed by ◊ionic bonds or by ◊covalent bonds.

halite mineral form of sodium chloride, NaCl. Common ◊salt is the mineral halite. When pure it is colourless and transparent, but it is often pink, red, or yellow. It is soft and has a low density.

Halite occurs naturally in evaporite deposits that have precipitated on evaporation of bodies of salt water. As rock salt, it forms beds within a sedimentary sequence; it can also migrate upwards through surrounding rocks to form salt domes. It crystallizes in the cubic system.

Hall effect production of a voltage across a conductor or semiconductor carrying a current at a right angle to a surrounding magnetic field. It was discovered in 1897 by the US physicist Edwin Hall (1855–1938). It is used in the **Hall probe** for measuring the strengths of magnetic fields and in magnetic switches.

Halley's comet comet that orbits the Sun about every 76 years, named after Edmond Halley who calculated its orbit. It is the brightest and most conspicuous of the periodic comets. Recorded

Halley, Edmond (1656–1742)

English astronomer. He not only identified the comet that was later to be known by his name, but also compiled a star catalogue, detected the proper motion of stars, using historical records, and began a line of research that, after his death, resulted in a reasonably accurate calculation of the astronomical unit.

Halley calculated that the comet sightings reported in 1456, 1531, 1607, and 1682 all represented reappearances of the same comet. He reasoned that the comet would follow a parabolic path and announced in 1705 in his Synopsis Astronomia Cometicae that it would reappear in 1758. When it did, public acclaim for the astronomer was such that his name was irrevocably attached to it.

He made many other notable contributions to astronomy, including the discovery of the proper motions of Aldebaran, Arcturus, and Sirius, and working out a method of obtaining the solar parallax by observations made during a transit of Venus. He was Astronomer Royal from 1720.

Mary Evans Picture Library

sightings go back over 2,000 years. It travels around the Sun in the opposite direction to the planets. Its orbit is inclined at almost 20° to the main plane of the Solar System and ranges between the orbits of Venus and Neptune. It will next reappear 2061.

The comet was studied by space probes at its last appearance in 1986. The European probe *Giotto* showed that the nucleus of Halley's comet is a tiny and irregularly shaped chunk of ice, measuring some 15 km/10 m long by 8 km/5 m wide, coated by a layer of very dark material, thought to be composed of carbon-rich compounds. This surface coating has a very low ◊albedo, reflecting just 4% of the light it receives from the Sun. Although the comet is one of the darkest objects known, it has a glowing head and tail produced by jets of gas from fissures in the outer dust layer. These vents cover 10% of the total surface area and become active only when exposed to the Sun. The force of these jets affects the speed of the comet's travel in its orbit.

HALLEY'S COMET

http://www.fis.uc.pt/astronomy/solar/halley.htm

Attractive site devoted to the comet – with facts and statistics, images, and information about the spacecraft that have visited it.

hallmark official mark stamped on British gold, silver, and (from 1913) platinum, instituted in 1327 (royal charter of London Goldsmiths) in order to prevent fraud. After 1363, personal marks of identification were added. Now tests of metal content are carried out at authorized assay offices in London, Birmingham, Sheffield, and Edinburgh; each assay office has its distinguishing mark, to which is added a maker's mark, date letter, and mark guaranteeing standard.

hallucinogen any substance that acts on the ◊central nervous system to produce changes in perception and mood and often hallucinations. Hallucinogens include ◊LSD, peyote, and ◊mescaline. Their effects are unpredictable and they are illegal in most countries.

In some circumstances hallucinogens may produce panic or even suicidal feelings, which can recur without warning several days or months after taking the drug. In rare cases they produce an irreversible psychotic state mimicking schizophrenia. Spiritual or religious experiences are common, hence the ritual use of hallucinogens in some cultures. They work by chemical interference with the normal action of neurotransmitters in the brain.

Reality is not only more fantastic than we think, but also much more fantastic than we imagine.

JBS Haldane British physiologist.
Attributed remark

halogen any of a group of five nonmetallic elements with similar chemical bonding properties: fluorine, chlorine, bromine, iodine, and astatine. They form a linked group in the ◊periodic table of the elements, descending from fluorine, the most reactive, to astatine, the least reactive. They combine directly with most metals to form salts, such as common salt (NaCl). Each halogen has seven electrons in its valence shell, which accounts for the chemical similarities displayed by the group.

halon organic chemical compound containing one or two carbon atoms, together with ◊bromine and other ◊halogens. The most commonly used are halon 1211 (bromochlorodifluoromethane) and halon 1301 (bromotrifluoromethane). The halons are gases and are widely used in fire extinguishers. As destroyers of the ◊ozone layer, they are up to ten times more effective than ◊chlorofluorocarbons (CFCs), to which they are chemically related.

Levels in the atmosphere are rising by about 25% each year, mainly through the testing of fire-fighting equipment. The use of halons in fire extinguishers was banned in 1994.

halophyte plant adapted to live where there is a high concentration of salt in the soil, for example, in salt marshes and mud flats.

hamadryad or ***king cobra*** or ***giant cobra*** large and poisonous cobra found from India to China and the Philippines, sometimes reaching a length of 5 m/16 ft. It is one of the longest and most venomous of snakes, and is yellow with black crossbands.
classification The hamadryad *Ophiophagus hannah* is in family Elapidae, suborder Serpentes, order Squamata, class Reptilia.

hammerhead any of several species of shark found in tropical seas, characterized by having eyes at the ends of flattened hammerlike extensions of the skull. Hammerheads can grow to 4 m/13 ft in length. (Genus *Sphyrna*, family Sphyrnidae.)

hamster any of a group of burrowing rodents with a thickset body, short tail, and cheek pouches to carry food. Several genera are found across Asia and in SE Europe. Hamsters are often kept as pets. (Genera include *Cricetus* and *Mesocricetus*, family Cricetidae.)

Species include the European and Asian **black-bellied** or **common hamster** (*C. cricetus*), about 25 cm/10 in long, which can be a crop pest and stores up to 90 kg/200 lb of seeds in its burrow. The **golden hamster** (*M. auratus*) lives in W Asia and SE Europe. All golden hamsters now kept as pets originated from one female and 12 young captured in Syria 1930.

hand unit used in measuring the height of a horse from front hoof to shoulder (withers). One hand equals 10.2 cm/4 in.

handfish very rare Tasmanian fish *Brachionichthys hirsutus* that moves along the seafloor on handlike fins. It is about 10 cm/4 in long and is found only in the coastal waters of S Tasmania.

handle in computing, term used on ◊Internet Relay Chat and other live chat services for a nickname.

A given user's handle may or may not be the same as his/her ◊user-ID; on many systems users are allowed to pick any name they like to use on chat systems as long as it is not already taken by another user.

Handles are also used on CB and ham radio, and hackers use handles, for cultural reasons as much as to disguise their real identities.

handshake in computing, an exchange of signals between two devices that establishes the communications channels and protocols necessary for the devices to send and receive data.

handwriting recognition in computing, ability of a computer to accept handwritten input and turn it into ◊digital data that can be processed and displayed or stored as ◊ASCII characters on the computer screen.

Handwriting recognition would free computer users from having to use the keyboard, but it is difficult to implement. A few machines, such as the Apple Newton, have the ability built in, but the technology is still at an early stage of development and such machines typically require users to train the machine by entering a sample alphabet. Technical limitations mean written input has to be printed in small boxes.

Hannover German fighter aircraft made by the *Hannoverische Wagenfabrik* from 1917. A two-seater biplane, the Hannover CLII, was also used for ground attack and as an escort for bombers. Improved as the CLIII A, it became a major part of the German Air Force, over 550 being built in 1917–18.

Hansa-Brandenburg German seaplanes, the most popular floatplanes with the German Navy in World War I. They continued in use after the war, and the chief designer, Ernst Heinkel, become famous as a manufacturer of warplanes during World War II.

haploid having a single set of ◊chromosomes in each cell. Most higher organisms are ◊diploid – that is, they have two sets – but their gametes (sex cells) are haploid. Some plants, such as mosses, liverworts, and many seaweeds, are haploid, and male honey bees are haploid because they develop from eggs that have not been fertilized. See also ◊meiosis.

hard copy computer output printed on paper.

hard disc in computing, a storage device usually consisting of a rigid metal ◊disc coated with a magnetic material. Data are read from and written to the disc by means of a disc drive. The hard disc may be permanently fixed into the drive or in the form of a disc pack that can be removed and exchanged with a different pack. Hard discs vary from large units with capacities of more than 3,000 megabytes, intended for use with mainframe computers, to small units with capacities as low as 20 megabytes, intended for use with microcomputers.

hardening of oils transformation of liquid oils to solid products by ◊hydrogenation.

Vegetable oils contain double covalent carbon-to-carbon bonds and are therefore examples of ◊unsaturated compounds. When hydrogen is added to these double bonds, the oils become saturated. The more saturated oils are waxlike solids.

hardness physical property of materials that governs their use. Methods of heat treatment can increase the hardness of metals. A scale of hardness was devised by German–Austrian mineralogist Friedrich Mohs in the 1800s, based upon the hardness of certain minerals from soft talc (Mohs' hardness 1) to diamond (10), the hardest of all materials.

hard-sectored disc floppy disc that is sold already formatted, so that ◊disc formatting is not necessary. Usually sectors are marked by holes near the hub of the disc. This system is now obsolete.

hardware the mechanical, electrical, and electronic components of a computer system, as opposed to the various programs, which constitute ◊software.

hard water water that does not lather easily with soap, and produces a deposit or 'scale' in kettles. It is caused by the presence of certain salts of calcium and magnesium.

Temporary hardness is caused by the presence of dissolved hydrogencarbonates (bicarbonates); when the water is boiled, they are converted to insoluble carbonates that precipitate as 'scale'. **Permanent hardness** is caused by sulphates and silicates, which are not affected by boiling. Water can be softened by ◊distillation, ◊ion exchange (the principle underlying commercial water softeners), addition of sodium carbonate or of large amounts of soap, or boiling (to remove temporary hardness).

Hardy–Weinberg equilibrium in population genetics, the theoretical relative frequency of different ◊alleles within a given population of a species, when the stable endpoint of evolution in an undisturbed environment is reached.

hare mammal closely related to the rabbit, similar in appearance but larger. Hares have very long black-tipped ears, long hind legs, and short upturned tails. (Genus *Lepus,* family Leporidae, order Lagomorpha.)

Throughout the long breeding season (June–August) there are chases and 'boxing matches' among males and females; the expression 'mad as a March hare' arises from this behaviour.

harebell perennial plant of the ◊bellflower family, with bell-shaped blue flowers, found on dry grassland and heaths. It is known in Scotland as the bluebell. (*Campanula rotundifolia,* family Campanulaceae.)

Hare's apparatus in physics, a specific kind of ◊hydrometer used to compare the relative densities of two liquids, or to find the density of one if the other is known. It was invented by US chemist Robert Hare (1781–1858).

It consists of a vertical E-shaped glass tube, with the long limbs dipping into the two liquids and a tap on the short limb. With the tap open, air is removed from the tops of the tubes and the liquids are pushed up the tubes by atmospheric pressure. When the tap is closed, the heights of the liquids are inversely proportional to their relative densities.

Harrier the only truly successful vertical takeoff and landing fixed-wing aircraft, often called the **jump jet**. It was built in Britain and made its first flight 1966. It has a single jet engine and a set of swivelling nozzles. These deflect the jet exhaust vertically downwards for takeoff and landing, and to the rear for normal flight. Designed to fly from confined spaces with minimal ground support, it refuels in midair.

harrier any of a group of birds of prey. Harriers have long wings and legs, a small head with a short beak, an owl-like frill of thickset feathers around the face, and soft plumage. They eat frogs, birds, snakes, and small mammals, and are found mainly in marshy areas throughout the world. (Genus *Circus,* family Accipitridae, order Falconiformes.)

harrier breed of hound, similar to a ◊foxhound but smaller, used in packs for hare-hunting.

harrow agricultural implement used to break up the furrows left by the ◊plough and reduce the soil to a fine consistency or tilth, and to cover the seeds after sowing. The traditional harrow consists of spikes set in a frame; modern harrows use sets of discs.

hartebeest large African antelope with lyre-shaped horns set close on top of the head in both sexes. It can grow to 1.5 m/5 ft tall at the rather humped shoulders and up to 2 m/6 ft long. Although they are clumsy-looking runners, hartebeest can reach speeds of 65 kph/40 mph. (Species *Alcelaphus buselaphus,* family Bovidae.)

hart's-tongue fern with straplike undivided fronds, up to 60 cm/24 in long, which have clearly visible brown spore-bearing organs on the undersides. The plant is native to Europe, Asia, and E North America, and is found on walls, in shady rocky places, and in woods. (*Phyllitis scolopendrium,* family Polypodiaceae.)

harvestman small animal (an ◊arachnid) related to spiders with very long, thin legs and a small body. Harvestmen are different from true spiders in that they do not have a waist or narrow part to the oval body. They feed on small insects and spiders, and lay their eggs in autumn, to hatch the following spring or early summer. They are found from the Arctic to the tropics. (Order Opiliones.)

harvest mite another name for the ◊chigger, a parasitic mite.

Harwell main research establishment of the United Kingdom Atomic Energy Authority, situated near the village of Harwell in Oxfordshire.

hash function in computing, an ◊algorithm that calculates a value from the content of a message which can then be used to detect alterations to the original message.

Similar to a ◊checksum but with greater security, hash functions play an important role in secure cryptographic systems (see ◊cryptography), where authentication is as important as hiding the data from third parties.

hashing in computing, the process used to convert a record, usually in a database, into a number that can be used to retrieve the record, or check its validity. The 'hashing algorithm', which may be based on manipulating the ASCII values of letters, will be devised so that different records give a useful range of results. Hashing is faster than storing things alphabetically, for example, where some areas may have lots of very similar records (for example, under c, s, or t) while others are little used (q, x, z).

hashish drug made from the resin contained in the female flowering tops of hemp (◊cannabis).

hash total in computing, a ◊validation check in which an otherwise meaningless control total is calculated by adding together numbers (such as payroll or account numbers) associated with a set of records. The hash total is checked each time data are input, in order to ensure that no entry errors have been made.

hassium synthesized, radioactive element of the ◊transactinide series, symbol Hs, atomic number 108, relative atomic mass 265. It was first synthesized in 1984 by the Laboratory for Heavy Ion Research in Darmstadt, Germany. Its temporary name was unniloctium.

haustorium (plural ***haustoria***) specialized organ produced by a parasitic plant or fungus that penetrates the cells of its host to absorb nutrients. It may be either an outgrowth of hyphae (see ◊hypha), as in the case of parasitic fungi, or of the stems of flowering parasitic plants, as in dodders (*Cuscuta*). The suckerlike haustoria of a dodder penetrate the vascular tissue of the host plant without killing the cells.

Havana cat breed of domestic shorthaired cat bred in Britain during the 1950s from a cross between two varieties of Siamese. It has a deep, rich-brown fur, wedge-shaped head, green eyes, long legs, and svelte build. In America, the Havana Brown is less Oriental in look than its British counterparts. It is sturdier with a medium-length body, rounder face, oval eyes, and longer fur. The name is derived from the colouring which resembles the Cuban cigar tobacco.

hawfinch European ◊finch, about 18 cm/7 in long. It feeds on berries and seeds, and can crack cherry stones with its large, powerful beak. The male bird has brown plumage, a black throat and black wings with a bold white shoulder stripe, a short white-tipped tail, and a broad band of grey at the back of the neck. (Species *Coccothraustes coccothraustes,* family Fringillidae, order Passeriformes.)

Hawfinches spend most of their time in the treetops, where they eat the fruits of pine, hornbeam, plum, cherry, hawthorn, laurel, and holly trees. They build their nests of twigs and mosses in lichen-covered trees, 2–10 m/6.5–33 ft above the ground. They are abundant in southern Europe and are also found in the temperate parts of Asia.

hawk any of a group of small to medium-sized birds of prey, belonging to the same family as eagles, kites, ospreys, and vultures.

HAWK

Some hawks have evolved a unique way of hanging on to their prey. The African harrier hawk and the Central and South American crane hawk can bend their legs both backwards and forwards from the middle joint. Their prey (mostly frogs, lizards, and baby birds) thus has great difficulty eluding them in even the trickiest crevices.

Hawks have short, rounded wings and a long tail compared with ◊falcons, and keen eyesight; the ◊sparrow hawk and ◊goshawk are examples. (Especially genera *Accipiter* and *Buteo,* family Accipitridae.)

Hawking, Stephen (William) (1942–)

English physicist whose work in general relativity – particularly gravitational field theory – led to a search for a quantum theory of gravity to explain black holes and the Big Bang, singularities that classical relativity theory does not adequately explain. His book *A Brief History of Time* **1988** gives a popular account of cosmology and became an international bestseller. His latest book is *The Nature of Space and Time*, written with Roger Penrose.

Hawking's objective of producing an overall synthesis of quantum mechanics and relativity theory began around the time of the publication in 1973 of his seminal book *The Large Scale Structure of Space-Time*, written with G F R Ellis. His most remarkable result, published in 1974, was that black holes could in fact emit particles in the form of thermal radiation – the so-called **Hawking radiation**.

If we find why it is that we and the universe exist, it would be the ultimate triumph of human reason – for then we would know the mind of God.

STEPHEN HAWKING English physicist.

hawk moth any member of a family of ◊moths with more than 1,000 species distributed throughout the world, but found mainly in tropical regions. Some South American hawk moths closely resemble hummingbirds. (Family Sphingidae.)

HAWK MOTH

The tongue of the Malagasy hawk moth is more than twice the length of its body. This enables it to feed from flowers without having to land on them, thus avoiding predators waiting in ambush.

hawthorn any of a group of shrubs or trees belonging to the rose family, growing abundantly in E North America, and also in Europe and Asia. All have alternate, toothed leaves and bear clusters of showy white, pink, or red flowers. Their small applelike fruits can be red, orange, blue, or black. Hawthorns are popular as ornamentals. (Genus *Crataegus,* family Rosaceae.)

hay preserved grass used for winter livestock feed. The grass is cut and allowed to dry in the field before being removed for storage in a barn.

The optimum period for cutting is when the grass has just come into flower and contains most feed value. During the natural drying process, the moisture content is reduced from 70–80% down to a safe level of 20%. In normal weather conditions, this takes from two to five days, during which time the hay is turned by machine to ensure even drying. Hay is normally baled before removal from the field.

Hayashi track in astronomy, a path on the ◊Hertzsprung–Russell diagram taken by protostars as they emerge from the clouds of dust and gas out of which they were born. A protostar appears on the right (cool) side of the Hertzsprung– Russell diagram and follows a Hayashi track until it arrives on the main sequence where hydrogen burning can start. It is named after the Japanese astrophysicist Chushiro Hayashi, who studied the theory of protostars in the 1960s.

hay fever allergic reaction to pollen, causing sneezing, with inflammation of the nasal membranes and conjunctiva of the eyes. Symptoms are due to the release of ◊histamine. Treatment is by antihistamine drugs.

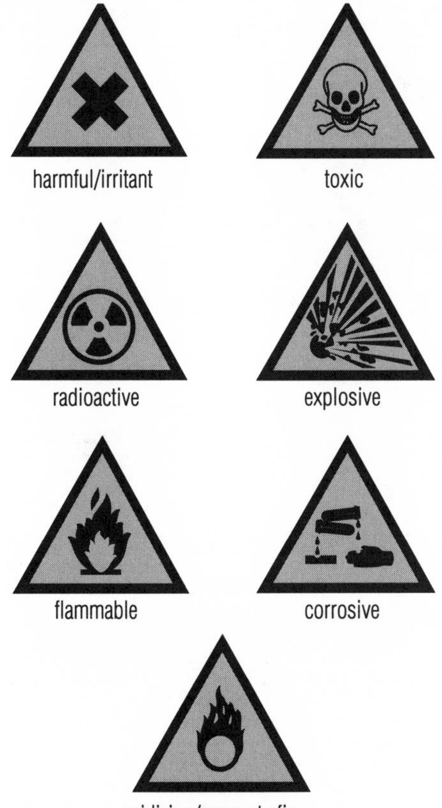

***hazard label** The internationally recognized symbols, warning of the potential dangers of handling certain substances.*

hazardous waste waste substance, usually generated by industry, that represents a hazard to the environment or to people living or working nearby. Examples include radioactive wastes, acidic resins, arsenic residues, residual hardening salts, lead from car exhausts, mercury, nonferrous sludges, organic solvents, asbestos, chlorinated solvents, and pesticides. The cumulative effects of toxic waste can take some time to become apparent (anything from a few hours to many years), and pose a serious threat to the ecological stability of the planet; its economic disposal or recycling is the subject of research.

haze factor unit of visibility in mist or fog. It is the ratio of the brightness of the mist compared with that of the object.

hazel any of a group of shrubs or trees that includes the European common hazel or cob (*C. avellana*), of which the filbert is the cultivated variety. North American species include the American hazel (*C. americana*). (Genus *Corylus,* family Corylaceae.)

HCI abbreviation for ◊human–computer interaction.

HDTV abbreviation for ◊high-definition television.

headache pain felt within the skull. Most headaches are caused by stress or tension, but some may be symptoms of brain or ◊systemic disease, including ◊fever.

Chronic daily headache may be caused by painkiller misuse, according to the European Headache Foundation in 1996. People who take daily analgesics to treat chronic headaches may actually be causing the headaches by doing so. See also ◊migraine.

header in computing, line or lines of text that appear at the beginning of each e-mail or USENET message sent across the Internet. The header includes important routing and identifying information, such as the sender's name, recipient's name (either a person or a newsgroup), date, time, and machine used when the message was composed, and the path by which the message arrived at its destination.

In the case of USENET postings, it also indicates if the message is intended for more than one group. The exact material is determined by ◊RFC (requests for comments) and discussion.

head louse parasitic insect that lives in human hair. See ◊louse.

health, world the health of people worldwide is monitored by the World Health Organization (WHO). Outside the industrialized world in particular, poverty and degraded environmental conditions mean that easily preventable diseases are widespread: WHO estimated in 1990 that 1 billion people, or 20% of the world's population, were diseased, in poor health, or malnourished. In North Africa and the Middle East, 25% of the population were ill.

vaccine-preventable diseases Every year, 46 million infants are not fully immunized; 2.8 million children die and 3 million are disabled due to vaccine-preventable diseases (polio, tetanus, diphtheria, whooping cough, tuberculosis, and measles).

diarrhoea Every year, there are 750 million cases in children, causing 4 million deaths. Oral rehydration therapy can correct dehydration and prevent 65% of deaths due to diarrhoeal disease. The basis of therapy is prepackaged sugar and salt. Treatment to cure the disease costs less than 20 cents, but fewer than one-third of children are treated in this way.

tuberculosis 1.6 billion people carry the bacteria, and there are 3 million deaths every year. Some 95% of all patients could be cured within six months using a specific antibiotic therapy which costs less than $30 per person.

prevention and cure Increasing health spending in industrialized countries by only $2 per head would enable immunization of all children to be performed, polio to be eradicated, and drugs provided to cure all cases of diarrhoeal disease, acute respiratory infection, tuberculosis, malaria, schistosomiasis, and most sexually transmitted diseases.

That physician will hardly be thought very careful of the health of others who neglects his own.

GALEN Greek physician and anatomist.
Of Protecting the Health bk V

hearing aid any device to improve the hearing of partially deaf people. Hearing aids usually consist of a battery-powered transistorized microphone/amplifier unit and earpiece. Some miniaturized aids are compact enough to fit in the ear or be concealed in the frame of eyeglasses.

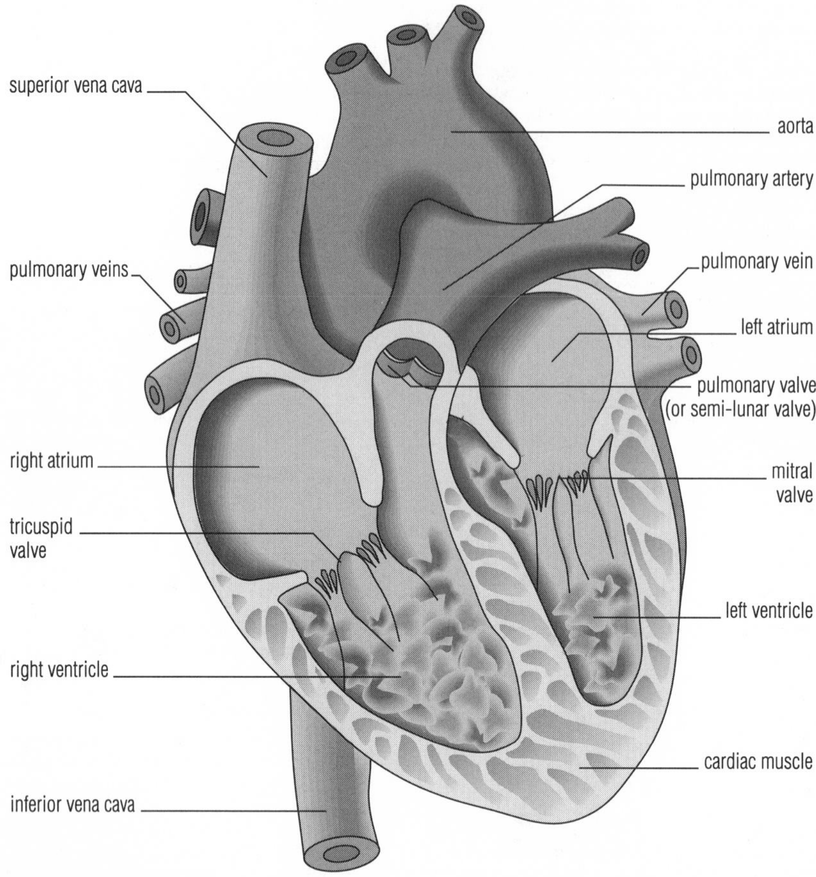

heart *The structure of the human heart. During an average lifetime, the human heart beats more than 2,000 million times and pumps 500 million l/110 million gal of blood. The average pulse rate is 70–72 beats per minute at rest for adult males, and 78–82 beats per minute for adult females.*

heart muscular organ that rhythmically contracts to force blood around the body of an animal with a circulatory system. Annelid worms and some other invertebrates have simple hearts consisting of thickened sections of main blood vessels that pulse regularly. An earthworm has ten such hearts. Vertebrates have one heart. A fish heart has two chambers – the thin-walled **atrium** (once called the auricle) that expands to receive blood, and the thick-walled **ventricle** that pumps it out. Amphibians and most reptiles have two atria and one ventricle; birds and mammals have two atria and two ventricles. The beating of the heart is controlled by the autonomic nervous system and an internal control centre or pacemaker, the **sinoatrial node**.

the cardiac cycle The cardiac cycle is the sequence of events during one complete cycle of a heart beat. This consists of the simultaneous contraction of the two atria, a short pause, then the simultaneous contraction of the two ventricles, followed by a longer pause while the entire heart relaxes. The contraction phase is called 'systole' and the relaxation phase which follows is called 'diastole'. The whole cycle is repeated 70–80 times a minute under resting conditions.

When the atria contract, the blood in them enters the two relaxing ventricles, completely filling them. The mitral and tricuspid valves, which were open, now begin to shut and as they do so, they create vibrations in the heart walls and tendons, causing the first heart sound. The ventricles on contraction push open the pulmonary and aortic valves and eject blood into the respective vessels. The closed mitral and tricuspid valves prevent return of blood into the atria during this phase. As the ventricles start to relax, the aortic and pulmonary valves close to prevent backward flow of blood, and their closure causes the second heart sound. By now, the atria have filled once again and are ready to start contracting to begin the next cardiac cycle.

heart attack or ***myocardial infarction*** sudden onset of gripping central chest pain, often accompanied by sweating and vomiting, caused by death of a portion of the heart muscle following obstruction of a coronary artery by thrombosis (formation of a blood clot). Half of all heart attacks result in death within the first two hours, but in the remainder survival has improved following the widespread use of thrombolytic (clot-buster) drugs.

After a heart attack, most people remain in hospital for seven to ten days, and may make a gradual return to normal activity over the following months. How soon a patient is able to return to work depends on the physical and mental demands of their job. Despite widespread fears to the contrary, it is safe to return to normal sexual activity within about a month of the attack.

AMERICAN HEART ASSOCIATION

http://www.amhrt.org/

Home page of the American Heart Association offers a risk assessment test, information about healthy living, including the effects of diet, and access to resources for both patients and carers.

heartbeat the regular contraction and relaxation of the heart, and the accompanying sounds. As blood passes through the heart a double beat is heard. The first is produced by the sudden closure of the valves between the atria and the ventricles. The second, slightly delayed sound, is caused by the closure of the valves found at the entrance to the major arteries leaving the heart. Diseased valves may make unusual sounds, known as heart murmurs.

heartburn burning sensation behind the breastbone (sternum). It results from irritation of the lower oesophagus (gullet) by excessively acid stomach contents, as sometimes happens during pregnancy and in cases of duodenal ulcer or obesity. It is often due to a weak valve at the entrance to the stomach that allows its contents to well up into the oesophagus.

heart–lung machine apparatus used during heart surgery to take over the functions of the heart and the lungs temporarily. It has a pump to circulate the blood around the body and is able to add oxygen to the blood and remove carbon dioxide from it. A heart–lung machine was first used for open-heart surgery in the USA in 1953.

heat form of energy possessed by a substance by virtue of the vibrating movement (kinetic energy) of its molecules or atoms. Heat energy is transferred by conduction, convection, and radiation. It always flows from a region of higher ◊temperature (heat intensity) to one of lower temperature. Its effect on a substance may be simply to raise its temperature, or to cause it to expand, melt (if a solid), vaporize (if a liquid), or increase its pressure (if a confined gas).
measurement Quantities of heat are usually measured in units of energy, such as joules (J) or calories (cal). The **specific heat** of a substance is the ratio of the quantity of heat required to raise the temperature of a given mass of the substance through a given range of temperature to the heat required to raise the temperature of an equal mass of water through the same range. It is measured by a ◊calorimeter.
conduction, convection, and radiation Conduction is the passing of heat along a medium to neighbouring parts with no visible motion accompanying the transfer of heat – for example, when the whole length of a metal rod is heated when one end is held in a fire. Convection is the transmission of heat through a fluid (liquid or gas) in currents – for example, when the air in a room is warmed by a fire or radiator. Radiation is heat transfer by infrared rays. It can pass through a vacuum, travels at the same speed as light, can be reflected and refracted, and does not affect the medium through which it passes. For example, heat reaches the Earth from the Sun by radiation.

For the transformation of heat, see ◊thermodynamics.

heat capacity in physics, the quantity of heat required to raise the temperature of an object by one degree. The **specific heat capacity** of a substance is the heat capacity per unit of mass, measured in joules per kilogram per kelvin ($J\ kg^{-1}\ K^{-1}$).

heat death in cosmology, a possible fate of the universe in which it continues expanding indefinitely while all the stars burn out and no new ones are formed. See ◊critical density.

heath in botany, any of a group of woody, mostly evergreen shrubs, including ◊heather, many of which have bell-shaped pendant flowers. They are native to Europe, Africa, and North America. (Common Old World genera *Erica* and *Calluna,* family Ericaceae.)

heather low-growing evergreen shrub of the ◊heath family, common on sandy or acid soil. The common heather (*Calluna vulgaris*) is a carpet-forming shrub, growing up to 60 cm/24 in high and bearing pale pink-purple flowers. It is found over much of Europe and has been introduced to North America.

heat of reaction alternative term for ◊energy of reaction.

heat pump machine, run by electricity or another power source, that cools the interior of a building by removing heat from interior air and pumping it out or, conversely, heats the inside by extracting energy from the atmosphere or from a hot-water source and pumping it in.

heat shield any heat-protecting coating or system, especially the coating (for example, tiles) used in spacecraft to protect the astronauts and equipment inside from the heat of re-entry when returning to Earth. Air friction can generate temperatures of up to 1,500°C/2,700°F on re-entry into the atmosphere.

heat storage any means of storing heat for release later. It is usually achieved by using materials that undergo phase changes, for example, Glauber's salt and sodium pyrophosphate, which melts at 70°C/158°F. The latter is used to store off-peak heat in the home: the salt is liquefied by cheap heat during the night and then freezes to give off heat during the day.

Other developments include the use of plastic crystals, which change their structure rather than melting when they are heated. They could be incorporated in curtains or clothing.

heatstroke or ***sunstroke*** rise in body temperature caused by excessive exposure to heat.

Mild heatstroke is experienced as feverish lassitude, sometimes with simple fainting; recovery is prompt following rest and replenishment of salt lost in sweat. Severe heatstroke causes collapse akin to that seen in acute ◊shock, and is potentially lethal without prompt treatment, including cooling the body carefully and giving fluids to relieve dehydration.

heat treatment in industry, the subjection of metals and alloys to controlled heating and cooling after fabrication to relieve internal stresses and improve their physical properties. Methods include ◊annealing, ◊quenching, and ◊tempering.

Heaviside's dolphin or **benguela dolphin** *Cephalorhynchus heavisidii* one of the least-known dolphins, confined to the coastal waters of Namibia. It is thought that about 100 a year are killed in purse seine nets from fishing boats, which could endanger this apparently rare species.

heavy horse powerful ◊horse specially bred for hauling wagons and heavy agricultural implements. After a decline following the introduction of the tractor, they are again being bred in increasing numbers and used for specialized work.

heavy industry industry that processes large amounts of bulky raw materials. Examples are the iron and steel industry, shipbuilding, and aluminium smelting. Heavy industries are often tied to locations close to their supplies of raw materials.

heavy water or ***deuterium oxide*** D_2O water containing the isotope deuterium instead of hydrogen (relative molecular mass 20 as opposed to 18 for ordinary water).

Its chemical properties are identical with those of ordinary water, but its physical properties differ slightly. It occurs in ordinary water in the ratio of about one part by mass of deuterium to 5,000 parts by mass of hydrogen, and can be concentrated by electrolysis, the ordinary water being more readily decomposed by this means than the heavy water. It has been used in the nuclear industry because it can slow down fast neutrons, thereby controlling the chain reaction.

hectare metric unit of area equal to 100 ares or 10,000 square metres (2.47 acres), symbol ha.

Trafalgar Square, London's only metric square, was laid out as one hectare.

hedge or ***hedgerow*** row of closely planted shrubs or low trees, generally acting as a land division and windbreak. Hedges also serve as a source of food and as a refuge for wildlife, and provide a ◊habitat not unlike the understorey of a natural forest.

hedgehog insectivorous mammal native to Europe, Asia, and Africa. The body, including the tail, is 30 cm/1 ft long. It is greyish brown in colour, has a piglike snout, and its back and sides are covered with sharp spines. When threatened it rolls itself into a ball bristling with spines. Hedgehogs feed on insects, slugs, mice, frogs, young birds, and carrion. Long-eared hedgehogs and desert hedgehogs are placed in different genera. (Genus *Erinaceus,* order Insectivora, family Erinaceidae.)

Hedgehogs normally shelter by day and go out at night. They find food more by smell and sound than by sight. The young are born in the late spring or early summer, and are blind, helpless, and covered with soft spines. For about a month they feed on their mother's milk, after which she teaches them to find their own food. In the autumn, hedgehogs make a nest of leaves and moss in the roots of a tree or in a hole in the ground and hibernate until spring.

hedge sparrow another name for the ◊dunnock, a small European bird.

height of a plane figure or solid, the perpendicular distance from the vertex to the base; see ◊altitude.

Heisenberg, Werner (Karl) (1901–1976)

German physicist who developed quantum theory and formulated the uncertainty principle, which concerns matter, radiation, and their reactions, and places absolute limits on the achievable accuracy of measurement. He was awarded a Nobel prize in 1932 for work he carried out when only 24.

Heisenberg was concerned not to try to picture what happens inside the atom but to find a mathematical system that explained it. His starting point was the spectral lines given by hydrogen, the simplest atom. Assisted by Max Born, Heisenberg presented his ideas in 1925 as a system called **matrix mechanics**. He obtained the frequencies of the lines in the hydrogen spectrum by mathematical treatment of values within matrices or arrays. His work was the first precise mathematical description of the workings of the atom and with it Heisenberg is regarded as founding quantum mechanics, which seeks to explain atomic structure in mathematical terms.

Heisenberg also was able to predict from studies of the hydrogen spectrum that hydrogen exists in two allotropes – orthohydrogen and para-hydrogen – in which the two nuclei of the atoms in a hydrogen molecule spin in the same or opposite directions respectively. The allotropes were discovered in 1929 (see allotropy).

In 1927, Heisenberg made the discovery of the **uncertainty principle**, for which he is best known. The uncertainty principle states that there is a theoretical limit to the precision with which a particle's position and momentum can be measured. In other words, it is impossible to specify precisely both the position and the simultaneous momentum (mass multiplied by velocity) of a particle. There is always a degree of uncertainty in either, and as one is determined with greater precision, the other can only be found less exactly. Heisenberg also formulated that multiplying the degrees of uncertainty of the position and momentum yields a value approximately equal to Planck's constant. The idea that the result of an action can be expressed only in terms of the probability of a certain effect was revolutionary, and it discomforted even Albert Einstein (1879–1955), but has remained valid.

In 1927, Heisenberg used the Pauli exclusion principle, which states that no two electrons can have all four quantum numbers the same, to show that ferromagnetism (the ability of some materials to acquire magnetism in the presence of an external magnetic field) is caused by electrostatic interaction between the electrons.

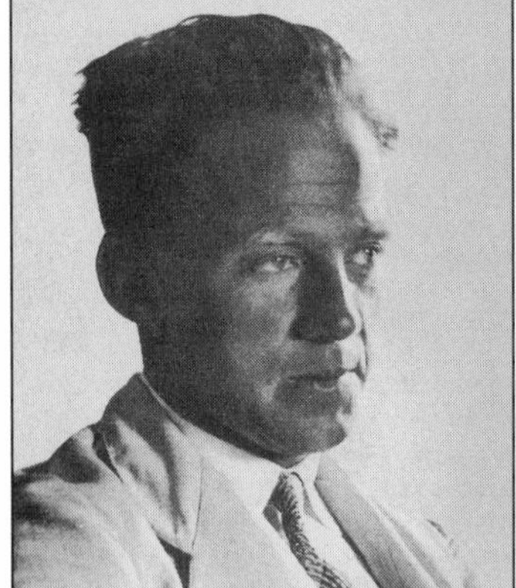

Mary Evans Picture Library

Helicobacter pylori spiral-shaped swimming bacterium that causes gastritis and stomach ◊ulcers when it colonizes the stomach lining. Without antibiotic treatment, infection can be permanent. *H. pylori* may also contribute towards stomach cancer.

Approximately 60% of 60-year-olds in the USA and western Europe are infected with *H. pylori;* the infection is rarely found in children. In developing countries 60–70% of children under 10 exhibit infection.

In 1997 scientists completed a full genetic blueprint (or genome) of *H. pylori.*

HELISPOT

http://www.helispot.com/

Helicopters of all shapes, sizes, and purposes are shown in photographs on this Web site. Police, military, news, and rescue helicopters are all featured in the hundreds of photographs listed. In addition there is an e-mail forum and many links to other helicopter resources

helicopter powered aircraft that achieves both lift and propulsion by means of a rotary wing, or rotor, on top of the fuselage. It can take off and land vertically, move in any direction, or remain stationary in the air. It can be powered by piston or jet engine. The ◊autogiro was a precursor.

The rotor of a helicopter has two or more blades of aerofoil cross-section like an aeroplane's wings. Lift and propulsion are achieved by angling the blades as they rotate. Experiments using the concept of helicopter flight date from the early 1900s, with the first successful liftoff and short flight in 1907. Ukrainian–US engineer Igor Sikorsky built the first practical single-rotor craft in the USA in 1939.

A single-rotor helicopter must also have a small tail rotor to counter the torque, or tendency of the body to spin in the opposite direction to the main rotor. Twin-rotor helicopters, like the Boeing Chinook, have their rotors turning in opposite directions to prevent the body from spinning. Helicopters are now widely used in passenger service, rescue missions on land and sea, police pursuits and traffic control, fire-fighting, and agriculture. In war they carry troops and equipment into difficult terrain, make aerial reconnaissance and attacks, and carry the wounded to aid stations. A fire-fighting helicopter was tested in Japan 1996, designed to reach skyscrapers beyond the reach of fire-engine ladders.

heliography old method of signalling, used by armies in the late 19th century, which employed sunlight reflected from a mirror to pass messages in ◊Morse code. On a clear day, a heliograph could send over distances in excess of 50 km/30 mi.

Also, an early photographic process by which a permanent image was formed on a glass plate.

helioseismology study of the Sun's structure by analysing vibrations and monitoring effects on the Sun's surface. Compare with ◊seismology.

heliosphere region of space through which the ◊solar wind flows outwards from the Sun. The **heliopause** is the boundary of this region, believed to lie about 100 astronomical units from the Sun, where the flow of the solar wind merges with the interstellar gas.

heliotrope decorative plant belonging to the borage family, with distinctive spikes of blue, lilac, or white flowers, including the Peruvian or cherry pie heliotrope (*H. peruvianum*). (Genus *Heliotropium,* family Boraginaceae.)

helium Greek *helios* 'Sun' colourless, odourless, gaseous, nonmetallic element, symbol He, atomic number 2, relative atomic mass 4.0026. It is grouped with the ◊inert gases, is nonreactive, and forms no compounds. It is the second-most abundant element (after hydrogen) in the universe, and has the lowest boiling (–268.9°C/–452°F) and melting points (–272.2°C/–458°F) of all the elements. It is present in small quantities in the Earth's atmosphere from gases issuing from radioactive elements (from ◊alpha decay) in the Earth's crust; after hydrogen it is the second lightest element.

Helium is a component of most stars, including the Sun, where the nuclear-fusion process converts hydrogen into helium with the

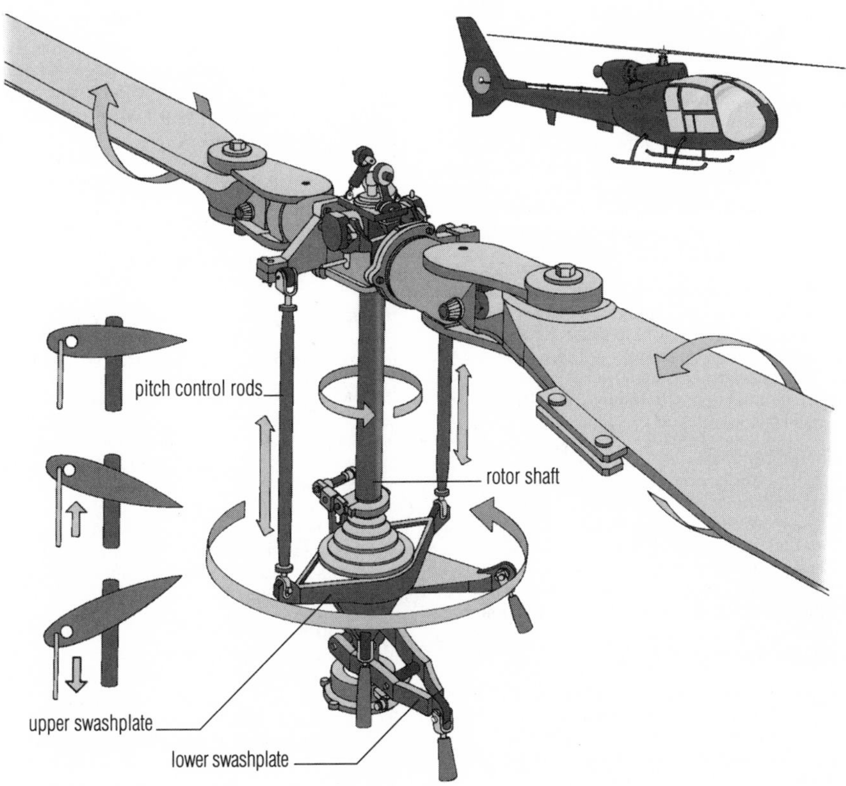

helicopter *The helicopter is controlled by varying the rotor pitch (the angle of the rotor blade as it moves through the air). For backwards flight, the blades in front of the machine have greater pitch than those behind the craft. This means that the front blades produce more lift and a backwards thrust. For forwards flight, the situation is reversed. In level flight, the blades have unchanging pitch.*

production of heat and light. It is obtained by compression and fractionation of naturally occurring gases. It is used for inflating balloons and as a dilutant for oxygen in deep-sea breathing systems. Liquid helium is used extensively in low-temperature physics (cryogenics).

helix in mathematics, a three-dimensional curve resembling a spring, corkscrew, or screw thread. It is generated by a line that encircles a cylinder or cone at a constant angle.

hellebore poisonous European ◊herbaceous plant belonging to the buttercup family. The stinking hellebore (*H. foetidus*) has greenish flowers early in the spring. (Genus *Helleborus*, family Ranunculaceae.)

helleborine one of several temperate Old World orchids, including the marsh helleborine (*E. palustris*) and the hellebore orchid (*E. helleborine*) introduced to North America. (Genera *Epipactis* and *Cephalanthera*, family Orchidaceae.)

helminth in medicine, collective name used to describe parasitic worms. There are several classes of helminth that can cause infections in humans, including ascarids (ascariasis), ◊tapeworms, and ◊threadworms.

helper application in computing, in Web ◊browsers, an external application that adds the ability to display certain types of files. Common helper applications include ◊RealAudio, which allows browsers to play live sound tracks such as radio broadcasts or recorded lectures; ◊Acrobat; and mIRC, which allows access to ◊Internet Relay Chat via the World Wide Web.

hematite principal ore of iron, consisting mainly of iron(III) oxide, Fe_2O_3. It occurs as **specular hematite** (dark, metallic lustre), **kidney ore** (reddish radiating fibres terminating in smooth, rounded surfaces), and a red earthy deposit.

Hemiptera large insect order consisting of the ◊bugs and containing about 55,000 species.

classification Hemiptera is in class Insecta, phylum Arthropoda.

The order is divided into two suborders.

suborder Homoptera These are the plant bugs. They are small to moderate-sized (from 3 mm/0.1 in to several centimetres/nearly an inch) insects with two pairs of wings usually present, held sloping over the body at rest. The forewings are usually evenly thickened with chitin; wingless forms are frequent. This suborder contains a large number of agricultural pests, some of which are vectors of plant viruses.

The important groups include the families Aleyrodidae, whiteflies; the Aphididae, greenflies; Cicadidae, cicadas; the Cicadellidae, leafhoppers; and the Psyllidae, plant lice. The superfamily Coccoidea, mealy bugs and scale insects, contains a further 16 families, many of which are important, including the lac insects from which shellac is obtained.

The plant bugs attack and destroy a wide range of plant life including grains, cereals, vegetables, fruit trees, and other trees. The aphids, one of the most important groups, transmit over 50 plant diseases.

suborder Heteroptera This suborder, characterized by having forewings unevenly thickened with chitin, is separated into two divisions: **Gymnocerata** have antennae that are usually longer than the head. They are terrestrial or water-skating forms. There are over 40 families, a few containing pests of agricultural importance. The Pyrrhocorridae, the cotton-stainers cause the most damage; the Coreidae, Pentastomidae, and Tingidae are of lesser importance. Most of the other families are predacious, feeding on other insects. Three families: Cimicidae, bedbugs; Polyctenidae; and Reduviidae, assassin bugs, are active bloodsuckers of mammals and birds. (Polyctenidae attacks only bats.)

suborder Cryptocerata Members of this suborder have antennae that are shorter than the head and are usually concealed. These bugs are usually predacious, and are truly aquatic, being adapted for swimming. This division includes the families Belostomatidae, giant water bugs; Corixidae, water boatmen; Nepidae, water-scorpions; and Notonectidae, backswimmers.

hemlock plant belonging to the carrot family, native to Europe, W Asia, and N Africa. It grows up to 2 m/6 ft high and produces delicate clusters of small white flowers. The whole plant, especially the root and fruit, is poisonous, causing paralysis of the nervous system. The name 'hemlock' is also given to some North American and Asiatic conifers (genus *Tsuga*) belonging to the pine family. (*Conium maculatum,* family Umbelliferae.)

hemp annual plant originally from Asia, now cultivated in most temperate countries for the fibres produced in the outer layer of the stem, which are used in ropes, twines, and, occasionally, in a type of linen or lace. The drug ◊cannabis is obtained from certain varieties of hemp. (*Cannabis sativa,* family Cannabaceae.)

The name 'hemp' is also given to other similar types of fibre: **sisal hemp** and **henequen** obtained from the leaves of *Agave* species native to Yucatán and cultivated in many tropical countries, and **manila hemp** obtained from *Musa textilis,* a plant native to the Philippines and the Maluku Islands, Indonesia.

henbane poisonous plant belonging to the nightshade family, found on waste ground throughout most of Europe and W Asia. It is a branching plant, up to 80 cm/31 in high, with hairy leaves and a sickening smell. The yellow flowers are bell-shaped. Henbane is used in medicine as a source of the drugs hyoscyamine and scopolamine. (*Hyoscyamus niger,* family Solanaceae.)

henna small shrub belonging to the loosestrife family, found in Iran, India, Egypt, and N Africa. The leaves and young twigs are ground to a powder, mixed to a paste with hot water, and applied to the fingernails and hair to give an orange-red hue. The colour may then be changed to black by applying a preparation of indigo. (*Lawsonia inermis,* family Lythraceae.)

Henna can also be used to dye both natural and synthetic textiles.

henry SI unit (symbol H) of ◊inductance (the reaction of an electric current against the magnetic field that surrounds it). One henry is the inductance of a circuit that produces an opposing voltage of one volt when the current changes at one ampere per second.

It is named after the US physicist Joseph Henry.

hepatitis any inflammatory disease of the liver, usually caused by a virus. Other causes include alcohol, drugs, gallstones, ◊lupus erythematous, and amoebic ◊dysentery. Symptoms include weakness, nausea, and jaundice.

Five different hepatitis viruses have been identified; A, B, C, D, and E. The hepatitis A virus (HAV) is the commonest cause of viral hepatitis, responsible for up to 40% of cases worldwide. It is spread by contaminated food. Hepatitis B, or serum hepatitis, is a highly contagious disease spread by blood products or in body fluids. It often culminates in liver failure, and is also associated with liver cancer, although only 5% of those infected suffer chronic liver damage. During 1995, 1.1 million people died of hepatitis B. Around 300 million people are ◊carriers. Vaccines are available against hepatitis A and B.

Hepatitis C is mostly seen in people needing frequent transfusions. Hepatitis D, which only occurs in association with hepatitis B, is common in the Mediterranean region. Hepatitis E is endemic in India and South America.

herb any plant (usually a flowering plant) tasting sweet, bitter, aromatic, or pungent, used in cooking, medicine, or perfumery; technically, a herb is any plant in which the aerial parts do not remain above ground at the end of the growing season.

HERB

The herb Catnip (*Nepeta cataria*) has a remarkable effect on cats. Members of the cat family roll over, extend their claws and twist in excitement when they smell the pungent odour of catnip. This reaction is believed to be caused by a chemical called trans-neptalacone, which is similar to a substance found in the female cat's urine.

herbaceous plant plant with very little or no wood, dying back at the end of every summer. The herbaceous perennials survive winters as underground storage organs such as bulbs and tubers.

herbalism in alternative medicine, the prescription and use of plants and their derivatives for medication. Herbal products are favoured by alternative practitioners as 'natural medicine', as opposed to modern synthesized medicines and drugs, which are regarded with suspicion because of the dangers of side effects and dependence.

Many herbal remedies are of proven efficacy both in preventing and curing illness. Medical herbalists claim to be able to prescribe for virtually any condition, except those so advanced that surgery is the only option.

herbarium collection of dried, pressed plants used as an aid to identification of unknown plants and by taxonomists in the ◊classification of plants. The plant specimens are accompanied by information, such as the date and place of collection, by whom collected, details of habitat, flower colour, and local names.

Herbaria range from small collections containing plants of a limited region, to the large university and national herbaria (some at ◊botanical gardens) containing millions of specimens from all parts of the world.

herbicide any chemical used to destroy plants or check their growth; see ◊weedkiller.

herbivore animal that feeds on green plants (or photosynthetic single-celled organisms) or their products, including seeds, fruit, and nectar. The most numerous type of herbivore is thought to be the zooplankton, tiny invertebrates in the surface waters of the oceans that feed on small photosynthetic algae. Herbivores are more numerous than other animals because their food is the most abundant. They form a vital link in the food chain between plants and carnivores.

herb Robert wild ◊geranium found throughout Europe and central Asia and naturalized in North America. About 30 cm/12 in high, it has hairy leaves and small pinkish to purplish flowers. (*Geranium robertianum,* family Geraniaceae.)

Herculaneum ancient city of Italy between Naples and Pompeii. Along with Pompeii, it was buried when Vesuvius erupted AD 79. It was excavated from the 18th century onwards.

Hercules in astronomy, the fifth-largest constellation, lying in the northern hemisphere. Despite its size it contains no prominent stars. Its most important feature is the best example in the northern hemisphere of a ◊globular cluster of stars 22,500 light years from Earth, which lies between Eta and Zeta Herculis.

Hercules beetle largest beetle in the world: males measure up to 17 cm/6.6 in in length; females are smaller. Hercules beetles are found mainly in the tropical and subtropical regions.

They are black, nocturnal, and exhibit extreme forms of sexual dimorphism (marked visual differences between males and females). Males have a dark-coloured, slender, curved horn of up to 10 mm/3.9 in long, on their heads.

classification Hercules beetles *Dynastes hercules* belong to the subfamily Dynastinae, family Scarabaeidae, order Coleoptera, class Insecta, phylum Arthropoda.

heredity in biology, the transmission of traits from parent to offspring. See also ◊genetics.

hermaphrodite organism that has both male and female sex organs. Hermaphroditism is the norm in such species as earthworms and snails, and is common in flowering plants. Cross-fertilization is the rule among hermaphrodites, with the parents functioning as male and female simultaneously, or as one or the other sex at different stages in their development. Human hermaphrodites are extremely rare.

hermit crab type of ◊crab.

hernia or ***rupture*** protrusion of part of an internal organ through a weakness in the surrounding muscular wall, usually in the groin. The appearance is that of a rounded soft lump or swelling.

heroin or ***diamorphine*** powerful ◊opiate analgesic, an acetyl derivative of ◊morphine. It is more addictive than morphine but causes less nausea. It has an important place in the control of severe pain in terminal illness, severe injuries, and heart attacks, but is widely used illegally.

Heroin was discovered in Germany in 1898.The major regions of opium production, for conversion to heroin, are the 'Golden Crescent' of Afghanistan, Iran, and Pakistan, and the 'Golden Triangle' across parts of Myanmar (Burma), Laos, and Thailand.

In 1971 there were 3,000 registered heroin addicts in the UK; in 1989 there were over 100,000.

heron large to medium-sized wading bird belonging to the same family as bitterns, egrets, night herons, and boatbills. Herons have sharp bills, broad wings, long legs, slender bodies, and soft plumage. They are found mostly in tropical and subtropical regions, but also in temperate zones, on lakes, fens, and mudflats, where they wade searching for prey. (Genera include *Ardea, Butorides,* and *Nycticorax;* family Ardeidae, order Ciconiiformes.)

They capture small animals, such as fish, molluscs, and worms, by spearing them with their long bills. Herons nest in trees or bushes, on ivy-covered rocks, or in reedbeds, making a loose fabric of sticks lined with grass or leaves; they lay greenish or drab-coloured eggs, varying in number from two to seven according to the different species.

herpes any of several infectious diseases caused by viruses of the herpes group. **Herpes simplex I** is the causative agent of a common inflammation, the cold sore. **Herpes simplex II** is responsible for genital herpes, a highly contagious, sexually transmitted disease characterized by painful blisters in the genital area. It can be transmitted in the birth canal from mother to newborn. **Herpes zoster** causes ◊shingles; another herpes virus causes chickenpox.

A number of antivirals treat these infections, which are particularly troublesome in patients whose immune systems have been suppressed medically; for example, after a transplant operation. The drug acyclovir, originally introduced for the treatment of genital herpes, has now been shown to modify the course of chickenpox and the related condition shingles, by reducing the duration of the illness.

herpetology the scientific study of ◊reptiles, including their classification, anatomy, physiology, behaviour, and ecology.

herring any of various marine fishes belonging to the herring family, but especially the important food fish *Clupea harengus.* A silvered greenish blue, it swims close to the surface, and may be 25–40 cm/10–16 in long. Herring travel in schools several kilometres long and wide. They are found in large quantities off the east coast of North America, and the shores of NE Europe. Overfishing and pollution have reduced their numbers. (Family Clupeidae.)

HERRING

The wolf herring *Chirocentrus dorab* is the largest fish in the herring order. It grows up to 3.7 m/12 ft long.

Herschel, (Frederick) William
(1738–1822)

German-born English astronomer. He was a skilled telescope-maker, and pioneered the study of binary stars and nebulae. He discovered the planet Uranus in 1781 and infrared solar rays in 1801. He catalogued over 800 double stars, and found over 2,500 nebulae, catalogued by his sister Caroline Herschel; this work was continued by his son John Herschel. By studying the distribution of stars, William established the basic form of our Galaxy, the Milky Way.

Herschel discovered the motion of binary stars around one another, and recorded it in his *Motion of the Solar System in Space* 1783. In 1789 he built, in Slough, Berkshire, a 1.2-m/4-ft telescope of 12 m/40 ft focal length (the largest in the world at the time), but he made most use of a more satisfactory 46-cm/18-in instrument. He discovered two satellites of Uranus and two of Saturn.

Mary Evans Picture Library

hertz SI unit (symbol Hz) of frequency (the number of repetitions of a regular occurrence in one second). Radio waves are often measured in megahertz (MHz), millions of hertz, and the ◊clock rate of a computer is usually measured in megahertz. The unit is named after Heinrich Hertz.

Hertz, Heinrich Rudolf
(1857–1894)

German physicist who studied electromagnetic waves, showing that their behaviour resembles that of light and heat waves.

Hertz confirmed James Clerk Maxwell's theory of electromagnetic waves. In 1888, he realized that electric waves could be produced and would travel through air, and he confirmed this experimentally. He went on to determine the velocity of these waves (which were later called radio waves) and, on showing that it was the same as that of light, devised experiments to show that the waves could be reflected, refracted, and diffracted.

Mary Evans Picture Library

Hertzsprung–Russell diagram in astronomy, a graph on which the surface temperatures of stars are plotted against their luminosities. Most stars, including the Sun, fall into a narrow band called the ◊main sequence. When a star grows old it moves from the main sequence to the upper right part of the graph, into the

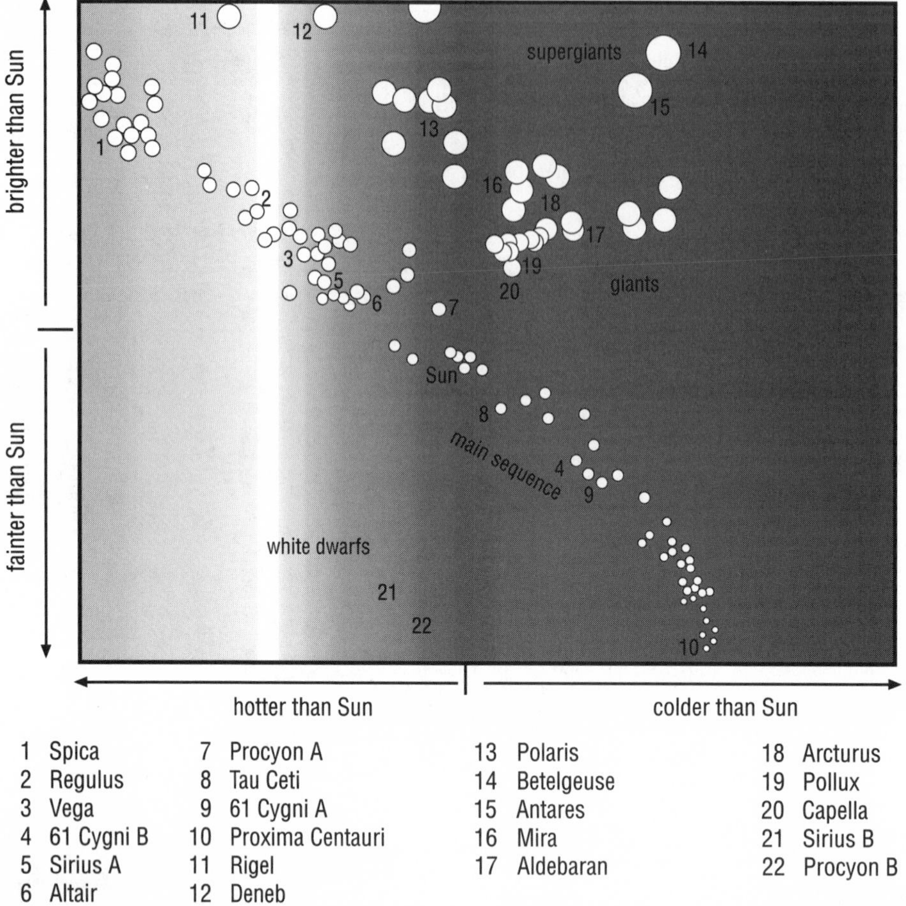

Hertzsprung–Russell diagram *The Hertzsprung–Russell diagram relates the brightness (or luminosity) of a star to its temperature. Most stars fall within a narrow diagonal band called the main sequence. A star moves off the main sequence when it grows old. The Hertzsprung–Russell diagram is one of the most important diagrams in astrophysics.*

Hertzsprung, Ejnar (1873–1967)

Danish astronomer and physicist. He introduced the concept of the absolute magnitude (brightness) of a star, and described the\ relationship between the absolute magnitude and the temperature of a star, formulating his results in the form of a diagram, known as the Hertzsprung–Russell diagram, that has become a standard reference.

His astronomical interests were very wide, but his observations were mainly of variable stars, double stars, and clusters.

area of the giants and supergiants. At the end of its life, as the star shrinks to become a white dwarf, it moves again, to the bottom left area. It is named after the Dane Ejnar Hertzsprung (1873–1967) and the American Henry Norris Russell (1877–1957), who independently devised it in the years 1911–13.

hessian fly or ***barley midge*** tiny black fly, a species of ◊gall midge that feeds on wheat and is considered a serious pest of winter wheat in the USA and New Zealand.

classification The hessian fly *Mayetiola destructor* belongs to the family Cecidomyiidae (suborder Nematocera) of order Diptera, class Insecta, phylum Arthropoda.

Hessian flies lay their eggs on the top surface of leaves of young wheat. The larvae feed on the leaf sheaths and also suck the plant sap. Wheat infested during the autumn appears stunted and the leaves are dark bluish-green. Intensely parasitized plants die during the winter.

The use of resistant wheat varieties in combination with delayed planting in the autumn (observing 'fly-safe' dates) has greatly reduced the damage caused by hessian flies in most wheat-producing areas of the USA.

Other allied pests include the sorghum midge *Contarinia sorghicola,* and the clover seed midge, *Dasyneura leguminicola.* The sorghum midge is a serious pest in the southern USA and the more humid areas of the Gulf States.

heterogeneous reaction in chemistry, a reaction where there is an interface between the different components or reactants. Examples of heterogeneous reactions are those between a gas and a solid, a gas and a liquid, two immiscible liquids, or two different solids.

heterosis or ***hybrid vigour*** improvement in physical capacities that sometimes occurs in the ◊hybrid produced by mating two genetically different parents.

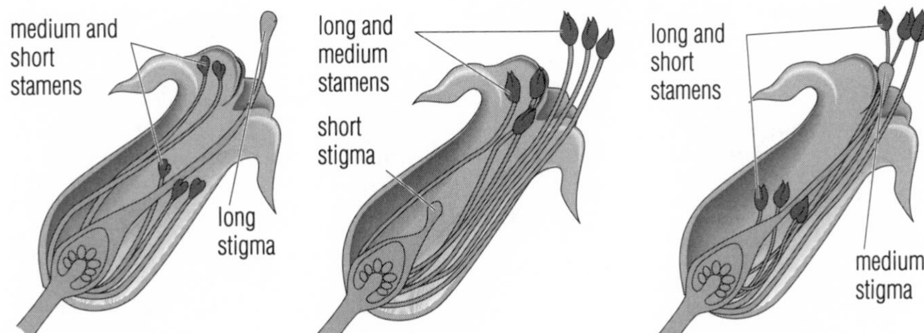

heterostyly *Heterostyly, in which lengths of the stamens and stigma differ in flowers of different plants of the same species. This is a device to ensure cross-pollination by visiting insects.*

The parents may be of different strains or varieties within a species, or of different species, as in the mule, which is stronger and has a longer life span than either of its parents (donkey and horse). Heterosis is also exploited in hybrid varieties of maize, tomatoes, and other crops.

heterostyly in botany, having ◊styles of different lengths.

Certain flowers, such as primroses (*Primula vulgaris*), have different-sized ◊anthers and styles to ensure cross-fertilization (through ◊pollination) by visiting insects.

heterotroph any living organism that obtains its energy from organic substances produced by other organisms. All animals and fungi are heterotrophs, and they include herbivores, carnivores, and saprotrophs (those that feed on dead animal and plant material).

heterozygous in a living organism, having two different ◊alleles for a given trait. In ◊homozygous organisms, by contrast, both chromosomes carry the same allele. In an outbreeding population an individual organism will generally be heterozygous for some genes but homozygous for others.

For example, in humans, alleles for both blue-and brown-pigmented eyes exist, but the 'blue' allele is ◊recessive to the dominant 'brown' allele.

Only individuals with blue eyes are predictably homozygous for this trait; brown-eyed people can be either homozygous or heterozygous.

heuristics in computing, a process by which a program attempts to improve its performance by learning from its own experience.

The separate branches of natural knowledge have a real and intimate connection.

ALEXANDER VON HUMBOLDT German botanist and geologist. *Cosmos* 1845

Hewlett-Packard (often abbreviated to *HP*) major manufacturer of computer and telecommunications hardware, founded 1939 by William Hewlett and David Packard and based in Palo Alto, California, USA. In 1996 the company was manufacturing more than 24,000 products, including medical equipment, analytical instruments, calculators, PCs, printers, workstations, and palmtops.

HP's sales grew dramatically from $13.2 billion in 1990 to $38.4 billion in 1996.

hexachlorophene $(C_6HCl_3OH)_2CH_2$ white, odourless bactericide, used in minute quantities in soaps and surgical disinfectants.

Trichlorophenol is used in its preparation, and, without precise temperature control, the highly toxic TCDD (tetrachlorodibenzodioxin; see ◊dioxin) may form as a by-product.

hexadecimal number system or ***hex*** number system to the base 16, used in computing. In hex the decimal numbers 0–15 are represented by the characters 0, 1, 2, 3, 4, 5, 6, 7, 8, 9, A, B, C, D, E, F.

Hexadecimal numbers are easy to convert to the computer's internal ◊binary code and are more compact than binary numbers.

Each place in a number increases in value by a power of 16 going from right to left; for instance, 8F is equal to $15 + (8 \times 16) = 143$ in decimal. Hexadecimal numbers are often preferred by programmers writing in low-level languages because they are more easily converted to the computer's internal binary (base-two) code than are decimal numbers, and because they are more compact than binary numbers and therefore more easily keyed, checked, and memorized.

hexagon six-sided ◊polygon.

HF in physics, abbreviation for **high** ◊frequency. HF radio waves have frequencies in the range 3–30 MHz.

HGV abbreviation for ***heavy goods vehicle***.

hibernation state of dormancy in which certain animals spend the winter. It is associated with a dramatic reduction in all metabolic processes, including body temperature, breathing, and heart rate. It is a fallacy that animals sleep throughout the winter.

The body temperature of the Arctic ground squirrel falls to below 0°C/32°F during hibernation. Hibernating bats may breathe only once every 45 minutes, and can go for up to 2 hours without taking a breath.

hibiscus any of a group of plants belonging to the mallow family. Hibiscuses range from large ◊herbaceous plants to trees. Popular as ornamental plants because of their brilliantly coloured, red to white, bell-shaped flowers, they include *H. syriacus* and *H. rosa-sinensis* of Asia and the rose mallow (*H. palustris*) of North America. (Genus *Hibiscus*, family Malvaceae.)

hickory tree belonging to the walnut family, native to North America and Asia. It provides a valuable timber, and all species produce nuts, though some are inedible. The pecan (*C. illinoensis*) is widely cultivated in the southern USA, and the shagbark (*C. ovata*) in the northern USA. (Genus *Carya*, family Juglandaceae.)

hidden file computer file in an ◊MS-DOS system that is not normally displayed when the directory listing command is given. Hidden files include certain system files, principally so that there is less chance of modifying or deleting them by accident, but any file can be made hidden if required.

hide or ***hyde*** Anglo-Saxon unit of measurement used to measure the extent of arable land; it varied from about 296 ha/120 acres in the east of England to as little as 99 ha/40 acres in Wessex. One hide was regarded as sufficient to support a peasant and his household; it was the area that could be ploughed in a season by one plough and one team of oxen.

The hide was the basic unit of assessment for taxation and military service; under Norman rule it became the basis for the feudal tax of hidage.

hierarchy in computing, on USENET, the structure for naming ◊newsgroups. All newsgroups on USENET are assigned to a major group. The ◊Big Seven hierarchies were the first to be set up, and setting up a new newsgroup in these involved following more or less formal procedures. The ◊alt hierarchy was set up to allow more flexibility. The biz hierarchy was set up 1994, after the first incidence of ◊spamming, to give advertising its own place.

A number of other hierarchies are available, set up for specific countries (**de** is Germany, **dk** is Denmark, **uk** is Britain); for Internet Service Providers (Demon, CompuServe, and AOL all have their own local groups); or for individual companies.

hi-fi (abbreviation for ***high-fidelity***) faithful reproduction of sound from a machine that plays recorded music or speech. A typical hi-fi system includes a turntable for playing vinyl records, a cassette tape deck to play magnetic tape recordings, a tuner to pick up radio broadcasts, an amplifier to serve all the equipment, possibly a compact-disc player, and two or more loudspeakers.

Advances in mechanical equipment and electronics, such as digital recording techniques and compact discs, have made it possible to eliminate many distortions in sound-reproduction processes.

Higgs boson or ***Higgs particle*** postulated ◊elementary particle whose existence would explain why particles have mass. The current theory of elementary particles, called the ◊standard model, cannot explain how mass arises. To overcome this difficulty, Peter Higgs (1929–) of the University of Edinburgh and Thomas Kibble (1932–) of Imperial College, London proposed in 1964 a new particle that binds to other particles and gives them their mass. The Higgs boson has not yet been detected experimentally.

high-definition television (HDTV) ◊television system offering a significantly greater number of scanning lines, and therefore a clearer picture, than that provided by conventional systems. Typically, HDTV has about twice the horizontal and vertical resolution of current 525-line (such as the American standard, NTSC) or 625-line standands (such as the British standard, PAL); a frame rate of at least 24 Hz; and a picture aspect ratio of 9:16 instead of the current 3:4. HDTV systems have been in development since the mid-1970s.

The Japanese HDTV system, or HiVision as it is trade-named in Japan, uses 1,125 scanning lines and an aspect ratio of 16:9 instead of the squarish 4:3 that conventional television uses. A European HDTV system, called HD-MAC, using 1,250 lines, is under development. In the USA, a standard incorporating digital techniques is being discussed.

highest common factor (HCF) in a set of numbers, the highest number that will divide every member of the set without leaving a remainder. For example, 6 is the highest common factor of 36, 48 and 72.

high-level language in computing, a programming language designed to suit the requirements of the programmer; it is independent of the internal machine code of any particular computer. High-level languages are used to solve problems and are often described as **problem-oriented languages** – for example, ◊BASIC was designed to be easily learnt by first-time programmers; ◊COBOL is used to write programs solving business problems; and ◊FORTRAN is used for programs solving scientific and mathematical problems. In contrast, low-level languages, such as ◊assembly languages, closely reflect the machine codes of specific computers, and are therefore described as **machine-oriented languages**.

Unlike low-level languages, high-level languages are relatively easy to learn because the instructions bear a close resemblance to everyday language, and because the programmer does not require a detailed knowledge of the internal workings of the computer. Each instruction in a high-level language is equivalent to several machine-code instructions. High-level programs are therefore more compact than equivalent low-level programs. However, each high-level instruction must be translated into machine code – by either a ◊compiler or an ◊interpreter program – before it can be executed by a computer. High-level languages are designed to be **portable** – programs written in a high-level language can be run on any computer that has a compiler or interpreter for that particular language.

high memory in computing, the first 64 kilobytes in the ◊extended memory of an ◊MS-DOS system. The operating system itself is usually installed in this area to allow more conventional memory (below 640 kilobytes) for applications.

High-Sierra format in computing, standard format for writing CD-ROM discs; see ◊ISO 9660.

high-tech industry any industry that makes use of advanced technology. The largest high-tech group is the fast-growing electronics industry and especially the manufacture of computers, microchips, and telecommunications equipment.

The products of these industries have low bulk but high value, as do their components. Silicon Valley in the USA and Silicon Glen in Scotland are two areas with high concentrations of such firms.

highway in Britain, any road over which there is a right of way. In the USA, any public road, especially a main road.

high-yield variety crop that has been specially bred or selected to produce more than the natural varieties of the same species. During the 1950s and 1960s, new strains of wheat and maize were developed to reduce the food shortages in poor countries (the ◊Green Revolution). Later, IR8, a new variety of rice that increased yields by up to six times, was developed in the Philippines. Strains of crops resistant to drought and disease were also developed. High-yield varieties require large amounts of expensive artificial fertilizers and sometimes pesticides for best results.

HII region in astronomy, a region of extremely hot ionized hydrogen, surrounding one or more hot stars, visible as a bright patch or emission ◊nebula in the sky. The gas is ionized by the intense ultraviolet radiation from the stars within it. HII regions are often associated with interstellar clouds in which new stars are being born. An example is the ◊Orion Nebula. It takes its name from a spectroscopic notation in which HI represents neutral hydrogen (H) and HII represents ionized hydrogen (H^+).

hill figure in Britain, any of a number of figures, usually of animals, cut from the turf to reveal the underlying chalk. Their origins are variously attributed to Celts, Romans, Saxons, Druids, or Benedictine monks, although most are of modern rather than ancient construction.

hillfort European Iron Age site with massive banks and ditches for defence, used as both a military camp and a permanent settlement. Examples found across Europe, in particular France, central Germany, and the British Isles, include Heuneberg near Sigmaringen, Germany, Spinans Hill in County Wicklow, Ireland, and Maiden Castle, Dorset, England.

Iron Age Germanic peoples spread the tradition of forts with massive defences, timberwork reinforcements, and sometimes elaborately defended gateways with guardrooms, the whole being overlooked from a rampart walk. The ramparts usually follow the natural line of a hilltop and are laid out to avoid areas of dead ground.

hinge joint in vertebrates, a joint where movement occurs in one plane only. Examples are the elbow and knee, which are controlled by pairs of muscles, the ◊flexors and ◊extensors.

hinterland area that is served by a port or settlement (the central place) and included in its sphere of influence. The city of Rotterdam, the Netherlands, is the hinterland of a port.

hinting in computing, a method of reducing the effects of ◊aliasing in the appearance of ◊outline fonts. Hinting makes use of a series of priorities so that noticeable distortions, such as uneven stem weight, are corrected. ◊PostScript Type 1 and ◊TrueType fonts are hinted.

Hipparcos (acronym for ***high precision parallax collecting satellite***) satellite launched by the European Space Agency in 1989. Named after the Greek astronomer Hipparchus, it is the world's first ◊astrometry satellite and is providing precise positions, distances, colours, brightnesses, and apparent motions for over 100,000 stars.

hippopotamus ***Greek 'river horse'*** large herbivorous, short-legged, even-toed hoofed mammal. The **common hippopotamus** (*Hippopotamus amphibius*) is found in Africa. It weighs up to 3,200 kg/7,040 lb, stands about 1.6 m/5.25 ft tall, and has a

Hippocrates
(c. 460–c. 377 BC)

Greek physician, often called the founder of medicine. Important Hippocratic ideas include cleanliness (for patients and physicians), moderation in eating and drinking, letting nature take its course, and living where the air is good. He believed that health was the result of the 'humours' of the body being in balance; imbalance caused disease. These ideas were later adopted by Galen.

He was born and practised on the island of Kos, where he founded a medical school. He travelled throughout Greece and Asia Minor, and died in Larisa, Thessaly. He is known to have discovered aspirin in willow bark. The *Corpus Hippocraticum/Hippocratic Collection,* a group of some 70 works, is attributed to him but was probably not written by him, although the works outline his approach to medicine. They include *Aphorisms* and the **Hippocratic Oath,** which embodies the essence of medical ethics.

Mary Evans Picture Library

HIPPOPOTAMUS

A hippopotamus can open its jaws to an angle of 150° – almost a straight line (180°).

brown or slate-grey skin. It is an endangered species. (Family Hippopotamidae.)

Hippos are social animals and live in groups. Because they dehydrate rapidly (at least twice as quickly as humans), they must stay close to water. When underwater, adults need to breath every 2–5 minutes and calves every 30 seconds. When out of water, their skin exudes an oily red fluid that protects them against the Sun's ultraviolet rays. The hippopotamus spends the day wallowing in rivers or waterholes, only emerging at night to graze. It can eat up to 25–40 kg/55–88 lb of grass each night. The **pygmy hippopotamus** (*Choeropsis liberiensis*) lives in W Africa.

There are an estimated 157,000 hippos in Africa (1993 figure), but they are under threat from hunters because of the value of their meat, hides, and large canine teeth (up to 0.5 m/1.6 ft long), which are used as a substitute for ivory.

HIPPOPOTAMUS

http://www.seaworld.org/animal_bytes/hippopotamusab.html

Illustrated guide to the hippopotamus including information about genus, size, life span, habitat, gestation, diet, and a series of fun facts.

Hispano-Suiza car designed by a Swiss engineer Marc Birkigt (1878–1947) who emigrated to Barcelona where he founded a factory which produced cars during the period 1900–38, legendary for their handling, elegance, and speed.

During World War I the Hispano-Suiza company produced a light-alloy aero-engine for the French air force.

histamine inflammatory substance normally released in damaged tissues, which also accounts for many of the symptoms of ◊allergy. It is an amine, $C_5H_9N_3$. Substances that neutralize its activity are known as ◊antihistamines. Histamine was first described in 1911 by British physiologist Henry Dale (1875–1968).

histogram in statistics, a graph showing frequency of data, in which the horizontal axis details discrete units or class boundaries, and the vertical axis represents the frequency. Blocks are drawn such that their areas (rather than their height as in a ◊bar chart) are proportional to the frequencies within a class or across several class boundaries. There are no spaces between blocks.

histology study of plant and animal tissue by visual examination, usually with a ◊microscope.

◊Stains are often used to highlight structural characteristics such as the presence of starch or distribution of fats.

histology in medicine, the laboratory study of cells and tissues.

history in computing, a list of sites visited by a Web ◊browser during the current session. The history is usually stored as a list of page titles and is accessed via the browser's menu system. The purpose is to make it easy for users to go back to a recently visited site.

hit in computing, request sent to a ◊file server.

Sites on the World Wide Web often measure their popularity in numbers of hits. However, this is misleading, as a single Web page may be made up of many files, each of which counts as a hit when a user downloads the whole page. Counting individual visits is a better indication of a site's success.

HIV (abbreviation for ***human immunodeficiency virus***) the infectious agent that is believed to cause ◊AIDS. It was first discovered in 1983 by Luc Montagnier of the Pasteur Institute in Paris, who called it lymphocyte-associated virus (LAV). Independently, US scientist Robert Gallo of the National Cancer Institute in Bethesda, Maryland, claimed its discovery in 1984 and named it human T-lymphocytotrophic virus 3 (HTLV-III).

transmission Worldwide, heterosexual activity accounts for three-quarters of all HIV infections. In addition to heterosexual men and women, high-risk groups are homosexual and bisexual men, prostitutes, intravenous drug-users sharing needles, and haemophiliacs and other patients treated with contaminated blood products. The virus has a short life outside the body, which makes transmission of the infection by methods other than sexual contact, blood transfusion, and shared syringes extremely unlikely.

US researchers in 1995 developed an explanation of why HIV is transmitted mainly by heterosexual sex in Africa and Asia, and by homosexual sex and intravenous drug use in Europe and the USA. They found that the HIV variant subtype B – responsible for 90% of European and US cases – did not grow well in reproductive tract cells, whereas subtype E – common in developing countries – did grow well. If subtype E becomes more prevalent in Europe and the USA, infection patterns will probably change. The first case of subtype E in Britain was documented in May 1996.

the development of HIV Many people who have HIV in their blood are not ill; in fact, it was initially thought that during the delay between infection with HIV and the development of AIDS the virus lay dormant. However, US researchers estimated in 1995 that HIV reproduces at a rate of a billion viruses a day, even in individuals with no symptoms, but is held at bay by the immune system producing enough white blood cells (CD4 cells) to destroy them. Gradually, the virus mutates so much that the immune system is unable to continue to counteract; people with advanced AIDS have virtually no CD4 cells remaining. These results indicate the importance of treating HIV-positive individuals before symptoms develop, rather than delaying treatment until the onset of AIDS.

About 15% of babies born to HIV-positive mothers are themselves HIV-positive. A very small number of these babies (less than 3%) test negative for the virus some months later, a phenomenon yet to be explained.

HIV INFOWEB

www.infoweb.org/

Up-to-date information about HIV and AIDS treatments and other important resources for patients and their families, such as housing.

HIV statistics In 1997 there were an estimated just under 30 million (1% of the world's adult population) HIV infections in the world. In Sub-Saharan Africa there were an estimated 20 million HIV sufferers, in S and SE Asia 6 million, in South America 1.3 million, in North America 860,000, and Western Europe 150,000 (figures released by the United Nations AIDS programme, UNAIDS).

hoatzin tropical bird found only in the Amazon, resembling a small pheasant in size and appearance. The beak is thick and the facial skin blue. Adults are olive-coloured with white markings above and red-brown below. The hoatzin is the only bird in its family. (Species *Opisthocomus hoatzin,* family Opisthocomidae, order Galliformes.)

The young are hatched naked, with claws on their wings, which they use to crawl reptile-fashion about the tree; these claws later fall off. They fly only reluctantly and prefer to climb among branches using their wings – they cannot grip with their feet. Hoatzin are chiefly arboreal, nesting on low trees or shrubs, and feeding on leaves and fruit.

hobby small ◊falcon found across Europe and N Asia. It is about 30 cm/1 ft long, with a grey-blue back, streaked front, and chestnut thighs. It is found in open woods and heaths, and feeds on insects and small birds. (Species *Falco subbuteo.*)

Hodgkin's disease or ***lymphadenoma*** rare form of cancer mainly affecting the lymph nodes and spleen. It undermines the immune system, leaving the sufferer susceptible to infection.

However, it responds well to radiotherapy and ◊cytotoxic drugs, and long-term survival is usual.

HODGKIN'S DISEASE INFORMATION

http://www.cancer.org/cidSpecificCancers/hodgkins/index.html

Comprehensive information on lymphadenoma from the American Cancer Society. Written in easily understandable language, this guide explains the normal functions of the lymphatic system before describing the disease. There is information on risk factors, causes, diagnosis, and treatment of Hodgkin's disease, and latest research news. Further sources of information are also indicated.

Hoffman, Albert

Swiss-born, US physician who, in 1943, accidentally discovered lysergic acid diethylamide (LSD), the most potent psychoactive drug ever known. LSD causes hallucinatory effects, paranoia, and depression, and is illegal except for research purposes.

Hoffman, together with Swiss chemist Arthur Stoll, produced lysergic acid diethylamide (LSD) in 1938 while trying to synthesize a new drug for the treatment of headaches. Since the new drug appeared to have no analgesic (pain-relieving) effect on laboratory animals, it remained untouched on a shelf for five years. Hoffman decided to perform further tests on LSD in 1943, during which he accidentally ingested an unknown amount of the drug. He described his first experience of LSD intoxication as 'a kind of drunkenness which was not unpleasant and which was characterized by extreme activity of the imagination'. LSD was later shown to block or inhibit the action of the neurotransmitter seratonin in the brain.

Hoffman's voltameter in chemistry, an apparatus for collecting gases produced by the ◊electrolysis of a liquid.

It consists of a vertical E-shaped glass tube with taps at the upper ends of the outer limbs and a reservoir at the top of the central limb. Platinum electrodes fused into the lower ends of the outer limbs are connected to a source of direct current. At the beginning of an experiment, the outer limbs are completely filled with electrolyte by opening the taps. The taps are then closed and the current switched on. Gases evolved at the electrodes bubble up the outer limbs and collect at the top, where they can be measured.

hog any member of the ◊pig family. The **river hog** (*Potamochoerus porcus*) lives in Africa, south of the Sahara. Reddish or black, up to 1.3 m/4.2 ft long plus tail, and 90 cm/3 ft at the shoulder, this gregarious animal roots for food in many types of habitat. The **giant forest hog** (*Hylochoerus meinerzthageni*) lives in thick forests of central Africa and grows up to 1.9 m/6 ft long. The ◊wart hog **is another African wild pig. The pygmy hog** *Sus salvanus,* the smallest of the pig family, is about 65 cm long (25 cm at the shoulder) and weighs 8–9 kg.

hognose North American colubrine, nonvenomous snake with a flattened head and a projecting snout for burrowing.

classification The hognose is in genus *Heterodon,* family Elapidae, suborder Serpentes, order Squamata, class Reptilia.

hogweed any of a group of plants belonging to the carrot family. The giant hogweed (*H. mantegazzianum*) grows over 3 m/9 ft high. (Genus *Heracleum,* family Umbelliferae.)

holdfast organ found at the base of many seaweeds, attaching them to the sea bed. It may be a flattened, suckerlike structure, or dissected and fingerlike, growing into rock crevices and firmly anchoring the plant.

holism in philosophy, the concept that the whole is greater than the sum of its parts.

holistic medicine umbrella term for an approach that virtually all alternative therapies profess, which considers the overall health and lifestyle profile of a patient, and treats specific ailments not primarily as conditions to be alleviated but rather as symptoms of more fundamental disease.

A physician is obligated to consider more than a diseased organ, more even than the whole man – he must view the man in his world.

HARVEY CUSHING US surgeon.
Quoted in René Dubos *Man Adapting*

holly any of a group of trees or shrubs that includes the English Christmas holly (*I. aquifolium*), an evergreen with spiny, glossy leaves, small white flowers, and poisonous scarlet berries on the female tree. Leaves of the Brazilian holly (*I. paraguayensis*) are used to make the tea **yerba maté**. (Genus *Ilex,* family Aquifoliaceae.)

hollyhock tall flowering plant belonging to the mallow family. *A. rosea,* originally a native of Asia, produces spikes of large white, yellow, pink, or red flowers, 3 m/10 ft high when cultivated as a biennial; it is a popular cottage garden plant. (Genus *Althaea,* family Malvaceae.)

holmium ***Latin*** *Holmia* ***'Stockholm'*** silvery, metallic element of the ◊lanthanide series, symbol Ho, atomic number 67, relative atomic mass 164.93. It occurs in combination with other rare-earth metals and in various minerals such as gadolinite. Its compounds are highly magnetic.

The element was discovered in 1878, spectroscopically, by the Swiss chemists J L Soret and Delafontaine, and independently in 1879 by Swedish chemist Per Cleve (1840–1905), who named it after Stockholm, near which it was found.

Holocene epoch of geological time that began 10,000 years ago, the second and current epoch of the Quaternary period. During this epoch the glaciers retreated, the climate became warmer, and humans developed significantly.

hologram three-dimensional image produced by holography. Small, inexpensive ◊holograms appear on credit cards and software licences to guarantee their authenticity.

holography method of producing three-dimensional (3-D) images, called ◊holograms, by means of ◊laser light. Holography uses a photographic technique (involving the splitting of a laser beam into two beams) to produce a picture, or hologram, that contains 3-D information about the object photographed. Some holograms show meaningless patterns in ordinary light and produce a 3-D image only when laser light is projected through them, but reflection holograms produce images when ordinary light is reflected from them (as found on credit cards).

Although the possibility of holography was suggested as early as 1947 (by Hungarian-born British physicist Dennis Gabor), it could not be demonstrated until a pure coherent light source, the laser, became available in 1963. The first laser-recorded holograms were created by Emmett Leith and Juris Upatnieks at the University of Michigan, USA, and Yuri Denisyuk in the Soviet Union.

The technique of holography is also applicable to sound, and bats may navigate by ultrasonic holography. Holographic techniques also have applications in storing dental records, detecting stresses and strains in construction and in retail goods, detecting forged paintings and documents, and producing three-dimensional body scans. The technique of detecting strains is of widespread application. It involves making two different holograms of an object on one plate, the object being stressed between exposures. If the object has distorted during stressing, the hologram will be greatly changed, and the distortion readily apparent.

Using holography, digital data can be recorded page by page in a crystal. In 1993 10,000 pages (100 megabytes) of digital data were stored in an iron-doped lithium nobate crystal measuring 1 cm^3.

homeopathy alternative spelling of ◊homoeopathy.

homeostasis maintenance of a constant internal state in an organism, particularly with regard to pH, salt concentration, temperature, and blood sugar levels. Stable conditions are important for the efficient functioning of the ◊enzyme reactions within the cells, which affect the performance of the entire organism.

homeothermy maintenance of a constant body temperature in endothermic (warm-blooded) animals, by the use of chemical processes to compensate for heat loss or gain when external temperatures change. Such processes include generation of heat by the breakdown of food and the contraction of muscles, and loss of heat by sweating, panting, and other means.

Mammals and birds are homeotherms, whereas invertebrates, fish, amphibians, and reptiles are cold-blooded or poikilotherms. Homeotherms generally have a layer of insulating material to retain heat, such as fur, feathers, or fat (see ◊blubber). Their metabolism functions more efficiently due to homeothermy, enabling them to remain active under most climatic conditions.

home page in computing, opening page on a particular site on the World Wide Web. The term is also used for the page which loads automatically when a user opens a Web ◊browser, and for a user's own personal Web pages.

Many Internet Service Providers provide free space to allow all their users to create and maintain their own home pages.

homoeopathy or ***homeopathy*** system of alternative medicine based on the principle that symptoms of disease are part of the body's self-healing processes, and on the practice of administering extremely diluted doses of natural substances found to produce in a healthy person the symptoms manifest in the illness being treated. Developed by German physician Samuel Hahnemann (1755–1843), the system is widely practised today as an alternative to allopathic (orthodox) medicine, and many controlled tests and

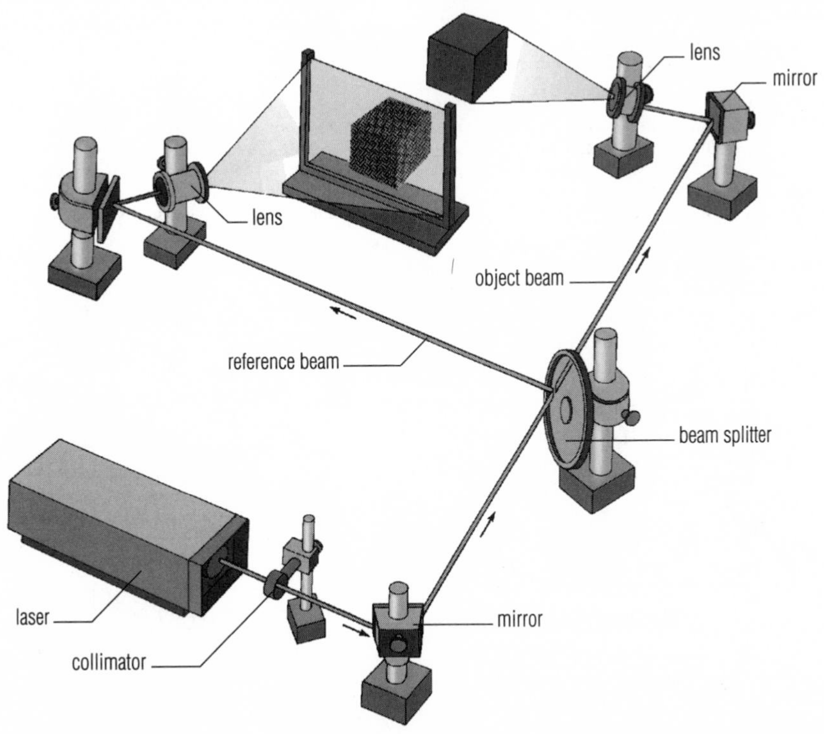

holography *Recording a transmission hologram. Light from a laser is divided into two beams. One beam goes directly to the photographic plate. The other beam reflects off the object before hitting the photographic plate. The two beams combine to produce a pattern on the plate which contains information about the 3-D shape of the object. If the exposed and developed plate is illuminated by laser light, the pattern can be seen as a 3-D picture of the object.*

achieved cures testify its efficacy.

In 1992, the German health authority, the *Bundesgesundheitsamt,* banned 50 herbal and homeopathic remedies containing ◊alkaloids because they are toxic, and set dose limits on 550 other natural remedies.

homogeneous reaction in chemistry, a reaction where there is no interface between the components. The term applies to all reactions where only gases are involved or where all the components are in solution.

Homo habilis tool-using hominid living about 2.5 million years ago in Africa; see ◊human species, origins of.

> *The Farmer will never be happy again; / He carries his heart in his boots; / For either the rain is destroying his grain / Or the drought is destroying his roots.*
>
> ALAN PATRICK HERBERT English writer and politician. 'The Farmer'

homologous in biology, a term describing an organ or structure possessed by members of different taxonomic groups (for example, species, genera, families, orders) that originally derived from the same structure in a common ancestor. The wing of a bat, the arm of a monkey, and the flipper of a seal are homologous because they all derive from the forelimb of an ancestral mammal.

homologous series any of a number of series of organic chemicals with similar chemical properties in which members differ by a constant relative molecular mass.

Alkanes (paraffins), alkenes (olefins), and alkynes (acetylenes) form such series in which members differ in mass by 14, 12, and 10 atomic mass units respectively. For example, the alkane homologous series begins with methane (CH_4), ethane (C_2H_6), propane (C_3H_8), butane (C_4H_{10}), and pentane (C_5H_{12}), each member differing from the previous one by a CH_2 group (or 14 atomic mass units).

homozygous in a living organism, having two identical ◊alleles for a given trait. Individuals homozygous for a trait always breed true; that is, they produce offspring that resemble them in appearance when bred with a genetically similar individual; inbred varieties or species are homozygous for almost all traits.

◊Recessive alleles are only expressed in the homozygous condition. See also ◊heterozygous.

honey sweet syrup produced by honey ◊bees from the nectar of flowers. It is stored in honeycombs and made in excess of their needs as food for the winter. Honey comprises various sugars, mainly laevulose and dextrose, with enzymes, colouring matter, acids, and pollen grains. It has antibacterial properties and was widely used in ancient Egypt, Greece, and Rome as a wound salve. It is still popular for sore throats, in hot drinks or in lozenges.

honeycomb moth another name for the ◊wax moth.

honeycomb worm colonial marine worm *Sabellaria alveolata* named after the hexagonal tubes made of cemented sand and shell fragments in which it lives low down on rocky sandy beaches. It feeds on organic material suspended in the water. It spends its larval stage as plankton.

honeyeater or ***honey-sucker*** any of a group of small, brightly coloured birds with long, curved beaks and long tails, native to Australia. They have a long tongue divided into four at the end to form a brush for collecting nectar from flowers. (Family Meliphagidae.)

Larger honeyeaters, such as the **blue-faced honeyeater** (*Entomyza cyanotis*) of NE Australia, which is 30 cm/12 in long, also eat insects and fruit. The blood-bird is a honeyeater.

Honeyeaters from Australasia colonized Hawaii, where four distinct species evolved of which only one, the *Kauaioo,* survives; it too was thought to be extinct but was rediscovered in 1960.

honey guide in botany, line or spot on the petals of a flower that indicate to pollinating insects the position of the nectaries (see ◊nectar) within the flower. The orange dot on the lower lip of the toadflax flower (*Linaria vulgaris*) is an example. Sometimes the markings reflect only ultraviolet light, which can be seen by many insects although it is not visible to the human eye.

honey possum or ***honey mouse*** or ***noolbenger*** tiny marsupial that is native of western Australia. It lives in trees, and feeds on insects and honey, which it extracts from flowers with its long extensile tongue.

classification The honey possum *Tarsipes spenserae* is the only member of the family Tarsipedidae, order Marsupialia, class Mammalia.

honeysuckle vine or shrub found in temperate regions of the world. The common honeysuckle or woodbine (*L. periclymenum*) of Europe is a climbing plant with sweet-scented flowers, reddish and yellow-tinted outside and creamy white inside; it now grows in the northeastern USA. (Genus *Lonicera,* family Caprifoliaceae.)

The North American trumpet honeysuckle (*L. sempervirens*) has unusual vaselike flowers and includes scarlet and yellow varieties.

hoof horny covering that protects the sensitive parts of the foot of an animal. The possession of hooves is characteristic of the orders Artiodactyla (even-toed ungulates such as deer and cattle), and Perissodactyla (horses, tapirs, and rhinoceroses).

alkane	alcohol	aldehyde	ketone	carboxylic acid	alkene
CH_4 methane	CH_3OH methanol	HCHO methanal	—	HCOOH methanoic acid	—
CH_3CH_3 ethane	CH_3CH_2OH ethanol	CH_3CHO ethanal	—	CH_3COOH ethanoic acid	CH_2CH_2 ethene
$CH_3CH_2CH_3$ propane	$CH_3CH_2CH_2OH$ propanol	CH_3CH_2CHO propanal	CH_3COCH_3 propanone	CH_3CH_2COOH propanoic acid	CH_2CHCH_3 propene
methane	methanol	methanal	propanone	methanoic acid	ethene

homologous series

The flexibility of the hoof is promoted by a fluid secreted by the keratogenous (horn-producing) membrane. The cloven hoof of the Artiodactyla has been evolved for walking and climbing on irregular surfaces by the formation of a separate hoof on each digit of the foot. Horses walk on the third digit of the foot, while cattle walk on the third and fourth.

Hooke, Robert (1635–1703)

English scientist and inventor, originator of Hooke's law, and considered the foremost mechanic of his time. His inventions included a telegraph system, the spirit level, marine barometer, and sea gauge. He coined the term 'cell' in biology.

He studied elasticity, furthered the sciences of mechanics and microscopy, invented the hairspring regulator in timepieces, perfected the air pump, and helped improve such scientific instruments as microscopes, telescopes, and barometers. His work on gravitation and in optics contributed to the achievements of his contemporary Isaac Newton.

Hooke's law law stating that the deformation of a body is proportional to the magnitude of the deforming force, provided that the body's elastic limit (see ◊elasticity) is not exceeded. If the elastic limit is not reached, the body will return to its original size once the force is removed. The law was discovered by Robert Hooke 1676.

For example, if a spring is stretched by 2 cm by a weight of 1 N, it will be stretched by 4 cm by a weight of 2 N, and so on; however, once the load exceeds the elastic limit for the spring, Hooke's law will no longer be obeyed and each successive increase in weight will result in a greater extension until finally the spring breaks.

hookworm parasitic roundworm (see ◊worm) with hooks around its mouth. It lives mainly in tropical and subtropical regions, but also in humid areas in temperate climates. The eggs are hatched in damp soil, and the larvae bore into the host's skin, usually through the soles of the feet. They make their way to the small intestine, where they live by sucking blood. The eggs are expelled with faeces, and the cycle starts again. The human hookworm causes anaemia, weakness, and abdominal pain. It is common in areas where defecation occurs outdoors. (Genus *Necator.*)

hoopoe bird slightly larger than a thrush, with a long, thin, slightly downward-curving bill and a bright pinkish-buff crest tipped with black that expands into a fan shape on top of the head. The wings and tail are banded with black and white, and the rest of the plumage is buff-coloured. The hoopoe is found throughout southern Europe and Asia down to southern Africa, India, Malaya. (Species *Upupa epops,* family Upupidae, order Coraciiformes.)

hoop pine softwood timber tree *Araucaria cunninghamii* of NE New South Wales and Queensland in Australia, and Papua New Guinea.

Hoover Dam highest concrete dam in the USA, 221 m/726 ft, on the Colorado River at the Arizona–Nevada border. It was built 1931–36. Known as **Boulder Dam** 1933–47, its name was restored by President Truman as the reputation of the former president, Herbert Hoover, was revived. It impounds Lake Mead, and has a hydroelectric power capacity of 1,300 megawatts.

hop in computing, on the Internet, an intermediate stage of the journey taken by a message travelling from one site to another.

Internet messages must travel through many machines to get to their destinations. The exact route is recorded in the ◊bang path.

Hope's apparatus in physics, an apparatus used to demonstrate the temperature at which water has its maximum density. It is named after Thomas Charles Hope (1766–1844).

It consists of a vertical cylindrical vessel fitted with horizontal thermometers through its sides near the top and bottom, and surrounded at the centre by a ledge that holds a freezing mixture (ice and salt). When the cylinder is filled with water, this gradually cools, the denser water sinking to the bottom; eventually the upper thermometer records 0°C/32°F (the freezing point of water) and the lower one has a constant reading of 4°C/39°F (the temperature at which water is most dense).

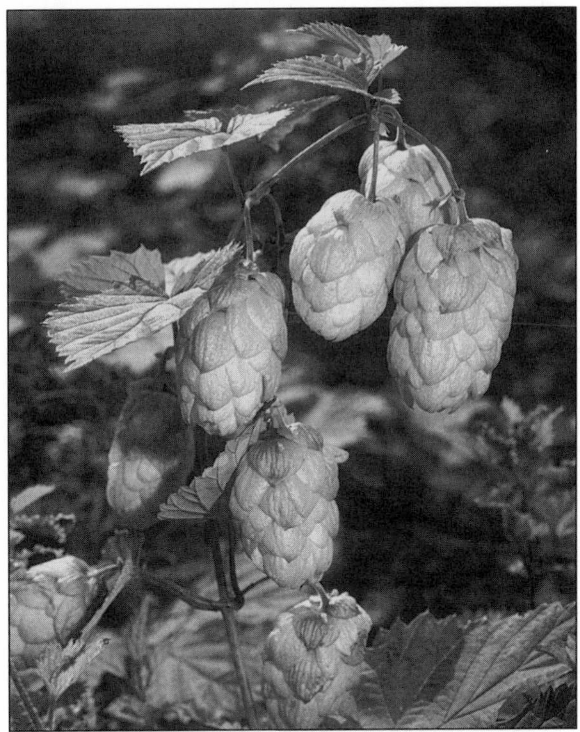

hops *A female hop plant showing the fruits which, in cultivated varieties, are used in brewing. The genus* Humulus *is a small one, with* H. lupulus *coming from Europe and W Asia and one species each from North America and E Asia.* *Premaphotos Wildlife*

hops female fruit heads of the hop plant *Humulus lupulus,* family Cannabiaceae; these are dried and used as a tonic and in flavouring beer. In designated areas in Europe, no male hops may be grown, since seedless hops produced by the unpollinated female plant contain a greater proportion of the alpha acid that gives beer its bitter taste.

horehound any of a group of plants belonging to the mint family. The white horehound (*M. vulgare*), found in Europe, N Africa, and W Asia and naturalized in North America, has a thick hairy stem and clusters of dull white flowers; it has medicinal uses. (Genus *Marrubium,* family Labiatae.)

horizon in astronomy, the ◊great circle dividing the visible part of the sky from the part hidden by the Earth.

horizon the limit to which one can see across the surface of the sea or a level plain, that is, about 5 km/3 mi at 1.5 m/5 ft above sea level, and about 65 km/40 mi at 300 m/1,000 ft.

hormone *Greek 'arousing'* secretion of the ◊endocrine glands, concerned with control of body functions. The major glands are the thyroid, parathyroid, pituitary, adrenal, pancreas, ovary, and testis. Hormones bring about changes in the functions of various organs according to the body's requirements. The ◊hypothalamus, which adjoins the pituitary gland, at the base of the brain, is a control centre for overall coordination of hormone secretion; the thyroid hormones determine the rate of general body chemistry; the adrenal hormones prepare the organism during stress for 'fight or flight'; and the sexual hormones such as oestrogen govern reproductive functions.

There are also hormone-secreting cells in the kidney, liver, gastrointestinal tract, thymus (in the neck), pineal (in the brain), and placenta. Many diseases due to hormone deficiency can be relieved with hormone preparations.

hormone-replacement therapy (HRT) use of ◊oestrogen and progesterone to help limit the unpleasant effects of the menopause in women. The treatment was first used in the 1970s.

At the menopause, the ovaries cease to secrete natural oestrogen. This results in a number of symptoms, including hot flushes, anxiety, and a change in the pattern of menstrual bleeding. It is also associated with osteoporosis, or a thinning of bones, leading to an increased incidence of fractures, frequently of the hip, in older women. Oestrogen preparations, taken to replace the decline in natural hormone levels, combined with regular exercise can help to maintain bone strength in women. In order to improve bone density, however, HRT must be taken for five years, during which time the woman will continue to menstruate. Many women do not find this acceptable.

horn broad term for a hardened processes on the heads of some members of order Artiodactyla: deer, antelopes, cattle, goats, and sheep; and the rhinoceroses in order Perissodactyla. They are used usually for sparring rather than serious fighting, often between members of the same species rather than against predators.

The structure of horn shows immense variation, some being primarily made of bone, as in the antlers of deer; others of the substance called horn, as in cattle or antelopes; and others of compressed hair, as in rhinoceroses. Antlers are usually shed and regrown every year, while true horns are grown for life.

In most horned species they are possessed by both sexes, but in some species horns are limited to males.

hornbeam any of a group of trees belonging to the birch family. They have oval leaves with toothed edges and hanging clusters of flowers, each with a nutlike seed attached to the base. The trunk is usually twisted, with smooth grey bark. (Genus *Carpinus,* family Betulaceae.)

hornbill any of a group of omnivorous birds found in Africa, India, and Malaysia. They are about 1 m/3 ft long, and have powerful down-curved beaks, usually surmounted by a bony growth or casque. During the breeding season, the female walls herself into a hole in a tree and does not emerge until the young are hatched. There are about 45 species. (Family Bucerotidae, order Coraciiformes.)

Hornbills feed chiefly on the ground, their food consisting of insects, small mammals, and reptiles. The **great hornbill** (*Buceros bicornis*) of SE Asia can reach up to 1.3 m/4.3 ft in length.

The **southern ground hornbill** lives in groups of about three to five birds (though sometimes as many as ten) with only one breeding pair, and the rest acting as helpers. On average, only one chick is reared successfully every nine years. Lifespan can be 40 years or more.

hornblende green or black rock-forming mineral, one of the amphiboles. It is a hydrous ◊silicate composed mainly of calcium, iron, magnesium, and aluminium in addition to the silicon and oxygen that are common to all silicates. Hornblende is found in both igneous and metamorphic rocks and can be recognized by its colour and prismatic shape.

horned toad or ***horned lizard*** common name for several species of lizard. Horned toads have large spines or horns on their heads and pointed scales, vary from 7–12 cm/3–5 in long, and are found in arid areas of North and Central America. An example is the desert-dwelling spiny moloch.

When attacked, horned toads inflate the body with air, gape, hiss, and bite.

classification Horned toads are in the genus *Phrynosoma,* family Iguanidae, suborder Sauria, order Squamata, class Reptilia.

horned viper northeast African snake. It is remarkable for the possession of a large spiky scale above each eye

classification The horned viper *Cerastes cornutus* belongs to the family Viperidae, suborder Serpentes, order Squamata, class Reptilia.

hornet type of ◊wasp.

hornfels ◊metamorphic rock formed by rocks heated by contact with a hot igneous body. It is fine-grained, brittle, and lacks foliation (a planar structure).

Hornfels may contain minerals only formed under conditions of great heat, such as andalusite, Al_2SiO_5, and cordierite, $(Mg,Fe)_2Al_4Si_5O_{18}$. This rock, originating from sedimentary rock strata, is found in contact with large igneous ◊intrusions where it represents the heat-altered equivalent of the surrounding clays. Its hardness makes it suitable for road building and railway ballast.

horn fly small fly that is a pest of cattle and other animals.

classification Horn flies are in the family Muscidae, class Insecta, phylum Arthropoda.

hornwort nonvascular plant (with no 'veins' to carry water and food), related to the ◊liverworts and ◊mosses. Hornworts are found in warm climates, growing on moist shaded soil. (Class Anthocerotae, order Bryophyta.)

The name is also given to a group of aquatic flowering plants which are found in slow-moving water. They have whorls of finely divided leaves and may grow up to 2 m/7 ft long. (Genus *Ceratophyllum,* family Ceratophyllaceae.)

Like liverworts and mosses, the bryophyte hornworts exist in two different reproductive forms, sexual and asexual, which appear alternately (see ◊alternation of generations). A leafy plant body, or gametophyte, produces gametes, or sex cells, and a small horned form, or sporophyte, which grows upwards from the gametophyte, produces spores. Unlike the sporophytes of mosses and liverworts, the hornwort sporophyte survives after the gametophyte has died.

horse hoofed, odd-toed, grazing mammal belonging to the same family as zebras and asses. The many breeds of domestic horse of Euro-Asian origin range in colour from white to grey, brown, and black. The yellow-brown **Mongolian wild horse**, or **Przewalski's horse** (*Equus przewalskii*), named after its Polish 'discoverer' about 1880, is the only surviving species of wild horse. (Species *Equus caballus,* family Equidae.)

Przewalski's horse became extinct in the wild because of hunting and competition with domestic animals for food; about 800 survive in captivity. However, in the late 1990s 55 Przewalski's horses were successfully reintroduced to the wild in Mongolia.

horse chestnut any of a group of trees, especially *A. hippocastanum,* originally from SE Europe but widely planted elsewhere. Horse chestnuts have large palmate (five-lobed) leaves, showy upright spikes of white, pink, or red flowers, and large, shiny, inedible seeds (**conkers**) in prickly green capsules. The horse chestnut is not related to the true chestnut. In North America it is called buckeye. (Genus *Aesculus,* family Hippocastanaceae.)

horsefly any of over 2,500 species of fly. The females suck blood from horses, cattle, and humans; the males live on plants and suck nectar. The larvae are carnivorous. (Family Tabanidae.)

horsefly *A female horsefly, or cleg,* Haematopota pluvialis *feeding on human blood. The bite of these insects is painful and in humans often produces a large swelling that can take a long time to heal. Premaphotos Wildlife*

HORSEFLY

There is a fly larva that eats toads. The horsefly larva *Tabanus punctifer* lives in the soft mud at the edges of ponds. It kills tiny, newly metamorphosed spadefoot toads by injecting them with venom, and then sucks out their body fluids.

horsepower imperial unit (abbreviation hp) of power, now replaced by the ◊watt. It was first used by the engineer James ◊Watt, who employed it to compare the power of steam engines with that of horses.

horseradish hardy perennial plant, native to SE Europe but naturalized elsewhere. The thick cream-coloured root is strong-tasting and is often made into a savoury sauce to accompany food. (*Armoracia rusticana,* family Cruciferae.)

horsetail plant related to ferns and club mosses; some species are also called **scouring rush**. There are about 35 living species, bearing their spores on cones at the stem tip. The upright stems are ribbed and often have spaced whorls of branches. Today they are of modest size, but hundreds of millions of years ago giant treelike forms existed. (Genus *Equisetum,* order Equisetales.)

horticulture art and science of growing flowers, fruit, and vegetables. Horticulture is practised in gardens and orchards, along with millions of acres of land devoted to vegetable farming. Some areas, like California, have specialized in horticulture because they have the mild climate and light fertile soil most suited to these crops.

host in biology, an organism that is parasitized by another. In ◊commensalism, the partner that does not benefit may also be called the host.

hot key in computing, a key stroke (or sequence of key strokes) that triggers a memory-resident program. Such programs are called ◊terminate and stay resident. Hot keys should be chosen so that they do not conflict with key sequences in commonly used applications.

hotlist in computing, stored list of favourite sites which allows users to move quickly to frequently used resources. See also ◊bookmark.

HOTOL (acronym for ***horizontal takeoff and landing***) reusable hypersonic spaceplane invented by British engineer Alan Bond in 1983 but never put into production.

HOTOL was to be a single-stage vehicle that could take off and land on a runway. It featured a revolutionary dual-purpose engine that enabled it to carry far less oxygen than a conventional spaceplane: it functioned as a jet engine during the initial stage of flight, taking in oxygen from the surrounding air; when the air became too thin, it was converted into a rocket, burning oxygen from an onboard supply. The project was developed by British Aerospace and Rolls-Royce but foundered for lack of capital in 1988.

hot spot in geology, isolated rising plume of molten mantle material that may rise to the surface of the Earth's crust creating features such as volcanoes, chains of ocean islands, seamounts, and rifts in continents. Hot spots occur beneath the interiors of tectonic plates and so differ from areas of volcanic activity at plate margins (see ◊plate tectonics). Examples of features made by hot spots are Iceland in the Atlantic Ocean, and in the Pacific Ocean the Hawaiian Islands and Emperor Seamount chain, and the Galápagos Islands.

Hot spots are responsible for large amounts of volcanic activity within tectonic plates rather than at plate margins. Volcanism from a hot spot formed the unique features of Yellowstone National Park, Wyoming, USA. The same hot spot that built Iceland atop the mid-Atlantic ridge in the North Atlantic Ocean also produced the voluminous volcanic rocks of the Isle of Skye, Scotland, at a time before these regions were rifted apart by the opening of the Atlantic Ocean.

Chains of volcanic seamounts trace the movements of tectonic plates as they pass over hot spots. Immediately above a hot spot on oceanic crust a volcano will form. This volcano is then carried away by plate tectonic movement, and becomes extinct. A new volcano forms beside it, again above the hot spot. The result is an active volcano and a chain of increasingly old and eroded extinct volcanoes stretching away along the line traced by the plate movement. The chain of volcanoes comprising the Hawaiian Islands and Emperor Seamounts formed in this way.

hot-swapping in computing, a technique that allows a user to exchange components without having to shut down the entire system.

The most common example of hot-swapping is ◊PCMCIA (personal computer memory card interface adapter) components: a user with only one PCMCIA slot can exchange a modem for a network card or hard disc while the machine is running. Special software recognizes the components and allows their immediate use.

hour period of time comprising 60 minutes; 24 hours make one calendar day.

housefly fly found in and around human dwellings, especially *M. domestica,* a common worldwide species. Houseflies are grey and have mouthparts adapted for drinking liquids and sucking moisture from food and manure. (Genus *Musca.*)

HOUSEFLY

In nine months, a housefly could lay enough eggs to produce a layer of flies that would cover all of Germany to a depth of 14 m/47 ft.

hovercraft vehicle that rides on a cushion of high-pressure air, free from all contact with the surface beneath, invented by British engineer Christopher Cockerell in 1959. Hovercraft need a smooth terrain when operating overland and are best adapted to use on waterways. They are useful in places where harbours have not been established.

Large hovercraft (SR-N4) operate a swift car-ferry service across the English Channel, taking only about 35 minutes between Dover and Calais. They are fitted with a flexible 'skirt' that helps maintain the air cushion.

A military version made of fibreglass, the M-10, is tough manoeuvrable, and less noisy. *See illustration on page 377.*

hoverfly brightly coloured winged insect. Hoverflies usually have spots, stripes, or bands of yellow or brown against a dark-coloured background, sometimes with dense hair covering the body surface. Many resemble bees, bumble bees, and wasps (displaying Batesian ◊mimicry) and most adults feed on nectar and pollen.

classification Hoverflies are members of the large family Syrphidae (numbering over 2,500 species), suborder Cyclorrhapha, order Diptera, class Insecta, phylum Arthropoda.

One of the most characteristic features of hoverflies is the presence of a longitudinal false vein in the wing.

larva The larvae show remarkable variations in appearance and feeding habits. They may feed externally on plants or they may be internal feeders, attacking the bulbs; for example the **narcissus fly**, *Merodon equestris.* Many are carnivorous, feeding on ◊scale insects, greenfly (◊aphids), and other insects that harm commercial crops.

The larvae may also feed on rotting wood or the decaying organic matter in stagnant pools; for example the **rat-tailed maggot**, larva of the drone fly *Eristalis tenax* is found in polluted pools. They breathe by extending their tail breathing tubes to reach the surface of the water.

howler monkey widely distributed large Central and South American monkey. Howler monkeys are tree-dwelling and feed on fruit and leaves. They have a prominent, hairless face and deep jaw, and the tail is long and prehensile.

Howler monkeys howl at dawn to demarcate territory. The howling is produced by the unusually developed egg-shaped hyoid bone at the upper end of the wind-pipe, in a swelling beneath the chin; the whole forms a hollow, resonant soundbox.
classification Howler monkeys are in genus *Alouatta,* family Cebidae, order Primates.

HP in computing, abbreviation for ◊Hewlett-Packard.

hp abbreviation for ◊horsepower.

HPGL (abbreviation for ***Hewlett Packard Graphics Language***) file format used in ◊vector graphics. HPGL is often generated by ◊CAD systems.

href in computing, a tag in HTML (hypertext markup language) that indicates that the following text is a link either to another portion of the same document or to an external document on the same or a remote site.

ht abbreviation for height.

HTML (abbreviation for ***Hypertext Markup Language***) standard for structuring and describing a document on the ◊World Wide Web. The HTML standard provides labels for constituent parts of a document (for example headings and paragraphs) and permits the inclusion of images, sounds, and 'hyperlinks' to other documents. A ◊browser program is then used to convert this information into a graphical document on-screen. The specifications for HTML version 4, called Dynamic HTML, were adopted at the end of 1997.

HTML is a specific example of ◊SGML (the international standard for text encoding). As such it is not a rigid standard but is constantly being improved to incorporate new features and allow greater freedom of design.

HTML extension in computing, any proprietary addition to the standard specification of HTML (hypertext markup language).

Both Microsoft and Netscape, publishers of the two leading Web ◊browsers, have built in such extensions, which are controversial as they clash with the basic ideal that the Net should operate on open standards which allow interoperability. In general, any browser should be able to log on to any site and be able to access most of its information, but the features implemented with proprietary extensions will only display correctly with a browser that supports those extensions.

HTTP (abbreviation for ***Hypertext Transfer Protocol***) in computing, the ◊protocol used for communications between client (the Web ◊browser) and ◊server on the World Wide Web.

hub in computing, central distribution point in a computer ◊network.

Hubble classification in astronomy, a scheme for classifying ◊galaxies according to their shapes, originally devised by the US astronomer Edwin Hubble in the 1920s.

Elliptical galaxies are classed from type E0 to E7, where the figure denotes the degree of ellipticity. An E0 galaxy appears circular to an observer, while an E7 is highly elliptical (this is based on the apparent shape; the true shape, distorted by foreshortening, may be quite different.) **Spiral galaxies** are classed as type Sa, Sb, or Sc, where Sa is a tightly wound spiral with a large central bulge and Sc is loosely wound with a small bulge. Intermediate types are denoted by Sab or Sbc. **Barred spiral galaxies**, which have a prominent bar across their centres, are similarly classed as type SBa, SBb, or SBc with intermediates SBab or SBbc. **Lenticular galaxies**, which have no spiral arms, are classed as type S0. **Irregular galaxies**, type Irr, can be subdivided into Irr I, which resemble poorly formed spirals, and Irr II which are otherwise

The Hubble classification was once believed to reveal an evolutionary sequence (from ellipticals to spirals) but this is now known not to be the case. Our own ◊Milky Way Galaxy is classified as type Sb or Sc, but may have a bar.

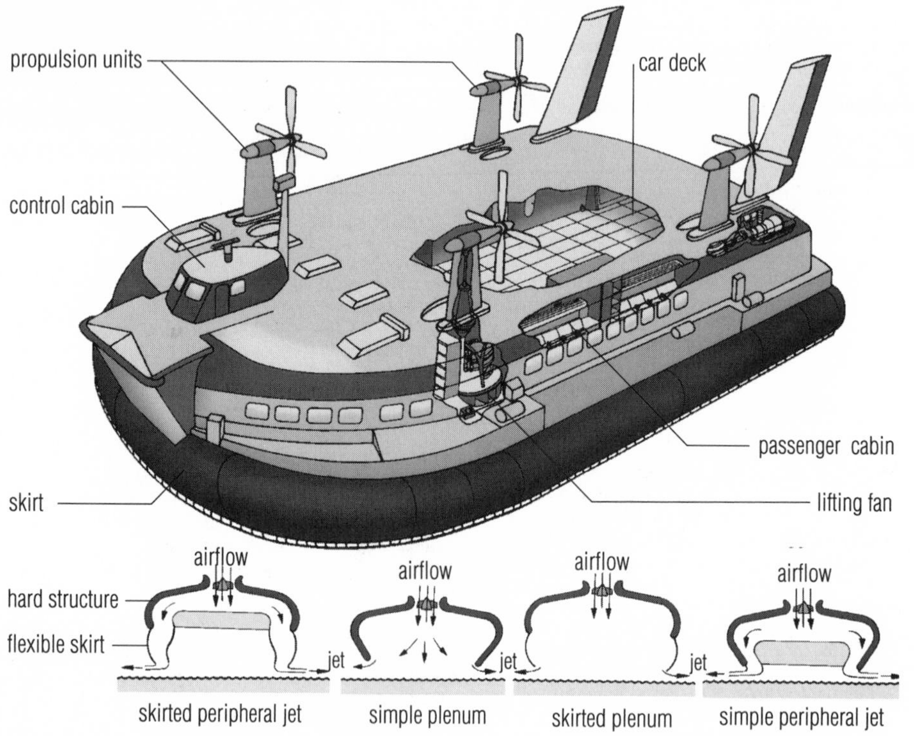

hovercraft *There are several alternative ways of containing the cushion of air beneath the hull of a hovercraft. The passenger-carrying hovercraft that sails across the English Channel has a flexible skirt; other systems are the open plenum and the peripheral jet.*

Hubble's constant in astronomy, a measure of the rate at which the universe is expanding, named after Edwin Hubble. Observations suggest that galaxies are moving apart at a rate of 50–100 kps/30–60 mps for every million ◊parsecs of distance. This means that the universe, which began at one point according to the ◊Big Bang theory, is between 10 billion and 20 billion years old (probably closer to 20). Observations by the Hubble Space Telescope in 1996 produced a revised constant of 73 kps/45 mps.

Hubble's law the law that relates a galaxy's distance from us to its speed of recession as the universe expands, announced in 1929 by Edwin Hubble. He found that galaxies are moving apart at speeds that increase in direct proportion to their distance apart. The rate of expansion is known as Hubble's constant.

Hubble Space Telescope (HST) space-based astronomical observing facility, orbiting the Earth at an altitude of 610 km/380 mi. It consists of a 2.4 m/94 in telescope and four complimentary scientific instruments, is roughly cylindrical, 13 m/43 ft long, and 4 m/13 ft in diameter, with two large solar panels. HST produces a wealth of scientific data, and allows astronomers to observe the birth of stars, find planets around neighbouring stars, follow the expanding remnants of exploding stars, and search for black holes in the centre of galaxies. HST is a cooperative programme between the European Space Agency (ESA) and the US agency NASA, and is the first spacecraft specifically designed to be serviced in orbit as a permanent space-based observatory. It was launched in 1990.

By having a large telescope above Earth's atmosphere, astronomers are able to look at the universe with unprecedented clarity. Celestial observations by HST are unhampered by clouds and other atmospheric phenomena that distort and attenuate starlight. In particular, the apparent twinkling of starlight caused by density fluctuations in the atmosphere limits the clarity of ground-based telescopes. HST performs at least ten times better than such telescopes and can see almost back to the edge of the universe and to the beginning of time (see ◊Big Bang).

Before HST could reach its full potential, a flaw in the shape of its main mirror, discovered two months after the launch, had to be corrected. In 1993, as part of a planned servicing and instrument upgrade mission, NASA astronauts aboard the space shuttle *Endeavor* installed a set of corrective lenses to compensate for the error in the mirror figure. COSTAR (corrective optics space telescope axial replacement), a device containing ten coin-sized mirrors, now feeds a corrected image from the main mirror to three of the HST's four scientific instruments. HST is also being used to detail the distribution of dust and stars in nearby galaxies, watch the collisions of galaxies in detail, infer the evolution of galaxies, and measure the age of the universe.

In December 1995 HST was trained on an 'empty' area of sky near the Plough, now termed the **Hubble Deep Field**. Around 1,500 galaxies, mostly new discoveries, were photographed.

Two new instruments were added in February 1997. The Near Infared Camera and Multi-Object Spectrometer (NICMOS) will enable Hubble to see things even further away (and therefore older) than ever before. The Space Telescope Imaging Spectograph will work 30 times faster than its predecessor as it can gather information about different stars at the same time. Three new cameras had to be fitted shortly afterwards as one of the original ones was found to be faulty.

In May 1997, three months after astronauts installed new equipment, US scientists reported that Hubble had made an extraordinary finding. Within 20 minutes of searching, it discovered evidence of a black hole 300 million times the mass of the Sun. It is located in the middle of galaxy M84 about 50 million light-years from Earth. Further findings in December 1997 concerned different shapes of dying stars. Previously, astronomers had thought that most stars die with a round shell of burning gas expanding into space. The photographs taken by the HST show shapes such as pinwheels and jet exhaust. This may be indicative of how the Sun will die.

huckleberry berry-bearing bush closely related to the ◊blueberry in the USA and bilberry in Britain. Huckleberry bushes have edible dark-blue berries. (Genus *Gaylussacia,* family Ericaceae.)

> *A human being: an ingenious assembly of portable plumbing.*
>
> Christopher Morley US editor, poet, and essayist. *Human Being*

human body the physical structure of the human being. It develops from the single cell of the fertilized ovum, is born at 40 weeks, and usually reaches sexual maturity between 11 and 18 years of age. The bony framework (skeleton) consists of more than 200 bones, over half of which are in the hands and feet. Bones are held together by joints, some of which allow movement. The circulatory system supplies muscles and organs with blood, which provides oxygen and food and removes carbon dioxide and other waste products. Body functions are controlled by the nervous system and hormones. In the upper part of the trunk is the thorax, which contains the lungs and heart. Below this is the abdomen, containing the digestive system (stomach and intestines); the liver, spleen, and pancreas; the urinary system (kidneys, ureters, and bladder); and, in women, the reproductive organs (ovaries, uterus, and vagina). In men, the prostate gland and seminal vesicles only of the reproductive system are situated in the abdomen, the testes being in the scrotum, which, with the penis, is suspended in front of and below the abdomen. The bladder empties through a small channel (urethra); in the female this opens in the upper end of the vulval cleft, which also contains the opening of the vagina, or birth canal; in the male, the urethra is continued into the penis. In both sexes, the lower bowel terminates in the anus, a ring of strong muscle situated between the buttocks.

skeleton The skull is mounted on the spinal column, or spine, a chain of 24 vertebrae. The ribs, 12 on each side, are articulated to the spinal column behind, and the upper seven meet the breastbone (sternum) in front. The lower end of the spine rests on the pelvic girdle, composed of the triangular sacrum, to which are attached the hipbones (ilia), which are fused in front. Below the sacrum is the tailbone (coccyx). The shoulder blades (scapulae) are held in place behind the upper ribs by muscles, and connected in front to the breastbone by the two collarbones (clavicles).

Each shoulder blade carries a cup (glenoid cavity) into which fits the upper end of the armbone (humerus). This articulates below with the two forearm bones (radius and ulna). These are articulated at the wrist (carpals) to the bones of the hand (metacarpals and phalanges). The upper end of each thighbone (femur) fits into a depression (acetabulum) in the hipbone; its lower end is articulated at the knee to the shinbone (tibia) and calf bone (fibula), which are articulated at the ankle (tarsals) to the bones of the foot (metatarsals and phalanges). At a moving joint, the end of each bone is formed of tough, smooth cartilage, lubricated by ◊synovial fluid. Points of special stress are reinforced by bands of fibrous tissue (ligaments).

Muscles are bundles of fibres wrapped in thin, tough layers of connective tissue (fascia); these are usually prolonged at the ends into strong, white cords (tendons, sinews) or sheets (aponeuroses), which connect the muscles to bones and organs, and by way of which the muscles do their work. Membranes of connective tissue also enfold the organs and line the interior cavities of the body. The thorax has a stout muscular floor, the diaphragm, which expands and contracts the lungs in the act of breathing.

The blood vessels of the **circulatory system**, branching into multitudes of very fine tubes (capillaries), supply all parts of the muscles and organs with blood, which carries oxygen and food necessary for life. The food passes out of the blood to the cells in a clear fluid (lymph); this is returned with waste matter through a system of lymphatic vessels that converge into collecting ducts that drain into large veins in the region of the lower neck. Capillaries join together to form veins which return blood, depleted of oxygen, to the heart.

A finely branching **nervous system** regulates the function of the muscles and organs, and makes their needs known to the controlling centres in the central nervous system, which consists of the brain and spinal cord. The inner spaces of the brain and the cord contain cerebrospinal fluid. The body processes are regulated both by the nervous system and by hormones secreted by the endocrine

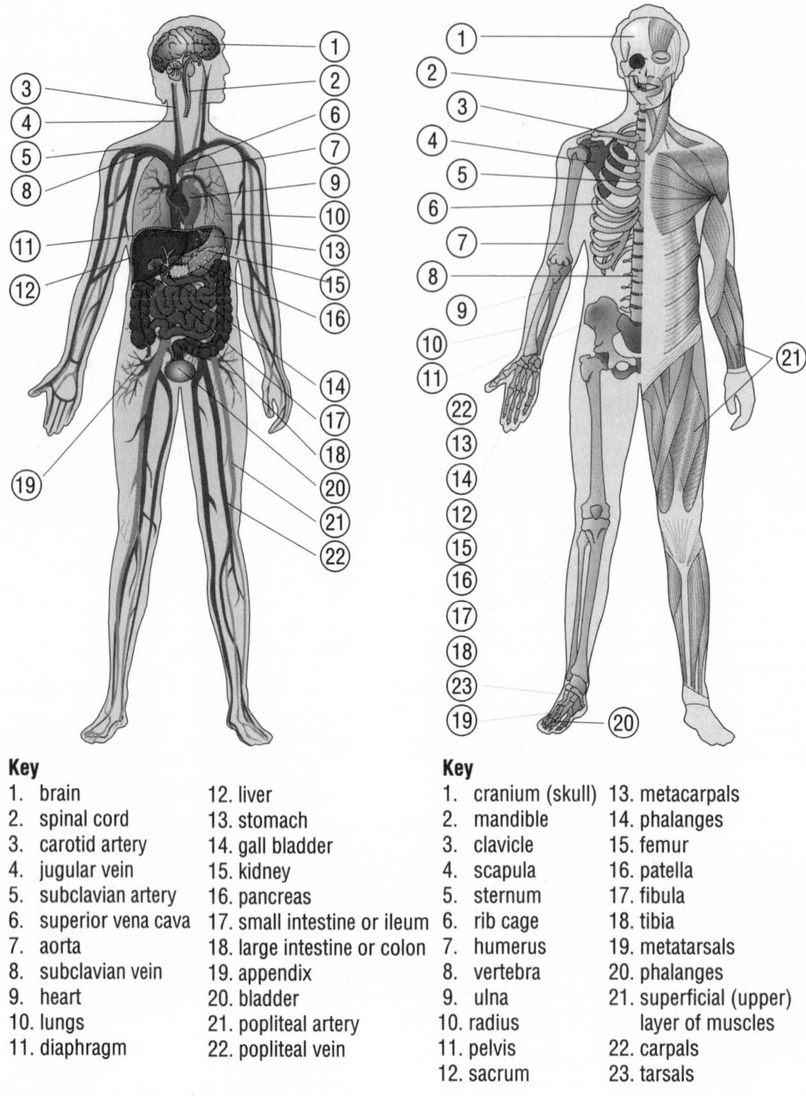

human body *The adult human body has approximately 650 muscles, 100 joints, 100,000 km/60,000 mi of blood vessels and 13,000 nerve cells. There are 206 bones in the adult body, nearly half of them in the hands and feet.*

glands. Cavities of the body that open onto the surface are coated with mucous membranes, which secrete a lubricating fluid (mucus).

The exterior surface of the body is covered with **skin**. Within the skin are the sebaceous glands, which secrete sebum, an oily fluid that makes the skin soft and pliable, and the sweat glands, which secrete water and various salts. From the skin grow hairs, chiefly on the head, in the armpits, and around the sexual organs; and nails shielding the tips of the fingers and toes; both hair and nails are modifications of skin tissue. The skin also contains nerve receptors for sensations of touch, pain, heat, and cold.

The human **digestive system** is nonspecialized and can break down a wide variety of foodstuffs. Food is mixed with saliva in the mouth by chewing and is swallowed. It enters the stomach, where it is gently churned for some time and mixed with acidic gastric juice. It then passes into the small intestine. In the first part of this, the duodenum, it is broken down further by the juice of the pancreas and duodenal glands, and mixed with bile from the liver, which splits up the fat. The jejunum and ileum continue the work of digestion and absorb most of the nutritive substances from the food. The large intestine completes the process, reabsorbing water into the body, and ejecting the useless residue as faeces.

The body, to be healthy, must maintain water and various salts in the right proportions; the process is called **osmoregulation**. The blood is filtered in the two kidneys, which remove excess water, salts, and metabolic wastes. Together these form urine, which has

HUMAN ANATOMY ONLINE

http://www.innerbody.com/indexbody.html

Fun, interactive, and educational site on the human body. The site is divided into many informative sections, including hundreds of images, and animations for Java compatible browsers.

a yellow pigment derived from bile, and passes down through two fine tubes (ureters) into the bladder, a reservoir from which the urine is emptied at intervals (micturition) through the urethra. Heat is constantly generated by the combustion of food in the muscles and glands, and by the activity of nerve cells and fibres. It is dissipated through the skin by conduction and evaporation of sweat, through the lungs in the expired air, and in other excreted substances. Average body temperature is about 38°C/100°F (37°C/98.4°F in the mouth).

human–computer interaction exchange of information between a person and a computer, through the medium of a ◊user interface, studied as a branch of ergonomics.

Human Genome Project research scheme, begun in 1988, to map the complete nucleotide (see ◊nucleic acid) sequence of human ◊DNA. There are approximately 80,000 different ◊genes in the human genome, and one gene may contain more than 2 million nucleotides. The programme aims to collect 10–15,000 genetic specimens from 722 ethnic groups whose genetic make-up is to be preserved for future use and study. The knowledge gained is expected to help prevent or treat many crippling and lethal diseases, but there are potential ethical problems associated with knowledge of an individual's genetic make-up, and fears that it will lead to genetic discrimination. Many indigenous people have condemned the project as 'bio-prospecting' – taking genetic material and exploiting it for economic gain – after attempts were made to patent Human T-Lymphotropic Virus Type 2 taken from a Guayami woman with leukaemia, in 1993.

The Human Genome Organization (HUGO) coordinating the project expects to spend $1 billion over the first five years, making this the largest research project ever undertaken in the life sciences. Work is being carried out in more than 20 centres around the world. By the beginning of 1991, about 2,000 genes had been mapped. By late 1994 a genetic map of the complete genome had been completed.

Concern that, for example, knowledge of an individual's genes may make that person an unacceptable insurance risk has led to planned legislation on genome privacy in the USA, and 3% of HUGO's funds have been set aside for researching and reporting on the ethical implications of the project.

Each strand of DNA carries a sequence of chemical building blocks, the nucleotides. There are only four different types, but the number of possible combinations is immense. The different combinations of nucleotides produce different proteins in the cell, and thus determine the structure of the body and its individual variations. To establish the nucleotide sequence, DNA strands are broken into fragments, which are duplicated (by being introduced into cells of yeast or the bacterium *Escherichia coli*) and distributed to the research centres.

Genes account for only a small amount of the DNA sequence. Over 90% of DNA appears not to have any function, although it is perfectly replicated each time the cell divides, and handed on to the next generation. Many higher organisms have large amounts of redundant DNA and it may be that this is an advantage, in that there is a pool of DNA available to form new genes if an old one is lost by mutation.

HUMAN GENETIC DISEASE: A LAYMANS APPROACH

http://mcrcr2.med.nyu.edu/murphp01/lysosome/hgd.htm

Comprehensive manual of cell biology for the family. It includes discussions of cell structure, DNA, chromosomes, and the detection of genetic defects. It also outlines the main goals of state-of-the-art genetic research.

human reproduction an example of ◊sexual reproduction, where the male produces sperm and the female eggs. These gametes contain only half the normal number of chromosomes, 23 instead of 46, so that on fertilization the resulting cell has the correct genetic complement. Fertilization is internal, which increases the chances of conception; unusually for mammals, copulation and pregnancy can occur at any time of the year. Human beings are also remarkable for the length of childhood and for the highly complex systems of parental care found in society. The use of contraception and the development of laboratory methods of insemination and fertilization are issues that make human reproduction more than a merely biological phenomenon.

human species, origins of evolution of humans from ancestral ◊primates. The African apes (gorilla and chimpanzee) are shown by anatomical and molecular comparisons to be the closest living relatives of humans. The oldest known **hominids** (of the human group), the australopithecines, found in Africa, date from 3.5–4.4 million years ago. The first to use tools came 2 million years later, and the first humanoids to use fire and move out of Africa appeared 1.7 million years ago. Neanderthals were not direct ancestors of the human species. Modern humans are all believed to descend from one African female of 200,000 years ago, although there is a rival theory that humans evolved in different parts of the world simultaneously.

Miocene apes Genetic studies indicate that the last common ancestor between chimpanzees and humans lived 5 to 10 million years ago. There are only fragmentary remains of ape and hominid fossils from this period. Dispute continues over the hominid status of *Ramapithecus,* the jaws and teeth of which have been found in India and Kenya in late Miocene deposits, dated between 14 and 10 million years. The lower jaw of a fossil ape found in the Otavi Mountains, Namibia, comes from deposits dated between 10 and 15 million years ago, and is similar to finds from E Africa and Turkey. It is thought to be close to the initial divergence of the great apes and humans.

Australopithecines Bones of the earliest known human ancestor, a hominid named *Australopithecus ramidus* 1994, were found in Ethiopia and dated as 4.4million years old. *A. afarensis,* found in Ethiopia and Kenya, date from 3.9 to 4.4 million years ago. These hominids walked upright and they were either direct ancestors or an offshoot of the line that led to modern humans. They may have been the ancestors of *Homo habilis* (considered by some to be a species of *Australopithecus*), who appeared about 2 million years later, had slightly larger bodies and brains, and were probably the first to use stone tools. Also living in Africa at the same time was *A. africanus,* a gracile hominid thought to be a meat-eater, and *A.robustus,* a hominid with robust bones, large teeth, heavy jaws, and thought to be a vegetarian. They are not generally considered to be our ancestors.

Homo erectus ***Over 1.7 million years ago,*** *Homo erectus,* believed by some to be descended from *H. habilis,* appeared in Africa. *H. erectus* had prominent brow ridges, a flattened cranium, with the widest part of the skull low down, and jaws with a rounded tooth row, but the chin, characteristic of modern humans, is lacking. They also had much larger brains (900–1,200 cu cm), and were probably the first to use fire and the first to move out of Africa. Their remains are found as far afield as China, W Asia, Spain, and S Britain. Modern human *H. sapiens sapiens* and the Neanderthals *H. sapiens neanderthalensis* are probably descended from *H. erectus.*

Neanderthals Neanderthals were large-brained and heavily built, probably adapted to the cold conditions of the ice ages. They lived in Europe and the Middle East, and disappeared about 40,000 years ago, leaving *H. sapiens sapiens* as the only remaining species of the hominid group. Possible intermediate forms between Neanderthals and *H.sapiens sapiens* have been found at Mount Carmel in Israel and at Broken Hill in Zambia, but it seems that *H.sapiens sapiens* appeared in Europe quite rapidly and either wiped out the Neanderthals or interbred with them.

modern humans There are currently two major views of human evolution: the **'out of Africa' model**, according to which *H. sapiens* emerged from *H.erectus,* or a descendant species, in Africa and then spread throughout the world; and the **multiregional model**, according to which selection pressures led to the emergence of similar advanced types of *H. sapiens* from *H. erectus* in different parts of the world at around the same time. Analysis of DNA in

Evolution: Out of Africa and the Eve Hypothesis

BY CHRIS STRINGER

Introduction

Most palaeoanthropologists recognize the existence of two human species during the last million years – *Homo erectus*, now extinct, and *Homo sapiens*, the species which includes recent or 'modern' humans. In general, they believe that *Homo erectus* was the ancestor of *Homo sapiens*. How did the transition occur?

The multiregional model

There are two opposing views. The multiregional model says that *Homo erectus* gave rise to *Homo sapiens* across its whole range, which, about 700,000 years ago, included Africa, China, Java (Indonesia), and, probably, Europe. *Homo erectus*, following an African origin about 1.7 million years ago, dispersed around the Old World, developing the regional variation that lies at the roots of modern 'racial' variation. Particular features in a given region persisted in the local descendant populations of today.

For example, Chinese *Homo erectus* specimens had the same flat faces, with prominent cheekbones, as modern Oriental populations. Javanese *Homo erectus* had robustly built cheekbones and faces that jutted out from the braincase, characteristics found in modern Australian Aborigines. No definite representatives of *Homo erectus* have yet been discovered in Europe. Here, the fossil record does not extend back as far as those of Africa and eastern Asia, although a possible *Homo erectus* jawbone more than a million years old was recently excavated in Georgia.

Nevertheless, the multiregional model claims that European *Homo erectus* did exist, and evolved into a primitive form of *Homo sapiens*. Evolution in turn produced the Neanderthals: the ancestors of modern Europeans. Features of continuity in this European lineage include prominent noses and midfaces.

Genetic continuity

The multiregional model was first described in detail by Franz Weidenreich, a German palaeoanthropologist. It was developed further by the American Carleton Coon, who tended to regard the regional lineages as genetically separate. Most recently, the model has become associated with such researchers as Milford Wolpoff (USA) and Alan Thorne (Australia), who have re-emphasized the importance of gene flow between the regional lines. In fact, they regard the continuity in time and space between the various forms of *Homo erectus* and their regional descendants to be so complete that they should be regarded as representing only one species – *Homo sapiens*.

The opposing view

The opposing view is that *Homo sapiens* had a restricted origin in time and space. This is an old idea. Early in the 20th century, workers such as Marcellin Boule (France) and Arthur Keith (UK) believed that the lineage of *Homo sapiens* was very ancient, having developed in parallel with that of *Homo erectus* and the Neanderthals. However, much of the fossil evidence used to support their ideas has been re-evaluated, and few workers now accept the idea of a very ancient and separate origin for modern *Homo sapiens*.

The Garden of Eden

Modern proponents of this approach focus on a recent and restricted origin for modern *Homo sapiens*. This was dubbed the 'Garden of Eden' or 'Noah's Ark' model by the US anthropologist William Howells in 1976 because of the idea that all modern human variation had a localized origin from one centre. Howells did not specify the centre of origin, but research since 1976 points to Africa as especially important in modern human origins.

The consequent 'Out of Africa' model claims that *Homo erectus* evolved into modern *Homo sapiens* in Africa about 100,000–150,000 years ago. Part of the African stock of early modern humans spread from the continent into adjoining regions and eventually reached Australia, Europe, and the Americas (probably by 45,000, 40,000, and 15,000 years ago respectively). Regional ('racial') variation only developed during and after the dispersal, so that there is no continuity of regional features between *Homo erectus* and present counterparts in the same regions.

Like the multiregional model, this view accepts that *Homo erectus* evolved into new forms of human in inhabited regions outside Africa, but argues that these non-African lineages became extinct without evolving into modern humans. Some, such as the Neanderthals, were displaced and then replaced by the spread of modern humans into their regions.

... and an African Eve?

In 1987, research on the genetic material called mitochondrial DNA (mtDNA) in living humans led to the reconstruction of a hypothetical female ancestor for all present-day humanity. This 'Eve' was believed to have lived in Africa about 200,000 years ago. Recent re-examination of the 'Eve' research has cast doubt on this hypothesis, but further support for an 'Out of Africa' model has come from genetic studies of nuclear DNA, which also point to a relatively recent African origin for present-day *Homo sapiens*.

Studies of fossil material of the last 50,000 years also seem to indicate that many 'racial' features in the human skeleton have developed only over the last 30,000 years, in line with the 'Out of Africa' model, and at odds with the million-year timespan one would expect from the multiregional model.

recent human populations suggests that *H. sapiens* originated about 200,000 years ago in Africa from a single female ancestor, 'Eve'. The oldest known fossils of *H.sapiens* also come from Africa, dating from 150,000–100,000 years ago. Separation of human populations would have occurred later, with separation of Asian, European, and Australian populations taking place between 100,000 and 50,000 years ago.

Humber Bridge suspension bridge with twin towers 163 m/535 ft high, which spans the estuary of the river Humber in NE England. When completed in 1980, it was the world's longest bridge with a span of 1,410 m/4,628 ft.

Built at a cost of £150 million, toll revenues over the following 15 years proved inadequate to pay even the interest on the debt.

humerus the upper bone of the forelimb of tetrapods. In humans, the humerus is the bone above the elbow.

humidity the quantity of water vapour in a given volume of the atmosphere (absolute humidity), or the ratio of the amount of water vapour in the atmosphere to the saturation value at the same temperature (relative humidity). At ◊dew point the relative humidity is 100% and the air is said to be saturated. Condensation (the conversion of vapour to liquid) may then occur. Relative humidity is measured by various types of ◊hygrometer.

hummingbird any of various small, brilliantly coloured birds found in the Americas. The name comes from the sound produced by the rapid vibration of their wings when hovering near flowers to feed. Hummingbirds have long, needlelike bills and tongues to obtain nectar from flowers and capture insects. They are the only birds able to fly backwards. The Cuban **bee hummingbird** (*Mellisuga helenae*), the world's smallest bird, is 5.5 cm/2 in long and weighs less than 2.5 g/0.1 oz. There are over 300 species. (Family Trochilidae, order Apodiformes.)

The long cleft tongue of a hummingbird is in the form of a double tube, which can be extended a considerable distance beyond the bill and withdrawn again very rapidly; the sternum (breastbone) is greatly developed, forming a suitable base for the wing muscles; the plumage has a metallic lustre.

hummingbird moth type of ◊hawk moth.

humours, theory of theory prevalent in the West in classical and medieval times that the human body was composed of four kinds of fluid: phlegm, blood, choler or yellow bile, and melancholy or black bile. Physical and mental characteristics were explained by different proportions of humours in individuals.

An excess of phlegm produced a 'phlegmatic', or calm, temperament; of blood a 'sanguine', or passionate, one; of yellow bile a 'choleric', or irascible, temperament; and of black bile a 'melancholy', or depressive, one. The Greek physician Galen connected the theory to that of the four elements (see ◊elements, the four): the phlegmatic was associated with water, the sanguine with air, the choleric with fire, and the melancholic with earth. An imbalance of the humours could supposedly be treated by diet.

humus component of ◊soil consisting of decomposed or partly decomposed organic matter, dark in colour and usually richer towards the surface. It has a higher carbon content than the original material and a lower nitrogen content, and is an important source of minerals in soil fertility.

hundredweight imperial unit (abbreviation cwt) of mass, equal to 112 lb (50.8 kg). It is sometimes called the long hundredweight, to distinguish it from the short hundredweight or **cental**, equal to 100 lb (45.4 kg).

hunting dog or ***painted dog*** wild dog that once roamed over virtually the whole of sub-Saharan Africa. A pack might have a range of almost 4,000 km/2,500 mi, hunting zebra, antelope, and other game. Individuals can run at 50 kph/30 mph for up to 5 km/3 mi, with short bursts of even higher speeds. The number of hunting dogs that survive has been reduced to a fraction of the original population. According to a 1997 International Union for the Conservation of Nature (IUCN) report, there were fewer than 3,000 hunting dogs remaining in the wild, with many existing populations too small to be viable. (Species *Lycaon pictus*, family Canidae.)

The maximum pack size found today is usually eight to ten, whereas in the past several hundred might have hunted together. Habitat destruction and the decline of large game herds have played a part in its decline, but the hunting dog has also suffered badly from the effects of distemper, a disease which was introduced into E Africa early in the 20th century.

Huntington's chorea rare hereditary disease of the nervous system that mostly begins in middle age. It is characterized by involuntary movements (◊chorea), emotional disturbances, and rapid mental degeneration progressing to ◊dementia. There is no known cure but the genetic mutation giving rise to the disease was located 1993, making it easier to test individuals for the disease and increasing the chances of developing a cure.

FACING HUNTINGTON'S DISEASE

http://neuro-chief-e.mgh.harvard.edu/MCMENEMY/facinghd.html

Excellent source of basic information about HD. Sympathetically presented by the British Huntington's Disease association, the guide covers how HD is passed on, how it is diagnosed, the risks to children conceived by couples at risk, and the course of this degenerative illness.

hurricane revolving storm in tropical regions, called **typhoon** in the N Pacific. It originates at latitudes between 5° and 20° N or S of the Equator, when the surface temperature of the ocean is above 27°C/80°F. A central calm area, called the eye, is surrounded by inwardly spiralling winds (anticlockwise in the northern hemisphere) of up to 320 kph/200 mph. A hurricane is accompanied by lightning and torrential rain, and can cause extensive damage. In meteorology, a hurricane is a wind of force 12 or more on the ◊Beaufort scale.

During 1995 the Atlantic Ocean region suffered 19 tropical storms, 11 of them hurricanes. This was the third-worst season since 1871, causing 137 deaths. The most intense hurricane recorded in the Caribbean/Atlantic sector was Hurricane Gilbert in 1988, with sustained winds of 280 kph/175 mph and gusts of over 320 kph/200 mph.

husky any of several breeds of sledge dog used in Arctic regions, growing to 70 cm/27.5 in high, and weighing about 50 kg/110 lbs, with pricked ears, thick fur, and a bushy tail. The Siberian husky is the best known.

Hutton, James
(1726–1797)

Scottish geologist, known as the 'founder of geology', who formulated the concept of uniformitarianism. In 1785 he developed a theory of the igneous origin of many rocks.

His *Theory of the Earth* 1788 proposed that the Earth was incalculably old. Uniformitarianism suggests that past events could be explained in terms of processes that work today. For example, the kind of river current that produces a certain settling pattern in a bed of sand today must have been operating many millions of years ago, if that same pattern is visible in ancient sandstones.

Mary Evans Picture Library

hyacinth any of a group of bulb-producing plants belonging to the lily family, native to the E Mediterranean and Africa. The cultivated hyacinth (*H. orientalis*) has large, scented, cylindrical heads of pink, white, or blue flowers. (Genus *Hyacinthus*, family Liliaceae.)

The ◊water hyacinth is unrelated, a floating plant from South America.

Hyades V-shaped cluster of stars that forms the face of the bull in the constellation ◊Taurus. It is 150 light years away and contains

HUYGENS, CHRISTIAAN

http://www-history.mcs.st-and.ac.uk/~history/Mathematicians/Huygens.html

Extensive biography of the great Dutch astronomer, physicist, and mathematician. The site contains a description of his contributions to astronomy, physics, and mathematics. Also included are the title page of his book *Horologium Oscillatorium* (1673) and the first page of his book *De Ratiociniis in Ludo Aleae* (1657). Several references for further reading are also listed, and the Web site also features a portrait of Huygens.

Huygens, Christiaan
(1629–1695)

or Huyghens Dutch mathematical physicist and astronomer. He proposed the wave theory of light, developed the pendulum clock in 1657, discovered polarization, and observed Saturn's rings. He made important advances in pure mathematics, applied mathematics, and mechanics, which he virtually founded. His work in astronomy was an impressive defence of the Copernican view of the Solar System.

mechanics Huygens' first studies in applied mathematics dealt with mechanics, the branch of physics pertaining to motions and forces. Working on impact and collision, Huygens used the idea of relative frames of reference, considering the motion of one body relative to the other. He anticipated the law of conservation of momentum stating that in a system of bodies under impact the centre of gravity is conserved. In *De Motu Corporum* 1656, he was also able to show that the quantity $\frac{1}{2}mv^2$ is conserved in an elastic collision.

Huygens also studied centrifugal force and showed, in 1659, its similarity to gravitational force, although he lacked the Newtonian concept of acceleration. He considered projectiles and gravity, developing the mathematically primitive ideas of Galileo. He found an accurate experimental value for the distance covered by a falling body in one second. In fact, his gravitational theories successfully deal with several difficult points that Newton carefully avoided. In the 1670s, Huygens studied motion in resisting media, becoming convinced by experiment that the resistance in such media as air is proportional to the square of the velocity.

the pendulum clock In 1657, Huygens developed a clock regulated by a pendulum, an idea that he published and patented. By 1658, major towns in Holland had pendulum tower clocks.

Mary Evans Picture Library

Huygens worked at the theory first of the simple pendulum and then of harmonically oscillating systems throughout the rest of his life, publishing the *Horologium Oscillatorium* 1673. He derived the relationship between the period of a simple pendulum and its length.

the theory of light The *Traité de la Lumière/Treatise on Light* 1678 contained Huygens' famous wave or pulse theory of light. Two years earlier, Huygens had been able to use his principle of secondary wave fronts to explain reflection and refraction, showing that refraction is related to differing velocities of light in media. He theorized that light is transmitted as a pulse moving through a medium, or ether, by setting up a whole train of vibrations in the ether in a serial displacement. His publication was partly a counter to Newton's particle theory of light. The thoroughness of Huygens' analysis of this model is impressive, but although he observed the effects due to polarization, he could not yet use his ideas to explain this phenomenon.

astronomy and the telescope Huygens' comprehensive study of geometric optics led to the invention of a telescope eyepiece that reduced chromatic aberration. It consisted of two thin plano-convex lenses, rather than one fat lens, with the field lens having a focal length three times greater than that of the eyepiece lens. Its main disadvantage was that cross-wires could not be fitted to measure the size of an image. Huygens then developed a micrometer to measure the angular diameter of celestial objects.

With a home-made telescope, he discovered Titan, one of Saturn's moons, in 1655. Later that year he observed that Titan's period of revolution was about 16 days and that it moved in the same plane as the so-called 'arms' of Saturn. This phenomenon had been somewhat of an enigma to many earlier astronomers, but because of Huygens' superior 7-m telescope, he partially unravelled the detail of Saturn's rings. In 1659, he published a Latin anagram that, when interpreted, read 'It (Saturn) is surrounded by a thin flat ring, nowhere touching and inclined to the ecliptic'. The theory behind Huygens' hypothesis followed later in *Systema Saturnium* 1659, which included observations on the planets, their satellites, the Orion nebula and the determination of the period of Mars, and provided further evidence for the Copernican view of the Solar System.

over 200 stars, although only about 12 are visible to the naked eye.

The Hyades is a much older cluster than the Pleiades, for not only have some of the brighter stars evolved into ◊red giants, some have gone even further and are now ◊white dwarfs. ◊Aldebaran, which marks the eye of the bull and which appears to be in the middle of the cluster, is not actually a member of the cluster. It is only 68 light years away, while the cluster is 130 light years away.

hybrid offspring from a cross between individuals of two different species, or two inbred lines within a species. In most cases, hybrids between species are infertile and unable to reproduce sexually. In plants, however, doubling of the chromosomes (see ◊polyploid) can restore the fertility of such hybrids.

hybridization the production of a ◊hybrid.

hydathode specialized pore, or less commonly, a hair, through which water is secreted by hydrostatic pressure from the interior of a plant leaf onto the surface. Hydathodes are found on many different plants and are usually situated around the leaf margin at vein endings. Each pore is surrounded by two crescent-shaped cells and resembles an open ◊stoma, but the size of the opening cannot be varied as in a stoma. The process of water secretion through hydathodes is known as ◊guttation.

Hydra in astronomy, the largest constellation, winding across more than a quarter of the sky between ◊Cancer and ◊Libra in the southern hemisphere. Hydra is named after the multiheaded monster slain by Hercules. Despite its size, it is not prominent; its brightest star is second-magnitude Alphard.

hydra in zoology, any of a group of freshwater polyps, belonging among the ◊coelenterates. The body is a double-layered tube (with six to ten hollow tentacles around the mouth), 1.25 cm/0.5 in long when extended, but capable of contracting to a small knob. Usually fixed to waterweed, hydras feed on minute animals that are caught and paralysed by stinging cells on the tentacles. (Genus *Hydra*, family Hydridae, phylum Coelenterata, subphylum Cnidaria.)

Hydras reproduce asexually in the summer and sexually in the winter. They have no specialized organs except those of reproduction.

hydrangea any of a group of flowering shrubs belonging to the saxifrage family, native to Japan. Cultivated varieties of *H. macrophylla* normally produce round heads of pink flowers, but these may be blue if there are certain chemicals in the soil, such as alum or iron. The name comes from the Greek for 'water vessel', after the cuplike seed capsules. (Genus *Hydrangea*, family Hydrangeaceae.)

hydrate chemical compound that has discrete water molecules combined with it. The water is known as **water of crystallization** and the number of water molecules associated with one molecule of the compound is denoted in both its name and chemical formula: for example, $CuSO_4.5H_2O$ is copper(II) sulphate pentahydrate.

hydration in chemistry, the combination of water and another substance to produce a single product. It is the opposite of ◊dehydration.

hydraulic radius measure of a river's ◊channel efficiency (its ability to discharge water), used by water engineers to assess the likelihood of flooding. The hydraulic radius of a channel is defined as the ratio of its cross-sectional area to its wetted perimeter (the part of the cross-section that is in contact with the water).

The greater the hydraulic radius, the greater the efficiency of the channel and the less likely the river is to flood. The highest values occur when channels are deep, narrow, and semi-circular in shape.

hydraulics field of study concerned with utilizing the properties of water and other liquids, in particular the way they flow and transmit pressure, and with the application of these properties in engineering. It applies the principles of ◊hydrostatics and hydrodynamics. The oldest type of hydraulic machine is the **hydraulic press**, invented by Joseph Bramah in England in 1795. The hydraulic principle of pressurized liquid increasing a force is commonly used on vehicle braking systems, the forging press, and the hydraulic systems of aircraft and excavators.

A hydraulic press consists of two liquid-connected pistons in cylinders, one of narrow bore, one of large bore. A force applied to the narrow piston applies a certain pressure (force per unit area) to the liquid, which is transmitted to the larger piston. Because the area of this piston is larger, the force exerted on it is larger. Thus the original force has been magnified, although the smaller piston must move a great distance to move the larger piston only a little.

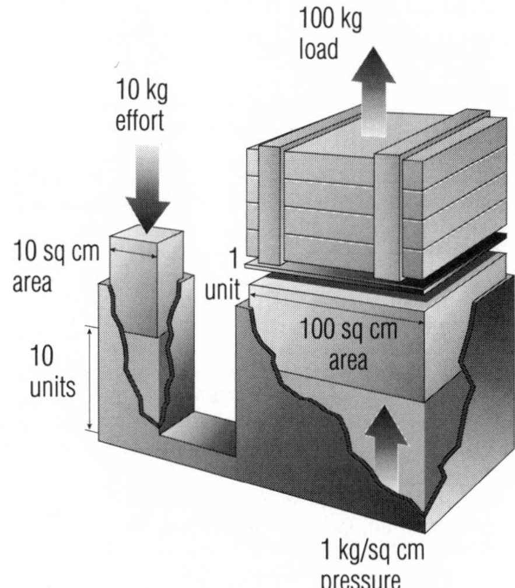

hydraulics The hydraulic jack transmits the pressure on a small piston to a larger one. A larger total force is developed by the larger piston but it moves a smaller distance than the small piston.

hydride chemical compound containing hydrogen and one other element, and in which the hydrogen is the more electronegative element (see ◊electronegativity).

Hydrides of the more reactive metals may be ionic compounds containing a hydride anion (H^-).

hydrocarbon any of a class of chemical compounds containing only hydrogen and carbon (for example, the alkanes and alkenes). Hydrocarbons are obtained industrially principally from petroleum and coal tar.

hydrocephalus potentially serious increase in the volume of cerebrospinal fluid (CSF) within the ventricles of the brain. In infants, since their skull plates have not fused, it causes enlargement of the head, and there is a risk of brain damage from CSF pressure on the developing brain.

Hydrocephalus may be due to mechanical obstruction of the outflow of CSF from the ventricles or to faulty reabsorption. Treatment usually involves surgical placement of a shunt system to drain the fluid into the abdominal cavity. In infants, the condition is often seen in association with ◊spina bifida. Hydrocephalus may occur as a consequence of brain injury or disease.

hydrochloric acid HCl solution of hydrogen chloride (a colourless, acidic gas) in water. The concentrated acid is about 35% hydrogen chloride and is corrosive. The acid is a typical strong, monobasic acid forming only one series of salts, the chlorides. It has many industrial uses, including recovery of zinc from galvanized scrap iron and the production of chlorine. It is also produced in the stomachs of animals for the purposes of digestion.

hydrocyanic acid or ***prussic acid*** solution of hydrogen cyanide gas (HCN) in water. It is a colourless, highly poisonous, volatile liquid, smelling of bitter almonds.

hydrodynamics branch of physics dealing with fluids (liquids and gases) in motion.

hydroelectric power electricity generated by moving water. In a typical scheme, water stored in a reservoir, often created by damming a river, is piped into water ◊turbines, coupled to electricity generators. In ◊pumped storage plants, water flowing through the turbines is recycled. A ◊tidal power station exploits the rise and fall of the tides. About one-fifth of the world's electricity comes from hydroelectric power.

Hydroelectric plants have prodigious generating capacities. The Grand Coulee plant in Washington State, USA, has a power output of around 10,000 megawatts. The Itaipu power station on the Paraná River (Brazil/Paraguay) has a potential capacity of 12,000 megawatts.

Work on the world's largest hydroelectric project, the Three Gorges Dam on the Chang Jiang, was officially inaugurated in 1994. By 1996, around 600,000 sq km/231,660 sq mi of land had been flooded worldwide for hydroelectric reservoirs.

hydrofoil wing that develops lift in the water in much the same way that an aeroplane wing develops lift in the air. A hydrofoil boat is one whose hull rises out of the water owing to the lift, and the boat skims along on the hydrofoils. The first hydrofoil was fitted to a boat 1906. The first commercial hydrofoil went into operation 1956. One of the most advanced hydrofoil boats is the Boeing ◊jetfoil. Hydrofoils are now widely used for fast island ferries in calm seas.

hydrogen ***Greek hydro + gen 'water generator'*** colourless, odourless, gaseous, nonmetallic element, symbol H, atomic number 1, relative atomic mass 1.00797. It is the lightest of all the elements and occurs on Earth chiefly in combination with oxygen as water. Hydrogen is the most abundant element in the universe, where it accounts for 93% of the total number of atoms and 76% of the total mass. It is a component of most stars, including the Sun, whose heat and light are produced through the nuclear-fusion process that converts hydrogen into helium. When subjected to a pressure 500,000 times greater than that of the Earth's atmosphere, hydrogen becomes a solid with metallic properties, as in one of the inner zones of Jupiter. Hydrogen's common and industrial uses include the hardening of oils and fats by hydrogenation, the creation of high-temperature flames for welding, and as rocket fuel. It has been proposed as a fuel for road vehicles.

> TO REMEMBER THE FOUR ELEMENTS THAT MAKE LIFE'S BUILDING BLOCKS:
>
> HONC IF YOU LIKE LIFE!
>
> HYDROGEN, OXYGEN, NITROGEN, CARBON

Its isotopes ◊deuterium and ◊tritium (half-life 12.5 years) are used in nuclear weapons, and deuterons (deuterium nuclei) are used in synthesizing elements. The element's name refers to the generation of water by the combustion of hydrogen, and was coined in 1787 by French chemist Louis Guyton de Morveau (1737–1816).

hydrogenation addition of hydrogen to an unsaturated organic molecule (one that contains ◊double bonds or ◊triple bonds). It is widely used in the manufacture of margarine and low-fat spreads by the addition of hydrogen to vegetable oils.

Vegetable oils contain double carbon-to-carbon bonds and are therefore examples of unsaturated compounds. When hydrogen is added to these double bonds, the oils become saturated and more solid in consistency.

hydrogen bomb bomb that works on the principle of nuclear ◊fusion. Large-scale explosion results from the thermonuclear release of energy when hydrogen nuclei are fused to form helium nuclei. The first hydrogen bomb was exploded at Enewetak Atoll in the Pacific Ocean by the USA in 1952.

In some sort of crude sense ... the physicists have known sin; and this is a knowledge which they cannot lose.

J Robert Oppenheimer US physicist.
On the hydrogen bomb, lecture at MIT
25 Nov 1947 *Physics in the Contemporary World*

---

hydrogen burning in astronomy, any of several processes by which hydrogen is converted to ◊helium by ◊nuclear fusion in the core of a star. In the Sun, the main process is the proton–proton chain, while in heavier stars the carbon cycle is more important. In both processes, four protons are converted to a helium nucleus with the emission of ◊positrons, ◊neutrinos, and gamma ◊rays. The temperature must exceed several million K for hydrogen burning to start and the least massive stars (◊brown dwarfs) never become hot enough.

hydrogen carbonate or ***bicarbonate*** compound containing the ion HCO_3^-, an acid salt of carbonic acid (solution of carbon dioxide in water). When heated or treated with dilute acids, it gives off carbon dioxide. The most important compounds are ◊sodium hydrogen carbonate (bicarbonate of soda), and ◊calcium hydrogen carbonate.

hydrogen cyanide HCN poisonous gas formed by the reaction of sodium cyanide with dilute sulphuric acid; it is used for fumigation.

The salts formed from it are cyanides – for example sodium cyanide, used in hardening steel and extracting gold and silver from their ores. If dissolved in water, hydrogen cyanide gives hydrocyanic acid.

hydrogen peroxide H_2O_2 in medicine, a liquid used, in diluted form, as an antiseptic. Oxygen is released when hydrogen peroxide is added to water and the froth helps to discharge dead tissue from wounds and ulcers. It is also used as a mouthwash and as a bleach.

hydrogen sulphate HSO_4^- compound containing the hydrogen sulphate ion. Hydrogen sulphates are ◊acid salts.

hydrogen sulphide H_2S poisonous gas with the smell of rotten eggs. It is found in certain types of crude oil where it is formed by decomposition of sulphur compounds. It is removed from the oil at the refinery and converted to elemental sulphur.

hydrogen trioxide H_2O_3 relatively stable compound of hydrogen and oxygen present in the atmosphere and possibly also in living tissue. It was first synthesized in 1994; previously it had been assumed to be too unstable.

It is produced in a reaction similar to that used for the commercial production of hydrogen peroxide (H_2O_2) but ozone (O_3) is used instead of oxygen. Hydrogen trioxide is stable at low temperatures but begins to decompose slowly at –40°C forming the high energy form of oxygen, singlet oxygen.

hydrograph graph showing how the discharge of a river varies with time. By studying hydrographs, water engineers can predict when flooding is likely and take action to prevent its taking place.

A hydrograph shows the time lag, or delay, between peak rainfall and the resultant peak in discharge, and the length of time taken for that discharge to peak. The shorter the time lag and the higher the peak, the more likely it is that flooding will occur. Factors likely to give short time lags and high peaks include heavy rainstorms, steep slopes, deforestation, poor soil quality, and the covering of surfaces with impermeable substances such as tarmac and concrete. Actions taken by water engineers to increase time lags and lower peaks include planting trees in the drainage basin of a river.

hydrography study and charting of Earth's surface waters in seas, lakes, and rivers.

hydrological cycle alternative name for the ◊water cycle, by which water is circulated between the Earth's surface and its atmosphere.

hydrology study of the location and movement of inland water, both frozen and liquid, above and below ground. It is applied to major civil engineering projects such as irrigation schemes, dams, and hydroelectric power, and in planning water supply.

hydrolysis chemical reaction in which the action of water or its ions breaks down a substance into smaller molecules. Hydrolysis occurs in certain inorganic salts in solution, in nearly all nonmetallic chlorides, in esters, and in other organic substances. It is one of the mechanisms for the breakdown of food by the body, as in the conversion of starch to glucose.

hydrometer in physics, an instrument used to measure the relative density of liquids (the density compared with that of water). A hydrometer consists of a thin glass tube ending in a sphere that leads into a smaller sphere, the latter being weighted so that the hydrometer floats upright, sinking deeper into less dense liquids than into denser liquids. Hydrometers are used in brewing and to test the strength of acid in car batteries.

The hydrometer is based on ◊Archimedes' principle.

hydrophilic ***Greek 'water-loving'*** in chemistry, a term describing ◊functional groups with a strong affinity for water, such as the carboxyl group (–COOH).

If a molecule contains both a hydrophilic and a ◊hydrophobic group (a group that repels water), it may have an affinity for both aqueous and nonaqueous molecules. Such compounds are used to stabilize ◊emulsions or as ◊detergents.

hydrophily type of ◊pollination where the pollen is transported by water. Water-pollinated plants occur in 31 genera in 11 different families. They are found in habitats as diverse as rainforests and seasonal desert pools. Pollen is either dispersed underwater or on the water's surface.

Pollen may be released directly onto the water's surface, as in the sea grass *Halodule pinifolia*, forming pollen rafts, or as in the freshwater plant *Vallisneria*, the pollen may be released within floating male flowers. In Caribbean turtle grass, *Thalassia testudinum*, pollen is released underwater embedded in strands of mucilage. Denser than water, it is carried by the current.

hydrophobia another name for the disease ◊rabies.

hydrophobic ***Greek 'water-hating'*** in chemistry, a term describing ◊functional groups that repel water (the opposite of hydrophilic).

hydrophone underwater ◊microphone and ancillary equipment capable of picking up waterborne sounds. It was originally developed to detect enemy submarines but is now also used, for example, for listening to the sounds made by whales.

hydrophyte plant adapted to live in water, or in waterlogged soil.

Hydrophytes may have leaves with a very reduced or absent ◊cuticle and no ◊stomata (since there is no need to conserve water), a reduced root and water-conducting system, and less supporting tissue since water buoys plants up. There are often numerous spaces between the cells in their stems and roots to make ◊gas exchange with all parts of the plant body possible. Many have highly divided leaves, which lessens resistance to flowing water; an example is spiked water milfoil *Myriophyllum spicatum*.

hydroplane on a submarine, a movable horizontal fin angled downwards or upwards when the vessel is descending or ascending. It is also a highly manoeuvrable motorboat with its bottom rising in steps to the stern, or a ◊hydrofoil boat that skims over the surface of the water when driven at high speed.

hydroponics cultivation of plants without soil, using specially prepared solutions of mineral salts. Beginning in the 1930s, large crops were grown by hydroponic methods, at first in California but since then in many other parts of the world.

Julius von Sachs (1832–1897), in 1860, and W Knop, in 1865, developed a system of plant culture in water whereby the relation of mineral salts to plant growth could be determined, but it was not until about 1930 that large crops could be grown. The term was first coined by US scientist W F Gericke.

hydrosphere the water component of the Earth, usually encompassing the oceans, seas, rivers, streams, swamps, lakes, groundwater, and atmospheric water vapour.

hydrostatics in physics, the branch of ◊statics dealing with fluids in equilibrium – that is, in a static condition. Practical applications include shipbuilding and dam design.

hydroxide any inorganic chemical compound containing one or more hydroxyl (OH) groups and generally combined with a metal. Hydroxides include sodium hydroxide (caustic soda, NaOH), potassium hydroxide (caustic potash, KOH), and calcium hydroxide (slaked lime, $Ca(OH)_2$).

hydroxyl group an atom of hydrogen and an atom of oxygen bonded together and covalently bonded to an organic molecule. Common compounds containing hydroxyl groups are alcohols and phenols.

In chemical reactions, the hydroxyl group (–OH) frequently behaves as a single entity.

hydroxypropanoic acid technical name for ◊lactic acid.

HYENA

The female spotted hyena has a higher level of the male sex hormone testosterone than the male. She is also up to 12% heavier than the male.

hyena any of three species of carnivorous doglike mammals living in Africa and Asia. Hyenas have extremely powerful jaws. They are scavengers, feeding on the remains of animals killed by predators such as lions, although they will also attack and kill live prey. (Genera *Hyaena* and *Crocuta*, family Hyaenidae, order Carnivora.)

The species are the **striped hyena** (*H. hyaena*) found from Asia Minor to India; the **brown hyena** (*H. brunnea*), found in S Africa; and the **spotted** or **laughing hyena** (*C. crocuta*), common south of the Sahara. The ◊aardwolf also belongs to the hyena family.

SPOTTED HYENAS

http://www.csulb.edu/~persepha/hyena.html

Facts about hyenas illustrated by a number of photos. There is also a highly informative 'Frequently Asked Questions' section dealing with questions such as 'Do they really laugh?' and 'Will they eat people?', as well as a folklore section dealing with the depiction of hyenas through history.

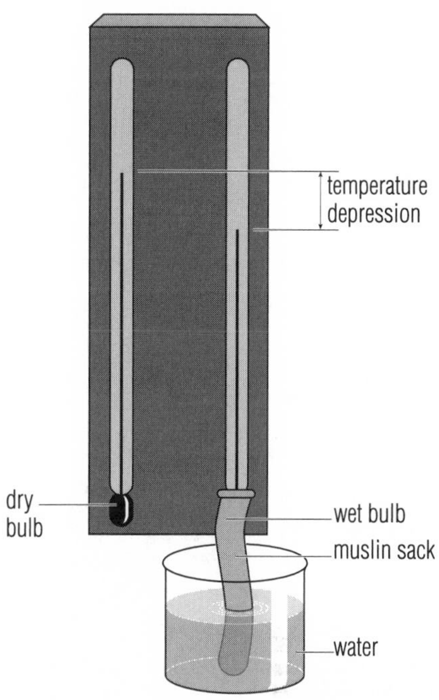

hygrometer *The most common hygrometer, or instrument for measuring the humidity of a gas, is the wet and dry bulb hygrometer. The wet bulb records a lower temperature because water evaporates from the muslin, taking heat from the wet bulb. The degree of evaporation and hence cooling depends upon the humidity of the surrounding air or other gas.*

hygrometer in physics, any instrument for measuring the humidity, or water vapour content, of a gas (usually air). A wet and dry bulb hygrometer consists of two vertical thermometers, with one of the bulbs covered in absorbent cloth dipped into water. As the water evaporates, the bulb cools, producing a temperature difference between the two thermometers. The amount of evaporation, and hence cooling of the wet bulb, depends on the relative humidity of the air.

Other hygrometers work on the basis of a length of natural fibre, such as hair or a fine strand of gut, changing with variations in humidity. In a ◊dew-point hygrometer, a polished metal mirror gradually cools until a fine mist of water (dew) forms on it. This gives a measure of the dew point, from which the air's relative humidity can be calculated.

hyoscine or ***scopolamine*** drug that acts on the autonomic nervous system and prevents muscle spasm. It is frequently included in premedication to dry up lung secretions and as a postoperative sedative. It is also used to treat ulcers, to relax the womb in labour, for travel sickness, and to dilate the pupils before an eye examination. It is an alkaloid, $C_{17}H_{21}NO_2$, obtained from various plants of the nightshade family (such as ◊belladonna).

hyperactivity condition of excessive activity in young children, combined with restlessness, inability to concentrate, and difficulty in learning. There are various causes, ranging from temperamental predisposition to brain disease. In some cases food additives have come under suspicion; in such instances modification of the diet may help. Mostly there is improvement at puberty, but symptoms may persist in the small proportion diagnosed as having ◊attention-deficit hyperactivity disorder.

hyperbola in geometry, a curve formed by cutting a right circular cone with a plane so that the angle between the plane and the base is greater than the angle between the base and the side of the cone. All hyperbolae are bounded by two asymptotes (straight

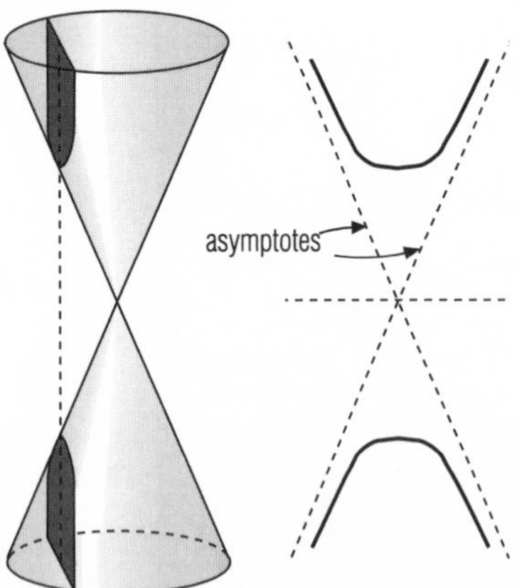

hyperbola The hyperbola is produced when a cone is cut by a plane. It is one of a family of curves called conic sections: the circle, ellipse, and parabola. These curves are produced when the plane cuts the cone at different angles and positions.

lines which the hyperbola moves closer and closer to but never reaches).

A hyperbola is a member of the family of curves known as ◊conic sections.

A hyperbola can also be defined as a path traced by a point that moves such that the ratio of its distance from a fixed point (focus) and a fixed straight line (directrix) is a constant and greater than 1; that is, it has an ◊eccentricity greater than 1.

Hypercard computer application developed for the Apple ◊Macintosh, in which data are stored as if on cards in a card-index system. A group of cards forms a stack. Additional features include the ability to link cards in different ways and, by the use of software buttons (icons that can be clicked or double clicked with a mouse), to access other data. Hypercard is very similar to ◊hypertext, although it does not conform to the rigorous definition of hypertext.

hypercharge in physics, a property of certain ◊elementary particles, analogous to electric charge, that accounts for the absence of some expected behaviour (such as decay).

hyperlink link from one document to another or, within the same document, from one place to another. It can be activated by clicking on the link with a ◊mouse. The link is usually highlighted in some way, for example by the inclusion of a small graphic. Documents linked in this way are described as ◊hypertext. Examples of programs that use hypertext and hyperlinks are ◊Windows help files, ◊Acrobat, and ◊Mosaic.

hypermedia in computing, system that uses links to lead users to related graphics, audio, animation, or video files in the same way that ◊hypertext systems link related pieces of text. The World Wide Web is an example of a hypermedia system, as is ◊HyperCard.

hyperon in physics, any of a group of highly unstable ◊elementary particles that includes all the baryons with the exception of protons and neutrons. They are all composed of three quarks. The lambda, xi, sigma, and omega particles are hyperons.

hypertension abnormally high ◊blood pressure due to a variety of causes, leading to excessive contraction of the smooth muscle cells of the walls of the arteries. It increases the risk of kidney disease, stroke, and heart attack.

Hypertension is one of the major public health problems of the developed world, affecting 15–20% of adults in industrialized countries (1996). It may be of unknown cause (**essential hypertension**), or it may occur in association with some other condition, such as kidney disease (**secondary or symptomatic hypertension**). It is controlled with a low-salt diet and drugs.

hypertext system for viewing information (both text and pictures) on a computer screen in such a way that related items of information can easily be reached. For example, the program might display a map of a country; if the user clicks (with a ◊mouse) on a particular city, the program will display information about that city.

hyperthyroidism or ***thyrotoxicosis*** overactivity of the thyroid gland due to enlargement or tumour. Symptoms include accelerated heart rate, sweating, anxiety, tremor, and weight loss. Treatment is by drugs or surgery.

hypha (plural ***hyphae***) delicate, usually branching filament, many of which collectively form the mycelium and fruiting bodies of a ◊fungus. Food molecules and other substances are transported along hyphae by the movement of the cytoplasm, known as 'cytoplasmic streaming'.

Typically hyphae grow by increasing in length from the tips and by the formation of side branches. Hyphae of the higher fungi (the ascomycetes and basidiomycetes) are divided by cross walls or septa at intervals, whereas those of lower fungi (for example, bread mould) are undivided. However, even the higher fungi are not truly cellular, as each septum is pierced by a central pore, through which cytoplasm, and even nuclei, can flow. The hyphal walls contain ◊chitin, a polysaccharide.

hypnosis artificially induced state of relaxation or altered attention characterized by heightened suggestibility. There is evidence that, with susceptible persons, the sense of pain may be diminished, memory of past events enhanced, and illusions or hallucinations experienced. Posthypnotic amnesia (forgetting what happened during hypnosis) and posthypnotic suggestion (performing an action after hypnosis that had been suggested during it) have also been demonstrated.

Hypnosis has a number of uses in medicine. Hypnotically induced sleep, for example, may assist the healing process, and hypnotic suggestion (hypnotherapy) may help in dealing with the symptoms of emotional and psychosomatic disorders. The Austrian physician Friedrich Anton Mesmer is said to be the discoverer of hypnosis, but he called it 'animal magnetism', believing it to be a physical force or fluid. The term 'hypnosis' was coined by James Braid (1795–1860), a British physician and surgeon who was the first to regard it as a psychological phenomenon. The Scottish surgeon James Esdaile (1805–1859), working in India, performed hundreds of operations in which he used hypnosis to induce analgesia (insensitivity to pain) or general anaesthesia (total insensitivity).

hypnotic any substance (such as ◊barbiturate, benzodiazepine, alcohol) that depresses brain function, inducing sleep. Prolonged use may lead to physical or psychological addiction.

hypo in photography, a term for sodium thiosulphate, discovered 1819 by John Herschel, and used as a fixative for photographic images since 1837.

hypocycloid in geometry, a cusped curve traced by a point on the circumference of a circle that rolls around the inside of another larger circle. (Compare ◊epicycloid.)

hypodermic syringe instrument used for injecting fluids beneath the skin into either muscles or blood vessels. It consists of a small graduated tube with a close-fitting piston and a nozzle onto which a hollow needle can be fitted.

hypogeal term used to describe seed germination in which the ◊cotyledons remain below ground. It can refer to fruits that develop underground, such as peanuts *Arachis hypogea.*

hypoglycaemia condition of abnormally low level of sugar (glucose) in the blood (below 60 g/100 ml), which starves the brain. It causes weakness, sweating, and mental confusion, sometimes fainting.

Hypoglycaemia is most often seen in ◊diabetes. Low blood sugar occurs when the diabetic has taken too much insulin. It is treated by administering glucose.

hypotenuse the longest side of a right-angled triangle, opposite the right angle. It is of particular application in Pythagoras' theorem (the square of the hypotenuse equals the sum of the squares of the other two sides), and in trigonometry where the ratios ◊sine and ◊cosine are defined as the ratios opposite/hypotenuse and adjacent/hypotenuse respectively.

hypothalamus region of the brain below the ◊cerebrum which regulates rhythmic activity and physiological stability within the body, including water balance and temperature. It regulates the production of the pituitary gland's hormones and controls that part of the ◊nervous system governing the involuntary muscles.

hypothermia condition in which the deep (core) temperature of the body falls below 35°C. If it is not discovered, coma and death ensue. Most at risk are the aged and babies (particularly if premature).

hypothesis in science, an idea concerning an event and its possible explanation. The term is one favoured by the followers of the philosopher Karl Popper, who argue that the merit of a scientific hypothesis lies in its ability to make testable predictions.

Historians will have to face the fact that natural selection determined the evolution of cultures in the same manner as it did that of species.

KONRAD LORENZ Austrian zoologist.
On Aggression 1966

hypothyroidism or ***myxoedema*** deficient functioning of the thyroid gland, causing slowed mental and physical performance, weight gain, sensitivity to cold, and susceptibility to infection.

This may be due to lack of iodine in the diet or a defect of the thyroid gland, both being productive of ◊goitre; or to the pituitary gland providing insufficient stimulus to the thyroid gland. Treatment of thyroid deficiency is by the hormone thyroxine. When present from birth, hypothyroidism can lead to cretinism if untreated.

hypsometer ***Greek hypsos 'height'*** instrument for testing the accuracy of a thermometer at the boiling point of water. It was originally used for determining altitude by comparing changes in the boiling point with changes in atmospheric pressure.

Hyracotherium extinct mammal belonging to the order Perissodactyla and considered to be an ancestor of the horse. It occurs in Eocene strata in Europe and was a small animal about 1 m/3.3 ft in length, with complete dentition, four digits on the forelimbs, and three on the hind-limbs, and orbits not enclosed by bone.

hyrax any of a group of small, rodentlike, herbivorous mammals that live among rocks in desert areas, and in forests in Africa, Arabia, and Syria. They are about the size of a rabbit, with a plump body, short legs, short ears, brownish fur, and long, curved front teeth. (Family Procaviidae, order Hyracoidea.)

They have four toes on the front limbs, and three on the hind limbs, each of which has a tiny hoof. There are nine species of hyrax. They are related to elephants.

hyssop aromatic herb belonging to the mint family, found in Asia, S Europe, and around the Mediterranean. It has blue flowers, oblong leaves, and stems that are woody near the ground but herbaceous (fleshy) above. (*Hyssopus officinalis,* family Labiatae.)

hysterectomy surgical removal of all or part of the uterus (womb). The operation is performed to treat fibroids (benign tumours growing in the uterus) or cancer; also to relieve heavy menstrual bleeding. A woman who has had a hysterectomy will no longer menstruate and cannot bear children.

hysteresis phenomenon seen in the elastic and electromagnetic behaviour of materials, in which a lag occurs between the application or removal of a force or field and its effect.

If the magnetic field applied to a magnetic material is increased and then decreased back to its original value, the magnetic field inside the material does not return to its original value. The internal field 'lags' behind the external field. This behaviour results in a loss of energy, called the **hysteresis loss**, when a sample is repeatedly magnetized and demagnetized. Hence the materials used in transformer cores and electromagnets should have a low hysteresis loss. Similar behaviour is seen in some materials when varying electric fields are applied (**electric hysteresis**). **Elastic hysteresis** occurs when a varying force repeatedly deforms an elastic material. The deformation produced does not completely disappear when the force is removed, and this results in energy loss on repeated deformations.

Hytelnet (contraction of ***hypertext browser for Telnet-accessible sites on the Internet***) in computing, program developed in 1990 which indexes Telnet-accessible sites on the Internet so that users can quickly look up the necessary access information.

Versions of Hytelnet exist for PCs, DEC VAXes, and UNIX machines. Hytelnet is distributed as ◊shareware; it is updated via the HYTEL-L electronic mailing list.

Hz in physics, the symbol for ◊hertz.

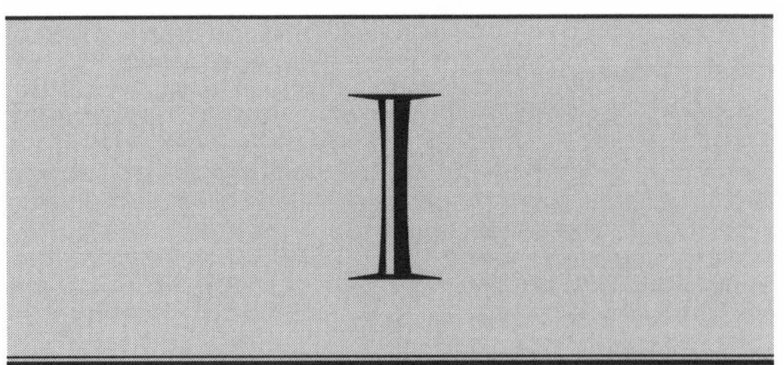

IAB in computing, abbreviation for ◊*Internet Architecture Board*.

IAEA abbreviation for ◊*International Atomic Energy Agency*.

ibex any of various wild goats found in mountainous areas of Europe, NE Africa, and Central Asia. They grow to 100 cm/3.5 ft, and have brown or grey coats and heavy horns. They are herbivorous and live in small groups.

ibis any of various wading birds, about 60 cm/2 ft tall, belonging to the same family as spoonbills. Ibises have long legs and necks, and long, downward-curved beaks, rather blunt at the end; the upper part is grooved. Their plumage is generally black and white. Various species occur in the warmer regions of the world. (Family Threskiornidae, order Ciconiiformes.)

The **scarlet ibis** (*Guara ruber*), a South American species, is brilliant scarlet with a few black patches. The scarlet colour is caused by an accumulation of pigment from the aquatic invertebrates that it feeds on.

IBM (abbreviation for ***International Business Machines***) multinational company, the largest manufacturer of computers in the world. The company is a descendant of the Tabulating Machine Company, formed 1896 by US inventor Herman Hollerith to exploit his punched-card machines. It adopted its present name in 1924. By 1991 it had an annual turnover of $64.8 billion and employed about 345,000 people, but in 1992 and 1993 it made considerable losses. The company acquired Lotus Development Corporation in 1995. By 1997 IBM had, under new management, recovered financially, with an annual turnover of $76 billion, which means it is still a dominant industry player.

Its aquisition of the Lotus Development Corporation gave IBM access to its wide range of innovative software, including the 1–2–3 spreadsheet and Notes, a market leader in groupware.

IBM-compatible in computing, a ◊clone of an IBM PC; synonymous with PC-compatible.

Although there were successful personal computers before the PC, IBM set the most common standard for these machines when it launched the PC in 1981. It created a clone industry by using readily available parts in the IBM PC, instead of developing proprietary parts itself. The success of the PC established Intel processors and Microsoft software as industry standards.

IC abbreviation for ◊integrated circuit.

Icarus in astronomy, an ◊Apollo asteroid 1.5 km/1 mi in diameter, discovered 1949. It orbits the Sun every 409 days at a distance of 28–300 million km/18–186 million mi (0.19–2.0 astronomical units). It was the first asteroid known to approach the Sun closer than does the planet Mercury. In 1968 it passed 6 million km/4 million mi from the Earth.

ice solid formed by water when it freezes. It is colourless and its crystals are hexagonal. The water molecules are held together by hydrogen bonds.

The freezing point of ice, used as a standard for measuring temperature, is 0° for the Celsius and Réaumur scales and 32° for the Fahrenheit. Ice expands in the act of freezing (hence burst pipes), becoming less dense than water (0.9175 at 5°C/41°F).

ice form of methamphetamine that is smoked for its stimulating effect; its use has been illegal in the USA since 1989. Its use may be followed by a period of depression and psychosis.

ANTARCTICA

The ice that covers Antarctica is 4,776 m/15,669 ft

ice age any period of glaciation occurring in the Earth's history, but particularly that in the Pleistocene epoch, immediately preceding historic times. On the North American continent, ◊glaciers reached as far south as the Great Lakes, and an ice sheet spread over N Europe, leaving its remains as far south as Switzerland.

There were several glacial advances separated by interglacial stages during which the ice melted and temperatures were higher than today.

Formerly there were thought to have been only three or four glacial advances, but recent research has shown about 20 major incidences. For example, ocean-bed cores record the absence or presence in their various layers of such cold-loving small marine animals as radiolaria, which indicate a fall in ocean temperature at regular intervals. Other ice ages have occurred throughout geological time: there were four in the Precambrian era, one in the Ordovician, and one at the end of the Carboniferous and beginning of the Permian. The occurrence of an ice age is governed by a combination of factors (the **Milankovitch hypothesis**): (1) the Earth's change of attitude in relation to the Sun, that is, the way it tilts in a 41,000-year cycle and at the same time wobbles on its axis in a 22,000-year cycle, making the time of its closest approach to the Sun come at different seasons; and (2) the 92,000-year cycle of eccentricity in its orbit round the Sun, changing it from an elliptical to a near circular orbit, the severest period of an ice age coinciding with the approach to circularity. There is a possibility that the Pleistocene ice age is not yet over. It may reach another maximum in another 60,000 years.

iceberg floating mass of ice, about 80% of which is submerged, rising sometimes to 100 m/300 ft above sea level. Glaciers that reach the coast become extended into a broad foot; as this enters the sea, masses break off and drift towards temperate latitudes, becoming a danger to shipping.

iceman nickname given to the preserved body of a prehistoric man discovered in a glacier on the Austrian–Italian border 1991. On the basis of the clothing and associated artefacts, the body was at first believed to be 4,000 years old, from the Bronze Age. Carbon dating established its age at about 5,300 years. The discovery led to a reappraisal of the boundary between the Bronze and the Stone Age.

ichneumon fly any of a large group of parasitic wasps. There are several thousand species in Europe, North America, and other regions. They have slender bodies, and the females have unusually long, curved ovipositors (egg-laying instruments) that can pierce several inches of wood. The eggs are laid in the eggs, larvae, or pupae of other insects, usually butterflies or moths. (Family Ichneumonidae.)

ichthyology the scientific study of ◊fish, including their classification, general biology, behaviour, ecology, and research into commercial fisheries.

ICHTHYOLOGY RESOURCES

http://muse.bio.cornell.edu/cgi-bin/hl?fish

Everything anyone should need for studying fish, including historical information about development, as well as up-to-date listings of currently endangered species. There is also a gallery of fish images and paintings for the less scientifically inclined.

icon in computing, a small picture on the computer screen, or ◊VDU, representing an object or function that the user may manipulate or otherwise use. It is a feature of ◊graphical user interface (GUI) systems. Icons make computers easier to use by allowing the user to point to and click with a ◊mouse on pictures, rather than type commands.

icosahedron (plural *icosahedra*) regular solid with 20 equilateral (equal-sided) triangular faces. It is one of the five regular ◊polyhedra, or Platonic solids.

id in Freudian psychology, the mass of motivational and instinctual elements of the human mind, whose activity is largely governed by the arousal of specific needs. It is regarded as the ◊unconscious element of the human psyche, and is said to be in conflict with the ◊ego and the ◊superego.

IDEA (acronym for ***International Data Encryption Algorithm***) in computing, an encryption ◊algorithm, developed in 1990 in Zürich, Switzerland. For reasons of speed, it is used in the encryption program ◊Pretty Good Privacy (PGP) along with ◊RSA.

identity in mathematics, a number or operation that leaves others unchanged when combined with them. Zero is the identity for addition; one is the identity for multiplication. For example:

$$7 + 0 = 7$$
$$7 \times 1 = 7$$

id Software computer software company that publishes popular games such as ◊*Doom* and ◊*Quake*, based in Texas, USA. An entire subculture has built up around id's games because of its habit of releasing ◊source code to enable fans to write their own additional game levels using settings of their own choice.

The company's first major product was the 1992 game *Wolfenstein 3-D*, in which players move around a series of complicated mazes retrieving treasure and shooting Nazi troops and guard dogs. *Quake*, released in 1996, uses complex, carefully styled 3-D graphics, adds vertical movement and underwater caves, and includes a gruesome collection of fierce aliens. Both *Doom* and *Quake* can be played competitively over networks, including the Internet.

IEEE abbreviation for ◊***Institute of Electrical and Electronic Engineers***, US institute which sets technical standards for electrical equipment and computer data exchange.

IETF in computing, abbreviation for Internet Engineering Task Force.

igneous rock rock formed from cooling magma or lava, and solidifying from a molten state. Igneous rocks are largely composed of silica (SiO_2) and they are classified according to their crystal size, texture, method of formation, or chemical composition, for example by the proportions of light and dark minerals.

ignis fatuus another name for ◊will-o'-the-wisp.

ignition coil ◊transformer that is an essential part of a petrol engine's ignition system. It consists of two wire coils wound around an iron core. The primary coil, which is connected to the car battery, has only a few turns. The secondary coil, connected via the ◊distributor to the ◊spark plugs, has many turns. The coil takes in a low voltage (usually 12 volts) from the battery and transforms it to a high voltage (about 15,000–20,000 volts) to ignite the engine.

When the engine is running, the battery current is periodically interrupted by means of the contact breaker in the distributor. The collapsing current in the primary coil induces a current in the secondary coil, a phenomenon known as ◊electromagnetic induction. The induced current in the secondary coil is at very high voltage, typically about 15,000–20,000 volts. This passes to the spark plugs to create sparks.

ignition temperature or ***fire point*** minimum temperature to which a substance must be heated before it will spontaneously burn independently of the source of heat; for example, ethanol has an ignition temperature of 425°C/798°F and a ◊flash point of 12°C/54°F.

iguana any of about 700 species of lizard, chiefly found in the Americas. The **common iguana** (*I. iguana*) of Central and South America is a vegetarian and may reach 2 m/6 ft in length. (Especially genus *Iguana*, family Iguanidae.)

iguanodon plant-eating ◊dinosaur whose remains are found in deposits of the Lower ◊Cretaceous age, together with the remains of other dinosaurs of the same order (ornithiscians) such as stegosaurus and◊ triceratops. It was 5–10 m/16–32 ft long and, when standing upright, 4 m/13 ft tall. It walked on its hind legs, using its long tail to balance its body. (Order *Ornithiscia.*)

ileum part of the small intestine of the ◊digestive system, between the duodenum and the colon, that absorbs digested food.

Its wall is muscular so that waves of contraction (peristalsis) can mix the food and push it forward. Numerous fingerlike projections, or villi, point inwards from the wall, increasing the surface area available for absorption. The ileum has an excellent blood supply, which receives the food molecules passing through the wall and transports them to the liver via the hepatic portal vein.

i.Link in computing, Sony Corporation's branded name for the IEEE ◊1394 serial port and bus. Sony has licensed the name and logo to other companies including Hitachi, Matsushita, Sharp, and Victor of Japan (JVC).

illumination or ***illuminance*** the brightness or intensity of light falling on a surface. It depends upon the brightness, distance, and angle of any nearby light sources. The SI unit is the ◊lux.

ILS abbreviation for ◊instrument landing system, **an automatic system for assisting aircraft landing at airports**.

IMA in computing, abbreviation for ◊***Interactive Multimedia Association***.

image in mathematics, a point or number that is produced as the result of a ◊transformation or mapping.

image picture or appearance of a real object, formed by light that passes through a lens or is reflected from a mirror. If rays of light actually pass through an image, it is called a **real image**. Real images, such as those produced by a camera or projector lens, can be projected onto a screen. An image that cannot be projected onto a screen, such as that seen in a flat mirror, is known as a **virtual image**.

image compression in computing, one of a number of methods used to reduce the amount of information required to represent an image, so that it takes up less computer memory and can be transmitted more rapidly and economically via telecommunications systems. It plays a major role in fax transmission and in videophone and multimedia systems.

image intensifier electronic device that brightens a dark image. Image intensifiers are used for seeing at night; for example, in military situations.

The intensifier first forms an image on a photocathode, which emits electrons in proportion to the intensity of the light falling on it. The electron flow is increased by one or more amplifiers. Finally, a fluorescent screen converts the electrons back into visible light, now bright enough to see.

image map in computing, on the World Wide Web, a large image with multiple hot spots on which users click to navigate around the site.

image processing technique for cleaning up and digitally retouching photographs.

A lot of the fundamental work involved in developing image processing techniques was done at the Jet Propulsion Laboratory in Pasadena, California, USA, which manages unmanned space flight for NASA. Pictures taken in-flight of planets have drop-out areas where data is missing due to static or other interference. These pictures are also often taken using parts of the spectrum which the human eye cannot see. Accordingly, computer ◊algorithms had to be developed to fill in the missing data and compute the correct colours. The images produced in this way are made available publicly and often appear in the media.

imaginary number term often used to describe the non-real element of a ◊complex number. For the complex number $(a + ib)$, ib is the imaginary number where $i = \sqrt{-1}$, and b any real number.

The imaginary number is a fine and wonderful recourse of the divine spirit, almost an amphibian between being and not being.

GOTTFRIED WILHELM LEIBNIZ German mathematician and philosopher. Attributed remark

imago sexually mature stage of an ◊insect.

immediate access memory in computing, ◊memory provided in the ◊central processing unit to store the programs and data in current use.

immersive in ◊virtual reality, term describing the sense that the user is completely surrounded by and immersed in the virtual world.

immiscible describing liquids that will not mix with each other, such as oil and water. When two immiscible liquids are shaken together, a turbid mixture is produced. This normally forms separate layers on being left to stand.

immunity the protection that organisms have against foreign microorganisms, such as bacteria and viruses, and against cancerous cells (see ◊cancer). The cells that provide this protection are called white blood cells, or leucocytes, and make up the immune system. They include neutrophils and ◊macrophages, which can engulf invading organisms and other unwanted material, and natural killer cells that destroy cells infected by viruses and cancerous cells. Some of the most important immune cells are the ◊B cells and ◊T cells. Immune cells coordinate their activities by means of chemical messengers or ◊lymphokines, including the antiviral messenger ◊interferon. The lymph nodes play a major role in organizing the immune response.

Immunity is also provided by a range of physical barriers such as the skin, tear fluid, acid in the stomach, and mucus in the airways. ◊AIDS is one of many viral diseases in which the immune system is affected.

immunization conferring immunity to infectious disease by artificial methods. The most widely used technique is ◊vaccination.

Immunization is an important public health measure. If most of the population has been immunized against a particular disease, it is impossible for an epidemic to take hold.

Vaccination against smallpox was developed by Edward ◊Jenner in 1796. In the late 19th century Louis ◊Pasteur developed vaccines against cholera, typhoid, typhus, plague, and yellow fever. In 1991, the WHO and UNICEF announced that four out of five children around the world are now immunized against six killer diseases: measles, tetanus, polio, diphtheria, whooping cough, and tuberculosis. Ten years ago this figure was only one in five children.

When meditating over a disease, I never think of finding a remedy for it, but, instead, a means of preventing it.

LOUIS PASTEUR French chemist and microbiologist. Address to the Fraternal Association of Former Students of the Ecole Centrale des Arts et Manufactures, Paris, 15 May 1884

immunocompromised lacking a fully effective immune system. The term is most often used in connection with infections such as ◊AIDS where the virus interferes with the immune response (see ◊immunity).

Other factors that can impair the immune response are pregnancy, diabetes, old age, malnutrition and extreme stress, making someone susceptible to infections by microorganisms (such as listeria) that do not affect normal, healthy people. Some people are immunodeficient; others could be on ◊immunosuppressive drugs.

immunodeficient lacking one or more elements of a working immune system. Immune deficiency is the term generally used for patients who are born with such a defect, while those who acquire such a deficiency later in life are referred to as ◊immunocompromised **or immunosuppressed.**

A serious impairment of the immune system is sometimes known as SCID, or Severe Combined Immune Deficiency. At one time children born with this condition would have died in infancy. They can now be kept alive in a germ-free environment, then treated with a bone-marrow transplant from a relative, to replace the missing immune cells. At present, the success rate for this type of treatment is still fairly low. See also ◊gene therapy.

immunoglobulin human globulin ◊protein that can be separated from blood and administered to confer immediate immunity on the recipient. It participates in the immune reaction as the antibody for a specific ◊antigen (disease-causing agent).

Normal immunoglobulin (gamma globulin) is the fraction of the blood serum that, in general, contains the most antibodies, and is obtained from plasma pooled from about a thousand donors. It is given for short-term (two to three months) protection when a person is at risk, mainly from hepatitis A (infectious hepatitis), or when a pregnant woman, not immunized against ◊German measles, is exposed to the rubella virus.

Specific immunoglobulins are injected when a susceptible (non-immunized) person is at risk of infection from a potentially fatal disease, such as hepatitis B (serum hepatitis), rabies, or tetanus. These immunoglobulins are prepared from blood pooled from donors convalescing from the disease.

immunosuppressive any drug that suppresses the body's normal immune responses to infection or foreign tissue. It is used in the treatment of autoimmune disease (see ◊autoimmunity); as part of chemotherapy for leukaemias, lymphomas, and other cancers; and to help prevent rejection following organ transplantation.

Immunosuppressed patients are at greatly increased risk of infection.

impact printer computer printer that creates characters by striking an inked ribbon against the paper beneath. Examples of impact printers are dot-matrix printers, daisywheel printers, and most types of line printer.

Impact printers are noisier and slower than nonimpact printers, such as ink-jet and laser printers, but can be used to produce carbon copies.

impala African ◊antelope found from Kenya to South Africa in savannas and open woodland. The body is sandy brown. Males have lyre-shaped horns up to 75 cm/2.5 ft long. Impalas grow up to 1.5 m/5 ft long and 90 cm/3 ft tall. They live in herds and spring high in the air when alarmed. (Species *Aepyceros melampus*, family Bovidae.)

impedance the total opposition of a circuit to the passage of alternating electric current. It has the symbol Z. For an ◊alternating current (AC) it includes the resistance R and the reactance X (caused by ◊capacitance or ◊inductance); the impedance can then be found using the equation $Z^2 = R^2 + X^2$.

Imperial College of Science, Technology, and Medicine (formerly ***Imperial College of Science and Technology***) institution established in South Kensington, London, 1907, for advanced scientific training and research, applied especially to industry. Part of the University of London, it comprises three separate colleges, the City and Guilds College (engineering faculty), the Royal College of Science (pure science), and the Royal School of Mines (mining). St Mary's Hospital Medical School was added in 1988, resulting in the change of name.

imperial system traditional system of units developed in the UK, based largely on the foot, pound, and second (f.p.s.) system.

implantation in mammals, the process by which the developing ◊embryo attaches itself to the wall of the mother's uterus and stimulates the development of the ◊placenta. In humans it occurs 6–8 days after ovulation.

Immunization: Vaccines in Foods

BY J M DUNWELL

Vaccines

◊Vaccines are ◊proteins that stimulate the immune response of animals, and help protect against infectious diseases caused by ◊viruses and ◊bacteria. More than 75 such diseases can now be prevented in this way and millions of deaths are prevented annually by the use of these products.

Oral immunization

Many infectious diseases are spread by contaminated water or food, and enter the body through the membranes of the ◊digestive system. Stimulating the immune system of the cells lining the digestive system best combats such diseases. Most people are familiar with the ◊polio vaccine provided on sugar cubes. This is probably the best example of vaccination provided by mouth (oral immunization) rather than by injection. The most obvious advantage of the oral route is that it does not require the use of sterile needles.

Need for new production methods

Like many pharmaceutical products, vaccines are relatively expensive to produce. Recently, it has been suggested that plants may be a useful new production system because large amounts of ◊antigen (the active protein component of the vaccine) could be produced at low cost, using agricultural methods rather than ◊cell culture-based systems that are expensive and complex. This would be particularly valuable for developing countries which often lack capital-intensive infrastructure, and where, for example, the problem of ◊diarrhoeal diseases of children is especially acute.

Transgenic plants as a production system

There are two potential methods for producing vaccines in plants. In the first, the ◊DNA fragment encoding the antigen could be introduced directly into the nuclear ◊chromosome of the plant, using any of the methods developed for the production of ◊transgenic plants. The transgenic plants containing the antigen would then be used directly as an oral vaccine, or the antigen could be purified and then consumed. Alternatively, the DNA could be incorporated into a specific virus that only infects plants; this virus could be multiplied within the plant chosen for production. The plant virus particles containing the antigen would then be purified prior to their being used as a vaccine.

Both methods have already been shown to be effective in primary studies, including some conducted on animals. Crops used for animal feed, such as ◊alfalfa, ◊cereals, and ◊legumes are obvious choices for animal vaccines. For humans, plants chosen for production include ◊potato and ◊banana; the latter species may be preferred for tropical countries since it would permit vaccine production in the regions of greatest need. It would also allow inexpensive storage of vaccine material without the need for costly refrigeration facilities.

Future prospects

In the next stage of development, the promising results must be confirmed in a wider range of animal and human studies, before such production systems can be approved for widespread use. Remaining challenges include maximizing the level of production of the antigenic protein, stabilizing this protein during post-harvest storage of plant material, and enhancing its immunogenic capacity. In addition, it will be necessary to determine whether 'edible vaccines' should be provided as a specific medical (or veterinary) product or as a routine food source.

In some species, such as seals and bats, implantation is delayed for several months, during which time the embryo does not grow; thus the interval between mating and birth may be longer than the ◊gestation period.

import file in computing, a file that can be read by a program even though it was produced as an ◊export file by a different program or make of computer.

imprinting in ◊ethology, the process whereby a young animal learns to recognize both specific individuals (for example, its mother) and its own species.

Imprinting is characteristically an automatic response to specific stimuli at a time when the animal is especially sensitive to those stimuli (the **sensitive period**). Thus, goslings learn to recognize their mother by following the first moving object they see after hatching; as a result, they can easily become imprinted on other species, or even inanimate objects, if these happen to move near them at this time. In chicks, imprinting occurs only between 10 and 20 hours after hatching. In mammals, the mother's attachment to her infant may be a form of imprinting made possible by a sensitive period; this period may be as short as the first hour after giving birth.

improper fraction ◊fraction whose numerator is larger than its denominator.

impulse in mechanics, the product of a force and the time over which it acts. An impulse applied to a body causes its ◊momentum to change and is equal to that change in momentum. It is measured in newton seconds (N s).

For example, the impulse J given to a football when it is kicked is given by:

$$J = Ft$$

where F is the kick force in newtons and t is the time in seconds for which the boot is in contact with the ball.

in abbreviation for ◊inch, **a measure of distance**.

inbreeding in ◊genetics, the mating of closely related individuals. It is considered undesirable because it increases the risk that offspring will inherit copies of rare deleterious ◊recessive alleles (genes) from both parents and so suffer from disabilities.

incandescence emission of light from a substance in consequence of its high temperature. The colour of the emitted light from liquids or solids depends on their temperature, and for solids generally the higher the temperature the whiter the light. Gases may become incandescent through ◊ionizing radiation, as in the glowing vacuum ◊discharge tube.

The oxides of cerium and thorium are highly incandescent and for this reason are used in gas mantles. The light from an electric filament lamp is due to the incandescence of the filament, rendered white-hot when a current passes through it.

inch imperial unit of linear measure, a twelfth of a foot, equal to 2.54 centimetres.

It was defined in statute by Edward II of England as the length of three barley grains laid end to end.

incisor sharp tooth at the front of the mammalian mouth. Incisors are used for biting or nibbling, as when a rabbit or a sheep eats grass. Rodents, such as rats and squirrels, have large continually-growing incisors, adapted for gnawing. The elephant tusk is a greatly enlarged incisor. In humans, the incisors are the four teeth at the front centre of each jaw.

inclination angle between the ◊ecliptic and the plane of the orbit of a planet, asteroid, or comet. In the case of satellites orbiting a planet, it is the angle between the plane of orbit of the satellite and the equator of the planet.

inclusive fitness in ◊genetics, the success with which a given variant (or allele) of a ◊gene is passed on to future generations by a particular individual, after additional copies of the allele in the individual's relatives and their offspring have been taken into account.

The concept was formulated by W D Hamilton as a way of explaining the evolution of ◊altruism in terms of ◊natural selection. See also ◊fitness and ◊kin selection.

incontinence failure or inability to control evacuation of the bladder or bowel (or both in the case of double incontinence). It may arise as a result of injury, childbirth, disease, or senility.

incremental backup in computing, a ◊backup copy of only those files that have been modified or created since the last incremental or full backup.

Independent Television Commission (ITC) (formerly the Independent Broadcasting Authority) public body responsible for licensing and regulating commercial television services in the UK, including ITV, Channel Four, and Channel Five, as well as Teletext and a number of cable and satellite services. It is not responsible for licensing S4C, the fourth Welsh channel. Its duties include implementing a code of practice, ensuring adequate quality of services, reporting on complaints, and ensuring competition. It is funded by payments from its licensees; it was paid £315 million in 1995. Members of the Commission are appointed by the Government.

indeterminacy principle alternative name for ◊uncertainty principle.

In effect, we have redefined the task of science to be the discovery of laws that will enable us to predict events up to the limits set by the uncertainty principle.

STEPHEN HAWKING English physicist.

index (plural ***indices***) ***Latin 'sign, indicator'*** in mathematics, another term for ◊exponent, the number that indicates the power to which a term should be raised.

indexed sequential file in computing, a type of file ◊access in which an index is used to obtain the address of the ◊block containing the required record.

indexing in computing, computerized service on the Internet that automatically scans ◊servers and compiles lists of the information they hold to make it easier for users to find what they are looking for.

Indexing servers for ◊FTP (File Transfer Protocol) are called ◊Archie servers. On the World Wide Web, the best-known indexing service is ◊Yahoo, which organizes sites by categories and subcategories, and also allows free-form searching.

Indian corn another name for ◊maize.

indicator in chemistry, a compound that changes its structure and colour in response to its environment. The commonest chemical indicators detect changes in ◊pH (for example, ◊litmus), or in the oxidation state of a system (redox indicators).

indicator species plant or animal whose presence or absence in an area indicates certain environmental conditions, such as soil type, high levels of pollution, or, in rivers, low levels of dissolved oxygen. Many plants show a preference for either alkaline or acid soil conditions, while certain trees require aluminium, and are found only in soils where it is present. Some lichens are sensitive to sulphur dioxide in the air, and absence of these species indicates atmospheric pollution.

indigo violet-blue vegetable dye obtained from various tropical plants such as the anil, but now replaced by a synthetic product. It was once a major export crop of India. (Plant genus *Indigofera*, family Leguminosae.)

indium ***Latin indicum 'indigo'*** soft, ductile, silver-white, metallic element, symbol In, atomic number 49, relative atomic mass 114.82. It occurs in nature in some zinc ores, is resistant to abrasion, and is used as a coating on metal parts. It was discovered in 1863 by German metallurgists Ferdinand Reich (1799–1882) and Hieronymus Richter (1824–1898), who named it after the two indigo lines of its spectrum.

indri largest living ◊lemur of Madagascar. It is black and white, almost tailless, with long arms and legs, and grows to 70 cm/2.3 ft long. It lives in the trees and is active by day. Its howl is doglike or human in tone. Like all lemurs, its survival is threatened by the widespread deforestation of Madagascar. (Species *Indri indri*, family Indriidae.)

induced current electric current that appears in a closed circuit when there is relative movement of its conductor in a magnetic field. The effect is known as the **dynamo effect**, and is used in all ◊dynamos and generators to produce electricity. See ◊electromagnetic induction.

There is no battery or other source of power in a circuit in which an induced current appears: the energy supply is provided by the relative motion of the conductor and the magnetic field. The magnitude of the induced current depends upon the rate at which the magnetic flux is cut by the conductor, and its direction is given by Fleming's right-hand rule (see ◊Fleming's rules).

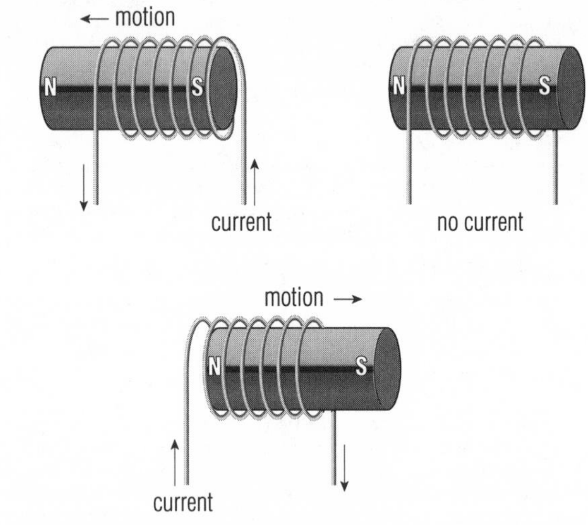

induced current

inductance in physics, the phenomenon where a changing current in a circuit builds up a magnetic field which induces an ◊electromotive force either in the same circuit and opposing the current (self-inductance) or in another circuit (mutual inductance). The SI unit of inductance is the henry (symbol H).

A component designed to introduce inductance into a circuit is called an ◊inductor (sometimes inductance) and is usually in the form of a coil of wire. The energy stored in the magnetic field of the coil is proportional to its inductance and the current flowing through it. See ◊electromagnetic induction.

induction in obstetrics, deliberate intervention to initiate labour before it starts naturally; then it usually proceeds normally.

Induction involves rupture of the fetal membranes (amniotomy) and the use of the hormone oxytocin to stimulate contractions of the womb. In biology, induction is a term used for various processes, including the production of an ◊enzyme in response to a particular chemical in the cell, and the ◊differentiation of cells in an ◊embryo in response to the presence of neighbouring tissues.

In obstetrics, induction is recommended as a medical necessity where there is risk to the mother or baby in waiting for labour to begin of its own accord.

induction in physics, an alteration in the physical properties of a body that is brought about by the influence of a field. See ◊electromagnetic induction and ◊magnetic induction.

induction coil type of electrical transformer, similar to an ◊ignition coil, that produces an intermittent high-voltage alternating current from a low-voltage direct current supply.

It has a primary coil consisting of a few turns of thick wire wound around an iron core and passing a low voltage (usually from a battery). Wound on top of this is a secondary coil made up of many turns of thin wire. An iron armature and make-and-break mechanism (similar to that in an ◊electric bell) repeatedly interrupts the current to the primary coil, producing a high, rapidly alternating current in the secondary circuit.

inductor device included in an electrical circuit because of its inductance.

Industrial Light & Magic (ILM) company that creates special effects for films and which has broken new ground in computer animation techniques (see ◊animation, computer). ILM was set up in 1975 by US director George Lucas to create special effects for his *Star Wars* films, and is based in San Rafael, California, USA.

The company's best-known computer-generated effects include the sea creature in *The Abyss* 1990, the liquid-metal man in *Terminator 2* 1991, and the dinosaurs in *Jurassic Park* 1993.

industry the extraction and conversion of raw materials, the manufacture of goods, and the provision of services. Industry can be either low technology, unspecialized, and labour-intensive, as in countries with a large unskilled labour force, or highly automated, mechanized, and specialized, using advanced technology, as in the industrialized countries. Major recent trends in industrial activity have been the growth of electronic, robotic, and microelectronic technologies, the expansion of the offshore oil industry, and the prominence of Japan and other Pacific-region countries in manufacturing and distributing electronics, computers, and motor vehicles.

Indus Valley civilization one of the four earliest ancient civilizations of the Old World (the other three being the Sumerian civilization 3500 BC; Egypt 3000 BC; and China 2200 BC), developing in the NW of the Indian subcontinent about 2500 BC.

Mohenjo Daro and Harappa were the two main city complexes, but many more existed along the Indus Valley, now in Pakistan. Remains include grid-planned streets with municipal drainage, public and private buildings, baths, temples, and a standardized system of weights and measures – all of which testify to centralized political control. Evidence exists for trade with Sumer and Akkad. The Aryan invasion of about 1500 BC probably led to its downfall.

inequality in mathematics, a statement that one quantity is larger or smaller than another, employing the symbols < and >. Inequalities may be solved by finding sets of numbers that satisfy them. For example, the solution set to the inequality $2x + 5 < 19$ consists of all values of x less than 7. Inequality relationships involving variables are sometimes called **inequations**.

inert gas or ***noble gas*** any of a group of six elements (helium, neon, argon, krypton, xenon, and radon), so named because they were originally thought not to enter into any chemical reactions. This is now known to be incorrect: in 1962, xenon was made to combine with fluorine, and since then, compounds of argon, krypton, and radon with fluorine and/or oxygen have been described.

The extreme unreactivity of the inert gases is due to the stability of their electronic structure. All the electron shells (◊energy levels) of inert gas atoms are full and, except for helium, they all have eight electrons in their outermost (◊valency) shell. The apparent stability of this electronic arrangement led to the formulation of the ◊octet rule to explain the different types of chemical bond found in simple compounds.

inertia in physics, the tendency of an object to remain in a state of rest or uniform motion until an external force is applied, as described by Isaac Newton's first law of motion (see ◊Newton's laws of motion).

inertial navigation navigation system that makes use of gyroscopes and accelerometers to monitor and measure a vehicle's movements. A computer calculates the vehicle's position relative to its starting position using the information supplied by the sensors. Inertial navigation is used in aircraft, submarines, spacecraft, and guided missiles.

infant mortality rate measure of the number of infants dying under one year of age, usually expressed as the number of deaths per 1,000 live births. Improved sanitation, nutrition, and medical care have considerably lowered figures throughout much of the world; for example in the 18th century in the USA and UK infant mortality was about 500 per thousand, compared with under 10 per thousand in 1989. The lowest infant mortality rate is in Japan, at 4.5 per 1,000 live births. In much of the Third World, however, the infant mortality rate remains high.

infection invasion of the body by disease-causing organisms (pathogens, or germs) that become established, multiply, and produce symptoms. Bacteria and viruses cause most diseases, but diseases are also caused by other microorganisms, protozoans, and other parasites.

Most pathogens enter and leave the body through the digestive or respiratory tracts. Polio, dysentery, and typhoid are examples of diseases contracted by ingestion of contaminated foods or fluids. Organisms present in the saliva or nasal mucus are spread by airborne or droplet infection; fine droplets or dried particles are inhaled by others when the affected individual talks, coughs, or sneezes. Diseases such as measles, mumps, and tuberculosis are passed on in this way.

A less common route of entry is through the skin, either by contamination of an open wound (as in tetanus) or by penetration of the intact skin surface, as in a bite from a malaria-carrying mosquito. Relatively few diseases are transmissible by skin-to-skin contact. Glandular fever and herpes simplex (cold sore) may be passed on by kissing, and the group now officially bracketed as sexually transmitted diseases (◊STDs) are mostly spread by intimate contact.

inferiority complex in psychology, a ◊complex or cluster of repressed fears, described by Alfred Adler, based on physical inferiority. The term is popularly used to describe general feelings of inferiority and the overcompensation that often ensues.

inferior planet planet (Mercury or Venus) whose orbit lies within that of the Earth, best observed when at its greatest elongation from the Sun, either at eastern elongation in the evening (setting after the Sun) or at western elongation in the morning (rising before the Sun).

inferno in astrophysics, a unit for describing the temperature inside a star. One inferno is 1 billion K, or approximately 1 billion °C.

infertility in medicine, inability to reproduce. In women, this may be due to blockage in the Fallopian tubes, failure of ovulation, a deficiency in sex hormones, or general ill health. In men, impotence, an insufficient number of sperm or abnormal sperm may be the cause of infertility. Clinical investigation will reveal the cause of the infertility in about 75% of couples and assisted conception may then be appropriate.

infinite series in mathematics, a series of numbers consisting of a denumerably infinite sequence of terms. The sequence $n, n^2, n^3,$ ... gives the series $n + n^2 + n^3 + \ldots$. For example, $1 + 2 + 3 + \ldots$ is a divergent infinite arithmetic series, and $8 + 4 + 2 + 1 + \frac{1}{2} + \ldots$ is a convergent infinite geometric series that has a sum to infinity of 16.

infinity mathematical quantity that is larger than any fixed assignable quantity; symbol ∞. By convention, the result of dividing any number by zero is regarded as infinity.

inflammation defensive reaction of the body tissues to disease or damage, including redness, swelling, and heat. Denoted by the suffix *-itis* (as in appendicitis), it may be acute or chronic, and may be accompanied by the formation of pus. This is an essential part of the healing process.

Inflammation occurs when damaged cells release a substance (◊histamine) that causes blood vessels to widen and leak into the surrounding tissues. This phenomenon accounts for the redness, swelling, and heat. Pain is due partly to the pressure of swelling and also to irritation of nerve endings. Defensive white blood cells congregate within an area of inflammation to engulf and remove foreign matter and dead tissue.

inflation in cosmology, a phase of extremely fast expansion thought to have occurred within 10–32 seconds of the ◊Big Bang and in which almost all the matter and energy in the universe was created. The inflationary model based on this concept accounts for the density of the universe being very close to the ◊critical density, the smoothness of the ◊cosmic background radiation, and the homogeneous distribution of matter in the universe. Inflation was proposed by US astronomer Alan Guth in the early 1980s.

inflorescence in plants, a branch, or system of branches, bearing two or more individual flowers. Inflorescences can be divided into two main types: cymose (or definite) and racemose (or indefinite). In a **cymose inflorescence**, the tip of the main axis produces a single flower and subsequent flowers arise on lower side branches, as in forget-me-not *Myosotis* and chickweed *Stellaria;* the oldest flowers are, therefore, found at the tip. A **racemose inflorescence** has an active growing region at the tip of its main axis, and bears flowers along its length, as in hyacinth *Hyacinthus;* the oldest flowers are found near the base or, in cases where the inflorescence is flattened, towards the outside.

The stalk of the inflorescence is called a peduncle; the stalk of each individual flower is called a pedicel.

Types of racemose inflorescence include the **raceme**, a spike of similar, stalked flowers, as seen in lupin *Lupinus.* A **corymb**, seen in candytuft *Iberis amara,* is rounded or flat-topped because the pedicels of the flowers vary in length, the outer pedicels being longer than the inner ones. A **panicle** is a branched inflorescence made up of a number of racemes; such inflorescences are seen in many grasses, for example, the oat *Avena.* The pedicels of an **umbel**, seen in members of the carrot family (Umbelliferae), all arise from the same point on the main axis, like the spokes of an umbrella. Other types of racemose inflorescence include the ◊catkin, a pendulous inflorescence, made up of many small stalkless flowers; the ◊spadix, **in which tiny flowers are borne on a fleshy axis; and the** ◊capitulum, in which the axis is flattened or rounded, bears many small flowers, and is surrounded by large petal-like bracts.

influenza any of various viral infections primarily affecting the air passages, accompanied by ◊systemic effects such as fever, chills, headache, joint and muscle pains, and lassitude. Treatment is with bed rest and analgesic drugs such as aspirin or paracetamol.

Depending on the virus strain, influenza varies in virulence and duration, and there is always the risk of secondary (bacterial) infection of the lungs (pneumonia). Vaccines are effective against known strains but will not give protection against newly evolving viruses. The 1918–19 influenza pandemic (see ◊epidemic) killed about 20 million people worldwide.

infobahn (from German autobahn 'motorway') in computing, short name for ◊information superhighway.

information service in computing, commercial online service which offers access to (usually high-priced) periodical databases and other information sources. The two major services are ◊America Online (AOL) and ◊CompuServe.

information superhighway popular collective name for the ◊Internet and other related large-scale computer networks. The term was first used in 1993 by US vice president Al Gore in a speech outlining plans to build a high-speed national data communications network.

information technology (IT) collective term for the various technologies involved in processing and transmitting information. They include computing, telecommunications, and microelectronics.

Word processing, databases, and spreadsheets are just some of the computing ◊software packages that have revolutionized work in the office environment. Not only can work be done more quickly than before, but IT has given decisionmakers the opportunity to consider far more data when making decisions.

infotainment (contraction of ***information and entertainment***) term applied to software that seeks to inform and entertain simultaneously. Many non-fiction ◊CD-ROM titles are classified as infotainment, such as multimedia encyclopedias or reference discs. Compare ◊edutainment.

infrared absorption spectrometry technique used to determine the mineral or chemical composition of artefacts and organic substances, particularly amber. A sample is bombarded by infrared radiation, which causes the atoms in it to vibrate at frequencies characteristic of the substance present, and absorb energy at those frequencies from the infrared spectrum, thus forming the basis for identification.

infrared astronomy study of infrared radiation produced by relatively cool gas and dust in space, as in the areas around forming stars. In 1983, the Infra-Red Astronomy Satellite (IRAS) surveyed the entire sky at infrared wavelengths. It found five new comets, thousands of galaxies undergoing bursts of star formation, and the possibility of planetary systems forming around several dozen stars.

Planets and gas clouds emit their light in the far and mid-infrared region of the spectrum. The Infrared Space Observatory (ISO), launched in 1995, observes a broad wavelength (3–200 micrometres) in this region. It is 10,000 times more sensitive than IRAS, and will search for ◊brown dwarfs (cool masses of gas smaller than the Sun).

infrared radiation invisible electromagnetic radiation of wavelength between about 0.75 micrometres and 1 millimetre – that is, between the limit of the red end of the visible spectrum and the shortest microwaves. All bodies above the ◊absolute zero of temperature absorb and radiate infrared radiation. Infrared radiation is used in medical photography and treatment, and in industry, astronomy, and criminology.

Infrared absorption spectra are used in chemical analysis, particularly for organic compounds. Objects that radiate infrared radiation can be photographed or made visible in the dark on specially sensitized emulsions. This is important for military purposes and in detecting people buried under rubble. The strong absorption by many substances of infrared radiation is a useful method of applying heat.

Infrared Space Observatory (ISO) orbiting telescope with a 60-cm/24-in diameter mirror. It was launched in November 1995 by the European Space Agency and will spend 18 months in an elongated orbit giving it a range from the Earth of 1,000–70,500 km/620–43,800 mi and keeping it as much as possible outside the radiation belts that would swamp its detectors.

Since its launch, ISO has made the first-ever discovery of water vapour from a source beyond the Solar System (in planetary nebula NGC 2027); has traced the spiral arms of the Whirlpool Galaxy and detected sites of star formation there; and obtained the first comprehensive spectrum of Saturn's atmosphere.

infrared telescope in astronomy, a ◊telescope designed to receive ◊electromagnetic waves in the infrared part of the spectrum. Infrared telescopes are always reflectors (glass lenses are opaque to infrared waves) and are normally of the ◊Cassegrain telescope type.

Since all objects at normal temperatures emit strongly in the infrared, careful design is required to ensure that the weak signals from the sky are not swamped by radiation from the telescope itself. Infrared telescopes are sited at high mountain observatories above the obscuring effects of water vapour in the atmosphere. Modern large telecopes are often designed to work equally well in both visible and infrared light.

infrastructure on the Internet, the underlying structure of telephone links, leased lines, and computer programs that makes communication possible.

ingestion process of taking food into the mouth. The method of food capture varies but may involve biting, sucking, or filtering. Many single-celled organisms have a region of their cell wall that acts as a mouth. In these cases surrounding tiny hairs (cilia) sweep food particles together, ready for ingestion.

inhibition, neural in biology, the process in which activity in one ◊nerve cell suppresses activity in another. Neural inhibition in networks of nerve cells leading from sensory organs, or to muscles, plays an important role in allowing an animal to make fine sensory discriminations and to exercise fine control over movements.

ink-jet printer computer printer that creates characters and graphics by spraying very fine jets of quick-drying ink onto paper. Ink-jet printers range in size from small machines designed to work with microcomputers to very large machines designed for high-volume commercial printing.

Because they produce very high-quality printing and are virtually silent, small ink-jet printers (along with ◊laser printers) are replacing impact printers, such as dot-matrix and daisywheel printers, for use with microcomputers.

in-line graphics on the ◊World Wide Web, images included in Web pages which can be downloaded and viewed on the fly. Web ◊browsers display these graphics automatically without any action required by the user. Those with slow connections, however, may choose to turn these off in the interests of speed and just view the text.

in-line video in computing, on the ◊World Wide Web, video files included in Web pages which can be played back on the fly. Web ◊browsers typically require a ◊helper application or ◊plug-in to be installed to play these files. Most sites which include in-line video have links to the necessary software for users who are not already equipped.

inoculation injection into the body of dead or weakened disease-carrying organisms or their toxins (◊vaccine) to produce immunity by inducing a mild form of a disease.

inorganic chemistry branch of chemistry dealing with the chemical properties of the elements and their compounds, excluding the more complex covalent compounds of carbon, which are considered in ◊organic chemistry.

The origins of inorganic chemistry lay in observing the characteristics and experimenting with the uses of the substances (compounds and elements) that could be extracted from mineral ores. These could be classified according to their chemical properties: elements could be classified as metals or nonmetals; compounds as acids or bases, oxidizing or reducing agents, ionic compounds (such as salts), or covalent compounds (such as gases). The arrangement of elements into groups possessing similar properties led to Mendeleyev's ◊periodic table of the elements, which prompted chemists to predict the properties of undiscovered elements that might occupy gaps in the table. This, in turn, led to the discovery of new elements, including a number of highly radioactive elements that do not occur naturally.

inorganic compound compound found in organisms that are not typically biological.

Water, sodium chloride, and potassium are inorganic compounds because they are widely found outside living cells. The term is also applied to those compounds that do not contain carbon and that are not manufactured by organisms. However, carbon dioxide is considered inorganic, contains carbon, and is manufactured by organisms during respiration. See ◊organic compound.

input device device for entering information into a computer. Input devices include keyboards, joysticks, mice, light pens, touch-sensitive screens, scanners, graphics tablets, speech-recognition devices, and vision systems. Compare ◊output device.

types of input device **Keyboards**, the most frequently used input devices, are used to enter instructions and data via keys. There are many variations on the layout and labelling of keys. Extra numeric keys may be added, as may special-purpose function keys, whose effects can be defined by programs in the computer.

The **graphics tablet** is an input device in which a stylus or cursor is moved, by hand, over a flat surface. The computer can keep track of the position of the stylus, enabling the operator to input drawings or diagrams into the computer. The **joystick** signals to a computer the direction and extent of displacement of a hand-held lever.

Light pens resemble ordinary pens and are used to indicate locations on a computer screen. With certain computer-aided design (◊CAD) programs, the light pen can be used to instruct the computer to change the shape, size, position, and colours of sections of a screen image.

Scanners produce a digital image of a document for input and storage in a computer, using technology similar to that of a photocopier. Small scanners can be passed over the document surface by hand; larger versions have a flat bed, like that of a photocopier, on which the input document is placed and scanned.

Input devices that are used commercially – for example, by banks, postal services, and supermarkets – must be able to read and capture large volumes of data very rapidly. Such devices include **document readers** for magnetic-ink character recognition (MICR), ◊optical character recognition (OCR), and optical mark recognition (OMR); mark-sense readers; bar-code scanners; magnetic-strip readers; and point-of-sale (POS) terminals. Punched-card and paper-tape readers were used in earlier commercial applications but are now obsolete.

insanity in medicine and law, any mental disorder in which the patient cannot be held responsible for their actions. The term is no longer used to refer to psychosis.

INSECT

The world's smallest winged insect is smaller than the eye of a house fly. It is the Tanzanian parasitic wasp, which has a wingspan of 0.2 mm/0.008 in.

insect any of a vast group of small invertebrate animals with hard, segmented bodies, three pairs of jointed legs, and, usually, two pairs of wings; they belong among the ◊arthropods and are distributed throughout the world. An insect's body is divided into three segments: head, thorax, and abdomen. On the head is a pair of feelers, or antennae. The legs and wings are attached to the thorax, or middle segment of the body. The abdomen, or end segment of the body, is where food is digested and excreted and where the reproductive organs are located.

Insects vary in size from 0.02 cm/0.007 in to 35 cm/13.5 in in length. The world's smallest insect is believed to be a 'fairy fly' wasp in the family Mymaridae, with a wingspan of 0.2 mm/0.008 in. (Class Insecta.)

Many insects hatch out of their eggs as ◊larvae (an immature stage, usually in the form of a caterpillar, grub, or maggot) and have to pass through further major physical changes (◊metamorphosis) before reaching adulthood. An insect about to go through metamorphosis hides itself or makes a cocoon in which to hide, then rests while the changes take place; at this stage the insect is called a ◊pupa, or a chrysalis if it is a butterfly or moth. When the changes are complete, the adult insect emerges.

The **classification** of insects is largely based upon characteristics of the mouthparts, wings, and metamorphosis. Insects are divided into two subclasses (one with two divisions) and 29 orders. More than 1 million species are known, and several thousand new ones are discovered each year.

The study of insects is called **entomology**.

TO REMEMBER THE PARTS OF AN INSECT'S LEG:

COCKROACHES TRAVEL FAST TOWARDS THEIR CHILDREN.

COXA / TROCHANTER / FEMUR / TIBIA / TARSUS / CLAW

INSECT CONTROL FAQ

http://res.agr.ca/lond/pmrc/faq/insect.html

Table of frequently asked questions about all kinds of insect control, including the Colorado potato beetle and aphids. The questions answered on this site include 'what are the most common insect pests?' and 'what alternatives are there to insecticides to control insects?'.

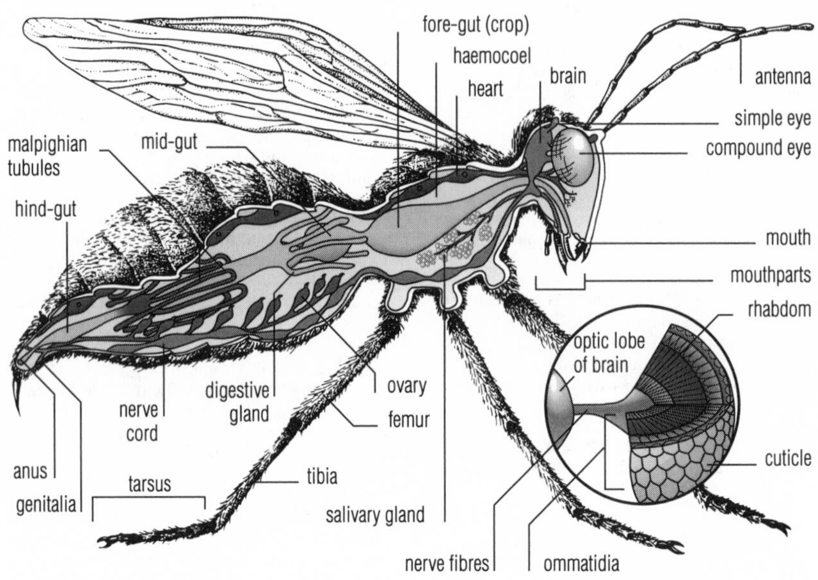

insect *Body plan of an insect. The general features of the insect body include a segmented body divided into head, thorax, and abdomen, jointed legs, feelers or antennae, and usually two pairs of wings. Insects often have compound eyes with a large field of vision.*

insecticide any chemical pesticide used to kill insects. Among the most effective insecticides are synthetic organic chemicals such as ◊DDT and dieldrin, which are chlorinated hydrocarbons. These chemicals, however, have proved persistent in the environment and are also poisonous to all animal life, including humans, and are consequently banned in many countries. Other synthetic insecticides include organic phosphorus compounds such as malathion. Insecticides prepared from plants, such as derris and pyrethrum, are safer to use but need to be applied frequently and carefully.

insectivore any animal whose diet is made up largely or exclusively of ◊insects. In particular, the name is applied to mammals of the order Insectivora, which includes the shrews, hedgehogs, moles, and tenrecs.

According to the Red List of endangered species published by the World Conservation Union (IUCN) for 1996, 36% of insectivore species are threatened with extinction.

insectivorous plant plant that can capture and digest live prey (normally insects), to obtain nitrogen compounds that are lacking in its usual marshy habitat. Some are passive traps, for example, the pitcher plants *Nepenthes* and *Sarracenia*. One pitcher-plant species has container-traps holding 1.6 l/3.5 pt of the liquid that 'digests' its food, mostly insects but occasionally even rodents. Others, for example, sundews *Drosera*, butterworts *Pinguicula*, and Venus flytraps *Dionaea muscipula*, have an active trapping mechanism. Insectivorous plants have adapted to grow in poor soil conditions where the number of microorganisms recycling nitrogen compounds is very much reduced. In these circumstances other plants cannot gain enough nitrates to grow. See also ◊leaf.

Near-carnivorous plants are unable to digest insects, but still trap them on their sticky coated leaves. The insects die and decay naturally, with the nutrients eventually becoming washed into the soil where they finally benefit the plant.

inselberg or ***kopje German 'island mountain'*** prominent steep-sided hill of resistant solid rock, such as granite, rising out of a plain, usually in a tropical area. Its rounded appearance is caused by so-called onion-skin ◊weathering, in which the surface is eroded in successive layers.

The Sugar Loaf in Rio de Janeiro harbour in Brazil, and Ayers Rock in Northern Territory, Australia, are famous examples.

insemination, artificial see ◊artificial insemination.

instinct in ◊ethology, behaviour found in all equivalent members of a given species (for example, all the males, or all the females with young) that is presumed to be genetically determined.

Examples include a male robin's tendency to attack other male robins intruding on its territory and the tendency of many female mammals to care for their offspring. Instincts differ from ◊reflexes in that they involve very much more complex actions, and learning often plays an important part in their development.

instruction register in computing, a special memory location used to hold the instruction that the computer is currently processing. It is located in the control unit of the ◊central processing unit, and receives instructions individually from the immediate-access memory during the fetch phase of the ◊fetch-execute cycle.

instruction set in computing, the complete set of machine-code instructions that a computer's ◊central processing unit can obey.

instrument landing system (ILS) landing aid for aircraft that uses ◊radio beacons on the ground and instruments on the flight deck. One beacon (localizer) sends out a vertical radio beam along the centre line of the runway. Another beacon (glide slope) transmits a beam in the plane at right angles to the localizer beam at the ideal approach-path angle. The pilot can tell from the instruments how to manoeuvre to attain the correct approach path.

insulation process or material that prevents or reduces the flow of electricity, heat or sound from one place to another.

Electrical insulation makes use of materials such as rubber, PVC, and porcelain, which do not conduct electricity, to prevent a current from leaking from one conductor to another or down to the ground. Insulation is a vital safety measure that prevents electric currents from being conducted through people and causing electric shock.

Double insulation is a method of constructing electrical appliances that provides extra protection from electric shock, and renders the use of an earth wire unnecessary. In addition to the usual cable insulation, an appliance that meets the double insulation standard is totally enclosed in an insulating plastic body or structure so that there is no direct connection between any external metal parts and the internal electrical components.

Thermal or **heat insulation** makes use of insulating materials such as fibreglass to reduce the loss of heat through the roof and walls of buildings. The U-value of an insulating layer is a measure of its ability to conduct heat – a material chosen as an insulator should therefore have a low ◊U-value. Air trapped between the fibres of clothes acts as a thermal insulator, preventing loss of body warmth.

insulator any poor ◊conductor of heat, sound, or electricity. Most substances lacking free (mobile) ◊electrons, such as non-metals, are electrical or thermal insulators. Usually, devices of glass or porcelain, called insulators, are used for insulating and supporting overhead wires.

insulin protein ◊hormone, produced by specialized cells in the islets of Langerhans in the pancreas, that regulates the metabolism (rate of activity) of glucose, fats, and proteins. Insulin was discovered by Canadian physician Frederick Banting and Canadian physiologist Charles Best, who pioneered its use in treating ◊diabetes.

Normally, insulin is secreted in response to rising blood sugar levels (after a meal, for example), stimulating the body's cells to store the excess. Failure of this regulatory mechanism in diabetes mellitus requires treatment with insulin injections or capsules taken by mouth. Types vary from pig and beef insulins to synthetic and bioengineered ones. They may be combined with other substances to make them longer-or shorter-acting. Implanted, battery-powered insulin pumps deliver the hormone at a preset rate, to eliminate the unnatural rises and falls that result from conventional, subcutaneous (under the skin) delivery. Human insulin has now been produced from bacteria by ◊genetic engineering techniques, but may increase the chance of sudden, unpredictable ◊hypoglycaemia, or low blood sugar. In 1990 the Medical College of Ohio developed gelatin capsules and an aspirinlike drug which helps the insulin pass into the bloodstream.

TO REMEMBER THE ROLE OF INSULIN:

REMEMBER THAT INSULIN GETS SUGAR INTO CELLS. WITHOUT INSULIN, A PERSON CAN HAVE EXCESS SUGAR IN HIS BLOOD YET DIE OF LACK OF SUGAR.

integer any whole number. Integers may be positive or negative; 0 is an integer, and is often considered positive. Formally, integers are members of the set $Z = \{... -3, -2, -1, 0, 1, 2, 3,... \}$. Fractions, such as $\frac{1}{2}$ and 0.35, are known as non-integral numbers ('not integers').

God made the integers, man made the rest.

LEOPOLD KRONECKER German mathematician. *Jahresberichte der deutschen Mathematiker Vereinigung* bk 2. In F Cajori *A History of Mathematics* 1919

integral calculus branch of mathematics using the process of ◊integration. It is concerned with finding volumes and areas and summing infinitesimally small quantities.

integrated circuit (IC), popularly called ***silicon chip***, a miniaturized electronic circuit produced on a single crystal, or chip, of a semiconducting material – usually silicon. It may contain many millions of components and yet measure only 5 mm/0.2 in square and 1 mm/0.04 in thick. The IC is encapsulated within a plastic or ceramic case, and linked via gold wires to metal pins with which it is connected to a ◊printed circuit board and the other components that make up such electronic devices as computers and calculators.

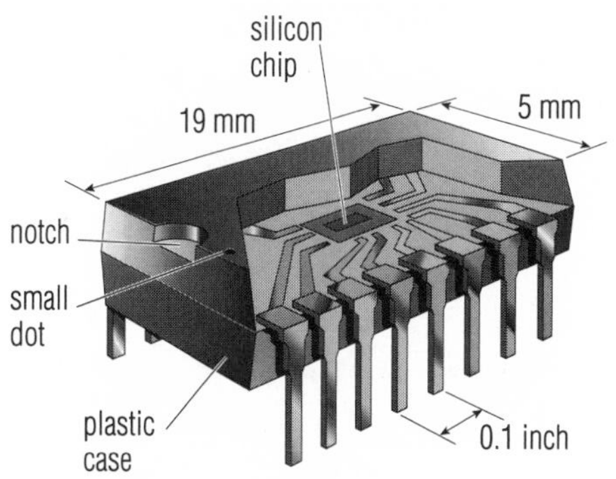

***integrated circuit** An integrated circuit (IC), or silicon chip. The IC is a piece of silicon, about the size of a child's fingernail, on which the components of an electrical circuit are etched. The IC is packed in a plastic container with metal legs that connect it to the circuit board.*

Integrated Services Digital Network (ISDN) internationally developed telecommunications system for sending signals in ◊digital format. It involves converting the 'local loop' – the link between the user's telephone (or private automatic branch exchange) and the digital telephone exchange – from an ◊analogue system into a digital system, thereby greatly increasing the amount of information that can be carried. The first large-scale use of ISDN began in Japan in 1988.

ISDN has advantages in higher voice quality, better quality faxes, and the possibility of data transfer between computers faster than current modems. With ISDN's **Basic Rate Access**, a multiplexer divides one voice telephone line into three channels: two B bands and a D band. Each B band offers 64 kilobits per second and can carry one voice conversation or 50 simultaneous data calls at 1,200 bits per second. The D band is a data-signalling channel operating at 16 kilobits per second. With **Primary Rate Access**, ISDN provides 30 B channels.

integrated steelworks modern industrial complex where all the steelmaking processes – such as iron smelting and steel shaping – take place on the same site.

integration in mathematics, a method in ◊calculus of determining the solutions of definite or indefinite integrals.

An example of a definite integral can be thought of as finding the area under a curve (as represented by an algebraic expression or function) between particular values of the function's variable. In practice, integral calculus provides scientists with a powerful tool for doing calculations that involve a continually varying quantity (such as determining the position at any given instant of a space rocket that is accelerating away from Earth). Its basic principles were discovered in the late 1660s independently by the German philosopher Leibniz and the British scientist ◊Newton.

integument in seed-producing plants, the protective coat surrounding the ovule. In flowering plants there are two, in gymnosperms only one. A small hole at one end, the micropyle, allows a pollen tube to penetrate through to the egg during fertilization.

Intel manufacturer of the microprocessors that form the basis of the IBM PC range and its clones. Intel developed the first ◊microprocessor, the 4004, in 1971, and has largely retained compatibility throughout the x86 range from the 8086 to the 80486 and the ◊Pentium or 586 released in 1993. Intel's current strategy is to promote the use of the Pentium II processor, introduced in 1997, while it is developing its next-generation chip, code-named Merced, in conjunction with Hewlett-Packard.

History of Insulin

BY PAULETTE PRATT

The term 'diabetes' (from the Ionian Greek 'to pass through'), together with a succinct clinical description of this once-fatal disease, was bequeathed to us by Aretaeus of Cappadocia. In the 2nd century AD he wrote: 'Diabetes is a dreadful affliction, not very frequent among men, being a melting down of the flesh and limbs into urine. The patients never stop making water and the flow is incessant, like the opening of aqueducts. Life is short, unpleasant and painful, thirst unquenchable, drinking excessive...'

'One cannot stop them either from drinking or making water. If for a while they abstain from drinking, their mouths become parched and their bodies dry; the viscera seem scorched up, the patients are affected by nausea, restlessness and a burning thirst, and within a short time they expire.'

Although Eastern physicians had noted the sweet taste of the urine in diabetes a thousand years earlier, in Europe the connection between sugar in the urine and diabetes was only made in 1670 by an English physician, Thomas Willis. In 1776, Liverpool physician Matthew Dobson showed that the blood serum of diabetic patients also contains a sweet-tasting substance. He proved that this is sugar and deduced that it is formed in the serum rather than in the kidneys. This was the first indication that diabetes is a systemic disease (pervading the whole body) rather than a specific kidney problem as some people had thought.

Soon after, another English physician, John Rollo, was among the first to attach the adjective 'mellitus' (from the Greek and Latin roots for 'honey') to distinguish diabetes from other conditions where there is copious urine output. The next major observation, published in the *London Medical Journal* in 1788, was that diabetes may ensue from damage to the pancreas. In Strasbourg a century later, Oskar Minkowski and Josef von Mering were able to produce experimental diabetes in a dog by removing its pancreas.

This firm association of diabetes with pancreatic deficiency prompted researchers to begin looking for the actual substance involved in order to develop a treatment. In 1893, a Frenchman, Edouard Laguesse, suggested that the pancreatic 'islets of Langerhans 'might be implicated. He named these after the distinguished German pathologist, Paul Langerhans, who, at the age of 22, had been the first person to describe them (1869).

A Belgian physician, Jean de Meyer, gave the name *insuline* (from the Latin insula, meaning island) to the as yet hypothetical blood sugar-lowering substance in 1909. The British physiologist Edward Sharpey Schafer, who argued that the islets must secrete a substance which governs carbohydrate metabolism, used the word 'insulin' for this notional substance in 1916, but the term did not immediately become current: Banting and Best and their collaborators, who discovered insulin in 192l, at first called it 'isletin'.

By the early years of this century then, it was known that diabetes mellitus arises from a lack of this unknown substance. Meanwhile, people developing the disease lived brief, wretched lives. Those who sought treatment were put on starvation diets. The effect of this was to lower blood glucose and produce emaciation; the extension it won to the patient's life was at best a few months.

At this time a number of scientists were on the track of insulin and an unknown Canadian doctor, 29-year-old Frederick Grant Banting, also developed an interest in the hormone. He approached J J R Macleod, then Professor of Physiology at the University of Toronto (and an expert on sugar metabolism), for facilities to conduct experiments in a bid to isolate insulin. Macleod made available laboratory space and experimental dogs for Banting's use; he also offered one of his students as an assistant, Charles H Best (who had won the opportunity to work alongside Banting on the toss of a coin). But it was the addition of biochemist James B. Collip which would ensure their success.

The first trial of the team's pancreatic extract was on 14-year-old Leonard Thompson, who was dying of diabetes in Toronto General Hospital, on January 1, 1922. This failed to relieve his symptoms and, moreover, caused an abscess to form at the injection site. However, a further extract, injected on January 23, brought the boy's blood sugar down to normal. In May, when the group reported the outcome of this modest trial to a meeting of the Association of American Physicians in Washington DC, they received a standing ovation.

From October 1923, once a commercially viable extraction process had been developed, insulin became widely available throughout North America and Europe. Now, for diabetic patients who would otherwise have been doomed, the issue was no longer one of survival but of quality of life on insulin treatment.

Among the people who witnessed the introduction of the life-saving extract into clinical use was a Portuguese doctor, Ernesto Roma, who was on a visit to Boston. Returning to Lisbon in 1926, he set up the World's first diabetic organisation, the Portuguese Association for the Protection of Poor Diabetics, which provided insulin free of charge. The British Diabetic Association was founded in 1934 by a doctor whose life had been saved by insulin, Robin Lawrence, and the writer H G Wells, who also had the disease.

Controversially, only Banting and Macleod received the Nobel prize for the discovery of insulin, in 1923 (in what was one of the Nobel committee's quickest ever recognitions). Despite the acrimony which had arisen within the group, the two men shared the award money with their collaborators. Frederick Banting, whose vision had driven the project, became a World hero and received a knighthood and a generous annuity from the Canadian government. He died in an air crash in Newfoundland in 194l.

Leonard Thompson, the original insulin 'guinea pig', survived until 1935 and at least two of the children who had been treated in Toronto in the trial period outlived all four of the men who had worked on the discovery of insulin. One of these, Ted Ryder, lived until 1993, reaching the age of 76.

Intel is thought to supply the processors for almost 90% of the world's personal computers.

intellectual property material such as computer software, magazine articles, songs, novels, or recordings which can be described as the expression of ideas fixed in a tangible form.

Generally, intellectual property is protected by copyright law, and distribution, sale, and copying of such material is restricted so that the creators can be paid for their work. On the Internet, intellectual property may include the words, graphics, audio files, and other material which comprise pages on the World Wide Web, as well as the words written by individuals in e-mail or on USENET.

intellectual property rights the right of control over the copying, distribution, and sale of ◊intellectual property which is codified in the copyright laws.

The future of intellectual property rights is unclear, as the Internet makes mass distribution and copying quick and easy. In the mid-1990s, many schemes were being considered for using encryption to mark computer files or prevent copying in an effort to safeguard these rights.

intelligence in psychology, a general concept that summarizes the abilities of an individual in reasoning and problem solving, particularly in novel situations. These consist of a wide range of verbal and nonverbal skills and therefore some psychologists dispute a unitary concept of intelligence.

Intelligence is quickness to apprehend as distinct from ability, which is capacity to act wisely on the thing apprehended.

ALFRED NORTH WHITEHEAD English philosopher and mathematician. *Dialogues* 15 Dec 1939

intelligence test test that attempts to measure innate intellectual ability, rather than acquired ability.

It is now generally believed that a child's ability in an intelligence test can be affected by his or her environment, cultural background, and teaching. There is scepticism about the accuracy of intelligence tests, but they are still widely used as a diagnostic tool when children display learning difficulties. 'Sight and sound' intelligence tests, developed by Christopher Brand in 1981, avoid cultural bias and the pitfalls of improvement by practice. Subjects are shown a series of lines being flashed on a screen at increasing speed, and are asked to identify in each case the shorter of a pair; and when two notes are relayed over headphones, they are asked to identify which is the higher. There is a close correlation between these results and other intelligence test scores.

intelligent agent in computing, another name for ◊agent.

intelligent terminal in computing, a ◊terminal with its own processor which can take some of the processing load away from the main computer.

Intelsat (acronym for ***International Telecommunications Satellite Organization***) organization established in 1964 to operate a worldwide system of communications satellites. In 1994 it had 134 member nations and 22 satellites in orbit. Its headquarters are in Washington DC. Intelsat satellites are stationed in geostationary orbit (maintaining their positions relative to the Earth) over the Atlantic, Pacific, and Indian Oceans. The first Intelsat satellite was *Early Bird,* launched in 1965.

intensity in physics, the power (or energy per second) per unit area carried by a form of radiation or wave motion. It is an indication of the concentration of energy present and, if measured at varying distances from the source, of the effect of distance on this. For example, the intensity of light is a measure of its brightness, and may be shown to diminish with distance from its source in accordance with the ◊inverse square law (its intensity is inversely proportional to the square of the distance).

interactive describing a computer system that will respond directly to data or commands entered by the user. For example, most popular programs, such as word processors and spreadsheet applications, are interactive. Multimedia programs are usually highly interactive, allowing users to decide what type of information to display (text, graphics, video, or audio) and enabling them (by means of ◊hypertext) to choose an individual route through the information.

interactive computing in computing, a system for processing data in which the operator is in direct communication with the computer, receiving immediate responses to input data. In ◊batch processing, by contrast, the necessary data and instructions are prepared in advance and processed by the computer with little or no intervention from the operator.

interactive digital video service alternative term for ◊video-on-demand.

interactive media in computing, new technology such as ◊CD-ROM and online systems which allow users to interact with other users or to choose their own path through the material.

The newest attempts to create interactive media are books published on the World Wide Web which allow readers to use ◊hyperlinks to move around the material at will in the order they choose. Other interactive media include plans for films and other projects which allow viewers to choose how to follow the story, which characters to focus on, or which plot threads to follow.

Interactive Multimedia Association (IMA) organization founded in 1987 to promote the growth of the multimedia industry. Based in Anapolis, Maryland, USA, the IMA runs special interest groups, summit meetings, conferences, and trade shows for its member companies.

interactive video (IV) computer-mediated system that enables the user to interact with and control information (including text, recorded speech, or moving images) stored on video disc. IV is most commonly used for training purposes, using analogue video discs, but has wider applications with digital video systems such as CD-I (Compact Disc Interactive, from Philips and Sony) which are based on the CD-ROM format derived from audio compact discs.

Intercast in computing, ◊Intel device that adds TV reception capability to a PC and uses blank lines to deliver data.

A number of leading PC manufacturers expect to bundle Intercast TV tuner boards with new computer systems.

intercostal in biology, the nerves, blood vessels, and muscles that lie between the ribs.

interface in computing, the point of contact between two programs or pieces of equipment. The term is most often used for the physical connection between the computer and a peripheral device, which is used to compensate for differences in such operating characteristics as speed, data coding, voltage, and power consumption. For example, a **printer interface** is the cabling and circuitry used to transfer data from a computer to a printer, and to compensate for differences in speed and coding.

Common standard interfaces include the **Centronics interface**, used to connect parallel devices, and the **RS232 interface**, used to connect serial devices. For example, in many microcomputer systems, an RS232 interface is used to connect the microcomputer to a modem, and a Centronics device is used to connect it to a printer.

interference in physics, the phenomenon of two or more wave motions interacting and combining to produce a resultant wave of larger or smaller amplitude (depending on whether the combining waves are in or out of ◊phase with each other).

Interference of white light (multiwavelength) results in spectral coloured fringes; for example, the iridescent colours of oil films seen on water or soap bubbles (demonstrated by ◊Newton's rings). Interference of sound waves of similar frequency produces the phenomenon of beats, often used by musicians when tuning an instrument. With monochromatic light (of a single wavelength), interference produces patterns of light and dark bands. This is the basis of ◊holography, for example. Interferometry can also be applied to radio waves, and is a powerful tool in modern astronomy.

interferometer in physics, a device that splits a beam of light into two parts, the parts being recombined after travelling different paths to form an interference pattern of light and dark bands.

Interferometers are used in many branches of science and industry where accurate measurements of distances and angles are needed.

In the Michelson interferometer, a light beam is split into two by a semisilvered mirror. The two beams are then reflected off fully silvered mirrors and recombined. The pattern of dark and light bands is sensitive to small alterations in the placing of the mirrors, so the interferometer can detect changes in their position to within one ten-millionth of a metre. Using lasers, compact devices of this kind can be built to measure distances, for example to check the accuracy of machine tools.

In radio astronomy, interferometers consist of separate radio telescopes, each observing the same distant object, such as a galaxy, in the sky. The signal received by each telescope is fed into a computer. Because the telescopes are in different places, the distance travelled by the signal to reach each differs and the overall signal is akin to the interference pattern in the Michelson interferometer. Computer analysis of the overall signal can build up a detailed picture of the source of the radio waves.

In space technology, interferometers are used in radio and radar systems. These include space-vehicle guidance systems, in which the position of the spacecraft is determined by combining the signals received by two precisely spaced antennae mounted on it.

interferometry in astronomy, any of several techniques used in astronomy to obtain high-resolution images of astronomical objects. See ◊speckle interferometry and ◊VLBI (very long baseline interferometry).

interferon naturally occurring cellular protein that makes up part of the body's defences against viral disease. Three types (alpha, beta, and gamma) are produced by infected cells and enter the bloodstream and uninfected cells, making them immune to virus attack.

Interferon was discovered in 1957 by Scottish virologist Alick Isaacs. Interferons are cytokines, small molecules that carry signals from one cell to another. They can be divided into two main types: **type I** (alpha, beta, tau, and omega) interferons are more effective at bolstering cells' ability to resist infection; **type II** (gamma) interferon is more important to the normal functioning of the immune system. Alpha interferon may be used to treat some cancers; interferon beta 1b has been found useful in the treatment of ◊multiple sclerosis.

interior angle one of the four internal angles formed when a transversal cuts two or more (usually parallel) lines. Also, one of the angles inside a ◊polygon.

interlacing technique for increasing resolution on computer graphic displays. The electron beam traces alternate lines on each pass, providing twice the number of lines of a non-interlaced screen. However, screen refresh is slower and screen flicker may be increased over that seen on an equivalent non-interlaced screen.

INTERMEDIATE TECHNOLOGY DEVELOPMENT GROUP

http://www.oneworld.org/itdg/

Full account of the work of the British aid organization working with rural poor to develop relevant and sustainable technologies. Reports of the low-tech projects supported by IT make fascinating reading. Of equal interest is work with other British aid agencies to develop approaches to project monitoring and evaluation which involve local people.

intermediate technology application of mechanics, electrical engineering, and other technologies, based on inventions and designs developed in scientifically sophisticated cultures, but utilizing materials, assembly, and maintenance methods found in technologically less advanced regions (known as the Third World).

Intermediate technologies aim to allow developing countries to benefit from new techniques and inventions of the 'First World', without the burdens of costly maintenance and supply of fuels and spare parts that in the Third World would represent an enormous and probably uneconomic overhead. See also ◊appropriate technology.

Science clears the fields on which technology can build.

WERNER CARL HEISENBERG German physicist.

intermediate vector boson alternative name for **weakon**, the elementary particle responsible for carrying the ◊weak nuclear force.

intermolecular force or ***van der Waals' force*** force of attraction between molecules. Intermolecular forces are relatively weak; hence simple molecular compounds are gases, liquids, or low-melting-point solids.

internal-combustion engine heat engine in which fuel is burned inside the engine, contrasting with an external-combustion engine (such as the steam engine) in which fuel is burned in a separate unit. The ◊diesel engine and ◊petrol engine are both internal-combustion engines. Gas ◊turbines and ◊jet and ◊rocket engines are also considered to be internal-combustion engines because they burn their fuel inside their combustion chambers.

internal modem in computing, a ◊modem that fits into a slot inside a personal computer. On older PCs, an internal modem may prove a better choice for high-speed data communications than an external modem, as it may have built-in features which make up for features missing in older computers. Internal modems are generally also cheaper, except for the small-sized ◊PCMCIA types.

The disadvantages are that an internal modems cannot easily be swapped from one computer to another, require greater skill to install (again except for PCMCIA), and have no external displays of lights to give users feedback.

internal resistance or ***source resistance*** the resistance inside a power supply, such as a battery of cells, that limits the current that it can supply to a circuit.

International Atomic Energy Agency (IAEA) agency of the United Nations established in 1957 to advise and assist member countries in the development and peaceful application of nuclear power, and to guard against its misuse. It has its headquarters in Vienna, and is responsible for research centres in Austria and Monaco, and the International Centre for Theoretical Physics, Trieste, Italy, established in 1964. It conducts inspections of nuclear installations in countries suspected of developing nuclear weapons, for example Iraq and North Korea.

international biological standards drugs (such as penicillin and insulin) of which the activity for a specific mass (called the international unit, or IU), prepared and stored under specific conditions, serves as a standard for measuring doses. For penicillin, one IU is the activity of 0.0006 mg of the sodium salt of penicillin, so a dose of a million units would be 0.6 g.

International Civil Aviation Organization agency of the United Nations, established in 1947 to regulate safety and efficiency and air law; headquarters Montréal, Canada.

INTERNATIONAL CIVIL AVIATION ORGANIZATION

http://www.icao.int

Site of the specialized UN agency regulating civil aviation. The role and history of the ICAO are well presented. There is information on rules of the air, international conventions, and standardization of safety standards. The ICAO tries to reassure nervous flyers that air travel is getting safer. There are links to all the online airlines, airports, and pilot training centres in the world.

International Date Line (IDL) imaginary line that approximately follows the 180° line of longitude. The date is put forward a day when crossing the line going west, and back a day when going east. The IDL was chosen at the International Meridian Conference 1884.

International Organization for Standardization (ISO) international organization founded in 1947 to standardize technical terms, specifications, units, and so on. Its headquarters are in Geneva.

International Telecommunication Union body belonging to the Economic and Social Council of the United Nations. It aims to extend international cooperation by improving telecommunications of all kinds.

International Telecommunications Union (ITU) international organization, based in Geneva, Switzerland, which manages telecommunications standards such as ◊modem speeds and ◊protocols. ITU activities include the coordination, development, regulation, and standardization of telecommunications.

The ITU has two permanent standards-making committes, the International Telegraph and Telephone Consultative Committee (CCITT) and the International Radio Consultative Committee (CCIR).

The Internal Combustion Engine

BY PETER LAFFERTY

The steam engine was the first reliable source of power. By the early 1800s, the steam engine had developed to the point where it could propel carriages along the road at reasonable speeds, and undertake long journeys. But the quest was on for a lighter, more powerful engine.

The idea of an internal combustion engine seems to have occurred around 1800 to French inventor Philippe Lebon. He argued that an engine that burnt fuel inside a cylinder would waste less heat and be more efficient than an engine, like the steam engine, which had a separate furnace in which the fuel was burnt. He proposed an engine in which a compressed mixture of gas and air was burnt in a cylinder, the heated gas driving a piston. Unfortunately, Lebon met an untimely end before he could build the engine. He was attacked and stabbed on the Champs Elysées in Paris and died of his wounds.

After Lebon, several inventors tried to build internal combustion engines but failed, mainly because of difficulties with ignition of the fuel–air mixture inside the cylinder.

In 1807 Swiss inventor Isaac de Rivas built an engine which he used to move a trolley. However, the engine was too inefficient to be of any use. In 1829, the Reverend William Cecil read a paper at Cambridge University about his experiments, and William Barnet in 1839 also laid claims to the invention. In 1853 Italians Eugenio Barsanti and Felice Mattecci patented a design, but they never built a working engine. It was not until 1860 that an efficient engine was built by Belgian engineer Etienne Lenoir.

Lenoir's engine consisted of a single cylinder with a storage battery for electrical ignition of the fuel–air mixture. It was a two-stroke engine, producing its power in two strokes, or movements, of the piston. It was fuelled by coal gas, as used then for domestic purposes and street lighting. The engine developed a feeble two horsepower. This was just enough power to drive a road vehicle and in 1863 Lenoir took a 10 km/6 mi journey in the first car powered by an internal combustion engine. The trip took 3 h to complete. The real value of the Lenoir engine was for powering small machines, and by 1865 more than 400 were in use in Paris, driving printing presses, lathes and water pumps. However, technical weaknesses, especially low compression, limited the potential of the Lenoir engine.

The next step forward was taken by German engineer Nikolaus Otto. In 1876, Otto patented the four- stroke engine, which produced its power using four movements of the piston. It used only half the fuel consumed by the Lenoir engine and was more powerful. The Otto engine was an immediate success; more than 35,000 were made in a few years. They were large engines and developed over 450 kW/600 hp.

Unfortunately for him, Otto's patent was invalidated in 1886 when his competitors dug up an earlier patent taken out by French inventor Alphonse Beau de Rochas in 1862. Rochas had described the four-stroke cycle in his patent. A court battle ensued, lasting two years, after which Otto's patent was declared invalid. This gave the go-ahead to other inventors to use the basic ideas without hindrance. German Karl Benz refined the Lenoir engine and introduced the use of liquid fuel, such as alcohol or petrol. He fitted his engine into a three-wheeled vehicle and in July 1886 at Mannheim the first petrol-driven motor car took to the roads. The trip covered about 1.6 km/1 mi mile at a speed of 14.5 kph/9 mph. Meanwhile, just 100 km/60 mi away in Cannstadt, Gottlieb Daimler was building his four-wheeled petrol-driven motor car. He completed a successful test run in August 1886.

A different type of internal combustion engine was invented by German engineer Karl Diesel in 1892. In the diesel engine, the compression used in the piston is much higher than in the petrol engine. This compression raises the temperature of air in the cylinder so high that electric ignition is not needed – the fuel ignites spontaneously when injected into the cylinder. This arrangement avoided the problems associated with electrical ignition and produced a simpler engine.

Working with such high pressures, Diesel was lucky to escape being killed when the cylinder head blew off one of his prototype engines. Undeterred he carried on to perfect the engine, and in 1899 he set up a factory to manufacture the engines. The factory flourished despite Diesel having little business sense. In 1913, at the height of his success, he vanished from the decks of a steamer crossing from Antwerp to England. His body was never found.

International Traffic in Arms Regulations US laws which prohibit the export of strong encryption by classifying it as a munition. Non-US users of common products such as ◊Netscape and ◊Lotus Notes are affected by these laws, as outside the USA American software suppliers must weaken the encryption built in to protect sensitive data.

In the mid-1990s several bills were introduced into the US Congress attempting to change these laws.

International Union for the Conservation of Nature (IUCN) organization established by the United Nations to promote the conservation of wildlife and habitats as part of the national policies of member states.

It has formulated guidelines and established research programmes (for example, International Biological Programme, IBP) and set up advisory bodies (such as Survival Commissions, SSC). In 1980, it launched the **World Conservation Strategy** to highlight particular problems, designating a small number of areas as **World Heritage Sites** to ensure their survival as unspoiled habitats (for example, Yosemite National Park in the USA, and the Simen Mountains in Ethiopia). It also compiles the **Red Data List of Threatened Animals**, classifying species according to their vulnerability to extinction.

According to its list of endangered species published in 1996, 25% of all mammal species (including 36% of insectivores and 33% of pigs and antelopes) and 11% of all bird species are threatened with extinction.

Internet global computer network connecting governments, companies, universities, and many other networks and users. ◊Electronic mail, conferencing, and chat services are all supported across the network, as is the ability to access remote computers and send and retrieve files. In 1997 around 55 million adults had access to the Internet in the USA alone.

The technical underpinnings of the Internet were developed as a project funded by the Advanced Research Project Agency (ARPA) to research how to build a network that would withstand bomb damage. The Internet itself began in 1984 with funding from the US National Science Foundation as a means to allow US universities to share the resources of five regional supercomputing centres. The number of users grew quickly, and in the early 1990s access became cheap enough for domestic users to have their own links on home personal computers. As the amount of information available via the Internet grew, indexing and search services such as Gopher, Archie, Veronica, and WAIS were created by Internet users to help both themselves and others. The newer World Wide Web allows seamless browsing across the Internet via ◊hypertext.

Internet Architecture Board (IAB) in computing, committee that coordinates the development of Internet ◊standards. Set up 1983, the IAB is a technical advisory group of the ◊Internet Society. Its responsibilities include architectural oversight for the ◊protocols and procedures used by the Internet, standards process oversight and appeal, editorial management and publication of ◊RFC (request for comments) documents, and advising the Internet

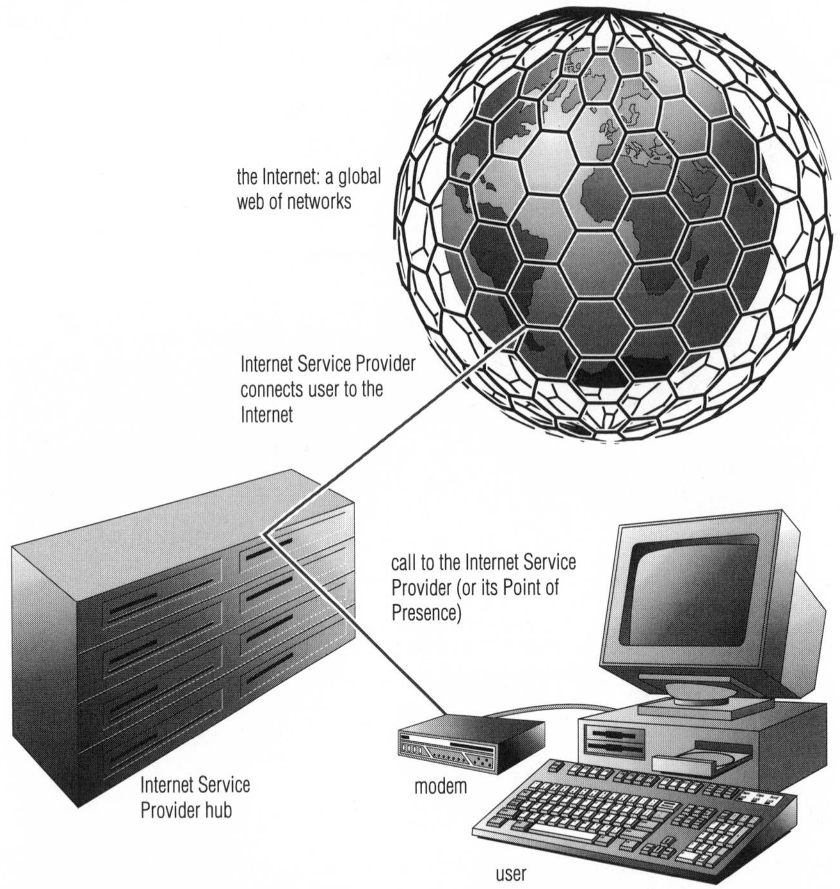

Internet *The Internet is accessed by users via a modem to the service provider's hub, which handles all connection requests. Once connected, the user can access a whole range of information from many different sources, including the World Wide Web.*

Society concerning technical, architectural, procedural, and some policy matters.

Internet-enabled in computing, facility that allows desktop applications to exchange information directly across the Internet. The most common Internet facility to build in is e-mail. Also popular is integrated Web access, so that a user can click on a ◊URL (uniform resource locator) from inside an application such as a word processor or personal information manager and be taken directly to that page on the World Wide Web.

Internet Engineering Task Force (IETF) in computing, international group which supervises the development of RFC (requests for comments), ◊protocols, and other engineering design for the Internet, reporting to the ◊Internet Architecture Board. It was formed 1986 and is based in Reston, Virginia, USA.

Internet Explorer in computing, Web ◊browser created by Microsoft 1995 to compete with ◊Netscape Navigator.Internet Explorer is given away free by Microsoft and bundled with its Windows 95 program. The US Justice Department sued Microsoft 1997 to prevent it from denying firms access to Windows 95 if they chose not to include Internet Explorer.

Internet Hunt in computing, monthly game played to test contestants' skills at finding information on the Internet.

Internet mail in computing, e-mail sent across the Internet. The distinction is primarily made on closed or commercial systems, where Internet mail comes from outside via a ◊gateway. Systems such as CompuServe used to charge extra for receiving or sending Internet mail, but such charges have been phased out.

Internet phone in computing, technology allowing users of the World Wide Web to talk to each other in more or less real time, via microphones and headsets. Network delays mean such connections are not as good quality as traditional telephone connections, but they are much cheaper for long-distance calls since users pay only for their local telephone connection to the Internet.

The earliest products were limited in that they only allowed users to talk to each other if both were logged on to the Vocaltec Web site at the same time. More recent products make it possible for a person using the Internet to dial any telephone in the world.

Internet Relay Chat (IRC) in computing, service that allows users connected to the Internet to chat with each other over many channels. There are probably hundreds of IRC channels active at any one time, covering a variety of topics. Many abbreviations are used to cut down on typing.

Internet Service Provider (ISP) in computing, any company that sells dial-up access to the Internet. Several types of company provide Internet access, including online information services such as ◊CompuServe and ◊America Online (AOL), electronic conferencing systems such as the ◊WELL and ◊Compulink Information eXchange, and local bulletin board systems (BBSs). Most recently founded ISPs, such as ◊Demon Internet and ◊PIPEX, offer only direct access to the Internet without the burden of running services of their own just for their members.

Such companies typically work out cheaper for their users, as they charge a low, flat rate for unlimited usage. By contrast, commercial online services typically charge by the hour or minute.

Internet Society (ISOC) global volunteer group that works to coordinate and develop the Internet and its underlying technology. It was founded 1992 and is based in Reston, Virginia, USA; the president (1996) is Vinton Cerf. Members include individuals, companies, nonprofit-making organizations, and government agencies.

Internet Talk Radio (also known as the ***Internet multicasting service***) service that broadcasts radio programmes of interest to the technical community, such as *Geek of the Week*. Based in Washington DC, USA, the service broadcasts via ◊MBONE.

Internet worm in computing, a virus; see ◊worm.

InterNIC in computing, service that administers ◊domain names and maintains a number of Internet user directories. Users interested in registering a particular domain name can use the InterNIC's resources to check if the domain name or a similar one is already in use.

interplanetary matter gas and dust thinly spread through the Solar System. The gas flows outwards from the Sun as the ◊solar wind.

Fine dust lies in the plane of the Solar System, scattering sunlight to cause the ◊zodiacal light. Swarms of dust shed by comets enter the Earth's atmosphere to cause ◊meteor showers.

interpolation mathematical technique for using two values to calculate intermediate values. It is used in ◊computer graphics to create smooth shadings.

interpreter computer program that translates and executes a program written in a high-level language. Unlike a ◊compiler, which produces a complete machine-code translation of the high-level program in one operation, an interpreter translates the source program, instruction by instruction, each time that program is run.

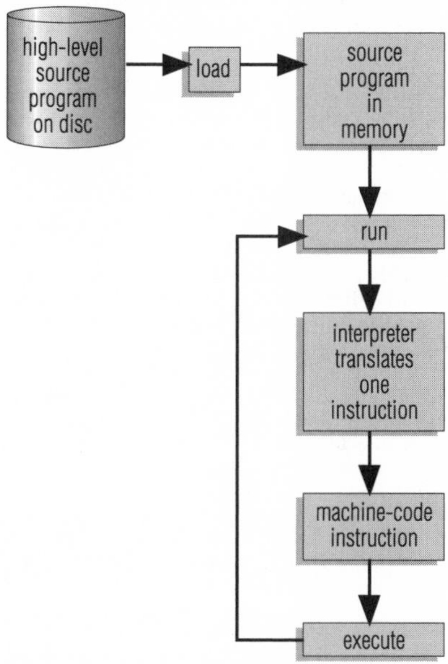

interpreter *The sequence of events when running an interpreter on a high-level language program. Instructions are translated one at a time, making the process a slow one; however, interpreted programs do not need to be compiled and may be executed immediately.*

> *Man is the interpreter of nature, science the right interpretation.*
>
> WILLIAM WHEWELL English physicist and philosopher. *The Philosophy of the Inductive Sciences* 1837

interquartile range in statistics, a measure of ◊dispersion in a frequency distribution, equalling the difference in value between the upper and lower ◊quartiles.

interrupt in computing, a signal received by the computer's central processing unit that causes a temporary halt in the execution of a program while some other task is performed. Interrupts may be generated by the computer's internal electronic clock (clock interrupt), by an input or output device, or by a software routine. After the computer has completed the task to which it was diverted, control returns to the original program.

For example, many computers, while printing a long document, allow the user to carry on with other work. When the printer is ready for more data, it sends an interrupt signal that causes the computer to halt work on the user's program and transmit more data to the printer.

intersection on a graph, the point where two lines or curves meet. The intersections of graphs provide the graphical solutions of equations.

intersection in set theory, the set of elements that belong to both set A and set B.

intersex individual that is intermediate between a normal male and a normal female in its appearance (for example, a genetic male that lacks external genitalia and so resembles a female).

interstellar cirrus in astronomy, wispy cloud-like structures discovered in the mid-1980s by the Infrared Astronomy Satellite (◊IRAS) and believed to be the remains of dust shells blown into space from cool giant or supergiant stars.

interstitial in biology, undifferentiated tissue that is interspersed with the characteristic tissue of an organ. It is often formed of fibrous tissue and supports the organ. Interstitial fluid refers to the fluid present in small amounts in the tissues of an organ.

intestine in vertebrates, the digestive tract from the stomach outlet to the anus. The human **small intestine** is 6 m/20 ft long, 4 cm/1.5 in in diameter, and consists of the duodenum, jejunum, and ileum; the **large intestine** is 1.5 m/5 ft long, 6 cm/2.5 in in diameter, and includes the caecum, colon, and rectum. Both are muscular tubes comprising an inner lining that secretes alkaline digestive juice, a submucous coat containing fine blood vessels and nerves, a muscular coat, and a serous coat covering all, supported by a strong peritoneum, which carries the blood and lymph vessels, and the nerves. The contents are passed along slowly by ◊peristalsis (waves of involuntary muscular action). The term intestine is also applied to the lower digestive tract of invertebrates.

intranet in computing, the use of software and other technology developed for the Internet on internal company ◊networks.

Many company networks (and those of other organizations) use the same ◊protocols as the Internet, namely ◊TCP/IP. Therefore the same technology that enables the World Wide Web can be used on an internal network to build an organization-wide web of internal documents that is familiar, easy to use, and comparatively inexpensive.

intrauterine device (IUD) or **coil**, a contraceptive device that is inserted into the womb (uterus). It is a tiny plastic object, sometimes containing copper. By causing a mild inflammation of the lining of the uterus it prevents fertilized eggs from becoming implanted.

IUDs are not usually given to women who have not had children. They are generally very reliable, as long as they stay in place, with a success rate of about 98%. Some women experience heavier and more painful periods, and there is a very slight risk of a pelvic infection leading to infertility.

intron or ***junk DNA*** in genetics, a sequence of bases in ◊DNA that carries no genetic information. Introns, discovered in 1977, make up 98% of DNA (the rest is made up of ◊exons). Their function is unknown.

10% of the human genome is made up of one base sequence, *Alu,* that occurs in about 1 million separate locations. It is made up of 283 nucleotides, has no determinable function (though some do have an effect on nearby genes), and is a ◊transposon ('jumping gene').

introversion in psychology, preoccupation with the self, generally coupled with a lack of sociability. The opposite of introversion is ◊extroversion.

The term was introduced by the Swiss psychiatrist Carl Jung 1924 in his description of ◊schizophrenia, where he noted that 'interest does not move towards the object but recedes towards the subject'. The term is also used within psychoanalysis to refer to the turning of the instinctual drives towards objects of fantasy rather than the pursuit of real objects. Another term for this sense is fantasy cathexis.

intrusion mass of ◊igneous rock that has formed by 'injection' of molten rock, or magma, into existing cracks beneath the surface of the Earth, as distinct from a volcanic rock mass which has erupted from the surface. Intrusion features include vertical cylindrical structures such as stocks, pipes, and necks; sheet structures such as dykes that cut across the strata and sills that push between them; laccoliths, which are blisters that push up the overlying rock; and batholiths, which represent chambers of solidified magma and contain vast volumes of rock.

intrusive rock ◊igneous rock formed beneath the Earth's surface. Magma, or molten rock, cools slowly at these depths to form coarse-grained rocks, such as granite, with large crystals. (◊Extrusive rocks, which are formed on the surface, are usually fine-grained.) A mass of intrusive rock is called an intrusion.

intuitionism in mathematics, the theory that propositions can be built up only from intuitive concepts that we all recognize easily, such as unity or plurality. The concept of ◊infinity, of which we have no intuitive experience, is thus not allowed.

There are children playing in the street who could solve some of my top problems in physics, because they have modes of sensory perception that I lost long ago.

J Robert Oppenheimer US physicist.
Attributed remark

Invar trademark for an alloy of iron containing 36% nickel, which expands or contracts very little when the temperature changes.

It is used to make precision instruments (such as pendulums and tuning forks) whose dimensions must not alter.

inverse function ◊function that exactly reverses the transformation produced by a function *f*; it is usually written as f^{-1}. For example $3x + 2$ and $(x - 2)/3$ are mutually inverse functions. Multiplication and division are inverse operations (see ◊reciprocals).

An inverse function is clearly demonstrated on a calculator by entering any number, pressing x^2, then pressing $\sqrt{x}$ to get the inverse. The functions on a scientific calculator can be inversed in a similar way.

inverse multiplexing in computing, technique for combining individual low-bandwidth channels into a single high-bandwidth channel. It is used to create high-speed telephone links for applications such as ◊videoconferencing which require the transmission of huge quantities of data.

inverse square law in physics, the statement that the magnitude of an effect (usually a force) at a point is inversely proportional to the square of the distance between that point and the object exerting the force.

Light, sound, electrostatic force (Coulomb's law), gravitational force (Newton's law) all obey the inverse square law.

inverse video or ***reverse video*** in computing, a display mode in which images on a display screen are presented as a negative of their normal appearance.

For example, if the computer screen normally displays dark images on a light background, inverse video will change all or part of the screen to a light image on a dark background.

Inverse video is commonly used to highlight parts of a display or to mark out text and pictures that the user wishes the computer to change in some way. For example, the user of a word-processing program might use a pointing device such as a ◊mouse to mark in inverse video a paragraph of text that is to be deleted from the document.

invertebrate animal without a backbone. The invertebrates comprise over 95% of the million or so existing animal species and include sponges, coelenterates, flatworms, nematodes, annelid worms, arthropods, molluscs, echinoderms, and primitive aquatic chordates, such as sea squirts and lancelets.

INVERTEBRATE

Every year, at least two species of British invertebrates become extinct.

inverted file in computing, a file that reorganizes the structure of an existing data file to enable a rapid search to be made for all records having one field falling within set limits.

For example, a file used by an estate agent might store records on each house for sale, using a reference number as the key field for ◊sorting. One field in each record would be the asking price of the house. To speed up the process of drawing up lists of houses falling within certain price ranges, an inverted file might be created in which the records are rearranged according to price. Each record would consist of an asking price, followed by the reference numbers of all the houses offered for sale at this approximate price.

in vitro fertilization (IVF; ***'fertilization in glass'***) allowing eggs and sperm to unite in a laboratory to form embryos. The embryos (properly called pre-embryos in their two- to eight-celled state) are stored by cooling to the temperature of liquid air (cryopreservation) until they are implanted into the womb of the otherwise infertile mother (an extension of ◊artificial insemination). The first baby to be produced by this method was born in 1978 in the UK. In cases where the Fallopian tubes are blocked, fertilization may be carried out by **intra-vaginal culture**, in which egg and sperm are incubated (in a plastic tube) in the mother's vagina, then transferred surgically into the uterus.

in vitro process biological experiment or technique carried out in a laboratory, outside the body of a living organism (literally 'in glass', for example in a test tube). By contrast, an in vivo process takes place within the body of an organism.

in vivo process biological experiment or technique carried out within a living organism; by contrast, an in vitro process takes place outside the organism, in an artificial environment such as a laboratory.

involuntary action behaviour not under conscious control, for example the contractions of the gut during peristalsis or the secretion of adrenaline by the adrenal glands. Breathing and urination reflexes are involuntary, although both can be controlled voluntarily to some extent. These processes are regulated by the ◊autonomic nervous system.

involute ***Latin 'rolled in'*** in geometry, ◊spiral that can be thought of as being traced by a point at the end of a taut nonelastic thread being wound onto or unwound from a spool.

I/O (abbreviation for ***input/output***) see ◊input devices and ◊output devices. The term is also used to describe transfer to and from disc – that is, disc I/O.

Io in astronomy, the third-largest moon of the planet Jupiter, 3,630 km/2,260 mi in diameter, orbiting in 1.77 days at a distance of 422,000 km/262,000 mi. It is the most volcanically active body in the Solar System, covered by hundreds of vents that erupt not lava but sulphur, giving Io an orange-coloured surface.

In July 1995 the Hubble Space Telescope revealed the appearance of a 320-km/200-mi yellow spot on the surface of Io, located on the volcano Ra Patera. Though clearly volcanic in origin, astronomers are unclear as to the exact cause of the new spot.

Using data gathered by the spacecraft *Galileo*, US astronomers concluded in 1996 that Io has a large metallic core. The *Galileo* space probe also detected a 10-megawatt beam of electrons flowing between Jupiter and Io.

In 1997 instruments aboard the spacecraft *Galileo* measured the temperature of Io's volcanoes and detected a minimum tmperature of 1,800 K (in comparison, Earth's hottest volcanoes only reach about 1,600 K).

iodide compound formed between iodine and another element in which the iodine is the more electronegative element (see ◊electronegativity, halide).

iodine ***Greek iodes 'violet'*** greyish-black nonmetallic element, symbol I, atomic number 53, relative atomic mass 126.9044. It is a member of the ◊halogen group. Its crystals give off, when heated, a violet vapour with an irritating odour resembling that of chlorine. It only occurs in combination with other elements. Its salts are known as iodides, which are found in sea water. As a mineral nutrient it is vital to the proper functioning of the thyroid gland, where it occurs in trace amounts as part of the hormone thyroxine. Absence of iodine from the diet leads to ◊goitre. Iodine is used in photography, in medicine as an antiseptic, and in making dyes.

Its radioactive isotope ^{131}I (half-life of eight days) is a dangerous fission product from nuclear explosions and from the nuclear reactors in power plants, since, if ingested, it can be taken up by the thyroid and damage it. It was discovered in 1811 by French chemist B Courtois (1777–1838).

iodoform (chemical name ***triiodomethane***) CHI_3, an antiseptic that crystallizes into yellow hexagonal plates. It is soluble in ether, alcohol, and chloroform, but not in water.

Iomega in computing, leading manufacturer of removable storage and back-up devices, in direct competition with ◊Syquest. Based in Roy, Utah, in the USA, Iomega's two most popular products are the Zip drive, which uses inexpensive 100Mb discs, and the Jaz drive, which uses 1Gb discs.

ion atom, or group of atoms, that is either positively charged (◊cation) or negatively charged (◊anion), as a result of the loss or gain of electrons during chemical reactions or exposure to certain forms of radiation.

ion engine rocket engine that uses ◊ions (charged particles) rather than hot gas for propulsion. Ion engines have been successfully tested in space, where they will eventually be used for gradual rather than sudden velocity changes. In an ion engine, atoms of mercury, for example, are ionized (given an electric charge by an electric field) and then accelerated at high speed by a more powerful electric field.

ion exchange process whereby an ion in one compound is replaced by a different ion, of the same charge, from another compound. It is the basis of a type of ◊chromatography in which the components of a mixture of ions in solution are separated according to the ease with which they will replace the ions on the polymer matrix through which they flow. The exchange of positively charged ions is called cation exchange; that of negatively charged ions is called anion exchange.

Ion-exchange is used in commercial water softeners to exchange the dissolved responsible for the water's hardness with others that do not have this effect. For example, when hard water is passed over an ion-exchange resin, the dissolved calcium and magnesium ions are replaced by either sodium or hydrogen ions, so the hardness is removed.

ion half equation equation that describes the reactions occurring at the electrodes of a chemical cell or in electrolysis. It indicates which ion is losing electrons (oxidation) or gaining electrons (reduction).

Examples are given from the electrolysis of dilute hydrochloric acid (HCl).

$$2Cl^- - 2e^- \rightarrow Cl_2 \text{ (positive electrode)}2H^+ + 2e^- \rightarrow H_2 \text{ (negative electrode)}$$

ionic bond or **electrovalent bond** bond produced when atoms of one element donate electrons to atoms of another element, forming positively and negatively charged ions respectively. The attraction between the oppositely charged ions constitutes the bond. Sodium chloride (Na^+Cl^-) is a typical ionic compound.

Each ion has the electronic structure of an inert gas (see ◊noble gas structure). The maximum number of electrons that can be gained is usually two.

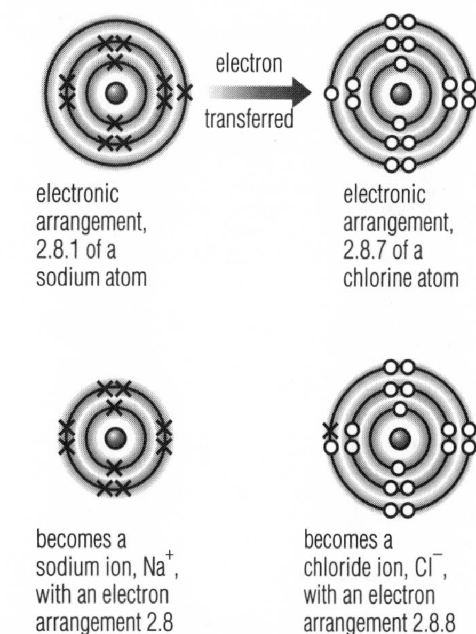

ionic bond *The formation of an ionic bond between a sodium atom and a chlorine atom to form a molecule of sodium chloride. The sodium atom transfers an electron from its outer electron shell (becoming the positive ion Na^+) to the chlorine atom (which becomes the negative chloride ion Cl^-). The opposite charges mean that the ions are strongly attracted to each other. The formation of the bond means that each atom becomes more stable, having a full quota of electrons in its outer shell.*

ionic compound substance composed of oppositely charged ions. All salts, most bases, and some acids are examples of ionic compounds. They possess the following general properties: they are crystalline solids with a high melting point; are soluble in water and insoluble in organic solvents; and always conduct electricity when molten or in aqueous solution. A typical ionic compound is sodium chloride (Na^+Cl^-).

ionic equation equation showing only those ions in a chemical reaction that actually undergo a change, either by combining together to form an insoluble salt or by combining together to form one or more molecular compounds. Examples are the precipitation of insoluble barium sulphate when barium and sulphate ions are combined in solution, and the production of ammonia and water from ammonium hydroxide.

$$Ba^{2+}_{(aq)} + SO_4{}^{2-}_{(aq)} \rightarrow BaSO_{4(s)} NH_4{}^+_{(aq)} + OH^-_{(aq)} \rightarrow NH_{3(g)} + H_2O_{(l)}$$

The other ions in the mixtures do not take part and are called ◊spectator ions.

ionization process of ion formation. It can be achieved in two ways. The first way is by the loss or gain of electrons by atoms to form positive or negative ions.

$$Na - e^- \rightarrow Na^+ 1/2Cl_2 + e^- \rightarrow Cl^-$$

In the second mechanism, ions are formed when a covalent bond breaks, as when hydrogen chloride gas is dissolved in water. One portion of the molecule retains both electrons, forming a negative ion, and the other portion becomes positively charged. This bond-fission process is sometimes called dissociation.

$$HCl_{(g)} + aq \leftrightarrow H^+_{(aq)} + Cl^-_{(aq)}$$

ionization chamber device for measuring ◊ionizing radiation. The radiation ionizes the gas in the chamber and the ions formed are collected and measured as an electric charge. Ionization chambers are used for determining the intensity of X-rays or the disintegration rate of radioactive materials.

ionization potential measure of the energy required to remove an ◊electron from an ◊atom. Elements with a low ionization potential readily lose electrons to form ◊cations.

ionization therapy enhancement of the atmosphere of an environment by instrumentally boosting the negative ion content of the air.

Fumes, dust, cigarette smoke, and central heating cause negative ion deficiency, which particularly affects sufferers from respiratory disorders such as bronchitis, asthma, and sinusitis. Symptoms are alleviated by the use of ionizers in the home or workplace. In severe cases, ionization therapy is used as an adjunct to conventional treatment.

ionizing radiation radiation that knocks electrons from atoms during its passage, thereby leaving ions in its path. Alpha and beta particles are far more ionizing in their effect than are neutrons or gamma radiation.

ionosphere ionized layer of Earth's outer ◊atmosphere (60–1,000 km/38–620 mi) that contains sufficient free electrons to modify the way in which radio waves are propagated, for instance by reflecting them back to Earth. The ionosphere is thought to be produced by absorption of the Sun's ultraviolet radiation.

ion plating method of applying corrosion-resistant metal coatings. The article is placed in argon gas, together with some coating metal, which vaporizes on heating and becomes ionized (acquires charged atoms) as it diffuses through the gas to form the coating. It has important applications in the aerospace industry.

IP address (abbreviation for ***Internet protocol address***) in computing, numbered ◊address assigned to an Internet ◊host. Traditionally, IP addresses are ◊32-bit, which means that numbered addresses have four sections separated by dots, each a decimal number between 0 and 255.

ipecacuanha or ***ipecac*** South American plant belonging to the madder family, the dried roots of which are used in medicine as an emetic (to cause vomiting) and to treat amoebic dysentery (infection of the intestine with amoebae). (*Psychotria ipecacuanha,* family Rubiaceae.)

IR or ***ir*** in physics, abbreviation for ***infrared***.

IRAS acronym for ***Infrared Astronomy Satellite*** joint US–UK–Dutch satellite launched in 1983 to survey the sky at infrared wavelengths, studying areas of star formation, distant galaxies, possible embryo planetary systems around other stars, and discovering five new comets in our own Solar System. It operated for 10 months.

IRC in computing, abbreviation for ◊***Internet Relay Chat***.

iridium ***Latin iridis 'rainbow'*** hard, brittle, silver-white, metallic element, symbol Ir, atomic number 77, relative atomic mass 192.2. It is resistant to tarnish and corrosion. Iridium is one of the so-called platinum group of metals; it occurs in platinum ores and as a free metal (◊native metal) with osmium in osmiridium, a natural alloy that includes platinum, ruthenium, and rhodium.

It is alloyed with platinum for jewellery and used for watch bearings and in scientific instruments. It was named in 1804 by English chemist Smithson Tennant (1761–1815) for its iridescence in solution.

iridium anomaly unusually high concentrations of the element iridium found world-wide in sediments which were deposited at the Cretaceous-Tertiary boundary (◊K-T boundary) 65 million years ago. Since iridium is more abundant in extraterrestrial material, its presence is thought to be evidence for a large meteor impact which may have caused the extinction of the dinosaurs.

iris in anatomy, the coloured muscular diaphragm that controls the size of the pupil in the vertebrate eye. It contains radial muscle that increases the pupil diameter and circular muscle that constricts the pupil diameter. Both types of muscle respond involuntarily to light intensity.

iris in botany, any of a group of perennial northern temperate flowering plants belonging to the iris family. The leaves are usually sword-shaped; the purple, white, or yellow flowers have three upright inner petals and three outward- and downward-curving ◊sepals. The wild yellow iris is called a flag. (Genus *Iris,* family Iridaceae.)

Irish terrier breed of large ◊terrier from the region of Cork and Ballymena. It has a thick, rough coat in reddish and wheaten hues and an athletic build. It stands about 45 cm/18 in at the shoulder.

Irish water spaniel breed of medium-sized gundog with a dark brown, thickly curling coat, used especially for hunting and retrieving waterfowl. It grows to 58.5 cm/23 in and is an ancestor of the smaller (up to 46 cm/18 in), but very similar, American water spaniel.

Irish wolfhound breed of hound used in Ireland for many centuries to hunt wolves and other large game. Of massive size (80 cm/32 in upwards) and powerful build, the wolfhound has a shaggy coat in a range of colours – wheaten, grey, brindled, black, red, or white.

In the 19th century the breed was revived when nearly extinct by crossing it with the ◊deerhound.

iron hard, malleable and ductile, silver-grey, metallic element, symbol Fe (from Latin *ferrum*), atomic number 26, relative atomic mass 55.847. It is the fourth most abundant element (the second most abundant metal, after aluminium) in the Earth's crust. Iron occurs in concentrated deposits as the ores hematite (Fe_2O_3), spathic ore ($FeCO_3$), and magnetite (Fe_3O_4). It sometimes occurs as a free metal, occasionally as fragments of iron or iron–nickel meteorites.

Iron is the most common and most useful of all metals; it is strongly magnetic and is the basis for ◊steel, an alloy with carbon and other elements (see also ◊cast iron). In electrical equipment it is used in all permanent magnets and electromagnets, and forms the cores of transformers and magnetic amplifiers. In the human body, iron is an essential component of haemoglobin, the molecule in red blood cells that transports oxygen to all parts of the body. A deficiency in the diet causes a form of anaemia.

Iron Age developmental stage of human technology when weapons and tools were made from iron. Preceded by the Stone and Bronze ages, it is the last technological stage in the Three Age System framework for prehistory. Iron was produced in Thailand about 1600 BC, but was considered inferior in strength to bronze until about 1000 BC, when metallurgical techniques improved, and the alloy steel was produced by adding carbon during the smelting process.

Ironworking was introduced into different regions over a wide time span, appearing in Thailand about 1600 BC, Asia Minor about 1200 BC, central Europe about 900 BC, China about 600 BC, and in remoter areas during exploration and colonization by the Old

World. It reached the Fiji Islands with an expedition in the late 19th century.

Iron Age cultures include Hallstatt (named after a site in Austria) and ◊La Tène (named after a site in Switzerland).

ironbark any species of ◊eucalyptus tree with hard, tough bark.

iron ore any mineral from which iron is extracted. The chief iron ores are ◊magnetite, **a black oxide**; ◊hematite, **or kidney ore, a reddish oxide**; **limonite**, brown, impure oxyhydroxides of iron; and **siderite**, a brownish carbonate.

Iron ores are found in a number of different forms, including distinct layers in igneous intrusions, as components of contact metamorphic rocks, and as sedimentary beds. Much of the world's iron is extracted in Russia, Kazakhstan, and the Ukraine. Other important producers are the USA, Australia, France, Brazil, and Canada; over 40 countries produce significant quantities of ore.

iron pyrites or *pyrite* FeS_2 common iron ore. Brassy yellow, and occurring in cubic crystals, it is often called 'fool's gold', since only those who have never seen gold would mistake it.

irradiation subjecting anything to radiation, including cancer tumours. See also ◊food irradiation.

irrational number a number that cannot be expressed as an exact ◊fraction. Irrational numbers include some square roots (for example, $\sqrt{2}$, $\sqrt{3}$, and $\sqrt{5}$ are irrational) and numbers such as π (the ratio of the circumference of a circle to its diameter, which is approximately equal to 3.14159) and e (the base of ◊natural logarithms, approximately 2.71828).

irregular galaxy in astronomy, a class of ◊galaxy with little structure, which does not conform to any of the standard shapes in the Hubble classification. The two satellite galaxies of the ◊Milky Way, the ◊Magellanic Clouds, are both irregulars. Some galaxies previously classified as irregulars are now known to be normal galaxies distorted by tidal effects or undergoing bursts of star formation (see ◊starburst galaxy).

irrigation artificial water supply for dry agricultural areas by means of dams and channels. Drawbacks are that it tends to concentrate salts at the surface, ultimately causing soil infertility, and that rich river silt is retained at dams, to the impoverishment of the land and fisheries below them.

Irrigation has been practised for thousands of years, in Eurasia as well as the Americas. An example is the channelling of the annual Nile flood in Egypt, which has been done from earliest times to its present control by the Aswan High Dam.

ISA bus (abbreviation for ***industry standard architecture bus***) in computing, 16-bit data ◊bus introduced in 1984 with the IBM PC AT and still in common use in PCs, alongside the superior ◊PCI bus. PC hardware and software manufacturers would like to get rid of the ISA bus as it is not compatible with ◊Plug and Play.

ISBN (abbreviation for ***International Standard Book Number***) code number used for ordering or classifying book titles. Every book printed now has a number on its back cover or jacket, preceded by the letters ISBN. It is a code to the country of origin and the publisher. The number is unique to the book, and will identify it anywhere in the world.

The final digit in each ISBN number is a check digit, which can be used by a computer program to validate the number each time it is input (see ◊validation).

ischaemic heart disease (IHD) disorder caused by reduced perfusion of the coronary arteries due to ◊atherosclerosis. It is the commonest cause of death in the Western world, leading to more than a million deaths each year in the USA and about 160,000 in the UK. See also ◊coronary artery disease.

Early symptoms of IHD include angina or palpitations, but sometimes a heart attack is the first indication that a person is affected.

ISDN abbreviation for ***◊Integrated Services Digital Network***, a telecommunications system.

island area of land surrounded entirely by water. Australia is classed as a continent rather than an island, because of its size.

Islands can be formed in many ways. **Continental islands** were once part of the mainland, but became isolated (by tectonic movement, erosion, or a rise in sea level, for example). **Volcanic islands**, such as Japan, were formed by the explosion of underwater volcanoes. **Coral islands** consist mainly of coral, built up over many years. An **atoll** is a circular coral reef surrounding a lagoon; atolls were formed when a coral reef grew up around a volcanic island that subsequently sank or was submerged by a rise in sea level. **Barrier islands** are found by the shore in shallow water, and are formed by the deposition of sediment eroded from the shoreline.

island arc curved chain of islands produced by volcanic activity at a destructive margin (where one tectonic plate slides beneath another). Island arcs are common in the Pacific where they ring the ocean on both sides; the Aleutian Islands off Alaska are an example.

Such island arcs are often later incorporated into continental margins during mountain-building episodes.

islets of Langerhans groups of cells within the pancreas responsible for the secretion of the hormone insulin. They are sensitive to the blood sugar, producing more hormone when glucose levels rise.

ISO abbreviation for ***◊International Organization for Standardization***.

ISO in photography, a numbering system for rating the speed of films, devised by the International Standards Organization.

ISO 9660 in computing, standard file format for ◊CD-ROM discs, synonymous with High Sierra format. This format is compatible with most systems, so the same disc can contain both Apple Macintosh and PC versions.

isobar line drawn on maps and weather charts linking all places with the same atmospheric pressure (usually measured in millibars).

When used in weather forecasting, the distance between the isobars is an indication of the barometric gradient (the rate of change in pressure).

Where the isobars are close together, cyclonic weather is indicated, bringing strong winds and a depression, and where far apart anticyclonic, bringing calmer, settled conditions.

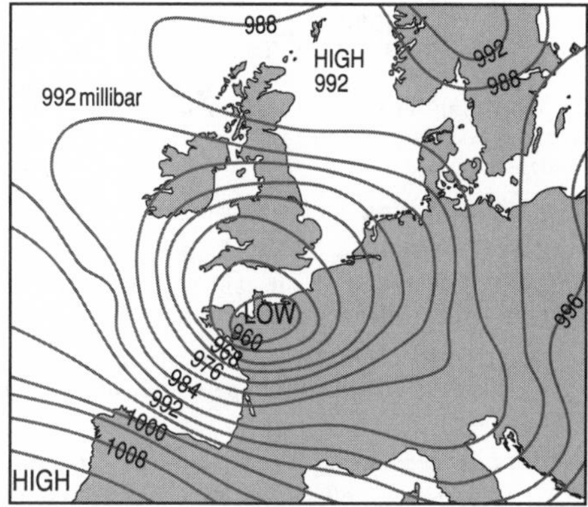

isobar The isobars around a low-pressure area or depression. In the northern hemisphere, winds blow anticlockwise around lows, approximately parallel to the isobars, and clockwise around highs. In the southern hemisphere, the winds blow in the opposite directions.

ISOC in computing, abbreviation for ***◊Internet Society***.

isomer chemical compound having the same molecular composition and mass as another, but with different physical or chemical properties owing to the different structural arrangement of its constituent atoms. For example, the organic compounds butane ($CH_3(CH_2)_2CH_3$) and methyl propane ($CH_3CH(CH_3)CH_3$) are isomers, each possessing four carbon atoms and ten hydrogen atoms but differing in the way that these are arranged with respect to each other.

butane $CH_3(CH_2)_2CH_3$

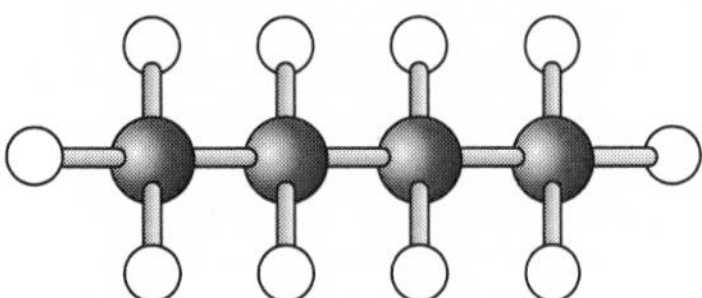

methyl propane $CH_3CH(CH_3)CH_3$

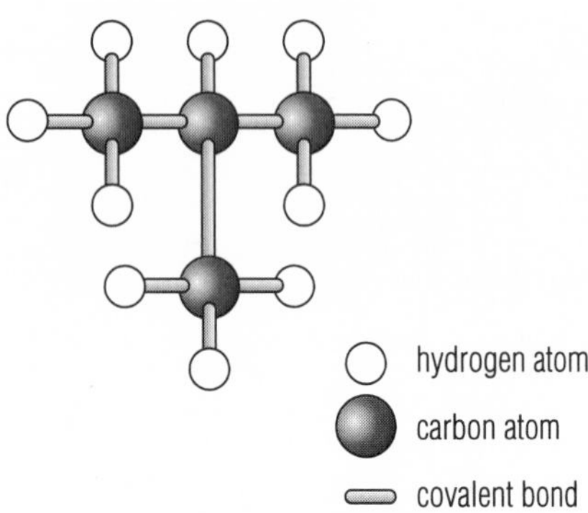

***isomer** The chemicals butane and methyl propane are isomers. Each has the molecular formula $CH_3CH(CH_3)CH_3$, but with different spatial arrangements of atoms in their molecules.*

Structural isomers have obviously different constructions, but **geometrical** and **optical isomers** must be drawn or modelled in order to appreciate the difference in their three-dimensional arrangement. Geometrical isomers have a plane of symmetry and arise because of the restricted rotation of atoms around a bond; optical isomers are mirror images of each other. For instance, 1,1-dichloroethene (CH_2=CCl_2) and 1,2-dichloroethene (CHCl=CHCl) are structural isomers, but there are two possible geometric isomers of the latter (depending on whether the chlorine atoms are on the same side or on opposite sides of the plane of the carbon–carbon double bond).

isometric transformation a ◊transformation in which length is preserved.

isomorphism the existence of substances of different chemical composition but with similar crystalline form.

isoprene $CH_2CHC(CH_3)CH_2$ (technical name ***methylbutadiene***) colourless, volatile fluid obtained from petroleum and coal, used to make synthetic rubber.

isosceles triangle a ◊triangle with two sides equal, hence its base angles are also equal. The triangle has an axis of symmetry which is an ◊altitude of the triangle.

isostasy the theoretical balance in buoyancy of all parts of the Earth's ◊crust, as though they were floating on a denser layer beneath. There are two theories of the mechanism of isostasy, the Airy hypothesis and the Pratt hypothesis, both of which have validity. In the **Airy hypothesis** crustal blocks have the same density but different depths: like ice cubes floating in water, higher mountains have deeper roots. In the **Pratt hypothesis**, crustal blocks have different densities allowing the depth of crustal material to be the same.

There appears to be more geological evidence to support the Airy hypothesis of isostasy. During an ◊ice age the weight of the ice sheet pushes that continent into the Earth's mantle; once the ice has melted, the continent rises again. This accounts for shoreline features being found some way inland in regions that were heavily glaciated during the Pleistocene period.

isotope one of two or more atoms that have the same atomic number (same number of protons), but which contain a different number of neutrons, thus differing in their atomic masses. They may be stable or radioactive, naturally occurring or synthesized. The term was coined by English chemist Frederick Soddy, pioneer researcher in atomic disintegration.

ISP in computing, abbreviation for ◊Internet Service Provider.

iteration in computing, a method of solving a problem by performing the same steps repeatedly until a certain condition is satisfied. For example, in one method of ◊sorting, adjacent items are repeatedly exchanged until the data are in the required sequence.

iteration in mathematics, method of solving ◊equations by a series of approximations which approach the exact solution more and more closely. For example, to find the square root of N, start with a guess n_1; calculate $N/n_1 = x_1$; calculate $(n_1 + x_1/2 = n_2$; calculate $N/n_1 = x_2$; calculate $(n_2 + x_2)/2 = n_3$. The sequence n_1, n_2, n_3 approaches the exact square root of

N. Iterative methods are particularly suitable for work with computers and programmable calculators.

iteroparity in biology, the repeated production of offspring at intervals throughout the life cycle. It is usually contrasted with ◊semelparity, where each individual reproduces only once during its life.

ITU abbreviation for ◊***International Telecommunications Union***, the standards-setting body for the communications industry.

IUE (acronym for ***International Ultraviolet Explorer***) joint NASA-ESA (US and European Space Agency) orbiting ultraviolet telescope with a 45-cm/18-in mirror, launched in 1978. It was switched off in September 1996.

IUPAC abbreviation for ***International Union of Pure and Applied Chemistry***, organization that recommends the nomenclature to be used for naming substances, the units to be used, and which conventions are to be adopted when describing particular changes.

IVF abbreviation for ◊***in vitro fertilization***.

ivory hard white substance of which the teeth and tusks of certain mammals are made. Among the most valuable are elephants' tusks, which are of unusual hardness and density. Ivory is used in carving and other decorative work, and is so valuable that poachers continue to illegally destroy the remaining wild elephant herds in Africa to obtain it.

Poaching for ivory has led to the decline of the African elephant population from 2 million to approximately 600,000, with the species virtually extinct in some countries. Trade in ivory was halted by Kenya in 1989, but Zimbabwe continued its policy of controlled culling to enable the elephant population to thrive and to release ivory for export. China and Hong Kong have refused to obey an international ban on ivory trading. In 1997, the 138 member nations of the Convention on International Trade in Endangered Species (◊CITES) voted in Harare, amidst much controversy, to remove the ban on trade in ivory in Botswana, Namibia, and Zimbabwe. These three countries would be allowed to sell a limited amount of ivory to Japan, and the money must be channelled into elephant conservation projects. Trade is scheduled to resume in 1999 and would only be allowed from the existing stockpiles of ivory.

Vegetable ivory is used for buttons, toys, and cheap ivory goods. It consists of the hard albumen of the seeds of a tropical palm (*Phytelephas macrocarpa*), and is imported from Colombia.

ivy any of an Old World group of woody climbing, trailing, or creeping evergreen plants. English or European ivy (*H. helix*) has shiny five-lobed leaves and clusters of small, yellowish-green flowers followed by black berries. It climbs by means of rootlike suckers put out from its stem, and causes damage to trees. (Genus *Hedera*, family Araliaceae.)

Ground ivy (*Glechoma hederacea*) is a small, originally European creeping plant belonging to the mint family; the North American poison ivy (*Rhus radicans*) belongs to the cashew family.

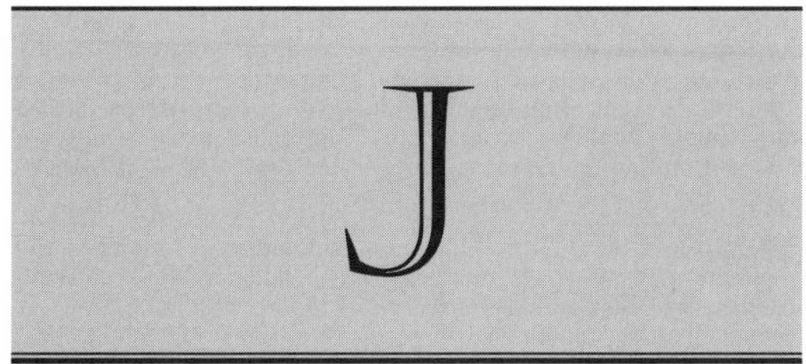

J in physics, the symbol for **joule**, the SI unit of energy.

jabiru stork found in Central and South America. It is 1.5 m/5 ft tall with white plumage. The head is black and red with a massive, slightly upturned bill. The neck is bare of feathers and can be puffed out, a manoeuvre which is probably used in social rituals. (Species *Jabiru mycteria,* family Ciconiidae, order Ciconiiformes.)

jaborandi plant belonging to the rue family, native to South America. It is the source of **pilocarpine**, used in medicine to contract the pupil of the eye. (*Pilocarpus microphyllus,* family Rutaceae.)

jacamar insect-eating bird related to the woodpeckers, found in dense tropical forest in Central and South America. It has a long, straight, sharply-pointed bill, a long tail, and paired toes. The plumage is golden bronze with a steely lustre. Jacamars are usually seen sitting motionless on trees from which they fly out to catch insects on the wing, then return to crack them on a branch before eating them. The largest species is *Jacamerops aurea,* which is nearly 30 cm/12 in long. (Family Galbulidae, order Piciformes.)

jacana or ***lily-trotter*** wading bird with very long toes and claws enabling it to walk on the floating leaves of water plants. There are seven species. Jacanas are found in Mexico, Central America, South America, Africa, S Asia, and Australia, usually in marshy areas. (Family Jacanidae, order Charadriiformes.)

The **Australian jacana** (*Irediparra gallinacea*) is so well adapted to life on water that the eggs are laid on floating vegetation and can themselves float.

jacaranda any of a group of tropical American trees belonging to the bignonia family, with fragrant wood and showy blue or violet flowers, commonly cultivated in the southern USA. (Genus *Jacaranda,* family Bignoniaceae.)

jack in computing, small plug allowing users to connect peripherals to CPUs (◊central processing units).

jack tool or machine for lifting, hoisting, or moving heavy weights, such as motor vehicles. A **screw jack** uses the principle of the screw to magnify an applied effort; in a car jack, for example, turning the handle many times causes the lifting screw to rise slightly, and the effort is magnified to lift heavy weights. A **hydraulic jack** uses a succession of piston strokes to increase pressure in a liquid and force up a lifting ram.

jackal any of several wild dogs found in S Asia, S Europe, and N Africa. Jackals can grow to 80 cm/2.7 ft long, and have greyish-brown fur and a bushy tail. (Genus *Canis.*)

The **golden jackal** (*C. aureus*) of S Asia, S Europe, and N Africa is 45 cm/1.5 ft high and 60 cm/2 ft long. It is greyish-yellow, and darker on the back. A nocturnal animal, it preys on smaller mammals and poultry, although packs will attack larger animals; it will also scavenge. The **side-striped jackal** (*C. adustus*) is found over much of Africa; the **black-backed jackal** (*C. mesomelas*) occurs only in the south of Africa.

jackdaw bird belonging to the crow family, native to Europe and Asia. It is mainly black, but greyish on the sides and back of the head, and about 33 cm/1.1 ft long. It nests in tree holes or on buildings. Usually it lays five bluish-white eggs, mottled with tiny dark brown spots. Jackdaws feed on a wide range of insects, molluscs, spiders, worms, birds' eggs, fruit, and berries. (Species *Corvus monedula,* family Corvidae, order Passeriformes.)

Jack Russell terrier or ***Parson Jack Russell terrier*** breed of small, short-legged, smooth-haired ◊terrier, which takes its name from its originator, the English clergyman and fox-hunting enthusiast John Russell (1795–1883). It was recognized by the UK Kennel Club 1990 as a distinct variant of the fox terrier, which it resembles in having a mainly white coat with brown patches.

jade semiprecious stone consisting of either jadeite, $NaAlSi_2O_6$ (a pyroxene), or nephrite, $Ca_2(Mg,Fe)_5Si_8O_{22}(OH,F)_2$ (an amphibole), ranging from colourless through shades of green to black according to the iron content. Jade ranks 5.5–6.5 on the Mohs' scale of hardness.

The early Chinese civilization discovered jade, bringing it from E Turkestan, and carried the art of jade-carving to its peak. The Olmecs, Aztecs, Maya, and the Maori have also used jade for ornaments, ceremony, and utensils.

jaggies in computing, 'stepped' appearance of curved or diagonal lines in computer graphics caused by ◊aliasing.

jaguar largest species of cat in the Americas, formerly ranging from the southwestern USA to southern South America, but now extinct in most of North America. It can grow up to 2.5 m/8 ft long including the tail. The background colour of the fur varies from creamy white to brown or black, and is covered with black spots. The jaguar is usually solitary. (Species *Panthera onca,* family Felidae.)

jaguarundi wild cat found in forests in Central and South America. Up to 1.1 m/3.5 ft long, it is very slim with rather short legs and short rounded ears. It is uniformly coloured dark brown or chestnut. A good climber, it feeds on birds and small mammals and, unusually for a cat, has been reported to eat fruit. (Species *Felis yaguoaroundi,* family Felidae.)

jansky unit of radiation received from outer space, used in radio astronomy. It is equal to 10^{-26} watts per square metre per hertz, and is named after US engineer Karl Jansky.

Jansky, Karl Guthe (1905–1950)

US radio engineer who in 1932 discovered that the Milky Way galaxy emanates radio waves; he did not follow up his discovery, but it marked the birth of radioastronomy.

jackal The black-backed jackal Canis mesomelas *is a common sight on the savannas of S Africa. It hunts singly for small animals and in packs for larger prey, often scavenging on carcasses left by larger predators such as lions. Premaphotos Wildlife*

Japan Current or ***Kuroshio*** warm ocean ◊current flowing from Japan to North America.

Japanese spaniel or **Japanese chin** ancient breed of toy dog introduced into Japan from China. Daintily built, it stands about 30 cm/12 in tall, and, like the pekingese, has a rounded head, drooping ears, and tail curved over its back. Its long, soft coat is always white, with either black or red markings.

jarrah type of ◊eucalyptus tree of W Australia, with durable timber.

Jarvik 7 the first successful artificial heart intended for permanent implantation in a human being. Made from polyurethane plastic and aluminium, it is powered by compressed air. Barney Clark became the first person to receive a Jarvik 7, in Salt Lake City, Utah, USA, 1982; it kept him alive for 112 days.

jasmine any of a group of subtropical plants with white or yellow flowers. The common jasmine (*J. officinale*) has fragrant pure white flowers that yield jasmine oil, used in perfumes; the Chinese winter jasmine (*J. nudiflorum*) has bright yellow flowers that appear before the leaves. (Genus *Jasminum,* family Oleaceae.)

jaundice yellow discoloration of the skin and whites of the eyes caused by an excess of bile pigment in the bloodstream. Approximately 60% of newborn babies exhibit some degree of jaundice, which is treated by bathing in white, blue, or green light that converts the bile pigment bilirubin into a water-soluble compound that can be excreted in urine. A serious form of jaundice occurs in rhesus disease (see ◊rhesus factor).

Bile pigment is normally produced by the liver from the breakdown of red blood cells, then excreted into the intestines. A build-up in the blood is due to abnormal destruction of red cells (as in some cases of ◊anaemia), impaired liver function (as in ◊hepatitis), or blockage in the excretory channels (as in gallstones or ◊cirrhosis). The jaundice gradually recedes following treatment of the underlying cause.

Java in computing, programming language much like C developed by James Gosling at ◊Sun Microsystems 1995. Java has been adopted as a multipurpose, cross-platform lingua franca for network computing, including the ◊World Wide Web. When users connect to a server that uses Java, they download a small program called an applet onto their computers. The ◊applet then runs on the computer's own processor via a ◊Java Virtual Machine program or JVM.

Java Virtual Machine (JVM) in computing, a program that sits on top of a computer's usual operating system and runs Java ◊applets.

Different computers require different JVMs but they should run the same Java code. This means that servers only need to provide one version of each applet, instead of different 'native code' versions for PCs, Apple Macintoshes, and UNIX workstations, as is the case with other plug-ins.

A JVM is commonly supplied as part of a Web browser but may be included as part of the operating system.

jaw one of two bony structures that form the framework of the mouth in all vertebrates except lampreys and hagfishes (the agnathous or jawless vertebrates). They consist of the upper jawbone (maxilla), which is fused to the skull, and the lower jawbone (mandible), which is hinged at each side to the bones of the temple by ◊ligaments.

jay any of several birds belonging to the crow family, generally brightly coloured and native to Europe, Asia, and the Americas. In the Eurasian **common jay** (*Garrulus glandarius*), the body is fawn with patches of white, blue, and black on the wings and tail. (Family Corvidae, order Passeriformes.)

Jays are shy and retiring in their habits, but have a screeching cry with the power to vary it by mimicking other birds. They feed chiefly on snails, insects, worms, and nuts, particularly acorns. They hide their nests in trees with thick foliage and lay about five or six eggs at a time.

The **blue jay** (*Cyanocitta cristata*), of the eastern and central USA, has a crest and is very noisy and bold.

Jeans mass in astronomy, the mass that a cloud (or part of a cloud) of interstellar gas must have before it can contract under its own weight to form a protostar. The Jeans mass is an expression of the **Jeans criterion**, which says that a cloud will contract when the gravitational force tending to drawing material towards its centre is greater than the opposing force due to gas pressure. It is named after English mathematician James Hopwood Jeans whose work focussed on the kinetic theory of gases and the origins of the cosmos.

jellyfish marine invertebrate, belonging among the ◊coelenterates, with an umbrella-shaped body made of a semi-transparent jellylike substance, often tinted with blue, red, or orange colours, and stinging tentacles that trail in the water. Most adult jellyfish move freely, but during parts of their life cycle many are polyplike and attached to rocks, the seabed, or another underwater surface. They feed on small animals that are paralysed by stinging cells in the jellyfish tentacles. (Phylum Coelenterata, subphylum Cnidaria.)

Most jellyfish cause no more discomfort to humans than a nettle sting, but contact with the tentacles of the subtropical Portuguese man-of-war (*Physalia physalis*) or the Australian box jellyfish (*Chironex fleckeri*) can be life-threatening.

Jenner, Edward
(1749–1823)

English physician who pioneered vaccination. In Jenner's day, smallpox was a major killer. His discovery in 1796 that inoculation with cowpox gives immunity to smallpox was a great medical breakthrough.

Jenner observed that people who worked with cattle and contracted cowpox from them never subsequently caught smallpox. In 1798 he published his findings that a child inoculated with cowpox, then two months later with smallpox, did not get smallpox. He coined the word 'vaccination' from the Latin word for cowpox, *vaccinia*.

Mary Evans Picture Library

Jentink's duiker small, shy ◊antelope that plunges into bushes when startled. It is acutely threatened by deforestation in its remaining habitat in W Africa, where it is also hunted. One captive breeding colony exists in Texas, USA, and there are hopes of establishing others as the immediate future for this species in the wild appears to be bleak. (Species *Cephalophus jentinki,* family Bovidae.)

jerboa any of a group of small nocturnal rodents with long and powerful hind legs developed for leaping. There are about 25 species of jerboa, native to desert areas of N Africa and SW Asia. (Family Dipodidae.)

The common N African jerboa (*Jaculus orientalis*) is a typical species. Its body is about 15 cm/6 in long and the tail is 25 cm/10 in long with a tuft at the tip. At speed it moves in a series of long jumps with its forefeet held close to its body.

Jerusalem artichoke a variety of ◊artichoke.

JET (abbreviation for ***Joint European Torus***) research facility at Culham, near Abingdon, Oxfordshire, UK, that conducts experiments on nuclear fusion. It is the focus of the European effort to produce a safe and environmentally sound fusion-power reactor. On 9 November 1991 the JET ◊tokamak, operating with a mixture of deuterium and iritium, produced a 1.7 megawatt pulse of power

JET WORLD WIDE WEB PAGE

http://www.jet.uk/

Web site of the Joint European Torus (JET) at Culham, UK, which includes an introduction to some aspects of nuclear fusion and an online tour of the project.

in an experiment that lasted two seconds. In 1997 isotopes of deuterium and tritium were fused to produce a record 21 megajoule of nuclear fusion power. JET has tested the first large-scale plant of the type needed to process and supply tritium in a future fusion power station.

jet in astronomy, a narrow luminous feature seen protruding from a star or galaxy, and representing a rapid outflow of material. See ◊active galaxy.

jet hard, black variety of lignite, a type of coal. It is cut and polished for use in jewellery and ornaments. Articles made of jet have been found in Bronze Age tombs.

jetfoil advanced type of ◊hydrofoil boat built by Boeing, propelled by water jets. It features horizontal, fully submerged hydrofoils fore and aft and has a sophisticated computerized control system to maintain its stability in all waters

Jetfoils have been in service worldwide since 1975. A jetfoil service operates across the English Channel between Dover and Ostend, Belgium, with a passage time of about 1.5 hours. Cruising speed of the jetfoil is about 80 kph/50 mph.

jet lag the effect of a sudden switch of time zones in air travel, resulting in tiredness and feeling 'out of step' with day and night. In 1989 it was suggested that use of the hormone melatonin helped to lessen the effect of jet lag by resetting the body clock. See also ◊circadian rhythm.

jet propulsion method of propulsion in which an object is propelled in one direction by a jet, or stream of gases, moving in the other. This follows from Isaac ◊Newton's third law of motion: 'To every action, there is an equal and opposite reaction.' The most widespread application of the jet principle is in the jet engine, the most common kind of aircraft engine

Jet Propulsion Laboratory NASA installation at Pasadena, California, operated by the California Institute of Technology. It is the command centre for NASA's deep-space probes such as the ◊Voyager, Magellan, and Galileo missions, with which it communicates via the Deep Space Network of radio telescopes at Goldstone, California; Madrid, Spain; and Canberra, Australia.

jet stream narrow band of very fast wind (velocities of over 150 kph/95 mph) found at altitudes of 10–16 km/6–10 mi in the upper troposphere or lower stratosphere. Jet streams usually occur about the latitudes of the Westerlies (35°–60°).

The jet stream may be used by high flying aircraft to speed their journeys. Their discovery of the existence of the jet stream allowed the Japanese to send gas-filled balloons carrying bombs to the northwestern US during World War II.

jigger or ***sandflea*** flea found in tropical and subtropical countries. The males of the species are free-living and measure about 1 mm/0.03 in in length. The females, which are slightly bigger, are parasites of humans and other animals.

Jiggers burrow into the skin, particularly the soft skin between the toes, and soon become enveloped within a skin fold. As they feed they become enlarged and distended and their legs degenerate; eventually a stage is reached when only the last two segments at the abdomen protrude from the skin fold. The eggs are then voided and fall on the soil or sand.

Apart from their presence within the host skin, which causes acute pain and the formation of ulcers, the fleas may be responsible for secondary infections. Preventive measures include ridding the host of the parasite, and destroying breeding places.

classification The jigger *Tunga penetrans* is in order Siphonaptera, class Insecta, phylum Arthropoda.

Jobs, Steven Paul (1955–)

US computer entrepreneur. He cofounded Apple Computer Inc with Steve Wozniak 1976, and founded NeXT Technology Inc in 1985. In 1986 he bought Pixar Animation Studios, the computer animation studio spun off from George Lucas's LucasFilm.

Jobs has been involved with the creation of three different types of computer: the Apple II personal computer 1977, the Apple Macintosh 1984 – marketed as 'the computer for the rest of us' – and the NeXT workstation 1988.

The NeXT was technically the most sophisticated and powerful design, but it was a commercial disaster, and in 1993 NeXT abandoned hardware manufacturing to concentrate on its highly-regarded UNIX-based object-oriented operating system, NextStep. Apple Computer bought NeXT at the end of 1996 to obtain NextStep, and Jobs returned to Apple in an advisory capacity. However, he soon took over as acting chief executive officer of the struggling firm 1997.

Jodrell Bank site in Cheshire, England, of the Nuffield Radio Astronomy Laboratories of the University of Manchester. Its largest instrument is the 76 m/250 ft radio dish (the Lovell Telescope), completed 1957 and modified 1970. A 38 x 25 m/125 x 82 ft elliptical radio dish was introduced 1964, capable of working at shorter wave lengths

These radio telescopes are used in conjunction with six smaller dishes up to 230 km/143 mi apart in an array called MERLIN (**m**ulti-**e**lement **r**adio-**l**inked **i**nterferometer **n**etwork) to produce detailed maps of radio sources.

JODRELL BANK HOME PAGE

http://www.jb.man.ac.uk/index.html

Comprehensive Web site describing the Nuffield Radio Astronomy Laboratories at Jodrell Bank, Cheshire, UK. The radar telescope has been used for astronomy for many years, this Web site describes some of the important discoveries it has led to and also hints at future developments.

John Dory marine bony fish also called a ◊dory.

Johnson Space Center NASA installation at Houston, Texas, home of mission control for crewed space missions. It is the main centre for the selection and training of astronauts.

joint in any animal with a skeleton, a point of movement or articulation. In vertebrates, it is the point where two bones meet. Some joints allow no motion (the sutures of the skull), others allow a very small motion (the sacroiliac joints in the lower back), but most allow a relatively free motion. Of these, some allow a gliding motion (one vertebra of the spine on another), some have a hinge action (elbow and knee), and others allow motion in all directions (hip and shoulder joints) by means of a ball-and-socket arrangement. The ends of the bones at a moving joint are covered with cartilage for greater elasticity and smoothness, and enclosed in an envelope (capsule) of tough white fibrous tissue lined with a membrane which secretes a lubricating and cushioning ◊synovial fluid. The joint is further strengthened by ligaments. In invertebrates with an ◊exoskeleton, the joints are places where the exoskeleton is replaced by a more flexible outer covering, the arthrodial membrane, which allows the limb (or other body part) to bend at that point.

Joint European Torus experimental nuclear-fusion machine, known as ◊JET.

jojoba desert shrub *Simmondsia chinensis* of southwest North America and Mexico, that grows to a height of around 6 m/20 ft. Its seeds are used as a source of jojoba oil, used as a substitute for sperm whale oil, and as a fragrance. It is increasingly grown as a commercial crop.

jonquil species of small ◊daffodil, with yellow flowers. It is native to Spain and Portugal, and is cultivated in other countries. (*Narcissus jonquilla,* family Amaryllidaceae.)

Josephson junction device used in 'superchips' (large and complex integrated circuits) to speed the passage of signals by a phenomenon called 'electron tunnelling'. Although these superchips respond a thousand times faster than the ◊silicon chip, they have the disadvantage that the components of the Josephson junctions operate only at temperatures close to ◊absolute zero. They are named after English theoretical physicist Brian Josephson.

joule SI unit (symbol J) of work and energy, replacing the ◊calorie (one joule equals 4.2 calories)

Joule, James Prescott (1818–1889)

English physicist. His work on the relations between electrical, mechanical, and chemical effects led to the discovery of the first law of thermodynamics.

He determined the mechanical equivalent of heat (Joule's equivalent) in 1843, and the SI unit of energy, the joule, is named after him. He also discovered Joule's law, which defines the relation between heat and electricity; and with Irish physicist Lord Kelvin in 1852 the Joule–Kelvin (or Joule–Thomson) effect.

Mary Evans Picture Library

Joule–Kelvin effect or *Joule–Thomson effect* in physics, the fall in temperature of a gas as it expands adiabatically (without loss or gain of heat to the system) through a narrow jet. It can be felt when, for example, compressed air escapes through the valve of an inflated bicycle tyre. It is the basic principle of most refrigerators.

joystick in computing, an input device that signals to a computer the direction and extent of displacement of a hand-held lever. It is similar to the joystick used to control the flight of an aircraft.

Joysticks are sometimes used to control the movement of a cursor (marker) across a display screen, but are much more frequently used to provide fast and direct input for moving the characters and symbols that feature in computer games. Unlike a ◊mouse, which can move a pointer in any direction, simple games joysticks are often capable only of moving an object in one of eight different directions.

JPEG (abbreviation for ***Joint Photographic Experts Group***) used to describe a compression standard set up by that group and now widely accepted for the storage and transmission of colour images. The JPEG compression standard reduces the size of image files considerably.

Jughead (acronymn for ***Jonzy's Universal Gopher Hierarchy Excavation and Display***) in computing, a ◊search engine enabling users of the Internet server ◊Gopher to find keywords in ◊Gopherspace directories.

jugular vein one of two veins in the necks of vertebrates; they return blood from the head to the superior (or anterior) ◊vena cava and thence to the heart.

jujube any of a group of trees belonging to the buckthorn family, with berrylike fruits. The common jujube (*Z. jujuba*) of Asia, Africa, and Australia, cultivated in S Europe and California, has fruit the size of small plums, known as Chinese dates when preserved in syrup. See also ◊lotus. (Genus *Zizyphus,* family Thamnaceae.)

Julian date in astronomy, a measure of time used in astronomy in which days are numbered consecutively from noon ◊GMT on 1 January 4713 BC. It is useful where astronomers wish to compare observations made over long time intervals. The Julian date (JD) at noon on 1 January 2000 will be 2451545.0. The modified Julian date (MJD), defined as MJD = JD - 2400000.5, is more commonly used since the date starts at midnight GMT and the smaller numbers are more convenient.

jumbo jet popular name for a generation of huge wide-bodied airliners including the **Boeing 747**, which is 71 m/232 ft long, has a wingspan of 60 m/196 ft, a maximum takeoff weight of nearly 400 tonnes, and can carry more than 400 passengers.

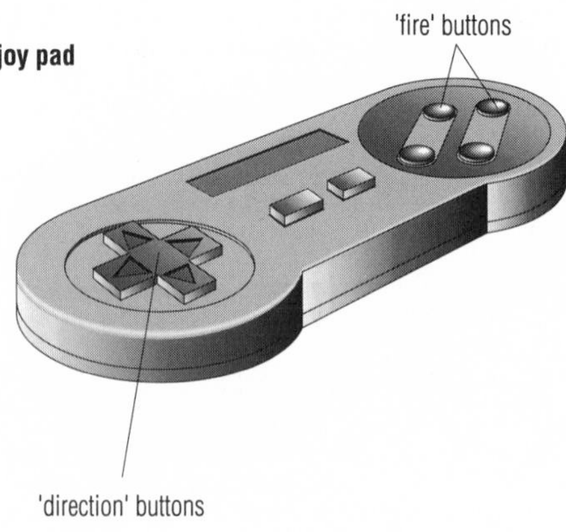

joystick *The directional and other controls on a conventional joystick may be translated to a joy pad, which enables all controls to be activated by buttons.*

jump in computing, a programming instruction that causes the computer to branch to a different part of a program, rather than execute the next instruction in the program sequence. Unconditional jumps are always executed; conditional jumps are only executed if a particular condition is satisfied.

jumper in computing, rectangular plug used to make connections on a circuit board. By pushing a jumper onto a particular set of pins on the board, or removing another, users can adjust the configuration of their computer's circuitry. Most home users, however, prefer to leave the insides of their machines with all the factory settings intact.

jumping hare or ***springhare*** either of two African species of long-eared rodents. The springhare (*P. capensis*) is about 40 cm/16 in long and resembles a small kangaroo with a bushy tail. It inhabits dry sandy country in E central Africa. (Genus *Pedetes*, family Pedetidae.)

Jung, Carl Gustav (1875–1961)

Swiss psychiatrist. He collaborated with Sigmund Freud from 1907 until their disagreement 1914 over the importance of sexuality in causing psychological problems. Jung studied myth, religion, and dream symbolism, saw the unconscious as a source of spiritual insight, and distinguished between introversion and extroversion.

Jung devised the word-association test in the early 1900s as a technique for penetrating a subject's unconscious mind. He also developed his theory concerning emotional, partly repressed ideas which he termed 'complexes'. In place of Freud's emphasis on infantile sexuality, Jung introduced the idea of a 'collective unconscious' which is made up of many archetypes or 'congenital conditions of intuition'.

Mary Evans Picture Library

jungle popular name for rainforest.

juniper any of a group of aromatic evergreen trees or shrubs of the cypress family, found throughout temperate regions. Its berries are used to flavour gin. Some junipers are mistakenly called cedars. (Genus *Juniperus*, family Cupressaceae.)

junk DNA another name for intron, a region of DNA that contains no genetic information.

Jupiter the fifth planet from the Sun, and the largest in the Solar System, with a mass equal to 70% of all the other planets combined, 318 times that of Earth's. It is largely composed of hydrogen and helium, liquefied by pressure in its interior, and probably with a rocky core larger than Earth. Its main feature is the Great Red Spot, a cloud of rising gases, 14,000 km/8,500 mi wide and 30,000 km/20,000 mi long, revolving anticlockwise.
mean distance from the Sun 778 million km/484 million mi
equatorial diameter 142,800 km/88,700 mi
rotation period 9 hr 51 min
year (complete orbit) 11.86 Earth years

JUPITER

http://www.hawastsoc.org/solar/eng/jupiter.htm

Full details of the planet and its moons including a chronology of exploration, various views of the planet and its moons, and links to other planets.

atmosphere consists of clouds of white ammonia crystals, drawn out into belts by the planet's high speed of rotation (the fastest of any planet). Darker orange and brown clouds at lower levels may contain sulphur, as well as simple organic compounds. Further down still, temperatures are warm, a result of heat left over from Jupiter's formation, and it is this heat that drives the turbulent weather patterns of the planet.
surface although largely composed of hydrogen and helium, Jupiter probably has a rocky core larger than Earth.

In 1995, the *Galileo* probe revealed Jupiter's atmosphere to consist of 0.2% water, less than previously estimated.
satellites Jupiter has 16 moons. The four largest moons, Io, Europa (which is the size of our Moon), Ganymede, and Callisto, are the **Galilean satellites**, discovered 1610 by Galileo (Ganymede, which is about the size of Mercury, is the largest moon in the Solar System). Three small moons were discovered 1979 by the Voyager space probes, as was a faint ring of dust around Jupiter's equator 55,000 km/34,000 mi above the cloud tops.

The Great Red Spot was first observed in 1664. Its top is higher than the surrounding clouds; its colour is thought to be due to red phosphorus. Jupiter's strong magnetic field gives rise to a large surrounding magnetic 'shell', or magnetosphere, from which bursts of radio waves are detected. The Southern Equatorial Belt in which the Great Red Spot occurs is subject to unexplained fluctuation. In 1989 it sustained a dramatic and sudden fading.

Comet Shoemaker-Levy 9 crashed into Jupiter July 1994. Impact zones were visible but are not likely to remain.

Jurassic period of geological time 208–146 million years ago; the middle period of the Mesozoic era. Climates worldwide were equable, creating forests of conifers and ferns; dinosaurs were abundant, birds evolved, and limestones and iron ores were deposited.

The name comes from the Jura Mountains in France and Switzerland, where the rocks formed during this period were first studied.

Till now man has been up against Nature, from now on he will be up against his own nature.

DENNIS GABOR Hungarian-born British physicist.
Inventing the Future

justification in printing and word processing, the arrangement of text so that it is aligned with either the left or right margin, or both.

jute fibre obtained from two plants of the linden family: *C. capsularis* and *C. olitorius*. Jute is used for sacks and sacking, upholstery, webbing (woven strips used to support upholstery), string, and stage canvas. (Genus *Corchorus*, family Tiliaceae.)

In the production of bulk packaging and tufted carpet backing, jute is now often replaced by synthetic polypropylene. The world's largest producer of jute is Bangladesh.

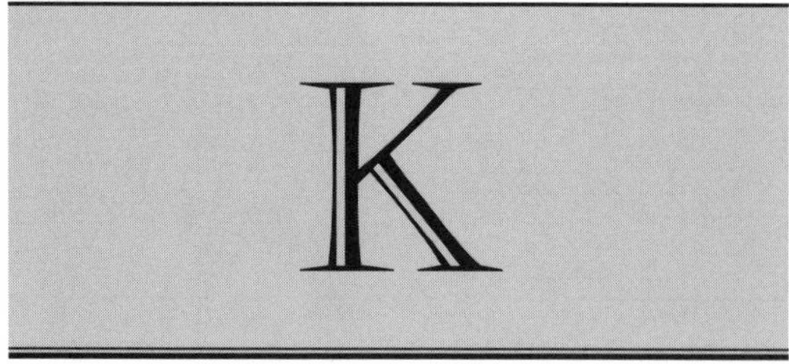

k symbol for **kilo-**, as in kg (kilogram) and km (kilometre).

K abbreviation for thousand, as in a salary of £30K.

K symbol for **kelvin**, a scale of temperature.

KA9Q in computing, ◊TCP/IP protocol named after the call sign of Philip Karn, the radio ham who wrote it for ◊packet radio. The system proved also to be useable on telephone connections, and so was adapted to several other computer platforms. It formed the basis of connections to ◊Demon Internet for many years.

Kagoshima Space Centre headquarters of Japan's Institute of Space and Astronautical Science (ISAS), situated in S Kyushu Island.

ISAS is responsible for the development of satellites for scientific research; other aspects of the space programme fall under the National Space Development Agency which runs the ◊Tanegashima Space Centre. Japan's first satellite was launched from Kagoshima 1970. By 1988 ISAS had launched 17 satellites and space probes.

kagu crested bird found in New Caledonia in the S Pacific. About 50 cm/1.6 ft long, it is virtually flightless and nests on the ground. The introduction of cats and dogs has endangered its survival. (Species *Rhynochetos jubatus,* order Gruiformes.)

kakapo nocturnal flightless parrot that lives in burrows in New Zealand. It is green, yellow, and brown with a disc of brown feathers round its eyes, like an owl. It weighs up to 3.5 kg/7.5 lb. When in danger, its main defence is to remain perfectly still. Because of the introduction of predators such as dogs, cats, rats, and ferrets, it is in danger of extinction; in 1997 there were only about 40 birds left. (Species *Strigops habroptilus,* order Psittaciformes.)

kale type of ◊cabbage.

kaleidoscope optical toy invented by the British physicist David Brewster in 1816. It usually consists of a pair of long mirrors at an angle to each other, and arranged inside a triangular tube containing pieces of coloured glass, paper, or plastic. An axially symmetrical (hexagonal) pattern is seen by looking along the tube, which can be varied infinitely by rotating or shaking the tube.

kangaroo any of a group of marsupials (mammals that carry their young in pouches) found in Australia, Tasmania, and New Guinea. Kangaroos are plant-eaters and most live in groups. They are adapted to hopping, the vast majority of species having very large, powerful back legs and feet compared with the small forelimbs. The larger types can jump 9 m/30 ft in a single bound. Most are nocturnal. Species vary from small rat kangaroos, only 30 cm/1 ft long, through the medium-sized wallabies, to the large red and great grey kangaroos, which are the largest living marsupials. These may be 1.8 m/5.9 ft long with 1.1 m/3.5 ft tails. (Family Macropodidae.)

In New Guinea and N Queensland, tree kangaroos (genus *Dendrolagus*) occur. These have comparatively short hind limbs. The great grey kangaroo (*Macropus giganteus*) produces a single young ('joey') about 2 cm/1 in long after a very short gestation, usually in early summer. At birth the young kangaroo is too young even to suckle. It remains in its mother's pouch, attached to a nipple which squirts milk into its mouth at intervals. It stays in the pouch, with excursions as it matures, for about 280 days.

A new species of kangaroo was discovered 1994 in New Guinea. Local people know it as 'bondegezou'. It weighs 15 kg/33 lb and is 1.2 m/3.9 ft in height. As it shows traits of both arboreal and ground-dwelling species, it may be a 'missing link'.

KANGAROO

A fully grown kangaroo can jump 13 m/14 yd. Mathematical calculations have shown that at speeds of over 29 kmph/18 mph, bouncing is a more energy-efficient way of moving for a kangaroo than running would be.

kangaroo paw bulbous plant *Anigozanthos manglesii,* family Hameodoraceae, with a row of small white flowers emerging from velvety green tubes with red bases. It is the floral emblem of Western Australia.

kaolin group of clay minerals, such as ◊kaolinite, $Al_2Si_2O_5(OH)_4$, derived from the alteration of aluminium silicate minerals, such as ◊feldspars and ◊mica. It is used in medicine to treat digestive upsets, and in poultices.

Kaolinite is economically important in the ceramic and paper industries. It is mined in the UK, the USA, France, and the Czech Republic.

kaolinite white or greyish ◊clay mineral, hydrated aluminium silicate, $Al_2Si_2O_5(OH)_4$, formed mainly by the decomposition of feldspar in granite. China clay (kaolin) is derived from it. It is mined in France, the UK, Germany, China, and the USA.

kapok silky hairs that surround the seeds of certain trees, particularly the **kapok tree** (*Bombax ceiba*) of India and Malaysia and the **silk-cotton tree** (*Ceiba pentandra*) of tropical America. Kapok is used for stuffing cushions and mattresses and for sound insulation; oil obtained from the seeds is used in food and soap.

karabash breed of large guard dog developed by the shepherds of Anatolia to protect their flocks. It is strongly built, stands up to 75 cm/29 in, and has a short grey, beige, or brindled coat with black on its muzzle and ears.

Karelian bear dog breed of medium-sized dog, used to protect Russian settlements from bears. About 60 cm/2 in high, the dog has a black or reddish-brown coat with white markings.

It was not exported until 1989, when some were sent to Yellowstone Park, USA, to keep bears away from tourists.

karri giant ◊eucalyptus tree *Eucalyptus diversifolia,* found in the extreme SW of Australia. It may reach over 120 m/400 ft. Its exceptionally strong timber is used for girders.

karst landscape characterized by remarkable surface and underground forms, created as a result of the action of water on permeable limestone. The feature takes its name from the Karst region on the Adriatic coast in Slovenia and Croatia, but the name is applied to landscapes throughout the world, the most dramatic of which is found near the city of Guilin in the Guangxi province of China.

Limestone is soluble in the weak acid of rainwater. Erosion takes place most swiftly along cracks and joints in the limestone and these open up into gullies called grikes. The rounded blocks left upstanding between them are called clints.

karyotype in biology, the set of ◊chromosomes characteristic of a given species. It is described as the number, shape, and size of the chromosomes in a single cell of an organism. In humans for example, the karyotype consists of 46 chromosomes, in mice 40, crayfish 200, and in fruit flies 8.

The diagrammatic representation of a complete chromosome set is called a **karyogram**.

katydid or ***bush cricket*** or ***longhorn grasshopper*** one of over 4,000 insect species, most of which are tropical, related to grasshoppers.

Members of this family have very long antennae and they tend to be wingless. The tympanal organs ('ears') are on the forelegs. They may be either plant-eating or carnivorous.

Some species are winged and the left forewing generally overlaps the right one; stridulation is produced by rubbing the forewings together. The winged species are usually green and are found among herbage, bushes, and trees where they often simulate the colour and shape of a leaf. Wingless forms inhabit places at ground-level, such as in the soil or under stones.

classification Katydids are in the family Tettigoniidae in order Orthoptera, class Insecta, phylum Arthropoda.

kauri pine New Zealand coniferous tree (see ◊conifer). Its fossilized gum deposits are valued in varnishes; the wood is used for carving and handicrafts. (*Agathis australis,* family Araucariaceae.)

kava narcotic, intoxicating beverage prepared from the roots or leaves of a variety of pepper plant, *Piper methysticum,* found in the South Pacific islands.

kayser unit of wave number (number of waves in a unit length), used in spectroscopy. It is expressed as waves per centimetre, and is the reciprocal of the wavelength. A wavelength of 0.1 cm has a wave number of 10 kaysers.

kcal symbol for **kilocalorie** (see ◊calorie).

kea hawklike greenish parrot found in New Zealand. It eats insects, fruits, and discarded sheep offal. The Maori name imitates its cry. (Species *Nestor notabilis,* family Psittacidae, order Psittaciformes.)

Keck Telescope world's largest optical telescope, situated on Mauna Kea, Hawaii. It has a primary mirror 10 m/33 ft in diameter, unique in that it consists of 36 hexagonal sections, each controlled and adjusted by a computer to generate single images of the objects observed. It received its first images in 1990.

An identical telescope next to it, named Keck II, became operational in 1996. It weighs 300 tonnes and has a 10-m/33-ft mirror comprised of 36 hexagons. Both telescopes are jointly owned by the California Institute of Technology and the University of California.

keeshond or ***Dutch barge dog*** sturdily built dog with erect ears and curled tail. It has a long grey top-coat, forming a mane around the neck, and a short, very thick undercoat, with darker 'spectacles' around the eyes. The ideal height is 46 cm/18 in for dogs; 43 cm/17 in for bitches.

keloid in medicine, overgrowth of fibrous tissue, usually produced at the site of a scar. Surgical removal is often unsuccessful, because the keloid returns.

kelp collective name for a group of large brown seaweeds. Kelp is also a term for the powdery ash of burned seaweeds, a source of iodine. (Typical families Fucaceae and Laminariaceae.)

The brown kelp (*Macrocystis pyrifera*), abundant in Antarctic and sub-Antarctic waters, is one of the fastest-growing living things, reaching lengths of up to 100 m/320 ft. It is farmed for the ◊alginate industry, its rapid surface growth allowing cropping several times a year, but it is an unwanted pest in N Atlantic waters.

kelpie breed of small herding dog also known as the Australian sheepdog. Bred from imported collie stock crossed with ◊dingo, it is much valued as a working dog. It has a coarse black or dark-coloured coat and is about 50 cm/20 in tall.

Do not imagine that mathematics is hard and crabbed, and repulsive to common sense. It is merely the etherealization of common sense.

WILLIAM KELVIN British physicist.
In S P Thomson *Life of Lord Kelvin* 1910

kelvin scale temperature scale used by scientists. It begins at ◊absolute zero (–273.15°C) and increases by the same degree intervals as the Celsius scale; that is, 0°C is the same as 273.15 K and 100°C is 373.15 K.

Kelvin, William Thomson, 1st Baron Kelvin (1824–1907)

Irish physicist who introduced the **Kelvin scale**, the absolute scale of temperature. His work on the conservation of energy in 1851 led to the second law of thermodynamics. Knighted 1866, Baron 1892.

Kelvin's knowledge of electrical theory was largely responsible for the first successful transatlantic telegraph cable. In 1847 he concluded that electrical and magnetic fields are distributed in a manner analogous to the transfer of energy through an elastic solid. From 1849 to 1859, Kelvin also developed the work of English scientist Michael Faraday into a full theory of magnetism, arriving at an expression for the total energy of a system of magnets.

Mary Evans Picture Library

Kennedy Space Center ◊NASA launch site on Merritt Island, near Cape Canaveral, Florida, used for *Apollo* and space-shuttle launches. The first flight to land on the Moon (1969) and *Skylab,* the first orbiting laboratory (1973), were launched here.

Kennelly–Heaviside layer former term for the ◊E layer of the ionosphere.

KENNEDY SPACE CENTRE

http://www.ksc.nasa.gov/

NASA's well-presented guide to the history and current operations of the USA's gateway to the universe. There is an enormous quantity of textual and multimedia information of interest for the general reader and for those who are technically minded.

Kepler's laws in astronomy, three laws of planetary motion formulated in 1609 and 1619 by the German mathematician and astronomer Johannes Kepler: (1) the orbit of each planet is an ellipse with the Sun at one of the foci; (2) the radius vector of each planet sweeps out equal areas in equal times; (3) the squares of the periods of the planets are proportional to the cubes of their mean distances from the Sun.

Kepler derived the laws after exhaustive analysis of numerous observations of the planets, especially Mars, made by Tycho ◊Brahe without telescopic aid. Isaac ◊Newton later showed that Kepler's Laws were a consequence of the theory of universal gravitation.

keratin fibrous protein found in the ◊skin of vertebrates and also in hair, nails, claws, hooves, feathers, and the outer coating of horns.

If pressure is put on some parts of the skin, more keratin is produced, forming thick calluses that protect the layers of skin beneath.

Kerberos in computing, system of symmetric ◊key cryptography developed at the Massachussetts Institute of Technology.

kermit in computing, a ◊file-transfer protocol, originally developed at Columbia University and made available without charge. Kermit is available as part of most communications packages and

Kepler, Johannes (1571–1630)

German mathematician and astronomer. He formulated what are now called **Kepler's laws** of planetary motion: (1) the orbit of each planet is an ellipse with the Sun at one of the foci; (2) the radius vector of each planet sweeps out equal areas in equal times; (3) the squares of the periods of the planets are proportional to the cubes of their mean distances from the Sun. Kepler's laws are the basis of our understanding of the Solar System, and such scientists as Isaac Newton built on his ideas.

Kepler was one of the first advocates of Sun-centred cosmology, as put forward by Copernicus. Unlike Copernicus and Galileo, Kepler rejected the Greek and medieval belief that orbits must be circular in order to maintain the fabric of the cosmos in a state of perfection.

early work Kepler also produced a calendar of predictions for the year 1595 which proved uncanny in its accuracy. In 1596, he published his *Prodromus dissertationum cosmographicarum seu mysterium cosmographicum* in which he demonstrated that the five Platonic solids (the only five regular polyhedrons) could be fitted alternately inside a series of spheres to form a 'nest'. The nest described quite accurately (within 5%) the distances of the planets from the Sun. Kepler regarded this discovery as a divine inspiration that revealed the secret of the Universe. Written in accordance with Copernican theories, it brought Kepler to the attention of all European astronomers.

Mary Evans Picture Library

In 1601, Kepler was bequeathed all of Tycho Brahe's data on planetary motion. He had already made a bet that, given Tycho's unfinished tables, he could find an accurate planetary orbit within a week. It was five years before Kepler obtained his first planetary orbit, that of Mars. His analysis of these data led to the discovery of his three laws. In 1604, his attention was diverted from the planets by his observation of the appearance of a new star, 'Kepler's nova'. Kepler had observed the first supernova visible since the one discovered by Brahe in 1572.

Kepler's laws Kepler's first two laws of planetary motion were published in *Astronomia Nova* 1609. The first law stated that planets travel in elliptical rather than circular, or epicyclic, orbits and that the Sun occupies one of the two foci of the ellipses. The second law established the Sun as the main force governing the orbits of the planets. It stated that the line joining the Sun and a planet traverses equal areas of space in equal periods of time, so that the planets move more quickly when they are nearer the Sun. He also suggested that the Sun itself rotates, a theory that was confirmed using Galileo's observations of sunspots, and he postulated that this established some sort of 'magnetic' interaction between the planets and the Sun, driving them in orbit. This idea, although incorrect, was an important precursor of Newton's gravitational theory.

Kepler's third law was published in *De Harmonices Mundi.* It described in precise mathematical language the link between the distances of the planets from the Sun and their velocities – specifically, that the orbital velocity of a planet is inversely proportional to its distance from the Sun.

Rudolphine Tables and other work Kepler finally completed and published the *Rudolphine Tables* 1627 based on Brahe's observations. These were the first modern astronomical tables, enabling astronomers to calculate the positions of the planets at any time in the past, present or future. The publication also included other vital information, such as a map of the world, a catalogue of stars, and the latest aid to computation, logarithms.

available on most operating systems, but it is now rarely used on the Internet.

kernel the inner, softer part of a ◊nut, or of a seed within a hard shell.

kerosene thin oil obtained from the distillation of petroleum; a highly refined form is used in jet aircraft fuel. Kerosene is a mixture of hydrocarbons of the ◊paraffin series.

Kerry blue terrier compact and sturdy dog, with a soft, full coat of bluish tone. It is 46 cm/18 in high and weighs 15–17 kg/33–37.4 lb. Its ears lie close to the head and it has a thin tail that is held erect.

kestrel or **windhover** small hawk that breeds in Europe, Asia, and Africa. About 30 cm/1 ft long, the male has a bluish grey head and tail and is light chestnut brown back with black spots on the back and pale with black spots underneath. The female is slightly larger and reddish brown above, with bars; she does not have the bluish grey head. The kestrel hunts mainly by hovering in midair while searching for prey. It feeds on small mammals, insects, frogs, and worms. (Species *Falco tinnunculus,* family Falconidae, order Falconiformes.)

It rarely builds its own nest, but uses those of other birds, such as crows and magpies, or scrapes a hole on a cliff-ledge. It is found all over Europe and Asia and most parts of Africa, and most birds migrate southwards in winter.

The **lesser kestrel** (*Falco naumanni*) is an inhabitant of southern Europe. The **American kestrel** or **sparrowhawk** (*F. sparverius*) is somewhat smaller, and occurs in most of North America. It is russet, grey, and tan in colour, with the male having more grey on its wings.

ketone member of the group of organic compounds containing the carbonyl group (C=O) bonded to two atoms of carbon (instead of one carbon and one hydrogen as in ◊aldehydes). Ketones are liquids or low-melting-point solids, slightly soluble in water.

An example is propanone (acetone, CH_3COCH_3), used as a solvent.

Kew Gardens popular name for the Royal Botanic Gardens, Kew, Surrey, England. They were founded 1759 by Augusta of Saxe-Coburg (1719–1772), the mother of King George III, as a small garden and passed to the nation by Queen Victoria 1840. By then they had expanded to almost their present size of 149 hectares/368 acres and since 1841 have been open daily to the public. They contain a collection of over 25,000 living plant species and many fine buildings. The gardens are also a centre for botanical research.

key in cryptography, the password needed to both encode and decipher a file. The key performs a sequence of operations on the original data. The recipient of the encoded file will need to apply another key in order to reverse all the operations in the correct order. Current encryption techniques such as ◊Pretty Good Privacy (PGP) make use of a ◊public key and a secret one.

keyboard in computing, an input device resembling a typewriter keyboard, used to enter instructions and data. There are many variations on the layout and labelling of keys. Extra numeric keys may be added, as may special-purpose function keys, whose effects can be defined by programs in the computer.

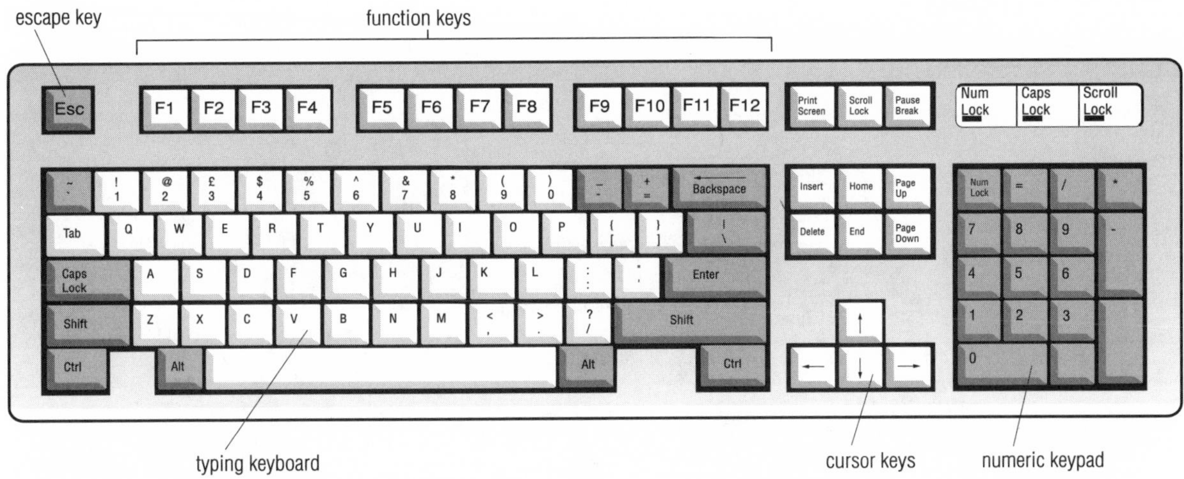

keyboard *A standard 102-key keyboard. As well as providing a QWERTY typing keyboard, the function keys (labelled F1–F12) may be assigned tasks specific to a particular system.*

key escrow in ◊public key cryptography, requirement that users store copies of their private keys with the government or other authorities for release to law enforcement officials upon production of the necessary legal documents.

Key escrow was first proposed in the USA, where it was built into the controversial ◊Clipper chip. In 1996, both the USA and the European Union were considering legislation requiring users of strong encryption to escrow their keys to protect law enforcement interests.

key field in computing, a selected field, or portion, of a record that is used to identify that record uniquely; in a file of records it is the field used as the basis for ◊sorting the file. For example, in a file containing details of a bank's customers, the customer account number would probably be used as the key field.

key frame in animation, a frame which was drawn by the user rather than generated by the computer. Animators feed a sequence of key frames into the computer, allowing the program to draw the intervening stages in a process known as **tweening**.

keyhole limpet primitive mollusc with a conical shell resembling that of the common limpet.

The shell is either cleft, as in *Fissurella,* or has a hole at the tip of the shell, as in *Diodora* (the rough keyhole limpet). A siphon is developed from the mantle and projects through this opening as the exhalant exit. Water is drawn over the gills from the forward end.
classification Keyhole limpets are of the superfamily Fissurellacea in subclass Prosobranchia, class Gastropoda, phylum Mollusca.

key-to-disc system or ***key-to-tape system*** in computing, a system that enables large amounts of data to be entered at a keyboard and transferred directly onto computer-readable discs or tapes.

Such systems are used in ◊batch processing, in which batches of data, prepared in advance, are processed by computer with little or no intervention from the user. The preparation of the data may be controlled by a minicomputer, freeing a larger, mainframe computer for the task of processing.

kg symbol for ◊kilogram.

kiang type of Asiatic wild ◊ass that lives in cold (below –40°C/–40°F in winter), high altitude (above 4,000 m/23,280 ft) deserts. Kiangs may be subspecies of the Asiatic wild ass *Equus hemionus,* or different species *E. kiang* There are three varieties: southern, western, and eastern. All are endangered and until recently the southern kiang was believed to be extinct.

The southern kiang, found between Sikkim in N India and the Tsangpo River in Tibet, has a shoulder height of 104–114 cm/41–45 in. Only about 100 remain. The western population, which ranges across Pakistan, India, and China, numbers around 1,500 in India; the eastern population is more numerous, with 10,000–30,000 in the protected Arjin Mountain Nature Reserves in China.

kidney in vertebrates, one of a pair of organs responsible for fluid regulation, excretion of waste products, and maintaining the ionic composition of the blood. The kidneys are situated on the rear wall of the abdomen. Each one consists of a number of long tubules; the outer parts filter the aqueous components of blood, and the inner parts selectively reabsorb vital salts, leaving waste products in the remaining fluid (urine), which is passed through the ureter to the bladder.

The action of the kidneys is vital, although if one is removed, the other enlarges to take over its function. A patient with two defective kidneys may continue near-normal life with the aid of a kidney machine or continuous ambulatory peritoneal ◊dialysis (CAPD); or a kidney transplant may be recommended.

kidney machine medical equipment used in ◊dialysis.

killer application a program so good or so compelling to certain potential users that they buy the computer that the program runs on for no other reason than to be able to use that program.

Killer applications are very rare. The most successful was VisiCalc, the first spreadsheet to run on a personal computer (the original Apple II microcomputer). VisiCalc succeeded as a killer application because it provided a unique tool for accountants to manipulate numbers easily without the need for programming skills. Another clear example is PageMaker, the first desktop publishing program, which was responsible for selling the Apple ◊Macintosh to the design and publishing community.

The ◊World Wide Web is the killer application for the Internet: by bringing visual excitement and ease of use to the Internet, it inspired people to buy new computers capable of supporting Web ◊browsers.

> TO REMEMBER THE SEVEN LAYERS OF THE OSI REFERENCE MODEL FOR COMPUTER NETWORKING:
>
> ACTIVE PENGUINS SEEK THE NEAREST DEEP POOL
>
> APPLICATION, PRESENTATION, SESSION, TRANSPORT, NETWORK, DATA-LINK, PHYSICAL

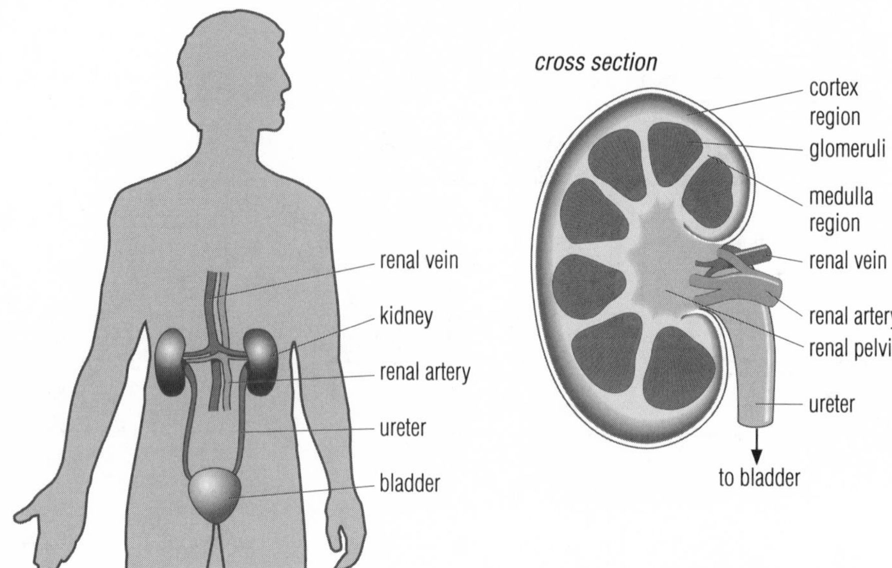

kidney *Blood enters the kidney through the renal artery. The blood is filtered through the glomeruli to extract the nitrogenous waste products and excess water that make up urine. The urine flows through the ureter to the bladder; the cleaned blood then leaves the kidney via the renal vein.*

KILLER WHALES

http://www.seaworld.org/killer_whale/killerwhales.html

Pictures and videos of this sea creature. There is also a lot of detailed biological information concerning, for example, the habitat, behaviour, and communication of killer whales. There are also plenty of activities and ideas to keep younger children entertained.

killer whale or ***orca*** toothed whale belonging to the dolphin family, found in all seas of the world. It is black on top, white below, and grows up to 9 m/30 ft long. It is the only whale that has been observed to prey on other whales, as well as on seals and seabirds. (Species *Orcinus orca,* family Delphinidae.)

killfile in computing, file specifying material that you do not wish to see when accessing a ◊newsgroup. By entering names, subjects or phrases into a killfile, users can make ◊USENET a more pleasant experience, filtering out tedious threads, offensive subject headings, ◊spamming or contributions from other irritating subscribers.

kiln high-temperature furnace used commercially for drying timber, roasting metal ores, or for making cement, bricks, and pottery. Oil- or gas-fired kilns are used to bake ceramics at up to 1,760°C/3,200°F; electric kilns do not generally reach such high temperatures.

kilo- prefix denoting multiplication by 1,000, as in kilohertz, a unit of frequency equal to 1,000 hertz.

kilobyte (K or KB) in computing, a unit of memory equal to 1,024 ◊bytes. It is sometimes used, less precisely, to mean 1,000 bytes.

In the metric system, the prefix 'kilo-' denotes multiplication by 1,000 (as in kilometre, a unit equal to 1,000 metres). However, computer memory size is based on the ◊binary number system, and the most convenient binary equivalent of 1,000 is 2^{10}, or 1,024.

kilogram SI unit (symbol kg) of mass equal to 1,000 grams (2.24 lb). It is defined as a mass equal to that of the international prototype, a platinum-iridium cylinder held at the International Bureau of Weights and Measures in Sèvres, France.

kilometre unit of length (symbol km) equal to 1,000 metres, equivalent to 3,280.89 ft or 0.6214 (about $\frac{5}{8}$) of a mile.

kilowatt unit (symbol kW) of power equal to 1,000 watts or about 1.34 horsepower.

kilowatt-hour commercial unit of electrical energy (symbol kWh), defined as the work done by a power of 1,000 watts in one hour and equal to 3.6 megajoules. It is used to calculate the cost of electrical energy taken from the domestic supply.

Kimball tag stock-control device commonly used in clothes shops, consisting of a small ◊punched card attached to each item offered for sale. The tag carries information about the item (such as its serial number, price, colour, and size), both in the form of printed details (which can be read by the customer) and as a pattern of small holes. When the item is sold, the tag (or a part of the tag) is removed and kept as a computer-readable record of sales.

kimberlite an igneous rock that is ultramafic (containing very little silica); a type of alkaline ◊peridotite with a porphyritic texture (larger crystals in a fine-grained matrix), containing mica in addition to olivine and other minerals. Kimberlite represents the world's principal source of diamonds.

Kimberlite is found in carrot-shaped pipelike ◊intrusions called **diatremes**, where mobile material from very deep in the Earth's crust has forced itself upwards, expanding in its ascent. The material, brought upwards from near the boundary between crust and mantle, often altered and fragmented, includes diamonds. Diatremes are found principally near Kimberley, South Africa, from which the name of the rock is derived, and in the Yakut area of Siberia, Russia.

kinesis (plural ***kineses***) in biology, a nondirectional movement in response to a stimulus; for example, woodlice move faster in drier surroundings. **Taxis** is a similar pattern of behaviour, but there the response is directional.

kinetic energy the energy of a body resulting from motion. It is contrasted with ◊potential energy.

kinetics the branch of chemistry that investigates the rates of chemical reactions.

kinetics branch of ◊dynamics dealing with the action of forces producing or changing the motion of a body; **kinematics** deals with motion without reference to force or mass.

kinetic theory theory describing the physical properties of matter in terms of the behaviour – principally movement – of its component atoms or molecules. The temperature of a substance is dependent on the velocity of movement of its constituent particles, increased temperature being accompanied by increased movement. A gas consists of rapidly moving atoms or molecules and, according to kinetic theory, it is their continual impact on the walls of the containing vessel that accounts for the pressure of the gas. The slowing of molecular motion as temperature falls, according to kinetic theory, accounts for the physical properties of liquids and solids, culminating in the concept of no molecular motion at ◊absolute zero (0K/–273°C).

By making various assumptions about the nature of gas molecules, it is possible to derive from the kinetic theory the various gas laws (such as ◊Avogadro's hypothesis, ◊Boyle's law, and ◊Charles's law).

King Charles spaniel breed of toy dog favoured by King Charles I of England. It has a characteristic domed head and upturned muzzle. It normally weighs less than 6 kg/13 lb. Different varieties are distinguished by the colours of the coat: King Charles (black with red markings); Prince Charles (white and black with red markings); Ruby (chestnut); Blenheim (white with chestnut markings).

king crab or ***horseshoe crab*** marine ◊arthropod found on the Atlantic coast of North America, and the coasts of Asia. The upper side of the body is entirely covered with a dark, rounded shell, and it has a long spinelike tail. It is up to 60 cm/2 ft long. It is unable to swim, and lays its eggs in the sand at the high-water mark. (Class Arachnida, subclass Xiphosura.)

There were approximately 500,000 *Paralithodes camtschatica* in the Barents Sea at the end of 1996. They were introduced by Russia as a potential food source. Norway claims they are unbalancing the marine ecosystem.

kingcup another name for ◊marsh marigold.

kingdom the primary division in biological ◊classification. At one time, only two kingdoms were recognized: animals and plants. Today most biologists prefer a five-kingdom system, even though it still involves grouping together organisms that are probably unrelated. One widely accepted scheme is as follows: **Kingdom Animalia** (all multicellular animals); **Kingdom Plantae** (all plants, including seaweeds and other algae, except blue-green); **Kingdom Fungi** (all fungi, including the unicellular yeasts, but not slime moulds); **Kingdom Protista** or **Protoctista** (protozoa, diatoms, dinoflagellates, slime moulds, and various other lower organisms with eukaryotic cells); and **Kingdom Monera** (all prokaryotes – the bacteria and cyanobacteria, or ◊blue-green algae). The first four of these kingdoms make up the eukaryotes.

When only two kingdoms were recognized, any organism with a rigid cell wall was a plant, and so bacteria and fungi were considered plants, despite their many differences. Other organisms, such as the photosynthetic flagellates (euglenoids), were claimed by both kingdoms. The unsatisfactory nature of the two-kingdom system became evident during the 19th century, and the biologist Ernst Haeckel was among the first to try to reform it. High-power microscopes have revealed more about the structure of cells; it has become clear that there is a fundamental difference between cells without a nucleus (◊prokaryotes) and those with a nucleus (◊eukaryotes). However, these differences are larger than those between animals and higher plants, and are unsuitable for use as kingdoms. At present there is no agreement on how many kingdoms there are in the natural world.

Although the five-kingdom system is widely favoured, some schemes have as many as 20.

The idea of man as a dominant animal of the earth whose whole behaviour tends to be dominated by his own desire for dominance gripped me. It seemed to explain almost everything.

MACFARLANE BURNET Australian physician.
Dominant Manual 1970

kingfisher any of a group of heavy-billed birds found near streams, ponds, and coastal areas around the world. The head is exceptionally large, and the long, angular bill is keeled; the tail and wings are relatively short, and the legs very short, with short toes. Kingfishers plunge-dive for fish and aquatic insects. The nest is usually a burrow in a riverbank. (Family Alcedinidae, order Coraciiformes.)

There are 88 species of kingfisher, the largest being the Australian ◊kookaburra. The Alcedinidae are sometimes divided into the subfamilies Daceloninae, Alcedininae, and Cerylinae.

kinkajou Central and South American carnivorous mammal belonging to the raccoon family. Yellowish-brown, with a rounded face and slim body, the kinkajou grows to 55 cm/1.8 ft with a 50 cm/1.6 ft tail, and has short legs with sharp claws. It spends its time in trees and has a prehensile tail, which it uses as an extra limb when moving from branch to branch. It feeds largely on fruit. (Species *Potos flavus,* family Procyonidae.)

kin selection in biology, the idea that ◊altruism shown to genetic relatives can be worthwhile, because those relatives share some genes with the individual that is behaving altruistically, and may continue to reproduce. See◊ inclusive fitness.

Alarm-calling in response to predators is an example of a behaviour that may have evolved through kin selection: relatives that are warned of danger can escape and continue to breed, even if the alarm caller is caught.

kiosk in computing, any computer that has been set up to act as an information centre in a public place. Users navigate the display using keyboards or ◊touch screens, but are never allowed to access the computer's operating system. A kiosk in a museum might show an interactive multimedia display, or one in a library might give readers access to catalogues.

Kirchhoff, Gustav Robert (1824–1887)

German physicist who with R W von Bunsen developed spectroscopic analysis in the 1850s and showed that all elements, heated to incandescence, have their individual spectra. In 1845 he derived the laws now known as Kirchhoff's laws that determine the value of the electric current and potential at any point in a network.

Mary Evans Picture Library

Kirchhoff's laws two laws governing electric circuits devised by the German physicist Gustav Kirchhoff. **Kirchhoff's first law** states that the total current entering any junction in a circuit is the same as the total current leaving it. This is an expression of the conservation of electric charge. **Kirchhoff's second law** states that the sum of the potential drops across each resistance in any closed loop in a circuit is equal to the total electromotive force acting in that loop. The laws are equally applicable to DC and AC circuits.

Kirkwood gaps in astronomy, regions of the ◊asteroid belt, between ◊Mars, and ◊Jupiter, where there are relatively few asteroids.

The orbital periods of particles in the gaps correspond to simple fractions, especially $\frac{1}{3}$, $\frac{2}{3}$, $\frac{3}{7}$, and $\frac{1}{2}$, of the orbital period of Jupiter, indicating that they are caused by the gravitational influence of the larger planet. The gaps are named after Daniel Kirkwood, the 19th century US astronomer who first drew attention to them.

kiss of life (***artificial ventilation***) in first aid, another name for ◊artificial respiration.

kite any of a group of birds of prey found in all parts of the world. Kites have long, pointed wings and, usually, a forked tail. There are about 20 species. (Family Accipitridae, order Falconiformes.)

kite quadrilateral with two pairs of adjacent equal sides. The geometry of this figure follows from the fact that it has one axis of symmetry.

Kitt Peak National Observatory observatory in the Quinlan Mountains near Tucson, Arizona, USA, operated by AURA (Association of Universities for Research into Astronomy). Its main telescopes are the 4-m/158-in Mayall reflector, opened in 1973, and the McMath Solar Telescope, opened in 1962, the world's largest of its type.

Among numerous other telescopes on the site is a 2.3-m/90-in reflector owned by the Steward Observatory of the University of Arizona.

KITT PEAK NATIONAL OBSERVATORY

http://www.noao.edu/kpno/kpno.html

Comprehensive information on the range of research carried out at Kitt Peak. In addition to scientific information of interest mainly to professional astronomers, there are details of current weather conditions at Kitts Peak and information for visitors. Visible and infrared images from satellites in geostationary orbits can be accessed.

kiwi flightless bird found only in New Zealand. It has long hairlike brown plumage, minute wings and tail, and a very long beak with nostrils at the tip. It is nocturnal and insectivorous. It lays two white eggs, each weighing up to 450 g/15.75 oz. (Species *Apteryx australis,* family Apterygidae, order Apterygiformes.)

All kiwi species have declined since European settlement of New Zealand, and the little spotted kiwi is most at risk. It survives only on one small island reservation, which was stocked with birds from the mainland.

KIWI

The kiwi produces the largest egg, proportionally to size, of any bird. The female lays one or two eggs, each weighing a quarter of her body weight.

kiwi fruit or ***Chinese gooseberry*** fruit of a vinelike plant grown commercially on a large scale in New Zealand. Kiwi fruits are egg-sized, oval, and similar in flavour to gooseberries, though much sweeter, with a fuzzy brown skin. (*Actinidithia chinensis,* family Actinidiaceae.)

kleptomania ***Greek kleptēs 'thief'*** behavioural disorder characterized by an overpowering desire to possess articles for which one has no need. In kleptomania, as opposed to ordinary theft, there is no obvious need or use for what is stolen and sometimes the sufferer has no memory of the theft.

kleptoparasitism habitual stealing of food from another organism. Skuas kleptoparasitize other seabirds, forcing them to relinquish their catches midflight. The Spanish slug *Deroceras hilbrandi* takes prey from the insect-eating plant *Pinguicula vallisneriifolia* whilst leaving the edible plant unharmed. Many small spiders are kleptoparasites living on the webs of bigger spiders.

km symbol for ◊kilometre.

knapweed any of several weedy plants belonging to the daisy family. In the common knapweed (*C. nigra*), also known as a **hardhead**, the hard, dark buds break open at the top into pale purple composite flowers. It is native to Europe and has been introduced to North America. (Genus *Centaurea,* family Compositae.)

knifefish any of a group of fishes in which the body is deep at the front and drawn to a narrow or pointed tail at the rear, the main fin being the well-developed long ventral (stomach) fin that completes the knifelike shape. The ventral fin is rippled for forward or backward movement. Knifefishes produce electrical fields, which they use for navigation. (Genus *Gymnotus* and other allied genera, family Gymnotidae.)

knocking in a spark-ignition petrol engine, a phenomenon that occurs when unburned fuel-air mixture explodes in the combustion chamber before being ignited by the spark. The resulting shock waves produce a metallic knocking sound. Loss of power occurs, which can be prevented by reducing the compression ratio, redesigning the geometry of the combustion chamber, or increasing the octane number of the petrol (usually by the use of tetraethyl lead anti-knock additives, or increasingly by MTBE – methyl tertiary butyl ether in unleaded petrol).

Knossos chief city of ◊Minoan Crete, near present-day Irákleion, 6 km/4 mi SE of Candia. The archaeological site, excavated by Arthur Evans 1899–1935, dates from about 2000–1400 BC, and includes the palace throne room, the remains of frescoes, and construction on more than one level.

Excavation of the palace of the legendary King Minos showed that the story of Theseus' encounter with the Minotaur in a labyrinth was possibly derived from the ritual 'bull-leaping' by young people depicted in the palace frescoes and from the maze-like layout of the palace.

knot wading bird belonging to the sandpiper family. It is about 25 cm/10 in long, with a short bill, neck, and legs. In the winter, it is grey above and white below, but in the breeding season, it is brick-red on the head and chest and black on the wings and back. It feeds on insects and molluscs. (Species *Calidris canutus,* family Scolopacidae, order Charadriiformes.)

Breeding in North American, European, and Asian arctic regions, knots travel widely in winter, to be found as far south as South Africa, Australasia, and southern parts of South America.

knot in navigation, unit by which a ship's speed is measured, equivalent to one ◊nautical mile per hour (one knot equals about 1.15 miles per hour). It is also sometimes used in aviation.

knotgrass annual plant belonging to the dock family. The bases of the small lance-shaped leaves enclose the slender stems, giving a superficial resemblance to grass. Small pinkish flowers are followed by seeds that are eaten by birds. Knotgrass grows worldwide except in the polar regions. (*Polygonum aviculare,* family Polygonaceae.)

knowbot in computing, a program that will search a system or a network, such as the Internet, seeking and retrieving information on behalf of a user and reporting back when it has found it. An example is the Knowbot Information Service, which can process users' queries by e-mail.

knowledge-based system (KBS) computer program that uses an encoding of human knowledge to help solve problems. It was discovered during research into ◊artificial intelligence that adding heuristics (rules of thumb) enabled programs to tackle problems that were otherwise difficult to solve by the usual techniques of computer science.

Chess-playing programs have been strengthened by including knowledge of what makes a good position, or of overall strategies, rather than relying solely on the computer's ability to calculate variations.

koala marsupial (mammal that carries its young in a pouch) found only in E Australia. It feeds almost entirely on eucalyptus shoots. It is about 60 cm/2 ft long, and resembles a bear (it is often incorrectly described as a 'koala bear'). The popularity of its greyish fur led to its almost complete extermination by hunters. Under protection since 1936, it rapidly increased in numbers, but recently numbers have fallen from 400,000 in 1985 to 40,000–80,000 in 1995. (Species *Phascolarctos cinereus,* family Phalangeridae.)

A three-year trial began in November 1996 in southern Australia, overpopulated by koalas, to bring their numbers under control by giving males vasectomies and females hormone implants preventing ovulation. In 1997, the programme of sterilization continued, and a relocation plan, following earlier trials, began.

KOALA

The fingerprints of koala bears are very similar to those of humans, with similar whorls, loop and arches. To avoid any confusion, Australian forensic scientists were warned, in 1996, to watch out for koalas at the scene of the crime.

Koch, (Heinrich Hermann) Robert (1843–1910)

German bacteriologist. Koch and his assistants devised the techniques for culturing bacteria outside the body, and formulated the rules for showing whether or not a bacterium is the cause of a disease. Nobel Prize for Physiology or Medicine 1905.

His techniques enabled him to identify the bacteria responsible for tuberculosis (1882), cholera (1883), and other diseases. He investigated anthrax bacteria in the 1870s and showed that they form spores which spread the infection.

Koch was a great teacher, and many of his pupils, such as Shibasaburo¯ Kitasato, Paul Ehrlich, and Emil von Behring, became outstanding scientists.

Mary Evans Picture Library

kohlrabi variety of kale, which is itself a variety of ◊cabbage; it is used for food and resembles a turnip. The leaves of kohlrabi shoot from a round swelling on the main stem. (*Brassica oleracea caulorapa* or *B. oleracea gongylodes,* family Cruciferae.)

kola alternative spelling of ◊cola, any of a group of tropical trees.

komondor breed of large herding dog originating in Hungary. It has a long, heavy, all-white coat with a rough 'corded' texture. Larger than the rather similar ◊puli, it stands about 80 cm/31.5 in tall.

Königsberg bridge problem long-standing puzzle that was solved by topology (the geometry of those properties of a figure which remain the same under distortion). In the city of Königsberg (now Kaliningrad in Russia), seven bridges connect the banks of the river Pregol'a and the islands in the river. For many years, people were challenged to cross each of the bridges in a single tour and return to their starting point. In 1736 Swiss mathematician Leonhard Euler converted the puzzle into a topological network, in which the islands and river banks were represented as nodes (junctions), and the connecting bridges as lines. By analysing this network he was able to show that it is not traversable – that is, it is impossible to cross each of the bridges once only and return to the point at which one started.

kookaburra or ***laughing jackass*** largest of the world's ◊kingfishers, found in Australia, with an extraordinary laughing call. It feeds on insects and other small creatures. The body and tail measure 45 cm/18 in, the head is greyish with a dark eye stripe, and the back and wings are flecked brown with grey underparts. It nests in shady forest regions, but will also frequent the vicinity of houses, and its cry is one of the most familiar sounds of the bush in E Australia. (Species *Dacelo novaeguineae,* family Alcedinidae, order Coraciiformes.)

Koonalda Cave cave in SW South Australia below the Nullarbor Plain. Anthropologists in the 1950s and 1960s discovered evidence of flint-quarrying and human markings that have been dated as 20,000 years old.

Korat breed of domestic shorthaired cat. It derives its name from the NE province of Korat in Thailand where it originated. It has a blue-grey coat with a silvery sheen with very thick fur.

It has a heart-shaped face with green eyes, and a lithe body.

Imported into the USA 1959, the breed was recognized there 1966, and in the UK in 1975.

kouprey wild ox native to the forests of N Cambodia. Only known to science since 1937, it is in great danger of extinction. Koupreys have cylindrical, widely separated horns and grow to 1.9 m/6 ft in height. (Species *Bos sauveli.*)

Kourou second-largest town of French Guiana, NW of Cayenne, site of the Guiana Space Centre of the European Space Agency; population (1996) 20,000 (20% of the total population of French Guiana).

Kow Swamp area in N Victoria, Australia, W of the town of Echuca, where the remains of about 40 humans have been found, buried in shallow graves. These bones have mostly been dated as 9,000–14,000 years old and were accompanied by human artefacts and objects such as shells. They are of a larger and more robust group of humans than those found from an earlier period at Lake Mungo and are similar to other finds from widely scattered sites in Australia such as Talgai in Queensland.

kph or ***km/h*** symbol for **kilometres per hour**.

krait highly venomous Indian snake related to the *cobra.*

Krebs, Hans Adolf (1900–1981)

German-born British biochemist. He discovered the citric acid cycle, also known as the ◊Krebs cycle, the final pathway by which food molecules are converted into energy in living tissues. For this work he shared the 1953 Nobel Prize for Physiology or Medicine. Knighted 1958.

Krebs first became interested in the process by which the body degrades amino acids. He discovered that nitrogen atoms are the first to be removed (deamination) and are then excreted as urea in the urine. He then investigated the processes involved in the production of urea from the removed nitrogen atoms, and by 1932 he had worked out the basic steps in the urea cycle.

Mary Evans Picture Library

TO REMEMBER THE KREBS CYCLE, ALSO KNOWN AS THE TCA (TRICARBOXYLIC ACID) CYCLE:

ACTORS IN KANSAS SHOULD SEE FOREIGN MOVIES, OF COURSE

ACONITATE, ISOCITRATE, α-KETOGLUTARATE, SUCCINYL-COA, SUCCINATE, FUMARATE, MALATE, OXALOACETATE, CITRATE

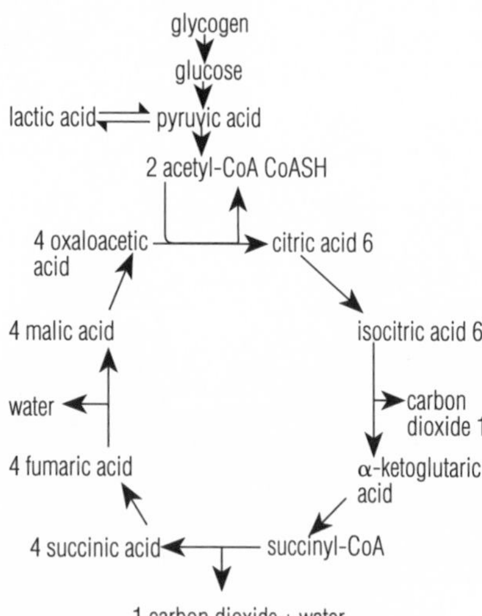

***Krebs cycle** The purpose of the Krebs (or citric acid) cycle is to complete the biochemical breakdown of food to produce energy-rich molecules, which the organism can use to fuel work. Acetyl coenzyme A (acetyl CoA) – produced by the breakdown of sugars, fatty acids, and some amino acids – reacts with oxaloacetic acid to produce citric acid, which is then converted in a series of enzyme-catalysed steps back to oxaloacetic acid. In the process, molecules of carbon dioxide and water are given off, and the precursors of the energy-rich molecules ATP are formed. (The numbers in the diagram indicate the number of carbon atoms in the principal compounds.)*

Krebs cycle or ***citric acid cycle*** or ***tricarboxylic acid cycle*** final part of the chain of biochemical reactions by which organisms break down food using oxygen to release energy (respiration). It takes place within structures called ◊mitochondria in the body's cells, and breaks down food molecules in a series of small steps, producing energy-rich molecules of ◊ATP.

krill any of several Antarctic ◊crustaceans, the most common species being *Euphausia superba.* Similar to a shrimp, it is up to 5 cm/2 in long, with two antennae, five pairs of legs, seven pairs of light organs along the body, and is coloured orange above and green beneath. It is the most abundant animal, numbering perhaps 600 trillion (million million). (Order Euphausiacea.)

Moving in enormous swarms, krill constitute the chief food of the baleen whales, and have been used to produce a protein concentrate for human consumption, and meal for animal feed.

KRILL

Approximately 600 trillion krill thrive in the Southern Ocean. Together they weigh more than the world's entire human population. The schools of shrimplike krill (moving at a rapid 20 cm/7.9 in per sec) form the base of many food chains; whales alone consume 150 million tonnes a year.

krypton ***Greek kryptos 'hidden'*** colourless, odourless, gaseous, nonmetallic element, symbol Kr, atomic number 36, relative atomic mass 83.80. It is grouped with the inert gases and was long believed not to enter into reactions, but it is now known to combine with fluorine under certain conditions; it remains inert to all other reagents. It is present in very small quantities in the air (about 114 parts per million). It is used chiefly in fluorescent lamps, lasers, and gas-filled electronic valves.

Krypton was discovered in 1898 in the residue from liquid air by British chemists William Ramsay and Morris Travers; the name refers to their difficulty in isolating it.

K-T boundary geologists' shorthand for the boundary between the rocks of the ◊Cretaceous and the ◊Tertiary periods 65 million years ago. It coincides with the end of the extinction of the dinosaurs and in many places is marked by a layer of clay or rock enriched in the element iridium. Extinction of the dinosaurs at the K-T boundary and deposition of the iridium layer are thought to be the result of either impact of a meteorite (or comet) that crashed into the Yucatán Peninsula (forming the **Chicxulub crater**) or the result of intense volcanism on the continent of India.

kudu either of two species of African antelope. The **greater kudu** (*T. strepsiceros*) is fawn-coloured with thin white vertical stripes, and stands 1.3 m/4.2 ft at the shoulder, with head and body 2.4 m/8 ft long. Males have long spiral horns. The greater kudu is found in bush country from Angola to Ethiopia. The similar **lesser kudu** (*T. imberbis*) lives in E Africa and is 1 m/3 ft at the shoulder. (Genus *Tragelaphus,* family Bovidae.)

kudzu Japanese creeper belonging to the ◊legume family, which helps fix nitrogen (see ◊nitrogen cycle) and can be used as a feed crop for animals, but became a pest in the southern USA when introduced to check soil erosion. (*Pueraria lobata,* family Leguminosae.)

Kuiper belt ring of small, icy bodies orbiting the Sun beyond the outermost planet. The Kuiper belt, named after US astronomer Gerard Kuiper who proposed its existence in 1951, is thought to be the source of comets that orbit the Sun with periods of less than 200 years. The first member of the Kuiper belt was seen in 1992. In 1995 the first comet-sized objects were discovered; previously the only objects found had diameters of at least 100 km/63 mi (comets generally have diameters of less than 10 km/6.3 mi).

Two new objects were discovered in the Kuiper belt in 1996. The first, 1996 TL66, is 500 km/300 mi in diameter and has an irregular orbit that takes it four–six times further from the Sun than Neptune. The second, 1996 RQ20, is slightly smaller, with an orbit that takes it about three times further from the Sun than Neptune. The orbits of both are at an angle of 20° to the plane of the Solar System.

kumquat small orange-yellow fruit of any of several evergreen trees native to E Asia and cultivated throughout the tropics. The trees grow 2.4–3.6 m/8–12 ft high and have dark green shiny leaves and white scented flowers. The fruit is eaten fresh (the skin is edible), preserved, or candied. The oval or Nagami kumquat is the most common variety. (Genus *Fortunella,* family Rutaceae.)

kurrajong tree widespread in E Australia *Brachychiton populneus* valued as fodder for stock particularly in drought conditions.

kuvasz breed of large guard dog native to Hungary, where it was formerly used to chase wolves and wild boar. Its medium-length, wavy coat is always white. It is strongly built and reaches 75 cm/29 in at the shoulder.

kW symbol for ◊kilowatt.

kwashiorkor severe protein deficiency in children under five years, resulting in retarded growth, lethargy, ◊oedema, diarrhoea, and a swollen abdomen. It is common in Third World countries with a high incidence of malnutrition.

kyanite aluminium silicate, Al_2SiO_5, a pale-blue mineral occurring as blade-shaped crystals. It is an indicator of high-pressure conditions in metamorphic rocks formed from clay sediments. Andalusite, kyanite, and sillimanite are all polymorphs (see ◊polymorphism).

What killed the dinosaurs?

BY EDWARD YOUNG

Sixty-five million years ago dinosaurs disappeared. With them went 70% of all species of the time. This 'mass extinction', one of many such events throughout Earth's history, marks the end of the ◊Cretaceous period and the beginning of the ◊Tertiary period, an interval of geological time known as the ◊K-T boundary (K for Kreide, German for Cretaceous). What killed the ◊dinosaurs? Two rival hypotheses dominate. One is that a huge asteroid or comet collided with Earth during K-T time, the other, is that voluminous volcanism in what is now western India was responsible. Distinguishing between these two hypotheses has proven difficult. In either case, the possible link between these events and the demise of the dinosaurs is forcing scientists to reexamine the role of catastrophe in Earth's history.

From Catastrophism to Uniformitarianism

Geology arose as a modern scientific discipline in the early 19th century with the fall of catastrophism, the notion that the history of our planet was shaped by successive catastrophic events and the rise of uniformitarianism, which holds that every-day processes, operating however slowly, are sufficient to explain the principle features of Earth's history.

Naturalists of the late 18th century understood that fossil marine animals and the sedimentary rock in which they were found represented ancient sea floors. But the cast accumulations of fossil-bearing rock revealed in the sides of mountains posed a time problem. The Earth is just 6,000 years old, it was believed, and any casual observer of the oceans could see that sediment did not accumulate fast enough to yield kilometre thicknesses of marine sediment (later turned to rock) unless normal processes were somehow accelerated by cataclysmic events. The great flood described in the Old Testament of the Bible was one catastrophe commonly invoked. Catastrophic upheavals were also called upon to explain mountains.

Near the end of the 18th century a Scottish scientist named James Hutton reasoned that all of the Earth's geological features could be explained by the slow and unchanging forces operating all around us *if* the Earth was very much older than had been previously imagined. This new view, ◊uniformitarianism, proved immensely successful in explaining geological observations, though not at first. Several decades later another Scot, Charles Lyell, refined and popularized Hutton's uniformitarianism. Lyell emphasized that human kind had existed for sufficient time as to bear witness to all kinds of processes that affect Earth history. Hutton and Lyell imagined Earth where the past looked much like the present, with no beginning nor an end. But it was their principle of uniformitarianism that allowed Charles Darwin to concieve of the evolution of species by natural selection and show that Earth's inhabitants at least, had changes irrevocably over geological time.

Without uniformitarianism there could have been no modern geology and no Darwinian theory of evolution and geologists have been understandably reluctant to dismiss the premise that 'the present is the key to the past'.

The new catastrophism

Was Lyell right? Have human beings actually witnessed all of the important agents of Earth change? Since the early years of uniformitarianism we have learned that Earth is 4.5 billion years old and that our ◊Solar System formed from the collapse of a fragment of molecular interstellar cloud approximately 4.6 billion years ago. Human history spans a mere one tenth of one thousandth of this interval and we would have been fortunate indeed if our existence had coincided with all of the forces that periodically effect our planet over millions and even billions of years. Therefore the most likely answer to the question: was Lyell right? must be *no*. Meteorite impact or volcanism on a massive scale may have killed off the dinosaurs. But both of these events, as it turns out, are normal in the course of the evolution of our planet. Should they be considered catastrophes in the context of Earth history?

In July of 1994 ◊comet Shoemaker-Levy 9 collided with ◊Jupiter. The impact was a catastrophe (for Jupiter) the like of which we have not seen before. Despite the fact that this event was unique in terms of human experiences, such colossal collisions are business-as-usual in astronomical terms. Numerous impact craters scar the rocky surfaces of most bodies in our solar system. These craters reveal that prior to 3.8 billion years ago, planets were routinely bombarded by meter to kilmetre-sized objects. The collisions constituted the final stages of rocky ◊accretion as the planets swept up the debris from which they were made. After 3.8 billion years accretion was essentially complete and impacts upon the planets became less frequent, but as Shoemaker-Levy 9 reminded us, they have not ceased entirely.

Impact structures dating back to the time of frequent bombardment have been destroyed on Earth by erosion and ◊tectonic processes that constantly deform and make over the crust. Nonetheless, scientists have thus far managed to identify more than 100 younger impact craters on Earth. It is estimated that, on average, ◊asteroids or ◊comets measuring 5 to 10 kilometres in diameter impact our planet every 50 to 100 million years. Kilometre-sized bodies are thought to hit roughly every million years. Objects in the order of 50 meters in diameter strike about once every 1000 years. For comparison, Shoemaker-Levy 9 was composed of several objects ranging from one to several kilometres in size, their collision with Jupiter released more energy than all of the nuclear weapons on Earth combined.

At present 150 asteroids are known to pass within one Earth orbit of the ◊Sun. They range in size from a few meters to 8 kilometres. A working group under the auspices of the ◊United States National Aeronautics and Space Administration (NASA) suggests that there may be 2100 such bodies in all. The impact of a single asteroid of 2 or more kilometres would have enough energy to profoundly affect Earth's ◊biosphere, hydrosphere, and ◊atmosphere. Fortunately, the likelihood of a collision of severe consequence in the next few hundred years is remote.

Not all catastrophes arrive from space. In 1783, just as catastrophism was about to give way to uniformitarianism, the Laki volcano erupted on Iceland. Unusually harsh winter conditions ensued in North America and Europe. Sulphuric acid rain destroyed Iceland's crops and livestock. Several events of comparable magnitude have confirmed that volcanic eruptions can bring about changes in climate. Have human's experienced the full extent of the influence of volcanism on Earth history? The geological record suggests probably not.

The impact hypothesis

In 1980, physicist and Nobel Prize laureate Luis W. Alvarez and his colleagues Walter Alvarez, Frank Asaro and Helen V. Michel suggested that the K-T mass extinction resulted from the impact of an asteroid or comet (the term bolide describes an impactor of any sort). A bolide greater than 10 kilometres in diameter and travelling 10 kilometres per second, they submitted, would liberate enough energy to trigger environmental disaster across the globe. The Earth would be plunged into months of darkness as the dust propelled into the air by the collision blocked the Sun's rays.

◊Photosynthesis would cease and plant-eating animals would be deprived of food, touching off a breakdown in the food chain. Temperatures would fall and as the shroud of dust prevented the Sun from warming Earth's surface, a phenomenon referred to as 'impact winter'. While land-dwelling animals were fighting starvation and the cold, marine creatures would have to battle acidification of the oceans; aerosols of debris and chemical reactions triggered by an atmospheric shock wave would result in nitric and sulphuric acid rain on a grand scale.

Alvarez and coworkers made their proposal on the basis of an unusual enrichment of the rare element ◊iridium in a layer of clay marking the K-T boundary in Italy. Iridium, chemically similar to ◊platinum and ◊gold, is rare on Earth but much more abundant in primitive rocky meteorites. Since their original report, the 'iridium anomaly', as it has come to be known, has since been found in rocks and sediments deposited at the K-T boundary around the world. There is other evidence supportive of an impact. Ratios of the isotope of the element ◊osmium, a platinum-group element like iridium, from some K-T samples are similar to primitive meteorites. Large amounts of soot in K-T boundary clay is thought to have come from large-scale burning of vegetation ignited by debris ejected from the atmosphere that fell back to earth like a hail of red-hot meteors. ◊Quartz grains shocked by pressures exceeding one hundred thousand atmospheres have been found in K-T deposits. Previously, shocked quartz had only been found at impact craters (Arizona's Meteor Crater for example) or sites where underground nuclear weapons were tested.

In 1991 a circular impact structure of K-T age was found buried beneath one kilometre of Tertiary carbonate rock in Mexico's Yucatan peninsula. The structure is referred to as the Chicxulub crater after the nearby town of Chicxulub Puerto. Experts agree that Chicxulub is the most spectacular crater on Earth and is the best candidate for the K-T impact site envisioned by Alvarez and co-workers. There are only two other impact structures of comparably large size and they are about 2 billion years old and poorly preserved. The precise size of Chicxulub has been debated. Estimates range from 180 to 300 kilometres in diameter. Most recent studies indicate that the hole upon impact was approximately 120 kilometres wide.

Despite its obvious attraction, the impact hypothesis is not without problems. Paleontologists find evidence that the K-T extinction was not instantaneous and may have begun up to a million years before K-T time and continued for tens of thousands of years after. Shocked quartz and even the iridium anomaly are found to occur just above and below the K-T sediment. Disastrous environmental conditions that would have besieged the Earth after impact of a large bolide should have lasted about a decade and so none of these observations is easily explained by the crash of a single asteroid or comet. To redress this apparent short-coming of the hypothesis, some proponents have argued that more than one bolide struck Earth at about K-T time.

The volcanism hypothesis

Another competing catastrophe theory has been put forward to explain not only the chemical and physical features of the K-T boundary but are also the protracted nature of the mass extinction. Beginning in the 1970s it was observed that the largest episode of ◊volcanism in the past 200 million years coincided with the K-T mass extinction. Remains of this volcanism are exposed today in the Deccan plateau region of western India. Here, vast quantities of ◊basalt (a type of dark volcanic rock) known as the Deccan Traps are exposed. Combined, the ancient flows are more than two kilometres thick and comprise roughly 3% of the entire Indian continent. Deccan volcanism lasted several hundreds of thousands of years and was most active at the time of the K-T mass extinction. American geologist Dewey M. McLean and French geophysicist Vincent Courtillot, among others, argue that it was the voluminous Deccan volcanism that was responsible for the K-T mass extinction. Recall the climatic effects of the Laki eruption? Imagine the effects of continuous large-scale volcanism for hundreds of thousands of years.

The chemical composition of Earth's ◊mantle is more like that of primitive meteorites than the crust. Deccan lavas came from the mantle. Thus instead of being derived from dust thrown up by an asteroid, the iridium anomaly and other chemical signatures of the K-T boundary could be the result of a deluge of volcanic dust. Similarly, shocked quartz, cited as critical evidence for bolide impact, can apparently be formed by eruption of some types of explosive volcanoes.

The environmental effects of large-scale volcanism and bolide impact may be similar. Volcanism, like impact, would loft large amounts of dust high into the atmosphere where it would be transported around the world. As with the impact hypothesis, the Earth might cool as the dust blocked the Sun's rays. Sulphur released by the volcanoes would cause rain to be acidic. Alternatively, McLean has argued that it was ◊carbon dioxide, a ◊greenhouse gas released during volcanism, that was the killer. Large amounts of carbon dioxide released in to the atmosphere would have changed the chemistry of the oceans and caused ◊global warming, both of which would be harmful to life.

An unlucky coincidence

New theoretical studies suggest that without a vulnerability to extinction, catastrophe may have little influence on the diversity of living organisms. Mass extinctions occur with a crude 30 million year periodicity. The largest, in which 90% of species disappeared, was at the end of the ◊Palaeozoic era approximately 250 million years ago. Smaller extinctions are more common. Theoreticians have shown recently that a pattern of frequent smaller extinctions and less frequent larger extinctions is the inevitable consequence of the dependence of living organisms on one another. The disappearance of an animal's prey, for example, may make the animal less fit for survival. The predator species might then vacate its ecological niche and in turn affect fitness of another species and so it goes until eventually an 'avalanche' of linked extinctions occurs. During an extinction 'avalanche' large numbers of species enter new habitats for which they are not well adapted. Mathematical simulations of such processes show that mass extinction requires the coincidence of *both* large numbers of vulnerable species due to an extinction avalanche, the result of normal evolutionary change, and an unusual amount of stress caused by an environmental catastrophe. Thus it seems the dinosaurs that lived during the Cretaceous period must have been ripe for expiration. Unfortunately for them, their vulnerability coincided with a particularly unlucky time in Earth's history when volcanism was rampant and a collision of the sort that occurs just once every 50 million years actually happened.

l symbol for ◊litre, **a measure of liquid volume**.

labelled compound or ***tagged compound*** chemical compound in which a radioactive isotope is substituted for a stable one. The path taken by such a compound through a system can be followed, for example by measuring the radiation emitted.

This powerful and sensitive technique is used in medicine, chemistry, biochemistry, and industry.

labellum lower petal of an orchid flower; it is a different shape from the two lateral petals and gives the orchid its characteristic appearance. The labellum is more elaborate and usually larger than the other petals. It often has distinctive patterning to encourage ◊pollination by insects; sometimes it is extended backwards to form a hollow spur containing nectar.

WIZARD'S LAB

http://library.advanced.org/11924/

Lots of fun, accessible science with spoken commentary for all those who love the Internet style of learning. A friendly 'wizard' leads surfers through the various corners of the virtual lab, so that they can learn about such topics as electricity, sound, light, energy, and magnetism. Each presentation concludes with useful summaries, particularly entertaining when given in the wizard's own voice. There is also a quiz section and a glossary of useful terms.

laboratory room or building equipped for scientific experiments, research, and teaching.

In Europe, private research laboratories have been used since the 16th century, and by the 18th century laboratories were also used for teaching. The German chemist Justus van Liebig established a laboratory 1826 in Giessen, Germany, where he not only instructed his students in the art of experimental chemistry, but also undertook chemical research with them.

A first-rate laboratory is one in which mediocre scientists can produce outstanding work.

PATRICK MAYNARD STUART BLACKETT British physicist. Quoted by M G K Menon in his commemoration lecture on H J Bhabha, Royal Institution 1967

Labrador retriever breed of dog. See ◊retriever.

laburnum any of a group of flowering trees or shrubs belonging to the pea family; the seeds develop in pealike pods but are poisonous. *L. anagyroides,* native to the mountainous parts of central Europe, is often grown as an ornamental tree. The flowers, in long drooping clusters, are bright yellow and appear in early spring; some varieties have purple or reddish flowers. (Genus *Laburnum,* family Leguminosae.)

labyrinthitis inflammation of the part of the inner ear responsible for the sense of balance (the labyrinth). It results in dizziness, which may then cause nausea and vomiting. It is usually caused by a viral infection of the ear (◊otitis), which resolves in a few weeks. The nausea and vomiting may respond to anti-emetic drugs.

lac resinous incrustation produced by the female of the lac insect (*Laccifer lacca*), which eventually covers the twigs of trees in India and the Far East. The gathered twigs are known as **stick lac**, and yield a useful crimson dye; **shellac**, which is used in varnishes, polishes, and leather dressings, is manufactured commercially by melting the separated resin and spreading it into thin layers or flakes.

laccolith intruded mass of igneous rock that forces apart two strata and forms a round lens-shaped mass many times wider than thick. The overlying layers are often pushed upward to form a dome. A classic development of laccoliths is illustrated in the Henry, La Sal, and Abajo mountains of SE Utah, USA, found on the Colorado plateau.

lacewing any of a group of insects found throughout the world. Lacewings take their name from the intricate veining of their two pairs of semitransparent wings. They have narrow bodies and long thin antennae. The larvae (called aphid lions) are predators, especially on aphids. (Families Hemerobiidae (brown lacewings) and Chrysopidae (green lacewings), order Neuroptera.)

The eggs of the golden-eye lacewing (*Chrysopa aculata*) are laid on the ends of plant stalks.

LACEWING

Green lacewing larvae disguise themselves to find their food. They feed on woolly alder aphids, but the aphids are guarded by ants who milk them for their honeydew. The larvae hoodwink the ants by plucking the white waxy fluff from the aphids and sticking it over themselves. With this disguise, they move among the aphids and eat them without the ants noticing.

lac insect small plant-sucking insect related to ◊scale insects and mealy bugs. The females of most species lack legs and have reduced antennae; their bodies are globular and enclosed within a dense resinous secretion called ◊lac. Lac insects are found mainly in the tropics and subtropics.

classification Lac insects are members of the family Lacciferidae, order Hemiptera (suborder Homoptera), class Insecta, phylum Arthropoda.

A number of species have two generations annually, in which two types of males occur: the first generation includes both winged and wingless males; the second generation is wingless.

Many species used to be of considerable commercial value, as they yield a dye. However, with the advent of synthetic dyes the demand for lac insects has decreased.

The Indian lac insect, *Laccifer lacca,* produces stick lac, a secretion from which shellac (used in varnishes and polishes) is prepared.

lactation secretion of milk in mammals, from the mammary glands. In late pregnancy, the cells lining the lobules inside the mammary glands begin extracting substances from the blood to produce milk. The supply of milk starts shortly after birth with the production of colostrum, a clear fluid consisting largely of water, protein, antibodies, and vitamins. The production of milk continues practically as long as the baby continues to suckle.

lacteal small vessel responsible for absorbing fat in the small intestine. Occurring in the fingerlike villi of the ◊ileum, lacteals have a milky appearance and drain into the lymphatic system.

Before fat can pass into the lacteal, bile from the liver causes its emulsification into droplets small enough for attack by the enzyme lipase. The products of this digestion form into even smaller droplets, which diffuse into the villi.

Large droplets re-form before entering the lacteal and this causes the milky appearance.

lactic acid or ***2-hydroxypropanoic acid*** $CH_3CHOHCOOH$ organic acid, a colourless, almost odourless liquid, produced by certain bacteria during fermentation and by active muscle cells when they are exercised hard and are experiencing ◊oxygen debt. An accumulation of lactic acid in the muscles may cause cramp. It occurs in yoghurt, buttermilk, sour cream, poor wine, and certain plant extracts, and is used in food preservation and in the preparation of pharmaceuticals.

lactose white sugar, found in solution in milk; it forms 5% of cow's milk. It is commercially prepared from the whey obtained in cheese-making. Like table sugar (sucrose), it is a disaccharide, consisting of two basic sugar units (monosaccharides), in this case, glucose and galactose. Unlike sucrose, it is tasteless.

ladybird or ***ladybug*** any of various small beetles, generally red or yellow in colour, with black spots. There are more than 5,200 species worldwide. As larvae and adults, they feed on aphids and scale-insect pests. (Family Coccinellidae, order Coleoptera.)

Ladybirds have been used as a form of ◊biological control since the 19th century and the US ladybird harvest was worth an annual $3–5 million by 1991.

lady's smock another name for the ◊cuckoo flower.

lagging material used for heat ◊insulation; it may be wrapped around hot-water tanks to reduce heat loss, or around water pipes to prevent freezing in winter.

lagoon coastal body of shallow salt water, usually with limited access to the sea. The term is normally used to describe the shallow sea area cut off by a ◊coral reef or barrier islands.

Lagrangian points five locations in space where the centrifugal and gravitational forces of two bodies neutralize each other; a third, less massive body located at any one of these points will be held in equilibrium with respect to the other two. Three of the points, L1–L3, lie on a line joining the two large bodies. The other two points, L4 and L5, which are the most stable, lie on either side of this line. Their existence was predicted in 1772 by French mathematician Joseph Louis Lagrange.

The **Trojan asteroids** lie at Lagrangian points L4 and L5 in Jupiter's orbit around the Sun. Clouds of dust and debris may lie at the Lagrangian points of the Moon's orbit around the Earth.

lahar mudflow formed of a fluid mixture of water and volcanic ash. During a volcanic eruption, melting ice may combine with ash to form a powerful flow capable of causing great destruction. The lahars created by the eruption of Nevado del Ruiz in Colombia, South America, in 1985 buried 22,000 people in 8 m/26 ft of mud.

lake body of still water lying in depressed ground without direct communication with the sea. Lakes are common in formerly glaciated regions, along the courses of slow rivers, and in low land near the sea. The main classifications are by origin: **glacial lakes**, formed by glacial scouring; **barrier lakes**, formed by landslides and glacial moraines; **crater lakes**, found in volcanoes; and **tectonic lakes**, occurring in natural fissures.

Crater lakes form in the calderas of extinct volcanoes, for example Crater Lake, Oregon. Subsidence of the roofs of limestone caves in karst landscape exposes the subterranean stream network and provides a cavity in which a lake can develop. Tectonic lakes form during tectonic movement, as when a rift valley is formed. Lake Tanganyika was created in conjunction with the East African Great Rift Valley. Glaciers produce several distinct types of lake, such as the lochs of Scotland and the Great Lakes of North America.

Lakes are mainly freshwater, but salt and bitter lakes are found in areas of low annual rainfall and little surface runoff, so that the rate of evaporation exceeds the rate of inflow, allowing mineral salts to accumulate. The Dead Sea has a salinity of about 250 parts per 1,000 and the Great Salt Lake, Utah, about 220 parts per 1,000. Salinity can also be caused by volcanic gases or fluids, for example Lake Natron, Tanzania.

In the 20th century large artificial lakes have been created in connection with hydroelectric and other works. Some lakes have become polluted as a result of human activity. Sometimes eutrophication (a state of overnourishment) occurs, when agricultural fertilizers leaching into lakes cause an explosion of aquatic life, which then depletes the lake's oxygen supply until it is no longer able to support life.

lake dwelling or ***pile dwelling*** prehistoric habitation built on piles driven into the bottom of a lake or at the edge of a lake or river. Such villages are found throughout Europe, in W Africa, South America, Borneo, and New Guinea.

Objects recovered from lake dwellings are often unusually well preserved by the mud or peat in which they are buried. Wooden items, wickerwork, woven fabrics, fruit, and pollen grains have been retrieved.

Lakeland terrier medium-sized wire-haired terrier weighing about 7–8 kg/15.5–17.5 lb with an ideal height of no more than 37 cm/14.5 in. Its skull is moderately broad, with small, V-shaped ears and dark eyes; the body is short and the tail traditionally docked.

Lamarck, Jean Baptiste de (1744–1829)

French naturalist. His theory of evolution, known as **Lamarckism,** was based on the idea that acquired characteristics (changes acquired in an individual's lifetime) are inherited by the offspring, and that organisms have an intrinsic urge to evolve into better-adapted forms. *Philosophie zoologique/Zoological Philosophy* 1809 outlined his 'transformist' (evolutionary) ideas.

Zoological Philosophy tried to show that various parts of the body developed because they were necessary, or disappeared because of disuse when variations in the environment caused a change in habit. If these body changes were inherited over many generations, new species would eventually be produced.

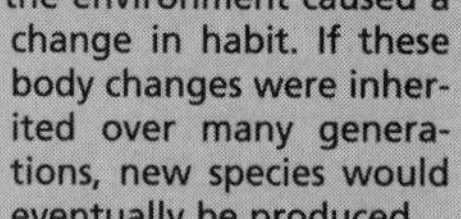

Lamarck was the first to distinguish vertebrate from invertebrate animals by the presence of a bony spinal column. He was also the first to establish the crustaceans, arachnids, and annelids among the invertebrates. It was Lamarck who coined the word 'biology'.

Mary Evans Picture Library

Lamarckism theory of evolution, now discredited, advocated during the early 19th century by French naturalist Jean Baptiste Lamarck.

Lamarckism is the theory that acquired characteristics were inherited. It differs from the Darwinian theory of evolution.

lambert unit of luminance (the light shining from a surface), equal to one ◊lumen per square centimetre. In scientific work the ◊candela per square metre is preferred.

lamina in flowering plants (◊angiosperms), the blade of the ◊leaf on either side of the midrib. The lamina is generally thin and flattened, and is usually the primary organ of ◊photosynthesis. It has a network of veins through which water and nutrients are conducted. More generally, a lamina is any thin, flat plant structure, such as the ◊thallus of many seaweeds.

lammergeier or ***bearded vulture*** Old World vulture with a wingspan of 2.7 m/9 ft. It ranges over S Europe, N Africa, and Asia, in wild mountainous areas. It feeds on offal and carrion and drops bones onto rocks to break them and so get at the marrow. (Species *Gypaetus barbatus,* family Accipitridae.)

lamp, electric device designed to convert electrical energy into light energy.

In a **filament lamp** such as a light bulb an electric current causes heating of a long thin coil of fine high-resistance wire enclosed at low pressure inside a glass bulb. In order to give out a good light the wire must glow white-hot and therefore must be made of a metal, such as tungsten, that has a high melting point. The efficiency of filament lamps is low because most of the electrical energy is converted to heat.

A **fluorescent lamp** uses an electrical discharge or spark inside a gas-filled tube to produce light. The inner surface of the tube is coated with a fluorescent material that converts the ultraviolet light generated by the discharge into visible light. Although a high voltage is needed to start the discharge, these lamps are far more efficient than filament lamps at producing light.

lamprey any of various eel-shaped jawless fishes. A lamprey feeds on other fish by fixing itself by its round mouth to its host and boring into the flesh with its toothed tongue. Lampreys breed in fresh water, and the young live as larvae for about five years before migrating to the sea. (Family Petromyzontidae.)

LAMPREY

King Henry I of England died from eating too many lampreys. Although lampreys always made him feel unwell, he was too fond of them to resist the temptation to eat them in large quantities.

LAN in computing, abbreviation for ◊local area network.

lancelet any of a variety of marine animals about 2.5 cm/1 in long. They have no skull, brain, eyes, heart, vertebral column, centralized brain, or paired limbs, but there is a notochord (a supportive rod) which runs from end to end of the body, a tail, and a number of gill slits. Found in all seas, lancelets burrow in the sand but when disturbed swim freely. (Genus *Amphioxus,* phylum Chordata, subphylum Cephalocordata.)

Taxonomically they are significant since the notochord may be regarded as the precursor of the backbone (spinal column).

Landsat series of satellites used for monitoring the Earth's resources. The first was launched in 1972.

landslide sudden downward movement of a mass of soil or rocks from a cliff or steep slope. Landslides happen when a slope becomes unstable, usually because the base has been undercut or because materials within the mass have become wet and slippery.

A **mudflow** happens when soil or loose material is soaked so that it no longer adheres to the slope; it forms a tongue of mud that reaches downhill from a semicircular hollow. A **slump** occurs when the material stays together as a large mass, or several smaller masses, and these may form a tilted steplike structure as they slide. A **landslip** is formed when ◊beds of rock dipping towards a cliff slide along a lower bed. Earthquakes may precipitate landslides.

langur any of various leaf-eating Old World monkeys that live in trees in S Asia. There are about 20 species. Langurs are related to the colobus monkey of Africa. (Genus *Presbytis* and other related genera.)

lanolin sticky, purified wax obtained from sheep's wool and used in cosmetics, soap, and leather preparation.

lanternfish any of about 300 species of small deep-sea bony fish. They are less than 15 cm/6 in long, with a large mouth, large eyes, and many luminous organs along the underside of the body, the function of which is not understood. They feed on plankton.
classification Lanternfish are in the order Myctophiformes, class Osteichthyes.

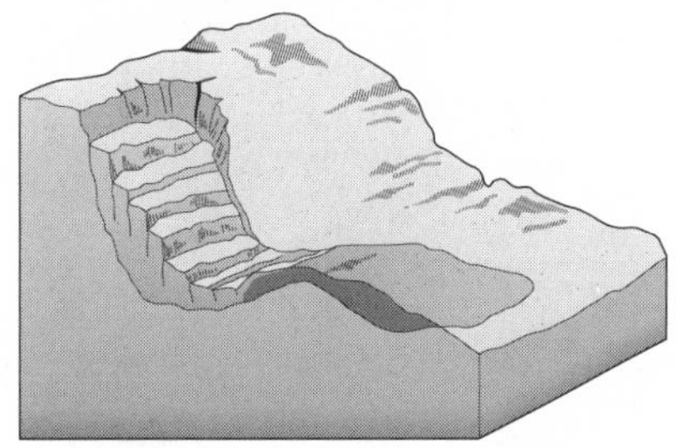

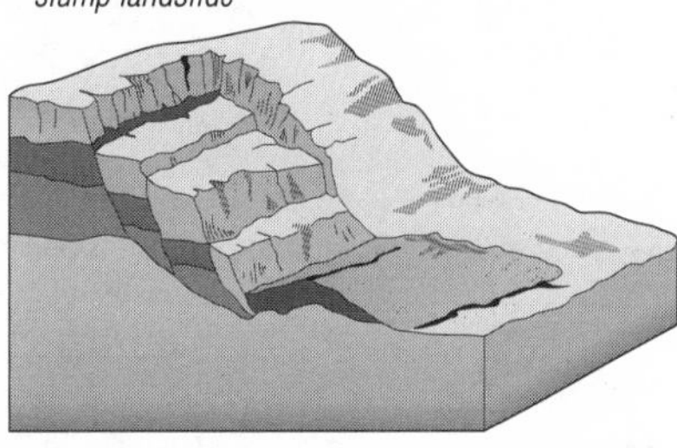

landslide *Types of landslide. A mudflow is a tongue of mud that slides downhill. A slump is a fall of a large mass that stays together after the fall. A landslip occurs when beds of rock move along a lower bed.*

Lanier, Jaron

US computing innovator who coined the term virtual reality (VR), and set up a small company, VPL Research Inc, to produce the first VR headsets and data gloves. The headsets enabled wearers to experience graphical worlds created by high-powered computers and to 'meet' in virtual spaces. In 1996 he was chief scientist at New Leaf Systems Inc, and visiting scholar at Columbia University's Department of Computer Science and New York University's Tisch School of the Arts. Lanier is also a musician, a composer and a painter

lantern fly one of a number of mainly tropical fly species, most of which have a narrow head that is drawn out into a long process. In some species this process looks like a lantern. Many lantern flies are large, with wing span up to 15 cm/6 in.

The head process contains a pouchlike diverticulum of the gut. The name lantern fly was originally given to the South American species *Lanternaria phosphorea.*
classification The lantern fly is a member of the family Fulgoridae, of suborder Homoptera, order Hemiptera, class Insecta, phylum Arthropoda.

langur A grey langur Presbytis entellus *exhibiting the leaf-eating habits of its kind. This animal is highly adapted to its diet and can digest leaves which are avoided by most other herbivorous mammals. Widespread in India and Sri Lanka, it is often found around human habitations as well as in forests. Premaphotos Wildlife*

lanthanide any of a series of 15 metallic elements (also known as rare earths) with atomic numbers 57 (lanthanum) to 71 (lutetium).

One of its members, promethium, is radioactive. All occur in nature. Lanthanides are grouped because of their chemical similarities (most are trivalent, but some can be divalent or tetravalent), their properties differing only slightly with atomic number.

Lanthanides were called rare earths originally because they were not widespread and were difficult to identify and separate from their ores by their discoverers. The series is set out in a band in the periodic table of the elements, as are the ◊actinides.

lanthanum ***Greek lanthanein 'to be hidden'*** soft, silvery, ductile and malleable, metallic element, symbol La, atomic number 57, relative atomic mass 138.91, the first of the lanthanide series. It is used in making alloys. It was named 1839 by Swedish chemist Carl Mosander (1797–1858).

laparoscope in medicine, another name for an endoscope.

laparotomy exploratory surgical procedure involving incision into the abdomen. The use of laparotomy, as of other exploratory surgery, has decreased sharply with advances in medical imaging and the direct-viewing technique known as ◊endoscopy.

lapis lazuli rock containing the blue mineral lazurite in a matrix of white calcite with small amounts of other minerals. It occurs in silica-poor igneous rocks and metamorphic limestones found in Afghanistan, Siberia, Iran, and Chile. Lapis lazuli was a valuable pigment of the Middle Ages, also used as a gemstone and in inlaying and ornamental work.

Laplink in computing, software that allows intelligent transfer of files between computers. Laplink is a key tool for those managing files across more than one computer, such as a mobile executive who has both a desktop computer at his office and a laptop for travelling. It is published by US company Traveling Software.

laptop computer portable microcomputer, small enough to be used on the operator's lap. It consists of a single unit, incorporating a keyboard, ◊floppy disc and ◊hard disc drives, and a screen. The screen often forms a lid that folds back in use. It uses a liquid-crystal or gas-plasma display, rather than the bulkier and heavier cathode-ray tubes found in most display terminals. A typical laptop computer measures about 210 x 297 mm/8.3 x 11.7 in (A4), is 5 cm/2 in in depth, and weighs less than 3 kg/6 lb 9 oz.

lapwing bird belonging to the plover family, also known as the **green plover** and, from its call, as the **peewit**. Bottle-green above and white below, with a long thin crest and rounded wings, it is about 30 cm/1 ft long. It inhabits moorland in Europe and Asia, making a nest scratched out of the ground, and is also often seen on farmland. (Species *Vanellus vanellus,* family Charadriidae.)

larch any of a group of trees belonging to the pine family. The common larch (*L. decidua*) grows to 40 m/130 ft. It is one of the few ◊conifers to shed its leaves annually. The small needlelike leaves are replaced every year by new bright-green foliage, which later darkens. (Genus *Larix,* family Pinaceae.)

Closely resembling it is the North American tamarack (*L. laricina*), and both are timber trees. The golden larch (*Pseudolarix amabilis*), a native of China, turns golden in autumn.

Large Electron Positron Collider (*LEP*) the world's largest particle ◊accelerator, in operation from 1989 at the CERN laboratories near Geneva in Switzerland. It occupies a tunnel 3.8 m/12.5 ft wide and 27 km/16.7 mi long, which is buried 180 m/590 ft underground and forms a ring consisting of eight curved and eight straight sections.

In June 1996, LEP resumed operation after a £210 million upgrade. The upgraded machine will be known as LEP2, and can generate collision energy of 161 gigaelectron volts.

Electrons and positrons enter the ring after passing through the Super Proton Synchrotron accelerator. They travel in opposite directions around the ring, guided by 3,328 bending magnets and kept within tight beams by 1,272 focusing magnets.

As they pass through the straight sections, the particles are accelerated by a pulse of radio energy. Once sufficient energy is accumulated, the beams are allowed to collide. Four giant detectors are used to study the resulting shower of particles.

In 1989 the LEP was used to measure the mass and lifetime of the Z particle, carrier of the weak nuclear force.

lark any of a group of songbirds found mainly in the Old World, but also in North America. Larks are brownish-tan in colour and usually about 18 cm/7 in long; they nest on the ground in the open. The **skylark** (*Alauda arvensis*) sings as it rises almost vertically in the air. It is light brown and 18 cm/7 in long. (Family Alaudidae, order Passeriformes.)

larkspur any of several plants included with the ◊delphiniums. (Genus *Delphinium,* family Ranunculaceae.).

larva stage between hatching and adulthood in those species in which the young have a different appearance and way of life from the adults. Examples include tadpoles (frogs) and caterpillars (butterflies and moths). Larvae are typical of the invertebrates, some of which (for example, shrimps) have two or more distinct larval stages. Among vertebrates, it is only the amphibians and some fishes that have a larval stage.

The process whereby the larva changes into another stage, such as a pupa (chrysalis) or adult, is known as ◊metamorphosis.

laryngitis inflammation of the larynx, causing soreness of the throat, a dry cough, and hoarseness. The acute form is due to a virus or other infection, excessive use of the voice, or inhalation of irritating smoke, and may cause the voice to be completely lost. With rest, the inflammation usually subsides in a few days.

larynx in mammals, a cavity at the upper end of the trachea (windpipe) containing the vocal cords. It is stiffened with cartilage and lined with mucous membrane. Amphibians and reptiles have much simpler larynxes, with no vocal cords. Birds have a similar

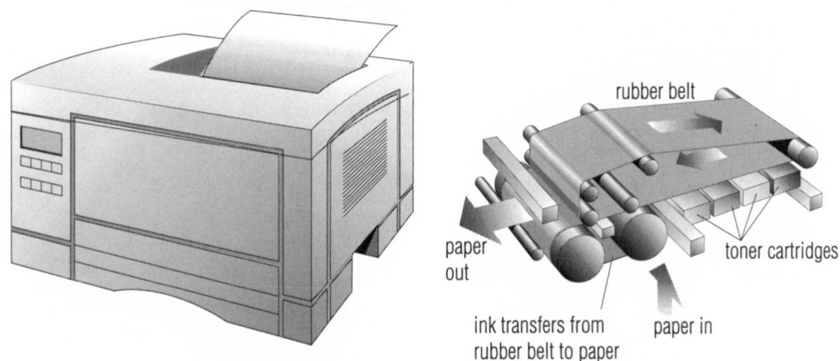

laser printer A laser printer works by transferring tiny ink particles contained in a toner cartridge to paper via a rubber belt. The image is produced by laser on a light-sensitive drum within the printer.

cavity, called the **syrinx**, found lower down the trachea, where it branches to form the bronchi. It is very complex, with well-developed vocal cords.

Las Campanas Observatory site in Chile of the 2.5-m/100-in Du Pont telescope of the Carnegie Institution of Washington, opened 1977.

laser (acronym for ***light amplification by stimulated emission of radiation***) device for producing a narrow beam of light, capable of travelling over vast distances without dispersion, and of being focused to give enormous power densities (10^8 watts per cm^2 for high-energy lasers). The laser operates on a principle similar to that of the ◊maser (a high-frequency microwave amplifier or oscillator). The uses of lasers include communications (a laser beam can carry much more information than can radio waves), cutting, drilling, welding, satellite tracking, medical and biological research, and surgery. Sound wave vibrations from the window glass of a room can be picked up by a reflected laser beam. Lasers are also used as entertainment in theatres, concerts, and light shows.

laser material Any substance the majority of whose atoms or molecules can be put into an excited energy state can be used as laser material. Many solid, liquid, and gaseous substances have been used, including synthetic ruby crystal (used for the first extraction of laser light in 1960, and giving a high-power pulsed output) and a helium–neon gas mixture, capable of continuous operation, but at a lower power.

applications Carbon dioxide gas lasers (CO_2 lasers) can produce a beam of 100 watts or more power in the infrared (wavelength 10.6 μm) and this has led to an important commercial application, the cutting of material for suits and dresses in hundreds of thicknesses at a time.

Dye lasers, in which complex organic dyes in solution are the lasing material, can be turned to produce light of any chosen wavelength over a range of a sizeable fraction of the visible spectrum.

laser mass spectroscopy forensic technique whereby a laser beam is used to scan a minute sample of evidence – such as particles of paint or hair. The beam releases a gas of charged ions, each of which can be identified by mass ◊spectroscopy.

laser printer computer printer in which the image to be printed is formed by the action of a laser on a light-sensitive drum, then transferred to paper by means of an electrostatic charge. Laser printers are page printers, printing a complete page at a time. The printed image, which can take the form of text or pictures, is made up of tiny dots, or ink particles. The quality of the image generated depends on the fineness of these dots – most laser printers can print up to 120 dots per cm/300 dots per in across the page.

A typical desktop laser printer can print about 4–20 pages per minute. The first low-cost laser printer suitable for office use appeared in 1984.

laser surgery use of intense light sources to cut, coagulate, or vaporize tissue. Less invasive than normal surgery, it destroys diseased tissue gently and allows quicker, more natural healing. It can be used by way of a flexible endoscope to enable the surgeon to view the diseased area at which the laser needs to be aimed.

Lassa fever acute disease caused by an arenavirus, first detected 1969, and spread by a species of rat found only in W Africa. It is classified as a haemorrhagic fever and characterized by high fever, headache, muscle pain, and internal bleeding. There is no known cure, the survival rate being less than 50%.

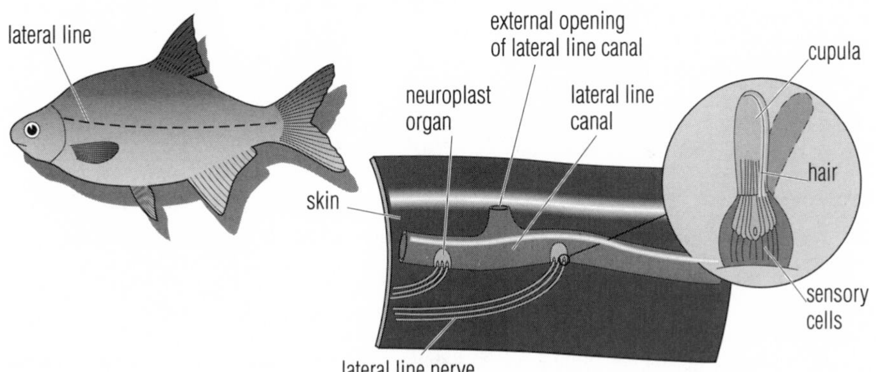

lateral line system In fishes, the lateral line system detects water movement. Arranged along a line down the length of the body are two water-filled canals, just under the skin. The canals are open to the outside, and water movements cause water to move in the canals. Nerve endings detect the movements.

La Tène prehistoric settlement at the east end of Lake Neuchâtel, Switzerland, which has given its name to a culture of the Iron Age dating from the 5th century BC to the Roman conquest.

The site was probably the crossing point of a river, no longer in existence, for most of the finds are associated with a wooden structure thought to be a bridge. The richness of metalwork found, in particular the swords and weapons, and a new style of decorative art recognized as the first Celtic art distinguish the culture, but little else changed from the preceding Hallstatt period.

latent heat in physics, the heat absorbed or released by a substance as it changes state (for example, from solid to liquid) at constant temperature and pressure.

lateral line system system of sense organs in fishes and larval amphibians (tadpoles) that detects water movement. It usually consists of a row of interconnected pores on either side of the body that divide into a system of canals across the head.

latex *Latin 'liquid'* fluid of some plants (such as the rubber tree and poppy), an emulsion of resins, proteins, and other organic substances. It is used as the basis for making rubber. The name is also applied to a suspension in water of natural or synthetic rubber (or plastic) particles used in rubber goods, paints, and adhesives.

lathe machine tool, used for **turning**. The workpiece to be machined, usually wood or metal, is held and rotated while cutting tools are moved against it. Modern lathes are driven by electric motors, which can drive the spindle carrying the workpiece at various speeds.

lathe shape in graphics software, a cross-sectional representation of a symmetrical three-dimensional object. The object's shape can be changed by using a mouse-operated tool, much as a piece of wood can be carved on a lathe.

latifundium *Latin for 'broad' and 'farm'* in ancient Rome, a large agricultural estate designed to make maximum use of cheap labour, whether free workers or slaves.

In present-day Italy, Spain, and South America, the term *latifondo* refers to a large agricultural estate worked by low-paid casual or semiservile labour in the interests of absentee landlords.

latitude and longitude imaginary lines used to locate position on the globe. Lines of latitude are drawn parallel to the Equator, with 0° at the Equator and 90° at the north and south poles. Lines of longitude are drawn at right angles to these, with 0° (the Prime Meridian) passing through Greenwich, England.

The 0-degree line of latitude is defined by Earth's equator, a characteristic definable by astronomical observation. It was determined as early as AD 150 by Egyptian astronomer ◊Ptolemy in his world atlas. The prime meridian, or 0-degree line of longitude, is a matter of convention rather than physics. Prior to the latter half of the 18th century, sailors navigated by referring to their position east or west of any arbitrary meridian. When Nevil Maskelyne (1732–1811), English astronomer and fifth Astronomer Royal, published the *Nautical Almanac* he referred all of his lunar–stellar distance tables to the Greenwich meridian. These tables were relied upon for computing longitudinal position and so the Greenwich meridian became widely accepted.

Chronometers, time keeping devices with sufficient accuracy for longitude determination, invented by English instrument-maker John Harrison (1693–1776) and perfected in 1759, would gradually replace the lunar distance method for navigation, but reliance on the Greenwich meridian persisted because the *Nautical Almanac* was used by sailors to verify their position. The Greenwich meridian was officially adopted as the prime meridian by the International Meridian Conference held in Washington, DC, in 1884.

lattice a network of straight lines.

lattice points the points of intersection of the lines in a lattice.

laudanum alcoholic solution (tincture) of the drug ◊opium. Used formerly as a narcotic and painkiller, it was available in the 19th century from pharmacists on demand in most of Europe and the USA.

laughing gas popular name for ◊nitrous oxide, an anaesthetic.

laughing jackass another name for the ◊kookaburra, an Australian kingfisher.

launch in computing, to start up a program. Many applications contain embedded programs (such as help screens or formatting options), with the result that users may launch programs without being aware they are doing so.

Laurasia northern landmass formed 200 million years ago by the splitting of the single world continent ◊Pangaea. (The southern landmass was ◊Gondwanaland.) It consisted of what was to become North America, Greenland, Europe, and Asia, and is believed to have broken up about 100 million years ago with the separation of North America from Europe.

laurel any of a group of European evergreen trees with glossy aromatic leaves, yellowish flowers, and black berries. The leaves of sweet bay or poet's laurel (*L. nobilis*) are used in cooking. Several species are cultivated worldwide. (Genus *Laurus*, family Lauraceae.)

laurustinus evergreen shrub belonging to the honeysuckle family, of Mediterranean origin. It has clusters of white flowers in winter. (*Viburnum tinus*, family Caprifoliaceae.)

lava molten rock (usually 800–1,100°C/1,500–2,000°F) that erupts from a ◊volcano and cools to form extrusive ◊igneous rock. It differs

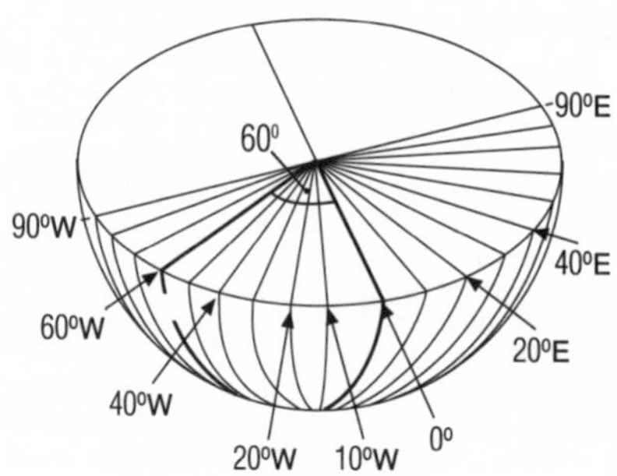

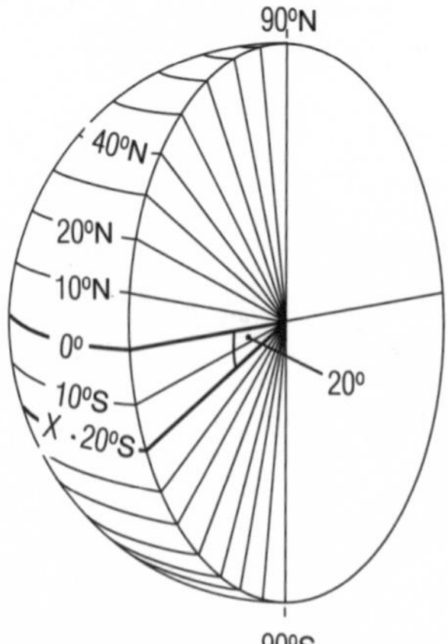

latitude and longitude *Locating a point on a globe using latitude and longitude. Longitude is the angle between the terrestrial meridian through a place and the standard meridian 0° passing through Greenwich, England. Latitude is the angular distance of a place from the equator.*

from magma in that it is molten rock on the surface; **magma** is molten rock below the surface. Lava that is viscous and sticky does not flow far; it forms a steep-sided conical composite volcano. Less viscous lava can flow for long distances and forms a broad flat shield volcano.

The viscosity of lava, and thus the form of volcano they form, depends on ◊silica content, temperature, and degree of solidification upon extrusion. It is often said that viscosity increases with silica content because silica polymerizes, but this rule can be misleading. Lavas having the composition of ◊basalt, which is low in silica content, tend to flow easily and form broad flat volcanoes as in the Hawaiian Islands. But some very silica-rich lavas of ◊rhyolite composition can also flow readily. Lavas that are especially viscous are often of andesite composition and intermediate in silica content. ◊Andesite lavas can therefore give rise to explosive volcanoes like the island of Montserrat, West Indies.

lavender sweet-smelling purple-flowering herb belonging to the mint family, native to W Mediterranean countries. The bushy low-growing species *L. angustifolia* has long, narrow, upright leaves of a silver-green colour. The small flowers, borne on spikes, vary in colour from lilac to deep purple and are covered with small fragrant oil glands. Lavender oil is widely used in pharmacy and perfumes. (Genus *Lavandula*, family Labiatae.)

laver any of several edible purplish-red seaweeds, including purple laver (*P. umbilicalis*). Growing on the shore and in the sea, attached to rocks and stones, laver forms thin, roundish sheets of tissue up to 20 cm/8 in across. It becomes almost black when dry. (Genus *Porphyra*, family Rhodophyceae.)

Lavoisier, Antoine Laurent (1743–1794)

French chemist. He proved that combustion needs only a part of the air, which he called oxygen, thereby destroying the theory of phlogiston (an imaginary 'fire element' released during combustion). With astronomer and mathematician Pierre de Laplace, he showed in 1783 that water is a compound of oxygen and hydrogen. In this way he established the basic rules of chemical combination.

Lavoisier established that organic compounds contain carbon, hydrogen, and oxygen. From quantitative measurements of the changes during breathing, he showed that carbon dioxide and water are normal products of respiration.

Mary Evans Picture Library

law of nature scientific generalization that both explains and predicts physical phenomena; laws of nature are generally assumed to be descriptive of, and applicable to, the world. The three laws of ◊thermodynamics are examples.

However, the first of Isaac ◊Newton's laws of motion discusses the behaviour of a moving body not acted on by a net force, and this neither applies to the world nor describes it, because there are no such bodies. Hence, some philosophers of science have argued that the laws of nature are rules governing scientists' expectations and so are prescriptive rather than descriptive. Others have argued that laws are idealized descriptions to which the world approximates, as triangles on a blackboard approximate to Euclidean triangles.

> *We have no right to assume that any physical laws exist, or if they have existed up to now, that they will continue to exist in a similar manner in the future.*
>
> MAX PLANCK German physicist. *The Universe in the Light of Modern Physics*

Lawrence, Ernest O(rlando) (1901–1958)

US physicist. His invention of the cyclotron particle accelerator pioneered the production of artificial radioisotopes and the synthesis of new transuranic elements. Nobel prize 1939.

During World War II, Lawrence was involved with the separation of uranium-235 and plutonium for the development of the atomic bomb, and he organized the Los Alamos Scientific Laboratories at which much of the work on this project was carried out. After the war, he continued as a believer in nuclear weapons and advocated the acceleration of their development.

Mary Evans Picture Library

lawrencium synthesized, radioactive, metallic element, the last of the actinide series, symbol Lr, atomic number 103, relative atomic mass 262. Its only known isotope, Lr-257, has a half-life of 4.3 seconds and was originally synthesized at the University of California at Berkeley in 1961 by bombarding californium with boron nuclei. The original symbol, Lw, was officially changed in 1963.

The element was named after Ernest Lawrence (1901–1958), the US inventor of the cyclotron.

laxative substance used to relieve constipation (infrequent bowel movement). Current medical opinion discourages regular or prolonged use. Regular exercise and a diet high in vegetable fibre are believed to be the best means of preventing and treating constipation.

> *The confidence and security of a people can be measured by their attitude towards laxatives.*
>
> FLORENCE KING US writer. *Reflections in a Jaundiced Eye*, 'Nice Guyism'

lb Latin 'libra' symbol for ◊pound **(weight)**.

LCD abbreviation for ◊liquid-crystal display.

LDAP (abbreviation for ***Lightweight Directory Access Protocol***) in computing, Internet standard that enables a client PC or workstation to look up an e-mail address on an LDAP server over a ◊TCP/IP network. LDAP is a simplified version of the 'heavyweight' X.500 directory access protocol in the ◊OSI (Open Systems Interconnection) standards suite.

L-dopa chemical, normally produced by the body, which is converted by an enzyme to dopamine in the brain. It is essential for integrated movement of individual muscle groups.

L-dopa is a left-handed isomer of an amino acid $C_9H_{11}NO_2$. As a treatment, it relieves the rigidity of ◊Parkinson's disease in 60% of sufferers, but may have significant side effects, such as extreme mood changes, hallucinations, and uncontrolled writhing movements. It is often given in combination with other drugs to improve its effectiveness at lower doses.

LDR abbreviation for ◊light-dependent resistor.

leaching process by which substances are washed through or out of the soil. Fertilizers leached out of the soil drain into rivers, lakes, and ponds and cause water pollution. In tropical areas, leaching of the soil after the destruction of forests removes scarce nutrients and can lead to a dramatic loss of soil fertility. The leaching of soluble minerals in soils can lead to the formation of distinct soil horizons as different minerals are deposited at successively lower levels.

lead heavy, soft, malleable, grey, metallic element, symbol Pb (from Latin *plumbum*), atomic number 82, relative atomic mass 207.19. Usually found as an ore (most often in galena), it occasionally occurs as a free metal (◊native metal), and is the final stable product of the decay of uranium. Lead is the softest and weakest of the commonly used metals, with a low melting point; it is a poor conductor of electricity and resists acid corrosion. As a cumulative poison, lead enters the body from lead water pipes, lead-based paints, and leaded petrol. (In humans, exposure to lead shortly after birth is associated with impaired mental health between the ages of two and four.) The metal is an effective shield against radiation and is used in batteries, glass, ceramics, and alloys such as pewter and solder.

lead–acid cell type of ◊accumulator (storage battery).

leaded petrol petrol that contains ◊antiknock, a mixture of the chemicals tetraethyl lead and dibromoethane. The lead from the exhaust fumes enters the atmosphere, mostly as simple lead compounds, which are poisonous to the developing nervous systems of children.

lead(II) nitrate $Pb(NO_3)_2$ one of only two common water-soluble compounds of lead. When heated, it decrepitates (see

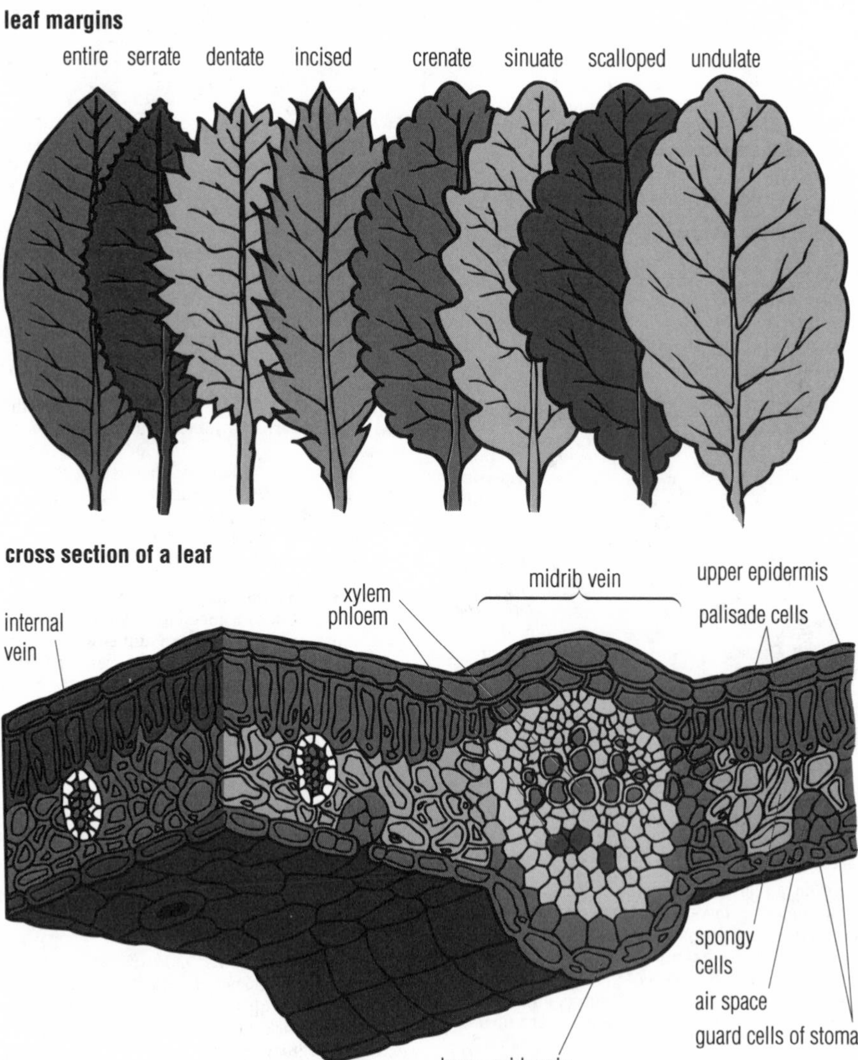

leaf *Leaf shapes and arrangements on the stem are many and varied; in cross section, a leaf is a complex arrangement of cells surrounded by the epidermis. This is pierced by the stomata through which gases enter and leave.*

◊decrepitation) and decomposes readily into oxygen, brown nitrogen(IV) oxide gas and the red-yellow solid lead(II) oxide.

$$2Pb(NO_3)_2 \rightarrow 2PbO + 4NO_2 + O_2$$

lead ore any of several minerals from which lead is extracted. The primary ore is galena or lead sulphite PbS. This is unstable, and on prolonged exposure to the atmosphere it oxidizes into the minerals cerussite $PbCO_3$ and anglesite $PbSO_4$. Lead ores are usually associated with other metals, particularly silver – which can be mined at the same time – and zinc, which can cause problems during smelting.

Most commercial deposits of lead ore are in the form of veins, where hot fluids have leached the ore from cooling ◊igneous masses and deposited it in cracks in the surrounding country rock, and in thermal ◊metamorphic zones, where the heat of igneous intrusions has altered the minerals of surrounding rocks. Lead is mined in over 40 countries, but half of the world's output comes from the USA, Canada, Russia, Kazakhstan, Uzbekistan, Canada, and Australia.

lead(II) oxide or *lead monoxide* PbO yellow or red solid, an amphoteric oxide (one that reacts with both acids and bases). The other oxides of lead are the brown solid lead(IV) oxide (PbO_2) and red lead (Pb_3O_4).

leaf lateral outgrowth on the stem of a plant, and in most species the primary organ of ◊photosynthesis. The chief leaf types are cotyledons (seed leaves), scale leaves (on underground stems), foliage leaves, and bracts (in the axil of which a flower is produced).

Typically leaves are composed of three parts: the sheath or leaf base, the petiole or stalk, and the lamina or blade. The lamina has a network of veins through which water and nutrients are conducted. Structurally the leaf is made up of ◊mesophyll cells surrounded by the epidermis and usually, in addition, a waxy layer, termed the cuticle, which prevents excessive evaporation of water from the leaf tissues by transpiration. The epidermis is interrupted by small pores, or stomata, through which gas exchange between the plant and the atmosphere occurs.

leaf-hopper any of numerous species of plant-sucking insects. They feed on the sap of leaves. Each species feeds on a limited range of plants. (Family Cicadellidae, order Homoptera.)

leaf insect any of various insects about 10 cm/4 in long, with a green, flattened body, remarkable for closely resembling the foliage on which they live. They are most common in SE Asia. (Genus *Phyllium,* order Phasmida.)

***leaf insect** This adult female* Phyllium *leaf insect, a newly discovered species when it was photographed in New Guinea, is mimicking a dead brown leaf. Other species are green and mimic living leaves. Premaphotos Wildlife*

Leakey, Richard Erskine Frere (1944–)

Kenyan palaeoanthropologist. In 1972 he discovered at Lake Turkana, Kenya, an apelike skull estimated to be about 2.9 million years old; it had some human characteristics and a brain capacity of 800 cu cm/49 cu in. In 1984 his team found an almost complete skeleton of Homo erectus some 1.6 million years old. He is the son of Louis and Mary Leakey.

He was appointed director of the Kenyan Wildlife Service 1988, waging a successful war against poachers and the ivory trade, but was forced to resign 1994 in the face of political interference. In 1995 he co-founded the Kenyan political party Safina (Swahili for Noah's Ark), which aims to clean up Kenya. The party was accused of racism and colonialism by President Daniel arap Moi.

learning theory in psychology, any theory or body of theories about how behaviour in animals and human beings is acquired or modified by experience. Two main theories are classical and operant ◊conditioning.

leased line in computing, permanent dedicated digital telephone link used for round-the-clock connection within a network or between offices. For example, a bank may use leased lines to carry financial data between branches and head office. The infrastructure of the Internet is a network of leased lines that deliver guaranteed ◊bandwidth at a fixed cost, regardless of how much traffic they carry. The enormous economies produced by the heavy use of such lines makes the Net a very cheap method of communication.

least action, principle of in physics, an alternative expression of Newton's laws of motion that states that a particle moving between two points under the influence of a force will follow the path along which its total action is least. Action is a quantity related to the average difference between the kinetic energy and the potential energy of the particle along its path. The principle is only true where no energy is lost from the system; for example an object moving in free fall in a gravitational field. It is closely related to ◊Fermat's principle of least time which governs the path taken by a ray of light.

leather material prepared from the hides and skins of animals, by tanning with vegetable tannins and chromium salts. Leather is a durable and water-resistant material, and is used for bags, shoes, clothing, and upholstery. There are three main stages in the process of converting animal skin into leather: cleaning, tanning, and dressing. Tanning is often a highly polluting process.

The skin, usually cattle hide, is dehydrated after removal to arrest decay. Soaking is necessary before tanning in order to replace the lost water with something that will bind the fibres together. The earliest practice, at least 7,000 years old, was to pound grease into the skin. In about 400 BC the Egyptians began to use vegetable extracts containing tannic acid, a method adopted in medieval Europe. Chemical tanning using mineral salts was introduced in the late 19th century.

leatherjacket larva of the ◊crane fly.

Le Chatelier's principle or *Le Chatelier-Braun principle* in science, the principle that if a change in conditions is imposed on a system in equilibrium, the system will react to counteract that change and restore the equilibrium.

First stated in 1884 by French chemist Henri le Chatelier (1850–1936), it has been found to apply widely outside the field of chemistry.

lecithin lipid (fat), containing nitrogen and phosphorus, that forms a vital part of the cell membranes of plant and animal cells. The name is from the Greek *lekithos* 'egg yolk', eggs being a major source of lecithin.

LED abbreviation for ◊*light-emitting diode*.

leech any of a group of ◊annelid worms. Leeches live in fresh water, and in tropical countries infest damp forests. As bloodsucking animals they are injurious to people and animals, to whom they attach themselves by means of a strong mouth adapted to sucking. (Class Hirudinea.)

Formerly, the **medicinal leech** (*Hirudo medicinalis*) was used extensively for 'bleeding' for a variety of ills. It is still cultivated as the source of the anticoagulant hirudin.

LEECH

In 1824, five million leeches were exported from France to England for therapeutic use. For centuries, it was believed that virtually all diseases could be at least partly relieved by leeching.

leek onionlike plant belonging to the lily family. The cultivated leek is a variety of the wild species *A. ampeloprasum* of the Mediterranean area and Atlantic islands. The lower leaf parts and white bulb are eaten as a vegetable. (Genus *Allium*, family Liliaceae.)

left-handedness using the left hand more skilfully and in preference to the right hand for most actions. It occurs in about 9% of the population, predominantly males. It is caused by dominance of the right side of the brain.

FAMOUS LEFT-HANDERS

http://www.indiana.edu/~primate/left.html

Thorough listing of famous left-handers. Among this list are the last four US Presidents, Joan of Arc, Charlemagne and Queen Victoria. On a more serious note, there are accounts of ordinary people being stigmatised for left-handedness and a plea for greater understanding. There are links to many other left-handedness sites.

left-hand rule in physics, a memory aid used to recall the relative directions of motion, magnetic field, and current in an electric motor. It was devised by English physicist John Fleming. (See ◊Fleming's rules).

legacy application in computing, inherited application, usually an old one that runs on a large minicomputer or mainframe, and that may be too important to scrap or too expensive to change. 'Legacy' implies that such applications are valuable and should be looked after. Those who want to be rid of legacy applications use different metaphors, such as 'slum clearance'.

legacy system in computing, old system with which new technology must be compatible.

legionnaires' disease pneumonia-like disease, so called because it was first identified when it broke out at a convention of the American Legion in Philadelphia in 1976. Legionnaires' disease is caused by the bacterium *Legionella pneumophila*, which breeds in warm water (for example, in the cooling towers of air-conditioning systems). It is spread in minute water droplets, which may be inhaled. The disease can be treated successfully with antibiotics, though mortality can be high in elderly patients.

legume plant of the family Leguminosae, which has a pod containing dry seeds. The family includes peas, beans, lentils, clover, and alfalfa (lucerne). Legumes are important in agriculture because of their specialized roots, which have nodules containing bacteria capable of fixing nitrogen from the air and increasing the fertility of the soil. The edible seeds of legumes are called **pulses**.

leishmaniasis any of several parasitic diseases caused by microscopic protozoans of the genus *Leishmania*, identified by William Leishman (1865–1926), and transmitted by sandflies.

It occurs in two main forms: **visceral** (also called kala-azar), in which various internal organs are affected, and **cutaneous**, where the disease is apparent mainly in the skin. Leishmaniasis occurs in the Mediterranean region, Africa, Asia, and Central and South America. There are 12 million cases of leishmaniasis annually.

In 1994 Indian researchers discovereda cheap and effective way of keeping sandfly populations under control, by plastering the walls of houses and outbuildings with mud and lime. The plaster deprives flies of the moist crevices in which they breed, and the lime kills any existing larvae. In trials, sandfly numbers dropped by 90%.

lek in biology, a closely spaced set of very small ◊territories each occupied by a single male during the mating season. Leks are found in the mating systems of several ground-dwelling birds (such as grouse) and a few antelopes.

The lek is a traditional site where both males and females congregate during the breeding season. The males display to passing females in the hope of attracting them to mate. Once mated, the females go elsewhere to lay their eggs or to complete gestation.

lemming any of a group of small rodents distributed worldwide in northern latitudes. They are about 12 cm/5 in long, with thick brownish fur, a small head, and a short tail. Periodically, when their population exceeds the available food supply, lemmings undertake mass migrations. (Genus *Lemmus* and other related genera, family Cricetidae.)

lemon sharp-tasting yellow citrus fruit of the small, evergreen, semitropical lemon tree. It may have originated in NW India, and was introduced into Europe by the Spanish Moors in the 12th or 13th century. It is now grown in Italy, Spain, California, Florida, South Africa, and Australia, and is widely used for flavouring and as a garnish. (*Citrus limon*, family Rutaceae.)

lemon balm perennial herb belonging to the mint family, with lemon-scented leaves. It is widely used in teas, liqueurs, and medicines. (*Melissa officinalis*, family Labiatae.)

lemur any of various prosimian ◊primates found in Madagascar and the Comoros Islands. There are about 16 species, ranging from mouse-sized to dog-sized animals; the pygmy mouse lemur (*Microcebus myoxinus*), weighing 30 g/1 oz, is the smallest primate. The diademed sifaka, weighing 7 kg/15 lb, is the largest species of lemur. Lemurs are arboreal, and some species are nocturnal. They have long, bushy tails, and feed on fruit, insects, and small animals. Many are threatened with extinction owing to loss of their forest habitat and, in some cases, from hunting. (Family Lemuridae.)

LEMUR

http://www.seaworld.org/animal_bytes/lemurab.html

Illustrated guide to the lemur including information about genus, size, life span, habitat, gestation, diet, and a series of fun facts.

lens in optics, a piece of a transparent material, such as glass, with two polished surfaces – one concave or convex, and the other plane, concave, or convex – that modifies rays of light. A convex lens brings rays of light together; a concave lens makes the rays diverge. Lenses are essential to spectacles, microscopes, telescopes, cameras, and almost all optical instruments.

The image formed by a single lens suffers from several defects or ◊aberrations, notably **spherical aberration** in which an image becomes blurred, and **chromatic aberration** in which an image in white light tends to have coloured edges. Aberrations are corrected by the use of compound lenses, which are built up from two or more lenses of different refractive index.

lens, gravitational see ◊gravitational lensing.

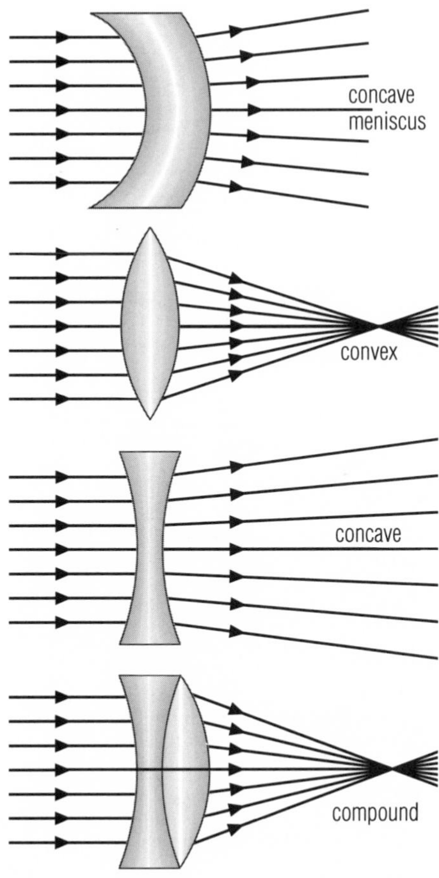

lens The passage of light through lenses. The concave lens diverges a beam of light from a distant source. The convex and compound lenses focus light from a distant source to a point. The distance between the focus and the lens is called the focal length. The shorter the focus, the more powerful the lens.

lenticel small pore on the stems of woody plants or the trunks of trees. Lenticels are a means of gas exchange between the stem interior and the atmosphere. They consist of loosely packed cells with many air spaces in between, and are easily seen on smooth-barked trees such as cherries, where they form horizontal lines on the trunk.

lenticular galaxy in astronomy, a lens-shaped ◊galaxy with a large central bulge and flat disc but no discernible spiral arms.

lentil annual Old World plant belonging to the pea family. The plant, which resembles vetch, grows 15–45 cm/6–18 in high and has white, blue, or purplish flowers. The seeds, contained in pods about 1.6 cm/0.6 in long, are widely used as food. (*Lens culinaris*, family Leguminosae.)

The most common varieties are the greyish French lentil and the red Egyptian lentil.

Lenz's law in physics, a law stating that the direction of an electromagnetically induced current (generated by moving a magnet near a wire or a wire in a magnetic field) will be such as to oppose the motion producing it. It is named after the German physicist Heinrich Friedrich Lenz (1804–1865), who announced it in 1833.

Leo zodiacal constellation in the northern hemisphere, represented as a lion. The Sun passes through Leo from mid-Aug to mid-Sept. Its brightest star is first-magnitude ◊Regulus at the base of a pattern of stars called the Sickle. In astrology, the dates for Leo are between about 23 July and 22 Aug (see ◊precession).

leopard or ***panther*** large wild cat found in Africa and Asia. The background colour of the coat is golden, and the black spots form rosettes that differ according to the variety; **black panthers** are simply a colour variation and retain the patterning as a 'watered-silk' effect. The leopard is 1.5–2.5 m/5–8 ft long, including the tail, which may measure 1 m/3 ft. (Species *Panthera pardus*, family Felidae.)

The **snow leopard** or **ounce** (*Panthera uncia*), which has irregular rosettes of much larger black spots on a light cream or grey background, is a native of mountains in central Asia. The **clouded leopard** (*Neofelis nebulosa*) is rather smaller, about 1.75 m/5.8 ft overall, with large blotchy markings rather than rosettes, and is found in SE Asia. There are seven subspecies, of which six are in danger of extinction, including the **Amur leopard** and the **South Arabian leopard**. One subspecies, the **Zanzibar leopard**, may already be extinct. The last **Judean desert leopard** died May 1995, although a small population survives in the Negev Desert.

Lepenski Vir prehistoric settlement site in the valley of the river Danube, where it runs through the Iron Gates gorge, in former Yugoslavia on the Romanian border. One of Europe's oldest farming settlements, dating from the 6th millennium BC, it is possibly the earliest and best preserved late Mesolithic to Neolithic (Middle to New Stone Age) site in the Balkans. The site is now submerged by an artificial lake.

A series of unusual trapezoidal dwellings were found, dating from the mid-6th millennium BC, associated with large limestone sculptures of fishlike human beings, belonging to a preceding camp of hunter-fisher people. All the dwellings had their wide end pointing towards the river, with limestone plaster floors and probably a wooden structure over. Hearths comprised limestone blocks inside elongated pits; in some cases human burials were made close by. The roofs of the dwellings may have been covered in hides or reed thatch. A larger central house may indicate social stratification.

Diet depended on fish and the development of fishing and boat technology. The life style of the inhabitants was sedentary but had arisen out of adaptation from a previous hunting tradition. Resources included catfish, carp, deer, and wild pigs.

lepidozamia palmlike plant of the ◊cycad order with two species both endemic to Australia. They are among the world's oldest plants and some specimens of *Lepidozamia peroffskyana* in Queensland are thought by some botanists to be about 10,000 years old.

Nature [is] that lovely lady to whom we owe polio, leprosy, smallpox, syphilis, tuberculosis, cancer.

STANLEY COHEN US biochemist.
Attributed remark

leprosy or ***Hansen's disease*** chronic, progressive disease caused by a bacterium *Mycobacterium leprae* closely related to that of tuberculosis. The infection attacks the skin and nerves. Once common in many countries, leprosy is now confined almost entirely to the tropics. It is controlled with drugs.

According to a World Health Organization estimate there were 1.3 million people with leprosy 1996; the year-2000 target for total elimination was declared unrealistic at an international leprosy conference in Delhi in 1996. There are two principal manifestations. **Lepromatous leprosy** is a contagious, progressive form distinguished by the appearance of raised blotches and lumps on the skin and thickening of the skin and nerves, with numbness, weakness, paralysis, and ultimately deformity of the affected parts. In **tuberculoid leprosy**, sensation is lost in some areas of the skin; sometimes there is loss of pigmentation and hair. The visible effects of long-standing leprosy (joint damage, paralysis, loss of fingers or toes) are due to nerve damage and injuries of which the sufferer may be unaware. Damage to the nerves remains, and the technique of using the patient's muscle material to encourage nerve regrowth is being explored.

lepton any of a class of light ◊elementary particles that are not affected by the strong nuclear force; they do not interact strongly with other particles or nuclei. The leptons are comprised of the ◊electron, ◊muon, and ◊tau, and their ◊neutrinos (the electron neutrino, muon neutrino, and tau neutrino), plus their six ◊antiparticles.

leptoquark in physics, a hypothetical particle made up of a ◊quark combined with a ◊lepton, or a new particle created by their interaction.

leptospermum shrub or small tree of tree of the genus *Leptospermum,* family Myrtaceae, mostly native to Australia and New Zealand.

leschenaultia shrub of the predominantly Australian genus *Leschenaultia,* family Goodenoviae, with species generally found in Western Australia and having tubular flowers of blue, red, orange, yellow, and pink. Best known is blue leschenaultia *L. biloba,* a spreading plant growing to 60 cm/2 ft.

lesion any change in a body tissue that is a manifestation of disease or injury.

letterpress method of printing from raised type, pioneered by Johann ◊Gutenberg in Europe in the 1450s.

lettuce annual plant whose large edible leaves are commonly used in salads. There are many varieties, including the cabbage lettuce, with round or loose heads, the Cos lettuce, with long, upright heads, and the Iceberg lettuce, with tight heads of crisp leaves. They are all believed to have been derived from the wild species *L. serriola.* (Genus *Lactuca,* especially *L. sativa,* family Compositae.)

leucine one of the nine essential ◊amino acids.

leucocyte another name for a ◊white blood cell.

leucotomy or ***lobotomy*** a brain operation to sever the connections between the frontal lobe and underlying structures. It was widely used in the 1940s and 1950s to treat severe psychotic or depressive illness. Though it achieved some success, it left patients dull and apathetic; there was also a considerable risk of epilepsy. It was largely replaced by the use of psychotropic drugs from the late 1950s.

Today, a limited amount of psychosurgery is performed in specialist centres under strict controls. It includes the creation of tiny, precise frontal lobe lesions to relieve severe conditions which have not responded to other treatments.

leukaemia any one of a group of cancers of the blood cells, with widespread involvement of the bone marrow and other blood-forming tissue. The central feature of leukaemia is runaway production of white blood cells that are immature or in some way abnormal. These rogue cells, which lack the defensive capacity of healthy white cells, overwhelm the normal ones, leaving the victim vulnerable to infection. Treatment is with radiotherapy and ◊cytotoxic drugs to suppress replication of abnormal cells, or by bone-marrow transplantation.

Abnormal functioning of the bone marrow also suppresses production of red blood cells and blood ◊platelets, resulting in ◊anaemia and a failure of the blood to clot.

Leukaemias are classified into acute or chronic, depending on their known rates of progression. They are also grouped according to the type of white cell involved.

leukotriene in biology, a group of naturally occurring substances that stimulate the activity, for example contraction, of smooth muscles.

levee naturally formed raised bank along the side of a river channel. When a river overflows its banks, the rate of flow is less than that in the channel, and silt is deposited on the banks. With each successive flood the levee increases in size so that eventually the river may be above the surface of the surrounding flood plain. Notable levees are found on the lower reaches of the Mississippi in the USA and the Po in Italy.

level or ***spirit level*** instrument for finding horizontal level, or adjusting a surface to an even level, used in surveying, building construction, and archaeology. It has a glass tube of coloured liquid, in which a bubble is trapped, mounted in an elongated frame. When the tube is horizontal, the bubble moves to the centre.

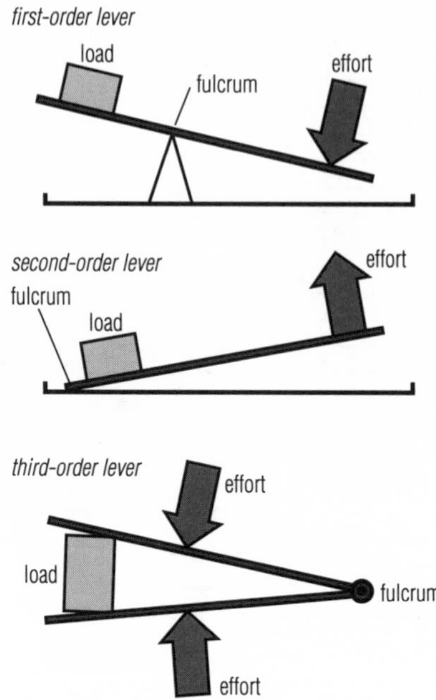

lever *Types of lever. Practical applications of the first-order lever include the crowbar, seesaw, and scissors. The wheelbarrow is a second-order lever; tweezers or tongs are third-order levers.*

lever simple machine consisting of a rigid rod pivoted at a fixed point called the fulcrum, used for shifting or raising a heavy load or applying force. Levers are classified into orders according to where the effort is applied, and the load-moving force developed, in relation to the position of the fulcrum.

A **first-order** lever has the load and the effort on opposite sides of the fulcrum – for example, a see-saw or pair of scissors. A **second-order** lever has the load and the effort on the same side of the fulcrum, with the load nearer the fulcrum – for example, nutcrackers or a wheelbarrow. A **third-order** lever has the effort nearer the fulcrum than the load, with both on the same side of it – for example, a pair of tweezers or tongs. The mechanical advantage of a lever is the ratio of load to effort, equal to the perpendicular distance of the effort's line of action from the fulcrum divided by the distance to the load's line of action. Thus tweezers, for instance, have a mechanical advantage of less than one.

Give me but one firm place on which to stand, and I will move the earth.

ARCHIMEDES Greek mathematician.
On the lever, quoted in *Pappus Alexander*

LF in physics, abbreviation for ◊***low frequency***. LF radio waves have frequencies in the range 30–300 kHz.

LH abbreviation for ◊***luteinizing hormone***.

Lhasa apso breed of toy dog from Tibet. It has a long coat, which may be solid-coloured (gold, dark grey, tawny) or bicoloured (black with white). It is similar in shape to a pekingese, having short legs, proportionately long body, and curled tail, but differs in having hair growing over its face. It grows up to 25 cm/10 in.

liana woody, perennial climbing plant with very long stems, which grows around trees right up to the top, where there is more sunlight. Lianas are common in tropical rainforests, where individual stems may grow up to 78 m/255 ft long. They have an unusual stem structure that makes them flexible, despite being woody.

Liberty engine US-manufactured aircraft engine based on a Rolls-Royce design, used in a number of aircraft and tanks in World War I. It was designed specifically for mass-production, in order to meet wartime needs for a reliable engine which could be turned out as quickly as the rest of an aircraft. A V-12, water-cooled engine, it developed 405 bhp (brake horsepower) at 1,650 rpm (revolutions per minute).

Liberty tank US name for the British Mark VIII tank, adopted by the Anglo-American Tank Committee for production in both the UK and USA in World War I. None were produced in time for the war, but about 100 were assembled in the USA after the Armistice.

libido in Freudian psychology, the energy of the sex instinct, which is to be found even in a newborn child. The libido develops through a number of phases, described by Sigmund Freud in his theory of infantile sexuality. The source of the libido is the ◊id.

The phases of the libido are identified by Freud as the **oral stage**, when a child tests everything by mouth, the **anal stage**, when the child gets satisfaction from control of its body, and the **genital stage**, when the libido becomes concentrated in the sex organs.

Loss of adult libido is seen in some diseases.

Libra faint zodiacal constellation on the celestial equator (see ◊celestial sphere) adjoining Scorpius, and represented as the scales of justice. The Sun passes through Libra during Nov. The constellation was once considered to be a part of Scorpius, seen as the scorpion's claws. In astrology, the dates for Libra are between about 23 September and 23 October (see ◊precession).

library program one of a collection, or library, of regularly used software routines, held in a computer backing store. For example, a programmer might store a routine for sorting a file into ◊key field order, and so could incorporate it easily into any new program being developed instead of having to rewrite it.

libration in astronomy, a slight, apparent wobble in the rotation of the Moon due to its variable speed of rotation and the tilt of its axis.

Generally, the Moon rotates on its axis in the same time as it takes to complete one orbit, causing it to keep one face turned permanently towards the Earth (see captured rotation). Its speed in orbit varies, however, because its orbit is not circular but elliptical, so at times the Moon's axial rotation appears to get either slightly ahead of or slightly behind its orbital motion, so that part of the 'dark side' of the Moon is visible around the east and west edges. This is known as **libration in longitude**.

Libration in latitude occurs because the Moon's axis is slightly tilted with respect to its orbital plane, so we can see over the north and south poles. In combination, these effects mean that a total of 59%of the Moon's surface is visible, rather than just 50% if libration did not occur.

lichen any organism of a unique group that consists of associations of a specific ◊fungus and a specific ◊alga living together in a mutually beneficial relationship. Found as coloured patches or spongelike masses on trees, rocks, and other surfaces, lichens flourish in harsh conditions. (Group Lichenes.)

Some lichens are edible, for example, reindeer moss and Iceland moss; others are a source of colour dyes, such as litmus, or are used in medicine. They are sensitive to pollution in the air (see ◊indicator species).

TO REMEMBER THAT **LICHEN** ARE MADE UP OF ALGAE AND **FUNGI**:

SHE WAS ALL GAL (**ALGAL**) AND HE WAS A FUN GUY (**FUNGI**). THEY TOOK A LIKIN' (**LICHEN**) TO EACH OTHER

FUN WITH LICHENS

http://mgd.orst.edu/hyperSQL/lichenland/index.html

Thorough guide to these unique fungus-alga combinations. Written by a lichen enthusiast at the University of Oregon, this is a good introduction to the subject. The textual content is well supported with photographs. There are sections suitable for the general reader, schoolchildren and professional botanists, ecologists, and foresters.

Lick Observatory observatory of the University of California and Mount Hamilton, California. Its main instruments are the 3.04-m/120-in Shane reflector, opened in 1959, and a 91-cm/36-in refractor, opened in 1988, the second-largest refractor in the world.

lie detector instrument that records graphically certain body activities, such as thoracic and abdominal respiration, blood pressure, pulse rate, and galvanic skin response (changes in electrical resistance of the skin). Marked changes in these activities when a person answers a question may indicate that the person is lying.

A living thing is distinguished from a dead thing by the multiplicity of the changes at any moment taking place in it.

HERBERT SPENCER English philosopher.
Principles of Biology pt 1, ch 4

life the ability to grow, reproduce, and respond to such stimuli as light, heat, and sound. Life on Earth may have began about 4 billion years ago when a chemical reaction produced the first organic substance. Over time, life has evolved from primitive single-celled organisms to complex multicellular ones. There are now some 10 million different species of plants and animals living on the Earth. The earliest fossil evidence of life is threadlike chains of cells discovered in 1980 in deposits in NW Australia; these have been dated as being 3.5 billion years old.

◊Biology is the study of living organisms – their evolution, structure, functioning, classification, and distribution – while ◊biochemistry is the study of the chemistry of living organisms. Biochemistry is especially concerned with the function of the chemical components of organisms such as proteins, carbohydrates, lipids, and nucleic acids.

Life probably originated in the primitive oceans. The original atmosphere, 4 billion years ago, consisted of carbon dioxide, nitrogen, and water. Laboratory experiments have shown that more complex organic molecules, such as ◊amino acids and ◊nucleotides, can be produced from these ingredients by passing electric sparks through a mixture. The climate of the early atmosphere was probably very violent, with lightning a common feature, and these conditions could have resulted in the oceans becoming rich in organic molecules, producing the so-called 'primeval soup'. These molecules may then have organized themselves into clusters capable of reproducing and eventually developing into simple cells. Soon after life developed, ◊photosynthesis would have become the primary source of energy for life. By this process, life would have substantially affected the chemistry of the atmosphere and, in turn, that of its own environment. Once the atmosphere had changed to its present composition, life could only be created by the replication of living organisms (a process called ◊biogenesis).

life cycle in biology, the sequence of developmental stages through which members of a given species pass. Most vertebrates have a simple life cycle consisting of ◊fertilization of sex cells or ◊gametes, a period of development as an ◊embryo, a period of juvenile growth after hatching or birth, an adulthood including ◊sexual reproduction, and finally death. Invertebrate life cycles are generally more complex and may involve major reconstitution of the individual's appearance (◊metamorphosis) and completely different styles of life. Plants have a special type of life cycle with two distinct phases, known as ◊alternation of generations. Many insects such as cicadas, dragonflies, and mayflies have a long larvae or pupae phase and a short adult phase. Dragonflies live an aquatic life as larvae and an aerial life during the adult phase. In many invertebrates and protozoa there is a sequence of stages in the life cycle, and in parasites different stages often occur in different host organisms.

life expectancy average lifespan that can be presumed of a person at birth. It depends on nutrition, disease control, environmental contaminants, war, stress, and living standards in general.

There is a marked difference between industrialized countries, which generally have an ageing population, and the poorest countries, where life expectancy is much shorter. In Bangladesh, life expectancy is currently 48; in Nigeria 49. In famine-prone Ethiopia it is only 41.

life sciences scientific study of the living world as a whole, a new synthesis of several traditional scientific disciplines including ◊biology, ◊zoology, and ◊botany, and newer, more specialized areas

Life expectancy

nation	*men*	*women*	*average*
Liechtenstein	78	83	81
Japan	76	82	79
Switzerland	74	82	78
Australia	75	80	78
Netherlands	74	81	78
Sweden	74	81	78
Iceland	74	80	77
Spain	74	80	77
Italy	73	80	77
Jamaica	75	78	77
Norway	73	80	77
Canada	72	79	76
USA	72	79	76
Belgium	72	78	75
Denmark	72	78	75
France	71	79	75
New Zealand	72	78	75
UK	72	78	75
Israel	73	76	75
Luxembourg	71	78	75
Malta	72	77	75
Portugal	71	78	75
Brunei	74	74	74
Kuwait	72	76	74
Singapore	71	77	74
Cyprus	72	76	74
Finland	70	78	74
Greece	72	76	74
Costa Rica	71	76	74
Cuba	72	75	74
San Marino	70	77	74
Austria	70	77	74
Panama	71	75	73
Ireland	70	76	73
Taiwan	70	75	73
Barbados	70	75	73
Yugoslavia (former)	69	75	72
Tonga	69	74	72
Uruguay	68	75	72
Czech Republic	68	75	72
Slovakia	68	75	72
Bulgaria	69	74	72
St Vincent and the Grenadines	69	74	72
Albania	69	73	71
Germany	68	74	71
St Lucia	68	73	71
St Christopher-Nevis	69	72	71
Hungary	67	74	71
United Arab Emirates	68	72	70
Qatar	68	72	70
Venezuela	67	73	70
Mexico	67	73	70
Korea, North	67	73	70
Trinidad and Tobago	68	72	70
Antigua and Barbuda	70	70	70
Poland	66	74	70
Romania	67	73	70
Paraguay	67	72	70
Tunisia	68	71	70
Sri Lanka	67	72	70
Argentina	66	73	70
Korea, South	66	73	70
Bahrain	67	71	69
Jordan	67	71	69
Vanuatu	67	71	69
Fiji	67	71	69
Grenada	69	69	69
Solomon Islands	66	71	69
Guyana	66	71	69
Chile	64	73	69
Surinam	66	71	69
Syria	67	69	68
China	67	69	68
Malaysia	65	70	68
Mauritius	64	71	68
Lebanon	65	70	68
Libya	64	69	67
Samoa, Western	64	69	67
Philippines	63	69	66
Seychelles	66	66	66
Saudi Arabia	64	67	66
Mongolia	63	67	65
Thailand	62	68	65
El Salvador	63	66	65
Turkey	63	66	65
Ecuador	62	66	64
Vietnam	62	66	64
Peru	61	66	64
Morocco	62	65	64
Colombia	61	66	64
Brazil	61	66	64
Dominican Republic	61	65	63
Iraq	62	63	63
Nicaragua	61	63	62
São Tomé Principe	62	62	62
Maldives	60	63	62
Tuvalu	60	63	62
Kenya	59	63	61
Zimbabwe	59	63	61
Algeria	59	62	61
Lesotho	59	62	61
Honduras	58	62	60
Belize	60	60	60
Botswana	59	59	59
Guatemala	57	61	59
Cape Verde	57	61	59
Egypt	57	60	59
Dominica	57	59	58
Iran	57	57	57
Oman	55	58	57
Zambia	54	57	56
India	56	55	56
Togo	53	57	55
Pakistan	54	55	55
Liberia	53	56	55
Myanmar	53	56	55
Ivory Coast	52	55	54
Papua New Guinea	53	54	54
Indonesia	52	55	54
Somalia	53	53	53
Sudan	51	55	53
Senegal	51	54	53
Zaire	51	54	53
Bolivia	51	54	53
Haiti	51	54	53
Ghana	50	54	52
Tanzania	49	54	52
Madagascar	50	53	52
Rwanda	49	53	51
Cameroon	49	53	51
Bangladesh	50	52	51
Swaziland	47	54	51
Djibouti	50	50	50
Uganda	49	51	50
Comoros	48	52	50
Nepal	50	49	50
Laos	48	51	50
Niger	48	50	49
Gabon	47	51	49
Yemen	47	50	49
Nigeria	47	49	48
Malawi	46	50	48
Burundi	45	48	47
Mozambique	45	48	47
Congo	45	48	47
Equatorial Guinea	44	48	46
Mauritania	43	48	46
Mali	44	47	46
Burkina Faso	44	47	46
Benin	42	46	44
Sierra Leone	41	47	44
Chad	42	45	44
Cambodia	42	45	44
Bhutan	44	43	44
Central African Republic	41	45	43
Angola	40	44	42
Guinea-Bissau	42	42	42
Gambia	42	42	42
Afghanistan	43	41	42
Guinea	39	42	41
Ethiopia	38	38	38

where separate figures are given for male and female life expectancy, the ranking is based on a simple average of the two

of study such as ◊biophysics and ◊sociobiology.

This approach has led to many new ideas and discoveries as well as to an emphasis on ◊ecology, the study of living organisms in their natural environments.

life table way of summarizing the probability that an individual will give birth or die during successive periods of life. From this, the proportion of individuals who survive from birth to any given age (**survivorship**) and the mean number of offspring produced (**net reproductive rate**) can be determined.

Insurance companies use life tables to estimate risks of death in order to set their premiums and governments use them to determine future needs for education and health services.

lift (US ***elevator***) device for lifting passengers and goods vertically between the floors of a building. US inventor Elisha Graves Otis developed the first passenger lift, installed in 1857. The invention of the lift allowed the development of the skyscraper from the 1880s.

A lift usually consists of a platform or boxlike structure suspended by motor-driven cables with safety ratchets along the sides of the shaft. At first steam powered the movement, but hydraulic and then electric lifts were common from the early 1900s. Lift operators worked controls and gates until lifts became automatic.

ligament strong, flexible connective tissue, made of the protein ◊collagen, which joins bone to bone at moveable joints and sometimes encloses the joints. Ligaments prevent bone dislocation (under normal circumstances) but allow joint flexion. The ligaments around the joints are composed of white fibrous tissue. Other ligaments are composed of yellow elastic tissue, which is adapted to support a continuous but varying stress, as in the ligament connecting the various cartilages of the ◊larynx (voice box).

ligand in chemistry, a group that bonds symmetrically to a central atom or ion of a metal; the result is called a **coordination complex**. An example of a neutral ligand is ammonia; the nitrosyl ion NO^+ is a charged ligand. An example of a coordination complex is hexamminocobalt chloride, $[Co(NH_3)_6]Cl_3$, in which the central cobalt ion (Co^{3+}) is surrounded by covalent bonds with six ammonia molecules and ionic bonds with three chloride ions.

Ligands are used in medicine as an antidote to heavy metal poisoning, removing the metal ions by attaching themselves to form a harmless compound.

light electromagnetic waves in the visible range, having a wavelength from about 400 nanometres in the extreme violet to about 770 nanometres in the extreme red. Light is considered to exhibit particle and wave properties, and the fundamental particle, or quantum, of light is called the photon. The speed of light (and of all electromagnetic radiation) in a vacuum is approximately 300,000 km/186,000 mi per second, and is a universal constant denoted by *c*.

Isaac ◊Newton was the first to discover, in 1666, that sunlight is composed of a mixture of light of different colours in certain proportions and that it could be separated into its components by dispersion. Before his time it was supposed that dispersion of light produced colour instead of separating already existing colours.

Light: Experiments to Determine its Nature

BY JULIAN ROWE

and all was light

Alexander Pope, the poet, wrote of Isaac Newton's work:

'Nature, and Nature's Laws lay hid in Night: God said,
Let Newton be! and All was **Light**.'

Newton discovers the spectrum

Isaac Newton, the English physicist and mathematician (1642–1727), would have been remembered as a great scientist for any one of his many discoveries. He made outstanding contributions to mathematics, astronomy, mechanics, and to understanding gravitation and the nature of light.

The first microscopes revealed the world of the very small to scientists for the very first time. They saw in great detail what microorganisms were really like. In the same way, at the other end of the scale, the first telescopes revealed to astronomers vast numbers of stars and the beauty of the Earth's planets. But there was a problem. Any image formed by the combination of the lenses then available to make microscopes or telescopes was surrounded by a colour fringe. This blurred the outline – an effect which became worse at higher magnifications.

from prisms and rainbows ...

People had long been familiar with the rainbow colours produced when light shone through a chandelier. Now, in order to improve their instruments, scientists needed to know why these colours were formed. Newton ground his own glass lenses and had, since he was an undergraduate student at Cambridge, been interested in the effect of a glass prism on sunlight.

Newton wrote: 'In the year 1666 (at which time I applied myself to the grinding of optick glass or other figures than spherical) I procured me a triangular glass prism, to try the celebrated phaenomena of colours.'

Newton made a small hole in the shutter covering the window in his room to let in a beam of sunlight. He placed the prism in front of this hole and viewed the vivid and intense spectrum of rainbow colours cast on the opposite wall.

Newton now examined these colours individually, using a second prism. He took two boards, each with a small hole in it. The first he placed behind the prism at the window. He positioned the second board so that only a single colour produced by the first prism fell on the hole in it. The second prism was placed so as to cast the light passing through the hole in the second board on to the wall. Newton saw at once that the coloured beam of light passing through the second prism was unchanged. This proved to be true for all the rainbow colours produced by the first prism.

Newton had performed the crucial experiment, because it had been assumed previously that light was basically white, and that colours could be added to it. Now it was clear that white light was a mixture of the colours of the rainbow; the prism simply split them up or refracted the light. A second prism could not 'split' them up further.

... to modern telescopes

In his book *Opticks*, published in 1704, Newton described a further experiment in which he used the second prism to recombine the rainbow colours of the spectrum to produce white light. Here for the first time was a simple explanation of the nature of light. The book had a great impact on 18th-century writers. What Newton had to say about what happened when white light passed through a prism could be immediately applied to rainbows, and this captured the imagination of artists and poets.

Because Newton suspected that the colour fringes or chromatic aberration produced by lenses in telescopes could not be avoided, in 1668 he designed a telescope that depended instead on the use of a curved mirror. Light reflected from a surface produces no colour effects, unlike light passing through a lens. Nowadays all large astronomical telescopes are of the reflecting type.

As a result of his elegant experiments with prisms and light, Newton also speculated about the ultimate nature of light itself. He proposed that light consisted of small 'corpuscules' (small particles) which are shot out from the source of light, rather in the same way that pellets are ejected from a shot gun. He was able to explain many of the known properties of light with this theory, which was widely accepted. Light has proved remarkably difficult to understand; nowadays it is regarded as having both particlelike and wavelike properties.

The ancients believed that light travelled at infinite speed; its finite speed was first discovered by Danish astronomer Ole Römer 1676.

My design in this book is not to explain the properties of light by hypotheses, but to propose and prove them by reason and experiments.

ISAAC NEWTON English physicist and mathematician. *Opticks*, 1704

---

light bulb incandescent filament lamp, first demonstrated by Joseph Swan in the UK in 1878 and Thomas Edison in the USA in 1879. The present-day light bulb is a thin glass bulb filled with an inert mixture of nitrogen and argon gas. It contains a filament made of fine tungsten wire. When electricity is passed through the wire, it glows white hot, producing light.

LIGHT BULBS

When Thomas Edison, inventor of the light bulb, died (on 18 October 1931), all non-essential electric lights in the USA – including the torch on the Statue of Liberty –

light curve in astronomy, a graph showing how the brightness of an astronomical object varies with time. Analysis of the light curves of variable stars, for example, gives information about the physical processes causing the variation.

light-dependent resistor (LDR) component of electronic circuits whose resistance varies with the level of illumination on its surface. Usually resistance decreases as illumination rises. LDRs are used in light-measuring or light-sensing instruments (for example, in the exposure-meter circuit of an automatic camera) and in switches (such as those that switch on street lights at dusk).

LDRs are made from ◊semiconductors, such as cadmium sulphide.

light-emitting diode (LED) an electronic component that converts electrical energy into light or infrared radiation in the range of 550 nm (green light) to 1300 nm (infrared). They are used for displaying symbols in electronic instruments and devices. An LED is a ◊diode made of ◊semiconductor material, such as gallium arsenide phosphide, that glows when electricity is passed through it. The first digital watches and calculators had LED displays, but many later models use ◊liquid-crystal displays.

In 1993 chemists at the University of Cambridge, England, developed LEDs from the polymer poly(*p*-phenylenevinyl) (PPV) that emit as much light as conventional LEDs and in a variety of colours.

A new generation of LEDs that can produce light in the mid-infrared range (300–1000 nm) safely and cheaply were developed by British researchers in 1995, using thin alternating layers of indium arsenide and indium arsenide antimonide.

lighthouse structure carrying a powerful light to warn ships or aeroplanes that they are approaching a place (usually land) dangerous or important to navigation. The light is magnified and directed out to the horizon or up to the zenith by a series of mirrors or prisms. Increasingly lighthouses are powered by electricity and automated rather than staffed; the more recent models also emit radio signals.
signals Lights may be either flashing (the dark period exceeding the light) or rotating (the dark period being equal or less); fixed lights are liable to cause confusion. The pattern of lighting is individually varied so that ships or aircraft can identify the lighthouse. In fog, sound signals are made (horns, sirens, explosives), and in the case of lightbuoys, fog bells and whistles are operated by the movement of the waves.
history Among early lighthouses were the Pharos of Alexandria (about 280 BC) and those built by the Romans at Ostia, Ravenna, Boulogne, and Dover. In England beacons burning in church towers served as lighthouses until the 17th century, and in the earliest lighthouses, such as the Eddystone, first built in 1698, open fires or candles were used.
modern developments Where reefs or sandbanks made erection of a lighthouse impossible, lightships were often installed; increasingly these are being replaced by fixed, small, automated lighthouses. Where it is impossible to install a fixed structure, unattended light-buoys equipped for up to a year's service may be used.

lightning high-voltage electrical discharge between two charged rainclouds or between a cloud and the Earth, caused by the build-up of electrical charges. Air in the path of lightning ionizes (becomes conducting), and expands; the accompanying noise is heard as thunder. Currents of 20,000 amperes and temperatures of 30,000°C/54,000°F are common.

LIGHTNING

Around the world there are a total of 70 to 100 lightning flashes every second.

lightning conductor device that protects a tall building from lightning strike by providing an easier path for current to flow to earth than through the building. It consists of a thick copper strip of very low resistance connected to the ground below. A good connection to the ground is essential and is made by burying a large metal plate deep in the damp earth. In the event of a direct lightning strike, the current in the conductor may be so great as to melt or even vaporize the metal, but the damage to the building will nevertheless be limited.

light pen in computing, a device resembling an ordinary pen, used to indicate locations on a computer screen. With certain computer-aided design (◊CAD) programs, the light pen can be used to instruct the computer to change the shape, size, position, and colours of sections of a screen image.

The pen has a photoreceptor at its tip that emits signals when light from the screen passes beneath it. From the timing of this signal and a gridlike representation of the screen in the computer memory, a computer program can calculate the position of the light pen.

light second unit of length, equal to the distance travelled by light in one second. It is equal to 2.997925×10^8 m/9.835592×10^8 ft. See ◊light year.

light watt unit of radiant power (brightness of light). One light watt is the power required to produce a perceived brightness equal to that of light at a wavelength of 550 nanometres and 680 lumens.

light year in astronomy, the distance travelled by a beam of light in a vacuum in one year, approximately 9.46 trillion (million million) km/5.88 trillion miles.

lignin naturally occurring substance produced by plants to strengthen their tissues. It is difficult for ◊enzymes to attack lignin, so living organisms cannot digest wood, with the exception of a few specialized fungi and bacteria. Lignin is the essential ingredient of all wood and is, therefore, of great commercial importance.

Chemically, lignin is made up of thousands of rings of carbon atoms joined together in a long chain. The way in which they are linked up varies along the chain.

lignite type of ◊coal that is brown and fibrous, with a relatively low carbon content. As a fuel it is less efficient because more of it must be burned to produce the same amount of energy generated by bituminous coal. Lignite also has a high sulphur content and is more polluting. It is burned to generate power in Scandinavia and some former eastern block countries because it is the only fuel resource available without importing.

lilac any of a group of flowering Old World shrubs, with clusters (panicles) of small, sweetly scented, white or purple flowers on the main stems. The common lilac (*S. vulgaris*) is a popular garden ornamental. (Genus *Syringa*, family Oleaceae.)

lilly pilly tree *Acmena smithii* with purplish white fruits, common along streams and in rainforests of E Australia.

lily any of a group of plants belonging to the lily family, of which there are about 80 species, most with showy, trumpet-shaped flowers growing from bulbs. The lily family includes hyacinths, tulips, asparagus, and plants of the onion genus. The name 'lily' is also applied to many lilylike plants of related genera and families. (Genus *Lilium*, family Liliaceae.)

lily of the valley plant belonging to the lily family, growing in woods in Europe, N Asia, and North America. The small bell-shaped white flowers hang downwards from short stalks attached to a central stem; they are strongly scented. The plant is often cultivated. (*Convallaria majalis*, family Liliaceae.)

lime or ***quicklime*** CaO (technical name ***calcium oxide***) white powdery substance used in making mortar and cement. It is made commercially by heating calcium carbonate ($CaCO_3$), obtained from limestone or chalk, in a ◊lime kiln. Quicklime readily absorbs water to become calcium hydroxide $Ca(OH)_2$, known as slaked lime, which is used to reduce soil acidity.

LIME

The theatrical expression 'in the limelight' comes from the 19th-century method of lighting the stage. From about 1838, a powerful flood of white light was produced by heating quicklime in a stream of oxygen – a dangerous chemical reaction.

lime sharp-tasting green or greenish-yellow citrus fruit of the small thorny lime bush, native to India. The white flowers are followed by the fruits, which resemble lemons but are more round in shape; they are rich in vitamin C. (*Citrus aurantifolia*, family Rutaceae.)

lime or ***linden*** any of a group of ◊deciduous trees native to the northern hemisphere. The leaves are heart-shaped and coarsely toothed, and the flowers are cream-coloured and fragrant. (Genus *Tilia*, family Tiliaceae.)

lime kiln oven used to make quicklime (calcium oxide, CaO) by heating limestone (calcium carbonate, $CaCO_3$) in the absence of air. The carbon dioxide is carried away to heat other kilns and to ensure that the reversible reaction proceeds in the right direction. $CaCO_3 \leftrightarrow CaO + CO_2$

limestone sedimentary rock composed chiefly of calcium carbonate $CaCO_3$, either derived from the shells of marine organisms or precipitated from solution, mostly in the ocean. Various types of limestone are used as building stone.

◊Marble is metamorphosed limestone. Certain so-called marbles are not in fact marbles but fine-grained fossiliferous limestones that take an attractive polish. Caves commonly occur in limestone. ◊Karst is a type of limestone landscape.

limewater common name for a dilute solution of slaked lime (calcium hydroxide, $Ca(OH)_2$). In chemistry, it is used to detect the presence of carbon dioxide.

If a gas containing carbon dioxide is bubbled through limewater, the solution turns milky owing to the formation of calcium carbonate ($CaCO_3$). Continued bubbling of the gas causes the limewater to clear again as the calcium carbonate is converted to the more soluble calcium hydrogencarbonate ($Ca(HCO_3)_2$).

limit in mathematics, in an infinite sequence, the final value towards which the sequence is tending. For example, the limit of the sequence $\frac{1}{2}, \frac{3}{4}, \frac{7}{8}, \frac{15}{16}$ ... is 1, although no member of the sequence will ever exactly equal 1 no matter how many terms are added together. The limit of the ratios of a Fibonacci sequence is $(\sqrt{5} + 1)/2$. This number is also the ◊golden section.

limiting factor in biology, any factor affecting the rate of a metabolic reaction. Levels of light or of carbon dioxide are limiting factors in ◊photosynthesis because both are necessary for the production of carbohydrates. In experiments, photosynthesis is observed to slow down and eventually stop as the levels of light decrease.

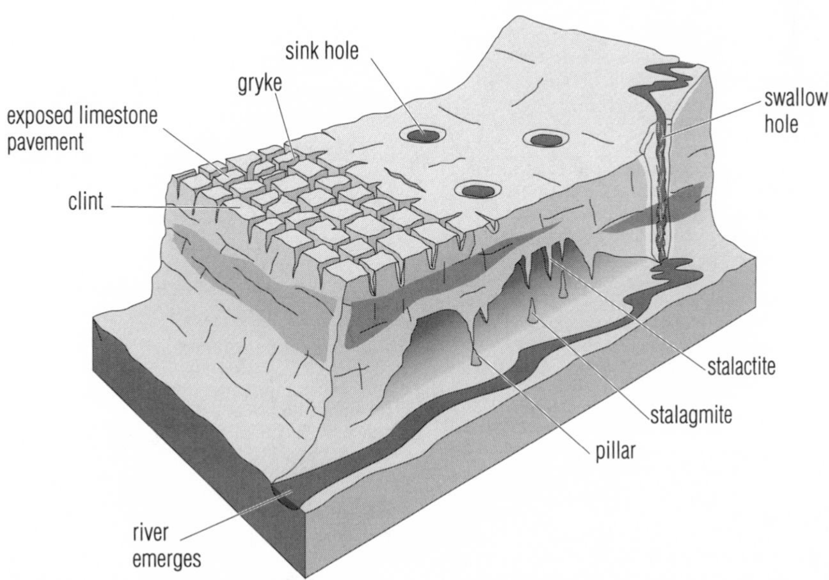

limestone *The physical weathering and erosion of a limestone landscape. The freezing and thawing of rain and its mild acidic properties cause cracks and joints to enlarge, forming limestone pavements, potholes, caves and caverns.*

It is believed that the concentrations of carbon dioxide building up in the atmosphere through the burning of fossil fuels will allow faster plant growth.

limnology study of lakes and other bodies of open fresh water, in terms of their plant and animal biology, chemistry, and physical properties.

limpet any of various marine ◊snails belonging to several families and genera, found in the Atlantic and Pacific oceans. A limpet has a conical shell and adheres firmly to rocks by its disclike foot. Limpets leave their fixed positions only to graze on seaweeds, always returning to the same spot. The **common limpet** (*P. vulgata*) can be seen on rocks at low tide. (Especially genera *Acmaea* and *Patella.*)

linac contraction of ◊linear accelerator, a type of particle accelerator in which the particles are accelerated along a straight tube.

Lindbergh, Charles A(ugustus) (1902–1974)

US aviator. He made the first solo nonstop flight in 33.5 hours across the Atlantic (Roosevelt Field, Long Island, New York, to Le Bourget airport, Paris) 1927 in the Spirit of St Louis, a Ryan monoplane designed by him.

Lindbergh was born in Detroit, Michigan. He was a barnstorming pilot before attending the US Army School in Texas 1924 and becoming an officer in the Army Air Service Reserve 1925. Learning that Raymond B Orteig had offered a prize of £25,000 for the person who first made a nonstop air flight between New York and Paris, he appealed to some St Louis businessmen who agreed to finance him.

Sachem

linden another name for the ◊lime tree.

Lindow Man remains of an Iron Age man discovered in a peat bog at Lindow Marsh, Cheshire, UK, in 1984. The chemicals in the bog had kept the body in an excellent state of preservation.

'Pete Marsh', as the archaeologists nicknamed him, had been knocked unconscious, strangled, and then had his throat cut before being thrown into the bog. He may have been a sacrificial victim, as Celtic peoples often threw offerings to the gods into rivers and marshes. His stomach contained part of an unleavened barley 'bannock' that might have been given as a sacrificial offering. His well-cared-for nails indicate that he might have been a Druid prince who became a willing sacrifice.

linear accelerator or ***linac*** in physics, a type of particle ◊accelerator in which the particles move along a straight tube. Particles pass through a linear accelerator only once – unlike those in a cyclotron (a ring-shaped accelerator), which make many revolutions, gaining energy each time.

The world's longest linac is the Stanford Linear Collider, in which electrons and positrons are accelerated along a straight track 3.2 km/2 mi long and then steered into a head-on collision with other particles.

The first linear accelerator was built in 1928 by Norwegian engineer Ralph Wideröe to investigate the behaviour of heavy ions (large atoms with one or more electrons removed), but devices capable of accelerating smaller particles such as protons and electrons could not be built until after World War II and the development of high-power radio-and microwave-frequency generators.

linear equation in mathematics, a relationship between two variables that, when plotted on Cartesian axes produces a straight-line graph; the equation has the general form $y = mx + c$, where m is the slope of the line represented by the equation and c is the y-intercept, or the value of y where the line crosses the y-axis in the ◊Cartesian coordinate system. Sets of linear equations can be used to describe the behaviour of buildings, bridges, trusses, and other static structures.

linear motor type of electric motor, an induction motor in which the fixed stator and moving armature are straight and parallel to each other (rather than being circular and one inside the other as in an ordinary induction motor). Linear motors are used, for example, to power sliding doors. There is a magnetic force between the stator and armature; this force has been used to support a vehicle, as in the experimental ◊maglev linear motor train.

linear programming in mathematics and economics, a set of techniques for finding the maxima or minima of certain variables governed by linear equations or inequalities. These maxima and minima are used to represent 'best' solutions in terms of goals such as maximizing profit or minimizing cost.

line input in audio systems, direct input to a tape recorder from a device such as another recorder, rather than a microphone.

linen yarn spun and the textile woven from the fibres of the stem of the ◊flax plant. Used by the ancient Egyptians, linen was introduced by the Romans to N Europe, where production became widespread. Religious refugees from the Low Countries in the 16th century helped to establish the linen industry in England, but here and elsewhere it began to decline in competition with cotton in the 18th century.

To get the longest possible fibres, flax is pulled, rather than cut by hand or machine, just as the ripened fruits, or bolls, are beginning to set. After preliminary drying, it is steeped in water so that the fibre can be more easily separated from the wood of the stem, then hackled (combed), classified, drawn into continuous fibres, and spun. Bleaching, weaving, and finishing processes vary according to the final product, which can be sailcloth, canvas, sacking, cambric, or lawn. Because of the length of its fibre, linen yarn has twice the strength of cotton, and yet is superior in delicacy, so that it is suitable for lace making. It mixes well with synthetic fibres.

line of force in physics, an imaginary line representing the direction of force at any point in a magnetic, gravitational, or electrical field.

line printer computer ◊printer that prints a complete line of characters at a time. Line printers can achieve very high printing speeds of up to 2,500 lines a minute, but can print in only one typeface, cannot print graphics, and are very noisy. Today, most users prefer ◊laser printers.

ling any of several deepwater long-bodied fishes of the cod family found in the N Atlantic. (Genus *Molva,* family Gadidae.)

ling another name for common ◊heather.

link in computing, an image or item of text in a ◊World Wide Web document that acts as a route to another Web page or file on the Internet. Links are created by using ◊HTML to combine an on-screen 'anchor' with a hidden Hypertext Reference (HRF), usually the ◊URL (Web address) of the item in question.

linkage in genetics, the association between two or more genes that tend to be inherited together because they are on the same chromosome.

The closer together they are on the chromosome, the less likely they are to be separated by crossing over (one of the processes of ◊recombination) and they are then described as being 'tightly linked'.

Linnaeus, Carolus (1707–1778)

Latinized form of Carl von Linné Swedish naturalist and physician. His botanical work *Systema naturae* 1735 contained his system for classifying plants into groups depending on shared characteristics (such as the number of stamens in flowers), providing a much-needed framework for identification. He also devised the concise and precise system for naming plants and animals, using one Latin (or Latinized) word to represent the genus and a second to distinguish the species.

For example, in the Latin name of the daisy, *Bellis perennis*, *Bellis* is the name of the genus to which the plant belongs, and *perennis* distinguishes the species from others of the same genus. By tradition the generic name always begins with a capital letter. The author who first described a particular species is often indicated after the name, for example, *Bellis perennis* Linnaeus, showing that the author was Linnaeus.

Mary Evans Picture Library

linnet small seed-eating bird belonging to the finch family, which is very abundant in Europe, Asia, and N W Africa. The male has a chestnut back with a pink breast and grey head, and a red breast and forehead during the breeding season; the female is mainly a dull brown. The linnet barely measures 13 cm/5 in in length, begins to breed in April, and generally chooses low-lying bush for its home. The eggs, ranging from four to six in number, are a delicate pale blue streaked with a purplish brown. (Species *Acanthis cannabina*, family Fringillidae, order Passeriformes.)

linoleum ***Latin lini oleum 'linseed oil'*** floor covering made from linseed oil, tall oil, rosin, cork, woodflour, chalk, clay, and pigments, pressed into sheets with a jute backing. Oxidation of the oil is accelerated by heating, so that the oil mixture solidifies into a tough, resilient material. Linoleum tiles have a backing made of polyester and glass.

Linoleum was invented in England in 1860 by Frederick Walton. In the early 20th century he invented a straight-line inlay machine which was able to produce patterned linoleum. Today, the manufacture of linoleum still follows the basic principles of Walton's process although production is much faster. Synthetic floor coverings are now popular and the use of linoleum has declined.

Linotype trademark for a typesetting machine once universally used for newspaper work, which sets complete lines (slugs) of hot-metal type as operators type the copy at a keyboard. It was invented in the USA in 1884 by German-born Ottmar Mergenthaler. It has been replaced by phototypesetting.

linsang nocturnal, tree-dwelling, carnivorous mammal of the civet family, about 75 cm/2.5 ft long. The African linsang (*Poiana richardsoni*) is a long, low, and lithe spotted animal about 33 cm/1.1 ft long with a 38 cm/1.25 ft tail. The two species of oriental linsang (genus *Prionodon*), found in Asia, are slightly larger. (Family Viverridae.)

linseed seeds of the flax plant, from which linseed oil is produced, the residue being used as cattle feed. The oil is used in paint, wood treatments and varnishes, and in the manufacture of linoleum floor coverings.

Linux (contraction of ***Linus UNIX***) in computing, operating system based on an original core program written by Linus Torvalds, a 22-year-old student at the University of Helsinki, Finland, 1991–92. Linux is a non-proprietary system, made up of freely-available ('open') code created over several years by ◊UNIX enthusiasts all over the world. Each programmer retains the copyright to his or her creation, but makes it freely available on the Internet. Linux retains the flexibility and many of the advanced programming features that make UNIX popular for technically-minded users, but can run on an ordinary PC instead an expensive UNIX workstation.

AFRICAN LION

http://www.seaworld.org/animal_bytes/lionab.html

Illustrated guide to the African lion including information about genus, size, life span, habitat, gestation, diet, and a series of fun facts.

lion large wild cat with a tawny coat. The young have darker spot markings to camouflage them; these usually disappear in the adult. The male has a heavy mane and a tuft at the end of the tail. Head and body measure about 2 m/6 ft, plus 1 m/3 ft of tail; lionesses are slightly smaller. Lions produce litters of two to six cubs, and often live in groups (prides) of several adult males and females with young. They are carnivores (meat-eaters) and are found only in Africa, south of the Sahara desert, and in the Gir Forest of northwest India.

behaviour Capable of short bursts of speed, lionesses do most of the hunting, working together to run down grazing animals. Females remain with the pride permanently; young males remain until they about three years old and one or more adult males (usually brothers) stay a couple of years or so until they are supplanted by a competing coalition of males. The incoming males, or male, kill all the cubs in a pride so that the lionesses become ready to breed again. When not hunting, lions spend most of their time dozing and sleeping. The average lifespan of a lion is 15–20 years in the wild and 20–25 years in captivity.

The Asiatic lion is listed on ◊CITES Appendix 1 (endangered); its total population numbered only 250–300 in 1996. 'Mountain lion' is a name for the ◊puma.

classification Lions belong to the animal phylum Chordata, subphylum Vertebrata, class Mammalia (mammals), order Carnivora (carnivores). They belong to the cat family, Felidae, genus *Panthera* (which also includes tigers, leopards, and jaguars), species *P. Leo.*

lion *Lions can sleep for over 18 hours a day, particularly after a large kill. Unlike other cats, lions live and hunt in groups (prides). Usually they kill only once or twice a week, hunting ruminants such as gazelles, zebra, and wildebeest. Premaphotos Wildlife*

lipase enzyme responsible for breaking down fats into fatty acids and glycerol. It is produced by the ◊pancreas and requires a slightly alkaline environment. The products of fat digestion are absorbed by the intestinal wall.

lipid any of a large number of esters of fatty acids, commonly formed by the reaction of a fatty acid with glycerol (see ◊glyceride). They are soluble in alcohol but not in water. Lipids are the chief constituents of plant and animal waxes, fats, and oils.

Phospholipids are lipids that also contain a phosphate group, usually linked to an organic base; they are major components of biological cell membranes.

lipophilic ***Greek 'fat-loving'*** in chemistry, a term describing ◊functional groups with an affinity for fats and oils.

lipophobic ***Greek 'fat-hating'*** in chemistry, a term describing ◊functional groups that tend to repel fats and oils.

liposome in medicine, a minute droplet of oil that is separated from a medium containing water by a ◊phospholipid layer. Drugs, such as cytotoxic agents, can be incorporated into liposomes and given by injection or by mouth. The liposomes allow the drug to reach the site of action, such as a tumour, without being broken down in the body.

Lippizaner pure white horse, named after its place of origin in Lippiza, Slovenia. They are trained at the Spanish Riding School of Vienna.

liquefaction the process of converting a gas to a liquid, normally associated with low temperatures and high pressures (see ◊condensation).

liquefaction in earth science, the conversion of a soft deposit, such as clay, to a jellylike state by severe shaking. During an earthquake buildings and lines of communication built on materials prone to liquefaction will sink and topple. In the Alaskan earthquake of 1964 liquefaction led to the destruction of much of the city of Anchorage.

liquefied petroleum gas (LPG) liquid form of butane, propane, or pentane, produced by the distillation of petroleum during oil refining. At room temperature these substances are gases, although they can be easily liquefied and stored under pressure in metal containers. They are used for heating and cooking where other fuels are not available: camping stoves and cigarette lighters, for instance, often use liquefied butane as fuel.

liquid state of matter between a ◊solid and a ◊gas. A liquid forms a level surface and assumes the shape of its container. Its atoms do not occupy fixed positions as in a crystalline solid, nor do they have freedom of movement as in a gas. Unlike a gas, a liquid is difficult to compress since pressure applied at one point is equally transmitted throughout (Pascal's principle). ◊Hydraulics makes use of this property.

liquid air air that has been cooled so much that it has liquefied. This happens at temperatures below about –196°C/–321°F. The various constituent gases, including nitrogen, oxygen, argon, and neon, can be separated from liquid air by the technique of ◊fractionation.

Air is liquefied by the **Linde process**, in which air is alternately compressed, cooled, and expanded, the expansion resulting each time in a considerable reduction in temperature. With the lower temperature the molecules move more slowly and occupy less space, so the air changes phase to become liquid.

liquid-crystal display (LCD) display of numbers (for example, in a calculator) or pictures (such as on a pocket television screen) produced by molecules of a substance in a semiliquid state with some crystalline properties, so that clusters of molecules align in parallel formations. The display is a blank until the application of an electric field, which 'twists' the molecules so that they reflect or transmit light falling on them. There two main types of LCD are **passive matrix** and **active matrix**.

liquorice perennial European herb belonging to the ◊legume family. The long sweet root yields an extract which is made into a hard black paste and used in confectionery and medicines. (*Glycyrrhiza glabra*, family Leguminosae.)

LISP (acronym for ***list processing***) high-level computer-programming language designed for manipulating lists of data items. It is used primarily in research into ◊artificial intelligence (AI).

Developed in the late 1950s, and until recently common only in university laboratories, LISP is used more in the USA than in Europe, where the language ◊PROLOG is often preferred for AI work.

listeriosis disease of animals that may occasionally infect humans, caused by the bacterium *Listeria monocytogenes*. The bacteria multiply at temperatures close to 0°C/32°F, which means they may flourish in precooked frozen meals if the cooking has not been thorough. Listeriosis causes flulike symptoms and inflammation of the brain and its surrounding membranes. It can be treated with penicillin.

LISTSERV in computing, program that receives incoming messages for a mailing list and redistributes them to subscribers. Listserv was originally written for IBM mainframes but there are now many alternatives for UNIX machines and PCs, such as ◊Majordomo.

litchi or *lychee* evergreen tree belonging to the soapberry family. The delicately flavoured egg-shaped fruit has a rough brownish outer skin and a hard seed. The litchi is native to S China, where it has been cultivated for 2,000 years. (*Litchi chinensis*, family Sapindaceae.)

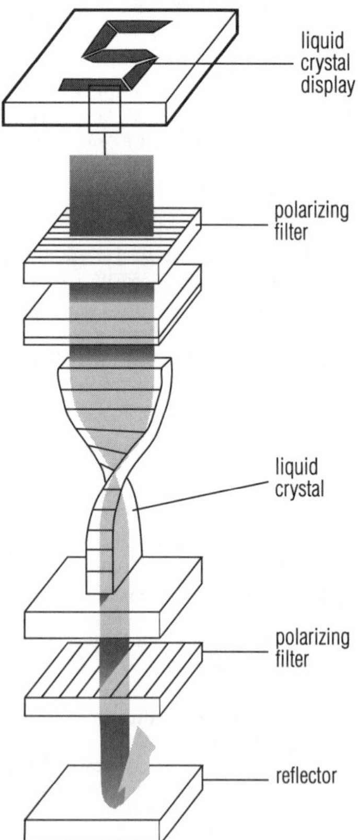

liquid-crystal display *A liquid-crystal display consists of a liquid crystal sandwiched between polarizing filters similar to polaroid sunglasses. When a segment of the seven-segment display is electrified, the liquid crystal twists the polarized light from the front filter, allowing the light to bounce off the rear reflector and illuminate the segment.*

lithification the conversion of an unconsolidated, newly deposited sediment into solid sedimentary rock by **compaction** of mineral grains that make up the sediment, new growth of the original mineral grains, and **cementation** by crystallization of new minerals from percolating aqueous solutions. The term is less commonly used to refer to solidification of molten lava or magma to form igneous rock.

lithium ***Greek lithos 'stone'*** soft, ductile, silver-white, metallic element, symbol Li, atomic number 3, relative atomic mass 6.941. It is one of the ◊alkali metals, has a very low density (far less than most woods), and floats on water (specific gravity 0.57); it is the lightest of all metals. Lithium is used to harden alloys, and in batteries; its compounds are used in medicine to treat manic depression.

Lithium was named 1818 by Swedish chemist Jöns Berzelius, having been discovered the previous year by his student Johan A Arfwedson (1792–1841). Berzelius named it after 'stone' because it is found in most igneous rocks and many mineral springs.

lithography printmaking technique invented in 1798 by Aloys Senefelder, based on the mutual repulsion of grease and water. A drawing is made with greasy crayon on an absorbent stone, which is then wetted. The wet stone repels ink (which is greasy) applied to the surface and the crayon absorbs it, so that the drawing can be printed. Lithographic printing is used in book production, posters, and prints, and this basic principle has developed into complex processes.

Many artists have made brilliant use of the process since the early 19th century, including Delacroix, Goya, Isabey, Bonington, Daumier, Gavarni, Whistler, Toulouse-Lautrec (who devised colour effects of the most striking and original kind), Bonnard, and Vuillard.

lithosphere topmost layer of the Earth's structure, forming the jigsaw of plates that take part in the movements of ◊plate tectonics. The lithosphere comprises the crust and a portion of the upper ◊mantle. It is regarded as being rigid and moves about on the more elastic and less rigid ◊asthenosphere. The lithosphere is about 100 km/63 mi thick.

litmus dye obtained from various ◊lichens and used in chemistry as an indicator to test the acidic or alkaline nature of aqueous solutions; it turns red in the presence of acid, and blue in the presence of alkali.

litre metric unit of volume (symbol l), equal to one cubic decimetre (1.76 imperial pints/2.11 US pints). It was formerly defined as the volume occupied by one kilogram of pure water at 4°C at standard pressure, but this is slightly larger than one cubic decimetre.

Little Dipper another name for the most distinctive part of the constellation ◊Ursa Minor, the Little Bear.

Little Willie prototype British tank built 1915. It consisted of little more than a rectangular box on two 'Creeping Grip' caterpillar tracks, with a two-wheeled steering unit connected to the rear, but it proved the viability of a tracked vehicle.

liver large organ of vertebrates, which has many regulatory and storage functions. The human liver is situated in the upper abdomen, and weighs about 2 kg/4.5 lb. It is divided into four lobes. The liver receives the products of digestion, converts glucose to glycogen (a long-chain carbohydrate used for storage), and breaks down fats. It removes excess amino acids from the blood, converting them to urea, which is excreted by the kidneys. The liver also synthesizes vitamins, produces bile and blood-clotting factors, and removes damaged red cells and toxins such as alcohol from the blood.

Livermore Valley valley in California, USA, site of the **Lawrence Livermore Laboratory**. Part of the University of California, it shares with Los Alamos Laboratory, New Mexico, all US military research into nuclear warheads and atomic explosives. It also conducts research into nuclear fusion, using high-integrity lasers.

liverwort nonvascular plant (with no 'veins' to carry water and food), related to ◊hornworts and mosses; it is found growing in damp places. (Class Hepaticae, order Bryophyta.)

The plant exists in two different reproductive forms, sexual and asexual, which appear alternately (see ◊alternation of generations). The main sexual form consists of a plant body, or ◊thallus, which may be flat, green, and lobed like a small leaf, or leafy and mosslike. The asexual, spore-bearing form is smaller, typically parasitic on the thallus, and produces a capsule from which spores are scattered.

lizard reptile generally distinguishable from snakes, which belong to the same order, by having four legs, moveable eyelids, eardrums, and a fleshy tongue, although some lizards are legless and snake-like in appearance. There are over 3,000 species of lizard worldwide. (Suborder Lacertilia, order Squamata.)

Like other reptiles, lizards are abundant in the tropics, although some species live as far north as the Arctic circle. There are about 20 families of lizards, including geckos, chameleons, skinks, monitors, agamas, and iguanas. The **common** or **viviparous lizard** (*Lacerta vivipara*), about 15 cm/6 in long, is found throughout Europe; in the far north, it hibernates through the long winter. Like many other species, it can shed its tail as a defence, later regrowing it. The **frilled lizard** (*Chlamydosaurus kingi*) of Australia has an erectile collar to frighten its enemies. There are two poisonous species of lizard, the **Mexican bearded lizard** and the **gila monster**. (For flying lizard see ◊flying dragon.)

llama South American even-toed hoofed mammal belonging to the camel family, about 1.2 m/4 ft high at the shoulder. Llamas can be white, brown, or dark, sometimes with spots or patches. They are very hardy, and require little food or water. They spit when annoyed. (Species *Lama glama*, family Camelidae.)

Llamas are used in Peru as beasts of burden, and also for their wool, milk, and meat. Llamas and alpacas are both domesticated forms of the ◊guanaco.

loach carplike freshwater fish with a long narrow body and no teeth in the small downward-pointing mouth, which is surrounded by barbels (sensitive bristles). Loaches are native to Asian and European waters. (Family Cobitidae.)

loam type of fertile soil, a mixture of sand, silt, clay, and organic material. It is porous, which allows for good air circulation and retention of moisture.

lobelia any of a group of temperate and tropical plants with white to mauve flowers. Lobelias may grow to shrub size but are mostly small annual plants. (Genus *Lobelia*, family Lobeliaceae.)

lobotomy another name for the former brain operation, ◊leucotomy.

The first rule of intelligent tinkering is to save all the parts.

PAUL EHRLICH German bacteriologist.
Saturday Review 5 June 1971

---

lobster any of various large marine ◊crustaceans. Lobsters are grouped with freshwater ◊crayfish in the suborder Reptantia ('walking'), although both lobsters and crayfish can also swim, using their fanlike tails. Lobsters have eyes on stalks and long antennae, and are mainly nocturnal. They scavenge and eat dead or dying fish. (Family Homaridae, order Decapoda.)

LOBSTER

When spiny lobsters migrate, they do so by walking in queues of up to 65 along the sea-bed, each clinging with its claws to the rear of the one in front. Scientific experiments with dead lobsters, weights and pulleys have shown that such an arrangement reduces drag and allows a 25% improvement in speed through the water.

True lobsters are distinguished by having very large 'claws' or pincers on their first pair of legs, and smaller ones on their second and third pairs. Spiny lobsters (family Palinuridae) have no large pincers. They communicate by means of a serrated pad at the base of their antennae, the 'sound' being picked up by sensory nerves located on hairlike outgrowths on their fellow lobsters up to 60 m/180 ft away.

lobworm marine annelid worm also called ◊lugworm.

local area network (*LAN*) in computing, a network restricted to a single room or building. Local area networks enable around 500 devices to be connected together.

local bus in computing, an extension of the central processing unit (CPU) ◊bus (electrical pathway), designed to speed up data transfer between the CPU, discs, graphics boards, and other devices. The ◊PCI bus has become the standard on PCs and more recently has been adopted for the Apple Macintosh.

Local Group in astronomy, a cluster of about 30 galaxies that includes our own, the Milky Way. Like other groups of galaxies, the Local Group is held together by the gravitational attraction among its members, and does not expand with the expanding universe. Its two largest galaxies are the Milky Way and the Andromeda galaxy; most of the others are small and faint.

local variable in computing, a ◊variable that can be accessed only by the instructions within a particular ◊subroutine.

lock construction installed in waterways to allow boats or ships to travel from one level to another. The earliest form, the **flash lock**, was first seen in the East in 1st-century-AD China and in the West in 11th-century Holland. By this method barriers temporarily dammed a river and when removed allowed the flash flood to propel the waiting boat through or over any obstacle. This was followed in 12th-century China and 14th-century Holland by the **pound lock**. In this system the lock has gates at each end. Boats enter through one gate when the levels are the same both outside and inside. Water is then allowed in (or out of) the lock until the level rises (or falls) to the new level outside the other gate.

Locks are important to shipping where canals link oceans of differing levels, such as the Panama Canal, or where falls or rapids are replaced by these adjustable water 'steps'.

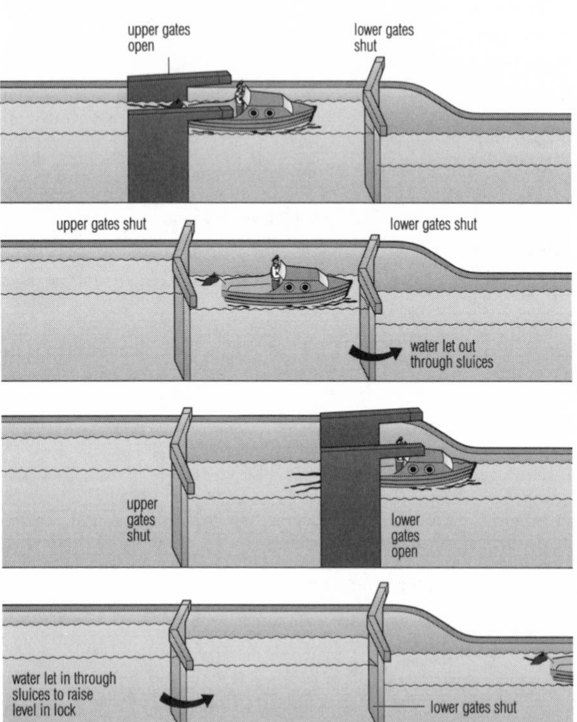

lock Travelling downstream, a boat enters the lock with the lower gates closed. The upper gates are then shut and the water level lowered by draining through sluices. When the water level in the lock reaches the downstream level, the lower gates are opened.

lock and key devices that provide security, usually fitted to a door of some kind. In 1778 English locksmith Robert Barron made the forerunner of the **mortise lock**, which contains levers that the key must raise to an exact height before the bolt can be moved. The **Yale lock**, a pin-tumbler cylinder design, was invented by US locksmith Linus Yale, Jr, in 1865. More secure locks include **combination locks**, with a dial mechanism that must be turned certain distances backwards and forwards to open, and **time locks**, which are set to be opened only at specific times.

Locks originated in the Far East over 4,000 years ago. The Romans developed the warded lock, which contains obstacles (wards) that the key must pass to turn.

Lockheed US aircraft manufacturer, the USA's largest military contractor. The company was founded in 1916 by two brothers, Allan and Malcolm Loughheed (they later changed the spelling of their name), who had built their first seaplane in 1913, with headquarters in Burbank, California. Lockheed built the Vega plane in 1926 (later used by Amelia Earhart in her solo transatlantic flight), the first fully pressurized aircraft, the XC-35, 1937, the P-38 Lightning fighter of World War II, and the TriStar passenger plane of the 1960s.

The P-38 Lightning shot down more Japanese aircraft than any other US fighter in the Pacific campaign. In 1974, the company was implicated in a scandal with the Japanese government, in which the then premier, Kakuei Tanake, was found guilty of accepting bribes from the Lockheed corporation and forced to resign.

After a merger the company became Lockheed Martin Aeronautical Systems.

lockjaw former name for ◊tetanus, a type of bacterial infection.

locomotion the ability to move independently from one place to another, occurring in most animals but not in plants. The development of locomotion as a feature of animal life is closely linked to another vital animal feature, that of nutrition. Animals cannot make their food, as can plants, but must find it first; often the food must be captured and killed, which may require great speed. Locomotion is also important in finding a mate, in avoiding predators, and in migrating to favourable areas.

locomotive engine for hauling railway trains. In 1804 Cornish engineer Richard Trevithick built the first steam engine to run on rails. Locomotive design did not radically improve until British engineer George Stephenson built the *Rocket* in 1829, which featured a multitube boiler and blastpipe, standard in all following **steam locomotives**. Today most locomotives are diesel or electric: **diesel locomotives** have a powerful diesel engine, and **electric locomotives** draw their power from either an overhead cable or a third rail alongside the ordinary track.

In a steam locomotive, fuel (usually coal, sometimes wood) is burned in a furnace. The hot gases and flames produced are drawn through tubes running through a huge water-filled boiler and heat up the water to steam. The steam is then fed to the cylinders, where it forces the pistons back and forth. Movement of the pistons is conveyed to the wheels by cranks and connecting rods. Diesel locomotives have a powerful diesel engine, burning oil.

The engine may drive a generator to produce electricity to power electric motors that turn the wheels, or the engine drives the wheels mechanically or through a hydraulic link. A number of **gas-turbine locomotives** are in use, in which a turbine spun by hot gases provides the power to drive the wheels.

locus ***Latin 'place'*** in mathematics, traditionally the path traced out by a moving point, but now defined as the set of all points on a curve satisfying given conditions. For example, the locus of a point that moves so that it is always at the same distance from another fixed point is a circle; the locus of a point that is always at the same distance from two fixed points is a straight line that perpendicularly bisects the line joining them.

LOCUST

Locust swarms can contain up to 10 billion individuals and cover a surface of 1,000 sq km/400 sq mi. The swarm can remain together for weeks, devastating crops and other vegetation for thousands of kilometres. Each square kilometre of locusts (up to 80 million) can consume 250 tonnes of food a day, the daily amount required to feed 80,000 people.

locust swarming grasshopper with short feelers, or antennae, and hearing organs on the abdomen (rear segment of the body). As winged adults, flying in swarms, locusts may be carried by the wind hundreds of miles from their breeding grounds; on landing they devour all vegetation. Locusts occur in nearly every continent. (Family Acrididae, order Orthoptera.)

locust tree another name for the ◊carob, a small tree of the Mediterranean region. It is also the name of several North American trees of the ◊legume family (Leguminosae).

lode geological deposit rich in certain minerals, generally consisting of a large vein or set of veins containing ore minerals. A system of veins that can be mined directly forms a lode, for example the mother lode of the California gold rush.

Lodes form because hot hydrothermal liquids and gases from magmas penetrate surrounding rocks, especially when these are limestones; on cooling, veins of ores formed from the magma then extend from the igneous mass into the local rock.

lodestar or ***loadstar*** a star used in navigation or astronomy, often ◊Polaris, the Pole Star.

loess yellow loam, derived from glacial meltwater deposits and accumulated by wind in periglacial regions during the ◊ice ages. Loess usually attains considerable depths, and the soil derived from it is very fertile. There are large deposits in central Europe (Hungary), China, and North America. It was first described in 1821 in the Rhine area, and takes its name from a village in Alsace.

log in mathematics, abbreviation for ◊***logarithm***.

log any apparatus for measuring the speed of a ship; also the daily record of events on board a ship or aircraft.

The log originally consisted of a piece of weighted wood attached to a line with knots at equal intervals that was cast from the rear of a ship. The vessel's speed was estimated by timing the passage of the knots with a sandglass (like an egg timer). Today logs use electromagnetism and sonar.

loganberry hybrid between a ◊blackberry and a ◊raspberry with large, tart, dull-red fruit. It was developed in 1881 by US judge James H Logan.

logarithm or ***log*** the ◊exponent or index of a number to a specified base – usually 10. For example, the logarithm to the base 10 of 1,000 is 3 because $10^3 = 1{,}000$; the logarithm of 2 is 0.3010 because $2 = 10^{0.3010}$. Before the advent of cheap electronic calculators, multiplication and division could be simplified by being replaced with the addition and subtraction of logarithms.

For any two numbers x and y (where $x = b^a$ *and* $y = b^c$) $x \times y = b^a \times b^c = b^{a+c}$; *hence we would add the logarithms of* x and y, and look up this answer in antilogarithm tables.

Tables of logarithms and antilogarithms are available that show conversions of numbers into logarithms, and vice versa.

For example, to multiply 6,560 by 980, one looks up their logarithms (3.8169 and 2.9912), adds them together (6.8081), then looks up the antilogarithm of this to get the answer (6,428,800). **Natural** or **Napierian logarithms** are to the base e, an ◊irrational number equal to approximately 2.7183.

The principle of logarithms is also the basis of the slide rule. With the general availability of the electronic pocket calculator, the need for logarithms has been reduced. The first log tables (to base e) were published by the Scottish mathematician John Napier in 1614. Base-ten logs were introduced by the Englishman Henry Briggs (1561–1631) and Dutch mathematician Adriaen Vlacq (1600–1667).

log file in computing, file that keeps a record of computer transactions. A log file might track the length and type of connection made to a network, or compile details of faxes sent by computer.

logic gate or ***logic circuit*** in electronics, one of the basic components used in building ◊integrated circuits. The five basic types of gate make logical decisions based on the functions NOT, AND, OR, NAND (NOT AND), and NOR (NOT OR). With the exception of the NOT gate, each has two or more inputs.

Information is fed to a gate in the form of binary-coded input signals (logic value 0 stands for 'off' or 'low-voltage pulse', logic 1 for 'on' or 'high-voltage'), and each combination of input signals yields a specific output (logic 0 or 1). An **OR** gate will give a logic 1 output if one or more of its inputs receives a logic 1 signal; however, an **AND** gate will yield a logic 1 output only if it receives a logic 1 signal through both its inputs. The output of a **NOT** or **inverter** gate is the opposite of the signal received through its single input, and a **NOR** or **NAND** gate produces an output signal that is the opposite of the signal that would have been produced by an OR or AND gate respectively. The properties of a logic gate, or of a combination of gates, may be defined and presented in the form of a diagram called a **truth table**, which lists the output that will be triggered by each of the possible combinations of input signals. The process has close parallels in computer programming, where it forms the basis of binary logic.

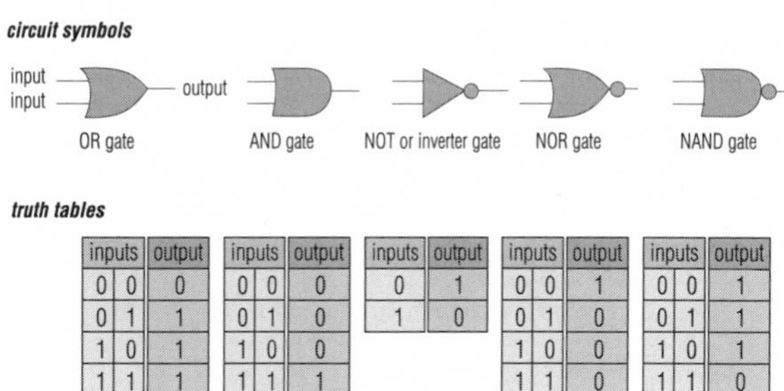

OR gate

inputs		output
0	0	0
0	1	1
1	0	1
1	1	1

AND gate

inputs		output
0	0	0
0	1	0
1	0	0
1	1	1

NOT gate

inputs	output
0	1
1	0

NOR gate

inputs		output
0	0	1
0	1	0
1	0	0
1	1	0

NAND gate

inputs		output
0	0	1
0	1	1
1	0	1
1	1	0

logic gate *The circuit symbols for the five basic types of logic gate: OR, AND, NOT, NOR, and NAND. The truth table displays the output results of each possible combination of input signal.*

LOGO ***Greek logos 'word'*** high-level computer programming language designed to teach mathematical concepts. Developed in about 1970 at the Massachusetts Institute of Technology, it became popular in schools and with home computer users because of its 'turtle graphics' feature. This allows the user to write programs that create line drawings on a computer screen, or drive a small mobile robot (a 'turtle' or 'buggy') around the floor.

LOGO encourages the use of languages in a logical and structured way, leading to 'microworlds', in which problems can be solved by using a few standard solutions.

log off or ***log out*** in computing, the process by which a user identifies himself or herself to a multiuser computer and leaves the system.

log on or ***log in*** in computing, the process by which a user identifies himself or herself to a multiuser computer and enters the system. Logging on usually requires the user to enter a password before access is allowed.

lomentum fruit similar to a pod but constricted between the seeds. When ripe, it splits into one-seeded units, as seen, for example, in the fruit of sainfoin *Onobrychis viciifolia* and radish *Raphanus raphanistrum*. It is a type of ◊schizocarp.

lone pair in chemistry, a pair of electrons in the outermost shell of an atom that are not used in bonding. In certain circumstances, they will allow the atom to bond with atoms, ions, or molecules (such as boron trifluoride, BF_3) that are deficient in electrons, forming coordinate covalent (dative) bonds in which they provide both of the bonding electrons.

longhorn beetle beetle with extremely long antennae, usually equalling the length of the entire body, and often twice its length. Their bodies are 2–150 mm/0.1–6 in long, usually cylindrical, and often mimic wasps, moss, or lichens. The larvae, white or yellow grubs, are wood-borers, mostly attacking decaying or dead wood, but they may bore into healthy trees causing much damage.

classification Longhorn beetles are in order Coleoptera, class Insecta, phylum Arthropoda.

longitude see ◊latitude and longitude.

The real scientist ... is ready to bear privations and, if need be, starvation rather than let anyone dictate to him which direction his work must take.

ALBERT SZENT-GYÖRGYI Hungarian-born US biochemist.
Science Needs Freedom 1943

longitudinal wave ◊wave in which the displacement of the medium's particles is in line with or parallel to the direction of travel of the wave motion.

long-sightedness or ***hypermetropia*** defect of vision in which a person is able to focus on objects in the distance, but not on close objects. It is caused by the failure of the lens to return to its normal rounded shape, or by the eyeball being too short, with the result that the image is focused on a point behind the retina. Long-sightedness is corrected by wearing spectacles fitted with ◊converging lenses, each of which acts like a magnifying glass.

loofah or **luffa** fibrous skeleton of the cylindrical fruit of the dishcloth gourd *Luffa cylindrica*, family Cucurbitaceae, used as a bath sponge.

look-and-feel in computing, the general appearance of a user interface (usually a ◊graphical user interface). The concept of look-and-feel was the subject of several court cases in the USA. ◊Apple sued ◊Microsoft on the basis that the look-and-feel of Microsoft ◊Windows infringed its copyright. The case was decided principally in Microsoft's favour.

loom any machine for weaving yarn or thread into cloth. The first looms were used to weave sheep's wool about 5000 BC. A loom is a frame on which a set of lengthwise threads (warp) is strung.

A second set of threads (weft), carried in a shuttle, is inserted at right angles over and under the warp.

In most looms the warp threads are separated by a device called a treddle to create a gap, or shed, through which the shuttle can be passed in a straight line. A kind of comb called a reed presses each new line of weave tight against the previous ones. All looms have similar features, but on the power loom, weaving takes place automatically at great speed. Mechanization of weaving began in 1733 when British inventor John Kay invented the flying shuttle. In 1785 British inventor Edmund Cartwright introduced a steam-powered loom. Among recent developments are shuttleless looms, which work at very high speed, passing the weft through the warp by means of 'rapiers', and jets of air or water.

loon North American name for the ◊diver bird.

loop in computing, short for ◊program loop.

loop the part of a curve which encloses a space when the curve crosses itself. In a ◊flow chart, a path which keeps on returning to the same question. In a ◊flow chart, a path which keeps on returning to the same question.

loopback in computing, any connection that sends an output signal to the same system's input. Loopback adaptors are used in electrical testing.

loosestrife any of several plants belonging to the primrose family, including the yellow loosestrife (*L. vulgaris*), with spikes of yellow flowers, and the low-growing creeping jenny (*L. nummularia*). The striking purple loosestrife (*Lythrum saclicaria*) belongs to a different family. (Genus *Lysimachia*, family Primulaceae; purple loosestrife family Lythraceae.)

loquat evergreen tree native to China and Japan, also known as the **Japan medlar**. The golden pear-shaped fruit has a delicate sweet-sour taste. (*Eriobotrya japonica*, family Rosaceae.)

Loran navigation system LOng-RAnge radio-based aid to Navigation. The current system (Loran C) consists of a master

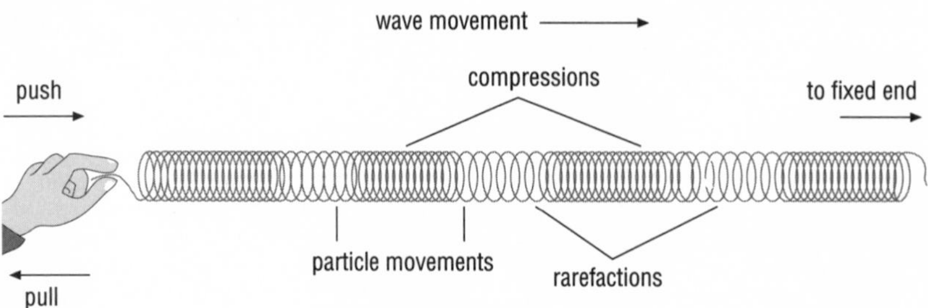

longitudinal wave *The diagram illustrates the motion of a longitudinal wave. Sound, for example, travels through air in longitudinal waves: the waves vibrate back and forth in the direction of travel. In the compressions the particles are pushed together, and in the rarefactions they are pulled apart.*

The Determination of Longitude

BY TONY JONES

Being lost at sea was one of the greatest fears of the early navigators. Although the system of latitude and longitude had been used since the time of Ptolemy in the 2nd century, it was not until the late 18th century that navigation became a reliable art.

The problem is that while the latitude of any point of the Earth – its angular distance north or south of the equator – can be determined by careful measurements of the altitude of the Sun or stars, longitude is a different matter. Longitude is measured east or west from an arbitrary prime meridian, connecting the Earth's poles. Until it settled on Greenwich in 1884, the prime meridian was often that of the ship's home port. To find longitude at sea, a navigator had to note the time when the Sun or a star appeared due south and compare it with the predicted time the same body appeared due south from the prime meridian. The difference in times (where 1 h of time is 15°), was the ship's longitude.

Unfortunately, there were no clocks which could keep time on board ships. Throughout the great voyages of discovery from the 15th–18th centuries sailors were largely ignorant of their longitude, which is why Columbus, sailing westwards along a line of latitude, had no idea where he was when he landed in the New World in 1492.

In 1610, Galileo Galilei (1564–1642) discovered the four large moons of Jupiter. Every now and then the moons would pass in and out of the shadow of Jupiter and Galileo saw that these eclipses could provide a celestial clock for navigators. All that was needed were accurate predictions for the eclipses for a number of ports. By observing theses eclipses, sailors would know the precise time at home and so be able calculate their longitude by noting which stars were then due south.

Astronomers put a great deal of effort into studying the motions of Jupiter's moons (one such, Danish, astronomer Ole Römer (1644–1710), found that the times of eclipses deviated systematically from predictions with the varying distance of Jupiter from the Earth, and so made the first measurement of the speed of light). However, the method was only usable when Jupiter was above the horizon in a dark, clear sky and an eclipse was imminent.

National observatories were founded in Paris (1667) and Greenwich (1675) with the prime purpose of developing astronomical methods of finding longitude. None the less, as the 18th century dawned no better method had come along and the increasing toll of lost ships and lives was causing growing concern. In a notorious accident in 1707, four Royal Navy ships, believing themselves to be in deeper water further east, were wrecked on the Scilly Isles with the loss of almost 2,000 lives.

Other ideas showed how desperate this problem had become. One proposal in 1713 would have stationed signal boats at 600-mile intervals across the Atlantic, delivering time signals in the form of exploding cannon shells.

Finally in 1714, under pressure from shipping and naval concerns, the British government set up a 'Board of Longitude' empowered to award a prize of £20,000 for a method of determining longitude at sea to a precision of half a degree.

The idea of a sea-going clock had been revived on several occasions since the 16th century, and Dutch astronomer Christiaan Huygens (1629–1695) had built and tested one in 1664. Yet no clock had been devised that could keep good time on a rolling ship through changes of temperature, barometric pressure and gravity while enduring the rigours of life at sea.

In 1735, a Lincolnshire clock-maker, John Harrison, presented his answer to the challenge. His sea-clock (known as H1) employed many novel features to ensure steady running and performed well in sea trials. Rather than claim the award, Harrison insisted on making an improved version, H2, which he delivered in 1741. An even better model, H3, was not completed until 1759, and in the intervening years another method was coming into contention.

The 'Board of Longitude' was dominated by astronomers who were hoping for a celestial rather than a mechanical solution. One such method, proposed as long ago as 1514, was to use the Moon as a clock. If the steadily shifting position of the Moon among the stars could be predicted, then precise measurements of its position should enable the time to be reckoned accurately enough for the determination of longitude. It was known as the lunar distance method. The problem was that the positions of the stars were poorly known, and sufficiently precise tables for the Moon's motion were not available.

While Harrison laboured on his clocks, these problems were gradually overcome. In 1725, former Astronomer Royal John Flamsteed's (1646–1719) catalogue of 3000 star positions was published and in 1757, cartographer Johann Tobias Mayer (1723–1762) of Nuremberg delivered accurate tables of the Moon's motion to the 'Board of Longitude'. Together with the recently invented sextant, navigators now had everything they needed to make use of the lunar distance method.

Shortly after completing H3, Harrison devised a dramatically different solution in the compact form of H4, an outsize pocket watch. H4 seemed to be the perfect solution to the longitude problem and performed exceedingly well in sea trials, losing only 5 s on its first transatlantic voyage in 1761. However, a leading advocate of the lunar distance method, astronomer Nevil Maskelyne (1732–1811), stalled the development of Harrison's clocks in the hope of gaining the award himself. In 1765, he became Astronomer Royal and took up his *ex officio* seat on the Board of Longitude. Under Maskelyne's influence, Harrison was denied his award for the next eight years while the Board prevaricated, demanding additional tests and the construction of more clocks.

Finally, in faltering health, Harrison appealed directly to King George III who intervened with the Board and ensured in 1773 that Harrison was given his just reward, three years before his death.

Between 1772 and 1779, James Cook (1728–1779) took several replicas of H4 on his voyages of discovery, and by the the turn of the century the 'marine chronometer' was in mass production by several clock-makers and had become a common sight on ocean-going ships.

radio transmitter and two to four secondary transmitters situated within 1,000–2,000 km/600–1,250 mi. Signals from the transmitters are detected by the ship or aircraft's navigation receiver, and slight differences (phase differences) between the master and secondary transmitter signals indicate the position of the receiver. The system is accurate to within 500 m/1,640 ft at a range of 2,000 km/1,250 mi, and covers the N Atlantic and N Pacific oceans, and adjacent areas such as the Mediterranean and Arabian Gulf.

The original Loran stem (Loran A) was used to guide bombers on night raids in Europe and N Africa in 1944.

lorikeet any of various small, brightly coloured parrots found in SE Asia and Australasia.

loris any of a group of small prosimian ◊primates native to S and SE Asia. Lorises are slow-moving, tree-dwelling, and nocturnal. They have very large eyes; true lorises have no tails. They climb without leaping, gripping branches tightly and moving on or hanging below them. (Family Lorisidae.)

The **slender loris** (*Loris tardigradus*) of S India and Sri Lanka is about 20 cm/8 in long. The tubbier **slow loris** (*Nycticebus coucang*) of SE Asia is 30 cm/1 ft.

The **angwantibo** (genus *Arctocebus*), **potto** (genus *Perodicticus*), and **galagos** or **bushbabies** (genera *Galago* and *Euoticus*) are similar African forms.

lory any of various small Australasian ◊parrots. Lories are very brightly coloured and characterized by a tongue with a brushlike tip adapted for feeding on pollen and nectar from flowers. (Subfamily Loriinae, order Psittaciformes.)

ANSWERS TO FREQUENTLY ASKED QUESTIONS ABOUT LORIES AND LORIKEETS

http://weber.u.washington.edu/~nyneve/loryFAQ.html

Comprehensive information on lories and lorikeets. Contents include a description of various breeds, their habitat, and efforts to conserve them. There is comprehensive advice on their housing and dietary requirements and photos of the most popular breeds. There is a bibliography of books about these parrots and a list of addresses of lori and parakeet clubs around the world.

Los Alamos town in New Mexico, USA, which has had a centre for atomic and space research since 1942. In World War II the first atom (nuclear fission) bomb was built there (under Robert ◊Oppenheimer); the ◊hydrogen bomb was also developed there.

lossless compression in computing, ◊data compression technique that reduces the number of ◊bits used to represent data in a file, thereby reducing its size while retaining all the original information. This makes it suitable for computer code and text files. Lossless compression typically achieves space savings of 30%.

lossy compression in computing, ◊data compression technique that dramatically reduces the size of a file by eliminating superfluous data. The lost information is either unnoticeable to the user, or can be recovered during decompression by extrapolation of the existing data. ◊JPEG and ◊MPEG are lossy methods that can reduce the size of graphics, audio, and video files by over 90%.

lotus any of several different plants, especially the **water lily** (*Nymphaea lotus*), frequent in Egyptian art, and the pink **Asiatic lotus** (*Nelumbo nucifera*), a sacred symbol in Hinduism and Buddhism, whose flower head floats erect above the water.

Others are those of the genus *Lotus* (family Leguminosae), including the **bird's foot trefoil** (*L. corniculatus*); the ◊jujube **shrub** (*Zizyphus lotus*), known to the ancient Greeks who used its fruit to make a type of bread and also a wine supposed to induce happy oblivion – hence **lotus-eaters**; and the **American lotus** (*Nelumbo lutea*), a pale yellow water lily of the southern USA.

LOTUS

The sacred lotus *Nelumbo nucifera* heats up when it is ready for pollination. For up to four days it maintains steamy temperatures of 30–35°C to attract insects and encourage them to move from one flower to another.

Lotus 1–2–3 ◊spreadsheet computer program, produced by Lotus Development Corporation. It first appeared in 1982 and its combination of spreadsheet, graphics display, and data management contributed to the rapid acceptance of the IBM Personal Computer in businesses.

Lotus Notes in computing, business software combining database and message facilities to help people in an organization to share information and work together. Notes is a very versatile ◊groupware program that can be customized to suit the needs of the organization.

loudness subjective judgement of the level or power of sound reaching the ear. The human ear cannot give an absolute value to the loudness of a single sound, but can only make comparisons between two different sounds. The precise measure of the power of a sound wave at a particular point is called its ◊intensity.

Accurate comparisons of sound levels may be made using sound-level meters, which are calibrated in units called ◊decibels.

loudspeaker electromechanical device that converts electrical signals into sound waves, which are radiated into the air. The most common type of loudspeaker is the **moving-coil speaker**. Electrical signals from, for example, a radio are fed to a coil of fine wire wound around the top of a cone. The coil is surrounded by a magnet. When signals pass through it, the coil becomes an electromagnet, which by moving causes the cone to vibrate, setting up sound waves.

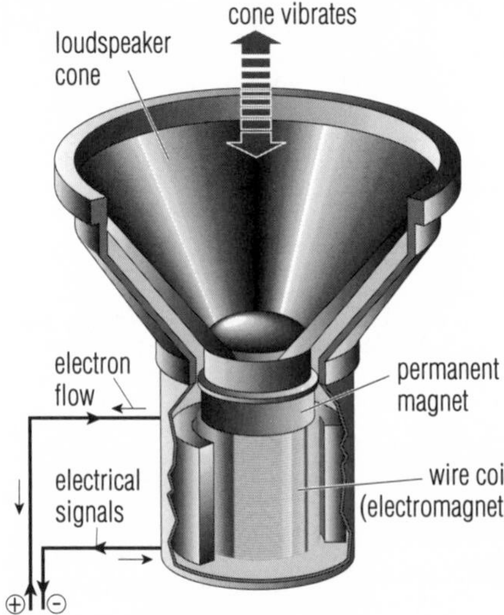

loudspeaker A moving-coil loudspeaker. Electrical signals flowing through the wire coil turn it into an electromagnet, which moves as the signals vary. The attached cone vibrates, producing sound waves.

louse parasitic insect that lives on mammals. It has a flat, segmented body without wings, and a tube attached to the head, used for sucking blood from its host. (Order Anoplura.)

Some lice occur on humans, including the **head louse** (*Pediculus capitis*) and the **body louse** (*P. corporis*), a typhus carrier. Pediculosis is a skin disease caused by infestation of lice. Most mammals have a species of lice adapted to living on them. Biting lice belong to a different order of insects (Mallophaga) and feed on the skin, feathers, or hair.

LOUSE

The human pubic (crab) louse, *Phthirus pubis*, lives on any coarse hair on the body, and may thus be found in eyebrows, beards, and armpits. It spends almost all its life attached to the same hair.

lovebird any of a group of birds belonging to the ◊parrot family, found in Africa south of the Sahara. They take their name from the affection the male displays towards the female. Lovebirds are generally just larger than sparrows (about 16 cm/6 in) and coloured green with red, yellow, and black markings on the head. (Genus *Agapornis,* family Psittacidae, order Psittaciformes.)

love-in-a-mist perennial plant of S Europe with fine leaves that create a soft haze around the delicate blue or white flowers; these are followed by large seedheads and, later, a profusion of new plants. (*Nigella damascena,* family Ranunculaceae.)

Lowell Observatory US astronomical observatory founded by Percival Lowell at Flagstaff, Arizona, with a 61-cm/24-in refractor opened in 1896. The observatory now operates other telescopes at a nearby site on Anderson Mesa including the 1.83-m/72-in Perkins reflector of Ohio State and Ohio Wesleyan universities.

lowest common denominator (lcd) the smallest number that is a multiple and thus divides exactly into each of the denominators of a set of fractions.

lowest common multiple (lcm) the smallest number that is a multiple of all of the numbers of a given set. See ◊lowest common denominator.

low-level language in computing, a programming language designed for a particular computer and reflecting its internal ◊machine code; low-level languages are therefore often described as **machine-oriented** languages. They cannot easily be converted to run on a computer with a different central processing unit, and they are relatively difficult to learn because a detailed knowledge of the internal working of the computer is required. Since they must be translated into machine code by an ◊assembler program, low-level languages are also called ◊assembly languages.

A mnemonic-based low-level language replaces binary machine-code instructions, which are very hard to remember, write down, or correct, with short codes chosen to remind the programmer of the instructions they represent. For example, the binary-code instruction that means 'store the contents of the accumulator' may be represented with the mnemonic STA.

In contrast, ◊high-level languages are designed to solve particular problems and are therefore described as **problem-oriented languages**.

LPG abbreviation for ***liquefied petroleum gas***.

LSD (abbreviation for ***lysergic acid diethylamide***) psychedelic drug, an ◊hallucinogen. Colourless, odourless, and easily synthesized, it is nonaddictive and nontoxic, but its effects are unpredictable. Its use is illegal in most countries.

The initials are from the German lyserg-säure-diäthylamid; the drug was first synthesized by a German chemist, Albert Hofmann, in 1943. In 1947 the US Central Intelligence Agency began experiments with LSD, often on unsuspecting victims. Many psychiatrists in North America used it in treatment in the 1950s. Its use as a means to increased awareness and enhanced perception was popularized in the 1960s by US psychologist Timothy Leary (1920–1997), novelist Ken Kesey, and chemist Augustus Owsley Stanley III. A series of laws to ban LSD were passed in the USA from 1965 (by which time 4 million Americans were estimated to have taken it) and in the UK in 1966; other countries followed suit. The drug had great influence on the hippie movement.

LSI (abbreviation for ***large-scale integration***) the technology that enables whole electrical circuits to be etched into a piece of semiconducting material just a few millimetres square.

By the late 1960s a complete computer processor could be integrated on a single chip, or ◊integrated circuit, and in 1971 the US electronics company Intel produced the first commercially available ◊microprocessor. Very large-scale integration (◊VLSI) results in even smaller chips.

lubricant substance used between moving surfaces to reduce friction. Carbon-based (organic) lubricants, commonly called grease and oil, are recovered from petroleum distillation.

Extensive research has been carried out on chemical additives to lubricants, which can reduce corrosive wear, prevent the accumulation of 'cold sludge' (often the result of stop-start driving in city traffic jams), keep pace with the higher working temperatures of aviation gas turbines, or provide radiation-resistant greases for nuclear power plants. Silicon-based spray-on lubricants are also used; they tend to attract dust and dirt less than carbon-based ones.

A solid lubricant is graphite, an allotropic form of carbon, either flaked or emulsified (colloidal) in water or oil.

lucerne another name for the plant ◊alfalfa.

lugworm any of a group of marine ◊annelid worms that grow up to 10 in/25 cm long. They are common burrowers between tidemarks and are useful for their cleansing and powdering of the beach sand, of which they may annually bring to the surface about 5,000 tonnes per hectare/2,000 tons per acre. (Genus *Arenicola.*)

lumbago pain in the lower region of the back, usually due to strain or faulty posture. If it occurs with ◊sciatica, it may be due to pressure on spinal nerves by a slipped disc. Treatment includes rest, application of heat, and skilled manipulation. Surgery may be needed in rare cases.

lumbar puncture or ***spinal tap*** insertion of a hollow needle between two lumbar (lower back) vertebrae to withdraw a sample of cerebrospinal fluid (CSF) for testing. Normally clear and colourless, the CSF acts as a fluid buffer around the brain and spinal cord. Changes in its quantity, colour, or composition may indicate neurological damage or disease.

lumen SI unit (symbol lm) of luminous flux (the amount of light passing through an area per second).

The lumen is defined in terms of the light falling on a unit area at a unit distance from a light source of luminous intensity of one ◊candela. One lumen at a wavelength of 5,550 angstroms equals 0.0014706 watts.

lumen in biology, the space enclosed by an organ, such as the bladder, or a tubular structure, such as the gastrointestinal tract.

luminescence emission of light from a body when its atoms are excited by means other than raising its temperature. Short-lived

Lumière

Auguste Marie Louis Nicolas (1862–1954) and Louis Jean (1864–1948) French brothers who pioneered cinematography. In February 1895 they patented their cinematograph, a combined camera and projector operating at 16 frames per second, screening short films for the first time on 22 March, and in December opening the world's first cinema in Paris. Among their first films were the simple documentaries *La Sortie des usines Lumière/Workers Leaving the Lumière Factory* 1895 and *L'Arrivée d'un train en gare de La Ciotat/The Arrival of a Train at Ciotat Station* 1895, and the comedy *L'Arroseur arrosé/The Hoser Hosed* 1895.

Between 1896 and 1900, the Lumiéres employed a number of camera operators to travel around the world and both demonstrate their invention and film new documentary shorts. Production was abandoned in 1900 after their films were displayed at the Paris Exposition. The brothers withdrew from filmmaking itself to concentrate on developing film technology and marketing their inventions.

Mary Evans Picture Library

luminescence is called fluorescence; longer-lived luminescence is called phosphorescence.

When exposed to an external source of energy, the outer electrons in atoms of a luminescent substance absorb energy and 'jump' to a higher energy level. When these electrons 'jump' back to their former level they emit their excess energy as light. Many different exciting mechanisms are possible: visible light or other forms of electromagnetic radiation (ultraviolet rays or X-rays), electron bombardment, chemical reactions, friction, and radioactivity. Certain living organisms produce bioluminescence.

luminosity or ***brightness*** in astronomy, the amount of light emitted by a star, measured in ◊magnitudes. The apparent brightness of an object decreases in proportion to the square of its distance from the observer. The luminosity of a star or other body can be expressed in relation to that of the Sun.

luminous paint preparation containing a mixture of pigment, oil, and a phosphorescent sulphide, usually calcium or barium. After exposure to light it appears luminous in the dark. The luminous paint used on watch faces contains radium, is radioactive and therefore does not require exposure to light.

lumpsucker marine bony fish so called from the frequent presence of a sucking disc formed from the united ventral fins. It is also distinguished by an absence of scales and the presence of spined plates along its side. Lumpsuckers feed mainly on small crustaceans and jellyfish.
classification The lumpsuckers belong to the genus *Cyclopterus,* family Cyclopteridae, order Scorpaeniformes, class Osteichthyes.

lung large cavity of the body, used for ◊gas exchange. It is essentially a sheet of thin, moist membrane that is folded so as to occupy less space. Most tetrapod (four-limbed) vertebrates have a pair of lungs occupying the thorax. The lung tissue, consisting of multitudes of air sacs and blood vessels, is very light and spongy, and functions by bringing inhaled air into close contact with the blood so that oxygen can pass into the organism and waste carbon dioxide can be passed out. The efficiency of lungs is enhanced by ◊breathing movements, by the thinness and moistness of their surfaces, and by a constant supply of circulating blood.

In humans, the principal diseases of the lungs are tuberculosis, pneumonia, bronchitis, emphysema, and cancer.

lungfish any of a group of fleshy-finned bony fishes found in South America, Australia, and Africa. They have elongated bodies,

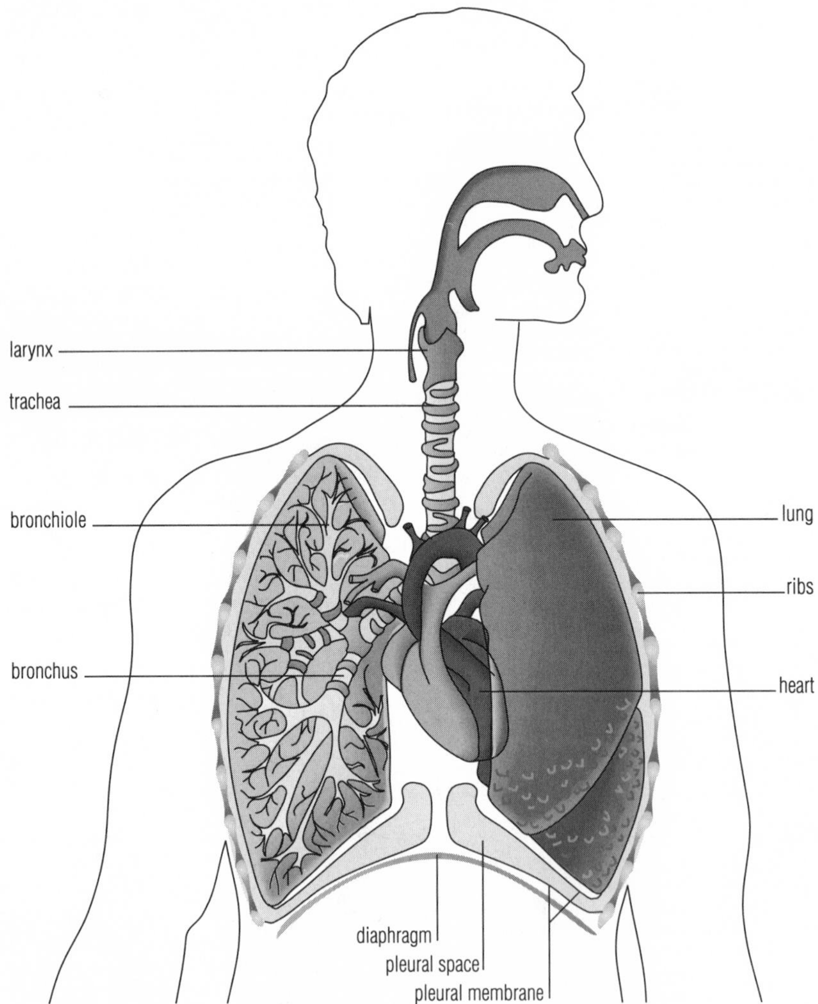

lung *The human lungs contain 300,000 million tiny blood vessels which would stretch for 2,400 km/1,500 mi if laid end to end. A healthy adult at rest breathes 12 times a minute; a baby breathes at twice this rate. Each breath brings 350 millilitres of fresh air into the lungs, and expels 150 millilitres of stale air from the nose and throat.*

and grow to about 2 m/6 ft, and in addition to gills have 'lungs' with which they can breathe air during periods of drought conditions. (Genera *Lepidosiren, Neoceratodus,* and *Protopterus,* subclass Dipnoi.)

Lungfish are related to the lobefins such as the ◊coelacanth, and were abundant 350 million years ago.

lupin any of a group of leguminous plants (see ◊legume) that comprises about 300 species. Lupins are native to Mediterranean regions and parts of North and South America, and some species are naturalized in Britain. Their spikes of pealike flowers may be white, yellow, blue, or pink. *L. albus* is cultivated in some places for cattle fodder and for green manuring; other varieties are cultivated in Europe as cottage garden plants. (Genus *Lupinus,* family Leguminosae.)

lupus in medicine, any of various diseases characterized by lesions of the skin. One form (lupus vulgaris) is caused by the tubercle bacillus (see ◊tuberculosis). The organism produces ulcers that spread and eat away the underlying tissues. Treatment is primarily with standard antituberculous drugs, but ultraviolet light may also be used.

Lupus erythematous (LE) has two forms: **discoid** LE, seen as red, scaly patches on the skin, especially the face; and **disseminated** or **systemic** LE, which may affect connective tissue anywhere in the body, often involving the internal organs. The latter is much more serious. Treatment is with ◊corticosteroids. LE is an ◊autoimmune disease.

lurcher British hunting dog of no established breed but of greyhound or deerhound type, often crossed with a collie. It was traditionally used by poachers to catch rabbits and hares, as it would hunt without drawing attention to itself by barking.

lurk in computing, to read a ◊USENET newsgroup without making a contribution. Before introducing themselves to the group, it is advisable for newcomers to lurk for a week or two in order to assess its members and their methods. That way, they can avoid posting an inappropriate message and attracting ◊flames.

luteinizing hormone ◊hormone produced by the pituitary gland. In males, it stimulates the testes to produce androgens (male sex hormones). In females, it works together with follicle-stimulating hormone to initiate production of egg cells by the ovary. If fertilization occurs, it plays a part in maintaining the pregnancy by controlling the levels of the hormones oestrogen and progesterone in the body.

lutetium *Latin Lutetia 'Paris'* silver-white, metallic element, the last of the ◊lanthanide series, symbol Lu, atomic number 71, relative atomic mass 174.97. It is used in the 'cracking', or breakdown, of petroleum and in other chemical processes. It was named by its discoverer, French chemist Georges Urbain, (1872–1938) after his native city.

lux SI unit (symbol lx) of illuminance or illumination (the light falling on an object). It is equivalent to one ◊lumen per square metre or to the illuminance of a surface one metre distant from a point source of one ◊candela.

LW abbreviation for ***long wave***, a radio wave with a wavelength of over 1,000 m/3,300 ft; one of the main wavebands into which radio frequency transmissions are divided.

lychee alternative spelling of ◊litchi, a fruit-bearing tree.

Lycos in computing, ◊search engine for the ◊World Wide Web. Lycos is a database compiled by Web ◊crawlers that comb the Internet for Web, ◊FTP and ◊Gopher sites, indexing them by title, headings, keywords, and text.

Lycos, named after a particularly voracious hunting spider, started as a research project at Carnegie Mellon University in Pittsburgh, USA, but became a commercial venture in 1995. By August 1996 Lycos had indexed over 60 million ◊URLs.

Lyddite British explosive used for filling artillery shells in World War I. Actually molten and cast picric acid, the name was adopted in order to conceal the nature of the substance and taken from the initial trials which were conducted at Lydd, in S England.

Lyell, Charles (1797–1875)

Scottish geologist. In his *Principles of Geology* 1830–33, he opposed the French anatomist Georges Cuvier's theory that the features of the Earth were formed by a series of catastrophes, and expounded the Scottish geologist James Hutton's view, known as uniformitarianism, that past events were brought about by the same processes that occur today – a view that influenced Charles Darwin's theory of evolution. Knighted 1848.

Lyell suggested that the Earth was as much as 240 million years old (in contrast to the 6,000 years of prevalent contemporary theory), and provided the first detailed description of the Tertiary period, dividing it into the Eocene, Miocene, and older and younger Pliocene periods. Darwin simply applied Lyell's geological method – explaining the past through what is observable in the present – to biology.

Mary Evans Picture Library

lymph fluid found in the lymphatic system of vertebrates.

Lymph is drained from the tissues by lymph capillaries, which empty into larger lymph vessels (lymphatics). These lead to lymph nodes (small, round bodies chiefly situated in the neck, armpit, groin, thorax, and abdomen), which process the ◊lymphocytes produced by the bone marrow, and filter out harmful substances and bacteria. From the lymph nodes, vessels carry the lymph to the thoracic duct and the right lymphatic duct, which drain into the large veins in the neck. Some vertebrates, such as amphibians, have a lymph heart, which pumps lymph through the lymph vessels.

lymph nodes small masses of lymphatic tissue in the body that occur at various points along the major lymphatic vessels. Tonsils and adenoids are large lymph nodes. As the lymph passes through them it is filtered, and bacteria and other microorganisms are engulfed by cells known as macrophages.

Lymph nodes are sometimes mistakenly called lymph 'glands', and the term 'swollen glands' refers to swelling of the lymph nodes caused by infection.

lymphocyte type of white blood cell with a large nucleus, produced in the bone marrow. Most occur in the ◊lymph and blood, and around sites of infection. **B lymphocytes** or ◊B cells are responsible for producing ◊antibodies. **T lymphocytes** or ◊T cells have several roles in the mechanism of ◊immunity.

lymphokines chemical messengers produced by lymphocytes that carry messages between the cells of the immune system (see ◊immunity). Examples include interferon, which initiates defensive reactions to viruses, and the interleukins, which activate specific ◊immune cells.

lynx wild cat found in rocky and forested regions of North America and Europe. About 1 m/3 ft in length, it has a short tail and tufted ears, and the long, silky fur is reddish brown or grey with dark spots. The North American **bobcat** or **bay lynx** (*Felix rufus*) looks similar but is smaller. Some zoologists place the lynx, the bobcat, and the ◊caracal in a separate genus, *Lynx.* (Species *Felis lynx,* family Felidae.)

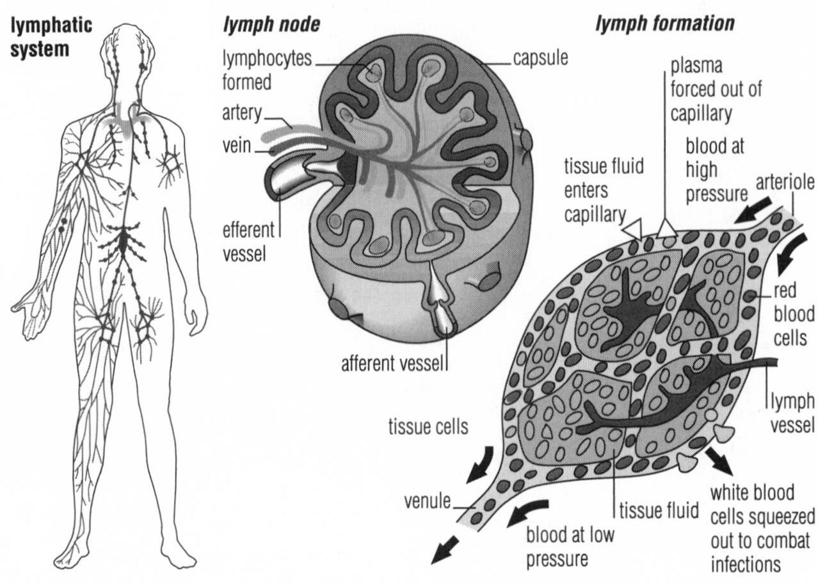

lymph Lymph is the fluid that carries nutrients and white blood cells to the tissues. Lymph enters the tissue from the capillaries (right) and is drained from the tissues by lymph vessels. The lymph vessels form a network (left) called the lymphatic system. At various points in the lymphatic system, lymph nodes (centre) filter and clean the lymph.

Lynx in computing, text-only Web browser for ◊UNIX computers.

lyophilization technical term for the ◊freeze-drying process used for foods and drugs and in the preservation of organic archaeological remains.

> *Progress in science depends on new techniques, new discoveries, and new ideas, probably in that order.*
>
> SYDNEY BRENNER South African-born British molecular biologist. *Nature* 1980

Lyra small but prominent constellation of the northern hemisphere, represented as the lyre of Orpheus. Its brightest star is ◊Vega.

Epsilon Lyrae is a system of four gravitationally linked stars. Beta Lyrae is an eclipsing binary. The Ring nebula, M57, is a ◊planetary nebula.

lyrebird either of two species of large birds found in SE Australia. They have very stout beaks and short, rounded wings; the tail has 16 feathers, and in the males the exterior pair of feathers are curved in the shape of a lyre; the tail of the female is long, broad, and normal in shape. Lyrebirds nest on the ground, and feed on insects, worms, and snails. (Genus *Menura,* family Menuridae, order Passeriformes.)

Lyrebirds live in the thick undergrowth, or sandy gullies of forests; they rarely fly, but run or strut with the tail spread horizontally. *M. superba* is 1 m/3 ft long, and of a brownish colour, with blue tinges; *M. alberti* is of a warmer, reddish colour.

lyretail African freshwater fish, 6 cm/2.4 in long, whose tail has two outward-curving fin supports for a central fin area which looks like the strings of a lyre. The male is bright blue with red markings; the less brightly coloured female has plainer fins. (Species *Aphyosemion australe.*)

Lyretails lay their eggs in mud at the bottom of swamps. In the event of a drought, the eggs usually survive in a dormant state and hatch with the next rainfall.

lysis in biology, any process that destroys a cell by rupturing its membrane or cell wall (see ◊lysosome).

lysosome membrane-enclosed structure, or organelle, inside a ◊cell, principally found in animal cells. Lysosomes contain enzymes that can break down proteins and other biological substances. They play a part in digestion, and in the white blood cells known as phagocytes the lysosome enzymes attack ingested bacteria.

m symbol for ◊metre.

MA abbreviation for ◊mechanical advantage.

McAdam, John Loudon
(1756–1836)

Scottish engineer, inventor of the macadam road surface. It originally consisted of broken granite bound together with slag or gravel, raised for drainage. Today, it is bound with tar or asphalt.

McAdam introduced a method of road building that raised the road above the surrounding terrain, compounding a surface of small stones bound with gravel on a firm base of large stones.

A camber, making the road slightly convex in section, ensured that rainwater rapidly drained off the road and did not penetrate the foundation. By the end of the 19th century, most of the main roads in Europe were built in this way.

Mary Evans Picture Library

macadamia edible nut of a group of trees native to Australia, especially *M. ternifolia*), and cultivated in Hawaii, South Africa, Zimbabwe, and Malawi. The nuts are slow-growing; they are harvested when they drop. (Genus *Macadamia*, family Proteaceae.)

macaque any of a group of medium-sized Old World monkeys. Various species live in forests from the Far East to N Africa. The ◊rhesus monkey and the ◊Barbary ape belong to this group. (Genus *Macaca*.)

Macaques range from long-tailed to tailless types, and have well-developed cheek pouches to carry food.

macaw any of a group of large, brilliantly coloured, long-tailed tropical American ◊parrots, such as the blue and yellow macaw *Ara ararauna*. They can be recognized by the massive beak, about half the size of the head, and by the extremely long tail. (Genera *Ara*, *Aratinga*, and *Anodorhynchus*.)

Every statement in physics has to state relations between observable quantities.

ERNST MACH Austrian physicist and philosopher.
Mach's Principle

Mach, Ernst
(1838–1916)

Austrian philosopher and physicist. He was an empiricist, believing that science is a record of facts perceived by the senses, and that acceptance of a scientific law depends solely on its standing the practical test of use; he opposed such concepts as Isaac GNewton's 'absolute motion'. GMach numbers are named after him.

McDonald Observatory observatory of the University of Texas on Mount Locke, Texas. It is the site of a 2.72-m/107-in reflector opened in 1969 and a 2.08-m/82-in reflector opened in 1939.

machine device that allows a small force (the effort) to overcome a larger one (the load). There are three basic machines: the inclined plane (ramp), the lever, and the wheel and axle. All other machines are combinations of these three basic types. Simple machines derived from the inclined plane include the wedge, the gear, and the screw; the spanner is derived from the lever; the pulley from the wheel.

The principal features of a machine are its ◊mechanical advantage, which is the ratio of load to effort, its ◊velocity ratio, and its ◊efficiency, which is the work done by the load divided by the work done by the effort; the latter is expressed as a percentage. In a perfect machine, with no friction, the efficiency would be 100%. All practical machines have efficiencies of less than 100%, otherwise perpetual motion would be possible.

One machine can do the work of fifty ordinary men. No machine can do the work of one extraordinary man.

ELBERT HUBBARD US writer.
A Thousand and One Epigrams

---

machine code in computing, a set of instructions that a computer's central processing unit (CPU) can understand and obey directly, without any translation. Each type of CPU has its own machine code. Because machine-code programs consist entirely of binary digits (bits), most programmers write their programs in an easy-to-use ◊high-level language. A high-level program must be translated into machine code – by means of a ◊compiler or ◊interpreter program – before it can be executed by a computer.

Where no suitable high-level language exists or where very efficient machine code is required, programmers may choose to write programs in a low-level, or assembly, language, which is eventually translated into machine code by means of an ◊assembler program.

Microprocessors (CPUs based on a single integrated circuit) may be classified according to the number of machine-code instructions that they are capable of obeying: ◊CISC (complex instruction set computer) microprocessors support up to 200 instructions, whereas ◊RISC (reduced instruction set computer) microprocessors support far fewer instructions but execute programs more rapidly.

machine-readable of data, readable directly by a computer without the need for retyping. The term is usually applied to files on disc or tape, but can also be applied to typed or printed text that can be scanned for ◊optical character recognition or ◊bar codes.

machine tool automatic or semi-automatic power-driven machine for cutting and shaping metals. Machine tools have powerful electric motors to force cutting tools into the metal: these are made from hardened steel containing heat-resistant metals such as tungsten and chromium. The use of precision machine tools in mass-production assembly methods ensures that all duplicate parts produced are virtually identical.

Many machine tools now work under computer control and are employed in factory ◊automation. The most common machine tool is the ◊lathe, which shapes shafts and similar objects. A milling machine cuts metal with a rotary toothed cutting wheel. Other machine tools cut, plane, grind, drill, and polish.

Mach number ratio of the speed of a body to the speed of sound in the undisturbed medium through which the body travels. Mach 1 is reached when a body (such as an aircraft) has a velocity greater than that of sound ('passes the sound barrier'), namely 331 m/1,087 ft per second at sea level. It is named after Austrian physicist Ernst Mach (1838–1916).

MACHO (abbreviation for ***massive astrophysical compact halo object***) component of the Galaxy's ◊dark matter. Most MACHOs are believed to be brown dwarfs, tiny failed stars with a mass of about 8% that of the Sun, but they may also include neutron stars left behind after supernova explosions. MACHOs are identifiable when they move in front of stars causing microlensing (magnification) of the star's light. Astronomers first identified MACHOs in 1993 and estimate that they account for 20% of the dark matter.

Macintosh range of microcomputers originally produced by Apple Computer. The Apple Macintosh, introduced 1984, was the first popular microcomputer with a ◊graphical user interface. The success of the Macintosh prompted other manufacturers and software companies to create their own graphical user interfaces. Most notable of these are Microsoft Windows, which runs on IBM PC-compatible microcomputers, and OSF/Motif, from the Open Software Foundation, which is used with many UNIX systems.

The success of PCs running Microsoft's Windows 3, launched in 1990, put pressure on Apple and the arrival of Windows 95 started Apple's decline. Apple's annual revenues peaked at $11.1 billion in 1995, and by 1997 had slumped to $7.1 billion. For comparison, Compaq, the market-leading PC supplier, increased its sales from $10.9 billion in 1995 to $18.1 billion in 1997. In 1997, however, Microsoft heavily invested in Apple.

mackerel any of various fish of the mackerel family, especially the **common mackerel** (*Scomber scombrus*) found in the N Atlantic and Mediterranean. It weighs about 0.7 kg/1.5 lb, and is blue with irregular black bands down its sides, the sides and under surface having a metallic sheen. Like all mackerels, it has a deeply forked tail, and a sleek, streamlined body form. (Family Scombroidia.)

The largest of the mackerels is the **tuna**, which weighs up to 700 kg/1,550 lb.

macro in computer programming, a new command created by combining a number of existing ones. For example, a word processing macro might create a letterhead or fax cover sheet, inserting words, fonts, and logos with a single keystroke or mouse click. Macros are also useful to automate computer communications – for example, users can write a macro to ask their computer to dial an **Internet Service Provider** (ISP), retrieve e-mail and ◊USENET articles, and then disconnect. A **macro key** on the keyboard combines the effects of pressing several individual keys.

macro- a prefix meaning on a very large scale, as opposed to micro.

macromolecule in chemistry, a very large molecule, generally a ◊polymer.

macrophage type of white ◊blood cell, or leucocyte, found in all vertebrate animals. Macrophages specialize in the removal of bacteria and other microorganisms, or of cell debris after injury. Like phagocytes, they engulf foreign matter, but they are larger than phagocytes and have a longer life span. They are found throughout the body, but mainly in the lymph and connective tissues, and especially the lungs, where they ingest dust, fibres, and other inhaled particles.

Macropodidae family of marsupials with large powerful hind feet, comprising all the ◊kangaroos.

Macrozamia genus of Australian ◊cycad with stiff, palm-like pinnate leaves. Macrozamias are an ancient group of plants and do not produce flowers; a pineapple-like seed cone develops from male and female cones which are on separate plants.

Madagascar teal or ***Bernier's teal*** a small duck apparently confined to a few small lakes and marshy areas in W Madagascar and now severely threatened with extinction. It is thought that there are at most a few hundred teal left alive and the opening of an airstrip nearby greatly increases the risk of sport shooting. (Species *Anas bernieri*.)

mad cow disease common name for ◊bovine spongiform encephalopathy, an incurable brain condition in cattle.

madder any of a group of plants bearing small funnel-shaped flowers, especially the perennial vine *R. tinctorum* which grows in Europe and Asia, the red root of which yields a red dye called alizarin (now made synthetically from coal tar). (Genus *Rubia*, family Rubiaceae.)

mafic rock plutonic rock composed chiefly of dark-coloured minerals containing abundant magnesium and iron, such as olivine and pyroxene. It is derived from **magnesium** and **ferric** (iron). The term **mafic** also applies to dark-coloured minerals rich in iron and magnesium as a group.

Magdalenian final cultural phase of the Palaeolithic (Old Stone Age) in W Europe, best known for its art, and lasting from c. 16,000–10,000 BC. It was named after the rock-shelter of La Madeleine in SW France.

Magellan NASA space probe to Venus, launched in May 1989; it went into orbit around ◊Venus Aug 1990 to make a detailed map of the planet by radar. It revealed volcanoes, meteorite craters, and fold mountains on the planet's surface. *Magellan* mapped 98% of Venus.

In Oct 1994 *Magellan* was instructed to self-destruct by entering the atmosphere around Venus where it burned up.

MAGELLAN MISSION TO VENUS

http://www.jpl.nasa.gov/magellan/

Details of the NASA Magellan project that sent a probe to Venus. It includes a full mission overview, technical details about the planet, many images, and an animated view of Venus.

Magellanic Clouds in astronomy, the two galaxies nearest to our own galaxy. They are irregularly shaped, and appear as detached parts of the ◊Milky Way, in the southern constellations ◊Dorado, Tucana, and Mensa.

The Large Magellanic Cloud spreads over the constellations of Dorado and Mensa. The Small Magellanic Cloud is in Tucana. The Large Magellanic Cloud is 169,000 light years from Earth, and about a third the diameter of our Galaxy; the Small Magellanic Cloud, 180,000 light years away, is about a fifth the diameter of our Galaxy. They are named after the navigator Ferdinand Magellan, who first described them.

maggot soft, plump, limbless ◊larva of flies, a typical example being the larva of the blowfly which is deposited as an egg on flesh.

MAGGOT

Wounds infested with maggots heal quickly and without spread of gangrene or other infection. This is because the maggots eat only the dead and suppurating flesh within a wound. This fact, first noted by World War I doctors in the trenches, is still used today in 'maggot therapy'.

magic bullet term sometimes used for a drug that is specifically targeted on certain cells or tissues in the body, such as a small collection of cancerous cells (see ◊cancer) or cells that have been invaded by a virus. Such drugs can be made in various ways, but ◊monoclonal antibodies are increasingly being used to direct the drug to a specific target.

The term was originally associated with the German chemist Paul Ehrlich (1854–1915) who discovered the first specific against ◊syphilis.

magic numbers in atomic physics certain numbers of ◊neutrons or ◊protons (2, 8, 20, 28, 50, 82, 126) in the nuclei of elements of outstanding stability, such as lead and helium.

Such stability is the result of neutrons and protons being arranged in completed 'layers' or 'shells'.

magic square in mathematics, a square array of numbers in which the rows, columns, and diagonals add up to the same total. A simple example employing the numbers 1 to 9, with a total of 15, has a first row of 6, 7, 2, a second row of 1, 5, 9, and a third row of 8, 3, 4.

maglev (acronym for ***magnetic levitation***) high-speed surface transport using the repellent force of superconductive magnets (◊see superconductivity) to propel and support, for example, a train above a track.

Technical trials on a maglev train track began in Japan in the 1970s, and a speed of 500 kph/310 mph has been reached, with a cruising altitude of 10 cm/4 in. The train is levitated by electromagnets and forward thrust is provided by linear motors aboard the cars, propelling the train along a reaction plate.

The German government approved a plan to build the world's first commercial maglev 1994. The Berlin–Hamburg line will cost DM8.9 billion (£3.5 billion). The three-hour journey time will be reduced by a third.

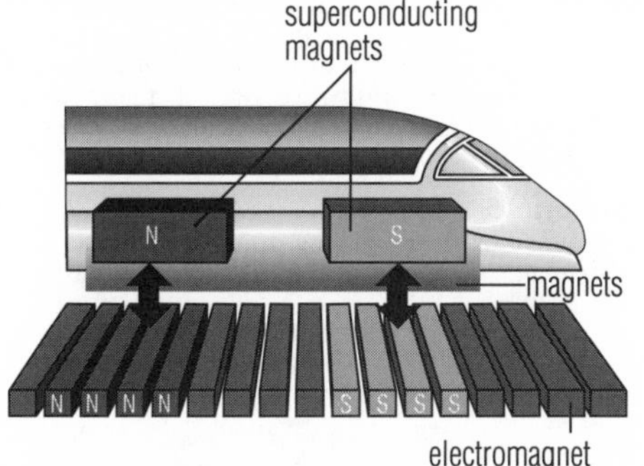

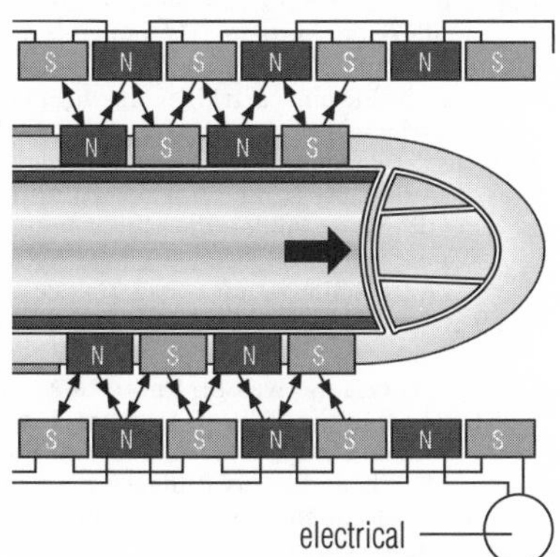

maglev The repulsion of superconducting magnets and electromagnets in the track keeps a maglev train suspended above the track. By varying the strength and polarity of the track electromagnets, the train can be driven forward.

magma molten rock material beneath the Earth's (or any of the terrestrial planets) surface from which ◊igneous rocks are formed. ◊Lava is magma that has extruded on to the surface.

magnesia common name for ◊magnesium oxide.

magnesium lightweight, very ductile and malleable, silver-white, metallic element, symbol Mg, atomic number 12, relative atomic mass 24.305. It is one of the alkaline-earth metals, and the lightest of the commonly used metals. Magnesium silicate, carbonate, and chloride are widely distributed in nature. The metal is used in alloys and flash photography. It is a necessary trace element in the human diet, and green plants cannot grow without it since it is an essential constituent of the photosynthetic pigment ◊chlorophyll ($C_{55}H_{72}MgN_4O_5$).

It was named after the ancient Greek city of Magnesia, near where it was first found. It was first recognized as an element by Scottish chemist Joseph Black 1755 and discovered in its oxide by English chemist Humphry Davy 1808. Pure magnesium was isolated 1828 by French chemist Antoine-Alexandre-Brutus Bussy.

magnesium oxide or ***magnesia*** MgO white powder or colourless crystals, formed when magnesium is burned in air or oxygen; a typical basic oxide. It is used to treat acidity of the stomach, and in some industrial processes; for example, as a lining brick in furnaces, because it is very stable when heated (refractory oxide).

magnet any object that forms a magnetic field (displays ◊magnetism), either permanently or temporarily through induction, causing it to attract materials such as iron, cobalt, nickel, and alloys of these. It always has ◊two magnetic poles, called north and south. The world's strongest magnet is at the Lawrence Berkeley National Laboratory in California. The magnet, which is a superconducting coil made of a niobium–tin alloy, has a field that is 250,000 times stronger than the Earth's magnetic field.

magnetic compass device for determining the direction of the horizontal component of the Earth's magnetic field. It consists of a magnetized needle with its north-seeking pole clearly indicated, pivoted so that it can turn freely in a plane parallel to the surface of the Earth (in a horizontal circle).

The needle will turn so that its north-seeking pole points towards the Earth's magnetic north pole. See also ◊compass.

Walkers, sailors, and other travellers use a magnetic compass to find their direction. The direction of the geographic, or true, North Pole is, however, slightly different from that of the magnetic north pole, and so the readings obtained from a compass of this sort must be adjusted using tables of magnetic corrections or information marked on local maps.

magnetic declination see ◊angle of declination.

magnetic dip see ◊dip, magnetic and ◊angle of dip.

magnetic dipole the pair of north and south magnetic poles, separated by a short distance, that makes up all magnets. Individual magnets are often called 'magnetic dipoles'. Single magnetic poles, or monopoles, have never been observed despite being searched for. See also magnetic ◊domain.

magnetic field region around a permanent magnet, or around a conductor carrying an electric current, in which a force acts on a moving charge or on a magnet placed in the field. The field can be represented by lines of force, which by convention link north and south poles and are parallel to the directions of a small compass needle placed on them. A magnetic field's magnitude and direction are given by the ◊magnetic flux density, expressed in ◊teslas. See also ◊polar reversal.

magnetic flux measurement of the strength of the magnetic field around electric currents and magnets. Its SI unit is the weber; one ◊weber per square metre is equal to one tesla.

The amount of magnetic flux through an area equals the product of the area and the magnetic field strength at a point within that area.

magnetic induction the production of magnetic properties in unmagnetized iron or other ferromagnetic material when it is brought close to a magnet. The material is influenced by the mag-

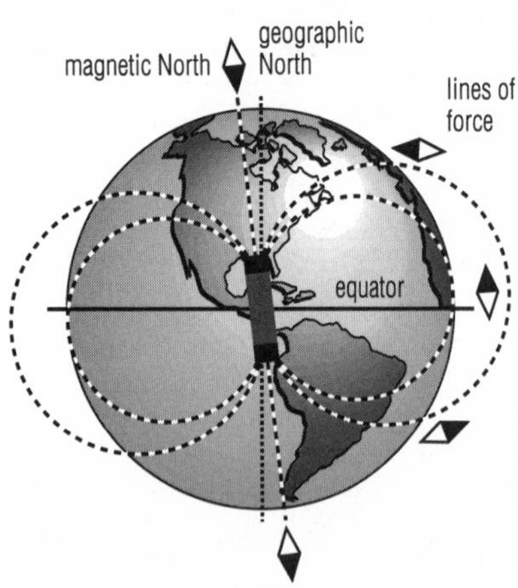

magnetic field The Earth's magnetic field is similar to that of a bar magnet with poles near, but not exactly at, the geographic poles. Compass needles align themselves with the magnetic field, which is horizontal near the equator and vertical at the magnetic poles.

net's magnetic field and the two are attracted. The induced magnetism may be temporary, disappearing as soon as the magnet is removed, or permanent depending on the nature of the iron and the strength of the magnet.

Electromagnets make use of temporary induced magnetism to lift sheets of steel: the magnetism induced in the steel by the approach of the electromagnet enables it to be picked up and transported. To release the sheet, the current supplying the electromagnet is temporarily switched off and the induced magnetism disappears.

magnetic-ink character recognition (MICR) in computing, a technique that enables special characters printed in magnetic ink to be read and input rapidly to a computer. MICR is used extensively in banking because magnetic-ink characters are difficult to forge and are therefore ideal for marking and identifying cheques.

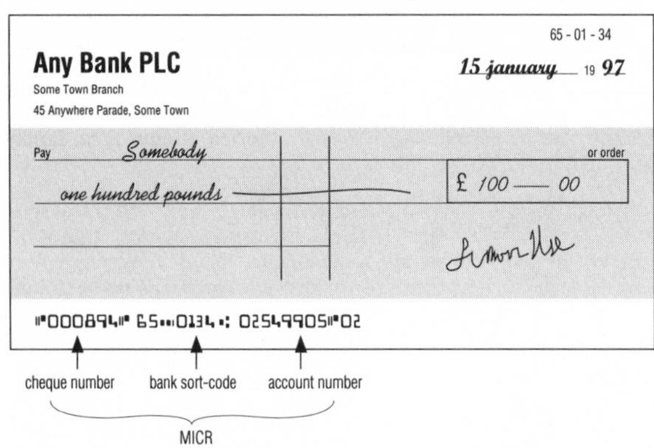

magnetic-ink character recognition An example of one of the uses of magnetic ink in automatic character recognition. Because of the difficulties in forging magnetic-ink characters, and the speed with which they can be read by computer systems, MICR is used extensively in banking.

magnetic material one of a number of substances that are strongly attracted by magnets and can be magnetized. These include iron, nickel, and cobalt, and all those ◊alloys that contain a proportion of these metals.

Soft magnetic materials can be magnetized very easily, but the magnetism induced in them (see ◊magnetic induction) is only temporary. They include Stalloy, an alloy of iron with 4% silicon used to make the cores of electromagnets and transformers, and the materials used to make 'iron' nails and paper clips.

Hard magnetic materials can be permanently magnetized by a strong magnetic field. Steel and special alloys such as Alcomax, Alnico, and Ticonal, which contain various amounts of aluminium, nickel, cobalt, and copper, are used to make permanent magnets. The strongest permanent magnets are ceramic, made under high pressure and at high temperature from powders of various metal oxides.

magnetic pole region of a magnet in which its magnetic properties are strongest. Every magnet has two poles, called north and south.

The north (or north-seeking) pole is so named because a freely suspended magnet will turn so that this pole points towards the Earth's magnetic north pole. The north pole of one magnet will be attracted to the south pole of another, but will be repelled by its north pole.

Unlike poles may therefore be said to attract, like poles to repel.

magnetic resonance imaging (MRI) diagnostic scanning system based on the principles of nuclear magnetic resonance. MRI yields finely detailed three-dimensional images of structures within the body without exposing the patient to harmful radiation. The technique is invaluable for imaging the soft tissues of the body, in particular the brain and the spinal cord.

Claimed as the biggest breakthrough in diagnostic imaging since the discovery of X-rays, MRI is a noninvasive technique based on a magnet which is many thousands of times stronger than the Earth's magnetic field. It causes nuclei within the atoms of the body to align themselves in one direction. When a brief radio pulse is beamed at the body the nuclei spin, emitting weak radio signals as they realign themselves to the magnet. These signals, which are characteristic for each type of tissue, are converted electronically into images on a viewing screen.

Also developed around magnetic technology, **magnetic resonance spectroscopy (MRS)** is a technique for investigating conditions in which there is a disturbance of the body's energy metabolism, including ischaemia and toxic damage due to drugs or other chemicals. MRS is also of value in diagnosing some cancers.

magnetic storm in meteorology, a sudden disturbance affecting the Earth's magnetic field, causing anomalies in radio transmissions and magnetic compasses. It is probably caused by ◊sunspot activity.

magnetic strip or ***magnetic stripe*** thin strip of magnetic material attached to a plastic card (such as a credit card) and used for recording data.

magnetic tape narrow plastic ribbon coated with an easily magnetizable material on which data can be recorded. It is used in sound recording, audiovisual systems (videotape), and computing. For mass storage on commercial mainframe computers, large reel-to-reel tapes are still used, but cartridges are becoming popular. Various types of cartridge are now standard on minis and PCs, while audio cassettes are sometimes used with home computers.

Magnetic tape was first used in **sound recording** in 1947, and made overdubbing possible, unlike the direct-to-disc system it replaced. Two-track tape was introduced in the 1950s and four-track in the early 1960s; today, studios use 16-, 24-, or 32-track tape, from which the tracks are mixed down to a stereo master tape.

In computing, magnetic tape was first used to record data and programs in 1951 as part of the UNIVAC 1 system. It was very popular as a storage medium for external memory in the 1950s and 1960s. Since then it has been largely replaced by magnetic ◊discs as a working medium, although tape is still used to make backup copies of important data. Information is recorded on the tape in binary form, with two different strengths of signal representing 1 and 0.

magnetism phenomena associated with ◊magnetic fields. Magnetic fields are produced by moving charged particles: in electromagnets, electrons flow through a coil of wire connected to a

battery; in permanent magnets, spinning electrons within the atoms generate the field.
susceptibility Substances differ in the extent to which they can be magnetized by an external field (susceptibility). Materials that can be strongly magnetized, such as iron, cobalt, and nickel, are said to be **ferromagnetic**; this is due to the formation of areas called ◊domains in which atoms, weakly magnetic because of their spinning electrons, align to form areas of strong magnetism. Magnetic materials lose their magnetism if heated to the ◊Curie temperature. Most other materials are **paramagnetic**, being only weakly pulled towards a strong magnet. This is because their atoms have a low level of magnetism and do not form domains. **Diamagnetic** materials are weakly repelled by a magnet since electrons within their atoms act as electromagnets and oppose the applied magnetic force. **Antiferromagnetic** materials have a very low susceptibility that increases with temperature; a similar phenomenon in materials such as ferrites is called **ferrimagnetism**.
application Apart from its universal application in dynamos, electric motors, and switch gears, magnetism is of considerable importance in advanced technology – for example, in particle ◊accelerators for nuclear research, memory stores for computers, tape recorders, and ◊cryogenics.

magnetite black, strongly magnetic opaque mineral, Fe_3O_4, of the spinel group, an important ore of iron. Widely distributed, magnetite is found in nearly all igneous and metamorphic rocks. Some deposits, called lodestone, are permanently magnetized. Lodestone has been used as a compass since the first millennium BC. Today the orientations of magnetite grains in rocks are used in the study of the Earth's magnetic field (see ◊palaeomagnetism).

Science can be introduced to children well or poorly. If poorly, children can be turned away from science; they can develop a lifelong antipathy; they will be in far worse condition than if they had never been introduced to science at all.

Isaac Asimov Russian-born US writer.

magneto simple electric generator, often used to provide the electricity for the ignition system of motorcycles and used in early cars.

It consists of a rotating magnet that sets up an electric current in a coil, providing the spark.

magnetohydrodynamics (MHD) field of science concerned with the behaviour of ionized gases or liquid in a magnetic field. Systems have been developed that use MHD to generate electrical power.

MND-driven ships have been tested in Japan. In 1991 two cylindrical thrusters with electrodes and niobium–titanium superconducting coils, soaked in liquid helium, were placed under the passenger boat *Yamato 1*. The boat, 30 m/100 ft long, was designed to travel at 8 knots. An electric current passed through the electrodes accelerates water through the thrusters, like air through a jet engine, propelling the boat forward.

magnetomotive force or ***magnetic potential*** the work done in carrying a unit magnetic pole around a magnetic circuit. The concept is analogous to ◊electromotive force in an electric circuit.

magnetosphere volume of space, surrounding a planet, controlled by the planet's magnetic field, and acting as a magnetic 'shell'. The Earth's magnetosphere extends 64,000 km/40,000 mi towards the Sun, but many times this distance on the side away from the Sun.

The extension away from the Sun is called the **magnetotail**. The outer edge of the magnetosphere is the **magnetopause**. Beyond this is a turbulent region, the **magnetosheath**, where the ◊solar wind is deflected around the magnetosphere. Inside the magnetosphere, atomic particles follow the Earth's lines of magnetic force. The magnetosphere contains the ◊Van Allen radiation belts. Other planets have magnetospheres, notably Jupiter.

magnetron thermionic ◊valve (electron tube) for generating very high-frequency oscillations, used in radar and to produce microwaves in a microwave oven. The flow of electrons from the tube's cathode to one or more anodes is controlled by an applied magnetic field.

magnification measure of the enlargement or reduction of an object in an imaging optical system. **Linear magnification** is the ratio of the size (height) of the image to that of the object.

Angular magnification is the ratio of the angle subtended at the observer's eye by the image to the angle subtended by the object when viewed directly.

magnifying glass the simplest optical instrument, a hand-held converging lens used to produce a magnified, erect and virtual image. The image, being virtual, or an illusion created by the ◊refraction of light rays in the lens, can only be seen by looking through the magnifying glass.

magnitude in astronomy, measure of the brightness of a star or other celestial object. The larger the number denoting the magnitude, the fainter the object. Zero or first magnitude indicates some of the brightest stars. Still brighter are those of negative magnitude, such as Sirius, whose magnitude is –1.46. **Apparent magnitude** is the brightness of an object as seen from Earth; **absolute magnitude** is the brightness at a standard distance of 10 parsecs (32.6 light years).

Each magnitude step is equal to a brightness difference of 2.512 times. Thus a star of magnitude 1 is $(2.512)^5$ or 100 times brighter than a sixth-magnitude star just visible to the naked eye. The apparent magnitude of the Sun is –26.8, its absolute magnitude +4.8.

magnitude size irrespective of sign, used especially for vectors irrespective of direction.

magnolia any of a group of trees or shrubs belonging to the magnolia family, native to North America and E Asia, and cultivated as ornamentals. Magnolias vary in height from 60 cm/2 ft to 30 m/150 ft. The large, fragrant single flowers are white, pink, or purple. The southern magnolia (*M. grandiflora*) of the USA grows up to 24 m/80 ft tall and has white flowers 23 cm/9 in across. (Genus *Magnolia*, family Magnoliaceae.)

Magnox early type of nuclear reactor used in the UK, for example in Calder Hall, the world's first commercial nuclear power station. This type of reactor uses uranium fuel encased in tubes of magnesium alloy called Magnox. Carbon dioxide gas is used as a coolant to extract heat from the reactor core. See also ◊nuclear energy.

magpie any of various birds belonging to the crow family. They feed on insects, snails, young birds, and carrion, and are found in Europe, Asia, N Africa, and W North America. (Genus *Pica*, family Corvidae, order Passeriformes.)

mahogany timber from any of several trees found in the Americas and Africa. Mahogany is a tropical hardwood obtained chiefly by rainforest logging. It has a warm red colour and can be highly polished. True mahogany comes mainly from *S. mahagoni* and *S. macrophylla*, but other types come from the Spanish and Australian cedars, the Indian redwood, and other trees of the mahogany family, native to Africa and the East Indies. (True mahogany genus *Swietenia*, family Meliaceae.)

S. mahagoni is under threat due to its popularity in the West for use in musical instruments, furniture, and veneers. There are attempts to make it the first hardwood tree listed under the CITES convention (the Convention on International Trade in Endangered Species).

maidenhair any of a group of ferns, especially *A. capillus-veneris*, with delicately hanging hairlike fronds ending in small kidney-shaped spore-bearing lobes. It is widely distributed in the Americas, and is sometimes found in the British Isles. (Genus *Adiantum*, family Polypodiaceae.)

maidenhair tree another name for the ◊ginkgo, a surviving member of an ancient group of plants.

mail-bombing or ***dumping*** in computing, sending large amounts of ◊e-mail to an individual or organization, usually in retaliation for a breach of ◊netiquette. The aim is to completely fill the recipient's ◊hard disc with immense, useless files, causing at best irritation, and at worst total computer failure. While mail-bombing often achieves its aim of annoying the individual concerned, it also inconveniences systems administrators and other users.

mailbox in computing, folder in which electronic mail is stored, typically divided into 'in' and 'out' trays. Users usually have two mailboxes: one on their PC, and another at their mail ◊server at the ◊Internet Service Provider (ISP), where incoming messages await collection.

mailbox name in an e-mail address, the name to the left of the @ sign, signifying the individual's mailbox for handling mail. All e-mail addresses appear in the form **mailbox name@** ◊domain **name**.

mail-enabled in computing, a piece of software that can generate ◊e-mail without launching a separate electronic mail program.

mailing list in computing, list of people who receive a given piece of ◊e-mail. Mailing lists are an easy way for people to share professional and technical information: hackers (see ◊hacking) often set up ad hoc mailing lists so that they can collaborate on a single piece of programming. It is also possible to join mailing lists devoted to special topics, social and leisure interests.

mail merge in computing, a feature offered by some word-processing packages that enables a list of personal details, such as names and addresses, to be combined with a general document outline to produce individualized documents.

For example, a club secretary might create a file containing a mailing list of the names and addresses of the club members. Whenever a letter is to be sent to all club members, a general letter outline is prepared with indications as to where individual names and addresses need to be added. The mail-merge feature then combines the file of names and addresses with the letter outline to produce and print individual letters addressed to each club member.

mail reflector in computing, an ◊e-mail address that acts as an ◊alias, redistributing all mail received to another address or to a ◊mailing list. Individuals use mail reflectors to hide their true identities or to forward messages following a change of e-mail address.

The same method can be used to address a particular group of people – for example, Bloggs College might create mail reflectors for all staff (**staff@bloggs.ac.uk**), for students (**students@bloggs.ac.uk**), former students (**alumni@bloggs.ac.uk**), and so on.

mail server software in client/server computing (see ◊client–server architecture), software that stores e-mail and distributes it only to the authorized recipient.

Maine Coon breed of domestic longhaired cat native to North America. It is the oldest American breed and one of the largest. Its fur is shaggy and uneven in length and of a coppery brown colour with black markings. It has a thick, bushy tail similar to the raccoon from which it gets its name.

The breed was registered in 1861, but was only officially recognized in the USA in 1976.

mainframe large computer used for commercial data processing and other large-scale operations. Because of the general increase in computing power, the differences between the mainframe, ◊supercomputer, minicomputer, and ◊microcomputer (personal computer) are becoming less marked.

Mainframe manufacturers include IBM, Amdahl, Fujitsu, and Hitachi. Typical mainframes have from 128 MB to 4 GB of memory and hundreds of gigabytes of disc storage.

mains electricity the domestic electricity-supply system. In the UK, electricity is supplied to houses, offices, and most factories as an ◊alternating current at a frequency of 50 hertz and a root-mean-square voltage of 230 volts. An advantage of having an alternating supply is that it may easily be changed, using a ◊transformer, to a lower and safer voltage, such as 9 volts, for operating toys and for recharging batteries.

main sequence in astronomy, the part of the ◊Hertzsprung–Russell diagram that contains most of the stars, including the Sun. It runs diagonally from the top left of the diagram to the lower right. The most massive (and hence brightest) stars are at the top left, with the least massive (coolest) stars at the bottom right.

maize (North American ***corn***) tall annual ◊cereal plant that produces spikes of yellow grains which are widely used as an animal feed. Grown extensively in all subtropical and warm temperate regions, its range has been extended to colder zones by hardy varieties developed in the 1960s. (*Zea mays*.)

Sweetcorn, a variety of maize in which the sugar is not converted to starch, is a familiar vegetable, known as corn on the cob; other varieties are made into hominy, polenta, popcorn, and corn bread. Sweetcorn is used in corn oil and fermented to make alcohol; its stalks are made into paper and hardboard.

It might seem unfair to reward a person for having so much pleasure over the years, asking the maize plant to solve specific problems and then watching its responses.

BARBARA MCCLINTOCK US geneticist.
On her lifelong research into the genetics
of the maize plant, *Newsweek* 24 Oct 1983

major arc the larger of the two arcs formed when a circle is divided into two unequal parts by a straight line or chord.

Majordomo in computing, ◊freeware mailing list processor for ◊UNIX systems.

mako large streamlined ◊shark.

malachite common ◊copper ore, basic copper carbonate, $Cu_2CO_3(OH)_2$. It is a source of green pigment and is used as an antifungal agent in fish farming, as well as being polished for use in jewellery, ornaments, and art objects.

malacology branch of zoology concerned with the study of ◊molluscs. It is distinguished from conchology, which is the study of mollusc shells only.

malamute breed of dog that takes its name from an Inuit people of Alaska. Stockily built and very hardy, it was prized as a sled dog. The malamute stands up to 63 cm/25 in tall, has a thick, bristly coat of grey or black with white markings, and carries its tail curved over its back.

It is similar in size, markings, and abilities to the Siberian ◊husky.

malaria infectious parasitic disease of the tropics transmitted by mosquitoes, marked by periodic fever and an enlarged spleen. When a female mosquito of the *Anopheles* genus bites a human who has malaria, it takes in with the human blood one of four malaria protozoa of the genus *Plasmodium*. This matures within the insect and is then transferred when the mosquito bites a new victim. Malaria affects about 267 million people in 103 countries, and in 1995 around 2.1 million people died of the disease. In sub-Saharan Africa alone between 1.5 and 2 million children die from malaria and its consequences each year.

infection Inside the human body the parasite settles first in the

FREQUENTLY ASKED QUESTIONS ABOUT MALARIA

http://www.outbreak.org/cgi-unreg/dynaserve.exe/Malaria/faq.html

Outbreak page covering frequently asked questions on malaria. The Web site contains answers to a comprehensive list of questions regarding the disease, including thorough descriptions of the virus and its related diseases.

liver, then multiplies to attack the red blood cells. Within the red blood cells the parasites multiply, eventually causing the cells to rupture and other cells to become infected. The cell rupture tends to be synchronized, occurring every 2–3 days, when the symptoms of malaria become evident.

In Brazil a malaria epidemic broke out among new settlers in the Amazon region, with 287,000 cases 1983 and 500,000 cases 1988. ***treatment*** ◊Quinine, the first drug used against malaria, has now been replaced by synthetics, such as chloroquine, used to prevent or treat the disease. However, chloroquine-resistant strains of the main malaria parasite, *Plasmodium fulciparum,* are spreading rapidly in many parts of the world.

The drug mefloquine (Lariam) is widely prescribed for use in areas where chloroquine-resistant malaria prevails. It is surrounded by controversy, however, as it has been linked to unpleasant side effects, including psychiatric disturbances such as anxiety and hallucinations, epileptic seizures, and memory loss.

Another drug, artemether, derived from the shrub wormwood, was found in 1996 trials to be as effective as quinine in the treatment of cerebral malaria.

An experimental malaria vaccine SPf66, developed by Colombian scientist Manuel Patarroyo, was trialled in 1994 in rural Tanzania, where villagers are bitten an average of 300 times a year by infected mosquitoes. It reduced the incidence of malaria by one third. However, further trials of SPf66 in the Gambia concluded in 1995 that the vaccine provided only 8% protection for young children. A further trial in Thailand in 1996 failed to provide any evidence of its effectiveness.

In 1993 research began into using chelating agents, which remove surplus iron from the blood, to treat malaria.

malic acid $HOOCCH_2CH(OH)COOH$ organic crystalline acid that can be extracted from apples, plums, cherries, grapes, and other fruits, but occurs in all living cells in smaller amounts, being one of the intermediates of the ◊Krebs cycle.

mallard common wild duck from which domestic ducks were bred, found almost worldwide. The male can grow to a length of 60 cm/2 ft and usually has a glossy green head, white collar, and chestnut brown breast with a pale grey body, while the female is mottled brown. Mallards are omnivorous dabbling ducks. (Species *Anas platyrhynchos,* subfamily Anatinae, order Anseriformes.)

mallee any of a group of small eucalyptus trees and shrubs with many small stems and thick underground roots that retain water. Before irrigation farming began, dense thickets of mallee characterized most of NW Victoria, Australia, known as the mallee region. (Genus *Eucalyptus,* family Myrtaceae.)

mallee fowl Australian bird *Leipoa ocellata,* family Megapodiidae. It is found in arid areas where the ◊mallee grows. Its young are born with feathers and are immediately independent, never needing any parental care. Mallee fowl grow to a length of around 60 cm/23 in.

The males have a unique method of incubating eggs by digging a pit in winter, then filling it with leaves and grass, and covering the resulting mound with sand. This compost heap then begins to rot and to generate heat. The female lays one egg every several days in a hole dug by the male, who then keeps the temperature at 33°C/91°F by testing the mound with his tongue, and adding or removing sand. When the chick hatches, it digs its way out.

mallow any flowering plant of the mallow family, including the European common mallow (*M. sylvestris*), the tree mallow (*L. arborea*), marsh mallow (*A. officinalis*), and hollyhock (*A. rosea*). Most mallows have pink or purple flowers. (Genera *Malva, Lavatera,* and *Althaea,* family Malvaceae.)

malnutrition condition resulting from a defective diet where certain important food nutrients (such as protein, vitamins, or carbohydrates) are absent. It can lead to deficiency diseases.

A related problem is ◊undernourishment. The World Health Organization estimated 1995 that one-third of the world's children are undernourished. According to UNICEF, in 1996 around 86 million children under the age of five (50% of all under-fives) in South Asia were malnourished, compared to 32 million (25%) in sub-Saharan Africa.

In a report released at the World Food Summit in Rome in 1996, the World Bank warned of an impending international food crisis. In 1996, more than 800 million people were unable to get enough food to meet their basic needs. Eighty-two countries, half of them in Africa, did not grow enough food for their own people; nor could they afford to import it. The World Bank calculated that food production would have to double over the next 30 years as the world population increases. Contrary to earlier predictions, food stocks and particularly grain stocks have fallen during the 1990s.

By 1996, 20 countries did not have enough water to meet people's needs, and water tables were falling in crucial regions such as the American Midwest, India, and China. Meanwhile, 90 million people are added to the planet's population every year. The increasingly prosperous and populous nations of East Asia are placing pressure on supplies; as people become wealthier they often eat more meat, which is a less efficient use of resources.

malt in brewing, grain (barley, oats, or wheat) artificially germinated and then dried in a kiln. Malts are fermented to make beers or lagers, or fermented and then distilled to produce spirits such as whisky.

maltase enzyme found in plants and animals that breaks down the disaccharide maltose into glucose.

Maltese-cross tube cathode-ray tube used to demonstrate some of the properties of cathode rays. The cathode rays, or electron streams, emitted by the tube's ◊electron gun are directed towards a fluorescent screen in front of which hangs a metal Maltese cross. Those electrons that hit the screen give up their kinetic energy and cause its phosphor coating to fluoresce. However, the sharply defined cross-shaped shadow cast on the screen shows that electrons are unable to pass through the Maltese cross. Cathode rays are thereby shown to travel in straight lines, and to be unable to pass through metal.

Maltese dog breed of long-coated lap dog. Its white coat is straight and silky and parted from head to tail and the short tail is doubled into the coat on the back. Maltese dogs have dark eyes, long drooping ears, and small feet. The ideal maximum height is 25 cm/10 in, and the weight is 3–4 kg/6.5–9 lb.

Maltese dogs are the most ancient lap-dog breed, their characteristics having been preserved for over 2,000 years.

maltose $C_{12}H_{22}O_{11}$ a ◊disaccharide sugar in which both monosaccharide units are glucose.

It is produced by the enzymic hydrolysis of starch and is a major constituent of malt, produced in the early stages of beer and whisky manufacture.

mamba either of two venomous snakes belonging to the cobra family, found in Africa south of the Sahara. Unlike cobras, they are not hooded. (Genus *Dendroaspis,* family Elapidae.)

The **green mamba** (*D. angusticeps*) is 1.5 m/5 ft long or more and lives in trees, feeding on birds and lizards. The **black mamba** (*D. polylepis*) is the largest venomous snake in Africa, occasionally as long as 3.4 m/11 ft, and spends more time on the ground.

mammal any of a large group of warm-blooded vertebrate animals characterized by having ◊mammary glands in the female; these are used for suckling the young. Other features of mammals are ◊hair (very reduced in some species, such as whales); a middle ear formed of three small bones (ossicles); a lower jaw consisting of two bones only; seven vertebrae in the neck; and no nucleus in the red blood cells. (Class Mammalia.)

Mammals are divided into three groups: **placental mammals,**

MAMMAL

Less than 3% of mammals are monogamous. Where monogamy is the norm, females usually synchronize their breeding as an extra precaution.

where the young develop inside the mother's body, in the ◊uterus, receiving nourishment from the blood of the mother via the ◊placenta; **marsupials**, where the young are born at an early stage of development and develop further in a pouch on the mother's body where they are attached to and fed from a nipple; and **monotremes**, where the young hatch from an egg outside the mother's body and are then nourished with milk.

The monotremes are the least evolved and have been largely displaced by more sophisticated marsupials and placentals, so that there are only a few types surviving (platypus and echidna). Placentals have spread to all parts of the globe, and where placentals have competed with marsupials, the placentals have in general displaced marsupial types. However, marsupials occupy many specialized niches in South America and, especially, Australasia.

According to the Red List of endangered species published by the World Conservation Union (IUCN) for 1996, 25% of mammal species are threatened with extinction.

The theory that marsupials succeed only where they do not compete with placentals was shaken 1992, when a tooth, 55 million years old and belonging to a placental mammal, was found in Murgon, Australia, indicating that placental animals appeared in Australia at the same time as the marsupials. The marsupials, however, still prevailed.

There are over 4,000 species of mammals, adapted to almost every way of life. The smallest shrew weighs only 2 g/0.07 oz, the largest whale up to 140 tonnes.

mammary gland in female mammals, a milk-producing gland derived from epithelial cells underlying the skin, active only after the production of young. In all but monotremes (egg-laying mammals), the mammary glands terminate in teats which aid infant suckling. The number of glands and their position vary between species. In humans there are 2, in cows 4, and in pigs between 10 and 14.

The hatched young of monotremes simply lick milk from a specialized area of skin on the mother's abdomen.

mammography X-ray procedure used to screen for breast cancer. It can detect abnormal growths at an early stage, before they can be seen or felt.

mammoth extinct elephant, remains of which have been found worldwide. Some were 50% taller than modern elephants; others were much samller. (Genus *Mammuthus* (or **Elephas**).)

The **woolly mammoth** (*M. primigenius*) of northern zones, the size of an Indian elephant, had long fur and large inward-curving tusks. Various species of mammoth were abundant in both the Old World and the New World in Pleistocene times, and were hunted by humans for food.

manakin any of a group of birds found in South and Central America, about 15 cm/6 in long and often brightly coloured. They feed on berries and other small fruits. The males of the genus *Manacus* clear a patch of the forest floor with a small tree as a display perch. (Family Pipridae, order Passeriformes.)

manatee any of a group of plant-eating aquatic mammals found in marine bays and sluggish rivers, usually in thick, muddy water. They have flippers as forelimbs, no hindlimbs, and a short rounded and flattened tail used for swimming. The marine manatees can grow up to about 4.5 m/15 ft long and weigh up to 600 kg/1,323 lb. (Genus *Trichechus,* family Trichechidae, order Sirenia.)

All three species of manatee are in danger of becoming extinct as a result of pollution and because they are hunted for food. They are the **Amazonian manatee** (*T. Inunguis*), found in the river Amazon; the **African manatee** (*T. Senegalensis*), which lives in the rivers and coastal areas of W Africa; and the **West Indian manatee** (*T. manatus*), which lives in the Caribbean Sea and along the east coasts of tropical North and South America. Only about 2,400 West Indian manatees remain in the main population around Florida; more than 200 died in 1996, poisoned by an algal toxin.

Manchester terrier breed of smooth-haired black-and-tan terrier. Manchester terriers have a long, wedge-shaped head, small dark eyes, and V-shaped ears, hanging close to the head. The usual weight is 8 kg/17.5 lb and the height 38–41 cm/15–16 in.

MANATEE FACTS

http://www.objectlinks.com/MANATEE/manfcts.htm

Information provided by the Save the Manatee Club of Florida, USA, describing the manatee and its habitat, behaviour, life span, and reproduction. Detailed information is also provided on conservation measures employed to protect the species.

The breed has a long neck tapering from the sloping shoulders to the head, and a narrow and deep chest. The legs are quite straight and the tail is thick where it joins the body, tapering to a point. The glossy coat should be jet black and rich mahogany tan on the head; the muzzle should be tanned to the nose, which, with the nasal bone, is jet black; the forelegs should be half tanned and the hind legs tanned on the inside, but not on the outside.

The earliest recognizable Manchester terrier is portrayed in an illuminated manuscript book of hours of the 15th century. It is generally accepted that the pure breed had its origin in and around Manchester, England.

mandarin type of small ◊orange.

mandragora or ***mandrake*** any of a group of almost stemless Old World plants with narcotic (pain-killing and sleep-inducing) properties, belonging to the nightshade family. They have large leaves, pale blue or violet flowers, and round berries known as devil's apples. (Genus *Mandragora,* family Solanaceae.)

The humanlike shape of the root of *M. officinarum* gave rise to the superstition that it shrieks when pulled from the ground.

mandrake another name for the plant ◊mandragora.

mandrill large W African forest-living baboon, active mainly on the ground. It has large canine teeth like the drill (*M. leucophaeus*), to which it is closely related. The nose is bright red and the cheeks are striped with blue; the thick skin of the buttocks is also red, and the fur is brown, apart from a yellow beard. (Species *Mandrillus sphinx.*)

Males are much larger than females, showing greater sexual dimorphism than any other primate. Males weigh up to 35 kg/77 lb and females usually less than 12 kg/26 lb. Females exhibit none of the bright coloration of the male. A single infant is born after 5 months' gestation; it is weaned at 6 months. Females reach sexual maturity at about three years; males at around ten years.

MANDRILL

The splendidly-coloured male mandrill is nearly three times heavier than his drab mate. No other primate exhibits such marked differences between the sexes. Females mature at about the age of three, whereas males may not reach maturity for ten years.

MANGABEYS

http://www.uni.edu/museum/cercopan/mangabey.html

Well-presented information on mangabeys from a conservation trust. Their life history, behaviour, and ecology is described, together with information about a conservation project in Nigeria. There are notes on the classification and distribution of the various subspecies.

mangabey any of a group of tropical African monkeys. The four species have long tails that can be used for support, although they are not fully prehensile (functional as additional limbs). They feed on shoots, leaves, fruit, and some animal food. (Genus *Cercocebus.*)

manganese hard, brittle, grey-white metallic element, symbol Mn, atomic number 25, relative atomic mass 54.9380. It resembles iron (and rusts), but it is not magnetic and is softer. It is used chiefly in making steel alloys, also alloys with aluminium and copper.

It is used in fertilizers, paints, and industrial chemicals. It is a necessary trace element in human nutrition. The name is old, deriving from the French and Italian forms of Latin for *magnesia* (MgO), the white tasteless powder used as an antacid from ancient times.

manganese ore any mineral from which manganese is produced. The main ores are the oxides, such as **pyrolusite**, MnO_2; **hausmannite**, Mn_3O_4; and **manganite**, MnO(OH).

Manganese ores may accumulate in metamorphic rocks or as sedimentary deposits, frequently forming nodules on the sea floor (since the 1970s many schemes have been put forward to harvest deep-sea manganese nodules). The world's main producers are Georgia, Ukraine, South Africa, Brazil, Gabon, and India.

manganese(IV) oxide or ***manganese dioxide*** MnO_2 brown solid that acts as a ◊depolarizer in dry batteries by oxidizing the hydrogen gas produced to water; without this process, the performance of the battery is impaired.

mangelwurzel or ***mangold*** variety of the common beet *Beta vulgaris* used chiefly as feed for cattle and sheep.

mango evergreen tree belonging to the cashew family, native to India but now widely cultivated for its large oval fruits in other tropical and subtropical areas, such as the West Indies. (*Mangifera indica,* family Anacardiaceae.)

mangold another name for ◊mangelwurzel.

mangrove any of several shrubs and trees, especially of the mangrove family, found in the muddy swamps of tropical and subtropical coastlines and estuaries. By sending down aerial roots from their branches, they rapidly form close-growing mangrove thickets. Their timber is resistant to water penetration and damage by marine worms. Mangrove swamps are rich breeding grounds for fish and shellfish, but these habitats are being destroyed in many countries. (Genera *Rhizophora* and *Avicennia,* families Rhizophoraceae (mangrove) and Avicenniaceae (related).)

mangrove swamp muddy swamp found on tropical coasts and estuaries, characterized by dense thickets of mangrove trees. These low trees are adapted to live in creeks of salt water and send down special breathing roots from their branches to take in oxygen from the air. The roots trap silt and mud, creating a firmer drier environment over time. Mangrove swamps are common in the Amazon delta and along the coasts of W Africa, N Australia, and Florida, USA.

manic depression or ***bipolar disorder*** mental disorder characterized by recurring periods of either ◊depression or mania (inappropriate elation, agitation, and rapid thought and speech) or both.

Sufferers may be genetically predisposed to the condition. Some cases have been improved by taking prescribed doses of ◊lithium.

manioc another name for the plant ◊cassava.

manometer instrument for measuring the pressure of liquids (including human blood pressure) or gases. In its basic form, it is a U-tube partly filled with coloured liquid. Greater pressure on the liquid surface in one arm will force the level of the liquid in the other arm to rise. A difference between the pressures in the two arms is therefore registered as a difference in the heights of the liquid in the arms.

manta another name for the ◊devil ray, a large fish.

mantis any of a group of carnivorous insects related to cockroaches. There are about 2,000 species of mantis, mainly tropical; some can reach a length of 20 cm/8 in. (Family Mantidae, order Dictyoptera.)

Mantises are often called 'praying mantises' because of the way they hold their front legs, adapted for grasping prey, when at rest. The eggs are laid in September and hatch early the following summer.

mantissa in mathematics, the decimal part of a ◊logarithm. For example, the logarithm of 347.6 is 2.5411; in this case, the 0.5411 is the mantissa, and the integral (whole number) part of the logarithm, the 2, is the ◊characteristic.

mantle intermediate zone of the Earth between the ◊crust and the core, accounting for 82% of Earth's volume. The boundary between the mantle and the crust above is the ◊Mohorovičić discontinuity, located at an average depth of 32 km/20 mi. The lower boundary with the core is the Gutenburg discontinuity at an average depth of 2,900 km/ 1813 mi.

The mantle is subdivided into **upper mantle**, **transition zone**, and **lower mantle**, based upon the different velocities with which seismic waves travel through these regions. The upper mantle includes a zone characterized by low velocities of seismic waves, called the **low velocity zone**, at 72 km/45 mi to 250 km/155 mi depth. This zone corresponds to the ◊aesthenosphere upon which Earth's tectonic plates of ◊lithosphere glide. Seismic velocities in the upper mantle are overall less than those in the transition zone and those of the transition zone are in turn less than those of the lower mantle. Faster propagation of seismic waves in the lower mantle implies that the lower mantle is more dense than the upper mantle.

The mantle is composed primarily of magnesium, silicon, and oxygen in the form of ◊silicate minerals. In the upper mantle, the silicon in silicate minerals, such as olivine, is surrounded by four oxygen atoms. Deeper in the transition zone greater pressures promote denser packing of oxygen such that some silicon is surrounded by six oxygen atoms, resulting in magnesium silicates with garnet and pyroxene structures. Deeper still, all silicon is surrounded by six oxygen atoms so that the new mineral $MgSiO_3$-perovskite predominates.

manufacturing industry or ***secondary industry*** industry that involves the processing of raw materials or the assembly of components. Examples are aluminium smelting, car assembly, and computer assembly. In the UK many traditional manufacturing industries, built up in the Industrial Revolution, are now declining in importance; for example, shipbuilding. Developing countries may lack the capital and expertise necessary for these industries.

Manx cat breed of domestic shorthaired cat originally bred in the Isle of Man, Britain. Its most distinctive feature is its nonexistent tail, the result of a natural mutation. The true Manx cat or 'rumpy' has a dimple at the base of the spine, while the variety with a residual tail or 'stumpy' is also recognized. The forelegs are short with longer hindlegs giving rise to the characteristic 'Manx hop', a rabbit-like gait. It has a strong, muscular body type. Most recognized colour combinations are permitted for the Manx.

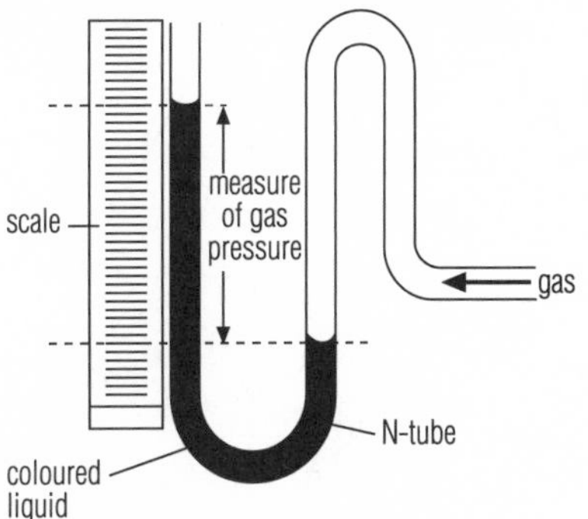

manometer *The manometer indicates gas pressure by the rise of liquid in the tube.*

map diagrammatic representation of an area – for example, part of the Earth's surface or the distribution of the stars. Modern maps of the Earth are made using satellites in low orbit to take a series of overlapping stereoscopic photographs from which a three-dimensional image can be prepared. The earliest accurate large-scale maps appeared about 1580.

Conventional aerial photography, laser beams, microwaves, and infrared equipment are also used for land surveying. Many different kinds of ◊map projection (the means by which a three-dimensional body is shown in two dimensions) are used in map-making. Detailed maps requiring constant updating are kept in digital form on computer so that minor revisions can be made without redrafting.

maple any of a group of deciduous trees with lobed leaves and green flowers, followed by two-winged fruits, or samaras. There are over 200 species, chiefly in northern temperate regions. (Genus *Acer*, family Aceraceae.)

map projection ways of depicting the spherical surface of the Earth on a flat piece of paper. Traditional projections include the **conic**, **azimuthal**, and **cylindrical**. The most famous cylindrical projection is the Mercator projection, which dates from 1569. The weakness of these systems is that countries in high latitudes are shown disproportionately large, and lines of longitude and latitude appear distorted.

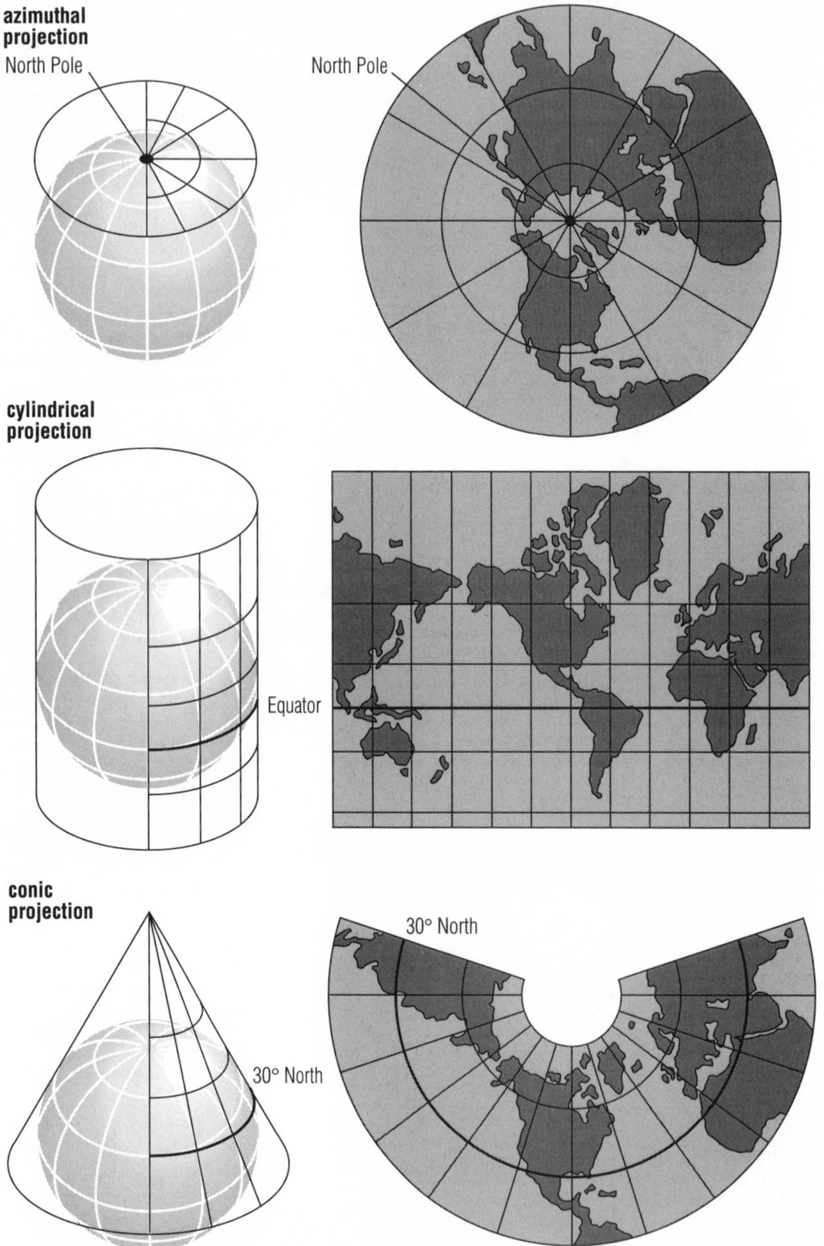

map projection *Three widely used map projections. If a light were placed at the centre of a transparent Earth, the shapes of the countries would be thrown as shadows on a sheet of paper. If the paper is flat, the azimuthal projection results; if it is wrapped around a cylinder or in the form of a cone, the cylindrical or conic projections result.*

In 1973 Germ.0an historian Arno Peters devised the **Peters projection** in which the countries of the world retain their relative areas. In 1992 the US physicist Mitchell Feigenbaum devised the **optimal conformal** projection, using a computer program designed to take data about the boundary of a given area and calculate the projection that produces the minimum of inaccuracies.

The theory behind traditional map projection is that, if a light were placed at the centre of a transparent Earth, the surface features could be thrown as shadows on a piece of paper close to the surface.

This paper may be flat and placed on a pole (azimuthal or zenithal), or may be rolled around the equator (cylindrical), or may be in the form of a tall cone resting on the equator (conical). The resulting maps differ from one another, distorting either area or direction, and each is suitable for a particular purpose. For example, projections distorting area the least are used for distribution maps, and those with least distortion of direction are used for navigation charts.

maquis general term for a largely evergreen type of vegetation common in many Mediterranean countries, consisting of scrub woodland with many low-growing tangled bushes and shrubs, typically including species of broom, gorse, and heather.

mara either of two species of rodents belonging to the guinea-pig family, found in Argentina, with long back limbs and a short tail. They can grow to 75 cm/2.5 ft long and are sometimes known as 'Patagonian cavies' or 'hares'. (Genus *Dolichotis,* family Caviidae.)

marabou African stork, about 120 cm/4 ft tall, with a bald head, long heavy bill, black back and wings and white underparts, and an inflatable throat pouch. It eats snakes, lizards, insects, and carrion. The bald head avoids blood clogging the plumage when the stork feeds on carcasses left by predators such as lions. (Species *Leptoptilos crumeniferus,* family Ciconiidae, order Ciconiiformes.)

marble rock formed by metamorphosis of sedimentary ◊limestone. It takes and retains a good polish, and is used in building and sculpture. In its pure form it is white and consists almost entirely of calcite $CaCO_3$. Mineral impurities give it various colours and patterns. Carrara, Italy, is known for white marble.

Marconi, Guglielmo (1874–1937)

Italian electrical engineer and pioneer in the invention and development of radio. In 1895 he achieved radio communication over more than a mile, and in England 1896 he conducted successful experiments that led to the formation of the company that became Marconi's Wireless Telegraph Company Ltd. He shared the Nobel Prize for Physics 1909.

After reading about radio waves, Marconi built a device to convert them into electrical signals. He then tried to transmit and receive radio waves over increasing distances. In 1898 he successfully transmitted signals across the English Channel, and in 1901 established communication with St John's, Newfoundland, from Poldhu in Cornwall, and in 1918 with Australia.

Mary Evans Picture Library

mare (plural ***maria***) dark lowland plain on the Moon. The name comes from Latin 'sea', because these areas were once wrongly thought to be water.

margay small wild cat living in forested areas from the southern USA to South America, where it hunts birds and small mammals. It is about 60 cm/2 ft long with a 40 cm/1.3 ft tail, and has a rounded head and yellowish-brown fur marked with black spots and blotches. (Species *Felis wiedi,* family Felidae.)

marginal land in farming, poor-quality land that is likely to yield a poor return. It is the last land to be brought into production and the first land to be abandoned. Examples are desert fringes in Africa and mountain areas in the UK.

marguerite European plant belonging to the daisy family. It is a shrubby perennial with white daisylike flowers. Marguerite is also the name of a cultivated variety of ◊chrysanthemum. (*Leucanthemum vulgare,* family Compositae.)

Mariana Trench lowest region on the Earth's surface; the deepest part of the sea floor. The trench is 2,400 km/1,500 mi long and is situated 300 km/200 mi E of the Mariana Islands, in the NW Pacific Ocean. Its deepest part is the gorge known as the Challenger Deep, which extends 11,034 m/36,210 ft below sea level.

marigold any of several plants belonging to the daisy family, including pot marigold (*C. officinalis*) and the tropical American *T. patula,* commonly known as French marigold. (Genera *Calendula* and *Tagetes,* family Compositae.)

marijuana dried leaves and flowers of the hemp plant ◊cannabis, used as a drug; it is illegal in most countries. Mexico is the world's largest producer.

Mariner spacecraft series of US space probes that explored the planets Mercury, Venus, and Mars 1962–75.

Mariner 1 (to Venus) had a failed launch. *Mariner 2* 1962 made the first fly-by of Venus, at 34,000 km/21,000 mi, confirmed the existence of ◊solar wind, and measured Venusian temperature. *Mariner 3* did not achieve its intended trajectory to Mars. *Mariner 4* 1965 passed Mars at a distance of 9,800 km/6,100 mi, and took photographs, revealing a dry, cratered surface. *Mariner 5* 1967 passed Venus at 4,000 km/2,500 mi, and measured Venusian temperature, atmosphere, mass, and diameter. *Mariner 6 and 7* 1969 photographed Mars' equator and southern hemisphere respectively, and also measured temperature, atmospheric pressure and composition, and diameter. *Mariner 8* (to Mars) had a failed launch. *Mariner 9* 1971 mapped the entire Martian surface, and photographed Mars' moons. Its photographs revealed the changing of the polar caps, and the extent of volcanism, canyons, and features, which suggested that there might once have been water on Mars. *Mariner 10* 1974–75 took close-up photographs of Mercury and Venus, and measured temperature, radiation, and magnetic fields.

marjoram aromatic herb belonging to the mint family. Wild marjoram (*O. vulgare*) is found both in Europe and Asia and has become naturalized in the Americas; the sweet marjoram (*O. majorana*) used in cooking is widely cultivated. (Genus *Origanum* or *Marjorana,* family Labiatae.)

market gardening farming system that specializes in the commercial growing of vegetables, fruit, or flowers. It is an intensive agriculture with crops often being grown inside greenhouses on small farms.

Market gardens may be located within easy access of markets, on the fringes of urban areas; for example, in the Home Counties for the London market. Such areas as the Channel Islands, where early crops can be grown outside because of a mild climate, are especially suitable.

markhor large wild goat with spirally twisted horns and a long shaggy coat. It is found in the Himalayas. (Species *Capra falconeri,* family Bovidae.)

Markov chain in statistics, an ordered sequence of discrete states (random variables) $x_1, x_2, ..., x_i, ..., x_n$ *such that the probability of* x_i *depends only on n* and/or the state x_{i-1} which has preceded it. If independent of *n,* the chain is said to be homogeneous.

mark sensing in computing, a technique that enables pencil marks made in predetermined positions on specially prepared forms to be rapidly read and input to a computer. The technique makes use of the fact that pencil marks contain graphite and therefore conduct electricity. A **mark sense reader** scans the form by passing small metal brushes over the paper surface. Whenever a brush touches a pencil mark a circuit is completed and the mark is detected.

marl crumbling sedimentary rock, sometimes called **clayey limestone**, including various types of calcareous ◊clays and fine-grained ◊limestones. Marls are often laid down in freshwater lakes and are usually soft, earthy, and of a white, grey, or brownish colour. They are used in cement-making and as fertilizer.

marlin or ***spearfish*** any of several open-sea fish known as billfishes. Some 2.5 m/7 ft long, they are found in warmer waters and have elongated snouts and high-standing dorsal (back) fins. Members of the family include the **sailfish** (*Istiophorus platypterus*), the fastest of all fishes over short distances – reaching speeds of 100 kph/62 mph – and the **blue marlin** (*Makaira nigricans*), highly prized as a 'game' fish. (Family Istiophoridae, order Perciformes.)

marlock medium-height tree, *Eucalyptus redunca*, with thick, narrow or elliptical leaves, horn-shaped buds, and mottled bark, found in SW Australia.

marmoset any of a group of small tree-dwelling monkeys found in South and Central America; some only reach a body length of 18 cm/7 in. Most species have characteristic tufted ears, clawlike nails, and a handsome tail, which is not prehensile (it cannot be used to grip branches in the same way as the arms and legs). Some marmosets are known as tamarins. (Genus *Callithrix* and related genera, family Callithricidae.)

Best-known is the **common marmoset** *C. jacchus* of Brazil, often kept there as a pet. The discovery of a new species of Brazilian marmoset, *C. saterei*, was announced in 1996. The black-capped dwarf marmoset was discovered in Brazil in 1997.

marmot any of several large burrowing rodents belonging to the squirrel family. There are about 15 species, distributed throughout Canada and the USA, and from the Alps to the Himalayas. They eat plants and some insects, and live in colonies, make burrows (one to each family), and hibernate in winter. In North America they are called **woodchucks** or **groundhogs**. (Genus *Marmota*, family Sciuridae.)

marram grass coarse perennial grass that flourishes in sandy areas. Because of its tough, creeping roots, it is widely used to hold coastal dunes in place. (*Ammophila arenaria*, family Gramineae.)

marri tree *Eucalyptus calophylla*, endemic to Western Australia, which, together with its hybrids with the flame gum *E. ficifolia*, is widely cultivated for its coloured flowers.

marrow or ***vegetable marrow*** trailing vine that produces large pulpy fruits, used as vegetables and in preserves; the young fruits of one variety are known as courgettes (US zucchini). (*Cucurbita pepo*, family Cucurbitaceae.)

Mars fourth planet from the Sun. It is much smaller than Venus or Earth, with a mass 0.11 that of Earth. Mars is slightly pear-shaped, with a low, level northern hemisphere, which is comparatively uncratered and geologically 'young', and a heavily cratered 'ancient' southern hemisphere.
mean distance from the Sun 227.9 million km/141.6 million mi
equatorial diameter 6,780 km/4,210 mi
rotation period 24 hr 37 min
year 687 Earth days
atmosphere 95% carbon dioxide, 3% nitrogen, 1.5% argon, and 0.15% oxygen. Red atmospheric dust from the surface whipped up by winds of up to 450 kph/280 mph accounts for the light pink sky. The surface pressure is less than 1% of the Earth's atmospheric pressure at sea level.
surface The landscape is a dusty, red, eroded lava plain. Mars has white polar caps (water ice and frozen carbon dioxide) that advance and retreat with the seasons.
satellites two small satellites: ◊Phobos and Deimos.

There are four enormous volcanoes near the equator, of which the largest is Olympus Mons 24 km/15 mi high, with a base 600 km/375 mi across, and a crater 65 km/40 mi wide. To the east of the four volcanoes lies a high plateau cut by a system of valleys, Valles Marineris, some 4,000 km/2,500 mi long, up to 200 km/120 mi wide and 6 km/4 mi deep; these features are apparently caused by faulting and wind erosion. Recorded temperatures vary from –100°C/–148°F to 0°C/32°F.

Mars may approach Earth to within 54.7 million km/34 million mi. The first human-made object to orbit another planet was *Mariner 9*. *Viking 1* and *Viking 2*, which landed, also provided much information. Studies in 1985 showed that enough water might exist to sustain prolonged missions by space crews.

In January 1997 NASA launched the *Mars Pathfinder*, which made a successful landing on Mars in July 1997 on a flood plain called Ares Vallis. After initial technical problems, its 0.3-m rover, Sojourner, began to explore the Martian landscape and to transmit data back to earth. Photographs from the *Mars Pathfinder* indicated that the planet is rusting. NASA announced this in July 1997 and said that a supercorrosive force was eroding rocks on the surface due to iron oxide in the soil.

In May 1997 American scientists announced that Mars is becoming increasingly colder and cloudier. Images from the Hubble Space Telescope showed that dust storms had covered areas of the planet that had been dark features in the early century, including one section as large as California.

The *Global Surveyor*, that entered Martian orbit in September 1997, revealed that Mars' magnetic field is a mere 800th that of the Earth.

MARS

http://www.hawastsoc.org/solar/eng/mars.htm

Detailed description of the planet Mars, commonly referred to as the Red Planet. It includes statistics and information about the surface, volcanoes, satellites, and clouds of the planet, supported by a good selection of images.

Mars Global Surveyor US spacecraft that went into orbit around ◊Mars on 12 September 1997 to conduct a detailed photographic survey of the planet commencing March 1998. The spacecraft used a previously untried technique called **aerobraking** to turn its initially highly elongated orbit into a 400 km/249 mi circular orbit by dipping into the outer atmosphere of the planet.

marsh low-lying wetland. Freshwater marshes are common wherever groundwater, surface springs, streams, or run-off cause frequent flooding or more or less permanent shallow water. A marsh is alkaline whereas a ◊bog is acid. Marshes develop on inorganic silt or clay soils. Rushes are typical marsh plants. Large marshes dominated by papyrus, cattail, and reeds, with standing water throughout the year, are commonly called◊ swamps. Near the sea, ◊salt marshes may form.

Marshall Space Flight Center NASA installation at Huntsville, Alabama, where the series of ◊Saturn rockets and the space-shuttle engines were developed. It also manages various payloads for the space shuttle, including the ◊Spacelab space station.

marsh gas gas consisting mostly of methane. It is produced in swamps and marshes by the action of bacteria on dead vegetation.

marsh marigold plant belonging to the buttercup family, known as the kingcup in the UK and as the cowslip in the USA. It grows in moist, sheltered places and has brilliant yellow five-sepalled flowers. (*Caltha palustris*, family Ranunculaceae.)

marsh rose shrub native to South Africa, which grows to 1–4 m/3–13 ft high. It is under threat, partly because its beautiful flowers are frequently picked, but also because of fungi, probably introduced by footwear or equipment, and by changes in management practice that have prevented periodic fires which are necessary for seed germination. Ironically, numbers of the shrub are now so low that uncontrolled fires could wipe out the remaining adult specimens. Although protected, they remain highly threatened. (*Orothamnus zeyheri.*)

Mars Observer NASA space probe launched in 1992 to orbit ◊Mars and survey the planet, its atmosphere, and the polar caps over two years. The probe was also scheduled to communicate information from the robot vehicles delivered by Russia's Mars 94 mission. The $1 billion project miscarried, however, when the probe unaccountably stopped transmitting in August 1993, three days before it was due to drop into orbit.

Mars Pathfinder US spacecraft that landed in the Ares Vallis region of Mars on 4 July 1997. It carried a small six-wheeled roving vehicle called **Sojourner** which examined rock and soil samples around the landing site. *Mars Pathfinder* was the first to use air bags instead of retro-rockets to cushion the landing

marsupial ***Greek marsupion 'little purse'*** mammal in which the female has a pouch where she carries her young (born tiny and immature) for a considerable time after birth. Marsupials include omnivorous, herbivorous, and carnivorous species, among them the kangaroo, wombat, opossum, phalanger, bandicoot, dasyure, and wallaby.

The Australian marsupial anteater known as the ◊numbat is an exception to the rule in that it has no pouch.

Marsupialia order of mammals consisting of the ◊marsupials.

marten small bushy-tailed carnivorous mammal belonging to the weasel family. Martens live in North America, Europe, and temperate regions of Asia, and are agile tree climbers. (Genus *Martes,* family Mustelidae.)

The **sable** (*M. zibellina*) lives in E Siberia, and provides the most valued fur. The largest marten is the **fisher** (*M. pennanti*) of North America, with black fur and reaching 125 cm/4 ft in length.

martin any of several species of birds belonging to the swallow family. (Family Hirundinidae, order Passeriformes.)

Martinsyde British aircraft manufacturer during World War I. Martinsyde began making monoplanes 1908 and after the outbreak of World War I produced several extremely good biplane scout-fighter aircraft for the Royal Flying Corps.

The F 4 Buzzard was a single-seat biplane powered by a 300 hp Hispano engine which had a top speed of 235 kph/145 mph, faster than any other single-seat aircraft of the period. The Buzzard was armed with two Vickers machine guns firing through the propeller arc.

maser (acronym for ***microwave amplification by stimulated emission of radiation***) in physics, a high-frequency microwave amplifier or oscillator in which the signal to be amplified is used to stimulate excited atoms into emitting energy at the same frequency. Atoms or molecules are raised to a higher energy level and then allowed to lose this energy by radiation emitted at a precise frequency. The principle has been extended to other parts of the electromagnetic spectrum as, for example, in the ◊laser.

The two-level ammonia-gas maser was first suggested in 1954 by US physicist Charles Townes at Columbia University, New York, and independently the same year by Nikolai Basov and Aleksandr Prokhorov in Russia. The solid-state three-level maser, the most sensitive amplifier known, was envisaged by Nicolaas Bloembergen (1920–) at Harvard in 1956. The ammonia maser is used as a frequency standard oscillator (see ◊clock), and the three-level maser as a receiver for satellite communications and radio astronomy.

mask in computing, restriction placed on the type of character that can be entered in a given field of a database or spreadsheet. For example, a 'dd-mm-yy' mask will only allow operators to enter a date in the field, and a field operating under a text mask will accept only letters, not numbers. See also ◊validation.

masochism desire to subject oneself to physical or mental pain, humiliation, or punishment, for erotic pleasure, to alleviate guilt, or out of destructive impulses turned inward. The term is derived from Leopold von Sacher-Masoch.

mass in physics, the quantity of matter in a body as measured by its inertia. Mass determines the acceleration produced in a body by a given force acting on it, the acceleration being inversely proportional to the mass of the body. The mass also determines the force exerted on a body by ◊gravity on Earth, although this attraction varies slightly from place to place. In the SI system, the base unit of mass is the kilogram.

At a given place, equal masses experience equal gravitational forces, which are known as the weights of the bodies. Masses may, therefore, be compared by comparing the weights of bodies at the same place.

The standard unit of mass to which all other masses are compared is a platinum-iridium cylinder of 1 kg, which is kept at the International Bureau of Weights and Measures in Sèvres, France.

mass action, law of in chemistry, a law stating that at a given temperature the rate at which a chemical reaction takes place is proportional to the product of the active masses of the reactants. The active mass is taken to be the molar concentration of the each reactant.

massage manipulation of the soft tissues of the body, the muscles, ligaments, and tendons, either to encourage the healing of specific injuries or to produce the general beneficial effects of relaxing muscular tension, stimulating blood circulation, and improving the tone and strength of the skin and muscles.

The benefits of massage were known to the ancient Chinese, Egyptian, and Greek cultures. The techniques most widely practised today were developed by the Swedish physician Per Henrik Ling (1776–1838).

> *A car can massage organs which no masseur can reach. It is the one remedy for the disorders of the great sympathetic nervous system.*
>
> JEAN COCTEAU French poet, dramatist, and film director. *Opium*

mass–energy equation Albert ◊Einstein's equation $E = mc^2$, denoting the equivalence of mass and energy, where E is the energy in joules, m is the mass in kilograms, and c is the speed of light, in a vacuum, in metres per second.

mass extinction an event that produces the extinction of many species at about the same time. One notable example is the boundary between the Cretaceous and Tertiary periods (known as the ◊K-T boundary) that saw the extinction of the dinosaurs and other big reptiles, and many of the marine invertebrates as well. Mass extinctions have taken place frequently during Earth's history.

The largest mass extinction occurred approximately 245 million years ago at the boundary between the Permian period of the Paleozoic era and the Triassic period of the Mesozoic era; 90% of all species became extinct.

mass number or ***nucleon number*** sum (symbol A) of the numbers of protons and neutrons in the nucleus of an atom. It is used along with the ◊atomic number (the number of protons) in ◊nuclear notation: in symbols that represent nuclear isotopes, such as ${}^{14}_{6}C$, the lower number is the atomic number, and the upper number is the mass number.

mass production manufacture of goods on a large scale, a technique that aims for low unit cost and high output. In factories mass production is achieved by a variety of means, such as division and specialization of labour and mechanization. These speed up production and allow the manufacture of near-identical, interchangeable parts. Such parts can then be assembled quickly into a finished product on an assembly line.

Division of labour means that a job is divided into a number of steps, and then groups of workers are employed to carry each step out, specializing and therefore doing the job in a routine way, producing more than if each individually had to carry out all the stages of manufacture. However, the system has been criticized for neglecting the skills of workers and removing their involvement with the end product.

Many of the machines now used in factories are robots (for example, on car-assembly lines): they work automatically under computer control. Such automation further streamlines production and raises output.

mass spectrometer in physics, an apparatus for analysing chemical composition. Positive ions (charged particles) of a substance are separated by an electromagnetic system, which permits accurate measurement of the relative concentrations of the various ionic masses present, particularly isotopes.

mastiff breed of powerful dog, usually fawn in colour, that was originally bred in Britain for hunting purposes. It has a large head, wide-set eyes, and broad muzzle. It can grow up to 90 cm/36 in at the shoulder, and weigh 100 kg/220 lb.

mastodon any of an extinct family of mammals belonging to the elephant order. They differed from elephants and mammoths in the structure of their grinding teeth. There were numerous species, among which the **American mastodon** (*Mastodon americanum*), about 3 m/10 ft high, of the Pleistocene era, is well known. They were hunted by humans for food. (Family Mastodontidae, order Proboscidae.)

matamata South American freshwater turtle or terrapin with a shell up to 40 cm/15 in long. The head is flattened, with a 'snorkel' nose, and the neck has many projections of skin. The movement of these in the water may attract prey, which the matamata catches by opening its mouth suddenly to produce an inrush of water. (Species *Chelys fimbriata.*)

match small strip of wood or paper, tipped with combustible material for producing fire. Friction matches containing phosphorus were first made in 1816 in France by François Derosne.

A **safety match** is one in which the oxidizing agent and the combustible body are kept apart, the former being incorporated into the striking surface on the side of the box, the latter into the match. Safety matches were patented by a Swede, J E Lundström in1855. Book matches were invented in the USA in 1892 by Joshua Pusey.

maté dried leaves of the Brazilian ◊holly (*Ilex paraguayensis*), an evergreen shrub that grows in Paraguay and Brazil. The roasted, powdered leaves are made into a tea. (Family Aquifoliaceae.)

mathematical induction formal method of proof in which the proposition $P(n + 1)$ is proved true on the hypothesis that the proposition $P(n)$ is true. The proposition is then shown to be true for a particular value of n, say k, and therefore by induction the proposition must be true for $n = k + 1, k + 2, k + 3, \dots$. In many cases $k = 1$, so then the proposition is true for all positive integers.

A theory with mathematical beauty is more likely to be correct than an ugly one that fits some experimental data. God is a mathematician of a very high order, and He used very advanced mathematics in constructing the universe.

PAUL DIRAC British physicist.
Scientific American May 1963

mathematics science of relationships between numbers, between spatial configurations, and abstract structures. The main divisions of **pure mathematics** include geometry, arithmetic, algebra, calculus, and trigonometry. Mechanics, statistics, numerical analysis, computing, the mathematical theories of astronomy, electricity, optics, thermodynamics, and atomic studies come under the heading of **applied mathematics**.

early history Prehistoric humans probably learned to count at least up to ten on their fingers. The ancient Egyptians (3rd millenium BC), Sumerians (2000–1500 BC), and Chinese (1500 BC) had systems for writing down numbers and could perform calculations using various types of ◊abacus. They used some fractions. Mathematicians in ancient Egypt could solve simple problems which involved finding a quantity that satisfied a given linear relationship. Sumerian mathematicians knew how to solve problems that involved quadratic equations. The fact that, in a right-angled triangle, the square of the longest side is equal to the sum of the squares of the other two sides (Pythagoras' theorem) was known in various forms in these cultures and also in Vedic India (1500 BC).

The first theoretical mathematician is held to be Thales of Miletus (c. 580 BC) who is believed to have proposed the first theorems in plane geometry. His disciple ◊Pythagoras established geometry as a recognized science among the Greeks. Pythagoras began to insist that mathematical statements must be proved using a logical chain of reasoning starting from acceptable assumptions. Undoubtedly the impetus for this demand for logical proof came from the discovery by this group of the surprising fact that the square root of 2 is a number which cannot be expressed as the ratio of two whole numbers. The use of logical reasoning, the methods of which were summarized by Aristotle, enabled Greek mathematicians to make general statements instead of merely solving individual problems as earlier mathematicians had done.

The spirit of Greek mathematics is typified in one of its most lasting achievements, the *Elements* by Euclid. This is a complete treatise on geometry in which the entire subject is logically deduced from a handful of simple assumptions. The ancient Greeks lacked a simple notation for numbers and nearly always relied on expressing problems geometrically. Although the Greeks were extremely successful with their geometrical methods they never developed a general theory of equations or any algebraic ideas of structure. However, they made considerable advances in techniques for solving particular kinds of equations and these techniques were summarized by Diophantus of Alexandria.

Medieval period When the Hellenic civilization declined, Greek mathematics (and the rest of Greek science) was kept alive by the Arabs, especially in the scientific academy at the court of the caliphs of Baghdad. The Arabs also learned of the considerable scientific achievements of the Indians, including the invention of a system of numerals (now called 'arabic' numerals) which could be used to write down calculations instead of having to resort to an abacus. One mathematician can be singled out as a bridge between the ancient and medieval worlds: al-Khwārizmī summarized Greek and Indian methods for solving equations and wrote the first treatise on the Indian numerals and calculating with them. Al-Khwarizmi's books and other Arabic works were translated into Latin and interest in mathematics in Western Europe began to increase in the 12th century. It was the demands of commerce which gave the major impetus to mathematical development and north Italy, the centre of trade at the time, produced a succession of important mathematicians beginning with Italian mathematician Leonardo Fibonacci who introduced Arabic numerals. The Italians made considerable advances in elementary arithmetic which was needed for money-changing and for the technique of double-entry bookkeeping invented in Venice. Italian mathematicians began to express equations in symbols instead of words. This algebraic notation made it possible to shift attention from solving individual equations to investigating the relationship between equations and their

MATHS PROBLEM OF THE MONTH

http://www.srl.rmit.edu.au/mav/PSTC/

Australian site, updated monthly, containing not just one, but several problems each month. They are each designed for different levels of difficulty. The main problems are divided into lower/middle primary, upper primary/lower secondary, and upper secondary levels. The site also includes a database of previous problems and a 'challenging problem of the month'. In other words, there is something to tease every level of mathematical brain.

Mathematics: chronology

BC

c. 2500 The people of Mesopotamia (now Iraq) developed a positional numbering (place-value) system, in which the value of a digit depends on its position in a number.

c. 2000 Mesopotamian mathematicians solved quadratic equations (algebraic equations in which the highest power of a variable is 2).

876 A symbol for zero was used for the first time, in India.

c. 550 Greek mathematician Pythagoras formulated a theorem relating the lengths of the sides of a right-angled triangle. The theorem was already known by earlier mathematicians in China, Mesopotamia, and Egypt.

c. 450 Hipparcos of Metapontum discovered that some numbers are irrational (cannot be expressed as the ratio of two integers).

300 Euclid laid out the laws of geometry in his book *Elements*, which was to remain a standard text for 2,000 years.

c. 230 Eratosthenes developed a method for finding all prime numbers.

c. 100 Chinese mathematicians began using negative numbers.

c. 190 Chinese mathematicians used powers of 10 to express magnitudes.

AD

c. 210 Diophantus of Alexandria wrote the first book on algebra.

c. 600 A decimal number system was developed in India.

829 Persian mathematician Muhammad ibn-M[umacr]s[amacr] al-Khwarizm[imacr] published a work on algebra that made use of the decimal number system.

1202 Italian mathematician Leonardo Fibonacci studied the sequence of numbers (1, 1, 2, 3, 5, 8, 13, 21, ...) in which each number is the sum of the two preceding ones.

1550 In Germany, Rheticus published trigonometrical tables that simplified calculations involving triangles.

1614 Scottish mathematician John Napier invented logarithms, which enable lengthy calculations involving multiplication and division to be carried out by addition and subtraction.

1623 Wilhelm Schickard invented the mechanical calculating machine.

1637 French mathematician and philosopher René Descartes introduced coordinate geometry.

1654 In France, Blaise Pascal and Pierre de Fermat developed probability theory.

1666 Isaac Newton developed differential calculus, a method of calculating rates of change.

1675 German mathematician Gottfried Wilhelm Leibniz introduced the modern notation for integral calculus, a method of calculating volumes.

1679 Leibniz introduced binary arithmetic, in which only two symbols are used to represent all numbers.

1684 Leibniz published the first account of differential calculus.

1718 Jakob Bernoulli in Switzerland published his work on the calculus of variations (the study of functions that are close to their minimum or maximum values).

1742 German mathematician Christian Goldbach conjectures that every even number greater than two can be written as the sum of two prime numbers. Goldbach's conjecture has still not been proven.

1746 In France, Jean le Rond d'Alembert developed the theory of complex numbers.

1747 D'Alembert used partial differential equations in mathematical physics.

1798 Norwegian mathematician Caspar Wessel introduced the vector representation of complex numbers.

1799 Karl Friedrich Gauss of Germany proved the fundamental theorem of algebra: the number of solutions of an algebraic equation is the same as the exponent of the highest term.

1810 In France, Jean Baptiste Joseph Fourier published his method of representing functions by a series of trigonometric functions.

1812 French mathematician Pierre Simon Laplace published the first complete account of probability theory.

1822 In the UK, Charles Babbage began construction of the first mechanical computer, the difference machine, a device for calculating logarithms and trigonometric functions.

1827 Gauss introduced differential geometry, in which small features of curves are described by analytical methods.

1829 In Russia, Nikolai Ivanovich Lobachevsky developed hyperbolic geometry, in which a plane is regarded as part of a hyperbolic surface, shaped like a saddle. In France, Evariste Galois introduced the theory of groups (collections whose members obey certain simple rules of addition and multiplication).

1844 French mathematician Joseph Liouville found the first transcendental number, which cannot be expressed as an algebraic equation with rational coefficients. In Germany, Hermann Grassmann studied vectors with more than three dimensions.

1854 George Boole in the UK published his system of symbolic logic, now called Boolean algebra.

1858 English mathematician Arthur Cayley developed calculations using ordered tables called matrices.

1865 August Ferdinand Möbius in Germany described how a strip of paper can have only one side and one edge.

1892 German mathematician Georg Cantor showed that there are different kinds of infinity and studied transfinite numbers.

1895 Jules Henri Poincaré published the first paper on topology, often called 'the geometry of rubber sheets'.

1931 In the USA, Austrian-born mathematician Kurt Gödel proved that any formal system strong enough to include the laws of arithmetic is either incomplete or inconsistent.

1937 English mathematician Alan Turing published the mathematical theory of computing.

1944 John Von Neumann and Oscar Morgenstern developed game theory in the USA.

1945 The first general purpose, fully electronic digital computer, ENIAC (electronic numerator, integrator, analyser, and computer), was built at the University of Pennsylvania, USA.

1961 Meteorologist Edward Lorenz at the Massachusetts Institute of Technology, USA, discovered a mathematical system with chaotic behaviour, leading to a new branch of mathematics – chaos theory.

1962 Benoit Mandelbrot in the USA invented fractal images, using a computer that repeats the same mathematical pattern over and over again.

1975 US mathematician Mitchell Feigenbaum discovered a new fundamental constant (approximately 4.669201609103), which plays an important role in chaos theory.

1980 Mathematicians worldwide completed the classification of all finite and simple groups, a task that took over a hundred mathematicians more than 35 years to complete and whose results took up more than 14,000 pages in mathematical journals.

1989 A team of US computer mathematicians at Amdahl Corporation, California, discovered the highest known prime number (it contains 65,087 digits).

1993 British mathematician Andrew Wiles published a 1,000-page proof of Fermat's last theorem, one of the most baffling challenges in pure mathematics.

1996 Wiles's proof was accepted after revision.

1997 The largest number to be fractorized to date has 167 digits: (3349–1)/2 was split into its 80- and 87-digit factors by a team of US mathematicians after 100,000 hours of computing.

solutions, and led eventually to the discovery of methods of solving cubic equations (about 1515) and quartic equations. They began to use the square roots of negative numbers (complex numbers) in their solutions to equations.

early modern period In the 17th century the focus of mathematical activity moved to France and Britain though continuing with the major themes of Italian mathematics: improvements in methods of calculation, development of algebraic symbolism, and the development of mathematical methods for use in physics and astronomy. Geometry was revitalized by the invention of coordinate geometry by René Descartes 1637; Blaise Pascal and Pierre de Fermat developed probability theory; John Napier invented logarithms; and Isaac Newton and Gottfried Leibniz invented calculus, later put on a more rigorous footing by Augustin Cauchy. In Russia, Nikolai Lobachevsky rejected Euclid's parallelism and developed a non-Euclidean geometry; this was subsequently generalized by Bernhard Riemann and later utilized by Einstein in his theory of relativity. In the mid-19th century a new major theme emerged: investigation of the logical foundations of mathematics. George Boole showed how logical arguments could be expressed in algebraic symbolism. Friedrich Frege and Giuseppe Peano considerably developed this symbolic logic.

the present In the 20th century, mathematics has become much more diversified. Each specialist subject is being studied in far greater depth and advanced work in some fields may be unintelligible to researchers in other fields. Mathematicians working in universities have had the economic freedom to pursue the subject for its own sake. Nevertheless, new branches of mathematics have been developed which are of great practical importance and which have basic ideas simple enough to be taught in secondary schools. Probably the most important of these is the mathematical theory of statistics in which much pioneering work was done by Karl Pearson. Another new development is operations research, which is concerned with finding optimum courses of action in practical situations, particularly in economics and management. As in the late medieval period, commerce began to emerge again as a major impetus for the development of mathematics.

Higher mathematics has a powerful tool in the high-speed electronic computer, which can create and manipulate mathematical 'models' of various systems in science, technology, and commerce.

Modern additions to school syllabuses such as sets, group theory, matrices, and graph theory are sometimes referred to as 'new' or 'modern' mathematics.

Et harum scientarum porta et clavis est Mathematica.
Mathematics is the door and the key to the sciences.

ROGER BACON English philosopher and scientist.
Opus Majus part 4 *Distinctia Prima*
cap 1, 1267 transl Robert Belle Burke, 1928

Mathilde rocky carbon-rich asteroid that is 53 km/33 mi in length. It is dominated by a huge 25-km/15.5 mi crater and its mass is one-millionth the mass of the Moon.

matrix in biology, usually refers to the ◊extracellular matrix.

matrix in mathematics, a square (n x n) or rectangular (m x n) array of elements (numbers or algebraic variables). They are a means of condensing information about mathematical systems and can be used for, among other things, solving simultaneous linear equations (see ◊simultaneous equations and ◊transformation).

Much early matrix theory was developed by the British mathematician Arthur Cayley, although the term was coined by his contemporary James Sylvester (1814–1897).

Matsushita Japanese electrical and electronics hardware company, the world's 12th-largest company in 1990 with annual revenues of $45 billion, controlling 87 companies in Japan and almost as many abroad, including film and record industries in the USA.

The company was founded in 1918 in Osaka by businessman Konosuke Matsushita (1894–1979).

Matsushita developed the VHS video format, which eventually conquered the market (though considered technically inferior to Sony's Betamax). Its electronics products are sold under the brand names National, Panasonic, Technics, and Quasar. Matsushita's US arm, the JVC corporation, earned over $6 billion in 1988. In 1989 Matsushita invested $100 million in a new Hollywood film studio, Largo, and in 1990 Matsushita bought MCA, the US entertainment conglomerate, for $6.5 billion; this includes MCA Records, Universal film and TV, the Putnam publishing group, music publishing, and theme park interests.

matter in physics, anything that has mass. All matter is made up of ◊atoms, which in turn are made up of ◊elementary particles; it exists ordinarily as a solid, liquid, or gas. The history of science and philosophy is largely taken up with accounts of theories of matter, ranging from the hard 'atoms' of Democritus to the 'waves' of modern quantum theory.

Mauna Kea astronomical observatory in Hawaii, USA, built on a dormant volcano at 4,200 m/13,784 ft above sea level. Because of its elevation high above clouds, atmospheric moisture, and artificial lighting, Mauna Kea is ideal for infrared astronomy. The first telescope on the site was installed in 1970.

Telescopes include the 2.24 m/88 in University of Hawaii reflector (1970). In 1979 three telescopes were erected: the 3.8 m/150 in United Kingdom Infrared Telescope (UKIRT) (also used for optical observations); the 3 m/120 in NASA Infrared Telescope Facility (IRTF); and the 3.6 m/142 in Canada–France–Hawaii Telescope (CFHT), designed for optical and infrared work. The 15 m/50 ft diameter UK/Netherlands James Clerk Maxwell Telescope (JCMT) is the world's largest telescope specifically designed to observe millimetre wave radiation from nebulae, stars, and galaxies. The JCMT is operated via satellite links by astronomers in Europe. The world's largest optical telescope, the ◊Keck Telescope, is also situated on Mauna Kea.

In 1996 the capacity of the JCMT was enhanced by the addition of SCUBA (Submillimetre Common-user Bolometer Array). SCUBA is a camera comprised of numerous detectors cooled to within a tenth of a degree of absolute zero (0 K) and is the world's most sensitive instrument at the 0.3–1.0 mm wavelength.

MAUNA KEA OBSERVATORIES

http://www.ifa.hawaii.edu/mko/mko.html

Official site of the renowned observatory. A clickable photo on the home page accesses information on the functions and findings of the group of telescopes atop Hawaii's highest peak. In addition to scientific data, there is information on access for visitors.

Maunder minimum in astronomy, the period 1645–1715 when ◊sunspots were rarely seen and no ◊aurorae ('northern lights') were recorded. The Maunder minimum coincided with a time of unusually low temperature on Earth, known as the Little Ice Age, and is often taken as evidence that changes in solar activity can affect Earth's climate. The Maunder minimum is named after the English astronomer E W Maunder, who drew attention to it.

maximum and minimum in ◊coordinate geometry, points at which the slope of a curve representing a ◊function changes from positive to negative (maximum), or from negative to positive (minimum). A tangent to the curve at a maximum or minimum has zero gradient.

Maxima and minima can be found by differentiating the function for the curve and setting the differential to zero (the value of the slope at the turning point). For example, differentiating the function for the parabola $y = 2x^2 - 8x$ gives $dy/dx = 4x - 8$. Setting this equal to zero gives $x = 2$, so that $y = -8$ (found by substituting $x = 2$ into the ◊parabola equation). Thus the function has a minimum at the point (2, –8).

maxwell c.g.s. unit (symbol Mx) of magnetic flux (the strength of a ◊magnetic field in an area multiplied by the area). It is now replaced by the SI unit, the ◊weber (one maxwell equals 10^{-8} weber).

The maxwell is a very small unit. It is equal to the flux through one square centimetre normal to a magnetic field with an intensity of one gauss.

Maxwell, James Clerk (1831–1879)

Scottish physicist. His main achievement was in the understanding of electromagnetic waves: Maxwell's equations bring together electricity, magnetism, and light in one set of relations. He studied gases, optics, and the sensation of colour, and his theoretical work in magnetism prepared the way for wireless telegraphy and telephony.

In developing the kinetic theory of gases, Maxwell gave the final proof that heat resides in the motion of molecules.

Studying colour vision, Maxwell explained how all colours could be built up from mixtures of the primary colours red, green, and blue. Maxwell confirmed English physicist Thomas Young's theory that the eye has three kinds of receptors sensitive to the primary colours, and showed that colour blindness is due to defects in the receptors. In 1861 he produced the first colour photograph to use a three-colour process.

Maxwell–Boltzmann distribution in physics, a statistical equation describing the distribution of velocities among the molecules of a gas. It is named after James Maxwell and Ludwig Boltzmann, who derived the equation, independently of each other, in the 1860s.

One form of the distribution is $n = Nexp(-E/RT)$, where N is the total number of molecules, n is the number of molecules with energy in excess of E, T is the absolute temperature (temperature in kelvin), R is the ◊gas constant, and *exp* is the exponential function.

Maxwell's screw rule in physics, a rule formulated by Scottish physicist James Maxwell that predicts the direction of the magnetic field produced around a wire carrying electric current. It states that if a right-handed screw is turned so that it moves forwards in the same direction as the conventional current, its direction of rotation will give the direction of the magnetic field.

mayfly any of a group of insects whose adult form lives only very briefly in the spring. The larval stage, which can last a year or more, is passed in water, the adult form developing gradually from the nymph through successive moults. The adult has transparent, net-veined wings. (Order Ephemerida.)

mayweed any of several species of the daisy family native to Europe and Asia and naturalized elsewhere, including the European dog fennel or stinking daisy (*Anthemis cotula*), naturalized in North America, and the pineapple mayweed (*Matricaria matricarioides*), found in Europe and Asia. All have finely divided leaves. (Family Compositae.)

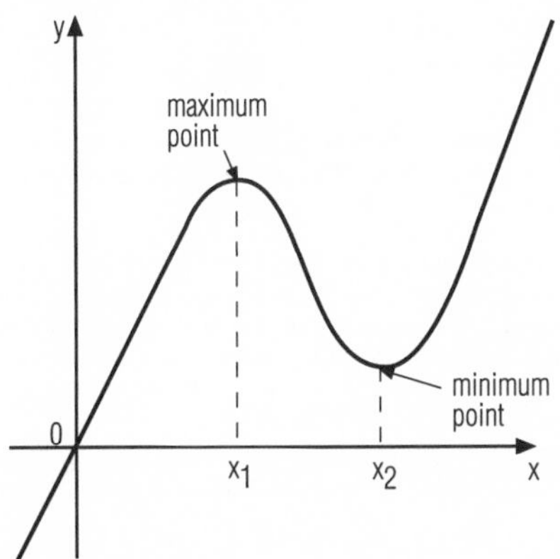

maximum and minimum *A maximum point on a curve is higher than the points immediately on either side of it; it is not necessarily the highest point on the curve. Similarly, a minimum point is lower than the points immediately on either side.*

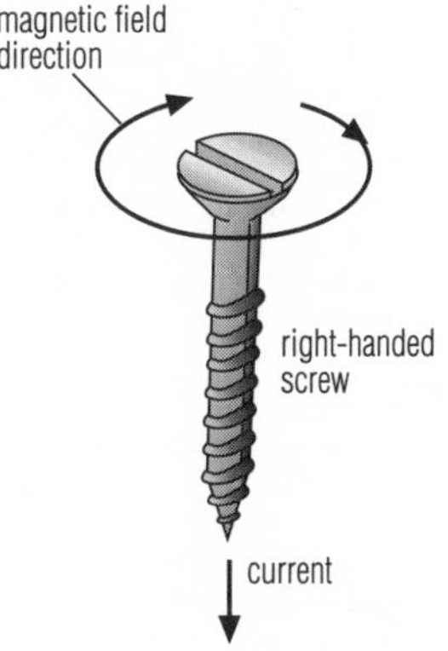

Maxwell's screw rule *Maxwell's screw rule, named after the physicist James Maxwell, predicts the direction of the magnetic field produced around a wire carrying electric current. If a right-handed screw is turned so that it moves forward in the same direction as the current, its direction of rotation will give the direction of the magnetic field.*

MBONE (contraction of ***multicast backbone***) in computing, layer of the Internet designed to deliver ◊packets of multimedia data, enabling video and audio communication. It can be used for telephony and video-conferencing – however, it can deliver a maximum of only five video frames per second, as opposed to television's 30. Large rock concerts are occasionally broadcast on the MBONE.

McDonnell Douglas US aircraft manufacturer that produces fighter planes and the DC-10 airbus. It was formed in 1967 in a merger. Douglas, founded in 1920 by Donald W Douglas (1892–1981), was known for its DC (Douglas Commercial) planes from the 1930s; McDonnell, founded in 1939 by James S McDonnell (1899–1980), was the first company to make jet-propelled planes to operate from aircraft carriers. The company's headquarters are in St Louis, Missouri. It came second place in the world number of planes ordered 1995.

The company announced in 1996 that it would merge with Boeing aircraft manufacturers and would operate under the ◊Boeing name.

MCI in computing, US-based long distance telecommunications company, active in Net communications since the 1980s, when it ran the backbone for the National Science Foundation's ◊NSFnet. In 1996 MCI announced Concert Internet Plus, a joint venture with British Telecom aiming to provide a single network spanning the globe.

MDMA (3,4-methylenedio-xymethamphetamine) psychedelic drug, also known as ◊ecstasy.

ME abbreviation for ***myalgic encephalomyelitis***, a popular name for ◊chronic fatigue syndrome.

meal-worm any larva of the beetle genus *Tenebrio*, especially *T. molitor*. Meal-worms are slender and round, about 2.5 cm/1 in long, and tawny with bright rusty bands. They are pests of stored grain.

The adult of *T. molitor* is black, measures about 1.3 cm/0.5 in in length, has stout legs, and antennae with 11 joints,

classification Meal-worms are in genus *Tenebrio* of the family Tenebrionidae, class Insecta, phylum Arthropoda.

mealy bug kind of ◊scale insect.

mean in mathematics, a measure of the average of a number of terms or quantities. The simple **arithmetic mean** is the average value of the quantities, that is, the sum of the quantities divided by their number. The **weighted mean** takes into account the frequency of the terms that are summed; it is calculated by multiplying each term by the number of times it occurs, summing the results and dividing this total by the total number of occurrences. The **geometric mean** of *n* quantities is the *n*

th root of their product. In statistics, it is a measure of central tendency of a set of data.

meander loop-shaped curve in a river flowing across flat country. As a river flows, any curve in its course is accentuated by the current. The current is fastest on the outside of the curve where it cuts into the bank; on the curve's inside the current is slow and deposits any transported material. In this way the river changes its course across the flood plain.

A loop in a river's flow may become so accentuated that it becomes cut off from the normal course and forms an ◊oxbow lake. The word comes from the river Menderes in Turkey.

mean deviation in statistics, a measure of the spread of a population from the ◊mean.

mean free path in physics, the average distance travelled by a particle, atom, or molecule between successive collisions. It is of importance in the ◊kinetic theory of gases.

mean life in nuclear physics, the average lifetime of a nucleus of a radioactive isotope equal to 1.44 times the ◊half-life. See ◊radioactivity.

measles acute virus disease (rubeola), spread by airborne infection.

Symptoms are fever, severe catarrh, small spots inside the mouth, and a raised, blotchy red rash appearing for about a week after two weeks' incubation. Prevention is by vaccination.

In industrialized countries it is not usually a serious disease, though serious complications may develop. More than 1 million children a year die of measles (1995); a high percentage of them are Third World children. The North and South American Indians died by the thousands in epidemics of the 17th, 18th, and 19th centuries.

CHILDHOOD INFECTIONS – MEASLES

http://kidshealth.org/parent/common/measles.html

Educational page on measles, providing information on the signs, symptoms and progress of the disease. It also addresses issues such as possible complications, vaccination, home treatment, and contagiousness.

mechanical advantage (MA) in physics, the number of times the load moved by a machine is greater than the effort applied to that machine. In equation terms: MA = load/effort.

The exact value of a working machine's MA is always less than its predicted value because there will always be some frictional resistance that increases the effort necessary to do the work.

TO REMEMBER THE DEFINITION OF MECHANICAL ADVANTAGE:

MEN ALWAYS LIKE EATING.

MA - LOAD OVER EFFORT (L/E)

mechanical equivalent of heat in physics, a constant factor relating the calorie (the c.g.s. unit of heat) to the joule (the unit of mechanical energy), equal to 4.1868 joules per calorie. It is redundant in the SI system of units, which measures heat and all forms of energy in ◊joules (so that the mechanical equivalent of heat is 1).

mechanics branch of physics dealing with the motions of bodies and the forces causing these motions, and also with the forces acting on bodies in ◊equilibrium. It is usually divided into ◊dynamics and ◊statics.

Quantum mechanics is the system based on the ◊quantum theory, which has superseded Newtonian mechanics in the interpretation of physical phenomena on the atomic scale.

mechanization the use of machines in place of manual labour or the use of animals. Until the 1700s there were few machines available to help people in the home, on the land, or in industry. There were no factories, only cottage industries, in which people carried out work, such as weaving, in their own homes for other people. The 1700s saw a long series of inventions, initially in the textile industry, that ushered in a machine age and brought about the Industrial Revolution.

Among the first inventions in the textile industry were those made by John Kay (flying shuttle, 1773), James Hargreaves (spinning jenny, 1764), and Richard Arkwright (water frame, 1769). Arkwright pioneered the mechanized factory system by installing many of his spinning machines in one building and employing people to work them.

media (singular ***medium***) in computing, the collective name for materials on which data can be recorded. For example, paper is a medium that can be used to record printed data; a floppy disc is a medium for recording magnetic data.

median in mathematics and statistics, the middle number of an ordered group of numbers. If there is no middle number (because there is an even number of terms), the median is the ◊mean (average) of the two middle numbers. For example, the median of the group 2, 3, 7, 11, 12 is 7; that of 3, 4, 7, 9, 11, 13 is 8 (the average of 7 and 9).

In geometry, the term refers to a line from the vertex of a triangle to the midpoint of the opposite side.

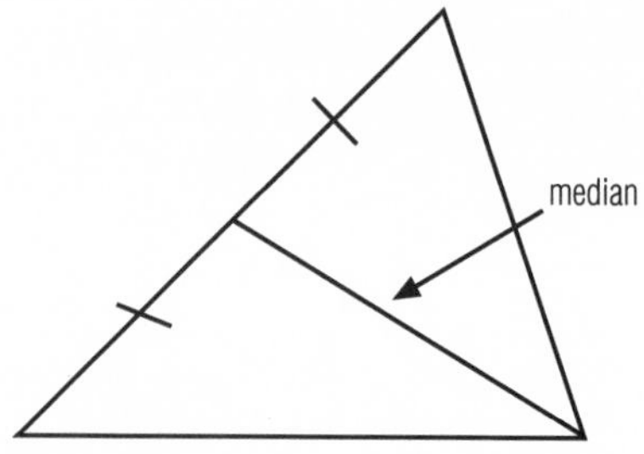

median *The median is the name given to a line from the vertex (corner) of a triangle to the mid-point of the opposite side.*

medical ethics moral guidelines for doctors governing good professional conduct. The basic aims are considered to be doing good, avoiding harm, preserving the patient's autonomy, telling the truth, and pursuing justice. Ethical issues provoke the most discussion in medicine where these five aims cannot be simultaneously achieved

MEDICINENET

http://www.medicinenet.com/

Immense US-based site dealing with all current aspects of medicine in plain language. There is a dictionary of diseases, cures, and medical terms. The site also includes an 'ask the experts' section, lots of current medical news, and last, but not least, some important first aid advice.

– for example, what is 'good' for a child may clash with his or her autonomy or that of the parents.

Traditionally these principles have been set out in the Hippocratic Oath (introduced by Greek physician ◊Hippocrates and including such injunctions as the command to preserve confidentiality, to help the sick to the best of one's ability, and to refuse fatal draughts), but in the late 20th century rapidly advancing technology has raised the question of how far medicine should intervene in natural processes.

MEDICINE

King Charles II of England died five days after medical treatment that was intended to cure him. He was bled, his scalp was cauterized (burned with a hot iron), and he was given an emetic, a rectal purge and numerous draughts and concoctions to drink.

medicine the practice of preventing, diagnosing, and treating disease, both physical and mental; also any substance used in the treatment of disease. The basis of medicine is anatomy (the structure and form of the body) and physiology (the study of the body's functions).

In the West, medicine increasingly relies on new drugs and sophisticated surgical techniques, while diagnosis of disease is more and more by noninvasive procedures. The time and cost of Western-type medical training makes it inaccessible to many parts of the Third World; where health care of this kind is provided it is often by auxiliary medical helpers trained in hygiene and the administration of a limited number of standard drugs for the prevalent diseases of a particular region.

One of the first duties of the physician is to educate the masses not to take medicine.

William Osler Canadian physician.
Aphorisms from his Bedside Teachings

medicine, alternative forms of medical treatment that do not use synthetic drugs or surgery in response to the symptoms of a disease, but aim to treat the patient as a whole (◊holism). The emphasis is on maintaining health (with diet and exercise) and on dealing with the underlying causes rather than just the symptoms of illness. It may involve the use of herbal remedies and techniques like ◊acupuncture, homeopathy, and ◊chiropractic. Some alternative treatments are increasingly accepted by orthodox medicine, but the absence of enforceable standards in some fields has led to the proliferation of eccentric or untrained practitioners.

medlar small shrub or tree native to SE Europe. It is widely cultivated for its fruits, resembling small brown-green pears or quinces. These are palatable when they have begun to decay. (*Mespilus germanica*, family Rosaceae.)

medulla central part of an organ. In the mammalian kidney, the medulla lies beneath the outer cortex and is responsible for the reabsorption of water from the filtrate. In plants, it is a region of packing tissue in the centre of the stem. In the vertebrate brain, the medulla is the posterior region responsible for the coordination of basic activities, such as breathing and temperature control.

medusa the free-swimming phase in the life cycle of a coelenterate, such as a ◊jellyfish or ◊coral. The other phase is the sedentary **polyp**.

Medicine, Western: chronology

c. 400 BC	Hippocrates recognized that disease had natural causes.
c. AD 200	Galen consolidated the work of the Alexandrian doctors.
1543	Andreas Vesalius gave the first accurate account of the human body.
1628	William Harvey discovered the circulation of the blood.
1768	John Hunter began the foundation of experimental and surgical pathology.
1785	Digitalis was used to treat heart disease; the active ingredient was isolated 1904.
1798	Edward Jenner published his work on vaccination.
1877	Patrick Manson studied animal carriers of infectious diseases.
1882	Robert Koch isolated the bacillus responsible for tuberculosis.
1884	Edwin Klebs isolated the diphtheria bacillus.
1885	Louis Pasteur produced a vaccine against rabies.
1890	Joseph Lister demonstrated antiseptic surgery.
1895	Wilhelm Röntgen discovered X-rays.
1897	Martinus Beijerinck discovered viruses.
1899	Felix Hoffman developed aspirin; Sigmund Freud founded psychiatry.
1900	Karl Landsteiner identified the first three blood groups, later designated A, B, and O.
1910	Paul Ehrlich developed the first specific antibacterial agent, Salvarsan, a cure for syphilis.
1922	Insulin was first used to treat diabetes.
1928	Alexander Fleming discovered penicillin.
1932	Gerhard Domagk discovered the first antibacterial sulphonamide drug, Prontosil.
1937	Electro-convulsive therapy (ECT) was developed.
1940s	Lithium treatment for manic-depressive illness was developed.
1950s	Antidepressant drugs and beta-blockers for heart disease were developed. Manipulation of the molecules of synthetic chemicals became the main source of new drugs. Peter Medawar studied the body's tolerance of transplanted organs and skin grafts.
1950	Proof of a link between cigarette smoking and lung cancer was established.
1953	Francis Crick and James Watson announced the structure of DNA. Jonas Salk developed a vaccine against polio.
1958	Ian Donald pioneered diagnostic ultrasound.
1960s	A new generation of minor tranquillizers called benzodiazepines was developed.
1967	Christiaan Barnard performed the first human heart-transplant operation.
1971	Viroids, disease-causing organisms even smaller than viruses, were isolated outside the living body.
1972	The CAT scan, pioneered by Godfrey Hounsfield, was first used to image the human brain.
1975	César Milstein developed monoclonal antibodies.
1978	World's first 'test-tube baby' was born in the UK.
1980s	AIDS (acquired immune-deficiency syndrome) was first recognized in the USA. Barbara McClintock's discovery of the transposable gene was recognized.
1980	The World Health Organization reported the eradication of smallpox.
1983	The virus responsible for AIDS, now known as human immunodeficiency virus (HIV), was identified by Luc Montagnier at the Institut Pasteur, Paris; Robert Gallo at the National Cancer Institute, Maryland, USA discovered the virus independently 1984.
1984	The first vaccine against leprosy was developed.
1987	The world's longest-surviving heart-transplant patient died in France, 18 years after his operation.
1989	Grafts of fetal brain tissue were first used to treat Parkinson's disease.
1990	Gene for maleness discovered by UK researchers.
1991	First successful use of gene therapy (to treat severe combined immune deficiency) was reported in the USA.
1993	First trials of gene therapy against cystic fibrosis took place in the USA.
1996	An Australian man, Ben Dent, was the first person to end his life by legally sanctioned euthanasia.

Complementary Therapy

by Pamela Morley

The term 'complementary therapy' is used to encompass any practice or system of beliefs about treatment that is not included in what is generally understood as Western scientific medicine. Science and much of Western medical practice is incompatible with many of the practices of complementary therapy, as such practices do not have a scientific basis, though this should not be seen as an obstacle to its understanding and acceptance. Practitioners of complementary therapy are seeing their role increasingly as offering something that Western scientific medicine does not, and something that adds to it without denying that scientific medicine has an essential role.

Medical intervention is restricted to qualified medical practitioners in many Western countries and a significant proportion of them use complementary therapy. Not all complementary practitioners are regulated and this has caused concern as complementary therapy grows in popularity. However, organizations concerned with the training and registration of complementary practitioners have developed at a rapid rate recently to meet the growing demands of the public for a pluralist, holistic, effective, and safe approach to health care.

Homeopathy

The roots of homeopathy lie in the work of Samuel Hahnemann, an 18th-century German physician. The brutalities of medical practice, which included purging, bleeding, and the use of poisons, were instrumental in his decision to explore other avenues in which he could use his skills. He was prompted to investigate the use of cinchona bark in the treatment of fever while he was working on a *Materia Medica*. Cinchona bark produced many of the symptoms associated with fever without inducing pyrexia. This led to him to speculate that a substance that was effective against a disease would produce symptoms resembling those of that disease if it was given to a healthy person.

Homeopathy recognizes a need for balance and harmony. Disturbances in the harmony of the body due to illness can precede the appearance of symptoms as the body reacts to the illness. Symptoms of the same illness differ between individuals, and the establishment of a detailed profile of the patient and a complete symptom picture are an essential part of the diagnosis. Homeopathic remedies are intended to stimulate the resources of the body to restore its natural harmony, following Hahnemann's principle that the appropriate treatment is one that produces the same symptoms in a healthy person. Many of these principles pose a problem to the scientist, but the greatest obstacle to scientific acceptance is the observation that homeopathic remedies become more potent when subject to serial dilution and mechanical shock in the process known as 'succussion'. Theories have been developed in an attempt to explain why more dilute preparations are more powerful, but none of these have yet been proven.

Herbal Medicine

A wide range of medical practices that use unrefined and refined plant materials for treatment is encompassed by the term 'herbal medicine'. They do not necessarily have a common belief system and they range from traditional herbal medicine to many ethnic medical systems, such as Chinese and Ayurvedic medicine.

Plants were used medicinally in China, Egypt, Greece, Rome, and other ancient civilizations up to 5,000 years ago. The central position of herbalism in health care was challenged by changes in medical thinking in Renaissance Europe, and by the consequent emphasis on the management of symptoms with specific remedies by the emerging medical establishment.

Samuel Thomson, an American physician, documented much of this early herbalist knowledge in the early 19th century, and he is now credited as the founder of Western herbal medicine. He developed a theory resembling that of the four humours, in which life and health were represented by heat; illness and death by cold; motion by air; and energy or life force by fire. He believed that the fever associated with infection was a healthy sign and, unlike his contemporaries, he wanted to facilitate it rather than to suppress it. He considered that coughing, vomiting, and diarrhoea were healthy signs of the body removing toxins.

The underlying belief in herbalism is that health depends on maintaining the natural state of the body. The natural state of the body, or 'vital pulse', is represented by the rhythmic variation in tissue and cell activity, which protects, regulates, and renews the body. A herbal remedy is a preparation of the entire plant rather than an active ingredient extracted from it. The constituent components may have many different activities that restore the balance of the body, which is lost with the onset of illness. They are not specific for a particular symptom and they are thought to act by stimulating the natural defences of the body and enhancing the elimination of toxins. Attention to diet is often used as an adjunct to treatment by herbalists.

Aromatherapy

The therapeutic use of volatile oils can be traced back to the ancient civilizations of India, China, Egypt, Babylon, and Greece, and their use in medicine survived until challenged by the advent of scientific chemistry in the 17th century.

Aromatherapists believe that health depends on a balance of mental, emotional, and physical processes which is disturbed in illness. A holistic approach is taken to diagnosis and treatment. The volatile oils used in aromatherapy are complex mixtures of chemicals that occur naturally in plants. Specific disorders are treated with particular oils. They are believed to be absorbed through the skin or by inhalation before exerting their subtle effects on physical symptoms and emotional well being. The pleasant smell and application of the oils by massage can enhance the beneficial effects of aromatherapy through reduction of tension and pain, increased relaxation, and improved circulation. Aromatherapy is widely used as an adjunct to conventional care in patients who are terminally ill.

Acupuncture

Traditional Chinese medicine is based on the fundamental principle that a life force known as *qi* flows around the body in 12 channels known as meridians. The flow of *qi* is important for good health. The balance between *yin* and *yang*, qualities possessed by all things including the internal functions and processes of the body and the meridians, is also vital to health. *Yin* is cold, dark, passive, and negative; *yin* organs include the heart, spleen, kidney, and liver. *Yang* is warm, light, active, and positive; *yang* organs include the small intestine, stomach, bladder, and gall bladder. Illness occurs when either *yin* or *yang* is dominant, and treatment helps to restore their balance.

Acupuncture is one form of treatment used in traditional Chinese medicine. It involves the insertion of fine needles into the skin at particular points on the body to correct the imbalances between *yin* and *yang*. There are about 2,000 acupoints that lie on the meridians through which *qi* flows. The imbalance between *yin* and *yang* may be associated with many factors, such as stress, emotion, diet, or injury, and these are considered in conjunction with the medical history of the patient, and examination of the 12 pulses and the condition of the tongue before a diagnosis is made. The acupoints to be stimulated are then selected and needles are inserted to a depth of about $\frac{1}{4}$ of an inch (6 mm) and rotated. The direction of insertion and rotation of the needles regulates the flow of *qi* and the collection or dispersion of energy.

Acupuncture can be used to treat a wide range of acute and chronic illnesses, such as pain, anxiety, asthma, migraine, menstrual disorders, and gastrointestinal complaints. It can also be used as an aid to dieting and giving up smoking.

Osteopathy

Osteopaths perceive the function of muscles and the skeletal system to be central to a range of health problems. Osteopathy was conceived as a system of diagnosis and treatment by Andrew Taylor Still in the USA in the 19th century. He believed that a lack of balance in the mechanical functioning of the body, such as muscle groups being too tense or joints moving incorrectly, may cause illness. He developed a range of manipulative techniques to correct the imbalances and claimed therapeutic success. These include massage, passive movement, and stretching of the limbs. Despite opposition from the medical profession, osteopathy has slowly achieved success because it can produce a dramatic improvement in disorders that are difficult to treat by conventional medicine, such as chronic back pain and sciatica.

These are just a few of the more popular forms of complementary therapy that are available today. There are many others: chiropractic, reflexology, and relaxation techniques such as hypnotherapy, to name but a few.

meerkat or ***suricate*** small mammal with long soft grey fur, which is found in southern Africa, and belongs to the mongoose family. A third of its length of 35 cm/14 in is occupied by the tail. It feeds on succulent bulbs, insects, and small vertebrates, and is sociable, living in large extended family groups.

The Madagascar cat and *Cynictis penicillata* are also termed meerkats.

classification Meerkats *Suricata suricatta* are in family Viverridae, order Carnivora.

meerschaum aggregate of minerals, usually the soft white clay mineral **sepiolite**, hydrous magnesium silicate. It floats on water and is used for making pipe bowls.

mega- prefix denoting multiplication by a million. For example, a megawatt (MW) is equivalent to a million watts.

megabyte (MB) in computing, a unit of memory equal to 1,024 ◊kilobytes.

It is sometimes used, less precisely, to mean 1 million bytes.

megalith ***Greek megas 'great', lithos 'stone'*** prehistoric stone monument of the late Neolithic (New Stone Age) or early Bronze Age. Most common in Europe, megaliths include single large uprights or ◊menhirs (for example, the Five Kings, Northumberland, England); rows or **alignments** (for example, Carnac, Brittany, France); stone circles; and the hutlike remains of burial chambers after the covering earth has disappeared, known as ◊dolmen (for example, Kits Coty, Kent, England, where only the entrance survives).

A number of explanations have been put forward for the building of megaliths during the Neolithic period in areas including Denmark, Ireland, NE Scotland, England, W France, and Spain. These range from economic reasons to expressions of dominance (neo-Marxist) and symbolism. The great stone monuments at ◊Carnac in W Brittany, France; in Jersey, such as La Hougue Bie; and in W Britain and Ireland, suggest possible cultural links through trade among megalith builders whose rural economy encompassed arable farming, stockrearing, and the development of pottery and weaving.

In the later Neolithic, in Wessex, S England, the construction of stone monuments such as ◊Avebury and ◊Stonehenge involved large numbers of working hours and considerable organization; possibly the stone was transported over a great distance, as has been suggested in the case of the bluestone at Stonehenge, although glacial deposition is another explanation.

Changes in social structure and diversification of labour probably caused the practice of megalith building to be abandoned.

Megalosaurus large bipedal carnivorous ◊dinosaur. Fragmentary fossil remains occur in European Jurassic deposits.

megamouth deep-sea shark that feeds on plankton. It has a bulbous head with protruding jaws and blubbery lips, is 4.5 m/15 ft long, and weighs 750 kg/1,650 lb. Although first discovered 1976, the first live specimen was found in 1992 off the coast of Los Angeles. The first female was found in 1994 in Hakata Bay, Kyushu, Japan; she was 4.8 m/16 ft long and weighed 790 kg/1,740 lb. (Species *Megachasma pelagios.*)

megapode *or* **mound-builder** any of a group of chickenlike birds found in the Malay Archipelago and Australia. They pile up large mounds of vegetable matter, earth, and sand 4 m/13 ft across, in which to deposit their eggs, then cover the eggs and leave them to be incubated by the heat produced by the rotting vegetation. There are 19 species, all large birds, 50–70 cm/20–27.5 in in length, with very large feet. They include brush turkeys. (Family Megapodiidae, order Galliformes.)

In some species the male bird feels the mound with his tongue and adds or takes away vegetation to provide the correct temperature.

MEGAPODE

The 'nests' in which scrub fowl lay their eggs are the largest structures created by any bird. These nests are in fact mounds of rotting vegetation, up to 5 m/16 ft in height and 12 m/40 ft in diameter. As the vegetation rots, it generates enough heat to incubate the eggs.

megathere any of a group of extinct giant ground ◊sloths of North and South America. Various species lived from about 7 million years ago until geologically recent times. They were plant-eaters, and some grew to 6 m/20 ft long. (Genus *Megatherium.*)

megaton one million (10^6) tons. Used with reference to the explosive power of a nuclear weapon, it is equivalent to the explosive force of one million tons of trinitrotoluene (TNT).

megavitamin therapy the administration of large doses of vitamins to combat conditions considered wholly or in part due to their deficiency.

Developed by US chemist Linus Pauling in the 1960s, and alternatively known as 'orthomolecular psychiatry', the treatment has proved effective with addicts, schizophrenics, alcoholics, and depressives.

meiosis in biology, a process of cell division in which the number of ◊chromosomes in the cell is halved. It only occurs in ◊eukaryotic cells, and is part of a life cycle that involves sexual reproduction because it allows the genes of two parents to be combined without the total number of chromosomes increasing.

In sexually reproducing ◊diploid animals (having two sets of chromosomes per cell), meiosis occurs during formation of the gametes (sex cells, sperm and egg), so that the ◊gametes are ◊haploid (having only one set of chromosomes). When the gametes unite during ◊fertilization, the diploid condition is restored. In plants, meiosis occurs just before spore formation. Thus the spores are haploid and in lower plants such as mosses they develop into a haploid plant called a gametophyte which produces the gametes (see ◊alternation of ◊generations). See also ◊mitosis.

> *We are inquiring into the deepest nature of our constitutions: How we inherit from each other. How we can change. How our minds think. How our will is related to our thoughts. How our thoughts are related to our molecules.*
>
> GERALD EDELMAN US biochemist. *Newsweek* 4 July 1976

meitnerium synthesized radioactive element of the ◊transactinide series, symbol Mt, atomic number 109, relative atomic mass 266. It was first produced in 1982 at the Laboratory for Heavy Ion Research in Darmstadt, Germany, by fusing bismuth and iron nuclei; it took a week to obtain a single new, fused nucleus. It was named in 1997 after the Austrian-born Swedish physicist Lise Meitner. Its temporary name was unnilennium.

melaleuca tree or shrub of the predominantly Australian genus *Melaleuca,* family Myrtaceae, many of which are found on river banks or in swamps; commonly known as paperbarks because of their papery and usually spongy bark.

melaleuca tree or ***paperbark*** tropical tree belonging to the myrtle family. The leaves produce **cajuput oil**, which is used in medicine. (*Melaleuca leucadendron,* family Myrtaceae.)

In favourable conditions, such as in the Florida Everglades, the tree reproduces rapidly. Attempts are being made to root out and destroy it because in a forest fire its crown becomes a ball of flame, rapidly spreading the blaze in all directions.

melamine $C_3H_6N_6$ ◊thermosetting polymer based on urea–formaldehyde. It is extremely resistant to heat and is also scratch-resistant. Its uses include synthetic resins.

melanin brown pigment that gives colour to the eyes, skin, hair, feathers, and scales of many vertebrates. In humans, melanin

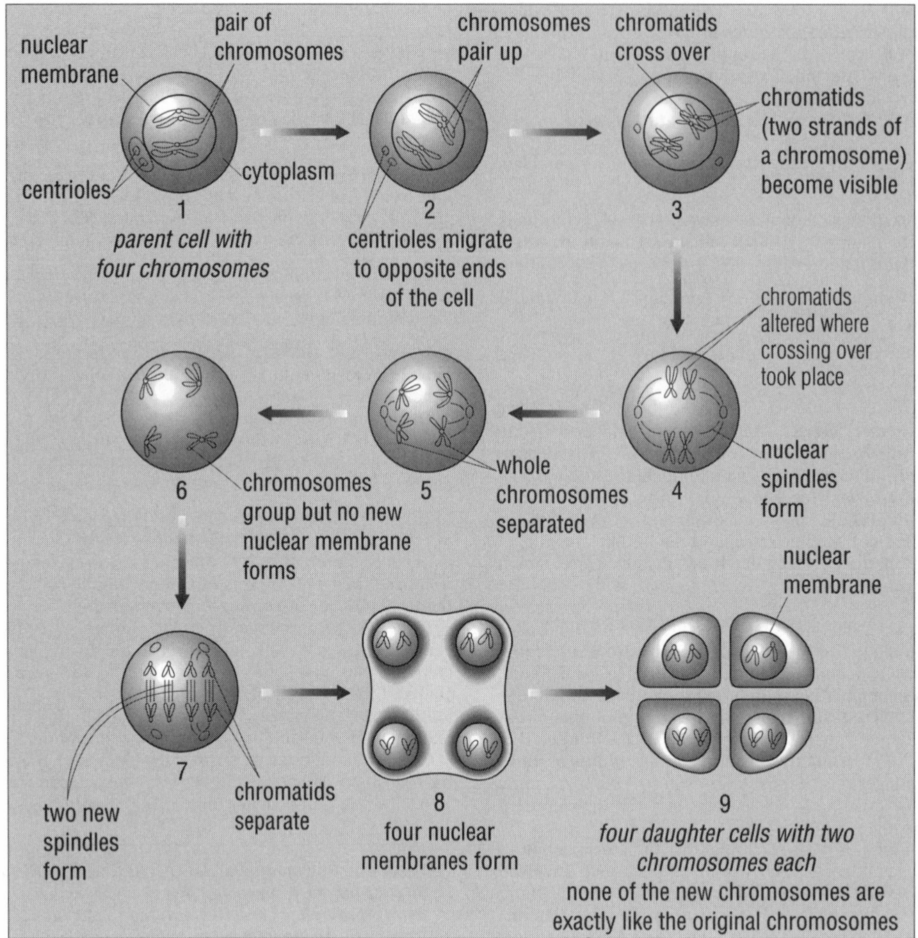

meiosis *Meiosis is a type of cell division that produces gametes (sex cells, sperm and egg). This sequence shows an animal cell but only four chromosomes are present in the parent cell (1). There are two stages in the division process. In the first stage (2–6), the chromosomes come together in pairs and exchange genetic material. This is called crossing over. In the second stage (7–9), the cell divides to produce four gamete cells, each with only one copy of each chromosome from the parent cell.*

helps protect the skin against ultraviolet radiation from sunlight. Both genetic and environmental factors determine the amount of melanin in the skin.

melanism black coloration of animal bodies caused by large amounts of the pigment melanin. Melanin is of significance in insects, because melanic ones warm more rapidly in sunshine than do pale ones, and can be more active in cool weather. A fall in temperature may stimulate such insects to produce more melanin. In industrial areas, dark insects and pigeons match sooty backgrounds and escape predation, but they are at a disadvantage in rural areas where they do not match their backgrounds. This is known as **industrial melanism**.

melanoma highly malignant tumour of the melanin-forming cells (melanocytes) of the skin. It develops from an existing mole in up to two thirds of cases, but can also arise in the eye or mucous membranes.

Malignant melanoma is the most dangerous of the skin cancers; it is associated with brief but excessive exposure to sunlight. It is easily treated if caught early but deadly once it has spread. There is a genetic factor in some cases.

Once rare, this disease is increasing at the rate of 7% in most countries with a predominantly fair-skinned population, owing to the increasing popularity of holidays in the sun. Most at risk are those with fair hair and light skin, and those who have had a severe sunburn in childhood. Cases of melanoma are increasing by 4% a year worldwide.

MELANOMA SKIN CANCER INFORMATION

http://www.cancer.org/cidSpecificCancers/melanomaskin/index.html

Comprehensive information on melanoma from the American Cancer Society. Written in easily understandable language, this guide explains the normal function of the skin and non-malignant cancers before turning to melanoma. There is information on risk factors, causes, diagnosis, treatment, latest research news, and prognosis for those with these highly malignant tumours. Further sources of information are also indicated.

melon any of several large, juicy (95% water), thick-skinned fruits of trailing plants of the gourd family. The muskmelon (*Cucumis melo*), of which the honeydew melon is a variety, and the large red ◊watermelon (*Citrullus vulgaris*) are familiar edible varieties. (Family Cucurbitaceae.)

Thought to have originated in Asia, the melon became naturalized in the Nile Valley and was introduced to Europe at the end of the 15th century.

meltdown the melting of the core of a nuclear reactor, due to overheating.

To prevent such accidents all reactors have equipment intended to flood the core with water in an emergency. The reactor is housed in a strong containment vessel, designed to prevent radiation escaping into the atmosphere. The result of a meltdown would be an area radioactively contaminated for 25,000 years or more.

At Three Mile Island, Pennsylvania, USA, in March 1979, a partial meltdown occurred caused by a combination of equipment failure and operator error, and some radiation was released into the air. In April 1986, a reactor at Chernobyl, near Kiev, Ukraine, exploded, causing a partial meltdown of the core. Radioactive ◊fallout was detected as far away as Canada and Japan.

melting point temperature at which a substance melts, or changes from solid to liquid form. A pure substance under standard conditions of pressure (usually one atmosphere) has a definite melting point. If heat is supplied to a solid at its melting point, the temperature does not change until the melting process is complete. The melting point of ice is 0°C or 32°F.

membrane in living things, a continuous layer, made up principally of fat molecules, that encloses a ◊cell or ◊organelles within a cell. Small molecules, such as water and sugars, can pass through the cell membrane by ◊diffusion. Large molecules, such as proteins, are transported across the membrane via special channels, a process often involving energy input. The ◊Golgi apparatus within the cell is thought to produce certain membranes.

In cell organelles, enzymes may be attached to the membrane at specific positions, often alongside other enzymes involved in the same process, like workers at a conveyor belt. Thus membranes help to make cellular processes more efficient.

memory in computing, the part of a system used to store data and programs either permanently or temporarily. There are two main types: immediate access memory and backing storage. Memory capacity is measured in ◊bytes or, more conveniently, in kilobytes (units of 1,024 bytes) or megabytes (units of 1,024 kilobytes).

Immediate access memory, or **internal memory**, describes the memory locations that can be addressed directly and individually by the central processing unit. It is either read-only (stored in ROM, PROM, and EPROM chips) or read/write (stored in RAM chips). Read-only memory stores information that must be constantly available and is unlikely to be changed. It is nonvolatile – that is, it is not lost when the computer is switched off. Read/write memory is volatile – it stores programs and data only while the computer is switched on.

Backing storage, or **external memory**, is nonvolatile memory, located outside the central processing unit, used to store programs and data that are not in current use. Backing storage is provided by such devices as magnetic ◊discs (floppy and hard discs), ◊magnetic tape (tape streamers and cassettes), optical discs (such as ◊CD-ROM), and ◊bubble memory. By rapidly switching blocks of information between the backing storage and the immediate-access memory, the limited size of the immediate-access memory may be increased artificially. When this technique is used to give the appearance of a larger internal memory than physically exists, the additional capacity is referred to as ◊virtual memory.

memory ability to store and recall observations and sensations. Memory does not seem to be based in any particular part of the brain; it may depend on changes to the pathways followed by nerve impulses as they move through the brain. Memory can be improved by regular use as the connections between nerve cells (neurons) become 'well-worn paths' in the brain. Events stored in **short-term memory** are forgotten quickly, whereas those in **long-term memory** can last for many years, enabling recall of information and recognition of people and places over long periods of time.

Short-term memory is the most likely to be impaired by illness or drugs whereas long-term memory is very resistant to such damage. Memory changes with age and otherwise healthy people may experience a natural decline after the age of about 40. Research is just beginning to uncover the biochemical and electrical bases of the human memory.

memory address in computing, number specifying the location of a particular item in a computer's ◊RAM.

memory resident present in the main (◊RAM) memory of the computer. For an application to be run, it has to be memory resi-

Mendel, Gregor Johann
(1822–1884)

Austrian biologist, founder of genetics. His experiments with successive generations of peas gave the basis for his theory of particulate inheritance rather than blending, involving dominant and recessive characters; see Mendelism. His results, published 1865–69, remained unrecognized until the early 20th century.

Mendel formulated two laws now recognized as fundamental laws of heredity: the law of segregation and the law of independent assortment of characters. Mendel concluded that each parent plant contributes a 'factor' to its offspring that determines a particular trait and that the pairs of factors in the offspring do not give rise to a blend of traits.

Mary Evans Picture Library

Much of his work was performed on the edible pea *Pisum*, which he grew in the monastery garden. He carefully self-pollinated and wrapped (to prevent accidental pollination by insects) each individual plant, collected the seeds produced by the plants, and studied the offspring of these seeds. Seeing that some plants bred true and others not, he worked out the pattern of inheritance of various traits.

He found that dwarf plants produced only dwarf offspring and that the seeds produced by this second generation also produced only dwarf offspring. With tall plants, however, he found that both tall and dwarf offspring were produced and concluded that there were two types of tall plants, those that bred true and those that did not. Next he cross-bred dwarf plants with true-breeding tall plants and found that all the offspring in the first generation were tall but that the offspring from subsequent generations were a mixture: one-quarter true-breeding dwarf plants, one-quarter true-breeding tall plants, and one-half non-true-breeding tall plants.

Mendel also studied other characteristics in pea plants, such as flower colour, seed shape and flower position, finding that, as with height, simple laws governed the inheritance of these traits. He reported his findings in 'Experiments with Plant Hybrids' 1866, but the importance of his work was not recognized at the time, even by the eminent botanist Karl Wilhelm von Naegeli, to whom Mendel sent a copy of his paper. It was not until 1900, when his work was rediscovered by Hugo De Vries, Carl Erich Correns, and Erich Tschermak von Seysenegg, that Mendel achieved fame – 16 years after his death.

MENDELWEB

http://www-hpcc.astro.washington.edu/mirrors/MendelWeb/

Hefty resource for anyone interested in Gregor Mendel, the origins of classical genetics, and the history and literature of science. View or download Mendel's original paper, with hypertext links to glossaries, biographical information, and exercises, or look up the essays, timeline, bibliography, and statistical tools.

dent. Some applications are kept in memory (see ◊terminate and stay resident), while most are deleted from the memory when their task is complete. However, the memory is usually not large enough to hold all applications and ◊swapping in and out of memory is necessary. This slows down the application.

menagerie small collection of wild animals kept in captivity for display. Rulers of early times used to bring back wild animals from abroad for public exhibition. Private collections later became common, and until the early 19th century one was maintained at the Tower of London, England. From these collections developed present-day ◊zoos.

mendelevium synthesized, radioactive metallic element of the ◊actinide series, symbol Md, atomic number 101, relative atomic mass 258. It was first produced by bombardment of Es-253 with helium nuclei. Its longest-lived isotope, Md-258, has a half-life of about two months. The element is chemically similar to thulium. It was named by the US physicists at the University of California at Berkeley who first synthesized it in 1955 after the Russian chemist Mendeleyev, who in 1869 devised the basis for the periodic table of the elements.

Mendeleyev, Dmitri Ivanovich (1834–1907)

Russian chemist who framed the periodic law in chemistry in 1869, which states that the chemical properties of the elements depend on their relative atomic masses. This law is the basis of the periodic table of the elements, in which the elements are arranged by atomic number and organized by their related groups.

Mendeleyev was the first chemist to understand that all elements are related members of a single ordered system. From his table he predicted the properties of elements then unknown, of which three (gallium, scandium, and germanium) were discovered in his lifetime. Meanwhile Lothar Meyer in Germany presented a similar but independent classification of the elements.

Mary Evans Picture Library

Mendelism in genetics, the theory of inheritance originally outlined by Austrian biologist Gregor Mendel. He suggested that, in sexually reproducing species, all characteristics are inherited through indivisible 'factors' (now identified with ◊genes) contributed by each parent to its offspring.

Discovery consists of seeing what everybody has seen, thinking what nobody has thought.

ALBERT SZENT-GYÖRGYI Hungarian-born US biochemist. Quoted in I G Good (ed) *The Scientist Speculates* 1962

menhaden or ***hardhead*** or ***mossbunker*** marine bony fish allied to ◊shads and common on the Atlantic coast of North America. It is employed as bait, but is chiefly valuable for its rich oil. The residue remaining after extraction is used as a fertilizer.
classification The menhaden *Brevoortia tyrannus* is in order Clupeiformes, class Osteichthyes.

menhir ***Breton 'long stone'*** prehistoric tall, upright stone monument or ◊megalith. Menhirs may be found singly as ◊monoliths or in groups. They have a wide geographical distribution in the Americas (mainly as monoliths), and in Europe, Asia, and Africa, and belong to many different periods. Most European examples were erected in the late Neolithic (New Stone Age) or early Bronze Age.

The menhirs at ◊Carnac in Brittany, NW France, are particularly impressive, one example standing about 10 m/39 ft high. In nearby Morbihan, Le Grand Menhir Brisé once stood almost 21 m/68 ft high.

In the British Isles, standing stones in England include the Devil's Arrows, Boroughbridge, W Yorkshire, and the Five Kings, Upper Coquerdale, Northumberland; and in Wales, Harold's Stones, Trelleck, Gwent. Numerous Irish examples, known as **goulaun**, **gallan**, **dallan**, or **liagan**, were built from the Neolithic to the early Christian period. In Scotland, groups of menhirs are often called **cat stones**, from Gaelic *cath* 'a battle'.

Ménière's disease or ***Ménière's syndrome*** recurring condition of the inner ear affecting mechanisms of both hearing and balance. It usually develops in the middle or later years. Symptoms, which include deafness, ringing in the ears, nausea, vertigo, and loss of balance, may be eased by drugs, but there is no cure.

meningitis inflammation of the meninges (membranes) surrounding the brain, caused by bacterial or viral infection. Bacterial meningitis, though treatable by antibiotics, is the more serious threat. Diagnosis is by ◊lumbar puncture.

Bacterial meningitis is caused by *Neisseria meningitidis*, a bacterium that colonizes the lining of the throat and is carried by 2–10% of the healthy population. Illness results if the bacteria enters the bloodstream, but normally the epithelial lining of the throat is a sufficient barrier.

Many common viruses can cause the occasional case of meningitis, although not usually in its more severe form. The treatment for viral meningitis is rest.

There are three strains of meningitis: serogroups A, B, and C. Vaccines exist only for A and C. However, they do not provide long-term protection nor are they suitable for children under the age of two. B is the most prevalent of the groups, causing over 50% of cases in Europe and the USA.

The severity of the disease varies from mild to rapidly lethal, and symptoms include fever, headache, nausea, neck stiffness, delirium, and (rarely) convulsions.

CHILDHOOD INFECTIONS – MENINGITIS

http://kidshealth.org/parent/common/meningitis.html

Useful information on the signs and symptoms, and appropriate treatment of meningitis in children. The site also discusses the incubation, duration, and contagiousness of the illness, as well as the preventive measures that can be taken in certain cases.

meniscus in physics, the curved shape of the surface of a liquid in a thin tube, caused by the cohesive effects of ◊surface tension (capillary action). When the walls of the container are made wet by the liquid, the meniscus is concave, but with highly viscous liquids (such as mercury) the meniscus is convex. Meniscus is also the name of a concavo-convex or convexo-concave lens.

meniscus in biology, the fibro-cartilage in joints, such as the knee joint.

menopause in women, the cessation of reproductive ability, characterized by menstruation (see ◊menstrual cycle) becoming irregular and eventually ceasing. The onset is at about the age of 50, but varies greatly. Menopause is usually uneventful, but some women suffer from complications such as flushing, excessive bleeding, and nervous disorders. Since the 1950s, ◊hormone-replacement therapy (HRT), using ◊oestrogen alone or with progestogen, a synthetic form of ◊progesterone, has been developed to counteract such effects.

Long-term use of HRT was previously associated with an increased risk of cancer of the uterus, and of clot formation in the blood vessels, but newer formulations using natural oestrogens are not associated with these risks. Without HRT there is increased risk of ◊osteoporosis (thinning of the bones) leading to broken bones, which may be indirectly fatal, particularly in the elderly.

The menopause is also known as the 'change of life'.

menstrual cycle cycle that occurs in female mammals of reproductive age, in which the body is prepared for pregnancy. At the beginning of the cycle, a Graafian (egg) follicle develops in the ovary, and the inner wall of the uterus forms a soft spongy lining. The egg is released from the ovary, and the uterus lining (endometrium) becomes vascularized (filled with blood vessels). If fertilization does not occur, the corpus luteum (remains of the Graafian follicle) degenerates, and the uterine lining breaks down, and is shed. This is what causes the loss of blood that marks menstruation. The cycle then begins again. Human menstruation takes place from puberty to menopause, except during pregnancy, occurring about every 28 days.

The cycle is controlled by a number of ◊hormones, including ◊oestrogen and ◊progesterone. If fertilization occurs, the corpus luteum persists and goes on producing progesterone.

MENSTRUAL CYCLE

The menstrual cycles of women living in close proximity to each other become synchronized. This could be due to pheromones released in the sweat and may have evolved as means of thwarting male infidelity.

mental disability arrested or incomplete development of mental capacities. It can be very mild, but in more severe cases is associated with social problems and difficulties in living independently. A person may be born with a mental disability (for example, ◊Down's syndrome) or may acquire it through brain damage. Between 90 and 130 million people in the world suffer from such disabilities.

Clinically, mental disability is graded as profound, severe, moderate, or mild, roughly according to IQ and the sufferer's ability to cope with everyday tasks. Among its many causes are genetic defect (phenylketonuria), chromosomal errors (Down's syndrome), infection before birth (◊rubella) or in infancy (◊meningitis), trauma (brain damage at birth or later), respiratory difficulties at the time of birth, toxins (lead poisoning), physical deprivation (lack of, or defective, ◊thyroid tissue, as in cretinism), and gross psychological deprivation. No clear cause of disability can be established for more than half of individuals with an IQ of less than 70.

mental illness disordered functioning of the mind. Since normal working cannot easily be defined, the borderline between mild mental illness and normality is a matter of opinion (not to be confused with normative behaviour). It is broadly divided into two categories: ◊neurosis, in which the patient remains in touch with reality; and ◊psychosis, in which perception, thought, and belief are disordered.

menu in computing, a list of options, displayed on screen, from which the user may make a choice – for example, the choice of services offered to the customer by a bank cash dispenser: withdrawal, deposit, balance, or statement. Menus are used extensively in ◊graphical user interface (GUI) systems, where the menu options are often selected using a pointing device called a ◊mouse.

Mercalli scale scale used to measure the intensity of an ◊earthquake. It differs from the ◊Richter scale, which measures **magnitude**. It is named after the Italian seismologist Giuseppe Mercalli (1850–1914).

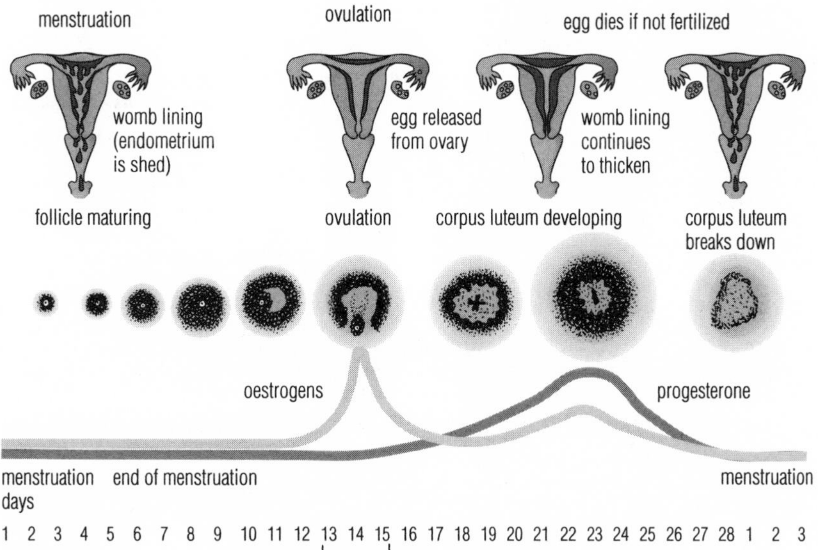

menstrual cycle *From puberty to the menopause, most women produce a regular rhythm of hormones that stimulate the various stages of the menstrual cycle. The change in hormone levels may cause premenstrual tension. This diagram shows an average menstrual cycle. The dates of each stage vary from woman to woman.*

The Mercalli scale

The Mercalli scale is a measure of the intensity of an earthquake. It differs from the Richter scale, which measures magnitude. It is named after the Italian seismologist Giuseppe Mercalli (1850–1914).

The scale shown here is the Modified Mercalli Intensity Scale, developed in 1931 by US seismologists Harry Wood and Frank Neumann.

Intensity value	*Description*
I	not felt except by a very few under especially favourable conditions
II	felt only by a few persons at rest, especially on upper floors of buildings
III	felt quite noticeably by persons indoors, especially on upper floors of buildings; many people do not recognize it as an earthquake; standing motor cars may rock slightly; vibrations similar to the passing of a truck; duration estimated
IV	felt indoors by many, outdoors by few during the day; at night, some awakened; dishes, windows, doors disturbed; walls make cracking sound; sensation like heavy truck striking building; standing motor cars rock noticeably
V	felt by nearly everyone; many awakened; some dishes, windows broken; unstable objects overturned; pendulum clocks may stop
VI	felt by all, many frightened; some heavy furniture moved; a few instances of fallen plaster; damage slight
VII	damage negligible in buildings of good design and construction; slight to moderate in well-built ordinary structures; considerable damage in poorly-built or badly-designed structures; some chimneys broken
VIII	damage slight in specially-designed structures; considerable damage in ordinary substantial buildings with partial collapse; damage great in poorly-built structures; fall of chimneys, factory stacks, columns, monuments, walls; heavy furniture overturned
IX	damage considerable in specially-designed structures; well-designed frame structures thrown out of plumb; damage great in substantial buildings, with partial collapse; buildings shifted off foundations
X	some well-built wooden structures destroyed; most masonry and frame structures destroyed with foundations; rails bent
XI	few, if any (masonry) structures remain standing; bridges destroyed; rails bent greatly
XII	damage total; lines of sight and level are distorted; objects thrown into the air

Intensity is a subjective value, based on observed phenomena, and varies from place to place with the same earthquake.

merchant navy the passenger and cargo ships of a country. Most are owned by private companies. To avoid strict regulations on safety, union rules on crew wages, and so on, many ships are today registered under 'flags of convenience', that is, flags of countries that do not have such rules.

During wartime, merchant shipping may be drafted by the national government for military purposes.

mercury or ***quicksilver Latin*** *mercurius* heavy, silver-grey, metallic element, symbol Hg (from Latin *hydrargyrum*), atomic number 80, relative atomic mass 200.59. It is a dense, mobile liquid with a low melting point (–38.87°C/–37.96°F). Its chief source is the mineral cinnabar, HgS, but it sometimes occurs in nature as a free metal.
uses Its alloys with other metals are called amalgams (a silver-mercury amalgam is used in dentistry for filling cavities in teeth). Industrial uses include drugs and chemicals, mercury-vapour lamps, arc rectifiers, power-control switches, barometers, and thermometers.
hazards Mercury is a cumulative poison that can contaminate the food chain, and cause intestinal disturbance, kidney and brain damage, and birth defects in humans. (The World Health Organization's 'safe' limit for mercury is 0.5 milligrams of mercury per kilogram of muscle tissue). The discharge into the sea by industry of organic mercury compounds such as dimethylmercury is the chief cause of mercury poisoning in the latter half of the 20th century. Between 1953 and 1975, 684 people in the Japanese fishing village of Minamata were poisoned (115 fatally) by organic mercury wastes that had been dumped into the bay and had accumulated in the bodies of fish and shellfish.

In a landmark settlement, a British multinational chemical company in April 1997 agreed to pay £1.3 million in compensation to 20 South African workers who were poisoned by mercury. Four of the black workers had died and a number of others were suffering severe brain and other neurological damage. The workers had accused Thor Chemical Holdings of adopting working practices in South Africa which would not have been allowed in Britain. The claimants had all worked at Thor's mercury plant at Cato Ridge in Natal. Thor had operated a mercury plant at Margate, in Kent, which during the 1980s was repeatedly criticised by the Health and Safety Executive (HSE) for bad working practices and over-exposure of British workers to mercury. Under pressure from the HSE, Thor closed down its mercury operations in Britain in 1987 and expanded them in South Africa.
history The element was known to the ancient Chinese and Hindus, and is found in Egyptian tombs of about 1500 BC. It was named by the alchemists after the fast-moving god, for its fluidity.

Mercury in astronomy, the closest planet to the Sun. Its mass is 0.056 that of Earth. On its sunward side the surface temperature reaches over 400°C/752°F, but on the 'night' side it falls to –170°C/–274°F.
mean distance from the Sun 58 million km/36 million mi
equatorial diameter 4,880 km/3,030 mi
rotation period 59 Earth days
year 88 Earth days
atmosphere Mercury has an atmosphere with minute traces of argon and helium.
surface composed of silicate rock often in the form of lava flows. In 1974 the US space probe *Mariner 10* showed that Mercury's surface is cratered by meteorite impacts.
satellites none

MERCURY

http://www.hawastsoc.org/solar/eng/mercury.htm

Detailed description of the planet Mercury. It includes statistics and information about the planet, along with a chronology of its exploration supported by a good selection of images.

mercury fulminate highly explosive compound used in detonators and percussion caps. It is a grey, sandy powder and extremely poisonous.

Mercury project US project to put a human in space in the one-seat Mercury spacecraft 1961–63.

The first two Mercury flights, on Redstone rockets, were short flights to the edge of space and back. The orbital flights, beginning with the third in the series (made by John Glenn), were launched by Atlas rockets.

merganser any of several diving ducks with long, slender, serrated bills for catching fish, widely distributed in the northern hemisphere. Most have crested heads. (Genus *Mergus*, family Anatidae.)

The male **common merganser** or **goosander** (*M. merganser*) has a greenish-black head, black back, and a pinkish-white breast and underparts; the male **red-breasted merganser** (*M. serrator*) drake has a crested glossy green head, white neck, red breast and black upper surface with white margins. The females of both are very similar, with crested chestnut heads, white underparts, and grey backs. *M. australis* is a rare species found only in the Auckland Islands.

meridian half a ◊great circle drawn on the Earth's surface passing through both poles and thus through all places with the same longitude. Terrestrial longitudes are usually measured from the Greenwich Meridian.

An astronomical meridian is a great circle passing through the celestial pole and the zenith (the point immediately overhead).

merino breed of sheep. Its close-set, silky wool is highly valued. Originally from Spain, the merino is now found all over the world, and is the breed on which the Australian wool industry is built.

meristem region of plant tissue containing cells that are actively dividing to produce new tissues (or have the potential to do so). Meristems found in the tip of roots and stems, the apical meristems, are responsible for the growth in length of these organs.

The ◊cambium is a lateral meristem that is responsible for increase in girth in perennial plants. Some plants also have intercalary meristems, as in the stems of grasses, for example. These are responsible for their continued growth after cutting or grazing has removed the apical meristems of the shoots.

Meristem culture involves growing meristems taken from shoots on a nutrient-containing medium, and using them to grow new plants.

It is used to propagate infertile plants or hybrids that do not breed true from seed and to generate virus-free stock, since viruses rarely infect apical meristems.

merlin small ◊falcon of Europe, Asia, and North America, where it is also called a **pigeon hawk**. The male, 26 cm/10 in long, has a grey-blue back and reddish-brown barred front; the female, 32 cm/13 in long, has a dark brown back and lighter front with streaks. Merlins fly relatively low over the ground when hunting and 'stoop' quickly onto their prey, which consists mainly of small birds. (Species *Falco columbarius,* order Falconiformes.)

They are found mainly on rocks and moors. On moorland the nest is generally built on a slope among the heather, and in other localities on rock ledges. The eggs are bluish-white, blotched with brown markings; four or five are laid.

MERLIN array radiotelescope network centred on ◊Jodrell Bank, N England.

mermaid's purse purse-shaped egg case of the ◊skates and many ◊sharks.

mesa Spanish ***'table'*** flat-topped, steep-sided plateau, consisting of horizontal weak layers of rock topped by a resistant formation; in particular, those found in the desert areas of the USA and Mexico. A small mesa is called a butte.

MYSTERY OF THE MESA: A SCIENCE DETECTIVE STORY

http://www.blm.gov/education/mesas/mesa.html

Sponsored by the US Bureau of Land Management, this site explores an archaeological discovery on a remote Alaskan mesa and explains how scientists study artefacts and draw conclusions about the ancient inhabitants of this land. Articles highlight the essential role of scientists in writing the earliest chapters of the USA's history.

mescaline psychedelic drug derived from a small, spineless cactus *Lophophora williamsii* of N Mexico and the SW USA, known as ◊peyote. The tops (called mescal buttons), which scarcely appear above ground, are dried and chewed, or added to alcoholic drinks. Mescaline is a crystalline alkaloid $C_{11}H_{17}NO_3$. It is used by some North American Indians in religious rites.

mesoglea layer of jelly-like noncellular tissue that separates the endoderm and ectoderm in jellyfish and other ◊coelenterates.

meson in physics, a group of unstable subatomic particles made up of two indivisible elementary particles called ◊quarks. It has a mass intermediate between that of the electron and that of the proton, is found in cosmic radiation, and is emitted by nuclei under bombardment by very high-energy particles.

The mesons form a subclass of the hadrons and include the kaons and pions. Their existence was predicted in 1935 by Japanese physicist Hideki Yukawa.

mesophyll the tissue between the upper and lower epidermis of a leaf blade (◊lamina), consisting of parenchyma-like cells containing numerous ◊chloroplasts.

In many plants, mesophyll is divided into two distinct layers.

The **palisade mesophyll** is usually just below the upper epidermis and is composed of regular layers of elongated cells. Lying below them is the **spongy mesophyll**, composed of loosely arranged cells of irregular shape. This layer contains fewer chloroplasts and has many intercellular spaces for the diffusion of gases (required for ◊respiration and ◊photosynthesis), linked to the outside by means of ◊stomata.

mesosphere layer in the Earth's ◊atmosphere above the stratosphere and below the thermosphere. It lies between about 50 km/31 mi and 80 km/50 mi above the ground.

Mesozoic era of geological time 245–65 million years ago, consisting of the Triassic, Jurassic, and Cretaceous periods. At the beginning of the era, the continents were joined together as Pangaea; dinosaurs and other giant reptiles dominated the sea and air; and ferns, horsetails, and cycads thrived in a warm climate worldwide. By the end of the Mesozoic era, the continents had begun to assume their present positions, flowering plants were dominant, and many of the large reptiles and marine fauna were becoming extinct.

message-ID in computing, special number given to every item of ◊e-mail as it travels across the Internet. Message-IDs are especially important for controlling traffic in ◊USENET. Articles are initially offered across the network by their message-IDs, enabling ◊news servers to check whether they have already received them and either take the rest of the message or move on to the next message-ID.

Messier catalogue in astronomy, a catalogue of 103 ◊galaxies, nebulas, and star clusters (the Messier objects) published in 1784 by French astronomer Charles Messier. Catalogue entries are denoted by the prefix 'M'. Well known examples include M31 (the ◊Andromeda galaxy), M42 (the ◊Orion Nebula), and M45 (the ◊Pleiades star cluster).

Messier compiled the catalogue to identify fuzzy objects that could be mistaken for ◊comets. The list was later extended to 109.

metabolism the chemical processes of living organisms enabling them to grow and to function. It involves a constant alternation of building up **(anabolism)** and breaking down **(catabolism)**. For example, green plants build up complex organic substances from water, carbon dioxide, and mineral salts (photosynthesis); by digestion animals partially break down complex organic substances, ingested as food, and subsequently resynthesize them for use in their own bodies.

metal any of a class of chemical elements with specific physical and chemical characteristics. Metallic elements compose about 75% of the 112 elements in the ◊periodic table of the elements.

Physical properties include a sonorous tone when struck, good conduction of heat and electricity, opacity but good reflection of light, malleability, which enables them to be cold-worked and rolled into sheets, ductility, which permits them to be drawn into thin wires, and the possible emission of electrons when heated (thermionic effect) or when the surface is struck by light (◊photoelectric effect).

The majority of metals are found in nature in a combined form only, as compounds or mineral ores; about 16 of them also occur in the elemental form, as ◊native metals. Their chemical properties are largely determined by the extent to which their atoms can lose one or more electrons and form positive ions (cations).

metal detector electronic device for detecting metal, usually below ground, developed from the wartime mine detector. In the head of the metal detector is a coil, which is part of an electronic circuit. The presence of metal causes the frequency of the signal in the circuit to change, setting up an audible note in the headphones worn by the user.

They are used to survey areas for buried metallic objects, occasionally by archaeologists. However, their indiscriminate use by treasure hunters has led to their being banned on recognized archaeological sites in some countries.

metal fatigue condition in which metals fail or fracture under relatively light loads, when these loads are applied repeatedly. Structures that are subject to flexing, such as the airframes of aircraft, are prone to metal fatigue.

metallic bond the force of attraction operating in a metal that holds the atoms together. In the metal the ◊valency electrons are able to move within the crystal and these electrons are said to be delocalized (see ◊electrons, delocalized). Their movement creates short-lived, positively charged ions. The electrostatic attraction between the delocalized electrons and the ceaselessly forming ions constitutes the metallic bond.

metallic character chemical properties associated with those elements classed as metals. These properties, which arise from the element's ability to lose electrons, are: the displacement of hydrogen from dilute acids; the formation of basic oxides; the formation of ionic chlorides; and their reducing reaction, as in the ◊thermite process (see ◊reduction).

In the periodic table of the elements, metallic character increases down any group and across a period from right to left.

metallic glass substance produced from metallic materials (non-corrosive alloys rather than simple metals) in a liquid state which, by very rapid cooling, are prevented from reverting to their regular metallic structure. Instead they take on the properties of glass, while retaining the metallic properties of malleability and relatively good electrical conductivity.

metalloid or ***semimetal*** any chemical element having some of but not all the properties of metals; metalloids are thus usually electrically semiconducting. They comprise the elements germanium, arsenic, antimony, and tellurium.

metallurgy the science and technology of producing metals, which includes extraction, alloying, and hardening. **Extractive**, or **process, metallurgy** is concerned with the extraction of metals from their ◊ores and refining and adapting them for use. **Physical metallurgy** is concerned with their properties and application. **Metallography** establishes the microscopic structures that contribute to hardness, ductility, and strength.

Metals can be extracted from their ores in three main ways: **dry processes**, such as smelting, volatilization, or amalgamation (treatment with mercury); **wet processes**, involving chemical reactions; and **electrolytic processes**, which work on the principle of ◊electrolysis.

The foundations of metallurgical science were laid about 3500 BC in Egypt, Mesopotamia, China, and India, where the art of ◊smelting metals from ores was discovered, starting with the natural alloy bronze. Later, gold, silver, copper, lead, and tin were worked in various ways, although they had been cold-hammered as native metals for thousands of years. The smelting of iron was discovered about 1500 BC. The Romans hardened and tempered iron into steel, using ◊heat treatment. From then until about AD 1400, advances in metallurgy came into Europe by way of Arabian chemists. ◊Cast iron began to be made in the 14th century in a crude blast furnace. The demands of the Industrial Revolution led to an enormous increase in ◊wrought iron production. The invention by British civil engineer Henry Bessemer of the ◊Bessemer process in 1856 made cheap steel available for the first time, leading to its present widespread use and the industrial development of many specialized steel alloys.

metal, porous lightweight metal made by melting metals such as copper, or iron alloys, in a sealed furnace filled with hydrogen, or other gas, under pressure. The formation of pores can be controlled by varying pressures and cooling times. They vary in density from 5% to 75% of the metal and in diameter from 5 micrometres (millionths of a metre) to 10 mm/0.39 in. The direction and positioning of the pores can also be controlled.

Porous metals were developed in the Ukraine in the 1960s and used in space rockets. Kerosene was forced through the pores to form a fine mist for optimum combustion.

metamorphic rock rock altered in structure and composition by pressure, heat, or chemically active fluids after original formation. (If heat is sufficient to melt the original rock, technically it becomes an igneous rock upon cooling.) The term was coined in 1833 by Scottish geologist Charles Lyell (1797–1875).

metamorphism geological term referring to the changes in rocks of the Earth's crust caused by increasing pressure and temperature. The resulting rocks are metamorphic rocks. All metamorphic changes take place in solid rocks. If the rocks melt and then harden, they become ◊igneous rocks.

metamorphosis period during the life cycle of many invertebrates, most amphibians, and some fish, during which the individual's body changes from one form to another through a major reconstitution of its tissues. For example, adult frogs are produced by metamorphosis from tadpoles, and butterflies are produced from caterpillars following metamorphosis within a pupa.

In classical thought and literature, metamorphosis is the transformation of a living being into another shape, either living or inanimate (for example Niobe). The Roman poet Ovid wrote about this theme.

metazoa another name for animals. It reflects an earlier system of classification, in which there were two main divisions within the animal kingdom, the multicellular animals, or metazoa, and the single-celled 'animals' or protozoa. The ◊protozoa are no longer included in the animal kingdom, so only the metazoa remain.

meteor flash of light in the sky, popularly known as a **shooting** or **falling star**, caused by a particle of dust, a **meteoroid**, entering the atmosphere at speeds up to 70 kps/45 mps and burning up by friction at a height of around 100 km/60 mi. On any clear night, several **sporadic meteors** can be seen each hour.

Several times each year the Earth encounters swarms of dust shed by comets, which give rise to a **meteor shower**.

This appears to radiate from one particular point in the sky, after which the shower is named; the Perseid meteor shower in August appears in the constellation Perseus. A brilliant meteor is termed a **fireball**. Most meteoroids are smaller than grains of sand. The Earth sweeps up an estimated 16,000 tonnes of meteoric material every year.

meteor-burst communications technique for sending messages by bouncing radio waves off the trails of ◊meteors. High-speed computer-controlled equipment is used to sense the presence of a meteor and to broadcast a signal during the short time that the meteor races across the sky.

The system, first suggested in the late 1920s, remained impracticable until data-compression techniques were developed, enabling messages to be sent in automatic high-speed bursts each time a meteor trail appeared. There are usually enough meteor trails in the sky at any time to permit continuous transmission of a message. The technique offers a communications link that is difficult to jam, undisturbed by storms on the Sun, and would not be affected by nuclear war.

meteorite piece of rock or metal from space that reaches the surface of the Earth, Moon, or other body. Most meteorites are thought to be fragments from asteroids, although some may be pieces from the heads of comets. Most are stony, although some are made of iron and a few have a mixed rock-iron composition.

Stony meteorites can be divided into two kinds: **chondrites** and **achondrites**. Chondrites contain chondrules, small spheres of the silicate minerals olivine and orthopyroxene, and comprise 85% of meteorites. Achondrites do not contain chondrules. Meteorites provide evidence for the nature of the Solar System and may be similar to the Earth's core and mantle, neither of which can be observed directly.

meteoroid chunk of rock in interplanetary space. There is no official distinction between meteoroids and asteroids, except that the term asteroid is generally reserved for objects larger than 1.6 km/1 mi in diameter, whereas meteoroids can range anywhere from pebble-size up.

Meteoroids are believed to result from the fragmentation of asteroids after collisions. Some meteoroids strike the Earth's atmosphere, and their fiery trails are called meteors. If they fall to Earth, they are named meteorites.

meteorology scientific observation and study of the ◊atmosphere, so that ◊weather can be accurately forecast.

Data from meteorological stations and weather satellites are collated by computer at central agencies, and forecast and weather maps based on current readings are issued at regular intervals. Modern analysis, employing some of the most powerful computers, can give useful forecasts for up to six days ahead.

At meteorological stations readings are taken of the factors determining weather conditions: atmospheric pressure, temperature, humidity, wind (using the ◊Beaufort scale), cloud cover (measuring both type of cloud and coverage), and precipitation such as rain, snow, and hail (measured at 12-hour intervals). ◊Satellites are used either to relay information transmitted from the Earth-based stations, or to send pictures of cloud development, indicating wind patterns, and snow and ice cover.

history Apart from some observations included by Aristotle in his book *Meteorologia*, meteorology did not become a precise science until the end of the 16th century, when Galileo and the Florentine academicians constructed the first thermometer of any importance, and when Evangelista Torricelli in 1643 discovered the principle of the barometer. Robert ◊Boyle's work on gases, and that of his assistant, Robert ◊Hooke, on barometers, advanced the physics necessary for the understanding of the weather. Gabriel ◊Fahrenheit's invention of a superior mercury thermometer provided further means for temperature recording.

weather maps In the early 19th century a chain of meteorological stations was established in France, and weather maps were constructed from the data collected. The first weather map in England, showing the trade winds and monsoons, was made in 1688, and the first telegraphic weather report appeared 31 Aug 1848. The first daily telegraphic weather map was prepared at the Great Exhibition in 1851, but the Meteorological Office was not established in London until 1855. The first regular daily collections of weather observations by telegraph and the first British daily weather reports were made in 1860, and the first daily printed maps appeared 1868.

collecting data Observations can be collected not only from land stations, but also from weather ships, aircraft, and self-recording and automatic transmitting stations, such as the ◊radiosonde. Radar may be used to map clouds and storms. Satellites have played an important role in televising pictures of global cloud distribution.

WORLD METEOROLOGICAL ORGANISATION

http://www.wmo.ch/

Internet voice of the World Meteorological Organisation, a UN division coordinating global scientific activity related to climate and weather. The site offers ample material on the long term objectives and immediate policies of the organization. It also disseminates important information on WMO's databases, training programmes, and satellite activities, as well as its projects related to the protection of the environment.

The great tragedy of Science – the slaying of a beautiful hypothesis by an ugly fact.

THOMAS HENRY HUXLEY English biologist. *Collected Essays*

meter any instrument used for measurement. The term is often compounded with a prefix to denote a specific type of meter: for example, ammeter, voltmeter, flowmeter, or pedometer.

methanal (common name ***formaldehyde***) HCHO gas at ordinary temperatures, condensing to a liquid at –21°C/–5.8°F. It has a powerful, penetrating smell. Dissolved in water, it is used as a biological preservative. It is used in the manufacture of plastics, dyes, foam (for example urea-formaldehyde foam, used in insulation), and in medicine.

methane CH_4 the simplest hydrocarbon of the paraffin series. Colourless, odourless, and lighter than air, it burns with a bluish flame and explodes when mixed with air or oxygen. It is the chief constituent of natural gas and also occurs in the explosive firedamp of coal mines. Methane emitted by rotting vegetation forms marsh gas, which may ignite by spontaneous combustion to produce the pale flame seen over marshland and known as ◊will-o'-the-wisp.

Methane causes about 38% of the warming of the globe through the ◊greenhouse effect; weight for weight it is 60–70 times more potent than carbon dioxide at trapping solar radiation in the atmosphere and so heating the planet. The amount of methane in the air is predicted to double over the next 60 years. An estimated 15% of all methane gas into the atmosphere is produced by cows and other cud-chewing animals, and 20% is produced by termites that feed on soil.

METHANE

The flatulence of a single sheep could power a small lorry for 40 km/25 mi a day. The digestive process produces methane gas, which can be burnt as fuel. According to one New Zealand scientist, the methane from 72 million sheep could supply the entire fuel needs of his country.

methanogenic bacteria one of a group of primitive microorganisms, the ◊Archaea. They give off methane gas as a by-product of their metabolism, and are common in sewage treatment plants and hot springs, where the temperature is high and oxygen is absent. Archaeons were originally classified as bacteria, but were found to be unique in 1996 following the gene sequencing of the deep-sea vent *Methanococcus jannaschii*.

methanoic acid (common name ***formic acid***) HCOOH, a colourless, slightly fuming liquid that freezes at 8°C/46.4°F and boils at 101°C/213.8°F. It occurs in stinging ants, nettles, sweat, and pine needles, and is used in dyeing, tanning, and electroplating.

methanol (common name ***methyl alcohol***) CH_3OH the simplest of the alcohols. It can be made by the dry distillation of wood (hence it is also known as wood alcohol), but is usually made from coal or natural gas. When pure, it is a colourless, flammable liquid with a pleasant odour, and is highly poisonous.

Methanol is used to produce formaldehyde (from which resins and plastics can be made), methyl-ter-butyl ether (MTB, a replacement for lead as an octane-booster in petrol), vinyl acetate (largely used in paint manufacture), and petrol. In 1993 Japanese engineers built an engine, made largely of ceramics, that runs on methanol. The prototype is lighter and has a cleaner exhaust than comparable metal, petrol-powered engines.

methionine one of the nine essential ◊amino acids. It is also used as an antidote to paracetamol poisoning.

methyl alcohol common name for ◊methanol.

methylated spirit alcohol that has been rendered undrinkable, and is used for industrial purposes, as a fuel for spirit burners or a solvent.

It is nevertheless drunk by some individuals, resulting eventually in death. One of the poisonous substances in it is ◊methanol, or methyl alcohol, and this gives it its name. (The 'alcohol' of alcoholic drinks is ethanol.)

methyl benzene alternative name for ◊toluene.

methyl bromide pesticide gas used to fumigate soil. It is a major ◊ozone depleter. Industry produces 50,000 tonnes of methyl bromide annually (1995). The European Union has promised a 25% reduction in manufacture by 1998, and the USA intends to ban use by 2001. The European Union (EU) proposed a total ban on usage by 2005 at a meeting in Sept 1997.

methyl orange $C_{14}H_{14}N_3NaO_3S$ orange-yellow powder used as an acid–base indicator in chemical tests, and as a stain in the preparation of slides of biological material. Its colour changes with pH; below pH 3.1 it is red, above pH 4.4 it is yellow.

metre SI unit (symbol m) of length, equivalent to 1.093 yards. It is defined by scientists as the length of the path travelled by light in a vacuum during a time interval of 1/299,792,458 of a second.

METRE

The metre was originally (in 1791) defined as one ten-millionth of the distance from the North Pole to the equator, on a line through Paris.

metric system system of weights and measures developed in France in the 18th century and recognized by other countries in the 19th century.

In 1960 an international conference on weights and measures recommended the universal adoption of a revised International System (Système International d'Unités, or SI), with seven prescribed 'base units': the metre (m) for length, kilogram (kg) for mass, second (s) for time, ampere (A) for electric current, kelvin (K) for thermodynamic temperature, candela (cd) for luminous intensity, and mole (mol) for quantity of matter.

supplementary units Two supplementary units are included in the SI system – the radian (rad) and steradian (sr) – used to measure plane and solid angles. In addition, there are recognized derived units that can be expressed as simple products or divisions of powers of the basic units, with no other integers appearing in the expression; for example, the watt.

non-SI units Some non-SI units, well established and internationally recognized, remain in use in conjunction with SI: minute, hour, and day in measuring time; multiples or submultiples of base or derived units which have long-established names, such as tonne for mass, the litre for volume; and specialist measures such as the metric carat for gemstones.

prefixes Prefixes used with metric units are tera (T) million million times; giga (G) billion (thousand million) times; mega (M) million times; kilo (k) thousand times; hecto (h) hundred times; deca (da) ten times; deci (d) tenth part; centi (c) hundredth part; milli (m) thousandth part; micro (μ) millionth part; nano (n) billionth part; pico (p trillionth part; femto (f) quadrillionth part; atto (a) quintillionth part.

C DISTANCES IN DESCENDING ORDER:

KIPPERS MAKE COLD MEALS

KILOMETRES / METR

Mexican hairless dog breed of dog remarkable for being without hair, except for tufts on its head and tail tip. Its skin may be grey or pinkish, and it stands about 40–50 cm/15–20 in tall. It may be descended from dogs of the ◊Chinese crested dog type that were brought to the New World by Spanish colonists at the end of the 16th century.

mg symbol for **milligram**.

MHD abbreviation for ◊magnetohydrodynamics .

mho SI unit of electrical conductance, now called the ◊siemens; equivalent to a reciprocal ohm.

mi symbol for ◊mile.

mica group of silicate minerals that split easily into thin flakes along lines of weakness in their crystal structure (perfect basal cleavage). They are glossy, have a pearly lustre, and are found in many igneous and metamorphic rocks. Their good thermal and electrical insulation qualities make them valuable in industry.

Their chemical composition is complicated, but they are silicates with silicon-oxygen tetrahedra arranged in continuous sheets, with weak bonding between the layers, resulting in perfect cleavage.

A common example of mica is muscovite (white mica), $KAl_2Si_3AlO_{10}(OH,F)_2$.

Michaelmas daisy popular name for a species of ◊aster, and also for the sea aster or starwort.

MICR abbreviation for ◊magnetic-ink character recognition.

micro- prefix (symbol μ) denoting a one-millionth part (10^{-6}). For example, a micrometre, μm, is one-millionth of a metre.

microbe another name for ◊microorganism.

MICROBE ZOO

http://commtechlab.msu.edu/sites/dlc-me/zoo/

Colourful and interactive zoo of some of the microbes that surround us. It includes sections on the 'domestic' microbes, the vampire ones that suck the life from other bacteria, the killers which destroy stone buildings, those in aquatic environments, and those that are to be found in beer, bread, chocolate, wine and other food. services and legal assistance.

microbilling in computing, technique of charging for software by usage. Instead of being sold to users in a box over the counter, programs are divided into small segments which can be quickly downloaded over a network on demand. Each time the program is used, the customer's account is debited by a small amount.

microbiology the study of microorganisms, mostly viruses and single-celled organisms such as bacteria, protozoa, and yeasts. The practical applications of microbiology are in medicine (since many microorganisms cause disease); in brewing, baking, and other food and beverage processes, where the microorganisms carry out fermentation; and in genetic engineering, which is creating increasing interest in the field of microbiology.

microchip popular name for the silicon chip, or ◊integrated circuit.

microclimate the climate of a small area, such as a woodland, lake, or even a hedgerow. Significant differences can exist between the climates of two neighbouring areas – for example, a town is usually warmer than the surrounding countryside (forming a heat island), and a woodland cooler, darker, and less windy than an area of open land.

Microclimates play a significant role in agriculture and horticulture, as different crops require different growing conditions.

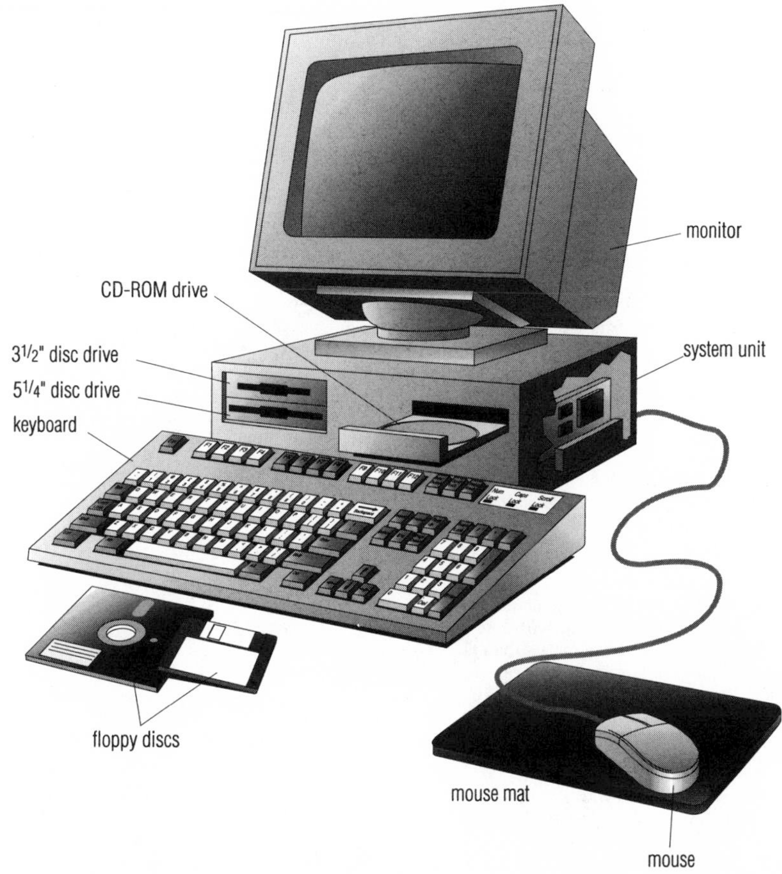

microcomputer The component parts of the microcomputer: the system unit contains the hub of the system, including the central processing unit (CPU), information on all of the computer's peripheral devices, and often a fixed disc drive. The monitor (or visual display unit) displays text and graphics, the keyboard and mouse are used to input data, and the floppy disc and CD-ROM drives read data stored on discs.

microcomputer or ***micro*** or ***personal computer*** small desktop or portable computer, typically designed to be used by one person at a time, although individual computers can be linked in a network so that users can share data and programs.

Its central processing unit is a ◊microprocessor, contained on a single integrated circuit.

Microcomputers are the smallest of the four classes of computer (the others are ◊supercomputer, mainframe, and ◊minicomputer). Since the appearance in 1975 of the first commercially available microcomputer, the Altair 8800, micros have become ubiquitous in commerce, industry, and education.

microfiche sheet of film on which printed text is photographically reduced. See ◊microform.

microform generic name for media on which text or images are photographically reduced. The main examples are **microfilm** (similar to the film in an ordinary camera) and **microfiche** (flat sheets of film, generally 105 mm/4 in x 148 mm/6 in, holding the equivalent of 420 standard pages). Microform has the advantage of low reproduction and storage costs, but it requires special devices for reading the text. It is widely used for archiving and for storing large volumes of text, such as library catalogues.

Computer data may be output directly and quickly in microform by means of COM (computer output on microfilm/microfiche) techniques.

microglia type of glial cell surrounding the nerve cells in the brain and spinal cord. They have an immune function.

micrometer instrument for measuring minute lengths or angles with great accuracy; different types of micrometer are used in astronomical and engineering work.

The type of micrometer used in astronomy consists of two fine wires, one fixed and the other movable, placed in the focal plane of a telescope; the movable wire is fixed on a sliding plate and can be positioned parallel to the other until the object appears between the wires.

The movement is then indicated by a scale on the adjusting screw.

micrometre one-millionth of a ◊metre (symbol μm).

microminiaturization reduction in size and weight of electronic components. The first size reduction in electronics was brought about by the introduction of the ◊transistor. Further reductions were achieved with ◊integrated circuits and the ◊silicon chip.

micron obsolete name for the micrometre, one millionth of a metre.

microorganism or ***microbe*** living organism invisible to the naked eye but visible under a microscope. Microorganisms include viruses and single-celled organisms such as bacteria, protozoa, yeasts, and some algae. The term has no taxonomic significance in biology. The study of microorganisms is known as microbiology.

microphone primary component in a sound-reproducing system, whereby the mechanical energy of sound waves is converted into electrical signals by means of a ◊transducer. One of the simplest is the telephone receiver mouthpiece, invented by Scottish–US inventor Alexander Graham Bell in 1876; other types of microphone are used with broadcasting and sound-film apparatus.

Telephones have a **carbon microphone**, which reproduces only a narrow range of frequencies. For live music, a **moving-coil microphone** is often used. In it, a diaphragm that vibrates with sound waves moves a coil through a magnetic field, thus generating an electric current. The **ribbon microphone** combines the diaphragm and coil. The **condenser microphone** is most commonly used in recording and works by a ◊capacitor. They are always used in telephones.

microprocessor complete computer ◊central processing unit contained on a single ◊integrated circuit, or chip. The appearance of the first microprocessor 1971 designed by Intel for a pocket calculator manufacturer heralded the introduction of the microcomputer. The microprocessor has led to a dramatic fall in the size and cost of computers, and ◊dedicated computers can now be found in washing machines, cars, and so on. Examples of microprocessors are the Intel Pentium family and the IBM/Motorola PowerPC, used by Apple Computer.

Texas Instruments introduced in January 1997 a digital-signal microprocessor chip that can process 1.6 billion instructions a second. This is about 40 times more powerful than a chip now found in today's computer modem. The new chip can reduce the time needed to download a file from the Internet from ten minutes to less than five seconds.

micropropagation the mass production of plants by placing tiny pieces of plant tissue in sterile glass containers along with nutrients. Perfect clones of superplants are produced in sterile cabinets, with filtered air and carefully controlled light, temperature, and humidity. The system is used for the house-plant industry and for forestry – micropropagation gives immediate results, whereas obtaining genetically homogenous tree seed by traditional means would take over 100 years.

micropyle in flowering plants, a small hole towards one end of the ovule. At pollination the pollen tube growing down from the ◊stigma eventually passes through this pore. The male gamete is contained within the tube and is able to travel to the egg in the interior of the ovule. Fertilization can then take place, with subsequent seed formation and dispersal.

microscope instrument for forming magnified images with high resolution for detail. Optical and electron microscopes are the ones chiefly in use; other types include acoustic, ◊scanning tunnelling, and ◊atomic force microscopes.

The **optical microscope** usually has two sets of glass lenses and an eyepiece. It was invented 1609 in the Netherlands by Zacharias Janssen (1580–c. 1638). **Fluorescence microscopy** makes use of fluorescent dyes to illuminate samples, or to highlight the presence of particular substances within a sample. Various illumination systems are also used to highlight details.

The ◊transmission electron microscope, developed from 1932, passes a beam of electrons, instead of a beam of light, through a specimen. Since electrons are not visible, the eyepiece is replaced with a fluorescent screen or photographic plate; far higher magnification and resolution are possible than with the optical microscope.

The Gscanning electron microscope (SEM), developed in the mid-1960s, moves a fine beam of electrons over the surface of a specimen, the reflected electrons being collected to form the image. The specimen has to be in a vacuum chamber.

The **acoustic microscope** passes an ultrasonic (ultrahigh-frequency sound) wave through the specimen, the transmitted sound being used to form an image on a computer screen.

The **scanned-probe microscope**, developed in the late 1980s, runs a probe, with a tip so fine that it may consist only of a single atom, across the surface of the specimen. In the **scanning tunnelling microscope**, an electric current that flows through the probe is used to construct an image of the specimen. In 1988 a scanning tunnelling microscope was used to photograph a single protein molecule for the first time. In the **atomic force microscope**, the force felt by the probe is measured and used to form the image. These instruments can magnify a million times and give images of single atoms.

Microsoft US corporation, now the world's largest software supplier. Microsoft's first major product was a version of Basic, written for the MITS Altair 1975, and adopted by most of the desktop computer industry. Through ◊MS-DOS, written for IBM, ◊Windows, and related applications it has steadily increased its hold on the personal computer market. Microsoft was founded by Bill ◊Gates and Paul Allen in 1975.

Together with ◊Intel, the company supplied operating systems and computer chips for about 90% of the world's personal computers in 1997.

In 1996, Microsoft launched another new operating system, Windows CE (Consumer Electronics), for handheld computers, pen-operated personal digital assistants, in-car systems and similar applications. Suppliers of CE-based HPCs (handheld personal computers) include Casio, Compaq, Hewlett-Packard, Philips and Sharp. Windows CE version 2 is also used in an improved version of WebTV: a set-top box that enables users to surf the Internet on their television sets. Microsoft purchased WebTV Networks for $425 million in 1997. The first companies to supply WebTV systems were Philips, Sony and Mitsubishi.

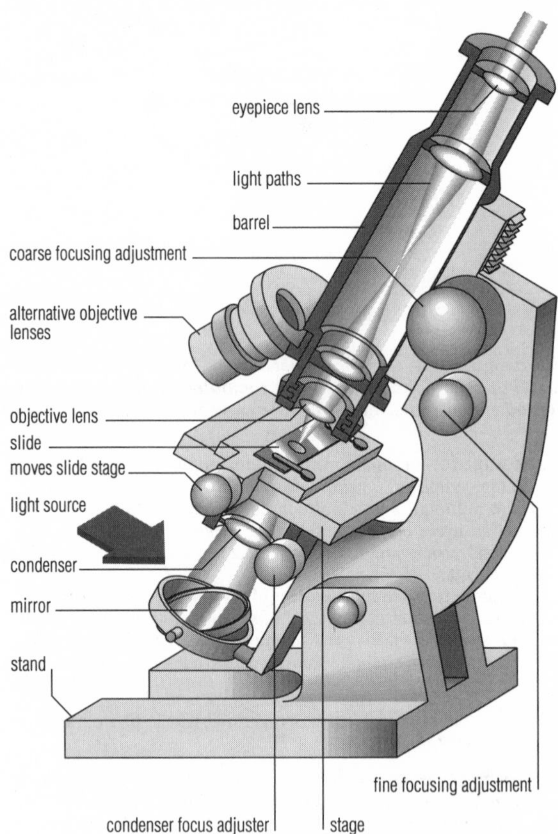

microscope *Terms used to describe an optical microscope. In essence, the optical microscope consists of an eyepiece lens and an objective lens, which are used to produce an enlarged image of a small object by focusing light from a light source. Optical microscopes can achieve magnifications of up to 1,500–2,000. Higher magnifications and resolutions are obtained by electron microscopes.*

A US federal probe into charges that Microsoft was engaging in anticompetitive behaviour was carried out 1990–93, from which date the US Justice Department launched its own investigations. Under a settlement reached in 1994, Microsoft agreed to end the uncompetitive practice 'per processor' pricing, whereby PC manufacturers paid a fee for each machine produced irrespective of the software to be installed. The Justice Department started another case in 1997, accusing Microsoft of breaking this settlement by tying the installation of Windows 95 to the installation of Microsoft's free Web browser, Internet Explorer. In December the company was ordered to change its marketing policy.

A science which hesitates to forget its founders is lost.

ALFRED NORTH WHITEHEAD English philosopher and mathematician. Attributed remark

Microsoft Network (MSN) in computing, online service operated by ◊Microsoft.

Microsoft Word in computing, versatile and powerful word processing program for ◊IBM-compatible and Apple ◊Macintosh PCs. The program began its life as an ◊MS-DOS program in 1983, and a year later it was released as one of the first programs for the Macintosh. The advanced features and ease of use of Version 6.0, released in 1994, established Word as the market leader in its field.

microsurgery part or all of an intricate surgical operation – rejoining a severed limb, for example – performed with the aid of a binocular microscope, using miniaturized instruments. Sewing of the nerves and blood vessels is done with a nylon thread so fine that it is only just visible to the naked eye.

The technique permits treatment of previously inaccessible lesions in the eye or brain.

microtubules tiny tubes found in almost all cells with a nucleus. They help to define the shape of a cell by forming scaffolding for cilia and they also form the fibres of mitotic spindle (see ◊mitosis).

microwave ◊electromagnetic wave with a wavelength in the range 0. 3 to 30 cm/0.1 in to 12 in, or 300–300,000 megahertz (between radio waves and ◊infrared radiation). Microwaves are used in radar, in radio broadcasting, and in microwave heating and cooking.

microwave heating heating by means of microwaves. Microwave ovens use this form of heating for the rapid cooking or reheating of foods, where heat is generated throughout the interior of the food. If food is not heated completely, there is a danger of bacterial growth that may lead to food poisoning. Industrially, microwave heating is used for destroying insects in grain and enzymes in processed food, pasteurizing and sterilizing liquids, and drying timber and paper.

Mid-Atlantic Ridge ◊ocean ridge, formed by the movement of plates described by ◊plate tectonics, that runs along the centre of the Atlantic Ocean, parallel to its edges, for some 14,000 km/8,800 mi – almost from the Arctic to the Antarctic.

The Mid-Atlantic Ridge is central because the ocean crust beneath the Atlantic Ocean has continually grown outwards from the ridge at a steady rate during the past 200 million years. Iceland straddles the ridge and was formed by volcanic outpourings.

midge common name for many insects resembling ◊gnats, generally divided into biting midges (family Ceratopogonidae) that suck blood and non-biting midges (family Chironomidae).

The larvae of some midges are the 'bloodworms' of stagnant water.

MIDI (acronym for ***musical instrument digital interface***) manufacturer's standard allowing different pieces of digital music equipment used in composing and recording to be freely connected.

The information-sending device (any electronic instrument) is called a controller, and the reading device (such as a computer) the sequencer. Pitch, dynamics, decay rate, and stereo position can all be transmitted via the interface. A computer with a MIDI interface can input and store the sounds produced by the connected instruments, and can then manipulate these sounds in many different ways. For example, a single keystroke may change the key of an entire composition. Even a full written score for the composition may be automatically produced.

midnight sun the constant appearance of the Sun (within the Arctic and Antarctic circles) above the ◊horizon during the summer.

midsummer the time of the summer ◊solstice, about 21 June. Midsummer Day, 24 June, is the Christian festival of St John the Baptist.

midwifery assistance of women in childbirth. Traditionally, it was undertaken by experienced specialists; in modern medical training it is a nursing speciality for practitioners called midwives.

The English physician William Harvey's 1653 work on generation contained an influential chapter on labour. Dr Peter Chamberlen II (1560–1631) made an important contribution to midwifery, particularly with his development of the first midwifery forceps.

mifepristone (RU486) anti-progesterone drug used, in combination with a ◊prostaglandin, to procure early ◊abortion (up to the tenth week in pregnancy). It is administered only in hospitals or recognized clinics and a success rate of 95% is claimed. Formerly known as RU486, it was developed and first used in France in 1989. It was licensed in the UK in 1991.

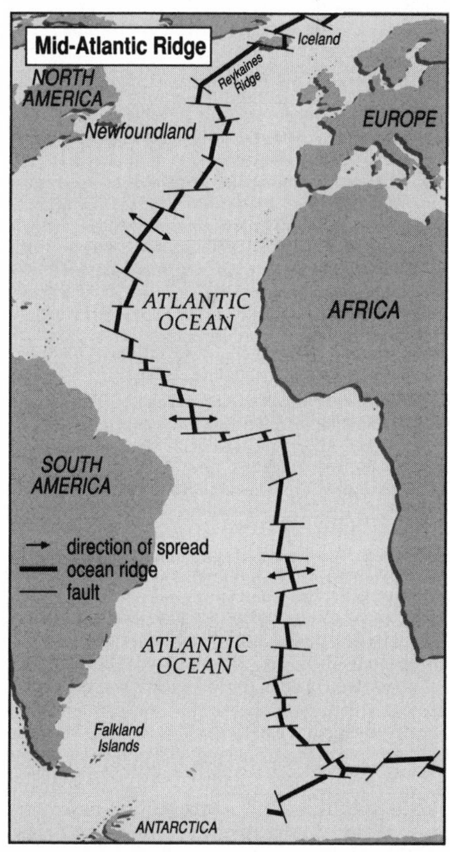

Mid-Atlantic Ridge *The Mid-Atlantic Ridge is the boundary between the crustal plates that form America, and Europe and Africa. An oceanic ridge cannot be curved since the material welling up to form the ridge flows at a right angle to the ridge. The ridge takes the shape of small straight sections offset by fractures transverse to the main ridge.*

By March 1991, 60,000 abortions had been carried out in France by this method.

mignonette sweet-scented plant, native to N Africa, with yellowish-green flowers in racemes (along the main stem) and abundant foliage; it is widely cultivated. (*Reseda odorata*, family Resedaceae.)

migraine acute, sometimes incapacitating headache (generally only on one side), accompanied by nausea, that recurs, often with advance symptoms such as flashing lights. No cure has been discovered, but ergotamine normally relieves the symptoms. Some sufferers learn to avoid certain foods, such as chocolate, which suggests an allergic factor.

MIGRATION

The grey whale migrates further than any other mammal. It makes a round trip of 20,400 km/12,500 mi between its summer feeding grounds in the Arctic and its winter breeding lagoons off the western coast

migration the movement, either seasonal or as part of a single life cycle, of certain animals, chiefly birds and fish, to distant breeding or feeding grounds.

The precise methods by which animals navigate and know where to go are still obscure. Birds have much sharper eyesight and better visual memory of ground clues than humans, but in long-distance flights appear to navigate by the Sun and stars, possibly in combination with a 'reading' of the Earth's magnetic field through an inbuilt 'magnetic compass', which is a tiny mass of tissue between the eye and brain in birds. Similar cells occur in 'homing' honeybees and in certain bacteria that use it to determine which way is 'down'. Leatherback turtles use the contours of underwater mountains and valleys to navigate by. Most striking, however, is the migration of young birds that have never flown a route before and are unaccompanied by adults. It is postulated that they may inherit as part of their genetic code an overall 'sky chart' of their journey that is triggered into use when they become aware of how the local sky pattern, above the place in which they hatch, fits into it. Similar theories have been advanced in the case of fish, such as eels and salmon, with whom vision obviously plays a lesser role, but for whom currents and changes in the composition and temperature of the sea in particular locations may play a part – for example, in enabling salmon to return to the precise river in which they were spawned. Migration also occurs with land animals; for example, lemmings and antelope.

Species migration is the spread of the home range of a species over many years, for example the spread of the collared dove (*Streptopelia decaocto*) from Turkey to Britain over the period 1920–52. Any journey which takes an animal outside of its normal home range is called **individual migration**; when the animal does not return to its home range it is called **removal migration**. An example of **return migration** is the movement of birds that fly south for the winter and return to their home ranges in the spring. Many types of whale also make return migrations. In **remigration**, the return leg of the migration is completed by a subsequent generation, for example locust swarms migrate, but each part of the circuit is completed by a different generation.

Related to migration is the homing ability of pigeons, bees, and other creatures.

Milankovitch hypothesis the combination of factors governing the occurrence of ◊ice ages proposed in 1930 by the Yugoslav geophysicist M Milankovitch (1879–1958). These include the variation in the angle of the Earth's axis, and the geometry of the Earth's orbit around the Sun.

mildew any ◊fungus that appears as a destructive growth on plants, paper, leather, or wood when they become damp for a certain length of time; such fungi usually form a thin white coating on the surface.

mile imperial unit of linear measure. A statute mile is equal to 1,760 yards (1.60934 km), and an international nautical mile is equal to 2,026 yards (1,852 m).

milfoil another name for the herb ◊yarrow. Water milfoils are unrelated; they have whorls of fine leaves and grow underwater. (Genus *Miriophyllum*, family Haloragidaceae.)

miljee small tree, *Acacia osswaldii*, widely distributed in inland Australia.

milk secretion of the ◊mammary glands of female mammals, with which they suckle their young (during ◊lactation). Over 85% is water, the remainder comprising protein, fat, lactose (a sugar), calcium, phosphorus, iron, and vitamins. The milk of cows, goats, and sheep is often consumed by humans, but regular drinking of milk after infancy is principally a Western practice.

milking machine machine that uses suction to milk cows. The first milking machine was invented in the USA by L O Colvin in 1860. Later it was improved so that the suction was regularly released by a pulsating device, since it was found that continuous suction is harmful to cows.

milk teeth or ***deciduous teeth*** teeth that erupt in childhood between the ages of 6 and 30 months. They are replaced by the permanent teeth, which erupt between the ages of 6 and 21 years. See also ◊dentition and ◊tooth.

Milky Way faint band of light crossing the night sky, consisting of stars in the plane of our Galaxy. The name Milky Way is often used for the Galaxy itself. It is a spiral◊ galaxy, 100,000 light years in diameter and 2,000 light years thick, containing at least 100 billion ◊stars. The Sun is in one of its spiral arms, about 25,000 light years from the centre, not far from its central plane.

The densest parts of the Milky Way, towards the Galaxy's centre, lie in the constellation ◊Sagittarius. In places, the Milky Way is interrupted by lanes of dark dust that obscure light from the stars beyond, such as the Coalsack ◊nebula in ◊Crux (the Southern Cross). It is because of these that the Milky Way is irregular in width and appears to be divided into two between Centaurus and Cygnus.

miller's thumb another name for ◊bullhead, a small fish.

millet any of several grasses of which the grains are used as a cereal food and the stems as animal fodder. Species include *Panicum miliaceum*, extensively cultivated in the warmer parts of Europe, and *Sorghum bicolor*, also known as durra. (Family Gramineae.)

milli- prefix (symbol m) denoting a one-thousandth part (10^{-3}).

For example, a millimetre, mm, is one thousandth of a metre.

millibar unit of pressure, equal to one-thousandth of a ◊bar.

millilitre one-thousandth of a litre (ml), equivalent to one cubic centimetre (cc).

millimetre of mercury unit of pressure (symbol mmHg), used in medicine for measuring blood pressure defined as the pressure exerted by a column of mercury one millimetre high, under the action of gravity.

millipede any of a group of ◊arthropods that have segmented bodies, each segment usually bearing two pairs of legs, and a pair of short clubbed antennae on the distinct head. Most millipedes are no more than 2.5 cm/1 in long; a few in the tropics are 30 cm/12 in. (Class Diplopoda.)

Millipedes live in damp, dark places, feeding mainly on rotting vegetation. Some species injure crops by feeding on tender roots, and some produce a poisonous secretion in defence. Certain orders have silk glands.

Mills Cross type of ◊radio telescope consisting of two rows of aerials at right angles to each other, invented in 1953 by the Australian radio astronomer Bernard Mills (1920–). The cross-shape produces a narrow beam useful for pinpointing the positions of radio sources.

Milstar (acronym for ***Military Strategic and Tactical Relay***) US communications satellite launched February 1994. It was designed to function in a nuclear war and broadcast orders to launch weapons. After the breakup of the Soviet Union the continuation of its development became controversial.

It consists of a network of four communications satellites and around 1,200 portable ground terminals. It will cost $17.3 billion. The second satellite was launched in 1995. The third satellite is due for launch in 1998.

MIME (acronymn for ***Multipurpose Internet Mail Extensions***) in computing, standard for transferring multimedia ◊e-mail messages and ◊World Wide Web ◊hypertext documents over the Internet. Under MIME, binary files (any file not in plain text, such as graphics and audio) are translated into a form of ◊ASCII before transmission, and then turned back into binary form by the recipient. See also ◊UUencode.

mimicry imitation of one species (or group of species) by another. The most common form is **Batesian mimicry** (named after English naturalist ◊H W Bates), where the mimic resembles a model that is poisonous or unpleasant to eat, and has aposematic, or warning, coloration; the mimic thus benefits from the fact that predators have learned to avoid the model. Hoverflies that resemble bees or wasps are an example. Appearance is usually the basis for mimicry, but calls, songs, scents, and other signals can also be mimicked.

In **Mullerian mimicry**, two or more equally poisonous or distasteful species have a similar colour pattern, thereby reinforcing the warning each gives to predators. In some cases, mimicry is not for protection, but allows the mimic to prey on, or parasitize, the model.

mimosa any of a group of leguminous trees, shrubs, or herbs belonging to the mimosa family, found in tropical and subtropical regions. They all have small, fluffy, golden, ball-like flowers. A similar but unrelated plant, *Acacia dealbata,* is sold as mimosa by European florists. (True mimosa genus *Mimosa,* family Mimosaceae.)

Certain species, such as the sensitive plant of Brazil *M. pudica,* shrink momentarily on being touched.

mineral naturally formed inorganic substance with a particular chemical composition and a regularly repeating internal structure. Either in their perfect crystalline form or otherwise, minerals are the constituents of ◊rocks. In more general usage, a mineral is any substance economically valuable for mining (including coal and oil, despite their organic origins).

Mineral forming processes include: melting of pre-existing rock and subsequent crystallization of a mineral to form magmatic or volcanic rocks; weathering of rocks exposed at the land surface, with subsequent transport and grading by surface waters, ice or wind to form sediments; and recrystallization through increasing temperature and pressure with depth to form metamorphic rocks.

Minerals are usually classified as magmatic, sedimentary, or metamorphic. The magmatic minerals include the feldspars, quartz, pyroxenes, amphiboles, micas, and olivines that crystallize from silica-rich rock melts within the crust or from extruded lavas.

The most commonly occurring sedimentary minerals are either pure concentrates or mixtures of sand, clay minerals, and carbonates (chiefly calcite, aragonite, and dolomite).

Minerals typical of metamorphism include andalusite, cordierite, garnet, tremolite, lawsonite, pumpellyite, glaucophane, wollastonite, chlorite, micas, hornblende, staurolite, kyanite, and diopside.

MINERAL GALLERY

`http://mineral.galleries.com/`

Collection of descriptions and images of minerals, organized by mineral name, class (sulphides, oxides, carbonates, and so on), and grouping (such as gemstones, birth stones, and fluorescent minerals).

mineral dressing preparing a mineral ore for processing. Ore is seldom ready to be processed when it is mined; it often contains unwanted rock and dirt. Therefore it is usually crushed into uniform size and then separated from the dirt, or gangue. This may be done magnetically (some iron ores), by washing (gold), by treatment with chemicals (copper ores), or by flotation.

mineral extraction recovery of valuable ores from the Earth's crust. The processes used include open-cast mining, shaft mining, and quarrying, as well as more specialized processes such as those used for oil and sulphur (see, for example, ◊Frasch process).

mineralogy study of minerals. The classification of minerals is based chiefly on their chemical composition and the kind of chemical bonding that holds these atoms together. The mineralogist also studies their crystallographic and physical characters, occurrence, and mode of formation.

Main Dietary Minerals

Mineral	*Main dietary sources*	*Major functions in the body*	*Deficiency symptoms*
Calcium	milk, cheese, green vegetables, dried legumes	constituent of bones and teeth; essential for nerve transmission, muscle contraction, and clotting	tetany
Chromium	vegetable oils, meat	involved in energy metabolism	impaired glucose metabolism
Copper	drinking water, meat	associated with iron metabolism	anaemia
Fluoride	drinking water, tea, seafoods	helps to keep bones and teeth healthy	increased rate of tooth decay
Iodine	seafoods, dairy products, many vegetables, iodized table salt	essential for healthy growth and development	goitre
Iron	meat (especially liver), legumes, green vegetables, whole grains, eggs	constituent of haemoglobin; involved in energy metabolism	anaemia
Magnesium	whole grains, green vegetables	involved in protein synthesis	growth failure, weakness, behavioural disturbances
Manganese	widely distributed in foods	involved in fat synthesis	not known in humans
Molybdenum	legumes, cereals, offal	constituent of some enzymes	not known in humans
Phosphorus	milk, cheese, meat, legumes, cereals	formation of bones and teeth, maintenance of acid–base balance	weakness, demineralization of bone
Potassium	milk, meat, fruits	maintenance of acid–base balance, fluid balance, nerve transmission	muscular weakness, paralysis
Selenium	seafoods, meat, cereals, egg yolk	role associated with that of vitamin E	not known in humans
Sodium	widely distributed in foods	as for potassium	cramp, loss of appetite, apathy
Zinc	widely distributed in foods	involved in digestion	growth failure, underdevelopment of reproductive organs

The systematic study of minerals began in the 18th century, with the division of minerals into four classes: earths, metals, salts, and bituminous substances, distinguished by their reactions to heat and water.

mineral oil oil obtained from mineral sources, for example coal or petroleum, as distinct from oil obtained from vegetable or animal sources.

mineral salt in nutrition, a simple inorganic chemical that is required by living organisms. Plants usually obtain their mineral salts from the soil, while animals get theirs from their food. Important mineral salts include iron salts (needed by both plants and animals), magnesium salts (needed mainly by plants, to make chlorophyll), and calcium salts (needed by animals to make bone or shell). A ◊trace element is required only in tiny amounts.

minicomputer multiuser computer with a size and processing power between those of a ◊mainframe and a ◊microcomputer. Nowadays almost all minicomputers are based on ◊microprocessors.

Minicomputers are often used in medium-sized businesses and in university departments handling ◊database or other commercial programs and running scientific or graphical applications.

Mini Disc digital audio disc that resembles a computer floppy disc in a 5 cm/2 in square case, with up to an hour's playing time. The system was developed by Sony for release in 1993.

Their small size makes Mini Discs particularly suitable for personal and car stereos, and the players are equipped with memory chips that store up to three seconds of music in order to compensate for any skips and jumps in playback.

mining extraction of minerals from under the land or sea for industrial or domestic uses. Exhaustion of traditionally accessible resources has led to development of new mining techniques; for example, extraction of oil from offshore deposits and from land shale reserves. Technology is also under development for the exploitation of minerals from entirely new sources such as mud deposits and mineral nodules from the sea bed.

Mud deposits are laid down by hot springs (about 350°C/660°F): sea water penetrates beneath the ocean floor and carries copper, silver, and zinc with it on its return. Such springs occur along the midocean ridges of the Atlantic and Pacific and in the geological rift between Africa and Arabia under the Red Sea.

Mineral nodules form on the ocean bed and contain manganese, cobalt, copper, molybdenum, and nickel; they stand out on the surface, and 'grow' by only a few millimetres every 100,000 years.

The deepest mine in Europe is a 1100 m deep working salt and potash mine at Boulby near Whitby on the northeast coast of England.

Minitel in computing, the dedicated terminal attached to France's teletext system, Teletel, which was launched in 1981 and has millions of users. Many Minitels – most of which have small black and white screens – were installed on free loan by France Telecom to subscribers who opted not to have telephone directories, and the online directory is still the most widely-used Minitel service. Erotic 'chat lines' have also proved very popular. Today in France, many PC users access Teletel using software that emulates a Minitel terminal.

mink either of two species of carnivorous mammals belonging to the weasel family, usually found in or near water. They have rich brown fur, and are up to 50 cm/1.6 ft long with bushy tails 20 cm/8 in long. They live in Europe and Asia (*M. lutreola*) and North America (*M. vison*). (Genus *Mustela.*)

They produce an annual litter of six in their riverbank burrows. The demand for their fur led to the establishment from the 1930s of mink ranches for breeding of the animals in a wide range of fur colours. In 1997 world production of mink skins was 26 million, which represented a 36% decline since 1986.

minnow any of various small freshwater fishes of the carp family, found in streams and ponds worldwide. Most species are small and dull in colour, but some are brightly coloured. They feed on larvae and insects. (Family Cyprinidae.)

Minoan civilization Bronze Age civilization on the Aegean island of Crete. The name is derived from Minos, the legendary king of Crete. The civilization is divided into three main periods: early Minoan, about 3000–2000 BC; middle Minoan, about 2000–1550 BC; and late Minoan, about 1550–1050 BC.

With the opening of the Bronze Age, about 3000 BC, the Minoan culture proper began. Each period was marked by cultural advances in copper and bronze weapons, pottery of increasingly intricate design, frescoes, and the construction of palaces and fine houses at Phaistos and Mallia, in addition to ◊Knossos. About 1400 BC, in the late Minoan period, the civilization was suddenly destroyed by earthquake or war. A partial revival continued until about 1100.

The earlier (Linear A) of two languages used in Crete remains undeciphered; Linear B, which is also found at sites on the mainland of Greece, was deciphered by Michael Ventris.

In religion the Minoans seem to have worshipped principally a great mother goddess with whom was associated a young male god. The tales of Greek mythology about Rhea, the mother of Zeus, and the birth of Zeus himself in a Cretan cave seem to be based on Minoan religion.

minor planet another name for an ◊asteroid.

Minsmere coastal marshland bird reserve (1948) near Aldeburgh, Suffolk, attracting a greater number of species than any other in Britain, and containing the Scrape, an artificial breeding habitat.

mint in botany, any aromatic plant of the mint family, widely distributed in temperate regions. The plants have square stems, creeping roots, and spikes of usually pink or purplish flowers. The family includes garden mint (*M. spicata*) and peppermint (*M. piperita*). (Genus *Mentha,* family Labiatae.)

minute unit of time consisting of 60 seconds; also a unit of angle equal to one sixtieth of a degree.

Miocene ***'middle recent'*** fourth epoch of the Tertiary period of geological time, 23.5–5.2 million years ago. At this time grasslands spread over the interior of continents, and hoofed mammals rapidly evolved.

mips (acronym for ***million instructions per second***) in computing, a measure of the speed of a processor. It does not equal the computer power in all cases.

Mir Russian ***'peace'*** or ***'world'*** Soviet space station, the core of which was launched on 20 February 1986. It is intended to be a permanently occupied space station.

A small wheat crop was harvested aboard the *Mir* space station on 6 December 1996. It was the first successful cultivation of a plant from seed in space.

Mira or ***Omicron Ceti*** brightest long-period pulsating ◊variable star, located in the constellation ◊Cetus. Mira was the first star discovered to vary periodically in brightness.

In 1596 Dutch astronomer David Fabricus noticed Mira as a third-magnitude object. Because it did not appear on any of the star charts available at the time, he mistook it for a ◊nova. The German astronomer Johann Bayer included it on his star atlas in 1603 and designated it Omicron Ceti. The star vanished from view again, only to reappear within a year. It was named 'Stella Mira', 'the wonderful star', by Hevelius, who observed it 1659–82.

It has a periodic variation between third or fourth magnitude and ninth magnitude over an average period of 331 days. It can sometimes reach second magnitude and once almost attained first magnitude 1779. At times it is easily visible to the naked eye, being the brightest star in that part of the sky, while at others it cannot be seen without a telescope.

mirage illusion seen in hot weather of water on the horizon, or of distant objects being enlarged. The effect is caused by the ◊refraction, or bending, of light.

Light rays from the sky bend as they pass through the hot layers of air near the ground, so that they appear to come from the horizon.

Because the light is from a blue sky, the horizon appears blue and watery. If, during the night, cold air collects near the ground, light can be bent in the opposite direction, so that objects below the horizon appear to float above it. In the same way, objects such as trees or rocks near the horizon can appear enlarged.

Reason, Observation and Experience – the Holy Trinity of Science.

ROBERT INGERSOLL US lawyer and orator. *The Gods*

mirror any polished surface that reflects light; often made from 'silvered' glass (in practice, a mercury-alloy coating of glass). A plane (flat) mirror produces a same-size, erect 'virtual' image located behind the mirror at the same distance from it as the object is in front of it. A spherical concave mirror produces a reduced, inverted real image in front or an enlarged, erect virtual image behind it (as in a shaving mirror), depending on how close the object is to the mirror. A spherical convex mirror produces a reduced, erect virtual image behind it (as in a car's rear-view mirror).

formula In a plane mirror the light rays appear to come from behind the mirror but do not actually do so. The inverted real image from a spherical concave mirror is an image in which the rays of light pass through it. The ◊focal length f of a spherical mirror is half the radius of curvature; it is related to the image distance v and object distance u by the equation $1/v + 1/u = 1/f$.

mirror site in computing, archive site which keeps a copy of another site's files for downloading by ◊FTP. Software archives such as those of the University of Michigan, and the many companies that distribute software by FTP, have several mirror sites around the world, so that users can choose the nearest site.

miscarriage spontaneous expulsion of a fetus from the womb before it is capable of independent survival. Often, miscarriages are due to an abnormality in the developing fetus.

missel thrush bird belonging to the ◊thrush family.

missile rocket-propelled weapon, which may be nuclear-armed. Modern missiles are often classified as surface-to-surface missiles (SSM), air-to-air missiles (AAM), surface-to-air missiles (SAM), or air-to-surface missiles (ASM). A **cruise missile** is in effect a pilotless, computer-guided aircraft; it can be sea-launched from submarines or surface ships, or launched from the air or the ground.

Rocket-propelled weapons were first used by the Chinese about AD 1100, and were encountered in the 18th century by the British forces. The rocket missile was then re-invented by William Congreve in England around 1805, and remained in use with various armies in the 19th century. The first wartime use of a long-range missile was against England in World War II, by the jet-powered German V1 (*Vergeltungswaffe*, 'revenge weapon' or Flying Bomb), a monoplane (wingspan about 6 m/18 ft, length 8.5 m/ 26 ft); the first rocket-propelled missile with a preset guidance system was the German V2, also launched by Germany against Britain in World War II.

Modern missiles are also classified as strategic or tactical: strategic missiles are the large, long-range **intercontinental ballistic missiles** (ICBMs, capable of reaching targets over 5,500 km/ 3,400 mi), and tactical missiles are the short-range weapons intended for use in limited warfare (with a range under 1,100 km/ 680 mi).

Not all missiles are large. There are many missiles that are small enough to be carried by one person. The Stinger, for example, is an anti-aircraft missile fired by a single soldier from a shoulder-held tube. Most fighter aircraft are equipped with missiles to use against enemy aircraft or against ground targets. Other small missiles are launched from a type of truck, called a MLRS (multiple-launch rocket system), that can move around a battlefield. Ship-to-ship missiles like the Exocet have proved very effective in naval battles.

The vast majority of missiles have systems that guide them to their target. The guidance system may consist of radar and computers, either in the missile or on the ground. These devices track the missile and determine the correct direction and distance required for it to hit its target. In the radio-guidance system, the computer is on the ground, and guidance signals are radio-transmitted to the missile. In the inertial guidance system, the computer is on board the missile. Some small missiles have heat-seeking devices fitted to their noses to seek out the engines of enemy aircraft, or are guided by laser light reflected from the target. Others (called TOW missiles) are guided by signals sent along wires that trail behind the missile in flight.

Outside the industrialized countries, 22 states had active ballistic-missile programmes by 1989, and 17 had deployed these weapons: Afghanistan, Argentina, Brazil, Cuba, Egypt, India, Iran, Iraq, Israel, North Korea, South Korea, Libya, Pakistan, Saudi Arabia, South Africa, Syria, and Taiwan. Non-nuclear short-range missiles were used during the Iran–Iraq War 1980–88 against Iraqi cities.

Battlefield missiles used in the 1991 Gulf War included antitank missiles and short-range attack missiles. NATO announced in 1990 that it was phasing out ground-launched nuclear battlefield missiles, and these are being replaced by types of tactical air-to-surface missile (TASM), also with nuclear warheads.

In the Falklands conflict in 1982, small, conventionally armed sea-skimming missiles were used (the French Exocet) against British ships by the Argentine forces, and similar small missiles have been used against aircraft and ships elsewhere.

Mississippian US term for the Lower or Early ◊Carboniferous period of geological time, 363–323 million years ago. It is named after the state of Mississippi.

mistletoe parasitic evergreen plant, native to Europe. It grows on trees as a small bush with translucent white berries. Used in many Western countries as a Christmas decoration, it also featured in the pagan religion Druidism. (*Viscum album*, family Loranthaceae.)

The seeds of the European mistletoe are dispersed by birds, but the dwarf mistletoe (*Arceuthobium pusillum*) of North America shoots out its ripe seeds at 100 kph/60 mph as far as 15 m/16 yd. Mistletoes lose water more than ten times as fast as other plants in order to draw nutrients to themselves; as a result, the dwarf mistletoe causes the loss of 20 million cubic metres of wood fibre a year.

mistral cold, dry, northerly wind that occasionally blows during the winter on the Mediterranean coast of France, particularly concentrated along the Rhône valley. It has been known to reach a velocity of 145 kph/90 mph.

mite minute ◊arachnid related to the ◊ticks. Some mites are free-living scavengers or predators. Some are parasitic, such as the **itch mite** (*Sarcoptes scabiei*), which burrows in skin causing scabies in humans and mange in dogs, and the **red mite** (*Dermanyssus gallinae*), which sucks blood from poultry and other birds. Others parasitize plants. (Order Acarina.)

The **harvest mite** (genus *Trombicula*) is harmless as an adult, but in the larval stage attacks people and animals, penetrating the skin and setting up great irritation. The **red spider mite** (*Tetranychus telarius*) is a troublesome pest in greenhouses as it feeds on plant juices. A number of mites live in cheese, flour, and other foodstuffs. They are conveyed from place to place in the larval stage by attaching themselves to flies. Some mites live entirely in the water, and many are parasitic on insects. See also ◊chigger.

MITE

Human eyelashes are home to whole colonies of tiny mites. The follicle mite is 0.33 mm/0.01 in long and lives head-down inside the hair follicle. These mites do not restrict themselves to eyelashes, however, but also frequent other parts of the human body with large sebaceous glands – such as nipples.

MIT media lab in computing, one of several important computer research centres at the Massachussetts Institute of Technology in Cambridge, Massachussetts, USA. The MIT media lab is at the forefront of multimedia technology.

mitochondria (singular ***mitochondrion***) membrane-enclosed organelles within ◊eukaryotic cells, containing enzymes responsible for energy production during ◊aerobic respiration. These rod-like or spherical bodies are thought to be derived from free-living bacteria that, at a very early stage in the history of life, invaded larger cells and took up a symbiotic way of life inside. Each still contains its own small loop of DNA called mitochondrial DNA, and new mitochondria arise by division of existing ones.

Mutations in mitochondrial genes are always inherited from the mother. These mutations have been linked to a number of disorders, mainly degenerative, including Alzheimer's disease and diabetes.

mitosis in biology, the process of cell division by which identical daughter cells are produced. During mitosis the DNA is duplicated and the chromosome number doubled, so new cells contain the same amount of DNA as the original cell.

The genetic material of ◊eukaryotic cells is carried on a number of chromosomes. To control movements of ◊chromosomes during cell division so that both new cells get the correct number, a system of protein tubules, known as the spindle, organizes the chromosomes into position in the middle of the cell before they replicate.

> TO REMEMBER THE FIVE SUB-PHASES OF THE PROPHASE OF MITOSIS:
>
> LAZY ZEBRAS PONDER DIRE DISASTERS
>
> LEPTOTENE, ZYGOTENE, POLYTENE, DIPLOTENE, DIAKINESIS

The spindle then controls the movement of chromosomes as the cell goes through the stages of division: **interphase**, **prophase**, **metaphase**, **anaphase**, and **telophase**. See also meiosis.

Mitsubishi world's largest electronics conglomerate and one of the big six cartels (*zaibatsu*) in Japan. Shipbuilding, banking, mineral-, and coalmining are among its activities.

The company began in 1870 as a shipping service, founded by Yatarō Iwasaki (1834–1885); after a series of name changes and a merger, the Mitsubishi Company was formed 1886. During World War II, the company was a major manufacturer of military aircraft, such as the high performance Zero naval fighter. There are now three distinct companies, all based in Tokyo: Mitsubishi Electric Corporation, Mitsubishi Motors Corporation, and Mitsubishi Heavy Industries Ltd.

mixed farming farming system where both arable and pastoral farming is carried out. Mixed farming is a lower-risk strategy than

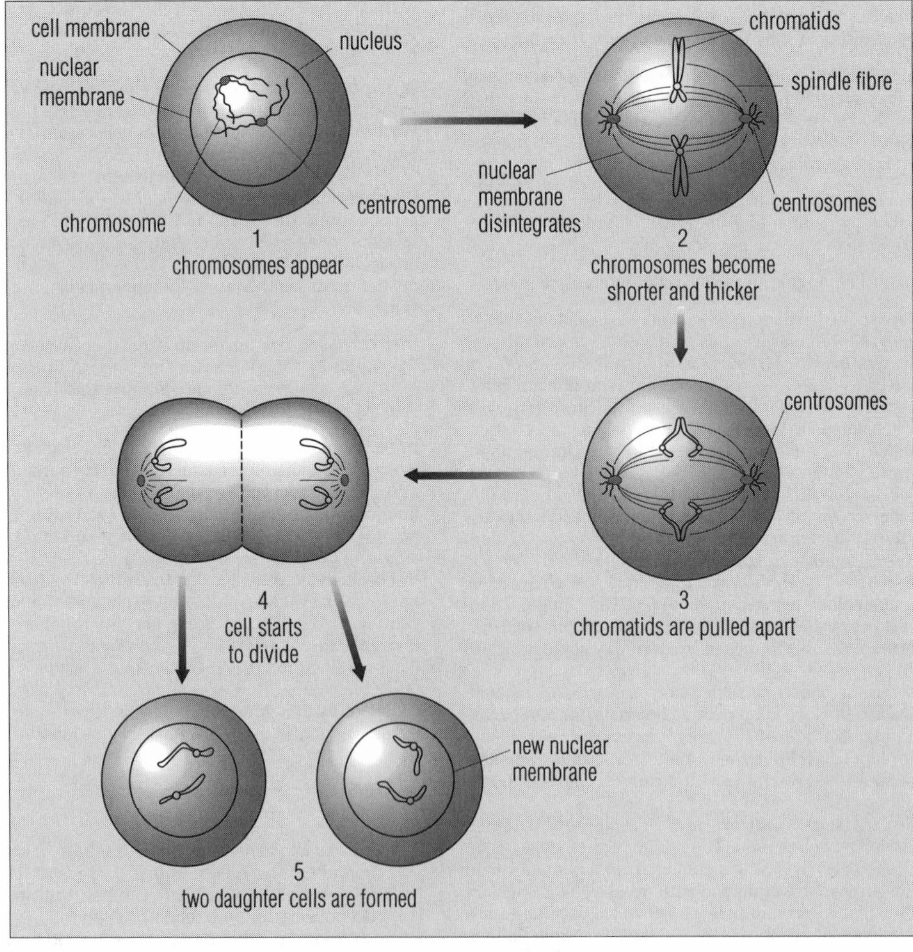

mitosis *The stages of mitosis, the process of cell division that takes place when a plant or animal cell divides for growth or repair. The two daughter cells each receive the same number of chromosomes as were in the original cell.*

◊monoculture. If climate, pests, or market prices are unfavourable for one crop or type of livestock, another may be more successful and the risk is shared. Animals provide manure for the fields and help to maintain soil fertility.

mixer in sound recording, equipment that allows an engineer to set a different volume level for each individual sound track so that solos can be highlighted and loud instruments can be kept from dominating softer ones. Multimedia systems that allow recording generally include similar, though not as sophisticated, functions through software. This is useful in applications such as adding background music to a scene where two people are talking and it is important to hear the voices clearly over the music.

mixture in chemistry, a substance containing two or more compounds that still retain their separate physical and chemical properties. There is no chemical bonding between them and they can be separated from each other by physical means (compare ◊compound).

m.k.s. system system of units in which the base units metre, kilogram, and second replace the centimetre, gram, and second of the ◊c.g.s. system. From it developed the SI system (see ◊SI units).

It simplifies the incorporation of electrical units into the metric system, and was incorporated in SI. For application to electrical and magnetic phenomena, the ampere was added, creating what is called the m.k.s.a. system.

ml symbol for **millilitre**.

mm symbol for **millimetre**.

mmHg symbol for ◊millimetre of mercury.

MMX in computing, umbrella name for improvements to the Intel Pentium line of processors in 1996, including 57 new instructions to handle multimedia and communications data. From 1997, all new Pentium chips included MMX as standard, such as the Pentium II range. MMX may be an abbreviation for MultiMedia eXtensions.

mnemonic in computing, a short sequence of letters used in low-level programming languages (see ◊low-level language) to represent a ◊machine code instruction.

moa any of a group of extinct flightless kiwi-like birds that lived in New Zealand. There were 19 species; they varied from 0.5 to 3.5 m/2 to 12 ft, with strong limbs, a long neck, and no wings. The largest species was *Dinornis maximus*. The last moa was killed in the 1800s. (Order Dinornithiformes.)

The Maori used them as food, and with the use of European firearms killed them in excessive numbers.

mobile ion in chemistry, an ion that is free to move; such ions are only found in the aqueous solutions or melts (molten masses) of an electrolyte. The mobility of the ions in an ◊electrolyte is what allows it to conduct electricity.

mobile phone in computing, cordless telephone linked to a digital cellular radio network. Mobile phones can connect to the Internet via a datacard, which converts computer data into a form that can be passed over the network and vice versa. Users can connect them to a ◊laptop computer and others incorporate a full pocket organizer. A trend for greater integration of phone and computer emerged in 1996.

Möbius strip structure made by giving a half twist to a flat strip of paper and joining the ends together. It has certain remarkable properties, arising from the fact that it has only one edge and one side. If cut down the centre of the strip, instead of two new strips of paper, only one long strip is produced. It was invented by the German mathematician August Möbius.

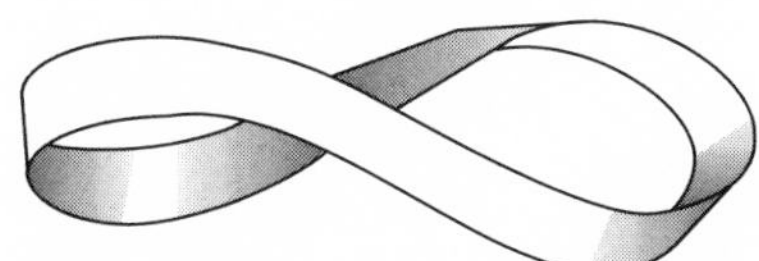

Möbius strip *The Möbius strip has only one side and one edge. It consists of a strip of paper connected at its ends with a half-twist in the middle.*

mockingbird North American songbird of the mimic thrush family, found in the USA and Mexico. About 25 cm/10 in long, it is brownish grey, with white markings on the black wings and tail. It is remarkable for its ability to mimic the songs of other species. (Species *Mimus polyglottos,* family Mimidae, order Passeriformes.)

mock orange or ***syringa*** any of a group of deciduous shrubs, including *P. coronarius,* which has white, strongly scented flowers similar to those of the orange tree. (Genus *Philadelphus,* family Philadelphaceae.)

mode in mathematics, the element that appears most frequently in a given set of data. For example, the mode for the data 0, 0, 9, 9, 9, 12, 87, 87 is 9.

model in computing, set of assumptions and criteria based on actual phenomena, used to conduct a ◊computer simulation. Models are used to predict the behaviour of a system such as the movement of a hurricane or the flow of goods from a store. In industry, they are an important tool for testing new products: engineers subject ◊virtual prototypes of aircraft or bridges to various scenarios to find out what adjustments are necessary to the design. However, a model is only as good as the assumptions that underlie it.

Models may run at the same speed of the real situation (**real-time models**) or run at faster or slower speeds.

Models are also the basis for ◊expert systems, which simulate the knowledge of a human expert.

> *A theory has only the alternative of being right or wrong. A model has a third possibility: it may be right, but irrelevant.*
>
> MANFRED EIGEN German physical chemist.
> Quoted in Jagdish Mehra (ed) *The Physicist's Conception of Nature* 1973

model simplified version of some aspect of the real world. Models are produced to show the relationships between two or more factors, such as land use and the distance from the centre of a town (for example, concentric-ring theory). Because models are idealized, they give only a general guide to what may happen.

modem (acronym for ***modulator/demodulator***) device for transmitting computer data over telephone lines. Such a device is necessary because the ◊digital signals produced by computers cannot, at present, be transmitted directly over the telephone network, which uses analogue signals. The modem converts the digital signals to ◊analogue, and back again.

Modems are used for linking remote terminals to central computers and enable computers to communicate with each other anywhere in the world. In 1997, the fastest standard modems transmitted data at a nominal rate of about 33,600 bps (bits per second), often abbreviated to 33.6K.

56K modems launched in 1997 achieve higher speeds by using a digital connection to the user's computer, while using a conventional analogue connection in the other direction. In theory the downstream link can transfer data at 56Kbps but in practice, speeds are usually 45–50K or less, depending on the quality of the phone line and other factors.

Initially there were two competing 56K systems – K56Flex from Rockwell and Lucent Technologies, and X2 from 3Com/US Robotics – with many users waiting for the ITU to agree a standard system.

modem tax in computing, urban legend that surfaces regularly on Internet bulletin boards. It says that the US government's Federal Communications Commission (FCC) is planning to introduce a telecommunications surcharge for using a modem on the public telephone network, and urges readers to write to the FCC to complain. The FCC, however, has no such plans.

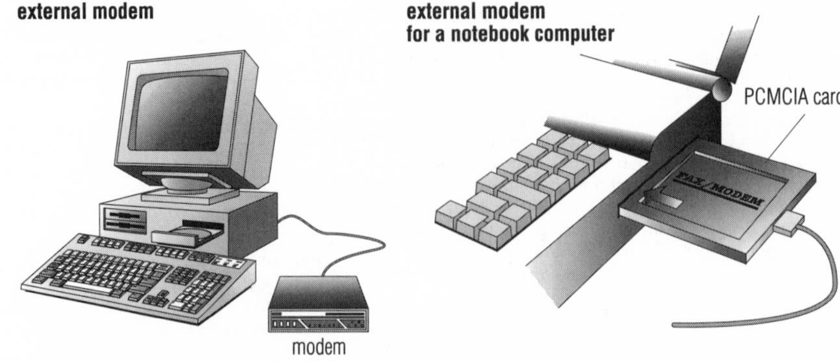

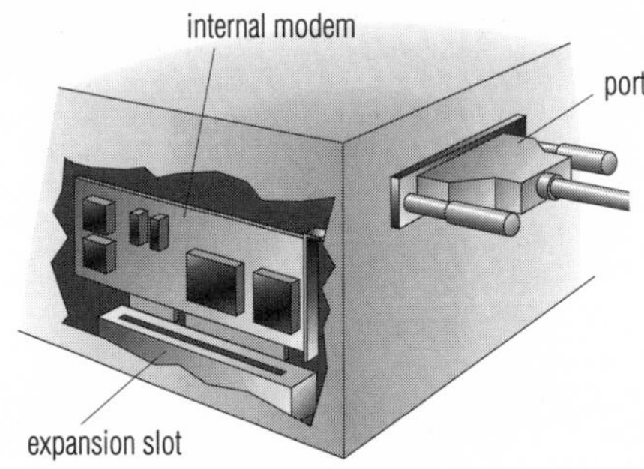

modem Modems are available in various forms: microcomputers may use an external device connected through a communications port, or an internal device, which takes the form of an expansion board inside the computer. Notebook computers use an external modem connected via a special interface card.

moderator in computing, person or group of people that screens submissions to certain ◊newsgroups and ◊mailing lists before passing them on for wider circulation. The aim of moderation is not to censor, but to ensure that the quality of debate is maintained by filtering out ◊spamming, irrelevant ('off-topic'), or gratuitously offensive postings.

moderator in a ◊nuclear reactor, a material such as graphite or heavy water used to reduce the speed of high-energy neutrons. Neutrons produced by nuclear fission are fast-moving and must be slowed to initiate further fission so that nuclear energy continues to be released at a controlled rate.

Slow neutrons are much more likely to cause ◊fission in a uranium-235 nucleus than to be captured in a U-238 (nonfissile uranium) nucleus. By using a moderator, a reactor can thus be made to work with fuel containing only a small proportion of U-235.

modulation in radio transmission, the variation of frequency, or amplitude, of a radio carrier wave, in accordance with the audio characteristics of the speaking voice, music, or other signal being transmitted. See ◊pulse-code modulation, AM (amplitude modulation), and ◊FM (frequency modulation).

module in construction, a standard or unit that governs the form of the rest. For example, Japanese room sizes are traditionally governed by multiples of standard tatami floor mats; today prefabricated buildings are mass-produced in a similar way. The components of a spacecraft are designed in coordination; for example, for the Apollo Moon landings the craft comprised a command module (for working, eating, sleeping), service module (electricity generators, oxygen supplies, manoeuvring rocket), and lunar module (to land and return the astronauts).

modulus in mathematics, a number that divides exactly into the difference between two given numbers. Also, the multiplication factor used to convert a logarithm of one base to a logarithm of another base. Also, another name for ◊absolute value.

Mohorovičić discontinuity also ***Moho*** or ***M-discontinuity*** boundary that separates the Earth's crust and mantle, marked by a rapid increase in the speed of earthquake waves. It follows the variations in the thickness of the crust and is found approximately 32 km/20 mi below the continents and about 10 km/6 mi below the oceans. It is named after the Yugoslav geophysicist Andrija Mohorovičić (1857–1936), who suspected its presence after analysing seismic waves from the Kulpa Valley earthquake in 1909.

Mohs' scale scale of hardness for minerals (in ascending order): 1 talc; 2 gypsum; 3 calcite; 4 fluorite; 5 apatite; 6 orthoclase; 7 quartz; 8 topaz; 9 corundum; 10 diamond.

The scale is useful in mineral identification because any mineral will scratch any other mineral lower on the scale than itself, and similarly it will be scratched by any other mineral higher on the scale.

> TO REMEMBER THE ORDER OF HARDNESS:
>
> TALL GYROSCOPES CAN FLY APART, ORBITING QUICKLY TO COMPLETE DISINTEGRATION.
>
> OR
>
> THOSE GIRLS CAN FLIRT AND OTHER QUEER THINGS CAN DO.
>
> TALC, GYPSUM OR ROCK SALT, CALCITE, FLUORITE, APATITE, ORTHACLASE, QUARTZ, TOPAZ, CORUNDUM, DIAMOND

molar one of the large teeth found towards the back of the mammalian mouth. The structure of the jaw, and the relation of the muscles, allows a massive force to be applied to molars. In herbivores the molars are flat with sharp ridges of enamel and are used for grinding, an adaptation to a diet of tough plant material. Carnivores have sharp powerful molars called carnassials, which are adapted for cutting meat.

molarity in chemistry, ◊concentration of a solution expressed as the number of ◊moles in grams of solute per cubic decimetre of solution.

molar solution in chemistry, solution that contains one ◊mole of a substance per litre of solvent.

molar volume volume occupied by one ◊mole (the molecular mass in grams) of any gas at standard temperature and pressure, equal to 2.24136×10^{-2} m^3.

mole SI unit (symbol mol) of the amount of a substance. It is defined as the amount of a substance that contains as many elementary entities (atoms, molecules, and so on) as there are atoms in 12 g of the ◊isotope carbon-12.

One mole of an element that exists as single atoms weighs as many grams as its ◊atomic number (so one mole of carbon weighs 12 g), and it contains 6.022045×10^{23} atoms, which is ◊Avogadro's number.

mole in construction, a mechanical device for boring horizontal holes underground without the need for digging trenches. It is used for laying pipes and cables.

mole small burrowing mammal with typically dark, velvety fur. Moles grow up to 18 cm/7 in long, and have acute senses of hearing, smell, and touch, but poor eyesight. They have short, muscular forelimbs and shovel-like, clawed front feet for burrowing in search of insects, grubs, and worms. Their fur lies without direction so that they can move forwards or backwards in their tunnels without discomfort. Moles are greedy eaters; they cannot live more than a few hours without food. (Family Talpidae, order Insectivora.)

North American moles differ from those of the Old World in having tusklike front upper incisor teeth. The same ecological role is taken in Africa by the **golden moles** (family Chrysochloridae), and in Australia by **marsupial moles** (genus *Notoryctes*, order Marsupialia).

Some members of the Talpidae family are aquatic, such as the **Russian desman** (*Desmana moschata*) and the North American **star-nosed mole** (*Condylura cristata*).

mole cricket dark brown burrowing insect about 35–50 mm/1.5–2 in long, covered with soft hairs. Over 50 species of mole crickets have been identified. They feed mainly on worms and other insects.

Mole crickets are particularly adapted for burrowing, the first pair of legs being large, flattened, and serrated for digging. The eyes are reduced, and the ovipositor (egg-laying organ) is vestigial. Some species have wings, which they use to fly at night. Other species have vestigial wings or the wings may be lacking.

Occasionally mole crickets may attack crops: for example the Puerto Rico mole cricket *Scapteriscus vicinus* is a serious pest.
classification Mole crickets are members of family Gryllotalpidae, order Orthoptera, class Insecta, phylum Arthropoda.

molecular biology study of the molecular basis of life, including the biochemistry of molecules such as DNA, RNA, and proteins, and the molecular structure and function of the various parts of living cells.

molecular clock use of rates of ◊mutation in genetic material to calculate the length of time elapsed since two related species diverged from each other during evolution. The method can be based on comparisons of the DNA or of widely occurring proteins, such as haemoglobin.

Since mutations are thought to occur at a constant rate, the length of time that must have elapsed in order to produce the difference between two species can be estimated. This information can be compared with the evidence obtained from palaeontology to reconstruct evolutionary events.

molecular cloud in astronomy, an enormous cloud of cool interstellar dust and gas containing hydrogen molecules and more complex molecular species. Giant molecular clouds (GMCs), about a million times as massive as the Sun and up to 300 light years in diameter, are regions in which stars are being born. The ◊Orion Nebula is part of a GMC.

molecular formula in chemistry, formula indicating the actual number of atoms of each element present in a single molecule of a chemical compound. This is determined by two pieces of information: the empirical ◊formula and the ◊relative molecular mass, which is determined experimentally.

molecular mass (also known as ***relative molecular mass***) the mass of a molecule, calculated relative to one-twelfth the mass of an atom of carbon-12. It is found by adding the relative atomic masses of the atoms that make up the molecule.

molecular solid in chemistry, solid composed of molecules that are held together by relatively weak ◊intermolecular forces. Such solids are low-melting and tend to dissolve in organic solvents. Examples of molecular solids are sulphur, ice, sucrose, and solid carbon dioxide.

molecule group of two or more ◊atoms bonded together. A molecule of an element consists of one or more like ◊atoms; a molecule of a compound consists of two or more different atoms bonded together. Molecules vary in size and complexity from the hydrogen molecule (H_2) to the large ◊macromolecules of proteins. They are held together by ionic bonds, in which the atoms gain or lose electrons to form ◊ions, or by covalent bonds, where electrons from each atom are shared in a new molecular orbital.

mole rat, naked small underground mammal, almost hairless, with a disproportionately large head. The mole rat is of importance to zoologists as one of the very few mammals that are eusocial, that is, living in colonies with sterile workers and one fertile female. (Species *Heterocephalus glaber*.)

The mole rat has the smallest brain relative to body size of any small mammal. Its underground colonies comprise one breeding female, some breeding males, and many functionally sterile workers of both sexes.

mollusc any of a group of invertebrate animals, most of which have a body divided into three parts: a head, a central mass containing the main organs, and a foot for movement; the more sophisticated octopuses and related molluscs have arms to capture their prey. The majority of molluscs are marine animals, but some live in fresh water, and a few live on dry land. They include clams, mussels, and oysters (bivalves), snails and slugs (gastropods), and cuttlefish, squids, and octopuses (cephalopods). The body is soft, without limbs (except for the cephalopods), and cold-blooded. There is no internal skeleton, but many species have a hard shell covering the body. (Phylum Mollusca.)

Molluscs have varying diets, the carnivorous species feeding mainly on other molluscs. Some are vegetarian. Reproduction is by means of eggs and is sexual; many species are hermaphrodite (having both male and female reproductive organs). The shells of molluscs take a variety of forms: single or univalve (like the snail), double or bivalve (like the clam), chambered (like the nautilus), and many other variations. In some cases (for example cuttlefish and squid), the shell is internal. Every mollusc has a fold of skin, the

MOLLUSC

The chiton, a species of marine shelled mollusc, uses magnetism to find its way home. The teeth on its tongue-like radulla contain magnetite, and enable the chiton to return to exactly the same place on its home rock after night-time feeding.

mantle, which covers either the whole body or only the back, and secretes the chalky substance that forms the shell. The lower ventral surface (belly area) of the body forms the foot, which enables the mollusc to move about.

Mollusca invertebrate animal phylum that contains the ◊molluscs.

molybdenite molybdenum sulphide, MoS_2, the chief ore mineral of molybdenum. It possesses a hexagonal crystal structure similar to graphite, has a blue metallic lustre, and is very soft (1–1.5 on Mohs' scale).

molybdenum Greek *molybdos 'lead'* heavy, hard, lustrous, silver-white, metallic element, symbol Mo, atomic number 42, relative atomic mass 95.94. The chief ore is the mineral molybdenite. The element is highly resistant to heat and conducts electricity easily. It is used in alloys, often to harden steels. It is a necessary trace element in human nutrition. It was named in 1781 by Swedish chemist Karl Scheele, after its isolation by P J Hjelm (1746–1813), for its resemblance to lead ore.

moment of a force in physics, measure of the turning effect, or torque, produced by a force acting on a body. It is equal to the product of the force and the perpendicular distance from its line of action to the point, or pivot, about which the body will turn. Its unit is the newton metre.

If the magnitude of the force is F newtons and the perpendicular distance is d metres then the moment is given by:

$$\text{moment} = Fd$$

See also ◊couple.

moment of inertia in physics, the sum of all the point masses of a rotating object multiplied by the squares of their respective distances from the axis of rotation. It is analogous to the ◊mass of a stationary object or one moving in a straight line.

In linear dynamics, Newton's second law of motion states that the force F on a moving object equals the products of its mass m and acceleration a ($F = ma$); the analogous equation in rotational dynamics is $T = I\alpha$, where T is the torque (the turning effect of a force) that causes an angular acceleration α and I is the moment of inertia. For a given object, I depends on its shape and the position of its axis of rotation.

momentum the product of the mass of a body and its velocity. If the mass of a body is m kilograms and its velocity is v m s^{-1}, then its momentum is given by:

$$\text{momentum} = mv$$

Its unit is the kilogram metre-per-second (kg m s^{-1}) or the newton second.

The momentum of a body does not change unless a resultant or unbalanced force acts on that body (see ◊Newton's laws of motion).

According to Newton's second law of motion, the magnitude of a resultant force F equals the rate of change of momentum brought about by its action, or:

$$F = (mv - mu)/t$$

where mu is the initial momentum of the body, mv is its final momentum, and t is the time in seconds over which the force acts. The change in momentum, or ◊impulse, produced can therefore be expressed as:

$$\text{impulse} = mv - mu = Ft$$

The law of conservation of momentum is one of the fundamental concepts of classical physics. It states that the total momentum of all bodies in a closed system is constant and unaffected by processes occurring within the system.

The **angular momentum** of an orbiting or rotating body of mass m travelling at a velocity v in a circular orbit of radius R is expressed as mvR. Angular momentum is conserved, and should any of the values alter (such as the radius of orbit), the other values (such as the velocity) will compensate to preserve the value of angular momentum, and that lost by one component is passed to another.

monazite mineral, $(Ce,La,Th)PO_4$, yellow to red, valued as a source of ◊lanthanides or rare earths, including cerium and europium; generally found in placer deposit (alluvial) sands.

mongolism former name (now considered offensive) for ◊Down's syndrome.

mongoose any of a group of carnivorous tropical mammals. The **Indian mongoose** (*H. mungo*) is greyish in colour and about 50 cm/1.5 ft long, with a long tail. It can be tamed and is often kept for its ability to kill snakes. Like the snakes themselves, the acetylcholine receptors connecting the mongooses' nerves and muscle cells are unaffected by the venom. (Genera *Herpestes, Ichneumia,* and other related genera, family Viverridae.)

Most mongooses are solitary, but the **banded mongoose** *Mungos mungo* is highly gregarious, living in groups of 15–40 individuals. They feed on small reptiles and invertebrates and spend about 60% of their day foraging.

The **white-tailed mongoose** (*I. albicauda*) of central Africa has a distinctive grey or white bushy tail.

mongoose *The ring-tailed mongoose* Galidia elegans *is found in Madagascar where it is active by day in both wet and dry forests. Like many mongooses, it has a very varied diet, including birds' eggs, snails, insects, lizards, and small mammals. Premaphotos Wildlife*

monitor or ***screen*** output device on which a computer displays information for the benefit of the operator user – usually in the form of a ◊graphical user interface such as ◊Windows. The commonest type is the ◊cathode-ray tube (CRT), which is similar to a television screen. Portable computers often use ◊liquid crystal display (LCD) screens. These are harder to read than CRTs, but require less power, making them suitable for battery operation.

monitor any of various lizards found in Africa, S Asia, and Australasia. Monitors are generally large and carnivorous, with well-developed legs and claws and a long powerful tail that can be swung in defence. (Family Varanidae.)

Monitors include the **Komodo dragon** (*Varanus komodoensis*), the largest of all lizards, and also the slimmer **Salvador's monitor** (*V. salvadorii*), which may reach 2.5 m/8 ft. Several other monitors, such as the **lace monitor** (*V. varius*), the **perentie** (*V. giganteus*) of Australia, and the **Nile monitor** (*V. niloticus*) of Africa, are up to 2 m/6 ft long.

monkey any of the various smaller, mainly tree-dwelling anthropoid ◊primates, excluding humans and the ◊apes. There are 125 species, living in Africa, Asia, and tropical Central and South America. Monkeys eat mainly leaves and fruit, and also small animals. Several species are endangered due to loss of forest habitat,

monkey *Temminck's red colobus monkey* Colobus badius temmincki *from the forests of W Africa is a typical Old World member of the family Cercopithecidae. Premaphotos Wildlife*

for example the woolly spider monkey and black saki of the Amazonian forest.

Old World monkeys (family Cercopithecidae) of tropical Africa and Asia are distinguished by their close-set nostrils and differentiated thumbs, some also having cheek pouches and rumps with bare patches (callosities) of hardened skin. They include ◊baboons, langurs, macaques, and guenons.

New World monkeys of Central and South America are characterized by wide-set nostrils, and some have highly sensitive prehensile tails that can be used as additional limbs, to grasp and hold branches or objects. They include two families:

(1) the family Cebidae, which includes the larger species saki, ◊capuchin, squirrel, howler, and spider monkeys;

(2) the family Callithricidae, which includes the small ◊marmosets and tamarins.

There are one hundred and ninety-three living species of monkeys and apes. One hundred and ninety-two are covered with hair. The exception is the naked ape self-named

Desmond Morris English anthropologist.
Homo sapiens. The Naked Ape 1967

---

monkey puzzle or ***Chilean pine*** coniferous evergreen tree, native to Chile; its branches, growing in circular arrangements (whorls) around the trunk and larger branches, are covered in prickly, leathery leaves. (*Araucaria araucana*, family Araucariaceae.)

Cut down for valuable timber, it is now listed as 'rare' on the Red Data list published by the International Union for the Conservation of Nature. International trade in any part of the tree is banned.

monkfish marine bony fish also known as ◊angelfish.

monocarpic or ***hapaxanthic*** describing plants that flower and produce fruit only once during their life cycle, after which they die. Most ◊annual plants and ◊biennial plants are monocarpic, but there are also a small number of monocarpic ◊perennial plants that flower just once, sometimes after as long as 90 years, dying shortly afterwards, for example, century plant *Agave* and some species of bamboo *Bambusa*. The general biological term related to organisms that reproduce only once during their lifetime is ◊semelparity.

monoclonal antibody (MAB) antibody produced by fusing an antibody-producing lymphocyte with a cancerous myeloma (bone-marrow) cell. The resulting fused cell, called a hybridoma, is immortal and can be used to produce large quantities of a single, specific antibody. By choosing antibodies that are directed against antigens found on cancer cells, and combining them with cytotoxic drugs, it is hoped to make so-called magic bullets that will be able to pick out and kill cancers.

It is the antigens on the outer cell walls of germs entering the body that provoke the production of antibodies as a first line of defence against disease. Antibodies 'recognize' these foreign antigens, and, in locking on to them, cause the release of chemical signals in the bloodstream to alert the immune system for further action. MABs are copies of these natural antibodies, with the same ability to recognize specific antigens. Introduced into the body, they can be targeted at disease sites.

The full potential of these biological missiles, developed by César Milstein and others at Cambridge University, England, 1975, is still under investigation. However, they are already in use in blood-grouping, in pinpointing viruses and other sources of disease, in tracing cancer sites, and in developing vaccines.

monocotyledon angiosperm (flowering plant) having an embryo with a single cotyledon, or seed leaf (as opposed to ◊dicotyledons, which have two). Monocotyledons usually have narrow leaves with parallel veins and smooth edges, and hollow or soft stems. Their flower parts are arranged in threes. Most are small plants such as orchids, grasses, and lilies, but some are trees such as palms.

monoculture farming system where only one crop is grown. In Third World countries this is often a ◊cash crop, grown on ◊plantations, for example, sugar and coffee. Cereal crops in the industrialized world are also frequently grown on a monoculture basis; for example, wheat in the Canadian prairies.

Monoculture allows the farmer to tailor production methods to the requirements of one crop, but it is a high-risk strategy since the crop may fail (because of pests, disease, or bad weather) and world prices for the crop may fall. Monoculture without ◊crop rotation is likely to result in reduced soil quality despite the addition of artificial fertilizers, and it contributes to ◊soil erosion.

monocyte in biology, type of white blood cell. They are found in the tissues, the lymphatic and circulatory systems where their purpose is to remove foreign particles, such as bacteria and tissue debris, by ingesting them.

monoecious having separate male and female flowers on the same plant. Maize (*Zea mays*), for example, has a tassel of male flowers at the top of the stalk and a group of female flowers (on the ear, or cob) lower down. Monoecism is a way of avoiding self-fertilization.

◊Dioecious plants have male and female flowers on separate plants.

monohybrid inheritance pattern of inheritance seen in simple ◊genetics experiments, where the two animals (or two plants) being crossed are genetically identical except for one gene.

This gene may code for some obvious external features such as seed colour, with one parent having green seeds and the other having yellow seeds. The offspring are monohybrids, that is, hybrids for one gene only, having received one copy of the gene from each parent. Known as the F1 generation, they are all identical, and usually resemble one parent, whose version of the gene (the dominant ◊allele) masks the effect of the other version (the recessive allele). Although the characteristic coded for by the recessive allele (for example, green seeds) completely disappears in this generation, it can reappear in offspring of the next generation if they have two recessive alleles. On average, this will occur in one out of four offspring from a cross between two of the monohybrids. The next generation (called F2) show a 3:1 ratio for the characteristic in question, 75% being like the original parent with the recessive allele. Austrian biologist Gregor ◊Mendel first carried out experiments of this type (crossing varieties of artificially bred plants, such as peas) and they revealed the principles of genetics. The same basic mechanism underlies all inheritance, but in most plants and animals there are so many genetic differences interacting to produce the external appearance (phenotype) that such simple, clear-cut patterns of inheritance are not evident.

monolith Greek *monos 'sole', lithos 'stone'* single isolated stone or column, usually standing and of great size, used as a form of monument. Some are natural features, such as the Buck Stone in the Forest of Dean, England. Other monoliths may be quarried, resited, finished, or carved; those in Egypt of about 3000 BC take the form of obelisks. They have a wide distribution including Europe, South America, N Africa, and the Middle East.

Apart from their ritual or memorial function, monoliths have been used as sundials and calendars in the civilizations of the Aztecs, Egyptians, and Chaldeans (ancient peoples of southern Babylonia). In landscape archaeology, monoliths are interpreted in a wider context, possibly as boundary markers. The largest cut stone, weighing about 1,500 tonnes, is sited in the ancient Syrian city of Baalbek.

monomer chemical compound composed of simple molecules from which ◊polymers can be made. Under certain conditions the simple molecules (of the monomer) join together (polymerize) to form a very long chain molecule (macromolecule) called a polymer. For example, the polymerization of ethene (ethylene) monomers produces the polymer polyethene (polyethylene).

$$2nCH_2 = CH_2 \rightarrow (CH_2\text{–}CH_2\text{–}CH_2\text{–}\ CH_2)n$$

Mononychus olecranus flightless bird from the Cretaceous period between 65 and 85 million years ago. Two well-preserved skeletons found in Mongolia 1987 and 1992 show *Mononychus* to have been about 1 m/3 ft in length wih a long neck and tail, slender hindlimbs, short, sturdy forelimbs, and teeth.

monorail railway that runs on a single rail; the cars can be balanced on it or suspended from it. It was invented in 1882 to carry light loads, and when run by electricity was called a **telpher**.

The Wuppertal Schwebebahn, which has been running in Germany since 1901, is a suspension monorail, where the passenger cars hang from an arm fixed to a trolley that runs along the rail. Today most monorails are of the straddle type, where the passenger cars run on top of the rail. They are used to transport passengers between terminals at some airports; Japan has a monorail (1964) running from the city centre to Hameda airport.

monosaccharide or ***simple sugar*** ◊carbohydrate that cannot be hydrolysed (split) into smaller carbohydrate units. Examples are glucose and fructose, both of which have the molecular formula $C_6H_{12}0_6$.

> TO REMEMBER THE MOLECULAR SHAPE OF FRUCTOSE AND GLUCOSE:
>
> THERE ARE TWO SIMPLE SUGARS (MONOSACCHARIDES) – FRUCTOSE AND GLUCOSE – WHICH COMBINE IN A SPECIFIC WAY TO FORM SUCROSE. REMEMBER THE MOLECULAR SHAPE OF FRUCTOSE HAS FIVE CARBONS (LETTER F STARTS BOTH WORDS) AND HEXAGON IS THE SHAPE OF GLUCOSE (LETTER G IN BOTH WORDS

monosodium glutamate (MSG) $NaC_5H_8NO_4$ a white, crystalline powder, the sodium salt of glutamic acid (an ◊amino acid found in proteins that plays a role in the metabolism of plants and animals). It has no flavour of its own, but enhances the flavour of foods such as meat and fish. It is used to enhance the flavour of many packaged and 'fast foods', and in Chinese cooking. Ill effects may arise from its overconsumption, and some people are very sensitive to it, even in small amounts. It is commercially derived from vegetable protein. It occurs naturally in soybeans and seaweed.

Monotremata order of mammals consisting of the ◊monotremes.

monotreme any of a small group of primitive egg-laying mammals, found in Australasia. They include the ◊echidnas (spiny anteaters) and the ◊platypus. (Order Monotremata.)

In 1995 Australian palaeontologists announced a new (extinct) family of monotreme, the Kollikodontidae, following the discovery of a 120-million-year-old jawbone in New South Wales.

monsoon wind pattern that brings seasonally heavy rain to S Asia; it blows towards the sea in winter and towards the land in summer. The monsoon may cause destructive flooding all over India and SE Asia from April to September, leaving thousands of people homeless each year.

The monsoon cycle is believed to have started about 12 million years ago with the uplift of the Himalayas.

monstera or ***Swiss cheese plant*** evergreen climbing plant belonging to the arum family, native to tropical America. *M. deliciosa* is grown as a house plant. Areas between the veins of the leaves dry up, forming deep notches and eventually holes. (Genus *Monstera*, family Araceae.)

montbretia plant belonging to the iris family, native to South Africa, with orange or reddish flowers on long stems. They are grown as ornamental pot plants. (*Tritonia crocosmiflora*, family Iridaceae.)

month unit of time based on the motion of the Moon around the Earth.

The time from one new or full Moon to the next (the **synodic** or **lunar month**) is 29.53 days. The time for the Moon to complete one orbit around the Earth relative to the stars (the **sidereal month**) is 27.32 days. The **solar month** equals 30.44 days, and is exactly one-twelfth of the solar or tropical year, the time taken for the Earth to orbit the Sun. The **calendar month** is a human invention, devised to fit the calendar year.

Montréal Protocol international agreement, signed in 1987, to stop the production of chemicals that are ◊ozone depleters by the year 2000.

Originally the agreement was to reduce the production of ozone depleters by 35% by 1999. The green movement criticized the agreement as inadequate, arguing that an 85% reduction in ozone depleters would be necessary just to stabilize the ozone layer at 1987 levels. The protocol (under the Vienna Convention for the Protection of the Ozone Layer) was reviewed in 1992. Amendments added another 11 chemicals to the original list of eight chemicals suspected of harming the ozone layer. A controversial amendment concerns a fund established to pay for the transfer of ozone-safe technology to poor countries.

MOO (abbreviation for ***MUD, object-oriented***) in computing, a ◊MUD (multi-user dungeon) that uses ◊object-oriented ◊programming, enabling participants to create their own personalized characters – which may well be specially equipped to attack the characters created by other players.

moon in astronomy, any natural ◊satellite that orbits a planet. Mercury and Venus are the only planets in the Solar System that do not have moons.

Moon natural satellite of Earth, 3,476 km/2,160 mi in diameter, with a mass 0.012 (approximately one-eightieth) that of Earth.

Its surface gravity is only 0.16 (one-sixth) that of Earth. Its average distance from Earth is 384,400 km/238,855 mi, and it orbits in a west-to-east direction every 27.32 days (the **sidereal month**). It

spins on its axis with one side permanently turned towards Earth. The Moon has no atmosphere and was thought to have no water till ice was discovered on its surface in 1998.
phases The Moon is illuminated by sunlight, and goes through a cycle of phases of shadow, waxing from **new** (dark) via **first quarter** (half Moon) to **full**, and waning back again to new every 29.53 days (the **synodic month**, also known as a **lunation**). On its sunlit side, temperatures reach 110°C/230°F, but during the two-week lunar night the surface temperature drops to –170°C/–274°F.
origins The origin of the Moon is still open to debate. Scientists suggest the following theories: that it split from the Earth; that it was a separate body captured by Earth's gravity; that it formed in orbit around Earth; or that it was formed from debris thrown off when a body the size of Mars struck Earth. Future exploration of the Moon may detect water permafrost, which could be located at the permanently shadowed lunar poles.
research The far side of the Moon was first photographed from the Soviet *Lunik 3* in October 1959. Much of our information about the Moon has been derived from this and other photographs and measurements taken by US and Soviet Moon probes, from geological samples brought back by US Apollo astronauts and by Soviet Luna probes, and from experiments set up by the US astronauts in 1969–72. The US probe, *Lunar Prospector*, launched January 1998, is intended to examine the composition of the lunar crust, record gamma rays, and map the lunar magnetic field.
composition The Moon's composition is rocky, with a surface heavily scarred by ◊meteorite impacts that have formed craters up to 240 km/150 mi across. Seismic observations indicate that the Moon's surface extends downwards for tens of kilometres; below this crust is a solid mantle about 1,100 km/688 mi thick, and below that a silicate core, part of which may be molten. Rocks brought back by astronauts show the Moon is 4.6 billion years old, the same age as Earth. It is made up of the same chemical elements as Earth, but in different proportions, and differs from Earth in that most of the Moon's surface features were formed within the first billion years of its history when it was hit repeatedly by meteorites.

The youngest craters are surrounded by bright rays of ejected rock. The largest scars have been filled by dark lava to produce the lowland plains called seas, or **maria** (plural of ◊mare). These dark patches form the so-called 'man-in-the-Moon' pattern. Inside some craters that are permanently in shadow is up to 300 million tonnes of ice existing as a thin layer of crystals.

One of the Moon's easiest features to observe is the mare **Plato**, which is about 100 km/62 mi in diameter and 2,700 m/8,860 ft deep, and at times is visible with the naked eye alone.

MOON

http://www.hawastsoc.org/solar/eng/moon.htm

Detailed description of the Moon. It includes statistics and information about the surface, eclipses, and phases of the Moon, along with details of the Apollo landing missions. The site is supported by a good selection of images.

Moon probe crewless spacecraft used to investigate the Moon. Early probes flew past the Moon or crash-landed on it, but later ones achieved soft landings or went into orbit. Soviet probes included the Luna/Lunik series. US probes (Ranger, Surveyor, Lunar Orbiter) prepared the way for the Apollo crewed flights.

moor in earth science, a stretch of land, usually at a height, which is characterized by a vegetation of heather, coarse grass, and bracken. A moor may be poorly drained and contain boggy hollows.

moorhen marsh bird belonging to the rail family, common in swamps, lakes, and ponds throughout Europe, Asia, Africa, and North and South America. It is about 33 cm/13 in long, brown above and dark grey below, with a red bill and forehead, a white stripe along the edge of the folded wings, a vivid white underside to the tail, and green legs. Its big feet are not webbed or lobed, but the moorhen can swim well. The nest is built by the waterside, and the eggs are buff-coloured with orange-brown spots. (Species *Gallinula chloropus*, family Rallidae, order Gruiformes.)

moose North American name for the ◊elk.

mopane worm caterpillar of the southern African emperor moth *Gonimbrasia belina* that is eaten in South Africa, either dried as a snack or rehydrated in stews. They grow to around 10 cm/4 in in length and are very high in protein.

moped lightweight motorcycle with pedals. Early mopeds (like the autocycle) were like motorized bicycles, using the pedals to start the bike and assist propulsion uphill. The pedals have little function in many mopeds today.

moraine rocky debris or ◊till carried along and deposited by a ◊glacier. Material eroded from the side of a glaciated valley and carried along the glacier's edge is called a **lateral moraine**; that worn from the valley floor and carried along the base of the glacier is called a **ground moraine**. Rubble dropped at the snout of a melting glacier is called a **terminal moraine**.

When two glaciers converge their lateral moraines unite to form a **medial moraine**. Debris that has fallen down crevasses and becomes embedded in the ice is termed an **englacial moraine**; when this is exposed at the surface due to partial melting it becomes ablation moraine.

moray eel with strong jaws armed with daggerlike teeth. The large species that hide in the crevices of coral reefs can inflict savage bites. Most species of moray are found in tropical seas.
classification Morays are in family Muraenidae belonging to the order Anguilliformes, class Osteichthyes.

morel any of a group of edible ◊mushrooms. The common morel (*M. esculenta*) grows in Europe and North America. The yellowish-brown cap is pitted with holes like a sponge and is about 2.5 cm/1 in long. It is used for seasoning gravies, soups, and sauces and is second only to the ◊truffle as the world's most sought-after mushroom. (Genus *Morchella*, order Pezizales.)

Morgan horse breed of riding and driving show horse originating in the USA in the 1780s from a single stallion named *Justin Morgan* after his owner. They are marked by high, curved necks and a high-stepping action. The breed is valued for its strength, endurance, and speed.

morning glory any of a group of twining or creeping plants native to tropical America, especially *I. purpurea*, with dazzling blue flowers. Small quantities of substances similar to the hallucinogenic drug LSD are found in the seeds of some species. (Genus *Ipomoea*, family Convolvulaceae.)

morphine narcotic alkaloid $C_{17}H_{19}NO_3$ derived from ◊opium and prescribed only to alleviate severe pain. Its use produces serious side effects, including nausea, constipation, tolerance, and addiction, but it is highly valued for the relief of the terminally ill.

The risk of addiction arising from the use of morphine for pain relief is much lower than for recreational use (about 1 in 3,000) as the drug is processed differently by the body when pain is present.

morphing the metamorphosis of one shape or object into another by computer-generated animation. First used in filmmaking in 1990, it has transformed cinema special effects. Conventional animation is limited to two dimensions; morphing enables the creation of three-dimensional transformations.

To create such effects, the start and end of the transformation must be specified on screen using a wire-frame model that mathematically defines the object. To make the object three-dimensional, the wire can be extruded from a cross-section or turned as on a lathe to produce an evenly turned surface. This is then rendered, or filled in and shaded. Once the beginning and end objects have been created, the computer can calculate the morphing process.

morphogen in medicine, one of a class of substances believed to be present in the growing embryo, controlling its growth pattern.

It is thought that variations in the concentration of morphogens in different parts of the embryo cause them to grow at different rates.

morphology in biology, the study of the physical structure and form of organisms, in particular their soft tissues.

Morse, Samuel Finley Breese (1791–1872)

US inventor. In 1835 he produced the first adequate electric telegraph (see telegraphy), and in 1843 was granted $30,000 by Congress for an experimental line between Washington DC and Baltimore. With his assistant Alexander Bain (1810–1877) he invented the Morse code.

Mary Evans Picture Library

Morse code international code for transmitting messages by wire or radio using signals of short (dots) and long (dashes) duration, originated by US inventor Samuel Morse for use on his invention, the telegraph (see ◊telegraphy).

The letters SOS (3 short, 3 long, 3 short) form the international distress signal, being distinctive and easily transmitted (popularly but erroneously save our souls). Its use was discontinued in 1997. By radio telephone the distress call is 'Mayday', for similar reasons (popularly alleged to derive from French *m'aidez*, help me).

A	B	C	D	E	F
·–	–···	–·–·	–··	·	··–·
G	H	I	J	K	L
––·	····	··	·–––	–·–	·–··
M	N	O	P	Q	R
––	–·	–––	·––·	––·–	·–·
S	T	U	V	W	X
···	–	··–	···–	·––	–··–
		Y	Z		
		–·––	––··		
1	2	3	4	5	
·––––	··–––	···––	····–	·····	
6	7	8	9	0	
–····	––···	–––··	––––·	–––––	

Morse code The Morse telegraph and workable code was first demonstrated in 1844. When a message was received, a series of short or long dashes ('dots' and 'dashes') were recorded onto a moving strip of paper. The pattern of the dots and dashes could be interpreted using Morse's Alphabetical Code.

Mosaic ◊browser program used for searching the ◊World Wide Web. It was distributed for free on the Internet as NCSA Mosaic, and made a significant contribution to the huge growth in the Internet's popularity.

Mosaic was developed at the National Center for Supercomputing Applications at the University of Illinois in 1993, and the team behind it went on to create ◊Netscape Navigator, which quickly became a ◊killer application for browsing the Web.

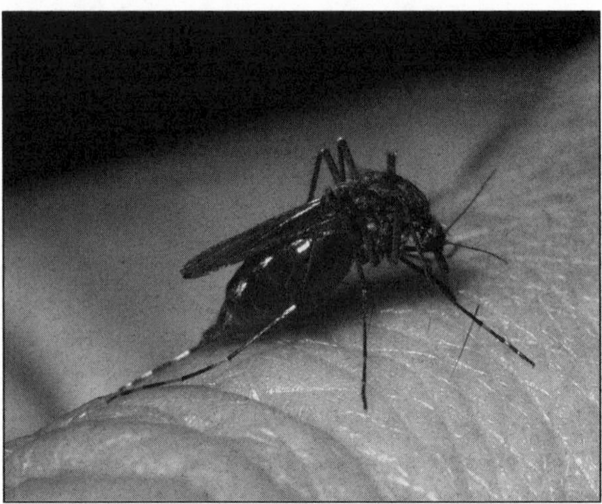

mosquito Though most of the more than 2,400 species of mosquito are tropical, they are found worldwide. The largest mosquito in the British Isles is the banded-legged Culiseta annulata*, seen here. Premaphotos Wildlife*

mosquito any of a group of flies in which the female has needle-like mouthparts and sucks blood before laying eggs. The males feed on plant juices. Some mosquitoes carry diseases such as ◊malaria. (Family Culicidae, order Diptera.)

Human odour in general is attractive to mosquitos, as well as the lactic acid in sweat and the heat of the human body at close range. Peoples' varying reactions to mosquito bites depend on their general allergic reaction and not on the degree of the bite; the allergic reaction is caused by the saliva injected from the mosquito's salivary glands to prevent the host's blood from clotting. The mosquito consumes 4 microlitres of blood when it feeds. Natural mosquito repellents include lavender oil, citronella (from lemon grass), thyme, and eucalyptus oils.

moss small nonflowering plant of the class Musci (10,000 species), forming with the ◊liverworts and the ◊hornworts the order Bryophyta. The stem of each plant bears ◊rhizoids that anchor it; there are no true roots. Leaves spirally arranged on its lower portion have sexual organs at their tips. Most mosses flourish best in damp conditions where other vegetation is thin.

The peat or bog moss *Sphagnum* was formerly used for surgical dressings. The smallest moss is the Cape pygmy moss *Ephemerum capensi*, only slightly larger than a pin head.

Mössbauer effect the recoil-free emission of gamma rays from atomic nuclei under certain conditions. The effect was discovered in 1958 by German physicist Rudolf Mössbauer, and used in 1960 to provide the first laboratory test of Einstein's general theory of relativity.

The absorption and subsequent re-emission of a gamma ray by an atomic nucleus usually causes it to recoil, so affecting the wavelength of the emitted ray. Mössbauer found that at low temperatures, crystals will absorb gamma rays of a specific wavelength and resonate so that the crystal as a whole recoils while individual nuclei do not. The wavelength of the re-emitted gamma rays is therefore virtually unaltered by recoil and may be measured to a high degree of accuracy. Changes in the wavelength may therefore be studied as evidence of the effect of, say, neighbouring electrons or gravity. For example, the effect provided the first verification of the general theory of relativity by showing that gamma-ray wavelengths become longer in a gravitational field, as predicted by Einstein.

moth any of a large number of mainly night-flying insects closely related to butterflies. Their wings are covered with microscopic scales. Most moths have a long sucking mouthpart (proboscis) for feeding on the nectar of flowers, but some have no functional mouthparts and rely instead upon stores of fat and other reserves

MOTH

Males of the US moth *Gluphisia septentrionis* spend up to three hours at a time 'puddling'. Puddling is like drinking, except that the water passes straight through the insect after its sodium has been extracted. As it puddles, the moth squirts out the unwanted liquid from its anus about 18 times per minute. It passes the water equivalent of 600 times its own body mass.

built up during the caterpillar stage. At least 100,000 different species of moth are known. (Order Lepidoptera.)

Moths feed chiefly on nectar and other fluid matter; some, like the ◊hawk moths, frequent flowers and feed while hovering. The females of some species (such as bagworm moths) have no wings at all or wings that are reduced to tiny flaps. Moths vary greatly in size: the minute Nepticulidae sometimes have a wingspread less than 3 mm/0.1 in, while the giant Noctuid or owlet moth (*Erebus agrippina*) measures about 280 mm/11 in across. In many cases the males are smaller and more brightly coloured than the females.

The larvae (caterpillars) have a well-developed head and three thoracic (middle) and ten abdominal (end) segments. Each thoracic segment has a pair of short legs, ending in single claws; a pair of suckerlike feet is present on segments three to six and ten of the end part of the body. In the family Geometridae the caterpillars have abdominal feet only on segments six and ten of the end part of the body. They move in a characteristic looping way and are known as 'loopers', 'inchworms', or geometers. Projecting from the middle of the lower lip of a caterpillar is a tiny tube or spinneret, through which silk is produced to make a cocoon within which the change to the pupa or chrysalis occurs. Silk glands are especially large in the ◊silkworm moth. Many caterpillars, including the geometers, which are hunted by birds, are protected by their resemblance in both form and colour to their immediate surroundings. Others, which are distasteful to such enemies, are brightly coloured or densely hairy.

The feeding caterpillars of many moths cause damage: the codling moth, for example, attacks fruit trees; and several species of clothes moth eat natural fibres.

motherboard ◊printed circuit board that contains the main components of a microcomputer. The power, memory capacity, and capability of the microcomputer may be enhanced by adding expansion boards to the motherboard.

mother-of-pearl or ***nacre*** the smooth lustrous lining in the shells of certain molluscs – for example pearl oysters, abalones, and mussels. When this layer is especially thick it is used commercially for jewellery and decorations. Mother-of-pearl consists of calcium carbonate. See ◊pearl.

motility the ability to move spontaneously. The term is often restricted to those cells that are capable of independent locomotion, such as spermatozoa. Many single-celled organisms are motile, for example, the amoeba. Research has shown that cells capable of movement, including vertebrate muscle cells, have certain biochemical features in common. Filaments of the proteins actin and myosin are associated with motility, as are the metabolic processes needed for breaking down the energy-rich compound ◊ATP (adenosine triphosphate).

motor anything that produces or imparts motion; a machine that provides mechanical power – for example, an ◊electric motor. Machines that burn fuel (petrol, diesel) are usually called engines, but the internal-combustion engine that propels vehicles has long been called a motor, hence 'motoring' and 'motorcar'. Actually the motor is a part of the car engine.

motorboat small, waterborne craft for pleasure cruising or racing, powered by a petrol, diesel, or gas-turbine engine. A boat not

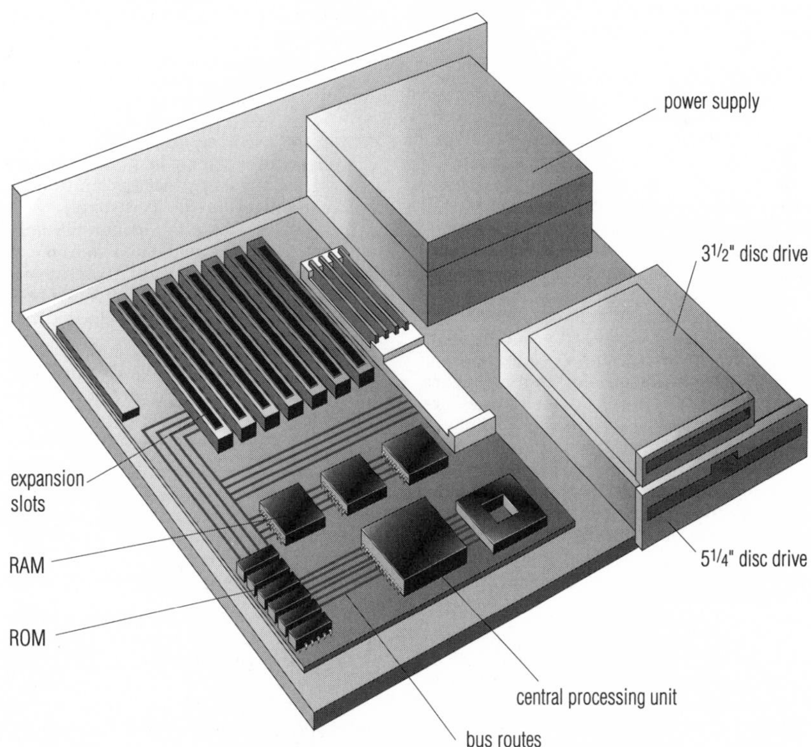

***motherboard** The position of a motherboard within a computer's system unit. The motherboard contains the central processing unit, Random Access Memory (RAM) chips, Read-Only Memory (ROM), and a number of expansion slots.*

equipped as a motorboat may be converted by a detachable outboard motor. For increased speed, such as in racing, motorboat hulls are designed to skim the water (aquaplane) and reduce frictional resistance. Plastics, steel, and light alloys are now used in construction as well as the traditional wood.

In recent designs, drag is further reduced with ◊hydrofins and hydrofoils, which enable the hull to rise clear of the water at normal speeds. Notable events in motorboat or 'powerboat' racing include the American Gold Cup in 1947 (over a 145 km/90 mi course) and the Round-Britain race in 1969.

motorcar another term for ◊car.

BRAVE NEW WORLD

Aldous Huxley's novel *Brave New World* is set in 632AF – that is, 632 years after Henry Ford mass-produced the motor car.

motorcycle or ***motorbike*** two-wheeled vehicle propelled by a ◊petrol engine. The first successful motorized bicycle was built in France in 1901, and British and US manufacturers first produced motorbikes 1903.

history In 1868 Ernest and Pierre Michaux in France experimented with a steam-powered bicycle, but the steam-power unit was too heavy and cumbersome. Gottlieb Daimler, a German engineer, created the first motorcycle when he installed his lightweight petrol engine in a bicycle frame 1886. Daimler soon lost interest in two wheels in favour of four and went on to pioneer the ◊car.

The first really successful two-wheel design was devised by Michael and Eugene Werner in France in 1901. They adopted the classic motorcycle layout with the engine low down between the wheels.

Harley Davidson in the USA and Triumph in the UK began manufacture in 1903. Road races like the Isle of Man TT (Tourist Trophy), established in 1907, helped improve motorcycle design and it soon evolved into more or less its present form. British bikes included the Vincent, BSA, and Norton.

industry In the 1970s British manufacturers were overtaken by Japanese ones, and such motorcycles as Honda, Kawasaki, Suzuki, and Yamaha now dominate the world market. They make a wide variety of machines, from ◊mopeds (lightweights with pedal assistance) to streamlined superbikes capable of speeds up to 250 kph/160 mph. There is still a smaller but thriving Italian motorcycle industry, making more specialist bikes. Laverda, Moto Guzzi, and Ducati continue to manufacture in Italy.

technical description The lightweight bikes are generally powered by a two-stroke petrol engine (see ◊two-stroke cycle), while bikes with an engine capacity of 250 cc or more are generally four-strokes (see ◊four-stroke cycle). However, many special-use larger bikes (such as those developed for off-road riding and racing) are two-stroke. Most motorcycles are air-cooled – their engines are surrounded by metal fins to offer a large surface area – although some have a water-cooling system similar to that of a car. Most small bikes have single-cylinder engines, but larger machines can have as many as six. The single-cylinder engine is economical and was popular in British manufacture, then the Japanese developed multiple-cylinder models, but there has recently been some return to single-cylinder engines. In the majority of bikes a chain carries the drive from the engine to the rear wheel, though some machines are now fitted with shaft drive.

motor effect tendency of a wire carrying an electric current in a magnetic field to move. The direction of the movement is given by the left-hand rule (see ◊Fleming's rules). This effect is used in the electric ◊motor. It also explains why streams of electrons produced, for instance, in a television tube can be directed by electromagnets.

motor nerve in anatomy, any nerve that transmits impulses from the central nervous system to muscles or organs. Motor nerves cause voluntary and involuntary muscle contractions, and stimulate glands to secrete hormones.

motor neuron disease or ***amyotrophic lateral sclerosis*** chronic disease in which there is progressive degeneration of the nerve cells which instigate movement. It leads to weakness, wasting, and loss of muscle function and usually proves fatal within two to three years of onset. Motor neuron disease occurs in both hereditary and sporadic forms but its causes remain unclear. A gene believed to be implicated in familial cases was discovered in 1993. In Britain some 1,200 new cases are diagnosed each year.

Results of a US trial in 1995 showed that the drug Myotrophin, a genetically engineered version of a chemical produced in the muscles, slowed deterioration in sufferers of MND by 25%.

Motorola US semiconductor and electronics company. In computing Motorola is best known for the 680x0 series of microprocessors used for many years by the Apple ◊Macintosh range and other computers. Its main microprocessor is the ◊PowerPC chip.

motorway main road for fast motor traffic, with two or more lanes in each direction, and with special access points (junctions) fed by slip roads. The first motorway (85 km/53 mi) ran from Milan to Varese, Italy, and was completed in 1924; by 1939 some 500 km/300 mi of motorway (*autostrada*) had been built, although these did not attain the standards of later express highways. In Germany some 2,100 km/1,310 mi of *Autobahnen* had been completed by 1942. After World War II motorways were built in a growing number of countries, for example the USA, France, and the UK. The most ambitious building programme was in the USA, which by 1974 had 70,800 km/44,000 mi of 'expressway'. Construction of new motorways causes much environmental concern.

mouflon wild sheep found in mountain areas of Cyprus, Corsica, and Sardinia. It has woolly underfur in winter, but this is covered by heavy guard hairs. The coat is brown with a white belly and rump. Males have strong, curving horns. (Species *Ovis ammon*, family Bovidae.)

mould furlike growth caused by any of a group of fungi (see ◊fungus) living on foodstuffs and other organic matter; a few are parasitic on plants, animals, or each other. Many moulds are of medical or industrial importance; for example, the antibiotic penicillin comes from a type of mould.

moulding use of a pattern, hollow form, or matrix to give a specific shape to something in a plastic or molten state. It is commonly used for shaping plastics, clays, and glass. When metals are used, the process is called ◊casting.

In **injection moulding**, molten plastic, for example, is injected into a water-cooled mould and takes the shape of the mould when it solidifies. In **blow moulding**, air is blown into a blob of molten plastic inside a hollow mould. In **compression moulding**, synthetic resin powder is simultaneously heated and pressed into a mould.

moulting periodic shedding of the hair or fur of mammals, feathers of birds, or skin of reptiles. In mammals and birds, moulting is usually seasonal and is triggered by changes of day length.

The term is also often applied to the shedding of the ◊exoskeleton of arthropods, but this is more correctly called ◊ecdysis.

mountain natural upward projection of the Earth's surface, higher and steeper than a hill. The process of mountain building (orogeny) consists of volcanism, folding, faulting, and thrusting, resulting from the collision and welding together of two tectonic plates (see ◊plate tectonics). This process deforms the rock and compresses it between the two plates into mountain chains.

mountain ash or ***rowan*** European flowering tree. It grows to 15 m/50 ft and has pinnate leaves (leaflets growing either side of the stem) and large clusters of whitish flowers, followed by scarlet berries in autumn. (*Sorbus aucuparia*, family Rosaceae.)

In Australia, the tallest growing hardwood species in the world (*Eucalyptus regnans*), found in forests of Victoria, is called mountain ash.

mountain devil woody shrub *Lambertia formosa*, family Proteaceae, of sandstone areas of New South Wales, Australia. It

Highest Mountains in the World, with First Ascents

Mountain	Location	Height m	ft	Year of first ascent	Expedition nationality/leader
Everest	China/Nepal	8,848	29,029	1953	British/New Zealander (J Hunt)
K2	Kashmir/Jammu	8,611	28,251	1954	Italian (A Desio)
Kangchenjunga	India/Nepal	8,598	28,208	1955	British (C Evans; by the southwest face)
Lhotse	China/Nepal	8,511	27,923	1956	Swiss (E Reiss)
Yalung Kang (formerly Kangchenjunga West Peak)	India/Nepal	8,502	27,893	1973	Japanese (Y Ageta)
Kangchenjunga South Peak	India/Nepal	8,488	27,847	1978	Polish (W Wröz)
Makalu I	China/Nepal	8,481	27,824	1955	French (J Couzy)
Kangchenjunga Middle Peak	India/Nepal	8,475	27,805	1973	Polish (W Wröz)
Lhotse Shar	China/Nepal	8,383	27,503	1970	Austrian (S Mayerl)
Dhaulagiri	Nepal	8,172	26,811	1960	Swiss/Austrian (K Diemberger)
Manaslu	Nepal	8,156	26,759	1956	Japanese (T Imanishi)
Cho Oyu	China/Nepal	8,153	26,748	1954	Austrian (H Tichy)
Nanga Parbat	Kashmir/Jammu	8,126	26,660	1953	German (K M Herrligkoffer)
Annapurna I	Nepal	8,078	26,502	1950	French (M Herzog)
Gasherbrum I	Kashmir/Jammu	8,068	26,469	1958	US (P K Schoening; by the southwest ridge)
Broad Peak	Kashmir/Jammu	8,047	26,401	1957	Austrian (M Schmuck)
Gasherbrum II	Kashmir/Jammu	8,034	26,358	1956	Austrian (S Larch; by the southwest spur)
Gosainthan	China	8,012	26,286	1964	Chinese (195-strong team; accounts are inconclusive)
Broad Peak (Middle)	Kashmir/Jammu	8,000	26,246	1975	Polish (K Glazek)
Gasherbrum III	Kashmir/Jammu	7,952	26,089	1975	Polish (J Onyskiewicz)
Annapurna II	Nepal	7,937	26,040	1960	British (C Bonington)
Gasherbrum IV	Kashmir/Jammu	7,923	25,994	1958	Italian (W Bonatti, C Mouri)
Gyachung Kang	Nepal	7,921	25,987	1964	Japanese (Y Kato, K Sakaizqwa)
Disteghil Shar	Kashmir	7,884	25,866	1960	Austrian (G Stärker, D Marchart)
Himalchuli	Nepal	7,864	25,800	1960	Japanese (M Harada, H Tanabe)
Nuptse	Nepal	7,841	25,725	1961	British (D Davis, C Bonington, L Brown)
Manaslu II	Nepal	7,835	25,705	1970	Japanese (H Watanabe, Lhakpa Tsering)
Masherbrum East	Kashmir	7,821	25,659	1960	Pakistani/US (G Bell, W Unsoeld)
Nanda Devi	India	7,817	25,646	1936	British (H W Tilman)
Chomo Lonzo	Nepal	7,815	25,639	1954	French (J Couzy, L Terry)

has a red, tubular flower which develops into a woody 'horned devil' seed pod.

mountain gorilla highly endangered ape found in bamboo and rainforest on the Rwanda, Congo (formerly Zaire), and Uganda borders in central Africa, with a total population of around 600 (1995). It is threatened by deforestation and illegal hunting for skins and the zoo trade. (Subspecies *Gorilla gorilla beringei.*)

mountain lion another name for the ◊puma.

MOUNTAIN LION

http://blackbox1.wittenberg.edu/academics/biol/courses/mammals/cougar.htm

Good profile of *Felis concolor*, largest cat in the USA. The contents include a description, information on habitat, diet, hunting technique, reproduction, and survival threats. Among the interesting facts in this well-written account is that there are some hundred indigenous names for this common wildcat and that the purr of the puma is 20 times louder that of the domestic cat.

Mount Palomar astronomical observatory, 80 km/50 mi NE of San Diego, California, USA. It has a 5-m/200-in diameter reflector called the Hale. Completed in 1948, it was the world's premier observatory during the 1950s.

Mount Stromlo Observatory astronomical observatory established in Canberra, Australia, in 1923. Important observations have been made there on the Magellanic Clouds, which can be seen clearly from southern Australia.

Mount Wilson site near Los Angeles, California, of the 2.5 m/100 in Hooker telescope, opened in 1917, with which Edwin Hubble discovered the expansion of the universe. Two solar telescopes in towers 18.3 m/60 ft and 45.7 m/150 ft tall, and a 1.5 m/60 in reflector opened in 1908, also operate there.

mouse in computing, an input device used to control a pointer on a computer screen. It is a feature of ◊graphical user interface (GUI) systems. The mouse is about the size of a pack of playing cards, is connected to the computer by a wire, and incorporates one or more buttons that can be pressed. Moving the mouse across a flat surface causes a corresponding movement of the pointer. In this way, the operator can manipulate objects on the screen and make menu selections.

The mouse was invented 1963 at the Stanford Research Institute, USA, by Douglas Engelbart, and developed by the Xerox Corporation in the 1970s. The first was made of wood; the Microsoft mouse was introduced in 1983, and the Apple Macintosh mouse in 1984. Mice work either mechanically (with electrical contacts to sense the movement in two planes of a ball on a level surface), or optically (photocells detecting movement by recording light reflected from a grid on which the mouse is moved).

MOUNT STROMLO AND SIDING SPRING OBSERVATORIES

http://msowww.anu.edu.au/

Searchable site of Australia's leading observatory. In addition to scientific data of interest only to astronomers, there is general information on the research work being undertaken, downloadable images of space, and information about the observatory.

mouse in zoology, one of a number of small rodents with small ears and a long, thin tail. The **house mouse** (*Mus musculus*) is distributed worldwide. It is 75 mm/3 in long, with a naked tail of the same length, and has a grey-brown body. (Family Muridae.)

mousebird any of a family of small crested birds found only in Africa. They have hairlike feathers, long tails, and move with a mouselike agility. The largest is the **blue-naped mousebird** (*Colius macrourus*), about 35 cm/14 in long. (Family Coliidae, order Coliiformes.)

Moustier, Le rock shelter in the Dordogne, SW France, with prehistoric remains. It gave the name Mousterian to a type of flint-tool culture associated with Neanderthal sites of 100,000–40,000 years ago.

mouth cavity forming the entrance to the digestive tract. In land vertebrates, air from the nostrils enters the mouth cavity to pass down the trachea. The mouth in mammals is enclosed by the jaws, cheeks, and palate.

moving-coil meter instrument used to detect and measure electrical current. A coil of wire pivoted between the poles of a permanent magnet is turned by the motor effect of an electric current (by which a force acts on a wire carrying a current in a magnetic field). The extent to which the coil turns can then be related to the magnitude of the current.

The sensitivity of the instrument depends directly upon the strength of the permanent magnet used, the number of turns making up the moving coil, and the coil's area. It depends inversely upon the strength of the controlling springs used to restrain the rotation of the coil. By the addition of a suitable resistor, a moving-coil meter can be adapted to read potential difference in volts.

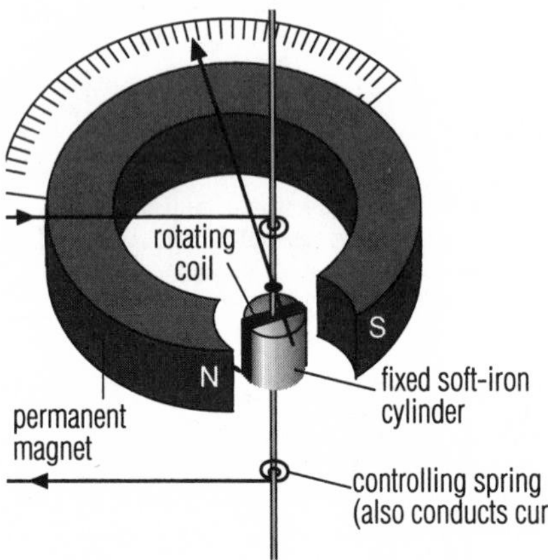

moving-coil meter A simple moving-coil meter. Direct electric current (DC) flowing through the wire coil combined with the presence of a magnetic field causes the coil to rotate; this in turn moves a pointer across a calibrated scale so that the degree of rotation can be related to the magnitude of the current.

mower an implement used to cut grass crops or lawns. Agricultural mowers used for haymaking have a long reciprocating knife leaving a broad swathe that will dry in the sun. Mowers used for cutting silage have one or more rotary blades that leave a deep pile of grass suitable for immediate loading. The rotary blade has also been adapted to lawnmowers, replacing the older mechanism of a cylinder with cutting bars attached.

mp in chemistry, abbreviation for ***melting point***.

MPC (abbreviation for ***Multimedia PC***) standard defining the minimum specification for developing and running CD-ROM software. It has been rendered largely obsolete by the fact that most of today's PCs include multimedia features as a matter of course. The current MPC specification, MPC III, requires at least 8 MB of RAM, a 75MHz Pentium processor, a VGA monitor, and a quad-speed CD-ROM disc drive.

MPEG (pronounced 'empeg'; acronym for ***Moving Picture Experts Group***) in computing, committee of the International Standards Organisation, formed in 1988, that sets standards for digital audio and video compression: hence, any file that has been compressed using those standards. The **MPEG-1** is the standard for the digital coding of video pictures for CD recording; **MPEG-2** is a common standard for broadcast-quality video; and **MPEG-4** for Internet telephony. (There is no MPEG-3 as it was absorbed into MPEG-2.)

MPR-II ***(Mat och ProvRad)*** in computing, Swedish standard that limits the amount of possibly harmful electromagnetic radiation that may be produced by visual display units (VDUs). A monitor tested for MPR-II compliance should have low emission rates.

MSCDEX.EXE (***Microsoft Compact Disc Extensions***) in computing, device driver used by Microsoft MS-DOS and Windows 3 to provide access to files on CD-ROM drives as though they were on a hard drive or floppy disc.

MS-DOS (abbreviation for ***Microsoft Disc Operating System***) computer ◊operating system produced by Microsoft Corporation, widely used on ◊microcomputers with Intel x 86 and Pentium family microprocessors. A version called PC-DOS is sold by IBM specifically for its personal computers. MS-DOS and PC-DOS are usually referred to as DOS. MS-DOS first appeared in 1981, and was similar to an earlier system from Digital Research called CP/M.

MTBF abbreviation for ***mean time between failures***, the statistically average time a component can be used before it goes wrong. The MTBF of a computer hard disc, for example, is around 150,000 hours.

mucous membrane thin skin lining all animal body cavities and canals that come into contact with the air (for example, eyelids, breathing and digestive passages, genital tract). It secretes mucus, a moistening, lubricating, and protective fluid.

mucus lubricating and protective fluid, secreted by mucous membranes in many different parts of the body. In the gut, mucus smooths the passage of food and keeps potentially damaging digestive enzymes away from the gut lining. In the lungs, it traps airborne particles so that they can be expelled.

MUD (acronym for ***multi-user dungeon*** or ***multi-user domain***) in computing, interactive multi-player game, played via the Internet or modem connection to one of the participating computers. MUD players typically have to solve puzzles, avoid traps, fight other participants and carry out various tasks to achieve their goals.

mudfish another name for the ◊bowfin.

mudnester any of an Australian group of birds that make their nests from mud, including the **apostle bird** (*Struthidea cinerea*) (so called from its appearance in little flocks of about 12), the **white-winged chough** (*Corcorax melanorhamphos*), and the **magpie lark** (*Grallina cyanoleuca*).

mudpuppy any of five species of brownish ◊salamanders, living in fresh water in North America. They all breathe in water using external gills. The species *N. maculatus* is about 20 cm/8 in long. Mudpuppies eat fish, snails, and other invertebrates. (Genus *Necturus*, family Proteidae.)

mudskipper any of a group of fishes belonging to the goby family, found in brackish water and shores in the tropics, except for the Americas. It can walk or climb over mudflats, using its strong pectoral (chest) fins as legs, and has eyes set close together on top of the head. It grows up to 30 cm/12 in long. (Genus *Periophthalmus*, family Gobiidae.)

MUDSKIPPER

There is a fish that can climb trees. The mudskipper spends three-quarters of its time out of water. Malaysian mudskippers live in mangrove swamps, where they climb among the tangled stems and roots, and sometimes into the branches.

mudstone fine-grained sedimentary rock made up of clay- to silt-sized particles (up to 0.0625 mm/0.0025 in).

mulberry any of a group of trees consisting of a dozen species, including the black mulberry (*M. nigra*). It is native to W Asia and has heart-shaped, toothed leaves and spikes of whitish flowers. It is widely cultivated for its compound fruits, which resemble raspberries. The leaves of the Asiatic white mulberry (*M. alba*) are those used in feeding silkworms. (Genus *Morus*, family Moraceae.)

mule hybrid animal, usually the offspring of a male ass and a female horse.

mulga Aboriginal name for various wattles and particularly *Acacia aneura* which covers large arid areas of inland Australia giving a characteristic greyness to the landscape and providing drought fodder for sheep.

Mullard Radio Astronomy Observatory radio observatory of the University of Cambridge, England. Its main instrument is the Ryle Telescope, eight dishes 12.8 m/42 ft wide in a line of 5 km/3 mi long, opened in 1972.

mullein any of a group of ◊herbaceous plants belonging to the figwort family. The great mullein (*V. thapsus*) has lance-shaped leaves 30 cm/12 in or more in length, covered in woolly down, and a large spike of yellow flowers. It is found in Europe and Asia and is naturalized in North America. (Genus *Verbascum*, family Scrophulariaceae.)

mullet either of two species of fish. The **red mullet** (*Mullus surmuletus*) is found in the Mediterranean and warm Atlantic as far north as the English Channel. It is about 40 cm/16 in long, red with yellow stripes, and has long barbels (sensitive bristles) round the mouth. (Family Mullidae.)

The **grey mullet** (*Crenimugil labrosus*) lives in ponds and estuaries. It is greyish above, with horizontal dark stripes, and grows to 60 cm/24 in. (Family Mugilidae.)

multicasting in computing, sending a simultaneous message across a ◊network to two or more workstations.

multimedia computerized method of presenting information by combining audio and video components using text, sound, and graphics (still, animated, and video sequences). For example, a multimedia database of musical instruments may allow a user not only to search and retrieve text about a particular instrument but also to see pictures of it and hear it play a piece of music. Multimedia applications emphasize interactivity between the computer and the user.

As graphics, video, and audio are extremely demanding of storage space, multimedia PCs are usually fitted with CD-ROM drives because of the high storage capacity of ◊CD-ROM discs.

In the mid-1990s developments in compression techniques and software made it possible to incorporate multimedia elements into Internet Web sites.

multiple birth in humans, the production of more than two babies from one pregnancy. Multiple births can be caused by more than two eggs being produced and fertilized (often as the result of hormone therapy to assist pregnancy), or by a single fertilized egg dividing more than once before implantation. See also ◊twin.

Multiple Mirror Telescope telescope on Mount Hopkins, Arizona, USA, opened in 1979, consisting of six 1.83 m/72 in mirrors mounted in a hexagon, the light-collecting area of which equals that of a single mirror of 4.5 m/176 in diameter. It is planned to replace the six mirrors with a single mirror 6.5 m/256 in wide.

multiple personality disorder (MPD) psychiatric disorder wherein the patient exhibits two or more personalities. Personalities can be widely differing, with the same patient switching between the personalities of children and adults of different ages, sexes, and temperaments. Each personality is distinct, and often unaware of the others. MPD may occur as a result of child abuse, though not all psychiatrists accept that it is a genuine disorder.

multiple proportions, law of in chemistry, the principle that if two elements combine with each other to form more than one compound, then the ratio of the masses of one of them that combine with a particular mass of the other is a small whole number.

multiple sclerosis (MS) or ***disseminated sclerosis*** incurable chronic disease of the central nervous system, occurring in young or middle adulthood. Most prevalent in temperate zones, it affects more women than men. It is characterized by degeneration of the myelin sheath that surrounds nerves in the brain and spinal cord.

Depending on where the demyelination occurs – which nerves are affected – the symptoms of MS can mimic almost any neurological disorder. Typically seen are unsteadiness, ataxia (loss of muscular coordination), weakness, speech difficulties, and rapid involuntary movements of the eyes. The course of the disease is episodic, with frequent intervals of ◊remission. Its cause is unknown, but it may be initiated in childhood by some environmental factor, such as infection, in genetically susceptible people. It has been shown that there is a genetic component: identical twins of MS sufferers have a 1 in 4 chance of developing the disease, compared to the 1 in 1,000 chance for the general population.

In 1993 interferon beta 1b became the first drug to be approved in the United States for treating MS. It reduces the number and severity of relapses, and slows the formation of brain lesions giving hope that it may slow down the progression of the disease.

MULTIPLE SCLEROSIS SUPPORT

http://www.infosci.org/MS-UK-MSSoc/

Embryonic site run by the British Multiple Sclerosis Society. There is information on the society itself and resources of help to sufferers and their families.

multiplexer in telecommunications, a device that allows a transmission medium to carry a number of separate signals at the same time – enabling, for example, several telephone conversations to be carried by one telephone line, and radio signals to be transmitted in stereo.

In **frequency-division multiplexing**, signals of different frequency, each carrying a different message, are transmitted.

Electrical frequency filters separate the message at the receiving station. In **time-division multiplexing**, the messages are broken into sections and the sections of several messages interleaved during transmission. ◊Pulse-code modulation allows hundreds of messages to be sent simultaneously over a single link.

multiplication one of the four basic operations of arithmetic, usually written in the form $a \times b$ or ab, and involving repeated addition in the sense that a is added to itself b times. Multiplication obeys commutative, associative, and distributive laws (the latter over addition) and every number (except 0) has a multiplicative inverse. The number 1 is the identity for multiplication.

multisession in computing, the ability of a compact disc or other ◊WORM ('write once, read many times') medium, to record information at different times. Multisession technology allows archives to be built up gradually, as in the ◊PhotoCD system, where users can progressively fill up a CD as they take pictures.

multistage rocket rocket launch vehicle made up of several rocket stages (often three) joined end to end. The bottom stage fires first, boosting the vehicle to high speed, then it falls away. The next stage fires, thrusting the now lighter vehicle even faster. The remaining stages fire and fall away in turn, boosting the vehicle's payload (cargo) to an orbital speed that can reach 28,000 kph/17,500 mph.

multitasking or ***multiprogramming*** in computing, a system in which one processor appears to run several different programs (or different parts of the same program) at the same time. All the programs are held in memory together and each is allowed to run for a certain period.

For example, one program may run while other programs are waiting for a peripheral device to work or for input from an operator.

The ability to multitask depends on the ◊operating system rather than the type of computer. UNIX is one of the commonest.

multi-threading in computing, executing two or more ◊threads, or sections, of a program at a time. Multi-threading is much faster than ◊multitasking because it switches very quickly between instructions.

multi-user dungeon in computing, interactive game usually abbreviated to ◊MUD.

multi-user shared hallucination in computing, interactive game usually abbreviated to ◊MUSH.

multiuser system or ***multiaccess system*** in computing, an operating system that enables several users to access centrally-stored data and programs simultaneously over a network. Each user has a terminal, which may be local (connected directly to the computer) or remote (connected to the computer via a modem and a telephone line).

Multiaccess is usually achieved by **time-sharing**: the computer switches very rapidly between terminals and programs so that each user has sole use of the computer for only a fraction of a second but can work as if she or he had continuous access.

Multi-user systems are becoming increasingly common in the workplace, and have many advantages – such as enabling employees to refer to and update a shared corporate database.

mummy any dead body, human or animal, that has been naturally or artificially preserved. Natural mummification can occur through freezing (for example, mammoths in glacial ice from 25,000 years ago), drying, or preservation in bogs or oil seeps. Artificial mummification may be achieved by embalming (for example, the mummies of ancient Egypt) or by freeze-drying.

MUMMY

Thousands of mummified cats were discovered in an underground cavern at Ben Hassan, Egypt, in 1889. Most were sold off for use as fertilizer.

mumps or ***infectious parotitis*** virus infection marked by fever, pain, and swelling of one or both parotid salivary glands (situated in front of the ears). It is usually shortlived in children, although meningitis is a possible complication. In adults the symptoms are more serious and it may cause sterility in men.

Mumps is the most common cause of ◊meningitis in children, but it follows a much milder course than bacterial meningitis, and a complete recovery is usual. Rarely, mumps meningitis may lead to deafness. An effective vaccine against mumps, measles, and rubella (MMR vaccine) is now offered for children aged 18 months.

Münchhausen's syndrome emotional disorder in which a patient feigns or invents symptoms to secure medical treatment. It is the chronic form of factitious disorder, which is more common, and probably underdiagnosed. In some cases the patient will secretly ingest substances to produce real symptoms. It was named after the exaggerated tales of Baron Münchhausen. Some patients invent symptoms for their children, a phenomenon known as Münchhausen's by proxy.

Munsterlander breed of gundog developed as two types – large (58–62 cm/23–24 in) and small (up to 56 cm/22 in) – in the early 20th century in Westphalia, Germany. The Small Munsterlander has a white coat with a brown head and brown patches and spots on the body. The Large Munsterlander has similar markings in black and white. Both have moderately long, wavy coats, drooping ears, and long tails.

muntjac any of about six species of small deer found in SE Asia. They live mostly in dense vegetation and do not form herds. The males have short spiked antlers and two sharp canine teeth forming tusks. They are sometimes called 'barking deer' because of their voices. (Genus *Muntiacus*.)

muon an ◊elementary particle similar to the electron except for its mass which is 207 times greater than that of the electron. It has a half-life of 2 millionths of a second, decaying into electrons and ◊neutrinos. The muon was originally thought to be a ◊meson and is thus sometimes called a mu meson, although current opinion is that it is a ◊lepton.

Murray cod Australian freshwater fish that grows to about 2 m/6 ft. It is is named after the river in which it is found. (Species *Maccullochella macquariensis*.)

> *The function of muscle is to pull and not to push, except in the case of the genitals and the tongue.*
>
> LEONARDO DA VINCI Italian painter, sculptor, architect, engineer, and scientist. *The Notebooks of Leonardo da Vinci* vol 1, ch 3

muscle contractile animal tissue that produces locomotion and power, and maintains the movement of body substances. Muscle is made of long cells that can contract to between one-half and one-third of their relaxed length.

Striped (or striated) muscles are activated by ◊motor nerves under voluntary control; their ends are usually attached via tendons to bones.

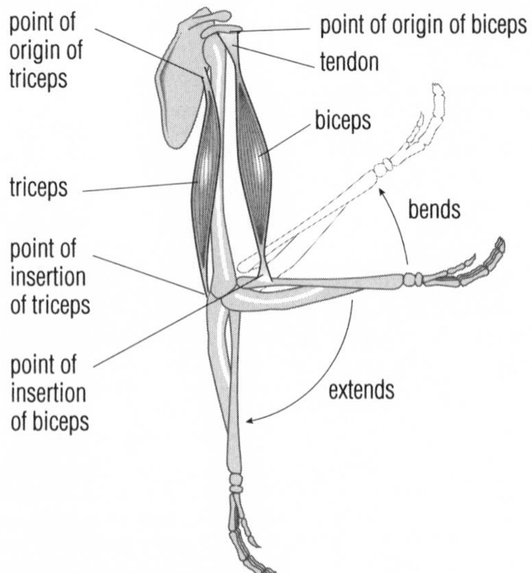

muscle The movements of the arm depend on two muscles, the biceps and the triceps. To lift the arm, the biceps shortens and the triceps lengthens. To lower the arm, the opposite occurs: the biceps lengthens and the triceps shortens.

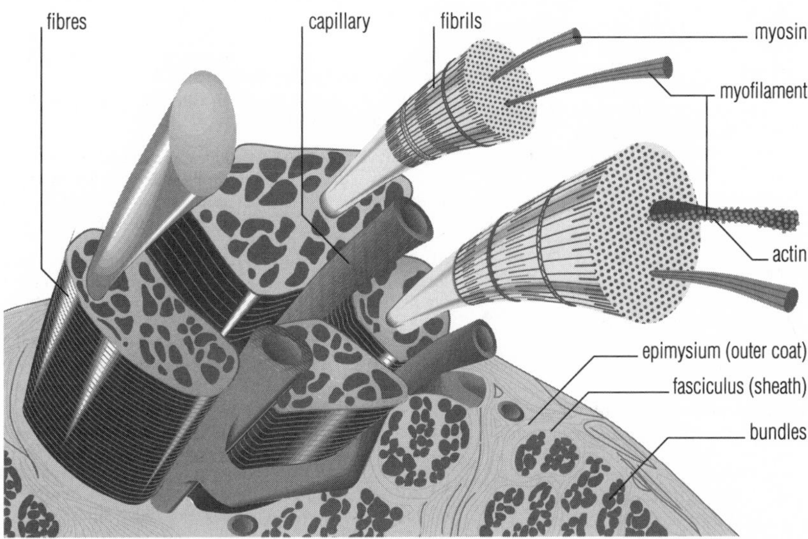

muscle Muscles make up 35–45% of our body weight; there are over 650 skeletal muscles. Muscle cells may be up to 20 cm/0.8 in long. They are arranged in bundles, fibres, fibrils, and myofilaments.

Involuntary or **smooth** muscles are controlled by ◊motor nerves of the autonomic nervous system, and are located in the gut, blood vessels, iris, and various ducts.

Cardiac muscle occurs only in the heart, and is also controlled by the autonomic nervous system.

muscovite white mica, $KAl_2Si_3AlO_{10}(OH,F)_2$, a common silicate mineral. It is colourless to silvery white with shiny surfaces, and like all micas it splits into thin flakes along its one perfect cleavage. Muscovite is a metamorphic mineral occurring mainly in schists; it is also found in some granites, and appears as shiny flakes on bedding planes of some sandstones.

muscular dystrophy any of a group of inherited chronic muscle disorders marked by weakening and wasting of muscle. Muscle fibres degenerate, to be replaced by fatty tissue, although the nerve supply remains unimpaired. Death occurs in early adult life.

The commonest form, Duchenne muscular dystrophy, strikes boys (1 in 3,000), usually before the age of four. The child develops a waddling gait and an inward curvature (lordosis) of the lumbar spine. The muscles affected by dystrophy and the rate of progress vary. There is no cure, but physical treatments can minimize disability. Death usually occurs before the age of 20.

MUSE (abbreviation for ***multi-user shared environment***) in computing, type of ◊MUD.

MUSH (acronym for ***multi-user shared hallucination***) in computing, a ◊MUD (multi-user dungeon) that can be altered by the players. Participants in a MUSH construct new environments or 'rooms' and devise new obstacles to challenge other players.

mushroom fruiting body of certain fungi (see ◊fungus), consisting of an upright stem and a spore-producing cap with radiating gills on the undersurface. There are many edible species belonging to the genus *Agaricus*, including the field mushroom (*A. campestris*). See also ◊toadstool.

musical instrument digital interface manufacturer's standard for digital music equipment; see ◊MIDI.

music therapy use of music as an adjunct to relaxation therapy, or in ◊psychotherapy to elicit expressions of suppressed emotions by prompting patients to dance, shout, laugh, cry, or whatever, in response.

Music therapists are most frequently called upon to help the mentally or physically disabled; for instance, patients suffering from speech difficulties or autism may be enabled to express themselves more effectively by making musical sounds, and music can help the physically disabled to develop better motor control.

musk in botany, perennial plant whose small oblong leaves give off the musky scent from which it takes its name; it is also called **monkey flower**. The name 'musk' is also given to several other plants with a similar scent, including the musk mallow (*Malva moschata*) and the musk rose (*Rosa moschata*). (*Mimulus moschatus*, family Scrophulariaceae.)

musk deer any of three species of small deer native to the mountains of central and NE Asia. A solitary animal, the musk deer is about 80–100 cm/30–40 in, sure-footed, and has large ears and no antlers. Males have long tusklike upper canine teeth. They are hunted and farmed for their musk (a waxy substance secreted by the male from a gland in the stomach area), which is used as medicine or perfume. (Genus *Moschus*.)

musk ox ruminant (cud-chewing) mammal native to the Arctic regions of North America. It has characteristics of both sheep and oxen, is about the size of a small domestic cow, and has long brown hair. At certain seasons it has a musky smell. (Species *Ovibos moschatus*, family Bovidae.)

Its underwool (**qiviut**) is almost as fine as that of the vicuna, and musk-ox farms have been established in Alaska, Quebec, and Norway to harvest this wool.

muskrat North American rodent, about 30 cm/12 in long, that lives beside streams, rivers, and lakes. It has webbed hind feet, a side-to-side flattened tail, and shiny, light-brown fur. It builds up a store of food, plastering it over with mud, for winter consumption. It is hunted for its fur. (Species *Ondatra zibethicus*, family Cricetidae.)

mussel any of a group of shellfish, some of which are edible, such as the **common mussel** (*Mytilus edulis*) which has a blue-black hinged shell and is found in clusters attached to rocks around the N Atlantic and American coasts. Mussels are bivalve ◊molluscs. (Class Bivalvia, phylum Mollusca.)

Freshwater pearl mussels, such as the species *Unio margaritiferus*, are found in some North American and European rivers. The larvae of the North American freshwater mussel *Lampsilis perovalis* are parasitic, living on the gills or fins of freshwater bass. The larvae of the British **swan mussel** (*Anodonta cygnea*) are also parasitic. *Margaritifera margaritifera* became a protected species in1991 having suffered from pollution and from amateur fishers who, unlike professionals, are not able to extract the pearl without killing the mussel itself. The **green-lipped mussel**, found only off New Zealand, produces an extract that is used in the treatment of arthritis.

MUSSEL

The European freshwater mussel *Margaritifera margaritifera* lives for at least 90 years.

mustard any of several annual plants belonging to the cress family, with seed-bearing pods and sweet-smelling yellow flowers. Brown and white mustard are cultivated as an accompaniment to food in Europe and North America. The seeds of brown mustard (*B. juncea*) and white mustard (*Sinapis alba*) are used in the preparation of table mustard. (Genus mainly *Brassica*, family Cruciferae.)

Brown mustard replaced black mustard (*B. nigra*) in commercial mustard products during the 1950s with the introduction of mechanized harvesting. *B. nigra* is unsuitable for mechanized harvesting since its pods split open to release their seeds; those of *B. juncea* do not. Table mustard is most often used as an accompaniment to meat, although it can also be used in sauces and dressings, and with fish. **English mustard** is made from finely milled brown and white mustard seed to which ground ◊turmeric is added for colour. French **Dijon mustard** contains brown mustard seed, verjuice (the juice of unripe grapes), oil, and white wine. Other varieties are made with vinegar, and may be flavoured with herbs or garlic. The seedlings of white mustard are used in salads. White mustard is also sometimes grown by farmers and ploughed back to enrich the soil. Brown mustard is grown on a large scale as an oilseed crop throughout India, China, and S Russia.

mutagen any substance that increases the rate of gene ◊mutation. A mutagen may also act as a ◊carcinogen.

mutation in biology, a change in the genes produced by a change in the ◊DNA that makes up the hereditary material of all living organisms. Mutations, the raw material of evolution, result from mistakes during replication (copying) of DNA molecules. Only a few improve the organism's performance and are therefore favoured by ◊natural selection. Mutation rates are increased by certain chemicals and by radiation.

Common mutations include the omission or insertion of a base (one of the chemical subunits of DNA); these are known as **point mutations**. Larger-scale mutations include removal of a whole segment of DNA or its inversion within the DNA strand. Not all mutations affect the organism, because there is a certain amount of redundancy in the genetic information. If a mutation is 'translated' from DNA into the protein that makes up the organism's structure, it may be in a nonfunctional part of the protein and thus have no detectable effect. This is known as a **neutral mutation**, and is of importance in ◊molecular clock studies because such mutations tend to accumulate gradually as time passes. Some mutations do affect genes that control protein production or functional parts of protein, and most of these are lethal to the organism.

mutton bird any of various shearwaters and petrels that breed in burrows on Australasian islands. The young are very fat, and are killed for food and oil.

mutual induction in physics, the production of an electromotive force (emf) or voltage in an electric circuit caused by a changing ◊magnetic flux in a neighbouring circuit. The two circuits are often coils of wire, as in a ◊transformer, and the size of the induced emf depends largely on the numbers of turns of wire in each of the coils.

mutualism or ◊***symbiosis*** an association between two organisms of different species whereby both profit from the relationship.

myall Aboriginal word for various wattle trees such as the weeping myall *Acacia pendula* found in semi-arid areas of the E states of Australia and the coastal myall *A. glaucescens* of New South Wales and Queensland.

myasthenia gravis in medicine, an uncommon condition characterized by loss of muscle power, especially in the face and neck. The muscles tire rapidly and fail to respond to repeated nervous stimulation. ◊Autoimmunity is the cause.

mycelium interwoven mass of threadlike filaments or ◊hyphae, forming the main body of most fungi. The reproductive structures, or 'fruiting bodies', grow from the mycelium.

Mycenaean civilization Bronze Age civilization that flourished in Crete, Cyprus, Greece, the Aegean Islands, and W Anatolia about 3000–1000 BC. During this period, magnificent architecture and sophisticated artefacts were produced.

◊Mycenean civilization was strongly influenced by the Minoan from Crete, from about 1600 BC. It continued to thrive, with its centre at Mycenae, after the decline of Crete in about 1400. It was finally overthrown by the Dorian invasions, about 1100. The system of government was by kings, who also monopolized priestly functions. The Mycenaeans have been identified with the Achaeans of Homer; they may also have been the marauding Sea Peoples of Egyptian records.

They used a form of Greek deciphered by Michael Ventris called Linear B, which has been discovered on large numbers of clay tablets containing administrative records. Their palaces were large and luxurious, and their tombs (known as beehive tombs) were massive and impressive monuments. Pottery, frescoes, and metalwork reached a high artistic level. Evidence of the civilization was brought to light by the excavations of Heinrich Schliemann at Troy, Mycenae, and Tiryns (a stronghold on the plain of Argolis) from 1870 onwards, and of Arthur Evans in Crete from 1899.

mycorrhiza mutually beneficial (mutualistic) association occurring between plant roots and a soil fungus. Mycorrhizal roots take up nutrients more efficiently than non-mycorrhizal roots, and the fungus benefits by obtaining carbohydrates from the plant or tree.

An **ectotrophic mycorrhiza** occurs on many tree species, which usually grow much better, most noticeably in the seeding stage, as a result. Typically the roots become repeatedly branched and coral-like, penetrated by hyphae of a surrounding fungal ◊mycelium. In an **endotrophic mycorrhiza**, the growth of the fungus is mainly inside the root, as in orchids. Such plants do not usually grow properly, and may not even germinate, unless the appropriate fungus is present.

Research by UK ecologists in 1996 showed that mycorrhizal fungi provides protection against ◊nematode worms that feed on plant roots, as well as pathogenic fungi.

myelin sheath insulating layer that surrounds nerve cells in vertebrate animals. It serves to speed up the passage of nerve impulses.

Myelin is made up of fats and proteins and is formed from up to a hundred layers, laid down by special cells, the **Schwann cells**.

mynah any of various tropical starlings found in SE Asia. The glossy black **hill mynah** (*Gracula religiosa*) of India can realistically mimic sounds and human speech. It is up to 40 cm/16 in long with yellow wattles (loose folds of skin) on the head, and a yellow bill and legs. (Family Sturnidae, order Passeriformes.)

myoglobin globular protein, closely related to ◊haemoglobin and located in vertebrate muscle. Oxygen binds to myoglobin and is released only when the haemoglobin can no longer supply adequate oxygen to muscle cells.

myopia or ***short-sightedness*** defect of the eye in which a person can see clearly only those objects that are close up. It is caused either by the eyeball being too long or by the cornea and lens system of the eye being too powerful, both of which cause the images of distant objects to be formed in front of the retina instead of on it. Nearby objects are sharply perceived. Myopia can be corrected by suitable glasses or contact lenses.

myopia, low-luminance poor night vision. About 20% of people have poor vision in twilight and nearly 50% in the dark. Low-luminance myopia does not show up in normal optical tests, but in 1989 a method was developed of measuring the degree of blurring by projecting images on a screen using a weak laser beam.

myrmecophyte plant that lives in association with a colony of ants and possesses specialized organs in which the ants live. For example, *Myrmecodia,* an epiphytic plant from Malaysia, develops root tubers containing a network of cavities inhabited by ants.

Several species of *Acacia* from tropical America have specialized hollow thorns for the same purpose. This is probably a mutualistic (mutually beneficial) relationship, with the ants helping to protect the plant from other insect pests and in return receiving shelter.

myrrh gum ◊resin produced by several small trees belonging to the bursera family, especially *C. myrrha,* found in Ethiopia and Arabia. In ancient times it was used for incense and perfume and in embalming dead bodies. (Genus *Commiphora,* family Burseraceae.)

myrtle any of a group of Old World evergreen shrubs belonging to the myrtle family. The commonly cultivated Mediterranean myrtle (*M. communis*) has oval opposite leaves and white flowers followed by purple berries, all of which are fragrant. (Genus *Myrtus,* family Myrtaceae.)

mystery reproductive syndrome *(MRS)* viral disease of pigs that causes sows to lose up to 10% of their litter. It was first seen in the USA in 1987 and in Europe in 1991. The symptoms are flu-like.

myxoedema thyroid-deficiency disease developing in adult life, most commonly in middle-aged women. The symptoms include loss of energy and appetite, weight gain, inability to keep warm, mental dullness, and dry, puffy skin. It is reversed by giving the thyroid hormone thyroxine. See also ◊hypothyroidism.

myxomatosis contagious, usually fatal, virus infection of rabbits which causes much suffering. It has been deliberately introduced in the UK and Australia since the 1950s to reduce the rabbit population.

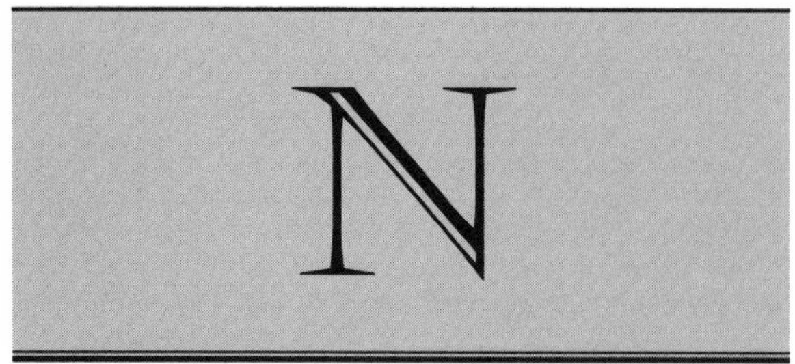

n in mathematics, variable used to denote an indefinite number.

nacre another name for ◊mother-of-pearl.

nadir the point on the celestial sphere vertically below the observer and hence diametrically opposite the **zenith**. The term is used metaphorically to mean the low point of a person's fortunes.

naevus mole, or patch of discoloration on the skin which has been present from birth. There are many different types of naevi, including those composed of a cluster of small blood vessels, such as the 'strawberry mark' (which usually disappears early in life), and the 'port-wine stain'.

A naevus of moderate size is harmless, and such marks can usually be disguised cosmetically unless they are extremely disfiguring, when they can sometimes be removed by cutting out, burning with an electric needle, freezing with carbon dioxide snow, or by argon laser treatment. In rare cases a mole may be a precursor of a malignant ◊melanoma. Any changes in a mole, such as enlargement, itching, soreness, or bleeding, should be reported to a doctor.

nagware in computing, another name for ◊guiltware.

nail in biology, a hard, flat, flexible outgrowth of the digits of primates (humans, monkeys, and apes). Nails are composed of ◊keratin.

name server (abbreviated from ***domain name server***) on the Internet, a type of ◊server which matches an Internet Protocol address to a ◊domain name and vice versa.

Humans remember names, but computers work with numbers. Domain name servers translate between the two, so that a human can type an email address such as **janedoe@anywhere.com** and the computer can route the message correctly.

NAND gate type of ◊logic gate.

nano- prefix used in ◊SI units of measurement, equivalent to a one-billionth part (10^{-9}). For example, a nanosecond is one-billionth of a second.

nanotechnology experimental technology using individual atoms or molecules as the components of minute machines, measured by the nanometre, or millionth of a millimetre. Nanotechnology research in the 1990s focused on testing molecular structures and refining ways to manipulate atoms using a scanning tunnelling microscope. The ultimate aim is to create very small computers and molecular machines which could perform vital engineering or medical tasks.

The ◊scanning electron microscope can be used to see and position single atoms and molecules, and to drill holes a nanometre (billionth of a metre) across in a variety of materials. The instrument can be used for ultrafine etching; the entire 28 volumes of the *Encyclopedia Britannica* could be engraved on the head of a pin. In the USA a complete electric motor has been built, which is less than 0.1 mm across with a top speed of 600,000 rpm. It is etched out of silicon, using the ordinary methods of chip manufacturers.

naphtha the mixtures of hydrocarbons obtained by destructive distillation of petroleum, coal tar, and shale oil. It is a raw material for the petrochemical and plastics industries. The term was originally applied to naturally occurring liquid hydrocarbons.

naphthalene $C_{10}H_8$ solid, white, shiny, aromatic hydrocarbon obtained from coal tar. The smell of moth-balls is due to their naphthalene content. It is used in making indigo and certain azo dyes, as a mild disinfectant, and as an insecticide.

Napier, John
(1550–1617)

8th Laird of Merchiston Scottish mathematician who invented logarithms in 1614 and 'Napier's bones', an early mechanical calculating device for multiplication and division.

It was Napier who first used and then popularized the decimal point to separate the whole number part from the fractional part of a number.

Mary Evans Picture Library

narcissism in psychology, an exaggeration of normal self-respect and self-involvement which may amount to mental disorder when it precludes relationships with other people.

narcissus any of a group of bulbous plants belonging to the amaryllis family. Species include the daffodil, jonquil, and narcissus. All have flowers with a cup or trumpet projecting from the centre. (Genus *Narcissus,* family Amaryllidaceae.)

narcotic pain-relieving and sleep-inducing drug. The term is usually applied to heroin, morphine, and other opium derivatives, but may also be used for other drugs which depress brain activity, including anaesthetic agents and ◊hypnotics.

narwhal toothed whale found only in the Arctic Ocean. It grows to 5 m/16 ft long, has a grey and black body, a small head, and short flippers. The male has a single spiral tusk growing straight out in front of its upper lip that can measure up to 2.7 m/9 ft long. (Species *Monodon monoceros,* family Monodontidae.)

NASA acronym for ***National Aeronautics and Space Administration***, US government agency for spaceflight and aeronautical research, founded in 1958 by the National Aeronautics and Space Act. Its headquarters are in Washington DC and its main installation is at the ◊Kennedy Space Center in Florida. NASA's early planetary and lunar programmes included Pioneer spacecraft from 1958, which gathered data for the later crewed missions, the most famous of which took the first people to the Moon in *Apollo 11* on 16–24 July 1969.

In the early 1990s, NASA moved towards lower-budget 'Discovery missions', which should not exceed a budget of $150 million (excluding launch costs), nor a development period of three years.

NASA HOME PAGE

http://www.nasa.gov/

Latest news from NASA, plus the most recent images from the Hubble Space Telescope, answers to questions about NASA resources and the space programme, and a gallery of video, audio clips, and still images.

nastic movement plant movement that is caused by an external stimulus, such as light or temperature, but is directionally independent of its source, unlike ◊tropisms. Nastic movements occur as a result of changes in water pressure within specialized cells or differing rates of growth in parts of the plant.

Examples include the opening and closing of crocus flowers following an increase or decrease in temperature (**thermonasty**), and the opening and closing of evening-primrose *Oenothera* flowers on exposure to dark and light (**photonasty**).

The leaf movements of the Venus flytrap *Dionaea muscipula* following a tactile stimulus, and the rapid collapse of the leaflets of the sensitive plant *Mimosa pudica* are examples of **haptonasty**. Sleep movements, where the leaves or flowers of some plants adopt a different position at night, are described as **nyctinasty**. Other movement types include **hydronasty**, in response to a change in the atmospheric humidity, and **chemonasty**, in response to a chemical stimulus.

nasturtium any of a group of plants that includes watercress (*N. officinale*), a perennial aquatic plant of Europe and Asia, grown as a salad crop. Belonging to a different family altogether, the South American trailing nasturtiums include the cultivated species *T. majus,* with orange, scarlet, or yellow flowers, and *T. minus,* which has smaller flowers. (Genus *Nasturtium,* family Cruciferae; South American genus *Tropaeolum,* family Tropaeolaceae.)

National Cash Register Company (NCR) US company founded in 1884 in Dayton, Ohio, by John H Patterson (1844–1922), originally as a business manufacturing 'thief-catchers' (devices to stop cashiers and sales clerks robbing tills). By 1910, largely due to Patterson's aggressive sales force, his factory was producing 90% of the USA's cash registers, and the company still retains its lead today.

National Computing Centre (NCC) UK centre set up in 1966 to offer advice and technical assistance to businesses on every aspect of information technology. The NCC is also the world's largest provider of escrow services for source code, a service necessary for businesses using custom-built software from a single supplier. It is based in Manchester.

National Education and Research Network in computing, communications backbone usually abbreviated to ◊NERN.

national grid the network of cables, carried overhead on pylons or buried under the ground, that connects consumers of electrical power to power stations, and interconnects the power stations. It ensures that power can be made available to all customers at any time, allowing demand to be shared by several power stations, and particular power stations to be shut down for maintenance work from time to time.

National Information Infrastructure (NII) in computing, US network, often referred to as the **information superhighway**, that embraces every component of the Internet – from the satellites that carry the data to the PCs and telephone links that Americans use to access the Net. The NII was a 1995 US government initiative, the implementation of which was left to the private sector. The project aims to give all Americans access to the country's information and computing resources.

National Institute of Standards and Technology (NIST) US body that plays an important role in setting computing and communications standards. NIST's Advanced Technology Program, which gives financial assistance to companies developing technologically advanced products during the research and development period, has played a considerable role in nurturing the US computer industry.

National Physical Laboratory (NPL) research establishment, set up in 1900 at Teddington, England, under the control of the Department of Industry; the chair of the visiting committee is the president of the Royal Society. In 1944 it began work on a project to construct a digital computer, called the ACE (Automatic Computing Engine), one of the first ever built. It was completed in 1950, embodying many of the ideas of British mathematician Alan ◊Turing. It was privatized in 1995.

National Rivers Authority (NRA) UK government agency launched in 1989. It had responsibility for managing water resources, investigating and regulating pollution, and taking over flood controls and land drainage from the former ten regional water authorities of England and Wales. In April 1996 the NRA was replaced by the Environment Agency, having begun to establish a reputation for being supportive to wildlife projects and tough on polluters.

Following a judicial review of the authority 1991 for allegedly failing to carry out its statutory duty to protect rivers and seas from pollution, river quality improved by 26% 1993–96.

native companion another name for the ◊brolga, so called because these birds are often seen in pairs.

native metal or *free metal* any of the metallic elements that occur in nature in the chemically uncombined or elemental form (in addition to any combined form). They include bismuth, cobalt, copper, gold, iridium, iron, lead, mercury, nickel, osmium, palladium, platinum, ruthenium, rhodium, tin, and silver. Some are commonly found in the free state, such as gold; others occur almost exclusively in the combined state, but under unusual conditions do occur as native metals, such as mercury. Examples of native nonmetals are carbon and sulphur.

Natural Environment Research Council (NERC) UK organization established by royal charter 1965 to undertake and support research in the earth sciences, to give advice both on exploiting natural resources and on protecting the environment, and to support education and training of scientists in these fields of study.

Research areas include geothermal energy, industrial pollution, waste disposal, satellite surveying, acid rain, biotechnology, atmospheric circulation, and climate. Research is carried out principally within the UK but also in Antarctica and in many developing countries. It comprises 13 research bodies.

natural frequency the frequency at which a mechanical system will vibrate freely. A pendulum, for example, always oscillates at the same frequency when set in motion. More complicated systems, such as bridges, also vibrate with a fixed natural frequency. If a varying force with a frequency equal to the natural frequency is applied to such an object the vibrations can become violent, a phenomenon known as ◊resonance.

natural gas mixture of flammable gases found in the Earth's crust (often in association with petroleum). It is one of the world's three main fossil fuels (with coal and oil). Natural gas is a mixture of ◊hydrocarbons, chiefly methane (80%), with ethane, butane, and propane. Natural gas is usually transported from its source by pipeline, although it may be liquefied for transport and storage and is, therefore, often used in remote areas where other fuels are scarce and expensive. Prior to transportation, butane and propane are removed and liquefied to form 'bottled gas'.

Natural History Museum British museum containing departments of zoology, entomology, geology, mineralogy, palaeontology, and botany. Based in London from 1856, the museum is housed in a building designed by Alfred Waterhouse and erected 1873–80 in South Kensington, London; it has no administrative connection with the British Museum. In 1985 the Natural History Museum was merged with the Geological Museum.

natural logarithm in mathematics, the ◊exponent of a number expressed to base e, where e represents the ◊irrational number 2.71828... .

Natural ◊logarithms are also called Napierian logarithms, after their inventor, the Scottish mathematician John Napier.

natural number one of the set of numbers used for counting. Natural numbers comprise all the positive integers, excluding zero.

natural radioactivity radioactivity generated by those radioactive elements that exist in the Earth's crust. All the elements from polonium (atomic number 84) to uranium (atomic number 92) are radioactive.

◊Radioisotopes of some lighter elements are also found in nature (for example potassium-40). See ◊background radiation.

natural selection the process whereby gene frequencies in a population change through certain individuals producing more descendants than others because they are better able to survive and reproduce in their environment.

The accumulated effect of natural selection is to produce ◊adaptations such as the insulating coat of a polar bear or the spadelike forelimbs of a mole. The process is slow, relying firstly on random variation in the genes of an organism being produced by ◊mutation and secondly on the genetic ◊recombination of sexual reproduction. It was recognized by Charles Darwin and English naturalist Alfred Russel Wallace as the main process driving ◊evolution.

nature the living world, including plants, animals, fungi, and all microorganisms, and naturally formed features of the landscape, such as mountains and rivers.

Whatever Nature has in store for mankind, unpleasant as it may be, man must accept, for ignorance is never better than knowledge.

Enrico Fermi Italian-born US physicist.
In Laura Fermi *Atoms in the Family* 1954

nature–nurture controversy or ***environment–heredity controversy*** long-standing dispute among philosophers and psychologists over the relative importance of environment, that is, upbringing, experience, and learning ('nurture'), and heredity, that is, genetic inheritance ('nature'), in determining the make-up of an organism, as related to human personality and intelligence.

One area of contention is the reason for differences between individuals; for example, in performing intelligence tests. The environmentalist position assumes that individuals do not differ significantly in their inherited mental abilities and that subsequent differences are due to learning, or to differences in early experiences. Opponents insist that certain differences in the capacities of individuals (and hence their behaviour) can be attributed to inherited differences in their genetic make-up.

nature reserve area set aside to protect a habitat and the wildlife that lives within it, with only restricted admission for the public. A nature reserve often provides a sanctuary for rare species. The world's largest is Etosha Reserve, Namibia; area 99,520 sq km/38,415 sq mi.

naturopathy in alternative medicine, facilitating of the natural self-healing processes of the body. Naturopaths are the general practitioners (GPs) of alternative medicine and often refer clients to other specialists, particularly in manipulative therapies, to complement their own work of seeking, through diet, the prescription of natural medicines and supplements, and lifestyle counselling, to restore or augment the vitality of the body and thereby its optimum health.

nautical mile unit of distance used in navigation, an internationally agreed-on standard (since 1959) equalling the average length of one minute of arc on a great circle of the Earth, or 1,852 m/6,076.12 ft. The term formerly applied to various units of distance used in navigation.

nautiloid fossil cephalopod mollusc with a straight or coiled chambered shell, and gently curved transverse septa. They range from Upper Cambrian to Recent periods. ◊Nautilus is the only living representative.
classification Nautiloids comprise the subclass Nautiloidea in class Cephalopoda, phylum Mollusca.

nautilus sea animal related to octopuses and squids, with many short, grasping tentacles surrounding a sharp beak, but different in that it has an outer shell. It is a ◊cephalopod, a type of ◊mollusc, and is found in the Indian and Pacific oceans. The well-known **pearly nautilus** (*N. pompilius*) has a chambered spiral shell about 20 cm/8 in in diameter. Its body occupies the outer chamber. (Genus *Nautilus*, class Cephalopoda.)

Paper nautilus is another name for the ◊argonaut, **a type of octopus**.

Nautilus the name of the world's first nuclear-powered submarine, launched by the USA in 1954; it sailed under the icecap to the North Pole.

navel or ***umbilicus*** small indentation in the centre of the abdomen of mammals, marking the site of attachment of the ◊umbilical cord, which connects the fetus to the ◊placenta.

navigate in computing, to find your way around hyperspace or a ◊hypertext document, especially when using a ◊browser.

BACTERIA

The freshwater bacterium *Aquaspirillium magnetotacticum* uses the Earth's magnetic field to navigate. The bacteria in the northern hemisphere travel north (downwards) if dislodged from the mud at the bottom of rivers and lakes; those in the southern hemisphere head south.

navigation the science and technology of finding the position, course, and distance travelled by a ship, plane, or other craft. Traditional methods include the magnetic ◊compass and ◊sextant. Today the gyrocompass is usually used, together with highly sophisticated electronic methods, employing beacons of radio signals, such as ◊Decca, Loran, and ◊Omega. Satellite navigation uses satellites that broadcast time and position signals.

The US ◊global positioning system (GPS) was introduced in 1992. When complete, it will feature 24 Navstar satellites that will enable users (including eventually motorists and walkers) to triangulate their position (from any three satellites) to within 15 m/50 ft.

In 1992, 85 nations agreed to take part in trials of a new navigation system which makes use of surplus military space technology left over from the Cold War. The new system, known as FANS or Future Navigation System, will make use of the 24 Russian Glonass satellites and the 24 US GPS satellites. Small computers will gradually be fitted to civil aircraft to process the signals from the satellite, allowing aircraft to navigate with pinpoint accuracy anywhere in the world. The signals from at least three satellites will guide the craft to within a few metres of accuracy. FANS will be used in conjunction with four Inmarsat satellites to provide worldwide communications between pilots and air-traffic controllers.

If sailing in unfamiliar waters, remember:

Brown brown, run aground White white, you might Green green, nice and clean Blue blue, run right through This allows you to estimate the depth of the water from shallowest to deepest, based on its colour

navigation, biological the ability of animals or insects to navigate. Although many animals navigate by following established routes or known landmarks, many animals can navigate without such aids; for example, birds can fly several thousand miles back to their nest site, over unknown terrain.

Such feats may be based on compass information derived from the position of the Sun, Moon, or stars, or on the characteristic patterns of Earth's magnetic field.

Biological navigation refers to the ability to navigate both in long-distance ◊migrations and over shorter distances when foraging (for example, the honey bee finding its way from the hive to a nectar site and back). Where reliant on known landmarks, birds may home on features that can be seen from very great distances (such as the cloud caps that often form above isolated mid-ocean islands). Even smells can act as a landmark. Aquatic species like salmon are believed to learn the characteristic taste of the river where they hatch and return to it, often many years later. Brain cells in some birds have been found to contain ◊magnetite and may therefore be sensitive to the Earth's magnetic field.

navigation map in computing, specialized tool to help users find their way around a Web site. Colourful graphics overlay a hidden grid, like that on a conventional map, containing ◊hypertext links. Users navigate by placing their cursor on an image and clicking the mouse, sending a 'map reference' back to the Web site which activates a link. Navigation maps give the designer more control over how the page will appear on the screen, and are more attractive than conventional links.

NBS abbreviation for ***National Bureau of Standards***, the US federal standards organization, on whose technical standards all US weights and measures are based.

NDA in computing, abbreviation for nondisclosure agreement.

near point the closest position to the eye to which an object may be brought and still be seen clearly. For a normal human eye the near point is about 25 cm; however, it gradually moves further away with age, particularly after the age of 40.

nebula cloud of gas and dust in space. Nebulae are the birthplaces of stars, but some nebulae are produced by gas thrown off from dying stars (see ◊planetary nebula; supernova). Nebulae are classified depending on whether they emit, reflect, or absorb light.

An **emission nebula**, such as the ◊Orion nebula, glows brightly because its gas is energized by stars that have formed within it. In a **reflection nebula**, starlight reflects off grains of dust in the nebula, such as surround the stars of the ◊Pleiades cluster. A **dark nebula** is a dense cloud, composed of molecular hydrogen, which partially or completely absorbs light behind it. Examples include the Coalsack nebula in ◊Crux and the Horsehead nebula in Orion.

WEB NEBULAE

http://www.vol.it/MIRROR/EN/ftp.seds.org/html/billa/twn/

Images of nebulae, plus a short account of the different types of nebulae, and a glossary of related terms.

neck structure between the head and the trunk in animals. In the back of the neck are the upper seven vertebrae of the spinal column, and there are many powerful muscles that support and move the head. In front, the neck region contains the ◊pharynx and ◊trachea, and behind these the oesophagus. The large arteries (carotid, temporal, maxillary) and veins (jugular) that supply the brain and head are also located in the neck. The ◊larynx (voice box) occupies a position where the trachea connects with the pharynx, and one of its cartilages produces the projection known as Adam's apple. The ◊thyroid gland lies just below the larynx and in front of the upper part of the trachea.

necrosis death or decay of tissue in a particular part of the body, usually due to bacterial poisoning or loss of local blood supply.

nectar sugary liquid secreted by some plants from a nectary, a specialized gland usually situated near the base of the flower. Nectar often accumulates in special pouches or spurs, not always in the same location as the nectary. Nectar attracts insects, birds, bats, and other animals to the flower for ◊pollination and is the raw material used by bees in the production of honey.

nectarine smooth, shiny-skinned variety of ◊peach, usually smaller than other peaches and with firmer flesh. It arose from a natural variation of the original form.

needlefish any of a group of bony marine fishes with an elongated body and long jaws lined with many sharp teeth. They live in warm, tropical seas. (Family Belonidae.)

Néel temperature the temperature at which the ◊susceptibility of an antiferromagnetic material has a maximum value; see also ◊magnetism.

negative/positive in photography, a reverse image, which when printed is again reversed, restoring the original scene. It was invented by Fox Talbot about 1834.

TO REMEMBER THE RELATIONSHIPS BETWEEN POSITIVE AND NEGATIVE:

'MINUS TIMES MINUS IS PLUS, THE REASON FOR THIS WE NEED NOT DISCUSS' W H AUDEN, A CERTAIN WORLD

OR

IMAGINE YOU'RE IN A TOWN IN THE WILD WEST. YOU'VE GOT GOOD GUYS (+) AND BAD GUYS (–), AND THEY CAN EITHER COME TO TOWN (+) OR LEAVE TOWN (–) IF THE GOOD GUYS (+) COME TO TOWN (+), THAT'S GOOD (+) IF THE BAD GUYS (–) COME TO TOWN (+), THAT'S BAD –) IF THE GOOD GUYS (+) LEAVE TOWN (–), THAT'S BAD (–) BUT IF THE BAD GUYS (–) LEAVE TOWN (–), THAT'S GOOD (+)

OR

POSITIVE TIMES NEGATIVE IS NEGATIVE: THE FRIENDS OF OUR ENEMIES ARE OUR ENEMIES NEGATIVE TIMES POSITIVE IS NEGATIVE: THE ENEMIES OF OUR FRIENDS ARE OUR ENEMIES NEGATIVE TIMES NEGATIVE IS POSITIVE: THE ENEMIES OF OUR ENEMIES ARE OUR FRIENDS POSITIVE TIMES POSITIVE IS POSITIVE: THE FRIENDS OF OUR FRIENDS ARE OUR FRIENDS

nematode any of a group of unsegmented ◊worms that are pointed at both ends, with a tough, smooth outer skin. They include many free-living species found in soil and water, including the sea, but a large number are parasites, such as the roundworms and pinworms that live in humans, or the eelworms that attack plant roots. They differ from ◊flatworms in that they have two openings to the gut (a mouth and an anus). (Phylum Nematoda.)

Most nematode species are found in deep-sea sediment. Around 13,000 species are known, but a 1995 study by the Natural History Museum, London, based on the analysis of sediment from 17 seabed sites worldwide, estimated that nematodes may make up as much as 75% of all species, with there being an estimated 100 million species. Some are anhydrobiotic, which means they can survive becoming dehydrated, entering a state of suspended animation until they are rehydrated.

nemesis theory theory of animal extinction, suggesting that a sister star to the Sun caused the extinction of the dinosaurs and other groups of animals.

The theory holds that the movement of this as yet undiscovered star disrupts the ◊Oort cloud of comets every 26 million years, resulting in the Earth suffering an increased bombardment from comets at these times. The theory was proposed in 1984 to explain the newly discovered layer of iridium – an element found in comets and meteorites – in rocks dating from the end of dinosaur times. However, many palaeontologists deny any evidence for a 26-million-year cycle of extinctions.

neo-Darwinism the modern theory of ◊evolution, built up since the 1930s by integrating the 19th-century English scientist Charles ◊Darwin's theory of evolution through natural selection with the theory of genetic inheritance founded on the work of the Austrian biologist Gregor ◊Mendel.

Neo-Darwinism asserts that evolution takes place because the environment is slowly changing, exerting a selection pressure on the individuals within a population. Those with characteristics that happen to adapt to the new environment are more likely to survive and have offspring and hence pass on these favourable characteristics. Over time the genetic make-up of the population changes and ultimately a new species is formed.

neodymium yellowish metallic element of the ◊lanthanide series, symbol Nd, atomic number 60, relative atomic mass 144.24. Its rose-coloured salts are used in colouring glass, and neodymium is used in lasers.

It was named in 1885 by Austrian chemist Carl von Welsbach (1858–1929), who fractionated it away from didymium (originally thought to be an element but actually a mixture of rare-earth metals consisting largely of neodymium, praesodymium, and cerium).

neon Greek *neos 'new'* colourless, odourless, nonmetallic, gaseous element, symbol Ne, atomic number 10, relative atomic mass 20.183. It is grouped with the ◊inert gases, is nonreactive, and forms no compounds. It occurs in small quantities in the Earth's atmosphere.

Tubes containing neon are used in electric advertising signs, giving off a fiery red glow; it is also used in lasers. Neon was discovered by Scottish chemist William Ramsay and the Englishman Morris Travers.

Neopilina deep-sea 'living fossil' occurring at great depths and feeding exclusively on radiolarians (marine protozoans).
classification *Neopilina* is in class Monoplacophora, phylum Mollusca.

neoplasm Greek *'new growth'* any lump or tumour, which may be benign or malignant (cancerous).

neoprene synthetic rubber, developed in the USA in 1931 from the polymerization of chloroprene. It is much more resistant to heat, light, oxidation, and petroleum than is ordinary rubber.

neoteny in biology, the retention of some juvenile characteristics in an animal that seems otherwise mature. An example is provided by the axolotl, a salamander that can reproduce sexually although still in its larval form.

neper unit used in telecommunications to express a ratio of powers and currents. It gives the attenuation of amplitudes as the natural logarithm of the ratio.

nephritis or ***Bright's disease*** general term used to describe inflammation of the kidney. The degree of illness varies, and it may be acute (often following a recent streptococcal infection), or chronic, requiring a range of treatments from antibiotics to ◊dialysis or transplant.

nephron microscopic unit in vertebrate kidneys that forms **urine**. A human kidney is composed of over a million nephrons. Each nephron consists of a knot of blood capillaries called a glomerulus, contained in the ◊Bowman's capsule, and a long narrow tubule enmeshed with yet more capillaries. Waste materials and water pass from the bloodstream into the tubule, and essential minerals and some water are reabsorbed from the tubule back into the bloodstream. The remaining filtrate (urine) is passed out from the body.

Neptune in astronomy, the eighth planet in average distance from the Sun. It is a giant gas (hydrogen, helium, methane) planet, with a mass 17.2 times that of Earth. It has the highest winds in the Solar System.
mean distance from the Sun 4.4 billion km/2.794 billion mi
equatorial diameter 48,600 km/30,200 mi
rotation period 16 hr 7 min
year 164.8 Earth years
atmosphere methane in its atmosphere absorbs red light and gives the planet a blue colouring. Consists primarily of hydrogen (85% with helium (13%) and methane (1–2%).
surface hydrogen, helium and methane. Its interior is believed to have a central rocky core covered by a layer of ice.
satellites of Neptune's eight moons, two (◊Triton and Nereid) are visible from Earth. Six were discovered by the *Voyager 2* probe in

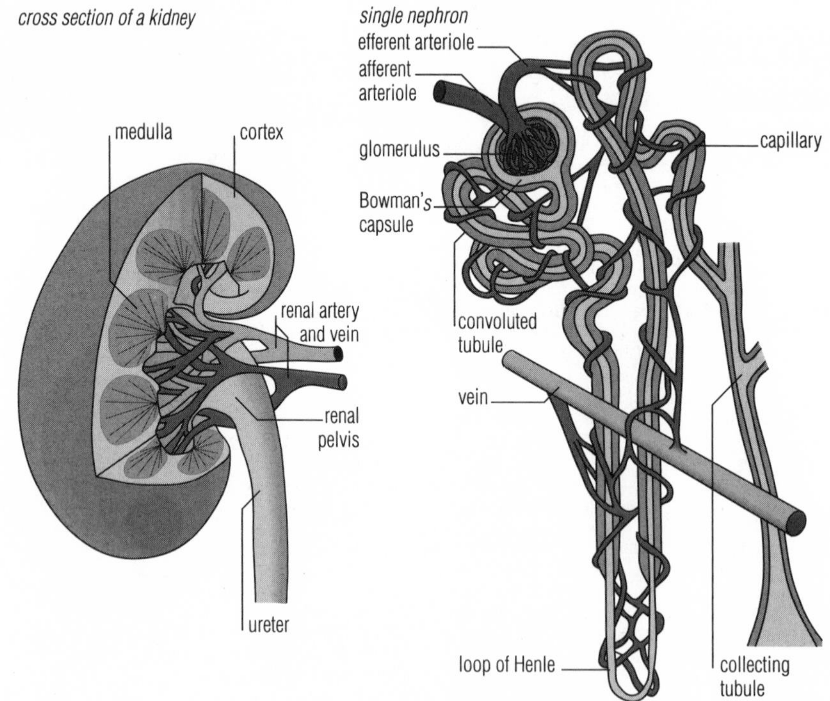

nephron *The kidney (left) contains more than a million filtering units, or nephrons (right), consisting of the glomerulus, Bowman's capsule, and the loop of Henle. Blood flows through the glomerulus – a tight knot of fine blood vessels from which water and metabolic wastes filter into the tubule. This filtrate flows through the convoluted tubule and loop of Henle where most of the water and useful molecules are reabsorbed into the blood capillaries. The waste materials are passed to the collecting tubule as urine.*

NEPTUNE

http://www.hawastsoc.org/solar/eng/neptune.htm

Detailed description of the planet Neptune. It includes a chronology of the exploration of the planet, along with statistics and information on its rings, moons, and satellites. Supported by a good selection of images.

1989, of which Proteus (diameter 415 km/260 mi) is larger than Nereid (300 km/200 mi).

rings there are four faint rings: Galle, Le Verrier, Arago, and Adams (in order from Neptune). Galle is the widest at 1,700 km/1,060 mi. Leverrier and Arago are divided by a wide diffuse particle band called the plateau.

Neptune was located 1846 by German astronomers Johan Galle and Heinrich d'Arrest (1822–1875) after calculations by English astronomer John Couch Adams and French mathematician Urbain Leverrier had predicted its existence from disturbances in the movement of Uranus. *Voyager 2,* which passed Neptune in Aug 1989, revealed various cloud features, notably an Earth-sized oval storm cloud, the Great Dark Spot, similar to the Great Red Spot on Jupiter, but images taken by the Hubble Space Telescope in 1994 show that the Great Dark Spot has disappeared. A smaller dark spot DS2 has also gone.

neptunium silvery, radioactive metallic element of the ◊actinide series, symbol Np, atomic number 93, relative atomic mass 237.048. It occurs in nature in minute amounts in ◊pitchblende and other uranium ores, where it is produced from the decay of neutron-bombarded uranium in these ores. The longest-lived isotope, Np-237, has a half-life of 2.2 million years. The element can be produced by bombardment of U-238 with neutrons and is chemically highly reactive.

It was first synthesized in 1940 by US physicists E McMillan (1907–) and P Abelson (1913–), who named it after the planet Neptune (since it comes after uranium as the planet Neptune comes after Uranus).

Neptunium was the first ◊transuranic element to be synthesized.

NERC abbreviation for ◊Natural Environment Research Council.

nerd in computing, slang term for someone who seems to spend more time interacting with computers than with human beings. The term was originally an abusive one, applied to weedy, diffident but studious US high school students by their more sporty and outgoing colleagues.

NERN (abbreviation for ***National Education and Research Network***) in computing, communications backbone capable of transferring data at the rate of one gigabit per second. It was designed for computer research, and is not accessible to the public.

Nernst, (Walther) Hermann (1864–1941)

German physical chemist who won a Nobel prize in1920 for work on heat changes in chemical reactions. He proposed in 1906 the principle known as the Nernst heat theorem or the third law of thermodynamics: chemical changes at the temperature of absolute zero involve no change of entropy (disorder).

Mary Evans Picture Library

nerve bundle of nerve cells enclosed in a sheath of connective tissue and transmitting nerve impulses to and from the brain and spinal cord. A single nerve may contain both motor and sensory nerve cells, but they function independently.

nerve cell or ***neuron*** elongated cell, the basic functional unit of the ◊nervous system that transmits information rapidly between different parts of the body. Each nerve cell has a cell body, containing the nucleus, from which trail processes called dendrites, responsible for receiving incoming signals. The unit of information is the **nerve impulse**, a travelling wave of chemical and electrical changes involving the membrane of the nerve cell. The cell's longest process, the ◊axon, carries impulses away from the cell body.

The impulse involves the passage of sodium and potassium ions across the nerve-cell membrane. Sequential changes in the permeability of the membrane to positive sodium (Na^+) ions and potassium (K^+) ions produce electrical signals called action potentials. Impulses are received by the cell body and passed, as a pulse of electric charge, along the axon. The axon terminates at the synapse, a specialized area closely linked to the next cell (which may be another nerve cell or a specialized effector cell such as a muscle). On reaching the ◊synapse, the impulse releases a chemical ◊neurotransmitter, which diffuses across to the neighbouring cell and there stimulates another impulse or the action of the effector cell.

Nerve impulses travel quickly – in humans, they may reach speeds of 160 m/525 ft per second.

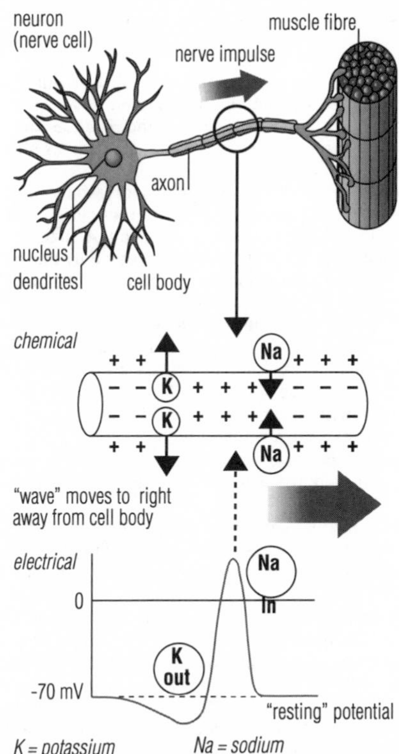

nerve cell *The anatomy and action of a nerve cell. The nerve cell or neuron consists of a cell body with the nucleus and projections called dendrites which pick up messages. An extension of the cell, the axon, connects one cell to the dendrites of the next. When a nerve cell is stimulated, waves of sodium (Na^+) and potassium (K^+) ions carry an electrical impulse down the axon.*

nervous breakdown popular term for a reaction to overwhelming psychological stress. There is no equivalent medical term. People said to be suffering from a nervous breakdown may be suffering from a neurotic illness, such as depression or anxiety, or a psychotic illness, such as schizophrenia.

nervous system the system of interconnected ◊nerve cells of most invertebrates and all vertebrates. It is composed of the ◊central and ◊autonomic nervous systems. It may be as simple as the nerve net of coelenterates (for example, jellyfishes) or as complex as the mammalian nervous system, with a central nervous system comprising ◊brain and ◊spinal cord and a peripheral nervous system connecting up with sensory organs, muscles, and glands.
human nervous system The human nervous system represents the product of millions of years of evolution, particularly in the degree of **encephalization** or brain complexity. It can be divided into central and peripheral parts for descriptive purposes, although there is both anatomical and functional continuity between the two parts. The central nervous system consists of the brain and the spinal cord. The peripheral nervous system is not so clearly subdivided, but its anatomical parts are: (1) the spinal nerves; (2) the cranial nerves; and (3) the autonomic nervous system.

NEUROSCIENCE FOR KIDS

http://weber.u.washington.edu/~chudler/neurok.html

Explore the nervous system – your brain, spinal cord, nerve cells, and senses – by means of this impressive site, designed for primary and secondary school students and teachers.

nest place chosen or constructed by a bird or other animal for incubation of eggs, hibernation, and shelter. Nests vary enormously, from saucerlike hollows in the ground, such as the scrapes of hares, to large and elaborate structures, such as the 4-m/13-ft diameter mounds of the ◊megapode birds.
birds' nests Birds that nest in slight depressions in the ground, such as terns and plovers, lay eggs that so closely resemble the ground that they generally escape detection. A slightly more elaborate nest is the burrow, such as that occupied by the sand-martin, kingfisher, or puffin. In many cases these underground nests are made in burrows left by rabbits or voles.

Many birds and some animals make their nests in the hollows of trees; the female of the Bornean rhinoceros hornbill is sealed up by the male for many weeks, until her chicks are almost ready to leave the nest. The mud nests of the ◊swallow family and other birds are built mainly with mud; some of these weigh over 2 kg/4.5 lb. Among the crudest nests that are made with collected material, such as sticks, leaves, blades of grass or hair, are those of the wood-pigeon, which are so loosely put together that the eggs are visible through them.

Swallows, martins, sparrows, and flycatchers prefer houses as nesting sites; the thrushes, finches, and linnets use evergreen bushes and hedges. Most species construct nests that are highly distinctive.
other nest-builders Amongst the fish, good examples of nest-builders are the three-spined stickleback *Gasterosteus aculeatus* and the Siamese fighting fish *Betta splendens*. The stickleback's nest is anchored to the river bed and constructed of algae and other aquatic plants stuck together by a secretion from the fish's kidneys. The nest of fighting fish is a floating bubble nest anchored to a piece of plant material into which the eggs are placed by the male after courtship.

Amongst the insects, nest-builders include the social insects, the ants, bees, and wasps, and their nests or hives, and the huge termite nests, up to 3 m/10 ft tall, found in the tropics.

Of the mammals, good examples are those of the harvest mouse (*Micromys minutus*) and the red squirrel (*Sciurus vulgaris*). The harvest mouse nest is a kind of ball made of interlaced leaves of grass that generally belong to the same plants that support it above the ground. The red squirrel's nest is composed of a layer of twigs with a layer of moss or bark fragments. The whole thing is usually placed at the base of a large branch.

Net abuse in computing, action that upsets participants in ◊USENET. Common forms include ◊spamming (advertising), cross-posting (sending the same message to several groups), scams (financial frauds), and attempts to rig or prevent discussions. In theory, ◊Internet Service Providers (ISPs) can punish Net abuse by blocking access to the Net, but in practice this sanction is very rarely invoked as the offender merely finds a new ISP.

Netcom in computing, major US-based Internet Service Provider (ISP), founded in 1988 to provide college students with off-campus access to university computer facilities. In 1996 the company claimed to be the world's largest ISP, with some 500,000 subscribers.

Netfind in computing, ◊search engine designed to locate personal ◊e-mail addresses. Users supply an individual's name and a possible domain name, and Netfind searches a database of ◊domain names, offering users a series of choices to help narrow down the range of options.

netiquette (derived from ***Internet etiquette***) behaviour guidelines evolved by users of the ◊Internet. The rules of netiquette include: no messages typed in upper case (considered to be the equivalent of shouting); new users, or new members of a ◊newsgroup, should read the frequently asked questions (FAQ) file before asking a question; no advertising via ◊USENET newsgroups.

Users who contravene netiquette can expect to receive ◊electronic mail flames (angry messages) pointing out the error of their ways. The Internet community is fiercely protective of netiquette.

net police (or ***net cops***) in computing, USENET readers who monitor and 'punish' postings which they find offensive or believe to be in breach of netiquette. Many unmoderated (see moderator) newsgroups are policed by these self-appointed guardians, whose attempts to enforce their vision of the group sometimes make them a target for 'punishment' themselves.

Netscape in computing, US software company that supplies Navigator, a World Wide Web browser, which is usually referred to as Netscape. (Netscape Communications was founded in 1994 as Mosaic Communications, and called its ◊browser Netscape. The names were changed in deference to the University of Illinois, where the Mosaic browser was written.)

Netscape gained widespread popularity by giving its browser away free for non-commercial use. Most of the company's revenues now come from sales of Netscape Communicator – a suite of software that includes a copy of Navigator – Web servers and intranet software with powerful groupware features. In 1996, it unveiled Netscape ONE (Open Network Environment), designed to help developers to create new online applications.

Net, the abbreviation for the ◊Internet. The term is often used to denote the entire community of people with with computer access to the Internet.

nettle any of a group of weedy plants with stinging hairs on oval, tooth-edged leaves; the hairs contain nerve poisons that penetrate the skin and cause a rash. The flowers are small and greenish, carried on spikes emerging at the same point where the leaves join the stem. The common nettle (*U. dioica*) grows on waste ground in Europe and North America, where it was introduced. (Genus *Urtica*, family Urticaceae.)

NETTLE

The hairs on stinging nettle leaves operate like mini hypodermic syringes. When the leaf is touched, the pressure in the hair falls as the fragile tip is broken away and a dose of nerve toxin is released.

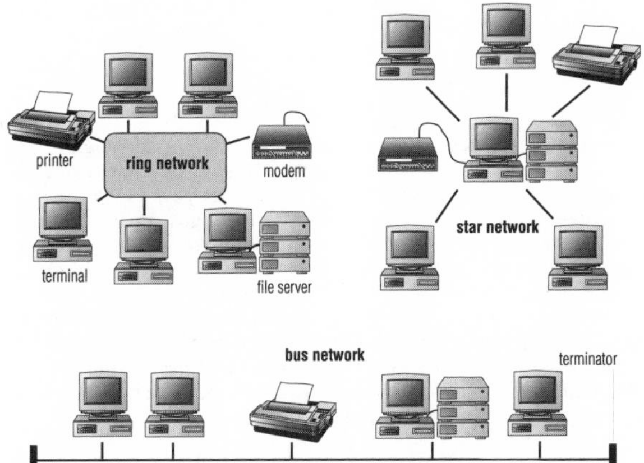

network *Local area networks can be connected together in a ring circuit or in a star arrangement. In the ring arrangement, signals from a terminal or peripheral circulate around the ring to reach the terminal or peripheral addressed. In the star arrangement, signals travel via a central controller. In a bus nework all elements are connected off a single cable that is terminated at each end.*

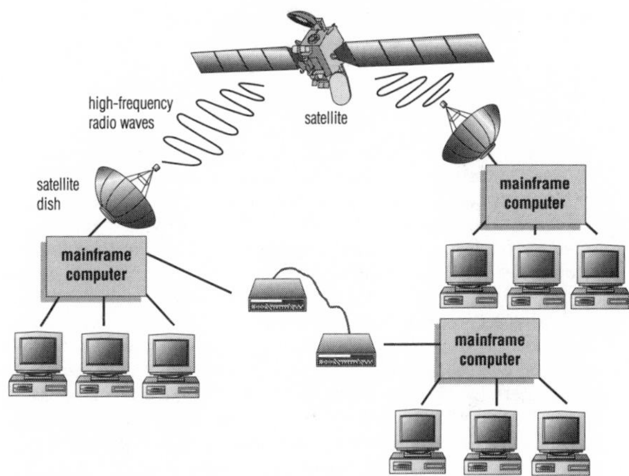

network *A wide area network is used to connect remote computers via telephone lines or satellite links. The ISDN (Integrated Services Digital Network) telecommunications network allows high-speed transfer of digital data.*

nettle rash popular name for the skin disorder ◊urticaria.

Netware leading ◊local area network operating system, supplied by Novell.

network in computing, a method of connecting computers so that they can share data and peripheral devices, such as printers. The main types are classified by the pattern of the connections – star or ring network, for example – or by the degree of geographical spread allowed; for example, **local area networks** (LANs) for communication within a room or building, and **wide area networks** (WANs) for more remote systems. Internet is the computer network that connects major English-speaking institutions throughout the world, with around 12 million users. Janet (joint academic network), a variant of Internet, is used in Britain. SuperJanet, launched in 1992, is an extension of this that can carry 1,000 million bits of information per second.

There is only one good, namely knowledge, and only one evil, namely ignorance.

PLATO Greek philosopher.
Dialogues

network computer (NC) simple computer consisting essentially of a microprocessor, a ◊RAM chip and a monitor. NCs are designed to function as part of a network, connected to a central ◊server via the Internet or an ◊intranet, downloading software (especially ◊object oriented programs) as required.

The absence of internal storage makes them much cheaper to buy and maintain than PCs, and they are easier to manage and upgrade, as all the software is stored in one place. Some commentators believe that the NC will eventually replace the networked PC as the standard computer setup for business, especially for tasks previously performed using dumb terminals.

network interface card (NIC) in computing, item of computer hardware that allows computers to be connected to a computer network.

network operating system (NOS) in computing, software designed to enable a LAN or other network to operate. The main task of every NOS is to tell both the central file server and the workstations connected to it how to communicate with each other. Network operating systems may also include security and backup features, remote access facilities, and a centralized database.

neuralgia sharp or burning pain originating in a nerve and spreading over its area of distribution. Trigeminal neuralgia, a common form, is a severe pain on one side of the face.

neural network artificial network of processors that attempts to mimic the structure of nerve cells (neurons) in the human brain. Neural networks may be electronic, optical, or simulated by computer software.

A basic network has three layers of processors: an input layer, an output layer, and a 'hidden' layer in between. Each processor is connected to every other in the network by a system of 'synapses'; every processor in the top layer connects to every one in the hidden layer, and each of these connects to every processor in the output layer. This means that each nerve cell in the middle and bottom layers receives input from several different sources; only when the amount of input exceeds a critical level does the cell fire an output signal.

The chief characteristic of neural networks is their ability to sum up large amounts of imprecise data and decide whether they match a pattern or not. Networks of this type may be used in developing robot vision, matching fingerprints, and analysing fluctuations in stock-market prices. However, it is thought unlikely by scientists that such networks will ever be able accurately to imitate the human brain, which is very much more complicated; it contains around 10 billion nerve cells, whereas current artificial networks contain only a few hundred processors.

neurohormone chemical secreted by nerve cells and carried by the blood to target cells. The function of the neurohormone is to act as a messenger; for example, the neurohormone ADH (antidiuretic hormone) is secreted in the pituitary gland and carried to the kidney, where it promotes water reabsorption in the kidney tubules.

neurology medical speciality concerned with the study and treatment of disorders of the brain, spinal cord, and peripheral nerves.

neuron another name for a ◊nerve cell.

neurosis in psychology, a general term referring to emotional disorders, such as anxiety, depression, and phobias. The main disturbance tends to be one of mood; contact with reality is relatively unaffected, in contrast to ◊psychosis.

neurotransmitter chemical that diffuses across a ◊synapse, and thus transmits impulses between ◊nerve cells, or between nerve

Neural Networks

by Peter Lafferty

Neural networks – strictly artificial neural networks – represent a radically different approach to computing. They are called neural networks because they are loosely modelled on the networks of neurons – nerve cells – that make up brains. Neural networks are characterized by their ability to learn, and can be described as trainable pattern recognizers. The study and use of neural networks is sometimes called neurocomputing.

Brains perform remarkable computational feats: recognizing music from just a few seconds of a recording, or faces seen only once before – accomplishments that defeat even the most modern computers. Yet brains stumble with arithmetic and make errors with simple logic. The reason for these anomalies might be found in the differences between brain and computer architecture – their internal structure and operating mechanisms.

Conventional computers possess distinct processing and memory units, controlled by programs, but animal nervous systems and neural networks are instead made up of highly interconnected webs of simple processing units. They have no specific memory locations, information instead being stored as patterns of interconnections between the processing units. Neural networks are not programmed, but are trained by example. They can, therefore, learn things that cannot easily be stated in programs, making them invaluable in a wide range of applications.

Although neurocomputing might seem a recent development, research started at around the same time as the early work on computers. In the 1940s scientists devised simple electrical networks, crudely modelled neural circuits, which could perform simple logical computations.

More sophisticated networks, called perceptrons, followed in the 1950s – the ancestors of modern neural networks. Perceptrons were just simple networks of amplifiers, but they could learn to recognize patterns. This generated tremendous excitement; however, significant limits to their abilities were soon discovered. Marvin Minsky and Seymour Papert of the Massachusetts Institute of Technology, USA, proved that certain problems could never be solved by perceptrons. When they published their results, research into neural networks effectively ceased for over a decade. At the end of the mid 1970s, however, theoretical breakthroughs made it possible for more complex neural networks to be developed, and by the mid 1980s they had become sufficiently sophisticated for general applications.

Neural networks are of interest to computer technologists because they have the potential to offer solutions to a range of problems that have proved difficult to solve using conventional computing approaches. These problems include pattern recognition, machine learning, time-series forecasting, machine vision and robot control. Underpinning all this is their ability to learn.

In a famous example, a neural network was trained to recognize speech – with eerily realistic results. The network, called NET-talk, was developed by T J Sejnowski and C R Rosenberg at Johns Hopkins University in the USA. It was linked to a computer that could produce synthetic speech, so its progress could be heard. After producing formless noise for a few hours, it started babbling like a baby. Overnight training improved its performance so that it could read text with a 95% accuracy. No conventionally programmed computer could do this.

cells and effector organs (for example, muscles). Common neurotransmitters are noradrenaline (which also acts as a hormone) and acetylcholine, the latter being most frequent at junctions between nerve and muscle. Nearly 50 different neurotransmitters have been identified.

neutral equilibrium the state of equilibrium possessed by a body that will stay at rest if moved into a new position; it will neither move back to its original position nor move on any further. A sphere placed on a horizontal surface is an example. See ◊stability.

neutralization in chemistry, a process occurring when the excess acid (or excess base) in a substance is reacted with added base (or added acid) so that the resulting substance is neither acidic nor basic.

In theory neutralization involves adding acid or base as required to achieve ◊pH 7. When the colour of an ◊indicator is used to test for neutralization, the final pH may differ from pH7 depending upon the indicator used. It will also differ from 7 in reactions between strong acids and weak bases and weak acids and strong bases, as the salt formed will have acid or basic properties respectively.

neutral oxide oxide that has neither acidic nor basic properties (see oxide). Neutral oxides are only formed by nonmetals. Examples are carbon monoxide, water, and nitrogen(I) oxide.

neutral solution solution of pH7, in which the concentrations of $H^+_{(aq)}$ and $OH^-_{(aq)}$ ions are equal.

neutrino in physics, any of three uncharged ◊elementary particles (and their antiparticles) of the ◊lepton class, having a mass too close to zero to be measured. The most familiar type, the antiparticle of the electron neutrino, is emitted in the beta decay of a nucleus. The other two are the muon and tau neutrinos.

neutron one of the three main subatomic particles, the others being the proton and the electron. The neutron is a composite particle, being made up of three ◊quarks, and therefore belongs to the ◊baryon group of the ◊hadrons. Neutrons have about the same mass as protons but no electric charge, and occur in the nuclei of all atoms except hydrogen. They contribute to the mass of atoms but do not affect their chemistry.

For instance, the ◊isotopes of a single element differ only in the number of neutrons in their nuclei but have identical chemical properties. Outside a nucleus, a free neutron is unstable, decaying with a half-life of 11.6 minutes into a proton, an electron, and an antineutrino. The neutron was discovered by the British chemist James Chadwick in 1932.

neutron beam machine nuclear reactor or accelerator producing a stream of neutrons, which can 'see' through metals. It is used in industry to check molecular changes in metal under stress.

neutron bomb or ***enhanced radiation weapon*** small hydrogen bomb for battlefield use that kills by radiation, with minimal damage to buildings and other structures.

neutron number (symbol N) the number of neutrons possessed by an atomic nucleus. ◊Isotopes are atoms of the same element possessing different neutron numbers.

neutron star very small, 'superdense' star composed mostly of ◊neutrons. They are thought to form when massive stars explode as ◊supernovae, during which the protons and electrons of the star's atoms merge, owing to intense gravitational collapse, to make neutrons. A neutron star may have the mass of up to three Suns, compressed into a globe only 20 km/12 mi in diameter.

NEUTRON STAR

Neutron stars are so condensed that a fragment the size of a sugar cube would weigh as much as all the people on Earth put together.

Neutrino: Discovery

by Peter Lafferty

Discovering the neutrino

Most fundamental particles are discovered experimentally. Some are predicted by theory, but are often not taken seriously until detected. The neutrino is an exception. Postulated in 1930, its existence was taken as an act of faith for 25 years.

There were good reasons for predicting the neutrino's existence. Unexplained energy losses in certain radioactive decays (called beta decay) suggested the laws of conservation of energy and angular momentum were invalid at subatomic level. The great Danish theoretical physicist Niels Bohr maintained these laws held only on average, not for each individual process. Austrian physicist Wolfgang Pauli explained it more simply: in beta decay, there was a previously undiscovered neutral particle carrying away the missing energy and momentum. He called it a 'neutron'. Italian physicist Enrico Fermi introduced the alternative term 'neutrino': Italian for 'little neutral one'. He constructed a successful theory of beta decay based on the neutrino's existence.

Reines and Cowan's explosive suggestion

Experimental observation of neutrinos proved difficult. They pass easily through solid material, penetrating lead 965 million million km/600 million million mi thick without being absorbed. This makes them extremely hard to detect. In the 1950s, US physicists Frederick Reines and Clyde Cowan put forward a far-fetched scheme using a nuclear weapon as neutrino source. Cowan described the proposed scheme several years later:

'We would dig a shaft near the centre of the explosion about 10 ft in diameter and about 150 ft deep. We would put a tank, 10 ft in diameter and 75 ft long on end at the bottom of the shaft. We would then suspend a detector from the top of the tank, along with its recording apparatus, and back-fill the shaft about the tank.'

'As the time for the explosion approached, we would start vacuum pumps and evacuate the tank as highly as possible. Then, when the countdown reached zero, we would break the suspension with a small explosive, allowing the detector to fall freely in the vacuum. For about two seconds, the falling detector would be seeing neutrinos and recording the pulses from them while the earth shock from the blast passed harmlessly by, rattling the tank mightily but not disturbing our falling detector. When all was relatively quiet, the detector would reach the bottom of the tank, landing on a thick pile of foam rubber and feathers.'

'We would return to the site of the shaft in a few days (when surface radioactivity had died away sufficiently), dig down to the tank, recover the detector and discover the truth about neutrinos.'

The crucial experiment

Before the spectacular experiment could be set up, Reines and Cowan realized that, with suitable modifications, they could utilize the much smaller neutrino flux from a nuclear reactor. They set up their experiment next to the Savannah River nuclear plant's reactor. The detector comprised a tank containing cadmium chloride dissolved in water. A neutrino passing through the tank reacts with protons in the water, producing a positron and a neutron. The positron combines with electrons, producing gamma rays. The neutron also produces gamma rays by reacting with the cadmium. When a gamma ray falls on a scintillation detector it produces a flash of light, detected using a photomultiplier and showing that a neutrino has passed through the tank.

At first, there were about 1.63 'events' (or signals) per hour with the reactor operating and 0.4 with it shut down. Subsequent experiments with various adjustments raised the rate to nearly three events per hour. The next task was to confirm that these signals were produced by neutrinos. This involved eliminating all other possible sources: principally neutrons, gamma rays, electrons, and protons from the reactor.

The water was in two plastic tanks, holding 200 l/40 gal, between large scintillation counters, and surrounded by 110 photomultipliers, with lead walls and floor 10 cm/4 in thick, and roof and doors 20 cm/8 in thick to eliminate radiation from the reactor. To prove the lead's effectiveness, tests were done with additional shields. One experiment involved packing wet sawdust in bags round the detectors to reduce spurious neutron flow. There was no appreciable change in signal, and so it was concluded that it was not due to radiation produced outside the detectors. The neutrino had indeed been detected.

Modern neutrino detection

Nowadays, neutrinos from space are routinely detected by underground 'telescopes' similar to the Reines and Cowan set-up. Some modern neutrino telescopes comprise large tanks of ultrapure water, weighing up to 3000 tonnes. The tank, in a mine, has walls lined with photoelectric detectors. An alternative type of telescope uses dry-cleaning fluid (carbon tetrachloride); when it captures a neutrino, it produces radioactive argon whose presence may be detected by analysis of the liquid. There are large-scale neutrino detectors in Japan, Russia, Italy, and the USA. In Feb 1987, when a supernova exploded in the Large Magellanic Cloud, these instruments detected neutrinos from the explosion 170,000 light-years away.

If its mass is any greater, its gravity will be so strong that it will shrink even further to become a ◊black hole. Being so small, neutron stars can spin very quickly. The rapidly flashing radio stars called ◊pulsars are believed to be neutron stars. The flashing is caused by a rotating beam of radio energy similar in behaviour to a lighthouse beam of light.

newbie in computing, insulting term for a new user of a ◊USENET newsgroup, whose naive or off-topic comments irritate established members of the group. A classic newbie *faux pas* is to post a question that is answered in the group's ◊FAQ (file of frequently asked questions).

Newcomen, Thomas
(1663–1729)

English inventor of an early steam engine. His 'fire engine' of 1712 was used for pumping water from mines until James Watt invented one with a separate condenser.

Newfoundland breed of large, gentle dog said to have originated in Newfoundland, Canada. Males can grow to 70 cm/27.5 in tall, and weigh 65 kg/145 lb; the females are slightly smaller. They have a dense, flat coat, usually dull black, and an oily, water-repellent undercoat, and they are excellent swimmers.

Newfoundlands that are black and white or brown and white are called **Landseers**.

New General Catalogue catalogue of star clusters and nebulae compiled by the Danish astronomer John Louis Emil Dreyer (1852–1926) and published in 1888. Its main aim was to revise, correct, and expand upon the *General Catalogue* compiled by English astronomer John Herschel, which appeared in 1864.

new media in computing, general term for ◊CD-ROM, the ◊World Wide Web, and other electronic media, including ◊multimedia.

Most publishing companies now have a 'new media' division which manages a Web site and studies how best to compete and exploit the company's assets in the electronic future.

newsgroup discussion group on the ◊Internet 's USENET. Newsgroups are organized in seven broad categories: **comp.** – computers and programming; **news.** – newsgroups themselves; **rec.** – sports and hobbies; **sci.** – scientific research and ideas; **talk.** – discussion groups; and **misc.** – everything else. In addition, there are alternative hierarchies such as the wide-ranging and anarchic **alt.** (alternative). Within these categories there is a hierarchy of subdivisions.

newsreader in computing, program that gives access to ◊USENET newsgroups, interpreting the standard commands understood by ◊news servers in a simple, user-friendly interface. Popular newsreaders include rn for ◊UNIX, Turnpike and Agent for PCs and NewsReader for Macintosh. It is also possible to access USENET with a ◊browser such as ◊Netscape Navigator.

news server computer that stores ◊USENET messages for access by users. Most ◊Internet Service Providers (ISPs) offer a news server as part of the service.

newt small ◊salamander found in Europe, Asia, NW Africa, and North America. (Family Salamandridae, order Urodela.)

NEWT

If a young newt loses one of its limbs it can grow another. Unfortunately, the ability to do this declines with age.

new technology collective term applied to technological advances made in such areas as ◊telecommunications, nuclear energy, space ◊satellites, and ◊computers.

New Technology Telescope optical telescope that forms part of the ◊European Southern Observatory, La Silla, Chile; it came into operationin 1991. It has a thin, lightweight mirror, 3.38 m/11.75 ft across, which is kept in shape by computer-adjustable supports to produce a sharper image than is possible with conventional mirrors. Such a system is termed **active optics**.

newton SI unit (symbol N) of ◊force. One newton is the force needed to accelerate an object with mass of one kilogram by one metre per second per second. The weight of a medium size (100 g/3 oz) apple is one newton.

Newton, Isaac
(1642–1727)

English physicist and mathematician who laid the foundations of physics as a modern discipline. During 1665–66, he discovered the binomial theorem, differential and integral calculus, and that white light is composed of many colours. He developed the three standard laws of motion and the universal law of gravitation, set out in *Philosophiae naturalis principia mathematica* 1687 (usually referred to as the *Principia*). Knighted 1705.

Newton's greatest achievement was to demonstrate that scientific principles are of universal application. He clearly defined the nature of mass, weight, force, inertia, and acceleration.

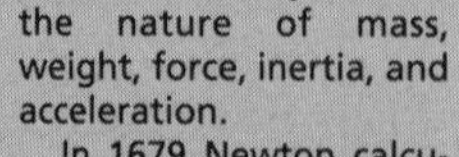

In 1679 Newton calculated the Moon's motion on the basis of his theory of gravity and also found that his theory explained the laws of planetary motion that had been derived by German astronomer Johannes Kepler on the basis of observations of the planets.

Mary Evans Picture Library

NEWTON, ISAAC

Among the lesser achievements of Isaac Newton were his career as a member of Parliament for Cambridge University – in which capacity his only recorded words were a request for a window to be opened – and his invention of the cat-flap (for a pet cat he kept at Woolsthorpe House).

Newton small portable computer, also called a ◊personal digital assistant (PDA), produced by Apple. The Newton combines many functions, including address book, diary, word processor, fax terminal, and e-mailing and Internet browsing facilities, in a pocket-sized unit. Its keyboardless interface and handwriting recognition software allow users to enter data using a stylus and a touch screen.

> *If I have seen farther it is by standing on the shoulders of giants.*
>
> Isaac Newton English physicist and mathematician. Letter to Robert Hooke, Feb 1675

Newtonian physics physics based on the concepts of the English scientist Isaac ◊Newton, before the formulation of quantum theory or relativity theory.

Newtonian telescope in astronomy, a simple reflecting ◊telescope in which light collected by a parabolic primary mirror is directed to a focus at the side of the tube by a flat secondary mirror placed at 45 degrees to the optical axis. It is named after ◊Isaac Newton, who constructed such a telescope in 1668.

Newton's laws of motion in physics, three laws that form the basis of Newtonian mechanics. (1) Unless acted upon by an unbalanced force, a body at rest stays at rest, and a moving body continues moving at the same speed in the same straight line. (2) An unbalanced force applied to a body gives it an acceleration proportional to the force (and in the direction of the force) and inversely proportional to the mass of the body. (3) When a body A exerts a force on a body B, B exerts an equal and opposite force on A; that is, to every action there is an equal and opposite reaction.

Newton's rings in optics, an ◊interference phenomenon seen (using white light) as concentric rings of spectral colours where light passes through a thin film of transparent medium, such as the wedge of air between a large-radius convex lens and a flat glass plate. With monochromatic light (light of a single wavelength), the rings take the form of alternate light and dark bands. They are caused by interference (interaction) between light rays reflected from the plate and those reflected from the curved surface of the lens.

NeXTStep ◊operating system and development environment, originally created for the ◊NeXT workstation, but later made available for other computers, including the IBM PC. NeXTStep is based on UNIX but contains a high level of ◊object orientation. Apple is using NeXTStep (more accurately, OpenStep) as the basis for its next-generation Macintosh operating system, codenamed Rhapsody 1997.

NeXT Technology Inc US computer manufacturer founded by Steve Jobs in 1985. NeXT's first product was an advanced workstation, the NeXT Cube, aimed at the higher education market. It sold poorly and NeXT abandoned hardware manufacturing to become a software company, Next Software Inc. This was taken over by Apple Computer for $400 million at the end of 1996.

NHS abbreviation for National Health Service, the UK state-financed health service.

niacin one of the 'B group' vitamins; see ◊nicotinic acid.

niche in ecology, the 'place' occupied by a species in its habitat, including all chemical, physical, and biological components, such as what it eats, the time of day at which the species feeds, temperature, moisture, the parts of the habitat that it uses (for example, trees or open grassland), the way it reproduces, and how it behaves.

It is believed that no two species can occupy exactly the same niche, because they would be in direct competition for the same resources at every stage of their life cycle.

Nichrome trade name for a series of alloys containing mainly nickel and chromium, with small amounts of other substances such as iron, magnesium, silicon, and carbon. Nichrome has a high melting point and is resistant to corrosion. It is therefore used in electrical heating elements and as a substitute for platinum in the ◊flame test.

nickel hard, malleable and ductile, silver-white metallic element, symbol Ni, atomic number 28, relative atomic mass 58.71. It occurs in igneous rocks and as a free metal (◊native metal), occasionally occurring in fragments of iron-nickel meteorites. It is a component of the Earth's core, which is held to consist principally of iron with some nickel. It has a high melting point, low electrical and thermal conductivity, and can be magnetized. It does not tarnish and therefore is much used for alloys, electroplating, and for coinage.

It was discovered in 1751 by Swedish mineralogist Axel Cronstedt (1722–1765) and the name given as an abbreviated form of *kopparnickel*, Swedish 'false copper', since the ore in which it is found resembles copper but yields none.

nickname in computing, an alternative ◊user-id, as used by participants in ◊MUDs, Internet Relay Chat and other interactive setups.

nicotine $C_{10}H_{14}N_2$ ◊alkaloid (nitrogenous compound) obtained from the dried leaves of the tobacco plant *Nicotiana tabacum* and used as an insecticide. A colourless oil, soluble in water, it turns brown on exposure to the air.

Nicotine in its pure form is one of the most powerful poisons known. It is the component of cigarette smoke that causes physical addiction. It is named after a 16th-century French diplomat, Jacques Nicot, who introduced tobacco to France.

Science is public, not private, knowledge.

ROBERT KING MERTON US sociologist.
Science, Technology and Society in Seventeenth-Century England 1938

---

nicotinic acid or ***niacin*** water-soluble ◊vitamin ($C_5H_5N.COOH$) of the B complex, found in meat, fish, and cereals; it can also be formed in small amounts in the body from the essential ◊amino acid tryptophan. Absence of nicotinic acid from the diet leads to the disease ◊pellagra.

nightingale songbird belonging to the thrush family; it sings with remarkable beauty by night as well as during the day. About 16.5 cm/6.5 in long, it is dull brown with a reddish-brown rounded tail; the breast is dull greyish-white, tinting to brown. It migrates in summer to Europe and winters in Africa. It feeds on insects, small animals, and occasionally fruit. It has a huge musical repertoire, built from about 900 melodic elements. (Species *Luscinia megarhyncos*, family Muscicapidae.)

The female is slightly smaller than the male, but the plumage is very similar. The nest is often built on the ground, made of dry grass and leaves, and four to six olive-green eggs are laid in it. The male's song continues until the young are hatched.

The **thrush nightingale** (*L. luscinia*) of eastern Europe, is a louder but less sweet songster. Both species also sing in their winter ranges in Africa.

nightjar any of about 65 species of night-hunting birds. They have wide, bristly mouths for catching flying insects. Their distinctive calls have earned them such names as 'whippoorwill' and 'church-will's-widow'. Some US species are called nighthawks. (Family Caprimulgidae, order Caprimulgiformes.)

The name 'nighthawk' most commonly refers to the Chordeiles species of North America, including *Chordeiles minor* which breeds widely as far north as southern Alaska, and migrates south to Argentina.

nightshade any of several plants in the nightshade family. They include the annual herbaceous black nightshade (*S. nigrum*), with white flowers similar to those of the potato plant and black berries; the perennial shrubby bittersweet or woody nightshade (*S. dulcamara*), with purple, potatolike flowers and scarlet berries; and, belonging to a different genus, deadly nightshade or ◊belladonna (*A. belladonna*). (Genera *Solanum* and *Atropa*, family Solanaceae.)

NII in computing, abbreviation for ◊National Information Infrastructure.

nilgai large antelope native to India. The bull has short conical horns and is bluish-grey. The female is brown. (Species *Boselaphus tragocamelus*.)

Nintendo Japanese ◊games console and software manufacturer. In 1996, the company introduced the N64 – the first 64-bit games console – using technology from workstation manufacturer Silicon Graphics Inc. Nintendo's most successful game is *Super Mario Brothers*.

niobium soft, grey-white, somewhat ductile and malleable, metallic element, symbol Nb, atomic number 41, relative atomic mass 92.906. It occurs in nature with tantalum, which it resembles in chemical properties. It is used in making stainless steel and other alloys for jet engines and rockets and for making superconductor magnets.

Niobium was discovered in 1801 by English chemist Charles Hatchett (1765–1847), who named it columbium (symbol Cb), a name that is still used in metallurgy. In 1844 it was renamed after Niobe by German chemist Heinrich Rose (1795–1864) because of its similarity to tantalum (Niobe is the daughter of Tantalus in Greek mythology).

NIST in computing, abbreviation for ◊National Institute of Standards and Technology.

nit egg case of the ◊louse, which is glued to the base of the host's hair.

nitrate salt or ester of nitric acid, containing the NO_3^- ion. Nitrates are used in explosives, in the chemical and pharmaceutical industries, in curing meat (see ◊nitre), and as fertilizers. They are the most water-soluble salts known and play a major part in the nitrogen cycle. Nitrates in the soil, whether naturally occurring or from inorganic or organic fertilizers, can be used by plants to make proteins and nucleic acids. However, runoff from fields can result in ◊nitrate pollution.

nitrate pollution the contamination of water by nitrates. Increased use of artificial fertilizers and land cultivation means that higher levels of nitrates are being washed from the soil into rivers, lakes, and aquifers. There they cause an excessive enrichment of the water (◊eutrophication), leading to a rapid growth of algae, which in turn darkens the water and reduces its oxygen content. The water is expensive to purify and many plants and animals die. High levels are now found in drinking water in arable areas. These may be harmful to newborn babies, and it is possible that they contribute to stomach cancer, although the evidence for this is unproven.

nitre or ***saltpetre*** potassium nitrate, KNO_3, a mineral found on and just under the ground in desert regions; used in explosives. Nitre occurs in Bihar, India, Iran, and Cape Province, South Africa. The salt was formerly used for the manufacture of gunpowder, but the supply of nitre for explosives is today largely met by making the salt from nitratine (also called Chile saltpetre, $NaNO_3$). Saltpetre is a ◊preservative and is widely used for curing meats.

nitric acid or ***aqua fortis*** HNO_3 fuming acid obtained by the oxidation of ammonia or the action of sulphuric acid on potassium nitrate. It is a highly corrosive acid, dissolving most metals, and a strong oxidizing agent. It is used in the nitration and esterification of organic substances, and in the making of sulphuric acid, nitrates, explosives, plastics, and dyes.

nitric oxide *or* **nitrogen monoxide** *(NO)* colourless gas released when metallic copper reacts with nitric acid and when nitrogen and oxygen combine at high temperatures. It is oxidized to nitrogen dioxide on contact with air. Nitric oxide has a wide range of functions in the body. It is involved in the transmission of nerve impulses and the protection of nerve cells against stress. It is released by macrophages in the immune system in response to viral and bacterial infection or to the proliferation of cancer cells. It is also important in the control of blood pressure.

nitrification process that takes place in soil when bacteria oxidize ammonia, turning it into nitrates. Nitrates can be absorbed by the roots of plants, so this is a vital stage in the ◊nitrogen cycle.

nitrite salt or ester of nitrous acid, containing the nitrite ion (NO_2^-). Nitrites are used as preservatives (for example, to prevent the growth of botulism spores) and as colouring agents in cured meats such as bacon and sausages.

nitrocellulose alternative name for ◊cellulose nitrate.

nitrogen ***Greek nitron 'native soda', sodium or potassium nitrate*** colourless, odourless, tasteless, gaseous, nonmetallic element, symbol N, atomic number 7, relative atomic mass 14.0067. It forms almost 80% of the Earth's atmosphere by volume and is a constituent of all plant and animal tissues (in proteins and nucleic acids). Nitrogen is obtained for industrial use by the liquefaction and fractional distillation of air. Its compounds are used in the manufacture of foods, drugs, fertilizers, dyes, and explosives.

Nitrogen has been recognized as a plant nutrient, found in manures and other organic matter, from early times, long before the complex cycle of ◊nitrogen fixation was understood. It was isolated in 1772 by English chemist Daniel Rutherford (1749–1819) and named in 1790 by French chemist Jean Chaptal (1756–1832).

nitrogen cycle the process of nitrogen passing through the ecosystem. Nitrogen, in the form of inorganic compounds (such as nitrates) in the soil, is absorbed by plants and turned into organic compounds (such as proteins) in plant tissue. A proportion of this nitrogen is eaten by ◊herbivores, with some of this in turn being passed on to the carnivores, which feed on the herbivores. The nitrogen is ultimately returned to the soil as excrement and when organisms die and are converted back to inorganic form by ◊decomposers.

Although about 78% of the atmosphere is nitrogen, this cannot be used directly by most organisms. However, certain bacteria and cyanobacteria (see ◊blue-green algae) are capable of nitrogen fixation. Some nitrogen-fixing bacteria live mutually with ◊leguminous plants (peas and beans) or other plants (for example, alder), where they form characteristic nodules on the roots. The presence of such plants increases the nitrate content, and hence the fertility, of the soil.

> *... the aim of science is not things themselves, as the dogmatists in their simplicity imagine, but the relations between things; outside those relations there is no reality knowable.*
>
> JULES HENRI POINCARÉ French mathematician. *Science and Hypothesis* 1905

nitrogen fixation the process by which nitrogen in the atmosphere is converted into nitrogenous compounds by the action of microorganisms, such as cyanobacteria (see ◊blue-green algae) and bacteria, in conjunction with certain ◊legumes. Several chemical processes duplicate nitrogen fixation to produce fertilizers; see ◊nitrogen cycle.

nitrogen oxide any chemical compound that contains only nitrogen and oxygen. All nitrogen oxides are gases. Nitrogen monoxide and nitrogen dioxide contribute to air pollution. See also ◊nitrous oxide.

Nitrogen oxide was discovered during the 1980s to act as a chemical messenger in small quantities within the human body, despite being toxic at higher concentrations, and its rapid reaction with oxygen. The medical condition of septic shock is linked to overproduction by the body of nitrogen oxide. Nitrogen oxide has an unpaired electron, which can be removed to produce the nitrosyl ion, NO^+·***nitrogen monoxide*** NO, or nitric oxide, is a colourless gas released when metallic copper reacts with concentrated ◊nitric acid. It is also produced when nitrogen and oxygen combine at high temperature. On contact with air it is oxidized to nitrogen dioxide. ***Nitrogen dioxide*** nitrogen(IV) oxide, NO_2, is a brown, acidic, pungent gas that is harmful if inhaled and contributes to the formation

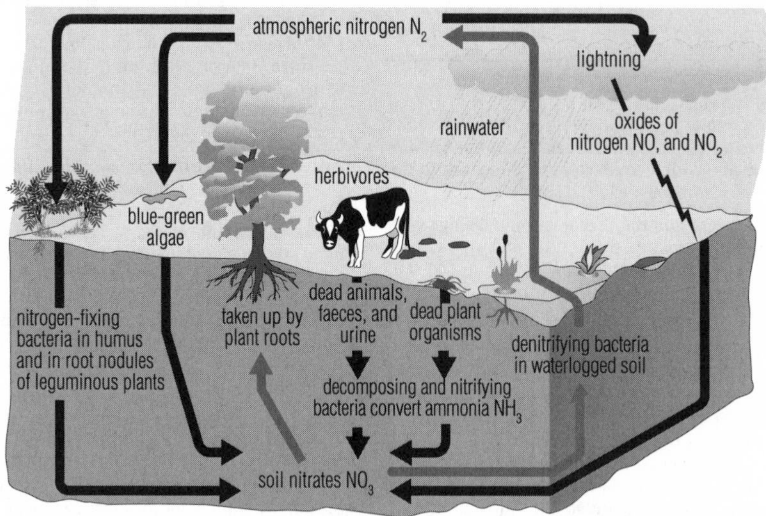

nitrogen cycle *The nitrogen cycle is one of a number of cycles during which the chemicals necessary for life are recycled. The carbon, sulphur, and phosphorus cycles are others. Since there is only a limited amount of these chemicals in the Earth and its atmosphere, the chemicals must be continuously recycled if life is to go on.*

of ◊acid rain, as it dissolves in water to form nitric acid. It is the most common of the nitrogen oxides and is obtained by heating most nitrate salts (for example ◊lead(II) nitrate, $Pb(NO_3)_2$). If liquefied, it gives a colourless solution (N_2O_4). It has been used in rocket fuels.

nitroglycerine $C_3H_5(ONO_2)_3$ flammable, explosive oil produced by the action of nitric and sulphuric acids on glycerol. Although poisonous, it is used in cardiac medicine. It explodes with great violence if heated in a confined space and is used in the preparation of dynamite, cordite, and other high explosives.

It was invented by the Italian Ascanio Soberro in 1846, and is unusual among explosives in that it is a liquid. Nitroglycerine is an effective explosive because it has low ◊activation energy, and produces little smoke when burned. However, it was initially so reactive it was virtually unusable. Alfred ◊Nobel's innovation was to purify nitroglycerine (using water, with which it is immiscible, to dissolve the impurities), and thereby make it more stable.

nitrous acid HNO_2 weak acid that, in solution with water, decomposes quickly to form nitric acid and nitrogen dioxide.

nitrous oxide or ***dinitrogen oxide*** N_2O colourless, nonflammable gas that, used in conjunction with oxygen, reduces sensitivity to pain. In higher doses it is an anaesthetic. Well tolerated, it is often combined with other anaesthetic gases to enable them to be used in lower doses. It may be self-administered; for example, in childbirth. It is a greenhouse gas; about 10% of nitrous oxide released into the atmosphere comes from the manufacture of nylon. It used to be known as 'laughing gas'.

NNTP (abbreviation for ***Network News Transfer Protocol***) in computing, set of standard procedures by which ◊USENET news is distributed across the Internet. NNTP governs both the way e-mailed messages travel between news servers and the way ◊newsreaders retrieve news from servers.

nobelium synthesized, radioactive, metallic element of the ◊actinide series, symbol No, atomic number 102, relative atomic mass 259. It is synthesized by bombarding curium with carbon nuclei.

It was named in 1957 after the Nobel Institute in Stockholm, Sweden, where it was claimed to have been first synthesized. Later evaluations determined that this was in fact not so, as the successful 1958 synthesis at the University of California at Berkeley produced a different set of data. The name was not, however, challenged. In 1992 the International Unions for Pure and Applied Chemistry and Physics (IUPAC and IUPAP) gave credit to Russian scientists in Dubna for the discovery of nobelium.

Nobel, Alfred Bernhard (1833–1896)

Swedish chemist and engineer. He invented dynamite in 1867, gelignite in 1875, and ballistite, a smokeless gunpowder, in 1887. Having amassed a large fortune from the manufacture of explosives and the exploitation of the Baku oilfields in Azerbaijan, near the Caspian Sea, he left this in trust for the endowment of five Nobel prizes.

Mary Evans Picture Library

Nobel prize annual international prize, first awarded in 1901 under the will of Alfred Nobel, Swedish chemist, who invented dynamite. The interest on the Nobel endowment fund is divided annually among the persons who have made the greatest contributions in the fields of physics, chemistry, medicine, literature, and world peace. The first four are awarded by academic committees based in Sweden, while the peace prize is awarded by a committee of the Norwegian parliament. A sixth prize, for economics, financed by the Swedish National Bank, was first awarded in 1969. The prizes have a large cash award and are given to organizations – such as the United Nations peacekeeping forces, which received the Nobel Peace Prize in 1988 – as well as individuals.

noble gas alternative name for ◊inert gas.

noble gas structure the configuration of electrons in noble or ◊inert gases (helium, neon, argon, krypton, xenon, and radon).

This is characterized by full electron shells around the nucleus of an atom, which render the element stable. Any ion, produced by the gain or loss of electrons, that achieves an electronic configuration similar to one of the inert gases is said to have a noble gas structure.

TO REMEMBER THE NOBLE GASES:

HE NEATLY **A**RRANGES **K**REMLIN **X**ECUTIVE **R**ANKS

HELIUM / NEON / ARGON / KRYPTON / XENON / RADON

NO CARRIER in computing, error message returned by a modem when the telephone line drops unexpectedly because of line noise or other interruptions.

node in computing, any device connected to a network, such as a ◊router, a ◊bridge, a ◊hub, and a ◊server. See also ◊host.

node in physics, a position in a ◊standing wave pattern at which there is no vibration. Points at which there is maximum vibration are called **antinodes**. Stretched strings, for example, can show nodes when they vibrate. Guitarists can produce special effects (harmonics) by touching a sounding string lightly to produce a node.

nodule in geology, a lump of mineral or other matter found within rocks or formed on the seabed surface; ◊mining technology is being developed to exploit them.

noise unwanted sound. Permanent, incurable loss of hearing can be caused by prolonged exposure to high noise levels (above 85 decibels). Over 55 decibels on a daily outdoor basis is regarded as an unacceptable level.

In scientific and engineering terms, a noise is any random, unpredictable signal.

noise pollution Noise is a recognized form of pollution, but is difficult to measure because the annoyance or discomfort caused varies between individuals. If the noise is in a narrow frequency band, temporary hearing loss can occur even though the level is below 85 decibels or exposure is only for short periods. Lower levels of noise are an irritant, but seem not to increase fatigue or affect efficiency to any great extent. Loss of hearing is a common complaint of people working on factory production lines or in the construction and road industry. Minor psychiatric disease, stress-related ailments including high blood pressure, and disturbed sleep patterns are regularly linked to noise, although the causal links are in most cases hard to establish. Loud noise is a major pollutant in towns and cities.

electronic noise Electronic noise takes the form of unwanted signals generated in electronic circuits and in recording processes by stray electrical or magnetic fields, or by temperature variations. In electronic recording and communication systems, **white noise** frequently appears in the form of high frequencies, or hiss. The main advantages of digital systems are their relative freedom from such noise and their ability to recover and improve noise-affected signals.

nomadic pastoralism farming system where animals (cattle, goats, camels) are taken to different locations in order to find fresh pastures. It is practised in the developing world; out of an estimated 30–40 million (1990) nomadic pastoralists worldwide, most are in central Asia and the Sahel region of W Africa. Increasing numbers of cattle may lead to overgrazing of the area and ◊desertification.

The increasing enclosure of land has reduced the area available for nomadic pastoralism and, as a result, this system of farming is under threat. The movement of farmers in this way contrasts with sedentary agriculture.

nondisclosure agreement (NDA) in computing, agreement signed with suppliers by manufacturers, programmers, journalists, and others, in exchange for detailed information or copies of new products in advance of their public launch. For example, a manufacturer might sign an NDA to get a copy of a new operating system in order to have compatible hardware ready for the program's launch. NDAs are often required in order to participate in beta (pre-launch) tests of important pieces of software.

nonlethal weapons weapons designed not to kill. See ◊weapons, nonlethal.

nonlinear video editing in computing, video editing method that processes compressed video data stored on a hard disc. This makes it much easier for editors to find their way around the material, and enables them to commence editing at any point in the tape – hence the name.

Editors use a computer to rearrange the material and produce an Edit Decision List (EDL) bearing all information on cuts, fades, and other effects. The EDL can then be used to create an automated final edit using the original tapes. The main video editing programs are Avid VideoShop for the Apple Macintosh and Tektronix Lightworks for PCs.

nonmetal one of a set of elements (around 20 in total) with certain physical and chemical properties opposite to those of metals. Nonmetals accept electrons (see ◊electronegativity) and are sometimes called electronegative elements.

nonrenewable resource natural resource, such as coal or oil, that takes thousands or millions of years to form naturally and can therefore not be replaced once it is consumed. The main energy sources used by humans are nonrenewable; ◊renewable resources, such as solar, tidal, and geothermal power, have so far been less exploited.

Nonrenewable resources have a high carbon content because their origin lies in the photosynthetic activity of plants millions of years ago. The fuels release this carbon back into the atmosphere as carbon dioxide. The rate at which such fuels are being burnt is thus resulting in a rise in the concentration of carbon dioxide in the atmosphere.

nonvolatile memory in computing, ◊memory that does not lose its contents when the power supply to the computer is disconnected.

noradrenaline in the body, a ◊catecholamine that acts directly on specific receptors to stimulate the sympathetic nervous system. Released by nerve stimulation or by drugs, it slows the heart rate mainly by constricting arterioles (small arteries) and so raising blood pressure. It is used therapeutically to treat ◊shock.

Norfolk terrier breed of dog identical to the ◊Norwich terrier except that the ears drop forward rather than being pricked.

NOR gate in electronics, a type of ◊logic gate.

normal distribution in statistics, a distribution widely used to model variation in a set of data which is symmetrical about its mean value. It can be expressed in the form:

$$f(x) = 1/\sigma\sqrt{2\pi}\,\exp\{-1/2(x-\mu/\sigma 1/2\}$$

where $f(x)$ is the relative frequency of data value x, σ is the ◊standard deviation, μ is the mean, exp is the exponential function, and π is a mathematical constant. The curve resulting when $f(x)$ is plotted against x is called the **normal distribution curve**.

An example of normal distribution can be found in the intelligence quotients (IQ) found in human populations, distributed around a mean value of 100. The distribution is also known as the Gaussian distribution after German mathematician Karl Gauss.

normal distribution curve the bell-shaped curve that results when a ◊normal distribution is represented graphically by plotting the distribution $f(x)$ against x. The curve is symmetrical about the mean value.

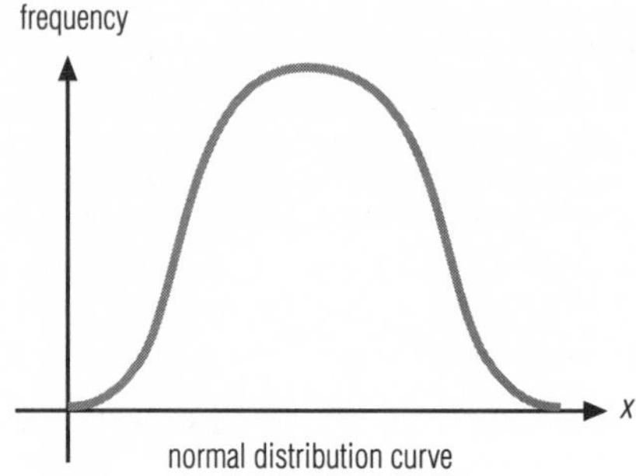

normal distribution

North Atlantic Drift warm ◊ocean current in the N Atlantic Ocean; an extension of the ◊Gulf Stream. It flows east across the Atlantic and has a mellowing effect on the climate of NW Europe, particularly the British Isles and Scandinavia.

northern lights common name for the ◊aurora borealis.

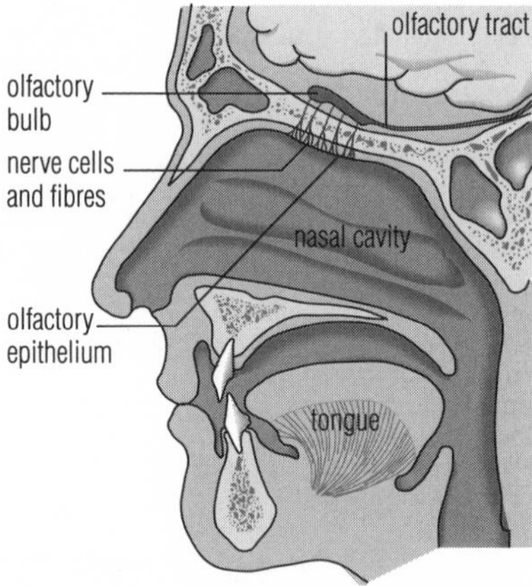

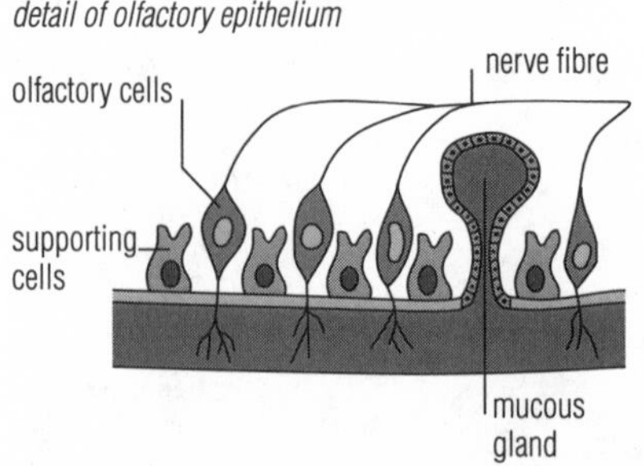

nose The structure of the nose. The organs of smell are confined to a small area in the roof of the nasal cavity. The olfactory cells are stimulated when certain molecules reach them. Smell is one of our most subtle senses: tens of thousands of smells can be distinguished. By comparison, taste, although closely related to smell, is a crude sensation. All the subtleties of taste depend upon smell.

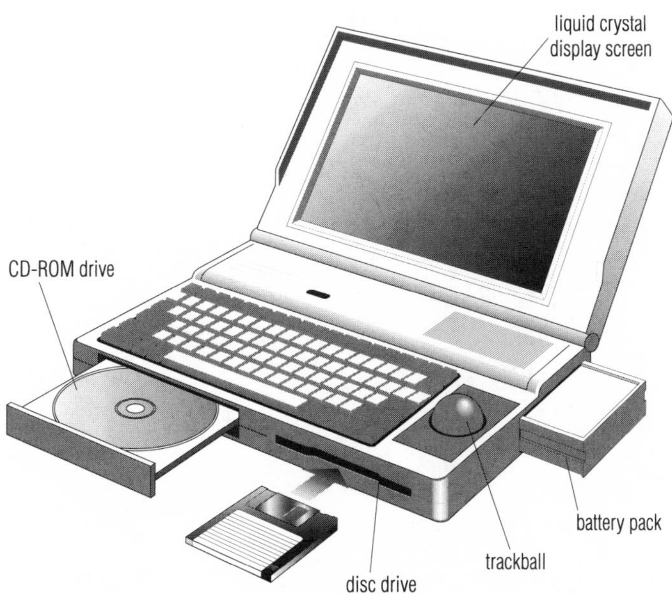

notebook computer *The component parts of a notebook computer. Although as powerful as a microcomputer, the battery pack enables the notebook to be used while travelling.*

Northrop US aircraft and military manufacturing company founded in 1939 by John K Northrop (1895–1981), an aircraft designer who had been a cofounder of Lockheed. Northrop makes uncrewed target aircraft and aircraft parts for other companies, and built the Black Widow night fighter used in World War II.

Norwich terrier small compact breed of terrier. It has a hard and wiry coat, that is close-lying and straight, and is coloured red, black, and tan; red grizzle; or grizzle and tan. Its head is rather foxlike, the muzzle being rather short and the skull wide between the erect ears. The legs are short, straight, and strong; the tail is traditionally docked. The height is usually 25 cm/10 in and the weight 5–6 kg/11–13 lb.

nose in humans, the upper entrance of the respiratory tract; the organ of the sense of smell. The external part is divided down the middle by a septum of ◊cartilage. The nostrils contain plates of cartilage that can be moved by muscles and have a growth of stiff hairs at the margin to prevent foreign objects from entering. The whole nasal cavity is lined with a ◊mucous membrane that warms and moistens the air as it enters and ejects dirt. In the upper parts of the cavity the membrane contains 50 million olfactory receptor cells (cells sensitive to smell).

nostril in vertebrates, the opening of the nasal cavity, in which cells sensitive to smell are located. (In fish, these cells detect water-borne chemicals, so they are effectively organs of taste.) In vertebrates with lungs, the nostrils also take in air. In humans, and most other mammals, the nostrils are located on the ◊nose.

notebook computer in computing, a small battery-powered portable about A4 in size and the thickness of a book. The first notebook computers, such as the Epson HX-20 and Tandy 100, became available in the early 1980s, with the first PC-compatible notebook, the Toshiba T1100, following in 1985. In the 1990s, the notebook format became the standard for portable PCs and Apple PowerBooks. Some manufacturers also offer smaller portable PCs called subnotebooks. See also ◊laptop computer.

NOT gate or ***inverter gate*** in electronics, a type of ◊logic gate.

notochord the stiff but flexible rod that lies between the gut and the nerve cord of all embryonic and larval chordates, including the vertebrates. It forms the supporting structure of the adult lancelet, but in vertebrates it is replaced by the vertebral column, or spine.

nova (plural ***novae***) faint star that suddenly erupts in brightness by 10,000 times or more, remains bright for a few days, and then fades away and is not seen again for very many years, if at all. Novae are believed to occur in close ◊binary star systems, where gas from one star flows to a companion ◊white dwarf. The gas ignites and is thrown off in an explosion at speeds of 1,500 kps/930 mps or more. Unlike a ◊supernova, the star is not completely disrupted by the outburst. After a few weeks or months it subsides to its previous state; it may erupt many more times.

Although the name comes from the Latin 'new', photographic records show that such stars are not really new, but faint stars undergoing an outburst of radiation that temporarily gives them an absolute magnitude in the range –6—10, at least 100,000 times brighter than the Sun. They fade away, rapidly at first and then more slowly over several years. Two or three such stars are detected in our Galaxy each year, but on average one is sufficiently close to us to become a conspicuous naked-eye object only about once in ten years. Novae very similar to those appearing in our own Galaxy have also been observed in other galaxies.

Novell US ◊network operating system specialist. Novell's ◊NetWare operating system for IBM-compatible PCs dominates the market for ◊local area networks and is used as an industry standard.

NSFnet (shorthand for ***National Science Foundation Network***) in computing, network funded by the US National Science Foundation, and an important part of the Internet backbone. In 1993 the National Science Foundation started building a very high speed Backbone Network Service (vBNS) to connect five government supercomputing centres at speeds of up to 2.5 gigabits per second – fast enough to transmit the entire contents of several public libraries every second.

NTP abbreviation for ***normal temperature and pressure***, the former name for **STP** (◊standard temperature and pressure).

NTSC (abbreviation for ***National Television Standards Committee***) in computing, the US ◊television standard signal format. Sometimes believed to stand for 'Never Twice the Same Colour'.

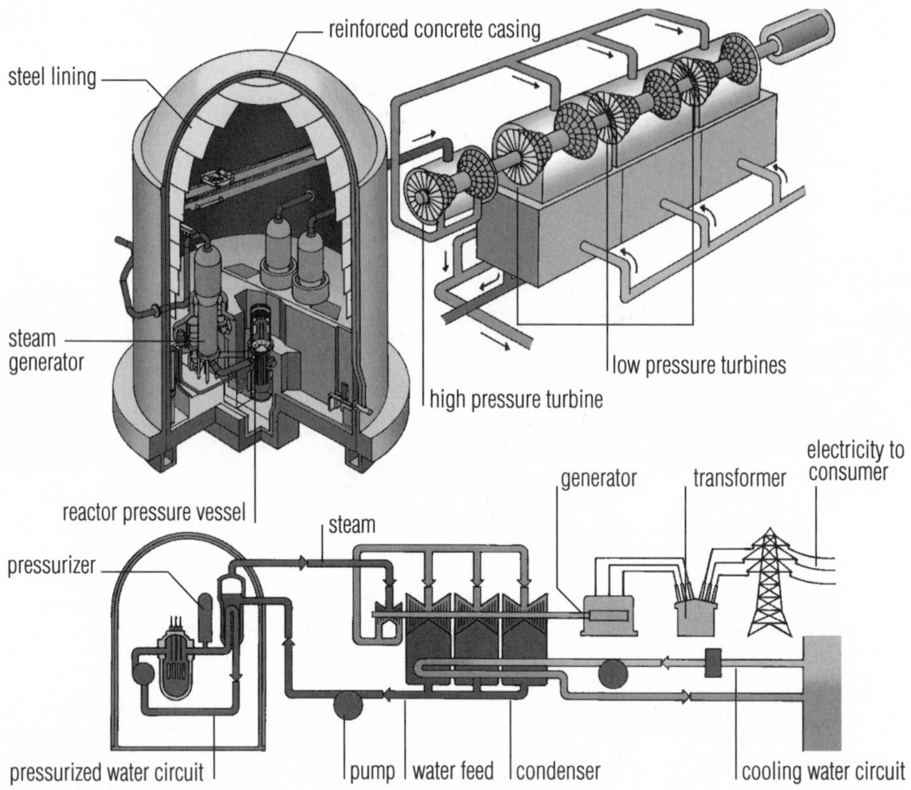

nuclear energy *A pressurized water nuclear power station. Water at high pressure is circulated around the reactor vessel where it is heated. The hot water is pumped to the steam generator where it boils in a separate circuit; the steam drives the turbines coupled to the electricity generator. This is the most widely used type of reactor. More than 20 countries have pressurized water reactors.*

nuclear energy or ***atomic energy*** energy released from the inner core, or ◊nucleus, of the atom. Energy produced by **nuclear** ◊fission **(the splitting of uranium or plutonium nuclei) has been harnessed since the 1950s to generate electricity, and research continues into the possible controlled use of** nuclear fusion **(the fusing, or combining, of atomic nuclei).**

In nuclear power stations, fission takes place in a nuclear reactor. The nuclei of uranium or, more rarely, plutonium are induced to split, releasing large amounts of heat energy. The heat is then removed from the core of the reactor by circulating gas or water, and used to produce the steam that drives alternators and turbines to generate electrical power. Unlike fossil fuels, such as coal and oil, which must be burned in large quantities to produce energy, nuclear fuels are used in very small amounts and supplies are therefore unlikely to be exhausted in the foreseeable future. However, the use of nuclear energy has given rise to concern over safety. Anxiety has been heightened by accidents such as the one at Chernobyl, Ukraine, in 1986. There has also been mounting concern about the production and disposal of toxic nuclear waste, which may have an active life of several thousand years, and the cost of maintaining nuclear power stations and decommissioning them at the end of their lives.

NUCLEAR ENERGY: FREQUENTLY ASKED QUESTIONS

http://www-formal.stanford.edu/jmc/progress/nuclear-faq.html

Answers to the most commonly asked questions about nuclear energy, particularly with a view to sustaining human progress. It contains many links to related pages and is a personal opinion that openly asks for comment from visitors.

nuclear fusion process whereby two atomic nuclei are fused, with the release of a large amount of energy. Very high temperatures and pressures are thought to be required in order for the process to happen. Under these conditions the atoms involved are stripped of all their electrons so that the remaining particles, which together make up a **plasma**, can come close together at very high speeds and overcome the mutual repulsion of the positive charges on the atomic nuclei. At very close range the strong nuclear force will come into play, fusing the particles together to form a larger nucleus. As fusion is accompanied by the release of large amounts of energy, the process might one day be harnessed to form the basis of commercial energy production. Methods of achieving controlled fusion are therefore the subject of research around the world.

Fusion is the process by which the Sun and the other stars produce their energy.

nuclear notation method used for labelling an atom according to the composition of its nucleus. The atoms or isotopes of a particular element are represented by the symbol ${}^{A}_{Z}X$ where A is the mass number of their nuclei, Z is their atomic number, and X is the chemical symbol for that element.

nuclear physics study of the properties of the nucleus of the ◊atom, including the structure of nuclei; nuclear forces; the interactions between particles and nuclei; and the study of radioactive decay. The study of elementary particles is ◊particle physics.

When we have found how the nuclei of atoms are built up we shall have found the greatest secret of all – except life. We shall have found the basis of everything – of the earth we walk on, of the air we breathe, of the sunshine, of our physical body itself, of everything in the world, however great or however small – except life.

ERNEST RUTHERFORD New Zealand physicist. *Passing Show* 24

nuclear reaction reaction involving the nuclei of atoms. Atomic nuclei can undergo changes either as a result of radioactive decay, as in the decay of radium to radon (with the emission of an alpha particle) or as a result of particle bombardment in a machine or device, as in the production of cobalt-60 by the bombardment of cobalt-59 with neutrons.

$$^{226}_{88}\text{Ra} \rightarrow {}^{222}_{86}\text{Rn} + {}^{4}_{2}\text{He} \quad {}^{59}_{27}\text{Co} + {}^{1}_{0}\text{n} \rightarrow {}^{60}_{27}\text{Co} + \gamma$$

Nuclear ◊fission and nuclear ◊fusion are examples of nuclear reactions. The enormous amounts of energy released arise from the mass–energy relation put forward by Einstein, stating that $E = mc^2$ (where E is energy, m is mass, and c is the velocity of light).

In nuclear reactions the sum of the masses of all the products (on the atomic mass unit scale) is less than the sum of the masses of the reacting particles. This lost mass is converted to energy according to Einstein's equation.

nuclear reactor device for producing ◊nuclear energy in a controlled manner. There are various types of reactor in use, all using nuclear ◊fission. In a **gas-cooled reactor**, a circulating gas under pressure (such as carbon dioxide) removes heat from the core of the reactor, which usually contains natural uranium. The efficiency of the fission process is increased by slowing neutrons in the core by using a ◊moderator such as carbon. The reaction is controlled with neutron-absorbing rods made of boron. An **advanced gas-cooled reactor** (AGR) generally has enriched uranium as its fuel. A **water-cooled reactor**, such as the steam-generating heavy water (deuterium oxide) reactor, has water circulating through the hot core. The water is converted to steam, which drives turbo-alternators for generating electricity. The most widely used reactor is the **pressurized-water reactor** (PWR), which contains a sealed system of pressurized water that is heated to form steam in heat exchangers in an external circuit. The **fast reactor** has no moderator and uses fast neutrons to bring about fission. It uses a mixture of plutonium and uranium oxide as fuel. When operating, uranium is converted to plutonium, which can be extracted and used later as fuel. It is also called the fast breeder because it produces more plutonium than it consumes. Heat is removed from the reactor by a coolant of liquid sodium.

Public concern over the safety of nuclear reactors has been intensified by explosions and accidental release of radioactive materials. The safest system allows for the emergency cooling of a reactor by automatically flooding an overheated core with water. Other concerns about nuclear power centre on the difficulties of reprocessing nuclear fuel and disposing safely of nuclear waste, and the cost of maintaining nuclear power stations and of decommissioning them at the end of their lives. The break up of the former USSR raised concerns about the ability of the new nation states to safely manage ageing reactors. In 1989, the UK government decided to postpone the construction of new nuclear power stations; in the USA, no new stations have been commissioned in over a decade. Rancho Seco, near Sacramento, California, was the first nuclear power station to be closed, by popular vote, in 1989. Sweden is committed to decommissioning its reactors. Some countries, such as France, are pressing ahead with their nuclear programmes.

It was reported in 1997 that there were 443 nuclear power plants in 31 countries, representing a net growth of 15 since the 1992 Rio Earth Summit, and a further 36 were under construction. This compares with a total of just over 100 reactors generating electricity in 15 countries in 1972. Nuclear power generates around 17% of the world's electricity.

Major accidents resulting in the release of large quantities of radiation occurred at Three Mile island in the USA in 1979 and Chernobyl, Ukraine, in 1986.

nuclear safety measures to avoid accidents in the operation of nuclear reactors and in the production and disposal of ◊nuclear weapons and of nuclear waste. There are no guarantees of the safety of any of the various methods of disposal.

Nuclear accidents **Windscale** (now Sellafield), Cumbria, England. In 1957, fire destroyed the core of a reactor, releasing large quantities of radioactive fumes into the atmosphere.

Ticonderoga, 130 km/80 mi off the coast of Japan. In 1965 a US Navy Skyhawk jet bomber fell off the deck of this ship, sinking in 4,900 m/16,000 ft of water. It carried a one-megaton hydrogen bomb. The accident was only revealed in 1989.

Three Mile Island, Harrisburg, Pennsylvania, USA. In 1979, a combination of mechanical and electrical failure, as well as operator error, caused a pressurized water reactor to leak radioactive matter.

Church Rock, New Mexico, USA. In July 1979, 380 million litres/100 million gallons of radioactive water containing uranium leaked from a pond into the Rio Purco, causing the water to become over 6,500 times as radioactive as safety standards allow for drinking water.

Chernobyl, Ukraine. In April 1986 there was an explosive leak, caused by overheating, from a nonpressurized boiling-water reactor, one of the largest in Europe. The resulting clouds of radioactive material spread as far as the UK. 31 people were killed in the explosion, and thousands of square kilometres of land were contaminated by fallout. By June 1992, seven times as many children in the Ukraine and Belarus were contracting thyroid cancer as before the accident, the incidence of leukemia was rising, and it was estimated that more than 6,000 people had died as a result of the accident, and that the death toll in the Ukraine alone would eventually reach 40,000.

Tomsk, Siberia, Russia. In April 1993 a tank exploded at a uranium reprocessing plant, sending a cloud of radioactive particles into the air.

nuclear waste the radioactive and toxic by-products of the nuclear-energy and nuclear-weapons industries. Nuclear waste may have an active life of several thousand years. Reactor waste is of three types: **high-level** spent fuel, or the residue when nuclear fuel has been removed from a reactor and reprocessed; **intermediate**, which may be long-or short-lived; and **low-level**, but bulky, waste from reactors, which has only short-lived radioactivity. Disposal, by burial on land or at sea, has raised problems of safety, environmental pollution, and security.

The issue of nuclear waste is becoming the central controversy threatening the future of generating electricity by nuclear energy. The dumping of nuclear waste at sea officially stopped in 1983, when a moratorium was agreed by the members of the London Dumping Convention (a United Nations body that controls disposal of wastes at sea). Covertly, the USSR continued dumping, and deposited thousands of tonnes of nuclear waste and three faulty reactors in the sea during 1964–86. The USSR and the Russian Federation between them dumped an estimated 12 trillion becquerels of radioactivity in the sea 1959–93. Russia has no way of treating nuclear waste and in 1993 announced its intention of continuing to dump it in the sea, in violation of international conventions, until 1997. Twenty reactors from Soviet nuclear-powered ships were dumped off the Arctic and Pacific coasts 1965–93, and some are leaking. Fish-spawning grounds off Norway are threatened by plutonium from abandoned Soviet nuclear warheads.

nucleic acid complex organic acid made up of a long chain of ◊nucleotides, present in the nucleus and sometimes the cytoplasm of the living cell. The two types, known as ◊DNA (deoxyribonucleic acid) and ◊RNA (ribonucleic acid), form the basis of heredity. The nucleotides are made up of a sugar (deoxyribose or ribose), a phosphate group, and one of four purine or pyrimidine bases. The order of the bases along the nucleic acid strand contains the genetic code.

nucleolus in biology, a structure found in the nucleus of eukaryotic cells. It produces the RNA that makes up the ◊ribosomes, from instructions in the DNA.

nucleon in particle physics, either a ◊proton or a ◊neutron, when present in the atomic nucleus. **Nucleon number** is an alternative name for the ◊mass number of an atom.

nucleon number or ***mass number*** (symbol A) the sum of the numbers of protons and neutrons in the nucleus of an atom. With the proton number, it is used in nuclear notation – for example, in the symbol $^{14}_{6}C$ representing the isotope carbon-14, the lower number is the ◊proton number, and the upper is the nucleon number.

nucleotide organic compound consisting of a purine (adenine or guanine) or a pyrimidine (thymine, uracil, or cytosine) base linked to a sugar (deoxyribose or ribose) and a phosphate group. ◊DNA and ◊RNA are made up of long chains of nucleotides.

To remember classes of nucleotides:

In DNA there are four nucleotides (cytosine, thymine, adenine, guanine) divided into two classes (pyrimidines and purines). The easiest way to remember which class they belong to is that the pyrimidines contain the letter y(cytosine and thymine)

nucleus in astronomy, the compact central core of a ◊galaxy, often containing powerful radio, X-ray and infrared sources. Active galaxies have extremely energetic nuclei.

nucleus in biology, the central, membrane-enclosed part of a eukaryotic cell, containing the chromosomes.

nucleus in physics, the positively charged central part of an ◊atom, which constitutes almost all its mass. Except for hydrogen nuclei, which have only protons, nuclei are composed of both protons and neutrons. Surrounding the nuclei are electrons, of equal and opposite charge to that of the protons, thus giving the atom a neutral charge.

The nucleus was discovered by New Zealand physicist Ernest Rutherford in 1911 as a result of experiments in passing alpha particles through very thin gold foil.

nuclide in physics, a species of atomic nucleus characterized by the number of protons (Z) and the number of neutrons (N). Nuclides with identical ◊proton number but differing ◊neutron number are called ◊isotopes.

nuée ardente a rapidly flowing, glowing white-hot cloud of ash and gas emitted by a volcano during a violent eruption. The ash and other pyroclastics in the lower part of the cloud behave like an ash flow. In 1902 a nuée ardente produced by the eruption of Mount Pelee in Martinique swept down the volcano in a matter of seconds and killed 28,000 people in the nearby town of St Pierre.

null character character with the ◊ASCII value 0. A null character is used by some programming languages, most notably C, to mark the end of a character string.

null-modem special cable that is used to connect the ◊serial interfaces of two computers, so as to allow them to exchange data.

null string in computing, a string, usually denoted by '–', containing nothing or a ◊null character. A null string is used in some programming languages to denote the last of a series of values.

numbat or ***banded anteater*** Australian ◊marsupial anteater. It is brown with white stripes on the back and has a long tubular tongue to gather termites and ants. The body is about 25 cm/10 in long, and the tongue can be extended 10 cm/4 in. It is different from other marsupials in that it has no pouch. (Species *Myrmecobius fasciatus.*)

number symbol used in counting or measuring. In mathematics, there are various kinds of numbers. The everyday number system is the decimal ('proceeding by tens') system, using the base ten. ◊Real numbers include all rational numbers (integers, or whole numbers, and fractions) and irrational numbers (those not expressible as fractions). ◊Complex numbers include the real and imaginary numbers (real-number multiples of the square root of –1). The ◊binary number system, used in computers, has two as its base. The ◊natural numbers, 0, 1, 2, 3, 4, 5, 6, 7, 8, and 9, give a counting system that, in the decimal system, continues 10, 11, 12, 13, and so on. These are whole numbers (integers), with fractions represented as, for example, $\frac{1}{4}$, $\frac{1}{2}$, $\frac{3}{4}$, or as decimal fractions (0.25, 0.5, 0.75). They are also **rational numbers**. **Irrational numbers** cannot be represented in this way and require symbols, such as $\sqrt{2}$, π, and e. They can be expressed numerically only as the (inexact) approximations 1.414, 3.142, and 2.718 (to three places of decimals) respectively. The symbols π and e are also examples of **transcendental numbers**, because they (unlike $\sqrt{2}$) cannot be derived by solving a ◊polynomial equation (an equation with one ◊variable quantity) with rational ◊coefficients (multiplying factors). Complex numbers, which include the real numbers as well as imaginary numbers, take the general form $a + bi$, where $i = \sqrt{-1}$ (that is, $i^2 = -1$), and a is the real part and bi the imaginary part.

evolution of number systems The ancient Egyptians, Greeks, Romans, and Babylonians all evolved number systems, although none had a ◊zero, which was introduced from India by way of Arab mathematicians in about the 8th century AD and allowed a place-value system to be devised on which the decimal system is based. Other number systems have since evolved and have found applications. For example, numbers to base two (binary numbers), using only 0 and 1, are commonly used in digital computers to represent the two-state 'on' or 'off' pulses of electricity. Binary numbers were first developed by German mathematician Gottfried Leibniz in the late 17th century.

Numbers constitute the only universal language.

Nathanael West US writer.
Miss Lonelyhearts 1933

number theory in mathematics, the abstract study of the structure of number systems and the properties of positive integers (whole numbers). For example, the theories of factors and prime numbers fall within this area, as do the work of mathematicians Giuseppe Peano (1858–1932), Pierre de Fermat, and Karl Gauss.

numerator the number or symbol that appears above the line in a vulgar fraction. For example, the numerator of 5/6 is 5. The numerator represents the fraction's dividend and indicates how many of the equal parts indicated by the denominator (number or symbol below the line) comprise the fraction.

nursing care of the sick, the very young, the very old, and the disabled. Organized training originated in 1836 in Germany, and was developed in Britain by the work of Florence Nightingale, who, during the Crimean War, established standards of scientific, humanitarian care in military hospitals. Nurses give day-to-day care and carry out routine medical and surgical duties under the supervision of medical staff.

In ancient times very limited care was associated with some temples, and in Christian times nursing became associated with the religious orders until the Reformation brought it into secular hands in Protestant countries. Many specialities and qualifications now exist in Western countries, standards being maintained by professional bodies and boards.

nut any dry, single-seeded fruit that does not split open to release the seed, such as the chestnut. A nut is formed from more than one carpel, but only one seed becomes fully formed, the remainder aborting. The wall of the fruit, the pericarp, becomes hard and woody, forming the outer shell.

Examples of true nuts are the acorn and hazelnut. The term also describes various hard-shelled fruits and seeds, including almonds and walnuts, which are really the stones of ◊drupes, and brazil nuts and shelled peanuts, which are seeds. The kernels of most nuts provide a concentrated, nutritious food, containing vitamins, minerals, and enzymes, about 50% fat, and 10–20% protein, although

Nucleus: Early Experiments to Determine Structure

by Julian Rowe

The most incredible event
What is an atom? Until about 100 years ago, scientists were pretty confident in regarding atoms as the permanent bricks of which the whole universe was built. All the changes of the universe amounted to nothing more drastic than simple rearrangements of permanent, indestructible atoms. Atoms seemed like the bricks in a child's box of toys, which could be used to build many different buildings in turn.

Chipped bricks ...
This comfortable picture was changed by the investigations of British physicist Joseph John Thomson (1856–1940) into cathode rays. Thomson showed conclusively that not only could atomic 'bricks' be chipped, but that the fragments produced were identical, no matter what atom they came from. They were of equal weight or mass, and carried the same negative electrical charge. The fragments were called electrons.

Thomson's experiments enabled him to calculate the ratio of the mass of the electron to its charge: it was about 1,000 times smaller than the value that had already been calculated for a hydrogen ion in the electrolysis of liquids. This was the proof, announced in April 1897, that electrons were fundamental particles of matter, far smaller than any atom. But atoms could not consist of negatively charged electrons alone. Particles with like electrical charge repel one another and, anyway, atoms are electrically neutral.

Thomson, who built up the Cavendish Laboratory at Cambridge into a great research school, was succeeded as professor by New Zealand physicist Ernest Rutherford (1871–1937), his pupil and one of the greatest pioneers of subatomic physics. Rutherford, while professor of physics at Manchester University, had shown that [alpha]-particles were doubly ionized helium atoms, using a Geiger–Müller counter. His assistant, German physicist Hans Wilhelm Geiger (1882–1945), with a colleague Walther Müller, invented this instrument, which is still used to measure ionizing radiation.

... And indestructible tissue paper?
Rutherford's idea for attacking the problem of the nature of an atom was to study the scattering of [alpha]-particles passing through thin metal foils. This painstaking work was carried out by Geiger in 1910 with his colleague Marsden, with astonishing results. They found that most of the particles were only slightly deflected as they passed through the foil. But a very small proportion, about 1 in 8,000, were widely deflected. Rutherford described this result as ' ... quite the most incredible event that has ever happened to me in my life ... It was almost as if you fired a 15 inch shell at a piece of tissue paper and it came back and hit you.'

The nuclear atom
Rutherford concluded when he published the results in 1911 that almost all the mass of the atom was concentrated in a very small region and that most of the atom was 'empty space'. This crucial experiment established the idea of the nuclear atom. The obstacle that deflected the [alpha]-particles could only be the missing positive charges of the atom. These were carried by the minute central nucleus. The electrons, Rutherford supposed, must be in motion around the nucleus, otherwise they would be drawn to it.

The number of positive charges in the nucleus equalled the number of electrons, and so accounted for the electrical neutrality of the atom. The proton, later discovered as part of the nucleus, carried an equal but opposite charge to the electron. But on theoretical grounds, Rutherfords's planetary model of the atom was unstable. Since electrons are charged particles, an atom ought to radiate energy by virtue of their motion. Danish theoretical physicist Niels Bohr (1885–1962), who was Rutherford's pupil, provided the theory that accounted for the stability of the atom. He showed that electrons must reside in 'stationary' orbits, in which they did not radiate energy.

---

a few, such as chestnuts, are high in carbohydrates and have only a moderate protein content of 5%. Nuts also provide edible and industrial oils. Most nuts are produced by perennial trees and shrubs. Whereas the majority of nuts are obtained from plantations, considerable quantities of pecans and brazil nuts are still collected from the wild. World production in the mid-1980s was about 4 million tonnes per year.

nut and bolt common method of fastening pieces of metal or wood together. The nut consists of a small block (usually metal) with a threaded hole in the centre for screwing on to a threaded rod or pin (bolt or screw). The method came into use at the turn of the 19th century, following Henry Maudslay's invention of a precision screw-cutting ◊lathe.

nutation in astronomy, a slight 'nodding' of the Earth in space, caused by the varying gravitational pulls of the Sun and Moon. Nutation changes the angle of the Earth's axial tilt (average 23.5°) by about 9 seconds of arc to either side of its mean position, a complete cycle taking just over 18.5 years.

nutation in botany, the spiral movement exhibited by the tips of certain stems during growth; it enables a climbing plant to find a suitable support. Nutation sometimes also occurs in tendrils and flower stalks.

The direction of the movements, clockwise or anticlockwise, is usually characteristic for particular species.

nutcracker either of two species of bird similar to a jay, belonging to the crow family. One species is found in the Old World and the other in the New World. (Genus *Nucifraga,* family Corvidae, order Passeriformes.)

nuthatch any of a group of small birds with short tails and pointed beaks. Nuthatches climb head first up, down, and around tree trunks and branches, foraging for insects and their larvae. (Family Sittidae, order Passeriformes.)

nutmeg kernel of the hard aromatic seed of the evergreen nutmeg tree, native to the Maluku Islands, Indonesia. Both the nutmeg and its secondary covering, known as **mace**, are used as spices in cookery. (*Myristica fragrans,* family Myristicaceae.)

nutrition the strategy adopted by an organism to obtain the chemicals it needs to live, grow, and reproduce. Also, the science of food, and its effect on human and animal life, health, and disease. Nutrition involves the study of the basic nutrients required to sustain life, their bioavailability in foods and overall diet, and the effects upon them of cooking and storage. It is also concerned with dietary deficiency diseases.

There are six classes of nutrients: water, carbohydrates, proteins, fats, vitamins, and minerals.

water Water is involved in nearly every body process. Animals and humans will succumb to water deprivation sooner than to starvation.

carbohydrates Carbohydrates are composed of carbon, hydrogen and oxygen. The major groups are starches, sugars, and cellulose and related material (or 'roughage'). The prime function of the carbohydrates is to provide energy for the body; they also serve as efficient sources of glucose, which the body requires for brain func-

> TO REMEMBER THE CLASSIFICATION OF FEEDING METHODS:
>
> ALL COUNTY PLAYERS HAVE HUNDREDS OF SHOTS PERFECTED.
>
> AUTOTROPHIC (I CHEMOSYNTHETIC II PHOTOSYNTHETIC) / HETEROTROPHIC (I HOLOZOIC II SAPROPHYTIC III PARASITIC)

tioning, utilization of foods, maintenance of body temperature. Roughage includes the stiff structural materials of vegetables, fruits, and cereal products.

proteins Proteins are made up of smaller units, amino acids. The primary function of dietary protein is to provide the amino acids required for growth and maintenance of body tissues. Both vegetable and animal foods are protein sources.

fats Fats serve as concentrated sources of energy, and protect vital organs such as the kidneys and skeleton. Saturated fats derive primarily from animal sources; unsaturated fats from vegetable sources such as nuts and seeds.

vitamins Vitamins are essential for normal growth, and are either fat-soluble or water-soluble. Fat-soluble vitamins include A, essential to the maintenance of mucous membranes, particularly the conjunctiva of the eyes; D, important to the absorption of calcium; E, an anti-oxidant; and K, which aids blood clotting. Water-soluble vitamins are the B complex, essential to metabolic reactions, and C, for maintaining connective tissue.

minerals Minerals are vital to normal development; calcium and iron are particularly important as they are required in relatively large amounts. Minerals required by the body in trace amounts include chromium, copper, fluoride, iodine, iron, magnesium, manganese, molybdenum, phosphorus, potassium, selenium, sodium, and zinc.

nyala antelope found in the thick bush of southern Africa. About 1 m/3 ft at the shoulder, it is greyish-brown with thin vertical white stripes. Males have horns up to 80 cm/2.6 ft long. (Species *Tragelaphus angasi*, family Bovidae.)

nylon synthetic long-chain polymer similar in chemical structure to protein. Nylon was the first all-synthesized fibre, made from petroleum, natural gas, air, and water by the Du Pont firm in 1938. It is used in the manufacture of moulded articles, textiles, and medical sutures. Nylon fibres are stronger and more elastic than silk and are relatively insensitive to moisture and mildew. Nylon is used for hosiery and woven goods, simulating other materials such as silks and furs; it is also used for carpets.

nymph in entomology, the immature form of insects that do not have a pupal stage; for example, grasshoppers and dragonflies. Nymphs generally resemble the adult (unlike larvae), but do not have fully formed reproductive organs or wings.

The Invention of Nylon

by Paul Meehan

Introduction

During the late 1920s, the Du Pont chemical company committed itself to a long-term programme of 'basic research', with particular emphasis on the development of new synthetic materials. In 1928, Wallace Hume Carothers (1896–1937), a young Harvard chemist, was appointed to lead the fledgling project. Within four years Carothers' team had developed and marketed neoprene, the first successful synthetic rubber; during the next decade numerous new materials were patented, culminating with the commercial release of nylon in October 1938, 18 months after Carothers' tragic death.

Polymer chemistry

By 1925, Du Pont had recognized the importance of the development of new materials; cheaper and better alternatives to expensive products such as silk were in great demand. Wallace Carothers, educated in Illinois and a teacher of chemistry at three Southern Universities, was plucked from Harvard to head Du Pont's research facility at Wilmington, Delaware, in 1928. The main goal of Carothers' team was to prepare and investigate organic compounds of high molecular weight; the group was then to develop ways in which each product's properties could be tailored to suit their desired final applications. This particular field, relatively unexplored at the time, was known as polymer chemistry; this branch of science was revolutionized by Carothers and his colleagues during the course of the next decade.

Carothers' first major contribution was the implementation of a technique known as 'condensation polymerization'. In this process, two compounds containing reactive groups at each end were combined in equimolar amounts to form a third complex, with the elimination of water as a by-product. The new complex, also containing reactive end-groups, could be further reacted, leading to the stepwise formation of a large polymeric material. The addition of a tiny amount of a 'termination agent', typically a monoacid or monoamine, halted the reaction, and prevented the generation of compounds of extremely high molecular weight, which would prove unmanageable. The final product could then be treated by one of several simple processes to produce polymers with specific properties.

Within three years the team had developed neoprene, the first commercially produced synthetic rubber. This was launched to great success in 1932. Subsequent experiments with polyesters proved moderately successful, but the company's overriding desire was to develop products which would emulate the properties of silk. For this reason Carothers turned to polyamide production. The reaction between dibasic acids and diamines generated a polymeric salt. Subsequent heating of this salt formed the polyamide resin. This process produced the series of products which would ultimately revolutionize materials science and make Du Pont's fortune – the nylons.

Nylon development

Upon production, the polyamides were treated by a process known as 'melt-spinning'. During this process, the hot, molten polymer is passed into a stream of cold air, whereupon it solidifies into a filament; depending on the final intended use of the product, this filament can range in size from finer than a human hair to thick bristles, akin to those used in toothbrushes. The filaments are then stretched, a process known as 'drawing', to make the component molecules pack more closely: this increase in the order, or crystallinity, of the material provides increased strength and elasticity in the resulting fibre. Nylon can be drawn to four times its original length.

Although nylon was the name given to the class of polyamide compounds produced by this process, commercial nylon is formed from the reaction between hexamethylenediamine and adipic acid; each component contains six carbon atoms, hence the systematic name nylon-6,6. The nylons as a group are strong, tough materials, adaptable to moulding. Although nylon has since been used in a huge variety of commercial applications, such as mechanical parts, carpets and home furnishings, the initial and most famous use of nylon was in ladies hosiery.

Commercial success

Carothers' life was blighted by a history of personal suffering; alcoholism and recurrent bouts of clinical depression ultimately led to his suicide, shortly after his 41st birthday in 1937. However, the development of nylon established his greatness as a chemical pioneer. When Charles Stine unveiled nylon to an unsuspecting world in New York, New York, on October 27th, 1938, the product was greeted by near-hysteria; on their first day of sales, a remarkable 5 million pairs of nylon stockings were bought by the public. Du Pont presently sells over 3 billion pounds worth of nylon annually, confirming the durability and importance of the product. However, Du Pont's legacy of success transcends nylon production. Carothers' research team pioneered modern polymer chemistry and sparked the materials revolution which has galvanized the chemical industry in the second half of the 20th century.

oak any of a group of trees or shrubs belonging to the beech family, with over 300 known species widely distributed in temperate zones. Oaks are valuable for timber, the wood being durable and straight-grained. Their fruits are called ◊acorns. (Genus *Quercus*, family Fagaceae.)

oarfish any of a group of deep-sea bony fish, found in warm parts of the Atlantic, Pacific, and Indian oceans. Oarfish are large, up to 9 m/30 ft long, elongated, and compressed, with a fin along the back and a manelike crest behind the head. They have a small mouth, no teeth or scales, and large eyes. They are often described as sea serpents. (Genus *Regalecidae*.)

oarweed or ***tangleweed*** any of several large, coarse, brown seaweeds found on the lower shore and below the low-tide mark, especially *L. digitata*. This species has fronds 1–2 m/3–6 ft long, a thick stalk, and a frond divided into flat fingers. In Japan and Korea it is cultivated and harvested commercially. (Especially genus *Laminaria*.)

oasis area of land made fertile by the presence of water near the surface in an otherwise arid region. The occurrence of oases affects the distribution of plants, animals, and people in the desert regions of the world.

oat type of annual grass, a ◊cereal crop. The plant has long narrow leaves and a stiff straw stem; the panicles of flowers (clusters around the main stem), and later of grain, hang downwards. The cultivated oat (*A. sativa*) is produced for human and animal food. (Genus *Avena*.)

obesity condition of being overweight (generally, 20% or more above the desirable weight for one's sex, build, and height). Obesity increases susceptibility to disease, strains the vital organs, and reduces life expectancy; it is usually remedied by controlled weight loss, healthy diet, and exercise.

In 1994 US researchers discovered a gene in mice, *ob*, which controls the production of leptin, a protein involved in appetite control; defects in this gene cause obesity. Research during 1995 showed that obese mice lost weight dramatically after a 4-week treatment with the protein. An almost identical gene is found in humans, but obese humans have been found to have too much leptin rather than too little, as was the case in mice, so leptin injections will not cure obesity in humans.

object linking and embedding (OLE) enhancement to ◊dynamic data exchange, which makes it possible not only to include live data from one application in another application, but also to edit the data in the original application without leaving the application in which the data has been included.

object-oriented programming (OOP) computer programming based on 'objects', in which data are closely linked to the procedures that operate on them. For example, a circle on the screen might be an object: it has data, such as a centre point and a radius, as well as procedures for moving it, erasing it, changing its size, and so on.

The technique originated with the Simula and Smalltalk languages in the 1960s and early 1970s, but it has now been incorporated into many general-purpose programming languages, including Java.

object program in computing, the ◊machine code translation of a program written in a ◊source language.

Oboe British radar-based blind bombing system of World War II adopted by the RAF 1942.

It used two transmitters based in the UK; one tracked the bomber, guiding it on a course across the target. The other also tracked the bomber and ordered it to drop its bombs at the computed bomb-release point. Since accuracy was of a very high order, bombing became very accurate, and the system was used by the Pathfinder force to drop marker bombs for the rest of a bombing force.

observation in science, the perception of a phenomenon – for example, examining the Moon through a telescope, watching mice to discover their mating habits, or seeing how a plant grows.

Traditionally, observation was seen as entirely separate from theory, free from preconceptions and therefore lending support to the idea of scientific objectivity. However, as the preceding examples show, observations are ordered according to a pre-existing theory; for instance, one cannot observe mating behaviour without having decided what mating behaviour might look like. In addition, many observations actually affect the behaviour of the observed (for instance, of mating mice).

When I am obliged to give up observation and experiment I shall die.

Charles Darwin British naturalist.
Quoted in A Moorhead, *Darwin and the Beagle*

observatory site or facility for observing astronomical or meteorological phenomena. The earliest recorded observatory was in Alexandria, N Africa, built by Ptolemy Soter in about 300 BC. The modern observatory dates from the invention of the telescope. Observatories may be ground-based, carried on aircraft, or sent into orbit as satellites, in space stations, and on the space shuttle.

The erection of observatories was revived in W Asia about AD 1000, and extended to Europe. The observatory built on the island of Hven (now Ven) in Denmark in 1576 for Tycho Brahe (1546–1601) was elaborate, but survived only to 1597. Later, observatories were built in Paris in 1667, ◊Greenwich (the ◊Royal Greenwich Observatory) in 1675, and Kew, England. Most early observatories were near towns, but with the advent of big telescopes, clear skies with little background light, and hence high, remote sites, became essential.

The most powerful optical telescopes covering the sky are at ◊Mauna ◊Kea, Hawaii; ◊Mount ◊Palomar, California; ◊Kitt Peak National Observatory, Arizona; La Palma, Canary Islands; ◊Cerro Tololo Inter-American Observatory, and the ◊European Southern Observatory, Chile; ◊Siding Spring Mountain, Australia; and Zelenchukskaya in the ◊Caucasus.

Radio astronomy observatories include ◊Jodrell Bank, Cheshire, England; the ◊Mullard Radio ◊Astronomy Observatory, Cambridge, England; ◊Arecibo, Puerto Rico; ◊Effelsberg, Germany; and ◊Parkes, Australia. The ◊Hubble Space Telescope was launched into orbit in 1990. The Very Large Telescope is under construction by the European Southern Observatory in the mountains of N Chile, for completion by 1997.

obsession persistently intruding thought, emotion, or impulse, often recognized by the sufferer as irrational, but nevertheless causing distress. It may be a brooding on destiny or death, or chronic doubts interfering with everyday life (such as fearing the gas is not turned off and repeatedly checking), or an impulse leading to repetitive action, such as continually washing one's hands.

In obsessive-compulsive neurosis, these intrusions compel the patient to perform rituals or ceremonies, albeit reluctantly, no matter how absurd or distasteful they may seem.

obsessive-compulsive disorder (OCD) in psychiatry, anxiety disorder that manifests itself in the need to check constantly that

Obesity, a Question of Inheritance

by Hilary Neve

At present, it is not possible to answer the question 'is obesity influenced by genetic factors?', as the roles of inherited (or genetic) factors in the development and maintenance of obesity are not yet understood fully, and the conclusions reported in many studies vary. They range from 'little genetic influence' to 'strong genetic influence', and depend on the specific factor investigated. This is because obesity itself is not merely just a simple disorder, but is in fact a complex mix of several varied disorders, each of which may be influenced by both genetic and nongenetic factors, and with interaction between different genes, and between genes and the environment.

Definition of Obesity

An individual is considered to be obese when they have a Body Mass Index (BMI) in excess of 30. The BMI is calculated by taking the individual's weight in kilogrammes and dividing this by the height in metres. Obesity occurs when energy intake exceeds the actual energy expended, so the unused energy is stored as body fat. A BMI of over 30 is a hazard to health and well being, and is now common enough in the Western world to constitute one of the most important medical and public health problems, putting the individual at high risk of degenerative disease or even death, and these risks increase as the BMI increases.

Obesity has been attributed to numerous causes including excessive intake, reactive eating due to stress or anxiety, low resting metabolic rate influencing the caloric value of energy expenditure, environmental effects, family behaviour problems, and genetic factors. Other influences include human biology, endocrine alterations, society, culture, and physical activity. It is a complex issue.

Genetic Influence

An individual's genetic composition (their genotype) has a specific influence on their sex, height, eye colour, and skeleton, and may also influence their body and muscular mass, as well as body fat and how this is regionally distributed. The variation in body fat distribution may also result from a complex interaction of physical, environmental, and social features, as well as from the genotype. Each gene may have a varying or specific influence with many genes each exerting a small effect, or perhaps a single rarer gene that plays a larger role over time, with inherited differences in the likelihood of developing obesity.

Each genotype may have its own particular influence, with a single gene defect influencing obesity, or it may exert several independent (polygenic) influences, including regulation of energy expenditure (or metabolism). For example, there may be a form of thrifty genotype that has developed over time, and which influences the more efficient use of energy intake. The body fat itself may consist mainly of enlarged fat cells, or there may be a larger number of smaller fat cells, each of which may have a specific genotype influence. Perhaps there is no particular gene that influences the development and/or maintenance of obesity, but probably several genes and aspects of human physiology that determine many aspects of weight, appetite, satiety, metabolism, and a predisposition to physical activity. Families may have shared genes, and they often share the same environment and particular eating patterns – also influential factors that need to be examined separately. With regard to body fat variation, the additive genetic effect on the amount of subcutaneous fat is considered to be quite low, but has been reported as highest for fat mass and regional distribution of the fat, which suggests that the genotype may be more influential on the visceral fat than the subcutaneous store. From the limited data available it appears that the genotype could account for up to 40 percent of the individual differences in the resting metabolic rate, the thermic effect of food, and the energy cost of light exercise, which would explain why some people become obese.

Studies

Studies of obesity in families show there is possibly a familial influence; for example, in a series of studies of the families of obese children, it was found that a child with one obese parent was at greater risk of developing obesity, but surprisingly also that those with two obese parents were at a lesser risk! This shows how complex this issue is and demonstrates the need for much more investigation.

Studies of adopted children and both their biological and adoptive parents suggest that inheritance plays an important role in the risk of developing obesity. Research has shown that there was no relationship between the BMI of the child and the adoptive parents, but that the BMI of the biological parents actually increased with that of the child whose weight was increasing.

Further evidence for the effect of the genotype and its influence has come from work examining the body weight of twins, where nearly two-thirds of the variability in BMI was attributed to genetic factors. The body weight of twins of the same sex (monozygotic) has been found to have identical genetic features and is more similar than the body weight of twins of different sexes (dizygotic). The genetic features of dizygotic twins are similar to those of other siblings.

Obesity appears to be more prevalent in the families of obese patients seeking surgical treatment for their condition than in a group of nonobese patients treated with other abdominal surgery. In approximately 10 percent of the families of the patients seeking help, more than one other member sought treatment. The incidence of obesity in the families of these patients was compared with that in a group of nonobese patients, and it was found that there were significantly more obese family members in the obese group. These included mothers and daughters, fathers and daughters, sisters and brothers, all with a BMI of over 35. This would suggest a genetic influence, and a need for further investigations into these factors.

There are also certain inherited syndromes where obesity is one of the characteristics. These include, in particular, Prader-Willi Syndrome, where children develop a ravenous appetite and a variety of food-seeking behaviours, with parents fighting a losing battle to control the child's intake. The Bardet-Biedl Syndrome is transmitted via an autosomal recessive trait, with obesity occurring in up to 80 percent of the cases.

There appears to be some single and polygenic influence on the transmission of obesity, although the genetic influence is more important in determining body fat distribution, and studies show that it may run in families, but one needs to examine separately the influences of the environment and the genes. The search for genetic members of the various obesity phenotypes does not appear to have been initiated to any extent as yet, but it appears likely to be increased in the future, as searches for influences on obesity continue.

certain acts have been performed 'correctly'. Sufferers may, for example, feel compelled to repeatedly wash themselves or return home again and again to check that doors have been unlocked and appliances switched off. They may also hoard certain objects and insist in these being arranged in a precise way or be troubled by intrusive and unpleasant thoughts. In extreme cases normal life is disrupted through the hours devoted to compulsive actions. Treatment involves ◊cognitive therapy and drug therapy with serotonin-blocking drugs such as Prozac.

There are approximately 1 million OCD sufferers in Britain and 5 million in the USA.

obsidian black or dark-coloured glassy volcanic rock, chemically similar to◊ granite, but formed by cooling rapidly on the Earth's surface at low pressure.

The glassy texture is the result of rapid cooling, which inhibits the growth of crystals. Obsidian was valued by the early civilizations of Mexico for making sharp-edged tools and ceremonial sculptures.

obstetrics medical speciality concerned with the management of pregnancy, childbirth, and the immediate postnatal period.

obtuse angle an angle greater than 90° but less than 180°.

occultation in astronomy, the temporary obscuring of a star by a body in the solar system. Occultations are used to provide information about changes in an orbit, and the structure of objects in space, such as radio sources.

The exact shapes and sizes of planets and asteroids can be found when they occult stars. The rings of Uranus were discovered when that planet occulted a star in 1977.

ocean great mass of salt water. Strictly speaking three oceans exist – the Atlantic, Indian, and Pacific – to which the Arctic is often added. They cover approximately 70% or 363,000,000 sq km/140,000,000 sq mi of the total surface area of the Earth. Water levels recorded in the world's oceans have shown an increase of 10–15 cm/4–6 in over the past 100 years.

depth (average) 3,660 m/12,000 ft, but shallow ledges (continental shelves) 180 m/600 ft run out from the continents, beyond which the continental slope reaches down to the ◊abyssal zone, the largest area, ranging from 2,000–6,000 m/6,500–19,500 ft. Only the ◊deep-sea trenches go deeper, the deepest recorded being 11,034 m/36,201 ft (by the *Vityaz*, USSR) in the Mariana Trench of the western Pacific in 1957

features deep trenches (off eastern and southeast Asia, and western South America), volcanic belts (in the western Pacific and eastern Indian Ocean), and ocean ridges (in the mid-Atlantic, eastern Pacific, and Indian Ocean)

temperature varies on the surface with latitude (–2°C to +29°C); decreases rapidly to 370 m/1,200 ft, then more slowly to 2,200 m/ 7,200 ft; and hardly at all beyond that

water contents salinity averages about 3%; minerals commercially extracted include bromine, magnesium, potassium, salt; those potentially recoverable include aluminium, calcium, copper, gold, manganese, silver.

pollution Oceans have always been used as a dumping area for human waste, but as the quantity of waste increases, and land areas for dumping it diminish, the problem is exacerbated. Today ocean pollutants include airborne emissions from land (33% by weight of total marine pollution); oil from both shipping and land-based sources; toxins from industrial, agricultural, and domestic uses; sewage; sediments from mining, forestry, and farming; plastic litter; and radioactive isotopes. Thermal pollution by cooling water from power plants or other industry is also a problem, killing coral and other temperature-sensitive sedentary species.

How inappropriate to call this planet Earth when quite clearly it is an Ocean.

ARTHUR C CLARKE British science and science-fiction writer. *Nature* 1990

oceanarium large display tank in which aquatic animals and plants live together much as they would in their natural environment. The first oceanarium was created by the explorer and naturalist W Douglas Burden in 1938 in Florida, USA.

ocean current fast-flowing ◊current of seawater generated by the wind or by variations in water density between two areas. Ocean currents are partly responsible for transferring heat from the Equator to the poles and thereby evening out the global heat imbalance.

Ocean Drilling Program (ODP, formerly the ***Deep-Sea Drilling Project 1968–85***) research project initiated in the USA to sample the rocks of the ocean ◊crust. Initially under the direction of Scripps Institution of Oceanography, the project was planned and administered by the Joint Oceanographic Institutions for Deep Earth Sampling (JOIDES). The operation became international in 1975, when Britain, France, West Germany, Japan, and the USSR also became involved.

Boreholes were drilled in all the oceans using the JOIDES ships *Glomar Challenger* and *Resolution*. Knowledge of the nature and history of the ocean basins was increased dramatically. The technical difficulty of drilling the seabed to a depth of 2,000 m/6,500 ft was overcome by keeping the ship in position with side-thrusting propellers and satellite navigation, and by guiding the drill using a radiolocation system. The project is intended to continue until 2005.

oceanography study of the oceans. Its subdivisions deal with each ocean's extent and depth, the water's evolution and composition, its physics and chemistry, the bottom topography, currents and wind effects, tidal ranges, the biology, and the various aspects of human use.

Oceanography involves the study of water movements – currents, waves, and tides – and the chemical and physical properties of the seawater. It deals with the origin and topography of the ocean floor – ocean trenches and ridges formed by ◊plate tectonics, and continental shelves from the submerged portions of the continents. Computer simulations are widely used in oceanography to plot the possible movements of the waters, and many studies are carried out by remote sensing.

ocean ridge mountain range on the seabed indicating the presence of a constructive plate margin (where tectonic plates are moving apart and magma rises to the surface; see ◊plate tectonics). Ocean ridges, such as the ◊Mid-Atlantic Ridge, consist of many segments offset along transform ◊faults, and can rise thousands of metres above the surrounding seabed.

Ocean ridges usually have a ◊rift valley along their crests, indicating where the flanks are being pulled apart by the growth of the plates of the ◊lithosphere beneath. The crests are generally free of sediment; increasing depths of sediment are found with increasing distance down the flanks.

ocean trench deep trench in the seabed indicating the presence of a destructive margin (produced by the movements of ◊plate tectonics). The subduction or dragging downwards of one plate of the◊lithosphere beneath another means that the ocean floor is pulled down. Ocean trenches are found around the edge of the Pacific Ocean and the NE Indian Ocean; minor ones occur in the Caribbean and near the Falkland Islands.

Ocean trenches represent the deepest parts of the ocean floor, the deepest being the ◊Mariana Trench which has a depth of 11,034 m/36,201 ft. At depths of below 6 km/3.6 mi there is no light and very high pressure; ocean trenches are inhabited by crustaceans, coelenterates (for example, sea anemones), polychaetes (a type of worm), molluscs, and echinoderms.

ocelot wild cat of the southwestern USA, Mexico, and Central and South America. It is up to 1 m/3 ft long with a 45 cm/1.5 ft tail, weighs about 18 kg/40 lb, and has a pale yellowish coat marked with horizontal stripes and blotches. As a result of being hunted for its fur, it is close to extinction. (Species *Felis pardalis*, family Felidae.)

OCELOT – *FELIS PARADALIS*

http://ananke.advanced.org/2878/tx_ocelot.html

Brief profile of the endangered wild cat. There is a description of the animal, its habitat and distribution, and the reasons why it is on the verge of extinction.

OCR abbreviation for optical character recognition.

octagon a ◊polygon with eight sides.

octahedron, regular regular solid with eight faces, each of which is an equilateral triangle. It is one of the five regular polyhedra or Platonic solids. The figure made by joining the midpoints of the faces is a perfect cube and the vertices of the octahedron are themselves the midpoints of the faces of a surrounding cube. For this reason, the cube and the octahedron are called dual solids.

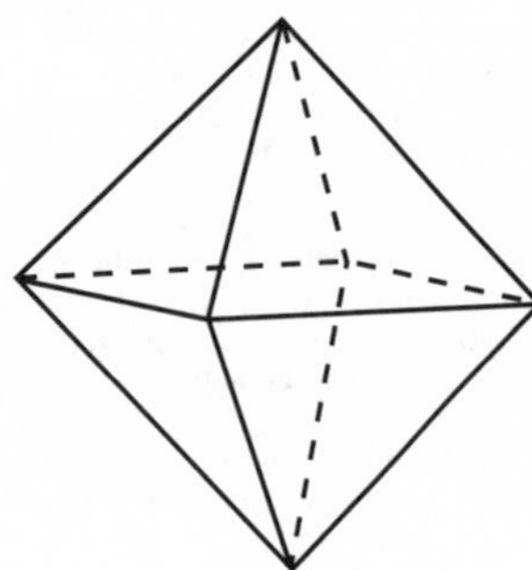

octahedron, regular An octahedron is a solid figure which has eight faces, each of which is an equilateral triangle.

octal number system number system to the base eight, used in computing. The highest digit that can appear in the octal system is seven. Whereas normal decimal, or base-ten, numbers may be considered to be written under column headings based on the number ten, octal, or base-eight, numbers can be thought of as written under column headings based on the number eight. The octal number 567 is therefore equivalent to the decimal number 375, since $(5 \times 64) + (6 \times 8) + (7 \times 1) = 375$.

The octal number system is sometimes used by computer programmers as an alternative to the ◊hexadecimal number system.

octane rating numerical classification of petroleum fuels indicating their combustion characteristics.

The efficient running of an ◊internal combustion engine depends on the ignition of a petrol–air mixture at the correct time during the cycle of the engine. Higher-rated petrol burns faster than lower-rated fuels. The use of the correct grade must be matched to the engine.

Octans faint constellation in the southern hemisphere, represented as an octant. It contains the southern celestial pole. The closest naked-eye star to the south celestial pole is fifth-magnitude Sigma Octantis.

octet rule in chemistry, rule stating that elements combine in a way that gives them the electronic structure of the nearest ◊inert gas. All the inert gases except helium have eight electrons in their outermost shell, hence the term octet.

octopus soft-bodied sea animal with a round or oval body and eight slender arms (tentacles) in a ring surrounding its mouth. They are solitary creatures, living alone in rocky dens. They feed on crabs and other small animals. There are about 50 different species of octopus living in all the oceans of the world. Some are small, having bodies only 8 cm/3 in long, but the largest deep-sea species can grow to lengths of 20 m/64 ft.

behaviour Octopuses can change colour to blend in with their surroundings and can swim using their arms or by a form of jet propulsion by squirting out water from their bodies. The octopus has rows of suckers along the length of each arm (or tentacle) which, as well as helping it swim and crawl around the ocean floor, allows it to search in cracks and crevices and grab prey. The octopus is a carnivore (flesh-eater), usually feeding on crabs, shrimps, and mussels, but the larger species of octopus have been known to hunt small sharks and dogfish. They trap the prey in their arms and drag it towards their powerful beaklike jaws. Once it has bitten its prey, the octopus injects it with a poisonous saliva to kill it. Sometimes, when frightened or to avoid enemies, they squirt out a black ink from their bodies which hides them and allows them to escape. If they lose an arm, they can grow another in its place. Octopuses are highly intelligent with two well developed eyes, similar to those of vertebrates (animals with backbones). They breathe using gills as fish do, but are unique in that they have three hearts.

classification Octopuses belong to the phylum Mollusca (◊molluscs), class Cephalopoda (◊cephalopods), subclass Coleoidea. They belong to the genus *Octopus* and there are about 50 known species including the **common octopus** (*O. vulgaris*), which may reach 2 m/6 ft in length; the Australian blue-ringed octopus (genus *Hapalochlaena*) that can kill a human being in 15 minutes as a result of its venomous bite; and the giant deep-sea octopus (*Architeuthis dux*) that can grow to 20 m/64 ft.

odd number any number not divisible by 2, thus odd numbers form the infinite sequence 1, 3, 5, 7 ... . Every square number n^2 is the sum of the first n odd numbers. For example, $49 = 7^2 = 1 + 3 + 5 + 7 + 9 + 11 + 13$.

oedema any abnormal accumulation of fluid in tissues or cavities of the body; waterlogging of the tissues due to excessive loss of ◊plasma through the capillary walls.

It may be generalized (the condition once known as dropsy) or confined to one area, such as the ankles.

Oedema may be mechanical – the result of obstructed veins or heart failure – or it may be due to increased permeability of the capillary walls, as in liver or kidney disease or malnutrition. Accumulation of fluid in the abdomen, a complication of cirrhosis, is known as **ascites**.

Oedipus complex in psychology, the unconscious antagonism of a son to his father, whom he sees as a rival for his mother's affection. For a girl antagonistic to her mother, as a rival for her father's affection, the term is **Electra complex**. The terms were coined by Sigmund ◊Freud.

Freud saw this as a universal part of childhood development, which in most children is resolved during late childhood. Contemporary theory places less importance on the Oedipus/Electra complex than did Freud and his followers.

OEM in computing, abbreviation for ◊original equipment manufacturer.

oersted c.g.s. unit (symbol Oe) of ◊magnetic field strength, now replaced by the SI unit ampere per metre. The Earth's magnetic field is about 0.5 oersted; the field near the poles of a small bar magnet is several hundred oersteds; and a powerful ◊electromagnet can have a field strength of 30,000 oersteds.

oesophagus muscular tube by which food travels from mouth to stomach. The human oesophagus is about 23 cm/9 in long. Its extends downwards from the ◊pharynx, immediately behind the windpipe. It is lined with a mucous membrane which secretes lubricant fluid to assist the downward movement of food (◊peristalsis).

oestrogen any of a group of hormones produced by the ◊ovaries of vertebrates; the term is also used for various synthetic hormones that mimic their effects. The principal oestrogen in mammals is oestradiol. Oestrogens control female sexual development, promote the growth of female secondary sexual characteristics, stimulate egg production, and, in mammals, prepare the lining of the uterus for pregnancy.

Oestrogens are used therapeutically for some hormone disorders and to inhibit lactation; they also form the basis of oral contraceptives. US researchers in 1995 observed that oestrogen plays a role in the healing of damaged blood vessels. It has also been found that women recover more quickly from strokes if given a low oestrogen dose.

oestrus in mammals, the period during a female's reproductive cycle (also known as the oestrus cycle or ◊menstrual cycle) when mating is most likely to occur. It usually coincides with ovulation.

office automation introduction of computers and other electronic equipment, such as fax machines, to support an office routine. Increasingly, computers are used to support administrative tasks such as document processing, filing, mail, and schedule management; project planning and management accounting have also been computerized.

office suite in computing, set of bundled programs designed especially for business use. An office suite will typically contain a ◊spreadsheet, scheduling and presentation software, a ◊word processor, a database, and e-mail facilities. The programs are set up to work individually and in concert, so that the user can (for example) create a report with charts created from a spreadsheet, and then e-mail the document to a list of clients selected from the database. Popular office suites include Lotus SmartSuite and Microsoft Office.

offline in computing, not connected, so that data cannot be transferred, for example, to a printer. The opposite of ◊on line.

offline browser in computing, program that downloads and copies Web pages onto a computer so that they can be viewed without being connected to the Internet. By taking advantage of off-peak hours, when telephone charges are low and the network responds faster, offline browsers are a thrifty way of using the ◊World Wide Web.

offline editing in video and film, process of editing a scratch copy of the footage rather than the expensively created footage itself. Once the edit has been finalized, the real footage is edited by a machine.

offline reader in computing, program that downloads information from ◊newsgroups, FTP servers or other Internet resources, storing it locally on a hard disc so that it can be read without running up a large telephone bill.

offset printing the most common method of ◊printing, which uses smooth (often rubber) printing plates. It works on the principle of ◊lithography: that grease and water repel one another.

The printing plate is prepared using a photographic technique, resulting in a type image that attracts greasy printing ink. On the printing press the plate is wrapped around a cylinder and wetted and inked in turn. The ink adheres only to the type area, and this image is then transferred via an intermediate blanket cylinder to the paper.

ogive in statistics, the curve on a graph representing ◊cumulative frequency.

ohm SI unit (symbol Ω) of electrical ◊resistance (the property of a conductor that restricts the flow of electrons through it).

It was originally defined with reference to the resistance of a column of mercury, but is now taken as the resistance between two points when a potential difference of one volt between them produces a current of one ampere.

> TO REMEMBER THE ORDER OF OHMIC VALUES IN RESISTORS:
>
> BILLY BROWN RELIES ON YOUR GIN BUT PREFERS GOOD WHISKEY.
>
> BLACK / BROWN / RED / ORANGE / YELLOW / GREEN / BLUE / PURPLE / GREY / WHITE

ohmic heating method of heating used in the food-processing industry, in which an electric current is passed through foodstuffs to sterilize them before packing. The heating effect is similar to that obtained by microwaves in that electrical energy is transformed into heat throughout the whole volume of the food, not just at the surface.

Ohmic heating is suitable for foods containing chunks of meat or fruit. It is an alternative to in-can sterilization and has been used to produce canned foods such as meat chunks, prawns, baked beans, fruit, and vegetables.

Ohm, Georg Simon (1789–1854)

German physicist who studied electricity and discovered the fundamental law that bears his name. The SI unit of electrical resistance, the **ohm**, is named after him, and the unit of conductance (the inverse of resistance) was formerly called the mho, which is 'ohm' spelled backwards.

Mary Evans Picture Library

Ohm's law law that states that the current flowing in a metallic conductor maintained at constant temperature is directly proportional to the potential difference (voltage) between its ends. The law was discovered by German physicist Georg Ohm in 1827.

If a current of I amperes flows between two points in a conductor across which the potential difference is V volts, then V/I is a constant called the ◊resistance R ohms between those two points. Hence:

$$V/I = R \text{ or } V = IR$$

Not all conductors obey Ohm's law; those that do are called **ohmic conductors**.

> TO REMEMBER ONE EXPRESSION OF THIS:
>
> VAMPIRES ARE RARE.
>
> VOLTS = AMPS × RESISTANCE

oil flammable substance, usually insoluble in water, and composed chiefly of carbon and hydrogen. Oils may be solids (fats and waxes) or liquids. The three main types are: **essential oils**, obtained from plants; **fixed oils**, obtained from animals and plants; and **mineral oils**, obtained chiefly from the refining of ◊petroleum.

Essential oils are volatile liquids that have the odour of their plant source and are used in perfumes, flavouring essences, and in ◊aromatherapy. Fixed oils are mixtures of ◊lipids, of varying consistency, found in both animals (for example, fish oils) and plants (in nuts and seeds); they are used as foods and as lubricants, and in the making of soaps, paints, and varnishes. Mineral oils are composed of a mixture of hydrocarbons, and are used as fuels and lubricants.

Eight of the 14 top-earning companies in the USA in 1990 (led by Exxon with $7 billion in sales) were in the global petroleum industry.

oil beetle another name for the ◊blister beetle.

oil, cooking fat that is liquid at room temperature, extracted from the seeds or fruits of certain plants and used for frying, salad dressings, and sauces and condiments such as mayonnaise and mustard. Plants used for cooking oil include sunflower, olive, maize (corn), soya, peanut, and rape. Vegetable oil is a blend of more than one type of oil. Most oils are hot-pressed and refined, a process that leaves them without smell or flavour. Cold-pressed, unrefined oils keep their flavour. Oils are generally low in cholesterol and contain a high proportion of polyunsaturated or monounsaturated fatty acids, although all except soya and corn oil become saturated when heated.

oil crop plant from whose seeds vegetable oils are pressed. Cool temperate areas grow rapeseed and linseed; warm temperate regions produce sunflowers, olives, and soya beans; tropical regions produce groundnuts (peanuts), palm oil, and coconuts.

Some of the major vegetable oils, such as soya bean oil, peanut oil, and cottonseed oil, are derived from crops grown primarily for other purposes. Most vegetable oils are used as both edible oils and as ingredients in industrial products such as soaps, varnishes, printing inks, and paints.

oil palm African ◊palm tree, the fruit of which yields valuable oils, used as food or processed into margarine, soaps, and livestock feeds. (*Elaeis guineensis.*)

oil refinery industrial complex where crude oil is processed into different products. The light volatile parts of the oil form ◊petroleum, while the heavier parts make bitumen and petrochemicals. Oil refineries are often located at deep-water ports or near their industrial markets. They need flat land and water for cooling.

oilseed rape either of two plants; see ◊rape.

oil spill oil released by damage to or discharge from a tanker or oil installation. An oil spill kills all shore life, clogging up the feathers of birds and suffocating other creatures. At sea toxic chemicals leach into the water below, poisoning sea life. Mixed with dust, the oil forms globules that sink to the seabed, poisoning sea life there as well. Oil spills are broken up by the use of detergents but such chemicals can themselves damage wildlife. The annual spillage of oil is 8 million barrels a year. At any given time tankers are carrying 500 million barrels.

In March 1989 the *Exxon Valdez* (belonging to the Exxon Corporation) spilled oil in Alaska's Prince William Sound, covering 12,400 sq km/4,800 sq mi and killing at least 34,400 sea birds, 10,000 sea otters, and up to 16 whales. The incident led to the US Oil Pollution Act of 1990, which requires tankers operating in US waters to have double hulls.

The world's largest oil spill was in the Persian Gulf in 1991 as a direct result of hostilities during the Gulf War. Around 6–8 million barrels of oil were spilled, polluting 675 km/420 mi of Saudi coastline. In some places, the oil was 30 cm/12 in deep in the sand.

In 1994 in the Komi region of N Russia, a broken pipeline leaking into the Pechora River was estimated to have caused one of the biggest oil spills since 1989.

okapi ruminant (cud-chewing) mammal related to the giraffe, although with a much shorter neck and legs, found in the tropical rainforests of central Africa. Its purplish brown body, creamy face, and black and white stripes on the legs and hindquarters provide excellent camouflage. Okapis have remained virtually unchanged for millions of years. (Species *Okapia johnstoni,* family Giraffidae.)

The okapi was unknown to Europeans until 1901; now only a few hundred are thought to survive.

okra plant belonging to the Old World hibiscus family. Its red-and-yellow flowers are followed by long, sticky, green fruits known as **ladies' fingers** or **bhindi**. The fruits are cooked in soups and stews. (*Hibiscus esculentus,* family Malvaceae.)

Olbers' paradox question put forward 1826 by Heinrich Olbers, who asked: If the universe is infinite in extent and filled with stars, why is the sky dark at night? The answer is that the stars do not live infinitely long, so there is not enough starlight to fill the universe. A wrong answer, frequently given, is that the expansion of the universe weakens the starlight.

Old English sheepdog breed of herding dog. It is grey or blue-grey, with white on its head, chest, and legs, and is about 62 cm/24 in at the shoulder. Its long, thick, rough hair grows abundantly over its face. It was formerly used widely in S England by shepherds and drovers, and its tail was traditionally docked to a stump to show that it was a working dog and so exempt from taxation. It is therefore sometimes known as a bobtail.

OLE in computing, abbreviation for ◊object linking and embedding

oleander or *rose bay* evergreen Mediterranean shrub belonging to the dogbane family, with pink or white flowers and aromatic leaves that produce and release the poison oleandrin. (*Nerium oleander,* family Apocynaceae.)

olefin common name for ◊alkene.

Oligocene third epoch of the Tertiary period of geological time, 35.5–3.25 million years ago. The name, from Greek, means 'a little recent', referring to the presence of the remains of some modern types of animals existing at that time.

oligodendrocyte type of glial cell surrounding the neurones in the brain and spinal cord. They produce the insulating ◊myelin sheath surrounding the nerve axon.

oligosaccharide ◊carbohydrate comprising a few ◊monosaccharide units linked together. It is a general term used to indicate that a carbohydrate is larger than a simple di- or trisaccharide but not as large as a polysaccharide.

olive evergreen tree belonging to the olive family. Native to Asia but widely cultivated in Mediterranean and subtropical areas, it grows up to 15 m/50 ft high and has twisted branches and lance-shaped silvery leaves that grow opposite each other. The white flowers are followed by small green oval fruits that turn bluish-black when ripe. They are preserved in brine or oil; dried; or pressed to make olive oil. (*Olea europaea,* family Oleaceae.)

The oil, which is a pale, greenish yellow, is widely consumed; it is also used in soaps and ointments, and as a lubricant.

olivenite basic copper arsenate, $Cu_2AsO_4(OH)$, occurring as a mineral in olive-green prisms.

olivine greenish mineral, magnesium iron silicate, $(Mg,Fe)_2SiO_4$. It is a rock-forming mineral, present in, for example, peridotite, gabbro, and basalt. Olivine is called **peridot** when pale green and transparent, and used in jewellery.

olm cave-dwelling aquatic ◊salamander. Olms are found in underground caves along the Adriatic seaboard in Italy, Croatia, and Yugoslavia. The adult is permanently larval in form, about 25 cm/10 in long, almost blind, with external gills and under-developed limbs. See ◊neoteny. (Species *Proteus anguinus,* family Proteidae.)

The olm is the only European member of its family; the other members are the North American ◊mudpuppies.

The olm can survive for 12 years without eating. It can also withstand subzero temperatures.

omega Ω a symbol for the mass density of the universe. If Ω is less than 1.0 the universe will expand forever; if it is more than 1.0 the gravitational pull of its mass will be strong enough to reverse its expansion and cause its eventual collapse. The value of Ω is estimated as probably being between 0.1 and 1.0.

Omega navigation system long-range radio-based aid to navigation, giving world-wide coverage. There are eight Omega transmitting stations, located in Norway, Liberia, Hawaii, Réunion, Argentina, Australia, USA, and Japan. The very-low-frequency signals from the transmitters are detected by a ship's navigation receiver, and slight differences (phase differences) between the signals indicate the position of the receiver. The system is accurate to within 4 km/2.5 mi during the day and 7 km/4 mi at night. See also ◊Decca navigation system.

omnivore animal that feeds on both plant and animal material. Omnivores have digestive adaptations intermediate between those of ◊herbivores and ◊carnivores, with relatively unspecialized digestive systems and gut microorganisms that can digest a variety of foodstuffs.

OMR abbreviation for optical mark recognition.

onager wild ass found in W Asia. Onagers are sandy brown, lighter underneath, and about the size of a small horse. (Species *Equus hemionus.*)

onchocerciasis or *river blindness* disease found in tropical Africa and Central America. It is transmitted by bloodsucking black flies, which infect the victim with parasitic filarial worms (genus *Onchocerca*), producing skin disorders and intense itching; some invade the eyes and may cause blindness.

It is treated with antiparasitic drugs known as filaricides.

oncogene gene carried by a virus that induces a cell to divide abnormally, giving rise to a cancer. Oncogenes arise from mutations in genes (proto-oncogenes) found in all normal cells. They are usually also found in viruses that are capable of transforming normal cells to tumour cells. Such viruses are able to insert their oncogenes into the host cell's DNA, causing it to divide uncontrollably. More than one oncogene may be necessary to transform a cell in this way.

In 1989 US scientists J Michael Bishop and Harold Varmus were jointly awarded the Nobel Prize for Physiology or Medicine for their concept of oncogenes, although credit for the discovery was claimed by a French cancer specialist, Dominique Stehelin.

oncology medical speciality concerned with the diagnosis and treatment of ◊neoplasms, especially cancer.

ONCOLINK – THE UNIVERSITY OF PENNSYLVANIA CANCER CENTRE RESOURCE

http://cancer.med.upenn.edu/

As the title of this page says, a broad resource of cancer-related information for sufferers and their families. It includes sections on 'causes, screening, and prevention', 'clinical trials', and 'conferences and meetings'.

onco-mouse mouse that has a human ◊oncogene (gene that can cause certain cancers) implanted into its cells by genetic engineering. Such mice are used to test anticancer treatments and were patented within the USA by Harvard University in 1988, thereby protecting its exclusive rights to produce the animal and profit from its research.

onion plant belonging to the lily family, whose bulb has a strong, distinctive smell and taste. Cultivated from ancient times, it may have originated in Asia. The bulb is edible; its pale concentric layers of leaf bases contain an oil that is released into the air when the onion is cut open, causing the eyes to water. Onions are used extensively in cooking. (*Allium cepa,* family Liliaceae.)

The onion is a biennial plant, the common variety producing a bulb in the first season and seeds in the second.

online in computing, connected, so that data can be transferred, for example, to a printer or from a network. The opposite of ◊offline.

Technology ... the knack of so arranging the world that we don't have to experience it.

MAX FRISCH Swiss dramatist.
In D J Boorstin *The Image*

online help in computing, guidance and assistance in using a program which is given by the software itself, instead of a manual or a customer services representative over the telephone.

online service in computing, commercial service like ◊America Online (AOL), ◊Compulink Information eXchange (CIX), or ◊CompuServe, which offers proprietary conferencing and other services to subscribers on top of access to the Internet.

online system in computing, originally a system that allows the computer to work interactively with its users, responding to each instruction as it is given and prompting users for information when necessary. Since almost all the computers used now work this way, 'online system' is now used to refer to large database, electronic mail, and conferencing systems accessed via a dial-up modem. These often have tens or hundreds of users from different places – sometimes from different countries – 'on line' at the same time.

on-site warranty in computing, after-sales service offered free by many hardware manufacturers for a limited period after purchase – usually one year. An on-site warranty entitles purchasers to a visit from an peripatetic engineer in case of problems.

ontogeny process of development of a living organism, including the part of development that takes place after hatching or birth. The idea that 'ontogeny recapitulates phylogeny' (the development of an organism goes through the same stages as its evolutionary history), proposed by the German scientist Ernst Heinrich Haeckel, is now discredited.

Onychophora phylum of invertebrates found in rainforest leaf-litter. See ◊velvet worm.

onyx semiprecious variety of chalcedonic ◊silica (SiO_2) in which the crystals are too fine to be detected under a microscope, a state known as cryptocrystalline. It has straight parallel bands of different colours: milk-white, black, and red.

Sardonyx, an onyx variety, has layers of brown or red carnelian alternating with lighter layers of onyx. It can be carved into cameos.

oocyte in medicine, an immature ovum. Only a fraction of the oocytes produced in the ovary survive until puberty and not all of these undergo meiosis to become an ovum that can be fertilized by a sperm.

oolite limestone made up of tiny spherical carbonate particles, called **ooliths**, cemented together. Ooliths have a concentric structure with a diameter up to 2 mm/0.08 in. They were formed by chemical precipitation and accumulation on ancient sea floors.

The surface texture of oolites is rather like that of fish roe. The late Jurassic limestones of the British Isles are mostly oolitic in nature.

Oort cloud spherical cloud of comets beyond Pluto, extending out to about 100,000 astronomical units (1.5 light years) from the Sun. The gravitational effect of passing stars and the rest of our Galaxy disturbs comets from the cloud so that they fall in towards the Sun on highly elongated orbits, becoming visible from Earth. As many as 10 trillion comets may reside in the Oort cloud, named after Dutch astronomer Jan Oort who postulated it in 1950.

oosphere another name for the female gamete, or ◊ovum, of certain plants such as algae.

ooze sediment of fine texture consisting mainly of organic matter found on the ocean floor at depths greater than 2,000 m/6,600 ft. Several kinds of ooze exist, each named after its constituents.

Siliceous ooze is composed of the ◊silica shells of tiny marine plants (diatoms) and animals (radiolarians). **Calcareous ooze** is formed from the calcite shells of microscopic animals (foraminifera) and floating algae (coccoliths).

opah or ***moonfish*** large marine bony fish. These fish may be up to 2 m/6.6 ft long and weigh approximately 200 kg/440 lb. They are widely distributed in warm seas, and feed on squids, crustaceans, and small fish.

classification Opahs are genus *Lampris*, family Lampridae, order Lampriformes.

opal form of hydrous ◊silica ($SiO_2.nH_2O$), often occurring as stalactites and found in many types of rock. The common opal is translucent, milk-white, yellow, red, blue, or green, and lustrous. Precious opal is opalescent, the characteristic play of colours being caused by close-packed silica spheres diffracting light rays within the stone.

Opal is cryptocrystalline, that is, the crystals are too fine to be detected under an optical microscope. Opals are found in Hungary; New South Wales, Australia (black opals were first discovered there in 1905); and Mexico (red fire opals).

Oparin, Alexandr Ivanovich (1894–1980)

Russian biochemist who in the 1920s developed one of the first of the modern theories about the origin of life on Earth, postulating a primeval soup of biomolecules.

opencast mining or ***open-pit mining*** or ***strip mining*** mining at the surface rather than underground. Coal, iron ore, and phosphates are often extracted by opencast mining. Often the mineral deposit is covered by soil, which must first be stripped off, usually by large machines such as walking draglines and bucket-wheel excavators. The ore deposit is then broken up by explosives.

One of the largest excavations in the world has been made by opencast mining at the Bingham Canyon copper mine in Utah, USA, measuring 790 m/2,590 ft deep and 3.7 km/2.3 mi across.

open cluster or ***galactic cluster*** in astronomy, a loose cluster of young stars. More than 1,200 open clusters have been catalogued, each containing between a dozen and several thousand stars. They are of interest to astronomers because they represent samples of stars that have been formed at the same time from similar material. Examples include the ◊Pleiades and the ◊Hyades. See also ◊globular cluster and ◊star cluster.

Open Group in computing, multivendor industry body formed in February 1996 through the merger of X/Open and the ◊Open Software Foundation. One of its functions is to test and brand with an X mark products that conform to open systems standards.

open-hearth furnace method of steelmaking, now largely superseded by the ◊basic–oxygen process. It was developed in 1864 in England by German-born William and Friedrich Siemens, and improved by Pierre and Emile Martin in France in the same year. In the furnace, which has a wide, saucer-shaped hearth and a low roof, molten pig iron and scrap are packed into the shallow hearth and heated by overhead gas burners using preheated air.

Open Software Foundation (OSF) in computing, software house created in 1988 by several major industry players (including Bull, DEC, Hewlett-Packard, IBM and Philips) to engineer a standard operating system and user interface for the ◊UNIX platform. The OSF joined with ◊X/Open to form The Open Group 1996.

open systems systems that conform to ◊Open Systems Interconnection or ◊POSIX standards. ◊UNIX was the original basis of open systems and most non-proprietary open systems still use this ◊operating system.

The term is also used more loosely to describe any system that can communicate with other systems and to describe other standards, such as ◊MS-DOS and ◊Windows. Open systems were developed partly to make better communication possible, but also to reduce users' dependence on (and lock-in to) suppliers of proprietary systems.

To remember the seven layers of the OSI Reference Model for computer networking:

Active penguins seek the nearest deep pool

Application, presentation, session, transport, network, data-link, physical

Open Systems Interconnection (OSI) in computing, ◊International Standards Organization standard, defining seven layers of communication protocols. Although OSI is an international standard, existing protocols, such as ◊TCP/IP and IBM's ◊Systems Network Architecture are more commonly used in commercial systems.

operating system (OS) in computing, a program that controls the basic operation of a computer. A typical OS controls the peripheral devices such as printers, organizes the filing system, provides a means of communicating with the operator, and runs other programs.

Many operating systems were written to run on specific computers, but some are available from third-party software houses and will run on machines from a variety of manufacturers. Examples include Microware's OS/9, Microsoft's MS-DOS and UNIX.

UNIX (developed at AT&T's Bell Laboratories) is the standard on workstations, minicomputers, and supercomputers; it is also used on desktop PCs and mainframes.

operational amplifier or ***op-amp*** electronic circuit that is used as a basic building block in electronic design. Operational amplifiers are used in a wide range of electronic measuring instruments. The name arose because they were originally designed to carry out mathematical operations and solve equations.

The voltage **gain** of an inverting operational amplifier is equal to the ratio of the resistance of the feedback resistor to the resistance of the input resistor.

operculum The thick calcareous plate that forms the operculum is clearly visible in this picture of a land winkle Pomatias elegans. *Premaphotos Wildlife*

operculum small cap covering the spore-producing body of many mosses. It is pushed aside when the spores are mature and ready to be ejected.

operon group of genes that are found next to each other on a chromosome, and are turned on and off as an integrated unit. They usually produce enzymes that control different steps in the same biochemical pathway. Operons were discovered in 1961 (by the French biochemists François Jacob and Jacques Monod) in bacteria.

They are less common in higher organisms where the control of metabolism is a more complex process.

Ophiuchus large constellation along the celestial equator (see ◊celestial sphere), known as the serpent bearer because the constellation ◊Serpens is wrapped around it. The Sun passes through Ophiuchus each December, but the constellation is not part of the zodiac. Ophiuchus contains ◊Barnard's star.

ophthalmia neonatorum form of ◊conjunctivitis mostly contracted during delivery by an infant whose mother is infected with ◊gonorrhoea. It can lead to blindness unless promptly treated.

ophthalmology medical speciality concerned with diseases of the eye and its surrounding tissues.

opiate, endogenous naturally produced chemical in the body that has effects similar to morphine and other opiate drugs; a type of neurotransmitter.

Examples include ◊endorphins and ◊encephalins.

opium drug extracted from the unripe seeds of the opium poppy (*Papaver somniferum*) of SW Asia. An addictive ◊narcotic, it contains several alkaloids, including **morphine**, one of the most powerful natural painkillers and addictive narcotics known, and **codeine**, a milder painkiller.

Heroin is a synthetic derivative of morphine and even more powerful as a drug. Opium is still sometimes given as a tincture, dissolved in alcohol and known as **laudanum**. Opium also contains the highly poisonous alkaloid **thebaine**.

opossum any of a family of marsupials (mammals that carry their young in a pouch) native to North and South America. Most opossums are tree-living, nocturnal animals, with prehensile tails that can be used as an additional limb, and hands and feet well adapted for grasping. They range from 10 cm/4 in to 50 cm/20 in in length and are insectivorous, carnivorous, or, more commonly, omnivorous. (Family Didelphidae.)

The name is also popularly applied to some of the similar-looking phalangers found in Australia.

opposition in astronomy, the moment at which a body in the Solar System lies opposite the Sun in the sky as seen from the Earth and crosses the ◊meridian at about midnight.

Although the ◊inferior planets cannot come to opposition, it is the best time for observation of the superior planets as they can then be seen all night.

optical aberration see ◊aberration, optical.

optical activity in chemistry, the ability of certain crystals, liquids, and solutions to rotate the plane of ◊polarized light as it passes through them. The phenomenon is related to the three-dimensional arrangement of the atoms making up the molecules concerned. Only substances that lack any form of structural symmetry exhibit optical activity.

optical character recognition (OCR) in computing, a technique for inputting text to a computer by means of a document reader. First, a ◊scanner produces a digital image of the text; then character-recognition software makes use of stored knowledge about the shapes of individual characters to convert the digital image to a set of internal codes that can be stored and processed by computer.

Oppenheimer, J(ulius) Robert (1904–1967)

US physicist. As director of the Los Alamos Science Laboratory 1943–45, he was in charge of the development of the atom bomb (the Manhattan Project). When later he realized the dangers of radioactivity, he objected to the development of the hydrogen bomb, and was alleged to be a security risk in 1953 by the US Atomic Energy Commission (AEC).

Investigating the equations describing the energy states of the atom, Oppenheimer showed in 1930 that a positively charged particle with the mass of an electron could exist. This particle was detected in 1932 and called the positron.

Sachem

OCR originally required specially designed characters but current devices can recognize most standard typefaces and even handwriting. OCR is used, for example, by gas and electricity companies to input data collected on meter-reading cards, and by ◊personal digital assistants to recognize users' handwriting.

optical computer computer in which both light and electrical signals are used in the ◊central processing unit. The technology is still not fully developed, but such a computer promises to be faster and less vulnerable to outside electrical interference than one that relies solely on electricity.

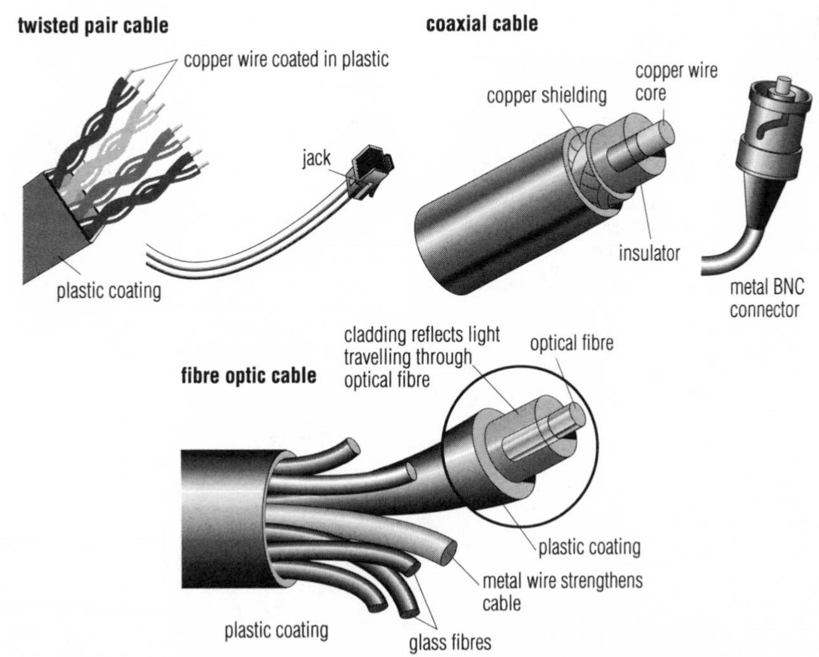

optical fibre *The major differences in construction between twisted pair (telephone), coaxial (Ethernet), and fibre optic cable.*

optical disc in computing, a storage medium in which laser technology is used to record and read large volumes of digital data. Types include ◊CD-ROM, ◊WORM, and erasable optical disc.

optical emission spectrometry another term for emission spectroscopy.

optical fibre very fine, optically pure glass fibre through which light can be reflected to transmit images or data from one end to the other. Although expensive to produce and install, optical fibres can carry more data than traditional cables, and are less susceptible to interference. Standard optical fibre transmitters can send up to 10 billion bits of information per second by switching a laser beam on and off.

Optical fibres are increasingly being used to replace metal communications cables, the messages being encoded as digital pulses of light rather than as fluctuating electric current. Current research is investigating how optical fibres could replace wiring inside computers.

Bundles of optical fibres are also used in endoscopes to inspect otherwise inaccessible parts of machines or of the living body (see ◊endoscopy). *See illustration on page 539.*

optical illusion scene or picture that fools the eye. An example of a natural optical illusion is that the Moon appears bigger when it is on the horizon than when it is high in the sky, owing to the ◊refraction of light rays by the Earth's atmosphere.

optical instrument instrument that makes use of one or more lenses or mirrors, or of a combination of these, in order to change the path of light rays and produce an image. Optical instruments such as magnifying glasses, ◊microscopes, and ◊telescopes are used to provide a clear, magnified image of the very small or the very distant. Others, such as ◊cameras, photographic enlargers, and film ◊projectors, may be used to store or reproduce images.

optical mark recognition (OMR) in computing, a technique that enables marks made in predetermined positions on computer-input forms to be detected optically and input to a computer. An **optical mark reader** shines a light beam onto the input document and is able to detect the marks because less light is reflected back from them than from the paler, unmarked paper.

optic nerve large nerve passing from the eye to the brain, carrying visual information. In mammals, it may contain up to a million nerve fibres, connecting the sensory cells of the retina to the optical centres in the brain. Embryologically, the optic nerve develops as an outgrowth of the brain.

optics branch of physics that deals with the study of ◊light and vision – for example, shadows and mirror images, lenses, microscopes, telescopes, and cameras. For all practical purposes light rays travel in straight lines, although Albert ◊Einstein demonstrated that they may be 'bent' by a gravitational field. On striking a surface they are reflected or refracted with some absorption of energy, and the study of this is known as geometrical optics.

optoelectronics branch of electronics concerned with the development of devices (based on the ◊semiconductor gallium arsenide) that respond not only to the ◊electrons of electronic data transmission, but also to ◊photons.

In 1989, scientists at IBM in the USA built a gallium arsenide microprocessor ('chip') containing 8,000 transistors and four photodetectors. The densest optoelectronic chip yet produced, this can detect and process data at a speed of 1 billion bits per second.

opuntia any ◊cactus belonging to the same group of plants as the ◊prickly pear. They all have showy flowers and fleshy, jointed stems. (Genus *Opuntia,* family Cactaceae.)

orange round orange-coloured juicy citrus fruit of several species of evergreen trees, which bear white blossom and fruits at the same time. Thought to have originated in SE Asia, orange trees are commercially cultivated in Spain, Israel, the USA, Brazil, South Africa, and elsewhere. The sweet orange (*C. sinensis*) is the one commonly eaten fresh; the Jaffa, blood, and navel orange are varieties of this species. (Genus *Citrus,* family Rutaceae.)

Tangerines and mandarins belong to a related species (*C. reticulata*). The sour or Seville orange (*C. aurantium*) is the bitter orange used in making marmalade. Oranges yield several essential oils.

orang-utan large ape found only in Borneo and Sumatra. Up to 1.65 m/5.5 ft in height, it is covered with long, red-brown hair and lives a largely solitary life in the trees, feeding mainly on fruit. Now an endangered species, it is officially protected because its habitat is being systematically destroyed by ◊deforestation. Less than 30,000 animals remain. (Species *Pongo pygmaeus.*)

There are two subspecies: *P. p. pygmaeus* found in Borneo, and the smaller *P. p. abelli* on the island of Sumatra. Their rate of reproduction is very slow, with an eight-year gap between births. Orang-utans are slow-moving and have been hunted for food, as well as by animal collectors. The name means 'man of the forest'.

ORANG-UTAN – QUINTESSENTIAL FOREST DWELLER

http://www.lpzoo.com/ark/orang_article.html

Well-written profile of the orang-utan. Among the interesting facts in this account of the behaviour, diet, and social life of the orang-utan is that they eat some 400 different kinds of food and that they are not solitary browsers but need to know that the company of other orang-utans is available. There is a picture, a map of the orang-utan's range, and even a bibliography.
services and legal assistance.

orbit path of one body in space around another, such as the orbit of Earth around the Sun, or the Moon around Earth. When the two bodies are similar in mass, as in a ◊binary star, both bodies move around their common centre of mass. The movement of objects in orbit follows Johann ◊Kepler's laws, which apply to artificial satellites as well as to natural bodies.

As stated by the laws, the orbit of one body around another is an ellipse. The ellipse can be highly elongated, as are comet orbits around the Sun, or it may be almost circular, as are those of some planets. The closest point of a planet's orbit to the Sun is called **perihelion**; the most distant point is **aphelion**. (For a body orbiting the Earth, the closest and furthest points of the orbit are called **perigee** and **apogee**.)

orbital, atomic region around the nucleus of an atom (or, in a molecule, around several nuclei) in which an electron is likely to be found. According to ◊quantum theory, the position of an ◊electron is uncertain; it may be found at any point. However, it is more likely to be found in some places than in others, and it is these that make up the orbital.

An atom or molecule has numerous orbitals, each of which has a fixed size and shape. An orbital is characterized by three numbers, called ◊quantum numbers, representing its energy (and hence size), its angular momentum (and hence shape), and its orientation. Each orbital can be occupied by one or (if their spins are aligned in opposite directions) two electrons.

TO REMEMBER THE ORDER OF ATOMIC ORBITALS:

SPIN PAIRS DON'T FORM - GO HIGHER.

THE PAULI SELECTION RULE STATES THAT TWO ELECTRONS OF LIKE SPIN MAY NOT BE PRESENT IN ANY ORBITAL IF THEY HAVE THE SAME SET OF QUANTUM NUMBERS. SINCE THE ELECTRONIC ORBITALS IN ATOMS ARE LISTED BY THE LETTERS S, P, D, F, G, H, IN ORDER OF ASCENDING ENERGY, THIS MNEMONIC ACTS AS A USEFUL REMINDER.

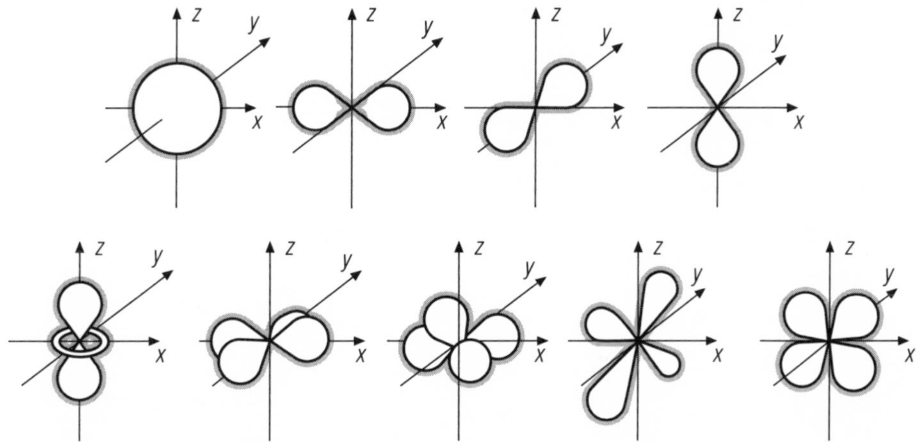

orbital *The shapes of atomic orbitals. An atomic orbital is a picture of the 'electron cloud' that surrounds the nucleus of an atom. There are four basic shapes for atomic orbitals: spherical, dumbbell, clover-leaf, and complex (shown at bottom left).*

orca another name for ◊killer whale.

orchid any plant of a large family that contains at least 15,000 species and 700 genera, distributed throughout the world except in the coldest areas, and most numerous in damp equatorial regions. The flowers are the most highly evolved of the plant kingdom; they have three ◊sepals and three petals and sometimes grow singly, but more usually appear with other flowers on spikes, growing up one side of the main stem, or all around the main stem, which may be upright or drooping. (Family Orchidaceae.)

order in biological classification, a group of related ◊families. For example, the horse, rhinoceros, and tapir families are grouped in the order Perissodactyla, the odd-toed ungulates, because they all have either one or three toes on each foot. The names of orders are not shown in italic (unlike genus and species names) and by convention they have the ending '-formes' in birds and fish; '-a' in mammals, amphibians, reptiles, and other animals; and '-ales' in fungi and plants. Related orders are grouped together in a ◊class.

ORCHID

The flowers of bee orchids resemble female bees so completely that they have the same shape, the same smell, and even the same degree of hairiness.

ordered pair in mathematics, any pair of numbers whose order makes a difference to their meaning. Coordinates are an ordered pair because the point (2,3) is not the same as the point (3,2). Vulgar fractions are ordered pairs because the top number gives the quantity of parts while the bottom gives the number of parts into which the unit has been divided.

ordinal number in mathematics, one of the series first, second, third, fourth, ... Ordinal numbers relate to order, whereas ◊cardinal numbers (1, 2, 3, 4, ...) relate to quantity, or count.

ordinate in coordinate geometry, the y ◊coordinate of a point; that is, the vertical distance of the point from the horizontal or x -axis. For example, a point with the coordinates (3,4) has an ordinate of 4. See ◊abscissa.

Ordnance Survey (OS) official body responsible for the mapping of Britain. It was established 1791 as the **Trigonometrical Survey** to continue work initiated in 1784 by Scottish military surveyor General William Roy (1726–1790). Its first accurate maps appeared in 1830, drawn to a scale of 1 in to the mile (1:63,000). In 1858 the OS settled on a scale of 1:2,500 for the mapping of Great Britain and Ireland (higher for urban areas, lower for uncultivated areas).

Subsequent revisions and editions include the 1:50,000 Landranger series of 1971–86. In 1989, the OS began using a computerized system for the creation and continuous revision of maps. Customers can now have maps drafted to their own specifications, choosing from over 50 features (such as houses, roads, and vegetation). Since 1988 the OS has had a target imposed by the government to recover all its costs from sales.

ORCHID HOUSE

http://sciserv2.uwaterloo.ca/orchids.html

Everything you could ever want to know about orchids can be found here. There is a very good introductory 'frequently asked questions' section, as well as information for the more experienced horticulturist. There is even an orchid-related short story and some pictures of orchids accompanied by soothing music.

Ordovician period of geological time 510–439 million years ago; the second period of the ◊Palaeozoic era. Animal life was confined to the sea: reef-building algae and the first jawless fish are characteristic.

The period is named after the Ordovices, an ancient Welsh people, because the system of rocks formed in the Ordovician period was first studied in Wales.

ore body of rock, a vein within it, or a deposit of sediment, worth mining for the economically valuable mineral it contains. The term is usually applied to sources of metals. Occasionally metals are found uncombined (native metals), but more often they occur as compounds such as carbonates, sulphides, or oxides. The ores often contain unwanted impurities that must be removed when the metal is extracted.

Commercially valuable ores include bauxite (aluminium oxide, Al_2O_3) hematite (iron(III) oxide, Fe_2O_3), zinc blende (zinc sulphide, ZnS), and rutile (titanium dioxide, TiO_2).

Hydrothermal ore deposits are formed from fluids such as saline water passing through fissures in the host rock at an elevated temperature. Examples are the 'porphyry copper' deposits of Chile and Bolivia, the submarine copper–zinc–iron sulphide deposits recently discovered on the East Pacific Rise, and the limestone lead–zinc deposits that occur in the southern USA and in the Pennines of Britain.

Other ores are concentrated by igneous processes, causing the ore metals to become segregated from a magma – for example, the chromite and platinum-metal-rich bands within the Bushveld, South Africa. Erosion and transportation in rivers of material from an existing rock source can lead to further concentration of heavy minerals in a deposit – for example, Malaysian tin deposits.

Weathering of rocks in situ can result in residual metal-rich soils, such as the nickel-bearing laterites of New Caledonia.

oregano any of several perennial herbs belonging to the mint family, especially the aromatic *O. vulgare*, also known as wild marjoram. It is native to the Mediterranean countries and W Asia and naturalized in the Americas. Oregano is extensively used to season Mediterranean cooking. (Genus *Origanum*, family Labiatae.)

orfe freshwater fish belonging to the carp family. It grows up to 50 cm/1.7 ft in length, and feeds on small aquatic animals. The species is generally greyish-black, but an ornamental variety is orange. It lives in rivers and lakes of Europe and NW Asia. (Species *Leuciscus idus*, family Cyprinidae.)

organ in biology, part of a living body, such as the liver or brain, that has a distinctive function or set of functions.

> *Man is a mind betrayed, not served, by his organs.*
>
> EDMOND AND JULES DE GONCOURT French writers. *The Goncourt Journals* 30 July 1861

organelle discrete and specialized structure in a living cell; organelles include mitochondria, chloroplasts, lysosomes, ribosomes, and the nucleus.

> *Organic chemistry just now is enough to drive one mad. It gives one the impression of a primeval, tropical forest full of the most remarkable things, a monstrous and boundless thicket, with no way of escape, into which one may well dread to enter.*
>
> FRIEDRICH WÖHLER German chemist. Letter to Berzelius 28 Jan 1835

organic chemistry branch of chemistry that deals with carbon compounds. Organic compounds form the chemical basis of life and are more abundant than inorganic compounds. In a typical organic compound, each carbon atom forms bonds covalently with each of its neighbouring carbon atoms in a chain or ring, and additionally with other atoms, commonly hydrogen, oxygen, nitrogen, or sulphur.

The basis of organic chemistry is the ability of carbon to form long chains of atoms, branching chains, rings, and other complex structures. Compounds containing only carbon and hydrogen are known as **hydrocarbons**.

> TO REMEMBER THE PREFIXES FOR NAMING CARBON CHAINS:
>
> MET ETHEL PROPERLY BUT MY PANTS HAD HOLES
>
> METH, ETH, PROP, BUT, PENT, HEX, HEPT (METHANE CAN ALSO BE REMEMBERED BY ME - ONE PERSON)

Formula	*Name*	*Atomic bonding*
CH_3	methyl	H–C(H)(H)–
CH_2CH_3	ethyl	–C(H)(H)–C(H)(H)–H
CC	double bond	>C=C<
CHO	aldehyde	–C(H)=O
CH_2OH	alcohol	–C(H)(H)–OH
CO	ketone	>C=O
COOH	acid	–C(=O)OH
CH_2NH_2	amine	–C(H)(H)–N(H)(H)
C_6H_6	benzene ring	H–C ring of six C atoms, each bonded to H

organic chemistry Common organic-molecule groupings. Organic chemistry is the study of carbon compounds, which make up over 90% of all chemical compounds. This diversity arises because carbon atoms can combine in many different ways with other atoms, forming a wide variety of loops and chains.

organic compound in chemistry, a class of compounds that contain carbon. The original distinction between organic and inorganic compounds was based on the belief that the molecules of living systems were unique, and could not be synthesized in the laboratory. Today it is routine to manufacture thousands of organic chemicals both in research and in the drug industry. Certain simple compounds of carbon, such as carbonates, oxides of carbon, carbon disulphide, and carbides are usually treated in inorganic chemistry.

organic farming farming without the use of synthetic fertilizers (such as ◊nitrates and phosphates) or ◊pesticides (herbicides, insecticides, and fungicides) or other agrochemicals (such as hormones, growth stimulants, or fruit regulators). Food produced by genetic engineering cannot be described as organic.

In place of artificial fertilizers, compost, manure, seaweed, or other substances derived from living things are used (hence the name 'organic'). Growing a crop of a nitrogen-fixing plant such as lucerne, then ploughing it back into the soil, also fertilizes the ground. Some organic farmers use naturally occurring chemicals such as nicotine or pyrethrum to kill pests, but control by non-chemical methods is preferred. Those methods include removal by hand, intercropping (planting with companion plants which deter pests), mechanical barriers to infestation, crop rotation, better cultivation methods, and ◊biological control. Weeds can be controlled by hoeing, mulching (covering with manure, straw, or black plastic), or burning off. Organic farming methods produce food with minimal pesticide residues and greatly reduce pollution of the environment. They are more labour intensive, and therefore more expensive, but use less fossil fuel. Soil structure is greatly improved by organic methods, and recent studies show that a conventional farm can lose four times as much soil through erosion as an organic farm, although the loss may not be immediately obvious.

organizer in embryology, a part of the embryo that causes changes to occur in another part, through ◊induction, thus 'organizing' development and ◊differentiation.

OR gate in electronics, a type of ◊logic gate.

origin in mathematics, the point where the x axis meets the y axis. The coordinates of the origin are (0,0).

original equipment manufacturer (OEM) in computing, company that manufactures equipment or, illogically, has equipment manufacturered for it by another company. The abbreviation is often used as a verb, as in: 'IBM OEMs PCs from Acer' (in other words, Acer makes PCs with IBM badges for IBM to sell).

orimulsion fuel made by mixing ◊bitumen and water that can be burnt in the same way as heavy oil. It is cheap to make but the smoke produced has a high sulphur content.

oriole any of several brightly coloured songbirds belonging to two families: New World orioles belong to the family Icteridae, and Old World orioles are members of the family Oriolidae. They eat insects, seeds, and fruit.

Orion in astronomy, a very prominent constellation in the equatorial region of the sky (see ◊celestial sphere), identified with the hunter of Greek mythology.

The bright stars Alpha (◊Betelgeuse), Gamma (Bellatrix), Beta (◊Rigel), and Kappa Orionis mark the shoulders and legs of Orion. Between them the belt is formed by Delta, Epsilon, and Zeta, three second-magnitude stars equally spaced in a straight line. Beneath the belt is a line of fainter stars marking Orion's sword. One of these, Theta, is not really a star but the brightest part of the ◊Orion nebula. Nearby is one of the most distinctive dark nebulae, the Horsehead.

Orion nebula luminous cloud of gas and dust 1,500 light years away, in the constellation Orion, from which stars are forming. It is about 15 light years in diameter, and contains enough gas to make a cluster of thousands of stars.

At the nebula's centre is a group of hot young stars, called the **Trapezium**, which make the surrounding gas glow. The nebula is visible to the naked eye as a misty patch below the belt of Orion.

ormolu *French or moulu 'ground gold'* alloy of copper, zinc, and sometimes tin, used for furniture decoration.

ornithology study of birds. It covers scientific aspects relating to their structure and classification, and their habits, song, flight, and value to agriculture as destroyers of insect pests. Worldwide scientific banding (or the fitting of coded rings to captured specimens) has resulted in accurate information on bird movements and distribution. There is an International Council for Bird Preservation with its headquarters at the Natural History Museum, London.

ornithophily ◊pollination of flowers by birds. Ornithophilous flowers are typically brightly coloured, often red or orange. They produce large quantities of thin, watery nectar, and are scentless because most birds do not respond well to smell. They are found mostly in tropical areas, with hummingbirds being important pollinators in North and South America, and the sunbirds in Africa and Asia.

orogeny or *orogenesis* the formation of mountains. It is brought about by the movements of the rigid plates making up the Earth's crust and upper-most mantle (described by ◊plate tectonics). Where two plates collide at a destructive margin rocks become folded and lifted to form chains of mountains (such as the Himalayas).

Processes associated with orogeny are faulting and thrusting (see ◊fault), folding, metamorphism, and plutonism (see ◊plutonic rock). However, many topographical features of mountains – cirques, u-shaped valleys – are the result of *non-orogenic* processes, such as weathering, erosion, and glaciation. ◊Isostasy (uplift due to the buoyancy of the Earth's crust) can also influence mountain physiography.

orrery mechanical device for demonstrating the motions of the heavenly bodies. Invented about 1710 by George Graham, it was named after his patron, the 4th Earl of Orrery. It is the forerunner of the planetarium.

orris root underground stem of a species of ◊iris grown in S Europe. It is violet-scented and is used in perfumery and herbal medicine.

orthochromatic photographic film or paper of decreased sensitivity, which can be processed with a red safelight. Using it, blue objects appear lighter and red ones darker because of increased blue sensitivity.

orthodontics branch of ◊dentistry concerned with ◊dentition, and with treatment of any irregularities, such as correction of malocclusion (faulty position of teeth).

orthopaedics Greek *orthos 'straight'; pais 'child'* medical speciality concerned with the correction of disease or damage in bones and joints.

The first orthopaedic hospital was founded 1780 at Orbe in Switzerland by Jean Venel. The first in England was founded 1817.

ortolan songbird belonging to the bunting family, common in Europe and W Asia, migrating to Africa in the winter. It is about 15 cm/6 in long and reddish-brown with black streaks on top, pinkish-buff below, and has an olive-green head and chest and a yellow throat; the female is paler with small dark streaks on the chest. The nest is built in the undergrowth, on the ground, or on banks. Long considered a delicacy among gourmets, it has become rare and is now a protected species. (Species *Emberiza hortulana*, family Emberizidae, order Passeriformes.)

oryx any of a group of large antelopes native to Africa and Asia. The **Arabian oryx** (*O. leucoryx*), at one time extinct in the wild, has been successfully reintroduced into its natural habitat using stocks bred in captivity. (Genus *Oryx*, family Bovidae.)

In 1997 the oryx reintroduction project was threatened because of poaching. The population was reduced to 370 compared with 410 in 1996.

The **scimitar-horned oryx** (*O. tao*) of the Sahara is also rare. The **Beisa oryx** (*O. beisa*) in E Africa and **gemsbok** (*O. gazella*) in the Kalahari are more common. In profile the two long horns appear as one, which may have given rise to the legend of the unicorn.

OS/2 single-user computer ◊operating system produced jointly by Microsoft Corporation and IBM for use on personal computers, particularly when attached to large IBM computers. Its main features were reliability – useful for running file servers – and a powerful object-oriented graphical user interface, Workplace Shell.

OS/2 was announced in 1987 but sales were dismal. Microsoft abandoned it in1992 to concentrate on Windows. IBM abandoned attempts to sell it on the mass market 1997, but supports its use as a corporate and network computer operating system.

oscillating universe in astronomy, a theory that states that the gravitational attraction of the mass within the universe will eventually slow down and stop the expansion of the universe. The outward motions of the galaxies will then be reversed, eventually resulting in a 'Big Crunch' where all the matter in the universe would be contracted into a small volume of high density. This could undergo a further ◊Big Bang, thereby creating another expansion phase. The theory suggests that the universe would alternately expand and collapse through alternate Big Bangs and Big Crunches.

oscillation one complete to-and-fro movement of a vibrating object or system. For any particular vibration, the time for one oscillation is called its ◊period and the number of oscillations in one second is called its ◊frequency. The maximum displacement of the vibrating object from its rest position is called the amplitude of the oscillation.

oscillator any device producing a desired oscillation (vibration). There are many types of oscillator for different purposes, involving various arrangements of thermionic ◊valves or components such as ◊transistors, inductors, capacitors, and ◊resistors.

An oscillator is an essential part of a radio transmitter, generating the high-frequency carrier signal necessary for radio communication. The ◊frequency is often controlled by the vibrations set up in a crystal (such as quartz).

oscillograph instrument for displaying or recording rapidly changing oscillations, electrical or mechanical.

oscilloscope or ***cathode-ray oscilloscope*** (CRO) instrument used to measure electrical voltages that vary over time and to display the waveforms of electrical oscillations or signals, by means of the deflection of a beam of ◊electrons. Readings are displayed graphically on the screen of a ◊cathode-ray tube.

OSI abbreviation for ◊Open ◊Systems ◊Interconnection.

osier any of several willow trees and shrubs, cultivated for their supple branches which are used in basket making; in particular, *S. viminalis.* (Genus *Salix.*)

osmium Greek *osme* ***'odour'*** hard, heavy, bluish-white, metallic element, symbol Os, atomic number 76, relative atomic mass 190.2. It is the densest of the elements, and is resistant to tarnish and corrosion. It occurs in platinum ores and as a free metal (see ◊native metal) with iridium in a natural alloy called osmiridium, containing traces of platinum, ruthenium, and rhodium. Its uses include pen points and light-bulb filaments; like platinum, it is a useful catalyst.

It was discovered in 1803 and named in 1804 by English chemist Smithson Tennant (1761–1815) after the irritating smell of one of its oxides.

osmoregulation process whereby the water content of living organisms is maintained at a constant level. If the water balance is disrupted, the concentration of salts will be too high or too low, and vital functions, such as nerve conduction, will be adversely affected.

In mammals, loss of water by evaporation is counteracted by increased intake and by mechanisms in the kidneys that enhance the rate at which water is resorbed before urine production. Both these responses are mediated by hormones, primarily those of the adrenal cortex (see ◊adrenal gland).

osmosis movement of solvent (usually water) through a semipermeable membrane separating solutions of different concentrations. The solvent passes from a less concentrated solution to a more concentrated solution until the two concentrations are equal. Applying external pressure to the solution on the more concentrated side arrests osmosis, and is a measure of the osmotic pressure of the solution.

Many cell membranes behave as semipermeable membranes, and osmosis is a vital mechanism in the transport of fluids in living organisms – for example, in the transport of water from the roots up the stems of plants.

osprey bird of prey, sometimes called 'fish hawk' because it plunges feet first into the water to catch fish. It is dark brown above and a striking white below, and measures 60 cm/2 ft with a 2 m/6 ft wingspan. The nest is often built in trees near the seashore or lakeside, and two or three white eggs, blotched with crimson, are laid. Ospreys occur on all continents except Antarctica and have faced extinction in several areas. (Species *Pandion haliaetus,* family Pandionidae, order Falconiformes.)

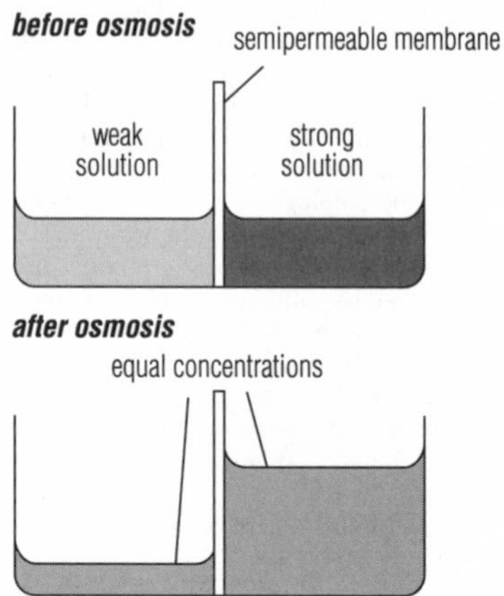

osmosis *Apparatus for measuring osmotic pressure. In 1877 German physicist Wilhelm Pfeffer used this apparatus to make the first ever measurement of osmotic pressure and show that osmotic pressure varies according to temperature and the strength of the solute (dissolved substance).*

ossification or ***osteogenesis*** process whereby bone is formed in vertebrate animals by special cells (**osteoblasts**) that secrete layers of ◊extracellular matrix on the surface of the existing ◊cartilage. Conversion to bone occurs through the deposition of calcium phosphate crystals within the matrix.

osteology part of the science of ◊anatomy, dealing with the structure, function, and development of bones.

osteomyelitis infection of bone, with spread of pus along the marrow cavity.

Now quite rare, it may follow from a compound fracture (where broken bone protrudes through the skin), or from infectious disease elsewhere in the body. It is more common in children whose bones are not yet fully grown.

The symptoms are high fever, severe illness, and pain over the limb. If the infection is at the surface of the bone it may quickly form an abscess; if it is deep in the bone marrow it may spread into the circulation and lead to blood poisoning. Most cases can be treated with immobilization, antibiotics, and surgical drainage.

osteopathy system of alternative medical practice that relies on physical manipulation to treat mechanical stress. It was developed over a century ago by US physician Andrew Taylor Still, who maintained that most ailments can be prevented or cured by techniques of spinal manipulation.

Osteopaths are generally consulted to treat problems of the musculo-skeletal structure such as back pain, and many doctors refer

OSTEOPATHIC HOME PAGE

http://www.concentric.net/~Ericdo/

Well-organized site dedicated to increasing public understanding of osteopathy. The theory behind the osteopaths' belief in the body's innate healing power and some of the healing techniques are fully explained. There is also an account of the origins and development of osteopathy and a selection of case histories attest to its success.

patients to them for such treatments. Although in the UK the wider applicability of their skills is not generally recognized, osteopathic doctors in the USA are also fully licensed to practice conventional medicine.

osteoporosis disease in which the bone substance becomes porous and brittle. It is common in older people, affecting more women than men. It may be treated with calcium supplements and etidronate. Approximately 1.7 million people worldwide, mostly women, suffer hip fractures, mainly due to osteoporosis. A single gene was discovered in 1993 to have a major influence on bone thinning.

Osteoporosis may occur in women whose ovaries have been removed, unless hormone-replacement therapy (HRT) is instituted; it may also occur in Cushing's syndrome and as a side effect of long-term treatment with ◊corticosteroids. Early menopause in women, childlessness, small body build, lack of exercise, heavy drinking, smoking, and hereditary factors may be contributory factors.

ostrich large flightless bird. There is only one species, found in Africa. The male may be about 2.5 m/8 ft tall and weigh 135 kg/300 lb, and is the largest living bird. It has exceptionally strong legs and feet (two-toed) that enable it to run at high speed, and are also used in defence. It lives in family groups of one cock with several hens, each of which lays about 14 eggs. (Species *Struthio camelus,* order Struthioniformes.)

The adult male's body is covered with black feathers, the plumes of the wings and tail being white; females and young males have grey feathers. The bill is wide and flat, the small head has large eyes, and the long neck has a sparse covering of downy feathers. The male incubates the eggs at night, but the female may sit on them during the day. Their eggs are the smallest in relation to the adult's body size of any bird. Ostriches eat mainly plant material and they can survive for a long time without water.

otitis inflammation of the ear. *Otitis externa,* occurring in the outer ear canal, is easily treated with antibiotics. Inflamed conditions of the middle ear (*otitis media*) or inner ear (*otitis interna*) are more serious, carrying the risk of deafness and infection of the brain. Treatment is with antibiotics or, more rarely, surgery.

otolith or ***ear stone*** tiny calcareous deposit found in the ears of fishes, which are in contact with the sensory cushions supplied by the acoustic nerves. Their function is as an organ of balance.

otosclerosis overgrowth of bone in the middle ear causing progressive deafness. This inherited condition is gradual in onset, developing usually before middle age. It is twice as common in women as in men.

The middle ear cavity houses the sound-conduction mechanism called the ossicular chain, consisting of three tiny bones (ossicles) that magnify vibrations received at the eardrum for onward transmission to the inner ear. In otosclerosis, extraneous growth of spongy bone immobilizes the chain, preventing the conduction of sound. Surgery is necessary to remove the diseased bone and reconstruct the ossicular chain.

otter any of various aquatic carnivores belonging to the weasel family, found on all continents except Australia. Otters have thick brown fur, short limbs, webbed toes, and long, compressed tails. They are social, playful, and agile.

otterhound breed of large dog developed during the Middle Ages from various French and British hound breeds to hunt otters. It is an excellent swimmer and has a rough, dense coat, longer than that of most hounds but in a similar range of colours. It grows to about 65 cm/26 in.

Otto cycle alternative name for the ◊four-stroke cycle, introduced by the German engineer Nikolaus Otto (1832–1891) in 1876. It improved on existing piston engines by compressing the fuel mixture in the cylinder before it was ignited.

Otto, Nikolaus August (1832–1891)

German engineer who in 1876 patented an effective internal-combustion engine and described the four-stroke cycle.

ounce another name for the snow ◊leopard.

ounce unit of mass, one-sixteenth of a pound ◊avoirdupois, equal to 437.5 grains (28.35 g); also one-twelfth of a pound troy, equal to 480 grains.

outback the inland region of Australia. Its main inhabitants are Aborigines, miners (including opal miners), and cattle ranchers. Its harsh beauty has been recorded by such artists as Sidney Nolan.

outlier in statistics, a highly atypical data value that distorts the ◊mean within a sample.

outline font ◊font in which the outline of each character is defined by a mathematical formula, making the font scalable to any size. Outline fonts can be output using the resolution of the output device, unlike ◊bit map fonts, which can be output at only one size and one resolution. The most common forms of outline fonts are ◊PostScript and ◊TrueType.

output device in computing, any device for displaying, in a form intelligible to the user, the results of processing carried out by a computer.

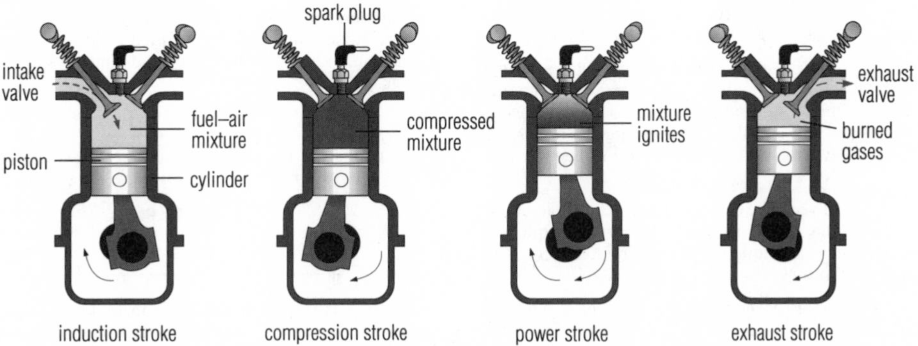

Otto cycle *The four-stroke cycle of a modern petrol engine. The cycle is called the Otto cycle after German engineer Nikolaus Otto, who introduced it in 1876. It improved on earlier engine cycles by compressing the fuel mixture before it was ignited.*

ouzel or *ousel* ancient name for the blackbird. The **ring ouzel** (*Turdus torquatus*) is similar to a blackbird, but has a white band across the breast. It is found in Europe in mountainous and rocky country. **Water ouzel** is another name for the ◊dipper.

ovary in female animals, the organ that generates the ◊ovum. In humans, the ovaries are two whitish rounded bodies about 25 mm/1 in by 35 mm/1.5 in, located in the lower abdomen to either side of the uterus. Every month, from puberty to the onset of the menopause, an ovum is released from the ovary. This is called ovulation, and forms part of the ◊menstrual cycle. In botany, an ovary is the expanded basal portion of the ◊carpel of flowering plants, containing one or more ◊ovules. It is hollow with a thick wall to protect the ovules. Following fertilization of the ovum, it develops into the fruit wall or pericarp.

The ovaries of female animals secrete the hormones responsible for the secondary sexual characteristics of the female, such as smooth, hairless facial skin and enlarged breasts. An ovary in a half-grown human fetus contains 5 million eggs, and so the unborn baby already possesses the female genetic information for the next generation.

In botany, the relative position of the ovary to the other floral parts is often a distinguishing character in classification; it may be either inferior or superior, depending on whether the petals and sepals are inserted above or below.

OverDrive chip in computing, a plug-in replacement for an Intel microprocessor, designed to speed up the PC in which it is used. Intel OverDrive chips are expensive but are cheaper than buying a new PC and offer a simpler upgrade path than replacing the computer's ◊motherboard.

overfishing fishing at rates that exceed the ◊sustained-yield cropping of fish species, resulting in a net population decline. For example, in the North Atlantic, herring has been fished to the verge of extinction and the cod and haddock populations are severely depleted. In thedeveloping world, use of huge factory ships, often by fisheries from industrialized countries, has depleted stocks for local people who cannot obtain protein in any other way. See also ◊fishing and fisheries.

Ecologists have long been concerned at the wider implications of overfishing, in particular the devastation wrought on oceanic ◊food chains. The United Nations Food and Agriculture Organization estimates that worldwide overfishing has damaged oceanic ecosystems to such an extent that potential catches are on average reduced by 20%. With better management of fishing programmes the fishing catch could in principle be increased; it is estimated that, annually, 20 million tonnes of fish are discarded from fishing vessels at sea, because they are not the species sought.

According to an estimate by the Food and Agriculture Organization in 1993, nine of the world's 17 main fishing grounds were suffering a potentially catastrophic decline in some species. In 1994 approximately 17% of fishing waters off the coast of New England, USA, was closed in an attempt to restore dwindling stocks. The area affected covered 17,000 sq km/6,600 sq mi and lay within the Georges Bank region of the Atlantic Ocean.

overflow error in computing, an ◊error that occurs if a number is outside the computer's range and is too large to deal with.

overlay in computing, set of specialized data for use with a larger database. A database of a particular country's geography, for example, that includes roads, towns, and natural features such as rivers and lakes might come with overlays that can be displayed or turned off at the user's command, such as the distribution of speed cameras.

overtone note that has a frequency or pitch that is a multiple of the fundamental frequency, the sounding body's ◊natural frequency. Each sound source produces a unique set of overtones, which gives the source its quality or timbre.

oviparous method of animal reproduction in which eggs are laid by the female and develop outside her body, in contrast to ovoviviparous and viviparous. It is the most common form of reproduction.

ovoviviparous method of animal reproduction in which fertilized eggs develop within the female (unlike oviparous), and the embryo gains no nutritional substances from the female (unlike viviparous). It occurs in some invertebrates, fishes, and reptiles.

ovulation in female animals, the process of releasing egg cells (ova) from the ◊ovary. In mammals it occurs as part of the ◊menstrual cycle.

ovule structure found in seed plants that develops into a seed after fertilization. It consists of an ◊embryo sac containing the female gamete (◊ovum or egg cell), surrounded by nutritive tissue, the nucellus. Outside this there are one or two coverings that provide protection, developing into the testa, or seed coat, following fertilization.

In ◊angiosperms (flowering plants) the ovule is within an ◊ovary, but in ◊gymnosperms (conifers and their allies) the ovules are borne on the surface of an ovuliferous (ovule-bearing) scale, usually within a ◊cone, and are not enclosed by an ovary.

ovum (plural *ova*) female gamete (sex cell) before fertilization. In animals it is called an egg, and is produced in the ovaries. In plants, where it is also known as an egg cell or oosphere, the ovum is produced in an ovule. The ovum is nonmotile. It must be fertilized by a male gamete before it can develop further, except in cases of ◊parthenogenesis.

owl any of a group of mainly nocturnal birds of prey found worldwide. They have hooked beaks, heads that can turn quickly and far round on their very short necks, and forward-facing immobile eyes, surrounded by 'facial discs' of rayed feathers; they fly silently and have an acute sense of hearing. Owls comprise two families: typical owls (family Strigidae), of which there are about 120 species, and barn owls (family Tytonidae), of which there are 10 species. (Order Strigiformes.)

They feed mainly on rodents, but sometimes also eat reptiles, fish, and insects, and some species have been seen feeding on carrion. All species lay white eggs, and begin incubation as soon as the first egg is laid. They regurgitate indigestible remains of their prey in pellets (castings).

ox castrated male of domestic cattle, used in developing countries for ploughing and other agricultural work. Also the extinct wild ox or ◊aurochs of Europe, and surviving wild species such as buffaloes and yaks.

oxalic acid $(COOH)_2.2H_2O$ white, poisonous solid, soluble in water, alcohol, and ether. Oxalic acid is found in rhubarb, and its salts (oxalates) occur in wood sorrel (genus *Oxalis,* family Oxalidaceae) and other plants. It also occurs naturally in human body cells. It is used in the leather and textile industries, in dyeing and bleaching, ink manufacture, metal polishes, and for removing rust and ink stains.

oxbow lake curved lake found on the flood plain of a river. Oxbows are caused by the loops of ◊meanders being cut off at times of flood and the river subsequently adopting a shorter course. In the USA, the term bayou is often used.

oxidation in chemistry, the loss of ◊electrons, gain of oxygen, or loss of hydrogen by an atom, ion, or molecule during a chemical reaction.

Oxidation may be brought about by reaction with another compound (oxidizing agent), which simultaneously undergoes ◊reduction, or electrically at the anode (positive electrode) of an electrolytic cell.

> TO REMEMBER THE DIFFERENCE BETWEEN OXIDATION AND REDUCTION WITH RELATION TO ELECTRONS:
>
> **OILRIG**
>
> OXIDATION IS LOSS; REDUCTION IS GAIN

oxidation number Roman numeral often seen in a chemical name, indicating the ◊valency of the element immediately before the number. Examples are lead(II) nitrate, manganese(IV) oxide, and potassium manganate(VII).

oxide compound of oxygen and another element, frequently produced by burning the element or a compound of it in air or oxygen.

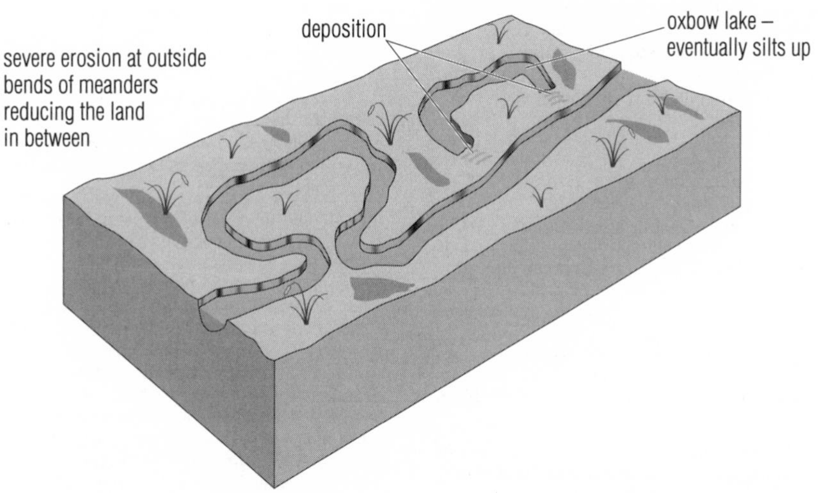

oxbow lake *The formation of an oxbow lake. As a river meanders across a flood plain, the outer bends are gradually eroded and the water channel deepens; as the loops widen, the neck of the loop narrows and finally gives way, allowing the water to flow in a more direct route, isolating the old water channel and forming an oxbow lake.*

Oxides of metals are normally ◊bases and will react with an acid to produce a ◊salt in which the metal forms the cation (positive ion). Some of them will also react with a strong alkali to produce a salt in which the metal is part of a complex anion (negative ion; see ◊amphoteric). Most oxides of nonmetals are acidic (dissolve in water to form an ◊acid). Some oxides display no pronounced acidic or basic properties.

oxide film thin film of oxide formed on the surface of some metals as soon as they are exposed to the air. This oxide film makes the metal much more resistant to a chemical attack. The considerable lack of reactivity of aluminium to most reagents arises from this property.

The thickness of the oxide film can be increased by ◊anodizing the aluminium.

oxidizing agent substance that will oxidize another substance (see ◊oxidation).

In a redox reaction, the oxidizing agent is the substance that is itself reduced. Common oxidizing agents include oxygen, chlorine, nitric acid, and potassium manganate(VII).

oxlip plant closely related to the ◊cowslip.

oxpecker or ***tick-bird*** either of two species of African birds belonging to the starling family. They climb around on the bodies of large mammals, feeding on ticks and other parasites and on cattle earwax. They are usually seen in groups of seven or eight, attending a herd of buffaloes or antelopes, and may help to warn the host of approaching dangers. (Species *Buphagus africana,* family Sturnidae, order Passeriformes.)

Both species have dingy brown plumage, a tawny undersurface and tail, and large laterally flattened colourful bills – one species has a red bill, the other a red and yellow bill.

oxyacetylene torch gas torch that burns ethyne (acetylene) in pure oxygen, producing a high-temperature flame (3,000°C/ 5,400°F). It is widely used in welding to fuse metals. In the cutting torch, a jet of oxygen burns through metal already melted by the flame.

oxyfuel fuel enriched with oxygen to decrease carbon monoxide (CO) emissions. Oxygen is added in the form of chemicals such as methyl tertiary butyl ether (MTBE) and ethanol.

Cars produce CO when there is insufficient oxygen present to convert all the carbon in the petrol to CO_2. This occurs mostly at low temperatures, such as during the first five minutes of starting the engine and in cold weather. CO emissions are reduced by the addition of oxygen-rich chemicals. The use of oxyfuels in winter is compulsory in 35 US cities. There are fears, however, that MTBE can cause health problems, including nausea, headaches, and skin rashes.

oxygen Greek *oxys* 'acid'; *genes* 'forming' colourless, odourless, tasteless, nonmetallic, gaseous element, symbol O, atomic number 8, relative atomic mass 15.9994. It is the most abundant element in the Earth's crust (almost 50% by mass), forms about 21% by volume of the atmosphere, and is present in combined form in water and many other substances. Oxygen is a by-product of ◊photosynthesis and the basis for ◊respiration in plants and animals.

Oxygen is very reactive and combines with all other elements except the ◊inert gases and fluorine. It is present in carbon dioxide, silicon dioxide (quartz), iron ore, calcium carbonate (limestone). In nature it exists as a molecule composed of two atoms (O_2); single atoms of oxygen are very short-lived owing to their reactivity. They can be produced in electric sparks and by the Sun's ultraviolet radiation in space, where they rapidly combine with molecular oxygen to form ozone (an allotrope of oxygen).

Oxygen is obtained for industrial use by the fractional distillation of liquid air, by the electrolysis of water, or by heating manganese (IV) oxide with potassium chlorate. It is essential for combustion, and is used with ethyne (acetylene) in high-temperature oxyacetylene welding and cutting torches.

The element was first identified by English chemist Joseph Priestley in 1774 and independently in the same year by Swedish chemist Karl Scheel. It was named by French chemist Antoine Lavoisier in 1777.

oxygen debt physiological state produced by vigorous exercise, in which the lungs cannot supply all the oxygen that the muscles need.

Oxygen is required for the release of energy from food molecules (aerobic ◊respiration). Instead of breaking food molecules down fully, muscle cells switch to a form of partial breakdown that does not require oxygen (anaerobic respiration) so that they can continue to generate energy. This partial breakdown produces ◊lactic acid, which results in a sensation of fatigue when it reaches certain levels in the muscles and the blood. Once the vigorous muscle movements cease, the body breaks down the lactic acid, using up extra oxygen to do so. Panting after exercise is an automatic mechanism to 'pay off' the oxygen debt.

oyster edible shellfish with a rough, irregular hinged shell, found on the sea bottom in coastal areas. Oysters are bivalve ◊molluscs; the upper valve (shell) is flat, the lower hollow, like a bowl, and the two are hinged by an elastic ligament. The mantle, a protective layer of skin, lies against the shell, shielding the inner body, which includes the organs for breathing, digesting food, and reproduction. Oysters commonly change their sex once a year, sometimes more often; females can release up to a million eggs during a spawning period. (Family Ostreidae.)

Oysters have been considered a delicacy since ancient times. Among the species commercially exploited for food today are the North American eastern oyster (*Crassostrea virginica*) of the Atlantic coast and the European oyster (*Ostrea edulis*). The former is oviparous (eggs are discharged straight into the water) and the latter is larviparous (eggs and larvae remain in the mantle cavity for a period before release). Oyster farming is increasingly practised, the beds being specially cleansed for the easy setting of the free-swimming larvae (known as 'spats'), and the oysters later properly spaced for growth and fattened.

Valuable ◊pearls are not obtained from members of the true oyster family; they occur in pearl oysters (family Pteriidae). There are also tree oysters (family Isognomonidae) and thorny oysters (family Spondylidae).

oyster catcher any of several quite large, chunky shorebirds, with a long, heavy bill which is flattened at the sides and used to prise open the shells of oysters, mussels, and other shellfish. (Family Haematopodidae, order Charadriiformes.)

oz abbreviation for ◊ounce.

Ozalid process trademarked copying process used to produce positive prints from drawn or printed materials or film, such as printing proofs from film images. The film is placed on top of chemically treated paper and then exposed to ultraviolet light. The image is developed dry using ammonia vapour.

ozone O_3 highly reactive pale-blue gas with a penetrating odour. Ozone is an allotrope of oxygen (see ◊allotropy), made up of three atoms of oxygen. It is formed when the molecule of the stable form of oxygen (O_2) is split by ultraviolet radiation or electrical discharge. It forms the ◊ozone layer in the upper atmosphere, which protects life on Earth from ultraviolet rays, a cause of skin cancer.

ozone depleter any chemical that destroys the ozone in the stratosphere. Most ozone depleters are chemically stable compounds containing chlorine or bromine, which remain unchanged for long enough to drift up to the upper atmosphere. The best known are ◊chlorofluorocarbons (CFCs), but many other ozone depleters are known, including halons, used in some fire extinguishers; methyl chloroform and carbon tetrachloride, both solvents; some CFC substitutes; and the pesticide methyl bromide.

CFCs accounted for approximately 75% of ozone depletion in 1995, whereas methyl chloroform (atmospheric concentrations of which had markedly decreased during 1990–94) accounted for an estimated 12.5%. The ozone depletion rate overall is now decreasing as international agreements to curb the use of ozone-depleting chemicals begin to take effect. In 1996 there was a decrease in ozone depleters in the lower atmosphere. This trend is expected to continue into the stratosphere over the next few years.

ozone layer thin layer of the gas ◊ozone in the upper atmosphere that shields the Earth from harmful ultraviolet rays. A continent-sized hole has formed over Antarctica as a result of damage to the ozone layer. This has been caused in part by ◊chlorofluorocarbons (CFCs), but many reactions destroy ozone in the stratosphere: nitric oxide, chlorine, and bromine atoms are implicated.

It is believed that the ozone layer is depleting at a rate of about 5% every 10 years over northern Europe, with depletion extending south to the Mediterranean and southern USA. However, ozone depletion over the polar regions is the most dramatic manifestation of a general global effect. Ozone levels over the Arctic in spring 1997 fell over 10% since 1987, despite the reduction in the concentration of CFCs and other industrial compounds which destroy the ozone when exposed to sunlight. It is thought that this may be because of an expanding vortex of cold air forming in the lower stratosphere above the Arctic, leading to increased ozone loss. It is expected that an Arctic hole as large as that over Antarctica could remain a threat to the northern hemisphere for several decades.

The hole in the ozone layer reached record dimensions in October 1997, with ozone depleted from an area of 22 million sq km.

CHEMISTRY OF THE OZONE LAYER

http://pooh.chem.wm.edu/chemWWW/courses/chem105/projects/group2/page1.html

Interesting step-by-step introduction to the ozone layer for those wishing to understand the chemistry of ozone depletion, the role of chlorofluorocarbons, the consequences of increased radiation for life on earth, and actions to tackle the problem. The information may be readily understood by those with a basic knowledge of chemistry.

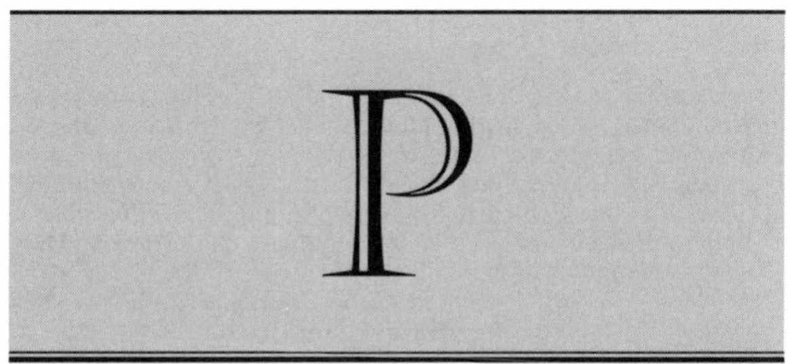

PA (abbreviation for ***public-address system***) amplification set-up for music or speech, usually employed in auditoriums or commercial venues.

paca large, tailless, nocturnal, burrowing ◊rodent, related to the agoutis. The paca, about 60 cm/2 ft long, is native to Central and South America. (Genus *Cuniculus,* family Dasyproctidae.)

pacemaker or ***sinoatrial node*** (SA node) in vertebrates, a group of muscle cells in the wall of the heart that contracts spontaneously and rhythmically, setting the pace for the contractions of the rest of the heart. The pacemaker's intrinsic rate of contraction is increased or decreased, according to the needs of the body, by stimulation from the ◊autonomic nervous system. The term also refers to a medical device implanted under the skin of a patient whose heart beats inefficiently. It delivers minute electric shocks to stimulate the heart muscles at regular intervals and restores normal heartbeat.

The latest pacemakers are powered by radioactive isotopes for long life and weigh no more than 15 g/0.5 oz.

Pacific Ocean world's largest ocean, extending from Antarctica to the Bering Strait; area 166,242,500 sq km/64,170,000 sq mi; average depth 4,188 m/13,749 ft; greatest depth of any ocean 11,034 m/36,210 ft in the ◊Mariana Trench.

That great sea, miscalled the Pacific.

Charles Darwin British naturalist. Attributed remark

packet in computing, unit of data sent across a network. As well as the actual substance of the message, every packet carries error-control information and details of its origin and its final target, enabling a ◊router to send it on to the intended recipient. This means that packets belonging to the same file can travel via different routes over the network, to be automatically reassembled in the correct sequence when they arrive at their destination. All traffic on the Internet consists of packets. See also ◊TCP/IP and ◊X.25.

packet radio in computing, the use of amateur (ham) radio, instead of telephones, to communicate between computers. A terminal node controller (TNC) replaces the modem, a radio transceiver takes the place of the telephone, and the phone system is replaced by radio waves. Packet radio, which works on several different frequencies, has a complete network of its own, complete with satellite links and terrestrial relays. It cannot be used to access the Internet, but it can be connected through the Internet.

packet switching in computing, a method of transmitting data between computers connected in a ◊network. A complete packet consists of the data being transmitted and information about which computer is to receive the data.

The packet travels around the network until it reaches the correct destination, just like a letter sent via the postal system (which is also a packet switching system). Packet switched networks are robust because different packets can take different routes to the same destination. In theory, the network should be able to survive particular circuits (connections) being bombed. The Internet, as a US Defense Department project, was originally designed as a packet switched network to withstand the effects of a nuclear strike.

paediatrics or ***pediatrics*** medical speciality concerned with the care of children.

paedomorphosis in biology, an alternative term for ◊neoteny.

page-description language in computing, a control language used to describe the contents and layout of a complete printed page. Page-description languages are frequently used to control the operation of ◊laser printers. The most popular page-description languages are Adobe Postscript and Hewlett-Packard Printer Control Language.

page printer computer printer that prints a complete page of text and graphics at a time. Page printers use electrostatic techniques, very similar to those used by photocopiers, to form images of pages, and range in size from small laser printers designed to work with microcomputers to very large machines designed for high-volume commercial printing.

paging method of increasing a computer's apparent memory capacity. See ◊virtual memory.

pain sense that gives an awareness of harmful effects on or in the body. It may be triggered by stimuli such as trauma, inflammation, and heat. Pain is transmitted by specialized nerves and also has psychological components controlled by higher centres in the brain. Drugs that control pain are known as painkillers or ◊analgesics.

A pain message to the brain travels along the sensory nerves as electrical impulses. When these reach the gap between one nerve and another, biochemistry governs whether this gap is bridged and may also either increase or decrease the attention the message receives or modify its intensity in either direction. The main type of pain transmitter is known simply as 'substance P', a neuropeptide concentrated in a certain area of the spinal cord. Substance P has been found in fish, and there is also evidence that the same substances that cause pain in humans (for example, bee venom) cause a similar reaction in insects and arachnids (for instance, spiders).

Since the sensation of pain is transmitted by separate nerves from that of fine touch, it is possible in diseases such as syringomyelia to have no sense of pain in a limb, yet maintain a normal sense of touch. Such a desensitized limb is at great risk of infection from unnoticed cuts and abrasions.

painkiller agent for relieving pain. Types of painkiller include analgesics such as ◊aspirin and aspirin substitutes, ◊morphine, ◊codeine, paracetamol, and synthetic versions of the natural inhibitors, the encephalins and endorphins, which avoid the side effects of the others.

Topical nerve irritants are also used in salves, such as camphor and eucalyptus; they cause the nerve endings to react to them, bringing increased blood flow to the areas and alleviating localized and joint pain.

paint any of various materials used to give a protective and decorative finish to surfaces or for making pictures. A paint consists of a pigment suspended in a vehicle, or binder, usually with added solvents. It is the vehicle that dries and hardens to form an adhesive film of paint. Among the most common kinds are cellulose paints (or lacquers), oil-based paints, emulsion (water-based) paints, and special types such as enamels and primers.

types of paint **Lacquers** consist of a synthetic resin (such as an acrylic resin or cellulose acetate) dissolved in a volatile organic solvent, which evaporates rapidly to give a very quick-drying paint. A typical **oil-based paint** has a vehicle of a natural drying oil (such as linseed oil), containing a prime pigment of iron, lead, titanium, or zinc oxide, to which coloured pigments may be added. The finish – gloss, semimatt, or matt – depends on the amount of inert pigment (such as clay or silicates). Oil-based paints can be thinned with, and brushes cleaned in, a solvent such as turpentine or white spirit (a petroleum product). **Emulsion paints**, sometimes called latex paints, consist of pigments dispersed in a water-based emulsion of a polymer (such as polyvinyl chloride [PVC] or acrylic resin). They can be thinned with water, which can also be used to wash the paint out of brushes and rollers. **Enamels** have little pigment, and they dry to an extremely hard, high-gloss film. **Primers** for the first coat on wood or metal, on the other hand, have a high pigment content (as do undercoat paints). Aluminium or bronze powder may be used for priming or finishing objects made of metal.

painted lady brownish-red and black butterfly that migrates to Britain from North Africa. The caterpillar feeds on thistles and other plants.
classification The painted lady *Vanessa cardui* is in family Nymphalidae, order Lepidoptera, class Insecta, phylum Arthropoda.

paint program in computing, program that enables users to 'paint' a picture on their computer screens, using a variety of brushes, spray-guns, and colours.

Paintshop Pro in computing, popular graphics or 'paint' program for Microsoft Windows created by US software house JASC Inc. It is distributed as shareware.

PAL (abbreviation for ***Phase Alternation by Line***) video standard used in Britain, other parts of Europe, and China. It has a higher definition and different screen format from the US NTSC standard. Running a television program written for PAL on an NTSC system can result in the bottom of the screen image being cut off.

Palaeocene Greek ***'old'*** + ***'recent'*** first epoch of the Tertiary period of geological time, 65–56.5 million years ago. Many types of mammals spread rapidly after the disappearance of the great reptiles of the Mesozoic. Flying mammals replaced the flying reptiles, swimming mammals replaced the swimming reptiles, and all the ecological niches vacated by the reptiles were adopted by mammals.

palaeomagnetism science of the reconstruction of the Earth's ancient magnetic field and the former positions of the continents from the evidence of **remnant magnetization** in ancient rocks; that is, traces left by the Earth's magnetic field in ◊igneous rocks before they cool. Palaeomagnetism shows that the Earth's magnetic field has reversed itself – the magnetic north pole becoming the magnetic south pole, and vice versa – at approximate half-million-year intervals, with shorter reversal periods in between the major spans.

Starting in the 1960s, this known pattern of magnetic reversals was used to demonstrate seafloor spreading or the formation of new ocean crust on either side of mid-oceanic ridges. As new material hardened on either side of a ridge, it would retain the imprint of the magnetic field, furnishing datable proof that material was spreading steadily outward. Palaeomagnetism is also used to demonstrate ◊continental drift by determining the direction of the magnetic field of dated rocks from different continents.

palaeoniscid member of a primitive order of freshwater ray-finned fish. They had a spindle-shaped body, scales of a characteristic structure known as ganoid, and a heterocercal (asymmetrical) tail. They lived from Devonian to Jurassic times, but were most abundant in the Carboniferous period.
classification Palaeoniscids are in class Osteichthyes.

There are approximately 37 families in this group, with a wide distribution, fossils having been found in the British Isles, South Africa, Australia, and North America. The shape of the fishes suggests that they were fast swimming predators, initially freshwater with later members moving into the seas.

MUSEUM OF PALAEONTOLOGY

http://www.ucmp.berkeley.edu/exhibit/exhibits.html

Large amount of detailed information on the subject in a carefully structured and carefully cross-referenced site. You can explore palaeontology through the three areas of phylogeny, geology, and evolution.

Cheirolepis canadensis, from the Upper Devonian era, is an example of the group.

palaeontology in geology, the study of ancient life, encompassing the structure of ancient organisms and their environment, evolution, and ecology, as revealed by their ◊fossils. The practical aspects of palaeontology are based on using the presence of different fossils to date particular rock strata and to identify rocks that were laid down under particular conditions; for instance, giving rise to the formation of oil.

The use of fossils to trace the age of rocks was pioneered in Germany by Johann Friedrich Blumenbach (1752–1830) at Göttingen, followed by Georges Cuvier and Alexandre Brongniart in France in 1811.

The term palaeontology was first used in 1834, during the period when the first ◊dinosaur remains were discovered.

Palaeozoic era of geological time 570–245 million years ago. It comprises the Cambrian, Ordovician, Silurian, Devonian, Carboniferous, and Permian periods. The Cambrian, Ordovician, and Silurian constitute the Lower or Early Palaeozoic; the Devonian, Carboniferous, and Permian make up the Upper or Late Palaeozoic. The era includes the evolution of hard-shelled multicellular life forms in the sea; the invasion of land by plants and animals; and the evolution of fish, amphibians, and early reptiles. The earliest identifiable fossils date from this era.

The climate at this time was mostly warm with short ice ages. The continents were very different from the present ones but, towards the end of the era, all were joined together as a single world continent called ◊Pangaea.

palate in mammals, the roof of the mouth. The bony front part is the hard palate, the muscular rear part the soft palate. Incomplete fusion of the two lateral halves of the palate (cleft palate) causes interference with speech.

palisade cell cylindrical cell lying immediately beneath the upper epidermis of a leaf. Palisade cells normally exist as one closely packed row and contain many chloroplasts. During the hours of daylight palisade cells are photosynthetic, using the energy of the sun to create carbohydrates from water and carbon dioxide.

palladium lightweight, ductile and malleable, silver-white, metallic element, symbol Pd, atomic number 46, relative atomic mass 106.4.

It is one of the so-called platinum group of metals, and is resistant to tarnish and corrosion. It often occurs in nature as a free metal (see ◊native metal) in a natural alloy with platinum. Palladium is used as a catalyst, in alloys of gold (to make white gold) and silver, in electroplating, and in dentistry.

It was discovered in 1803 by British physicist William Wollaston (1766–1828), and named after the asteroid Pallas (found 1802).

palliative in medicine, any treatment given to relieve symptoms rather than to cure the underlying cause. In conditions that will resolve of their own accord (for instance, the common cold) or that are incurable, the entire treatment may be palliative.

palm any of a group of large treelike plants with a single tall stem that has a thick cluster of large palmate (five-lobed) leaves or pinnate leaves (leaflets either side of the stem) at the top. Most of the numerous species are tropical or subtropical. Some, such as the coconut, date, sago, and oil palms, are important economically. (Family Palmae.)

pampas grass any of a group of large grasses native to South America, especially *C. argentea,* which is grown in gardens and has tall leaves and large clusters of feathery white flowers growing around the tips of the flower-bearing stems. (Genus *Cortaderia.*)

panchromatic in photography, a term describing highly sensitive black-and-white film made to render all visible spectral colours in correct grey tones. Panchromatic film is always developed in total darkness.

pancreas in vertebrates, an accessory gland of the digestive system located close to the duodenum. When stimulated by the

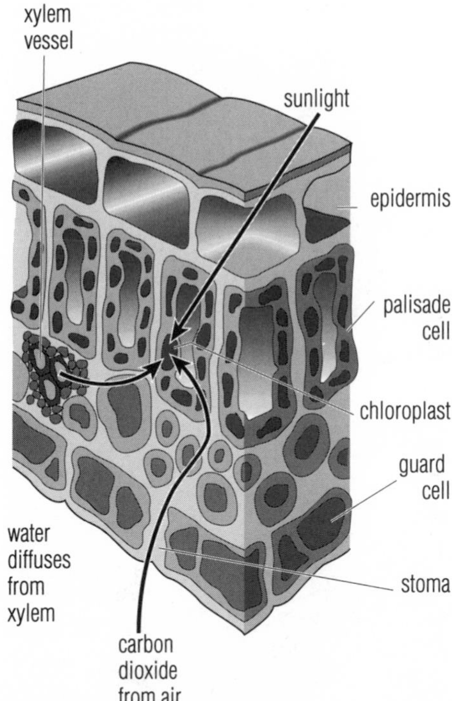

palisade cell *Palisade cells are closely packed, columnar cells, lying in the upper surfaces of leaves. They contain many chloroplasts (where photosynthesis takes place) and are well adapted to receive and process the components necessary for photosynthesis – carbon dioxide, water, and sunlight. For instance, their vertical arrangement means that there are few cross-walls to interfere with the passage of sunlight.*

hormone secretin, it releases enzymes into the duodenum that digest starches, proteins, and fats. In humans, it is about 18 cm/7 in long, and lies behind and below the stomach. It contains groups of cells called the **islets of Langerhans**, which secrete the hormones insulin and glucagon that regulate the blood sugar level.

panda one of two carnivores of different families, native to NW China and Tibet. The **giant panda** *Ailuropoda melanoleuca* has black-and-white fur with black eye patches and feeds mainly on bamboo shoots, consuming about 8 kg/17.5 lb of bamboo per day. It can grow up to 1.5 m/4.5 ft long, and weigh up to 140 kg/300 lb. It is an endangered species. The **lesser**, or **red**, **panda** *Ailurus fulgens,* of the raccoon family, is about 50 cm/1.5 ft long, and is black and chestnut, with a long tail.

Pandas' bamboo diet is of low nutritional value, being about 90% water. This makes it impossible for them to hibernate, since although they spend about 12 hours of every day eating, they cannot accumulate the necessary reserves of fat. There is some dispute about whether they should be included in the bear family or the raccoon family, or classified as a family of their own.

Destruction of the giant pandas' natural habitats threatens to make them extinct in the wild, and they are the focus of conservation efforts; there were only 1,200 giant pandas in 1996.

Pangaea or ***Pangea*** Greek ***'all-land'*** single land mass, made up of all the present continents, believed to have existed between 300 and 200 million years ago; the rest of the Earth was covered by the Panthalassa ocean. Pangaea split into two land masses – ◊Laurasia in the north and ◊Gondwanaland in the south – which subsequently broke up into several continents. These then drifted slowly to their present positions (see ◊continental drift).

The existence of a single 'supercontinent' was proposed by German meteorologist Alfred Wegener in 1912.

pangolin or ***scaly anteater*** toothless mammal of tropical Africa and SE Asia. They are long-tailed and covered with large, overlapping scales, except on the muzzle, sides of the head, throat, chest, and belly. They have an elongated skull and a long, extensible tongue. Pangolins measure 30–100 cm/12–39 in long, exclusive of the prehensile tail, which is about twice as long as the body.

Some are arboreal and others are terrestrial. All live on ants and termites. Pangolins comprise the order Pholidota. There is only one genus (*Manis*) and family Manidae, with seven species.

The lower gums of the mouth form two thickened horny ridges separated by a groove along which the cylindrical wormlike tongue slips in and out. The feet are strongly clawed, especially on the third toe of the forefoot, which is used in burrowing and in climbing. The extreme tip of the tail is free from scales and padded with thick skin. To deter predators a powerful stench is emitted by the entire surface of the skin, and its bony overlapping scales protect it when it rolls up into a ball.

pansy cultivated plant derived from the European wild pansy (*Viola tricolor*) and including many different varieties and strains. The flowers are usually purple, yellow, or cream, or a mixture of these colours, and there are many highly developed varieties bred for size, colour, or special markings. Several of the 400 different species are scented. (Family Violaceae.)

Panthalassa ocean that covered the surface of the Earth not occupied by the world continent ◊Pangaea between 300 and 200 million years ago.

panther another name for the ◊leopard.

Pantone Matching System trade name for a standard set of colours used in graphics and printing, precisely graded and numbered using a universal system. Colours shown on monitors and computer printers are not reliable enough for most designers, so print graphics programs usually include the facility to specify the desired Pantone colours.

pantothenic acid water-soluble ◊vitamin ($C_9H_{17}NO_5$) of the B complex, found in a wide variety of foods. Its absence from the diet can lead to dermatitis, and it is known to be involved in the breakdown of fats and carbohydrates.

papaya tropical evergreen tree, native from Florida to South America. Varieties are grown throughout the tropics. The edible fruits are like melons, with orange-coloured flesh and large numbers of blackish seeds in the centre; they can weigh up to 9 kg/20 lb. (*Carica papaya,* family Caricaceae.)

The fruit juice and the tree sap contain papain, an ◊enzyme used to tenderize meat and help digestion.

paper thin, flexible material made in sheets from vegetable fibres (such as wood pulp) or rags and used for writing, drawing, printing, packaging, and various household needs. The name comes from papyrus, a form of writing material made from water reed, used in ancient Egypt. The invention of true paper, originally made of pulped fishing nets and rags, is credited to Tsai Lun, Chinese minister of agriculture, in AD 105.

Paper came to the West with Arabs who had learned the secret from Chinese prisoners of war in Samarkand in 768. It spread from Morocco to Moorish Spain and to Byzantium in the 11th century,

YOU CAN MAKE PAPER

http://www.beakman.com/paper/paper.html

Fun and environmentally conscious project aiming to teach children about paper and how to make their own home-made paper. Friendly chatting follows the step-by-step instructions. The site also offers an interactive on cellular phones, gravity, smoking and our lungs, relativity, magnets, and more. Children (and adults) can post their questions to a query box.

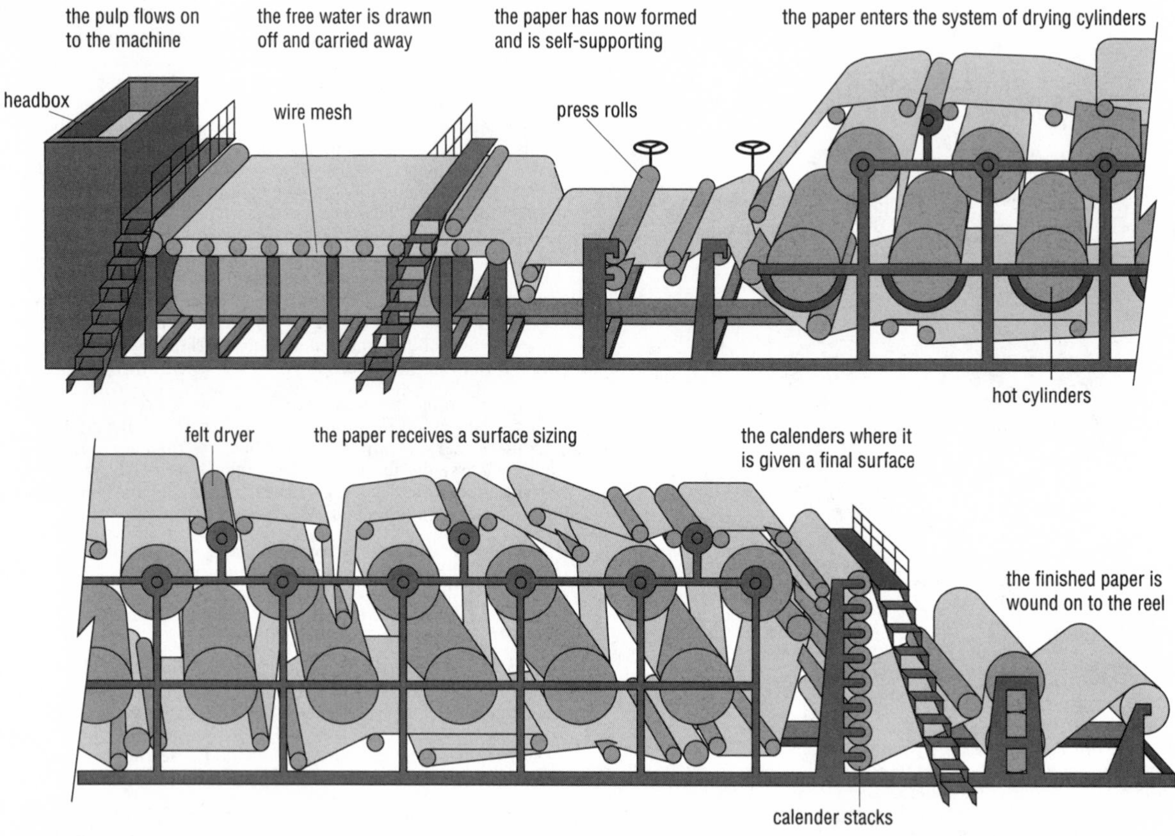
the pulp flows on to the machine
the free water is drawn off and carried away
the paper has now formed and is self-supporting
the paper enters the system of drying cylinders
headbox
wire mesh
press rolls
hot cylinders
felt dryer
the paper receives a surface sizing
the calenders where it is given a final surface
the finished paper is wound on to the reel
calender stacks

paper *Today's fully automatic papermaking machines can be 200 m/640 ft long and produce over 1,000 m/3,200 ft of paper in a minute. The most common type of papermaking machine is the Fourdrinier, named after two British stationer brothers who invented it in 1803. Their original machine deposited the paper on pieces of felt, after which it was finished by hand.*

then to the rest of Europe. All early paper was handmade within frames.

With the spread of literacy there was a great increase in the demand for paper. Production by hand of single sheets could not keep pace with this demand, which led to the invention, by Louis Robert (1761–1828) in 1799, of a machine to produce a continuous reel of paper. The process was developed and patented in 1801 by François Didot, Robert's employer. Today most paper is made from ◊wood pulp on a Fourdrinier machine, then cut to size; some high grade paper is still made from esparto or rag. Paper products absorb 35% of the world's annual commercial wood harvest; recycling avoids some of the enormous waste of trees, and most papermakers plant and replant their own forests of fast-growing stock.

paper nautilus another name for the ◊argonaut.

paper sizes standard European sizes for paper, designated by a letter (A, B, or C) and a number (0–6). The letter indicates the size of the basic sheet at manufacture; the number is how many times it has been folded. A4 is obtained by folding an A3 sheet, which is half an A2 sheet, in half, and so on.

papillon French ***'butterfly'*** breed of French toy spaniel that has pricked ears with plumes of hair, giving its head a butterfly-like appearance. It is less than 28 cm/11 in tall, and its fine, wavy, long coat is mainly white with coloured patches, especially on the ears.

pappus (plural *pappi*) in botany, a modified ◊calyx comprising a ring of fine, silky hairs, or sometimes scales or small teeth, that persists after fertilization. Pappi are found in members of the daisy family (Compositae) such as the dandelions *Taraxacum,* where they form a parachutelike structure that aids dispersal of the fruit.

Pap test or ***Pap smear*** common name for ◊cervical smear.

parabola in mathematics, a curve formed by cutting a right circular cone with a plane parallel to the sloping side of the cone. A parabola is one of the family of curves known as ◊conic sections. The graph of $y = x^2$ is a parabola.

It can also be defined as a path traced out by a point that moves in such a way that the distance from a fixed point (focus) is equal to its distance from a fixed straight line (directrix); it thus has an ◊eccentricity of 1.

The trajectories of missiles within the Earth's gravitational field approximate closely to parabolas (ignoring the effect of air resistance). The corresponding solid figure, the paraboloid, is formed by rotating a parabola about its axis. It is a common shape for headlight reflectors, dish-shaped microwave and radar aerials, and radiotelescopes, since a source of radiation placed at the focus of a paraboloidal reflector is propagated as a parallel beam.

paracetamol analgesic, particularly effective for musculoskeletal pain. It is as effective as aspirin in reducing fever, and less irritating to the stomach, but has little anti-inflammatory action. An overdose can cause severe, often irreversible or even fatal, liver and kidney damage.

parachute any canopied fabric device strapped to a person or a package, used to slow down descent from a high altitude, or returning spent missiles or parts to a safe speed for landing, or sometimes to aid (through braking) the landing of a plane or mis-

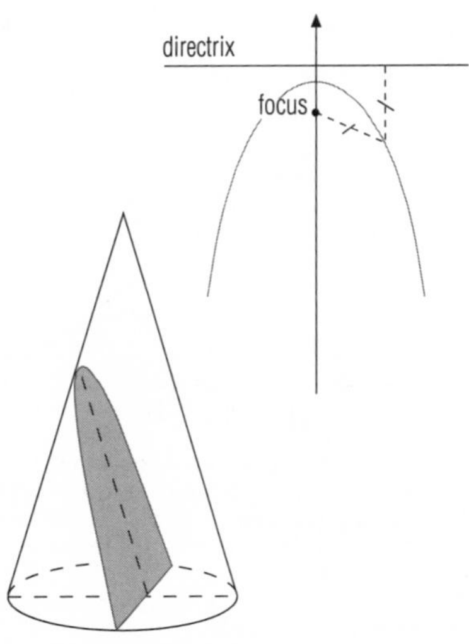

parabola The parabola is a curve produced when a cone is cut by a plane. It is one of a family of curves called conic sections, which also includes the circle, ellipse, and hyperbole. These curves are produced when the plane cuts the cone at different angles and positions.

sile. Modern designs enable the parachutist to exercise considerable control of direction, as in skydiving.

Leonardo da Vinci sketched a parachute design, but the first descent, from a balloon at a height of 670 m/2,200 ft over Paris, was not made until 1797 by André-Jacques Garnerin (1769–1823). The first descent from an aircraft was made by Capt Albert Berry in 1912 from a height of 457 m/1,500 ft over Missouri.

A parachute is typically folded into a pack from which it is released by a rip cord or other device. It originally consisted of some two dozen panels of silk (later nylon) in a circular canopy with shroud lines to a harness. Modern parachutes are variously shaped, often small and rectangular.

In **parascending** the parachuting procedure is reversed, the canopy (parafoil) to which the person is attached being towed behind a vehicle to achieve an ascent.

paradigm all those factors, both scientific and sociological, that influence the research of the scientist. The term, first used by the US historian of science Thomas Kuhn, has subsequently spread to social studies and politics.

> *Nevertheless, paradigm changes do cause scientists to see the world of their research-engagement differently. In so far as their only recourse to that world is through what they see and do, we may want to say that after a revolution scientists are responding to a different world.*
>
> THOMAS SAMUEL KUHN US philosopher and historian of science. *The Structure of Scientific Revolutions* 1970

paradisefish small freshwater fish found in ditches and paddy fields in Asia.

As in the related ◊fighting fish (*Betta*), the males, when in breeding colours, are very pugnacious.

classification The paradisefish *Macropodus opercularis* is in the family Anabantidae, order Perciformes, class Osteichthyes.

paraffin common name for ◊alkane, any member of the series of hydrocarbons with the general formula $Cn_{H2}n_{+2}$. The lower members are gases, such as methane (marsh or natural gas). The middle ones (mainly liquid) form the basis of petrol, kerosene, and lubricating oils, while the higher ones (paraffin waxes) are used in ointment and cosmetic bases.

parakeet any of various small long-tailed ◊parrots, order Psittaciformes, with a moderate beak. They include the **ring-necked parakeets**, genus *Psittacula,* which are very common in India and Africa, and ◊cockatiels, and ◊budgerigars, natives of Australia. The **king parakeet** is about the size of a magpie and has a red head and breast and green wings.

paraldehyde common name for ◊ethanal trimer.

parallax the change in the apparent position of an object against its background when viewed from two different positions. In astronomy, nearby stars show a shift owing to parallax when viewed from different positions on the Earth's orbit around the Sun. A star's parallax is used to deduce its distance from the Earth.

Nearer bodies such as the Moon, Sun, and planets also show a parallax caused by the motion of the Earth. **Diurnal parallax** is caused by the Earth's rotation.

parallax in ◊virtual reality, the distance between the viewer's left and right eyes in the virtual world.

This difference is what creates the impression of depth. Right and left images of distant objects look the same; but left and right images of nearby objects look markedly different owing to the difference of perspective. Manipulating this variable in a virtual world helps make objects look large or small.

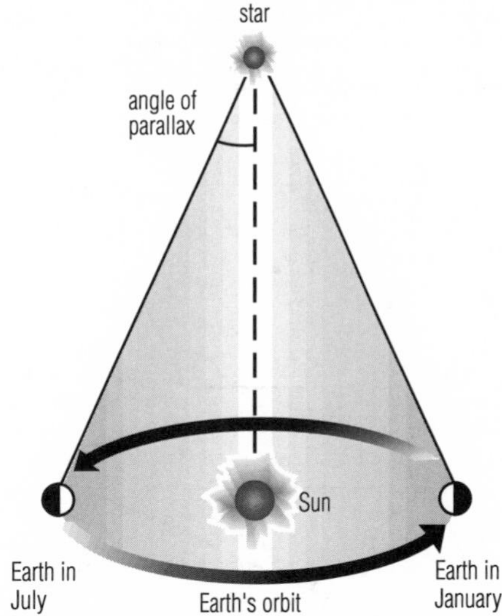

parallax The parallax of a star, the apparent change of its position during the year, can be used to find the star's distance from the Earth. The star appears to change its position because it is viewed at a different angle in July and January. By measuring the angle of parallax, and knowing the diameter of the Earth's orbit, simple geometry can be used to calculate the distance to the star.

parallel circuit electrical circuit in which the components are connected side by side. The current flowing in the circuit is shared by the components. The division of the current across each conductor is in the ratio of their resistances.

parallel device in computing, a device that communicates binary data by sending the bits that represent each character simultaneously along a set of separate data lines, unlike a ◊serial device.

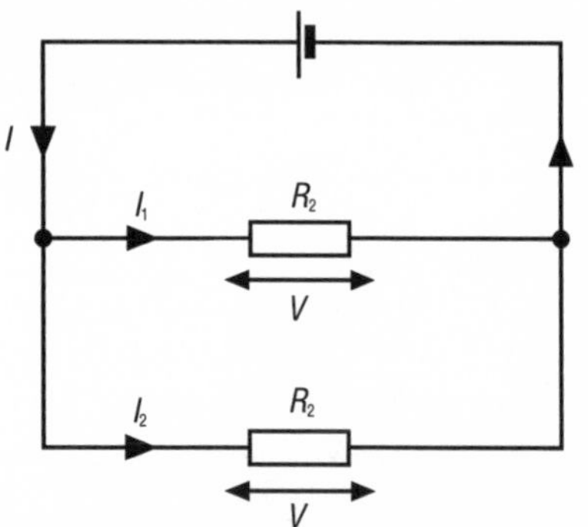

parallel circuit In a parallel circuit, the components are connected side by side, so that the current is split between two or more parallel paths or conductors.

parallel lines and parallel planes in mathematics, straight lines or planes that always remain a constant distance from one another no matter how far they are extended. This is a principle of Euclidean geometry. Some non-Euclidean geometries, such as elliptical and hyperbolic geometry, however, reject Euclid's parallel axiom.

parallelogram in mathematics, a quadrilateral (four-sided plane figure) with opposite pairs of sides equal in length and parallel, and opposite angles equal. The diagonals of a parallelogram bisect each other. Its area is the product of the length of one side and the perpendicular distance between this and the opposite side. In the special case when all four sides are equal in length, the parallelogram is known as a rhombus, and when the internal angles are right angles, it is a rectangle or square.

(i) opposite sides and angles are equal

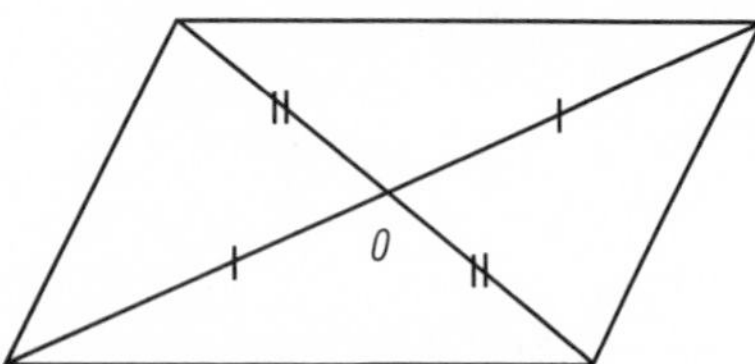

(ii) diagonals bisect each other at *0*

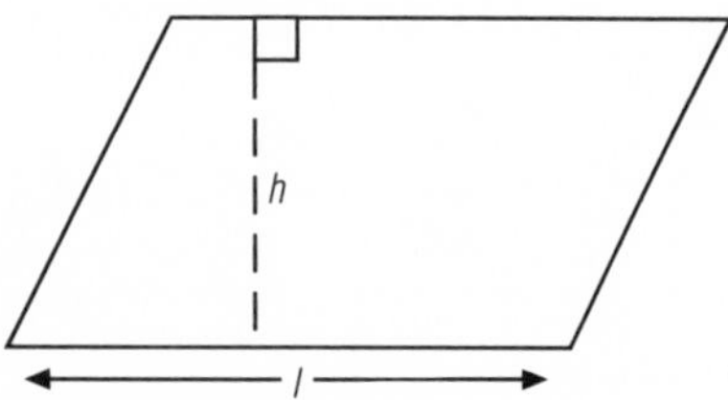

(iii) area of a parallelogram *l* x *h*

parallelogram Some properties of a parallelogram.

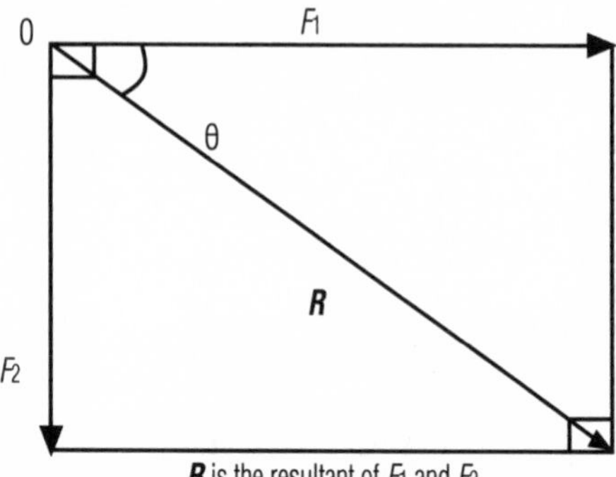

parallelogram of forces The diagram shows how the parallelogram of forces can be used to calculate the resultant (combined effect) of two different forces acting together on an object. The two forces are represented by two lines drawn at an angle to each other. By completing the parallelogram (of which the two lines are sides), a diagonal may be drawn from the original angle to the opposite corner to represent the resultant force vector.

parallelogram of forces in physics and applied mathematics, a method of calculating the resultant (combined effect) of two different forces acting together on an object. Because a force has both magnitude and direction it is a ◊vector quantity and can be represented by a straight line. A second force acting at the same point in a different direction can be represented by another line drawn at an angle to the first. By completing the parallelogram (of which the two lines are sides) a diagonal may be drawn from the original angle to the opposite corner to represent the resultant force vector.

parallel processing emerging computer technology that allows more than one computation at the same time. Although in the 1980s this technology enabled only a small number of computer processor units to work in parallel, in theory thousands or millions of processors could be used at the same time.

Parallel processing, which involves breaking down computations into small parts and performing thousands of them simultaneously, rather than in a linear sequence, offers the prospect of a vast improvement in working speed for certain repetitive applications.

parallel running in computing, a method of implementing a new computer system in which the new system and the old system are run together for a short while. The old system is therefore available to take over from its replacement should any faults arise. An alternative method is ◊pilot running.

paralysis loss of voluntary movement due to failure of nerve impulses to reach the muscles involved. It may result from almost any disorder of the nervous system, including brain or spinal cord injury, poliomyelitis, stroke, and progressive conditions such as a tumour or multiple sclerosis. Paralysis may also involve loss of sensation due to sensory nerve disturbance.

paramagnetic material material that is weakly pulled towards a strong magnet. The effect is caused by unpaired electrons in the atoms of the material, which cause the atoms to act as weak magnets. A paramagnetic material has a fairly low magnetic susceptibility that is inversely proportional to temperature. See magnetism.

Paramecium genus of protozoa. It is unicellular and has a large nucleus (meganucleus) and one or more small nuclei (micronuclei), and an arrangement of cilia (hairlike organs) by which it moves about.

There are also two contractile vacuoles which function alternately and act as osmotic organs; water is constantly absorbed by osmosis, and these vacuoles collect and forcibly expel it. *Paramecium* directs a current of water into its mouth by the movements of its cilia. The cilia also move the animal through the water.

Reproduction is by fission and by conjugation. In the former

case, first the smaller nucleus, then the larger, become constricted and divide into two by oblique division, and the missing organs in either part are quickly regenerated. Frequent multiplication by fission diminishes the vitality of the organism and is succeeded by conjugation, when two individuals exchange part of the substance of their nuclear apparatus. When conditions become unfavourable the animals enclose themselves in cysts.
classification *Paramecium* belongs to the subclass Hymenostomatia, class Oligohymenophora, phylum Ciliophora.

parameter variable factor or characteristic. For example, length is one parameter of a rectangle; its height is another. In computing, it is frequently useful to describe a program or object with a set of variable parameters rather than fixed values.

For example, if a programmer writes a routine for drawing a rectangle using general parameters for the length, height, line thickness, and so on, any rectangle can be drawn by this routine by giving different values to the parameters.

Similarly, in a word-processing application that stores parameters for font, page layout, type of ◊justification, and so on, these can be changed by the user.

paranoia mental disorder marked by delusions of grandeur or persecution. In popular usage, paranoia means baseless or exaggerated fear and suspicion.

In **chronic paranoia**, patients exhibit a rigid system of false beliefs and opinions, believing themselves, for example, to be followed by the secret police, to be loved by someone at a distance, or to be of great importance or in special relation to God. There are no hallucinations and patients are in other respects normal.

In **paranoid states**, the delusions of persecution or grandeur are present but not systematized.

In **paranoid** ◊schizophrenia, the patient suffers from many unsystematized and incoherent delusions, is extremely suspicious, and experiences hallucinations and the feeling that external reality has altered.

paranormal not within the range of, or explicable by, established science. Paranormal phenomena include ◊extrasensory perception **(ESP) which takes in clairvoyance, precognition, and telepathy**; **telekinesis**, the movement of objects from one position to another by human mental concentration; and **mediumship**, supposed contact with the spirits of the dead, usually via an intermediate 'guide' in the other world. ◊Parapsychology is the study of such phenomena.

Paranormal phenomena are usually attributed to the action of an unknown factor, ◊psi.

There have been many reports of sporadic paranormal phenomena, the most remarkable being reports by one person, or occasionally more, of apparitions or hallucinatory experiences associated with another person's death.

paraplegia paralysis of the lower limbs, involving loss of both movement and sensation; it is usually due to spinal injury.

parapsychology Greek *para* ***'beyond'*** study of ◊paranormal phenomena, which are generally subdivided into two types: ◊extrasensory perception (ESP), or the paracognitive; and psychokinesis (PK), telekinesis, or the paraphysical – movement of an object without the use of physical force or energy.

Most research into parapsychology has been experimental. The first Society for Psychical Research was established in London in 1882 by scientists, philosophers, classical scholars, and spiritualists. Despite continued scepticism within the scientific establishment, a chair of parapsychology was establishedin in 1984 at Edinburgh University, endowed by the Hungarian author Arthur Koestler.

paraquat $CH_3(C_5H_4N)_2CH_3.2CH_3SO_4$ (technical name **1,1-dimethyl-4,4-dipyridylium**) nonselective herbicide (weedkiller). Although quickly degraded by soil microorganisms, it is deadly to human beings if ingested.

parasite organism that lives on or in another organism (called the host) and depends on it for nutrition, often at the expense of the host's welfare. Parasites that live inside the host, such as liver flukes and tapeworms, are called **endoparasites**; those that live on the exterior, such as fleas and lice, are called **ectoparasites**.

parathyroid one of a pair of small ◊endocrine glands. Most tetrapod vertebrates, including humans, possess two such pairs, located behind the ◊thyroid gland. They secrete parathyroid hormone, which regulates the amount of calcium in the blood.

parenchyma plant tissue composed of loosely packed, more or less spherical cells, with thin cellulose walls. Although parenchyma often has no specialized function, it is usually present in large amounts, forming a packing or ground tissue. It usually has many intercellular spaces.

parental care in biology, the time and energy spent by a parent in order to rear its offspring to maturity. Among animals, it ranges from the simple provision of a food supply for the hatching young at the time the eggs are laid (for example, many wasps) to feeding and protection of the young after hatching or birth, as in birds and mammals. In the more social species, parental care may include the teaching of skills – for example, female cats teach their kittens to hunt.

parental generation in genetic crosses, the set of individuals at the start of a test, providing the first set of gametes from which subsequent generations (known as the F1 and F2) will arise.

parity of a number, the state of being either even or odd. In computing, the term refers to the number of 1s in the binary codes used to represent data. A binary representation has **even parity** if it contains an even number of 1s and **odd parity** if it contains an odd number of 1s.

For example, the binary code 1000001, commonly used to represent the character 'A', has even parity because it contains two 1s, and the binary code 1000011, commonly used to represent the character 'C', has odd parity because it contains three 1s. A **parity bit** (0 or 1) is sometimes added to each binary representation to give all the same parity so that a ◊validation check can be carried out each time data are transferred from one part of the computer to another. So, for example, the codes 1000001 and 1000011 could have parity bits added and become **0**1000001 and **1**1000011, both with even parity. If any bit in these codes should be altered in the course of processing the parity would change and the error would be quickly detected.

parity check a form of validation of data.

Parkes site in New South Wales of the Australian National Radio Astronomy Observatory, featuring a radio telescope of 64 m/210 ft aperture, run by the Commonwealth Scientific and Industrial Research Organization. It received a NASA-funded upgrade in 1996 to enable it to track the space probe *Galileo*.

Parkinson's disease or ***parkinsonism*** or ***paralysis agitans*** degenerative disease of the brain characterized by a progressive loss of mobility, muscular rigidity, tremor, and speech difficulties. The condition is mainly seen in people over the age of 50.

Parkinson's disease destroys a group of cells called the *substantia nigra* ('black substance') in the upper part of the ◊brainstem. These cells are concerned with the production of a neurotransmitter known as dopamine, which is essential to the control of voluntary movement. The almost total loss of these cells, and of their chemical product, produces the disabling effects. A defective gene responsible for 1 in 20 cases was identified in 1992.

The disease occurs in two forms: **multiple system atrophy (MSA)**, which is a failure of the central nervous system and accounts for 1 in 5 cases; and **pure autonomic failure (PAF)**, a deficit in the peripheral nerves. Symptoms, particularly in the early

PARASITE

Birds support a vast variety of parasites. A curlew may carry over 1,000 feather lice, and a single grouse can harbour 10,000 nematode worms within its intestines.

PARKINSON'S DISEASE: HOPE THROUGH RESEARCH

http://www.ninds.nih.gov/healinfo/disorder/parkinso/pdhtr.htm

Extensive background information on Parkinson's disease. Amongst other issues, it discusses the causes and symptoms of the disorder, the diagnostic methods used and the treatments and medications that are available, the role of surgery in the treatment of the disease, and that of diet and exercise as ways of achieving alleviation of its symptoms.

stages, can be identical. In 1997, an estimated 1.5 million Americans and over 120,000 Britons were suffering with Parkinson's.

The introduction of the drug ◊L-dopa in the 1960s seemed at first the answer to Parkinson's disease. However, it became evident that long-term use brings considerable problems. At best, it postpones the terminal phase of the disease. Brain grafts with dopamine-producing cells were pioneered in the early 1980s, and attempts to graft Parkinson's patients with fetal brain tissue have been made. This experimental surgery brought considerable improvement to some PAF patients, but is ineffective in the MSA form. In 1989 a large US study showed that the drug deprenyl may slow the rate at which disability progresses in patients with early Parkinson's disease.

parrot tropical bird found mainly in Australia and South America. These colourful birds have been valued as pets in the Western world for many centuries. Parrots have the ability to imitate human speech. They are mainly vegetarian, and range in size from the 8.5 cm/3.5 in pygmy parrot to the 100 cm/40 in Amazon parrot. The smaller species are commonly referred to as ◊parakeets. The plumage is often very colourful, and the call is usually a harsh screech. In most species the sexes are indistinguishable. Several species are endangered. Parrots are members of the family Psittacidae, of the order Psittaciformes.

Parrots all have powerful hooked bills and feet adapted for tree climbing. The bill, with its elongated tip, is well adapted in most parrots for tearing up fruit and cracking nuts, and in a number of species the tongue is highly specialized for extracting honey by means of a brushlike tip.

The talent for imitating human speech is marked in the grey parrot *Psittacus erithacus* of Africa. Alex, a 20-year-old African grey taking part in a long-term language project at the University of Arizona during 1996, can count up to six, name 100 objects and describe their colour, texture, and shape. Parrots were among the first items to be traded between natives and European settlers and merchants.

unusual parrots The ◊kakapo of New Zealand is flightless and usually lives on the ground, though it can still climb trees. The ◊kea, another New Zealand parrot, differs from the rest of the group in having developed carnivorous habits.

PARROT

http://www.seaworld.org/animal_bytes/parrotsab.html

Illustrated guide to the parrot including information about genus,

parrot fish or ***parrot wrasse*** member of a family of marine bony fish. The teeth of this group have fused to form extremely hard beaks that are able to bite off pieces of coral; these, with seaweed and molluscs, form the principal food. The fish are all brilliantly coloured, and some may grow up to 1 m/3.3 ft in length.

classification Parrot fish comprise the family Scaridae, order Perciformes, class Osteichthyes.

parse in computing, software facility for breaking down a data stream into individual pieces of information that can be acted upon. On the World Wide Web, for example, data entered by a user can be sent to a database program for storage and later analysis; the ability to do this depends on being able to feed the right bit of data into the right record field.

parsec in astronomy, a unit (symbol pc) used for distances to stars and galaxies. One parsec is equal to 3.2616 ◊light years, 2.063×10^5 astronomical units, and 3.086×10^{13} km.

It is the distance at which a star would have a ◊parallax (apparent shift in position) of one second of arc when viewed from two points the same distance apart as the Earth's distance from the Sun; or the distance at which one astronomical unit subtends an angle of one second of arc.

parsley herb belonging to the carrot family, cultivated for flavouring and garnishing in cookery and for its nutrient value, being rich in vitamin C and minerals. It can grow up to 45 cm/1.5 ft high and has aromatic, curled or flat pinnate leaves (leaflets either side of the stem) and delicate open clusters of yellow flowers. It is a biennial plant. (*Petroselinum crispum*, family Umbelliferae.)

parsnip temperate biennial plant belonging to the carrot family, found in Europe and Asia, and cultivated for its tapering, creamy-white, aromatic root, which is much used as a winter vegetable. (*Pastinaca sativa*, family Umbelliferae.)

parthenocarpy in botany, the formation of fruits without seeds. This phenomenon, of no obvious benefit to the plant, occurs naturally in some plants, such as bananas. It can also be induced in some fruit crops, either by breeding or by applying certain plant hormones.

parthenogenesis development of an ovum (egg) without any genetic contribution from a male. Parthenogenesis is the normal means of reproduction in a few plants (for example, dandelions) and animals (for example, certain fish). Some sexually reproducing species, such as aphids, show parthenogenesis at some stage in their life cycle to accelerate reproduction to take advantage of good conditions.

parthenogenesis *During spring and summer female aphids such as this* Macrosiphum cholodkovskyi *produce a continuous succession of offspring by parthenogenesis, but mate and lay eggs before the onset of winter. Premaphotos Wildlife*

particle detector one of a number of instruments designed to detect subatomic particles and track their paths; they include the cloud chamber, bubble chamber, spark chamber, and multiwire chamber.

The earliest particle detector was the ◊cloud chamber, which contains a super-saturated vapour in which particles leave a trail of droplets, in much the same way that a jet aircraft leaves a trail of vapour in the sky. A bubble chamber contains a superheated liquid in which a particle leaves a trail of bubbles. A spark chamber contains a series of closely-packed parallel metal plates, each at a high voltage. As particles pass through the chamber, they leave a visible spark between the plates. A modern multiwire chamber consists of an array of fine, closely-packed wires, each at a high voltage. As a particle passes through the chamber, it produces an electrical signal in the wires. A computer analyses the signal and reconstructs the path of the particles. Multiwire detectors can be used to detect X-ray and gamma rays, and are used as detectors in ◊positron emission tomography (PET).

particle physics study of the particles that make up all atoms, and of their interactions. More than 300 subatomic particles have now been identified by physicists, categorized into several classes according to their mass, electric charge, spin, magnetic moment, and interaction. Subatomic particles include the◊ elementary particles (◊quarks, ◊leptons, and ◊gauge bosons), which are believed to be indivisible and so may be considered the fundamental units of matter; and the ◊hadrons (baryons, such as the proton and neutron, and mesons), which are composite particles, made up of two or three quarks. The proton, electron, and neutrino are the only stable particles (the neutron being stable only when in the atomic nucleus). The unstable particles decay rapidly into other particles, and are known from experiments with particle accelerators and cosmic radiation. See ◊atomic structure.

Pioneering research took place at the Cavendish laboratory, Cambridge, England. In 1897 English physicist Joseph John Thomson discovered that all atoms contain identical, negatively charged particles (◊electrons), which can easily be freed. By 1911 New Zealand physicist Ernest Rutherford had shown that the electrons surround a very small, positively-charged ◊nucleus. In the case of hydrogen, this was found to consist of a single positively charged particle, a ◊proton. The nuclei of other elements are made up of protons and uncharged particles called ◊neutrons.

1932 saw the discovery of a particle (whose existence had been predicted by British theoretical physicist Paul Dirac in 1928) with the mass of an electron, but an equal and opposite charge – the ◊positron. This was the first example of ◊antimatter; it is now believed that all particles have corresponding antiparticles. In 1934 Italian-born US physicist Enrico Fermi argued that a hitherto unsuspected particle, the ◊neutrino, must accompany electrons in beta-emission.

particles and fundamental forces By the mid-1930s, four types of fundamental ◊force interacting between particles had been identified. The ◊electromagnetic force acts between all particles with electric charge, and is thought to be related to the exchange between these particles of ◊gauge bosons called ◊photons, packets of electromagnetic radiation.

In 1935 Japanese physicist Hideki Yukawa suggested that the ◊strong nuclear force (binding protons and neutrons together in the nucleus) was transmitted by the exchange of particles with a mass about one-tenth of that of a proton; these particles, called ◊pions (originally pi mesons), were found by British physicist Cecil Powell in 1946. Yukawa's theory was largely superseded from 1973 by the theory of ◊quantum chromodynamics, which postulates that the strong nuclear force is transmitted by the exchange of gauge bosons called ◊gluons between the ◊quarks and antiquarks making up protons and neutrons. Theoretical work on the ◊weak nuclear force began with Enrico Fermi in the 1930s. The existence of the gauge bosons that carry this force, the ◊weakons (W and Z particles), was confirmed in 1983 at CERN, the European nuclear research organization. The fourth fundamental force, ◊gravity, is experienced by all matter; the postulated carrier of this force has been named the ◊graviton.

leptons The electron, muon, tau, and their neutrinos comprise the ◊leptons – light particles with half-integral spin that 'feel' the weak nuclear and electromagnetic force but not the strong force. The muon (found by US physicist Carl Anderson in cosmic radiation in 1937) produces the muon neutrino when it decays; the tau, a surprise discovery of the 1970s, produces the tau neutrino when it decays.

mesons and baryons The hadrons (particles that 'feel' the strong nuclear force) were found in the 1950s and 1960s. They are classified into ◊mesons, with whole-number or zero spins, and ◊baryons (which include protons and neutrons), with half-integral spins. It was shown in the early 1960s that if hadrons of the same spin are represented as points on suitable charts, simple patterns are formed. This symmetry enabled a hitherto unknown baryon, the omega-minus, to be predicted from a gap in one of the patterns; it duly turned up in experiments.

quarks In 1964, US physicists Murray Gell-Mann and George Zweig suggested that all hadrons were built from three 'flavours' of a new particle with half-integral spin and a charge of magnitude either $\frac{1}{3}$ or $\frac{2}{3}$ that of an electron; Gell-Mann named the particle the **quark**.

Mesons are quark–antiquark pairs (spins either add to one or cancel to zero), and baryons are quark triplets. To account for new mesons such as the psi (J) particle the number of quark flavours had risen to six by 1985.

If I could remember the names of all these particles I'd be a botanist.

Enrico Fermi Italian-born US physicist.
Quoted in R L Weber *More Random Walks in Science*

particle size in chemistry the size of the grains that make up a powder. The grain size has an effect on certain properties of a substance.

Finely divided powders have a greater surface area for contact; they therefore react more quickly, dissolve more readily, and are of increased efficiency as catalysts compared with their larger-sized counterparts.

particle, subatomic in physics, a particle that is smaller than an atom; see ◊particle physics.

partridge any of various medium-sized ground-dwelling fowl of the family Phasianidae, order Galliformes, that also includes pheasants, quail, and chickens. Partridges are Old World birds, some of which have become naturalized in North America.

Partridges pair very early in the year, the males, like the males of most gallinaceous species, being very pugnacious. The nest is made with a minimum of trouble on the ground in fields or hedgerows, and contains 10–20 olive brown eggs. The hen hatches them, but the male is attentive to her during incubation. The young are fed chiefly on ant pupae, and other insects when these are not available; these and snails and slugs form a considerable proportion of the food of older birds, but in addition grain and other seeds are consumed in great quantity when obtainable. The young remain with their parents for some months, forming coveys of about 20 birds. In the morning and evening they search the stubble and pastures for food, but during the day they hide wherever safe cover may be found.

PASCAL (French acronym for ***program appliqué à la selection et la compilation automatique de la littérature***) a high-level computer-programming language. Designed by Niklaus Wirth (1934–) in the 1960s as an aid to teaching programming, it is still widely used as such in universities, and as a good general-purpose programming language. Most professional programmers, however, now use ◊C or ◊C++. Pascal was named after 17th-century French mathematician Blaise Pascal.

pascal SI unit (symbol Pa) of pressure, equal to one newton per square metre. It replaces ◊bars and millibars (10^5 Pa equals one bar). It is named after the French mathematician Blaise Pascal.

In the field of observation, chance only favours those minds which have been prepared.

Louis Pasteur French chemist and microbiologist.
Encyclopaedia Britannica 1911, 11th edn, vol 20

Pascal, Blaise
(1623–1662)

French philosopher and mathematician. He contributed to the development of hydraulics, calculus, and the mathematical theory of probability.

mathematics Pascal's work in mathematics widened general understanding of conic sections, introduced an algebraic notational system that rivalled that of Descartes and made use of the arithmetical triangle (called Pascal's triangle) in the study of probabilities.

Together with Fermat, Pascal studied two specific problems of probability: the first concerned the probability that a player will obtain a certain face of a dice in a given number of throws; and the second was to determine the portion of the stakes returnable to each player of several if a game is interrupted. Pascal used the arithmetical triangle to derive combinational analysis. **Pascal's triangle** is a triangular array of numbers in which each number is the sum of the pair of numbers above it. In general the *n*th ($n = 0, 1, 2, ...$) row of the triangle gives the binomial coefficients $n^{C}r$, with $r = 0, 1, ..., n$.

In 1657–59, Pascal also perfected his 'theory of indivisibles' – the forerunner of integral calculus –, which enabled him to study problems involving infinitesimals, such as the calculations of areas and volumes.

Mary Evans Picture Library

hydrostatics,* Pascal's principle *and hydraulics Pascal's work in hydrostatics involved repeating the experiment by Italian physicist Evangelista Torricelli to prove that air pressure supports a column of mercury. He confirmed that a vacuum must exist in the space at the top of the tube, and set out to prove that the column of mercury is held up by the weight of air exerted on the container of liquid at the base of the tube. Pascal suggested that at high altitudes there would be less air above the tube and that the column would be lower. Poor health prevented him from undertaking the experiment himself, so he entrusted it to his brother-in-law who obtained the expected results using a mercury column in the mountains of the Puy de Dôme in 1648. This led rapidly to investigations of the use of the mercury barometer in weather forecasting.

Pascal then turned to a study of pressure in liquids and gases, and found that pressure is transmitted equally in all directions throughout a fluid and is always exerted perpendicular to any surface in or containing the fluid. Propounded in a treatise on hydrostatics in 1654, **Pascal's principle** is fundamental to applications of hydrostatics and governs the operation of hydraulic machines, such as the hydraulic press and jack.

calculating machine Between 1642 and 1645, Pascal constructed a machine to carry out the processes of addition and subtraction, and then organized the manufacture and sale of these first calculating machines. At least seven of these 'computers' still exist. One was presented to Queen Christina of Sweden in 1652.

PASCAL, BLAISE

http://www.nd.edu/StudentLinks/akoehl/Pascal.html

Biography and photograph of the philosopher and mathematician Blaise Pascal. His philosophy and mathematics are briefly discussed. There is also a link to Pascal's *Pensées*.

Pascal's triangle triangular array of numbers (with 1 at the apex), in which each number is the sum of the pair of numbers above it. It is named after French mathematician Blaise Pascal, who used it in his study of probability. When plotted at equal distances along a horizontal axis, the numbers in the rows give the binomial probability distribution (with equal probability of success and failure) of an event, such as the result of tossing a coin.

```
              1
            1   1
          1   2   1
        1   3   3   1
      1   4   6   4   1
    1   5  10  10   5   1
  1   6  15  20  15   6   1
1   7  21  35  35  21   7   1
```

Pascal's triangle *In Pascal's triangle, each number is the sum of the two numbers immediately above it, left and right – for example, 2 is the sum of 1 and 1, and 4 is the sum of 3 and 1. Furthermore, the sum of each row equals a power of 2 – for example, the sum of the 3rd row is* $4 = 2^2$*; the sum of the 4th row is* $8 = 2^3$.

paspalum grass of the genus *Paspalum*, especially *P. dilatatum*, native to S America and now one of the most widespread grasses in the higher-rainfall areas of Australia. It is a useful pasture grass in subtropical coastal areas, but a weed of crops, citrus orchards, and lawns.

pasqueflower plant belonging to the buttercup family. A low-growing hairy perennial, it has feathery leaves and large purple bell-shaped flowers that are upright at first, then droop. Found in Europe and Asia, it grows on grassland on limy soil. (*Pulsatilla vulgaris*, family Ranunculaceae.)

passion flower any of a group of tropical American climbing plants. They have distinctive flowers consisting of a saucer-shaped petal base, a fringelike corona or circle of leafy outgrowths inside the ring of petals, and a central stalk bearing five pollen-producing ◊stamens and three pollen-receiving ◊stigmas. The flowers can be yellow, greenish, purple, or red. Some species produce edible fruit. (Genus *Passiflora*, family Passifloraceae.)

Parts of the flower were said by Jesuit missionaries to South America to resemble symbols of Christ's crucifixion, for example the crown of thorns, the five wounds, and the three nails; hence the name, referring to the suffering, or passion, of Christ on the cross.

passive matrix display or ***passive matrix LCD*** in computing, ◊liquid crystal display (LCD) produced by passing a current between an array of electrodes set between glass plates. Passive matrix screens lack the transistors that enhance the performance of ◊active matrix LCDs, which makes them relatively inexpensive, but lacking in contrast and slow to react.

passive smoking inhalation of tobacco smoke from other people's cigarettes; see ◊smoking.

password secret combination of characters used in computing to control access and thus to ensure ◊data security.

Pasteur, Louis
(1822–1895)

French chemist and microbiologist who discovered that fermentation is caused by microorganisms and developed the germ theory of disease. He also created a vaccine for rabies, which led to the foundation of the Pasteur Institute in Paris in 1888.

stereoisomers Pasteur first gained recognition through his early work on the optical activity of stereo isomers. In 1848 he presented a paper to the Paris Academy of Sciences in which he reported that there are two molecular forms of tartaric acid, one that rotates plane polarized light to the right and another (a mirror image of the first) that rotates it to the left. In addition, he showed that one form can be assimilated by living microorganisms whereas its optical antipode cannot.

fermentation A query from an industrialist about wine- and beer-making prompted Pasteur's research into fermentation. Using a microscope he found that properly aged wine contains small spherical globules of yeast cells whereas sour wine contains elongated yeast cells. He proved that fermentation does not require oxygen, yet it involves living microorganisms, and that, to produce the correct type of fermentation (alcohol-producing rather than lactic acid-producing), it is necessary to use the correct type of yeast. Pasteur also realized that, after wine has formed, it must be gently heated to about 50°C/122°F – pasteurized – to kill the yeast and thereby prevent souring during the ageing process.

spontaneous generation and the germ theory of disease Pasteur then turned his attention to spontaneous generation, a problem that had once again become a matter of controversy. Pasteur showed that dust in the air contains spores of living organisms that reproduce when introduced into a nutrient broth. Then he boiled the broth in a container with a U-shaped tube that allowed air to reach the broth but trapped dust in the U-bend. He found that the broth remained free of living organisms, disproving the theory of spontaneous generation.

In the mid-1860s, the French silk industry was seriously threatened by a disease that killed silkworms and Pasteur was commissioned by the government to investigate the disease. He announced in 1868 that he had found a minute parasite that infects the silkworms, and recommended that all infected silkworms be destroyed. His advice was followed and the disease eliminated. This stimulated his interest in infectious diseases and, from the results of his previous work on fermentation, spontaneous generation, and the silkworm disease, Pasteur developed the **germ theory of disease**. This theory was probably the most important single medical discovery of all time, because it provided both a practical method of combating disease by disinfection and a theoretical foundation for further research.

the prevention of disease Continuing his research into disease, in 1881 Pasteur developed a method for reducing the virulence of certain pathogenic microorganisms. By heating a preparation of anthrax bacilli he attenuated their virulence but found that they still brought about the full immune response when injected into sheep. Using a similar method, Pasteur then inoculated fowl against chicken cholera, following the work of Edward Jenner (who first vaccinated against cowpox in 1796).

In 1882, Pasteur began what proved to be his most spectacular research: the prevention of rabies. He demonstrated that the causative microorganism (actually a virus, although the existence of viruses was not known at that time) infects the nervous system and then, using the dried tissues of infected animals, he succeeded in obtaining an attenuated form of the virus suitable for the inoculation of human beings. The culmination of this work came on 6 July 1885, when Pasteur used his vaccine to save the life of a young boy who had been bitten by a rabid dog. The success of this experiment brought Pasteur even greater acclaim and led to the establishment of the Pasteur Institute in 1888.

Mary Evans Picture Library

PASTEUR, LOUIS

More germs are transmitted when shaking hands than when kissing. Louis Pasteur, the pioneer of hygienic methods, refused to shake hands with acquaintances for fear of infection.

pasteurization treatment of food to reduce the number of microorganisms it contains and so protect consumers from disease. Harmful bacteria are killed and the development of others is delayed. For milk, the method involves heating it to 72°C/161°F for 15 seconds followed by rapid cooling to 10°C/50°F or lower. The process also kills beneficial bacteria and reduces the nutritive property of milk.

The experiments of Louis Pasteur on wine and beer in the 1850s and 1860s showed how heat treatment slowed the multiplication of bacteria and thereby the process of souring. Pasteurization of milk made headway in the dairy industries of Scandinavia and the USA before 1900 because of the realization that it also killed off bacteria associated with the diseases of tuberculosis, typhoid, diphtheria, and dysentery.

patch in computing, modification or update made to a program, consisting of a short segment of additional code. Developers often correct bugs or fine-tune software by releasing a patch which rewrites existing codes and adds new material.

patchouli soft-wooded E Indian shrub belonging to the mint family; the leaves are the source of the perfume patchouli. (*Pogostemon heyneanus,* family Labiateae.)

patella or ***kneecap*** flat bone embedded in the knee tendon of birds and mammals, which protects the joint from injury.

pathogen Greek ***'disease producing'*** in medicine, any microorganism that causes disease. Most pathogens are ◊parasites, and the diseases they cause are incidental to their search for food or shelter inside the host. Nonparasitic organisms, such as soil bacteria or those living in the human gut and feeding on waste foodstuffs, can also become pathogenic to a person whose immune system or liver is damaged. The larger parasites that can cause disease, such as nematode worms, are not usually described as pathogens.

pathology medical speciality concerned with the study of disease processes and how these provoke structural and functional changes in the body.

Pauli exclusion principle in physics, a principle of atomic structure. See ◊exclusion principle.

Pauli, Wolfgang
(1900–1958)

Austrian-born Swiss physicist who originated the exclusion principle: in a given system no two fermions (electrons, protons, neutrons, or other elementary particles of half-integral spin) can be characterized by the same set of quantum numbers. He also predicted the existence of neutrinos. He won the Nobel Prize for Physics in 1945.

The exclusion principle, announced 1925, involved adding a fourth quantum number to the three already used (n, l, and m). This number, s, would represent the spin of the electron and would have two possible values. The principle also gave a means of determining the arrangement of electrons into shells around the nucleus, which explained the classification of elements into related groups by their atomic number.

Mary Evans Picture Library

Pauling, Linus Carl
(1901–1994)

US theoretical chemist and biologist. His ideas on chemical bonding are fundamental to modern theories of molecular structure. He also investigated the properties and uses of vitamin C as related to human health. He won the Nobel Prize for Chemistry in 1954 and the Nobel Peace Prize in 1962, having campaigned for a nuclear-test ban.work Pauling's work on the nature of the chemical bond included much new information about interatomic distances. Applying his knowledge of molecular structure to proteins in blood, he discovered that many proteins have structures held together with hydrogen bonds, giving them helical shapes.

He was a pioneer in the application of quantum-mechanical principles to the structures of molecules, relating them to interatomic distances and bond angles by X-ray and electron diffraction, magnetic effects, and thermochemical techniques. In 1928, Pauling introduced the concept of hybridization of bonds. This provided a clear, basic insight into the framework structure of all carbon compounds; that is, of the whole of organic chemistry. He also studied electronegativity of atoms and polarization (movement of electrons) in chemical bonds. Electronegativity values can be used to show why certain substances, such as hydrochloric acid, are acid, whereas others, such as sodium hydroxide, are alkaline. Much of this work was consolidated in his book The Nature of the Chemical Bond 1939.

Mary Evans Picture Library

Pavlov, Ivan Petrovich
(1849–1936)

Russian physiologist who studied conditioned reflexes in animals (see conditioning). His work had a great impact on behavioural theory (see behaviourism) and learning theory. Nobel Prize for Physiology or Medicine 1904.

Mary Evans Picture Library

pawpaw or ***papaw*** small tree belonging to the custard-apple family, native to the eastern USA. It produces oblong fruits 13 cm/5 in long with yellowish edible flesh. The name 'pawpaw' is also used for the ◊papaya. (*Asimina triloba*, family Annonaceae.)

PC card standard for 'credit card' memory and device cards used in ◊portable computers. As well as providing ◊flash memory, PC cards can provide either additional disc storage, or modem or fax functionality.

PCI ***(abbreviation for* peripheral component interconnect)** form of ◊local bus connection between external devices and the main ◊central processing unit. Developed (but not owned) by ◊Intel, it was available as 32-bit in 1993, but is now available as 64-bit.

PCL ◊page description language, developed by Hewlett Packard for use on Laserjet laser printers. Versions PCL 1 to PCL 4 used ◊raster graphics fonts; PCL 5 uses ◊outline fonts.

PCM abbreviation for ◊pulse-code ◊modulation.

PCMCIA (abbreviation for ***Personal Computer Memory Card International Association***) in computing, another name for a **PC card**.

PCP abbreviation for **phencyclidine hydrochloride**, a drug popularly known as angel dust.

PCX in computing, bitmapped graphics file format, originally developed by Z-Soft for use with PC-Paintbrush, but now used and generated by many applications and hardware such as scanners.

pd abbreviation for potential difference.

PDF (abbreviation for ***portable document format***) in computing, file format created by Adobe's Acrobat system that retains the entire content of an electronic document (including layouts, graphics, styled text, and navigation features) regardless of the computer system on which it is viewed. Because they are platform-independent, PDF files are a good way to send documents over the Internet.

pea climbing leguminous plant (see ◊legume) with pods of round green edible seeds, grown since prehistoric times for food. The pea is a popular vegetable and is eaten fresh, canned, frozen, or dried. The **sweet pea** (*Lathyrus odoratus*) of the same family is grown for its scented red, purple, pink, and white butterfly-shaped flowers; it is a popular cottage garden plant. (Edible pea *Pisum sativum*, family Leguminosae.)

PeaceNet computer network dedicated to the cause of world peace and social justice. PeaceNet carries specialist news and information services which are used by many human rights and disarmament organizations. Compare ◊GreenNet.

peach yellow-reddish round edible fruit of the peach tree, which is cultivated for its fruit in temperate regions and has oval leaves and small, usually pink, flowers. The fruits have thick velvety skins; nectarines are a smooth-skinned variety. (*Prunus persica,* family Rosaceae.)

peacock technically, the male of any of various large ◊pheasants, order Galliformes. The name is most often used for the common peacock *Pavo cristatus,* a bird of the pheasant family, native to S Asia. It is rather larger than a pheasant. The male has a large fan-shaped tail, brightly coloured with blue, green, and purple 'eyes' on a chestnut background, that is raised during courtship displays. The female (peahen) is brown with a small tail.

The hen lays 4–8 eggs in the spring, and incubation takes 30 days. She remains with her chicks eight months. The green peacock, *P. muticus,* native to SE Asia, breeds freely with the common peacock. A third species, *Afropavus congensis,* was discovered in the late 1930s in the Congo forests. These are much smaller than the common peacock and do not have erectile tail coverts.

peacock butterfly butterfly measuring about 5 cm/2 in across the wings, which are a dull deep or brownish-red, and each of which bears an 'eye' rather like those in the peacock's tail.
classification The peacock butterfly *Vanessa io* is in family Nymphalidae, order Lepidoptera, class Insecta, phylum Arthropoda.

The butterfly hibernates through the winter, and in early spring lays its eggs on stinging nettles; they hatch into black and yellow caterpillars, with six rows of black spines and a series of white dots arranged transversely on each segment.

peanut or ***groundnut*** or ***monkey nut*** South American vinelike annual plant. After flowering, the flower stalks bend and force the pods into the earth to ripen underground. The nuts are a staple food in many tropical countries and are widely grown in the southern USA. They provide a valuable edible oil and are the basis for a large number of processed foods. (*Arachis hypogaea,* family Leguminosae.)

pear succulent, gritty-textured edible fruit of the pear tree, native to temperate regions of Europe and Asia. White flowers precede the fruits, which have a greenish-yellow and brown skin and taper towards the stalk. Pear trees are cultivated for their fruit which are eaten fresh or canned; a wine known as perry is made from pear juice. (*Pyrus communis,* family Rosaceae.)

pearl shiny, hard, rounded abnormal growth composed of nacre (or mother-of-pearl), a chalky substance. Nacre is secreted by many molluscs, and deposited in thin layers on the inside of the shell around a parasite, a grain of sand, or some other irritant body. After several years of the mantle (the layer of tissue between the shell and the body mass) secreting this nacre, a pearl is formed.

Although commercially valuable pearls are obtained from freshwater mussels and oysters, most precious pearls come from the various species of the family Pteriidae (the pearl oysters) found in tropical waters off N and W Australia, off the Californian coast, in the Persian Gulf, and in the Indian Ocean. Because of their rarity, large mussel pearls of perfect shape are worth more than those from oysters.

Artificial pearls were first cultivated in Japan in 1893. A tiny bead of shell from a clam, plus a small piece of membrane from another pearl oyster's mantle (to stimulate the secretion of nacre) is inserted in oysters kept in cages in the sea for three years, and then the pearls are harvested.

peat fibrous organic substance found in bogs and formed by the incomplete decomposition of plants such as sphagnum moss. N Asia, Canada, Finland, Ireland, and other places have large deposits, which have been dried and used as fuel from ancient times. Peat can also be used as a soil additive.

Peat bogs began to be formed when glaciers retreated, about 9,000 years ago. They grow at the rate of only a millimetre a year, and large-scale digging can result in destruction both of the bog and of specialized plants growing there. The destruction of peat bogs is responsible for diminishing fish stocks in coastal waters; the run off from the peatlands carries high concentrations of iron, which affects the growth of the plankton on which the fish feed.

pecan nut-producing ◊hickory tree (*C. illinoensis* or *C. pecan*), native to the central USA and N Mexico and now widely cultivated. The trees grow to over 45 m/150 ft, and the edible nuts are smooth-shelled, the kernel resembling a smooth, oval walnut. (Genus *Carya,* family Juglandaceae.)

peccary one of two species of the New World genus *Tayassu* of piglike hoofed mammals. A peccary has a gland in the middle of its back which secretes a strong-smelling substance. Peccaries are blackish in colour, covered with bristles, and have tusks that point downwards. Adults reach a height of 40 cm/16 in, and a weight of 25 kg/60 lb.

peck obsolete unit of dry measure, equalling eight quarts or a quarter bushel (9.002 litres).

pectoral relating to the upper area of the thorax associated with the muscles and bones used in moving the arms or forelimbs, in vertebrates. In birds, the *pectoralis major* is the very large muscle used to produce a powerful downbeat of the wing during flight.

pedestrianization the closing of an area to traffic, making it more suitable for people on foot. It is now common in many town shopping centres, since cars and people often obstruct one another. This restricts accessibility and causes congestion. Sometimes service vehicles (such as buses and taxis) are allowed access.

pedicel the stalk of an individual flower, which attaches it to the main floral axis, often developing in the axil of a bract.

pedometer small portable instrument for counting the number of steps taken, and measuring the approximate distance covered by a person walking. Each step taken by the walker sets in motion a swinging weight within the instrument, causing the mechanism to rotate, and the number of rotations are registered on the instrument face.

peepul another name for the ◊bo tree.

peer-to-peer networking in computing, method of file sharing in which computers are linked to each other as opposed to being linked to a central file server.

pegasid or ***sea moth*** or ***sea robin*** marine fish of the family Pegasidae, the only family within the order Pegasiformes. Pegasids are 5–15 cm/2–6 in long with armoured bodies and large winglike pectoral fins. There are five species and they are found only in the Indo-Pacific.

Pegasids are under threat due to demands for their use in Chinese medicine as a treatment for respiratory diseases and cancers.

Pegasus in astronomy, a constellation of the northern hemisphere, near Cygnus, and represented as the winged horse of Greek mythology.

pegmatite extremely coarse-grained ◊igneous rock of any composition found in veins; pegmatites are usually associated with large granite masses.

pekan *or* **fisher marten** North American marten (carnivorous mammal) *Martes penanti* about 1.2 m/4 ft long, with a doglike face, and brown fur with white patches on the chest. It eats porcupines.

pekingese breed of small long-haired dog first bred at the Chinese court as the 'imperial lion dog'. It has a flat skull and flat face, is typically less than 25 cm/10 in tall, and weighs less than 5 kg/11 lb.

Peking man Chinese representative of an early species of human, found as fossils, 500,000–750,000 years old, in the cave of Choukoutien in 1927 near Beijing (Peking). Peking man used chipped stone tools, hunted game, and used fire. Similar varieties of early human have been found in Java and E Africa.

Their classification is disputed: some anthropologists classify them as *Homo erectus,* others as *Homo sapiens pithecanthropus.*

pelargonium (commonly called ***geranium***) any of a group of shrubby, tender flowering plants belonging to the geranium family, grown extensively for their colourful white, pink, scarlet, and black-purple flowers. They are the familiar summer bedding and pot 'geraniums'. Ancestors of the garden hybrids came from southern Africa. (Genus *Pelargonium,* family Geraniaceae.)

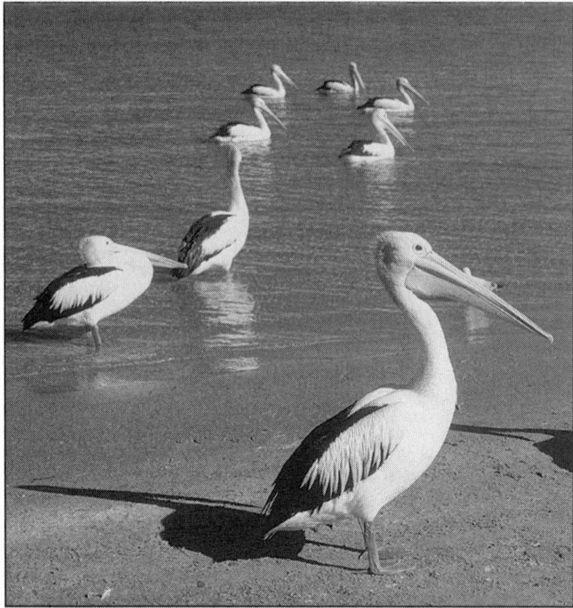

pelican The pale pink pouch beneath the large bill is clearly visible in these Australian black-backed pelicans. When not fishing, they spend much of the day in shallow water, preening to keep their feathers well oiled. Premaphotos Wildlife

pelican large water bird of family Pelecanidae, order Pelecaniformes, remarkable for the pouch beneath the bill, which is used as a fishing net and temporary store for catches of fish. Some species grow up to 1.8 m/6 ft and have wingspans of 3 m/10 ft.

The legs are short and the feet large, with four webbed toes; the tail is short and rounded, and the neck long. The wings are long and expansive, and the birds are capable of rapid flight. The species are widely distributed, frequenting the seashore and margins of lakes, and feeding almost exclusively on fish, which are deposited in the pouch for subsequent digestion.

Oh, a wondrous bird is the pelican! / His beak holds more than his belican. / He takes in his beak / Food enough for a week. / But I'll be darned if I know how the helican.

DIXON MERRITT US writer.
Nashville Banner 22 Apr 1913

pellagra chronic disease mostly seen in subtropical countries in which the staple food is maize. It is caused by deficiency of ◊nicotinic acid (one of the B vitamins), which is contained in protein foods, beans and peas, and yeast. Symptoms include diarrhoea, skin eruptions, and mental disturbances.

pellitory-of-the-wall plant belonging to the nettle family, found growing in cracks in walls and rocks and also on banks in W and S Europe; it is widely cultivated in gardens. The stems are up to 1 m/3 ft tall and reddish, the leaves are lance-shaped, and the greenish male and female flowers grow separately but on the same plant. (*Parietaria judaica,* family Urticaceae.)

Peltier effect in physics, a change in temperature at the junction of two different metals produced when an electric current flows through them. The extent of the change depends on what the conducting metals are, and the nature of change (rise or fall in temperature) depends on the direction of current flow. It is the reverse of the ◊Seebeck effect. It is named after the French physicist Jean Charles Peltier (1785–1845) who discovered it in 1834.

pelvis in vertebrates, the lower area of the abdomen featuring the bones and muscles used to move the legs or hindlimbs. The **pelvic girdle** is a set of bones that allows movement of the legs in relation to the rest of the body and provides sites for the attachment of relevant muscles.

pen hand-held implement for writing. Pens have existed since ancient Egyptian times. Quill pens were developed by the Romans, and the technology remained unchanged until the 18th-century development of the steel nib. The fountain pen, which ensured a steady supply of ink, was invented in the 1880s. Today the dominant types of pen are the ballpoint, which became widespread in the 1940s and 1950s, and the felt-tip pen, dating from the 1960s.

pen-based computer computer (usually portable), for which input is by means of a pen or stylus, rather than a keyboard. It incorporates handwriting recognition software, although prior to the release of the Apple ◊Newton and similar models, this had effectively meant using separate characters rather than 'joined-up' writing.

pendulum weight (called a 'bob') swinging at the end of a rod or cord. The regularity of a pendulum's swing was used in making the first really accurate clocks in the 17th century. Pendulums can be used for measuring the acceleration due to gravity (an important constant in physics).

Specialized pendulums are used to measure velocities (ballistic pendulum) and to demonstrate the Earth's rotation (Foucault's pendulum).

penetration technology the development of missiles that have low radar, infrared, and optical signatures and thus can penetrate an enemy's defences undetected. In 1980 the USA announced that it had developed such a piloted aircraft, known as Stealth. It comes in both fighter and bomber versions. The Stealth bomber saw action in the Gulf War.

penguin marine flightless bird, family Spheniscidae, order Sphenisciformes, mostly black and white, found in the southern hemisphere. They comprise 18 species in six genera. Males are usually larger than the females. Penguins range in size from 40 cm/1.6 ft to 1.2 m/4 ft tall, and have thick feathers to protect them from the intense cold. They are awkward on land (except on snow slopes down which they propel themselves at a rapid pace), but their wings have evolved into flippers, making them excellent swimmers. Penguins congregate to breed in 'rookeries', and often spend many months incubating their eggs while their mates are out at sea feeding. They feed on a mixture of fish, squid, and krill.

The wing is long and has no covert or quill feathers, and always remains open. The feathers are tiny, with very broad shafts and but little vane or web. The legs of the birds are placed far back, and in the water the feet are stretched out straight behind and held motionless, the wings working rapidly as if being used in flight. Moult in penguins is general and areas of feathers are lost at once. It is usually a rapid process unlike the ordered progressive moult of flying birds. Penguins generally moult once a year, and have to stay out of the water during this time, without feeding.

The nest is often no more than a slight hollow in the ground, but some penguins, especially the Adelie penguins *Pygoscelis adeliae,* collect stones, with which they bank the nest round. One or two eggs are laid, and both birds, but chiefly the male, attend to their incubation. Both parents are very devoted to the young, one always staying to guard them, the other bringing them sea crustaceans and other small animals, which the young take by pushing their beaks far down the parent's throat.

They are very social birds, living together, and usually breed in vast colonies, always returning to the same rookery (breeding group). The young gather in groups while the parents are foraging

Penicillin: Discovery

by Julian Rowe

Chance favours the prepared mind

'I think the discovery and development of penicillin may be looked on as quite one of the luckiest accidents that have occurred in medicine.' With these words, Professor Howard Florey (1898–1968), an Australian pathologist, concluded a lecture he gave in 1943 at the Royal Institution. The topic was penicillin: the first, and still perhaps overall the best of a range of natural chemotherapeutic agents called antibiotics.

Together with Ernst Chain (1906–1979), Howard Florey had made the practical exploitation of penicillin possible on a worldwide scale.

A chance discovery

The story of the discovery of penicillin started with a chance observation made by British bacteriologist Alexander Fleming (1881–1955), while he was working in 1928 in his laboratory at St Mary's Hospital in London.

Fleming was doing research on staphylococcus, a species of bacterium that can cause disease in humans and animals. In the laboratory such bacteria are grown in dishes containing a culture medium – a jelly-like substance which contains their food. Fleming noticed that one of his dishes had been accidentally contaminated with a mould. The mould could have entered the laboratory through an open window. All around where the mould was growing, the staphylococci had disappeared.

Fleming investigates the mould

Intrigued, because he had correctly concluded that the mould must contain a substance that killed the bacterium, Fleming isolated the mould and grew more of it in a culture broth. He found that the broth acquired a high antibacterial activity. He tested the action of the broth with a wide variety of pathogenic bacteria, and found that many of them were quickly destroyed.

Fleming was also able to demonstrate that the white corpuscles in human blood were not sensitive to the broth. This suggested to him that other human cells in the body would not be affected by it.

Penicillin is discovered

The mould that Fleming's acute powers of observation had noted in a single culture dish, was found to be *Penicillium notatum*. Fleming named the drug penicillin after this mould.

There the matter rested for 15 years. At the time that penicillin was discovered, it would have been extremely difficult to isolate and purify the drug using the chemical techniques then available. It would also have been quite easily destroyed by them. Without any of the pure substance, Fleming had no way of knowing its extraordinarily high antibacterial activity and its almost negligible toxicity. In fact, penicillin diluted 80,000,000 times will still inhibit the growth of staphylococcus. To translate this number of noughts into something tangible: if one drop of water is diluted 80,000,000 times it would fill over 6,000 whisky bottles.

The first practical application

Then in 1935, German–British biochemist Ernst Chain joined Professor Florey at Oxford. There in 1939 he began a survey of antimicrobial substances. One of the first he looked at was Fleming's mould. It was chosen because it was already known to be active against staphylococcus, and because, since it was difficult to purify, it represented a biochemical challenge.

A method of purification using primitive apparatus was discovered, and an experiment using penicillin to treat infected mice was carried out with remarkable success. Eventually, enough penicillin was made to treat the first human patient in the terminal stage of a generalized infection. The patient showed an astonishing, although temporary, recovery. Five more seriously ill patients were successfully treated.

Because these patients had already failed to respond to sulphonamide drugs, the value of penicillin was now clearly apparent. For although suphonamides are much more toxic to bacteria than to leucocytes (white blood cells), they do have some poisonous action on the whole human organism.

The new lifesaver

England, then in the midst of World War II, had insufficient resources to manufacture the new wonder drug on a sufficiently large scale. Florey went to the USA to try to interest the large pharmaceutical companies in penicillin. As a result of an outstanding effort, enough penicillin was produced in time to treat all the battle casualties of the Normandy landings in 1944. The use of penicillin in wartime saved countless lives, as it has continued to do ever since.

for food. When the parents return, the chicks often have to chase for food, with the stronger chick being fed first. They spend much time preening themselves and each other (allopreening).

It was estimated in 1997 that the penguin population fell 20% in 10 years. Zoologists blame over-fishing, particularly by large trawling fleets.

penicillin any of a group of ◊antibiotic (bacteria killing) compounds obtained from filtrates of moulds of the genus *Penicillium* (especially *P. notatum*) or produced synthetically. Penicillin was the first antibiotic to be discovered (by Alexander ◊Fleming); it kills a broad spectrum of bacteria, many of which cause disease in humans.

The use of the original type of penicillin is limited by the increasing resistance of ◊pathogens and by allergic reactions in patients. Since 1941, numerous other antibiotics of the penicillin family have been discovered which are more selective against, or resistant to, specific microorganisms.

penis male reproductive organ containing the ◊urethra, the channel through which urine and ◊semen are voided. It transfers sperm to the female reproductive tract to fertilize the ovum. In mammals, the penis is made erect by vessels that fill with blood, and in most mammals (but not humans) is stiffened by a bone.

Snakes and lizards have a paired structure that serves as a penis; other reptiles have a single organ. A few birds, mainly ducks and geese, also have a type of penis, as do snails, barnacles, and some other invertebrates. Many insects have a rigid, nonerectile male organ, usually referred to as an intromittent organ.

PENIS

The penis of the male Antarctic opossum shrimp is almost the same length as his entire body. Moreover, he has not just one penis but two.

pennyroyal European perennial plant belonging to the mint family, with oblong leaves and clusters or whorls of purplish flowers growing around the stem at intervals. It is found in wet places on sandy soil. (*Mentha pulegium,* family Labiatae.)

pentadactyl limb typical limb of the mammals, birds, reptiles, and amphibians. These vertebrates (animals with backbone) are all descended from primitive amphibians whose immediate ancestors were fleshy-finned fish. The limb which evolved in those amphibians had three parts: a 'hand/foot' with five digits (fingers/toes), a lower limb containing two bones, and an upper limb containing one bone.

This basic pattern has persisted in all the terrestrial vertebrates, and those aquatic vertebrates (such as seals) which are descended from them. Natural selection has modified the pattern to fit different ways of life. In flying animals (birds and bats) it is greatly altered and in some vertebrates, such as whales and snakes, the limbs are greatly reduced or lost. Pentadactyl limbs of different species are an example of ◊homologous organs.

pentagon five-sided plane figure. The regular pentagon has golden section proportions between its sides and diagonals. The five-pointed star formed by drawing all the diagonals of a regular pentagon is called a **pentagram**. This star has further golden sections.

pentanol $C_5H_{11}OH$ (common name ***amyl alcohol***) clear, colourless, oily liquid, usually having a characteristic choking odour. It is obtained by the fermentation of starches and from the distillation of petroleum.

Pentium in computing, microprocessor produced by ◊Intel in 1993. The Pentium followed on from the 486 processor and would have been called the 586, but Intel was unable to register numbers as a trademark. The Pentium family was extended by the Pentium Pro in 1995 and the Pentium II in 1997, and also by the addition of MMX instructions 1996. All members of the family are 32-bit chips with 64-bit data buses for faster access to memory and the ◊PCI expansion bus.

The original Pentium had about 3.1 million transistors, the Pentium Pro about 5.5 million, and the Pentium II about 7.5 million. The slowest Pentium ran at 60 MHz, but in 1997 speeds reached 300 MHz in PCs and 450 MHz under laboratory conditions.

penumbra the region of partial shade between the totally dark part (umbra) of a ◊shadow and the fully illuminated region outside. It occurs when a source of light is only partially obscured by a shadow-casting object. The darkness of a penumbra varies gradually from total darkness at one edge to full brightness at the other. In astronomy, a penumbra is a region of the Earth from which only a partial ◊eclipse of the Sun or Moon can be seen.

peony any of a group of perennial plants native to Europe, Asia, and North America, remarkable for their large, round, brilliant white, pink, or red flowers. Most popular in gardens are the common peony (*P. officinalis*), the white peony (*P. lactiflora*), and the taller tree peony (*P. suffruticosa*). (Genus *Paeonia*, family Paeoniaceae.)

pepper climbing plant native to the East Indies. When gathered green, the berries are crushed to release the seeds for the spice called black pepper. When the berries are ripe, the seeds are removed and their outer skin is discarded, to produce white pepper. Chilli pepper, cayenne or red pepper, and the sweet peppers used as a vegetable come from ◊capsicums native to the New World. (*Piper nigrum*, family Piperaceae.)

peppermint perennial herb of the mint family, native to Europe, with oval aromatic leaves and purple flowers. Oil of peppermint is used in medicine and confectionery. (*Mentha piperita*, family Labiatae.)

pepsin enzyme that breaks down proteins during digestion. It requires a strongly acidic environment and is present in the stomach.

peptide molecule comprising two or more ◊amino acid molecules (not necessarily different) joined by **peptide bonds**, whereby the acid group of one acid is linked to the amino group of the other (–CO.NH). The number of amino acid molecules in the peptide is indicated by referring to it as a di-, tri-, or polypeptide (two, three, or many amino acids).

Proteins are built up of interacting polypeptide chains with various types of bonds occurring between the chains. Incomplete hydrolysis (splitting up) of a protein yields a mixture of peptides, examination of which helps to determine the sequence in which the amino acids occur within the protein.

peptide bond bond that joins two peptides together within a protein. The carboxyl (–COOH) group on one ◊amino acid reacts with the amino ($-NH_2$) group on another amino acid to form a peptide bond (–CO–NH–) with the elimination of water. Peptide bonds are broken by hydrolytic enzymes called peptidases.

perborate any salt formed by the action of hydrogen peroxide on borates.

Perborates contain the radical BO_3.

percentage way of representing a number as a ◊fraction of 100. Thus 45 percent (45%) equals $\frac{45}{100}$, and 45% of 20 is $\frac{45}{100}$ x 20 = 9.

In general, if a quantity x changes to y, the percentage change is $100(x - y)/x$. Thus, if the number of people in a room changes from 40 to 50, the percentage increase is (100 x 10)/40 = 25%. To express a fraction as a percentage, its denominator must first be converted to 100 – for example, $\frac{1}{8}$ = 12.5/100 = 12.5%. The use of percentages often makes it easier to compare fractions that do not have a common denominator.

The percentage sign is thought to have been derived as an economy measure when recording in the old counting houses; writing in the numeric symbol for $\frac{25}{100}$ of a cargo would take two lines of parchment, and hence the '100' denominator was put alongside the 25 and rearranged to '%'.

percentile in a cumulative frequency distribution, one of the 99 values of a variable that divide its distribution into 100 parts of equal frequency. In practice, only certain of the percentiles are used. They are the ◊median (or 50th percentile), the lower and the upper ◊quartiles (respectively, the 25th and 75th percentiles), the 10th percentile which cuts off the bottom 10% of a frequency distribution, and the 90th which cuts off the top 10%. The 5th and 95th are also sometimes used.

perch any of the largest order of spiny-finned bony fishes, the Perciformes, with some 8,000 species. This order includes the sea basses, cichlids, damselfishes, mullets, barracudas, wrasses, and gobies. Perches of the freshwater genus *Perca* are found in Europe, Asia, and North America. They have varied shapes and are usually a greenish colour. They are very prolific, spawning when about three years old, and have voracious appetites.

perch, climbing freshwater bony fish that is often found in stagnant poorly oxygenated water. It is able to breathe air and so can travel short distances on land, between water sources, by pulling itself along by its fins. Climbing perch are in the genus *Anabas*.

peregrine falcon species of ◊falcon.

perennating organ in plants, that part of a ◊biennial plant or herbaceous perennial that allows it to survive the winter; usually a root, tuber, rhizome, bulb, or corm.

perennial plant plant that lives for more than two years. Herbaceous perennials have aerial stems and leaves that die each autumn. They survive the winter by means of an underground storage (perennating) organ, such as a bulb or rhizome. Trees and shrubs or woody perennials have stems that persist above ground throughout the year, and may be either ◊deciduous or ◊evergreen. See also ◊annual plant, biennial plant.

perfume fragrant essence used to scent the body, cosmetics, and candles. More than 100 natural aromatic chemicals may be blended from a range of 60,000 flowers, leaves, fruits, seeds, woods, barks, resins, and roots, combined by natural animal fixatives and various synthetics. Favoured ingredients include ◊balsam, civet (from the African civet cat) hyacinth, jasmine, lily of the valley, musk (from the ◊musk deer), orange blossom, rose, and tuberose.

Culture of the cells of fragrant plants, on membranes that are constantly bathed in a solution to carry the essential oils away for separation, is now being adopted to reduce costs.

perianth in botany, a collective term for the outer whorls of the flower, which protect the reproductive parts during development.

In most ◊dicotyledons the perianth is composed of two distinct whorls, the calyx of sepals and the corolla of ◊petals, whereas in many ◊monocotyledons the sepals and petals are indistinguishable and the segments of the perianth are then known individually as tepals.

periastron in astronomy, the point at which an object travelling in an elliptical orbit around a star is at its closest to the star; the point at which it is furthest is known as the apastron.

pericarp wall of a ◊fruit. It encloses the seeds and is derived from the ◊ovary wall. In fruits such as the acorn, the pericarp becomes dry and hard, forming a shell around the seed. In fleshy fruits the pericarp is typically made up of three distinct layers. The **epicarp**, or **exocarp**, forms the tough outer skin of the fruit, while the **mesocarp** is often fleshy and forms the middle layers. The innermost layer or **endocarp**, which surrounds the seeds, may be membranous or thick and hard, as in the ◊drupe (stone) of cherries, plums, and apricots.

peridotite rock consisting largely of the mineral olivine; pyroxene and other minerals may also be present. Peridotite is an ultramafic rock containing less than 45% silica by weight. It is believed to be one of the rock types making up the Earth's upper mantle, and is sometimes brought from the depths to the surface by major movements, or as inclusions in lavas.

perigee the point at which an object, travelling in an elliptical orbit around the Earth, is at its closest to the Earth. The point at which it is furthest from the Earth is the apogee.

perihelion the point at which an object, travelling in an elliptical orbit around the Sun, is at its closest to the Sun. The point at which it is furthest from the Sun is the aphelion.

perimeter or ***boundary*** line drawn around the edge of an area or shape. For example, the perimeter of a rectangle is the sum of its four sides; the perimeter of a circle is known as its **circumference**.

period in chemistry, a horizontal row of elements in the ◊periodic table. There is a gradation of properties along each period, from metallic (group I, the alkali metals) to nonmetallic (group VII, the halogens).

period another name for menstruation; see ◊menstrual cycle.

period in physics, the time taken for one complete cycle of a repeated sequence of events. For example, the time taken for a pendulum to swing from side to side and back again is the period of the pendulum. The period is the reciprocal of the ◊frequency.

TO REMEMBER THE ELEMENTS IN THEIR CORRECT ORDER IN THE FIRST THREE PERIODS OF THE TABLE (HYDROGEN BEING OMITTED AND POTASSIUM INCLUDED):

HERE LIES BENJAMIN BOLD CRY NOT OLD FRIEND NEEDLESSLY NATURE MAGNIFIES ALL SIMPLE PEOPLE SOMETIMES, CLOTS AND KINGS.

HYDROGEN, HELIUM, LITHIUM, BERYLLIUM, BORON, CARBON, NITROGEN, OXYGEN, FLUORINE, NEON, SODIUM, MAGNESIUM, ALUMINIUM, SILICON, PHOSPHORUS, SULPHUR, CHLORINE, ARGON, POTASSIUM **(H, HE, LI, BE, B, C, N, O, F, NE, NA, MG, AL, SI, P, S, CL, A, K)**

periodic table of the elements in chemistry, a table in which the elements are arranged in order of their atomic number. The table summarizes the major properties of the elements and enables

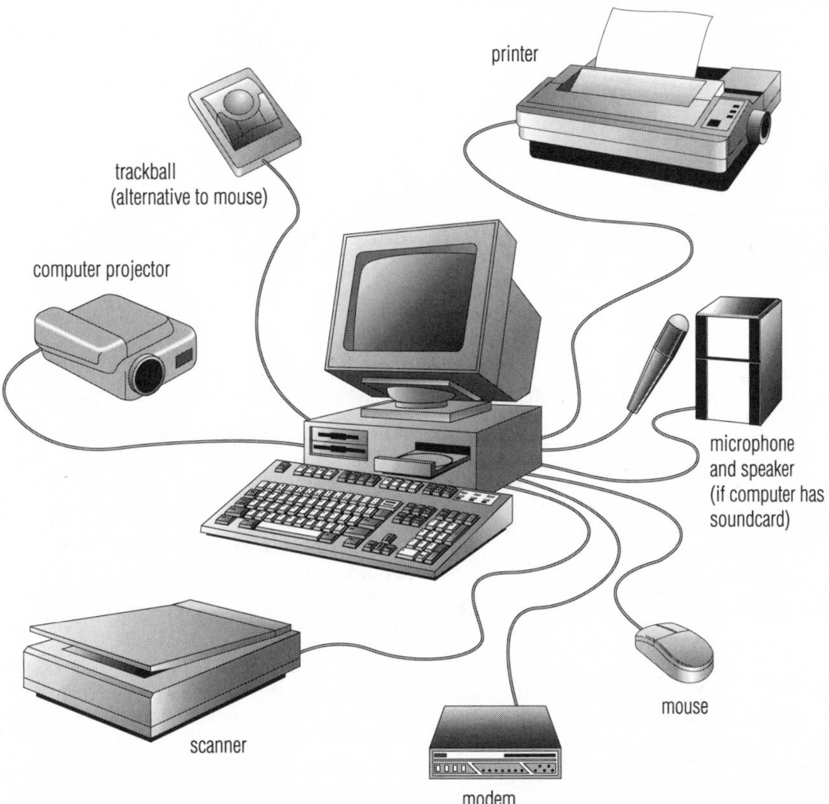

peripheral device *Some of the types of peripheral device that may be connected to a computer include printers, scanners, and modems.*

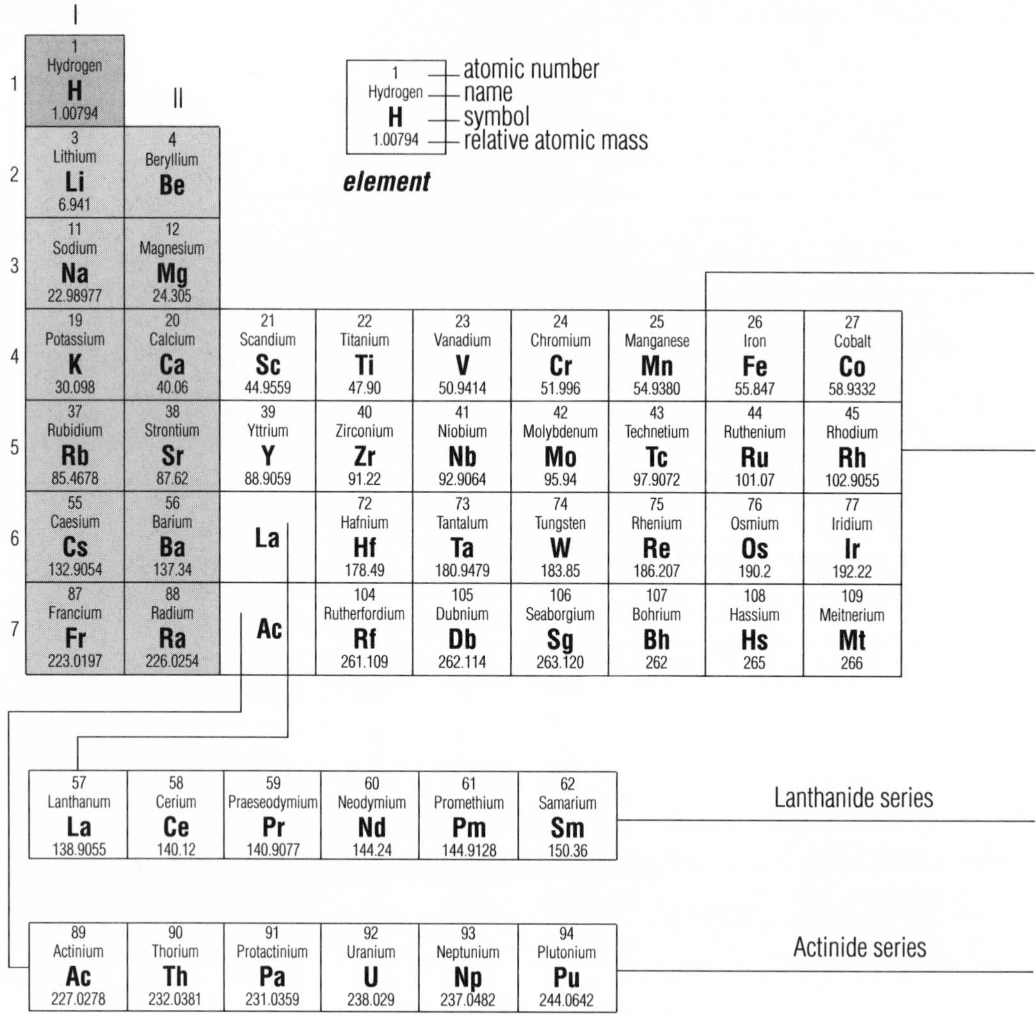

periodic table of the elements

predictions to be made about their behaviour.

There are striking similarities in the chemical properties of the elements in each of the vertical columns (called **groups**), which are numbered I–VII and 0 to reflect the number of electrons in the outermost unfilled shell and hence the maximum ◊valency. A gradation (trend) of properties may be traced along the horizontal rows (called **periods**). Metallic character increases across a period from right to left, and down a group. A large block of elements, between groups II and III, contains the transition elements, characterized by displaying more than one valency state.

PERIODIC TABLE OF THE ELEMENTS

http://domains.twave.net/users/yinon/default.html

Elements in the periodic table are discussed in depth. Information regarding the date of discovery, symbol, classification, atomic number, mass, melting and boiling points, number of protons, electrons and neutrons, crystal structure, and more is given for each element. Elements can be arranged by atomic number, name, chemical symbol, or date of discovery.

periodontal disease (formerly known as ***pyorrhoea***) disease of the gums and bone supporting the teeth, caused by the accumulation of plaque and microorganisms; the gums recede, and the teeth eventually become loose and may drop out unless treatment is sought. Bacteria can eventually erode the bone that supports the teeth, so that surgery becomes necessary.

peripatus invertebrate found in rainforest leaf-litter. See ◊velvet worm.

peripheral device in computing, any item connected to a computer's ◊central processing unit (CPU). Typical peripherals include keyboard, mouse, monitor and printer. Users who enjoy playing games might add a ◊ joystick or a ◊trackball; others might connect a ◊modem, scanner, or ◊integrated services digital network (ISDN) terminal to their machines. *See illustration on page 565.*

periscope optical instrument designed for observation from a concealed position such as from a submerged submarine. In its basic form it consists of a tube with parallel mirrors at each end, inclined at 45° to its axis. The periscope attained prominence in naval and military operations of World War I.

			III	IV	V	VI	VII	0
								2 Helium **He** 4002.60
			5 Boron **B** 10.81	6 Carbon **C** 12.011	7 Nitrogen **N** 14.0067	8 Oxygen **O** 15.9994	9 Fluorine **F** 18.99840	10 Neon **Ne** 20.179
			13 Aluminium **Al** 26.98154	14 Silicon **Si** 28.066	15 Phosphorus **P** 30.9738	16 Sulphur **S** 32.06	17 Chlorine **Cl** 35.453	18 Argon **Ar** 39.948
28 Nickel **Ni** 58.70	29 Copper **Cu** 63.546	30 Zinc **Zn** 65.38	31 Gallium **Ga** 69.72	32 Germanium **Ge** 72.59	33 Arsenic **As** 74.9216	34 Selenium **Se** 78.96	35 Bromine **Br** 79.904	36 Krypton **Kr** 83.80
46 Palladium **Pd** 106.4	47 Silver **Ag** 107.868	48 Cadmium **Cd** 112.40	49 Indium **In** 114.82	50 Tin **Sn** 118.69	51 Antimony **Sb** 121.75	52 Tellurium **Te** 127.75	53 Iodine **I** 126.9045	54 Xenon **Xe** 131.30
78 Platinum **Pt** 195.09	79 Gold **Au** 196.9665	80 Mercury **Hg** 200.59	81 Thallium **Tl** 204.37	82 Lead **Pb** 207.37	83 Bismuth **Bi** 207.2	84 Polonium **Po** 210	85 Astatine **At** 211	86 Radon **Rn** 222.0176
110 Ununnilium **Uun** 269	111 Unununium **Uuu** 272							

63 Europium **Eu** 151.96	64 Gadolinium **Gd** 157.25	65 Terbium **Tb** 158.9254	66 Dysprosium **Dy** 162.50	67 Holmium **Ho** 164.9304	68 Erbium **Er** 167.26	69 Thulium **Tm** 168.9342	70 Ytterbium **Yb** 173.04	71 Lutetium **Lu** 174.97
95 Americium **Am** 243.0614	96 Curium **Cm** 247.0703	97 Berkelium **Bk** 247	98 Californium **Cf** 251.0786	99 Einsteinium **Es** 252.0828	100 Fermium **Fm** 257.0951	101 Mendelevium **Md** 258.0986	102 Nobelium **No** 259.1009	103 Lawrencium **Lr** 260.1054

Although most often thought of as a submarine observation device, periscopes were widely used in the trenches during World War I to allow observation without exposing the observer, and special versions were also developed to be attached to rifles.

Perissodactyla one of the orders of hoofed mammals, characterized by the possession of an odd number of toes on the hind foot, and by the presence of a third trochanter (projection) on the femur or thigh bone. There are three living families of Perissodactyla: Equidae (horses); Tapiridae (tapirs); and Rhinocerotidae (rhinoceroses). In addition there are a number of extinct forms.

peristalsis wavelike contractions, produced by the contraction of smooth muscle, that pass along tubular organs, such as the intestines. The same term describes the wavelike motion of earthworms and other invertebrates, in which part of the body contracts as another part elongates.

peritoneum membrane lining the abdominal cavity and digestive organs of vertebrates. **Peritonitis**, inflammation within the peritoneum, can occur due to infection or other irritation. It is sometimes seen following a burst appendix and quickly proves fatal if not treated.

periwinkle in botany, any of several trailing blue-flowered evergreen plants of the dogbane family, native to Europe and Asia. They range in length from 20 cm/8 in to 1 m/3 ft. (Genus *Vinca*, family Apocynaceae.)

The related Madagascar periwinkle (*Catharanthus roseus*) produces chemicals that prevent the division of cells and are used to treat leukaemia.

periwinkle in zoology, any marine snail of the family Littorinidae, found on the shores of Europe and E North America. Periwinkles have a conical spiral shell, and feed on algae.

permafrost condition in which a deep layer of soil does not thaw out during the summer. Permafrost occurs under periglacial conditions. It is claimed that 26% of the world's land surface is permafrost.

Permafrost gives rise to a poorly drained form of grassland typical of N Canada, Siberia, and Alaska known as ◊tundra.

permanent hardness hardness of water that cannot be removed by boiling (see ◊hard water).

permeability in physics, the degree to which the presence of a substance alters the magnetic field around it. Most substances have

The Periodic Table

by Gordon Woods

Introduction

Think how difficult it would be to assemble a jigsaw of which about 35 of the pieces were missing and roughly 20 of the 65 you had were too damaged to fit properly. Could you work out the shapes of some of the missing pieces? These are exactly the processes carried out by Mendeleyev in 1869 when he produced the first Periodic Table.

Earlier attempts

Several 19th century scientists had sought earlier to identify patterns in the properties of chemical elements linked to the weights of the atoms. Dobereiner had noticed sets of three similar elements (triads) for which the average weight of the lightest and heaviest was close to the weight of the middle one (try chlorine 35.5, bromine 80 and iodine 127). British chemist Newlands wrote the elements in order of increasing weight, noting that an element resembled the eighth following. His 'Law of Octaves' soon broke down because of missing elements from a fundamentally correct law. He was ridiculed (why not list the elements alphabetically!), flung out of 'The Royal Society', Britain's top scientific institution, only to be reinstated when it was realized that he had nearly beaten Mendeleyev.

Who was Mendeleyev?

Dmitri Ivanovitch Mendeleyev was born in Tobolsk (Siberia) in 1834 and brought to St Petersburg, capital of Tzarist Russia, for his secondary education by his ambitious mother who had realized her youngest son's potential. After research throughout Europe he was appointed Chemistry Professor at St Petersburg in 1865. His first marriage foundered because of all the time he spent researching; later he married a young student. After discontent among the university students Mendeleyev took their petition to the education minister who sacked him from his professorial chair. Later both Oxford and Cambridge awarded him honorary doctorates. Aged 53 he made a solo balloon ascent to view a solar eclipse. A Periodic Table was carried aloft in his funeral procession in February 1907.

Mendeleyev's special contribution

Mendeleyev is said to have been playing patience when he suddenly visualized the arrangement of the elements in the patterns of the cards. It is certainly true that 20 years of previous education had equipped him to formulate the 'Periodic Law' which he developed for the remaining 40 years of his life. It stated that the elements display periodic (i.e. regularly repeating) properties when listed in order of increasing atomic weight.

Accurate atomic weights were needed for all 19th century element patterns. Mendeleyev correctly recalculated some values better to fit his table. However iodine and tellurium provided a problem since iodine was chemically similar to bromine yet the heavier element tellurium fitted below bromine according to the weight order. Mendeleyev's solution was to have his research assistants redetermine tellurium's atomic weight to be the smaller. Thus he correctly positioned the two elements but for the wrong reason. Today we know that the elements are listed in order of increasing atomic number which only differs from the atomic weight order in three instances.

A stroke of genius was to leave spaces for elements yet to be discovered and to boldly predict properties for five such elements. Good scientists explain known information, great ones correctly predict unknown facts. Fortunately three of these missing elements were found within 20 years and their properties matched predictions to a remarkable degree.

Modern periodic tables

Note the plural. There are many different formats, some are three-dimensional but all show the elements in order of increasing atomic number. Most have vertical columns called groups and horizontal rows called periods. The underlying reason for the arrangement is the electron arrangement of the atoms of the elements. All elements in the same group have the same number of electrons in the outermost shell which governs the chemical nature of an element, hence their chemical similarity. Elements in the same period have the same number of electron shells, an extra electron being added for each increase in the atomic number.

Metals and nonmetals

Crossing from left to right elements become more nonmetallic and descending they become more metallic. Thus moving diagonally down to the right, elements are comparable in their metallic/nonmetallic nature. This can be shown by a staircase, or better, as a diagonal line through the boxes of those elements which cannot be clearly classified either as a metal or a nonmetal. For example the use of silicon in computers stems from it being a semi-conductor. Metals are conductors, nonmetals are insulators so semi-conductors are both. Science is not black and white but shades of grey.

Using the Periodic Table

The group number is given in Roman numerals above the main groups. For groups I–IV the group number is the sole valency. For groups V–VII, the main valency is (8–group number) with a less common valency of the group number from the third period onwards. Group 0 (there is no Roman numeral for zero) on the far right is called the noble gases. Their valency is regarded as 0. These elements were once called inert gases but to the astonishment of chemists Bartlett made compounds between fluorine, xenon and krypton. The Periodic Table is less helpful with transition metals which have a valency of 2 and usually other(s).

One can copy Mendeleyev's work by making predictions about 'unknown' elements. Knowing that both sodium and potassium react with water producing hydrogen and an alkali, it is reasonable to predict the same behaviour for rubidium and caesium directly below them. Since potassium is more reactive than sodium, it is likely that caesium will be the most reactive of the four. It is! When added to a bowl of water it shatters the container! Incidentally caesium is one of three elements which have different spelling in North America and the UK. Which are the others?

Are there more elements to discover?

By 1950 all the elements for which Mendeleyev had left gaps had been discovered. Some are extremely rare and were identified from the radioactive decay of other elements, sometimes in the debris of atomic bomb tests (1944–1950). However elements with atomic numbers above 92 have been created by bombarding atoms of uranium with neutrons, carbon nuclei, and other subatomic particles. These synthetic elements are all identified from their radioactivity. As the atomic number increases it becomes harder to make the elements, so less of the element exists... and it is decaying all the time. It is possible to identify 10–18 g but there is less than 1 g of the elements with atomic number greater than 100.

The discoverer of an element has the right to name it. Some chose their country (gallium, francium), or a property (chromium has compounds in many colours), or the place of discovery (such as strontium, named after the Scottish village of Strontian). Only three places in the world have the facilities to make the synthetic elements. Both the USSR and the USA claimed initial discovery of elements 104 and 105 but each country gave them different names (for example 104 to the Russians was Kurschatovium (Ku) but to the Americans was Rutherfordium (Rf). This scientific argument was initially solved by giving them artificial temporary names, unnilquadium (a hundredandfourium), and unnilpentium. A committee sat for years to decide officially who were the discoverers.

Symbols and names
Element symbols are internationally agreed but the name differs with the language. This difference is only slight with elements discovered since 1850. Less reactive metals, isolated for hundreds of years may have very different names. Petrol is unleaded in the UK, bleifrei in Germany, sans plomb in France, senza piomba in Italy, sin plomo in Spain. Note how the last three names relate to the Latin plumbum from which the symbol Pb is derived, as are plumber and plumbline.

Unusual formats
Hundreds of versions exist of the Periodic Table. For example: some show the physical state (solid, liquid or gas) of the element; in the UK only, the metal mercury and the nonmetal bromine are liquids; three-dimensional varieties divide up the Periodic Table into its four blocks labelled s, p, d and f according to the shape of the outer electron cloud round the nucleus.

The Periodic Table today is the most recognizable logo of chemistry. Despite the range of formats they are all related to Mendeleyev's original formulation. Element 101 is named after him but strangely he never won a Nobel prize.

a small constant permeability. When the permeability is less than 1, the material is a ◊diamagnetic material; when it is greater than 1, it is a ◊paramagnetic material. Ferrimagnetic materials have very large permeabilities. See also ◊magnetism.

Permian period of geological time 290–245 million years ago, the last period of the Palaeozoic era. Its end was marked by a significant change in marine life, including the extinction of many corals and trilobites. Deserts were widespread, terrestrial amphibians and mammal-like reptiles flourished, and cone-bearing plants (gymnosperms) came to prominence. In the oceans, 49% of families and 72% of genera vanished in the late Permian. On land, 78% of reptile families and 67% of amphibian families disappeared.

permutation in mathematics, a specified arrangement of a group of objects.

It is the arrangement of *a* distinct objects taken *b* at a time in all possible orders. It is given by $a!/(a - b)!$, where '!' stands for ◊factorial. For example, the number of permutations of four letters taken from any group of six different letters is 6!/2! = (1 x 2 x 3 x 4 x 5 x 6)/(1 x 2) = 360. The theoretical number of four-letter 'words' that can be made from an alphabet of 26 letters is 26!/22! = 358,800.

perovskite a yellow, brown or greyish-black orthorhombic mineral, $CaTiO_3$, which sometimes contains cerium. Other minerals that have a similar structure are said to have the **perovskite structure**. The term also refers to $MgSiO_3$ with the perovskite structure, the principle mineral that makes up the Earth's lower ◊mantle.

$CaTiO_3$ perovskite occurs primarily as a minor constituent of some igneous rocks in Earth's crust and mantle and in some meteorites. $MgSiO_3$ perovskite has the same chemical composition as pyroxene, a principal constituent of the upper mantle. But the extreme pressures in the lower mantle cause the oxygen atoms to be packed more tightly together than in pyroxene, giving rise to the perovskite form of $MgSiO_3$ in the lower mantle.

The perovskite structure of $MgSiO_3$ was discovered in diamond-anvil cell experiments in which upper mantle materials that are stable at the Earth's surface, such as the mineral pyroxene, are squeezed at high pressures to simulate the Earth's interior. Although this mineral does not occur naturally at the Earth's surface it is thought to be the most abundant mineral in the mantle, and therefore Earth's most abundant mineral.

perpendicular in mathematics, at a right angle; also, a line at right angles to another or to a plane. For a pair of ◊skew lines (lines in three dimensions that do not meet), there is just one common perpendicular, which is at right angles to both lines; the nearest points on the two lines are the feet of this perpendicular.

perpetual motion the idea that a machine can be designed and constructed in such a way that, once started, it will continue in motion indefinitely without requiring any further input of energy (motive power). Such a device would contradict at least one of the two laws of thermodynamics that state that (1) energy can neither be created nor destroyed (the law of conservation of energy) and (2) heat cannot by itself flow from a cooler to a hotter object. As a result, all practical (real) machines require a continuous supply of energy, and no heat engine is able to convert all the heat into useful work.

Perseus in astronomy, a bright constellation of the northern hemisphere, near ◊Cassiopeia. It is represented as the mythological hero; the head of the decapitated Gorgon, Medusa, is marked by ◊Algol (Beta Persei), the best known of the eclipsing binary stars.

Perseus lies in the Milky Way and contains the Double Cluster, a twin cluster of stars called h and Chi Persei. They are just visible to the naked eye as two hazy patches of light close to one another.

Persian cat or ***Longhair*** breed of domestic longhaired cat. The modern longhair pedigree is descended from cats imported to Britain in the late 19th century from Turkey or Persia. The typical Persian has a cobby (sturdy and rounded) body, a round head and eyes, short nose, with long, luxuriant fur. They occur in many colours and colour combinations.

In the USA, most longhaired cats are classified as Persian with the colours listed as varieties; in Britain, they are called Longhairs and each colour is listed as a separate breed.

persicaria any of a group of plants belonging to the dock family, found growing in waste places and arable land, often near water. Common persicaria (*P. persicaria*) is sprawling in shape and has lance-shaped, black-spotted leaves and spikes of pink flowers. Pale persicaria (*P. lapathifolium*) is slightly larger, with pale dots on the leaves, and heads of usually white flowers. Both are found throughout much of the northern hemisphere. (Genus *Polygonum*, family Polygonaceae.)

persimmon any of a group of tropical trees belonging to the ebony family, especially the common persimmon (*D. virginiana*) of the southeastern USA. Growing up to 19 m/60 ft high, the persimmon has alternate oval leaves and yellow-green flowers. The small, sweet, orange fruits are edible. (Genus *Diospyros*, family Ebenaceae.)

The Japanese persimmon (*D. kaki*) has larger fruits and is widely cultivated.

personal computer (PC) another name for ◊microcomputer. The term is also used, more specifically, to mean the IBM Personal Computer and computers compatible with it.

The first IBM PC was introduced in 1981; it had 64 kilobytes of random access memory (RAM) and one floppy-disc drive. It was followed in 1983 by the XT (with a hard-disc drive) and in 1984 by the AT (based on a more powerful ◊microprocessor). Many manufacturers have copied the basic design, which is now regarded as a standard for business microcomputers. Computers designed to function like an IBM PC are **IBM-compatible computers**.

personal digital assistant (PDA) handheld computer designed to store names, addresses, and diary information, and to send and receive faxes and e-mail. They aim to provide a more flexible and powerful alternative to the Filofax or diary.

The market for PDAs with keyboards is being fought between the Psion Series 3 and 5 (strongest in Europe), the Sharp Zaurus range (strongest in Asia), and HPCs (Handheld PCs) running Microsoft's Windows CE operating system. However, by far the best-selling PDA in 1997 was the Palm Pilot, a very small stylus-operated machine made by US Robotics, a division of 3Com.

personal identification device (PID) device, such as a magnetic card, carrying machine readable identification, which provides authorization for access to a computer system. PIDs are often used in conjunction with a ◊PIN.

personality individual's characteristic way of behaving across a wide range of situations. Two broad dimensions of personality are ◊extroversion and neuroticism. A number of more specific personal traits have also been described, including ◊psychopathy (antisocial behaviour).

personal productivity software in computing, work-oriented software such as ◊word processors, spreadsheets, or ◊databases.

perspective the realistic representation of a three-dimensional object in two dimensions. In a perspective drawing, vertical lines are drawn parallel from the top of the page to the bottom. Horizontal lines, however, are represented by straight lines which meet at one of two perspective points. These perspective points lie to the right and left of the drawing at a distance which depends on the view being taken of the object.

Perspex trade name for a clear, lightweight, tough plastic first produced in 1930. It is widely used for watch glasses, advertising signs, domestic baths, motorboat windscreens, aircraft canopies, and protective shields. Its chemical name is polymethylmethacrylate (PMMA). It is manufactured under other names: Lucite, Acrylite, and Rhoplex (in the USA), and Oroglas (in Europe).

perspiration excretion of water and dissolved substances from the ◊sweat glands of the skin of mammals. Perspiration has two main functions: body cooling by the evaporation of water from the skin surface, and excretion of waste products such as salts.

Genius is one per cent inspiration and ninety-nine per cent perspiration.

THOMAS ALVA EDISON US scientist and inventor. *Life* ch 24

pertussis medical name for ◊whooping cough, an infectious disease mainly seen in children.

Peru Current formerly known as ***Humboldt Current*** cold ocean ◊current flowing north from the Antarctic along the W coast of South America to S Ecuador, then west. It reduces the coastal temperature, making the W slopes of the Andes arid because winds are already chilled and dry when they meet the coast.

pessary medical device designed to be inserted into the vagina either to support a displaced womb or as a contraceptive. The word is also used for a vaginal suppository used for administering drugs locally, made from glycerol or oil of theobromine, which melts within the vagina to release the contained substance – for example, a contraceptive, antibiotic, antifungal agent, or ◊prostaglandin (to induce labour).

pest in biology, any insect, fungus, rodent, or other living organism that has a harmful effect on human beings, other than those that directly cause human diseases. Most pests damage crops or livestock, but the term also covers those that damage buildings, destroy food stores, and spread disease.

pesticide any chemical used in farming, gardening, or indoors to combat pests. Pesticides are of three main types: **insecticides** (to kill insects), **fungicides** (to kill fungal diseases), and **herbicides** (to kill plants, mainly those considered weeds). Pesticides cause a number of pollution problems through spray drift onto surrounding areas, direct contamination of users or the public, and as residues on food.

The safest pesticides include those made from plants, such as the insecticides pyrethrum and derris.

Pyrethrins are safe and insects do not develop resistance to them. Their impact on the environment is very small as the ingredients break down harmlessly.

More potent are synthetic products, such as chlorinated hydrocarbons. These products, including DDT and dieldrin, are highly toxic to wildlife and often to human beings, so their use is now restricted by law in some areas and is declining. Safer pesticides such as malathion are based on organic phosphorus compounds, but they still present hazards to health. The aid organization Oxfam estimates that pesticides cause about 10,000 deaths worldwide every year.

Pesticides were used to deforest SE Asia during the Vietnam War, causing death and destruction to the area's ecology and lasting health and agricultural problems.

pet animal kept for companionship and occasionally for status. Research suggests that interaction with a pet induces relaxation (slower heart rate and lower blood pressure). In 16th–17th century Europe, keeping animals in this way was thought suggestive of witchcraft.

AnAustralian study in 1992 found that pet owners had lower cholesterol levels than non-pet owners with comparable lifestyles.

petal part of a flower whose function is to attract pollinators such as insects or birds. Petals are frequently large and brightly coloured and may also be scented. Some have a nectary at the base and markings on the petal surface, known as honey guides, to direct pollinators to the source of the nectar. In wind-pollinated plants, however, the petals are usually small and insignificant, and sometimes absent altogether. Petals are derived from modified leaves, and are known collectively as a corolla.

Some insect-pollinated plants also have inconspicuous petals, with large colourful ◊bracts (leaflike structures) or ◊sepals taking over their role, or strong scents that attract pollinators such as flies.

petiole in botany, the stalk attaching the leaf blade, or ◊lamina, to the stem. Typically it is continuous with the midrib of the leaf and attached to the base of the lamina, but occasionally it is attached to the lower surface of the lamina, as in the nasturtium (a peltate leaf). Petioles that are flattened and leaflike are termed phyllodes. Leaves that lack a petiole are said to be sessile.

petit Brabançon smooth-haired form of the ◊griffon ◊Bruxelloise.

petrel any of various families of seabirds in the order Procellariiforme, including the worldwide **storm petrels** (family Hydrobatidae), which include the smallest seabirds (some only 13 cm/5 in long), and the **diving petrels** (family Pelecanoididae) of the southern hemisphere. All have a hooked bill, rudimentary hind toes, tubular nostrils, and feed by diving underwater. They include ◊fulmars and ◊shearwaters.

Like other ground-nesting or burrow-nesting seabirds, petrels are vulnerable to predators such as rats that take eggs and nestlings. Several island species are in danger of extinction, including the **Bermuda petrel** *Pterodroma cahow* and the **Freira petrel** of Madeira *P. madeira*.

petrochemical chemical derived from the processing of petroleum (crude oil).

Petrochemical industries are those that obtain their raw materials from the processing of petroleum and natural gas. Polymers, detergents, solvents, and nitrogen fertilizers are all major products of the petrochemical industries. Inorganic chemical products include carbon black, sulphur, ammonia, and hydrogen peroxide.

petrol mixture of hydrocarbons derived from petroleum, mainly used as a fuel for internal-combustion engines. It is colourless and highly volatile. **Leaded petrol** contains antiknock (a mixture of tetraethyl lead and dibromoethane), which improves the combustion of petrol and the performance of a car engine. The lead from the exhaust fumes enters the atmosphere, mostly as simple lead compounds. There is strong evidence that it can act as a nerve poison on young children and cause mental impairment. This has prompted a gradual switch to the use of **unleaded petrol** in the UK.

The changeover from leaded petrol gained momentum from 1989 owing to a change in the tax on petrol, making it cheaper to buy unleaded fuel. Unleaded petrol contains a different mixture of hydrocarbons, and has a lower ◊octane rating than leaded petrol. Leaded petrol cannot be used in cars fitted with a ◊catalytic converter.

In the USA, petrol is called gasoline, and unleaded petrol has been used for some years.

petrol engine the most commonly used source of power for motor vehicles, introduced by the German engineers Gottlieb Daimler and Karl Benz in 1885. The petrol engine is a complex piece of machinery made up of about 150 moving parts. It is a reciprocating piston engine, in which a number of pistons move up and down in cylinders. A mixture of petrol and air is introduced to the space above the pistons and ignited. The gases produced force the pistons down, generating power. The engine-operating cycle is repeated every four strokes (upward or downward movement) of the piston, this being known as the ◊four-stroke cycle. The motion of the pistons rotate a crankshaft, at the end of which is a heavy flywheel. From the flywheel the power is transferred to the car's driving wheels via the transmission system of clutch, gearbox, and final drive.

The parts of the petrol engine can be subdivided into a number of systems. The **fuel system** pumps fuel from the petrol tank into the carburettor. There it mixes with air and is sucked into the engine cylinders. (With electronic fuel injection, it goes directly from the tank into the cylinders by way of an electronic monitor.) The **ignition system** supplies the sparks to ignite the fuel mixture in the cylinders. By means of an ignition coil and contact breaker, it boosts the 12-volt battery voltage to pulses of 18,000 volts or more. These go via a distributor to the spark plugs in the cylinders, where they create the sparks. (Electronic ignitions replace these parts.) Ignition of the fuel in the cylinders produces temperatures of 700°C/1,300°F or more, and the engine must be cooled to prevent overheating.

Most engines have a **water-cooling system**, in which water circulates through channels in the cylinder block, thus extracting the heat. It flows through pipes in a radiator, which are cooled by fan-blown air. A few cars and most motorbikes are air-cooled, the cylinders being surrounded by many fins to present a large surface area to the air. The **lubrication system** also reduces some heat, but its main job is to keep the moving parts coated with oil, which is pumped under pressure to the camshaft, crankshaft, and valve-operating gear.

petroleum or ***crude oil*** natural mineral oil, a thick greenish-brown flammable liquid found underground in permeable rocks. Petroleum consists of hydrocarbons mixed with oxygen, sulphur, nitrogen, and other elements in varying proportions. It is thought to be derived from ancient organic material that has been converted by, first, bacterial action, then heat, and pressure (but its origin may be chemical also).

From crude petroleum, various products are made by distillation and other processes; for example, fuel oil, petrol, kerosene, diesel, and lubricating oil. Petroleum products and chemicals are used in large quantities in the manufacture of detergents, artificial fibres, plastics, insecticides, fertilizers, pharmaceuticals, toiletries, and synthetic rubber.

Petroleum was formed from the remains of marine plant and animal life which existed many millions of years ago (hence it is known as a fossil fuel). Some of these remains were deposited along with rock-forming sediments under the sea where they were decomposed anaerobically (without oxygen) by bacteria which changed the fats of the sediments into fatty acids which were then changed into an asphaltic material called kerogen. This was then converted over millions of years into petroleum by the combined action of heat and pressure. At an early stage the organic material was squeezed out of its original sedimentary mud into adjacent sandstones. Small globules of oil collected together in the pores of the rock and eventually migrated upwards through layers of porous rock by the action of the oil's own surface tension (capillary action), by the force of water movement within the rock, and by gas pressure. This migration ended either when the petroleum emerged through a fissure as a seepage of gas or oil on to the Earth's surface, or when it was trapped in porous reservoir rocks, such as sandstone or limestone, in anticlines and other traps below impervious rock layers.

The modern oil industry originates in the discovery of oil in western Ontario in 1857 followed by Edwin Drake's discovery in Pennsylvania in 1859. Drake used a steam engine to drive a punching tool to 21 m/68 ft below the surface where he struck oil and started an oil boom. Rapid development followed in other parts of

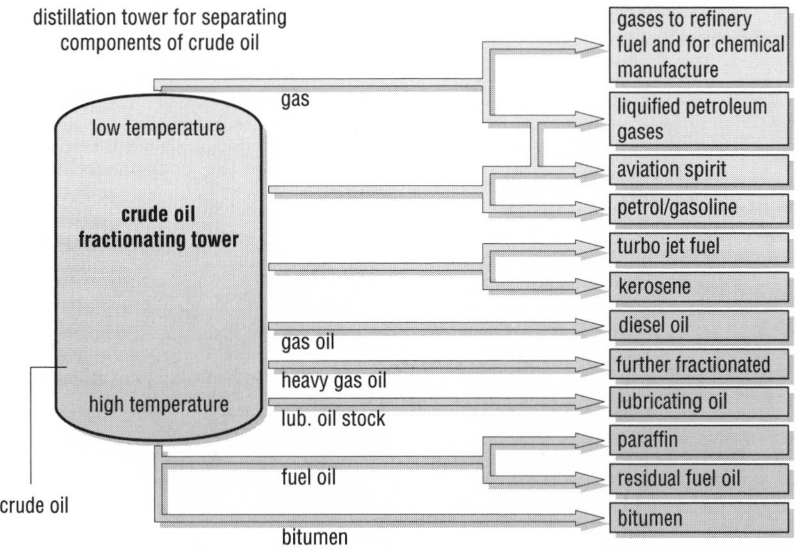

petroleum *Refining petroleum using a distillation column. The crude petroleum is fed in at the bottom of the column where the temperature is high. The gases produced rise up the column, cooling as they travel. At different heights up the column, different gases condense to liquids called fractions, and are drawn off.*

the USA, Canada, Mexico, and then Venezuela where commercial production began in 1878. Oil was found in Romania in 1860, Iran in 1908, Iraq in 1923, Bahrain in 1932, and Saudi Arabia and Kuwait in 1938.

The USA led in production until the 1960s, when the Middle East outproduced other areas, their immense reserves leading to a worldwide dependence on cheap oil for transport and industry. In 1961 the Organization of the Petroleum Exporting Countries (OPEC) was established to avoid exploitation of member countries; after OPEC's price rises in 1973, the International Energy Agency (IEA) was established in 1974 to protect the interests of oil-consuming countries. New technologies were introduced to pump oil from offshore and from the Arctic (the Alaska pipeline) in an effort to avoid a monopoly by OPEC. Global consumption of petroleum in 1993 was 23 billion barrels.

As shallow-water oil reserves dwindle, multinational companies have been developing deep-water oilfields at the edge of the continental shelf in the Gulf of Mexico. Shell has developed Mars, a 500-million barrel oilfield, in 900 m/2,940 ft of water, and the oil companies now have the technology to drill wells at up to 3,075 m/10,000 ft under the sea. It is estimated that the deep waters of Mexico could yield 8–15 million barrels in total; it could overtake the North Sea in importance as an oil source.

In Asia, the oil pipeline from Azerbaijan through Russia to the West, which is the only major pipeline from the Caspian sea, closed during Russia's conflict with Chechnya but reopened in 1997.

pollution The burning of petroleum fuel is one cause of air pollution. The transport of oil can lead to catastrophes – for example, the *Torrey Canyon* tanker lost off SW England in 1967, which led to an agreement by the international oil companies in 1968 to pay compensation for massive shore pollution. The 1989 oil spill in Alaska from the *Exxon Valdez* damaged the area's fragile environment, despite clean-up efforts. Drilling for oil involves the risks of accidental spillage and drilling-rig accidents. The problems associated with oil have led to the various alternative energy technologies.

A new kind of bacterium was developed during the 1970s in the USA, capable of 'eating' oil as a means of countering oil spills.

petrology branch of geology that deals with the study of rocks, their mineral compositions, and their origins.

Peugeot France's second-largest car manufacturer, founded in 1885 when Armand Peugeot (1849–1915) began making bicycles; the company bought the rival firm Citroên in 1974 and the European operations of the American Chrysler Company in 1978.

In 1889 Armand Peugeot produced his first steam car and in 1890 his first petrol-driven car, with a Daimler engine. Peugeot's cars did well in races and were in demand from the public, and by 1900 he was producing a range of models. In the 1930s Peugeot sporting family cars sold widely. In 1978, after the acquisition of Chrysler in Europe, the Talbot marque was reintroduced.

pewter any of various alloys of mostly tin with varying amounts of lead, copper, or antimony. Pewter has been known for centuries and was once widely used for domestic utensils but is now used mainly for ornamental ware.

peyote spineless cactus of N Mexico and the southwestern USA. It has white or pink flowers. Its buttonlike tops contain **mescaline**, which causes hallucinations and is used by American Indians in religious ceremonies. (*Lophopora williamsii,* family Cactaceae.)

PGP abbreviation for the encryption program ◊Pretty Good Privacy.

pH scale from 0 to 14 for measuring acidity or alkalinity. A pH of 7.0 indicates neutrality, below 7 is acid, while above 7 is alkaline. Strong acids, such as those used in car batteries, have a pH of about 2; strong alkalis such as sodium hydroxide are pH 13.

Acidic fruits such as citrus fruits are about pH 4. Fertile soils have a pH of about 6.5 to 7.0, while weak alkalis such as soap are 9 to 10.

phage another name for a ◊bacteriophage, a virus that attacks bacteria.

phagocyte type of white blood cell, or ◊leucocyte, that can engulf a bacterium or other invading microorganism. Phagocytes are found in blood, lymph, and other body tissues, where they also ingest foreign matter and dead tissue. A ◊macrophage differs in size and life span.

phalanger name given to members of the family Phalangeridae (possums) found in New Guinea and Sulawesi. The ◊cuscus is an example.

phalarope any of a genus *Phalaropus* of small, elegant shorebirds in the sandpiper family (Scolopacidae). They have the habit of spinning in the water to stir up insect larvae. They are native to North America, the UK, and the polar regions of Europe.

The male phalarope is courted by the female and hatches the eggs. The female is always larger and more colourful.

phanerogam obsolete term for a plant that bears flowers or cones and reproduces by means of seeds, that is an ◊angiosperm and ◊gymnosperm, or a◊seed plant. Plants such as mosses, fungi, and ferns were known as **cryptogams**.

Phanerozoic Greek *phanero* ***'visible'*** eon in Earth history, consisting of the most recent 570 million years. It comprises the Palaeozoic, Mesozoic, and Cenozoic eras. The vast majority of fossils come from this eon, owing to the evolution of hard shells and internal skeletons. The name means 'interval of well-displayed life'.

pharaoh hound breed of hunting dog known from tomb paintings to have existed in ancient Egypt. It has a long head, large pricked ears, and short red coat with small white markings on the muzzle, chest, toes, and tail tip. Wiry in build, it grows to about 56 cm/22 in tall.

Dogs of the pharaoh hound type are thought to have been introduced into Europe in antiquity by Phoenician traders.

pharmacognosy branch of pharmacology concerned with the identification of drugs extracted from plant and animal tissues.

pharmacology study of the properties of drugs and their effects on the human body.

> *Ali Asuli writing ... 900 years ago divided his pharmacopeia into ... 'Diseases of the Rich' and 'Diseases of the Poor'.*
>
> ABDUS SALAM Pakistani physicist.
> *Scientific World* No 3 1967

pharmacy the preparation and dispensing of drugs; as an area of study, pharmacy includes an understanding of the origins, nature, and action of drugs. The place where a pharmacist dispenses drugs is also referred to as a pharmacy.

pharynx muscular cavity behind the nose and mouth, extending downwards from the base of the skull. Its walls are made of muscle strengthened with a fibrous layer and lined with mucous membrane. The internal nostrils lead backwards into the pharynx, which continues downwards into the oesophagus and (through the epiglottis) into the windpipe. On each side, a Eustachian tube enters the pharynx from the middle ear cavity.

The upper part (nasopharynx) is an airway, but the remainder is a passage for food. Inflammation of the pharynx is named pharyngitis.

phase in astronomy, the apparent shape of the Moon or a planet when all or part of its illuminated hemisphere is facing the Earth.

The Moon undergoes a full cycle of phases from new (when between the Earth and the Sun) through first quarter (when at 90° eastern elongation from the Sun), full (when opposite the Sun), and last quarter (when at 90° western elongation from the Sun).

The Moon is gibbous (more than half but less than fully illuminated) when between first quarter and full or full and last quarter. Mars can appear gibbous at quadrature (when it is at right angles to the Sun in the sky). The gibbous appearance of Jupiter is barely noticeable.

The planets whose orbits lie within that of the Earth can also undergo a full cycle of phases, as can an asteroid passing inside the Earth's orbit.

phase in chemistry, a physical state of matter: for example, ice and liquid water are different phases of water; a mixture of the two is termed a two-phase system.

phase in physics, a stage in an oscillatory motion, such as a wave motion: two waves are in phase when their peaks and their troughs coincide. Otherwise, there is a **phase difference**, which has consequences in ◊interference phenomena and ◊alternating current electricity.

pheasant any of various large, colourful Asiatic fowls of the family Phasianidae, order Galliformes, which also includes grouse, quail, and turkey. The typical pheasants are in the genus *Phasianus,* which has two species: the Japanese pheasant, *P. versicolor,* found in Japan, and the Eurasian ring-necked or common pheasant, *P. colchicus,* also introduced to North America. The genus is distinguished by the very long wedge-shaped tail and the absence of a crest. The plumage of the male common pheasant is richly tinted with brownish-green, yellow, and red markings, but the female is a camouflaged brownish colour. The nest is made on the ground. The male is polygamous.

Among the more exotically beautiful pheasants of other genera, often kept as ornamental birds, are the **golden pheasant** *Chrysolophus pictus* and **Lady Amherst's pheasant** *Chrysolophus amherstiae,* both from China, and the **argus pheasant** *Argusianus argus* of Malaysia, which has metallic spots or 'eyes' on the wings.

Reeves's pheasant *Symaticus reevesii,* a native of China, is over 2 m/6.6 ft in length, and has yellow and brown spangled plumage.

phenol member of a group of aromatic chemical compounds with weakly acidic properties, which are characterized by a hydroxyl (OH) group attached directly to an aromatic ring. The simplest of the phenols, derived from benzene, is also known as phenol and has the formula C_6H_5OH. It is sometimes called **carbolic acid** and can be extracted from coal tar.

Pure phenol consists of colourless, needle-shaped crystals, which take up moisture from the atmosphere. It has a strong and characteristic smell and was once used as an antiseptic. It is, however, toxic by absorption through the skin.

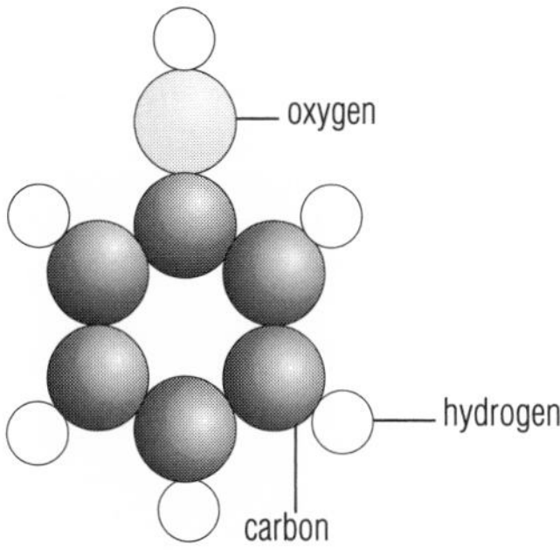

phenol The phenol molecule with its ring of six carbon atoms and a hydroxyl (OH) group attached. Phenol was first extracted from coal tar in 1834. It is used to make phenolic and epoxy resins, explosives, pharmaceuticals, perfumes, and nylon.

phenolphthalein acid–base indicator that is clear below pH 8 and red above pH 9.6. It is used in titrating weak acids against strong bases.

phenotype in genetics, visible traits, those actually displayed by an organism. The phenotype is not a direct reflection of the ◊genotype because some alleles are masked by the presence of other, dominant alleles (see ◊dominance). The phenotype is further modified by the effects of the environment (for example, poor nutrition stunts growth).

phenylanaline one of the nine essential amino acids. Phenylketonuria is a rare genetic disease which results from the inability to metabolize the phenylalanine present in food.

pheromone chemical signal (such as an odour) that is emitted by one animal and affects the behaviour of others. Pheromones are used by many animal species to attract mates.

phlebitis inflammation of the wall of a vein. It is sometimes associated with ◊varicose veins or with a blockage by a blood clot (◊thrombosis), in which case it is more accurately described as thrombophlebitis.

Phlebitis may occur as a result of the hormonal changes associated with pregnancy, or due to long-term use of contraceptive pills, or following prolonged immobility (which is why patients are mobilized as soon as possible after surgery). If a major vein is involved, nearly always in a leg, the part beyond the blockage swells and may remain engorged for weeks. It is very painful. Treatment is with ◊anticoagulant drugs and sometimes surgery, depending on the cause.

phloem tissue found in vascular plants whose main function is to conduct sugars and other food materials from the leaves, where they are produced, to all other parts of the plant.

Phloem is composed of sieve elements and their associated companion cells, together with some ◊sclerenchyma and ◊parenchyma cell types. Sieve elements are long, thin-walled cells joined end to end, forming sieve tubes; large pores in the end walls allow the continuous passage of nutrients. Phloem is usually found in association with ◊xylem, the water-conducting tissue, but unlike the latter it is a living tissue.

phlogiston hypothetical substance formerly believed to have been produced during combustion. The term was invented by the German chemist Georg Stahl. The phlogiston theory was replaced by the theory of oxygen gain and loss, first enunciated by the French chemist Antoine Lavoisier.

phlox any of a group of plants native to North America and Siberia. Phloxes are small with alternate leaves and clusters of showy white, pink, red, or purple flowers. (Genus *Phlox,* family Polemoniaceae.)

phobia excessive irrational fear of an object or situation – for example, agoraphobia (fear of open spaces and crowded places), acrophobia (fear of heights), and claustrophobia (fear of enclosed places). ◊Behaviour therapy is one form of treatment.

A **specific phobia** is a severe dislike of a particular thing, including objects, animals or situations. Specific phobias start in childhood (particularly animal phobias) and early adulthood. They are more common in women than men.

Complex phobias have more complicated contributing factors and include agoraphobia and social phobia. These phobias are more disabling. Agoraphobia typically starts between the ages of 18 and 28. Social phobia usually onsets between 11 and 16 years.

Phobos one of the two moons of Mars, discovered 1877 by the US astronomer Asaph Hall (1829–1907). It is an irregularly shaped lump of rock, cratered by ◊meteorite impacts. Phobos is 27 x 22 x 19 km/17 x 13 x 12 mi across, and orbits Mars every 0.32 days at a distance of 9,400 km/5,840 mi from the planet's centre. It is thought to be an asteroid captured by Mars' gravity.

Pholus or ***5145 Pholus*** in astronomy, a red centaur discovered 1991.

phon unit of loudness, equal to the value in decibels of an equally loud tone with frequency 1,000 Hz. The higher the frequency, the louder a noise sounds for the same decibel value; thus an 80-decibel tone with a frequency of 20 Hz sounds as loud as 20 decibels at 1,000 Hz, and the phon value of both tones is 20. An aircraft engine has a loudness of around 140 phons.

phong shading in computing, type of shading used in animation and 3-D graphics, based on a computerized model of how light is reflected from surfaces.

Phobias

Fear	*Name of phobia*
Animals	zoophobia
Bacteria	bacteriophobia, bacillophobia
Beards	pogonophobia
Bees	apiphobia, melissophobia
Being alone	monophobia, autophobia, eremophobia
Being buried alive	taphophobia
Being seen by others	scopophobia
Being touched	haphephobia, aphephobia
Birds	ornithophobia
Blood	h(a)ematophobia, hemophobia
Blushing	ereuthrophobia, e(y)rythrophobia
Books	bibliophobia
Cancer	cancerophobia, carcinophobia
Cats	ailurophobia, gatophobia
Chickens	alektorophobia
Childbirth	tocophobia, parturiphobia
Children	paediphobia
Cold	cheimatophobia, frigophobia
Colour	chromatophobia, chromophobia, psychrophobia
Comets	cometophobia
Computers	computerphobia, cyberphobia
Contamination	misophobia, coprophobia
Criticism	enissophobia
Crossing bridges	gephyrophobia
Crossing streets	dromophobia
Crowds	demophobia, ochlophobia
Darkness	achulophobia, nyctophobia, scotophobia
Dawn	eosophobia
Daylight	phengophobia
Death, corpses	necrophobia, thanatophobia
Defecation	rhypophobia
Deformity	dysmorphophobia
Demons	demonophobia
Dirt	mysophobia
Disease	nosophobia, pathophobia
Disorder	ataxiophobia
Dogs	cynophobia
Draughts	anemophobia
Dreams	oneirophobia
Drinking	dipsophobia
Drugs	pharmacophobia
Duration	chronophobia
Dust	amathophobia, koniphobia
Eating	phagophobia
Enclosed spaces	claustrophobia
Everything	pan(t)ophobia
Facial hair	trichopathophobia
Faeces	coprophobia
Failure	kakorrphiaphobia
Fatigue	kopophobia, ponophobia
Fears	phobophobia
Fever	febriphobia
Fire	pyrophobia
Fish	ichthyophobia
Flying, the air	aerophobia
Fog	homichlophobia
Food	sitophobia
Foreign languages	xenoglossophobia
Freedom	eleutherophobia
Fun	cherophobia
Germs	spermophobia, bacillophobia
Ghosts	phasmophobia
Glass	hyalophobia
God	theophobia
Going to bed	clinophobia
Graves	taphophobia
Hair	chaetophobia, trichophobia, hypertrichophobia
Heart conditions	cardiophobia
Heat	thermophobia
Heaven	ouranophobia
Heights	acrophobia, altophobia
Hell	hadephobia, stygiophobia
Home	domatophobia, oikophobia
Homosexuality	homophobia
Horses	hippophobia
Human beings	anthrophobia
Ice, frost	cryophobia
Ideas	ideophobia
Illness	nosemaphobia, nosophobia
Imperfection	atelophobia
Infection	mysophobia
Infinity	apeirophobia
Injustice	dikephobia
Inoculations, injections	trypanophobia
Insanity	lyssophobia, maniaphobia
Insects	entomophobia
Itching	acarophobia, scabiophobia
Jealousy	zelophobia
Knowledge	epistemophobia
Lakes	limnophobia
Large objects	macrophobia
Leaves	phyllophobia
Left side	levophobia
Leprosy	leprophobia
Lice	pediculophobia
Lightning	astraphobia
Machinery	mechanophobia
Many things	polyphobia
Marriage	gamophobia
Meat	carnophobia
Men	androphobia
Metals	metallophobia
Meteors	meteorophobia
Mice	musophobia
Mind	psychophobia
Mirrors	eisoptrophobia, catotrophobia
Money	chrometophobia
Monsters, monstrosities	teratophobia
Motion	kinesophobia, kinetophobia
Music	musicophobia
Names	onomatophobia
Narrowness	anginaphobia
Needles	belonophobia
Night, darkness	achluophobia
Noise	phonophobia
Novelty	cainophobia, cenotophobia, neophobia
Nudity	gymnotophobia
Number 13	triskaidekaphobia, terdekaphobia
Odours	osmophobia
Open spaces	agoraphobia
Pain	algophobia, odynophobia
Parasites	parasitophobia
Physical love	erotophobia
Pins	enetophobia
Places	topophobia
Pleasure	hedonophobia
Pointed instruments	aichmophobia
Poison	toxiphobia, toxophobia, iophobia
Poverty	peniaphobia
Precipices	cremnophobia
Pregnancy	maieusiophobia
Punishment	poinephobia
Rain	ombrophobia
Reptiles	batrachophobia
Responsibility	hypegiaphobia
Ridicule	katagalophobia
Rivers	potamophobia
Robbery	harpaxophobia
Ruin	atephobia
Rust	iophobia
Sacred things	hierophobia
Satan	satanophobia
School	scholionophobia
Sea	thalassophobia
Semen	spermatophobia
Sex	genophobia
Sexual intercourse	coitophobia
Shadows	sciophobia
Sharp objects	belonephobia
Shock	hormephobia
Sin	hamartiophobia
Sinning	peccatophobia
Skin	dermatophobia
Sleep	hypnophobia
Small objects	microphobia
Smell	olfactophobia
Smothering, choking	pnigerophobia
Snakes	ophidiophobia, ophiophobia
Snow	chionophobia
Soiling	rypophobia
Solitude	eremitophobia, eremophobia
Sound	akousticophobia
Sourness	acerophobia
Speaking aloud	phonophobia
Speed	tachophobia
Spiders	arachn(e)ophobia
Standing	stasiphobia
Standing erect	stasibasiphobia
Stars	siderophobia
Stealing	kleptophobia
Stillness	eremophobia
Stings	cnidophobia
Strangers	xenophobia
Strong light	photophobia
Stuttering	laliophobia, lalophobia
Suffocation	anginophobia
Sun	heliophobia
Symbols	symbolophobia
Taste	geumaphobia
Teeth	odontophobia
Thinking	phronemophobia
Thrown objects	ballistophobia
Thunder	astraphobia, brontophobia, keraunophobia
Touch	aphephobia, haptophobia, haphephobia
Travel	hodophobia
Travelling by train	siderodromophobia
Trees	dendrophobia
Trembling	tremophobia
Vehicles	amaxophobia, ochophobia
Venereal disease	cypridophobia
Void	kenophobia
Vomiting	emetophobia
Walking	basiphobia
Wasps	spheksophobia
Water	hydrophobia, aquaphobia
Weakness	asthenophobia
Wind	ancraophobia
Women	gynophobia
Words	logophobia
Work	ergophobia, ergasiophobia
Worms	helminthophobia
Wounds, injury	traumatophobia
Writing	graphophobia

phonograph the name US inventor Thomas ◊Edison gave to his sound-recording apparatus, which developed into the record player. The word 'phonograph' is still used in the USA.

phosphate salt or ester of phosphoric acid. Incomplete neutralization of ◊phosphoric acid gives rise to acid phosphates (see ◊acid salts and ◊buffer). Phosphates are used as fertilizers, and are required for the development of healthy root systems. They are involved in many biochemical processes, often as part of complex molecules, such as ◊ATP.

phosphate analysis the regular sampling and chemical analysis of phosphorus levels in the soil around archaeological sites in order to locate concentrations of human bone and excrement, and hence areas of human activity, settlements, and burial grounds.

phospholipid any ◊lipid consisting of a glycerol backbone, a phosphate group, and two long chains. Phospholipids are found everywhere in living systems as the basis for biological membranes.

One of the long chains tends to be hydrophobic and the other hydrophilic (that is, they interrelate with water in opposite ways). This means that phospholipids will line up the same way round when in solution.

phosphor any substance that is phosphorescent, that is, gives out visible light when it is illuminated by a beam of electrons or ultraviolet light. The television screen is coated on the inside with phosphors that glow when beams of electrons strike them. Fluorescent lamp tubes are also phosphor-coated. Phosphors are also used in Day-Glo paints, and as optical brighteners in detergents.

phosphorescence in physics, the emission of light by certain substances after they have absorbed energy, whether from visible light, other electromagnetic radiation such as ultraviolet rays or X-rays, or cathode rays (a beam of electrons). When the stimulating energy is removed phosphorescence ceases, although it may persist for a short time after (unlike ◊fluorescence, which stops immediately).

phosphoric acid acid derived from phosphorus and oxygen. Its commonest form (H_3PO_4) is also known as orthophosphoric acid, and is produced by the action of phosphorus pentoxide (P_2O_5) on water. It is used in rust removers and for rust-proofing iron and steel.

phosphorus Greek *phosphoros 'bearer of light'* highly reactive, nonmetallic element, symbol P, atomic number 15, relative atomic mass 30.9738. It occurs in nature as phosphates (commonly in the form of the mineral ◊apatite), and is essential to plant and animal life. Compounds of phosphorus are used in fertilizers, various organic chemicals, for matches and fireworks, and in glass and steel.

Phosphorus was first identified in 1674 by German alchemist Hennig Brand (born c. 1630), who prepared it from urine. The element has three allotropic forms: a black powder; a white-yellow, waxy solid that ignites spontaneously in air to form the poisonous gas phosphorus pentoxide; and a red-brown powder that neither ignites spontaneously nor is poisonous.

PhotoCD picture storage and viewing system developed by Kodak and Philips. The aim of Kodak's PhotoCD is to allow the user to put up to 100 photos onto compact disc: images are transferred from film to a PhotoCD disc and can then be viewed by means of Kodak's own PhotoCD player, which plugs into a television set, or by using suitable software on a multimedia PC.

PhotoCD is based on **multisession** ◊WORM (write-once read many times) technology. The images can be written to the disc in multiple recording sessions.

photocell or ***photoelectric cell*** device for measuring or detecting light or other electromagnetic radiation, since its electrical state is altered by the effect of light. In a **photoemissive** cell, the radiation causes electrons to be emitted and a current to flow (◊photoelectric effect); a **photovoltaic** cell causes an ◊electromotive force to be generated in the presence of light across the boundary of two substances. A **photoconductive** cell, which contains a semiconductor, increases its conductivity when exposed to electromagnetic radiation.

Photocells are used for photographers' exposure meters, burglar and fire alarms, automatic doors, and in solar energy arrays.

photochemical reaction any chemical reaction in which light is produced or light initiates the reaction. Light can initiate reactions by exciting atoms or molecules and making them more reactive: the light energy becomes converted to chemical energy. Many photochemical reactions set up a ◊chain reaction and produce ◊free radicals.

This type of reaction is seen in the bleaching of dyes or the yellowing of paper by sunlight. It is harnessed by plants in ◊photosynthesis and by humans in ◊photography.

Chemical reactions that produce light are most commonly seen when materials are burned. Light-emitting reactions are used by living organisms in ◊bioluminescence. One photochemical reaction is the action of sunlight on car exhaust fumes, which results in the production of ozone. Some large cities, such as Los Angeles, and Santiago, Chile, now suffer serious pollution due to photochemical smog.

photocopier machine that uses some form of photographic process to reproduce copies of documents or illustrations. Most modern photocopiers, as pioneered by the Xerox Corporation, use electrostatic photocopying, or ◊xerography ('dry writing').

Additional functions of photocopiers include enlargement and reduction, copying on both sides of the sheet of paper, copying in colour, collating, and stapling.

photodiode semiconductor ◊p–n junction diode used to detect light or measure its intensity. The photodiode is encapsulated in a transparent plastic case that allows light to fall onto the junction. When this occurs, the reverse-bias resistance (high resistance in the opposite direction to normal current-flow) drops and allows a larger reverse-biased current to flow through the device. The increase in current can then be related to the amount of light falling on the junction.

Photodiodes that can detect small changes in light level are used in alarm systems, camera exposure controls, and optical communication links.

photoelectric cell alternative name for ◊photocell.

photoelectric effect in physics, the emission of ◊electrons from a substance (usually a metallic surface) when it is struck by ◊photons (quanta of electromagnetic radiation), usually those of visible light or ultraviolet radiation.

photography process for reproducing images on sensitized materials by various forms of radiant energy, including visible light, ultraviolet, infrared, X-rays, atomic radiations, and electron beams.

Photography was developed in the 19th century; among the pioneers were Louis Daguerre in France and Fox Talbot in the UK. Colour photography dates from the early 20th century.

The most familiar photographic process depends upon the fact that certain silver compounds (called ◊halides) are sensitive to light. A photographic film is coated with these compounds and, in a camera, is exposed to light. An image, or picture, of the scene

EXPOSURE: A BEGINNERS GUIDE TO PHOTOGRAPHY

http://www.88.com/exposure/index.htm

Introduction to the world of photography including a 'crash course', as well as sections with a 'few easy tricks to jazz up your pictures' and an explanation of exposure theory. To help out with the latter, there is a 'sim-cam', allowing you to experiment with f-number and shutter speed for an image and see the results without wasting a lot of film.

Photography: chronology

1515 Leonardo da Vinci described the camera obscura.
1750 The painter Canaletto used a camera obscura as an aid to his painting in Venice.
1790 Thomas Wedgwood in England made photograms –placing objects on leather, sensitized using silver nitrate.
1826 Nicéphore Niepce, a French doctor, produced the world's first photograph from nature on pewter plates with a camera obscura and an eight-hour exposure.
1838 As a result of his earlier collaboration with Niepce, L J M Daguerre produced the first daguerreotype camera photograph.
1839 Daguerre was awarded an annuity by the French government and his process given to the world.
1840 Invention of the Petzval lens, which reduced exposure time by 90%. Herschel discovered sodium thiosulphate as a fixer for silver halides.
1841 Fox Talbot's calotype process was patented – the first multicopy method of photography using a negative/positive process, sensitized with silver iodide.
1844–46 Fox Talbot published the first photographic book, *The Pencil of Nature.*
1845 Hill and Adamson began to use calotypes for portraits in Edinburgh, Scotland.
1851 Fox Talbot used a one-thousandth of a second exposure to demonstrate high-speed photography. Invention of the wet-collodion-on-glass process and the waxed-paper negative. Photographs were displayed at the Great Exhibition in London, England.
1852 The London Society of Arts exhibited 779 photographs.
1855 Roger Fenton made documentary photographs of the Crimean War from a specially constructed caravan with portable darkroom.
1858 Nadar took the first aerial photographs from a balloon.
1859 Nadar in Paris made photographs underground using battery-powered arc lights.
1860 Queen Victoria was photographed by Mayall. Abraham Lincoln was photographed by Mathew Brady for political campaigning.
1861 The single-lens reflex plate camera was patented by Thomas Sutton. The principles of three-colour photography were demonstrated by Scottish physicist James Clerk Maxwell.
1870 Julia Margaret Cameron used long lenses for her distinctive portraits.
1871 Gelatin-silver bromide was developed.
1878 In the USA Eadweard Muybridge analysed the movements of animals through sequential photographs, using a series of cameras.
1879 The photogravure process was invented.
1880 A silver bromide emulsion was fixed with hypo. Photographs were first reproduced in newspapers in New York using the half-tone engraving process. The first twin-lens reflex camera was produced in London. Gelatin-silver chloride paper was introduced.
1884 George Eastman produced flexible negative film.
1889 The Eastman Company in the USA produced the Kodak No 1 camera and roll film, facilitating universal, hand-held snapshots.
1891 The first telephoto lens. The interference process of colour photography was developed by the French doctor Gabriel Lippmann.
1897 The first issue of Alfred Stieglitz's *Camera Notes* in the USA.
1902 In Germany, Deckel invented a prototype leaf shutter and Zeiss introduced the Tessar lens.
1904 The autochrome colour process was patented by the Lumière brothers.
1905 Alfred Stieglitz opened the gallery '291' in New York promoting photography. Lewis Hine used photography to expose the exploitation of children in American factories, causing protective laws to be passed.
1907 The autochrome process began to be factory-produced.
1914 Oskar Barnack designed a prototype Leica camera for Leitz in Germany.
1924 Leitz launched the first 35mm camera, the Leica, delayed because of World War I. It became very popular with photojournalists because it was quiet, small, dependable, and had a range of lenses and accessories.
1929 Rolleiflex produced a twin-lens reflex camera in Germany.
1935 In the USA, Mannes and Godowsky invented Kodachrome transparency film, which produced sharp images and rich colour quality. Electronic flash was invented in the USA.
1936 *Life* magazine, significant for its photojournalism, was first published in the USA.
1938 *Picture Post* magazine was introduced in the UK.
1940 Multigrade enlarging paper by Ilford was made available in the UK.
1942 Kodacolour negative film was introduced.
1945 The zone system of exposure estimation was published in the book *Exposure Record* by Ansel Adams.
1947 Polaroid black and white instant process film was invented by Dr Edwin Land, who set up the Polaroid corporation in Boston, Massachusetts. The principles of holography were demonstrated in England by Dennis Gabor.
1955 Kodak introduced Tri-X, a black and white 200 ASA film.
1959 The zoom lens was invented by the Austrian firm of Voigtlander.
1960 The laser was invented in the USA, making holography possible. Polacolor, a self-processing colour film, was introduced by Polaroid, using a 60-second colour film and dye diffusion technique.
1963 Cibachrome, paper and chemicals for printing directly from transparencies, was made available by Ciba-Geigy of Switzerland. One of the most permanent processes, it is marketed by Ilford in the UK.
1966 The International Center of Photography was established in New York.
1969 Photographs were taken on the Moon by US astronauts.
1970 A charge-coupled device was invented at Bell Laboratories in New Jersey, USA, to record very faint images (for example in astronomy). Rencontres Internationales de la Photographie, the annual summer festival of photography with workshops, was founded in Arles, France.
1971 Opening of the Photographers' Gallery, London, and the Photo Archive of the Bibliothéque Nationale, Paris.
1972 The SX70 system, a single-lens reflex camera with instant prints, was produced by Polaroid.
1975 The Center for Creative Photography was established at the University of Arizona.
1980 Ansel Adams sold an original print, *Moonrise: Hernandez*, for $45,000, a record price, in the USA. *Voyager 1* sent photographs of Saturn back to Earth across space.
1983 The National Museum of Photography, Film and Television opened in Bradford, England.
1985 The Minolta Corporation in Japan introduced the Minolta 7000 – the world's first body-integral autofocus single-lens reflex camera.
1988 The electronic camera, which stores pictures on magnetic disc instead of on film, was introduced in Japan.
1990 Kodak introduced PhotoCD which converts 35mm camera pictures (on film) into digital form and stores them on compact disc (CD) for viewing on TV.
1992 Japanese company Canon introduced a camera with autofocus controlled by the user's eye. The camera focuses on whatever the user is looking at. *Girl with a Leica* by Russian photographer Aleksandr Rodchenko sold for £115,500 at Christie's, London – a world-record price for a photograph.
1996 Corbis, a company owned by Bill Gates, bought the exclusive rights to 2,500 photographs by Ansel Adams.

before the camera is formed on the film because the silver halides become activated (light-altered) where light falls but not where light does not fall. The image is made visible by the process of ◊developing, made permanent by fixing, and, finally, is usually printed on paper. Motion-picture photography uses a camera that exposes a roll of film to a rapid succession of views that, when developed, are projected in equally rapid succession to provide a moving image.

photogravure ◊printing process that uses a plate prepared photographically, covered with a pattern of recessed cells in which the ink is held. See ◊gravure.

photoluminescence see ◊luminescence.

photolysis chemical reaction that is driven by light or ultraviolet radiation. For example, the light reaction of photosynthesis (the process by which green plants manufacture carbohydrates from carbon dioxide and water) is a photolytic reaction.

photometer instrument that measures luminous intensity, usually by comparing relative intensities from different sources. Bunsen's grease-spot photometer of 1844 compares the intensity of a light source with a known source by each illuminating one half of a translucent area. Modern photometers use ◊photocells, as in a photographer's exposure meter. A photomultiplier can also be used as a photometer.

photomultiplier instrument that detects low levels of electromagnetic radiation (usually visible light or ◊infrared radiation) and amplifies it to produce a detectable signal.

One type resembles a ◊photocell with an additional series of coated ◊electrodes (dynodes) between the ◊cathode and ◊anode. Radiation striking the cathode releases electrons (primary emission) which hit the first dynode, producing yet more electrons (◊secondary emission), which strike the second dynode. Eventually this produces a measurable signal up to 100 million times larger than the original signal by the time it leaves the anode. Similar devices, called image intensifiers, are used in television camera tubes that 'see' in the dark.

photon in physics, the ◊elementary particle or 'package' (quantum) of energy in which light and other forms of electromagnetic radiation are emitted. The photon has both particle and wave properties; it has no charge, is considered massless but possesses momentum and energy. It is one of the ◊gauge bosons, and is the carrier of the ◊electromagnetic force, one of the fundamental forces of nature.

According to ◊quantum theory the energy of a photon is given by the formula $E = hf$, where h is Planck's constant and f is the frequency of the radiation emitted.

photoperiodism biological mechanism that determines the timing of certain activities by responding to changes in day length. The flowering of many plants is initiated in this way. Photoperiodism in plants is regulated by a light-sensitive pigment, **phytochrome**. The breeding seasons of many temperate-zone animals are also triggered by increasing or declining day length, as part of their ◊biorhythms.

Autumn-flowering plants (for example, chrysanthemum and soya bean) and autumn-breeding mammals (such as goats and deer) require days that are shorter than a critical length; spring-flowering and spring-breeding ones (such as radish and lettuce, and birds) are triggered by longer days.

photosphere visible surface of the Sun, which emits light and heat. About 300 km/200 mi deep, it consists of incandescent gas at a temperature of 5,800K (5,530°C/9,980°F).

Rising cells of hot gas produce a mottling of the photosphere known as **granulation**, each granule being about 1,000 km/620 mi in diameter. The photosphere is often marked by large, dark patches called ◊sunspots.

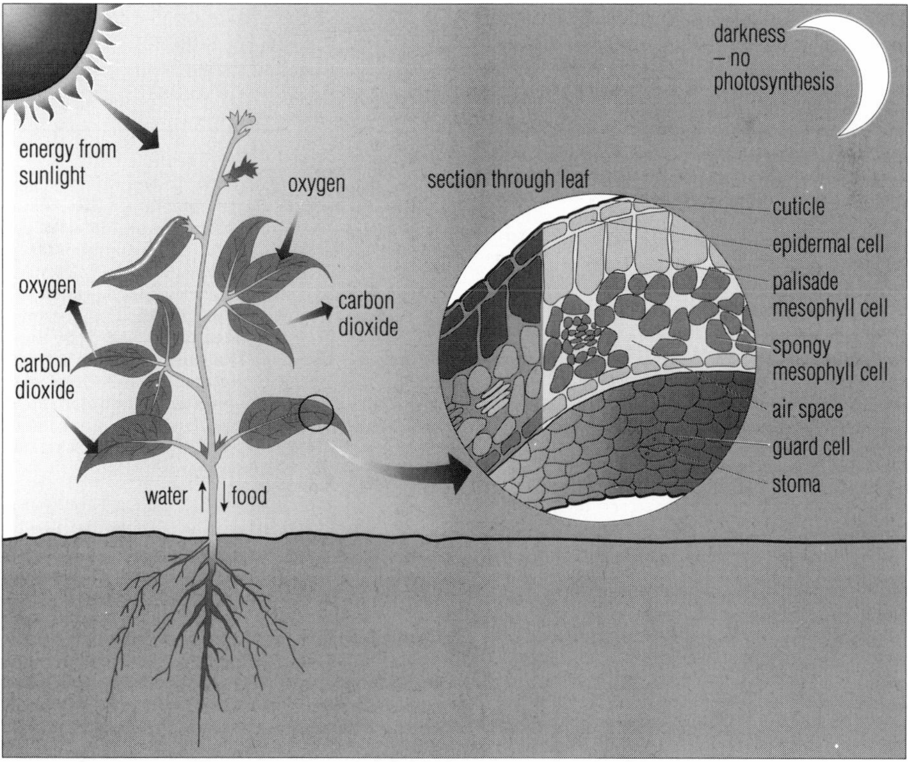

photosynthesis *Process by which green plants and some bacteria manufacture carbohydrates from water and atmospheric carbon dioxide, using the energy of sunlight. Photosynthesis depends on the ability of chlorophyll molecules within plant cells to trap the energy of light to split water molecules, giving off oxygen as a by-product. The hydrogen of the water molecules is then used to reduce carbon dioxide to simple carbohydrates.*

photosynthesis process by which green plants trap light energy from the Sun. This energy is used to drive a series of chemical reactions which lead to the formation of carbohydrates. The carbohydrates occur in the form of simple sugar, or glucose, which provides the basic food for both plants and animals. For photosynthesis to occur, the plant must possess ◊chlorophyll and must have a supply of carbon dioxide and water. Photosynthesis takes place inside ◊chloroplasts which are found mainly in the leaf cells of plants.

The by-product of photosynthesis, oxygen, is of great importance to all living organisms, and virtually all atmospheric oxygen has originated by photosynthesis.

Chloroplasts contain the enzymes and chlorophyll necessary for photosynthesis, and the leaf structure of plants is specially adapted to this purpose.

leaf structure In the lower epidermis on the leaf underside are stomata (pores; see ◊stoma), each of which is surrounded by a pair of ◊guard cells t hat control their opening and closing. These guard cells contain chloroplasts. The central layer of the leaf between the layers of epidermis is called the mesophyll, and all the cells in this tissue contain chloroplasts. Running through the mesophyll are the veins, each of which contains large, thick-walled ◊xylem vessels for carrying water, and smaller, thin-walled ◊phloem tubes for transporting the food produced by the leaf. Most of the glucose that forms during photosynthesis is stored in the chloroplasts as starch. As plant-eating animals eat the leaves they too are dependent on plant photosynthesis to supply their basic energy needs.

chemical process The chemical reactions of photosynthesis occur in two stages. During the **light reaction** sunlight is used to split water (H_2O) into oxygen (O_2), protons (hydrogen ions, H^+), and electrons, and oxygen is given off as a by-product. In the **dark reaction**, for which sunlight is not required, the protons and electrons are used to convert carbon dioxide (CO_2) into carbohydrates ($C_m(H_2O)_n$). *So the whole processcan be summarized by the equation.*

$$CO_2 + 2H_2O \rightarrow C_m(H_2O)_n + H_2O + O_2$$

Photosynthesis depends on the ability of chlorophyll to capture the energy of sunlight and to use it to split water molecules. The initial charge separation occurs in less than a billionth of a second, a speed that compares with current computers.

Plant pigments Photosynthetic pigments are the plant pigments responsible for capturing light energy during photosynthesis. The primary pigment is chlorophyll, which absorbs blue and red light. Other pigments, such as ◊carotenoids, are accessory pigments which also capture light energy and pass it on to chlorophyll. Photosynthesis by cyanobacteria was responsible for the appearance of oxygen in the Earth's atmosphere 2 billion years ago, and photosynthesis by plants maintains the oxygen levels today.

PHOTOSYNTHESIS DIRECTORY

http://esg-www.mit.edu:8001/esgbio/ps/psdir.html

A wealth of scientific information concerning photosynthesis, its stages and its importance from MIT in Boston, USA. The site discusses issues such as the evolution and discovery of photosynthesis, the chloroplast, and the chlorophyll, and all steps of the light and dark reactions that take place during photosynthesis. The site also offers detailed diagrams of the procedures discussed.

phototropism movement of part of a plant toward or away from a source of light. Leaves are positively phototropic, detecting the source of light and orientating themselves to receive the maximum amount.

phreaking in computing, using computer technology to make free long-distance phone calls, charge them to another account, or otherwise illegally access the telephone network. In the 1980s, phreaking was semi-respectable among hackers (see ◊hacking, but it is now less reputable – and thanks to improved security in the phone network, much more difficult. The case of Kevin Mitnick did much to bring phreaking to public attention.

phyllotaxis the arrangement of leaves on a plant stem. Leaves are nearly always arranged in a regular pattern and in the majority of plants they are inserted singly, either in a **spiral** arrangement up the stem, or on **alternate** sides. Other principal forms are opposite leaves, where two arise from the same node, and whorled, where three or more arise from the same node.

phylloxera plant-eating insect of the family Phylloxeridae, closely related to the aphids.

The grape, or vine phylloxera *Phylloxera vitifolia,* a native of North America, is a notorious pest of grapevines, forming galls on roots and leaves, which damage the plant. European vines are markedly susceptible and many French vineyards suffered from the arrival of the pest in Europe in the late 19th century, when nearly 2 million hectares of vineyards were destroyed. In 1993 infestation became apparent in Californian vineyards, threatening a loss of 20,000 hectares by the end of the century. Phylloxera is very resistant to treatment, as there are no natural enemies and it is difficult to treat with pesticide because of its depth within the soil. Phylloxera insects (hemipterans) may be destroyed by spraying with carbon disulphide or petroleum.

phylogeny historical sequence of changes that occurs in a given species during the course of its evolution. It was once erroneously associated with ontogeny (the process of development of a living organism).

TREE OF LIFE

http://phylogeny.arizona.edu/tree/phylogeny.html

Project designed to present information about the phylogenetic relationships and characteristics of organisms, illustrating the diversity and unity of living organisms.

phylum (plural ***phyla***) major grouping in biological classification. Mammals, birds, reptiles, amphibians, fishes, and tunicates belong to the phylum Chordata; the phylum Mollusca consists of snails, slugs, mussels, clams, squid, and octopuses; the phylum Porifera contains sponges; and the phylum Echinodermata includes starfish, sea urchins, and sea cucumbers. In classifying plants (where the term 'division' often takes the place of 'phylum'), there are between four and nine phyla depending on the criteria used; all flowering plants belong to a single phylum, Angiospermata, and all conifers to another, Gymnospermata. Related phyla are grouped together in a ◊kingdom; phyla are subdivided into ◊classes.

There are 36 different phyla. The most recently identified is the Cycliophora described in 1995. It contains a single known species, *Symbion pandora,* that lives on lobsters.

physical change in chemistry, a type of change that does not produce a new chemical substance, does not involve large energy changes, and that can be easily reversed (the opposite of a ◊chemical change). Boiling and melting are examples of physical change.

physical chemistry branch of chemistry concerned with examining the relationships between the chemical compositions of substances and the physical properties that they display. Most chemical reactions exhibit some physical phenomenon (change of state, temperature, pressure, or volume, or the use or production of electricity), and the measurement and study of such phenomena has led to many chemical theories and laws.

physics branch of science concerned with the laws that govern the structure of the universe, and the investigation of the properties of matter and energy and their interactions. For convenience,

Recent Progress in Physics

by Peter Rodgers

Atom lasers
Quantum mechanics predicts that particles can behave like waves. The wavelength of a particle gets shorter as the particle moves faster. For atoms this wavelength is usually much smaller than the size of the atom itself. However, if the atom is moving very slowly its wavelength can become quite large and the waves of nearby atoms begin to overlap. When this happens the atoms form a new state of matter known as a Bose–Einstein condensate. This new state of matter was created for the first time by American physicists in 1995. Bose–Einstein condensates have completely different properties from the other four states of matter: solid, liquid, gas and plasma.

To form a Bose–Einstein condensate it is necessary to trap a gas of atoms and then cool them to just a fraction of a degree above absolute zero. This is done using a combination of lasers and magnetic fields. By carefully releasing the atoms from the trap it is possible to make what is known as an atom laser. In an atom laser all the atoms travel in the same direction with the same speed – just like the photons (particles of light) in a conventional laser. American physicists used sodium atoms to make the first ever atom laser in 1996. Atom lasers could be used as a tool in other physics experiments, in atomic clocks or to print tiny circuits in electronics

Quantum information technology
Recent years have seen exciting progress in a new field of physics called quantum information technology. Quantum information technology essentially involves three subjects: quantum computation, quantum cryptography and quantum communication.

In conventional computers, information is handled as a series of bits which can either be one or zero. Quantum computation is based on the ability of quantum particles to be in two or more places at the same time. This allows information to be handled as a series of 'qubits' which can be both one and zero at the same time. Therefore quantum computers can, in theory, work much faster than ordinary computers. So far physicists have built simple quantum logic gates and developed theoretical schemes to deal with the errors that can arise during computation.

Quantum cryptography allows two people, usually called Alice and Bob, to exchange information with complete security. Researchers in Switzerland and the UK have demonstrated that quantum cryptography can be made to work over distances greater than 10 km. In quantum communication Alice and Bob use the properties of quantum mechanics to communicate in ways that are not possible classically. Both quantum cryptography and quantum communication rely on a property of quantum mechanics called entanglement. Physicists in Austria and Italy have used entanglement to 'teleport' single photons in the laboratory.

Most work so far has concentrated on pairs of entangled photons. Entanglement means that certain properties of the photons are very closely related, even when the photons are very far apart. For example, if the polarization of the first photon is measured to be vertical, then the polarization of the second photon will instantly become horizontal. This happens even though the second photon could have had any value of polarization before the measurement on the first photon. Einstein called this 'spooky action at a distance'.

Neutrino masses
Neutrinos are the most mysterious particles in the 'Standard Model of Particle Physics'. They have no charge and are thought to have no mass; and since neutrinos only experience one of the four fundamental forces, the weak force, they are difficult to detect.

One particular mystery concerns neutrinos from the Sun. The Sun produces energy by converting 600 tonnes of hydrogen into helium every second. According to theory this should result in 65 billion solar neutrinos bombarding every sq cm/0.15 sq in of the Earth's surface every second. To test this theory physicists have built massive experiments in underground mines. However none of these experiments has been able to detect any more than half the number of neutrinos predicted by theory.

One possible explanation for this shortage is that neutrinos do in fact have mass. This would allow the electron neutrinos produced in the centre of the Sun to oscillate into either muon or tau neutrinos on their journey to the surface. Existing experiments can only detect electron neutrinos although a Canadian experiment that can detect all three types is began in 1998.

To confirm that neutrinos do indeed oscillate, physicists are planning to send beams of muon neutrinos from high-energy accelerators to the various underground experiments. If electron neutrinos are detected in these beams it will provide conclusive evidence for oscillation and hence neutrino mass. One proposal for such an experiment would involve sending a beam from CERN in Switzerland to the Gran Sasso laboratory some 730 km/450 mi away in Italy. Similar experiments have been proposed in the USA and Japan.

Proof of neutrino mass would be a major breakthrough in particle physics. It might also help solve the 'dark matter' problem – the fact that less than 10% of the mass of the universe is visible – in astrophysics.

---

physics is often divided into branches such as atomic physics, nuclear physics, particle physics, solid-state physics, molecular physics, electricity and magnetism, optics, acoustics, heat, thermodynamics, quantum theory, and relativity. Before the 20th century, physics was known as **natural philosophy**.

All science is either physics or stamp collecting.

Ernest Rutherford New Zealand physicist.
Quoted in J B Birks *Rutherford at Manchester*

physiology branch of biology that deals with the functioning of living organisms, as opposed to anatomy, which studies their structures.

physiotherapy treatment of injury and disease by physical means such as exercise, heat, manipulation, massage, and electrical stimulation.

HOW THINGS WORK

http://howthingswork.virginia.edu/

Well-organized site to provide answers to any question relating to physics. There is a large database of previously asked questions which may be readily accessed. The site is provided by the Professor of Physics at the University of Virginia, USA. It is an essential point of reference for school science teachers and anybody with an interest in physics.

phytomenadione one form of vitamin K, a fat-soluble chemical found in green vegetables. It is involved in the production of prothrombin, which is essential in blood clotting. It is given to newborns to prevent potentially fatal brain haemorrhages.

phytophthora soil fungus *Phytophthora cinnamoni* which has assumed epidemic proportions in S Australia killing stands of jarrah, stringybark eucalypts, and native shrubs.

Physics: chronology

c. 400 BC The first 'atomic' theory was put forward by Democritus.
c. 250 Archimedes' principle of buoyancy was established.
AD 1600 Magnetism was described by William Gilbert.
1608 Hans Lippershey invented the refracting telescope.
c. 1610 The principle of falling bodies descending to earth at the same speed was established by Galileo.
1642 The principles of hydraulics were put forward by Blaise Pascal.
1643 The mercury barometer was invented by Evangelista Torricelli.
1656 The pendulum clock was invented by Christiaan Huygens.
1662 Boyle's law concerning the behaviour of gases was established by Robert Boyle.
c. 1665 Isaac Newton put forward the law of gravity, stating that the Earth exerts a constant force on falling bodies.
1690 The wave theory of light was propounded by Christiaan Huygens.
1704 The corpuscular theory of light was put forward by Isaac Newton.
1714 The mercury thermometer was invented by Daniel Fahrenheit.
1764 Specific and latent heats were described by Joseph Black.
1771 The link between nerve action and electricity was discovered by Luigi Galvani.
c. 1787 Charles's law relating the pressure, volume, and temperature of a gas was established by Jacques Charles.
1795 The metric system was adopted in France.
1798 The link between heat and friction was discovered by Benjamin Rumford.
1800 Alessandro Volta invented the Voltaic cell.
1801 Interference of light was discovered by Thomas Young.
1808 The 'modern' atomic theory was propounded by John Dalton.
1811 Avogadro's hypothesis relating volumes and numbers of molecules of gases was proposed by Amedeo Avogadro.
1814 Fraunhofer lines in the solar spectrum were mapped by Joseph von Fraunhofer.
1815 Refraction of light was explained by Augustin Fresnel.
1820 The discovery of electromagnetism was made by Hans Oersted.
1821 The dynamo principle was described by Michael Faraday; the thermocouple was discovered by Thomas Seebeck.
1822 The laws of electrodynamics were established by André Ampère.
1824 Thermodynamics as a branch of physics was proposed by Sadi Carnot.
1827 Ohm's law of electrical resistance was established by Georg Ohm; Brownian movement resulting from molecular vibrations was observed by Robert Brown.
1829 The law of gaseous diffusion was established by Thomas Graham.
1831 Electromagnetic induction was discovered by Faraday.
1834 Faraday discovered self-induction.
1842 The principle of conservation of energy was observed by Julius von Mayer.
c. 1847 The mechanical equivalent of heat was described by James Joule.
1849 A measurement of speed of light was put forward by French physicist Armand Fizeau (1819–1896).
1851 The rotation of the Earth was demonstrated by Jean Foucault.
1858 The mirror galvanometer, an instrument for measuring small electric currents, was invented by William Thomson (Lord Kelvin).
1859 Spectrographic analysis was made by Robert Bunsen and Gustav Kirchhoff.
1861 Osmosis was discovered.
1873 Light was conceived as electromagnetic radiation by James Maxwell.
1877 A theory of sound as vibrations in an elastic medium was propounded by John Rayleigh.
1880 Piezoelectricity was discovered by Pierre Curie.
1887 The existence of radio waves was predicted by Heinrich Hertz.
1895 X-rays were discovered by Wilhelm Röntgen.
1896 The discovery of radioactivity was made by Antoine Becquerel.
1897 Joseph Thomson discovered the electron.
1899 Ernest Rutherford discovered alpha and beta rays.
1900 Quantum theory was propounded by Max Planck; the discovery of gamma rays was made by French physicist Paul-Ulrich Villard (1860–1934).
1902 Oliver Heaviside discovered the ionosphere.
1904 The theory of radioactivity was put forward by Rutherford and Frederick Soddy.
1905 Albert Einstein propounded his special theory of relativity.
1908 The Geiger counter was invented by Hans Geiger and Rutherford.
1911 The discovery of the atomic nucleus was made by Rutherford.
1913 The orbiting electron atomic theory was propounded by Danish physicist Niels Bohr.
1915 X-ray crystallography was discovered by William and Lawrence Bragg.
1916 Einstein put forward his general theory of relativity; mass spectrography was discovered by William Aston.
1924 Edward Appleton made his study of the Heaviside layer.
1926 Wave mechanics was introduced by Erwin Schrödinger.
1927 The uncertainty principle of quantum physics was established by Werner Heisenberg.
1931 The cyclotron was developed by Ernest Lawrence.
1932 The discovery of the neutron was made by James Chadwick; the electron microscope was developed by Vladimir Zworykin.
1933 The positron, the antiparticle of the electron, was discovered by Carl Anderson.
1934 Artificial radioactivity was developed by Frédéric and Irène Joliot-Curie.
1939 The discovery of nuclear fission was made by Otto Hahn and Fritz Strassmann.
1942 The first controlled nuclear chain reaction was achieved by Enrico Fermi.
1956 The neutrino, an elementary particle, was discovered by Clyde Cowan and Fred Reines.
1960 The Mössbauer effect of atom emissions was discovered by Rudolf Mössbauer; the first laser and the first maser were developed by US physicist Theodore Maiman (1927–).
1964 Murray Gell-Mann and George Zweig discovered the quark.
1967 Jocelyn Bell (now Bell Burnell) and Antony Hewish discovered pulsars (rapidly rotating neutron stars that emit pulses of energy).
1971 The theory of superconductivity was announced, where electrical resistance in some metals vanishes above absolute zero.
1979 The discovery of the asymmetry of elementary particles was made by US physicists James W Cronin and Val L Fitch.
1982 The discovery of processes involved in the evolution of stars was made by Subrahmanyan Chandrasekhar and William Fowler.
1983 Evidence of the existence of weakons (W and Z particles) was confirmed at CERN, validating the link between the weak nuclear force and the electromagnetic force.
1986 The first high-temperature superconductor was discovered, able to conduct electricity without resistance at a temperature of −238°C/−396°F.
1989 CERN's Large Electron Positron Collider (LEP), a particle accelerator with a circumference of 27 km/16.8 mi, came into operation.
1991 LEP experiments demonstrated the existence of three generations of elementary particles, each with two quarks and two leptons.
1995 Top quark discovered at Fermilab, the US particle-physics laboratory, near Chicago. US researchers announce the discovery of a material which is superconducting at the temperature of liquid nitrogen – a much higher temperature than previously achieved.
1996 CERN physicists created the first atoms of antimatter (nine atoms of antihydrogen). The Lawrence Livermore National Laboratory, California, USA, produces a laser of 1.3 petawatts (130 trillion watts).
1997 A new subatomic particle, an exotic meson, was possibly discovered at Brookhaven National Laboratory, Upton, New York, USA. The exotic meson is made up of either a quark, an antiquark and a gluon, or two quarks and two antiquarks. US physicists display the first atomic laser. It emits atoms that act like lightwaves.

PI

In 1853, the English mathematician William Shanks published the value of pi to 707 decimal places. The calculation had taken him 15 years and was surpassed only in 1945, when computations made on an early desk calculator showed that the last 180 decimal places he had calculated were incorrect.

pi symbol π, the ratio of the circumference of a circle to its diameter. The value of pi is 3.1415926, correct to seven decimal places. Common approximations to pi are $\frac{22}{7}$ and 3.14, although the value 3 can be used as a rough estimation.

In mathematics you don't understand things. You just get used to them.

John Von Neumann Hungarian-born US mathematician. Attributed remark

picric acid $C_6H_2(NO_2)_3OH$ (technical name **2,4,6-trinitrophenol**) strong acid that is used to dye wool and silks yellow, for the treatment of burns, and in the manufacture of explosives. It is a yellow, crystalline solid.

PICS (abbreviation for Platform for Internet Content Selection) in computing, method of classifying data according to its content. Under PICS, the creator and the reader of a file can add descriptive electronic labels to it, making it possible for users to sort documents according to keywords on the label. The system, introduced 1996, aims to help parents to control what their children can see on the Internet, for example by blocking access to pornographic or violent material; it also enables people to highlight subjects in which they are especially interested.

PICT in computing, object-oriented file format used on the Apple ◊Macintosh computer. The format uses ◊QuickDraw and is supported by almost all graphics applications on the Macintosh.

pie chart method of displaying proportional information by dividing a circle up into different-sized sectors (slices of pie). The angle of each sector is proportional to the size, expressed as a percentage, of the group of data that it represents.

For example, data from a traffic survey could be presented in a pie chart in the following way:

(1) convert each item of data to a percentage figure;
(2) 100% will equal 360 degrees of the circle, therefore each 1% = 360/100 = 3.6 degrees;
(3) calculate the angle of the segment for each item of data by multiplying the percentage by 3.6, and plot this on the circle.

The diagram may be made clearer by adding colours or shadings to each group, together with a key.

pier structure built out into the sea from the coastline for use as a landing place or promenade.

piezoelectric effect property of some crystals (for example, quartz) to develop an electromotive force or voltage across opposite faces when subjected to tension or compression, and, conversely, to expand or contract in size when subjected to an electromotive force. Piezoelectric crystal ◊oscillators are used as frequency standards (for example, replacing balance wheels in watches), and for producing ultrasound.

pig any even-toed hoofed mammal of the family Suidae. They are omnivorous, and have simple, non-ruminating stomachs and thick hides. The Middle Eastern **wild boar** *Sus scrofa* is the ancestor of domesticated breeds; it is 1.5 m/4.5 ft long and 1 m/3 ft high, with formidable tusks, but not naturally aggressive. The smallest member of the pig family is the **pygmy hog** *Sus salvanus.*

Wild pigs include the ◊babirusa **and the** ◊wart hog. The farming of domesticated pigs was practised during the Neolithic in the Middle East and China at least 11,000 years ago and the pig was a common farm animal in ancient Greece and Rome. Over 400 breeds evolved over the centuries, many of which have all but disappeared in more recent times with the development of intensive rearing systems; however, different environments and requirements have ensured the continuation of a variety of types. The Berkshire, Chester White, Poland, China, Saddleback, Yorkshire, Duroc, and Razorback are the main surviving breeds. Modern indoor rearing methods favour the large white breeds, such as the Chester White and the originally Swedish Landrace, over coloured varieties, which tend to be hardier and can survive better outdoors. Since 1960, hybrid pigs, produced by crossing two or more breeds, have become popular for their heavy but lean carcasses.

pigeon or ***dove*** bird of the family Columbidae, order Columbiformes, distinguished by its large crop, which becomes glandular in the breeding season and secretes a milky fluid ('pigeon's milk') that aids digestion of food for the young. There are many species, and they are found worldwide.

New World species include the mourning-doves, which live much of the time on the ground. The fruit pigeons of Australasia and the Malay regions are beautifully coloured. In the USA, there were once millions of passenger pigeons *Ectopistes migratorius,* but they have been extinct since 1914.

pigeon hawk another name for the merlin, a small ◊falcon.

pigeon pea woody, perennial legume *Cajanus cajan,* grown as a crop in many parts of Africa, Asia, and Latin America. It constitutes about 5% of world legume production (3.5 million hectares). Pigeon peas have a growing season of 6–9 months and are either harvested dry and used mainly in dahl soup, or harvested earlier and eaten as a green vegetable. They are highly nutritious containing up to 28% protein, and 10 times more fat, 5 times more vitamin A, and 3 times more vitamin C than ordinary peas. Cultivating pigeon pea also replenishes the soil with nitrates.

pig iron or ***cast iron*** the quality of iron produced in a ◊blast furnace. It contains around 4% carbon plus some other impurities.

pika or ***mouse-hare*** any small mammal of the family Ochotonidae, belonging to the order Lagomorpha (rabbits and hares). The single genus *Ochotona* contains about 15 species, most of which live in mountainous regions of Asia, although two species are native to North America.

Pikas have short, rounded ears, and most species are about 20 cm/8 in long, with greyish-brown fur and no visible tail. Their warning call is a sharp whistle. They are vegetarian and in late summer cut grasses and other plants and place them in piles to dry as hay, which is then stored for the winter.

Pikas can be divided into rock pikas and burrowing pikas. Rock pikas live in rocky territory alone or in pairs. Population densities are low and lifespan is about six years. Females have two or three young per year. Burrowing pikas are social animals and live in family groups at high densities in meadows or steppes, with a much shorter lifespan, of less than two years. Females have as many as twenty young per year, in several large litters.

Pikas do not hibernate, but stay mostly in their burrows, feeding on the hay piles that they have stocked up during the summer.

pike any of a family Esocidae in the order Salmoniformes, of slender, freshwater bony fish with narrow pointed heads and sharp, pointed teeth. The northern pike *Esox lucius,* of North America and Eurasia, may reach a length of 2.2 m/7 ft and a weight of 9 kg/20 lb.

Other kinds of pike include muskellunges, up to 2.2 m/7 ft long, and the smaller pickerels, both in the genus *Esox.*

pikeperch any of various freshwater members of the perch family, resembling pikes, especially the walleye *Stizostedion vitreum,* common in Europe, W Asia, and North America. It reaches over 1 m/3 ft.

pike-perch freshwater bony fish. It is common in the rivers and lakes of Europe and western Asia, and also found in North

America. It may reach as much as 1 m/3.3 ft in length. Pike-perch feed on other fish.

classification Pike-perch *Lucioperca lucioperca* are in order Perciformes, class Osteichthyes.

pilchard any of various small, oily members of the herring family, Clupeidae, especially the commercial sardine of Europe *Sardina pilchardus,* and the California sardine *Sardinops sagax.*

In March 1995 a mystery virus or toxin began causing the deaths of millions of pilchards in the oceans south of Australia, killing adults over 12 cm/4.7 in long, but not appearing to harm fish feeding on the pilchards. In April a slick of dead pilchards 40 km/25 mi long was observed off Tasmania.

Pill, the commonly used term for the contraceptive pill, based on female hormones. The combined pill, which contains synthetic hormones similar to oestrogen and progesterone, stops the production of eggs, and makes the mucus produced by the cervix hostile to sperm. It is the most effective form of contraception apart from sterilization, being more than 99% effective.

The **minipill** or progesterone-only pill prevents implantation of a fertilized egg into the wall of the uterus. The minipill has a slightly higher failure rate, especially if not taken at the same time each day, but has fewer side effects and is considered safer for long-term use. Possible side effects of the Pill include migraine or headache and high blood pressure. More seriously, oestrogen-containing pills can slightly increase the risk of a clot forming in the blood vessels. This risk is increased in women over 35 if they smoke. Controversy surrounds other possible health effects of taking the Pill. The evidence for a link with cancer is slight (and the Pill may protect women from some forms of cancer). Once a woman ceases to take it, there is an increase in the likelihood of conceiving identical twins.

pilotfish small marine fish *Naucrates ductor* of the family Carangidae, which also includes pompanos. It hides below sharks, turtles, or boats, using the shade as a base from which to prey on smaller fish. It is found in all warm oceans and grows to about 36 cm/1.2 ft.

pilot running in computing, a method of implementing a new computer system in which the work is gradually transferred from the old system to the new system over a period of time. This ensures that any faults in the new system are resolved before the old system is withdrawn. An alternative method is ◊parallel running.

pimento or ***allspice*** any of several evergreen trees belonging to the myrtle family, found in tropical parts of the New World. The dried berries of the species *P. dioica* are used as a spice (see ◊allspice). Also, a sweet variety of ◊capsicum pepper (more correctly spelled **pimiento**). (Pimento genus *Pimenta,* family Myrtaceae.)

pimpernel any of a group of plants belonging to the primrose family, comprising about 30 species mostly native to W Europe. The European scarlet pimpernel (*A. arvensis*) grows in cornfields, the small star-shaped flowers opening only in full sunshine. It is naturalized in North America. (Genus *Anagallis,* family Primulaceae.)

PIN (acronym for ***personal identification number***) in banking, a unique number used as a password to establish the identity of a customer using an automatic cash dispenser. The PIN is normally encoded into the magnetic strip of the customer's bank card and is known only to the customer and to the bank's computer. Before a cash dispenser will issue money or information, the customer must insert the card into a slot in the machine (so that the PIN can be read from the magnetic strip) and enter the PIN correctly at a keyboard. This helps to prevent stolen cards from being used to obtain money from cash dispensers.

pine any of a group of coniferous, ◊resin-producing trees with evergreen needle-shaped leaves; there are about 70–100 species of pines, making them the largest family of ◊conifers. (Genus *Pinus,* family Pinaceae.)

The oldest living species is probably the bristlecone pine (*P. aristata*), native to California, of which some specimens are said to be 4,600 years old.

Pine (acronym for ***program for Internet news and e-mail***) electronic mail program for ◊UNIX and ◊MS-DOS. Pine grew out of ◊Elm, an older UNIX e-mailer, and includes online help and a user-friendly text editor called Pico.

pineal body or ***pineal gland*** a cone-shaped outgrowth of the vertebrate brain. In some lower vertebrates, it develops a rudimentary lens and retina, which show it to be derived from an eye, or pair of eyes, situated on the top of the head in ancestral vertebrates. In fishes that can change colour to match their background, the pineal perceives the light level and controls the colour change. In birds, the pineal detects changes in daylight and stimulates breeding behaviour as spring approaches. Mammals also have a pineal gland, but it is located deeper within the brain. It secretes a hormone, melatonin, thought to influence rhythms of activity. In humans, it is a small piece of tissue attached by a stalk to the rear wall of the third ventricle of the brain.

pineapple large, juicy fruit of the pineapple plant, which belongs to the bromeliad family and is native to South and Central America but now cultivated in many other tropical areas, such as Hawaii and Queensland, Australia. The plant's mauvish flowers are produced in the second year, and afterwards join with their bracts (specialized leaves protecting the buds) to form the fleshy fruit, which looks like a giant cone. (*Ananas comosus,* family Bromeliaceae.)

For export to world markets the fruits are cut unripe and lack the sweet juiciness typical of the canned pineapple (usually the smoother-skinned Cayenne variety), which is allowed to mature fully.

pine marten species of ◊marten, a small mammal.

pine siskin streaked, tan, black, and yellow ◊finch *Carduelis pinus* of North America, about 12 cm/5 in long.

PING (contraction of ***Packet Internet Groper***) in computing, short message sent over a network by one computer to check whether another is correctly connected to it. By extension, one can 'ping' other people – for example, checking addresses on a ◊mailing list by sending an ◊e-mail to all members requesting an acknowledgement.

pinhole camera the simplest type of camera, in which a pinhole rather than a lens is used to form an image. Light passes through the pinhole at one end of a box to form a sharp inverted image on the inside surface of the opposite end. The image is equally sharp for objects placed at different distances from the camera because only one ray from a particular distance or direction can enter through the tiny pinhole, and so only one corresponding point of light will be produced on the image. A photographic film or plate fitted inside the box will, if exposed for a long time, record the image.

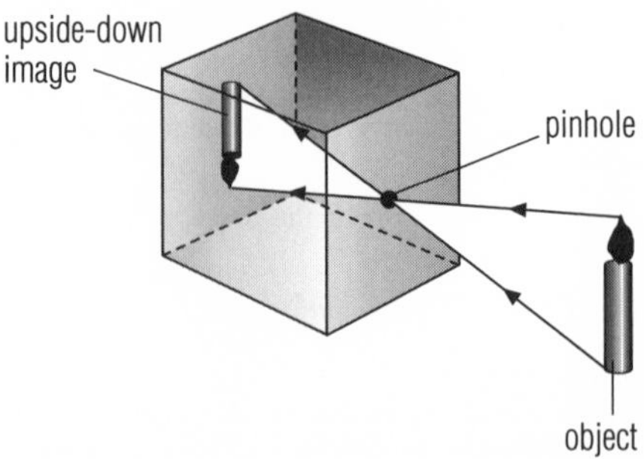

pinhole camera *A pinhole camera has no lens but can nevertheless produce a sharp inverted image because only one ray from a particular point can enter the tiny pinhole aperture, and so no blurring takes place. However, the very low amount of light entering the camera also means that the film at the back must be exposed for a long time before a photographic image is produced; the camera is therefore only suitable for photographing stationary objects.*

pink any of a group of annual or perennial plants that have stems with characteristic swellings (nodes) and scented flowers ranging in colour from white through pink to purple. Members of the pink family include carnations, sweet williams, and baby's breath (*Gypsophila paniculata*). (Genus *Dianthus,* family Carophyllaceae.)

Deptford pink (*D. armeria*), which has deep pink flowers with pale dots, is native to Europe and naturalized in the USA.

pinna in botany, the primary division of a ◊pinnate leaf. In mammals, the pinna is the external part of the ear.

pinnate leaf leaf that is divided up into many small leaflets, arranged in rows along either side of a midrib, as in ash trees (*Fraxinus*). It is a type of compound leaf. Each leaflet is known as a **pinna**, and where the pinnae are themselves divided, the secondary divisions are known as pinnules.

pint imperial dry or liquid measure of capacity equal to 20 fluid ounces, half a quart, one-eighth of a gallon, or 0.568 litre. In the US, a liquid pint is equal to 0.473 litre, while a dry pint is equal to 0.550 litre.

pinworm ◊nematode worm *Enterobius vermicularis,* an intestinal parasite of humans.

pion or ***pi meson*** in physics, a subatomic particle with a neutral form (mass 135 MeV) and a positively charged form (mass 139 MeV). The charged pion decays into muons and neutrinos and the neutral form decays into gamma-ray photons. They belong to the ◊hadron class of ◊elementary particles.

The mass of a positive pion is 273 times that of an electron; the mass of a neutral pion is 264 times that of an electron.

Pioneer probe any of a series of US Solar-System space probes 1958–78. The probes *Pioneer 4–9* went into solar orbit to monitor the Sun's activity during the 1960s and early 1970s. *Pioneer 5,* launched in 1960, was the first of a series to study the solar wind between the planets. *Pioneer 10,* launched March in 1972, was the first probe to reach Jupiter (December 1973) and to leave the Solar System in 1983. *Pioneer 11,* launched April 1973, passed Jupiter December 1974, and was the first probe to reach Saturn (September 1979), before also leaving the Solar System.

Pioneer 10 and *11* carry plaques containing messages from Earth in case they are found by other civilizations among the stars. Pioneer Venus probes were launched May and August 1978. One orbited Venus, and the other dropped three probes onto the surface. The orbiter finally burned up in the atmosphere of Venus 1992. In 1992 *Pioneer 10* was more than 8 billion km/4.4 billion mi from the Sun. Both it and *Pioneer 11* were still returning data measurements of starlight intensity to Earth.

Pioneer 1, 2, and *3,* launched in 1958, were intended Moon probes, but *Pioneer 2's* launch failed, and *1* and *3* failed to reach their target, although they did measure the ◊Van Allen radiation belts. *Pioneer 4* began to orbit the Sun after passing the Moon.

pioneer species in ecology, those species that are the first to colonize and thrive in new areas. Coal tips, recently cleared woodland, and new roadsides are areas where pioneer species will quickly appear. As the habitat matures other species take over, a process known as **succession**.

pipefish any of various long-snouted, thin, pipelike marine fish in the same family (Syngnathidae) as seahorses. The great pipefish *Syngnathus acus* grows up to 50 cm/1.6 ft, and the male has a brood pouch for eggs and developing young, which hatch as tiny versions of the adults in five to six weeks: there is no larval stage.

PIPEFISH

When pipefish mate it is the female who penetrates the male. She inserts her eggs into his internal pouch using her protruding ovarian duct. He then fertilizes the eggs and carries them as they develop.

pipeline any extended line of conduits for carrying water, oil, gas, or other material over long distances. Pipelines are widely used in water-supply and oil- and gas-distribution schemes. The USA has 2.4 million km/1.5 million mi of pipeline (including over 300,000 km/200,000 mi of oil pipeline). One of the longest is the Trans-Alaskan Pipeline in Alaska.

The first gas pipeline between North Africa and Europe opened in 1996, bringing gas from Algeria to Spain and eventually to France and Portugal. Financed largely by the European Union, it will help diversify the supply of gas throughout Europe and bring transport costs down. The 1,400 km/875 mi pipeline brings gas from Algeria via Morocco and the Strait of Gibraltar to the city of Cordoba in southern Spain, where it will be channelled into Spain's natural-gas network. It should supply nearly half of Spain's gas needs by 2000. Construction of the pipeline took almost five years, at a cost of $2.3 billion. It was the most complicated project of its kind in the world, since 45 km/30 mi of the pipe had to be laid on the geologically complex floor of the Strait of Gibraltar, the site of treacherously strong currents.

Piper Alpha disaster accident aboard the North Sea oil platform Piper Alpha on 6 July 1988, in which 167 people died. The rig was devastated by a series of explosions, caused initially by a gas leakage. An official inquiry held into the disaster highlighted the vulnerability of offshore rigs.

pipette device for the accurate measurement of a known volume of liquid, usually for transfer from one container to another, used in chemistry and biology laboratories.

A pipette is a glass tube, often with an enlarged bulb, which is calibrated in one or more positions, or it may be a plastic device with an adjustable plunger, fitted with one or more disposable plastic tips.

PIPEX (contraction of ***public Internet protocol exchange***) in computing, UK-based Internet provider which started operations in 1992, specializing in serving the commercial sector. The company became one of the UK's major ◊backbone providers and was acquired by ◊UUNET 1996.

pipit any of various sparrow-sized ground-dwelling songbirds of the genus *Anthus* of the family Motacillidae, order Passeriformes.

piranha any South American freshwater fish of the genus *Serrusalmus,* in the same order as cichlids. They can grow to 60 cm/2 ft long, and have razor-sharp teeth; some species may rapidly devour animals, especially if attracted by blood.

Pisces inconspicuous zodiac constellation, mainly in the northern hemisphere between ◊Aries and ◊Aquarius, near ◊Pegasus. It is represented as two fish tied together by their tails. The Circlet, a delicate ring of stars, marks the head of the western fish in Pisces. The constellation contains the **vernal equinox**, the point at which the Sun's path around the sky (the **ecliptic**) crosses the celestial equator (see ◊celestial sphere). The Sun reaches this point around 21 March each year as it passes through Pisces from mid-March to late April. In astrology, the dates for Pisces are between about 19 Feb and 20 March (see ◊precession).

Piscis Austrinus or ***Southern Fish*** constellation of the southern hemisphere near ◊Capricornus. Its brightest star is the first-magnitude ◊Fomalhaut.

pistachio deciduous tree of the cashew family, native to Europe and Asia, whose green nuts are eaten salted or used to enhance and flavour food, especially ice cream. (*Pistacia vera,* family Anacardiaceae.)

pistil general term for the female part of a flower, either referring to one single ◊carpel or a group of several fused carpels.

pistol any small firearm designed to be fired with one hand.

Pistols were in use from the early 15th century.

The problem of firing more than once without reloading was tackled by using many combinations of multiple barrels, both stationary and revolving. A breech-loading, multichambered revolver from 1650 still survives; the first practical solution, however, was

Samuel Colt's six-gun 1847. Behind a single barrel, a short six-chambered cylinder was rotated by cocking the hammer and a fresh round of ammunition brought into firing position. The automatic pistol, operated by gas or recoil, was introduced in Germany in the 1890s. Both revolvers and automatics remain in widespread military use.

piston barrel-shaped device used in reciprocating engines (steam, petrol, diesel oil) to harness power. Pistons are driven up and down in cylinders by expanding steam or hot gases. They pass on their motion via a connecting rod and crank to a crankshaft, which turns the driving wheels. In a pump or compressor, the role of the piston is reversed, being used to move gases and liquids. See also ◊internal-combustion engine.

pit bull terrier or ***American pit bull terrier*** variety of dog that was developed in the USA solely as a fighting dog. It usually measures about 50 cm/20 in at the shoulder and weighs roughly 23 kg/50 lb, but there are no established criteria since it is not recognized as a breed by either the American or British Kennel Clubs. Selective breeding for physical strength and aggression has created a dog unsuitable for life in the modern community.

pitch in chemistry, a black, sticky substance, hard when cold, but liquid when hot, used for waterproofing, roofing, and paving. It is made by the destructive distillation of wood or coal tar, and has been used since antiquity for caulking wooden ships.

pitch in mechanics, the distance between the adjacent threads of a screw or bolt. When a screw is turned through one full turn it moves a distance equal to the pitch of its thread. A screw thread is a simple type of machine, acting like a rolled-up inclined plane, or ramp (as may be illustrated by rolling a long paper triangle around a pencil). A screw has a ◊mechanical advantage greater than one.

pitchblende or ***uraninite*** brownish-black mineral, the major constituent of uranium ore, consisting mainly of uranium oxide (UO_2). It also contains some lead (the final, stable product of uranium decay) and variable amounts of most of the naturally occurring radioactive elements, which are products of either the decay or the fissioning of uranium isotopes. The uranium yield is 50–80%; it is also a source of radium, polonium, and actinium. Pitchblende was first studied by Pierre and Marie ◊Curie, who found radium and polonium in its residues in 1898.

pitcher plant any of various ◊insectivorous plants, the leaves of which are shaped like a pitcher and filled with a fluid that traps and digests insects. (Genera especially *Nepenthes* and *Sarracenia*, family Sarraceniaceae.)

Pitot tube instrument that measures fluid (gas and liquid) flow. It is used to measure the speed of aircraft, and works by sensing pressure differences in different directions in the airstream.

It was invented in the 1730s by the French scientist Henri Pitot (1695–1771).

pitta tropical bird of order Passeriformes, genus *Pitta*, forming the family Pittidae. Some 20 species are native to SE Asia, W Africa, and Australia. They have round bodies, big heads, are often brightly coloured, and are silent. They live on the ground and in low undergrowth, and can run from danger. They feed on insects.

pittosporum tree or shrub of the large genus *Pittosporum*, family Pittosporaceae, of Asia, Africa, and Australia. Of the Australian species, some are found in moist rainforest areas while one species grows in the dry inland. *P. undulatum* of the eastern mainland states has cream bell-shaped flowers and orange fruit.

pituitary gland major ◊endocrine gland of vertebrates, situated in the centre of the brain. It is attached to the ◊hypothalamus by a stalk. The pituitary consists of two lobes. The posterior lobe is an extension of the hypothalamus, and is in effect nervous tissue. It stores two hormones synthesized in the hypothalamus: ◊ADH and oxytocin. The anterior lobe secretes six hormones, some of which control the activities of other glands (thyroid, gonads, and adrenal cortex); others are direct-acting hormones affecting milk secretion and controlling growth.

pituri Australian shrub *Duboisia hopwoodii*, the leaves and twigs of which are used by Aborigines as a narcotic.

Pixar Hollywood animation company bought by Steve Jobs in 1986. In 1995 Pixar, together with Walt Disney, released *Toy Story*, the first ever feature-length computer-animated cartoon film.

pixel (derived from ***picture element***) single dot on a computer screen. All screen images are made up of a collection of pixels, with each pixel being either off (dark) or on (illuminated, possibly in colour). The number of pixels available determines the screen's resolution. Typical resolutions of microcomputer screens vary from 320 x 200 pixels to 640 x 480 pixels, but screens with 1,024 x 768 pixels are now common for high-quality graphic (pictorial) displays.

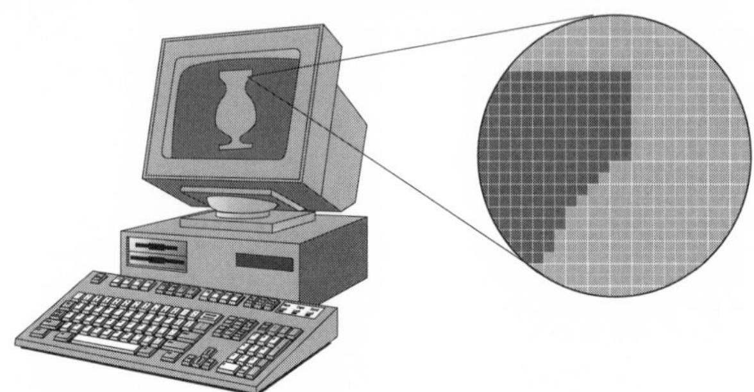

pixel *Computer screen images are made of a number of pixels('dots'). The greater the number of pixels the greater the resolution of the image; most computer screens are set at 640 × 480 pixels, although higher resolutions are available.*

PKZIP in computing, widely-used shareware file compression utility. Files created with PKZIP (often posted to ◊newsgroups and ◊bulletin boards) bear the suffix .zip and are said to be 'zipped'.

placebo Latin ***'I will please'*** any harmless substance, often called a 'sugar pill', that has no active ingredient, but may nevertheless bring about improvement in the patient's condition.

The use of placebos in medicine is limited to drug trials, where a placebo is given alongside the substance being tested,to compare effects. The 'placebo effect', first named in 1945, demonstrates the control mind exerts over matter, bringing changes in blood pressure, perceived pain, and rates of healing. Recent research points to the release of certain neurotransmitters in the production of the placebo effect.

placenta organ that attaches the developing ◊embryo or ◊fetus to the ◊uterus in placental mammals (mammals other than marsupials, platypuses, and echidnas). Composed of maternal and embryonic tissue, it links the blood supply of the embryo to the blood supply of the mother, allowing the exchange of oxygen, nutrients, and waste products. The two blood systems are not in direct contact, but are separated by thin membranes, with materials diffusing across from one system to the other. The placenta also produces hormones that maintain and regulate pregnancy. It is shed as part of the afterbirth.

It is now understood that a variety of materials, including drugs and viruses, can pass across the placental membrane. HIV, the virus that causes ◊AIDS, can be transmitted in this way.

The tissue in plants that joins the ovary to the ovules is also called a placenta.

place value the value given to a digit because of its position within a number. For example, in the decimal number 2,465 the 2 represents two thousands, the 4 represents four hundreds, the 6 represents six tens, and the 5 represents five units.

plage in astronomy, a bright patch in the ◊chromosphere above a group of ◊sunspots, occasionally seen on images of the Sun in hydrogen light.

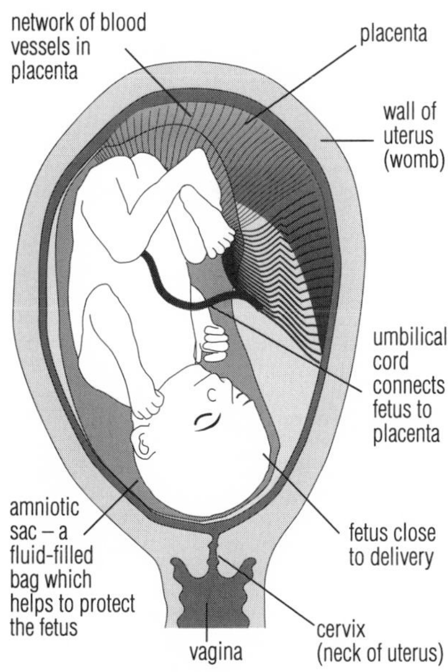

placenta *The placenta is a disc-shaped organ about 25 cm/10 in in diameter and 3 cm/1 in thick. It is connected to the fetus by the umbilical cord.*

PLAGUE

http://www.outbreak.org/cgi-unreg/dynaserve.exe/Plague/index.html

Basic medical details of the biological weapon version of plague viruses and bacteria. The Web site contains brief sections covering characteristics of the diseases including its toxicology, the symptoms they cause, cautions and precautions, first aid therapy for victims of the diseases, and a list of neutralization and decontamination methods.

plague term applied to any epidemic disease with a high mortality rate, but it usually refers to the bubonic plague. This is a disease transmitted by fleas (carried by the black rat) which infect the sufferer with the bacillus *Yersinia pestis.* An early symptom is swelling of lymph nodes, usually in the armpit and groin; such swellings are called 'buboes'. It causes virulent blood poisoning and the death rate is high.

Rarer but more virulent forms of plague are **septicaemic** and **pneumonic**; both still exert a formidable mortality. Outbreaks of plague still occur, mostly in poor countries, but never to the extent seen in the late Middle Ages. According to a World Health Organization report published in 1996, the incidence of plague is on the increase. It was reported in 13 states of the USA between 1984 and 1994, in comparison with just 3 states in the 1940s.

PLAGUE

In 1666, to help counter the spread of plague, the British Parliament decreed that all bodies had to be wrapped in a woollen shroud for burial. This decree provided wool-makers with a constant source of business for nearly 150 years.

plaice fish *Pleuronectes platessa* belonging to the flatfish group, abundant in the N Atlantic. It is white beneath and brownish with orange spots on the 'eyed' side. It can grow to 75 cm/2.5 ft long, and weigh about 2 kg/4.5 lb.

plain or ***grassland*** land, usually flat, upon which grass predominates. The plains cover large areas of the Earth's surface, especially between the deserts of the tropics and the rainforests of the Equator, and have rain in one season only. In such regions the climate belts move north and south during the year, bringing rainforest conditions at one time and desert conditions at another. Temperate plains include the North European Plain, the High Plains of the USA and Canada, and the Russian Plain also known as the steppe.

plaintext in computing, another name for ◊cleartext..

plan in computing, file publicly accessible on UNIX systems that holds whatever information users wish to make public about themselves.

On other services such records may be called a resumé, bio, or directory entry. The purpose is generally the same, to allow users of the same system to find out a little more about the real-world identity of the people with whom they are interacting.

planarian nonparasitic flatworm. Planarians are usually small, flat, soft creatures, common both in fresh water and in the sea, where they may be found under rocks and stones in pools. Some of them are brilliantly coloured. They feed on insects, small molluscs, and worms.

The mouth is on the underside of the body, the digestive system varies from a simple bulblike pharynx to a many-branched intestine. The skin is covered with protective vibrating cilia ('hairs'). Planarians multiply sexually and also by division.

classification Planarians form the class Turbellaria, which, with Monogenea, Digenea, and Cestoda, comprise the phylum Platyhelminthes.

Planck's constant in physics, a fundamental constant (symbol h) that relates the energy (E) of one quantum of electromagnetic radiation (the smallest possible 'packet' of energy; see quantum theory) to the frequency (f) of its radiation by $E = hf$.

Its value is 6.6261×10^{-34} joule seconds.

plane in botany, any of several trees belonging to the plane family. Species include the oriental plane (*P. orientalis*), a favourite plantation tree of the Greeks and Romans, and the American plane or buttonwood (*P. occidentalis*). A hybrid of these two is the London plane (*P. x acerifolia*), with palmate, usually five-lobed leaves, which is widely planted in cities for its resistance to air pollution. (Genus *Platanus*, family Platanaceae.)

All species have hanging burlike fruits and can grow to 30 m/100 ft high.

plane figure in geometry, a two-dimensional figure. All ◊polygons are plane figures.

It will free man from the remaining chains, the chains of gravity which still tie him to this planet.

WERNHER VON BRAUN German-born US rocket engineer.
On space travel, *Time* 10 Feb 1958

planet Greek ***'wanderer'*** large celestial body in orbit around a star, composed of rock, metal, or gas. There are nine planets in the ◊Solar System: Mercury, Venus, Earth, Mars, Jupiter, Saturn, Neptune, Uranus, and Pluto. The inner four, called the **terrestrial planets**, are small and rocky, and include the planet Earth. The outer planets, with the exception of Pluto, are called the **major planets**, and consist of large balls of rock, liquid, and gas; the largest is Jupiter, which contains a mass equivalent to 70% of all the other planets combined. Planets do not produce light, but reflect the light of their parent star.

As seen from the Earth, all the historic planets are conspicuous

Planck, Max Karl Ernst (1858–1947)

German physicist who framed the quantum theory in 1900. His research into the manner in which heated bodies radiate energy led him to report that energy is emitted only in indivisible amounts, called 'quanta', the magnitudes of which are proportional to the frequency of the radiation. His discovery ran counter to classical physics and is held to have marked the commencement of the modern science. He was awarded the Nobel Prize for Physics in 1918.

Measurements of the frequency distribution of black body radiation by Wilhelm Wien (1864–1928) in 1893 showed the peak value of energy occurring at a higher frequency with greater temperature. This may be observed in the varying colour produced by a glowing object. At low temperatures, it glows red but as the temperature rises the peak energy is emitted at a greater frequency, and the colour become yellow and then white.

Mary Evans Picture Library

Wien attempted to derive a radiation law that would relate the energy to frequency and temperature but discovered a radiation law in 1896 that was valid only at high frequencies. Lord Rayleigh (1842–1919) later found a similar equation that held for radiation emitted at low frequencies. Planck was able to combine these two radiation laws, arriving at a formula for the observed energy of the radiation at any given frequency and temperature. This entailed making the assumption that the energy consists of the sum of a finite number of discrete units of energy that he called quanta, and that the energy ϵ of each quantum is given by the equation: $\epsilon = hv$, where v is the frequency of the radiation and h is a constant now recognized to be a fundamental constant of nature, called Planck's constant. By directly relating the energy of a radiation to its frequency, an explanation was found for the observation that radiation of greater energy has a higher frequency distribution.

Planck's idea that energy must consist of indivisible particles, not waves, was revolutionary because it totally contravened the accepted belief that radiation consisted of waves. It soon found rapid acceptance: Albert Einstein in 1905 used Planck's quantum theory as an explanation for photoelectricity and in 1913 Danish physicist Niels Bohr successfully applied the quantum theory to the atom. This was later developed into a full system of quantum mechanics in the 1920s, when it also became clear that energy and matter have both a particle and a wave nature.

Planck's constant, a fundamental constant (symbol h), is the energy of one quantum of electromagnetic radiation divided by the frequency of its radiation.

naked-eye objects moving in looped paths against the stellar background. The size of these loops, which are caused by the Earth's own motion round the Sun, are inversely proportional to the planet's distance from the Earth.

new discoveries In 1995 Italian astronomers believed they had detected a new planet around 51 Pegasi in the constellation Pegasus. It was named 51 Pegasi B and is thought to have a mass comparable to that of Jupiter. The gravitational pull thought to be that of the planet may be caused by pulsation in the parent star.

The discovery of three further new planets was announced at the American Astronomical Society meeting in January 1996. All are outside the Solar System, but two are only about 35 light years from Earth and orbit stars visible with the naked eye. One, 70 Vir B, is in the constellation Virgo, and the other, 47 UMa B, is in Ursa Major. The third, ß Pictoris, is about 50 light years away in the southern constellation Pictor.

In April 1996 another planet was discovered, orbiting Rho Cancri in the constellation Cancer. Yet another was found in June 1996, this time orbiting the star Tau Bootis. By July 1996 the total of new planets discovered since October 1995 had risen to 10.

The discovery of a new planet with an orbit which is more irregular than that of any other was discovered by US astronomers October 1996. The new planet has 1.6 times the mass of Jupiter and orbits the star 16 Cygni B. Its distance from the star 16 Cygni B varies from 90 million km to 390 million km.

NINE PLANETS

http://seds.lpl.arizona.edu/nineplanets/nineplanets/nineplanets.html

Multimedia tour of the Solar System, with descriptions of each of the planets and major moons, and appendices on such topics as astronomical names and how they're assigned, the origin of the Solar System, and hypothetical planets.

To remember the order of the planets, outwards from the Sun:

My very educated mother just served us nine pies.

Mercury, Venus, Earth, Mars, Jupiter, Saturn, Uranus, Neptune, Pluto

planetarium optical projection device by means of which the motions of stars and planets are reproduced on a domed ceiling representing the sky.

planetary embryo in astronomy, one of numerous massive bodies thought to have formed from the accretion of planetesimals during the formation of the Solar System. Embryos in the region of the Earth's orbit would have been about 1,023 kg/ 2,251 lb in mass, and about 10–100 of them would have coalesced to make the Earth.

planetary nebula shell of gas thrown off by a star at the end of its life. Planetary nebulae have nothing to do with planets. They were named by William Herschel, who thought their rounded shape resembled the disc of a planet. After a star such as the Sun has expanded to become a ◊red giant, its outer layers are ejected into space to form a planetary nebula, leaving the core as a ◊white dwarf at the centre.

planimeter simple integrating instrument for measuring the area of a regular or irregular plane surface. It consists of two hinged arms: one is kept fixed and the other is traced around the boundary of the area. This actuates a small graduated wheel; the area is calculated from the wheel's change in position.

planisphere in astronomy, a graphical device for determining the aspect of the sky for any date and time in the year. It consists of two discs mounted concentrically so that the upper disc, which has an aperture corresponding to the horizon of the observer, can rotate over the lower disc, which is printed with a map of the sky centred

Discovery of the Major Planets

by Tony Jones

Other than the Earth, there are eight major planets in the solar system. Five of them – Mercury, Venus, Mars, Jupiter and Saturn – have been known since antiquity. Looking like bright stars, they reveal their true nature by moving slowly from night to night against the background of the constellations. Indeed, the word 'planet' comes from the ancient Greek for 'wanderer'.

Venus is unmistakable. Shining brilliant white, it is by far the brightest object in the sky after the Sun and Moon and is often visible in daylight. Every few months it is an arresting sight in the evening or morning sky. Jupiter, Mars and Saturn are also prominent, and Mercury may escape attention only because it is close to the Sun and never seen in darkness. These five, together with the Sun and Moon, were familiar sights in the heavens throughout recorded history and have been woven into religious and astrological myth since ancient times.

The world was taken by surprise then, when a humble music teacher discovered a new member of the Sun's family of planets in 1781. William Herschel (1738–1822) was a committed amateur astronomer and a skilled telescope maker. He had built a series of superb telescopes at his home in Bath, England. On 13 March, while conducting a survey of the night sky, he came across a curious star that appeared as a disk rather than a point of light. A few nights later it had changed position and within months the astronomical world had confirmed that Herschel's object was a new planet far beyond the orbit of Saturn, then the outermost known member of the solar system.

Herschel wanted to call it George's Star, in honour of King George III, but the name Uranus, after the Greek sky god and father of Cronos (Saturn), was eventually accepted. The King was dazzled none the less, and Herschel, the first person ever to discover a new planet, became a favourite at the royal court and soon the most influential astronomer of his day.

Uranus, though faint, is actually visible to the naked eye under good conditions. It was later found that the planet had been recorded on at least 20 occasions as far back as 1690 and mistaken for a star each time. The earlier observers had not had the benefit of Herschel's powerful telescopes which were able to discern the greenish disc of the planet.

Some years later astronomers were having problems with the orbit of Mercury, the planet closest to the Sun. Its movements could not be completely accounted for by Newton's laws of gravity. A French astronomer, Urbain Leverrier (1811–1877), proposed in 1845 that the discrepancy could be explained by the gravitational attraction of an undiscovered planet, which he called Vulcan, orbiting within the orbit of Mercury only 30 million km from the Sun. All attempts to find Vulcan failed, and the Mercury problem remained unsolved until 1915, when Albert Einstein (1879–1955) showed that the discrepancies in the orbit were a consequence of the general theory of relativity.

Leaving astronomers to search for Vulcan, Leverrier turned his attention to Uranus which was also deviating from its predicted path. Again, he attributed the perturbation to another planet, this time beyond the orbit of Uranus, and predicted where in the sky it would be found. Johann Galle (1812–1910) at the Berlin Observatory pointed a telescope at Leverrier's position on 23 September 1846 and almost at once discovered the new planet only one degree from the predicted location. It became known as Neptune, after the Roman god of the sea.

It turned out that a young Cornish mathematician, John Couch Adams (1819–1892) had predicted the position of Neptune a year earlier but had been unable to persuade the Astronomer Royal, George Airy (1801–1892) to take it seriously. When Airy finally asked James Challis (1803–1882) at Cambridge Observatory to search for the planet, Challis saw it on two occasions more than a month before Galle but failed to recognize it.

Buoyed by this outstanding triumph of Newtonian mechanics, astronomers soon suspected that Neptune in turn was being affected by the pull of a still more distant planet. One of the scientists who attempted to calculate its position was US businessman and astronomer Percival Lowell (1855–1916). He built his own observatory in 1895 at Flagstaff in Arizona but failed to track down the mystery planet. It was not until 18 February 1930, 14 years after Lowell's death, that Clyde Tombaugh (1906–1997), an assistant at the observatory, finally stumbled across the planet. He had ignored the predictions of the mathematicians and had systematically worked his way through the zodiac, the band of sky in which the planets move, comparing pairs of photographs taken on different nights and looking for a 'star' that had moved.

The planet, which was named Pluto after the god of the underworld, was much fainter than expected and was later found on several photographs taken during earlier searches.

Though astronomers continue to discover asteroids, comets and other small bodies in the outer solar system, modern search techniques are so thorough that there is little chance of more major planets lying unseen beyond the orbit of Pluto.

---

on the north or south celestial pole. In use, the observer aligns the time of day marked around the edge of the upper disc with the date marked around the edge of the lower disc. The aperture then shows which stars are above the horizon.

plankton small, often microscopic, forms of plant and animal life that live in the upper layers of fresh and salt water, and are an important source of food for larger animals. Marine plankton is concentrated in areas where rising currents bring mineral salts to the surface.

plant organism that carries out ◊photosynthesis, has cellulose cell walls and complex cells, and is immobile. A few parasitic plants have lost the ability to photosynthesize but are still considered to be plants.

Plants are ◊autotrophs, that is, they make carbohydrates from water and carbon dioxide, and are the primary producers in all food chains, so that all animal life is dependent on them. They play a vital part in the carbon cycle, removing carbon dioxide from the atmosphere and generating oxygen. The study of plants is known as ◊botany.

levels of complexity Many of the lower plants (the algae and bryophytes) consist of a simple body, or thallus, on which the organs of reproduction are borne. Simplest of all are the threadlike algae, for example *Spirogyra*, which consist of a chain of cells.

The seaweeds (algae) and mosses and liverworts (bryophytes) represent a further development, with simple, multicellular bodies that have specially modified areas in which the reproductive organs are carried. Higher in the morphological scale are the ferns, club mosses, and horsetails (pteridophytes). Ferns produce leaflike fronds bearing sporangia on their undersurface in which the spores are carried. The spores are freed and germinate to

PLANT

Plants can communicate with each other. A wounded plant may release a gaseous hormone that warns its neighbours to prepare their defences for insect attack, thus limiting potential damage.

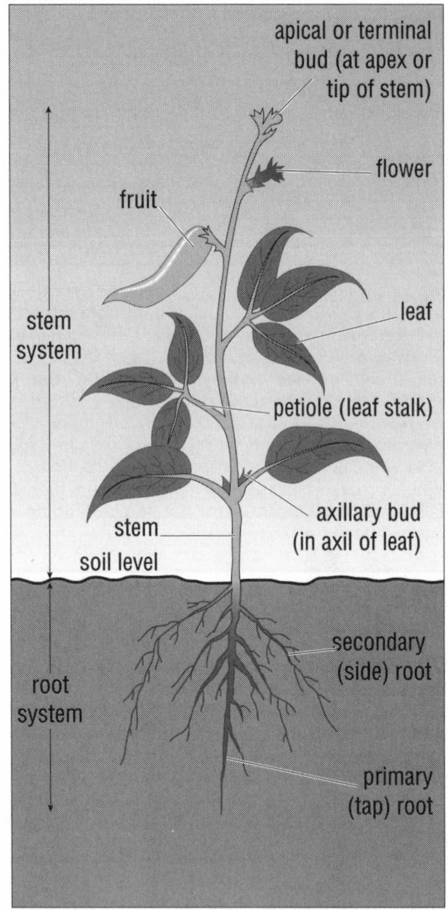

plant *Stem and root systems of a typical seed plant. The root system may sometimes be more extensive than the part of the plant visible above ground.*

produce small independent bodies carrying the sexual organs; thus the fern, like other pteridophytes and some seaweeds, has two quite separate generations in its life cycle (see ◊alternation of generations).

The pteridophytes have special supportive water-conducting tissues, which identify them as vascular plants, a group which includes all seed plants, that is the gymnosperms (conifers, yews, cycads, and ginkgos) and the angiosperms (flowering plants).

seed plants The seed plants are the largest group, and structurally the most complex. They are usually divided into three parts: root, stem, and leaves. Stems grow above or below ground. Their cellular structure is designed to carry water and salts from the roots to the leaves in the ◊xylem, and sugars from the leaves to the roots in the ◊phloem. The leaves manufacture the food of the plant by means of photosynthesis, which occurs in the ◊chloroplasts they contain. Flowers and cones are modified leaves arranged in groups, enclosing the reproductive organs from which the fruits and seeds result.

SURVEY OF THE PLANT KINGDOMS

http://www.mancol.edu/science/biology/plants_new/intro/start.html

Systematic guide to the non-animal kingdoms (plants, fungi, protista, and monera) – their major groups, classification, and anatomy.

plantain any of a group of northern temperate plants. The great plantain (*P. major*) is low-growing with large oval leaves close to the ground, grooved stalks, and spikes of green flowers with purple anthers (in which the pollen matures) followed by seeds, which are used in bird food. (Genus *Plantago,* family Plantaginaceae.)

The most common introduced species is the ribwort plantain (*P. lanceolata*), native to Europe and Asia and a widespread weed in Australia, Europe, and America. Many other species are troublesome weeds.

A type of ◊banana is also known as plantain.

plantation large farm or estate where commercial production of one crop – such as rubber (in Malaysia), palm oil (in Nigeria), or tea (in Sri Lanka) – is carried out. Plantations are usually owned by large companies, often multinational corporations, and run by an estate manager. Many plantations were established in countries under colonial rule, using slave labour.

plant classification taxonomy or classification of plants. Originally the plant kingdom included bacteria, diatoms, dinoflagellates, fungi, and slime moulds, but these are not now thought of as plants. The groups that are always classified as plants are the bryophytes (mosses and liverworts), pteridophytes (ferns, horsetails, and club mosses), gymnosperms (conifers, yews, cycads, and ginkgos), and angiosperms (flowering plants). The angiosperms are split into monocotyledons (for example, orchids, grasses, lilies) and dicotyledons (for example, oak, buttercup, geranium, and daisy).

The basis of plant classification was established by the Swedish naturalist Carolus ◊Linnaeus. Among the angiosperms, it is largely based on the number and arrangement of the flower parts.

The unicellular algae, such as *Chlamydomonas,* are often now put with the protists (single-celled organisms) instead of the plants. Some classification schemes even classify the multicellular algae (seaweeds and freshwater weeds) in a new kingdom, the Protoctista, along with the protists.

plant hormone substance produced by a plant that has a marked effect on its growth, flowering, leaf fall, fruit ripening, or some other process. Examples include ◊auxin, gibberellin, ethylene, and ◊cytokinin.

Unlike animal hormones, these substances are not produced by a particular area of the plant body, and they may be less specific in their effects. It has therefore been suggested that they should not be described as hormones at all.

plant propagation production of plants. Botanists and horticulturalists can use a wide variety of means for propagating plants. There are the natural techniques of ◊vegetative reproduction, together with ◊cuttings, grafting, and ◊micropropagation. The range is wide because most plant tissue, unlike animal tissue, can give rise to the complete range of tissue types within a particular species.

plaque any abnormal deposit on a body surface, especially the thin, transparent film of sticky protein (called mucin) and bacteria on tooth surfaces. If not removed, this film forms tartar (calculus), promotes tooth decay, and leads to gum disease. Another form of plaque is a deposit of fatty or fibrous material in the walls of blood vessels causing ◊atheroma.

Plaskett's star the most massive ◊binary star known, consisting of two supergiants of about 40 and 50 solar masses, orbiting each other every 14.4 days. Plaskett's star lies in the constellation Monoceros and is named after Canadian astronomer John S Plaskett (1865–1941), who identified it as a binary star and discovered its massive nature in 1922.

plasma in biology, the liquid component of the ◊blood.

plasma in physics, an ionized gas produced at extremely high temperatures, as in the Sun and other stars, which contains positive and negative charges in equal numbers. It is a good electrical conductor. In thermonuclear reactions the plasma produced is confined through the use of magnetic fields.

plasma display type of flat display, which uses an ionized gas between two panels containing grids of wires. When current flows through the wires a ◊pixel is charged causing it to light up.

plasmapheresis technique for acquiring plasma from blood. Blood is withdrawn from the patient and separated into its components (plasma and blood cells) by centrifugal force in a continuous-flow cell separator. Once separated, the plasma is available for specific treatments. The blood cells are transfused back into the patient.

plasma torch cutting device used mainly in metallurgy. It works by passing a strong electric current through a rarefied gas, ionizing it to produce temperatures on impact of up to 8,000°C/4,500°F.

plasmid small, mobile piece of ◊DNA found in bacteria and used in ◊genetic engineering. Plasmids are separate from the bacterial chromosome but still multiply during cell growth. Their size ranges from 3% to 20% of the size of the chromosome. There is usually only one copy of a single plasmid per cell, but occasionally several are found. Some plasmids carry 'fertility genes' that enable them to move from one bacterium to another and transfer genetic information between strains. Plasmid genes determine a wide variety of bacterial properties including resistance to antibiotics and the ability to produce toxins.

plasmolysis the separation of the plant cell cytoplasm from the cell wall as a result of water loss. As moisture leaves the vacuole the total volume of the cytoplasm decreases while the cell itself, being rigid, hardly changes. Plasmolysis is induced in the laboratory by immersing a plant cell in a strongly saline or sugary solution, so that water is lost by osmosis. Plasmolysis is unlikely to occur in the wild except in severe conditions.

plaster of Paris form of calcium sulphate, obtained from gypsum; it is mixed with water for making casts and moulds.

plastic any of the stable synthetic materials that are fluid at some stage in their manufacture, when they can be shaped, and that later set to rigid or semi-rigid solids. Plastics today are chiefly derived from petroleum. Most are polymers, made up of long chains of identical molecules.

environmental influence Since plastics have afforded an economical replacement for ivory in the manufacture of piano keys and billiard balls, the industrial chemist may well have been responsible for the survival of the elephant.

Most plastics cannot be broken down by microorganisms, so cannot easily be disposed of. Incineration leads to the release of toxic fumes, unless carried out at very high temperatures.

plastic surgery surgical speciality concerned with the repair of congenital defects and the reconstruction of tissues damaged by disease or injury, including burns. If a procedure is undertaken solely for reasons of appearance, for example, the removal of bags under the eyes or a double chin, it is called **cosmetic surgery**.

A doctor is a man who can distinguish the possible from the impossible.

HEROPHILUS OF CHALCEDON Greek scientist.
Quoted in John Stobaeus *Florilegium* bk 4, ch 38

plastid general name for a cell ◊organelle of plants that is enclosed by a double membrane and contains a series of internal membranes and vesicles. Plastids contain ◊DNA and are produced by division of existing plastids. They can be classified into two main groups: the **chromoplasts**, which contain pigments such as carotenes and chlorophyll, and the **leucoplasts**, which are colourless; however, the distinction between the two is not always clear-cut.

◊Chloroplasts are the major type of chromoplast. They contain chlorophyll, are responsible for the green coloration of most plants, and perform ◊photosynthesis. Other chromoplasts give flower petals and fruits their distinctive colour. Leucoplasts are food-storage bodies and include amyloplasts, found in the roots of many plants, which store large amounts of starch.

plate or tectonic plate, one of several sections of ◊lithosphere approximately 100 km/60 mi thick and at least 200 km/120 mi across, which together comprise the outermost layer of the Earth like the pieces of the cracked surface of a hard-boiled egg.

The plates are made up of two types of crustal material: oceanic crust (sima) and continental crust (sial), both of which are underlain by a solid layer of ◊mantle. Dense **oceanic crust** lies beneath Earth's oceans and consists largely of ◊basalt. **Continental crust**, which underlies the continents and their continental shelves, is thicker, less dense, and consists of rocks rich in silica and aluminium.

Due to convection in the Earth's mantle (see ◊plate tectonics) these pieces of lithosphere are in motion, riding on a more plastic layer of the mantle, called the aesthenosphere. Mountains, volcanoes, earthquakes, and other geological features and phenomena all come about as a result of interaction between the plates.

plateau elevated area of fairly flat land, or a mountainous region in which the peaks are at the same height. An **intermontane plateau** is one surrounded by mountains. A **piedmont plateau** is one that lies between the mountains and low-lying land. A **continental plateau** rises abruptly from low-lying lands or the sea. Examples are the Tibetan Plateau and the Massif Central in France.

platelet tiny disc-shaped structure found in the blood, which helps it to clot. Platelets are not true cells, but membrane-bound cell fragments without nuclei that bud off from large cells in the bone marrow.

They play a vital role in blood clotting as they release blood clotting factors at the site of a cut. Over twelve clotting factors have been discovered and they produce a complex series of reactions which ultimately leads to fibrinogen, the inactive blood sealant always found in the plasma, being converted into fibrin. Fibrin aggregates into threads which form the fabric of a blood clot.

plate tectonics theory formulated in the 1960s to explain the phenomena of ◊continental drift and seafloor spreading, and the formation of the major physical features of the Earth's surface. The Earth's outermost layer, the ◊lithosphere, is regarded as a jigsaw puzzle of rigid major and minor plates that move relative to each other, probably under the influence of convection currents in the mantle beneath. At the margins of the plates, where they collide or move apart, major landforms such as fold mountains, volcanoes, ocean trenches, and ocean ridges are created. The rate of drift is at most 15 cm/6 in per year.

The concept of plate tectonics brings together under one unifying theory many previously unrelated phenomena observed in the Earth's crust. The size of the crust plates is variable, as they are constantly changing, but six or seven large plates now cover much of the Earth's surface, the remainder being occupied by a number of smaller plates. Each large plate may include both continental and ocean crust. As a result of seismic studies it is known that the lithosphere is a rigid layer extending to depths of 50–100 km/30–60 mi, overlying the upper part of the mantle (the ◊asthenosphere), which is composed of rocks very close to melting point, with a low shear strength. This zone of mechanical weakness allows the

PLATE TECTONICS

http://www.seismo.unr.edu/ftp/pub/louie/class/100/plate-tectonics.html

Well-illustrated site on this geological phenomenon. As well as the plentiful illustrations, this site also has a good clear manner of explaining the way the plates of the Earth's crust interact to produce seismic activity.

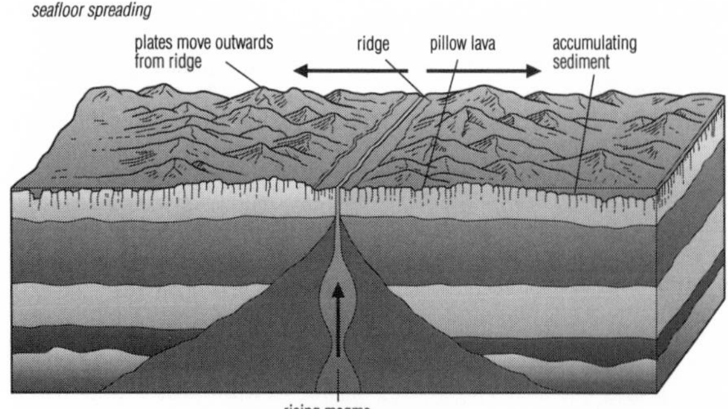

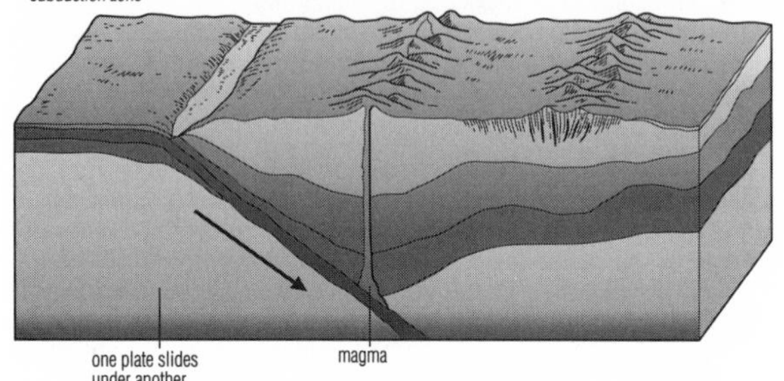

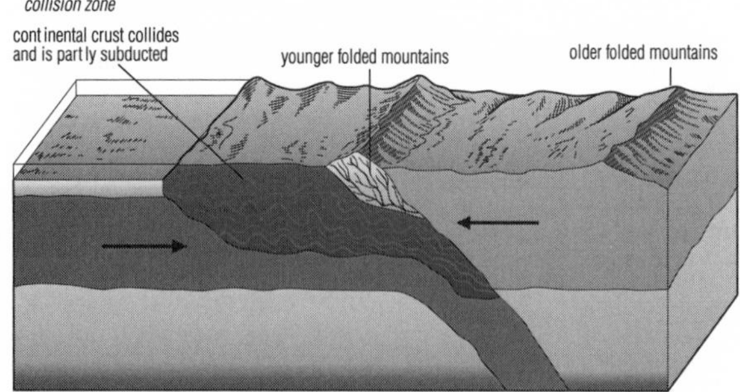

***plate tectonics** The three main types of action in plate tectonics. (top) Seafloor spreading. The upwelling of magma forces apart the crust plates, producing new crust at the joint. Rapid extrusion of magma produces a domed ridge; more gentle spreading produces a central valley. (middle) The drawing downwards of an oceanic plate beneath a continent produces a range of volcanic fold mountains parallel to the plate edge. (bottom) Collision of continental plates produces immense fold mountains, such as the Himalayas. Younger mountains are found near the coast with older ranges inland. The plates of the Earth's lithosphere are always changing in size and shape of each plate as material is added at constructive margins and removed at destructive margins. The process is extremely slow, but it means that the tectonic history of the Earth cannot be traced back further than about 200 million years.*

movement of the overlying plates. The margins of the plates are defined by major earthquake zones and belts of volcanic and tectonic activity, which have been well known for many years. Almost all earthquake, volcanic, and tectonic activity is confined to the margins of plates, and shows that the plates are in constant motion.

platform the ◊operating system, together with the ◊hardware on which it runs.

Platform for Internet Content Selection in computing, method of classifying data, usually abbreviated to ◊PICS.

platinum Spanish *platina* 'little silver' *(plata* 'silver') heavy, soft, silver-white, malleable and ductile, metallic element, symbol Pt, atomic number 78, relative atomic mass 195.09. It is the first of a group of six metallic elements (platinum, osmium, iridium, rhodium, ruthenium, and palladium) that possess similar traits, such as resistance to tarnish, corrosion, and attack by acid, and that often occur as free metals (◊native metals). They often occur in natural alloys with each other, the commonest of which is osmiridium. Both pure and as an alloy, platinum is used in dentistry, jewellery, and as a catalyst.

Platonic solid in geometry, another name for a regular ◊polyhedron, one of five possible three-dimensional figures with all its faces the same size and shape.

Platyhelminthes invertebrate phylum consisting of the ◊flatworms.

platypus monotreme, or egg-laying, mammal *Ornithorhynchus anatinus,* found in Tasmania and E Australia. Semiaquatic, it has small eyes and no external ears, and jaws resembling a duck's beak. It lives in long burrows along river banks, where it lays two eggs in a rough nest. It feeds on water worms and insects, and when full-grown is 60 cm/2 ft long.

According to research by Australian scientists in 1995, platypuses locate their prey by detecting the small electric fields produced by their nerve and muscle activity.

REMARKABLE PLATYPUS

http://www.anca.gov.au/plants/manageme/platintr.htm

Comprehensive information on the shy monotreme presented by the Australian Natural Conservation Agency. Findings of latest research into platypuses is presented, together with recommendations to help preserve the species.

Platyrrhini New World monkeys, including the the families Callitrichidae (marmosets and tamarins) and Cebidae (including capuchin, spider, and howler monkeys). The term is now rarely used.

Platyrrhines are characterized by having nostrils that are widely spaced and face sideways. Compare with the Old World ◊Catarrhini.

PlayStation in computing, market-leading ◊games console made by ◊Sony.

Pleiades in astronomy, an open star cluster about 400 light years away in the constellation Taurus, represented as the Seven Sisters of Greek mythology. Its brightest stars (highly luminous, blue-white giants only a few million years old) are visible to the naked eye, but there are many fainter ones.

It is a young cluster, and the stars of the Pleiades are still surrounded by traces of the reflection ◊nebula from which they formed, visible on long-exposure photographs.

pleiotropy process whereby a given gene influences several different observed characteristics of an organism. For example, in the fruit fly *Drosophila* the vestigial gene reduces the size of wings, modifies the halteres, changes the number of egg strings in the ovaries, and changes the direction of certain bristles. Many human syndromes are caused by pleiotropic genes, for example Marfan's syndrome where the slender physique, hypermobility of the joints, elongation of the limbs, dislocation of the lens, and susceptibility to heart disease are all caused by one gene.

Pleistocene first epoch of the Quaternary period of geological time, beginning 1.64 million years ago and ending 10,000 years ago. The polar ice caps were extensive and glaciers were abundant during the ice age of this period, and humans evolved into modern *Homo sapiens sapiens* about 100,000 years ago.

Plesetsk rocket-launching site 170 km/105 mi S of Archangel, Russia. From 1966 the USSR launched artificial satellites from here, mostly military.

plesiosaur prehistoric carnivorous marine reptile of the Jurassic and Cretaceous periods, which reached a length of 12 m/36 ft, and had a long neck and paddlelike limbs. The pliosaurs evolved from the plesiosaurs.

pleuracanth extinct freshwater sharklike fish with a diphycercal (symmetrical) tail and a long fin down the back. They existed from Devonian to Triassic times, and were abundant in the Carboniferous period. Little is known of their ancestry.

pleurisy inflammation of the pleura, the thin, secretory membrane that covers the lungs and lines the space in which they rest. Pleurisy is nearly always due to bacterial or viral infection, but may also be a complication of other diseases.

Normally the two lung surfaces move easily on one another, lubricated by small quantities of fluid. When the pleura is inflamed, the surfaces may dry up or stick together, making breathing difficult and painful. Alternatively, a large volume of fluid may collect in the pleural cavity, the space between the two surfaces, and pus may accumulate.

Plimsoll line loading mark painted on the hull of merchant ships, first suggested by English politician Samuel Plimsoll. It shows the depth to which a vessel may be safely (and legally) loaded.

Pliocene ***'almost recent'*** fifth and last epoch of the Tertiary period of geological time, 5.2–1.64 million years ago. The earliest hominid, the humanlike ape *Australopithecines,* evolved in Africa.

pliosaur prehistoric carnivorous marine reptile, descended from the plesiosaurs, but with a shorter neck, and longer head and jaws. It was approximately 5 m/15 ft long. In 1989 the skeleton of one of a previously unknown species was discovered in N Queensland, Australia. A hundred million years ago, it lived in the sea that once covered the Great Artesian Basin.

plotter or ***graph plotter*** device that draws pictures or diagrams under computer control.

Plotters are often used for producing business charts, architectural plans, and engineering drawings. **Flatbed plotters** move a pen up and down across a flat drawing surface, whereas **roller plotters** roll the drawing paper past the pen as it moves from side to side.

Plough, the in astronomy, a popular name for the most prominent part of the constellation ◊Ursa Major.

plough agricultural implement used for tilling the soil. The plough dates from about 3500 BC, when oxen were used to pull a simple wooden blade, or ard. In about 500 BC the iron ploughshare came into use. By about AD 1000 horses as well as oxen were being used to pull wheeled ploughs, equipped with a ploughshare for cutting a furrow, a blade for forming the walls of the furrow (called a coulter), and a mouldboard to turn the furrow. In the 18th century an innovation introduced by Robert Ransome (1753–1830), led to a reduction in the number of animals used to draw a plough: from 8–12 oxen, or 6 horses, to a 2- or 4-horse plough.

Steam ploughs came into use in some areas in the 1860s, superseded half a century later by tractor-drawn ploughs. The modern plough consists of many 'bottoms', each comprising a curved ploughshare and angled mouldboard. The bottom is designed so that it slices into the ground and turns the soil over.

plover any shore bird of the family Charadriidae, order Charadriiformes, found worldwide. Plovers are usually black or brown above and white below, and have short bills. The European **golden plover** *Pluviatilis apricaria,* of heathland and sea coast, is about 28 cm/11 in long. In winter the upper parts are a sooty black with large yellow spots, and white throat and underparts, changing to black in the spring. It nests on the ground, laying four yellowish eggs blotched with brown.

The **ringed plover** *Charadrius hiaticula,* with a black and white face, and black band on the throat, is found on British shores, nesting in a scrape on a beach or amongst shingle. The largest of the ringed plovers is the **killdeer** *Charadrius vociferus,* so called because of its cry.

plug and play in computing, item of hardware or software that configures itself and the user's system automatically when first installed. Having been thus 'plugged' in, it can be used ('played' with) immediately. In the PC industry, suppliers have adopted a form of Plug and Play (PnP) developed by Microsoft and Intel in 1993.

plug-in in computing, small add-on file which enhances the operation of an application program, often by enabling it to launch, display or interpret a file created using another one. The first plug-ins were made for graphics programs in the 1980s, but the practice became very popular in the mid-1990s, when a range of plug-ins became available to enhance the multimedia capabilites of ◊Netscape's Navigator ◊browser. Plug-ins are often created and distributed by independent developers rather than the manufacturer of the program they extend.

plug, three-pin insulated device with three metal projections used to connect the wires in the cable of an electrical appliance

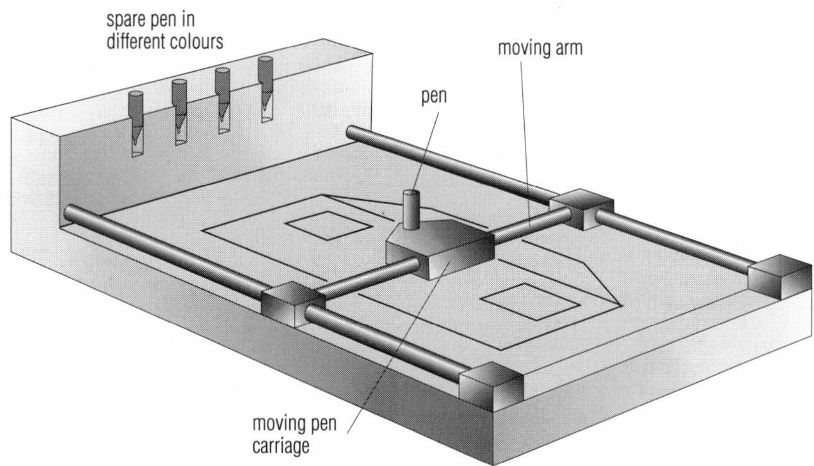

plotter *A flatbed plotter, which may be used to produce plans, graphs, and other drawings. The moving arm, holding a pen of the appropriate colour, travels over the surface of the paper.*

with the wires of a mains supply socket. In the UK, plugs have pins of rectangular section, and must comply with the British Standard BS 1363 laid down by the British Standards Institute. A plug must be designed carefully with regard to construction, labelling, clearance between components, accessibility of live parts, earthing (see ◊earth), and terminal design. Before being approved, it is tested for the resistance of its insulation, temperature rise while in use, anchorage of cables, mechanical strength, and susceptibility to damage by heat and rust.

plum smooth-skinned, oval, reddish-purple or green edible fruit of the plum tree. There are many varieties, including the Victoria, czar, egg-plum, greengage, and damson; the wild sloe (*P. spinosa*), which is the fruit of the ◊blackthorn, is closely related. Dried plums are known as prunes. (*Prunus domestica*, family Rosaceae.)

plumbago alternative name for the mineral ◊graphite.

plumule part of a seed embryo that develops into the shoot, bearing the first true leaves of the plant. In most seeds, for example the sunflower, the plumule is a small conical structure without any leaf structure. Growth of the plumule does not occur until the ◊cotyledons have grown above ground. This is ◊epigeal germination. However, in seeds such as the broad bean, a leaf structure is visible on the plumule in the seed. These seeds develop by the plumule growing up through the soil with the cotyledons remaining below the surface. This is known as ◊hypogeal germination.

Pluto in astronomy, the smallest and, usually, outermost planet of the Solar System. The existence of Pluto was predicted by calculation by Percival Lowell and the planet was located by Clyde Tombaugh in 1930. Its highly elliptical orbit occasionally takes it within the orbit of Neptune, as in 1979–99. Pluto has a mass about 0.002 of that of Earth.
mean distance from the Sun 5.8 billion km/3.6 billion mi
equatorial diameter 2,300 km/1,438 mi
rotation period 6.39 Earth days
year 248.5 Earth years
atmosphere thin atmosphere with small amounts of methane gas
surface low density, composed of rock and ice, primarily frozen methane; there is an ice cap at Pluto's north pole
satellites one moon, Charon

PLUTO AND CHARON

http://www.hawastsoc.org/solar/eng/pluto.htm

Site devoted to our most distant planet and its satellite. It contains a table of statistics, photographs, and an animation of their rotation. You can also find out about NASA's planned mission to Pluto and Charon in 2010.

plutonic rock igneous rock derived from magma that has cooled and solidified deep in the crust of the Earth; granites and gabbros are examples of plutonic rocks.

plutonium silvery-white, radioactive, metallic element of the ◊actinide series, symbol Pu, atomic number 94, relative atomic mass 239.13. It occurs in nature in minute quantities in ◊pitchblende and other ores, but is produced in quantity only synthetically. It has six allotropic forms (see ◊allotropy) and is one of three fissile elements (elements capable of splitting into other elements – the others are thorium and uranium). The element has awkward physical properties and is the most toxic substance known.

plywood manufactured panel of wood widely used in building. It consists of several thin sheets, or plies, of wood, glued together with the grain (direction of the wood fibres) of one sheet at right angles to the grain of the adjacent plies. This construction gives plywood equal strength in every direction.

PLYWOOD

Many people know that Alfred Nobel, founder of the prizes that bear his name, was the inventor of dynamite. However, it is less well known that his father, Immanuel Nobel, was the inventor of plywood.

pneumatic drill drill operated by compressed air, used in mining and tunnelling, for drilling shot holes (for explosives), and in road repairs for breaking up pavements. It contains an air-operated piston that delivers hammer blows to the drill bit many times a second. The French engineer Germain Sommeiller (1815–1871) developed the pneumatic drill in 1861 for tunnelling in the Alps.

pneumatophore erect root that rises up above the soil or water and promotes ◊gas exchange. Pneumatophores, or breathing roots, are formed by certain swamp-dwelling trees, such as mangroves, since there is little oxygen available to the roots in waterlogged conditions. They have numerous pores or ◊lenticels over their surface, allowing gas exchange.

pneumoconiosis disease of the lungs caused by an accumulation of dust, especially from coal, asbestos, or silica. Inhaled particles make the lungs gradually fibrous and the victim has difficulty breathing. Over many years the condition causes severe disability.

pneumonectomy surgical removal of all or part of a lung.

pneumonia inflammation of the lungs, generally due to bacterial or viral infection but also to particulate matter or gases. It is characterized by a build-up of fluid in the alveoli, the clustered air sacs (at the ends of the air passages) where oxygen exchange takes place.

Symptoms include fever and pain in the chest. With widespread availability of antibiotics, infectious pneumonia is much less common than it was. However, it remains a dire threat to patients whose immune systems are suppressed (including transplant recipients and AIDS and cancer victims) and to those who are critically ill or injured. Pneumocystis pneumonia is a leading cause of death in AIDS.

pneumothorax the presence of air in the pleural cavity, between a lung and the chest wall. It may be due to a penetrating injury of the lung or to lung disease, or it may occur without apparent cause (spontaneous pneumothorax) in an otherwise healthy person. Prevented from expanding normally, the lung is liable to collapse.

p–n junction diode in electronics, another name for semiconductor diode.

pochard any of various diving ducks found in Europe and North America, especially the genus *Aythya*. They feed largely on water plants. The nest is made in long grass on the borders of lakes and pools.

pod in botany, a type of fruit that is characteristic of legumes (plants belonging to the Leguminosae family), such as peas and beans. It develops from a single ◊carpel and splits down both sides when ripe to release the seeds.

In certain species the seeds may be ejected explosively due to uneven drying of the fruit wall, which sets up tensions within the fruit. In agriculture, the name 'legume' is used for the crops of the pea and bean family. 'Grain legume' refers to those that are grown mainly for their dried seeds, such as lentils, chick peas, and soya beans.

podzol or ***podsol*** type of light-coloured soil found predominantly under coniferous forests and on moorlands in cool regions where rainfall exceeds evaporation. The constant downward movement of water leaches nutrients from the upper layers, making podzols poor agricultural soils.

The leaching of minerals such as iron, lime, and alumina leads to the formation of a bleached zone, often also depleted of clay.

These minerals can accumulate lower down the soil profile to form a hard, impermeable layer which restricts the drainage of water through the soil.

poikilothermy the condition in which an animal's body temperature is largely dependent on the temperature of the air or water in which it lives. It is characteristic of all animals except birds and mammals, which maintain their body temperatures by ◊homeothermy (they are 'warm-blooded').

Poikilotherms have behavioural means of temperature control; they can warm themselves up by basking in the sun, or shivering, and can cool themselves down by sheltering from the Sun under a rock or by bathing in water.

Poikilotherms are often referred to as 'cold-blooded animals', but this is not really correct: their internal temperatures, regulated by behavioural means, are often as high as those of birds and mammals during the times they need to be active for feeding and reproductive purposes, and may be higher, for example in very hot climates. The main difference is that their body temperatures fluctuate more than those of homeotherms.

poinsettia or ***Christmas flower*** winter-flowering shrub with large red leaves encircling small greenish-yellow flowers. It is native to Mexico and tropical America and is a popular houseplant in North America and Europe. (*Euphorbia pulcherrima,* family Euphorbiaceae.)

point in geometry, a basic element, whose position in the Cartesian system may be determined by its ◊coordinates.

Mathematicians have had great difficulty in defining the point, as it has no size, and is only the place where two lines meet. According to the Greek mathematician Euclid, (i) a point is that which has no part; (ii) the straight line is the shortest distance between two points.

point and click in computing, basic method of navigating a ◊Web page or a multimedia CD-ROM. The user points at an object using a cursor and a mouse, and clicks to activate it.

pointer any of several breeds of gun dog, bred especially to scent the position of game and indicate it by standing, nose pointed towards it, often with one forefoot raised, in silence. English pointers have smooth coats, mainly white mixed with black, tan, or dark brown. They stand about 60 cm/24 in tall, and weigh 28 kg/62 lb.

A very similar breed, the German short-haired pointer, was developed in the 19th century to point and also to pursue game.

The Weimeraner is another pointing breed.

point of sale (POS) in business premises, the point where a sale is transacted, for example, a POS terminal such as a supermarket checkout. In conjunction with electronic funds transfer, point of sale is part of the terminology of 'cashless shopping', enabling buyers to transfer funds directly from their bank accounts to the shop's.

point-of-sale terminal (POS terminal) computer terminal used in shops to input and output data at the point where a sale is transacted; for example, at a supermarket checkout. The POS terminal inputs information about the identity of each item sold, retrieves the price and other details from a central computer, and prints out a fully itemized receipt for the customer. It may also input sales data for the shop's computerized stock-control system.

A POS terminal typically has all the facilities of a normal till, including a cash drawer and a sales register, plus facilities for the direct capture of sales information – commonly, a laser scanner for reading bar codes. It may also be equipped with a device to read customers' bank cards, so that payment can be transferred electronically from the customers' bank accounts to the shop's (see ◊EFTPOS).

Point-to-Point Protocol in computing, method of connecting a computer to the Internet; usually abbreviated to PPP.

poise c.g.s. unit (symbol P) of dynamic ◊viscosity (the property of liquids that determines how readily they flow). It is equal to one dyne-second per square centimetre. For most liquids the centipoise (one hundredth of a poise) is used. Water at 20°C/68°F has a ◊viscosity of 1.002 centipoise.

Poiseuille's formula in physics, a relationship describing the rate of flow of a fluid through a narrow tube. For a capillary (very narrow) tube of length l and radius r with a pressure difference p between its ends, and a liquid of viscosity η, the velocity of flow expressed as the volume per second is $\pi pr^4/8l\eta$. The formula was devised in 1843 by French physicist Jean Louis Poiseuille (1799–1869).

poison or ***toxin*** any chemical substance that, when introduced into or applied to the body, is capable of injuring health or destroying life.

The liver removes some poisons from the blood. The majority of poisons may be divided into **corrosives**, such as sulphuric, nitric, and hydrochloric acids; **irritants**, including arsenic and copper sulphate; **narcotics** such as opium, and carbon monoxide; and **narcotico-irritants** from any substances of plant origin including carbolic acid and tobacco.

how poisons work Corrosives all burn and destroy the parts of the body with which they come into contact; irritants have an irritating effect on the stomach and bowels; narcotics affect the brainstem and spinal cord, inducing a stupor; and narcotico-irritants can cause intense irritations and finally act as narcotics.

FROG

There is a species of frog found in Colombia that produces enough poison to kill 1,500 people. Pharmacologists are keen to see if the venom of *Phyllobates terribilis* might be the basis of a new painkiller.

polar coordinates in mathematics, a way of defining the position of a point in terms of its distance r from a fixed point (the origin) and its angle θ to a fixed line or axis. The coordinates of the point are $(r\theta)$.

Often the angle is measured in ◊radians, rather than degrees. The system is useful for defining positions on a plane in programming the operations of, for example, computer-controlled cloth- and metal-cutting machines.

polarimetry in astronomy, any technique for measuring the degree of polarization of radiation from stars, galaxies, and other objects.

Polaris or ***Pole Star*** or ***North Star*** bright star closest to the north celestial pole, and the brightest star in the constellation ◊Ursa Minor. Its position is indicated by the 'pointers' in ◊Ursa Major. Polaris is a yellow ◊supergiant about 500 light years away. It is also known as **Alpha Ursae Minoris**.

It currently lies within 1° of the north celestial pole; ◊precession (Earth's axial wobble) will bring Polaris closest to the celestial pole (less than 0.5° away) in about AD 2100. Then its distance will start to increase, reaching 1° in 2205 and 47° in 28000. Other bright stars that have been, or will be close to the north celestial pole are Alpha Draconis (3000 BC), Gamma Cephei (AD 4000), Alpha Cephei (AD 7000), and ◊Vega (AD 14000).

polarized light light in which the electromagnetic vibrations take place in one particular plane. In ordinary (unpolarized) light, the electric fields vibrate in all planes perpendicular to the direction of propagation. After reflection from a polished surface or transmission through certain materials (such as Polaroid), the electric fields are confined to one direction, and the light is said to be **linearly polarized**. In **circularly polarized** and **elliptically polarized** light, the electric fields are confined to one direction, but the direction rotates as the light propagates. Polarized light is used to test the strength of sugar solutions, to measure stresses in transparent materials, and to prevent glare.

polarography electrochemical technique for the analysis of oxidizable and reducible compounds in solution. It involves the diffusion of the substance to be analyzed onto the surface of a small electrode, usually a bead of mercury, where oxidation or reduction occurs at an electric potential characteristic of that substance.

Polaroid camera instant-picture camera, invented by Edwin Land in the USA in 1947. The original camera produced black-and-white prints in about one minute. Modern cameras can produce black-and-white prints in a few seconds, and colour prints in less than a minute. An advanced model has automatic focusing and exposure.

It ejects a piece of film on paper immediately after the picture has been taken.

The film consists of layers of emulsion and colour dyes together with a pod of chemical developer. When the film is ejected the pod bursts and processing occurs in the light, producing a paper-backed print.

polar reversal change in polarity of Earth's magnetic field. Like all magnets, Earth's magnetic field has two opposing regions, or poles, one of attraction and one of repulsion, positioned approximately near geographical North and South Poles. During a period of normal polarity the region of attraction corresponds with the North Pole. Today, a compass needle, like other magnetic materials, aligns itself parallel to the magnetizing force and points to the North Pole. During a period of reversed polarity, the region of attraction would change to the South Pole and the needle of a compass would point south.

Studies of the magnetism retained in rocks at the time of their formation (like little compasses frozen in time) have shown that the polarity of the magnetic field has reversed repeatedly throughout geological time.

Polar reversals are a random process. Although the average time between reversals over the last ten million years has been 250,000 years, the rate of reversal has changed continuously over geological time. The most recent reversal was 700,000 years ago; scientists have no way of predicting when the next reversal will occur. The reversal process takes about a thousand years. Movements of Earth's molten core are thought to be responsible for the magnetic field and its polar reversals. Dating rocks using distinctive sequences of magnetic reversals is called palaeomagnetic stratigraphy.

polder area of flat reclaimed land that used to be covered by a river, lake, or the sea. Polders have been artificially drained and protected from flooding by building dykes. They are common in the Netherlands, where the total land area has been increased by nearly one-fifth since AD 1200. Such schemes as the Zuider Zee project have provided some of the best agricultural land in the country.

pole either of the geographic north and south points of the axis about which the Earth rotates. The geographic poles differ from the magnetic poles, which are the points towards which a freely suspended magnetic needle will point.

In 1985 the magnetic north pole was some 350 km/218 mi NW of Resolute Bay, Northwest Territories, Canada. It moves northwards about 10 km/6 mi each year, although it can vary in a day about 80 km/50 mi from its average position. It is relocated every decade in order to update navigational charts.

It is thought that periodic changes in the Earth's core cause a reversal of the magnetic poles (see ◊polar reversal, magnetic field). Many animals, including migrating birds and fish, are believed to orient themselves partly using the Earth's magnetic field. A permanent scientific base collects data at the South Pole.

polecat Old World weasel *Mustela putorius* with a brown back and dark belly and two yellow face patches. The body is about 50 cm/20 in long and it has a strong smell from anal gland secretions. It is native to Asia, Europe, and N Africa. In North America, ◊skunks are sometimes called polecats. A ferret is a domesticated polecat.

pole, magnetic see ◊magnetic pole.

Pole Star another name for ◊Polaris, the northern pole star. There is no bright star near the southern celestial pole.

polio (poliomyelitis) viral infection of the central nervous system affecting nerves that activate muscles. The disease used to be known as infantile paralysis. Two kinds of vaccine are available, one injected (see ◊Salk) and one given by mouth. The Americas were declared to be polio-free by the Pan American Health Organization in 1994. In 1997 the World Health Organization reported that causes of polio had dropped by nearly 90% since 1988 when the organization began its programme to eradicate the disease by the year 2000. Most cases remain in Africa and south-east Asia.

The polio virus is a common one and its effects are mostly confined to the throat and intestine, as with influenza or a mild digestive upset. There may also be muscle stiffness in the neck and back. Paralysis is seen in about 1% of cases, and the disease is life-threatening only if the muscles of the throat and chest are affected. Cases of this kind, once entombed in an 'iron lung', are today maintained on a respirator.

It is courage based on confidence, not daring, and it is confidence based on experience.

JONAS SALK US physician and microbiologist. On administering the then-experimental polio vaccine to himself and his family, 1955

---

pollack marine fish *Pollachius virens* of the cod family, growing to 75 cm/2.5 ft, and found close to the shore on both sides of the N Atlantic.

pollarding type of pruning whereby the young branches of a tree are severely cut back, about 2–4 m/6–12 ft above the ground, to produce a stumplike trunk with a rounded, bushy head of thin new branches. It is similar to ◊coppicing.

pollen the grains of ◊seed plants that contain the male gametes. In ◊angiosperms (flowering plants) pollen is produced within

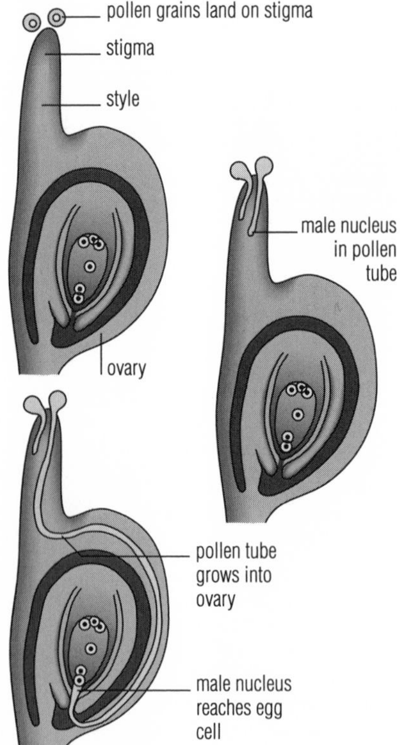

pollen *Pollination, the process by which pollen grains transfer their male nuclei (gametes) to the ovary of a flower. The pollen grains land on the stigma and form a pollen tube that grows down into the ovary. The male nuclei travel along the pollen tube.*

◊anthers; in most ◊gymnosperms (cone-bearing plants) it is produced in male cones. A pollen grain is typically yellow and, when mature, has a hard outer wall. Pollen of insect-pollinated plants (see ◊pollination) is often sticky and spiny and larger than the smooth, light grains produced by wind-pollinated species.

The outer wall of pollen grains from both insect-pollinated and wind-pollinated plants is often elaborately sculptured with ridges or spines so distinctive that individual species or genera of plants can be recognized from their pollen. Since pollen is extremely resistant to decay, useful information on the vegetation of earlier times can be gained from the study of fossil pollen. The study of pollen grains is known as palynology.

pollen tube outgrowth from a pollen grain that grows towards the ◊ovule, following germination of the grain on the ◊stigma. In ◊angiosperms (flowering plants) the pollen tube reaches the ovule by growing down through the style, carrying the male gametes inside. The gametes are discharged into the ovule and one fertilizes the egg cell.

pollination the process by which pollen is transferred from one plant to another. The male ◊gametes are contained in pollen grains, which must be transferred from the anther to the stigma in ◊angiosperms (flowering plants), and from the male cone to the female cone in ◊gymnosperms (cone-bearing plants). Fertilization (not the same as pollination) occurs after the growth of the pollen tube to the ovary. Self-pollination occurs when pollen is transferred to a stigma of the same flower, or to another flower on the same plant; cross-pollination occurs when pollen is transferred to another plant. This involves external pollen-carrying agents, such as wind (see ◊anemophily), water (see ◊hydrophily), insects, birds (see ◊ornithophily), bats, and other small mammals.

Animal pollinators carry the pollen on their bodies and are attracted to the flower by scent, or by the sight of the petals. Most

Southeast Asia: Eco-Disaster 1997

by Charles Arthur

This was probably the biggest short-term eco-disaster modern humanity has ever witnessed. It began with an agricultural practice that has been followed for centuries in Indonesia. Late in August, villagers there began clearing land by setting fire to the forest. But they were joined by companies eager to create new space for rubber and palm oil plantations. Overall, hundreds of individual fires were purposely set in the expectation that the monsoon rains would quickly come and put them out, leaving the land easy to clear. A combination of events led to the fires going out of control. They were not stopped when they were small because of the commercial desire to keep them going. The peat and lignite began to burn underneath the soil, which was dry from the summer. The monsoon, nature's own fire extinguisher, was late and unusually small. Winds whipped up the flames, giving the fires new life and blowing the ashes overseas.

Smoke and haze

Singapore was one of the countries on the receiving end of the smoke and haze. Within a month of the fires starting, the sun became invisible during the day. The haze pollution index, issued daily, went above 500 – the level at which it is officially hazardous. An index of between 0 and 50 is considered 'good', between 50 and 100 is 'moderate,' and 100 to 200 is 'unhealthy'.

By the end of September, Britain was preparing to evacuate diplomats' families and issued health warnings to tourists in the affected area. One journalist described the first effects of standing amidst the 'darkness at noon: an acrid taste around the mouth, next a stinging sensation in the eyes and the pervasive reek of carbonized wood. After a few minutes, a tightening in the chest.'

Meanwhile, a convoy of more than 1,200 firemen set off in what turned out to be a vain attempt to fight the fires, reckoned by then to have consumed 1.5 million acres of forest. Countries affected by the smog, which was now clearly visible in satellite photographs as a swathe across the ocean and land, included Malaysia, Indonesia, Singapore, the Philippines, Brunei, and Thailand.

Human toll

The pollution then began to have a more direct effect. On the night of 26 September, two cargo ships collided, killing 29 crewmen, in the Straits of Malacca – an accident blamed on poor visibility caused by the haze. The following day, an A300B4 Airbus on a Garuda Airlines internal flight in Indonesia, from Jakarta to the city of Medan on Sumatra, crashed into a rice field in a mountainous area of northern Sumatra. The 222 passengers and 12 crew were all killed. The crash was initially blamed on the smog haze, a suspicion that intensified the next day when the visibility at Medan airport remained so poor that relatives of the crash victims were unable to leave for it from Jakarta aboard a Boeing 747 jumbo jet that the airline had made available. However, the transcript of the conversation between the pilot and the control tower subsequently showed that the pilot mistook left for right, and turned in the wrong direction for landing. Whether this was compounded by the lowered visibility remains an open question. But in subsequent weeks the Indonesian government cancelled some domestic internal flights because, from the air, the pilots could not see the airports where they were meant to land.

By this time, two people had also died directly from smoke inhalation, while on Borneo and Sumatra, where the fires were raging, hospitals had treated at least 32,000 victims of smoke inhalation. On Borneo, which is shared between Indonesia, Malaysia, and Brunei, normal life came to a halt while people waited, and hoped, for the monsoon.

Climate change

The delay in the monsoon – which the original land-burners had expected – was pinned on a reversal in the direction of El Niño, an enormous ocean current in the Pacific which normally brings warm, wet air from the south. Instead it brought drier air and little rain. It was not only humans or plants that suffered as the fires raged. The habitats of orang-utans and other rare species in Borneo fell to the flames, and hundreds of other species, including insects, animals, and birds, faced threats to their supply of food and water, and to the valuable nesting space for their young.

At last, on 30 September, Kuala Lumpur received the first downpours – though only enough to drop its pollution index to near 100, from 155. The peak reading for the whole period was at Sarawak, in Indonesia, which recorded a level of 835. The haze did not disappear in October: Kuala Lumpur was still reporting visibility down to a few hundred metres at ground level at noon in the middle of the month. The problem persisted until November, when the monsoon arrived in full. By then, though, some of the smoke had reached northern Australia.

Lasting effects

The long-term effects of the fire are hard to predict. The ecological effects are impossible to estimate, because forest species – both animal and plant – often prove remarkably resilient to fire, recolonizing burnt areas more quickly than scientists predict. The revenues lost from tourism amounted to millions of dollars. Almost as soon as the smoke began to clear, the country was plunged into a foreign exchange crisis on the international markets, partly sparked by fears about the strength of its economy following the fires.

flowers are adapted for pollination by one particular agent only. Bat-pollinated flowers tend to smell of garlic, rotting vegetation, or fungus. Those that rely on animals generally produce nectar, a sugary liquid, or surplus pollen, or both, on which the pollinator feeds. Thus the relationship between pollinator and plant is an example of mutualism, in which both benefit. However, in some plants the pollinator receives no benefit (as in ◊pseudocopulation), while in others, nectar may be removed by animals that do not effect pollination.

polling in computing, a technique for transferring data from a terminal to the central computer of a ◊multiuser system. The computer automatically makes a connection with each terminal in turn, interrogates it to check whether it is holding data for transmission, and, if it is, collects the data.

pollinium group of pollen grains that is transported as a single unit during pollination. Pollinia are common in orchids.

polluter-pays principle the idea that whoever causes pollution is responsible for the cost of repairing any damage. The principle is accepted in British law but has in practice often been ignored; for example, farmers causing the death of fish through slurry pollution have not been fined the full costs of restocking the river.

pollution the harmful effect on the environment of by-products of human activity, principally industrial and agricultural processes – for example, noise, smoke, car emissions, chemical and radioactive effluents in air, seas, and rivers, pesticides, radiation, ◊sewage (see sewage disposal), and household waste. Pollution contributes to the ◊greenhouse effect. See also ◊air pollution.

Pollution control involves higher production costs for the industries concerned, but failure to implement adequate controls may result in irreversible environmental damage and an increase in the incidence of diseases such as cancer. Radioactive pollution results from inadequate ◊nuclear safety.

Transboundary pollution is when the pollution generated in one country affects another, for example as occurs with ◊acid rain. Natural disasters may also cause pollution; volcanic eruptions, for example, cause ash to be ejected into the atmosphere and deposited on land surfaces.

> *As cruel a weapon as the cave man's club, the chemical barrage has been hurled against the fabric of life.*
>
> RACHEL CARSON US marine biologist and writer. *The Silent Spring*

Pollux or ***Beta Geminorum*** the brightest star in the constellation ◊Gemini, and the 17th-brightest star in the sky. Pollux is a yellow star with a true luminosity 45 times that of the Sun. It is 35 light years away.

The first-magnitude Pollux and the second-magnitude ◊Castor, Alpha Geminorum, mark the heads of the Gemini twins. It is thought that the two stars may have changed their relative brightness since Bayer named them, as Alpha is usually assigned to the brightest star in a constellation.

polonium radioactive, metallic element, symbol Po, atomic number 84, relative atomic mass 210. Polonium occurs in nature in small amounts and was isolated from ◊pitchblende. It is the element having the largest number of isotopes (27) and is 5,000 times as radioactive as radium, liberating considerable amounts of heat. It was the first element to have its radioactive properties recognized and investigated.

Polonium was isolated in 1898 from the pitchblende residues analyzed by French scientists Pierre and Marie ◊Curie, and named after Marie Curie's native Poland.

polyanthus cultivated variety of ◊primrose, with several flowers on one stalk, bred in a variety of colours. (Family Primulaceae)

polychlorinated biphenyl (PCB) any of a group of chlorinated isomers of biphenyl $(C_6H_5)_2$. They are dangerous industrial chemicals, valuable for their fire-resisting qualities. They constitute an environmental hazard because of their persistent toxicity. Since 1973 their use has been limited by international agreement.

polyester synthetic resin formed by the ◊condensation of polyhydric alcohols (alcohols containing more than one hydroxyl group) with dibasic acids (acids containing two replaceable hydrogen atoms). Polyesters are thermosetting ◊plastics, used in making synthetic fibres, such as Dacron and Terylene, and constructional plastics. With glass fibre added as reinforcement, polyesters are used in car bodies and boat hulls.

polyethylene or ***polyethene*** polymer of the gas ethylene (technically called ethene, C_2H_4). It is a tough, white, translucent, waxy thermoplastic (which means it can be repeatedly softened by heating). It is used for packaging, bottles, toys, wood preservation, electric cable, pipes and tubing.

Polyethylene is produced in two forms: low-density polyethylene, made by high-pressure polymerization of ethylene gas, and high-density polyethylene, which is made at lower pressure by using catalysts. This form, first made in 1953 by German chemist Karl Ziegler, is more rigid at low temperatures and softer at higher temperatures than the low-density type. Polyethylene was first made in the 1930s at very high temperatures by ICI.

polygon in geometry, a plane (two-dimensional) figure with three or more straight-line sides. Common polygons have names which define the number of sides (for example, triangle, quadrilateral, pentagon).

These are all convex polygons, having no interior angle greater than 180°. The sum of the internal angles of a polygon having n sides is given by the formula $(2n - 4) \times 90°$; therefore, the more sides a polygon has, the larger the sum of its internal angles and, in the case of a convex polygon, the more closely it approximates to a circle.

polygraph technical name for a ◊lie detector.

PAVILION OF POLYHEDREALITY

http://www.li.net/~george/pavilion.html

Collection of images and instructions on how to make various polyhedrals, some from quite surprising materials.

polyhedron in geometry, a solid figure with four or more plane faces. The more faces there are on a polyhedron, the more closely it approximates to a sphere. Knowledge of the properties of polyhedra is needed in crystallography and stereochemistry to determine the shapes of crystals and molecules.

There are only five types of regular polyhedron (with all faces the same size and shape), as was deduced by early Greek

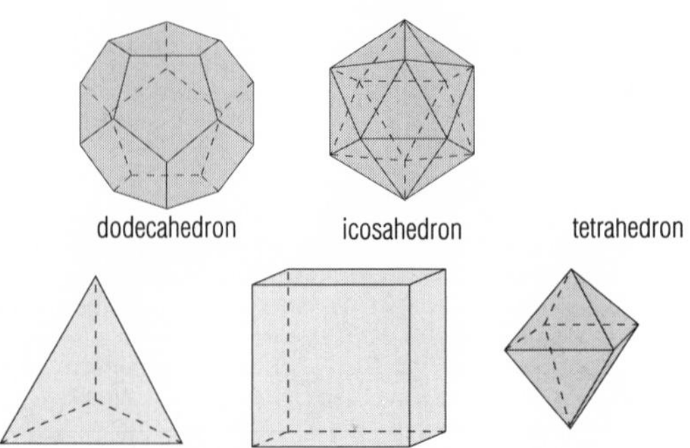

polyhedron *The five regular polyhedra or Platonic solids.*

mathematicians; they are the tetrahedron (four equilateral triangular faces), cube (six square faces), octahedron (eight equilateral triangles), dodecahedron (12 regular pentagons) and icosahedron (20 equilateral triangles).

polymer compound made up of a large long-chain or branching matrix composed of many repeated simple units (**monomers**). There are many polymers, both natural (cellulose, chitin, lignin) and synthetic (polyethylene and nylon, types of plastic). Synthetic polymers belong to two groups: thermosoftening and thermosetting (see ◊plastic).

The size of the polymer matrix is determined by the amount of monomer used; it therefore does not form a molecule of constant molecular size or mass.

POLYMERS AND LIQUID CRYSTALS

http://plc.cwru.edu/

Online tutorial about two modern physical wonders. The site is divided into a 'virtual textbook' and a 'virtual laboratory', with corresponding explanations and experiments.

polymerase chain reaction (PCR) technique developed during the 1980s to clone short strands of DNA from the ◊genome of an organism. The aim is to produce enough of the DNA to be able to sequence and identify it. It was developed by US biochemist Kary Mullis of San Diego in 1983.

polymerization chemical union of two or more (usually small) molecules of the same kind to form a new compound. **Addition polymerization** produces simple multiples of the same compound. **Condensation polymerization** joins molecules together with the elimination of water or another small molecule.

Addition polymerization uses only a single monomer (basic molecule); condensation polymerization may involve two or more different monomers (**co-polymerization**).

polymorphism in genetics, the coexistence of several distinctly different types in a ◊population (groups of animals of one species). Examples include the different blood groups in humans, different colour forms in some butterflies, and snail shell size, length, shape, colour, and stripiness.

polymorphism in mineralogy, the ability of a substance to adopt different internal structures and external forms, in response to different conditions of temperature and/or pressure. For example, diamond and graphite are both forms of the element carbon, but they have very different properties and appearance.

Silica (SiO_2) also has several polymorphs, including quartz, tridymite, cristobalite, and stishovite (the latter a very high pressure form found in meteoritic impact craters).

polynomial in mathematics, an algebraic expression that has one or more ◊variables (denoted by letters). A polynomial of degree one, that is, whose highest ◊power of x is 1, as in $2x + 1$, is called a linear polynomial; $3x^2 + 2x + 1$ is quadratic; $4x^3 + 3x^2 + 2x + 1$ is cubic.

polyp or ***polypus*** small 'stalked' benign tumour, usually found on mucous membrane of the nose or bowels. Intestinal polyps are usually removed, since some have been found to be precursors of cancer.

polyp *Corals such as this* Galaxea fascicularis *from the Indian Ocean off Kenya, E Africa, are composed of countless individual polyps. Premaphotos Wildlife*

polyp in zoology, the sedentary stage in the life cycle of a coelenterate (such as a ◊coral or ◊jellyfish), the other being the free-swimming **medusa**.

polypeptide long-chain ◊peptide.

polyploid in genetics, possessing three or more sets of chromosomes in cases where the normal complement is two sets (◊diploid). Polyploidy arises spontaneously and is common in plants (mainly among flowering plants), but rare in animals. Many crop plants are natural polyploids, including wheat, which has four sets of chromosomes per cell (durum wheat) or six sets (common wheat).

Plant breeders can induce the formation of polyploids by treatment with a chemical, colchicine.

polypropylene plastic made by the polymerization, or linking together, of ◊propene molecules (CH_2=CH-CH_3). It is used as a moulding material.

polysaccharide long-chain ◊carbohydrate made up of hundreds or thousands of linked simple sugars (monosaccharides) such as glucose and closely related molecules.

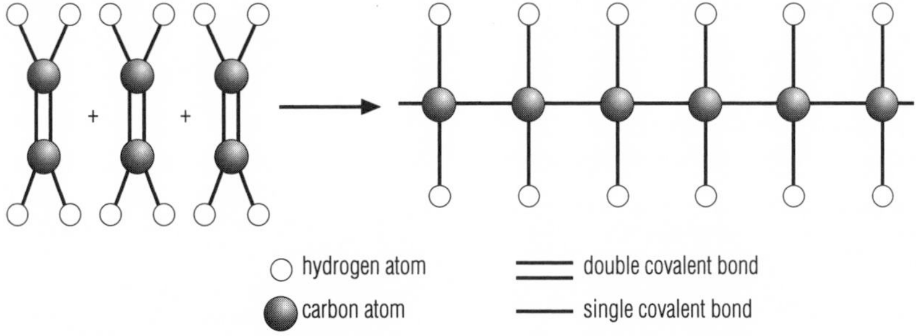

polymerization *In polymerization, small molecules (monomers) join together to make large molecules (polymers). In the polymerization of ethene to polyethene, electrons are transferred from the carbon–carbon double bond of the ethene molecule, allowing the molecules to join together as a long chain of carbon–carbon single bonds.*

oxygen CH$_2$OH OH OH OH carbon hydrogen CH$_2$OH OH CH$_2$OH OH OH OH CH$_2$OH

polysaccharide A typical polysaccharide molecule, glycogen (animal starch), is formed from linked glucose ($C_6H_{12}O_6$) molecules. A glycogen molecule has 100–1,000 linked glucose units.

The polysaccharides are natural polymers. They either act as energy-rich food stores in plants (starch) and animals (glycogen), or have structural roles in the plant cell wall (cellulose, pectin) or the tough outer skeleton of insects and similar creatures (chitin). See also ◊carbohydrate.

polystyrene type of plastic used in kitchen utensils or, in an expanded form, in insulation and ceiling tiles. CFCs are used to produce expanded polystyrene so alternatives are being sought.

polytetrafluoroethene (PTFE) polymer made from the monomer tetrafluoroethene (CF_2CF_2). It is a thermosetting plastic with a high melting point that is used to produce 'non-stick' surfaces on pans and to coat bearings. Its trade name is Teflon.

Polythene trade name for a variety of ◊polyethylene.

polyunsaturate type of ◊fat or oil containing a high proportion of triglyceride molecules whose ◊fatty acid chains contain several double bonds. By contrast, the fatty-acid chains of the triglycerides in saturated fats (such as lard) contain only single bonds. Medical evidence suggests that polyunsaturated fats, used widely in margarines and cooking fats, are less likely to contribute to cardiovascular disease than saturated fats, but there is also some evidence that they may have adverse effects on health.

The more double bonds the fatty-acid chains contain, the lower the melting point of the fat. Unsaturated chains with several double bonds produce oils, such as vegetable and fish oils, which are liquids at room temperature. Saturated fats, with no double bonds, are solids at room temperature. The polyunsaturated fats used for margarines are produced by taking a vegetable or fish oil and turning some of the double bonds to single bonds, so that the product is semi-solid at room temperature. This is done by bubbling hydrogen through the oil in the presence of a catalyst, such as platinum. The catalyst is later removed.

Monounsaturated oils, such as olive oil, whose fatty-acid chains contain a single double bond, are probably healthier than either saturated or polyunsaturated fats. Butter contains both saturated and unsaturated fats, together with ◊cholesterol, which also plays a role in heart disease.

polyurethane polymer made from the monomer urethane. It is a thermoset ◊plastic, used in liquid form as a paint or varnish, and in foam form for upholstery and in lining materials (where it may be a fire hazard).

polyvinyl chloride (PVC) type of ◊plastic used for drainpipes, floor tiles, audio discs, shoes, and handbags. It is derived from vinyl chloride (CH_2=CHCl).

Swedish scientists identified a link between regular exposure to PVC and testicular cancer, in 1998, increasing the demand for a ban on PVC in commercial products.

pome type of ◊pseudocarp, or false fruit, typical of certain plants belonging to the Rosaceae family. The outer skin and fleshy tissues are developed from the ◊receptacle (the enlarged end of the flower stalk) after fertilization, and the five ◊carpels (the true fruit) form the pome's core, which surrounds the seeds. Examples of pomes are apples, pears, and quinces.

pomegranate round, leathery, reddish-yellow fruit of the pomegranate tree, a deciduous shrub or small tree native to SW Asia but cultivated widely in tropical and subtropical areas. The fruit contains a large number of seeds that can be eaten fresh or made into wine. (*Punica granatum,* family Punicaceae.)

pomeranian breed of toy dog, about 15 cm/6 in high, weighing about 3 kg/6.5 lb. It has long straight hair with a neck frill, and the tail is carried over the back.

pomeron in physics, hypothetical object with energy and momentum, but no colour or electrical charge, produced when an electron strikes a proton. Pomerons were first suggested in 1958 by Russian physicist Isaac Pomeranchuk.

pompano warm-water, marine fish. It is silver and grows up to 90 cm/35 in. Pompanos are a valuable edible fish.
classification Pompanos are in the genus *Trachinotus,* in order Perciformes of class Osteichthyes.

Pompeii ancient city in Italy, near the volcano ◊Vesuvius, 21 km/13 mi SE of Naples.

In AD 63 an earthquake destroyed much of the city, which had been a Roman port and pleasure resort; it was completely buried beneath volcanic ash when Vesuvius erupted in AD 79. Over 2,000 people were killed. Pompeii was rediscovered in 1748 and the systematic excavation begun in 1763 still continues.

pond-skater water ◊bug (insect of the Hemiptera order with piercing mouth parts) that rows itself across the surface by using its middle legs. It feeds on smaller insects.

pondweed any of a group of aquatic plants that either float on the surface of the water or are submerged. The leaves of floating pondweeds are broad and leathery, whereas leaves of the submerged forms are narrower and translucent; the flowers grow in green spikes. (Genus *Potamogeton,* family Potamogetonaceae.)

pony small ◊horse under 1.47 m/4.5 ft (14.2 hands) shoulder height. Although of Celtic origin, all the pony breeds have been crossed with thoroughbred and Arab stock, except for the smallest – the hardy Shetland, which is less than 105 cm/42 in shoulder height.

poodle breed of gun dog, including standard (above 38 cm/15 in at shoulder), miniature (below 38 cm/15 in), and toy (below 28 cm/11 in) varieties. The dense curly coat, usually cut into an elaborate style, is often either black or white, although greys and browns are also bred.

The poodle probably originated in Russia, was naturalized in Germany, where it was used for retrieving ducks and gained its name (from the German *pudeln,* 'to splash'), and became a luxury dog in France.

PoP (acronym for ***point of presence***) in computing, place where users can access a network via a telephone connection. A PoP is a collection of modems and other equipment which are permanently connected to the network. Compare ◊vPoP.

POP3 (abbreviation for ***Post Office Protocol***) on the Internet, one of the two most common mail ◊protocols.

Internet Service Providers (ISPs) offer ◊SMTP, POP3, or both. The primary difference to most users is the choice of software available. SMTP is older and more flexible, but POP3 is generally simpler for those accessing the Internet via a dial-up account.

poplar any of a group of deciduous trees with characteristically broad leaves. The white poplar (*P. alba*) has a smooth grey trunk and leaves with white undersides. (Genus *Populus,* family Salicaceae.)

Other varieties are the aspen (*P. tremula*), grey poplar (*P. canescens*), and black poplar (*P. nigra*). Most species are tall; they are often grown as windbreaks in commercial orchards.

poppy any of a group of plants belonging to the poppy family. They have brightly coloured mainly red and orange flowers, often with dark centres, and yield a milky sap. Species include the crimson European field poppy (*P. rhoeas*) and the Asian opium poppy (*P. somniferum*), source of the drug ◊opium. Closely related are the California poppy (*Eschscholtzia californica*) and the yellow horned or sea poppy (*Glaucium flavum*). (Poppy genus *Papaver,* family Papaveraceae.)

population in biology and ecology, a group of animals of one species, living in a certain area and able to interbreed; the members of a given species in a ◊community of living things.

population in statistics, the universal set from which a sample of data is selected. The chief object of statistics is to find out population characteristics by taking samples.

population control measures taken by some governments to limit the growth of their countries' populations by trying to reduce birth rates. Propaganda, freely available contraception, and tax disincentives for large families are some of the measures that have been tried.

The population-control policies introduced by the Chinese government are the best known. In 1979 the government introduced a 'one-child policy' that encouraged ◊family planning and penalized couples who have more than one child. It has been only partially successful since it has been difficult to administer, especially in rural areas, and has in some cases led to the killing of girls in favour of sons as heirs.

population cycle in biology, regular fluctuations in the size of a population, as seen in lemmings, for example. Such cycles are often caused by density-dependent mortality: high mortality due to overcrowding causes a sudden decline in the population, which then gradually builds up again. Population cycles may also result from an interaction between a predator and its prey.

population genetics the branch of genetics that studies the way in which the frequencies of different ◊alleles (alternative forms of a gene) in populations of organisms change, as a result of natural selection and other processes.

pop-up menu in computing, a menu that appears in a (new) window when an option is selected with a mouse or key-stroke sequence in a ◊graphical user ◊interface (GUI), such as Windows 95. Compare with ◊pull-down menu.

porbeagle medium-sized ◊shark.

porcupine any ◊◊rodent with quills on its body, belonging to either of two families: Old World porcupines (family Hystricidae), terrestrial in habit and having long black-and-white quills; or New World porcupines (family Erethizontidae), tree-dwelling, with prehensile tails and much shorter quills.

porcupine fish another name for the puffer fish.

pore in biology, a pore is a small opening in the skin that releases sweat and sebum. Sebum acts as a natural lubricant and protects the skin from the effects of moisture or excessive dryness.

pornography, Internet material of an explicitly sexual nature, whether it be text, photographs, graphics, audio, or video available on the Internet.

The amount of pornography and the ease of finding it has been exaggerated by both politicians and mass media. Nonetheless, there is material available on the Internet to offend almost everyone, and most governments are either attempting or considering some means of censorship.

porphyria group of rare genetic disorders caused by an enzyme defect. Porphyria affects the digestive tract, causing abdominal distress; the nervous system, causing psychotic disorder, epilepsy, and weakness; the circulatory system, causing high blood pressure; and the skin, causing extreme sensitivity to light. No specific treatments exist.

In porphyria the body accumulates and excretes (rather than utilizes) one or more porphyrins, the pigments that combine with iron to form part of the oxygen-carrying proteins haemoglobin and myoglobin; because of this urine turns reddish brown on standing. It is known as the 'royal disease' because sufferers are believed to have included Mary Queen of Scots, James I, and George III.

porphyry any ◊igneous rock containing large crystals in a finer matrix.

porpoise any small whale of the family Delphinidae that, unlike dolphins, have blunt snouts without beaks. Common porpoises of the genus *Phocaena* can grow to 1.8 m/6 ft long; they feed on fish and crustaceans.

port in computing, a socket that enables a computer processor to communicate with an external device. It may be an **input port**

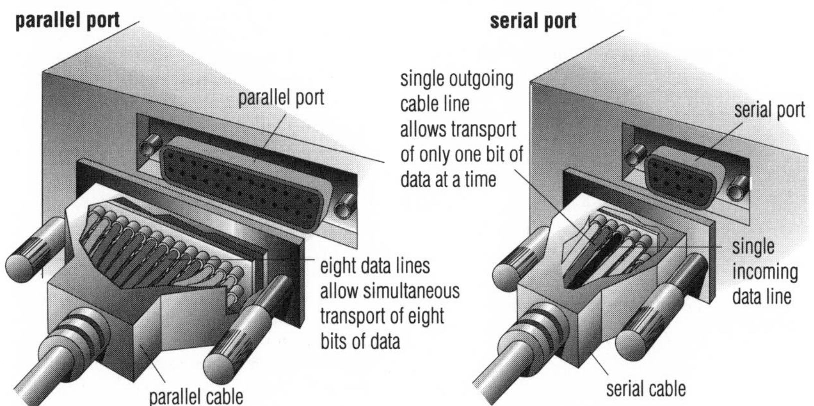

port *The two types of communications port in a microcomputer. The parallel port enables up to eight bits of data to travel through it at any one time; the serial port enables only one.*

(such as a joystick port), or an **output port** (such as a printer port), or both (an **i/o port**).

Microcomputers may provide ports for cartridges, televisions and/or monitors, printers, and modems, and sometimes for hard discs and musical instruments (MIDI, the musical-instrument digital interface). Ports may be serial or parallel.

port point where goods are loaded or unloaded from a water-based to a land-based form of transport. Most ports are coastal, though inland ports on rivers also exist. Ports often have specialized equipment to handle cargo in large quantities (for example, container or ◊roll-on/roll-off facilities).

portability in computing, the characteristic of certain programs that enables them to run on different types of computer with minimum modification. Programs written in a ◊high-level language can usually be run on any computer that has a compiler or interpreter for that particular language.

portable computer computer that can be carried from place to place. The term embraces a number of very different computers – from those that would be carried only with some reluctance to those, such as ◊laptop computers and ◊notebook computers, that can be comfortably carried and used in transit.

port address on the Internet, a way for a host system to specify which ◊server a particular application will use.

Portuguese man-of-war any of a genus *Physalia* of phylum *Coelenterata* (see ◊coelenterate). They live in the sea, in colonies, and have a large air-filled bladder (or 'float') on top and numerous hanging tentacles made up of feeding, stinging, and reproductive individuals. The float can be 30 cm/1 ft long.

position vector a vector that defines the position of a point with respect to the origin.

positive integer any whole number from 0 upwards. 0 is included so that the properties of positive integers include those related to the ◊identity for addition.

positron in physics, the antiparticle of the electron; an ◊elementary particle having the same mass as an electron but exhibiting a positive charge. The positron was discovered in 1932 by US physicist Carl Anderson at Caltech, USA, its existence having been predicted by the British physicist Paul Dirac in 1928.

positron emission tomography (PET) an imaging technique which enables doctors to observe the metabolic activity of the human body by following the progress of a radioactive chemical that has been inhaled or injected, detecting ◊gamma radiation given out when ◊positrons emitted by the chemical are annihilated. The technique has been used to study a wide range of conditions, including schizophrenia, Alzheimer's disease and Parkinson's disease.

POSIX (acronym for ***portable operating system interface for UNIX***) ◊ANSI standard, developed to describe how the programming interfaces and other features of ◊UNIX worked, in order to remove control from the developers, AT&T Bell Laboratories. Subsequently many other (proprietary) ◊operating systems were modified in order to become POSIX-compliant, that is, they provide an open systems interface, so that they can communicate with other POSIX-compliant systems, even though the operating systems themselves are internally quite different. See also ◊open systems interconnection.

possum another name for the ◊opossum, a marsupial animal with a prehensile tail found in North, Central and South America. The name is also used for many of the smaller marsupials found in Australia.

post in computing, to send a message to a ◊newsgroup or ◊bulletin board for others to read.

POS terminal acronym for ◊point of sale terminal, a cash register linked to a computer.

posting in computing, another word for article.

postmaster in computing, ◊systems administrator in charge of a mail server. The term is especially used for people who manage the electronic mail system in a ◊local area network (LAN) or other local network.

postmortem or ***autopsy*** Latin ***'after death'*** dissection of a dead body to determine the cause of death.

postnatal depression mood change occurring in many mothers a few days after the birth of a baby, also known as 'baby blues'. It is usually a shortlived condition but can sometimes persist; one in five women suffer a lasting depression after giving birth. The most severe form of post-natal depressive illness, **puerperal psychosis**, requires hospital treatment.

In mild cases, antidepressant drugs and hormone treatment may help, although no link has been established between hormonal levels and postnatal depression. Research by UK psychologists 1996 showed that the mourning of a lost lifestyle may be a contributory factor.

PostScript in computing, a page-description language developed by Adobe that has become a standard. PostScript is primarily a language for printing documents on laser printers, but it can be adapted to produce images on other types of devices.

PostScript is an object-oriented language, meaning that it treats images, including fonts, as collections of geometrical objects rather than as ◊bit maps. PostScript fonts are ◊outline fonts stored in the computer memory as a set of instructions for drawing the circles, straight lines and curves that make up the outline of each character. This means they are also scalable. Given a single typeface definition, a PostScript printer can thus produce a multitude of fonts.

potash general name for any potassium-containing mineral, most often applied to potassium carbonate (K_2CO_3) or potassium hydroxide (KOH). Potassium carbonate, originally made by roasting plants to ashes in earthenware pots, is commercially produced from the mineral sylvite (potassium chloride, KCl) and is used mainly in making artificial fertilizers, glass, and soap.

The potassium content of soils and fertilizers is also commonly expressed as potash, although in this case it usually refers to potassium oxide (K_2O).

potassium Dutch *potassa* ***'potash'*** soft, waxlike, silver-white, metallic element, symbol K (Latin *kalium*), atomic number 19, relative atomic mass 39.0983. It is one of the ◊alkali metals and has a very low density – it floats on water, and is the second lightest metal (after lithium). It oxidizes rapidly when exposed to air and reacts violently with water. Of great abundance in the Earth's crust, it is widely distributed with other elements and found in salt and mineral deposits in the form of potassium aluminium silicates.

Potassium is the main base ion of the fluid in the body's cells. Along with ◊sodium, it is important to the electrical potential of the nervous system and, therefore, for the efficient functioning of nerve and muscle. Shortage, which may occur with excessive fluid loss (prolonged diarrhoea, vomiting), may lead to muscular paralysis; potassium overload may result in cardiac arrest. It is also required by plants for growth. The element was discovered and named in 1807 by English chemist Humphry Davy, who isolated it from potash in the first instance of a metal being isolated by electric current.

potassium-argon dating or ***K-Ar dating*** isotopic dating method based on the radioactive decay of potassium-40 (40K) to the stable isotope argon-40 (40Ar). Ages are based on the known half-life of 40K, and the ratio of 40K to 40Ar. The method is routinely applied to rock samples about 100,000 to 30 million years old.

The method is used primarily to date volcanic layers in stratigraphic sequences with archaeological deposits, and the palaeomagnetic-reversal timescale. Complicating factors, such as sample contamination by argon absorbed from the atmosphere, and argon gas loss by diffusion out of the mineral, limit the application of this technique.

potassium dichromate $K_2Cr_2O_7$ orange, crystalline solid, soluble in water, that is a strong ◊oxidizing agent in the presence of dilute sulphuric acid. As it oxidizes other compounds it is itself reduced to potassium chromate (K_2CrO_4), which is green. Industrially it is used in the manufacture of dyes and glass and in tanning, photography, and ceramics.

potassium manganate(VII) $KMnO_4$ or ***potassium permanganate*** dark purple, crystalline solid, soluble in water, that is a strong oxidizing agent in the presence of dilute sulphuric acid. In the process of oxidizing other compounds it is itself reduced to manganese(II) salts (containing the Mn^{2+} ion), which are colourless.

potato perennial plant with edible tuberous roots that are rich in starch and are extensively eaten as a vegetable. Used by the Andean Indians for at least 2,000 years before the Spanish Conquest, the potato was introduced to Europe by the mid-16th century, and reputedly to England by the explorer Walter Raleigh. (*Solanum tuberosum,* family Solanaceae.)

In Ireland, the potato famine of 1845, caused by a parasitic fungus, resulted in many thousands of deaths from starvation, and led to large-scale emigration to the USA.

potato blight disease of the potato caused by a parasitic fungus *Phytophthora infestans.* It was the cause of the 1845 potato famine in Ireland. New strains of *P. infestans* continue to arise. The most virulent version so far is *P. infestans US-8,* which arose in Mexico 1992 , spreading to N America 1994. It remained resistant to known fungicides 1996.

potential difference (pd) difference in the electrical potential (see ◊potential, electric) of two points, being equal to the electrical energy converted by a unit electric charge moving from one point to the other. The SI unit of potential difference is the volt (V). The potential difference between two points in a circuit is commonly referred to as voltage. See also ◊Ohm's law.

potential divider ***or*** **voltage divider** two resistors connected in series in an electrical circuit in order to obtain a fraction of the potential difference, or voltage, across the battery or electrical source. The potential difference is divided across the two resistors in direct proportion to their resistances.

potential, electric in physics, the potential at a point is equal to the energy required to bring a unit electric charge from infinity to the point. The SI unit of potential is the volt (V). Positive electric charges will flow 'downhill' from a region of high potential to a region of low potential. See ◊potential difference.

potential energy ◊energy possessed by an object by virtue of its relative position or state (for example, as in a compressed spring). It is contrasted with kinetic energy, the form of energy possessed by moving bodies.

potentiometer in physics, an electrical ◊resistor that can be divided so as to compare, measure, or control voltages. In radio circuits, any rotary variable resistance (such as volume control) is referred to as a potentiometer.

A simple type of potentiometer consists of a length of uniform resistance wire (about 1 m/3 ft long) carrying a constant current provided by a battery connected across the ends of the wire. The source of potential difference (voltage) to be measured is connected (to oppose the cell) between one end of the wire, through a ◊galvanometer (instrument for measuring small currents), to a contact free to slide along the wire. The sliding contact is moved until the galvanometer shows no deflection. The ratio of the length of potentiometer wire in the galvanometer circuit to the total length of wire is then equal to the ratio of the unknown potential difference to that of the battery.

potto arboreal, nocturnal, African prosimian primate *Perodicticus potto* belonging to the ◊loris family. It has a thick body, strong limbs, and grasping feet and hands, and grows to 40 cm/16 in long, with horny spines along its backbone, which it uses in self-defence. It climbs slowly, and eats insects, snails, fruit, and leaves.

poultry domestic birds such as chickens, turkeys, ducks, and geese. They were domesticated for meat and eggs by early farmers in China, Europe, Egypt, and the Americas. Chickens were domesticated from the SE Asian jungle fowl *Gallus gallus* and then raised in the East as well as the West. Turkeys are New World birds, domesticated in ancient Mexico. Geese and ducks were domesticated in Egypt, China, and Europe.

Good egg-laying breeds of chicken are Leghorns, Minorcas, and Anconas; varieties most suitable for eating are Dorkings, Australorps, Brahmas, and Cornish; those useful for both purposes are Orpingtons, Rhode Island Reds, Wyandottes, Plymouth Rocks, and Jersey White Giants. Most farm poultry are hybrids, selectively crossbred for certain characteristics, including feathers and down.

factory farming Since World War II, the development of battery-produced eggs and the intensive breeding of broiler fowls and turkeys has roused a public outcry against 'factory' methods of farming. The birds are often kept constantly in small cages, have their beaks and claws removed to prevent them from pecking their neighbours, and are given feed containing growth hormones and antibacterial drugs, which eventually make their way up the food chain to humans. Factory farming has led to a growing interest in deep-litter and free-range systems, although these account for only a small percentage of total production.

POULTRY BREEDS

http://www.ansi.okstate.edu/poultry/

Masses of information on poultry breeds from all over the world, offered by the Department of Animal Science of Oklahoma State University. It includes photos and elaborate descriptions of about a hundred different species of chickens, ducks, geese, turkeys, and other poultry. Other experts on ornithology are invited to contribute textual and visual material.

standard potential divider

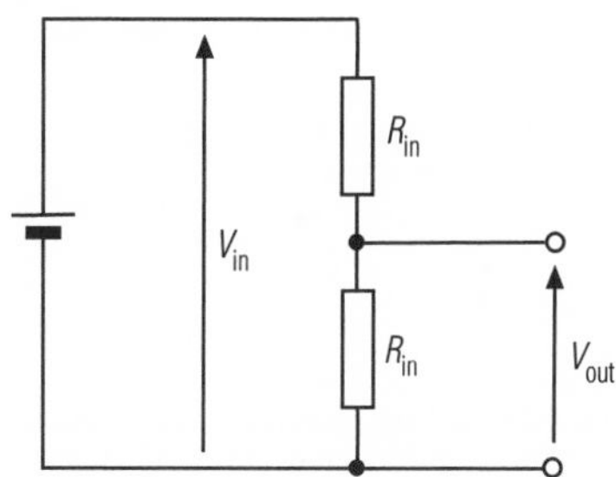

potentiometer used as a potential divider

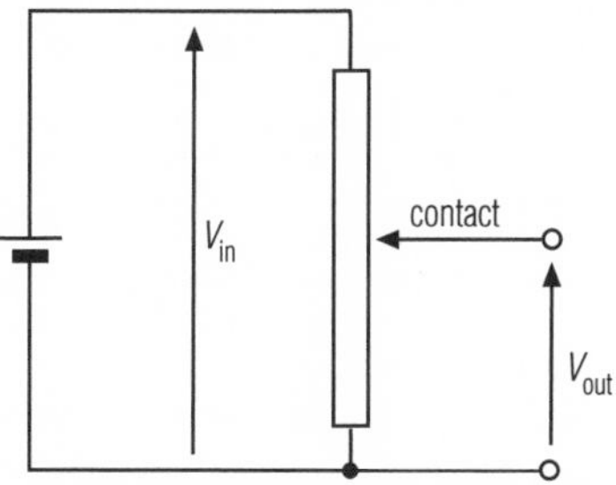

potential divider *A potential divider is a resistor or a chain of resistors connected in series in an electrical circuit. It is used to obtain a known fraction of the total voltage across the whole resistor or chain. When a variable resistor, or potentiometer, is used as a potential divider, the output voltage can be varied continuously by sliding a contact along the resistor. Devices like this are used in electronic equipment to to vary volume, tone, and brightness control.*

pound imperial unit (abbreviation lb) of mass. The commonly used avoirdupois pound, also called the **imperial standard pound** (7,000 grains/0.45 kg), differs from the **pound troy** (5,760 grains/0.37 kg), which is used for weighing precious metals. It derives from the Roman *libra,* which weighed 0.327 kg.

poundal imperial unit (abbreviation pdl) of force, now replaced in the SI system by the ◊newton. One poundal equals 0.1383 newtons.

It is defined as the force necessary to accelerate a mass of one pound by one foot per second per second.

powan British species of ◊whitefish.

powder metallurgy method of shaping heat-resistant metals such as tungsten. Metal is pressed into a mould in powdered form and then sintered (heated to very high temperatures).

powder post beetle dark, small (2–3 mm/0.08–0.12 in long), elongate beetles, which attack both freshly-cut and old timber. Over 90 species have been described.

classification Powder post beetles are in the family Lyctidae of order Coleoptera, class Insecta, phylum Arthropoda.

The eggs are laid in the vessels in the sapwood of hardwoods. Softwoods, such as pine, are never attacked because the vessels are not of the right size, nor will heartwood be attacked as it does not have the right starch and sugar content. The life cycle takes about one year, the winter being spent in the larval condition. The larvae are commonly called ◊woodworm

The adults' exit holes are distinctly visible on the surface of wood, and often a very fine wood powder is noticeable around them. There are various measures which can be taken to prevent infestation: painting and varnishing the wood surface prevents the adult females from laying their eggs in the wood; and chemical treatment of the wood may help.

power in mathematics, that which is represented by an ◊exponent or index, denoted by a superior small numeral. A number or symbol raised to the power of 2 – that is, multiplied by itself – is said to be squared (for example, 3^2, x^2), and when raised to the power of 3, it is said to be cubed (for example, 2^3, y^3).

power in optics, a measure of the amount by which a lens will deviate light rays. A powerful converging lens will converge parallel rays steeply, bringing them to a focus at a short distance from the lens. The unit of power is the **dioptre**, which is equal to the reciprocal of focal length in metres. By convention, the power of a converging (or convex) lens is positive and that of a diverging (or concave) lens negative.

power in physics, the rate of doing work or consuming energy. It is measured in watts (joules per second) or other units of work per unit time.

PowerPC in computing, ◊microprocessor produced by IBM and ◊Motorola, originally as a challenger to Intel, though now being directed towards industrial uses.

The PowerPC was based on IBM's multichip POWER (Performance Optimization With Enhanced Risc) architecture introduced with the RS/6000 line of UNIX workstations and servers 1990. When Apple decided to switch to PowerPC processor, its previous chip supplier, Motorola, switched from its own 88000 ◊RISC processor to join a triumvirate backing the PowerPC. However, the group failed to make any impact on Intel and Apple's sales declined 1995–97.

PowerPoint in computing, ◊presentation graphics program made by ◊Microsoft and sold mainly as part of Microsoft Office.

power station building where electrical energy is generated from a fuel or from another form of energy. Fuels used include fossil fuels such as coal, gas, and oil, and the nuclear fuel uranium. Renewable sources of energy include ◊gravitational potential energy, used to produce ◊hydroelectric power, and ◊wind power.

The energy supply is used to turn ◊turbines either directly by means of water or wind pressure, or indirectly by steam pressure, steam being generated by burning fossil fuels or from the heat released by the fission of uranium nuclei. The turbines in their turn spin alternators, which generate electricity at very high voltage.

The world's largest power station is Turukhansk, on the Lower Tunguska river, Russia, with a capacity of 20,000 megawatts.

I can therefore see no justification for the introduction of a system which has no element of permanency and every element of danger to life and property.

THOMAS EDISON US Scientist and inventor.

power transmission transfer of electrical power from one location, such as a power station, to another. Electricity is conducted along cables at a high voltage (up to 500 kV on the super grid) in order to reduce the current in the wires, and hence minimize the amount of energy wasted from them as heat.

◊Transformers are needed to step down these voltages before power can be supplied to consumers. High voltages require special insulators to prevent current from leaking to the ground and these may clearly be seen on the pylons that carry overhead wires.

PRAIRIE NET

http://dolphin.upenn.edu/~bdp/index.html

Clearing house of information on the prairies. Contents include a catalogue of prairie fauna and flora, reports of conservation efforts to protect America's grasslands, and a photo gallery. There are reports of exhibitions on the prairies and links to other prairie sites.

prairie the central North American plain, formerly grass-covered, extending over most of the region between the Rocky Mountains on the west and the Great Lakes and Ohio River on the east.

prairie dog any of the North American genus *Cynomys* of burrowing rodents in the squirrel family (Sciuridae). They grow to 30 cm/12 in, plus a short 8 cm/3 in tail. Their 'towns' can contain up to several thousand individuals. Their barking cry has given them their name. Persecution by ranchers has brought most of the five species close to extinction.

PRAIRIE DOG

http://ngp.ngpc.state.ne.us/wildlife/pdogs.html

Well-written profile of this sociable burrowing rodent from the Nebraskan wildlife. In addition to information on its diet and habitat, it looks at the ecological importance of preserving prairie dog towns.

prairie wolf another name for the ◊coyote.

praseodymium Greek *prasios 'leek-green'* + *didymos 'twin'* silver-white, malleable, metallic element of the ◊lanthanide series, symbol Pr, atomic number 59, relative atomic mass 140.907. It occurs in nature in the minerals monzanite and bastnaesite, and its green salts are used to colour glass and ceramics. It was named in 1885 by Austrian chemist Carl von Welsbach (1858–1929).

He fractionated it from dydymium (originally thought to be an element but actually a mixture of rare-earth metals consisting largely of neodymium, praseodymium, and cerium), and named it for its green salts and spectroscopic line.

prawn any of various ◊shrimps of the suborder Natantia ('swimming'), of the crustacean order Decapoda, as contrasted with lobsters and crayfishes, which are able to 'walk'. Species called prawns are generally larger than species called shrimps.

praying mantis another name for ◊mantis.

preadaptation in biology, the fortuitous possession of a character that allows an organism to exploit a new situation. In many cases, the character evolves to solve a particular problem that a species encounters in its preferred habitat, but once evolved may allow the organism to exploit an entirely different situation. The ability to extract oxygen directly from the air evolved in some early fishes, probably in response to life in stagnant, deoxygenated pools; this later made it possible for their descendants to spend time on land, so giving rise eventually to the air-breathing amphibians.

Precambrian in geology, the time from the formation of Earth (4.6 billion years ago) up to 570 million years ago. Its boundary with the succeeding Cambrian period marks the time when animals first developed hard outer parts (exoskeletons) and so left abundant fossil remains. It comprises about 85% of geological time and is divided into two periods: the Archaean, in which no life existed, and the Proterozoic, in which there was life in some form.

precession slow wobble of the Earth on its axis, like that of a spinning top. The gravitational pulls of the Sun and Moon on the Earth's equatorial bulge cause the Earth's axis to trace out a circle on the sky every 25,800 years. The position of thecelestial poles (see ◊celestial sphere) is constantly changing owing to precession, as are the positions of the equinoxes (the points at which the celestial equator intersects the Sun's path around the sky). The **precession of the equinoxes** means that there is a gradual westward drift in the ecliptic – the path that the Sun appears to follow – and in the coordinates of objects on the celestial sphere.

This is why the dates of the astrological signs of the zodiac no longer correspond to the times of year when the Sun actually passes through the constellations. For example, the Sun passes through Leo from mid-Aug to mid-Sept, but the astrological dates for Leo are between about 23 July and 22 Aug.

Precession also occurs in other planets. Uranus has the Solar System's fastest known precession (264 days) determined in 1995.

precipitation in chemistry, the formation of an insoluble solid in a liquid as a result of a reaction within the liquid between two or more soluble substances. If the solid settles, it forms a **precipitate**; if the particles of solid are very small, they will remain in suspension, forming a **colloidal precipitate** (see ◊colloid).

precipitation in meteorology, water that falls to the Earth from the atmosphere. It includes rain, snow, sleet, hail, dew, and frost.

precocial animals that are active and mobile from birth. Examples include antelopes, ostriches, and crocodiles.

predator any animal that hunts, kills, and eats another animal (the prey). Examples of predators include lions, who prey on antelope and zebra, and owls, who prey on mice and rats.

Predators are usually bigger and more powerful than their prey (although a stoat preys on a rabbit, which may be four or five times its size), and their population is smaller – if the predator became more widespread than the prey, the population of the predator would inevitably fall. Other relationships between species include parasitism, in which the host is not necessarily killed by the ◊parasite, and ◊symbiosis, in which both species benefit from the relationship.

pre-eclampsia or ***toxaemia of pregnancy*** potentially serious condition developing in the third trimester and marked by high blood pressure and fluid retention. Arising from unknown causes, it disappears when pregnancy is over. It may progress to ◊eclampsia if untreated.

prefabricated building in architecture and construction, the manufacture of large elements, such as walls, floors, and roofs, or even entire buildings, for assembly at the site. Prefabrication is widely used for constructing housing and other buildings, either to meet tight construction deadlines or, as in the UK during the reconstruction following World War II and the housing boom of the 1960s, when there is a large demand for buildings but labour supply is limited.

history Modern prefabrication began when the Industrial Revolution brought about large-scale production of iron. From 1750, iron framing was developed for factories, as in the flax-spinning mill at Ditherington near Shrewsbury, built in 1796.

Joseph Paxton's 'Crystal Palace' of 1851 was entirely prefabricated from cast-iron and glass to meet a nine-month construction deadline. This style was further developed by Buckminster Fuller's ◊geodesic domes in the 1960s. During the 1930s, Jean Prouvé (1901–1984) developed a system of wall components for lightweight housing and further developed the 'curtain wall' as well as other components for prefabricated construction.

Prefabrication really came into its own from 1945, when there was a shortage of labour to carry out the massive building programmes being undertaken in the wake of World War II. In the UK, entire houses and other buildings were fully made up at the factory and then delivered and assembled on site.

pregnancy in humans, the period during which an embryo grows within the womb. It begins at conception and ends at birth, and the normal length is 40 weeks. Menstruation usually stops on conception. About one in five pregnancies fails, but most of these failures occur very early on, so the woman may notice only that her period is late. After the second month, the breasts become tense and tender, and the areas round the nipples become darker. Enlargement of the uterus can be felt at about the end of the third month, and thereafter the abdomen enlarges progressively. Fetal movement can be felt at about 18 weeks; a heart-beat may be heard during the sixth month. Pregnancy in animals is called ◊gestation.

complications Occasionally the fertilized egg implants not in the womb but in the ◊Fallopian tube (the tube between the ovary and the uterus), leading to an ectopic ('out of place') pregnancy. This will cause the woman severe abdominal pain and vaginal bleeding. If the growing fetus ruptures the tube, life-threatening shock may ensue. Toxaemia is characterized by rising blood pressure, and if left untreated, can result in convulsions leading to coma.

According to 1996 World Health Organization (WHO) figures, 585,000 women die annually from pregnancy-related causes; 99% of these deaths occur in developing countries. The highest rate of maternal death is in Sierra Leone with 1,800 deaths per 100,000 live births, compared with an average of 27 for industrialized countries.

prehistoric art art that predates written records. The history of the fine arts – painting, engraving, and sculpture – begins around 40,000 BC in the Palaeolithic period (Old Stone Age). The oldest known rock engravings are in Australia, but within the next 30,000 years art occurs on every continent. The earliest surviving artefacts in Europe date from approximately 30,000–10,000 BC, a period of hunter-gatherer cultures. Small sculptures are generally of fecund female nudes and relate to the cult of the Mother Goddess; for example, the stone *Willendorf Venus* (Kunsthistorisches Museum, Vienna) about 21,000 BC. The murals of the caves of Lascaux, France, and Altamira, Spain, depict mostly animals.

During the Neolithic period (New Stone Age) 10,000–2,000 BC, settled communities were established, which led to a greater technical and aesthetic sophistication in tools, ceramic vessels, jewellery, and human and animal figures. Human figures appear more often in wall paintings, and are skilfully composed into groups. The period 4,000–2,000 BC saw the erection of the great ◊megalith monuments, such as those at Carnac, France, and Stonehenge, England, and the production of ceramic pots and figurines with decorative elements that were later to be developed in Celtic art.

prehistoric life the diverse organisms that inhabited Earth from the origin of life about 3.5 billion years ago to the time when humans began to keep written records, about 3500 BC. During the course of evolution, new forms of life developed and many other forms, such as the dinosaurs, became extinct. Prehistoric life evolved over this vast timespan from simple bacteria-like cells in the oceans to algae and protozoans and complex multicellular forms such as worms, molluscs, crustaceans, fishes, insects, land plants, amphibians, reptiles, birds, and mammals. On a geological

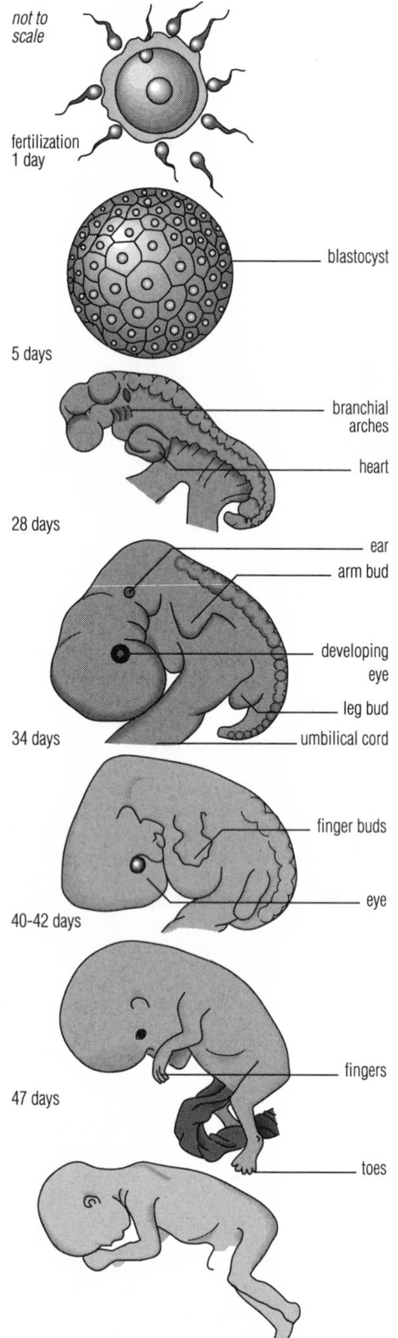

***pregnancy** The development of a human embryo. Division of the fertilized egg, or ovum, begins within hours of conception. Within a week a ball of cells –a blastocyst – has developed. After the third week, the embryo has changed from a mass of cells into a recognizable shape. At four weeks, the embryo is 3 mm/0.1 in long, with a large bulge for the heart and small pits for the ears. At six weeks, the embryo is 1.5 cm/0.6 in with a pulsating heart and ear flaps. At the eighth week, the embryo is 2.5 cm/1 in long and recognizably human, with eyelids, small fingers, and toes. From the end of the second month, the embryo is almost fully formed and further development is mainly by growth. After this stage, the embryo is termed a fetus.*

timescale human beings evolved relatively recently, about 4 million years ago, although the exact dating is a matter of some debate. See also ◊geological time.

prehistory human cultures before the use of writing. The study of prehistory is mainly dependent on archaeology. General chronological dividing lines between prehistoric eras, or history and prehistory, are difficult to determine because communities have developed at differing rates. The Three Age System of classification (published in 1836 by the Danish archaeologist Christian Thomsen) is based on the predominant materials used by early humans for tools and weapons: ◊Stone Age, ◊Bronze Age, and ◊Iron Age.

Human prehistory begins with the emergence of early modern hominids (see ◊human species, origins of). *Homo habilis,* the first tool user, was in evidence around 2 million years ago, and found at such sites as Koobi Fora, Kenya and Olduvai Gorge, Tanzania.

Stone Age Stone was the main material used for tools and weapons. The Stone Age is divided into:

Old Stone Age (Palaeolithic) 3,500,000–8500 BC. Stone and bone tools were chipped into shape by early humans or hominids from Africa, Asia, the Middle East, and Europe, as well as later Neanderthal and Cro-Magnon people; the only domesticated animals were dogs. Some Asians crossed the Bering land bridge to inhabit the Americas. ◊Prehistoric art was being produced 20,000 years ago in many parts of the world; for example, at Altamira in Spain, Lascaux in France, in southern Africa, and in Australia.

Middle Stone Age (Mesolithic) and **New Stone Age** (Neolithic). Bone tools and stone or flint implements were used. In Neolithic times, agriculture and the domestication of goats, sheep, and cattle began. Stone Age cultures survived in the Americas, Asia, Africa, Oceania, and Australia until the 19th and 20th centuries.

Bronze Age Bronze tools and weapons appeared approximately 5000 BC in the Far East, and continued in the Middle East until about 1200 BC; in Europe this period lasted from about 2000 to 500 BC.

Iron Age Iron was hardened (alloyed) by the addition of carbon, so that it superseded bronze for tools and weapons; in the Old World generally from about 1000 BC.

prematurity the condition of an infant born before the full term. In obstetrics, an infant born before 37 weeks' gestation is described as premature.

Premature babies are often at risk. They lose heat quickly because they lack an insulating layer of fat beneath the skin; there may also be breathing difficulties. In hospitals with advanced technology, specialized neonatal units can save some babies born as early as 23 weeks.

premenstrual tension (PMT) or ***premenstrual syndrome*** medical condition caused by hormone changes and comprising a number of physical and emotional features that occur cyclically before menstruation and disappear with its onset. Symptoms include mood changes, breast tenderness, a feeling of bloatedness, and headache.

premolar in mammals, one of the large teeth toward the back of the mouth. In herbivores they are adapted for grinding. In carnivores they may be carnassials. Premolars are present in milk ◊dentition as well as permanent dentition.

presbyopia vision defect, an increasing inability with advancing age to focus on near objects. It is caused by thickening and loss of elasticity in the lens, which is no longer able to relax to the near-spherical shape required for near vision.

prescription in medicine, an order written in a recognized form by a practitioner of medicine, dentistry, or veterinary surgery to a pharmacist for a preparation of medications to be used in treatment.

By tradition it used to be written in Latin, except for the directions addressed to the patient. It consists of (1) the superscription *recipe* ('take'), contracted to Rx; (2) the inscription or body, containing the names and quantities of the drugs to be dispensed; (3) the subscription, or directions to the pharmacist; (4) the signature, followed by directions to the patient; and (5) the patient's name, the date, and the practitioner's name.

presentation graphics in computing, program that helps users to create presentations such as visual aids, handouts, and overhead slides. Presentation graphics programs process artwork, graphics, and text to produce a series of 'slides' – images which help speakers to get their message across. Leading programs include Microsoft ◊PowerPoint and (for ◊multimedia presentations, incorporating moving pictures and sounds) Macromedia Director.

preservative substance (additive) added to a food in order to inhibit the growth of bacteria, yeasts, moulds, and other microorganisms, and therefore extend its shelf life. The term sometimes refers to ◊anti-oxidants (substances added to oils and fats to prevent their becoming rancid) as well. All preservatives are potentially damaging to health if eaten in sufficient quantity. Both the amount used, and the foods in which they can be used, are restricted by law.

Alternatives to preservatives include faster turnover of food stocks, refrigeration, better hygiene in preparation, sterilization, and pasteurization (see ◊food technology).

pressure in a fluid, the force that would act normally (at right angles) per unit surface area of a body immersed in the fluid. The SI unit of pressure is the pascal (Pa), equal to a pressure of one newton per square metre. In the atmosphere, the pressure declines with height from about 100 kPa at sea level to zero where the atmosphere fades into space. Pressure is commonly measured with a ◊barometer, manometer, or ◊Bourdon gauge. Other common units of pressure are the bar and the torr.

Absolute pressure is measured from a vacuum; **gauge pressure** is the difference between the absolute pressure and the local ◊atmospheric pressure. In a liquid, the pressure at a depth h is given by ρgh where ρ is the density and g is the acceleration of free fall.

pressure cooker closed pot in which food is cooked in water under pressure, where water boils at a higher temperature than normal boiling point (100°C/212°F) and therefore cooks food quickly. The modern pressure cooker has a quick-sealing lid and a safety valve that can be adjusted to vary the steam pressure inside.

The French scientist Denis Papin invented the pressure cooker in England in 1679.

pressure law law stating that the pressure of a fixed mass of gas at constant volume is directly proportional to its absolute temperature.

The law may be expressed as:

pressure/temperature = constant or, more usefully, as: $P_1/T_1 = P_2/T_2$where P_1 and T_1 are the initial pressure and temperature in kelvin of a gas, and P_2 and T_2 are its final pressure and temperature. See also ◊gas laws.

pressurized water reactor (PWR) a ◊nuclear reactor design used in nuclear power stations in many countries, and in nuclear-powered submarines. In the PWR, water under pressure is the coolant and ◊moderator. It circulates through a steam generator, where its heat boils water to provide steam to drive power ◊turbines.

Prestel ◊viewdata service that provides information on the television screen via the telephone network. The service was first offered to the public by British Telecom – then a division of the General Post Office – in 1979. It never lived up to expectations and British Telecom sold off what remained in 1995.

Prestel On-Line is now a Scottish telecommmunications company specializing in Internet access and content provision

Pretty Good Privacy (PGP) in computing, strong encryption program that runs on personal computers and is distributed on the Net free of charge. It was written by Phil Zimmermann and released to the Net in 1991 amid growing fears that the USA would pass a law requiring all secure communications systems to incorporate a 'back door' to make it easy for law enforcement officials to read encrypted messages.

PGP is based on the RSA ◊algorithm and uses ◊public-key cryptography; its source code has been released to the cryptographic community for study and testing. Since version 1.0, its development has proceeded in multiple locations around the world to avoid conflicts with the US laws banning the export of strong encryption. A companion product, PGPfone, released in 1996, runs across the Internet to give users the equivalent of a military grade secure telephone.

prickly pear any of several cacti (see ◊cactus) native to Central and South America, mainly Mexico and Chile, but naturalized in S Europe, N Africa, and Australia, where it is a pest. The common prickly pear (*O. vulgaris*) is low-growing, with flat, oval stem joints, bright yellow flowers, and prickly, oval fruit; the flesh and seeds of the peeled fruit have a pleasant taste. (Genus *Opuntia*, family Cactaceae.)

primary data information that has been collected at first hand. It involves measurement of some sort, whether by taking readings off instruments, sketching, counting, or conducting interviews (using questionnaires).

primary sexual characteristic the endocrine gland producing maleness and femaleness. In males, the primary sexual characteristic is the ◊testis; in females it is the ◊ovary. Both are endocrine glands that produce hormones responsible for secondary sexual characteristics, such as facial hair and a deep voice in males and breasts in females.

primate in zoology, any member of the order of mammals that includes monkeys, apes, and humans (together called **anthropoids**), as well as lemurs, bushbabies, lorises, and tarsiers (together called **prosimians**).

Generally, they have forward-directed eyes, gripping hands and feet, opposable thumbs, and big toes. They tend to have nails rather than claws, with gripping pads on the ends of the digits, all adaptations to the arboreal, climbing mode of life.

In 1996 a new primate genus (probably extinct) was identified by a US anthropologist from a collection of bones believed to belong to a ◊potto. The animal has been named *Pseudopotto martini*.

According to the Red List of endangered species published by the World Conservation Union (IUCN) for 1996, 46% of primate species are threatened with extinction.

> *He is proud that he has the biggest brain of all the primates, but attempts to conceal the fact that he also has the biggest penis.*
>
> DESMOND MORRIS English anthropologist. *The Naked Ape*, Introduction

prime number number that can be divided only by 1 or itself, that is, having no other factors. There is an infinite number of primes, the first ten of which are 2, 3, 5, 7, 11, 13, 17, 19, 23, and 29 (by definition, the number 1 is excluded from the set of prime numbers). The number 2 is the only even prime because all other even numbers have 2 as a factor.

Over the centuries mathematicians have sought general methods (algorithms) for calculating primes, from ◊Eratosthenes' sieve to programs on powerful computers.

The largest prime, 2^{859433}–1 (258,716 digits long) was discovered in 1993. It is the thirty-third **Mersenne prime**. All Mersenne primes are in the form $2q^{-1}$, where q is also a prime.

LARGEST KNOWN PRIMES

http://www.utm.edu/research/primes/largest.html#contents

Everything you ever wanted to know about prime numbers, including the top ten recorded primes and Euclid's proof that the largest prime can never be reached.

Prime numbers

All the Prime Numbers between 1 and 1,000

2	71	167	271	389	503	631	757	883
3	73	173	277	397	509	641	761	887
5	79	179	281	401	521	643	769	907
7	83	181	283	409	523	647	773	911
11	89	191	293	419	541	653	787	919
13	97	193	307	421	547	659	797	929
17	101	197	311	431	557	661	809	937
19	103	199	313	433	563	673	811	941
23	107	211	317	439	569	677	821	947
29	109	223	331	443	571	683	823	953
31	113	227	337	449	577	691	827	967
37	127	229	347	457	587	701	829	971
41	131	233	349	461	593	709	839	977
43	137	239	353	463	599	719	853	983
47	139	241	359	467	601	727	857	991
53	149	251	367	479	607	733	859	997
59	151	257	373	487	613	739	863	
61	157	263	379	491	617	743	877	
67	163	269	383	499	619	751	881	

primrose any of a group of plants belonging to the primrose family, with showy five-lobed flowers. The common primrose (*P. vulgaris*) is a woodland plant, native to Europe, with abundant pale yellow flowers in spring. Related to it is the ◊cowslip. (Genus *Primula*, family Primulaceae.)

principal focus in optics, the point at which incident rays parallel to the principal axis of a ◊lens converge, or appear to diverge, after refraction. The distance from the lens to its principal focus is its ◊focal length.

print in computing, to transfer data to a ◊printer, to a screen or to another file.

printed circuit board (PCB) electrical circuit created by laying (printing) 'tracks' of a conductor such as copper on one or both sides of an insulating board. The PCB was invented in 1936 by Austrian scientist Paul Eisler, and was first used on a large scale in 1948.

Components such as integrated circuits (chips), resistors and capacitors can be soldered to the surface of the board (surface-mounted) or, more commonly, attached by inserting their connecting pins or wires into holes drilled in the board. PCBs include ◊motherboards, expansion boards, and adaptors.

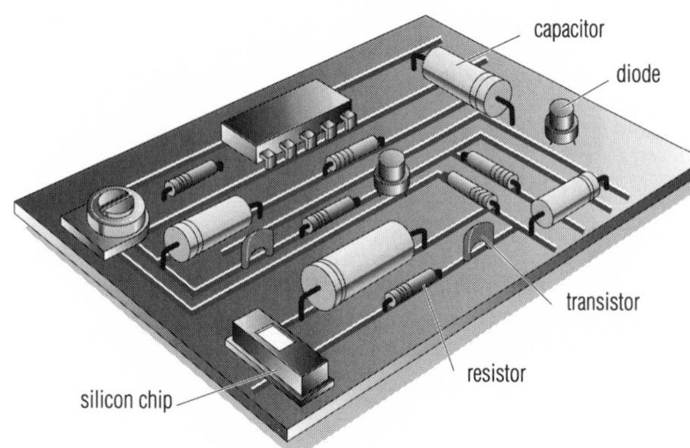

printed circuit board *A typical microcomputer printed circuit board (PCB). The PCB contains sockets for the integrated circuits, or chips, and the connecting tracks.*

printer in computing, an output device for producing printed copies of text or graphics. Types include the **◊daisywheel printer**, which produces good-quality text but no graphics; the **◊dot matrix** printer, which produces text and graphics by printing a pattern of small dots; the **◊ink-jet printer**, which creates text and graphics by spraying a fine jet of quick-drying ink onto the paper; and the **◊laser printer**, which uses electrostatic technology very similar to that used by a photocopier to produce high-quality text and graphics.

Printers may be classified as **impact printers** (such as daisywheel and dot-matrix printers), which form characters by striking an inked ribbon against the paper, and **nonimpact printers** (such as ink-jet and laser printers), which use a variety of techniques to produce characters without physical impact on the paper.

A further classification is based on the basic unit of printing, and categorizes printers as character printers, line printers, or page printers, according to whether they print one character, one line, or a complete page at a time.

printing reproduction of multiple copies of text or illustrative material on paper, as in books or newspapers, or on an increasing variety of materials; for example, on plastic containers. The first printing used woodblocks, followed by carved wood type or moulded metal type and hand-operated presses. Modern printing is effected by electronically controlled machinery. Current printing processes include electronic phototypesetting with ◊offset printing, and ◊gravure print.

origins In China the art of printing from a single wooden block was known by the 6th century AD, and movable type was being used by the 11th century. In Europe printing was unknown for another three centuries, and it was only in the 15th century that movable type was reinvented, traditionally by Johannes ◊Gutenberg in Germany. From there printing spread to Italy, France, and England, where it was introduced by William Caxton.

steam power, linotype, and monotype There was no further substantial advance until, in the 19th century, steam power replaced hand-operation of printing presses, making possible long 'runs'; hand-composition of type (each tiny metal letter was taken from the case and placed individually in the narrow stick that carried one line of text) was replaced by machines operated by a keyboard. **Linotype**, a hot-metal process (it produced a line of type in a solid slug) used in newspapers, magazines, and books, was invented by Ottmar Mergenthaler 1886 and commonly used until the 1980s. The **Monotype**, used in bookwork (it produced a series of individual characters, which could be hand-corrected), was invented by Tolbert Lanston (1844–1913) in the USA 1889.

Important as these developments were, they represented no fundamental change but simply a faster method of carrying out the same basic typesetting operations. The actual printing process still involved pressing the inked type on to paper, by ◊letterpress.

20th-century developments In the 1960s, letterpress began to face increasing competition from ◊offset printing, **a method that prints from an inked flat surface, and from the** ◊gravure **method (used for high-circulation magazines), which uses recessed plates. The introduction of electronic phototypesetting machines, also in the 1960s, allowed the entire process of setting and correction to be done in the same way that a typist operates, thus eliminating the hot-metal composing room (with its hazardous fumes, lead scraps, and noise) and leaving only the making of plates and the running of the presses to be done traditionally**.

By the 1970s some final steps were taken to plateless printing, using various processes, such as a computer-controlled laser beam, or continuous jets of ink acoustically broken up into tiny equal-sized drops, which are electrostatically charged under computer control. Pictures can be fed into computer typesetting systems by optical ◊scanners.

print spooler in computing, ◊utility program that stores information in a temporary file before sending it on to a printer. Print spoolers help computers to work efficiently, allowing the ◊central processing unit (CPU) to carry on with other work while a document is being printed.

prion (acronym for ***proteinaceous infectious particle***) exceptionally small microorganism, a hundred times smaller than a virus.

Composed of protein, and without any detectable amount of nucleic acid (genetic material), it is thought to cause diseases such as scrapie in sheep, and certain degenerative diseases of the nervous system in humans. How it can operate without nucleic acid is not yet known.

prism in mathematics, a solid figure whose cross section is constant in planes drawn perpendicular to its axis. A cube, for example, is a rectangular prism with all faces (bases and sides) the same shape and size.

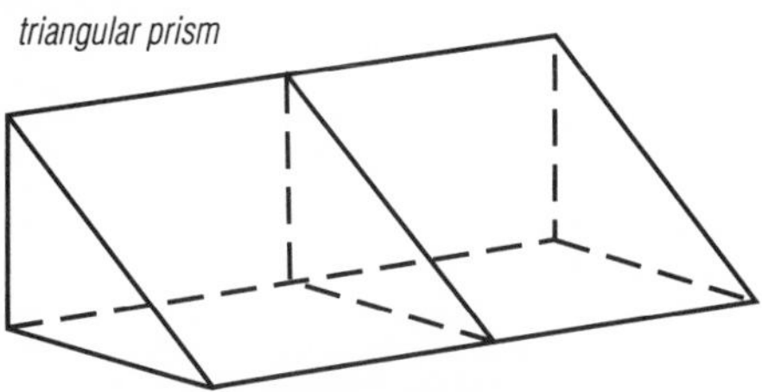

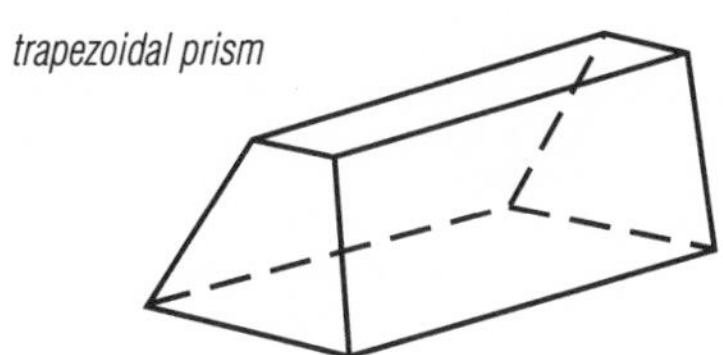

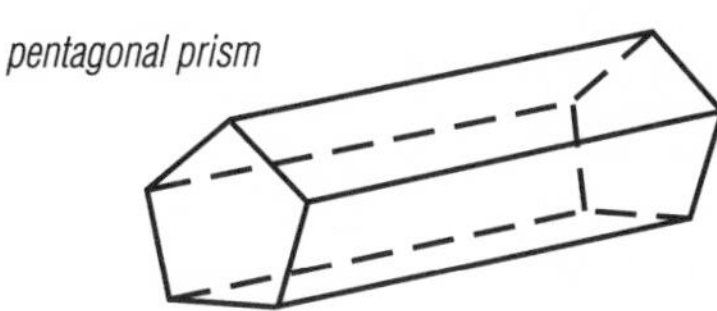

prism

prism in optics, a triangular block of transparent material (plastic, glass, silica) commonly used to 'bend' a ray of light or split a beam into its spectral colours. Prisms are used as mirrors to define the optical path in binoculars, camera viewfinders, and periscopes. The dispersive property of prisms is used in the ◊spectroscope.

privacy on the Internet, generally used to mean the right to control who has access to the personal information generated by interaction with computers.

The right to privacy is one of the most hotly debated issues on the Internet, as commercial suppliers seek to gather more and more information about their customers. The most common approaches to securing the right to privacy are technological, via encryption, and legislative, via laws such as Britain's Data Protection Act. A third approach is to use services such as ◊anonymous remailers to strip identifying information from individual messages when posting contentious or sensitive material.

privacy enhanced mail (PEM) in computing, Internet protocol that gives a degree of confidentiality to ◊e-mail, using various ◊public-key cryptography methods.

privet any of a group of evergreen shrubs with dark green leaves, belonging to the olive family. They include the European common privet (*L. vulgare*) with white flowers and black berries, naturalized in North America, and the native North American California privet (*L. ovalifolium*), also known as hedge privet. (Genus *Ligustrum*, family Oleaceae.)

probability likelihood, or chance, that an event will occur, often expressed as odds, or in mathematics, numerically as a fraction or decimal.

In general, the probability that n particular events will happen out of a total of m possible events is n/m. A certainty has a probability of 1; an impossibility has a probability of 0. Empirical probability is defined as the number of successful events divided by the total possible number of events.

In tossing a coin, the chance that it will land 'heads' is the same as the chance that it will land 'tails', that is, 1 to 1 or even; mathematically, this probability is expressed as $\frac{1}{2}$ or 0.5. The odds against any chosen number coming up on the roll of a fair die are 5 to 1; the probability is $\frac{1}{6}$ or 0.1666... . If two dice are rolled there are 6 x 6 = 36 different possible combinations. The probability of a double (two numbers the same) is $\frac{6}{36}$ or $\frac{1}{6}$ since there are six doubles in the 36 events: (1,1), (2,2), (3,3), (4,4), (5,5), and (6,6).

Probability theory was developed by the French mathematicians Blaise Pascal and Pierre de Fermat in the 17th century, initially in response to a request to calculate the odds of being dealt various hands at cards. Today probability plays a major part in the mathematics of atomic theory and finds application in insurance and statistical studies.

> *At any rate, I am convinced that He [God] does not play dice.*
>
> ALBERT EINSTEIN German-born US physicist.
> Letter to Max Born 4 Dec 1926

proboscis monkey large, leaf-eating monkey found only in mangrove swamps in Borneo. The male's nose is bulbous and prolonged to hang below the upper lip.
classification Proboscis monkeys *Nasalis larvatus*, are in family Cercopithecidae, order Primates.

procedural programming programming in which programs are written as lists of instructions for the computer to obey in sequence. It closely matches the computer's own sequential operation.

procedure in computing, a small part of a computer program that performs a specific task, such as clearing the screen or sorting a file. A **procedural language**, such as BASIC, is one in which the programmer describes a task in terms of how it is to be done, as opposed to a **declarative language**, such as PROLOG, in which it is described in terms of the required result. See ◊programming.

Careful use of procedures is an element of ◊structured programming. In some programming languages there is an overlap between procedures, ◊functions, and ◊subroutines.

process control automatic computerized control of a manufacturing process, such as glassmaking. The computer receives ◊feedback information from sensors about the performance of the machines involved, and compares this with ideal performance data stored in its control program. It then outputs instructions to adjust automatically the machines' settings.

Because the computer can monitor and reset each machine hundreds of times each minute, performance can be maintained at levels that are very close to the ideal.

processing cycle in computing, the sequence of steps performed repeatedly by a computer in the execution of a program. The computer's central processing unit (CPU) continuously works through a loop, involving fetching a program instruction from memory, fetching any data it needs, operating on the data, and storing the result in the memory, before fetching another program instruction.

There are no things, only processes.

DAVID BOHM US-born British physicist.
In C H Waddington *The Evolution of an Evolutionist* 1975

processor in computing, another name for the ◊central processing unit or ◊microprocessor of a computer.

Procyon or ***Alpha Canis Minoris*** brightest star in the constellation ◊Canis Minor and the eighth-brightest star in the sky. Procyon is a first-magnitude white star 11.4 light years from Earth, with a mass of 1.7 Suns. It has a ◊white dwarf companion that orbits it every 40 years.

The name, derived from Greek, means 'before the dog', and reflects the fact that in midnorthern latitudes Procyon rises shortly before ◊Sirius, the Dog Star. Procyon and Sirius are sometimes called 'the Dog Stars'. Both are relatively close to us and have white dwarf companions.

Prodigy in computing, online (originally, viewdata) service launched in 1988 by a partnership of ◊IBM and leading US retailer Sears Roebuck; bought in 1996 by the global communications company International Wireless, which relaunched it as an Internet service.

Even though Prodigy has been lavishly funded, thoughout its history it has lagged behind ◊CompuServe and ◊America Online (AOL). By 1996, it had 1.4 million subscribers, but had never marketed itself outside North America. In late 1996, Prodigy announced it would launch a Spanish-language service in Mexico.

productivity, biological in an ecosystem, the amount of material in the food chain produced by the primary producers (plants) that is available for consumption by animals. Plants turn carbon dioxide and water into sugars and other complex carbon compounds by means of photosynthesis. Their net productivity is defined as the quantity of carbon compounds formed, less the quantity used up by the respiration of the plant itself.

progesterone ◊steroid hormone that occurs in vertebrates. In mammals, it regulates the menstrual cycle and pregnancy. Progesterone is secreted by the corpus luteum (the ruptured Graafian follicle of a discharged ovum).

prograde or ***direct motion*** in astronomy, the orbit or rotation of a planet, or ◊satellite if the sense of rotation is the same as the general sense of rotation of the Solar System. On the ◊celestial sphere, it refers to motion from west to east against the background of stars.

program in computing, a set of instructions that controls the operation of a computer. There are two main kinds: ◊applications programs, which carry out tasks for the benefit of the user – for example, word processing; and ◊systems programs, which control the internal workings of the computer. A ◊utility program is asystems program that carries out specific tasks for the user. Programs can be written in any of a number of ◊programming languages but are always translated into machine code before they can be executed by the computer.

program counter in computing, an alternative name for ◊sequence-control register.

program documentation ◊documentation that provides a complete technical description of a program, built up as the software is written, and is intended to support any later maintenance or development of the program.

program files in computing, files which contain the code used by a computer program.

program flow chart type of ◊flow chart used to describe the flow of data through a particular computer program.

program loop part of a computer program that is repeated several times. The loop may be repeated a fixed number of times (**counter-controlled loop**) or until a certain condition is satisfied (**condition-controlled loop**). For example, a counter-controlled loop might be used to repeat an input routine until exactly ten numbers have been input; a condition-controlled loop might be used to repeat an input routine until the ◊data terminator 'XXX' is entered.

programmer job classification for ◊computer personnel. Programmers write the software needed for any new computer system or application.

programming writing instructions in a programming language for the control of a computer. **Applications programming** is for end-user programs, such as accounts programs or word-processing packages. **Systems programming** is for operating systems and the like, which are concerned more with the internal workings of the computer.

There are several programming styles:

procedural programming, in which programs are written as lists of instructions for the computer to obey in sequence, is by far the most popular. It is the 'natural' style, closely matching the computer's own sequential operation; **declarative programming**, as used in the programming language PROLOG, does not describe how to solve a problem, but rather describes the logical structure of the problem. Running such a program is more like proving an assertion than following a procedure; **functional programming** is a style based largely on the definition of functions. There are very few functional programming languages, HOPE and ML being the most widely used, though many more conventional languages (for example C) make extensive use of functions; **object-oriented programming**, the most recently developed style, involves viewing a program as a collection of objects that behave in certain ways when they are passed certain 'messages'. For example, an object might be defined to represent a table of figures, which will be displayed on screen when a 'display' message is received.

programming language in computing, a special notation in which instructions for controlling a computer are written. Programming languages are designed to be easy for people to write and read, but must be capable of being mechanically translated (by a ◊compiler or an ◊interpreter) into the ◊machine code that the computer can execute. Programming languages may be classified as ◊high-level languages or ◊low-level languages. See also◊ source language.

program trading in finance, buying and selling a group of shares using a computer program to generate orders automatically whenever there is an appreciable movement in prices.

One form in use in the USA in 1989 was **index arbitrage**, in which a program traded automatically whenever there was a difference between New York and Chicago prices of an equivalent number of shares. Program trading comprised some 14% of daily trading on the New York Stock Exchange by volume in September 1989, but was widely criticized for lessening market stability. It has been blamed, among other factors, for the Stock Market crashes of 1987 and 1989.

progression sequence of numbers each occurring in a specific relationship to its predecessor. An **arithmetic progression** has numbers that increase or decrease by a common sum or difference (for example, 2, 4, 6, 8); a **geometric progression** has numbers each bearing a fixed ratio to its predecessor (for example, 3, 6, 12, 24); and a **harmonic progression** has numbers whose ◊reciprocals are in arithmetical progression, for example 1, $\frac{1}{2}$, $\frac{1}{3}$, $\frac{1}{4}$.

Project Gutenberg an electronic 'library' containing hundreds of 'etexts' – books made freely accessible via the ◊World Wide Web and downloadable via FTP. The project started in 1971 at the University of Illinois. For copyright reasons, most of the books available are classics dating from before the 20th century, but there are also some current reference books – including the current *CIA factbook*.

projectile particle that travels with both horizontal and vertical motion in the Earth's gravitational field. If the frictional forces of air resistance are ignored, the two components of its motion can be analyzed separately: its vertical motion will be accelerated due to its

Programming Languages

Language	Main uses	Description
Ada	defence applications	high-level
assembler languages	jobs needing detailed control of the hardware, fast execution, and small program size	fast and efficient but require considerable effort and skill
ALGOL (algorithmic language)	mathematical work	high-level with an algebraic style; no longer in current use, but has influenced languages such as Ada an PASCAL
BASIC (beginners' all-purpose symbolic instruction code)	mainly in education, business, and the home, and among non-professional programmers, such as	easy to learn; early versions lacked the features of other languages
C	engineerssystems and general programming	fast and efficient; widely used as a general-purpose language; especially popular among professional programmers
C++	systems and general programming; commercial software development	developed from C, adding the advantages of object-oriented programming
COBOL (common business-oriented language)	business programming	strongly oriented towards commercial work; easy to learn but very verbose; widely used on mainframes
FORTH	control applications	reverse Polish notation language
FORTRAN (formula translation)	scientific and computational work	based on mathematical formulae; popular among engineers, scientists, and mathematicians
Java	developed for consumer electronics; used for many interactive Web sites	multipurpose, cross-platform, object-oriented language with similar features to C and C++ but simpler
LISP (list processing)	artificial intelligence	symbolic language with a reputation for being hard to learn; popular in the academic and research communities
LOGO	teaching of mathematical concepts	high-level; popular with schools and home computer users
Modula-2	systems and real-time programming; general programming highly-structured	intended to replace PASCAL for 'real-world' applications
OBERON	general programming	small, compact language incorporating many of the features of PASCAL and Modula-2
PASCAL (program appliqué à la sélection et la compilation automatique de la littérature)	general-purpose language	highly-structured; widely used for teaching programming in universities
Perl (pathological eclectic rubbish lister)	systems programming and Web development especially in UNIX environment	easy manipulation of text, files, and processes,
PROLOG (programming in logic)	artificial intelligence	symbolic-logic programming system, originally intended for theorem solving but now used more generally in artificial intelligence

weight in the gravitational field; its horizontal motion may be assumed to be at constant velocity. In a uniform gravitational field and in the absence of frictional forces the path of a projectile is a parabola.

projection of the earth on paper, see ◊map projection.

projector any apparatus that projects a picture on to a screen. In a **slide projector**, a lamp shines a light through the photographic slide or transparency, and a projection ◊lens throws an enlarged image of the slide onto the screen. A **film projector** has similar optics, but incorporates a mechanism that holds the film still while light is transmitted through each frame (picture). A shutter covers the film when it moves between frames. A **television projector**, often used at sports events, produces an enlarged image of the television screen. It shines an intense light through a small LCD (liquid crystal display) throwing the television picture onto a large screen.

prokaryote in biology, an organism whose cells lack organelles (specialized segregated structures such as nuclei, mitochondria, and chloroplasts). Prokaryote DNA is not arranged in chromosomes but forms a coiled structure called a **nucleoid**. The prokaryotes comprise only the **bacteria** and **cyanobacteria** (see ◊blue-green algae); all other organisms are eukaryotes.

prolapse displacement of an organ due to the effects of strain in weakening the supporting tissues. The term is most often used with regard to the rectum (due to chronic bowel problems) or the uterus (following several pregnancies).

PROLOG (contraction of ***programming in logic***) high-level computer-programming language based on logic. Invented in 1971 at the University of Marseille, France, it did not achieve widespread use until more than ten years later. It is used mainly for ◊artificial intelligence programming.

PROM (acronym for ***programmable read-only memory***) in computing, a memory device in the form of an integrated circuit (chip) that can be programmed after manufacture to hold information permanently. PROM chips are empty of information when manufactured, unlike ROM (read-only memory) chips, which have information built into them. Other memory devices are ◊EPROM (erasable programmable read-only memory) and ◊RAM (random-access memory).

promethium radioactive, metallic element of the ◊lanthanide series, symbol Pm, atomic number 61, relative atomic mass 145.

It occurs in nature only in minute amounts, produced as a fission product/by-product of uranium in ◊pitchblende and other uranium ores; for a long time it was considered not to occur in nature. The longest-lived isotope has a half-life of slightly more than 20 years.

Promethium is synthesized by neutron bombardment of neodymium, and is a product of the fission of uranium, thorium, or plutonium; it can be isolated in large amounts from the fission-product debris of uranium fuel in nuclear reactors. It is used in phosphorescent paints and as an X-ray source.

prominence bright cloud of gas projecting from the Sun into space 100,000 km/60,000 mi or more. **Quiescent prominences** last for months, and are held in place by magnetic fields in the Sun's corona. **Surge prominences** shoot gas into space at speeds of 1,000 kps/600 mps.

Loop prominences are gases falling back to the Sun's surface after a solar ◊flare.

prompt symbol displayed on a screen indicating that the computer is ready for input. The symbol used will vary from system to system and application to application. The current cursor position is normally next to the prompt. Generally prompts only appear in ◊command line interfaces.

pronghorn ruminant mammal *Antilocapra americana* constituting the family Antilocapridae, native to the W USA. It is not a true antelope. It is light brown and about 1 m/3 ft high. It sheds its horns annually and can reach speeds of 100 kph/60 mph. The loss of prairies to agriculture, combined with excessive hunting, has brought this unique animal close to extinction.

PRONGHORN

http://eco.bio.lmu.edu/WWW_Nat_History/mammals/arti/anti_am.htm

Profile of the pronghorn, its characteristics, and distribution. There is a high-resolution photo of America's fastest native mammal.

proof in mathematics, a set of arguments used to deduce a mathematical theorem from a set of axioms.

Some proofs command assent. Others woo and charm the intellect. They evoke delight and an overpowering desire to say 'Amen, Amen'.

JOHN WILLIAM STRUTT, 3RD BARON RAYLEIGH English physicist.
H E Hunter *The Divine Proportion* 1970

proof spirit numerical scale used to indicate the alcohol content of an alcoholic drink. Proof spirit (or 100% proof spirit) acquired its name from a solution of alcohol in water which, when used to moisten gunpowder, contained just enough alcohol to permit it to burn.

propane C_3H_8 gaseous hydrocarbon of the ◊alkane series, found in petroleum and used as fuel.

propanol or ***propyl alcohol*** third member of the homologous series of ◊alcohols. Propanol is usually a mixture of two isomeric compounds (see ◊isomer): propan-1-ol ($CH_3CH_2CH_2OH$) and propan-2-ol ($CH_3CHOHCH_3$). Both are colourless liquids that can be mixed with water and are used in perfumery.

propanone CH_3COCH_3 (common name ***acetone***) colourless flammable liquid used extensively as a solvent, as in nail-varnish remover. It boils at 56.5°C/133.7°F, mixes with water in all proportions, and has a characteristic odour.

propellant substance burned in a rocket for propulsion. Two propellants are used: oxidizer and fuel are stored in separate tanks and pumped independently into the combustion chamber. Liquid oxygen (oxidizer) and liquid hydrogen (fuel) are common propellants, used, for example, in the space-shuttle main engines. The explosive charge that propels a projectile from a gun is also called a propellant.

propeller screwlike device used to propel some ships and aeroplanes. A propeller has a number of curved blades that describe a helical path as they rotate with the hub, and accelerate fluid (liquid or gas) backwards during rotation. Reaction to this backward movement of fluid sets up a propulsive thrust forwards. The marine screw propeller was developed by Francis Pettit Smith in the UK and Swedish-born John Ericson in the USA and was first used in 1839.

propene $CH_3CH{=}CH_2$ (common name **propylene**) second member of the alkene series of hydrocarbons. A colourless, flammable gas, it is widely used by industry to make organic chemicals, including polypropylene plastics.

propenoic acid $H_2C{=}CHCOOH$ (common name **acrylic acid**) acid obtained from the aldehyde propenal (acrolein) derived from glycerol or fats. Glasslike thermoplastic resins are made by polymerizing ◊esters of propenoic acid or methyl propenoic acid and used for transparent components, lenses, and dentures. Other acrylic compounds are used for adhesives, artificial fibres, and artists' acrylic paint.

proper motion gradual change in the position of a star that results from its motion in orbit around our Galaxy, the Milky Way. Proper motions are slight and undetectable to the naked eye, but can be accurately measured on telescopic photographs taken many years apart.

Barnard's Star is the star with the largest proper motion, 10.3 arc seconds per year.

properties in chemistry, the characteristics a substance possesses by virtue of its composition.

Physical properties of a substance can be measured by physical means, for example boiling point, melting point, hardness, elasticity, colour, and physical state. **Chemical properties** are the way it reacts with other substances; whether it is acidic or basic, an oxidizing or a reducing agent, a salt, or stable to heat, for example.

prophylaxis any measure taken to prevent disease, including exercise and ◊vaccination. Prophylactic (preventive) medicine is an aspect of public-health provision that is receiving increasing attention.

proportion the relation of a part to the whole (usually expressed as a fraction or percentage). In mathematics two variable quantities x and y are proportional if, for all values of x, $y = kx$, where k is a constant. This means that if x increases, y increases in a linear fashion.

A graph of x against y would be a straight line passing through the origin (the point $x = 0$, $y = 0$). y is inversely proportional to x if the graph of y against $1/x$ is a straight line through the origin. The corresponding equation is $y = k/x$. Many laws of science relate quantities that are proportional (for example, ◊Boyle's law).

proportional font font in which individual letters of the alphabet take up different amounts of space according to their shape.

Computer **fixed fonts** are designed so that each letter has the same width and takes up the same amount of space on a line. A letter 'l', however, logically is thinner than a letter 'o'. Proportional fonts allow spacing according to these differences, and are therefore easier to read. Until the advent of personal computers and font software such as Adobe ◊PostScript, proportional spacing was the province of professional typography, used in books, newspapers, magazines, and other commercial publishing.

proprioceptor in biology, one of the sensory nerve endings that are located in muscles, tendons, and joints. They relay information on the position of the body and the state of muscle contraction.

prop root or ***stilt root*** modified root that grows from the lower part of a stem or trunk down to the ground, providing a plant with extra support. Prop roots are common on some woody plants, such as mangroves, and also occur on a few herbaceous plants, such as maize. **Buttress roots** are a type of prop root found at the base of tree trunks, extended and flattened along the upper edge to form massive triangular buttresses; they are common on tropical trees.

propyl alcohol common name for ◊propanol.

propylene common name for ◊propene.

prosimian or ***primitive primate*** in zoology, any animal belonging to the suborder Strepsirhin of ◊primates. Prosimians are characterized by a wet nose with slitlike nostrils, the tip of the nose having a prominent vertical groove. Examples are lemurs, pottos, tarsiers, and the aye-aye.

prostaglandin any of a group of complex fatty acids present in the body that act as messenger substances between cells. Effects include stimulating the contraction of smooth muscle (for example, of the womb during birth), regulating the production of stomach acid, and modifying hormonal activity. In excess, prostaglandins may produce inflammatory disorders such as arthritis. Synthetic prostaglandins are used to induce labour in humans and domestic animals.

The analgesic actions of substances such as aspirin are due to inhibition of prostaglandin synthesis.

prostate cancer in medicine, ◊cancer of the ◊prostate gland. It is a slow progressing cancer and about 60% of cases are detected before metastasis (spreading) so it can be successfully treated by surgical removal of the gland and radiotherapy. It is, however, the second commonest cancer-induced death in males (after lung cancer).

Symptoms include a frequent need to urinate, with weak, painful, and interrupted urine flow.

prostatectomy surgical removal of the prostate gland. In many men over the age of 60 the prostate gland enlarges, causing obstruction to the urethra. This causes the bladder to swell with retained urine, leaving the sufferer more prone to infection of the urinary tract.

The treatment of choice is transurethral resection of the prostate, in which the gland is removed by passing an endoscope (slender optical instrument) up the urethra and using diathermy to burn away the prostatic tissue. This procedure has now largely replaced 'open' prostatectomy, in which the prostate is removed via an incision in the abdomen.

prostate gland gland surrounding and opening into the ◊urethra at the base of the ◊bladder in male mammals.

The prostate gland produces an alkaline fluid that is released during ejaculation; this fluid activates sperm, and prevents their clumping together. Older men may develop **benign prostatic hyperplasia** (BHP), a painful condition in which the prostate becomes enlarged and restricts urine flow. This can cause further problems of the bladder and kidneys. It is treated by ◊prostatectomy.

PROSTHETIC HISTORY PAGE

http://pele.repoc.nwu.edu/nupoc/prosHistory.html

History of prosthetics from prehistory to modern times. The Web site describes artificial limbs in historical terms, citing many cases from classical texts. The Web site lacks the graphics which would make it much more interesting, but the text descriptions made are reasonably lengthy and complete.

prosthesis artificial device used to substitute for a body part which is defective or missing. Prostheses include artificial limbs, hearing aids, false teeth and eyes, heart ◊pacemakers and plastic heart valves and blood vessels.

Prostheses in the form of artificial limbs, such as wooden legs and metal hooks for hands, have been used for centuries, although artificial limbs are now more natural-looking and comfortable to wear. The comparatively new field of ◊bionics has developed myoelectric, or bionic, arms, which are electronically operated and worked by minute electrical impulses from body muscles.

protactinium Latin *protos 'before'* + *aktis 'first ray'* silver–grey, radioactive, metallic element of the ◊actinide series, symbol Pa, atomic number 91, relative atomic mass 231.036. It occurs in nature in very small quantities, in ◊pitchblende and other uranium ores. It has 14 known isotopes; the longest-lived, Pa-231, has a half-life of 32,480 years.

protandry in a flower, the state where the male reproductive organs reach maturity before those of the female. This is a common method of avoiding self-fertilization. See also ◊protogyny.

protease general term for a digestive enzyme capable of splitting proteins. Examples include pepsin, found in the stomach, and trypsin, found in the small intestine.

protected mode operating mode of ◊Intel microprocessors (80286 and above), which allows multitasking and provides other features such as ◊extended memory and ◊virtual memory (above 1 Gbyte). Protected mode operation also improves ◊data security.

INTRODUCTION TO PROTEINS

http://biotech.chem.indiana.edu/pages/protein_intro.html

Lucid introduction to the world of proteins with discussions of their structures and sequences, as well as descriptions of some major kinds of proteins. The site also includes a useful glossary and offers a variety of photographic shots.

protein complex, biologically important substance composed of amino acids joined by ◊peptide bonds. Proteins are essential to all living organisms. As **enzymes** they regulate all aspects of metabolism. Structural proteins such as **keratin** and **collagen** make up the skin, claws, bones, tendons, and ligaments; **muscle** proteins produce movement; **haemoglobin** transports oxygen; and **membrane** proteins regulate the movement of substances into and out of cells. For humans, protein is an essential part of the diet, and is found in

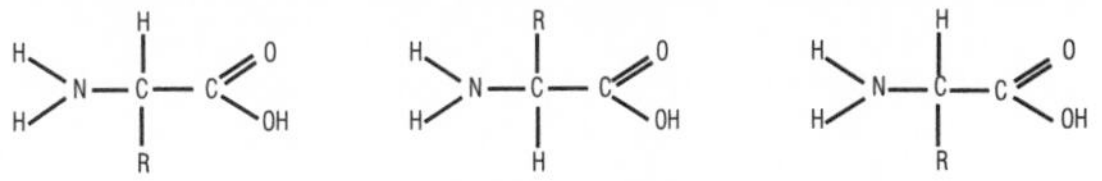

amino acids, where R is one of many possible side chains

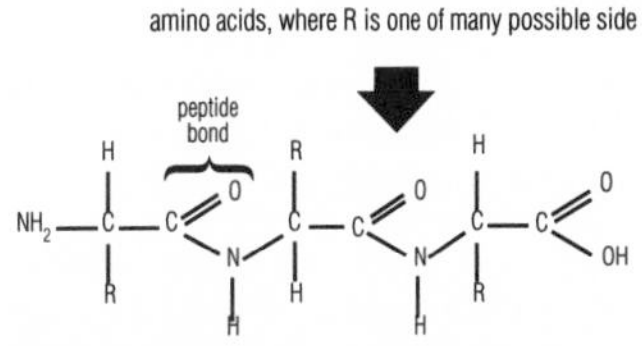

peptide bond

peptide – this is one made of just three amino acid units. Proteins consist of very large numbers of amino acid units in long chains, folded up in specific ways

***protein** A protein molecule is a long chain of amino acids linked by peptide bonds. The properties of a protein are determined by the order, or sequence, of amino acids in its molecule, and by the three-dimensional structure of the molecular chain. The chain folds and twists, often forming a spiral shape.*

greatest quantity in soya beans and other grain legumes, meat, eggs, and cheese.

Other types of bond, such as sulphur–sulphur bonds, hydrogen bonds, and cation bridges between acid sites, are responsible for creating the protein's characteristic three-dimensional structure, which may be fibrous, globular, or pleated. Protein provides 4 kcal of energy per gram (60 g per day is required).

protein engineering the creation of synthetic proteins designed to carry out specific tasks. For example, an enzyme may be designed to remove grease from soiled clothes and remain stable at the high temperatures in a washing machine.

protein synthesis manufacture, within the cytoplasm of the cell, of the proteins an organism needs. The building blocks of proteins are amino acids, of which there are 20 types. The pattern in which the ◊amino acids are linked decides what kind of protein is produced. In turn it is the genetic code, contained within ◊DNA, that determines the precise order in which the amino acids are linked up during protein manufacture.

Interestingly, DNA is found only in the nucleus, yet protein synthesis occurs only in the cytoplasm. The information necessary for making the proteins is carried from the nucleus to the cytoplasm by another nucleic acid, ◊RNA.

Proterozoic eon of geological time, 3.5 billion to 570 million years ago, the second division of the Precambrian. It is defined as the time of simple life, since many rocks dating from this eon show traces of biological activity, and some contain the fossils of bacteria and algae.

prothallus in botany, a short-lived gametophyte of many ferns and other ◊pteridophytes (such as horsetails or clubmosses). It bears either the male or female sex organs, or both. Typically it is a small, green, flattened structure that is anchored in the soil by several ◊rhizoids (slender, hairlike structures, acting as roots) and needs damp conditions to survive. The reproductive organs are borne on the lower surface close to the soil. See also ◊alternation of generations.

protist in biology, a single-celled organism which has a eukaryotic cell, but which is not a member of the plant, fungal, or animal kingdoms. The main protists are ◊protozoa.

Single-celled photosynthetic organisms, such as diatoms and dinoflagellates, are classified as protists or algae. Recently the term has also been used for members of the kingdom Protista, which features in certain five-kingdom classifications of the living world (see also ◊plant classification). This kingdom may include slime moulds, all algae (seaweeds as well as unicellular forms), and protozoa.

protocol in computing, an agreed set of **standards** for the transfer of data between different devices. They cover transmission speed, format of data, and the signals required to synchronize the transfer. See also ◊interface.

protogyny in a flower, the state where the female reproductive organs reach maturity before those of the male. Like protandry, in which the male organs reach maturity first, this is a method of avoiding self-fertilization, but it is much less common.

proton Greek *'first'* in physics, a positively charged subatomic particle, a constituent of the nucleus of all atoms. It belongs to the ◊baryon subclass of the ◊hadrons. A proton is extremely long-lived, with a lifespan of at least 10^{32} years. It carries a unit positive charge equal to the negative charge of an ◊electron. Its mass is almost 1,836 times that of an electron, or 1.67×10^{-27} kg. Protons are composed of two up ◊quarks and one down quark held together by ◊gluons. The number of protons in the atom of an element is equal to the atomic number of that element.

protonema in botany, a young ◊gametophyte of a moss, which develops from a germinating spore (see ◊alternation of generations). Typically it is a green, branched, threadlike structure that grows over the soil surface bearing several buds that develop into the characteristic adult moss plants.

proton number alternative name for ◊atomic number.

Proton rocket Soviet space rocket introduced in 1965, used to launch heavy satellites, space probes, and the *Salyut* and *Mir* space stations.

Proton consists of up to four stages as necessary. It has never been used to launch humans into space.

protoplasm contents of a living cell. Strictly speaking it includes all the discrete structures (organelles) in a cell, but it is often used simply to mean the jellylike material in which these float. The contents of a cell outside the nucleus are called ◊cytoplasm.

protostar in astronomy, early formation of a star that has recently condensed out of an interstellar cloud and which is not yet hot enough for hydrogen burning to start. Protostars derive their energy from gravitational contraction. See ◊Hayashi track.

prototheria subclass of mammals made up of the egg-laying monotremes. It contains only the echidna (spiny anteater) and the platypus.

prototype in technology, any of the first few machines of a new design. Prototypes are tested for performance, reliability, economy, and safety; then the main design can be modified before full-scale production begins.

protozoa group of single-celled organisms without rigid cell walls. Some, such as amoeba, ingest other cells, but most are ◊saprotrophs or parasites. The group is polyphyletic (containing organisms which have different evolutionary origins).

protractor instrument used to measure a flat ◊angle.

provitamin any precursor substance of a vitamin. Provitamins are ingested substances that become converted to active vitamins within the organism. One example is ergosterol (provitamin D_2), which through the action of sunlight is converted to calciferol (vitamin D_2); another example is beta-carotene, which is hydrolysed in the liver to vitamin A.

Proxima Centauri the closest star to the Sun, 4.2 light years away. It is a faint ◊red dwarf, visible only with a telescope, and is a member of the Alpha Centauri triple-star system.

It is called Proxima because it is about 0.1 light years closer to us than its two partners.

proxy server on the ◊World Wide Web, a server which 'stands in' for another server, storing and forwarding files on behalf of a computer which might be slower or too busy to deal with the request itself. Many ◊URLs (Web addresses) redirect the enquirer to a proxy server which then supplies the requested page.

In 1996, the authorities in Singapore imposed a legal requirement on local Internet providers to filter all traffic via a government-run proxy server that can block access to various sites – the first serious government attempt to censor the Internet.

prussic acid former name for ◊hydrocyanic acid.

pseudocarp in botany, a fruitlike structure that incorporates tissue that is not derived from the ovary wall. The additional tissues may be derived from floral parts such as the ◊receptacle and ◊calyx. For example, the coloured, fleshy part of a strawberry develops from the receptacle and the true fruits are small ◊achenes – the 'pips' embedded in its outer surface. Rose hips are a type of pseudocarp that consists of a hollow, fleshy receptacle containing a number of achenes within. Different types of pseudocarp include pineapples, figs, apples, and pears.

A **coenocarpium** is a fleshy, multiple pseudocarp derived from an ◊inflorescence rather than a single flower. The pineapple has a thickened central axis surrounded by fleshy tissues derived from the receptacles and floral parts of many flowers. A fig is a type of pseudocarp called a **syconium**, formed from a hollow receptacle with small flowers attached to the inner wall. After fertilization the ovaries of the female flowers develop into one-seeded achenes.

Apples and pears are ◊pomes, another type of pseudocarp.

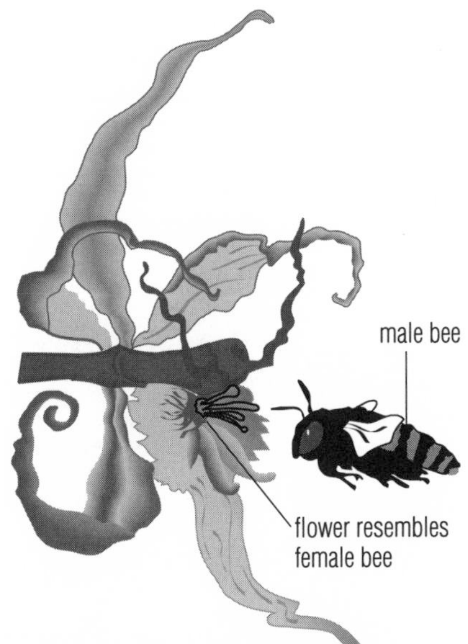

pseudocopulation The male bee, attracted to the orchid because of its resemblance to a female bee, attempts to mate with the flower. The bee's efforts cover its body with pollen, which is carried to the next flower it visits.

pseudocopulation attempted copulation by a male insect with a flower. It results in ◊pollination of the flower and is common in the orchid family, where the flowers of many species resemble a particular species of female bee. When a male bee attempts to mate with a flower, the pollinia (groups of pollen grains) stick to its body. They are transferred to the stigma of another flower when the insect attempts copulation again.

pseudomorph mineral that has replaced another *in situ* and has retained the external crystal shape of the original mineral.

pseudonym in computing, name adopted by someone on the Internet, especially to participate in ◊USENET or discussions using IRC (◊Internet Relay Chat). Pseudonyms are often jokey or witty, and are sometimes used to conceal the user's gender or identity.

psi in parapsychology, a hypothetical faculty common to humans and other animals, said to be responsible for ◊extrasensory perception, telekinesis, and other paranormal phenomena.

psoriasis chronic, recurring skin disease characterized by raised, red, scaly patches, on the scalp, elbows, knees, and elsewhere. Tar preparations, steroid creams, and ultraviolet light are used to treat it, and sometimes it disappears spontaneously. Psoriasis may be accompanied by a form of arthritis (inflammation of the joints).

PSORIASIS

http://biomed.nus.sg/nsc/psoriasi.html

Well-presented practical information about psoriasis from Singapore's National Skin Centre. The condition is explained in simple language supported by a picture. There are details of various treatment regimes.

PSTN (abbreviation for ***Public Switched Telephone Network***) telephone network used by the general public, and sometimes used as the medium to link ◊LANs. PSTNs are minor roads which lead to the ◊information superhighway.

psychedelic drug any drug that produces hallucinations or altered states of consciousness. Such sensory experiences may be in the auditory, visual, tactile, olfactory, or gustatory fields or in any combination. Among drugs known to have psychedelic effects are LSD (lysergic acid diethylamide), mescaline, and, to a mild degree, marijuana, along with a number of other plant-derived or synthetically prepared substances.

psychiatry branch of medicine dealing with the diagnosis and treatment of mental disorder, normally divided into the areas of **neurotic conditions**, including anxiety, depression, and hysteria, and **psychotic disorders**, such as schizophrenia. Psychiatric treatment consists of drugs, analysis, or electroconvulsive therapy.

In practice there is considerable overlap between psychiatry and ◊clinical psychology, the fundamental difference being that psychiatrists are trained medical doctors (holding an MD degree) and may therefore prescribe drugs, whereas psychologists may hold a PhD but do not need a medical qualification to practise. See also ◊psychoanalysis.

psychoanalysis theory and treatment method for neuroses, developed by Sigmund ◊Freud in the 1890s. Psychoanalysis asserts that the impact of early childhood sexuality and experiences, stored in the ◊unconscious, can lead to the development of adult emotional problems. The main treatment method involves the free association of ideas, and their interpretation by patient and analyst, in order to discover these long-buried events and to grasp their significance to the patient, linking aspects of the patient's historical past with the present relationship to the analyst. Psychoanalytic treatment aims to free the patient from specific symptoms and from irrational inhibitions and anxieties.

concepts As a theoretical system, psychoanalysis rests on three basic concepts. The central concept is that of the **unconscious**, a reservoir within one's mental state which contains elements and experiences of which one is unaware, but which may to some extent be brought into preconscious and conscious awareness, or inferred from aspects of behaviour. The second and related basic concept is that of **resistance**, a process by which unconscious elements are forcibly kept out of the conscious awareness by an active repressive force. Freud came to experience the third basic concept in his work, known as **transference**, with his earliest patients, who transferred to him aspects of their past relationships with others, so that their relationship with him was coloured by their previous feelings. The analysis of the transference in all its manifestations has become a vital aspect of current psychoanalytic practice.

id, ego, and superego Freud proposed a model of human psychology based on the concept of the conflicting ◊id, ego, and ◊superego. The id is the mind's instinctual element which demands pleasure and satisfaction; the ego is the conscious mind which deals with the demands of the id and superego; the superego is the ethical element which acts as a conscience and may produce feelings of guilt. The conflicts between these three elements can be used to explain a range of neurotic symptoms.

other schools In the early 1900s a group of psychoanalysts gathered around Freud. Some of these later broke away and formed their own schools, notably Alfred Adler in 1911 and ◊Carl Jung in 1913. The significance of early infantile experience has been further elaborated in the field of child analysis, particularly in the work of Melanie Klein and her students, who pay particular attention to the development of the infant in the first six to eight months of life.

psychology systematic study of human and animal behaviour. The first psychology laboratory was founded in 1879 by Wilhelm Wundt at Leipzig, Germany. The subject includes diverse areas of study and application, among them the roles of instinct, heredity, environment, and culture; the processes of sensation, perception, learning, and memory; the bases of motivation and emotion; and the functioning of thought, intelligence, and language. Significant psychologists have included Gustav Fechner, founder of psychophysics; Wolfgang Köhler, one of the ◊Gestalt or 'whole' psychologists; Sigmund Freud and his associates Carl Jung and Alfred Adler; William James, Jean Piaget; Carl Rogers; Hans Eysenck; J B Watson; and B F Skinner.

Experimental psychology emphasizes the application of rigorous

Psychology: chronology

1846	E H Weber reported on his pioneering quantitative investigations of touch in *On Touch and Common Sensibility.*
1860	G T Fechner published *Elements of Psychophysics,* in which he presented the first statistical treatment of psychological data.
1879	Wilhelm Wundt founded the first psychological laboratory in Leipzig.
1885	H Ebbinghaus published his experimental research into memory.
1890	William James published the first comprehensive psychology text, *Principles of Psychology.*
1895	Joseph Breuer and Sigmund Freud published *Studies on Hysteria,* containing the first writings on psychoanalysis.
1896	The first psychology clinic was founded by Lightner Witner at the University of Pennsylvania; the first use of the term 'clinical psychology'.
1900	Freud's *Interpretation of Dreams* published.
1905	Alfred Binet and Théodore Simon developed the first effective intelligence test.
1906	Ivan Pavlov first lectured in the West on conditioned reflexes in animals.
1908	The first textbook of social psychology was published by William McDougall and E A Ross.
1911	Max Wertheimer, Wolfgang Köhler, and Kurt Koffka founded the Gestalt School in Frankfurt.
1913	John B Watson's article 'Psychology as a behaviorist views it' was published and the behaviourist movement thus launched.
1923	Jean Piaget's *The Language and the Thought of the Child* published, the first of his many books on the development of thinking.
1927	C Spearman proposed in *The Abilities of Man* that intelligence comprises two kinds of factors, a general factor ('g') and specific factors.
1929	H Berger published his findings on the electroencephalogram (EEG).
1938	B F Skinner published *The Behavior of Organisms,* detailing his study of operant conditioning and his radical behaviourism.
1943	C L Hull published his influential book *Principles of Behavior,* the most rigorous account of conditioning and learning from the perspective of behaviourism.
1947	Hans Eysenck published *Dimensions of Personality,* a large-scale study of neuroticism and extraversion.
1948	Norbert Wiener coined the term 'cybernetics' and published *Cybernetics: Control and Communication in the Animal and Machine.*
1949	D O Hebb's *Organization of Behaviour* re-emphasized the role of central (brain) processes in the explanation of behaviour.
1950	Alan Turing proposed his test of whether a machine can be said to think, in the article 'Computing Machinery and Intelligence'. *The Authoritarian Personality* by Theodor Adorno and others published.
1953	E Aserinksy and N Kleitman published the first account of REM (rapid eye movement) sleep.
1957	Noam Chomsky published *Syntactic Structures,* a seminal work of psycholinguistics, which revolutionized the study of language. L Festinger published *A Theory of Cognitive Dissonance.*
1958	A Newell and H A Simon, with J C Shaw, published their article on human problem-solving, the first account of the information-processing approach to human psychology.
1958	Donald E Broadbent published *Perception and Communication,* a detailed account of information-processing psychology.
1960	G A Miller, E Galanter, and K Pribam applied the idea of a hierarchically structured computer program to the whole of psychology in their *Plans and the Structure of Behaviour.*
1961	A Newell and H A Simon published their pioneering computational model of human problem-solving, the General Problem Solver.
1962	M S Gazzaniga, J E Bogen, and R W Sperry first reported on the 'split brain' phenomenon in epileptic patients.
1963	Stanley Milgram published his first studies of obedience and the conditions under which individuals will inflict harm when so instructed.
1967	Konovski published *Integrative Activity of the Brain,* a melding of conditioning principles with sensation and motivation. Ulrich Neisser's *Cognitive Psychology* marked renewed interest in the study of cognition after years in which behaviourism had dominated.
1968	R C Atkinson and R M Shiffin developed their theory of interacting memory systems in cognitive processing.
1970	T Shallice and E K Warrington provided the first of much evidence from brain-damaged patients that short-term memory is parallel with long-term memory and is best viewed as a collection of separate processing modules.
1972	E Tulving distinguished episodic memory (for personal experience) and semantic memory (for general knowledge and facts about the world).
1983	J A Fodor published *The Modularity of Mind,* dividing the mind into independent cognitive processors and defining their activity.
1985	A new view of intelligence proposed by Robert J Sternberg in *Beyond IQ: A Triarchic Theory of Intelligence.*
1986	J L McClelland and D E Rumelhart developed complex computational networks using parallel processing to simulate human learning and categorization.
1989	The mathematician Roger Penrose, in *The Emperor's New Mind,* argued that the computational account of the mind is incomplete, particularly concerning consciousness.
1992	The philosopher John Searle, in *The Rediscovery of the Mind,* argued for the return of consciousness to its position as the central topic in psychology and cognitive science.

and objective scientific methods to the study of a wide range of mental processes and behaviour, whereas **social psychology** concerns the study of individuals within their social environment; for example, within groups and organizations. This has led to the development of related fields such as **occupational psychology**, which studies human behaviour at work, and **educational psychology**. **Clinical psychology** concerns the understanding and treatment of mental health disorders, such as anxiety, phobias, or depression; treatment may include behaviour therapy, cognitive therapy, counselling, psychoanalysis, or some combination of these.

Modern studies have been diverse; for example, the psychological causes of obesity; the nature of religious experience; and the underachievement of women seen as resulting from social pressures. Other related subjects are the nature of sleep and dreams, and the possible extensions of the senses, which leads to the more contentious ground of ◊parapsychology.

psychometrics measurement of mental processes. This includes intelligence and aptitude testing to help in job selection and in the clinical assessment of cognitive deficiencies resulting from brain damage.

psychopathy personality disorder characterized by chronic antisocial behaviour (violating the rights of others, often violently) and an absence of feelings of guilt about the behaviour.

Because the term 'psychopathy' has been misused to refer to any severe mental disorder, many psychologists now prefer the term 'antisocial personality disorder', though this also includes cases in which absence or a lesser degree of guilt is not a characteristic feature.

psychosis or ***psychotic disorder*** general term for a serious mental disorder where the individual commonly loses contact with reality and may experience hallucinations (seeing or hearing things that do not exist) or delusions (fixed false beliefs). For example, in a paranoid psychosis, an individual may believe that others are plotting against him or her. A major type of psychosis is ◊schizophrenia.

psychosomatic of a physical symptom or disease thought to arise from emotional or mental factors.

The term 'psychosomatic' has been applied to many conditions, including asthma, migraine, hypertension, and peptic ulcers. Whereas it is unlikely that these and other conditions are wholly due to psychological factors, emotional states such as anxiety or depression do have a distinct influence on the frequency and severity of illness.

psychosurgery operation to relieve severe mental illness. See ◊leucotomy.

psychotherapy any treatment for psychological problems that involves talking rather than surgery or drugs. Examples include ◊cognitive therapy and ◊psychoanalysis.

psychotic disorder another name for ◊psychosis.

pt symbol for ◊pint.

ptarmigan hardy, northern ground-dwelling bird of genus *Lagopus,* family Phasianidae (which also includes ◊grouse), with feathered legs and feet.

The willow ptarmigan *L. lagopus,* found in bushes and heather in northern parts of North America, Europe, and Asia, grows to 38 cm/15 in and turns white in the winter.

pteridophyte simple type of ◊vascular plant. The pteridophytes comprise four classes: the Psilosida, including the most primitive vascular plants, found mainly in the tropics; the Lycopsida, including the club mosses; the Sphenopsida, including the horsetails; and the Pteropsida, including the ferns. They do not produce seeds.

They are mainly terrestrial, non-flowering plants characterized by the presence of a vascular system; the possession of true stems, roots, and leaves; and by a marked ◊alternation of generations, with the sporophyte forming the dominant generation in the life cycle. The pteridophytes formed a large and dominant flora during the Carboniferous period, but many are now known only from fossils.

pterodactyl genus of ◊pterosaur.

pterosaur extinct flying reptile of the order Pterosauria, existing in the Mesozoic age. They ranged from the size of a starling to the 12 m/39 ft wingspan of *Arambourgiania philadelphiae;* the largest of the pterosaurs discovered so far. Some had horns on their heads that, when in flight, made a whistling to roaring sound.

Pterosaurs were formerly assumed to be smooth-skinned gliders, but recent discoveries show that at least some were furry, probably warm-blooded, and may have had muscle fibres and blood vessels on their wings, stiffened by moving the hind legs, thus allowing controlled and strong flapping flight.

Ptolemy
(c. AD 100–c. AD 170)

(Claudius Ptolemaeus) Egyptian astronomer and geographer. His *Almagest* developed the theory that Earth is the centre of the universe, with the Sun, Moon, and stars revolving around it. In 1543 the Polish astronomer Copernicus proposed an alternative to the **Ptolemaic system.** Ptolemy's *Geography* was a standard source of information until the 16th century.

The *Almagest* (he called it *Syntaxis*) contains all his works on astronomical themes, the only authoritative works until the time of Copernicus. Probably inspired by Plato, Ptolemy began with the premise that the Earth was a perfect sphere. All planetry orbits were circular, but those of Mercury and Venus, and possibly Mars (Ptolemy was not sure), were epicyclic (the planets orbited a point that itself was orbiting the Earth). The sphere of the stars formed a dome with points of light attached or pricked through.

Mary Evans Picture Library

PTFE abbreviation for ◊polytetrafluoroethene.

ptomaine any of a group of toxic chemical substances (alkaloids) produced as a result of decomposition by bacterial action on proteins.

puberty stage in human development when the individual becomes sexually mature. It may occur from the age of ten upwards. The sexual organs take on their adult form and pubic hair grows. In girls, menstruation begins, and the breasts develop; in boys, the voice breaks and becomes deeper, and facial hair develops.

pubes lowest part of the front of the human trunk, the region where the external generative organs are situated. The underlying bony structure, the pubic arch, is formed by the union in the midline of the two pubic bones, which are the front portions of the hip bones. In women this is more prominent than in men, to allow more room for the passage of the child's head at birth, and it carries a pad of fat and connective tissue, the *mons veneris* (mount of Venus), for its protection.

public-domain software any computer program that is not under copyright and can therefore be used freely without charge. Much of this software has been written in US universities, under government contract. Public-domain software should not be confused with ◊shareware, which is under copyright.

public key in ◊public-key cryptography, a string of ◊bits that is associated with a particular person and that may be used to decrypt messages from that person or to encrypt messages to him/her.

public-key cryptography system that allows remote users to exchange encrypted data without the need to transmit a secret key in advance. Under this system, first proposed by Whitfield Diffie and Martin Hellman in a widely read and influential paper 'New Directions in Cryptography' 1976, each party has a personal pair of keys, one private and one public. The private key is kept secret and not given out to anyone. The public key, however, is distributed widely, to friends, business partners, and even to public key servers – computers which store many users' public keys so that anyone can obtain a copy. Each user asks as many people as possible to sign his/her public key, to verify that it is actually his/hers.

The two keys are complementary. The sender of a message – usually known as Bob – encrypts his message with his private key and sends it to the recipient, usually called Alice. She decrypts it with her public key and by doing so verifies that the message came from him. If Bob wants the message to be unreadable by anyone but Alice, he encrypts it with her public key so it can only be decrypted with her private key, which she is keeping secret. Using both sets of keys authenticates the message and ensures its privacy.

Several ◊algorithms in common use apply public-key cryptography, including the ◊RSA algorithm, published in 1977 in *Scientific American* and named after its inventors, Ronald Rivest, Adi Shamir, and Leonard Adleman, and the Skipjack algorithm used in the ◊Clipper chip. The disadvantage is that it is extremely slow, so it is common on the Net to see ◊Pretty Good Privacy (PGP), which uses RSA, being used only to encrypt a digest of the message generated using a ◊hash function. This is appended to the end of the message along with a listing of the user's public key.

public news server in computing, site, often provided by an institution, which provides free access to ◊USENET. Public news servers offer an alternative to taking a news feed from an ◊Internet Service Provider (ISP).

puddle clay clay, with sand or gravel, that has had water added and mixed thoroughly so that it becomes watertight. The term was coined in 1762 by the canal builder James Brindley, although the use of such clay in dams goes back to Roman times.

puff adder variety of ◊adder, a poisonous snake.

puffball ball-shaped fruiting body of certain fungi (see ◊fungus) that cracks open when it ripens, releasing the enclosed spores in the form of a brown powder; for example, the common puffball (*L. perlatum*). (Genera *Lycoperdon* and *Calvatia.*)

PUFFBALL

The giant puffball fungus can grow up to 1.8 m/6 ft in circumference.

puffer fish fish of the family Tetraodontidae. As a means of defence it inflates its body with water until it becomes spherical and the skin spines become erect. Puffer fish are mainly found in warm waters, where they feed on molluscs, crustaceans, and coral.

There are approximately 120 puffer fish species. They vary in size, up to 50 cm/20 in long. To allow inflation, they have elastic skin and no ribs. The skin of some puffer fish is poisonous (25 times more toxic than cyanide). In Japan, where they are called *fugu,* they are prized as a delicacy after the poison has been removed. Nevertheless, the death of about 100 diners is recorded each year.

puffin any of various sea birds of the genus *Fratercula* of the ◊auk family, found in the N Atlantic and Pacific. The puffin is about 35 cm/14 in long, with a white face and front, red legs, and a large deep bill, very brightly coloured in summer. Having short wings and webbed feet, puffins are poor fliers but excellent swimmers. They nest in rock crevices, or make burrows, and lay a single egg.

pug breed of small dog with short wrinkled face, hanging ears, chunky body, and tail curled over the hip. It weighs 6–8 kg/13–18 lb. Its short coat may be black, beige or grey; the beige or grey dogs have black on the face and ears.

Pugwash group of scientists working towards nuclear disarmament. It came into being 1954 following a suggestion by Bertrand ◊Russell to Polish physicist Joseph Rotblat. The name derives from the Nova Scotian town where the first meeting was held. Pugwash shared the 1995 Nobel Peace Prize with Rotblat.

The Pugwash conference in 1961 included both the US presidential science adviser and the vice president of the Soviet Academy of Sciences and led to a follow-on discussion with President Kennedy on a nuclear test ban (a test-ban treaty was signed in 1963).

puli breed of herding dog originating in Hungary. It has a long black or dark grey coat with a rough 'corded' texture. The puli stands about 44 cm/17 in tall. Its head is rounded, with a short muzzle, drooping ears, and its tail is curved back.

pull-down menu in computing, a list of options provided as part of a ◊graphical user interface. The presence of pull-down menus is normally indicated by a row of single words at the top of the screen. When the user points at a word with a ◊mouse, a full menu appears (is pulled down) and the user can then select the required option. Compare with ◊pop-up menu.

In some graphical user interfaces the menus appear from the bottom of the screen and in others they may appear at any point on the screen when a special menu button is pressed on the mouse.

pulley simple machine consisting of a fixed, grooved wheel, sometimes in a block, around which a rope or chain can be run. A simple pulley serves only to change the direction of the applied effort (as in a simple hoist for raising loads). The use of more than one pulley results in a mechanical advantage, so that a given effort can raise a heavier load.

The mechanical advantage depends on the arrangement of the pulleys. For instance, a block and tackle arrangement with three ropes supporting the load will lift it with one-third of the effort needed to lift it directly (if friction is ignored), giving a mechanical advantage of three.

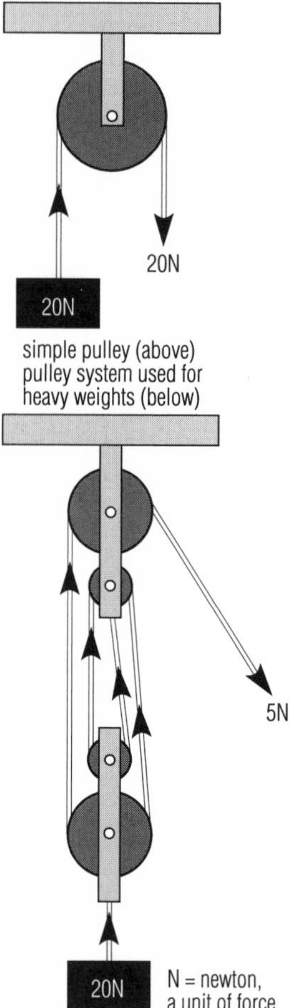

pulley The mechanical advantage of a pulley increases with the number of rope strands. If a pulley system has four ropes supporting the load, the mechanical advantage is four, and a 5 Newton force will lift a 20 Newton load.

pulmonary pertaining to the ◊lungs.

pulsar celestial source that emits pulses of energy at regular intervals, ranging from a few seconds to a few thousandths of a second. Pulsars are thought to be rapidly rotating ◊neutron stars, which flash at radio and other wavelengths as they spin. They were discovered in 1967 by Jocelyn ◊Bell Burnell and Antony Hewish at the Mullard Radio Astronomy Observatory, Cambridge, England. Over 500 radio pulsars are now known in our Galaxy, although a million or so may exist.

LITTLE GREEN MEN, WHITE DWARFS, OR PULSARS?

http://www.bigear.org/vol1no1/burnell.htm

Entertaining first-hand history of the discovery of pulsars. This is the text of an after-dinner speech given by Bell Burnell. It gives an intimate account of the excitement and challenges of gamma and X-ray astronomy. There is also a brief biography of the pioneering astronomer.

Pulsar: Discovery

by Peter Lafferty

Little green men?

Making a major scientific discovery is not as many people imagine; often, there is no 'eureka moment' or single instant of discovery. Discovery is more often a process of checking and rechecking, of gradually eliminating spurious effects, until the truth is apparent. The discovery of the first pulsar shows this process in action.

Luck played a part in the discovery. In 1967 Antony Hewish at the Mullard Radio Astronomy Laboratory, Cambridge, England, constructed a new type of radio telescope – a large array of 2,048 aerials covering an area of 1.8 hectares/4.4 acres – to study the 'twinkling' or scintillation of radio galaxies. This is caused by clouds of ionized gas ejected from the Sun. It is most noticeable at metre wavelengths, so the new telescope had to be sensitive to radiation of this wavelength. Most radio telescopes achieve high sensitivity by averaging incoming signals for several seconds, and so are unsuitable for studying rapidly varying signals. They collect radiation with wavelengths of around a centimetre. The new telescope's ability to detect rapidly varying signals of metre wavelength was just what was needed to detect a pulsar.

Twinkle, twinkle, little galaxy

The telescope began work in July 1967. Its first task was to locate all radio galaxies twinkling in the area of sky accessible to it. Each day, as the Earth rotated, the telescope swept its radio eye across a band of sky. A complete scan took four days. Initially a graduate student, Jocelyn Bell, ran the survey and analysed the results, output on about 30 m/100 ft of chart paper each day.

After a few weeks, Bell noticed an unusual signal: not a single blip, but an untidy bunch of squiggles on the chart. It was nothing like the signals she was looking for, so she marked a query on the chart and did not investigate further. Later, when she saw the same signal on another chart, she realized it merited closer attention. The signal came from a part of the sky where scintillations were normally weak. It occurred at night, and scintillations are strongest during the day. A faster chart recorder was installed for a more detailed look at the signal. It would stretch out the signal over a longer chart, like a photographic enlargement.

What was going on?

For a while, Bell and Hewish's efforts were frustrated – the signal weakened and vanished. For a month, there was no sign of it. The researchers feared that they had seen a one-off event: possibly a star flaring brightly for a short time. If so, they had missed the chance to study it in detail. However, on 28 November, it returned. This time, the new recorder revealed the true nature of the signal. It was a series of short pulses about 1.3 seconds apart. Timing the pulses more accurately showed that they were in step to within one-millionth of a second. Their short duration indicated that they were coming from a very small object. Something peculiar was going on, but what?

The task now was to rule out spurious effects. Did the signal result from a machine malfunction? Was it caused by a satellite signal? Or a radar echo from the Moon? The fact that the signal appeared at regular intervals hinted that it was not a machine malfunction. Having calculated when the signal would next appear, at the appointed time the research team stood around the recorder. Nothing! Hewish and the others began to wander away. But before they reached the door, they were called back. 'Here it is!' said a student. They had miscalculated when the signal would be picked up. They knew now that it came from outside the laboratory.

Is there anybody there?

Further study established that the signal rotated with the stars, and came from beyond the Solar System, but from within our galaxy. At one stage, Hewish thought that the signal might be a message from an extraterrestrial civilization. It was given the name 'LGM', for 'little green men'. However, this possibility was ruled out. Other beings must live on a planet circling round a star. The planetary motion would show up as a slight variation in the pulse rate. After carefully timing the pulses for several weeks, the idea of a planetary origin was given up.

On 21 December 1967 Bell discovered a second signal elsewhere in the sky. This clinched the reality of the phenomenon, and the name 'pulsar' was quickly coined to describe the object radiating the pulsation. The results were published in February 1968; within a year it was generally accepted that the signals came from rapidly spinning neutron stars. Since then more than 500 pulsars have been discovered. Antony Hewish shared the 1974 Nobel Prize for physics with British radio astronomer Martin Ryle for their work in radio astronomy and, in particular, the discovery of pulsars.

Pulsars slow down as they get older, and eventually the flashes fade. Of the 500 known radio pulsars, 20 are millisecond pulsars (flashing 1,000 times a second). Such pulsars are thought to be more than a billion years old. Two pulsars, one (estimated to be 1,000 years old) in the Crab nebula and one (estimated to be 11,000 years old) in the constellation Vela, give out flashes of visible light.

pulse impulse transmitted by the heartbeat throughout the arterial systems of vertebrates. When the heart muscle contracts, it forces blood into the ◊aorta (the chief artery). Because the arteries are elastic, the sudden rise of pressure causes a throb or sudden swelling through them. The actual flow of the blood is about 60 cm/2 ft a second in humans. The average adult pulse rate is generally about 70 per minute. The pulse can be felt where an artery is near the surface, for example in the wrist or the neck.

pulse crop such as peas and beans. Pulses are grown primarily for their seeds, which provide a concentrated source of vegetable protein, and make a vital contribution to human diets in poor countries where meat is scarce, and among vegetarians. Soya beans are the major temperate protein crop in the West; most are used for oil production or for animal feed. In Asia, most are processed into soya milk and beancurd. Peanuts dominate pulse production in the tropical world and are generally consumed as human food.

Pulses play a useful role in ◊crop rotation as they help to raise soil nitrogen levels as well as acting as break crops. In the mid-1980s, world production was about 50 million tonnes a year.

pulse-code modulation (PCM) in physics, a form of digital ◊modulation in which microwaves or light waves (the carrier waves) are switched on and off in pulses of varying length according to a binary code. It is a relatively simple matter to transmit data that are already in binary code, such as those used by computer, by these means. However, if an analogue audio signal is to be transmitted, it must first be converted to a **pulse-amplitude modulated** signal (PAM) by regular sampling of its amplitude. The value of the amplitude is then converted into a binary code for transmission on the carrier wave.

puma also called ***cougar*** or ***mountain lion*** large wild cat *Felis concolor* found in North and South America. Tawny-coated, it is 1.5 m/4.5 ft long with a 1-m/3-ft tail. Cougars live alone, with each male occupying a distinct territory; they eat deer, rodents, and cattle. Although in some areas they have been hunted nearly to extinction, in California puma populations have grown, with numbers reaching an estimated 5,000–6,000 by 1996.

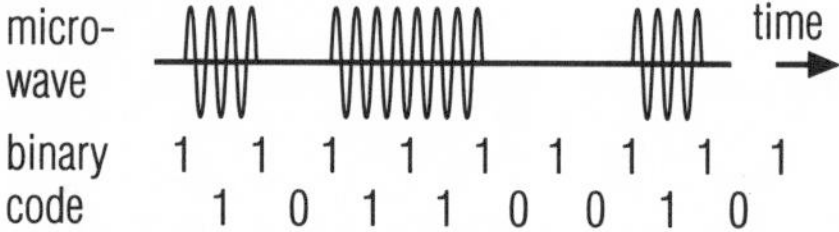

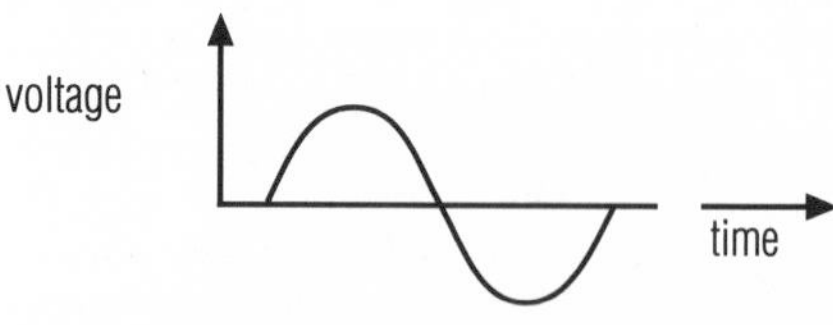

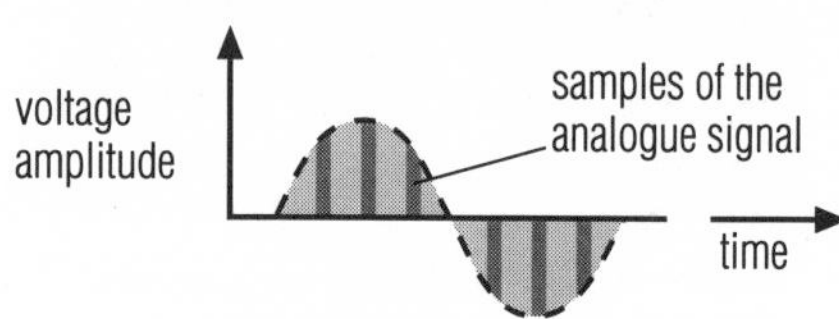

***pulse-code modulation** The amplitude, duration, position and presence of a series of pulses are controlled in pulse-code modulation, which is relatively simple for digital data already in binary code. Analogue signals need to be converted into a recognizable binary code (a pulse-amplitude modulated signal) by regular sampling of its amplitude. Morse code is a very simple example of pulse-code modulation.*

pumice light volcanic rock produced by the frothing action of expanding gases during the solidification of lava. It has the texture of a hard sponge and is used as an abrasive.

pump any device for moving liquids and gases, or compressing gases.

Some pumps, such as the traditional **lift pump** used to raise water from wells, work by a reciprocating (up-and-down) action. Movement of a piston in a cylinder with a one-way valve creates a partial vacuum in the cylinder, thereby sucking water into it.

Gear pumps, used to pump oil in a car's lubrication system, have two meshing gears that rotate inside a housing, and the teeth move the oil. **Rotary pumps** contain a rotor with vanes projecting from it inside a casing, sweeping the liquid round as they move.

pumped storage hydroelectric plant that uses surplus electricity to pump water back into a high-level reservoir. In normal working conditions the water flows from this reservoir through the turbines to generate power for feeding into the grid. At times of low power demand, electricity is taken from the grid to turn the ◊turbines into pumps that then pump the water back again. This ensures that there is always a maximum 'head' of water in the reservoir to give the maximum output when required.

pumpkin creeping plant whose large round fruit has a thick orange rind, pulpy flesh, and many seeds. Pumpkins are used in cookery (especially pies and soups) and are hollowed out to form candle lanterns at Hallowe'en. (*Cucurbita pepo*, family Cucurbitaceae.)

punched card in computing, an early form of data storage and input, now almost obsolete. The 80-column card widely used in the 1960s and 1970s was a thin card, measuring 190 mm x 84 mm/7.5 in x 3.33 in, holding up to 80 characters of data encoded as small rectangular holes.

The punched card was invented by French textile manufacturer Joseph-Marie Jacquard (1752–1834) about 1801 to control weaving looms. The first data-processing machine using punched cards was developed by US inventor Herman Hollerith in the 1880s for the US census.

punctuated equilibrium model evolutionary theory developed by Niles Eldredge and US palaeontologist Stephen Jay Gould in 1972 to explain discontinuities in the fossil record. It claims that periods of rapid change alternate with periods of relative stability (stasis), and that the appearance of new lineages is a separate process from the gradual evolution of adaptive changes within a species.

The pattern of stasis and more rapid change is now widely accepted, but the second part of the theory remains unsubstantiated.

The **turnover pulse hypothesis** of US biologist Elisabeth Vrba postulates that the periods of rapid evolutionary change are triggered by environmental changes, particularly changes in climate.

punnett square graphic technique used in genetics for determining the likely outcome, in statistical terms, of a genetic cross. It resembles a game of noughts and crosses, in which the genotypes of the parental generation gametes are entered first, so that the subsequent combinations can then be calculated.

pupa nonfeeding, largely immobile stage of some insect life cycles, in which larval tissues are broken down, and adult tissues and structures are formed.

In many insects, the pupa is **exarate**, with the appendages (legs, antennae, wings) visible outside the pupal case; in butterflies and moths, it is called a chrysalis, and is **obtect**, with the appendages developing inside the case.

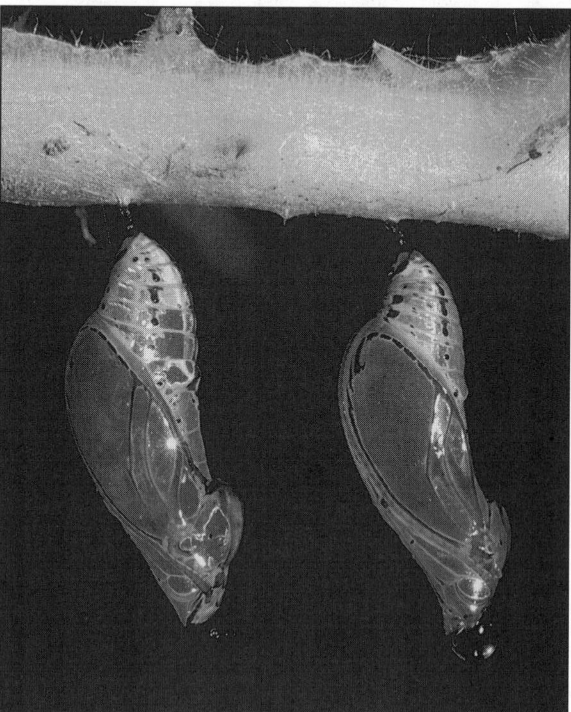

***pupa** The pupae or chrysalises produced by many butterflies inhabiting tropical rainforests often bear a striking resemblance to a large drop of water. In an environment where water drips almost constantly from leaves, this makes them less conspicuous to predators. Premaphotos Wildlife*

Purkinje, Jan Evangelista (1787–1869)

Czech physiologist who made pioneering studies of vision, the functioning of the brain and heart, pharmacology, embryology, and cells and tissue. In 1819 Purkinje described the visual phenomenon in which different-coloured objects of equal brightness in certain circumstances appear to the eye to be unequally bright; this is now called the Purkinje effect.

purple emperor handsome high-flying butterfly, with rusty black wings, lustrous in the male, and with seven white spots and a transverse white band.
classification The purple emperor *Apatura iris* is in order Lepidoptera, class Insecta, phylum Arthropoda.

purpura condition marked by purplish patches on the skin or mucous membranes due to localized spontaneous bleeding. It may be harmless, as sometimes with the elderly, or linked with disease, allergy, or drug reactions.

pus yellowish fluid that forms in the body as a result of bacterial infection; it includes white blood cells (leucocytes), living and dead bacteria, dead tissue, and serum. An enclosed collection of pus is called an abscess.

push-button in computing, in a ◊dialog box or ◊toolbar, a square, oval, or oblong button which presents the user with an option. By clicking on the button, the user opts to initiate an action such as centering text or saving a file. Most programs offer keyboard ◊shortcuts as an alternative to using a push-button, for example one can often hit the return key instead of clicking the 'OK' button in a dialogue box. Compare ◊radio button.

putrefaction decomposition of organic matter by microorganisms.

PVC abbreviation for ◊polyvinyl chloride.

P-wave (abbreviation of ***primary wave***) in seismology, a class of seismic wave that passes through the Earth in the form of longitudinal pressure waves at speeds of 6–7 kps/3.7–4.4 mps in the crust and up to 13 kps/8 mps in deeper layers. P–waves from an earthquake travel faster than S–waves and are the first to arrive at monitoring stations (hence primary waves). They can travel both through solid rock and the liquid outer core of the Earth.

PWR abbreviation for ◊pressurized water reactor, **a type of nuclear reactor**.

pyelitis inflammation of the renal pelvis, the central part of the kidney where urine accumulates before discharge. It is caused by bacterial infection and is more common in women than in men.

pyramid in geometry, a three-dimensional figure with triangular side-faces meeting at a common vertex (point) and with a ◊polygon as its base. The volume V of a pyramid is given by $V = \frac{1}{3}Bh$, where B is the area of the base and h is the perpendicular height.

Pyramids are generally classified by their bases. For example, the Egyptian pyramids have square bases, and are therefore called square pyramids. Triangular pyramids are also known as tetrahedra ('four sides').

pyramid of numbers in ecology, a diagram that shows how many plants and animals there are at different levels of a ◊food chain.

There are always far fewer individuals at the top of the chain than at the bottom because only about 10% of the food an animal eats is turned into flesh, so the amount of food flowing through the chain drops at each step. In a pyramid of numbers, the primary producers (usually plants) are represented at the bottom by a broad band, the plant-eaters are shown above by a narrower band, and the animals that prey on them by a narrower band still. At the top of the pyramid are the 'top carnivores' such as lions and sharks, which are present in the smallest number.

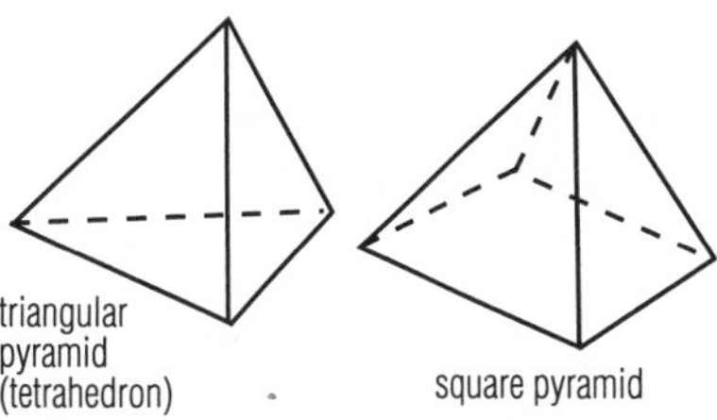

Types of pyramid.

pyrethrum popular name for several cultivated chrysanthemums. The ornamental species *C. coccineum,* and hybrids derived from it, are commonly grown in gardens. Pyrethrum powder, made from the dried flower heads of some species, is a powerful pesticide for aphids and mosquitoes. (Genus *Chrysanthemum,* family Compositae.)

pyridine C_5H_5N a heterocyclic compound (see ◊cyclic compounds). It is a liquid with a sickly smell and occurs in coal tar. It is soluble in water, acts as a strong ◊base, and is used as a solvent, mainly in the manufacture of plastics.

pyridoxine or ***vitamin*** B_6 $C_8H_{11}NO_3$ water-soluble ◊vitamin of the B complex. There is no clearly identifiable disease associated with deficiency but its absence from the diet can give rise to malfunction of the central nervous system and general skin disorders. Good sources are liver, meat, milk, and cereal grains. Related compounds may also show vitamin B_6 activity.

pyrite iron sulphide FeS_2; also called **fool's gold** because of its yellow metallic lustre. Pyrite has a hardness of 6–6.5 on the Mohs' scale. It is used in the production of sulphuric acid.

pyrogallol $C_6H_3OH_3$ (technical name **trihydroxybenzene**) derivative of benzene, prepared from gallic acid. It is used in gas analysis for the measurement of oxygen because its alkaline solution turns black as it rapidly absorbs oxygen. It is also used as a developer in photography.

pyrolysis decomposition of a substance by heating it to a high temperature in the absence of air. The process is used to burn and dispose of old tyres, for example, without contaminating the atmosphere.

pyrometer in physics, any instrument used for measuring high temperatures by means of the thermal radiation emitted by a hot object. In a **radiation pyrometer** the emitted radiation is detected by a sensor such as a thermocouple. In an **optical pyrometer** the colour of an electrically heated filament is matched visually to that of the emitted radiation. Pyrometers are especially useful for measuring the temperature of distant, moving or inaccessible objects.

pyroxene any one of a group of minerals, silicates of calcium, iron, and magnesium with a general formula X,YSi_2O_6, found in igneous and metamorphic rocks. The internal structure is based on single chains of silicon and oxygen. Diopside (X = Ca, Y = Mg) and

PYTHAGORAS' THEOREM

http://www-groups.dcs.st-and.ac.uk/~history/Diagrams/PythagorasTheorem.gif

Simple site giving visual proof of Pythagoras's famous theorem.

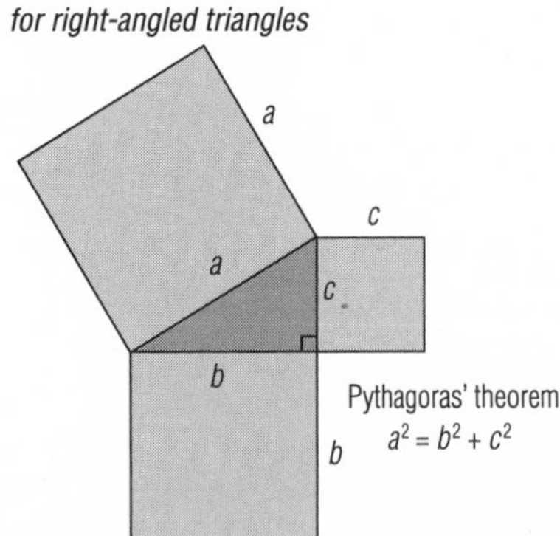

Pythagoras' theorem *Pythagoras' theorem for right-angled triangles is likely to have been known long before the time of Pythagoras. It was probably used by the ancient Egyptians to lay out the pyramids.*

Pythagoras
(c. 580–500 BC)

Greek mathematician and philosopher who formulated Pythagoras' theorem.

Much of Pythagoras' work concerned numbers, to which he assigned mystical properties. For example, he classified numbers into triangular ones (1, 3, 6, 10, ...), which can be represented as a triangular array, and square ones (1, 4, 9, 16, ...), which form squares. He also observed that any two adjacent triangular numbers add to a square number (for example, $1 + 3 = 4$; $3 + 6 = 9$; $6 + 10 = 16$).

Mary Evans Picture Library

augite (X = Ca, Y = Mg,Fe,Al) are common pyroxenes.

Jadeite ($NaAlSi_2O_6$), which is considered the more valuable form of jade, is also a pyroxene.

Pythagoras' theorem in geometry, a theorem stating that in a right-angled triangle, the area of the square on the hypotenuse (the longest side) is equal to the sum of the areas of the squares drawn on the other two sides. If the hypotenuse is h units long and the lengths of the other sides are a and b, then $h^2 = a^2 + b^2$.

The theorem provides a way of calculating the length of any side of a right-angled triangle if the lengths of the other two sides are known. It is also used to determine certain trigonometrical relationships such as $\sin^2 \theta + \cos^2 \theta = 1$.

python any constricting snake of the Old World subfamily Pythoninae of the family Boidae, which also includes ◊boas and the ◊anaconda. Pythons are found in the tropics of Africa, Asia, and Australia. Unlike boas, they lay eggs rather than produce living young. Some species are small, but the reticulated python *Python reticulatus* of SE Asia can grow to 10 m/33 ft.

A healthy adult can survive from six to twelve months without food. When food is scarce females do not ovulate so energy is not used up in reproducing.

qat or ***kat*** or ***khat*** evergreen shrub with white flowers belonging to the staff-tree family, native to Africa and Asia. The leaves are chewed as a mild narcotic drug in some Arab countries. Its use was banned in Somalia 1983. (*Catha edulis,* family Celastraceae.)

quadrat in environmental studies, a square structure used to study the distribution of plants in a particular place, for instance a field, rocky shore, or mountainside. The size varies, but is usually 0.5 or 1 metre square, small enough to be carried easily. The quadrat is placed on the ground and the abundance of species estimated. By making such measurements a reliable understanding of species distribution is obtained.

QUADRATIC, CUBIC, AND QUARTIC EQUATIONS

http://ww-history.mcs.st-and.ac.uk/~history/HistTopics/Quadratic_etc_equations.html

History and usage of quadratic equations in mathematics. The site chronicles the discovery and development of this area of mathematics, and also provides biographical background information on those mathematicians responsible.

quadratic equation in mathematics, a polynomial equation of second degree (that is, an equation containing as its highest power the square of a variable, such as x^2). The general formula of such equations is $ax^2 + bx + c = 0$, in which *a, b,* and *c* are real numbers, and only the coefficient *a* cannot equal 0.

In ◊coordinate geometry, a quadratic function represents a ◊parabola.

Some quadratic equations can be solved by factorization, or the values of *x* can be found by using the formula for the general solution $x = [-b \pm \sqrt{(b^2 - 4ac)}]/2a$. Depending on the value of the discriminant $b^2 - 4ac$, a quadratic equation has two real, two equal, or two complex roots (solutions). When $b^2 - 4ac > 0$, there are two distinct real roots. When $b^2 - 4ac = 0$, there are two equal real roots. When $b^2 - 4ac < 0$, there are two distinct complex roots.

quadrature position of the Moon or an outer planet where a line between it and Earth makes a right angle with a line joining Earth to the Sun.

quadrilateral plane (two-dimensional) figure with four straight sides. The following are all quadrilaterals, each with distinguishing properties: **square** with four equal angles and sides, four axes of symmetry; **rectangle** with four equal angles, opposite sides equal, two axes of symmetry; **rhombus** with four equal sides, two axes of symmetry; **parallelogram** with two pairs of parallel sides, rotational symmetry; and **trapezium** one pair of parallel sides.

quad speed in computing, a ◊CD-ROM drive that transfers data at 600 ◊kilobytes per second – four times as fast as the first CD-ROM drives on the market. Because ◊access time remains a key factor in the movement of data, the extra speed does not necessarily translate into a fourfold improvement in performance.

quagga South African zebra that became extinct in the 1880s. It was brown, with a white tail and legs, and unlike surviving zebra species, had stripes only on its head, neck, and forequarters. An intriguing attempt to recreate the quagga by breeding from a zebra with poorly developed stripes began in 1991.

quail any of several genera of small ground-dwelling birds of the family Phasianidae, which also includes grouse, pheasants, bobwhites, and prairie chickens. Species are found in Africa, India, Australia, North America, and Europe.

species The **common** or **European quail** *Coturnix coturnix* is about 18 cm/7 in long, reddish-brown, with a white throat with a black

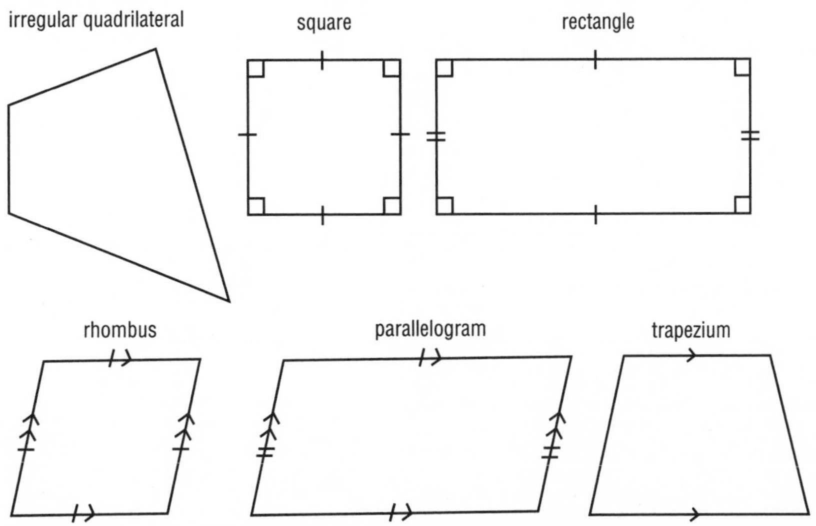

quadrilateral *A quadrilateral is a plane figure with four straight sides. The diagram shows different types of quadrilateral, each with distinguishing properties. A square has four equal angles, four axes of symmetry; a rectangle has four equal angles, two axes of symmetry; a rhombus has four equal sides, two axes of symmetry; a parallelogram has two pairs of parallel sides, rotational symmetry; and a trapezium has one pair of parallel sides.*

patch at the bottom, and a yellowish belly. It is found in Europe, Asia, and Africa, and has been introduced to North America. The nest is a small hollow in the ground, and in it are laid about ten yellowish-white eggs blotched with brown. The bird feeds upon grain seeds and insects.

Quake computer game released 1996 as a successor to ◊*Doom* and produced by id Software. It is a strategy game using ◊3-D graphics.

Players navigate their way around 32 levels of mazes, uncovering secrets and combatting alien enemies. A command line console system allows players to enter ◊source code to enhance play.

qualitative analysis in chemistry, a procedure for determining the identity of the component(s) of a single substance or mixture. A series of simple reactions and tests can be carried out on a compound to determine the elements present.

quantitative analysis in chemistry, a procedure for determining the precise amount of a known component present in a single substance or mixture. A known amount of the substance is subjected to particular procedures.

Gravimetric analysis determines the mass of each constituent present; ◊**volumetric analysis** determines the concentration of a solution by titration against a solution of known concentration.

quantum chromodynamics (QCD) in physics, a theory describing the interactions of ◊quarks, the ◊elementary particles that make up all ◊hadrons (subatomic particles such as protons and neutrons). In quantum chromodynamics, quarks are considered to interact by exchanging particles called gluons, which carry the ◊strong nuclear force, and whose role is to 'glue' quarks together.

The mathematics involved in the theory is complex, and, although a number of successful predictions have been made, the theory does not compare in accuracy with ◊quantum electrodynamics, upon which it is modelled. See ◊forces, fundamental.

quantum electrodynamics (QED) in physics, a theory describing the interaction of charged subatomic particles within electric and magnetic fields. It combines ◊quantum theory and ◊relativity, and considers charged particles to interact by the exchange of photons. QED is remarkable for the accuracy of its predictions; for example, it has been used to calculate the value of some physical quantities to an accuracy of ten decimal places, a feat equivalent to calculating the distance between New York and Los Angeles to within the thickness of a hair. The theory was developed by US physicists Richard Feynman and Julian Schwinger, and by Japanese physicist Sin-Itiro Tomonaga in 1948.

quantum mechanics branch of physics dealing with the interaction of ◊matter and ◊radiation, the structure of the atom, the motion of atomic particles, and with related phenomena (see ◊elementary particle and ◊quantum theory).

This problem of getting the interpretation proved to be rather more difficult than just working out the equations.

PAUL DIRAC British physicist.
Hungarian Academy of Sciences Report (on quantum mechanics)

quantum number in physics, one of a set of four numbers that uniquely characterize an ◊electron and its state in an ◊atom. The **principal quantum number** *n* defines the electron's main energy level. The **orbital quantum number** *l* relates to its angular momentum. The **magnetic quantum number** *m* describes the energies of electrons in a magnetic field. The **spin quantum number** m_s gives the spin direction of the electron.

The principal quantum number, defining the electron's energy level, corresponds to shells (energy levels) also known by their spectroscopic designations K, L, M, and so on. The orbital quantum number gives rise to a series of subshells designated *s, p, d, f,* and so on, of slightly different energy levels. The magnetic quantum number allows further subdivision of the subshells (making three subdivisions p_x, p_y, and p_z in the *p* subshell, for example, of the same energy level). No two electrons in an atom can have the same set of quantum numbers (the ◊Pauli exclusion principle).

quantum simulation the use of ◊computer simulation to study the quantum behaviour of matter. Simulations based on just 50 or 60 atoms are able to mimic the properties of real matter. If a small group of atoms is surrounded by other identical groups every atom behaves as if it were part of a larger material. This makes it is possible, for example, to simulate the behaviour of solids and liquids at high temperatures, and to study chemical reactions at surfaces to aid in the design of better catalysts.

QUANTUM AGE BEGINS

http://www-history.mcs.st-and.ac.uk/~history/HistTopics/The_Quantum_age_begins.html

St Andrews University-run Web site chronicling the discovery of quantum theory. Biographical details of the mathematicians and physicists involved is also provided. The site also includes links to many other history of mathematics related Web resources.

quantum theory or ***quantum mechanics*** in physics, the theory that ◊energy does not have a continuous range of values, but is, instead, absorbed or radiated discontinuously, in multiples of definite, indivisible units called quanta. Just as earlier theory showed how light, generally seen as a wave motion, could also in some ways be seen as composed of discrete particles (◊photons), quantum theory shows how atomic particles such as electrons may also be seen as having wavelike properties. Quantum theory is the basis of particle physics, modern theoretical chemistry, and the solid-state physics that describes the behaviour of the silicon chips used in computers.

The theory began with the work of Max Planck in 1900 on radiated energy, and was extended by Albert Einstein to electromagnetic radiation generally, including light. Danish physicist Niels Bohr used it to explain the ◊spectrum of light emitted by excited hydrogen atoms. Later work by Erwin Schrödinger, Werner Heisenberg, Paul Dirac, and others elaborated the theory to what is called quantum mechanics (or wave mechanics).

Our task is not to penetrate into the essence of things, the meaning of which we don't know anyway, but rather to develop concepts which allow us to talk in a productive way about phenomena in nature.

NIELS BOHR Danish physicist.
Letter to H P E Hansen 20 July 1935

quarantine from French *quarantaine* '40 days' any period for which people, animals, plants, or vessels may be detained in isolation to prevent the spread of contagious disease.

quark in physics, the ◊elementary particle that is the fundamental constituent of all hadrons (subatomic particle that experiences the strong nuclear force and divided into baryons, such as neutrons and protons, and mesons). Quarks have electric charges that are fractions of the electronic charge ($+\frac{2}{3}$ or $-\frac{1}{3}$ of the electronic charge). There are six types, or 'flavours': up, down, top, bottom, strange, and charmed, each of which has three varieties, or 'colours': red, green, and blue (visual colour is not meant, although the analogy is useful in many ways). To each quark there is an antiparticle, called an antiquark. See ◊quantum chromodynamics.

The Top Quark

BY PETER RODGERS

The standard model

All forms of matter are made from two types of particles called quarks and leptons. These particles interact with each other through four forces: gravity, electromagnetism, and the strong and weak nuclear forces. All these forces are thought to be carried by other particles known as gauge bosons. This model of fundamental particles and their interactions is known as the *standard model of particle physics.*

Particle families

Quarks and leptons come in families. The lightest family contains the up quark, the down quark, the electron and the electron neutrino. The up quark has an electric charge of $+\frac{2}{3}$, the down quark has a charge of $-\frac{1}{3}$ and the electron has a charge of –1. The neutrino has no mass (i.e. it does not weigh anything) and no charge. Everyday matter is made up of up and down quarks and electrons. Single quarks have never been observed in experiments – they always combine in twos and threes to form other particles known as mesons and baryons. Each particle in the standard model also has an antiparticle with the same mass but opposite electric charge. One of the biggest mysteries in particle physics is why the universe is made of matter rather than antimatter.

Heavy particles

By the middle of 1980 physicists knew that there were only three families of particles. The second family comprised the charm and strange quarks, the muon, and the muon neutrino. These particles had the same pattern of behaviour as the particles in the first family but were heavier: the muon, for example, was 212 times heavier than the electron. The particles were also short-lived and decayed into lighter particles. The particles in the third family were heavier still and even more short-lived. The third family included the bottom quark and the tau lepton, both discovered in the mid 1970s. A sixth quark was needed to complete the picture but the top quark remained elusive until it was discovered at FermiLab in the US in 1995.

How to make new particles

The top quark was the last quark to be discovered because it was the heaviest. Physicists discover new particles by colliding high-energy beams of other particles together: the more energetic the collisions, the heavier the particles that can be discovered. The top quark turned out to have a mass of 175 gigaelectronvolts – as heavy as an atom of gold.

What next?

The top quark is not the end of the story. Physicists now hope to find the particle (or particles) which could explain why all the fundamental particles have very different masses. This particle is named after the British theoretical physicist Peter Higgs. Physicists hope to discover the Higgs particle at the large hadron collider (LHC), which is due to start in 2005 at the CERN laboratory near Geneva. The LHC will collide beams of high-energy protons in a circular particle accelerator with a circumference of 27 km/17 mi. LHC physicists also hope to discover supersymmetric particles. Supersymmetry is a theory which predicts that the two types of fundamental particles – quarks and leptons – are in fact related.

quart imperial liquid or dry measure, equal to two pints or 1.136 litres. In the USA, a liquid quart is equal to 0.946 litre, while a dry quart is equal to 1.101 litres.

quartile in statistics, any one of the three values of a variable that divide its distribution into four parts of equal frequency. They comprise the **lower quartile** (or 25th ◊percentile), below which lies the lowest 25% frequency distribution of a variable; the ◊median (or 50th percentile), which forms the dividing line between the upper, middle 25% and the lower, middle 25%; and the upper **quartile** (or 75th percentile), above which lies the top 25%. The difference of value between the upper and lower quartiles is known as the interquartile range, which is a useful measure of the dispersion of a statistical distribution because it is not affected by freak extreme values (see ◊range).

quartz crystalline form of ◊silica SiO_2, one of the most abundant minerals of the Earth's crust (12% by volume). Quartz occurs in many different kinds of rock, including sandstone and granite. It ranks 7 on the Mohs' scale of hardness and is resistant to chemical or mechanical breakdown. Quartzes vary according to the size and purity of their crystals. Crystals of pure quartz are coarse, colourless, transparent, show no cleavage, and fracture unevenly; this form is usually called rock crystal. Impure coloured varieties, often used as gemstones, include ◊agate, citrine quartz, and ◊amethyst. Quartz is also used as a general name for the cryptocrystalline and noncrystalline varieties of silica, such as chalcedony, chert, and opal.

Three quarks for Muster Mark!

JAMES JOYCE Irish novelist.
Supposedly the source of the name 'quark': *Finnegan's Wake* 1939

Quartz is used in ornamental work and industry, where its reaction to electricity makes it valuable in electronic instruments (see ◊piezoelectric effect). Quartz can also be made synthetically.

Crystals that would take millions of years to form naturally can now be 'grown' in pressure vessels to a standard that allows them to be used in optical and scientific instruments and in electronics, such as quartz wristwatches.

quartzite ◊metamorphic rock consisting of pure quartz sandstone that has recrystallized under increasing heat and pressure.

quasar *(from* **quasi-stell**ar *object or QSO)* one of the most distant extragalactic objects known, discovered in 1963. Quasars appear starlike, but each emits more energy than 100 giant galaxies. They are thought to be at the centre of galaxies, their brilliance emanating from the stars and gas falling towards an immense ◊black hole at their nucleus.

Quasar light shows a large ◊red shift, indicating that they are very distant. Some quasars emit radio waves (see ◊radio astronomy), which is how they were first identified, but most are radio-quiet. The furthest are over 10 billion light years away.

quasi-atom particle assemblage resembling an atom, in which particles not normally found in atoms become bound together for a brief period.

Quasi-atoms are generally unstable structures, either because they are subject to matter–antimatter annihilation (positronium), or because one or more of their constituents is unstable (muonium).

quassia any of a group of tropical American trees with bitter bark and wood. The heartwood of *Q. amara* is a source of quassiin, an infusion of which was formerly used as a tonic; it is now used in insecticides. (Genus *Quassia,* family Simaroubaceae.)

The quassia family includes the Asian ailanthus (*Ailanthus altissima*), also called the tree of heaven.

Quaternary period of geological time that began 1.64 million years ago and is still in process. It is divided into the ◊Pleistocene and ◊Holocene epochs.

quebracho any of several South American trees belonging to the cashew family, with very hard, tannin-rich wood; chiefly the red quebracho (*S. lorentzii*), used in the tanning of leather. (Genus *Schinopsis,* family Anacardiaceae.)

quenching ◊heat treatment used to harden metals. The metals are heated to a certain temperature and then quickly plunged into cold water or oil.

? wild card character standing for any single character in most operating systems. It allows a user to specify a group of files whose names differ by only one character for mass handling. Typing 'dir part?.doc' in a DOS directory would display a list of files such as part1.doc, party.doc, and so on. The letter 'x' is often used to mean the same thing.

questionnaire a question list submitted to a certain number of people whose answers are then used to compile quantitative or qualitative statistical information. Questionnaires are a means of obtaining ◊primary data and are useful in market research, for example.

quetzal long-tailed Central American bird *Pharomachus mocinno* of the ◊trogon family, order Trogoniformes. The male is brightly coloured, with green, red, blue, and white feathers. It has a train of blue-green plumes (tail coverts) that hang far beyond the true tail feathers. There is a crest on the head and decorative drooping feathers on the wings. It is about 1.3 m/4.3 ft long including tail. The female is smaller and lacks the tail and plumage.

The quetzal eats fruit, insects, and small frogs and lizards. It is the national emblem of Guatemala, and was considered sacred by the Mayans and the Aztecs. The quetzal's forest habitat is rapidly being destroyed, and hunting of birds for trophies or souvenirs also threatens its survival.

queue in computing, backup of ◊packets of data awaiting processing, or of ◊e-mail waiting to be read.

QuickDraw object-based graphics display system used by the Apple ◊Macintosh range of microcomputers. The use of QuickDraw gives most Macintosh applications the same ◊look-and-feel.

quicksilver another name for the element ◊mercury.

QuickTime multimedia utility developed by Apple, initially for the ◊Macintosh, but now also available for ◊Windows. Allows multimedia, such as sound and video, to be embedded in other documents, including Web pages.

quince small tree native to western Asia but widely cultivated elsewhere. The bitter, yellow, pear-shaped fruit is used in preserves. Flowering quinces are cultivated mainly for their attractive flowers. (*Cydonia oblonga;* flowering quince genus *Chaenomeles;* family Rosaceae.)

quinine antimalarial drug extracted from the bark of the cinchona tree. Peruvian Indians taught French missionaries how to use the bark in 1630, but quinine was not isolated until 1820. It is a bitter alkaloid, with the formula $C_{20}H_{24}N_2O_2$.

Other antimalarial drugs have since been developed with fewer side effects, but quinine derivatives are still valuable in the treatment of unusually resistant strains.

quoting in computing, common practice in electronic communications. When replying to an e-mail, or adding to a ◊newsgroup thread, users quote all or part of the original message in their response. The usual method of doing this is by preceding each quoted line with the symbol >.

QWERTY standard arrangement of keys on a UK or US typewriter or computer keyboard. Q, W, E, R, T, and Y are the first six keys on the top alphabetic line. The arrangement was made in the days of mechanical keyboards in order that the keys would not jam together. Other European countries use different arrangements, such as AZERTY and QWERTZ, which are more appropriate to the language of the country.

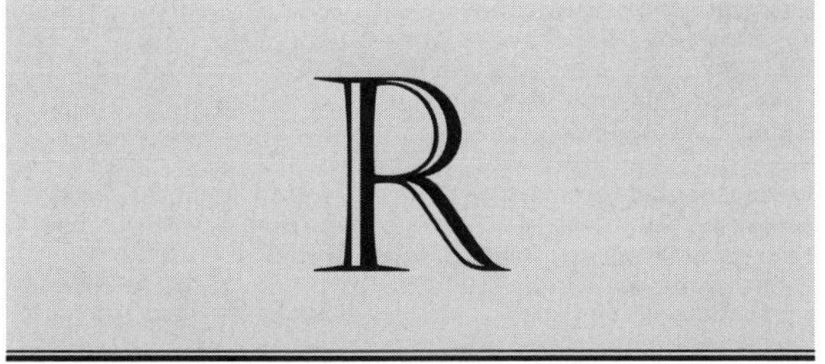

rabbit any of several genera of hopping mammals of the order Lagomorpha, which together with hares constitute the family Leporidae. Rabbits differ from ◊hares in bearing naked, helpless young and in occupying burrows.

The Old World rabbit (*Oryctolagus cuniculus*), originally from S Europe and N Africa, has now been introduced worldwide. It is bred for meat and for its fur, which is usually treated to resemble more expensive furs. It lives in interconnected burrows called 'warrens', unlike cottontails (genus *Sylvilagus*), of which 13 species are native to North and South America.

PAULSON'S RABBIT WORLD

http://pages.prodigy.com/NTMX83A/

Comprehensive guide to keeping these active and gregarious animals as pets. If you are contemplating getting a bunny this is the site to visit. There is advice on providing accommodation (while giving the rabbit the run of the house), protecting rabbits from household dangers, toilet training, diet, and common rabbit ailments. There are useful links to the House Rabbit Society and other rabbit sites.

RABBIT

Rabbits eat some of their droppings. This behaviour, called refection, is similar to chewing the cud in cows, and ensures that food is fully digested.

rabies or ***hydrophobia*** Greek 'fear of water' viral disease of the central nervous system that can afflict all warm-blooded creatures. It is caused by a lyssavirus. It is almost invariably fatal once symptoms have developed. Its transmission to humans is generally by a bite from an infected animal. Rabies continues to kill hundreds of thousands of people every year; almost all these deaths occur in Asia, Africa, and South America.

After an incubation period, which may vary from ten days to more than a year, symptoms of fever, muscle spasm, and delirium develop. As the disease progresses, the mere sight of water is enough to provoke convulsions and paralysis. Death is usual within four or five days from the onset of symptoms. Injections of rabies vaccine and antiserum may save those bitten by a rabid animal from developing the disease. Louis ◊Pasteur was the first to produce a preventive vaccine, and the Pasteur Institute was founded to treat the disease.

As a control measure for foxes and other wild animals, vaccination (by bait) is recommended. In France, Germany, and the border areas of Austria and the Czech Republic, foxes are now vaccinated against rabies with capsules distributed by helicopter; as a result, rabies has been virtually eradicated in Western Europe, and no-one has died of the disease in the European Union since 1973. In spring 1994, around 6 million vaccination baits were scattered across the border areas of Poland, Slovenia, Slovakia, and Hungary to extend the vaccination area within Europe.

RACCOONS

http://www.loomcom.com/raccoons

Compiled with obvious enthusiasm and providing facts brought to life with images, sounds, and animations. It also includes a section on raccoons in the media, links to other sites of interest, and an interactive bulletin board for raccoon-related discussion.

raccoon any of several New World species of carnivorous mammals of the genus *Procyon*, in the family Procyonidae. The common raccoon *P. lotor* is about 60 cm/2 ft long, with a grey-brown body, a black-and-white ringed tail, and a black 'mask' around its eyes. The crab-eating raccoon *P. cancrivorus* of South America is slightly smaller and has shorter fur.

raceme in botany, a type of ◊inflorescence.

rack railway railway, used in mountainous regions, that uses a toothed pinion running in a toothed rack to provide traction. The rack usually runs between the rails. Ordinary wheels lose their grip even on quite shallow gradients, but rack railways, like that on Mount Pilatus in Switzerland, can climb slopes as steep as 50% (1 in 2).

rad unit of absorbed radiation dose, now replaced in the SI system by the ◊gray (one rad equals 0.01 gray), but still commonly used. It is defined as the dose when one kilogram of matter absorbs 0.01 joule of radiation energy (formerly, as the dose when one gram absorbs 100 ergs).

radar (acronym for ***radio direction and ranging***) device for locating objects in space, direction finding, and navigation by means of transmitted and reflected high-frequency radio waves.

The direction of an object is ascertained by transmitting a beam of short-wavelength (1–100 cm/0.5–40 in), short-pulse radio waves, and picking up the reflected beam. Distance is determined by timing the journey of the radio waves (travelling at the speed of light) to the object and back again. Radar is also used to detect objects underground, for example service pipes, and in archaeology. Contours of remains of ancient buildings can be detected down to 20 m/66 ft below ground. Radar is essential to navigation in darkness, cloud, and fog, and is widely used in warfare to detect enemy aircraft and missiles. To avoid detection, various devices, such as modified shapes (to reduce their radar cross-section), radar-absorbent paints and electronic jamming are used. To pinpoint small targets laser ◊'radar', instead of microwaves, has been developed.

Developed independently in Britain, France, Germany, and the USA in the 1930s, it was first put to practical use for aircraft detection by the British, who had a complete coastal chain of radar sets installed by September 1938. It proved invaluable in the Battle of Britain 1940, when the ability to spot incoming German aircraft did away with the need to fly standing patrols. Chains of ground radar stations are used to warn of enemy attack – for example, North Warning System 1985, consisting of 52 stations across the Canadian Arctic and N Alaska. Radar is also used in ◊meteorology and ◊astronomy.

RADAR

http://chide.museum.org.uk/radar.index.html

Radar information ranging from biographies and reminiscences of the people involved in developing the technology, to pictures of radar exhibits at the Centre of the History of Electronic Defence. A brief history of the development of radar is also included, which gives credit to British researchers for their role in the winning of the Battle of Britain.

radar astronomy bouncing of radio waves off objects in the Solar System, with reception and analysis of the 'echoes'. Radar contact with the Moon was first made in 1945 and with Venus in 1961. The travel time for radio reflections allows the distances of objects to be determined accurately. Analysis of the reflected beam reveals the rotation period and allows the object's surface to be mapped. The rotation periods of Venus and Mercury were first determined by radar. Radar maps of Venus were obtained first by Earth-based radar and subsequently by orbiting space probes.

radial artery in biology, artery that passes down the forearm and supplies blood to the hand and the fingers. The brachial artery, a large artery supplying blood to the arm, divides at the elbow to form the radial and ulnar arteries. The pulsation of blood through the radial artery can be felt at the wrist. This is generally known as the pulse.

radial circuit circuit used in household electric wiring in which all electrical appliances are connected to cables that radiate out from the main supply point or fuse box. In more modern systems, the appliances are connected in a ring, or ◊ring circuit, with each end of the ring connected to the fuse box.

radial nerve in biology, the nerve in the upper arm. Nervous impulses to regulate the function of the muscles which extend the arm, the wrist, and some fingers pass along these nerves. They also relay sensation to parts of the arm and hand. The radial nerve arises from the brachial plexus (network of nerves supplying the arm) in the armpit and descends the upper arm before dividing into the superficial radial and interosseous nerves.

radial velocity in astronomy, the velocity of an object, such as a star or galaxy, along the line of sight, moving towards or away from an observer. The amount of ◊Doppler shift (apparent change in wavelength) of the light reveals the object's velocity. If the object is approaching, the Doppler effect causes a ◊blue shift in its light. That is, the wavelengths of light coming from the object appear to be shorter, tending toward the blue end of the ◊spectrum. If the object is receding, there is a ◊red shift, meaning the wavelengths appear to be longer, toward the red end of the spectrum.

radian SI unit (symbol rad) of plane angles, an alternative unit to the ◊degree. It is the angle at the centre of a circle when the centre is joined to the two ends of an arc (part of the circumference) equal in length to the radius of the circle. There are 2π (approximately 6.284) radians in a full circle (360°).

One radian is approximately 57°, and 1° is $\pi/180$ or approximately 0.0175 radians. Radians are commonly used to specify angles in ◊polar coordinates.

radiant heat energy that is radiated by all warm or hot bodies. It belongs to the ◊infrared part of the electromagnetic ◊spectrum and causes heating when absorbed. Radiant heat is invisible and should not be confused with the red glow associated with very hot objects, which belongs to the visible part of the spectrum.

Infrared radiation can travel through a vacuum and it is in this form that the radiant heat of the Sun travels through space. It is the trapping of this radiation by carbon dioxide and water vapour in the atmosphere that gives rise to the ◊greenhouse effect.

radiata pine softwood timber tree *Pinus radiata* native to California; in Australia it is the most widely cultivated softwood, covering many thousands of hectares.

radiation in physics, emission of radiant ◊energy as particles or waves – for example, heat, light, alpha particles, and beta particles (see ◊electromagnetic waves and ◊radioactivity). See also ◊atomic radiation.

Of the radiation given off by the Sun, only a tiny fraction of it, called insolation, reaches the Earth's surface; much of it is absorbed and scattered as it passes through the ◊atmosphere. The radiation given off by the Earth itself is called **ground radiation**.

radiation biology study of how living things are affected by radioactive (ionizing) emissions (see ◊radioactivity) and by electromagnetic (nonionizing) radiation (◊electromagnetic waves). Both are potentially harmful and can cause mutations as well as leukaemia and other cancers; even low levels of radioactivity are very dangerous. Both however, are used therapeutically, for example to treat cancer, when the radiation dose is very carefully controlled (◊radiotherapy **or X-ray therapy**).

Radioactive emissions are more harmful. Exposure to high levels produces radiation burns and radiation sickness, plus genetic damage (resulting in birth defects) and cancers in the longer term. Exposure to low-level ionizing radiation can also cause genetic damage and cancers, particularly leukaemia.

Electromagnetic radiation is usually harmful only if exposure is to high-energy emissions, for example close to powerful radio transmitters or near radar-wave sources. Such exposure can cause organ damage, cataracts, loss of hearing, leukaemia and other cancers, or premature ageing. It may also affect the nervous system and brain, distorting their electrical nerve signals and leading to depression, disorientiation, headaches, and other symptoms. Individual sensitivity varies and some people are affected by electrical equipment, such as televisions, computers, and refrigerators.

Background radiation is the natural radiation produced by cosmic rays and radioactive rocks such as granite, and this must be taken into account when calculating the effects of nuclear accidents or contamination from power stations.

radiation monitoring system network of monitors to detect any rise in background gamma radiation and to warn of a major nuclear accident within minutes of its occurrence. The accident at Chernobyl in Ukraine in 1986 prompted several W European countries to begin installation of such systems locally, and in 1994 work began on a pilot system to provide a **gamma curtain**, a dense net of radiation monitors, throughout E and W Europe.

radiation sickness sickness resulting from exposure to radiation, including X-rays, gamma rays, neutrons, and other nuclear radiation, as from weapons and fallout. Such radiation ionizes atoms in the body and causes nausea, vomiting, diarrhoea, and other symptoms. The body cells themselves may be damaged even by very small doses, causing leukaemia and other cancers.

Science has nothing to be ashamed of, even in the ruins of Nagasaki.

JACOB BRONOWSKI Polish-born scientist, broadcaster, and writer.
Science and Human Values 1978

---

radiation units units of measurement for radioactivity and radiation doses. In SI units, the activity of a radioactive source is measured in becquerels (symbol Bq), where one becquerel is equal to one nuclear disintegration per second (an older unit is the curie). The exposure is measured in coulombs per kilogram (C kg^{-1}); the amount of ionizing radiation (X-rays or gamma rays) which produces one coulomb of charge in one kilogram of dry air (replacing the roentgen). The absorbed dose of ionizing radiation is measured in grays (symbol Gy) where one gray is equal to one joule of energy being imparted to one kilogram of matter (the rad is the previously used unit). The dose equivalent, which is a measure of the effects of radiation on living organisms, is the absorbed dose multiplied by a suitable factor which depends upon the type of radiation. It is measured in sieverts (symbol Sv), where one sievert is a dose equivalent of one joule per kilogram (an older unit is the rem).

radical in chemistry, a group of atoms forming part of a molecule, which acts as a unit and takes part in chemical reactions without disintegration, yet often cannot exist alone for any length of time; for example, the methyl radical $-CH_3$, or the carboxyl radical $-COOH$.

radicle part of a plant embryo that develops into the primary root. Usually it emerges from the seed before the embryonic shoot, or ◊plumule, its tip protected by a root cap, or calyptra, as it pushes through the soil. The radicle may form the basis of the entire root system, or it may be replaced by adventitious roots (positioned on the stem).

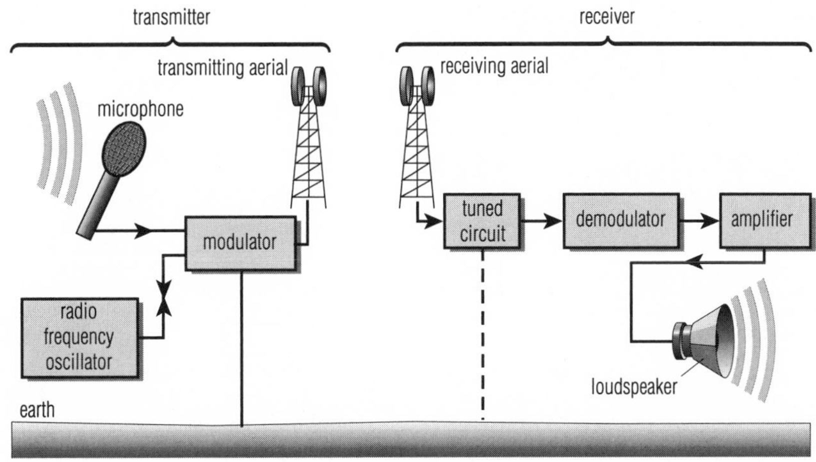

radio *Radio transmission and reception. The radio frequency oscillator generates rapidly varying electrical signals, which are sent to the transmitting aerial. In the aerial, the signals produce radio waves (the carrier wave), which spread out at the speed of light. The sound signal is added to the carrier wave by the modulator. When the radio waves fall on the receiving aerial, they induce an electrical current in the aerial. The electrical current is sent to the tuning circuit, which picks out the signal from the particular transmitting station desired. The demodulator separates the sound signal from the carrier wave and sends it, after amplification, to the loudspeaker.*

radio transmission and reception of radio waves. In radio transmission a microphone converts ◊sound waves (pressure variations in the air) into ◊electromagnetic waves that are then picked up by a receiving aerial and fed to a loudspeaker, which converts them back into sound waves.

The theory of electromagnetic waves was first developed by Scottish physicist James Clerk ◊Maxwell 1864, given practical confirmation in the laboratory in 1888 by German physicist Heinrich ◊Hertz, and put to practical use by Italian inventor Guglielmo ◊Marconi, who in 1901 achieved reception of a signal in Newfoundland, Canada, transmitted from Cornwall, England.

To carry the transmitted electrical signal, an ◊oscillator produces a carrier wave of high frequency; different stations are allocated different transmitting carrier frequencies. A modulator superimposes the audiofrequency signal on the carrier. There are two main ways of doing this: ◊amplitude modulation **(AM)**, used for long- and medium-wave broadcasts, in which the strength of the carrier is made to fluctuate in time with the audio signal; and ◊frequency modulation (FM), as used for VHF broadcasts, in which the frequency of the carrier is made to fluctuate. The transmitting aerial emits the modulated electromagnetic waves, which travel outwards from it.

In radio reception a receiving aerial picks up minute voltages in response to the waves sent out by a transmitter. A tuned circuit selects a particular frequency, usually by means of a variable ◊capacitor connected across a coil of wire. A demodulator disentangles the audio signal from the carrier, which is now discarded, having served its purpose. An amplifier boosts the audio signal for feeding to the loudspeaker. In a ◊superheterodyne receiver, the incoming signal is mixed with an internally-generated signal of fixed frequency so that the amplifier circuits can operate near their optimum frequency.

radioactive decay process of disintegration undergone by the nuclei of radioactive elements, such as radium and various isotopes of uranium and the transuranic elements. This changes the element's atomic number, thus transmuting one element into another, and is accompanied by the emission of radiation. Alpha and beta decay are the most common forms.

In **alpha decay** (the loss of a helium nucleus – two protons and two neutrons) the atomic number decreases by two; in **beta decay** (the loss of an electron) the atomic number increases by one. Certain lighter artificially created isotopes also undergo radioactive decay. The associated radiation consists of alpha rays, beta rays, or gamma rays (or a combination of these), and it takes place at a constant rate expressed as a specific half-life, which is the time taken for half of any mass of that particular isotope to decay completely. Less commonly occurring decay forms include heavy-ion emission, electron capture, and spontaneous fission (in each of these the atomic number decreases).

The original nuclide is known as the parent substance, and the product is a daughter nuclide (which may or may not be radioactive). The final product in all modes of decay is a stable element.

radioactive tracer any of various radioactive ◊isotopes used in labelled compounds; see ◊tracer.

radioactive waste any waste that emits radiation in excess of the background level. See ◊nuclear waste.

radioactivity spontaneous alteration of the nuclei of radioactive atoms, accompanied by the emission of radiation. It is the property exhibited by the radioactive ◊isotopes of stable elements and all isotopes of radioactive elements, and can be either natural or induced. See ◊radioactive decay.

the discovery of radioactivity Radioactivity was first discovered in 1896, when Becquerel observed that some photographic plates, although securely wrapped up, became blackened when placed near certain uranium compounds. A closer investigation showed that thin metal coverings were unable to prevent the blackening of the plates. It was clear that the uranium compounds emitted radiation that was able to penetrate the metal coverings. Pierre and Marie ◊Curie soon succeeded in isolating other radioactive elements. One of these was radium, which was found to be over 1 million times more radioactive than uranium.

radioactive radiations Further investigation of the nature of ◊radiation by Ernest Rutherford revealed that there are three types of radiation: ◊alpha particles, beta particles, and gamma rays. Alpha particles are positively charged, high-energy particles emitted from the nucleus of a radioactive atom. They consist of two neutrons and two protons and are thus identical to the nucleus of a helium atom. Because of their large mass, alpha particles have a short range of only a few centimetres in air, and can be stopped by a sheet of paper. Beta particles are more penetrating and can travel through a 3-mm/0.1-in sheet of aluminium or up to 1 m/3 ft of air. They consist of high-energy electrons emitted at high velocity from a radioactive atom that is undergoing spontaneous disintegration.

Digital Radio

BY BARRY FOX

Conventional radio is broadcast as an analogue signal, using either amplitude modulation (AM) or frequency modulation (FM). The sound suffers interference from other stations and 'multipath' reflections from hills and buildings. If the signal is weak and the receiver is straining to pick it up, the sound is polluted with background hiss.

If analogue sound is converted into digital code before transmission, as long as the signal is strong enough to decode, it is immune from interference and free from hiss. Less transmitter power is needed to cover the same area as an analogue signal. However, if reflections are as strong as the code, the receiver does not work at all. Also, when analogue sound is converted into digits, the raw code takes up more space on the airwaves than the analogue signal.

There is more space in the satellite bands, and some broadcasters and music delivery services have transmitted CD quality digital sound from space. But the satellite bands are now crowding. Also, the signals can only be received with a dish aerial, mounted in a fixed position.

Digital Audio Broadcasting (DAB) lets a receiver work with a simple rod aerial, even when moving. It also reduces the number of digital bits needed so that the signal takes up less space than an analogue transmission. Although DAB signals can be transmitted from satellites, they will initially come from conventional terrestrial transmitters.

Pan-European Eureka research team number 147 developed a DAB system, and this has been adopted as the standard for Europe. The only difference between countries is in the transmission frequencies to be used; high VHF in some and L band at 1,500 MHz in others.

The Eureka system combines two processes. Analogue sound is first converted into digital code and compressed by a system known as 'Musicam'. When there are two sounds of similar frequency, but different volume level, the 'Musicam' encoder ignores the quieter sound. This can reduce the number of bits by a factor of ten, without the ear noticing.

The bitstream is then split into several hundred parallel channels, so that each carries only slow- moving bits of data. The many channels are broadcast simultaneously on closely neighbouring frequencies. The receiver recombines the channels and rebuilds the sound. Because the bits in each channel are travelling slowly, the receiver can distinguish between wanted signals which arrive direct from the transmitter, and unwanted 'multipath' reflections which arrive later.

The introduction of DAB does not take anything away from existing listeners, but a new radio is needed to listen to new digital broadcasts. These radios will often tune to all possible DAB bands, so that owners can use them anywhere in Europe.

The Eureka system is on offer to other countries, and Canada looks likely to adopt it. The situation in the USA is still fluid, because rival systems use 'in-band, on-channel' (IBOC) technology. IBOC transmits digital code at very low level, underneath a conventional analogue radio broadcast. So conventional AM and FM radio analogue receivers should continue working as normal, while a new digital radio retrieves the low-level signal and decodes it to deliver high-quality sound.

So new frequencies are not needed for IBOC, but critics say it may be susceptible to 'multipath' reflections and interference. There may be no single agreed standard for the USA, with open market competition left to create a *de facto* standard – like VHS versus Beta home video.

Britain's BBC started regular Eureka DAB transmissions in September 1995, and the commercial stations soon followed, along with most other countries in Europe. At first the only receivers were bulky engineering test prototypes. Compact radios are expected during 1998, with the prices falling to consumer levels by the end of the century.

Gamma rays comprise very high-frequency electromagnetic radiation. Gamma rays are stopped only by direct collision with an atom and are therefore very penetrating; they can, however, be stopped by about 4 cm/1.5 in of lead.

When alpha, beta, and gamma radiation pass through matter they tend to knock electrons out of atoms, ionizing them. They are therefore called ionizing radiation. Alpha particles are the most ionizing, being heavy, slow moving and carrying two positive charges. Gamma rays are weakly ionizing as they carry no charge. Beta particles fall between alpha and gamma radiation in ionizing potential.

detection of radioactivity Detectors of ionizing radiation make use of the ionizing properties of radiation to cause changes that can be detected and measured. A ◊Geiger counter detects the momentary current that passes between electrodes in a suitable gas when ionizing radiation causes the ionization of that gas. The device is named after the German physicist Hans ◊Geiger. The ◊activity of a radioactive source describes the rate at which nuclei are disintegrating within it. One ◊becquerel (1 Bq) is defined as a rate of one disintegration per second.

radioactive decay Radioactive decay occurs when an unstable nucleus emits alpha, beta, or gamma radiation in order to become more stable. The energy given out by disintegrating atoms is called ◊atomic radiation. An alpha particle consists of two protons and two neutrons. When ◊alpha decay occurs (the emission of an alpha particle from a nucleus) it results in the formation of a new nucleus. An atom of uranium isotope of mass 238, on emitting an alpha particle, becomes an atom of thorium,mass 234. ◊Beta decay, the loss of an electron from an atom, is accomplished by the transformation of a neutron into a proton, thus resulting in an increase in the atomic number of one. For example, the decay of the carbon 314 isotope results in the formation of an atom of nitrogen (mass 14, atomic number 7) and the emission of an electron. Gamma emission usually occurs as part of alpha or beta emission. High-speed electromagnetic radiation is emitted from the nucleus in order to make it more stable during the loss of an alpha or beta particle.

◊Isotopes of an element have different atomic masses. They have the same number of protons but different numbers of neutrons in the nucleus. For example, uranium 235 and uranium 238 both have 92 protons but the latter has three more neutrons than the former. Some isotopes are naturally radioactive (see ◊radioisotopes) while others are not. Radioactive decay can take place either as a one-step decay, or through a series of steps that transmute one element into another. This is called a decay series or chain, and sometimes produces an element more radioactive than its predecessor. For example, uranium 238 decays by alpha emission to thorium 234; thorium 234 is a beta emitter and decays to give protactinium 234. This emits a beta particle to form uranium 234, which in turn undergoes alpha decay to form thorium 230. A further alpha decay yields the isotope radium 226.

the rate of radioactive decay The emission of radioactivity by an atom occurs spontaneously and quite unpredictably. However, in a sample containing many radioactive atoms, the overall rate of decay appears to be governed by the number of nuclei left undecayed. The time taken for half the radioactive atoms in a sample to decay remains constant and is called the ◊half-life. Radioactive substances decay exponentially with time, and the value of the half-life for a substance can vary from a fraction of a second to billions of years.

health hazards We are surrounded by radioactive substances. Our food contains traces of radioactive isotopes and our own bodies are made of naturally radioactive matter. In addition, we are bombarded by streams of high-energy charged particles from outer space. Radiation present in the environment is known as ◊background radiation and we should take this into account when considering the risk of exposure to other sources.

Alpha, beta, and gamma radiation are dangerous to body tissues because of their ionizing properties, especially if a radioactive substance is ingested or inhaled. Illness resulting from exposure to radioactive substances can take various forms, which are collectively known as ◊radiation sickness.

radioactivity in use Radioactivity has a number of uses in modern science, but its use should always be carefully controlled and monitored to minimize the risk of harm to living things. In science, a small quantity of a radioactive tracer can be used to follow the path of a chemical reaction or a physical or biological process. ◊Radiocarbon dating is a technique for measuring the age of organic materials. Another application is in determining the age of rocks. This is based on the fact that in many uranium and thorium ores, all of which have been decaying since the formation of the rock, the alpha particles released during decay have been trapped as helium atoms in the rock. The age of the rock can be assessed by calculating the relative amounts of helium, uranium, and thorium in it. This calculation can help to estimate the age of the Earth at around 4.6 billion years.

In medicine, radioactive emissions and electromagnetic radiation can be used therapeutically; for example, to treat cancer, when the radiation dose is very carefully controlled (see ◊radiotherapy).

nuclear fission and fusion ◊Fission of a nucleus occurs when the nucleus splits into two approximately equal fragments. The fission of the nucleus results in the release of neutrons and a large amount of energy. In a nuclear reactor, the fission of uranium 235 is caused by bombarding it with neutrons. A nuclear chain reaction is caused as neutrons released by the splitting of atomic nuclei themselves go on to split other nuclei, releasing even more neutrons. In a nuclear reactor this process is carefully controlled to release ◊nuclear energy.

In ◊nuclear fusion, two light nuclei combine to form a bigger nucleus. As fusion is accompanied by the release of large amounts of energy, the process might one day be harnessed to form the basis of commercial energy production. So far, no successful fusion reactor has been built.

RADIOACTIVITY IN NATURE

http://www.sph.umich.edu/group/eih/UMSCHPS/natural.htm

Detailed explanation of the different types of radiation found naturally on Earth and in its atmosphere, as well as those produced by humans. It includes tables of the breakdown of nuclides commonly found in soil, the oceans, the air, and even the human body.

radio astronomy study of radio waves emitted naturally by objects in space, by means of a ◊radio telescope. Radio emission comes from hot gases (**thermal radiation**); electrons spiralling in magnetic fields (**synchrotron radiation**); and specific wavelengths (**lines**) emitted by atoms and molecules in space, such as the 21-cm/8-in line emitted by hydrogen gas.

Radio astronomy began in 1932 when US astronomer Karl ◊Jansky detected radio waves from the centre of our Galaxy, but the subject did not develop until after World War II. Radio astronomy has greatly improved our understanding of the evolution of stars, the structure of galaxies, and the origin of the universe. Astronomers have mapped the spiral structure of the Milky Way from the radio waves given out by interstellar gas, and they have detected many individual radio sources within our Galaxy and beyond.

Among radio sources in our Galaxy are the remains of ◊supernova explosions, such as the ◊Crab nebula and ◊pulsars. Short-wavelength radio waves have been detected from complex molecules in dense clouds of gas where stars are forming. Searches have been undertaken for signals from other civilizations in the Galaxy, so far without success.

Strong sources of radio waves beyond our Galaxy include ◊radio galaxies and ◊quasars. Their existence far off in the universe demonstrates how the universe has evolved with time. Radio astronomers have also detected weak **background radiation** thought to be from the ◊Big Bang explosion that marked the birth of the universe.

radio beacon radio transmitter in a fixed location, used in marine and aerial ◊navigation. Ships and aircraft pinpoint their positions by reference to continuous signals given out by two or more beacons.

radio button in computing, in a ◊dialog box, a round button denoting an option. Users are offered a choice of radio buttons, and can choose only one.

radiocarbon dating *or* **carbon dating** method of dating organic materials (for example, bone or wood), used in archaeology. Plants take up carbon dioxide gas from the atmosphere and incorporate it into their tissues, and some of that carbon dioxide contains the radioactive isotope of carbon, ^{14}C or carbon-14. As this decays at a known rate (half of it decays every 5,730 years), the time elapsed since the plant died can be measured in a laboratory. Animals take carbon-14 into their bodies from eating plant tissues and their remains can be similarly dated. After 120,000 years so little carbon-14 is left that no measure is possible (see ◊half-life).

Radiocarbon dating was first developed 1949 by the US chemist Willard Libby. The method yields reliable ages back to about 50,000 years, but its results require correction since Libby's assumption that the concentration of carbon-14 in the atmosphere was constant through time has subsequently been proved wrong. Discrepancies were noted between carbon-14 dates for Egyptian tomb artefacts and construction dates recorded in early local texts. Radiocarbon dates from tree rings (see ◊dendrochronology) showed that material before 1000 BC had been exposed to greater concentrations of carbon-14. Now radiocarbon dates are calibrated against calendar dates obtained from tree rings, or, for earlier periods, against uranium/thorium dates obtained from coral. The carbon-14 content is determined by counting beta particles with either a proportional gas or a liquid scintillation counter for a period of time. A new advance, accelerator mass spectrometry, requires only tiny samples and counts the atoms of carbon-14 directly, disregarding their decay.

radio, cellular portable telephone system; see ◊cellular phone.

radiochemistry chemical study of radioactive isotopes and their compounds (whether produced from naturally radioactive or irradiated materials) and their use in the study of other chemical processes.

When such isotopes are used in labelled compounds, they enable the biochemical and physiological functioning of parts of the living body to be observed. They can help in the testing of new drugs, showing where the drug goes in the body and how long it stays there. They are also useful in diagnosis – for example cancer, fetal abnormalities, and heart disease.

radio frequencies and wavelengths classification of, see ◊electromagnetic waves.

radio galaxy galaxy that is a strong source of electromagnetic waves of radio wavelengths. All galaxies, including our own, emit some radio waves, but radio galaxies are up to a million times more powerful.

In many cases the strongest radio emission comes not from the visible galaxy but from two clouds, invisible through an optical telescope, that can extend for millions of light years either side of the galaxy. This double structure at radio wavelengths is also shown by some ◊quasars, suggesting a close relationship between the two types of object. In both cases, the source of energy is thought to be a massive black hole at the centre. Some radio galaxies are thought to result from two galaxies in collision or recently merged.

radiography branch of science concerned with the use of radiation (particularly ◊X-rays) to produce images on photographic film or fluorescent screens. X-rays penetrate matter according to its nature, density, and thickness. In doing so they can cast shadows on photographic film, producing a radiograph. Radiography is widely used in medicine for examining bones and tissues and in industry for examining solid materials; for example, to check welded seams in pipelines

radioisotope (contraction of ***radioactive isotope***) in physics, a naturally occurring or synthetic radioactive form of an element. Most radioisotopes are made by bombarding a stable element with neutrons in the core of a nuclear reactor. The radiations given off by radioisotopes are easy to detect (hence their use as ◊tracers), can in some instances penetrate substantial thicknesses of materials, and have profound effects (such as genetic ◊mutation) on living matter. Although dangerous, radioisotopes are used in the fields of medicine, industry, agriculture, and research.

radioisotope scanning use of radioactive materials (radioisotopes or radionucleides) to pinpoint disease. It reveals the size and shape of the target organ and whether any part of it is failing to take up radioactive material, usually an indication of disease.

The speciality known as nuclear medicine makes use of the affinity of different chemical elements for certain parts of the body. Iodine, for instance, always makes its way to the thyroid gland. After being made radioactive, these materials can be given by mouth or injected, and then traced on scanners working on the Geiger-counter principle. The diagnostic record gained from radioisotope scanning is known as a **scintigram**.

radiology medical speciality concerned with the use of radiation, including X-rays, and radioactive materials in the diagnosis and treatment of injury and disease.

radiometric dating method of dating rock by assessing the amount of ◊radioactive decay of naturally occurring ◊isotopes. The dating of rocks may be based on the gradual decay of uranium into lead. The ratio of the amounts of 'parent' to 'daughter' isotopes in a sample gives a measure of the time it has been decaying, that is, of its age. Different elements and isotopes are used depending on the isotopes present and the age of the rocks to be dated. Once-living matter can often be dated by ◊radiocarbon dating, employing the half-life of the isotope carbon-14, which is naturally present in organic tissue.

Radiometric methods have been applied to the decay of long-lived isotopes, such as potassium-40, rubidium-87, thorium-232, and uranium-238, which are found in rocks. These isotopes decay very slowly and this has enabled rocks as old as 3,800 million years to be dated accurately. Carbon dating can be used for material between 1,000 and 100,000 years old. **Potassium** dating is used for material more than 100,000 years old, **rubidium** for rocks more than 10 million years old, and **uranium** and **thorium** dating is suitable for rocks older than 20 million years.

radiosonde balloon carrying a compact package of meteorological instruments and a radio transmitter, used to 'sound', or measure, conditions in the atmosphere. The instruments measure temperature, pressure, and humidity, and the information gathered is transmitted back to observers on the ground. A radar target is often attached, allowing the balloon to be tracked.

radio telescope instrument for detecting radio waves from the universe in ◊radio astronomy. Radio telescopes usually consist of a metal bowl that collects and focuses radio waves the way a concave mirror collects and focuses light waves. Radio telescopes are much larger than optical telescopes, because the wavelengths they are detecting are much longer than the wavelength of light. The largest single dish is 305 m/1,000 ft across, at Arecibo, Puerto Rico.

A large dish such as that at◊Jodrell Bank, England, can see the radio sky less clearly than a small optical telescope sees the visible sky. **Interferometry** is a technique in which the output from two dishes is combined to give better resolution of detail than with a single dish. **Very long baseline interferometry** (VBLI) uses radio telescopes spread across the world to resolve minute details of radio sources.

In **aperture synthesis**, several dishes are linked together to simulate the performance of a very large single dish. This technique was pioneered by Martin Ryle at Cambridge, England, site of a radio telescope consisting of eight dishes in a line 5 km/3 mi long. The ◊Very Large Array in New Mexico, USA, consists of 27 dishes arranged in a Y-shape, which simulates the performance of a single dish 27 km/17 mi in diameter. Other radio telescopes are shaped like long troughs, and some consist of simple rod-shaped aerials.

radiotherapy treatment of disease by ◊radiation from X-ray machines or radioactive sources. Radiation, which reduces the activity of dividing cells, is of special value for its effect on malignant tissues, certain nonmalignant tumours, and some diseases of the skin.

Generally speaking, the rays of the diagnostic X-ray machine are not penetrating enough to be efficient in treatment, so for this purpose more powerful machines are required, operating from 10,000 to over 30 million volts. The lower-voltage machines are similar to conventional X-ray machines; the higher-voltage ones may be of special design; for example, linear accelerators and betatrons. Modern radiotherapy is associated with fewer side effects than formerly, but radiotherapy to the head can cause temporary hair loss, and if the treatment involves the gut, diarrhoea and vomiting may occur. Much radiation now given uses synthesized ◊radioisotopes. Radioactive cobalt is the most useful, since it produces gamma rays, which are highly penetrating, and it is used instead of very high-energy X-rays.

radio wave electromagnetic wave possessing a long wavelength (ranging from about 10^{-3} to 10^4 m) and a low frequency (from about 10^5 to 10^{11} Hz). Included in the radio-wave part of the spectrum are ◊microwaves, used for both communications and for cooking; ultra high- and very high-frequency waves, used for television and FM (frequency modulation) radio communications; and short, medium, and long waves, used for AM (amplitude modulation) radio communications. Radio waves that are used for communications have all been modulated (see ◊modulation) to carry information. Certain astronomical objects emit radio waves, which may be detected and studied using vradio telescopes.

radish annual herb native to Europe and Asia, and cultivated for its fleshy, pungent, edible root, which is usually reddish but sometimes white or black; it is eaten raw in salads. (*Raphanus sativus*, family Cruciferae.)

radium Latin *radius* 'ray' white, radioactive, metallic element, symbol Ra, atomic number 88, relative atomic mass 226.02. It is one of the valkaline-earth metals, found in nature in ◊pitchblende and other uranium ores. Of the 16 isotopes, the commonest, Ra-226, has a half-life of 1,620 years. The element was discovered and named in 1898 by Pierre and Marie ◊Curie, who were investigating the residues of pitchblende.

Radium decays in successive steps to produce radon (a gas), polonium, and finally a stable isotope of lead. The isotope Ra-223 decays through the uncommon mode of heavy-ion emission, giving off carbon-14 and transmuting directly to lead. Because radium luminesces, it was formerly used in paints that glowed in the dark; when the hazards of radioactivity became known its use was abandoned, but factory and dump sites remain contaminated and many former workers and neighbours contracted fatal cancers.

It would be impossible, it would go against the scientific spirit .... Physicists should always publish their researches completely. If our discovery has a commercial future that is a circumstance from which we should not profit. If radium is to be used in the treatment of disease, it is impossible for us to take advantage of that.

MARIE CURIE Polish-born French scientist.
On the patenting of radium. Discussion with her husband, Pierre, quoted in Eve Curie *The discovery of radium* in *Marie Curie* transl V Sheean 1938

radius in biology, one of the two bones in the lower forelimb of tetrapod (four-limbed) vertebrates.

radius in mathematics, a straight line from the centre of a circle to its circumference, or from the centre to the surface of a sphere.

radon colourless, odourless, gaseous, radioactive, nonmetallic element, symbol Rn, atomic number 86, relative atomic mass 222. It is grouped with the ◊inert gases and was formerly considered nonreactive, but is now known to form some compounds with fluorine. Of the 20 known isotopes, only three occur in nature; the longest half-life is 3.82 days (Rn-222).
discovery Radon is the densest gas known and occurs in small amounts in spring water, streams, and the air, being formed from the natural radioactive decay of radium. Ernest Rutherford discovered the isotope Rn-220 in 1899, and Friedrich Dorn (1848–1916) in 1900; after several other chemists discovered additional isotopes, William Ramsay and R W Whytlaw-Gray isolated the element, which they named niton in 1908. The name radon was adopted in the 1920s.

rafflesia ***or* stinking corpse lily** any of a group of parasitic plants without stems, native to Malaysia, Indonesia, and Thailand. There are 14 species, several of which are endangered by the destruction of the forests where they grow. The fruit is used locally for medicine. The largest flowers in the world are produced by *R. arnoldiana*. About 1 m/3 ft across, they exude a smell of rotting flesh, which attracts flies to pollinate them. (Genus *Rafflesia*, family Rafflesiaceae.)

RAFFLESIA

The world's largest flower smells of rotting flesh. The flower of the parasitic *Rafflesia* has a diameter of up to 1 m/3.3 ft and attracts pollinating insects by mimicking the smell of decomposing corpses. It flowers only once every ten years.

ragworm marine bristle-worm (polychaete), characterized by its prominent parapodia (lateral, paired 'paddles' found on each of its segments). Ragworms are usually well adapted to an active existence, with large muscle blocks and stout parapodia for swimming as well as crawling and burrowing, and a large head complete with complex sense organs. Some, such as *Nereis virens*, reach several metres in length, but most are 2–10 cm/1–4 in long.

Ragworms can be found on the seashore at low tide sheltering from dehydration and high temperatures under rocks, in crevices, or shallow burrows and are often brightly coloured. They are often scavengers feeding on general animal debris or are active predators possessing a large proboscis and stout jaws for feeding on other soft-bodied invertebrates; some feed on algae.
classification The ragworm is in genus *Nereis*, a member of class Polychaeta in phylum Annelida.

ragwort any of several European perennial plants, usually with yellow flower heads; some are poisonous. (Genus *Senecio*, family Compositae.)

Raid (acronym for ***redundant array of independent*** (or ***inexpensive***) ***discs***) in computing, arrays of discs, each connected to a bus, that can be configured in different ways, depending on the application. Raid 1 is, for example, disc mirroring, while Raid 5 spreads every character between discs. Raid is intended to improve performance and data security.

rail any wading bird of the family Rallidae, including the rails proper (genus *Rallus*), coots, moorhens, and gallinules. Rails have dark plumage, a short neck and wings, and long legs. They are 10–45 cm/4–18 in long.

Many oceanic islands have their own species of rail, often flightless, such as the Guam rail *R. owstoni* and Auckland Island rail *R. muelleri*. Several of these species have declined sharply, usually because of introduced predators such as rats and cats.

railway method of transport in which trains convey passengers and goods along a twin rail track. Following the work of English steam pioneers such as Scottish engineer James ◊Watt, English engineer George ◊Stephenson built the first public steam railway, from Stockton to Darlington, England, in 1825. This heralded extensive railway building in Britain, continental Europe, and North America, providing a fast and economical means of transport and communication. After World War II, steam engines were replaced by electric and diesel engines. At the same time, the growth of road building, air services, and car ownership destroyed the supremacy of the railways.
growth years Four years after building the first steam railway, Stephenson opened the first steam passenger line, inaugurating it with his locomotive *Rocket*, which achieved speeds of 50 kph/30 mph. The railway construction that followed resulted in 250 separate companies in Britain, which resolved into four systems 1921 and became the nationalized British Railways in 1948, known as British Rail from 1965. In North America the growth of railways during the 19th century made shipping from the central and western territories economical and helped the North to win the American Civil War; US rail travel reached its peak in 1929. Railways were extended into Asia, the Middle East, Africa, and Latin America in the late 19th century and were used for troop and supply transport in both world wars. ***gauge*** Railway tracks were at first made of wood but later of iron or steel, with ties wedging them apart and keeping them parallel. The distance between the wheels is known as the gauge. Since much of the early development of the railway took place in Tyneside, England, the gauge of local coal wagons, 1.24 m/4 ft 8.5 in, was adopted 1824 for the Stockton–Darlington railway, and most other early railways followed suit. The main exception was the Great Western Railway (GWR) of Isambard Kingdom ◊Brunel, opened in 1841, with a gauge of 2.13 m/7 ft. The narrow gauge won legal backing in the UK 1846, but parts of GWR carried on with Brunel's broad gauge until 1892. British engineers building railways overseas tended to use the narrow gauge, and it became the standard in the USA from 1885. Other countries, such as Ireland and Finland, favoured the broad gauge. Although expensive, it offers a more comfortable journey. ***decline of railways*** With the increasing use of private cars and government-encouraged road haulage after World War II, and the demise of steam, rising costs on the railways meant higher fares, fewer passengers, and declining freight traffic. In the UK many rural rail services closed down on the recommendations of the Beeching Report 1963, reducing the size of the network by more than 20% between 1965 and 1970, from a peak of 24,102 km/14,977 mi. In the 1970s, national railway companies began investing in faster intercity services: in the UK, the diesel high-speed train (HST) was introduced. Elsewhere such trains run on specially built tracks; for example, the ◊Shinkansen (Japan) and ◊TGV (France) networks.

rain form of ◊precipitation in which separate drops of water fall to the Earth's surface from clouds. The drops are formed by the accumulation of fine droplets that condense from water vapour in the air. The condensation is usually brought about by rising and subsequent cooling of air.

Rain can form in three main ways – frontal (or cyclonic) rainfall, orographic (or relief) rainfall, and convectional rainfall. **Frontal rainfall** takes place at the boundary, or ◊front, between a mass of warm air from the tropics and a mass of cold air from the poles. The water vapour in the warm air is chilled and condenses to form clouds and rain.

Orographic rainfall occurs when an airstream is forced to rise over a mountain range. The air becomes cooled and precipitation takes place. In the UK, the Pennine hills, which extend southwards from Northumbria to Derbyshire in N England, interrupt the path of the prevailing southwesterly winds, causing orographic rainfall. Their presence is partly responsible for the west of the UK being wetter than the east. **Convectional rainfall**, associated with hot climates, is brought about by rising and abrupt cooling of air that has been warmed by the extreme heat of the ground surface. The

Railways: chronology

1500s	Tramways – wooden tracks along which trolleys ran – were in use in mines.
1789	Flanged wheels running on cast-iron rails were first introduced; cars were still horse-drawn.
1804	Richard Trevithick built the first steam locomotive, and ran it on the track at the Pen-y-darren ironworks in South Wales.
1825	George Stephenson in England built the first public railway to carry steam trains – the Stockton and Darlington line – using his engine *Locomotion*.
1829	Stephenson designed his locomotive *Rocket*.
1830	Stephenson completed the Liverpool and Manchester Railway, the first steam passenger line. The first US-built locomotive, *Best Friend of Charleston*, went into service on the South Carolina Railroad.
1835	Germany pioneered steam railways in Europe, using *Der Adler*, a locomotive built by Stephenson.
1863	Robert Fairlie, a Scot, patented a locomotive with pivoting driving bogies, allowing tight curves in the track (this was later applied in the Garratt locomotives). London opened the world's first underground railway, powered by steam.
1869	The first US transcontinental railway was completed at Promontory, Utah, when the Union Pacific and the Central Pacific railroads met. George Westinghouse of the USA invented the compressed-air brake.
1879	Werner von Siemens demonstrated an electric train in Germany. Volk's Electric Railway along the Brighton seafront in England was the world's first public electric railway.
1883	Charles Lartique built the first monorail, in Ireland.
1885	The trans-Canada continental railway was completed, from Montréal in the east to Port Moody, British Columbia, in the west.
1890	The first electric underground railway opened in London.
1901	The world's longest-established monorail, the Wuppertal Schwebebahn, went into service in Germany.
1912	The first diesel locomotive took to the rails in Germany.
1938	The British steam locomotive *Mallard* set a steam-rail speed record of 203 kph/126 mph.
1941	Swiss Federal Railways introduced a gas-turbine locomotive.
1964	Japan National Railways inaugurated the 515 km/320 mi New Tokaido line between Osaka and Tokyo, on which the 210 kph/130 mph 'bullet' trains run.
1973	British Rail's High Speed Train (HST) set a diesel-rail speed record of 229 kph/142 mph.
1979	Japan National Railways' maglev test vehicle ML-500 attained a speed of 517 kph/321 mph.
1981	France's Train à Grande Vitesse (TGV) superfast trains began operation between Paris and Lyons, regularly attaining a peak speed of 270 kph/168 mph.
1987	British Rail set a new diesel-traction speed record of 238.9 kph/148.5 mph, on a test run between Darlington and York; France and the UK began work on the Channel Tunnel, a railway link connecting the two countries, running beneath the English Channel.
1988	The West German Intercity Experimental train reached 405 kph/252 mph on a test run between Würzburg and Fulda.
1990	A new rail-speed record of 515 kph/320 mph was established by a French TGV train, on a stretch of line between Tours and Paris.
1991	The British and French twin tunnels met 23 km/14 mi out to sea to form the Channel Tunnel.
1993	British Rail privatization plans announced; government investment further reduced.
1994	Rail services start through the Channel Tunnel.

water vapour carried by the air condenses and so rain falls heavily. Convectional rainfall is usually accompanied by a thunderstorm, and it can be intensified over urban areas due to higher temperatures.

rainbow arch in the sky displaying the colours of the ◊spectrum formed by the refraction and reflection of the Sun's rays through rain or mist. Its cause was discovered by Theodoric of Freiburg in the 14th century.

ABOUT RAINBOWS

http://www.unidata.ucar.edu/staff/blynds/rnbw.html

Wealth of information on rainbows with fact sheets and lucid diagrams, answers to a series of standard questions, an experiment section, and extensive bibliographies.

rainforest dense forest usually found on or near the ◊Equator where the climate is hot and wet. Heavy rainfall results as the moist air brought by the converging tradewinds rises because of the heat. Over half the tropical rainforests are in Central and South America, the rest in SE Asia and Africa. They provide the bulk of the oxygen needed for plant and animal respiration. Tropical rainforest once covered 14% of the Earth's land surface, but are now being destroyed at an increasing rate as their valuable timber is harvested and the land cleared for agriculture, causing problems of ◊deforestation. Although by 1991 over 50% of the world's rainforest had been removed, they still comprise about 50% of all growing wood on the planet, and harbour at least 40% of the Earth's species (plants and animals).

Tropical rainforests are characterized by a great diversity of species, usually of tall broad-leafed evergreen trees, with many climbing vines and ferns, some of which are a main source of raw materials for medicines. A tropical forest, if properly preserved, can yield medicinal plants, oils (from cedar, juniper, cinnamon, sandalwood), spices, gums, resins (used in inks, lacquers, linoleum), tanning and dyeing materials, forage for animals, beverages, poisons, green manure, rubber, and animal products (feathers, hides, honey). Other rainforests include montane, upper montane or cloud, mangrove, and subtropical.

Rainforests comprise some of the most complex and diverse ecosystems on the planet and help to regulate global weather patterns. When deforestation occurs, the microclimate of the mature forest disappears; soil erosion and flooding become major problems since rainforests protect the shallow tropical soils. Once an area is cleared it is very difficult for shrubs and bushes to re-establish because soils are poor in nutrients. This causes problems for plans to convert rainforests into agricultural land – after two or three years the crops fail and the land is left bare. Clearing of the rainforests may lead to a global warming of the atmosphere, and contribute to the ◊greenhouse effect.

raisin dried grape, for eating as a fruit and also used in baking and confectionery. The chief kinds are the seedless raisin, the sultana, and the currant. The main producers are the Mediterranean area, California, Mexico, and Australia.

Grapes may be dried in the sun or artificially, using hot air. The dark colour of the dried fruit comes from the caramelization of natural sugars during the drying process. Drying reduces grapes to 25% of their original weight, while retaining almost all the nutritional value of the fresh fruit.

RAM (acronym for ***random-access memory***) in computing, a memory device in the form of a collection of integrated circuits (chips), frequently used in microcomputers. Unlike ◊ROM (read-only memory) chips, RAM chips can be both read from and written to by the computer, but their contents are lost when the power is switched off.

Many modern commercial programs require a great deal of RAM to work efficiently. While Windows 95 will run in 8 megabytes (MB) of RAM and is usable with 16 MB, 32 MB is better and many people now fit more.

RAMdisc ◊RAM that has been configured to appear to the operating system as a disc. It is much faster to access than an actual hard disc and therefore can be used for applications that need frequent read-and-write operations. However, as the data is stored in RAM, it will be lost when the computer is turned off.

ramjet simple jet engine (see under ◊jet propulsion) used in some guided missiles. It only comes into operation at high speeds. Air is then 'rammed' into the combustion chamber, into which fuel is sprayed and ignited.

Ramón y Cajal, Santiago (1852–1934)

Spanish cell biologist and anatomist whose research revealed that the nervous system is based on units of nerve cells (neurons). He shared the 1906 Nobel Prize for Physiology or Medicine.

ramp another name for an inclined plane, a slope used as a simple machine.

random access in computing, an alternative term for ◊direct access.

random event in statistics, an event that is not affected by either previous or future events. For example, if a new book is opened at random, all page numbers are equally likely.

random number one of a series of numbers having no detectable pattern. Random numbers are used in ◊computer simulation and ◊computer games. It is impossible for an ordinary computer to generate true random numbers, but various techniques are available for obtaining pseudo-random numbers – close enough to true randomness for most purposes.

range in statistics, a measure of dispersion in a frequency distribution, equalling the difference between the largest and smallest values of the variable. The range is sensitive to extreme values in the sense that it will give a distorted picture of the dispersion if one measurement is unusually large or small. The ◊interquartile range is often preferred.

range check in computing, a ◊validation check applied to a numerical data item to ensure that its value falls in a sensible range.

rangefinder instrument for determining the range or distance of an object from the observer; used to focus a camera or to sight a gun accurately. A **rangefinder camera** has a rotating mirror or prism that alters the image seen through the viewfinder, and a secondary window. When the two images are brought together into one, the lens is sharply focused.

rape in botany, either of two plant species of the mustard family grown for their seeds, which yield a pungent edible oil. The common turnip is a variety of *B. rapa* and the swede turnip is a variety of of *B. napus*. (*Brassica rapa* and *B. napus*, family Cruciferae.)

Oilseed rape, or canola, is the world's third most important oilseed crop. Plant breeders developed it from the 'weed' rapeseed (*B. napus oleifera*). The first variety was marketed 1974, and the bright yellow fields of oilseed rape in flower are now a familiar sight in the countryside.

Rape methyl ester provides a renewable replacement for diesel fuel that gives off fewer sooty particles and none of the sulphur dioxide that causes acid rain.

RARE (abbreviation for ***Réseaux Associés pour la Recherche Européenne***) association of national and international European computer networks and their users.

rare-earth element alternative name for ◊lanthanide.

rare gas alternative name for ◊inert gas.

rash in medicine, eruption on the surface of the skin. It is usually raised and red or it may contain vesicles filled with fluid. It may also be scaly or crusty. Characteristic rashes are produced by infectious diseases, such as chickenpox, measles, German measles, and scarlet fever. The severity of the rash usually reflects the severity of the disease. Rashes are also produced as an allergic response to stings from insects and plants. These are often alleviated by antihistamines and they usually resolve within a few days.

Chronic rashes are present in patients with some skin diseases, such as ◊eczema and ◊psoriasis.

raspberry any of a group of prickly cane plants native to Europe, Asia, and North America, and widely cultivated. They have white flowers followed by hollow red composite fruits, which are eaten fresh as a delicacy and used for making jam and wine. (Genus *Rubus*, family Rosaceae.)

raster graphics computer graphics that are stored in the computer memory by using a map to record data (such as colour and intensity) for every ◊pixel that makes up the image. When transformed (enlarged, rotated, stretched, and so on), raster graphics become ragged and suffer loss of picture resolution, unlike ◊vector graphics. Raster graphics are typically used for painting applications, which allow the user to create artwork on a computer screen much as if they were painting on paper or canvas.

raster image processor full name for printer program ◊RIP.

rat any of numerous long-tailed ◊rodents (especially of the families Muridae and Cricetidae) larger than mice and usually with scaly, naked tails. The genus *Rattus* in the family Muridae includes the rats found in human housing.

The **brown rat** *R. norvegicus* is about 20 cm/8 in long with a tail of almost equal length. It is believed to have originated in central Asia, and is now found worldwide after being transported from Europe by ships. Female brown rats become sexually receptive at the age of 8–12 weeks. If food is plentiful, litters of up to 12 are born every few months. The **black rat** *R. rattus*, responsible for the ◊plague, is smaller than the brown rat, but has larger ears and a longer, more pointed snout. It does not interbreed with brown rats. The **pack rat** or **wood rat**, genus *Neotoma*, is common throughout North America and there are seven different species. Their dens, made of partly eaten plants, dung, and miscellaneous objects, are known as middens and can be up to 2 m/6.5 ft across and 20–30 cm/8–12 in high. The rats' crystallized urine preserves the midden, in some cases for up to 40,000 years.

ratemeter instrument used to measure the count rate of a radioactive source. It gives a reading of the number of particles emitted from the source and captured by a detector in a unit of time (usually a second).

rate of reaction the speed at which a chemical reaction proceeds. It is usually expressed in terms of the concentration (usually in ◊moles per litre) of a reactant consumed, or product formed, in unit time; so the units would be moles per litre per second (mol l^{-1} s^{-1}). The rate of a reaction may be affected by the concentration of the reactants, the temperature of the reactants, and the presence of a catalyst. If the reaction is entirely in the gas state, the rate is affected by pressure, and, for solids, it is affected by the particle size.

During a reaction at constant temperature the concentration of the reactants decreases and so the rate of reaction decreases.

These changes can be represented by drawing graphs.

The rate of reaction is at its greatest at the beginning of the reaction and it gradually slows down. For an ◊endothermic reaction (one

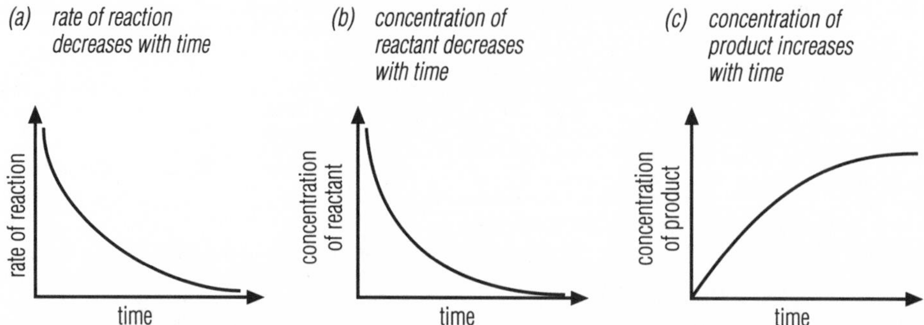
(a) rate of reaction decreases with time
(b) concentration of reactant decreases with time
(c) concentration of product increases with time
rate of reaction
concentration of reactant
concentration of product
time
time
time

rate of reaction *The rate of reaction decreases with time whilst the concentration of product increases.*

that absorbs heat) increasing the temperature may produce large increases in the rate of reaction. A 10°C rise can double the rate while a 40°C rise can produce a 50–100-fold increase in the rate.

◊Collision theory is used to explain these effects. Increasing the concentration or the pressure of a gas means there are more particles per unit volume, therefore there are more collisions and more fruitful collisions. Increasing the temperature makes the particles move much faster, resulting in more collisions per unit time and more fruitful collisions; consequently the rate increases.

ratio measure of the relative size of two quantities or of two measurements (in similar units), expressed as a proportion. For example, the ratio of vowels to consonants in the alphabet is 5:21; the ratio of 500 m to 2 km is 500:2,000, or 1:4.

rationalized units units for which the defining equations conform to the geometry of the system. Equations involving circular symmetry contain the factor 2π; those involving spherical symmetry 4π. ◊SI units are rationalized, ◊c.g.s. units are not.

rational number in mathematics, any number that can be expressed as an exact fraction (with a denominator not equal to 0), that is, as $a \div b$ where a and b are integers. For example, $\frac{2}{1}$, $\frac{1}{4}$, $\frac{15}{4}$, $-\frac{3}{5}$ are all rational numbers, whereas π (which represents the constant 3.141592 ...) is not. Numbers such as π are called ◊irrational numbers.

ratite flightless bird that has a breastbone without the keel to which flight muscles are attached. Examples are ◊ostrich, rhea, emu, cassowary, and ◊kiwi.

rat-tail *or* **grenadier** any fish of the family Macrouridae of deep-sea bony fishes. They have stout heads and bodies, and long tapering tails. They are common in deep waters on the continental slopes. Some species have a light-emitting organ in front of the anus.

Also known as rat-tails are some of the ◊chimaeras.

rattlesnake any of various New World pit ◊vipers of the genera *Crotalus* and *Sistrurus* (the massasaugas and pygmy rattlers), distinguished by horny flat segments of the tail, which rattle when vibrated as a warning to attackers. They can grow to 2.5 m/8 ft long. The venom injected by some rattlesnakes can be fatal.

There are 31 species distributed from S Canada to central South America. The eastern diamondback *C. adamanteus* 0.9–2.5 m/2.8–8 ft long, is found in the flat pinelands of the southern USA.

Raunkiaer system method of classification devised by the Danish ecologist Christen Raunkiaer (1860–1938) whereby plants are divided into groups according to the position of their ◊perennating (overwintering) buds in relation to the soil surface. For example, plants in cold areas, such as the tundra, generally have their buds protected below ground, whereas in hot, tropical areas they are above ground and freely exposed. This scheme is useful for comparing vegetation types in different parts of the world.

The main divisions are **phanerophytes** with buds situated well above the ground; **chamaephytes** with buds borne within 25 cm/10 in of the soil surface; **hemicryptophytes** with buds at or immediately below the soil surface; and **cryptophytes** with their buds either beneath the soil (**geophyte**) or below water (**hydrophyte**).

raven any of several large ◊crows, genus *Corvus*, of the Corvidae family, order Passeriformes. The common raven *C. corax* is about 60 cm/2 ft long with a wingspan of nearly 1 m/3 ft, and has black, lustrous plumage; the beak and mouth, tongue, legs, and feet are also black. It is a scavenger, and is found only in the northern hemisphere.

The nest is built in cliffs or in the fork of a tall tree, and is a bulky structure. In it are laid four or five pale-green eggs spotted with brown. Incubation by the female lasts about 21 days.

Ravens are traditionally associated with death, probably from their practice of gathering in large numbers around a carcass, despite being by habit a solitary species.

ray any of several orders (especially Ragiformes) of cartilaginous fishes with a flattened body, winglike pectoral fins, and a whiplike tail.

Species include the stingray, for example the Southern stingray *Dasyatis americana*, which has a serrated, poisonous spine on the tail, and the ◊torpedo fish.

ray, electric another name for the torpedo.

rayon any of various shiny textile fibres and fabrics made from ◊cellulose. It is produced by pressing whatever cellulose solution is used through very small holes and solidifying the resulting filaments. A common type is ◊viscose, which consists of regenerated filaments of pure cellulose. Acetate and triacetate are kinds of rayon consisting of filaments of cellulose acetate and triacetate.

rays original name for radiation of all types, such as ◊X-rays and gamma rays.

ray-tracing in computer graphics, method of rendering sharp, detailed images. Designers specify the size, shape, colour, and texture of objects and the type and location of light sources, and use a program to devise a mathematical model tracing how light rays would bounce off the surfaces. The results, complete with shading, shadows, and reflections, depict 'virtual worlds' with near-photographic clarity.

razorbill North Atlantic sea bird *Alca torda* of the auk family, order Charadriiformes, which breeds on cliffs and migrates south in winter. It is about 40 cm/16 in long, has a large curved beak, and is black above and white below. It uses its wings as paddles when diving. Razorbills make no nest; the female lays a single egg, which is white with brown markings. They are common off Newfoundland.

razor-shell or ***razor-fish***; US name ***razor clam*** any bivalve mollusc in two genera *Ensis* and *Solen* with narrow, elongated shells, resembling an old-fashioned razor handle and delicately coloured. They can burrow rapidly into sand and are good swimmers.

reactance property of an alternating current circuit that together with any ◊resistance makes up the vimpedance (the total opposition of the circuit to the passage of a current).

The reactance of an inductance L is wL and that of the capacitance is $1/wC$. Reactance is measured in vohms.

reaction in chemistry, the coming together of two or more atoms, ions, or molecules with the result that a ◊chemical change takes place. The nature of the reaction is portrayed by a chemical equation.

reaction force in physics, the equal and opposite force described by Newton's third law of motion that arises whenever one object applies a force (**action force**) to another. For example, if a magnet attracts a piece of iron, then that piece of iron will also attract the magnet with a force that is equal in magnitude but opposite in direction. When any object rests on the ground the downwards contact force applied to the ground always produces an equal, upwards reaction force.

reaction principle principle stated by ◊Newton as his third law of motion: to every action, there is an equal and opposite reaction.

In other words, a force acting in one direction is always accompanied by an equal force acting in the opposite direction. This explains how rocket and ◊jet propulsion works and why a gun recoils after firing.

reactivity series chemical series produced by arranging the metals in order of their ease of reaction with reagents such as oxygen, water, and acids. This arrangement aids the understanding of the properties of metals, helps to explain differences between them, and enables predictions to be made about a metal's behaviour, based on a knowledge of its position or properties.

read-only storage in computing, a permanent means of storing data so that it can be read any number of times but cannot be modified. CD-ROM is a read-only storage medium; CD-ROMs come with the data already encoded on them.

RealAudio in computing, software system for broadcasting sound over the Internet in real time. Broadcasters use an encoder and a special server to provide content, and members of the 'audience' can listen to live radio or create a customized news broadcast which they can download whenever they wish. RealAudio software is supplied by RealNetworks Inc (formerly called Progressive Networks). Its RealPlayer software plays RealAudio and RealVideo.

real number in mathematics, any of the ◊rational numbers (which include the integers) or ◊irrational numbers. Real numbers exclude vimaginary numbers, found in ◊complex numbers of the general form $a + bi$ where $i = \sqrt{-1}$, although these do include a real component a.

real-time system in computing, a program that responds to events in the world as they happen. For example, an automatic-pilot program in an aircraft must respond instantly in order to correct deviations from its course. Process control, robotics, games, and many military applications are examples of real-time systems.

receiver, radio component of a radio communication system that receives and processes radio waves. It detects and selects modulated radio waves (see ◊modulation) by means of an aerial and tuned circuit, and then separates the transmitted information from the carrier wave by a process that involves rectification. The receiver device will usually also include the amplifiers that produce the audio signals (signals that are heard).

receptacle the enlarged end of a flower stalk to which the floral parts are attached. Normally the receptacle is rounded, but in some plants it is flattened or cup-shaped. The term is also used for the region on that part of some seaweeds which becomes swollen at certain times of the year and bears the reproductive organs.

receptor in biology, receptors are discrete areas of cell membranes or areas within cells with which neurotransmitters, hormones, and drugs interact. Such interactions control the activities of the body. For example, adrenaline transmits nervous impulses to receptors in the sympathetic nervous system which initiates the characteristic response to excitement and fear in an individual.

Other types of receptors, such as the proprioceptors, are located in muscles, tendons, and joints. They relay information on the position of the body and the state of muscle contraction to the brain.

recessive gene in genetics, an ◊allele (alternative form of a gene) that will show in the ◊phenotype (observed characteristics of an organism) only if its partner allele on the paired chromosome is similarly recessive. Such an allele will not show if its partner is dominant, that is if the organism is ◊heterozygous for a particular characteristic. Alleles for blue eyes in humans, and for shortness in pea plants are recessive. Most mutant alleles are recessive and therefore are only rarely expressed (see ◊haemophilia and ◊sickle-cell disease).

Natural selection has no vision, no foresight, no sight at all. If it can be said to play the role of watchmaker in nature, it is the blind watchmaker.

RICHARD DAWKINS English zoologist.
The Blind Watchmaker 1986

---

reciprocal in mathematics, the result of dividing a given quantity into 1. Thus the reciprocal of 2 is $\frac{1}{2}$; of $\frac{2}{3}$ is $\frac{3}{2}$; of x^2 is $\frac{1}{x^2}$ or x^{-2}. Reciprocals are used to replace division by multiplication, since multiplying by the reciprocal of a number is the same as dividing by that number.

recombinant DNA in genetic engineering, ◊DNA formed by splicing together genes from different sources into new combinations.

recombination in genetics, any process that recombines, or 'shuffles', the genetic material, thus increasing genetic variation in the offspring. The two main processes of recombination both occur during meiosis (reduction division of cells). One is ◊crossing over, in which chromosome pairs exchange segments; the other is the random reassortment of chromosomes that occurs when each gamete (sperm or egg) receives only one of each chromosome pair.

record in computing, a collection of related data items or **fields**. A record usually forms part of a ◊file.

recording any of a variety of techniques used to capture, store, and reproduce music, speech, and other information carried by sound waves. A microphone first converts the sound waves into an electrical signal which varies in proportion to the loudness of the sound. The signal can be stored in digital or analogue form, or on magnetic tape.

analogue recording In an analogue recording, the pattern of the signal is copied into another form. In a **vinyl** gramophone record, for example, a continuous spiral groove is cut into a plastic disc by vibrating needle. The recording is replayed by a stylus which follows the undulations in the groove, so reproducing the vibrations which are amplified and turned back into sound. In a **magnetic tape** recording, the signal is recorded as a pattern of magnetization on a plastic tape coated with a magnetic powder. When the tape is played back, the magnetic patterns create an electrical signal which, as with the gramophone record, is used to recreate the original sound. All analogue recording techniques suffer from background noise and the quality of reproduction is gradually degraded as the disc or tape wears.

digital recording In digital recording, the signals picked up by the microphone are converted into a stream of numbers which can then be stored in several ways. The most well-known of these is the ◊compact disc, in which numbers are coded as a string of tiny pits pressed into a 12-cm plastic disc. When the recording is played back, using a laser, the exact values are retrieved and converted into a varying electrical signal and then back into sound. Digital recording is relatively immune to noise and interference and gives a very high quality of reproduction. It is also suitable for storing information to be processed by computers.

record player device for reproducing recorded sound stored as a spiral groove on a vinyl disc. A motor-driven turntable rotates the record at a constant speed, and a stylus or needle on the head of a pick-up is made to vibrate by the undulations in the record groove. These vibrations are then converted to electrical signals by a ◊transducer in the head (often a ◊piezoelectric crystal). After amplification, the signals pass to one or more loudspeakers, which convert them into sound. Alternative formats are ◊compact disc and magnetic ◊tape recording.

The pioneers of the record player were Thomas ◊Edison, with his ◊phonograph, and Emile Berliner (1851–1929), who invented the predecessor of the vinyl record 1896. More recent developments are stereophonic sound and digital recording on compact disc.

rectangle quadrilateral (four-sided plane figure) with opposite sides equal and parallel and with each interior angle a right angle (90°). Its area A is the product of the length l and height h; that is, $A = l \times h$. A rectangle with all four sides equal is a ◊square.

A rectangle is a special case of a ◊parallelogram. The diagonals of a rectangle are equal and bisect each other.

rectangular axis another name for ◊Cartesian coordinates.

rectangular hyperbola the graph of the ◊function $y = 1/x$. The x and y axes are ◊asymptotes to this curve.

rectangular prism another name for a ◊cuboid.

rectifier in electrical engineering, a device used for obtaining one-directional current (DC) from an alternating source of supply (AC). (The process is necessary because almost all electrical power is generated, transmitted, and supplied as alternating current, but many devices, from television sets to electric motors, require direct current.) Types include plate rectifiers, thermionic ◊diodes, and ◊semiconductor diodes.

rectum lowest part of the large intestine of animals, which stores faeces prior to elimination (defecation).

recurring decimal any fraction that cannot be represented in the decimal system by a finite decimal. All fractions will result in recurring decimals unless the denominator of the fraction is either a power of 2 or 5, or a multiple of these. For example, $\frac{1}{4}$ is 0.25 but $\frac{1}{6}$ (= $\frac{1}{2}$ x 3) is 0.1666... .

recursion in computing and mathematics, a technique whereby a ◊function or ◊procedure calls itself into use in order to enable a complex problem to be broken down into simpler steps. For example, a function that finds the factorial of a number n (calculates the product of all the whole numbers between 1 and n) would obtain its result by multiplying n by the factorial of $n - 1$.

recycling processing of industrial and household waste (such as paper, glass, and some metals and plastics) so that the materials can be reused. This saves expenditure on scarce raw materials, slows down the depletion of ◊nonrenewable resources, and helps to reduce pollution.

The USA recycles only around 13% of its waste, compared to around 33% in Japan. However, all US states encourage or require local recycling programmes to be set up. It was estimated 1992 that 4,000 cities collected waste from 71 million people for recycling. Most of these programmes were set up 1989–92. Around 33% of newspapers, 22% of office paper, 64% of aluminium cans, 3% of plastic containers, and 20% of all glass bottles and jars were recycled.

Aluminium is frequently recycled because of its value and special properties that allow it to be melted down and re-pressed without loss of quality, unlike paper and glass, which deteriorate when recycled.

RECYCLE CITY

http://www.epa.gov/recyclecity/

Child-friendly site of the US Environmental Protection Agency designed to help people to live more ecologically. The site includes a host of fun games and activities to encourage children to think about waste disposal issues.

red admiral butterfly butterfly with black wings crossed by scarlet bands and marked with white and blue spots. The spiny black caterpillar feeds on nettles.
classification The red admiral butterfly *Vanessa atalanta* is in order Lepidoptera, lass Insecta, phylum Arthropoda.

red blood cell or ***erythrocyte*** the most common type of blood cell, responsible for transporting oxygen around the body. It contains haemoglobin, which combines with oxygen from the lungs to form oxyhaemoglobin. When transported to the tissues, these cells are able to release the oxygen because the oxyhaemoglobin splits into its original constituents.

Mammalian erythrocytes are disc-shaped with a depression in the centre and no nucleus; they are manufactured in the bone marrow and, in humans, last for only four months before being destroyed in the liver and spleen. Those of other vertebrates are oval and nucleated.

red cedar tree *Toona australis* native to New Guinea and E Australia. It is a deciduous rainforest tree and is valued for its beautiful red timber. Much early Australian colonial furniture came from this species.

redcurrant in botany, type of ◊currant.

Red Data List report published by the World Conservation Union (IUCN) and regularly updated that lists animal species by their conservation status. Categories of risk include **extinct in the wild**, **critically endangered**, **endangered**, **vulnerable**, and **lower risk** (divided into three subcategories). The list was updated 1996.

red deer large deer widely distributed throughout Europe, Asia and North Africa. A full-grown male (stag or hart) stands 1.2 m/4 ft at the withers, and typical antlers measure about 80 cm/31 in in length with a spread of about the same. During the breeding season the colour is a rich brown, turning grey at the approach of winter. The young are spotted with white.

The antlers are shed in April or May, and a few days afterwards the new growth shows. While the new antlers are developing they are covered with a thick velvet, and while in this condition are very sensitive. They are full-grown in about 12 weeks, and the 'velvet' is then rubbed off. Hornless stags sometimes occur.
classification The red deer *Cervus elaphus* is in family Cervidae, order Artiodactyla.

red dwarf any star that is cool, faint, and small (about one-tenth the mass and diameter of the Sun). Red dwarfs burn slowly, and have estimated lifetimes of 100 billion years. They may be the most abundant type of star, but are difficult to see because they are so faint. Two of the closest stars to the Sun, ◊Proxima Centauri and ◊Barnard's Star, are red dwarfs.

The whole history of particle physics, or of physics, is one of getting down the number of concepts to as few as possible.

ABDUS SALAM Pakistani physicist.
L Wolpert and A Richards *A Passion for Science* 1988

red giant any large bright star with a cool surface. It is thought to represent a late stage in the evolution of a star like the Sun, as it runs out of hydrogen fuel at its centre. Red giants have diameters between 10 and 100 times that of the Sun. They are very bright because they are so large, although their surface temperature is lower than that of the Sun, about 2,000–3,000K (1,700–2,700°C/3,000–5,000°F). See also Red ◊supergiants.

red-hot poker any of a group of perennial plants native to Africa, in particular *K. uvaria*, with a flame-coloured spike of flowers. (Genus *Kniphofia*, family Liliaceae.)

redox reaction chemical change where one reactant is reduced and the other reactant oxidized. The reaction can only occur if both reactants are present and each changes simultaneously. For example, hydrogen reduces copper(II) oxide to copper while it is itself oxidized to water. The corrosion of iron and the reactions taking place in electric and electrolytic cells are just a few instances of redox reactions.

red pepper red fruit of various ◊capsicums.

red setter breed of dog. See ◊setter.

redshank wading bird *Tringa totanus* of N Europe and Asia, a type of sandpiper. It nests in swampy areas, rarely in Europe, since most redshanks winter in the south. It is greyish and speckled black, and has long red legs.

red shift in astronomy, the lengthening of the wavelengths of light from an object as a result of the object's motion away from us. It is an example of the ◊Doppler effect. The red shift in light from galaxies is evidence that the universe is expanding.

Lengthening of wavelengths causes the light to move or shift towards the red end of the ◊spectrum, hence the name. The amount of red shift can be measured by the displacement of lines in an object's spectrum. By measuring the amount of red shift in light from stars and galaxies, astronomers can tell how quickly these objects are moving away from us. A strong gravitational field can also produce a red shift in light; this is termed **gravitational red shift**.

redstart any bird of the genus *Phoenicurus*, a member of the thrush family Muscicapidae, order Passeriformes. It winters in Africa and spends the summer in Eurasia. The **American redstart** *Setophaga ruticulla* belongs to the family Parulidae.

Redstone rocket short-range US military missile, modified for use as a space launcher. Redstone rockets launched the first two flights of the ◊Mercury project. A modified Redstone, *Juno 1*, launched the first US satellite, *Explorer 1*, in 1958.

> TO REMEMBER THE PRINCIPLES OF OXIDATION AND REDUCTION:
>
> REMEMBER THAT **LEO** THE LION GOES '**GER**'
>
> **L**OSE **E**LECTRONS – **O**XIDATION, **G**AIN **E**LECTRONS – **R**EDUCTION

reduction in chemistry, the gain of electrons, loss of oxygen, or gain of hydrogen by an atom, ion, or molecule during a chemical reaction.

Reduction may be brought about by reaction with another compound, which is simultaneously oxidized (reducing agent), or electrically at the cathode (negative electrode) of an electric cell.

redundancy in computing, duplication of information. Redundancy is often used as a check, when an additional check digit or bit is included. See also ◊validation.

redwing type of thrush *Turdus iliacus*, family Muscicapidae, order Passeriformes. It is smaller than the song thrush, with reddish wing and body markings, and there is a distinct white line over the eye. It breeds in the north of Europe and Asia, flying south in winter.

redwood giant coniferous tree, one of the two types of ◊sequoia.

reed any of various perennial tall, slender grasses found growing in wet or marshy environments; also the hollow, jointed stalks of any of these plants. The common reed (*P. australis*) reaches a height of 3 m/10 ft, having stiff, upright leaves and straight stems with a plume of purplish flowers at the top. (Especially species of the genera *Phragmites* and *Arundo*, family Gramineae.)

reed switch switch containing two or three thin iron strips, or reeds, inside a sealed glass tube. When a magnet is brought near the switch, it induces magnetism in the reeds, which then attract or repel each other according to the positions of their induced magnetic poles. Electric current is switched on or off as the reeds make or break contact.

A simple burglar alarm can be constructed by inserting a magnet into the closing edge of a door, and a reed switch into the part of the doorframe facing the magnet: when the door is closed the magnet remains close to the switch, keeping a circuit open; when the door is opened the magnet moves away, closing the switch and setting off an alarm.

re-entrant polygon a ◊polygon that is not completely convex. It has at least one interior angle greater than 180°.

reflecting telescope in astronomy, a ◊telescope in which light is collected and brought to a focus by a concave mirror. ◊Cassegrain telescope and ◊Newtonian telescope are examples.

referee in science, one who reads and comments on a scientific paper before its publication, normally a scientist of at least equal standing to the author(s).

refining any process that purifies or converts something into a more useful form. Metals usually need refining after they have been extracted from their ores by such processes as ◊smelting. Petroleum, or crude oil, needs refining before it can be used; the process involves fractional ◊distillation, the separation of the substance into separate components or 'fractions'.

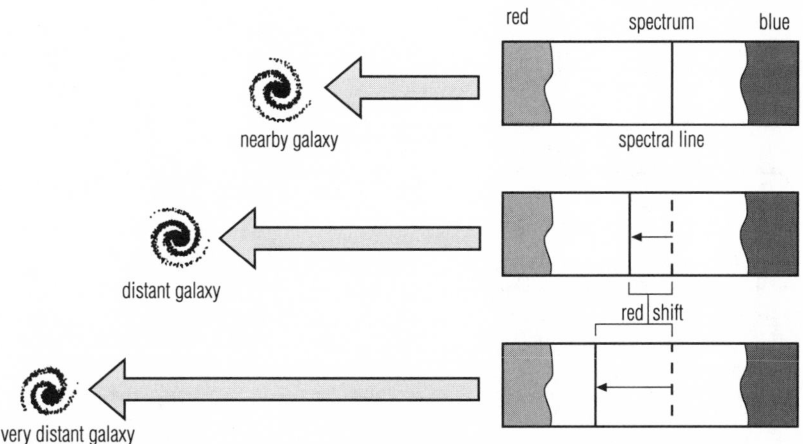

***red shift** The red shift causes lines in the spectra of galaxies to be shifted towards the red end of the spectrum. More distant galaxies have greater red shifts than closer galaxies. The red shift indicates that distant galaxies are moving apart rapidly, as the universe expands.*

Electrolytic metal-refining methods use the principle of ◊electrolysis to obtain pure metals. When refining petroleum, or crude oil, further refinery processes after fractionation convert the heavier fractions into more useful lighter products. The most important of these processes is ◊cracking; others include ◊polymerization, hydrogenation, and reforming.

reflection in geometry, a ◊transformation that maps a shape across a line so that the line forms an axis of reflectional symmetry. Reflections in two perpendicular axes produce a rotation of 180° (a half turn). Reflections can be used to deduce many properties of shapes.

reflection in physics, the throwing back or deflection of waves, such as ◊light or ◊sound waves, when they hit a surface. The **law of reflection** states that the angle of incidence (the angle between the ray and a perpendicular line drawn to the surface) is equal to the angle of reflection (the angle between the reflected ray and a perpendicular to the surface).

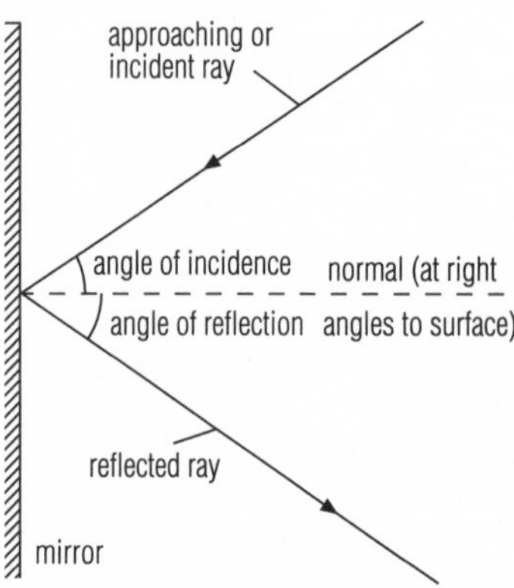

reflection *The law of reflection: the angle of incidence of a light beam equals the angle of reflection of the beam.*

reflex in animals, a very rapid involuntary response to a particular stimulus. It is controlled by the ◊nervous system. A reflex involves only a few nerve cells, unlike the slower but more complex responses produced by the many processing nerve cells of the brain.

A **simple reflex** is entirely automatic and involves no learning. Examples of such reflexes include the sudden withdrawal of a hand in response to a painful stimulus, or the jerking of a leg when the kneecap is tapped. Sensory cells (receptors) in the knee send signals to the spinal cord along a sensory nerve cell. Within the spine a **reflex arc** switches the signals straight back to the muscles of the leg (effectors) via an intermediate nerve cell and then a motor nerve cell; contraction of the leg occurs, and the leg kicks upwards. Only three nerve cells are involved, and the brain is only aware of the response after it has taken place. Such reflex arcs are particularly common in lower animals, and have a high survival value, enabling organisms to take rapid action to avoid potential danger. In higher animals (those with a well-developed ◊central nervous system) the simple reflex can be modified by the involvement of the brain – for instance, humans can override the automatic reflex to withdraw a hand from a source of pain.

A **conditioned reflex** involves the modification of a reflex action in response to experience (learning). A stimulus that produces a simple reflex response becomes linked with another, possibly unrelated, stimulus. For example, a dog may salivate (a reflex action) when it sees its owner remove a tin-opener from a drawer because it has learned to associate that stimulus with the stimulus of being fed.

Experiment alone crowns the efforts of medicine, experiment limited only by the natural range of the powers of the human mind. Observation discloses in the animal organism numerous phenomena existing side by side, and interconnected now profoundly, now indirectly, or accidentally. Confronted with a multitude of different assumptions the mind must guess the real nature of this connection.

IVAN PAVLOV Russian physiologist.
Experimental Psychology and Other Essays, Pt X

reflex angle an angle greater than 180° but less than 360°.

reflex camera camera that uses a mirror and prisms to reflect light passing through the lens into the viewfinder, showing the photographer the exact scene that is being shot. When the shutter button is released the mirror springs out of the way, allowing light to reach the film. The most common type is the single-lens reflex (◊SLR) camera. The twin-lens reflex (TLR) camera has two lenses: one has a mirror for viewing, the other is used for exposing the film.

reflexology in alternative medicine, manipulation and massage of the feet to ascertain and treat disease or dysfunction elsewhere in the body.

Correspondence between reflex points on the feet and remote organic and physical functions were discovered early in the 20th century by US physician William Fitzgerald, who also found that pressure and massage applied to these reflex points beneficially affect the related organ or function.

refraction the bending of a wave when it passes from one medium to another. Refraction occurs because waves travel at different velocities in different media.

refraction *Refraction is the bending of a light beam when it passes from one transparent medium to another. This is why a spoon appears bent when standing in a glass of water and pools of water appear shallower than they really are. The quantity* $\frac{\sin i}{\sin r}$ *has a constant value, for each material, called the refractive index.*

refractive index measure of the refraction of a ray of light as it passes from one transparent medium to another. If the angle of incidence is i and the angle of refraction is r, the ratio of the two refractive indices is given by $\frac{n_1}{n_2} = \frac{\sin i}{\sin r}$. It is also equal to the speed of light in the first medium divided by the speed of light in the second, and it varies with the wavelength of the light.

refractor in astronomy, ◊telescope in which light is collected and brought to a focus by a convex lens (the object lens or objective).

refractory (of a material) able to resist high temperature, for example ceramics made from clay, minerals, or other earthy materials. Furnaces are lined with refractory materials such as silica and dolomite.

Alumina (aluminium oxide) is an excellent refractory, often used for the bodies of spark plugs. Titanium and tungsten are often called refractory metals because they are temperature resistant. ◊Cermets are refractory materials made up of ceramics and metals.

refresh in computing, to redraw the image on a ◊VDU. All such images are a series of frames created by a device – in the case of a cathode ray tube, an electron beam – which 'paints' the image on the screen, ◊pixel bypixel. This process is too rapid for the human eye to detect, although a high **refresh rate** (number of times a screen is redrawn per second) is said to reduce eye strain.

refrigeration use of technology to transfer heat from cold to warm, against the normal temperature gradient, so that a body can remain substantially colder than its surroundings. Refrigeration equipment is used for the chilling and deep-freezing of food in ◊food technology, and in air conditioners and industrial processes.

Refrigeration is commonly achieved by a vapour-compression cycle, in which a suitable chemical (the refrigerant) travels through a long circuit of tubing, during which it changes from a vapour to a liquid and back again. A compression chamber makes it condense, and thus give out heat. In another part of the circuit, called the evaporator coils, the pressure is much lower, so the refrigerant evaporates, absorbing heat as it does so. The evaporation process takes place near the central part of the refrigerator, which therefore becomes colder, while the compression process takes place near a ventilation grille, transferring the heat to the air outside. The most commonly used refrigerants in modern systems were ◊chlorofluorocarbons, but these are now being replaced by coolants that do not damage the ozone layer.

REFRIGERATION

The philosopher Francis Bacon was probably the first person whose death was caused by frozen food. Experimenting with the idea of preserving meat by freezing, he stuffed a chicken with snow. Unfortunately the experiment resulted in his catching a chill, then bronchitis, which led to his death.

regelation phenomenon in which water refreezes to ice after it has been melted by pressure at a temperature below the freezing point of water. Pressure makes an ice skate, for example, form a film of water that freezes once again after the skater has passed.

regeneration in biology, regrowth of a new organ or tissue after the loss or removal of the original. It is common in plants, where a new individual can often be produced from a 'cutting' of the original. In animals, regeneration of major structures is limited to lower organisms; certain lizards can regrow their tails if these are lost, and new flatworms can grow from a tiny fragment of an old one. In mammals, regeneration is limited to the repair of tissue in wound healing and the regrowth of peripheral nerves following damage.

The human body is an energy system ... which is never a complete structure; never static; is in perpetual inner self-construction and self-destruction; we destroy in order to make it new.

NORMAN O BROWN US philosopher. *Love's Body* ch 8

register in computing, a memory location that can be accessed rapidly; it is often built into the computer's central processing unit.

Some registers are reserved for special tasks – for example, an **instruction register** is used to hold the machine-code command that the computer is currently executing, while a **sequence-control register** keeps track of the next command to be executed. Other registers are used for holding frequently used data and for storing intermediate results.

registration in computing, informing a manufacturer that you have bought their product. For computer hardware, registration brings the consumer benefits such as on-site service and access to a free telephone helpline. Software houses also give registered customers telephone support and may supply them with upgrades and new product information.

For ◊shareware, registration is virtually synonymous with payment. Programs are supplied save-disabled, incomplete, or with frequent, annoying built-in reminders to register. Only by sending the small fee requested can the user obtain a code to release the program's full potential, as well as the legal right to continue using it.

regolith the surface layer of loose material that covers most bedrock. It consists of eroded rocky material, volcanic ash, river alluvium, vegetable matter, or a mixture of these known as ◊soil.

regular of geometric figures, having all angles and sides equal. Also, of solids, having bases comprised of regular ◊polygons.

Regulus or ***Alpha Leonis*** the brightest star in the constellation Leo, and the 21st brightest star in the sky. First-magnitude Regulus has a true luminosity 100 times that of the Sun, and is 69 light years from Earth.

Regulus was one of the four royal stars of ancient Persia marking the approximate positions of the Sun at the equinoxes and solstices. The other three were ◊Aldebaran, Antares, and ◊Fomalhaut.

reindeer or ***caribou*** deer *Rangifer tarandus* of Arctic and subarctic regions, common to North America and Eurasia. About 1.2 m/4 ft at the shoulder, it has a thick, brownish coat and broad hooves well adapted to travel over snow. It is the only deer in which both sexes have antlers; these can grow to 1.5 m/5 ft long, and are shed in winter.

The Old World reindeer have been domesticated by the Lapps of Scandinavia for centuries. There are two types of North American caribou: the large woodland caribou of the more southerly regions, and the barren-ground caribou of the far north. Reindeer migrate south in winter, moving in large herds. They eat grass, small plants, and lichens.

relational database ◊database in which data are viewed as a collection of linked tables. It is the most popular of the three basic database models, the others being **network** and **hierarchical**.

relative in computing (of a value), variable and calculated from a base value. For example, a **relative address** is a memory location that is found by adding a variable to a base (fixed) address, and a **relative cell reference** locates a cell in a spreadsheet by its position relative to a base cell – perhaps directly to the left of the base cell or three columns to the right of the base cell. The opposite of relative is ◊absolute.

relative atomic mass the mass of an atom relative to one-twelfth the mass of an atom of carbon-12. It depends primarily on the number of protons and neutrons in the atom, the electrons having negligible mass. If more than one ◊isotope of the element is present, the relative atomic mass is calculated by taking an average that takes account of the relative proportions of each isotope, resulting in values that are not whole numbers. The term **atomic weight**, although commonly used, is strictly speaking incorrect.

relative biological effectiveness (RBE) the relative damage caused to living tissue by different types of radiation. Some radiations do much more damage than others; alpha particles, for example, cause 20 times as much destruction as electrons (beta particles).

The RBE is defined as the ratio of the absorbed dose of a standard amount of radiation to the absorbed dose of 200 kV X-rays that produces the same amount of biological damage.

relative density the density (at 20°C/68°F) of a solid or liquid relative to (divided by) the maximum density of water (at 4°C/39.2°F). The relative density of a gas is its density divided by the density of hydrogen (or sometimes dry air) at the same temperature and pressure.

relative humidity the concentration of water vapour in the air. It is expressed as the ratio of the partial pressure of the water vapour to its saturated vapour pressure at the same temperature. The higher the temperature, the higher the saturated vapour pressure.

relative molecular mass the mass of a molecule, calculated relative to one-twelfth the mass of an atom of carbon-12. It is found by adding the relative atomic masses of the atoms that make up the molecule.

The term **molecular weight** is often used, but strictly this is incorrect.

relativity in physics, the theory of the relative rather than absolute character of motion and mass, and the interdependence of matter, time, and space, as developed by German-born US physicist Albert ◊Einstein in two phases:

special theory of relativity (1905) Starting with the premises that (1) the laws of nature are the same for all observers in unaccelerated motion, and (2) the speed of light is independent of the motion of its source, Einstein arrived at some rather unexpected consequences. Intuitively familiar concepts, like mass, length, and time, had to be modified. For example, an object moving rapidly past the observer will appear to be both shorter and heavier than when it is at rest (that is, at rest relative to the observer), and a clock moving rapidly past the observer will appear to be running slower than when it is at rest. These predictions of relativity theory seem to be foreign to everyday experience merely because the changes are quite negligible at speeds less than about 1,500 km s^{-1}, and they only become appreciable at speeds approaching the speed of light.

general theory of relativity (1915) The geometrical properties of space-time were to be conceived as modified locally by the presence of a body with mass. A planet's orbit around the Sun (as observed in three-dimensional space) arises from its natural trajectory in modified space-time; there is no need to invoke, as Isaac ◊Newton did, a force of ◊gravity coming from the Sun and acting on the planet. Einstein's general theory accounts for a peculiarity in the behaviour of the motion of the perihelion of the orbit of the planet Mercury that cannot be explained in Newton's theory. The new theory also said that light rays should bend when they pass by a massive object. The predicted bending of starlight was observed during the eclipse of the Sun 1919. A third corroboration is found in the shift towards the red in the spectra of the Sun and, in particular, of stars of great density – white dwarfs such as the companion of Sirius.

Einstein showed that, for consistency with the above premises (1) and (2), the principles of dynamics as established by Newton needed modification; the most celebrated new result was the equation $E = mc^2$, which expresses an equivalence between mass (m) and ◊energy (E), c being the speed of light in a vacuum. In 'relativistic mechanics', conservation of mass is replaced by the new concept of conservation of 'mass-energy'.

General relativity is central to modern ◊astrophysics and ◊cosmology; it predicts, for example, the possibility of ◊black holes. General relativity theory was inspired by the simple idea that it is impossible in a small region to distinguish between acceleration and gravitation effects (as in a lift one feels heavier when the lift accelerates upwards), but the mathematical development of the idea is formidable. Such is not the case for the special theory, which a nonexpert can follow up to $E = mc^2$ and beyond.

relay in electrical engineering, an electromagnetic switch. A small current passing through a coil of wire wound around an iron core attracts an ◊armature whose movement closes a pair of sprung contacts to complete a secondary circuit, which may carry a large current or activate other devices. The solid-state equivalent is a thyristor switching device.

relay neuron nerve cell in the spinal cord, connecting motor neurons to sensory neurons. Relay neurons allow information to pass straight through the spinal cord, bypassing the brain. In humans such reflex actions, which are extremely rapid, cause the sudden removal of a limb from a painful stimulus.

reload in computing, command which asks a ◊browser to reopen a currently-displayed ◊URL. Reloading may 'unstall' a partially-loaded page or bring a faster download from a busy server.

rem (acronym of ***roentgen equivalent man***) unit of radiation dose equivalent.

remission in medicine, temporary disappearance of symptoms during the course of a disease.

remora any of a family of warm-water fishes that have an adhesive disc on the head, by which they attach themselves to whales, sharks, and turtles. These provide the remora with shelter and transport, as well as food in the form of parasites on the host's skin.

remote imaging photographing the Earth's surface with orbiting satellites. With a simple aerial, receiver and software it is possible to download images straight on to a personal computer – helping amateur meteorologists, for example, to make weather forecasts.

remote sensing gathering and recording information from a distance. Space probes have sent back photographs and data about planets as distant as Neptune. In archaeology, surface survey techniques provide information without disturbing subsurface deposits.

Satellites such as *Landsat* have surveyed all the Earth's surface from orbit. Computer processing of data obtained by their scanning instruments, and the application of so-called false colours (generated by the computer), have made it possible to reveal surface features invisible in ordinary light. This has proved valuable in agriculture, forestry, and urban planning, and has led to the discovery of new deposits of minerals.

REMOTE SENSING IN HISTORY

http://observe.ivv.nasa.gov/nasa/exhibits/history/history_0.html

Brief timeline with some often not appreciated landmarks in the history of remote sensing and an engaging investigation into the long-held desire of people to look further and further away from them.

remote terminal in computing, a terminal that communicates with a computer via a modem (or acoustic coupler) and a telephone line.

REM sleep (acronym for ***rapid-eye-movement sleep***) phase of sleep that recurs several times nightly in humans and is associated with dreaming. The eyes flicker quickly beneath closed lids.

Renault France's largest motor-vehicle manufacturer, founded 1898. In Nov 1994 the French government began to implement

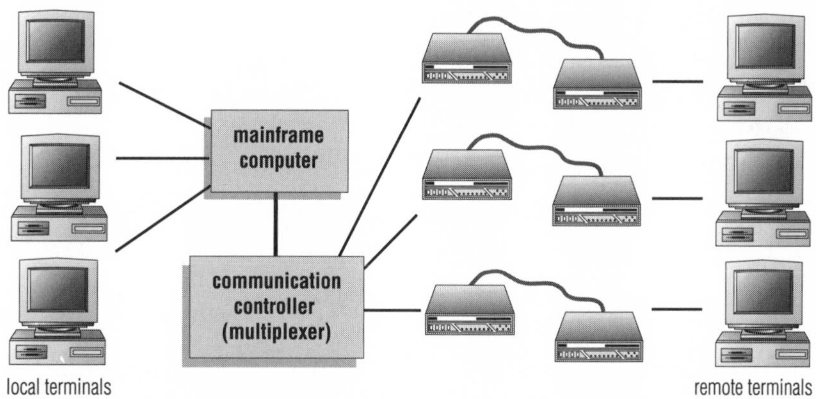

remote terminal *Remote computer terminals communicate with the central mainframe via modems and telephone lines. The controller allocates computer time to the terminals according to predetermined priority rules. The multiplexor allows more than one terminal to use the same communications link at the same time (multiplexing).*

plans to privatize the company, which had been nationalized from 1944.

Louis Renault (1877–1944) formed the company with his brothers Fernand and Marcel. In 1899 they began motor racing, which boosted the sales of their cars, and by 1908 they were producing 5,000 cars a year. The company produced tanks for the French army in both world wars.

rendering using a computer to draw an image on a computer screen. In graphics, this often means using ◊ray-tracing, phong shading, or a similar program to turn an outline sketch into a detailed image of a solid object.

renewable energy power from any source that replenishes itself. Most renewable systems rely on ◊solar energy directly or through the weather cycle as ◊wave power, hydroelectric power, or ◊wind power via wind turbines, or solar energy collected by plants (alcohol fuels, for example). In addition, the gravitational force of the Moon can be harnessed through ◊tidal power stations, and the heat trapped in the centre of the Earth is used via ◊geothermal energy systems.

renewable resource natural resource that is replaced by natural processes in a reasonable amount of time. Soil, water, forests, plants, and animals are all renewable resources as long as they are properly conserved. Solar, wind, wave, and geothermal energies are based on renewable resources.

rennet extract, traditionally obtained from a calf's stomach, that contains the enzyme rennin, used to coagulate milk in the cheese-making process. The enzyme can now be chemically produced.

rennin or ***chymase*** enzyme found in the gastric juice of young mammals, used in the digestion of milk.

repellent anything whose smell, taste, or other properties discourages nearby creatures. **Insect repellent** is usually a chemical substance that keeps, for example, mosquitoes at bay; natural substances include citronella, lavender oil, and eucalyptus oils. A device that emits ultrasound waves is also claimed to repel insects and small mammals.

repetitive strain injury (RSI) inflammation of tendon sheaths, mainly in the hands and wrists, which may be disabling. It is found predominantly in factory workers involved in constant repetitive movements, and in those who work with computer keyboards. The symptoms include aching muscles, weak wrists, tingling fingers and in severe cases, pain and paralysis. Some victims have successfully sued their employers for damages.

REPETITIVE STRAIN INJURY

http://engr-www.unl.edu/ee/eeshop/rsi.html

Unofficial, but very informative and extensively-linked, site produced by a sufferer of RSI. It includes a section on the symptoms, as well as diagrams and photos of how to type without straining your back or hands. The site is largely focused upon prevention rather than cure.

replication in biology, production of copies of the genetic material DNA; it occurs during cell division (◊mitosis and ◊meiosis). Most mutations are caused by mistakes during replication.

During replication the paired strands of DNA separate, exposing the bases. Nucleotides floating in the cell matrix pair with the exposed bases, adenine pairing with thymine, and cytosine with guanine.

repression in psychology, a mental process that ejects and excludes from consciousness ideas, impulses, or memories that would otherwise threaten emotional stability.

In the Austrian psychiatrist Sigmund Freud's early writing, repression is controlled by the censor, a hypothetical mechanism or agency that allows ideas, memories, and so on from the unconscious to emerge into consciousness only if distorted or disguised, as for example in dreams.

reproduction in biology, process by which a living organism produces other organisms similar to itself. There are two kinds: ◊asexual reproduction and ◊sexual reproduction. The ability to reproduce is considered one of the fundamental attributes of living things.

reproduction rate *or* **fecundity** in ecology, the rate at which a population or species reproduces itself.

reptile any member of a class (Reptilia) of vertebrates. Unlike amphibians, reptiles have hard-shelled, yolk-filled eggs that are laid on land and from which fully formed young are born. Some snakes and lizards retain their eggs and give birth to live young. Reptiles are cold-blooded, and their skin is usually covered with scales. The metabolism is slow, and in some cases (certain large snakes) intervals between meals may be months. Reptiles date back over 300 million years.

Many extinct forms are known, including the orders Pterosauria, Plesiosauria, Ichthyosauria, and Dinosauria. The chief living orders are the Chelonia (tortoises and turtles), Crocodilia (alligators and crocodiles), and Squamata, divided into three suborders: Lacertilia (lizards), Ophidia or Serpentes (snakes), and Amphisbaenia (worm lizards). The order Rhynchocephalia has one surviving species, the lizardlike tuatara of New Zealand.

A four-year study of rainforest in E Madagascar revealed 26 new reptile species 1995.

Reptilia class of vertebrates that comprises the ◊reptiles.

request for comments in computing, the expansion of the abbreviation RFC.

research the primary activity in science, a combination of theory and experimentation directed towards finding scientific explanations of phenomena. It is commonly classified into two types: **pure research**, involving theories with little apparent relevance to human concerns; and **applied research**, concerned with finding solutions to problems of social or commercial importance – for instance in medicine and engineering. The two types are linked in that theories developed from pure research may eventually be found to be of great value to society.

financing research Scientific research is most often funded by government and industry, and so a nation's wealth and priorities are likely to have a strong influence on the kind of work undertaken.

In 1989 the European Community (now the European Union) Council adopted a revised programme on research and technological development for the period 1990–94, requiring a total EC finance of 5,700 million ECUs, to be apportioned as follows: information and communications technology 2,221 million; industrial and materials technologies 888 million; life sciences and technologies 741 million; energy 814 million; human capacity and mobility 518 million; environment 518 million.

reserved word word that has a meaning special to a programming language. For example, 'if' and 'for' are reserved words in most high-level languages.

residual current device or ***earth leakage circuit breaker*** device that protects users of electrical equipment from electric shock by interrupting the electricity supply if a short circuit or current leakage occurs.

It contains coils carrying current to and from the electrical equipment. If a fault occurs, the currents become unbalanced and the residual current trips a switch. Residual current devices are used to protect household gardening tools as well as electrical equipment in industry.

residue in chemistry, a substance or mixture of substances remaining in the original container after the removal of one or more components by a separation process.

The nonvolatile substance left in a container after ◊evaporation of liquid, the solid left behind after removal of liquid by filtration, and the substances left in a distillation flask after removal of components by ◊distillation, are all residues.

resin substance exuded from pines, firs, and other trees in gummy drops that harden in air. Varnishes are common products of the hard resins, and ointments come from the soft resins.

Rosin is the solid residue of distilled turpentine, a soft resin. The name 'resin' is also given to many synthetic products manufactured by polymerization; they are used in adhesives, plastics, and varnishes.

resistance in physics, that property of a conductor that restricts the flow of electricity through it, associated with the conversion of electrical energy to heat; also the magnitude of this property. Resistance depends on many factors, such as the nature of the material, its temperature, dimensions, and thermal properties; degree of impurity; the nature and state of illumination of the surface; and the frequency and magnitude of the current. The SI unit of resistance is the ohm.

resistivity in physics, a measure of the ability of a material to resist the flow of an electric current. It is numerically equal to the ◊resistance of a sample of unit length and unit cross-sectional area, and its unit is the ohm metre (symbol Ωm). A good conductor has a low resistivity (1.7×10^{-8} [Ωm for copper); an insulator has a very high resistivity (10^{15} Ωm for polyethane).

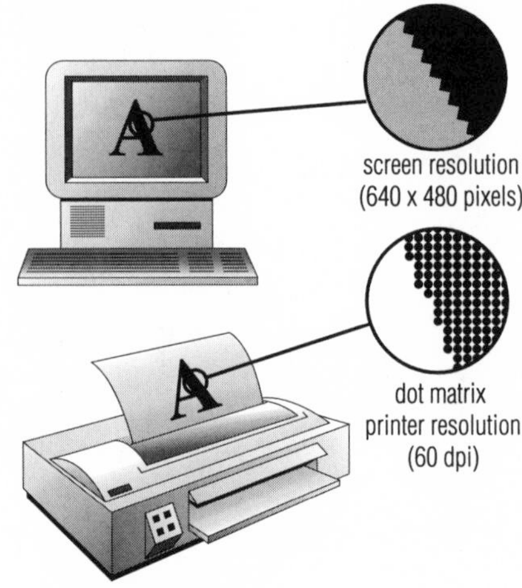

resolution *An example of typical resolutions of screens and printers. The resolution of a screen image when printed can only be as high as the resolution supported by the printer itself.*

resistor in physics, any component in an electrical circuit used to introduce ◊resistance to a current. Resistors are often made from wire-wound coils or pieces of carbon. ◊Rheostats and ◊potentiometers are variable resistors.

When resistors R_1, R_2, R_3,... are connected in a ◊series circuit, the total resistance of the circuit is $R_1 + R_2 + R_3 + \ldots$. When resistors R_1, R_2, R_3,... are connected in a ◊parallel circuit, the total resistance of the circuit is R, given by $1/R = 1/R_1 + 1/R_2 + 1/R_3 + \ldots$.

resolution in computing, the number of dots per unit length in which an image can be reproduced on a screen or printer. A typical screen resolution for colour monitors is 75 dpi (dots per inch). A ◊laser printer will typically have a printing resolution of 300 dpi, and ◊dot matrix printers typically have resolutions from 60 dpi to 180 dpi. Photographs in books and magazines have a resolution of 1,200 dpi or 2,400 dpi.

resolution of forces in mechanics, the division of a single force into two parts that act at right angles to each other. The two parts of a resolved force, called its **components**, have exactly the same effect when acting together on an object as the single force which they replace.

For example, the weight W of an object on a slope, tilted at an angle θ, can be resolved into two components: one acting at a right angle to the slope, equal to $W\cos\theta$, and one acting parallel to and down the slope, equal to $W\sin\theta$. The component acting down the slope (minus any friction force that may be acting in the opposite direction) is responsible for the acceleration of the object.

resolver in computing, see ◊name server.

resonance rapid amplification of a vibration when the vibrating object is subject to a force varying at its ◊natural frequency. In a trombone, for example, the length of the air column in the instrument is adjusted until it resonates with the note being sounded. Resonance effects are also produced by many electrical circuits. Tuning a radio, for example, is done by adjusting the natural frequency of the receiver circuit until it coincides with the frequency of the radio waves falling on the aerial.

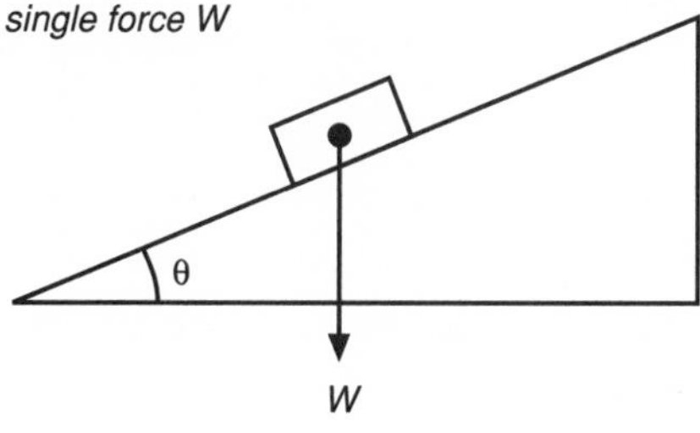

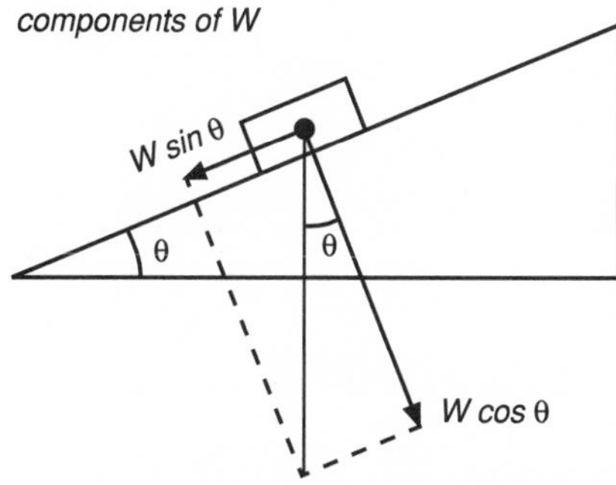

***resolution of forces** In mechanics, the resolution of forces is the division of a single force into two parts that act at right angles to each other. In the diagram, the weight W of an object on a slope, tilted at an angle Θ, can be resolved into two parts or components: one acting at a right angle to the slope, equal to W cos Θ, and one acting parallel to and down the slope, equal to W sin Θ.*

Resonance has many physical applications. Children use it to increase the size of the movement on a swing, by giving a push at the same point during each swing. Soldiers marching across a bridge in step could cause the bridge to vibrate violently if the frequency of their steps coincided with its natural frequency.

Resonance was the cause of the collapse of the Tacoma Narrows Bridge, USA, 1940, when the frequency of the wind gusts coincided with the natural frequency of the bridge.

resources materials that can be used to satisfy human needs. Because human needs are diverse and extend from basic physical requirements, such as food and shelter, to ill-defined aesthetic needs, resources encompass a vast range of items. The intellectual resources of a society – its ideas and technologies – determine which aspects of the environment meet that society's needs, and therefore become resources. For example, in the 19th century, uranium was used only in the manufacture of coloured glass. Today, with the advent of nuclear technology, it is a military and energy resource. Resources are often categorized into **human resources**, such as labour, supplies, and skills, and **natural resources**, such as climate, fossil fuels, and water. Natural resources are divided into ◊nonrenewable resources and ◊renewable resources.

Nonrenewable resources include minerals such as coal, copper ores, and diamonds, which exist in strictly limited quantities. Once consumed they will not be replenished within the time span of human history. In contrast, water supplies, timber, food crops, and similar resources can, if managed properly, provide a steady yield virtually forever; they are therefore replenishable or renewable resources. Inappropriate use of renewable resources can lead to their destruction, as for example the cutting down of rainforests, with secondary effects, such as the decrease in oxygen and the increase in carbon dioxide and the ensuing ◊greenhouse effect. Some renewable resources, such as wind or solar energy, are continuous; supply is largely independent of people's actions.

Demands for resources made by rich nations are causing concern that the present and future demands of industrial societies cannot be sustained for more than a century or two, and that this will be at the expense of the Third World and the global environment. Other authorities believe that new technologies will emerge, enabling resources that are now of little importance to replace those being exhausted.

respiration biochemical process whereby food molecules are progressively broken down (oxidized) to release energy in the form of ◊ATP. In most organisms this requires oxygen, but in some bacteria the oxidant is the nitrate or sulphate ion instead. In all higher organisms, respiration occurs in the ◊mitochondria. Respiration is also used to mean breathing, in which oxygen is exchanged for carbon dioxide in the lung alveoli, though this is more accurately described as a form of ◊gas exchange.

respiratory surface area used by an organism for the exchange of gases, for example the lungs, gills or, in plants, the leaf interior. The gases oxygen and carbon dioxide are both usually involved in respiration and photosynthesis. Although organisms have evolved different types of respiratory surface according to need, there are certain features in common. These include thinness and moistness, so that the gas can dissolve in a membrane and then diffuse into the body of the organism. In many animals the gas is then transported away from the surface and towards interior cells by the blood system.

response any change in an organism occurring as a result of a stimulus. There are many different types of response, some involving the entire organism, others only groups of cells or tissues. Examples include the muscular contractions in an animal, the movement of leaves towards the light, and the onset of hibernation by small mammals at the start of winter.

response time in computing, the delay between entering a command and seeing its effect.

rest mass in physics, the mass of a body when its velocity is zero. For subatomic particles, it is their mass at rest or at velocities considerably below that of light. According to the theory of ◊relativity, at very high velocities, there is a relativistic effect that increases the mass of the particle.

restriction enzyme bacterial ◊enzyme that breaks a chain of DNA into two pieces at a specific point; used in ◊genetic engineering. The point along the DNA chain at which the enzyme can work is restricted to places where a specific sequence of base pairs occurs. Different restriction enzymes will break a DNA chain at different points. The overlap between the fragments is used in determining the sequence of base pairs in the DNA chain.

resultant force in mechanics, a single force acting on a particle or body whose effect is equivalent to the combined effects of two or more separate forces. The resultant of two forces acting at one point on an object can be found using the ◊parallelogram of forces method.

resuscitation steps taken to revive anyone on the brink of death. The most successful technique for life-threatening emergencies, such as electrocution, near-drowning, or heart attack, is mouth-to-mouth resuscitation. Medical and paramedical staff are trained in cardiopulmonary resuscitation (CPR): the use of specialized equipment and techniques to attempt to restart the breathing and/or heartbeat and stabilize the patient long enough for more definitive treatment. CPR has a success rate of less than 30%.

retina light-sensitive area at the back of the ◊eye connected to the brain by the optic nerve. It has several layers and in humans contains over a million rods and cones, sensory cells capable of converting light into nervous messages that pass down the optic nerve to the brain.

The **rod cells**, about 120 million in each eye, are distributed throughout the retina. They are sensitive to low levels of light, but do not provide detailed or sharp images, nor can they detect colour. The **cone cells**, about 6 million in number, are mostly concentrated in a central region of the retina called the **fovea**, and provide both detailed and colour vision. The cones of the human eye contain three visual pigments, each of which responds to a different primary colour (red, green, or blue). The brain can interpret the varying signal levels from the three types of cone as any of the different colours of the visible spectrum.

The image actually falling on the retina is highly distorted; research into the eye and the optic centres within the brain has shown that this poor quality image is processed to improve its quality. The retina can become separated from the wall of the eyeball as a result of a trauma, such as a boxing injury. It can be reattached by being 'welded' into place by a laser.

retinol *or* **vitamin A** fat-soluble chemical derived from ß-carotene and found in milk, butter, cheese, egg yolk, and liver. Lack of retinol in the diet leads to the eye disease **xerophthalmia**.

retriever any of several breeds of hunting dogs, often used as guide dogs for the blind. The commonest breeds are the **Labrador retriever**, large, smooth-coated, and usually black or yellow; and the **golden retriever**, with either flat or wavy coat. They can grow to 60 cm/2 ft high and weigh 40 kg/90 lb.

Retrievers were originally developed for retrieving birds and other small game. Their gentle, even-tempered nature makes them popular companion dogs, and Labradors are also used in police work.

retrograde in astronomy, the orbit or rotation of a ◊planet or ◊satellite if the sense of rotation is opposite to the general sense of rotation of the Solar System. On the ◊celestial sphere, it refers to motion from east to west against the background of stars.

retrovirus any of a family of ◊viruses (Retroviridae) containing the genetic material ◊RNA rather than the more usual ◊DNA.

For the virus to express itself and multiply within an infected cell, its RNA must be converted to DNA. It does this by using a built-in enzyme known as reverse transcriptase (since the transfer of genetic information from DNA to RNA is known as ◊transcription, and retroviruses do the reverse of this). Retroviruses include those causing AIDS and some forms of leukaemia. See ◊immunity.

Retroviruses are used as vectors in ◊genetic engineering, but they cannot be used to target specific sites on the chromosome. Instead they incorporate their genes at random sites.

return-to-base warranty in computing, a warranty on a piece of hardware that requires the owner to return it to the retailer or the factory for service. Compare ◊on-site warranty.

reuse multiple use of a product (often a form of packaging), by returning it to the manufacturer or processor each time. Many such returnable items are sold with a deposit which is reimbursed if the item is returned. Reuse is usually more energy- and resource-efficient than ◊recycling unless there are large transport or cleaning costs.

reverberation in acoustics, the multiple reflections, or echoes, of sounds inside a building that merge and persist a short time (up to a few seconds) before fading away. At each reflection some of the sound energy is absorbed, causing the amplitude of the sound wave and the intensity of the sound to reduce a little.

Too much reverberation causes sounds to become confused and indistinct, and this is particularly noticeable in empty rooms and halls, and such buildings as churches and cathedrals where the hard, unfurnished surfaces do not absorb sound energy well. Where walls and surfaces absorb sound energy very efficiently, too little reverberation may cause a room or hall to sound dull or 'dead'. Reverberation is a key factor in the design of theatres and concert halls, and can be controlled by lining ceilings and walls with materials possessing specific sound-absorbing properties.

reverse engineering in computing, analysing an existing piece of computer hardware or software by finding out what it does and then working out how it does it. Companies perform this process on their own products in order to iron out faults, and on their competitors' products in order to find out how they work. For example, the microchips in the first IBM PCs were reverse engineered by other computer firms to make compatible machines without infringing IBM's copyright.

reverse osmosis the movement of solvent (liquid) through a semipermeable membrane from a more concentrated solution to a more dilute solution. The solvent's direction of movement is opposite to that which it would experience during ◊osmosis, and is achieved by applying an external pressure to the solution on the more concentrated side of the membrane. The technique is used in desalination plants, when water (the solvent) passes from brine (a salt solution) into fresh water via a semipermeable filtering device.

reverse video alternative term for ◊inverse video.

reversible reaction chemical reaction that proceeds in both directions at the same time, as the product decomposes back into reactants as it is being produced. Such reactions do not run to completion, provided that no substance leaves the system. Examples include the manufacture of ammonia from hydrogen and nitrogen, and the oxidation of sulphur dioxide to sulphur trioxide.

Rex cat two breeds of domestic cat with short, curly coats. The Cornish Rex was bred in 1950 in Cornwall, England. It has a wedge-shaped head, large ears, slender body with a naturally arched back, and very long legs. The Devon Rex, bred since 1966 in Devon, has a shorter wedge-shaped head than the Cornish, more pronounced cheekbones, and has less curl in its fur. The body is muscular and broad-chested. Apart from bicoloured, all coat colours and patterns are recognized.

It derives its name from the Rex curly-haired mutation in rabbits. Rex cats were recognized in Britain 1967.

Reynolds number number used in ◊fluid mechanics to determine whether fluid flow in a particular situation (through a pipe or around an aircraft body or a fixed structure in the sea) will be turbulent or smooth. The Reynolds number is calculated using the flow velocity, density and viscosity of the fluid, and the dimensions of the flow channel. It is named after British engineer Osborne Reynolds.

RFC (abbreviation for ***request for comments***) in computing, discussion document on the subject of standards for the Internet. RFCs start as technical proposals lodged with the Internet Architecture Board by computer engineers. The proposals are published on the Internet, where they are subject to general review. After any necessary amendments are made, RFCs become agreed procedures across the network.

RGB (abbreviation of ***red–green–blue***) method of connecting a colour screen to a computer, involving three separate signals: red, green, and blue. All the colours displayed by the screen can be made up from these three component colours.

rhe unit of fluidity equal to the reciprocal of the ◊poise.

rhea one of two flightless birds of the family Rheidae, order Rheiformes. The common rhea *Rhea americana* is 1.5 m/5 ft high and is distributed widely in South America. The smaller Darwin's rhea *Pterocnemia pennata* occurs only in the south of South America and has shorter, feathered legs, and mottled plumage. Rheas differ from the ostrich in their smaller size and in having a feathered neck and head, three-toed feet, and no plumelike tail feathers.

rhenium Latin *Rhenus* 'Rhine' heavy, silver-white, metallic element, symbol Re, atomic number 75, relative atomic mass 186.2. It has chemical properties similar to those of manganese and a very high melting point (3,180°C/5,756°F), which makes it valuable as an ingredient in alloys.

It was identified and named 1925 by German chemists W Noddack (1893–1960), I Tacke, and O Berg from the Latin name for the river Rhine.

Both the man of science and the man of action live always at the edge of mystery, surrounded by it.

J Robert Oppenheimer US physicist.
Address at Columbia University, New York, Dec 1954

rheostat in physics, a variable ◊resistor, usually consisting of a high-resistance wire-wound coil with a sliding contact. It is used to vary electrical resistance without interrupting the current (for example, when dimming lights). The circular type in electronics (which can be used, for example, as the volume control of an amplifier) is also known as a ◊potentiometer.

rhesus factor group of ◊antigens on the surface of red blood cells of humans which characterize the rhesus blood group system. Most individuals possess the main rhesus factor (Rh+), but those without this factor (Rh–) produce ◊antibodies if they come into contact with it. The name comes from rhesus monkeys, in whose blood rhesus factors were first found.

If an Rh– mother carries an Rh+ fetus, she may produce antibodies if fetal blood crosses the ◊placenta. This is not normally a problem with the first infant because antibodies are only produced slowly. However, the antibodies continue to build up after birth, and a second Rh+ child may be attacked by antibodies passing from mother to fetus, causing the child to contract anaemia, heart failure, or brain damage. In such cases, the blood of the infant has to be changed for Rh– blood; a badly affected fetus may be treated in the womb (see ◊fetal therapy). The problem can be circumvented by giving the mother anti-Rh globulin just after the first pregnancy, preventing the formation of antibodies.

rhesus monkey macaque monkey *Macaca mulatta* found in N India and SE Asia. It has a pinkish face, red buttocks, and long, straight, brown-grey hair. It can grow up to 60 cm/2 ft long, with a 20 cm/8 in tail.

rheumatic fever or ***acute rheumatism*** acute or chronic illness characterized by fever and painful swelling of joints. Some victims also experience involuntary movements of the limbs and head, a form of ◊chorea. It is now rare in the developed world.

Rheumatic fever, which strikes mainly children and young adults, is always preceded by a streptococcal infection such as ◊scarlet fever or a severe sore throat, usually occurring a couple of weeks beforehand. It is treated with bed rest, antibiotics, and painkillers. The most important complication of rheumatic fever is damage to the heart and its valves, producing rheumatic heart disease many years later, which may lead to disability and death.

rheumatism nontechnical term for a variety of ailments associated with inflammation and stiffness of the joints and muscles.

rheumatoid arthritis inflammation of the joints; a chronic progressive disease, it begins with pain and stiffness in the small joints of the hands and feet and spreads to involve other joints, often with severe disability and disfigurement. There may also be damage to the eyes, nervous system, and other organs. The disease is treated with a range of drugs and with surgery, possibly including replacement of major joints.

Rheumatoid arthritis most often develops between the ages of 30 and 40, and is three times more common in women than men. It is an ◊autoimmune disease and new hope has come for sufferers with the announcement in 1994 of an experimental drug which deactivates part of the immune system responsible for tissue damage. The drug, a ◊monoclonal antibody, has performed well in preliminary trials, reducing pain and stiffness and improving mobility.

In the West it affects 2–3% of women and nearly 1% of men; an estimated 165 million people worldwide suffered from rheumatoid arthritis in 1995. In children rheumatoid arthritis is known as Still's disease.

rhim or ***sand gazelle*** smallish gazelle *Gazella leptocerus* that has already disappeared over most of its former range of north Africa. Populations are fragmented and often isolated. It is one of several highly threatened gazelle species in northern Africa and the Sahara.

rhinoceros large grazing mammal with one or more horns on its snout. Rhinoceroses have thick, loose skin with little hair, stumpy, powerful legs with three toes on each foot. The largest species (the one-horned Indian rhinoceros) can grow up to 2 m/6 ft high at the shoulder and weigh 2,300–4,000 kg/5,060–8,800 lb. Rhinoceroses eat grass, leafy twigs, and shrubs, and are solitary. They have poor eyesight but excellent hearing and smell. Although they look clumsy, rhinos can reach speeds of 56 kph/35 mph. In the wild they are thought to live for about 25 years, and up to 47 in captivity. There are five species: three Asian and two African, all in danger of extinction.

species The largest rhinoceros is the **one-horned Indian rhinoceros** *Rhinoceros unicornis,* which has a rough skin, folded into shield-like pieces; the African rhinoceroses are smooth-skinned and two-horned. The African **black rhinoceros** *Diceros bicornis* is 1.5 m/5 ft high, with a prehensile (grasping) upper lip for feeding on shrubs, and sometimes a smaller third horn. The **broad-lipped ('white') rhinoceros** *Ceratotherium simum* is actually slaty-grey, with a squarish mouth for browsing grass. The **Javan rhinoceros** *R. sondaicus* is near extinction, as is the **two-horned Sumatran rhinoceros** *Dicerorhinus sumatrensis.*

in danger The Javan rhino is now one of the world's rarest mammals, and is included on the ◊CITES list of endangered species. In 1996, its total population numbered only 57–70, of which about 50 were in Java's Ujong Kulon National Park, and a small number, perhaps 15, in Vietnam. The total population of Indian rhinoceroses consisted of about 2,000 in 1995.

huge ancestor An extinct hornless species, the baluchithere (genus *Baluchitherium*), reached 4.5 m/15 ft high.

classification Rhinoceroses belong to the phylum Chordata, subphylum Vertebrata, class Mammalia (mammal), order Perissodactyla (odd-toed ungulates), suborder Ceratomorpha, family Rhinocerotidae. Today there are four genera with five remaining species: the great Indian rhinoceros (*Rhinoceros unicornis*), the Javan or lesser one-horned rhinoceros (*R. sondaicus*), the Sumatran or Asiatic two-horned or hairy rhinoceros (*Dicerorhinus sumatrensis*), the African black rhinoceros (*Diceros bicornis*) and the African white rhinoceros (*Ceratotherium simum*).

RHINOCEROS

The white rhino is not white, but a dirty grey. The name is a mistranslation of the Afrikaans word *weit,* which means 'wide'. The white rhino has a wider face and body than the more common black rhino.

rhinoceros *The Indian rhinoceros* Rhinoceros unicornis, *the largest of the Asiatic species, weighs up to two tons and has only one horn. Its skin is deeply creased at the neck, shoulders, and legs, resembling armour plating. Now restricted to areas of Nepal, Assam, and Bengal, the Indian rhinoceros, like nearly all rhinoceroses, is an endangered species. Premaphotos Wildlife*

RHINOCEROS

http://www.cm-net.com/rhino/

Page about the ecological plight of the rhinoceros, with text and pictures describing the various species, and the differing criteria threatening them with extinction. There is also a quiz and projects to get involved in.

rhizoid hairlike outgrowth found on the ◊gametophyte generation of ferns, mosses, and liverworts. Rhizoids anchor the plant to the substrate and can absorb water and nutrients.

They may be composed of many cells, as in mosses, where they are usually brownish, or may be unicellular, as in liverworts, where they are usually colourless. Rhizoids fulfil the same functions as the ◊roots of higher plants but are simpler in construction.

rhizome or ***rootstock*** horizontal underground plant stem. It is a ◊perennating organ in some species, where it is generally thick and fleshy, while in other species it is mainly a means of ◊vegetative reproduction, and is therefore long and slender, with buds all along it that send up new plants. The potato is a rhizome that has two distinct parts, the tuber being the swollen end of a long, cordlike rhizome.

rhm (abbreviation of ***roentgen-hour-metre***) the unit of effective strength of a radioactive source that produces gamma rays. It is used for substances for which it is difficult to establish radioactive disintegration rates.

Rhodesian ridgeback breed of large dog developed by European settlers in the late 19th and early 20th centuries in Zimbabwe (formerly Rhodesia) to pursue and hold at bay lions and other big game. Bred partly from European gundogs and mastiffs, it has the distinguishing feature of a ridge of hair that runs back up its spine towards the shoulders. It has a strong build, stands up to 69 cm/27 in tall, and has a smooth red-gold or honey-coloured coat.

rhodium ***Greek rhodon 'rose'*** hard, silver-white, metallic element, symbol Rh, atomic number 45, relative atomic mass 102.905. It is one of the so-called platinum group of metals and is resistant to tarnish, corrosion, and acid. It occurs as a free metal in the natural alloy osmiridium and is used in jewellery, electroplating, and thermocouples.

rhododendron any of numerous, mostly evergreen shrubs belonging to the heath family. The leaves are usually dark and leathery, and the large funnel-shaped flowers, which grow in tight clusters, occur in all colours except blue. They thrive on acid soils. ◊Azaleas belong to the same genus. (Genus *Rhododendron*, family Ericaceae.)

rhombic sulphur allotropic form of sulphur. At room temperature, it is the stable ◊allotrope, unlike monoclinic sulphur.

rhombus in geometry, an equilateral (all sides equal) ◊parallelogram. Its diagonals bisect each other at right angles, and its area is half the product of the lengths of the two diagonals. A rhombus whose internal angles are 90° is called a ◊square.

rhubarb perennial plant grown for its pink edible leaf stalks. The large leaves contain ◊oxalic acid, and are poisonous. There are also wild rhubarbs native to Europe and Asia. (*Rheum rhaponticum*, family Polygonaceae.)

RHUBARB COMPENDIUM

http://www.clark.net/pub/dan/rhubarb/rhubarb.html

Pictures, history, recipes, the list of information included at this site goes on an on; it even includes a section on rhubarb being a possible key to CFC control. It is impossible to believe you would need to know something about rhubarb that this site doesn't tell you.

Rhynchocephalia order of primitive reptiles that lived in Triassic times. The ◊tuatara is the only survivor of this ancient group.

rhyolite ◊igneous rock, the fine-grained volcanic (extrusive) equivalent of granite.

rhythm method method of natural contraception that relies on refraining from intercourse during ◊ovulation.

The time of ovulation can be worked out by the calendar (counting days from the last period), by temperature changes, or by inspection of the cervical mucus. All these methods are unreliable because it is possible for ovulation to occur at any stage of the menstrual cycle.

rib long, usually curved bone that extends laterally from the ◊spine in vertebrates. Most fishes and many reptiles have ribs along most of the spine, but in mammals they are found only in the chest area. In humans, there are 12 pairs of ribs. The ribs protect the lungs and heart, and allow the chest to expand and contract easily.

At the rear, each pair is joined to one of the vertebrae of the spine. The upper seven ('true' or vertebro-sternal ribs) are joined by ◊cartilage directly to the breast bone (sternum). The next three ('false' or vertebro-costal ribs) are joined by cartilage to the end of the rib above. The last two ('floating ribs') are not attached at the front. The diaphragm and muscles between adjacent ribs are responsible for the respiratory movements which fill the lungs with air.

Every great scientific truth goes through three stages. First, people say it conflicts with the Bible. Next they say it had been discovered before. Lastly they say they always believed it.

Louis Agassiz Swiss palaeontologist.
Attributed remark

ribbonfish member of a family of marine fish. They have elongated and compressed bodies which have a ribbonlike appearance. They are pelagic (open sea) fishes.

There is no anal fin, but the dorsal fin is as long as the body, and the ventral fins have from one long ray to nine smaller ones. Ribbonfish are seldom found alive, and are usually seen floating dead on the surface of the ocean.

The **dealfish** *Trachypterus arcticus*, occurs in the north Atlantic. The ◊oarfish also belongs to this family.

classification Ribbonfish are in the family Trachypteridae, order Lampridiformes, class Osteichthyes.

riboflavin or ***vitamin*** B_2 ◊vitamin of the B complex important in cell respiration. It is obtained from eggs, liver, and milk. A deficiency in the diet causes stunted growth.

ribonucleic acid full name of RNA.

ribosome in biology, the protein-making machinery of the cell. Ribosomes are located on the endoplasmic reticulum (ER) of eukaryotic cells, and are made of proteins and a special type of ◊RNA, ribosomal RNA. They receive messenger RNA (copied from the ◊DNA) and ◊amino acids, and 'translate' the messenger RNA by using its chemically coded instructions to link amino acids in a specific order, to make a strand of a particular protein.

rice principal ◊cereal of the wet regions of the tropics, derived from wild grasses probably native to India and SE Asia. Rice is unique among cereal crops in that it is grown standing in water. The yield is very large, and rice is said to be the staple food of one-third of the world's population. (*Oryza sativa*.)

cultivation Rice takes 150–200 days to mature in warm, wet conditions. During its growing period, it needs to be flooded either by the heavy monsoon rains or by irrigation. This restricts the cultivation of swamp rice, the usual kind, to level land and terraces. A poorer variety, known as hill rice, is grown on hillsides. Outside Asia, there is some rice production in the Po Valley in Italy and in Louisiana, the Carolinas, and California in the USA.

In 1994 the International Rice Research Institute announced a new rice variety that can potentially increase rice yields by 25%. It produces more seed heads than the standard crop and each seed head contains 200 rice grains, compared with the present 100. The plant is also more compact, enabling it to be planted more densely.

nutrition Rice contains 8–9% protein. Brown, or unhusked, rice has valuable B-vitamins that are lost in husking or polishing. Most of the rice eaten in the world is, however, sold in the polished white form.

history Rice has been cultivated since prehistoric days in the East. New varieties with greatly increased protein content have been developed by gamma radiation for commercial cultivation, and yields are now higher than ever before (see ◊green revolution).

by-products Rice husks when burned provide a ◊silica ash that, mixed with lime, produces an excellent cement.

Richter scale scale based on measurement of seismic waves, used to determine the magnitude of an ◊earthquake at its epicentre. The magnitude of an earthquake differs from its intensity, measured by the ◊Mercalli scale, which is subjective and varies from place to place for the same earthquake. The scale is named after US seismologist Charles Richter.

An earthquake's magnitude is a function of the total amount of energy released, and each point on the Richter scale represents a thirtyfold increase in energy over the previous point. The greatest earthquake ever recorded, in 1920 in Gansu, China, measured 8.6 on the Richter scale.

rich text format in computing, file format usually abbreviated to ◊RTF.

ricin extremely poisonous extract from the seeds of the castor-oil plant. When incorporated into ◊monoclonal antibodies, ricin can attack cancer cells, particularly in the treatment of lymphoma and leukaemia.

rickets defective growth of bone in children due to an insufficiency of calcium deposits. The bones, which do not harden adequately, are bent out of shape. It is usually caused by a lack of vitamin D and insufficient exposure to sunlight. Renal rickets, also a condition of malformed bone, is associated with kidney disease.

rift valley valley formed by the subsidence of a block of the Earth's ◊crust between two or more parallel ◊faults. Rift valleys are steep-sided and form where the crust is being pulled apart, as at ◊ocean ridges, or in the Great Rift Valley of E Africa.

The Richter scale

The Richter scale is based on measurement of seismic waves, used to determine the magnitude of an earthquake at its epicenter. The magnitude of an earthquake differs from its intensity, measured by the Mercalli scale, which is subjective and varies from place to place for the same earthquake. The Richter scale was named after US seismologist Charles Richter (1900–1985).

Magnitude	*Relative amount of energy released*	*Examples*	*Year*
1	1		
2	31		
3	960		
4	30,000	Carlisle, England (4.7)	1979
5	920,000	Wrexham, Wales (5.1)	1990
6	29,000,000	San Fernando (CA) (6.5)	1971
		northern Armenia (6.8)	1988
7	890,000,000	Loma Prieta (CA) (7.1)	1989
		Kobe, Japan (7.2)	1995
		Rasht, Iran (7.7)	1990
		San Francisco (CA) (7.7–7.9)[1]	1906
8	28,000,000,000	Tangshan, China (8.0)	1976
		Gansu, China (8.6)	1920
		Lisbon, Portugal (8.7)	1755
9	850,000,000,000	Prince William Sound (AK) (9.2)	1964

[1] Richter's original estimate of a magnitude of 8.3 has been revised by two recent studies carried out by the California Institute of Technology and the US Geological Survey.

Rigel or ***Beta Orionis*** brightest star in the constellation Orion. It is a blue-white supergiant, with an estimated diameter 50 times that of the Sun. It is 900 light years from Earth, and is intrinsically the brightest of the first-magnitude stars, its luminosity being about 100,000 times that of the Sun. It is the seventh-brightest star in the sky.

right-angled triangle triangle in which one of the angles is a right angle (90°). It is the basic form of triangle for defining trigonometrical ratios (for example, sine, cosine, and tangent) and for which ◊Pythagoras' theorem holds true. The longest side of a right-angled triangle is called the hypotenuse; its area is equal to half the product of the lengths of the two shorter sides.

Any triangle constructed with its hypotenuse as the diameter of a circle, with its opposite vertex (corner) on the circumference, is a

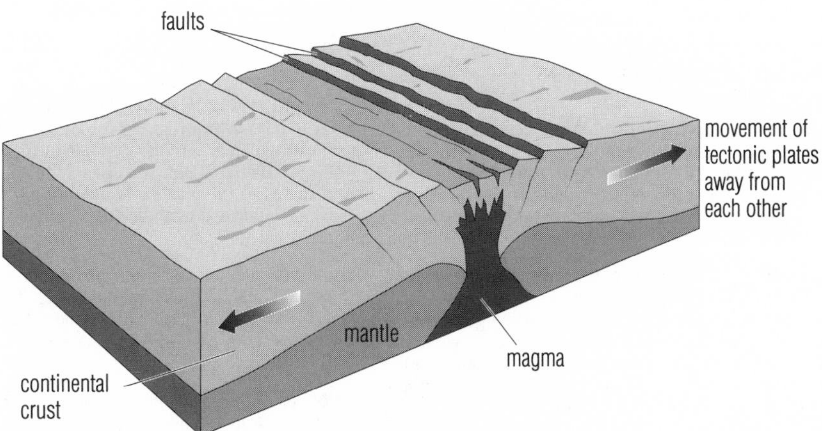

rift valley *The subsidence of rock resulting from two or more parallel rocks moving apart is known as a graben. When this happens on a large scale, with tectonic plates moving apart, a rift valley is created.*

right-angled triangle. This is a fundamental theorem in geometry, first credited to the Greek mathematician Thales about 580 BC.

right ascension in astronomy, the coordinate on the ◊celestial sphere that corresponds to longitude on the surface of the Earth. It is measured in hours, minutes, and seconds eastwards from the point where the Sun's path, the ecliptic, once a year intersects the celestial equator; this point is called the **vernal equinox**.

right click in computing, on IBM-compatible PCs, a click on the right-hand button of the mouse that brings up a context-sensitive menu presenting a range of options relevant to the user's current activity.

right-hand rule in physics, a memory aid used to recall the relative directions of motion, magnetic field, and current in an electric generator. It was devised by English physicist John Fleming. See ◊Fleming's rules.

rigor medical term for shivering or rigidity. **Rigor mortis** is the stiffness that ensues in a corpse soon after death, owing to chemical changes in muscle tissue.

ring circuit household electrical circuit in which appliances are connected in series to form a ring with each end of the ring connected to the power supply. It superseded the ◊radial circuit.

ring ouzel mountain songbird *Turdus torquatus* with brownish-black plumage and a broad white patch on the throat. It nests in heather or on banks in moorland districts. It belongs to the thrush family Muscicapidae, order Passeriformes.

ringworm any of various contagious skin infections due to related kinds of fungus, usually resulting in circular, itchy, discoloured patches covered with scales or blisters. The scalp and feet (athlete's foot) are generally involved. Treatment is with antifungal preparations.

RIP (abbreviation for ***raster image processor***) program in a laser printer (or other high-resolution printer) that converts the stream of printing instructions from a computer into the pattern of dots that make up the printed page. A separate program is required for each type of printer and for each page description language (such as ◊PostScript or ◊PCL).

RIPs are very demanding programs because of the complexity of a typical printed page. It is not unusual for RIPs to run on extremely fast and powerful ◊RISC ◊microprocessors, which are sometimes more powerful than the processor in the computer attached to the printer.

RiPEM (contraction of ***Riordan's Internet Privacy Enhanced Mail***) in computing, ◊public domain software for sending and receiving e-mail using ◊Pretty Good Privacy (PGP) for improved security. The name refers to Mark Riordan, who wrote most of the program.

ripple tank in physics, shallow water-filled tray used to demonstrate various properties of waves, such as reflection, refraction, diffraction, and interference.

RISC (acronym for ***reduced instruction-set computer***) in computing, a microprocessor (processor on a single chip) that carries out fewer instructions than other (◊CISC) microprocessors in common use in the 1990s. Because of the low number and the regularity of ◊machine code instructions, the processor carries out those instructions very quickly.

ritualization in ethology, a stereotype that occurs in certain behaviour patterns when these are incorporated into displays. For example, the exaggerated and stylized head toss of the goldeneye drake during courtship is a ritualization of the bathing movement used to wet the feathers; its duration and form have become fixed. Ritualization may make displays clearly recognizable, so ensuring that individuals mate only with members of their own species.

river large body of water that flows down a slope along a channel restricted by adjacent banks and ◊levées. A river originates at a point called its **source**, and enters a sea or lake at its **mouth**. Along its length it may be joined by smaller rivers called **tributaries**; a river and its tributaries are contained within a drainage basin. The point at which two rivers join is called the confluence.

Major rivers of the world include the Ganges, the Mississippi, and the Nile, the world's longest river. A river follows the path of least resistance downhill, and deepens, widens and lengthens its channel by ◊erosion.

Longest Rivers in the World

River	*Location*	*Approximate length km*	*mi*
Nile	Africa	6,695	4,160
Amazon	South America	6,570	4,083
Chang Jiang (Yangtze)	China	6,300	3,915
Mississippi–Missouri–Red Rock	USA	6,020	3,741
Huang He (Yellow River)	China	5,464	3,395
Ob–Irtysh	China/Kazakhstan/Russia	5,410	3,362
Amur–Shilka	Asia	4,416	2,744
Lena	Russia	4,400	2,734
Congo–Zaire	Africa	4,374	2,718
Mackenzie–Peace–Finlay	Canada	4,241	2,635
Mekong	Asia	4,180	2,597
Niger	Africa	4,100	2,548
Yenisei	Russia	4,100	2,548
Parana	Brazil	3,943	2,450
Mississippi	USA	3,779	2,348
Murray–Darling	Australia	3,751	2,331
Missouri	USA	3,726	2,315
Volga	Russia	3,685	2,290
Madeira	Brazil	3,241	2,014
Purus	Brazil	3,211	1,995
São Francisco	Brazil	3,199	1,988
Yukon	USA/Canada	3,185	1,979
Rio Grande	USA/Mexico	3,058	1,900
Indus	Tibet/Pakistan	2,897	1,800
Danube	eastern Europe	2,858	1,776
Japura	Brazil	2,816	1,750
Salween	Myanmar/China	2,800	1,740
Brahmaputra	Asia	2,736	1,700
Euphrates	Iraq	2,736	1,700
Tocantins	Brazil	2,699	1,677
Zambezi	Africa	2,650	1,647
Orinoco	Venezuela	2,559	1,590
Paraguay	Paraguay	2,549	1,584
Amu Darya	Tajikistan/Turkmenistan/Uzbekistan	2,540	1,578
Ural	Russia/Kazakhstan	2,535	1,575
Kolyma	Russia	2,513	1,562
Ganges	India/Bangladesh	2,510	1,560
Arkansas	USA	2,344	1,459
Colorado	USA	2,333	1,450
Dnieper	eastern Europe	2,285	1,420
Syr Darya	Asia	2,205	1,370
Irrawaddy	Myanmar	2,152	1,337
Orange	South Africa	2,092	1,300

river red gum large tree *Eucalyptus camaldulensis* found lining the banks of Australian inland rivers. It usually branches low and is often wide spreading, with smooth bark on the upper trunk and branches. It is one of Australia's best-known and most valuable timber trees.

riveting method of joining metal plates. A hot metal pin called a rivet, which has a head at one end, is inserted into matching holes in two overlapping plates, then the other end is struck and formed into another head, holding the plates tight. Riveting is used in building construction, boilermaking, and shipbuilding.

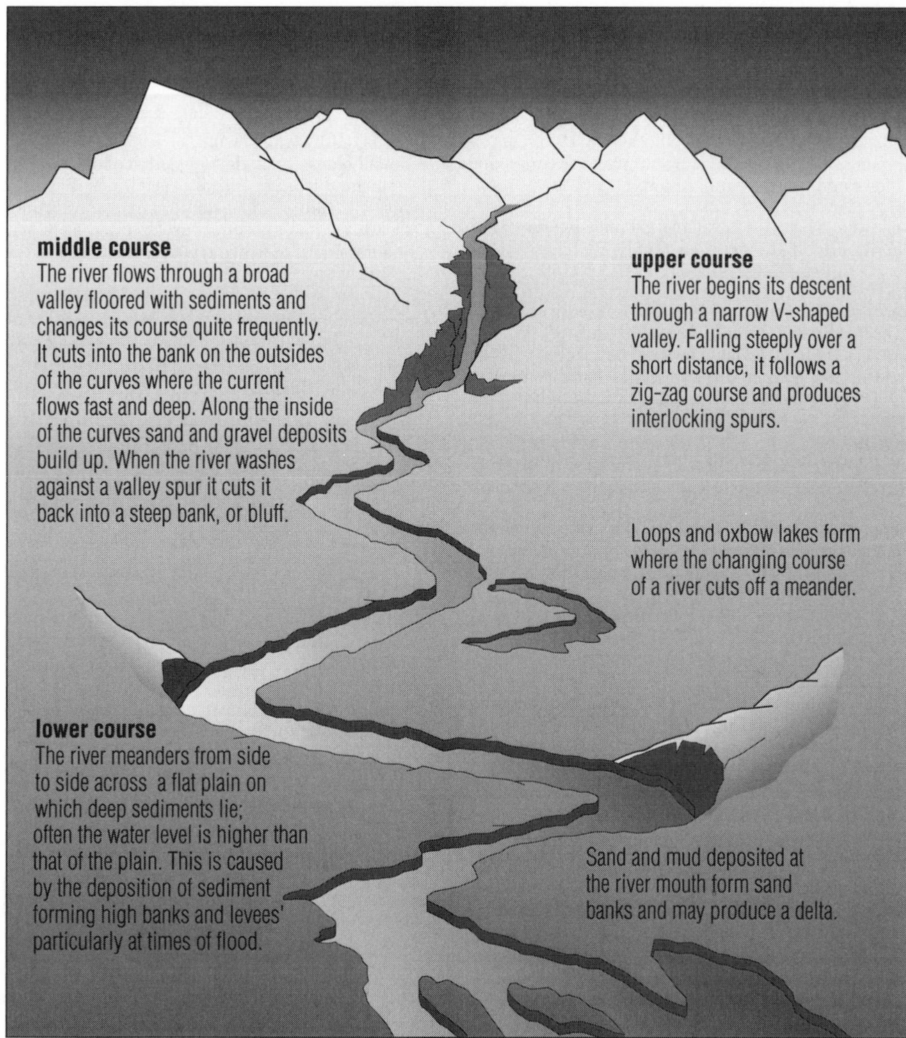
middle course
The river flows through a broad valley floored with sediments and changes its course quite frequently. It cuts into the bank on the outsides of the curves where the current flows fast and deep. Along the inside of the curves sand and gravel deposits build up. When the river washes against a valley spur it cuts it back into a steep bank, or bluff.
upper course
The river begins its descent through a narrow V-shaped valley. Falling steeply over a short distance, it follows a zig-zag course and produces interlocking spurs.
Loops and oxbow lakes form where the changing course of a river cuts off a meander.
lower course
The river meanders from side to side across a flat plain on which deep sediments lie; often the water level is higher than that of the plain. This is caused by the deposition of sediment forming high banks and levees' particularly at times of flood.
Sand and mud deposited at the river mouth form sand banks and may produce a delta.

river *The course of a river from its source of a spring or melting glacier, through to maturity where it flows into the sea.*

RL (abbreviation of ***real life***) in computing, the opposite of ◊virtual reality.

rlogin (contraction of ***remote login***) in computing, ◊UNIX program that enables users to log in on another computer via the Internet. Compare ◊Telnet.

rms in physics, abbreviation for ◊root-mean-square.

RNA (abbreviation for ***ribonucleic acid***) nucleic acid involved in the process of translating the genetic material ◊DNA into proteins. It is usually single-stranded, unlike the double-stranded DNA, and consists of a large number of nucleotides strung together, each of which comprises the sugar ribose, a phosphate group, and one of four bases (uracil, cytosine, adenine, or guanine). RNA is copied from DNA by the formation of ◊base pairs, with uracil taking the place of thymine.

> To remember that although DNA and RNA are both nucleic acids, they do different jobs in the cell:
>
> DNA DELIVERS THE BLUEPRINT, RNA READS IT

RNA occurs in three major forms, each with a different function in the synthesis of protein molecules. **Messenger RNA** (mRNA) acts as the template for protein synthesis. Each ◊codon (a set of three bases) on the RNA molecule is matched up with the corresponding amino acid, in accordance with the ◊genetic code. This process (translation) takes place in the ribosomes, which are made up of proteins and **ribosomal RNA** (rRNA). **Transfer RNA** (tRNA) is responsible for combining with specific amino acids, and then matching up a special 'anticodon' sequence of its own with a codon on the mRNA.

This is how the genetic code is translated.

Although RNA is normally associated only with the process of protein synthesis, it makes up the hereditary material itself in some viruses, such as ◊retroviruses.

roach any freshwater fish of the Eurasian genus *Rutilus*, of the carp family, especially *R. rutilus* of N Europe. It is dark green above, whitish below, with reddish lower fins; it grows to 35 cm/1.2 ft.

road specially constructed route for wheeled vehicles to travel on.

Reinforced tracks became necessary with the invention of wheeled vehicles in about 3000 BC and most ancient civilizations had some form of road network. The Romans developed engineering techniques that were not equalled for another 1,400 years.

Until the late 18th century most European roads were haphazardly maintained, making winter travel difficult. In the UK the turnpike system of collecting tolls created some improvement. The Scottish engineers Thomas Telford and John ◊McAdam introduced sophisticated construction methods in the early 19th century. Recent developments have included durable surface compounds and machinery for rapid ground preparation.

roadrunner crested North American ground-dwelling bird *Geococcyx californianus* of the ◊cuckoo family, found in the SW USA and Mexico. It can run at a speed of 25 kph/15 mph.

robin migratory songbird *Erithacus rubecula* of the thrush family Muscicapidae, order Passeriformes, found in Europe, W Asia, Africa, and the Azores. About 13 cm/5 in long, both sexes are olive brown with a red breast. Two or three nests are constructed during the year in sheltered places, and from five to seven white freckled eggs are laid.

The larger North American robin *Turdus migratorius* belongs to the same family. In Australia members of several unrelated genera are called robins, and may have white, yellowish, or red breasts.

robot any computer-controlled machine that can be programmed to move or carry out work. Robots are often used in industry to transport materials or to perform repetitive tasks. For instance, robotic arms, fixed to a floor or workbench, may be used to paint machine parts or assemble electronic circuits. Other robots are designed to work in situations that would be dangerous to humans – for example, in defusing bombs or in space and deep-sea exploration.

Some robots are equipped with sensors, such as touch sensors and video cameras, and can be programmed to make simple decisions based on the sensory data received. As robots do not suffer from fatigue or become distracted, researchers in robotics aim to produce robots that can carry out sophisticated tasks more efficiently than humans, for example a voice-operated robot able to carry out some heart operations was tested successfully on a cow in the USA in 1998.

ROBOT

The word 'robot' originated in the theatre. It was invented by the Czech playwright Karel Capek in his 1921 play *R.U.R.* (Rossum's Universal Robots).

Roche limit in astronomy, the distance from a planet within which a large moon would be torn apart by the planet's gravitational force, creating a set of rings. The Roche limit lies at approximately 2.5 times the planet's radius (the distance from its centre to its surface).

rock constituent of the Earth's crust composed of ◊minerals or materials of organic origin that have consolidated into hard masses as ◊igneous, sedimentary, or ◊metamorphic rocks. Rocks are formed from a combination (or aggregate) of minerals, and the property of a rock will depend on its components. Where deposits of economically valuable minerals occur they are termed ◊ores. As a result of ◊weathering, rock breaks down into very small particles that combine with organic materials from plants and animals to form ◊soil. In ◊geology the term 'rock' can also include unconsolidated materials such as ◊sand, mud, ◊clay, and ◊peat.

Igneous rock is formed by the cooling and solidification of ◊magma, the molten rock material that originates in the lower part of the Earth's crust, or ◊mantle, where it reaches temperatures as high as 1,000°C. The rock may form on or below the Earth's surface and is usually crystalline in texture. Larger ◊crystals are more common in rocks such as ◊granite which have cooled slowly within the Earth's crust; smaller crystals form in rocks such as ◊basalt which have cooled more rapidly on the surface. Because of their acidic composition, igneous rocks such as granite are particularly susceptible to ◊acid rain.

Sedimentary rocks are formed by the compression of particles deposited by water, wind, or ice. They may be created by the erosion of older rocks, the deposition of organic materials, or they may be formed from chemical precipitates. For example, ◊sandstone is derived from sand particles, ◊limestone from the remains of sea creatures, and gypsum is precipitated from evaporating sea water. Sedimentary rocks are typically deposited in distinct layers or strata and many contain ◊fossils.

Metamorphic rocks are formed through the action of high pressure or heat on existing igneous or sedimentary rocks, causing changes to the composition, structure, and texture of the rocks. For example,◊ marble is formed by the effects of heat and pressure on limestone, while granite may be metamorphosed into ◊gneiss, a coarse-grained foliated rock.

rock crawler wingless insects with long antennae and either reduced eyes or none. Rock crawlers are generally found only at higher altitudes (450–2,000 m/1,480–6,550 ft), in the mountains of Japan, western North America and eastern Siberia, and prefer low temperature conditions. They live under logs and stones and are omnivorous and nocturnal.

Rock crawlers were discovered in the Canadian Rockies, as late as 1914. Their order, Grylloblattodea, contains three genera and only 16 species, and appears to exemplify the only modern representatives of the primitive insects from which the cockroaches (Blattodea) and grasshoppers and crickets (Orthoptera) have evolved.

long lifespan Eggs have an incubation period of approximately one year; the eight nymphal stages occupy a further five years; and the adult female then lives a further year before laying eggs.

classification Rock crawlers are in order Grylloblattodea in subclass Pterygota, class Insecta, phylum Arthropoda.

rocket projectile driven by the reaction of gases produced by a fast-burning fuel. Unlike jet engines, which are also reaction engines, modern rockets carry their own oxygen supply to burn their fuel and do not require any surrounding atmosphere. For warfare, rocket heads carry an explosive device.

Rockets have been valued as fireworks over the last seven centuries, but their intensive development as a means of propulsion to high altitudes, carrying payloads, started only in the interwar years with the state-supported work in Germany (primarily by Wernher von Braun) and of Robert Hutchings Goddard (1882–1945) in the USA. Being the only form of propulsion available that can function in a vacuum, rockets are essential to exploration in outer space. ◊Multistage rockets have to be used, consisting of a number of rockets joined together.

Two main kinds of rocket are used: one burns liquid propellants, the other solid propellants. The fireworks rocket uses gunpowder as a solid propellant. The ◊space shuttle's solid rocket boosters use a mixture of powdered aluminium in a synthetic rubber binder. Most rockets, however, have liquid propellants, which are more powerful and easier to control. Liquid hydrogen and kerosene are common fuels, while liquid oxygen is the most common oxygen provider, or oxidizer. One of the biggest rockets ever built, the Saturn V Moon rocket, was a three-stage design, standing 111 m/365 ft high. It weighed more than 2,700 tonnes/3,000 tons

ONLINE ROCKETRY

http://www.rocketryonline.com/

Searchable site with reference materials, organizations, clubs, upcoming launches, products, books, and clubs devoted to rocketry.

on the launch pad, developed a takeoff thrust of some 3.4 million kg/7.5 million lb, and could place almost 140 tonnes/150 tons into low Earth orbit. In the early 1990s, the most powerful rocket system was the Soviet Energiya, capable of placing 100 tonnes/110 tons into low Earth orbit. The US space shuttle can put only 24 tonnes/26 tons into orbit. See ◊missile.

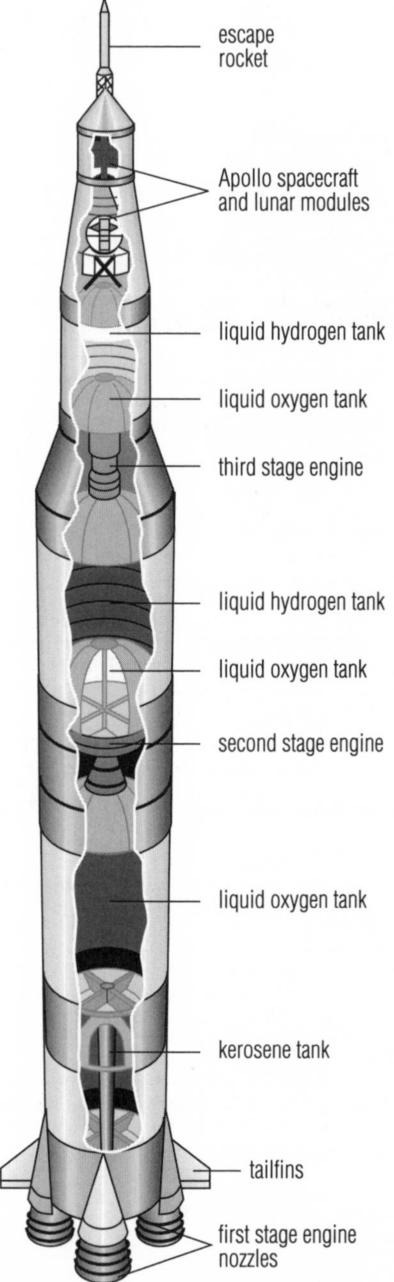

rocket *The three-stage Saturn V rocket used in the Apollo moonshots of the 1960s and 1970s. It stood 111 m/365 ft high, as tall as a 30-storey skyscraper, weighed 2,700 tonnes/3,000 tons when loaded with fuel, and developed a power equivalent to 50 Boeing 747 jumbo jets.*

rock salmon another name for ◊dogfish.

Rocky Mountain goat species of ruminant that occurs in North America. It is intermediate in position between a goat and an antelope. It resembles a goat in size and has long white hair with woolly undercoat, black, hollow horns, compressed at the base, and short ears.
classification The Rocky Mountain goat *Oreamnos americanus* is a member of the family Bovidae, order Artiodactyla.

rod a type of light-sensitive cell in the ◊retina of most vertebrates. Rods are highly sensitive and provide only black and white vision. They are used when lighting conditions are poor and are the only type of visual cell found in animals active at night.

rodent any mammal of the worldwide order Rodentia, making up nearly half of all mammal species. Besides ordinary 'cheek teeth', they have a single front pair of incisor teeth in both upper and lower jaw, which continue to grow as they are worn down.

RODENT

Once attached to their mother's nipple, the young of some rodent species simply do not let go. This prevents any rival sibling from muscling in on the young rodent's food supply, and also enables it to hang on if the mother is forced to run away from a predator. Tenacious clinging is characteristic of 44 rodent species, all in the mouse family.

roebuck male of the Eurasian roe ◊deer.

roe deer or ***roebuck*** small deer (the buck stands about 66 cm/ 26 in at the shoulder, and is 1.2 m/ 4 ft in length from the nose to the tiny tail). Roe deer are reddish-brown in summer (in winter the redness disappears), and the underparts are yellowish-grey. The horns average about 20 cm/8 in in length.

The mating season is in July to August and the young are born in the following May and June. They are at first reddish-brown with white spots.

Roe deer occur over central and southern Europe, and other races range as far east as China.
classification The roe deer *Capreolus capreolus* is in family Cervidae, order Artiodactyla.

roentgen or ***röntgen*** unit (symbol R) of radiation exposure, used for X-rays and gamma rays. It is defined in terms of the number of ions produced in one cubic centimetre of air by the radiation. Exposure to 1,000 roentgens gives rise to an absorbed dose of about 870 rads (8.7 grays), which is a dose equivalent of 870 rems (8.7 sieverts).

rogue value in computing, another name for ◊data terminator.

roller any brightly coloured bird of the Old World family Coraciidae, resembling crows but in the same order as kingfishers and hornbills. Rollers grow up to 32 cm/13 in long. The name is derived from the habit of some species of rolling over in flight.

rolling common method of shaping metal. Rolling is carried out by giant mangles, consisting of several sets, or stands, of heavy rollers positioned one above the other. Red-hot metal slabs are rolled into sheet and also (using shaped rollers) girders and rails. Metal sheets are often cold-rolled finally to impart a harder surface.

roll-on/roll-off *or* **ro-ro** method of loading and unloading cargo ships. Lorries drive straight on board a specially designed vessel and then drive off at the ship's destination without unloading their cargo. This saves time and money, although valuable cargo space is taken up by the lorries and special ◊port facilities are needed. Ro-ro is best suited to shorter journeys where handling costs are proportionately higher. Cross-Channel traffic between the UK and France and Belgium is an example.

Rolls-Royce industrial company manufacturing cars and aeroplane engines, founded 1906 by Henry Royce and Charles Rolls. The Silver Ghost car model was designed 1906, and produced until 1925, when the Phantom was introduced. In 1914 Royce designed the Eagle aircraft engine, used extensively in World War I. Royce also designed the Merlin engine, used in Spitfires and Hurricanes in World War II. Jet engines followed, and became an important part of the company.

From 1994, BMW of Germany were to build a percentage of the engines for Rolls-Royce and Bentley cars, as well as providing engineering consultation.

ROM (acronym for ***read-only memory***) in computing, a memory device in the form of a collection of integrated circuits (chips), frequently used in microcomputers. ROM chips are loaded with data and programs during manufacture and, unlike ◊RAM (random-access memory) chips, can subsequently only be read, not written to, by computer. However, the contents of the chips are not lost when the power is switched off, as happens in RAM.

ROM is used to form a computer's permanent store of vital information, or of programs that must be readily available but protected from accidental or deliberate change by a user. For example, a microcomputer ◊operating system is often held in ROM memory.

Roman numerals ancient European number system using symbols different from Arabic numerals (the ordinary numbers 1, 2, 3, 4, 5, and so on). The seven key symbols in Roman numerals, as represented today, are I (1), V (5), X (10), L (50), C (100), D (500), and M (1,000). There is no zero, and therefore no place-value as is fundamental to the Arabic system. The first ten Roman numerals are I, II, III, IV (or IIII), V, VI, VII, VIII, IX, and X. When a Roman symbol is preceded by a symbol of equal or greater value, the values of the symbols are added (XVI = 16).

When a symbol is preceded by a symbol of less value, the values are subtracted (XL = 40). A horizontal bar over a symbol indicates a multiple of 1,000 ($\bar{X}$= 10,000). Although addition and subtraction are fairly straightforward using Roman numerals, the absence of a zero makes other arithmetic calculations (such as multiplication) clumsy and difficult.

To remember the values of Roman numerals:

X shall stand for playmates Ten, **V** for Five stout stalwart men, **I** for One, as I'm alive, **C** for Hundred and **D** for Five. **M** for a Thousand soldiers true, and **L** for Fifty, I'll tell you.

Röntgen, Wilhelm Konrad (1845–1923)

Mary Evans Picture Library

(or **Roentgen**) German physicist. He discovered X-rays 1895. While investigating the passage of electricity through gases, he noticed the fluorescence of a barium platinocyanide screen. This radiation passed through some substances opaque to light, and affected photographic plates. Developments from this discovery revolutionized medical diagnosis. He won the Nobel Prize for Physics 1901.

röntgen alternative spelling for ◊roentgen, unit of X- and gamma-ray exposure.

rook gregarious European ◊crow *Corvus frugilegus*. The plumage is black and lustrous and the face bare; the legs, toes, and claws are also black. A rook can grow to 45 cm/18 in long. Rooks nest in colonies (rookeries) at the tops of trees. They feed mainly on invertebrates found just below the soil surface. The last 5 mm/0.2 in of beak tip is mostly cartilage containing lots of nerve endings to enable the rook to feel for hidden food.

The nest is a large structure made of twigs and straw, and in it are laid four to six bluish-green eggs blotched with greenish-brown. Feathers round the base of the beak are present in young birds but do not grow again after the second moult.

root in computing, the account used by system administrators and other superusers in ◊UNIX systems. Users logged in as root (or in some systems, avatar) have permission to access and change all the files in the system.

root the part of a plant that is usually underground, and whose primary functions are anchorage and the absorption of water and dissolved mineral salts. Roots usually grow downwards and towards water (that is, they are positively geotropic and hydrotropic; see ◊tropism). Plants such as epiphytic orchids, which grow above ground, produce aerial roots that absorb moisture from the atmosphere. Others, such as ivy, have climbing roots arising from the stems, which serve to attach the plant to trees and walls.

The absorptive area of roots is greatly increased by the numerous slender root hairs formed near the tips. A calyptra, or root cap, protects the tip of the root from abrasion as it grows through the soil.

Symbiotic associations occur between the roots of certain plants, such as clover, and various bacteria that fix nitrogen from the air (see ◊nitrogen fixation). Other modifications of roots include ◊contractile roots, pneumatophores, taproots, and ◊prop roots.

evolution The evolution of root systems by land plants was very fast, in evolutionary terms. The earliest plants (410 million years ago) had tiny roots only a few millimetres in length, but within 20 million years, roots were as long as 50 cm/20 in.

root of an equation, a value that satisfies the equality. For example, $x = 0$ and $x = 5$ are roots of the equation $x^2 -5x = 0$.

root cap cap at the tip of a growing root. It gives protection to the zone of actively dividing cells as the root pushes through the soil.

root crop plant cultivated for its swollen edible root (which may or may not be a true root). Potatoes are the major temperate root crop; the major tropical root crops are cassava, yams, and sweet potatoes. Root crops are second in importance only to cereals as human food. Roots have a high carbohydrate content, but their protein content rarely exceeds 2%. Consequently, communities relying almost exclusively upon roots may suffer from protein deficiency. Food production for a given area from roots is greater than from cereals.

In the mid-1980s, world production of potatoes, cassava, and yams was just under 600 million tonnes. Root crops are also used as animal feed, and may be processed to produce starch, glue, and alcohol. Sugar beet has largely replaced sugar cane as a source of sugar in Europe.

root directory in computing, the top directory in a ◊tree-and-branch filing system. It contains all the other directories.

root hair tiny hairlike outgrowth on the surface cells of plant roots that greatly increases the area available for the absorption of water and other materials. It is a delicate structure, which survives for a few days only and does not develop into a root.

New root hairs are continually being formed near the root tip, one of the places where plants show the most active growth to replace the ones that are lost. The majority of land plants have

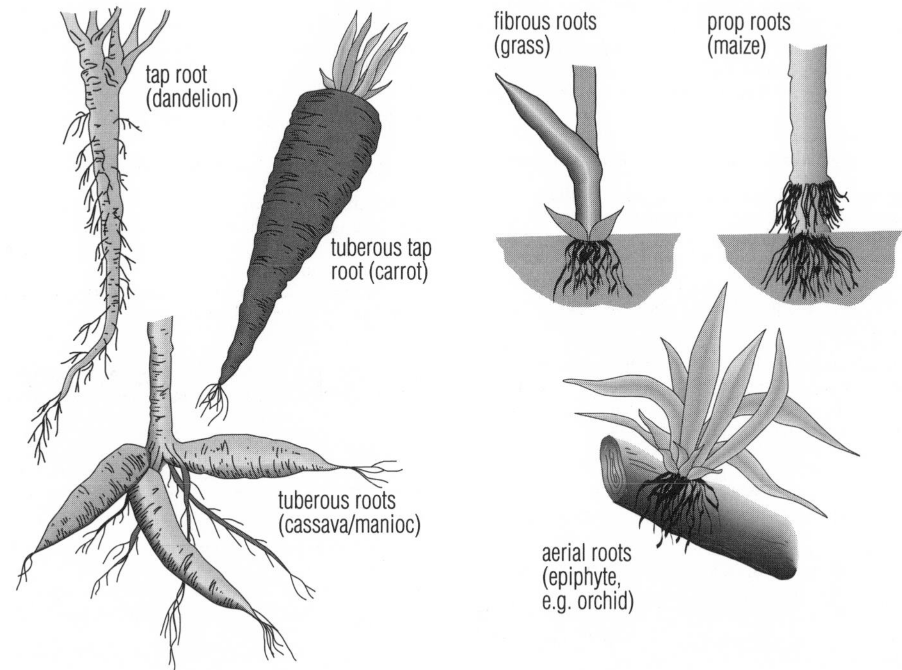

root *Types of root. Many flowers (dandelion) and vegetables (carrot) have swollen tap roots with smaller lateral roots. The tuberous roots of the cassava are swollen parts of an underground stem modified to store food. The fibrous roots of the grasses are all of equal size. Prop roots grow out from the stem and then grow down into the ground to support a heavy plant. Aerial roots grow from stems but do not grow into the ground; many absorb moisture from the air.*

root hairs. The layer of the root's epidermis that produces root hairs is known as the **piliferous layer**.

root mean square (rms) in mathematics, value obtained by taking the ◊square root of the mean of the squares of a set of values; for example the rms value of four quantities *a, b, c,* and *d* is $\sqrt{[(a^2 + b^2 + c^2 + d^2)/4]}$.

root-mean-square (rms) measure of the effective magnitude of a cyclic or randomly varying quantity whose average value is zero. For a cyclic quantity, it is equal to the square root of the average of the squares of the quantity at each instant over a complete cycle; where the variation is a ◊sine wave, the rms value is equal to the peak value divided by $\sqrt{2}$. In electrical engineering, for example, the rms value of the current or voltage in an AC circuit is used in power calculations. The rms value is also used as measure of the amplitude of randomly varying quantities, such as the noise in a telecommunications channel.

root nodule clearly visible swelling that develops in the roots of members of the bean family, the Leguminosae. The cells inside this tumourous growth have been invaded by the bacteria Rhizobium, a soil microbe capable of converting gaseous nitrogen into nitrate. The nodule is therefore an association between a plant and a bacterium, with both partners benefiting. The plant obtains nitrogen compounds while the bacterium obtains nutrition and shelter.

Nitrogen fixation by bacteria is one of the main ways by which the nitrogen in the atmosphere is cycled back into living things. The economic value of the process is so great that research has been carried out into the possibility of stimulating the formation of root nodules in crops such as wheat, which do not normally form an association with rhizobium.

rootstock another name for ◊rhizome, an underground plant organ.

rope stout cordage with circumference over 2.5 cm/1 in. Rope is made similarly to thread or twine, by twisting yarns together to form strands, which are then in turn twisted around one another in the direction opposite to that of the yarns. Although ◊hemp is still used to make rope, nylon is increasingly used.

rorqual any of a family (Balaenopteridae) of baleen ◊whales, especially the genus *Balaenoptera,* which includes the blue whale *B. musculus,* the largest of all animals, measuring 30 m/100 ft and more. The common rorqual or fin whale *B. physalus* is slate-coloured and not quite so long.

The sei whale *B. borealis,* the minke whale *B. acutorostrata,* Bryde's whale *B. edeni,* and the humpback whale *Megaptera novaeangliae* also belong to this family. All are long-bodied whales with pleated throats.

Rorschach test in psychology, a method of diagnosis involving the use of inkblot patterns that subjects are asked to interpret, to help indicate personality type, degree of intelligence, and emotional stability. It was invented by the Swiss psychiatrist Hermann Rorschach (1884–1922).

ROSAT joint US/German/UK satellite launched 1990 to study cosmic sources of X-rays and extremely short ultraviolet wavelengths, named after Wilhelm Röntgen, the discoverer of X-rays.

rose any shrub or climbing plant belonging to the rose family, with prickly stems and fragrant flowers in many different colours. Numerous cultivated forms have been derived from the sweetbrier or eglantine (*R. rubiginosa*) and dogrose (*R. canina*) native to Europe and Asia. There are many climbing varieties, but the forms most commonly grown in gardens are bush roses and standards (cultivated roses grafted on to a brier stem). (Genus *Rosa,* family Rosaceae.)

rosebay willowherb common perennial weed. See ◊willowherb.

rose beetle another name for ◊rose chafer.

rose chafer *or* **rose beetle** brightly coloured insect occurring mainly in the tropics.

In the adult stage rose chafers feed on tender shoots and floral parts of plants or on the sap exuded from trees. In contrast, the larvae are generally found in soil, where they attack the roots of most plants, and hence are agricultural pests. Some also inhabit decaying wood, leaf litter, and other plant refuse. There are about 2,500 species.
classification The rose chafer is in subfamily Cetoniinae, family Scarabaeidae, order Coleoptera, class Insecta, phylum Arthropoda.

rosemary evergreen shrub belonging to the mint family, native to the Mediterranean and W Asia, with small, narrow, scented leaves and clusters of pale blue or purple flowers. It is widely cultivated as a herb for use in cooking and for its aromatic oil, used in perfumery and pharmaceuticals. Rosemary is a traditional symbol of remembrance. (*Rosemarinus officinalis,* family Labiatae.)

Rosetta in astronomy, a project of the ◊European Space Agency, due for launch in 2003, to send a spacecraft to Comet Wirtanen. *Rosetta* is expected to go into orbit around the comet in 2011 and land two probes on the nucleus a year later. The spacecraft will stay with the comet as it makes its closest approach to the Sun in October 2013.

rotation in geometry, a ◊transformation in which a figure is turned about a given point, known as the **centre of rotation**. A rotation of 180° is known as a half turn.

rotifer any of the tiny invertebrates, also called 'wheel animalcules', of the phylum Rotifera. Mainly freshwater, some marine, rotifers have a ring of ◊cilia that carries food to the mouth and also provides propulsion. They are the smallest of multicellular animals - few reach 0.05 cm/0.02 in.

Rottweiler breed of dog originally developed in Rottweil, Germany, as a herding and guard dog, and subsequently used as a police dog. Powerfully built, the dog is about 63–66 cm/25–27 in high at the shoulder, black with tan markings. It has a short coat and docked tail.

roughage alternative term for dietary ◊fibre, material of plant origin that cannot be digested by enzymes normally present in the human ◊gut.

rough collie breed of herding dog originating in Scotland. It has a long, thick coat which may be sable, blue merle, or tri-coloured, all with white markings. Its head is narrow, with a pointed muzzle and pricked ears that fold down at the tips. Of slender build, it grows to about 62 cm/24 in. The smooth collie is identical, except that its coat is short.

rounding process by which a number is approximated to the nearest above or below with one or more fewer decimal places. For example, 34.3583 might be rounded to 34.358, whereas 34.3587 would be rounded to 34.359. Similarly, 3,587 might be rounded to the nearest thousand, giving 4,000. When unwanted decimals are simply left out, the process is known as **truncating**.

Rounding can produce considerable errors, especially when the rounded numbers are multiplied by other rounded numbers. For example, if the volume of a cuboid is calculated as 3 x 4 x 5 when the true dimensions are 3.4 x 4.4 x 5.4, the rounding error is 20.784 out of 80.784, an error of over 25%.

roundworm parasitic ◊nematode worm, genus *Toxocara,* found in dogs, cats, and other animals.

router in computing, a device that pushes traffic through a packet-switched network. On the Internet, traffic travels through a series of routers that relay each **packet** of data to its destination by the best possible route.

rove beetle any of a number of beetles with characteristic very short elytra (wing cases) that conceal large, well developed wings that are intricately folded away. When required the wings can unfold very rapidly, for almost instantaneous flight. The family includes some 20,000 species.
classification The rove beetle is in family Staphylinidae in order Coleoptera class Insecta, phylum Arthropoda.

Most of these beetles are small and inconspicuous, except the ◊devil's coach horse, which is about 3 cm/1.2 in. Some species are predatory; others live in association with ant and termite colonies.

rowan another name for the European ◊mountain ash tree.

Royal Aeronautical Society oldest British aviation body, formed in 1866. Its members discussed and explored the possibilities of flight long before its successful achievement.

royal antelope small nocturnal African antelope, inhabitants of dense jungle. They are the smallest of all antelopes, being no more than 30 cm/12 in high, and are slenderly built with very thin legs, no thicker than a pencil; they are generally brown in colour.
classification The royal antelope *Neotragus pygmaeus* is in family Bovidae, in order Artiodactyla.

ROYAL BOTANIC GARDENS, KEW

http://www.rbgkew.org.uk/

Kew Gardens' home page, with general visitor information, a history of the gardens, a guide to the main plant collections, and a searchable database.

Royal Botanic Gardens, Kew botanic gardens in Richmond, Surrey, England, popularly known as ◊Kew Gardens.

The history of the living world can be summarised as the elaboration of ever more perfect eyes within a cosmos in which there is always something more to be seen.

PIERRE TEILHARD DE CHARDIN French Jesuit theologian, palaeontologist, and philosopher. *The Phenomenon of Man* 1955

Royal Greenwich Observatory the national astronomical observatory of the UK, founded in 1675 at Greenwich, SE London, England, to provide navigational information for sailors. After World War II it was moved to Herstmonceux Castle, Sussex; in 1990 it was transferred to Cambridge. It also operates telescopes on La Palma in the Canary Islands, including the 4.2-m/165-in William Herschel Telescope, commissioned 1987.

In 1998 the Particle Physics and Astronomy Research Council decided to return some of the Royal Observatory's work back to the original Greenwich site from Cambridge (other technical work will go to a new UK Astronomy Technology Centre in Edinburgh).

The observatory was founded by King Charles II. The eminence of its work resulted in Greenwich Time and the Greenwich Meridian being adopted as international standards of reference in 1884.

ROYAL GREENWICH OBSERVATORY

http://www.ast.cam.ac.uk/RGO/

Official and searchable site of the world's most famous observatory. In addition to an excellent history and guide for visitors to the observatory's museum, there are comprehensive details of current RGO research (no longer carried out in Greenwich). This is an important site both for students of astronomy and for those seeking information on latest research.

Royal Horticultural Society British society established in 1804 for the improvement of horticulture. The annual Chelsea Flower Show, held in the grounds of the Royal Hospital, London, is also a social event, and another flower show is held at Vincent Square,

ROYAL HORTICULTURAL SOCIETY

http://www.rhs.org.uk/index_f.html

Large source of information on horticulture in the UK. The contents include a guide to RHS gardens, the society's scientific and educational work, RHS publications, and information about the annual Chelsea Flower Show and other events.

London. There are gardens, orchards, and trial grounds at Wisley, Surrey, and the Lindley Library has one of the world's finest horticultural collections.

Royal Institution of Great Britain organization for the promotion, diffusion, and extension of science and knowledge, founded in London 1799 by the Anglo-American physicist Count Rumford (1753–1814).

Royal Society oldest and premier scientific society in Britain, originating in 1645 and chartered in 1662; Robert vBoyle, Christopher Wren, and Isaac ◊Newton were prominent early members. Its Scottish equivalent is the **Royal Society of Edinburgh** 1783.

Royal Society of Chemistry society formed in the UK in 1980, merging the Chemical Society (founded 1841) and the Royal Institute of Chemistry (founded 1877). The society's object, as stated in its royal charter, is the general advancement of chemical science and its applications, serving to that end as a learned society, a professional body, and a representative body. It is recognized in the UK and internationally as an authoritative voice of chemistry and chemists.

RS-232 interface standard type of computer vinterface used to connect computers to serial devices. It is used for modems, mice, screens, and serial printers.

RSA in computing, name of both an encryption valgorithm and the company (RSA Inc) set up to exploit that algorithm in commercial encryption products. First described 1977 by its inventors, Ronald Rivest, Adi Shamir, and Leonard Adelman, and published in *Scientific American,* the RSA algorithm is used in the free program ◊Pretty Good Privacy (PGP) and in commercial products released by RSA Laboratories.

RSI (abbreviation for ◊***repetitive strain injury***), a condition affecting workers, such as typists, who repeatedly perform certain movements with their hands and wrists.

RSPB abbreviation for ***Royal Society for the Protection of Birds***.

ROYAL SOCIETY FOR THE PROTECTION OF BIRDS

http://birdcare.com/bin/showpage/birdaction/rspb

Home page of the RSPB. The Web site includes a vast amount of information on birds and bird watching in the UK, with descriptions, sketches and photographs of every common UK bird. The site also holds information on how to join the society, and lists the society's sites and activities around the country.

RSUP (abbreviation for ***Reliable SAP Update Protocol***) in computing, bandwidth-saving protocol for Novell networks developed by router manufacturer Cisco Systems.

RTF (abbreviation for ***Rich Text Format***) in computing, file format designed to facilitate the exchange of documents between different word processing programs. RTF text files make it possible to transfer formatting such as font styles or paragraph indents from one program to another.

RU486 another name for ◊mifepristone, an abortion pill.

rubber slang term for a ◊condom.

rubber coagulated ◊latex of a variety of plants, mainly from the New World. Most important is Para rubber, which comes from the tree *Hevea brasiliensis,* belonging to the spurge family. It was introduced from Brazil to SE Asia, where most of the world supply is now produced, the chief exporters being Peninsular Malaysia, Indonesia, Sri Lanka, Cambodia, Thailand, Sarawak, and Brunei. At about seven years the tree, which may grow to 20 m/60 ft, is ready for tapping. Small cuts are made in the trunk and the latex drips into collecting cups. In pure form, rubber is white and has the formula $(C_5H_8)n$.***plant rubber*** Other sources of rubber are the Russian dandelion *Taraxacum koksagyz,* which grows in temperate climates and can yield about 45 kg/100 lb of rubber per tonne of roots, and guayule *Parthenium argentatum,* a small shrub which grows in the southwestern USA and Mexico.
treatment Early uses of rubber were limited by its tendency to soften on hot days and harden on colder ones, a tendency that was eliminated by Charles Goodyear's invention of ◊vulcanization 1839.
synthetic rubber In the 20th century, world production of rubber increased a hundredfold, and World War II stimulated the production of synthetic rubber to replace the supplies from Malaysian sources overrun by the Japanese. There are an infinite variety of synthetic rubbers adapted to special purposes, but economically foremost is SBR (styrene-butadiene rubber). Cheaper than natural rubber, it is preferable for some purposes, for example in car tyres, where its higher abrasion resistance is useful, and it is either blended with natural rubber or used alone for industrial moulding and extrusions, shoe soles, hoses, and latex foam.

rubber plant Asiatic tree belonging to the mulberry family, native to Asia and N Africa, which produces vlatex in its stem. It has shiny, leathery, oval leaves, and young specimens are grown as house plants. (*Ficus elastica,* family Moraceae.)

rubella technical term for ◊German measles.

rubidium Latin *rubidus* 'red' soft, silver-white, metallic element, symbol Rb, atomic number 37, relative atomic mass 85.47. It is one of the valkali metals, ignites spontaneously in air, and reacts violently with water. It is used in photocells and vacuum-tube filaments.

Rubidium was discovered spectroscopically by German physicists Robert Bunsen and Gustav Kirchhoff 1861, and named after the red lines in its spectrum.

ruby the red transparent gem variety of the mineral ◊vcorundum Al_2O_3, aluminium oxide. Small amounts of chromium oxide, Cr_2O_3, substituting for aluminium oxide, give ruby its colour. Natural rubies are found mainly in Myanmar (Burma), but rubies can also be produced artificially and such synthetic stones are used in ◊lasers.

ruby-tailed cuckoo wasp *or* **ruby-tailed fly** insect in the family Chrysididae.

rudd or ***red eye*** freshwater bony fish allied to the ◊roach. It is tinged with bronze, and has reddish fins, the dorsal being farther back than that of the roach. It is found in British and European lakes and sluggish streams. The largest weigh over 1 kg/2.2 lb and may be as much as 45 cm/18 in long.
classification The rudd *Scardinius erythropthalmus* belongs to the order Cypriniformes, class Osteichthyes.

rue shrubby perennial herb native to S Europe and temperate Asia. It bears clusters of yellow flowers. An oil extracted from the strongly scented blue-green leaves is used in perfumery. (*Ruta graveolens,* family Rutaceae.)

ruff bird *Philomachus pugnax* of the sandpiper family Scolopacidae. The name is taken from the frill of erectile purple-black feathers developed in the breeding season around the neck of the male. The females (reeves) have no ruff; they lay four spotted green eggs in a nest of coarse grass made amongst reeds or rushes. The ruff is found across N Europe and Asia, and migrates south in winter. It is a casual migrant throughout North America.

ruffe *or* **pope** European freshwater perchlike fish. The dorsal fin is continuous in the ruffe, whereas in the perch there are two separate fins.
classification The ruff *Acerina cernua* is in family Percidae in order Perciformes, class Osteichthyes.

ruminant any even-toed hoofed mammal with a rumen, the 'first stomach' of its complex digestive system. Plant food is stored and fermented before being brought back to the mouth for chewing (chewing the cud) and then is swallowed to the next stomach. Ruminants include cattle, antelopes, goats, deer, and giraffes, all with a four-chambered stomach. Camels are also ruminants, but they have a three-chambered stomach.

Rumpler Berlin aircraft company which made aircraft for the German Army in World War I.

runner *or* **stolon** in botany, aerial stem that produces new plants.

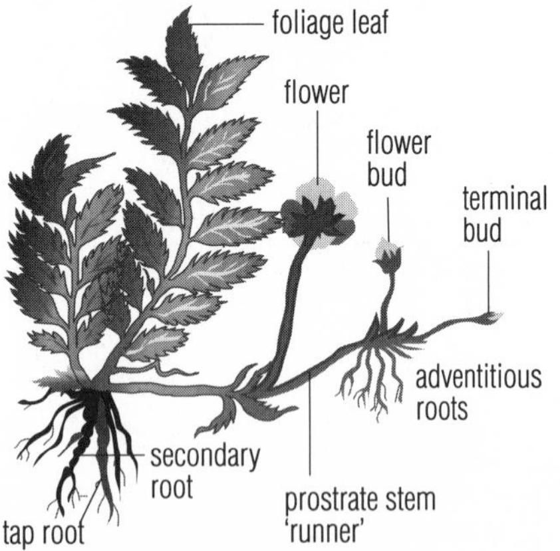

***runner** A runner, or stolon, grows horizontally near the base of some plants, such as the strawberry. It produces roots along its length and new plants grow at these points.*

run-time system in computing, programs that must be stored in memory while an application is executed.

run-time version in computing, copy of a program that is provided with another application, so that the latter can be run, although it does not provide the full functionality of the program. An example is the provision of run-time versions of Microsoft ◊Windows with Windows applications for those users who do not have the full version of Windows.

rupture in medicine, another name for ◊hernia.

rush any of a group of grasslike plants found in wet places in cold and temperate regions. The round stems and flexible leaves of some species have been used for making mats and baskets since ancient times. (Genus *Juncus*, family Juncaceae.)

Three passions, simple but overwhelmingly strong, have governed my life: the longing for love, the search for knowledge, and unbearable pity for the suffering of mankind.

BERTRAND RUSSELL English philosopher and mathematician. *Autobiography*, Prologue

Russell, Bertrand Arthur William (1872–1970)

3rd Earl Russell British philosopher and mathematician. He contributed to the development of modern mathematical logic and wrote about social issues. His works include *Principia Mathematica* 1910–13 (with A N Whitehead), in which he attempted to show that mathematics could be reduced to a branch of logic; *The Problems of Philosophy* 1912; and *A History of Western Philosophy* 1946. He was an outspoken liberal pacifist. Earl 1931. Nobel Prize for Literature 1950.

Russell was born in Monmouthshire, the grandson of Prime Minister John Russell. He studied mathematics and philosophy at Trinity College, Cambridge, where he became a lecturer in 1910. His pacifist attitude in World War I lost him the lectureship, and he was imprisoned for six months for an article he wrote in a pacifist journal. His *Introduction to Mathematical Philosophy* 1919 was written in prison. He and his wife ran a progressive school 1927–32. After visits to the USSR and China, he went to the USA in 1938 and taught at many universities. In 1940, a US court disqualified him from teaching at City College of New York because of his liberal moral views. He later returned to England and resumed his fellowship at Trinity College.

Russell was a life-long pacifist except during World War II. From 1949 he advocated nuclear disarmament and until 1963 was on the Committee of 100, an offshoot of the Campaign for Nuclear Disarmament.

Among his other works are *Principles of Mathematics* 1903, *Principles of Social Reconstruction* 1917, *Marriage and Morals* 1929, *An Enquiry into Meaning and Truth* 1940, *New Hopes for a Changing World* 1951, and *Autobiography* 1967–69.

Mary Evans Picture Library

Russian Academy of Sciences society founded 1725 by Catherine the Great in St Petersburg. The academy has been responsible for such achievements as the ◊Sputnik satellite, and has daughter academies in the Ukraine (welding, cybernetics), Armenia (astrophysics), and Georgia (mechanical engineering).

Russian Blue breed of domestic shorthaired cat, probably not of Russian origin. Long and elegant in form, it has a flattish head and broad face, and its slanting eyes are green. The undercoat is thick and upstanding, and its blue-grey colour is slightly silvered by light grey tips to the overlying guard hairs.

russula any of a large group of fungi (see ◊fungus), containing many species. They are medium-to-large mushrooms with flattened caps, and many are brightly coloured. (Genus *Russula*.)

R. emetica is a common species found in damp places under conifer trees. Up to 9 cm/3.5 in across, the cap is scarlet, fading to cherry, and the gills are white. This mushroom tastes acrid and causes vomiting eaten raw, but some russulas are edible.

rust in botany, common name for a group of minute parasitic fungi (see ◊fungus) that appear on the leaves of their hosts as orange-red spots, later becoming darker. The commonest is the wheat rust (*Puccinia graminis*). (Order Uredinales.)

rust reddish-brown oxide of iron formed by the action of moisture and oxygen on the metal. It consists mainly of hydrated iron(III) oxide ($Fe_2O_3.H_2O$) and iron(III) hydroxide ($Fe(OH)_3$).

Paints that penetrate beneath any moisture, and plastic compounds that combine with existing rust to form a protective coating, are used to avoid rusting.

Rutherford, Ernest, 1st Baron Rutherford of Nelson (1871–1937)

New Zealand-born British physicist. He was a pioneer of modern atomic science. His main research was in the field of radioactivity, and he discovered alpha, beta, and gamma rays. He was the first to recognize the nuclear nature of the atom 1911. Nobel prize 1908. Knighted 1914, Baron 1931.

Rutherford produced the first artificial transformation, changing one element to another, 1919, bombarding nitrogen with alpha particles and getting hydrogen and oxygen. After further research he announced that the nucleus of any atom must be composed of hydrogen nuclei; at Rutherford's suggestion, the name 'proton' was given to the hydrogen nucleus 1920. He speculated that uncharged particles (neutrons) must also exist in the nucleus.

In 1934, using heavy water, Rutherford and his co-workers bombarded deuterium with deuterons and produced tritium. This may be considered the first nuclear fusion reaction.

Mary Evans Picture Library

ruthenium hard, brittle, silver-white, metallic element, symbol Ru, atomic number 44, relative atomic mass 101.07. It is one of the so-called platinum group of metals; it occurs in platinum ores as a free metal and in the natural alloy osmiridium. It is used as a hardener in alloys and as a catalyst; its compounds are used as colouring agents in glass and ceramics.

rutherfordium synthesized, radioactive, metallic element, symbol Rf. It is the first of the transactinide series, atomic number 104, relative atomic mass 262. It is produced by bombarding californium with carbon nuclei and has ten isotopes, the longest-lived of which, Rf-262, has a half-life of 70 seconds.

Two institutions claim to be the first to have synthesized it: the Joint Institute for Nuclear Research in Dubna, Russia, in 1964; and the University of California at Berkeley, USA, in 1969.

rutile titanium oxide mineral, TiO_2, a naturally occurring ore of titanium. It is usually reddish brown to black, with a very bright (adamantine) surface lustre. It crystallizes in the tetragonal system. Rutile is common in a wide range of igneous and metamorphic rocks and also occurs concentrated in sands; the coastal sands of E and W Australia are a major source. It is also used as a pigment that gives a brilliant white to paint, paper, and plastics.

Rydberg constant in physics, a constant that relates atomic spectra to the ◊spectrum of hydrogen. Its value is 1.0977×10^7 per metre.

rye tall annual ◊cereal grass grown extensively in N Europe and other temperate regions. The flour is used to make dark-coloured ('black') breads. Rye is grown mainly as a food crop for animals, but the grain is also used to make whisky and breakfast cereals. (*Secale cereale.*)

S abbreviation for ***south***.

SAA abbreviation for ◊systems application architecture.

sabin unit of sound absorption, used in acoustical engineering. One sabin is the absorption of one square foot (0.093 square metre) of a perfectly absorbing surface (such as an open window).

Sabin, Albert Bruce (1906–1993)

Russian-born US microbiologist who developed a highly effective, live vaccine against polio. The earlier vaccine, developed by physicist Jonas Salk, was based on heat-killed viruses. Sabin was convinced that a live form would be longer-lasting and more effective, and in 1957 he succeeded in weakening the virus so that it lost its virulence. The vaccine can be given by mouth.

sable marten *Martes zibellina,* about 50 cm/20 in long and usually brown. It is native to N Eurasian forests, but now found mainly in E Siberia. The sable has diminished in numbers because of its valuable fur, which has long attracted hunters.

Conservation measures and sable farming have been introduced to save it from extinction.

saccharide another name for a ◊sugar molecule.

saccharin or ***ortho-sulpho benzimide*** $C_7H_5NO_3S$ sweet, white, crystalline solid derived from coal tar and substituted for sugar. Since 1977 it has been regarded as potentially carcinogenic. Its use is not universally permitted and it has been largely replaced by other sweetening agents.

Sachs, Julius von (1832–1897)

German botanist and plant physiologist who developed several important experimental techniques and showed that photosynthesis occurs in the chloroplasts (the structure in a plant cell containing the green pigment chlorophyll) and produces oxygen. He was especially gifted in his experimental approach; some of his techniques are still in use today, such as the simple iodine test, which he used to show the existence of starch in a whole leaf.

sacred baboon or ***hamadryas*** medium-sized ◊baboon *Papio hamadryas* that was once sacred in Egypt but has since become extinct there owing to competition for land. It occurs in troops of up to 500. It is still found in Ethiopia on dry savannah where there are rocky cliffs and hillsides, but is threatened by habitat changes and perhaps also hunting.

sadism tendency to derive pleasure (usually sexual) from inflicting physical or mental pain on others. The term is derived from the Marquis de Sade.

sadomasochism sexual behaviour that combines ◊sadism and vmasochism. The term was coined 1907 by sexologist Richard von Krafft-Ebing.

safety glass glass that does not splinter into sharp pieces when smashed. **Toughened glass** is made by heating a glass sheet and then rapidly cooling it with a blast of cold air; it shatters into rounded pieces when smashed. **Laminated glass** is a 'sandwich' of a clear plastic film between two glass sheets; when this is struck, it simply cracks, the plastic holding the glass in place.

safety lamp portable lamp designed for use in places where flammable gases such as methane may be encountered; for example, in coal mines. The electric head lamp used as a miner's working light has the bulb and contacts in protected enclosures. The flame safety lamp, now used primarily for gas detection, has the wick enclosed within a strong glass cylinder surmounted by wire gauzes. English chemist Humphrey Davy 1815 and English engineer George ◊Stephenson each invented flame safety lamps.

Saffir–Simpson damage-potential scale scale of potential damage from wind and sea when a hurricane is in progress: 1 is minimal damage, 5 is catastrophic.

safflower thistlelike Asian plant with large orange-yellow flowers. It is widely grown for the oil from its seeds, which is used in cooking, margarine, and paints and varnishes; the leftovers are used as cattle feed. (*Carthamus tinctorius,* family Compositae.)

saffron crocus plant belonging to the iris family, probably native to SW Asia, and formerly widely cultivated in Europe; also the dried orange-yellow ◊stigmas of its purple flowers, used for colouring and flavouring in cookery. (*Crocus sativus,* family Iridaceae.)

sage perennial herb belonging to the mint family, with grey-green aromatic leaves used for flavouring in cookery. It grows up to 50 cm/20 in high and has bluish-lilac or pink flowers. (*Salvia officinalis,* family Labiatae.)

Sagittarius bright zodiac constellation in the southern hemisphere, represented as a centaur aiming a bow and arrow at neighbouring Scorpius. The Sun passes through Sagittarius from mid-Dec to mid-Jan, including the winter solstice, when it is farthest south of the Equator. The constellation contains many nebulae and ◊globular clusters, and open ◊star clusters. Kaus Australis and Nunki are its brightest stars. The centre of our Galaxy, the ◊Milky Way, is marked by the radio source Sagittarius A. In astrology, the dates for Sagittarius are about 22 Nov–21 Dec (see ◊precession).

sago starchy material obtained from the pith of the sago palm *Metroxylon sagu.* It forms a nutritious food and is used for manufacturing glucose and sizing textiles.

Sahel Arabic *sahil* 'coast' marginal area to the south of the Sahara, from Senegal to Somalia, which experiences desert-like conditions during periods of low rainfall. The desertification is partly due to climatic fluctuations but has also been caused by the pressures of a rapidly expanding population, which has led to overgrazing and the destruction of trees and scrub for fuelwood. In recent years many famines have taken place in the area.

saiga antelope *Saiga tartarica* of E European and W Asian steppes and deserts. Buff-coloured, whitish in winter, it stands 75 cm/30 in at the shoulder, with a body about 1.5 m/5 ft long. Its nose is unusually large and swollen, an adaptation which may help warm and moisten the air inhaled, and keep out the desert dust. The saiga can run at 80 kph/50 mph.

Only the male has horns, which are straight and up to 30 cm/1 ft long. The saiga is threatened by the demand for its horn for use in traditional Chinese medicine. Once a vanishing species, it is now protected; in 1994 it was listed in Appendix II of ◊CITES, requiring a special permit for trade. The total 1995 population was about 1 million.

The Miner's Safety lamp

BY PETER LAFFERTY

In 1793, the headmaster at Penzance Grammar School, Cornwall, England, told Humphry Davy that he was lazy. Yet Davy went on to become one of the best-known chemists of his time. He discovered six previously unknown elements, sodium, potassium, magnesium, calcium, barium, and strontium. He won many scientific honours, and was knighted in 1812 by Prince Regent – the King, George III, was insane and could not carry out the investiture. He was even awarded a prize established by Napoleon Bonaparte, at a time when England and France were at war. He became wealthy – in 1811 he was paid a very large sum of money for a course of lectures in Ireland. Not bad for a lazy schoolboy!

Davy became a household name when he solved the problem of explosions in coal mines. The only illumination in the coal mines of the time was naked flames in lamps. The danger of explosions in some mines was very real, especially as mines were worked at deeper levels underground. The heat of the flame would ignite the mixture of air, coal dust and fire damp (methane) found in the mines, causing an explosion. In 1815, within six months of being asked to devise a safe lamp, Davy had the solution. He discovered that the heat of a candle flame would not pass along a narrow metal tube, as the metal conducted the heat away. This meant that a mixture of air and coal dust at one end of the tube could not be ignited by a candle at the other end. Applying this discovery, Davy completely surrounded the flame of a lamp with a piece of metal gauze. The gauze acted as a huge number of short metal tubes and conducted the heat of the flame away from the explosive gas outside the lamp. The gas was not heated by the lamp and did not explode. The gauze did not block the light from the lamp. The new lamp was adopted widely and saved many lives. In appreciation, the mine owners of Tyne and Wear in Northeast England honoured Davy with a valuable gold plate. The Davy lamp meant that they could work coal seams previously thought too dangerous.

Numerous other achievements can be attributed to this great scientist. He investigated the effect of breathing the gas nitrous oxide. It was thought at the time that the gas had the power to spread diseases. Davy decided to test the gas on himself and breathed two quarts from a silk bag. He found that the gas made him feel drunk, in a pleasant sort of way. When his friends breathed the gas, some laughed uncontrollably, so the gas became known as laughing gas. Davy also noticed that the gas eased the pain of a toothache he had been suffering. He commented: 'as nitrous oxide appears to destroy pain it may probably be used to advantage during surgical operations'. This suggestion was not taken up for another 45 years, when it was used by an American dentist, Horace Wells, as an anaesthetic.

Davy also introduced a chemical approach to agriculture, the tanning industry and mineralogy; he designed an arc lamp for illumination, an electrolytic process for the desalination of sea water and a method of cathodic protection for the copper-clad ships of the day by connecting them to zinc plates. But his genius has been described as flawed. At his best, he was a scientist of great perception, a painstaking laboratory worker and a brilliant lecturer. At other times, he was disorganized, readily distracted and prone to hasty decisions and arguments. He was snobbish, over-excitable, suspicious and ungenerous to those he saw as scientific rivals. In 1824 he tried to block the election of his protégé Michael Faraday to the Royal Society, even after Faraday had demonstrated his genius by devising the first simple electric motor and discovering benzene. Ironically, many regard Faraday as Davy's finest discovery.

In 1824, the people of Penzance decided to honour Davy. The local newspaper reported: 'At the general meeting in Penzance it was unaminously resolved that a public dinner be given to Sir Humphry Davy at the Union Hotel in Chapel Street, and that the Mayor be required to wait on him forthwith.' Later they wrote: 'Every heart, tongue and eye were as one to do honour to him who had not only rendered the name of their town as famous and imperishable as science itself, but (who had added lustre to the intellectual character of their country and)... who is one of the happy few who can claim to be permanent benefactors to the human race.' It is not recorded whether his old headmaster was present!

sailfish marine bony fish. The snout is long and pointed and the dorsal fin is unusually large. It is blue above, silver below, and over 3 m/10 ft long. It can swim up to 100 km/60 mi in pursuit of the fish it eats.
classification Sailfish belong to genus *Istiophorus* in the order Perciformes, class Osteichthyes.

St Bernard breed of large, heavily built dog, named after the monks of Grand St Bernard Hospice, Switzerland, who kept them for finding lost travellers in the Alps and to act as guides. They are 70 cm/30 in high at the shoulder, and weigh about 70 kg/154 lb. They have pendulous ears and lips, large feet, and drooping lower eyelids. They are usually orange and white.

St Elmo's fire bluish, flamelike electrical discharge that sometimes occurs above ships' masts and other pointed objects or about aircraft in stormy weather. Although high voltage, it is low current and therefore harmless. St Elmo (or St Erasmus) is the patron saint of sailors.

saki New World tree-dwelling monkey with a long, non-prehensile tail. There are four species: the white-faced saki, monk saki, black bearded saki, and white-nosed bearded saki. They are found only in the Amazon valley and Guiana.
classification Sakis are in the genera *Pithecia* and *Chiropotes* (bearded sakis) in the family Cebidae, order Primates.

salamander tailed amphibian of the order Urodela. They are sometimes confused with lizards, but unlike ◊lizards they have no

Sakharov, Andrei Dmitrievich (1921–1989)

Soviet physicist. He was an outspoken human-rights campaigner, who with Igor Tamm (1895–1971) developed the hydrogen bomb. He later protested against Soviet nuclear tests and was a founder of the Soviet Human Rights Committee 1970, winning the Nobel Peace Prize 1975. For criticizing Soviet action in Afghanistan, he was in internal exile 1980–86.

Sakharov was elected to the Congress of the USSR People's Deputies 1989, where he emerged as leader of its radical reform grouping before his death later the same year.

Mary Evans Picture Library

scales or claws. Salamanders have smooth or warty moist skin. The order includes some 300 species, arranged in nine families, found mainly in the northern hemisphere. Salamanders include hellbenders, ◊mudpuppies, olms, waterdogs, sirens, mole salamanders, ◊newts, and lungless salamanders (dusky, woodland, and spring salamanders).

They eat insects and worms, and live in water or in damp areas in the northern temperate regions, mostly feeding at night and hiding during the day, and often hibernating during the winter. Fertilization is either external or internal, often taking place in water. The larvae have external gills. Some remain in the larval form, although they become sexually mature and breed; this is called neoteny. The Mexican ◊axolotl and the mud puppy *Necturus maculosus* of North America are neotenic.

According to fossil evidence, giant salamanders were once common throughout Europe, and reached up to 2.3 m in length.

sal ammoniac former name for ◊ammonium chloride.

salicylic acid HOC_6H_4COOH the active chemical constituent of aspirin, an analgesic drug. The acid and its salts (salicylates) occur naturally in many plants; concentrated sources include willow bark and oil of wintergreen.

When purified, salicylic acid is a white solid that crystallizes into prismatic needles at 318°F/159°C. It is used as an antiseptic, in food preparation and dyestuffs, and in the preparation of aspirin.

saliva in vertebrates, an alkaline secretion from the salivary glands that aids the swallowing and digestion of food in the mouth. In mammals, it contains the enzyme amylase, which converts starch to sugar. The salivary glands of mosquitoes and other blood-sucking insects produce ◊anticoagulants.

SALIVA

The Chinese delicacy of bird's nest soup is in fact a bowl of coagulated swiftlet saliva. Asian cave swiftlets make their tiny cup-shaped nests from layer upon layer of their quick drying saliva.

salivary gland or ***parotid gland*** in mammals, one of two glands situated near the mouth responsible for the manufacture of saliva and its secretion into the mouth. The salivary glands are stimulated to produce saliva during a meal. Saliva contains an enzyme, ptyalin, and mucous which are essential for the mastication and initial digestion of food.

Salk, Jonas Edward (1914–1995)

US physician and microbiologist. In 1954 he developed the original vaccine that led to virtual eradication of paralytic polio in industrialized countries. He was director of the Salk Institute for Biological Studies, University of California, San Diego, 1963–75.

sally certain Australian eucalypts and wattles thought to resemble the ◊willow (genus *Salix*) in habit or foliage. Two species recognized in the timber industry are the black sally *Eucalyptus stellulata* found in New South Wales and Victoria and the white sally *Eucalyptus pauciflora* of South Australia, Tasmania, Victoria, and New South Wales.

salmon any of the various bony fishes of the family Salmonidae. More specifically the name is applied to several species of game fishes of the genera Salmo and Oncorhynchus of North America and Eurasia that mature in the ocean but, to spawn, return to the freshwater streams where they were born. Their normal colour is silvery with a few dark spots, but the colour changes at the spawning season.

life cycle The spawning season is between Sept and Jan, although they occasionally spawn at other times. The orange eggs, about 6 mm/0.25 in in diameter, are laid on the river bed, fertilized by the male, and then covered with gravel by the female. The incubation period is from five weeks to five months. The young hatched fish are known as **alevins**, and when they begin feeding they are called **parr**. At about two years old, the coat becomes silvery, and they are then **smolts**. Depending on the species, they may spend up to four years at sea before returning to their home streams to spawn (at this stage called **grilse**), often overcoming great obstacles to get there and die.

salmon farming Salmon are increasingly farmed in cages, and 'ranched' (selectively bred, hatched, and fed before release to the sea). Stocking rivers indiscriminately with hatchery fish may destroy the precision of their homing instinct by interbreeding between those originating in different rivers.

salmonella any of a very varied group of bacteria, genus *Salmonella* that colonize the intestines of humans and some animals. Some strains cause typhoid and paratyphoid fevers, while others cause salmonella ◊food poisoning, which is characterized by stomach pains, vomiting, diarrhoea, and headache. It can be fatal in elderly people, but others usually recover in a few days without antibiotics. Most cases are caused by contaminated animal products, especially poultry meat.

Human carriers of the disease may be well themselves but pass the bacteria on to others through unhygienic preparation of food. Domestic pets can also carry the bacteria while appearing healthy.

Salmonidae important family of fishes, with a small adipose fin, without fin rays, between the dorsal fin and the tail. Many species live in the sea, but enter fresh water to spawn, afterwards returning to the sea. The salmon, trout, char, and whitefish are included in this family.

classification Salmonidae are in order Salmoniformes, class Osteichthyes.

salsify ***or*** **vegetable oyster** hardy biennial plant native to the Mediterranean region. Its white fleshy roots and spring shoots are cooked and eaten; the roots are said to taste like oysters. (*Tragopogon porrifolius*, family Compositae.)

salt in chemistry, any compound formed from an acid and a base through the replacement of all or part of the hydrogen in the acid by a metal or electropositive radical. **Common salt** is sodium chloride (see ◊salt, common).

A salt may be produced by chemical reaction between an acid and a base, or by the displacement of hydrogen from an acid by a metal (see ◊displacement activity). As a solid, the ions normally adopt a regular arrangement to form crystals. Some salts only form stable crystals as hydrates (when combined with water). Most inorganic salts readily dissolve in water to give an electrolyte (a solution that conducts electricity).

TO CREATE A SALT:

IF A SOLUBLE SALT YOU WISH TO PROVIDE, YOU FIRST ON THE ACID SETTLE; THEN NEUTRALIZE WITH THE PROPER OXIDE, HYDROXIDE, CARBONATE OR METAL BUT IF THE SALT WILL NOT DISSOLVE, A SIMPLER MEANS YOU'LL TRY: PRECIPITATE IT, YOU RESOLVE, THEN FILTER, WASH AND DRY

saltation Latin *saltare* 'to leap' in biology, the idea that an abrupt genetic change can occur in an individual, which then gives rise to a new species. The idea has now been largely discredited, although the appearance of ◊polyploid individuals can be considered an example.

saltbush any of a group of drought-resistant plants belonging to the goosefoot family, especially the widespread genus *Atriplex*, used as grazing plants in arid, saline, and alkaline parts of North America, Australia, and S Africa, and the Australian and New Zealand genus *Rhagodia*. Where saltbush is the predominant vegetation, as in SW South Australia, the whole area is referred to as the saltbush. (Family Chenopodiaceae.)

salt, common or ***sodium chloride*** NaCl white crystalline solid, found dissolved in sea water and as rock salt (the mineral halite) in large deposits and salt domes. Common salt is used extensively in the food industry as a preservative and for flavouring, and in the chemical industry in the making of chlorine and sodium.

salt marsh wetland with halophytic vegetation (tolerant to sea water). Salt marshes develop around estuaries and on the sheltered side of sand and shingle spits. Salt marshes usually have a network of creeks and drainage channels by which tidal waters enter and leave the marsh.

saltpetre former name for potassium nitrate (KNO_3), the compound used in making gunpowder (from about 1500). It occurs naturally, being deposited during dry periods in places with warm climates, such as India.

saluki ancient breed of hunting dog resembling the greyhound. It is about 65 cm/26 in high and has a silky coat, which is usually fawn, cream, or white.

The saluki is a gazehound (hunts by sight) and is descended from the hound of the African desert Bedouins.

Salvarsan historical proprietary name for arsphenamine (technical name 3,3-diamino-4,4-dihydroxyarsenobenzene dichloride), the first specific antibacterial agent, discovered by German bacteriologist Paul Ehrlich in 1909. Because of its destructive effect on *Spirochaeta pallida*, it was used in the treatment of syphilis before the development of antibiotics.

sal volatile another name for ◊smelling salts.

Salyut Russian 'salute' series of seven space stations launched by the USSR 1971–82. Salyut was cylindrical in shape, 15 m/50 ft long, and weighed 19 tonnes/21 tons. It housed two or three cosmonauts at a time, for missions lasting up to eight months.

Salyut 1 was launched 19 April 1971. It was occupied for 23 days in June 1971 by a crew of three, who died during their return to Earth when their ◊Soyuz ferry craft depressurized. In 1973 *Salyut 2* broke up in orbit before occupation. The first fully successful Salyut mission was a 14-day visit to *Salyut 3* July 1974. In 1984–85 a team of three cosmonauts endured a record 237-day flight in *Salyut 7*. In 1986 the Salyut series was superseded by ◊*Mir*, an improved design capable of being enlarged by additional modules sent up from Earth.

samara in botany, a winged fruit, a type of ◊achene.

samarium hard, brittle, grey-white, metallic element of the vlanthanide series, symbol Sm, atomic number 62, relative atomic mass 150.4. It is widely distributed in nature and is obtained commercially from the minerals monzanite and bastnaesite. It is used only occasionally in industry, mainly as a catalyst in organic reactions. Samarium was discovered by spectroscopic analysis of the mineral samarskite and named 1879 by French chemist Paul Lecoq de Boisbaudran (1838–1912) after its source.

samoyed breed of dog originating in Siberia. It weighs about 25 kg/60 lb and is 58 cm/23 in tall. It resembles a ◊chow chow, but has a more pointed face and a white or cream coat.

samphire or ***glasswort*** or ***sea asparagus*** perennial plant found on sea cliffs and coastlines in Europe. The aromatic, salty leaves are fleshy and sharply pointed; the flowers grow in yellow-green open clusters. Samphire is used in salads, or pickled. (*Crithmum maritimum*, family Umbelliferae.)

sampling measurement of an ◊analogue signal (such as an audioor video signal) at regular intervals. The result of the measurement can be converted into a ◊digital signal that can be electronically enhanced, edited or processed.

San Andreas fault geological fault stretching for 1,125 km/700 mi NW–SE through the state of California, USA. It marks a conservative plate margin, where two plates slide past each other (see ◊plate tectonics).

Friction is created as the coastal Pacific plate moves northwest, rubbing against the American continental plate, which is moving slowly southeast. The relative movement is only about 5 cm/2 in a year, which means that Los Angeles will reach San Francisco's latitude in 10 million years. The friction caused by the tectonic movement gives rise to frequent, destructive ◊earthquakes. For example, in 1906 an earthquake originating from the fault almost destroyed San Francisco and killed about 700 people.

SAN ANDREAS FAULT AND BAY AREA

http://sepwww.stanford.edu/oldsep/joe/fault_images/BayAreaSanAndreasFault.html

Detailed tour of the San Andreas Fault and the San Francisco Bay area, with information on the origination of the fault. The site is supported by a full range of area maps.

sand loose grains of rock, sized 0.0625–2.00 mm/0.0025–0.08 in in diameter, consisting most commonly of ◊quartz, but owing their varying colour to mixtures of other minerals. Sand is used in cement-making, as an abrasive, in glass-making, and for other purposes.

Sands are classified into marine, freshwater, glacial, and terrestrial. Some 'light' soils contain up to 50% sand. Sands may eventually consolidate into ◊sandstone.

sandalwood fragrant heartwood of any of several Asiatic and Australian trees, used for ornamental carving, in perfume, and burned as incense. (Genus *Santalum*, family Santalaceae.)

sandbar ridge of sand built up by the currents across the mouth of a river or bay. A sandbar may be entirely underwater or it may form an elongated island that breaks the surface. A sandbar stretching out from a headland is a **sand spit**.

Coastal bars can extend across estuaries to form **bay bars**.

sand eel small, carnivorous fish found near the coasts of temperate seas of the northern hemisphere. Their bodies are covered with small scales, the swimbladder is absent, and they have long, sharply pointed snouts with which they bury themselves in the sand.

classification Sand eels are in genus *Ammodytes* in the family Ammodytidae, belonging to the order Perciformes, class Osteichthyes.

sandflea another name for ◊jigger.

sandgrouse any bird of the family Pteroclidae, order Columbiformes. They look like long-tailed grouse, but are actually closely related to pigeons. They live in warm, dry areas of Europe,

SANDGROUSE

A sandgrouse can hold about 9,000 seeds in its crop (that part of its anatomy used to store food). This is useful, as ground-feeding is a risky business and the birds need to feed rapidly as they move about.

Asia, and Africa and have long wings, short legs and bills, a wedge-shaped tail, and thick skin. They are sandy coloured and feed on vegetable matter and insects.

Sandgrouse may travel long distances to water to drink, and some carry water back to their young by soaking the breast feathers. The **pin-tailed sandgrouse** *Pterocles alchata* is a desert bird living in southern Europe, Africa, and Asia.

sand hopper or ***beachflea*** any of various small crustaceans belonging to the order Amphipeda, with laterally compressed bodies, that live in beach sand and jump like fleas. The eastern sand hopper *Orchestia agilis* of North America is about 1.3 cm/0.5 in long.

sand lizard lizard found on sandy heaths in Britain and central Europe, growing to nearly 20 cm/8 in in length. The male is brownish above, and in the spring a bright green on the flanks and belly. The female is brownish or greyish and mottled all over. They are active burrowers.
classification The sand lizard *Lacerta agilis* is in the suborder Sauria, order Squamata, class Reptilia.

sandpiper shorebird with a long, slender bill, which is compressed and grooved at the tip. They belong to the family Scolopacidae, which includes godwits, ◊curlews, and ◊snipes, order Charadriiformes.

sandstone ◊sedimentary rocks formed from the consolidation of sand, with sand-sized grains (0.0625–2 mm/0.0025–0.08 in) in a matrix or cement. Their principal component is quartz. Sandstones are commonly permeable and porous, and may form freshwater ◊aquifers. They are mainly used as building materials.

Sandstones are classified according to the matrix or cement material (whether derived from clay or silt; for example, as calcareous sandstone, ferruginous sandstone, siliceous sandstone).

sans-serif font typeface, such as Helvetica or Gill Sans, the strokes of which terminate in plain ends. Such fonts are very clear – hence their use in posters and signposts – but many designers believe that in running text, ◊serif fonts are easier to read.

sap the fluids that circulate through ◊vascular plants, especially woody ones. Sap carries water and food to plant tissues. Sap contains alkaloids, protein, and starch; it can be milky (as in rubber trees), resinous (as in pines), or syrupy (as in maples).

saponification in chemistry, the ◊hydrolysis (splitting) of an ◊ester by treatment with a strong alkali, resulting in the liberation of the alcohol from which the ester had been derived and a salt of the constituent fatty acid. The process is used in the manufacture of soap.

sapphire deep-blue, transparent gem variety of the mineral ◊corundum Al_2O_3, aluminium oxide. Small amounts of iron and titanium give it its colour. A corundum gem of any colour except red (which is a ruby) can be called a sapphire; for example, yellow sapphire.

saprophyte in botany, an obsolete term for a ◊saprotroph, an organism that lives in dead or decaying matter.

saprotroph (formerly ***saprophyte***) organism that feeds on the excrement or the dead bodies or tissues of others. They include most fungi (the rest being parasites); many bacteria and protozoa; animals such as dung beetles and vultures; and a few unusual plants, including several orchids. Saprotrophs cannot make food for themselves, so they are a type of ◊heterotroph. They are useful scavengers, and in sewage farms and refuse dumps break down organic matter into nutrients easily assimilable by green plants.

Sarcodina subphylum of protozoa containing the ◊amoebae.

sarcoidosis chronic disease of unknown cause involving enlargement of the lymph nodes and the formation of small fleshy nodules in the lungs. It may also affect the eyes, and skin, and (rarely) other tissue. Many cases resolve spontaneously or may be successfully treated using ◊corticosteroids.

sarcoma malignant◊ tumour arising from the fat, muscles, bones, cartilage, or blood and lymph vessels and connective tissues. Sarcomas are much less common than ◊carcinomas.

sardine common name for various small fishes (◊pilchards) in the herring family.

sarin poison gas 20 times more lethal to humans than potassium cyanide. It cripples the central nervous system, blocking the action of an enzyme that removes acetylcholine, the chemical that transmits signals. Sarin was developed in Germany during World War II.

Sarin was used 1995 in a terrorist attack on the Tokyo underground by a Japanese sect. It is estimated that the USA had a stockpile of 15,000 tonnes of sarin, and more than 1,000 US rockets with sarin warheads were found to be leaking 1995. There are no known safe disposal methods.

SARIN

http://www.outbreak.org/cgi-unreg/dynaserve.exe/cb/sarin.html

Outbreak page on the nerve agent sarin. The Web site contains sections on the characteristics of sarin, its toxicology, symptoms it causes, cautions and precautions, first aid therapy for victims of the gas, and a list of neutralization and decontamination methods.

The human race has today the means for annihilating itself.

MAX BORN German-born British physicist.
Bulletin of the Atomic Scientists June 1957

satellite any small body that orbits a larger one, either natural or artificial. Natural satellites that orbit planets are called moons. The first **artificial satellite**, *Sputnik 1*, was launched into orbit around the Earth by the USSR in 1957. Artificial satellites are used for scientific purposes, communications, weather forecasting, and military applications. The brightest artificial satellites can be seen by the naked eye.

At any time, there are several thousand artificial satellites orbiting the Earth, including active satellites, satellites that have ended their working lives, and discarded sections of rockets. Artificial satellites eventually re-enter the Earth's atmosphere. Usually they burn up by friction, but sometimes debris falls to the Earth's surface, as with ◊*Skylab* and ◊*Salyut 7*. In 1997 there were 300 active artificial satellites in orbit around Earth, the majority used in communications.

satellite applications the uses to which artificial satellites are put. These include:
scientific experiments and observation Many astronomical observations are best taken above the disturbing effect of the atmosphere. Satellite observations have been carried out by *IRAS* (*Infrared Astronomical Satellite*, 1983) which made a complete infrared survey of the skies, and *Solar Max* 1980, which observed solar flares. The *Hipparcos* satellite, launched 1989, measured the positions of many stars. The *ROSAT* (Roentgen Satellite), launched June 1990, examined UV and X-ray radiation. In 1992, the COBE (Cosmic Background Explorer) satellite detected details of the Big Bang that mark the first stage in the formation of galaxies. Medical experiments have been carried out aboard crewed satellites, such as the Soviet *Mir* and the US *Skylab*.
reconnaissance, land resource, and mapping applications Apart from military use and routine mapmaking, the US *Landsat*, the French *SPOT*, and equivalent USSR satellites have provided much useful information about water sources and drainage, vegetation, land use, geological structures, oil and mineral locations, and snow and ice.

weather monitoring The US NOAA series of satellites, and others launched by the European space agency, Japan, and India, provide continuous worldwide observation of the atmosphere.
navigation The US Global Positioning System uses 24 Navstar satellites that enable users (including walkers and motorists) to find their position to within 100 m/328 ft. The US military can make full use of the system, obtaining accuracy to within 1.5 m/4 ft 6 in. The Transit system, launched in the 1960s, with 12 satellites in orbit, locates users to within 100 m/328 ft.
communications A complete worldwide communications network is now provided by satellites such as the US-run ◊Intelsat system.

satellite television transmission of broadcast signals through artificial communications satellites. Mainly positioned in ◊geostationary orbit, satellites have been used since the 1960s to relay television pictures around the world.

Higher-power satellites have more recently been developed to broadcast signals to cable systems or directly to people's homes.

saturated compound organic compound, such as propane, that contains only single covalent bonds. Saturated organic compounds can only undergo further reaction by ◊substitution reactions, as in the production of chloropropane from propane.

saturated fatty acid ◊fatty acid in which there are no double bonds in the hydrocarbon chain.

saturated solution in physics and chemistry, a solution obtained when a solvent (liquid) can dissolve no more of a solute (usually a solid) at a particular temperature. Normally, a slight fall in temperature causes some of the solute to crystallize out of solution. If this does not happen the phenomenon is called supercooling, and the solution is said to be **supersaturated**.

Saturn in astronomy, the second-largest planet in the Solar System, sixth from the Sun, and encircled by bright and easily visible equatorial rings. Viewed through a telescope it is ochre. Its polar diameter is 12,000 km/7,450 mi smaller than its equatorial diameter, a result of its fast rotation and low density, the lowest of any planet. Its mass is 95 times that of Earth, and its magnetic field 1,000 times stronger.
mean distance from the Sun 1.427 billion km/0.886 billion mi
equatorial diameter 120,000 km/75,000 mi
rotational period 10 hr 14 min at equator, 10 hr 40 min at higher latitudes
year 29.46 Earth years
atmosphere visible surface consists of swirling clouds, probably made of frozen ammonia at a temperature of –170°C/–274°F, although the markings in the clouds are not as prominent as Jupiter's. The space probes *Voyager 1* and *2* found winds reaching 1,800 kph/1,100 mph
surface Saturn is believed to have a small core of rock and iron, encased in ice and topped by a deep layer of liquid hydrogen
satellites 18 known moons, more than for any other planet. The largest moon, ◊Titan, has a dense atmosphere. Other satellites include Epimetheus, Janus, Pandor, and Prometheus. The rings visible from Earth begin about 14,000 km/9,000 mi from the planet's cloudtops and extend out to about 76,000 km/47,000 mi. Made of small chunks of ice and rock (averaging 1 m/3 ft across), they are 275,000 km/170,000 mi rim to rim, but only 100 m/300 ft thick. The Voyager probes showed that the rings actually consist of thousands of closely spaced ringlets, looking like the grooves in a gramophone record.

SATURN

http://www.hawastsoc.org/solar/eng/saturn.htm

How many rings does Saturn have? How many satellites? Find out this and more at this site, which also features a video of a storm in the planet's atmosphere.

Saturn rocket family of large US rockets, developed by Wernher von Braun (1912–1977) for the ◊Apollo project. The two-stage *Saturn IB* was used for launching Apollo spacecraft into orbit around the Earth. The three-stage *Saturn V* sent Apollo spacecraft to the Moon, and launched the *Skylab* ◊space station. The liftoff thrust of a *Saturn V* was 3,500 tonnes. After Apollo and *Skylab*, the Saturn rockets were retired in favour of the ◊space shuttle.

sausage tree tropical African tree, which grows up to 12 m/40 ft tall and has purplish flowers. Its gourdlike fruits hang from stalks and look like thick sausages; they can be up to 60 cm/2 ft long and weigh 2–5 kg/5–12 lb. (*Kigelia pinnata*, family Bignoniaceae.)

savanna or ***savannah*** extensive open tropical grasslands, with scattered trees and shrubs. Savannas cover large areas of Africa, North and South America, and N Australia. The soil is acidic and sandy and generally considered suitable only as pasture for low-density grazing.

A new strain of rice suitable for savanna conditions was developed 1992. It not only grew successfully under test conditions in Colombia but also improved pasture quality so grazing numbers could be increased twentyfold.

sawfish any fish of the order Pristiformes of large, sharklike ◊rays, characterized by a flat, sawlike snout edged with teeth. The common sawfish *Pristis pectinatus*, also called the smalltooth, is more than 6 m/19 ft long. It has some 24 teeth along an elongated snout (2 m/6 ft) that can be used as a weapon.

sawfly any of several families of insects of the order Hymenoptera, related to bees, wasps, and ants, but lacking a 'waist' on the body. The egg-laying tube (ovipositor) of the female is surrounded by a pair of sawlike organs, which it uses to make a slit in a plant stem to lay its eggs. Horntails are closely related.

sawshark member of two genera of sharks. They grow to 1 m/3.3 ft long including the long, sawlike, toothed snout, which is used to attack prey. They are not dangerous to humans.

Although they resemble the sawfish, a ray, their gill-slits are on the sides of the head instead of underneath, and the front edge of the pectoral fins are free, not fused to the head and body.
classification *Pliotrema* and *Pristiophorus*, are in the family Pristiophoridae of order Pristiophoriformes, subclass Elasmobranchii, class Chondrichthyes.

saxifrage any of a group of plants belonging to the saxifrage family, found growing in rocky, mountainous, and alpine areas in the northern hemisphere. They are low plants with groups of small white, pink, or yellow flowers. (Genus *Saxifraga*, family Saxifragaceae.)

SCABIES

http://biomed.nus.sg/nsc/scabies.html

Well-presented information about scabies from Singapore's National Skin Centre. There is a picture of the condition and information on its transmission and treatment.

scabies contagious infection of the skin caused by the parasitic itch mite *Sarcoptes scabiei*, which burrows under the skin to deposit eggs. Treatment is by antiparasitic creams and lotions.

scabious any of a group of plants belonging to the teasel family, native to Europe and Asia, with many small, usually purplish-blue flowers borne in a single head on a tall stalk. The small scabious (*S. columbaria*) and the Mediterranean sweet scabious (*S. atropurpurea*) are often cultivated. (Genus *Scabiosa*, family Dipsacaceae.)

scalable font font that can be used at any size and any resolution, on a screen or hard-copy device, such as a laser printer or image setter. Scalable fonts are always ◊outline fonts.

scalar quantity in mathematics and science, a quantity that has magnitude but no direction, as distinct from a ◊vector quantity, which has a direction as well as a magnitude. Temperature, mass, and volume are scalar quantities.

scale the numerical relationship, expressed as a ◊ratio, between the actual size of an object and the size of an image that represents it on a map, plan, or diagram.

scale in chemistry, ◊calcium carbonate deposits that form on the inside of a kettle or boiler as a result of boiling ◊hard water.

scale insect any small plant-sucking insect, order Homoptera, of the superfamily Coccoidea. Some species are major pests – for example, the citrus mealy bug (genus *Pseudococcus*), which attacks citrus fruits in North America. The female is often wingless and legless, attached to a plant by the head and with the body covered with a waxy scale. The rare males are winged.

scaler instrument that counts the number of radioactive particles passing through a radiation detector such as a Geiger–Müller tube (the scaler and tube together form a ◊Geiger counter). It gives the total, or cumulative, number of particles counted whereas a ◊ratemeter gives the number of particles detected in a unit of time.

scallop any marine bivalve ◊mollusc of the family Pectinidae, with a fan-shaped shell. There are two 'ears' extending from the socketlike hinge. Scallops use water-jet propulsion to move through the water to escape predators such as starfish. The giant Pacific scallop found from Alaska to California can reach 20 cm/8 in width.

scaly anteater another name for the ◊pangolin.

scandium silver-white, metallic element of the ◊lanthanide series, symbol Sc, atomic number 21, relative atomic mass 44.956.

Its compounds are found widely distributed in nature, but only in minute amounts. The metal has little industrial importance.

Scandium is relatively more abundant in the Sun and other stars than on Earth. Scandium oxide (scandia) is used as a catalyst, in making crucibles and other ceramic parts, and scandium sulphate (in very dilute aqueous solution) is used in agriculture to improve seed germination.

scanner in computing, a device that can produce a digital image of a document for input and storage in a computer. It uses technology similar to that of a photocopier. Small scanners can be passed over the document surface by hand; larger versions have a flat bed, like that of a photocopier, on which the input document is placed and scanned.

Scanners are widely used to input graphics for use in ◊desktop publishing. If text is input with a scanner, the image captured is seen by the computer as a single digital picture rather than as separate characters. Consequently, the text cannot be processed by, for example, a word processor unless suitable optical character-recognition software is available to convert the image to its constituent characters. Scanners vary in their resolution, typical hand-held scanners ranging from 75 to 300 dpi. Types include flatbed, drum, and overhead.

scanner device, usually electronic, used to sense and reproduce an image.

◊Magnetic resonance imaging (MRI) was being used in 1990 to tell stale food from fresh: the image of a fresh vegetable is different from that of one frozen and thawed. It is also used in medical diagnosis.

scanning in medicine, the noninvasive examination of body organs to detect abnormalities of structure or function. Detectable waves – for example, ◊ultrasound, gamma, or ◊X-rays – are passed through the part to be scanned. Their absorption pattern is recorded, analysed by computer, and displayed pictorially on a screen.

scanning electron microscope (SEM) electron microscope that produces three-dimensional images, magnified 10–200,000 times. A fine beam of electrons, focused by electromagnets, is moved, or scanned, across the specimen. Electrons reflected from the specimen are collected by a detector, giving rise to an electrical signal, which is then used to generate a point of brightness on a television-like screen. As the point moves rapidly over the screen, in phase with the scanning electron beam, an image of the specimen is built up.

The resolving power of an SEM depends on the size of the electron beam – the finer the beam, the greater the resolution. Present-day instruments typically have a resolution of 7–10 nm.

The first scanning electron picture was produced in 1935 by Max Knoll of the German company Telefunken, though the first commercial SEM (produced by the Cambridge Instrument Company in the UK) did not go on sale until 1965.

scanning transmission electron microscope (STEM) electron microscope that combines features of the ◊scanning electron microscope (SEM) and the transmission electron microscope (TEM). First built in the USA in 1966, the microscope has both the SEM's contrast characteristics and lack of aberrations and the high resolution of the TEM. Magnifications of over 90 million times can be achieved, enough to image single atoms.

A fine beam of electrons, 0.3 nm in diameter, moves across the specimen, as in an SEM. However, because the specimen used is a thin slice, the beam also passes through the specimen (as in a TEM). The reflected electrons and those that penetrated the specimen are collected to form an electric signal, which is interpreted by computer to form an image on screen.

scanning tunnelling microscope (STM) microscope that produces a magnified image by moving a tiny tungsten probe across the surface of the specimen. The tip of the probe is so fine that it may consist of a single atom, and it moves so close to the specimen surface that electrons jump (or tunnel) across the gap between the tip and the surface.

The magnitude of the electron flow (current) depends on the distance from the tip to the surface, and so by measuring the current, the contours of the surface can be determined. These can be used to form an image on a computer screen of the surface, with individual atoms resolved. Magnifications up to 100 million times are possible.

The STM was invented 1981 by Gerd Binning from Germany and Heinrich Rohrer from Switzerland at the IBM Zurich Research Laboratory. With Ernst Ruska, who invented the transmission electron microscope in 1933, they were awarded the Nobel Prize for Physics in 1986.

scapula or ***shoulder blade*** large, flat, triangular bone which lies over the second to seventh ribs on the back, forming part of the pectoral girdle, and assisting in the articulation of the arm with the chest region. Its flattened shape allows a large region for the attachment of muscles.

scarab any of a family Scarabaeidae of beetles, often brilliantly coloured, and including ◊cockchafers, June beetles, and dung beetles. The *Scarabeus sacer* was revered by the ancient Egyptians as the symbol of resurrection.

scarlet fever or ***scarlatina*** acute infectious disease, especially of children, caused by the bacteria in the *Streptococcus pyogenes* group. It is marked by fever, vomiting, sore throat, and a bright red rash spreading from the upper to the lower part of the body. The rash is followed by the skin peeling in flakes. It is treated with antibiotics.

scarp and dip in geology, the two slopes formed when a sedimentary bed outcrops as a landscape feature. The scarp is the slope that cuts across the bedding plane; the dip is the opposite slope which follows the bedding plane. The scarp is usually steep, while the dip is a gentle slope.

scatter diagram or ***scattergram*** diagram whose purpose is to establish whether or not a relationship or ◊correlation exists between two variables; for example, between life expectancy and gross national product. Each observation is marked with a dot in a position that shows the value of both variables. The pattern of dots is then examined to see whether they show any underlying trend by means of a **line of best fit** (a straight line drawn so that its distance from the various points is as short as possible).

scattering in physics, the random deviation or reflection of a stream of particles or of a beam of radiation such as light, by the particles in the matter through which it passes.
alpha particles Alpha particles scattered by a thin gold foil provided the first convincing evidence that atoms had very small, very dense, positive nuclei. From 1906 to 1908 Ernest Rutherford carried out a series of experiments from which he estimated that the closest approach of an alpha particle to a gold nucleus in a head-on collision was about 10^{-14} m. He concluded that the gold nucleus must be no larger than this. Most of the alpha particles fired at the gold foil passed straight through undeviated; however, a few were scattered in all directions and a very small fraction bounced back towards the source. This result so surprised Rutherford that he is reported to have commented: 'It was almost as if you fired a 15-inch shell at a piece of tissue paper and it came back and hit you'.
light Light is scattered from a rough surface, such as that of a sheet of paper, by random reflection from the varying angles of each small part of the surface. This is responsible for the dull, flat appearance of such surfaces and their inability to form images (unlike mirrors). Light is also scattered by particles suspended in a gas or liquid. The red and yellow colours associated with sunrises and sunsets are due to the fact that red light is scattered to a lesser extent than is blue light by dust particles in the atmosphere. When the Sun is low in the sky, its light passes through a thicker, more dusty layer of the atmosphere, and the blue light radiated by it is scattered away, leaving the red sunlight to pass through to the eye of the observer.

scent gland gland that opens onto the outer surface of animals, producing odorous compounds that are used for communicating between members of the same species (◊pheromones), or for discouraging predators.

scheltopusik another name for the vglass snake.

schipperke ***Dutch 'little boatman' from its use on canal barges*** breed of small dog originally bred in Flanders as a hunter of rats. It has a short, thick, bristly, all-black coat. Of sturdy build, it has a small head with pointed ears; its tail is often completely docked. Schipperkes come in two sizes, the smaller weighing up to 5 kg/11 lb, the larger up to 9 kg/20 lb.

schist ◊metamorphic rock containing mica or another platy or elongate mineral, whose crystals are aligned to give a foliation (planar texture) known as schistosity. Schist may contain additional minerals such as ◊garnet.

schizocarp dry vfruit that develops from two or more carpels and splits, when mature, to form separate one-seeded units known as mericarps.

The mericarps may be dehiscent, splitting open to release the seed when ripe, as in *Geranium*, or indehiscent, remaining closed once mature, as in mallow *Malva* and plants of the Umbelliferae family, such as the carrot *Daucus carota* and parsnip *Pastinaca sativa*.

schizophrenia mental disorder, a psychosis of unknown origin, which can lead to profound changes in personality, behaviour, and perception, including delusions and hallucinations. It is more common in males and the early-onset form is more severe than when the illness develops in later life. Modern treatment approaches include drugs, family therapy, stress reduction, and rehabilitation.

Schizophrenia implies a severe divorce from reality in the patient's thinking. Although the causes are poorly understood, it is now recognized as an organic disease, associated with structural anomalies in the brain. Canadian researchers 1995 identified a protein in the brain, PSA-NCAM, that plays a part in filtering sensory information. The protein is significantly reduced in the brains of schizophrenics, supporting the idea that schizophrenia occurs when the brain is overwhelmed by sensory information.

There is some evidence that early trauma, either in the womb or during delivery, may play a part in causation. There is also a genetic contribution.

There is an enormous inter-country variation in the symptoms of schizophrenia and in the incidence of the main forms of the disease, according to a 1997 report by American investigators. **Paranoid schizophrenia**, characterized by feeling of persecution, is 50% more common in developed countries, whereas **catatonic schizophrenia**, characterized by total immobility, is six times more frequent in developing countries. **Hebephrenic schizophrenia**, characterized by disorganized behaviour and speech and emotional bluntness, is four times more prevalent in developed countries overall but is rare in the USA.

SCHIZOPHRENIA

http://www.pslgroup.com/SCHIZOPHR.HTM

Facts about schizophrenia – causes and symptoms, the different types of the disease, how it affects sufferers' family members, available treatments, and new developments. It includes a list of available support resources.

Schmidt Telescope reflecting telescope used for taking wide-angle photographs of the sky. Invented 1930 by Estonian astronomer Bernhard Schmidt (1879–1935), it has an added corrector lens to help focus the incoming light. Examples are the 1. 2-m/48-in Schmidt telescope on ◊Mount Palomar and the UK Schmidt telescope, of the same size, at ◊Siding Spring.

schnauzer breed of dog originating in Germany and now found in three sizes: miniature, standard, and giant. All have a coarse coat, either all black or pepper and salt in colour, with a strong, square muzzle and bristly hair on the face. The standard schnauzer (about 48 cm/18 in tall) is used as a general-purpose guard and farm dog; the giant (up to 65 cm/25.5 in) is used as a police and guard dog; the miniature (under 35 cm/14 in) is kept as a pet.

Schneider Trophy aviation trophy presented by Jacques Schneider in 1913 for competition between seaplanes of any nation. From the first holder, M Prévost in 1913, who averaged 73.62 kph/45.75 mph, the trophy changed hands several times before being won outright by Britain, after victories in 1927, 1929 and 1931, the last creating a world record of 547.30 kph/340.08 mph.

Schwarzschild radius in ◊astrophysics, the radius of the event horizon surrounding a vblack hole within which light cannot escape its gravitational pull.

For a black hole of mass M, the Schwarzschild radius Rs is given by Rs = $2gm/c^2$, where g is the gravitational constant and c is the speed of light. The Schwarzschild radius for a black hole of solar mass is about 3 km/1.9 mi. It is named after Karl Schwarzschild, the German mathematician who deduced the possibility of black holes from ◊Einstein's general theory of relativity in 1916.

sciatica persistent pain in the back and down the outside of one leg, along the sciatic nerve and its branches. Causes of sciatica include inflammation of the nerve or pressure of a displaced disc on a nerve root leading out of the lower spine.

[Science doesn't deal with facts; indeed] fact is an emotion-loaded word for which there is little place in scientific debate. Science is above all a cooperative enterprise.

HERMANN BONDI Austrian-born British scientist and mathematician. *Nature* 1977

science Latin *scientia* 'knowledge' any systematic field of study or body of knowledge that aims, through experiment, observation, and deduction, to produce reliable explanations of phenomena, with reference to the material and physical world.
history Activities such as healing, star-watching, and engineering have been practised in many societies since ancient times. Pure science, especially physics (formerly called natural philosophy), had traditionally been the main area of study for philosophers. The European scientific revolution between about 1650 and 1800 replaced speculative philosophy with a new combination of observation, experimentation, and rationality.
philosophy of science Today, scientific research involves an interaction between tradition, experiment and observation, and deduction. The subject area called philosophy of science investigates the nature of this complex interaction, and the extent of its ability to gain access to the truth about the material world. It has long been recognized that induction from observation cannot give explanations based on logic. In the 20th century Karl Popper has described ◊scientific method as a rigorous experimental testing of a scientist's ideas or ◊hypotheses (see hypothesis). The origin and role of these ideas, and their interdependence with observation, have been examined, for example, by the US thinker Thomas S Kuhn, who places them in a historical and sociological setting.
sociology of science The sociology of science investigates how scientific theories and laws are produced, and questions the possibility of objectivity in any scientific endeavour. One controversial point of view is the replacement of scientific realism with scientific relativism, as proposed by Paul K Feyerabend. Questions concerning the proper use of science and the role of science education are also restructuring this field of study.

MAD SCIENTIST NETWORK

http://medinfo.wustl.edu/~ysp/MSN/

Indispensable resource for school science teachers and children in need of answers to scientific questions. The Mad Scientist network is a group of scientists prepared to field queries on a vast range of subjects. There is an excellent online archive of previous questions and answers, and helpful guides to accessing other general interest Web science sites.

science park site near a university on which high-technology industrial businesses are housed, so that they can benefit from the research expertise of the university's scientists. Science parks originated in the USA in the 1950s.

scientific law in science, principles that are taken to be universally applicable.

Laws (for instance, ◊Boyle's law and ◊Newton's laws of motion) form the basic theoretical structure of the physical sciences, so that the rejection of a law by the scientific community is an almost inconceivable event. On occasion a law may be modified, as was the case when Einstein showed that Newton's laws of motion do not apply to objects travelling at speeds close to that of light.

scientific method in science, the belief that experimentation and observation, properly understood and applied, can avoid the influence of cultural and social values and so build up a picture of a reality independent of the observer.

Techniques and mechanical devices that improve the reliability of measurements may seem to support this theory; but the realization that observations of subatomic particles influence their behaviour has undermined the view that objectivity is possible in science (see ◊uncertainty principle).

scientific notation alternative term for ◊standard form.

scilla any of a group of bulbous plants belonging to the lily family, with blue, pink, or white flowers; they include the spring ◊squill (*S. verna*). (Genus *Scilla*, family Liliaceae.)

scimitar oryx medium-sized ◊oryx *Oryx dammah*. Its startling, swept-back horns have made it a prime target for hunters. It was once found over virtually the whole of the Sahel. Numbers started to decline sharply in the 1950s and the animals were reduced to scattered groups by the 1970s, then reached the edge of extinction by the 1980s. The initial cause of decline was the destruction of grasslands, but savage hunting annihilated the remainder. There are captive breeding herds and plans to reintroduce the species in Tunisia.

scintillation counter instrument for measuring very low levels of radiation. The radiation strikes a scintillator (a device that emits a unit of light when a charged elementary particle collides with it), whose light output is 'amplified' by a ◊photomultiplier; the current pulses of its output are in turn counted or added by a scaler to give a numerical reading.

sclerenchyma plant tissue whose function is to strengthen and support, composed of thick-walled cells that are heavily lignified (toughened). On maturity the cell inside dies, and only the cell walls remain.

Sclerenchyma may be made up of one or two types of cells: **sclereids**, occurring singly or in small clusters, are often found in the hard shells of fruits and in seed coats, bark, and the stem cortex; **fibres**, frequently grouped in bundles, are elongated cells, often with pointed ends, associated with the vascular tissue (◊xylem and ◊phloem) of the plant.

Some fibres provide useful materials, such as flax from *Linum usitatissimum* and hemp from *Cannabis sativa*.

sclerosis any abnormal hardening of body tissues, especially the nervous system or walls of the arteries. See ◊multiple sclerosis and vatherosclerosis.

scoliosis lateral (sideways) deviation of the spine. It may be congenital or acquired (through bad posture, illness, or other deformity); or it may be idopathic (of unknown cause). Treatments include mechanical or surgical correction, depending on the cause.

Scombridae important family of bony fish, which include the bonito, mackerel, tuna or tunny, and wahoo.

Fossil forms of Scombridae are found in the Eocene and Miocene strata.
classification Scombridae is in order Perciformes, class Osteichthyes.

Scorpio alternative term for ◊Scorpius.

SCORPION

If disturbed, whip scorpions emit a spray that is 84% acetic acid (the acid in vinegar). The spray also contains a powerful solvent to ensure that the irritant acid penetrates its target fully.

scorpion any arachnid of the order Scorpiones, common in the tropics and subtropics. Scorpions have four pairs of walking legs, large pincers, and long tails ending in upcurved poisonous stings,

WELCOME TO THE SCORPION EMPORIUM

http://wrbu.si.edu/www/stockwell/emporium/emporium.html

Complete source of information on the nippy creepy crawlies. There is an interesting list of frequently asked questions about scorpions. A gallery of photos aids identification of a particular species. There is advice on looking after scorpions and even what to do if they turn on you.

though the venom is not usually fatal to a healthy adult human. Some species reach 25 cm/10 in. There are about 600 different species.

They are nocturnal in habit, hiding during the day beneath stones and under the loose bark of trees. The females are viviparous (producing live young), the eggs being hatched in the enlarged oviducts. Scorpions sometimes prey on each other, but their main food is the woodlouse. They seize their prey with their powerful claws or palpi. They are also able to survive for a long time without eating; one scorpion managed to survive for 17 months on a single housefly.

scorpion fly any insect of the order Mecoptera. They have a characteristic downturned beak with jaws at the tip, and many males have a scorpion-like upturned tail, giving them their common name. Most feed on insects or carrion. They are an ancient group with relatively few living representatives.

Scorpius bright zodiacal constellation in the southern hemisphere between ◊Libra and ◊Sagittarius, represented as a scorpion. The Sun passes briefly through Scorpius in the last week of Nov. The heart of the scorpion is marked by the bright red supergiant star ◊Antares. Scorpius contains rich ◊Milky Way star fields, plus the strongest ◊X-ray source in the sky, Scorpius X-1. The whole area is rich in clusters and nebulae. In astrology, the dates for Scorpius are about 24 Oct–21 Nov (see ◊precession).

Scottish Fold cat breed of domestic shorthaired cat with distinctive folded ears. Developed in Scotland in the 1960s from a mutation, it was imported into the USA from the early 1970s. The folded ear flaps either droop forward or forward and downward with the tip almost touching the head. The head is round and set on a well rounded body. The coat, which is short and dense, is acceptable in almost any colour.

The breed was recognized in Britain 1976.

Scottish terrier breed of short-legged ◊terrier used originally to kill foxes and rodents. Its coarse, thick coat is usually black, but may also be brindled or wheaten, and grows long underneath the body; the long bristling hairs around its muzzle and over its eyes are characteristic. It stands about 28 cm/11 in at the shoulder and carries its ears and thick, pointed tail upright.

scrambling circuit in radiotelephony, a transmitting circuit that renders signals unintelligible unless received by the corresponding unscrambling circuit.

scraper earth-moving machine used in road construction. Self-propelled or hauled by a ◊bulldozer, a scraper consists of an open bowl, with a cutting blade at the lower front edge. When moving, the blade bites into the soil, which is forced into the bowl.

scrapie fatal disease of sheep and goats that attacks the central nervous system, causing deterioration of the brain cells, and leading to the characteristic staggering gait and other behavioural abnormalities, before death. It is caused by the presence of an abnormal version of the brain protein PrP and is related to ◊bovine spongiform encephalopathy, the disease of cattle known as 'mad cow disease', and Creutzfeldt–Jakob disease in humans. It is a transmissible spongiform encephalopathy.

In 1996 Dutch researchers announced a test for detecting abnormal PrP in the tonsils of affected sheep before the symptoms of scrapie become apparent.

screamer any South American marsh-dwelling bird of the family Anhimidae, order Anseriformes; there are only three species, all in the genus *Anhima.* They are about 80 cm/30 in long, with short curved beaks, long toes, dark plumage, spurs on the fronts of the wings, and a crest or horn on the head.

Screamers wade in wet forests and marshes, although their feet are scarcely webbed. They are related to ducks and are placed in the same order. The **horned screamer** *A. cornuta* is found in certain parts of Central and South America, and has glossy black plumage with a white abdomen; it has a long, slender, yellowish horn on its head.

scree pile of rubble and sediment that collects at the foot of a mountain range or cliff. The rock fragments that form scree are usually broken off by the action of frost (◊freeze-thaw weathering).

With time, the rock waste builds up into a heap or sheet of rubble that may eventually bury even the upper cliffs, and the growth of the scree then stops. Usually, however, erosional forces remove the rock waste so that the scree stays restricted to lower slopes.

screen in computing, another name for monitor.

screen dump in computing, the process of making a printed copy of the current VDU screen display. The screen dump is sometimes stored as a data file instead of being printed immediately.

screen grabber in computing, software which can take a snapshot of the contents of a computer screen and save it as a picture file. Screen grabbers are useful for creating the screen shots seen in many computer magazines to illustrate software reviews and instructions.

screening or ***health screening*** the systematic search for evidence of a disease, or of conditions that may precede it, in people who are at risk but not suffering from any symptoms. The aim of screening is to try to limit ill health from preventable diseases that might otherwise go undetected in the early stages. Examples are hypothyroidism and phenylketonuria, for which all newborn babies in Western countries are screened; breast cancer (◊mammography) and cervical cancer; and stroke, for which high blood pressure is a known risk factor.

The criteria for a successful screening programme are that the disease should be important and treatable, the population at risk identifiable, the screening test acceptable, accurate, and cheap, and that the results of screening should justify the costs involved.

screen saver in computing, program designed to prevent a static image from 'burning' itself into the phosphor screen of an idle computer monitor. If the user leaves the computer alone for more than a few minutes, the screen saver automatically displays a moving or changing image – perhaps a sequence of random squiggles, or an animation of flying toasters – on the screen. When the user touches any key, the computer returns to its previous state.

screw in construction, cylindrical or tapering piece of metal or plastic (or formerly wood) with a helical groove cut into it. Each turn of a screw moves it forward or backwards by a distance equal to the pitch (the spacing between neighbouring threads).

Its mechanical advantage equals $2r/P$, where P is the pitch and r is the radius of the thread. Thus the mechanical advantage of a tapering wood screw, for example, increases as it is rotated into the wood.

script in communications, a series of instructions for a computer. For example, when users log on to an ISP (Internet Service Provider) or other service, their computers follow a script containing passwords and other information to tell the ISP's server who they are.

scrollback in computing, the automatic scrolling of messages down the screen as they are received in ◊Internet Relay Chat (IRC), ◊bulletin boards or similar forums,.

scrollbar in computing, a narrow box along two sides of a ◊window, enabling users to move its contents up, down, left or right. Each end of the scrollbar represents the same end of the document on display, and the vmouse is used to move a small 'scrollbox' up and down the bar to scroll the contents or to click on the directional arrows.

scrolling in computing, the action by which data displayed on a VDU screen are automatically moved upwards and out of sight as new lines of data are added at the bottom.

scrub bird one of two Australian birds of the genus *Atrichornis,* order Passeriformes. Both are about 18 cm/7 in long, rather wrenlike but long-tailed. Scrub birds are good mimics.

The noisy scrub bird *Atrichornis clamosus* was feared to be extinct, but has been rediscovered, although numbers are still low. The other species is the rufous scrub bird *A. rufescens.*

SCSI (abbreviation for ***small computer system interface***) in computing, standard method for connecting peripheral devices (such as printers, scanners and CD-ROM drives) to a computer. A group of peripherals linked in series to a single SCSI port is called a **daisy-chain**.

scuba (acronym for ***self-contained underwater breathing apparatus***) another name for ◊aqualung.

scurvy disease caused by deficiency of vitamin C (ascorbic acid), which is contained in fresh vegetables and fruit. The signs are weakness and aching joints and muscles, progressing to bleeding of the gums and other spontaneous haemorrhage, and drying-up of the skin and hair. It is reversed by giving the vitamin.

scurvy grass plant found growing in salt marshes and on banks by the sea in the northern hemisphere. Shoots may grow low, or more upright, up to 50 cm/20 in, with fleshy heart-shaped lower leaves; the flowers are white and have four petals. The edible, sharp-tasting leaves are a good source of vitamin C and were formerly eaten by sailors as a cure for the disease scurvy. (*Cochlearia officinalis,* family Cruciferae.)

scythe harvesting tool with long wooden handle and sharp, curving blade.

It is similar to a◊ sickle. The scythe was in common use in the Middle East and Europe from the dawn of agriculture until the early 20th century, by which time it had generally been replaced by machinery.

Until the beginning of the 19th century, the scythe was used in the hayfield for cutting grass, but thereafter was applied to cereal crops as well, because it was capable of a faster work rate than the sickle. One person could mow 0.4 hectares/1 acre of wheat in a day with a scythe. Next came a team of workers to gather and bind the crop into sheaves and stand them in groups, or stooks, across the field.

SDK (abbreviation for ***software development kit***) in computing, suite of programs supplied to software developers to help them develop applications for environments such as Microsoft Windows and Microsoft Office.

sea anemone invertebrate marine animal of the phylum Cnidaria with a tubelike body attached by the base to a rock or shell. The other end has an open 'mouth' surrounded by stinging tentacles, which capture crustaceans and other small organisms. Many sea anemones are beautifully coloured, especially those in tropical waters.

***sea anemone** Distributed along the west coasts of the British Isles, the snakelocks anemone* Anemonia sulcata *is found on the middle and lower shores. Along with the common beadlet anemone, it is the sea anemone most likely to be discovered by the casual observer. Premaphotos Wildlife*

sea bass any marine fish of the family Serranidae, of perchlike appearance. Striped bass *Roccus saxatilis* of the E North American coast, is the best known.

seaborgium synthesized radioactive element of the ◊transactinide series, symbol Sg, atomic number 106, relative atomic mass 263. It was first synthesized 1974 in the USA and given the temporary name unnilhexium. The discovery was not confirmed until 1993. It was officially named 1997 after US nuclear chemist Glenn Seaborg.

The University of California, Berkeley, bombarded californium with oxygen nuclei to get isotope 263; the Joint Institute for Nuclear Research, Dubna, Russia, bombarded lead with chromium nuclei to obtain isotopes 259 and 260.

sea butterfly or ***pteropod*** member of a group of molluscs comprising about 100 species that swim freely in the ocean, having a pair of fins developed from the sides of the mouth and neck, enabling the animal to progress by flapping.
classifiation Sea butterflies belong to order Thecosomata in subclass Opisthobranchia, class Gastropoda, phylum Mollusca.

sea cucumber any echinoderm of the class Holothuroidea with a cylindrical body that is tough-skinned, knobbed, or spiny. The body may be several feet in length. Sea cucumbers are sometimes called 'cotton-spinners' from the sticky filaments they eject from the anus in self-defence.

The dried flesh of sea cucumbers is a delicacy in Japan and Taiwan, and overfishing has threatened some populations. A high density is vital to sustain a population as they reproduce by releasing sperm or ova into the water; other sea cucumbers must also be releasing sperm or ova nearby.

seafloor spreading growth of the ocean ◊crust outwards (sideways) from ocean ridges. The concept of seafloor spreading has been combined with that of continental drift and incorporated into ◊plate tectonics.

Seafloor spreading was proposed 1960 by US geologist Harry Hess (1906–1969), based on his observations of ocean ridges and the relative youth of all ocean beds. In 1963, British geophysicists Fred Vine and Drummond Matthews observed that the floor of the Atlantic Ocean was made up of rocks that could be arranged in strips, each strip being magnetized either normally or reversely (due to changes in the Earth's polarity when the North Pole becomes the South Pole and vice versa, termed ◊polar reversal). These strips were parallel and formed identical patterns on both sides of the ocean ridge. The implication was that each strip was formed at some stage in geological time when the magnetic field was polarized in a certain way. The seafloor magnetic-reversal patterns could be matched to dated magnetic reversals found in terrestrial rock. It could then be shown that new rock forms continuously and spreads away from the ocean ridges, with the oldest rock located farthest away from the midline. The observation was made independently 1963 by Canadian geologist Lawrence Morley, studying an ocean ridge in the Pacific near Vancouver Island.

seagull common name for a number of ◊gull species.

sea hare marine mollusc widely distributed around Britain that occurs offshore amongst kelps.

The sea hare comes on shore during the summer to spawn. The shell is greatly reduced and internal and the animal relies for protection on its cryptic coloration (matching the background) that it acquires from the algae upon which it feeds. When disturbed, it releases a purple fluid that acts as a smoke screen and allows it to escape, either by crawling, or swimming by means of winglike projections developed from the mantle.
classifiation Sea hares are in order Anaspidea in the subclass Opisthobranchia, class Gastropoda, phylum Mollusca.

sea horse any marine fish of several related genera, especially *Hippocampus,* of the family Syngnathidae, which includes the ◊pipefishes. The body is small and compressed and covered with bony plates raised into tubercles or spines. The tail is prehensile, and the tubular mouth sucks in small shellfish and larvae as food.

The head and foreparts, usually carried upright, resemble those of a horse. They swim vertically and beat their fins up to 70 times a second.

Unusually for fish, sea horses are monogamous and have a relatively long courtship, from 3–7 days. The female deposits her eggs, from dozens to hundreds, in a special pouch in the male. The male fertilizes the eggs whilst they are in his pouch, and nourishes them for six weeks or so until they are finally released as young fish.

SEA HORSE

The largest sea horse is the Australian leafy sea horse, which grows to 30 cm/12 in.

seakale perennial European coastal plant with broad, fleshy leaves and white flowers; it is cultivated in Europe and the young shoots are eaten as a vegetable. (*Crambe maritima,* family Cruciferae.)

seal aquatic carnivorous mammal of the families Otariidae and Phocidae (sometimes placed in a separate order, the Pinnipedia). The eared seals or sea lions (Otariidae) have small external ears, unlike the true seals (Phocidae). Seals have a streamlined body with thick blubber for insulation, and front and hind flippers. They are able to close their nostrils as they dive, and obtain oxygen from their blood supply while under water. They feed on fish, squid, or crustaceans, and are commonly found in Arctic and Antarctic seas, but also in Mediterranean, Caribbean, and Hawaiian waters.

sea lily any ◊echinoderm of the class Crinoidea. In most, the rayed, cuplike body is borne on a sessile stalk (permanently attached to a rock) and has feathery arms in multiples of five encircling the mouth. However, some sea lilies are free-swimming and unattached.

sea lion any of several genera of ◊seals of the family Otariidae (eared seals), which also includes the fur seals. These streamlined animals have large fore flippers which they use to row themselves through the water. The hind flippers can be turned beneath the body to walk on land.

There are two species of sea lion in the northern hemisphere, and three in the south. They feed on fish, squid, and crustaceans. **Steller's sea lion** *Eumetopias jubatus* lives in the N Pacific, large numbers breeding on the Aleutian Islands. Males may be up to 3.4 m/11 ft long, with a thick neck with a characteristic mane, and weigh up to one tonne. Females are one-third the weight. The **Californian sea lion** *Zalophus californianus* only reaches 2.3 m/7 ft, and is the species most often seen in zoos and as a 'performing seal'.

The **Australian sea lion** *Neophoca cinerea* is found only in southern Australian waters, especially on offshore islands such as Kangaroo Island. It is one of the larger sea lions; males weigh up to 300 kg/660 lb, three times as much as females, and are 2 m/6.5 ft long. The **New Zealand sea lion** *Phocarctos hookeri,* of similar size, is found mainly on Auckland Island, 322 km/200 mi S of New Zealand.

Sealyham breed of terrier dog, named after the place in Pembrokeshire, Wales, where it originated in the 19th century as a cross between the Welsh and Jack Russell terriers. It has a coarse white coat and reaches a height of 30 cm/12 in.

sea mouse any of a genus *Aphrodite* of large marine ◊annelid worms (polychaetes), with oval bodies covered in bristles and usually found on muddy sea floors.

seaplane aeroplane capable of taking off from, and landing on, water. There are two major types, floatplanes and flying boats. The floatplane is similar to an ordinary aeroplane but has floats in place of wheels; the flying boat has a broad hull shaped like a boat and may also have floats attached to the wing tips.

Seaplanes depend on smooth water for a good landing, and since World War II few have been built, although they were widely used in both world wars and the first successful international airlines, such as Pan Am, relied on a fleet of flying boats in the 1920s and 1930s.

sea potato yellow-brown sea urchin *Echinocardium cordatum* covered in short spines, and found burrowing in sand from the lower shore downwards.

search engine in computing, remotely accessible program to help users find information on the Internet. Commercial search engines such as ◊AltaVista and ◊Lycos comprise databases of documents, ◊URLs, ◊USENET articles and more, which can be searched by keying in a key word or phrase. The databases are compiled by a mixture of automated agents (◊spiders) and ◊webmasters registering their sites. However, only about 50% of Web pages can be accessed by search engines.

searching in computing, extracting a specific item from a large body of data, such as a file or table. The method used depends on how the data are organized. For example, a binary search, which requires the data to be in sequence, involves first deciding which half of the data contains the required item, then which quarter, then which eighth, and so on until the item is found.

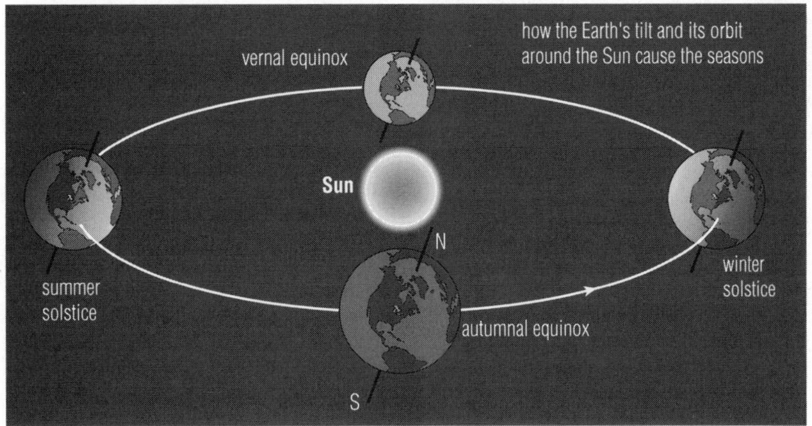

***season** The cause of the seasons. As the Earth orbits the Sun, its axis of rotation always points in the same direction. This means that, during the northern hemisphere summer solstice (21 June), the Sun is overhead in the northern hemisphere. At the northern hemisphere winter solstice (22 December), the Sun is overhead in the southern hemisphere.*

search request in computing, a structured request by a user for information from a ◊database. This may be a simple request for all the entries that have a single field meeting a certain condition. For example, a user searching a file of car-registration details might request a list of all the records that have 'VOLKSWAGEN' in the ◊field recording the make of car. In more complex examples, the user may construct a search request using operators like AND, OR, NOT, CONTAINING, and BETWEEN.

sea robin any of a family (Triglidae) of spine-finned coastal fishes, especially the slender sea robin *Prionotus scitulus* of the Gulf and SE North American coast. They have large heads and creep along the sea bottom by means of three fingerlike appendages detached from the pectoral fins.

Sears Tower skyscraper in Chicago, USA, rising 110 storeys to a height of 443 m/1,454 ft. Topped out in 1973, it was then the world's tallest building. It was built as the headquarters of Sears, Roebuck & Co, to provide office accommodation for more than 16,000 people.

sea slug any of an order (Nudibranchia) of marine gastropod molluscs in which the shell is reduced or absent. The order includes some very colourful forms, especially in the tropics. They are largely carnivorous, feeding on hydroids and ◊sponges.

Most are under 2.5 cm/1 in long, and live on the sea bottom or on vegetation, although some live in open waters. Tentacles on the back help take in oxygen.

sea snake one of a number of aquatic venomous snakes. Their tails are compressed laterally, and form powerful swimming organs. The eyes are extremely small, have round pupils, and the snakes are practically blind when out of water. The poison secreted by the animals is very virulent, and is used by them to kill the fish on which they feed.

All the species are viviparous (the young develop inside the mother), and inhabit the Indian and Pacific Oceans. A considerable number of human deaths each year are caused by these animals, particularly in the Indian Ocean.

classification Sea snakes are all members of family Hydrophiidae, order Squamata, class Reptilia.

season period of the year having a characteristic climate. The change in seasons is mainly due to the change in attitude of the Earth's axis in relation to the Sun, and hence the position of the Sun in the sky at a particular place. In temperate latitudes four seasons are recognized: spring, summer, autumn (fall), and winter. Tropical regions have two seasons – the wet and the dry. Monsoon areas around the Indian Ocean have three seasons: the cold, the hot, and the rainy.

The northern temperate latitudes have summer when the southern temperate latitudes have winter, and vice versa. During winter, the Sun is low in the sky and has less heating effect because of the oblique angle of incidence and because the sunlight has further to travel through the atmosphere. The differences between the seasons are more marked inland than near the coast, where the sea has a moderating effect on temperatures. In polar regions the change between summer and winter is abrupt; spring and autumn are hardly perceivable. In tropical regions, the belt of rain associated with the trade winds moves north and south with the Sun, as do the dry conditions associated with the belts of high pressure near the tropics. The monsoon's three seasons result from the influence of the Indian Ocean on the surrounding land mass of Asia in that area.

seasonal affective disorder (SAD) form of depression that occurs in winter and is relieved by the coming of spring. Its incidence decreases closer to the Equator. One type of SAD is associated with increased sleeping and appetite.

It has been suggested that SAD may be caused by changes in the secretion of melatonin, a hormone produced by the ◊pineal body in the brain. Melatonin secretion is inhibited by bright daylight.

sea squirt or ***tunicate*** any solitary or colonial-dwelling saclike ◊chordate of the class Ascidiacea. A pouch-shaped animal attached to a rock or other base, it draws in food-carrying water through one siphon and expels it through another after straining it through numerous gill slits. The young are free-swimming tadpole-shaped organisms, which, unlike the adults, have a ◊notochord.

Sea squirts have transparent or translucent tunics made of cellulose. They vary in size from a few millimetres to 30 cm/12 in in length and are cylindrical, circular, or irregular in shape. Their defences against predators include sulphuric acid secretion and the accumulation of vanadium, a toxic heavy metal.

seat belt safety device in a motor vehicle or aeroplane that is designed to reduce the risk of injury to a passenger from sudden changes in velocity, such as during a collision or when brakes are applied sharply. In an emergency, it extends the time over which the decelerating force acts on a passenger thereby reducing that force to a safe level. It also spreads the force over a broad band across the chest and over the hip bone, reducing the pressure applied to the person.

sea urchin any of various orders of the class Echinoidea among the ◊echinoderms. They all have a globular body enclosed with plates of lime and covered with spines. Sometimes the spines are anchoring organs, and they also assist in locomotion. Sea urchins feed on seaweed and the animals frequenting them, and some are edible, as is their roe.

sea water the water of the seas and oceans, covering about 70% of the Earth's surface and comprising about 97% of the world's water (only about 3% is fresh water). Sea water contains a large amount of dissolved solids, the most abundant of which is sodium chloride (almost 3% by mass); other salts include potassium chloride, bromide, and iodide, magnesium chloride, and magnesium sulphate. It also contains a large amount of dissolved carbon dioxide, and thus acts as a carbon 'sink' that may help to reduce the greenhouse effect.

seaweed any of a vast group of simple multicellular plant forms belonging to the ◊algae and found growing in the sea, brackish estuaries, and salt marshes, from about the high-tide mark to depths of 100–200 m/300–600 ft. Many seaweeds have holdfasts (attaching them to rocks or other surfaces), stalks, and fronds, sometimes with air bladders to keep them afloat, and are green, blue-green, red, or brown.

Some have traditionally been gathered for food, such as purple laver (*Porphyra umbilicalis*), green vlaver (*Ulva lactuca*), and ◊carragheen (*Chondrus crispus*). From the 1960s, seaweeds have been farmed, and the ◊alginates (salts) which are extracted are used in convenience foods, ice cream, and animal feeds, as well as in toothpaste, soap, and the manufacture of iodine and glass.

sea urchin *The bony skeleton of the sea urchin is often washed up in large numbers on beaches. Known as a test, and often sold as an ornament, it has a relatively smooth surface as the urchin's spines are quickly detached once the animal dies. Premaphotos Wildlife*

The ribbonlike seaweed *Undaria,* which arrived in the Mediterranean in the 1980s from Japan attached to imported oysters, is now being grown by the French for export to the Asian market.

seborrhoeic eczema common skin disease affecting any sebum- (natural oil) producing area of the skin. It is thought to be caused by the yeast *Pityrosporum,* and is characterized by yellowish-red, scaly areas on the skin, and dandruff. Antidandruff shampoos are often helpful.

sebum oily secretion from the sebaceous glands that acts as a skin lubricant. ◊Acne is caused by inflammation of the sebaceous glands and over-secretion of sebum.

sec or s abbreviation for **second**, a unit of time.

SECAM (acronym for ***Système Electronique Couleur Avec Mémoire***) television and video standard used in France, some states in Eastern Europe, and a few other countries. It is broadly similar to the PAL system used in most of Europe.

secant in trigonometry, the function of a given angle in a right-angled triangle, obtained by dividing the length of the hypotenuse (the longest side) by the length of the side adjacent to the angle. It is the ◊reciprocal of the ◊cosine (sec = 1/cos). See illustration on page 672.

second basic ◊SI unit (symbol sec or s) of time, one-sixtieth of a minute. It is defined as the duration of 9,192,631,770 cycles of regulation (periods of the radiation corresponding to the transition between two hyperfine levels of the ground state) of the caesium-133 isotope. In mathematics, the second is a unit (symbol ') of angular measurement, equalling one-sixtieth of a minute, which in turn is one-sixtieth of a degree.

secondary data information that has been collected by another agency. Examples of secondary data include government reports and statistics, company reports and accounts, and weather reports in newspapers.

secondary emission in physics, an emission of electrons from the surface of certain substances when they are struck by high-speed electrons or other particles from an external source. It can be detected with a ◊photomultiplier.

secondary growth or ***secondary thickening*** increase in diameter of the roots and stems of certain plants (notably shrubs and trees) that results from the production of new cells by the ◊cambium. It provides the plant with additional mechanical support and new conducting cells, the secondary vxylem and ◊phloem. Secondary growth is generally confined to ◊gymnosperms and, among the ◊angiosperms, to the dicotyledons. With just a few exceptions, the monocotyledons (grasses, lilies) exhibit only primary growth, resulting from cell division at the apical ◊meristems.

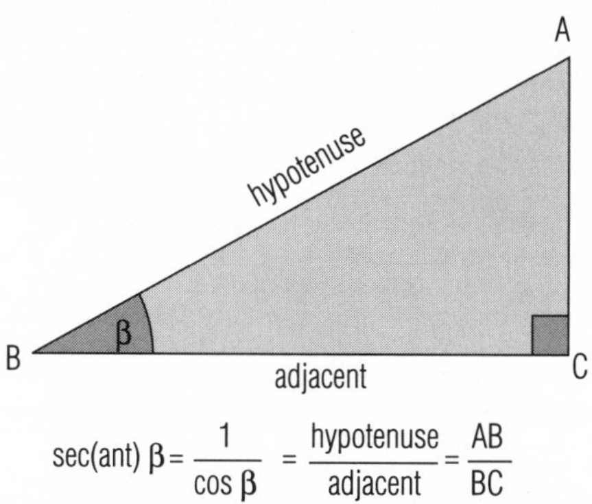

$$\sec(\text{ant})\,\beta = \frac{1}{\cos\beta} = \frac{\text{hypotenuse}}{\text{adjacent}} = \frac{AB}{BC}$$

secant *The secant of an angle is a function used in the mathematical study of the triangle. If the secant of angle B is known, then the hypotenuse can be found given the length of the adjacent side, or the adjacent side can be found from the hypotenuse.*

secondary sexual characteristic in biology, an external feature of an organism that is indicative of its gender (male or female), but not the reproductive organs themselves. They include facial hair in men and breasts in women, combs in cockerels, brightly coloured plumage in many male birds, and manes in male lions. In many cases, they are involved in displays and contests for mates and have evolved by ◊sexual selection. Their development is stimulated by sex hormones.

secretary bird ground-hunting, long-legged, mainly grey-plumaged bird of prey *Sagittarius serpentarius.* It is about 1.2 m/4 ft tall, with an erectile head crest tipped with black. It is protected in southern Africa because it eats poisonous snakes.

It gets its name from the fact that its head crest supposedly looks like a pen behind a clerk's ear. It is the only member of the family Sagittariidae, in the same order (Falconiformes) as vultures, eagles, and hawks.

secretin ◊hormone produced by the small intestine of vertebrates that stimulates the production of digestive secretions by the pancreas and liver.

secretion in biology, any substance (normally a fluid) produced by a cell or specialized gland, for example, sweat, saliva, enzymes, and hormones. The process whereby the substance is discharged from the cell is also known as secretion.

sector in computing, part of the magnetic structure created on a disc surface during ◊disc formatting so that data can be stored on it. The disc is first divided into circular tracks and then each circular track is divided into a number of sectors.

sector in geometry, part of a circle enclosed by two radii and the arc that joins them.

secure HTTP in computing, communications protocol that provides the basis for privacy-enhanced or encrypted communications between a Web ◊browser and a server. Secure HTTP enables users to send private information such as credit card numbers and addresses over the Internet.

secure socket layer (SSL) in computing, standard protocol built into Web ◊browsers such as Netscape and Internet Explorer, which provides an encrypted channel for private information such as credit card numbers and passwords

Considered a key technology to allow commerce across the World Wide Web, SSL began appearing on the Net in 1995.

security protection against loss or misuse of data; see vdata security.

sedative any drug that has a calming effect, reducing anxiety and tension.

Sedatives will induce sleep in larger doses. Examples are ◊barbiturates, narcotics, and ◊benzodiazepines.

sedge any of a group of perennial grasslike plants, usually with three-cornered solid stems, common in low water or on wet and marshy ground. (Genus *Carex,* family Cyperaceae.)

> TO TELL THE DIFFERENCE BETWEEN GRASSES AND SEDGES:
>
> 'SEDGES HAVE EDGES'. UNLIKE GRASSES, SEDGES HAVE THREE-SIDED STEMS IN CROSS-SECTION; ALSO, SEDGES GROW IN WET SPOTS, OFTEN ALONG MARSH EDGES WHEREAS GRASSES PREFER DRIER UPLAND AREAS

sediment any loose material that has 'settled' – deposited from suspension in water, ice, or air, generally as the water current or wind speed decreases. Typical sediments are, in order of increasing coarseness, clay, mud, silt, sand, gravel, pebbles, cobbles, and boulders.

Sediments differ from sedimentary rocks in which deposits are fused together in a solid mass of rock by a process called ◊lithification. Pebbles are cemented into ◊conglomerates; sands become sandstones; muds become mudstones or shales; peat is transformed into coal.

sedimentary rock rock formed by the accumulation and cementation of deposits that have been laid down by water, wind, ice, or gravity. Sedimentary rocks cover more than two-thirds of the Earth's surface and comprise three major categories: clastic, chemically precipitated, and organic (or biogenic). Clastic sediments are the largest group and are composed of fragments of pre-existing rocks; they include clays, sands, and gravels.

Chemical precipitates include some limestones and evaporated deposits such as gypsum and halite (rock salt). Coal, oil shale, and limestone made of fossil material are examples of organic sedimentary rocks.

Most sedimentary rocks show distinct layering (stratification), caused by alterations in composition or by changes in rock type. These strata may become folded or fractured by the movement of the Earth's crust, a process known as **deformation**.

Seebeck effect in physics, the generation of a voltage in a circuit containing two different metals, or semiconductors, by keeping the junctions between them at different temperatures. Discovered by the German physicist Thomas Seebeck (1770–1831), it is also called the thermoelectric effect, and is the basis of the ◊thermocouple. It is the opposite of the ◊Peltier effect (in which current flow causes a temperature difference between the junctions of different metals).

seed the reproductive structure of higher plants (◊angiosperms and ◊gymnosperms). It develops from a fertilized ovule and consists of an embryo and a food store, surrounded and protected by an outer seed coat, called the testa. The food store is contained either in a specialized nutritive tissue, the ◊endosperm, or in the cotyledons of the embryo itself. In angiosperms the seed is enclosed within a ◊fruit, whereas in gymnosperms it is usually naked and unprotected, once shed from the female cone.

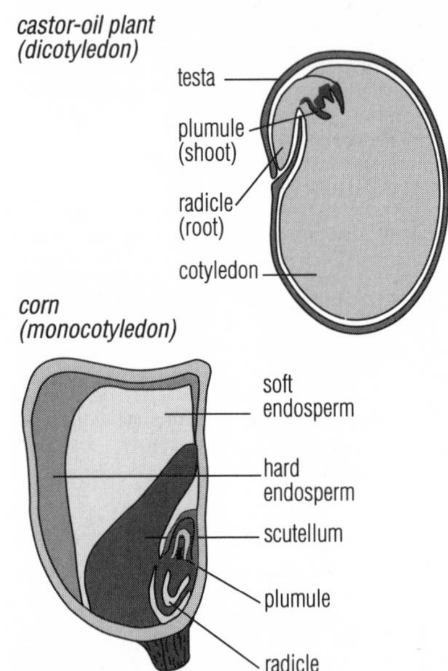

seed The structure of seeds. The castor is a dicotyledon, a plant in which the developing plant has two leaves, developed from the cotyledon. In maize, a monocotyledon, there is a single leaf developed from the scutellum.

Following ◊germination the seed develops into a new plant.

Seeds may be dispersed from the parent plant in a number of different ways. Agents of dispersal include animals, as with ◊burs and fleshy edible fruits, and wind, where the seed or fruit may be winged or plumed. Water can disperse seeds or fruits that float, and various mechanical devices may eject seeds from the fruit, as in the pods of some leguminous plants (see ◊legume).

There may be a delay in the germination of some seeds to ensure that growth occurs under favourable conditions (see ◊after-ripening, dormancy). Most seeds remain viable for at least 15 years if dried to about 5% water and kept at –20°C/–4°F, although 20% of them will not survive this process.

SEEDS OF LIFE

http://www.vol.it/mirror/SeedsOfLife/home.html

Wealth of information about seeds and fruits, with information about the basic structure of a seed, fruit types, how seeds are dispersed, and seeds and humans, plus a mystery seed contest.

seed plant any seed-bearing plant; also known as a **spermatophyte**.

The seed plants are subdivided into two classes: the ◊angiosperms, or flowering plants, and the ◊gymnosperms, principally the cycads and conifers.

Together, they comprise the major types of vegetation found on land.

Angiosperms are the largest, most advanced, and most successful group of plants at the present time, occupying a highly diverse range of habitats. There are estimated to be about 250,000 different species. Gymnosperms differ from angiosperms in their ovules which are borne unprotected (not within an ◊ovary) on the scales of their cones.

The arrangement of the reproductive organs, and their more simplified internal tissue structure, also distinguishes them from the flowering plants. In contrast to the gymnosperms, the ovules of angiosperms are enclosed within an ovary and many species have developed highly specialized reproductive structures associated with vpollination by insects, birds, or bats.

seek time in computing, time taken for a read-write head to reach a particular item of data on a ◊disc track.

Sega Japanese ◊games console and software manufacturer. Sega's most successful game is *Sonic the Hedgehog*.

segment in geometry, part of a circle cut off by a straight line or ◊chord, running from one point on the circumference to another. All angles in the same segment are equal.

seismic wave energy wave generated by an ◊earthquake or an artificial explosion. There are two types of seismic waves: **body waves** that travel through the Earth's interior, and **surface waves** that travel through the surface layers of the crust and can be felt as the shaking of the ground, as in an earthquake.

body waves There are two types of body waves: P-waves and S-waves, so-named because they are the primary and secondary waves detected by a seismograph. **P-waves** are longitudinal waves (wave motion in the direction the wave is travelling), whose compressions and rarefactions resemble those of a sound wave. **S-waves** are transverse waves or shear waves, involving a back-and-forth shearing motion at right angles to the direction the wave is travelling (see ◊wave).

Because liquids have no resistance to shear and cannot sustain a shear wave, S-waves cannot travel through liquid material. The Earth's outer core is believed to be liquid because S-waves disappear at the mantle-core boundary, while P-waves do not.

surface waves Surface waves travel in the surface and subsurface layers of the crust. **Rayleigh waves** travel along the free surface (the uppermost layer) of a solid material. The motion of particles is

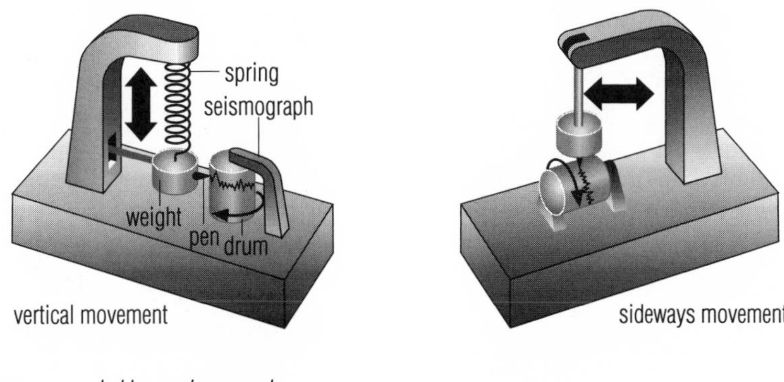

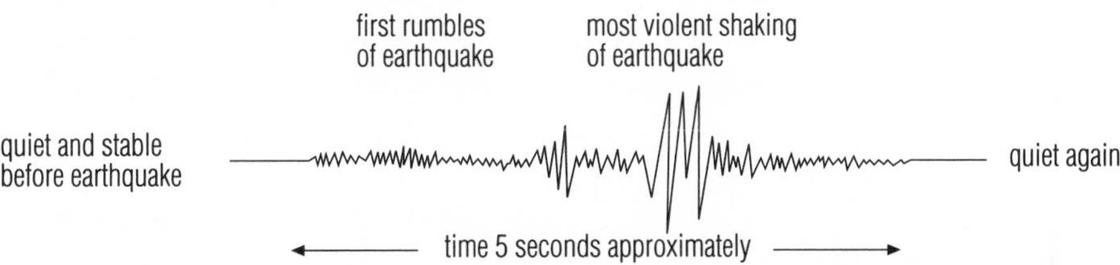

***seismograph** A seismogram, or recording made by a seismograph. Such recordings are used to study earthquakes and in prospecting.*

elliptical, like a water wave, creating the rolling motion often felt during an earthquake. **Love waves** are transverse waves trapped in a subsurface layer due to different densities in the rock layers above and below. They have a horizontal side-to-side shaking motion transverse (at right angles) to the direction the wave is travelling.

seismograph instrument used to record the activity of an earthquake. A heavy inert weight is suspended by a spring and attached to this is a pen that is in contact with paper on a rotating drum. During an earthquake the instrument moves causing the pen to record a zigzag line on the paper; the pen doesn't move.

seismology study of earthquakes and how their shock waves travel through the Earth. By examining the global pattern of waves produced by an earthquake, seismologists can deduce the nature of the materials through which they have passed. This leads to an understanding of the Earth's internal structure.

On a smaller scale, artificial earthquake waves, generated by explosions or mechanical vibrators, can be used to search for subsurface features in, for example, oil or mineral exploration. Earthquake waves from underground nuclear explosions can be distinguished from natural waves by their shorter wavelength and higher frequency.

seismosaurus plant-eating sauropod dinosaur, *Seismosaurus hallorum,* related to ◊diplodocus. It is believed to be the longest dinosaur, with a length of 39–52 m, and a mass of around 100 tonnes. One incomplete skeleton was discovered in the New Mexican desert 1985.

selenium Greek *Selene* 'Moon' grey, nonmetallic element, symbol Se, atomic number 34, relative atomic mass 78.96. It belongs to the sulphur group and occurs in several allotropic forms that differ in their physical and chemical properties. It is an essential trace element in human nutrition.

Obtained from many sulphide ores and selenides, it is used as a red colouring for glass and enamel.

Because its electrical conductivity varies with the intensity of light, selenium is used extensively in photoelectric devices. It was discovered in 1817 by Swedish chemist Jöns Berzelius and named after the Moon because its properties follow those of tellurium, whose name derives from Latin *Tellus* 'Earth'.

self-inductance or ***self-induction*** in physics, the creation of an electromotive force opposing the current. See ◊inductance.

Sellafield site of a nuclear power station on the coast of Cumbria, NW England. It was known as **Windscale** until 1971, when the management of the site was transferred from the UK Atomic Energy Authority to British Nuclear Fuels Ltd. It reprocesses more than 1,000 tonnes of spent fuel from nuclear reactors annually. The plant is the world's greatest discharger of radioactive waste: between 1968 and 1979, 180 kg/400 lb of plutonium was discharged into the Irish Sea.

In 1996, British Nuclear Fuels was fined £25,000 after admitting 'serious and significant' failures in safety that left a Sellafield plant worker contaminated with radioactivity.

In 1998, the Norwegian environment minister called for a ban on the release of technetium-99 into the sea. It is being released from Sellafield and causing raised concentrations along the coast of Norway.

For accidents, see ◊nuclear safety.

semelparity in biology, the occurrence of a single act of reproduction during an organism's lifetime. Most semelparous species produce very large numbers of offspring when they do reproduce, and normally die soon afterwards. Examples include the Pacific salmon and the pine looper moth. Many plants are semelparous, or ◊monocarpic. Repeated reproduction is called ◊iteroparity.

semen fluid containing ◊sperm from the testes and secretions from various sex glands (such as the prostate gland) that is ejaculated by male animals during copulation. The secretions serve to nourish and activate the sperm cells, and prevent them clumping together.

semicircular canal one of three looped tubes that form part of the labyrinth in the inner ◊ear. They are filled with fluid and detect changes in the position of the head, contributing to the sense of balance.

semiconductor material with electrical conductivity intermediate between metals and insulators and used in a wide range of electronic devices. Certain crystalline materials, most notably silicon and germanium, have a small number of free electrons that have escaped from the bonds between the atoms. The atoms from which they have escaped possess vacancies, called holes, which are similarly able to move from atom to atom and can be regarded as positive charges. Current can be carried by both electrons (negative carriers) and holes (positive carriers). Such materials are known as **intrinsic semiconductors**.

Conductivity of a semiconductor can be enhanced by doping the material with small numbers of impurity atoms which either release free electrons (making an **n-type semiconductor** with more electrons than holes) or capture them (a **p-type semiconductor** with more holes than electrons). When p-type and n-type materials are brought together to form a p–n junction, an electrical barrier is formed which conducts current more readily in one direction than the other. This is the basis of the ◊semiconductor diode, used for rectification, and numerous other devices including ◊transistors, rectifiers, and ◊integrated circuits (silicon chips).

semiconductor diode or ***p–n junction diode*** in electronics, a two-terminal semiconductor device that allows electric current to flow in only one direction, the **forward-bias** direction. A very high resistance prevents current flow in the opposite, or **reverse-bias**, direction. It is used as a ◊rectifier, converting alternating current (AC) to direct current (DC).

seminiferous tubule in male vertebrates, one of a number of tightly packed, highly coiled tubes in the testis. The tubes are lined with germinal epithelium cells, from which ◊sperm are produced by cell division (◊meiosis) and in the midst of which the sperm mature, nourished and protected in the folds of large Sertoli cells. After maturation, the sperm are stored in a long tube called the epididymis.

sendmail in computing, UNIX program for sending ve-mail via ◊TCP/IP (Transport Control Protocol/Internet Protocol) using ◊SMTP (simple mail transfer protocol).

senescence in biology, the deterioration in physical and (sometimes) mental capacities that occurs with ◊ageing.

senile dementia ◊dementia associated with old age, often caused by ◊Alzheimer's disease.

sense in mathematics, the orientation of a vector. Each vector has an equivalent vector of the opposite sense. The combined effect of two vectors of opposite sense is a zero vector.

sense organ any organ that an animal uses to gain information about its surroundings. All sense organs have specialized receptors (such as light receptors in the eye) and some means of translating their response into a nerve impulse that travels to the brain. The main human sense organs are the eye, which detects light and colour (different wavelengths of light); the ear, which detects sound (vibrations of the air) and gravity; the nose, which detects some of the chemical molecules in the air; and the tongue, which detects some of the chemicals in food, giving a sense of taste. There are also many small sense organs in the skin, including pain, temperature, and pressure sensors, contributing to our sense of touch.

animal senses Research suggests that our noses may also be sensitive to magnetic forces, giving us an innate sense of direction. This sense is well developed in other animals, as are a variety of senses that we do not share. Some animals can detect small electrical discharges, underwater vibrations, minute vibrations of the ground, or sounds that are below (infrasound) or above (ultrasound) our range of hearing. Sensitivity to light varies greatly. Most mammals cannot distinguish different colours, whereas some birds can detect the polarization of light. Many insects can see light in the ultraviolet range, which is beyond our spectrum, while snakes can form images of infrared radiation (radiant heat). In many animals, light is also detected by another organ, the pineal body, which 'sees' light filtering through the skull, and measures the length of the day to keep track of the seasons.

Science is nothing but trained and organized common sense.

THOMAS HENRY HUXLEY English biologist.
Collected Essays, 'The Method of Zadig'

---

sensitivity the ability of an organism, or part of an organism, to detect changes in the environment. Although all living things are capable of some sensitivity, evolution has led to the formation of highly complex mechanisms for detecting light, sound, chemicals, and other stimuli. It is essential to an animal's survival that it can process this type of information and make an appropriate response.

sensor in computing, a device designed to detect a physical state or measure a physical quantity, and produce an input signal for a computer. For example, a sensor may detect the fact that a printer has run out of paper or may measure the temperature in a kiln.

The signal from a sensor is usually in the form of an analogue voltage, and must therefore be converted to a digital signal, by means of an ◊analogue-to-digital ◊converter, before it can be input.

sepal part of a flower, usually green, that surrounds and protects the flower in bud. The sepals are derived from modified leaves, and are collectively known as the ◊calyx.

In some plants, such as the marsh marigold *Caltha palustris,* where true ◊petals are absent, the sepals are brightly coloured and petal-like, taking over the role of attracting insect pollinators to the flower.

sepsis general term for infectious change in the body caused by bacteria or their toxins.

septicaemia general term for any form of ◊blood poisoning.

septic shock life-threatening fall in blood pressure caused by blood poisoning (septicaemia). Toxins produced by bacteria infecting the blood induce a widespread dilation of the blood vessels throughout the body, and it is this that causes the patient's collapse (see shock). Septic ◊shock can occur following bowel surgery, after a penetrating wound to the abdomen, or as a consequence of infection of the urinary tract. It is usually treated in an intensive care unit and has a high mortality rate.

sequence-control register or ***program counter*** in computing, a special memory location used to hold the address of the next instruction to be fetched from the immediate access memory for execution by the computer (see ◊fetch–execute cycle). It is located in the control unit of the ◊central processing unit.

sequencing in biochemistry, determining the sequence of chemical subunits within a large molecule. Techniques for sequencing amino acids in proteins were established in the 1950s, insulin being the first for which the sequence was completed. The ◊Human Genome Project is attempting to determine the sequence of the 3 billion base pairs within human ◊DNA.

sequential file in computing, a file in which the records are arranged in order of a ◊key field and the computer can use a searching technique, like a ◊binary search, to access a specific record. See ◊file access.

sequoia either of two species of ◊conifer tree belonging to the redwood family, native to the western USA. The **redwood** (*Sequoia sempervirens*) is a long-living timber tree, and one specimen, the Howard Libbey Redwood, is the world's tallest tree at 110 m/361 ft, with a trunk circumference of 13.4 m/44 ft. The **giant sequoia** (*Sequoiadendron giganteum*) reaches up to 30 m/100 ft in circumference at the base of the trunk, and grows almost as tall as the redwood. It is also (except for the bristlecone pine) the oldest living tree, some specimens being estimated at over 3,500 years of age. (Family Taxodiaceae.)

sere plant ◊succession developing in a particular habitat. A **lithosere** is a succession starting on the surface of bare rock. A **hydrosere** is a succession in shallow freshwater, beginning with planktonic vegetation and the growth of pondweeds and other aquatic plants, and ending with the development of swamp. A **plagiosere** is the sequence of communities that follows the clearing of the existing vegetation.

serial device in computing, a device that communicates binary data by sending the bits that represent each character one by one along a single data line, unlike a ◊parallel device.

serial file in computing, a file in which the records are not stored in any particular order and therefore a specific record can be accessed only by reading through all the previous records. See ◊file access.

serial interface in computing, an ◊interface through which data is transmitted one bit at a time.

Serial Line Internet Protocol in computing, method of connecting a computer to the Internet; usually abbreviated to ◊SLIP.

seriema flesh-eating bird of the order Gruiformes, found in the grasslands of northern Argentina, eastern Bolivia, Paraguay, and parts of Brazil. There are two species: the **red-legged seriema** *Cariama cristata* and the **black-legged** or **Burmeister's seriema** *Chunga burmeisteri*.

The birds are about 0.7m/2.3 ft tall wth long legs and neck. They are poor fliers but excellent runners, reaching speeds of about 60 kph/37 mph. They eat small mammals, reptiles, insects, and other birds. Prey is beaten on the ground until senseless, then swallowed whole.

series circuit electrical circuit in which the components are connected end to end, so that the current flows through them all one after the other. See illustration on page 676.

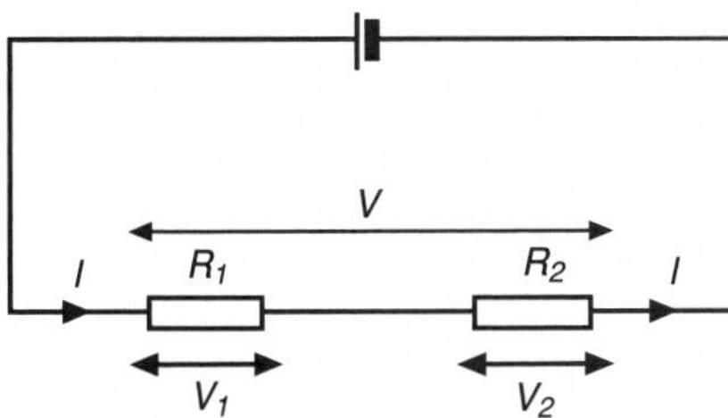

series circuit *In a series circuit, the components of the circuit are connected end to end, so that the current passes through each component one after the other, without division or branching into parallel circuits.*

serif font typeface, such as Times or Palatino, the strokes of which terminate in ornamental curves or cross-strokes. These are said to aid legibility.

Serpens constellation on the celestial equator (see ◊celestial sphere), represented as a serpent coiled around the body of ◊Ophiuchus. It is the only constellation divided into two halves: **Serpens Caput**, the head (on one side of Ophiuchus), and **Serpens Cauda**, the tail (on the other side). Its main feature is the Eagle nebula.

serpentine group of minerals, hydrous magnesium silicate, $Mg_3Si_2O_5(OH)_4$, occurring in soft ◊metamorphic rocks and usually dark green. The fibrous form **chrysotile** is a source of ◊asbestos; other forms are **antigorite** and **lizardite**. Serpentine minerals are formed by hydration of ultramafic rocks during metamorphism. Rare snake-patterned forms are used in ornamental carving.

serum clear fluid that separates out from clotted blood. It is blood plasma with the anticoagulant proteins removed, and contains ◊antibodies and other proteins, as well as the fats and sugars of the blood. It can be produced synthetically, and is used to protect against disease.

serval African wild cat *Felis serval*. It is a slender, long-limbed cat, about 1 m/3 ft long, with a yellowish-brown, black-spotted coat. It has large, sensitive ears, with which it locates its prey, mainly birds and rodents.

Servals weigh about 11–13 kg/24–28 lb. They are solitary animals, except for females with young. The young are born (after a gestation of 65–75 days) in litters of four to six and are independent after a year. Sexual maturity is reached at the age of about 2 years, and lifespan is 13–20 years.

server computer used as a store of software and data for use by other computers on a ◊network. See ◊file server.

service tree deciduous tree (*S. domestica*) with alternate pinnate leaves (leaflets growing either side of the stem), creamy white flowers, and small, brown, edible, oval fruits, native to Europe and Asia. The European wild service tree (*S. torminalis*) has oblong rather than pointed leaflets. It is related to the vmountain ash. (Genus *Sorbus*, family Rosaceae.)

servomechanism automatic control system used in aircraft, motor cars, and other complex machines. A specific input, such as moving a lever or joystick, causes a specific output, such as feeding current to an electric motor that moves, for example, the rudder of the aircraft. At the same time, the position of the rudder is detected and fed back to the central control, so that small adjustments can continually be made to maintain the desired course.

sesame annual ◊herbaceous plant, probably native to SE Asia, and widely cultivated in India. It produces oily seeds used in cooking and soap making. (*Sesamum indicum*, family Pedaliaceae.)

sessile in botany, a leaf, flower, or fruit that lacks a stalk and sits directly on the stem, as with the sessile acorns of certain ◊oaks. In zoology, it is an animal that normally stays in the same place, such as a barnacle or mussel. The term is also applied to the eyes of ◊crustaceans when these lack stalks and sit directly on the head.

set or ***class*** in mathematics, any collection of defined things (elements), provided the elements are distinct and that there is a rule to decide whether an element is a member of a set. It is usually denoted by a capital letter and indicated by curly brackets {}.

For example, L may represent the set that consists of all the letters of the alphabet. The symbol $\in$ stands for 'is a member of'; thus $p \in L$ means that p belongs to the set consisting of all letters, and $4 \notin L$ means that 4 does not belong to the set consisting of all letters.

There are various types of sets. A **finite set** has a limited number of members, such as the letters of the alphabet; an **infinite set** has an unlimited number of members, such as all whole numbers; an **empty** or **null set** has no members, such as the number of people who have swum across the Atlantic Ocean, written as {} or ø; a **single-element set** has only one member, such as days of the week beginning with M, written as {Monday}. **Equal sets** have the same members; for example, if W = {days of the week} and S = {Sunday, Monday, Tuesday, Wednesday, Thursday, Friday, Saturday}, it can be said that $W = S$. Sets with the same number of members are **equivalent sets**. Sets with some members in common are **intersecting sets**; for example, if R = {red playing cards} and F = {face cards}, then R and F share the members that are red face cards. Sets with no members in common are **disjoint sets**. Sets contained within others are **subsets**; for example, V = {vowels} is a subset of L = {letters of the alphabet}.

Sets and their interrelationships are often illustrated by a ◊Venn diagram.

SETI (abbreviation for ***search for extra-terrestrial intelligence***) in astronomy, a programme originally launched by ◊NASA in 1992, using powerful◊ radio telescopes to search the skies for extra-terrestrial signals. NASA cancelled the SETI project in 1993, but other privately funded SETI projects continue.

setter any of various breeds of gun dog, called 'setters' because they were trained to crouch or 'set' on the sight of game to be pursued. They stand about 66 cm/26 in high and weigh about 25 kg/55 lb. They have a long, smooth coat, feathered tails, and spaniel-like faces.

The Irish setter is a rich red, the English setter is usually white with black, tan, or liver markings, and the Gordon setter is black and brown.

set-top box box containing decoding equipment for satellite or cable television broadcasts. Such boxes represent a means of linking television sets to a network such as the ◊Internet, enabling people to browse the ◊World Wide Web using their televisions as the monitor, or to view ◊video-on-demand.

Seven Wonders of the World in antiquity, the ◊pyramids of Egypt, the Hanging Gardens of Babylon, the temple of Artemis at Ephesus, the Greek sculptor Phidias' chryselephantine statue of Zeus at Olympia, the Mausoleum at Halicarnassus, the Colossus of Rhodes, and the lighthouse on the island of Pharos in the Bay of Alexandria.

sewage disposal the disposal of human excreta and other waterborne waste products from houses, streets, and factories. Conveyed through sewers to sewage works, sewage has to undergo a series of treatments to be acceptable for discharge into rivers or the sea, according to various local laws and ordinances. Raw sewage, or sewage that has not been treated adequately, is one serious source of water pollution and a cause of ◊eutrophication.

In the industrialized countries of the West, most industries are responsible for disposing of their own wastes. Government agencies establish industrial waste-disposal standards. In most countries, sewage works for residential areas are the responsibility of local authorities. The solid waste (sludge) may be spread over fields as a fertilizer or, in a few countries, dumped at sea. A significant proportion of bathing beaches in densely populated regions have unacceptably high bacterial content, largely as a result of untreated sewage being discharged into rivers and the sea. This can, for example, cause stomach upsets in swimmers.

The use of raw sewage as a fertilizer (long practised in China) has the drawback that disease-causing microorganisms can survive in the soil and be transferred to people or animals by consumption of subsequent crops. Sewage sludge is safer, but may contain dangerous levels of heavy metals and other industrial contaminants.

sewing machine apparatus for the mechanical sewing of cloth, leather, and other materials by a needle, powered by hand, treadle, or belted electric motor. The popular lockstitch machine, using a double thread, was invented independently in the USA by both Walter Hunt in 1834 and Elias Howe in 1846. Howe's machine was the basis of the machine patented in 1851 by US inventor Isaac ◊Singer.

In modern microprocessor-controlled sewing machines, as many as 25 different stitching patterns can be selected by push button.

sex chromosome chromosome that differs between the sexes and that serves to determine the sex of the individual. In humans, females have two X chromosomes and males have an X and a Y chromosome.

sex determination process by which the sex of an organism is determined. In many species, the sex of an individual is dictated by the two sex chromosomes (X and Y) it receives from its parents. In mammals, some plants, and a few insects, males are XY, and females XX; in birds, reptiles, some amphibians, and butterflies the reverse is the case. In bees and wasps, males are produced from unfertilized eggs, females from fertilized eggs.

Environmental factors can affect some fish and reptiles, such as turtles, where sex is influenced by the temperature at which the eggs develop. In 1991 it was shown that maleness is caused by a single gene, 14 base pairs long, on the Y chromosome.

sex hormone steroid hormone produced and secreted by the gonads (testes and ovaries). Sex hormones control development and reproductive functions and influence sexual and other behaviour.

sex linkage in genetics, the tendency for certain characteristics to occur exclusively, or predominantly, in one sex only. Human examples include red-green colour blindness and haemophilia, both found predominantly in males. In both cases, these characteristics are ◊recessive and are determined by genes on the ◊X chromosome.

Since females possess two X chromosomes, any such recessive ◊allele on one of them is likely to be masked by the corresponding allele on the other. In males (who have only one X chromosome paired with a largely inert ◊Y chromosome) any gene on the X chromosome will automatically be expressed. Colour blindness and haemophilia can appear in females, but only if they are ◊homozygous for these traits, due to inbreeding, for example.

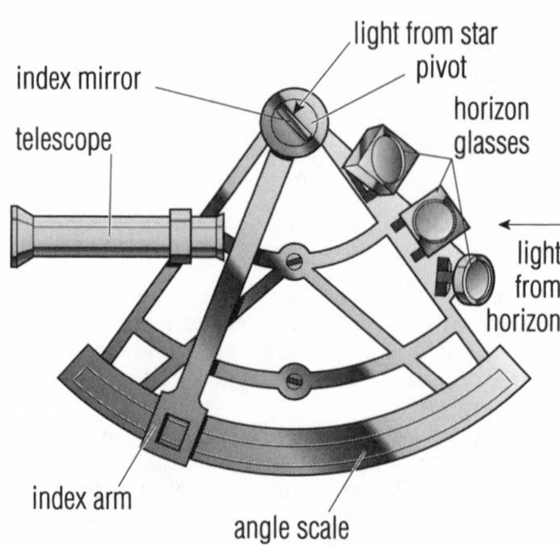

sextant *The geometry of the sextant. When the light from a star can be seen at the same time as light from the horizon, the angle A can be read from the position of the index arm on the angle scale.*

sextant navigational instrument for determining latitude by measuring the angle between some heavenly body and the horizon. It was invented in 1730 by John Hadley (1682–1744) and can be used only in clear weather.

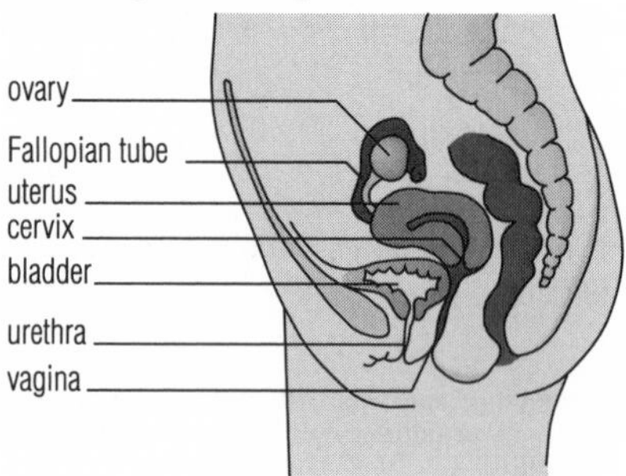

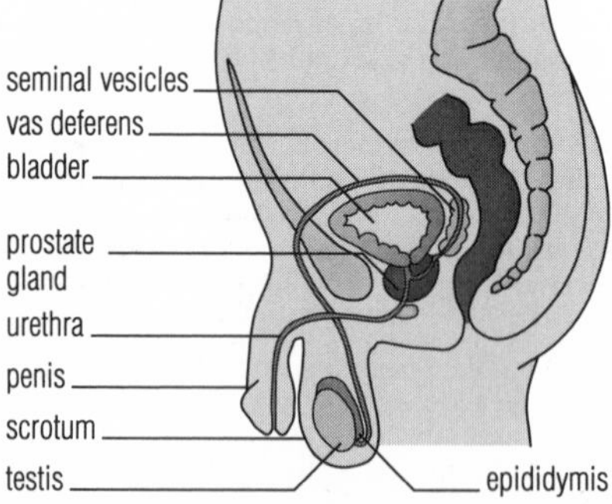

sexual reproduction *The human reproductive organs. In the female, gametes called ova are released regularly in the ovaries after puberty. The Fallopian tubes carry the ova to the uterus or womb, in which the baby will develop. In the male, sperm is produced inside the testes after puberty; about 10 million sperm cells are produced each day, enough to populate the world in six months. The sperm duct or vas deferens, a continuation of the epididymis, carries sperm to the urethra during ejaculation.*

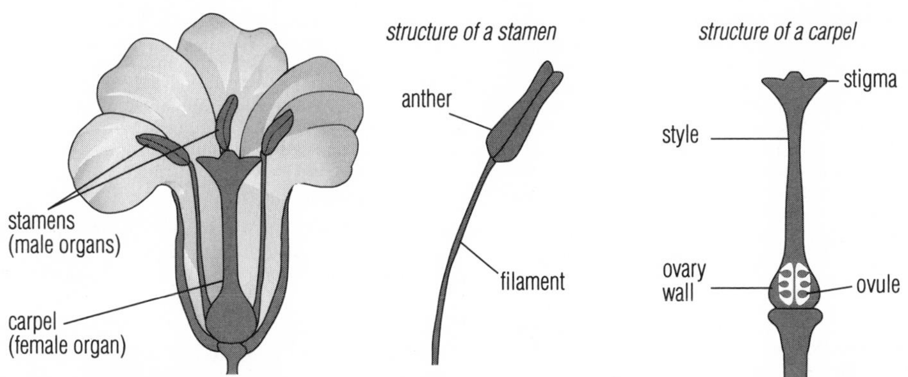

sexual reproduction *Reproductive organs in flowering plants. The stamens are the male parts of the plant. Each consists of a stalklike filament topped by an anther. The anther contains four pollen sacs which burst to release tiny grains of pollen, the male sex cells. The carpels are the female reproductive parts. Each carpel has a stigma which catches the pollen grain. The style connects the stigma to the ovary. The ovary contains one or more ovules, the female sex cells. Buttercups have many ovaries; the lupin has only one.*

When the horizon is viewed through the right-hand side **horizon glass**, which is partly clear and partly mirrored, the light from a star can be seen at the same time in the mirrored left-hand side by adjusting an **index mirror**. The angle of the star to the horizon can then be read on a calibrated scale.

sexton beetle or ***burying beetle*** carrion-feeding orange and black beetle of the genus *Nicrophorus.* Before laying eggs, sexton beetles must locate an animal carcass and bury it. Once buried, the beetles construct a 'crypt' around the carcass. After laying their eggs in the surrounding soil, they roll the carcass into a ball and coat it with antibacterial secretions. When the larvae hatch 2–3 days later their parents guide them to the carrion that is their food source.

The beetles can bury a mouse carcass within an hour. If the soil beneath the carcass is too hard, the beetles must move the carcass, as they bury the carcass by displacing the soil beneath it. Though the larvae can usually complete their development unassisted, the parents remain and help them to feed by regurgitating food.

sexually transmitted disease (STD) any disease transmitted by sexual contact, involving transfer of body fluids. STDs include not only traditional ◊venereal disease, but also a growing list of conditions, such as ◊AIDS and scabies, which are known to be spread primarily by sexual contact. Other diseases that are transmitted sexually include viral ◊hepatitis. The WHO estimate that there are 356,000 new cases of STDs daily worldwide (1995).

sexual reproduction reproductive process in organisms that requires the union, or ◊fertilization, of gametes (such as eggs and sperm). These are usually produced by two different individuals, although self-fertilization occurs in a few ◊hermaphrodites such as tapeworms. Most organisms other than bacteria and cyanobacteria (◊blue-green algae) show some sort of sexual process. Except in some lower organisms, the gametes are of two distinct types called eggs and sperm. The organisms producing the eggs are called

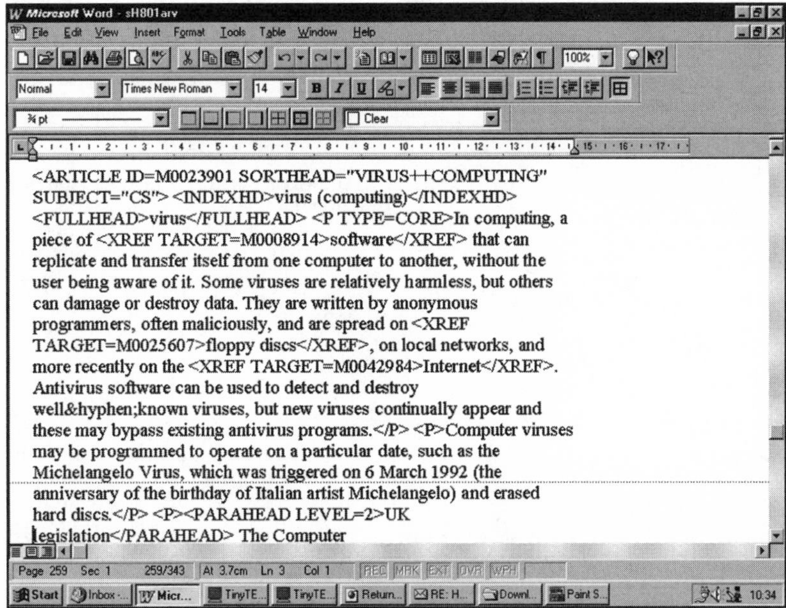

SGML *An example of an SGML source file. No on-screen formatting is used; headings and paragraphs are tagged as such and only appear in a different typeface in the final display.*

females, and those producing the sperm, males. The fusion of a male and female gamete produces a **zygote**, from which a new individual develops.

sexual selection process similar to ◊natural selection but relating exclusively to success in finding a mate for the purpose of sexual reproduction and producing offspring. Sexual selection occurs when one sex (usually but not always the female) invests more effort in producing young than the other. Members of the other sex compete for access to this limited resource (usually males competing for the chance to mate with females).

Sexual selection often favours features that increase a male's attractiveness to females (such as the pheasant's tail) or enable males to fight with one another (such as a deer's antlers). More subtly, it can produce hormonal effects by which the male makes the female unreceptive to other males, causes the abortion of fetuses already conceived, or removes the sperm of males who have already mated with a female.

Seyfert galaxy galaxy whose small, bright centre is caused by hot gas moving at high speed around a massive central object, possibly a ◊black hole. Almost all Seyferts are spiral galaxies. They seem to be closely related to ◊quasars, but are about 100 times fainter. They are named after their discoverer Carl Seyfert (1911–1960).

SGML (abbreviation for ***Standard Generalized Markup Language***) ◊International Standards Organization standard describing how the structure (features such as headers, columns, margins, and tables) of a text can be identified so that it can be used, probably via ◊filters, in applications such as ◊desktop publishing and ◊electronic publishing. HTML and VRML are both types of SGML.

shackle obsolete unit of length, used at sea for measuring cable or chain. One shackle is 15 fathoms (90 ft/27 m).

shad any of several marine fish, especially the genus *Alosa*, the largest (60 cm/2 ft long and 2.7 kg/6 lb in weight) of the herring family (Clupeidae). They migrate in shoals to breed in rivers.

shadoof or ***shaduf*** machine for lifting water, consisting typically of a long, pivoted wooden pole acting as a lever, with a weight at one end. The other end is positioned over a well, for example. The shadoof was in use in ancient Egypt and is still used in Arab countries today.

shadow area of darkness behind an opaque object that cannot be reached by some or all of the light coming from a light source in front. Its presence may be explained in terms of light rays travelling in straight lines and being unable to bend round obstacles. A point source of light produces an ◊umbra, a completely black shadow with sharp edges. An extended source of light produces both a central umbra and a ◊penumbra, a region of semidarkness with blurred edges where darkness gives way to light.

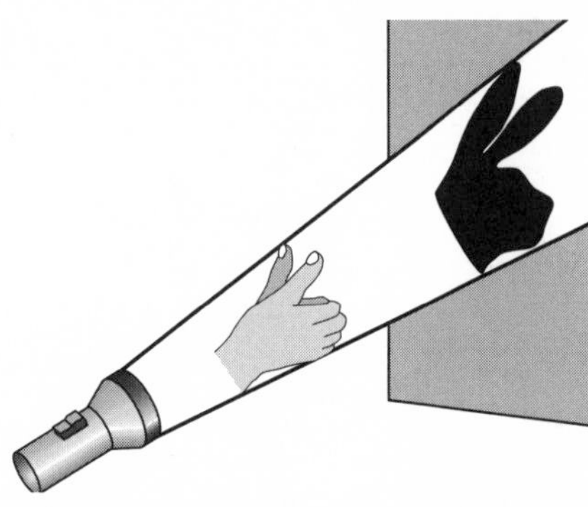

shadow *Shadows are created as light travels in straight lines and so cannot bend around objects, and is therefore blocked.*

◊Eclipses are caused by the Earth passing into the Moon' s shadow or the Moon passing into the Earth's shadow.

shag waterbird *Phalacrocorax aristoclis*, order Pelecaniformes, related to the ◊cormorant. It is smaller than the cormorant, with a green tinge to its plumage and in the breeding season has a crest. Its food consists mainly of sand eels for which it dives, staying underwater for up to 54 seconds. It breeds on deeply fissured cliffs, and on rocky parts of isolated islands.

shale fine-grained and finely layered ◊sedimentary rock composed of silt and clay. It is a weak rock, splitting easily along bedding planes to form thin, even slabs (by contrast, mudstone splits into irregular flakes). Oil shale contains kerogen, a solid bituminous material that yields ◊petroleum when heated.

shallot small onion in which bulbs are clustered like garlic; it is used for cooking and in pickles. (*Allium ascalonicum*, family Liliaceae.)

shamrock any of several leguminous plants (see ◊legume) whose leaves are divided into three leaflets, including ◊clovers. St Patrick is said to have used one to illustrate the doctrine of the Holy Trinity, and it was made the national badge of Ireland. (Family Leguminosae.)

sharecropping farming someone else's land, where the farmer gives the landowner a proportion of the crop instead of money. This system of rent payment was common in the USA, especially the South, until after World War II. It is still common in parts of the developing world; for example, in India. Often the farmer is left with such a small share of the crop that he or she is doomed to poverty.

shared memory bus architecture (SMBA) in computing, system of ◊buses that allows parallel computers to share ◊RAM for greater processing power.

SHAREWARE.COM

http://www.shareware.com/

Access to a whole host of add-ons, new applications, upgrades, and games available as free downloads from the Internet. There is a wide variety here, so fortunately, as well as a list of new items and a search engine, the shareware is also organized by the most popular requests from the previous week.

shareware software distributed free via the Internet or on discs given away with magazines. Users have the opportunity to test its functionality and ability to meet their requirements before paying a small registration fee directly to the author. This may bring additional functionality, documentation, and occasional upgrades. Shareware is not copyright-free. Compare with ◊public-domain software.

SHARK

Despite their reputation, about 90% of all species of shark present no threat to humans. They are too small, have inadequate teeth, or live at too great a depth beneath the water.

shark any member of various orders of cartilaginous fish (class Chondrichthyes), found throughout the oceans of the world. There are about 400 known species of shark. They have tough, usually grey skin covered in denticles (small toothlike scales). A shark's streamlined body has side pectoral fins, a high dorsal fin, and a forked tail with a large upper lobe. Five open gill slits are visible on each side of the generally pointed head. They shed and replace their teeth continually, even before birth. Teeth may be replaced as frequently as every week. Most sharks are fish-eaters, and a few will attack humans. They range from several feet in length to the **great white shark** *Carcharodon carcharias*, 9 m/30 ft long, and the harmless plankton-feeding **whale shark** *Rhincodon typus*, over 15 m/50 ft in length.

Relatively few attacks on humans lead to fatalities, and research suggests that the attacking sharks are not searching for food, but attempting to repel perceived rivals from their territory.

endangered species An estimated 100 million sharks are killed each year for their meat, skin, and oil (basking shark). Some species, such as the great white shark, the tiger shark, and the hammerhead, are now endangered and their killing has been banned in US waters since July 1991. Other species will be protected by catch quotas. The Convention on International trade in Endangered Species (CITES) agreed in 1994 to investigate the extent of the shark trade.

The fins of 90% of sharks caught are traded, almost all destined for Asia, to be made into soup. Many sharks are 'finned': the fins are sliced from live sharks, which are then thrown back to die. Finning was banned in US Atlantic waters in 1993, and by Canada in 1994. As most sharks tend to be long-lived, not reaching sexual maturity till the age of almost 30, and produce small numbers of young with a high juvenile mortality rate, they are ill-equipped to withstand high levels of fishing.

SHARK

http://www.seaworld.org/animal_bytes/sharkab.html

Illustrated guide to the shark including information about genus, size, life span, habitat, gestation, diet, and a series of fun facts.

shearwater any sea bird of the genus *Puffinus*. All the species are oceanic, and either dark above and white below or all dark. Shearwaters are members of the same family (Procellariidae), as the diving ◊petrels, order Procellariiformes. They get their name from their habit of skimming low over the sea on still wings.

The **sooty shearwater** *P. griseus* is common on both North Atlantic coasts. The **muttonbird** or **whalebird** *P. tenuirostris* breeds in Australia but for the rest of the year moves over the Pacific; it is killed for meat and oil. The shearwater population around the Californian coast declined by 90% between 1987 and 1994. In a 1997 report, US biologists attributed the loss of the majority of four million birds to global warming because increased water temperatures affect the plankton that shearwaters feed on.

sheath another name for a ◊condom.

sheathbill white-plumaged shore bird of the southern hemisphere, family Chionididae. The snowy or greater sheathbill *Chionis alba* occurs in the Antarctic region and grows to a length of 39 cm/15 in. It feeds on penguin and seal excrement, and by stealing what it can from penguins feeding their young with half-digested krill.

At breeding times, sheathbills eat unattended penguin eggs. Their own nests are conglomerations of litter – bone, guano, and the remains of dead chicks. They lay two or three eggs but only raise a single chick, probably sacrificing the weaker chick as food for the stronger. Sheathbills are unique as Antarctica's only genuine land-bird, spending most of their time scavenging in penguin colonies.

sheep any of several ruminant, even-toed, hoofed mammals of the family Bovidae. Wild species survive in the uplands of central and eastern Asia, North Africa, southern Europe and North America. The domesticated breeds are all classified as *Ovis aries*.

Various breeds of sheep are reared worldwide for meat, wool, milk, and cheese, and for rotation on arable land to maintain its fertility.

sheepdog any of several breeds of dog, bred originally for herding sheep. The dog now most commonly used by shepherds and farmers in Britain to tend sheep is the ◊border collie. Non-pedigree dogs of the border collie type, though more variable in size and colour, are referred to as working sheepdogs. Other recognized British breeds are the Old English and ◊Shetland sheepdogs. Many countries have their own breeds of sheepdog, such as the ◊Belgian sheepdog, Australian ◊kelpie, and Hungarian puli.

sheep ked wingless insect that is an external parasite of sheep, feeding on their blood.

Adult keds are particularly well-adapted to clinging to their hosts; they are flattened dorso-ventrally and their legs end in claws. The female fly, which lacks wings, deposits 10–15 larvae which she cements to the sheep's fleece. The oval-shaped, non-motile larvae pupate almost instantaneously while still attached to the host. The newly emerged adults suck the sheep's blood. The sheep react to these irritations by scratching and thus damage their wool. In addition the keds defecate on the wool, which lowers its quality. Dipping the sheep regularly removes the keds.

classification The sheep ked *Melophagus ovinus* is in family Hippoboscidae, suborder Cyclorrhapha, order Diptera, class Insecta, phylum Arthropoda.

sheep scab highly contagious disease of sheep, caused by mites that penetrate the animal's skin. Painful irritation, infection, loss of fleece, and death may result. The disease is notifiable in the UK.

shelduck duck *Tadorna tadorna* of family Anatidae, order Anseriformes. It has a dark-green head and red bill, with the rest of the plumage strikingly marked in black, white, and chestnut. The drake is about 60 cm/24 in long. Widely distributed in Europe and Asia, it lays 10–12 white eggs in rabbit burrows on sandy coasts, and is usually seen on estuary mudflats.

shelf sea relatively shallow sea, usually no deeper than 200 m/650 ft, overlying the continental shelf around the coastlines. Most fishing and marine mineral exploitations are carried out in shelf seas.

shell in computing, program that mediates access to a particular system or server. Windows 95 is a shell that interposes a ◊graphical user interface and other utilities between the operator and ◊MS-DOS. In DOS itself, the file COMMAND.COM is a shell that makes the operating system display a ◊prompt and enables it to interpret user instructions. Shells can also be used to improve computer security.

shell the hard outer covering of a wide variety of invertebrates. The covering is usually mineralized, normally with large amounts of calcium. The shell of birds' eggs is also largely made of calcium.

shellac resin derived from secretions of the ◊lac insect.

shell account in computing, cheap method of accessing the ◊Internet via another computer, usually a ◊UNIX machine. Users with a shell account are given text-only access (via the telephone) to another computer connected to the Net.

shellfish popular name for molluscs and crustaceans, including the whelk and periwinkle, mussel, oyster, lobster, crab, and shrimp.

shell script in computing, the UNIX equivalent of batch files created for a program◊ shell. Essentially, shell scripts allow users to create their own commands by creating a file that contains the sequence of commands they want to run and then designating the file as executable. Thereafter, typing the name of the file executes the sequence of commands.

shell shock or ***combat neurosis*** or ***battle fatigue*** any of the various forms of mental disorder that affect soldiers exposed to heavy explosions or extreme ◊stress. Shell shock was first diagnosed during World War I.

Sheltie breed of dog. See ◊Shetland sheepdog.

shepherd's purse annual plant distributed worldwide in temperate zones. It is a persistent weed with white flowers followed by heart-shaped, seed-containing pouches, which give the plant its name. (*Capsella bursa-pastoris,* family Cruciferae.)

Shetland sheepdog or ***Sheltie*** breed of small herding dog native to the Shetlands islands of Scotland. Similar to a ◊rough collie, it has a long coat with a variety of colours and markings, narrow head, pricked ears folded at the tips, and dainty build, but reaches only 36 cm/14 in in height.

SHF in physics, abbreviation for **superhigh** ◊frequency. SHF radio waves have frequencies in the range 3–30 GHz.

shiatsu in alternative medicine, Japanese method of massage derived from ◊acupuncture and sometimes referred to as 'acupressure', which treats organic or physiological dysfunctions by applying finger or palm pressure to parts of the body remote from the affected part.

SHIATSU – JAPANESE MASSAGE

http://www1.tip.nl/~t283083/e_index.htm

Well-written introduction to the theoretical underpinnings and the practice of shiatsu. The origins of this ancient Japanese pressure technique are explained with reference to the theory of yin and yang. Diagrams are used to explain techniques. There is a bibliography and list of addresses of shiatsu therapists. services and legal assistance.

shield in geology, alternative name for ◊craton, the ancient core of a continent.

shield in technology, any material used to reduce the amount of radiation (electrostatic, electromagnetic, heat, nuclear) reaching from one region of space to another, or any material used as a protection against falling debris, as in tunnelling.

Electrical conductors are used for electrostatic shields, soft iron for electromagnetic shields, and poor conductors of heat for heat shields. Heavy materials, such as lead, and concrete are used for protection against X-rays and nuclear radiation. See also ◊biological shield and ◊heat shield.

shifting cultivation farming system where farmers move on from one place to another when the land becomes exhausted. The most common form is **slash-and-burn** agriculture: land is cleared by burning, so that crops can be grown. After a few years, soil fertility is reduced and the land is abandoned. A new area is cleared while the old land recovers its fertility.

Slash-and-burn is practised in many tropical forest areas, such as the Amazon region, where yams, cassava, and sweet potatoes can be grown. This system works well while population levels are low, but where there is overpopulation, the old land will be reused before soil fertility has been restored. A variation of this system, found in parts of Africa, is rotational bush fallowing that involves a more permanent settlement and crop rotation.

shih tzu breed of small dog originating in China. It has short legs and a maximum height of 26 cm/10.5 in. Its long, dense coat may be any colour, and it carries its plumy tail over its back. The long hair growing from the top of its muzzle and falling either side of its face gives it its characteristic expression.

Shimbel index a mathematical measurement of the accessibility of a transportation network. It is the total of the number of links or edges that form the shortest path between each ◊node (junctions or places) and all other nodes in the network.

shingles common name for ◊herpes zoster, a disease characterized by infection of sensory nerves, with pain and eruption of blisters along the course of the affected nerves.

SHINGLES

http://biomed.nus.sg/nsc/shingles.html

Excellent guide to diagnosing and treating herpes zoster from Singapore's National Skin Centre. There are pictures to illustrate the condition.

Shinkansen Japanese 'new trunk line' fast railway network operated by Japanese Railways, on which the 'bullet' trains run. The network, opened 1964, uses specially built straight and level track, on which average speeds of 160 kph/100 mph are attained.

The Shinkansen between Tokyo and Osaka carried 270,000 passengers a day by 1990.

The new Japanese bullet train, *Nozomi*-503, March 1997 hit an average speed of 261.8 kph/163 mph between Hiroshima and Kokura, breaking the current rail speed record. Equipped with a long-nose lead carriage and new sound-proofing for a faster, quieter ride, the *Nozomi*-503 carried 1,300 passengers in 16 carriages from Osaka to Fukuoka, hitting speeds of up to 300 kph/187 mph. The official record for average speed between two stations of 252.6 kph/157 mph had been held by the French TGV. The *Nozomi* also matched the top speed reached by the TGV.

ship large seagoing vessel. The Greeks, Phoenicians, Romans, and Vikings used ships extensively for trade, exploration, and warfare. The 14th century was the era of European exploration by sailing ship, largely aided by the invention of the compass. In the 15th century Britain's Royal Navy was first formed, but in the 16th–19th centuries Spanish and Dutch fleets dominated the shipping lanes of both the Atlantic and Pacific.

The ultimate sailing ships, the fast US and British tea clippers, were built in the 19th century. Also in the 19th century, iron was first used for some shipbuilding instead of wood. Steam-propelled ships of the late 19th century were followed by compound engine and turbine-propelled vessels from the early 20th century.

origins The earliest vessels were rafts or dug-out canoes, many of which have been found in Britain, and date from prehistoric times. The Greeks and Phoenicians built wooden ships, propelled by oar or sail. The Romans and Carthaginians built war galleys equipped with rams and several tiers of rowers. The double-ended oak ships of the Vikings were built for rough seas.

development of sailing ships The invention of the stern rudder during the 12th century, together with the developments made in sailing during the Crusades, enabled the use of sails to almost completely supersede that of oars. Following the invention of the compass, and with it the possibilities of exploration, the development of sailing ships advanced quickly during the 14th century. In the 15th century Henry VIII built the *Great Harry,* the first double-decked English warship.

In the 16th century ships were short and high-sterned, and despite Pett's three-decker in the 17th century, English ships did not bear comparison with the Spanish and Dutch until the early 19th century. In the 1840s iron began replacing wood in shipbuilding, pioneered by British engineer Isambard Kingdom Brunel's *Great Britain* in 1845. Throughout the 19th century, improvements were made in warships, including the evolution of the elliptical stern. However, increased rivalry between US and British owners for possession of the Chinese and Indian tea trade led to improvements also being made to the merchant vessel.

The first clipper, the *Ann McKim,* was built in Baltimore in 1832, and Britain soon adopted this type of fast-sailing ship. One of the finest of the tea clippers, the *Sir Launcelot,* was built in 1865 and marked the highest development of the sailing ship. The US ship *Champion of the Seas* was one of the fastest of its time, averaging speeds of 20 knots.

Ships: chronology

8000-7000 BC	Reed boats were developed in Mesopotamia and Egypt; dugout canoes were used in northwest Europe.
4000-3000	The Egyptians used single-masted square-rigged ships on the Nile.
1200	The Phoenicians built keeled boats with hulls of wooden planks.
1st century BC	The Chinese invented the rudder.
AD 200	The Chinese built ships with several masts.
200-300	The Arabs and Romans developed fore-and-aft rigging that allowed boats to sail across the direction of wind.
800-900	Square-rigged Viking longboats crossed the North Sea to Britain, the Faroe Islands, and Iceland.
1090	The Chinese invented the magnetic compass.
1400-1500	Three-masted ships were developed in western Europe, stimulating voyages of exploration.
1620	Dutch engineer Cornelius Drebbel invented the submarine.
1776	US engineer David Bushnell built a hand-powered submarine, *Turtle*, with buoyancy tanks.
1777	The first boat with an iron hull was built in Yorkshire, England.
1783	Frenchman Jouffroy d'Abbans built the first paddle-driven steamboat.
1802	Scottish engineer William Symington launched the first stern paddle-wheel steamer, the *Charlotte Dundas*.
1807	The first successful steamboat, the *Clermont*, designed by US engineer and inventor Robert Fulton, sailed between New York and Albany.
1836	The screw propeller was patented, by Francis Pettit Smith in the UK.
1838	British engineer Isambard Kingdom Brunel's *Great Western*, the first steamship built for crossing the Atlantic, sailed from Bristol to New York in 15 days.
1845	*Great Britain*, also built by Isambard Kingdom Brunel, became the first propeller-driven iron ship to cross the Atlantic.
1845	The first clipper ship, *Rainbow*, was launched in the USA.
1863	*Plongeur*, the first submarine powered by an air-driven engine, was launched in France.
1866	The British clippers *Taeping* and *Ariel* sailed, laden with tea, from China to London in 99 days.
1886	German engineer Gottlieb Daimler built the first boat powered by an internal-combustion engine.
1897	English engineer Charles Parson fitted a steam turbine to *Turbinia*, making it the fastest boat of the time.
1900	Irish-American John Philip Holland designed the first modern submarine *Holland VI*, fitted with an electric motor for underwater sailing and an internal-combustion engine for surface travel; E Forlanini of Italy built the first hydrofoil.
1902	The French ship *Petit-Pierre* became the first boat to be powered by a diesel engine.
1955	The first nuclear-powered submarine, *Nautilus*, was built in the USA; the hovercraft was patented by British inventor Christopher Cockerell.
1959	The first nuclear-powered surface ship, the Soviet ice-breaker *Lenin*, was commissioned; the US *Savannah* became the first nuclear-powered merchant (passenger and cargo) ship.
1980	Launch of the first wind-assisted commercial ship for half a century, the Japanese tanker *Shin-Aitoku-Maru*.
1983	German engineer Ortwin Fries invented a hinged ship designed to bend into a V-shape in order to scoop up oil spillages in its jaws.
1989	*Gentry Eagle* set a record for the fastest crossing of the Atlantic in a power vessel, taking 2 days, 14 hours, and 7 minutes.
1990	*Hoverspeed Great Britain*, a wave-piercing catamaran, crossed the Atlantic in 3 days, 7 hours, and 52 minutes, setting a record for the fastest crossing by a passenger vessel. The world's largest car and passenger ferry, the *Silja Serenade*, entered service between Stockholm and Helsinki, carrying 2,500 passengers and 450 cars.
1992	Japanese propellerless ship *Yamato* driven by magnetohydrodynamics completes its sea trials. The ship uses magnetic forces to suck in and eject sea water like a jet engine.
1997	The biggest cruise ship ever, the *Carnival Destiny*, was launched. It is as long as three football pitches, taller than the Statue of Liberty, and too wide to pass through the Panama Canal. US researchers tested a new type of submersible (small submarine) with wings, which can turn, dive, and roll like an aeroplane.

steamships Early steamers depended partly on sails for auxiliary power. In 1802 the paddle-wheel steamer *Charlotte Dundas*, constructed by William Symington, was launched on the Forth and Clyde Canal, Scotland. However, the effort was halted amid fears that the wash produced by the paddle would damage the canal banks. In 1812 the *Comet*, built in Scotland 1804 by Bell, Napier, and Robertson, was launched. This ship, which had a paddle on each side, was a commercial success, and two others were built for service from Glasgow. From this time the steamship-building industry rapidly developed on the banks of the Clyde.

The first steamship to cross the Atlantic was the Dutch vessel *Curaçao*, a wooden paddler built at Dover 1826, which left Rotterdam in April 1827, and took one month to cross. The next transatlantic steamer, the *Royal William*, crossed from Quebec to London in 17 days in 1833. Britain's entry into the transatlantic efforts began with Brunel's *Great Western* paddle-steamer, which achieved recognition when it completed the journey from Bristol to New York in 15 days – three days faster than a clipper.

The first great iron steamship, *Rainbow*, was launched 1838. In the following year, Pettit Smith designed the *Archimedes*, the first steamer to use a screw propeller, followed quickly by Brunel's *Great Britain*, which crossed from Liverpool to New York in 14.5 days 1845.

In 1862 the Cunard Company obtained permission to fit mail steamers with propellers, which suffered less from the rolling of the ship, and the paddle-wheel was relegated to comparatively smooth water. The opening of the Suez Canal in 1869, together with the simultaneous introduction of the compound engine, raised steamships to superiority over sailing ships. In 1902 the turbine engine was employed on passenger steamers on the Clyde, and in 1905 was applied to the transatlantic service. This was followed by the introduction of the internal combustion engine.

the Blue Riband of the Atlantic The trophy for the fastest Atlantic crossing, the 'Blue Riband', has been held by many passenger liners, including the Cunarder *Mauretania* (1909–30), the *Queen Mary* (1938–52), and the *United States* (1952–89).

tankers Following World War II, when reconstruction and industrial development created a great demand for oil, the tanker was developed to carry supplies to the areas of consumption. The shipyards of the world were flooded with orders for tankers; due to economic demands, the size of the tankers became increasingly large. The Suez Canal crisis 1956, with its disruption of the free flow of the world's oil supplies, focused attention on the possibility of working giant tankers over the Cape route. The prolonged closure of the Suez Canal after 1967 and the great increase in oil consumption led to the development of the very large tanker, or 'supertanker'.

shock in medicine, circulatory failure marked by a sudden fall of blood pressure and resulting in pallor, sweating, fast (but weak) pulse, and sometimes complete collapse. Causes include disease, injury, and psychological trauma.

In shock, the blood pressure falls below that necessary to supply the tissues of the body, especially the brain. Treatment depends on the cause. Rest is needed, and, in the case of severe blood loss, restoration of the normal circulating volume.

shock absorber in technology, any device for absorbing the shock of sudden jarring actions or movements. Shock absorbers are used in conjunction with coil springs in most motor-vehicle suspension systems and are usually of the telescopic type, consisting of a piston in an oil-filled cylinder. The resistance to movement of the piston through the oil creates the absorbing effect.

shock wave narrow band or region of high pressure and temperature in which the flow of a fluid changes from subsonic to supersonic.

Shock waves are produced when an object moves through a fluid at a supersonic speed. See ◊sonic boom.

Shockwave in computing, ◊application that enables interactive and multimedia features, such as movies, sounds, and animations, to be embedded in Web pages. Unlike ◊Java , which achieves these effects by using a special programming language, Shockwave allows developers to add items created with conventional ◊authoring tools such as ◊Director or Freehand.

shoebill or ***whale-headed stork*** large, grey, long-legged, swamp-dwelling African bird *Balaeniceps rex.* Up to 1.5 m/5 ft tall, it has a large wide beak 20 cm/8 in long, with which it scoops fish, molluscs, reptiles, and carrion out of the mud. It is the only species in the family Balaenicipitidae of the order Ciconiiformes.

shoot in botany, the parts of a ◊vascular plant growing above ground, comprising a stem bearing leaves, buds, and flowers. The shoot develops from the ◊plumule of the embryo.

shooting star another name for a ◊meteor.

Short British aircraft manufacturers. The Type 184 seaplane in 1914 was the first aircraft to carry a torpedo and, during the World War I Gallipoli campaign, was the first aircraft to sink an enemy ship with a torpedo.

The firm began by making balloons in 1898 and only turned to aircraft in 1908. The company also manufactured a number of airships for the Royal Flying Corps and Royal Naval Air Service in their Bedford factory.

short circuit unintended direct connection between two points in an electrical circuit.

Its relatively low resistance means that a large current flows through it, bypassing the rest of the circuit, and this may cause the circuit to overheat dangerously.

shortcut in computing, keyboard combination or icon which activates a procedure otherwise available only through pull-down menus and ◊dialog boxes. Most commercial software comes with built-in keyboard shortcuts and ◊pushbuttons, and many allow users to create their own custom shortcuts. In Windows 95, a shortcut is an icon that launches a program direct from the desktop.

short-sightedness nontechnical term for ◊myopia.

shoveler fresh-water duck *Anas clypeata,* family Anatidae, order Anseriformes, so named after its long and broad flattened beak used for filtering out small organisms from sand and mud. The male has a green head, white and brown body plumage, black and white wings, greyish bill, orange feet, and can grow up to 50 cm/20 in long. The female is speckled brown. Spending the summer in N Europe or North America, it winters further south.

shovelware in computing, material used to fill (usually) a large-capacity disc, such as a CD-ROM, by 'shovelling it in' without changing or updating it to suit the new format. The term is also used for a disc that is full of old or low-cost material, such as shareware programs or the texts of out-of-copyright books

shredder machine for disposing of confidential documents or computer discs. Paper is shredded into strips or, in high-security machines, into confetti; magnetic discs are cut to pieces or pulverized.

SHREW

The number of chromosomes in the cells of common shrews varies from 20–25 in females and 21–27 in males. They are the only mammals not to have a constant number of chromosomes.

shrew insectivorous mammal of the family Soricidae, order Insectivora, found in the Americas and Eurasia. It is mouselike, but with a long nose and pointed teeth. Its high metabolic rate means that it must eat almost constantly.

The **common shrew** *Sorex araneus* is about 7.5 cm/3 in long with a long, supple, pointed snout bearing numerous stiff hairs projecting beyond the lower jaw; its fur is reddish-grey above and greyish beneath. It has glands which secrete a strong, unpleasant odour as a means of defence. It feeds on insects, worms, and often on members of its own kind killed after a fight.

SHREW(-ISTS) SITE

http://members.vienna.at/shrew/index.html

Splendid site for the shrew enthusiast that includes images, details of current research, a newsletter, and facts, stories and myths about this animal. There is even a shrew gift shop!

shrike or ***butcher-bird*** bird of the family Laniidae, of which there are over 70 species, living mostly in Africa, but also in Eurasia and North America. They often impale insects and small vertebrates on thorns. They can grow to 35 cm/14 in long, have grey, black, or brown plumage, sharply clawed feet, and hooked beaks.

shrimp crustacean related to the ◊prawn. It has a cylindrical, semi-transparent body, with ten jointed legs. Some shrimps grow as large as 25 cm/10 in long.

The European common shrimp *Crangon vulgaris* is greenish, translucent, has its first pair of legs ending in pincers, possesses no rostrum (the beaklike structure which extends forwards from the head in some crustaceans), and has comparatively shorter antennae than the prawn. *Synalpheus regalis,* a shrimp that lives within sponges in the coral reefs of Belize, was discovered in 1996 to live in social colonies with a structure resembling that of social insects, such as ants. All are the offspring of a single reproductive female; care of young is cooperative; and larger individuals act to defend the colony.

shrub perennial woody plant that typically produces several separate stems, at or near ground level, rather than the single trunk of most trees. A shrub is usually smaller than a tree, but there is no clear distinction between large shrubs and small trees.

shunt in electrical engineering, a conductor of very low resistance that is connected in parallel to an ◊ammeter in order to enable it to measure larger electric currents. Its low resistance enables it to act like a bypass, diverting most of the current through itself and away from the ammeter.

SI (abbreviation for ***Système International d'Unités***) (French 'International System of Metric Units'); see ◊SI units.

sial in geochemistry and geophysics, the substance of the Earth's continental ◊crust, as distinct from the ◊sima of the ocean crust.

The name, now used rarely, is derived from **si**lica and **al**umina, its two main chemical constituents. Sial is often rich in granite.

siamang the largest ◊gibbon *Symphalangus syndactylus,* native to Malaysia and Sumatra. Siamangs have a large throat pouch to amplify the voice, making the territorial 'song' extremely loud.

They are black-haired, up to 90 cm/3 ft tall, with very long arms (a span of 150 cm/5 ft).

Siamese cat breed of domestic shorthaired cat originating in Thailand. Siamese were imported into Britain in the 1880s and into the US shortly afterwards. It has large pointed ears on a wedge-shaped head, blue eyes, and a long, slender body. In the Seal-point, the original and most popular variety, the fur is cream with dark brown ears, face, tail, legs, and feet. There are now many varieties.

Developed from a Siamese mutant, the Balinese differs from the original only in the length of its coat, which is long. It appeared first in the USA in the late 1940s and recognized there in 1970.

Siamese fighting fish beautiful freshwater fish noted for its colour and elaborate behavioural displays. The male builds a nest of bubbles and looks after the eggs.
classification The Siamese fighting fish *Betta splendens* is in family Belontidae, order Perciformes, class Osteichthyes.

sick building syndrome malaise diagnosed in the early 1980s among office workers and thought to be caused by such pollutants as formaldehyde (from furniture and insulating materials), benzene (from paint), and the solvent trichloroethene, concentrated in air-conditioned buildings. Symptoms include headache, sore throat, tiredness, colds, and flu. Studies have found that it can cause a 40% drop in productivity and a 30% rise in absenteeism.

Work on improving living conditions of astronauts showed that the causes were easily and inexpensively removed by potplants in which interaction is thought to take place between the plant and microorganisms in its roots. Among the most useful are chrysanthemums (counteracting benzene), English ivy and the peace lily (trichloroethene), and the spider plant (formaldehyde).

sickle harvesting tool of ancient origin characterized by a curving blade with serrated cutting edge and short wooden handle. It was widely used in the Middle East and Europe for cutting wheat, barley, and oats from about 10,000 BC to the 19th century.

sickle-cell disease hereditary chronic blood disorder common among people of black African descent; also found in the E Mediterranean, parts of the Persian Gulf, and in NE India. It is characterized by distortion and fragility of the red blood cells, which are lost too rapidly from the circulation. This often results in ◊anaemia.

People with this disease have abnormal red blood cells (sickle cells), containing a defective ◊haemoglobin. The presence of sickle cells in the blood is called **sicklemia**.

The disease is caused by a recessive allele. Those with two copies of the allele suffer debilitating anaemia; those with a single copy paired with the normal allele, suffer with only mild anaemia and have a degree of protection against ◊malaria because fewer normal red blood cells are available to the parasites for infection.

In the US there were approximately 65,000 African Americans suffering from sickle-cell disease in 1996; there were about 5,500 British sufferers. Worldwide, 100,000 babies are born with the disease annually. Those born in developing countries are unlikely to survive for long.

Bone marrow transplantation can provide a cure, but the risks (a fatality rate of 10% and a complications rate of 20% are so great that it is only an option for the severely ill. US researchers announced in April 1995 that patients treated with a drug called hydroxyurea showed a reduction in the number of sickle cells. The drug works by reducing the amount of defective haemoglobin produced, and reviving the production of fetal haemoglobin. Fetal haemoglobin is not affected by sickling.

sidereal period the orbital period of a planet around the Sun, or a moon around a planet, with reference to a background star. The sidereal period of a planet is in effect a 'year'. A ◊synodic period is a full circle as seen from Earth.

sidereal time in astronomy, time measured by the rotation of the Earth with respect to the stars. A sidereal day is the time taken by the Earth to turn once with respect to the stars, namely 23 h 56 min 4 s. It is divided into sidereal hours, minutes, and seconds, each of which is proportionally shorter than the corresponding SI unit.

sidewinder rattlesnake *Crotalus cerastes* that lives in the deserts of the SW USA and Mexico, and moves by throwing its coils into a sideways 'jump' across the sand. It can grow up to 75 cm/30 in long.

Siding Spring Mountain peak 400 km/250 mi NW of Sydney, site of the UK Schmidt Telescope, opened 1973, and the 3.9-m/154-in **Anglo-Australian Telescope**, opened in 1975, which was the first big telescope to be fully computer-controlled. It is one of the most powerful telescopes in the southern hemisphere.

SIDS (acronym for ***sudden infant death syndrome***) the technical name for ◊cot death.

siemens SI unit (symbol S) of electrical conductance, the reciprocal of the ◊resistance of an electrical circuit. One siemens equals one ampere per volt. It was formerly called the mho or reciprocal ohm.

Siemens multinational industrial empire founded in Germany by Ernst Werner von Siemens and expanded by his brothers. **William** (Karl Wilhelm) (1823–1883) moved to the UK in 1843; he perfected the open-hearth production of steel, pioneered the development of the electric locomotive and the laying of transoceanic cables, and improved the electric generator. The company now operates in the electrical and electronic sector.

sievert SI unit (symbol Sv) of radiation dose equivalent. It replaces the rem (1 Sv equals 100 rem). Some types of radiation do more damage than others for the same absorbed dose – for example, an absorbed dose of alpha radiation causes 20 times as much biological damage as the same dose of beta radiation. The equivalent dose in sieverts is equal to the absorbed dose of radiation in grays multiplied by the relative biological effectiveness. Humans can absorb up to 0.25 Sv without immediate ill effects; 1 Sv may produce radiation sickness; and more than 8 Sv causes death.

sight the detection of light by an ◊eye, which can form images of the outside world.

Sigma Octantis the star closest to the south celestial pole (see ◊celestial sphere), in effect the southern equivalent of ◊Polaris, although far less conspicuous. Situated just less than 1° from the south celestial pole in the constellation Octans, Sigma Octantis is 120 light years away.

signal any sign, gesture, sound, or action that conveys information. Examples include the use of flags (semaphore), light (traffic and railway signals), radio telephony, radio telegraphy (◊Morse code), and electricity (telecommunications and computer networks).

The International Code of Signals used by shipping was drawn up by an international committee and published 1931. The codes and abbreviations used by aircraft are dealt with by the International Civil Aviation Organization, established in 1944.

signal processing in computing, the digitizing of an ◊analogue signal such as a voice stream.

signal-to-noise ratio ratio of the power of an electrical signal to that of the unwanted noise accompanying the signal. It is expressed in ◊decibels.

In general, the higher the signal-to-noise ratio, the better. For a telephone, an acceptable ratio is 40 decibels; for television, the acceptable ratio is 50 decibels.

signature (or *.sig*) in computing, personal information appended to a message by the sender of an ◊e-mail message or ◊USENET posting in order to add a human touch. Signatures, which are optional, usually carry the sender's real name and e-mail address, and may also include the writer's occupation, telephone number, and the ◊URL of his or her ◊home page. Many have a short quote, motto or slogan, and a few incorporate ◊ASCII art. .Sig is the name of the file in which signature information is stored on a UNIX system.

significant figures the figures in a number that, by virtue of their place value, express the magnitude of that number to a specified degree of accuracy. The final significant figure is rounded up if the following digit is greater than 5. For example, 5,463,254 to three significant figures is 5,460,000; 3.462891 to four significant figures is 3.463; 0.00347 to two significant figures is 0.0035.

silage fodder preserved through controlled fermentation in a ◊silo, an airtight structure that presses green crops. It is used as a winter feed for livestock. The term also refers to stacked crops that may be preserved indefinitely.

Silbury Hill artificial mound of the Neolithic (New Stone Age) period, around 2800 BC, situated just south of ◊Avebury, Wiltshire, England. Steep and rounded, it towers 40 m/130 ft high with a surrounding ditch approximately 6 m/20 ft deep, made when quarrying for the structure. It is the largest ancient artificial mound in Europe.

Excavation has revealed that it is not a burial mound, as was previously thought, but its purpose is still unclear. The main mound was built in a series of horizontal layers over a primary mound about 25 m/82 ft in diameter. It may have initially been about a third higher and the sides were originally terraced.

The mound is estimated to have required 18 million hours of labour to complete, which suggests considerable organization of workforce in keeping with a social structure regarded as later Neolithic, with a paramount chief in control of the territory.

silencer (North American ***muffler***) device in the exhaust system of cars and motorbikes. Gases leave the engine at supersonic speeds, and the exhaust system and silencer are designed to slow them down, thereby silencing them.

Some silencers use baffle plates (plates with holes, which disrupt the airflow), others use perforated tubes and an expansion box (a large chamber that slows down airflow).

silica silicon dioxide, SiO_2, the composition of the most common mineral group, of which the most familiar form is quartz. Other silica forms are ◊chalcedony, chert, opal, tridymite, and cristobalite.

Common sand consists largely of silica in the form of quartz.

silicate one of a group of minerals containing silicon and oxygen in tetrahedral units of SiO_4, bound together in various ways to form specific structural types. Silicates are the chief rock-forming minerals. Most rocks are composed, wholly or in part, of silicates (the main exception being limestones). Glass is a manufactured complex polysilicate material in which other elements (boron in borosilicate glass) have been incorporated.

Generally, additional cations are present in the structure, especially Al^{3+}, Fe^{2+}, Mg^{2+}, Ca^{2+}, Na^{+}, K^{+}, but quartz and other polymorphs of SiO_2 are also considered to be silicates; stishovite (a high-pressure form of SiO_2) is a rare exception to the usual tetrahedral coordination of silica and oxygen.

In **orthosilicates**, the oxygens are all ionically bonded to cations such as Mg^{2+} or Fe^{2+} (as olivines), and are not shared between tetrahedra. All other silicate structures involve some degree of oxygen sharing between adjacent tetrahedra. For example, beryl is a **ring silicate** based on tetrahedra linked by sharing oxygens to form a circle. Pyroxenes are single **chain silicates**, with chains of linked tetrahedra extending in one direction through the structure; amphiboles are similar but have double chains of tetrahedra. In micas, which are **sheet silicates**, the tetrahedra are joined to form continuous sheets that are stacked upon one another. **Framework silicates**, such as feldspars and quartz, are based on three-dimensional frameworks of tetrahedra in which all oxygens are shared.

silicon Latin *silex* 'flint' brittle, nonmetallic element, symbol Si, atomic number 14, relative atomic mass 28.086. It is the second-most abundant element (after oxygen) in the Earth's crust and occurs in amorphous and crystalline forms. In nature it is found only in combination with other elements, chiefly with oxygen in silica (silicon dioxide, SiO_2) and the silicates. These form the mineral ◊quartz, which makes up most sands, gravels, and beaches.

Pottery glazes and glassmaking are based on the use of silica sands and date from prehistory. Today the crystalline form of silicon is used as a deoxidizing and hardening agent in steel, and has become the basis of the electronics industry because of its ◊semiconductor properties, being used to make 'silicon chips' for microprocessors.

The element was isolated by Swedish chemist Jöns Berzelius in 1823, having been named in 1817 by Scottish chemist Thomas Thomson by analogy with boron and carbon because of its chemical resemblance to these elements.

silicon chip ◊integrated circuit with microscopically small electrical components on a piece of silicon crystal only a few millimetres square.

One chip may contain more than a million components. A chip is mounted in a rectangular plastic package and linked via gold wires to metal pins, so that it can be connected to a printed circuit board for use in electronic devices, such as computers, calculators, television sets, car dashboards, and domestic appliances.

Silicon Glen area in central Scotland, around Glenrothes new town, where there are many electronics firms. By 1986 Glenrothes had over 21% of its workforce employed in electrical engineering, especially high-tech firms. Many of the firms here are owned by US and other foreign companies.

Silicon Graphics, Inc (SGI) manufacturer of high-performance workstations and software designed primarily for graphics and image processing.

Silicon Valley nickname given to a region of S California, approximately 32 km/20 mi long, between Palo Alto and San Jose. It is the site of many high-technology electronic firms, whose prosperity is based on the silicon chip.

SILICON VALLEY

http://www.internetvalley.com/introduction.html

Brief exploration of the history of California's Silicon Valley, which was named after the brittle metalloid used in the manufacture of microprocessors.

silicosis chronic disease of miners and stone cutters who inhale ◊silica dust, which makes the lung tissues fibrous and less capable of aerating the blood. It is a form of ◊pneumoconiosis.

silk-screen printing or ***serigraphy*** method of ◊printing based on stencilling. It can be used to print on most surfaces, including paper, plastic, cloth, and wood. An impermeable stencil (either paper or photosensitized gelatin plate) is attached to a finely meshed silk screen that has been stretched on a wooden frame, so that the ink passes through to the area beneath only where an image is required. The design can also be painted directly on the screen with varnish. A series of screens can be used to add successive layers of colour to the design.

The process was developed in the early 20th century for commercial use and adopted by many artists from the 1930s onwards, most notably Andy Warhol.

silkworm usually the larva of the **common silkworm moth** *Bombyx mori*. After hatching from the egg and maturing on the leaves of white mulberry trees (or a synthetic substitute), it spins a protective cocoon of fine silk thread 275 m/900 ft long. To keep the thread intact, the moth is killed before emerging from the cocoon, and several threads are combined to form the commercial silk thread woven into textiles.

Other moths produce different fibres, such as **tussah** from *Antheraea mylitta*. The raising of silkworms is called **sericulture** and began in China about 2000 BC. Chromosome engineering and artificial selection practised in Japan have led to the development of different types of silkworm for different fibres.

SILKWORM

It takes about 1,700 silkworm cocoons to make a silk dress and 350 to make a pair of stockings.

silo in farming, an airtight tower in which ◊silage is made by the fermentation of freshly cut grass and other forage crops. In military technology, a silo is an underground chamber for housing and launching a ballistic missile.

Silurian period of geological time 439–409 million years ago, the third period of the Palaeozoic era. Silurian sediments are mostly marine and consist of shales and limestone. Luxuriant reefs were built by coral-like organisms. The first land plants began to evolve during this period, and there were many ostracoderms (armoured jawless fishes). The first jawed fishes (called acanthodians) also appeared.

silver white, lustrous, extremely malleable and ductile, metallic element, symbol Ag (from Latin *argentum*), atomic number 47, relative atomic mass 107.868. It occurs in nature in ores and as a free metal; the chief ores are sulphides, from which the metal is extracted by smelting with lead. It is one of the best metallic conductors of both heat and electricity; its most useful compounds are the chloride and bromide, which darken on exposure to light and are the basis of photographic emulsions.

Silver is used ornamentally, for jewellery and tableware, for coinage, in electroplating, electrical contacts, and dentistry, and as a solder. It has been mined since prehistory; its name is an ancient non-Indo-European one, *silubr*, borrowed by the Germanic branch as *silber*.

silverberry North American shrub *Eleagnus commutata* of the oleaster family, having twigs marked with brown and silver scales and bearing silvery yellow, fragrant flowers. The silvery berrylike fruits are edible.

silverfish wingless insect, a type of ◊bristletail.

silver plate silverware made by depositing a layer of silver on another metal, usually copper, by the process of ◊electroplating.

sima in geochemistry and geophysics, the substance of the Earth's oceanic ◊crust, as distinct from the ◊sial of the continental crust. The name, now used rarely, is derived from **si**lica and **ma**gnesia, its two main chemical constituents.

simple harmonic motion (SHM) oscillatory or vibrational motion in which an object (or point) moves so that its acceleration towards a central point is proportional to its distance from it. A simple example is a pendulum, which also demonstrates another feature of SHM, that the maximum deflection is the same on each side of the central point.

A graph of the varying distance with respect to time is a sine curve, a characteristic of the oscillating current or voltage of an alternating current (AC), which is another example of SHM.

Simple Mail Transfer Protocol in computing, protocol for transferring electronic mail between computers, commonly abbreviated to ◊SMTP.

Simple Network Management Protocol in computing, agreed method of managing a computer network, commonly abbreviated to ◊SNMP.

simplify of a fraction, to reduce to lowest terms by dividing both numerator and denominator by any number that is a factor of both, until there are no common factors between the numerator and denominator. Also, in algebra, to condense an algebraic expression by grouping similar terms and reducing constants to their lowest terms. For example, the expression $a + 2b + b + 2a - 2(a + b)$ can be simplified to $a + b$.

Science may be described as the art of systematic over-simplification.

KARL POPPER Austrian philosopher of science. Remark, Aug 1982

simulation short for ◊computer simulation.

simultaneous equations in mathematics, one of two or more algebraic equations that contain two or more unknown quantities that may have a unique solution. For example, in the case of two linear equations with two unknown variables, such as (i) $x + 3y = 6$ and (ii) $3y - 2x = 4$, the solution will be those unique values of x and y that are valid for both equations. Linear simultaneous equations can be solved by using algebraic manipulation to eliminate one of the variables, ◊coordinate geometry, or matrices (see ◊matrix).

For example, by using algebra, both sides of equation (i) could be multiplied by 2, which gives $2x + 6y = 12$. This can be added to equation (ii) to get $9y = 16$, which is easily solved: $y = \frac{16}{9}$. The variable x can now be found by inserting the known y value into either original equation and solving for x. Another method is by plotting the equations on a graph, because the two equations represent straight lines in coordinate geometry and the coordinates of their point of intersection are the values of x and y that are true for both of them. A third method of solving linear simultaneous equations involves manipulating matrices. If the equations represent either two parallel lines or the same line, then there will be no solutions or an infinity of solutions respectively.

sine in trigonometry, a function of an angle in a right-angled triangle which is defined as the ratio of the length of the side opposite the angle to the length of the hypotenuse (the longest side).

Various properties in physics vary sinusoidally; that is, they can be represented diagrammatically by a sine wave (a graph obtained by plotting values of angles against the values of their sines). Examples include ◊simple harmonic motion, such as the way alternating current (AC) electricity varies with time.

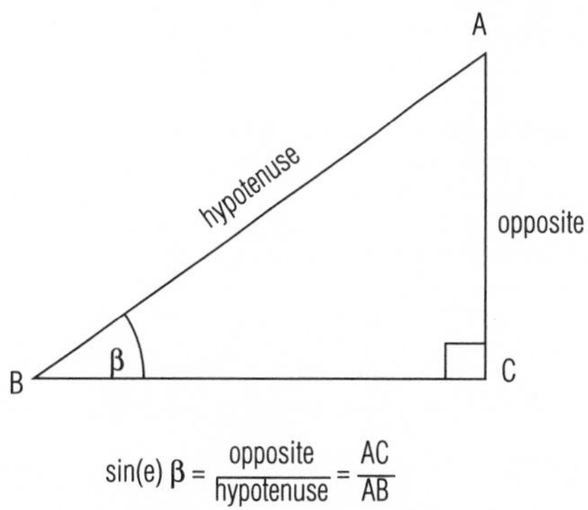

$$\sin(e)\ \beta = \frac{\text{opposite}}{\text{hypotenuse}} = \frac{AC}{AB}$$

sine *(left) The sine of an angle; (right) constructing a sine wave. The sine of an angle is a function used in the mathematical study of the triangle. If the sine of angle β is known, then the hypotenuse can be found given the length of the opposite side, or the opposite side can be found from the hypotenuse. Within a circle of unit radius (left), the height P_1A_1 equals the sine of angle P_1OA_1. This fact and the equalities below the circle allow a sine curve to be drawn, as on the right.*

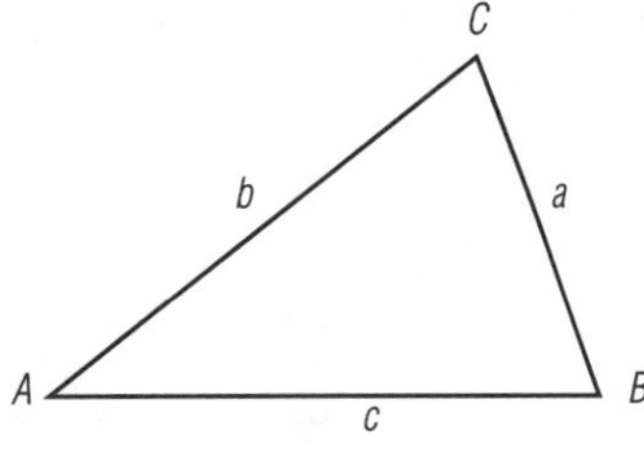

the sine rule states that

$$\frac{a}{\sin A} = \frac{b}{\sin B} = \frac{c}{\sin C}$$

or

$$\frac{\sin A}{a} = \frac{\sin B}{b} = \frac{\sin C}{c}$$

sine rule *The sine rule relates the sides and angles of a triangle, stating that the ratio of the length of each side and the sine of the angle opposite is constant.*

sine rule in trigonometry, a rule that relates the sides and angles of a triangle, stating that the ratio of the length of each side and the sine of the angle opposite is constant (twice the radius of the circumscribing circle). If the sides of a triangle are a, b, and c, and the angles opposite are A, B, and C, respectively, then the sine rule may be expressed as

$$a/\sin A = b/\sin B = c/\sin C.$$

Singer, Isaac Merrit
(1811–1875)

US inventor of domestic and industrial sewing machines. Within a few years of opening his first factory in 1851, he became the world's largest sewing-machine manufacturer (despite infringing the patent of Elias Howe), and by the late 1860s more than 100,000 Singer sewing machines were in use in the USA alone.

Single European Act 1986 update of the Treaty of Rome (signed in 1957) that provides a legal basis for action by the European Union in matters relating to the environment. The act requires that environmental protection shall be a part of all other Union policies. Also, it allows for agreement by a qualified majority on some legislation, whereas before such decisions had to be unanimous.

single-sideband transmission radio-wave transmission using either the frequency band above the carrier wave frequency, or below, instead of both (as now).

singularity in astrophysics, the point in ◊space-time at which the known laws of physics break down. Singularity is predicted to exist at the centre of a black hole, where infinite gravitational forces compress the infalling mass of a collapsing star to infinite density. It is also thought, according to the Big Bang model of the origin of the universe, to be the point from which the expansion of the universe began.

sinusitis painful inflammation of one of the sinuses, or air spaces, that surround the nasal passages. Most cases clear with antibiotics and nasal decongestants, but some require surgical drainage.

Sinusitis most frequently involves the maxillary sinuses, within the cheek bones, producing pain around the eyes, toothache, and a nasal discharge.

SIPC (abbreviation for ***simply interactive PC***) in computing, easy-to-use and cheaply-priced computer planned by ◊Microsoft, Intel, and Toshiba for release 1997. The SIPC will be sealed unit that can be connected to the telephone, television, hi-fi and other domestic electronic appliances.

siphon tube in the form of an inverted U with unequal arms. When it is filled with liquid and the shorter arm is placed in a tank or reservoir, liquid flows out of the longer arm provided that its exit is below the level of the surface of the liquid in the tank.

The liquid flows through the siphon because low pressure develops at the apex as liquid falls freely down the long arm. The difference between the pressure at the tank surface (atmospheric pressure) and the pressure at the apex causes liquid to rise in the short arm to replace that falling from the long arm.

siphonogamy plant reproduction in which a pollen tube grows to enable male gametes to pass to the ovary without leaving the protection of the plant.

Siphonogamous reproduction is found in all angiosperms and most gymnosperms, and has enabled these plants to reduce their dependency on wet conditions for reproduction, unlike the zoidogamous plants (see ◊zoidogamy).

Sirius or ***Dog Star*** or ***Alpha ◊Canis Majoris*** the brightest star in the night sky, 8.6 light years from Earth in the constellation Canis Major. Sirius is a white star with a mass 2.3 times that of the Sun, a diameter 1.8 times that of the Sun, and a luminosity of 23 Suns. It is orbited every 50 years by a ◊white dwarf, Sirius B, also known as the Pup.

Sirius is a double star with an orbital period of 50 years. Its eighth-magnitude companion is sometimes known as 'the Dark Companion' as it was first detected by Friedrich Bessel from its gravitational effect on the proper motion of Sirius. It was seen for the first time in 1862 but it was only in the 1920s that it was recognized as the first known example of a white dwarf.

sirocco hot, normally dry and dust-laden wind that blows from the deserts of N Africa across the Mediterranean into S Europe. It occurs mainly in the spring. The name 'sirocco' is also applied to any hot oppressive wind.

sisal strong fibre made from various species of ◊agave, such as *Agave sisalina*.

siskin North American finch *Carduelis pinus* with yellow markings or greenish-yellow bird *Carduelis spinus* about 12 cm/5 in long, found in Eurasia. They are members of the finch family Fringillidae, order Passeriformes.

sitatunga herbivorous antelope *Tragelaphus spekei* found in several swamp regions in Central Africa. Its hooves are long and splayed to help progress on soft surfaces. It grows to about 1.2 m/4 ft high at the shoulder; the male has thick horns up to 90 cm/3 ft long.

Males are dark greyish-brown, females and young are chestnut, all with whitish markings on the rather shaggy fur.

site location at which computers are used. If a company uses only ◊IBM computers, for example, it is known as an IBM site. The term is also used for a computer which acts as a ◊server for files that can be accessed via the ◊World Wide Web,also called a **Web site**.

site licence in computing, licence issued with commercial software entitling the purchaser to install the program on a fixed number of computers.

site of special scientific interest (SSSI) in the UK, land that has been identified as having animals, plants, or geological features that need to be protected and conserved. From 1991 these sites were designated and administered by English Nature, Scottish

Natural Heritage, and the Countryside Council for Wales.

Numbers fluctuate, but there were over 5,000 SSSIs in 1991, covering about 6% of Britain. Although SSSIs enjoy some legal protection, this does not in practice always prevent damage or destruction; during 1992, for example, 40% of SSSIs were damaged by development, farming, public access, and neglect. A report by English Nature estimated that a quarter of the total area of SSSIs, over 1 million acres, had been damaged by acid rain. Around 1% of SSSIs are irreparably damaged each year. In 1995–96 7% of Welsh SSSIs and 4.2% of English SSSIs experienced damage.

SI units (French ***Système International d'Unités***) standard system of scientific units used by scientists worldwide.

Originally proposed in 1960, it replaces the ◊m.k.s., ◊c.g.s., and ◊f.p.s. systems. It is based on seven basic units: the metre (m) for length, kilogram (kg) for mass, second (s) for time, ampere (A) for electrical current, kelvin (K) for temperature, mole (mol) for amount of substance, and candela (cd) for luminosity.

16-bit in computing, term describing the ability to process 16 ◊bits at a time. The Intel 286 series of microprocessors are examples of 16-bit processors.

The term is used slightly differently to specify the quality of the sound produced by ◊sound cards, where it refers to digital audio resolution; the quality of sound produced by a 16-bit sound card is roughly equivalent to that produced by a compact disc.

64-bit in computing, term describing the ability to process 64 ◊bits simultaneously. DEC's Alpha processor is the best known 64-bit chip. However, Intel and Hewlet-Packard are jointly developing new 32-bit and 64-bit processors, code-named Merced, that will be compatible with the 32-bit Pentium range.

Sizewell nuclear power station in Suffolk, eastern England, 3 km/ 2 mi east of Leiston. Sizewell A, a Magnox nuclear power station, came into operation in 1966. Sizewell B, Britain's first pressurized-water nuclear reactor (PWR) and among the most advanced nuclear power stations in the world, reached full load in June

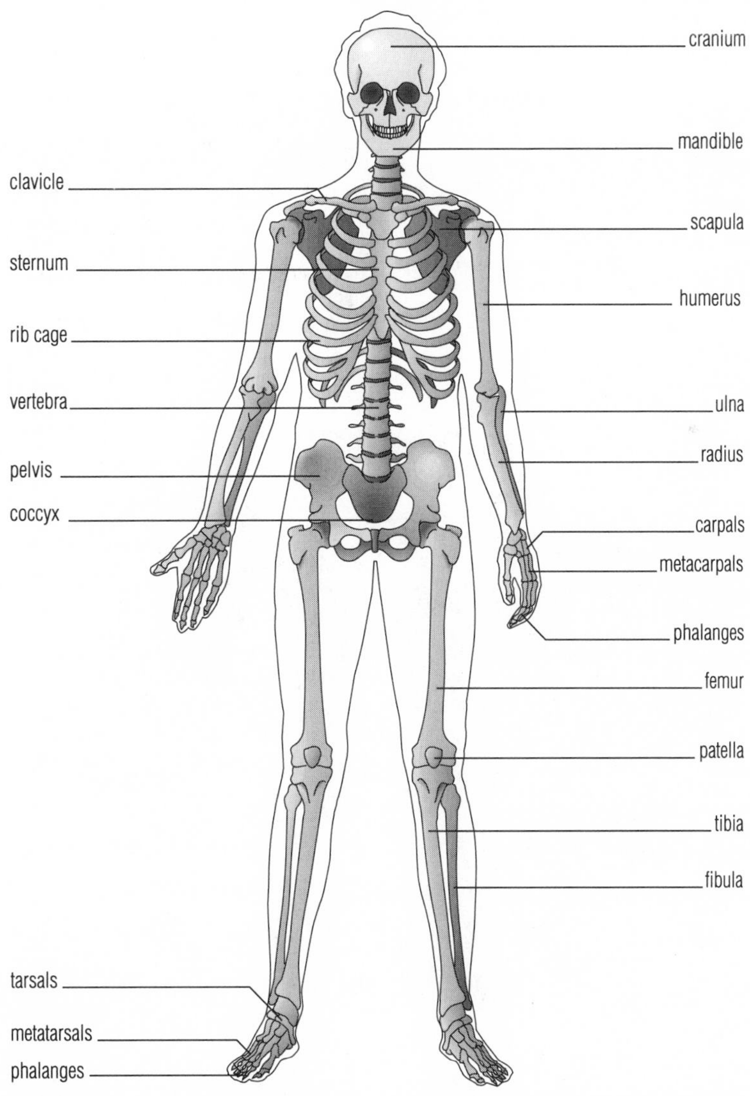

skeleton *The human skeleton is made up of 206 bones and provides a strong but flexible supportive framework for the body.*

1995. Plans to build Sizewell C were abandoned by the British government in December 1995.

Sizewell B has an electrical output of 1,188 MW. It cost £2,030 million to construct (in 1987).

skate any of several species of flatfish of the ray group. The common skate *Raja batis* is up to 1.8 m/6 ft long and greyish, with black specks. Its egg cases ('mermaids' purses') are often washed ashore by the tide.

skeleton the rigid or semirigid framework that supports and gives form to an animal's body, protects its internal organs, and provides anchorage points for its muscles. The skeleton may be composed of bone and cartilage (vertebrates), chitin (arthropods), calcium carbonate (molluscs and other invertebrates), or silica (many protists). The human skeleton is composed of 206 bones, with the ◊vertebral column (spine) forming the central supporting structure.

A skeleton may be internal, forming an ◊endoskeleton, or external, forming an ◊**exoskeleton**, as in the shells of insects or crabs. Another type of skeleton, found in invertebrates such as earthworms, is the hydrostatic skeleton. This gains partial rigidity from fluid enclosed within a body cavity. Because the fluid cannot be compressed, contraction of one part of the body results in extension of another part, giving peristaltic motion. See illustration on page 687.

skew distribution in statistics, a distribution in which frequencies are not balanced about the mean. For example, low wages are earned by a great number of people, while high wages are earned by very few. However, because the high wages can be very high they pull the average up the scale, making the average wage look unrepresentatively high.

skew lines straight lines that are not parallel and yet do not meet since they lie in a different plane. Every pair of skew lines has a minimum distance between them, which is the length of their common perpendicular.

skin the covering of the body of a vertebrate. In mammals, the outer layer (epidermis) is dead and its cells are constantly being rubbed away and replaced from below; it helps to protect the body from infection and to prevent dehydration. The lower layer (dermis) contains blood vessels, nerves, hair roots, and sweat and sebaceous glands, and is supported by a network of fibrous and elastic cells. The medical speciality concerned with skin diseases is called dermatology.

Skin grafting is the repair of injured skin by placing pieces of skin, taken from elsewhere on the body, over the injured area.

SKIN

Each person sheds an average of 18 kg/40lb of skin in a lifetime. The outer layer of skin – the epidermis – consists entirely of dead cells that fall off and are replaced by the level below.

skink lizard of the family Scincidae, a large family of about 700 species found throughout the tropics and subtropics. The body is usually long and the legs are reduced. Some skinks are legless and rather snakelike. Many are good burrowers, or can 'swim' through sand, like the **sandfish** genus *Scincus* of North Africa. Some skinks lay eggs, others bear live young.

Skinks include the **three-toed skink** *Chalcides chalcides* of S Europe and northwest Africa, up to 40 cm/16 in long, of which half is tail, and the **stump-tailed skink** *Tiliqua rugosa* of Australia, which stores fat in its triangular tail, looks the same at either end, and feeds on fruit as well as small animals. A new skink genus was identified in the rainforest of the Philippine Islands and described

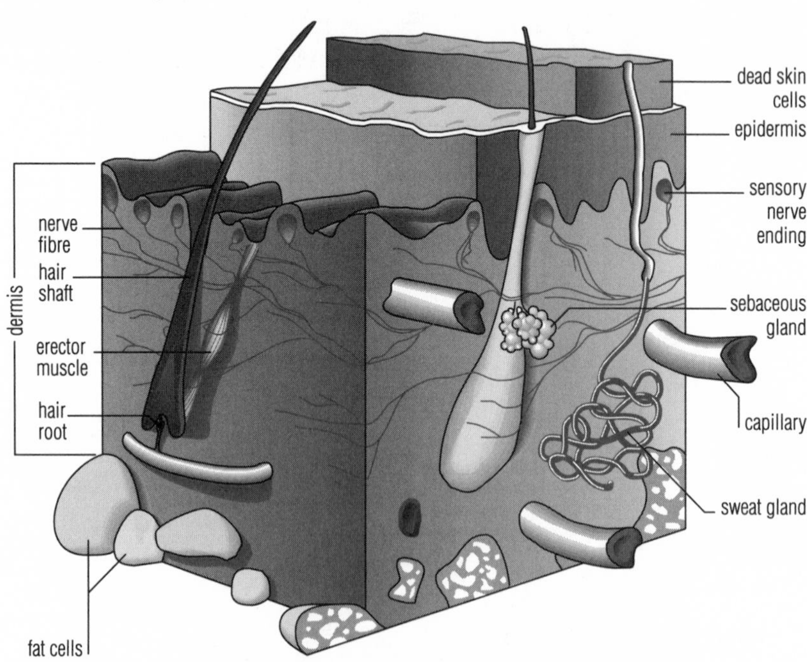

skin The skin is composed of two layers: the epidermis, a layer of dead cells; and the living dermis. The skin of an adult man covers about 1.9 sq m/20 sq ft; a woman's skin covers about 1.6 sq m/17 sq ft.

in 1997. There are two species of **moist forest skink** *Parvoscinus*. They lack external ear openings and females have only one oviduct and lay a single egg.

skua dark-coloured gull-like seabird, living in Arctic and Antarctic waters. Skuas can grow up to 60 cm/2 ft long, with long, well-developed wings and short, stout legs; in colour they are greyish above and white below. They are aggressive scavengers, and seldom fish for themselves but force gulls to disgorge their catch, and also eat chicks of other birds. Skuas are in the family Stercorariidae, order Charadriiformes.

The largest species is the **great skua** *Stercorarius skua* of the N Atlantic, 60 cm/2 ft long and dark brown on the upper parts.

Antarctic skuas *Catharacta antarctica* nest near the penguin colonies they feed on, and are as agressive in defending their own nests as they are in defending their local penguin colony from other predators. They fly north during the Antarctic winter.

skull in vertebrates, the collection of flat and irregularly shaped bones (or cartilage) that enclose the brain and the organs of sight, hearing, and smell, and provide support for the jaws. In most mammals, the skull consists of 22 bones joined by fibrous immobile joints called sutures. The floor of the skull is pierced by a large hole (*foramen magnum*) for the spinal cord and a number of smaller apertures through which other nerves and blood vessels pass.

The skull comprises the cranium (brain case) and the bones of the face, which include the upper jaw, enclosing the sinuses, and form the framework for the nose, eyes, and the roof of the mouth cavity. The lower jaw is hinged to the middle of the skull at its lower edge. The opening to the middle ear is located near the jaw hinge. The plate at the back of the head is jointed at its lower edge with the upper section of the spine. Inside, the skull has various shallow cavities into which fit different parts of the brain.

TO REMEMBER THE BONES OF THE SKULL:

OLD PEOPLE FROM TEXAS EAT SPIDERS

OCCIPITAL, PARIETAL, FRONTAL, TEMPORAL, EPHNOID, SPHENOID

skunk North American mammal of the weasel family. The common skunk *Mephitis mephitis* has a long, arched body, short legs, a bushy tail, and black fur with white streaks on the back. In self-defence, it discharges a foul-smelling fluid.

SKUNK AND OPOSSUM PAGE

http://elvis.neep.wisc.edu/~firmiss/mephitis-didelphis.html

Lively site providing all the information you could possibly want about skunks and opossums – photos, a guide to identifying their tracks, common misconceptions, advice on keeping them as pets, stories featuring the animals, and even a recipe!

skunk cabbage either of two disagreeably smelling North American plants of the arum family Araceae: *Symplocarpus foetidus*, of the E, growing in wet soils and having large, cabbage-like leaves and a fleshy blunt spike of tiny flowers in a purple, hooded sheath; or *Lysichiton americanum* of the W, having similar appearance except that the sheath enclosing a more elongated flower spike is yellow.

Skye terrier breed of short-legged ◊terrier from the island of Skye and adjoining areas of Scotland, bred originally as a killer of rodents. Its long, thick coat may be black, grey, fawn, or cream. It is about 25 cm/10 in at the shoulder and its body is long in proportion.

Skylab US space station, launched 14 May 1973, made from the adapted upper stage of a Saturn V rocket. At 75 tonnes/82.5 tons, it was the heaviest object ever put into space, and was 25.6 m/84 ft long. *Skylab* contained a workshop for carrying out experiments in weightlessness, an observatory for monitoring the Sun, and cameras for photographing the Earth's surface.

Damaged during launch, it had to be repaired by the first crew of astronauts. Three crews, each of three astronauts, occupied *Skylab* for periods of up to 84 days, at that time a record duration

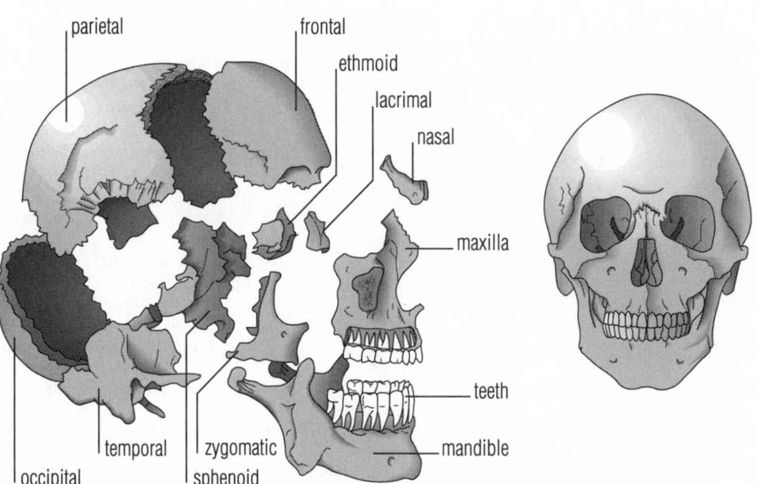

skull *The skull is a protective box for the brain, eyes, and hearing organs. It is also a framework for the teeth and flesh of the face. The cranium has eight bones: occipital, two temporal, two parietal, frontal, sphenoid, and ethmoid. The face has 14 bones, the main ones being two maxillae, two nasal, two zygoma, two lacrimal, and the mandible.*

for human spaceflight. *Skylab* finally fell to Earth on 11 July 1979, dropping debris on Western Australia.

PROJECT SKYLAB

http://www.ksc.nasa.gov/history/skylab/skylab.html

Official NASA archive of the project that launched the USA's first experimental space station. There are comprehensive details (technical and of general interest) on all the experiments included in the project. There is also a selection of photos and videos and a search engine

skylark a type of ◊lark.

slag in chemistry, the molten mass of impurities that is produced in the smelting or refining of metals.

The slag produced in the manufacture of iron in a ◊blast furnace floats on the surface above the molten iron. It contains mostly silicates, phosphates, and sulphates of calcium. When cooled, the solid is broken up and used as a core material in the foundations of roads and buildings.

slaked lime $Ca(OH)_2$ (technical name ***calcium hydroxide***) substance produced by adding water to quicklime (calcium oxide, CaO). Much heat is given out and the solid crumbles as it absorbs water. A solution of slaked lime is called ◊limewater.

slash and burn simple agricultural method whereby natural vegetation is cut and burned, and the clearing then farmed for a few years until the soil loses its fertility, whereupon farmers move on and leave the area to regrow. Although this is possible with a small, widely dispersed population, it becomes unsustainable with more people and is now a cause of ◊deforestation.

slate fine-grained, usually grey metamorphic rock that splits readily into thin slabs along its ◊cleavage planes. It is the metamorphic equivalent of ◊shale.

Slate is highly resistant to atmospheric conditions and can be used for writing on with chalk (actually gypsum). Quarrying slate takes such skill and time that it is now seldom used for roof and sill material except in restoring historic buildings.

sleep state of natural unconsciousness and activity that occurs at regular intervals in most mammals and birds, though there is considerable variation in the amount of time spent sleeping. Sleep differs from hibernation in that it occurs daily rather than seasonally, and involves less drastic reductions in metabolism. The function of sleep is unclear. People deprived of sleep become irritable, uncoordinated, forgetful, hallucinatory, and even psychotic.

In humans, sleep is linked with hormone levels and specific brain electrical activity, including delta waves, quite different from the brain's waking activity. REM (rapid eye movement) phases, associated with dreams, occur at regular intervals during sleep, when the eyes move rapidly beneath closed lids.

SLEEP

The koala sleeps on average 22 hours a day. It is the only animal more slothful than the sloth, which sleeps only 20 hours a day. Some say that the koala's diet of eucalyptus leaves means that it is in an almost permanently drugged sleep.

sleeping pill any ◊sedative that induces sleep; in small doses, such drugs may relieve anxiety.

sleeping sickness infectious disease of tropical Africa, a form of ◊trypanosomiasis. Early symptoms include fever, headache, and chills, followed by ◊anaemia and joint pains. Later, the disease attacks the central nervous system, causing drowsiness, lethargy, and, if left untreated, death. Sleeping sickness is caused by either of two trypanosomes, *Trypanosoma gambiense* or *T. rhodesiense*. Control is by eradication of the tsetse fly, which transmits the disease to humans.

Sleeping sickness in cattle is called nagana.

slide rule mathematical instrument with pairs of logarithmic sliding scales, used for rapid calculations, including multiplication, division, and the extraction of square roots. It has been largely superseded by the electronic calculator.

It was invented in 1622 by the English mathematician William Oughtred. A later version was devised by the French army officer Amédée Mannheim (1831–1906).

slide show in computing ◊presentation graphics programs, facility to display a presentation electronically instead of outputting it onto film or paper. The program displays the images ('slides') using the computer's full screen or an overhead projector. Slide shows are a versatile display method: presenters can customize timings to suit what they have to say and incorporate sound and movies into their presentations.

slime mould or ***myxomycete*** extraordinary organism that shows some features of ◊fungus and some of ◊protozoa. Slime moulds are not closely related to any other group, although they are often classed, for convenience, with the fungi. There are two kinds, cellular slime moulds and plasmodial slime moulds, differing in their complex life cycles.

Cellular slime moulds go through a phase of living as single cells, looking like amoebae, and feed by engulfing the bacteria found in rotting wood, dung, or damp soil. When a food supply is exhausted, up to 100,000 of these amoebae form into a colony resembling a single sluglike animal and migrate to a fresh source of bacteria. The colony then takes on the aspect of a fungus, and forms long-stalked fruiting bodies which release spores. These germinate to release amoebae, which repeat the life cycle.

Plasmodial slime moulds have a more complex life cycle involving sexual reproduction. They form a slimy mass of protoplasm with no internal cell walls, which slowly spreads over the bark or branches of trees.

SLIME MOULD

Single-celled slime moulds can clump together to form a multicellular organism when times get tough. If food is becoming scarce, the unicellular slime mould releases a chemical to attract others. As they group together, they begin to produce spores that can then be dispersed to more fruitful areas.

SLIP (abbreviation for ***serial line Internet protocol***) in computing, the older of two standard methods for connecting a computer to the Internet via a modem and telephone line. Unlike PPP (Point-to-Point Protocol), a SLIP connection needs to have its ◊IP address reset every time it is used, and offers no ◊error detection.

sloe fruit of the ◊blackthorn bush.

slope another name for ◊gradient.

sloth slow-moving South American mammal, about 70 cm/2.5 ft long, family Bradypodidae, order Edentata. Sloths are greyish brown and have small rounded heads, rudimentary tails, and prolonged forelimbs. Each foot has long curved claws adapted to clinging upside down from trees. On the ground the animals cannot walk, but drag themselves along. They are vegetarian.

The hair is brown, long, coarse and shaggy. An alga lives in it, and in damp weather turns the hair green, which helps the animal to blend in with its leafy background. Sloths are nocturnal animals. They usually live alone in the treetops, eating leaves. They give birth to one young at a time, which spends its first few weeks clinging to its mother's hair.

slow-worm harmless species of lizard *Anguis fragilis,* once common in Europe, now a protected species in Britain. Superficially resembling a snake, it is distinguished by its small mouth and movable eyelids. It is about 30 cm/1 ft long, and eats worms and slugs.

SLR (abbreviation for ***single-lens reflex***) a type of ◊camera in which the image can be seen through the lens before a picture is taken. A small mirror directs light entering the lens to the viewfinder.

When a picture is taken the mirror moves rapidly aside to allow the light to reach the film. The SLR allows different lenses, such as close-up or zoom lenses, to be used because the photographer can see exactly what is being focused on.

slug obsolete unit of mass, equal to 14.6 kg/32.17 lb. It is the mass that will have an acceleration of one foot per second when under a force of one pound weight.

slug soft-bodied land-living gastropod (type of ◊mollusc) related to the snails, but without a shell, or with a much reduced shell. All slugs have a protective coat of slime and a distinctive head with protruding tentacles. The eyes are at the end of the tentacles, which are also used to smell and locate food. Slugs eat dead animal matter and plants; some species are carnivorous and eat other slugs, snails, and earthworms. Slugs are hermaphrodite (having both male and female organs). They can fertilize themselves, but usually mate with another. Slugs can live for up to three years, and are invertebrates (animals without backbones).
behaviour Water can quickly be lost from the slug's body, so, to prevent drying out, slugs normally come out to feed only at night or when it is wet. During dry weather they shelter in crevices, hide under rocks or go underground. The slug moves by gliding its flattened body (foot) over the ground, leaving a slimy mucus trail.
types of slug Land slugs belong to two groups, the roundbacks and the keeled slugs. Roundbacks, such as the slugs found in gardens, are usually about 2–3cm/0.7–1 in long and have soft fleshy sausage-shaped bodies. Keeled slugs, such as the great grey slug, are usually longer, growing up to 20 cm/6.4 in long, and they have a ridge or keel along their backs.
classification Slugs belong to the animal phylum Mollusca (molluscs), class Gastropoda (slugs and snails). There are over 40,000 species of gastropod and most land and freshwater slugs belong to a group called the pulmonates. The great number of land species include the common garden slug (*Arion hortensis*) and the great grey slug (*Limax maximus*).

slurry form of manure composed mainly of liquids. Slurry is collected and stored on many farms, especially when large numbers of animals are kept in factory units (see ◊factory farming). When slurry tanks are accidentally or deliberately breached, large amounts can spill into rivers, killing fish and causing ◊eutrophication. Some slurry is spread on fields as a fertilizer.

smack slang term for ◊heroin, an addictive depressant drug.

small arms one of the two main divisions of firearms: guns that can be carried by hand. The first small arms were portable handguns in use in the late 14th century, supported on the ground and ignited by hand. Today's small arms range from breech-loading single-shot rifles and shotguns to sophisticated automatic and semiautomatic weapons. In 1990, 10,567 people were killed by handguns in the USA, compared with 91 in Switzerland, 87 in Japan, 68 in Canada, and 13 in Sweden. From 1988 guns accounted for more deaths among teenage US males than all other causes put together.

The matchlock, which evolved during the 15th century, used a match of tow and saltpetre gripped by an S-shaped lever, which was rocked towards the touch hole with one finger, enabling the gun to be held, aimed, and fired in much the same way as today. Front and back sights, followed by a curved stock that could be held against the shoulder (in the hackbut or Hookgun), gave increased precision. The difficulty of keeping a match alight in wet weather was overcome by the introduction of the wheel lock, in about 1515, in which a shower of sparks was produced by a spring-drawn steel wheel struck by iron pyrites. This cumbersome and expensive mechanism evolved into the simpler flintlock in about 1625, operated by flint striking steel and in general use for 200 years until a dramatic advance, the 'percussion cap', invented in 1810 by a sport-loving Scottish cleric, Alexander Forsyth (1769–1843), removed the need for external igniters. From then on, weapons were fired by a small explosive detonator placed behind or within the base of the bullet, struck by a built-in hammer.

The principles of rifling, breech-loading, and the repeater, although known since the 16th century, were not successfully exploited until the 19th century. It was known that imparting a spin made the bullet's flight truer, but the difficulty of making the bullet bite the grooves had until then prevented the use of rifling. The Baker rifle, issued to the British Rifle Brigade in 1800, was loaded from the front of the barrel (muzzle) and had a mallet for hammering the bullets into the grooves. The first breechloader was von Dreyse's 'needle gun', issued to the Prussian army in 1842, in which the detonator was incorporated with the cartridge. By 1870 breech-loading was in general use, being quicker, and sweeping the barrel out after each firing. An early rifle with bolt action was the Lee-Metford of 1888, followed by the Lee-Enfield, both having a magazine beneath the breech, containing a number of cartridges. A modified model is still used by the British army. US developments favoured the repeater (such as the Winchester) in which the fired case was extracted and ejected, the hammer cocked, and a new charge inserted into the chamber, all by one reciprocation of a finger lever. In the semiautomatic, part of the explosion energy performs the same operations: the Garand, long used by the US army, is of this type. Completely automatic weapons were adopted during World War II. Improvements since then have concentrated on making weapons lighter and faster-firing, as with the M-16, extensively used by US troops in the Vietnam War.

SMALLPOX

http://www.outbreak.org/cgi-unreg/dynaserve.exe/Smallpox.html

Story of the eradication of the smallpox virus. The Web site covers the eradication program from its earliest stages to the final destruction of the virus, described by the WHO as 'Man's greatest achievement'. A photograph of the virus is included on the Web site via a hypertext link, and an interview with John Scott Porterfield, one of the workers responsible for the virus' destruction, is also available here.

smallpox acute, highly contagious viral disease, marked by aches, fever, vomiting, and skin eruptions leaving pitted scars. Widespread vaccination programmes have eradicated this often fatal disease.

It was endemic in Europe until the development of vaccination by Edward ◊Jenner about 1800, and remained so in Asia, where a virulent form of the disease (variola major) entailed a fatality rate of 30% until the World Health Organization (WHO) campaign from 1967, which resulted in its virtual eradication by 1980. The campaign was estimated to have cost $300 million/£200 million, and was the organization's biggest health success to date.

The deviation of man from the state in which he was originally placed by nature seems to have proved him to be a prolific source of diseases.

Edward Jenner English physician.
An Inquiry into the Causes and Effects of the Variolae Vaccinae, or Cow-pox

Smalltalk the first high-level programming language used in ◊object-oriented applications.

smart in computing, term for any piece of equipment that works with the help of a microprocessor: a 'smart' carburetter, for example, maintains the correct proportion of air-to-petrol vapour in a car engine by electronically monitoring engine temperature, acceleration, and other variables. Designers are incorporating smart technology into an increasing range of products, such as smart toasters, which can prevent toast from burning. Smart furniture, such as chairs with cushions that adjust themselves according the size and weight of the person sitting in them, is a typical area of current research.

Architects are already making smart buildings, especially large office blocks and hospitals. Such buildings are wired with sensors to monitor heating, lighting, and air quality. A central computer automatically performs simple tasks such as turning lights out when there is nobody in a room, adjusting air conditioning and even darkening photoelectric windows to counteract bright sunlight.

smart card plastic card with an embedded microprocessor and memory. It can store, for example, personal data, identification, and bank-account details, to enable it to be used as a credit or debit card. The card can be loaded with credits, which are then spent electronically, and reloaded as needed. Possible other uses range from hotel door 'keys' to passports.

The smart card was invented by French journalist Juan Moreno in 1974. It is expected that by the year 2000 it will be possible to make cards with as much computing power as the leading personal computers of 1990.

smart drug any drug or combination of nutrients (vitamins, amino acids, minerals, and sometimes herbs) said to enhance the functioning of the brain, increase mental energy, lengthen the span of attention, and improve the memory. As yet there is no scientific evidence to suggest that these drugs have any significant effect on healthy people.

Some smart drugs consist of food additives which are precursors of the neurotransmitter ◊acetylcholine. Most, however, are experimental drugs devised by pharmaceutical companies to treat aspects of dementia, in particular, memory loss. The description is also applied to existing drugs claimed to improve mental performance but which are legally prescribed for other purposes. These include beta-blockers (prescribed for some heart disease), phenytoin (epilepsy), and L-dopa (Parkinson's disease).

smart fluid or ***electrorheological fluid*** liquid suspension that solidifies to form a jellylike solid when a high-voltage electric field is applied across it and that returns to the liquid state when the field is removed. Most smart fluids are ◊zeolites or metals coated with polymers or oxides.

SMELL

The great white shark is so sensitive to the smell of blood that it can detect a single drop in 4,600,000 litres of water. Two-thirds of the shark's brain governs sense of smell.

smell sense that responds to chemical molecules in the air. It works by having receptors for particular chemical groups, into which the airborne chemicals must fit to trigger a message to the brain.

A sense of smell is used to detect food and to communicate with other animals (see ◊pheromone and ◊scent gland). Humans can distinguish between about 10,000 different smells. Aquatic animals can sense chemicals in water, but whether this sense should be described as 'smell' or 'taste' is debatable. See also ◊nose.

MYSTERY OF SMELL

http://www.hhmi.org/senses/d/d110.htm

As part of a much larger site called 'Seeing, Hearing, and Smelling the World', here is a page examining the way our sense of smell works. It is divided into four sections called 'the vivid world of odours', 'finding the odourant receptors', 'how rats and mice – and probably humans – recognize odours', and 'the memory of smells'. This site makes good use of images and animations to help with the explanations, so it is best viewed with an up-to-date browser.

smelling salts or ***sal volatile*** a mixture of ammonium carbonate, bicarbonate, and carbamate together with other strong-smelling substances, formerly used as a restorative for dizziness or fainting.

smelt small fish, usually marine, although some species are freshwater.

They occur in Europe and North America. The most common European smelt is the sparling *Osmerus eperlanus*.

smelting processing a metallic ore in a furnace to produce the metal. Oxide ores such as iron ore are smelted with coke (carbon), which reduces the ore into metal and also provides fuel for the process.

A substance such as limestone is often added during smelting to facilitate the melting process and to form a slag, which dissolves many of the impurities present.

smiley alternative term for ◊emoticon, named after the original smiling face :-).

Smithsonian Institution academic organization in Washington DC, USA, founded in 1846 with money left by British chemist and mineralogist James Smithson. The Smithsonian Institution, 'an establishment for the increase and diffusion of knowledge', undertakes scientific research but is also the parent organization of a collection of museums.

The Smithsonian Institution's second curator, the naturalist Spencer Baird (1823–87), at the expense of research, increased funds for collection and exploration, thereby securing its role as a leading museum.

smog natural fog containing impurities, mainly nitrogen oxides (NO_x) and volatile organic compounds (VOCs) from domestic fires, industrial furnaces, certain power stations, and internal-combustion engines (petrol or diesel). It can cause substantial illness and loss of life, particularly among chronic bronchitics, and damage to wildlife.

photochemical smog is mainly prevalent in the summer as it is caused by chemical reaction between strong sunlight and vehicle exhaust fumes. Such smogs create a build-up of ozone and nitrogen oxides which cause adverse symptoms, including coughing and eye irritation, and in extreme cases can kill.

The London smog of 1952 lasted for five days and killed more than 4,000 people from heart and lung diseases. The use of smokeless fuels, the treatment of effluent, and penalties for excessive smoke from poorly maintained and operated vehicles can be effective in reducing smog but it still occurs in many cities throughout the world.

smokeless fuel fuel that does not give off any smoke when burned, because all the carbon is fully oxidized to carbon dioxide (CO_2). Natural gas, oil, and coke are smokeless fuels.

smoking method of preserving fresh oily meats (such as pork and goose) or fish (such as herring and salmon). Before being smoked, the food is first salted or soaked in brine, then hung to dry. Meat is hot-smoked over a fast-burning wood fire, which is covered with sawdust, producing thick smoke and partly cooking the meat. Fish may be hot-smoked or cold-smoked over a slow-burning wood fire, which does not cook it. Modern refrigeration techniques mean that food does not need to be smoked to help it keep, so factory-smoked foods tend to be smoked just enough to give them a smoky flavour, with colours added to give them the appearance of traditionally smoked food.

smoking inhaling the fumes from burning substances, generally ◊tobacco in the form of cigarettes. The practice is habit-forming and is dangerous to health, since carbon monoxide and other toxic materials result from the combustion process. A direct link between lung cancer and tobacco smoking was established in 1950; the habit is also linked to respiratory and coronary heart diseases. In the West, smoking is now forbidden in many public places because even **passive smoking** – breathing in fumes from other people's cigarettes – can be harmful.

smooth collie breed of dog. See ◊rough collie.

smoothing capacitor large electronic ◊capacitor connected across the output of a rectifier circuit that has the effect of smoothing out the voltage variations to give a nearly steady DC voltage supply.

The voltage and current output from a rectifier circuit fitted with a smoothing capacitor is similar to that provided by a battery.

smooth muscle involuntary muscle capable of slow contraction over a period of time. It is present in hollow organs, such as the intestines, stomach, bladder, and blood vessels. Its presence in the wall of the alimentary canal allows slow rhythmic movements known as ◊peristalsis, which cause food to be mixed and forced along the gut. Smooth muscle has a microscopic structure distinct from other forms.

smooth snake common nonvenomous snake found in southern and central Europe It grows to a length of 60 cm/24 in, and it is brownish-red or grey in colour, with dark-brown spots along its back. It is ovoviviparous, producing live young that free themselves from their shells immediately.
classification The smooth snake *Coronella austriaca* is in family Colubridae, suborder Serpentes, order Squamata, class Reptilia.

SMPTE (abbreviation for the ***Society of Motion Picture and Television Engineers***) US organization founded 1916 to advance the theory and application of motion-imaging technology including film, television, video, computer imaging, and telecommunications.

The SMPTE has 8,500 members in 72 countries, including engineers, executives, technical directors, camerapeople, editors, and consultants. It is based in White Plains, New York.

SMTP (abbreviation for ***simple mail transfer protocol***) in computing, the basic protocol for transferring electronic mail between computers. SMTP is an agreed procedure for identifying the ◊host, sending and receiving data and checking e-mail addresses.

smut in botany, any of a group of parasitic fungi (see ◊fungus) that infect flowering plants, particularly cereal grasses. (Order Ustilaginales.)

SNA abbreviation for IBM's ◊Systems Network Architecture.

snail air-breathing gastropod mollusc with a spiral shell. There are thousands of species, on land and in water. The typical snails of the genus *Helix* have two species in Europe. The common garden snail *H. aspersa* is very destructive to plants.

snail mail in the computing community, nickname for the conventional postal service. E-mail can deliver messages within minutes while conventional postal services take at least a day. One's postal address is therefore a 'snail mail address'.

snake reptile of the suborder Serpentes of the order Squamata, which also includes lizards. Snakes are characterized by an elongated limbless body, possibly evolved because of subterranean ancestors. However, a team of US and Israeli palaeontologists rediscovered a fossil collection in 1996 which suggested that snakes evolved from sea-dwelling predators.

One of the striking internal modifications is the absence or greatly reduced size of the left lung. The skin is covered in scales, which are markedly wider underneath where they form. There are 3,000 species found in the tropical and temperate zones, but none in New Zealand, Ireland, Iceland, and near the poles. Only three species are found in Britain: the adder, smooth snake, and grass snake.
locomotion In all except a few species, scales are an essential aid to locomotion. A snake is helpless on glass where scales can effect no 'grip' on the surface; progression may be undulant, 'concertina', or creeping, or a combination of these.
senses Detailed vision is limited at a distance, though movement is immediately seen; hearing is restricted to ground vibrations (sound waves are not perceived); the sense of touch is acute; besides the sense of smell through the nasal passages, the flickering tongue picks up airborne particles which are then passed to special organs in the mouth for investigation; and some (rattlesnakes) have a cavity between eye and nostril which is sensitive to infrared rays (useful in locating warm-blooded prey in the dark).
reproduction Some are oviparous and others ovoviviparous, that is, the eggs are retained in the oviducts until development is complete; in both cases the young are immediately self-sufficient.
species The majority of snakes belong to the Colubridae, chiefly harmless, such as the common grass snake of Europe, but including the deadly African boomslang *Dispholidus typus*. The venomous families include the Elapidae, comprising the true ◊cobras, the New World coral snakes, and the Australian taipan, copperhead, and death adder; the Viperidae (see ◊viper); and the Hydrophiidae, aquatic sea-snakes.

Among the more primitive snakes are the Boidae, which still show links with the lizards and include the boa constrictor, anaconda, and python. These kill by constriction but their victims are usually comparatively small animals.

All snakes are carnivorous, and often camouflaged for better concealment in hunting as well as for their own protection.
treatment of snakebite The serums used to treat snakebites are called antivenins. Antivenins are produced by injecting animals (horses and sheep are used) with venom, extracting their blood, now containing antibodies to the venom, and removing the red blood cells. However, in addition to the desired venom antibodies, many other antibodies and proteins are contained within the serum. These often cause 'serum sickness' in the patient, as a result of a severe allergenic reaction.

As antivenins are expensive to prepare and store, and specific to one snake species, experiments have been carried out using more widely valid treatments, for example, trypsin, a powerful protein-degrading enzyme, effective against the cobra/mamba group.

In 1993 Japanese and Brazilian researchers independently identified a protein in the blood of a venomous snake that neutralizes its own venom. In laboratory tests in Australia, this protein, named *Notechis scutatus* inhibitor (NSI) after the tiger snake from the whose blood it was isolated, was effective against the venom of six other snakes.

SNAKES AND OTHER SLITHERING THINGS

http://fovea.retina.net/~gecko/herps/snakes/

Guide to different snakes and tips on keeping them as pets. Emergency guidelines in case of being bitten by a snake are given, and light relief is provided in the form of an ode to snakes.

snake fly elongate insect found in wooded regions, among flowers or tree-trunks. More than 80 species are known.

The adult insects have an unusually long prothorax (region immediately behind the head) which forms a kind of 'neck' and the entire body is elongate, ending in a drawn out slender egg-laying apparatus (ovipositor), hence their name. The female inserts the eggs, with its long ovipositor, into slits in the bark of trees, especially of conifers. The larva forages under the loose bark, preying on soft-bodied insects.
classification The snake fly is in family Raphidiidae, in suborder Megaloptera of order Neuroptera, class Insecta, phylum Arthropoda.

snapdragon perennial ◊herbaceous plant belonging to the figwort family, with spikes of brightly coloured two-lipped flowers. (*Antirrhinum majus,* family Scrophulariaceae.)

snapper one of a number of tropical, carnivorous fish, about 60 cm/24 in or more in length. Many are red, but the species come in many colours. They are valuable edible fishes, especially the red snapper *Lutjanus blackfordi.*
classification Snappers are in the family Lutjanidae of order Perciformes, class Osteichthyes.

snellen unit expressing the visual power of the eye.

Snell's law of refraction in optics, the rule that when a ray of light passes from one medium to another, the sine of the angle of incidence divided by the sine of the angle of refraction is equal to the ratio of the indices of refraction in the two media. For a ray passing from medium 1 to medium 2:by $\frac{n_2}{n_1} = \frac{\sin i}{\sin r}$ where n_1 and n_2 are the refractive indices of the two media. The law was devised by the Dutch physicist Willebrord Snell.

sniffer in computing, software tool that analyses the transport data attached to ◊packets sent across a network, used to monitor the network's efficiency and level of usage. Hackers (see ◊hacking) also use sniffers to collect people's passwords for ◊Telnet connections.

snipe marsh bird of the family Scolopacidae, order Charadriiformes closely related to the ◊woodcock. Snipes use their long, straight bills to probe marshy ground for worms, insects, and molluscs. Their nests are made on the grass, and they lay four eggs.

The cry of the birds resembles the sound 'scape-scape', and during the breeding season they make a peculiar drumming or bleating noise in their downward flight. A gamebird, the snipe has a swift and darting flight, making it a difficult target.

SNMP (abbreviation for ***Simple Network Management Protocol***) in computing, agreed method of managing a computer network. SNMP governs the overall structure of the Internet, in particular its arrangement around ◊hubs and ◊nodes.

snook or ***robalo*** or ***sea pike*** US bony fish found in coastal and brackish waters. They can reach up to 1.4 m/4.6 ft and feed mainly on fish and crustaceans.
classification The snook *Centropomus undecimalis* is in the family Serranidae, order Perciformes and so is closely related to the perches.

snoring loud noise during sleep made by vibration of the soft palate (the rear part of the roof of the mouth), caused by streams of air entering the nose and mouth at the same time. It is most common when the nose is partially blocked.

Sleep apnoea causes loud snoring that wakes the sufferer repeatedly throughout the night, causing chronic tiredness.

snowdrop small bulbous European plant; its white bell-shaped hanging flowers, tinged with green, are among the first to appear in early spring. (*Galanthus nivalis,* family Amaryllidaceae.)

snow gum small to medium eucalypt growing at high altitudes in Australia with white smooth bark and open habit, especially *Eucalyptus pauciflora.*

snow leopard a type of ◊leopard.

SNR (abbreviation for ***supernova remnant***) in astronomy, the glowing remains of a star that has been destroyed in a◊ supernova explosion. The brightest and most famous example is the ◊Crab Nebula.

soap mixture of the sodium salts of various ◊fatty acids: palmitic, stearic, and oleic acid. It is made by the action of sodium hydroxide (caustic soda) or potassium hydroxide (caustic potash) on fats of animal or vegetable origin. Soap makes grease and dirt disperse in water in a similar manner to a ◊detergent.

Soap was mentioned by Galen in the 2nd century for washing the body, although the Romans seem to have washed with a mixture of sand and oil. Soap was manufactured in Britain from the 14th century, but better-quality soap was imported from Castile or Venice. The Soapmakers' Company, London, was incorporated in 1638. Soap was taxed in England from the time of Cromwell in the 17th century to 1853.

soapstone compact, massive form of impure ◊talc.

social behaviour in zoology, behaviour concerned with altering the behaviour of other individuals of the same species. Social behaviour allows animals to live harmoniously in groups by establishing hierarchies of dominance to discourage disabling fighting. It may be aggressive or submissive (for example, cowering and other signals of appeasement), or designed to establish bonds (such as social grooming or preening).

The social behaviour of mammals and birds is generally more complex than that of lower organisms, and involves relationships with individually recognized animals. Thus, courtship displays allow individuals to choose appropriate mates and form the bonds necessary for successful reproduction. In the social systems of bees, wasps, ants, and termites, an individual's status and relationships with others are largely determined by its biological form, as a member of a caste of workers, soldiers, or reproductives; see ◊eusociality.

It is his ability to communicate with his fellows and train his offspring that has probably been the chief agency in the rapid social evolution of man.

THOMAS HUNT MORGAN US geneticist.
The Scientific Basis of Evolution 1932

---

sociobiology study of the biological basis of all social behaviour, including the application of ◊population genetics to the evolution of behaviour. It builds on the concept of ◊inclusive fitness, contained in the notion of the 'selfish gene'. Contrary to some popular interpretations, it does not assume that all behaviour is genetically determined.

socket in computing, mechanism for creating a connection to an application on another computer. A socket combines an ◊IP address (denoting the host computer on a network) with a port number describing the application (perhaps ◊FTP or ◊SMTP) the user requires.

soda ash former name for ◊sodium carbonate.

soda lime powdery mixture of calcium hydroxide and sodium hydroxide or potassium hydroxide, used in medicine and as a drying agent.

sodium soft, waxlike, silver-white, metallic element, symbol Na (from Latin *natrium*), atomic number 11, relative atomic mass 22.989. It is one of the ◊alkali metals and has a very low density, being light enough to float on water. It is the sixth-most abundant element (the fourth-most abundant metal) in the Earth's crust. Sodium is highly reactive, oxidizing rapidly when exposed to air and reacting violently with water. Its most familiar compound is sodium chloride (common salt), which occurs naturally in the oceans and in salt deposits left by dried-up ancient seas.

Sir Humphrey Davy detested gravy. He lived in the odium of having discovered Sodium.

EDMUND CLERIHEW BENTLEY English author.
Biography for Beginners 1925

---

sodium carbonate or ***soda ash*** Na_2CO_3 anhydrous white solid. The hydrated, crystalline form ($Na_2CO_3.10H_2O$) is also known as washing soda.

It is made by the ◊Solvay process and used as a mild alkali, as it is hydrolysed in water.

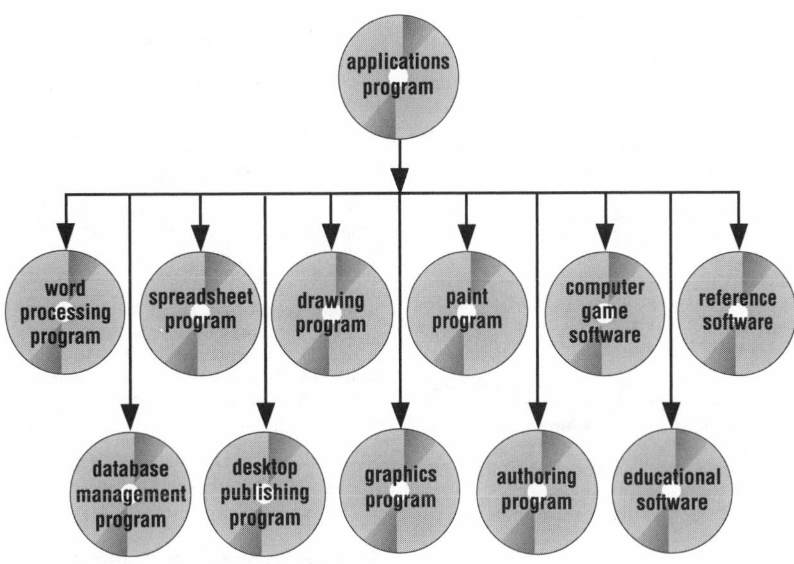

software *The various types of software application program that are available for computer systems.*

$$CO_3{}^{2-}{}_{(aq)} + H_2O_{(l)} \rightarrow HCO_3{}^{-}{}_{(aq)} + OH^{-}{}_{(aq)}$$

It is used to neutralize acids, in glass manufacture, and in water softening.

sodium chloride or ***common salt*** or ***table salt*** NaCl white, crystalline compound found widely in nature. It is a typical ionic solid with a high melting point (801°C/1,474°F); it is soluble in water, insoluble in organic solvents, and is a strong electrolyte when molten or in aqueous solution. Found in concentrated deposits, it is widely used in the food industry as a flavouring and preservative, and in the chemical industry in the manufacture of sodium, chlorine, and sodium carbonate.

sodium hydrogen carbonate chemical name for ◊bicarbonate of soda.

sodium hydroxide *or* **caustic soda** NaOH the commonest alkali. The solid and the solution are corrosive. It is used to neutralize acids, in the manufacture of soap, and in oven cleaners. It is prepared industrially from sodium chloride by the ◊electrolysis of concentrated brine.

soft-sectored disc another name for an unformatted blank disc; see ◊disc formatting.

software in computing, a collection of programs and procedures for making a computer perform a specific task, as opposed to ◊hardware, the physical components of a computer system. Software is created by programmers and is either distributed on a suitable medium, such as the ◊floppy disc, or built into the computer in the form of ◊firmware. Examples of software include ◊operating systems, compilers, and applications programs such as payrolls or word processors. No computer can function without some form of software.

To function, computers need two types of software: application software and systems software. **Application software**, such as a payroll system or a ◊word processor, is designed for the benefit of the end user. **Systems software** performs tasks related to the operation and performance of the computer system itself. For example, a systems program might control the operation of the display screen, or control and organize backing storage.

software agent in computing, see ◊intelligent agent

software piracy in computing, unauthorized duplication of computer software. Although some software piracy is done by companies for financial gain, most piracy is done by private individuals who lend discs to friends or copy programs from the workplace to their computers at home.

Software manufacturers' attempts to protect their property – for example, by using special codes to prevent programs from being installed more than once from each set of discs – have proved unpopular with users and bypassable by determined copiers. Because computer data is so easy to duplicate, and the use of unauthorized software is so hard to detect, it appears nigh impossible to enforce anti-piracy law. The only sure way to prevent it appears to be for manufacturers to sell each copy of their software with a ◊dongle – a coded plug that must actually be fitted to the computer for the software to function.

software project life cycle various stages of development in the writing of a major program (software), from the identification of a requirement to the installation, maintenance, and support of the finished program. The process includes ◊systems analysis and systems design.

software suite in computing, a set of complementary programs which can be bought separately, or (at a considerable saving) as a bundled package. ◊office suites are an especially common form of software suite.

Examples include: Adobe's graphics software which includes Photoshop (for processing photographs), Pagemaker (for page layout), and Illustrator (for creating illustrations); and Macromedia's multimedia software, which comprises Director (for creating presentations), xRes2 (for editing images), SoundEdit (for editing sound) and Extreme 3D (for 3D modelling and animation).

soft water water that contains very few dissolved metal ions such as calcium (Ca^{2+}) or magnesium (Mg^{2+}). It lathers easily with soap, and no ◊scale is formed inside kettles or boilers. It has been found that the incidence of heart disease is higher in soft-water areas.

softwood any coniferous tree (see conifer), or the wood from it. In general this type of wood is softer and easier to work, but in some cases less durable, than wood from flowering (or angiosperm) trees.

SOHO (abbreviation for **Solar and Heliospheric Observatory**) space probe launched in 1995 by the ◊European Space Agency to study the ◊solar wind of atomic particles streaming towards the Earth from the Sun. It also observes the Sun in ultraviolet and visible light, and measures slight oscillations on the Sun's surface that can reveal details of the structure of the Sun's interior. It is positioned 1.5 million km/938,000 mi from Earth towards the Sun. SOHO is operated jointly with NASA and costs $1.2 billion.

Soho carries equipment for 11 separate experiments, including the study of the Sun's corona, measurement of its magnetic field, and of solar winds. The **Coronal Diagnostic Spectrometer** (CDS) detects radiation at extreme ultraviolet wavelengths and allows the study of the Sun's atmosphere. The **Michelson Doppler Imager** (MDI) measures Doppler shifts in light wavelengths and can detect winds caused by convention beneath the Sun's surface. The **Extreme-Ultraviolet Imaging Telescope** (EIT) investigates the mechanisms that heat the Sun's corona. The **Large-Angle Spectroscopic Coronagraph** (LASCO) images the corona by detecting sunlight scattered by the coronal gases.

soil loose covering of broken rocky material and decaying organic matter overlying the bedrock of the Earth's surface. Various types of soil develop under different conditions: deep soils form in warm wet climates and in valleys; shallow soils form in cool dry areas and on slopes. **Pedology**, the study of soil, is significant because of the relative importance of different soil types to agriculture.

The organic content of soil is widely variable, ranging from zero in some desert soils to almost 100% in peats.

TO REMEMBER THE CHIEF CONSTITUENTS OF SOIL:

ALL HAIRY MEN WILL BUY RAZORS.

AIR / HUMUS / MINERAL SALTS / WATER / BACTERIA / ROCK PARTICLES

SOIL PH – WHAT IT MEANS

http://www.esf.edu/pubprog/brochure/soilph/soilph.htm

Explanation of soil pH. The Web site also describes how to measure the pH of soil using simple experimental equipment, and goes on to describe methods that may be used to modify the acidity of alkalinity of your soil.

soil creep gradual movement of soil down a slope in response to gravity. This eventually results in a mass downward movement of soil on the slope.

Evidence of soil creep includes the formation of terracettes (steplike ridges along the hillside), leaning walls and telegraph poles, and trees that grow in a curve to counteract progressive leaning.

soil erosion the wearing away and redistribution of the Earth's soil layer.

It is caused by the action of water, wind, and ice, and also by improper methods of ◊agriculture. If unchecked, soil erosion results in the formation of deserts (◊desertification). It has been estimated that 20% of the world's cultivated topsoil was lost between 1950 and 1990.

If the rate of erosion exceeds the rate of soil formation (from rock and decomposing organic matter), then the land will become infertile. The removal of forests (◊deforestation) or other vegetation often leads to serious soil erosion, because plant roots bind soil, and without them the soil is free to wash or blow away, as in the American ◊dust bowl. The effect is worse on hillsides, and there has been devastating loss of soil where forests have been cleared from mountainsides, as in Madagascar.

Improved agricultural practices such as contour ploughing are needed to combat soil erosion. Windbreaks, such as hedges or strips planted with coarse grass, are valuable, and organic farming can reduce soil erosion by as much as 75%.

Soil degradation and erosion are becoming as serious as the loss of the rainforest. It is estimated that more than 10% of the world's soil lost a large amount of its natural fertility during the latter half of the 20th century. Some of the worst losses are in Europe, where 17% of the soil is damaged by human activity such as mechanized farming and fallout from acid rain. Mexico and Central America have 24% of soil highly degraded, mostly as a result of deforestation.

soil mechanics branch of engineering that studies the nature and properties of the soil. Soil is investigated during construction work to ensure that it has the mechanical properties necessary to support the foundations of dams, bridges, and roads.

Sokoke scops owl small African ◊owl *Otus ieneae* thought to be entirely confined to the threatened Arabuko Sokoke Forest in Kenya. Only discovered in 1965, the owl is typical of many of the continent's little-known species, confined to a few limited and specialized habitats and thus extremely vulnerable to change. There are currently efforts to establish a national park in the forest.

sol ◊colloid of very small solid particles dispersed in a liquid that retains the physical properties of a liquid.

solan goose another name for the ◊gannet.

Solar and Heliospheric Observatory (SOHO) European Space Agency spacecraft usually abbreviated to ◊SOHO.

solar cycle in astronomy, the variation of activity on the ◊Sun over an 11-year period indicated primarily by the number of ◊sunspots visible on its surface. The next period of maximum activity is expected around 2001.

solar energy energy derived from the Sun's radiation. The amount of energy falling on just 1 sq km/0.3861 sq mi is about 4,000 megawatts, enough to heat and light a small town. In one second the Sun gives off 13 million times more energy than all the electricity used in the USA in one year. **Solar heaters** have industrial or domestic uses. They usually consist of a black (heat-absorbing) panel containing pipes through which air or water, heated by the Sun, is circulated, either by thermal convection or by a pump.

Solar energy may also be harnessed indirectly using **solar cells** (photovoltaic cells) made of panels of ◊semiconductor material (usually silicon), which generate electricity when illuminated by sunlight. Although it is difficult to generate a high output from solar energy compared to sources such as nuclear or fossil fuels, it is a major nonpolluting and renewable energy source used as far north as Scandinavia as well as in the SW USA and in Mediterranean countries.

A solar furnace, such as that built in 1970 at Odeillo in the French Pyrenees, had thousands of mirrors to focus the Sun's rays; it produced uncontaminated intensive heat (up to 3,000°C/5,4000°F) for industrial and scientific or experimental purposes. The world's first solar power station connected to a national grid opened in 1991 at Adrano in Sicily. Scores of giant mirrors move to follow the Sun throughout the day, focusing the rays into a boiler. Steam from the boiler drives a conventional turbine. The plant generates up to 1 megawatt. A similar system, called Solar 1, has been built in the Mojave Desert near Daggett, California, USA. It consists of 1,818 computer-controlled mirrors arranged in circles around a central boiler tower 91 m/300 ft high. Advanced schemes have been proposed that would use giant solar reflectors in space to harness solar energy and beam it down to Earth in the form of ◊microwaves.

In March 1996 the first solar power plant capable of storing heat was switched on in California's Mojave Desert. Solar 2, part of a three-year government-sponsored project, consists of 2,000 motorized mirrors that will focus the Sun's rays on to a 91-m/300 ft metal tower containing molten nitrate salt. When the salt reaches 565°C/1049°F it boils water to drive a 10-megawatt steam turbine. The molten salt retains its heat for up to 12 hours.

Despite their low running costs, their high installation cost and low power output have meant that solar cells have found few applications outside space probes and artificial satellites. Solar heating is, however, widely used for domestic purposes in many parts of the world, and is an important renewable source of energy.

If sunbeams were weapons of war, we would have had solar energy long ago.

George Porter British physical chemist. *Observer* 1973

Solar Maximum Mission satellite launched by the US agency NASA in 1980 to study solar activity, which discovered that the Sun's luminosity increases slightly when sunspots are most numerous. It was repaired in orbit by astronauts from the space shuttle in 1984 and burned up in the Earth's atmosphere in 1989.

solar pond natural or artificial 'pond', such as the Dead Sea, in which salt becomes more soluble in the Sun's heat. Water at the bottom becomes saltier and hotter, and is insulated by the less salty water layer at the top. Temperatures at the bottom reach about 100°C/212°F and can be used to generate electricity.

solar radiation radiation given off by the Sun, consisting mainly of visible light, ◊ultraviolet radiation, and infrared radiation, although the whole spectrum of ◊electromagnetic waves is present, from radio waves to X-rays. High-energy charged particles, such as electrons, are also emitted, especially from solar ◊flares. When these reach the Earth, they cause magnetic storms (disruptions of the Earth's magnetic field), which interfere with radio communications.

Solar System the ◊Sun (a star) and all the bodies orbiting it: the ◊nine planets (Mercury, Venus, Earth, Mars, Jupiter, Saturn, Uranus, Neptune, and Pluto), their moons, the asteroids, and the comets. The Sun contains 99.86% of the mass of the Solar System.

The Solar System gives every indication of being a strongly unified system having a common origin and development. It is isolated in space; all the planets go round the Sun in orbits that are nearly circular and coplanar, and in the same direction as the Sun itself rotates; moreover this same pattern is continued in the regular system of satellites that accompany Jupiter, Saturn, and Uranus. It is thought to have formed by condensation from a cloud of gas and dust in space about 4.6 billion years ago.

SOLAR SYSTEM

http://www.hawastsoc.org/solar/eng/

Educational tour of the Solar System. It contains information and statistics about the Sun, Earth, planets, moons, asteroids, comets, and meteorites found within the Solar System, supported by images.

solar time in astronomy, the time of day as determined by the position of the ◊Sun in the sky.

Apparent solar time, the time given by a sundial, is not uniform because of the varying speed of the Earth in its elliptical orbit. **Mean solar time** is a uniform time that coincides with apparent solar time at four instants through the year. The difference between them is known as the equation of time, and is greatest in early November when the Sun is more than 16 minutes fast on mean solar time. Mean solar time on the Green meridian is known as ◊Greenwich Mean Time and is the basis of civil timekeeping.

solar wind stream of atomic particles, mostly protons and electrons, from the Sun's corona, flowing outwards at speeds of between 300 kps/200 mps and 1,000 kps/600 mps.

The fastest streams come from 'holes' in the Sun's corona that lie over areas where no surface activity occurs. The solar wind pushes the gas of comets' tails away from the Sun, and 'gusts' in the solar wind cause geomagnetic disturbances and aurorae on Earth.

solder any of various alloys used when melted for joining metals such as copper, its common alloys (brass and bronze), and tin-plated steel, as used for making food cans.

Soft solders (usually alloys of tin and lead, sometimes with added antimony) melt at low temperatures (about 200°C/392°F), and are widely used in the electrical industry for joining copper wires. Hard (or brazing) solders, such as silver solder (an alloy of copper, silver, and zinc), melt at much higher temperatures and form a much stronger joint. ◊Printed circuit boards for computers are assembled by soldering.

A necessary preliminary to making any solder joint is thorough cleaning of the surfaces of the metal to be joined (to remove oxide) and the use of a flux (to prevent the heat applied to melt the solder from reoxidizing the metal).

soldier beetle reddish beetle with soft, black elytra (wing cases) and a black patch and black legs. It reaches a length of 15 mm/0.5 in and can be found in the daytime during the months of April to July on field, garden, and forest plants. It feeds particularly on aphids. Its larvae are black, and are to be found in the soil or among moss.

classification The soldier beetle is in family Cantharidae, order Coleoptera, class Insecta, phylum Arthropoda.

sole flatfish found in temperate and tropical waters. The **common sole** *Solea solea*, also called **Dover sole**, is found in the southern seas of NW Europe. Up to 50 cm/20 in long, it is a prized food fish, as is the **sand** or **French sole** *Pegusa lascaris* further south.

solenodon rare insectivorous shrewlike mammal, genus *Solenodon*. There are two species, one each on Cuba and Hispaniola. They are about 30 cm/12 in long with a 25 cm/10 in naked tail, shaggy hair, long, pointed snouts, and strong claws, and they produce venomous saliva. They are slow-moving, come out mostly at night, and eat insects, worms, and other invertebrate animals. They are threatened with extinction owing to introduced predators.

solenoid coil of wire, usually cylindrical, in which a magnetic field is created by passing an electric current through it (see ◊electromagnet). This field can be used to move an iron rod placed on its axis.

Mechanical valves attached to the rod can be operated by switching the current on or off, so converting electrical energy into mechanical energy. Solenoids are used to relay energy from the battery of a car to the starter motor by means of the ignition switch.

solid in physics, a state of matter that holds its own shape (as opposed to a liquid, which takes up the shape of its container, or a gas, which totally fills its container). According to ◊kinetic theory, the atoms or molecules in a solid are not free to move but merely vibrate about fixed positions, such as those in crystal lattices.

solidification change of state from liquid (or vapour) to solid that occurs at the ◊freezing point of a substance.

solid-state circuit electronic circuit where all the components (resistors, capacitors, transistors, and diodes) and interconnections are made at the same time, and by the same processes, in or on one piece of single-crystal silicon. The small size of this construction accounts for its use in electronics for space vehicles and aircraft.

soliton solitary wave that maintains its shape and velocity, and does not widen and disperse in the normal way. The mathematical equations that sum up the behaviour of solitons are being used to further research in nuclear fusion and superconductivity.

Solomon's seal any of a group of perennial plants belonging to the lily family, native to Europe and found growing in moist, shady woodland areas. They have drooping bell-like white or greenish-white flowers which appear just above the point where the leaves join the arching stems, followed by blue or black berries. (Genus *Polygonatum*, family Liliaceae.)

solstice either of the days on which the Sun is farthest north or south of the celestial equator each year. The **summer solstice**, when the Sun is farthest north, occurs around 21 June; the **winter solstice** around 22 December.

solubility measure of the amount of solute (usually a solid or gas) that will dissolve in a given amount of solvent (usually a liquid) at a particular temperature. Solubility may be expressed as grams of solute per 100 grams of solvent or, for a gas, in parts per million (ppm) of solvent.

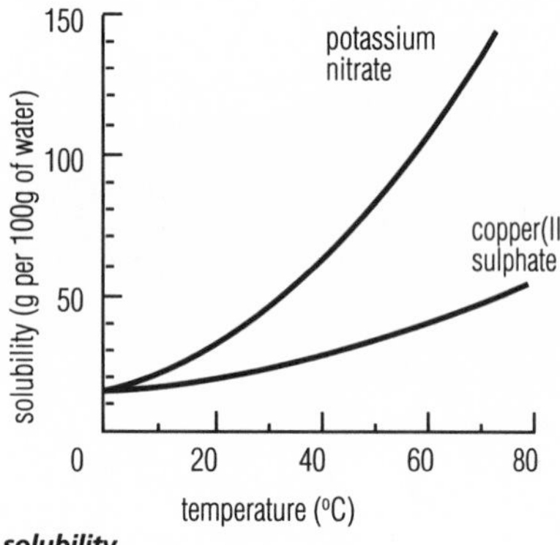

solubility

solubility curve graph that indicates how the solubility of a substance varies with temperature. Most salts increase their solubility with an increase in temperature, as they dissolve endothermically. These curves can be used to predict which salt, and how much of it, will crystallize out of a mixture of salts.

solute substance that is dissolved in another substance (see ◊solution).

solution two or more substances mixed to form a single, homogenous phase. One of the substances is the **solvent** and the others **(solutes)** are said to be dissolved in it.

The constituents of a solution may be solid, liquid, or gaseous. The solvent is normally the substance that is present in greatest quantity; however, if one of the constituents is a liquid this is considered to be the solvent even if it is not the major substance.

solution in earth science, the dissolving in water of minerals within a rock. It may result in weathering (for example, when weakly acidic rainfall causes carbonation) and erosion (when flowing water passes over rocks).

Solution commonly affects limestone and chalk, and may be responsible for forming features such as sink holes.

solution in algebra, the value of a variable that satisfies a given equation; see ◊root.

solution set the set of values that satisfies an ◊inequality relationship, or equation(s).

Solvay process industrial process for the manufacture of sodium carbonate.

It is a multistage process in which carbon dioxide is generated from limestone and passed through ◊brine saturated with ammonia. Sodium hydrogen carbonate is isolated and heated to yield sodium carbonate. All intermediate by-products are recycled so that the only ultimate by-product is calcium chloride.

solvent substance, usually a liquid, that will dissolve another substance (see ◊solution). Although the commonest solvent is water, in popular use the term refers to low-boiling-point organic liquids, which are harmful if used in a confined space. They can give rise to respiratory problems, liver damage, and neurological complaints.

Typical organic solvents are petroleum distillates (in glues), xylol (in paints), alcohols (for synthetic and natural resins such as shellac), esters (in lacquers, including nail varnish), ketones (in cellulose lacquers and resins), and chlorinated hydrocarbons (as paint stripper and dry-cleaning fluids). The fumes of some solvents, when inhaled (◊glue-sniffing), affect mood and perception. In addition to damaging the brain and lungs, repeated inhalation of solvent from a plastic bag can cause death by asphyxia.

sonar (acronym for ***sound navigation and ranging***) method of locating underwater objects by the reflection of ultrasonic waves. The time taken for an acoustic beam to travel to the object and back to the source enables the distance to be found since the velocity of sound in water is known. Sonar devices, or **echo sounders**, were developed in 1920, and are the commonest means of underwater navigation.

sone unit of subjective loudness. A tone of 40 decibels above the threshold of hearing with a frequency of 1,000 hertz is defined as one sone; any sound that seems twice as loud as this has a value of two sones, and so on. A loudness of one sone corresponds to 40 ◊phons.

sonic boom noise like a thunderclap that occurs when an aircraft passes through the ◊sound barrier, or begins to travel faster than the speed of sound. It happens when the cone-shaped shock wave caused by the plane touches the ground.

sonochemistry branch of chemistry based on the properties of chemicals when subjected to high-intensity ultrasound. The ultrasound causes bubbles to form, grow, and implode. The implosion generates intense local heat and extreme pressure, but for less than a millionth of a second. Light is also emitted (◊sonoluminescence).

Applications include the production of amorphous metals, molten metals cooled so fast they freeze before crystals have a chance to form properly. This gives them unique electromagnetic properties and resistance to corrosion.

sonoluminescence emission of light by a liquid that is subjected to high-frequency sound waves. The rapid changes of pressure induced by the sound cause minute bubbles to form in the liquid, which then collapse. Light is emitted at the final stage of the collapse, probably because it squeezes and heats gas inside the bubbles.

Sony Japanese electronics company that produced the ◊Walkman, the first easily portable cassette player with headphones, in 1980. It diversified into entertainment by the purchase of CBS Records 1988 and Columbia Pictures in 1989. Sony made the 3.5 in disc drives for the Apple Macintosh in 1984, and also manufactures microchips and ◊games consoles, amongst other things.

During the 1970s Sony developed the Betamax video-cassette format, which technicians rated as more advanced than the rival VHS system developed by the ◊Matsushita Corporation, but the latter eventually triumphed in the marketplace. Sony's former chair, Akio Morita, is co-author of *A Japan That Can Say No* 1989 and sequels.

Sony Corporation's sales for the year to March 31 1997 were 5,663 billion yen ($45,670 million), at which time it had 22,000 employees.

sorbic acid $CH_3CH{=}CHCH{=}CHCOOH$ tasteless acid found in the fruit of the mountain ash (genus *Sorbus*) and prepared synthetically. It is widely used in the preservation of food – for example, cider, wine, soft drinks, animal feeds, bread, and cheese.

sorghum or ***great millet*** or ***Guinea corn*** any of a group of ◊cereal grasses native to Africa but cultivated widely in India, China, the USA, and S Europe. The seeds are used for making bread. ◊Durra is a member of the genus. (Genus *Sorghum.*)

Around 58 million tonnes of sorghum are grown worldwide on 44 million hectares. It is vulnerable to the fungus ◊ergot, which can destroy whole crops. In 1994 a simple fungicidal spray of garlic and water was found to be nearly 100% successful in combatting ergot.

sorrel Old French *sur* 'sour' any of several plants belonging to the buckwheat family. *R. acetosa* is grown for its bitter salad leaves. ◊Dock plants are of the same genus. (Genus *Rumex,* family Polygonaceae.)

sorting in computing, arranging data in sequence. When sorting a collection, or file, of data made up of several different ◊fields, one must be chosen as the **key field** used to establish the correct sequence. For example, the data in a company's mailing list might include fields for each customer's first names, surname, address, and telephone number. For most purposes the company would wish the records to be sorted alphabetically by surname; therefore, the surname field would be chosen as the key field.

The choice of sorting method involves a compromise between running time, memory usage, and complexity. Those used include **selection sorting**, in which the smallest item is found and exchanged with the first item, the second smallest exchanged with the second item, and so on; **bubble sorting**, in which adjacent items are continually exchanged until the data are in sequence; and **insertion sorting**, in which each item is placed in the correct position and subsequent items moved down to make a place for it.

sorus in ferns, a group of sporangia, the reproductive structures that produce ◊spores. They occur on the lower surface of fern fronds.

sound physiological sensation received by the ear, originating in a vibration that communicates itself as a pressure variation in the air and travels in every direction, spreading out as an expanding sphere. All sound waves in air travel with a speed dependent on the temperature; under ordinary conditions, this is about 330 m/1,070 ft per second. The pitch of the sound depends on the number of vibrations imposed on the air per second, but the speed is unaffected. The loudness of a sound is dependent primarily on the amplitude of the vibration of the air.

The lowest note audible to a human being has a frequency of about 20 ◊hertz (vibrations per second), and the highest one of about 20,000 Hz; the lower limit of this range varies little with the person's age, but the upper range falls steadily from adolescence onwards.

sound absorption in acoustics, the conversion of sound energy to heat energy when sound waves strike a surface. The process reduces the amplitude of each reflected sound wave (echo) and thus the degree to which ◊reverberation takes place. Materials with good sound-absorbing properties are often fitted on walls and ceilings in buildings such as offices, factories, and concert halls in order to reduce or control sound levels.

sound barrier concept that the speed of sound, or sonic speed (about 1,220 kph/760 mph at sea level), constitutes a speed limit to flight through the atmosphere, since a badly designed aircraft suffers severe buffeting at near sonic speed owing to the formation of shock waves. US test pilot Chuck Yeager first flew through the 'barrier' in 1947 in a Bell X-1 rocket plane. Now, by careful design, such aircraft as Concorde can fly at supersonic speed with ease, though they create in their wake a ◊sonic boom.

SoundBlaster in computing, the most popular type of ◊sound card for IBM-compatible PCs. SoundBlaster cards are made by ◊Creative Labs.

sound card printed circuit board that, coupled with a set of speakers, enables a computer to reproduce music and sound effects. 16-bit sound cards give better reproduction than 8-bit sound cards, and usually offer stereo sound.

sound-level indicator instrument used to measure the intensity or loudness of sound.

Readings are given on a ◊decibel (dB) scale that compares the sound level with the threshold of human hearing (standardized as an intensity of 1.0×10^{-12} watts per square metre). A specialised scale called the dBA scale gives a weighted reading that takes into account the ear's sensitivity to different frequencies.

sound synthesis the generation of sound (usually music) by electronic synthesizer.

sorus Heaps of bright yellow spore-producing sporangia grouped to form sori are clearly visible beneath this frond of common polypody fern. Premaphotos Wildlife

soundtrack band at one side of a cine film on which the accompanying sound is recorded. Usually it takes the form of an optical track (a pattern of light and shade). The pattern is produced on the film when signals from the recording microphone are made to vary the intensity of a light beam. During playback, a light is shone through the track on to a photocell, which converts the pattern of light falling on it into appropriate electrical signals. These signals are then fed to loudspeakers to recreate the original sounds.

sound wave the longitudinal wave motion with which sound energy travels through a medium. It carries energy away from the source of the sound without carrying the material itself with it. Sound waves are mechanical; unlike electromagnetic waves, they require vibration of their medium's molecules or particles, and this is why sound cannot travel through a vacuum.

source code in computing, the original instructions written by computer programmers. Before these instructions can be understood, they must be processed by a ◊compiler and turned into ◊machine code.

source language in computing, the language in which a program is written, as opposed to ◊machine code, which is the form in which the program's instructions are carried out by the computer. Source languages are classified as either ◊high-level languages or ◊low-level languages, according to whether each notation in the source language stands for many or only one instruction in machine code.

Programs in high-level languages are translated into machine code by either a ◊compiler or an ◊interpreter program. Low-level programs are translated into machine code by means of an ◊assembler program. The program, before translation, is called the **source program**; after translation into machine code it is called the **object program**.

source program in computing, a program written in a ◊source language.

source resistance alternative term for ◊internal resistance, the resistance inside an electric power supply.

souring change that occurs to wine on prolonged exposure to air. The ethanol in the wine is oxidized by the air (oxygen) to ethanoic acid. It is the presence of the ethanoic (acetic) acid that produces the sour taste.

$$CH_3CH_2OH_{(aq)} + O_{2(g)} \rightarrow CH_3COOH_{(aq)} + H_2O_{(l)}$$

The Year in Space – 1997

BY TIM FURNISS

Space in 1997 has been dominated by three events: the landing on the planet Mars of the NASA *Mars Pathfinder* and its tiny rover, the Sojourner, on 4 July; the hyped-up, infamous incidents on the Russian *Mir* space station; and the successful test flight of Europe's *Ariane 5* rocket.

Mars Pathfinder *Lands*

The landing of the low-cost *Mars Pathfinder* and the images it returned – 21 years after the last touchdowns on the Red Planet by the *Vikings 1* and *2* – was made all the more spectacular by the access to its pictures by users of the Internet. The Web revolution even resulted in home-based addicts getting daily weather reports from Mars. The Sojourner, about the size of a microwave oven and the precursor of slightly larger and more sophisticated rovers on future missions in the Mars Surveyor programme, caught the imagination of the public with its explorations and analysis of rocks with such names as Yogi and Barnacle Bill.

Both craft continued to operate well beyond their design lives and provided more evidence that water once flowed across the now barren, ruddy coloured, rocky surface. The mission formally ended in November after four months.

Mir *Space Station*

Closer to home, the remarkable Russian *Mir 1* space station continued manned operations – also beyond its design life – providing a wealth of data and experience about operating larger space stations. The Russians' invaluable expertise in this area of space utilization was sadly underplayed by the extraordinary media reaction to certain incidents on the station, which were highlighted because US astronauts were on board at the time.

A fire that broke out in February was not the first to occur on the station, but the collision of the *Progress* tanker craft with the *Spektr* module in June could have been a disaster. The collision was more of a glancing blow, but the *Spektr* module lost the use of a solar panel and was depressurized as a result. The incident was a reminder that space travel is dangerous, and risks have to be accepted. Most of the media attention was given to the age of the *Mir* station, and the fact that it was apparently a 'wreck'. In fact, while the core module of *Mir* was launched in 1986, the final module of the space complex was launched in 1996! Running a space station for that long is bound to involve things breaking down, but part of the Russian way of working is to treat these events as operational, not emergency, situations, which is a different culture altogether from NASA Space Shuttle missions. Regular spacewalks and maintenance on the *Mir* station will contribute towards keeping the *Mir* in working order and ready to house many more crews until it is retired, perhaps in 1999.

During spacewalks in 1997 and early 1998, the veteran Russian cosmonaut Anatoli Solovyov became the first to make 14 spacewalks, all outside the *Mir* station on various missions. He has accumulated 63 hours of spacewalk time, compared with the individual US record of 29 hours. Another *Mir* spacewalk marked the first by a Russian and US astronaut together, an occasion later repeated aboard the Space Shuttle. Once the International Space Station is operational, NASA and the other partners will owe a debt to the operational space-station experience database provided by Russia.

Ariane 5 *Launched*

The successful flight of the *Ariane 5* from Kourou on 31 October was a great relief to the European space industry. The first *Ariane 5* failed dramatically in an explosion in June 1996, and another problem could have been a disaster. It is now hoped that *Ariane 5* can go on to forge a successful commercial career, allowing the old workhorse, the *Ariane 4*, to retire in about 2003. Eleven *Ariane 4*s made successful commercial flights in 1997.

Notable Satellite Launches

Brazil, making its first attempt to join the 'space league' of nations that have launched national satellites on indigenously-developed boosters, failed when its VLS booster had to be destroyed after an engine fault. A spectacular failure of a US Delta rocket, which had people running for cover at Cape Canaveral in January, illustrated that losses can be experienced by veteran space nations as well. Another Delta featured in the successful launch of the first in a series of satellites, opening a new era in communications. Sixty-six iridium satellites will eventually enable users of mobile telephones to make a call from anywhere in the world to anywhere in the world. By the end of the year, 41 iridiums had been launched, and the network should be completed in mid-1998.

Successes and Some Failures

A new era in planetary exploration began in 1997, too, with the launch in November of the first spacecraft, the *Cassini/Huygens*, to orbit the planet Saturn in 2004 after its long route around the solar system. The *Huygens* lander is to touch down on the surface of the Saturnian moon, Titan. Another planetary spacecraft, the Mars Global Surveyor, reached Mars orbit in September, but its manoeuvring to operational mapping orbit was interrupted by some malfunctions and, as a result, its mission may be limited.

The launch of a new crew to operate a shift aboard the *Mir* space station in July marked the 200th manned spaceflight launch in history since April 1961 (not including the failed Challenger Shuttle mission in 1986). The USA also launched eight Space Shuttle missions in 1997, three of them to dock with the *Mir* space station to deliver a new astronaut and return one home. As the year closed, the US resident *Mir* astronaut was David Wolf, who clambered aboard the *Mir* in October and was replaced by another astronaut early in 1998.

The year also marked a Shuttle record. One mission, STS 83, had to be aborted after three days due to a fuel cell failure but was reflown in July with the entire crew returning to space in a record 84 days. The Russian *Proton* launcher completed its second commercial launch in May 1997, carrying a *Telstar* satellite into orbit for the joint US/Russian International Launch Services (ILS). The company's link-up with the USA has transformed the commercial career of the *Proton*, which is now fully booked until 2001 for commercial launches but the *Proton* blotted the copy book by failing on the 25 December. Overall, in 1997, there were 86 satellite launches, 38 by the USA, 28 by Russia, 12 by Europe, 6 by China, 2 by Japan and 1 by India, involving almost 140 satellites.

Not all the satellites performed well, however. A Japanese earth-observation satellite suffered a solar panel malfunction and was lost, two US Earth observation satellites were also lost, and a communications satellite stranded in the wrong orbit.

One of the 28 Russian satellite launches inaugurated a new launch site at Svobodny in far-eastern Russia. The former top-secret military base and missile launch complex has been converted into a launch base for small satellites into low earth orbit, using converted military missiles. In the business world, the proposed merger of the UK/French Matra Marconi Space company and Germany's Diamler-Benz Aerospace space division, announced in 1997, will result in the formation of a large pan-European company to compete on equal terms with the giant US satellite manufacturers, Hughes, Lockheed Martin, and Space Systems Loral. 1998 promises to be a very significant year in the history of space exploration – the start of the assembly of the first International Space Station.

Space Flight: chronology

1903	Russian scientist Konstantin Tsiolkovsky published the first practical paper on astronautics.
1926	US engineer Robert Goddard launched the first liquid-fuel rocket.
1937-45	In Germany, Wernher von Braun developed the V2 rocket.
1957	4 Oct: The first space satellite, *Sputnik 1* (USSR, Russian 'fellow-traveller'), orbited the Earth at a height of 229-898 km/142-558 mi in 96.2 min. 3 Nov: *Sputnik 2* was launched carrying a dog, 'Laika'; it died on board seven days later.
1958	31 Jan: *Explorer 1*, the first US satellite, discovered the Van Allen radiation belts.
1961	12 April: the first crewed spaceship, *Vostok 1* (USSR), with Yuri Gagarin on board, was recovered after a single orbit of 89.1 min at a height of 142-175 km/88-109 mi.
1962	20 Feb: John Glenn in *Friendship 7* (USA) became the first American to orbit the Earth. *Telstar* (USA), a communications satellite, sent the first live television transmission between the USA and Europe.
1963	16-19 June: Valentina Tereshkova in *Vostok 1* (USSR) became the first woman in space.
1967	27 Jan: US astronauts Virgil Grissom, Edward White, and Roger Chaffee were killed during a simulated countdown when a flash fire swept through the cabin of *Apollo 1*. 24 April: Vladimir Komarov was the first person to be killed on a mission, when his ship, *Soyuz 1* (USSR), crash-landed on the Earth.
1969	20 July: Neil Armstrong of *Apollo 11* (USA) was the first person to walk on the Moon.
1970	10 Nov: *Luna 17* (USSR) was launched; its space probe, *Lunokhod*, took photographs and made soil analyses of the Moon's surface.
1971	19 April: *Salyut 1* (USSR), the first orbital space station, was established; it was later visited by the *Soyuz 11* crewed spacecraft.
1973	*Skylab 2*, the first US orbital space station, was established.
1975	15-24 July: *Apollo 18* (USA) and *Soyuz 19* (USSR) made a joint flight and linked up in space.
1979	The European Space Agency's satellite launcher, *Ariane 1*, was launched.
1981	12 April: The first reusable crewed spacecraft, the space shuttle *Columbia* (USA), was launched.
1986	Space shuttle *Challenger* (USA) exploded shortly after take-off, killing all seven crew members.
1988	US shuttle programme resumed with launch of *Discovery*. Soviet shuttle *Buran* was launched from the rocket *Energiya*. Soviet cosmonauts Musa Manarov and Vladimir Titov in space station *Mir* spent a record 365 days 59 min in space.
1990	April: Hubble Space Telescope (USA) was launched from Cape Canaveral.
1991	5 April: The Gamma Ray Observatory was launched from the space shuttle *Atlantis* to survey the sky at gamma-ray wavelengths. 18 May: Astronaut Helen Sharman, the first Briton in space, was launched with Anatoli Artsebarsky and Sergei Krikalev to *Mir* space station, returning to Earth 26 May in *Soyuz TM-11* with Viktor Afanasyev and Musa Manarov. Manarov set a record for the longest time spent in space, 541 days, having also spent a year aboard *Mir* 1988.
1992	European satellite *Hipparcos*, launched 1989 to measure the position of 120,000 stars, failed to reach geostationary orbit and went into a highly elliptical orbit, swooping to within 500 km/308 mi of the Earth every ten hours. The mission was later retrieved. 16 May: Space shuttle *Endeavour* returned to Earth after its first voyage. During its mission, it circled the Earth 141 times and travelled 4 million km/2.5 million mi. 23 Oct: *LAGEOS II* (Laser Geodynamics Satellite) was released from the space shuttle *Columbia* into an orbit so stable that it will still be circling the Earth in billions of years. Dec: Space shuttle *Endeavour* successfully carried out mission to replace the Hubble Space Telescope's solar panels and repair its mirror.
1994	4 Feb: Japan's heavy-lifting *H-2* rocket was launched successfully, carrying an uncrewed shuttle craft.
1995	June: the US space shuttle *Atlantis* docked with *Mir*, exchanging crew members.
1996	4 June: the *Ariane 5* rocket disintegrated almost immediately after takeoff, destroying the four Cluster satellites.
1997	April: NASA ceased operations using the space probe *Pioneer 10* after 25 years of sending signals from the edge of the Solar System. July: *Mir* underwent increasing difficulties, following a collision with a cargo ship in June that depressurized one of its modules, Spektr.

South African Astronomical Observatory national observatory of South Africa at Sutherland, founded 1973 after the merger of the Royal Observatory, Cape Town, and the Republic Observatory, Johannesburg, and operated by the Council for Scientific and Industrial Research of South Africa. Its main telescope is a 1.88-m/74-in reflector formerly at the Radcliffe Observatory, Pretoria.

Southern Cross popular name for the constellation ◊Crux.

southern lights common name for the ◊aurora australis, coloured light in southern skies.

Southern Ocean corridor linking the Pacific, Atlantic, and Indian oceans, all of which receive cold polar water from the world's largest ocean surface current, the Antarctic Circumpolar Current, which passes through the Southern Ocean.

soya bean leguminous plant (see ◊legume) native to E Asia, in particular Japan and China. Originally grown as a food crop for animals, it is increasingly used for human consumption in cooking oils and margarine, as a flour, soya milk, soy sauce, or processed into tofu, miso, or textured vegetable protein (◊TVP). (*Glycine max.*)

Soya is the richest natural vegetable food. The dried bean is 18–22% fat, 35% carbohydrate, and one hectare of soya beans yields 162 kg/357 lb of protein (compared with 9 kg/20 lb per hectare for beef). There are more than 1,000 varieties. The plant has been cultivated in Asia for about 5,000 years, and first became known in Europe when brought back from Japan by German botanist Engelbert Kaenfer in 1692. Today the USA produces more soya beans than Asia.

Miso is soya beans fermented with cereal grains, water, and salt, used in soups and sauces; **soy sauce** is beans fermented with salt; and **tamari** is similar to soy sauce but stronger, having been matured for up to two years.

Soyuz Russian *'union'* Soviet series of spacecraft, capable of carrying up to three cosmonauts. Soyuz spacecraft consist of three parts: a rear section containing engines; the central crew compartment; and a forward compartment that gives additional room for working and living space. They are now used for ferrying crews up to space stations, though they were originally used for independent space flight.

space or ***outer space*** the void that exists beyond Earth's atmosphere. Above 120 km/75 mi, very little atmosphere remains, so objects can continue to move quickly without extra energy. The space between the planets is not entirely empty, but filled with the tenuous gas of the ◊solar wind as well as dust specks.

Space Probe: chronology

1959	(13 Sept) *Luna 2* (USSR) hit the Moon, the first craft to do so.
	(10 Oct) *Luna 3* photographed the far side of the Moon.
1962	(14 Dec) *Mariner 2* (USA) flew past Venus; launch date 26 Aug 1962.
1964	(31 July) *Ranger 7* (USA) hit the Moon, having sent back 4,316 pictures before impact.
1965	(14 July) *Mariner 4* flew past Mars; launch date 28 Nov 1964.
1966	(3 Feb) *Luna 9* achieved the first soft landing on the Moon, having transmitted 27 close up panoramic photographs; launch date 31 Jan 1966.
	(2 June) *Surveyor 1* (USA) landed softly on the Moon and returned 11,150 pictures; launch date 30 May 1965.
1971	(13 Nov) *Mariner 9* entered orbit of Mars; launch date 30 May 1971.
1973	(3 Dec) *Pioneer 10* (USA) flew past Jupiter; launch date 3 March 1972.
1974	(29 March) *Mariner 10* flew past Mercury; launch date 3 Nov 1973.
1975	(22 Oct) *Venera 9* (USSR) landed softly on Venus and returned its first pictures; launch date 8 June 1975.
1976	(20 July) *Viking 1* (USA) first landed on Mars; launch date 20 Aug 1975.
	(3 Sept) *Viking 2* transmitted data from the surface of Mars.
1977	(20 Aug) *Voyager 2* (USA) launched. (5 Sept) *Voyager 1* launched.
1978	(4 Dec) *Pioneer-Venus 1* (USA) orbited Venus; launch date 20 May 1978.
1979	(5 March and 9 July) *Voyager 1* and *Voyager 2* encountered Jupiter, respectively.
1980	(12 Nov) *Voyager 1* reached Saturn.
1981	(25 Aug) *Voyager 2* flew past Saturn.
1982	(1 March) *Venera 13* transmitted its first colour pictures of the surface of Venus; launch date 30 Oct 1981.
1983	(10 Oct) *Venera 15* mapped the surface of Venus from orbit; launch date 2 June 1983.
1985	(2 July) *Giotto* (European Space Agency) launched to Halley's comet.
1986	(24 Jan) *Voyager 2* encountered Uranus.
	(13-14 March) *Giotto* met Halley's comet, closest approach 596 km/370 mi, at a speed 50 times faster than that of a bullet.
1989	(4 May) *Magellan* (USA) launched from space shuttle *Atlantis* on a 15-month cruise to Venus across 15 million km/9 million mi of space.
	(25 Aug) *Voyager 2* reached Neptune (4,400 million km/2,700 million mi from Earth), approaching it to within 4,850 km/ 3,010 mi.
	(18 Oct) *Galileo* (USA) launched from space shuttle Atlantis for six-year journey to Jupiter.
1990	(10 Aug) *Magellan* arrived at Venus and transmitted its first pictures 16 Aug 1990.
	(6 Oct) *Ulysses* (European Space Agency) launched from space shuttle *Discovery*, to study the Sun.
1991	(29 Oct) *Galileo* made the closest-ever approach to an asteroid, Gaspra, flying within 1,600 km/990 mi.
1992	(8 Feb) *Ulysses* flew past Jupiter at a distance of 380,000 km/236,000 mi from the surface, just inside the orbit of Io and closer than 11 of Jupiter's 16 moons.
	(10 July) *Giotto* (USA) flew at a speed of 14 kms/8.5 mps to within 200 km/124 mi of comet Grigg-Skellerup, 12 light years (240 million km/150 mi) away from Earth.
	(25 Sept) *Mars Observer* (USA) launched from Cape Canaveral, the first US mission to Mars for 17 years.
	(10 Oct) *Pioneer-Venus 1* burned up in the atmosphere of Venus.
1993	(21 Aug) *Mars Observer* disappeared three days before it was due to drop into orbit around Mars.
	(28 Aug) *Galileo* flew past the asteroid Ida.
1995	(Dec) *Galileo's* probe entered the atmosphere of Jupiter. It radioed information back to the orbiter for 57 minutes before it was destroyed by atmospheric pressure.
1996	NASA's Near Earth Asteroid Rendezvous (NEAR) was launched to study Eros.
1997	The US spacecraft *Mars Pathfinder* landed on Mars. Two days later the probe's rover *Sojourner*, a six-wheeled vehicle that was controlled by an Earth-based operator, began to explore the area around the spacecraft.
1997	The US space probe *Galileo* began orbiting Jupiter's moons. It took photographs of Europa for a potential future landing site, and detected molecules containing carbon and nitrogen on Callisto, suggesting that life once existed there.
1997	The US *Near Earth Asteroid Rendezvous* (NEAR) spacecraft flew within 1,200 km/746 mi of the asteroid Mathilde, taking high-resolution photographs and revealing a 25-km/15.5-mi crater covering the 53-km/33-mi asteroid.
1997	The US spacecraft *Mars Global Surveyor* went into orbit around Mars to conduct a detailed photographic survey of the planet, commencing in March 1998, and reported the discovery of bacteria on Mars.
1998	The US probe *Lunar Prospector* was launched to go into low orbits around the Moon and transmit data on the composition of its crust, record gamma rays, and map its magnetic field. The satellite detected 11 million tonnes of water on the Moon in the form of ice.
1998	Analysis of high resolution images from the *Galileo* spacecraft suggested that the icy crust of Europa, Jupiter's fourth largest moon, may hide a vast ocean warm enough to support life.
1998	(4 July) Japan's Planet-B was launched to study Mars.

Space isn't remote at all. It's only an hour's drive away if your car could go straight upwards.

FRED HOYLE English astronomer and writer. *Observer* Sept 1979

Spacelab small space station built by the European Space Agency, carried in the cargo bay of the US space shuttle, in which it remains throughout each flight, returning to Earth with the shuttle. Spacelab consists of a pressurized module in which astronauts can work, and a series of pallets, open to the vacuum of space, on which equipment is mounted.

Spacelab is used for astronomy, Earth observation, and experiments utilizing the conditions of weightlessness and vacuum in orbit. The pressurized module can be flown with or without pallets, or the pallets can be flown on their own, in which case the astronauts remain in the shuttle's own crew compartment. All the sections of Spacelab can be reused many times. The first Spacelab mission, consisting of a pressurized module and pallets, lasted ten days November–December 1983.

space probe any instrumented object sent beyond Earth to collect data from other parts of the Solar System and from deep space. The first probe was the Soviet *Lunik 1,* which flew past the Moon in 1959. The first successful planetary probe was the US *Mariner 2,* which flew past Venus in 1962, using ◊transfer orbit. The first space probe to leave the Solar System was *Pioneer 10* in 1983. Space probes include *Galileo, Giotto, Magellan, Mars Observer, Ulysses,* the ◊Moon probes, and the Mariner, Pioneer, Viking, and Voyager series.

space programme the systematic exploration and utilization of space; see ◊space probe and ◊space shuttle.

space shuttle reusable crewed spacecraft. The first was launched 12 April 1981 by the USA. It was developed by NASA to reduce the cost of using space for commercial, scientific, and military purposes. After leaving its payload in space, the space-shuttle orbiter can be flown back to Earth to land on a runway, and is then available for reuse.

Four orbiters were built: *Columbia, Challenger, Discovery,* and *Atlantis. Challenger* was destroyed in a midair explosion just over a minute after its tenth launch 28 January 1986, killing all seven crew members, the result of a failure in one of the solid rocket boosters. Flights resumed with redesigned boosters in Sept 1988. A replacement orbiter, *Endeavour,* was built, which had its maiden flight in May 1992. At the end of the 1980s, an average of $375 million had been spent on each space-shuttle mission.

The USSR produced a shuttle of similar size and appearance to the US one. The first Soviet shuttle, *Buran,* was launched without a crew by the Energiya rocket 15 Nov 1988. In Japan, development of a crewless shuttle began in 1986.

NASA SHUTTLE WEB

http://shuttle.nasa.gov/reference/

Official NASA site for all shuttle missions. There is extensive technical and nontechnical information, both textual and graphic. Questions can be sent to shuttle crew members during missions. If they are not answered there is an extensive list of frequently asked questions. There are helpful links to related sites and even a plain English explanation of NASA's bewildering jargon and acronyms.

space sickness or *space adaptation syndrome* feeling of nausea, sometimes accompanied by vomiting, experienced by about 40% of all astronauts during their first few days in space. It is akin to travel sickness, and is thought to be caused by confusion of the body's balancing mechanism, located in the inner ear, by weightlessness. The sensation passes after a few days as the body adapts.

space station any large structure designed for human occupation in space for extended periods of time. Space stations are used for carrying out astronomical observations and surveys of Earth, as well as for biological studies and the processing of materials in weightlessness. The first space station was ◊*Salyut 1,* and the USA has launched ◊*Skylab.*

NASA plans to build a larger space station, to be called *Alpha* in cooperation with other countries, including the European Space Agency, which is building a module called *Columbus;* Russia and Japan are also building modules.

space suit protective suit worn by astronauts and cosmonauts in space. It provides an insulated, air-conditioned cocoon in which people can live and work for hours at a time while outside the spacecraft. Inside the suit is a cooling garment that keeps the body at a comfortable temperature even during vigorous work. The suit provides air to breathe, and removes exhaled carbon dioxide and moisture. The suit's outer layers insulate the occupant from the extremes of hot and cold in space (–150°C/–240°F in the shade to +180°C/+350°F in sunlight), and from the impact of small meteorites. Some space suits have a jet-propelled backpack, which the wearer can use to move about.

space-time in physics, combination of space and time used in the theory of relativity. When developing ◊relativity, Albert Einstein showed that time was in many respects like an extra dimension (or direction) to space. Space and time can thus be considered as entwined into a single entity, rather than two separate things.

Space-time is considered to have four dimensions: three of space and one of time. In relativity theory, events are described as occurring at points in space-time. The **general theory of relativity** describes how space-time is distorted by the presence of material bodies, an effect that we observe as gravity.

spadix The numerous tiny stalkless flowers on the spadix of the sweet flag Acorus calamus. *A plant of watersides, the sweet flag is native to S Asia and North America but is now widely naturalized in Europe, including the British Isles. Premaphotos Wildlife*

spadix in botany, an ◊inflorescence consisting of a long, fleshy axis bearing many small, stalkless flowers. It is partially enclosed by a large bract or ◊spathe. A spadix is characteristic of plants belonging to the family Araceae, including the arum lily *Zantedeschia aethiopica.*

spamming advertising on the ◊Internet by broadcasting to many or all ◊newsgroups regardless of relevance. Spamming is contrary to netiquette, the Net's conduct code, and is likely to result in the advertiser being bombarded by flames (angry messages), and 'dumping' (the downloading of large, useless files).

spaniel any of several breeds of small and medium-sized gundog, characterized by large, drooping ears and a wavy, long, silky coat. Spaniels are divided into two groups: those that are still working gundogs – ◊Clumber, cocker, Irish water, springer, and ◊Sussex – and the toy breeds that are kept as pets – including the◊Japanese, King Charles, papillon, and◊ Tibetan.

The working breeds usually have docked tails.

Spanish fly alternative name for a European blister ◊beetle *Lytta vesicatoria,* once used in powdered form as a dangerous diuretic and supposed aphrodisiac.

spark chamber electronic device for recording tracks of charged subatomic particles, decay products, and rays. In combination with a stack of photographic plates, a spark chamber enables the point where an interaction has taken place to be located, to within a cubic centimetre. At its simplest, it consists of two smooth thread-like ◊electrodes that are positioned 1–2 cm/0.5–1 in apart, the space between being filled by an inert gas such as neon. Sparks jump through the gas along the ionized path created by the radiation. See ◊particle detector.

spark plug plug that produces an electric spark in the cylinder of a petrol engine to ignite the fuel mixture. It consists essentially of two electrodes insulated from one another. High-voltage (18,000 V) electricity is fed to a central electrode via the distributor. At the base of the electrode, inside the cylinder, the electricity jumps to another electrode earthed to the engine body, creating a spark. See also ◊ignition coil.

sparrow any of a family (Passeridae) of small Old World birds of the order Passeriformes with short, thick bills, but applied particularly to the different members of the genus *Passer* in the family Ploceidae, order Passeriformes.

Many numbers of the New World family Emberizidae, which includes vwarblers, orioles, and buntings, are also called sparrows; for example, the North American song sparrow *Melospize melodia.*

sparrow hawk small woodland ◊hawk *Accipiter nisus,* of the family Falconidae, order Falconiformes, found in Eurasia and N Africa. It is bluish-grey, with brown and white markings, and has a long tail and short wings. The male grows to 28 cm/11 in long, and the female to 38 cm/15 in. It hunts small birds and mice.

spastic term applied generally to limbs with impaired movement, stiffness, and resistance to passive movement, and to any body part (such as the colon) affected with spasm.

spathe in flowers, the single large bract surrounding the type of inflorescence known as a ◊spadix. It is sometimes brightly coloured and petal-like, as in the brilliant scarlet spathe of the flamingo plant *Anthurium andreanum* from South America; this serves to attract insects.

spawn extruded egg mass of such egg-laying animals as fish, amphibians, and molluscs.

Spawn is produced in very variable quantities (for example, the ◊ling lays about 150,000,000 eggs, and the American oyster 60,000,000 eggs) and is much preyed upon, even, as in the case of the stickleback, by the female herself. A variety of means have been devised for its protection.

In fish, spawning is the reproductive phase, variously involving aggregation of the fish, courtship, extrusion of eggs and sperm into the water, and fertilization of the eggs. Large migrations may precede spawning, as in salmon and herring. In some groups the spawn is not released, fertilization being internal.

The name is also sometimes given to the mycelium of mushrooms and other fungi, seen as white threads in decaying matter.

spearmint perennial herb belonging to the mint family, with aromatic leaves and spikes of purple flowers; the leaves are used for flavouring in cookery. (*Mentha spicata,* family Labiatae.)

speciation emergence of a new species during evolutionary history. One cause of speciation is the geographical separation of populations of the parent species, followed by reproductive isolation and selection for different environments so that they no longer produce viable offspring when they interbreed. Other causes are ◊assortative mating and the establishment of a ◊polyploid population.

species in biology, a distinguishable group of organisms that resemble each other or consist of a few distinctive types (as in ◊polymorphism), and that can all interbreed to produce fertile offspring. Species are the lowest level in the system of biological classification.

Related species are grouped together in a genus. Within a species there are usually two or more separate ◊populations, which may in time become distinctive enough to be designated subspecies or varieties, and could eventually give rise to new species through ◊speciation. Around 1.4 million species have been identified so far, of which 750,000 are insects, 250,000 are plants, and 41,000 are vertebrates. In tropical regions there are roughly two species for each temperate-zone species. It is estimated that one species becomes extinct every day through habitat destruction.

specific gravity alternative term for ◊relative density.

specific heat capacity in physics, quantity of heat required to raise unit mass (1 kg) of a substance by one ◊kelvin (1 K). The unit of specific heat capacity in the SI system is the ◊joule per kilogram kelvin (J kg^{-1} K^{-1}).

specific latent heat in physics, the heat that changes the physical state of a unit mass (one kilogram) of a substance without causing any temperature change.

The **specific latent heat of fusion** of a solid substance is the heat required to change one kilogram of it from solid to liquid without any temperature change. The **specific latent heat of vaporization** of a liquid substance is the heat required to change one kilogram of it from liquid to vapour without any temperature change.

speckle interferometry technique whereby large telescopes can achieve high resolution of astronomical objects despite the adverse effects of the atmosphere through which light from the object under study must pass. It involves the taking of large numbers of images, each under high magnification and with short exposure times. The pictures are then combined to form the final picture. The technique was introduced by the French astronomer Antoine Labeyrie in 1970.

spectacles pair of lenses fitted in a frame and worn in front of the ◊eyes to correct or assist defective vision. Common defects of the eye corrected by spectacle lenses are short sight (myopia) by using concave (spherical) lenses, long sight (hypermetropia) by using convex (spherical) lenses, and astigmatism by using cylindrical lenses.

Spherical and cylindrical lenses may be combined in one lens. Bifocal spectacles correct vision both at a distance and for reading by combining two lenses of different curvatures in one piece of glass. Varifocal spectacles have the same effect without any visible line between the two types of lens.

Spectacles are said to have been invented in the 13th century by a Florentine monk. Few people found the need for spectacles until printing was invented, when the demand for them increased rapidly. Using photosensitive glass, lenses can be produced that darken in glare and return to normal in ordinary light conditions. Lightweight plastic lenses are also common. The alternative to spectacles is contact lenses.

spectator ion in a chemical reaction that takes place in solution, an ion that remains in solution without taking part in the chemical change. For example, in the precipitation of barium sulphate from barium chloride and sodium sulphate, the sodium and chloride ions are spectator ions.

$$BaCl_{2\,(aq)} + Na_2SO_{4\,(aq)} \rightarrow BaSO_{4\,(s)} + 2NaCl_{(aq)}$$

spectral classification in astronomy, the classification of stars according to their surface temperature and ◊luminosity, as determined from their spectra. Stars are assigned a spectral type (or class) denoted by the letters O, B, A, F, G, K, and M, where O stars (about 40,000 K) are the hottest and M stars (about 3,000 K) are the coolest.

Each letter may be further divided into ten subtypes, B0, B1, B2, etc. Stars are also assigned a luminosity class denoted by a Roman numeral attached to the spectral type: I (◊supergiants), II (bright giants), III (giants), IV (subgiants), V (main sequence), VI (subdwarfs), or VII (◊white dwarfs). The Sun is classified as type G2V. See also ◊Hertzsprung–Russell diagram.

spectrometer in physics and astronomy, an instrument used to study the composition of light emitted by a source. The range, or ◊spectrum, of wavelengths emitted by a source depends upon its constituent elements, and may be used to determine its chemical composition.

The simpler forms of spectrometer analyse only visible light. A **collimator** receives the incoming rays and produces a parallel beam, which is then split into a spectrum by either a ◊diffraction grating or a prism mounted on a turntable. As the turntable is rotated each of the constituent colours of the beam may be seen through a **telescope**, and the angle at which each has been deviated may be measured on a circular scale. From this information the wavelengths of the colours of light can be calculated.

Spectrometers are used in astronomy to study the electromagnetic radiation emitted by stars and other celestial bodies. The spectral information gained may be used to determine their chemical composition, or to measure the ◊red shift of colours associated with the expansion of the universe and thereby calculate the speed with which distant stars are moving away from the Earth.

spectrometry in analytical chemistry, a technique involving the measurement of the spectrum of energies (not necessarily electromagnetic radiation) emitted or absorbed by a substance.

spectroscopy study of spectra (see ◊spectrum) associated with atoms or molecules in solid, liquid, or gaseous phase. Spectroscopy can be used to identify unknown compounds and is an invaluable tool in science, medicine, and industry (for example, in checking the purity of drugs).

Emission spectroscopy is the study of the characteristic series of sharp lines in the spectrum produced when an ◊element is heated. Thus an unknown mixture can be analysed for its component elements. Related is **absorption spectroscopy**, dealing with atoms and molecules as they absorb energy in a characteristic way. Again, dark lines can be used for analysis. More detailed structural information can be obtained using **infrared spectroscopy** (concerned with molecular vibrations) or **nuclear magnetic resonance (NMR) spectroscopy** (concerned with interactions between adjacent atomic nuclei). **Supersonic jet laser beam spectroscopy** enables the isolation and study of clusters in the gas phase. A laser vaporizes a small sample, which is cooled in helium, and ejected into an evacuated chamber. The jet of clusters expands supersonically, cooling the clusters to near absolute zero, and stabilizing them for study in a ◊mass spectrometer.

spectrum (plural *spectra*) in physics, an arrangement of frequencies or wavelengths when electromagnetic radiations are separated into their constituent parts. Visible light is part of the ◊electromagnetic spectrum and most sources emit waves over a range of wavelengths that can be broken up or 'dispersed'; white light can be separated into red, orange, yellow, green, blue, indigo, and violet. The visible spectrum was first studied by Isaac ◊Newton, who showed in 1672 how white light could be broken up into different colours.

> TO REMEMBER THE ORDER OF COLOURS:
>
> RICHARD OF YORK GAINED BATTLES IN VAIN.
>
> OR
>
> ROLL OUT YOUR GUINNESS, BOYS, IN VATS.
>
> OR
>
> REAL OLD YOKELS GUZZLE BEER IN VOLUME.
>
> RED, ORANGE, YELLOW, GREEN, BLUE, INDIGO, VIOLET

speech chip in computing, see ◊DSP.

speech recognition or ***voice input*** in computing, any technique by which a computer can understand ordinary speech. Spoken words are divided into 'frames', each lasting about one-thirtieth of a second, which are converted to a wave form. These are then compared with a series of stored frames to determine the most likely word. Research into speech recognition started in 1938, but the technology did not become sufficiently developed for commercial applications until the late 1980s.

There are three types: **separate word recognition** for distinguishing up to several hundred separately spoken words; **connected speech recognition** for speech in which there is a short pause between words; and **continuous speech recognition** for normal but carefully articulated speech.

speech synthesis or ***voice output*** computer-based technology for generating speech. A speech synthesizer is controlled by a computer, which supplies strings of codes representing basic speech sounds (phonemes); together these make up words. Speech-synthesis applications include children's toys, car and aircraft warning systems, and talking books for the blind.

speech writing system computing system that enables data to be input by voice. It includes a microphone, and ◊sound card that plugs into the computer and converts the analogue signals of the voice to digital signals. Examples include DragonDictate, and IBM's Personal Dictation System released in 1994.

The user must read sample sentences to the computer on first use to familiarize it with individual pronunciation. Early speech writers were very inaccurate and slow but by the mid-1990s speeds of 80 words per minute with 95–99% accuracy were achievable.

speed common name for ◊amphetamine, a stimulant drug.

speed the rate at which an object moves. The average speed v of an object may be calculated by dividing the distance s it has travelled by the time t taken to do so, and may be expressed as:

$$v = \frac{s}{t}$$

The usual units of speed are metres per second or kilometres per hour.

Speed is a scalar quantity in which direction of motion is unimportant (unlike the vector quantity ◊velocity, in which both magnitude and direction must be taken into consideration). See also ◊distance-time graph and ◊speed-time graph.

speed of light speed at which light and other ◊electromagnetic waves travel through empty space. Its value is 299,792,458 m/ 186,281 mi per second. The speed of light is the highest speed possible, according to the theory of ◊relativity, and its value is independent of the motion of its source and of the observer. It is impossible to accelerate any material body to this speed because it would require an infinite amount of energy.

> TO REMEMBER THE SPEED OF LIGHT:
>
> THE SPEED OF LIGHT IS 299,792,458 M/S, WHICH CAN BE REMEMBERED FROM THE NUMBER OF LETTERS IN EACH WORD OF THE FOLLOWING PHRASE: WE GUARANTEE CERTAINTY, CLEARLY REFERRING TO THIS LIGHT MNEMONIC

speed of reaction alternative term for ◊rate of reaction.

speed of sound speed at which sound travels through a medium, such as air or water. In air at a temperature of 0°C/32°F, the speed of sound is 331 m/1,087 ft per second. At higher temperatures, the speed of sound is greater; at 18°C/64°F it is 342 m/1,123 ft per second.

It is greater in liquids and solids; for example, in water it is around 1,440 m/4,724 ft per second, depending on the temperature.

speedometer instrument attached to the transmission of a vehicle by a flexible drive shaft, which indicates the speed of the vehicle in miles or kilometres per hour on a dial easily visible to the driver.

speed–time graph graph used to describe the motion of a body by illustrating how its speed or velocity changes with time. The gradient of the graph gives the object's acceleration: if the gradient is zero (the graph is horizontal) then the body is moving with constant speed or uniform velocity; if the gradient is constant, the body is moving with uniform acceleration. The area under the graph gives the total distance travelled by the body.

speedwell any of a group of flowering plants belonging to the snapdragon family. Of the many wild species, most are low-growing with small bluish flowers. (Genus *Veronica,* family Scrophulariaceae.)

speleology scientific study of caves, their origin, development, physical structure, flora, fauna, folklore, exploration, mapping, photography, cave-diving, and rescue work. **Potholing**, which involves following the course of underground rivers or streams, has become a popular sport.

Speleology first developed in France in the late 19th century, where the Société de Spéléologie was founded in 1895.

sperm or ***spermatozoon*** in biology, the male ◊gamete of animals. Each sperm cell has a head capsule containing a nucleus, a middle portion containing ◊mitochondria (which provide energy), and a long tail (flagellum). See ◊sexual reproduction.

In most animals, the sperm are motile, and are propelled by a long flagellum, but in some (such as crabs and lobsters) they are nonmotile. Sperm cells are produced in the testes (see ◊testis). From there they pass through the sperm ducts via the seminal vesicles and the ◊prostate gland, which produce fluids called semen that give the sperm cells energy and keep them moving after they leave the body. Hundreds of millions of sperm cells are contained in only a small amount of semen. The human sperm is 0.005 mm/0.0002 in long and can survive inside the female for 2–9 days. Mammalian sperm have receptor cells identical to some of those found in the lining of the nose. These may help in navigating towards the egg.

The term is sometimes applied to the motile male gametes (◊antherozoids) of lower plants.

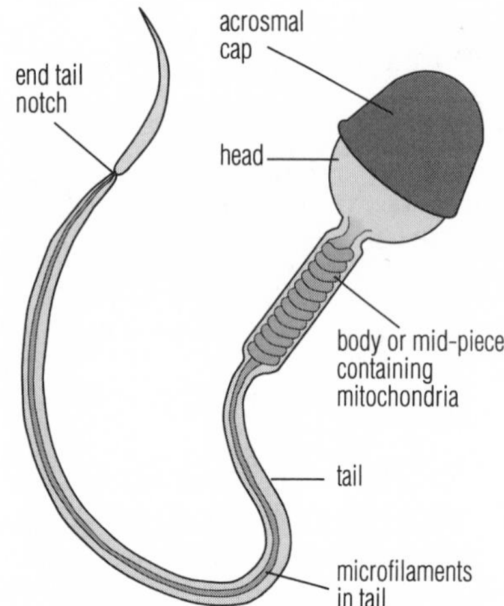

sperm Only a single sperm is needed to fertilize an egg, or ovum. Yet up to 500 million may start the journey towards the egg. Once a sperm has fertilized an egg, the egg's wall cannot be penetrated by other sperm. The unsuccessful sperm die after about three days.

spermaceti glistening waxlike substance, not a true oil, contained in the cells of the huge, almost rectangular 'case' in the head of the sperm whale, amounting to about 2.8 tonnes/3 tons. It rapidly changes in density with variations in temperature. It was formerly used in lubricants and cosmetics, but in 1980 a blend of fatty acids and esters from tallow and coconut oil was developed as a substitute.

spermatophore small capsule containing ◊sperm and other nutrients produced in invertebrates, newts, and cephalopods.

spermatophyte in botany, another name for a ◊seed plant.

sperm competition competition between the sperm of rival males within the body of the female. This may involve actual removal of a rival's sperm before mating, for example the penis of a male dragonfly is shaped to scoop out existing sperm; or internal competition between rival sperm cells.

spermicide any cream, jelly, pessary, or other preparation that kills the ◊sperm cells in semen. Spermicides are used for contraceptive purposes, usually in combination with a ◊condom or ◊diaphragm. Sponges impregnated with spermicide have been developed but are not yet in widespread use. Spermicide used alone is only 75% effective in preventing pregnancy.

sphalerite mineral composed of zinc sulphide with a small proportion of iron, formula (Zn,Fe)S. It is the chief ore of zinc. Sphalerite is brown with a nonmetallic lustre unless an appreciable amount of iron is present (up to 26% by weight). Sphalerite usually occurs in ore veins in limestones, where it is often associated with galena. It crystallizes in the cubic system but does not normally form perfect cubes.

sphere in mathematics, a perfectly round object with all points on its surface the same distance from the centre. This distance is the radius of the sphere. For a sphere of radius r, the volume $V = 4/3\pi r^3$ and the surface area $A = 4\pi r^2$.

There is geometry in the humming of the strings. There is music in the spacings of the spheres.

PYTHAGORAS
Quoted in Aristotle *Metaphysics*

sphincter ring of muscle, such as is found at various points in the ◊alimentary canal, that contracts and relaxes to open and close the canal and control the movement of food. The **pyloric sphincter**, at the base of the stomach, controls the release of the gastric contents into the ◊duodenum. After release the sphincter contracts, closing off the stomach. The **external anal sphincter** closes the ◊anus; the **internal anal sphincter** constricts the rectum; the **sphincter vesicae** controls the urethral orifice of the bladder. In the eye the **sphincter pupillae** contracts the pupil in response to bright light.

sphygmomanometer instrument for measuring blood pressure. Consisting of an inflatable arm cuff joined by a rubber tube to a pressure-recording device (incorporating a column of mercury with a graduated scale), it is used, together with a stethoscope, to measure arterial blood pressure.

Sphynx cat or ***Canadian Hairless*** breed of domestic hairless cat bred in Ontario, Canada, since 1966. It is bald apart from a fine down on the face, ears, feet, and tail, and the skin is wrinkled on the face, body, and legs. It has very large ears, a short nose, and no whiskers.

The Sphynx has not yet been recognized by many cat associations. Hairless cats are said to have been bred by the Aztecs and have also been recorded at the turn of the 20th century in New Mexico, USA. However, the 'Mexican Hairless' has now become extinct.

Spica or ***Alpha Virginis*** the brightest star in the constellation Virgo and the 16th brightest star in the sky. First-magnitude Spica has a true luminosity of over 1,500 times that of the Sun, and is 140 light years from Earth. It is also a spectroscopic binary star, the components of which orbit each other every four days.

spice any aromatic vegetable substance used as a condiment and for flavouring food. Spices are mostly obtained from tropical plants, and include pepper, nutmeg, ginger, and cinnamon. They have little food value but increase the appetite and may help digestion.

spicebush aromatic E North American shrub *Lindera benzoin* of the laurel family Lauraceae, with leathery, elliptical leaves.

Its red, aromatic berries can be dried and crushed for use as a spice and its leaves for tea.

spicules, solar in astronomy, short-lived jets of hot gas in the upper ◊chromosphere of the Sun. Spiky in appearance, they move at high velocities along lines of magnetic force to which they owe their shape, and last for a few minutes each. Spicules appear to disperse material into the ◊corona.

spider any arachnid (eight-legged animal) of the order Araneae. There are about 30,000 known species, mostly a few centimetres

SPIDER

Spider silk is up to 200 times finer than the finest human hair and is highly elastic. It can be stretched to over 20% of its length and retains its elasticity at temperatures as low as –40°C.

in size, although a few tropical forms attain great size, for example, some bird-eating spiders attain a body length of 9 cm/3.5 in. Spiders produce silk, and many spin webs to trap their prey. They are found everywhere in the world except Antarctica. Many species are found in woods and dry commons; a few are aquatic. Spiders are predators; they bite their prey, releasing a powerful toxin from poison glands which causes paralysis, together with digestive juices. They then suck out the juices and soft parts.

spider in computing, program that combs the ◊Internet for new documents such as Web pages and ◊FTP files. Spiders start their work by retrieving a document such as a Web page and then following all the links and references contained in it. They repeat the process with the followed links, supplying all the references they find to a database that can be searched via a ◊search engine.

spider monkey species of monkey found in Central and South America. Spider monkeys have long and very flexible limbs and a long, prehensile tail that is much used in climbing. The thumb is either absent or vestigial (much reduced).

species There are two species in the genus *Ateles*: the **black spider monkey** (or coaita) *A. paniscus* lives in Brazil and the **long-haired spider monkey** (or marimonda) *A. belzebuth* lives in Guiana. The single species in the genus *Brachyteles* is the **woolly spider monkey** *B. arachnoides,* characterized by its long, woolly hair. It is quite large and varies from grey to brown or even yellow in colour.

classification Spider monkeys are in the family Cebidae, order Primates.

spider plant African plant belonging to the lily family. Two species (*C. comosum* and *C. elatum*) are popular house plants. They have long, narrow, variegated leaves and produce flowering shoots from which the new plants grow, hanging below the main plant. The flowers are small and white. Spider plants absorb toxins from the air and therefore help to purify the atmosphere around them. (Genus *Chlorophytum,* family Liliaceae.)

spikelet in botany, one of the units of a grass ◊inflorescence. It comprises a slender axis on which one or more flowers are borne.

Each individual flower or floret has a pair of scalelike bracts, the glumes, and is enclosed by a membranous lemma and a thin, narrow palea, which may be extended into a long, slender bristle, or **awn**.

spikenard either of two plants: a Himalayan plant belonging to the valerian family whose underground stems produce a perfume used in Eastern aromatic oils; or a North American plant of the ginseng family, with fragrant roots. (Himalayan *Nardostachys jatamansi,* family Valerianaceae; North American *Aralia racemosa,* family Araliaceae.)

spin in physics, the intrinsic ◊angular momentum of a subatomic particle, nucleus, atom, or molecule, which continues to exist even when the particle comes to rest. A particle in a specific energy state has a particular spin, just as it has a particular electric charge and mass. According to ◊quantum theory, this is restricted to discrete and indivisible values, specified by a spin ◊quantum number. Because of its spin, a charged particle acts as a small magnet and is affected by magnetic fields.

spina bifida congenital defect in which part of the spinal cord and its membranes are exposed, due to incomplete development of the spine (vertebral column). It is a neural tube defect.

Spina bifida, usually present in the lower back, varies in severity. The most seriously affected babies may be paralysed below the waist. There is also a risk of mental retardation and death from hydrocephalus, which is often associated. Surgery is performed to close the spinal lesion shortly after birth, but this does not usually cure the disabilities caused by the condition. Spina bifida can be diagnosed prenatally.

spinach annual plant belonging to the goosefoot family. It is native to Asia and widely cultivated for its leaves, which are eaten as a vegetable. (*Spinacia oleracea,* family Chenopodiaceae.)

spinal cord major component of the ◊central nervous system in vertebrates, encased in the spinal column. It consists of bundles of nerves enveloped in three layers of membrane (the meninges).

spinal tap another term for ◊lumbar puncture, a medical test.

spine backbone of vertebrates. In most mammals, it contains 26 small bones called vertebrae, which enclose and protect the spinal cord (which links the peripheral nervous system to the brain).

The spine articulates with the skull, ribs, and hip bones, and provides attachment for the back muscles.

In humans it is made up of individual vertebrae, separated by intervertebral discs. In the adult there are seven cervical **vertebrae** in the neck; twelve thoracic in the upper trunk; five lumbar in the lower back; the sacrum (consisting of five rudimentary vertebrae fused together, joined to the hipbones); and the coccyx (four vertebrae, fused into a tailbone). The human spine has four curves (front to rear), which allow for the increased size of the chest and pelvic cavities, and permit springing, to minimize jolting of the internal organs. *See illustration on page 708.*

spinel any of a group of 'mixed oxide' minerals consisting mainly of the oxides of magnesium and aluminium, $MgAl_2O_4$ and $FeAl_2O_4$. Spinels crystallize in the cubic system, forming octahedral crystals. They are found in high-temperature igneous and metamorphic rocks. The aluminium oxide spinel contains gem varieties, such as the ruby spinels of Sri Lanka and Myanmar (Burma).

spinifex spiny grass chiefly found in Australia, growing on the coastal sand dunes. It is often planted to bind sand along the seashore. The term also refers to porcupine grass, any of a group of spiny-leaved, tussock-forming grasses of inland Australia. (Genus *Spinifex;* porcupine grass genus *Triodia.*)

spinone breed of medium-sized gundog developed in Italy from various ancient hunting breeds. Its rough coat, mainly white with orange-brown patches and flecks, is ideal for hunting in wooded areas. It has a sturdy build and grows to about 65 cm/25.5 in.

spiny anteater alternative name for ◊echidna.

spiracle in insects, the opening of a ◊trachea, through which oxygen enters the body and carbon dioxide is expelled. In cartilaginous fishes (sharks and rays), the same name is given to a circular opening that marks the remains of the first gill slit.

In tetrapod vertebrates, the spiracle of early fishes has evolved into the Eustachian tube, which connects the middle ear cavity with the pharynx.

***spiracle** The spiracles of this large* Dirphia avia *moth caterpillar from Trinidad are visible as a line of white ovals outlined with a black rim. Premaphotos Wildlife*

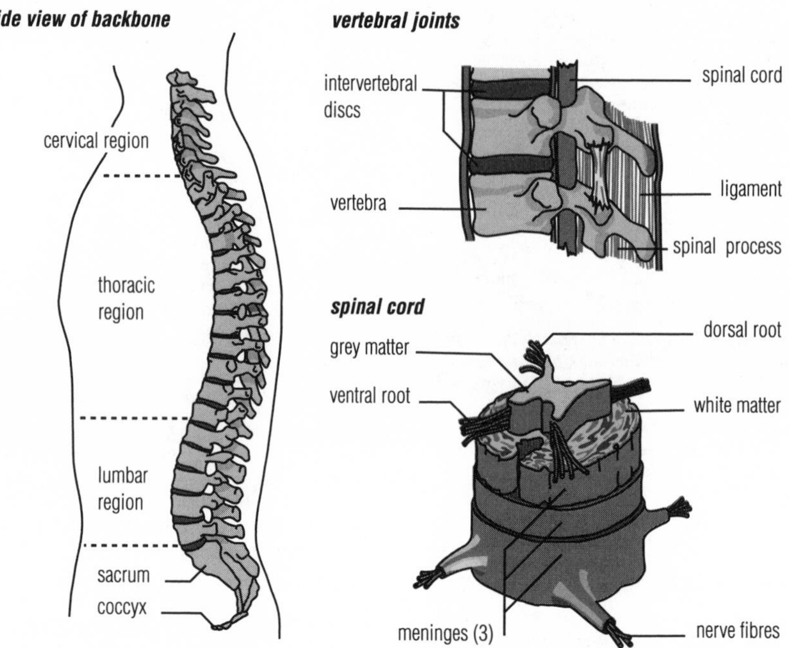

spine *The human spine extends every night during sleep. During the day, the cartilage discs between the vertebra are squeezed when the body is in a vertical position, standing or sitting, but at night, with pressure released, the discs swell and the spine lengthens by about 8 mm/0.3 in.*

spiraea any of a group of ◊herbaceous plants or shrubs, which includes many cultivated species with ornamental sprays of white or pink flowers; their delicate appearance has given rise to the popular name bridal wreath. (Genus *Spiraea*, family Rosaceae.)

spiral a plane curve formed by a point winding round a fixed point from which it distances itself at regular intervals, for example the spiral traced by a flat coil of rope. Various kinds of spirals can be generated mathematically – for example, an equiangular or logarithmic spiral (in which a tangent at any point on the curve always makes the same angle with it) and an ◊involute. Spirals also occur in nature as a normal consequence of accelerating growth, such as the spiral shape of the shells of snails and some other molluscs.

spiral aloe or ***kharetsa*** a perennial succulent plant *Aloe polyphylla* confined to mountains in Lesotho. An attractive species valued by the horticultural trade, this succulent has been endangered by uprooting for sale to collectors. It is now legally protected and is known from about 50 localities, but remains vulnerable.

spiral galaxy in astronomy, one of the main classes of ◊galaxy in the Hubble classification comprising up to 30% of known galaxies. Spiral galaxies are characterized by a central bulge surrounded by a flattened disc containing (normally) two spiral arms composed of hot young stars and clouds of dust and gas. In about half of spiral galaxies (barred spirals) the arms originate at the ends of a bar across the central bulge. The bar is not a rigid object but consists of stars in motion about the centre of the galaxy.

spirits of salts former name for ◊hydrochloric acid.

Formerly, when religion was strong and science weak, men mistook magic for medicine; now, when science is strong and religion weak, men mistake medicine for magic.

THOMAS SZASZ Hungarian-born US psychiatrist.
'Science and Scientism'

spiritual healing or ***psychic healing*** transmission of energy from or through a healer, who may practise hand healing or absent healing through prayer or meditation.

In religions worldwide, from shamanism to latter-day charismatic Christianity, healing powers have been attributed to gifted individuals, and sometimes to particular locations (Delphi, Lourdes) or objects (religious relics), and the anecdotal evidence for the reality of spiritual healing is substantial and cross-cultural. Since both healers and beneficiaries can only adduce metaphysical explanations for the effects, medical science remains sceptical, at most allowing that in exceptional cases faith and will may bring about inexplicable cures or remissions, which, however, also occur in cases where no spiritual contribution is claimed.

spirochaete spiral-shaped bacterium. Some spirochaetes are free-living in water, others inhabit the intestines and genital areas of animals. The sexually transmitted disease syphilis is caused by a spirochaete.

spit ridge of sand or shingle projecting from the land into a body of water. It is deposited by waves carrying material from one direction to another across the mouth of an inlet (longshore drift). Deposition in the brackish water behind a spit may result in the formation of a ◊salt marsh.

spittle alternative name for ◊saliva and ◊cuckoo spit.

spittlebug alternative name for ◊froghopper.

spleen organ in vertebrates, part of the reticuloendothelial system, which helps to process ◊lymphocytes. It also regulates the number of red blood cells in circulation by destroying old cells, and stores iron. It is situated on the left side of the body, behind the stomach.

sponge any saclike simple invertebrate of the phylum Porifera, usually marine. A sponge has a hollow body, its cavity lined by cells

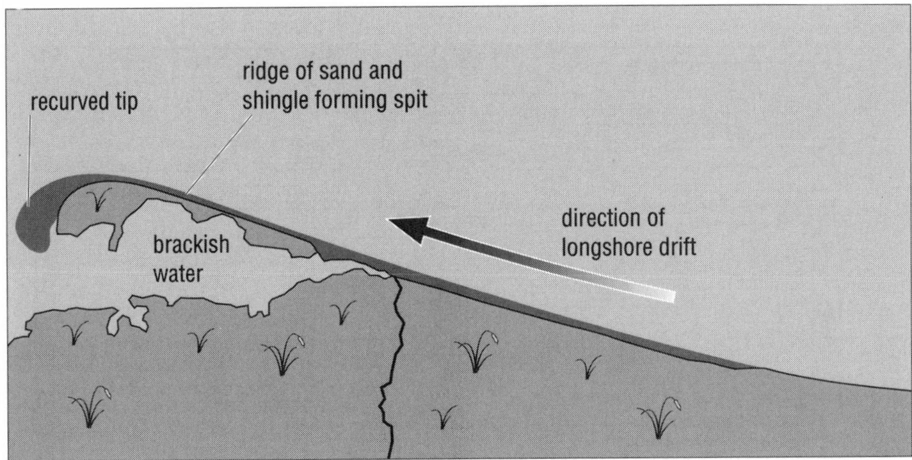

spit *Longshore drift carries sand and shingle up coastlines. Deposited material gradually builds up over time at headlands forming a new stretch of land called a spit. A spit that extends across a bay is known as a bar.*

bearing flagellae, whose whiplike movements keep water circulating, bringing in a stream of food particles. The body walls are strengthened with protein (as in the bath sponge) or small spikes of silica, or a framework of calcium carbonate.

A deep-sea sponge found in 1994 is the first carnivorous sponge to be identified. The 15-mm/0.6-in high sponge, of the family Cladorhizidae, traps small crustaceans by entangling them in thin filaments. Epithelial cells then migrate towards the prey and envelop it.

spontaneous combustion burning that is not initiated by the direct application of an external source of heat. A number of materials and chemicals, such as hay and sodium chlorate, can react with their surroundings, usually by oxidation, to produce so much internal heat that combustion results.

Special precautions must be taken for the storage and handling of substances that react violently with moisture or air. For example, phosphorus ignites spontaneously in the presence of air and must therefore be stored under water; sodium and potassium are stored under kerosene in order to prevent their being exposed to moisture.

spontaneous generation or ***abiogenesis*** erroneous belief that living organisms can arise spontaneously from nonliving matter. This survived until the mid-19th century, when the French chemist Louis Pasteur demonstrated that a nutrient broth would not generate microorganisms if it was adequately sterilized. The theory of ◊biogenesis holds that spontaneous generation cannot now occur; it is thought, however, to have played an essential role in the origin of ◊life on this planet 4 billion years ago.

spooling in computing, the process in which information to be printed is stored temporarily in a file, the printing being carried out later. It is used to prevent a relatively slow printer from holding up the system at critical times, and to enable several computers or programs to share one printer.

spoonbill any of several large wading birds of the ibis family Threskiornithidae, order Ciconiiformes, characterized by a long, flat bill, dilated at the tip in the shape of a spoon. Spoonbills are white or pink, and up to 90 cm/3 ft tall. Their feet are adapted for wading, and the birds obtain their food, consisting chiefly of fish, frogs, molluscs, and crustaceans, from shallow water.

sporangium structure in which ◊spores are produced.

spore small reproductive or resting body, usually consisting of just one cell. Unlike a ◊gamete, it does not need to fuse with another cell in order to develop into a new organism. Spores are produced by the lower plants, most fungi, some bacteria, and certain protozoa. They are generally light and easily dispersed by wind movements.

Plant spores are haploid and are produced by the sporophyte, following ◊meiosis; see ◊alternation of generations.

sporophyte diploid spore-producing generation in the life cycle of a plant that undergoes valternation of generations.

sprat small marine bony fish common around the British Isles. It is 7–15 cm/2.8–6 in long, with smooth scales and a prominent lower jaw. It has a sharp, toothed edge to its belly.
classification The sprat *Clupea sprattus* is a small member of the herring genus, order Clupeiformes, class Osteichthyes.

spreadsheet in computing, a program that mimics a sheet of ruled paper, divided into columns and rows. The user enters values in the sheet, then instructs the program to perform some operation on them, such as totalling a column or finding the average of a series of numbers.

Highly complex numerical analyses may be built up from these simple steps.

Spreadsheets are widely used in business for forecasting and financial control. The first spreadsheet program, Software Arts' VisiCalc, appeared 1979. The best known include ◊Lotus 1–2–3 and Microsoft ◊Excel.

spring device, usually a metal coil, that returns to its original shape after being stretched or compressed. Springs are used in some machines (such as clocks) to store energy, which can be released at a controlled rate. In other machines (such as engines) they are used to close valves.

In vehicle-suspension systems, springs are used to cushion passengers from road shocks. These springs are used in conjunction with ◊shock absorbers to limit their amount of travel. In bedding and upholstered furniture springs add comfort.

spring in geology, a natural flow of water from the ground, formed at the point of intersection of the water table and the ground's surface. The source of water is rain that has percolated through the overlying rocks. During its underground passage, the water may have dissolved mineral substances that may then be precipitated at the spring (hence, a mineral spring).

A spring may be continuous or intermittent, and depends on the position of the water table and the topography (surface features).

spring balance instrument for measuring weight that relates the weight of an object to the extent to which it stretches or

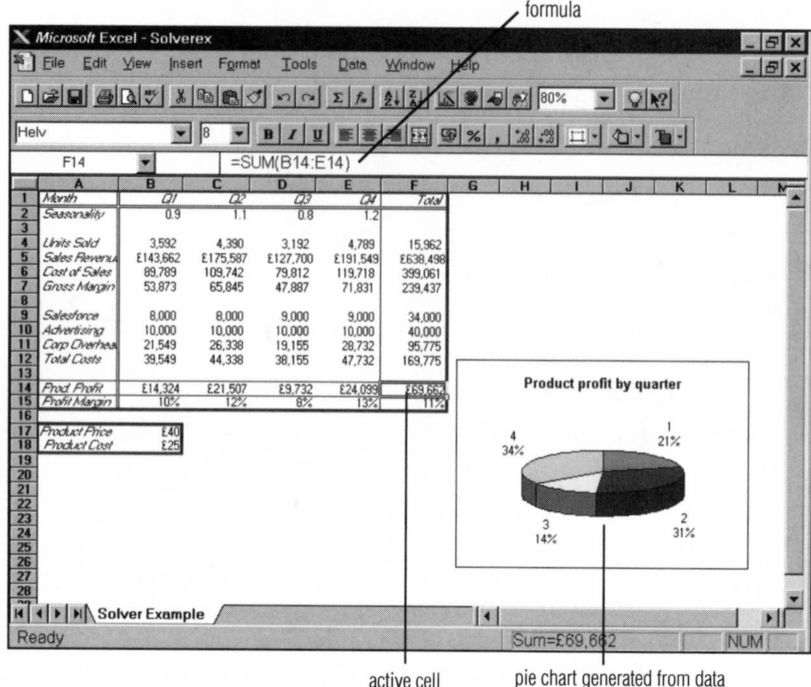

	A	B	C	D	E	F
1	Month	Q1	Q2	Q3	Q4	Total
2	Seasonality	0.9	1.1	0.8	1.2	
3						
4	Units Sold	3,592	4,390	3,192	4,789	15,962
5	Sales Revenu	£143,662	£175,587	£127,700	£191,549	£638,498
6	Cost of Sales	89,789	109,742	79,812	119,718	399,061
7	Gross Margin	53,873	65,845	47,887	71,831	239,437
8						
9	Salesforce	8,000	8,000	9,000	9,000	34,000
10	Advertising	10,000	10,000	10,000	10,000	40,000
11	Corp Overhea	21,549	26,338	19,155	28,732	95,775
12	Total Costs	39,549	44,338	38,155	47,732	169,775
13						
14	Prod Profit	£14,324	£21,507	£9,732	£24,099	£69,662
15	Profit Margin	10%	12%	8%	13%	11%
16						
17	Product Price	£40				
18	Product Cost	£25				

spreadsheet *A typical spreadsheet software package. The data it contains may be output in a graphical form, enabling the production of charts and diagrams.*

compresses a vertical spring. According to ◊Hooke's law, the extension or compression will be directly proportional to the weight, providing that the spring is not overstretched. A pointer attached to the spring indicates the weight on a scale, which may be calibrated in newtons (the SI unit of force) for physics experiments, or in grams, kilograms, or pounds (units of mass) for everyday use.

springbok South African antelope *Antidorcas marsupialis* about 80 cm/30 in at the shoulder, with head and body 1.3 m/4 ft long. It may leap 3 m/10 ft or more in the air when startled or playing, and has a fold of skin along the middle of the back which is raised to a crest in alarm. Springboks once migrated in herds of over a million, but are now found only in small numbers where protected.

springer spaniel breed of medium-sized gundog bred in England and Wales for 'springing' (flushing out) game. The Welsh springer is red and white and used mainly for upland game; the English is brown and white, or black and white, or a variety of solid colours,

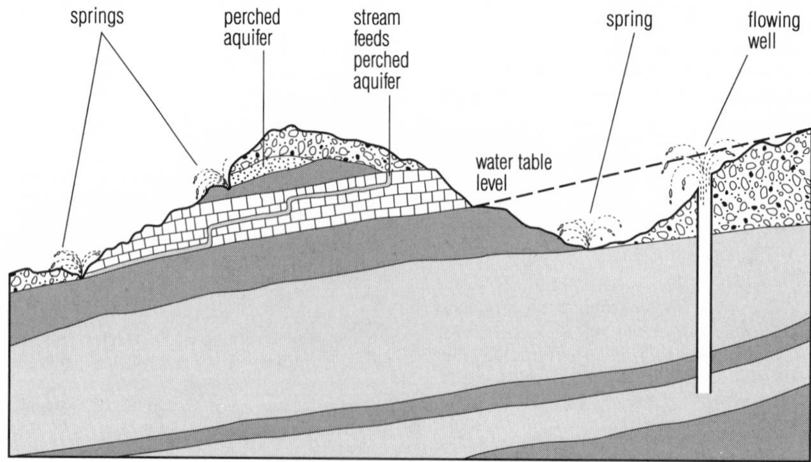

spring *Springs occur where water-laden rock layers (aquifers) reach the surface. Water will flow from a well whose head is below the water table.*

and will spring game and retrieve from water. Both types weigh up to about 20 kg/45 lb and stand about 50 cm/20 in tall.

Springfield rifle US Army service rifle, adopted in 1903 and retained in service until the 1940s.

Of 0.30 in calibre, it used a Mauser bolt mechanism and five-shot magazine. The name came from the Springfield, Massachusetts, arsenal where it was designed and originally manufactured.

springtail small wingless insect. The maximum size is 6 mm/0.2 in in length. Springtails are extremely widespread and can be found in soil, decaying vegetable matter, under the bark of trees, in ant and termite nests, and on the surface of fresh water. There are about 1,500 species of springtail and some species are, unusually for insects, marine.

Springtails have mandibulate mouthparts (adapted for chewing), which are withdrawn into the head when not in use. They do not have compound eyes, but simple eyes may be present. The antennae are usually four-segmented, and the abdomen is six-segmented with, usually, three pairs of appendages, the most important being the forked springing organ attached to the under surface of segment number four. There is, usually, no tracheal (respiratory tube) system and the insects breathe through the cuticle. They usually, therefore, inhabit moist situations.

classification Springtails are in order Collembola, class Insecta, phylum Arthropoda.

Sprint US telecommunications company supplying data and long-distance voice connections. It was founded in 1899 as the Brown Telephone Company.

Sprint began offering long distance service under the Sprint brand name in 1986. The company was the first to connect coast-to-coast fibre-optic transmissions.

sprite in computing, a graphics object made up of a pattern of ◊pixels (picture elements) defined by a computer programmer. Some ◊high-level languages and ◊applications programs contain routines that allow a user to define the shape, colours, and other characteristics of individual graphics objects. These objects can then be manipulated and combined to produce animated games or graphic screen displays.

spruce coniferous tree belonging to the pine family, found over much of the northern hemisphere. Pyramidal in shape, spruces have rigid, prickly needles and drooping, leathery cones. Some are important forestry trees, such as the sitka spruce (*P. sitchensis*), native to W North America, and the Norway spruce (*P. abies*), now planted widely in North America. (Genus *Picea*, family Pinaceae.)

Sputnik Russian 'fellow traveller' series of ten Soviet Earth-orbiting satellites. *Sputnik 1* was the first artificial satellite, launched 4 October 1957. It weighed 84 kg/185 lb, with a 58 cm/23 in diameter, and carried only a simple radio transmitter which allowed scientists to track it as it orbited Earth. It burned up in the atmosphere 92 days later. Sputniks were superseded in the early 1960s by the Cosmos series.

Sputnik 2, launched 3 November 1957, weighed about 500 kg/1,100 lb including the dog Laika, the first living creature in space. Unfortunately, there was no way to return the dog to Earth, and it died in space. Later Sputniks were test flights of the ◊Vostok spacecraft.

sq abbreviation for **square** (measure).

SQL (abbreviation for ***structured query language***) high-level computer language designed for use with ◊relational databases. Although it can be used by programmers in the same way as other languages, it is often used as a means for programs to communicate with each other. Typically, one program (called the 'client') uses SQL to request data from a database 'server'.

Although originally developed by IBM, SQL is now widely used on many types of computer.

Squamata order of reptiles comprising the snakes and lizards.

square in geometry, a quadrilateral (four-sided) plane figure with all sides equal and each angle a right angle. Its diagonals bisect each other at right angles. The area A of a square is the length l of one side multiplied by itself ($A = l \times l$).

Also, any quantity multiplied by itself is termed a square, represented by an ◊exponent of power 2; for example, $4 \times 4 = 4^2 = 16$ and $6.8 \times 6.8 = 6.8^2 = 46.24$.

An algebraic term is squared by doubling its exponent and squaring its coefficient if it has one; for example, $(x^2)^2 = x^4$ and $(6y^3)^2 = 36y^6$. A number that has a whole number as its ◊square root is known as a **perfect square**; for example, 25, 144 and 54,756 are perfect squares (with roots of 5, 12, and 234, respectively).

square root in mathematics, a number that when squared (multiplied by itself) equals a given number. For example, the square root of 25 (written $\sqrt{25}$) is ± 5, because $5 \times 5 = 25$, and $(-5) \times (-5) = 25$. As an ◊exponent, a square root is represented by $\frac{1}{2}$, for example, $16^{\frac{1}{2}} = 4$.

Negative numbers (less than 0) do not have square roots that are ◊real numbers. Their roots are represented by ◊complex numbers, in which the square root of –1 is given the symbol i (that is, $\pm i^2 = -1$). Thus the square root of –4 is $\sqrt{[(-1) \times 4]} = \sqrt{-1} \times \sqrt{4} = 2i$.

SQUID

The eyes of the giant squid – at a diameter of 37 cm/15 in – are the size of dustbin lids. They are the largest in the animal kingdom.

squid marine mollusc of the class Cephalopoda. See ◊cephalopod.

IN SEARCH OF GIANT SQUID

http://seawifs.gsfc.nasa.gov/OCEAN_PLANET/HTML/squid_opening.html

Exhibition about the world's largest invertebrates presented by the Smithsonian's National Museum of Natural History. It includes a large number of photos, discussion of stories and myths surrounding giant squid, a fascinating comparison of squid and snails, and informative sections on anatomy, food, movement, and defence systems.

squill bulb-forming perennial plant belonging to the lily family, found growing in dry places near the sea in W Europe. Cultivated species usually bear blue flowers, either singly or in clusters, at the top of the stem. (Genus *Scilla*, family Liliaceae.)

squint or ***strabismus*** common condition in which one eye deviates in any direction. A squint may be convergent (with the bad eye turned inwards), divergent (outwards), or, in rare cases, vertical. A convergent squint is also called **cross-eye**.

There are two types of squint: **paralytic**, arising from disease or damage involving the extraocular muscles or their nerve supply; and **nonparalytic**, which may be inherited or due to some refractive error within the eye. Nonparalytic (or concomitant) squint is the typical condition seen in small children. It is treated by corrective glasses, exercises for the eye muscles, or surgery.

squirrel rodent of the family Sciuridae. Squirrels are found worldwide except for Australia, Madagascar, and polar regions. Some are tree dwellers; these generally have bushy tails, and some, with membranes between their legs, are called ◊flying squirrels. Others are terrestrial, generally burrowing forms called ground squirrels; these include chipmunks, gophers, marmots, and prairie dogs.

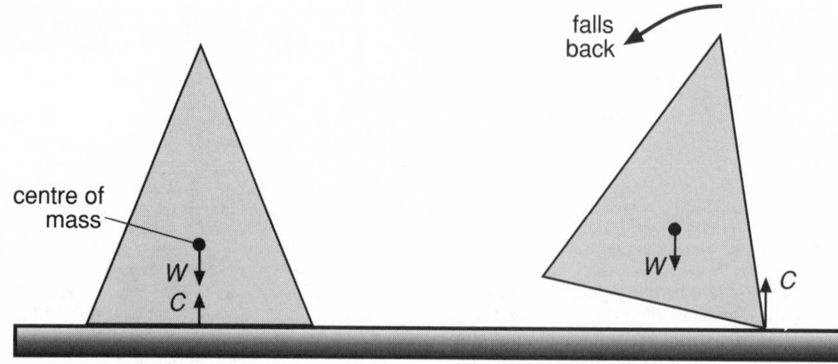

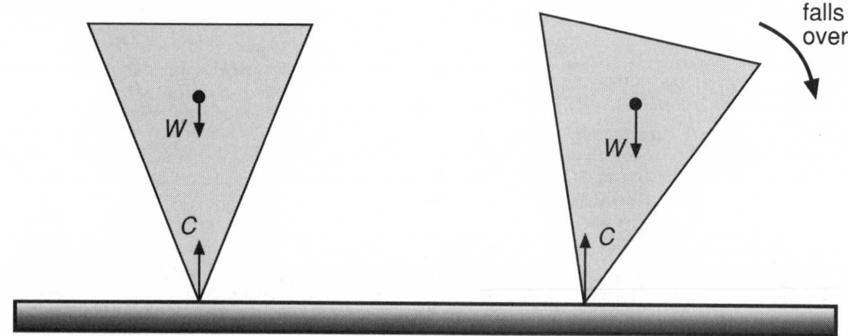

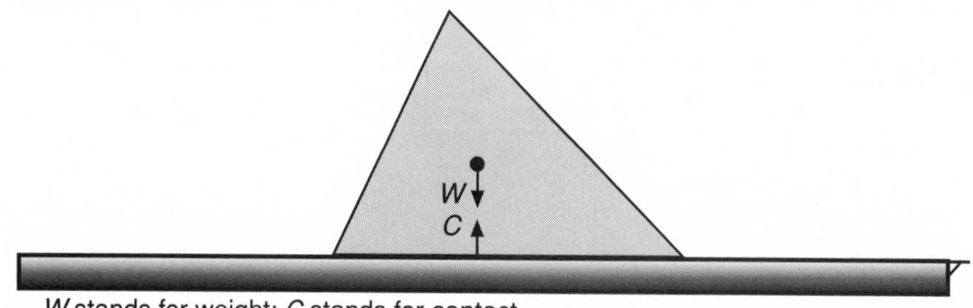

stability

squirrel monkey small, tree-dwelling New World monkey that eats mainly fruit, with some insects. They have long, non-prehensile tails and live in groups of as many as 200 individuals.

classification Squirrel monkeys are in genus *Saimiri* family Cebidae, order Primates.

SRAM (acronym for ***static random-access memory***) computer memory device in the form of a silicon chip used to provide ◊immediate access memory. SRAM is faster but more expensive than ◊DRAM (dynamic random-access memory).

DRAM loses its contents unless they are read and rewritten every 2 milliseconds or so. This process is called **refreshing** the memory. SRAM does not require such frequent refreshing.

SSSI abbreviation for ◊Site of Special Scientific Interest.

Staaken German heavy bombing aircraft of World War I made by the *Zeppelin Werke Staaken*.

stability measure of how difficult it is to move an object from a position of balance or ◊equilibrium with respect to gravity.

An object displaced from equilibrium does not remain in its new position if its weight, acting vertically downwards through its ◊centre of mass, no longer passes through the line of action of the ◊contact force (the force exerted by the surface on which the object is resting), acting vertically upwards through the object's new base. If the lines of action of these two opposite but equal forces do not coincide they will form a couple and create a moment (see ◊moment of a force) that will cause the object either to return to its original rest position or to topple over into another position.

An object in **stable equilibrium** returns to its rest position after being displaced slightly. This form of equilibrium is found in objects that are difficult to topple over; these usually possess a relatively wide base and a low centre of mass – for example, a cone resting on its flat base on a horizontal surface. When such an object is tilted slightly its centre of mass is raised and the line of action of its weight no longer coincides with that of the contact force exerted by its new, smaller base area. The moment created will tend to lower the centre of mass and so the cone will fall back to its original position.

An object in **unstable equilibrium** does not remain at rest if displaced, but falls into a new position; it does not return to its original rest position. Objects possessing this form of equilibrium are easily toppled and usually have a relatively small base and a high centre of mass – for example, a cone balancing on its point, or apex, on a horizontal surface. When an object such as this is given the slightest push its centre of mass is lowered and the displacement of the line of action of its weight creates a moment. The moment will tend to lower the centre of mass still further and so the object will fall on to another position.

An object in **neutral equilibrium** stays at rest if it is moved into a new position – neither moving back to its original position nor on any further. This form of equilibrium is found in objects that are able to roll, such as a cone resting on its curved side placed on a horizontal surface. When such an object is rolled its centre of mass remains in the same position, neither rising nor falling, and the line of action of its weight continues to coincide with the contact force; no moment is created and so its equilibrium is maintained.

stabilizer one of a pair of fins fitted to the sides of a ship, especially one governed automatically by a ◊gyroscope mechanism, designed to reduce side-to-side rolling of the ship in rough weather.

stable equilibrium the state of equilibrium possessed by a body that will return to its original rest position if displaced slightly. See ◊stability.

stack in computing, a method of storing data in which the most recent item stored will be the first to be retrieved. The technique is commonly called 'last in, first out'.

Stacks are used to solve problems involving nested structures; for example, to analyse an arithmetical expression containing subexpressions in parentheses, or to work out a route between two points when there are many different paths.

Staffordshire bull terrier breed of dog developed in England as a cross between the bulldog and the terrier. Like the related ◊bull terrier, it was formerly used for bull-baiting and is still used for illegal dogfighting. It has a sturdy, muscular build, with a heavy, square head, and powerful jaws. It stands up to about 40 cm/15 in at the shoulder and weighs in the range 10.5–17 kg/24–38 lb. Common colours are red-brown, fawn, or brindle, often with white markings.

stag beetle any of a number of large dark brown beetles, the males of which possess enormous mandibles, or jaws, shaped rather like the antlers of a stag. There are over 900 species within this family.

The males are much bigger than the females and very often the length of their mandibles equals the length of the rest of the body. The mandibles appear to be largely ornamental and cannot be moved by the jaw muscles. Another characteristic feature is the smooth appearance of the chestnut-coloured wing cases, which are devoid of ridges. The larvae inhabit the rotting wood or the roots of trees, such as oak.

classification The stag beetle is in family Lucanidae of the superfamily Scarabaeoidea, order Coleoptera, class Insecta, phylum Arthropoda.

stain in chemistry, a coloured compound that will bind to other substances. Stains are used extensively in microbiology to colour microorganisms and in histochemistry to detect the presence and whereabouts in plant and animal tissue of substances such as fats, cellulose, and proteins.

stainless steel widely used ◊alloy of iron, chromium, and nickel that resists rusting. Its chromium content also gives it a high tensile strength. It is used for cutlery and kitchen fittings, and in surgical instruments. Stainless steel was first produced in the UK in 1913 and in Germany in 1914.

stalactite and stalagmite cave structures formed by the deposition of calcite dissolved in ground water. **Stalactites** grow downwards from the roofs or walls and can be icicle-shaped, straw-shaped, curtain-shaped, or formed as terraces. **Stalagmites** grow upwards from the cave floor and can be conical, fir-cone-shaped, or resemble a stack of saucers. Growing stalactites and stalagmites may meet to form a continuous column from floor to ceiling.

Stalactites are formed when ground water, hanging as a drip, loses a proportion of its carbon dioxide into the air of the cave. This reduces the amount of calcite that can be held in solution, and a small trace of calcite is deposited. Successive drips build up the stalactite over many years. In stalagmite formation the calcite comes out of the solution because of agitation – the shock of a drop of water hitting the floor is sufficient to remove some calcite from the drop. The different shapes result from the splashing of the falling water.

stamen male reproductive organ of a flower. The stamens are collectively referred to as the ◊androecium. A typical stamen consists of a stalk, or filament, with an anther, the pollen-bearing organ, at its apex, but in some primitive plants, such as *Magnolia,* the stamen may not be markedly differentiated.

The number and position of the stamens are significant in the classification of flowering plants. Generally the more advanced plant families have fewer stamens, but they are often positioned more effectively so that the likelihood of successful pollination is not reduced.

stand-alone computer self-contained computer, usually a microcomputer, that is not connected to a network of computers and can be used in isolation from any other device.

standard atmosphere alternative term for ◊atmosphere, a unit of pressure.

standard deviation in statistics, a measure (symbol σ or s) of the spread of data. The deviation (difference) of each of the data items from the mean is found, and their values squared. The mean value of these squares is then calculated. The standard deviation is the square root of this mean.

If n is the number of items of data, x is the value of each item, and $\bar{x}$ is the mean value, the standard deviation σ may be given by the formula

$$\sigma = \sqrt{[\sigma(x - \bar{x})^2/n]}$$

where Σ indicates that the differences between the value of each item of data and the mean should be summed.

To simplify the calculations, the formula may be rearranged to $\sigma = \sqrt{[\Sigma x^2/n - \bar{x}^2]}$. As a result, it becomes necessary only to calculate Σx and Σx^2.

For example, if the ages of a set of children were 4, 4.5, 5, 5.5, 6, 7, 9, and 11, Σx would be 52, $\bar{x}$ would be $52/n = 52/8 = 6.5$, and Σx^2 would be 378.5 ($= 4^2 + 4.5^2 + 5^2 + 5.5^2 + 6^2 + 7^2 + 9^2 + 11^2$). Therefore, the standard deviation σ would be $\sqrt{[378.5/8 - (6.5)^2]} = \sqrt{5.0625} = 2.25$.

standard form or ***scientific notation*** method of writing numbers often used by scientists, particularly for very large or very small numbers. The numbers are written with one digit before the decimal point and multiplied by a power of 10. The number of digits given after the decimal point depends on the accuracy required. For example, the ◊speed of light is 2.9979×10^8 m/1.8628×10^5 mi per second.

standard gravity acceleration due to gravity, generally taken as 9.81274 m/32.38204 ft per second per second. See also g *scale.*

standard illuminant any of three standard light intensities, A, B, and C, used for illumination when phenomena involving colour are measured. A is the light from a filament at 2,848K (2,575°C/4,667°F), B is noon sunlight, and C is normal daylight. B and C are defined with respect to A. Standardization is necessary because colours appear different when viewed in different lights.

standard model in physics, the modern theory of ◊elementary particles and their interactions. According to the standard model, elementary particles are classified as leptons (light particles, such as electrons), ◊hadrons (particles, such as neutrons and protons, that are formed from quarks), and gauge bosons. Leptons and hadrons interact by exchanging ◊gauge bosons, each of which is responsible for a different fundamental force: photons mediate the electromagnetic force, which affects all charged particles; gluons mediate the strong nuclear force, which affects quarks; gravitons mediate the force of gravity; and the weakons (intermediate vector bosons) mediate the weak nuclear force. See also ◊forces, fundamental, quantum electrodynamics, and ◊quantum chromodynamics.

standards in computing, any agreed system or protocol that helps different pieces of software or different computers to work together.

In the fast-moving area of computer technology, standards have sometimes developed haphazardly: market forces brought about de facto standards such as the ◊MS-DOS operating system for PCs, or the 3.5 in floppy disc. If computers are to communicate over a network, however, standards must be co-ordinated: the ◊World Wide Web, for example, works because everybody who uses it agrees to follow the same conventions, such as using ◊HTML to build Web documents. Other standards, like ◊SMTP – the procedure for sending e-mail – exist to make cross-platform communication (for example between a ◊UNIX machine and a ◊Macintosh) possible. Bodies involved with this process include: the ◊Internet Architecture Board, which lays down basic procedures by promulgating RFCs, the W3 Consortium, which looks after HTML, and the International Standards Organization.

standard temperature and pressure (STP) in chemistry, a standard set of conditions for experimental measurements, to enable comparisons to be made between sets of results. Standard temperature is 0°C/32°F (273K) and standard pressure 1 atmosphere (101,325 Pa).

standard volume in physics, the volume occupied by one kilogram molecule (the molecular mass in kilograms) of any gas at standard temperature and pressure. Its value is approximately 22.414 cubic metres.

standing wave in physics, a wave in which the positions of ◊nodes (positions of zero vibration) and antinodes (positions of maximum vibration) do not move. Standing waves result when two similar waves travel in opposite directions through the same space.

For example, when a sound wave is reflected back along its own path, as when a stretched string is plucked, a standing wave is formed. In this case the antinode remains fixed at the centre and the nodes are at the two ends. Water and ◊electromagnetic waves can form standing waves in the same way.

staphylococcus spherical bacterium that occurs in clusters. It is found on the skin and mucous membranes of humans and other animals. It can cause abscesses and systemic infections that may prove fatal.

Staphylococcus aureus is a very common bacterium, present in the nose in 30% of people. Normally it gives no trouble, but, largely due to over-prescribing of antibiotics, strains have arisen that are resistant to the drugs used to treat them, principally methicillin, a semisynthetic form of penicillin. Methicillin-resistant *S. aureus* (MRSA) strains represent a serious hazard to the critically ill or immunosuppressed.

MRSA normally responds to two antibiotics which are considered too toxic for use in any but life-threatening infections (vancomycin and teicoplanin) but it still causes fatalities.

STARS AND CONSTELLATIONS

http://www.astro.wisc.edu/~dolan/constellations/constellations.html

Hugely informative site on stars and constellations. It includes star charts of all major stars and constellations, details of the origins of the various names, photographs of the galaxy and the milky way, and details on what stars can be seen at any given time.

star luminous globe of gas, mainly hydrogen and helium, which produces its own heat and light by nuclear reactions. Although stars shine for a very long time – many billions of years – they are not eternal, and have been found to change in appearance at different stages in their lives.

The smallest mass possible for a star is about 8% that of the Sun (80 times that of ◊Jupiter), otherwise nuclear reactions do not occur. Objects with less than this critical mass shine only dimly, and are termed **brown dwarfs**.

I ask you to look both ways. For the road to a knowledge of the stars leads through the atom; and important knowledge of the atom has been reached through the stars.

ARTHUR STANLEY EDDINGTON British astronomer.

starburst galaxy in astronomy, a spiral galaxy that appears unusually bright in the infrared part of the spectrum due to a recent burst of star formation, possibly triggered by the gravitational influence of a nearby companion galaxy.

starch widely distributed, high-molecular-mass ◊carbohydrate, produced by plants as a food store; main dietary sources are cereals, legumes, and tubers, including potatoes. It consists of varying proportions of two ◊glucose polymers (◊polysaccharides): straight-chain (amylose) and branched (amylopectin) molecules.

Purified starch is a white powder used to stiffen textiles and paper and as a raw material for making various chemicals. It is used in the food industry as a thickening agent. Chemical treatment of starch gives rise to a range of 'modified starches' with varying properties. Hydrolysis (splitting) of starch by acid or enzymes generates a variety of 'glucose syrups' or 'liquid glucose' for use in the food industry. Complete hydrolysis of starch with acid generates the ◊monosaccharide glucose only. Incomplete hydrolysis or enzymic hydrolysis yields a mixture of glucose, maltose, and non-hydrolysed fractions called dextrins.

star cluster group of related stars, usually held together by gravity. Members of a star cluster are thought to form together from one large cloud of gas in space. **Open clusters** such as the ◊Pleiades contain from a dozen to many hundreds of young stars, loosely scattered over several light years. ◊Globular clusters are larger and much more densely packed, containing perhaps 100,000 old stars.

The more conspicuous clusters were originally catalogued with the nebulae, and are usually known by their Messier or NGC numbers. A few clusters like the Pleiades, ◊Hyades, and Praesepe are also known by their traditional names.

stardust US project to obtain a sample of dust and gas from the head of a comet. Due for launch in February 1999, the *Stardust* space probe will fly through the head Comet Wild 2 in January 2004, passing within 100 km/62 mi of the 4 km/2.5 mi nucleus. It will return to Earth with its samples in January 2006.

starfish or ***sea star*** any vechinoderm of the subclass Asteroidea with arms radiating from a central body. Usually there are five arms, but some species have more. They are covered with spines and small pincerlike organs. There are also a number of small tubular processes on the skin surface that assist in locomotion and respiration. Starfish are predators, and vary in size from 1.2 cm/0.5 in to 90 cm/3 ft.

Some species use their suckered tube feet to pull open the shells of bivalve molluscs, then evert their stomach to surround and digest the animal inside. The poisonous and predatory crown-of-thorns of the Pacific is very destructive to coral and severely damaged Australia's Great Barrier Reef when it multiplied prolifically in the 1960s–70s. Although it had practically disappeared by 1990, in 1996 another outbreak along the Great Barrier Reef was officially declared.

Another destructive species, *Asteria amurensis*, spread round the coast of Tasmania in 1993, and could reach as far as Sydney. It is normally found only in the northern Pacific and was probably introduced into Tasmania in the ballast water of a ship travelling from Japan.

starfish The large starfish Stichaster striatus *on the rocky Pacific coastline of Peru. Starfish live along shorelines and on seabeds, feeding mainly on molluscs and crustaceans. They have the ability to regenerate an arm if one is broken off. Premaphotos Wildlife*

star fruit fruit of the ◊carambola tree.

starling any member of a large widespread Old World family (Sturnidae) of chunky, dark, generally gregarious birds of the order Passeriformes. The European starling *Sturnus vulgaris*, common in N Eurasia, has been naturalized in North America from the late 19th century. The black, speckled plumage is glossed with green and purple. The feathers on the upper parts are tipped with buff, and the wings are greyish-black, with a reddish-brown fringe. The female is less glossy and lustrous than the male. Its own call is a bright whistle, but it is a mimic of the songs of other birds. It is about 20 cm/8 in long.

Strikingly gregarious in feeding, flight, and roosting, it often becomes a pest in large cities, where it becomes attached to certain buildings as 'dormitories', returning each night from omnivorous foraging in the countryside, feeding principally on worms, snails, and insects. Nests are made almost anywhere, and about five pale blue eggs are laid. If disturbed, starlings have been known to lay eggs in the nests of other birds before starting a new nest with their mate elsewhere.

start bit ◊bit used in ◊asynchronous communications to indicate the beginning of a piece of data.

startup screen in computing, screen displayed by a PC while it loads its voperating system and other resident software. Well-known startup screens include the Windows 95 'flying window' motif and the Macintosh 'smiling face'. It is also possible to create a custom start-up screen, perhaps incorporating a favourite image or corporate logo.

states of matter forms (solid, liquid, or gas) in which material can exist. Whether a material is solid, liquid, or gaseous depends on its temperature and the pressure on it. The transition between states takes place at definite temperatures, called melting point and boiling point.

◊Kinetic theory describes how the state of a material depends on the movement and arrangement of its atoms or molecules.

The atoms or molecules of **gases** move randomly in otherwise empty space, filling any size or shape of container. Gases can be liquefied by cooling as this lowers the speed of the molecules and enables attractive forces between them to bind them together.

A **liquid** forms a level surface and assumes the shape of its container; its atoms or molecules do not occupy fixed positions, nor do they have total freedom of movement.

Solids hold their own shape as their atoms or molecules are not free to move about but merely vibrate about fixed positions, such as those in ◊crystal lattices. *See illustration on page 716.*

state symbol symbol used in chemical equations to indicate the physical state of the substances present. The symbols are: (s) for solid, (l) for liquid, (g) for gas, and (aq) for aqueous.

static electricity ◊electric charge that is stationary, usually acquired by a body by means of electrostatic induction or friction. Rubbing different materials can produce static electricity, as seen in the sparks produced on combing one's hair or removing a nylon shirt. In some processes static electricity is useful, as in paint spraying where the parts to be sprayed are charged with electricity of opposite polarity to that on the paint droplets, and in ◊xerography.

static IP address (abbreviation for ***static Internet Protocol address***) in computing, an ◊IP address which is permanently assigned to a particular user. Most Internet Service Providers (ISPs) use ◊dynamic IP addressing for their customers. Static IP addressing is, however, generally used by businesses or any organization running its own site and is also available for individuals from some ISPs, such as Demon Internet, allowing them to set up ◊FTP or Web sites on their home computers. Static IP addressing also allows a higher degree of tracking an individual user's actions on the Internet.

statics branch of mechanics concerned with the behaviour of bodies at rest and forces in equilibrium, and distinguished from ◊dynamics.

statistical mechanics branch of physics in which the properties of large collections of particles are predicted by considering the motions of the constituent particles. It is closely related to vthermodynamics.

statistics branch of mathematics concerned with the collection and interpretation of data. For example, to determine the ◊mean age of the children in a school, a statistically acceptable answer might be obtained by calculating an average based on the ages of a representative sample, consisting, for example, of a random tenth of the pupils from each class. ◊Probability is the branch of statistics dealing with predictions of events.

mean, median, and mode The mean, median, and mode are different ways of finding a 'typical' or 'central' value of a set of data. The ◊mean is obtained by adding up all the observed values and dividing by the number of values; it is the number which is commonly used as an average value. The ◊median is the middle value, that is, the value which is exceeded by half the items in the sample. The ◊mode is the value which occurs with greatest frequency the most common value. The mean is the most useful measure for the purposes of statistical theory. The idea of the median may be extended and a distribution can be divided into four quartiles. The first quartile is the value which is exceeded by three-quarters of

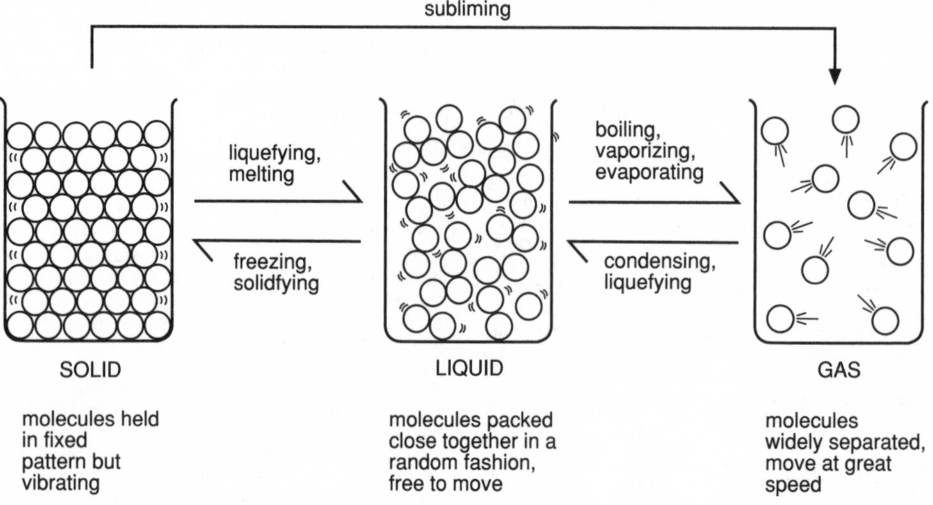

state of matter *Matter changes state when heat energy is absorbed or released.*

the items; the second quartile is the same as the median; the third quartile is the value that is exceeded by one-quarter of the items.

standard deviation and other measures of dispersion The mean is a very incomplete summary of a group of observations; it is useful to know also how closely the individual members of a group approach the mean, and this is indicated by various measures of dispersion. The **range** is the difference between the maximum and minimum values of the group; it is not very satisfactory as a measure of dispersion. The **mean deviation** is the arithmetic mean of the differences between the mean and the individual values, the differences all being taken as positive. However, the **mean deviation** also does not convey much useful information about a group of observations. The most useful measure of dispersion is the **variance**, which is the arithmetic mean of the squares of the deviations from the mean. The positive square root of the variance is called the ◊standard deviation, a measure (symbol σ or s) of the spread of data. The deviation (difference) of each of the data items from the mean is found, and their values squared. The mean value of these squares is then calculated. The standard deviation is the square root of this mean.

It is usual to standardize the measurements by working in units of the standard deviation measured from the mean of the distributions, enabling statistical theories to be generalized. A standardized distribution has a mean of zero and a standard deviation of unity. Another useful measure of dispersion is the semi-interquartile range, which is one-half of the distance between the first and third quartiles, and can be considered as the average distance of the quartiles from the median. In many typical distributions the semi-interquartile range is about two-thirds of the standard deviation and the mean deviation is about four-fifths of the standard deviation.

applications One of the most important uses of statistical theory is in testing whether experimental data support hypotheses or not. For example, an agricultural researcher arranges for different groups of cows to be fed different diets and records the milk yields. The milk-yield data are analysed and the means and standard deviations of yields for different groups vary. The researcher can use statistical tests to assess whether the variation is of an amount that should be expected because of the natural variation in cows or whether it is larger than normal and therefore likely to be influenced by the difference in diet.

correlation Correlation measures the degree to which two quantities are associated, in the sense that a variation in one quantity is accompanied by a predictable variation in the other. For example, if the pressure on a quantity of gas is increased then its volume decreases. If observations of pressure and volume are taken then statistical correlation analysis can be used to determine whether the volume of a gas can be completely predicted from a knowledge of the pressure on it.

STD abbreviation for ◊sexually transmitted disease.

steady-state theory in astronomy, a rival theory to that of the ◊Big Bang, which claims that the universe has no origin but is expanding because new matter is being created continuously throughout the universe. The theory was proposed in 1948 by Hermann Bondi, Thomas Gold (1920–), and Fred Hoyle, but was dealt a severe blow in 1965 by the discovery of ◊cosmic background radiation (radiation left over from the formation of the universe) and is now largely rejected.

steam in chemistry, a dry, invisible gas formed by vaporizing water.

The visible cloud that normally forms in the air when water is vaporized is due to minute suspended water particles. Steam is widely used in chemical and other industrial processes and for the generation of power.

steam engine engine that uses the power of steam to produce useful work. It was the principal power source during the British Industrial Revolution in the 18th century. The first successful steam engine was built 1712 by English inventor Thomas Newcomen at Dudley, West Midlands; it was developed further by Scottish mining engineer James Watt from 1769 and by English mining engineer Richard Trevithick, whose high-pressure steam engine of 1802 led to the development of the steam locomotive.

In Newcomen's engine, steam was admitted to a cylinder as a piston moved up, and was then condensed by a spray of water, allowing air pressure to force the piston downwards. James Watt improved Newcomen's engine in 1769 by condensing the steam outside the cylinder (thus saving energy formerly used to reheat the cylinder) and by using steam to force the piston upwards. Watt also introduced the **double-acting engine**, in which steam is alter-

STEAM ENGINE

http://www.easystreet.com/pnwc/museum/Steam_Locomotive.html

Basic guide to the principles behind the steam engine. It includes a labelled diagram and explanatory text of the engine in its most well-known form – the steam locomotive.

nately sent to each side of the piston. The **compound engine** (1781) uses the exhaust from one cylinder to drive the piston of another. A later development was the steam ◊turbine, still used today to power ships and generators in power stations. In other contexts, the steam engine was superseded by the ◊internal-combustion engine.

stearic acid $CH_3(CH_2)_{16}COOH$ saturated long-chain ◊fatty acid, soluble in alcohol and ether but not in water. It is found in many fats and oils, and is used to make soap and candles and as a lubricant. The salts of stearic acid are called stearates.

stearin mixture of stearic and palmitic acids, used to make soap.

steel alloy or mixture of iron and up to 1.7% carbon, sometimes with other elements, such as manganese, phosphorus, sulphur, and silicon. The USA, Russia, Ukraine, and Japan are the main steel producers. Steel has innumerable uses, including ship and car manufacture, skyscraper frames, and machinery of all kinds.

Steels with only small amounts of other metals are called **carbon steels**. These steels are far stronger than pure iron, with properties varying with the composition. **Alloy steels** contain greater amounts of other metals. Low-alloy steels have less than 5% of the alloying material; high-alloy steels have more. Low-alloy steels containing up to 5% silicon with relatively little carbon have a high electrical resistance and are used in power transformers and motor or generator cores, for example. **Stainless steel** is a high-alloy steel containing at least 11% chromium. Steels with up to 20% tungsten are very hard and are used in high-speed cutting tools. About 50% of the world's steel is now made from scrap.

Steel is produced by removing impurities, such as carbon, from raw or pig iron, produced by a ◊blast furnace. The main industrial process is the ◊basic-oxygen process, in which molten pig iron and scrap steel is placed in a container lined with heat-resistant, alkaline (basic) bricks. A pipe or lance is lowered near to the surface of the molten metal and pure oxygen blown through it at high pressure. The surface of the metal is disturbed by the blast and the impurities are oxidized (burned out). The ◊open-hearth process is an older steelmaking method in which molten iron and limestone are placed in a shallow bowl or hearth (see open-hearth furnace). Burning oil or gas is blown over the surface of the metal, and the impurities are oxidized. High-quality steel is made in an **electric furnace**. A large electric current flows through electrodes in the furnace, melting a charge of scrap steel and iron. The quality of the steel produced can be controlled precisely because the temperature of the furnace can be maintained exactly and there are no combustion by-products to contaminate the steel. Electric furnaces are also used to refine steel, producing the extra-pure steels used, for example, in the petrochemical industry.

The steel produced is cast into ingots, which can be worked when hot by hammering (forging) or pressing between rollers to produce sheet steel. Alternatively, the **continuous-cast process**, in which the molten metal is fed into an open-ended mould cooled by water, produces an unbroken slab of steel.

Stefan–Boltzmann law in physics, a law that relates the energy, *E*, radiated away from a perfect emitter (a ◊black body), to the temperature, *T*, of that body. It has the form $E = \sigma T^4$, where *E* is the energy radiated per unit area per second, *T* is the temperature, and σ is the **Stefan–Boltzmann constant**. Its value is 5.6705×10^{-8} W m^{-2} K^{-4}. The law was derived by Austrian physicists Joseph Stefan and Ludwig Boltzmann.

steganography in computing, camouflaging messages in large computer files, especially those carrying audio, video, or graphics, by appropriating a small percentage of their constituent data. For example, a graphics file measuring 500 × 500 ◊pixels, using 32 ◊bits to represent each pixel, contains 8 million bits. A single bit of each pixel (perhaps the 1st, the 15th or the 32nd) could be used to insert some 5,000 words of text, chopped into individual bits, without making any perceptible difference to the image. The text message itself can be encrypted using ◊Pretty Good Privacy (PGP) for added security.

Stegosaurus genus of late Jurassic North American dinosaurs of the order Ornithischia. They were ungainly herbivores, with very small heads, a double row of triangular plates along the back, and spikes on the tail.

steinbok or ***steenbok*** southern African antelope. It is reddish-brown and about 60 cm/23.5 in high at the shoulder.
classification The steinbok *Raphicerus campestris* is in family Bovidae, in order Artiodactyla.

stellar population in astronomy, a classification of stars according to their chemical composition as determined by ◊spectroscopy.

Population I stars have a relatively high abundance of elements heavier than hydrogen and helium, and are confined to the spiral arms and disc of the Galaxy. They are believed to be young stars formed from material that has already been enriched with elements created by ◊nuclear fusion in earlier generations of stars. Examples include open clusters and ◊supergiants. **Population II** stars have a low abundance of heavy elements and are found throughout the Galaxy but especially in the central bulge and outer halo. They are among the oldest objects in the Galaxy, and include ◊globular clusters. The Sun is a Population I star.

Steller's sea cow extinct member of the order Sirenia (today consisting of dugongs and manatees) discovered in 1741. They weighed approximately 10 tonnes, fed on kelp, and lived in shallow waters around the Bering Sea. Hunted relentlessly for their meat, they died out within 27 years of their discovery. The reduction in their kelp food supply may also have contributed to their extinction.

Stephenson, George (1781–1848)

English engineer. He built the first successful steam locomotive. He also invented a safety lamp independently of Humphrey Davy in 1815. He was appointed engineer of the Stockton and Darlington Railway, the world's first public railway, in 1821, and of the Liverpool and Manchester Railway in 1826. In 1829 he won a prize with his locomotive *Rocket*.

Experimenting with various gradients, Stephenson found that a slope of 1 in 200, common enough on roads, reduced the haulage power of a locomotive by 50% (on a completely even surface, a tractive force of less than 5 kg/11 lb would move a tonne). Friction was virtually independent of speed. It followed that railway gradients should always be as low as possible, and cuttings, tunnels, and embankments were therefore necessary. He also advocated the use of malleable iron rails instead of cast iron. The gauge for the Stockton and Darlington railway was set by Stephenson at 1.4 m/4 ft 8 in, which became the standard gauge for railways in most of the world.

Mary Evans Picture Library

stem main supporting axis of a plant that bears the leaves, buds, and reproductive structures; it may be simple or branched. The plant stem usually grows above ground, although some grow underground, including ◊rhizomes, corms, rootstocks, and ◊tubers. Stems contain a continuous vascular system that conducts water and food to and from all parts of the plant.

The point on a stem from which a leaf or leaves arise is called a node, and the space between two successive nodes is the internode.

In some plants, the stem is highly modified; for example, it may form a leaf-like ◊cladode or it may be twining (as in many climbing plants), or fleshy and swollen to store water (as in cacti and other succulents). In plants exhibiting ◊secondary growth, the stem may become woody, forming a main trunk, as in trees, or a number of branches from ground level, as in shrubs.

steppe the temperate grasslands of Europe and Asia. Sometimes the term refers to other temperate grasslands and semi-arid desert edges.

stepper motor electric motor that can be precisely controlled by signals from a computer. The motor turns through a precise angle each time it receives a signal pulse from the computer. By varying the rate at which signal pulses are produced, the motor can be run at different speeds or turned through an exact angle and then stopped. Switching circuits can be constructed to allow the computer to reverse the direction of the motor.

By combining two or more motors, complex movement control becomes possible. For example, if stepper motors are used to power the wheels of a small vehicle, a computer can manoeuvre the vehicle in any direction.

Stepper motors are commonly used in small-scale applications where computer-controlled movement is required. In larger applications, where greater power is necessary, pneumatic or hydraulic systems are usually preferred.

step rocket another term for ◊multistage rocket.

steradian SI unit (symbol sr) of measure of solid (three-dimensional) angles, the three-dimensional equivalent of the ◊radian. One steradian is the angle at the centre of a sphere when an area on the surface of the sphere equal to the square of the sphere's radius is joined to the centre.

stereocilium sensory hair cell found on the ◊cochlea in the inner ◊ear. When the cochlear fluid vibrates in response to sound the hairs move together pushing on protein molecules on their surface. On each stereocilium the protein molecule triggers the opening of an ion gate that enables the flow of potassium ions through the hair. The ion flow causes an electrical signal to be transmitted to the brain as a nerve impulse, where it is interpreted as sound.

stereophonic sound system of sound reproduction using two complementary channels leading to two loudspeakers, which gives a more natural depth to the sound. Stereo recording began with the introduction of two-track magnetic tape in the 1950s. See ◊hi-fi.

Stereo is more democratic, mono more totalitarian.

JEAN-LUC GODARD French filmmaker and writer. Opening a cinema in Dolby stereo in Moscow, Feb 1992

sterilization the killing or removal of living organisms such as bacteria and fungi. A sterile environment is necessary in medicine, food processing, and some scientific experiments. Methods include heat treatment (such as boiling), the use of chemicals (such as disinfectants), irradiation with gamma rays, and filtration. See also ◊asepsis.

sterilization in medicine, any surgical operation to terminate the possibility of reproduction. In women, this is normally achieved by sealing or tying off the ◊Fallopian tubes (tubal ligation) so that fertilization can no longer take place. In men, the transmission of sperm is blocked by ◊vasectomy.

According to the results of a long-term US study released in 1996, the failure rate for female sterilization is 1 in 50, higher than previously believed, with some pregnancies occurring as long as 14 years after the operation.

Sterilization may be encouraged by governments to limit population growth or as part of a selective-breeding policy (see ◊eugenics).

STERILIZATION

In 1632, the weekly food ration for each child in a children's hospital in Norwich, England, included two gallons of beer. In the days before reliable water-purification systems, the potential bad effects of alcohol were far outweighed by its sterilizing properties.

sterling silver ◊alloy containing 925 parts of silver and 75 parts of copper. The copper hardens the silver, making it more useful.

sternum or ***breastbone***, the large flat bone, 15–20 cm/5.9–7.8 in long in the adult, at the front of the chest, joined to the ribs. It gives protection to the heart and lungs. During open-heart surgery the sternum must be split to give access to the thorax.

steroid in biology, any of a group of cyclic, unsaturated alcohols (lipids without fatty acid components), which, like sterols, have a complex molecular structure consisting of four carbon rings. Steroids include the sex hormones, such as ◊testosterone, the corticosteroid hormones produced by the ◊adrenal gland, bile acids, and ◊cholesterol.

The term is commonly used to refer to ◊anabolic steroid. In medicine, synthetic steroids are used to treat a wide range of conditions.

Steroids are also found in plants. The most widespread are the **brassinosteroids**, necessary for normal plant growth.

sterol any of a group of solid, cyclic, unsaturated alcohols, with a complex structure that includes four carbon rings; cholesterol is an example. Steroids are derived from sterols.

stethoscope instrument used to ascertain the condition of the heart and lungs by listening to their action. It consists of two earpieces connected by flexible tubes to a small plate that is placed against the body. It was invented in 1819 in France by René Théophile Hyacinthe Laënnec.

stick insect insect of the order Phasmida, closely resembling a stick or twig. The eggs mimic plant seeds. Many species are wingless. The longest reach a length of 30 cm/1 ft.

Fossilized eggs were identified in 1995, and are thought to be around 44 million years old.

stickleback any fish of the family Gasterosteidae, found in marine and fresh waters of the northern hemisphere. It has a long body that can grow to 18 cm/7 in. The spines along a stickleback's back take the place of the first dorsal fin, and can be raised to make the

stick insect *The Brazilian* Phibalosoma phyllinum, *which is 30 cm/1 ft long, spends the day resting in cryptic pose in trees and bushes. Stick insects do not always rest among twigs. Many species from tropical rainforests rest on top of large leaves such as palms, where they resemble a fallen twig.* *Premaphotos Wildlife*

fish difficult to eat for predators. After the eggs have been laid the female takes no part in rearing the young: the male builds a nest for the eggs, which he then guards and rears for the first two weeks.

The common three-spined stickleback *Gasterosteus aculeatus*, up to 10 cm/4 in, is found in freshwater habitats and also in brackish estuaries.

stigma in a flower, the surface at the tip of a ◊carpel that receives the ◊pollen. It often has short outgrowths, flaps, or hairs to trap pollen and may produce a sticky secretion to which the grains adhere.

stimulant any substance that acts on the brain to increase alertness and activity; for example, ◊amphetamine. When given to children, stimulants may have a paradoxical, calming effect. Stimulants cause liver damage, are habit-forming, have limited therapeutic value, and are now prescribed only to treat narcolepsy and severe obesity.

stimulus any agency, such as noise, light, heat, or pressure, that can be detected by an organism's receptors.

stingray cartilaginous fish that is a species of ◊ray.

stinkhorn any of a group of foul-smelling European fungi (see ◊fungus), especially *P. impudicus;* they first appear on the surface as white balls. (Genus *Phallus*, order Phallales.)

The spores of the stinkhorn are dispersed by flies. The flies are attracted by the its corpselike aroma and feed on the spore-containing slime at its tip. This give them diarrhoea almost immediately, so the spores are spread but still likely to end up in suitable habitat.

stinkwood any of various trees with unpleasant-smelling wood. The S African tree *O. bullata* has offensive-smelling wood when newly felled, but fine, durable timber used for furniture. Another stinkwood is *G. augusta* from tropical America. (Genera *Ocotea*, family Lauraceae; *Gustavia*.)

stipule outgrowth arising from the base of a leaf or leaf stalk in certain plants. Stipules usually occur in pairs or fused into a single semicircular structure.

Stirling engine hot-air external combustion engine invented by Scottish priest Robert Stirling 1816. The engine operates by adapting to the fact that the air in its cylinders heats up when it is compressed and cools when it expands. The engine will operate on any fuel, is nonpolluting and relatively quiet. It was used fairly widely in the 19th century before the appearance of small, powerful, and reliable electric motors. Attempts have also been made in recent times to use Stirling's engine to power a variety of machines.

stoat carnivorous mammal *Mustela erminea* of the northern hemisphere, in the weasel family, about 37 cm/15 in long including the black-tipped tail. It has a long body and a flattened head. The upper parts and tail are red-brown, and the underparts are white. In the colder regions, the coat turns white (ermine) in winter. Its young are called kits.

The stoat is an efficient predator, killing its prey (typically rodents and rabbits) by biting the back of the neck. It needs to consume the equivalent of almost a third of its body weight each day. Females are about half the size of males, and males and females live in separate territories. Stoats live in Europe, Asia, and North America; they have been introduced to New Zealand.

stock in botany, any of a group of ◊herbaceous plants commonly grown as garden ornamentals. Many cultivated varieties, including simple-stemmed, queen's, and ten-week stocks, have been derived from the wild stock (*M. incana*); night-scented (or evening) stock (*M. bicornis*) becomes aromatic at night. (Genus *Matthiola*, family Cruciferae.)

stokes c.g.s. unit (symbol St) of kinematic viscosity (a liquid's resistance to flow).

Liquids with higher kinematic viscosity have higher turbulence than those with low kinematic viscosity. It is found by dividing the dynamic viscosity in ◊poise by the density of the liquid.

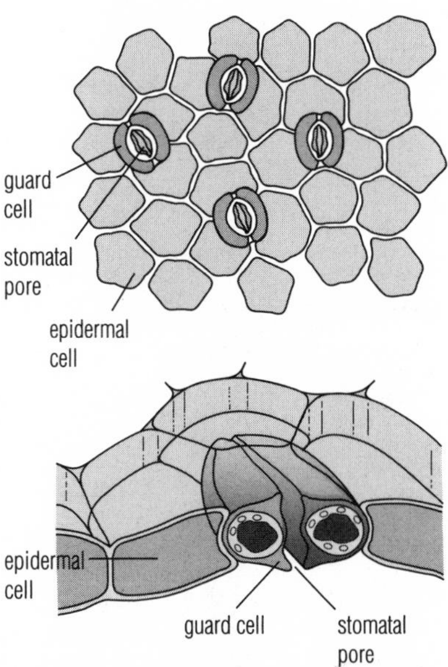

***stoma** The stomata, tiny openings in the epidermis of a plant, are surrounded by pairs of crescent-shaped cells, called guard cells. The guard cells open and close the stoma by changing shape.*

STOL (acronym for ***short takeoff and landing***) aircraft fitted with special devices on the wings (such as sucking flaps) that increase aerodynamic lift at low speeds. Small passenger and freight STOL craft may become common with the demand for small airports, especially in difficult terrain.

stolon in botany, a type of ◊runner.

stolport (acronym for ***short take off and landing port***) airport that can be used by planes adapted to a shorter than normal runway. Such planes tend to have a restricted flying range. Stolport sites are found in built-up areas where ordinary planes would not be able to land safely.

stoma (plural ***stomata***) in botany, a pore in the epidermis of a plant. Each stoma is surrounded by a pair of guard cells that are crescent-shaped when the stoma is open but can collapse to an oval shape, thus closing off the opening between them. Stomata allow the exchange of carbon dioxide and oxygen (needed for ◊photosynthesis and ◊respiration) between the internal tissues of the plant and the outside atmosphere. They are also the main route by which water is lost from the plant, and they can be closed to conserve water, the movements being controlled by changes in turgidity of the guard cells.

stomach the first cavity in the digestive system of animals. In mammals it is a bag of muscle situated just below the diaphragm. Food enters it from the oesophagus, is digested by the acid and ◊enzymes secreted by the stomach lining, and then passes into the duodenum. Some plant-eating mammals have multichambered stomachs that harbour bacteria in one of the chambers to assist in the digestion of ◊cellulose. *See illustration on page 718.*

The gizzard is part of the stomach in birds.

stone (plural ***stone***) imperial unit (abbreviation st) of mass. One stone is 14 pounds (6.35 kg).

Stone Age the developmental stage of humans in ◊prehistory before the use of metals, when tools and weapons were made chiefly of stone, especially flint. The Stone Age is subdivided into the Old or **Palaeolithic**, when flint implements were simply chipped

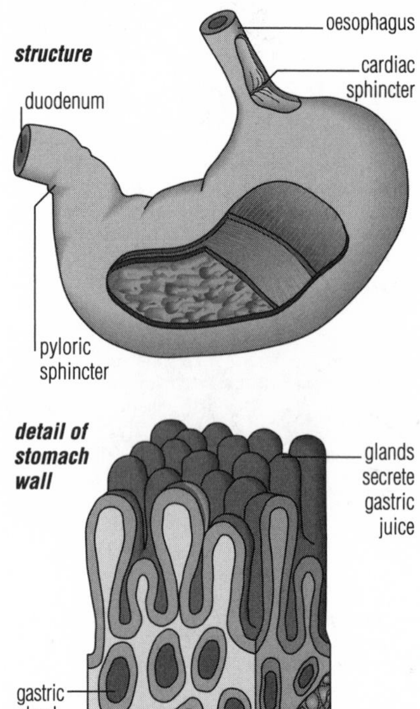

stomach The human stomach can hold about 1.5 l/2.6 pt of liquid. The digestive juices are acidic enough to dissolve metal. To avoid damage, the cells of the stomach lining are replaced quickly – 500,000 cells are replaced every minute, and the whole stomach lining every three days.

into shape; the Middle or **Mesolithic**; and the New or **Neolithic**, when implements were ground and polished. Palaeolithic people were hunters and gatherers; by the Neolithic period people were taking the first steps in agriculture, the domestication of animals, weaving, and pottery.

Recent research has been largely directed towards the relationship of the Palaeolithic period to ◊geochronology (the measurement of geological time) and to the clarification of an absolute chronology based upon geology. The economic aspects of the Neolithic cultures have attracted as much attention as the typology of the implements and pottery, and the study of chambered tombs.

stonechat small insectivorous ◊thrush *Saxicola torquata*, family Muscicapidae, order Passeriformes, frequently found in Eurasia and Africa on open land with bushes. The male has a black head and throat, tawny breast, and dark back; the female is browner. It is about 13 cm/5 in long.

stonecrop any of a group of plants belonging to the orpine family, succulent herbs with fleshy leaves and clusters of red, yellow, or white starlike flowers. Stonecrops are characteristic of dry, rocky places and some grow on walls. (Genus *Sedum*, family Crassulaceae.)

stonefish any of a family (Synanceiidae) of tropical marine bony fishes with venomous spines and bodies resembling encrusted rocks.

stonefly any insect of the order Plecoptera, with a long tail and antennae and two pairs of membranous wings. Stoneflies live near fresh water. There are over 1,300 species.

STONEFISH

Stonefish are the most poisonous of all fish. The needle-like spines along their backs contain sufficient venom to kill within six hours anyone unlucky enough to tread upon them.

Stonehenge Old English 'hanging stones' megalithic monument on Salisbury Plain, 3 km/1.9 mi W of Amesbury, Wiltshire, England. The site developed over various periods from a simple henge (earthwork circle and ditch), dating from about 3000 BC, to a complex stone structure, from about 2100 BC, which included a circle of 30 upright stones, their tops linked by lintel stones to form a continuous circle about 30 m/100 ft across.

Within this sarsen **peristyle** was a horseshoe arrangement of five sarsen **trilithons** (two uprights plus a lintel, set as five separate entities), and the so-called 'Altar Stone' – an upright pillar – on the axis of the horseshoe at the open, NE end, which faces in the direction of the rising sun. A further horseshoe and circle within the sarsen peristyle were constructed from bluestone relocated from previous outer circles.

It has been suggested that Stonehenge was constructed as an observatory.

stop bit ◊bit used in ◊asynchronous communications to indicate the end of a piece of data.

stopping distance the minimum distance in which a vehicle can be brought to rest in an emergency from the moment that the driver notices danger ahead. It is the sum of the thinking distance and the braking distance.

store-and-forward technology in computing, general term for systems like ◊UUCP and e-mail, which work by storing data that has been received and then forwarding it on demand to the authorized recipient. Most of the Internet is based on store-and-forward technology.

stork any of the 17 species of the Ciconiidae, a family of long-legged, long-necked wading birds with long, powerful wings, and long conical bills used for spearing prey. Some species grow up to 1.5 m/5 ft tall.

species Species include the Eurasian **white stork** *Ciconia ciconia*, which is encouraged to build on rooftops as a luck and fertility symbol. It feeds on reptiles, small mammals, and insects. Its plumage is greyish white, its quills and longest feathers on the wing coverts black, and the beak and legs red. It migrates to Africa in winter. The **jabiru** *Jabiru mycteria* of the Americas is up to 1.5 m/5 ft high, and is white plumaged, with a black and red head. In the **black stork** *C. nigra*, the upper surface is black and the lower parts are white. It is widely found in southern and central Europe, Asia, and parts of Africa. The adjutant bird, ◊ibis, ◊heron, and ◊spoonbill are related birds.

STORK

Dissatisfied white stork chicks sometimes switch nests. A wandering chick is initially greeted with aggression at its new home, but is soon accepted. The most attractive nests are those where the resident chicks are younger than the new arrival, who will therefore not have to battle for food with older siblings.

story board in film and television, technique for reviewing a particular story or scene before it is expensively filmed, animated, or scripted.

The scene is broken down into key frames or moments, and sketched in varying detail onto boards with accompanying text outlining the plot's progress.

STP abbreviation for ◊standard temperature and pressure.

straight line a line that does not bend or curve. The graph of a linear relationship is a straight line and is often presented in the form $y = mx + c$, where m is the slope, or gradient, of the line and c is the y-intercept (the point at which the line cuts the y-axis).

strain in the science of materials, the extent to which a body is distorted when a deforming force (stress) is applied to it. It is a ratio of the extension or compression of that body (its length, area, or volume) to its original dimensions (see ◊Hooke's law. For example, linear strain is the ratio of the change in length of a body to its original length.

stratigraphy branch of geology that deals with the sequence of formation of ◊sedimentary rock layers and the conditions under which they were formed. Its basis was developed by William Smith, a British canal engineer. The basic principle of superimposition establishes that upper layers or deposits have accumulated later in time than the lower ones.

Stratigraphy involves both the investigation of sedimentary structures to determine past environments represented by rocks, and the study of fossils for identifying and dating particular beds of rock. A body of rock strata with a set of unifying characteristics indicative of an environment is called a ◊facies.

Stratigraphic units can be grouped in terms of time or lithology (rock type). Strata that were deposited at the same time belong to a single **chronostratigraphic unit** but need not be the same lithology. Strata of a specific lithology can be grouped into a **lithostratigraphic unit** but are not necessarily the same age.

Stratigraphy in the interpretation of archaeological excavations provides a relative chronology for the levels and the artefacts within rock beds. It is the principal means by which the context of archaeological deposits is evaluated.

stratosphere that part of the atmosphere 10–40 km/6–25 mi from the Earth's surface, where the temperature slowly rises from a low of −55°C/−67°F to around 0°C/32°F. The air is rarefied and at around 25 km/15 mi much ◊ozone is concentrated.

strawberry low-growing perennial plant widely cultivated for its red, fleshy fruits, which are rich in vitamin C. Commercial cultivated forms bear one crop of fruit in summer, with the berries resting on a bed of straw to protect them from the damp soil, and multiply by runners. The flowers are normally white, although pink-flowering varieties are cultivated as ornamentals. (Genus *Fragaria*, family Rosaceae.)

streaming in computing, sending data, for example video frames or radio broadcasts, in a steady flow over the Internet. Streaming requires data to pass through a special channel or dedicated connection; conventional ◊packets, which travel by a multiplicity of routes, may arrive in the wrong order or be duplicated on the way. ◊RealAudio and ◊CU-SeeMe make use of streaming.

streamlining shaping a body so that it offers the least resistance when travelling through a medium such as air or water. Aircraft, for example, must be carefully streamlined to reduce air resistance, or ◊drag.

High-speed aircraft must have swept-back wings, supersonic craft a sharp nose and narrow body.

strength of acids and bases in chemistry, the ability of ◊acids and ◊bases to dissociate in solution with water, and hence to produce a low or high ◊pH, respectively.

A strong acid is fully ◊dissociated in aqueous solution, whereas a weak acid is only partly dissociated. Since the dissociation of acids generates hydrogen ions, a solution of a strong acid will have a high concentration of hydrogen ions and therefore a low pH. A strong base will have a high pH, whereas a weaker base will not dissociate completely and will have a pH of nearer 7.

streptomycin antibiotic drug discovered in 1944, active against a wide range of bacterial infections.

Streptomycin is derived from a soil bacterium *Streptomyces griseus* or synthesized.

stress in psychology, any event or situation that makes heightened demands on a person's mental or emotional resources. Stress can be caused by overwork, anxiety about exams, money, job security, unemployment, bereavement, poor relationships, marriage breakdown, sexual difficulties, poor living or working conditions, and constant exposure to loud noise.

Many changes that are apparently 'for the better', such as being promoted at work, going to a new school, moving to a new house, and getting married, are also a source of stress. Stress can cause, or aggravate, physical illnesses, among them psoriasis, eczema, asthma, and stomach and mouth ulcers. Apart from removing the source of stress, acquiring some control over it and learning to relax when possible are the best responses.

stress and strain in the science of materials, measures of the deforming force applied to a body (stress) and of the resulting change in its shape (◊strain). For a perfectly elastic material, stress is proportional to strain (◊Hooke's law).

stress protein one of a group of proteins produced by a cell when it is under stress. Stress proteins are created in response to a wide variety of stresses including illness, high temperatures, alcohol, and poisons. They act as a buffer for the cell and repair damage.

stridulatory organs in insects, organs that produce sound when rubbed together. Crickets rub their wings together, but grasshoppers rub a hind leg against a wing. Stridulation is thought to be used for attracting mates, but may also serve to mark territory.

strike the compass direction of a horizontal line on a planar structural surface, such as a fault plane, bedding plane, or the trend of a structural feature, such as the axis of a fold. Strike is 90° from dip.

string in computing, a group of characters manipulated as a single object by the computer. In its simplest form a string may consist of a single letter or word – for example, the single word SMITH might be established as a string for processing by a computer. A string can also consist of a combination of words, spaces, and numbers – for example, 33 HIGH STREET ANYTOWN ALLSHIRE could be established as a single string.

Most high-level languages have a variety of string-handling functions. For example, functions may be provided to read a character from any given position in a string or to count automatically the number of characters in a string.

string theory mathematical theory developed in the 1980s to explain the behaviour of ◊elementary particles; see ◊superstring theory.

string, vibrations of the standing waves set up in a stretched string or wire when it is plucked, or stroked with a bow. They are formed by the reflection of progressive waves at the fixed ends of the string. Waves of many different ◊frequencies can be established on a string at the same time. Those that match the natural frequencies of the string will, by a process called ◊resonance, produce large-amplitude vibrations. The vibration of lowest frequency is called the ◊fundamental vibration; vibrations of frequencies that are multiples of the fundamental frequency are called harmonics.

strip mining another term for ◊opencast mining.

strobilus in botany, a reproductive structure found in most ◊gymnosperms and some ◊pteridophytes, notably the club mosses. In conifers the strobilus is commonly known as a cone.

stroboscope instrument for studying continuous periodic motion by using light flashing at the same frequency as that of the motion; for example, rotating machinery can be optically 'stopped' by illuminating it with a stroboscope flashing at the exact rate of rotation.

stroke or ***cerebrovascular accident*** or ***apoplexy*** interruption of the blood supply to part of the brain due to a sudden bleed in the brain (cerebral haemorrhage) or ◊embolism or ◊thrombosis. Strokes vary in severity from producing almost no symptoms to proving rapidly fatal. In between are those (often recurring) that leave a wide range of impaired function, depending on the size and location of the event.

Strokes involving the right side of the brain, for example, produce weakness of the left side of the body. Some affect speech. Around 80% of strokes are **ischaemic strokes**, caused by a blood clot blocking an artery transporting blood to the brain. Transient ischaemic attacks, or 'mini-strokes', with effects lasting only briefly (less than 24 hours), require investigation to try to forestall the possibility of a subsequent full-blown stroke.

The disease of the arteries that predisposes to stroke is ◊atherosclerosis. High blood pressure (◊hypertension) is also a precipitating factor – a worldwide study in 1995 estimated that high blood pressure before middle age gives a tenfold increase in the chance of having a stroke later in life.

Strokes can sometimes be prevented by surgery (as in the case of some ◊aneurysms), or by use of vanticoagulant drugs or vitamin E or daily aspirin to minimize the risk of stroke due to blood clots. According to the results of a US trial announced in December 1995, the clot-buster drug tPA, if administered within three hours of a stroke, can cut the number of stroke victims experiencing lasting disability by 50%.

stromatolite mound produced in shallow water by mats of algae that trap mud particles. Another mat grows on the trapped mud layer and this traps another layer of mud and so on. The stromatolite grows to heights of a metre or so. They are uncommon today but their fossils are among the earliest evidence for living things – over 2,000 million years old.

strong nuclear force one of the four fundamental ◊forces of nature, the other three being the electromagnetic force, gravity, and the weak nuclear force. The strong nuclear force was first described by Japanese physicist Hideki Yukawa in 1935. It is the strongest of all the forces, acts only over very small distances (within the nucleus of the atom), and is responsible for binding together ◊quarks to form ◊hadrons, and for binding together protons and neutrons in the atomic nucleus. The particle that is the carrier of the strong nuclear force is the ◊gluon, of which there are eight kinds, each with zero mass and zero charge.

strontium soft, ductile, pale-yellow, metallic element, symbol Sr, atomic number 38, relative atomic mass 87.62. It is one of the ◊alkaline-earth metals, widely distributed in small quantities only as a sulphate or carbonate. Strontium salts burn with a red flame and are used in fireworks and signal flares.

The radioactive isotopes Sr-89 and Sr-90 (half-life 25 years) are some of the most dangerous products of the nuclear industry; they are fission products in nuclear explosions and in the reactors of nuclear power plants. Strontium is chemically similar to calcium and deposits in bones and other tissues, where the radioactivity is damaging. The element was named in 1808 by English chemist Humphry Davy, who isolated it by electrolysis, after Strontian, a mining location in Scotland where it was first found.

strophanthus any of a group of tropical plants belonging to the dogbane family, native to Africa and Asia. Seeds of the handsome climber *S. gratus* yield a poison, strophantin, which is used on arrowheads in hunting, and in medicine as a heart stimulant. (Genus *Strophanthus,* family Apocynaceae.)

structured programming in computing, the process of writing a program in small, independent parts. This makes it easier to control a program's development and to design and test its individual component parts. Structured programs are built up from units called **modules**, which normally correspond to single ◊procedures or ◊functions. Some programming languages, such as PASCAL and Modula-2, are better suited to structured programming than others.

strychnine $C_{21}H_{22}O_2N_2$ bitter-tasting, poisonous alkaloid. It is a poison that causes violent muscular spasms, and is usually obtained by powdering the seeds of plants of the genus *Strychnos* (for example *S. nux vomica*). Curare is a related drug.

sturgeon any of a family of large, primitive, bony fishes with five rows of bony plates, small sucking mouths, and chin barbels used for exploring the bottom of the water for prey.

Sturgeons take 6–25 years to reach sexual maturity. The population in the Caspian Sea is threatened by pollution and intensive fishing for caviar; there was a 75% decline in the catch 1984–94. It has been estimated that sturgeon will vanish from the Caspian Sea by 2007 as a result of poaching and smuggling of the fish. Rising pollution levels and the damming of rivers also mean that fewer sturgeon are returning to rivers to spawn. A million sturgeon used to go to the Ural river to spawn, but now there are only 200,000. Some 90% of the caviar taken from the Caspian Sea is smuggled, and poachers often catch the females before they are mature enough to produce eggs, thus further decimating the stocks. In an effort to preserve Acipenseridae, all sturgeon species valued for their caviar were added in 1997 to the Convention on International Trade in Endangered Species (◊CITES) Appendix 2 (classed as vulnerable).

Sturt's desert pea scarlet pea-shaped flower with prominent black 'eye' *Clianthus formosus.* It is the floral emblem of South Australia.

style in flowers, the part of the ◊carpel bearing the ◊stigma at its tip. In some flowers it is very short or completely lacking, while in others it may be long and slender, positioning the stigma in the most effective place to receive the pollen.

Style, Old and New forms of dating, see ◊calendar.

style sheet in computing, pre-set group of formats used in word processing, presentation graphics and page layout programs. Style sheets impose margins, fonts, point sizes, alignments, and other criteria to give text a uniform appearance. In a page layout program, designers might use different style sheets for headings, picture captions, and main text.

subatomic particle in physics, a particle that is smaller than an atom. Such particles may be indivisible ◊elementary particles, such as the ◊electron and ◊quark, or they may be composites, such as the ◊proton, neutron, and alpha particle. See also ◊particle physics.

subduction zone region where two plates of the Earth's rigid lithosphere collide, and one plate descends below the other into the weaker asthenosphere. Subduction occurs along ocean trenches, most of which encircle the Pacific Ocean; portions of the ocean plate slide beneath other plates carrying continents.

Ocean trenches are usually associated with volcanic ◊island arcs and deep-focus earthquakes (more than 300 km/185 mi below the surface), both the result of disturbances caused by the plate subduction. The Aleutian Trench bordering Alaska is an example of an active subduction zone, which has produced the Aleutian Island arc.

subject drift in computing, tendency for postings in ◊UseNet, and sometimes entire newsgroups, to wander away from their original subject matter. As threads accumulate in response to a posting, the subject heading is retained, but the discussions can rapidly go off at a tangent. Thus a thread headed 'Re: Ice cream – favourite flavours' might actually be a long-running discussion about Napoleon.

sublimation in chemistry, the conversion of a solid to vapour without passing through the liquid phase.

Sublimation depends on the fact that the boiling-point of the solid substance is lower than its melting-point at atmospheric pressure. Thus by increasing pressure, a substance which sublimes can be made to go through a liquid stage before passing into the vapour state.

Some substances that do not sublime at atmospheric pressure can be made to do so at low pressures. This is the principle of freeze-drying, during which ice sublimes at low pressure.

submarine underwater warship. The first underwater boat was constructed in 1620 for James I of England by the Dutch scientist Cornelius van Drebbel (1572–1633). A naval submarine, or submersible torpedo boat, the *Gymnote,* was launched by France in 1888. The conventional submarine of World War I was driven by diesel engine on the surface and by battery-powered electric motors underwater.

The diesel engine also drove a generator that produced electricity to charge the batteries.

history In the 1760s, the American David Bushnell (1742–1824) designed a submarine called *Turtle* for attacking British ships, and in 1800 Robert Fulton designed a submarine called *Nautilus* for Napoleon for the same purpose. John P Holland, an Irish emigrant to the USA, designed a submarine about 1875, which was used by both the US and the British navies at the turn of the century. Submarine warfare was really established as a distinct form of naval tactics during World War I and submarines, from the ocean-going vessels to the midget type, played a vital role in both world wars. In particular, German U-boats caused great difficulty to Allied merchant shipping, until the radio codes were broken in 1942.

nuclear submarines In 1954 the USA launched the first nuclear-powered submarine, the *Nautilus*. The US nuclear submarine *Ohio*, in service from 1981, is 170 m/560 ft long and carries 24 Trident missiles, each with 12 independently targetable nuclear warheads. The nuclear warheads on US submarines have a range that is being extended to 11,000 km/6,750 mi. Three Vanguard-class Trident missile-carrying submarines, which when armed will each wield more firepower than was used in the whole of World War II, are being built in the 1990s in the UK. Operating depth is usually up to 300 m/1,000 ft, and nuclear-powered speeds of 30 knots (55 kph/34 mph) are reached. As in all nuclear submarines, propulsion is by steam turbine driving a propeller. The steam is raised using the heat given off by the nuclear reactor (see ◊nuclear energy). In oceanography, salvage, and pipe-laying, smaller submarines called **submersibles** are used. They are also being developed for tourism.

submersible vessel designed to operate under water, especially a small submarine used by engineers and research scientists as a ferry craft to support diving operations. The most advanced submersibles are the so-called lock-out type, which have two compartments: one for the pilot, the other to carry divers. The diving compartment is pressurized and provides access to the sea.

subnotebook in computing, a portable computer, usually a PC-compatible, that is smaller than a notebook computer but larger than a handheld computer. Subnotebooks often leave out features such as floppy disc and CD-ROM drives. One example is the Toshiba Libretto.

subroutine in computing, a small section of a program that is executed ('called') from another part of the program. Subroutines provide a method of performing the same task at more than one point in the program, and also of separating the details of a program from its main logic. In some computer languages, subroutines are similar to ◊functions or ◊procedures.

substitute in mathematics, to put values in the place of variables in an algebraic expression or formula. An algebraic expansion or simplification can be checked by substituting simple values for each variable. For example, to check that$x^3 + y^3 = (x + y)(x^2 + y^2 - xy)$ the value $x = 1$ and $y = 2$ might be substituted in both sides of the expression, giving left-hand side: $1^3 + 2^3 = 1 + 8 = 9$ right-hand side: $(1 + 2)(1^2 + 2^2 - 2) = 3 \times 3 = 9$.

The two sides are the same, so the expansion of $x^3 + y^3$ is correct.

substitution reaction in chemistry, the replacement of one atom or ◊functional group in an organic molecule by another.

substrate in biochemistry, a compound or mixture of compounds acted on by an enzyme. The term also refers to a substance such as ◊agar that provides the nutrients for the metabolism of microorganisms. Since the enzyme systems of microorganisms regulate their metabolism, the essential meaning is the same.

substring in computing, a portion of a ◊string. In searching a text database, for example, specifying that a sequence of letters is a substring will widen the search from just matching words to other words in which that sequence of letters appears. For example, searching a database on the string 'computer' will not retrieve entries which use 'computing' or 'compute'. Searching on the substring 'comput' however, will retrieve all three. The technique adds flexibility when the exact syntax of the search term is unknown.

subsystem in computing, hardware and/or software that performs a specific function within a larger system. ◊Silicon Graphics, for example, uses subsystems to perform the many calculations needed for computer animation.

subtraction taking one number or quantity away from another, or finding the difference between two quantities; it is one of the four basic operations of arithmetic. Subtraction is neither commutative: $a - b \neq b - a$ nor associative: $a - (b - c) \neq (a - b) - c$. For example, $8 - 5 \neq 5 - 8$ $7 - (4 - 3) \neq (7 - 4) - 3$.

subway North American term for ◊underground railway.

succession in ecology, a series of changes that occur in the structure and composition of the vegetation in a given area from the time it is first colonized by plants (**primary succession**), or after it has been disturbed by fire, flood, or clearing (**secondary succession**).

If allowed to proceed undisturbed, succession leads naturally to a stable ◊climax community (for example, oak and hickory forest or savannah grassland) that is determined by the climate and soil characteristics of the area.

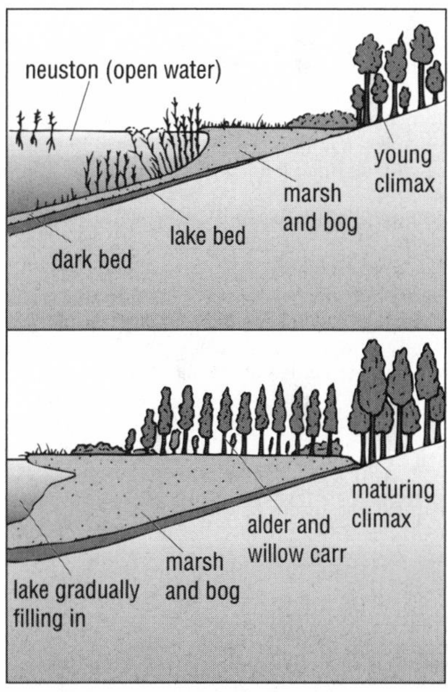

succession The succession of plant types along a lake. As the lake gradually fills in, a mature climax community of trees forms inland from the shore. Extending out from the shore, a series of plant communities can be discerned with small, rapidly growing species closest to the shore.

succulent plant thick, fleshy plant that stores water in its tissues; for example, cacti and stonecrops *Sedum*. Succulents live either in areas where water is very scarce, such as deserts, or in places where it is not easily obtainable because of the high concentrations of salts in the soil, as in salt marshes. Many desert plants are◊ xerophytes.

sucker fish another name for ◊remora.

suckering in plants, reproduction by new shoots (suckers) arising from an existing root system rather than from seed. Plants that produce suckers include elm, dandelion, and members of the rose family.

SUCCULENT PLANT

The flowers of the stapeliads of Africa and southern Asia look very like dung or decaying meat. This is because they rely on carrion-feeding beetles to pollinate them. So convincing are the flowers that they are often covered with maggots that have hatched from eggs mistakenly laid on them.

sucrase enzyme capable of digesting sucrose into its constituent molecules of glucose and fructose.

In mammals this action takes place within the wall of the intestine, the products of the reaction being liberated into the lumen. This is an example of intracellular digestion.

sucrose or ***cane sugar*** or ***beet sugar*** $C_{12}H_{22}O_{11}$ a sugar found in the pith of sugar cane and in sugar beets. It is popularly known as ◊sugar.

Sucrose is a disaccharide sugar, each of its molecules being made up of two simple sugar (monosaccharide) units: glucose and fructose.

sudden infant death syndrome (SIDS) in medicine, the technical term for ◊cot death.

sugar or ***sucrose*** sweet, soluble, crystalline carbohydrate found in the pith of sugar cane and in sugar beet. It is a **disaccharide** sugar, each of its molecules being made up of two simple-sugar (**monosaccharide**) units: glucose and fructose. Sugar is easily digested and forms a major source of energy in humans, being used in cooking and in the food industry as a sweetener and, in high concentrations, as a preservative. A high consumption is associated with obesity and tooth decay. In the UK, sucrose may not be used in baby foods.

The main sources of sucrose sugar are tropical sugar cane *Saccharum officinarum,* which accounts for two-thirds of production, and temperate sugar beet *Beta vulgaris.* Minor quantities are produced from the sap of maple trees, and from sorghum and date palms. Raw sugar crystals obtained by heating the juice of sugar canes are processed to form brown sugars, such as Muscovado and Demerara, or refined and sifted to produce white sugars, such as granulated, caster, and icing sugar. The syrup that is drained away from the raw sugar is molasses; it may be processed to form golden syrup or treacle, or fermented to form rum. Molasses obtained from sugar beet juice is too bitter for human consumption. The fibrous residue of sugar cane, called bagasse, is used in the manufacture of paper, cattle feed, and fuel; and new types of cane are being bred for low sugar and high fuel production.

Approximately 9 million hectares/22.25 million acres of beet, mostly in Europe, Russia, Ukraine, Georgia, Belarus, and Armenia, and 13 million hectares/32 million acres of cane, grown in tropical and subtropical countries, together produce 100 million tonnes of raw sugar each year. Cane usually yields over 20 tonnes of sugar per hectare/9 tons per acre per year; sugar beet rarely exceeds 7 tonnes per hectare/3 tons per acre per year.

Of the 100 sugar cane-producing countries, India and Brazil are the largest, with 3 million and 2.5 million hectares/7.5 million acres and 6 million acres respectively. In many smaller countries, such as Barbados and Mauritius, sugar production is a vital component of the national economy. However, subsidies given to European beet-sugar producers by the European Union have affected world markets and the export earnings of many Third World sugar-producing countries.

sugar maple E North American ◊maple tree.

sulphate SO_4^{2-} salt or ester derived from sulphuric acid. Most sulphates are water soluble (the exceptions are lead, calcium, strontium, and barium sulphates), and require a very high temperature to decompose them.

The commonest sulphates seen in the laboratory are copper(II) sulphate ($CuSO_4$), iron(II) sulphate ($FeSO_4$), and aluminium sulphate ($Al_2(SO_4)_3$). The ion is detected in solution by using barium chloride or barium nitrate to precipitate the insoluble sulphate.

sulphide compound of sulphur and another element in which sulphur is the more ◊electronegative element (see electronegativity). Sulphides occur in a number of minerals. Some of the more volatile sulphides have extremely unpleasant odours (hydrogen sulphide smells of bad eggs).

sulphite SO_3^{2-} salt or ester derived from sulphurous acid.

sulphonamide any of a group of compounds containing the chemical group sulphonamide (SO_2NH_2) or its derivatives, which were, and still are in some cases, used to treat bacterial diseases. Sulphadiazine ($C_{10}H_{10}N_4O_2S$) is an example.

Sulphonamide was the first commercially available antibacterial drug, the forerunner of a range of similar drugs. Toxicity and increasing resistance have limited their use chiefly to the treatment of urinary-tract infection.

sulphur brittle, pale-yellow, nonmetallic element, symbol S, atomic number 16, relative atomic mass 32.064. It occurs in three allotropic forms: two crystalline (called rhombic and monoclinic, following the arrangements of the atoms within the crystals) and one amorphous. It burns in air with a blue flame and a stifling odour. Insoluble in water but soluble in carbon disulphide, it is a good electrical insulator. Sulphur is widely used in the manufacture of sulphuric acid (used to treat phosphate rock to make fertilizers) and in making paper, matches, gunpowder and fireworks, in vulcanizing rubber, and in medicines and insecticides.

It is found abundantly in nature in volcanic regions combined with both metals and nonmetals, and also in its elemental form as a crystalline solid. It is a constituent of proteins, and has been known since ancient times.

sulphur dioxide SO_2 pungent gas produced by burning sulphur in air or oxygen. It is widely used for disinfecting food vessels and equipment, and as a preservative in some food products. It occurs in industrial flue gases and is a major cause of ◊acid rain.

sulphuric acid or ***oil of vitriol*** H_2SO_4 a dense, viscous, colourless liquid that is extremely corrosive. It gives out heat when added to water and can cause severe burns. Sulphuric acid is used extensively in the chemical industry, in the refining of petrol, and in the manufacture of fertilizers, detergents, explosives, and dyes. It forms the acid component of car batteries.

sulphurous acid H_2SO_3 solution of sulphur dioxide (SO_2) in water. It is a weak acid.

sulphur trioxide SO_3 colourless solid prepared by reacting sulphur dioxide and oxygen in the presence of a vanadium(V) oxide catalyst in the ◊contact process. It reacts violently with water to give sulphuric acid.

The violence of its reaction with water makes it extremely dangerous. In the contact process, it is dissolved in concentrated sulphuric acid to give oleum ($H_2S_2O_7$).

sumac any bush or tree of the genus *Rhus* of the cashew family, having pinnate compound leaves and clusters of small reddish fruits. Staghorn sumac *Rhus typhina,* growing to 36 ft/11 m tall, is common in North America. Included too are several poisonous plants (sometimes referred to collectively as the genus *Toxicodendron*), such as poison ◊ivy, poison sumac, and certain Japanese sumacs.

summer time practice introduced in the UK in 1916 whereby legal time from spring to autumn is an hour in advance of Greenwich mean time.

Continental Europe 'puts the clock back' a month earlier than the UK in autumn. British summer time was permanently in force February 1940–October 1945 and February 1968–October 1971. Double summer time (2 hours in advance) was in force during the summers of 1941–45 and 1947.

In North America the practice is known as **daylight saving time**.

... in my studies of astronomy and philosophy I hold this opinion about the universe, that the Sun remains fixed in the centre of the circle of heavenly bodies, without changing its place: and the Earth, turning upon itself moves round the Sun.

GALILEO Italian physicist.
Letter to Cristina di Lorena 1615

Sun the ◊star at the centre of the Solar System. Its diameter is 1,392,000 km/865,000 mi; its temperature at the surface is about 5,800K (5,500°C/9,900°F), and at the centre 15,000,000K (about 15,000,000°C/27,000,000°F). It is composed of about 70% hydrogen and 30% helium, with other elements making up less than 1%. The Sun's energy is generated by nuclear fusion reactions that turn hydrogen into helium at its centre. The gas core is far denser than mercury or lead on Earth. The Sun is about 4.7 billion years old, with a predicted lifetime of 10 billion years.

SUN

http://www.hawastsoc.org/solar/eng/sun.htm

All you every wanted to know about our closest star, including cross sections, photographs, a history of exploration, animations of eclipses, and much more. You can also take a multimedia tour of the Sun or find out what today's weather is like on the Sun.

sun-and-planet gear another term for ◊epicyclic gear.

sundew any of a group of insectivorous plants found growing in bogs; sticky hairs on the leaves catch and digest insects that land on them. (Genus *Drosera*, family Droseraceae.)

sundial instrument measuring time by means of a shadow cast by the Sun. Almost completely superseded by the proliferation of clocks, it survives ornamentally in gardens. The dial is marked with the hours at graduated distances, and a style or gnomon (parallel to Earth's axis and pointing to the north) casts the shadow.

sunfish marine fish *Mola mola* with disc-shaped body 3 m/10 ft long found in all temperate and tropical oceans. The term also applies to fish of the North American freshwater Centrarchidae family, which have compressed, almost circular bodies, up to 80 cm/30 in long, and are nestbuilders and avid predators.

sunflower tall, thick-stemmed plant with a large, single, yellow-petalled flower, belonging to the daisy family. The common or giant sunflower (*H. annuus*), probably native to Mexico, can grow up to 4.5 m/15 ft high. It is commercially cultivated in central Europe, the USA, Russia, Ukraine, and Australia for the oil-bearing seeds that ripen in the central disc of the flower head; sunflower oil is widely used as a cooking oil and in margarine. (Genus *Helianthus*, family Compositae.)

Sun Microsystems (named after the ***Stanford University Network***) US-based computer manufacturer founded in 1982 with the motto 'the network is the computer'. Sun specializes in office networks, workstations, and servers running Solaris, a version of the UNIX operating system. Sun pioneered the concept of open systems – technology that is available to other manufacturers – and in 1995 released Java, a platform-independent programming language.

sunspot dark patch on the surface of the Sun, actually an area of cooler gas, thought to be caused by strong magnetic fields that block the outward flow of heat to the Sun's surface. Sunspots consist of a dark central **umbra**, about 4,000K (3,700°C/6,700°F), and a lighter surrounding **penumbra**, about 5,500K (5,200°C/9,400°F). They last from several days to over a month, ranging in size from 2,000 km/1,250 mi to groups stretching for over 100,000 km/62,000 mi.

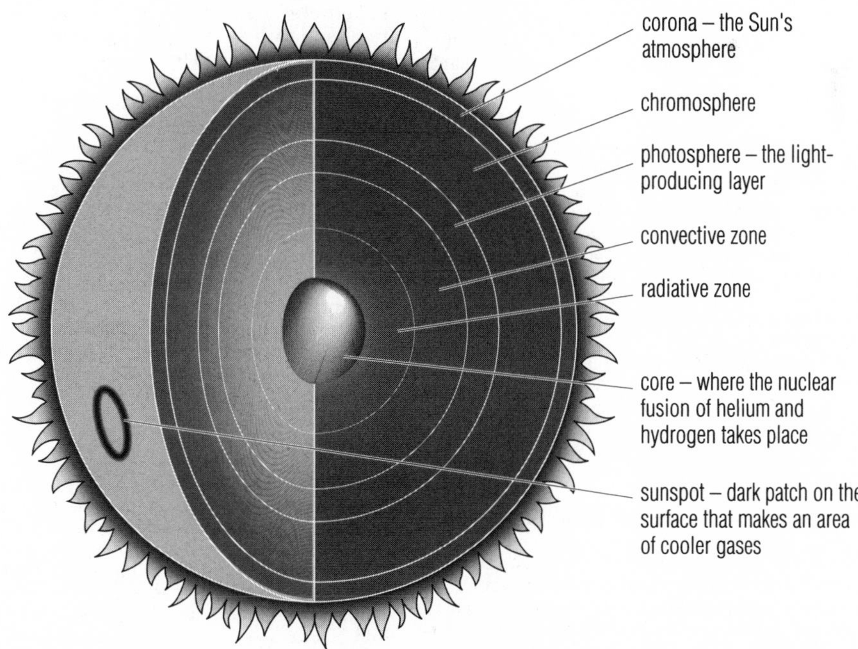

Sun *The structure of the Sun. Nuclear reactions at the core releases vast amounts of energy in the form of light and heat that radiate out to the photosphere and corona. Surges of glowing gas rise as prominences from the surface of the Sun and cooler areas, known as sunspots appear as dark patches on the giant stars surface.*

SUNSPOTS

http://athena.wednet.edu/curric/space/sun/sunspot.html

Well-written and easily understandable explanation of sunspots. There is a high-resolution image of a group of sunspots and a link for further sunspot pictures. There is information on how to observe sunspots and the Sun's cycle of magnetic activity. For more detailed information, there are links to solar observatories.

Sunspots are more common during active periods in the Sun's magnetic cycle, when they are sometimes accompanied by nearby flares. The number of sunspots visible at a given time varies from none to over 100, in a cycle averaging 11 years. There was a lull in sunspot activity, known as the Maunder minimum, 1645–1715, that coincided with a cold spell in Europe.

Sunyaev-Zel'dovich effect slight dip in the ◊cosmic background radiation when observed through the gas that surrounds clusters of galaxies.

First mapped in 1993 by British astronomers around the Abell 2218 galaxy cluster. The size of the Sunyaev-Zel'dovich effect is a measure of the gas thickness the cosmic background radiation passes through.

superactinide any of a theoretical series of superheavy, radioactive elements, starting with atomic number 113, that extend beyond the ◊transactinide series in the periodic table. They do not occur in nature and none has yet been synthesized.

It is postulated that this series has a group of elements that have half-lives longer than those of the transactinide series.

This group, centred on element 114, is referred to as the 'island of stability', based on the nucleon arrangement. The longer half-lives will, it is hoped, allow enough time for their chemical and physical properties to be studied when they have been synthesized.

supercluster in astronomy, a grouping of several clusters of galaxies to form a structure about 100–300 million light years across. Our own Galaxy and its neighbours lie on the edge of the local supercluster of which the ◊Virgo cluster is the dominant member.

supercomputer the fastest, most powerful type of computer, capable of performing its basic operations in picoseconds (thousand-billionths of a second), rather than nanoseconds (billionths of a second), like most other computers.

To achieve these extraordinary speeds, supercomputers use several processors working together and techniques such as cooling processors down to nearly ◊absolute zero temperature, so that their components conduct electricity many times faster than normal. Supercomputers are used in weather forecasting, fluid dynamics, and aerodynamics. Manufacturers include Cray Research, Fujitsu, and NEC.

Of the world's 500 most powerful supercomputers 232 are in the USA, 109 in Japan, and 140 in Europe, with 23 in the UK. In 1992 Fujitsu announced the launch of the first computer capable of performing 300 billion calculations a second. In 1996 University of Tokyo researchers completed a computer able to perform 1.08 trillion floating-point operations per second.

superconductivity in physics, increase in electrical conductivity at low temperatures. The resistance of some metals and metallic compounds decreases uniformly with decreasing temperature until at a critical temperature (the superconducting point), within a few degrees of absolute zero (0K/–273.15°C/–459.67°F), the resistance suddenly falls to zero. The phenomenon was discovered by Dutch scientist Heike Kamerlingh Onnes in 1911.

Some metals, such as platinum and copper, do not become superconductive; as the temperature decreases, their resistance decreases to a certain point but then rises again. Superconductivity can be nullified by the application of a large magnetic field.

In the superconducting state, an electric current will continue indefinitely once started, provided that the material remains below the superconducting point. In 1986 IBM researchers achieved superconductivity with some ceramics at –243°C/–405°F), opening up the possibility of **'high-temperature' superconductivity**; Paul Chu at the University of Houston, Texas, achieved superconductivity at –179°C/–290°F, a temperature that can be sustained using liquid nitrogen.

In 1993 Swiss researchers produced an alloy of mercury, barium, and copper which becomes superconducting at 133 K (–140°C/–220°F). A high-temperature semiconductor material, called bismuth ceramic, which is superconducting at 100 K, became commercially available in 1997.

supercooling the cooling of a liquid below its freezing point without freezing taking place; or the cooling of a ◊saturated solution without crystallization taking place, to form a supersaturated solution. In both cases supercooling is possible because of the lack of solid particles around which crystals can form. Crystallization rapidly follows the introduction of a small crystal (seed) or agitation of the supercooled solution.

supercritical fluid fluid that combines the properties of a gas and a liquid, see ◊fluid, supercritical.

superego in Freudian psychology, the element of the human mind concerned with the ideal, responsible for ethics and self-imposed standards of behaviour. It is characterized as a form of conscience, restraining the ◊ego, and responsible for feelings of guilt when the moral code is broken.

superfluid fluid that flows without viscosity or friction and has a very high thermal conductivity. Liquid helium at temperatures below 2K (–271°C/–456°F) is a superfluid: it shows unexpected behaviour; for instance, it flows uphill in apparent defiance of gravity and, if placed in a container, will flow up the sides and escape.

supergiant the largest and most luminous type of star known, with a diameter of up to 1,000 times that of the Sun and absolute magnitudes of between –5 and –9. Supergiants are likely to become ◊supernovae.

superheterodyne receiver the most widely used type of radio receiver, in which the incoming signal is mixed with a signal of fixed frequency generated within the receiver circuits. The resulting signal, called the intermediate-frequency (i.f.) signal, has a frequency between that of the incoming signal and the internal signal. The intermediate frequency is near the optimum frequency of the amplifier to which the i.f. signal is passed.

This arrangement ensures greater gain and selectivity. The superheterodyne system is also used in basic television receivers.

superior planet planet that is farther away from the Sun than the Earth is: that is, Mars, Jupiter, Saturn, Uranus, Neptune, and Pluto.

supernova the explosive death of a star, which temporarily attains a brightness of 100 million Suns or more, so that it can shine as brilliantly as a small galaxy for a few days or weeks. Very approximately, it is thought that a supernova explodes in a large galaxy about once every 100 years. Many supernovae – astronomers estimate some 50% – remain undetected because of obscuring by interstellar dust.

The name 'supernova' was coined by US astronomers Fritz Zwicky and Walter Baade in 1934. Zwicky was also responsible for the division into types I and II. **Type I** supernovae are thought to occur in ◊binary star systems, in which gas from one star falls on to a ◊white dwarf, causing it to explode. **Type II** supernovae occur in stars ten or more times as massive as the Sun, which suffer runaway internal nuclear reactions at the ends of their lives, leading to explosions. These are thought to leave behind ◊neutron stars and ◊black holes. Gas ejected by such an explosion causes an expanding radio source, such as the ◊Crab nebula. Supernovae are thought to be the main source of elements heavier than hydrogen and helium.

superphosphate phosphate fertilizer made by treating apatite (calcium phosphate mineral) with sulphuric or phosphoric acid.

The commercial mixture contains largely monocalcium phosphate. Single-superphosphate obtained from apatite and sulphuric acid contains 16–20% available phosphorus, as P_2O_5; triple-superphosphate, which contains 45–50% phosphorus, is made by treating apatite with phosphoric acid.

supersaturation in chemistry, the state of a solution that has a higher concentration of ◊solute than would normally be obtained in a ◊saturated solution.

Many solutes have a higher ◊solubility at high temperatures. If a hot saturated solution is cooled slowly, sometimes the excess solute does not come out of solution. This is an unstable situation and the introduction of a small solid particle will encourage the release of excess solute.

supersonic speed speed greater than that at which sound travels, measured in ◊Mach numbers. In dry air at 0°C/32°F, sound travels at about 1,170 kph/727 mph, but decreases its speed with altitude until, at 12,000 m/39,000 ft, it is only 1,060 kph/658 mph.

When an aircraft passes the◊sound barrier, shock waves are built up that give rise to ◊sonic boom, often heard at ground level. US pilot Captain Charles Yeager was the first to achieve supersonic flight, in a Bell VS-1 rocket plane on 14 October 1947.

superstring theory in physics, a mathematical theory developed in the 1980s to explain the properties of ◊elementary particles and the forces between them (in particular, gravity and the nuclear forces) in a way that combines ◊relativity and ◊quantum theory.

In string theory, the fundamental objects in the universe are not pointlike particles but extremely small stringlike objects. These objects exist in a universe of ten dimensions, although, for reasons not yet understood, only three space dimensions and one dimension of time are discernible.

There are many unresolved difficulties with superstring theory, but some physicists think it may be the ultimate 'theory of everything' that explains all aspects of the universe within one framework.

supersymmetry in physics, a theory that relates the two classes of elementary particle, the ◊fermions and the ◊bosons. According to supersymmetry, each fermion particle has a boson partner particle, and vice versa. It has not been possible to marry up all the known fermions with the known bosons, and so the theory postulates the existence of other, as yet undiscovered fermions, such as the photinos (partners of the photons), gluinos (partners of the gluons), and gravitinos (partners of the gravitons). Using these ideas, it has become possible to develop a theory of gravity – called **supergravity** – that extends Einstein's work and considers the gravitational, nuclear, and electromagnetic forces to be manifestations of an underlying superforce. Supersymmetry has been incorporated into the◊ superstring theory, and appears to be a crucial ingredient in the 'theory of everything' sought by scientists.

support in computing, a particular type of hardware or ◊software that is compatible with a relevant standard or another type of hardware or software. A given printer might, for example, support 600 dpi (dots per inch) resolution, or a particular computer system might support SVGA graphics.

support environment in computing, a collection of programs (software) used to help people design and write other programs. At its simplest, this includes a ◊text editor (word-processing software) and a ◊compiler for translating programs into executable form; but it can also include interactive debuggers for helping to locate faults, data dictionaries for keeping track of the data used, and rapid prototyping tools for producing quick, experimental mock-ups of programs.

suprachiasmatic nucleus one of two small regions in the ◊hypothalamus that play a part in controlling ◊circadian rhythm.

suprarenal gland alternative name for the ◊adrenal gland.

surd expression containing the root of an ◊irrational number that can never be exactly expressed – for example, $\sqrt{3} = 1.732050808...$.

surface area the area of the outside surface of a solid. *See illustration on page 728.*

surface-area-to-volume ratio the ratio of an animal's surface area (the area covered by its skin) to its total volume. This is high for small animals, but low for large animals such as elephants.

The ratio is important for endothermic (warm-blooded) animals because the amount of heat lost by the body is proportional to its surface area, whereas the amount generated is proportional to its volume. Very small birds and mammals, such as hummingbirds and shrews, lose a lot of heat and need a high intake of food to maintain their body temperature. Elephants, on the other hand, are in danger of overheating, which is why they have no fur.

surface tension in physics, the property that causes the surface of a liquid to behave as if it were covered with a weak elastic skin; this is why a needle can float on water. It is caused by the exposed surface's tendency to contract to the smallest possible area because of cohesive forces between ◊molecules at the surface. Allied phenomena include the formation of droplets, the concave profile of a meniscus, and the ◊capillary action by which water soaks into a sponge.

surfactant (contraction of ***surface-active agent***) substance added to a liquid in order to increase its wetting or spreading properties. Detergents are examples.

surfing in computing, exploring the ◊Internet. The term is derived from 'channel surfing', or flicking rapidly through the dozens of channels typically available on cable TV networks.

surgeon fish any fish of the tropical marine family Acanthuridae. It has a flat body up to 50 cm/20 in long, is brightly coloured, and has a movable spine on each side of the tail that can be used as a weapon.

SURGERY

An English surgeon received £3,000 and a knighthood for removing a bladder stone from Leopold I, uncle to Queen Victoria. The surgeon, Henry Thompson, removed the stone using a lithotrite – an instrument inserted into the bladder through the penis, which crushes the stone so that it can be expelled naturally.

surgery branch of medicine concerned with the treatment of disease, abnormality, or injury by operation. Traditionally it has been performed by means of cutting instruments, but today a number of technologies are used to treat or remove lesions, including ultrasonic waves and laser surgery.

Surgery is carried out under sterile conditions using an ◊anaesthetic. There are many specialized fields, including cardiac (heart), orthopaedic (bones and joints), ophthalmic (eye), neuro (brain and nerves), thoracic (chest), and renal (kidney) surgery; other specialities include plastic and reconstructive surgery, and ◊transplant surgery.

Historically, surgery for abscesses, amputation, dental problems, trepanning, and childbirth was practised by the ancient civilizations of both the Old World and the New World.

During the Middle Ages, Arabic surgeons passed their techniques on to Europe, where, during the Renaissance, anatomy and physiology were pursued. By the 19th century, anaesthetics and Joseph Lister's discovery of antiseptics became the basis for successful surgical practices. The 20th century's use of antibiotics and blood ◊transfusions has made surgery safer and more effective.

Some early operations, such as thoracoplasty (causing partial collapse of a lung) for tuberculosis, have been replaced by other treatments. Also, the need for exploratory surgery has been reduced by the introduction of noninvasive imaging techniques,

surface area of common three-dimensional shapes

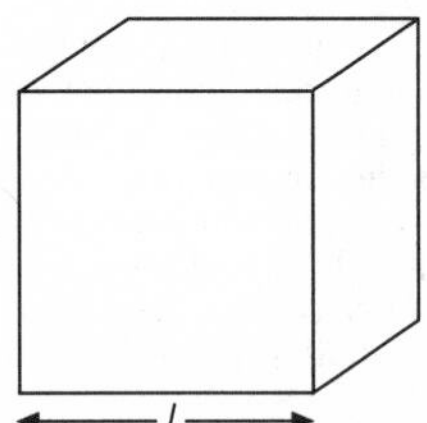

surface area of a ***cube***
(faces are identical)
= 6 × area of each surface
$= 6\,l^2$

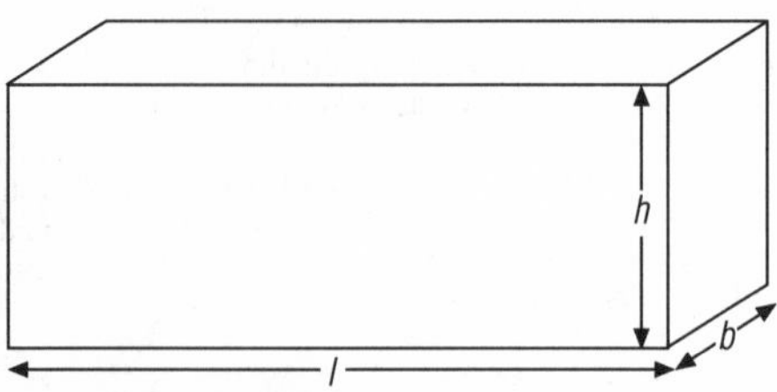

surface area of a ***cuboid***
(opposite faces are identical)
= area of two end faces + area of two sides + area of top and base
$= 2lh + 2hb + 2lb$
$= 2(lh + hb + lb)$

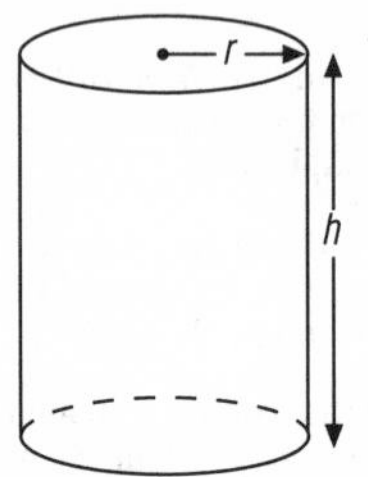

surface area of a ***cylinder***
= area of a curved surface + area of top and base
= 2π × (radius of cross-section × height) + 2π (radius of cross-section)^2
$= 2\pi rh + 2\pi r^2$
$= 2\pi r(h + r)$

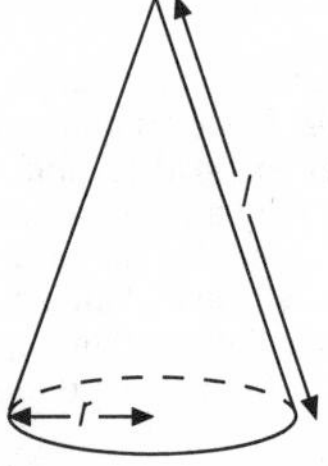

surface area of a ***cone***
= area of a curved surface + area base
= π × (radius of cross-section × slant height) + π (radius of cross-section)^2
$= \pi rl + \pi r^2$
$= \pi r(l + r)$

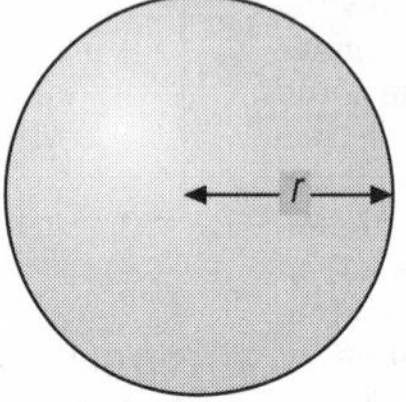

surface area of a ***sphere***
= 4π × radius^2
$= 4\pi r^2$

surface area *Surface areas of common three-dimensional shapes.*

such as ◊ultrasound and ◊CAT scans. The practice of endoscopy (examination of the interior of the body by direct viewing) has enabled the development of minimally invasive keyhole surgery.

Sine experientia nihil sufficienter sciri potest.
Without experience nothing can be known sufficiently.

ROGER BACON English philosopher and scientist.
Opus Majus, 1267–68

surgical spirit ◊ethanol to which has been added a small amount of methanol to render it unfit to drink. It is used to sterilize surfaces and to cleanse skin abrasions and sores.

surrogacy practice whereby a woman is sought, and usually paid, to bear a child for an infertile couple or a single parent.

survey in statistics, a method of collecting data in which people are asked to answer a number of questions (usually in the form of a questionnaire). An opinion poll is a survey. The reliability of a survey's results depends on whether the sample from which the information has been collected is free from bias and sufficiently large.

surveying the accurate measuring of the Earth's crust, or of land features or buildings. It is used to establish boundaries, and to evaluate the topography for engineering work. The measurements used are both linear and angular, and geometry and trigonometry are applied in the calculations.

susceptibility in physics, ratio of the intensity of magnetization produced in a material to the intensity of the magnetic field to which the material is exposed. It measures the extent to which a material is magnetized by an applied magnetic field. ◊Diamagnetic materials have small negative susceptibilities; ◊paramagnetic materials have small positive susceptibilities; ◊ferromagnetic materials have large positive susceptibilities. See also ◊magnetism.

suslik small Eurasian ground ◊squirrel *Citellus citellus.*

suspension mixture consisting of small solid particles dispersed in a liquid or gas, which will settle on standing. An example is milk of magnesia, which is a suspension of magnesium hydroxide in water.

suspension bridge ◊bridge in which the spanning roadway or railway is supported by a system of steel ropes suspended from two or more tall towers.

suspensory ligament in the ◊eye, a ring of fibre supporting the lens. The ligaments attach to the ciliary muscles, the circle of muscle mainly responsible for changing the shape of the lens during ◊accommodation. If the ligaments are put under tension, the lens becomes flatter, and therefore able to focus on objects in the far distance.

Sussex spaniel breed of small gundog, originating at Rosehill Park, Sussex, England. Weighing only about 23 kg/50 lb and standing 40 cm/15 in tall, it is characterized by its golden liver-coloured coat.

sustainable capable of being continued indefinitely. For example, the sustainable yield of a forest is equivalent to the amount that grows back. Environmentalists made the term a catchword, in advocating the sustainable use of resources.

SUSTAINABLE DEVELOPMENT

http://iisd1.iisd.ca/

Tackles a complex issue from many different points of view. There are sections on trade and key topics such as forests and oceans. The site also reports on global initiatives to encourage sustainability. One of the major advantages of this site, though, is that it makes this issue easy to understand for beginners through its 'contents and principles' section.

sustained-yield cropping in ecology, the removal of surplus individuals from a ◊population of organisms so that the population maintains a constant size. This usually requires selective removal of animals of all ages and both sexes to ensure a balanced ◊population structure. Taking too many individuals can result in a population decline, as in overfishing.

Excessive cropping of young females may lead to fewer births in following years, and a fall in population size. Appropriate cropping frequencies can be determined from an analysis of a ◊life table.

SUSY in physics, an abbreviation for ◊supersymmetry.

SVGA (abbreviation for ***super video graphics array***) in computing, a graphic display standard providing higher resolution than ◊VGA. SVGA screens have resolutions of either 800 × 600 or 1,024 × 768.

swallow any bird of the family Hirundinidae of small, insect-eating birds in the order Passeriformes, with long, narrow wings, and deeply forked tails. Swallows feed while flying, capturing winged insects in the mouth, which is lined with bristles made viscid (sticky) by a salivary secretion.

SWALLOW

Most birds have fleas; there are 17 species of flea found only on swallows and martins.

swamp region of low-lying land that is permanently saturated with water and usually overgrown with vegetation; for example, the everglades of Florida, USA. A swamp often occurs where a lake has filled up with sediment and plant material. The flat surface so formed means that runoff is slow, and the water table is always close to the surface. The high humus content of swamp soil means that good agricultural soil can be obtained by draining.

swamp cypress or ***bald cypress*** deciduous tree belonging to the redwood family, found growing in or near water in the southeastern USA and Mexico; it is a valuable timber tree. (*Taxodium distichum,* family Taxodiaceae.)

swan large water bird, with a long slender neck and webbed feet, closely related to ducks and geese. The four species of swan found in the northern hemisphere are white; the three species found in the southern hemisphere are all or partly black. The male (cob) and female (pen) are similar in appearance, and they usually pair for life. They nest on or near water in every continent, except Africa and Antarctica. Swans produce a clutch of 4–6 greenish coloured eggs and their young are known as cygnets. Cygnets are covered with a grey down and only become fully feathered and able to fly after 14–16 weeks.

Swans feed mainly on aquatic plants. They are among the largest and heaviest birds that can fly and because of this require large areas of water to take off. They fly with a slow, graceful wing beat and when migrating, fly in a distinctive V-shaped flock.

The **mute swan** is the most common species. It is native to northern Europe and Asia, but has been introduced and is now widespread in North America. The mute swan has white feathers, black legs and a bright orange flattened bill with a black knob on the upper bill, near the eyes. It may be as long as 150 cm/5 ft in length and weigh as much as 14 kg/30 lb. It hisses loudly when angry.

classification Swans belong to animal phylum Chordata, class Aves (birds), order Anseriformes, family Anatidae. They belong to the genus *Cygnus.* There are seven species: the mute swan (*Cygnus olor*), the whooper swan (*C. cygnus*), Bewick's swan (*C. bewicki*), the tundra (whistling) swan (*C. columbianus*), the North American trumpeter swan (*C. buccinator*), the black swan of Australia (*C. atratus*), and the South American black-necked swan (*C. melanocoryphus*). The North American trumpeter swan is the largest, with a wingspan of 2.4 m/8 ft.

swap in computing, to move segments of data in and out of memory. For fast operation as much data as possible is required in main memory, but it is generally not possible to include all data at the same time. Swapping is the operation of writing and reading from the backup store, often a special space on the disc.

S-wave (abbreviation of ***secondary wave***) in seismology, a class of seismic wave that passes through the Earth in the form of transverse shear waves. S-waves from an earthquake travel at roughly half the speed of P-waves and arrive later at monitoring stations (hence secondary waves) though with greater amplitude. They can travel through solid rock but not through the liquid outer core of the Earth.

sweat gland ◊gland within the skin of mammals that produces surface perspiration. In primates, sweat glands are distributed over the whole body, but in most other mammals they are more localized; for example, in cats and dogs they are restricted to the feet and around the face.

swede annual or biennial plant widely cultivated for its edible root, which is purple, white, or yellow. It is similar in taste to the turnip but is of greater food value, firmer fleshed, and can be stored for a longer time. (*Brassica napus,* family Cruciferae.)

sweet cicely plant belonging to the carrot family, native to S Europe; the root is eaten as a vegetable, and the aniseed-flavoured leaves are used in salads. (*Myrrhis odorata,* family Umbelliferae.)

sweetener any chemical that gives sweetness to food. Caloric sweeteners are various forms of ◊sugar; noncaloric, or artificial, sweeteners are used by dieters and diabetics and provide neither energy nor bulk. Questions have been raised about the long-term health effects from several artificial sweeteners.

Sweeteners are used to make highly processed foods attractive, whether sweet or savoury. Most of the noncaloric sweeteners do not have E numbers. Some are banned for baby foods and for young children: thaumatin, aspartame, acesulfame-K, sorbitol, and mannitol. Cyclamate is banned in the UK and the USA; acesulfame-K is banned in the USA.

In 1997, Japanese geneticists engineered a strain of yeast that produces a protein, called monellin, which is 3,000 times as sweet as sugar and 15 times sweeter than aspartame. Monellin occurs naturally in the berries of a West African plant, *Dioscoreophyllum cumminisii* and, as a protein, it contains only 4 kilocalories per gram.

sweet pea plant belonging to the ◊pea family.

sweet potato tropical American plant belonging to the morning-glory family; the white-orange tuberous root is used as a source of starch and alcohol and eaten as a vegetable. (*Ipomoea batatas,* family Convolvulaceae.)

sweet william biennial to perennial plant belonging to the pink family, native to S Europe. It is grown for its fragrant red, white, and pink flowers. (*Dianthus barbatus,* family Caryophyllaceae.)

swift fast-flying, short-legged bird of the family Apodidae, order Apodiformes, of which there are about 75 species, found largely in the tropics. They are 9–23 cm/4–11 in long, with brown or grey plumage, long, pointed wings, and usually a forked tail. They are capable of flying at 110 kph/70 mph.

The nests of the **grey-rumped swiftlet** *Collocalia francica* of Borneo consist almost entirely of solidified saliva, and are harvested for bird's-nest soup. The increasing removal of nests for commercial purposes is endangering the birds.

swim bladder thin-walled, air-filled sac found between the gut and the spine in bony fishes. Air enters the bladder from the gut or from surrounding capillaries (see ◊capillary), and changes of air pressure within the bladder maintain buoyancy whatever the water depth.

In evolutionary terms, the swim bladder of higher fishes is a derivative of the lungs present in all primitive fishes (not just lungfishes).

swing wing correctly ***variable-geometry wing*** aircraft wing that can be moved during flight to provide a suitable configuration for either low-speed or high-speed flight. The British engineer Barnes Wallis developed the idea of the swing wing, first used on the US-built Northrop X-4, and since used in several aircraft, including the US F-111, F-114, and the B-1, the European Tornado, and several Soviet-built aircraft.

These craft have their wings projecting nearly at right angles for takeoff and landing and low-speed flight, and swung back for high-speed flight.

Swiss cheese plant common name for ◊monstera, a plant belonging to the arum family.

swordfish marine bony fish *Xiphias gladius,* the only member of its family (Xiphiidae), characterized by a long swordlike beak protruding from the upper jaw. It may reach 4.5 m/15 ft in length and weigh 450 kg/1,000 lb.

sycamore deciduous tree native to Europe. The leaves are five-lobed, and the hanging clusters of flowers are followed by winged fruits. The timber is used for furniture making. (*Acer pseudoplatanus.*)

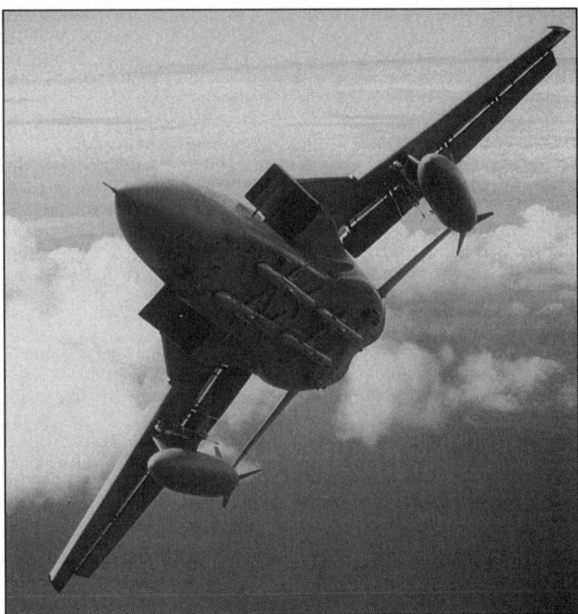

swing wing A British Aerospace Tornado F2 swing-wing (variable-geometry) fighter-bomber. It is flying at a relatively low speed and the wings are fully extended. British Aerospace

syenite grey, crystalline, plutonic (intrusive) ◊igneous rock, consisting of feldspar and hornblende; other minerals may also be present, including small amounts of quartz.

symbiosis any close relationship between two organisms of different species, and one where both partners benefit from the association. A well-known example is the pollination relationship between insects and flowers, where the insects feed on nectar and carry pollen from one flower to another. This is sometimes known as ◊mutualism.

symbol in chemistry, letter or letters used to represent a chemical element, usually derived from the beginning of its English or Latin name. Symbols derived from English include B, boron; C, carbon; Ba, barium; and Ca, calcium. Those derived from Latin include Na, sodium (Latin *natrium*); Pb, lead (Latin *plumbum*); and Au, gold (Latin *aurum*).

symbolic address in computing, a symbol used in ◊assembly language programming to represent the binary ◊address of a memory location.

symbolic processor computer purpose-built to run so-called symbol-manipulation programs rather than programs involving a great deal of numerical computation. They exist principally for the ◊artificial intelligence language ◊LISP, although some have also been built to run ◊PROLOG.

symmetry exact likeness in shape about a given line (axis), point, or plane. A figure has symmetry if one half can be rotated and/or reflected onto the other. (Symmetry preserves length, angle, but not necessarily orientation.) In a wider sense, symmetry exits if a change in the system leaves the essential features of the system unchanged; for example, reversing the sign of electric charges does not change the electrical behaviour of an arrangement of charges.

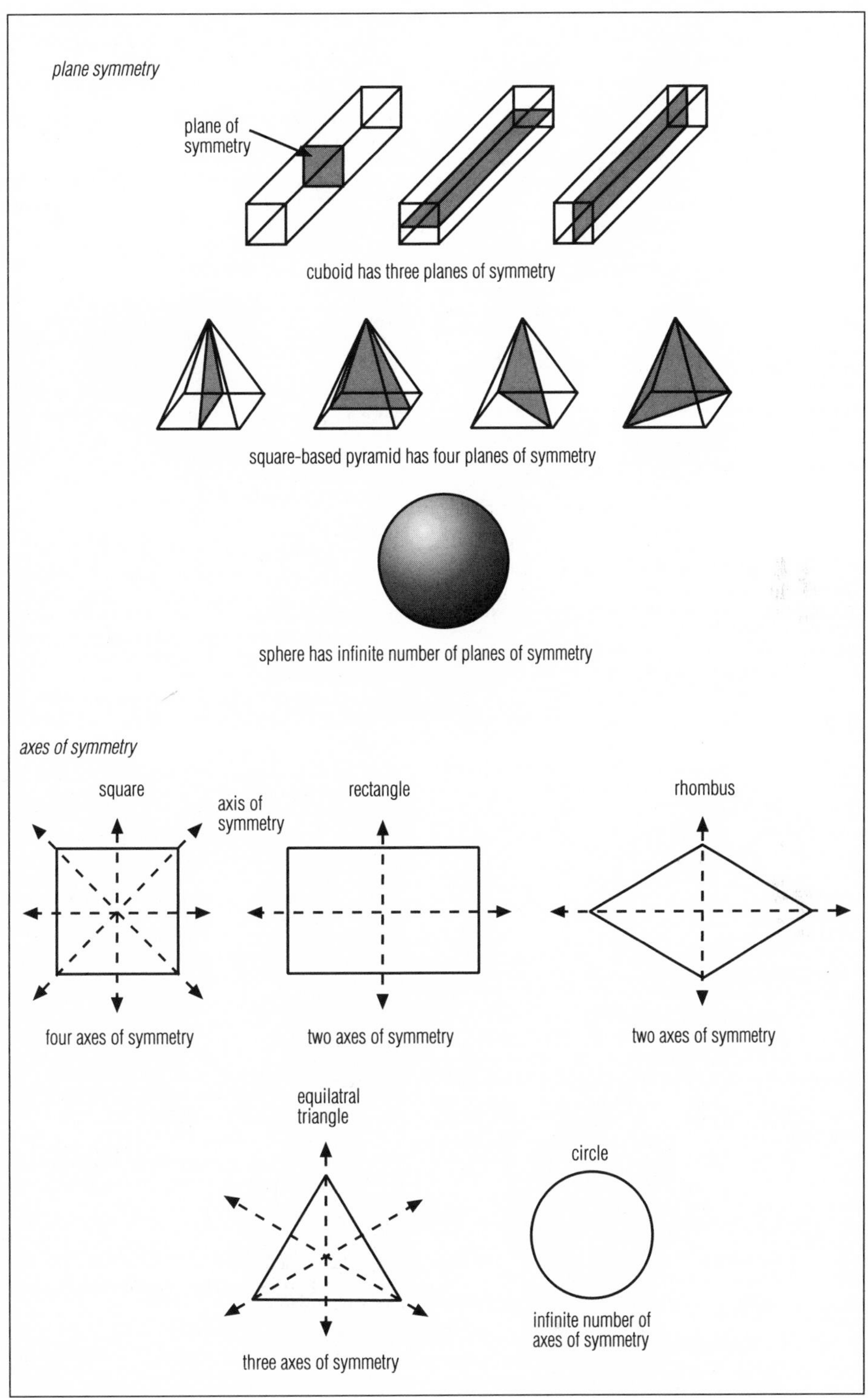

symmetry *The planes of symmetry of some common three-dimensional shapes and the axes of symmetry of some common two-dimensional ones.*

There will come a time, when the world will be filled with one science, one truth, one industry, one brotherhood, one friendship with nature ... this is my belief, it progresses, it grows stronger, this is worth living for, this is worth waiting for.

DMITRI IVANOVICH MENDELEYEV Russian chemist.
In Y A Urmantsev *The Symmetry of Nature and the Nature of Symmetry* 1974

symptom any change or manifestation in the body suggestive of disease as perceived by the sufferer. Symptoms are subjective phenomena. In strict usage, **symptoms** are events or changes reported by the patient; **signs** are noted by the doctor during the patient's examination.

synapse junction between two ◊nerve cells, or between a nerve cell and a muscle (a neuromuscular junction), across which a nerve impulse is transmitted. The two cells are separated by a narrow gap called the **synaptic cleft**. The gap is bridged by a chemical ◊neurotransmitter, released by the nerve impulse.

The threadlike extension, or ◊axon, of the transmitting nerve cell has a slightly swollen terminal point, the **synaptic knob**. This forms one half of the synaptic junction and houses membrane-bound vesicles, which contain a chemical neurotransmitter. When nerve impulses reach the knob, the vesicles release the transmitter and this flows across the gap and binds itself to special receptors on the receiving cell's membrane. If the receiving cell is a nerve cell, the other half of the synaptic junction will be one or more extensions called ◊dendrites; these will be stimulated by the neurotransmitter to set up an impulse, which will then be conducted along the length of the nerve cell and on to its own axons. If the receiving cell is a muscle cell, it will be stimulated by the neurotransmitter to contract.

Synapsida group of mammal-like reptiles living 315–195 million years ago, whose fossil record is largely complete, and who were for a while the dominant land animals, before being replaced by the dinosaurs. The true mammals are their descendants.

synchronous regular. Most communication within a computer system is synchronous, controlled by the computer's own internal clock, while communication between computers is usually ◊asynchronous. Synchronous telecommunications are, however, becoming more widely used.

synchronous orbit another term for ◊geostationary orbit.

synchronous rotation in astronomy, another name for ◊captured rotation.

synchrotron particle ◊accelerator in which particles move, at increasing speed, around a hollow ring. The particles are guided around the ring by electromagnets, and accelerated by electric fields at points around the ring. Synchrotrons come in a wide range of sizes, the smallest being about a metre across while the largest is 27 km across. The Tevatron synchrotron at ◊Fermilab is some 6 km in circumference and accelerates protons and antiprotons to 1 TeV.

The European Synchrotron Radiation Facility (ESRF) opened in Grenoble, France, in September 1994, funded by £400 million from 12 European countries.

syncline geological term for a fold in the rocks of the Earth's crust in which the layers or beds dip inwards, thus forming a trough-like structure with a sag in the middle. The opposite structure, with the beds arching upwards, is an ◊anticline.

syndrome in medicine, a set of signs and symptoms that always occur together, thus characterizing a particular condition or disorder.

synergy in medicine, the 'cooperative' action of two or more drugs, muscles, or organs; applied especially to drugs whose combined action is more powerful than their simple effects added together.

synodic period the time taken for a planet or moon to return to the same position in its orbit as seen from the Earth; that is, from one ◊opposition to the next. It differs from the ◊sidereal period because the Earth is moving in orbit around the Sun.

synovial fluid viscous colourless fluid that bathes movable joints between the bones of vertebrates. It nourishes and lubricates the ◊cartilage at the end of each bone.

Synovial fluid is secreted by a membrane, the synovium, that links movably jointed bones. The same kind of fluid is found in bursae, the membranous sacs that buffer some joints, such as in the shoulder and hip region.

synthesis in chemistry, the formation of a substance or compound from more elementary compounds. The synthesis of a drug can involve several stages from the initial material to the final product; the complexity of these stages is a major factor in the cost of production.

synthetic any material made from chemicals. Since the 1900s, more and more of the materials used in everyday life are synthetics, including plastics (polythene, polystyrene), ◊synthetic fibres (nylon, acrylics, polyesters), synthetic resins, and synthetic rubber. Most naturally occurring organic substances are now made synthetically, especially pharmaceuticals.

synthetic fibre fibre made by chemical processes, unknown in nature. There are two kinds. One is made from natural materials that have been chemically processed in some way; ◊rayon, for example, is made by processing the cellulose in wood pulp. The other type is the true synthetic fibre, made entirely from chemicals. ◊Nylon was the original synthetic fibre, made from chemicals obtained from petroleum (crude oil).

Fibres are drawn out into long threads or filaments, usually by so-called spinning methods, melting or dissolving the parent material and then forcing it through the holes of a perforated plate, or spinneret.

syphilis sexually transmitted disease caused by the spiral-shaped bacterium (spirochete) *Treponema pallidum*. Untreated, it runs its course in three stages over many years, often starting with a painless hard sore, or chancre, developing within a month on the area of infection (usually the genitals). The second stage, months later, is a rash with arthritis, hepatitis, and/or meningitis. The third stage, years later, leads eventually to paralysis, blindness, insanity, and death. The Wassermann test is a diagnostic blood test for syphilis.

With widespread availability of antibiotics, syphilis is now increasingly treatable in the industrialized world, at least to the extent that the final stage of the disease is rare. The risk remains that the disease may go undiagnosed or that it may be transmitted by a pregnant woman to her fetus.

SYPHILIS

Undergarments with a mercury coating to protect the wearer against syphilis were sometimes worn as a precautionary measure in 17th-century Italy.

Syquest manufacturer of removable ◊hard disc drives and high-capacity floppy disc drives, which may be used to transport large files from one location to another.

syringa common, but incorrect, name for the ◊mock orange. The genus *Syringa* includes ◊lilacs, and is not related to the mock orange.

syrinx the voice-producing organ of a bird. It is situated where the trachea divides in two and consists of vibrating membranes, a reverberating capsule, and numerous controlling muscles.

sysop (contraction of ***system operator***) in computing, the operator of a ◊bulletin board system (BBS).

system administrator (or ***sysadmin***) in computing, person who runs and maintains a computer system, especially a ◊local area network (LAN). The responsibilities of a systems administrator typically include installing hardware and software, supervising system security, fixing faults, and organizing training.

systematics science of naming and identifying species, and determining their degree of relatedness. It plays an important role in preserving ◊biodiversity; only a small fraction of existing species have been named and described. See also ◊classification.

Système International d'Unités official French name for ◊SI units.

system flow chart type of ◊flow chart used to describe the flow of data through a particular computer system.

systemic in medicine, relating to or affecting the body as a whole. A systemic disease is one where the effects are present throughout the body, as opposed to local disease, such as ◊conjunctivitis, which is confined to one part.

system implementation in computing, the process of installing a new computer system.

To ensure that a system's implementation takes place as efficiently and with as little disruption as possible, a number of tasks are necessary. These include ordering and installing new equipment, ordering new stationery and storage media, training personnel, converting data files into new formats, drawing up an overall implementation plan, and preparing for a period of either ◊parallel running or ◊pilot running.

SYSTEM.INI (abbreviation for ***System Initialization***) in computing, file used by Microsoft Windows to store information about which parts of Windows to load and how to set itself up on the PC on which it is running, for example SYSTEM.INI specifies drivers for the keyboard, graphics card, and sound card, if any.

system requirements in computing, minimum specification necessary in order to use a particular piece of hardware or software.

systems analysis in computing, the investigation of a business activity or clerical procedure, with a view to deciding if and how it can be computerized. The analyst discusses the existing procedures with the people involved, observes the flow of data through the business, and draws up an outline specification of the required computer system. The next step is ◊systems design.

Systems in use in the 1990s include Yourdon, SSADM (Structured Systems Analysis and Design Methodology), and Soft Systems Methodology.

Systems Application Architecture (SAA) in computing, IBM model for client–server computing, introduced in 1987. SAA was a grandiose attempt to reduce the incompatibilities between IBM's many ranges of hardware, including mainframes, minicomputers, and PCs. It uses ◊CUA (common user access) standards to ensure that commands and keystrokes are used consistently in different applications.

systems design in computing, the detailed design of an ◊applications package. The designer breaks the system down into component programs, and designs the required input forms, screen layouts, and printouts. Systems design forms a link between systems analysis and ◊programming.

Systems Network Architecture (SNA) a set of communication protocols developed by IBM and incorporated in hardware and software implementations. See also ◊TCP/IP and ◊Open Systems Interconnection (OSI).

systems program in computing, a program that performs a task related to the operation and performance of the computer system itself. For example, a systems program might control the operation of the display screen, or control and organize backing storage. In contrast, an ◊applications program is designed to carry out tasks for the benefit of the computer user.

System X in communications, a modular, computer-controlled, digital switching system used in telephone exchanges.

systole in biology, the contraction of the heart. It alternates with diastole, the resting phase of the heart beat.

syzygy in astronomy, the alignment of three celestial bodies, usually the ◊Sun, Earth, and ◊Moon or the Sun, Earth, and another planet. A syzygy involving the Sun, Earth, and Moon usually occurs during solar and lunar ◊eclipses.

The term also refers to the Moon or another planet when it is in ◊conjunction or opposition.

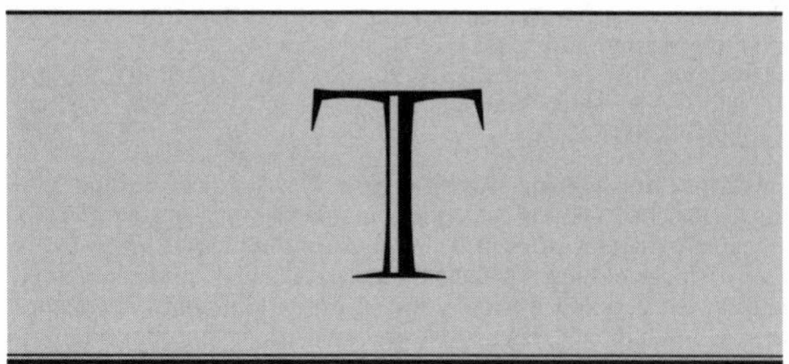

t symbol for ◊tonne, ton.

T1 link digital telephone line which can transfer data at 1.544 megabits per second. T1 lines are a type of ◊Integrated Services Digital Network (ISDN) communication.

T3 digital telephone standard that transmits data at 44.736 megabits per second, widely used for ◊Integrated Services Digital Network (ISDN) lines.

tabby cat breed of short- or long-haired domestic cat. The distinctive patterning of the coat is inherited from the cat's predomesticated ancestors. It is believed that all colour variations of short-haired cats have been bred from the tabby. The coat's ground colour is either grey or golden-brown overlaid with stripes ('mackerel'), blotches ('classic'), or (less frequently) spots. There are many varieties.

The name is derived from the striped watered silk, known in Britain as tabbi silk, produced by the weavers of the Attabiya district of Baghdad.

tachograph combined speedometer and clock that records a vehicle's speed (on a small card disc, magnetic disc, or tape) and the length of time the vehicle is moving or stationary. It is used to monitor a lorry driver's working hours.

taiga or ***boreal forest*** Russian name for the forest zone south of the ◊tundra, found across the northern hemisphere. Here, dense forests of conifers (spruces and hemlocks), birches, and poplars occupy glaciated regions punctuated with cold lakes, streams, bogs, and marshes. Winters are prolonged and very cold, but the summer is warm enough to promote dense growth.

The varied fauna and flora are in delicate balance because the conditions of life are so precarious. This ecology is threatened by mining, forestry, and pipeline construction.

taipan species of small-headed cobra *Oxyuranus scutellatus,* found in NE Australia and New Guinea. It is about 3 m/10 ft long, and has a brown back and yellow belly. Its venom is fatal within minutes.

takahe flightless bird *Porphyrio mantelli* of the rail family, order Gruiformes, native to New Zealand. It is about 60 cm/2 ft tall and weighs just over 2 kg/4.4 lb, with blue and green plumage and a red bill. The takahe was thought to have become extinct at the end of the 19th century, but in 1948 small numbers were rediscovered in the tussock grass of a mountain valley on South Island.

talc $Mg_3Si_4O_{10}(OH)_2$, mineral, hydrous magnesium silicate. It occurs in tabular crystals, but the massive impure form, known as **steatite** or **soapstone**, is more common. It is formed by the alteration of magnesium compounds and is usually found in metamorphic rocks. Talc is very soft, ranked 1 on the Mohs' scale of hardness. It is used in powdered form in cosmetics, lubricants, and as an additive in paper manufacture.

French chalk and potstone are varieties of talc. Soapstone has a greasy feel to it, and is used for carvings such as Inuit sculptures.

Talgai skull cranium of a pre-adult male, dating from 10,000–20,000 years ago, found at Talgai station, S Queensland, Australia. It was one of the earliest human archaeological finds in Australia, having been made in 1886. Its significance was not realized, however, until the work of Edgeworth David and others after 1914. The skull is large with heavy eyebrow ridges and cheekbones.

tallowwood large tree *Eucalyptus microcorys,* family Myrtaceae, of New South Wales and Queensland, Australia, growing in coastal forests and yielding a strong timber. Its nectar is much prized by apiarists.

tamandua tree-living toothless anteater *Tamandua tetradactyla* found in tropical forests and tree savanna from S Mexico to Brazil. About 56 cm/1.8 ft long with a prehensile tail of equal length, it has strong foreclaws with which it can break into nests of tree ants and termites, which it licks up with its narrow tongue.

tamarack coniferous tree native to boggy soils in North America, where it is used for timber. It is a type of larch. (*Larix laricina,* family Pinaceae.)

tamarind evergreen tropical tree native to the Old World, with pinnate leaves (leaflets either side of the stem) and reddish-yellow flowers, followed by pods. The pulp surrounding the seeds is used in medicine and as a flavouring. (*Tamarindus indica,* family Leguminosae.)

tamarisk any of a group of small trees or shrubs that flourish in warm, salty, desert regions of Europe and Asia where no other vegetation is found. The common tamarisk *T. gallica,* which grows in European coastal areas, has small, scalelike leaves on feathery branches and produces spikes of small pink flowers. (Genus *Tamarix,* family Tamaricaceae.)

tanager New World bird of the family Emberizidae, order Passeriformes. There are about 230 species in forests of Central and South America, all brilliantly coloured. They are 10–20 cm/4–8 in long, with plump bodies and conical beaks. The tanagers of North America all belong to the genus *Piranga.*

Species include the **paradise tanager** *Tangara chilensis.* Its plumage has a metallic lustre; the head is sea-green in colour, the breast is violet, and there is a flame-coloured patch on the lower part of the back. It feeds on fruit and insects. The **scarlet tanager** *Piranga olivacea* is about 18 cm/7 in long, and has brilliant scarlet plumage in the male with black wings and tail. In autumn its plumage changes to a dull green, like that of the female.

Tanegashima Space Centre Japanese rocket-launching site on a small island off S Kyushu.

Tanegashima is run by the National Space Development Agency (NASDA), responsible for the practical applications of Japan's space programme (research falls under a separate organization based at ◊Kagoshima Space Centre). NASDA, founded in 1969, has headquarters in Tokyo; a tracking and testing station, the Tsukuba Space Centre, in E central Honshu; and an Earth observation centre near Tsukuba.

tangent in geometry, a straight line that touches a curve and gives the gradient of the curve at the point of contact. At a maximum, minimum, or point of inflection, the tangent to a curve has zero ◊gradient. Also, in trigonometry, a function of an acute angle in a right-angled triangle, defined as the ratio of the length of the side opposite the angle to the length of the side adjacent to it; a way of expressing the gradient of a line.

tangerine small type of ◊orange.

tangram puzzle made by cutting up a square into seven pieces.

tannic acid *or* **tannin** $C_{14}H_{10}O_9$ yellow astringent substance, composed of several ◊phenol rings, occurring in the bark, wood, roots, fruits, and galls (growths) of certain trees, such as the oak. It precipitates gelatin to give an insoluble compound used in the manufacture of leather from hides (tanning).

tanning treating animal skins to preserve them and make them into leather. In vegetable tanning, the prepared skins are soaked in tannic acid. Chrome tanning, which is much quicker, uses solutions of chromium salts.

tansy perennial herb belonging to the daisy family, native to Europe. The yellow flower heads grow in clusters on stalks up to

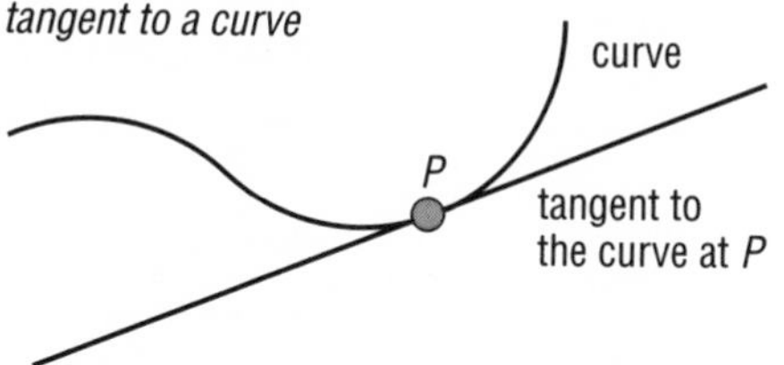

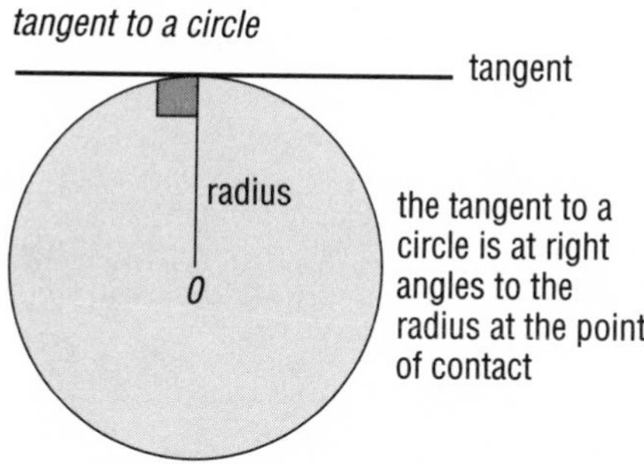

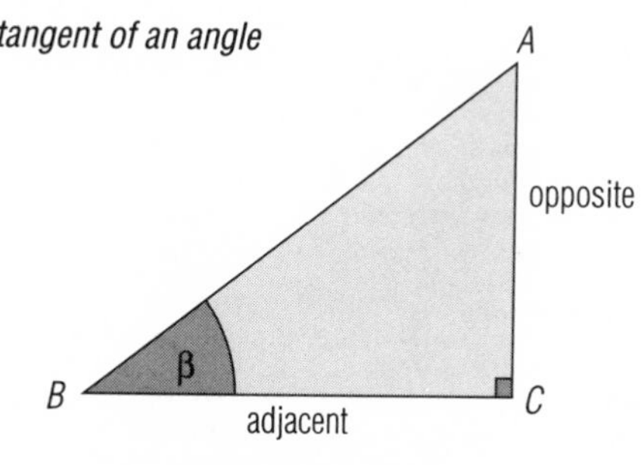

$$\text{tangent } \beta = \frac{\sin\beta}{\cos\beta} = \frac{\text{opposite}}{\text{adjacent}} = \frac{AC}{BC}$$

tangent *The tangent of an angle is a mathematical function used in the study of right-angled triangles. If the tangent of an angle ß is known, then the length of the opposite side can be found given the length of the adjacent side, or vice versa.*

120 cm/4 ft tall, and the aromatic leaves are used in cookery. (*Tanacetum vulgare,* family Compositae.)

tantalum hard, ductile, lustrous, grey-white, metallic element, symbol Ta, atomic number 73, relative atomic mass 180.948. It occurs with niobium in tantalite and other minerals. It can be drawn into wire with a very high melting point and great tenacity, useful for lamp filaments subject to vibration. It is also used in alloys, for corrosion-resistant laboratory apparatus and chemical equipment, as a catalyst in manufacturing synthetic rubber, in tools and instruments, and in rectifiers and capacitors.

It was discovered and named in 1802 by Swedish chemist Anders Ekeberg (1767–1813) after the mythological Greek character Tantalos.

tape recording, magnetic method of recording electric signals on a layer of iron oxide, or other magnetic material, coating a thin plastic tape. The electrical signals from the microphone are fed to the electromagnetic recording head, which magnetizes the tape in accordance with the frequency and amplitude of the original signal. The impulses may be audio (for sound recording), video (for television), or data (for computer). For playback, the tape is passed over the same, or another, head to convert magnetic into electrical signals, which are then amplified for reproduction. Tapes are easily demagnetized (erased) for reuse, and come in cassette, cartridge, or reel form.

tape streamer in computing, a backing storage device consisting of a continuous loop of magnetic tape. Tape streamers are largely used to store dumps (rapid backup copies) of important data files (see ◊data security).

tapeworm any of various parasitic flatworms of the class Cestoda. They lack digestive and sense organs, can reach 15 m/50 ft in length, and attach themselves to the host's intestines by means of hooks and suckers. Tapeworms are made up of hundreds of individual segments, each of which develops into a functional hermaphroditic reproductive unit capable of producing numerous eggs. The larvae of tapeworms usually reach humans in imperfectly cooked meat or fish, causing anaemia and intestinal disorders.

TAPI ***(abbreviation for*** **Telephony Application Programming Interface**) in computing, program included in ◊Windows 95 to enable applications to use the telephone. The TAPI standard was developed by Microsoft and Intel in 1993.

tapir any of the odd-toed hoofed mammals (perissodactyls) of the single genus *Tapirus,* now constituting the family Tapiridae. There are four species living in the American and Malaysian tropics. They reach 1 m/3 ft at the shoulder and weigh up to 350 kg/770 lb. Their survival is in danger because of destruction of the forests.

Tapirs have thick, hairy, black skin, short tails, and short trunks. They are vegetarian, harmless, and shy. They are related to the ◊rhinoceros, and slightly more distantly to the horse.

The Malaysian tapir *T. indicus* is black with a large white patch on the back and hindquarters. The three South American species are dark to reddish brown; the **Brazilian tapir** *T. terrestris* is the most widespread. **Baird's tapir** *T. bairdii* is rare and found only in Central America.

The **mountain tapir** *T. pinchaque* is the rarest tapir (less than 2,500 remaining), and is found only in the northern Andes. It weighs 150–200 kg/330–440 lb and is about 80 cm/32 in tall. It is mainly solitary except when breeding. The gestation period is 13 months and the single young remains with the mother for 18 months. Mountain tapirs are strong swimmers.

taproot in botany, a single, robust, main ◊root that is derived from the embryonic root, or ◊radicle, and grows vertically downwards, often to considerable depth. Taproots are often modified for food storage and are common in biennial plants such as the carrot *Daucus carota,* where they act as ◊perennating organs.

tar dark brown or black viscous liquid obtained by the destructive distillation of coal, shale, and wood. Tars consist of a mixture of hydrocarbons, acids, and bases. ◊Creosote and ◊paraffin are produced from wood tar. See also ◊coal tar.

TAR in computing, UNIX-based compression routine in common use on the Internet.

tarantula wolf spider *Lycosa tarantula* (family Lycosidae) with a 2.5 cm/1 in body. It spins no web, relying on its speed in hunting to

AMERICAN TARANTULA SOCIETY

http://www.concentric.net/~Dmartin/ats/about.html

Information on tarantulas, other spiders, and scorpions from the world's largest arachnid society. There are articles on buying, feeding, looking after, and breeding tarantulas. Tarantula owners exchange experiences and there is a listing of other arachnid sites.

tarantula The mygalomorph bird-eating spider Stichoplastus incei *and related species are generally described as tarantulas. Native to tropical America, they are largely nocturnal and feed mainly on insects, but will also attack larger prey such as mice and birds. Their bite is painful but not fatal. Premaphotos Wildlife*

catch its prey. The name 'tarantula' is also used for any of the numerous large, hairy spiders of the family Theraphosidae, with large poison fangs, native to the SW USA and tropical America.

The theraphosid *Aphonopelma* has a body length of 5 cm/2 in and a leg span of 12.5 cm/5 in. They are no more poisonous than other spiders of similar size. They burrow in the ground and catch their prey by pouncing on it and not by means of a web.

In the Middle Ages, the wolf spider's bite was thought to cause hysterical ailments or **tarantism** for which dancing was the cure, hence the name 'tarantula' and its popular association with the dance 'tarantella'

tare common name for any of the plants known as ◊vetches.

taro *or* **eddo** plant belonging to the arum family, native to tropical Asia; the tubers (underground stems) are edible and are the source of Polynesian poi (a fermented food). (*Colocasia esculenta,* family Araceae.)

tarpon large silver-sided fish *Tarpon atlanticus* of the family Megalopidae. It reaches 2 m/6 ft and may weigh 135 kg/300 lb. It lives in warm W Atlantic waters.

tarragon perennial bushy herb belonging to the daisy family, native to the Old World. It grows up to 1.5 m/5 ft tall and has narrow leaves and small green-white flower heads arranged in groups. Tarragon contains an aromatic oil; its leaves are used to flavour salads, pickles, and tartar sauce. It is closely related to wormwood. (*Artemisia dracunculus,* family Compositae.)

tarsier any of three species of the prosimian primates, genus *Tarsius,* of the East Indies and the Philippines. These survivors of early primates are about the size of a rat with thick, light-brown fur, very large eyes, and long feet and hands. They are nocturnal, arboreal, and eat insects and lizards.

tartaric acid $HOOC(CHOH)_2COOH$ organic acid present in vegetable tissues and fruit juices in the form of salts of potassium, calcium, and magnesium. It is used in carbonated drinks and baking powders.

tartrazine *(E102)* yellow food colouring produced synthetically from petroleum. Many people are allergic to foods containing it. Typical effects are skin disorders and respiratory problems. It has been shown to have an adverse effect on hyperactive children.

taskbar in computing, strip at the bottom of a ◊Windows 95 or NT 4 screen containing icons ('task buttons') of all programs launched in the current session. The taskbar makes it possible to switch between applications simply by clicking the mouse on a task button.

Tasmanian devil carnivorous marsupial *Sarcophilus harrisii,* in the same family (Dasyuridae) as native 'cats'. It is about 65 cm/2.1 ft long with a 25 cm/10 in bushy tail. It has a large head, strong teeth, and is blackish with white patches on the chest and hind parts. It is nocturnal, carnivorous, and can be ferocious when cornered. It has recently become extinct in Australia and survives only in remote parts of Tasmania.

TASMANIAN DEVIL

http://www.cyberdata.com.au/currumbin/page29.html

Profile of the largest of Australia's surviving marsupial carnivores. There is a picture of a devil, details of its appearance and behaviour, and explanation of how it became extinct on the Australian mainland. There is an accompanying note about the demise of the Tasmanian tiger.

Tasmanian wolf or ***thylacine*** carnivorous marsupial *Thylacinus cynocephalus,* in the family Dasyuridae. It is doglike in appearance with a long tail, characteristic dark stripes on back and hindquarters, and measures nearly 2 m/6 ft from nose to tail tip. It was hunted to probable extinction in the 1930s, but there are still occasional unconfirmed reports of sightings, both on the Australian mainland and in the Tasmanian mountains, its last known habitat.

taste sense that detects some of the chemical constituents of food. The human ◊tongue can distinguish only four basic tastes (sweet, sour, bitter, and salty) but it is supplemented by the sense of smell. What we refer to as taste is really a composite sense made up of both taste and smell.

tau ◊elementary particle with the same electric charge as the electron but a mass nearly double that of a proton. It has a lifetime of around 3×10^{-13} seconds and belongs to the ◊lepton family of particles – those that interact via the electromagnetic, weak nuclear, and gravitational forces, but not the strong nuclear force.

Taube German military aircraft of World War I. At the outbreak of war it was the principal aircraft of the German Army and performed useful service as a scout, notably in the detection of Russian movements which resulted in Hindenburg's victory at the Battle of Tannenberg in 1914.

Tau Ceti one of the nearest stars visible to the naked eye, 11.9 light years from Earth in the constellation Cetus. It has a diameter slightly less than that of the Sun, and an actual luminosity of about 45% of the Sun's. Its similarity to the Sun is sufficient to suggest that Tau Ceti may possess a planetary system, although observations have yet to reveal evidence of this.

Taurus conspicuous zodiacal constellation in the northern hemisphere near ◊Orion, represented as a bull. The Sun passes through Taurus from mid-May to late June. In astrology, the dates for Taurus are between about 20 April and 20 May (see ◊precession).

The V-shaped ◊Hyades open ◊star cluster forms the bull's head, with ◊Aldebaran as the red eye. The ◊Pleiades open cluster is in the shoulder. Taurus also contains the ◊Crab nebula, the remnants of the supernova of AD 1054, which is a strong radio and X-ray source and the location of one of the first ◊pulsars to be discovered.

tautomerism form of isomerism in which two interconvertible ◊isomers are in equilibrium. It is often specifically applied to an equilibrium between the keto ($-CH_2-C=O$) and enol ($-CH=C-OH$) forms of carbonyl compounds.

taxis *(plural* **taxes)** *or* **tactic movement** in botany, the movement of a single cell, such as a bacterium, protozoan, single-celled alga, or gamete, in response to an external stimulus. A movement directed towards the stimulus is described as positive taxis, and away from it as negative taxis. The alga *Chlamydomonas,* for example, demonstrates positive **phototaxis** by swimming towards a light source to increase the rate of photosynthesis.

Chemotaxis is a response to a chemical stimulus, as seen in many bacteria that move towards higher concentrations of nutrients.

taxonomy another name for the ◊classification of living organisms.

Tay–Sachs disease inherited disorder, due to a defective gene, causing an enzyme deficiency that leads to blindness, retardation, and death in infancy. It is most common in people of E European Jewish descent.

TB abbreviation for the infectious disease ◊tuberculosis.

TB RESOURCES: ABOUT TUBERCULOSIS

http://www.cpmc.columbia.edu/tbcpp/abouttb.html

Basic and useful information about tuberculosis. The fact sheet includes presentations on the signs and tests for TB, an explanation of TB infection and the ways TB is spread, and an assessment of the importance of drugs for the cure of the disease.

TBT (abbreviation for ***tributyl tin***) chemical used in antifouling paints that has become an environmental pollutant.

T cell or ***T lymphocyte*** immune cell (see ◊immunity and ◊lymphocyte) that plays several roles in the body's defences. T cells are so called because they mature in the ◊thymus.

There are three main types of T cells: T helper cells (Th cells), which allow other immune cells to go into action; T suppressor cells (Ts cells), which stop specific immune reactions from occurring; and T cytotoxic cells (Tc cells), which kill cells that are cancerous or infected with viruses. Like ◊B cells, to which they are related, T cells have surface receptors that make them specific for particular antigens.

TCP/IP (abbreviation for ***transport control protocol/Internet protocol***) set of network protocols, developed principally by the US Department of Defense. TCP/IP is widely used, particularly in ◊UNIX and on the ◊Internet and it is now incorporated into operating systems, such as Microsoft Windows 95.

tea evergreen shrub or small tree whose fermented, dried leaves are soaked in hot water to make a refreshing drink, also called tea. Known in China as early as 2737 BC, tea was first brought to Europe AD 1610 and rapidly became a popular drink. In 1823 the shrub was found growing wild in N India, and plantations were later established in Assam and Sri Lanka; producers today include Africa, South America, Georgia, Azerbaijan, Indonesia, and Iran. (*Camellia sinensis,* family Theaceae.)

the tea plant In the wild the tea plant can grow as tall as 12 m/40 ft, but in cultivation it is kept down to a bush 1.5 m/4 ft high. The young shoots and leaves are picked every five days.

processing Once plucked, the young leaves are spread out on shelves in withering lofts and allowed to wither (dry and shrivel up) in a current of air for 4–18 hours. **Black teas** (from Sri Lanka and India) are macerated (soaked and softened) in rolling machines to release the essential oils, allowed to ferment, and then dried and graded. The fermentation gives them a blackish-brown colour. **Green teas** (from China, Taiwan, and Japan) are steamed or heated and then rolled, dried, and finally graded. They are green or partly green in colour.

Some teas are scented with plant oils: Earl Grey, for example, is flavoured with oil of ◊bergamot.

grading Grading is carried out according to the size of leaf. For example, some Sri Lankan (Ceylon) tea grades are orange pekoe, flowery pekoe, broken orange pekoe, broken pekoe, and fannings. The latter grades are mostly the black teas sold in tea bags. Black teas make up 75% of the world's trade in tea.

tea customs Methods of drinking tea vary in different countries: in Japan special teahouses and an elaborate tea ceremony have evolved, and in Tibet, hard slabs of compressed tea are used as money before being finally brewed.

teak tropical Asian timber tree with yellowish wood used in furniture and shipbuilding. (*Tectona grandis,* family Verbenaceae.)

teal any of various small, short-necked dabbling ducks of the genus *Anas,* order Anseriformes, but particularly *A. crecca.* The male is dusky grey; its tail feathers ashy grey; the crown of its head deep cinnamon or chestnut; its eye is surrounded by a black band, glossed with green or purple, which unites on the nape; its wing markings are black and white; and its bill is black and resembles that of the widgeon. The female is mottled brown. The total length is about 35cm/14 in.

The **blue-winged teal** *A. discors* is a brillantly coloured bird 35–42 cm/14–17 in long, with bright blue wing coverts. It is a native of North America, and migrates in winter to South America.

tear gas any of various volatile gases that produce irritation and watering of the eyes, used by police against crowds and used in chemical warfare. The gas is delivered in pressurized, liquid-filled canisters or grenades, thrown by hand or launched from a specially adapted rifle. Gases (such as Mace) cause violent coughing and blinding tears, which pass when the victim breathes fresh air, but there are no lasting effects.

tears salty fluid exuded by lacrimal glands in the eyes. The fluid contains proteins that are antibacterial, and also absorbs oils and mucus. Apart from cleaning and disinfecting the surface of the eye, the fluid supplies nutrients to the cornea, which does not have a blood supply.

If insufficient fluid is produced, as sometimes happens in older people, the painful condition of 'dry-eye' results and the eye may be damaged.

teasel upright prickly biennial herb, native to Europe and Asia. It grows up to 1.5 m/5 ft, has prickly stems and leaves, and a large prickly head of purple flowers. The dry, spiny seed heads were once used industrially to tease or fluff up the surface fibres of cloth. (*Dipsacus fullonum,* family Dipsacaceae.)

tea tree shrub or small tree native to Australia and New Zealand. It is thought that some species of tea tree were used by the explorer Captain Cook to brew tea; it was used in the first years of settlement for this purpose. (Genus *Leptospermum,* family Myrtaceae.)

technetium Greek *technetos* 'artificial' silver-grey, radioactive, metallic element, symbol Tc, atomic number 43, relative atomic mass 98.906. It occurs in nature only in extremely minute amounts, produced as a fission product from uranium in ◊pitchblende and other uranium ores. Its longest-lived isotope, Tc-99, has a half-life of 216,000 years. It is a superconductor and is used as a hardener in steel alloys and as a medical tracer.

It was synthesized in 1937 (named in 1947) by Italian physicists Carlo Perrier and Emilio Segrè, who bombarded molybdenum with deuterons, looking to fill a missing spot in the ◊periodic table of the elements (at that time it was considered not to occur in nature). It was later isolated in large amounts from the fission product debris of uranium fuel in nuclear reactors.

technology the use of tools, power, and materials, generally for the purposes of production. Almost every human process for getting food and shelter depends on complex technological systems, which have been developed over a 3-million-year period. Significant milestones include the advent of the ◊steam engine in 1712, the introduction of ◊electricity and the ◊internal combustion engine in the mid-1870s, and recent developments in communications, ◊electronics, and the nuclear and space industries. The **advanced technology** (highly automated and specialized) on which modern industrialized society depends is frequently contrasted

Communications

BY PETER LAFFERTY

Introduction

Early 1998 saw a remarkable demonstration of the power of modern communications technology. Signals were received from the most distant spaceprobe, *Voyager 1*, launched by the US in 1977. In February 1998, *Voyager 1* was over 10.5 billion km/ 6.5 billion mi from the Earth, a distance so great that data from the probe took almost 9 h to reach the Earth, travelling at the speed of light. This was the longest distance over which a radio message has been received.

Of course, radio astronomers might argue that they routinely receive data from far greater distances, from stellar objects at the edge of the universe. They are correct, which again illustrates the wonderful sensitivity of modern radio receivers. The World's largest radio telescope is at Arecibo in Puerto Rico. Its dish is 305 m/1,000 ft across, wider than three football fields. It can pick up signals as weak as one ten-thousandth of a millionth of a millionth of the power of a household light bulb.

Worldwide mobile phones

On Earth, a new generation of communications network based on low-orbit satellites is being put in place. Because the new satellites are much nearer the Earth than current communications satellites, it will not be necessary to own a huge receiver dish to collect the signal. A hand-held mobile phone will communicate directly with an overhead satellite and route the call through other satellites, to the receiver. The first such system, called Iridium, got under way with the launch of five satellites in May 1997; seven more satellites were launched in June 1997. The Iridium system will eventually consist of 66 satellites which will fly in 11 polar orbits, 675 km/ 420 mi high. The satellites will blanket the globe – there will be a satellite overhead at all times wherever you are. You will be able to phone anyone, anywhere on the planet, even if they are in the middle of the Sahara Desert. Initially, the Iridium handsets are expected to be expensive, although the price should come down once several similar systems are competing for the market. A rival operator, Teledesic, plans to launch 288 satellites which will provide a worldwide high- speed data and phone service.

Fibre optics

Conventional Earth-bound telephony has also progressed. A plan to build a worldwide optical fibre network took a step forward in 1997 when the Fibreoptic Link Around the Globe (FLAG) was completed. It links Britain and the Far East, a distance of 27,000 km/17,000 mi. However, with FLAG barely completed, an even more ambitious enterprise got underway.

In 1998 more than 300 international telecommunications companies signed up for a scheme called Project Oxygen. This project will involve laying 320,000 km/200,000 mi of optical fibre to link 171 countries, with the first cables being in place by the year 2000 and the rest completed by 2003. The cable would be able to carry 320 billion bits of information each second – existing submarine cables carry less than 10 billion bits per second. Cables that do not require optical amplifiers would be able to carry 1 trillion bits per second.

The enormous capacity of fibre optic cable links arises because the cable can carry more than one signal at once. The cables can carry signals at different wavelength (or colour) without interference. In the past year, telephone companies have started to install cables that can carry four separate signals at different wavelengths. The cable planned for Project Oxygen will carry eight signals at the same time. But this is not the limit to this technology: research at Lucent Technology, New Jersey and NTT in Japan, indicates that up to 100 signals could be transmitted.

'Beam me up, Scottie'

Telephones as small as buttons – reminescent of James Kirk's communicator in 'Star Trek' – are promised by the Dutch electronics firm Philips. Philips have developed a method of miniaturizing radio receivers. The secret is to fix the miniature radio components to an insulating base. If a silicon base is used – the usual process in modern electronics – the components interfere with each other via electronic conduction in the base. With an insulator there is no interference, and the power needed to work the device is 10 times less.

Internet radio and telephones

A wide variety of material is now being transmitted over the Internet, including images and audio and video files. One of the interesting new media services on the Internet is digitized audio. Audio- digitizing chips and add-in boards are available for most computer systems. The most popular products for PCs are Soundblaster boards, and many computers have sound equipment as a standard feature.

Audio files have been transmitted over the Internet for some time, but now we have Internet telephony and Internet radio. Internet telephony uses the Internet to send audio between two or more computer users in real time, so the users can converse. Vocaltec introduced the first internet telephony software in 1995. Running a multimedia PC, the Vocaltec Internet Phone lets users speak into their microphones and listen via their speakers. Internet radio transmits audio and music programs produced for traditional radio broadcasts over the Internet for playing through the user's computer speakers.

The problem with Internet telephony and radio is that transfer of audio files can be rather slow. The result is that, even with a fast modem, audio files will be transferred at a rate slightly greater than real time – a 5-min audio file will take over 5 min to transfer. Moreover, if someone else is also using the Internet link, or a slow modem is being used, the problem is even worse. The delay experienced in Internet telephony is typically 10 times that on the public telephone networks. Web radio concentrates at present on spoken programmes, rather than music. Programmes broadcast by the Canadian Broadcasting Commission include a science magazine show, a variety show and documentaries. The audio quality is far from that achieved by compact discs, but is equivalent or better than a standard telephone service. Moreover, for this type programme, the quality is usually acceptable.

Internet music broadcasters use a technology called streaming. This technique transmits music in 2-s blocks, with one block being downloaded while the preceding block is being played. In this way, it is not necessary to download an entire song before playing it.

Digital television

Digital television will be launched late in 1998 in Europe and the USA. In digital television, information is broadcast as a complex series of on/off signals, known as a digital signal. Existing television programmes are transmitted as continuous signals, known as analogue signals. The analogue signals build up a television picture made up of 625 lines. Digital television will double that, providing pictures of much better quality. Viewers will also be able to control the picture on the screen by cropping it, zooming in on a detail, or choosing which viewing angle they want at a sports event, for example. However, the biggest effect of digital television will be to greatly increase the number of channels available. Digital signals are much more compressed than analogue signals, so more channels can be transmitted.

A question waiting for an answer is whether television broadcasters will choose to use their digital frequencies for a single high-definition channel or will transmit up to five standard definition programmes (this is called multi-casting). Cable TV operators are faced with a similar dilemma. The debate between high-definition and multi-casting is the most important single issue facing the television industry in 1998.

In the USA, the largest cable television operator, TCI, started testing its digital service in 1997. The service delivers more channels (over 150 channels of audio and video), and provides a high- quality picture. This may be part of an attempt by the cable industry to force broadcasters to devote their entire frequency spectrum to high-definition broadcasts rather than providing a multi-channel service which would compete with cable operators.

Interactive television
Interactive television is another road forward for television. This system allows the viewer to access services such as home banking and shopping through their television sets. It can also give viewers access to movies, games, children's TV and local information. In the UK, Sky TV has an interactive channel called Intertext, and British Telecom has tested an interactive channel. Similar trials in the USA cast doubt over the future of interactive TV, as there seemed to be no real demand for such services, causing Bell Atlantic and TCI/Microsoft to scale back their trials. Time Warner has announced that it is shutting down its interactive service in Orlando, Florida. The service, which began with much hype, has been plagued by technical difficulties.

Pay-per-view TV
Pay-per-view TV is a system by which viewers pay an additional fee, usually by credit card, to watch specific programmes. This has proved successful in the USA, particularly for films and sporting events. In the UK, BSkyB has experimented with the idea and is set to screen more programmes in this way. With the introduction of digital TV, the main terrestrial television stations are expected to introduce pay-per-view.

with the **low technology** (labour-intensive and unspecialized) that characterizes some developing countries. ◊Intermediate technology is an attempt to adapt scientifically advanced inventions to less developed areas by using local materials and methods of manufacture. ◊Appropriate technology refers to simple and small-scale tools and machinery of use to developing countries.

power In human prehistory, the only power available was muscle power, augmented by primitive tools, such as the wedge or lever.

The domestication of animals about 8500 BC and invention of the wheel about 2000 BC paved the way for the water mill (1st century BC) and later the windmill (12th century AD). Not until 1712 did an alternative source of power appear in the form of the first working steam engine, constructed by English inventor Thomas Newcomen; subsequent modifications improved its design. English chemist and physicist Michael Faraday's demonstration of the dynamo in 1831 revealed the potential of the electrical motor, and in 1876 the German scientist Nikolaus Otto introduced the four-stroke cycle used in the modern internal combustion engine. The 1940s saw the explosion of the first atomic bomb and the subsequent development of the nuclear power industry. Latterly concern over the use of nonrenewable power sources and the ◊pollution caused by the burning of fossil fuels has caused technologists to turn increasingly to exploring renewable sources of energy, in particular ◊solar energy, wind energy, and ◊wave power.

materials The earliest materials used by humans were wood, bone, horn, shell, and stone. Metals were rare and/or difficult to obtain, although forms of bronze and iron were in use from 6000 BC and 1000 BC respectively. The introduction of the blast furnace in the 15th century enabled cast iron to be extracted, but this process remained expensive until English ironmaker Abraham Darby substituted coke for charcoal in 1709, thus ensuring a plentiful supply of cheap iron at the start of the Industrial Revolution. Rubber, glass, leather, paper, bricks, and porcelain underwent similar processes of trial and error before becoming readily available. From the mid-1800s, entirely new materials, synthetics, appeared. First dyes, then plastic and the more versatile celluloid, and later drugs were synthesized, a process continuing into the 1980s with the growth of ◊genetic engineering, which enabled the production of synthetic insulin and growth hormones.

production The utilization of power sources and materials for production frequently lagged behind their initial discovery. The ◊lathe, known in antiquity in the form of a pole powered by a foot treadle, was not fully developed until the 18th century when it was used to produce objects of great precision, ranging from astronomical instruments to mass-produced screws. The realization that gears, cranks, cams, and wheels could operate in harmony to perform complex motion made ◊mechanization possible. Early attempts at ◊automation include Scottish engineer James Watt's introduction of the fly-ball governor into the steam engine in 1769 to regulate the machine's steam supply automatically, and French textile maker Joseph Marie Jacquard's demonstration in 1804 of how looms could be controlled automatically by punched cards. The first moving assembly line appeared in 1870 in meat-packing factories in Chicago, USA, transferring to the motor industry in 1913. With the perfection of the programmable electronic computer in the 1960s, the way lay open for fully automatic plants. The 1960s–90s saw extensive developments in the electronic and microelectronic industries (initially in the West, later joined by Japan and the Pacific region) and in the field of communications.

Any sufficiently advanced technology is indistinguishable from magic.

ARTHUR C CLARKE English science and science-fiction writer. *The Lost Worlds of 2001*

technology education training for the practical application of science in industry and commerce. Britain's Industrial Revolution preceded that of the rest of Europe by half a century and its prosperity stimulated other countries to encourage technological education.

tectonics in geology, the study of the movements of rocks on the Earth's surface. On a small scale tectonics involves the formation of ◊folds and ◊faults, but on a large scale ◊plate tectonics deals with the movement of the Earth's surface as a whole.

Teflon trade name for polytetrafluoroethene (PTFE), a tough, waxlike, heat-resistant plastic used for coating nonstick cookware and in gaskets and bearings.

tektite **Greek** *tektos* 'molten' small, rounded glassy stone, found in certain regions of the Earth, such as Australasia. Tektites are probably the scattered drops of molten rock thrown out by the impact of a large ◊meteorite.

telco in computing slang, contraction of ***telecommunications company***.

TeleAdapt company that specializes in supplying worldwide telephone and power adaptor plugs for portable computer users.

telecommunications communications over a distance, generally by electronic means. Long-distance voice communication was pioneered in 1876 by Scottish scientist Alexander Graham Bell when he invented the telephone. Today it is possible to communicate internationally by telephone cable or by satellite or microwave link, with over 100,000 simultaneous conversations and several television channels being carried by the latest satellites.

history The first mechanical telecommunications systems were semaphore and the heliograph (using flashes of sunlight), invented in the mid-19th century, but the forerunner of the present telecommunications age was the electric telegraph. The earliest practicable telegraph instrument was invented by William Cooke and Charles Wheatstone in Britain in 1837 and used by railway companies. In the USA, Samuel Morse invented a signalling code, ◊Morse code, which is still used, and a recording telegraph, first used commercially between England and France in 1851.

Following German physicist Heinrich ◊Hertz's discovery of elec-

Telecommunications: chronology

1794	Claude Chappe in France built a long-distance signalling system using semaphore.
1839	Charles Wheatstone and William Cooke devised an electric telegraph in England.
1843	Samuel Morse transmitted the first message along a telegraph line in the USA, using his Morse code of signals – short (dots) and long (dashes).
1858	The first transatlantic telegraph cable was laid.
1876	Alexander Graham Bell invented the telephone.
1877	Thomas Edison invented the carbon transmitter for the telephone.
1878	The first telephone exchange was opened at New Haven, Connecticut.
1884	The first long-distance telephone line was installed, between Boston and New York.
1891	A telephone cable was laid between England and France.
1892	The first automatic telephone exchange was opened, at La Porte, Indiana.
1894	Guglielmo Marconi pioneered wireless telegraphy in Italy, later moving to England.
1900	Reginald Fessenden in the USA first broadcast voice by radio.
1901	Marconi transmitted the first radio signals across the Atlantic.
1904	John Ambrose Fleming invented the thermionic valve.
1907	Charles Krumm introduced the forerunner of the teleprinter.
1920	Stations in Detroit and Pittsburgh began regular radio broadcasts.
1922	The BBC began its first radio transmissions, for the London station 2LO.
1932	The Telex was introduced in the UK.
1956	The first transatlantic telephone cable was laid.
1962	Telstar pioneered transatlantic satellite communications, transmitting live TV pictures.
1966	Charles Kao in England advanced the idea of using optical fibres for telecommunications transmissions.
1969	Live TV pictures were sent from astronauts on the Moon back to Earth.
1975	Prestel, the world's first viewdata system, using the telephone lines to link a computer data bank with the TV screen, was introduced in the UK.
1977	The first optical fibre cable was installed in California.
1984	First commercial cellphone service started in Chicago, USA.
1988	International Services Digital Network (ISDN), an international system for sending signals in digital format along optical fibres and coaxial cable, launched in Japan.
1989	The first transoceanic optical fibre cable, capable of carrying 40,000 simultaneous telephone conversations, was laid between Europe and the USA.
1991	ISDN introduced in the UK.
1992	Videophones, made possible by advances in image compression and the development of ISDN, introduced in the UK.
1993	Electronic version of the *Guardian* newspaper, for those with impaired vision, launched in the UK. The newspaper is transmitted to the user's home and printed out in braille or spoken by a speech synthesizer.
1995	The USA's main carrier of long-distance telecommunications, AT&T, processed 160 million calls daily, an increase of 50% since 1990.
1996	Researchers in Tokyo and California used lasers to communicate with an orbiting satellite, the first time lasers have been used to provide two-way communications with space.
1996	Work began on laying the world's longest fibreoptic cable, which will follow a 17,000-mi/27,300-km route around the globe from Europe, through the Suez Canal, across the Indian Ocean, and around the Pacific.
1996	Computer scientists in Japan and the USA transmitted information along optical fibre at a rate of one trillion bits. At this rate, 300 years' worth of a daily newspaper could be transmitted in one second.
1997	There were 300 active artificial satellites in orbit around Earth, the majority of which were used for communications purposes.
1998	US vice president Al Gore announced plans for Internet2 a high-speed data communications network that would serve the main US research universities, and bypass the congestion on the Internet.

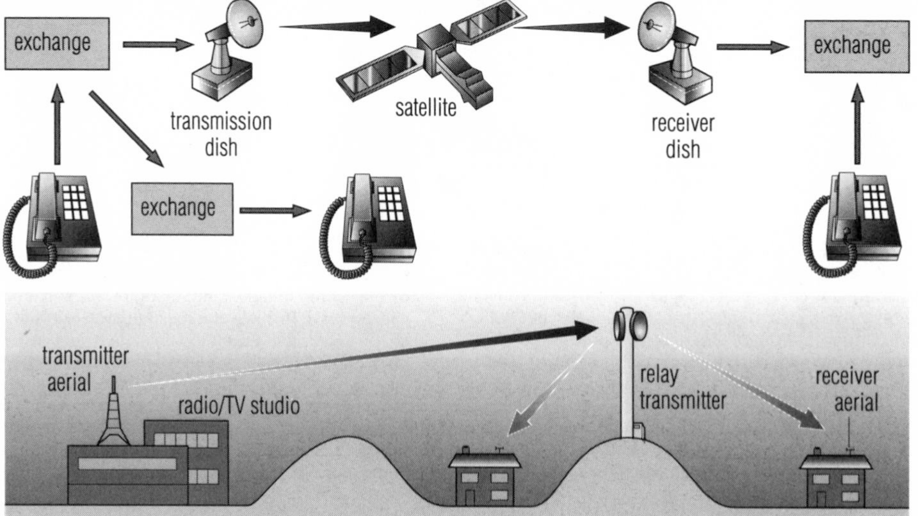

telecommunications *The international telecommunications system relies on microwave and satellite links for long-distance international calls. Cable links are increasingly made of optical fibres. The capacity of these links is enormous. The TDRS-C (tracking data and relay satellite communications) satellite, the world's largest and most complex satellite, can transmit in a single second the contents of a 20-volume encyclopedia, with each volume containing 1,200 pages of 2,000 words. A bundle of optical fibres, no thicker than a finger, can carry 10,000 phone calls – more than a copper wire as thick as an arm.*

tromagnetic waves, Italian inventor Guglielmo ◊Marconi pioneered a 'wireless' telegraph, ancestor of the radio. He established wireless communication between England and France in 1899 and across the Atlantic in 1901.

The modern telegraph uses teleprinters to send coded messages along telecommunications lines. Telegraphs are keyboard-operated machines that transmit a five-unit Baudot code (see ◊baud). The receiving teleprinter automatically prints the received message. The modern version of the telegraph is ◊electronic mail in which text messages are sent electronically from computer to computer via network connections such as the ◊Internet.

communications satellites The chief method of relaying long-distance calls on land is microwave radio transmission.The drawback to long-distance voice communication via microwave radio transmission is that the transmissions follow a straight line from tower to tower, so that over the sea the system becomes impracticable. A solution was put forward 1945 by the science-fiction writer Arthur C Clarke, when he proposed a system of communications satellites in an orbit 35,900 km/22,300 mi above the Equator, where they would circle the Earth in exactly 24 hours, and thus appear fixed in the sky. Such a system is now in operation internationally, by ◊Intelsat. The satellites are called geostationary satellites (syncoms). The first to be successfully launched, by Delta rocket from Cape Canaveral, was *Syncom 2* in July 1963. Many such satellites are now in use, concentrated over heavy traffic areas such as the Atlantic, Indian, and Pacific oceans. Telegraphy, telephony, and television transmissions are carried simultaneously by high-frequency radio waves. They are beamed to the satellites from large dish antennae or Earth stations, which connect with international networks.

◊Integrated Services Digital Network (ISDN) makes videophones and high-quality fax possible; the world's first large-scale centre of ISDN began operating in Japan in 1988. ISDN is a system that transmits voice and image data on a single transmission line by changing them into digital signals.

Fibre-optic cables consisting of fine glass fibres present an alternative to the usual copper cables for telephone lines. The telecommunications signals are transmitted along the fibres in digital form as pulses of laser light.

telecommuting working from home using a telephone, fax, and ◊modem to keep in touch with the office of the employing company. In the mid 1990s, it was estimated that 5% of US workers and 2.3% (600,000) of the British workforce were telecommuters.

Most telecommuters are self-employed, or sales people spending much of their time on the road. However, the number of part-time telecommuters, for example working one day per week at home, is growing.

Telecom Tower formerly *Post Office Tower* building in London, 189 m/620 ft high. Completed in 1966, it is a microwave relay tower capable of handling up to 150,000 simultaneous telephone conversations and over 40 television channels.

telegraphy transmission of messages along wires by means of electrical signals. The first modern form of telecommunication, it now uses printers for the transmission and receipt of messages. Telex is an international telegraphy network.

Overland cables were developed in the 1830s, but early attempts at underwater telegraphy were largely unsuccessful until the discovery of the insulating gum gutta-percha in 1843 enabled a cable to be laid across the English Channel in 1851. **Duplex telegraph** was invented in the 1870s, enabling messages to be sent in both directions simultaneously. Early telegraphs were mainly owned by the UK: 72% of all submarine cables were British-owned in 1900.

telemedicine in computing, the use of computer communications to improve medical practice and training.

> **TELEMEDICINE: A GUIDE TO ASSESSING TELECOMMUNICATIONS FOR HEALTH CARE**
>
> http://www.nap.edu/readingroom/books/telemed/summary.html
>
> Overview of the development of telemedicine and summary of a US report into its future direction. The difficulties of evaluating telemedicine are set out.

telemetry measurement at a distance, in particular the systems by which information is obtained and sent back by instruments on board a spacecraft. See ◊remote sensing.

telepathy form of ◊extrasensory perception defined as 'the communication of impressions of any kind from one mind to another, independently of the recognized channels of sense', by the English essayist F W H Myers (1843–1901), cofounder in 1882 of the Psychical Research Society, who coined the term.

telephone instrument for communicating by voice along wires, developed by Scottish inventor Alexander Graham ◊Bell in 1876. The transmitter (mouthpiece) consists of a carbon microphone, with a diaphragm that vibrates when a person speaks into it. The

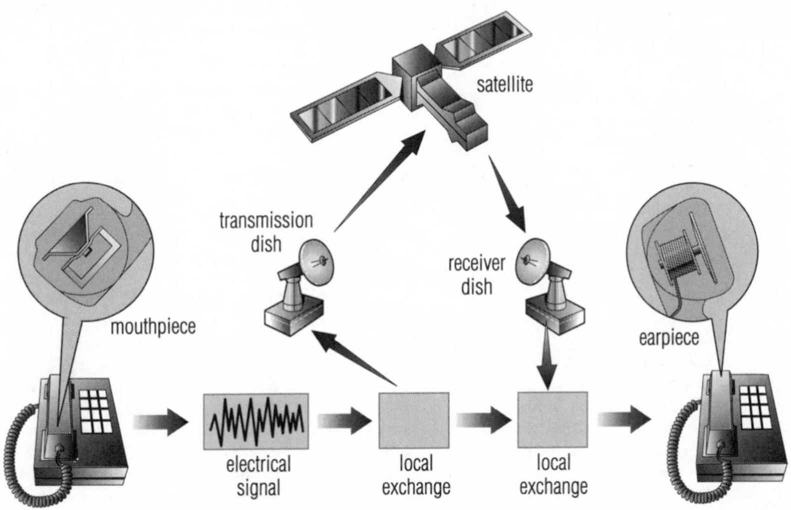

telephone *In the telephone, sound vibrations are converted to an electric signal and back again. The mouthpiece contains a carbon microphone that produces an electrical signal which varies in step with the spoken sounds. The signal is routed to the receiver via local or national exchanges. The earpiece contains an electromagnetic loudspeaker which reproduces the sounds by vibrating a diaphragm.*

diaphragm vibrations compress grains of carbon to a greater or lesser extent, altering their resistance to an electric current passing through them. This sets up variable electrical signals, which travel along the telephone lines to the receiver of the person being called. There they cause the magnetism of an electromagnet to vary, making a diaphragm above the electromagnet vibrate and give out sound waves, which mirror those that entered the mouthpiece originally.

The standard instrument has a handset, which houses the transmitter (mouthpiece), and receiver (earpiece), resting on a base, which has a dial or push-button mechanism for dialling a telephone number. Some telephones combine a push-button mechanism and mouthpiece and earpiece in one unit. A cordless telephone is of this kind, connected to a base unit not by wires but by radio. It can be used at distances up to about 100 m/330 ft from the base unit. In 1988 Japan and in 1991 Britain introduced an ◊Integrated Services Digital Network (see ◊telecommunications), providing fast transfer of computerized information.

The art of dialling has replaced the art of dialogue.

GITA MEHTA Indian writer.
Karma Cola VIII 2

---

telephone tapping *or* **telephone bugging** listening in on a telephone conversation, without the knowledge of the participants; in the UK and the USA this is a criminal offence if done without a warrant or the consent of the person concerned.

Telephony Application Programming Interface in computing, Windows 95 program, commonly abbreviated to TAPI.

teleprinter or ***teletypewriter*** transmitting and receiving device used in telecommunications to handle coded messages. Teleprinters are automatic typewriters keyed telegraphically to convert typed words into electrical signals (using a five-unit Baudot code, see ◊baud) at the transmitting end, and signals into typed words at the receiving end.

telescope optical instrument that magnifies images of faint and distant objects; any device for collecting and focusing light and other forms of electromagnetic radiation. It is a major research tool in astronomy and is used to sight over land and sea; small telescopes can be attached to cameras and rifles. A telescope with a large aperture, or opening, can distinguish finer detail and fainter objects than one with a small aperture. The **refracting telescope** uses lenses, and the **reflecting telescope** uses mirrors. A third type, the **catadioptric telescope**, is a combination of lenses and mirrors. See also ◊radio telescope.

refractor In a refractor, light is collected by a ◊lens called the **object glass** or **objective**, which focuses light down a tube, forming an image magnified by an **eyepiece**. Invention of the refractor is attributed to a Dutch optician, Hans Lippershey, in 1608. Hearing of the invention in 1609, ◊Galileo quickly constructed one for himself and went on to produce a succession of such instruments which he used from 1610 onwards for astronomical observations. The largest refracting telescope in the world, at ◊Yerkes Observatory, Wisconsin, USA, has an aperture of 102 cm/40 in.

reflector In a reflector, light is collected and focused by a concave mirror. The first reflector was built about 1670 by Isaac ◊Newton. Large mirrors are cheaper to make and easier to mount than large lenses, so all the largest telescopes are reflectors. The largest reflector with a single mirror, 6 m/236 in, is at ◊Zelenchukskaya, Russia. Telescopes with larger apertures composed of numerous smaller segments have been built, such as the ◊Keck Telescope on ◊Mauna Kea. A **multiple-mirror telescope** was installed on Mount Hopkins, Arizona, USA, in 1979. It consists of six mirrors of 1.8 m/72 in aperture, which perform like a single 4.5-m/176-in mirror. ◊**Schmidt telescopes** are used for taking wide-field photographs of the sky. They have a main mirror plus a thin lens at the front of the tube to increase the field of view.

The **liquid-mirror telescope** is a reflecting telescope constructed with a rotating mercury mirror. In 1995 NASA completed a

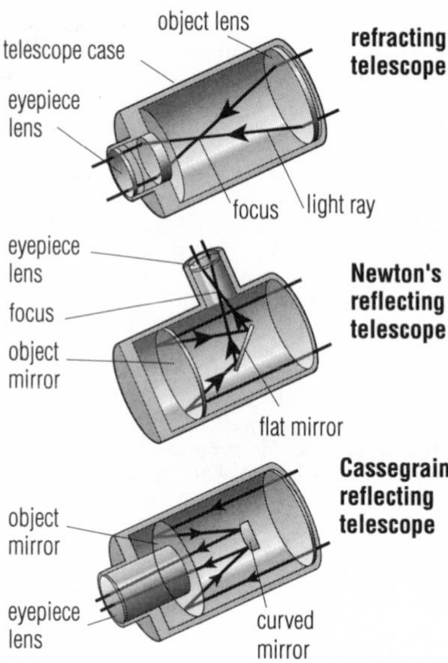

telescope *Three kinds of telescope. The refracting telescope uses a large objective lens to gather light and form an image which the smaller eyepiece lens magnifies. A reflecting telescope uses a mirror to gather light. The Schmidt telescope uses a corrective lens to achieve a wide field of view. It is one of the most widely used tools of astronomy.*

3-m/9.8-ft liquid mirror telescope at its Orbital Debris Observatory in New Mexico, USA.

telescopes in space Large telescopes can now be placed in orbit above the distorting effects of the Earth's atmosphere. Telescopes in space have been used to study infrared, ultraviolet, and X-ray radiation that does not penetrate the atmosphere but carries much information about the births, lives, and deaths of stars and galaxies. The 2.4-m/94-in ◊Hubble Space Telescope, launched in 1990, can see the sky more clearly than can any telescope on Earth.

In 1996 an X-ray telescope was under development by UK, US, and Australian astronomers, based on the structure of a lobster's eye, which has thousands of square tubes reflecting light onto the retina. The £4 million Lobster Eye telescope will contain millions of tubes 10–20 micrometres across and is intended for use on a satellite.

teletext broadcast system of displaying information on a television screen. The information – typically about news items, entertainment, sport, and finance – is constantly updated. Teletext is a form of ◊videotext, pioneered in Britain by the British Broadcasting Corporation (BBC) with Ceefax and by Independent Television with Teletext.

television **(TV)** reproduction of visual images at a distance using radio waves. For transmission, a television camera converts the pattern of light it takes in into a pattern of electrical charges. This is scanned line by line by a beam of electrons from an electron gun, resulting in variable electrical signals that represent the picture. These signals are combined with a radio carrier wave and broadcast as electromagnetic waves. The TV aerial picks up the wave and feeds it to the receiver (TV set). This separates out the vision signals, which pass to a cathode-ray tube where a beam of electrons is made to scan across the screen line by line, mirroring the action of the electron gun in the TV camera. The result is a recreation of the pattern of light that entered the camera. Twenty-five pictures are built up each second with interlaced scanning in Europe (30 in North America), with a total of 625 lines (525 lines in North America and Japan).

receiving aerials Because the wavelength of any television signal is short a resonant ◊aerial becomes possible, and this usually con-

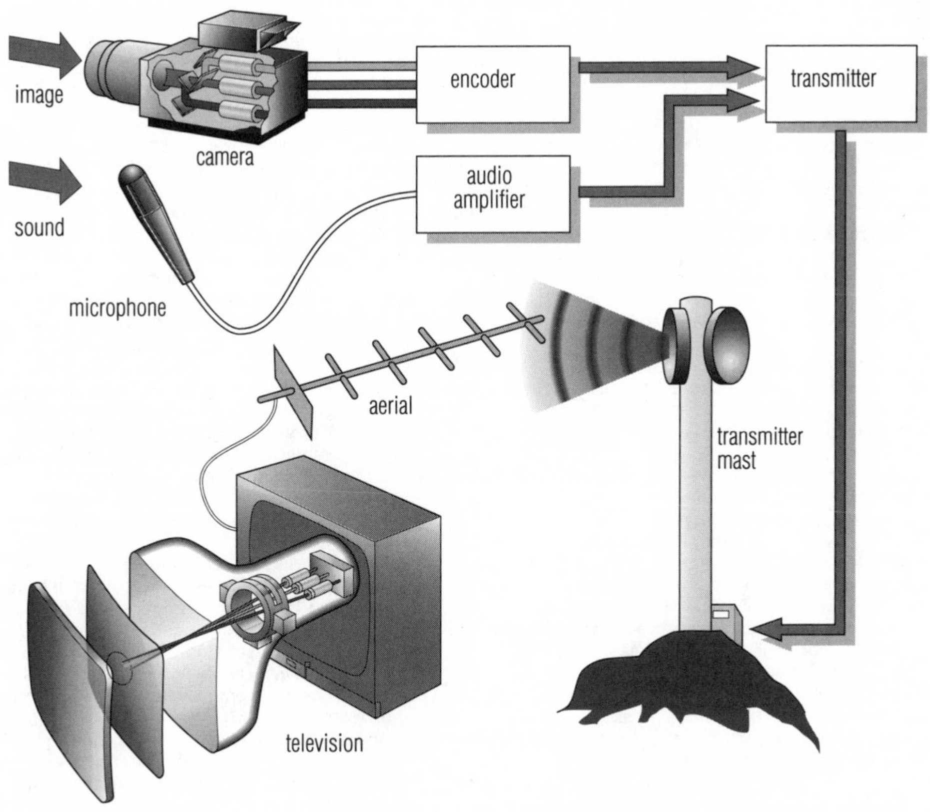

television *Simplified block diagram of a complete colour television system – transmitting and receiving. The camera separates the picture into three colours – red, blue, green – by using filters and different camera tubes for each colour. The audio signal is produced separately from the video signal. Both signals are transmitted from the same aerial using a special coupling device called a diplexer. There are four sections in the receiver: the aerial, the tuners, the decoders, and the display. As in the transmitter, the audio and video signals are processed*

sists of a half-wave aerial made of light alloy or steel tube, fed at the centre with low-impedance coaxial or balanced cable. Greater gain is obtained if a reflector element is added, and quite complicated arrays are used in areas of weak signal strength.

These aerials are mounted either vertically or horizontally to conform with the polarization of the transmitting aerials. Tubing is used for the elements, since an aerial made of wire would be too sharply resonant, with resulting loss of bandwidth, and therefore poor picture definition.

television channels In addition to transmissions received by all viewers, the 1970s and 1980s saw the growth of pay-television cable networks, which are received only by subscribers, and of devices, such as those used in the Qube system (USA), which allow the viewers' opinions to be transmitted instantaneously to the studio via a response button, so that, for example, a home viewing audience can vote in a talent competition. The number of programme channels continues to increase, following the introduction of satellite-beamed TV signals.

Further use of TV sets has been brought about by ◊videotext and the use of video recorders to tape programmes for playback later or to play pre-recorded video cassettes, and by their use as computer screens and for security systems. Extended-definition television gives a clear enlargement from a microscopic camera and was first used in 1989 in neurosurgery to enable medical students to watch brain operations.

history In 1873 it was realized that, since the electrical properties of the nonmetallic chemical element selenium vary according to the amount of light to which it is exposed, light could be converted into electrical impulses, making it possible to transmit such impulses over a distance and then reconvert them into light. The chief difficulty was seen to be the 'splitting of the picture' so that the infinite variety of light and shade values might be transmitted and reproduced. In 1908 it was found that cathode-ray tubes would best effect transmission and reception. Mechanical devices were used at the first practical demonstration of television, given by Scottish electrical engineer John Logie ◊Baird in London on 27 January 1926, and cathode-ray tubes were used experimentally in the UK from 1934.

The world's first public television service was started from the BBC station at Alexandra Palace in N London, on 2 November 1936. In the USA, TV technology was pioneered by David Sarnoff and Philo Taylor Farnsworth (1906–1971) and sets became available in the 1930s, but few performances were televised until the late 1940s, when local and network shows were scheduled in major cities and, by coaxial cable, across the nation. Live performances gave way to videotaped shows by the late 1950s, and colour sets became popular from the 1960s.

colour television Baird was an early pioneer in this area, and one of the first techniques developed employed a system whereby the normal frame frequency was increased by a factor of three, each successive frame containing the material for one primary colour. The receiver used revolving colour discs in front of the viewing screen, synchronized with the correct frame colours at the camera. A similar system replaced the colour discs by three superimposed projected pictures corresponding to the three primary colours. Baird demonstrated colour TV in London in 1928, but it was not until December 1953 that the first successful system was adopted for broadcasting, in the USA. This was called the NTSC system,

Digital Television

BY BARRY FOX

An analogue television station needs up to 8 MHz of frequency space. Two terrestrial transmitters cannot use the same frequency within several hundred kilometres of each other because even weak signals from one will interfere with strong signals from the other. Therefore, each country can only have a few television channels.

A satellite can transmit more channels, but its transmitters cover a wide geographical area. So the satellite usually delivers a handful of channels in different languages to several adjacent countries.

Converting a transmission system from analogue to digital multiplies the number of programme channels it can deliver, by up to ten. The bitstream can be used to carry a few programmes with better-than-analogue picture quality or many programmes with compromised clarity.

Digital television needs only one-hundredth the transmission power of analogue television. As a result, the digital signals can slot between the analogue frequencies, in the so-called 'taboo' channels which cannot be used for analogue broadcasting because of interference risks. Because the digital terrestrial frequencies are similar to existing analogue frequencies, existing aerials should be able to receive new digital broadcasts.

Once digital television is ubiquitous, broadcasters can plan the end of analogue broadcasting. This will release more frequencies either for digital broadcasting or mobile radio.

Initially, viewers will use a set-top box which converts the digital signals into analogue television, which an existing television set displays. New television sets will incorporate the digital circuitry. They will also have a wide format screen, with 16:9 aspect ratio to do justice to movies and widescreen sports broadcasts. Conventional television sets, with 4:3 screens, will show a slight letterboxing effect with black borders at the top and bottom of the picture.

National broadcasters will usually 'simulcast' existing 4:3 analogue programmes in digital widescreen, 'free to air'. Extra programmes will be encrypted, and available only if the viewer pays a fee, either by subscription or special event payment. Pay viewing will be controlled by a smart card, a credit card with a microchip that slots into the receiver to authorize decoding.

The digital television system for Europe was developed in the 1990s by an independent voluntary industry group, the Digital Video Broadcasting Group (DVB). The DVB's standards were then simply rubber-stamped by Europe's governments and official bodies. Some services will start before the year 2000.

The impetus for DVB came from the commercial failure of the high-definition television system developed in the 1980s as an official European research project, Eureka 95. High Definition Multiplexed Analogue Components (HD-MAC) was a hybrid system; the transmitted pictures were analogue but they travelled with digitally coded 'helper' signals which a suitable television set could use to make the images much wider and clearer than for conventional television. Although HD-MAC worked, high-definition receivers were prohibitively expensive.

There are three main DVB standards, for cable, satellite and terrestrial broadcasting. All are based on MPEG-2 coding, the digital compression standard set by the Motion Picture Experts Group of the International Electrotechnical Commission (IEC) and the International Standards Organisation (ISO). The main differences are in the way the compressed signal is packaged for transmission.

Terrestrial digital television uses a system similar to that developed for digital radio. Instead of transmitting one wide channel, the broadcaster transmits several thousand narrow sub-channels, packed tightly together. The digital code is split into a similar number of streams, so each channel carries fewer bits of code each second, and the bits in each channel are widely spaced apart in time. Unwanted reflections arrive in the gaps and the receiver rejects them.

The USA already has a commercial digital satellite service, called DSS, and existing networks will broadcast terrestrial digital television. The European DVB and North American systems are not compatible. The main difference is that the American system was designed to bridge the gap between televisions and computers, with emphasis on high-definition viewing, whereas the European system is aimed primarily at squeezing more programme channels into available frequency space.

Some observers fear that although the basic systems follow agreed standards, there is room for individual broadcasters to use their own proprietary systems to control pay viewing. This could block the design of a single receiver that works with rival satellite or terrestrial services.

since it was developed by the National Television System Committee, and variations of it have been developed in Europe; for example, SECAM (sequential and memory) in France and Eastern Europe, and PAL (phase alternation by line) in most of Western Europe. The three differ only in the way colour signals are prepared for transmission, the scanning rate, and the number of lines used. When there was no agreement on a universal European system in 1964, in 1967 the UK, West Germany, the Netherlands, and Switzerland adopted PAL while France and the USSR adopted SECAM. In 1989 the European Community (now the European Union) agreed to harmonize TV channels from 1991, allowing any station to show programmes anywhere in the EC.

The method of colour reproduction is related to that used in colour photography and printing. It uses the principle that any colours can be made by mixing the primary colours red, green, and blue in appropriate proportions. (This is different from the mixing of paints, where the primary colours are red, yellow, and blue.) In colour television the receiver reproduces only three basic colours: red, green, and blue. The effect of yellow, for example, is reproduced by combining equal amounts of red and green light, while white is formed by a mixture of all three basic colours.

Signals indicate the amounts of red, green, and blue light to be generated at the receiver. To transmit each of these three signals in the same way as the single brightness signal in black and white television would need three times the normal band width and reduce the number of possible stations and programmes to one-third of that possible with monochrome television. The three signals are therefore coded into one complex signal, which is transmitted as a more or less normal black and white signal and produces a satisfactory – or compatible – picture on black and white receivers. A fraction of each primary red, green, and blue signal is added together to produce the normal brightness, or luminance, signal. The minimum of extra colouring information is then sent by a special subcarrier signal, which is superimposed on the brightness signal. This extra colouring information corresponds to the hue and saturation of the transmitted colour, but without any of the fine detail of the picture. The impression of sharpness is conveyed only by the brightness signal, the colouring being added as a broad colour wash. The various colour systems differ only in the way in which the colouring information is sent on the subcarrier signal. The colour receiver has to amplify the complex signal and decode it back to the basic red, green, and blue signals; these primary signals are then applied to a colour cathode-ray tube.

The colour display tube is the heart of any colour receiver. Many designs of colour picture tubes have been invented; the most successful of these is known as the 'shadow mask tube'. It operates on similar electronic principles to the black and white television picture tube, but the screen is composed of a fine mosaic of over 1 mil-

Television: chronology

1878	William Crookes in England invented the Crookes tube, which produced cathode rays.
1884	Paul Nipkow in Germany built a mechanical scanning device, the Nipkow disc, a rotating disc with a spiral pattern of holes in it.
1897	Karl Ferdinand Braun, also in Germany, modified the Crookes tube to produce the ancestor of the TV receiver picture tube.
1906	Boris Rosing in Russia began experimenting with the Nipkow disc and cathode-ray tube, eventually succeeding in transmitting some crude TV pictures.
1923	Vladimir Zworykin in the USA invented the first electronic camera tube, the iconoscope.
1926	John Logie Baird demonstrated a workable TV system, using mechanical scanning by Nipkow disc.
1928	Baird demonstrated colour TV.
1929	The BBC began broadcasting experimental TV programmes, using Baird's system.
1931	US physicist Allen Balcom Du Mont perfected the first practical, low-cost cathode ray tube.
1936	The BBC began regular broadcasting from Alexandra Palace, London, using a high-definition all-electronic system developed by EMI. This marked the end of the BBC's usage of Baird's system.
1938	Allen Balcom Du Mont manufactured the first all-electronic receiver to be marketed in the USA. It used a huge 35 cm/14 in cathode ray tube.
1939	The NBC (National Broadcasting Company) began the first regular television broadcasting service in the USA.
1940	Experimental colour TV transmission began in the USA, as CBS in New York City made colour broadcasts using a semi-mechanical method called the 'field sequential system'.
1953	Successful colour TV transmissions began in the USA, using the NTSC (National Television Systems Committee) system. This system is used today throughout the American continents and Japan.
1956	The first videotape recorder was produced in California by the Ampex Corporation.
1962	TV signals were transmitted across the Atlantic via the Telstar satellite.
1970	The first videodisc system was announced by Decca in Britain and AEG-Telefunken in Germany, but it was not perfected until the 1980s, when laser scanning was used for playback.
1973	The BBC and Independent Television in the UK introduced the world's first teletext systems, Ceefax and Oracle, respectively.
1975	Sony introduced their videocassette tape-recorder system, Betamax, for domestic viewers, six years after their professional U-Matic system. The UK Post Office (now British Telecom) announced their Prestel viewdata system.
1979	Matsushita in Japan developed a pocket-sized, flat-screen TV set, using a liquid-crystal display.
1986	Data broadcasting using digital techniques was developed; an enhancement of teletext was produced.
1989	The Japanese began broadcasting high-definition television; satellite television was introduced in the UK.
1990	The BBC introduced a digital stereo sound system (NICAM); MAC, a European system allowing greater picture definition, more data, and sound tracks, was introduced.
1992	All-digital high-definition television demonstrated in the USA.
1993	A worldwide standard for digital television agreed at meeting of manufacturers and broadcasters in Sydney, Australia. The Japanese electronics company NEC announced the development of a flat thin screen that produces full-colour high resolution pictures, without a cathode ray tube. Television in the form of wraparound 'Sport' television glasses went on sale in the USA, enabling the wearer to watch television whilst walking.
1995	US House of Representatives voted in favour of including a chip in all TV sets that will allow parents to censor and block out certain categories of programmes that they consider unsuitable for their children's viewing.

lion dots arranged in an orderly fashion. One-third of the dots glow red when bombarded by electrons, one-third glow green, and one-third blue. There are three sources of electrons, respectively modulated by the red, green, and blue signals. The tube is arranged so that the shadow mask allows only the red signals to hit red dots, the green signals to hit green dots, and the blue signals to hit blue dots. The glowing dots are so small that from a normal viewing distance the colours merge into one another and a picture with a full range of colours is seen.

teleworking *or* **telecommuting** working from home rather than in an office, typically using a telephone and a personal computer connected to the office via a modem. The term was introduced in the 1980s.

Convenient for employers as it reduces overheads, it also facilitates working part-time for those with such commitments as young children. However, it has proved more costly to administer than many advocates had anticipated in the 1980s. Teleworking is most successful when combined with some attendance at the workplace. In 1991 an estimated 500,000 people in Britain were employed full time in this way, with a further 1.5 million part-time. According to a 1997 estimate, about 2% of the US population were teleworking on any one day.

telex **(acronym for *teleprinter exchange*)** international telecommunications network that handles telegraph messages in the form of coded signals. It uses ◊teleprinters for transmitting and receiving, and makes use of land lines (cables) and radio and satellite links to make connections between subscribers.

tellurium **Latin** *Tellus* **'Earth'** silver-white, semi-metallic (◊metalloid) element, symbol Te, atomic number 52, relative atomic mass 127.60. Chemically it is similar to sulphur and selenium, and it is considered one of the sulphur group. It occurs naturally in telluride minerals, and is used in colouring glass blue-brown, in the electrolytic refining of zinc, in electronics, and as a catalyst in refining petroleum.

It was discovered in 1782 by Austrian mineralogist Franz Müller (1740–1825), and named in 1798 by German chemist Martin Klaproth.

Teller, Edward
(1908–)

Hungarian-born US physicist known as the father of the hydrogen bomb. He worked on the fission bomb – the first atomic bomb – 1942–46 (the Manhattan Project) and on the fusion bomb, or H-bomb, 1946–52. In the 1980s he was one of the leading supporters of the Star Wars programme (Strategic Defense Initiative).

He was a key witness against his colleague Robert Oppenheimer at the security hearings in 1954. Teller was widely believed to be the model for the leading character in Stanley Kubrick's 1964 film *Dr Strangelove*. It was also Teller who convinced President Reagan of the feasibility of the Star Wars project for militarizing space with fission-bomb-powered X-ray lasers. Millions of dollars were spent before the project was discredited. Teller then suggested 'brilliant pebbles' – thousands of missile-interceptors based in space – and the use of nuclear explosions to prevent asteroids hitting the Earth. He opposed all test-ban treaties.

EDWARD TELLER PROFILE

http://www.achievement.org/autodoc/page/tel0pro-1

Description of the life and work of the 'father of the hydrogen bomb', physicist Edward Teller. The Web site contains not only a profile and biographical information, but also holds a lengthy interview with Teller from 1990 accompanied by a large number of photographs, video sequences, and audio clips.

Telnet in computing, Internet utility that enables a user to work on a remote computer as if directly connected. Telnet connections to a remote computer system are typically much cheaper than long-distance telephone calls; the user makes a local call to an Internet access provider and the rest of the connection is handled via the Internet at no additional cost. ◊Bulletin board systems usually work via Telnet.

telomere Greek *telos* 'end'; *meros* 'part' chromosome tip. Telomeres prevent chromosomes sticking together. Like DNA they are made up of nucleotides, usually rich in thymine and guanine. Every time a cell divides, the telomeres shorten. They trigger the cell's senescence (inability to reproduce) when they reach a threshold length. This process is prevented from happening during the replication of cancer cells by the presence of the enzyme **telomerase**. Telomerase replaces the segments of the telomeres, maintaining their length so that cell replication is no longer controlled.

Telstar US communications satellite, launched on 10 July 1962, which relayed the first live television transmissions between the USA and Europe. *Telstar* orbited the Earth in 158 minutes, and so had to be tracked by ground stations, unlike the geostationary satellites of today.

temperature degree or intensity of heat of an object and the condition that determines whether it will transfer heat to another object or receive heat from it, according to the laws of ◊thermodynamics. The temperature of an object is a measure of the average kinetic energy possessed by the atoms or molecules of which it is composed. The SI unit of temperature is the kelvin (symbol K) used with the Kelvin scale. Other measures of temperature in common use are the Celsius scale and the Fahrenheit scale.

The normal temperature of the human body is about 36.9°C/98.4°F. Variation by more than a degree or so indicates ill health, a rise signifying excessive activity (usually due to infection), and a decrease signifying deficient heat production (usually due to lessened vitality).

TO UNDERSTAND TEMPERATURE ON THE CELSIUS SCALE FOR THOSE USED TO FAHRENHEIT TEMPERATURES:

30 IS HOT; 20 IS NICE; 10 IS COLD; 0 IS ICE

temperature regulation the ability of an organism to control its internal body temperature; in warm-blooded animals this is known as ◊homeothermy.

Although some plants have evolved ways of resisting extremes of temperature, sophisticated mechanisms for maintaining the correct temperature are found in multicellular animals. Such mechanisms may be behavioural, as when a lizard moves into the shade in order to cool down, or internal, as in mammals and birds, where temperature is regulated by the ◊medulla.

tempering heat treatment for improving the properties of metals, often used for steel alloys. The metal is heated to a certain temperature and then cooled suddenly in a water or oil bath.

template in computing, file that lays down a document's format. Templates are used in word processing, spreadsheet, and other programs to specify all the styles used in a document, such as fonts, margins, macros, formulas and so on. They are widely used to automate the production of documents such as memos, mailings and reports, making sure that they have a uniform appearance.

temporary hardness hardness of water that is removed by boiling (see ◊hard water).

tench European freshwater bony fish *Tinca tinca*, a member of the carp family, now established in North America. It is about 45 cm/18 in long, weighs 2 kg/4.5 lb, and is coloured olive-green above and grey beneath. The scales are small and there is a barbel at each side of the mouth.

tendon or ***sinew*** in vertebrates, a cord of very strong, fibrous connective tissue that joins muscle to bone. Tendons are largely composed of bundles of fibres made of the protein collagen, and because of their inelasticity are very efficient at transforming muscle power into movement.

tendril in botany, a slender, threadlike structure that supports a climbing plant by coiling around suitable supports, such as the stems and branches of other plants. It may be a modified stem, leaf, leaflet, flower, leaf stalk, or stipule (a small appendage on either side of the leaf stalk), and may be simple or branched. The tendrils of Virginia creeper *Parthenocissus quinquefolia* are modified flower heads with suckerlike pads at the end that stick to walls, while those of the grapevine *Vitis* grow away from the light and thus enter dark crevices where they expand to anchor the plant firmly.

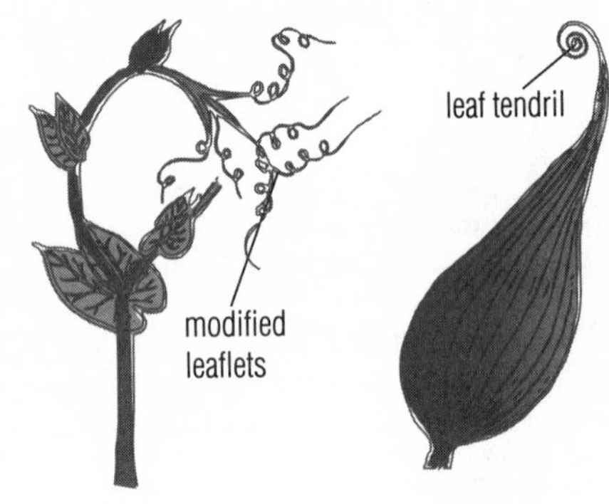

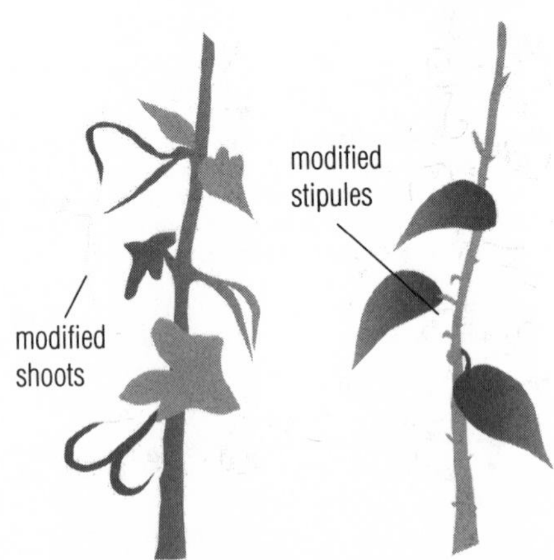

tendril *Tendrils are specially modifed leaves, shoots, or stems. They support the plant by twining around the stems of other plants nearby, as in the pea, or they may attach themselves to suitable surfaces by means of suckers, as in the virginia creeper.*

tension in physics, the stress (force) set up in a stretched material. In a stretched string or wire it exerts a pull that is equal in magnitude but opposite in direction to the stress being applied at the string ends. Tension is measured in newtons.

terabyte in computing, 1,024 ◊gigabytes, or 1,099,511,627,776 ◊bytes.

teratogen any substance or agent that can induce deformities in the fetus if absorbed by the mother during pregnancy. Teratogens include some drugs (notably alcohol and thalidomide), other chemicals, certain disease organisms, and radioactivity.

terbium soft, silver-grey, metallic element of the ◊lanthanide series, symbol Tb, atomic number 65, relative atomic mass 158.925. It occurs in gadolinite and other ores, with yttrium and ytterbium, and is used in lasers, semiconductors, and television tubes. It was named in 1843 by Swedish chemist Carl Mosander (1797–1858) for the town of Ytterby, Sweden, where it was first found.

terminal in computing, a device consisting of a keyboard and display screen (◊VDU) to enable the operator to communicate with the computer. The terminal may be physically attached to the computer or linked to it by a telephone line (remote terminal). A 'dumb' terminal has no processor of its own, whereas an 'intelligent' terminal has its own processor and takes some of the processing load away from the main computer.

terminal emulation in computing, communications program such as ◊Telnet that allows a computer to emulate a terminal or workstation of a remote host. The host accepts instructions from the remote computer as if it were one of its own workstations.

terminal moraine linear, slightly curved ridge of rocky debris deposited at the front end, or snout, of a glacier. It represents the furthest point of advance of a glacier, being formed when deposited material (till), which was pushed ahead of the snout as it advanced, became left behind as the glacier retreated.

terminal velocity *or* **terminal speed** the maximum velocity that can be reached by a given object moving through a fluid (gas or liquid) under the action of an applied force. As the speed of the object increases so does the total magnitude of the forces resisting its motion. Terminal velocity is reached when the resistive forces exactly balance the applied force that has caused the object to accelerate; because there is now no resultant force, there can be no further acceleration.

For example, an object falling through air will reach a terminal velocity and cease to accelerate under the influence of gravity when the air resistance equals the object's weight.

Parachutes are designed to increase air resistance so that the acceleration of a falling person or package ceases more rapidly, thereby limiting terminal velocity to a safe level.

terminal voltage the potential difference (pd) or voltage across the terminals of a power supply, such as a battery of cells. When the supply is not connected in circuit its terminal voltage is the same as its ◊electromotive force (emf); however, as soon as it begins to supply current to a circuit its terminal voltage falls because some electric potential energy is lost in driving current against the supply's own ◊internal resistance. As the current flowing in the circuit is increased the terminal voltage of the supply falls.

terminate and stay resident (TSR) term given to an MS-DOS program that remains in the memory – for example, a clock, calculator, or thesaurus. The program is installed by the use of a ◊hot key.

terminating decimal decimal fraction with a finite number of digits (a ◊recurring decimal, by contrast, has an infinite number of digits). Only those fractions with denominators that are powers of two and five can be converted into terminating decimals.

termite any member of the insect order Isoptera. Termites are soft-bodied social insects living in large colonies which include one or more queens (of relatively enormous size and producing an egg every two seconds), much smaller kings, and still smaller soldiers, workers, and immature forms. Termites build galleried nests of soil particles that may be 6 m/20 ft high.

One group, the Macrotermitinae, constructs fungus gardens from its own faeces by infecting them with a special fungus that digests the faeces and renders them edible. Termites may dispose of a quarter of the vegetation litter of an area, and their fondness for wood (as in houses and other buildings) brings them into conflict with humans. The wood is broken down in their stomachs by numerous microorganisms living in ◊symbiosis with their hosts. Some species construct adjustable air vents in their nests, and one species moistens the inside of the nest with water to keep it cool. Fossilized termite nests found in Arizona, USA, have been estimated to be about 220 million years old.

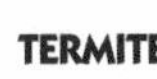

TERMITE

Termite nests may house 2 million termites and reach heights of up to 6 m/6.6 yd. A skyscraper built to the same scale would be 8 km/5 mi high.

tern any of various lightly built seabirds in the gull family Laridae, order Charadriiformes, with pointed wings and bill, and usually a forked tail. Terns plunge-dive after aquatic prey. They are 20–50 cm/8–20 in long, and usually coloured in combinations of white and black. They are extensively distributed, especially in temperate climates.

species The **common tern** *Sterna hirundo* has white underparts, grey upper wings, and a black crown on its head. The **Arctic tern** *Sterna paradisea* migrates from northern parts of Greenland, North America, and Europe to the Antarctic, thereby ensuring most of its life is spent in daylight. The **Antarctic tern** *Sterna vittata* has a striking blood-red beak; it does not migrate.

terrapin member of some species of the order Chelonia (◊turtles and ◊tortoises). Terrapins are small to medium-sized, aquatic or semi-aquatic, and are found widely in temperate zones. They are omnivorous, but generally eat aquatic animals. Some species are in danger of extinction owing to collection for the pet trade; most of the animals collected die in transit.

Species include the **diamondback terrapin** *Malaclemys terrapin* of the eastern USA, the **yellow-bellied terrapin**, and the **red-eared terrapin** *Pseudemys scripta elegans.*

terrestrial planet in astronomy, any of the four small, rocky inner ◊planets of the Solar System: ◊Mercury, Venus, Earth, and ◊Mars. The Moon is sometimes also included, although it is a satellite of the Earth and not strictly a planet.

terrier any of various breeds of highly intelligent, active dogs. They are usually small. Types include the bull, cairn, fox, Irish, Scottish, Sealyham, Skye, and Yorkshire terriers. They were originally bred for hunting rabbits and following quarry such as foxes down into burrows.

The small Parson Jack Russell terrier was recognized by the Kennel Club in 1990 as a variant of the fox terrier.

territorial behaviour in biology, any behaviour that serves to exclude other members of the same species from a fixed area or ◊territory. It may involve aggressively driving out intruders, marking the boundary (with dung piles or secretions from special scent glands), conspicuous visual displays, characteristic songs, or loud calls.

territory in animal behaviour, a fixed area from which an animal or group of animals excludes other members of the same species. Animals may hold territories for many different reasons; for example, to provide a constant food supply, to monopolize potential mates, or to ensure access to refuges or nest sites.

The size of a territory depends in part on its function: some nesting and mating territories may be only a few square metres, whereas feeding territories may be as large as hundreds of square kilometres.

terror bird or ***phorusrhacoid*** member of an extinct group of flightless, carnivorous birds that lived 62–2.5 million years ago in South America. During this time they were the dominant predators. From fossils, 25 species of terror bird have been recognized, ranging in height from 1–3 m/3.3–9.8 ft. Their closest living relative is the ◊seriema.

Tertiary period of geological time 65–1.64 million years ago, divided into five epochs: Palaeocene, Eocene, Oligocene, Miocene, and Pliocene. During the Tertiary period, mammals took over all the ecological niches left vacant by the extinction of the dinosaurs, and became the prevalent land animals. The continents took on their present positions, and climatic and vegetation zones as we know them became established. Within the geological time column the Tertiary follows the Cretaceous period and is succeeded by the Quaternary period.

Terylene trade name for a synthetic polyester fibre produced by the chemicals company ICI. It is made by polymerizing ethylene glycol and terephthalic acid. Cloth made from Terylene keeps its shape after washing and is hard-wearing.

Terylene was the first wholly synthetic fibre invented in Britain. It was created by the chemist J R Whinfield of Accrington in 1941. In 1942 the rights were sold to ICI (Du Pont in the USA) and bulk production began in 1955. Since 1970 it has been the most widely produced synthetic fibre, often under the generic name polyester. In 1989 8.4 million tonnes were produced, constituting over 50% of world synthetic fibre output.

tesla SI unit (symbol T) of ◊magnetic flux density. One tesla represents a flux density of one ◊weber per square metre, or 10^4 ◊gauss. It is named after the Croatian-born US engineer Nikola Tesla.

Tesla, Nikola
(1856–1943)

Croatian-born US physicist and electrical engineer who invented fluorescent lighting, the Tesla induction motor (1882–87), and the Tesla coil, and developed the alternating current (AC) electrical supply system.

The **Tesla coil** is an air core transformer with the primary and secondary windings tuned in resonance to produce high-frequency, high-voltage electricity. Using this device, Tesla produced an electric spark 40m/135 ft long in 1899. He also lit more than 200 lamps over a distance of 40 km/25 mi without the use of intervening wires. Gas-filled tubes are readily energized by high-frequency currents and so lights of this type were easily operated within the field of a large Tesla coil. Tesla soon developed all manner of coils which have since found numerous applications in electrical and electronic devices.

Mary Evans Picture Library

TESLA, NIKOLA

http://www.neuronet.pitt.edu/~bogdan/tesla/

Short biography of the electrical inventor plus quotations by and about Tesla, anecdotes, a photo gallery, and links to other sites of interest.

testa the outer coat of a seed, formed after fertilization of the ovule. It has a protective function and is usually hard and dry. In some cases the coat is adapted to aid dispersal, for example by being hairy. Humans have found uses for many types of testa, including the fibre of the cotton seed.

test cross in genetics, a breeding experiment used to discover the genotype of an individual organism. By crossing with a double recessive of the same species, the offspring will indicate whether the test individual is homozygous or heterozygous for the characteristic in question. In peas, a tall plant under investigation would be crossed with a double recessive short plant with known genotype tt. The results of the cross will be all tall plants if the test plant is TT. If the individual is in fact Tt then there will be some short plants (genotype tt) among the offspring.

test data data designed to test whether a new computer program is functioning correctly. The test data are carefully chosen to ensure that all possible branches of the program are tested. The expected results of running the data are written down and are then compared with the actual results obtained using the program.

testis *(plural* testes) the organ that produces ◊sperm in male (and hermaphrodite) animals. In vertebrates it is one of a pair of oval structures that are usually internal, but in mammals (other than elephants and marine mammals), the paired testes (or testicles) descend from the body cavity during development, to hang outside the abdomen in a scrotal sac. The testes also secrete the male sex hormone ◊androgen.

test message in computing, a message in ◊USENET that is posted simply to make sure that one's software or network connections are working properly.

testosterone in vertebrates, hormone secreted chiefly by the testes, but also by the ovaries and the cortex of the adrenal glands. It promotes the development of secondary sexual characteristics in males. In animals with a breeding season, the onset of breeding behaviour is accompanied by a rise in the level of testosterone in the blood.

Synthetic or animal testosterone is used to treat inadequate development of male characteristics or (illegally) to aid athletes' muscular development. Like other sex hormones, testosterone is a ◊steroid.

tetanus *or* **lockjaw** acute disease caused by the toxin of the bacillus *Clostridium tetani,* which usually enters the body through a wound. The bacterium is chiefly found in richly manured soil. Untreated, in seven to ten days tetanus produces muscular spasm and rigidity of the jaw spreading to other parts of the body, convulsions, and death. There is a vaccine, and the disease may be treatable with tetanus antitoxin and antibiotics.

CHILDHOOD INFECTIONS – TETANUS

http://kidshealth.org/parent/common/tetanus.html

Important information on the signs and symptoms of tetanus, the incubation, duration, and treatment of the illness. Specific reference is made to neonatal tetanus that affects new born infants as a result of inefficient surgical techniques during delivery.

Tethys Sea sea that once separated ◊Laurasia from Gondwanaland. It has now closed up to become the Mediterranean, the Black, the Caspian, and the Aral seas.

tetra any of various brightly coloured tropical freshwater bony fishes of the family Characidae, formerly placed in the genus *Tetragonopterus.* Tetras are found mainly in tropical South America, and also in Africa.

tetrachloromethane CCl_4 or **carbon tetrachloride** chlorinated organic compound that is a very efficient solvent for fats and greases, and was at one time the main constituent of household dry-cleaning fluids and of fire extinguishers used with electrical and petrol fires. Its use became restricted after it was discovered to be carcinogenic and it has now been largely removed from educational and industrial laboratories.

tetracycline one of a group of antibiotic compounds having in common the four-ring structure of chlortetracycline, the first member of the group to be isolated. They are prepared synthetically or obtained from certain bacteria of the genus *Streptomyces*. They are broad-spectrum antibiotics, effective against a wide range of disease-causing bacteria.

tetraethyl lead $Pb(C_2H_5)_4$ compound added to leaded petrol as a component of ◊antiknock to increase the efficiency of combustion in car engines. It is a colourless liquid that is insoluble in water but soluble in organic solvents such as benzene, ethanol, and petrol.

tetrahedron (plural *tetrahedra*) in geometry, a solid figure (◊polyhedron) with four triangular faces; that is, a ◊pyramid on a triangular base. A regular tetrahedron has equilateral triangles as its faces.

In chemistry and crystallography, tetrahedra describe the shapes of some molecules and crystals; for example, the carbon atoms in a crystal of diamond are arranged in space as a set of interconnected regular tetrahedra.

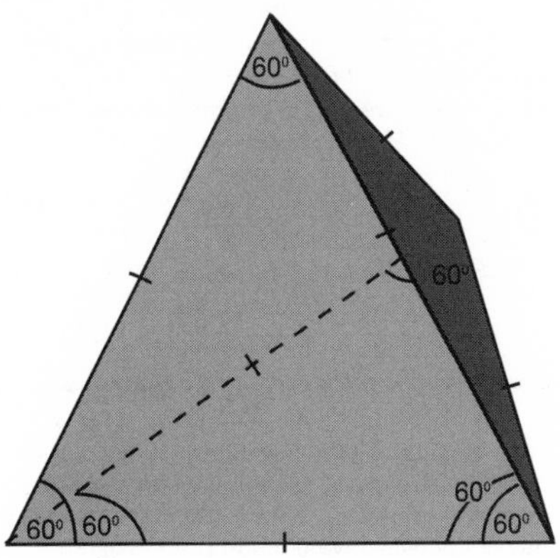

tetrahedron *A regular tetrahedron is a pyramid on a triangular base with all its sides equal in length.*

tetrapod Greek 'four-legged' type of ◊vertebrate. The group includes mammals, birds, reptiles, and amphibians. Birds are included because they evolved from four-legged ancestors, the forelimbs having become modified to form wings. Even snakes are tetrapods, because they are descended from four-legged reptiles.

T$_E$X (pronounced 'tek') ◊public domain text formatting and typesetting system, developed by Donald Knuth and widely used for producing mathematical and technical documents. Unlike ◊desktop publishing applications, T$_E$X is not ◊WYSIWYG, although in some implementations a screen preview of pages is possible.

text editor in computing, a program that allows the user to edit text on the screen and to store it in a file. Text editors are similar to ◊word processors, except that they lack the ability to format text into paragraphs and pages and to apply different typefaces and styles.

textured vegetable protein manufactured meat substitute; see ◊TVP.

TFT display another name for ◊active matrix LCD.

TGV (abbreviation for ***train à grande vitesse***) (French 'high-speed train') French electrically powered train that provides the world's fastest rail service. Since it began operating in 1981, it has carried more than 100 million passengers between Paris and Lyon, at average speeds of 214 kph/133 mph. In 1990, a TGV broke the world speed record, reaching a speed of 515.3 kph/320.2 mph (about half that of a passenger jet aircraft) on a stretch of line near Tours.

In 1990 a second service, the Atlantique, was launched, running from Paris to Le Mans and Tours. A third linking Paris with the Channel Tunnel, Brussels, and Cologne opened in 1993. The TGV network now extends to the Mediterranean, Switzerland, and Britanny. A new route is planned eastwards to Strasbourg, opening in 2006.

thalassaemia or ***Cooley's anaemia*** any of a group of chronic hereditary blood disorders that are widespread in the Mediterranean countries, Africa, the Far East, and the Middle East. They are characterized by an abnormality of the red blood cells and bone marrow, with enlargement of the spleen. The genes responsible are carried by about 100 million people worldwide. The diseases can be diagnosed prenatally.

thallium Greek *thallos* 'young green shoot' soft, bluish-white, malleable, metallic element, symbol Tl, atomic number 81, relative atomic mass 204.38. It is a poor conductor of electricity. Its compounds are poisonous and are used as insecticides and rodent poisons; some are used in the optical-glass and infrared-glass industries and in photocells.

Discovered spectroscopically by its green line, thallium was isolated and named by William Crookes in 1861.

thallus any plant body that is not divided into true leaves, stems, and roots. It is often thin and flattened, as in the body of a seaweed, lichen, or liverwort, and the gametophyte generation (◊prothallus) of a fern.

Some flowering plants (◊angiosperms) that are adapted to an aquatic way of life may have a very simple plant body which is described as a thallus (for example, duckweed *Lemna*).

Thames barrier movable barrier built across the river Thames at Woolwich, London, UK, as part of the city's flood defences. Completed in 1982, the barrier comprises curved flood gates which are rotated 90° into position from beneath the water to form a barrier when exceptionally high tides are expected.

THAMES BARRIER

http://www.environment-agency.gov.uk/info/barrier.html

Interesting and comprehensive description from Britain's environment ministry of the functions of the world's largest movable flood barrier and how it saves London from flooding. There is a comprehensive history of the Barrier, description of how surge tides are generated, and information for visitors.

thaumatin naturally occurring, non-carbohydrate sweetener derived from the bacterium *Thaumatococcus danielli*. Its sweetness is not sensed as quickly as that of other sweeteners, and it is not as widely used in the food industry.

thebaine $C_{19}H_{21}NO_3$ highly poisonous extract of ◊opium.

theodolite instrument for the measurement of horizontal and vertical angles, used in surveying. It consists of a small telescope mounted so as to move on two graduated circles, one horizontal and the other vertical, while its axes pass through the centre of the circles. See also ◊triangulation.

theorem mathematical proposition that can be deduced by logic from a set of axioms (basic facts that are taken to be true without proof). Advanced mathematics consists almost entirely of theorems and proofs, but even at a simple level theorems are important.

It is also a good rule not to put too much confidence in experimental results until they have been confirmed by theory.

ARTHUR STANLEY EDDINGTON British astrophysicist. Quoted in R L Weber *More Random Walks in Science*

theory in science, a set of ideas, concepts, principles, or methods used to explain a wide set of observed facts. Among the major theories of science are ◊relativity, quantum theory, evolution, and ◊plate tectonics.

Theory of Everything (ToE) another name for ◊grand unified theory.

therm unit of energy defined as 10^5 British thermal units; equivalent to 1.055×10^8 J. It is no longer in scientific use.

thermal capacity another name for ◊heat capacity

thermal conductivity in physics, the ability of a substance to conduct heat. Good thermal conductors, like good electrical conductors, are generally materials with many free electrons (such as metals).

Thermal conductivity is expressed in units of joules per second per metre per kelvin ($J\ s^{-1}\ m^{-1}\ K^{-1}$). For a block of material of cross-sectional area a and length l, with temperatures T_1 and T_2 at its end faces, the thermal conductivity λ equals $Hl/at(T_2 - T_1)$, where H is the amount of heat transferred in time t.

thermal dissociation reversible breakdown of a compound into simpler substances by heating it (see ◊dissociation). The splitting of ammonium chloride into ammonia and hydrogen chloride is an example. On cooling, they recombine to form the salt.

thermal expansion in physics, expansion that is due to a rise in temperature. It can be expressed in terms of linear, area, or volume expansion.

The coefficient of linear expansion α is the fractional increase in length per degree temperature rise; area, or superficial, expansion β is the fractional increase in area per degree; and volume, or cubic, expansion γ is the fractional increase in volume per degree. To a close approximation, $\beta = 2\alpha$ and $\gamma = 3\alpha$.

thermal prospection an expensive remote-sensing method used in aerial reconnaissance, based on weak variations in temperature which can be found above buried structures whose thermal properties are different from those of their surroundings.

thermal reactor nuclear reactor in which the neutrons released by fission of uranium-235 nuclei are slowed down in order to increase their chances of being captured by other uranium-235 nuclei, and so induce further fission. The material (commonly graphite or heavy water) responsible for doing so is called a **moderator**. When the fast newly-emitted neutrons collide with the nuclei of the moderator's atoms, some of their kinetic energy is lost and their speed is reduced. Those that have been slowed down to a speed that matches the thermal (heat) energy of the surrounding material are called **thermal neutrons**, and it is these that are most likely to induce fission and ensure the continuation of the chain reaction. See ◊nuclear reactor and ◊nuclear energy.

thermic lance cutting tool consisting of a tube of mild steel, enclosing tightly packed small steel rods and fed with oxygen. On ignition, temperatures above 3,000°C/5,400°F are produced and the thermic lance becomes its own sustaining fuel. It rapidly penetrates walls and a 23-cm/9-in steel door can be cut through in less than 30 seconds.

thermionics branch of electronics dealing with the emission of electrons from matter under the influence of heat.

thermistor semiconductor device whose electrical ◊resistance falls as temperature rises. The current passing through a thermistor increases rapidly as its temperature rises, and so they are used in electrical thermometers.

thermite process method used in incendiary devices and welding operations. It uses a powdered mixture of aluminium and (usually) iron oxide, which, when ignited, gives out enormous heat. The oxide is reduced to iron, which is molten at the high temperatures produced. This can be used to make a weld. The process was discovered in 1895 by German chemist Hans Goldschmidt (1861–1923).

thermocouple electric temperature measuring device consisting of a circuit having two wires made of different metals welded together at their ends. A current flows in the circuit when the two junctions are maintained at different temperatures (◊Seebeck effect). The electromotive force generated – measured by a millivoltmeter – is proportional to the temperature difference.

thermodynamics branch of physics dealing with the transformation of heat into and from other forms of energy. It is the basis of the study of the efficient working of engines, such as the steam and internal combustion engines. The three laws of thermodynamics are: (1) energy can be neither created nor destroyed, heat and mechanical work being mutually convertible; (2) it is impossible for an unaided self-acting machine to convey heat from one body to another at a higher temperature; and (3) it is impossible by any procedure, no matter how idealized, to reduce any system to the ◊absolute zero of temperature (0K/–273°C/–459°F) in a finite number of operations. Put into mathematical form, these laws have widespread applications in physics and chemistry.

If someone points out to you that your pet theory of the universe is in disagreement with Maxwell's equations – then so much the worse for Maxwell's equations. If it is found to be contradicted by observation – well, these experimentalists do bungle things sometimes. But if your theory is found to be against the second law of thermodynamics I can give you no hope; there is nothing for it but to collapse in deepest humiliation.

ARTHUR STANLEY EDDINGTON British astronomer.

thermography photographic recording of heat patterns. It is used medically as an imaging technique to identify 'hot spots' in the body – for example, tumours, where cells are more active than usual. Thermography was developed in the 1970s and 1980s by the military to assist night vision by detecting the body heat of an enemy or the hot engine of a tank. It uses a photographic method (using infrared radiation) employing infrared-sensitive films.

thermoluminescence (TL) release, in the form of a light pulse, of stored nuclear energy (electrons) in a mineral substance when heated to 500°C by ◊irradiation. The energy results from the radioactive decay of uranium and thorium, which is absorbed by crystalline inclusions within the mineral matrix, such as quartz and feldspar. The release of TL from these crystalline substances is used in archaeology to date pottery, and by geologists in studying terrestrial rocks and meteorites.

thermoluminescent dating Crystalline substances find their way into the clay fabric of ancient pottery as additives designed to strengthen the material and allow it to breathe during kiln-firing at 600°C and above. Firing erases the huge level of TL energy accrued in geological times and sets a 'time-zero' for fresh energy accumulation over archaeological times, the TL intensity measured today being proportional to the pottery's age. TL can date inorganic materials, including stone tools left as burnt flint, older than about 50,000–80,000 years, although it is regarded as less precise in its accuracy than radiocarbon dating.

thermometer instrument for measuring temperature. There are many types, designed to measure different temperature ranges to varying degrees of accuracy. Each makes use of a different physical effect of temperature. Expansion of a liquid is employed in common **liquid-in-glass thermometers**, such as those containing mercury or alcohol. The more accurate **gas thermometer** uses the effect of temperature on the pressure of a gas held at constant

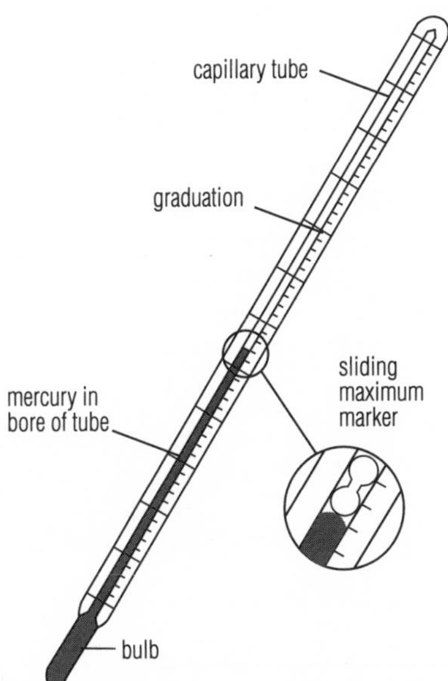

thermometer *Maximum and minimum thermometers are universally used in weather-reporting stations. The maximum thermometer, shown here, includes a magnet that fits tightly inside a capillary tube and is moved up it by the rising mercury. When the temperature falls, the magnet remains in position, thus enabling the maximum temperature to be recorded.*

volume. A **resistance thermometer** takes advantage of the change in resistance of a conductor (such as a platinum wire) with variation in temperature. Another electrical thermometer is the ◊thermocouple. Mechanically, temperature change can be indicated by the change in curvature of a bimetallic strip (as commonly used in a ◊thermostat).

thermopile instrument for measuring radiant heat, consisting of a number of ◊thermocouples connected in series with alternate junctions exposed to the radiation. The current generated (measured by an ◊ammeter) is proportional to the radiation falling on the device.

thermoplastic *or* **thermosoftening plastic** type of plastic that always softens on repeated heating. Thermoplastics include polyethylene (polyethene), polystyrene, nylon, and polyester.

Thermos trade name for a type of ◊vacuum flask.

thermoset type of◊plastic that remains rigid when set, and does not soften with heating. Thermosets have this property because the long-chain polymer molecules cross-link with each other to give a rigid structure. Examples include Bakelite, resins, melamine, and urea–formaldehyde resins.

thermosphere layer in the Earth's ◊atmosphere above the mesosphere and below the exosphere. Its lower level is about 80 km/50 mi above the ground, but its upper level is undefined. The ionosphere is located in the thermosphere. In the thermosphere the temperature rises with increasing height to several thousand degrees Celsius. However, because of the thinness of the air, very little heat is actually present.

thermostat temperature-controlling device that makes use of feedback. It employs a temperature sensor (often a bimetallic strip) to operate a switch or valve to control electricity or fuel supply. Thermostats are used in central heating, ovens, and car engines.

At the required preset temperature (for example of a room or gas oven), the movement of the sensor switches off the supply of electricity to the room heater or gas to the oven. As the room or oven cools down, the sensor turns back on the supply of electricity or gas.

thiamine or ***vitamin*** B_1 a water-soluble vitamin of the B complex. It is found in seeds and grain. Its absence from the diet causes the disease ◊beriberi.

1394 in computing, high speed external serial ◊bus system designed to connect computers and consumer electronics devices such as camcorders, digital television sets, DVD players, scanners, and colour printers. One 1394 port can connect up to 63 devices.

1394 is being specified as a standard by an Institute of Electronic and Electrical Engineers committee, IEEE.1394. The system started life at Apple Computer as FireWire, and is called i.Link by Sony Corporation. 1394 was designed in part to replace the ◊SCSI bus.

35 mm width of photographic film, the most popular format for the camera today. The 35-mm camera falls into two categories, the ◊SLR and the ◊rangefinder.

32-bit in computing, term describing the ability to process 32 ◊bits at a time. The Intel 386 and 486 series of microprocessors are examples of 32-bit processors.

The term is also used to specify the quality of sound produced by ◊sound cards, where increased speed indicates the ability to produce more fully detailed (and therefore more realistic) sound. Windows NT, OS/2, and Windows 95 are all examples of 32-bit operating systems.

thistle any of a group of prickly plants with spiny stems, soft cottony purple flower heads, and deeply indented leaves with prickly edges. The thistle is the national emblem of Scotland. (Genera include *Carduus, Carlina, Onopordum,* and *Cirsium;* family Compositae.)

thorax in four-limbed vertebrates, the part of the body containing the heart and lungs, and protected by the ribcage; in arthropods, the middle part of the body, between the head and abdomen.

In mammals the thorax is separated from the abdomen by the muscular diaphragm. In insects the thorax bears the legs and wings. The thorax of spiders and crustaceans, such as lobsters, is fused with the head, to form the cephalothorax.

thorium dark-grey, radioactive, metallic element of the ◊actinide series, symbol Th, atomic number 90, relative atomic mass 232.038. It occurs throughout the world in small quantities in minerals such as thorite and is widely distributed in monazite beach sands. It is one of three fissile elements (the others are uranium and plutonium), and its longest-lived isotope has a half-life of 1.39 $\times 10^{10}$ years. Thorium is used to strengthen alloys. It was discovered by Jöns Berzelius in 1828 and was named by him after the Norse god Thor.

Monomer I	*Monomer II*	*Polymer name*	*Uses*
formaldehyde (methanal)	phenol	PF resins (Bakelites)	electrical fittings, radio cabinets
formaldehyde	urea	UF resins	electrical fittings, insulation, adhesives
formaldehyde	melamine	melamines	laminates for furniture

thermoset *Unlike thermoplastics, thermosets remain rigid when set and do not soften when heated.*

Monomer	Polymer	Name	Uses
$CH_2=CH_2$ ethene	$[CH_2-CH_2]_n$	poly(ethene), polythene	bottles, packaging, insulation, pipes
$CH_2=CH-CH_3$ propene	$[CH_2-CH]_n$ with CH_3 side group	poly(propene), polypropylene	mouldings, film, fibres
$CH_2=CH-CL$ chloroethene (vinyl chloride)	$[CH_2-CH]_n$ with Cl side group	polyvinylchloride (PVC), poly(chloroethene)	insulation, flooring, household fabric
$CH_2=CH-C_6H_5$ phenylethene (styrene)	$[CH_2-CH]_n$ with C_6H_5 side group	polystyrene, poly(phenylethene)	insulation, packaging
$CF_2=CF_2$ tetrafluoroethene	$[CF_2-CF_2]_n$ ($n = 1000+$)	poly(tetrafluoroethene) (PTFE)	high resistance to chemical and electrical reaction, low-friction applications

thermoplastic *Examples of thermosoftening plastics, their basic monomer origins, polymer trade names, and everyday uses.*

thorn apple or ***jimson weed*** annual plant belonging to the nightshade family, native to America and naturalized worldwide. It grows to 2 m/6 ft in northern temperate and subtropical areas and has white or violet trumpet-shaped flowers followed by capsulelike fruits that split to release black seeds. All parts of the plant are poisonous. (*Datura stramonium*, family Solanaceae.)

thread in computing, subject line of electronic messages within an online topic or conference. Most online conferencing systems use some kind of threading; one advantage is that it makes it easy for readers of a particular conference or forum to skip over sections that do not interest them. Threading is an important feature of off-line readers, as otherwise it is difficult to tell how individual messages relate to one another.

threadworm kind of ◊nematode.

3-D graphics in computing, graphics defined by width, height, and depth (in mathematical terms, *x*, *y*, and *z* axes). In **business applications** such as spreadsheets, 3-D graphics allow users to display complex relationships between several different types of data. In **computer animation**, 3-D graphics allow animators to create characters which look rounded and real enough to interact with humans, such as the cartoon characters in the film *Who Framed Roger Rabbit?* in 1988 or the liquid-metal man in *Terminator 2* in 1991.

thrift or ***sea pink*** any of several perennial low-growing coastal plants. The common sea pink *A. maritima* occurs in clumps on seashores and cliffs throughout Europe. The leaves are small and linear and the dense round heads of pink flowers rise on straight stems. (Genus *Armeria*, family Plumbaginaceae.)

thrips any of a number of tiny insects of the order Thysanoptera, usually with feathery wings. Many of the 3,000 species live in flowers and suck their juices, causing damage and spreading disease. Others eat fungi, decaying matter, or smaller insects.

throat in human anatomy, the passage that leads from the back of the nose and mouth to the ◊trachea and ◊oesophagus. It includes the ◊pharynx and the ◊larynx, the latter being at the top of the trachea. The word 'throat' is also used to mean the front part of the neck, both in humans and other vertebrates; for example, in describing the plumage of birds. In engineering, it is any narrowing entry, such as the throat of a carburettor.

thrombosis condition in which a blood clot forms in a vein or artery, causing loss of circulation to the area served by the vessel. If it breaks away, it often travels to the lungs, causing pulmonary embolism.

Thrombosis in veins of the legs is often seen in association with ◊phlebitis, and in arteries with ◊atheroma. Thrombosis increases the risk of heart attack and stroke. It is treated by surgery and/or anticoagulant drugs.

thrush any bird of the large family Turdidae, order Passeriformes, found worldwide and known for their song. Thrushes are usually brown with speckles of other colours. They are 12–30 cm/5–12 in long.

thrush infection usually of the mouth (particularly in infants), but also sometimes of the vagina, caused by a yeastlike fungus (◊*Candida*). ◊It is seen as white patches on the mucous membranes.

Thrush, also known as **candidiasis**, may be caused by antibiotics removing natural antifungal agents from the body. It is treated with a further antibiotic.

Thrust 2 jet-propelled car in which British driver Richard Noble set a world land speed record in the Black Rock desert of Nevada, USA, on 4 October 1983. The record speed was 1,019.4 kph/633.468 mph. In 1996 Noble attempted to break the sound barrier in *Thrust SCC*. *Thrust SCC* has two Rolls-Royce Spey engines (the same kind used in RAF Phantom jets) that provide 110,000 horsepower; it weighs 6,350 kg/13,970 lb, and is 16.5 m/54 ft in length. It was driven by RAF fighter pilot Andy Green to break the sound barrier in September 1997, setting a speed of 1,149.272 kph/714.144 mph.

thulium soft, silver-white, malleable and ductile, metallic element of the ◊lanthanide series, symbol Tm, atomic number 69, relative atomic mass 168.94. It is the least abundant of the rare earth metals, and was first found in gadolinite and various other minerals. It is used in arc lighting.

The X-ray-emitting isotope Tm-170 is used in portable X-ray units. Thulium was named by French chemist Paul Lecoq de Boisbaudran in 1886 after the northland, Thule.

thumbnail in computing, a small version of a larger image used for reference. A ◊PhotoCD or ◊clip art collection might initially present images as thumbnails, while publishing programs include the facility for designers to produce thumbnail page layouts.

Thrust: Breaking the Land Speed Record

BY CHARLES ARTHUR

The attempt to break the sound barrier in a car, and in doing so establish a new land speed record, began in 1991. The idea was sparked off in the mind of Richard Noble, the UK driver who had established a new record of 960.9 kph/600.6 mph, when Craig Breedlove – the US rival whose record Noble had just broken – announced that he intended to break the sound barrier. Noble recalled later: 'From that moment, I knew we had to mount a challenge. I could not let Breedlove beat me to what is the last great challenge to man.'

The History Behind Land Speed Record Attempts

The history of the land speed record began on 18 December 1898, when Gaston Chasseloup-Laubat of France, driving an electric vehicle at Acheres, achieved 62.792 kph/39.245 mph. Since 15 September 1924, it has been held either by a Briton or an American – increasing 32 times from its value then of 234 kph/146 mph.

How the Speed Is Measured

The measurement process has become increasingly precise: it now uses laser interferometry for timing and distance. Today, a valid attempt must be made twice over a measured mile. The two runs, one in each direction, must be completed within one hour; the final speed is the average of the two runs. For a jet-fuelled car such as Noble's, or Craig Breedlove's *Spirit of America*, that 'turnaround' time represented a considerable challenge, even though covering the distance itself takes only a few seconds.

Work Begins on Thrust

In June 1994 work started on *Thrust SSC* ('SuperSonic Car'). By the time Noble had succeeded in his mission, it had cost £5 million. In many ways it was a revolutionary design, but the black *Thrust SSC* could hardly be called pretty. The Rolls-Royce jet engines, with their long tubular intakes and afterburners mounted either side of the needle-shaped body, came from a Phantom jet fighter. The steering was done by the rear wheels – a bit like a supermarket shopping trolley or forklift truck – the feasibility of which was first tested on a Mini. The car was driven by Andy Green, normally a Tornado jet pilot with the UK Royal Air Force.

The Team Heads for Nevada

After testing during June 1997 in the Jordanian desert, the *Thrust SSC* team left for Black Rocks, Nevada, in September. They were short of cash – a call for £200,000 was made as the team left – but determined to break the record. Also heading there was Craig Breedlove, with the *Spirit of America II*. He too intended to break the record and go supersonic. The thin air of Black Rock's high-altitude setting, and its flat, dry desert provides the ideal location for speed attempts, even though the teams had to drive more than 160 km/100 mi every day from their lodgings to the site.

Craig Breedlove's Many Attempts and Successes at Breaking the Record

Breedlove has a long history of setting the land speed record: he broke the 640 kph/400 mph, 800 kph/500 mph, and 960 kph/600 mph barriers. In October 1996 his car was hurtling across the Black Rock desert at 1,080 kph/675 mph, within seconds of setting a new record, when it crashed. Breedlove survived. The car didn't.

Craig Breedlove's 1997 version was powered by a single 48,000 horsepower fighter jet engine. In early testing he managed 549 kph/343 mph. But there was intense speculation among observers and engineers about whether Breedlove's car was stable enough. He admitted that if he was not confident enough to ride in it, he would try to pilot the car by a remote control link at up to 1,120 kph/700 mph – an idea that Noble insisted was dangerous.

Testing, Checking, and Repairing

Because the tiniest fault could be deadly at high speeds, the teams spent long hours checking and repairing any problems that turned up in low-speed testing. Such is the sophistication of modern cars that some of the 'repairs' involved computer code – controlling the suspension and engines – rather than anything physical. But after nearly a month, the *Thrust SSC*, driven by Green, was ready to make a serious attempt.

Thrust Goes Supersonic

The attempt to break the record succeeded on 25 September when the car broke Noble's 1993 record of 1,013 kph/633 mph by the remarkable margin of 130 kph/81 mph, as Green drove the car at 1,120/700mph on the first run and 1,165 kph/728 mph on the second for a 1,142 kph/714 mph average. The Queen sent her congratulations from Buckingham Palace. But the team had greater aims. The car had only been using 70 % of its power: they were convinced it could go supersonic.

The media were interested in what the experience was like. Green replied: 'The world looks the same at that speed. The mountains are still in the distance, the ground just moves past you a little faster.'

The training runs went on. Then on Monday 13 October the car broke the speed of sound on each run – but a parachute failure meant the car rolled more than a mile past its intended stopping place. It took 61 minutes to complete the second run – rendering it invalid as a record by 60 seconds, according to the international rules. The speeds were 1,222.669 kph/764.168 mph – or 1.007 % above the speed of sound – and 1,216.245 kph/760.153 mph.

But on Wednesday 15 October, during the first run at 9.07 a.m. local time, the car hit 1,214.932 kph/759.333mph. The return speed of 1,225.774 kph/766.109 mph, completed in the time limit, set the new record at 1,220.354 kph/762.721 mph.

Congratulations for the Team

Among the first to congratulate the team was the UK Prime Minister Tony Blair, who sent a message calling it 'a triumph in which the nation can share and take pride. This success is an excellent example of Britain at its best'.

Noble flew back to the UK, and welcomed the team when they returned with the car on 30 October. 'I think we were all actually quite pleased that it went so smoothly,' he said. And did he have any more plans – for 800 mph and upwards, perhaps? He refused to be drawn. 'We have got something planned but there's a lot of research to do first,' he replied.

thunderstorm severe storm of very heavy rain, thunder, and lightning. Thunderstorms are usually caused by the intense heating of the ground surface during summer. The warm air rises rapidly to form tall cumulonimbus clouds with a characteristic anvil-shaped top. Electrical charges accumulate in the clouds and are discharged to the ground as flashes of lightning. Air in the path of lightning becomes heated and expands rapidly, creating shock waves that are heard as a crash or rumble of thunder.

The rough distance between an observer and a lightning flash can be calculated by timing the number of seconds between the flash and the thunder. A gap of three seconds represents about a kilometre; five seconds represents about a mile.

thylacine another name for the ◊Tasmanian wolf.

thyme any of several herbs belonging to the mint family. Garden thyme *T. vulgaris,* native to the Mediterranean, grows to 30 cm/1 ft high and has small leaves and pinkish flowers. Its aromatic leaves are used for seasoning in cookery. (Genus *Thymus,* family Labiatae.)

thymus organ in vertebrates, situated in the upper chest cavity in humans. The thymus processes ◊lymphocyte cells to produce T-lymphocytes (T denotes 'thymus-derived'), which are responsible for binding to specific invading organisms and killing them or rendering them harmless.

The thymus reaches full size at puberty, and shrinks thereafter; the stock of T-lymphocytes is built up early in life, so this function diminishes in adults, but the thymus continues to function as an ◊endocrine gland, producing the hormone thymosin, which stimulates the activity of the T-lymphocytes.

thyristor type of ◊rectifier, an electronic device that conducts electricity in one direction only. The thyristor is composed of layers of ◊semiconductor material sandwiched between two electrodes called the anode and cathode. The current can be switched on by using a third electrode called the gate.

Thyristors are used to control mains-driven motors and in lighting dimmer controls.

thyroid ◊endocrine gland of vertebrates, situated in the neck in front of the trachea. It secretes several hormones, principally thyroxine, an iodine-containing hormone that stimulates growth, metabolism, and other functions of the body. The thyroid gland may be thought of as the regulator gland of the body's metabolic rate. If it is overactive, as in ◊hyperthyroidism, the sufferer feels hot and sweaty, has an increased heart rate, diarrhoea, and weight loss. Conversely, an underactive thyroid leads to **myxoedema**, a condition characterized by sensitivity to the cold, constipation, and weight gain. In infants, an underactive thyroid leads to **cretinism**, a form of mental retardation.

thyrotoxicosis synonym for ◊hyperthyroidism.

thyroxine in medicine, a hormone containing iodine that is produced by the thyroid gland. It is used to treat conditions that are due to deficiencies in thyroid function, such as myxoedema.

Tibetan mastiff large breed of dog regarded as the ancestor of many present breeds. It is a very powerful animal with a long black or black and tan coat. It is about 71 cm/28 in in height and 60 kg/132 lb in weight.

Tibetan mastiffs were used in Tibet as watchdogs and are mentioned in old Chinese literature and by Marco Polo.

Tibetan spaniel breed of miniature dog from the valleys of Tibet. Standing up to 28 cm/11 in tall, it has a fine, silky coat in a range of solid or broken colours. Its tail curves over its back.

Tibetan terrier breed of small herding dog used by the nomads of Tibet to gather and guard their flocks. It has a long, wavy coat that may be black, white, grey, beige, or any range of colours in between. Its tail curves over its back. It reaches a height of about 43 cm/17 in.

The name 'Tibetan terrier' is misleading as it has nothing in common with the terrier group of dogs and resembles a small Old English sheepdog.

tibia the anterior of the pair of bones in the leg between the ankle and the knee. In humans, the tibia is the shinbone. It articulates with the ◊femur above to form the knee joint, the ◊fibula externally at its upper and lower ends, and with the talus below, forming the ankle joint.

tick any of the arachnid family Ixodoidae, order Acarina, of large bloodsucking mites. They have flat bodies protected by horny shields. Many carry and transmit diseases to mammals (including humans) and birds.

life cycle During part of their existence they parasitize animals and birds, for which they have developed a rostrum or beak composed of two barbed harpoons above and a dart below. Their eggs are laid on rough herbage and hatch into white six-legged larvae, which climb up the legs of passing animals and in some species complete their life history on the animal's skin, but in others return to the grass for a period, dropping from the host when engorged with blood.

Ticks cause irritation and anaemia, and can also transmit ◊typhus, Lyme disease, rickettsia, and relapsing fever.

tidal energy energy derived from the tides. The tides mainly gain their potential energy from the gravitational forces acting between the Earth and the Moon. If water is trapped at a high level during high tide, perhaps by means of a barrage across an estuary, it may then be gradually released and its associated ◊gravitational potential energy exploited to drive turbines and generate electricity. Several schemes have been proposed for the Bristol Channel, in SW England, but environmental concerns as well as construction costs have so far prevented any decision from being taken.

tidal heating in astrophysics, a process in which one body is heated internally by tidal stresses set up by the gravitational pull of another body. Tidal heating is common among the moons of the giant planets, and is the heat source for volcanic activity on ◊Io, one of the moons of ◊Jupiter.

tidal power station ◊hydroelectric power plant that uses the 'head' of water created by the rise and fall of the ocean tides to spin the water turbines. The world's only large tidal power station is located on the estuary of the river Rance in the Gulf of St Malo, Brittany, France, and has been in use since 1966. It produces 240 megawatts and can generate electricity on both the ebb and flow of the tide.

tidal wave common name for a ◊tsunami.

Tidbinbilla space tracking station and nature reserve in Australia, just S of Canberra. It provides tracking facilities and command transmissions in support of NASA manned and unmanned spacecraft including the ◊Voyager probes.

tide the rhythmic rise and fall of the sea level in the Earth's oceans and their inlets and estuaries due to the gravitational attraction of the Moon and, to a lesser extent, the Sun, affecting regions of the Earth unequally as it rotates. Water on the side of the Earth nearest the Moon feels the Moon's pull and accumulates directly below it producing high tide.

High tide occurs at intervals of 12 hr 24 min 30 sec. The maxi-

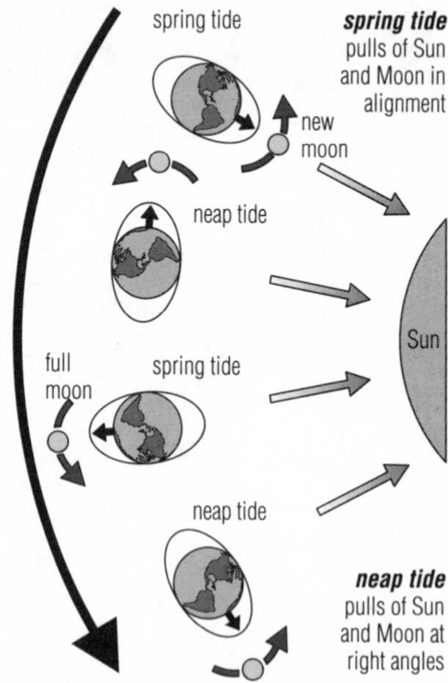

tide The gravitational pull of the Moon is the main cause of the tides. Water on the side of the Earth nearest the Moon feels the Moon's pull and accumulates directly under the Moon. When the Sun and the Moon are in line, at new and full moon, the gravitational pull of Sun and Moon are in line and produce a high spring tide. When the Sun and Moon are at right angles, lower neap tides occur.

mum high tides, or spring tides, occur at or near new and full Moon when the Moon and Sun are in line and exert the greatest combined gravitational pull. Lower high tides, or neap tides, occur when the Moon is in its first or third quarter and the Moon and Sun are at right angles to each other.

TIFF (acronym for ***t**agged **i**mage **f**ile **f**ormat)* a ◊graphics file format.

tiger largest of the great cats, *Panthera tigris* (family Felidae, order Carnivora), formerly found in much of central and S Asia, from Siberia south to Sumatra, but nearing extinction (5,000 in 1997) because of hunting and the high prices paid for the pelt, as well as the destruction of its natural habitat.

The male tiger can grow to 3.6 m/12 ft long, while the female averages about 2.6 m/8.5 ft. It weighs up to 300 kg/660 lbs, and has a yellow-orange coat with black stripes. Tigers are solitary, and largely nocturnal. They will eat carrion, but generally kill for themselves. Their food consists mainly of deer, antelopes, and smaller animals, but they sometimes kill wild boar. Human-eating tigers are rare and are the result of weakened powers or shortage of game.

TIGER

http://www.fws.gov/~r9extaff/biologues/bio_tige.html

Important addition to the ecological sites on the Web: this page offers descriptions of several types of tigers with details of their anatomy, hunting methods, habitats, the pressures they are under, and the measures taken to protect them.
services and legal assistance.

tiger beetle brightly coloured beetle with long legs and antennae. The most striking feature is their large eyes. Most adult tiger beetles are in shades of blue, bronze, or green, with yellow or white markings. They are typically found on sand or dry soils. Some 2,000 species have been recorded, mostly in the tropics.

The adults move rapidly and fly readily. The larvae live in burrows in the soil, where they lie in wait with their powerful mandibles, or jaws, ready to grab any insect that passes by.

classification Tiger beetles are members of the family Cicindelidae, order Coleoptera, class Insecta, phylum Arthropoda. The main genus is *Cicindela.*

tiling in computing, arrangement of ◊windows in a ◊graphical user interface system so that they do not overlap.

till or ***boulder clay*** deposit of clay, mud, gravel, and boulders left by a ◊glacier. It is unsorted, with all sizes of fragments mixed up together, and shows no stratification; that is, it does not form clear layers or ◊beds.

tilt-rotor aircraft type of vertical takeoff aircraft, also called a ◊convertiplane.

timber wood used in construction, furniture, and paper pulp. **Hardwoods** include tropical mahogany, teak, ebony, rosewood, temperate oak, elm, beech, and eucalyptus. All except eucalyptus are slow-growing, and world supplies are almost exhausted. **Softwoods** comprise the ◊conifers (pine, fir, spruce, and larch), which are quick to grow and easy to work but inferior in quality of grain. **White woods** include ash, birch, and sycamore; all have light-coloured timber, are fast-growing, and can be used as veneers on cheaper timber.

time continuous passage of existence, recorded by division into hours, minutes, and seconds. Formerly the measurement of time was based on the Earth's rotation on its axis, but this was found to be irregular. Therefore the second, the standard SI unit of time, was redefined in 1956 in terms of the Earth's annual orbit of the Sun, and in 1967 in terms of a radiation pattern of the element caesium.

time out in computing, pre-set period of time during which a computer waits for a response from a device or another computer. For example, when sending a fax, a computer will time out the telephone call if the receiving fax machine fails to answer.

Times Beach town in Missouri, USA, that accidentally became contaminated with ◊dioxin, and was bought by the Environmental Protection Agency in 1983 for cleansing.

time-sharing in computing, a way of enabling several users to access the same computer at the same time. The computer rapidly switches between user ◊terminals and programs, allowing each user to work as if he or she had sole use of the system.

Time-sharing was common in the 1960s and 1970s before the spread of cheaper computers, and might make a comeback in the late 1990s, with the advent of **network computing**.

timestamp in computing, ◊digital signature that 'fixes' a document in time, so that any later alterations can be readily detected.

tin soft, silver-white, malleable and somewhat ductile, metallic element, symbol Sn (from Latin *stannum*), atomic number 50, relative atomic mass 118.69. Tin exhibits ◊allotropy, having three forms: the familiar lustrous metallic form above 13.2°C/55.8°F; a brittle form above 161°C/321.8°F; and a grey powder form below 13.2°C/55.8°F (commonly called tin pest or tin disease). The metal is quite soft (slightly harder than lead) and can be rolled, pressed, or hammered into extremely thin sheets; it has a low melting point. In nature it occurs rarely as a free metal. It resists corrosion and is therefore used for coating and plating other metals.

Tin and copper smelted together form the oldest desired alloy, bronze; since the Bronze Age (3500 BC) that alloy has been the basis of both useful and decorative materials. Tin is also alloyed with metals other than copper to make solder and pewter. It was recognized as an element by Antoine Lavoisier, but the name is very old and comes from the Germanic form *zinn*. The mines of Cornwall were the principal western source of tin until the 19th century, when rich deposits were found in South America, Africa, SE Asia, and Australia. Tin production is concentrated in Malaysia, Indonesia, Brazil, and Bolivia.

tinamou fowl-like bird of the family Tinamidae, in the South American order Tinamiformes, of which there are some 45 species. They are up to 40 cm/16 in long, and their drab colour provides good camouflage. They are excellent runners but poor flyers and are thought to be related to the ◊ratites (flightless birds). Tinamous are mainly vegetarian, but sometimes eat insects. They escape predators by remaining still or by burrowing through dense cover.

Several females lay eggs in one nest; one hen may also lay eggs in nests guarded by different males. The males build the nests and incubate the eggs.

tinnitus in medicine, constant buzzing or ringing in the ears. The phenomenon may originate from prolonged exposure to noisy conditions (drilling, machinery, or loud music) or from damage to or disease of the middle or inner ear. The victim may become overwhelmed by the relentless noise in the head.

In some cases there is a hum at a frequency of about 40 Hz, which resembles that heard by people troubled by environmental hum but may include whistles and other noises resembling a machine workshop. Being in a place where external noises drown the internal ones gives some relief, and devices may be worn that create pleasant, soothing sounds to override them.

Objective tinnitus is a very rare form in which other people can also hear the noises. This may be caused by muscle spasms in the inner ear or throat, or abnormal resonance of the eardrum and ossicles.

tin ore mineral from which tin is extracted, principally cassiterite, SnO_2. The world's chief producers are Malaysia, Thailand, and Bolivia.

tinplate milled steel coated with tin, the metal used for most 'tin' cans. The steel provides the strength, and the tin provides the corrosion resistance, ensuring that the food inside is not contaminated. Tinplate may be made by ◊electroplating or by dipping in a bath of molten tin.

TinyMUD in computing, one of the oldest and most popular ◊MUDs, named for the efficiency of its program code.

TinySex in computing, cybersex on ◊TinyMUD.

TIR abbreviation for ***Transports Internationaux Routiers*** (French 'International Road Transport').

tire US spelling of ◊tyre.

tissue in biology, any kind of cellular fabric that occurs in an organism's body. Several kinds of tissue can usually be distinguished, each consisting of cells of a particular kind bound together by cell walls (in plants) or extracellular matrix (in animals). Thus, nerve and muscle are different kinds of tissue in animals, as are ◊parenchyma and ◊sclerenchyma in plants.

tissue culture process by which cells from a plant or animal are removed from the organism and grown under controlled conditions in a sterile medium containing all the necessary nutrients. Tissue culture can provide information on cell growth and differentiation, and is also used in plant propagation and drug production.

tissue plasminogen activator (tPA) naturally occurring substance in the body tissues that activates the enzyme plasmin that is able to dissolve blood clots. Human tPA, produced in bacteria by genetic engineering, has, like streptokinase, been used to dissolve blood clots in the coronary arteries of heart attack victims. It has been shown to be more effective than streptokinase when used in conjunction with heparin, but it is much more expensive.

tit or ***titmouse*** any of 65 species of insectivorous, acrobatic bird of the family Paridae, order Passeriformes. Tits are 8–20 cm/3–8 in long and have grey or black plumage, often with blue or yellow markings. They are found in Eurasia and Africa, and also in North America, where they are called **chickadees**.

TIT

Birds are not the only inhabitants of bird nests. A Finnish study of 56 bird species found that their nests harboured 529 different kinds of invertebrates (including 228 species of mite). One great tit's nest was home to 3,469 arthropods.

Titan in astronomy, largest moon of the planet Saturn, with a diameter of 5,150 km/3,200 mi and a mean distance from Saturn of 1,222,000 km/759,000 mi. It was discovered in 1655 by Dutch mathematician and astronomer Christiaan ◊Huygens, and is the second largest moon in the Solar System (Ganymede, of Jupiter, is larger).

Titan is the only moon in the Solar System with a substantial atmosphere (mostly nitrogen), topped with smoggy orange clouds that obscure the surface, which may be covered with liquid ethane lakes. Its surface atmospheric pressure is greater than Earth's. Radar signals suggest that Titan has dry land as well as oceans (among the planets, only Earth has both in the Solar System).

titanium strong, lightweight, silver-grey, metallic element, symbol Ti, atomic number 22, relative atomic mass 47.90. The ninth-most abundant element in the Earth's crust, its compounds occur in practically all igneous rocks and their sedimentary deposits. It is very strong and resistant to corrosion, so it is used in building high-speed aircraft and spacecraft; it is also widely used in making alloys, as it unites with almost every metal except copper and aluminium. Titanium oxide is used in high-grade white pigments.

Titanium bonds with bone in a process called **osseointegration**. As the body does not react to the titanium it is valuable for permanent implants such as prostheses.

The element was discovered in 1791 by English mineralogist William Gregor (1761–1817) and was named by German chemist Martin Klaproth in 1796 after the Titans, the giants of Greek mythology. It was not obtained in pure form until 1925.

titanium ore any mineral from which titanium is extracted, principally ilmenite ($FeTiO_3$) and rutile (TiO_2). Brazil, India, and Canada are major producers. Both these ore minerals are found either in rock formations or concentrated in heavy mineral sands.

Titan rocket family of US space rockets, developed from the Titan intercontinental missile. Two-stage Titan rockets launched the ◊Gemini crewed missions. More powerful Titans, with additional stages and strap-on boosters, were used to launch spy satellites and space probes, including the ◊Viking and ◊Voyager probes and *Mars Observer*.

titration in analytical chemistry, a technique to find the concentration of one compound in a solution by determining how much of it will react with a known amount of another compound in solution.

One of the solutions is measured by ◊pipette into the reaction vessel. The other is added a little at a time from a ◊burette. The end-point of the reaction is determined with an ◊indicator or an electrochemical device.

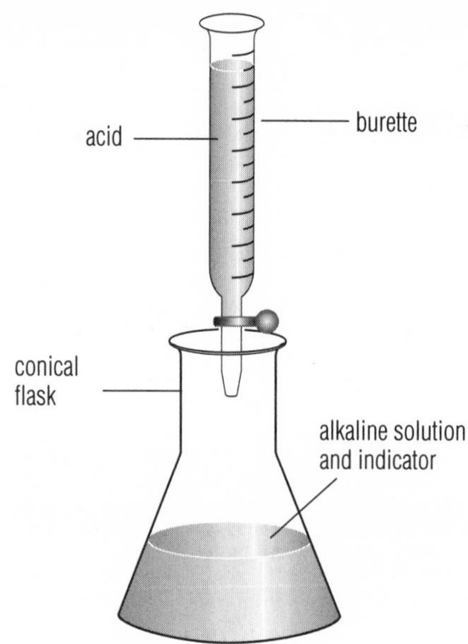

titration *A method used to find the concentration of an acid or an alkali. Typically a burette is filled with an acid of unknown concentration which is slowly (drop by drop) added to an alkali of a known concentration, mixed with an indicator (such as phenolphthalein). The volume of acid need to neutralize the alkali in the flask can be used to calculate the concentration of the acid.*

TLA (abbreviation for ***three letter acronym***) hackers' self-fulfilling reference to the apparent ubiquity of three-letter abbreviations (all popularly and wrongly referred to as acronyms) in the computing world. Anyone who has used a DOS-based CPU and a ◊VGA or ◊LCD ◊VDU (or, indeed, an ◊IBM ◊MPC) to create ◊GIFs, WAVs or ◊PDF files, or who has hooked up to an ISP (◊Internet Service Provider) to access IRC, WWW, a BBS or a ◊MUD, or to get an ◊FAQ by ◊FTP, will be familiar with this syndrome.

Some hackers are so addicted to using TLAs that a four-letter acronym is known mockingly as an 'ETLA' – **Extended Three-Letter Acronym**.

TN3270 in computing, variation of ◊Telnet used to connect to IBM mainframes.

TNT (abbreviation for ***trinitrotoluene***) $CH_3C_6H_2(NO_2)_3$, a powerful high explosive. It is a yellow solid, prepared in several isomeric forms from ◊toluene by using sulphuric and nitric acids.

toad any of the more terrestrial warty-skinned members of the tailless amphibians (order Anura). The name commonly refers to members of the genus *Bufo,* family Bufonidae, which are found worldwide, except for Australia (where the marine or ◊cane toad *B. marinus* has been introduced), Madagascar, and Antarctica. They differ from ◊frogs chiefly by the total absence of teeth, and in certain other anatomical features.

toadflax any of a group of small plants belonging to the snapdragon family, native to W Europe and Asia. Toadflaxes have spurred, two-lipped flowers, commonly purple or yellow, and grow 20–80 cm/8–32 in tall. (Genus *Linaria,* family Scrophulariaceae.)

toadstool common name for many umbrella-shaped fruiting bodies of fungi (see ◊fungus). The term is normally applied to those that are inedible or poisonous.

tobacco any of a group of large-leaved plants belonging to the nightshade family, native to tropical parts of the Americas. The species *N. tabacum* is widely cultivated in warm, dry climates for use in cigars and cigarettes, and in powdered form as snuff. (Genus *Nicotiana,* family Solanaceae.)

The leaves are cured, or dried, and matured in storage for two to three years before use. Introduced to Europe as a medicine in the 16th century, tobacco has been recognized from the 1950s as a major health hazard; see ◊cancer. The leaves also yield **nicotine**, a colourless oil, one of the most powerful poisons known, and addictive in humans. It is used in insecticides.

Worldwide, the tobacco conglomerations make a net profit of $6 billion each year. A US Supreme Court decision in 1992 ruled that tobacco companies can be held legally responsible for the dangerous effects of smoking on health; conglomerations spend $50 million a year on legal advice to avoid paying out compensation to victims. However, in March 1996 the Liggett Group became the first tobacco company to agree to settle smoking-related claims.

In early 1998 a court case in Minnesota, USA, revealed that the tobacco industry was aware of the carcinogenic effects of smoking cigarettes in 1958 when British scientists informed manufacturers (British American Tobacco) of the link between smoking and lung cancer. By the end of the 1970s tobacco companies were considering producing nicotine-containing merchandise other than cigarettes, should they become socially unacceptable. The research involved identifying a pattern of repeat consumption; a product that involved repeated handling; nicotine (or a 'direct' substitute) as the main constituent; the product being non-ignitable. At that time, tobacco manufacturers were aware that nicotine was the addictive, though not the most harmful, element in cigarettes.

When I was young, I kissed my first woman, and smoked my first cigarette on the same day. Believe me, never since have I wasted any more time on tobacco.

ARTURO TOSCANINI Italian conductor.
Attributed remark 1957

tocopherol *or* **vitamin E** fat-soluble chemical found in vegetable oils. Deficiency of tocopherol leads to multiple adverse effects on health. In rats, vitamin E deficiency has been shown to cause sterility.

tog unit of measure of thermal insulation used in the textile trade; a light summer suit provides 1.0 tog.

The tog value of an object is equal to ten times the temperature difference (in °C) between its two surfaces when the flow of heat is equal to one watt per square metre; one tog equals 0.645 ◊clo.

toggle in computing, to switch between two settings. In software a toggle is usually triggered by the same code, so it is important that this code only has two meanings. An example is the use of the same character in a text file to indicate both opening and closing quotation marks; if the same character is also used to mean an apostrophe, then conversion, via a toggle switch, for a ◊desktop publishing system that uses different opening and closing quotation marks, will not be carried out correctly.

toilet place where waste products from the body are excreted. Simple latrines, with sewers to carry away waste, have been found in the Indus Valley and ancient Babylon; the medieval garderobe is essentially the same, even though flushing lavatories had been known to Roman civilizations.

tokamak Russian acronym for toroidal magnetic chamber, an experimental machine conceived by Soviet physicist Andrei ◊Sakharov and developed in the Soviet Union to investigate controlled nuclear fusion. It consists of a doughnut-shaped chamber surrounded by electromagnets capable of exerting very powerful magnetic fields. The fields are generated to confine a very hot (millions of degrees) ◊plasma of ions and electrons, keeping it away from the chamber walls. See also ◊JET.

Token Ring protocol for ◊local area networks, developed by IBM in 1985.

toluene *or* **methyl benzene** $C_6H_5CH_3$ colourless, inflammable liquid, insoluble in water, derived from petroleum. It is used as a solvent, in aircraft fuels, in preparing phenol (carbolic acid, used in making resins for adhesives, pharmaceuticals, and as a disinfectant), and the powerful high explosive ◊TNT.

tomato annual plant belonging to the nightshade family, native to South America. It is widely cultivated for its shiny, round, red fruit containing many seeds (technically a berry), which is widely used in salads and cooking. (*Lycopersicon esculentum,* family Solanaceae.)

A genetically engineered tomato, the first genetically engineered food for sale, appeared in shops in California and Chicago in May 1994.

tomography the technique of using X-rays or ultrasound waves to procure images of structures deep within the body for diagnostic purposes. In modern medical imaging there are several techniques, such as the ◊CAT scan (computerized axial tomography).

ton imperial unit of mass. The **long ton**, used in the UK, is 1,016 kg/2,240 lb; the **short ton**, used in the USA, is 907 kg/2,000 lb. The **metric ton** or **tonne** is 1,000 kg/2,205 lb.

ton in shipping, unit of volume equal to 2.83 cubic metres/100 cubic feet. **Gross tonnage** is the total internal volume of a ship in tons; **net register tonnage** is the volume used for carrying cargo or passengers. **Displacement tonnage** is the weight of the vessel, in terms of the number of imperial tons of seawater displaced when the ship is loaded to its load line; it is used to describe warships.

tongue in tetrapod vertebrates, a muscular organ usually attached to the floor of the mouth. It has a thick root attached to a U-shaped bone (hyoid), and is covered with a ◊mucous membrane containing nerves and taste buds. It is the main organ of taste. The tongue directs food to the teeth and into the throat for chewing and swallowing. In humans, it is crucial for speech; in other animals, for lapping up water and for grooming, among other functions. In some animals, such as frogs, it can be flipped forwards to catch insects; in others, such as anteaters, it serves to reach for food found in deep holes.

tonka South American tree *Dipteryx odorata,* family Leguminosae. The fruit, a dry fibrous pod, encloses a black aromatic bean used in flavouring, perfumery, and the manufacture of snuff and tobacco.

tonne the metric ton of 1,000 kg/2,204.6 lb; equivalent to 0.9842 of an imperial ◊ton.

tonsillitis inflammation of the ◊tonsils.

tonsils in higher vertebrates, masses of lymphoid tissue situated at the back of the mouth and throat (palatine tonsils), and on the rear surface of the tongue (lingual tonsils). The tonsils contain many ◊lymphocytes and are part of the body's defence system against infection.

The ◊adenoids are sometimes called pharyngeal tonsils.

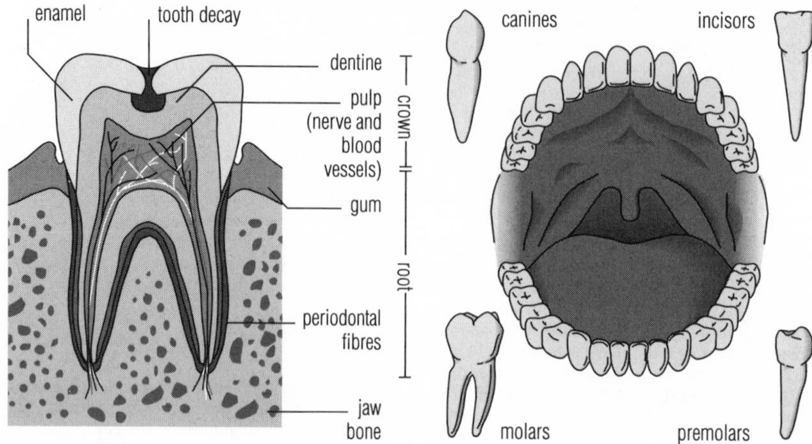

tooth *Adults have 32 teeth: two incisors, one canine, two premolars, and three molars on each side of each jaw. Each tooth has three parts: crown, neck, and root. The crown consists of a dense layer of mineral, the enamel, surrounding hard dentine with a soft centre, the pulp.*

toolbar in computing, area at the top or side of a screen with ◊push-buttons and other features to perform frequently-used tasks. For example, the toolbar of a ◊paint program might offer quick access to different brushes, spraycans, erasers, and other useful tools.

ToolBook in computing, multimedia authoring tool created by the US company Asymetrix for Microsoft Windows.

tooth in vertebrates, one of a set of hard, bonelike structures in the mouth, used for biting and chewing food, and in defence and aggression. In humans, the first set (20 milk teeth) appear from age six months to two and a half years. The permanent ◊dentition replaces these from the sixth year onwards, the wisdom teeth (third molars) sometimes not appearing until the age of 25 or 30. Adults have 32 teeth: two incisors, one canine (eye tooth), two premolars, and three molars on each side of each jaw. Each tooth consists of an enamel coat (hardened calcium deposits), dentine (a thick, bonelike layer), and an inner pulp cavity, housing nerves and blood vessels. Mammalian teeth have roots surrounded by cementum, which fuses them into their sockets in the jawbones.

The neck of the tooth is covered by the ◊gum, while the enamel-covered crown protrudes above the gum line.

The chief diseases of teeth are misplacements resulting from defect or disturbance of the tooth-germs before birth, eruption out of their proper places, and caries (decay).

A genetically engineered protein able to stimulate the recovery of tooth tissue in decayed teeth was undergoing trials in 1993.

TOOTH

About one in every 2,000 babies is born with a tooth. Louis XIV of France was born with two teeth, which may explain why he had had eight wet-nurses by the time he moved on to solid foods.

topaz mineral, aluminium fluorosilicate, $Al_2(F_2SiO_4)$. It is usually yellow, but pink if it has been heated, and is used as a gemstone when transparent. It ranks 8 on the Mohs' scale of hardness.

tope slender shark *Galeorhinus galeus* ranging through temperate and tropical seas. Dark grey above and white beneath, it reaches 2 m/6 ft in length. The young are born well-formed, sometimes 40 at a time.

topi *or* **korrigum** antelope *Damaliscus korrigum* of equatorial Africa, head and body about 1.7 m/5.5 ft long, 1.1 m/3.5 ft high at the shoulder, with a chocolate-brown coat.

topography the surface shape and composition of the landscape, comprising both natural and artificial features, and its study. Topographical features include the relief and contours of the land; the distribution of mountains, valleys, and human settlements; and the patterns of rivers, roads, and railways.

topology in computing, the arrangement of devices in a ◊network. Common topologies include **star networks**, where a central computer manages network access, and **ring networks**, where users can establish direct connections with other workstations.

topology branch of geometry that deals with those properties of a figure that remain unchanged even when the figure is trans-

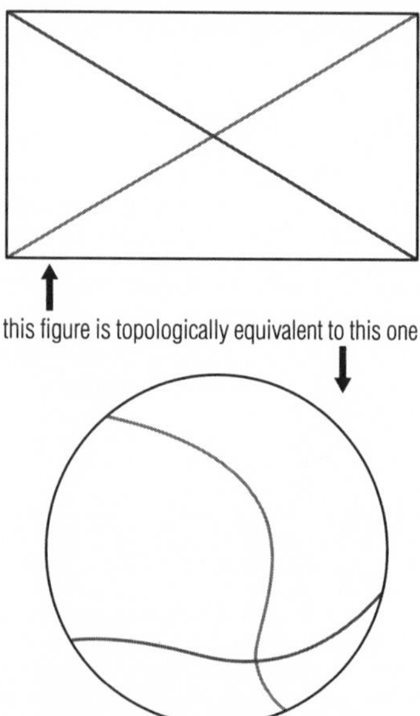

topology *A topological oddity, the Klein bottle is a bottle in name only because it has only one surface and no outside or inside.*

transition in computing, way in which one image changes to another in a ◊slide show, animation or multimedia presentation.

Different transitions have a different effect on the viewer: slow mixes (fades) are gentler on the eye than sudden blackouts, and wipes – in which one scene replaces the next like a blind being pulled across the screen – are an especially dynamic type of transition.

transition metal any of a group of metallic elements that have incomplete inner electron shells and exhibit variable valency – for example, cobalt, copper, iron, and molybdenum. They are excellent conductors of electricity, and generally form highly coloured compounds.

translation in living cells, the process by which proteins are synthesized. During translation, the information coded as a sequence of nucleotides in messenger ◊RNA is transformed into a sequence of amino acids in a peptide chain. The process involves the 'translation' of the ◊genetic code. See also ◊transcription.

translation program in computing, a program that translates another program written in a high-level language or assembly language into the machine-code instructions that a computer can obey. See ◊assembler, compiler, and vinterpreter.

translocation in genetics, the exchange of genetic material between chromosomes. It is responsible for congenital abnormalities, such as Down's syndrome.

transmission electron microscope (TEM) the most powerful type of ◊electron microscope, with a resolving power ten times better than that of a ◊scanning electron microscope and a thousand times better than that of an optical microscope. A fine electron beam passes through the specimen, which must therefore be sliced extremely thinly – typically to about one-thousandth of the thickness of a sheet of paper (100 nanometres). The TEM can resolve objects 0.001 micrometres (0.04 millionth of an inch) apart, a gap that is 100,000 times smaller than the unaided eye can see.

A TEM consists of a tall evacuated column at the top of which is a heated filament that emits electrons. The electrons are accelerated down the column by a high voltage (around 100,000 volts) and pass through the slice of specimen at a point roughly half-way down. Because the density of the specimen varies, the 'shadow' of the beam falls on a fluorescent screen near the bottom of the column and forms an image. A camera is mounted beneath the screen to record the image.

The electron beam is controlled by magnetic fields produced by electric coils, called electron lenses. One electron lens, called the condenser, controls the beam size and brightness before it strikes the specimen. Another electron lens, called the objective, focuses the beam on the specimen and magnifies the image about 50 times. Other electron lenses below the specimen then further magnify the image.

The **high voltage transmission electron microscope** (HVEM) uses voltages of up to 3 million volts to accelerate the electron beam. The largest of these instruments is as tall as a three-storey building.

The first experimental TEM was built in 1931 by German scientists Max Knoll and Ernest Ruska of the Technische Hochschule, Berlin, Germany. They produced a picture of a platinum grid magnified 117 times. The first commercial electron microscope was built in England in 1936.

transparency in photography, a picture on slide film. This captures the original in a positive image (direct reversal) and can be used for projection or printing on positive-to-positive print material, for example by the Cibachrome or Kodak R-type process.

Slide film is usually colour but can be obtained in black and white.

transpiration the loss of water from a plant by evaporation. Most water is lost from the leaves through pores known as ◊stomata, whose primary function is to allow ◊gas exchange between the plant's internal tissues and the atmosphere. Transpiration from the leaf surfaces causes a continuous upward flow of water from the roots via the ◊xylem, which is known as the transpiration stream.

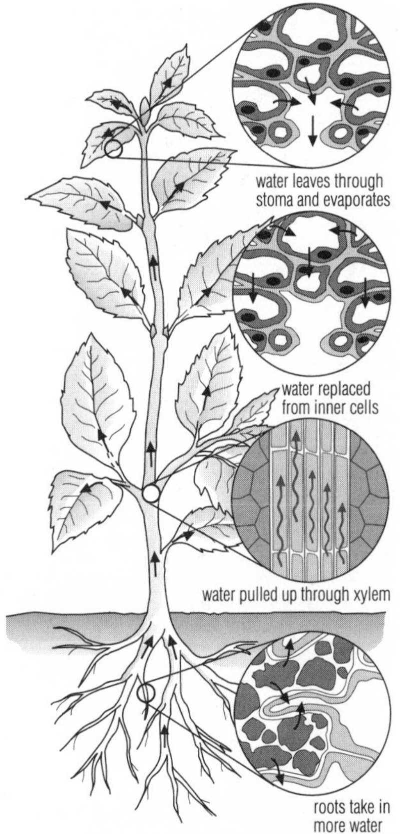
water leaves through stoma and evaporates
water replaced from inner cells
water pulled up through xylem
roots take in more water

***transpiration** The loss of water from a plant by evaporation is known as transpiration. Most of the water is lost through the surface openings, or stomata, on the leaves. The evaporation produces what is known as the transpiration stream, a tension that draws water up from the roots through the xylem, water-carrying vessels in the stem.*

transplant in medicine, the transfer of a tissue or organ from one human being to another or from one part of the body to another (skin grafting). In most organ transplants, the operation is for life-saving purposes, although the immune system tends to reject foreign tissue. Careful matching and immunosuppressive drugs must be used, but these are not always successful.

Corneal grafting, which may restore sight to a diseased or damaged eye, was pioneered in 1905, and is the oldest successful human transplant procedure. Of the internal organs, kidneys were first transplanted successfully in the early 1950s and remain most in demand. Modern transplantation also encompasses the heart, lungs, liver, pancreatic tissue, bone, and bone-marrow. In the USA 19,017 people received organ transplants in 1994.

Most transplant material is taken from cadaver donors, usually those suffering death of the ◊brainstem, or from frozen tissue

TRANSPLANTATION AND DONATION

http://monroe.mcit.med.umich.edu/trans/transweb/

This site includes organ and tissue transplantation and donation, the latest research developments, answers to commonly asked questions, and information about donation. It is supported by articles and reports from medical professionals.

Transplant: chronology

1682	A Russian doctor used bone from a dog to repair the skull of an injured nobleman. The graft was reportedly successful, though it angered the Russian Orthodox church.
1771	Scottish surgeon John Hunter describes his experiments in the transplantation of tissues, including a human tooth into a cock's comb in *Treatise on the Natural History of Human Teeth*
1905	Corneal grafting, which may restore sight to a diseased or damaged eye, was pioneered.
1950s	The kidneys were first transplanted successfully; kidney transplants were pioneered by British surgeon Roy Calne. Peter Medawar conducted vital research into the body's tolerance of transplanted organs and skin grafts.
1964	Chimpanzee kidneys were transplanted into humans in the USA, but with little success; in the UK a pig's heart valve was transplanted successfully and the operation became routine.
1967	South African surgeon Christiaan Barnard performed the first human heart transplant. The 54-year-old patient lived for 18 days.
1969	The world's first heart and lung transplant is performed at the Stanford Medical Centre, California, USA.
1970	The first successful nerve transplant is achieved in West Germany.
1978	Cyclosporin, an immunosuppressive drug derived from a fungus revolutionized transplant surgery by reducing the incidence and severity of rejection of donor organs.
1982	Jarvik 7, an artificial heart made of plastic and aluminium was transplanted; the recipient lived another 112 days.
1986	British surgeons John Wallwork and Roy Calne perform the first triple transplant – heart, lung, and liver – at Papworth Hospital, Cambridge, England.
1987	The world's longest-surviving heart-transplant patient died in France, 18 years after his operation. A three-year-old girl in the USA receives a new liver, pancreas, small intestine, and parts of the stomach and colon; the first successful five-organ transplant.
1989	Grafts of fetal brain tissue were first used to treat Parkinson's disease.
1990	Nobel Prize for Medicine or Physiology was awarded to two US surgeons, Donnall Thomas and Joseph Murray, for their pioneering work on organ and tissue transplantation.
1995	The first experiments to use genetically altered animal organs in humans were given US government approval July – genetically altered pig livers were attached to the circulatory systems of patients whose livers had failed. An AIDS patient received a bone marrow transplant from a baboon but the graft failed to take.
1997	Fetal nerve cells from pigs were injected into the brains of Parkinson's patients. In one case the cells survived for seven months.
1998	(23 June) Cultured human neural cells were injected into the brain of a stroke victim. This was the first transplant of brain tissue used in stroke treatment and the first use of cultured cells rather than fetal tissue.

banks. In rare cases, kidneys, corneas, and part of the liver may be obtained from living donors. Besides the shortage of donated material, the main problem facing transplant surgeons is rejection of the donated organ by the recipient's body. The 1990 Nobel Prize for Medicine or Physiology was awarded to two US surgeons, Donnall Thomas and Joseph Murray, for their pioneering work on organ and tissue transplantation.

The first experiments to use genetically altered animal organs in humans were given US government approval in July 1995 – genetically altered pig livers were attached to the circulatory systems of patients who were near death or whose livers had failed. Need for the tests had arisen due to a shortage of human organs available for transplant.

It is infinitely better to transplant a heart than to bury it to be eaten by worms.

CHRISTIAAN BARNARD South African surgeon. *Time* 31 October 1969

transposon or ***jumping gene*** segment of DNA able to move within or between chromosomes. Transposons trigger changes in gene expression by shutting off genes or causing insertion ◊mutations.

The origins of transposons are obscure, but geneticists believe some may be the remnants of viruses that have permanently integrated their genes with those of their hosts. They were first identified by US geneticist Barbara McClintock in 1947.

transputer in computing, a member of a family of microprocessors designed for parallel processing, developed in the UK by Inmos. In the circuits of a standard computer the processing of data takes place in sequence; in a transputer's circuits processing takes place in parallel, greatly reducing computing time for those programs that have been specifically written for it.

The transputer implements a special programming language called OCCAM, which Inmos based on CSP (communicating sequential processes), developed by C A R Hoare of Oxford University Computing Laboratory.

Though backed by the British government, Inmos was not commercially successful. It was taken over by UK company Thorn-EMI in 1984 and traded to the French–Italian electronics company SGS-Thomson in 1989.

transsexual person who identifies himself or herself completely with the opposite sex, believing that the wrong sex was assigned at birth. Unlike **transvestites**, who desire to dress in clothes traditionally worn by the opposite sex; transsexuals think and feel emotionally in a way typically considered appropriate to members of the opposite sex, and may undergo surgery to modify external sexual characteristics.

In 1995 Dutch researchers identified a structural difference between the brains of transsexual men and other men. Within the brain a small cluster of cells, the bed nucleus of the stria terminalis (BST), is smaller in women than men. Transsexual males in the study were found to have a female-sized BST. Research is continuing into the significance of this finding.

Trans-Siberian Railway the world's longest single-service railway, connecting the cities of European Russia with Omsk, Novosibirsk, Irkutsk, and Khabarovsk, and terminating at Nakhodka on the Pacific coast east of Vladivostok. The line was built between 1891 and 1915, and has a total length of 9,289 km/5,772 mi, from Moscow to Vladivostok.

The greater part of the Trans-Siberian Railway was completed in record time in the period 1891–99. The line opened up the regions of Siberia and the Far East to extensive Russian colonization. It also enabled large-scale geological prospecting of the Kuznetsk, Karaganda, Ekibastuz and Cheremkhovo coal basins and of the Amur and Kolyma gold deposits to be carried out, which laid the basis for the economic development of Siberia. The Trans-Mongolian Railway branches off at Lake Baikal and travels via the Mongolian capital Ulan-Bator to Beijing. At Tarskaya, almost 3,000 km west of Vladivostok, the Trans-Siberian meets the Trans-Manchurian Railway, which reaches Beijing via Harbin. A new northern rail route across Siberia, the Baikal–Amur Mainline (BAM), stretching 3,102 km/1,928 mi from Ust-Kut to the Pacific, was officially opened in 1991 after seventeen years' work.

transuranic element or ***transuranium element*** chemical element with an atomic number of 93 or more – that is, with a greater number of protons in the nucleus than has uranium. All transuranic elements are radioactive. Neptunium and plutonium are found in nature; the others are synthesized in nuclear reactions.

First Organ Transplants

BY PAULETTE PRATT

Although transplantation may sound wholly contemporary, it is not really all that new. The term 'transplant', for instance, is thought to have been coined by the renowned 18th-century Scottish surgeon John Hunter (1728–93) in describing animal experiments. The oldest transplant procedure is corneal grafting, pioneered by an eye surgeon called Eduard Zirm in the small town of Olmutz in Moravia in 1905.

Throughout the early years of this century experimentation continued in animals. An early pioneer was the French-American surgeon Alexis Carrel, working at the Rockefeller Institute in New York. Besides switching around dogs' hearts, he developed the techniques of surgical anastomosis – reconnecting severed blood vessels – which would be essential to major surgery in general and certainly to transplant operations.

Carrel received the Nobel prize for this work in 1912 and, two years later, informed the International Surgical Association: 'The surgical side of transplantation of organs is completed as we are now able to perform transplantation of organs with perfect ease... All our efforts must now be directed toward the biological methods which will prevent the reaction of the organism against foreign tissue.'

However, almost two decades were to pass before anyone tried transplanting organs in human beings. Between 1933 and 1939 the Russian surgeon Voronoy, working in the Ukraine, made six attempts to graft cadaver kidneys into very sick patients, all of which failed. Next, in 1946, US surgeons used a cadaver graft in a bid to save a patient who was in acute kidney failure due to septicaemia. This worked only in that the patient's own kidneys resumed their function within two days.

The major problem was that of rejection, the body's destructive response to 'foreign' tissue. Although the phenomenon was widely recognized by the mid 20th century, no one understood how it came about. So, in 1953, when surgeons in Paris made the first attempt at grafting a kidney from a living donor – mother to son – the organ functioned well for three weeks, until rejection set in.

Finally, the world's first truly successful organ transplant took place in December 1954, when surgeons at the Peter Bent Brigham Hospital in Boston opted for the only formula where rejection does not occur: a transplant between identical twins. They removed one of Robert Herrick's kidneys and grafted it into his brother, Richard, who was dying of kidney failure. Robert made an uneventful recovery and lived quite normally with a single kidney; Richard lived for a further eight years.

This historic operation established the procedure still in use today, whereby in most cases the non-functioning kidneys are left in place and the donor kidney is inserted in the recipient's lower abdomen, usually on the right-hand side; it is connected via the ureter to the bladder. Once the blood vessels are anastomosed (connected together) and circulation is established, the grafted kidney may begin producing urine before the surgeons have had time to close (though some may not function for several weeks).

However, following the success in Boston, further attempts at kidney grafting ended in failure, except in the case of identical twins. The survival rate hardly improved even when patients were exposed to total body irradiation to knock out the immune system and given anti-cancer drugs against rejection. Now, with their own body defences obliterated, most kidney recipients died from infection.

A number of developments in the early 1960s however, began to transform renal grafting from an experimental procedure into a viable option for end-stage kidney disease. First came the introduction of tissue typing – matching donor and recipient for compatibility in order to minimize the strength of the immune response. Then, in 1962, came the major breakthrough: the appearance of azathioprine, the first effective anti-rejection drug. The following year a steroid drug, prednisone, was added and the two-drug combination formed the basis of immunosuppressive treatment for many years.

Meanwhile, pioneering attempts to transplant other organs proved considerably more problematic. The first human being to undergo liver transplantation, a three-year-old boy with biliary atresia, died on the operating table in Denver, Colorado, in 1963. Few patients undergoing this formidable procedure – one of the most challenging in the entire surgical repertoire – survived in the early years.

In 1967, researchers at Stanford University in California, who had been experimenting with cardiac transplantation for years, were pipped at the post when the South African surgeon Christiaan Barnard performed the world's first human heart transplant. The patient, 54-year-old Louis Washkansky, seemed to spend most of the remaining 18 days of his life in front of television cameras before finally dying from pneumonia. Further attempts were made at various centres but the results were so disastrous that heart transplantation had to virtually be abandoned for more than a decade.

Still the twin spectres haunting the transplant scene were infection and rejection. It was very hard to get the formula right. Except in the case of kidney grafting, where there was the fall-back of dialysis, if organ recipients received insufficient immunosuppression they died of rejection; or, if the immune system was knocked out completely, they succumbed to infection. It was mainly the arrival of the powerful new anti-rejection drug cyclosporin – available from 1980 onwards – that transformed the picture.

Today there is a whole range of life-saving transplants available – kidney, liver, heart, lung(s), pancreas and small bowel. Except for kidney transplants, none of these procedures would be possible without the life-support technology developed over the last few decades. Ventilators, for instance, are used to maintain the brainstem-dead donors who are the main source of organs for grafting; the ventilator, too, sustains the recipient's breathing during and immediately after surgery. The heart–lung machine, introduced in 1953, is essential in major transplants where the recipient's own circulation has to be interrupted.

With all this high-profile activity, too often overlooked are the more humdrum grafts – of tissues such as skin, bone, joints, nerves and corneas – which can restore mobility, sensation or sight or prevent loss of a limb. Other than blood, bone is now the most frequently grafted tissue worldwide.

transverse wave ◊wave in which the displacement of the medium's particles is at right-angles to the direction of travel of the wave motion.

transverse wave The diagram illustrates the motion of a transverse wave. Light waves are examples of transverse waves: they undulate at right angles to the direction of travel and are characterized by alternating crests and troughs. Simple water waves, such as the ripples produced when a stone is dropped into a pond, are also examples of transverse waves.

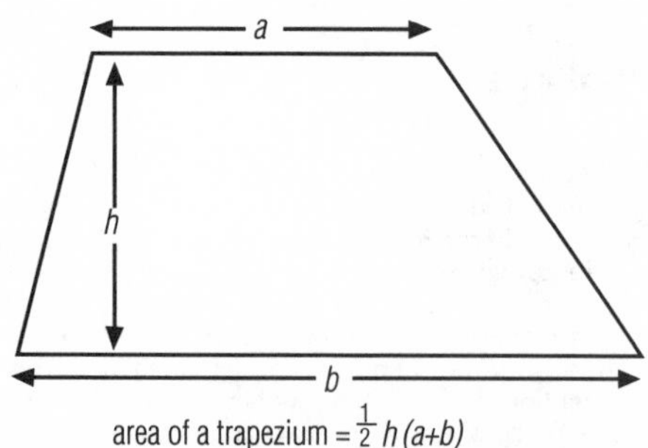

trapezium A trapezium is a four-sided plane figure with two of its sides parallel.

trapezium (US *trapezoid*) in geometry, a four-sided plane figure (quadrilateral) with two of its sides parallel. If the parallel sides have lengths a and b and the perpendicular distance between them is h (the height of the trapezium), its area $A = \frac{1}{2}h(a + b)$.

An isosceles trapezium has its sloping sides equal, and is symmetrical about a line drawn through the midpoints of its parallel sides.

travel graph type of ◊distance–time graph which shows the stages of a journey. Stops on the journey are shown as horizontal lines. Travel graphs can be used to find out where vehicles will overtake each other or meet if travelling in opposite directions.

travel sickness nausea and vomiting caused by the motion of cars, boats, or other forms of transport. Constant vibration and movement may stimulate changes in the fluid of the semicircular canals (responsible for balance) of the inner ear, to which the individual fails to adapt, and to which are added visual and psychological factors. Some proprietary remedies contain ◊antihistamine drugs.

Space sickness is a special case: in weightless conditions normal body movements result in unexpected and unfamiliar signals to the brain. Astronauts achieve some control of symptoms by wedging themselves in their bunks.

tree perennial plant with a woody stem, usually a single stem (trunk), made up of ◊wood and protected by an outer layer of ◊bark. It absorbs water through a ◊root system. There is no clear dividing line between shrubs and trees, but sometimes a minimum achievable height of 6 m/20 ft is used to define a tree.

angiosperms A treelike form has evolved independently many times in different groups of plants. Among the ◊angiosperms, or flowering plants, most trees are ◊dicotyledons. This group includes trees such as oak, beech, ash, chestnut, lime, and maple, and they are often referred to as broad-leaved trees because their leaves are broader than those of conifers, such as pine and spruce. In temperate regions angiosperm trees are mostly ◊deciduous (that is, they lose their leaves in winter), but in the tropics most angiosperm trees are evergreen. There are fewer trees among the ◊monocotyledons, but the palms and bamboos (some of which are treelike) belong to this group.

gymnosperms The ◊gymnosperms include many trees and they are classified into four orders: Cycadales (including cycads and sago palms), Coniferales (the conifers), Ginkgoales (including only one living species, the ginkgo, or maidenhair tree), and Taxales (including yews). Apart from the ginkgo and the larches (conifers), most gymnosperm trees are evergreen.

tree ferns There are also a few living trees in the ◊pteridophyte group, known as tree ferns. In the swamp forests of the Carboniferous era, 300 million years ago, there were giant treelike horsetails and club mosses in addition to the tree ferns.

oldest trees The world's oldest living trees are found in the Pacific forest of North America, some more than 2,000 years old.

tree-and-branch filing system in computing, a filing system where all files are stored within directories, like folders in a filing cabinet. These directories may in turn be stored within further directories. The root directory contains all the other directories and may be thought of as equivalent to the filing cabinet. Another way of picturing the system is as a tree with branches from which grow smaller branches, ending in leaves (individual files).

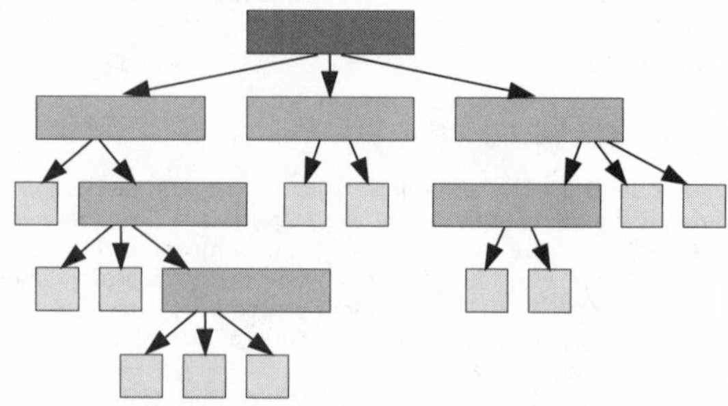

tree-and-branch filing system The directory filing structure used by computers. The structure can be likened to an upside-down tree, with the root at the top, branching downwards and outwards into sub-directories.

tree creeper small, short-legged bird of the family Certhiidae, which spirals with a mouselike movement up tree trunks searching for food with its thin down-curved beak.

The **common tree creeper** *Certhia familiaris* is 12 cm/5 in long, brown above, white below, and is found across Europe, N Asia, and North America.

tree diagram in probability theory, a branching diagram consisting only of arcs and nodes (but not loops curving back on themselves), which is used to establish probabilities.

tree rings rings visible in the wood of a cut tree; see ◊annual rings.

trefoil any of several ◊clover plants of a group belonging to the pea family, the leaves of which are divided into three leaflets. The name is also used for other plants with leaves divided into three lobes. (Genus *Trifolium*, family Leguminosae.)

Bird's-foot trefoil *Lotus corniculatus*, also belonging to the pea family, is a low-growing perennial found in grassy places throughout Europe, N Asia, parts of Africa, and Australia. It has five leaflets to each leaf, but the first two are bent back so it appears to have only three. The yellow flowers, often tinged orange or red, are borne in heads with only a few blooms. Hop trefoil *T. campestre* has leaves with only three leaflets and tight-packed round heads of yellow flowers about 1.5 cm/0.6 in across. It also grows in grassy places throughout Europe, W Asia, N Africa, and North America. In Australia, Austral trefoil *Lotus australis* is a widespread native with pink or white flowers. It is suspected of being poisonous.

trematode parasitic flatworm with an oval non-segmented body, of the class Trematoda, including the ◊fluke.

tremor minor ◊earthquake.

trepang ◊sea cucumbers used as food.

triangle in geometry, a three-sided plane figure, the sum of whose interior angles is 180°. Triangles can be classified by the relative lengths of their sides. A **scalene triangle** has three sides of unequal length; an **isosceles triangle** has at least two equal sides; an **equilateral triangle** has three equal sides (and three equal angles of 60°).

triangle of forces method of calculating the force (the resultant) produced by two other forces. It is based on the fact that if three forces acting at a point can be represented by the sides of a triangle, the forces are in equilibrium. See ◊parallelogram of forces.

triangulation technique used in surveying and navigation to determine distances, using the properties of the triangle. To begin, surveyors measure a certain length exactly to provide a base line. From each end of this line they then measure the angle to a distant point, using a ◊theodolite. They now have a triangle in which they know the length of one side and the two adjacent angles. By simple trigonometry they can work out the lengths of the other two sides.

To make a complete survey of the region, they repeat the process, building on the first triangle.

Triassic period of geological time 245–208 million years ago, the first period of the Mesozoic era. The continents were fused together to form the world continent ◊Pangaea. Triassic sediments contain remains of early dinosaurs and other reptiles now extinct. By late Triassic times, the first mammals had evolved.

tribology the science of friction, lubrication, and lubricants. It studies the origin of frictional forces, the wearing of interacting surfaces, and the problems of efficient lubrication.

tributyl tin (TBT) chemical used in antifouling paints on ships' hulls and other submarine structures to deter the growth of barnacles. The tin dissolves in sea water and enters the food chain. It can cause reproductive abnormalities – exposed female whelks develop penises; the use of TBT has therefore been banned in many countries, including the UK.

triceratops any of a genus *Triceratops* of massive, horned dinosaurs of the order Ornithischia. They had three horns and a neck frill and were up to 8 m/25 ft long; they lived in the Cretaceous period.

trichloromethane technical name for ◊chloroform.

triconodonta one of the oldest orders of fossil mammals. Triconodonts lived in Jurassic times and were small in size. They had a characteristic dentition, with each tooth bearing three conical cusps.

tricuspid valve flap of tissue situated on the right side of the ◊heart between the atrium and the ventricle. It prevents blood flowing backwards when the ventricle contracts.

As in all valves, its movements are caused by pressure changes during the beat rather than by any intrinsic muscular activity. As the valve snaps shut, a vibration passes through the chest cavity and is detectable as the first sound of the heartbeat.

triggerfish any marine bony fish of the family Balistidae, with a laterally compressed body, up to 60 cm/2 ft long, and a deep belly. They have small mouths but strong jaws and teeth. The first spine on the dorsal fin locks into an erect position, allowing them to fasten themselves securely in crevices for protection; it can only be moved by depressing the smaller third ('trigger') spine.

There are many species, found mainly in warm waters, and some are very colourful.

trigger plant any of a group of grasslike plants, with most species occurring in Australia. Flowers of the trigger plant are fertilized by insects trapped by a touch-sensitive column within the flower. In struggling to free themselves, the insects become covered in pollen, which they then spread to other flowers after escaping. (Genus *Stylidium*, family Stylidiaceae.)

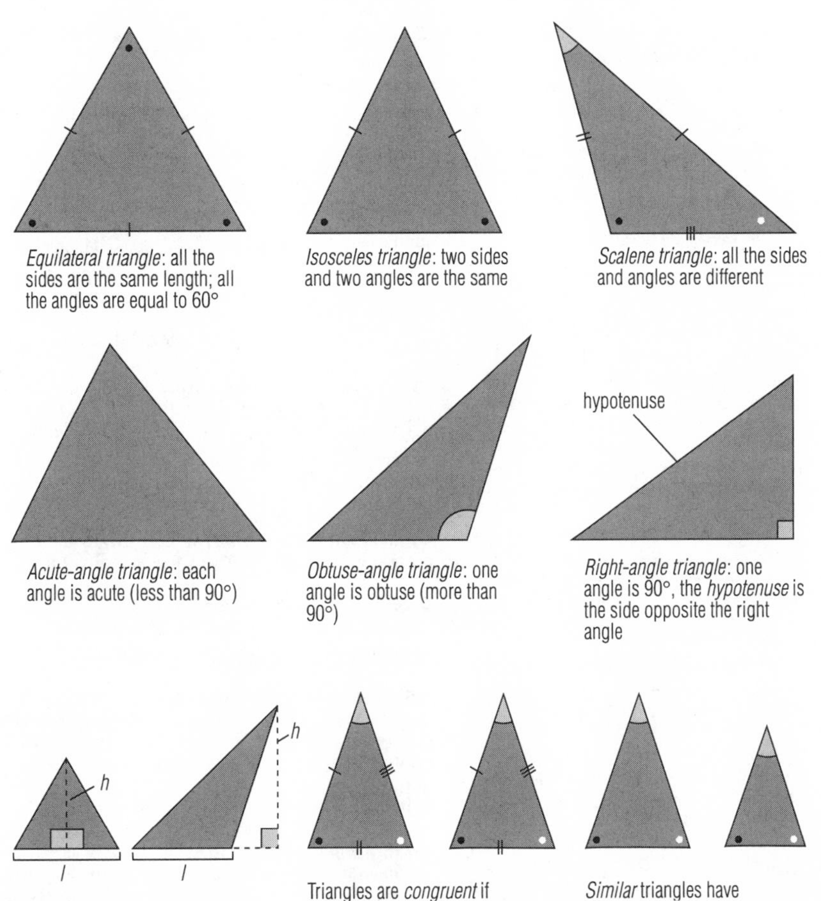
Equilateral triangle: all the sides are the same length; all the angles are equal to 60°
Isosceles triangle: two sides and two angles are the same
Scalene triangle: all the sides and angles are different
Acute-angle triangle: each angle is acute (less than 90°)
Obtuse-angle triangle: one angle is obtuse (more than 90°)
hypotenuse
Right-angle triangle: one angle is 90°, the *hypotenuse* is the side opposite the right angle
h
h
l
l
Triangles are *congruent* if
Similar triangles have

triangle *Types of triangle.*

triglyceride chemical name for ◊fat comprising three fatty acids reacted with a glycerol.

trigonometry branch of mathematics that solves problems relating to plane and spherical triangles. Its principles are based on the fixed proportions of sides for a particular angle in a right-angled triangle, the simplest of which are known as the ◊sine, ◊cosine, and ◊tangent (so-called trigonometrical ratios). Trigonometry is of practical importance in navigation, surveying, and simple harmonic motion in physics.

Using trigonometry, it is possible to calculate the lengths of the sides and the sizes of the angles of a right-angled triangle as long as one angle and the length of one side are known, or the lengths of two sides. The longest side, which is always opposite to the right angle, is called the **hypotenuse**. The other sides are named depending their position relating to the angle that is to be found or used: the side opposite this angle is always termed **opposite** and that adjacent is the **adjacent**. So the following trigonometrical ratios are used:

$$\text{sine} = \frac{\text{opposite}}{\text{hypotenuse}}$$

$$\text{cosine} = \frac{\text{adjacent}}{\text{hypotenuse}}$$

$$\text{tangent} = \frac{\text{opposite}}{\text{adjacent}}$$

TRIGONOMETRIC FUNCTIONS

http://www-history.mcs.st-and.ac.uk/~history/HistTopics/Trigonometric_functions.html

History of the development of the trigonometric functions in mathematics. The site also explains the basic principles of the use of these functions and details the role they have played in the advancement of other branches of mathematics. Biographical details of the mathematicians chiefly responsible for the discovery of trigonometry are also available here.

triiodomethane technical name for ◊iodoform.

trillium any of a group of perennial herbaceous woodland plants belonging to the lily family, native to Asia and North America. They have a circle, or whorl, of three leaves around the stem, at the end of which the single flower has three green ◊sepals and three usually maroon or white petals. The nodding trillium *T. cernuum* ranges across most of the eastern half of North America. (Genus *Trillium*, family Liliaceae.)

trilobite any of a large class (Trilobita) of extinct, marine, invertebrate arthropods of the Palaeozoic era, with a flattened, oval body, 1–65 cm/0.4–26 in long. The hard-shelled body was divided by two deep furrows into three lobes. There existed more than 1,500 genera of trilobites.

Some were burrowers, others were swimming and floating forms. Their worldwide distribution, many species, and the immense quantities of their remains make them useful in geological dating.

Trinitron in computing, ◊monitor based on a ◊cathode-ray tube developed by ◊Sony, designed to give a sharper image and more uniform brightness than conventional monitors.

triode three-electrode thermionic ◊valve containing an anode and a cathode (as does a ◊diode) with an additional negatively biased control grid. Small variations in voltage on the grid bias result in

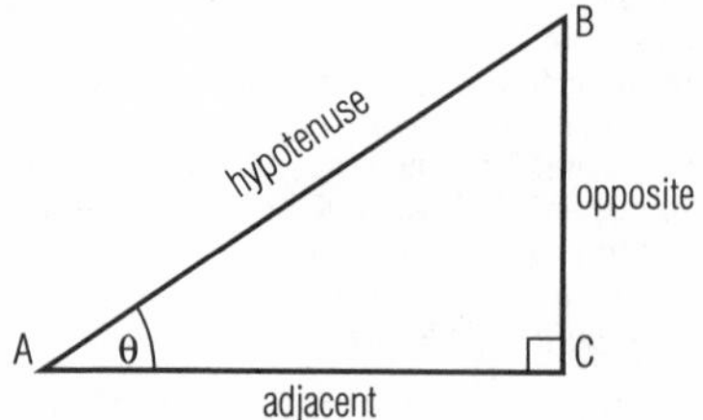

for any right-angled triangle with angle θ as shown the trigonometrical ratios are

$$\sin(e)\,\theta = \frac{BC}{AB} = \frac{\text{opposite}}{\text{hypotenuse}}$$

$$\cos\theta = \frac{AC}{AB} = \frac{\text{adjacent}}{\text{hypotenuse}}$$

$$\tan\theta = \frac{BC}{AC} = \frac{\text{opposite}}{\text{adjacent}}$$

trigonometry *At its simplest level, trigonometry deals with the relationships between the sides and angles of triangles. Unknown angles or lengths are calculated by using trigonometrical ratios such as sine, cosine, and tangent. The earliest applications of trigonometry were in the fields of navigation, surveying, and astronomy, and usually involved working out an inaccessible distance such as the distance of the Earth from the Moon.*

large variations in the current. The triode was commonly used in amplifiers but has now been almost entirely superseded by the ◊transistor.

triple bond three covalent bonds between adjacent atoms, as in the ◊alkynes (–C ≡ C–).

triple nose-leaf bat one of many threatened bats in Africa, *Triaenops persicus* is found scattered along much of the coastal regions of E Africa and faces threats from disturbance of the caves in which it breeds. Tourism development, resulting in disturbance to coral caves which the bats inhabit, is a particular problem.

triploblastic in biology, having a body wall composed of three layers. The outer layer is the **ectoderm**, the middle layer the **mesoderm**, and the inner layer the **endoderm**. This pattern of development is shown by most multicellular animals (including humans).

triticale cereal crop of recent origin that is a cross between wheat *Triticum* and rye *Secale*. It can produce heavy yields of high-protein grain, principally for use as animal feed.

tritium radioactive isotope of hydrogen, three times as heavy as ordinary hydrogen, consisting of one proton and two neutrons. It has a half-life of 12.5 years.

Triton in astronomy, the largest of Neptune's moons. It has a diameter of 2,700 km/1,680 mi, and orbits Neptune every 5.88 days in a retrograde (east to west) direction. It takes the same time to rotate about its own axis as it does to make one revolution of Neptune.

It is slightly larger than the planet Pluto, which it is thought to resemble in composition and appearance. Probably Triton was formerly a separate body like Pluto but was captured by Neptune. Triton was discovered in 1846 by British astronomer William Lassell (1799–1880) only weeks after the discovery of Neptune. Triton's surface, as revealed by the *Voyager 2* space probe, has a temperature of 38K (–235°C/–391°F), making it the coldest known place in the solar system. It is covered with frozen nitrogen and methane, some of which evaporates to form a tenuous atmosphere with a pressure only 0.00001 that of the Earth at sea level. Triton has a pink south polar cap, probably coloured by the effects of solar radiation on methane ice. Dark streaks on Triton are thought to be formed by geysers of liquid nitrogen. The surface has few impact craters (the largest is the Mazomba, with a diameter of 27 km/17 mi), indicating that many of the earlier craters have been erased by the erupting and freezing of water (cryovulcanism).

trogon Greek *trogein* 'to gnaw' any species of the family Trogonidae, order Trogoniformes, of tropical birds, up to 50 cm/1.7 ft long, with resplendent plumage, living in the Americas, Africa, and Asia. They are primarily birds of forest or woodland, living in trees. Their diet consists mainly of insects and other arthropods, and sometimes berries and other fruit. Most striking is the ◊quetzal.

troilite FeS, probable mineral of the Earth's core, abundant in meteorites.

Trojan in computing, a program that looks as though it will do something entertaining or useful but actually does something else, such as reformatting the user's hard disc. Trojans are named after the Trojan horse in Greek mythology. A virus is not a Trojan, but inserting a virus into another program – such as virus checker – would make that program a Trojan.

trolling in computing, mischievously posting a deliberately erroneous or obtuse message to a ◊newsgroup in order to tempt others to reply – usually in a way that makes them appear gullible, intemperate or foolish.

tropical cyclone another term for ◊hurricane.

tropical disease any illness found mainly in hot climates. The most important tropical diseases worldwide are ◊malaria, ◊leishmaniasis, ◊sleeping sickness, lymphatic filiarasis, and schistosomiasis. Other major scourges are ◊Chagas's disease, leprosy, and river blindness. Malaria kills about 1.5 million people each year, and produces chronic anaemia and tiredness in 100 times as many, while schistosomiasis is responsible for 1 million deaths a year. All the main tropical diseases are potentially curable, but the facilities for diagnosis and treatment are rarely adequate in the countries where they occur.

tropics the area between the tropics of Cancer and Capricorn, defined by the parallels of latitude approximately 23°30' N and S of the Equator. They are the limits of the area of Earth's surface in which the Sun can be directly overhead. The mean monthly temperature is over 20°C/68°F.

Climates within the tropics lie in parallel bands. Along the Equator is the intertropical convergence zone, characterized by high temperatures and year-round heavy rainfall. Tropical rainforests are found here. Along the tropics themselves lie the tropical high-pressure zones, characterized by descending dry air and desert conditions. Between these, the conditions vary seasonally between wet and dry, producing the tropical grasslands.

tropine $C_8H_{15}NO$ poisonous crystalline solid formed by the hydrolysis of the ◊alkaloid atropine.

tropism or ***tropic movement*** the directional growth of a plant, or part of a plant, in response to an external stimulus such as gravity or light. If the movement is directed towards the stimulus it is described as positive; if away from it, it is negative. **Geotropism** for example, the response of plants to gravity, causes the root (positively geotropic) to grow downwards, and the stem (negatively geotropic) to grow upwards.

Phototropism occurs in response to light, **hydrotropism** to water, **chemotropism** to a chemical stimulus, and **thigmotropism**, or **haptotropism**, to physical contact, as in the tendrils of climbing plants when they touch a support and then grow around it.

Tropic movements are the result of greater rate of growth on one side of the plant organ than the other. Tropism differs from a ◊nastic movement in being influenced by the direction of the stimulus.

troposphere lower part of the ◊Earth's atmosphere extending about 10.5 km/6.5 mi from the Earth's surface, in which temperature decreases with height to about –60°C/–76°F except in local layers of temperature inversion. The **tropopause** is the upper boundary of the troposphere, above which the temperature increases slowly with height within the atmosphere. All of the Earth's weather takes place within the troposphere.

trout any of various bony fishes in the salmon family, popular for sport and food, usually speckled and found mainly in fresh water. They are native to the northern hemisphere. Trout have thick bodies and blunt heads, and vary in colour. The common trout *Salmo trutta* is widely distributed in Europe, occurring in British fresh and coastal waters. Sea trout are generally silvery and river trout olive-brown, both with spotted fins and sides.

In the USA, the name 'trout' is given to various species, notably to the rainbow trout *S. gairdneri,* which has been naturalized in many other countries.

Troy (Latin ***Ilium***) ancient city (now Hissarlik or Hisarlih in Turkey) of Asia Minor, just S of the Dardanelles, besieged in the legendary ten-year Trojan War (mid-13th century BC), as described in Homer's *Iliad.* According to the legend, the city fell to the Greeks, who first used the stratagem of leaving behind, in a feigned retreat, a large wooden horse containing armed infiltrators to open the city's gates. Believing it to be a religious offering, the Trojans took it within the walls.

Nine cities found one beneath another were originally excavated by Heinrich Schliemann 1874–90. Recent research suggests that the seventh, sacked and burned about 1250 BC, is probably the Homeric Troy, which was succeeded by a shanty town which was sacked after 800 BC. The later city of Ilium was built on the same site in the 7th century BC, and survived to the Roman period. It has been suggested that Homer's tale of war might have a basis in fact, for example, a conflict arising from trade rivalry (Troy was on a tin trade route), which might have been triggered by such an incident as Paris running off with Helen. The wooden horse may have been a votive offering for Poseidon (whose emblem was a horse) left behind by the Greeks after an earthquake had opened breaches in the city walls.

troy system system of units used for precious metals and gems. The pound troy (0.37 kg) consists of 12 ounces (each of 120 carats) or 5,760 grains (each equal to 65 mg).

TrueType scalable font system, jointly developed by Apple and Microsoft. It allows scalable fonts to be used by non-PostScript printers. Such printers are usually cheaper.

truffle any of a group of underground fungi (see ◊fungus), certain of which are highly valued as edible delicacies; in particular, the species *Tuber melanosporum,* generally found growing under oak trees. It is native to the Périgord region of France but is cultivated in other areas as well. It is rounded, blackish-brown, externally covered with warts, and has blackish flesh. (Order Tuberales.)

Dogs and pigs are traditionally used to sniff out truffles, but in 1990 an artificial 'nose' developed at the University of Manchester Institute of Science and Technology, England, proved more effective in tests in Bordeaux.

Trumpet in computing, popular shareware ◊TCP/IP program for Windows or ◊MS-DOS.

trumpeter any South American bird of the genus *Psophia,* family Psophiidae, order Gruiformes, up to 50 cm/20 in tall, related to the cranes. Trumpeters have long legs, a short bill, and dark plumage. The trumpeter ◊swan is unrelated.

P. crepitans is a bird of lustrous and brilliantly-coloured plumage and is often domesticated. There are three species; very little is known about any of them in the wild.

Tropical Diseases (and How to Avoid Them)

BY KEITH WALLBANKS

The concept of 'tropical disease' first arose when Victorian Europeans explored the tropics and encountered diseases, in areas such as the 'white man's grave' in West Africa, with which they were unfamiliar. However, it now usually encompasses all the diseases of the tropics, including those, such as tuberculosis, which are also common in temperate regions.

It is difficult for most of us to grasp the impact of tropical diseases on the human race because the numbers are so large. Of the 52 million deaths in 1996, for example, 40 million occurred in the developing world and 17 million of these (nearly three times the number killed by cancers worldwide) were caused by infectious or parasitic disease. Such disease accounts for 45% of all deaths in developing countries, compared with just over 1% in the rest of the world.

Disease in the tropics may be caused by poor nutrition, environmental factors and/or by living organisms such as fungi (ringworm, athlete's foot), viruses (polio, hepatitis A and B, yellow fever, some forms of meningitis), bacteria (travellers' diarrhoea, typhoid, cholera, tetanus, tuberculosis, leprosy, legionnaires' disease, other forms of meningitis), the single-celled organisms known as protozoa (malaria, sleeping sickness, amoebic dysentery, Chagas's disease, leishmaniasis) and the worms known as nematodes (elephantiasis, river blindness, Guinea worm, hookworm, *Strongyloides*), trematodes (bilharzia) and cestodes (tapeworms, hydatid disease). Each of the living organisms has to get below the surface of the skin to survive. Some of the fungi live in the keratin just below the surface but the other pathogens need to get deeper, often into the bloodstream or gut. Several of them (the bacteria causing typhoid, cholera, other causes of diarrhoea, the amoebae causing dysentery, the *Ascaris* roundworm, Guinea worm, hepatitis A virus and tapeworms) rely on us to swallow them in food or water or to ingest them accidentally as we touch our mouths with unclean hands. Other pathogens (some hepatitis B and human immunodeficiency viruses (HIV)) rely on openings in the skin, caused by accident or injection, to gain access to the bloodstream, although HIV, hepatitis B and gonorrhoea are mainly spread by sexual contact between men and women. As 30% of the populations of some towns in the tropics now carry HIV, sex (particularly unprotected sex) with a new partner is a life-threatening gamble. The bacteria causing tuberculosis are drawn into our lungs from the air and those causing leprosy are mostly passed on in sneezes. A few parasites have stages in their life cycles which simply burrow into our skin, either from the soil (hookworm, *Strongyloides*) or water (bilharzia). Some of the most successful parasites of humans (those causing malaria, sleeping sickness, river blindness, elephantiasis, yellow fever and leishmaniasis) spend part of their life cycle in insects (called the vectors of the pathogens) which distribute the parasites and later transmit them to humans as the insects feed. The parasites causing malaria and elephantiasis use mosquitoes in this way, the nematodes of river blindness use blackflies (which breed in rivers, hence the name) and the trypanosomes of sleeping sickness and Chagas's disease use tsetse flies and bugs, respectively. Clean insects acquire the parasites when they feed on an infected individual. Most of the parasites do not simply use the vectors for distribution but also multiply and develop within them, the vectors acting as intermediate hosts of the parasites and humans as the definitive hosts. Freshwater snails act as the intermediate hosts of the schistosomes causing bilharzia, and pork and beef tapeworms use pigs and cattle, respectively, in a similar way.

Malaria remains one of the most important human parasitic diseases. More than two-fifths of the world's population live in the 100 countries where transmission of malaria occurs and there are about 400 million clinical cases of malaria each year (1.5–2.7 million of them fatal). Human malaria may be caused by any of four species: *Plasmodium falciparum*, *Plasmodium vivax* and the rarer *Plasmodium ovale* and *Plasmodium malariae*. Although only one of these species (*P. falciparum*) causes fatal infections, it is this species which is the most common and widespread, being present in 92 of the 100 countries were malaria transmission occurs. In fact, *P. falciparum* may cause more illness and deaths in humans than any other pathogen on Earth.

The malarial parasite injected by a feeding mosquito passes to the liver and multiplies there for a week or two. It then emerges, invades the red blood cells and multiplies again until the blood cells rupture and the released parasites invade more cells. It is the rupture of the infected red cells, which occurs more or less at the same time (every 2–3 days), that causes the first symptom of malaria: intermittent fever. After a while, some of the parasites breaking out of the blood cells develop into the sexual forms which are capable of infecting mosquitoes. Liver and kidney failure, severe anaemia, convulsions, coma and/or death may develop in falciparum malaria. As malarial parasites in the liver are not affected by the majority of anti-malarial drugs in the bloodstream, any traveller who is infected in the last few days of their trip returns home with viable parasites. All travellers at risk of malaria must therefore continue to take anti-malarials for 4 weeks after leaving a malarious area, so that parasites emerging from the liver to infect the blood cells are killed. Two species causing human malaria (*P. vivax* and *P. ovale*) have special stages, called hypnozoites, which can lie dormant in the liver for months and sometimes years, and cause attacks of malaria when they eventually become active.

The relationship between an individual's natural resistance to disease (their level of immunity) and the severity of their suffering is an important one. Those who live in countries where tropical diseases are common are often exposed to the diseases many times and those that survive may have high levels of immunity to them. One individual infected with *P. falciparum* may stay healthy whereas another, infected in exactly the same way but without any immunity to the infection, may die within 24 h. This is why a traveller to such countries may suffer when all around appear healthy.

The recent increase in the numbers of visitors to the tropics has meant that more of those from the developed world are putting themselves at risk of acquiring a tropical disease and of taking it home. Although there is usually little risk of the returned traveller passing on their disease, there is a major risk that it will not be diagnosed or treated correctly, simply because local physicians are unfamiliar with its signs and symptoms or fail to consider it. The symptoms and signs of malaria are so non-specific that local physicians often take them to indicate influenza or gastritis unless the sick traveller mentions that they have visited a malarious area in the last year or more. Of those returning to the UK or USA and eventually dying of falciparum malaria, for example, almost 50% are misdiagnosed as cases of influenza or of another viral infection when first examined by their physicians. Fatal infectious or parasitic disease is fortunately rare in travellers to the tropics and accounts for only a small proportion of deaths in this group (most of the deaths are caused by accidents, especially road traffic accidents, while the travellers are drunk or by cardiovascular disease in the older traveller). The commonest afflictions the traveller to a developing country is likely to suffer are, in descending frequency, sunburn, diarrhoea and vomiting (usually caused by *Escherichia coli* and of a few days' duration), malaria, acute infection of the respiratory tract (with fever) and hepatitis A. The chances of acquiring some of the perhaps better known diseases, such as leprosy, are virtually nil.

Anyone from a temperate country planning to visit a tropical country can take many steps to reduce their chances of developing a health problem as a result (prevention is always better than cure, particularly when the disease involved may be rapidly fatal and difficult to treat). It is important to be aware of the risks and how to avoid or minimize them. People should educate themselves by contacting local travel health clinics, reading recent guides or exploring the World Wide Web; one of the best Web sites on travel health is run by the 'Centers for Disease Control' in the USA (**http://www.cdc.gov**). Just in case a severe problem arises, travel insurance should be enough to cover the expenses of repatriation. Travellers must take appropriate advice on what drugs and other measures they should take to protect themselves against malaria. As the malarial parasites continue to develop resistance to the drugs used against them, it is important to seek up-to-date information on the best drug or drugs to use in any particular area. Use of a bednet (preferably one impregnated with insecticide), keeping the skin covered and using an insect repellent (preferably one containing DEET) and insecticides (in mosquito coils or from electronic vaporizers) not only reduces the risk of being bitten by mosquitoes carrying malarial parasites but also limits the nuisance and loss of sleep caused by other biting insects. It is possible to be vaccinated against several tropical diseases (hepatitis A and B, yellow fever, polio, typhoid) before travel. Every traveller should be immunized against tetanus but the most common cholera vaccine is no longer generally recommended as it is not very effective (a new, more effective one is now on the market). As vaccination may take several weeks it is important to seek health advice early. Once in the tropics, personal hygiene is important and care should be taken with any food or drink. Any food should be cooked adequately and preferably eaten immediately after cooking (shellfish, ice cream and any raw foods, including salads and unpasteurized milk, are particularly hazardous). Any water to be drunk, if from a local source, is best boiled or sterilized chemically. Skin contact with fresh water should be avoided as much as possible as the water may contain the schistosome stages (cercariae) which can burrow into skin and lying directly on sand or walking barefoot should also be avoided. Most bouts of diarrhoea only last a few days even if untreated, but plenty of safe fluids should be drunk (and the use of oral rehydration salts which can be bought and taken with the traveller should also be considered) to prevent dehydration. Ice cubes (which may be made with contaminated water) are best avoided.

truncation error in computing, an ◊error that occurs when a decimal result is cut off (truncated) after the maximum number of places allowed by the computer's level of accuracy.

truth table in electronics, a diagram showing the effect of a particular ◊logic gate on every combination of inputs.

Every possible combination of inputs and outputs for a particular gate or combination of gates is described, thereby defining their action in full. When logic value 1 is written in the table, it indicates a 'high' (or 'yes') input of perhaps 5 volts; logic value 0 indicates a 'low' (or 'no') input of 0 volts.

trypanosomiasis any of several debilitating long-term diseases caused by a trypanosome (protozoan of the genus *Trypanosoma*). They include sleeping sickness in Africa, transmitted by the bites of ◊tsetse flies, and ◊Chagas's disease in Central and South America, spread by assassin bugs.

Trypanosomes can live in the bloodstream of humans and other vertebrates. Millions of people are affected in warmer regions of the world; the diseases also affect cattle, horses, and wild animals, which form a reservoir of infection.

trypsin an enzyme in the vertebrate gut responsible for the digestion of protein molecules. It is secreted by the pancreas but in an inactive form known as trypsinogen. Activation into working trypsin occurs only in the small intestine, owing to the action of another enzyme enterokinase, secreted by the wall of the duodenum. Unlike the digestive enzyme pepsin, found in the stomach, trypsin does not require an acid environment.

tsetse fly any of a number of blood-feeding African flies of the genus *Glossina*, some of which transmit the disease nagana to cattle and sleeping sickness to human beings. Tsetse flies may grow up to 1.5 cm/0.6 in long.

There are 22 species of tsetse fly in sub-Saharan Africa.

TSR abbreviation for ◊terminate and stay resident.

tsunami (Japanese 'harbour wave') ocean wave generated by vertical movements of the sea floor resulting from ◊earthquakes or volcanic activity. Unlike waves generated by surface winds, the entire depth of water is involved in the wave motion. In the open ocean the tsunami takes the form of several successive waves, rarely in excess of 1 m/3 ft in height but travelling at speeds of 650–800 kph/400–500 mph. In the coastal shallows tsunamis slow down and build up producing huge swells over 15 m/45 ft high in some cases and over 30 m/90 ft in rare instances. The waves sweep inland causing great loss of life and property. On 26 May 1983, an earthquake in the Pacific Ocean caused tsunamis up to 14 m/42 ft high, which killed 104 people along the western coast of Japan near Minehama, Honshu.

Before each wave there may be a sudden withdrawal of water from the beach. Used synonymously with tsunami, the popular term 'tidal wave' is misleading: tsunamis are not caused by the gravitational forces that affect ◊tides.

TSUNAMI!

http://www.geophys.washington.edu/tsunami/intro.html

Description of many aspects of tsunamis. Included are details on how a tsunami is generated and how it propagates, how they have affected humans, and how people in coastal areas are warned about them. The site also discusses if and how you may protect yourself from a tsunami and provides 'near real-time' tsunami information bulletins.

TTL abbreviation for ◊transistor–transistor logic, **a family of integrated circuits**.

TTY in computing, contraction of teletype.

tuatara lizardlike reptile of the genus *Sphenodon*. It grows up to 70 cm/2.3 ft long, is greenish black, and has a spiny crest down its back. On the top of its head is the ◊pineal body, or so-called 'third eye', linked to the brain, which probably acts as a kind of light meter. It is the sole survivor of the reptilian order Rhynchocephalia. It lays eggs in burrows that it shares with seabirds, and has the longest incubation period of all reptiles (up to 15 months).

S. punctatus is found on about 30 small islands off New Zealand, whereas *S. guntheri* has survived on one island only, and numbers around 300 individuals. In an attempt to found a second colony of *S. guntheri*, 50 4–6 year olds, reared in semi-natural captivity, along with 20 adults from the existing population, were released on to a new island November 1995.

tuber swollen region of an underground stem or root, usually modified for storing food. The potato is a **stem tuber**, as shown by the presence of terminal and lateral buds, the 'eyes' of the potato. **Root tubers**, for example dahlias, developed from ◊adventitious roots (growing from the stem, not from other roots) lack these. Both types of tuber can give rise to new individuals and so provide a means of ◊vegetative reproduction.

Unlike a bulb, a tuber persists for one season only; new tubers developing on a plant in the following year are formed in different places. See also ◊rhizome.

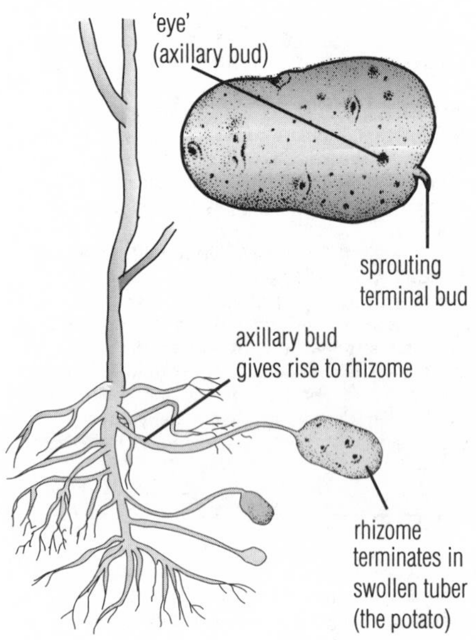

tuber *Tubers are produced underground from stems, as in the potato, or from roots, as in the dahlia. Tubers can grow into new plants.*

tuberculosis (TB) formerly known as ***consumption*** or ***phthisis*** infectious disease caused by the bacillus *Mycobacterium tuberculosis.* It takes several forms, of which pulmonary tuberculosis is by far the most common. A vaccine, ◊BCG, was developed around 1920 and the first antituberculosis drug, streptomycin, in 1944. The bacterium is mostly kept in check by the body's immune system; about 5% of those infected develop the disease. Treatment of patients with a combination of anti-TB medicines for 6–8 months produces a cure rate of 80%.

In pulmonary TB, a patch of inflammation develops in the lung, with formation of an abscess. Often, this heals spontaneously, leaving only scar tissue. The dangers are of rapid spread through both lungs (what used to be called 'galloping consumption') or the development of miliary tuberculosis (spreading in the bloodstream to other sites) or tuberculous ◊meningitis.

Over the last 15 years there has been a sharp resurgence in countries where the disease was in decline. The increase has been most marked in deprived inner city areas, particularly in the USA, and here there is a clear link between TB and HIV, the virus which causes AIDS. TB is the main cause of death in HIV positive individuals.

According to a World Health Organization (WHO) report in 1995, TB is responsible for more than a quarter of all adult deaths in developing countries; worldwide there are 20 million with the disease and approximately 1.9 billion infected with the TB bacterium but not displaying symptoms. TB caused around 3.1 million deaths during 1995.

The last decade has seen the spread of drug-resistant strains of the TB bacterium. Many strains are now resistant to the two front-line drugs, isoniazid and rifampicin, and some are multi-drug resistant (MDR). Rare until its recent appearance in the USA, MDR TB is now spreading through a number of developing countries. It is untreatable and many of its victims have died. According to a 1996 WHO estimate there may be as many as 50 million people worldwide with the drug-resistant form of TB (Britain had its first case in 1995).

tuberose Mexican flowering plant belonging to the ◊agave family, grown as a sweet-smelling greenhouse plant. It has spikes of scented white flowers like lilies. (*Polianthes tuberosa,* family Agavaceae.)

Tucana constellation of the southern hemisphere, represented as a toucan. It contains the second most prominent ◊globular cluster in the sky, 47 Tucanae, and the Small ◊Magellanic Cloud.

Tucana is one of the 11 constellations named by Johann Bayer early in the 17th century to complement the 65 constellations delineated in ancient times.

tucu-tuco any member of the genus *Ctenomys,* a burrowing South American rodent about 20 cm/8 in long with a 7 cm/3 in tail. It has a large head, sensitive ears, and enormous incisor teeth.

Tucu-tucos spend most of their time below ground in a burrow system, generally one animal to a burrow. The name tucu-tuco is an attempt to imitate the bubbling call.

tufa or ***travertine*** soft, porous, ◊limestone rock, white in colour, deposited from solution from carbonate-saturated ground water around hot springs and in caves.

Undersea tufa columns, such as those in the Ikka Fjord in SW Greenland, that form over alkaline springs, can reach 20 m/65 ft in height and grow at about 50 cm/20 in per year. They provide a habitat for a wide variety of marine life.

tulip any of a group of spring-flowering bulbous plants belonging to the lily family, usually with single goblet-shaped flowers on the end of an upright stem and narrow oval leaves with pointed ends. Tulips come in a large range of shapes, sizes, and colours and are widely cultivated as a garden flower. (Genus *Tulipa,* family Liliaceae.)

T. gesnerana, from which most of the garden cultivars have been derived, probably originated in Asia Minor. It was quickly adopted in Europe from Turkey during the 16th century, and tulip collecting became a craze in 17th-century Holland – it was the subject of a novel, *The Black Tulip,* by Alexandre Dumas (*père*) in 1850. Today tulips are commercially cultivated on a large scale in the Netherlands and East Anglia, England.

The **tulip tree** (*Liriodendron tulipifera*) of the eastern USA is a member of the magnolia family, with large, tulip-shaped blooms.

TULIP BOOK

http://www.bib.wau.nl/tulips/

Online version of P Cos's manuscript catalogue of tulips, published in 1637.

tumour overproduction of cells in a specific area of the body, often leading to a swelling or lump. Tumours are classified as **benign** or **malignant** (see cancer). Benign tumours grow more slowly, do not invade surrounding tissues, do not spread to other parts of the body, and do not usually recur after removal. However, benign tumours can be dangerous in areas such as the brain. The most familiar types of benign tumour are warts on the skin. In some cases, there is no sharp dividing line between benign and malignant tumours.

US doctors managed to halt tumour growth in mice by firing gold beads coated with DNA from a gene gun in 1995.

tuna any of various large marine bony fishes of the mackerel family, especially the genus *Thunnus,* popular as food and game. **Albacore** *T. alalunga,* **bluefin tuna** *T. thynnus,* and **yellowfin tuna** *T. albacares* are commercially important.

Tuna fish gather in shoals and migrate inshore to breed, where they are caught in large numbers. The increasing use by Pacific tuna fishers of enormous driftnets, which kill dolphins, turtles, and other marine creatures as well as catching the fish, has caused protests by environmentalists; tins labelled 'dolphin-friendly' contain tuna not caught by driftnets. Thailand is a major tuna-importing and canning country.

Overfishing is causing a reduction in tuna stocks around the world. In spite of the introduction of quotas in Australia in the 1980s, the country's catch of southern bluefin tuna in 1990–91 was

5,000 tonnes – the lowest since 1962, and the species could be in danger of extinction. Tuna stocks in the Atlantic declined by almost 90% during 1970–92.

tundra region of high latitude almost devoid of trees, resulting from the presence of ◊permafrost. The vegetation consists mostly of grasses, sedges, heather, mosses, and lichens. Tundra stretches in a continuous belt across N North America and Eurasia. Tundra is also used to describe similar conditions at high altitudes.

tung oil oil used in paints and varnishes, obtained from tung trees native to China. (Genus *Aleurites,* family Euphorbiaceae.)

tungsten Swedish *tung sten* 'heavy stone' hard, heavy, grey-white, metallic element, symbol W (from German *Wolfram*), atomic number 74, relative atomic mass 183.85. It occurs in the minerals wolframite, scheelite, and hubertite. It has the highest melting point of any metal (3,410°C/6,170°F) and is added to steel to make it harder, stronger, and more elastic; its other uses include high-speed cutting tools, electrical elements, and thermionic couplings. Its salts are used in the paint and tanning industries.

Tungsten was first recognized in 1781 by Swedish chemist Karl Scheele in the ore scheelite. It was isolated in 1783 by Spanish chemists Fausto D'Elhuyar (1755–1833) and his brother Juan José (1754–1796).

tungsten ore either of the two main minerals, wolframite $(FeMn)WO_4$ and scheelite, $CaWO_4$, from which tungsten is extracted. Most of the world's tungsten reserves are in China, but the main suppliers are Bolivia, Australia, Canada, and the USA.

Tunguska Event explosion at Tunguska, central Siberia, Russia, in June 1908, which devastated around 6,500 sq km/2,500 sq mi of forest. It is thought to have been caused by either a cometary nucleus or a fragment of ◊Encke's comet about 200 m/220 yards across, or possibly an asteroid. The magnitude of the explosion was equivalent to an atom bomb (10–20 megatons) and produced a colossal shock wave; a bright falling object was seen 600 km/375 mi away and was heard up to 1,000 km/625 mi away.

tunicate any marine ◊chordate of the subphylum Tunicata (Urochordata), for example the ◊sea squirt. Tunicates have transparent or translucent tunics made of cellulose. They vary in size from a few millimetres to 30 cm/1 ft in length, and are cylindrical, circular, or irregular in shape. There are more than 1,000 species.

> *We live today in a world in which poets and historians and men of affairs are proud that they wouldn't even begin to consider thinking about learning anything of science, regarding it as the far end of a tunnel too long for any wise man to put his head into.*
>
> J ROBERT OPPENHEIMER US physicist. *The Open Mind* 1955

tunnel passageway through a mountain, under a body of water, or underground. Tunnelling is a significant branch of civil engineering in both mining and transport. The difficulties naturally increase with the size, length, and depth of tunnel, but with the mechanical appliances now available no serious limitations are imposed. Granite or other hard rock presents little difficulty to modern power drills. In recent years there have been notable developments in linings (for example, concrete segments and steel liner plates), and in the use of rotary diggers and cutters and explosives.

tunny another name for ◊tuna.

turbine engine in which steam, water, gas, or air (see ◊windmill) is made to spin a rotating shaft by pushing on angled blades, like a fan. Turbines are among the most powerful machines. Steam turbines are used to drive generators in power stations and ships' propellers; water turbines spin the generators in hydroelectric power plants; and gas turbines (as jet engines; see ◊jet propulsion) power most aircraft and drive machines in industry.

The high-temperature, high-pressure steam for **steam turbines** is raised in boilers heated by furnaces burning coal, oil, or gas, or by nuclear energy. A steam turbine consists of a shaft, or rotor, which rotates inside a fixed casing (stator). The rotor carries 'wheels' consisting of blades, or vanes. The stator has vanes set between the vanes of the rotor, which direct the steam through the rotor vanes at the optimum angle. When steam expands through the turbine, it spins the rotor by reaction. The steam engine of Hero of Alexandria (130 BC), called the *aeolipile,* was the prototype of this type of turbine, called a **reaction turbine**. Modern development of the reaction turbine is largely due to English engineer Charles Parsons. Less widely used is the **impulse turbine**, patented in 1882 by Carl Gustaf Patrick de Laval (1845–1913). It works by directing a jet of steam at blades on a rotor. Similarly there are reaction and impulse water turbines: impulse turbines work on the same principle as the water wheel and consist of sets of buckets arranged around the edge of a wheel; reaction turbines look much like propellers and are fully immersed in the water.

In a **gas turbine** a compressed mixture of air and gas, or vaporized fuel, is ignited, and the hot gases produced expand through the turbine blades, spinning the rotor. In the industrial gas turbine, the rotor shaft drives machines. In the jet engine, the turbine drives the compressor, which supplies the compressed air to the engine, but most of the power developed comes from the jet exhaust in the form of propulsive thrust.

turbocharger turbine-driven device fitted to engines to force more air into the cylinders, producing extra power. The turbocharger consists of a 'blower', or ◊compressor, driven by a turbine, which in most units is driven by the exhaust gases leaving the engine.

turbofan jet engine of the type used by most airliners, so called because of its huge front fan. The fan sends air not only into the engine for combustion but also around the engine for additional thrust. This results in a faster and more fuel-efficient propulsive jet (see ◊jet propulsion).

turbojet jet engine that derives its thrust from a jet of hot exhaust gases. Pure turbojets can be very powerful but use a lot of fuel.

A single-shaft turbojet consists of a shaft (rotor) rotating in a casing. At the front is a multiblade ◊compressor, which takes in and compresses air and delivers it to one or more combustion chambers. Fuel (kerosene) is then sprayed in and ignited. The hot gases expand through a nozzle at the rear of the engine after spinning a turbine. The ◊turbine drives the compressor. Reaction to the backward stream of gases produces a forward propulsive thrust.

turboprop jet engine that derives its thrust partly from a jet of exhaust gases, but mainly from a propeller powered by a turbine in the jet exhaust. Turboprops are more economical than turbojets but can be used only at relatively low speeds.

A turboprop typically has a twin-shaft rotor. One shaft carries the compressor and is spun by one turbine, while the other shaft carries a propeller and is spun by a second turbine.

turbot any of various flatfishes of the flounder group prized as food, especially *Scophthalmus maximus* found in European waters. It grows up to 1 m/3 ft long and weighs up to 14 kg/30 lb. It is brownish above and whitish underneath.

turbulence irregular fluid (gas or liquid) flow, in which vortices and unpredictable fluctuations and motions occur. ◊Streamlining reduces the turbulence of flow around an object, such as an aircraft, and reduces drag. Turbulent flow of a fluid occurs when the ◊Reynolds number is high.

turgor the rigid condition of a plant caused by the fluid contents of a plant cell exerting a mechanical pressure against the cell wall. Turgor supports plants that do not have woody stems.

Turing machine abstract model of an automatic problem-solving machine, formulated by Alan Turing in 1937. It provides the theoretical basis of modern digital computing.

Turing, Alan Mathison (1912–1954)

English mathematician and logician. In 1936 he described a 'universal computing machine' that could theoretically be programmed to solve any problem capable of solution by a specially designed machine. This concept, now called the Turing machine, foreshadowed the digital computer.

Turing is believed to have been the first to suggest (in 1950) the possibility of machine learning and artificial intelligence. His test for distinguishing between real (human) and simulated (computer) thought is known as the Turing test: with a person in one room and the machine in another, an interrogator in a third room asks questions of both to try to identify them. When the interrogator cannot distinguish between them by questioning, the machine will have reached a state of humanlike intelligence.

ALAN TURING HOME PAGE

http://www.turing.org.uk/turing/

Authoritative illustrated biography of the computer pioneer, plus links to related sites. This site contains information on his origins and his code-breaking work during World War II, as well as several works written by Turing himself.

turkey any of several large game birds of the pheasant family, Meleagrididae, order Galliformes, native to the Americas. The wild turkey *Meleagris galloparvo* reaches a length of 1.3 m/4.3 ft, and is native to North and Central American woodlands. The domesticated turkey derives from the wild species. The ocellated turkey *Agriocharis ocellata* is found in Central America; it has eyespots on the tail.

The domesticated turkey was introduced to Europe in the 16th century. Since World War II, it has been intensively bred, in the same way as the chicken. It is gregarious, except at breeding time.

turmeric perennial plant belonging to the ginger family, native to India and the East Indies; also the ground powder from its tuberous rhizomes (underground stems), used in curries to give a yellow colour and as a dyestuff. (*Curcuma longa*, family Zingiberaceae.)

In India it is traditionally applied in the form of a paste of powder to aid healing of cuts and grazes.

turnip biennial plant widely cultivated in temperate regions for its edible white- or yellow-fleshed root and young leaves, which are used as a green vegetable. Closely allied to it is the ◊swede (*B. napus*). (*Brassica rapa*, family Cruciferae.)

turnkey system in computing, a system that the user has only to switch on to have direct access to application software that is usually specific to a particular application area. Turnkey systems often use menus. The user is expected to follow instructions on the screen and to have no knowledge of how the system operates.

turnpike road road with a gate or barrier preventing access until a toll had been paid, common from the mid-16th–19th centuries. In 1991, a plan for the first turnpike road to be built in the UK since the 18th century was announced: the privately funded Birmingham northern relief road, 50 km/31 mi long.

turnstone any small wading shorebirds of the genus *Arenaria*, order Charadriiformes, especially the ruddy turnstone *A. interpres*, which breeds in the Arctic and migrates to the southern hemisphere. It is seen on rocky beaches, turning over stones for small crustaceans and insects. It is about 23 cm/9 in long and has a summer plumage of black and chestnut above, white below; it is duller in winter.

turpentine solution of resins distilled from the sap of conifers, used in varnish and as a paint solvent but now largely replaced by ◊white spirit.

turquoise mineral, hydrous basic copper aluminium phosphate, $CuAl_6(PO_4)_4(OH)_8 5H_2O$. Blue-green, blue, or green, it is a gemstone. Turquoise is found in Australia, Egypt, Ethiopia, France, Germany, Iran, Turkestan, Mexico, and southwestern USA. It was originally introduced into Europe through Turkey, from which its name is derived.

turtle small computer-controlled wheeled robot. The turtle's movements are determined by programs written by a computer user, typically using the high-level programming language ◊LOGO.

turtle freshwater or marine reptile whose body is protected by a shell. Turtles are related to tortoises, and some species can grow to a length of up to 2.5 m/8 ft. Turtles often travel long distances to lay their eggs on the beaches where they were born. Many species have suffered through destruction of their breeding sites as well as being hunted for food and their shells. Unlike tortoises, turtles cannot retract their heads into their shells.

Marine turtles are generally herbivores, feeding mainly on sea grasses. Freshwater turtles eat a range of animals including worms, frogs, and fish. They are excellent swimmers, having legs that are modified to oarlike flippers but which make them awkward on land. The shell is more streamlined and lighter than that of the tortoise.

Species include the **green turtle** *Chelonia mydas;* the **loggerhead** *Caretta caretta;* the **giant leathery** or **leatherback turtle** *Dermochelys coriacea,* which can weigh half a tonne; and the **hawksbill** *Eretmochelys imbricata,* which is hunted for its shell which provides tortoiseshell, used in jewellery and ornaments, and is now endangered. Other turtles suffer because their eggs are taken by collectors and their breeding sites are regularly destroyed, often for tourist developments.

The use of radiotransmitters has shown that migrating leatherback turtles navigate by following the contours of the Earth's crust along existing pathways. The identification and protection of these pathways could substantially reduce the number of leatherback turtles drowned in driftnets or caught on fishing lines.

TURTLES

http://www.turtles.org

Site full of information about turtles. There are pictures, information on current research programmes, a kids corner, and stills from an underwater video camera.

tussock moth type of ◊moth. Several species are major forest pests, both in Europe and in North America, for example, the **gypsy moth** *Lymantria dispar,* the **nun moth** *L. monacha,* and the browntail moth *Nygmia phaeorrhoea.* The caterpillars have tufts (tussocks) of long hairs.

In some species, such as the white-marked tussock moth *Hemerocampa leucostigma,* the females are wingless.

classification Tussock moths are in the family Lymantriidae, order Lepidoptera, class Insecta, phylum Arthropoda.

TVP (abbreviation for ***texturized vegetable protein***) meat substitute usually made from soya beans. In manufacture, the soyabean solids (what remains after oil has been removed) are ground finely and mixed with a binder to form a sticky mixture. This is forced through a spinneret and extruded into fibres, which are treated with salts and flavourings, wound into hanks, and then chopped up to resemble meat chunks.

TWAIN (acronym for ***technology without an interesting name***) in computing, software standard allowing images to be taken directly from a ◊scanner or digital camera into any image processing application. Before TWAIN, users were restricted to the scanners explicitly supported by their software; now, the only necessity is that both items follow the TWAIN standard.

24-bit colour in computing, term specifying that a ◊video adapter is able to display more than 16 million colours simultaneously. The human eye processes 16 million colours with every blink, and a computer needs the same number of colours to be able to display pictures of a photographic quality. Powerful microprocessors, large amounts of ◊RAM, and mass storage media are needed to handle the large computer files involved in holding such complex data.

twin one of two young produced from a single pregnancy. Human twins may be genetically identical (monozygotic), having been formed from a single fertilized egg that splits into two cells, both of which became implanted. Nonidentical (fraternal or dizygotic) twins are formed when two eggs are fertilized at the same time.

twitch another common name for ◊couch grass.

2-D graphics in computing, graphics defined only by width and height (in mathematical terms, x and y axes). Examples of 2-D graphics are the graphics generated by spreadsheets or animated characters with no shading.

256-colour in computing, term specifying the number of colours that an 8-bit ◊video adapter or ◊VGA screen is able to display simultaneously. The earliest VGA screens could handle only 16 colours. By 1996 most new computer systems came equipped with a video adapter and display that could handle 256 colours, allowing the use of more detailed and complex graphics. The extra depth is useful for applications such as games and multimedia encyclopedias.

two's complement number system number system, based on the ◊binary number system, that allows both positive and negative numbers to be conveniently represented for manipulation by computer.

In the two's complement system the most significant column heading (the furthest to the left) is always taken to represent a negative number.

For example, the four-column two's complement number 1101 stands for –3, since: –8 + 4 + 1 = –3.

two-stroke cycle operating cycle for internal combustion piston engines. The engine cycle is completed after just two strokes (up or down) of the piston, which distinguishes it from the more common ◊four-stroke cycle. Power mowers and lightweight motorcycles use two-stroke petrol engines, which are cheaper and simpler than four-strokes.

Most marine diesel engines are also two-stroke. In a typical two-stroke motorcycle engine, fuel mixture is drawn into the crankcase as the piston moves up on its first stroke to compress the mixture above it. Then the compressed mixture is ignited, and hot gases are produced, which drive the piston down on its second stroke. As it moves down, it uncovers an opening (port) that allows the fresh fuel mixture in the crankcase to flow into the combustion space above the piston. At the same time, the exhaust gases leave through another port.

type metal ◊alloy of tin, lead, and antimony, for making the metal type used by printers.

typesetting means by which text, or copy, is prepared for ◊printing, now usually carried out by computer.

Text is keyed on a typesetting machine in a similar way to typing. Laser or light impulses are projected on to light-sensitive film that, when developed, can be used to make plates for printing.

typewriter keyboard machine that produces characters on paper. The earliest known typewriter design was patented by Henry Mills in England in 1714. However, the first practical typewriter was built in 1867 in Milwaukee, Wisconsin, USA, by Christopher Sholes, Carlos Glidden, and Samuel Soulé. By 1873 Remington and Sons, US gunmakers, had produced under contract the first typing machines for sale and in 1878 they patented the first with lower-case as well as upper-case (capital) letters.

The first typewriter patented by Sholes included an alphabetical layout of keys, but Remington's first commercial typewriter had the ◊QWERTY keyboard, designed by Sholes to slow down typists who were too fast for their mechanical keyboards.

Other layouts include the Dvorak keyboard developed by John Dvorak in 1932, in which the most commonly used letters are evenly distributed between left and right, and are positioned under the strongest fingers. Later developments included tabulators from about 1898, portable machines about 1907, the gradual introduction of electrical operation (allowing increased speed, since the keys are touched, not depressed), proportional spacing in 1940, and the rotating typehead with stationary plates in 1962. More recent typewriters work electronically, are equipped with a memory, and can be given an interface that enables them to be connected to a computer. The ◊wordprocessor has largely replaced the typewriter for typing letters and text.

If my doctor told me I only had six months to live, I wouldn't brood. I'd type a little faster.

Isaac Asimov Russian-born US writer.
Life

---

typhoid fever acute infectious disease of the digestive tract, caused by the bacterium *Salmonella typhi,* and usually contracted through a contaminated water supply. It is characterized by bowel haemorrhage and damage to the spleen. Treatment is with antibiotics.

The symptoms begin 10–14 days after ingestion and include fever, headache, cough, constipation, and rash. The combined TAB vaccine protects both against typhoid and the milder, related condition known as **paratyphoid fever**.

typhoon violent revolving storm, a ◊hurricane in the W Pacific Ocean.

typhus any one of a group of infectious diseases caused by bacteria transmitted by lice, fleas, mites, and ticks. Symptoms include fever, headache, and rash. The most serious form is epidemic typhus, which also affects the brain, heart, lungs, and kidneys and is associated with insanitary overcrowded conditions. Treatment is by antibiotics.

The small bacteria responsible are of the genus *Rickettsia,* especially *R. pronazekii.* A preventive vaccine exists.

TYPHUS

Typhus claimed fewer victims in World War II than fighting. This was the first war in which this was the case since the first documented typhus epidemic in 1489.

tyrannosaurus any of a genus *Tyrannosaurus* of gigantic flesh-eating ◊dinosaurs, order Saurischia, that lived in North America and Asia about 70 million years ago. They had two feet, were up to 15 m/50 ft long, 6.5 m/20 ft tall, weighed 10 tonnes, and had teeth 15 cm/6 in long.

Only a few whole skeletons are known; the most complete was discovered in 1989 in Hell Creek, Montana, and preserved in the Museum of the Rockies, Bozeman, Montana, USA.

US archaeologists proved in February 1997 that tyrannosaurus had a biting force of 1,400 kg/3,000 lb, by analysing bite marks in the fossil skeleton of a triceratops and using these to create replica teeth. They then measured the force necessary to reproduce the marks in a cow skeleton using the replica teeth.

tyre (US ***tire***) inflatable rubber hoop fitted round the rims of bicycle, car, and other road-vehicle wheels. The first pneumatic rubber tyre was patented in 1845 by the Scottish engineer Robert William Thomson (1822–73), but it was Scottish inventor John Boyd Dunlop of Belfast who independently reinvented pneumatic tyres for use with bicycles in 1888–89. The rubber for car tyres is hardened by ◊vulcanization.

Tyuratam site of the ◊Baikonur Cosmodrome in Kazakhstan.

uakari any of several rare South American monkeys of the genus *Cacajao.* There are three species, all with bald faces and long fur. About 55 cm/1.8 ft long in head and body, and with a comparatively short 15 cm/6 in tail, they rarely leap, but are good climbers, remaining in the tops of the trees in swampy forests and feeding largely on fruit. The black uakari is in danger of extinction because it is found in such small numbers already, and the forests where it lives are fast being destroyed.

UART (abbreviation for ***universal synchronous receiver–transmitter***) in computing, integrated circuit that converts computer data into ◊asynchronous signals suitable for transmission via a telephone line, and vice versa. UARTs combine a transmitter (parallel-to-serial converter) and a receiver (serial-to-parallel converter) to provide a 'bridge' between the parallel signals used by the computer and the serial signals used by communications networks.

UHF (abbreviation for ***ultra high frequency***) referring to radio waves of very short wavelength, used, for example, for television broadcasting.

UHT abbreviation for ***ultra-heat treated*** or ◊ultra-heat treatment.

UKAEA abbreviation for ◊United Kingdom Atomic Energy Authority.

ULA abbreviation for ◊uncommitted logic array, **a type of integrated circuit**.

ulcer any persistent breach in a body surface (skin or mucous membrane). It may be caused by infection, irritation, or tumour and is often inflamed. Common ulcers include aphthous (mouth), gastric (stomach), duodenal, decubitus ulcers (pressure sores), and those complicating varicose veins.

Treatment of ulcers depends on the site. Drugs are the first line of attack against peptic ulcers (those in the digestive tract), though surgery may become necessary. Bleeding stomach ulcers can be repaired without an operation by the use of endoscopy: a flexible fibre-optic tube is passed into the stomach and under direct vision fine instruments are used to repair the tissues.

ULCER

Headless bedbugs were applied to ulcers in the 16th century, and crushed bedbugs were still believed to be effective in treating ulcers in 18th-century China. It was not until this century that positive evidence was found of the antibacterial properties of insect haemolymph.

ulna one of the two bones found in the lower limb of the tetrapod (four-limbed) vertebrate. It articulates with the shorter ◊radius and ◊humerus (upper arm bone) at one end and with the radius and wrist bones at the other.

ultrafiltration process by which substances in solution are separated on the basis of their molecular size. A solution is forced through a membrane with pores large enough to permit the passage of small solute molecules but not large ones.

Ultrafiltration is a vital mechanism in the vertebrate kidney: the cell membranes lining the Bowman's capsule act as semipermeable membranes, allowing water and substances of low molecular weight such as urea and salts to pass through into the urinary tubules but preventing the larger proteins from being lost from the blood.

ultra-heat treatment (UHT) preservation of milk by raising its temperature to 132°C/269°F or more. It uses higher temperatures than pasteurization, and kills all bacteria present, giving the milk a long shelf life but altering the flavour.

ultrasonics branch of physics dealing with the theory and application of ultrasound: sound waves occurring at frequencies too high to be heard by the human ear (that is, above about 20 kHz).

The earliest practical application of ultrasonics was the detection of submarines during World War I by reflecting pulses of sound from them (see vsonar). Similar principles are now used in industry for nondestructive testing of materials and in medicine to produce images of internal organs and developing fetuses (◊ultrasound scanning). High-power ultrasound can be used for cleaning, welding plastics, and destroying kidney stones without surgery.

ultrasound scanning or ***ultrasonography*** in medicine, the use of ultrasonic pressure waves to create a diagnostic image. It is a safe, noninvasive technique that often eliminates the need for exploratory surgery.

The sound waves transmitted through the body are absorbed and reflected to different degrees by different body tissues.

ultraviolet astronomy study of cosmic ultraviolet emissions using artificial satellites. The USA launched a series of satellites for this purpose, receiving the first useful data in 1968. Only a tiny percentage of solar ultraviolet radiation penetrates the atmosphere, this being the less dangerous longer-wavelength ultraviolet. The dangerous shorter-wavelength radiation is absorbed by gases in the ozone layer high in the Earth's upper atmosphere.

The US Orbiting Astronomical Observatory (OAO) satellites provided scientists with a great deal of information regarding cosmic ultraviolet emissions. *OAO-1,* launched in 1966, failed after only three days, although *OAO-2,* put into orbit in 1968, operated for four years instead of the intended one year, and carried out the first ultraviolet observations of a supernova and also of Uranus. *OAO-3* (*Copernicus*), launched in 1972, continued transmissions into the 1980s and discovered many new ultraviolet sources. The *International Ultraviolet Explorer (IUE),* which was launched in January 1978 and ceased operation in September 1996, observed all the main objects in the Solar System (including Halley's comet), stars, galaxies, and the interstellar medium.

ultraviolet radiation electromagnetic radiation invisible to the human eye, of wavelengths from about 400 to 4 nm (where the ◊X-ray range begins). Physiologically, ultraviolet radiation is extremely powerful, producing sunburn and causing the formation of vitamin D in the skin.

Levels of ultraviolet radiation have risen an average of 6.8% a decade in the northern hemisphere and 9.9% in the southern hemisphere 1972–96, according to data gathered by the Total Ozone Mapping Spectrometer on the *Nimbus 7* satellite.

Ultraviolet rays are strongly germicidal and may be produced artificially by mercury vapour and arc lamps for therapeutic use. The radiation may be detected with ordinary photographic plates or films. It can also be studied by its fluorescent effect on certain materials. The desert iguana *Disposaurus dorsalis* uses it to locate the boundaries of its territory and to find food.

Ulysses space probe to study the Sun's poles, launched in 1990 by a US space shuttle. It is a joint project by NASA and the European Space Agency. In February 1992, the gravity of Jupiter swung *Ulysses* on to a path that looped it first under the Sun's south pole in 1994 and then over its north pole in 1995 to study the Sun and solar wind at latitudes not observable from the Earth.

umbilical cord connection between the ◊embryo and the ◊placenta of placental mammals. It has one vein and two arteries, transporting oxygen and nutrients to the developing young, and removing waste products. At birth, the connection between the young and the placenta is no longer necessary. The umbilical cord drops off or is severed, leaving a scar called the navel.

umbra central region of a ◊shadow that is totally dark because no light reaches it, and from which no part of the light source can be seen (compare ◊penumbra). In astronomy, it is a region of the Earth from which a complete ◊eclipse of the Sun or Moon can be seen.

umbrella bird any of three species of bird of tropical South and Central America, family Cotingidae, order Passeriformes, about 45 cm/18 in long. The Amazonian species *Cephalopterus ornatus*, the **ornate umbrella bird**, has an inflatable wattle at the neck to amplify its humming call, and in display elevates a long crest (12 cm/4 in) lying above the bill so that it rises umbrella-like above the head. These features are less noticeable in the female, which is brownish, while the male is blue-black.

In the **long-wattled umbrella bird** *C. penduliger*, the wattle is covered with black feathers and may reach a length of 28 cm/11 in. The wattle of *C. glabricollis* is short, bare, and red.

umbrella tree tree native to Queensland and the Northern Territory, Australia, with large shiny leaves each made up of leaflets arranged like an open hand, and small raspberrylike clusters of red flowers at the ends of branches. It is common as an indoor plant in many countries. (*Schefflera actinophylla.*)

unbundling in computing, marketing or selling products, usually hardware and software, separately rather than as a single package.

uncertainty principle or ***indeterminacy principle*** in quantum mechanics, the principle that it is impossible to know with unlimited accuracy the position and momentum of a particle. The principle arises because in order to locate a particle exactly, an observer must bounce light (in the form of a ◊photon) off the particle, which must alter its position in an unpredictable way.

It was established by German physicist Werner ◊Heisenberg, and gave a theoretical limit to the precision with which a particle's momentum and position can be measured simultaneously: the more accurately the one is determined, the more uncertainty there is in the other.

uncommitted logic array (ULA) or ***gate array*** in computing, a type of semicustomized integrated circuit in which the logic gates are laid down to a general-purpose design but are not connected to each other. The interconnections can then be set in place according to the requirements of individual manufacturers. Producing ULAs may be cheaper than using a large number of TTL (◊transistor–transistor logic) chips or commissioning a fully customized chip.

unconformity surface of erosion or nondeposition eventually overlain by younger ◊sedimentary rock strata and preserved in the geologic record. A surface where the ◊beds above and below lie at different angles is called an **angular unconformity**. The boundary between older igneous or metamorphic rocks that are truncated by erosion and later covered by younger sedimentary rocks is called a **nonconformity**.

unconscious in psychoanalysis, a part of the personality of which the individual is unaware, and which contains impulses or urges that are held back, or repressed, from conscious awareness.

> *My unconscious knows more about the consciousness of the psychologist than his consciousness knows about my unconscious.*
>
> KARL KRAUS Austrian dramatist and critic. *Die Fackel* 18 January 1917

undelete in computing, a command that allows a user to reinstate deleted text or files. See also ◊delete.

underflow error in computing, an ◊error that occurs if a number is outside the computer's range and is too small to deal with.

underground (US ***subway***) rail service that runs underground. The first underground line in the world was in London, opened in 1863; it was essentially a roofed-in trench. The London Underground is still the longest, with over 400 km/250 mi of routes. Many large cities throughout the world have similar systems, and Moscow's underground, the Metro, handles up to 6.5 million passengers a day.

undernourishment condition that results from consuming too little food over a period of time. Like **malnutrition** – the result of a diet that is lacking in certain nutrients (such as protein or vitamins) – undernourishment is common in poor countries. Both lead to a reduction in mental and physical efficiency, a lowering of resistance to disease in general, and often to deficiency diseases such as beriberi or anaemia. In the Third World, lack of adequate food is a common cause of death.

In 1996, an estimated 195 million children under the age of five were undernourished in the world. Undernourishment is not just a problem of the developing world: there were an estimated 12 million children eating inadequately in the USA in 1992. According to UN figures there were 200 million Africans suffering from undernourishment in 1996.

ungulate general name for any hoofed mammal. Included are the odd-toed ungulates (perissodactyls) and the even-toed ungulates (artiodactyls), along with subungulates such as elephants.

In 1996 the fossil jaws and teeth of an early ungulate were discovered in Russia. The fossils are believed to be 85 million years old, indicating that ungulates were in existence 20 million years before the extinction of the dinosaurs.

UNGULATE

The aardvark, the hyrax, and the elephant look completely unalike, but in fact are more closely related to each other than to any other mammal. They are all primitive ungulates (hoofed grazing mammals).

unicellular organism animal or plant consisting of a single cell. Most are invisible without a microscope but a few, such as the giant ◊amoeba, may be visible to the naked eye. The main groups of unicellular organisms are bacteria, protozoa, unicellular algae, and unicellular fungi or yeasts. Some become disease-causing agents, ◊pathogens.

Unicode 16-bit character encoding system, intended to cover all characters in all languages (including Chinese and similar languages) and to be backwards compatible with ◊ASCII.

Unlike ASCII, which is 8-bit and can therefore represent only 256 characters – insufficient for many diacritics outside the English language – Unicode can represent 65,536 characters, big enough to handle almost all written languages, including Japanese, Tibetan, and the International Phonetic Alphabet (IPA). It was created in the 1980s by Apple and Xerox in the US.

unidentified flying object or ***UFO*** any light or object seen in the sky whose immediate identity is not apparent. Despite unsubstantiated claims, there is no evidence that UFOs are alien spacecraft. On investigation, the vast majority of sightings turn out to have been of natural or identifiable objects, notably bright stars and planets, meteors, aircraft, and satellites, or to have been perpetrated by pranksters. The term **flying saucer** was coined in 1947.

unified field theory in physics, the theory that attempts to explain the four fundamental forces (strong nuclear, weak nuclear, electromagnetic, and gravity) in terms of a single unified force (see ◊particle physics).

Research was begun by Albert Einstein, and by 1971 a theory developed by US physicists Steven Weinberg and Sheldon Glashow, Pakistani physicist Abdus Salam, and others, had demonstrated the link between the weak and electromagnetic forces. The next stage is to develop a theory (called the ◊grand unified theory) that combines the strong nuclear force with the electroweak force. The final stage will be to incorporate gravity into the scheme. Work on the ◊superstring theory indicates that this may be the ultimate 'theory of everything'.

What God hath put asunder, no man shall ever join.

WOLFGANG PAULI Austrian-born Swiss physicist. On Einstein's attempts at a unified field theory, quoted in J P S Uberoi *Culture and Science*

uniformitarianism in geology, the principle that processes that can be seen to occur on the Earth's surface today are the same as those that have occurred throughout geological time. For example, desert sandstones containing sand-dune structures must have been formed under conditions similar to those present in deserts today. The principle was formulated by James ◊Hutton and expounded by Charles ◊Lyell.

uninterruptible power supply (UPS) power supply that includes a battery, so that in the event of a power failure, it is possible to continue operations. UPSs are normally used to provide time either for a system to be shut down in the usual way (so that files are not corrupted) or for an alternative power supply to be connected. For large systems these operations are usually carried out automatically.

unit standard quantity in relation to which other quantities are measured. There have been many systems of units. Some ancient units, such as the day, the foot, and the pound, are still in use. ◊SI units, the latest version of the metric system, are widely used in science.

United Kingdom Atomic Energy Authority (UKAEA) UK national authority, established in 1954 to be responsible for research and development of all nonmilitary aspects of nuclear energy. The authority also provided private industry with contract research and development, and specialized technical and advanced engineering services. The research function was split off into a new company, **AEA Technology**, which was put up for sale in September 1996 as part of the government's privatization programme. UKAEA now manages its nuclear installations and is responsible for decommissioning and maximizing the return on property.

The main areas of research are: thermal reactors, fast reactors, fusion, decommissioning of plants and radioactive waste management, nuclear fuels, and environmental and energy technology. The principal establishments are at the Atomic Energy Research Establishment, Harwell, Oxfordshire; the Culham Laboratory, Oxfordshire; Dounreay, Scotland; Risley, Cheshire; and Winfrith, Dorset.

United Kingdom Infrared Telescope (UKIRT) 3.8-m/150-in reflecting telescope for observing at infrared wavelengths, opened in 1978 on ◊Mauna Kea and operated by the Royal Observatory, Edinburgh.

universal indicator in chemistry, a mixture of ◊pH indicators, used to gauge the acidity or alkalinity of a solution. Each component changes colour at a different pH value, and so the indicator is capable of displaying a range of colours, according to the pH of the test solution, from red (at pH 1) to purple (at pH 13).

universal joint flexible coupling used to join rotating shafts; for example, the drive shaft in a car. In a typical universal joint the ends of the shafts to be joined end in U-shaped yokes. They dovetail into each other and pivot flexibly about an X-shaped spider. This construction allows side-to-side and up-and-down movement, while still transmitting rotary motion.

Universal Serial Bus (USB) in computing, a royalty-free connector intended to replace the out-of-date COM and parallel printer ports that have been used in PCs since 1981. The USB allows up to 127 peripherals – including joysticks, scanners, printers, and keyboards – to be daisy-chained from a single socket, offering higher speeds and improved plug-and-play facilities.

The USB includes hardware and software specifications controlled by the multivendor USB-IF (Universal Serial Bus Implementors Forum) formed in March 1995. Some PC motherboards have included USB connectors since October 1996, and Release 2 of Windows 95 supports USB as long as peripherals come with their own drivers. Microsoft provided full software support for USB in Windows 98.

universal time (UT) another name for ◊Greenwich Mean Time. It is based on the rotation of the Earth, which is not quite constant. Since 1972, UT has been replaced by **coordinated universal time** (UTC), which is based on uniform atomic time; see ◊time.

I have no doubt that in reality the future will be vastly more surprising than anything I can imagine. Now my own suspicion is that the universe is not only queerer than we suppose, but queerer than we can suppose.

J B S HALDANE British physiologist. *Possible Worlds and Other Papers* 1927 Attributed remark

universe all of space and its contents, the study of which is called ◊cosmology. The universe is thought to be between 10 billion and 20 billion years old, and is mostly empty space, dotted with ◊galaxies for as far as telescopes can see. The most distant detected galaxies and ◊quasars lie 10 billion light years or more from Earth, and are moving farther apart as the universe expands. Several theories attempt to explain how the universe came into being and evolved; for example, the ◊Big Bang theory of an expanding universe originating in a single explosive event, and the contradictory ◊steady-state theory.

Apart from those galaxies within the ◊Local Group, all the galaxies we see display ◊red shifts in their spectra, indicating that they are moving away from us. The farther we look into space, the greater are the observed red shifts, which implies that the more distant galaxies are receding at ever greater speeds.

This observation led to the theory of an expanding universe, first proposed by Edwin Hubble in 1929, and to Hubble's law, which states that the speed with which one galaxy moves away from another is proportional to its distance from it. Current data suggest that the galaxies are moving apart at a rate of 50–100 kps/30–60 mps for every million ◊parsecs of distance.

INQUIRER'S GUIDE TO THE UNIVERSE

http://sln.fi.edu/planets/planets.html

Web site designed for teachers and school students, with pages on 'space science fact' – the universe as humans know it today, and 'space science fiction' – the universe as humans imagine it might be. Features include planetary fact sheets, information about planets outside the Solar System, virtual trips to black holes and neutron stars, space quotes, and a course in spaceship design.

UNIX multiuser ◊operating system designed for minicomputers but becoming increasingly popular on microcomputers, workstations, mainframes, and supercomputers.

UNIX was developed by AT&T's Bell Laboratories in the USA during the late 1960s, using the programming language C. It could therefore run on any machine with a C compiler, so ensuring its wide portability. Its wide range of functions and flexibility, together with the fact that it was available free 1976–1983, have made it widely used by universities and in commercial software.

In the 1990s, AT&T's Unix System Laboratories was taken over by Novell, which later sold it to the Santa Cruz Operation.

unleaded petrol petrol manufactured without the addition of ◊antiknock. It has a slightly lower octane rating than leaded petrol, but has the advantage of not polluting the atmosphere with lead compounds. Many cars can be converted to run on unleaded petrol by altering the timing of the engine, and most new cars are designed to do so.

Cars fitted with a ◊catalytic converter must use unleaded fuel.

Aromatic hydrocarbons and alkenes are added to unleaded petrol instead of lead compounds to increase the octane rating. After combustion the hydrocarbons produce volatile organic compounds. These have been linked to cancer, and are involved in the formation of phytochemical smog. A low-lead fuel is less toxic than unleaded petrol for use in cars that are not fitted with a catalytic converter.

The use of unleaded petrol has been standard in the USA for some years.

unnilennium temporary name assigned to the element ◊◊meitnerium, atomic number 109.

unnilhexium temporary name assigned to the element ◊seaborgium 1974–97.

unniloctium temporary name assigned to the element ◊hassium, atomic number 108.

unnilpentium temporary name assigned to the element ◊dubnium.

unnilquadium temporary name assigned to the element ◊rutherfordium 1964–97.

unnilseptium temporary name assigned to the element ◊bohrium 1964–97.

unsaturated compound chemical compound in which two adjacent atoms are linked by a double or triple covalent bond.

Examples are ◊alkenes and ◊alkynes, where the two adjacent atoms are both carbon, and ◊ketones, where the unsaturation exists between atoms of different elements (carbon and oxygen). The laboratory test for unsaturated compounds is the addition of bromine water; if the test substance is unsaturated, the bromine water will be decolorized.

unsaturated solution solution that is capable of dissolving more solute than it already contains at the same temperature.

unshielded twisted pair (UTP) form of cabling used for ◊local area networks, now commonly used as an alternative to ◊coaxial cable.

unstable equilibrium the state of equilibrium possessed by a body that will not remain at rest if displaced slightly, but will topple over into a new position; it will not return to its original rest position. See ◊stability.

ununnilium synthesized radioactive element of the ◊transactinide series, symbol Uun, atomic number 110, relative atomic mass 269. It was discovered in October 1994, detected for a millisecond, at the GSI heavy-ion cyclotron, Darmstadt, Germany, while lead atoms were bombarded with nickel atoms.

unununium synthesized radioactive element of the ◊transactinide series, symbol Uuu, atomic number 111, relative atomic mass 272. It was detected at the GSI heavy-ion cyclotron, Darmstadt, Germany, in December 1994, when bismuth-209 was bombarded with nickel.

upas tree SE Asian tree *Antiaris toxicaria* of the mulberry family Moraceae, with a poisonous latex used for arrows, and traditionally reputed to kill all who fell asleep under it.

upgrade in computing, improved version of an existing software program. Upgrades are sometimes available free or at low cost to registered owners of previous versions.

In an office environment, it is important to carry out software upgrades simultaneously on all machines. Files created using upgrades can rarely be opened by users running older programs.

UPS abbreviation for ◊uninterruptible power supply.

upthrust upward force experienced by all objects that are totally or partially immersed in a fluid (liquid or gas). It acts against the weight of the object, and, according to Archimedes' principle, is always equal to the weight of the fluid displaced by that object. An object will float when the upthrust from the fluid is equal to its weight (see ◊floating).

uraninite uranium oxide, UO_2, an ore mineral of uranium, also known as **pitchblende** when occurring in massive form. It is black or brownish-black, very dense, and radioactive. It occurs in veins and as massive crusts, usually associated with granite rocks.

uranium hard, lustrous, silver-white, malleable and ductile, radioactive, metallic element of the ◊actinide series, symbol U, atomic number 92, relative atomic mass 238.029. It is the most abundant radioactive element in the Earth's crust, its decay giving rise to essentially all radioactive elements in nature; its final decay product is the stable element lead. Uranium combines readily with most elements to form compounds that are extremely poisonous. The chief ore is ◊pitchblende, in which the element was discovered by German chemist Martin Klaproth in 1789; he named it after the planet Uranus, which had been discovered in 1781.

Small amounts of certain compounds containing uranium have been used in the ceramics industry to make orange-yellow glazes and as mordants in dyeing; however, this practice was discontinued when the dangerous effects of radiation became known.

Uranium is one of three fissile elements (the others are thorium and plutonium). It was long considered to be the element with the highest atomic number to occur in nature. The isotopes U-238 and U-235 have been used to help determine the age of the Earth.

Uranium-238, which comprises about 99% of all naturally occurring uranium, has a half-life of 4.51×10^9 years. Because of its abundance, it is the isotope from which fissile plutonium is produced in breeder nuclear reactors. The fissile isotope U-235 has a half-life of 7.13×10^8 years and comprises about 0.7% of naturally occurring uranium; it is used directly as a fuel for ◊nuclear reactors and in the manufacture of nuclear weapons.

WHAT IS URANIUM?

http://www.uic.com.au/uran.htm

Comprehensive and informative page on uranium, its properties and uses, mainly in nuclear reactors and weapons, provided by the Uranium Information Council.

uranium ore material from which uranium is extracted, often a complex mixture of minerals. The main ore is uraninite (or pitchblende), UO_2, which is commonly found with sulphide minerals. The USA, Canada, and South Africa are the main producers in the West.

Uranus the seventh planet from the Sun, discovered by William ◊Herschel in 1781. It is twice as far out as the sixth planet, Saturn. Uranus has a mass 14.5 times that of Earth. The spin axis of Uranus is tilted at 98°, so that one pole points towards the Sun, giving extreme seasons.

URANUS

http://www.hawastsoc.org/solar/eng/uranus.htm

Did you know that Uranus tipped on its side? Find out more about Uranus, its rings, and its moons at this site. Also included are a table of statistics about the planet, photographs, and animations of it rotating.

mean distance from the Sun 2.9 billion km/1.8 billion mi
equatorial diameter 50,800 km/31,600 mi
rotation period 17.2 hr
year 84 Earth years
atmosphere deep atmosphere composed mainly of hydrogen and helium
surface composed primarily of hydrogen and helium but may also contain heavier elements, which might account for Uranus's mean density being higher than Saturn's
satellites 17 moons (two discovered in 1997); 11 thin rings around the planet's equator were discovered in 1977.

Uranus has a peculiar magnetic field, whose axis is tilted at 60° to its axis of spin, and is displaced about a third of the way from the planet's centre to its surface. Uranus spins from east to west, the opposite of the other planets, with the exception of Venus and possibly Pluto. The rotation rate of the atmosphere varies with latitude, from about 16 hours in mid-southern latitudes to longer than 17 hours at the equator.

Uranus's equatorial ring system comprises 11 rings. The ring furthest from the planet centre (51,000 km/31,800 mi), Epsilon, is 100 km/62 mi at its widest point. In 1995, US astronomers determined the ring particles contained long-chain hydrocarbons. Looking at the brightest region of Epsilon, they were also able to calculate the ◊precession of Uranus as 264 days, the fastest known precession in the Solar System.

urea $CO(NH_2)_2$ waste product formed in the mammalian liver when nitrogen compounds are broken down. It is filtered from the blood by the kidneys, and stored in the bladder as urine prior to release. When purified, it is a white, crystalline solid. In industry it is used to make urea-formaldehyde plastics (or resins), pharmaceuticals, and fertilizers.

ureter tube connecting the kidney to the bladder. Its wall contains fibres of smooth muscle whose contractions aid the movement of urine out of the kidney.

urethra in mammals, a tube connecting the bladder to the exterior. It carries urine and, in males, semen.

urial or ***Punjab wild sheep*** or ***shapu*** wild sheep that ranges from sea level near the Caspian Sea to 4,200 m/13,860 ft in Tibet. The male has massive horns up to 1 m/3.3 ft long.
classification The urial *Ovis vignei* is in family Bovidae, in order Artiodactyla.

uric acid $C_5H_4N_4O_3$ nitrogen-containing waste substance, formed from the breakdown of food and body protein.

It is only slightly soluble in water. Uric acid is the normal means by which most land animals that develop in a shell (birds, reptiles, insects, and land gastropods) deposit their waste products. The young are unable to get rid of their excretory products while in the shell and therefore store them in this insoluble form.

Humans and other primates produce some uric acid as well as urea, the normal nitrogenous waste product of mammals, adult amphibians, and many marine fishes. If formed in excess and not excreted, uric acid may be deposited in sharp crystals in the joints and other tissues, causing gout; or it may form stones (calculi) in the kidneys or bladder.

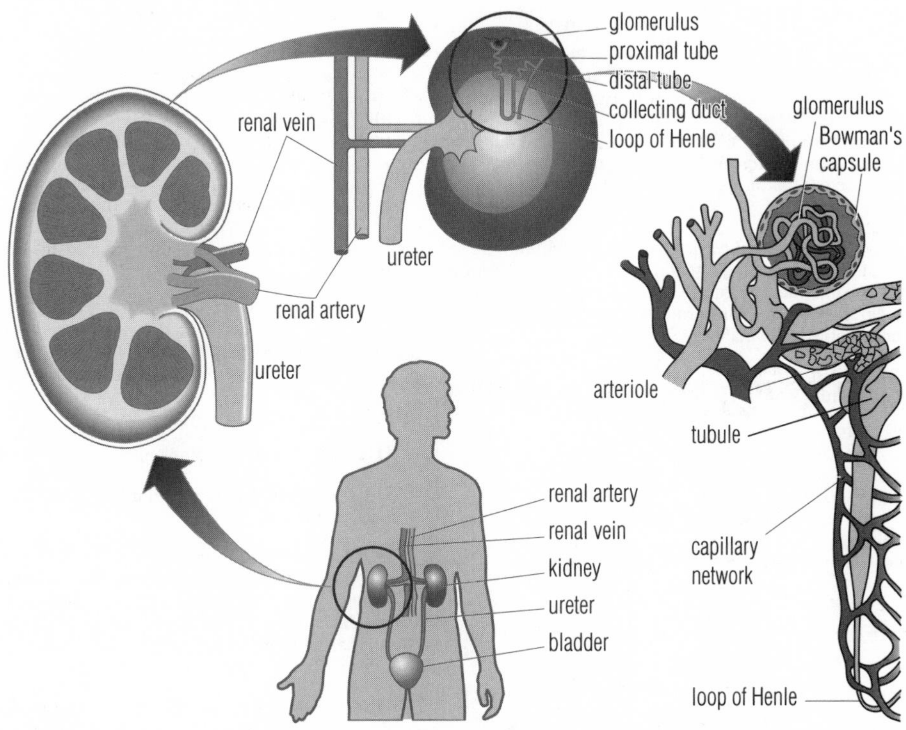

urinary system *The human urinary system. At the bottom right, the complete system in outline; on the left, the arrangement of blood vessels connected to the kidney; at the top right, a detail of the network of vessels within a kidney.*

urinary system system of organs that removes nitrogenous waste products and excess water from the bodies of animals. In vertebrates, it consists of a pair of kidneys, which produce urine; ureters, which drain the kidneys; and (in bony fishes, amphibians, some reptiles, and mammals) a bladder that stores the urine before its discharge. In mammals, the urine is expelled through the urethra; in other vertebrates, the urine drains into a common excretory chamber called a ◊cloaca, and the urine is not discharged separately.

urine amber-coloured fluid filtered out by the kidneys from the blood. It contains excess water, salts, proteins, waste products in the form of urea, a pigment, and some acid.

The kidneys pass it through two fine tubes (ureters) to the bladder, which may act as a reservoir for up to 0.7 l/1.5 pt at a time. In mammals, it then passes into the urethra, which opens to the outside by a sphincter (constricting muscle) under voluntary control. In reptiles and birds, nitrogenous wastes are discharged as an almost solid substance made mostly of ◊uric acid, rather than urea.

URL (abbreviation for ***Uniform Resource Locator***) series of letters and/or numbers specifying the location of a document on the ◊World-Wide Web. Every URL consists of a domain name, a description of the document's location within the host computer and the name of the document itself, separated by full stops and backslashes. Thus *The Times* Web site can be found at http://www.the-times.co.uk/news/pages/home.html, and a tribute to Elvis Presley is at http:///www.mit.edu:8001/activities/41West/elvis.html. The complexity of URLs explains why bookmarks and links, which save the user from the chore of typing them in, are so popular.

Ursa Major Latin 'Great Bear' the third largest constellation in the sky, in the north polar region. Its seven brightest stars make up the familiar shape or asterism of the **Big Dipper** or **Plough**. The second star of the handle of the dipper, called Mizar, has a companion star, Alcor.

Two stars forming the far side of the bowl act as pointers to the north pole star, ◊Polaris. Dubhe, one of them, is the constellation's brightest star.

Ursa Minor Latin 'Little Bear' small constellation of the northern hemisphere. It is shaped like a dipper, with the bright north pole star ◊Polaris at the end of the handle.

Two other bright stars in this group, Beta and Gamma Ursae Minoris, are called 'the Guards' or 'the Guardians of the Pole'. The constellation also contains the orange subgiant Kochab, about 95 light years from Earth.

urticaria or ***nettle rash*** or ***hives*** irritant skin condition characterized by itching, burning, stinging, and the spontaneous appearance of raised patches of skin. Treatment is usually by ◊antihistamines or steroids taken orally or applied as lotions. Its causes are varied and include allergy and stress.

URTICARIA

http://biomed.nus.sg/nsc/urticari.html

Excellent practical information about hives from Singapore's National Skin Centre. Information about its causes includes advice about diet. There are three photos of the condition and advice about treatment.

USB in computing, abbreviation for ◊Universal Serial Bus.

USENET (contraction of ***users' network***) the world's largest ◊bulletin board system, which brings together people with common interests to exchange views and information. It consists of ◊e-mail messages and articles organized into ◊newsgroups. USENET is uncensored and governed by the rules of ◊netiquette.

user-friendly term used to describe the ease of use of a computer system, particularly for those with little understanding or familiarity with computers. Even for experienced users, user-friendly programs are quicker to learn.

user ID (contraction of ***user identification***) name or nickname that identifies the user of a computer system or network. See also ◊password.

user interface in computing, the procedures and methods through which the user operates a program. These might include ◊menus, input forms, error messages, and keyboard procedures. A ◊graphical user interface (GUI or WIMP) is one that makes use of icons (small pictures) and allows the user to make menu selections with a mouse.

A **command line interface** is a character-based interface in which a prompt is displayed on the screen at which the user types a command, followed by ◊carriage return, at which point the command, if valid, is executed.

In a **graphical user interface** programs and files appear as icons (small pictures), user options are selected from pull-down menus, and data are displayed in windows (rectangular areas), which the operator can manipulate in various ways. The operator uses a pointing device, typically a ◊mouse, to make selections and initiate actions.

The study of the ways in which people interact with computers is a subbranch of ergonomics. It aims to make it easier for people to use computers effectively and comfortably, and has become a focus of research for many national and international programmes.

US Naval Observatory US government observatory in Washington DC, which provides the nation's time service and publishes almanacs for navigators, surveyors, and astronomers. It contains a 66-cm/26-in refracting telescope opened in 1873. A 1.55-m/61-in reflector for measuring positions of celestial objects was opened in 1964 at Flagstaff, Arizona.

UTC abbreviation for **coordinated universal time**, the standard measurement of ◊time.

uterus hollow muscular organ of female mammals, located between the bladder and rectum, and connected to the Fallopian tubes above and the vagina below. The embryo develops within the uterus, and in placental mammals is attached to it after implantation via the ◊placenta and umbilical cord. The lining of the uterus changes during the ◊menstrual cycle. In humans and other higher primates, it is a single structure, but in other mammals it is paired.

The outer wall of the uterus is composed of smooth muscle, capable of powerful contractions (induced by hormones) during childbirth.

utility program in computing, a systems program designed to perform a specific task related to the operation of the computer when requested to do so by the computer user. For example, a utility program might be used to complete a screen dump, format a disc, or convert the format of a data file so that it can be accessed by a different applications program.

UTP abbreviation for ◊unshielded twisted pair.

U-tube U-shaped tube that may be partly filled with liquid and used as a ◊manometer.

UUCP (abbreviation for ***UNIX to UNIX Copy Program***) in computing, protocol which allows ◊UNIX users to share files, read ◊USENET articles and exchange ◊e-mail. The system is based on computers regularly 'polling' (connecting to) each other to swap data. Polling can take place via an ordinary telephone connection or over the Internet.

UUencode in computing, ◊utility program that converts a ◊binary file (typically, a program or graphics file) into ◊ASCII text suitable for inclusion in ◊e-mail or ◊USENET messages. The recipient then **UUdecodes** the text file, reconverting it from ASCII to the original binary file.

UUNET Technologies, Inc US-based provider of Internet access. UUNET was the first commercial Internet Service Provider, founded in 1987; the company now has an international network of ◊PoPs and is a major ◊backbone provider. It acquired ◊PIPEX from Unipalm in 1996 and is now itself part of WorldCom Inc.

UV in physics, abbreviation for **ultraviolet**.

U-value measure of a material's heat-conducting properties. It is used in the building industry to compare the efficiency of insulating products, a good insulator having a low U-value. The U-value of a material is defined as the rate at which heat is conducted through it per unit surface area per unit temperature-difference between its two sides; it is measured in watts per square metre per kelvin (W m^{-2} K^{-1}). In mathematical terms, it may be calculated as the rate of loss of heat/surface area × temperature difference.

uvula muscular structure descending from the soft palate. Its length is variable (5–20 mm/0.2–0.8 in in humans). It is raised during swallowing and is sometimes used in the production of speech sounds.

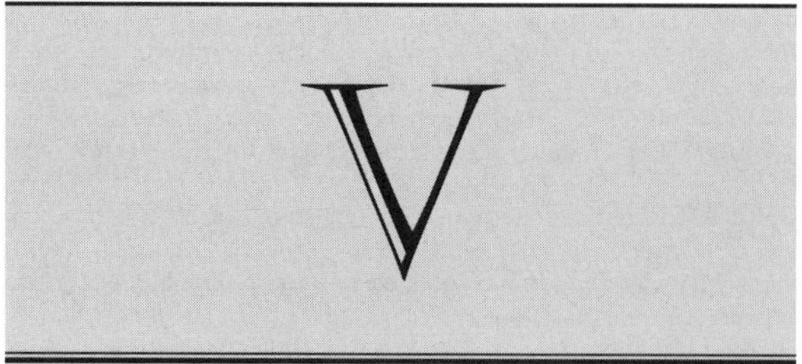

v in physics, symbol for velocity.

V Roman numeral for *five*; in physics, symbol for ◊volt.

vaccine any preparation of modified pathogens (viruses or bacteria) that is introduced into the body, usually either orally or by a hypodermic syringe, to induce the specific ◊antibody reaction that produces ◊immunity against a particular disease.

In 1796, Edward ◊Jenner was the first to inoculate a child successfully with cowpox virus to produce immunity to smallpox. His method, the application of an infective agent to an abraded skin surface, is still used in smallpox inoculation.

The people – could you patent the Sun?

JONAS SALK US physician and microbiologist.
On being asked who owned the patent on his polio vaccine

Vactor (contraction of ***virtual actor***) in computing, animated character moved and voiced by an actor behind the scenes using a ◊Waldo and dataglove to control the character.

vacuole in biology, a fluid-filled, membrane-bound cavity inside a cell. It may be a reservoir for fluids that the cell will secrete to the outside, or may be filled with excretory products or essential nutrients that the cell needs to store.

vacuum in general, a region completely empty of matter; in physics, any enclosure in which the gas pressure is considerably less than atmospheric pressure (101,325 pascals).

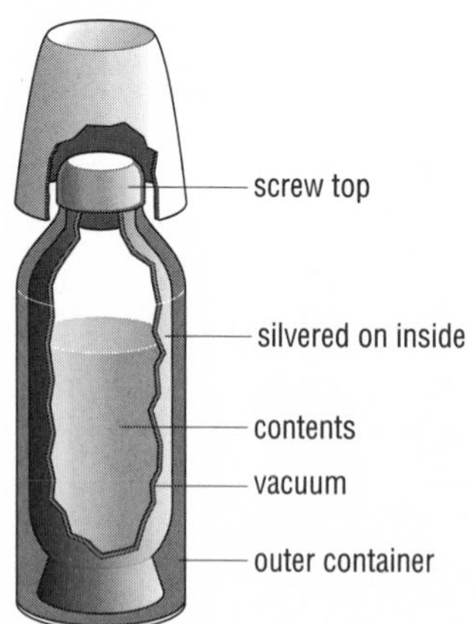

vacuum flask *The vacuum flask allows no heat to escape from or enter its contents. It has double walls with a vacuum between to prevent heat loss by conduction. Radiation is prevented by silvering the walls. The vacuum flask was invented by Scottish chemist James Dewar in about 1872.*

We must first discuss the nature of the vacuum; some writers deny its existence, but through experiments we will provide a true account.

HERON OF ALEXANDRIA Greek scientist.
Pneumatics bk1, ch 1

vacuum cleaner cleaning device invented in 1901 by the Scot Hubert Cecil Booth. Having seen an ineffective dust-blowing machine, he reversed the process so that his machine (originally on wheels, and operated from the street by means of tubes running into the house) operated by suction.

vacuum flask or ***Dewar flask*** or ***Thermos flask*** container for keeping things either hot or cold. It has two silvered glass walls with a vacuum between them, in a metal or plastic outer case. This design reduces the three forms of heat transfer: radiation (prevented by the silvering), conduction, and convection (both prevented by the vacuum). A vacuum flask is therefore equally efficient at keeping cold liquids cold or hot liquids hot.

vagina the lower part of the reproductive tract in female mammals, linking the uterus to the exterior. It admits the penis during sexual intercourse, and is the birth canal down which the baby passes during delivery.

valence electron in chemistry, an electron in the outermost shell of an ◊atom. It is the valence electrons that are involved in the formation of ionic and covalent bonds (see ◊molecule). The number of electrons in this outermost shell represents the maximum possible valence for many elements and matches the number of the group that the element occupies in the ◊periodic table of the elements.

valency in chemistry, the measure of an element's ability to combine with other elements, expressed as the number of atoms of hydrogen (or any other standard univalent element) capable of uniting with (or replacing) its atoms. The number of electrons in the outermost shell of the atom dictates the combining ability of an element.

The elements are described as uni-, di-, tri-, and tetravalent when they unite with one, two, three, and four univalent atoms respectively. Some elements have **variable valency**: for example, nitrogen and phosphorus have a valency of both three and five. The valency of oxygen is two: hence the formula for water, H_2O (hydrogen being univalent).

valency shell in chemistry, outermost shell of electrons in an ◊atom. It contains the ◊valence electrons. Elements with four or more electrons in their outermost shell can show variable valency. Chlorine can show valencies of 1, 3, 5, and 7 in different compounds.

valerian any of a group of perennial plants native to the northern hemisphere, with clustered heads of fragrant tubular flowers in red, white, or pink. The root of the common valerian or garden heliotrope *V. officinalis* is used in medicine to relieve wind and to soothe or calm patients. (Genera *Valeriana* and *Centranthus*, family Valerianaceae.)

validation in computing, the process of checking input data to ensure that it is complete, accurate, and reasonable. Although it would be impossible to guarantee that only valid data are entered into a computer, a suitable combination of validation checks should ensure that most errors are detected.

Common validation checks include:

character-type check Each input data item is checked to ensure that it does not contain invalid characters.

For example, an input name might be checked to ensure that it contains only letters of the alphabet, or an input six-figure date might be checked to ensure it contains only numbers.

field-length check The number of characters in an input field is checked to ensure that the correct number of characters has been entered. For example, a six-figure date field might be checked to ensure that it does contain exactly six digits.

Vaccine: the First Vaccination

BY JULIAN ROWE

Introduction

Today, during their first few months of life, infants are routinely vaccinated against diphtheria, tetanus, whooping cough, and poliomyelitis. After one year, vaccination against measles, mumps, and rubella is also recommended. Thanks to such preventive medicine and to proper nutrition, the common infectious diseases of childhood have largely disappeared from the developed world; if they do occur, the consequences are not usually serious.

Vaccinations

The regular use of vaccination began in 1796 as a result of the pioneering work of Edward Jenner, a British physician (1749–1823). In the 18th century, smallpox was one of the commonest and most deadly diseases. Most people contracted it, and a face completely unscarred by the disease was rare. In 17th-century London, some 10% of all deaths were due to smallpox.

Because the disease was so common, it was well known that an earlier, nonfatal attack of smallpox conferred immunity in any following epidemics. In Eastern countries, people were deliberately exposed to mild forms of the disease. This method was brought back to England in 1721 by Lady Mary Wortley Montagu, wife of the British Ambassador to Turkey. She had her own children 'vaccinated' (the procedure was then called **variolation**), encountering much prejudice as a result.

Kill or cure?

In England, an epidemic of smallpox swept Gloucestershire in 1788, and variolation was widely practised. It involved scratching a vein in the arm of a healthy person, and working into it a small of amount of matter from a smallpox pustule taken from a person with a mild attack of the disease. This risky procedure had two major disadvantages. The inoculated subject, unless isolated, was likely to start a fresh smallpox epidemic; and if the dose was too virulent, the resulting disease was fatal.

Edward Jenner had a country medical practice, and was familiar with both human and animal diseases. He noted that milkmaids often caught the disease cowpox, and inquired further. He saw that milking was regularly done by both men and maidservants. The men, after changing the dressings on horses suffering from a disease called 'the grease', went on to milk the cows, thus infecting them at the same time. In due course, the cows became diseased, and in turn the milkmaids who milked them caught cowpox.

Jenner's observations

Jenner wrote: 'Thus the disease makes its progress from the horse to the nipple of the cow, and from the cow to the human subject.' He went on: 'What makes the cowpox virus so extremely singular is that the person who has been thus affected is for ever secure from the infection of the smallpox.' Jenner then describes a great number of instances, in proof of his observations. Here are some of them.

Case I. Joseph Merret, the undergardener to the Earl of Berkeley, had been a farmer's servant in 1770, and sometimes helped with the milking. He also attended the horses. Merret caught cowpox. In April 1795, he was treated during a general inoculation that took place. Jenner found that despite repeatedly inserting variolous matter into Merret's arm, it was impossible to infect him with smallpox. During the whole time his family had smallpox, Merret stayed with them, and remained perfectly healthy. Jenner was at pains to make sure that Merret had at no time previously caught smallpox.

Case II. Sarah Portlock nursed one of her own children who, in 1792, accidentally caught smallpox. She considered herself safe from infection, for as a farmer's servant 27 years previously, she had contracted cowpox. She remained in the same room as her child, and as in the previous case, variolation produced no disease.

Jenner then performed the experiment that was to make him famous, and give medicine vaccination, one of the most powerful weapons against disease.

The first vaccination

Case XVII. On 14 May 1796, Jenner selected a healthy eight-year-old boy and inoculated him with cowpox, taken from a sore in the hand of a dairymaid. He inserted the infected matter in two incisions, each about 25 mm/1 in long. The boy showed only mild symptoms: on the seventh day he complained of a slight headache, became a little chilly and suffered loss of appetite.

Then on 1 July 1796, Jenner inoculated the boy with variolous matter, inserting it in several slight punctures and incisions in both arms. No disease followed. The only symptoms the boy showed were those of someone who had recovered from smallpox, or had previously suffered from cowpox. Several months later, the boy was inoculated again with similar results.

Jenner published his results privately on the advice of Fellows of the Royal Society, who considered that he should not risk his reputation by presenting anything 'so much at variance with established knowledge'. However, in a few years, vaccination was a widespread practice.

control-total check The arithmetic total of a specific field from a group of records is calculated – for example, the hours worked by a group of employees might be added together – and then input with the data to which it refers. The program recalculates the control total and compares it with the one entered to ensure that entry errors have not been made.
hash-total check An otherwise meaningless control total is calculated – for example, by adding together account numbers. Even though the total has no arithmetic meaning, it can still be used to check the validity of the input account numbers.
parity check Parity bits are added to binary number codes to ensure that each number in a set of data has the ◊same parity (that each binary number has an even number of 1s, for example). The binary numbers can then be checked to ensure that their parity remains the same. This check is often applied to data after they have been transferred from one part of the computer to another; for example, from a disc drive into the immediate-access memory.
check digit A digit is calculated from the digits of a code number and then added to that number as an extra digit. For example, in the ISBN (International Standard Book Number) 0 631 90057 8, the 8 is a check digit calculated from the book code number 063190057 and then added to it to make the full ISBN. When the full code number is input, the computer recalculates the check digit and compares it with the one entered. If the entered and calculated check digits do not match, the computer reports that an entry error of some kind has been made.
range check An input numerical data item is checked to ensure that its value falls in a sensible range. For example, an input two-digit day of the month might be checked to ensure that it is in the range 01 to 31.

Valley of Ten Thousand Smokes valley in SW Alaska, on the Alaska Peninsula, where in 1912 Mount Katmai erupted in one of the largest volcanic explosions ever known, although without loss of human life since the area was uninhabited. The valley was filled with ash to a depth of 200 m/660 ft. It was dedicated as the Katmai National Monument in 1918. Thousands of fissures on the valley floor continue to emit steam and gases.

valve in animals, a structure for controlling the direction of the blood flow. In humans and other vertebrates, the contractions of the beating heart cause the correct blood flow into the arteries because a series of valves prevents back flow. Diseased valves, detected as 'heart murmurs', have decreased efficiency. The tendency for low-pressure venous blood to collect at the base of limbs under the influence of gravity is counteracted by a series of small valves within the veins. It was the existence of these valves that prompted the 17th-century physician William Harvey to suggest that the blood circulated around the body.

valve or ***electron tube*** in electronics, a glass tube containing gas at low pressure, which is used to control the flow of electricity in a circuit. The electron tube valve was invented by US radio engineer Lee de Forest (1873–1961). Three or more metal electrodes are inset into the tube. By varying the voltage on one of them, called the **grid electrode**, the current through the valve can be controlled, and the valve can act as an amplifier.

Valves have been replaced for most applications by ◊transistors. However, they are still used in high-power transmitters and amplifiers, and in some hi-fi systems.

valve device that controls the flow of a fluid. Inside a valve, a plug moves to widen or close the opening through which the fluid passes.

Common valves include the cone or needle valve, the globe valve, and butterfly valve, all named after the shape of the plug. Specialized valves include the one-way valve, which permits fluid flow in one direction only, and the safety valve, which cuts off flow under certain conditions.

valvular heart disease damage to the heart valves, leading to either narrowing of the valve orifice when it is open (stenosis) or leaking through the valve when it is closed (regurgitation).

Worldwide, rheumatic fever is the commonest cause of damage to the heart valves, but in industrialized countries it is being replaced by bacterial infection of the valves themselves (infective endocarditis) and ischaemic heart disease as the main causes. Valvular heart disease is diagnosed by hearing heart murmurs with a stethoscope, or by cardiac ◊ultrasound.

vampire bat South and Central American bat of the family Desmodontidae, of which there are three species. The **common vampire** *Desmodus rotundus* is found from N Mexico to central Argentina; its head and body grow to 9 cm/3.5 in. Vampire bats feed on the blood of birds and mammals; they slice a piece of skin from a sleeping animal with their sharp incisor teeth and lap up the flowing blood. They chiefly approach their prey by flying low then crawling and leaping.

Vampire bats feed on all kinds of mammals including horses, cattle, and occasionally humans. The bite is painless and the loss of blood is small (about 1 cubic cm/0.06 cubic in); the victim seldom comes to any harm. Vampire bats are intelligent and among the few mammals to show altruistic behaviour (they adopt orphans and help other bats in need).

The other species are *Diaemus youngi*, the **white-winged vampire**, and *Diphylla ecaudata*, the **hairy-legged vampire**.

vanadium silver-white, malleable and ductile, metallic element, symbol V, atomic number 23, relative atomic mass 50.942. It occurs in certain iron, lead, and uranium ores and is widely distributed in small quantities in igneous and sedimentary rocks. It is used to make steel alloys, to which it adds tensile strength.

Spanish mineralogist Andrés del Rio (1764–1849) and Swedish chemist Nils Sefström (1787–1845) discovered vanadium independently, the former in 1801 and the latter in 1831. Del Rio named it 'erythronium', but was persuaded by other chemists that he had not in fact discovered a new element; Sefström gave it its present name, after the Norse goddess of love and beauty, Vanadis (or Freya).

Van Allen, James Alfred (1914–)

US physicist whose instruments aboard the first US satellite *Explorer 1* in 1958 led to the discovery of the Van Allen belts, two zones of intense radiation around the Earth. He pioneered high-altitude research with rockets after World War II.

vanadium(V) oxide Va_2O_5 or **vanadium pentoxide** crystalline compound used as a catalyst in the ◊contact process for the manufacture of sulphuric acid.

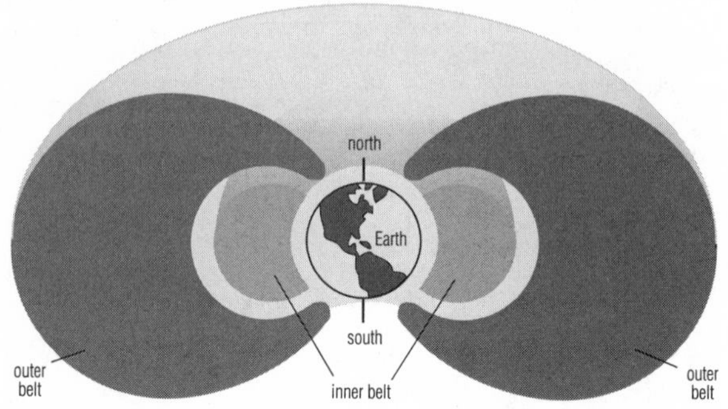

Van Allen radiation belts *The Van Allen belts of trapped charged particles are a hazard to spacecraft, affecting on-board electronics and computer systems. Similar belts have been discovered around the planets Mercury, Jupiter, Saturn, Uranus, and Neptune.*

Van Allen radiation belts two zones of charged particles around the Earth's magnetosphere, discovered in 1958 by US physicist James Van Allen. The atomic particles come from the Earth's upper atmosphere and the ◊solar wind, and are trapped by the Earth's magnetic field. The inner belt lies 1,000–5,000 km/620–3,100 mi above the Equator, and contains ◊protons and ◊electrons. The outer belt lies 15,000–25,000 km/9,300–15,500 mi above the Equator, but is lower around the magnetic poles. It contains mostly electrons from the solar wind.

van de Graaff, Robert Jemison (1901–1967)

US physicist who from 1929 developed a high-voltage generator, which in its modern form can produce more than a million volts.

van de Graaff generator electrostatic generator capable of producing a voltage of over a million volts. It consists of a continuous vertical conveyor belt that carries electrostatic charges (resulting from friction) up to a large hollow sphere supported on an insulated stand. The lower end of the belt is earthed, so that charge accumulates on the sphere. The size of the voltage built up in air depends on the radius of the sphere, but can be increased by enclosing the generator in an inert atmosphere, such as nitrogen.

van der Waals' law modified form of the ◊gas laws that includes corrections for the non-ideal behaviour of real gases (the molecules of ideal gases occupy no space and exert no forces on each other). It is named after Dutch physicist J D van der Waals (1837–1923).

The equation derived from the law states that:

$$(P + \frac{a}{V^2})(V - b) = RT$$

where P, V, and T are the pressure, volume, and temperature (in kelvin) of the gas, respectively; R is the ◊gas constant; and a and b are constants for that particular gas.

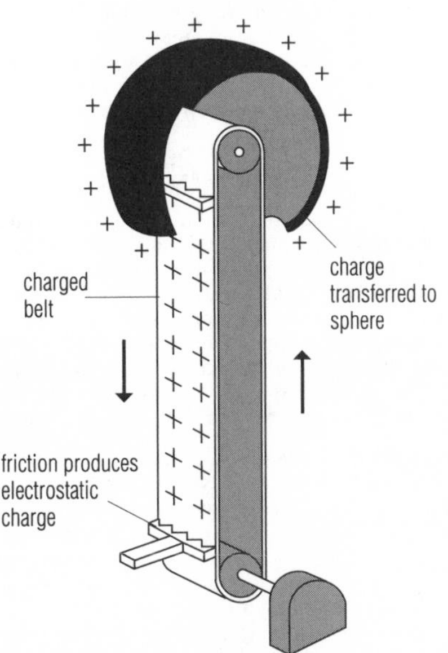

***van de Graaff generator** US physicist Robert Jemison van de Graaff developed this high-powered generator that can produce more than a million volts. Experiments involving charged particles make use of van de Graaff generators as particle accelerators.*

Vanguard early series of US Earth-orbiting satellites and their associated rocket launcher. *Vanguard 1* was the second US satellite, launched on 17 March 1958 by the three-stage Vanguard rocket. Tracking of its orbit revealed that the Earth is slightly pear-shaped. The series ended in September 1959 with *Vanguard 3*.

vanilla any of a group of climbing orchids native to tropical America but cultivated elsewhere, with large, fragrant white or yellow flowers. The dried and fermented fruit, or podlike capsules, of the species *V. planifolia* are the source of the vanilla flavouring used in cookery and baking. (Genus *Vanilla*.)

Annual world production of vanilla pods is estimated at 1,500 tonnes. Vanilla flavouring (**vanillin**) can now be produced artificially from waste sulphite liquor, a by-product of paper pulp-making.

vapour one of the three states of matter (see also ◊solid and ◊liquid). The molecules in a vapour move randomly and are far apart, the distance between them, and therefore the volume of the vapour, being limited only by the walls of any vessel in which they might be contained. A vapour differs from a ◊gas only in that a vapour can be liquefied by increased pressure, whereas a gas cannot unless its temperature is lowered below its ◊critical temperature; it then becomes a vapour and may be liquefied.

vapour density density of a gas, expressed as the ◊mass of a given volume of the gas divided by the mass of an equal volume of a reference gas (such as hydrogen or air) at the same temperature and pressure. It is equal approximately to half the relative molecular weight (mass) of the gas.

vapour pressure pressure of a vapour given off by (evaporated from) a liquid or solid, caused by vibrating atoms or molecules continuously escaping from its surface. In an enclosed space, a maximum value is reached when the number of particles leaving the surface is in equilibrium with those returning to it; this is known as the **saturated vapour pressure** or **equilibrium vapour pressure**.

variable in computing, a quantity that can take different values. Variables can be used to represent different items of data in the course of a program.

A computer programmer will choose a symbol to represent each variable used in a program. The computer will then automatically assign a memory location to store the current value of each variable, and use the chosen symbol to identify this location.

For example, the letter *P* might be chosen by a programmer to represent the price of an article. The computer would automatically reserve a memory location with the symbolic address *P* to store the price being currently processed.

Different programming languages place different restrictions on the choice of symbols used to represent variables. Some languages only allow a single letter followed, where required, by a single number. Other languages allow a much freer choice, allowing, for example, the use of the full word 'price' to represent the price of an article.

A **global variable** is one that can be accessed by any program instruction; a **local variable** is one that can only be accessed by the instructions within a particular subroutine.

variable in mathematics, a changing quantity (one that can take various values), as opposed to a ◊constant. For example, in the algebraic expression $y = 4x^3 + 2$, the variables are x and y, whereas 4 and 2 are constants.

A variable may be dependent or independent. Thus if y is a function of x, written $y = f(x)$, such that $y = 4x^3 + 2$, the domain of the function includes all values of the **independent variable** x while the range (or co-domain) of the ◊function is defined by the values of the **dependent variable** y.

variable-geometry wing technical name for what is popularly termed a ◊swing wing, a type of movable aircraft wing.

variable star in astronomy, a star whose brightness changes, either regularly or irregularly, over a period ranging from a few hours to months or years. The ◊Cepheid variables regularly expand and contract in size every few days or weeks.

Stars that change in size and brightness at less precise intervals include **long-period variables**, such as the red giant ◊Mira in the constellation ◊Cetus (period about 330 days), and **irregular variables**, such as some red supergiants. **Eruptive variables** emit sudden outbursts of light. Some suffer flares on their surfaces, while others, such as a ◊nova, result from transfer of gas between a close pair of stars. A ◊supernova is the explosive death of a star. In an ◊**eclipsing binary**, the variation is due not to any change in the star itself, but to the periodic eclipse of a star by a close companion. The different types of variability are closely related to different stages of stellar evolution.

variance in statistics, the square of the ◊standard deviation, the measure of spread of data. Population and sample variance are denoted by σ^2 or s^2, respectively. Variance provides a measure of the dispersion of a set of statistical results about the mean or average value.

variation in biology, a difference between individuals of the same species, found in any sexually reproducing population. Variations may be almost unnoticeable in some cases, obvious in others, and can concern many aspects of the organism. Typically, variations in size, behaviour, biochemistry, or colouring may be found. The cause of the variation is genetic (that is, inherited), environmental, or more usually a combination of the two. The origins of variation can be traced to the recombination of the genetic material during the formation of the gametes, and, more rarely, to mutation.

> *I have called this principle, by which each slight variation, if useful, is preserved, by the term of Natural Selection.*
>
> CHARLES DARWIN British naturalist.
> *On the Origin of Species* 1859

varicose veins or ***varicosis*** condition where the veins become swollen and twisted. The veins of the legs are most often affected; other vulnerable sites include the rectum (◊haemorrhoids) and testes.

Some people have an inherited tendency to varicose veins, and the condition often appears in pregnant women, but obstructed blood flow is the direct cause. They may cause a dull ache or may be the site for ◊thrombosis, infection, or ulcers. The affected veins can be injected with a substance that causes them to shrink, or surgery may be needed.

variegation description of plant leaves or stems that exhibit patches of different colours. The term is usually applied to plants that show white, cream, or yellow on their leaves, caused by areas of tissue that lack the green pigment ◊chlorophyll. Variegated plants are bred for their decorative value, but they are often considerably weaker than the normal, uniformly green plant. Many will not breed true and require ◊vegetative reproduction.

The term is sometimes applied to abnormal patchy colouring of petals, as in the variegated petals of certain tulips, caused by a virus infection. A mineral deficiency in the soil may also be the cause of variegation.

varve in geology, a pair of thin sedimentary beds, one coarse and one fine, representing a cycle of thaw followed by an interval of freezing, in lakes of glacial regions.

Each couplet thus constitutes the sedimentary record of a year, and by counting varves in glacial lakes a record of absolute time elapsed can be determined. Summer and winter layers often are distinguished also by colour, with lighter layers representing summer deposition, and darker layers being the result of dark clay settling from water while the lake is frozen.

vascular bundle in botany, strand of primary conducting tissue (a 'vein') in vascular plants, consisting mainly of water-conducting tissues, metaxylem and protoxylem, which together make up the primary xylem, and nutrient-conducting tissue, phloem. It extends from the roots to the stems and leaves. Typically the phloem is situated nearest to the epidermis and the xylem towards the centre of the bundle. In plants exhibiting ◊secondary growth, the ◊xylem and ◊phloem are separated by a thin layer of vascular ◊cambium, which gives rise to new conducting tissues.

vascular plant plant containing vascular bundles. ◊Pteridophytes (ferns, horsetails, and club mosses), ◊gymnosperms (conifers and cycads), and ◊angiosperms (flowering plants) are all vascular plants.

vas deferens in male vertebrates, a tube conducting sperm from the testis to the urethra. The sperm is carried in a fluid secreted by various glands, and can be transported very rapidly when the smooth muscle in the wall of the vas deferens undergoes rhythmic contraction, as in sexual intercourse.

vasectomy male sterilization; an operation to cut and tie the ducts (see ◊vas deferens) that carry sperm from the testes to the penis. Vasectomy does not affect sexual performance, but the semen produced at ejaculation no longer contains sperm.

Some surgical attempts to reopen the duct have been successful, and some have opened spontaneously, thus making conception possible. Initially there were concerns of lower life expectancy due to increased risks of testicular or prostate cancer. However, a large-scale study in Boston in 1992 found that an increased rate of lung cancer was offset by a reduced rate of cardiovascular disease.

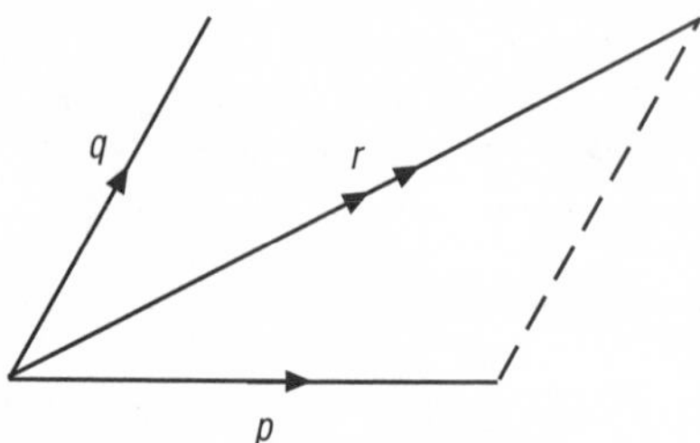

vector quantity A parallelogram of vectors. Vectors can be added graphically using the parallelogram rule. According to the rule, the sum of vectors p *and* q *is the vector* r *which is the diagonal of the parallelogram with sides* p *and* q

VBLA *(abbreviation for* **very long baseline array**) in astronomy, a group of ten 25-m/82.5 ft ◊radio telescopes spread across North America and Hawaii which operate as a single instrument using the technique of very long baseline interferometry (VBLI). The longest baseline (distance between pairs of telescopes) is about 8,000 km/4,970 mi.

VDU abbreviation for ◊visual display unit.

vector graphics computer graphics that are stored in the computer memory by using geometric formulas. Vector graphics can be transformed (enlarged, rotated, stretched, and so on) without loss of picture resolution. It is also possible to select and transform any of the components of a vector-graphics display because each is separately defined in the computer memory. In these respects vector graphics are superior to ◊raster graphics. Vector graphics are typically used for drawing applications, allowing the user to create and modify technical diagrams such as designs for houses or cars.

vector quantity any physical quantity that has both magnitude and direction (such as the velocity or acceleration of an object) as distinct from ◊scalar quantity (such as speed, density, or mass), which has magnitude but no direction. A vector is represented either geometrically by an arrow whose length corresponds to its magnitude and points in an appropriate direction, or by two or three numbers representing the magnitude of its components.

Vectors can be added graphically by constructing a ◊parallelogram of vectors (such as the parallelogram of forces commonly employed in physics and engineering).

If two forces p and q are acting on a body at A, then the parallelogram of forces is drawn to determine the resultant force and direction r. p, q, and r are vectors. In technical writing, a vector is denoted by **bold** type, underlined AB, or overlined AB.

Vega *or* **Alpha Lyrae** brightest star in the constellation ◊Lyra and the fifth brightest star in the night sky. It is a blue-white star, 25 light years from Earth, with a luminosity 50 times that of the Sun.

In 1983 the Infrared Astronomy Satellite (IRAS) discovered a ring of dust around Vega, possibly a disc from which a planetary system is forming.

vegetative reproduction type of ◊asexual ◊reproduction in plants that relies not on spores, but on multicellular structures formed by the parent plant. Some of the main types are ◊stolons and runners, ◊gemmae, bulbils, sucker shoots produced from roots (such as in the creeping thistle *Cirsium arvense*), ◊tubers, bulbs, corms, and ◊rhizomes. Vegetative reproduction has long been exploited in horticulture and agriculture, with various methods employed to multiply stocks of plants. See also ◊plant propagation.

vein in animals with a circulatory system, any vessel that carries blood from the body to the heart. Veins contain valves that prevent the blood from running back when moving against gravity. They always carry deoxygenated blood, with the exception of the veins leading from the lungs to the heart in birds and mammals, which carry newly oxygenated blood.

The term is also used more loosely for any system of channels that strengthens living tissues and supplies them with nutrients – for example, leaf veins (see ◊vascular bundle), and the veins in insects' wings.

Vela bright constellation of the southern hemisphere near Carina, represented as the sails of a ship. It contains large wisps of gas – called the Gum nebula after its discoverer, the Australian astronomer Colin Gum (1924–1960) – believed to be the remains of one or more ◊supernovae. Vela also contains the second optical ◊pulsar (a pulsar that flashes at a visible wavelength) to be discovered.

Vela was originally regarded as part of Argo. Its four brightest stars are second-magnitude, one of them being Suhail, about 490 light years from Earth.

veldt subtropical grassland in South Africa, equivalent to the Pampas of South America.

velocity speed of an object in a given direction. ◊Velocity is a vector quantity, since its direction is important as well as its magnitude (or speed).

The velocity at any instant of a particle travelling in a curved path is in the direction of the tangent to the path at the instant considered. The velocity v of an object travelling in a fixed direction may be calculated by dividing the distance s it has travelled by the time t taken to do so, and may be expressed as:

$$v = \frac{s}{t}$$

velocity ratio (VR) or ***distance ratio*** in a machine, the distance moved by the input force, or effort, divided by the distance moved by the output force, or load, in the same time. It follows that the velocities of the effort and the load are in the same ratio. Velocity ratio has no units. See also ◊mechanical advantage and efficiency.

velvet worm or ***peripatus*** invertebrate with soft body (15–150 mm/0.5–5.9 in in length), velvety skin and paired unsegmented legs. They are found in leaf-litter in rainforests in Africa, Australia, Indonesia, Malaysia, and S America, and feed on small invertebrates. They are unlike any other invertebrates and so the 200 species occupy their own phylum, Onychophora. Velvet worms date back 400 million years and may be a 'missing link' between the arthropods (insects and crustaceans) and annelids (soft-bodied segmented worms, including earthworms). The 20–40 million-year-old fossils of two new kinds of velvet worm were discovered by US palaeontologists in 1996.

VELVET WORM

The mating technique of African velvet worms is bizarre. The male places sperm bundles anywhere along the female's body. Beneath the sperm bundle the skin dissolves forming a hole. The sperm can thus enter the female's body cavity, where it makes its way to her ovaries.

vena cava either of the two great veins of the trunk, returning deoxygenated blood to the right atrium of the ◊heart. The **superior vena cava**, beginning where the arches of the two innominate veins join high in the chest, receives blood from the head, neck, chest, and arms; the **inferior vena cava**, arising from the junction of the right and left common iliac veins, receives blood from all parts of the body below the diaphragm.

venereal disease (VD) any disease mainly transmitted by sexual contact, although commonly the term is used specifically for gonorrhoea and syphilis, both occurring worldwide, and chancroid ('soft sore') and lymphogranuloma venerum, seen mostly in the tropics. The term ◊sexually transmitted disease **(STD)** is more often used to encompass a growing list of conditions passed on primarily, but not exclusively, by sexual contact.

Venn, John
(1834–1923)

English logician whose diagram, known as the Venn diagram, is much used in the teaching of elementary mathematics.

Venn diagram in mathematics, a diagram representing a ◊set or sets and the logical relationships between them. The sets are drawn as circles. An area of overlap between two circles (sets) contains elements that are common to both sets, and thus represents a third set. Circles that do not overlap represent sets with no elements in common (disjoint sets). The method is named after the British logician John ◊Venn.

ventral surface the front of an animal. In vertebrates, the side furthest from the backbone; in invertebrates, the side closest to the ground. The positioning of the main nerve pathways on the ventral side is a characteristic of invertebrates.

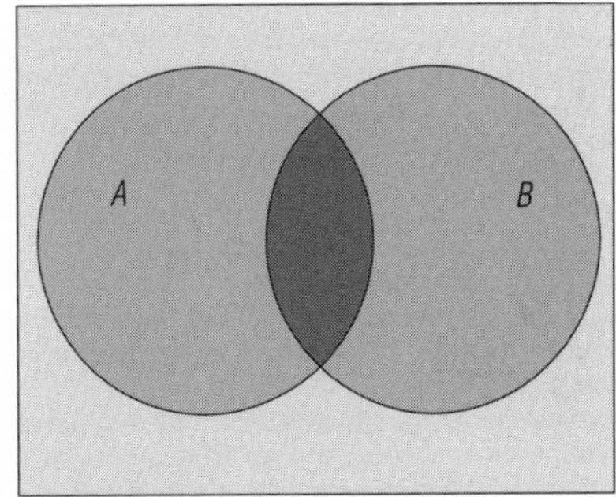

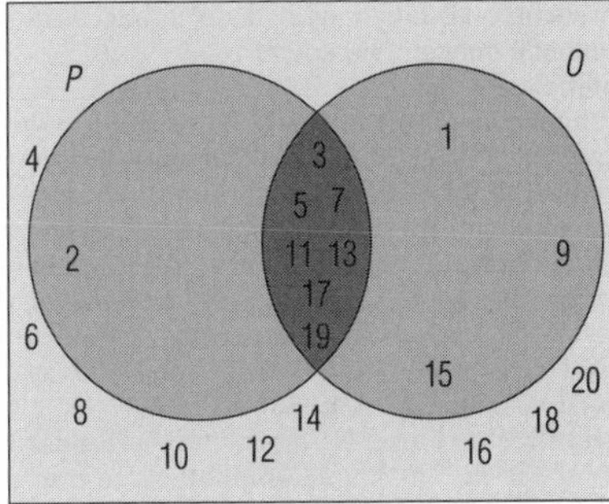

ξ = set of whole numbers from 1 to 20
O = set of odd numbers
P = set of prime numbers

Venn diagram *Sets and their relationships are often represented by Venn diagrams. The sets are drawn as circles – the area of overlap between the circles shows elements that are common to each set, and thus represent a third set. Here (a) is a Venn diagram of two intersecting sets and (b) a Venn diagram showing the set of whole numbers from 1 to 20 and the subsets P and O of prime and odd numbers, respectively. The intersection of P and O contains all the prime numbers that are also odd.*

ventricle in zoology, either of the two lower chambers of the heart that force blood to circulate by contraction of their muscular walls. The term also refers to any of four cavities within the brain in which cerebrospinal fluid is produced.

Venturi tube device for measuring the rate of fluid flow through a pipe. It consists of a tube with a constriction (narrowing) in the middle of its length. The constriction causes a drop in pressure in the fluid flowing in the pipe. A pressure gauge attached to the constriction measures the pressure drop and this is used to find the rate of fluid flow.

Venturi tubes are also used in the carburettor of a motor car to draw petrol into the engine.

Venus second planet from the Sun. It can approach Earth to within 38 million km/24 million mi, closer than any other planet. Its mass is 0.82 that of Earth. Venus rotates on its axis more slowly

FACE OF VENUS HOME PAGE

http://www.eps.mcgill.ca/~bud/craters/FaceOfVenus.html

Overview and description of the surface of the planet Venus. It includes interactive databases of corona and craters, and many images.

than any other planet, from east to west, the opposite direction to the other planets (except Uranus and possibly Pluto).
mean distance from the Sun 108.2 million km/67.2 million mi
equatorial diameter 12,100 km/7,500 mi
rotation period 243 Earth days
year 225 Earth days
atmosphere Venus is shrouded by clouds of sulphuric acid droplets that sweep across the planet from east to west every four days. The atmosphere is almost entirely carbon dioxide, which traps the Sun's heat by the ◊greenhouse effect and raises the planet's surface temperature to 480°C/900°F, with an atmospheric pressure of 90 times that at the surface of the Earth.
surface consists mainly of silicate rock and may have an interior structure similar to that of Earth: an iron–nickel core, a ◊mantle composed of more mafic rocks (rocks made of one or more ferromagnesian, dark-coloured minerals), and a thin siliceous outer ◊crust. The surface is dotted with deep impact craters. Some of Venus's volcanoes may still be active.
satellites no moons

The first artificial object to hit another planet was the Soviet probe *Venera 3,* which crashed on Venus on 1 March 1966. Later Venera probes parachuted down through the atmosphere and landed successfully on its surface, analysing surface material and sending back information and pictures. In December 1978 a US ◊Pioneer Venus probe went into orbit around the planet and mapped most of its surface by radar, which penetrates clouds. In 1992 the US space probe *Magellan* mapped 99% of the planet's surface to a resolution of 100 m/ 330 ft.

The largest highland area is Aphrodite Terra near the equator, half the size of Africa. The highest mountains are on the northern highland region of Ishtar Terra, where the massif of Maxwell Montes rises to 10,600 m/35,000 ft above the average surface level. The highland areas on Venus were formed by volcanoes.

Venus has an ion-packed tail 45 million km/28 million mi in length that stretches away from the Sun and is caused by the bombardment of the ions in Venus's upper atmosphere by the solar wind. It was first discovered in the late 1970s but it was not until 1997 that the Solar Heliospheric Observatory (SOHO) revealed its immense length.

Venus flytrap insectivorous plant belonging to the sundew family, native to the southeastern USA. Its leaves have two hinged surfaces that rapidly close together to trap any insect which brushes against the sensitive leaf hairs; digestive juices then break down the insect body so that it can be absorbed by the plant. (*Dionaea muscipula,* family Droseraceae.)

verbena any of a group of plants containing about 100 species, mostly found in the American tropics. The leaves are fragrant and the tubular flowers are arranged in close spikes in colours ranging from white to rose, violet, and purple. The garden verbena is a hybrid annual. (Genus *Verbena,* family Verbenaceae.)

verdigris green-blue coating of copper ethanoate that forms naturally on copper, bronze, and brass. It is an irritating, poisonous compound made by treating copper with ethanoic acid, and was formerly used in wood preservatives, antifouling compositions, and green paints.

verification in computing, the process of checking that data being input to a computer have been accurately copied from a source document.

This may be done visually, by checking the original copy of the data against the copy shown on the VDU screen. A more thorough method is to enter the data twice, using two different keyboard operators, and then to check the two sets of input copies against each other. The checking is normally carried out by the computer itself, any differences between the two copies being reported for correction by one of the keyboard operators.

Where large quantities of data have to be input, a separate machine called a **verifier** may be used to prepare fully verified tapes or discs for direct input to the main computer.

vermilion HgS red form of mercuric sulphide; a scarlet that occurs naturally as the crystalline mineral ◊cinnabar.

vermin general term for animals destructive of crops and game, such as rats, mice, moles, weasels, and foxes. The word is also used of the insect parasites of people, such as lice and fleas.

vernal equinox see spring ◊equinox.

vernalization the stimulation of flowering by exposure to cold. Certain plants will not flower unless subjected to low temperatures during their development. For example, winter wheat will flower in summer only if planted in the previous autumn. However, by placing partially germinated seeds in low temperatures for several days, the cold requirement can be supplied artificially, allowing the wheat to be sown in the spring.

vernier device for taking readings on a graduated scale to a fraction of a division. It consists of a short divided scale that carries an index or pointer and is slid along a main scale. It was invented by Pierre Vernier.

Veronica software tool for searching for files on the ◊Internet. Veronica is broadly similar to ◊Archie, but whereas the latter searches anonymous ◊ftp sites, Veronica searches Gopher servers.

verruca growth on the skin; see wart.

vertebra in vertebrates, an irregularly shaped bone that forms part of the ◊vertebral column. Children have 33 vertebrae, 5 of which fuse in adults to form the sacrum and 4 to form the coccyx.

Vesalius, Andreas
(1514–1564)

Belgian physician who revolutionized anatomy by performing postmortem dissections and making use of illustrations to teach anatomy. Vesalius upset the authority of Galen, and his book – the first real textbook of anatomy – marked the beginning of biology as a science.

Vesalius was taught anatomy in the Galenist tradition. Galen had never dissected a human body – all his accounts of the human anatomy were based on his research of the Barbary ape – although he was regarded as infallible and was venerated until the Renaissance. Vesalius was therefore taught principles of anatomy that had not been questioned for 1,300 years.

Dissatisfied with the instruction he had received, Vesalius resolved to make his own observations. His dissections of the human body (then illegal) enabled him to discover that Galen's system of medicine was based on fundamental anatomical errors. Vesalius disproved the widely held belief that men had one rib less than women. He also believed, contrary to Aristotle's theory of the heart being the centre of the mind and emotion, that the brain and the nervous system were the centre.

Vesalius's book *De humani corporis fabrica/On the Structure of the Human Body* of 1543 employed talented artists to provide the illustrations and is one of the great books of the 16th century. The quality of anatomical depiction introduced a new standard into all illustrated works, especially into medical books, and highlighted the need to introduce scientific method into the study of anatomy. Together with the main work of astronomer Copernicus, published in the same year, *On the Structure of the Human Body* marked the dawn of modern science.

Mary Evans Picture Library

VISUAL PATHWAY

http://www.hhmi.org/senses/b/b150.htm

As part of a much larger site called 'Seeing, Hearing, and Smelling the World', here is a page explaining the way light travels from the eye to the brain and how it is converted into images our brain can understand. This site makes good use of images and animations to help with the explanations, so it is best viewed with an up-to-date browser.

visual display unit (VDU) computer terminal consisting of a keyboard for input data and a screen for displaying output. The oldest and most popular type of VDU screen is the ◊cathode-ray tube (CRT), which uses essentially the same technology as a television screen. Other types use plasma display technology and ◊liquid-crystal displays.

visualization in computing, turning numerical data into graphics. A simple example is to create a bar chart from a set of sales figures; more complex types of visualization include ◊fractals and other forms of computer-generated art.

visual programming in computing, programming method that uses a system of graphics, instead of text, to build software.

vitalism the idea that living organisms derive their characteristic properties from a universal life force. In the 20th century, this view is associated with the French philosopher Henri Bergson.

vitamin any of various chemically unrelated organic compounds that are necessary in small quantities for the normal functioning of the human body. Many act as coenzymes, small molecules that enable ◊enzymes to function effectively. Vitamins must be supplied by the diet because the body cannot make them. They are normally present in adequate amounts in a balanced diet. Deficiency of a vitamin may lead to a metabolic disorder ('deficiency disease'), which can be remedied by sufficient intake of the vitamin. They are generally classified as **water-soluble** (B and C) or **fat-soluble** (A, D, E, and K). See separate entries for individual vitamins, also ◊nicotinic acid, folic acid, and ◊pantothenic acid.

Scurvy (the result of vitamin C deficiency) was observed at least 3,500 years ago, and sailors from the 1600s were given fresh sprouting cereals or citrus-fruit juices to prevent or cure it. The

Vitamins

Vitamin	*Name*	*Main dietary sources*	*Established benefit*	*Deficiency symptoms*
A	retinol	dairy products, egg yolk, liver; also formed in body from ß-carotene, a pigment present in some leafy vegetables	aids growth; prevents night blindness and xerophthalmia (a common cause of blindness among children in developing countries); helps keep the skin and mucous membranes resistant to infection	night blindness; rough skin; impaired bone growth
B_1	thiamin	germ and bran of seeds and grains, yeast	essential for carbohydrate metabolism and health of nervous system	beriberi; Korsakov's syndrome
B_2	riboflavin	eggs, liver, milk, poultry, broccoli, mushrooms	involved in energy metabolism; protects skin, mouth, eyes, eyelids, mucous membranes	inflammation of tongue and lips; sores in corners of the mouth
B_6	pyridoxine/pantothenic acid/biotin	meat, poultry, fish, fruits, nuts, whole grains, leafy vegetables, yeast extract	important in the regulation of the central nervous system and in protein metabolism; helps prevent anaemia, skin lesions, nerve damage	dermatitis; neurological problems; kidney stones
B_{12}	cyanocobalamin	liver, meat, fish, eggs, dairy products, soybeans	involved in synthesis of nucleic acids, maintenance of myelin sheath around nerve fibres; efficient use of folic acid	anaemia; neurological disturbance
folic acid	nicotinic acid (or niacin)	green leafy vegetables, liver, peanuts; cooking and processing can cause serious losses in food	involved in synthesis of nucleic acids; helps protect against cervical dysplasia (precancerous changes in the cells of the uterine cervix)	megaloblastic anaemia
C		meat, yeast extract, some cereals; also formed in the body from the amino acid tryptophan	maintains the health of the skin, tongue, and digestive system	pellagra
D	ascorbic acid	citrus fruits, green vegetables, tomatoes, potatoes; losses occur during storage and cooking	prevents scurvy, loss of teeth; fights haemorrhage; important in synthesis of collagen (constituent of connective tissue); aids in resistance to some types of virus and bacterial infections	scurvy
E	calciferol, cholecalciferol	liver, fish oil, dairy products, eggs; also produced when skin is exposed to sunlight	promotes growth and mineralization of bone	rickets in children; osteomalacia in adults
K	tocopherol	vegetable oils, eggs, butter, some cereals, nuts	prevents damage to cell membranes	anaemia
	phytomenadione, menaquinone	green vegetables, cereals, fruits, meat, dairy products	essential for blood clotting	haemorrhagic problems

concept of scurvy as a deficiency disease, however, caused by the absence of a specific substance, emerged later. In the 1890s a Dutch doctor, Christiaan Eijkman, discovered that he could cure hens suffering from a condition like beriberi by feeding them on whole-grain, rather than polished, rice. In 1912 Casimir Funk, a Polish-born biochemist, had proposed the existence of what he called 'vitamines' (vital amines), but it was not fully established until about 1915 that several deficiency diseases were preventable and curable by extracts from certain foods. By then it was known that two groups of factors were involved, one being water-soluble and present, for example, in yeast, rice-polishings, and wheat germ, and the other being fat-soluble and present in egg yolk, butter, and fish-liver oils. The water-soluble substance, known to be effective against beriberi, was named vitamin B. The fat-soluble vitamin complex was at first called vitamin A. As a result of analytical techniques these have been subsequently separated into their various components, and others have been discovered.

vitamin A another name for ◊retinol.

vitamin B$_1$ another name for ◊thiamine.

vitamin B$_{12}$ another name for ◊cyanocobalamin.

vitamin B$_2$ another name for ◊riboflavin.

vitamin B$_6$ another name for ◊pyridoxine.

vitamin C another name for ◊ascorbic acid.

vitamin D another name for ◊cholecalciferol.

vitamin E another name for ◊tocopherol.

vitamin H another name for ◊biotin.

vitamin K another name for ◊phytomenadione.

vitreous humour transparent jellylike substance behind the lens of the vertebrate ◊eye. It gives rigidity to the spherical form of the eye and allows light to pass through to the retina.

vitriol any of a number of sulphate salts. Blue, green, and white vitriols are copper, ferrous, and zinc sulphate, respectively. **Oil of vitriol** is sulphuric acid.

viviparous in animals, a method of reproduction in which the embryo develops inside the body of the female from which it gains nourishment (in contrast to ◊oviparous and ◊ovoviviparous). Vivipary is best developed in placental mammals, but also occurs in some arthropods, fishes, amphibians, and reptiles that have placentalike structures. In plants, it is the formation of young plantlets or bulbils instead of flowers. The term also describes seeds that germinate prematurely, before falling from the parent plant.

Premature germination is common in mangrove trees, where the seedlings develop sizable spearlike roots before dropping into the swamp below; this prevents their being washed away by the tide.

vivisection literally, cutting into a living animal. Used originally to mean experimental surgery or dissection practised on a live subject, the term is often used by antivivisection campaigners to include any experiment on animals, surgical or otherwise.

There are people who do not object to eating mutton chop – people who do not even object to shooting pheasant with the considerable chance that it may be only wounded and may have to die after lingering pain, unable to obtain its proper nutriment – and yet consider it something monstrous to introduce under the skin of a guinea pig a little inoculation of some microbe to ascertain its action. These seem to me the most inconsistent views.

JOSEPH LISTER English surgeon.
British Medical Journal 1897

VLBI (abbreviation for ***very long baseline interferometry***) in radio astronomy, a method of obtaining high-resolution images of astronomical objects by combining simultaneous observations made by two or more radio telescopes thousands of kilometres apart. The maximum resolution that can be achieved is proportional to the longest baseline in the array (the distance between any pair of telescopes), and inversely proportional to the radio wavelength being used.

VLF in physics, abbreviation for **very low** ◊frequency. VLF radio waves have frequencies in the range 3–30 kHz.

VLSI (abbreviation for ***very large-scale integration***) in electronics, the early-1990s level of advanced technology in the microminiaturization of ◊integrated circuits, and an order of magnitude smaller than ◊LSI (large-scale integration).

VMS in computing, operating system created in 1978 by ◊DEC for its VAX minicomputers. VMS was for many years a popular operating system for hackers (see ◊hacking), although it has now been largely eclipsed by ◊UNIX.

V numbers in computing, series of ◊protocols issued by the CCITT defining the rate at which modems transfer data. The numbers have come to designate a modem's speed: V.32 modems transmit at up to 9,600 ◊bits per second (bps); V.32bis at up to 14,400 bps and V.34 at up to 28,800 bps.

vocal cords the paired folds, ridges, or cords of tissue within a mammal's larynx, and a bird's syrinx. Air constricted between the folds or membranes makes them vibrate, producing sounds. Muscles in the larynx change the pitch of the sounds produced, by adjusting the tension of the vocal cords.

voice sound produced through the mouth and by the passage of air between the ◊vocal cords. In humans the sound is much amplified by the hollow sinuses of the face, and is modified by the movements of the lips, tongue, and cheeks.

voice input in computing and electronics, an alternative name for ◊speech recognition.

voice mail ◊electronic mail including spoken messages and audio. Messages can also be generated electronically using ◊speech synthesis. In offices, voice mail systems are often included in computerized telephone switchboards.

voice modem in computing, ◊modem which handles voice as well as data communications, so that it can be used to add the capabilities of a ◊voice mail system to a personal computer.

Primarily aimed at small and home-based businesses, voice modems use a built-in ◊DSP and typically also include fax facilities.

voice output in computing and electronics, an alternative name for ◊speech synthesis.

voice-to-MIDI converter microphone which sends human vocal input to a synthesizer. This system of singing to run a synthesizer does not work well unless the singer has perfect pitch, so it is not commonly used.

vol abbreviation for **volume**.

volatile in chemistry, term describing a substance that readily passes from the liquid to the vapour phase. Volatile substances have a high ◊vapour pressure.

volatile memory in computing, ◊memory that loses its contents when the power supply to the computer is disconnected.

volcanic rock another name for ◊extrusive rock, igneous rock formed on the Earth's surface.

volcano crack in the Earth's crust through which hot magma (molten rock) and gases well up. The magma is termed lava when it reaches the surface. A volcanic mountain, usually cone shaped with a crater on top, is formed around the opening, or vent, by the

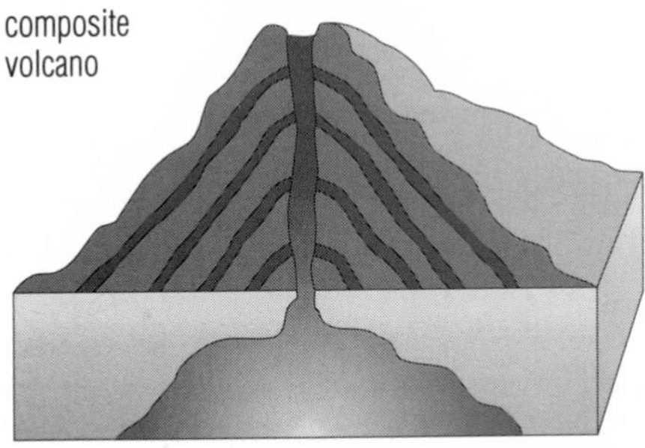

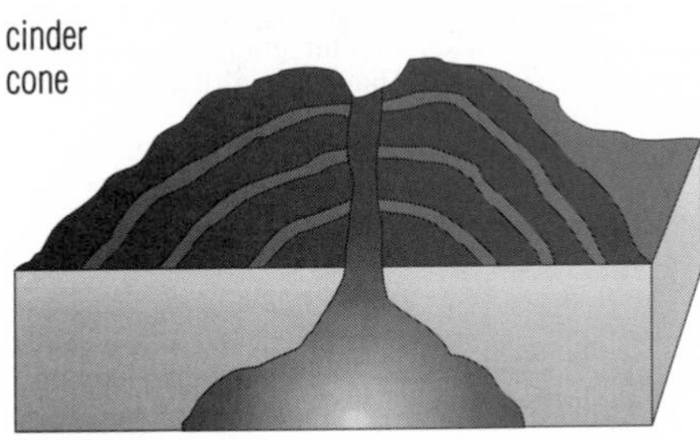

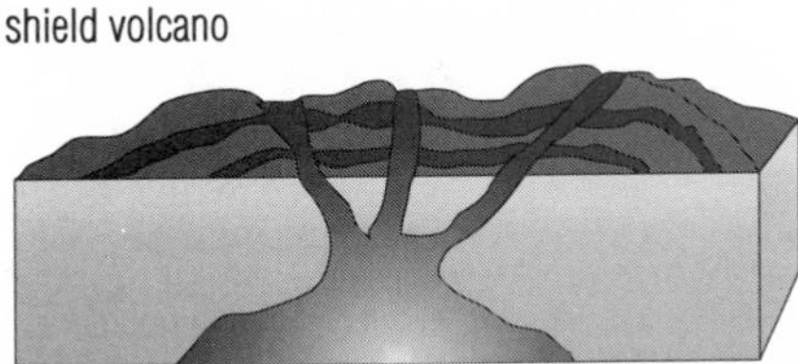

***volcano** There are two main types of volcano, but three distinctive cone shapes. Composite volcanoes emit a stiff, rapidly solidifying lava which forms high, steep-sided cones. Volcanoes that regularly throw out ash build up flatter domes known as cinder cones. The lava from a shield volcano is not ejected violently, flowing over the crater rim forming a broad low profile.*

build-up of solidified lava and ashes (rock fragments). Most volcanoes arise on plate margins (see ◊plate tectonics), where the movements of plates generate magma or allow it to rise from the mantle beneath. However, a number are found far from plate-margin activity, on 'hot spots' where the Earth's crust is thin.

There are two main types of volcano:

Composite volcanoes, such as Stromboli and Vesuvius in Italy, are found at destructive plate margins (areas where plates are being pushed together), usually in association with island arcs and coastal mountain chains. The magma is mostly derived from plate material and is rich in silica. This makes a very stiff lava such as andesite, which solidifies rapidly to form a high, steep-sided volcanic mountain. The magma often clogs the volcanic vent, causing violent eruptions as the blockage is blasted free, as in the eruption of Mount St Helens, USA, in 1980. The crater may collapse to form a ◊caldera.

Shield volcanoes, such as Mauna Loa in Hawaii, are found along the rift valleys and ocean ridges of constructive plate margins (areas where plates are moving apart), and also over hot spots. The magma is derived from the Earth's mantle and is quite free-flowing. The lava formed from this magma – usually basalt – flows for some distance over the surface before it sets and so forms broad low volcanoes. The lava of a shield volcano is not ejected violently but simply flows over the crater rim.

The type of volcanic activity is also governed by the age of the volcano. The first stages of an eruption are usually vigorous as the magma forces its way to the surface. As the pressure drops and the vents become established, the main phase of activity begins, composite volcanoes giving pyroclastic debris and shield volcanoes giving lava flows. When the pressure from below ceases, due to exhaustion of the magma chamber, activity wanes and is confined to the emission of gases and in time this also ceases. The volcano then enters a period of quiescence, after which activity may resume after a period of days, years, or even thousands of years. Only when the root zones of a volcano have been exposed by erosion can a volcano be said to be truly extinct.

Many volcanoes are submarine and occur along mid-ocean ridges. The chief terrestrial volcanic regions are around the Pacific rim (Cape Horn to Alaska); the central Andes of Chile (with the world's highest volcano, Guallatiri, 6,060 m/19,900 ft); North Island, New Zealand; Hawaii; Japan; and Antarctica. There are more than 1,300 potentially active volcanoes on Earth. Volcanism has helped shape other members of the Solar System, including the Moon, Mars, Venus, and Jupiter's moon Io.

MTU VOLCANOES PAGE

`http://www.geo.mtu.edu/volcanoes/`

Excellent volcano page provided by Michigan Technological University. Includes a world map of volcanic activity with information on recent eruptions, the latest research in remote sensing of volcanoes, and many spectacular photographs.

vole any of various rodents of the family Cricetidae, subfamily Microtinae, distributed over Europe, Asia, and North America, and related to hamsters and lemmings. They are characterized by stout bodies and short tails. They have brown or grey fur, and blunt noses, and some species reach a length of 30 cm/12 in. They feed on grasses, seeds, aquatic plants, and insects. Many show remarkable fluctuations in numbers over 3–4 year cycles.

The most common genus is *Microtus*, which includes 45 species distributed across North America and Eurasia.

Volkswagen (VW) German 'the people's car' German car manufacturer. The original VW, with its distinctive beetle shape, was

Volta, Alessandro, Guseppe Antonio Anastasio, Count (1745–1827)

Italian physicist who invented the first electric cell (the voltaic pile, in 1800), the electrophorus (an early electrostatic generator, in 1775), and an electroscope.

studies of gas and vapour In 1776 Volta discovered methane by examining marsh gas found in Lago Maggiore. He then made the first accurate estimate of the proportion of oxygen in the air by exploding air with hydrogen to remove the oxygen. In about 1795, Volta recognized that the vapour pressure of a liquid is independent of the pressure of the atmosphere and depends only on temperature.

Mary Evans Picture Library

Major Volcanoes Active in the 20th Century by Region

Volcano	*Height* *m*	*ft*	*Location*	**Date*
Africa				
Cameroon	4,096	13,353	isolated mountain, Cameroon	1986
Nyiragongo	3,470	11,385	Virungu, Democratic Republic of Congo	1994
Nyamuragira	3,056	10,028	Democratic Republic of Congo	1994
Ol Doinyo Lengai	2,886	9,469	Tanzania	1993
Lake Nyos	918	3,011	Cameroon	1986
Erta-Ale	503	1,650	Ethiopia	1995
Antarctica				
Erebus	4,023	13,200	Ross Island, McMurdo Sound	1995
Deception Island	576	1,890	South Shetland Island	1970
Asia				
Kerinci	3,800	12,467	Sumatra, Indonesia	1987
Rindjani	3,726	12,224	Lombok, Indonesia	1966
Semeru	3,676	12,060	Java, Indonesia	1995
Slamet	3,428	11,247	Java, Indonesia	1989
Raung	3,322	10,932	Java, Indonesia	1993
Agung	3,142	10,308	Bali, Indonesia	1964
On-Taka	3,063	10,049	Honshu, Japan	1991
Merapi	2,911	9,551	Java, Indonesia	1998
Marapi	2,891	9,485	Sumatra, Indonesia	1993
Asama	2,530	8,300	Honshu, Japan	1990
Nigata Yake-yama	2,475	8,111	Honshu, Japan	1989
Mayon	2,462	8,084	Luzon, Philippines	1993
Canlaon	2,459	8,070	Negros, Philippines	1993
Chokai	2,225	7,300	Honshu, Japan	1974
Galunggung	2,168	7,113	Java, Indonesia	1984
Azuma	2,042	6,700	Honshu, Japan	1977
Sangeang Api	1,935	6,351	Lesser Sunda Island, Indonesia	1988
Pinatubo	1,759	5,770	Luzon, Philippines	1995
Kelut	1,730	5,679	Java, Indonesia	1990
Unzen	1,360	4,462	Japan	1996
Krakatoa	818	2,685	Sumatra, Indonesia	1996
Taal	300	984	Philippines	1977
Atlantic Ocean				
Pico de Teide	3,716	12,192	Tenerife, Canary Islands, Spain	1909
Fogo	2,835	9,300	Cape Verde Islands	1995
Beerenberg	2,277	7,470	Jan Mayen Island, Norway	1985
Hekla	1,491	4,920	Iceland	1991
Krafla	654	2,145	Iceland	1984
Helgafell	215	706	Iceland	1973
Surtsey	174	570	Iceland	1967
Caribbean				
La Grande Soufrière	1,467	4,813	Basse-Terre, Guadeloupe	1977
Pelée	1,397	4,584	Martinique	1932
La Soufrière St Vincent	1,234	4,048	St Vincent and the Grenadines	1979
Soufriere Hills/ Chances Peak	968	3,176	Montserrat	1997
Central America				
Acatenango	3,960	12,992	Sierra Madre, Guatemala	1972
Fuego	3,835	12,582	Sierra Madre, Guatemala	1991
Tacana	3,780	12,400	Sierra Madre, Guatemala	1988
Santa Maria	3,768	12,362	Sierra Madre, Guatemala	1993
Irazú	3,452	11,325	Cordillera Central, Costa Rica	1992
Turrialba	3,246	10,650	Cordillera Central, Costa Rica	1992
Póas	2,721	8,930	Cordillera Central, Costa Rica	1994
Pacaya	2,543	8,346	Sierra Madre, Guatemala	1996
San Miguel	2,131	6,994	El Salvador	1986
Arenal	1,552	5,092	Costa Rica	1996
Europe				
Kliuchevskoi	4,750	15,584	Kamchatka Peninsula, Russia	1997
Koryakskaya	3,456	11,339	Kamchatka Peninsula, Russia	1957
Sheveluch	3,283	10,771	Kamchatka Peninsula, Russia	1997
Etna	3,236	10,625	Sicily, Italy	1998
Bezymianny	2,882	9,455	Kamchatka Peninsula, Russia	1997
Alaid	2,335	7,662	Kurile Islands, Russia	1986
Tiatia	1,833	6,013	Kurile Islands, Russia	1981
Sarychev Peak	1,512	4,960	Kurile Islands, Russia	1989
Vesuvius	1,289	4,203	Italy	1944
Stromboli	931	3,055	Lipari Islands, Italy	1996
Santorini (Thera)	584	1,960	Cyclades, Greece	1950
Indian Ocean				
Karthala	2,440	8,000	Comoros	1991
Piton de la Fournaise (Le Volcan)	1,823	5,981	Réunion Island, France	1998
mid-Pacific				
Mauna Loa	4,170	13,681	Hawaii, USA	1984
Kilauea	1,247	4,100	Hawaii, USA	1998
North America				
Popocatépetl	5,452	17,887	Altiplano de México, Mexico	1997
Colima	4,268	14,003	Altiplano de México, Mexico	1994
Spurr	3,374	11,070	Alaska Range (AK) USA	1953
Lassen Peak	3,186	10,453	California, USA	1921
Redoubt	3,108	10,197	Alaska Range (AK) USA	1991
Iliamna	3,052	10,016	Alaska Range (AK) USA	1978
Shishaldin	2,861	9,387	Aleutian Islands (AK) USA	1997
St Helens	2,549	8,364	Washington, USA	1995
Pavlof	2,517	8,261	Alaska Range (AK) USA	1997
Veniaminof	2,507	8,225	Alaska Range (AK) USA	1995
Novarupta (Katmai)	2,298	7,540	Alaska Range (AK) USA	1931
El Chichon	2,225	7,300	Altiplano de México, Mexico	1982
Makushin	2,036	6,680	Aleutian Islands (AK) USA	1987
Oceania				
Ruapehu	2,796	9,175	New Zealand	1997
Ulawun	2,296	7,532	Papua New Guinea	1993
Ngauruhoe	2,290	7,515	New Zealand	1977
Bagana	1,998	6,558	Papua New Guinea	1993
Manam	1,829	6,000	Papua New Guinea	1997
Lamington	1,780	5,844	Papua New Guinea	1956
Karkar	1,499	4,920	Papua New Guinea	1979
Lopevi	1,450	4,755	Vanuatu	1982
Ambrym	1,340	4,376	Vanuatu	1991
Tarawera	1,149	3,770	New Zealand	1973
Langila	1,093	3,586	Papua New Guinea	1996
Rabaul	688	2,257	Papua New Guinea	1997
Pagan	570	1,870	Mariana Islands	1993
White Island	328	1,075	New Zealand	1995
South America				
San Pedro	6,199	20,325	Andes, Chile	1960
Guallatiri	6,060	19,882	Andes, Chile	1993
Lascar	5,990	19,652	Andes, Chile	1995
San José	5,919	19,405	Andes, Chile	1931
Cotopaxi	5,897	19,347	Andes, Ecuador	1975
Tutupaca	5,844	19,160	Andes, Ecuador	1902
Ubinas	5,710	18,720	Andes, Peru	1969
Tupungatito	5,640	18,504	Andes, Chile	1986
Islunga	5,566	18,250	Andes, Chile	1960
Nevado del Ruiz	5,435	17,820	Andes, Colombia	1992
Tolima	5,249	17,210	Andes, Colombia	1943
Sangay	5,230	17,179	Andes, Ecuador	1996

*Date of last eruption

produced in Germany in 1938, to a design by Ferdinand Porsche. It was still in production in Latin America in the late 1980s, by which time it had exceeded 20 million sales.

volt SI unit of electromotive force or electric potential, symbol V. A small battery has a potential of 1.5 volts, whilst a high-tension transmission line may carry up to 765,000 volts. The domestic electricity supply in the UK is 230 volts (lowered from 240 volts in 1995); it is 110 volts in the USA.

The absolute volt is defined as the potential difference necessary to produce a current of one ampere through an electric circuit with a resistance of one ohm. It can also be defined as the potential difference that requires one joule of work to move a positive charge of one coulomb from the lower to the higher potential. It is named after the Italian scientist Alessandro Volta.

voltage commonly used term for ◊potential difference (pd) or ◊electromotive force (emf).

voltage amplifier electronic device that increases an input signal in the form of a voltage or ◊potential difference, delivering an output signal that is larger than the input by a specified ratio.

voltmeter instrument for measuring potential difference (voltage). It has a high internal resistance (so that it passes only a small current), and is connected in parallel with the component across which potential difference is to be measured. A common type is constructed from a sensitive current-detecting moving-coil ◊galvanometer placed in series with a high-value resistor (multiplier). To measure an AC (◊alternating current) voltage, the circuit must usually include a rectifier; however, a moving-iron instrument can be used to measure alternating voltages without the need for such a device.

volume in geometry, the space occupied by a three-dimensional solid object. A prism (such as a cube) or a cylinder has a volume equal to the area of the base multiplied by the height. For a pyra-

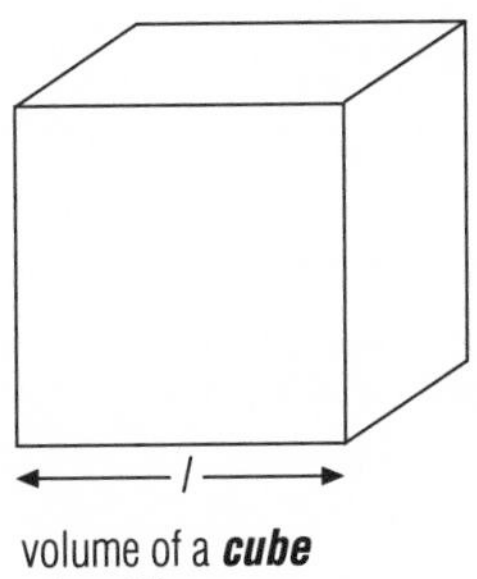

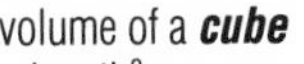

volume of a ***cube***
= length^3
= l^3

volume of a ***cuboid***
= length × breadth × height
= $l \times b \times h$

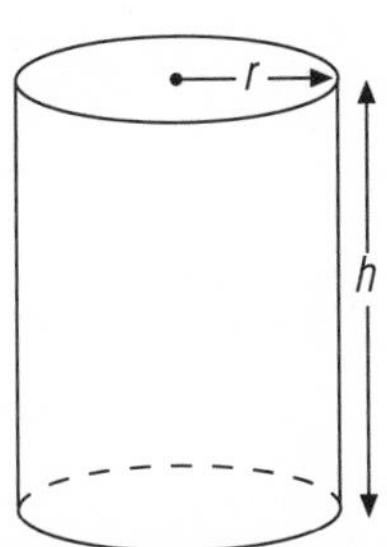

volume of a ***cylinder***
= π × (radius of cross section)^2 × height
= $\pi r^2 h$

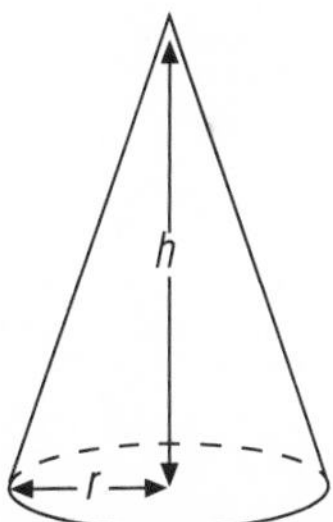

volume of a ***cone***
= $\frac{1}{3}\pi$ × (radius of cross section)^2 × height
= $\frac{1}{3}\pi r^2 h$

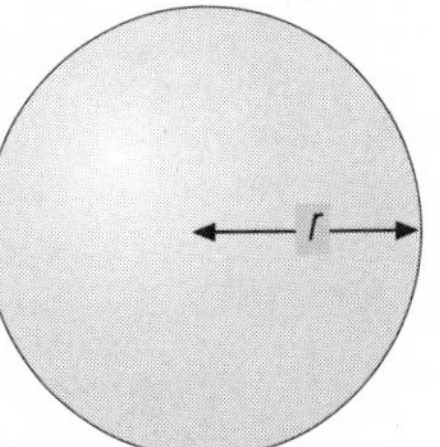

volume of a ***sphere***
= $\frac{4}{3}\pi$ radius^3
= $\frac{4}{3}\pi r^3$

volume *Volume of common three-dimensional shapes.*

TO REMEMBER THAT IF AN OBJECT FLOATS, IT DISPLACES WATER EQUAL TO ITS MASS, BUT IF IT SINKS, IT DISPLACES WATER EQUAL TO ITS VOLUME.

THINK OF A PEBBLE, MADE OF NEUTRONIUM. IT IS SMALL, BUT IT WEIGHS A LOT. IF IT WERE TO DISPLACE WATER EQUAL TO ITS MASS, THEN WHEN YOU THREW THIS LITTLE PEBBLE INTO A SWIMMING POOL, ALL THE WATER WOULD HAVE TO JUMP OUT OF THE SWIMMING POOL. SO IT MUST ONLY DISPLACE WATER EQUAL TO ITS VOLUME.

mid or cone, the volume is equal to one-third of the area of the base multiplied by the perpendicular height. The volume of a sphere is equal to $\frac{4}{3} \times \pi r^3$, where r is the radius. Volumes of irregular solids may be calculated by the technique of ◊integration. See illustration on page 795.

volumetric analysis procedure used for determining the concentration of a solution. A known volume of a solution of unknown concentration is reacted with a solution of known concentration (standard). The standard solution is delivered from a ◊burette so the volume added is known. This technique is known as ◊titration. Often an indicator is used to show when the correct proportions have reacted. This procedure is used for acid–base, ◊redox, and certain other reactions involving solutions.

Volvox genus of small, colonial, chlorophyll-containing, flagellate protozoa, common in ponds, and resembling green algae.
classification *Volvox* belongs to order Volvocida, class Phytomastigophora, subphylum Mastigophora, phylum Sarcomastigophora.

Voskhod Russian 'ascent' Soviet spacecraft used in the mid-1960s; it was modified from the single-seat Vostok, and was the first spacecraft capable of carrying two or three cosmonauts. During *Voskhod 2's* flight in 1965, Aleksi Leonov made the first space walk.

Vostok Russian 'east' first Soviet spacecraft, used 1961–63. Vostok was a metal sphere 2.3 m/7.5 ft in diameter, capable of carrying one cosmonaut. It made flights lasting up to five days. *Vostok 1* carried the first person into space, Yuri Gagarin.

Voyager probes two US space probes. *Voyager 1*, launched on 5 September 1977, passed Jupiter in March 1979, and reached Saturn in November 1980. *Voyager 2* was launched earlier, on 20 August 1977, on a slower trajectory that took it past Jupiter in July 1979, Saturn in August 1981, Uranus in January 1986, and Neptune in August 1989. Like the ◊Pioneer probes, the *Voyagers* are on their way out of the Solar System; at the start of 1995, *Voyager 1* was 8.8 billion km/5.5 billion mi from Earth, and *Voyager 2* was 6.8 billion km/4.3 billion mi from Earth. Their tasks now include helping scientists to locate the position of the heliopause, the boundary at which the influence of the Sun gives way to the forces exerted by other stars.

Both *Voyagers* carry specially coded long-playing records called *Sounds of Earth* for the enlightenment of any other civilizations that might find them.

vPoP (acronym for ***virtual point of presence***) telephone link which enables users to connect to a distant point of presence (◊PoP) for the price of a local call.

VR abbreviation for ◊velocity ratio.

VRAM (acronym for ***video random-access memory***) form of ◊RAM that allows simultaneous access by two different devices, so that graphics can be handled at the same time as data are updated. VRAM improves graphic display performance.

VR browser in computing, application that enables PC users to 'walk through' a ◊virtual reality scene on their monitors.

VRML (acronym for ***Virtual Reality Modelling Language***) in computing, method of displaying three-dimensional images on a ◊Web page. VRML, which functions as a counterpart to ◊HTML, is a platform-independent language that creates a ◊virtual reality scene which users can 'walk' through and follow links much like a conventional Web page.

In some contexts, VRML can replace conventional computer interfaces with their icons, menus, files, and folders. It is possible to use VRML to create, for example, a virtual museum with all the elements of a real museum, including corridors, display cases and multimedia demonstrations. Other possibilities include a Web market containing stalls with goods that can be 'handled' using a mouse, or a virtual library of 'books' which can be taken off 'shelves'.

VSTOL (abbreviation for ***vertical/short takeoff and landing***) aircraft capable of taking off and landing either vertically or using a very short length of runway (see ◊STOL). Vertical takeoff requires a vector-control system that permits the thrust of the aircraft engine to be changed from horizontal to vertical for takeoff and back again to horizontal to permit forward flight. An alternative VSTOL technology developed in the USA involves tilting the wings of the aircraft from vertical to horizontal and along with them the aircraft propellers, thus changing from vertical lift to horizontal thrust.

The first VSTOL was US Convair XFY-1 in 1954. The British ◊Harrier fighter bomber is the most successful VSTOL aircraft. It is now manufactured under licence in the USA and provides integral air support for the US Marines. In addition to the UK's Royal Air Force and Royal Navy, the Indian, Spanish, and Italian navies are equipped with the Harrier. It was used in the 1982 Falklands conflict and the 1991 Gulf War.

VT-100 in computing, type number of a simple character-based computer terminal originally supplied by ◊DEC (Digital Equipment Corporation). VT-100 terminal emulation is commonly provided in personal computer communications software and may be useful for logging on to minicomputers and networks via the Internet.

vulcanization technique for hardening rubber by heating and chemically combining it with sulphur. The process also makes the rubber stronger and more elastic. If the sulphur content is increased to as much as 30%, the product is the inelastic solid known as ebonite. More expensive alternatives to sulphur, such as selenium and tellurium, are used to vulcanize rubber for specialized products such as vehicle tyres. The process was discovered accidentally by US inventor Charles Goodyear in 1839 and patented in 1844.

Accelerators can be added to speed the vulcanization process, which takes from a few minutes for small objects to an hour or more for vehicle tyres. Moulded objects are often shaped and vulcanized simultaneously in heated moulds; other objects may be vulcanized in hot water, hot air, or steam.

Vulpecula small constellation in the northern hemisphere just south of ◊Cygnus, represented as a fox. It contains a major planetary ◊nebula, the Dumbbell, and the first ◊pulsar (pulsating radio source) to be discovered.

vulture any of various carrion-eating birds of prey in the order Falconiformes, with naked heads and necks, strong hooked bills, and keen senses of sight and smell. Vultures are up to 1 m/3.3 ft long, with wingspans of up to 3.7 m/12 ft. The plumage is usually dark, and the head brightly coloured.

The vulture's eyes are adapted to give an overall view with a magnifying area in the centre, enabling it to locate possible food sources and see the exact site in detail.

W abbreviation for **west**; in physics, symbol for **watt**.

W3 Consortium (W3C) computing industry group which seeks to promote standards and co-ordinate developments in the World Wide Web. Founded in 1994 and based at the Massachusetts Institute of Technology (MIT), the Consortium is directed by Tim Berners-Lee, inventor of the Web. The W3 Consortium is behind many initiatives, including the HTML (hypertext markup language) standard for building Web pages and the ◊PICS content rating system.

wadi in arid regions of the Middle East, a steep-sided valley containing an intermittent stream that flows in the wet season.

wafer in microelectronics, a 'superchip' some 8–10 cm/3–4 in in diameter, for which wafer-scale integration (WSI) is used to link the equivalent of many individual ◊silicon chips, improving reliability, speed, and cooling.

wagtail slim, narrow-billed bird of the genus *Motacilla*, in the family Motacillidae, order Passeriformes, about 18 cm/7 in long, with a characteristic flicking movement of the tail. There are about 30 species, found mostly in Eurasia and Africa.

WAIS (abbreviation for ***Wide Area Information Server***) software tool for searching for and retrieving information from a range of archives on the ◊Internet.

wait state situation when the ◊central processing unit or a ◊bus is idle. Wait states are necessary because system components run at different speeds.

Waldo in computing, a mechanical device, such as a gripper arm, that follows the movements of a human limb. Waldos were developed by the nuclear industry in the 1940s for handling hazardous substances at a safe distance, and were named after a 1942 story by science-fiction writer Robert Heinlein.

Waldsterben German 'forest death' tree decline related to air pollution, common throughout the industrialized world. It appears to be caused by a mixture of pollutants; the precise chemical mix varies between locations, but it includes acid rain, ozone, sulphur dioxide, and nitrogen oxides.

Waldsterben was first noticed in the Black Forest of Germany during the late 1970s, and is spreading to many Third World countries, such as China.

Walkman trade name of a personal stereo manufactured by the Sony corporation. Introduced in 1980, it was the first easily portable cassette player with headphones, and the name Walkman is often used as a generic term.

walkthrough in computing, another name for ◊flythrough.

wall artificial barrier of brick or stone. Walls are normally built to protect property, but in upland areas they frequently replace hedges or fences as field boundaries.

wallaby any of various small and medium-sized members of the ◊kangaroo family.

Wallace line imaginary line running down the Lombok Strait in SE Asia, between the island of Bali and the islands of Lombok and Sulawesi. It was identified by English naturalist Alfred Russel Wallace as separating the S Asian (Oriental) and Australian biogeographical regions, each of which has its own distinctive animals.

Subsequently, others have placed the boundary between these two regions at different points in the Malay archipelago, owing to overlapping migration patterns.

wallflower European perennial cottage garden plant with fragrant spikes of red, orange, yellow, brown, or purple flowers in spring. (*Cheiranthus cheiri*, family Cruciferae.)

wallpaper in computing, design used as a background 'desktop pattern' on ◊graphical user interfaces (GUIs), such as Microsoft Windows or Apple's Mac OS, and visible when no ◊windows are open. Users can choose from a range of different wallpapers, including plain colours, textures and repeating patterns, or design their own.

wall pressure in plants, the mechanical pressure exerted by the cell contents against the cell wall. The rigidity (turgor) of a plant often depends on the level of wall pressure found in the cells of the stem. Wall pressure falls if the plant cell loses water.

walnut deciduous tree, probably originating in SE Europe and now widely cultivated elsewhere. It can grow up to 30 m/100 ft high, and produces a full crop of edible nuts about twelve years after planting; the timber is used in furniture and the oil is used in cooking. (*Juglans regia*, family Juglandaceae.)

walrus Arctic marine carnivorous mammal *Odobenus rosmarus* of the same family (Otaridae) as the eared ◊seals. It can reach 4 m/13 ft in length, and weigh up to 1,400 kg/3,000 lb. It has webbed flippers, a bristly moustache, and large tusks. It is gregarious except at breeding time and feeds mainly on molluscs. It has been hunted for its ivory tusks, hide, and blubber; the Alaskan walrus is close to extinction.

WALRUS

http://www.seaworld.org/animal_bytes/walrusab.html

Illustrated guide to the walrus including information about genus, size, life span, habitat, gestation, diet, and a series of fun facts.

WAN abbreviation for **wide area** ◊network.

wand in ◊virtual reality, simple input device to allow users to interact with onscreen objects in three dimensions.

Wankel engine rotary petrol engine developed by the German engineer Felix Wankel (1902–1988) in the 1950s. It operates according to the same stages as the ◊four-stroke petrol engine cycle, but these stages take place in different sectors of a figure-eight chamber in the space between the chamber walls and a triangular rotor. Power is produced once on every turn of the rotor. The Wankel engine is simpler in construction than the four-stroke piston petrol engine, and produces rotary power directly (instead of via a crankshaft). Problems with rotor seals have prevented its widespread use.

wapiti or ***elk*** species of deer *Cervus canadensis*, native to North America, Europe, and Asia, including New Zealand. It is reddish-brown in colour, about 1.5 m/5 ft at the shoulder, weighs up to 450 kg/1,000 lb, and has antlers up to 1.2 m/4 ft long. It is becoming increasingly rare.

waratah Australian shrub or tree of the family Proteaceae, including the crimson-flowered *Telopea speciosissima*, floral emblem of New South Wales.

warble fly large, brownish, hairy flies, with mouthparts that are reduced or vestigial. The larva is a large maggot covered with spines. They cause myiasis (invasion of the tissues by fly larvae) in animals.

In agriculture, warble flies are pests, causing damage to livestock, where their presence can retard growth, reduce milk and meat yield, and render hides worthless.

The larvae of *Oestrus ovis* normally invade the nasal cavities of sheep and goats, and those of *Hypoderma* are skin parasites of cattle and other animals, causing 'ulcers' in the skin, a condition called warbles. In humans *Oestrus* invasion is rare, except for shepherds and goatherds, and the larva is more often noticed attempting to penetrate the eye than the nasal cavities. *Hypoderma* attempts to follow its normal pattern, migrating from the site of the bite to the shoulders or neck.

classification Warble flies are in family Oestridae, order Diptera, class Insecta, phylum Arthropoda.

warbler any of two families of songbirds, order Passeriformes. The Old World warblers are in the family Sylviidae, while the New World warblers are members of the Parulidae.

American or wood warblers (family Parulidae) are small, insect-eating birds, often brightly coloured, such as the yellow warbler, prothonatory warbler, and dozens of others. This group is sometimes placed in the same family (Emberizidae) as sparrows and ◊orioles. Old World warblers (family Sylviidae) are typically slim and dull-plumaged above, lighter below, insectivorous, and fruit-eating, overwhelmingly represented in Eurasia and Africa. These are sometimes considered a subgroup of the same family (Muscicapidae) that includes thrushes.

wAreZ in computing, slang for pirated games or other applications that can be downloaded using ◊FTP.

warfarin poison that induces fatal internal bleeding in rats; neutralized with sodium hydroxide, it is used in medicine as an anticoagulant in the treatment of ◊thrombosis: it prevents blood clotting by inhibiting the action of vitamin K. It can be taken orally and begins to act several days after the initial dose.

Warfarin is a crystalline powder, $C_{19}H_{16}O_4$. Heparin may be given in treatment at the same time and discontinued when warfarin takes effect. It is often given as a preventive measure, to reduce the risk of ◊thrombosis or ◊embolism after major surgery.

warning coloration in biology, an alternative term for ◊aposematic coloration.

VIRAL WARTS

http://biomed.nus.sg/nsc/viral.html

Excellent practical information about warts from Singapore's National Skin Centre. Various treatment methods, none of them foolproof, are described. There is advice for patients who have cryotherapy and reassurance to suffers that warts are not cancerous. There are three photos of various kinds of warts.

wart protuberance composed of a local overgrowth of skin. The common wart (*Verruca vulgaris*) is due to a virus infection. It usually disappears spontaneously within two years, but can be treated with peeling applications, burning away (cautery), freezing (cryosurgery), or laser treatment.

wart hog African wild ◊pig *Phacochoerus aethiopicus*, which has a large head with a bristly mane, fleshy pads beneath the eyes, and four large tusks. It has short legs and can grow to 80 cm/2.5 ft at the shoulder.

washing soda $Na_2CO_3.10H_2O$ (chemical name **sodium carbonate decahydrate**) substance added to washing water to 'soften' it (see ◊hard water).

Washington Convention alternative name for ◊CITES, the international agreement that regulates trade in endangered species.

WASP

Wasps use tools. After laying her eggs, the female sand wasp sometimes uses a small pebble to smooth sand over the entrance to her nest to seal it.

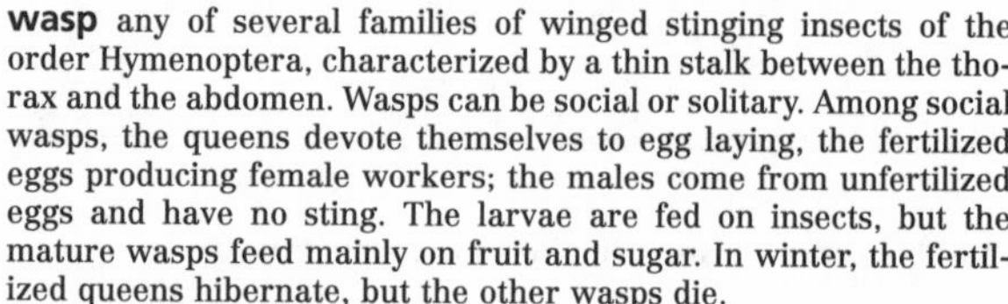

wasp any of several families of winged stinging insects of the order Hymenoptera, characterized by a thin stalk between the thorax and the abdomen. Wasps can be social or solitary. Among social wasps, the queens devote themselves to egg laying, the fertilized eggs producing female workers; the males come from unfertilized eggs and have no sting. The larvae are fed on insects, but the mature wasps feed mainly on fruit and sugar. In winter, the fertilized queens hibernate, but the other wasps die.

waste materials that are no longer needed and are discarded. Examples are household waste, industrial waste (which often contains toxic chemicals), medical waste (which may contain organisms that cause disease), and ◊nuclear waste (which is radioactive). By ◊recycling, some materials in waste can be reclaimed for further use. In 1990 the industrialized nations generated 2 billion tonnes of waste. In the USA, 40 tonnes of solid waste are generated annually per person, roughly twice as much as in Europe or Japan.

There has been a tendency to increase the amount of waste generated per person in industrialized countries, particularly through the growth in packaging and disposable products, creating a 'throwaway society'.

waste disposal depositing of waste. Methods of waste disposal vary according to the materials in the waste and include incineration, burial at designated sites, and dumping at sea. Organic waste can be treated and reused as fertilizer (see ◊sewage disposal). ◊Nuclear waste and ◊toxic waste are usually buried or dumped at sea, although this does not negate the danger.

environmental pollution Waste disposal is an increasing problem in the late 20th century. Environmental groups, such as Greenpeace and Friends of the Earth, are campaigning for more recycling, a change in lifestyle so that less waste (from packaging and containers, to nuclear materials) is produced, and safer methods of disposal.

Although incineration cuts down on landfill and can produce heat as a useful by-product it is still a wasteful method of disposal in comparison with recycling. For example, recycling a plastic bottle saves twice as much energy as is obtained by burning it.

waste disposal, USA The USA burns very little of its rubbish as compared with other industrialized countries. Most of its waste, 80%, goes into landfills. Many of the country's landfill sites will have to close in the 1990s because they do not meet standards to protect groundwater.

watch portable timepiece. In the early 20th century increasing miniaturization, mass production, and convenience led to the watch moving from the pocket to the wrist. Watches were also subsequently made waterproof, antimagnetic, self-winding, and shock-resistant. In 1957 the electric watch was developed, and in the 1970s came the digital watch, which dispensed with all moving parts.

history Traditional mechanical watches with analogue dials (hands) are based on the invention by Peter Henlein (1480–1542) of the mainspring as the energy store. By 1675 the invention of the balance spring allowed watches to be made small enough to move from waist to pocket. By the 18th century pocket-watches were

WARTHOG

http://www.seaworld.org/animal_bytes/warthogab.html

Illustrated guide to the warthog including information about genus, size, life span, habitat, gestation, diet, and a series of fun facts.

accurate, and by the 20th century wristwatches were introduced. In the 1950s battery-run electromagnetic watches were developed; in the 1960s electronic watches were marketed, which used the ◊piezoelectric oscillations of a quartz crystal to mark time and an electronic circuit to drive the hands. In the 1970s quartz watches without moving parts were developed – the solid-state watch with a display of digits. Some included a tiny calculator and such functions as date, alarm, stopwatch, and reminder beeps.

water H_2O liquid without colour, taste, or odour. It is an oxide of hydrogen with a relative molecular mass of 18. Water begins to freeze at 0°C or 32°F, and to boil at 100°C or 212°F. When liquid, it is virtually incompressible; frozen, it expands by $\frac{1}{11}$ of its volume. At 4°C/39.2°F, one cubic centimetre of water has a mass of one gram; this is its maximum density, forming the unit of specific gravity. It has the highest known specific heat, and acts as an efficient solvent, particularly when hot. Most of the world's water is in the sea; less than 0.01% is fresh water.

Water covers 70% of the Earth's surface and occurs as standing (oceans, lakes) and running (rivers, streams) water, rain, and vapour and supports all forms of life on Earth.

According to two UN reports in January 1997 large areas of the globe will start running critically short of water in the next 30 years. Total worldwide water consumption has been growing at 2.5% a year, roughly twice as fast as population, and by 1997 had reached 4,200 cubic kilometres annually. Water consumption has risen sixfold during the 20th century. Growing demands for this resource could lead to future conflicts as many rivers cross national boundaries.

water beetle aquatic beetle with an oval, flattened, streamlined shape. The head is sunk into the thorax and the hindlegs are flattened into flippers for swimming; there is a wide variation in size within the species; they are usually dark or black in colour and the entire body has a resplendent sheen. Both the adults and larvae are entirely aquatic, and are common in still, fresh waters such as ponds and lakes.

classification Water beetles are in family Dytiscidae is in the order Coleoptera, class Insecta, phylum Arthropoda.

Both adults and larvae are carnivorous. The larvae have a particularly fierce appearance with sickle-shaped mandibles, or jaws. These mandibles have holes at their tips through which the larva secretes digestive enzymes when it catches its prey. So to a great extent digestion is external, the body fluids of its victim being sucked up via the holes and the channels in the mandibles. The pupal stage is terrestrial, being spent under the soil. There are some 4,000 species within this family.

The adult beetles return to the water surface periodically to replenish their supply of air, which is trapped under their wing cases.

water boatman any water ◊bug of the family Corixidae that feeds on plant debris and algae. It has a flattened body 1.5 cm/0.6 in long, with oarlike legs.

The name is sometimes also used for the backswimmers, genus *Notonecta,* which are superficially similar, but which can fly and which belong to a different family (Notonectidae) of bugs.

water-borne disease disease associated with poor water supply. In the Third World four-fifths of all illness is caused by water-borne diseases, with diarrhoea being the leading cause of childhood death. Malaria, carried by mosquitoes dependent on stagnant water for breeding, affects 400 million people every year and kills 5 million. Polluted water is also a problem in industrialized nations, where industrial dumping of chemical, hazardous, and radioactive wastes causes a range of diseases from headache to cancer.

waterbuck any of several African ◊antelopes of the genus *Kobus* which usually inhabit swampy tracts and reedbeds. They vary in size from about 1.8m/6 ft to 2.1 m/7.25 ft long, are up to 1.4 m/4.5 ft tall at the shoulder, and have long brown fur. The large curved horns, normally carried only by the males, have corrugated surfaces. Some species have white patches on the buttocks. Lechwe, kor, and defassa are alternative names for some of the species.

water bug any of a number of aquatic ◊bugs where all stages of the life cycle (adult, larval, and egg) occur in the water; the eggs are usually attached to the stems or leaves of water plants. In contrast to the land bugs, which have quite distinctly noticeable antennae, the antennae of water bugs are hidden. In general, water bugs are also less brightly coloured; they are usually varying shades of black or brown, and tend to inhabit the bottom strata of ponds, lakes, and streams. They may or may not have wings.

classification Water bugs belong to the suborder Heteroptera, order Hemiptera, class Insecta, phylum Arthropoda.

The largest water bugs, giant waterbugs, belong to the family Belostomatidae. They found in Australia, India, China, and South America. They are over 10 cm/4 in long, and prey on insects, tadpoles, and small fish.

water closet (WC) alternative name for ◊toilet.

watercress perennial aquatic plant found in Europe and Asia and cultivated for its pungent leaves which are used in salads. (*Nasturtium officinale,* family Cruciferae.)

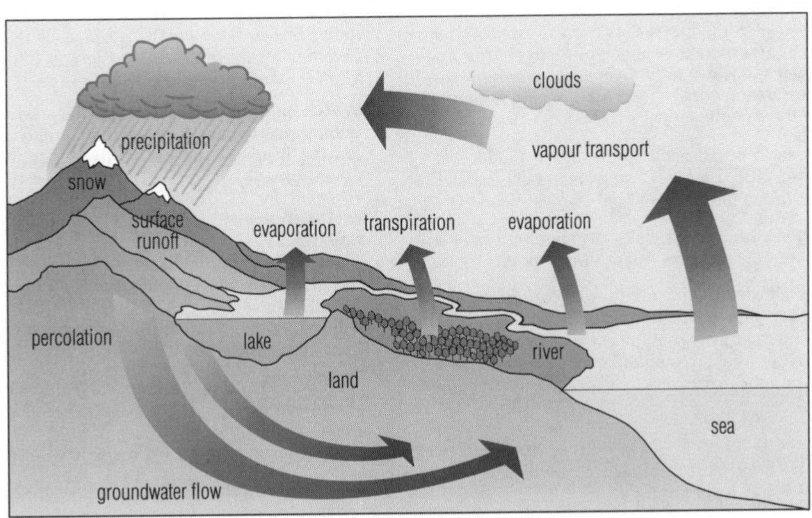

water cycle *About one-third of the solar energy reaching the Earth is used in evaporating water. About 380,000 cubic km/95,000 cubic mi is evaporated each year. The entire contents of the oceans would take about one million years to pass through the water cycle.*

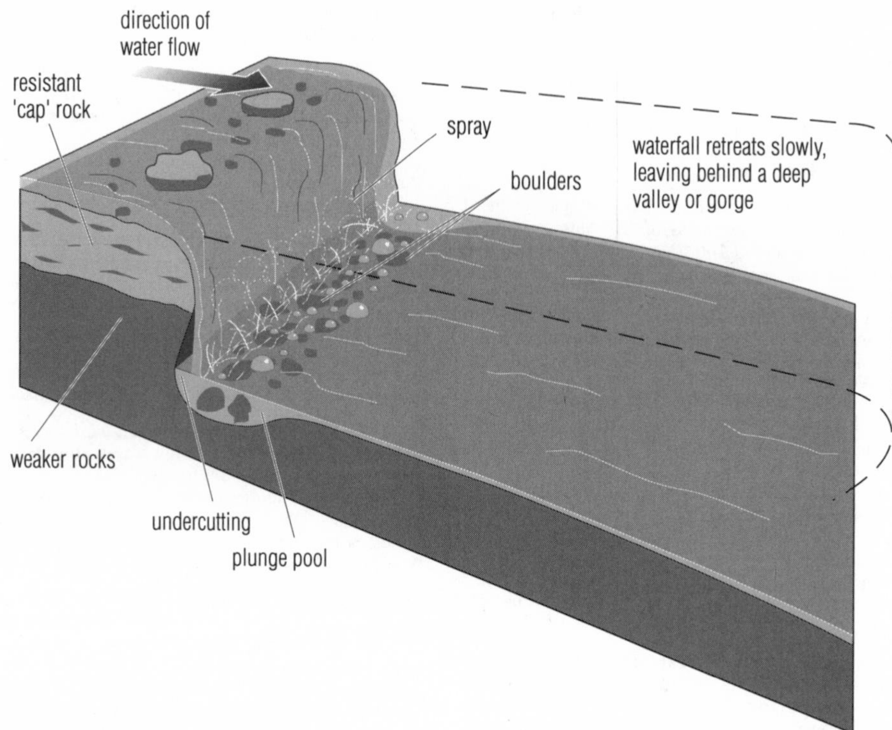

waterfall *When water flows over hard rock and soft rock, the soft rocks erode creating waterfalls. As the erosion processes continue, the falls move backwards, in the opposite direction of the water*

water cycle *or* **hydrological cycle** in ecology, the natural circulation of water through the ◊biosphere. Water is lost from the Earth's surface to the atmosphere either by evaporation caused by the Sun's heat on the surface of lakes, rivers, and oceans, or through the transpiration of plants. This atmospheric water is carried by the air moving across the Earth, and condenses as the air cools to form clouds, which in turn deposit moisture on the land and sea as rain or snow. The water that collects on land flows to the ocean in streams and rivers. *See illustration on page 803.*

waterfall cascade of water in a river or stream. It occurs when a river flows over a bed of rock that resists erosion; weaker rocks downstream are worn away, creating a steep, vertical drop and a plunge pool into which the water falls. Over time, continuing erosion causes the waterfall to retreat upstream forming a deep valley, or ◊gorge.

water flea any aquatic crustacean in the order Cladocera, of which there are over 400 species. The commonest species is *Daphnia pulex,* used in the pet trade to feed tropical fish.

waterfowl any water bird, but especially any member of the family Anatidae, which consists of ducks, geese, and swans.

water gas fuel gas consisting of a mixture of carbon monoxide and hydrogen, made by passing steam over red-hot coke. The gas was once the chief source of hydrogen for chemical syntheses such as the Haber process for making ammonia, but has been largely superseded in this and other reactions by hydrogen obtained from natural gas.

water glass common name for sodium metasilicate (Na_2SiO_3). It is a colourless, jellylike substance that dissolves readily in water to give a solution used for preserving eggs and fireproofing porous materials such as cloth, paper, and wood. It is also used as an adhesive for paper and cardboard and in the manufacture of soap and silica gel, a substance that absorbs moisture.

water hyacinth tropical aquatic plant belonging to the pickerelweed family. In one growing season 25 plants can produce 2 million new plants. It is liable to choke waterways, removing nutrients from the water and blocking out the sunlight, but it can be used to purify sewage-polluted water as well as in making methane gas, compost, concentrated protein, paper, and baskets. Originating in South America, it now grows in more than 50 countries. (*Eichhornia crassipes,* family Pontederiaceae.)

water lily any of a group of aquatic plants belonging to the water lily family. The fleshy roots are embedded in mud and the large round leaves float on the surface of the water. The cup-shaped flowers may be white, pink, yellow, or blue. (Genera *Nymphaea* and *Nuphar,* family Nymphaeaceae.)

water meadow irrigated meadow. By flooding the land for part of each year, increased yields of hay are obtained. Water meadows were common in Italy, Switzerland, and England (from 1523) but have now largely disappeared.

water measurer slender long-legged wingless bug found on the water surface or on vegetation skirting the water. They are carnivorous, feeding on animals such as water fleas. They walk slowly and gracefully on the water surface using their long legs, their bodies held above the surface film.
classification The water measurers belong to the family Hydrometridae order Hemiptera class Insecta, phylum Arthropoda.

watermelon large ◊melon belonging to the gourd family, native to tropical Africa, with a dark green rind and reddish juicy flesh studded with a large number of black seeds. It is widely cultivated in subtropical regions. (*Citrullus vulgaris,* family Cucurbitaceae.)

water mill machine that harnesses the energy in flowing water to produce mechanical power, typically for milling (grinding) grain. Water from a stream is directed against the paddles of a water wheel to make it turn. Simple gearing transfers this motion to the millstones. The modern equivalent of the water wheel is the water turbine, used in ◊hydroelectric power plants.

Although early step wheels were used in ancient China and Egypt, and parts of the Middle East, the familiar vertical water wheel came into widespread use in Roman times. There were two types: **undershot**, in which the wheel simply dipped into the stream, and the more powerful **overshot**, in which the water was directed at the top of the wheel. The Domesday Book records over 7,000 water mills in Britain. Water wheels remained a prime source of mechanical power until the development of a reliable steam engine in the 1700s, not only for milling, but also for metal-working, crushing and grinding operations, and driving machines in the early factories. The two were combined to form paddlewheel steamboats in the 18th century.

water of crystallization water chemically bonded to a salt in its crystalline state. For example, in copper(II) sulphate, there are five moles of water per mole of copper sulphate: hence its formula is $CuSO_4.5H_2O$. This water is responsible for the colour and shape of the crystalline form. When the crystals are heated gently, the water is driven off as steam and a white powder is formed.

$$CuSO_4.5H_2O_{(s)} \rightarrow CuSO_{4\,(s)} + 5H_2O_{(g)}$$

water pollution any addition to fresh or sea water that disrupts biological processes or causes a health hazard. Common pollutants include nitrates, pesticides, and sewage (see ◊sewage disposal), although a huge range of industrial contaminants, such as chemical byproducts and residues created in the manufacture of various goods, also enter water – legally, accidentally, and through illegal dumping.

In 1980 the UN launched the 'Drinking Water Decade', aiming for cleaner water for all by 1990. However, in 1994 it was estimated that approximately half of all people in the developing world did not have safe drinking water. A 1995 World Bank report estimated that some 10 million deaths in developing countries were caused annually by contaminated water.

water scorpion water bug in which the first pair of legs are modified into prehensile organs for grasping prey. They are carnivorous and feed on smaller insects. The prey is held securely between their first pair of legs while the water scorpion sucks up its body fluids.
classification Water scorpion are in family Nepidae in order Hemiptera, class Insecta, phylum Arthropoda.

Another characteristic feature of these bugs is their respiratory tube. While the bug remains at the bottom of the water, the respiratory tube reaches up to the surface, thus renewing its supply of air. The respiratory tube itself has quite a complex structure. It is made up of two grooved canals locked together by minute hairs or bristles, which give it the appearance of a single tube. At the base of the tube there are two respiratory spiracles or 'air-diffusing holes'. This respiratory tube is often wrongly believed to be a stinging organ, hence the name of water scorpion.

water softener any substance or unit that removes the hardness from water. Hardness is caused by the presence of calcium and magnesium ions, which combine with soap to form an insoluble scum, prevent lathering, and cause deposits to build up in pipes and cookware (kettle fur). A water softener replaces these ions with sodium ions, which are fully soluble and cause no scum.

waterspout funnel-shaped column of water and cloud that is drawn from the surface of the sea or a lake by a ◊tornado.

water supply distribution of water for domestic, municipal, or industrial consumption. Water supply in sparsely populated regions usually comes from underground water rising to the surface in natural springs, supplemented by pumps and wells. Urban sources are deep artesian wells, rivers, and reservoirs, usually formed from enlarged lakes or dammed and flooded valleys, from which water is conveyed by pipes, conduits, and aqueducts to filter beds. As water seeps through layers of shingle, gravel, and sand, harmful organisms are removed and the water is then distributed by pumping or gravitation through mains and pipes.
water treatment Often other substances are added to the water, such as chlorine and fluoride; aluminium sulphate, a clarifying agent, is the most widely used chemical in water treatment. In towns, domestic and municipal (road washing, sewage) needs account for about 135 l/30 gal per head each day. In coastal desert areas, such as the Arabian peninsula, desalination plants remove salt from sea water. The Earth's waters, both fresh and saline, have been polluted by industrial and domestic chemicals, some of which are toxic and others radioactive (see ◊water pollution).
drought A period of prolonged dry weather can disrupt water supply and lead to drought. The area of the world subject to serious droughts, such as the Sahara, is increasing because of destruction of forests, overgrazing, and poor agricultural practices. A World Bank report in 1995 warned that a global crisis was imminent: chronic water shortages were experienced by 40% of the world's population, notably in the Middle East, northern and sub-Saharan Africa, and central Asia. 1.4 billion people (25 % of the population) had no access to safe drinking water in 1997.

water table the upper level of ground water (water collected underground in porous rocks). Water that is above the water table will drain downwards; a spring forms where the water table cuts the surface of the ground. The water table rises and falls in response to rainfall and the rate at which water is extracted, for example, for irrigation and industry.

In many irrigated areas the water table is falling due to the extraction of water. Below N China, for example, the water table is sinking at a rate of 1 m/3 ft a year. Regions with high water tables and dense industrialization have problems with ◊pollution of the water table. In the USA, New Jersey, Florida, and Louisiana have water tables contaminated by both industrial ◊wastes and saline seepage from the ocean.

Watson, James Dewey (1928–)

Mary Evans Picture Library

US biologist. His research on the molecular structure of DNA and the genetic code, in collaboration with Francis Crick, earned him a shared Nobel prize in 1962. Based on earlier works, they were able to show that DNA formed a double helix of two spiral strands held together by base pairs.

Crick and Watson published their work on the proposed structure of DNA in 1953, and explained how genetic information could be coded.

It is necessary to be slightly underemployed if you want to do something significant.

JAMES WATSON US biologist.
The Eighth Day of Creation

watt SI unit (symbol W) of power (the rate of expenditure or consumption of energy) defined as one joule per second. A light bulb, for example, may use 40, 60, 100, or 150 watts of power; an electric heater will use several kilowatts (thousands of watts). The watt is named after the Scottish engineer James Watt.

Watt, James
(1736–1819)

Scottish engineer who developed the steam engine in the 1760s, making Thomas Newcomen's engine vastly more efficient by cooling the used steam in a condenser separate from the main cylinder. He eventually made a double-acting machine that supplied power with both directions of the piston and developed rotary motion. He also invented devices associated with the steam engine, artistic instruments and a copying process, and devised the horsepower as a description of an engine's rate of working. The modern unit of power, the watt, is named after him.

At Glascow University, Watt was asked to repair a small working model of Newcomen's steam engine, which was temperamental and difficult to operate without air entering the cylinder and destroying the vacuum. It was also extremely costly to run in terms of the coal required to keep a sufficient head of steam in a practical engine. In Newcomen's engine, the steam in the cylinder was condensed by a jet of water, creating a vacuum. The vacuum, in turn, was filled during the power stroke by the atmosphere pressing the piston to the bottom of the cylinder. On each stroke the cylinder was heated by the steam and cooled by the injected water, thus absorbing a tremendous amount of heat. Watt investigated the properties of steam and made measurements of boilers and pistons. He had the idea of a separate condenser (separate from the piston) that would allow the cylinder to be kept hot, and the condenser fairly cold by lagging, thus improving the thermal efficiency.

Mary Evans Picture Library

Working with manufacturer Matthew Boulton in 1782, Watt improved his machine by making it double-acting. Using a mechanical linkage known as 'parallel motion' and an extra set of valves, the engine was made to drive on both the forward and backward strokes of the piston, and a 'sun-and-planet' gear (also devised by Watt) allowed rotatory motion to be produced. This new and highly adaptable engine was quickly adopted by cotton and woollen mills.

During the period 1775–90, Watt invented an automatic centrifugal governor, which cut off the steam when the engine began to work too quickly and turned it on again when it had slowed sufficiently. He also devised a steam engine indicator that showed steam pressure and the degree of vacuum within the cylinder. Because of the secretarial duties connected with his business, Watt invented a way of copying letters and drawings with a chemical process that was displaced only with the advent of the typewriter and photocopier.

Watt devised a rational method to rate the capability of his engines by considering the rate at which horses worked. After many experiments, he concluded that a 'horsepower' was 33,000 lb (15,000 kg) raised through 1 ft (0.3 m) each minute. The English-speaking world used horsepower to describe the capability of an engine until recent years.

The absolute watt is defined as the power used when one joule of work is done in one second. In electrical terms, the flow of one ampere of current through a conductor whose ends are at a potential difference of one volt uses one watt of power (watts = volts × amperes).

wattle any of certain species of ◊acacia in Australia, where their fluffy golden flowers are the national emblem. The leathery leaves are adapted to drought conditions and avoid loss of water through ◊transpiration by turning their edges to the direct rays of the sun. Wattles are used for tanning leather and in fencing.

WAV (abbreviation of ***Windows WAVeform***) in computing, audio file format for ◊IBM-compatible PCs, widely used to distribute sounds over the Internet. WAV files, which contain a digitized recording of a sound, bear the suffix .wav.

wave in the oceans, a ridge or swell formed by wind or other causes. The power of a wave is determined by the strength of the wind and the distance of open water over which the wind blows (the fetch). Waves are the main agents of ◊coastal erosion and deposition: sweeping away or building up beaches, creating ◊spits and berms, and wearing down cliffs by their hydraulic action and by the corrosion of the sand and shingle that they carry. A ◊tsunami (misleadingly called a 'tidal wave') is formed after a submarine earthquake.

As a wave approaches the shore it is forced to break as a result of friction with the sea bed. When it breaks on a beach, water and sediment are carried up the beach as **swash**; the water then drains back as **backwash**.

A **constructive wave** causes a net deposition of material on the shore because its swash is stronger than its backwash. Such waves tend be low and have crests that spill over gradually as they break. The backwash of a **destructive wave** is stronger than its swash, and therefore causes a net removal of material from the shore. Destructive waves are usually tall and have peaked crests that plunge downwards as they break, trapping air as they do so.

If waves strike a beach at an angle the beach material will be gradually moved along the shore (longshore drift), causing a deposition of material in some areas and erosion in others.

Atmospheric instability caused by the ◊greenhouse effect and global warming appears to be increasing the severity of Atlantic storms and the heights of the ocean waves. Waves in the South Atlantic are shrinking – they are on average half a metre smaller than in the mid-1980s – and those in the Northeast Atlantic have doubled in size over the last 40 years. As the height of waves affects the supply of marine food, this could affect fish stocks, and there are also implications for shipping and oil and gas rigs in the North Atlantic, which will need to be strengthened if they are to avoid damage.

wave in physics, a disturbance travelling through a medium (or space). There are two types: in a ◊longitudinal wave, such as a sound wave, the disturbance is parallel to the wave's direction of travel; in a ◊transverse wave, such as an electromagnetic wave, it is perpendicular. The medium (for example the Earth, for seismic waves) is not permanently displaced by the passage of a wave. See also ◊standing wave.

> *Physicists use the wave theory on Mondays, Wednesdays and Fridays, and the particle theory on Tuesdays, Thursdays and Saturdays.*
>
> WILLIAM HENRY BRAGG British physicist. Attributed remark

wave-cut platform gently sloping rock surface found at the foot of a coastal cliff. Covered by water at high tide but exposed at low tide, it represents the last remnant of an eroded headland (see ◊coastal erosion).

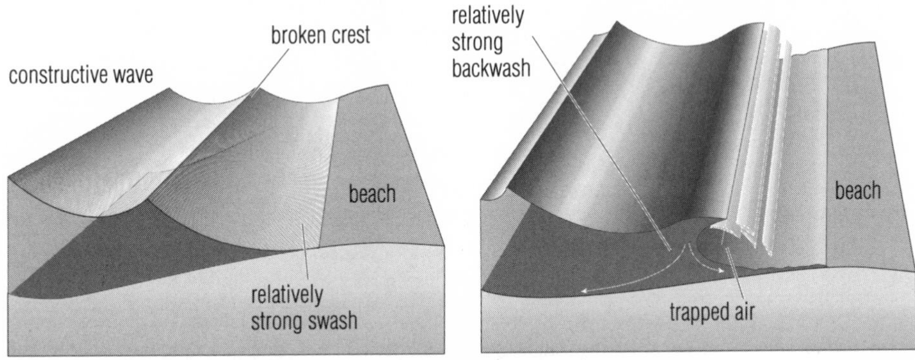

wave The low gentle crests of a constructive wave, with the energy of the wave flowing up the beach in a strong swash and depositing material, contrasts with the high steep crested more forceful motions of destructive waves which crash in at an angle to the beach directing all their energy into plunging waves which tear up the sand and shingle and carry it out with the strong backwash.

waveguide hollow metallic tube, either empty or containing a ◊dielectric used to guide a high-frequency electromagnetic wave (microwave) travelling within it. The wave is reflected from the internal surfaces of the guide. Waveguides are extensively used in radar systems.

wavelength the distance between successive crests of a ◊wave. The wavelength of a light wave determines its colour; red light has a wavelength of about 700 nanometres, for example. The complete range of wavelengths of electromagnetic waves is called the electromagnetic ◊spectrum.

wave power power obtained by harnessing the energy of water waves. Various schemes have been advanced since 1973, when oil prices rose dramatically and an energy shortage threatened. In 1974 the British engineer Stephen Salter developed the duck – a floating boom whose segments nod up and down with the waves. The nodding motion can be used to drive pumps and spin generators. Another device, developed in Japan, uses an oscillating water column to harness wave power. A major breakthrough will be required if wave power is ever to contribute significantly to the world's energy needs, although several ideas have reached prototype stage.

A 75-kW wave-power generator off the Scottish island of Islay is one of only three in the world connected to a power grid. Since 1987 the British government has invested £1 million into this generator as a trial for a large-scale plant. In 1994 the Department of Trade and Industry announced that it would not help to fund a 600-kW version because the technology had 'limited potential', but a European grant rescued the project, and a second example is to be built.

wavetable synthesizer ◊MIDI synthesizer that uses sampling – recordings of actual musical instruments – to create sounds. The authenticity of the sound source means that wavetable synthesizers can achieve very realistic results.

wax solid fatty substance of animal, vegetable, or mineral origin.

Waxes are composed variously of ◊esters, fatty acids, free ◊alcohols, and solid hydrocarbons.

Mineral waxes are obtained from petroleum and vary in hardness from the soft petroleum jelly (or petrolatum) used in ointments to the hard paraffin wax employed for making candles and waxed paper for drinks cartons.

Animal waxes include beeswax, the wool wax lanolin, and spermaceti from sperm-whale oil; they are used mainly in cosmetics, ointments, and polishes. Another animal wax is tallow, a form of suet obtained from cattle and sheep's fat, once widely used to make candles and soap. Sealing wax is made from lac or shellac, a resinous substance obtained from secretions of ◊scale insects.

Vegetable waxes, which usually occur as a waterproof coating on plants that grow in hot, arid regions, include carnauba wax (from the leaves of the carnauba palm) and candelilla wax, both of which are components of hard polishes such as car waxes.

waxbill any of a group of small, mainly African, seed-eating birds in the family Estrildidae, order Passeriformes, which also includes the grass finches of Australia. Waxbills grow to 15 cm/6 in long, are brown and grey with yellow, red, or brown markings, and have waxy-looking red or pink beaks.

They sometimes raise the young of ◊whydahs, who lay their eggs in waxbill nests.

waxflower name given to Australian wildflowers of the genus *Eriostemon*.

wax moth greyish-brown moth with a wing span of about 3 cm/1.2 in that is a pest of beehives.

The adult female moth penetrates the hive and lays her eggs directly on the comb. The larvae feed on the wax, the pollen, and even, if there are many larvae, on the host's brood.

Proper care of the hive, and fumigating the combs before storing them, tends to keep wax moths under control.

classification Wax moths *Galleria mellonella* are in family Pyralidae, order Lepidoptera, class Insecta, phylum Arthropoda.

wax myrtle evergreen bush or tree *Myrica cerifera* of the barberry family, native to SE North America. Its fruit consists of greyish nutlets coated with a wax that is collected for making scented candles; 0.5 kg/1 lb of nutlets immersed in hot water yields about 115 g/4 oz of wax. The fruit is eaten by ground-dwelling birds such as the bobwhite and wild turkey.

waxwing any of several fruit-eating birds of the family Bombycillidae, order Passeriformes. They are found in the northern hemisphere. The Bohemian waxwing *Bombycilla garrulus* of North America and Eurasia is about 18 cm/7 in long, and is greyish-brown above with a reddish-chestnut crest, black streak at the eye, and variegated wings. It undertakes mass migrations in some years.

wayfaring tree European shrub belonging to the honeysuckle family, with clusters of fragrant white flowers, found on limy soils; it is naturalized in the northeastern USA. (*Viburnum lantana*, family Caprifoliaceae.)

weak acid acid that only partially ionizes in aqueous solution (see ◊dissociation). Weak acids include ethanoic acid and carbonic acid. The pH of such acids lies between pH 3 and pH 6.

weak base base that only partially ionizes in aqueous solution (see ◊dissociation); for example, ammonia. The pH of such bases lies between pH 8 and pH 10.

weak nuclear force *or* **weak interaction** one of the four fundamental forces of nature, the other three being gravity, the electromagnetic force, and the strong force. It causes radioactive beta decay and other subatomic reactions. The particles that carry the weak force are called ◊weakons (or intermediate vector bosons) and comprise the positively and negatively charged W particles and the neutral Z particle.

weakon or ***intermediate vector boson*** in physics, a ◊gauge boson that carries the weak nuclear force, one of the fundamental forces of nature. There are three types of weakon, the positive and negative W particle and the neutral Z particle.

The assumption of a state of matter more finely subdivided than the atom of an element is a somewhat startling one.

J J Thomson English physicist.
Royal Institution Lecture 1897

weapon any implement used for attack and defence, from simple clubs, spears, and bows and arrows in prehistoric times to machine guns and nuclear bombs in modern times. The first revolution in warfare came with the invention of ◊gunpowder and the development of cannons and shoulder-held guns. Many other weapons now exist, such as grenades, shells, torpedoes, rockets, and guided missiles. The ultimate in explosive weapons are the atomic (fission) and hydrogen (fusion) bombs. They release the enormous energy produced when atoms split or fuse together. There are also chemical and bacteriological weapons, which release poisons or disease.

There floated through my mind a line from the Bhagavad Gita in which Krishna is trying to persuade the Prince to do his duty: 'I am become death, the shatterer of worlds'.

J Robert Oppenheimer US physicist.
On seeing the first atomic bomb explosion, quoted in
P Goodchild *Oppenheimer: The Father of the Atomic Bomb* 1983

weapons, nonlethal weapons designed to disable enemy troops or weaponry without fatalities.

The US nonlethal weapons programme is highly secretive but research in 1994 was believed to include low frequency noise to disorient troops, a highly adhesive foam to impede both machinery and people, and lasers to cause temporary blindness; production of these laser weapons was stopped in the USA in 1995, and the United Nations stated it was considering a ban on all such weapons.

The taser, a nonlethal stun weapon, is available commercially in the USA. It fires two darts connected to a wire that delivers a voltage sufficiently great to cause muscles to spasm, thereby temporarily disabling the target.

weasel any of various small, short-legged, lithe carnivorous mammals with bushy tails, especially the genus *Mustela,* found worldwide except Australia. They feed mainly on small rodents although some, like the mink *M. vison,* hunt aquatic prey. Most are 12–25 cm/5–10 in long, excluding the tail.

Included in this group are the North American long-tailed weasel, the northern hemisphere ermine or stoat, the Eurasian polecat, and the endangered North American black-footed ferret. In cold regions the coat colour of several species changes to white during the winter.

weather day-to-day variation of climatic and atmospheric conditions at any one place, or the state of these conditions at a place at any one time. Such conditions include humidity, precipitation, temperature, cloud cover, visibility, and wind. To a meteorologist the term 'weather' is limited to the state of the sky, precipitation, and visibility as affected by fog or mist. A region's ◊climate is derived from the average weather conditions over a long period of time. See also ◊meteorology.

Weather forecasts, in which the likely weather is predicted for a particular area, based on meteorological readings, may be short-range (covering a period of one or two days), medium-range (five to seven days), or long-range (a month or so). Readings from a series of scattered recording stations are collected and compiled on a weather map. Such a procedure is called synoptic forecasting. The weather map uses conventional symbols to show the state of the sky, the wind speed and direction, the kind of precipitation, and other details at each gathering station. Points of equal atmospheric pressure are joined by lines called isobars (lines joining places of equal pressure). The trends shown on such a map can be extrapolated to predict what weather is coming.

DAN'S WILD WILD WEATHER PAGE

http://www.whnt19.com/kidwx/index.html

Excellent introduction to the weather for kids. It has pages dealing with everything from climate to lightning, from satellite forecasting to precipitation; all explained in a lively style with plenty of pictures.

weather area any of the divisions of the sea around the British Isles for the purpose of weather forecasting for shipping. The areas are used to indicate where strong or gale-force winds are expected.

weathering process by which exposed rocks are broken down on the spot by the action of rain, frost, wind, and other elements of the weather. It differs from ◊erosion in that no movement or transportion of the broken-down material takes place. Two types of weathering are recognized: physical (or mechanical) and chemical. They usually occur together.
physical weathering This includes such effects as freeze–thaw (the splitting of rocks by the alternate freezing and thawing of water trapped in cracks) and exfoliation, or onion-skin weathering (flaking caused by the alternate expansion and contraction of rocks in response to extreme changes in temperature).
chemical weathering Involving a chemical change in the rocks affected, the most common form is caused by rainwater that has absorbed carbon dioxide from the atmosphere and formed a weak carbonic acid. This then reacts with certain minerals in the rocks and breaks them down. Examples are the solution of caverns in limestone terrains, and the breakdown of feldspars in granite to form china clay or kaolin.

Although physical and chemical weathering normally occur together, in some instances it is difficult to determine which type is involved. For example, exfoliation, which produces rounded ◊inselbergs in arid regions, such as Ayers Rock in central Australia, may be caused by the daily physical expansion and contraction of the surface layers of the rock in the heat of the Sun, or by the chemical reaction of the minerals just beneath the surface during the infrequent rains of these areas.

Weathering

physical weathering	
temperature changes	weakening rocks by expansion and contraction
frost	wedging rocks apart by the expansion of water on freezing
unloading	the loosening of rock layers by release of pressure after the erosion and removal of those layers above
chemical weathering	
carbonation	the breakdown of calcite by reaction with carbonic acid in rainwater
hydrolysis	the breakdown of feldspar into china clay by reaction with carbonic acid in rainwater
oxidation	the breakdown of iron-rich minerals due to rusting
hydration	the expansion of certain minerals due to the uptake of water

weaver any small bird of the family Ploceidae, order Passeriformes; they are mostly about 15 cm/6 in long. The majority of weavers are African, a few Asian. The males use grasses to weave elaborate globular nests in bushes and trees. The nests are entered from beneath, and the male hangs from it calling and flapping his wings to attract a female. Their bodies are somewhat elongated and the tails long, and the prominent conical bill is very powerful. They eat insects and may eat cultivated grain. Males are often more brightly coloured than females.

Many kinds are polygamous, so build several nests, and some species build large communal nests with many chambers. One species, the red-billed African quelea *Quelea quelea,* lives and breeds in flocks numbering many thousands of individuals; the flocks migrate to follow food sources. Their destructive power can equal that of locusts.

Web authoring tool in computing, software for creating ◊Web pages. The basic Web authoring tool is ◊HTML, the source code that determines how a Web page is constructed and how it looks. Other programs, such as Java and ◊VRML, can also be incorporated to enhance Web pages with animations and interactive features. Commercial authoring tools include HoTMetaL PRO, NetObjects' Fusion, and Microsoft's Front Page.

Web browser in computing, client software that allows access to the World-Wide Web. See ◊browser.

weber SI unit (symbol Wb) of ◊magnetic flux (the magnetic field strength multiplied by the area through which the field passes). It is named after German chemist Wilhelm Weber. One weber equals 10^8 ◊maxwells.

A change of flux at a uniform rate of one weber per second in an electrical coil with one turn produces an electromotive force of one volt in the coil.

Webmaster in computing, ◊system administrator for a server on the ◊World Wide Web.

Web page in computing, a ◊hypertext document on the ◊World Wide Web.

webspinner gregarious webspinning insects that construct and live in silken tunnels. They are generally found living under stones or bark. There are 140 species, mainly tropical.

Webspinners are small and either brown or yellowish-brown, with smoky wings. The female is wingless and the males, usually, have two pairs of wings. ◊Metamorphosis is absent in the females and slight in the males. The females take care of the eggs and young.

classification Webspinners are in order Embioptera, class Insecta, phylum Arthropoda.

webzine magazine published on the Web, instead of on paper. Notable examples include *FEED* (about culture and technology), *Slate* (a serious periodical funded by ◊Microsoft), and *Suck* (satire).

wedge block of triangular cross-section that can be used as a simple machine. An axe is a wedge: it splits wood by redirecting the energy of the downward blow sideways, where it exerts the force needed to split the wood.

weedkiller *or* **herbicide** chemical that kills some or all plants. Selective herbicides are effective with cereal crops because they kill all broad-leaved plants without affecting grasslike leaves. Those that kill all plants include sodium chlorate and ◊paraquat; see also ◊Agent Orange. The widespread use of weedkillers in agriculture has led to an increase in crop yield but also to pollution of soil and water supplies and killing of birds and small animals, as well as creating a health hazard for humans.

weever fish any of a family (Trachinidae) of marine bony fish of the perch family, especially the genus *Trachinus,* with poison glands on the dorsal fin and gill cover that can give a painful sting. It grows up to 5 cm/2 in long, has eyes near the top of the head, and lives on sandy seabeds.

weevil any of a superfamily (Curculionoidea) of ◊beetles, usually less than 6 mm/0.25 in long, and with a head prolonged into a downward beak, which is used for boring into plant stems and trees for feeding.

The larvae are usually white and the adults green, black, or

WWW address (URL)

icons link to required audio and video plug-ins

hot spots

user clicks on 'Enter' - a hypertext link to . . .

. . . a menu page of graphic hotspots . . .

. . . and selects an interactive game

web page *An example of how pages on the World Wide Web may be linked to take the user to additional pages of information.*

weevil *The long down-turned snout or beak typical of the weevils is clearly seen on this* Rhinastus latesternus *from the rainforests of Peru. This is a giant of its kind; most European weevils would fit comfortably on the tip of its snout. The larvae develop inside tree branches.* *Premaphotos Wildlife*

brown. The grain weevil *Sitophilus granarius* is a serious pest of stored grain and the boll weevil *Anthonomus grandis* damages cotton crops.

Wegener, Alfred Lothar (1880–1930)

German meteorologist and geophysicist whose theory of continental drift, expounded in Origin of Continents and Oceans in 1915, was originally known as 'Wegener's hypothesis'. His ideas can now be explained in terms of plate tectonics, the idea that the Earth's crust consists of a number of plates, all moving with respect to one another.

Mary Evans Picture Library

weight the force exerted on an object by ◊gravity. The weight of an object depends on its mass – the amount of material in it – and the strength of the Earth's gravitational pull, which decreases with height. Consequently, an object weighs less at the top of a mountain than at sea level. On the surface of the Moon, an object has only one-sixth of its weight on Earth, because the Moon's surface gravity is one-sixth that of the Earth.

weightlessness the apparent loss in weight of a body in ◊free fall. Astronauts in an orbiting spacecraft do not feel any weight because they are falling freely in the Earth's gravitational field. It is incorrect to attribute weightlessness to the astronauts being beyond the influence of Earth's gravity. The same phenomenon can be experienced in a falling lift or in an aircraft deliberately imitating the path of a freely falling object.

weights and measures see under ◊c.g.s. system, f.p.s. system, m.k.s. system, SI units.

God has ordered all his creation by Weight and Measure.

JUSTUS VON LIEBIG German chemist.
Notice above entrance to Liebig's laboratory

Weil's disease or ***leptospirosis*** infectious disease of animals that is occasionally transmitted to human beings, usually by contact with water contaminated with rat urine. It is characterized by acute fever, and infection may spread to the brain, liver, kidneys, and heart. It has a 10% mortality rate.

The usual form occurring in humans is caused by a spiral-shaped bacterium (spirochete) that is a common parasite of rats. The condition responds poorly to antibiotics, and death may result.

Weimaraner breed of large gundog bred in the German state of Weimar at the end of the 18th century as a pointer. Its smooth coat is a striking silvery grey. It has an athletic build, stands up to 69 cm/27.5 in tall, and its tail is docked.

Weimaraners are unusual in having pale amber or even blue-grey eyes.

weir low wall built across a river to raise the water level.

welding joining pieces of metal (or nonmetal) at faces rendered plastic or liquid by heat or pressure (or both). The principal processes today are gas and arc welding, in which the heat from a gas flame or an electric arc melts the faces to be joined. Additional 'filler metal' is usually added to the joint.

Forge (or hammer) welding, employed by blacksmiths since early times, was the only method available until the late 19th century. Resistance welding is another electric method in which the weld is formed by a combination of pressure and resistance heating from an electric current. Recent developments include electric-slag, electron-beam, high-energy laser, and the still experimental radio-wave energy-beam welding processes.

WELL, the (acronym for ***Whole Earth 'Lectronic Link***) San Francisco-based electronic conferencing system. It was founded in 1984 by Stewart Brand, with Larry Brilliant, Matthew McClure, and Kevin Kelly (later founding editor of ◊*Wired* magazine). The WELL includes among its 11,000 members a mix of leading journalists and writers, Grateful Dead fans, and technological inventors.

The WELL featured in the 1995 arrest of hacker Kevin Mitnick, and was the site where the first few Computers, Freedom, and Privacy conferences (annual gatherings to discuss the future impact of technology) were planned. The WELL was bought in 1994 by Reebok founder Bruce Katz.

Welsh corgi breed of dog with a foxlike head and pricked ears, originally bred for cattle herding. The coat is dense, with several varieties of colouring. Corgis are about 30 cm/12 in at the shoulder, and weigh up to 12 kg/27 lb.

There are two types of corgi, the Pembrokeshire and the Cardiganshire. The Pembrokeshire has a finely textured coat, yellowish or reddish brown, or sometimes black and tan, and has almost no tail. The Cardiganshire corgi has a short, rough coat, usually red and white, and a long furry tail. Their small size was an advantage because cattle were unable to bend low enough to gore them.

welwitschia woody plant found in the deserts of SW Africa. It has a long, water-absorbent taproot and can live for up to 100 years. (*Welwitschia mirabilis*, order Gnetales.)

Westerlies prevailing winds from the west that occur in both hemispheres between latitudes of about 35° and 60°. Unlike the ◊trade winds, they are very variable and produce stormy weather.

The Westerlies blow mainly from the SW in the northern hemisphere and the NW in the southern hemisphere, bringing moist weather to the W coast of the landmasses in these latitudes.

West Highland terrier breed of small, stockily-built ◊terrier from Scotland with short legs and fairly long pure white coat. It stands about 28 cm/11 in tall.

weta flightless insect *Deinacrida rugosa,* 8.5 cm/3.5 in long, resembling a large grasshopper, found on offshore islands of New Zealand.

wetland permanently wet land area or habitat. Wetlands include areas of ◊marsh, fen, ◊bog, flood plain, and shallow coastal areas. Wetlands are extremely fertile. They provide warm, sheltered waters for fisheries, lush vegetation for grazing livestock, and an abundance of wildlife. Estuaries and seaweed beds are more than 16 times as productive as the open ocean.

The term is often more specifically applied to a naturally flooding area that is managed for agriculture or wildlife. A water meadow, where a river is expected to flood grazing land at least once a year thereby replenishing the soil, is a traditional example.

WHALE

A whale's skull is made up of 30 bones (compared with 22 in the human skull).

whale any marine mammal of the order Cetacea. The only mammals to have adapted to living entirely in water, they have front limbs modified into flippers and no externally visible traces of hind limbs. They have horizontal tail flukes. When they surface to breathe, the hot air they breathe out condenses to form a 'spout' through the blowhole (single or double nostrils) in the top of the head. Whales are intelligent and have a complex communication system, known as 'songs'. They occur in all seas of the world.

The order is divided into two groups: the toothed whales (Odontoceti) and the baleen whales (Mysticeti). Toothed whales are predators, feeding on fish and squid. They include ◊dolphins and ◊porpoises, along with large forms such as sperm whales. The largest whales are the baleen whales, with plates of modified mucous membrane called baleen (whalebone) in the mouth; these strain the food, mainly microscopic plankton, from the water. Baleen whales include the finback and right whales, and the blue whale, the largest animal that has ever lived, of length up to 30 m/100 ft.

Whales have been hunted for hundreds of years (see ◊whaling); today they are close to extinction. Of the 11 great whale species, 7 were listed as either endangered or vulnerable in 1996. Whale-watching, as an economic alternative to whaling, generated $121 million worldwide in 1994.

whaling the hunting of whales. Whales have been killed by humans since at least the middle ages. There were hundreds of thousands of whales at the beginning of the 20th century, but the invention of the harpoon in 1870 and improvements in ships and mechanization have led to the near-extinction of several species of whale. Commercial whaling was largely discontinued in 1986, although Norway and Japan have continued commercial whaling.

Traditional whaling areas include the coasts of Greenland and Newfoundland, but the Antarctic, in the summer months, supplies the bulk of the catch.

Practically the whole of the animal can be utilized in one form or another: whales are killed for whale oil (made from the thick layer of fat under the skin called 'blubber'), which is used as a lubricant, or for making soap, candles, and margarine; for the large reserve of oil in the head of the sperm whale, used in the leather industry; and for **ambergris**, a waxlike substance from the intestines of the sperm whale, used in making perfumes. Whalebone was used by corset manufacturers and in the brush trade; there are now synthetic substitutes for all these products. Whales have also been killed for use in petfood manufacture in the USA and Europe, and as a food in Japan. The flesh and ground bones are used as soil fertilizers.

wheat cereal plant derived from the wild *Triticum,* a grass native to the Middle East. It is the chief cereal used in breadmaking and is widely cultivated in temperate climates suited to its growth. Wheat is killed by frost, and damp makes the grains soft, so warm, dry regions produce the most valuable grain.

The main wheat-producing areas of the world are the Ukraine, the prairie states of the USA, the Punjab in India, the prairie provinces of Canada, parts of France, Poland, S Germany, Italy, Argentina, and SE Australia. Flour is milled from the nutritious tissue surrounding the embryonic plant in the grain (the ◊endosperm); the coatings of the grain produce bran. Semolina is also prepared from wheat; it is a by-product from the manufacture of fine flour.

wheatear small (15 cm/6 in long) migratory bird *Oenanthe oenanthe* of the family Muscicapidae, order Passeriformes (which includes thrushes). Wheatears are found throughout the Old World and also breed in far northern parts of North America. The plumage is light grey above and white below with a buff tinge on the breast, a black face-patch, and black and white wings and tail. In flight a white patch on the lower back and tail is conspicuous. The wheatear's food consists chiefly of insects.

whelk any of various families of large marine snails with a thick spiral shell, especially the family Buccinidae. Whelks are scavengers, and also eat other shellfish. The largest grow to 40 cm/16 in long. Tropical species, such as the conches, can be very colourful.

whey watery by-product of the cheesemaking process, which is drained off after the milk has been heated and ◊rennet (a curdling agent) added to induce its coagulation.

In Scandinavia, especially Norway, whey is turned into cheese, *mysost* and (from goat's whey) *gjetost.* The flavour of whey cheese is sweet from added brown sugar and is an acquired taste.

whimbrel wading bird *Numenius phaeopus,* order Charadriiformes, with a medium-sized down-curved bill, streaked brown plumage, and striped head. About 40 cm/1.3 ft long, it breeds in the Arctic, and winters in Africa, S North America, South America, and S Asia. It is related to the ◊curlew.

whiplash injury damage to the neck vertebrae and their attachments caused by a sudden backward jerk of the head and neck. It is most often seen in vehicle occupants as a result of the rapid deceleration experienced in a crash.

whippet breed of dog resembling a small greyhound. It grows to 56 cm/22 in at the shoulder, and 9 kg/20 lb in weight.

whippoorwill North American ◊nightjar *Caprimulgus vociferus,* order Caprimulgiformes, so called from its cry during the nights of its breeding season. It is about 25 cm/10 in long, mottled tawny brown in colour, with a white collar on the throat, and long, stiff bristles at the base of the bill.

whip snake or ***coachwhip*** any of the various species of nonpoisonous slender-bodied tree-dwelling snakes of the New World genus *Masticophis,* family Colubridae. They are closely allied to members of the genus *Coluber* of SW North America, Eurasia, Australasia, and N Africa, some of which are called whip snakes in the Old World, but racers in North America.

Whip snakes grow to about 1.5 m/5 ft in length, move very quickly, and are partially tree-dwelling. They feed on rodents, small birds, lizards, sucker frogs, and insects. All lay eggs.

whirligig beetle aquatic steel-black beetle with an oval, flattened body. The second and third pairs of legs are exceptionally

short and broad, and are used for paddling in the water. About 400 species have been recorded.
classification The whirligig beetle is in the family Gyrinidae of order Coleoptera, class Insecta, phylum Arthropoda.

Whirligig beetles are usually found in groups whirling around on the water surface. When disturbed they dart into the water. Both adults and larvae are carnivorous, feeding on small insects that fall onto the water. The adults have well developed wings and are capable of flying from one pond to the next.

whirling disease parasitic disease of trout. The parasite *Myxobolus cerebralis* spends part of its life cycle in tubifex worms, before moving to trout where it consumes the cartilage causing eventual death. Infected fish start to swim in circles after their spines have been destroyed, hence the name.

whirlwind rapidly rotating column of air, often synonymous with a ◊tornado. On a smaller scale it produces the dust-devils seen in deserts.

whitebait any of the fry (young) of various silvery fishes, especially ◊herring. It is also the name for a Pacific smelt *Osmerus mordax*.

whitebeam tree native to S Europe, usually found growing on chalk or limestone. It can reach 20 m/60 ft in height. It takes its name from the dense coat of short white hairs on the underside of the leaves. (*Sorbus aria,* family Rosaceae.)

white blood cell or *leucocyte* one of a number of different cells that play a part in the body's defences and give immunity against disease. Some (◊phagocytes and ◊macrophages) engulf invading microorganisms, others kill infected cells, while ◊lymphocytes produce more specific immune responses. White blood cells are colourless, with clear or granulated cytoplasm, and are capable of independent amoeboid movement. They occur in the blood, ◊lymph, and elsewhere in the body's tissues.

Unlike mammalian red blood cells, they possess a nucleus. Human blood contains about 11,000 leucocytes to the cubic millimetre – about one to every 500 red cells.

White blood cell numbers may be reduced (leucopenia) by starvation, pernicious anaemia, and certain infections, such as typhoid and malaria. An increase in their numbers (leucocytosis) is a reaction to normal events such as digestion, exertion, and pregnancy, and to abnormal ones such as loss of blood, cancer, and most infections.

white dwarf small, hot ◊star, the last stage in the life of a star such as the Sun. White dwarfs make up 10% of the stars in the Galaxy; most have a mass 60% of that of the Sun, but only 1% of the Sun's diameter, similar in size to the Earth. Most have surface temperatures of 8,000°C/14,400°F or more, hotter than the Sun. Yet, being so small, their overall luminosities may be less than 1% of that of the Sun. The Milky Way contains an estimated 50 billion white dwarfs.

whitefish any of various freshwater fish, genera *Coregonus* and *Prosopium,* of the salmon family, found in lakes and rivers of North America and Eurasia. They include the **whitefish** *C. clupeaformis* and **cisco** *C. artedi.*

whitefly tiny four-winged insect related to aphids and scale insects. The adults barely exceed a length of 3 mm/0.12 in; their wings are dusted with a powdery white wax which they secrete. In temperate countries they may be found in glasshouses, where they are pests of plants, such as cucumber and tomato. They are widely distributed in the tropics, where they attack citrus trees. They injure the plant by feeding on the sap and excreting honeydew, which encourages sooty black mould to grow.
classification Whiteflies are in family Aleyrodidae in order Hemiptera, class Insecta, phylum Arthropoda.
development In general the eggs are laid on the undersurface of leaves in a characteristic circular or arch-shape, and are attached to the leaves by means of a stalk. Each female lays about 100 eggs that hatch into first-instar larvae, which are oval-shaped, have antennae, walking legs, and feed actively by means of their stylets and proboscis. The mobile first-instar larva moults into a rather immobile second-instar larva, which is similar in shape, but has much shorter legs and antennae; third and fourth instars follow; the fourth feeds initially, but then stops and secretes a case around itself which bears waxy filaments. The case splits along a characteristic T-shaped line of suture (dorsally) and the adult whitefly emerges.

whiteout 'fog' of grains of dry snow caused by strong winds in temperatures of between –18°C/0°F and –1°C/30°F. The uniform whiteness of the ground and air causes disorientation in humans.

white spirit colourless liquid derived from petrol; it is used as a solvent and in paints and varnishes.

whitethroat any of several Old World warblers of the genus *Sylvia* in the family Muscicapidae, order Passeriformes. They are found in scrub, hedges, and wood clearings of Eurasia in summer, migrating to Africa in winter. They are about 14 cm/5.5 in long.

whiting predatory fish *Merlangius merlangus* common in shallow sandy N European waters. It grows to 70 cm/2.3 ft.

Whittle, Frank
(1907–1996)

British engineer. He patented the basic design for the turbojet engine in 1930. In the Royal Air Force he worked on jet propulsion 1937–46. In May 1941 the Gloster E 28/39 aircraft first flew with the Whittle jet engine. Both the German (first operational jet planes) and the US jet aircraft were built using his principles. He was knighted in 1948.

WHO acronym for ***World Health Organization***.

whois in computing, searchable database of every registered ◊domain and the names of their users. A special application, also called Whois, is needed to search the database.

whooping cough or ***pertussis*** acute infectious disease, seen mainly in children, caused by colonization of the air passages by the bacterium *Bordetella pertussis.* There may be catarrh, mild fever, and loss of appetite, but the main symptom is violent coughing, associated with the sharp intake of breath that is the characteristic 'whoop', and often followed by vomiting and severe nose bleeds. The cough may persist for weeks.

Although debilitating, the disease is seldom serious in older children, but infants are at risk both from the illness itself and from susceptibility to other conditions, such as ◊pneumonia. During 1995, there were 355,000 deaths from whooping cough. Immunization lessens the incidence and severity of the disease: the whole cell (or 'killed') vaccine has been replaced by an acellular version, which is made up from the bacteria *Bordetella pertussis,* and has fewer side effects than its predecessor.

A new strain of the bacterium *Bordetella pertussis,* which had first appeared in about 1985, spread across Europe in 1997. It arose in the Netherlands and by October there were 2,785 cases there compared with 321 in 1995.

whortleberry a form of ◊bilberry.

whydah any of various African birds of the genus *Vidua,* order Passeriformes, of the weaver family. They lay their eggs in the nests of waxbills, which rear the young. Young birds resemble young ◊waxbills, but the adults do not resemble adult waxbills. Males have long tail feathers used in courtship displays.

wide-angle lens photographic lens of shorter focal length than normal, taking in a wider angle of view.

wide area network in computing, a ◊network that connects computers distributed over a wide geographical area.

widget plastic device inserted into beer cans to give the beer a creamier head. Pressurized gas, trapped in the widget during canning, is released through a tiny nozzle when the can is opened. The first widget, introduced by Guinness in 1989, released pressurized nitrogen.

Wien's displacement law in physics, a law of radiation stating that the wavelength carrying the maximum energy is inversely proportional to the absolute temperature of a ◊black body: the hotter a body is, the shorter the wavelength. It has the form $\lambda_{max}T$ = constant, where λ_{max} is the wavelength of maximum intensity and T is the temperature. The law is named after German physicist Wilhelm Wien.

wigeon either of two species of dabbling duck of genus *Anas*, order Anseriformes. The **American wigeon** *A. americana*, about 48 cm/19 in long, is found along both coasts in winter and breeds inland. Males have a white-capped head and a green eye stripe.

wild card in computing, character which represents 'any character' in a search or command. When comparing ◊strings, the computer does not seek a precise match for a wild card character. The most useful wildcards are ?, which matches any single character, and *, which matches any number of characters, including zero. Hence the ◊DOS commands DEL *.* – delete all files – and COPY *.DOC – copy all files with the filename extension 'DOC'.

wildebeest or ***gnu*** either of two species of African ◊antelope, with a cowlike face, a beard and mane, and heavy curved horns in both sexes. The body is up to 1.3 m/4.2 ft high at the shoulder and slopes away to the hindquarters. (Genus *Connochaetes.*)

The **brindled wildebeest** *C. taurinus* is silver-grey with a dark face, mane, and tail tuft, and is found from Kenya southwards. Vast herds move together on migration. The **white-tailed wildebeest** *C. gnou* of South Africa almost became extinct, but was saved by breeding on farms.

wilderness area of uninhabited land that has never been disturbed by humans, usually located some distance from towns and cities. According to estimates by US group Conservation International, 52% (90 million sq km/35 million sq mi) of the Earth's total land area was still undisturbed in 1994.

wildebeest *The brindled wildebeest* Connochaetes taurinus *is known for the huge migratory herds which can be observed each year in the Serengeti–Masai Mara plains in E Africa. It is a close grazer, so relies heavily on the renewal of the long grasses through regular burning. Premaphotos Wildlife*

The self-eulogizing attempts of expatriates to impose the notion of wildlife as a treasured legacy overlook the reality that to most of a local impoverished and inert populace wildlife is considered an obstacle ...

DIAN FOSSEY US primatologist.
Gorillas in the Mist

wildlife trade international trade in live plants and animals, and in wildlife products such as skins, horns, shells, and feathers. The trade has made some species virtually extinct, and whole ecosystems (for example, coral reefs) are threatened. Wildlife trade is to some extent regulated by ◊CITES (Convention on International Trade in Endangered Species).

Species almost eradicated by trade in their products include

Threatened Plants and Animals from the World Wildlife Trade

Common name	*Scientific name*	*Range*	*Reason threatened*
alligator snapping turtle	*Macroclemys temminckii*	North America	used in canned turtle soup, a delicacy in some countries; also sold as pets
beluga sturgeon	*Huso huso*	Caspian Sea	caviar is a delicacy in many countries; the long life cycle of the fish makes the population more vulnerable
big leaf mahogany	*Swietenia macrophylla king*	Central and South America	mahogany wood is used for furniture in many countries
black rhino	*Diceros bicornis*	Africa	hunted for their horns, which are used in powdered form in oriental medicine
giant panda	*Ailuropoda melanaleca*	China	destruction of the bamboo forests, the natural habitat for pandas, makes the population more vulnerable; as does poaching and demand as zoo animals
goldenseal	*Hydrastis canadensis*	North America	used in herbal medicine as a 'natural antibiotic'; demand has increased as herbal medicine becomes more widespread
green-cheeked parrot	*Amazona viridiginohs*	Mexico	hunted and captured for pet trade; many birds die in transit
hawksbill turtle	*Eretmochelys imbricata*	tropical seas	the shell is used as tortoiseshell, although under an official ban in most places; the slow reproductive cycle of the turtle makes the population more vunerable
mako shark	*Isurus oxyrinchus*	Atlantic, Pacific, and Indian oceans	shark meat is a delicacy in some countries; the slow reproductive cycle makes the population more vulnerable
tiger	*Panthera tigris*	Asia	destruction of jungle; hunted for bones and other parts for use in oriental medicine

Source: Convention on International Trade in Endangered Species, World Wide Fund for Nature

many of the largest whales, crocodiles, marine turtles, and some wild cats. Until recently, some 2 million snake skins were exported from India every year. Populations of black rhino and African elephant have collapsed because of hunting for their horns and tusks (◊ivory), and poaching remains a problem in cases where trade is prohibited.

wild type in genetics, the naturally occurring gene for a particular character that is typical of most individuals of a given species, as distinct from new genes that arise by mutation.

will-o'-the-wisp light sometimes seen over marshy ground, believed to be burning gas containing methane from decaying organic matter.

An Australian scientist put forward the hypothesis in 1995 that the phenomenon may be caused by barn owls, which sometimes develop a ghostly glow due to a light-emitting honey fungus that they pick up from rotting trees.

willow any of a group of trees or shrubs containing over 350 species, found mostly in the northern hemisphere, flourishing in damp places. The leaves are often lance-shaped, and the male and female catkins are borne on separate trees. (Genus *Salix,* family Salicaceae.)

willowherb any of a group of perennial flowering plants belonging to the evening primrose family. The **rosebay willowherb** or **fireweed** *C. angustifolium* is common in woods and wasteland. It grows to 1.2 m/4 ft with tall upright spikes of red or purplish flowers. (Genera *Epilobium* and *Chamaenerion,* family Onagraceae.)

willow warbler bird *Phylloscopus trochilus,* family Muscicapidae, order Passeriformes. It is about 11 cm/4 in long, similar in appearance to the chiffchaff, but with a distinctive song. It is found in woods and shrubberies, and migrates from N Eurasia to Africa.

wilting the loss of rigidity (◊turgor) in plants, caused by a decreasing wall pressure within the cells making up the supportive tissues. Wilting is most obvious in plants that have little or no wood.

WIMP (abbreviation for ***weak interacting massive particle***) ◊hypothetical subatomic particle found in the Galaxy's dark matter. These particles could constitute the 80% of dark matter unaccounted for by ◊MACHOs (massive astrophysical compact halo objects).

WIMP (acronym for ***windows, icons, menus, pointing device***) in computing, another name for ◊graphical user interface (GUI).

Winchester drive in computing, an old-fashioned term for ◊hard disc.

WinCode in computing, program developed by US company Snappy Inc, that uses a process known as bit-shifting to UUencode and ◊UUdecode binary programs and files in 7-bit ASCII text so that they can be transmitted via online systems and over the Internet. Several other coding systems are also used, and recent versions of WinCode can handle most of the common formats. WinCode is a copyright program distributed as ◊freeware.

wind the lateral movement of the Earth's atmosphere from high-pressure areas (anticyclones) to low-pressure areas (depression). Its speed is measured using an ◊anemometer or by studying its effects on, for example, trees by using the ◊Beaufort scale. Although modified by features such as land and water, there is a basic worldwide system of ◊trade winds, ◊westerlies, and polar easterlies.

A belt of low pressure (the ◊doldrums) lies along the Equator. The trade winds blow towards this from the horse latitudes (areas of high pressure at about 30° N and 30° S of the Equator), blowing from the NE in the northern hemisphere, and from the SE in the southern. The Westerlies (also from the horse latitudes) blow north of the Equator from the SW and south of the Equator from the NW.

Cold winds blow outwards from high-pressure areas at the poles. More local effects result from landmasses heating and cooling faster than the adjacent sea, producing onshore winds in the daytime and offshore winds at night.

The ◊monsoon is a seasonal wind of S Asia, blowing from the SW in summer and bringing the rain on which crops depend. It blows from the NE in winter.

Famous or notorious warm winds include the **chinook** of the eastern Rocky Mountains, North America; the **föhn** of Europe's Alpine valleys; the **sirocco** (Italy)/**khamsin** (Egypt)/**sharav** (Israel), spring winds that bring warm air from the Sahara and Arabian deserts across the Mediterranean; and the **Santa Ana**, a periodic warm wind from the inland deserts that strikes the California coast.

The dry northerly **bise** (Switzerland) and the **mistral**, which strikes the Mediterranean area of France, are unpleasantly cold winds.

NATIONAL WIND TECHNOLOGY CENTRE

http://www.nrel.gov/wind/

Source of information on the importance of tapping wind power and how to do it. This US Department of Energy site has reports on latest research. For children there is a wind energy quiz and details of educational materials. There is information about a number of authorities generating energy from wind power in various parts of world.

wind-chill factor *or* **wind-chill index** estimate of how much colder it feels when a wind is blowing. It is the sum of the temperature (in °F below zero) and the wind speed (in miles per hour). So for a wind of 15 mph at an air temperature of –5°F, the wind-chill factor is 20.

wind farm array of windmills or ◊wind turbines used for generating electrical power. The world's largest wind farm at Altamont Pass, California, USA, consists of 6,000 wind turbines generating 1 TWh of electricity per year. Wind farms supply about 1.5% of California's electricity needs. To produce 1,200 megawatts of electricity (an output comparable with that of a nuclear power station), a wind farm would need to occupy around 370 sq km/140 sq mi.

Denmark has built the world's first offshore wind farm, off Vindeby on Lolland Island in the North Sea.

windmill mill with sails or vanes that, by the action of wind upon them, drive machinery for grinding corn or pumping water, for example. Wind turbines, designed to use wind power on a large scale, usually have a propeller-type rotor mounted on a tall shell tower. The turbine drives a generator for producing electricity.

Windmills were used in the East in ancient times, and in Europe they were first used in Germany and the Netherlands in the 12th century. The main types of traditional windmill are the **post mill**, which is turned around a post when the direction of the wind changes, and the **tower mill**, which has a revolving turret on top. It usually has a device (fantail) that keeps the sails pointing into the wind. In the USA windmills were used by the colonists and later a light type, with steel sails supported on a long steel girder shaft, was introduced for use on farms.

window in computing, a rectangular area on the screen of a graphical user interface. A window is used to display data and can be manipulated in various ways by the computer user.

Windows ◊graphical user interface (GUI) from Microsoft that has become the standard for IBM PCs and clones.

There are three versions of Windows. **Windows 95** is designed for homes and offices and retains maximum compatibility with programs written for the ◊MS-DOS operating system. **Windows NT** is a 32-bit ◊multiuser and ◊multitasking operating system designed for business use, especially on workstations and server computers, where it is seen as a rival to ◊UNIX. **Windows CE** is a small operating system that supports a subset of the Windows applications programming interface. It is designed for handheld personal computers (HPCs) and consumer electronics products. Windows 95 is limited to Intel and x86-compatible processors but both NT and CE run on a variety of chips from different manufacturers.

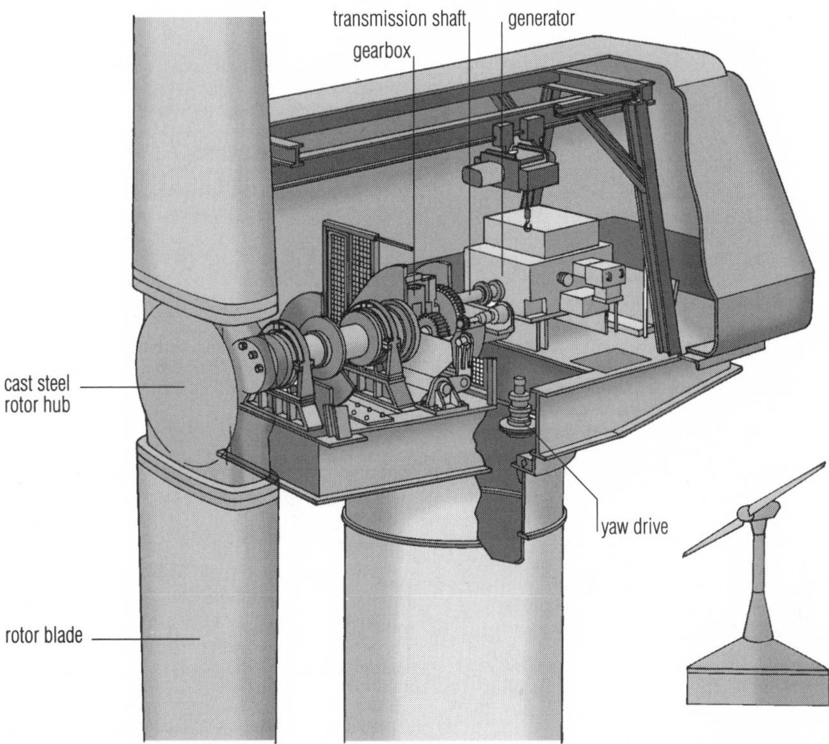

***wind power** The wind turbine is the modern counterpart of the windmill. The rotor blades are huge – up to 100 m/330 ft across – in order to extract as much energy as possible from the wind. Inside the turbine head, gears are used to increase the speed of the turning shaft so that the electricity generation is as efficient as possible.*

Windows WAVeform in computing, audio file format commonly abbreviated to ◊WAV.

wind power the harnessing of wind energy to produce power. The wind has long been used as a source of energy: sailing ships and windmills are ancient inventions. After the energy crisis of the 1970s ◊wind turbines began to be used to produce electricity on a large scale.

wind tunnel test tunnel in which air is blown over, for example, a stationary model aircraft, motor vehicle, or locomotive to simulate the effects of movement. Lift, drag, and airflow patterns are observed by the use of special cameras and sensitive instruments. Wind-tunnel testing assesses aerodynamic design, prior to full-scale construction.

wind turbine windmill of advanced aerodynamic design connected to an electricity generator and used in wind-power installations. Wind turbines can be either large propeller-type rotors mounted on a tall tower, or flexible metal strips fixed to a vertical axle at top and bottom.

The world's largest wind turbine is on Hawaii, in the Pacific Ocean. It has two blades 50 m/160 ft long on top of a tower 20 storeys high. An example of a propeller turbine is found at Tvind in Denmark and has an output of some 2 MW. Other machines use novel rotors, such as the 'egg-beater' design developed at Sandia Laboratories in New Mexico, USA.

WIND TURBINES

http://www.nrel.gov/wind/turbines.html

Reports on latest wind turbine research. There are technical details of a variety of experimental turbines, information on the work of companies active in research and development, and speculation about the configurations of the kinds of turbines likely to become significant contributors to energy resources in the next century.

wing in biology, the modified forelimb of birds and bats, or the membranous outgrowths of the ◊exoskeleton of insects, which give the power of flight. Birds and bats have two wings. Bird wings have feathers attached to the fused digits ('fingers') and forearm bones, while bat wings consist of skin stretched between the digits. Most insects have four wings, which are strengthened by wing veins.

The wings of butterflies and moths are covered with scales. The hind pair of a fly's wings are modified to form two knoblike balancing organs (halteres).

WIN.INI (acronym for ***Windows Initialization***) in computing, file used by Microsoft Windows to store a range of settings that in general govern the appearance of Windows and some Windows 3 applications. Changes made via Windows 3's Control Panel program are often stored in WIN.INI. In Windows 95 and later versions, control has been moved to the Registry.

Winsock (contraction of ***Windows socket***) in computing, program that supplies an interface between Windows software and a ◊TCP/IP application.

wintergreen any of a group of plants belonging to the heath family, especially the species *G. procumbens* of NE North America, which creeps underground and sends up tiny shoots. Oil of wintergreen, used in treating rheumatism, is extracted from its leaves. Wintergreen is also the name for various plants belonging to the wintergreen family Pyrolaceae, including the green pipsissewa *C. maculata* of N North America, Europe, and Asia. (Genus *Gaultheria*, family Ericaceae; also genera *Pyrola, Chimaphila, Orthilia*, and *Moneses*, family Pyrolaceae.)

wire thread of metal, made by drawing a rod through progressively smaller-diameter dies. Fine-gauge wire is used for electrical power transmission; heavier-gauge wire is used to make load-bearing cables.

Gold, silver, and bronze wire has been found in the ruins of Troy and in ancient Egyptian tombs. From early times to the 14th century, wire was made by hammering metal into sheets, cutting thin strips, and making the strips round by hammering them. The Romans made wire by hammering heated metal rods.

Wire drawing was introduced in Germany in the 14th century. In this process, a metal rod is pulled (drawn) through a small hole in a mould (die). Until the 19th century this was done by hand; now all wire is drawn by machine. Metal rods are pulled through a series of progressively smaller tungsten carbide dies to produce large-diameter wire, and through diamond dies for very fine wire. The die is funnel-shaped, with one opening smaller than the diameter of the rod. The rod, which is pointed at one end, is coated with a lubricant to allow it to slip through the die. Pincers pull the rod through until it can be wound round a drum. The drum then rotates, drawing the wire through the die and winding it into a coil.

There are many kinds of wire for different uses: galvanized wire (coated with zinc), which does not rust; ◊barbed wire and wire mesh for fencing; and wire cable, made by weaving thin wires into ropes. Needles, pins, nails, and rivets are made from wire.

Wired US computing magazine founded in 1993 by Jane Metcalfe and Louis Rossetto to serve as the voice of the 'digital revolution'. It is based in San Francisco.

wired gloves in computing, interface worn on the hands for ◊virtual reality applications. The gloves detect the movement of the hands, enabling the user to 'touch' and 'move' objects in a virtual environment.

wire frame in computing, method of creating three-dimensional computerized animations by drawing a series of frames showing the moving image in outline, like a moving skeleton. When the designer is satisfied with the action of the wire-frame figure, he or she adds the 'skin', superimposing textures to give the final effect.

wireless original name for a radio receiver. In early experiments with transmission by radio waves, notably by Italian inventor Guglielmo ◊Marconi in Britain, signals were sent in Morse code, as in telegraphy. Radio, unlike the telegraph, used no wires for transmission, and the means of communication was termed 'wireless telegraphy'.

wireworm larva of some species of ◊click beetle. Wireworms are considered agricultural pests as they attack the seeds of many crops.

wisent another name for the European ◊bison.

wisteria any of a group of climbing leguminous shrubs (see ◊legume), including *W. sinensis*, native to the eastern USA and E Asia. Wisterias have hanging clusters of bluish, white, or pale mauve flowers, and pinnate leaves (leaflets on either side of the stem). They are grown against walls as ornamental plants. (Genus *Wisteria*, family Leguminosae.)

witch hazel any of a group of flowering shrubs or small trees belonging to the witch hazel family, native to North America and E Asia, especially *H. virginiana*. An astringent extract prepared from the bark or leaves is used in medicine as an eye lotion and a liniment to relieve pain or stiffness. (Genus *Hamamelis*, family Hamamelidaceae.)

wizard in computing, interactive tool developed by ◊Microsoft that 'talks' users of a program through a complex operation, such as creating a ◊template or a presentation. The wizard presents the user with a series of ◊dialog boxes asking simple questions in ordinary language, which the user answers by choosing ◊radio buttons, checking boxes and entering information by keyboard.

The term wizard stems from programmers' slang, where it means an expert in a particular piece of software or hardware, capable of answering all manner of queries, fixing faults and dealing with emergencies.

woad biennial plant native to Europe, with arrow-shaped leaves and clusters of small yellow flowers. It was formerly cultivated for a blue dye extracted from its leaves. Ancient Britons used the blue dye as a body paint in battle. (*Isatis tinctoria*, family Cruciferae.)

wolf any of two species of large wild dogs of the genus *Canis*. The **grey** or **timber wolf** *C. lupus*, of North America and Eurasia, is highly social, measures up to 90 cm/3 ft at the shoulder, and weighs up to 45 kg/100 lb. It has been greatly reduced in numbers except for isolated wilderness regions. The **red wolf** *C. rufus*, generally more slender and smaller (average weight about 15 kg/35 lb) and tawnier in colour, may not be a separate species, but a grey wolf–coyote hybrid. It used to be restricted to S central USA, but is now thought to be extinct in the wild.

WILD WOLVES

http://www.pbs.org/wgbh/nova/wolves/

'What's in a wolf's howl – a calling card, a warning, or an invitation? Hear the call of the wild, find out how wolves are making a comeback, and discover the ancient connection between dogs and wolves at this Web site.'

wolffish carnivorous marine fish in the genus *Anarrhichas*.

wolfram alternative name for ◊tungsten.

wolframite iron manganese tungstate, $(Fe,Mn)WO_4$, an ore mineral of tungsten. It is dark grey with a submetallic surface lustre, and often occurs in hydrothermal veins in association with ores of tin.

wolverine *Gulo gulo*, largest land member of the weasel family (Mustelidae), found in Europe, Asia, and North America.

It is stocky in build, and about 1 m/3.3 ft long. Its long, thick fur is dark brown on the back and belly and lighter on the sides. It covers food that it cannot eat with an unpleasant secretion. Destruction of habitat and trapping for its fur have greatly reduced its numbers.

womb common name for the ◊uterus.

wombat any of a family (Vombatidae) of burrowing, herbivorous marsupials, native to Tasmania and S Australia. They are about 1 m/3.3 ft long, heavy, with a big head, short legs and tail, and coarse fur.

The two living species include the **common wombat** *Vombatus ursinus* of Tasmania and SE Australia, and *Lasiorhirnus latifrons*, the **plains wombat** of S Australia.

wood the hard tissue beneath the bark of many perennial plants; it is composed of water-conducting cells, or secondary ◊xylem, and gains its hardness and strength from deposits of ◊lignin. **Hardwoods**, such as oak, and **softwoods**, such as pine, have commercial value as structural material and for furniture.

The central wood in a branch or stem is known as **heartwood** and is generally darker and harder than the outer wood; it consists only of dead cells. As well as providing structural support, it often contains gums, tannins, or pigments which may impart a characteristic colour and increased durability. The surrounding **sapwood** is the functional part of the xylem that conducts water.

The **secondary xylem** is laid down by the vascular ◊cambium which forms a new layer of wood annually, on the outside of the existing wood and visible as an ◊annual ring when the tree is felled; see ◊dendrochronology.

Commercial wood can be divided into two main types: hardwood, containing xylem vessels and obtained from angiosperms (for example, oak), and softwood, containing only ◊tracheids, obtained from gymnosperms (for example, pine). Although in general softwoods are softer than hardwoods, this is not always the case: balsa, the softest wood known, is a hardwood, while pitch pine, very dense and hard, is a softwood. A superhard wood is produced in wood–plastic combinations (WPC), in which wood is impregnated with liquid plastic (monomer) and the whole is then bombarded with gamma rays to polymerize the plastic.

woodcock either of two species of wading birds, genus *Scolopax*, of the family Scolopacidae, which have barred plumage and long bills, and live in wet woodland areas. They belong to the long-billed section of the snipes, order Charadriiformes.

woodland area in which trees grow more or less thickly; generally smaller than a forest. Temperate climates, with four distinct seasons a year, tend to support a mixed woodland habitat, with some conifers but mostly broad-leaved and deciduous trees, shedding their leaves in autumn and regrowing them in spring. In the Mediterranean region and parts of the southern hemisphere, the trees are mostly evergreen.

Temperate woodlands grow in the zone between the cold coniferous forests and the tropical forests of the hotter climates near the Equator. They develop in areas where the closeness of the sea keeps the climate mild and moist.

Old woodland can rival tropical rainforest in the number of species it supports, but most of the species are hidden in the soil. A study in Oregon, USA, in 1991 found that the soil in a single woodland location contained 8,000 arthropod species (such as insects, mites, centipedes, and millipedes), compared with only 143 species of reptile, bird, and mammal in the woodland above.

woodlouse crustacean of the order Isopoda. Woodlice have segmented bodies, flattened undersides, and 14 legs. The eggs are carried by the female in a pouch beneath the thorax. They often live in high densities: up to as many as 8,900 per sq m.

The hatchlings, called mancas, have only 12 legs and must moult twice before gaining their final pair of legs.

Common in Britain are the genera *Oniscus* and *Porcellio*.

WEIRD AND WONDERFUL WORLD OF WOODLICE

http://www.dryad.demon.co.uk/julies/woodlice.htm

Comprehensive and entertaining guide to woodlice. Information is provided on history, predators, physiology, reproduction, behaviour, colour variations, recommended reading, and there are even tips on keeping them as pets.

woodmouse or ***long-tailed field mouse*** *Apodemus sylvaticus*, rodent that lives in woodlands, hedgerows, and sometimes open fields in Britain and Europe. About 9 cm/3.5 in long, with a similar length of tail, it is yellow-brown above, white below, and has long oval ears.

It is nocturnal and feeds largely on seeds, but eats a range of foods, including some insects.

woodpecker bird of the family Picidae, order Piciformes. They are adapted for climbing up the bark of trees, and picking out insects to eat from the crevices. The feet, though very short, are usually strong; the nails are broad and crooked and the toes placed in pairs, two forward and two backward. As an additional support their tail feathers terminate in points, and are uncommonly hard. Woodpeckers have a long extensile tongue, which has muscles enabling the bird to dart it forth and to retract it again quickly. There are about 200 species worldwide.

wood pitch by-product of charcoal manufacture, made from **wood tar**, the condensed liquid produced from burning charcoal gases. The wood tar is boiled to produce the correct consistency. It has been used since ancient times for caulking wooden ships (filling in the spaces between the hull planks to make them watertight).

wood pulp wood that has been processed into a pulpy mass of fibres. Its main use is for making paper, but it is also used in making ◊rayon and other cellulose fibres and plastics.

There are two methods of making wood pulp: mechanical and chemical. In the former, debarked logs are ground with water (to prevent charring) by rotating grindstones; the wood fibres are physically torn apart. In the latter, log chips are digested with chemicals (such as sodium sulphite). The chemicals dissolve the material holding the fibres together.

wood wasp *or* **horntail** moderately large wasp that is black or metallic blue, often with yellow bandings. The long lancelike ovipositor (egg-laying organ) of the female wood wasp is used for drilling holes into wood. Usually a single egg is deposited into each hole, and the larva on hatching bores through the heart wood causing much damage.

classification The wood wasp is in the family Siricidae, suborder Symphyta, order Hymenoptera, class Insecta, phylum Arthropoda.

The common wood wasp *Sirex juvencus* is about 30 mm/1.1 in long and blue-black with a metallic sheen. The male may be distinguished from the female by its short triangular spine or horn at the tip of its abdomen and also by a brown-red stripe on its back. The female lays her eggs in conifers.

woodworm common name for the larval stage of certain wood-boring beetles. Dead or injured trees are their natural target, but they also attack structural timber and furniture.

Included are the furniture beetle *Anobium punctatum*, which attacks older timber; the powder-post beetle genus *Lyctus*, which attacks newer timber; the ◊deathwatch beetle, whose presence always coincides with fungal decay; and wood-boring ◊weevils. Special wood preservatives have been developed to combat woodworm infestation, which has markedly increased since about 1950.

wool the natural hair covering of the sheep, and also of the llama, angora goat, and some other ◊mammals. The domestic sheep *Ovis aries* provides the great bulk of the fibres used in textile production. Lanolin is a by-product.

history Sheep have been bred for their wool since ancient times. Hundreds of breeds were developed in the Middle East, Europe, and Britain over the centuries, several dozen of which are still raised for their wool today. Most of the world's finest wool comes from the merino sheep, originally from Spain. In 1797 it was introduced into Australia, which has become the world's largest producer of merino wool; South Africa and South America are also large producers. Wools from crossbred sheep (usually a cross of one of the British breeds with a merino) are produced in New Zealand. Since the 1940s, blendings of wool with synthetic fibres have been developed for textiles.

woolly bear larva of the ◊carpet beetle.

word in computing, a group of bits (binary digits) that a computer's central processing unit treats as a single working unit. The size of a word varies from one computer to another and, in general, increasing the word length leads to a faster and more powerful computer. In the late 1970s and early 1980s, most microcomputers were 8-bit machines. During the 1980s 16-bit microcomputers were introduced and 32-bit microcomputers are now available. Mainframe computers may be 32-bit or 64-bit machines.

Word word processing program for the PCs and Apple ◊Macintoshes. See ◊Microsoft Word.

WordPerfect word processing program for various computers produced by US software company WordPerfect Corp. It was first released in 1982 and by 1987 was the dominant ◊MS-DOS word processor, rapidly eclipsing the previous leader, WordStar, by offering many more features, despite having the reputation of being difficult to learn.

WordPerfect Corp was slow to release a version of WordPerfect for ◊Windows, and when it did appear 1992 it suffered in comparison with Microsoft ◊Word. WordPerfect Corp was taken over by Novell, but the union was not a success, and most of its software was sold on cheaply to Corel.

word processing storage and retrieval of written text by computer. Word-processing software packages enable the writer to key in text and amend it in a number of ways. A print-out can be obtained or the text could be sent to another person or organization on disc or via ◊electronic mail. Word processing has revolutionized the task of a typing secretary. Word-processing packages can be used with databases or graphics packages, and desktop publishing packages are available too.

word processor in computing, a program that allows the input, amendment, manipulation, storage, and retrieval of text; or a computer system that runs such software. Since word-processing programs became available to microcomputers, the method has largely replaced the typewriter for producing letters or other text. Typical facilities include insert, delete, cut and paste, reformat, search and replace, copy, print, mail merge, and spelling check.

The leading word-processing programs include Microsoft Word, the market leader, Lotus WordPro, and Corel WordPerfect.

work in physics, a measure of the result of transferring energy from one system to another to cause an object to move. Work should not be confused with ◊energy (the capacity to do work, which is also measured in joules) or with power (the rate of doing work, measured in joules per second).

Work is equal to the product of the force used and the distance moved by the object in the direction of that force. If the force is F newtons and the distance moved is d metres, then the work W is given by:

$$W = Fd$$

For example, the work done when a force of 10 newtons moves an object 5 metres against some sort of resistance is 50 joules (50 newton-metres).

workgroup in computing, small group of computer users who need to share data and computer facilities.

workstation high-performance desktop computer with strong graphics capabilities, traditionally used for engineering (◊CAD and ◊CAM), scientific research, and desktop publishing. From 1985–95, workstations were frequently based on fast RISC (reduced instruction-set computer) chips running the UNIX operating system. However, the market is under attack from 'Wintel' PCs with Intel Pentium processors running Microsoft Windows NT, which are cheaper and run PC software as well as workstation programs. By 1997, four of the five leading workstation manufacturers – DEC, Hewlett-Packard, IBM and Silicon Graphics Inc, but not Sun Microsystems – had committed to supporting NT.

World Wide Fund for Nature (WWF, formerly the ***World Wildlife Fund***) international organization established in 1961 to raise funds for conservation by public appeal. Projects include conservation of particular species, for example, the tiger and giant panda, and special areas, such as the Simen Mountains, Ethiopia.

World-Wide Web (WWW) ◊hypertext system for publishing information on the ◊Internet. World-Wide Web documents ('Web pages') are text files coded using ◊HTML to include text and graphics, and are stored on a Web server connected to the Internet.

Web pages may also contain dynamic objects and Java applets for enhanced animation, video, sound, and interactivity.

The Web server can be any computer, from the simplest Apple Macintosh to the largest mainframe, if Web server software is available.

Every Web page has a ◊URL (Uniform Resource Locator) – a unique address (usually starting with http://www) which tells a ◊browser program (such as Netscape Navigator or Microsoft Internet Explorer) where to find it. An important feature of the World-Wide Web is that most documents contain links enabling readers to follow whatever aspects of a subject interest them most. These links may connect to different computers all over the world. Interlinked or nested Web pages belonging to a single organization are known as a 'Web site'.

WORM WORLD

http://www.nj.com/yucky/worm/index.html

Lively guide for children, with information on topics such as worms' bodies, how to make a worm bin, and different types of worm, plus an art gallery and some worm jokes.

worm any of various elongated limbless invertebrates belonging to several phyla. Worms include the ◊flatworms, such as ◊flukes and ◊tapeworms; the roundworms or ◊nematodes, such as the eelworm and the hookworm; the marine ribbon worms or nemerteans; and the segmented worms or ◊annelids.

In 1979, giant sea worms about 3 m/10 ft long, living within tubes created by their own excretions, were discovered in hydrothermal vents 2,450 m/8,000 ft beneath the Pacific NE of the Galápagos Islands.

WORM (acronym for ***write once read many times***) in computing, a storage device, similar to a ◊CD-ROM. The computer can write to the disc directly, but cannot later erase or overwrite the same area. WORMs are mainly used for archiving and backup copies.

worm in computing, ◊virus designed to spread from computer to computer across a network. Worms replicate themselves while 'hiding' in a computer's memory, causing systems to 'crash' or slow down, but do not infect other programs or destroy data directly.

The most celebrated worm was the 'Internet worm' of November 1988. Released onto the Internet by Robert Morris, Jr., a graduate student at Cornell University, it infected some 6,000 systems via a loophole in ◊UNIX e-mail and finger procedures. Morris claimed that a programming bug had caused the worm to replicate far more virulently than he had intended, and took swift measures to publish an 'antidote' on the network – but by then, many machines had already been disconnected from it. Morris was later convicted, fined, and sentenced to 400 hours community service.

wormwood any of a group of plants belonging to the daisy family and mainly found in northern temperate regions, especially the aromatic herb *A. absinthium*, the leaves of which are used in the alcoholic drink absinthe. Tarragon is closely related to wormwood. (Genus *Artemisia*, family Compositae.)

W particle in physics, an ◊elementary particle, one of the weakons responsible for transmitting the ◊weak nuclear force.

wrack any of the large brown ◊seaweeds characteristic of rocky shores. The bladder wrack *F. vesiculosus* has narrow, branched

wrack *Bladder wrack* Fucus vesiculosus *and flat wrack* F. spiralis *often grow together to form dense mats on rocks on the middle shore around the coasts of W Europe.* *Premaphotos Wildlife*

fronds up to 1 m/3.3 ft long, with oval air bladders, usually in pairs on either side of the midrib or central vein. (Genus *Fucus.*)

wrasse any bony fish of the family Labridae, found in temperate and tropical seas. They are slender and often brightly coloured, with a single long dorsal fin. They have elaborate courtship rituals, and some species can change their colouring and sex. Species vary in size from 5 cm/2 in to 2 m/6.5 ft.

wren any of the family Troglodytidae of small birds of the order Passeriformes, with slender, slightly curved bills, and uptilted tails.

WREN

The testes of the tiny male Australian fairy wren account for one-tenth of his body weight. He can produce more sperm than any other bird, and ejaculates 8.3 billion sperm at a time. (A human male manages about 4 million.)

write-once technology in computing, technology that allows a user to write data onto an optical disc once. After that the data are permanent and can be read any number of times.

write protection device on discs and tapes that provides ◊data security by allowing data to be read but not deleted, altered, or overwritten.

wrought iron fairly pure iron containing some beads of slag, widely used for construction work before the days of cheap steel. It is strong, tough, and easy to machine. It is made in a puddling furnace, invented by Henry Colt in England in 1784. Pig iron is remelted and heated strongly in air with iron ore, burning out the carbon in the metal, leaving relatively pure iron and a slag containing impurities. The resulting pasty metal is then hammered to remove as much of the remaining slag as possible. It is still used in fences and gratings.

Wright brothers Orville (1871–1948) and Wilbur (1867–1912)

US inventors; brothers who pioneered piloted, powered flight. Inspired by Otto Lilienthal's gliding, they perfected their piloted glider in 1902. In 1903 they built a powered machine, a 12-hp 341-kg/750-lb plane, and became the first to make a successful powered flight, near Kitty Hawk, North Carolina. Orville flew 36.6 m/120 ft in 12 seconds; Wilbur, 260 m/852 ft in 59 seconds.

Mary Evans Picture Library

wt abbreviation for **weight**.

WWF abbreviation for ◊World Wide Fund for Nature (formerly ***World Wildlife Fund***).

WYSIWYG (acronym for ***what you see is what you get***) in computing, a program that attempts to display on the screen a faithful representation of the final printed output. For example, a WYSIWYG ◊word processor would show actual page layout – line widths, page breaks, and the sizes and styles of type.

x in computing, ◊wild card character often used to describe versions of hardware or software. One might, therefore, refer to Windows 3.x (any version of Windows, from 3.0 to 3.31), or an x86 chip (any of the chips manufactured by ◊Intel with serial numbers ending in 86).

X.25 in computing, communications protocol for sending ◊packets of data over a network.

X.400 in computing, standard maintained by the ITU (International Telecommunications Union, formerly the ◊CCITT) which forms the basis for a message handling system. X.400 is used as a shorthand term for a number of recommendations and standards involved in running some electronic mail systems over telecommunications lines.

X.500 directory standards for network addresses, issued by the ◊Comité Consultatif International Téléphonique et Télégraphique (CCITT).

xanthophyll yellow pigment in plants that, like ◊chlorophyll, is responsible for the production of carbohydrates by photosynthesis.

X chromosome larger of the two sex chromosomes, the smaller being the ◊Y chromosome. These two chromosomes are involved in ◊sex determination. Females have two X chromosomes, males have an X and a Y. Genes carried on the X chromosome produce the phenomenon of sex linkage.

Early in the development of a female embryo, one of the X chromosomes becomes condensed so that most of its genes are inactivated. If this inactivation is incomplete, skeletal defects and mental retardation result.

xenon Greek *xenos* 'stranger' colourless, odourless, gaseous, non-metallic element, symbol Xe, atomic number 54, relative atomic mass 131.30. It is grouped with the ◊inert gases and was long believed not to enter into reactions, but is now known to form some compounds, mostly with fluorine. It is a heavy gas present in very small quantities in the air (about one part in 20 million).

Xenon is used in bubble chambers, light bulbs, vacuum tubes, and lasers. It was discovered in 1898 in a residue from liquid air by Scottish chemists William Ramsay and Morris Travers.

xerography dry, electrostatic method of producing images, without the use of negatives or sensitized paper, invented in the USA by Chester Carlson in 1938 and applied in the Xerox ◊photocopier.

An image of the document to be copied is projected on to an electrostatically charged photo-conductive plate. The charge remains only in the areas corresponding to its image. The latent image on the plate is then developed by contact with ink powder, which adheres only to the image, and is then usually transferred to ordinary paper or some other flat surface, and quickly heated to form a permanent print.

Applications include document copying, enlarging from microfilm, preparing printing masters for offset litho printing and dyeline machines, making X-ray pictures, and printing high-speed computer output.

xerophyte plant adapted to live in dry conditions. Common adaptations to reduce the rate of ◊transpiration include a reduction of leaf size, sometimes to spines or scales; a dense covering of hairs over the leaf to trap a layer of moist air (as in edelweiss); water storage cells; sunken stomata; and permanently rolled leaves or leaves that roll up in dry weather (as in marram grass). Many desert cacti are xerophytes.

Xerox PARC Xerox Corporation's Palo Alto Research Center in California. During the 1970s and 1980s, Xerox PARC spawned a series of major computing innovations, including ◊Ethernet networks and ◊graphical user interfaces (GUIs). Laser printing, ◊Smalltalk, and the first (never-manufactured) personal computer were also developed there.

Xerox never capitalized on these inventions, leaving entrepreneurs such as Steve Jobs and Bill ◊Gates to bring them into the marketplace, but Xerox PARC remains at the cutting edge of computer innovations.

XGA (abbreviation for ***extended graphics array***) in computing, colour display system which provides either 256 colours on screen and a resolution of 1,024 × 768 ◊pixels or 25,536 colours with a resolution of 640 × 480. This gives a much sharper image than, for example, ◊VGA, which can display only 16 colours at 480 lines of 640 pixels.

XML (abbreviation for ***eXtensible Markup Language***) in computing, a simplified subset of SGML for defining languages for specific purposes or specific industries for use on the World Wide Web. XML is more powerful than HTML but less cumbersome than SGML. XML has been developed through the ◊W3 Consortium, and both Microsoft and Netscape are expected to support it in their version 5 browsers.

Xmodem in computing, an ◊FTP ◊protocol designed to make transmitting files via telephone speedy and error-free.

XON/XOFF in computing, control commands used when two devices ◊handshake using a modem connection. XON starts or resumes transmission of data and XOFF pauses it. XON and XOFF can be manually activated by control-Q and control-S respectively.

X/Open in computing, multivendor computer industry body formed in 1984 to ratify and support the use of UNIX as an open operating system. In February 1996, X/Open merged with the Open Software Foundation to form The Open Group.

XOR (contraction of ***exclusive or***) in computing, search filter meaning 'A or B, but not both'. Thus a search for 'chocolate xor biscuit' might yield 'chocolate', 'biscuit', 'chocolate cake' and 'shortbread biscuit' but never 'chocolate biscuit'. See also ◊Boolean algebra.

X-ray band of electromagnetic radiation in the wavelength range 10^{-11} to 10^{-9} m (between gamma rays and ultraviolet radiation; see ◊electromagnetic waves). Applications of X-rays make use of their short wavelength (as in ◊X-ray diffraction) or their penetrating power (as in medical X-rays of internal body tissues). X-rays are dangerous and can cause cancer.

X-rays with short wavelengths pass through most body tissues, although dense areas such as bone prevent their passage, showing up as white areas on X-ray photographs. The X-rays used in ◊radiotherapy have very short wavelengths that penetrate tissues deeply and destroy them.

X-rays were discovered by German experimental physicist Wilhelm Röntgen in 1895 and formerly called roentgen rays. They are produced when high-energy electrons from a heated filament

X-RAY

http://www.nobel.se/laureates/physics-1901-1-bio.html

Biography of Wilhelm Conrad Röntgen, the German physicist who first realized the huge potential of the electromagnetic field of X-rays. The presentation includes sections on Röntgen's early years and education, his academic career and scientific experiments, and the miraculous coincidences that led him to his great discovery of X-rays.

What is Medical Imaging?

BY CATHY WALSH

Wilhelm Conrad Röntgen, a physicist at the university of Wirzburg, Germany, discovered 'a new kind of ray' on 8 November 1895. He called this radiation X-rays.

Röntgen was investigating the behaviour of cathode rays (electrons) in cathode ray tubes. The tube consisted of a glass envelope and when a high voltage discharge was passed through this tube, a faint light was produced. Röntgen had enclosed his cathode tube in black cardboard to prevent this light from escaping. He then darkened his laboratory room to be sure that there were no light leaks in the cardboard cover. Upon passing a high tension electric discharge through the tube, he noticed a faint light glowing. The source of the light was the fluorescence of a small piece of paper coated with barium platinocyanide. His conclusion was that some unknown type of ray was produced when the tube was energized. Thus, the great discovery of X-rays was made.

There is no doubt that Röntgen's scientific contemporaries were startled by his discovery, but you can imagine the reaction of the non-scientific population when they learned of the new ray that could see through solid objects! It has even been reported that shy Victorian ladies of the period started bathing with their clothes on because they suspected 'those wicked scientists' of watching through the walls.

Medical practitioners, however, soon realized the potential of the X-ray and its value for diagnosis. Developments in ultrasound and nuclear medicine mean that X-rays are no longer the only method of producing diagnostic images. The technological changes and scientific developments have led to the X-ray Department becoming a Medical Imaging Department.

There is a wide variety of imaging techniques undertaken in the modern Medical Imaging Department including those listed below.

Radiography
Images produced by X-rays for diagnosis. These images can be 'plain', showing only bony structures, or they can be 'contrast studies', showing soft tissue such as arteries and veins or organs such as the stomach or kidneys by means of an iodine or barium-based contrast agent introduced by an injection into a vein or by drinking a solution of the contrast agent. The final product, the 'radiograph' or 'X-ray', results when an X-ray cassette placed under the area of interest is exposed to a certain amount of X-ray energy. Once exposed a latent image is formed on the X-ray film within the cassette and requires processing to produce the actual image. The processing of radiographic film is rather like developing film from a standard camera – it involves the film being placed in a bath of developer at a certain temperature and for a certain amount of time, then it requires washing, fixing, washing again, and finally drying. This procedure has traditionally been done manually, but in the last 15–20 years it has become automated and in some departments a darkroom is no longer required.

Computed radiography
A technique for replacing conventional film systems with a digital image which can be viewed, stored and transmitted electronically.

Computed tomography (CT)
Images are again produced by X-rays but as their name suggests the images are computerized and show transverse sectional views through the human body. This is a very precise form of radiography and the thickness of the sectional image produced can range from 2 to 12 mm. The whole body can be imaged this way.

Magnetic resonance imaging
Images are produced by a strong magnet and radio waves rather than by X-rays. The patient is placed inside the magnet and radio waves are applied. Once the radio waves are stopped the patient gives off a signal which is transmitted to a computer which then produces the image. Once again the whole body can be examined with this method of image production. However, should the patient have metal implants such as plates or joints, they cannot be placed into the magnet.

Ultrasound scans
Images are produced by sound waves similar to sonar rather than X-rays. Ultrasound is used to image soft tissue structures such as the liver, gall bladder, spleen, kidneys and unborn babies in their mother's womb.

Nuclear medicine scans
Images are produced by the effect of a radioisotope taken by the patient, on different parts of the body. A computer detects the amount of isotope in the patient's body and an image showing the concentration of isotope is then produced. This form of imaging can be used to image bone, lungs and soft tissue organs such as the liver and spleen.

Technological advances have not only increased the number of imaging techniques available but have also enhanced how images are produced and how they are stored and distributed. Picture Archive and Communication Systems (PACS) enables images which are produced digitally, such as MRI, CT, and Nuclear Medicine images, to be stored on optical disc or digital linear tape. This in turn enables the images to be viewed on workstations which sit on the same network, whether those workstations are within the imaging department, on a ward or clinic in the hospital, or in a doctor's home or surgery.

The information obtained from these examinations can differentiate between different organs without the need for the patient to undergo surgical procedures. The ability to send images to the place where they are required as soon as they are produced saves time and personnel, which in these times of cost savings and the need to cut surgical waiting lists increases the importance of the Medical Imaging Department.

---

cathode strike the surface of a target (usually made of tungsten) on the face of a massive heat-conducting anode, between which a high alternating voltage (about 100 kV) is applied. *See illustration on page 822.*

One does not, by knowing all the physical laws as we know them today, immediately obtain an understanding of anything much.

RICHARD FEYNMAN US physicist.
The Character of Physical Law

X-ray astronomy detection of X-rays from intensely hot gas in the universe. Such X-rays are prevented from reaching the Earth's surface by the atmosphere, so detectors must be placed in rockets and satellites. The first celestial X-ray source, Scorpius X-1, was discovered by a rocket flight in 1962.

Since 1970, special satellites have been put into orbit to study X-rays from the Sun, stars, and galaxies. Many X-ray sources are believed to be gas falling on to ◊neutron stars and ◊black holes.

X-ray diffraction method of studying the atomic and molecular structure of crystalline substances by using ◊X-rays. X-rays directed at such substances spread out as they pass through the crystals owing to ◊diffraction (the slight spreading of waves around the

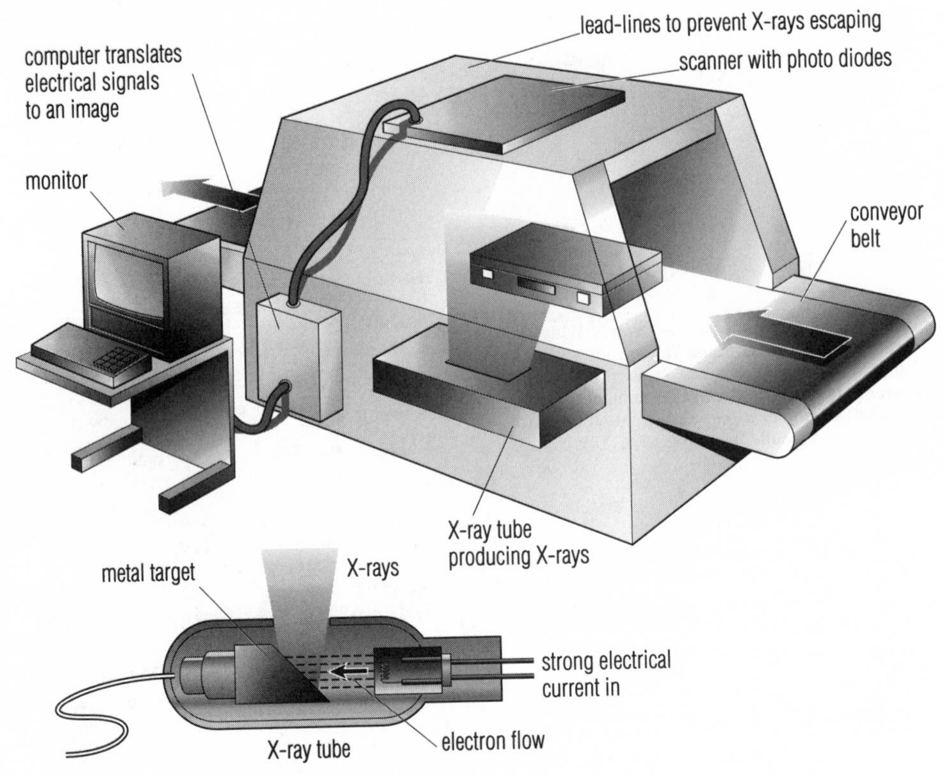

X-ray *An X-ray image. The X-rays are generated by high-speed electrons impinging on a tungsten target. The rays pass through the specimen and on to a photographic plate or imager.*

edge of an opaque object) of the rays around the atoms. By using measurements of the position and intensity of the diffracted waves, it is possible to calculate the shape and size of the atoms in the crystal. The method has been used to study substances such as ◊DNA that are found in living material.

X-ray diffraction analysis the use of X-rays to study the atomic and molecular structure of crystalline substances such as ceramics, stone, sediments, and weathering products on metals. The sample, as a single crystal or ground to powder, is exposed to X-rays at various angles; the diffraction patterns produced are then compared with reference standards for identification.

X-ray fluorescence spectrometry technique used to determine the major and trace elements in the chemical composition of such materials as ceramics, obsidian, and glass. A sample is bombarded with X-rays, and the wavelengths of the released energy, or fluorescent X-rays, are detected and measured. Different elements have unique wavelengths, and their concentrations can be estimated from the intensity of the released X-rays. This analysis may, for example, help an archaeologist in identifying the source of the material.

X-ray telescope in astronomy, a ◊telescope designed to receive ◊electromagnetic waves in the X-ray part of the spectrum. X-rays cannot be focused by lenses or mirrors in the same way as visible light, and a variety of alternative techniques is used to form images. Because X-rays cannot penetrate the Earth's atmosphere, X-ray telescopes are mounted on ◊satellites, ◊rockets, or ◊high-flying balloons.

X Windows in computing, a networked window management system developed as part of Project Athena at the Massachusetts Institute of Technology in 1984. It has been adopted as a standard by the UNIX community but is platform-independent and versions exist for many different operating systems. X Windows enables a user to open windows into a number of different computers at the same time, either using an X Terminal or via X software running on a PC, a UNIX workstation or another computer. Although X Windows is not a graphical user interface, it provides software tools to support such interfaces: Motif is a popular UNIX GUI built on X.

X got its name because it started from an earlier MIT development called W. X Window System is now a trademark of The Open Group.

xylem tissue found in ◊vascular plants, whose main function is to conduct water and dissolved mineral nutrients from the roots to other parts of the plant. Xylem is composed of a number of different types of cell, and may include long, thin, usually dead cells known as ◊tracheids; fibres (schlerenchyma); thin-walled ◊parenchyma cells; and conducting vessels.

In most ◊angiosperms (flowering plants) water is moved through these vessels. Most ◊gymnosperms and ◊pteridophytes lack vessels and depend on tracheids for water conduction.

Non-woody plants contain only primary xylem, derived from the procambium, whereas in trees and shrubs this is replaced for the most part by secondary xylem, formed by ◊secondary growth from the actively dividing vascular ◊cambium. The cell walls of the secondary xylem are thickened by a deposit of ◊lignin, providing mechanical support to the plant; see ◊wood.

Yahoo! in computing, ◊search engine for the ◊World Wide Web, based on a catalogue of indexed resources. Yahoo!, for some time the only search engine on the Web, was created at Stanford University by post-graduate students David Filo and Jerry Yang.

The name – from Swift's *Gulliver's Travels* but found by searching a dictionary – is supposed to stand for **Yet Another Hierarchical Officious Oracle**.

yak species of cattle *Bos grunniens,* family Bovidae, which lives in wild herds at high altitudes in Tibet. It stands about 2 m/6 ft at the shoulder and has long shaggy hair on the underparts. It has large, upward-curving horns and humped shoulders. It is in danger of becoming extinct.

In the wild, the yak is brown or black, but the domesticated variety, which is half the size of the wild form, may be white. It is used for milk, meat, leather, and as a beast of burden. The yak is protected from extremes of cold by its thick coat and by the heat produced from the fermentation in progress in its stomach.

Yale lock trademark for a key-operated pin-tumbler cylinder lock invented by US locksmith Linus Yale Jr (1821–1868) in 1865 and still widely used.

yam any of a group of climbing plants cultivated in tropical regions; the starchy tubers (underground stems) are eaten as a vegetable. The Mexican yam (*D. composita*) contains a chemical that is used in the contraceptive pill. (Genus *Dioscorea,* family Dioscoreaceae.)

yapok nocturnal ◊opossum *Chironectes minimus* found in tropical South and Central America. It is about 33 cm/1.1 ft long, with a 40 cm/1.3 ft tail. It has webbed hind feet and thick fur, and is the only aquatic marsupial. The female has a watertight pouch.

yard unit (symbol yd) of length, equivalent to 3 feet (0.9144 m).

In the USA, it is sometimes used to denote a cubic yard (0.7646 cubic meters), as of topsoil.

YARD

The foot, yard and inch owe their length to Henry I of England. He decreed that one yard was the length of his extended arm, measured from nose to fingertip.

yardang ridge formed by wind erosion from a dried-up riverbed or similar feature, as in Chad, China, Peru, and North America. On the planet Mars yardangs occur on a massive scale.

yarran small tree *Acacia homalophylla* found in E Australia useful as fodder and for firewood and fence posts.

yarrow *or* **milfoil** perennial herb belonging to the daisy family, with feathery, scented leaves and flat-topped clusters of white or pink flowers. It is native to Europe and Asia. (*Achillea millefolium,* family Compositae.)

yaws contagious tropical disease common in the West Indies, W Africa, and some Pacific islands, characterized by red, raspberry-like eruptions on the face, toes, and other parts of the body, sometimes followed by lesions of the bones; these may progress to cause gross disfigurement. It is caused by a spirochete (*Treponema pertenue*), a bacterium related to the one that causes ◊syphilis. Treatment is by antibiotics.

Y chromosome smaller of the two sex chromosomes. In male mammals it occurs paired with the other type of sex chromosome (X), which carries far more genes. The Y chromosome is the smallest of all the mammalian chromosomes and is considered to be largely inert (that is, without direct effect on the physical body). See also ◊sex determination.

In humans, about one in 300 males inherits two Y chromosomes at conception, making him an XYY triploid. Few if any differences from normal XY males exist in these individuals, although at one time they were thought to be emotionally unstable and abnormally aggressive. In 1989 the gene determining that a human being is male was found to occur on the X as well as on the Y chromosome; however, it is not activated in the female.

yd abbreviation for ◊yard.

year unit of time measurement, based on the orbital period of the Earth around the Sun. The **tropical year**, from one spring ◊equinox to the next, lasts 365.2422 days. It governs the occurrence of the seasons, and is the period on which the calendar year is based. The **sidereal year** is the time taken for the Earth to complete one orbit relative to the fixed stars, and lasts 365.2564 days (about 20 minutes longer than a tropical year). The difference is due to the effect of ◊precession, which slowly moves the position of the equinoxes. The **calendar year** consists of 365 days, with an extra day added at the end of February each leap year. **Leap years** occur in every year that is divisible by four, except that a century year is not a leap year unless it is divisible by 400. Hence 1900 was not a leap year, but 2000 will be.

other types of year A **historical year** begins on 1 January, although up to 1752, when the Gregorian calendar was adopted in England, the civil or legal year began on 25 March. The English **fiscal/financial year** still ends on 5 April, which is 25 March plus the 11 days added under the reform of the calendar in 1752. The **regnal year** begins on the anniversary of the sovereign's accession; it is used in the dating of acts of Parliament.

The **anomalistic year** is the time taken by any planet in making one complete revolution from perihelion to perihelion; for the Earth this period is about five minutes longer than the sidereal year due to the gravitational pull of the other planets.

year 2000 in computing, problem faced by computer professionals, the industry, and users towards the close of the 20th century because most computers use only 6 digits to record the date. Thus, 10 August 1962 is recorded as 10/08/62, 081062 , or a similar format. Because the year is represented by only two characters, computers all over the world need reprogramming to prevent them assuming that the figures 00 stand for 1900 rather than 2000.

The consequences could be devastating, including pension funds and payrolls being unable to make payments, accounting systems refusing to issue cheques, landlords crediting tenants with 99 years rent and many companies going out of business. Action to minimize these problems started in the mid 1990s.

Science is built up with facts, as a house is with stones. But a collection of facts is no more a science than a heap of stones is a house.

JULES HENRI POINCARÉ French mathematician.
Science and Hypothesis 1905
Attributed remark

yeast one of various single-celled fungi (see ◊fungus) that form masses of tiny round or oval cells by budding. When placed in a sugar solution the cells multiply and convert the sugar into alcohol and carbon dioxide. Yeasts are used as fermenting agents in baking, brewing, and the making of wine and spirits. Brewer's yeast (*S.*

cerevisiae) is a rich source of vitamin B. (Especially genus *Saccharomyces;* also other related genera.)

yeast artificial chromosome *(YAC)* fragment of ◊DNA from the human genome inserted into a yeast cell. The yeast replicates the fragment along with its own DNA. In this way the fragments are copied to be preserved in a gene library. YACs are characteristically between 250,000 and 1 million base pairs in length. A ◊cosmid works in the same way.

yeheb nut small tree found in Ethiopia and Somalia, formerly much valued for its nuts as a food source. Although cultivated as a food crop in Kenya and Sudan, it is now critically endangered in the wild and is only known to survive at three sites. Overgrazing by cattle and goats has prevented regrowth, and the taking of nuts for consumption prevents reseeding. Although reintroduction would be possible from cultivated trees, the continuing grazing pressure would make establishment unlikely without proper management. (*Cordeauxia adulis.*)

yellow archangel flowering plant belonging to the mint family, found over much of Europe. It grows up to 60 cm/2 ft tall and has nettlelike leaves and rings, or whorls, of yellow flowers growing around the main stem; the lower lips of the flowers are streaked with red in early summer. (*Lamiastrum galeobdolon,* family Labiatae.)

yellow fever or ***yellow jack*** acute tropical viral disease, prevalent in the Caribbean area, Brazil, and on the west coast of Africa. The yellow fever virus is an arbovirus transmitted by mosquitoes. Its symptoms include a high fever, headache, joint and muscle pains, vomiting, and yellowish skin (jaundice, possibly leading to liver failure); the heart and kidneys may also be affected. Mortality is high in serious cases.

Before the arrival of Europeans, yellow fever was not a problem because indigenous people had built up an immunity. The disease was brought under control after the discovery that it is carried by the mosquito *Aêdes aegypti.* The first effective vaccines were produced by Max Theiler (1899–1972) of South Africa, for which he was awarded the 1951 Nobel Prize for Medicine. The World Health Organization estimates there are about 200,000 cases of yellow fever each year in Africa, with 30,000 deaths (1993).

YELLOW FEVER

http://www.outbreak.org/cgi-unreg/dynaserve.exe/YellowFever/index.html

Outbreak page on yellow fever. The Web site contains a section on frequently asked questions about the disease, and a section on current and recent outbreaks. The outbreaks section is updated regularly, often giving numbers of casualties and descriptions of operations by the World Health Organization to curb the spread of any outbreak.

yellowhammer Eurasian bird *Emberiza citrinella* of the bunting family Emberizidae, order Passeriformes. About 16.5 cm/6.5 in long, the male has a yellow head and underside, a chestnut rump, and a brown-streaked back. The female is duller.

yellow star-of-Bethlehem rare flowering plant *Gagea lutea.* It has clusters of stalked yellow flowers that appear in very early spring, and is found in damp ◊loam, usually by woodland streams, mainly in N England.

Yerkes Observatory astronomical centre in Wisconsin, USA, founded by George Hale in 1897. It houses the world's largest refracting optical ◊telescope, with a lens of diameter 102 cm/40 in.

yew any of a group of evergreen coniferous trees native to the northern hemisphere. The dark green flat needlelike leaves and bright red berrylike seeds are poisonous; the wood is hard and close-grained. (Genus *Taxus,* family Taxaceae.)

The western or Pacific yew (*T. brevifolia*) is native to North America. English yew (*T. baccata*) is widely cultivated as an ornamental tree. The wood was formerly used to make longbows.

The anticancer drug taxol is synthesized from the bark of the Pacific yew.

yield point *or* **elastic limit** the stress beyond which a material deforms by a relatively large amount for a small increase in stretching force. Beyond this stress, the material no longer obeys ◊Hooke's law.

yolk store of food, mostly in the form of fats and proteins, found in the ◊eggs of many animals. It provides nourishment for the growing embryo.

yolk sac sac containing the yolk in the egg of most vertebrates. The term is also used for the membranous sac formed below the developing mammalian embryo and connected with the umbilical cord.

Yorkshire terrier breed of toy dog from N England. Its long, straight coat is blue-black on the body and red or tan on the head, chest, and legs. It weighs just 3 kg/6.5 lb, and its body is long in proportion to its short legs.

ytterbium soft, lustrous, silvery, malleable and ductile element of the ◊lanthanide series, symbol Yb, atomic number 70, relative atomic mass 173.04. It occurs with (and resembles) yttrium in gadolinite and other minerals, and is used in making steel and other alloys.

In 1878 Swiss chemist Jean-Charles de Marignac gave the name ytterbium (after the Swedish town of Ytterby, near where it was found) to what he believed to be a new element. French chemist Georges Urbain (1872–1938) discovered in 1907 that this was in fact a mixture of two elements: ytterbium and lutetium.

yttrium silver-grey, metallic element, symbol Y, atomic number 39, relative atomic mass 88.905. It is associated with and resembles the rare earth elements (◊lanthanides), occurring in gadolinite, xenotime, and other minerals. It is used in colour-television tubes and to reduce steel corrosion.

The name derives from the Swedish town of Ytterby, near where it was first discovered in 1788. Swedish chemist Carl Mosander (1797–1858) isolated the element in 1843.

yucca any of a group of plants belonging to the lily family, with over 40 species found in Latin America and the southwestern USA. The leaves are stiff and sword-shaped and the flowers, which grow on upright central spikes, are white and bell-shaped. (Genus *Yucca,* family Liliaceae.)

Yuccas grow in dry soils where nitrate salts, required for protein manufacture, are in short supply. They have therefore evolved the ability to use ammonia, absorbed from animal urine, instead. Feeding extracts of yucca to livestock has been shown to reduce unpleasant ammoniacal smells from factory farms.

Yukawa, Hideki
(1907–1981)

Japanese physicist. In 1935 he discovered the strong nuclear force that binds protons and neutrons together in the atomic nucleus, and predicted the existence of the subatomic particle called the meson. He was awarded a Nobel prize in 1949.

Mary Evans Picture Library

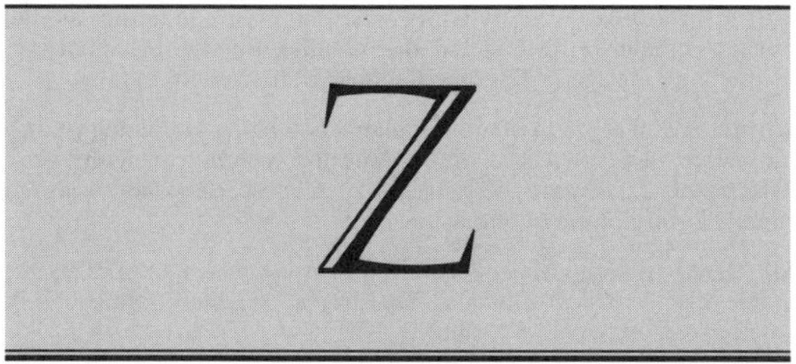

Z in physics, the symbol for **impedance** (electricity and magnetism).

zander fish *Stizostedion lucioperca,* a cross between the ◊pike and the ◊perch. It has a grey-green back, white underside, two dorsal fins and a wide mouth with fangs. It is about 60 cm/24 in long and weighs about 7.5 kg. It is a solitary and voracious predator and lays up to 2 million eggs per year on vegetation in slow-flowing or still water.

z-buffer in computing, ◊buffer for storing depth information for displaying three-dimensional graphics. (Two-dimensional images may be displayed using *x, y* coordinates but the third dimension implies *x, y,* and *z*.) In a graphics card, z-buffer memory keeps track of which onscreen elements are visible and which are hidden behind other objects.

zebra black and white striped member of the horse genus *Equus* found in Africa; the stripes serve as camouflage or dazzle and confuse predators. It is about 1.5 m/5 ft high at the shoulder, with a stout body and a short, thick mane. Zebras live in family groups and herds on mountains and plains, and can run at up to 60 kph/40 mph. Males are usually solitary.

The **mountain zebra** *E. zebra* was once common in Cape Colony and Natal and still survives in parts of South Africa and Angola. It has long ears and is silvery-white with black or dark-brown markings. **Grevy's zebra** *E. grevyi,* at 1.6 m and 450 kg, is the largest member of the horse family. It has finer and clearer markings than the mountain zebra and inhabits Ethiopia and Somalia. Whereas other zebra species have a harem system, Grevy's males defend territories that females pass through to graze. The species is classified as endangered. **Burchell's** or the **common zebra** *E. burchelli* is medium in size, has white ears, a long mane, and a full tail; it roams the plains north of the Orange River in South Africa.

zebra *The Cape mountain zebra* Equus Hippotigris zebra zebra. *It now survives mainly in the Mountain Zebra National Park near Cradock in South Africa, having been saved from near extinction (numbers had been reduced to about 40 individuals). Hartmann's mountain zebra is more widely distributed in the semi-deserts of Namibia.* Premaphotos Wildlife

zebu any of a species of ◊cattle *Bos indicus* found domesticated in E Asia, India, and Africa. It is usually light-coloured, with large horns and a large fatty hump near the shoulders. It is used for pulling loads, and is held by some Hindus to be sacred. There are about 30 breeds.

Zebus have been crossbred with other species of cattle in hot countries to pass on their qualities of heat tolerance and insect resistance. In the USA, they are called Brahman cattle.

zeitgeber German 'time giver' in biology, signal that synchronizes ◊circadian rhythms ensuring that internal and external time are linked. In most species the most important zeitgeber is light and dark changes during the cycle of night and day.

Zelenchukskaya site of the world's largest single-mirror optical telescope, with a mirror of 6 m/236 in diameter, in the Caucasus Mountains of Russia. At the same site is the RATAN 600 radio telescope, consisting of radio reflectors in a circle of 600 m/2,000 ft diameter. Both instruments are operated by the Academy of Sciences in St Petersburg.

zenith uppermost point of the celestial horizon, immediately above the observer; the nadir is below, diametrically opposite. See ◊celestial sphere.

zeolite any of the hydrous aluminium silicates, also containing sodium, calcium, barium, strontium, or potassium, chiefly found in igneous rocks and characterized by a ready loss or gain of water. Zeolites are used as 'molecular sieves' to separate mixtures because they are capable of selective absorption. They have a high ion-exchange capacity and can be used to make petrol, benzene, and toluene from low-grade raw materials, such as coal and methanol.

Zeppelin, Ferdinand Adolf August Heinrich, Count von Zeppelin (1838–1917)

German airship pioneer. His first airship was built and tested in 1900. During World War I a number of zeppelins bombed England. They were also used for luxury passenger transport but the construction of hydrogen-filled airships with rigid keels was abandoned after several disasters in the 1920s and 1930s. Zeppelin also helped to pioneer large multi-engine bomber planes.

Mary Evans Picture Library

zero the number (written 0) that when added to any number leaves that number unchanged. It results when any number is subtracted from itself, or when any number is added to its negative. The product of any number with zero is itself zero.

zero wait state term applied to ◊central processing units that run without wait states – that is, without waiting for slower chips.

Zhubov scale scale for measuring ice coverage, developed in the USSR. The unit is the **ball**; one ball is 10% coverage, two balls 20%, and so on.

zidovudine (formerly *AZT*) antiviral drug used in the treatment of ◊AIDS. It is not a cure for AIDS but is effective in prolonging life; it does not, however, delay the onset of AIDS in people carrying the virus.

Zidovudine was developed in the mid-1980s and approved for use by 1987. Taken every four hours, night and day, it reduces the risk of opportunistic infection and relieves many neurological complications. However, frequent blood monitoring is required to control anaemia, a potentially life-threatening side effect of zidovudine. Blood transfusions are often necessary, and the drug must be withdrawn if bone-marrow function is severely affected.

A US trial in 1994 showed that the drug does provide some protection to babies born to HIV-positive mothers. The number of babies infected was reduced by two-thirds where mothers received zidovudine during pregnancy. Long-term affects of zidovudine on the babies' health remain to be determined.

ZIF socket (acronym for ***zero insertion force socket***) socket on a computer's ◊motherboard that enables a chip to be easily removed or inserted by use of a lever. ZIF sockets are usually only used for expensive ◊microprocessors that are designed to be upgraded.

ZIFT (abbreviation for ***zygote inter-Fallopian transfer***) modified form of ◊in vitro fertilization in which the fertilized ovum is reintroduced into the mother's ◊Fallopian tube before the ovum has undergone its first cell division. This mimics the natural processes of fertilization (which normally occurs in the Fallopian tube) and implantation more effectively than older techniques.

Zimbabwe or **Great Zimbabwe** ***Shona*** zimbabwe (***'house of stone'***) extensive stone architectural ruins 27 km/17 mi SE of Victoria in Mashonaland, Zimbabwe. The site was occupied from the 3rd century AD, but the massive stone structures date from the 10th–15th centuries AD. They were probably the work of the Shona people, who established their rule in about AD 1000 and mined minerals for trading.

The new state of Zimbabwe took its name from these ruins, and the national emblem is a bird derived from soapstone sculptures of fish eagles found there. The site comprises hill ruins with the earliest dwellings (10th century AD), a series of stone-walled enclosures on a granite outcrop known as the Acropolis, a massive elliptical building, or Great Enclosure, with 10-m/30-ft stone walls, a ritual or political site known as the Temple, and a conical tower built in a later phase.

Porcelain of the Ming period and golden ornaments have been found in the ruins. Gold, copper, tin, and iron were all mined by the Shona.

zinc Germanic *zint* 'point' hard, brittle, bluish-white, metallic element, symbol Zn, atomic number 30, relative atomic mass 65.37. The principal ore is sphalerite or zinc blende (zinc sulphide, ZnS). Zinc is hardly affected by air or moisture at ordinary temperatures; its chief uses are in alloys such as brass and in coating metals (for example, galvanized iron). Its compounds include zinc oxide, used in ointments (as an astringent) and cosmetics, paints, glass, and printing ink.

Zinc is an essential trace element in most animals; adult humans have 2–3 g/0.07–0.1 oz zinc in their bodies. There are more than 300 known enzymes that contain zinc.

Zinc has been used as a component of brass since the Bronze Age, but it was not recognized as a separate metal until 1746, when it was described by German chemist Andreas Sigismund Marggraf (1709–1782). The name derives from the shape of the crystals on smelting.

zinc ore mineral from which zinc is extracted, principally sphalerite (Zn,Fe)S, but also zincite, ZnO_2, and smithsonite, $ZnCO_3$, all of which occur in mineralized veins. Ores of lead and zinc often occur together, and are common worldwide; Canada, the USA, and Australia are major producers.

zinc oxide ZnO white powder, yellow when hot, that occurs in nature as the mineral zincite. It is used in paints and as an antiseptic in zinc ointment; it is the main ingredient of calamine lotion.

zinc sulphide ZnS yellow-white solid that occurs in nature as the mineral sphalerite (also called zinc blende). It is the principal ore of zinc, and is used in the manufacture of fluorescent paints.

zinnia any of a group of annual plants belonging to the daisy family, native to Mexico and South America; notably the cultivated hybrids of *Z. elegans* with brightly coloured daisylike flowers. (Genus *Zinnia*, family Compositae.)

Zip drive in computing, portable disc drive manufactured by or under license from ◊Iomega. Zip drives can store almost 100 ◊megabytes on each 3.5-in disc.

zip fastener fastening device used in clothing, invented in the USA by Whitcomb Judson in 1891, originally for doing up shoes. It has two sets of interlocking teeth, meshed by means of a slide that moves up and down. It did not become widely used in the clothing industry until the 1930s.

zipped file in computing, a file that has been compressed using the ◊PKZIP program.

zircon zirconium silicate, $ZrSiO_4$, a mineral that occurs in small quantities in a wide range of igneous, sedimentary, and metamorphic rocks. It is very durable and is resistant to erosion and weathering. It is usually coloured brown, but can be other colours, and when transparent may be used as a gemstone.

Zircons contain abundant radioactive isotopes of uranium and so are useful for uranium–lead dating to determine the ages of rocks.

zirconium Germanic *zircon*, from Persian *zargun* 'golden' lustrous, greyish-white, strong, ductile, metallic element, symbol Zr, atomic number 40, relative atomic mass 91.22. It occurs in nature as the mineral zircon (zirconium silicate), from which it is obtained commercially. It is used in some ceramics, alloys for wire and filaments, steel manufacture, and nuclear reactors, where its low neutron absorption is advantageous.

It was isolated in 1824 by Swedish chemist Jöns Berzelius. The name was proposed by English chemist Humphry Davy in 1808.

Zmodem in computing, ◊FTP ◊protocol for transferring files across the ◊Internet or other communications link. It offers the facility to use ◊wild cards to search files and to resume interrupted transfers where they left off.

zodiac zone of the heavens containing the paths of the Sun, Moon, and planets. When this was devised by the ancient Greeks, only five planets were known, making the zodiac about 16° wide. In astrology, the zodiac is divided into 12 signs, each 30° in extent: Aries, Taurus, Gemini, Cancer, Leo, Virgo, Libra, Scorpio, Sagittarius, Capricorn, Aquarius, and Pisces. These do not cover the same areas of sky as the astronomical constellations.

The 12 astronomical constellations are uneven in size and do not between them cover the whole zodiac, or even the line of the ecliptic, much of which lies in the constellation of ◊Ophiuchus.

zodiacal light cone-shaped light sometimes seen extending from the Sun along the ◊ecliptic, visible after sunset or before sunrise. It is due to thinly spread dust particles in the central plane of the Solar System. It is very faint, and requires a dark, clear sky to be seen.

zoidogamy type of plant reproduction in which male gametes (antherozoids) swim in a film of water to the female gametes. Zoidogamy is found in algae, bryophytes, pteridophytes, and some gymnosperms (others use◊ siphonogamy).

zone therapy alternative name for ◊reflexology.

zoo (abbreviation for ***zoological gardens***) place where animals are kept in captivity. Originally created purely for visitor entertainment and education, zoos have become major centres for the breeding of endangered species of animals; a 1984 report identified 2,000 vertebrate species in need of such maintenance. The Arabian oryx has already been preserved in this way; it was captured in 1962, bred in captivity, and released again in the desert in 1972, where it has flourished.

ZOONET IMAGE ARCHIVES

http://www.mindspring.com/~zoonet/gallery.html

Comprehensive collection of indexes to zoo galleries, with or without detailed text, and links to other animal pictures.

Notable zoos exist in New York, San Diego, Toronto, Chicago, London, Paris, Berlin, Moscow, and Beijing (Peking). Many groups object to zoos because they keep animals in unnatural conditions alien to their habitat.

Anyone who has got any pleasure at all should try to put something back. Life is like a superlative meal and the world is like the maitre d'hotel. What I am doing is the equivalent of leaving a reasonable tip.

GERALD DURRELL British conservationist. *Guardian* 1971

zoological colony in zoology, colony formed when an organism gives rise to several buds which adhere to the parent and continue to reproduce by budding. Such colonies are common among sponges and corals.

The freshwater hydra forms a temporary colony, while many other forms, including most corals, are permanently colonial. In many cases the individuals that make up a colony perform identical functions, but in the condition known as polymorphism, the functions are specialized and allotted to various members. Thus the individuality of the members is frequently lost, and they become almost like organs instead of whole living creatures; this happens, for instance in the ◊Portuguese man-of-war.

zoology branch of biology concerned with the study of animals. It includes any aspect of the study of animal form and function – description of present-day animals, the study of evolution of animal forms, ◊anatomy, physiology, embryology, behaviour, and geographical distribution.

TO REMEMBER THE MAJOR CHARACTERISTICS OF LIVING ORGANISMS:

NEWMARKET RUNS EVERY GREAT RACE IN MAY.

NUTRITION, RESPIRATION, EXCRETION, GROWTH, REPRODUCTION, IRRITABILITY (RESPONSE TO CONDITIONS), MOVEMENT

zoom lens photographic lens that, by variation of focal length, allows speedy transition from long shots to close-ups.

zoonosis any infectious disease that can be transmitted to humans by other vertebrate animals. Probably the most feared example is ◊rabies. The transmitted microorganism sometimes causes disease only in the human host, leaving the animal host unaffected.

Z particle in physics, an ◊elementary particle, one of the weakons responsible for carrying the ◊weak nuclear force.

zucchini another name for the courgette, a type of ◊marrow.

zwitterion ion that has both a positive and a negative charge, such as an ◊amino acid in neutral solution. For example, glycine contains both a basic amino group (NH_2) and an acidic carboxyl group (COOH); when these are both ionized in aqueous solution, the acid group loses a proton to the amino group, and the molecule is positively charged at one end and negatively charged at the other.

zygote ◊ovum (egg) after ◊fertilization but before it undergoes cleavage to begin embryonic development.

What counts ... in science is to be not so much the first as the last.

ERWIN CHARGAFF Czech-born US biochemist. *Science* 1971

APPENDICES

Scientific Discoveries

Discovery	Date	Discoverer	Nationality
Absolute zero, concept	1851	William Thomson, 1st Baron Kelvin	Irish
Adrenalin, isolation	1901	Jokichi Takamine	Japanese
Alizarin, synthesized	1869	William Perkin	English
Allotropy (in carbon)	1841	Jöns Jakob Berzelius	Swedish
Alpha rays	1899	Ernest Rutherford	New Zealand-born British
Alternation of generations (ferns and mosses)	1851	Wilhelm Hofmeister	German
Aluminium, extraction by electrolysis of aluminium oxide	1886	Charles Hall, Paul Héroult	US, French
Aluminium, improved isolation	1827	Friedrich Wöhler	German
Anaesthetic, first use (ether)	1842	Crawford Long	US
Anthrax vaccine	1881	Louis Pasteur	French
Antibacterial agent, first specific (Salvarsan for treatment of syphilis)	1910	Paul Ehrlich	German
Antiseptic surgery (using phenol)	1865	Joseph Lister	English
Argon	1892	William Ramsay	Scottish
Asteroid, first (Ceres)	1801	Giuseppe Piazzi	Italian
Atomic theory	1803	John Dalton	English
Australopithecus	1925	Raymond Dart	Australian-born South African
Avogadro's hypothesis	1811	Amedeo Avogadro	Italian
Bacteria, first observation	1683	Anton van Leeuwenhoek	Dutch
Bacteriophages	1916	Felix D'Herelle	Canadian
Bee dance	1919	Karl von Frisch	Austrian
Benzene, isolation	1825	Michael Faraday	English
Benzene, ring structure	1865	Friedrich Kekulé	German
Beta rays	1899	Ernest Rutherford	New Zealand-born British
Big-Bang theory	1948	Ralph Alpher, George Gamow	US
Binary arithmetic	1679	Gottfried Leibniz	German
Binary stars	1802	William Herschel	German-born English
Binomial theorem	1665	Isaac Newton	English
Blood, circulation	1619	William Harvey	English
Blood groups, ABO system	1900	Karl Landsteiner	Austrian-born US
Bode's law	1772	Johann Bode, Johann Titius	German
Bohr atomic model	1913	Niels Bohr	Danish
Boolean algebra	1854	George Boole	English
Boyle's law	1662	Robert Boyle	Irish
Brewster's law	1812	David Brewster	Scottish
Brownian motion	1827	Robert Brown	Scottish
Cadmium	1817	Friedrich Strohmeyer	German
Caesium	1861	Robert Bunsen	German
Carbon dioxide	1755	Joseph Black	Scottish
Charles' law	1787	Jacques Charles	French
Chlorine	1774	Karl Scheele	Swedish
Complex numbers, theory	1746	Jean d'Alembert	French
Conditioning	1902	Ivan Pavlov	Russian
Continental drift	1912	Alfred Wegener	German
Coriolis effect	1834	Gustave-Gaspard Coriolis	French
Cosmic radiation	1911	Victor Hess	Austrian
Decimal fractions	1576	François Viète	French
Dinosaur fossil, first recognized	1822	Mary Ann Mantell	English
Diphtheria bacillus, isolation	1883	Edwin Krebs	US
DNA	1869	Johann Frederick Miescher	Swiss
DNA and RNA	1909	Phoebus Levene	Russian-born US
DNA, double-helix structure	1953	Francis Crick, James Watson	English, US
Doppler effect	1842	Christian Doppler	Austrian
Earth's magnetic pole	1546	Gerardus Mercator	Flemish

Scientific Discoveries (continued)

Discovery	*Date*	*Discoverer*	*Nationality*
Earth's molten core	1916	Albert Michelson	German-born US
Earth's molten core, proof	1906	Richard Oldham	Welsh
Earth's rotation, demonstration	1851	Léon Foucault	French
Eclipse, prediction	585 BC	Thales of Miletus	Greek
Electrolysis, laws	1833	Michael Faraday	English
Electromagnetic induction	1831	Michael Faraday	English
Electromagnetism	1819	Hans Christian Oersted	Danish
Electron	1897	J J Thomson	English
Electroweak unification theory	1967	Sheldon Lee Glashow, Abdus Salam, Steven Weinberg	US, Pakistani, US
Endorphins	1975	John Hughes	US
Enzyme, first animal (pepsin)	1836	Theodor Schwann	German
Enzyme, first (diastase from barley)	1833	Anselme Payen	French
Enzymes, 'lock and key' hypothesis	1899	Emil Fischer	German
Ether, first anaesthetic use	1842	Crawford Long	US
Eustachian tube	1552	Bartolomeo Eustachio	Italian
Evolution by natural selection	1858	Charles Darwin	English
Exclusion principle	1925	Wolfgang Pauli	Austrian-born Swiss
Fallopian tubes	1561	Gabriello Fallopius	Italian
Fluorine, preparation	1886	Henri Moissan	French
Fullerines	1985	Harold Kroto, David Walton	English
Gay-Lussac's law	1808	Joseph-Louis Gay-Lussac	French
Geometry, Euclidean	300 BC	Euclid	Greek
Germanium	1886	Clemens Winkler	German
Germ theory	1861	Louis Pasteur	French
Global temperature and link with atmospheric carbon dioxide	1896	Svante Arrhenius	Swedish
Gravity, laws	1687	Isaac Newton	English
Groups, theory	1829	Evariste Galois	French
Gutenberg discontinuity	1914	Beno Gutenberg	German-born US
Helium, production	1896	William Ramsay	Scottish
Homo erectus	1894	Marie Dubois	Dutch
Homo habilis	1961	Louis Leakey, Mary Leakey	Kenyan, English
Hormones	1902	William Bayliss, Ernest Starling	English
Hubble's law	1929	Edwin Hubble	US
Hydraulics, principles	1642	Blaise Pascal	French
Hydrogen	1766	Henry Cavendish	English
Iapetus	1671	Giovanni Cassini	Italian-born French
Infrared solar rays	1801	William Herschel	German-born English
Insulin, isolation	1921	Frederick Banting, Charles Best	Canadian
Insulin, structure	1969	Dorothy Hodgkin	English
Interference of light	1801	Thomas Young	English
Irrational numbers	450 BC	Hipparcos	Greek
Jupiter's satellites	1610	Galileo	Italian
Kinetic theory of gases	1850	Rudolf Clausius	German
Krypton	1898	William Ramsay, Morris Travers	Scottish, English
Lanthanum	1839	Carl Mosander	Swedish
Lenses, how they work	1039	Ibn al-Haytham Alhazen	Arabic
Light, finite velocity	1675	Ole Römer	Danish
Light, polarization	1678	Christiaan Huygens	Dutch
Linnaean classification system	1735	Linnaeus	Swedish
'Lucy', hominid	1974	Donald Johanson	US
Magnetic dip	1576	Robert Norman	English
Malarial parasite in *Anopheles* mosquito	1897	Ronald Ross	British
Malarial parasite observed	1880	Alphonse Laveran	French
Mars, moons	1877	Asaph Hall	US
Mendelian laws of inheritance	1866	Gregor Mendel	Austrian
Messenger RNA	1960	Sydney Brenner, François Jacob	South African, French
Microorganisms as cause of fermentation	1856	Louis Pasteur	French
Monoclonal antibodies	1975	César Milstein, George Köhler	Argentinean-born British, German
Motion, laws	1687	Isaac Newton	English
Natural selection	1859	Charles Darwin	English
Neon	1898	William Ramsay, Morris Travers	Scottish, English
Neptune	1846	Johann Galle	German
Neptunium	1940	Edwin McMillan, Philip Abelson	US
Nerve impulses, electric nature	1771	Luigi Galvani	Italian
Neutron	1932	James Chadwick	English
Nitrogen	1772	Daniel Rutherford	Scottish

Scientific Discoveries (continued)

Discovery	*Date*	*Discoverer*	*Nationality*
Normal distribution curve	1733	Abraham De Moivre	French
Nuclear atom, concept	1911	Ernest Rutherford	New Zealand-born British
Nuclear fission	1938	Otto Hahn, Fritz Strassman	German
Nucleus, plant cell	1831	Robert Brown	Scottish
Ohm's law	1827	Georg Ohm	German
Organic substance, first synthesis (urea)	1828	Friedrich Wöhler	German
Oxygen	1774	Joseph Priestley	English
Oxygen, liquefaction	1894	James Dewar	Scottish
Ozone layer	1913	Charles Fabry	French
Palladium	1803	William Hyde Wollaston	English
Pallas (asteroid)	1802	Heinrich Olbers	German
Pendulum, principle	1581	Galileo	Italian
Penicillin	1928	Alexander Fleming	Scottish
Penicillin, widespread preparation	1940	Ernst Chain, Howard Florey	German, Australian
Pepsin	1836	Theodor Schwann	German
Periodic law for elements	1869	Dmitri Mendeleyev	Russian
Period–luminosity law	1912	Henrietta Swan	US
Phosphorus	1669	Hennig Brand	German
Piezoelectric effect	1880	Pierre Curie	French
Pi meson (particle)	1947	Cecil Powell, Giuseppe Occhialini	English, Italian
Pistils, function	1676	Nehemiah Grew	English
Planetary nebulae	1790	William Herschel	German-born English
Planets, orbiting Sun	1543	Copernicus	Polish
Pluto	1930	Clyde Tombaugh	US
Polarization of light by reflection	1808	Etienne Malus	French
Polio vaccine	1952	Jonas Salk	US
Polonium	1898	Marie and Pierre Curie	French
Positron	1932	Carl Anderson	US
Potassium	1806	Humphry Davy	English
Probability theory	1654	Blaise Pascal, Pierre de Fermat	French
Probability theory, expansion	1812	Pierre Laplace	French
Proton	1914	Ernest Rutherford	New Zealand-born British
Protoplasm	1846	Hugo von Mohl	German
Pulsar	1967	Jocelyn Bell Burnell	English
Pythagoras' theorem	550 BC	Pythagoras	Greek
Quantum chromodynamics	1972	Murray Gell-Mann	US
Quantum electrodynamics	1948	Richard Feynman, Seymour Schwinger, Shin'chiro Tomonaga	US, US, Japanese
Quark, first suggested existence	1963	Murray Gell-mann, George Zweig	US
Quasar	1963	Maarten Schmidt	Dutch-born US
Rabies vaccine	1885	Louis Pasteur	French
Radioactivity	1896	Henri Becquerel	French
Radio emissions, from Milky Way	1931	Karl Jansky	US
Radio waves, production	1887	Heinrich Hertz	German
Radium	1898	Marie and Pierre Curie	French
Radon	1900	Friedrich Dorn	German
Refraction, laws	1621	Willibrord Snell	Dutch
Relativity, general theory	1915	Albert Einstein	German-born US
Relativity, special theory	1905	Albert Einstein	German-born US
Rhesus factor	1940	Karl Landsteiner, Alexander Wiener	Austrian, US
Rubidium	1861	Robert Bunsen	German
Sap circulation	1846	Giovanni Battista	Italian
Sap flow in plants	1733	Stephen Hales	English
Saturn, 18th moon	1990	Mark Showalter	US
Saturn's satellites	1656	Christiaan Huygens	Dutch
Smallpox inoculation	1796	Edward Jenner	English
Sodium	1806	Humphry Davy	English
Stamens, function	1676	Nehemiah Grew	English
Stars, luminosity sequence	1905	Ejnar Hertzsprung	Danish
Stereochemistry, foundation	1848	Louis Pasteur	French
Stratosphere	1902	Léon Teisserenc	French
Sunspots	1611	Galileo, Christoph Scheiner	Italian, German
Superconductivity	1911	Heike Kamerlingh-Onnes	Dutch
Superconductivity, theory	1957	John Bardeen, Leon Cooper, John Schrieffer	US
Thermodynamics, second law	1834	Benoit-Pierre Clapeyron	French
Thermodynamics, third law	1906	Hermann Nernst	German
Thermoelectricity	1821	Thomas Seebeck	German

Scientific Discoveries (continued)

Discovery	*Date*	*Discoverer*	*Nationality*
Thorium-X	1902	Ernest Rutherford, Frederick Soddy	New Zealand-born British, English
Titius–Bode law	1772	Johan Bode, Johann Titius	German
Tranquillizer, first (reserpine)	1956	Robert Woodward	US
Transformer	1831	Michael Faraday	English
Troposphere	1902	Léon Teisserenc	French
Tuberculosis bacillus, isolation	1883	Robert Koch	German
Tuberculosis vaccine	1923	Albert Calmette, Camille Guérin	French
Uranus	1781	William Herschel	German-born English
Urea cycle	1932	Hans Krebs	German
Urease, isolation	1926	James Sumner	US
Urea, synthesis	1828	Friedrich Wöhler	German
Valves, in veins	1603	Geronimo Fabricius	Italian
Van Allen radiation belts	1958	James Van Allen	US
Virus, first identified (tobacco mosaic disease, in tobacco plants)	1898	Martinus Beijerinck	Dutch
Vitamin A, isolation	1913	Elmer McCollum	US
Vitamin A, structure	1931	Paul Karrer	Russian-born Swiss
Vitamin B, composition	1955	Dorothy Hodgkin	English
Vitamin B, isolation	1925	Joseph Goldberger	Austrian-born US
Vitamin C	1928	Charles Glen King, Albert Szent-Györgi	US, Hungarian-born US
Vitamin C, isolation	1932	Charles Glen King	US
Vitamin C, synthesis	1933	Tadeus Reichstein	Polish-born Swiss
Wave mechanics	1926	Erwin Schrödinger	Austrian
Xenon	1898	William Ramsay, Morris Travers	Scottish, English
X-ray crystallography	1912	Max von Laue	German
X-rays	1895	Wilhelm Röntgen	German

Greek Language: Alphabet

Α	α	alpha	Η	η	eta	Ν	ν	nu	Τ	τ	tau
Β	β	beta	Θ	θ	theta	Ξ	ξ	xi	Υ	υ	upsilon
Γ	γ	gamma	Ι	ι	iota	Ο	ο	omicron	Φ	φ	phi
Δ	δ	delta	Κ	κ	kappa	Π	π	pi	Χ	χ	chi
Ε	ϵ	epsilon	Λ	λ	lambda	Ρ	ρ	rho	Ψ	ψ	psi
Ζ	ζ	zeta	Μ	μ	mu	Σ	σ	sigma	Ω	ω	omega

Inventions

Invention	*Date*	*Inventor*	*Nationality*
Achromatic lens	1733	Chester Moor Hall	English
Adding machine	1642	Blaise Pascal	French
Aeroplane, powered	1903	Orville and Wilbur Wright	US
Air conditioning	1902	Willis Carrier	US
Air pump	1654	Otto Guericke	German
Airship, first successful	1852	Henri Giffard	French
Airship, rigid	1900	Ferdinand von Zeppelin	German
Amniocentesis test	1952	Douglas Bevis	English
Aqualung	1943	Jacques Cousteau	French
Arc welder	1919	Elihu Thomson	US
Armillary ring	125	Zhang Heng	Chinese
Aspirin	1899	Felix Hoffman	German
Assembly line	1908	Henry Ford	US
Autogiro	1923	Juan de la Cierva	Spanish
Automatic pilot	1912	Elmer Sperry	US
Babbitt metal	1839	Isaac Babbitt	US
Bakelite, first synthetic plastic	1909	Leo Baekeland	US
Ballpoint pen	1938	Lazlo Biró	Hungarian
Barbed wire	1874	Joseph Glidden	US
Bar code system	1970	Monarch Marking, Plessey Telecommunications	US, English
Barometer	1642	Evangelista Torricelli	Italian

Invention	*Date*	*Inventor*	*Nationality*
Bathysphere	1934	Charles Beebe	US
Bessemer process	1856	Henry Bessemer	British
Bicycle	1839	Kirkpatrick Macmillan	Scottish
Bifocal spectacles	1784	Benjamin Franklin	US
Binary calculator	1938	Konrad Zuse	German
Bottling machine	1895	Michael Owens	US
Braille	1837	Louis Braille	French
Bunsen burner	1850	Robert Bunsen	German
Calculator, pocket	1971	Texas Instruments	US
Camera film (roll)	1888	George Eastman	US
Camera obscura	1560	Battista Porta	Italian
Carbon fibre	1963	Leslie Phillips	English
Carbon-zinc battery	1841	Robert Bunsen	German
Carburettor	1893	Wilhelm Maybach	German
Car, four-wheeled	1887	Gottlieb Daimler	German
Car, petrol-driven	1885	Karl Benz	German
Carpet sweeper	1876	Melville Bissell	US
Cash register	1879	James Ritty	US
Cassette tape	1963	Philips	Dutch
Catapult	*c.* 400 BC	Dionysius of Syracuse	Greek
Cathode ray oscilloscope	1897	Karl Braun	German
CD-ROM	1984	Sony, Fujitsu, Philips	Japanese, Japanese, Dutch

Inventions (continued)

Invention	Date	Inventor	Nationality
Cellophane	1908	Jacques Brandenberger	Swiss
Celluloid	1869	John Wesley Hyatt	US
Cement, Portland	1824	Joseph Aspidin	English
Centigrade scale	1742	Anders Celsius	Swedish
Chemical symbols	1811	Jöns Jakob Berzelius	Swedish
Chronometer, accurate	1762	John Harrison	English
Cinematograph	1895	Auguste and Louis Lumière	French
Clock, pendulum	1656	Christiaan Huygens	Dutch
Colt revolver	1835	Samuel Colt	US
Compact disc	1972	RCA	US
Compact disc player	1984	Sony, Philips	Japanese, Dutch
Compass, simple	1088	Shen Kua	Chinese
Computer, bubble memory	1967	A H Bobeck and Bell Telephone Laboratories team	US
Computer, first commercially available (UNIVAC 1)	1951	John Mauchly, John Eckert	US
Computerized axial tomography (CAT) scanning	1972	Godfrey Hounsfield	English
Contraceptive pill	1954	Gregory Pincus	US
Cotton gin	1793	Eli Whitney	US
Cream separator	1878	Carl de Laval	Swedish
Crookes tube	1878	William Crookes	English
Cyclotron	1931	Ernest O Lawrence	US
DDT	1940	Paul Müller	Swiss
Diesel engine	1892	Rudolf Diesel	German
Difference engine (early computer)	1822	Charles Babbage	English
Diode valve	1904	Ambrose Fleming	English
Dynamite	1866	Alfred Nobel	Swedish
Dynamo	1831	Michael Faraday	English
Electric cell	1800	Alessandro Volta	Italian
Electric fan	1882	Schuyler Wheeler	US
Electric generator, first commercial	1867	Zénobe Théophile Gramme	French
Electric light bulb	1879	Thomas Edison	US
Electric motor	1821	Michael Faraday	English
Electric motor, alternating current	1888	Nikola Tesla	Croatian-born US
Electrocardiography	1903	Willem Einthoven	Dutch
Electroencephalography	1929	Hans Berger	German
Electromagnet	1824	William Sturgeon	English
Electron microscope	1933	Ernst Ruska	German
Electrophoresis	1930	Arne Tiselius	Swedish
Fahrenheit scale	1714	Gabriel Fahrenheit	Polish-born Dutch
Felt-tip pen	1955	Esterbrook	English
Floppy disc	1970	IBM	US
Flying shuttle	1733	John Kay	English
FORTRAN	1956	John Backus, IBM	US
Fractal images	1962	Benoit Mandelbrot	Polish-born French
Frozen food	1929	Clarence Birdseye	US
Fuel cell	1839	William Grove	Welsh
Galvanometer	1820	Johann Schwiegger	German
Gas mantle	1885	Carl Welsbach	Austrian
Geiger counter	1908	Hans Geiger, Ernest Rutherford	German, New Zealand-born British
Genetic fingerprinting	1985	Alec Jeffreys	British
Glider	1877	Otto Lilienthal	German
Gramophone	1877	Thomas Edison	US
Gramophone (flat discs)	1887	Emile Berliner	German
Gyrocompass	1911	Elmer Sperry	US
Gyroscope	1852	Jean Foucault	French
Heart, artificial	1982	Robert Jarvik	US
Heart-lung machine	1953	John Gibbon	US
Helicopter	1939	Igor Sikorsky	US
Holography	1947	Dennis Gabor	Hungarian-born British
Hovercraft	1955	Christopher Cockerell	English
Hydrogen bomb	1952	US government scientists	US
Hydrometer	1675	Robert Boyle	Irish
Iconoscope	1923	Vladimir Zworykin	Russian-born US
Integrated circuit	1958	Jack Kilby, Texas Instruments	US
Internal-combustion engine, four-stroke	1877	Nikolaus Otto	German
Internal-combustion engine, gas-fuelled	1860	Etienne Lenoir	Belgian
In vitro fertilization	1969	Robert Edwards	Welsh
Jet engine	1930	Frank Whittle	English
Jumbo jet	1969	Joe Sutherland and Boeing team	US
Laser, prototype	1960	Theodore Maiman	US
Lightning rod	1752	Benjamin Franklin	US
Linoleum	1860	Frederick Walton	English
Liquid crystal display (LCD)	1971	Hoffmann-LaRoche Laboratories	Swiss
Lock (canal)	980	Ciao Wei-yo	Chinese
Lock, Yale	1851	Linus Yale	US
Logarithms	1614	John Napier	Scottish
Loom, power	1785	Edmund Cartwright	English
Machine gun	1862	Richard Gatling	US
Magnifying glass	1250	Roger Bacon	English
Map	c. 510BC	Hecataeus	Greek
Map, star	c. 350BC	Eudoxus	Greek
Maser	1953	Charles Townes and Arthur Schawlow	US
Mass-spectrograph	1918	Francis Aston	English
Microscope	1590	Zacharias Janssen	Dutch
Miners' safety lamp	1813	Humphry Davy	English
Mohs' scale for mineral hardness	1822	Frederick Mohs	German
Morse code	1838	Samuel Morse	US
Motorcycle	1885	Gottlieb Daimler	German
Neutron bomb	1977	US military	US
Nylon	1934	Wallace Carothers	US
Paper chromatography	1944	Archer Martin, Richard Synge	English
Paper, first	105	Ts'ai Lun	Chinese
Particle accelerator	1932	John Cockcroft, Ernest Walton	English, Irish
Pasteurization (wine)	1864	Louis Pasteur	French
Pen, fountain	1884	Lewis Waterman	US
Photoelectric cell	1904	Johann Elster	German
Photograph, first colour	1881	Frederic Ives	US
Photograph, first (on a metal plate)	1827	Joseph Niepce	French
Piano	1704	Bartelommeo Cristofori	Italian
Planar transistor	1959	Robert Noyce	US
Plastic, first (Parkesine)	1862	Alexander Parkes	English
Plough, cast iron	1785	Robert Ransome	English
Punched-card system for carpet-making loom	1805	Joseph-Marie Jacquard	French
Radar, first practical equipment	1935	Robert Watson-Watt	Scottish
Radio	1901	Guglielmo Marconi	Italian
Radio interferometer	1955	Martin Ryle	English
Radio, transistor	1952	Sony	Japanese
Razor, disposable safety	1895	King Gillette	US

Inventions (continued)

Invention	Date	Inventor	Nationality
Recombinant DNA, technique	1973	Stanley Cohen, Herbert Boyer	US
Refrigerator, domestic	1918	Nathaniel Wales, E J Copeland	US
Richter scale	1935	Charles Richter	US
Road locomotive, steam	1801	Richard Trevithick	English
Road vehicle, first self-propelled (steam)	1769	Nicolas-Joseph Cugnot	French
Rocket, powered by petrol and liquid oxygen	1926	Robert Goddard	US
Rubber, synthetic	1909	Karl Hoffman	German
Scanning tunnelling microscope	1980	Heinrich Rohrer, Gerd Binning	Swiss, German
Seed drill	1701	Jethro Tull	English
Seismograph	1880	John Milne	English
Shrapnel shell	1784	Henry Shrapnel	English
Silicon transistor	1954	Gordon Teal	US
Silk, method of producing artificial	1887	Hilaire, Comte de Chardonnet	French
Spinning frame	1769	Richard Arkwright	English
Spinning jenny	1764	James Hargreaves	English
Spinning mule	1779	Samuel Crompton	English
Stainless steel	1913	Harry Brearley	English
Steam engine	50 BC	Heron of Alexandria	Greek
Steam engine, first successful	1712	Thomas Newcomen	English
Steam engine, improved	1765	James Watt	Scottish
Steam locomotive, first effective	1814	George Stephenson	English
Steam turbine, first practical	1884	Charles Parsons	English
Steel, open-hearth production	1864	William Siemens, Pierre Emile Martin	German, French
Submarine	1620	Cornelius Drebbel	Dutch
Superheterodyne radio receiver	1918	Edwin Armstrong	US
Tank	1914	Ernest Swinton	English
Telephone	1876	Alexander Graham Bell	Scottish-born US
Telescope, binocular	1608	Johann Lippershey	Dutch
Telescope, reflecting	1668	Isaac Newton	English
Television	1926	John Logie Baird	Scottish
Terylene (synthetic fibre)	1941	John Whinfield, J T Dickson	English
Thermometer	1607	Galileo	Italian
Thermometer, alcohol	1730	Réné Antoine Ferchault de Réaumur	French
Thermometer, mercury	1714	Gabriel Fahrenheit	Polish-born Dutch
TNT	1863	J Willbrand	German
Toaster, pop-up	1926	Charles Strite	US
Toilet, flushing	1778	Joseph Bramah	English
Transistor	1948	John Bardeen, Walter Brattain, William Shockley	US
Triode valve	1906	Lee De Forest	US
Tunnel diode	1957	Leo Esaki, Sony	Japanese
Tupperware	1944	Earl Tupper	US
Type, movable earthenware	1045	Pi Shêng	Chinese
Type, movable metal	1440	Johannes Gutenberg	German
Ultrasound, first use in obstetrics	1958	Ian Donald	Scottish
Velcro	1948	Georges de Mestral	Swiss
Video, home	1975	Matsushita, JVC, Sony	Japanese
Viscose	1892	Charles Cross	English
Vulcanization of rubber	1839	Charles Goodyear	US
Wind tunnel	1932	Ford Motor Company	US
Wireless telegraphy	1895	Guglielmo Marconi	Italian
Word processor	1965	IBM	US
Zinc-carbon battery	1868	George Leclanché	French
Zip	1891	Whitcombe Judson	US

Nobel Prize: Introduction

The Nobel Prizes were first awarded in 1901 under the will of Alfred B Nobel (1833–96), a Swedish chemist, who invented dynamite. The interest on the Nobel endowment fund is divided annually among the persons who have made the greatest contributions in the fields of physics, chemistry, medicine, literature, and world peace. The first four are awarded by academic committees based in Sweden, while the peace prize is awarded by a committee of the Norwegian parliament. A sixth prize, for economics, financed by the Swedish National Bank, was first awarded in 1969. The prizes have a large cash award and are given to organizations – such as the United Nations peacekeeping forces, which received the Nobel Peace Prize in 1988 – as well as to individuals.

Nobel Prize for Chemistry

Year	Winner(s)[1]	Awarded for
1901	Jacobus van't Hoff (Netherlands)	laws of chemical dynamics and osmotic pressure
1902	Emil Fischer (Germany)	sugar and purine syntheses
1903	Svante Arrhenius (Sweden)	theory of electrolytic dissociation
1904	William Ramsay (UK)	discovery of inert gases in air and their locations in the periodic table
1905	Adolf von Baeyer (Germany)	work in organic dyes and hydroaromatic compounds
1906	Henri Moissan (France)	isolation of fluorine and adoption of electric furnace
1907	Eduard Buchner (Germany)	biochemical research and discovery of cell-free fermentation
1908	Ernest Rutherford (UK)	work in atomic disintegration, and the chemistry of radioactive substances
1909	Wilhelm Ostwald (Germany)	work in catalysis, and principles of equilibria and rates of reaction
1910	Otto Wallach (Germany)	work in alicyclic compounds
1911	Marie Curie (France)	discovery of radium and polonium, and the isolation and study of radium
1912	Victor Grignard (France)	discovery of Grignard reagent
	Paul Sabatier (France)	finding method of catalytic hydrogenation of organic compounds
1913	Alfred Werner (Switzerland)	work in bonding of atoms within molecules
1914	Theodore Richards (USA)	accurate determination of the atomic masses of many elements
1915	Richard Willstäter (Germany)	research into plant pigments, especially chlorophyll
1916	no award	
1917	no award	

Nobel Prize for Chemistry (continued)

Year	*Winner(s)*[1]	*Awarded for*
1918	Fritz Haber (Germany)	synthesis of ammonia from its elements
1919	no award	
1920	Walther Nernst (Germany)	work in thermochemistry
1921	Frederick Soddy (UK)	work in radioactive substances, especially isotopes
1922	Francis Aston (UK)	work in mass spectrometry of isotopes of radioactive elements, and enunciation of the whole-number rule
1923	Fritz Pregl (Austria)	method of microanalysis of organic substances
1924	no award	
1925	Richard Zsigmondy (Austria)	elucidation of heterogeneity of colloids
1926	Theodor Svedberg (Sweden)	investigation of dispersed systems
1927	Heinrich Wieland (Germany)	research on constitution of bile acids and related substances
1928	Adolf Windaus (Germany)	research on constitution of sterols and related vitamins
1929	Arthur Harden (UK) and Hans von Euler-Chelpin (Sweden)	work on fermentation of sugar, and fermentative enzymes
1930	Hans Fischer (Germany)	analysis of haem (the iron-bearing group in haemoglobin) and chlorophyll, and the synthesis of haemin (a compound of haem)
1931	Carl Bosch (Germany) and Friedrich Bergius (Germany)	invention and development of chemical high-pressure methods
1932	Irving Langmuir (USA)	discoveries and investigations in surface chemistry
1933	no award	
1934	Harold Urey (USA)	discovery of deuterium (heavy hydrogen)
1935	Irène and Frédéric Joliot-Curie (France)	synthesis of new radioactive elements
1936	Peter Debye (Netherlands)	work in molecular structures by investigation of dipole moments and the diffraction of X-rays and electrons in gases
1937	Norman Haworth (UK)	work in carbohydrates and ascorbic acid (vitamin C)
	Paul Karrer (Switzerland)	work in carotenoids, flavins, retinol (vitamin A) and riboflavin (vitamin B_2)
1938	Richard Kuhn (Germany) (declined)	carotenoids and vitamins research
1939	Adolf Butenandt (Germany) (declined)	work in sex hormones
	Leopold Ruzicka (Switzerland)	polymethylenes and higher terpenes
1940	no award	
1941	no award	
1942	no award	
1943	Georg von Hevesy (Hungary)	use of isotopes as tracers in chemical processes
1944	Otto Hahn (Germany)	discovery of nuclear fission
1945	Artturi Virtanen (Finland)	work in agriculture and nutrition, especially fodder preservation
1946	James Sumner (USA)	discovery of crystallization of enzymes
	John Northrop (USA) and Wendell Stanley (USA)	preparation of pure enzymes and virus proteins
1947	Robert Robinson (UK)	investigation of biologically important plant products, especially alkaloids
1948	Arne Tiselius (Sweden)	researches in electrophoresis and adsorption analysis, and discoveries concerning serum proteins
1949	William Giauque (USA)	work in chemical thermodynamics, especially at very low temperatures
1950	Otto Diels (West Germany) and Kurt Alder (West Germany)	discovery and development of diene synthesis
1951	Edwin McMillan (USA) and Glenn Seaborg (USA)	discovery and work in chemistry of transuranic elements
1952	Archer Martin (UK) and Richard Synge (UK)	development of partition chromatography
1953	Hermann Staudinger (West Germany)	discoveries in macromolecular chemistry
1954	Linus Pauling (USA)	study of nature of chemical bonds, especially in complex substances
1955	Vincent du Vigneaud (USA)	investigations into biochemically important sulphur compounds, and the first synthesis of a polypeptide hormone
1956	Cyril Hinshelwood (UK) and Nikolay Semenov (USSR)	work in mechanism of chemical reactions
1957	Alexander Todd (UK)	work in nucleotides and nucleotide coenzymes
1958	Frederick Sanger (UK)	determination of the structure of proteins, especially insulin
1959	Jaroslav Heyrovsk[yacute] (Czechoslovakia)	discovery and development of polarographic methods of chemical analysis
1960	Willard Libby (USA)	development of radiocarbon dating in archaeology, geology, and geography
1961	Melvin Calvin (USA)	study of assimilation of carbon dioxide by plants
1962	Max Perutz (UK) and John Kendrew (UK)	determination of structures of globular proteins
1963	Karl Ziegler (West Germany) and Giulio Natta (Italy)	chemistry and technology of high polymers
1964	Dorothy Crowfoot Hodgkin (UK)	crystallographic determination of the structures of biochemical compounds, notably penicillin and cyanocobalamin (vitamin B_{12})
1965	Robert Woodward (USA)	organic synthesis
1966	Robert Mulliken (USA)	molecular orbital theory of chemical bonds and structures
1967	Manfred Eigen (West Germany), Ronald Norrish (UK), and George Porter (UK)	investigation of rapid chemical reactions by means of very short pulses of energy
1968	Lars Onsager (USA)	discovery of reciprocal relations, fundamental for the thermodynamics of irreversible processes
1969	Derek Barton (UK) and Odd Hassel (Norway)	concept and applications of conformation
1970	Luis Federico Leloir (Argentina)	discovery of sugar nucleotides and their role in carbohydrate biosynthesis
1971	Gerhard Herzberg (Canada)	research on electronic structure and geometry of molecules, particularly free radicals
1972	Christian Anfinsen (USA), Stanford Moore (USA), and William Stein (USA)	work in amino-acid structure and biological activity of the enzyme ribonuclease

Nobel Prize for Chemistry (continued)

Year	*Winner(s)*[1]	*Awarded for*
1973	Ernst Fischer (West Germany) and Geoffrey Wilkinson (UK)	work in chemistry of organometallic sandwich compounds
1974	Paul Flory (USA)	studies of physical chemistry of macromolecules
1975	John Cornforth (UK)	work in stereochemistry of enzyme-catalysed reactions
	Vladimir Prelog (Switzerland)	work in stereochemistry of organic molecules and their reactions
1976	William Lipscomb (USA)	study of structure and chemical bonding of boranes (compounds of boron and hydrogen)
1977	Ilya Prigogine (Belgium)	work in thermodynamics of irreversible and dissipative processes
1978	Peter Mitchell (UK)	formulation of a theory of biological energy transfer and chemiosmotic theory
1979	Herbert Brown (USA) and Georg Wittig (West Germany)	use of boron and phosphorus compounds, respectively, in organic syntheses
1980	Paul Berg (USA)	biochemistry of nucleic acids, especially recombinant DNA
	Walter Gilbert (USA) and Frederick Sanger (UK)	base sequences in nucleic acids
1981	Kenichi Fukui (Japan) and Roald Hoffmann (USA)	theories concerning chemical reactions
1982	Aaron Klug (UK)	determination of crystallographic electron microscopy: structure of biologically important nucleic-acid–protein complexes
1983	Henry Taube (USA)	study of electron-transfer reactions in inorganic chemical reactions
1984	Bruce Merrifield (USA)	development of chemical syntheses on a solid matrix
1985	Herbert Hauptman (USA) and Jerome Karle (USA)	development of methods of determining crystal structures
1986	Dudley Herschbach (USA), Yuan Lee (USA), and John Polanyi (Canada)	development of dynamics of chemical elementary processes
1987	Donald Cram (USA), Jean-Marie Lehn (France), and Charles Pedersen (USA)	development of molecules with highly selective structure-specific interactions
1988	Johann Deisenhofer (West Germany), Robert Huber (West Germany), and Hartmut Michel (West Germany)	discovery of three-dimensional structure of the reaction centre of photosynthesis
1989	Sidney Altman (USA) and Thomas Cech (USA)	discovery of catalytic function of RNA
1990	Elias James Corey (USA)	new methods of synthesizing chemical compounds
1991	Richard Ernst (Switzerland)	improvements in the technology of nuclear magnetic resonance (NMR) imaging
1992	Rudolph Marcus (USA)	theoretical discoveries relating to reduction and oxidation reactions
1993	Kary Mullis (USA)	invention of the polymerase chain reaction technique for amplifying DNA
	Michael Smith (Canada)	invention of techniques for splicing foreign genetic segments into an organism's DNA in order to modify the proteins produced
1994	George Olah (USA)	development of technique for examining hydrocarbon molecules
1995	F Sherwood Rowland (USA), Mario Molina (USA), and Paul Crutzen (Netherlands)	explaining the chemical process of the ozone layer
1996	Robert Curl, Jr (USA), Harold Kroto (UK), and Richard Smalley (USA)	discovery of fullerenes
1997	John Walker (UK), Paul Boyer (USA), and Jens Skou (Denmark)	study of the enzymes involved in the production of adenosine triphospate (ATP), which acts as a store of energy in bodies called mitochondria inside cells

[1] Nationality given is the citizenship of recipient at the time award was made.

Nobel Prize for Physics

Year	*Winner(s)*[1]	*Awarded for*
1901	Wilhelm Röntgen (Germany)	discovery of X-rays
1902	Hendrik Lorentz (Netherlands) and Pieter Zeeman (Netherlands)	influence of magnetism on radiation phenomena
1903	Henri Becquerel (France)	discovery of spontaneous radioactivity
	Pierre Curie (France) and Marie Curie (France)	research on radiation phenomena
1904	John Strutt (Lord Rayleigh, UK)	densities of gases and discovery of argon
1905	Philipp von Lenard (Germany)	work on cathode rays
1906	Joseph J Thomson (UK)	theoretical and experimental work on the conduction of electricity by gases
1907	Albert Michelson (USA)	measurement of the speed of light through the design and application of precise optical instruments such as the interferometer
1908	Gabriel Lippmann (France)	photographic reproduction of colours by interference
1909	Guglielmo Marconi (Italy) and Karl Ferdinand Braun (Germany)	development of wireless telegraphy
1910	Johannes van der Waals (Netherlands)	equation describing the physical behaviour of gases and liquids
1911	Wilhelm Wien (Germany)	laws governing radiation of heat
1912	Nils Dalén (Sweden)	invention of light-controlled valves, which allow lighthouses and buoys to operate automatically
1913	Heike Kamerlingh Onnes (Netherlands)	studies of properties of matter at low temperatures
1914	Max von Laue (Germany)	discovery of diffraction of X-rays by crystals
1915	William Bragg (UK) and Lawrence Bragg (UK)	X-ray analysis of crystal structures
1916	no award	
1917	Charles Barkla (UK)	discovery of characteristic X-ray emission of the elements
1918	Max Planck (Germany)	formulation of quantum theory

Nobel Prize for Physics (continued)

Year	*Winner(s)*[1]	*Awarded for*
1919	Johannes Stark (Germany)	discovery of Doppler effect in rays of positive ions, and splitting of spectral lines in electric fields
1920	Charles Guillaume (Switzerland)	discovery of anomalies in nickel-steel alloys
1921	Albert Einstein (Switzerland)	theoretical physics, especially law of photoelectric effect
1922	Niels Bohr (Denmark)	discovery of the structure of atoms and radiation emanating from them
1923	Robert Millikan (USA)	discovery of the electric charge of an electron, and study of the photoelectric effect
1924	Karl Siegbahn (Sweden)	X-ray spectroscopy
1925	James Franck (Germany) and Gustav Hertz (Germany)	discovery of laws governing the impact of an electron upon an atom
1926	Jean Perrin (France)	confirmation of the discontinuous structure of matter
1927	Arthur Compton (USA)	transfer of energy from electromagnetic radiation to a particle
	Charles Wilson (UK)	invention of the Wilson cloud chamber, by which the movement of electrically charged particles may be tracked
1928	Owen Richardson (UK)	work on thermionic phenomena and associated law
1929	Louis Victor de Broglie (France)	discovery of the wavelike nature of electrons
1930	Chandrasekhara Raman (India)	discovery of the scattering of single-wavelength light when it is passed through a transparent substance
1931	no award	
1932	Werner Heisenberg (Germany)	creation of quantum mechanics
1933	Erwin Schrödinger (Austria) and Paul Dirac (UK)	development of quantum mechanics
1934	no award	
1935	James Chadwick (UK)	discovery of the neutron
1936	Victor Hess (Austria)	discovery of cosmic radiation
	Carl Anderson (USA)	discovery of the positron
1937	Clinton Davisson (USA) and George Thomson (UK)	diffraction of electrons by crystals
1938	Enrico Fermi (Italy)	use of neutron irradiation to produce new elements, and discovery of nuclear reactions induced by slow neutrons
1939	Ernest Lawrence (USA)	invention and development of the cyclotron, and production of artificial radioactive elements
1940	no award	
1941	no award	
1942	no award	
1943	Otto Stern (USA)	molecular-ray method of investigating elementary particles, and discovery of magnetic moment of proton
1944	Isidor Isaac Rabi (USA)	resonance method of recording the magnetic properties of atomic nuclei
1945	Wolfgang Pauli (Austria)	discovery of the exclusion principle
1946	Percy Bridgman (USA)	development of high-pressure physics
1947	Edward Appleton (UK)	physics of the upper atmosphere
1948	Patrick Blackett (UK)	application of the Wilson cloud chamber to nuclear physics and cosmic radiation
1949	Hideki Yukawa (Japan)	theoretical work predicting existence of mesons
1950	Cecil Powell (UK)	use of photographic emulsion to study nuclear processes, and discovery of pions (pi mesons)
1951	John Cockcroft (UK) and Ernest Walton (Ireland)	transmutation of atomic nuclei by means of accelerated subatomic particles
1952	Felix Bloch (USA) and Edward Purcell (USA)	precise nuclear magnetic measurements
1953	Frits Zernike (Netherlands)	invention of phase-contrast microscope
1954	Max Born (UK)	statistical interpretation of wave function in quantum mechanics
	Walther Bothe (West Germany)	coincidence method of detecting the emission of electrons
1955	Willis Lamb (USA)	structure of hydrogen spectrum
	Polykarp Kusch (USA)	determination of magnetic moment of the electron
1956	William Shockley (USA), John Bardeen (USA), and Walter Houser Brattain (USA)	study of semiconductors, and discovery of the transistor effect
1957	Tsung-Dao Lee (China) and Chen Ning Yang (China)	investigations of weak interactions between elementary particles
1958	Pavel Cherenkov (USSR), Ilya Frank (USSR), and Igor Tamm (USSR)	discovery and interpretation of Cherenkov radiation
1959	Emilio Segrè (USA) and Owen Chamberlain (USA)	discovery of the antiproton
1960	Donald Glaser (USA)	invention of the bubble chamber
1961	Robert Hofstadter (USA)	scattering of electrons in atomic nuclei, and structure of protons and neutrons
	Rudolf Mössbauer (West Germany)	resonance absorption of gamma radiation
1962	Lev Landau (USSR)	theories of condensed matter, especially liquid helium
1963	Eugene Wigner (USA)	discovery and application of symmetry principles in atomic physics
	Maria Goeppert-Mayer (USA) and Hans Jensen (Germany)	discovery of the shell-like structure of atomic nuclei
1964	Charles Townes (USA), Nikolai Basov (USSR), and Aleksandr Prokhorov (USSR)	work on quantum electronics leading to construction of oscillators and amplifiers based on maser–laser principle
1965	Shin'ichiro Tomonaga (Japan), Julian Schwinger (USA), and Richard Feynman (USA)	basic principles of quantum electrodynamics
1966	Alfred Kastler (France)	development of optical pumping, whereby atoms are raised to higher energy levels by illumination
1967	Hans Bethe (USA)	theory of nuclear reactions, and discoveries concerning production of energy in stars

Nobel Prize for Physics (continued)

Year	Winner(s)[1]	Awarded for
1968	Luis Alvarez (USA)	elementary-particle physics, and discovery of resonance states, using hydrogen bubble chamber and data analysis
1969	Murray Gell-Mann (USA)	classification of elementary particles, and study of their interactions
1970	Hannes Alfvén (Sweden)	work in magnetohydrodynamics and its applications in plasma physics
	Louis Néel (France)	work in antiferromagnetism and ferromagnetism in solid-state physics
1971	Dennis Gabor (UK)	invention and development of holography
1972	John Bardeen (USA), Leon Cooper (USA), and John Robert Schrieffer (USA)	theory of superconductivity
1973	Leo Esaki (Japan) and Ivar Giaever (USA)	tunnelling phenomena in semiconductors and superconductors
	Brian Josephson (UK)	theoretical predictions of the properties of a supercurrent through a tunnel barrier
1974	Martin Ryle (UK) and Antony Hewish (UK)	development of radioastronomy, particularly the aperture-synthesis technique, and the discovery of pulsars
1975	Aage Bohr (Denmark), Ben Mottelson (Denmark), and James Rainwater (USA)	discovery of connection between collective motion and particle motion in atomic nuclei, and development of theory of nuclear structure
1976	Burton Richter (USA) and Samuel Ting (USA)	discovery of the psi meson
1977	Philip Anderson (USA), Nevill Mott (UK), and John Van Vleck (USA)	contributions to understanding electronic structure of magnetic and disordered systems
1978	Pyotr Kapitsa (USSR)	invention and application of low-temperature physics
	Arno Penzias (USA) and Robert Wilson (USA)	discovery of cosmic background radiation
1979	Sheldon Glashow (USA), Abdus Salam (Pakistan), and Steven Weinberg (USA)	unified theory of weak and electromagnetic fundamental forces, and prediction of the existence of the weak neutral current
1980	James W Cronin (USA) and Val Fitch (USA)	violations of fundamental symmetry principles in the decay of neutral kaon mesons
1981	Nicolaas Bloembergen (USA) and Arthur Schawlow (USA)	development of laser spectroscopy
	Kai Siegbahn (Sweden)	high-resolution electron spectroscopy
1982	Kenneth Wilson (USA)	theory for critical phenomena in connection with phase transitions
1983	Subrahmanyan Chandrasekhar (USA)	theoretical studies of physical processes in connection with structure and evolution of stars
	William Fowler (USA)	nuclear reactions involved in the formation of chemical elements in the universe
1984	Carlo Rubbia (Italy) and Simon van der Meer (Netherlands)	contributions to the discovery of the W and Z particles (weakons)
1985	Klaus von Klitzing (West Germany)	discovery of the quantized Hall effect
1986	Erns Ruska (West Germany)	electron optics, and design of the first electron microscope
	Gerd Binnig (West Germany) and Heinrich Rohrer (Switzerland)	design of scanning tunnelling microscope
1987	Georg Bednorz (West Germany) and Alex Müller (Switzerland)	superconductivity in ceramic materials
1988	Leon M Lederman (USA), Melvin Schwartz (USA), and Jack Steinberger (USA)	neutrino-beam method, and demonstration of the doublet structure of leptons through discovery of muon neutrino
1989	Norman Ramsey (USA)	measurement techniques leading to discovery of caesium atomic clock
	Hans Dehmelt (USA) and Wolfgang Paul (Germany)	ion-trap method for isolating single atoms
1990	Jerome Friedman (USA), Henry Kendall (USA), and Richard Taylor (Canada)	experiments demonstrating that protons and neutrons are made up of quarks
1991	Pierre-Gilles de Gennes (France)	work on disordered systems including polymers and liquid crystals; development of mathematical methods for studying the behaviour of molecules in a liquid on the verge of solidifying
1992	Georges Charpak (France)	invention and development of detectors used in high-energy physics
1993	Joseph Taylor (USA) and Russell Hulse (USA)	discovery of first binary pulsar (confirming the existence of gravitational waves)
1994	Clifford Shull (USA) and Bertram Brockhouse (Canada)	development of technique known as 'neutron scattering' which led to advances in semiconductor technology
1995	Frederick Reines (USA)	discovery of the neutrino
	Martin Perl (USA)	discovery of the tau lepton
1996	David Lee (USA), Douglas Osheroff (USA), and Robert Richardson (USA)	discovery of superfluidity in helium-3
1997	Claude Cohen-Tannoudji (France), William Phillips (USA), and Steven Chu (USA)	discovery of a way to slow down individual atoms using lasers for study in a near-vacuum

[1] Nationality given is the citizenship of recipient at the time award was made.

Nobel Prize for Physiology or Medicine

Year	Winner(s)[1]	Awarded for
1901	Emil von Behring (Germany)	discovery that the body produces antitoxins, and development of serum therapy for diseases such as diphtheria
1902	Ronald Ross (UK)	work on the role of the *Anopheles* mosquito in transmitting malaria
1903	Niels Finsen (Denmark)	discovery of the use of ultraviolet light to treat skin diseases
1904	Ivan Pavlov (Russia)	discovery of the physiology of digestion
1905	Robert Koch (Germany)	investigations and discoveries in relation to tuberculosis

Nobel Prize for Physiology or Medicine (continued)

Year	*Winner(s)*[1]	*Awarded for*
1906	Camillo Golgi (Italy) and Santiago Ramón y Cajal (Spain)	discovery of the fine structure of the nervous system
1907	Charles Laveran (France)	discovery that certain protozoa can cause disease
1908	Ilya Mechnikov (Russia) and Paul Ehrlich (Germany)	work on immunity
1909	Emil Kocher (Switzerland)	work on the physiology, pathology, and surgery of the thyroid gland
1910	Albrecht Kossel (Germany)	study of cell proteins and nucleic acids
1911	Allvar Gullstrand (Sweden)	work on the refraction of light through the different components of the eye
1912	Alexis Carrel (France)	work on the techniques for connecting severed blood vessels and transplanting organs
1913	Charles Richet (France)	work on allergic responses
1914	Robert Bárány (Austria-Hungary)	work on the physiology and pathology of the equilibrium organs of the inner ear
1915	no award	
1916	no award	
1917	no award	
1918	no award	
1919	Jules Bordet (Belgium)	work on immunity
1920	August Krogh (Denmark)	discovery of the mechanism regulating the dilation and constriction of blood capillaries
1921	no award	
1922	Archibald Hill (UK)	work in the production of heat in contracting muscle
	Otto Meyerhof (Germany)	work in the relationship between oxygen consumption and metabolism of lactic acid in muscle
1923	Frederick Banting (Canada) and John Macleod (UK)	discovery and isolation of the hormone insulin
1924	Willem Einthoven (Netherlands)	invention of the electrocardiograph
1925	no award	
1926	Johannes Fibiger (Denmark)	discovery of a parasite ***Spiroptera carcinoma*** that causes cancer
1927	Julius Wagner-Jauregg (Austria)	use of induced malarial fever to treat paralysis caused by mental deterioration
1928	Charles Nicolle (France)	work on the role of the body louse in transmitting typhus
1929	Christiaan Eijkman (Netherlands)	discovery of a cure for beriberi, a vitamin-deficiency disease
	Frederick Hopkins (UK)	discovery of trace substances, now known as vitamins, that stimulate growth
1930	Karl Landsteiner (USA)	discovery of human blood groups
1931	Otto Warburg (Germany)	discovery of respiratory enzymes that enable cells to process oxygen
1932	Charles Sherrington (UK) and Edgar Adrian (UK)	discovery of function of neurons (nerve cells)
1933	Thomas Morgan (USA)	work on the role of chromosomes in heredity
1934	George Whipple (USA), George Minot (USA), and William Murphy (USA)	work on treatment of pernicious anaemia by increasing the amount of liver in the diet
1935	Hans Spemann (Germany)	organizer effect in embryonic development
1936	Henry Dale (UK) and Otto Loewi (Germany)	chemical transmission of nerve impulses
1937	Albert Szent-Györgyi (Hungary)	investigation of biological oxidation processes and of the action of ascorbic acid (vitamin C)
1938	Corneille Heymans (Belgium)	mechanisms regulating respiration
1939	Gerhard Domagk (Germany)	discovery of the first antibacterial sulphonamide drug
1940	no award	
1941	no award	
1942	no award	
1943	Henrik Dam (Denmark)	discovery of vitamin K
	Edward Doisy (USA)	chemical nature of vitamin K
1944	Joseph Erlanger (USA) and Herbert Gasser (USA)	transmission of impulses by nerve fibres
1945	Alexander Fleming (UK)	discovery of the bactericidal effect of penicillin
	Ernst Chain (UK) and Howard Florey (Australia)	isolation of penicillin and its development as an antibiotic drug
1946	Hermann Muller (USA)	discovery that X-ray irradiation can cause mutation
1947	Carl Cori (USA) and Gerty Cori (USA)	production and breakdown of glycogen (animal starch)
	Bernardo Houssay (Argentina)	function of the pituitary gland in sugar metabolism
1948	Paul Müller (Switzerland)	discovery of the first synthetic contact insecticide DDT
1949	Walter Hess (Switzerland)	mapping areas of the midbrain that control the activities of certain body organs
	Antonio Egas Moniz (Portugal)	therapeutic value of prefrontal leucotomy in certain psychoses
1950	Edward Kendall (USA), Tadeus Reichstein (Switzerland), and Philip Hench (USA)	structure and biological effects of hormones of the adrenal cortex
1951	Max Theiler (South Africa)	discovery of a vaccine against yellow fever
1952	Selman Waksman (USA)	discovery of streptomycin, the first antibiotic effective against tuberculosis
1953	Hans Krebs (UK)	discovery of the Krebs cycle
	Fritz Lipmann (USA)	discovery of coenzyme A, a nonprotein compound that acts in conjunction with enzymes to catalyse metabolic reactions leading up to the Krebs cycle
1954	John Enders (USA), Thomas Weller (USA), and Frederick Robbins (USA)	cultivation of the polio virus in the laboratory
1955	Hugo Theorell (Sweden)	work on the nature and action of oxidation enzymes

Nobel Prize for Physiology or Medicine (continued)

Year	*Winner(s)*[1]	*Awarded for*
1956	André Cournand (USA), Werner Forssmann (West Germany), and Dickinson Richards (USA)	work on the technique for passing a catheter into the heart for diagnostic purposes
1957	Daniel Bovet (Italy)	discovery of synthetic drugs used as muscle relaxants in anaesthesia
1958	George Beadle (USA) and Edward Tatum (USA)	discovery that genes regulate precise chemical effects
	Joshua Lederberg (USA)	work on genetic recombination and the organization of bacterial genetic material
1959	Severo Ochoa (USA) and Arthur Kornberg (USA)	discovery of enzymes that catalyse the formation of RNA (ribonucleic acid) and DNA (deoxyribonucleic acid)
1960	Macfarlane Burnet (Australia) and Peter Medawar (UK)	acquired immunological tolerance of transplanted tissues
1961	Georg von Békésy (USA)	investigations into the mechanism of hearing within the cochlea of the inner ear
1962	Francis Crick (UK), James Watson (USA), and Maurice Wilkins (UK)	discovery of the double-helical structure of DNA and of the significance of this structure in the replication and transfer of genetic information
1963	John Eccles (Australia), Alan Hodgkin (UK), and Andrew Huxley (UK)	ionic mechanisms involved in the communication or inhibition of impulses across neuron (nerve cell) membranes
1964	Konrad Bloch (USA) and Feodor Lynen (West Germany)	work on the cholesterol and fatty-acid metabolism
1965	François Jacob (France), André Lwoff (France), and Jacques Monod (France)	genetic control of enzyme and virus synthesis
1966	Peyton Rous (USA)	discovery of tumour-inducing viruses
	Charles Huggins (USA)	hormonal treatment of prostatic cancer
1967	Ragnar Granit (Sweden), Haldan Hartline (USA), and George Wald (USA)	physiology and chemistry of vision
1968	Robert Holley (USA), Har Gobind Khorana (USA), and Marshall Nirenberg (USA)	interpretation of genetic code and its function in protein synthesis
1969	Max Delbrück (USA), Alfred Hershey (USA), and Salvador Luria (USA)	replication mechanism and genetic structure of viruses
1970	Bernard Katz (UK), Ulf von Euler (Sweden), and Julius Axelrod (USA)	work on the storage, release, and inactivation of neurotransmitters
1971	Earl Sutherland (USA)	discovery of cyclic AMP, a chemical messenger that plays a role in the action of many hormones
1972	Gerald Edelman (USA) and Rodney Porter (UK)	work on the chemical structure of antibodies
1973	Karl von Frisch (Austria), Konrad Lorenz (Austria), and Nikolaas Tinbergen (UK)	work in animal behaviour patterns
1974	Albert Claude (USA), Christian de Duve (Belgium), and George Palade (USA)	work in structural and functional organization of the cell
1975	David Baltimore (USA), Renato Dulbecco (USA), and Howard Temin (USA)material of the cell	work on interactions between tumour-inducing viruses and the genetic
1976	Baruch Blumberg (USA) and Carleton Gajdusek (USA)	new mechanisms for the origin and transmission of infectious diseases
1977	Roger Guillemin (USA) and Andrew Schally (USA)	discovery of hormones produced by the hypothalamus region of the brain
	Rosalyn Yalow (USA)	radioimmunoassay techniques by which minute quantities of hormone may be detected
1978	Werner Arber (Switzerland), Daniel Nathans (USA), and Hamilton Smith (USA)	discovery of restriction enzymes and their application to molecular genetics
1979	Allan Cormack (USA) and Godfrey Hounsfield (UK)	development of the computed axial tomography (CAT) scan
1980	Baruj Benacerraf (USA), Jean Dausset (France), and George Snell (USA)	work on genetically determined structures on the cell surface that regulate immunological reactions
1981	Roger Sperry (USA)	functional specialization of the brain's cerebral hemispheres
	David Hubel (USA) and Torsten Wiesel (Sweden)	work on visual perception
1982	Sune Bergström (Sweden), Bengt Samuelsson (Sweden), and John Vane (UK)	discovery of prostaglandins and related biologically active substances
1983	Barbara McClintock (USA)	discovery of mobile genetic elements
1984	Niels Jerne (Denmark-UK), Georges Köhler (West Germany), and César Milstein (Argentina)cific, monoclonal antibodies	work on immunity and discovery of a technique for producing highly spe
1985	Michael Brown (USA) and Joseph L Goldstein (USA)	work on the regulation of cholesterol metabolism
1986	Stanley Cohen (USA) and Rita Levi-Montalcini (USA-Italy)	discovery of factors that promote the growth of nerve and epidermal cells
1987	Susumu Tonegawa (Japan)	work on the process by which genes alter to produce a range of different antibodies
1988	James Black (UK), Gertrude Elion (USA), and George Hitchings (USA)	work on the principles governing the design of new drug treatment
1989	Michael Bishop (USA) and Harold Varmus (USA)	discovery of oncogenes, genes carried by viruses that can trigger cancerous growth in normal cells
1990	Joseph Murray (USA) and Donnall Thomas (USA)	pioneering work in organ and cell transplants
1991	Erwin Neher (Germany) and Bert Sakmann (Germany)	discovery of how gatelike structures (ion channels) regulate the flow of ions into and out of cells
1992	Edmond Fisher (USA) and Edwin Krebs (USA)	isolating and describing the action of the enzyme responsible for reversible protein phosphorylation, a major biological control mechanism
1993	Phillip Sharp (USA) and Richard Roberts (UK)	discovery of split genes (genes interrupted by nonsense segments of DNA)
1994	Alfred Gilman (USA) and Martin Rodbell (USA)	discovery of a family of proteins (G-proteins) that translate messages – in the form of hormones or other chemical signals – into action inside cells
1995	Edward Lewis (USA), Eric Wieschaus (USA), and Christiane Nüsslein-Volhard (Germany)ment	discovery of genes which control the early stages of the body's develop
1996	Peter Doherty (Australia) and Rolf Zinkernagel (Switzerland)	discovery of how the immune system recognizes virus-infected cells
1997	Stanley Prusiner (USA)	discoveries, including the 'prion' theory, that could lead to new treatments of dementia-related diseases, including Alzheimer's and Parkinson's diseases

Roman Numerals

Roman	Arabic	Roman	Arabic	Roman	Arabic
I	1	IX	9	LX	60
II	2	X	10	XC	90
III	3	XI	11	C	100
IV	4	XIX	19	CC	200
V	5	XX	20	CD	400
VI	6	XXX	30	D	500
VII	7	XL	40	CM	900
VIII	8	L	50	M	1,000

SI Units

Quantity	SI unit	Symbol
absorbed radiation dose	gray	Gy
amount of substance	mole*	mol
electric capacitance	farad	F
electric charge	coulomb	C
electric conductance	siemens	S
electric current	ampere*	A
energy or work	joule	J
force	newton	N
frequency	hertz	Hz
illuminance	lux	lx
inductance	henry	H
length	metre*	m
luminous flux	lumen	lm
luminous intensity	candela*	cd
magnetic flux	weber	Wb
magnetic flux density	tesla	T
mass	kilogram*	kg
plane angle	radian	rad
potential difference	volt	V
power	watt	W
pressure	pascal	Pa
radiation dose equivalent	sievert	Sv
radiation exposure	roentgen	R
radioactivity	becquerel	Bq
resistance	ohm	Ω
solid angle	steradian	sr
sound intensity	decibel	dB
temperature	°Celsius	°C
temperature, thermodynamic	kelvin*	K
time	second*	s

* SI base unit.